May 6–11, 2017
Denver, CO, USA

Association for
Computing Machinery

Advancing Computing as a Science & Profession

CHI'17

Proceedings of the 2017 ACM SIGCHI Conference on Human Factors in Computing Systems

Sponsored by:

ACM SIGCHI

Supported by:

Bloomberg, Facebook, Google, IBM Research, Microsoft, & NSF

Association for
Computing Machinery

Advancing Computing as a Science & Profession

The Association for Computing Machinery
2 Penn Plaza, Suite 701
New York, New York 10121-0701

Notice to Past Authors of ACM-Published Articles
ACM intends to create a complete electronic archive of all articles and/or other material previously published by ACM. If you have written a work that has been previously published by ACM in any journal or conference proceedings prior to 1978, or any SIG Newsletter at any time, and you do NOT want this work to appear in the ACM Digital Library, please inform permissions@acm.org, stating the title of the work, the author(s), and where and when published.

ISBN: 978-1-4503-4655-9 (Digital)

ISBN: 978-1-4503-5468-4 (Print)

Additional copies may be ordered prepaid from:

ACM Order Department
PO Box 30777
New York, NY 10087-0777, USA

Phone: 1-800-342-6626 (USA and Canada)
+1-212-626-0500 (Global)
Fax: +1-212-944-1318
E-mail: acmhelp@acm.org
Hours of Operation: 8:30 am – 4:30 pm ET

Printed in the USA

CHI 2017 is the premier international conference for the field of Human-Computer Interaction (HCI). This year it was held in Denver, bordering the beautiful Rocky Mountain region in the U.S., and reflected in our logo. The CHI 2017 conference began with two days of workshops and symposia, followed by four days of a technical program with 17 parallel sessions of provocative papers, panels, case studies, SIGs (Special Interest Groups), courses, and the popular student research, design, and game competitions. The growing alt.chi forum, now in its twelfth year, presented stimulating new ideas in HCI. The Interactivity forum showcased cutting-edge technology. For its second year, the CHI Art Exhibit merged art and technology in fascinating ways.

This innovative work can be found in the Proceedings and Extended Abstracts, archived in the ACM Digital Library. For papers, the conference received 2400 submissions which were rigorously reviewed, resulting in 600 accepted papers. To ensure a better fit with reviewers, new subcommittees were created. Across all tracks, CHI received nearly 5000 submissions and accepted over 1000.

Our conference theme this year, *Explore, Innovate, Inspire*, informed our planning process. A new venue held this year was CHI Stories. We generally know little of the personalities that drive the research presented at CHI. CHI Stories is a chance for CHI community members to share personal stories of inspiration, challenge, successes and failures, and grit. We also focused on inclusion this year. Hundreds of CHI attendees volunteered their skills in a Day of Service partnering with non-profit organizations. Inclusion was also manifest throughout the conference, for example, in the Diversity and Inclusion Lunch and by using telepresence robots to enable people with disabilities to participate remotely in the conference. Our keynote speakers were chosen to reflect our conference theme. The speakers were Neri Oxman, who combines computational design, digital fabrication, materials science and synthetic biology; Ben Shneiderman a founder of the CHI conference who, along with some key CHI personalities, gave a perspective on CHI's history and future; Wael Ghonim, credited with starting the Arab Spring and nominated for the Nobel Peace Prize; and best-selling author Nicholas Carr who challenges us to examine the unforeseen impacts of technology, particularly with automation.

The world has experienced a dramatic change this past year. We live in extraordinary times and this calls for extraordinary thinking, something that the CHI community excels at. One of the challenges the community faced this year was responding to a U.S. executive order to ban citizens of certain countries from entering the country to attend CHI. As CHI is committed to inclusion, we decided to hold events at the conference to discuss and plan how we can continue our commitment to inclusion. The conference held a panel to discuss impacts of current political events on science, and hastily organized a panel to promote a conversation of civil liberties in science and a SIG on how the CHI community can participate in change. We are proud to have expanded telepresence options through the use of robots to enable people to participate in the conference remotely if they were physically unable to enter the country. We had a keynote speaker who inspired us on the topic of Internet activism. Our art exhibit, *I'll Be Watching You,* examined the contemporary issue of surveillance.

We are extremely grateful to a legion of volunteers who made CHI 2017 possible, including over 7000 reviewers across all areas of the technical program, 254 senior members of the papers program committee, over 100 members of the CHI 2017 conference organization committee and importantly, the more than 175 student volunteers. We also thank SIGCHI (the Special Interest Group on Computer-Human Interaction of ACM) as well as the ACM itself for its continued support.

Gloria Mark, University of California Irvine, CHI 2017 General Conference Co-Chair

Susan Fussell, Cornell University, CHI 2017 General Conference Co-Chair

Cliff Lampe, University of Michigan, CHI 2017 Technical Program Chair

m.c. schraefel, University of Southampton, CHI 2017 Technical Program Chair

Juan Pablo Hourcade, University of Iowa, CHI 2017 Papers Co-Chair

Caroline Appert, Université Paris-Sud, CHI 2017 Papers Co-Chair

Daniel Wigdor, University of Toronto, CHI 2017 Papers Co-Chair

Loren Terveen, University of Minnesota, President, ACM SIGCHI Executive Committee

Scooter Morris, University of San Francisco, ACM SIGCHI Liaison

Table of Contents

ix CHI 2017 Organization

Session: Innovative Sensing

1 **Electrick: Low-Cost Touch Sensing Using Electric Field Tomography**
Yang Zhang, Gierad Laput, Chris Harrison, *Carnegie Mellon University*

15 **GhostID: Enabling Non-Persistent User Differentiation in Frequency-Division Capacitive Multi-Touch Sensors**
Sidharth Sahdev, *University of Toronto & Tactual Labs*
Clifton Forlines, Ricardo Jota, *Tactual Labs*
Bruno De Araujo, *University of Toronto & Tactual Labs*
Braon Moseley, Jonathan Deber, Steven Sanders, Darren Leigh, *Tactual Labs*
Daniel Wigdor, *University of Toronto*

28 **Essence: Olfactory Interfaces for Unconscious Influence of Mood and Cognitive Performance**
Judith Amores, Pattie Maes, *Masschusetts Institute of Technology*

35 **Group Touch: Distinguishing Tabletop Users in Group Settings via Statistical Modeling of Touch Pairs**
Abigail C. Evans, Katie Davis, James Fogarty, Jacob O. Wobbrock, *University of Washington*

Session: Interruptions and Email

48 **What Makes Live Events Engaging on Facebook Live, Periscope, and Snapchat**
Oliver L. Haimson, *Microsoft Research & University of California, Irvine*
John C. Tang, *Microsoft Research*

61 **Reducing Interruptions at Work: A Large-Scale Field Study of FlowLight**
Manuela Züger, *University of Zurich*
Christopher Corley, *ABB Corporate Research*
André N. Meyer, *University of Zurich*
Boyang Li, *ABB Corporate Research*
Thomas Fritz, *University of Zurich*
David Shepherd, Vinay Augustine, Patrick Francis, Nicholas Kraft, Will Snipes, *ABB Corporate Research*

73 **MyriadHub: Efficiently Scaling Personalized Email Conversations with Valet Crowdsourcing**
Nicolas Kokkalis, Chengdiao Fan, Johannes Roith, Michael S. Bernstein, *Stanford University*
Scott Klemmer, *University of California, San Diego*

85 **"If a person is emailing you, it just doesn't make sense": Exploring Changing Consumer Behaviors in Email**
Frank Bentley, Nediyana Daskalova, Nazanin Andalibi, *Yahoo*

Session: Learning to be Makers

96 **'Maker' within Constraints: Exploratory Study of Young Learners using Arduino at a High School in India**
Sowmya Somanath, Lora Oehlberg, *University of Calgary*
Janette Hughes, *University of Ontario Institute of Technology*
Ehud Sharlin, Mario Costa Sousa, *University of Calgary*

109 ***'I Make, Therefore I Am':* The Effects of Curriculum-Aligned Making on Children's Self-Identity**
Sharon Lynn Chu, Rebecca Schlegel, Francis Quek, Andrew Christy, Kaiyuan Chen, *Texas A&M University*

121 **"It's a Bomb!" – Material Literacy and Narratives of Making**
Sophie Landwehr Sydow, *Södertörn University & Stockholm University*
Jakob Tholander, *Stockholm University*
Martin Jonsson, *Södertörn University*

133 **MakerWear: A Tangible Approach to Interactive Wearable Creation for Children**
Majeed Kazemitabaar, Jason McPeak, Alexander Jiao, Liang He, Thomas Outing, Jon E. Froehlich, *University of Maryland, College Park*

Session: Mental Health

146 **Self Harmony: Rethinking Hackathons to Design and Critique Digital Technologies for Those Affected by Self-Harm**
Nataly Birbeck, *Newcastle University*
Shaun Lawson, *Northumbria University*
Kellie Morrissey, Tim Rapley, Patrick Olivier, *Newcastle University*

158 **Changing Moods: How Manual Tracking by Family Caregivers Improves Caring and Family Communication**
Naomi Yamashita, *NTT Communication Science Labs*
Hideaki Kuzuoka, *University of Tsukuba*
Keiji Hirata, *Future University Hakodate*
Takashi Kudo, *Osaka University*
Eiji Aramaki, *Nara Institute of Science and Technology*
Kazuki Hattori, *University of Tsukuba*

170 **Modeling and Understanding Visual Attributes of Mental Health Disclosures in Social Media**
Lydia Manikonda, *Arizona State University*
Munmun De Choudhury, *Georgia Institute of Technology*

182 **The Social Lives of Individuals with Traumatic Brain Injury**
Jessica L. Feuston, Charlotte G. Marshall-Fricker, Anne Marie Piper, *Northwestern University*

Session: Perceptions of Visualizations

195 **User-Guided Synthesis of Interactive Diagrams**
John Sarracino, *University of California, San Diego*
Odaris Barrios-Arciga, *Scripps College*
Jasmine Zhu, Noah Marcus, *Harvey Mudd College*
Sorin Lerner, *University of California, San Diego*
Ben Wiedermann, *Harvey Mudd College*

Table of Contents

208 Peripheral Popout: The Influence of Visual Angle and Stimulus Intensity on Popout Effects
Carl Gutwin, *University of Saskatchewan*
Andy Cockburn, *University of Canterbury*
Ashley Coveney, *University of Saskatchewan*

220 Attention Allocation Aid for Visual Search
Arturo Deza, Jeffrey R. Peters, *University of California, Santa Barbara*
Grant S. Taylor, *U.S. Army Aviation Development Directorate*
Amit Surana, *United Technologies Research Center*
Miguel P. Eckstein, *University of California, Santa Barbara*

Session: Targets and Paths

232 Steering Through Sequential Linear Path Segments
Shota Yamanaka, *Meiji University & Japan Society for the Promotion of Science*
Wolfgang Stuerzlinger, *Simon Fraser University*
Homei Miyashita, *Meiji University*

244 Modeling User Performance on Curved Constrained Paths
Mathieu Nancel, *University of Waterloo, Aalto University, & Inria Lille*
Edward Lank, *University of Waterloo & University of Lille*

255 Free the Hands! Enhanced Target Selection via a Variable-Friction Shoe
Daniel Horodniczy, Jeremy R. Cooperstock, *McGill University*

260 *To Miss is Human*: Information-Theoretic Rationale for Target Misses in Fitts' Law
Julien Gori, Olivier Rioul, Yves Guiard, *Université Paris-Saclay*

Session: Technology & Adoption

265 Implications for Adoption
Joseph Lindley, Paul Coulton, Miriam Sturdee, *Lancaster University*

278 UX Design Innovation: Challenges for Working with Machine Learning as a Design Material
Graham Dove, Kim Halskov, *Aarhus University*
Jodi Forlizzi, John Zimmerman, *Carnegie Mellon University*

289 Technology Maintenance: A New Frame for Studying Poverty and Marginalization
Amy Gonzales, *Indiana University*

Session: Telepresence and Robots

301 Someone to Read with: Design of and Experiences with an In-Home Learning Companion Robot for Reading
Joseph E. Michaelis, Bilge Mutlu, *University of Wisconsin–Madison*

313 Robotic Telepresence at Scale
Irene Rae, *Microsoft & Google*
Carman Neustaedter, *Simon Fraser University*

325 Movement Matters: Effects of Motion and Mimicry on Perception of Similarity and Closeness in Robot-Mediated Communication
Mina Choi, Rachel Kornfield, *University of Wisconsin, Madison*
Leila Takayama, *University of California, Santa Cruz*
Bilge Mutlu, *University of Wisconsin–Madison*

336 A Simple Nod of the Head: The Effect of Minimal Robot Movements on Children's Perception of a Low-Anthropomorphic Robot
Cristina Zaga, Roelof A. J. de Vries, Jamy Li, Khiet P. Truong, Vanessa Evers, *Universiteit Twente*

342 My Student is a Robot: How Schools Manage Telepresence Experiences for Students
Veronica Ahumada Newhart, Judith S. Olson, *University of California, Irvine*

Session: Authentication and Access Control

348 How Do System Administrators Resolve Access-Denied Issues in the Real World?
Tianyin Xu, Han Min Naing, Le Lu, Yuanyuan Zhou, *University of California, San Diego*

362 User Interactions and Permission Use on Android
Kristopher Micinski, Daniel Votipka, Rock Stevens, Nikolaos Kofinas, Michelle L. Mazurek, Jeffrey S. Foster, *University of Maryland, College Park*

374 Where Usability and Security Go Hand-in-Hand: Robust Gesture-Based Authentication for Mobile Systems
Can Liu, Gradeigh D. Clark, Janne Lindqvist, *Rutgers University*

387 I'm too Busy to Reset my LinkedIn Password: On the Effectiveness of Password Reset Emails
Jun Ho Huh, *Honeywell ACS Labs*
Hyoungshick Kim, *Sungkyunkwan University*
Swathi S.V.P. Rayala, Rakesh B. Bobba, *Oregon State University*
Konstantin Beznosov, *University of British Columbia*

Session: Cars and Automation

392 Priming Drivers before Handover in Semi-Autonomous Cars
Remo M.A. van der Heiden, *Utrecht University*
Shamsi T. Iqbal, *Microsoft Research*
Christian P. Janssen, *Utrecht University*

405 Toward Measurement of Situation Awareness in Autonomous Vehicles
David Sirkin, Nikolas Martelaro, Mishel Johns, Wendy Ju, *Stanford University*

416 The Trouble with Autopilots: Assisted and Autonomous Driving on the Social Road
Barry Brown, *University of Stockholm*
Eric Laurier, *University of Edinburgh*

430 Understanding the Cost of Driving Trips
Caleb Southern Yunnuo Cheng, Cheng Zhang, Gregory D. Abowd, *Georgia Institute of Technology*

Table of Contents

Session: Design Theory

435 Making Ritual Machines: The Mobile Phone as a Networked Material for Research Products
David Chatting, , *Newcastle University*
David S. Kirk, Abigail C. Durrant, *Northumbria University*
Chris Elsden, *Newcastle University*
Paulina Yurman, *Goldsmiths University of London*
Jo-Anne Bichard, *Royal College of Art*

448 Products as Agents: Metaphors for Designing the Products of the IoT Age
Nazli Cila, *Amsterdam University of Applied Sciences*
Iskander Smit, *Info.nl*
Elisa Giaccardi, *Delft University of Technology*
Ben Kröse, *Amsterdam University of Applied Sciences*

460 Pause: A Multi-lifespan Design Mechanism
Batya Friedman, Daisy Yoo, *University of Washington*

465 Interdependent Wearables (for Play): A Strong Concept for Design
Katherine Isbister, *University of California, Santa Cruz*
Kaho Abe, Michael Karlesky, *New York University*

472 How Methods Make Designers
Seyram Avle, Silvia Lindtner, *University of Michigan*
Kaiton Williams, *Cornell University*

Session: Fabrication via 3D Printing

484 Consumer to Creator: How Households Buy Furniture to Inform Design and Fabrication Interfaces
Bokyung Lee, Gyeol Han, Jundong Park, Daniel Saakes, *Korea Advanced Institute of Science and Technology*

497 Stretching the Bounds of 3D Printing with Embedded Textiles
Michael L. Rivera, *Carnegie Mellon University*
Melissa Moukperian, Daniel Ashbrook, *Rochester Institute of Technology*
Jennifer Mankoff, Scott E. Hudson, *Carnegie Mellon University*

509 WeaveMesh: A Low-Fidelity and Low-Cost Prototyping Approach for 3D Models Created by Flexible Assembly
Ye Tao, Guanyun Wang, Caowei Zhang, Nannan Lu, Xiaolian Zhang, Cheng Yao, Fangtian Ying, *Zhejiang University*

Session: Learning and Reading

519 A Framework for Speechreading Acquisition Tools
Benjamin M. Gorman, David R. Flatla, *University of Dundee*

531 FLight: A Low-Cost Reading and Writing System for Economically Less-Privileged Visually-Impaired People Exploiting Ink-based Braille System
Tusher Chakraborty, Taslim Arefin Khan, A. B. M. Alim Al Islam, *Bangladesh University of Engineering and Technology*

541 Teaching Language and Culture with a Virtual Reality Game
Alan Cheng, Lei Yang, Erik Andersen, *Cornell University*

550 Identifying how Visually Impaired People Explore Raised-line Diagrams to Improve the Design of Touch Interfaces
Sandra Bardot, Marcos Serrano, *University of Toulouse & CNRS*
Bernard Oriola, Christophe Jouffrais, *CNRS & University of Toulouse*

Session: Robots at Work & Home

556 Sensing and Handling Engagement Dynamics in Human-Robot Interaction Involving Peripheral Computing Devices
Mingfei Sun, Zhenjie Zhao, Xiaojuan Ma, *Hong Kong University of Science and Technology*

568 Managing Uncertainty in Time Expressions for Virtual Assistants
Xin Rong, *University of Michigan & Microsoft Research*
Adam Fourney, *Microsoft Research*
Robin N. Brewer, *Northwestern University & Microsoft Research*
Meredith Ringel Morris, Paul N. Bennett, *Microsoft Research*

580 Comparing Social Robot, Screen and Voice Interfaces for Smart-Home Control
Michal Luria, *Interdisciplinary Center Herzliya*
Guy Hoffman, *Cornell University*
Oren Zuckerman, *Interdisciplinary Center Herzliya*

Session: Self-tracking Mental Health

629 Self-tracking for Mental Wellness: Understanding Expert Perspectives and Student Experiences
Christina Kelley, *Georgia Institute of Technology*
Bongshin Lee, *Microsoft Research*
Lauren Wilcox, *Georgia Institute of Technology*

642 "It's Definitely Been a Journey": A Qualitative Study on How Women with Eating Disorders Use Weight Loss Apps
Elizabeth V. Eikey, *Pennsylvania State University*
Madhu C. Reddy, *Northwestern University*

655 Conflict in Comments: Learning but Lowering Perceptions, with Limits
W. Ben Towne, Carolyn P. Rosé, James D. Herbsleb, *Carnegie Mellon University*

667 Identification and Classification of Usage Patterns in Long-Term Activity Tracking
Jochen Meyer, Merlin Wasmann, Wilko Heuten, *OFFIS Institute for Information Technology*
Abdallah El Ali, Susanne C.J. Boll, *Carl von Ossietzky University*

Session: Smartwatch Interactions and Displays

679 AirPanes: Two-Handed Around-Device Interaction for Pane Switching on Smartphones
Khalad Hasan, *University of Manitoba*
David Ahlström, *Alpen-Adria-Universität Klagenfurt*
Junhyeok Kim, Pourang Irani, *University of Manitoba*

692 Float: One-Handed and Touch-Free Target Selection on Smartwatches
Ke Sun, Yuntao Wang, Chun Yu, Yukang Yan, Hongyi Wen, Yuanchun Shi, *Tsinghua University*

Table of Contents

705 COMPASS: Rotational Keyboard on Non-Touch Smartwatches
Xin Yi, Chun Yu, Weijie Xu, *Tsinghua University*
Xiaojun Bi, *Stony Brook University*
Yuanchun Shi, *Tsinghua University*

716 WatchThru: Expanding Smartwatch Displays with Mid-air Visuals and Wrist-worn Augmented Reality
Dirk Wenig, Johannes Schöning, *University of Bremen*
Alex Olwal, *Google, Inc.*
Mathias Oben, *Hasselt University*
Rainer Malaka, *University of Bremen*

722 Evaluation of Korean Text Entry Methods for Smartwatches
Ivaylo Ilinkin, Sunghee Kim, *Gettysburg College*

Session: Social & Collaborative Technologies

727 "WhatsApp is for family; Messenger is for friends": Communication Places in App Ecosystems
Midas Nouwens, Carla F. Griggio, Wendy E. Mackay, *University Paris-Sud, CNRS, Inria, Université Paris-Saclay*

736 I Need Your Encouragement! Requesting Supportive Comments on Social Media Reduces Test Anxiety
Robert Deloatch, Brian P. Bailey, Alex Kirlik, Craig Zilles, *University of Illinois at Urbana Champaign*

748 Goodbye Text, Hello Emoji: Mobile Communication on WeChat in China
Rui Zhou, *Georgia Institute of Technology*
Jasmine Hentschel, *THRIVE*
Neha Kumar, *Georgia Institute of Technology*

760 A Kaleidoscope of Languages: When and How Non-Native English Speakers Shift between English and Their Native Language during Multilingual Teamwork
Ge Gao, Susan R. Fussell, *Cornell University*

Session: Sustainability and Public Service

773 The (Un)sustainability of Imagined Future Information Societies
Daniel Pargman, Elina Eriksson, Mattias Höjer, Ulrika Gunnarsson Östling, Luciane Aguiar Borges, *KTH Royal Institute of Technology*

786 Means and Ends in Human-Computer Interaction: Sustainability through Disintermediation
Barath Raghavan, *International Computer Science Institute*
Daniel Pargman, *KTH Royal Institute of Technology*

797 Crowdfunding Platforms and the Design of Paying Publics
Ann Light, *University of Sussex*
Jo Briggs, *University of Northumbria at Newcastle*

810 Reappropriating Hackathons: The Production Work of the CHI4Good Day of Service
Emily Porter, Chris Bopp, *University of Colorado, Boulder*
Elizabeth Gerber, *Northwestern University*
Amy Voida, *University of Colorado, Boulder*

Session: Understanding Data Visualization

815 Understanding Concept Maps: A Closer Look at How People Organise Ideas
Stefano Padilla, Thomas S. Methven, David A. Robb, Mike J. Chantler, *Heriot Watt University*

828 Increasing Users' Confidence in Uncertain Data by Aggregating Data from Multiple Sources
Miriam Greis, Emre Avci, Albrecht Schmidt, Tonja Machulla, *University of Stuttgart*

841 Bottom-up vs. Top-down: Trade-offs in Efficiency, Understanding, Freedom and Creativity with InfoVis Tools
Gonzalo Gabriel Méndez, *University of St Andrews & Escuela Superior Politécnica del Litoral*
Uta Hinrichs, Miguel A. Nacenta, *University of St Andrews*

853 What Happened in my Home?: An End-User Development Approach for Smart Home Data Visualization
Nico Castelli, *Bonn-Rhein-Sieg University of Applied Sciences & University of Siegen*
Corinna Ogonowski, *University of Siegen*
Timo Jakobi, *Bonn-Rhein-Sieg University of Applied Sciences & University of Siegen*
Martin Stein, *University of Siegen & Fraunhofer Institute for Applied Information Technology (FIT)*
Gunnar Stevens, *Bonn-Rhein-Sieg University of Applied Sciences & University of Siegen*
Volker Wulf, *University of Siegen and Fraunhofer Institute for Applied Information Technology (FIT)*

Session: Clinical Settings

867 Opportunities and Design Considerations for Peer Support in a Hospital Setting
Shefali Haldar, Sonali R. Mishra, Maher Khelifi, *University of Washington*
Ari H. Pollack, *University of Washington & Seattle Children's Hospital*
Wanda Pratt, *University of Washington*

880 Patient Strategies as Active Adaptation: Understanding Patient Behaviors During an Emergency Visit
Sun Young Park, *University of Michigan*
Yunan Chen, *University of California, Irvine*

893 Itchtector: A Wearable-based Mobile System for Managing Itching Conditions
Jongin Lee, *Korea Advanced Institute of Science & Technology*
Daeki Cho, *NEC Laboratories America, Inc.*
Junhong Kim, Eunji Im, JinYeong Bak, *Korea Advanced Institute of Science & Technology*
Kyung ho Lee, *The Catholic University of Korea*
Kwan Hong Lee, *AcademicMerit*
John Kim, *Korea Advanced Institute of Science & Technology*

Table of Contents

Session: Digital Privacy & Security

906 Privacy, Security, and Surveillance in the Global South: A Study of Biometric Mobile SIM Registration in Bangladesh
Syed Ishtiaque Ahmed, *Cornell University*
Md. Romael Haque, *Bangladesh University of Engineering and Technology*
Shion Guha, *Marquette University*
Md. Rashidujjaman Rifat, *University of Colorado, Boulder*
Nicola Dell, *Cornell Tech*

919 Youth Perspectives on Critical Data Literacies
Samantha Hautea, *University of Washington*
Sayamindu Dasgupta, *University of Washington & Massachusetts Institute of Technology*
Benjamin Mako Hill, *University of Washington*

931 Where is the Digital Divide? A Survey of Security, Privacy, and Socioeconomics
Elissa M. Redmiles, *University of Maryland*
Sean Kross, *John Hopkins University*
Michelle L. Mazurek, *University of Maryland*

Session: Educational Assessment

937 A Unified Framework for Knowledge Assessment and Progression Analysis and Design
Shuhan Wang, *Cornell University*
Fang He, *Peking University*
Erik Andersen, *Cornell University*

949 HOBIT: Hybrid Optical Bench for Innovative Teaching
David Furió, *Université de Bordeaux*
Stéphanie Fleck, *Université de Lorraine*
Bruno Bousquet, Jean-Paul Guillet, Lionel Canioni, *Université de Bordeaux*
Martin Hachet, *Inria*

960 PathViewer: Visualizing Pathways through Student Data
Yiting Wang, Walker M. White, Erik Andersen, *Cornell University*

Session: Fabricating New Materials

965 WireFab: Mix-Dimensional Modeling and Fabrication for 3D Mesh Models
Min Liu, Yunbo Zhang, *Purdue University*
Jing Bai, *Beifang University of Nationalities*
Yuanzhi Cao, Jeffrey M. Alperovich, Karthik Ramani, *Purdue University*

977 Digital Mechanical Metamaterials
Alexandra Ion, Ludwig Wall, Robert Kovacs, Patrick Baudisch, *Hasso Plattner Institute*

989 Organic Primitives: Synthesis and Design of pH-Reactive Materials using Molecular I/O for Sensing, Actuation, and Interaction
Viirj Kan, Emma Vargo, Noa Machover, Hiroshi Ishii, Serena Pan, Weixuan Chen, *Massachusetts Institute of Technology*
Yasuaki Kakehi, *Massachusetts Institute of Technology & Keio University*

1001 Flexibles: Deformation-Aware 3D-Printed Tangibles for Capacitive Touchscreens
Martin Schmitz, *Technische Universität Darmstadt*
Jürgen Steimle, *Saarland University*
Jochen Huber, *Synaptics*
Niloofar Dezfuli, Max Mühlhäuser, *Technische Universität Darmstadt*

Session: Human Factors

This session was journal presentations. See conference program.

Session: Motivation in Games

1015 Towards Personality-driven Persuasive Health Games and Gamified Systems
Rita Orji, Lennart E. Nacke, Chrysanne Di Marco, *University of Waterloo*

1028 Is Difficulty Overrated? The Effects of Choice, Novelty and Suspense on Intrinsic Motivation in Educational Games
J. Derek Lomas, *University of California, San Diego & Carnegie Mellon University*
Kenneth Koedinger, Nirmal Patel, Sharan Shodhan, Nikhil Poonwala, Jodi L. Forlizzi, *Carnegie Mellon University*

1040 Why is This Happening to Me? How Player Attribution can Broaden our Understanding of Player Experience
Ansgar E. Depping, Regan L. Mandryk, *University of Sakatchewan*

1053 Keeping Users Engaged through Feature Updates: A Long-Term Study of Using Wearable-Based Exergames
Zhao Zhao, Ali Arya, Anthony Whitehead, Gerry Chan, S. Ali Etemad, *Carleton University*

Session: Self-Monitored Healthcare

1065 Supporting the Self-Management of Chronic Pain Conditions with Tailored Momentary Self-Assessments
Phil Adams, Elizabeth L. Murnane, Michael Elfenbein, Elaine Wethington, Geri Gay, *Cornell University*

1078 Supporting Self-Care of Adolescents with Nut Allergy Through Video and Mobile Educational Tools
Neil Alexander Davidson, *Newcastle University & Great North Children's Hospital*
John Vines, *Northumbria University*
Tom Bartindale, *Newcastle University*
Selina Sutton, David Philip Green, *Northumbria University*
Rob Comber, Madeline Balaam, Patrick Olivier, *Newcastle University*
Gillian Vance, *Newcastle University & Great North Children's Hospital*

Session: Toolkits and UIs

1093 AVUI: Designing a Toolkit for Audiovisual Interfaces
Nuno N. Correia, *University of Madeira*
Atau Tanaka, *University of London*

Table of Contents

1105 **Suggesting API Usage to Novice Programmers with the Example Guru**
Michelle Ichinco, Wint Yee Hnin, Caitlin L. Kelleher, *Washington University in St. Louis*

1118 **Toward Everyday Gaze Input: Accuracy and Precision of Eye Tracking and Implications for Design**
Anna Maria Feit, *Aalto University & Microsoft Research*
Shane Williams, *Microsoft Research*
Arturo Toledo, *Microsoft Research & Toledo Design*
Ann Paradiso, Harish Kulkarni, *Microsoft Research*
Shaun Kane, *Microsoft Research & University of Colorado*
Meredith Ringel Morris, *Microsoft Research*

1131 **Heat-Nav: Using Temperature Changes as Navigation Cues**
Jordan Tewell, Jon Bird, *City University of London*
George R. Buchanan, *University of Melbourne*

1136 **CodePilot: Scaffolding End-to-End Collaborative Software Development for Novice Programmers**
Jeremy Warner, *University of California, Berkeley*
Philip J. Guo, *University of California, San Diego*

Session: Uniqueness of Geographic Information

1142 **Crowdsourcing GO: Effect of Worker Situation on Mobile Crowdsourcing Performance**
Kazushi Ikeda, Keiichiro Hoashi, *KDDI Research, Inc.*

1154 **Understanding "Death by GPS": A Systematic Study of Catastrophic Incidents Associated with Personal Navigation Technologies**
Allen Yilun Lin, *Northwestern University*
Kate Kuehl, *University of Minnesota*
Johannes Schöning, *University of Bremen*
Brent Hecht, *Northwestern University*

1167 **The Effect of Population and "Structural" Biases on Social Media-based Algorithms – A Case Study in Geolocation Inference Across the Urban-Rural Spectrum**
Isaac Johnson, *Northwestern University*
Connor McMahon, *University of Minnesota*
Johannes Schöning, *University of Bremen*
Brent Hecht, *Northwestern University*

1179 **The Geography of Pokémon GO: Beneficial and Problematic Effects on Places and Movement**
Ashley Colley, *University of Lapland*
Jacob Thebault-Spieker, *University of Minnesota*
Allen Yilun Lin, *Northwestern University*
Donald Degraen, *Saarland University*
Benjamin Fischman, *University of Minnesota*
Jonna Häkkilä, *University of Lapland*
Kate Kuehl, *University of Minnesota*
Valentina Nisi, Nuno Jardim Nunes, *Madeira Interactive Technologies Institute*
Nina Wenig, Dirk Wenig, *University of Bremen*
Brent Hecht, *Northwestern University*
Johannes Schöning, *University of Bremen*

Session: Visual Perception based Decisions

1193 **Empirical Analysis of the Subjective Impressions and Objective Measures of Domain Scientists' Visual Analytic Judgments**
Aritra Dasgupta, Susannah Burrows, Kyungsik Han, Philip J. Rasch, *Pacific Northwest National Lab*

1205 **A Cognitive Model of How People Make Decisions Through Interaction with Visual Displays**
Xiuli Chen, Sandra Dorothee Starke, Andrew Howes, Chris Baber, *University of Birmingham*

1217 **Building with Data: Architectural Models as Inspiration for Data Physicalization**
Carmen Hull, Wesley Willett, *University of Calgary*

Session: All about Data

1265 **Variolite: Supporting Exploratory Programming by Data Scientists**
Mary Beth Kery, *Carnegie Mellon University*
Amber Horvath, *Oregon State Unviersity*
Brad Myers, *Carnegie Mellon University*

1277 **The Trials and Tribulations of Working with Structured Data - a Study on Information Seeking Behaviour**
Laura M. Koesten, Emilia Kacprzak, *The Open Data Institute & University of Southampton*
Jenifer F. A. Tennison, *The Open Data Institute*
Elena Simperl, *University of Southampton*

1290 **Same Stats, Different Graphs: Generating Datasets with Varied Appearance and Identical Statistics through Simulated Annealing**
Justin Matejka, George Fitzmaurice, *Autodesk Research*

1295 **Inferring Cognitive Models from Data using Approximate Bayesian Computation**
Antti Kangasrääsiö, Kumaripaba Athukorala, *Aalto University*
Andrew Howes, *University of Birmingham*
Jukka Corander, *University of Oslo*
Samuel Kaski, Antti Oulasvirta, *Aalto University*

1307 **Effects of Frequency Distribution on Linear Menu Performance**
Wanyu Liu, *CNRS, Telecom ParisTech,Université Paris-Saclay & University Paris-Sud, Inria*
Gilles Bailly, *CNRS, Telecom ParisTech, Université Paris-Saclay & Sorbonne Universités*
Andrew Howes, *University of Birmingham*

Session: Design and Cognitive Impairment

1313 **DemYouth: Co-Designing and Enacting Tools to Support Young People's Engagement with People with Dementia**
Roisin McNaney, *Lancaster University*
John Vines, *Northumbria University*
Jamie Mercer, Leon Mexter,, *Youth Focus North East*
Daniel Welsh, Tony Young, *Newcastle University*

Table of Contents

1326 **The Value of Experience-Centred Design Approaches in Dementia Research Contexts**
Kellie Morrissey, *Newcastle University*
John McCarthy, Nadia Pantidi, *University College Cork*

1339 **Connecting Those That Care: Designing for Transitioning, Talking, Belonging and Escaping**
Kiel Long, *Newcastle University*
Lyndsey L. Bakewell, *Loughborough University*
Roisin C. McNaney, *Lancaster University*
Konstantina Vasileiou, *University of Bath*
Mark Atkinson, Manuela Barreto, *University of Exeter*
Julie Barnett, *University of Bath*
Michael Wilson, *Loughborough University*
Shaun Lawson, John Vines, *Northumbria University*

1352 **Designing Game-Based Myoelectric Prosthesis Training**
Aaron Tabor, Scott Bateman, Erik Scheme, *University of New Brunswick*
David R. Flatla, *University of Dundee*
Kathrin Gerling, *University of Lincoln*

Session: Evaluating Visual Perceptions

1364 **Affective Color in Visualization**
Lyn Bartram, Abhisekh Patra,, *Simon Fraser University*
Maureen Stone, *Tableau Software*

1375 **Explaining the Gap: Visualizing One's Predictions Improves Recall and Comprehension of Data**
Yea-Seul Kim, Katharina Reinecke, Jessica Hullman, *University of Washington*

1387 **Regression by Eye: Estimating Trends in Bivariate Visualizations**
Michael Correll, Jeffrey Heer, *University of Washington*

1397 **Evaluating Perceptually Complementary Views for Network Exploration Tasks**
Chunlei Chang, Benjamin Bach, Tim Dwyer, Kim Marriott, *Monash University*

Session: HCI/UX Education and Industry

1408 **How Design-inclusive UXR Influenced the Integration of Project Activities: Three Design Cases from Industry**
Janne van Kollenburg, *Philips Design & Eindhoven University of Technology*
Sander Bogers, *Eindhoven University of Technology & Philips Design*
Eva Deckers, *Philips Design*
Joep Frens, Caroline Hummels, *Eindhoven University of Technology*

1419 **Augmented Studio: Projection Mapping on Moving Body for Physiotherapy Education**
Thuong Hoang, Martin Reinoso, Zaher Joukhadar, Frank Vetere, David Kelly *University of Melbourne*

1431 **Facilitating Development of Pragmatic Competence through a Voice-driven Video Learning Interface**
Gabriel Culbertson, Solace Shen, Malte Jung, Erik Andersen, *Cornell University*

1441 **Advancing UX Education: A Model for Integrated Studio Pedagogy**
Mihaela Vorvoreanu, Colin M. Gray, Paul Parsons, Nancy Rasche, *Purdue University*

Session: Novel Game Interfaces

1447 **Bendtroller: An Exploration of In-Game Action Mappings with a Deformable Game Controller**
Paden Shorey, Audrey Girouard, *Carleton University*

1459 **Inner Garden: Connecting Inner States to a Mixed Reality Sandbox for Mindfulness**
Joan Sol Roo, Renaud Gervais, *Inria*
Jeremy Frey, *University of Bordeaux*
Martin Hachet, *Inria*

1471 **Providing Haptics to Walls & Heavy Objects in Virtual Reality by Means of Electrical Muscle Stimulation**
Pedro Lopes, Sijing You, Lung-Pan Cheng, Sebastian Marwecki, Patrick Baudisch, *Hasso Plattner Institute*

1483 **It wasn't really about the Pokémon: Parents' Perspectives on a Location-Based Mobile Game**
Kiley Sobel, Arpita Bhattacharya, Alexis Hiniker, Jin Ha Lee, Julie A. Kientz, Jason C. Yip, *University of Washington*

Session: Novel Interfaces

1497 **Placing and Recalling Virtual Items on the Skin**
Joanna Bergstrom-Lehtovirta, Sebastian Boring, Kasper Hornbæk, *University of Copenhagen*

1508 **FLIPPIN' : Exploring a Paper-based Book UI Design in a Public Space**
Koichi Yoshino, Koichi Obata, *Toppan Printing Co., Ltd.*
Satoru Tokuhisa, *Yamaguchi University*

1518 **Designing Interactive Advertisements for Public Displays**
Hasibullah Sahibzada, Eva Hornecker, Florian Echtler, Patrick Tobias Fischer, *Bauhaus-Universität Weimar*

Session: Players, Spectators, Communities

1530 **Don't Talk Dirty to Me: How Sexist Beliefs Affect Experience in Sexist Games**
Jason T. Bowey, Ansgar E. Depping, Regan L. Mandryk, *University of Saskatchewan*

1544 **Understanding Gaming Perceptions and Experiences in a Women's College Community**
Orit Shaer, Lauren Westendorf, Nicholas A. Knouf, *Wellesley College*
Claudia Pederson, *Wichita State University*

1558 **Ways of Spectating: Unravelling Spectator Participation in Kinect Play**
Burak S. Tekin, *University of Basel*
Stuart Reeves, *The University of Nottingham*

1571 **Expanding Video Game Live-Streams with Enhanced Communication Channels: A Case Study**
Pascal Lessel, *Saarland Informatics Campus*
Alexander Vielhauer, *Saarland University*
Antonio Krüger, *Saarland Informatics Campus*

Table of Contents

1577 **"These are not my hands!": Effect of Gender on the Perception of Avatar Hands in Virtual Reality**
Valentin Schwind, Pascal Knierim, Cagri Tasci, Patrick Franczak, Nico Haas, Niels Henze, *University of Stuttgart*

Session: Smart Monitoring in Physical Spaces

1583 **Looking Inside the Wires: Understanding Museum Visitor Learning with an Augmented Circuit Exhibit**
Elham Beheshti, David Kim, Gabrielle Ecanow, Michael S. Horn, *Northwestern University*

1595 **Log it While it's Hot: Designing Human Interaction with Smart Thermostats for Shared Work Environments**
Stephen Snow, Frederik Auffenberg, m.c. schraefel, *University of Southampton*

1607 **Community-Empowered Air Quality Monitoring System**
Yen-Chia Hsu, Paul Dille, Jennifer Cross, Beatrice Dias, Randy Sargent, Illah Nourbakhsh, *Carnegie Mellon University*

1620 **The Catch(es) with Smart Home – Experiences of a Living Lab Field Study**
Timo Jakobi, *Bonn-Rhein-Sieg University of Applied Science & University of Siegen*
Corinna Ogonowski, *University of Siegen*
Nico Castelli, Gunnar Stevens, *Bonn-Rhein-Sieg University of Applied Science & University of Siegen*
Volker Wulf, *University of Siegen & Fraunhofer Institute for Applied Information Technology*

Session: Social Computing and Health

1634 **A Social Media Based Index of Mental Well-Being in College Campuses**
Shrey Bagroy, Ponnurangam Kumaraguru,, *IIIT-Delhi*
Munmun De Choudhury, *Georgia Institute of Technology*

1647 **When Fitness Meets Social Networks: Investigating Fitness Tracking and Social Practices on WeRun**
Xinning Gui, Yu Chen, Clara Caldeira, *University of California, Irvine*
Dan Xiao, *Shenzhen Polytechnic*
Yunan Chen, *University of California, Irvine*

1660 **Be Grateful You Don't Have a Real Disease": Understanding Rare Disease Relationships"**
Haley MacLeod, Grace Bastin, Leslie S. Liu, Katie Siek, Kay Connelly, *Indiana University*

1674 **When Personal Tracking Becomes Social: Examining the Use of Instagram for Healthy Eating**
Chia-Fang Chung, Elena Agapie, Jessica Schroeder, Sonali Mishra, James Fogarty, Sean Munson, *University of Washington*

Session: Supporting Local Space

1688 **Participatory Media: Creating Spaces for Storytelling in Neighbourhood Planning**
Jennifer Manuel, Geoff Vigar, Tom Bartindale, Rob Comber, *Newcastle University*

1702 **Block Party: Synchronized Planning and Navigation Views for Neighbourhood Expeditions**
Huiyuan Zhou, Aisha Edrah, Bonnie MacKay, Derek Reilly, *Dalhousie University*

1714 **Designing for Cohabitation: Naturecultures, Hybrids, and Decentering the Human in Design**
Nancy Smith, Shaowen Bardzell, Jeffrey Bardzell, *Indiana University*

1726 **Stranger Searching in a Strange Land: The Impact of Familiarity on Local Search**
Isaac Johnson, *Northwestern University*
Victoria Schwanda Sosik, Kacey Ballard, *Google, Inc.*

Session: Temperature Interfaces

1731 **Ambiotherm: Enhancing Sense of Presence in Virtual Reality by Simulating Real-World Environmental Conditions**
Nimesha Ranasinghe, Pravar Jain, Shienny Karwita, David Tolley, *National University of Singapore*
Ellen Yi-Luen Do, *National University of Singapore & Georgia Institute of Technology*

1743 **Multi-moji: Combining Thermal, Vibrotactile & Visual Stimuli to Expand the Affective Range of Feedback**
Graham Wilson, Stephen A. Brewster, *University of Glasgow*

1756 **The Heat is On: A Temperature Display for Conveying Affective Feedback**
Jordan Tewell, Jon Bird, *City University of London*
George R. Buchanan, *The University of Melbourne*

1768 **Exploring Novice Approaches to Smartphone-based Thermographic Energy Auditing: A Field Study**
Matthew Louis Mauriello, Manaswi Saha, Erica Brown Brown, Jon E. Froehlich, *University of Maryland*

Session: Behavior in Online Communities

1781 **"People Are Either Too Fake or Too Real": Opportunities and Challenges in Tie-Based Anonymity**
Xiao Ma, *Cornell Tech*
Nazanin Andalibi, *Drexel University*
Louise Barkhuus, *The IT University of Copenhagen*
Mor Naaman, *Cornell Tech*

Session: Connect, Move, Touch, Build

1794 **Environment-Scale Fabrication: Replicating Outdoor Climbing Experiences**
Emily Whiting, *Dartmouth College*
Nada Ouf, *University of Pennsylvania*
Liane Makatura, Christos Mousas, *Dartmouth College*
Zhenyu Shu, *Zhejiang University*
Ladislav Kavan, *University of Utah*

1805 **Why Tangibility Matters: A Design Case Study of At-Risk Children Learning to Read and Spell**
Min Fan, Alissa N. Antle, Maureen Hoskyn, Carman Neustaedter, Emily S. Cramer, *Simon Fraser University*

Table of Contents

1817 **WeBuild: Automatically Distributing Assembly Tasks Among Collocated Workers to Improve Coordination**
C. Ailie Fraser, *Autodesk Research & University of California, San Diego*
Tovi Grossman, George Fitzmaurice, *Autodesk Research*

1831 **Pressure-Based Gain Factor Control for Mobile 3D Interaction using Locally-Coupled Devices**
Lonni Besançon, *Inria & Université Paris Saclay*
Mehdi Ammi, *LIMSI-CNRS*
Tobias Isenberg, *Inria*

Session: Crowd-powered Systems

1843 **The Effect of Peripheral Micro-tasks on Crowd Ideation**
Victor Girotto, Erin Walker, *Arizona State University*
Winslow Burleson, *New York University*

1855 **Respeak: A Voice-based, Crowd-powered Speech Transcription System**
Aditya Vashistha, Pooja Sethi, Richard Anderson
University of Washington

1867 **Subcontracting Microwork**
Meredith Ringel Morris, *Microsoft Research*
Jeffrey P. Bigham, *Carnegie Mellon University*
Robin Brewer, *Northwestern University*
Jonathan Bragg, *University of Washington*
Anand Kulkarni, *University of California, Berkeley*
Jessie Li, *Carnegie Mellon University*
Saiph Savage, *West Virginia University*

1877 **Scalable Annotation of Fine-Grained Categories Without Experts**
Timnit Gebru, Jonathan Krause, *Stanford University*
Jia Deng, *University of Michigan*
Li Fei-Fei, *Stanford University*

1882 **The Effect of Performance Feedback on Social Media Sharing at Volunteer-Based Online Experiment Platforms**
Bernd Huber, *Harvard University*
Katharina Reinecke, *University of Washington*
Krzysztof Z. Gajos, *Harvard University*

Session: Gesture as Input

1887 **Toward Realistic Hands Gesture Interface: Keeping it Simple for Developers and Machines**
Eyal Krupka, Kfir Karmon, Noam Bloom, Daniel Freedman, Ilya Gurvich, Aviv Hurvitz, Ido Leichter, Yoni Smolin, Yuval Tzairi, Alon Vinnikov, *Microsoft Research*
Aharon Bar-Hillel, *Ben-Gurion University*

1899 **Memory in Motion: The Influence of Gesture- and Touch-Based Input Modalities on Spatial Memory**
Johannes Zagermann, Ulrike Pfeil, Daniel Fink, Philipp von Bauer, Harald Reiterer, *University of Konstanz*

1911 ***EarFieldSensing*: A Novel In-Ear Electric Field Sensing to Enrich Wearable Gesture Input through Facial Expressions**
Denys J.C. Matthies, Bernhard A. Strecker, *Fraunhofer IGD Rostock*
Bodo Urban, *Fraunhofer IGD Rostock*

1923 **EchoFlex: Hand Gesture Recognition using Ultrasound Imaging**
Jess McIntosh, Asier Marzo, Mike Fraser, *University of Bristol*
Carol Phillips, *University Hospitals Bristol NHS Foundation Trust*

Session: Human Performance Gaming

1935 **Virtuosos on the Screen: Playing Virtual Characters Like Instruments in Competitive Super Smash Bros. Melee**
Colin M. Ford, *University of California, Irvine*

1949 **Designing Leaderboards for Gamification: Perceived Differences Based on User Ranking, Application Domain, and Personality Traits**
Yuan Jia, Yikun Liu, Xing Yu, *Indiana University at Indianapolis*
Stephen Voida, *University of Colorado, Boulder*

1961 **Inferring Motion Direction using Commodity Wi-Fi for Interactive Exergames**
Kun Qian, Chenshu Wu, *Tsinghua University*
Zimu Zhou, *Eidgenössische Technische Hochschule (ETH)*
Yue Zheng, Zheng Yang, Yunhao Liu, *Tsinghua University*

1973 **Be Me or Be Mii?: A Study of Self-Presentation and Interaction in the Miitomo Mobile Application**
Anna Kasunic, Geoff Kaufman, *Carnegie Mellon University*

1978 **Why Players use Pings and Annotations in Dota 2**
Jason Wuertz, Scott Bateman, *University of New Brunswick*
Anthony Tang, *University of Calgary*

Session: Interdisciplinary Techniques

2019 **Unpacking Visible Light Communication as a Material for Design**
Charles Windlin, *KTH Royal Institute of Technology*
Jarmo Laaksolahti, *KTH Royal Institute of Technology & Mobile Life @ SICS*

2024 **Tobiko: A Contact Array for Self-Configuring, Surface-Powered Sensors**
C. K. Harnett, *University of Louisville*

2029 **Live Physiological Sensing and Visualization Ecosystems: An Activity Theory Analysis**
Tamara Clegg, Leyla Norooz, Seokbin Kang, Monica Katzen, Virginia Byrne, Rafael Valez, Angelisa Plane, Vanessa Oguamanam, Thomas Outing, *University of Maryland, College Park*
Jason Yip, *University of Washington*
Elizabeth Bonsignore, Jon Froehlich, *University of Maryland, College Park*

2042 **Thin Grey Lines: Confrontations With Risk on Colorado's Front Range**
Robert Soden, Leah Sprain, Leysia Palen, *University of Colorado, Boulder*

Table of Contents

2054 Deconstructing Cosmetic Virtual Goods Experiences in Dota 2
Ilya Musabirov, Denis Bulygin, *National Research University Higher School of Economics*
Paul Okopny, *Uppsala University*
Alexander Sirotkin, *National Research University Higher School of Economics*

2059 Shift+Tap or Tap+LongPress? The Upper Bound of Typing Speed on InScript
Sanjay Ghosh, Anirudha Joshi, Manjiri Joshi, Nagraj Emmadi, Girish Dalvi, Shashank Ahire, Swati Rangale, *Indian Institute of Technology, Bombay*

Session: It Could Be This Way

2064 Evaluation of Prototypes and the Problem of Possible Futures
Antti Salovaara, *University of Helsinki & Aalto University*
Antti Oulasvirta, *Aalto University*
Giulio Jacucci, *University of Helsinki*

2078 Situated Dissemination through an HCI Workplace
Ko-Le Chen, *Newcastle University*
Rachel Clarke, *Twisted Digits*
Teresa Almeida, Matthew Wood, *Newcastle University*
David S. Kirk, *Northumbria University*

2091 A Survey of the Trajectories Conceptual Framework: Investigating Theory Use in HCI
Raphael Velt, Steve Benford, Stuart Reeves, *The University of Nottingham*

2106 ProtoMold: An Interactive Vacuum Forming System for Rapid Prototyping
Junichi Yamaoka, Yasuaki Kakehi, *Keio University*

Session: Methods and Theories

2116 Extracting Gait Velocity and Stride Length from Surrounding Radio Signals
Chen-Yu Hsu, *Massachusetts Institute of Technology*
Yuchen Liu, *Hong Kong University of Science and Technology*
Zachary Kabelac, Rumen Hristov, Dina Katabi, *Massachusetts Institute of Technology*
Christine Liu, *Boston University School of Medicine*

2127 Personas and Behavioral Theories: A Case Study Using Self-Determination Theory to Construct Overweight Personas
Arne Jansen, Maarten Van Mechelen, Karin Slegers, *KU Leuven - imec*

Session: Perspectives on Cognitive Impairment

2137 Designing for the "Universe of One": Personalized Interactive Media Systems for People with the Severe Cognitive Impairment Associated with Rett Syndrome
Anthony Hornof, Haley Whitman, Marah Sutherland, Samuel Gerendasy *University of Oregon*
Joanna McGrenere, *University of Brisith Columbia*

2149 Supporting People with Dementia in Digital Social Sharing
Amanda Lazar, *Northwestern University*
Caroline Edasis, *Mather LifeWays*
Anne Marie Piper, *Northwestern University*

2163 Care and Connect: Exploring Dementia-Friendliness Through an Online Community Commissioning Platform
Kellie Morrissey, Andrew Garbett, Peter Wright, Patrick Olivier, Edward Ian Jenkins, *Newcastle University*
Katie Brittain, *Northumbria University*

2175 A Critical Lens on Dementia and Design in HCI
Amanda Lazar, *Northwestern University*
Caroline Edasis, *Mather LifeWays*
Anne Marie Piper, *Northwestern University*

Session: Precautionary Behaviors

2189 Stories from Survivors: Privacy & Security Practices when Coping with Intimate Partner Abuse
Tara Matthews, Kathleen O'Leary, Anna Turner, Manya Sleeper, Jill Palzkill Woelfer, Martin Shelton, *Google*
Cori Manthorne, *Community Overcoming Relationship Abuse*
Elizabeth F. Churchill, Sunny Consolvo, *Google*

2202 Self-Confidence Trumps Knowledge: A Cross-Cultural Study of Security Behavior
Yukiko Sawaya, *KDDI Research, Inc.*
Mahmood Sharif, Nicolas Christin, *Carnegie Mellon University*
Ayumu Kubota, Akihiro Nakarai, Akira Yamada, *KDDI Research, Inc.*

2215 What Do We Really Know about How Habituation to Warnings Occurs Over Time? A Longitudinal fMRI Study of Habituation and Polymorphic Warnings
Anthony Vance, Brock Kirwan, Daniel Bjorn, Jeffrey Jenkins, Bonnie Brinton Anderson, *Brigham Young University*

2228 Can People Self-Report Security Accurately? Agreement Between Self-Report and Behavioral Measures
Rick Wash, Emilee Rader, Chris Fennell, *Michigan State University*

2233 Toward Harmonizing Self-reported and Logged Social Data for Understanding Human Behavior
Vivek K. Singh, *Rutgers University*
Arushi Jain, *Indian Institute of Technology*

Session: Second Screen

2239 HeartChat: Heart Rate Augmented Mobile Chat to Support Empathy and Awareness
Mariam Hassib, *University of Stuttgart & LMU Munich*
Daniel Buschek, *LMU Munich*
Paweł W. Woźniak, *University of Stuttgart*
Florian Alt, *LMU Munich*

Table of Contents

2252 "I've been manipulated!": Designing Second Screen Experiences for Critical Viewing of Reality TV
Tom Feltwell, Gavin Wood, *Northumbria University*
Kiel Long, *Newcastle University*
Phillip Brooker, *University of Bath*
Tom Schofield, *Newcastle University*
Ioannis Petridis, *Northumbria University*
Julie Barnett, *University of Bath*
John Vines, Shaun Lawson, *Northumbria University*

2264 Interaction with a TV Companion App as Synopsis and Supplement
John Dowell, Edward Anstead, *University College London*

2269 Social Printers: A Physical Social Network for Political Debates
Katerina Gorkovenko, Nick Taylor, Jon Rogers, *University of Dundee*

Session: Civic Technology

2282 A City in Common: A Framework to Orchestrate Large-scale Citizen Engagement around Urban Issues
Mara Balestrini, Yvonne Rogers, *University College London*
Carolyn Hassan, *Knowle West Media Centre*
Javi Creus, *Ideas for Change*
Martha King, *Knowle West Media Centre*
Paul Marshall, *University College London*

2295 Creating a Sociotechnical API: Designing City-Scale Community Engagement
Mariam Asad, Christopher A. Le Dantec, *Georgia Institute of Technology*
Becky Nielsen, *IT University of Copenhagen*
Kate Diedrick, *Solidarity Research Cooperative*

2306 Empowered Participation: How Citizens Use Technology in Local Governance
Sheena Erete, *DePaul University*
Jennifer O. Burrell, *MadX, LLC.*

2320 Community Conversational: Supporting and Capturing Political Deliberation in Local Consultation Processes
Ian G. Johnson, *Newcastle University*
Alistair MacDonald, *Northumbria University & Newcastle University*
Jo Briggs, *Northumbria University*
Jennifer Manuel, *Newcastle University*
Karen Salt, *Nottingham University*
Emma Flynn, *Durham University*
John Vines, *Northumbria University*

Session: Crowdfunding and Crowdsourcing

2334 Revolt: Collaborative Crowdsourcing for Labeling Machine Learning Datasets
Joseph Chee Chang, *Carnegie Mellon University*
Saleema Amershi, Ece Kamar, *Microsoft Research*

2347 VoxPL: Programming with the Wisdom of the Crowd
Daniel W. Barowy, *University of Massachusetts*
Emery D. Berger, *University of Massachusetts, Amherst*
Daniel G. Goldstein, Siddharth Suri, *Microsoft Research*

2359 Embedding a Crowd inside a Relay Baton: A Case Study in a Non-Competitive Sporting Activity
Franco Curmi, Maria Angela Ferrario, Jon Whittle, *Lancaster University*

2371 Prioritizing Flexibility and Intangibles: Medical Crowdfunding for Stigmatized Individuals
Amy Gonzales, Nicole Fritz, *Indiana University*

2376 Understanding the Effects of Endorsements in Scientific Crowdfunding
Sanorita Dey, *University of Illinois at Urbana-Champaign*
Karrie Karahalios, *University of Illinois at Urbana-Champaign & Adobe Systems*
Wai-Tat Fu, *University of Illinois at Urbana-Champaign*

Session: Designing for the Workplace

2382 Calendar.help: Designing a Workflow-Based Scheduling Agent with Humans in the Loop
Justin Cranshaw, Emad Elwany, Todd Newman, *Microsoft Research*
Rafal Kocielnik, *University of Washington*
Bowen Yu, *University of Minnesota*
Sandeep Soni, *Georgia Institute of Technology*
Jaime Teevan, Andrés Monroy-Hernandez, *Microsoft Research*

2394 Conversational Chat Circles: Being All Here Without Having to Hear It All
Matthew K. Miller, *Microsoft Research & University of Saskatchewan*
John C. Tang, Gina Venolia, *Microsoft Research*
Gerard Wilkinson, *Microsoft Resaerch & Newcastle University*
Kori Inkpen, *Microsoft Research*

2405 A Predictive Model of Emergency Physician Task Resumption Following Interruptions
Allan Fong, *National Center for Human Factors in Healthcare*
A. Zachary Hettinger, *Georgetown University School of Medicine*
Raj M. Ratwani, *National Center for Human Factors in Healthcare & Georgetown University School of Medicine*

2411 Undertanding and Detecting Divided Attention in Mobile MOOC Learning
Xiang Xiao, Jingtao Wang, *University of Pittsburgh*

Session: Designing Haptic Interfaces

2416 PinPad: Touchpad Interaction with Fast and High-Resolution Tactile Output
Jingun Jung, Eunhye Youn, Geehyuk Lee, *Korea Advanced Institute of Science and Technology*

2426 Agency in Mid-air Interfaces
Patricia Cornelio Martinez, Silvana De Pirro, Chi Thanh Vi, Sriram Subramanian, *University of Sussex*

2440 Frozen Suit: Designing a Changeable Stiffness Suit and its Application to Haptic Games
Ahmed Al Maimani, Anne Roudaut, *University of Bristol*

Table of Contents

2449 Haptic-Enabled Handheld Mobile Robots: Design and Analysis
Ayberk Özgür Wafa Johal, Francesco Mondada, Pierre Dillenbourg, *École Polytechnique Fédérale de Lausanne*

Session: Exertion, Sport, Bodies

2462 A Thing of Beauty: Steering Behavior in an Interactive Playground
Robby van Delden, Alejandro Moreno, Ronald Poppe, Dennis Reidsma, Dirk Heylen, *University of Twente*

2473 Five Lenses for Designing Exertion Experiences
Florian 'Floyd' Mueller, Damon Young, *RMIT University*

2488 Recording and Sharing Non-Visible Information on Body Movement while Skateboarding
Hyung Kun Park, HyeonBeom Yi, Woohun Lee, *Korea Advanced Institute of Science and Technology*

2493 The Pokémon GO Experience: A Location-Based Augmented Reality Mobile Game Goes Mainstream
Janne Paavilainen, Hannu Korhonen, Kati Alha, Jaakko Stenros, Elina Koskinen, Frans Mayra, *University of Tampere*

Session: Human Computer Integration

2499 Manifesting the Cyborg through Techno-Body Modification: From Human-Computer Interaction to Integration
Lauren M. Britton, Bryan Semaan, *Syracuse University*

2511 Factors in Fairness and Emotion in Online Case Resolution Systems
Youyang Hou, Cliff Lampe, Maximilian Bulinski, J.J. Prescott, *University of Michigan*

2523 Us vs. Them: Understanding Artificial Intelligence Technophobia over the Google DeepMind Challenge Match
Changhoon Oh, Taeyoung Lee, Yoojung Kim, SoHyun Park, *Seoul National University*
Sae bom Kwon, *Sogang University*
Bongwon Suh, *Seoul National University*

Session: Improving Gaze Mechanisms

2535 Tell Me Where to Look: Investigating Ways for Assisting Focus in 360° Video
Yen-Chen Lin, Yung-Ju Chang, Hou-Ning Hu, Hsien-Tzu Cheng, Chi-Wen Huang, Min Sun, *National Tsing Hua University*

2546 ScreenGlint: Practical, In-situ Gaze Estimation on Smartphones
Michael Xuelin Huang, Jiajia Li, Grace Ngai, Hong Va Leong, *The Hong Kong Polytechnic University*

2558 Improving Dwell-Based Gaze Typing with Dynamic, Cascading Dwell Times
Martez E. Mott, *University of Washington*
Shane Williams, *Microsoft Research*
Jacob O. Wobbrock, *University of Washington*
Meredith Ringel Morris, *Microsoft Research*

2571 Looking Coordinated: Bidirectional Gaze Mechanisms for Collaborative Interaction with Virtual Characters
Sean Andrist, *Microsoft Research*
Michael Gleicher, Bilge Mutlu, *University of Wisconsin-Madison*

Session: Innovative Fabrication Techniques

2583 Pineal: Bringing Passive Objects to Life with Embedded Mobile Devices
David Ledo, *Autodesk Research & University of Calgary*
Fraser Anderson, Ryan Schmidt, *Autodesk Research*
Lora Oehlberg, Saul Greenberg, *University of Calgary*
Tovi Grossman, *Autodesk Research*

2594 CalibMe: Fast and Unsupervised Eye Tracker Calibration for Gaze-Based Pervasive Human-Computer Interaction
Thiago Santini, Wolfgang Fuhl, Enkelejda Kasneci, *University of Tübingen*

2606 TrussFab: Fabricating Sturdy Large-Scale Structures on Desktop 3D Printers
Robert Kovacs, Anna Seufert, Ludwig Wall, Hsiang-Ting Chen, Florian Meinel, Willi Müller, Sijing You, Maximilian Brehm, Jonathan Striebel, Yannis Kommana, Alexander Popiak, Thomas Bläsius, Patrick Baudisch, *Hasso-Plattner-Institute*

2617 StretchEBand: Enabling Fabric-based Interactions through Rapid Fabrication of Textile Stretch Sensors
Anita Vogl, Patrick Parzer, Teo Babic, Joanne Leong, *University of Applied Sciences Upper Austria*
Alex Olwal, *Google, Inc.*
Michael Haller, *University of Applied Sciences Upper Austria*

Session: Intelligent Visualization Systems

2628 GraphScape: A Model for Automated Reasoning about Visualization Similarity and Sequencing
Younghoon Kim, Kanit Wongsuphasawat, Jessica Hullman, Jeffrey Heer, *University of Washington*

2639 GIAnT: Visualizing Group Interaction at Large Wall Displays
Ulrich von Zadow, Raimund Dachselt, *Technische Universität Dresden*

2648 Voyager 2: Augmenting Visual Analysis with Partial View Specifications
Kanit Wongsuphasawat, Zening Qu, Dominik Moritz, Riley Chang, Felix Ouk, *University of Washington*
Anushka Anand, Jock Mackinlay, *Tableau Research*
Bill Howe, Jeffrey Heer, *University of Washington*

2660 TouchPivot: Blending WIMP & Post-WIMP Interfaces for Data Exploration on Tablet Devices
Jaemin Jo, Sehi L'Yi, *Seoul National University*
Bongshin Lee, *Microsoft Research*
Jinwook Seo, *Seoul National University*

Table of Contents

Session: Mindfulness and Reflection

2672 A Framework for Interactive Mindfulness Meditation Using Attention-Regulation Process
Kavous Salehzadeh Niksirat, Chaklam Silpasuwanchai, *Kochi University of Technology*
Mahmoud Mohamed Hussien Ahmed, *Kochi University of Technology & South Valley University*
Peng Cheng, *PauseAble ApS*
Xiangshi Ren, *Kochi University of Technology*

2685 Designing Digital Mindfulness: Presence-In and Presence-With versus Presence-Through
Bin Zhu, *KTH Royal Institute of Technology & China Academy of Art*
Anders Hedman, Haibo Li, *KTH Royal Institute of Technology*

2696 Reflective Practicum: A Framework of Sensitising Concepts to Design for Transformative Reflection
Petr Slovák, Christopher Frauenberger, Geraldine Fitzpatrick, *Vienna University of Technology*

2708 mHealth for Maternal Mental Health: Everyday Wisdom in Ethical Design
Marguerite Barry, Kevin Doherty, *Trinity College Dublin*
Jose Marcano Belisario, Josip Car, *Imperial College London*
Cecily Morrison, *Imperial College London & Microsoft Research*
Gavin Doherty, *Trinity College Dublin*

Session: Supporting Low Resource Communities

2757 Uncovering the Values and Constraints of Real-time RideSharing for Low-resource Populations
Tawanna R. Dillahunt, Vaishnav Kameswaran, Linfeng Li, Tanya Rosenblat, *University of Michigan*

2770 Supporting Community Health Workers in India through Voice- and Web-Based Feedback
Brian DeRenzi, *University of Cape Town*
Nicola Dell, *Cornell Tech*
Jeremy Wacksman, *Dimagi, Inc*
Scott Lee, *Harvard University*
Neal Lesh, *Dimagi, Inc*

2782 We Play We Learn: Exploring the Value of Digital Educational Games in Rural Egypt
Shaimaa Lazem, Hussein Aly Jad, *City for Scientific Research and Technological Applications*

2792 Sidestepping the Elephant in the Classroom: Using Culturally Localized Technology to Teach Around Taboos
Piya Sorcar, Benjamin Strauber, Prashant Loyalka, *Stanford University*
Neha Kumar, *Georgia Institute of Technology*
Shelley Goldman, *Stanford University*

Session: Technology Augmented Driving

2805 What Can Be Predicted from Six Seconds of Driver Glances?
Lex Fridman, *Massachusetts Institute of Technology*
Heishiro Toyoda, *Toyota Collaborative Safety Research Center*
Sean Seaman, Bobbie Seppelt, Linda Angell, *Touchstone Evaluations*
Joonbum Lee, Bruce Mehler, Bryan Reimer, *Massachusetts Institute of Technology*

2814 Using Advisory 3D Sound Cues to Improve Drivers' Performance and Situation Awareness
MinJuan Wang, *Chalmers University of Technology*
Sus Lundgren Lyckvi, *Chalmers University of Technology & University of Gothenburg*
Chenhui Chen, *Chalmers University of Technology*
Palle Dahlstedt, *Chalmers University of Technology & University of Gothenburg*
Fang Chen, *Chalmers University of Technology*

2826 Designing Gamified Applications that Make Safe Driving More Engaging
Fabius Steinberger, Ronald Schroeter, Marcus Foth, Daniel Johnson, *Queensland University of Technology*

2840 Tunneled In: Drivers with Active Secondary Tasks Need More Time to Transition from Automation
Brian Mok, Mishel Johns, David Miller, Wendy Ju, *Stanford University*

2845 An Evaluation of Input Controls for In-Car Interactions
Alexander Ng, Stephen A. Brewster, *University of Glasgow*
Frank Beruscha, Wolfgang Krautter, *Robert Bosch GmbH*

Session: Autism, Disabilities and Assistive Technology

2853 When Empathy Is Not Enough: Assessing the Experiences of Autistic Children with Technologies
Katharina Spiel, *Vienna University of Technology*
Christopher Frauenberger, *Vienna University of Technology*
Eva Hornecker, *Bauhaus Universität Weimar*
Geraldine Fitzpatrick, *Vienna University of Technology*

2865 ProCom: Designing and Evaluating a Mobile and Wearable System to Support Proximity Awareness for People with Autism
LouAnne E. Boyd, *University of California, Irvine*
Xinlong Jiang, *University of Chinese Academy of Sciences*
Gillian R. Hayes, *University of California, Irvine*

2878 Smartphone-Based Gaze Gesture Communication for People with Motor Disabilities
Xiaoyi Zhang, *University of Washington*
Harish Kulkarni, Meredith Ringel Morris, *Microsoft Research*

Table of Contents

2890 Exploring the Design Space of AAC Awareness Displays
Kiley Sobel, Alexander Fiannaca, *University of Washington & Microsoft Research*
Jon Campbell, Harish Kulkarni, Ann Paradiso, Ed Cutrell, Meredith Ringel Morris *Microsoft Research*

Session: Big Data Intelligent Visualization Systems

2904 Trust, but Verify: Optimistic Visualizations of Approximate Queries for Exploring Big Data
Dominik Moritz, *University of Washington*
Danyel Fisher, Bolin Ding, Chi Wang, *Microsoft Research*

2916 iSphere: Focus+Context Sphere Visualization for Interactive Large Graph Exploration
Fan Du, *University of Maryland*
Nan Cao, *Tongji University*
Yu-Ru Lin, *University of Pittsburgh*
Panpan Xu, *Hong Kong University of Science and Technology*
Hanghang Tong, *Arizona State University*

2928 TagRefinery: A Visual Tool for Tag Wrangling
Christoph Kralj, *University of Vienna*
Mohsen Kamalzadeh, *Simon Fraser University*
Torsten Möller, *University of Vienna*

2940 TopoGroups: Context-Preserving Visual Illustration of Multi-Scale Spatial Aggregates
Jiawei Zhang, Abish Malik, Benjamin Ahlbrand, *Purdue University*
Niklas Elmqvist, *University of Maryland, College Park*
Ross Maciejewski, *Arizona State University*
David S. Ebert, *Purdue University*

Session: Data as Design Material

2952 A Design Perspective on Data
Melanie Feinberg, *University of North Carolina at Chapel Hill*

2964 Bitbarista: Exploring Perceptions of Data Transactions in the Internet of Things
Larissa Pschetz, Ella Tallyn, Rory Gianni, Chris Speed, *University of Edinburgh*

2976 Centralized, Parallel, and Distributed Information Processing during Collective Sensemaking
Peter Krafft, *Masschusetts Institute of Technology*
Kaitlyn Zhou, Isabelle Edwards, Kate Starbird, Emma S. Spiro, *University of Washington*

2988 Quietto: An Interactive Timepiece Molded in Concrete and Milled Wood
Kyung-Ryong Lee, Geon-il Goh, Young-Woo Park, *Ulsan National Institute of Science and Technology*

2993 Locked or Not? Mental Models of IoT Feature Interaction
Lana Yarosh, *University of Minnesota, Twin Cities*
Pamela Zave, *AT&T Labs Research*

Session: Designing Gaze-based Gestures and Features

2998 Robust Gaze Features for Enabling Language Proficiency Awareness
Jakob Karolus, Paweł W. Woźniak, *University of Stuttgart*
Lewis L. Chuang, *Max Planck Institute for Biological Cybernetics*
Albrecht Schmidt, *University of Stuttgart*

3011 A Multifaceted Study on Eye Contact based Speaker Identification in Three-party Conversations
Yu Ding, Yuting Zhang, *University of Houston*
Meihua Xiao, *East China Jiaotong University*
Zhigang Deng, *University of Houston*

3022 Supporting Making Fixations and the Effect on Gaze Gesture Performance
Howell Istance, Aulikki I. Hyrskykari, *University of Tampere*

3034 GazeEverywhere: Enabling Gaze-only User Interaction on an Unmodified Desktop PC in Everyday Scenarios
Simon Schenk, Marc Dreiser, Gerhard Rigoll, Michael Dorr, *Technische Universität München*

Session: Enabling Healthy Behaviors

3045 Trajectories of Engagement and Disengagement with a Story-Based Smoking Cessation App
Wally Smith, *The University of Melbourne*
Bernd Ploderer, *Queensland University of Technology*
Greg Wadley, Sarah Webber, *University of Melbourne*
Ron Borland, *Cancer Council Victoria*

3057 Lessons from Practice: Designing Tools to Facilitate Individualized Support for Quitting Smoking
Arpita Bhattacharya, *University of Washington*
Roger Vilardaga, *Duke University*
Julie A. Kientz, Sean A. Munson, *University of Washington*

3071 Toward Usable Evidence: Optimizing Knowledge Accumulation in HCI Research on Health Behavior Change
Predrag Klasnja, *Group Health Research Institute*
Eric B. Hekler, Elizabeth V. Korinek, John Harlow, *Arizona State University*
Sonali R. Mishra, *University of Washington*

Session: Haptics on Skin

3083 Investigating Haptic Perception of and Physiological Responses to Air Vortex Rings on a User's Cheek
Yuka Sato, Ryoko Ueoka, *Kyushu University*

3095 SkinMarks: Enabling Interactions on Body Landmarks Using Conformal Skin Electronics
Martin Weigel, Aditya Shekhar Nittala, *Saarland University*
Alex Olwal, *Google, Inc.*
Jürgen Steimle, *Saarland University*

Table of Contents

3106 tactoRing: A Skin-Drag Discrete Display
Seungwoo Je, Brendan Rooney, *Korea Advanced Institute of Science & Technology*
Liwei Chan, *National Chiao Tung University*
Andrea Bianchi, *Korea Advanced Institute of Science & Technology*

3115 Fingertip Tactile Devices for Virtual Object Manipulation and Exploration
Samuel B. Schorr, Allison M. Okamura, *Stanford University*

3120 BrushTouch: Exploring an Alternative Tactile Method for Wearable Haptics
Evan Strasnick, *Stanford University*
Jessica R. Cauchard, *Stanford University & Interdisciplinary Center, Herzliya*
James A. Landay, *Stanford University*

Session: HCI and Collective Action

3126 HCI, Solidarity Movements and the Solidarity Economy
Vasillis Vlachokyriakos, Clara Crivellaro, Pete Wright, *Newcastle University*
Evika Karamagioli, Eleni-Revekka Staiou, Dimitris Gouscos, *University of Athens*
Rowan Thorpe, *Open Lab: Athens*
Antonio Krüger, *Saarland Informatics Campus*
Johannes Schöning, *University of Bremen*
Matt Jones, *Swansea University*
Shaun Lawson, *Northumbria University*
Patrick Olivier, *Newcastle University*

3138 Environmental Protection and Agency: Motivations, Capacity, and Goals in Participatory Sensing
Paul Aoki, Allison Woodruff, *Independent*
Baladitya Yellapragada, *University of California, Berkeley*
Wesley Willett, *University of Calgary*

3151 Providing Online Crisis Information: An Analysis of Official Sources during the 2014 Carlton Complex Wildfire
Apoorva Chauhan, Amanda L. Hughes, *Utah State University*

3163 "Algorithms ruin everything": #RIPTwitter Folk Theories and Resistance to Algorithmic Change in Social Media
Michael A. DeVito, Darren Gergle, Jeremy Birnholtz, *Northwestern University*

Session: Online Content

3175 The Bag of Communities: Identifying Abusive Behavior Online with Preexisting Internet Data
Eshwar Chandrasekharan, *Georgia Institute of Technology*
Mattia Samory, *University of Padua*
Anirudh Srinivasan, Eric Gilbert, *Georgia Institute of Technology*

3187 PersaLog: Personalization of News Article Content
Eytan Adar, Carolyn Gearig, *University of Michigan, Ann Arbor*
Ayshwarya Balasubramanian, *Deloitte*
Jessica Hullman, *University of Washington*

3201 You Want Me to Work with *Who*? Stakeholder Perceptions of Automated Project-based Courses
Farnaz Jahanbakhsh, Wai-Tat Fu, Karrie Karahalios, Darko Marinov, Brian Bailey, *University of Illinois at Urbana Champaign*

3213 Multimodal Classification of Moderated Online Pro-Eating Disorder Content
Stevie Chancellor, *Georgia Institute of Technology*
Yannis Kalantidis, *Yahoo Research*
Jessica A. Pater, Munmun De Choudhury, *Georgia Institute of Technology*
David A. Shamma, *Centrum Wiskunde & Informatica (CWI)*

Session: Pens, Ink, Input

3227 *WritLarge*: Ink Unleashed by Unified Scope, Action, & Zoom
Haijun Xia, *Microsoft Research & University of Toronto*
Ken Hinckley, Michel Pahud, Xiao Tu, Bill Buxton, *Microsoft Research*

3241 *As We May Ink?* Learning from Everyday Analog Pen Use to Improve Digital Ink Experiences
Yann Riche, *Riche Design*
Nathalie Henry Riche, Ken Hinckley, Sheri Panabaker, *Microsoft*
Sarah Fuelling, *Percipient Research Microsoft*
Sarah Williams, *Auspicious Kitten Design*

3254 Thumb + Pen Interaction on Tablets
Ken Pfeuffer, *Microsoft Research & Lancaster University*
Ken Hinckley, Michel Pahud, Bill Buxton, *Microsoft Research*

3267 Experimental Analysis of Mode Switching Techniques in Touch-based User Interfaces
Hemant Bhaskar Surale, Fabrice Matulic, Daniel Vogel, *University of Waterloo*

Session: Sensing and Input

3281 ForceEdge: Controlling Autoscroll on Both Desktop and Mobile Computers Using the Force
Axel Antoine, *Inria & Université de Lille*
Sylvain Malacria, *Inria*
Géry Casiez, *Université de Lille*

3293 Finding Common Ground: A Survey of Capacitive Sensing in Human-Computer Interaction
Tobias Grosse-Puppendahl, Christian Holz, Gabe Cohn, *Microsoft Research*
Raphael Wimmer, *University of Regensburg*
Oskar Bechtold, *Technische Universität Darmstadt*
Steve Hodges, *Microsoft Research*
Matthew S. Reynolds, Joshua R. Smith, *University of Washington*

3316 bioSync: A Paired Wearable Device for Blending Kinesthetic Experience
Jun Nishida, Kenji Suzuki, *University of Tsukuba*

3328 Modeling Cumulative Arm Fatigue in Mid-Air Interaction based on Perceived Exertion and Kinetics of Arm Motion
Sujin Jang, *Purdue University*
Wolfgang Stuerzlinger, *Simon Fraser University*
Satyajit Ambike, Karthik Ramani, *Purdue University*

Table of Contents

Session: Social Justice

3340 Women's Safety in Public Spaces: Examining the Efficacy of Panic Buttons in New Delhi
Naveena Karusala, Neha Kumar, *Georgia Institute of Technology*

3352 Technologies & Social Justice Outcomes in Sex Work Charities: Fighting Stigma, Saving Lives
Angelika Strohmayer, *Newcastle University*
Mary Laing, *Northumbria University*
Rob Comber, *Newcastle University*

3365 A Human-Centered Approach to Algorithmic Services: Considerations for Fair and Motivating Smart Community Service Management that Allocates Donations to Non-Profit Organizations
Min Kyung Lee, Ji Tae Kim, *Carnegie Mellon University*
Leah Lizarondo, *412 Food Rescue*

3377 Class Confessions: Restorative Properties in Online Experiences of Socioeconomic Stigma
Eugenia Ha Rim Rho, Oliver L. Haimson, *University of California, Irvine*
Nazanin Andalibi, *Drexel University*
Melissa Mazmanian, Gillian R. Hayes, *University of California, Irvine*

Session: Wild Methods

3390 Activity as the Ultimate Particular of Interaction Design
Annika Waern, Jon Back, *Uppsala University*

3403 Intuition in Design: Reflections on the Iterative Aesthetics of Form
Haakon Faste, *California College of the Arts*

3414 Understanding Public Evaluation: Quantifying Experimenter Intervention
Julie R. Williamson, John Williamson, *University of Glasgow*

3426 Challenges in Public Display Deployments: A Taxonomy of External Factors
Ville Mäkelä, Sumita Sharma, Jaakko Hakulinen, *University of Tampere*
Tomi Heimonen, *University of Wisconsin-Stevens Point*
Markku Turunen, *University of Tampere*

Session: Chatbot Interfaces

3476 Typefaces and the Perception of Humanness in Natural Language Chatbots
Heloisa Candello, Claudio Pinhanez, *IBM Research – Brazil*
Flavio Figueiredo, *Universidade Federal de Minas Gerais*

3488 "Could You Define That in Bot Terms?": Requesting Creating and Using Bots on Reddit
Kiel Long, *Newcastle University*
John Vines, Selina Sutton, *Northumbria University*
Phillip Brooker, *University of Bath*
Tom Feltwell, *Northumbria University*
Ben Kirman, *University of York*
Julie Barnett, *University of Bath*
Shaun Lawson, *Northumbria University*

3501 Response Times when Interpreting Artificial Subtle Expressions are Shorter than with Human-like Speech Sounds
Takanori Komatsu, *Meiji University*
Kazuki Kobayashi, *Shinshu University*
Seiji Yamada, *National Institute of Informatics & SOKENDAI*
Kotaro Funakoshi, *Honda Research Institute Japan Co., Ltd.*
Mikio Nakano, *Ltd.*

3506 A New Chatbot for Customer Service on Social Media
Anbang Xu, Zhe Liu, Yufan Guo, Vibha Sinha, Rama Akkiraju, *IBM Research - Almaden*

Session: Collaborative Crowdwork

3511 CrowdVerge: Predicting If People Will Agree on the Answer to a Visual Question
Danna Gurari, Kristen Grauman, *University of Texas at Austin*

3523 Flash Organizations: Crowdsourcing Complex Work by Structuring Crowds As Organizations
Melissa A. Valentine, Daniela Retelny, *Stanford University*
Alexandra To, *Carnegie Mellon University*
Negar Rahmati, Tulsee Doshi, Michael S. Bernstein, *Stanford University*

3538 Facilitating Pervasive Community Policing on the Road with Mobile Roadwatch
Sangkeun Park, Emilia-Stefania Ilincai, Jeungmin Oh, Sujin Kwon, *Korea Advanced Institute of Science and Technology*
Rabeb Mizouni, *Khalifa University*
Uichin Lee, *Korea Advanced Institute of Science and Technology*

3551 ReTool: Interactive Microtask and Workflow Design through Demonstration
Chen Chen, Xiaojun Meng, Shengdong Zhao, *National University of Singapore*
Morten Fjeld, *Chalmers University of Technology*

Session: Contextual Smartwatch Use

3557 Always On(line)? User Experience of Smartwatches and their Role within Multi-Device Ecologies
Marta E. Cecchinato, Anna L. Cox, *University College London*
Jon Bird, *City University London*

3569 Quantifying Sources and Types of Smartwatch Usage Sessions
Aku Visuri, *University of Oulu*
Zhanna Sarsenbayeva, *University of Oulu & University of Melbourne*
Niels van Berkel, Jorge Goncalves, *University of Melbourne & University of Oulu*
Reza Rawassizadeh, *Dartmouth College*
Vassilis Kostakos, *University of Melbourne & University of Oulu*
Denzil Ferreira, *University of Oulu*

Table of Contents

3582 Situating Wearables: Smartwatch Use in Context
Donald McMillan, Barry Brown, Airi Lampinen, Moira McGregor, *Stockholm University*
Eve Hoggan, *Aarhus University*
Stefania Pizza, *Sapienza University of Rome*

3595 BreakSense: Combining Physiological and Location Sensing to Promote Mobility during Work-Breaks
Scott A. Cambo, *FXPAL & Northwestern University*
Daniel Avrahami, Matthew L. Lee, *FX Palo Alto Laboratory, Inc.*

Session: Data Culture

3608 Disempowered by Data: Nonprofits, Social Enterprises, and the Consequences of Data-Driven Work
Chris Bopp, Ellie Harmon, Amy Voida, *University of Colorado*

3620 Scratch Community Blocks: Supporting Children as Data Scientists
Sayamindu Dasgupta, *Massachusetts Institute of Technology & University of Washington*
Benjamin Mako Hill, *University of Washington*

3632 Supporting the Use of User Generated Content in Journalistic Practice
Peter Tolmie, *The University of Nottingham & University of Warwick*
Rob Procter, *Warwick University*
David William Randall, *University of Siegen*
Mark Rouncefield, *Lancaster University*
Christian Burger, Geraldine Wong Sak Hoi, *SwissInfo.ch*
Arkaitz Zubiaga, Maria Liakata, *University of Warwick*

3645 How Data Workers Cope with Uncertainty: A Task Characterisation Study
Nadia Boukhelifa, Marc-Emmanuel Perrin, Samuel Huron, James Eagan, *Université Paris-Saclay*

Session: Fabrication and DIY

3657 Cardboard Machine Kit: Modules for the Rapid Prototyping of Rapid Prototyping Machines
Nadya Peek, *Massachusetts Institute of Technology*

3669 Printflatables: Printing Human-Scale, Functional and Dynamic Inflatable Objects
Harpreet Sareen, Udayan Umapathi, Patrick Shin, *Massachusetts Institute of Technology*

3681 Sketching CuddleBits: Coupled Prototyping of Body and Behaviour for an Affective Robot Pet
Paul Bucci, Xi Laura Cang, Anasazi Valair, David Marino, Lucia Tseng, *University of British Columbia*
Merel Jung, *University of Twente*
Jussi Rantala, *University of Tampere*
Oliver S. Schneider, Karon E. MacLean, *University of British Columbia*

3693 WireDraw: 3D Wire Sculpturing Guided with Mixed Reality
Ya-Ting Yue, Xiaolong Zhang, *The University of Hong Kong*
Yongliang Yang, *University of Bath*
Gang Ren, *Xiamen University of Technology*
Yi-King Choi, Wenping Wang, *The University of Hong Kong*

Session: FnT: Personal Fabrication

This session was journal presentations. See conference program.

Session: Haptic Feedback

3705 Sparkle: Hover Feedback with Touchable Electric Arcs
Daniel Spelmezan, *University of Sussex*
Deepak Ranjan Sahoo, *University of Sussex & Swansea University*
Sriram Subramanian, *University of Sussex*

3718 Sparse Haptic Proxy: Touch Feedback in Virtual Environments Using a General Passive Prop
Lung-Pan Cheng, *Hasso Plattner Institute & Microsoft Research*
Eyal Ofek, Christian Holz, Hrvoje Benko, Andrew D. Wilson, *Microsoft Research*

3729 HapticHead: A Spherical Vibrotactile Grid around the Head for 3D Guidance in Virtual and Augmented Reality
Oliver Beren Kaul, Michael Rohs, *University of Hannover*

3741 Passive yet Expressive TouchTokens
Rafael Morales González, Caroline Appert, *Université Paris-Saclay*
Gilles Bailly, *Université Paris-Saclay & Sorbonne Universités*
Emmanuel Pietriga, *Université Paris-Saclay*

3746 Enhancing Pen-based Interaction using Electrovibration and Vibration Haptic Feedback
Qinglong Wang, *Kochi University of Technology & Jilin University*
Xiangshi Ren, *Kochi University of Technology*
Xiaoying Sun, *Jilin University*

Session: Passwords and Authentication

3751 Stay Cool! Understanding Thermal Attacks on Mobile-based User Authentication
Yomna Abdelrahman, *University of Stuttgart*
Mohamed Khamis, *LMU Munich*
Stefan Schneegass, *University of Stuttgart*
Florian Alt, *LMU Munich*

3764 Thumprint: Socially-Inclusive Local Group Authentication Through Shared Secret Knocks
Sauvik Das, Gierad Laput, Jason I. Hong, Chris Harrison, *Carnegie Mellon University*

3775 Design and Evaluation of a Data-Driven Password Meter
Blase Ur, *University of Chicago*
Felicia Alfieri, Maung Aung, Lujo Bauer, Nicolas Christin, Jessica Colnago, Lorrie Faith Cranor, Henry Dixon, Pardis Emami Naeini, Hana Habib, Noah Johnson, William Melicher, *Carnegie Mellon University*

Table of Contents

3787 Can Unicorns Help Users Compare Crypto Key Fingerprints?
Joshua Tan, Lujo Bauer, *Carnegie Mellon University*
Joseph Bonneau, *Stanford University*
Lorrie Faith Cranor, Jeremy Thomas, *Carnegie Mellon University*
Blase Ur, *University of Chicago*

Session: Social Media Privacy

3799 FDVT: Data Valuation Tool for Facebook Users
José González Cabañas, Ángel Cuevas, Rubén Cuevas, *Universidad Carlos III de Madrid*

3810 Characterizing Social Insider Attacks on Facebook
Wali Ahmed Usmani, *The University of British Columbia*
Diogo Marques, *University of Lisbon*
Ivan Beschastnikh, Konstantin Beznosov, *The University of British Columbia*
Tiago Guerreiro, Luís Carriço, *University of Lisbon*

3821 Photo Privacy Conflicts in Social Media: A Large-scale Empirical Study
Jose M. Such, *King's College, London*
Joel Porter, *Lancaster University*
Sören Preibusch, *Google, Inc.*
Adam Joinson, *University of Bath*

3833 Towards Understanding Differential Privacy: When Do People Trust Randomized Response Technique?
Brooke Bullek, Stephanie Garboski, Darakhshan J. Mir, Evan M. Peck, *Bucknell University*

3838 Was my message read?: Privacy and Signaling on Facebook Messenger
Roberto Hoyle, *Oberlin College*
Srijita Das, *Indiana University*
Apu Kapadia, *Indiana University Bloomington*
Adam J. Lee, *University of Pittsburgh*
Kami Vaniea, *The University of Edinburgh*

Session: Technology & Spatial Landmarks

3843 The Effects of Artificial Landmarks on Learning and Performance in Spatial-Memory Interfaces
Md. Sami Uddin, Carl Gutwin, *University of Saskatchewan*
Andy Cockburn, *University of Canterbury*

3856 Studying Space Use: Bringing HCI Tools to Architectural Projects
Himanshu Verma, Hamed S. Alavi, Denis Lalanne, *University of Fribourg*

3867 Locating the Internet in the Parks of Havana
Michaelanne Dye, *Georgia Institute of Technology*
David Nemer, *University of Kentucky*
Laura R. Pina, *University of Washington*
Nithya Sambasivan, *Google*
Amy S. Bruckman, Neha Kumar, *Georgia Institute of Technology*

Session: Wearable Technology

3879 TriTap: Identifying Finger Touches on Smartwatches
Hyunjae Gil, DoYoung Lee, *Ulsan National Institute of Science and Technology*
Seunggyu Im, *Jacobs University*
Ian Oakley, *Ulsan National Institute of Science and Technology*

3891 WatchSense: On- and Above-Skin Input Sensing through a Wearable Depth Sensor
Srinath Sridhar, *Max Planck Institute for Informatics*
Anders Markussen, *University of Copenhagen*
Antti Oulasvirta, *Aalto University*
Christian Theobalt, *Max Planck Institute for Informatics*
Sebastian Boring, *University of Copenhagen*

3903 Supporting Everyday Function in Chronic Pain Using Wearable Technology
Aneesha Singh, Nadia Bianchi-Berthouze, Amanda CdeC Williams, *University College London*

3916 SoPhy: A Wearable Technology for Lower Limb Assessment in Video Consultations of Physiotherapy
Deepti Aggarwal, Weiyi Zhang, Thuong Hoang, *University of Melbourne*
Bernd Ploderer, *University of Melbourne & Queensland University of Technology*
Frank Vetere, *University of Melbourne*
Mark Bradford, *Royal Children's Hospital*

Session: Camera-based Tracking

3929 EagleSense: Tracking People and Devices in Interactive Spaces using Real-Time Top-View Depth-Sensing
Chi-Jui Wu, *University College London*
Steven Houben, *Lancaster University*
Nicolai Marquardt, *University College London*

3943 Interactive Visual Calibration of Volumetric Head-Tracked 3D Displays
Andrew John Wagemakers, Dylan Brodie Fafard, Ian Stavness, *University of Saskatchewan*

3954 Changing the Appearance of Real-World Objects By Modifying Their Surroundings
David Lindlbauer, *Technical University of Berlin*
Jörg Mueller, *Aarhus University*
Marc Alexa, *Technical University of Berlin*

3966 HeadPhones: Ad Hoc Mobile Multi-Display Environments through Head Tracking
Jens Grubert, *Coburg University*
Matthias Kranz, *University of Passau*

Session: Ubiquitous Sensing

3972 Zensei: Embedded, Multi-electrode Bioimpedance Sensing for Implicit, Ubiquitous User Recognition
Munehiko Sato, *Massachusetts Institute of Technology & The University of Tokyo*
Rohan S. Puri, *Massachusetts Institute of Technology*
Alex Olwal, *Massachusetts Institute of Technology & Google, Inc.*
Yosuke Ushigome, Lukas Franciszkiewicz, *Takram London*
Deepak Chandra, Ivan Poupyrev, *Google Inc.*
Ramesh Raskar, *Massachusetts Institute of Technology*

Table of Contents

3986 Synthetic Sensors: Towards General-Purpose Sensing
Gierad Laput, Yang Zhang, Chris Harrison, *Carnegie Mellon University*

4000 Deus EM Machina: On-Touch Contextual Functionality for Smart IoT Appliances
Robert Xiao, Gierad Laput, Yang Zhang, Chris Harrison, *Carnegie Mellon University*

4009 Seeing, Sensing and Recognizing Laban Movement Qualities
Sarah Fdili Alaoui, *Universit Paris-Saclay*
Jules Françoise, Thecla Schiphorst, *Simon Fraser University*
Karen Studd, *Laban Institute of Movement Studies*
Frederic Bevilacqua, *IRCAM*

Session: Experiences with Virtual Reality

4021 ShareVR: Enabling Co-Located Experiences for Virtual Reality between HMD and Non-HMD Users
Jan Gugenheimer, Evgeny Stemasov, Julian Frommel, Enrico Rukzio, *Ulm University*

4034 CarVR: Enabling In-Car Virtual Reality Entertainment
Philipp Hock, Sebastian Benedikter, Jan Gugenheimer, Enrico Rukzio, *Ulm University*

4045 Effects of Sharing Physiological States of Players in a Collaborative Virtual Reality Gameplay
Arindam Dey, Thammathip Piumsomboon, *University of South Australia*
Youngho Lee, *Mokpo National University*
Mark Billinghurst, *University of South Australia*

4057 VRRRRoom: Virtual Reality for Radiologists in the Reading Room
Maurício Sousa, Daniel Mendes, *INESC-ID & University of Lisbon*
Soraia Paulo, *INESC-ID*
Nuno Matela, *Instituto de Biofísica e Engenharia Biomédica & Faculdade de Ciências da Universidade de Lisboa*
Joaquim Jorge, *INESC-ID/IST/U Lisboa & University of Lisbon*
Daniel Simões Lopes, *INESC-ID*

4063 Handsfree Omnidirectional VR Navigation using Head Tilt
Sam Tregillus, Majed Al Zayer, Eelke Folmer, *University of Nevada*

Session: Food & Nutrition

4069 Rice Today, Roti Tomorrow: Diets and Diabetes in Urban Indian Households
Jasmine Hentschel, *THRIVE*
Samyukta Manjayya Sherugar, Rui Zhou, *Georgia Institute of Technology*
Vaishnav Kameswaran, *University of Michigan*
Rajesh Chandwani, *Indian Institute of Management*
Neha Kumar, *Georgia Institute of Technology*

4082 Monster Appetite: Effects of Subversive Framing on Nutritional Choices in a Digital Game Environment
Maria L. Hwang, Lena Mamykina, *Columbia University Medical Center*

4097 The Role of Explanations in Casual Observational Learning about Nutrition
Marissa Burgermaster, *Columbia University Medical Center*
Krzysztof Z. Gajos, *Harvard University*
Patricia Davidson, *West Chester University*
Lena Mamykina, *Columbia University*

Session: Impaired Vision and Navigation

4146 Audible Beacons and Wearables in Schools: Helping Young Visually Impaired Children Play and Move Independently
Euan Freeman, Graham Wilson, Stephen Brewster, *University of Glasgow*
Gabriel Baud-Bovy, *Italian Institute of Technology*
Charlotte Magnusson, Hector Caltenco, *Lund University*

4158 Embracing Errors: Examining How Context of Use Impacts Blind Individuals' Acceptance of Navigation Aid Errors
Ali Abdolrahmani, William Easley, Michele Williams, Stacy Branham, Amy Hurst, *University of Maryland, Baltimore County*

4170 Understanding Low Vision People's Visual Perception on Commercial Augmented Reality Glasses
Yuhang Zhao, Michele Hu, Shafeka Hashash, Shiri Azenkot, *Cornell Tech*

4182 Synthesizing Stroke Gestures Across User Populations: A Case for Users with Visual Impairments
Luis A. Leiva, *Sciling*
Daniel Martín-Albo, *Universitat Politècnica de València*
Radu-Daniel Vatavu, *University Stefan cel Mare of Suceava*

Session: Innovative Text Entry Systems

4194 Investigating Tilt-based Gesture Keyboard Entry for Single-Handed Text Entry on Large Devices
Hui-Shyong Yeo, *University of St Andrews*
Xiao-Shen Phang, *NEC Corporation of Malaysia*
Steven J. Castellucci, *York University*
Per Ola Kristensson, *University of Cambridge*
Aaron Quigley, *University of St Andrews*

4203 Modelling Learning of New Keyboard Layouts
Jussi P. P. Jokinen, *Aalto University*
Sayan Sarcar, *Kochi University of Technology*
Antti Oulasvirta, *Aalto University*
Chaklam Silpasuwanchai, Zhenxin Wang, Xiangshi Ren, *Kochi University of Technology*

4216 Word Clarity as a Metric in Sampling Keyboard Test Sets
Xin Yi, Chun Yu, Weinan Shi, *Tsinghua University*
Xiaojun Bi, *Stony Brook University*
Yuanchun Shi, *Tsinghua University*

Table of Contents

4229 Quantifying Aversion to Costly Typing Errors in Expert Mobile Text Entry
Nikola Banovic, *Carnegie Mellon University*
Varun Rao, *PES Institute of Technology & Carnegie Mellon University*
Abinaya Saravanan, *Coimbatore Institute of Technology & Carnegie Mellon University*
Anind K. Dey, Jennifer Mankoff, *Carnegie Mellon University*

Session: Models of Use and Gestures

4242 High Costs and Small Benefits: A Field Study of How Users Experience Operating System Upgrades
Francesco Vitale, *Université Paris-Saclay*
Joanna McGrenere, *University of British Columbia*
Aurélien Tabard, *Université Lyon 1*
Michel Beaudouin-Lafon, Wendy E. Mackay, *Université Paris-Saclay*

4254 Understanding Shoulder Surfing in the Wild: Stories from Users and Observers
Malin Eiband, Mohamed Khamis, Emanuel von Zezschwitz, Heinrich Hussmann, Florian Alt, *LMU Munich*

4266 Fieldward and Pathward: Dynamic Guides for Defining Your Own Gestures
Joseph Malloch, Carla F. Griggio, *Université Paris-Saclay*
Joanna McGrenere, *University of British Columbia*
Wendy E. Mackay, *Université Paris-Saclay*

4278 Gesture Interfaces: Minor Change in Effort, Major Impact on Appeal
Xiaoxing Liu, Geb W. Thomas, *University of Iowa*

4284 MoveMeant: Anonymously Building Community Through Shared Location Histories
Emily Sun, Ross McLachlan, Mor Naaman, *Cornell Tech*

Session: Sound of Music

4290 MuEns: A Multimodal Human-Machine Music Ensemble for Live Concert Performance
Akira Maezawa, *Yamaha Corporation*
Kazuhiko Yamamoto, *Yamaha Corporation & The University of Tokyo*

4302 Playing Fast and Loose with Music Recognition
Chris Greenhalgh, Steve Benford, Adrian Hazzard, Alan Chamberlain, *University of Nottingham*

4314 Holographic Whisper: Rendering Audible Sound Spots in Three-dimensional Space by Focusing Ultrasonic Waves
Yoichi Ochiai, Takayuki Hoshi, *University of Tokyo & Pixie Dust Technologies, Inc.*
Ippei Suzuki, *University of Tsukuba*

4326 EnseWing: Creating an Instrumental Ensemble Playing Experience for Children with Limited Music Training
Fei Lyu, *Chinese Academy of Sciences & Beijing University of Posts and Telecommunications*
Feng Tian, *Chinese Academy of Sciences*
Wenxin Feng, *Boston University*
Xiang Cao, *Xiaoxiaoniu Creative Technologies*
Xiaolong (Luke) Zhang, *Pennsylvania State University*
Guozhong Dai, Hongan Wang, *Chinese Academy of Sciences*

Session: Technology Enabled Commerce

4331 Market Design for HCI: Successes and Failures of Peer-to-Peer Exchange Platforms
Airi Lampinen, Barry Brown, *Stockholm University*

4344 Community Commerce: Facilitating Trust in Mom-to-Mom Sale Groups on Facebook
Carol Moser, Paul Resnick, Sarita Schoenebeck, *University of Michigan*

4358 No Such Thing as Too Much Chocolate: Evidence Against Choice Overload in E-Commerce
Carol Moser, Chanda Phelan, Paul Resnick, Sarita Y. Schoenebeck, *University of Michigan*
Katharina Reinecke, *University of Washington*

4370 Why Users Disintermediate Peer-to-Peer Marketplaces
Victoria Bellotti, *Palo Alto Research Center & University of California, Santa Cruz*
Dan Turner, Kamila Demkova, *Palo Alto Research Center*
Alexander Ambard, *Google*
Amanda Waterman, *Palo Alto Research Center*

Session: Unusual Displays

4383 MistForm: Adaptive Shape Changing Fog Screens
Yutaka Tokuda, Mohd Adili Norasikin, Sriram Subramanian, Diego Martinez Plasencia, *University of Sussex*

4396 The Object Inside: Assessing 3D Examination with a Spherical Handheld Perspective-Corrected Display
Francois Berard, Thibault Louis, *University Grenoble Alpes*

4405 Visual Composition of Graphical Elements on Non-Rectangular Displays
Marcos Serrano, *University of Toulouse*
Anne Roudaut, *University of Bristol*
Pourang Irani, *University of Manitoba*

4417 Effects of Tactile Feedback on the Perception of Virtual Shapes on Non-Planar DisplayObjects
Juan Pablo Carrascal, Roel Vertegaal, *Queen's University.*

4424 BreathScreen – Design and Evaluation of an Ephemeral UI
Ismo Alakärppä, Elisa Jaakkola, Ashley Colley, Jonna Häkkilä, *University of Lapland*

Table of Contents

Session: User Perceptions in Sociotechnical Systems

A Quantified Past: Toward Design for Remembering With Personal Informatics
Chris Elsden, *Newcastle University*
David S. Kirk, Abigail Durrant, *Northumbria University*

4430 **Foreign-language Reviews: Help or Hindrance?**
Scott A. Hale, *University of Oxford & The Alan Turing Institute*
Irene Eleta, *ISGlobal Barcelona Institute for Global Health &*

4443 **Getting Something for Nothing? A User-Centric Perspective on Loyalty Card Schemes**
Annika Hupfeld, *Eindhoven University of Technology*
Chris Speed, *Edinburgh University*

4454 **Online Feedback Exchange: A Framework for Understanding the Socio-Psychological Factors**
Eureka Foong, *Northwestern University*
Steven P. Dow, *University of California, San Diego*
Brian P. Bailey, *University of Illinois at Urbana-Champaign*
Elizabeth M. Gerber, *Northwestern University*

Session: 360 Video

4468 **The Geometry of Storytelling: Theatrical Use of Space for 360-degree Videos and Virtual Reality**
Vanessa C. Pope, *Queen Mary University*
Robert Dawes, Florian Schweiger, *BBC Research & Development*
Alia Sheikh, *BBC Research & Development North*

4479 **Tap, Dwell or Gesture?: Exploring Head-Based Text Entry Techniques for HMDs**
Chun Yu, Yizheng Gu, Zhican Yang, Xin Yi, *Tsinghua University*
Hengliang Luo, *Samsung Beijing R&D Center*
Yuanchun Shi, *Tsinghua University*

4489 **Videos of Things: Speculating on, Anticipating and Synthesizing Technological Mediations**
Doenja Oogjes, *Simon Fraser University*
Ron Wakkary, *Simon Fraser University & Eindhoven University of Technology*

4501 **Watching 360° Videos Together**
Anthony Tang, Omid Fakourfar, *University of Calgary*

Session: Civic Engagement

4507 **Revisiting The American Voter on Twitter**
Huyen T. Le, G.R. Boynton, *University of Iowa*
Yelena Mejova, *Qatar Computing Research Institute*
Zubair Shafiq, Padmini Srinivasan, *University of Iowa*

4520 **Managing Uncertainty: Using Social Media for Risk Assessment during a Public Health Crisis**
Xinning Gui, *University of California, Irvine*
Yubo Kou, *Purdue University*
Kathleen H. Pine, *Arizona State University*
Yunan Chen, *University of California, Irvine*

4534 **Theory-Driven Collocated CMC: A Study of Collocated Mediated Interaction as a Public Sphere**
Matti Nelimarkka, *University of Helsinki & Aalto University*
Antti Salovaara, *University of Helsinki*
Bryan Semaan, *Syracuse University*
Giulio Jacucci, *HIIT, Aalto University & University of Helsinki*

Session: Cross Device Interaction

4548 **Is Two Enough?! Studying Benefits, Barriers, and Biases of Multi-Tablet Use for Collaborative Visualization**
Thomas Plank, Hans-Christian Jetter, *University of Applied Sciences Upper Austria*
Roman Rädle, Clemens N. Klokmose, *Aarhus University*
Thomas Luger, *University of Applied Sciences Upper Austria*
Harald Reiterer, *University of Konstanz*

4561 **LetsPic: Supporting In-situ Collaborative Photography over a Large Physical Space**
Auk Kim, Sungjoon Kang, Uichin Lee, *Korea Advanced Institute of Science and Technology*

4574 **XDBrowser 2.0: Semi-Automatic Generation of Cross-Device Interfaces**
Michael Nebeling, *University of Michigan*

Improv: An Input Framework for Improvising Cross-Device Interaction By Demonstration
Xiang 'Anthony' Chen, *Carnegie Mellon University & Google Research*
Yang Li, *Google Research*

Session: Crowdwork

4585 **Low-Wage Precarious Workers' Sociotechnical Practices Working Towards Addressing Wage Theft**
Lynn Dombrowski, Adriana Alvarado Garcia, Jessica Despard, *Indiana University-Purdue University Indianapolis*

4599 **Examining Crowd Work and Gig Work Through The Historical Lens of Piecework**
Ali Alkhatib, Michael S. Bernstein, Margaret Levi, *Stanford University*

4617 **Leveraging Complementary Contributions of Different Workers for Efficient Crowdsourcing of Video Captions**
Yun Huang, Yifeng Huang, Na Xue, *Syracuse University*
Jeffrey P. Bigham, *Carnegie Mellon University*

4627 **Critique Style Guide: Improving Crowdsourced Design Feedback with a Natural Language Model**
Markus Krause, *University of California, Berkeley*
Tom Garncarz, *Carnegie Mellon University*
JiaoJiao Song, *Huazhong University of Science and Technology*
Elizabeth M. Gerber, *Northwestern University*
Brian P. Bailey, *University of Illinois at Urbana-Champaign*
Steven P. Dow, *University of California, San Diego*

Table of Contents

Session: Improving Touch Interfaces

4640 **ProbUI: Generalising Touch Target Representations to Enable Declarative Gesture Definition for Probabilistic GUIs**
Daniel Buschek, Florian Alt, *University of Munich (LMU))*

4654 **BackXPress: Using Back-of-Device Finger Pressure to Augment Touchscreen Input on Smartphones**
Christian Corsten, Bjoern Daehlmann, Simon Voelker, Jan Borchers, *RWTH Aachen University*

4667 **Improving Gesture Recognition Accuracy on Touch Screens for Users with Low Vision**
Radu-Daniel Vatavu, *University Stefan cel Mare of Suceava*

4680 **Understanding Grip Shifts: How Form Factors Impact Hand Movements on Mobile Phones**
Rachel Eardley, *Cardiff Metropolitan University*
Anne Roudaut, *University of Bristol*
Steve Gill, Stephen Thompson, *Cardiff Metropolitan University*

Session: Innovative Input Techniques

4692 **Structured Input Improves Usability and Precision for Solving Geometry-based Algebraic Problems**
Bo Kang, Joseph J. LaViola Jr., Pamela Wisniewski, *University of Central Florida*

4703 **Genie: Input Retargeting on the Web through Command Reverse Engineering**
Amanda Swearngin, Andrew J. Ko, James Fogarty, *University of Washington*

4715 **IconHK: Using Toolbar button Icons to Communicate Keyboard Shortcuts**
Emmanouil Giannisakis, *Université Paris-Saclay*
Gilles Bailly, *Université Paris-Saclay & UPMC Univ Paris 06*
Sylvain Malacria, Fanny Chevalier, *Inria*

4727 **Mouse, Tactile, and Tangible Input for 3D Manipulation**
Lonni Besançon, Paul Issartel, *Université Paris-Saclay*
Mehdi Ammi, *LIMSI-CNRS*
Tobias Isenberg, *INRIA*

Session: Markets in the Global South

4741 **Market Practices and the Bazaar: Technology Consumption in ICT Markets in the Global South**
Priyank Chandra, *University of Michigan*
Syed Ishtiaque Ahmed, *Cornell University*
Joyojeet Pal, *University of Michigan*

4753 **Cinehacking Cape Town - Embracing Informality in Pursuit of High Quality Media**
David Philip Green, *Northumbria University & Newcastle University*
Guy Schofield, *University of York*
Gary Pritchard, *University of Surrey*
Patrick Olivier, Peter Wright, *Newcastle University*

4765 **Informality and Invisibility: Traditional Technologies as Tools for Collaboration in an Informal Market**
Priyank Chandra, *University of Michigan*

4776 **From Margins to Seams: Imbrication, Inclusion, and Torque in the Aadhaar Identification Project**
Ranjit Singh, Steven J. Jackson, *Cornell University*

Session: Performative Interactions

4825 **Performing Research: Four Contributions to HCI**
Robyn Taylor, *Newcastle University*
Jocelyn Spence, Brendan Walker, *University of Nottingham*
Bettina Nissen, *University of Edinburgh*
Peter Wright, *Newcastle University*

4838 **MagicFace: Stepping into Character through an Augmented Reality Mirror**
Ana Javornik, *Newcastle University*
Yvonne Rogers, Delia Gander, *University College London*
Ana Moutinho, *Holition Ltd*

4850 **Interactive Performance as a Means of Civic Dialogue**
Chiara Rossitto, *Stockholm University*
Maria Normark, *Södertörn University*
Louise Barkhuus, *The IT University of Copenhagen*

4863 **The Game of Performing Play: Understanding Streaming as Cultural Production**
Anthony J. Pellicone, *University of Maryland*
June Ahn, *New York University*

Session: Serious + Educational + Exer Games

4875 **Finding the Right Fit: Understanding Health Tracking in Workplace Wellness Programs**
Chia-Fang Chung, *University of Washington*
Nanna Jensen, Irina A. Shklovski, *IT University of Copenhagen*
Sean Munson, *University of Washington*

4887 **Mastery Learning of Second Language through Asynchronous Modeling of Native Speakers in a Collaborative Mobile Game**
Xiangmin Fan, Wencan Luo, Jingtao Wang, *University of Pittsburgh*

4899 **Misrepresentation of Health Research in Exertion Games Literature**
Joe Marshall, *University of Nottingham*
Conor Linehan, *University College Cork*

4911 **Teaching Programming with Gamified Semantics**
Ian Arawjo, Cheng-Yao Wang, Andrew C. Myers, Erik Andersen, François Guimbretière, *Cornell University*

Table of Contents

Session: Technology in Households

4924 **Investigating the Suitability of the Asynchronous, Remote, Community-based Method for Pregnant and New Mothers**
Annu Sible Prabhakar, *Indiana University & University of Cincinnati*
Lucia Guerra-Reyes, *Indiana University –Bloomington*
Vanessa M. Kleinschmidt, *National Institute for Public Safety Health*
Ben Jelen, Haley MacLeod, Kay Connelly, Katie A. Siek, *Indiana University -Bloomington*

4935 **Has Instagram Fundamentally Altered the 'Family Snapshot'?**
Effie Le Moignan, Shaun Lawson, *Northumbria University*
Duncan A. Rowland, *Independent Researcher*
Jamie Mahoney, Pam Briggs, *Northumbria University*

4948 **Internet Search Roles of Adults in their Homes**
Jinyoung Kim, *University of Maryland, College Park & Seoul National University*
Brenna McNally, Leyla Norooz, Allison Druin, *University of Maryland, College Park*

4960 **Understanding the Role of Human Senses in Interactive Meditation**
Mahmoud Mohamed Hussien Ahmed, *Kochi University of Technology & South Valley University*
Chaklam Silpasuwanchai, Kavous Salehzadeh Niksirat, Xiangshi Ren, *Kochi University of Technology*

4966 **Gender Norms and Attitudes about Childcare Activities Presented on Father Blogs**
Kai Lukoff, *University of Washington*
Carol Moser, Sarita Schoenebeck, *University of Michigan*

Session: Textures and Haptics

4972 **WAVES: A Wearable Asymmetric Vibration Excitation System for Presenting Three-Dimensional Translation and Rotation Cues**
Heather Culbertson, Julie M. Walker, Michael Raitor, Allison M. Okamura, *Stanford University*

4983 **Magnetic Plotter: A Macrotexture Design Method Using Magnetic Rubber Sheets**
Kentaro Yasu, *Nippon Telegraph and Telephone (NTT)*

4994 **Generating Haptic Textures with a Vibrotactile Actuator**
Paul Strohmeier, Kasper Hornbæk, *University of Copenhagen*

5006 **Localized Haptic Texture: A Rendering Technique based on Taxels for High Density Tactile Feedback**
Yosra Rekik, Eric Vezzoli, Laurent Grisoni, Frédéric Giraud, *University of Lille Sci. & Tech, CNRS, & INRIA*

Session: Design and Games

5016 **Supporting Easy Physical-to-Virtual Creation of Mobile VR Maze Games: A New Genre**
Wei Gai, Chenglei Yang, Yulong Bian, *Shandong University*
Chia Shen, *National Science Foundation*
Xiangxu Meng, Lu Wang, Juan Liu, Mingda Dong, Chengjie Niu, Cheng Lin, *Shandong University*

5029 **The UX of Avatar Customization**
Victoria McArthur, *University of Toronto Mississauga*

5034 **To Three or not to Three: Improving Human Computation Game Onboarding with a Three-Star System**
Jacqueline Gaston, *Carnegie Mellon University*
Seth Cooper, *Northeastern University*

Session: Design Frameworks

5040 **What Is Interaction?**
Kasper Hornbæk, *University of Copenhagen*
Antti Oulasvirta, *Aalto University*

5053 **Beyond Grids: Interactive Graphical Substrates to Structure Digital Layout**
Nolwenn Maudet, Ghita Jalal, Philip Tchernavskij, Michel Beaudouin-Lafon, Wendy E. Mackay, *Université Paris-Saclay*

5065 **Expressive Fused Deposition Modeling by Controlling Extruder Height and Extrusion Amount**
Haruki Takahashi, Homei Miyashita, *Meiji University*

5075 **shiftIO: Reconfigurable Tactile Elements for Dynamic Affordances and Mobile Interaction**
Evan Strasnick, Jackie Yang, Kesler Tanner, *Stanford University*
Alex Olwal, *Google, Inc.*
Sean Follmer, *Stanford University*

Session: Difficulty and Challenge in Games

5087 **A Good Reason to Die: How Avatar Death and High Challenges Enable Positive Experiences**
Serge Petralito, Florian Brühlmann, *University of Basel*
Glena Iten, Elisa D. Mekler, *University of Waterloo*
Klaus Opwis, *University of Basel*

5098 **How Human Am I? EEG-based Evaluation of Virtual Characters**
Maryam Mustafa, *Technical University of Braunschweig*
Stefan Guthe, *Technische Universität Darmstadt*
Jan-Philipp Tauscher, *Technical University of Braunschweig*
Michael Goesele, *Technische Universität Darmstadt*
Marcus Magnor, *Technical University of Braunschweig & University of New Mexico*

5109 **Testing Incremental Difficulty Design in Platformer Games**
Rina R. Wehbe, Elisa D. Mekler, Mike Schaekermann, Edward Lank, Lennart E. Nacke, *University of Waterloo*

5114 **EngageMeter: A System for Implicit Audience Engagement Sensing Using Electroencephalography**
Mariam Hassib, *LMU Munich & University of Stuttgart*
Stefan Schneegass, *University of Stuttgart*
Philipp Eiglsperger, *LMU Munich*
Niels Henze, Albrecht Schmidt, *University of Stuttgart*
Florian Alt, *LMU Munich*

Table of Contents

5117 **Can I Think of Something Else when Using a BCI? Cognitive Demand of an SSVEP-based BCI**
Andéol Evain, *Université de Rennes 1*
Ferran Argelaguet, Nicolas Roussel, *Inria*
Géry Casiez, *Université de Lille*
Anatole Lécuyer, *Inria*

5123 **"Not another Z piece!" Adaptive Difficulty in TETRIS**
Katharina Spiel, *Vienna University of Technology & Bauhaus-Universität Weimar*
Sven Bertel, *Bauhaus-Universität Weimar*
Fares Kayali, *Vienna University of Technology*

Session: Embodied Interaction

5129 **The World-as-Support: Embodied Exploration, Understanding and Meaning-Making of the Augmented World**
Laura Malinverni, Julian Maya, Marie-Monique Schaper, Narcis Pares, *Universitat Pompeu Fabra*

5145 **Extending the Body for Interaction with Reality**
Tiare Feuchtner, Jörg Müeller, *Aarhus University*

5158 **Embodied Design Ideation Methods: Analysing the Power of Estrangement**
Danielle Wilde, *University of Southern Denmark*
Anna Vallgårda, *IT University of Copenhagen*
Oscar Tomico, *Eindhoven University of Technology & ELISAVA*

5171 **Designing for Kinesthetic Awareness: Revealing User Experiences through Second-Person Inquiry**
Jules Françoise, Yves Candau, *Simon Fraser University*
Sarah Fdili Alaoui, *Université Paris Sud*
Thecla Schiphorst, *Simon Fraser University*

Session: Emerging Privacy

5184 **Chameleon Devices: Investigating More Secure and Discreet Mobile Interactions via Active Camouflaging**
Jennifer Pearson, Simon Robinson, Matt Jones, *Swansea University*
Anirudha Joshi, Shashank Ahire, *IIT Bombay*
Deepak Sahoo, *Swansea University & University of Sussex*
Sriram Subramanian, *University of Sussex*

5197 **Toys that Listen: A Study of Parents, Children, and Internet-Connected Toys**
Emily McReynolds, Sarah Hubbard, Timothy Lau, Aditya Saraf, Maya Cakmak, Franziska Roesner, *University of Washington*

5208 **Better the Devil You Know: Exposing the Data Sharing Practices of Smartphone Apps**
Max Van Kleek, *University of Oxford*
Ilaria Liccardi, *Massachusetts Institute of Technology*
Reuben Binns, Jun Zhao, *University of Oxford*
Daniel J. Weitzner, *Massachusetts Institute of Technology*
Nigel Shadbolt, *University of Oxford*

5221 **Parents' and Children's Preferences about Parents Sharing about Children on Social Media**
Carol Moser, Tianying Chen, Sarita Y. Schoenebeck, *University of Michigan*

5226 **Challenges of using Personal Data to Drive Personalised Electronic Programme Guides**
Neelima Sailaja, Andy Crabtree, *University of Nottingham*
Phil Stenton, *BBC R&D*

Session: Family Health

5232 **Reflective Informatics Through Family Storytelling: Self-discovering Physical Activity Predictors**
Herman Saksono, Andrea G. Parker, *Northeastern University*

5245 **Supporting Families in Reviewing and Communicating about Radiology Imaging Studies**
Matthew K. Hong, Clayton Feustel, Meeshu Agnihotri, Max Silverman, *Georgia Institute of Technology*
Stephen F. Simoneaux, *Children's Healthcare of Atlanta*
Lauren Wilcox, *Georgia Institute of Technology*

5257 **How Values Shape Collaboration Between Patients with Multiple Chronic Conditions and Spousal Caregivers**
Andrew B. L. Berry, Catherine Lim, Andrea L. Hartzler, Tad Hirsch, *University of Washington*
Edward H. Wagner, Evette Ludman, James D. Ralston, *Group Health Research Institute*

Session: Improving Video Communication

5271 **Through the Looking Glass: The Effects of Feedback on Self-Awareness and Conversational Behaviour during Video Chat**
Matthew K. Miller, Regan L. Mandryk, Max V. Birk, Ansgar E. Depping, Tushita Patel, *University of Saskatchewan*

5284 **Gestures From the Point of View of an Audience: Towards Anticipatable Interaction of Presenters With 3D Content.**
Andrey Krekhov, Katharina Emmerich, Maxim Babinski, Jens Krüger, *University Duisburg-Essen*

5295 **Showing Objects: Holding and Manipulating Artefacts in Video-mediated Collaborative Settings**
Christian Licoppe, *Université Paris-Saclay*
Paul K. Luff, Christian Heath, *King's College*
Hideaki Kuzuoka, Naomi Yamashita, *NTT Communication Science Laboratories*
Sylvaine Tuncer, *CNRS, Télécom ParisTech, Université Paris-Saclay*

5307 **ThirdEye: Simple Add-on Display to Represent Remote Participant's Gaze Direction in Video Communication**
Mai Otsuki, Taiki Kawano, Keita Maruyama, Hideaki Kuzuoka, *University of Tsukuba*
Yusuke Suzuki, *OKI Electric Industry Co., Ltd.*

Table of Contents

5313 **FaceShare: Mirroring with Pseudo-Smile Enriches Video Chat Communications**
Keita Suzuki, *University of Tokyo*
Masanori Yokoyama, *University of Tokyo & NTT Service Evolution Laboratories*
Shigeo Yoshida, *University of Tokyo*
Takayoshi Mochizuki, Tomohiro Yamada, *NTT Service Evolution Laboratories*
Takuji Narumi, Tomohiro Tanikawa, Michitaka Hirose, *University of Tokyo*

Session: Online and On-the-go

5318 **Squeezeback: Pneumatic Compression for Notifications**
Henning Pohl, Peter Brandes, Hung Ngo Quang, Michael Rohs, *University of Hannover*

5331 **Cito: An Actuated Smartwatch for Extended Interactions**
Jun Gong, *Dartmouth College*
Lan Li, *South China University of Technology*
Daniel Vogel, *University of Waterloo*
Xing-Dong Yang, *Dartmouth College*

5346 **How Busy Are You? Predicting the Interruptibility Intensity of Mobile Users**
Fengpeng Yuan, Xianyi Gao, Janne Lindqvist, *Rutgers University*

5361 **Demand Around the Clock: Time Use and Data Demand of Mobile Devices in Everyday Life**
Kelly Widdicks, Oliver Bates, Mike Hazas, Adrian Friday, *Lancaster University*
Alastair R. Beresford, *University of Cambridge*

Session: Speculation & Storytelling

5373 **Reworking the Gaps between Design and Ethnography**
Vera Khovanskaya, Phoebe Sengers, *Cornell University*
Melissa Mazmanian, *University of California, Irvine*
Charles Darrah, *San Jose State University*

5386 **On Speculative Enactments**
Chris Elsden, David Chatting, *Newcastle University*
Abigail C. Durrant, *Northumbria University*
Andrew Garbett, *Newcastle University*
Bettina Nissen, *University of Edinburgh*
John Vines, David S. Kirk, *Northumbria University*

5400 **Research Fiction: Storytelling, Plot and Design**
Mark Blythe, *Northumbria University*

5412 **Intersectional HCI: Engaging Identity through Gender, Race, and Class**
Ari Schlesinger, W. Keith Edwards, Rebecca E. Grinter, *Georgia Institute of Technology*

Session: Virtual Reality

5428 **Vremiere: In-Headset Virtual Reality Video Editing**
Cuong Nguyen, *Portland State University*
Stephen DiVerdi, Aaron Hertzmann, *Adobe Research*
Feng Liu, *Portland State University*

5439 **"They're Just Tixel Pits Man": Disputing the 'Reality' of Virtual Reality Pornography through the Story Completion Method**
Matthew Wood, *Newcastle University*
Gavin Wood, *Northumbria University*
Madeline Balaam, *Newcastle University*

5452 **ThermoVR: Exploring Integrated Thermal Haptic Feedback with Head Mounted Displays**
Roshan Lalintha Peiris, Wei Peng, Zikun Chen, *Keio University*
Liwei Chan, *National Chiao Tung University*
Kouta Minamizawa, *Keio University*

5457 **Efficient Typing on a Visually Occluded Physical Keyboard**
James Walker, Bochao Li, Keith Vertanen, Scott Kuhl, *Michigan Technological University*

Session: Visualization for the People

5462 **Showing People Behind Data: Does Anthropomorphizing Visualizations Elicit More Empathy for Human Rights Data?**
Jeremy Boy, *United Nations*
Anshul Vikram Pandey, John Emerson, Margaret Satterthwaite, Oded Nov, Enrico Bertini, *New York University*

5475 **Narratives in Crowdsourced Evaluation of Visualizations: A Double-Edged Sword?**
Evanthia Dimara, *INRIA*
Anastasia Bezerianos, *Univ Paris Sud, CNRS & INRIA*
Pierre Dragicevic, *INRIA*

5485 **Visualization Literacy at Elementary School**
Basak Alper, *NASA Jet Propulsion Laboratory (JPL)*
Nathalie Henry Riche, *Microsoft Research*
Fanny Chevalier, *Inria*
Jeremy Boy, *United Nations*
Metin Sezgin, *Koc University*

5498 **Finding Similar People to Guide Life Choices: Challenge, Design, and Evaluation**
Fan Du, Catherine Plaisant, Neil Spring, Ben Shneiderman, *University of Maryland*

Session: Classroom Tools

5545 **Better Organization or a Source of Distraction? Introducing Digital Peer Feedback to a Paper-Based Classroom**
Amy Shannon, Alex Sciuto, Danielle Hu, *Carnegie Mellon University*
Steven P. Dow, *University of California, San Diego*
Jessica Hammer, *Carnegie Mellon University*

5556 **Group Spinner: Recognizing and Visualizing Learning in the Classroom for Reflection, Communication, and Planning**
Ahmed Kharrufa, Sally Rix, Timur Osadchiy, *Newcastle University*
Anne Preston, *Kingston University*
Patrick Olivier, *Newcastle University*

Table of Contents

5568 ViVo: Video-Augmented Dictionary for Vocabulary Learning
Yeshuang Zhu, Yuntao Wang, Chun Yu, Shaoyun Shi, Yankai Zhang, Shuang He, Shuang He, Peijun Zhao, *Tsinghua University*
Xiaojuan Ma, *Hong Kong University of Science and Technology*
Yuanchun Shi, *Tsinghua University*

5580 From in the Class or in the Wild? Peers Provide Better Design Feedback Than External Crowds
Helen Wauck, Yu-Chun (Grace) Yen, Wai-Tat Fu, *University of Illinois at Urbana-Champaign*
Elizabeth Gerber, *Northwestern University*
Steven P. Dow, *University of California at San Diego*
Brian P. Bailey, *University of Illinois at Urbana-Champaign*

Session: Finger and Pen

5592 Collection Objects: Enabling Fluid Formation and Manipulation of Aggregate Selections
Haijun Xia, Bruno Araujo, Daniel Wigdor, *University of Toronto*

5605 IllumiPaper: Illuminated Interactive Paper
Konstantin Klamka, Raimund Dachselt, *Technische Universität Dresden*

5619 Does Practice Make Perfect?: Learning to Deal with Latency in Direct-Touch Interaction
Elie Cattan, Amélie Rochet-Capellan, Pascal Perrier, François Bérard, *University Grenoble Alpes & CNRS*

5630 MarkPad: Augmenting Touchpads for Command Selection
Bruno Fruchard, *CNRS, Telecom ParisTech, Université Paris-Saclay, Inria Université Paris-Sud*
Eric Lecolinet, *CNRS, Telecom ParisTech, Université Paris-Saclay*
Olivier Chapuis, *Université Paris-Sud, CNRS, Inria, Université Paris-Saclay*

Session: Interactions in Virtual Reality

5643 Experimental Evaluation of Sketching on Surfaces in VR
Rahul Arora, *University of Toronto & Autodesk Research*
Rubaiat Habib Kazi, Fraser Anderson, Tovi Grossman, *Autodesk Research*
Karan Singh, *University of Toronto*
George Fitzmaurice, *Autodesk Research*

5655 I Am The Passenger: How Visual Motion Cues Can Influence Sickness For In-Car VR
Mark McGill, Alexander Ng, Stephen Brewster, *University of Glasgow*

5669 VaiR: Simulating 3D Airflows in Virtual Reality
Michael Rietzler, Katrin Plaumann, Taras Kränzle, Marcel Erath, Alexander Stahl, Enrico Rukzio, *Ulm University*

Session: Mobility and Navigation in Many Forms

5678 Collaborative Map Making: A Reflexive Method for Understanding Matters of Concern in Design Research
Hee Rin Lee, Selma Šabanović, *Indiana University*
Sonya S. Kwak, *Ewha Womans University*

5690 Toward Principles for the Design of Navigation Affordances in Code Editors: An Empirical Investigation
Austin Z. Henley, Scott D. Fleming, Maria V. Luong, *University of Memphis*

5703 Follow-My-Lead: Intuitive Indoor Path Creation and Navigation Using Interactive Videos
Quentin Roy, *Singapore Management University*
Simon T. Perrault, *Yale-NUS College*
Shengdong Zhao, *National University of Singapore*
Richard C. Davis, *Act8 Design Pte. Ltd.*
Anuroop Pattena Vaniyar, *Singapore Management University*
Velko Vechev, *National University of Singapore & Chalmers University of Technology*
Youngki Lee, Archan Misra, *Singapore Management University*

5716 Mobility in Later Life – Appropriation of an Integrated Transportation Platform
Martin Stein, *University of Siegen & Fraunhofer Institute for Applied Information Technology (FIT)*
Johanna Meurer, *University of Siegen*
Alexander Boden, *Fraunhofer Institute for Applied Information Technology (FIT)*
Volker Wulf, *University of Siegen & Fraunhofer Institute for Applied Information Technology (FIT)*

Session: Participant Design with Children

5730 Gains from Participatory Design Team Membership as Perceived by Child Alumni and their Parents
Brenna McNally, Matthew Louis Mauriello, Mona Leigh Guha, Allison Druin, *University of Maryland*

5742 Examining Adult-Child Interactions in Intergenerational Participatory Design
Jason C. Yip, Kiley Sobel, Caroline Pitt, Kung Jin Lee, Sijin Chen, Kari Nasu, Laura R. Pina, *University of Washington*

5755 Participatory Evaluation with Autistic Children
Katharina Spiel, *Vienna University of Technology*
Laura Malinverni, *Universitat Pompeu Fabra*
Judith Good, *University of Sussex*
Christopher Frauenberger, *Vienna University of Technology & University of Sussex*

5767 Co-Designing with Preschoolers Using Fictional Inquiry and Comicboarding
Alexis Hiniker, Kiley Sobel, *Microsoft Research & University of Washington*
Bongshin Lee, *Microsoft Research*

Table of Contents

Session: Patient-generated Data in the Clinic

5773 **Making Space for the Quality Care: Opportunities for Technology in Cognitive Behavioral Therapy for Insomnia**
Haining Zhu, Yuhan Luo, Eun Kyoung Choe, *Pennsylvania State University*

5787 **Prescribing 10,000 Steps Like Aspirin: Designing a Novel Interface for Data-Driven Medical Consultations**
Yoojung Kim, *Seoul National University*
Eunyoung Heo, *Seoul National University Bundang Hospital*
Hyunjeong Lee, Sookyoung Ji, Jueun Choi, *Seoul National Universtiy*
Jeong-Whun Kim, *Seoul National University Bundang Hospital*
Joongseek Lee, *Seoul National University*
Sooyoung Yoo, *Seoul National University Bundang Hospital*

5800 **Crafting a View of Self-Tracking Data in the Clinical Visit**
Helena M. Mentis, Anita Komlodi, *University of Maryland Baltimore County*
Katrina Schrader, Michael Phipps, Ann Gruber-Baldini, Karen Yarbrough, Lisa Shulman, *University of Maryland School of Medicine*

5813 **What Happens to Digital Feedback?: Studying the Use of a Feedback Capture Platform by Care Organisations**
Andy Dow, *Newcastle University*
John Vines, *Northumbria University*
Toby Lowe, Rob Comber, Rob Wilson, *Newcastle University*

Session: Personal Object Recognizers: Feasibility and Challenges

5826 **Facade: Auto-generating Tactile Interfaces to Appliances**
Anhong Guo, *Carnegie Mellon University*
Jeeeun Kim, *University of Colorado, Boulder*
Xiang 'Anthony' Chen, *Carnegie Mellon University*
Tom Yeh, *University of Colorado, Boulder*
Scott E. Hudson, Jennifer Mankoff, Jeffrey P. Bigham, *Carnegie Mellon University*

5839 **People with Visual Impairment Training Personal Object Recognizers: Feasibility and Challenges**
Hernisa Kacorri, Kris M. Kitani, Jeffrey P. Bigham, Chieko Asakawa, *Carnegie Mellon University*

5850 **Jackknife: A Reliable Recognizer with Few Samples and Many Modalities**
Eugene M. Taranta II, Amirreza Samiei, Mehran Maghoumi, Pooya Khaloo, Corey R. Pittman, Joseph J. LaViola Jr., *University of Central Florida*

5862 **Ubiquitous Accessibility for People with Visual Impairments: Are We There Yet?**
Syed Masum Billah, Vikas Ashok, *Stony Brook University*
Donald E. Porter, *University of North Carolina at Chapel Hill*
I.V. Ramakrishnan, *Stony Brook University*

Session: Spatial Manipulation and Navigation

5869 **BIGnav: Bayesian Information Gain for Guiding Multiscale Navigation**
Wanyu Liu, *CNRS, Telecom ParisTech, Université Paris-Saclay, Inria*
Rafael Lucas D'Oliveira, *University of Campinas*
Michel Beaudouin-Lafon, *University Paris-Sud, CNRS, Inria, Université Paris-Saclay*
Olivier Rioul, *CNRS, Telecom ParisTech, Université Paris-Saclay*

5881 **Design and Evaluation of a Handheld-based 3D User Interface for Collaborative Object Manipulation**
Jerônimo Gustavo Grandi, *Universidade Federal do Rio Grande do Sul*
Henrique Galvan Debarba, *École Polytechnique Fédérale de Lausanne & Artanim Foundation*
Luciana Nedel, Anderson Maciel, *Universidade Federal do Rio Grande do Sul*

5892 **TDome: A Touch-Enabled 6DOF Interactive Device for Multi-Display Environments**
Houssem Saidi, Marcos Serrano, *University of Toulouse-IRIT*
Pourang Irani, *University of Manitoba*
Emmanuel Dubois, *University of Toulouse-IRIT*

5905 **A Field Experiment of Spatially-Stable Overviews for Document Navigation**
Carl Gutwin, *University of Saskatchewan*
Andy Cockburn, *University of Canterbury*
Nickolas Gough, *University of Saskatchewan*

Session: Technology Use Around the Globe

5917 **Imagined Connectivities: Synthesized Conceptions of Public Wi-Fi in Urban India**
Nithya Sambasivan, Paul M. Aoki, *Google Inc.*

5929 **Agency in Assistive Technology Adoption: Visual Impairment and Smartphone Use in Bangalore**
Joyojeet Pal, *University of Michigan*
Anandhi Viswanathan, *Independent Researcher*
Priyank Chandra, *University of Michigan, Ann Arbor*
Anisha Nazareth, *International Institute of Information Technology*
Vaishnav Kameswaran, Hariharan Subramonyam, *University of Michigan, Ann Arbor*
Aditya Johri, *George Mason University*
Mark S. Ackerman, Sile O'Modhrain, *University of Michigan, Ann Arbor*

5941 **Money, God, and SMS: Explorations in Supporting Social Action Through a Bangladeshi Mosque**
Md. Rashidujjaman Rifat, *University of Colorado, Boulder*
Jay Chen, *New York University - Abu Dhabi*
Kentaro Toyama, *University of Michigan*

5954 **Negotiating Absent Practices and Dormant Features: Discourse as a Means of Shaping the Implementation of a Global Enterprise System to Meet Local Work Culture**
George Kandathil, *Indian Institute of Management*
Erica L. Wagner, *Portland State University*

Table of Contents

Session: What Things Look Like

5966 Hybrid HFR Depth: Fusing Commodity Depth and Color Cameras to Achieve High Frame Rate, Low Latency Depth Camera Interactions
Jiajun Lu, *University of Illinois at Urbana Champaign & Microsoft Research*
Hrvoje Benko, Andrew D. Wilson, *Microsoft Research*

5976 Understanding the Aesthetic Evolution of Websites: Towards a Notion of Design Periods
Wen Chen, David J. Crandall, Norman Makoto Su, *Indiana University, Bloomington*

5988 Understanding Blind People's Experiences with Computer-Generated Captions of Social Media Images
Haley MacLeod, *Indiana University, Bloomington*
Cynthia L. Bennett, *University of Washington*
Meredith Ringel Morris, Edward Cutrell, *Microsoft Research*

6000 Time Travel with One Click: Effects of Digital Filters on Perceptions of Photographs
Yilang Peng, *University of Pennsylvania*

Session: Accessibility

6012 ForgetMeNot: Active Reminder Entry Support for Adults with Acquired Brain Injury
Matthew Jamieson, *University of Glasgow*
Brian O'Neill, *Graham Anderson House*
Breda Cullen, Marilyn Lennon, *University of Strathclyde*
Stephen Brewster, Jonathan Evans, *University of Glasgow*

6024 Interaction Proxies for Runtime Repair and Enhancement of Mobile Application Accessibility
Xiaoyi Zhang, Anne Spencer Ross, Anat Caspi, James Fogarty, Jacob O. Wobbrock, *University of Washington*

6038 SUGILITE: Creating Multimodal Smartphone Automation by Demonstration
Toby Jia-Jun Li, *Carnegie Mellon University*
Amos Azaria, *Ariel University*
Brad A. Myers, *Carnegie Mellon University*

6050 Automated Detection of Facial Expressions during Computer-Assisted Instruction in Individuals on the Autism Spectrum
Alex A. Ahmed, Matthew S. Goodwin, *Northeastern University*

6056 Comparing Touchscreen and Mouse Input Performance by People With and Without Upper Body Motor Impairments
Leah Findlater, *University of Maryland*
Karyn Moffatt, *McGill University*
Jon E. Froehlich, Meethu Malu, Joan Zhang, *University of Maryland*

Session: Cultural Heritage

6062 Designing Cultural Values into Interaction
Reese Muntean, Alissa N. Antle, Brendan Matkin, Kate Hennessy, *Simon Fraser University*
Susan Rowley, Jordan Wilson, *University of British Columbia*

6075 Kinecting with Orangutans: Zoo Visitors' Empathetic Responses to Animals' Use of Interactive Technology
Sarah Webber, Marcus Carter, Sally Sherwen, Wally Smith, Zaher Joukhadar, Frank Vetere, *University of Melbourne*

6089 Reconsidering Nature: The Dialectics of Fair Chase in the Practices of American Midwest Hunters
Norman Makoto Su, EunJeong Cheon, *Indiana University, Bloomington*

6101 Exploring Seasonality in Mobile Cultural Heritage
David McGookin, Koray Tahiroğlu, Tuomas Vaittinen, Mikko Kytö, Beatrice Monastero, Juan Carlos Vasquez, *Aalto University*

6106 Where No One Has Gone Before: A Meta-Dataset of the World's Largest Fanfiction Repository
Kodlee Yin, Cecilia Aragon, Sarah Evans, Katie Davis, *University of Washington*

Session: Explorative Engineering

6111 Illumination Aesthetics: Light as a Creative Material within Computational Design
Cesar Torres, Jasper O'Leary, Molly Nicholas, Eric Paulos, *University of California, Berkeley*

6123 Transformative Appetite: Shape-Changing Food Transforms from 2D to 3D by Water Interaction through Cooking
Wen Wang, Lining Yao, *Massachusetts Institute of Technology*
Teng Zhang, *Syracuse University*
Chin-Yi Cheng, Daniel Levine, Hiroshi Ishii, *Massachusetts Institute of Technology*

6133 Emotion Actuator: Embodied Emotional Feedback through Electroencephalography and Electrical Muscle Stimulation
Mariam Hassib, *University of Munich (LMU) & University of Stuttgart*
Max Pfeiffer, *University of Hannover & University of Münster*
Stefan Schneegass, *University of Stuttgart*
Michael Rohs, *University of Hannover*
Florian Alt, *University of Munich (LMU)*

6147 Understanding the Role Fluidity of Stakeholders During Assistive Technology Research "In the Wild"
LouAnne E. Boyd, *University of California, Irvine*
Kyle Rector, *University of Iowa*
Halley P. Profita, Abigale J. Stangl, *University of Colorado, Boulder*
Annuska Zolyomi, *University of Washington*
Shaun K. Kane, *University of Colorado, Boulder*
Gillian R. Hayes, *University of California, Irvine*

Session: Health Volunteers

6159 Video Consumption Patterns for First Time Smartphone Users: Community Health Workers in Lesotho
Maletsabisa Molapo, Melissa Densmore, Brian DeRenzi, *University of Cape Town*

Table of Contents

6171 **Experiences of Delivering a Public Health Data Service**
Emma Simpson, Rob Comber, Andrew Garbett, Ed Ian Jenkins, Madeline Balaam, *Newcastle University*

6184 **Understanding Volunteer AT Fabricators: Opportunities and Challenges in DIY-AT for Others in e-NABLE**
Jeremiah Parry-Hill, *Rochester Institute of Technology*
Patrick C. Shih, *Indiana University, Bloomington*
Jennifer Mankoff, *Carnegie Mellon University*
Daniel Ashbrook, *Rochester Institute of Technology*

6195 **VITA: Towards Supporting Volunteer Interactions with Long-Term Care Residents with Dementia**
Pin Sym Foong, Shengdong Zhao, *National University of Singapore*
Kelsey Carlson, *Ludwig-Maximilians-Universität*
Zhe Liu, *National University of Singapore*

Session: Helping Software Developers

6208 **Micro-Versioning Tool to Support Experimentation in Exploratory Programming**
Hiroaki Mikami, Daisuke Sakamoto, Takeo Igarashi, *University of Tokyo*

6220 **Codeon: On-Demand Software Development Assistance**
Yan Chen, Sang Won Lee, Yin Xie, YiWei Yang, Walter S. Lasecki, Steve Oney, *University of Michigan, Ann Arbor*

6232 **PFIS-V: Modeling Foraging Behavior in the Presence of Variants**
Sruti Srinivasa Ragavan, Bhargav Pandya, *Oregon State University*
David Piorkowski, *Oregon State University & IBM Research*
Charles Hill, *Oregon State University*
Sandeep Kaur Kuttal, *University of Tulsa*
Anita Sarma, Margaret Burnett, *Oregon State University*

6245 **Improving Communication Between Pair Programmers Using Shared Gaze Awareness**
Sarah D'Angelo, *Northwestern Univeristy*
Andrew Begel, *Microsoft Research*

Session: Interactive Design Methodologies

6291 **Post-userism**
Eric P. S. Baumer, *Lehigh University*
Jed R. Brubaker, *University of Colorado Boulder*

6304 **Tap the "Make This Public" Button: A Design-Based Inquiry into Issue Advocacy and Digital Civics**
Mariam Asad, Christopher A. Le Dantec, *Georgia Institute of Technology*

6317 **Enabling Polyvocality in Interactive Documentaries through 'Structural Participation'**
David Philip Green, *Northumbria University & Newcastle University*
Simon Bowen, *Newcastle University*
Jonathan Hook, *University of York*
Peter Wright, *Newcastle University*

6330 **Supporting Expressive Procedural Art Creation through Direct Manipulation**
Jennifer Jacobs, *Massachusetts Institute of Technology & Adobe Research*
Sumit Gogia, *Massachusetts Institute of Technology*
Radomir Mech, Joel R. Brandt,, *Adobe Research*

Session: Motivation in Peer-production Communities

6342 **Crowd Diversity and Performance in Wikipedia: The Mediating Effects of Task Conflict and Communication**
Ruqin Ren, Bei Yan, *University of Southern California*

6352 **Freedom versus Standardization: Structured Data Generation in a Peer Production Community**
Andrew Hall, Sarah McRoberts, Jacob Thebault-Spieker, *University of Minnesota*
Yilun Lin, *Northwestern University*
Shilad Sen, *Macalester College*
Brent Hecht, *Northwestern University*
Loren Terveen, *University of Minnesota*

6363 **Commitment of Newcomers and Old-timers to Online Health Support Communities**
Diyi Yang, Robert Kraut, *Carnegie Mellon University*
John M. Levine, *University of Pittsburgh*

6376 **Starting Online Communities: Motivations and Goals of Wiki Founders**
Jeremy Foote, Darren Gergle, Aaron Shaw, *Northwestern University*

6381 **Investigating the Motivational Paths of Peer Production Newcomers**
Martina Balestra, *New York University*
Coye Cheshire, *University of California, Berkeley*
Ofer Arazy, *University of Haifa*
Oded Nov, *New York University*

Session: Older Adults and Computers

6386 **Traversing Boundaries: Understanding the Experiences of Ageing Saudis**
Soud Nassir, Tuck Wah Leong, *University of Technology Sydney*

6398 **Transitions in Digital Personhood: Online Activity in Early Retirement**
Abigail Durrant, David Kirk *Northumbria University*
Diego Trujillo Pisanty, *Newcastle University*
Wendy Moncur, Kathryn Orzech, *University of Dundee*
Tom Schofield, Chris Elsden, David Chatting, Andrew Monk, *Newcastle University*

6412 **Dissecting Spear Phishing Emails for Older vs Young Adults: On the Interplay of Weapons of Influence and Life Domains in Predicting Susceptibility to Phishing**
Daniela Oliveira, Harold Rocha, Huizi Yang, Donovan Ellis, Sandeep Dommaraju, *University of Florida*
Melis Muradoglu, *University of Florida & New York University*
Devon Weir, Adam Soliman, Tian Lin, Natalie Ebner, *University of Florida*

Table of Contents

6425 Privacy Considerations when Designing Social Network Systems to Support Successful Ageing
Andrew R. McNeill, Lynne Coventry, Jake Pywell, Pam Briggs *Northumbria University*

Session: Spatial & Temporal Design

6438 Malleable Embodiment: Changing Sense of Embodiment by Spatial-Temporal Deformation of Virtual Human Body
Shunichi Kasahara, *SonyCSL*
Keina Konno, Richi Owaki, Tsubasa Nishi, Akiko Takeshita, Takayuki Ito, *Yamaguchi Center for Arts and Media*
Shoko Kasuga, Junichi Ushiba, *Keio University*

6449 Sensitizing Concepts for Socio-spatial Literacy in HCI
Peter Gall Krogh, Marianne Graves Petersen, *Aarhus University*
Kenton O'Hara, *Microsoft Research*
Jens Emil Grenbæk, *Aarhus University*

6461 Situational When: Designing for Time Across Cultures
Jennyfer Lawrence Taylor, Alessandro Soro, Paul Roe, Anita Lee Hong, Margot Brereton, *Queensland University of Technology*

6475 Modeling Sub-Document Attention Using Viewport Time
Max Grusky, *Cornell University*
Jeiran Jahani, Josh Schwartz, Dan Valente, *Chartbeat, Inc.*
Yoav Artzi, *Cornell Tech & Cornell University*
Mor Naaman, *Cornell Tech*

6481 Remote Collaboration With Mixed Reality Displays: How Shared Virtual Landmarks Facilitate Spatial Referencing
Jens Müller, *University of Konstanz*
Roman Rädle, *Aarhus University*
Harald Reiterer, *University of Konstanz*

Session: The Infrastructure of Trust

6487 Growing the Blockchain Information Infrastructure
Karim Jabbar, Pernille Bjørn, *University of Copenhagen*

6499 Design for Trust: An Exploration of the Challenges and Opportunities of Bitcoin Users
Corina Sas, *Lancaster University*
Irni Eliana Khairuddin, *Universiti Teknologi MARA*

6511 Infrastructure as Creative Action: Online Buying, Selling, and Delivery in Phnom Penh
Margaret Jack, *Cornell University*
Jay Chen, *New York University - Abu Dhabi*
Steven J. Jackson, *Cornell University*

6523 Supporting Cultures of Making: Technology, Policy, Visions, and Myths
Shaowen Bardzell, Jeffrey Bardzell, Sarah Ng, *Indiana University Bloomington*

Session: Video Smart" Viewers"

6536 EgoScanning: Quickly Scanning First-Person Videos with Egocentric Elastic Timelines
Keita Higuchi, Ryo Yonetani, Yoichi Sato, *The University of Tokyo*

6547 Retargeting Video Tutorials Showing Tools With Surface Contact to Augmented Reality
Peter Mohr, David Mandl, *Graz University of Technology*
Markus Tatzgern, *Salzburg University of Applied Sciences*
Eduardo Veas, *Know Center GmbH*
Dieter Schmalstieg, Denis Kalkofen, *Graz University of Technology*

6559 Close to the Action: Eye-Tracking Evaluation of Speaker-Following Subtitles
Kuno Kurzhals, Emine Cetinkaya, *University of Stuttgart*
Yongtao Hu, Wenping Wang, *The University of Hong Kong*
Daniel Weiskopf, *University of Stuttgart*

6569 Responsive Action-based Video Synthesis
Corneliu Ilisescu, Halil Aytac Kanaci, Matteo Romagnoli, *University College London*
Neill D. F. Campbell, *University of Bath & University College London*
Gabriel J. Brostow, *University College London*

Session: 3D Tangibles

6581 Co-3Deator: A Team-First Collaborative 3D Design Ideation Tool
Cecil Piya, Vinayak, *Purdue University*
Senthil Chandrasegaran, Niklas Elmqvist, *University of Maryland*
Karthik Ramani, *Purdue University*

6593 *EdiPulse*: Investigating a Playful Approach to Self-monitoring through 3D Printed Chocolate Treats
Rohit Ashok Khot, *Royal Melbourne Institute of TechonologY*
Deepti Aggarwal, *University of Melbourne*
Ryan Pennings, Larissa Hjorth, Florian 'Floyd' Mueller *Royal Melbourne Institute of Techonology University*

6608 Investigating Cross-Device Interaction between a Handheld Device and a Large Display
Jeni Paay, Dimitrios Raptis, Jesper Kjeldskov, Mikael B. Skov, Eric V. Ruder, Bjarke M. Lauridsen, *Aalborg University*

Session: Appropriation and Individuation

6620 Competent Men and Warm Women: Gender Stereotypes and Backlash in Image Search Results
Jahna Otterbacher, *Open University*
Jo Bates, Paul Clough, *The University of Sheffield*

6632 Technology Individuation: The Foibles of Augmented Everyday Objects
Aloha Hufana Ambe, Margot Brereton, Alessandro Soro, Paul Roe, *Queensland University of Technology*

Table of Contents

6645 **Social Consequences of Grindr Use: Extending the Internet-Enhanced Self-Disclosure Hypothesis**
Samuel Hardman Taylor, Jevan Alexander Hutson, Tyler Richard Alicea, *Cornell University*

6658 **Gender-Inclusiveness Personas vs. Stereotyping: Can We Have it Both Ways?**
Charles G. Hill, *Oregon State University*
Maren Haag, *Heilbronn University*
Alannah Oleson, Chris Mendez, *Oregon State University*
Nicola Marsden, *Heilbronn University*
Anita Sarma, Margaret Burnett, *Oregon State University*

Session: Data Extraction

6672 **SEER: Auto-Generating Information Extraction Rules from User-Specified Examples**
Maeda F. Hanafi, Azza Abouzied, *Abu Dhabi*
Laura Chiticariu, Yunyao Li, *IBM Research - Almaden*

6683 **Leveraging Human Routine Models to Detect and Generate Human Behaviors**
Nikola Banovic, Anqi Wang, *Carnegie Mellon University*
Yanfeng Jin, *Middlebury College & Carnegie Mellon University*
Christie Chang, Julian Ramos, Anind Dey, Jennifer Mankoff, *Carnegie Mellon University*

6695 **Interactive Vectorization**
Jun Xie, *University of Washington*
Holger Winnemöller, Wilmot Li, Stephen Schiller, *Adobe Systems, Inc.*

6705 **ChartSense: Interactive Data Extraction from Chart Images**
Daekyoung Jung, Wonjae Kim, Hyunjoo Song, Jeong-in Hwang, *Seoul National University*
Bongshin Lee, *Microsoft Research*
Bohyoung Kim, *Hankuk University of Foreign Studies*
Jinwook Seo, *Seoul National University*

Session: Displays and Collaboration

6718 **CamRay: Camera Arrays Support Remote Collaboration on Wall-Sized Displays**
Ignacio Avellino, Cédric Fleury, Wendy E. Mackay, Michel Beaudouin-Lafon, *University Paris-Sud, CNRS, Inria, Université Paris-Saclay*

6730 **CoReach: Cooperative Gestures for Data Manipulation on Wall-sized Displays**
Can Liu, *University Paris-Sud, CNRS, Inria, Université Paris-Saclay & University College London*
Olivier Chapuis, *University Paris-Sud, CNRS, Inria, Université Paris-Saclay*
Michel Beaudouin-Lafon, *Inria & Université Paris-Saclay*
Eric Lecolinet, *CNRS, Telecom ParisTech, Université Paris-Saclay*

6742 **Turbulent Touch: Touchscreen Input for Cockpit Flight Displays**
Andy Cockburn, *University of Canterbury*
Carl Gutwin, *University of Saskatchewan*
Philippe Palanque, *Université Paul Sabatier Toulouse 3*
Yannick Deleris, *Airbus Operations*
Catherine Trask, Ashley Coveney, Marcus Yung, *University of Saskatchewan*
Karon MacLean, *University of British Columbia*

6754 **AlterNail: Ambient, Batteryless, Stateful, Dynamic Displays at your Fingertips**
Christine Dierk, Tomás Vega Galvez, Eric Paulos, *University of California, Berkeley*

6760 **Subtle and Personal Workspace Requirements for Visual Search Tasks on Public Displays**
James R. Wallace, Ariel Weingarten, Edward Lank, *University of Waterloo*

Session: Drones

6765 **"Spiders in the Sky": User Perceptions of Drones Privacy and Security**
Victoria Chang, Pramod Chundury, *University of Maryland College Park*
Marshini Chetty, *Princeton University*

6777 **Privacy Mechanisms for Drones: Perceptions of Drone Controllers and Bystanders**
Yaxing Yao, Huichuan Xia, Yun Huang, Yang Wang, *Syracuse University*

6789 **Free to Fly in Public Spaces: Drone Controllers' Privacy Perceptions and Practices**
Yaxing Yao, Huichuan Xia, Yun Huang, Yang Wang, *Syracuse University*

6794 **Drone & Wo: Cultural Influences on Human-Drone Interaction Techniques**
Jane L. E, *Stanford University*
Ilene L. E, *West Windsor-Plainsboro High School South*
James A. Landay, *Stanford University*
Jessica R. Cauchard, *Stanford University & Interdisciplinary Center Herzliya*

Session: Online Experiments

6800 **Citizen Science Opportunities in Volunteer-Based Online Experiments**
Nigini Oliveira, *University of Washington & Universidade Federal de Campina Grande*
Eunice Jun, Katharina Reinecke, *University of Washington*

6813 **Differences in Crowdsourced vs. Lab-based Mobile and Desktop Input Performance Data**
Leah Findlater, Joan Zhang, Jon E. Froehlich, *University of Maryland*
Karyn Moffatt, *McGill University*

6825 **Gut Instinct: Creating Scientific Theories with Online Learners**
Vineet Pandey, Amnon Amir, Justine Debelius, Embriette R. Hyde, Tomasz Kosciolek, Rob Knight, Scott Klemmer, *University of California, San Diego*

6837 **Self-Experimentation for Behavior Change: Design and Formative Evaluation of Two Approaches**
Jisoo Lee, Erin Walker, *Arizona State University*
Winslow Burleson, *New York University*
Matthew Kay, *University of Washington*
Matthew Buman, Eric B. Hekler, *Arizona State University*

Table of Contents

Session: Personal Informatics & Self-Tracking

6850 TummyTrials: A Feasibility Study of Using Self-Experimentation to Detect Individualized Food Triggers
Ravi Karkar, Jessica Schroeder, Daniel A. Epstein, Laura R. Pina, Jeffrey Scofield, James Fogarty, Julie A. Kientz, Sean A. Munson, *University of Washington*
Roger Vilardaga, *Duke University*
Jasmine Zia, *University of Washington*

6864 Making Sense of Sleep Sensors: How Sleep Sensing Technologies Support and Undermine Sleep Health
Ruth Ravichandran, Sang-Wha Sien, Shwetak N. Patel, Julie A. Kientz, Laura R. Pina, *University of Washington*

6876 Examining Menstrual Tracking to Inform the Design of Personal Informatics Tools
Daniel A. Epstein, *University of Washington*
Nicole B. Lee, *Independent Researcher*
Jennifer H. Kang, Elena Agapie, Jessica Schroeder, Laura R. Pina, *University of Washington*
James Fogarty, *Computer Science & Engineering*
Julie A. Kientz, Sean Munson, *University of Washington*

6889 Quantifying the Body and Caring for the Mind: Self-Tracking in Multiple Sclerosis
Amid Ayobi, Paul Marshall, Anna L. Cox, *University College London*
Yunan Chen, *University of California, Irvine*

Session: Presentation in Online Communities

6902 Share First, Save Later: Performance of Self through Snapchat Stories
Sarah McRoberts, Haiwei Ma, Andrew Hall, Svetlana Yarosh, *University of Minnesota*

6912 Situated Anonymity: Impacts of Anonymity, Ephemerality, and Hyper-Locality on Social Media
Ari Schlesinger, Eshwar Chandrasekharan, Amy S. Bruckman, W. Keith Edwards, Rebecca E. Grinter, *Georgia Institute of Technology*

6925 Relational Distancing and Termination between Online Friends: An Application of the Investment Model
Christopher J. Carpenter, *Western Illinois University*
Stephanie Tom Tong, *Wayne State University*

6936 Enhancing Personal Informatics Through Social Sensemaking
Aare Puussaar, *Newcastle University*
Adrian K. Clear, *Northumbria University*
Peter Wright, *Newcastle University*

6943 Sizing Up the Troll: A Quantitative Characterization of Moderator-Identified Trolling in an Online Forum
Mattia Samory, Enoch Peserico, *University of Padua*

Session: Sharing, People and Communities

6948 Building a Maker Community Around an Open Hardware Platform
Fabio Morreale, Giulio Moro, *Queen Mary University of London*
Alan Chamberlain, Steve Benford, *The University of Nottingham*
Andrew P. McPherson, *Queen Mary University of London*

6960 Celebratory Technology to Orchestrate the Sharing of Devices and Stories during Family Mealtimes
Hasan Shahid Ferdous, Frank Vetere, *The University of Melbourne*
Hilary Davis, *The University of Melbourne & Swinburne University of Technology*
Bernd Ploderer, *Queensland University of Technology*
Kenton O'Hara, *Microsoft Research*
Rob Comber, *Newcastle University*
Geremy Farr-Wharton, *Newcastle University*

6973 Exploring Topic-Based Sharing Mechanisms
Manya Sleeper, Lorrie Faith Cranor, Sarah K. Pearman, *Carnegie Mellon University*

6986 HCI and Environmental Public Policy: Opportunities for Engagement
Vanessa Thomas, *Lancaster University*
Christian Remy, *University of Zurich*
Mike Hazas, Oliver Bates, *Lancaster University*

Session: Technology in the Workplace

6993 Utilizing Experience Goals in Design of Industrial Systems
Virpi Roto, *Aalto University*
Eija Kaasinen, *VTT Technical Research Centre of Finland Ltd.*
Tomi Heimonen, *University of Wisconsin-Stevens Point*
Hannu Karvonen, *VTT Technical Research Centre of Finland Ltd.*
Jussi P. P. Jokinen, Petri Mannonen, *Aalto University*
Hannu Nousu, *KONE Corporation*
Jaakko Hakulinen, *University of Tampere*
Yichen Lu, *Design and Architecture*
Pertti O. Saariluoma, *University of Jyväskylä*
Tiina Kymäläinen, *VTT Technical Research Centre of Finland Ltd.*
Tuuli Keskinen, Markku Turunen, *University of Tampere*
Hanna Maria Kaarina Koskinen, *VTT Technical Research Centre of Finland Ltd.*

7005 Evaluating Digital Creativity Support to Improve Health-and-Safety in a Manufacturing Plant
Neil Maiden, Konstantinos Zachos, James Lockerbie, *City University London*
Sergio Levis, *FCA Group*
Kasia Camargo, Shaun Hoddy, Gianluca Allemandi, *CNH Industrial*

Table of Contents

7015 **The Design Fictions of Philanthropic IT: Stuck Between an Imperfect Present and an Impossible Future**
Ellie Harmon, Chris Bopp, Amy Voida, *University of Colorado, Boulder*

7029 **Proxemic Transitions: Designing Shape-Changing Furniture for Informal Meetings**
Jens Emil Grønbæk, Henrik Korsgaard, Marianne Graves Petersen, Morten Henriksen Birk, Peter Gall Krogh, *Aarhus University*

Session: Technology Use Challenges for Older Adults

7042 **Successful Leisure in Independent Living Communities: Understanding Older Adults' Motivations to Engage in Leisure Activities**
Amanda Lazar, *Northwestern University*
David H. Nguyen, *Accenture Labs*

7057 **Navigating Relationships and Boundaries: Concerns around ICT-uptake for Elderly People**
Dominik Hornung, Claudia Müller, *University of Siegen*
Irina Shklovski, *IT University of Copenhagen*
Timo Jakobi, Volker Wulf, *University of Siegen*

7070 **Older Adults Learning Computer Programming: Motivations, Frustrations, and Design Opportunities**
Philip J. Guo, *University of California, San Diego*

7084 **Author Index**

CHI 2017 Organization

Conference Chairs
Gloria Mark, University of California, Irvine
Susan Fussell, Cornell University

Assistants to General Chairs
Yiran Wang, University of California, Irvine
Ge Gao, Cornell University

Senior Technical Program Chair
Cliff Lampe, University of Michigan

Technical Program Chair
m.c. schraefel, University of Southampton

Assistant to the Technical Program Chairs
Lindsay Blackwell, University of Michigan

Papers Chairs
Caroline Appert, Univ. Paris-Sud & CNRS
Juan Pablo Hourcade, University of Iowa
Daniel Wigdor, University of Toronto

Assistant to Papers Chairs
Michael Glueck, University of Toronto

alt.chi Chairs
Karrie Karahalios, University of Illinois at Urbana – Champaign
Jessa Lingel, University of Pennsylvania
Janet Vertesi, Princeton University

Case Studies Chairs
Stephen Snow, University of Southampton
Jessica Tsimeris, Google

Courses Chairs
Erik Andersen, Cornell University
Hilary Hutchinson, Google
Max Wilson, University of Nottingham

Demos Chairs
Ido Guy, Yahoo
Stephen Voida, University of Colorado Boulder

Doctoral Consortium Chairs
Anna Cox, University College London
Jeff Bigham, Carnegie Mellon University
Kenton O'Hara, Microsoft Research, UK

Interactive Installations Chairs
Adrian Friday, Lancaster University
Shengdong Zhao, National University of Singapore

Late Breaking Work Chairs
Sharon Ding, Fudan University
Ingrid Erikson, Rutgers University
Bryan Semaan, Syracuse University
Fanis Tsandilas, INRIA

Panels Chairs
Sarita Schoenebeck, University of Michigan
Jude Yew, National University of Singapore

Student Design Competition Chairs
Joonhwan Lee, Seoul National University
Scott Minneman, California College of Arts

Student Game Competition Chairs
Floyd Mueller, RMIT University
Josh Tanenbaum, University of California, Irvine

Student Research Competition Chairs
Jeremy Birnholtz, Northwestern University
Jenn Thom, Spotify

Special Interest Groups Chairs
Lindsay Reynolds, Facebook
Bert Scerbo, Disney

Systems Chairs
Michael Stewart, Virginia Tech
Dorota Filipczuk, University of Southampton

Symposia Chair
Lana Yarosh, University of Minnesota

Video Showcase Chairs
Danyel Fisher, Microsoft Research
Catherine Letondal, ENAC

Workshops Chairs
Duncan Brumby, University College London
Christopher Frauenberger, Vienna University of Technology, Austria
Shamsi Iqbal, Microsoft Research

Art Chairs
Jiffer Harriman, University of Colorado
Andruid Kerne, Texas A&M University
HyunJoo Oh, University of Colorado Boulder
Thecla Schiphorst, Simon Fraser University

CHI Stories Chairs
Nazanin Andalibi, Drexel University
Nick Diakopoulos, University of Maryland, College Park
Andrea Forte, Drexel University
Misa Maruyama, University of Hawaii at Manoa
Scott Robertson, University of Hawaii at Manoa

Career Development Workshop Chairs
Luigina Ciolfi, Sheffield Hallam University
Michael Muller, IBM Research

Journals Chair
Hrvoje Benko, Microsoft Research

Remix Chairs
Susan Dray, Dray & Associates
Amy Voida, University of Colorado Boulder

Student Volunteer Chairs
Patrick Carrington, University of Maryland, Baltimore County (UMBC)
Anna Kötteritzsch, Universität der Bundeswehr München

Video Previews Chair
Carla Griggio, Inria

Awards Chair
Steven Drucker, Microsoft

Accessibility Chairs
Erin Brady, Indiana University – Purdue University Indianapolis
Sean Goggins, Missouri University
Shaun Kane, University of Colorado Boulder

Data Chair
Boyu Gao, Konkuk University
Toni-Jan Keith Monserrat, University of the Philippines Los Baños

Diversity and Inclusivity Lunch Chairs
Anke Brock, Inria Bordeaux
Allison Druin, University of Maryland
Gopinaath Kannabiran, Indiana University, Bloomington

Language Inclusion Chair
Tilman Dingler, University of Stuttgart

Local Arrangements Chairs
Jed Brubaker, University of Colorado Boulder
Tom Yeh, University of Colorado Boulder

Social Impact Chairs
Kathy Baxter, Salesforce
Elizabeth Gerber, Northwestern University
Jill Woelfer, Google

Social Media Chairs
Dan Afergan, Google
Bart Knijnenburg, Clemson University
Vicky McArthur, University of Toronto Mississauga

Telepresence Chairs
Min Kyung Lee, Carnegie Mellon University
Carman Neustaedter, Simon Fraser University

Translations Chairs
Hao-Chuan Wang, National Tsing Hua University
Naomi Yamashita, Nippon Telegraph and Telephone

Design Director
Donghee Yvette Wohn, New Jersey Institute of Technology

Logo Design/Artwork
Jia Zhang, MIT Media Lab

Web Designer
Xiying Wang, Cornell University

Webmaster
Xiying Wang, Cornell University

ACM Liaison
Farrah Khan, ACM

SIGCHI Liaison
Scooter Morris, University of California, San Francisco

Conference Management
Paul Henning, Conference & Logistics Consultants, Inc.
Stacey Ogren, Conference & Logistics Consultants, Inc.
Lois Sarfo-Mensah, Conference & Logistics Consultants, Inc.
Michael O'Connell, Conference & Logistics Consultants, Inc.

Registration
Taylor Vick, Executive Events, Inc.

Sponsorship and Exhibits
Carol Klyver, Foundations of Excellence

Technical Liaison
Sara Drenner, BI WORLDWIDE

Better Organization or a Source of Distraction? Introducing Digital Peer Feedback to a Paper-Based Classroom

Amy Shannon
Carnegie Mellon University
Pittsburgh, USA
amyshann@andrew.cmu.edu

Alex Sciuto
Carnegie Mellon University
Pittsburgh, USA
sciutoalex@gmail.com

Danielle Hu
Carnegie Mellon University
Pittsburgh, USA
daniellh@andrew.cmu.edu

Steven P. Dow
University of California, San Diego
San Diego, USA
spdow@ucsd.edu

Jessica Hammer
Carnegie Mellon University
Pittsburgh, USA
hammerj@andrew.cmu.edu

ABSTRACT

Peer feedback is a central activity for project-based design education. The prevalence of devices carried by students and the emergence of novel peer feedback systems enables the possibility of collecting and sharing feedback immediately between students during class. However, pen and paper is thought to be more familiar, less distracting for students, and easier for instructors to implement and manage. To evaluate the efficacy of in-class digital feedback systems, we conducted a within-subjects study with 73 students during two weeks of a game design course. After short student presentations, while instructors provided verbal feedback, peers provided feedback either on paper or through a device. The study found that both methods yielded comments of similar quality and quantity, but the digital approach provided additional ways for students to participate and required less effort from the instructors. While both methods produced similar behaviors, students held inaccurate perceptions about their behavior with each method. We discuss design implications for technologies to support in-class feedback exchange.

Author Keywords

In-class activities, peer feedback; interactive learning techniques; computer-supported collaborative learning

ACM Classification Keywords

K.3.1. Computer Uses in Education: Collaborative Learning; H.5.3 Group and Organization Interfaces: Computer-supported cooperative work.

INTRODUCTION

Learning to give and receive feedback helps students build a core skillset for project-based education [1,5]. Feedback from instructors can help students align their work with evaluation rubrics [26] and think critically about how others view their work [7]. Many instructors use peer feedback to help students receive more feedback, and in a more timely manner than from the instructor alone (e.g. [13]).

Classrooms currently implement peer feedback in a variety of ways, but each of these methods have challenges. Verbal feedback techniques, such as question & answer periods or open design critiques, allow the entire group to hear all the feedback given. However, in many classes, whether due to time constraints or social anxiety, not everyone gets to speak. Verbal feedback can also be easy to forget unless written down or recorded.

Written feedback, such as typing comments into an email or filling out paper evaluation forms, allows every peer to give feedback privately and in parallel, so the time required to give feedback does not need to scale to accommodate larger classes. However, these strategies do not give peers the ability to see feedback already given by other peers. Further, handwritten feedback can sometimes be illegible and difficult to organize.

A number of digital peer feedback systems have emerged to help collect and organize written feedback [5,13,21]. Courses typically use peer feedback systems outside of class time, which creates extra work for students and can take time away from reflecting on and improving their work [13]. As a solution for this, some researchers have explored using feedback systems *during* class to gather relevant, copious, timely, and diverse feedback [6,20]. However, prior work has not sufficiently explored the potential drawbacks of digital in-class peer feedback. For example, bringing new technologies into a classroom might be distracting for students and unwieldy for instructors.

Instructors lack guidance on the efficacy of using devices to facilitate in-class peer feedback and how this compares to other real-time feedback methods. Therefore, this study investigates if a digital peer feedback system produces feedback of equal or better quality and quantity compared to a paper-based method during class, if the digital system distracts students, and if the digital system provides additional benefits.

We conducted a within-subjects study in a project-based course with 73 students. During two consecutive weeks of project presentations, peers provided feedback either on

ACM 978-1-4503-4655-9/17/05...$15.00
DOI: http://dx.doi.org/10.1145/3025453.3025564

paper or through a digital device. To facilitate digital feedback exchange, we used a peer feedback system for web and mobile where students can enter feedback and read/upvote comments written by others. Students provided feedback (either on paper or a device) while the instructors gave verbal feedback, keeping with the culture of this particular course.

Our study examined the quantity and quality of feedback provided with each method, student perceptions of each method, and differences between student and instructor feedback. We found that both methods yielded a similar number of unique open-ended comments, although the digital approach led to more student participation overall when accounting for upvotes. Students generally felt they had better feedback exchanges on paper, although assessments on the feedback by instructors indicated no difference in quality. Surveys and interviews with students revealed split opinions. Students who preferred paper liked the ability to create sketches; others appreciated the social awareness and dynamics afforded by the digital method.

This research contributes: 1) empirical evidence that digital systems can be equally as effective as paper-based methods for eliciting student feedback during class, 2) design implications for peer feedback systems, and 3) a discussion on how classroom culture and student expectations might affect the implementation and use of an in-class peer feedback system.

RELATED WORK

The peer feedback process is valued by researchers and educators because it allows students to get a larger quantity of feedback than if the instructor were the only feedback provider [22]. It also allows students to receive feedback faster than if every student was waiting on the instructor. This is particularly important given that a recent study found peer feedback helped students improve their grades, but only if delivered within a timely manner [13].

Peer feedback also improves student learning. Students who reflect on peer feedback and revise their work improve their self-regulated learning skills [3] and self-assessment abilities [15]. Students who provide feedback can learn to focus on students' work and performance, rather than on the students themselves or their personal characteristics [9]. This process also helps students understand the desired criteria (relevant), compare their actual performance with these criteria (critical), and engage in action that closes this gap (actionable) [16,18]. We use those criteria—relevant, critical, and actionable—as metrics to evaluate the feedback given during this study.

Student and Instructor Feedback

Multiple researchers have shown that novice peer feedback can be as effective as receiving feedback from an expert, such as the instructor. Topping [22] found that peer assessment, where students provide a grade in addition to feedback, can improve student performance at least as much as instructor feedback. Cho and Schunn [5] used their SWoRD system for providing feedback on writing assignments to show that students receiving feedback from a group of novices had greater improvement on their next draft than students receiving feedback from a single expert, perhaps because students consider peer feedback carefully rather than blindly adhering to expert suggestions. Yuan et al [25] found that when students used rubrics to give critiques, their feedback was perceived to be as useful as expert feedback.

While experts have deep domain knowledge, peers have the advantage of sharing the experiences and challenges of the student. Experts often poorly estimate what feedback is most helpful to novices [12], in part because experts tend to reference concepts and information that novices do not yet possess [4]. Peers, on the other hand, share concepts and skills with the student receiving the feedback, as they are at a similar level of expertise [5]. Even if the content of the feedback is less expert, it may be easier for students to process and understand. Peer feedback can therefore supplement expert feedback, as each has different strengths and weaknesses.

Real-Time Technology in the Classroom

Bringing technology into the classroom may reveal challenges related to classroom culture and technology adoption that are not a factor when using paper to collect feedback. Technology can be a distraction to students during class [8], not only to the students using the system, but also to instructors or students who present to an inattentive audience. Instructors may also be hesitant to introduce an unfamiliar technology into a live class [2].

Although many advocate for the benefits of using paper instead of digital or electronic information (e.g. [19]), researchers have started investigating the effects of using digital systems in the classroom. Piper and Hollan [17] found that students were more engaged with educational material presented on a tabletop display than with the same material presented on paper. The study found students who used the tabletop display solved problems on their own before resorting to answer keys and repeated activities more often than students who used paper documents.

Peer Feedback Systems

Most peer feedback systems are designed for use outside of class, typically by requiring students to review a certain number of peer assignments before they receive their own feedback [13]. As demonstrated in prior work, this design choice creates a burden on students to find additional time outside of class and limits the number of perspectives represented in the feedback a student receives [13]. These challenges may be mitigated by an in-class peer feedback system that mimics the process used when providing written feedback during class [20]. The open question that we explore in this research is how in-class digital peer feedback systems compare with other methods.

Figure 1. Screenshot from a game created by students in the final presentation.

METHOD

Participants

We conducted a study with 73 students in a graduate-level project-based course on designing virtual environments and games (see Figure 1 for an example). The instructor divided students into fifteen teams to complete course projects, each lasting around two weeks. Teams were randomized between projects. The course, offered at a mid-western university in the United States, was divided into two sections—one in the morning and one in the afternoon. Students were assigned to present their work in a particular session, but they could also attend the other session to provide feedback, and often did. Each section met for three hours twice a week. All fifteen teams presented designs to the class each week, either as a work in progress or as a finished product. Half of the teams presented in the morning section and half in the afternoon section; in both sections, the entire class session was devoted to presenting work and receiving feedback.

Classroom Setting

Before our comparative study, we observed the class for one week to establish a baseline before introducing the digital system. We also briefly interviewed the two course instructors prior to our observation using a semi-structured interview process to gain insights on their development of the existing peer feedback techniques used in this course.

As part of the regular feedback process in the course, the class used a paper-based system. Before class, the teaching assistants would leave a pile of notecards on each chair in the classroom. Students were expected to write feedback on one notecard per presenting team. Figure 2 shows an example paper notecard. After each student presentation, the course instructors would give public verbal feedback to the presenting team. Students could provide written feedback at any point; there were no restrictions on when they could and could not write. At the end of class, notecards were handed directly to a representative from each presenting team. Instructors and teaching assistants never saw what was written on the notecards, and did not record or grade participation in the feedback process.

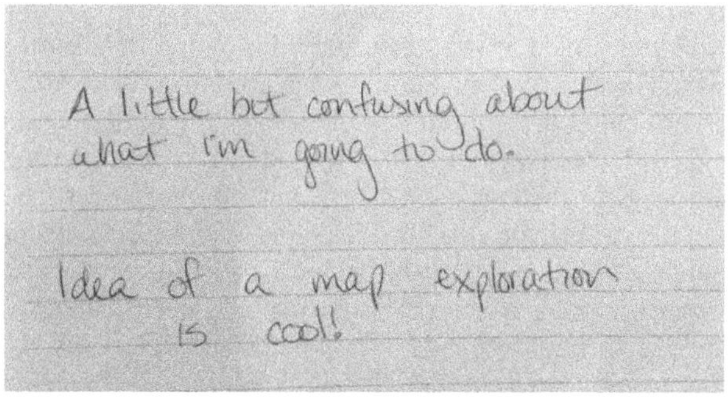

Figure 2. Example of a paper notecard.

Despite the existence of a formal feedback process, the course instructors did not feel students were successfully learning peer feedback skills. Instructors commented that students would not give helpful or high-quality feedback to each other. Further, the instructors felt the teams were not sufficiently reflecting on the instructors' or peers' feedback. One instructor pointed out that they had recently implemented a new assignment to "make them at least read [the feedback]".

An instructor said that "the class is defined by students showing work off to each other" and that they believe students have a "strong desire to share and discuss what's being done." We observed students paying close attention during student presentations, so much so that they would often audibly react to the game demos. After each presentation, instructors would spend up to twenty minutes giving verbal feedback. During this time, students would spend no more than five minutes writing feedback on their notecards, and we observed how students would drift towards Facebook, mobile phones, or other off-topic distractions until the next presentation began. We frequently observed students falling asleep between presentations while instructors were speaking.

The Digital Feedback System

For a digital comparison to the paper feedback process, we used an open source peer feedback system designed to be used in real-time during the class session [20]. With this system, students access presentations on either a laptop or a mobile device using a short sharable link. Students choose a username for each presentation. There are no requirements or restrictions on what can be chosen as a username. Students can type multiple responses into a text box in real-time during the presentation. Students can view and upvote the responses given by other students in real-time on a separate tab of the system interface. Voting students cannot see the author's username, but that information is available to the presenting team. Afterwards, the presenting team can view all their feedback and sort, tag, and filter comments to organize the feedback received. Screenshots of this system are shown in Figure 3.

Procedure

We implemented a two-week study during the final project. During the first week, the morning section gave feedback on paper, and the afternoon section used the digital system to provide feedback. For the second week, the afternoon section gave feedback on paper, and the morning section used the digital system. Each team presented for about four minutes, followed by 10-20 minutes of instructors' verbal feedback, during which time students provided feedback on paper or through their devices. For these two weeks, if a class section was in the digital condition, the teaching assistant for the course transcribed all the instructors' verbal comments into the digital system for later comparison with student comments. The research team had extra devices available in case students did not have access to technology, but the students never needed them.

Students were given a pre-survey before the study asking their opinions on the paper process, challenges they faced when giving or receiving feedback on paper, and their current process of reflecting on feedback. The pre-survey consisted primarily of Likert-scale questions for agreement: for example, "How much do you agree/disagree with the following statement: I can say everything I want to say using the paper notecards". Students were also given a post survey at the end of the study asking them to compare the paper process to the digital system by reporting perceived differences between each method with multiple-choice questions (PeerPresents, Notecard Rodeo, or No preference). We also asked students to express their preferences on open-ended questions, which we analyzed to extract themes and interesting comments.

Measures and Analysis

Student Participation

From system logs, we collected the usernames used by students, the responses and timestamps of those responses, and a list of usernames that voted on each response. We collected and transcribed the notecards and counted how many notecards included drawings.

To measure how long students stayed engaged with paper-based peer feedback, a researcher observed two class sessions before the digital system was introduced. The researcher sat such that she could unobtrusively observe all students. The researcher recorded the times when each presentation started, when the majority of students had stopped writing, when all students had stopped writing, and when the instructors stopped talking. Length of engagement with the digital system was computed using system logs.

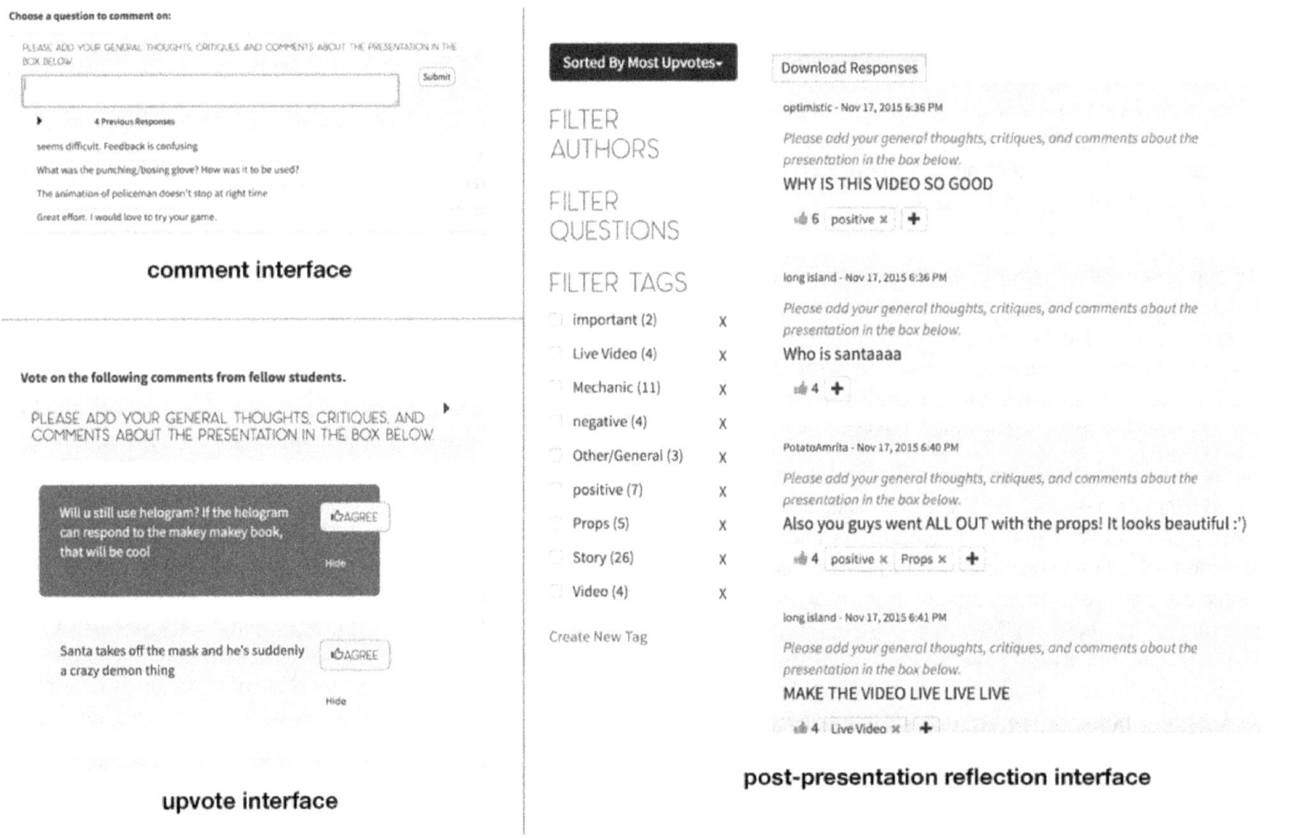

Figure 3. Screenshots of the digital system. Peers use the "comment interface" (upper left) to provide feedback. Peers can switch to the "upvote interface" (lower left) to review other students' comments. The "reflection interface" (right) allows presenters to organize their feedback after the presentation.

Feedback Quality

We surveyed students on the perceived quality of the feedback exchange with each method. We also asked students for their opinions on the strengths and weaknesses of each method. Finally, we randomly selected 10 comments each from two digital condition presentations and two paper condition presentations and asked instructors to rate the quality of comments on a scale from 1 to 5. Instructors were blind to condition; the comments were a random sample of 10-15% of comments from 25% of the teams, as instructors were under tight time constraints and could not rate all comments.

Content Analysis

To further investigate the content of written responses, we segmented responses into individual comments and coded them into categories. We divided responses into individual comments primarily based on physical markers such as bullet points or numbers, separate sentences or sentence clauses, and skipped lines between items. We coded feedback into categories based on relevance, form, and sentiment (see [16,18]).

For relevance, comments were coded as On Topic (focused on content), On Topic (focused on communication skills), Emotional Support, or Off Topic. Comments were also coded as either Praise, Criticism, Neither praise nor criticism, or Both praise and criticism. Comments were also coded as Descriptive, Actionable, Question, or None of the above. Descriptive comments were stating observations or describing the game. Actionable comments were offering specific suggestions or giving instructions. Questions were comments where students asked the presenters a question. Table 1 lists examples of each type of comment. Three independent coders categorized 10% of the data and achieved moderate agreement. After discussion and retraining on all categories, coding agreement on an additional 5% of the data reached an acceptable agreement of ICC 0.85.

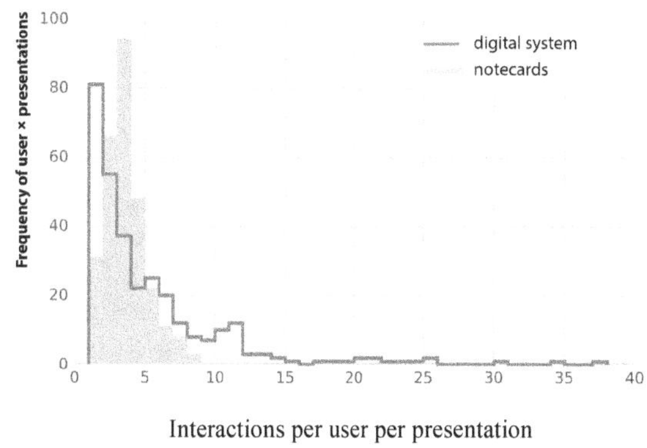

Figure 4. Distribution of interactions per user per presentation shows some students interacted much more with the digital system.

RESULTS

The overall results show that students wrote a similar number of comments on paper as the digital condition, and instructors rated comments from both conditions to be equal in quality. Students in the digital condition interacted in more diverse ways and for a longer period of time than with paper, despite students expressing a preference for paper.

In both the paper and digital condition, there was an average of 20 respondents per presentation (approximately 2/3 of the class; the other 1/3 chose not to participate). Each respondent gave an average of three comments per presentation (an average of 57 comments per presentation). About half (56%) of students' digital responses received at least 1 upvote. Across all presentations in the digital system, 44% of students were active voters (more than 3 upvotes), and 1 student voted on every presentation but did not provide any written comments. 13% of paper notecards had drawings.

Comment Relevance	On Topic: Content	"Music could have been more intense"
	On Topic: Communication	"It's interesting how it's only one person responding to questions, and the same person standing apart from the team…
	Emotional Support	"Great effort"; "I would love to try your game"
	Off Topic	"Shooting lazers!!!"
Comment Form	Descriptive	"health bar looks like a shield"
	Actionable	"Could add sound effect for teacher turning around"
	Question	"What was the punching/bosing glove? How was it to be used?"
	None of the Above	"RIP mama bird"
Comment Sentiment	Praise	"Whoa nice lighting effects"
	Criticism	"The animation of policeman doesn't stop at right time"
	Neither	"How to lose the game?"

Table 1. Example comments for each coding category.

No Difference in Number of Comments per Condition
Students produced a similar number of textual comments on paper as they did on their devices (for paper, M=61.5 (SD=18.75); for digital, M=53.2 (SD=17.42)), and there was no significant difference between conditions in the average length of comments (for paper, M=50.07 (SD=38.92); for digital, M=55.94 (SD=48.45)). There was also no significant difference in the number of comments per presentation (for paper, M=3.04 (SD=1.45); for digital, M=2.86 (SD=1.85)). Based on our observations and from our discussions with students, students did not give verbal feedback to other teams at any time outside of class.

No Difference in Quality of Comments per Condition
Based on instructors' blind-to-condition ratings on a scale of 1 to 5, there was no significant difference in comment quality between conditions (for paper, M=2.7 (SD=0.77); for digital, M=2.5 (SD=0.65)).

More Ways to Interact in Digital Condition
The digital system provided an additional way for students to interact through upvotes. Figure 4 shows the distribution of interactions per user over time. With the digital system, many students made only one interaction, while one made as many as 37 interactions in one presentation.

Longer Length of Engagement in Digital Condition
In our observations of the paper system, the majority of students began writing comments after the presentation ended and stopped participating in the feedback process within five minutes (M= 3.75 minutes (SD=0.96)). With the digital system, students stayed engaged longer and spent more time giving comments, as shown in Figure 5, some continuing to comment for more than 20 minutes.

Students Thought Paper Produced More Feedback
On the post survey, students reported feeling that they received more feedback from paper notecards, $X^2(1,N=73)=17.31$, $p<0.05$. Students did not report a significant difference between paper and digital in terms of what led them to participate more during class, or what led them to give more feedback during class.

Students Perceived Paper Produced Better Feedback
Students believed they gave higher quality feedback on paper, $t(73)=8.33$, $p < 0.05$ Students also believed they received higher quality feedback from paper notecards, $t(73) = 35.0$, $p < 0.05$. However, as noted above, there was no significant difference in comment quality between conditions.

More Content-Related Comments Using Paper
There was a significantly different distribution of comments among relevance categories, X^2 (3,N=1659) = 55.60, $p<0.05$ (see Table 2). Students in the paper condition had more On-Topic-Content comments, fewer On-Topic-Communication comments, and fewer Off-Topic comments than students in the digital condition. There were a similar number of Emotional-Support comments, Critical comments, and Actionable comments between conditions.

Faculty Gave More Critical and Actionable Feedback
Instructors gave more relevant comments, less praise, more criticism, and more actionable comments compared to students in either condition (see Table 2). This aligns closely with the prior work's definition of "good" feedback as relevant, critical, and actionable [16,18].

Student Opinions
Open-ended questions on the survey asked students to describe the strengths and weaknesses of each feedback method. Students provided opinions on four key aspects.

Physical Constraints on Paper and Devices
Students said that it was hard to read handwriting on the notecards, and we observed students ignoring cards they could not read in team discussions. Students said it was difficult to write in the dark classroom, and they frequently forgot to bring a pen. Students also believed they ran out of space on the cards.

		Student notecards	Student digital	Faculty
Comment Relevance	On Topic: Content	793 (92.1%)	666 (82.5%)	149 (98%)
	On Topic: Communication	20 (2.3%)	35 (4.4%)	2 (1.3%)
	Emotional Support	43 (5.0%)	33 (4.1%)	1 (0.1%)
	Off Topic	5 (0.5%)	64 (8.0%)	0 (0%)
Comment Form	Descriptive	642 (74.6%)	535 (67.0%)	96 (63.1%)
	Actionable	113 (13.1%)	109 (13.7%)	44 (29.0%)
	Question	75 (8.7%)	91 (11.4%)	12 (7.9%)
	None of the Above	31 (3.6%)	63 (7.9%)	0 (0%)
Comment Sentiment	Praise	406 (47.2%)	311 (39.0%)	30 (19.7%)
	Criticism	227 (26.4%)	200 (25.1%)	53 (34.9%)
	Neither	269 (31.2%)	318 (39.8%)	75 (49.3%)

Table 2. Distribution of comment type for students in each condition and for instructors.

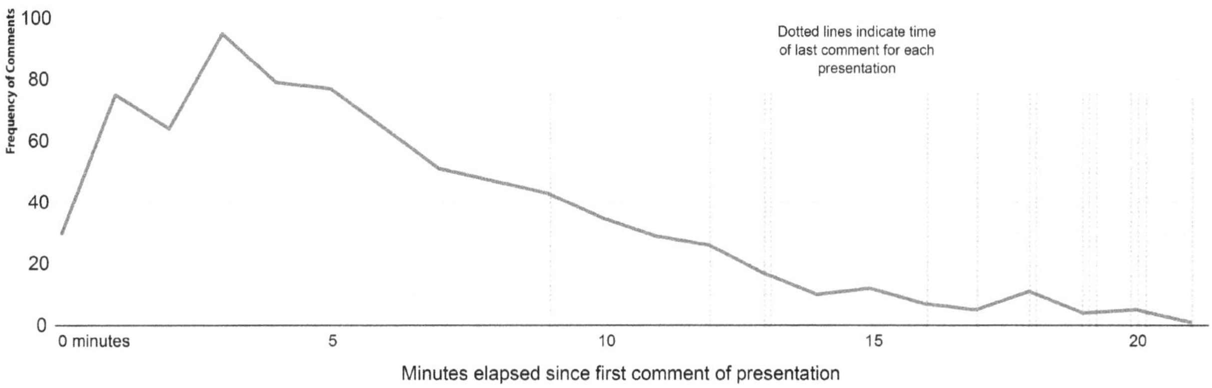

Figure 5. Digital comments peaked around 4 minutes, but continued for up to 20 minutes for some presentations.

When using the digital system, students said that not everyone has a laptop, and the mobile view of the system was not always sufficient. Students expressed the inability to draw as a major shortcoming of the digital system.

Digital Supported a Social Atmosphere

Students felt that the digital system was "fun", "funny", and "social." Students commented that they liked being able to see other students' opinions during class. However, some students felt the social atmosphere had drawbacks. Students felt the comments turned into more of a group chat than a meaningful critique, and that some students were "performing" by trying to write the funniest or most provocative comments, rather than trying to give the most helpful feedback.

Anonymity and Criticism

A few students commented that they felt uncomfortable being critical when the entire class could see their comments, even when the comment did not have their name on it. Students also disagreed on which method felt more anonymous. Some felt notecards were "completely anonymous", even though we observed that students often recognized each other's handwriting and drawing style. Others appreciated that the digital system allowed them to choose an anonymous username, and that the username was only visible to the presenting team.

Organization in Both Conditions

There were dissenting opinions among students about which method better supported feedback organization after class. Some felt notecards were easier to organize because all team members could see them without needing a device. Others preferred the sorting and tagging features provided in the digital system. Others did not organize their feedback with either method.

DISCUSSION

This within-subjects study compared different media—paper and digital—for collecting peer feedback in a classroom setting. We found that contrary to popular opinion, technology does not detract from the peer feedback process, as long as it is used appropriately. Students wrote a similar number of comments with both methods, and instructors rated comments from both conditions to be equal in quality. Students in the digital condition interacted in more diverse ways and for a longer period of time than with paper. However, students generally preferred the paper notecards, and believed that they received more feedback and gave higher quality feedback on paper than online. Here we discuss the discrepancy between students' perceptions and reality, the ancillary benefits of going digital, the effects on classroom culture, and the pedagogical affordances of each approach. Finally, we deliberate on the design implications, study limitations, and future work.

Student Perceptions vs. Reality

Students accurately believed that they *gave* the same amount of feedback with each approach. However, they inaccurately believed they *received* more feedback from paper notecards, even though there was no significant difference in the average numbers of comments per presentation between conditions or the average length of comments. Our observations revealed that some students did not bring a device to the team meetings when students discussed their feedback, which may account for this discrepancy. Even though an equal amount of feedback was available, some students may not have seen it.

Students also believed they gave and received higher quality feedback on paper, and that the digital system was more of a social group chat than a meaningful critique. However, the instructors' ratings indicate no difference in comment quality between conditions. This misconception may be due to the different distribution of comments for each method, as students in the paper condition gave more content-related comments, fewer communication-related comments, and fewer off-topic comments than in the digital condition. This misconception could relate to the students' perspective that peers were acting like "performers" on the digital system. The public nature of commenting may have led students to believe they received more off-topic comments than was actually the case.

Ancillary Benefits of the Digital System

Paper notecards and the digital system perform equally well at generating useful comments. However, there are additional advantages to using a digital approach.

Facilitating Diverse Input and Social Interactions

The ability to comment quickly, endlessly, and in real-time seems to have encouraged students to give feedback on in-the-moment observations such as presentation style, which they were less inclined to comment on when using paper, perhaps because of their perception of a limited response space. The digital system allowed students to comment anonymously if they chose, which students valued.

Importantly, the digital system allowed multiple types of interactions during class, a strategy supported by the theory of legitimate peripheral participation [14]. Students who felt less inclined to comment could still participate by reading and voting on other comments. This additional method of participation could explain why students stayed engaged with the digital system for so much longer than observed when writing on the paper notecards.

Students remarked on some negative aspects of the social atmosphere they experienced in the digital system, and there were more off-topic comments in the digital version. We expect this is related to the sense of immediacy the system provides, allowing students to capture their transient thoughts and ideas more easily than when writing feedback on a notecard. When students feel free to respond with what's on their mind, they produce more off-topic comments, but also more comments related to in-the-moment observations such as communication style or points of confusion that might later be resolved.

Providing Organization Support

The digital system offered organization support for students to sort and tag their feedback. While not all students chose to utilize those features, the ones that did found the process valuable to their reflection, which has been shown to be an essential aspect of peer feedback by prior researchers [16].

However, while some teams valued the organization provided by the digital system, the sorting and tagging functionality did not support every team's reflection process. Some teams relied on physically sorting and grouping notecards in a way that could not be captured with the digital system. The digital system had a "Download Responses" button that allowed students to print out their comments, but students did not use this feature.

Handling the Logistics of Peer Feedback

The digital system also provided support for instructors. The system made the logistics of giving and receiving feedback easier, which is a factor teachers value when implementing in-class technology [2]. Teaching assistants did not have to hand out piles of notecards to every chair, team leaders did not have to gather cards from every student, and feedback was never lost in the way a misplaced notecard would be. In larger classes, the paper notecard process would be unmanageable from a logistics standpoint, but the digital system scales.

Effects on Classroom Culture

The instructors commented on the investment students had in their peers' projects. The faculty believed every student was writing notecard feedback, when really only two-thirds of the class participated on paper. Introducing the digital system did not change the number of participants in class.

The digital system did increase the length of time students were engaged in the peer feedback process, but faculty may have been unaware of this difference. When we observed instructors giving verbal feedback before introducing the digital system, they stood at the front of the room facing the presenters, with their backs to the rest of the class. Thus, they could not see when students became disengaged with the feedback process and turned to Facebook or fell asleep.

It is important to note that giving students a specific task to do on their devices kept their attention on course content for a longer period of time than asking them to put their devices away and comment on paper. Students did not report feeling distracted when using the digital system either as a presenter or as a feedback provider. Using a digital system also did not change the quality of the student feedback. The classroom culture around peer feedback did not significantly change because of our two-week system intervention.

Pedagogical Affordances of Digital and Paper

Although students valued the paper feedback more, instructors should choose a peer feedback system that provides the most pedagogically effective approach for a given classroom context. To understand the pedagogical differences between the paper and digital systems, we examined the affordances each provides. Paper provides better tangibility, spatial awareness, and flexibility [11]. The digital system builds on the affordances of social media, including visibility, editability, persistence, and association [23].

In our study, the tangibility of the paper notecards may have made that feedback more salient to students during reflection sessions. Students valued the flexibility to "break the rules" by providing drawings as feedback. Some groups relied on physically organizing the paper notecards, although it created a burden for the instructors and TAs.

The visibility of the digital system influenced students' social behavior, causing some of them to "perform" for the class. Visibility also allowed people to react to each other's comments by voting. The persistence afforded by the digital system meant students could see comments after the fact, promoting a longer length of engagement with the peer feedback process.

Students responded positively to the tangibility of the physical system, even when it created an extra burden for the instructors and TAs. On the other hand, the visibility of the digital system significantly influenced student behavior in both helpful and potentially distracting ways.

Students engaged with the affordances of each system in ways that revealed their needs in the feedback process. Paper sketching indicates that students desire to be expressive (which was further validated by their survey responses) while the use of upvoting suggests students' desire to be social (which was further validated by their "off-topic" comments in the digital condition). Future work can explore how to accomplish both these goals, as well as increase the quality of peer feedback.

Design Implications for Peer Feedback Systems

Future designs for in-class peer feedback systems can explore how visibility can improve student experience with the system, mitigate the perception of social performance, and increase the quality of peer feedback.

Expressiveness

Students took advantage of having multiple ways to interact with the digital feedback, particularly with low-effort upvotes. Students also enjoyed the social aspect of the system. They missed not being able to give expressive feedback through drawings. Supporting such expressive forms of interaction can help accommodate for a lack of nonverbal cues, a known issue in computer-mediated communication [24]. Future peer feedback systems could design other interactions that allow students to make their social self and emotional state visible in a helpful way. For example, a system could allow students to click on their mood throughout the presentation (confused, bored, engaged, etc.) or even add a meme to give feedback.

Mutual Awareness

In the digital condition, students were highly aware of the audience for comments, which produced concerns about "performing." However, mutual awareness also provided benefits such as the ability to learn from and vote on other students' comments. Future systems could explore more granular control of feedback visibility to support providing good feedback and reflecting on feedback received. For example, other students' comments might only become visible after a student has made a comment themselves.

Modeling Expert Behavior

In our study, instructors gave more criticism, less praise, and more actionable comments than students. Prior research has noted that students benefit from being more critical of each other when giving feedback [10]. However, listening to an expert give good feedback is not enough for students to improve their feedback skills. Future systems could explore other ways to model expert behavior and encourage relevant, critical, and actionable comments from students. For instance, many recent peer feedback systems explore the use of expert rubrics to scaffold the process [13,25]. Another idea would be to delegate to a student or a teaching assistant the job of transcribing the instructors' verbal comments, making them visible and available for further discussion in the digital system.

LIMITATIONS

The course setup provided constraints for our experiment design. We chose a within-subjects experiment because students could attend both the morning and afternoon sessions of the course. A between-subjects design would have required half the class to use only paper and half to use digital within the same session. This would have made it difficult not only for the instructors to manage, but also for the presenting students to reflect on feedback coming from both notecards and the system. Since both methods (paper and digital) supported anonymity, we were not able to perform within-subjects analysis on an individual basis.

In addition, while we did ask students to rate their feedback as a whole, we did not ask students to individually rate the quality of feedback they received. This information could have been valuable, and we intend to collect student ratings of individual comments in future studies. Future studies should also ask instructors to rate all comments rather than only a subset to better compare to student perspectives.

Finally, our system was deployed for only two weeks, which means that the novelty of the system may have affected our results. Future studies can explore how practices evolve in a digital feedback system over time.

FUTURE WORK

We chose to compare the digital system to a written feedback process rather than a verbal feedback process because written feedback is given in parallel, asynchronously, and in real time, which is more similar to the digital system than a verbal feedback process. This choice also allowed us to examine specific processes only available in the digital system, such as voting on other students' comments. In the future, we would like to make additional comparative evaluations of in-class peer feedback systems to better understand affordances of different in-class peer feedback approaches. For example, the digital system used in this study or another system could be compared to a verbal feedback process, such as a Q&A period. We also want to compare our in-class peer feedback system to a traditional out-of-class peer feedback system.

Digital feedback systems also provide a platform for future interventions. Additional comparisons could be done with versions of this digital system to discover effective interventions, or to mitigate the negative aspects of a social atmosphere. For example, we could make variations of the interface that encourage different levels of awareness of other student comments to see the effects of prioritizing commenting or voting in different educational settings.

We could also use the digital system to investigate attention management during class. Students in this study were more likely to remain attentive to course material when they were given a specific digital task. Future tools could investigate what tasks help students remain attentive, how long additional tasks can keep students' attention, how students decide when to disengage from the class, and what makes digital tasks more appealing than paper tasks.

Finally, future studies can explore methods for scaffolding peer feedback to look more like expert feedback. For example, we could investigate how to help students frame their own questions as part of a rubric. Another angle is to examine whether different levels of anonymity might encourage more critical feedback.

CONCLUSION

This research presented empirical evidence that shows digital methods can be at least as effective as paper at encouraging student interaction during class while offering logistical benefits for instructors. This work also indicates that students and professors may be overrating the benefits of paper-based feedback and overestimating potential negative effects of technology during class. We also developed design implications for in-class peer feedback systems to enable more expressiveness, to model expert behavior, and to explore different levels of awareness. We also discuss how factors such as classroom culture and student expectations might affect the implementation of an in-class peer feedback system to guide future designers of such systems.

ACKNOWLEDGEMENTS

We would like to thank the students, TAs, and instructors in Building Virtual Worlds for their participation. NSF grants #1122206 and #1122320 funded this research. The research reported here was supported, in whole or in part, by the Institute of Education Sciences, U.S. Department of Education, through Grant R305B150008 to Carnegie Mellon University. The opinions expressed are those of the authors and do not represent the views of the Institute or the U.S. Department of Education

REFERENCES

1. Hugh Beyer and Karen Holtzblatt. 1997. *Contextual Design: Defining Customer-Centered Systems*. Elsevier. Retrieved September 24, 2015 from https://books.google.com/books?hl=en&lr=&id=JxQaQgOONGIC&pgis=1

2. Charles Buabeng-Andoh. 2012. Factors influencing teachers' adoption and integration of information and communication technology into teaching: A review of the literature. *International Journal of Education and Development using Information and Communication Technology* 8, 1: 136–155. Retrieved September 24, 2015 from http://search.proquest.com/openview/938bbe87db68135bee298a6845a43dd9/1?pq-origsite=gscholar

3. Deborah L. Butler and Phillip H. Winne. 1995. Feedback and self-regulated learning: A theoretical synthesis. *Review of educational research.* Retrieved June 24, 2015 from http://rer.sagepub.com/content/65/3/245.short

4. C. Camerer, G. Lowenstein, and M. Weber. 1989. The curse of knowledge in economic settings: an experimental analysis. *Journal of Political Economy*, 97: 1232–1254.

5. Kwangsu Cho and Christian D. Schunn. 2007. Scaffolded writing and rewriting in the discipline: A web-based reciprocal peer review system. *Computers & Education* 48, 3: 409–426. http://doi.org/10.1016/j.compedu.2005.02.004

6. Matthew W. Easterday, Daniel Rees Lewis, Colin Fitzpatrick, and Elizabeth M. Gerber. 2014. Computer supported novice group critique. *Proceedings of the 2014 conference on Designing interactive systems - DIS '14*, ACM Press, 405–414. http://doi.org/10.1145/2598510.2600889

7. Peggy A. Ertmer, Jennifer C. Richardson, Brian Belland, et al. 2007. Using Peer Feedback to Enhance the Quality of Student Online Postings: An Exploratory Study. *Journal of Computer-Mediated Communication* 12, 2: 412–433. http://doi.org/10.1111/j.1083-6101.2007.00331.x

8. Carrie B. Fried. 2008. In-class laptop use and its effects on student learning. *Computers & Education* 50, 3: 906–914. http://doi.org/10.1016/j.compedu.2006.09.006

9. Graham Gibbs and Claire Simpson. 2004. Conditions under which assessment supports students' learning. *Learning and teaching in higher education.* Retrieved June 24, 2015 from http://www2.glos.ac.uk/offload/tli/lets/lathe/issue1/issue1.pdf#page=5

10. Sarah Gielen, Elien Peeters, Filip Dochy, Patrick Onghena, and Katrien Struyven. 2010. Improving the effectiveness of peer feedback for learning. *Learning and Instruction* 20, 4: 304–315. http://doi.org/10.1016/j.learninstruc.2009.08.007

11. Gunnar Harboe and Elaine M. Huang. 2015. Real-World Affinity Diagramming Practices. *Proceedings of the 33rd Annual ACM Conference on Human Factors in Computing Systems - CHI '15*, ACM Press, 95–104. http://doi.org/10.1145/2702123.2702561

12. Pamela Hinds and Mark Mortensen. 2005. Understanding Conflict in Geographically Distributed Teams. *Organization Science.* Retrieved March 23, 2015 from http://web.stanford.edu/~phinds/PDFs/Hinds-Mortensen-OS05.pdf

13. Chinmay Kulkarni, Michael S. Bernstein, and Scott

Klemmer. 2015. PeerStudio: Rapid Peer Feedback Emphasizes Revision and Improves Performance. *Proceedings from The Second (2015) ACM Conference on Learning @ Scale*: 75–84. Retrieved June 10, 2015 from https://hci.stanford.edu/publications/2015/PeerStudio/Peerstudio.pdf

14. Jean Lave and Etienne Wenger. 1991. *Situated Learning: Legitimate Peripheral Participation.* Cambridge University Press. Retrieved October 28, 2014 from http://books.google.com/books?hl=en&lr=&id=CAVIOrW3vYAC&pgis=1

15. Ngar-Fun Liu and David Carless. 2006. Peer feedback: the learning element of peer assessment. *Teaching in Higher education.* Retrieved June 10, 2015 from http://www.tandfonline.com/doi/abs/10.1080/13562510600680582

16. David J. Nicol and Deborah Macfarlane-Dick. 2006. Formative assessment and self-regulated learning: A model and seven principles of good feedback practice. *Studies in Higher Education.* Retrieved June 24, 2015 from http://ewds.strath.ac.uk/REAP/public/Papers/DN_SHE_Final.pdf

17. Anne Marie Piper and James D. Hollan. 2009. Tabletop displays for small group study. *Proceedings of the 27th international conference on Human factors in computing systems - CHI 09*, ACM Press, 1227. http://doi.org/10.1145/1518701.1518885

18. D. Royce Sadler. 1989. Formative assessment and the design of instructional systems. *Instructional Science* 18, 2: 119–144. http://doi.org/10.1007/BF00117714

19. Abigail J. Sellen and Richard H.R. Harper. 2003. *The Myth of the Paperless Office.* MIT Press, Cambridge, MA, USA.

20. Amy Shannon, Jessica Hammer, Hassler Thurston, Natalie Diehl, and Steven P. Dow. 2016. PeerPresents: A Web-Based System for In-Class Peer Feedback during Student Presentations. *Designing Interactive Systems*, 447–458.

21. David Tinapple, Loren Olson, and John Sadauskas. 2013. CritViz: Web-based software supporting peer critique in large creative classrooms. *Bulletin of the IEEE Technical Committee on Learning Technology.* Retrieved June 10, 2015 from http://www.ieeetclt.org/issues/january2013/Tinapple.pdf

22. Kieth Topping. 1998. Peer assessment between students in colleges and universities. *Review of educational Research.* Retrieved September 24, 2015 from http://rer.sagepub.com/content/68/3/249.short

23. Jeffrey W. Treem and Paul M. Leonardi. 2013. Social Media Use in Organizations: Exploring the Affordances of Visibility, Editability, Persistence, and Association. *Annals of the International Communication Association* 36, 1: 143–189. http://doi.org/10.1080/23808985.2013.11679130

24. J. B. Walther. 1996. Computer-Mediated Communication: Impersonal, Interpersonal, and Hyperpersonal Interaction. *Communication Research* 23, 1: 3–43. http://doi.org/10.1177/009365096023001001

25. A Yuan, K Luther, and M Krause. 2016. Almost an Expert: The Effects of Rubrics and Expertise on Perceived Value of Crowdsourced Design Critiques. *(CSCW'16) Proceedings of the 19th ACM Conference on Computer-Supported Cooperative Work & Social Computing*: 1005–1017. Retrieved May 26, 2016 from https://www.kurtluther.com/pdf/CrowdCrit_CSCW_2016_camera.pdf

26. Haiyi Zhu, Steven P. Dow, Robert E. Kraut, and Aniket Kittur. 2014. Reviewing versus doing. *Proceedings of the 17th ACM conference on Computer supported cooperative work & social computing - CSCW '14*, ACM Press, 1445–1455. http://doi.org/10.1145/2531602.2531718

Group Spinner: Recognizing & Visualizing Learning in the Classroom for Reflection, Communication & Planning

Ahmed Kharrufa[1], Sally Rix[2], Timur Osadchiy[1], Anne Preston[3], Patrick Olivier[1]

[1]Open Lab, Newcastle University
Newcastle upon Tyne, UK
{ahmed.kharrufa, t.osadchiy, patrick.olivier}@newcastle.ac.uk

[2]Newcastle University
Newcastle upon Tyne, UK
s.rix@newcastle.ac.uk

[3]Kingston University,
Kingston upon Thames, UK
a.preston@kingston.ac.uk

ABSTRACT

Group Spinner is a digital visual tool intended to help teachers observe and reflect on children's collaborative technology-enhanced learning activities in the classroom. We describe the design of Group Spinner, which was informed by activity theory, previous work and teachers' focus group feedback. Based on a radar chart and a set of indicators, Group Spinner allows teachers to record in-class observations as to different aspects of group learning and learning behaviors, beyond the limited knowledge acquisition measures. Our exploratory study involved 6 teachers who used the tool for a total of 23 classes in subjects ranging from Maths and Geography to Sociology and Art. Semi-structured interviews with these teachers revealed a number of different uses of the tool. Depending on their experience and pedagogy, teachers considered Group Spinner to be a valuable tool to support awareness, reflection, communication, and/or planning.

Author Keywords

Technology enhanced learning; collaboration; reflection; schools/educational setting; radar-chart; observation.

ACM Classification Keywords

H.5.0 Information Interfaces and Presentation: General

INTRODUCTION

For the past two decades there has been an increasing pressure on schools to focus more on the teaching of 21st century skills [17], integrate more technology in the classroom [30] and adapt to changing ideas about knowledge and learning [44]. This dynamic educational landscape has given rise to significant challenges in recognizing the impact of such changes on students' learning. Standardized assessments facilitated by 'high stakes' testing "encourage engagement with learning only insofar that it serves the achievement of the outcome" [21].

CHI 2017, May 06-11, 2017, Denver, CO, USA
ACM 978-1-4503-4655-9/17/05.
http://dx.doi.org/10.1145/3025453.3025679

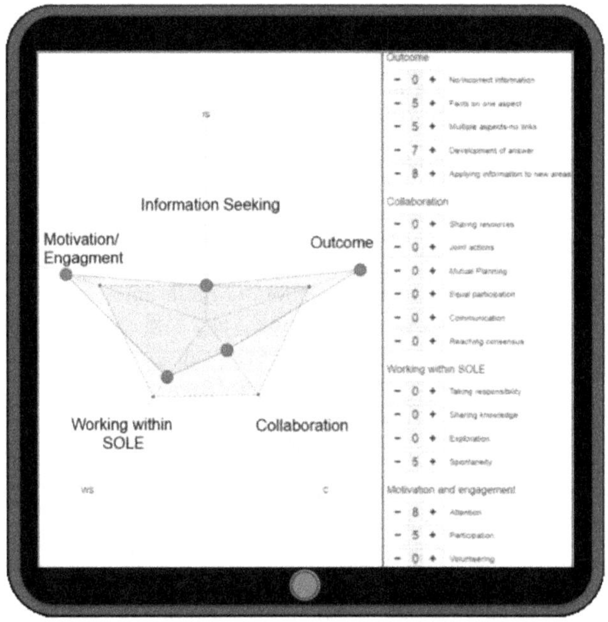

Figure 1. Annotated crop of Group Spinner's interface showing current and previous session graphs along with some indicators.

When it comes to technology based learning interventions, attempts to identify the impact of the use of technology within education must go beyond input-output tests and measure the broader pattern of use [8]. What is measured by standardized tests is, to a large extent, shaped by concepts of learning and knowledge developed prior to the digital age [44]. Technology's expected role – as a tool, a learning support or as an agent of change – and its expected contributions must be taken into consideration [35]. As McFarlane highlights, while some learning technologies may not (or are not intended to) support the acquisition of knowledge, their positive effects are on the development of 'skills' such as problem-solving, critical thinking, autonomy, confidence and information-building – highly desirable skills for members of modern society.

Thus a challenge for teachers is to incorporate and evidence a wider variety of learning opportunities in the classroom. New approaches and tools are needed to support teachers to reflect on their practice in these new settings, as well as recognize development in students' learning and learning behaviors beyond basic subject knowledge.

We describe the design process and present an exploratory study of Group Spinner, an interactive visualization tool based on a radar-chart and a set of indicators that allows teachers to record in-class observations of different aspects of group learning and learning behaviors. Group Spinner allows teachers (and potentially students) to tag positive observable behaviors according to a predefined rubric. These tags are incorporated in a radar-chart diagram that allows a quick recording and visualization of each group's performance with respect to the rubric (see Figure 1). With repeated use, Group Spinner can help teachers to track changes in students' learning/learning behavior with a view to visually communicate these changes to students and to inform planning and even pedagogy of future sessions.

Our research goals evolved during the research process from designing an evaluation tool for recognizing/ visualizing learning, to exploring its general use for teachers. We therefore conducted an exploratory study with six teachers, who used the tool for a total of 23 classes in subjects ranging from Mathematics and Geography to Sociology and Art. Our contribution is three-fold: 1) the introduction of Group Spinner as a digital tool to support teachers in technology-enhanced group learning activities; 2) the identification of insights into different use cases and the potential benefits of Group Spinner based on teachers' feedback in an exploratory study; and, 3) an understanding of teacher practices and concerns in technology-enhanced group-based lessons.

RELATED WORK

Collaborative technology in the classroom

Existing research on educational technology has mainly focused on understanding the role of technology from researchers' perspectives. That is, it overlooked how teachers can observe and understand the role of technology with regards to students' learning and behavior. This is unsurprising as evaluating learning resulting from the use of technologies targeting collaboration or higher level skills is not straight forward, and is normally done through extensive qualitative analysis (e.g. [19,26,28]). Dillenbourg and Jermann's work on classroom orchestration [9] aimed at providing a model for analyzing (and designing) technology use in the classroom. The model brings researchers' attention to a wide range of factors under the themes of teacher centrism, cross-plane integration, sequentiality, time management and physicality. However, its focus is more on how teachers orchestrate (manage) the classroom in the presence of technology than on students' learning side of things. Accordingly, while this model has been used by researchers looking at collaborative technology for the classroom (e.g. [24,34]), its use meant that it focused the analysis on understanding technology's role in supporting teachers in their 'orchestration' activities.

Taxonomies for assessing learning

A number of taxonomies have been developed to help teachers in assessing students' learning. The SOLO taxonomy (Structure of the Observed Learning Outcome) provides a framework which enables teachers to focus on quality of learning rather than quantity. It is defined as "a systematic way of describing how a learner's performance grows in complexity when mastering many academic tasks." [4:87]. SOLO is widely used by teachers as an effective tool to evaluate the learning outcome of an open task, where students are empowered to construct their own learning as opposed to reconstructing, or regurgitating, information they have already been given. Despite this, SOLO is still clearly focused on learning outcomes: that is, the knowledge and understanding of content. The learning processes that students engage in are disregarded, meaning that learning remains a knowledge-driven pursuit and the behaviors that enable students to effectively acquire that knowledge and understanding are ignored.

Bloom's Taxonomy of Educational Objectives [5,27] and its subsequent revisions [1] widens the scope of behaviors to observe. The usefulness of this template lies in it being able to support teachers in the design of curricula and classes which integrate plans for learning behaviors across three domains (Cognitive, Affective and Psychomotor) and to structure learning objectives in a progressive linear sequence moving from simple (remembering) to more complex (evaluating) behaviors. The increased use of digital technology in the classroom led to the development of Bloom's Digital Taxonomy [7], whereby different digital tools are aligned to the types of behaviors they can facilitate and where collaboration is a common thread running throughout. However, neither taxonomy recognizes the complex and dynamic nature of learning processes and, where technology is concerned, student-driven appropriation of the different tools available to them. The Digital Taxonomy also reduces characterizations of learning to a limited number of descriptors and tools, where the ultimate goal is assessment rather than leveraging the affordances of technology for learning design.

Starkey [44] highlighted shortcomings in both SOLO and Bloom's taxonomies and proposed the 'digital age learning matrix'. Her main criticism of SOLO taxonomy was its narrow focus on knowledge within the learner and that it did not pay due regard to knowledge creation and the connected nature of learning in the digital world. While Bloom's taxonomy addressed knowledge creation, it was considered too linear and not appropriate for use as a holistic tool. Starkey's matrix was developed as a research tool for the analysis and evaluation of teachers' activities that incorporates the use of technologies in the classroom. The matrix combines elements of observed use of technology (accessing information, presenting, processing information, and gaming) with levels of learning (doing, thinking about connection, thinking about concepts, critiquing and evaluating, knowledge creation and knowledge sharing). While more holistic, Starkey's matrix is still knowledge-oriented and does not adapt to the new rules/culture of more innovative classrooms by incorporating subjective aspects of learning (such as motivation and engagement) and, in regards to collaboration, only takes the perspective of knowledge sharing.

Other dedicated frameworks do exist for several different desirable learning skills and behaviours. For example, Limberg's [31] typology enables us to understand the characteristics of students' Information Seeking behaviour, and Guilloteaux et al. [18] addresses motivation and engagement. However, these do not address how such processes might coexist in students' learning experience.

Studies to assess learning

In an attempt to examine the impact of a statewide technology coaching program for teachers, Lowther et al's [33] mixed methods study found that while data based on students assessment and achievement records showed that gains in high-stakes tests were mixed, it was the classroom observations that revealed the changes in students' behavior. Such behaviors included more frequent engagement in research, project-based learning and use of technology. However, the classroom observations were carried out by researchers trained for a specific observation protocol of computer use, one that involved counting the number of times certain activities (such as cooperative learning and hands-on activity) occurred.

Moving from collecting data to presenting data, Ikuta and Gotoh [22] and Narumi and Gotoh [39] described the development and evaluation of a tool for visualizing learning outcomes. Their approach used radar chart visualizations of four learning outcomes: knowledge and understanding, domain-specific skills, generic skills and attitude. The approach has a superficial similarity to Group Spinner, but is in fact a highly structured and restricted *output-only* set of radar charts that are intended to create a visual summary of students' formal assessment results over the course of their undergraduate studies. The graphs are drawn automatically, created through a complex process of mapping proportions of different module assessment to each learning outcome and aggregating all the students' assessment results. The visualizations formed part of the students' e-portfolios and were intended to help students reflect on their learning, establish their own learning targets and become more independent in their learning.

While such approaches expand the measure of learning beyond domain-knowledge, the reliance on performance assessments serves to enforce the traditional emphasis on formal assessment. Dintzner et al. [10] used radar charts and curriculum mapping to visualize how the different courses in a pharmacy doctoral program contribute to the programmatic "big picture". This again is used as an organizational, output-only, visual tool to compare the contribution of the different courses to different competences rather than a tool for teachers or students.

Activity Theory

Unlike taxonomies and tools that are developed with specific goals in mind, Activity Theory (AT) [38,42] can provide a holistic framework for a wider exploration of learning processes. Developed originally as a general framework for studying human practices as a development process both at the individual and social level, it has been widely used in education where learning becomes the practice being studied [2,12,23,43]. AT's conceptualization of learning has three main elements: a subject (the learners); the object (task or activity); and a tool/instrument (a computer or a skill) [23]. Engeström, in his book 'Learning by Expanding' [11] developed the application of AT for education by incorporating the community (stakeholders in the learning process), the rules that govern the subject behavior within the community and the learning context, and the division of labor to achieve the objective (see Figure 2). While providing a framework for exploration, the abstract nature of AT makes it difficult to operationalize as a tool for teachers in their daily practice.

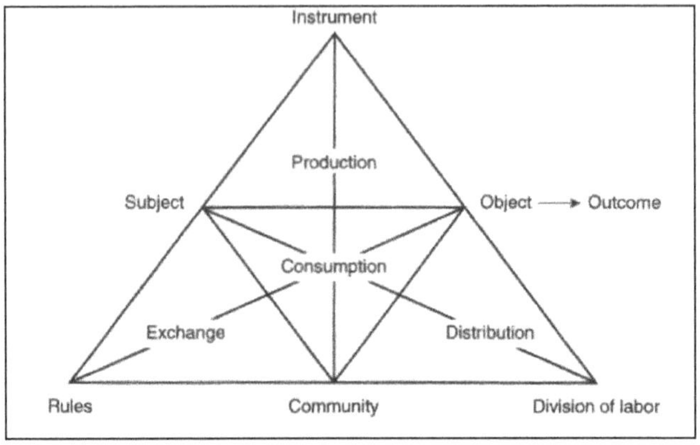

Figure 2. The structure of a human activity system [11:63]

Finally, most previous research fails to accommodate student development over time, focusing instead on providing snapshots of students' performance – typically of one learning task. Indeed, the literature identifies a lack of teacher-oriented practical tools to scaffold the provision of more holistic views of students' learning and learning behavior; this is the key motivation for Group Spinner.

GROUP SPINNER: DESIGN AND DEVELOPMENT

Group Spinner's original motivation was to help teachers recognize and record progress in students learning and learning behaviors beyond the limited scope of assessment of knowledge acquisition. We drew on: 1) AT's view on learning [11] to provide a frame for identifying relevant observable behaviors; 2) the use of the radar-chart (e.g. [10,22,39]) as a tool to visualize measures of diverse behaviors in one chart as well as the change of these measures over time; and 3) existing taxonomies and guidelines to inform the development of a structured observation protocol for each behavior (a rubric). The design of Group Spinner was undertaken in five phases: 1) the development of the radar chart and its axes; 2) a focus group with teachers; 3) the development of an exemplar rubric; 4) a paper-based prototype trial; and 5) development of a fully functional digital prototype.

Activity Theory	Mapping to Group Spinner
Tool/Instrument	Skills in tool use: language, ICT, and thinking skills
Subject	Subjective factors affecting learning: motivation, behavior, confidence (identity)
Rules	Classroom dynamics
Community	Organization process
Division of labor	Collaboration
Object-outcome	Learning outcome

Table 1. Initial mapping of Activity Theory's concepts to Group Spinner axes.

Phase 1: The radar chart and its axes.

Table 1 shows our mapping of key elements of Engeström's characterization of the human activity system to the context of a technology-enhanced group learning activities. With the tool element, the aim has been to focus on the set of skills that students utilize when using the technology, as well as language and thinking skills, as tools to achieve their objective. AT views learning as a by-product of motives and goals, with subject-related factors such as motivation being considered as "integral to cognition, knowing, and learning, not some independent or peripheral factors that affect cognition" [42]. Accordingly, we initially mapped the subject element to a number of subjective factors including motivation, behavior, and confidence.

This mapping is then used as a basis of the first paper-version of the Group Spinner radar chart (Figure 3). It had five categories and a superset of 10 axes. The expected scenario of use was that teachers could select the axes on which they wish to focus on and create a copy for each group in the classroom. Through observation, the teacher could then place points on the different axes based on how well the performance of the groups were with respect to properties represented by the axes. These points are then joined together to form the first plot for each group in the class. In following sessions, teachers are to repeat the process for each group, based on the performance of previous sessions as well as observations of the current one. With repeated use, the teachers will be 'spinning' a web that visualizes each group's development over time.

Phase 2: Focus group

To gain early insights on the concepts behind Group Spinner, we conducted a focus group with a number of teachers from a local 'state' high school where group-based, technology-supported classes (in this case Self-Organized Learning Environment sessions, or SOLEs) are common practice. In SOLEs – a learning approach that is being used internationally (www.theschoolinthecloud.org) – students are asked a difficult open question, then given access to the Internet through a standard web browser and invited to work in groups to come up with an answer. Students work with no direct teacher intervention and are normally expected to

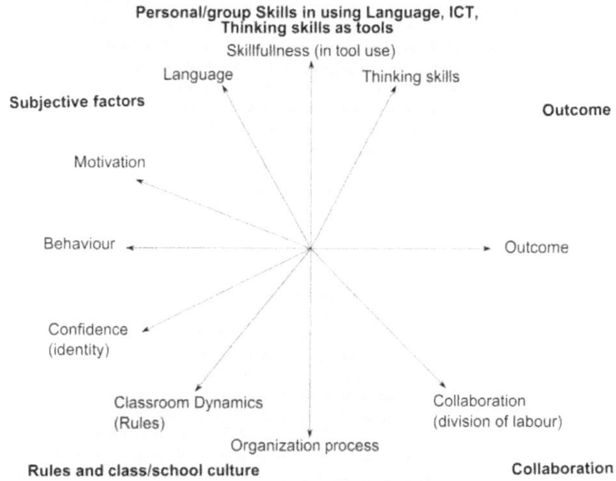

Figure 3. First version radar chart; superset of all possible axes as inspired by Activity Theory's activity triangle.

present their answer at the end of the session, discussing it with both the teacher and other students [36,37]. The focus group, with six experienced teachers from this school, was conducted to understand how teachers evaluated such non-traditional sessions and to solicit their feedback on the first paper-version of Group Spinner. The discussion was audio recorded and transcribed. The transcript was thematically analyzed separately by two researchers (from technical and high school teaching backgrounds). Notes were then compared to identify key common themes. The main points highlighted by the teachers with regards to running non-traditional, self-organized sessions were:

- *Outcomes:* the focus on outcomes is a major concern and impacts on their teaching and assessment.
- *Skills:* teachers, however, are still seeking to develop the students' ability to learn independently (individually or in groups) and to be able to evaluate different opinions (i.e., critical thinking skills).
- *Group dynamics* and the ability of students to switch groups and share ideas are seen as a positive thing.
- *Motivation* and moving from external to internal gratification are important factors for learning.
- The *culture of the class* (as set by the teacher and the school policy) plays an important role in the success or failure of any non-traditional teaching approach.

After introducing the paper prototype in Figure 3, the main points arising from the discussion were:

- *Awareness*: the different axes are important in making teachers and students 'aware' that there are outcomes that need to be considered alongside the traditional learning one. Having a 'debrief' using the tool or even hanging the diagram on the wall would be of benefit.
- *Reflection*: the tool can help teachers be more 'self-reflective'.

- *Communication*: the tool could be used as a "*good communication device, to communicate in your learning and get, for own personal target setting*". One suggested use case was to stop halfway through a session and have discussions such as "*Look at this. Which are we best at? Which are we worst at? Where are we making best progress? Where's the change?*"
- *Planning*: the tool could be used to plan sessions based on the previous ones to "*move things forward*".
- *Need for a rubric*: a taxonomy is desirable. The SOLO taxonomy was suggested as an example to help identify where to place a certain point on the axes.
- *Generalizability*: the potential benefits of the tools were seen as applicable for any group task, not confined to the self-organized learning environment context.

Finally, the teachers identified two major points of concern with the tool: *(1) Complexity*: There is a need to reduce the number of axes, to make it relevant to the activity at hand and increase its usability; 2) *Workload*: there was a concern about the additional effort required to use it in class, with one experienced teacher explaining that Group Spinner would just be "another layer" of work.

The focus group confirmed our view that too much emphasis is put on assessing traditional learning outcomes. It also confirmed the importance of the identified axes including subjective factors (motivation), skills (critical thinking), group dynamics (collaboration) and classroom culture. In addition to validating some of our motivations and design choices, the insights from the focus group changed how we viewed the potential use of the tool and accordingly our overall research goals. We no longer aimed to study Group Spinner simply as an evaluation tool, but to explore its general use to support teachers. Most importantly, the notion of using it as a reflection tool for the teacher and a communication tool to discuss and reflect on progress with students during or after sessions. Teachers also talked about using Group Spinner as a planning tool based on previous observations. This led us to make two important design decisions: 1) identify a core set of axes, and 2) provide a clear rubric for each axis.

Phase 3: An exemplar rubric

Self-Organized Learning Environment sessions present a good context to identify core axes and rubrics needed for Group Spinner, given its collaborative nature, reliance on the use of technology as a mediating tool (the Internet), its view of learning as extending beyond knowledge acquisition, and its need for minimum teacher scaffolding (allowing teachers to observe the class). For this context we used five axes: 1) *Information Seeking* (the use of the Internet/critical thinking as tools); 2) *Outcome*; 3) *Collaboration* (division of labour); 4) *Working within SOLEs* (context-specific culture/rules); and 5) *Motivation and Engagement* (subjective factors). These axes, along with their rubric, link to most of the main aspects covered by AT and reflect the key points raised in the focus group. The underlined numbered points in the following descriptions show the rubric's main observable indicators:

(1) Information Seeking

Students are increasingly relying on the use of the Internet in their assignments and in the classroom, making information seeking a key 21st century skill. In settings that promote learner independence, this is done with no—or minimal—guidance [36]. However, students are not necessarily equipped with effective information seeking skills, often stopping at the first information they encounter and building answers from the most readily available information rather than the most accurate or persuasive [20]. An inability to navigate the Internet to answer difficult questions and attendant frustration have been apparent in SOLE research [41]. Limberg's typology [31,32] was adopted as a criteria for observing effective information seeking. It reflects a clear progression of the sophistication of information management from: (1) Fact Finding, to (2) Balancing Information to find a position and finally to (3) Scrutinizing and Analyzing. This model is also applicable to digital environments because the affective and constructive elements of the process remain the same [29]. Moreover, these behaviors are easily observable by watching students and listening to their conversations.

(2) Outcome

Evaluating outcomes can be difficult for teachers in settings where diversity of information and outcomes are welcome. It is appropriate to consider both how much and how well students have learned, with Biggs and Collis [3] suggesting that the latter is much more challenging. Limberg [31] found that there was significant overlap between how students experienced information seeking and what learning outcome was achieved: students who predominantly worked within the simple fact finding stage typically obtained an outcome best described as fragmentary knowledge, while those scrutinizing and analyzing information showed critical assessment grounded in understanding and evaluation. This approach to constructing answers worked well with SOLO taxonomy [3], as it offers a framework within which teachers can evaluate the quality of an answer that they could not have anticipated. SOLO begins at the prestructural level, whereby students present: (1) No or Incorrect Information, to the unistructural, where they focus on (2) Facts on One Aspect, to multistructural where they offer (3) Multiple Aspects but with No Links, relational, where they show (4) Development of an Answer and finally extended abstract, in which they go beyond the information they found to (5) Apply Information to New Areas. Within this evaluative framework, students can gain credit for quantitative increases in knowledge up to the third level, at which point qualitative increases in understanding are required [4].

(3) Collaboration

When the teacher is not expected to be directly involved during group activities, students rely on their peers for support. A model examining the use of digital technology must therefore address the collaborative nature of knowledge creation and use [44]. However, as Wiener [45] puts it

"*Students put into groups are only students grouped and are not collaborators, unless a task that demands consensual learning unifies the group activity*". Students may appear to be working together to find a common answer by sharing some resources and doing actions together. However, when asked separately they may give different answers, indicating an absence of true attempts to engage in discussions aiming to reach a common ground and a consensus. Thus, reaching consensus is one of the key elements expected from effective group collaboration [45]. There are a number of observable behaviors that give positive indications that some type of collaboration is happening [13,15,45] of which we selected: (1) Sharing Resources; (2) Joint Actions; (3) Mutual Planning; (4) Equal Participation; (5) Communication; and (6) Reaching Consensus.

(4) Context-Specific: Working within SOLE

The rubric for 'Working with SOLE' was developed on the basis of numerous observations of SOLE sessions, the majority of which were at secondary school level (11-18 years). Over the course of more than 50 such observations it was clear both that students found the adjustment from 'traditional' lessons to SOLE challenging (see also [41]), and that teachers were also unsure of how this different style of learning might look in practice. This served as further evidence of the need for context-specific axes for Group Spinner. In self-organized settings, full responsibility for learning is handed over to students. Indeed, it can be difficult for them to understand how to deal with such an extreme change in their learning environment and we observed a default behavior of asking the teacher for help. The rubric for this axis was designed to address these key aspects of SOLE activities: (1) Taking Responsibility for their learning. The move from "knowledge hoarding" to (2) Knowledge Sharing [14] was also problematic for students as they often saw learning as a competition. Observations showed that students were typically happy to produce 'an' answer, regardless of whether they fully understood it or believed it was the best answer. Yet the concept of learning as a process of (3) Exploration, in which students could satisfy their curiosity, is central to SOLE. Another defining element of self-organized learning is (4) Spontaneity, although in our observations of students the rules and rituals of the traditional classroom were so entrenched that students would more readily adopt these in other settings rather than do something different.

(5) Motivation and Engagement

In learning sciences, motivation is an individual difference variable used interchangeably to describe why a student does something, for how long they are willing to do it and how hard they are going to pursue it. In terms of classroom practice, motivation is treated by teachers and students as associated with particular behavioral characteristics. The associated term 'engagement' is also often used to refer to different types of 'motivated behavior'. Teachers and students have very personalized definitions of these constructs that may or may not be rooted in something which is evidenced or recognized behaviorally. However, teachers' and students' use the terms generally to refer to: 'why, how long, how hard, how well, how proactively and in what way students engage in the learning process'. To provide some guidance through which motivation might be manifested in action, we draw on Guilloteaux and Dornyei's work on the Motivational Orientation of Language Teaching (MOLT) Observation Scheme [18]. MOLT was devised to gain information on students' 'situation-specific' motivation. It formulates an observation scheme, with specific descriptors of motivated and motivational-relevant behavior to help identify the quality of motivational experiences as they 'happen in time'. The observable 'motivated behavior' [16,18] includes three main variables/measures: (1) Attention and not displaying inattentive or disruptive behavior; (2) Participation and actively taking part in discussion linked to the activity; and (3) Volunteering to help students, groups and the teacher.

Phase 4: Paper-based classroom trial

A member of the research team used a paper-based version of Group Spinner (a radar chart with the five axes of the rubric only along with the rubric) to further inform the first digital version of Group Spinner. The researcher, who has experience in teaching, running and observing SOLE sessions, attended two such sessions to observe students and record these observations on the paper-based radar chart. The two main insights from this lightweight face-validity evaluation of the design were: (1) that the rubrics' details of observable behaviors were valuable in drawing the observer's attention to important and easily observable aspects of students behavior that may be otherwise missed; and (2) trying to keep a mental record of these behaviors and translating them into points on the graph was cognitively challenging. Functionality to tag behaviors as they are observed, which could then inform the graph, was seen as essential for the successful use of the tool.

Phase 5: Design and development of the digital tool

The focus group and the paper trial helped shape the original design ideas, and led to the following five additional design features for the digital version of Group Spinner (see Figure 4 and Figure 5):

1. *Two clear modes of operation*: (a) a rubric-based indicators mode, focused on tagging behaviors as they happen (setting indicator values, Figure 5); and a (b) graph mode which allows viewing and manipulating points on the graph (while optionally viewing the indicator values, Figure 4)
2. *Navigation*: (a) quick navigation between the axes and their indicators in indicators mode, reducing the need for scrolling by displaying main headlines for the indicators (and help for each indicator through a help icon); and (b) quick scrolling to a specific axis indicator using navigation links on the sidebar (Figure 5).
3. *Incremental control*: allow incrementing or decrementing a value for each indicator representing

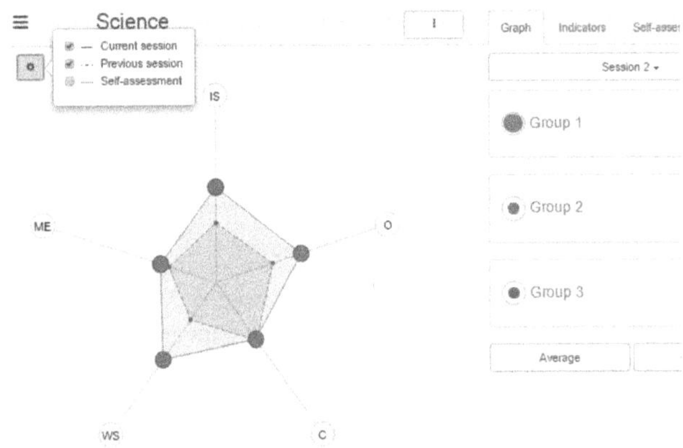

Figure 4. The graph mode shows the current/previous session graphs. The current graph points can be changed by dragging the control points along the axes. The right side allows changing sessions/ and groups as well as switching to the indicators mode.

either the number of times a behavior is observed, its quality, or both (depending on how teachers want to use it) (Figure 5).

4. *Making comparison*: (a) display the graph from the previous session for reference (Figure 4); (b) support comparing and averaging graphs for all groups for a certain session, or for all sessions for a certain group.
5. *Support multiple groups* (or students) per session with a quick way to switch between groups; allow the creation of new classes, sessions, and groups (Figure 4).

Group Spinner was designed to be available on most smartphones, tablets and PCs. It was developed as a responsive web-app using HTML5, CSS and JavaScript on the client side with Bootstrap 3, AngularJS and D3.js frameworks. The server side was built using Python with Pyramid framework and SQLAlchemy as an Object Relational Mapper. PostgreSQL was used for the database.

The tool was trialed with one teacher (T1) for two sessions before making it available to the other teachers. T1 provided early feedback which led to improvements in switching between the indicators and graph modes, and better presentation and navigation in the indicators mode.

GROUP SPINNER: USER STUDY

Group Spinner was used over 23 sessions in total (average of 50 minutes per session) by six participants, one primary school teacher (T1), four secondary school teachers from the same school (T2-T5), and a practitioner from the research team (T6) (Table 2). T2-T5 where from the school in which we conducted the focus group (only T4 had taken part in the focus group). Training teachers to use Group Spinner took approximately 10-15 minutes. Teachers ranged in experience, from one year of teaching with infrequent use of SOLEs to 10 years of teaching with regular use of SOLES over the past three years. We conducted semi-structured interviews (averaging 25 minutes each) individually with the

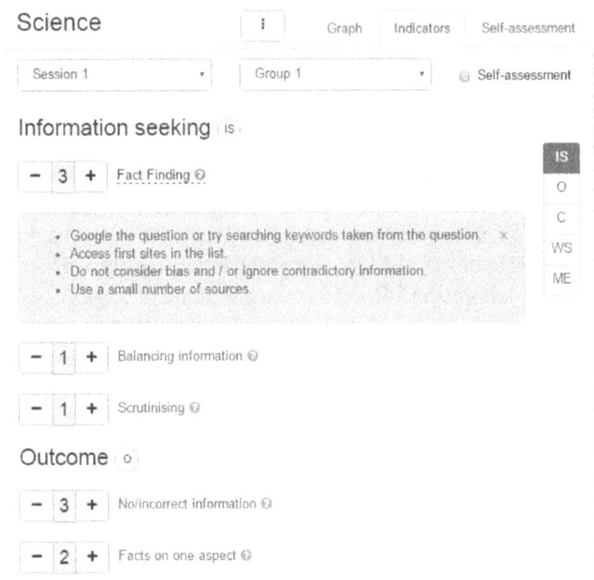

Figure 5. The indicators mode allows teachers to change the value of each indicator as well as display a clear description for each (help icon). The bar to the right allows for quick navigation to the desired set of indicators.

teachers, except for T6 (a member of the research team) who provided her feedback in written form. Interviews were audio recorded and transcribed for analysis.

Our goal was to explore both the different ways in which teachers use Group Spinner as well as its identified benefits to teachers and learners. This guided the questions of the interview, where teachers were asked about how they used Group Spinner, its perceived value, their perception of associated workload and their feedback on the ease of understanding the axes/rubric and the tool itself. The interview transcripts were analyzed separately by two researchers (from technical and high school teaching backgrounds) as with the focus group transcript. The analysis was first informed by pre-determined themes driven by the interview questions and subthemes emerging from the focus group & interview transcripts. We were keen to see if the teachers' feedback addressed the same themes that emerged from the focus group (awareness, reflection, communication, and planning).

A quote from T5 summarized much of the feedback we received: "*I think as a teacher it does* ***allow you to focus on those subdivisions*** *within what kids are doing in SOLE and* ***really think about them****...I think that* ***does then maybe alter your pedagogy*** *around what you do, what you ask kids to do. As I say one thing that came out for me was something that I was suspecting anyway, which is I think we need to ban that presentation, hard presentation methods. But I think, the crucial thing is what I would have done with it long-term around the data that is gathered. So then* ***have a really powerful conversation*** *with the kids*", then added "*It is a tool to allow you to* ***improve pedagogy and debrief***".

	Sessions	Age	Subject
T1	7	6-7	Art and SOLE
T2	3 x 2classes	11-12	Math
T3	2	13-14	Geography
T4	2	13-14	Sociology
T5	2	11-12	Geography
T6	4	10-15	Digital & foreign language skills (summer school)

Table 2. Sessions with Group Spinner

How? Observed use cases

(H1) *Post-class tagging (T1):* T1 struggled with the idea of using the interface "in situ" and settled on an approach where she would look at the indicators after the session: "*did I think they had done those things or not?*" She would then do the tagging, giving values based on memory and translating these into points on the graph. This is potentially a consequence of her being a tester for an earlier Group Spinner prototype, in which the navigation design had not been optimized. None of the other teachers reported difficulties using Group Spinner during a class.

(H2) *Tagging during the class (T2, T3, T6):* Teachers tagged behaviors as they were observed for each of the groups, on their tablets while walking around the class and talking to groups. T2 and T3 drew the graphs at the end or immediately after the sessions, based on the tags and their memory. T6 worked on the graph and the indicators during the session.

(H3) *Working on the graph directly (T2, T4):* Teachers walked around the class and talked to groups as normal, but adjusted the graph directly without using the indicators. T2 used Group Spinner for the first few sessions as in (H2), but once she got familiar with the indicators she switched to (H3). Similarly, T4 said that she initially used the criteria to help her understand what is related to each axis. T4 said that the process of tagging would take too much lesson time when she would rather be talking with students, whereas working directly on the graph was quite quick.

(H4) *Systematic observation cycles (T5):* T5 did systematic cycles around the six groups in his class every 10 minutes. This involved stopping at each group and asking them questions to identify and tag students' learning and learning behavior, and adjusting the graph accordingly at the end of each cycle. He reported that this was very intensive but he wanted to capture the rise and fall in students' performance throughout the session and not just have a final outcome (even though the tool only maintains the final state). This approach prompted discussions with groups such as "*I was really pushing that axis, I'm dragging it down again to get you to think about why that might be happening.*"

For all teachers, judgment for the tagging was based on both the quantity and the quality of the observed behaviors.

Why? Value for teachers and learners

(W1) *Awareness*: All teachers referred to the value of the tool in increasing their awareness about what was happening in the class. T1, T3, and T4 said that it brought their attention to, or made them "*more aware*" (T4) of things they may not think about (T1: "*I had never assessed any of those things that are on the spinner before.*") T3 initially questioned the value of the tool, but later said that she found that it helped her become aware of, and analyze, what each group was doing as well as concentrate on skills/behaviors that she might not think about otherwise. T1: "*...you have got the immediate impact of the graph. Then you have got your bits, statements down the side to back up what has been put on there*" (Figure 1 shows one of T1's graphs for sessions 6 with some of the indicators).

(W2) *Reflection*: T1, T2, and T5 described using the tool to help them think of, or 'reflect' on, their teaching and identify areas for development. T5: "*there is that obvious ability to then reflect on what you have done, the quality of your question. How you might adapt SOLE accordingly.*" However, T2 emphasized the importance of the tool at first use (to be aware of, and think about, the different aspects in the session) and not necessarily for longitudinal use (due to limited time, and the independent nature of her sessions).

(W3) *Communication:* While T1 (who taught 6 to 7 year olds), T3, and T6 did not use the tool to mediate discussions with the students, T2, T4 and T5 suggested that this could be one of the most important benefits of the tool. T4 mentioned that using the tool as a communication device helped students be "*reflective on how they've done*" across sessions and made them aware of what was happening with other groups. She emphasized that the tool helped make students aware of the process as "*it isn't an evaluation of what they did at the end, it's an evaluation of what they did throughout*". She also stressed the importance and benefits of the 'visual' representation in discussions with students: "*Sometimes there was things that I hadn't even picked up on that they then gave value to, which hopefully just having that conversation, but we would have had that conversation, it might have changed the focus of it potentially.*" T5 echoed T4's view on the importance of using the visual tool over a number of sessions to stimulate discussions with students and ask questions about what might be the reason for changes of the points on different axes. According to T5 "*I think that is perhaps its biggest strength actually. Predictably I think that would be where many teachers would find it to be really useful, the idea that they have got an evidence base, to talk to individual groups or even whole groups*". T2 only talked in terms of potential benefits. T1 and T4 saw potential in using the tool to talk to school's management "*to show that SOLE is a worthwhile thing to do*" [T1] as the tool helped look "*at the whole child*" rather than just ticking objectives.

(W4) *Track/Inform/Plan*: One of the most interesting comments was from T5 (quoted earlier) that the tool encouraged him to rethink how he facilitates self-organized

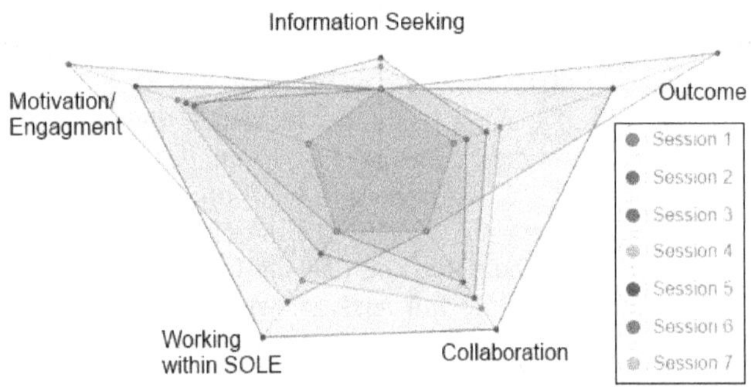

Figure 6. Graphs of 6 sessions by T1 with the yet unmodified graph of session 7.

sessions. According to T1, T3, and T5 the tool helped in recognizing progress, and thus could assist in identifying areas for development. "*I was able to use the spinner tool to show progress, then retract it... You would normally get an overall feeling for the direction of travel without seeing some of those barriers or red traffic lights.*" [T5]. T6 however, said that she used the tool at check points just to 'document things'.

(W5)** Repeated use*: T1 who talked the most about the value of repeated use, used Group Spinner for seven sessions with the same class. "when I look back I can see immediately what the focus of that session was**... I need to make sure there are opportunities for making sure it is balanced all the way round*" (Figure 6). Other teachers who have used the tool two or three times with the same class talked about the benefits of comparing to a previous lesson, and the potential benefits for both the teacher in recognizing development, reflection, and planning (T1, T3, T5) and the students during post-session debriefings (T4, T5). T1 and T2 drew the graphs independently of previous sessions and then looked at the previous sessions for comparisons. Conversely, T3 made use of the graph from the previous session when creating a new one.

Did it add to your workload?

Teachers had different views regarding workload, correlating the load to their use of the tool in the study and how they may use it in the future. T1 said "*Well it is interesting to fill in so it is something I would be thinking about anyway.*" T3 said "*kind of did it within the lesson so not much*". T4 said that it was "*dead easy to use*", but might have thought otherwise had she worked on the indicators rather than the graphs directly. T6 claimed it would only add to the workload if she wanted to study the data and graphs afterwards. On the other hand, T2 and T5 said that the use of the tool did add to their workload, either because they wanted to have conversations with the students (T2) or because of a systematic approach to visiting and talking to each group (T5).

Ease of understanding and use

Whilst the feedback was mostly that the axes made sense and were easy to understand, the participants raised several issues: T1 said that she struggled with the outcome axis; T2 found the 'working within SOLE' indicator quite difficult, as she found the definition of a 'perfect scenario' unclear; and T5 said that he was not fully convinced by the motivation and engagement axis. Otherwise, apart from reports from three teachers about a few cases where updates where not saved (due to internet connection or multiple login issues), there were no comments on any usability issues with the app.

Challenges and teachers' wish list

The main challenge teachers reported relates to time management. T2 stated that she would be hesitant to use the tool in the future, as she would not be able to find the time to use it to engage with students, where she perceived that the tool was of most value. T3 stated that because in the beginning she was not fully used to the tool, she felt like at times it held her back from fully engaging with the students. T3 also expressed concerns in using it with classes that have behavior issues, where using the tool and managing behavior may come into conflict.

T2 and T5 wanted to have a record of the changing values for each tag during the session, enabling discussions with students about changes in their behavior/performance within it. T2 wanted a below zero indicator value for recording negative behavior. T4 asked for the ability to have school-wide customizations of axes. Finally, T1 and T6 talked about there being value in providng the ability to attach notes/photos to the graph axes (or the indicators). According to T1 "*a lot of early years programs work like that.*"

DISCUSSION

During the design process, the focus of the tool shifted from a tool to help with evaluation to a tool to recognize and reflect on learning. The focus group and study then extended this to include communication and planning. Even though only T4 took part in the study and focus group, the six teachers' comments from the study confirmed the same 'value' themes of awareness, reflection, communication and planning. T4, who was skeptical in the focus group and expressed concerns that the tool would only add another layer of work, became much more positive about it. She mentioned that working directly on the graph was 'dead easy' and she was among those who particularly valued the visualizations as a tool to scaffold conversations with the students. The feedback from the teachers highlighted a great variety in how teachers have or would use Group Spinner in terms of breadth, depth, and frequency/time span. Four different use cases were identified, mostly determined by the teachers' pedagogical approach, their goals behind using Group Spinner, and the time/effort they were willing to invest in using it.

An interesting conclusion that can be drawn from the study is that teachers' experience in settings like SOLE, their pedagogy and the age of the students involved could be linked to the extent to which the teachers perceived the main value of the tool as a student development tool, or a personal (teacher) development tool. T2-T5 (all having at least one year experience running SOLE sessions) focused more developing students over and above traditional learning outcomes. The visual nature of the graphs and the overlay with previous sessions was seen as a way to support meaningful conversations with the students. Students were debriefed about their learning by *connecting the outcome to the process*, which the tool can help to identify as a series of ups and downs rather than an overall direction of travel. T1's interpretation of the tool, on the other hand, seems to be more evaluative than developmental, and more for her own purpose than for the students – potentially due to her working with younger students. It's likely that this view would also apply to other teachers who may be less experienced in playing a scaffolding role in non-traditional classes. However, even experienced teachers mentioned that the tool could have an impact on their planning and pedagogy, because reflection on their own practice would inevitably follow from recognising how students were developing. Even using the tool for only two sessions helped T5 reshape his future pedagogy. In this way, and even for these teachers, Group Spinner becomes a development tool for them as well.

In addition to visualizations being powerful tools to enhance communication [6,40], there was a recognition of the fact that the indicators provided a useful language to communicate with students about their learning. However, there was some concern about the need/time required to 'train' students in this language. This would be most powerful where the whole school 'buys in' to the language together, so that students understand that the behaviours they develop are transferable. The rubrics could be particularly useful here, bringing clarity to what the behaviours look like in practice and making them tangible. In general, the teachers' feedback highlighted the need for tools that allows visual representation of students' performance and behavior to allow for more effective teacher-student dialogue. These need not necessarily be in the form of separate tools, but as features integrated into other technologies developed for the classroom as highlighted by previous work on classroom orchestration [9] and recommendations for designing technologies for the classroom [25].

A limitation of our study is that some teachers only managed to use the tool for two sessions. However, T1, who had a chance to use Group Spinner for seven sessions, was the most enthusiastic about Group Spinner's long-term benefits with repeated use as she saw this firsthand. Furthermore, our initial focus was on group activities for two reasons: 1) students thinking and learning is more visible, and thus observable through their discussions when they work in groups, and 2) it is easier for the teacher to observe a limited number of groups than every student in a large class. This limits the use of the tool to group activities where groups are maintained across sessions. However, T1 decided to focus on a number of individual students who, while still working within groups, are representative of the whole class. In this sense, and if the teacher's objective in using the tool is personal (reflection and planning) then this can be a useful alternative to observing and tracking groups. Due to the limited time that the teachers were able to use the tool, none of them used the students' self-assessment feature (apart from one teacher who only experimented with it). However, T2, T3, T4, and T6 commented on its potential to inform discussions based on comparisons between student and teacher graphs.

As the teachers themselves identified, the tool is not only for use in SOLE-based learning activities (and was not designed as such) but rather for any context where there is need to recognize students' development beyond subject knowledge. This applies to technology-free contexts and to traditional group learning activities, in which case information-seeking can be replaced by the most relevant skill for that activity. Accordingly, our future plans are to allow teachers to create, share and use different templates (axes and rubrics) based on their context of use (a functionality repeatedly requested by T4) and look at the benefits/practical challenges of long-term use. Two other interesting directions of enquiry are exploring the tool's use for reciprocal-communication when students use the tool for self-evaluation in addition to the teacher, and looking at the effects of different visualization options on the quality of such communication (e.g. sliders to navigate through the different layers in time, or reformatting the visualizations to show the value of each aspect across a time axes).

CONCLUSION

We presented the design process and findings from an exploratory study of Group Spinner, a digital tool to help teachers recognize the impact of collaborative technology-enhanced learning activities in the classroom. All six teachers who used the tool over 23 session in total confirmed that they saw value in using the tool in their classroom around the themes of increased awareness, reflection, communication and/or planning. Teachers' experience and pedagogy as well as external factors such as time limitations and students' age can be linked to whether the tool was mainly perceived as a development tool for the student or the teacher. The feedback showed that the tool was flexible enough to allow for different styles of use depending on teachers' goals behind using the tool. Teachers' feedback also shows that technology to support teachers should not only be focused on content delivery, assessment, and administration, but rather expand in scope to address their wider challenges and needs in the classroom as exemplified by the values associated with Group Spinner.

ACKNOWLEDGMENTS

This work was funded by EPSRC awards EP/M023001/1. Data supporting this publication is openly available under an 'Open Data Commons Open Database License'. Additional metadata are available at: http://dx.doi.org/10.17634/141304-6. Please contact Newcastle Research Data Service at rdm@ncl.ac.uk for access instructions.

REFERENCES

1. L.W. Anderson and D. Krathwohl. 2001. *A Taxonomy for Learning, Teaching and Assessing: a Revision of Bloom's Taxonomy of Educational Objectives*. Longman, New York.
2. Sasha Barab, Steve Schatz, and Rebecca Scheckler. 2004. Using Activity Theory to Conceptualize Online Community and Using Online Community to Conceptualize Activity Theory. *Mind, Culture, and Activity* 11, 1: 25–47. https://doi.org/10.1207/s15327884mca1101
3. John B Biggs and K. F. Collis. 2014. *Evaluating the quality of learning: the SOLO taxonomy (Structure of the Observed Learning Outcome)*. Academic Press, Cambridge.
4. John B Biggs and Catherine Tang. 2011. *Teaching For Quality Learning At University*.
5. B. S. Bloom and D. R. Krathwohl. 1956. *Taxonomy of Educational Objectives: The classification of educational goals. Handbook I: Cognitive Domain*. Longmans, New York.
6. SK Card, JD Mackinlay, and B Shneiderman. 1999. *Readings in information visualization: using vision to think*.
7. Andrew. Churches. 2009. Bloom's digital taxonomy. *Educational origami*.
8. C Crook. 1996. *Computers and the collaborative experience of learning*. Psychology Press.
9. Pierre Dillenbourg and Patrick Jermann. 2010. Technology for Classroom Orchestration. In *New Science of Learning*. Springer New York, New York, NY, 525–552. https://doi.org/10.1007/978-1-4419-5716-0_26
10. Matthew R Dintzner, Eric C Nemec, Kim Tanzer, and Beth Welch. 2015. Using Radar Plots for Curricular Mapping to Visualize Assessment in a New Doctor of Pharmacy Program. *American journal of pharmaceutical education* 79, 8: 121. https://doi.org/10.5688/ajpe798121
11. Yrjö Engeström. 2014. *Learning by Expanding*. Cambridge University Press.
12. Yrno Engestrom. 2001. Expansive Learning at Work: toward an activity theoretical reconceptualization. *Journal of Education and Work* 14, 1: 133–156. https://doi.org/10.1080/13639080020028747
13. Cresencia Fong. 2009. Guidance and Career Education Course rubric.
14. Dianne P. Ford and Sandy Staples. 2010. Are full and partial knowledge sharing the same? *Journal of Knowledge Management 14*, 394–409. https://doi.org/10.1108/13673271011050120
15. Leonardo Giusti, Massimo Zancanaro, Eynat Gal, and Patrice L. (Tamar) Weiss. 2011. Dimensions of collaboration on a tabletop interface for children with autism spectrum disorder. In *Proceedings of the 2011 annual conference on Human factors in computing systems - CHI '11*, 3295. https://doi.org/10.1145/1978942.1979431
16. T. Good and J. Brophy. 2003. *Looking in Classrooms*. Boston: Allyn & Bacon.
17. Jiangyue Gu and Brian R. Belland. 2015. Preparing Students with 21st Century Skills: Integrating Scientific Knowledge, Skills, and Epistemic Beliefs in Middle School Science Curricula. In *Emerging Technologies for STEAM Education*. Springer International Publishing, Cham, 39–60. https://doi.org/10.1007/978-3-319-02573-5_3
18. Marie J Guilloteaux, Zoltán Dörnyei, and Zoltàn Dôrnyei. 2008. Motivating Language Learners: A Classroom-Oriented Investigation of the Effects of Motivational Strategies on Student Motivation. *Source: TESOL Quarterly* 42, 1: 55–77.
19. P. Heslop, A. Preston, A. Kharrufa, M. Balaam, D. Leat, and P. Olivier. 2015. *Evaluating digital tabletop collaborative writing in the classroom*. https://doi.org/10.1007/978-3-319-22668-2_41
20. Wendy Holliday and Qin Li. 2004. Understanding the millennials: updating our knowledge about students. *Reference Services Review* 32, 4: 356–366. https://doi.org/10.1108/00907320410569707
21. Desmond Hunter. 2006. Assessing collaborative learning. *British Journal of Music Education* 23, 1: 75. https://doi.org/10.1017/S0265051705006753
22. T Ikuta and Y Gotoh. 2014. Development of Visualization of Learning Outcomes Using Curriculum Mapping Takashi Ikuta and Yasushi Gotoh. In *Digital Systems for Open Access to Formal and Informal Learning*, D. G. Sampson et al (ed.). Springer International Publishing, 69–82. https://doi.org/10.1007/978-3-319-02264-2_6
23. K. Isssroff and E. Scanlon. 2002. Using technology in Higher Education: an Activity Theory perspective. *Journal of Computer Assisted Learning* 18, 1: 77–83. https://doi.org/10.1046/j.0266-4909.2001.00213.x
24. Ahmed Kharrufa, Madeline Balaam, Phil Heslop, David Leat, Paul Dolan, and Patrick Olivier. 2013. Tables in the Wild: Lessons Learned from a Large-Scale Multi-Tabletop Deployment. In *Proceedings of the SIGCHI Conference on Human Factors in Computing Systems - CHI '13*, 1021.

https://doi.org/10.1145/2470654.2466130

25. Ahmed Kharrufa, Roberto Martinez-Maldonado, Judy Kay, and Patrick Olivier. 2013. Extending tabletop application design to the classroom. In *Proceedings of the 2013 ACM international conference on Interactive tabletops and surfaces - ITS '13*, 115–124. https://doi.org/10.1145/2512349.2512816
26. Ahmed N S Kharrufa, Patrick Olivier, and David Leat. 2010. Learning Through Reflection at the Tabletop: A Case Study with Digital Mysteries. In *EdMedia: World Conference on Educational Media and Technology*, 665–674.
27. D. R. Krathwohl, B. S. Bloom, and B. B. Masia. 1964. *Taxonomy of Educational Objectives: The classification of educational goals. Handbook II: Affective Domain*. David McKay Company, New York.
28. Stefan Kreitmayer, Yvonne Rogers, Robin Laney, and Stephen Peake. 2013. UniPad: orchestrating collaborative activities through shared tablets and an integrated wall display. In *Proceedings of the 2013 ACM international joint conference on Pervasive and ubiquitous computing - UbiComp '13*, 801. https://doi.org/10.1145/2493432.2493506
29. Carol C. Kuhlthau, Jannica Heinström, and Ross J. Todd. 2008. The "information search process" revisited: is the model still useful? *Information Research* 13: 45–45. https://doi.org/Article
30. Cher Ping Lim, Yong Zhao, Jo Tondeur, Ching Sing Chai, and Chin-Chung Tsai. 2013. Bridging the gap: technology trends and use of technology in schools. *Educational Technology & Society* 16, 2: 59–69.
31. Louise Limberg. 1999. Three Conceptions of Information Seeking and Use. *Proceedings of the Second international conference on research in Information Needs, seeking and use in different contexts*, September 1999: 1–16.
32. Louise Limberg. 1999. Experiencing information seeking and learning: A study of the interaction between two phenomena. *Information Research 5*, 50–67.
33. DL Lowther, FA Inan, and J Daniel Strahl. 2008. Does technology integration "work" when key barriers are removed? *Educational Media International* 45, 3: 195–213.
34. Roberto Martinez Maldonado, Yannis Dimitriadis, Judy Kay, Kalina Yacef, and Marie-Theresa Edbauer. 2012. Orchestrating a multi-tabletop classroom: from activity design to enactment and reflection. In *Proceedings of the 2012 ACM international conference on Interactive tabletops and surfaces - ITS '12*, 119. https://doi.org/10.1145/2396636.2396655
35. A. McFarlane. 2001. Perspectives on the relationships between ICT and assessment. *Journal of Computer Assisted Learning* 17, 3: 227–234. https://doi.org/10.1046/j.0266-4909.2001.00177.x
36. Sugata Mitra. 2014. SOLE Toolkit. *Newcastle University*.
37. Sugata Mitra. 2014. The future of schooling: Children and learning at the edge of chaos. *Prospects* 44, 4: 547–558. https://doi.org/10.1007/s11125-014-9327-9
38. BA Nardi. 1996. *Context and consciousness: activity theory and human-computer interaction*. MIT Press.
39. Takatsune Narumi and Yasushi Gotoh. 2014. Students' Reflections Using Visualized Learning Outcomes and E-Portfolios. *International Association for Development of the Information Society*.
40. Karen Renaud and Judy Van Biljon. 2016. The role of knowledge visualisation in supporting postgraduate dissertation assessment. *British Journal of Educational Technology*. https://doi.org/10.1111/bjet.12494
41. S Rix and S McElwee. 2016. What happens if students are asked to learn Geography content, specifically Population, through SOLE? *Other Education: The Journal of Educational Alternatives* 5, 1: 30–54.
42. W.-M. Roth and Y.-J. Lee. 2007. "Vygotsky's Neglected Legacy": Cultural-Historical Activity Theory. *Review of Educational Research* 77, 2: 186–232. https://doi.org/10.3102/0034654306298273
43. Wolff-Michael Roth. 2004. Introduction: "Activity Theory and Education: An Introduction." *Mind, Culture, and Activity* 11, 1: 1–8. https://doi.org/10.1207/s15327884mca1101_1
44. Louise Starkey. 2011. Evaluating learning in the 21st century: a digital age learning matrix. *Technology, Pedagogy and Education* 20, 1: 19–39. https://doi.org/10.1080/1475939X.2011.554021
45. Harvey S. Wiener. 1986. Collaborative Learning in the Classroom: A Guide to Evaluation. *College English* 48, 1: 52. https://doi.org/10.2307/376586

ViVo: Video-Augmented Dictionary for Vocabulary Learning

Yeshuang Zhu[1], Yuntao Wang[1], Chun Yu[1†], Shaoyun Shi[1], Yankai Zhang[1], Shuang He[1], Peijun Zhao[1], Xiaojuan Ma[2], Yuanchun Shi[1]
Key Laboratory of Pervasive Computing, Ministry of Education
Tsinghua National Laboratory for Information Science and Technology
[1]Department of Computer Science and Technology, Tsinghua University, Beijing, 100084, China
[2]Hong Kong University of Science and Technology, Hong Kong
zhu-ys13@mails.tsinghua.edu.cn, {yuntaowang, chunyu, shiyc}@tsinghua.edu.cn, mxj@cse.ust.hk

Figure 1. An overview of ViVo's interface. (A) The interface consists of the following main parts: a list of word definitions with the in-context sense in the video scene highlighted, a video area accompanied by the subtitles in the video's original language and optional dual subtitles, metadata of the current clip being played, and a clip navigation panel that supports filtering clips by meanings (C) or by movies (D). (B) As the clip is playing, bilingual keywords are automatically aligned and highlighted, and learners can interact with the clip by switching the subtitle's language and voting for a clip.

ABSTRACT

Research on Computer-Assisted Language Learning (CALL) has shown that the use of multimedia materials such as images and videos can facilitate interpretation and memorization of new words and phrases by providing richer cues than text alone. We present *ViVo*, a novel video-augmented dictionary that provides an inexpensive, convenient, and scalable way to exploit huge online video resources for vocabulary learning. ViVo automatically generates short video clips from existing movies with the target word highlighted in the subtitles. In particular, we apply a word sense disambiguation algorithm to identify the appropriate movie scenes with adequate contextual information for learning. We analyze the challenges and feasibility of this approach and describe our interaction design. A user study showed that learners were able to retain nearly 30% more new words with ViVo than with a standard bilingual dictionary days after learning. They preferred our video-augmented dictionary for its benefits in memorization and enjoyable learning experience.

†Denotes the corresponding author.

CHI 2017, May 06-11, 2017, Denver, CO, USA
 ISBN 978-1-4503-4655-9/17/05...$15.00
DOI: http://dx.doi.org/10.1145/3025453.3025779

Author Keywords

Subtitles; movie clips; dictionary; vocabulary learning

ACM Classification Keywords

H.5.2. Information Interfaces and Presentation (e.g. HCI): Graphical User Interfaces (GUI)

INTRODUCTION

Learner dictionaries, which rely on textual definitions and example sentences to illustrate words, are an important means for foreign language learning. However, learning with dictionaries is tedious and ineffective due to the monotonous textual illustration [5]. To improve the learning experience, researchers have explored and studied the use of multimedia to supplement dictionaries by coupling images, audios, and videos (e.g., [24]). Besides, modern online dictionaries such as *Bing Dictionary* already present word definitions together with images retrieved from the Internet. According to previous studies, multimedia contents provide abundant and multi-sensory contextual information through audible and visual data; they not only help to interpret the subtle usages of vocabulary but also provide rich cues for later recall [25, 29].

In this paper, we describe an inexpensive, convenient, and scalable video-augmented dictionary. The idea behind is to automatically retrieve short video clips from existing subtitled movies or TV genres to illustrate the keywords of interest, and incorporate them into a dictionary to facilitate vocabulary learning. The goal introduces major challenges such as to what extent the scenes and contexts in existing video resources are rich and helpful to promote vocabulary learning, and how to extract appropriate video clips to illustrate individual words from large numbers of videos. Specifically, existing video resources contain contexts of vocabulary usage but without conveying the explicit definition of words; polysemous words render this problem even more challenging. Moreover, it is important to ask how one should model the user interface for video-augmented dictionaries in order to promote the learning effect. After carefully analyzing the feasibility and iteratively designing the user interface, we finally present *ViVo*, an online dictionary system augmented with movie videos. A user study shows that ViVo can improve learners' mid-term performance of vocabulary learning by 30% compared with a traditional dictionary.

This paper makes four main contributions:

- A quantitative analysis of vocabulary richness in existing subtitled movies and TV genres, which reveals an unrecognized opportunity for vocabulary learning.
- Accurately interpreting word meanings in video scenes to achieve dictionary-like illustrations of word senses by applying an effective word sense disambiguation (WSD) algorithm based on word embedding.
- A novel dictionary interface augmented with video clips to encourage learning from video contexts, highlight the bilingual contents for additional learning cues, and select the scenes with adequate contextual information.
- A user study that sheds light on the advantage of learning from movie videos as well as learners' interaction behavior with the video-augmented dictionary.

Captions and Subtitles

In this paper, two types of subtitles are examined: captions, a.k.a. transcripts in its original language (which means a foreign language for learners), and dual subtitles where both transcripts and its translations are shown. We will refer to both as subtitles in the following part of this paper, e.g., English subtitles and Chinese-English dual subtitles. In subtitles, a long dialog sentence is usually separated into short phrases called *lines* in order to display it properly. Besides, dual subtitles are often translated non-literally and only on phrase level rather than on individual words, as they are aimed at providing foreign audiences with a better comprehension of the movie plot. These facts pose challenges to constructing a video-augmented dictionary from subtitled videos.

RELATED WORK

A substantial body of work has been carried out to promote foreign language learning. Here, we review related work on contextual language learning, video-based language learning, and illustrating words with multimedia materials.

Contextual Language Learning

The core idea of contextual learning is to enable learners to acquire language knowledge with associated context. For example, Edge et al. proposed *Micromandarin* [10], which automatically provided contextually relevant content for language learning according to learner's location. Dearman and Truong [6] evaluated the learning effect of a live wallpaper on mobile phones and found that participants were much better at learning contextually relevant vocabulary than learning contextually independent ones. Edge et al. proposed *SpatialEase* [9], which contextualized the learning process of space- and motion-related vocabulary in body movements. Cai et al. [4] proposed the concept of wait-learning, which allowed learning conversation-related words during waiting for responses when chatting via instant messaging tools.

Although effective, one drawback of contextual language learning is that learning materials have to be heavily dependent on learner's context and thus are often limited and unpredictable. In contrast, our approach is based on another kind of context - the context in existing movies and TV genres - that can be analyzed and customized in advance to support dedicated and goal-directed learning. Learners can hence fully determine the vocabulary to learn according to their needs.

Language Learning via Subtitled Videos

Dual subtitles, which display subtitles in both the viewer's native language and the language of the video, are considered one of the best ways to present videos to language learners [22]. However, subtitles are usually comprehension oriented with non-literal, phrase-level translations, and interactions are poorly supported. Various kinds of enhancements have been attempted in order to make subtitles more suitable for language learning. For example, Zhou et al. [31] extended subtitles in a foreign language to contain an additional list of keywords contained in the current line together with definitions, memory skills, and so on. Similarly, *Gliflix* [23] added translations to monolingual subtitles for selected vocabulary words that appeared in the dialog. The purpose was to reduce the cognitive load on the viewers to discern and match specific vocabulary in two languages while comprehending the storyline. Kovacs et al. [15] designed interactive *Smart Subtitles* that showed word definitions and pronunciations on hover and supported dialog-based navigation by clicking on subtitle lines. Compared with dual subtitles, users could learn more vocabulary using Smart Subtitles with the same view time, understanding of the plot, and enjoyment.

However, current approaches to subtitle-aided language learning have focused on equipping the natural process of watching videos with more chances of incidental learning, i.e., they adopted a video to vocabulary workflow. In contrast to learning while watching videos, our research explores a vocabulary to video workflow: we gear our system design more toward dedicated learning by embedding video clips into a dictionary, with the purpose of providing rich contextual information for comprehending and remembering new words.

Illustrating Words with Multimedia Materials

In a dictionary, textual definitions and example sentences are usually insufficient for learners to grasp various and subtle differences in word meanings or emotions, especially for polysemous and synonymous vocabulary [5]. To overcome this, researchers have explored the use of multimedia contents (e.g. images, voices, and videos) as additional materials to illustrate words [2, 26, 20, 12]. Furthermore, other than manually collecting and compiling learning materials,

Savva et al. [24] proposed *TransPhoner*, which applied computational methods to transform a keyword in a foreign language into phonetically similar, highly imageable keywords in the learner's first language serving as memorable pronunciation guides, namely mnemonic keywords. A user experiment showed that TransPhoner could generate keywords with comparable quality to manually selected keywords, and was especially helpful for learners' memory of complex words.

To the best of our knowledge, existing work has relied on either static images or video clips generated from images to illustrate words. However, images have been found less capable than videos of creating learning materials, especially for abstract words [14]. In our research, we exploit the richness of existing movies and TV genres and propose computational approaches to generating appropriate video clips for learning, which are context-rich and scalable as we will show in the remainder of this paper.

The creation of a video-augmented dictionary for language learners requires three essential parts of work: 1) validating the feasibility of using existing subtitles as a resource for the dictionary in terms vocabulary richness; 2) filling the gap between the sense-based video scenes and the word-based entries in the dictionary; 3) properly designing the interface that optimizes the video-based learning effect. In the following three sections, we will address the three issues step by step.

ANALYSIS OF VOCABULARY IN SUBTITLES

While existing subtitles contain rich vocabularies with contextual information, it remains unknown to what extent they can be used as a resource for augmenting the dictionary. Specifically, what is the range, frequency, and distribution of the vocabulary in all subtitles and in each one alone? To answer these questions, we analyzed the vocabulary use in more than ten thousand subtitles of English movies and TV genres.

Data Resources

We randomly crawled a corpus of publicly available subtitles contributed by voluntary users[1]. For each subtitle, we also collected the metadata necessary for this study including genre, language, IMDb rating, and etc., utilizing the OMDb API[2]. Finally, we obtained 11,447 unique subtitle files in English. Each file corresponded to a movie or an episode of TV series. Among all subtitles most were for TV episodes, and only a tiny portion (about 5%) were for movies.

As for the words of interest, we considered the TOEFL and GRE word lists. These two lists represent everyday and professional language use respectively, and are targeted at the large number of English learners around the world who can basically understand the lines in the movies but still need to learn more new words. The TOEFL word list contained 2,859 essential vocabulary words [18] and the GRE list had 6,194 words [30]. These two lists shared 1,608 words in common, which meant there were 7,445 unique words in total. All words in the subtitles were lemmatized using Stanford CoreNLP [17] and counted against the two word lists.

[1] `http://www.zimuzu.tv/`

[2] `http://www.omdbapi.com/`

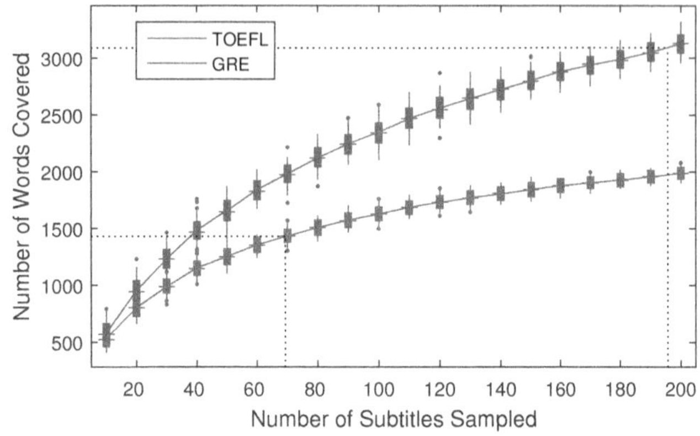

Figure 2. Curves and box plots for the coverages of TOEFL and GRE vocabularies in the subtitles. The dashed lines denote the estimated numbers of videos needed to cover half of the two word lists respectively.

Results and Findings

Existing videos are a rich resource of vocabulary use. In general, the subtitles covered almost all the TOEFL and GRE words (98% and 94% respectively), meaning that almost all these words could be illustrated by at least one video scene.

Furthermore, we estimated the growth of vocabulary coverage over the number of subtitles by randomly sampling N subtitles and counting the number of distinct vocabulary words in them. The sampling process was repeated 100 times for each N to obtain more reliable results. The growth curves with variances are shown in Figure 2. It can be seen that the word coverage grows unexpectedly rapidly with the number of subtitles. In particular, only 70 subtitles are sufficient to cover about 1,500 vocabulary words, which account for half of the TOEFL words or 1/3 of the GRE words. Moreover, vocabulary contained in a single subtitle can be quite rich. As an example, we found that the subtitle containing the most vocabulary words corresponded to the movie *Hamlet*[3], with 372 TOEFL words and 472 GRE words respectively in this 150-minute movie. It is encouraging news for language learners that hundreds of hard words can be illustrated with a live and coherent context of a single movie.

Moreover, the high vocabulary coverage was not a coincidental result of a small number of verbose subtitles. First, Figure 2 reveals the variance of the coverage at each point to be relatively small. Second, to further eliminate the possibility of the extreme case where a minority of subtitles would contribute to a main body of the vocabulary, we also analyzed the subtitle-vocabulary histograms and found that the distribution of the number of vocabulary words in each subtitle alone was nearly normal ($mean = 57$, $sd = 26$). These facts indicate that almost every movie or TV episode can be highly supportive of creating video-based learning materials.

It is worth noting that such a high vocabulary coverage in the subtitles is not an initially anticipated result, as the words used in speaking like movie dialogs tend to be shorter and less abstract than in writing [7, 1]. But in our analysis, for GRE words, which are usually considered to be formal and

[3] IMDb link: `http://www.imdb.com/title/tt0116477/`

academic, numerous occurrences have been found in the subtitles. The findings suggest that existing movies and TV genres are a viable resource to illustrate words, both in quantity and in diversity.

WORD SENSE DISAMBIGUATION

We have revealed the abundance of vocabulary in the subtitles. However, each word occurrence in one video scene can only illustrate one specific meaning of the word, as opposed to the fact that polysemy is common and is well presented in traditional dictionaries. It remains unknown to us whether the contexts in the subtitles are rich enough to illustrate the various polysemous words as a dictionary does. Hence in this section, we focus on identifying word senses by employing an effective, unsupervised word sense disambiguation (WSD) algorithm based on word embedding, with the ultimate goal of filling the gap between the sense-based video scenes and the word-based entries in our video-augmented dictionary.

WSD Based on Word Embedding

WSD is the task of determining the meaning of a word given its context in a sentence, which can be difficult as there are various cases of polysemy such as extended meanings (e.g. nominal and verbal usages) and nuanced meanings (e.g. analogy and sarcasm). To accurately calculate the likelihood of a word's meaning in a given sentence, we describe em-Lesk, an unsupervised WSD method based on the Lesk WSD algorithm [16] and word embedding [19].

The Lesk algorithm follows the distributional hypothesis in language semantics that words used in similar contexts tend to share similar meanings [13]. With the help of a standard dictionary, WSD can be achieved by finding the most closely matched meaning from the definition list of a given keyword.

To measure the semantic similarity between a keyword's context and each definition entry in the dictionary, we take advantage of word embedding. Word embedding is a way of word representation that also follows the distributional hypothesis and where each word is represented as a normalized vector of real numbers. By maximizing the dot product of a word vector and the vectors of its neighbors in a training corpus, the cosine similarity between two resulting word vectors is able to indicate the semantic similarity between the two corresponding words. This approach has previously been successfully applied to semantic analysis tasks such as in [11].

As for our em-Lesk algorithm for WSD, we first retrieve the word vectors pre-trained on a large text corpus. After averaging these vectors weighted by TF-IDF, we obtain the vector representing the keyword's whole context. The same process is also applied to each definition entry of the keyword to obtain the vector of each word meaning. The final similarity score between the keyword and each definition entry is calculated as the cosine similarity between the two corresponding vectors. The above approach is not language-specific but applicable to a variety of languages where a dictionary and a training corpus can be obtained.

For the implementation of em-Lesk, we used the word2vec tool to train word vectors on a 100-billion-word news corpus based on the skip-gram model with negative sampling [19], in coordination with a Collins Dictionary with bilingual definitions and example sentences for Chinese English learners[4]. Besides, as each word instance in a sentence and each meaning entry in the dictionary have a part-of-speech (POS) tag, em-Lesk also utilized the POS information to eliminate irrelevant senses so that the candidate list could be narrowed down. POS tags were obtained via the Stanford POS Tagger [27].

	TOEFL		GRE	
	Strict	General	Strict	General
MFS	.306	.434	.326	.521
POS-MFS	.367	.518	.390	.609
Em-Lesk	**.600**	**.670**	**.648**	**.745**

Table 1. Accuracy of em-Lesk compared with the baselines.

Evaluation of Em-Lesk

We compared our em-Lesk algorithm with two baselines to show its effectiveness: the most frequent sense (*MFS*) that always chose the first and also the most frequent sense of the keyword in the dictionary, and *POS-MFS* that always chose the most frequent sense that shared the same POS tag with the keyword to be disambiguated. The MFS baseline was considered to be quite competitive in the field of WSD [3].

Example sentences given for each word sense in the Collins Dictionary provided us with a handy dataset for automatically evaluating our em-Lesk algorithm. The examples were all selected from a corpus of real-world text curated from fictions, broadcasts, recorded conversations, etc. As a large part of the examples were also dialog sentences, they were representative of the sentences in the subtitles for our purpose of an initial evaluation. We constructed two test sets from the TOEFL and the GRE word lists respectively, with a total of 14,345 pairs of mapping from an example sentence to the corresponding word sense. We also considered two test conditions, i.e., *strict* and *general*. In the *general* condition, we took all the test data into account, whereas in the *strict* condition, we considered only the words with ambiguous senses under the same POS, i.e., the words that had at least two definitions with the same POS. We ran the three WSD methods on the test data and computed the WSD accuracy.

As shown in Table 1, em-Lesk outperformed the two baselines and could correctly disambiguate up to 74% ambiguous GRE words in the *general* condition. Note that the evaluation took only the mapping of example sentence to its belonging definition as correct. In practice, the performance would be even higher as many different senses of a word were no more than the same meaning used in different contexts and were too trivial for learners to distinguish, such as *abandon* (somebody) versus *abandon* (a thing or place). Hence, em-Lesk was sufficient for our goal of analyzing senses in the subtitles and building a video-augmented dictionary.

There are several directions to improve our current WSD method. First, we trained word embedding on an external corpus due to the lack of sufficient amount of text in existing subtitles. It will be better to begin with the embedding trained

[4] `http://www.collinsdictionary.com/`

on the external corpus and then adapt the vectors to the context of movies according to the text from subtitles. Second, we found that in the evaluation, a large part of WSD errors made by em-Lesk could be attributed to POS tagging: if a word instance received an incorrect POS tag, then it was impossible for em-Lesk to tell its correct meaning. This can be alleviated by jointly considering the POS score and the context similarity score. Third, we can utilize the sentence-sense pairs in existing dictionaries as labeled data to train a supervised WSD model. However, these improvements are beyond the scope of this paper. Besides, in the automatic evaluation, we used example sentences from a dictionary as a ground-truth, which could potentially lead to performance bias for em-Lesk if the context around a keyword contained the same words as its associated definition. Since the evaluation was an initial one, a manual examination in the context of subtitles was desired in the future.

Sense Richness in Subtitles

We applied our em-Lesk algorithm described above to testing the sense diversity of our subtitle corpus. Among all the 15,518 distinct senses of the TOEFL and GRE words in the dictionary, 93.5% were covered by the subtitles. Hence, we draw the conclusion that there are not only abundant word occurrences in movie subtitles but also a high diversity of word meanings due to different contexts of use.

INTERACTION DESIGN

An Overview

The richness of vocabulary and contextual information in existing videos motivates us to design ViVo, a novel video-augmented dictionary for language learners. ViVo enhances traditional dictionary by illustrating words with short video clips automatically excerpted from movies. As shown in Figure 1, ViVo presents textual information of the looked-up word like in a dictionary, which includes the vocabulary level, pronunciation, and bilingual definitions. At the same time, ViVo fetches the associated video clips as example sentences where the keyword is enunciated and the subtitles are given.

However, the interface design involves several usability challenges, e.g., how to encourage learning from the video contexts other than the textual contents, how the learning contents should be properly highlighted in both subtitles and videos, and how to segment and filter the clips to identify the best ones for learning. In this section, we describe how our design of ViVo can address these considerations. The techniques supporting the design will be later elaborated in the Implementation section.

Encouraging Video-Based Learning

In order to emphasize on the video-based learning feature and encourage vocabulary learning from the context of use, two key design decisions are made.

First, textual definitions are delayed to show up until one of the video clips has finished. Once a clip is selected, it will automatically start playing with subtitles (Figure 1B). Once finished, it will jump back to the start and wait for learners to repeat it. Then a text layer is shown to teach learners the exact word meanings in the dictionary, along with the whole dialog sentence just being played (Figure 1A). This design encourages a process of learning from guessing where learners attempt to guess or recall the word meaning by means of the videos before they are exposed to the exact definitions [26, 20].

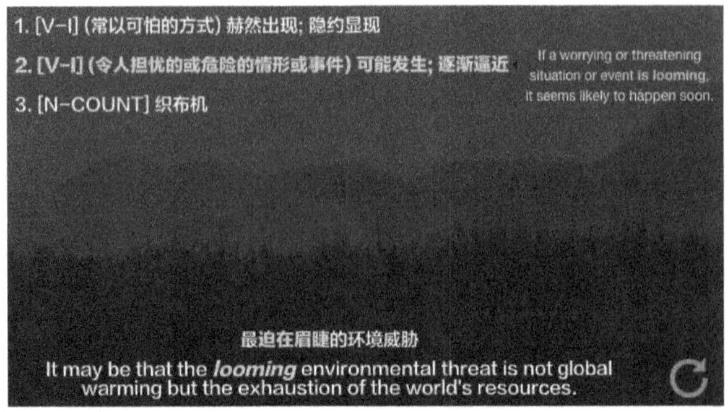

Figure 3. An example of ViVo's keyword highlighting. Learners can acquire word meanings from both the rigorous definitions in the dictionary and the in-context uses in the video scene.

Second, Chinese subtitles are initially hidden from the interface and are only shown on user's demand. ViVo presents the English-only subtitles by default, although users can switch between the monolingual subtitle and the bilingual ones by clicking the subtitle button. This design also facilitates the process of learning from guessing and more importantly, it avoids learners' tendency to shift their attention from the word itself and other information in the foreign language when bilingual information is given [15].

With the above design of learning flow, learners are guided to concentrate on both the textual information and the scenes in the movies.

Sense and Keyword Highlighting

As shown in Figure 3, given a keyword in a video clip, ViVo identifies and highlights its best-matched sense in the dictionary. Other definitions in Chinese are also presented as supplements for learners to gain an overview of the various different meanings of the word. When a user hovers on each meaning, a detailed definition in English is shown.

Moreover, as has been discussed before, the translation in the subtitles is usually non-literal and dependent on the context, which in turn offers an alternative explanation for the word in addition to the rigorous definitions in the dictionary. In order to exploit such an additional opportunity for learning, the English keyword and its translated Chinese counterpart are both highlighted to draw learners' attention (Figure 1B and Figure 3). The highlighted translation in the subtitles, in combination with the accurate dictionary definition, provides two translations for the same keyword, which has been proved to help users notice the differences and infer the meaning from uncertain translations [28].

Clip Segmentation, Selection, and Navigation

Previous research has revealed the benefits of reviewing a word in different contexts on learner's retention of the word [5]. Moreover, viewing the same word across multiple video clips can exploit the phenomenon of dual coding

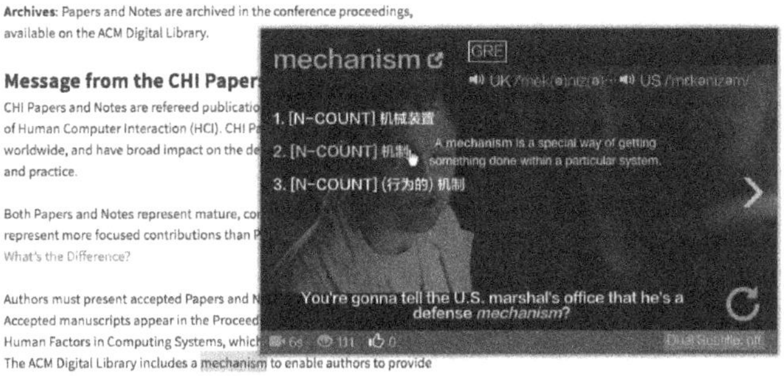

Figure 4. ViVo's pop-up search interface. While reading online, the user selects a word to immediately view its meaning in the context, illustrated by one of the best-matched movie clips.

which helps guard against the negative effects of encoding specificity [21]. Guaranteed by the richness of context in the subtitles, ViVo can retrieve an adequate number of clips to illustrate a single word. However, the issue of longer time cost arises when learners are faced with multiple, context-rich clips. We alleviate this issue by excerpting the clips at the length of a complete sentence, like the example sentences in the dictionary. Clips that last too long (more than 20 seconds) are also filtered out. The design is a trade-off between learning efficiency and contextual richness. With sentence-length clips, learners can still understand a large part of the video context while at the same time exploring multiple clips with a relatively high efficiency.

Furthermore, ViVo provides navigation features that help learners quickly scan through the clips without actually playing them one by one. All clips associated with the keyword are listed on the right panel of ViVo. Learners decide which clips to view according to the metadata including image previews, length in seconds, view times, and votes by other learners. In particular, votes and view times enable social interaction among users. If a learner finds a clip to be helpful for remembering a word, she/he can also vote it up. Learners can further explore the clips by meanings and by movies (Figure 1C and Figure 1D). To facilitate browsing by meanings, a concise definition of the keyword is provided in the learner's native language over the preview image of each clip. For browsing by movies, metadata is shown for each movie and TV episode including title, year, poster, as well as the quality of both the video content (IMDb rating) and its richness in vocabulary for learning (the numbers of TOEFL and GRE words covered).

Pop-up Search Interface

Apart from the use for dedicated vocabulary learning, ViVo can also be tailored as a pop-up search interface to facilitate vocabulary lookup and review at reading, as shown in Figure 4. While reading, users select a word in the document to inspect its meanings in a pop-up window. The interface analyzes the context of the word to determine its in-context definition to highlight, i.e. the definition in the dictionary that best matches the usage in current reading context. If no contextual information is detected, the most common sense of the word will be presented. As in ViVo's main interface, the textual definition is presented along with an associated video clip. However, in the pop-up interface, definitions are shown prior to the videos as understanding is the primary goal for readers. Whether to further review the word in the video's context is optional to the user. If the user clicks the play button or stays in the definition page for a time longer than a preset limit (five seconds in our case), the recommended clip will start playing automatically. Learners can replay it or jump to the next clip by pressing a corresponding button, or else they can simply click outside the pop-up window to close it and continue the reading process. Besides, a previous study has shown that when an unfamiliar word is re-looked up, it will enhance vocabulary learning by reminding learners of its contextual information learned in previous encounters [5]. The pop-up interface can yield this benefit by prioritizing those clips that the user has previously viewed.

IMPLEMENTATION

We implemented ViVo as an online application based on the HTML5 video elements, and implemented ViVo's pop-up search interface as a Google Chrome extension that monitors user's word selection activity. ViVo required all the videos to have no subtitles embedded in the frames. Each video was accompanied by two standalone subtitles: an English version and a Chinese-English dual version. We converted all the videos into H.264 format and all the subtitles into WebVTT format[5] so that they could be natively supported by HTML5 video players. In this section, we describe how we addressed the technical challenges in the implementation of ViVo.

Clip Generation

After all vocabulary words in the subtitles are indexed, each subtitle line containing the target word can be retrieved along with the timestamps indicating the start and the end of the clip in the whole video. However, in subtitles, a longer sentence of dialog usually spans multiple lines. To restore a full sentence from the lines, we design regular expression rules to traverse forward and backward starting from the central line to determine the actual sentence boundaries. Then a grammatically legitimate sentence is obtained by concatenating the lines within the boundaries. Furthermore, in order to avoid cutting off an ongoing speech at length, we opt to truncate the clip at the middle point of the interval between two consecutive sentences. The spared time offers extra benefits for learners to get prepared to focus on the target word and its context. Eventually, each clip is associated with a complete dialog sentence in both languages along with length in time, metadata of movie, a screenshot, the corresponding sense in the dictionary, etc. The sense is determined by performing our em-Lesk WSD algorithm.

Highlighting Bilingual Keywords

Since all English words in the subtitles have been lemmatized before being indexed, it is straightforward to locate and highlight an English keyword even in the sentences where the word is morphed. A particular issue arises when locating the Chinese counterpart of an English keyword in the translated subtitles, especially when the translation is non-literal and paraphrased. Therefore, given a pair of bilingual sentences, we first perform word segmentation. In particular, for

[5] `https://w3c.github.io/webvtt/`

languages without explicit boundaries between words, such as Chinese in our case, the segmentation is done based on a dictionary and word frequency[6]. Then we employ a statistical bilingual word aligner[7] to align the two lists of tokens, while the salience of the highlight is bound to the confidence score of the aligner in order to accommodate the uncertainty. The following snippet illustrates how bilingual keyword alignment can help learners to grasp word senses:

- *Transcription*: `I will` **`avert`** `my eyes.`
- *Translation*: 我会非礼勿视的

In the translation above, the word *avert (eyes)* is liberally translated as the Chinese idiom *to see no evil* with a little bit of humor. Our procedure successfully aligns the keyword to its Chinese counterpart and creates an impressive mnemonic of one specific use of the keyword.

We manually examined the quality of keyword highlighting on a set of 60 keyword-line pairs. For 37 of the pairs, our method correctly located the Chinese counterpart of the given English keywords. For 19 pairs, no Chinese counterpart was found. Only in four cases, the translation was highlighted in a wrong way. Missing or erroneous alignment was mainly caused by the limitation of the aligner we used: the aligner was not specifically trained on movie dialogs. However, as such cases are relatively rare and the missing highlighting of translated keywords has limited impact on learners, the above highlighting method is sufficient for our system.

Clip Ranking

ViVo tries to pick out those clips from the matched candidates that best highlight the keyword to learn. We adopt heuristics to rank the clips based on the observation that a keyword is better enunciated in a scene if the subtitle line containing the keyword stays longer on the screen while the remaining lines taking up less of the total time. On the one hand, as the number of words in a subtitle line is fairly limited by the width of the frame, a longer presence time of a subtitle line indicates a slower and clearer speech. On the other hand, given a fixed presence time of the keyword, a shorter clip lowers learner's cognitive load and wait time to be exposed to the target word. Therefore, we round the time span of all clips into intervals of every two seconds, and then sort them by the longest time of the matched line, and then by the shortest total length.

In the future, we will take into consideration more factors to further identify the clips that are better suited for learning, such as to reward the lines with no other difficult words around the keyword, or to incorporate a grammar checker to filter out those incomplete, informal sentences. Besides, we also take social interaction into consideration. The clips that have received more votes or views are ranked higher.

EVALUATION

We conducted a user study with 22 Chinese-native speakers who learned and used English as a foreign language. The goal of the study was to examine the effectiveness of ViVo for memorizing new word meanings, compared with a full-featured online dictionary - Youdao[8]. The Youdao Dictionary was widely used by English learners in China and was already equipped with a few multimedia features such as related images retrieved from the web and synthesized speech of example sentence. Given a list of words to be learned, we measured participants' short-term and mid-term retention performance, as well as learning time and learning strategy.

Video and Subtitle Resources

From the IMDb Top 250 list[9], we sampled 61 movies that were produced in English and later than the year 1960. These movies covered a wide range of genres, including science fiction, drama, history, and etc. Altogether, they contained 1,666 TOEFL and 2,448 GRE vocabulary words. Note that the coverage was higher than the results shown in Figure 2, as all the subtitles here were for movies, which were usually twice in length compared with the subtitles for TV genres.

Vocabulary

As the vocabulary size of each participant varied, we took a two-step process to determine the appropriate learning task for each participant. First, we created a long list of 140 vocabulary words from the TOEFL and GRE vocabulary sets; all the words were chosen by two non-native English speakers in a way that both of them were unfamiliar with the words. For each word, at least one occurrence could be found in the movie collection (4 on average). Then a day before the study, we asked each participant to filter the long list to obtain 36 completely unfamiliar words for the learning task. By "completely unfamiliar", the words that were guessable or seemingly seen before by the participant were excluded. We did not use a pretest here as participants might forget the exact meanings of the words they had seen before but would quickly pick them up if they encountered the words again.

Participants

Twenty-two undergraduate and graduate students with an engineering background were recruited for our study. The subjects aged from 20 to 34 ($mean = 23.8$, $sd = 3.1$) and seven of them were female. They were all Chinese-native with self-evaluated English proficiency as intermediate and had been learning and using English for years. Specifically, they all had previous experience with reading and writing academic papers in English. Seven of them had taken TOEFL or GRE exams before. Besides, they were unfamiliar with a majority of the selected movies prior to the study.

Experimental Design and Procedure

The 36 words were equally and randomly divided into three sessions, and in each session, half were learned with ViVo and the other half with the dictionary. Participants learned the words once and were tested twice for short-term and mid-term retention respectively. Word orders were all randomized for both learning and testing. Note that the interweaving of the two learning methods in each session prevented participants from establishing a global context of the movies and hence the result could more closely reflect the actual learning effect of local contexts provided by the short video clips.

[6] `http://www.xunsearch.com/scws/api.php`

[7] `http://nlp.csai.tsinghua.edu.cn/~ly/systems/TsinghuaAligner/TsinghuaAligner.html`

[8] `http://dict.youdao.com/`

[9] `http://www.imdb.com/chart/top`

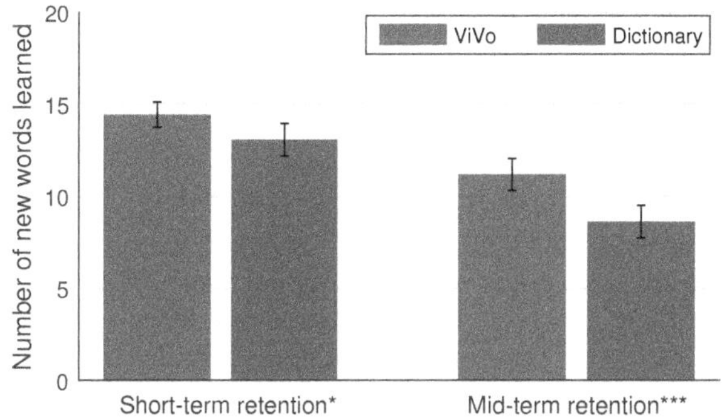

Figure 5. The performance of vocabulary learning, with standard error bars. (*: p <.01, ***: p <.0001)

Upon beginning the study, participants first did a warm-up exercise to get familiar with the interfaces of ViVo and Youdao Dictionary. Then came the three sessions of learning and post-learning test. The words came out one after another. For each word, participants could learn as much time as they liked until they felt satisfied and proceeded by clicking the next button. The next word would show up after a five-second intervention of a distractor image. After one learning session was finished, participants took a test to recall Chinese definitions for the 12 word they had just learned. The questions were free-response and had no time limit. Participants were told not to guess the meanings. The above procedure of learning and testing was repeated twice. Participants took a five-minute rest between each two consecutive sessions. Finally, the first day of the study ended with a questionnaire. Participants were told to refrain from either reviewing the 36 words or actively learning new words by other means in the subsequent days. Two days later, they did a second test of all the 36 words learned and took part in an informal interview.

RESULTS

Vocabulary Gain

Participants' learning outcome was measured by the number of words correctly defined after learning. Any answer that was semantically relevant was counted as correct. For polysemous words, participants only had to recall one of the meanings they had encountered. Two raters independently marked the answers according to the meanings in the dictionary and then discussed with each other until a consensus was reached.

Figure 5 shows participants' vocabulary gain right after learning and two days later. On the whole, participants could remember more new words after learning with movie clips than using a standard dictionary. A paired t-test showed that with ViVo there were significantly more new words correctly defined ($t_{21} = 3.14$, $p < .01$) right after learning. From a longer-term perspective, the advantage of learning with ViVo enlarged by 30% more words successfully recalled than learning with a dictionary ($t_{21} = 6.95$, $p < .0001$).

Furthermore, note that the mid-term result is more reliable than the short-term one: as the post-learning test happened right after the learning process, it was not difficult for the participants with certain English proficiency to temporarily remember all the 12 words in each session, which led to a smaller difference in the test scores. Hence, the improvement

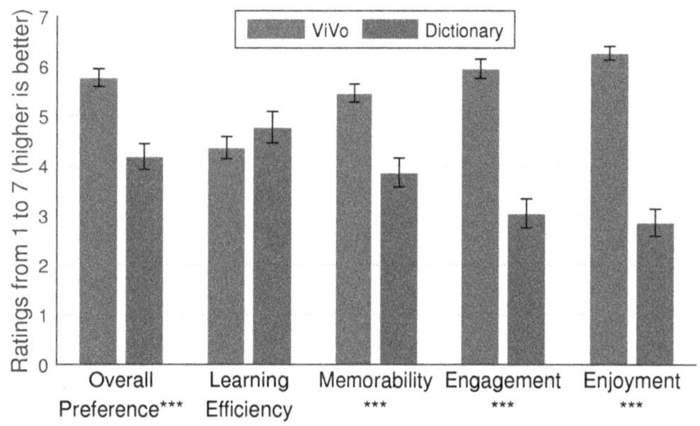

Figure 6. Subjective ratings of interface preferences, with standard error bars. (*: p <.0001)**

in learning with ViVo was pronounced enough to conclude that vocabulary learning based on movie clips is more effective compared with traditional dictionaries. Although we did not conduct a long-term study, according to the forgetting curve [8], without any revision after learning, the retention decays exponentially and remains at a relatively stable level after two days. Hence, the mid-term result could speak for the long-term learning effect of ViVo.

Learning Time and User Interaction

The mean time for learning each word was 50 seconds ($sd = 23$) in ViVo versus 37 seconds ($sd = 23$) in the dictionary respectively. Time spent on ViVo was 35% higher and a significant difference was observed in the amount of learning time ($t_{21} = 7.39$, $p < .0001$). Note that in the learning stage of our study, we allowed participants to freely browse the materials for each word and did not impose any time limit, which represented a natural way of learning. It was therefore reasonable to expect that participants had taken equally self-initiative to devote adequate time to both learning conditions. We confirmed the hypothesis by running a Wilcoxon signed-rank test on participants' self-evaluated learning efficiency for both interfaces (see Learning Efficiency in Figure 6) and no significant difference was found ($Z = -22.5$, $p = .43$). Namely, the increase in learning time with ViVo is not evident enough to be perceived by learners.

Furthermore, different learning strategies adopted in both interfaces can be revealed by our system's interaction log and participants' self-assessed time allocation. In ViVo, learners intensively interacted with the video clips both in depth and in breadth: in order to learn each word, they actively viewed more than four clips averagely (the mean clip duration was about six seconds); for each distinct clips the learners had viewed, they would repeat it once again on average, with more than half of the clips were played at least twice. Besides, in ViVo, learners spent 2/3 of the time on video-related contents such as viewing the clips, reading the subtitles, and browsing the movies. In the dictionary condition, however, they paid little attention to the example sentences but spent more than half of the time reading the word definitions. The above evidence indicates that ViVo's design attracts learners to engage themselves in the video-based learning process. Such initiative in repetitive practice enhances

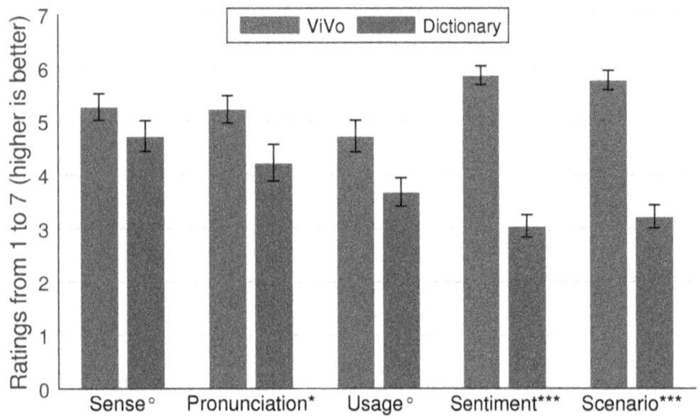

Figure 7. Subjective ratings of learning outcomes, with standard error bars. (°: <.05, *: p <.01, ***: p <.0001)

learners' long-term retention [8] and is exclusive to video-based learning [31], even if more time may be needed.

Subjective Feedback

Figure 6 shows participants' preference on the whole and on several aspects. We ran Wilcoxon signed-rank tests on the 7-point scale ratings. Results confirmed that learners preferred ViVo to the dictionary for vocabulary learning. Specifically, they felt significantly more engaged and joyful in the learning experience with ViVo, and considered the memorization of new words learned from video contexts would last longer.

Subjective feedback on the learning outcomes is shown in Figure 7. The learning outcomes of ViVo learners went beyond only the vocabulary gain. Statistical tests showed that users of ViVo significantly learned more about a word than that of the dictionary. In particular, the sentiment and use scenarios of the word were considered to be exclusive advantages of vocabulary learning based on video scenes, which benefited from the rich pragmatic context in movies as we will discuss below.

Furthermore, in the free-form feedback, learners agreed that learning with ViVo "*made remembering words much more interesting*" and "*created impressive cues by associating the words with the scenes*". Subjects stated that they were attracted to repeat viewing or explore multiple clips: "*I would like to repeat a clip until I could understand the word meanings all by myself*" (P5); "*I wanted to explore more scenarios where a word is used as different meanings*" (P16). The repetition, which might potentially cost longer time, also indicates learners' willingness and engagement in learning with ViVo. More importantly, learning from multiple clips provided richer cues for later recall and was especially beneficial to longer-term memorization: "*The video-based learning was more like the way I learned my native language where new words were gained in practical use*" (P11); "*There were many times during the posttests when I could clearly remember the scenes associated with the words*" (P9). P21 even correctly contextualized most of his answers in the scenes although not required in the tests. In contrast, dictionary learners tend to get weary with the textual information and are unwilling to explore more of a word even given enough learning time: "*There were too many example sentences but I was just tired to read them*" (P1); "*I thought the dictionary to be more efficient for word lookup and understanding, but poor information was provided for vocabulary learning*" (P5).

DISCUSSION

Proper Scenes for Learning

In the interview after the study, we asked participants to identify impressive words learned from movie scenes and provide reasons. From their feedback, we summarized several types of impressive scenes that are particularly helpful for illustrating and learning. Four typical categories are shown in Figure 8 and discussed below.

- **Repeated**: A word repeated in the same movie indicates its importance or relevance to the movie context and can inculcate a strong memory of it. P6 even expressed that he would *"never forget the word **sergeant** for the rest of life as it is repeated in too many scenes in Forrest Gump"*.
- **Self-explanatory**: Self-explanatory scenes are easy for learners to interpret without much text or plot. A thing, an activity, or a feeling can all be intuitively illustrated by the items or characters' performance in movies. For example, *tuck* reminded P3 of how an officer ordered a soldier and *hassle* reminded P18 of how a prisoner was regarded.
- **Humorous**: The dialogs containing a joke, a metaphor, or an exaggerated action can draw learners' interest, even if only a conversation setting is depicted visually. For example, a joking dialog impressed P14 and P15 with how the word *raccoon* was pronounced, even though the scene *"has nothing to do with raccoons"*.
- **Emotive**: Dialogs with an intense emotion, e.g., provocative and irritating, can convey an emotional impact on learners. P22 said, *"I can contextualize several words learned in the scenes depicting a debate"*. And P10 was particularly instilled by the line *"We can not **falter**!"*.

Impressive scenes usually combine multiple features above. In the future, we can further refine the clips for learning by incorporating semantic features of the subtitles and the scenes, other than emphasizing the keyword based on dwell time in our current stage. Moreover, superficial features like sentence terminators and video metadata might be helpful enough to indicate the visual content and semantic in a scene. For example, lines ending with exclamations or questions can serve as indicators of emotive scenes, and scenes excerpted from comedies are likely to contain humorous performance.

Effect of Familiarity

For each word learned via ViVo, we asked participants to label whether they were familiar with the associated clips before and then calculated the mean of vocabulary gain for each participant under both familiarity conditions. However, a t-test revealed no significant difference. The result can be partly attributed to the movie collection used in our study: the movies were not popular and 2/3 of them were unfamiliar to participants. A further study is needed in order to draw conclusions about the effects of familiarity on learning outcomes. From another perspective, the advantage of video-augmented learning with ViVo might not be limited by the familiarity with the movie. The choice of presenting clips at a sentence

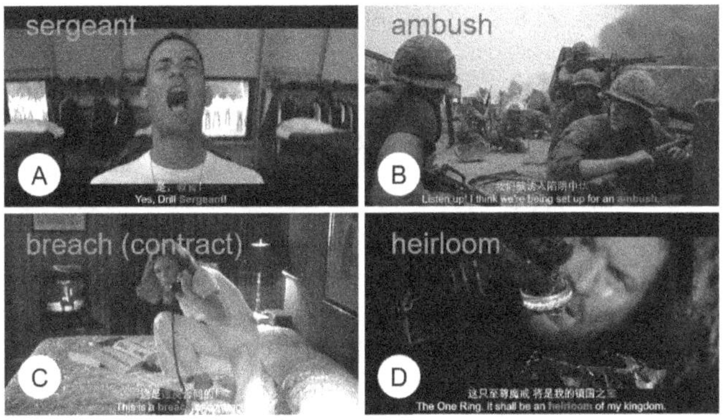

Figure 8. Examples types of impressive scenes for learning, including the ones that are repeated (A and D), self-explanatory (B and D), humorous (A), and emotive (A and C).

level eliminates the need for learners' prior knowledge about the whole movie.

However, according to the subjective feedback, participants preferred to view the clips from the movies that were familiar to them. Five participants explicitly showed great interest in learning with clips from movies they were familiar with. In the future, it will be better to allow learners to choose videos of interest or upload their own video collections in order to create a personalized learning environment. Moreover, the number and level of vocabulary words contained can serve as a new criterion for recommending movies to learners. By tracking the viewing history of each individual learner, a personalized watchlist can be automatically generated to maximize the learner's exposure to new words.

The Vocabulary-Media Workflow

Many previous video-based learning approaches (e.g., [23] and [15]) used a media-vocabulary workflow. However, accurately mastering the usage of vocabulary in a foreign language needs much more dedicated learning effort. Dedicated learners usually have learning tasks and schedule in advance and wish to gain anticipated learning outcomes, which cannot be met in a learning process directed primarily by video watching. In contrast, ViVo adopted a vocabulary-media workflow which can bring multiple video clips together to illustrate a single word for learning while pertaining the advantages of multimedia materials. Moreover, as it is expensive to manually create multimedia materials for learning that meets the learner's level and goal, our vocabulary-media approach exploits rich language knowledge and context in existing online videos which are inexpensive, convenient, and scalable.

Both the vocabulary-media workflow and its reverse have their use scenarios and are hence complementary to each other. In the future, a system combining both with blended reference, consumption, and review modes might ultimately be a very promising and engaging way for language learning.

Limitations and Future Work

Our current lab study only focused on learners' vocabulary gain after one round of learning and hence suffers several limitations. First, the longer learning time could be due to a potential novelty effect in our lab study. A long-term, in-situ study is needed to explore how ViVo can become integrated into the learning process in practice, including the word look-up function at reading. Second, the vocabulary tests were not sufficient to reflect the learning outcomes in depth. As the outcomes of video-based learning tend to be compound, further studies are needed to quantify the learning effects in term of word pronunciation, usage, mood, and etc. Third, the movies used in our study were not customized for each subject. It is an interesting direction to let the user specify a collection of preferred movies and explore the effect of familiarity on video-based vocabulary learning.

Moreover, our video-based approach can be generalized, both to different levels of learners and to learning other languages. On the one hand, learning difficulty can be manipulated by picking out the lines with only words below a specific level. On the other hand, the proposed approach of providing rich movie contexts for language learning is not restricted to specific language. Although currently we did not analyze the vocabulary coverage in movies in other languages, we expect a similar result as movies reflect human life where language is used. However, several challenges need to be addressed for scaling-up, including accommodating the noises of online subtitles, obtaining subtitles in less-spoken languages, and video license issues.

CONCLUSION

We have presented ViVo, a novel video-augmented dictionary that makes the abundant language knowledge and usage context in movies easy-to-access by learners. In order to automatically generate illustrative video clips for learning at scale, we first verified the feasibility of utilizing existing movies with respect to the coverage range and spread of words in subtitles. Furthermore, we identified the scenes with adequate contextual information for learning the diverse word senses using a WSD algorithm. Based on the findings, we described the design and implementation of ViVo, which focused on encouraging learning from understanding the context and choosing clips that best highlighted the keywords and senses through both visual effects and proper length of time. Finally, the results of a lab study confirmed ViVo's advantage over the dictionary by a 30% increase in the mid-term vocabulary retention. Learners gained better interpretation and memorization of new words from the rich cues in the videos and they strongly preferred ViVo for its efficient and enjoyable learning experience. ViVo offers an inexpensive, convenient, and scalable way to exploit huge online multimedia resources for language learning.

ACKNOWLEDGEMENT

This work is supported by the National Key Research and Development Plan under Grant No. 2016YFB1001200, the Natural Science Foundation of China under Grant No. 61272230, Tsinghua University Research Funding No. 20151080408. This work is also funded by the NExT Research Centre, supported by the National Research Foundation, Prime Minister's Office, Singapore under its IRC@SG Funding Initiative.

REFERENCES

1. Akinnaso, F. N. On the differences between spoken and written language. *Language and speech 25*, 2 (1982), 97–125.
2. Amemiya, S., Hasegawa, K., Kaneko, K., Miyakoda, H., and Tsukahara, W. Long-term memory of foreign-word learning by short movies for ipods. In *Advanced Learning Technologies, 2007. ICALT 2007. Seventh IEEE International Conference on*, IEEE (2007), 561–563.
3. Bhingardive, S., Singh, D., V, R., Redkar, H., and Bhattacharyya, P. Unsupervised most frequent sense detection using word embeddings. In *Proceedings of the 2015 Conference of the North American Chapter of the Association for Computational Linguistics: Human Language Technologies*, ACL (2015), 1238–1243.
4. Cai, C. J., Guo, P. J., Glass, J. R., and Miller, R. C. Wait-learning: Leveraging wait time for second language education. In *Proceedings of the 33rd Annual ACM Conference on Human Factors in Computing Systems*, CHI '15, ACM (2015), 3701–3710.
5. Dang, T.-D., Chen, G.-D., Dang, G., Li, L.-Y., et al. Rolo: A dictionary interface that minimizes extraneous cognitive load of lookup and supports incidental and incremental learning of vocabulary. *Computers & Education 61* (2013), 251–260.
6. Dearman, D., and Truong, K. Evaluating the implicit acquisition of second language vocabulary using a live wallpaper. In *Proceedings of the SIGCHI Conference on Human Factors in Computing Systems*, ACM (2012), 1391–1400.
7. DeVito, J. A. Levels of abstraction in spoken and written language. *Journal of Communication 17*, 4 (1967), 354–361.
8. Ebbinghaus, H. *Memory: A contribution to experimental psychology*. No. 3. University Microfilms, 1913.
9. Edge, D., Cheng, K.-Y., and Whitney, M. Spatialease: Learning language through body motion. In *Proceedings of the SIGCHI Conference on Human Factors in Computing Systems*, CHI '13, ACM (2013), 469–472.
10. Edge, D., Searle, E., Chiu, K., Zhao, J., and Landay, J. A. Micromandarin: Mobile language learning in context. In *Proceedings of the SIGCHI Conference on Human Factors in Computing Systems*, CHI '11, ACM (2011), 3169–3178.
11. Fast, E., Chen, B., and Bernstein, M. S. Empath: Understanding topic signals in large-scale text. In *Proceedings of the 2016 CHI Conference on Human Factors in Computing Systems*, ACM (2016), 4647–4657.
12. Han, C.-H., Yang, C.-L., and Wang, H.-C. Supporting second language reading with picture note-taking. In *CHI '14 Extended Abstracts on Human Factors in Computing Systems*, CHI EA '14, ACM (2014), 2245–2250.
13. Harris, Z. S. Distributional structure. *Word 10*, 2-3 (1954), 146–162.
14. Kayama, T., Kaneko, K., Miyakoda, H., and Ishikawa, M. Effective materials for abstract words in foreign vocabulary learning. In *Wireless, Mobile and Ubiquitous Technologies in Education (WMUTE), 2010 6th IEEE International Conference on*, IEEE (2010), 207–209.
15. Kovacs, G., and Miller, R. C. Smart subtitles for vocabulary learning. In *Proceedings of the SIGCHI Conference on Human Factors in Computing Systems*, CHI '14, ACM (2014), 853–862.
16. Lesk, M. Automatic sense disambiguation using machine readable dictionaries: how to tell a pine cone from an ice cream cone. In *Proceedings of the 5th annual international conference on Systems documentation*, ACM (1986), 24–26.
17. Manning, C. D., Surdeanu, M., Bauer, J., Finkel, J., Bethard, S. J., and McClosky, D. The Stanford CoreNLP natural language processing toolkit. In *Association for Computational Linguistics (ACL) System Demonstrations* (2014), 55–60.
18. Matthiesen, S. J. *Essential Words for the TOEFL*. Barron's Educational Series, 2014.
19. Mikolov, T., Sutskever, I., Chen, K., Corrado, G. S., and Dean, J. Distributed representations of words and phrases and their compositionality. In *Advances in neural information processing systems* (2013), 3111–3119.
20. Miyakoda, H., Kaneko, K.-i., and Ishikawa, M. Effective learning material for mobile devices. *JLCL 26*, 1 (2011), 39–51.
21. Paivio, A. Dual coding theory: Retrospect and current status. *Canadian Journal of Psychology/Revue canadienne de psychologie 45*, 3 (1991), 255.
22. Raine, P. Incidental learning of vocabulary through authentic subtitled videos. *JALT-The Japan Association for Language Teaching* (2012).
23. Sakunkoo, N., and Sakunkoo, P. Gliflix: Using movie subtitles for language learning. In *UIST 2013 Adjunct*, ACM (2013).
24. Savva, M., Chang, A. X., Manning, C. D., and Hanrahan, P. Transphoner: Automated mnemonic keyword generation. In *Proceedings of the SIGCHI Conference on Human Factors in Computing Systems*, CHI '14, ACM (2014), 3725–3734.
25. Secules, T., Herron, C., and Tomasello, M. The effect of video context on foreign language learning. *The Modern Language Journal 76*, 4 (1992), 480–490.
26. Takigiku, Y., Kaneko, K., Ishikawa, M., and Miyakoda, H. Short movie materials based on tessellation for foreign vocabulary learning. In *Information Technology Based Higher Education and Training (ITHET), 2010 9th International Conference on*, IEEE (2010), 284–291.

27. Toutanova, K., Klein, D., Manning, C. D., and Singer, Y. Feature-rich part-of-speech tagging with a cyclic dependency network. In *Proceedings of the 2003 Conference of the North American Chapter of the Association for Computational Linguistics on Human Language Technology-Volume 1*, Association for Computational Linguistics (2003), 173–180.

28. Xu, B., Gao, G., Fussell, S. R., and Cosley, D. Improving machine translation by showing two outputs. In *Proceedings of the SIGCHI Conference on Human Factors in Computing Systems*, ACM (2014), 3743–3746.

29. Yeh, Y., and Wang, C.-w. Effects of multimedia vocabulary annotations and learning styles on vocabulary learning. *Calico Journal* (2003), 131–144.

30. Yu, M. *New Oriental GRE Vocabulary Selection*. Qunyan Press, 2005.

31. Zhou, J., Dai, X., and Wang, P. Foreign language learning based on video scenes. In *Education Technology and Computer (ICETC), 2010 2nd International Conference on*, vol. 2, IEEE (2010), V2–350.

From in the Class or in the Wild? Peers Provide Better Design Feedback Than External Crowds

Helen Wauck[1], Yu-Chun Yen[1], Wai-Tat Fu[1], Elizabeth Gerber[2], Steven P. Dow[3], Brian P. Bailey[1]

[1]University of Illinois at Urbana
{wauck2, yyen4, wfu, bpbailey}
@illinois.edu

[2]Northwestern University
egerber@northwestern.edu

[3]University of California at
San Diego
spdow@ucsd.edu

ABSTRACT
As demand for design education increases, instructors are struggling to provide timely, personalized feedback for student projects. Gathering feedback from classroom peers and external crowds offer scalable approaches, but there is little evidence of how they compare. We report on a study in which students (n=127) created early- and late-stage prototypes as part of nine-week projects. At each stage, students received feedback from peers and external crowds: their own social networks, online communities, and a task market. We measured the quality, quantity and valence of the feedback and the actions taken on it, and categorized its content using a taxonomy of critique discourse. The study found that peers produced feedback that was of higher perceived quality, acted upon more, and longer compared to the crowds. However, crowd feedback was found to be a viable supplement to peer feedback and students preferred it for projects targeting specialized audiences. Feedback from all sources spanned only a subset of the critique categories. Instructors may fill this gap by further scaffolding feedback generation. The study contributes insights for how to best utilize different feedback sources in project-based courses.

Author Keywords
Feedback; design methods; learning; crowdsourcing.

ACM Classification Keywords
H.5.3 [Information Interface and Presentation]: Group and Organization Interfaces--Collaborative computing.

INTRODUCTION
Formative feedback is a critical aspect of project-based design courses because it helps students assess and improve their in-progress work [11]. Without it, students learn less effectively and the quality of their project solutions suffers [14, 35]. However, instructors struggle to deliver timely, personalized feedback due to increasing student demand for design courses coupled with significant long-term resource constraints faced by many public institutions [2].

CHI 2017, May 06-11, 2017, Denver, CO, USA
© 2017 ACM. ISBN 978-1-4503-4655-9/17/05…$15.00
DOI: http://dx.doi.org/10.1145/3025453.3025477

Researchers have explored two approaches for scaling feedback generation in project-based design courses. The first engages classroom peers in feedback exchange [19]. Peer feedback has learning benefits for the recipient and the provider [8, 28], and there is a shared context to ground the exchange [6]. However, peer feedback can be narrow since students are learning the same course material and typically share similar demographics [11]. Peer feedback can also be affected by friendship and competition between the students [36], and the increased workload it imposes on them [22]. These issues could affect the quality of the feedback and students' willingness to act on it. Further, students depend on instructors to orchestrate the exchange.

The second approach engages online crowds external to the classroom. Students receive feedback from people in social networks, online communities, and task markets. External crowds may include more authentic, specialized audiences that would be hard to access in class. This might increase students' perceived value of and willingness to act on the feedback. Students can also gather feedback from external crowds as often as their time and resources allow. Planning for feedback aids self-regulation skills, which is critical for career readiness [43]. However, feedback from such crowds can be noisy due to the lack of a shared context [5], among many factors, and requires social or financial capital [41].

Despite the availability of both approaches in project-based courses, there is little knowledge of how they compare. Do students perceive differences in quality between feedback received from classroom peers and external crowds? Do they act on the feedback differently? Do these sources yield different categories of feedback that would be more or less suitable at different design stages? Investigating these questions will provide deeper empirical understanding of the relation between the feedback source and output, and help instructors devise scalable feedback strategies to provide the most help at different stages of student projects.

We conducted a study in which students (n=127) completed user interface design projects of their choice over nine weeks. Early- and late-stage prototypes were created during the projects. Students received feedback at each stage from three to six classroom peers and three crowds: their own social networks, online communities, and a task market. Students—blind to the source—rated the perceived quality and selected the action taken on each feedback response. We measured the number of responses, length, and valence of the feedback, and categorized the content using a critique taxonomy [4]. We also surveyed and interviewed students to gauge their perceptions of the feedback sources.

Our study has three main findings. First, classroom peers produced feedback that was of higher perceived quality, was acted upon more, and was longer compared to the feedback from the external crowds. This is likely due to the multiple incentives peers have for giving feedback: course grades, social ties in the classroom, and interest in the topic since this was an elective course.

Second, results show that feedback from external crowds is a viable supplement to peer feedback. This is supported by the findings that students perceived the crowd feedback to be of comparable quality (μ=4.1 vs. μ=5.0 for peers; 7-pt scale), students did not report feeling uncomfortable sharing their work with online crowds, and they preferred external crowds for accessing specialized audiences. Instructors can thus have increased confidence when appropriating the use of external crowds for design feedback in the classroom.

Finally, most of the feedback produced across all sources focused on recommending improvements, assessing design quality, and sense-making, while missing other categories of critique discourse (e.g., brainstorming possibilities and offering comparisons to existing solutions). Instructors should be mindful of this gap, especially at the early design stage, when the content from these missing categories may be most beneficial. Instructors can fill this content gap by further scaffolding the feedback generation process.

Our work makes three contributions to the CHI community. First, we offer deeper empirical knowledge of the relation between the source of the feedback provider and the quality, quantity, and content of their feedback. Second, our results offer guidance as to how instructors can better orchestrate feedback from different sources to benefit learning and improve project quality (e.g., organize peer feedback at project milestones and leverage external crowds for feedback in-between the milestones or to access specialized user audiences). These results can also inform how professional HCI designers consider the tradeoffs in obtaining feedback from colleagues or external crowds. Third, our study provides implications for improving the effectiveness of crowd platforms for feedback exchange.

RELATED WORK

We discuss tradeoffs of receiving design feedback from instructors, end users, classroom peers, and external crowds in large project-based courses. We highlight how the use of external crowds and classroom peers can address issues of scale and offer learning benefits. We also situate our work in context of prior HCI-related studies of these approaches.

Instructor and End User Feedback

Historically, instructor feedback has been considered an integral component of design education [37]. Instructors question the intent and effectiveness of the students' design work (sketches, renderings, 3D models); and students use the feedback to inform next steps [24]. Instructors can also draw from the literature to tailor the feedback to improve its learning benefit [31, 32]. However, it is difficult for instructors to provide personalized feedback to dozens of student projects in parallel given their many professional responsibilities (preparing course content, conducting research, academic service, etc.) [8]. This may be one reason students widely report dissatisfaction with the written feedback actually received from instructors [27].

To supplement their feedback, instructors teach students to seek feedback from potential end users who might use the design solution [12, 13]. For example, students might seek people with dietary restrictions to give feedback on the design of an app that filters restaurants based on the menu items. However, it can be difficult for students to quickly locate users who match the target audience, and who can commit the time needed to give feedback on the project [5].

Classroom Peer Feedback

Peer feedback asks people similar in ability to assess each other's in-progress work [23]. Peer feedback is scalable and also offers learning benefits. For example, it supports skill assessment and learning through exposure to different solution strategies [14, 18, 28, 31] and can lead to improved solution quality [9, 29]. Given its benefits, educators have applied peer feedback in a variety of classroom settings, from small studio courses to large online courses [23]. Researchers continue to improve the quality of peer review by studying interface features of the review platforms [15], rubrics [23], and characteristics of the review content [31].

However, peer feedback may be influenced by friendship, competition [36], and course workload [22]. Feedback could also be narrow due to students' exposure to the same learning material and their similar demographics [11, 17]. These limitations could affect the perceived quality of the feedback and students' willingness to act on it. It is therefore unclear how students would perceive feedback generated by classroom peers relative to external audiences.

External Crowd Feedback in the Classroom

Another alternative for scaling feedback generation is to have students solicit feedback from external crowds, such as social media (e.g. Facebook), online communities (e.g. Reddit), and paid task markets (e.g. MTurk) [17]. External crowds can quickly provide personalized feedback on many projects in parallel [5, 17]. Students may perceive the feedback favorably due to its authenticity [33] and potential insights outside the course material [17]. Being responsible for knowing when and how to gather feedback can also help students learn to be more self-directed in their work [7].

Researchers have begun to assess feedback from external crowds in the classroom. Xu et al. showed that students can apply the feedback from a task market to make non-trivial revisions to their graphic designs [40]. Other work has shown that the feedback from a task market can be of high quality and is perceived to improve the design process [25].

Hui et al. showed students can leverage social media to receive feedback and improve their work [16]. However, getting feedback from external crowds can require social capital [30], community membership, or payment [20]. Students may also be reluctant to share work online [16].

Our study contributes to this thread of work by providing empirical knowledge of how the *source* of the feedback (classroom peers or external crowds) affects its content, quantity, perceived quality, and actions taken.

External Crowd Feedback Outside the Classroom

Yen et al. [41] performed the only study we are aware of that compared the design feedback from different external crowds, including online communities, social media, and task markets. The study found that the feedback from different sources was of similar perceived quality; however, online communities offered more process feedback, task markets offered more design suggestions, and social media offered the most responses without payment. Most participants in the study had professional design experience.

Our study extends this prior work in two ways. First, Yen et al compared feedback between external crowds, whereas our study compares external crowd feedback to that of classroom peers. It is critical for instructors to know how the feedback differs between these sources so that they can choose the source best suited to their students' projects. Second, our study generates the external feedback using the same platforms as in [41] but in the context of a course where students are learning about design and have little or no prior design experience. Our focus on students differs from the prior study which had more experienced designers.

RESEARCH QUESTIONS

Our study was designed to answer the following questions:

RQ1: How does the source (peers and external crowds) and stage of the design (early vs. late) affect students' **(a)** perceived value of and **(b)** action taken on the feedback?

RQ2: How do the source of the feedback and stage of the design affect the content of the design feedback generated?

RQ3: What do students perceive as the benefits and limits of leveraging peers and external audiences for feedback?

These questions were posed to help design educators understand how various sources of feedback could be effectively leveraged at different stages of the process. For example, external crowds may be more detail-oriented, which may be less helpful for early-stage prototypes. Answers to these questions will also provide a deeper understanding of how crowds driven by different incentives provide different types of feedback, which instructors can take advantage of when choosing which feedback.

METHOD

To answer these research questions, we conducted a study in a project-based user interface (UI) design course at the University of Illinois, a large public university in the U.S.

Design Course and Projects

The UI design course targeted upper-level undergraduate and beginning graduate students in computer science, but about 10% of the students came from engineering, psychology, and the arts. For most students, this was their first course on UI design. The instructor organized students into teams (4-6 students) to balance skill sets. There were 188 students (44 female) and 40 teams in the course. The lecture topics included user research, ideation, prototyping, and evaluation. The teams applied these topics to a UI design project of their choice. Example projects included a mobile route-finding app, a web app to render online news in the style of a print newspaper, and an app for managing vacation packing lists.

The projects were structured as a design process. Each stage corresponded to a project deliverable submitted for a grade. Two key deliverables were targeted in this study: *early-* and *late-stage* prototypes. An early-stage prototype consisted of drawn sketches representing the direction of the proposed project solution. A late-stage prototype was a programming implementation of a team's revised early stage design.

These two design stages represented major milestones and would especially benefit from formative feedback. Early-stage prototypes may benefit from feedback about goals, scope and approach; late-stage prototypes may benefit from feedback about implementation choices and aesthetics; and both may benefit from perspectives beyond the course staff. At each stage, teams received feedback from classroom peers and the external crowds. The feedback was generated as part of a course assignment. All students were required to complete the assignment at each stage, since learning to gather feedback online and write constructive feedback are important learning goals [1, 10]. Other project deliverables such as the proposals and user research reports received feedback only from the course staff. We adapted an existing online review platform (described in [41]) to collect and present feedback from each source and design stage. Figure 1 shows an example of a project team's early- and late-stage prototypes and some of the feedback they received.

Peer and External Crowd Feedback

Project teams received feedback from four sources:

Peers: Each student was randomly assigned a design from another project team for feedback. Each team therefore received feedback from three to six peers at each stage. The links to the feedback forms were sent by email from the course staff as part of an individual assignment. Students entered their feedback on our platform and submitted it for grading by the course staff on a two-point scale: specific and helpful (2), too generic or short (1), or none given (0). Students were aware of the rubric prior to giving feedback.

Online community: Each project team posted the feedback link for their design to an online community of their choice, with instructions to target a relevant audience. This was performed as a group task to reduce a wave of requests to

Early-stage Prototype **Late-stage Prototype**

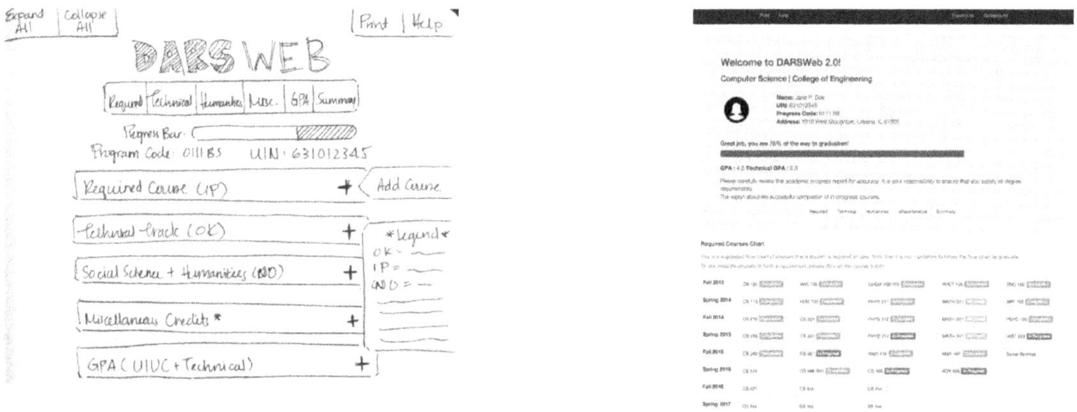

Peers: "It looks really convenient! I like the idea of having the flexibility to add courses and check if they fulfil requirements. I also like the color coding feature. One thing that is not clear in the image is whether there will be a percentage indicator on the progress bar to get an accurate idea of the progress. Also, in my opinion, the buttons Expand All and Collapse All should be on the right side '+' button is located on the right side too. The Print and Help button can be on the left side. You could also add the option to save the report as a PDF."

Online Communities: "I like the idea you guys have implemented. A more UI friendly way of viewing your academic progress would definitely be a welcome development for us students. One thing I do want to say is that with your idea, obtaining information is going to be very tedious. I am sure you don't currently have a way to access each student's academic record. As a result, I assume, you would request all of this information from the user themselves…"

Task Market: "I think you have a great concept going. When you do finally add colors, I would add bright colors to make the page really pop."

Social Media: "Great work! Looks clean and interface looks user-friendly."

Peers: "Should the required courses be divided by year? I don't imagine courses need to be taken at particular times. Also I'm seeing the Required, Miscellaneous and Summary sections but where are the Technical and Humanities requirements? Is there a general overview of the courses taken already? seems like only a portion of the completed classes are displayed in the summary area. I do appreciate the clarity of the design, though it seems to be missing some information I think would really add to it."

Online Communities: "You might want to signify the number of hours a certain class fills and/or completed during each semester. Also keep in mind that some people complete classes over winter or summer semesters."

Task Market: "Overall, it's pretty clear. I would like to see all the boxes the same size. Maybe use different colors to differentiate courses too."

Social Media: "Your navbar is pushed in compared to your divs. This kinda looks asymmetrical / pyramid-like. I'd rather it be square."

Figure 1: An example of a project team's early- and late-stage prototypes for an online course planning interface and the anonymous feedback received from the four sources studied. Some of the feedback was omitted for brevity.

any one community. As a default, the course staff suggested the Reddit forum /r/design_critiques, a popular resource for online design critique. The team submitted a screen shot of the post and rationale for the community selected.

Social network: Each project team member posted the feedback link for their design to an online social network (Facebook or Twitter) using their own account. This was an individual task to smooth differences in each team's total network size [16]. Students submitted a screenshot as proof of their post. Students were not required to perform this task if they did not have a social media account or were uncomfortable using it for this purpose.

Paid task market: The research team posted the link to each team's design to Amazon.com's Mechanical Turk (MTurk) for feedback. Five pieces of feedback were solicited for each design to be consistent with the volume of peer responses. The feedback tasks paid $0.40, which, based on pilot data, equated to a wage at or above U.S. minimum wage. The task prompt stated: "*We are collecting feedback on a [design stage] design for a user interface. The user interface design project is part of a course project at a university.*" The research team posted all feedback tasks for the teams to eliminate the need for students to create accounts on MTurk and to have consistency in the configuration of the MTurk tasks across each project team.

All feedback was left anonymously, though the platform logged the source. We chose these sources because they are readily available and because they differ in terms of the incentives for giving feedback – course credit (peers), topical interest (online communities), social relations (social media), and financial gain (paid task market).

Procedure

The procedure consisted of two phases summarized in Figure 2. The first phase began two weeks before the due date for the early-stage prototypes, at the midpoint of the course. The corresponding homework assignment generated feedback from all four sources for early-stage prototypes.

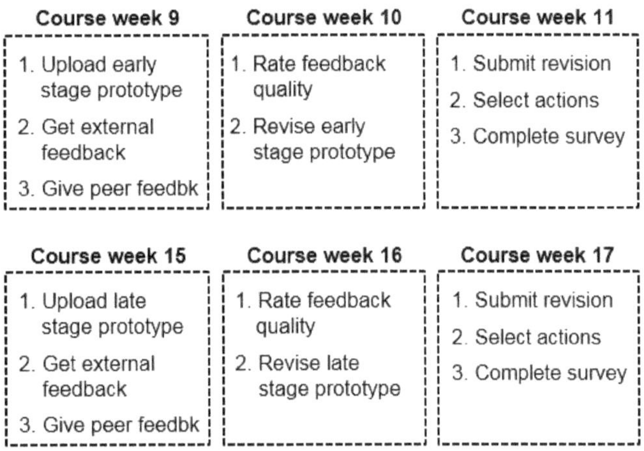

Figure 2: Summary of the nine-week experimental procedure. The early-stage prototype phase began in course week 9 (top row). The late-stage prototype phase began in course week 15 (bottom row). Prototypes were created in the weeks preceding the respective phase of the experiment.

For the assignment, each team uploaded an image or scan of their early-stage prototype to our platform along with a title and description. The platform created a link to the feedback form for the design and then stepped the team through posting the link to an online community and social network. Meanwhile, the research team posted the link to the paid task market for feedback. Students received individual emails with the links for giving peer feedback. Feedback generation lasted one week and all feedback was aggregated on our platform.

Teams had one week to iterate on the design after receiving feedback. After iterating, teams returned to our platform, selected the action taken for each feedback response, and completed a feedback reflection form (see Measures). The revised early-stage prototype was then submitted as part of the project requirements, completing the assignment.

For the second phase, the same procedure was repeated for the late stage prototypes. These prototypes were uploaded as a screenshot of the implemented user interface. This phase occurred near the final weeks of the course.

All students participated in the team projects and completed the two assignments as part of the course. At the end of the course, we distributed a consent form to the students. Only students who gave consent to use their data were included in our analysis. The study required coordination between the research team and course staff, which had no overlap. The study was approved by the IRB at our institution.

Measures

We measured the perceived quality, action taken, valence, content category, and length of each feedback response. We also collected demographics from the providers: gender, age, design expertise, and their reason for leaving feedback.

Teams collectively rated perceived quality of each feedback response on a 7-point scale (7=highest). After iterating on their design, teams selected the action taken on each piece of feedback: implemented fully, implemented partially, thought about it, or ignored it. All feedback was presented blind to condition to control for biases toward the feedback sources. These measures allowed us to gauge not only perceptions of the feedback, but also how it was applied.

The valence of feedback indicates its affective tone [34]. Given the size of the data set, we recruited two judges to rate the valence of each response on a 5-point Likert scale (1=Very Negative, 3=Neutral, 5=Very Positive). Judges were recruited from MTurk and were paid $0.12 per task. For a majority (56%) of the responses, judges agreed on the rating, which became the rating assigned. Of the disagreements, 82% of the responses differed by only one Likert scale point. In this and the remaining cases, a member of the research team cast the deciding vote.

To categorize content, the responses were partitioned into idea units, and the units were categorized using a taxonomy of critique discourse (e.g. judgement, brainstorming, and process) [4]. Details of the categorization are in Results. The word count of each response was also measured.

At the end of each design stage, teams completed a feedback reflection form. Teams rated the overall quality of the feedback received on a 7-point scale (1=Low, 7=High) and their comfort level sharing their design with each of the three external crowds (1=Very Uncomfortable, 7=Very Comfortable). The form also asked teams to select which source they expected to provide the highest quality feedback (or indicate that they expected the same quality from all sources) and to write a free response characterizing the strengths and weaknesses of the feedback.

Student Interviews

At the completion of the course, we conducted 45-minute semi-structured interviews with 10 students. Participants were recruited through a message distributed to the course roster. Each participant got $10 as remuneration. Interviews were audio recorded and then transcribed for analysis.

Interview questions focused on perceptions of soliciting the feedback from external crowds ("What do you think is the largest benefit [and weakness] of getting feedback from external crowds?") and which method they would prefer in a future course ("Which approach [peers or external crowds] would you prefer to leverage in similar engineering design courses?"). We used a bottom-up analysis to code emergent themes in the interview data [3]

RESULTS

Our study examined how the source (peers and external crowds) and design stage (early vs. late) affect students' perceived value of and action taken on the feedback received (RQ1); how the source and design stage affects the content of the feedback (RQ2); and student perceptions of receiving feedback from peers and external crowds (RQ3).

	OC	TM	SM	Peers
Early stage	34	199	280	93
Late stage	39	211	127	94
Total	73	410	407	187

Table 1: Number of feedback responses per source and design stage. OC = Online Communities, TM = Task Market, SM = Social Media, Peers = Classroom Peers.

Quantity of Feedback

We collected 1159 feedback responses across all sources and design stages. In total, 127 out of 188 peers in the course consented to participate in the study, a 68% response rate. We removed ten of the feedback responses due to inappropriate content. The remaining responses were filtered for double submissions (50) and omissions (32), leaving 1077 responses for analysis. The distribution of responses between source and design stage is summarized in Table 1. This pattern was consistent across both design stages. However, the number of social media responses was greater in the early stage (280) than in the late stage (127) (χ^2=113.5, p<0.001). This may reflect the social cost of requesting feedback from one's online social network [30].

Peer Feedback Has Higher Perceived Quality (RQ1a)

Figure 3 summarizes students' perceived quality ratings. We performed an ANCOVA with Source (peers vs. external crowds) and Stage (early vs. late) as factors. The provider's self-reported gender, age category, and design expertise (1-5, 5=expert) were added as co-variates. The ANCOVA showed that feedback from peers (μ=5.03) was rated higher than from the external crowds (μ=4.10; F(1,1065)=38.1; p<0.001). As shown in Figure 3, peer feedback was rated about 20% higher than that of external crowds. One explanation is that peers were more likely to identify issues relevant to the learning goals of the course. For instance, during an interview, one student stated, "*the peer source [addressed] issues we learned about in class*".

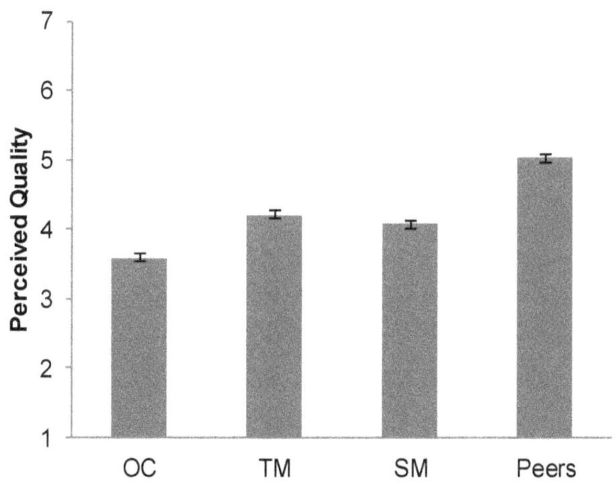

Figure 3: The means of the perceived quality ratings. OC = Online Community, TM = Task Market, SM = Social Media. Error bars show pooled standard error (0.06).

Stage did not have a main effect, there were no interactions, and no effects of interest were found for the covariates.

Pairwise comparisons using Tukey's method showed that feedback from peers (μ=5.03) was rated higher than from online communities (μ=3.6, p<0.001), social media (μ=4.08, p<0.001), and the task market (μ=4.20, p<0.001). Feedback from online communities was perceived to be the lowest quality, which may be due to the cursory nature of the feedback typically received from this source [38, 39]. No other differences were detected for perceived quality.

Peer Feedback is Implemented More (RQ1b)

We compared the counts of the project teams' selected actions on the feedback using Source and Stage as factors. Feedback responses without a selected action (n=19) were removed from the analysis. Peer feedback was implemented more (23% *implement partially*), thought about more (34% *think about it*) and ignored less (14% *ignore*) relative to the feedback from external crowds (16% *implement partially*, χ^2=5.2, p=0.022; 22% *think about it*, χ^2= 12.0, p<0.001; and 35% *ignore*, χ^2=28.8, p<0.001). There were no other differences detected, and no differences between stages.

Peers Write Longer Feedback

We analyzed the length of the feedback using the same model as for perceived quality, except with length as the dependent measure. The ANCOVA showed an interaction effect (F(1,1065)=19.04, p<0.001): feedback from peers and online communities was longer for early-stage designs (μ=108 and 74 words, respectively) than for late-stage designs (u=70 and 46, respectively; p<0.001 in both cases). Feedback from social media and the task market was similar in length between stages. Social media feedback had a mean length of 40 words at the early stage and 45 words at the late stage, while task market feedback had a mean of 43 words for the early stage and 47 words for the late stage. The ANCOVA also showed that peers wrote more content (μ=89 words) than providers in online communities (μ=59), the task market (μ=45), and social media (μ=43) (p<0.001 all cases). No other covariates of interest were significant. A regression analysis showed a small correlation between length and perceived quality (R^2=0.14, p<0.001), corroborating that students value longer feedback [42].

Valence is More Negative for Late-Stage Prototypes

The valence of the feedback was analyzed using the same model as for perceived quality, with valence as the dependent measure. The ANCOVA showed a main effect of Stage (F(1,1065)=4.34, p=0.037): feedback at the late stage (μ=2.92) exhibited more negative valence than at the early stage (μ=3.04, p=0.036). This may be because late-stage prototypes have specific graphic design elements that elicit specific critiques [37]. Source did not have a main effect, and none of the covariates had a significant effect.

Content Focuses on Assessment and Analysis (RQ2)

To categorize the content, we first partitioned the feedback in our dataset into idea units. An idea unit represents a coherent unit of thought and may be comprised of a phrase,

Category	Definition	Example Idea Units
Judgement	Critic reacts to what they see and renders some assessment of its quality.	"I like the color scheme."
Process-Oriented	Critic makes statements or asks questions about the process that students might have used or could use to create the design.	"Use animations for more polished prototypes."
Brainstorming	Critic asks questions or makes rhetorical statements about future imagined possibilities for the design.	"Also, this would be great for use within Airports for travelers."
Interpretation	Critic reacts to what they see and tries to make sense of the concept or product.	"I have no idea what is going on with this page, it doesn't make any sense."
Direct Recommendation	Critic gives specific advice about a particular aspect of design. Feedback is focused, purposeful, and specific.	"The picture could use annotations on the controls for screen cropping."
Investigation	Critic requests information (typically by questioning) about the design or the design process.	"What other information will you include to help students take their desired courses?"
Free Association	Critic makes reactive, associative statements about the design.	"it doesn't seem that different than similar products right now."
Comparison	Critic contrasts the design or design process with something else in a focused, intentional way.	"Though I can see this is a preliminary design, it is very similar to DropBox -- how do you plan on differentiating it?"
Identity-Invoking	Critic makes statements or asks questions to suggest that students consider the larger picture of themselves as designers in a future professional community.	"seems you have learned little or nothing from [the design course]."
Support	Generic praise and support of the designer, not the design.	"keep up the great work guys!!!."

Table 2: Categories used for feedback content analysis, adapted from [4].

sentence, or group of sentences. The partitioning yielded a total of 3116 idea units; 282 from online communities, 1046 from MTurk, 1022 from social media, and 766 from peers.

Given the size of our dataset and the unequal distribution of the responses, we sampled the idea units to ensure that each source was equally represented. Online communities gave the fewest responses, with 282 idea units. Therefore, we randomly sampled 282 idea units from each of the other sources, giving a total of 1128 (282 x 4) units for analysis.

Idea units were categorized using a taxonomy of critique discourse in design [4]. The taxonomy has nine categories: *judgement, process-oriented, brainstorming, interpretation, direct recommendation, investigation, free association, comparison*, and *identity-invoking*. After reviewing the data set, we added a category for *support* (the idea unit offered praise or encouragement). Definitions and examples of each category are shown in Table 2.

We trained two independent labelers outside our research team on 10% of the dataset (n=106 idea units). After several iterations, Krippendorff's α, a measure of inter-rater reliability [21], did not exceed 0.6. Thus, both labelers categorized all idea units independently. We aggregated the resulting category assignments, and the labelers worked together to resolve disagreement. If agreement was not reached, a member of our research team cast the final vote.

The distribution of categories across the sources and stages is summarized in Table 3. The most noticeable pattern was that the vast majority (90%) of idea units fell into four categories: *direct recommendation (40%), judgement (31%), interpretation (12%),* and *investigation (7%)*. This was consistent across sources and design stages. These four categories are most useful for the late stage, when there is more emphasis on the design representation and its quality.

However, these categories may be less suitable for the early stage. At this stage, students may benefit most from reflecting on how they approached the design, how the design compares to other solutions, and how it fits in a broader social and cultural context [37]. Feedback in the categories *brainstorming (3%), comparison (3%), process-oriented (2%), free association (2%),* and *identity-invoking (<1%)* would best speak to those issues, but these categories were rarely addressed by any of the four sources.

Student Perceptions (RQ3)

In this section, we report results from the project team surveys collected at the early stage (n=40) and late stage (n=40) and the individual interviews (n=10). Quotations are reported with a T for team survey responses and an S for individual student interview responses.

Peers Expected to Be Highest Quality Source

Teams selected which source they expected to provide the highest quality feedback. Expectations for the highest quality source differed at both the early stage (χ^2=16.0, p=0.0031) and late stage (χ^2=29.7, p<0.001). Overall, 45% of teams expected peer feedback to be of highest quality and 40% expected external crowds to be of highest quality. The remaining 15% expected them to be the same quality.

At the late stage, more teams expected peer feedback to be of highest quality (50%) than online communities (18%, p= 0.0460), the task market (8%, p=0.005), and social media (15%, p=0.019). At the early stage, teams' preferences were not as strong, with the only difference being between peer feedback (40%) and the task market (5%, p=0.005).

	Early-Stage Prototypes				Late-Stage Prototypes			
	OC	TM	SM	Peers	OC	TM	SM	Peers
Judgement	38 (29%)	38 (31%)	53 (29%)	48 (29%)	53 (36%)	52 (32%)	26 (29%)	32 (29%)
Process-Oriented	3 (2%)	2 (2%)	4 (2%)	2 (1%)	1 (1%)	4 (2%)	0 (0%)	2 (2%)
Brainstorming	2 (2%)	5 (4%)	6 (3%)	2 (1%)	5 (3%)	6 (4%)	1 (1%)	1 (1%)
Interpretation	21 (16%)	8 (6%)	24 (13%)	29 (17%)	13 (9%)	14 (9%)	10 (11%)	19 (17%)
Direct Recommendation	43 (33%)	61 (49%)	73 (39%)	59 (35%)	48 (33%)	76 (47%)	42 (46%)	40 (36%)
Investigation	16 (12%)	2 (2%)	10 (5%)	18 (11%)	8 (5%)	2 (1%)	5 (5%)	16 (14%)
Free Association	2 (2%)	4 (3%)	0 (0%)	2 (1%)	6 (4%)	3 (2%)	1 (1%)	0 (0%)
Comparison	4 (3%)	2 (2%)	7 (4%)	8 (5%)	6 (4%)	3 (2%)	2 (2%)	1 (1%)
Identity-Invoking	1 (1%)	0 (0%)	0 (0%)	0 (0%)	2 (1%)	0 (0%)	1 (1%)	0 (0%)
Support	0 (0%)	1 (1%)	6 (3%)	0 (0%)	0 (0%)	0 (0%)	1 (1%)	0 (0%)

Table 3: The distribution of occurrences across critique categories for each source and design stage. OC = Online Communities, TM = Task Market, and SM = Social Media. Percents do not sum to 100 because some idea units did not fit into any category.

Students Somewhat Comfortable Sharing Designs Online

Project teams rated their comfort level sharing their designs with each external crowd (1=Very Uncomfortable, 7=Very Comfortable). Students reported being neutral to somewhat comfortable sharing their designs online. The distributions were μ=5.0, σ=1.90 for online communities; μ=4.2, σ=1.99 for social media; and μ=4.0, σ=1.60 for the task market.

A repeated measures ANOVA with Source and Stage as factors and level of comfort rating as the measure showed that Source had a main effect ($F(2,197)=7.55$, $p=0.0007$). Post-hoc tests revealed that teams were less comfortable with having their designs shared on the task market (μ=4.0) than with online communities (μ=5.0, $p=0.0047$). This difference may be due to students being less familiar with the task market, since the researchers posted the designs on their behalf. There was no difference detected in comfort level between the early- and late-stage prototypes.

Strengths and Weaknesses of the Feedback

Project teams were asked to characterize the strengths and weaknesses of the feedback they received at both stages. Since students were blind to condition, they reported on the feedback holistically. We discuss the responses in aggregate since they were similar between the two stages. We use *n* to indicate the number of responses citing a given theme.

The most commonly cited strengths of the feedback were that it brought new issues to the team's attention through specific, useful suggestions (*n*=28), it was more honest and unfiltered due to anonymity (*n*=6), and it produced diverse perspectives by including access to broader audiences (*n*=5). A team building a web-based weather application described the usefulness of specific suggestions:

> *"Having people outside our groups reviewing our design, we are able to receive some insights into things we previously overlooked. For example, we originally did not think that precipitation was important, but now we know that most people look at precipitation when they want to find out the weather."* (T21)

Students valued not only specific feedback, but also feedback based on diverse perspectives. A team working on a mobile route finding app explained:

> *"The strength is that we learned a lot from people with different background and opinions from different perspectives. A lot of them are quite useful."* (T11)

Students also valued the honesty of the feedback. A team working on a multi-thread messaging platform noted:

> *"Since the feedback is anonymous, people can very easily troll you. ...However, the same anonymity allows people to provide honest feedback, which is totally worth the tradeoff."* (T2)

While students appreciated many aspects of the feedback, they struggled with vague or irrelevant content (*n*=28). For instance, teams building a mobile restaurant finding app and a course management system for university students said, respectively:

> *Very vague feedback. Some of it was not even feedback."* (T6)

> *"A lot of feedback was just 'good job' with no actual suggestions for improving the platform."* (T15)

This also manifested for some teams as a low signal to noise ratio. One team working on a mobile home meal sharing app explained:

> *"While it was good to hear the compliments about the app, it was also a lot to filter through to find the main design points that were important to change."* (T19)

Teams also reported frustration when the providers appeared to misunderstand the context of the design

(n=10). For example, one team developing a mobile work scheduling app stated:

> *"Generally a lot of the feedback was questions about how the prototype worked as opposed to giving substantial feedback."* (T37)

Students See Tradeoffs for Different Feedback Sources

Interviewees (9 of 10) believed the choice between all of the sources of design feedback depended on the source's knowledge of the topic and design domain, and how well the source represented the target user audience. Interviewees perceived the non-expert nature of external crowds as both a strength and a weakness. When non-expertise was viewed as a strength, interviewees pointed to situations where external crowds could provide fresh insights. For example, one interviewee remarked that having external crowds critique his team's re-design of an online course management tool was useful due to their novel perspective:

> *"Since we had a student focused design, to have people that are possibly not students, like from Reddit, was one of the greatest strengths of it...because they point out a lot of things that we didn't notice, because with a student, they know how Compass runs, so they're looking for the same functions in our design. But someone who hasn't used it, it's completely new to them."* (S2). Another interviewee shared a similar view: *"Sometimes [external crowds] will provide some more feedback...from a non-designer's perspective, from practical use."* (S5)

In other situations, non-expertise was seen as a weakness. One interviewee said,

> *"The purpose of the design is to make a design that's going to function the best. I want someone who could help me with functionality as opposed to just looks."* (S2)

In these cases, peers or online communities were seen as the most expert source. Another interviewee explained why:

> *"For the peers, they will give more technical advice... The people who are on Reddit, they might be more expert, and they focus more on the details than our peers-our friends, for example. So, they might give more advanced ideas or constructive ideas."* (S6)

Finally, interviewees felt it would be most helpful to get feedback from the source most representative of their target audience. For instance, one interviewee's group was designing an interface for chemistry lab equipment and felt they needed feedback from this specialized user audience:

> *"It depends on what the functionality of the project is and the target users. For myself, I have a project where we're designing a switch...for a chemistry lab...the users are mostly scientists, [so] the crowd user may not be really helpful."* (S1)

DISCUSSION AND FUTURE WORK

A goal of our study was to compare the feedback from classroom peers and external crowds at different design stages for student projects. Our results showed that peers produced feedback that was of higher perceived quality, was acted on more, and was longer than the feedback from the external crowds. Students also expected the feedback from peers to be of higher quality than from any of the external crowds. One reason for this pattern was that even though peers were anonymous to each other, they were accountable to the course staff for completing the feedback assignments. Though the feedback assignments were only part of the coursework, our experience as instructors is that receiving a grade is a strong incentive for students to perform the work. Students also had incentives that overlapped with the external crowds: classroom peers typically have some social ties with each other, and given that this was an elective course, many students registered due to an interest in the topic.

Our results showed that crowd feedback is still a viable option for student projects since the feedback was perceived to be of comparable quality (μ=4.1 vs. μ=5.0 for peers). External crowd feedback could therefore supplement peer feedback received at key project milestones or replace it when tight schedules or an already high student workload make peer feedback less desirable. Instructors could also use external crowds to help students learn to become more self-directed in planning for and acquiring feedback [7], as this is an essential skill for innovation careers [11]. Finally, external crowds can be helpful for accessing specialized user audiences, as mentioned by student interviewees.

All sources produced feedback that primarily spanned four of the nine categories of the critique taxonomy: suggestions for improvement (*direct recommendation*), assessments of quality (*judgement*), and sense-making statements (*investigation* and *interpretation*). These categories are especially beneficial for designs at the late stage [37]. The other categories (e.g., *brainstorm*, *process*, and *comparison*) may be more suitable for early-stage designs because the content would likely address how teams approached the design problem, how the solution path compares to alternatives, and how it fits in a larger context. To fill these categories, instructors may need to scaffold the feedback generation process with appropriate prompts (e.g. as in [26]) or provide this type of feedback themselves.

The design stage had minimal effects in our study. With Stage as a factor, our analysis did not detect differences in perceived quality of the feedback, actions taken, content categories, or comfort sharing, and showed only minimal effects for expectation of quality. Instructors may therefore weigh the stage of the design less than other factors when considering which sources to use for feedback.

Students reported feeling comfortable sharing their designs (all means > 4 on a 7-point scale) with all three external crowds. This may be due the anonymous feedback context our experimental design created. Due to an omission in our survey, we did not collect comfortableness ratings for sharing designs with classroom peers.

In our study, students benefited from the work performed by feedback providers recruited from online communities and social media, but did not reciprocate that effort. In the future, if an instructor wishes to leverage these platforms, s/he should consider requiring students to pay forward that effort. This may also help students understand how to approach these platforms when later requesting feedback.

Our results for external crowds can be compared to a study by Yen et al that used similar platforms to generate feedback for design projects outside of a classroom context [41]. Both studies found that average perceived quality for all crowds was just above 4 on a 7-point scale with minimal or no differences between crowds. For the crowds where the number of responses were not controllable, Yen et al observed that online communities produced more responses than social networks, whereas our results showed the opposite pattern. In our study, student teams utilized their collective social networks, as in Hui et al. [16], which may have increased responses due to a larger network size. Also, all the feedback requests were posted to online communities in parallel, which may have caused feedback providers to give less attention to each posted design. Using the same taxonomy, both studies found that *judgements* and *direct recommendations* were most common in the feedback.

Our results also produced two main design implications for improving the effectiveness of crowd-based platforms for feedback exchange. First, the prototypes in our study were represented on our platform as a single image. This approach supports any implementation (e.g., mobile, desktop, and Web), and mimics existing feedback platforms (e.g., Reddit). However, students reported that this constraint caused the feedback to focus more on aesthetics rather than usability at the late stage. Enabling richer design representations, such as design images organized into tasks or videos of prototype use, could help focus feedback on other important aspects of the late stage design. Second, students mentioned the desire to have a dialogue with their feedback providers. Enabling this dialogue during feedback generation could help clarify the issues raised, answer questions, and promote a longer-term relationship between the providers and designers throughout the project.

In addition to the issues already discussed, we see several opportunities for future work. First, this paper viewed external crowds and peers as separate sources. Future work could examine how external crowds and peers could work together to produce feedback that is of higher quality than either could produce alone. Second, the external crowds in our study provided a large, broad audience from which to generate feedback. Future work could explore how online technologies might connect students with a smaller group of target users from external audiences for the duration of their design projects. Finally, as prior work has shown that feedback helps students learn [23], a future study should investigate how the feedback received from peers and external crowds affects learning and project outcomes.

LIMITATIONS

One limitation of our study is that we conducted it in a single university course. Future work is needed to test the generalizability of our findings in additional course settings. Second, we did not scaffold feedback generation, instead using a similar open-ended prompt for each source to be consistent across conditions. However, previous work has shown that scaffolding using rubrics [43], pre-authored statements [24], task decomposition [40], and framing features of the review platform [14] can improve feedback from non-experts. Future work should test how different scaffolding and framing techniques affect the pattern of results reported in this paper. Third, while limiting the use of peer feedback reduces student workload, we did not measure the additional student effort required to gather external crowd feedback. Future work comparing the relative effort required for each activity is needed to understand the extent to which crowd feedback reduces student workload. Finally, we measured feedback quality based on student perceptions. Future work should include additional measures such as expert evaluation to create a more complete profile of feedback quality.

CONCLUSION

This paper compares the feedback generated by classroom peers and three external crowds at different stages of the design process in a project-based design course. Our results show that while peers outperformed the external crowds on certain measures, such as perceived quality of the feedback and actions taken on it, getting feedback from external crowds is still a viable option when peer feedback is not desirable, and may be preferred for projects that target specialized audiences. Our analysis also points to the need to broaden the scope of the feedback (e.g. to include more process-oriented and conceptual feedback, and comparisons to existing design solutions) offered by all four sources. Our results will help instructors know how to better coordinate the use of classroom peers and external crowds in a way that is most beneficial to learning and student projects at different stages of the design process.

ACKNOWLEDGEMENTS

This work was funded in part by the National Science Foundation under awards 1530818, 1462693, 1122206 and 1122320, the first author's NSF Graduate Research Fellowship under award 1144245, and an award received by the last author from the Grants for the Advancement of Teaching Engineering program at the University of Illinois.

REFERENCES

1. Phyllis C. Blumenfeld, Elliot Soloway, Ronald W. Marx, Joseph S. Krajcik, Mark Guzdial and Annemarie Palincsar. 1991. Motivating project-based learning: Sustaining the doing, supporting the learning. *Educational Psychologist*, 26

(3-4). 369-398.
http://dx.doi.org/10.1080/00461520.1991.9653139

2. Donald J. Boyd. 2015. Public Research Universities: Changes in State Funding. *American Academy of Arts and Sciences*.
3. Juliet Corbin and Anselm Strauss. 2014. *Basics of Qualitative Research; Techniques and Procedures for Developing Grounded Theory*. Sage Publications.
4. Deanna P. Dannels and Kelly N. Martin. 2008. Critiquing Critiques: A Genre Analysis of Feedback Across Novice to Expert Design Studios. *Journal of Business and Technical Communication*, 22 (2). 135-159. http://dx.doi.org/10.1177/1050651907311923
5. Steven P. Dow, Elizabeth Gerber and Audris Wong. 2013. A Pilot Study of Using Crowds in the Classroom. in *Proceedings of the ACM Conference on Human Factors in Computing Systems*, 227-236. http://dx.doi.org/10.1145/2470654.2470686
6. Matthew Easterday, Daniel Rees-Lewis, Colin Fitzpatrick and Elizabeth M. Gerber. 2014. Computer supported novice group critique. in *Proceedings of the ACM Conference on Designing Interactive Systems*, ACM, 405-414. http://dx.doi.org/10.1145/2598510.2600889
7. Matthew Easterday, Daniel Rees-Lewis and Elizabeth Gerber. 2013. Formative feedback in Digital Lofts: Learning environments for real world innovation. in *AIED Workshops*.
8. Peggy Ertmer, Jennifer C. Richardson, Brian Belland, Denise Camin, Patrick Connolly, Glen Coulthard, Kimfong Lei and Christopher Mong. 2007. Using peer feedback to enhance the quality of student online postings: An exploratory study. *Journal of Computer-Mediated Communication*, 12 (2). 412-433. http://dx.doi.org/10.1111/j.1083-6101.2007.00331.x
9. Edmund Burke Feldman. 1981. *Varieties of Visual Experience: Art as Image and Idea*. Prentice-Hall, Englewood Cliffs, N.J.
10. Sebastian K. Fixson. 2009. Teaching Innovation through Interdisciplinary Courses and Programmes in Product Design and Development: An Analysis at 16 US Schools. *Creativity & Innovation Management*, 18 (3). 199-208. http://dx.doi.org/10.1111/j.1467-8691.2009.00523.x
11. Elizabeth M. Gerber, Jeanne Marie Olson and Rebecca L. D. Komarek. 2012. Extracurricular design-based learning: Preparing students for careers in innovation. *International Journal of Engineering Education*, 28 (2). 317-324.
12. John D. Gould. 1995. How to Design Usable Systems. in Baecker, R.M., Buxton, W., Grudin, J. and Greenberg, S. eds. *Readings in Human-Computer Interaction: Toward the Year 2000*, 93-121.
13. John D. Gould and C. Lewis. 1985. Designing for Usability: Key Principles and What Designers Think. *Communications of the ACM*, 28 (3). 300-311. http://dx.doi.org/10.1145/3166.3170
14. John Hattie and Helen Timperley. 2007. The power of feedback. *Review of Educational Research*, 77 (1). 81-112. http://dx.doi.org/10.3102/003465430298487
15. Catherine M Hicks, Vineet Pandey, C Ailie Fraser and Scott Klemmer. 2016. Framing Feedback: Choosing Review Environment Features that Support High Quality Peer Assessment. in *Proceedings of the 2016 CHI Conference on Human Factors in Computing Systems*, ACM, 458-469. http://dx.doi.org/10.1145/2858036.2858195
16. Julie Hui, Amos Glenn, Rachel Jue, Elizabeth Gerber and Steven Dow. 2015. Using Anonymity and Communal Efforts to Improve Quality of Crowdsourced Feedback. in *Third AAAI Conference on Human Computation and Crowdsourcing*.
17. Julie S. Hui, Elizabeth M. Gerber and Steven P. Dow. 2014. Crowd-based design activities: helping students connect with users online. in *Proceedings of the ACM Conference on Designing Interactive Systems*, 875-884. http://dx.doi.org/10.1145/2598510.2598538
18. Christopher Hundhausen, Anukrati Agrawal, Dana Fairbrother and Michael Trevisan. 2009. Integrating pedagogical code reviews into a CS 1 course: an empirical study. in *Proceedings of the ACM Technical Symposium on Computer Science Education*, ACM, 291-295. 10.1145/1508865.1508972
19. Christopher D. Hundhausen, Dana Fairbrother and Marian Petre. 2012. An Empirical Study of the "Prototype Walkthrough": A Studio-Based Activity for HCI Education. *ACM Transactions on Computer-Human Interaction*, 19 (4). 1-36. http://dx.doi.org/10.1145/2395131.2395133
20. Aniket Kittur, Ed H. Chi and Bongwon Suh. 2008. Crowdsourcing user studies with Mechanical Turk. in *Proceedings of the ACM conference on Human Factors in Computing Systems*, ACM, 453-456. http://dx.doi.org/10.1145/1357054.1357127
21. Klaus Krippendorff. 2007. Computing Krippendorff's alpha reliability *Departmental papers (ASC)*.
22. Chinmay E Kulkarni, Michael S Bernstein and Scott R Klemmer. 2015. PeerStudio: Rapid Peer Feedback Emphasizes Revision and Improves Performance. in *Proceedings of the Second ACM Conference on Learning@ Scale*, ACM, 75-84. http://dx.doi.org/10.1145/2724660.2724670
23. Chinmay Kulkarni, Koh Pang Wei, Huy Le, Daniel Chia, Kathryn Papadopoulos, Justin Cheng, Daphne Koller and Scott R Klemmer. 2013. Peer and self assessment in massive online classes. *ACM Transactions on Computer-Human Interaction (TOCHI)*, 20 (6). 1-31. http://dx.doi.org/10.1145/2505057
24. Micah Lande and Larry Leifer. 2010. Difficulties student engineers face designing the future. *International Journal of Engineering Education*, 26 (2). 271.
25. Kurt Luther, Jari-lee Tolentino, Wei Wu, Amy Pavel, Brian P. Bailey, Maneesh Agrawala, Björn Hartmann and Steven P. Dow. 2015. Structuring, Aggregating, and Evaluating Crowdsourced Design Critique. in *Proceedings of the ACM Conference on Computer Supported Cooperative Work*, 473-485. http://dx.doi.org/10.1145/2675133.2675283
26. Xiaojuan Ma, Yu Li, Jodi Forlizzi and Steven P. Dow. 2015. Exiting the Design Studio: Leveraging Online Participants

for Early-Stage Design Feedback. in *Proceedings of the ACM Conference on Computer Supported Cooperative Work*, 676-685. http://dx.doi.org/10.1145/2675133.2675174

27. David Nicol. 2010. From monologue to dialogue: improving written feedback processes in mass higher education. *Assessment & Evaluation in Higher Education*, 35 (5). 501-517. http://dx.doi.org/10.1080/02602931003786559

28. Ken Reily, Pam Ludford Finnerty and Loren Terveen. 2009. Two Peers are Better Than One: Aggregating Peer Reviews for Computing Assignments is Surprisingly Accurate. in *Proceedings of the ACM International Conference on Supporting Group Work*, 115-124. http://dx.doi.org/10.1145/1531674.1531692

29. Howard Risatti. 1987. Art criticism in discipline-based art education. *Journal of Aesthetic Education*, 21 (2). 217-225. http://dx.doi.org/10.2307/3332751

30. Jeffrey M Rzeszotarski and Meredith Ringel Morris. 2014. Estimating the social costs of friendsourcing. in *Proceedings of the ACM Conference on Human Factors in Computing Systems*, ACM, 2735-2744. http://dx.doi.org/10.1145/2556288.2557181

31. D Royce Sadler. 1989. Formative assessment and the design of instructional systems. *Instructional Science*, 18 (2). 119-144. http://dx.doi.org/10.1007/BF00117714

32. D. Royce Sadler. 2010. Beyond feedback: developing student capability in complex appraisal. *Assessment & Evaluation in Higher Education*, 35 (5). 535-550. http://dx.doi.org/10.1080/02602930903541015

33. David Williamson Shaffer and Mitchel Resnick. 1999. "Thick" Authenticity: New Media and Authentic Learning. *Journal of Interactive Learning Research*, 10 (2). 195-215.

34. Mostafa Al Masum Shaikh, Helmut Prendinger and Mitsuru Ishizuka. 2008. Sentiment assessment of text by analyzing linguistic features and contextual valence assignment. *Applied Artificial Intelligence*, 22 (6). 558-601. http://dx.doi.org/10.1080/08839510802226801

35. Valerie Shute. 2007. Focus on Formative Feedback. *Educational Testing Service*, Research report RR-07-11.

36. Holly Smith, Ali Cooper and Les Lancaster. 2002. Improving the Quality of Undergraduate Peer Assessment: A Case for Student and Staff Development. *Innovations in Education and Teaching International*, 39 (1). 71-81. http://dx.doi.org/10.1080/13558000110102904

37. Maryam Tohidi, William Buxton, Ronald Baecker and Abigail Sellen. 2006. Getting the right design and the design right. in *Proceedings of the ACM Conference on Human Factors in Computing Systems*, 1243-1252. http://dx.doi.org/10.1145/1124772.1124960

38. Wesley Willett, Jeffrey Heer and Maneesh Agrawala. 2012. Strategies for crowdsourcing social data analysis. in *Proceedings of the ACM conference on Human Factors in Computing Systems*, ACM, 227-236. http://dx.doi.org/10.1145/2207676.2207709

39. Anbang Xu and Brian P. Bailey. 2012. What Do You Think? A Case Study of Benefit, Expectation, and Interaction in a Large Online Critique Community in *CSCW*, 295-304. http://dx.doi.org/10.1145/2145204.2145252

40. Anbang Xu, Huaming Rao, Steven P Dow and Brian P Bailey. 2015. A Classroom Study of Using Crowd Feedback in the Iterative Design Process. in *Proceedings of the 18th ACM Conference on Computer Supported Cooperative Work & Social Computing*, ACM, 1637-1648. http://dx.doi.org/10.1145/2675133.2675140

41. Yu-Chun (Grace) Yen, Steven P. Dow, Elizabeth Gerber and Brian P. Bailey. 2016. Social Network, Web Forum, or Task Market? Comparing Different Crowd Genres for Design Feedback Exchange in *Proceedings of the ACM Conference on Designing Interactive Systems*. http://dx.doi.org/10.1145/2901790.2901820

42. Alvin Yuan, Kurt Luther, Markus Krause, Sophie Vennix, Steven P Dow and Björn Hartmann. 2016. Almost an Expert: The Effects of Rubrics and Expertise on Perceived Value of Crowdsourced Design Critiques. in *Proceedings of the ACM Conference on Computer Supported Cooperative Work and Social Computing*, 1005-1017. http://dx.doi.org/10.1145/2818048.2819953

43. Haoqi Zhang, Matthew W. Easterday, Elizabeth M. Gerber, Daniel Rees Lewis and Leesha Maliakal. 2017. Agile Research Studios: Orchestrating Communities of Practice to Advance Research Training. in *Proceedings of Computer Supported Cooperative Work*, to appear. http://dx.doi.org/10.1145/2998181.2998199

Collection Objects: Enabling Fluid Formation and Manipulation of Aggregate Selections

Haijun Xia, Bruno Araujo, Daniel Wigdor
University of Toronto
{haijunxia | brar | daniel}@dgp.toronto.edu

Figure 1. A drawing of a lightbulb, comprised of a number of drawing objects, is manipulated using Collection Objects. Left: the thickness of all strokes is adjusted simultaneously. Right: The color of the "rays" is harmonized with a single gesture.

ABSTRACT

Despite the long development of Graphical User Interfaces, working with multiple graphical objects remains a challenge, due to the difficulties of forming complex selections, ambiguities of operations, and tediousness of repetitively unselect-reselect or ungroup-regroup objects. Instead of tackling them as individual problems, we attribute it to the lack of system support to the general selection-action cycles. We propose Collection Objects to not only support a single fast selection-action cycle but also allow multiple cycles to be chained together into a fluid workflow. Collection Objects unifies selection, grouping, and manipulation of aggregate selections into a single object, with which selection can be composed with various techniques, modified for later actions, grouped with objects inside still directly accessible, and quasi-moded for less context switching. We implemented Collection Object in the context of a vector drawing application with simultaneous pen and touch input. Results of an expert evaluation show that Collection Objects holds considerable promises for fluid interaction with multiple objects.

CHI 2017, May 06-11, 2017, Denver, CO, USA
 ISBN 978-1-4503-4655-9/17/05...$15.00
DOI: http://dx.doi.org/10.1145/3025453.3025554

INTRODUCTION

Direct-touch and pen input offer several advantages over traditional indirect input, including mobility and the replacement of dedicated control surfaces with larger screens [17]. Due to these advantages, direct touch has achieved near ubiquity in higher-end mobile devices. As these devices have become popular, UIs have been adapted for direct touch. The use of direct physical manipulation, enabling control through translation, rotation, and scaling with simple gestures, rather than by selecting and manipulating offset controls, is now nearly universal in such devices. One particular advantage of gesture-based systems is the ability to *phrase* object selection, operations, and additional parameters into a single gestural stroke, resulting in fewer mental steps [10]. Although desirable, it is brittle: mental flow breaks whenever any step requires excessive cognitive effort. Surprisingly, a key operation has resisted being made fluid: multiple object selection. Such selections have been called-out as a particularly tedious subtask in direct touch UIs [14, 27].

Problems with selecting and manipulating multiple objects have been identified since the dawn of the direct manipulation paradigm [13, 37]; it is perhaps, therefore, unsurprising that improving selection has been a focus of considerable effort in research. Less studied, however, has been the user's experience immediately before and after engaging a particular selection technique, and how well the technique flows as part of a phrase of related gestures. It is the thesis of the present work that no matter how sophisticated a technique may be, users suffer if it requires a significant shift in focus from their primary activity.

In its most common form, selection is a transient state, and each newly made selection replaces the previous one. While this reduces the use of modes, it can also cause significant frustration. For example, a user may lose the work performed theretofore that they composed a large aggregate selection due to an error late in the process [30]. Commonly, selections may be saved as groups for later reuse, but rigid group structures often force users to constantly select and reselect, as well as ungroup and regroup while switching attention among objects [32]. There is an opportunity, therefore, to improve workflows by changing selection to be more object-like, while simultaneously providing more flexibility.

In addition to the difficulties of selecting multiple objects, the WIMP UI also falls short when visualizing and interacting with the selected objects. In noun and verb pairings enabled by toolbars, which act as the core of WIMP UIs, when two objects have different values for a field, the field is typically left blank. This creates ambiguity within the interface [19]. Moreover, select+toolbar also fails to provide support for simple workflows when working with multiple objects. If a user wants to share the color of an object to a set of selected objects, for example, she will have to 1) deselect the set of objects, 2) select the object which has the color, 3) look up and copy its color value, 4) reselect the objects, and 5) finally apply the change.

Our goal is to facilitate interaction with multiple objects on touchscreen devices, while maintaining the direct physical manipulation paradigm. We approach this from two directions. First, we seek to replace transient selection and rigid groups with an embodiment that can be manipulated directly, resulting in lower penalties for erroneous selections and easier reuse. Second, we seek to explore how various selection, grouping, and manipulation techniques can be encapsulated within such an embodiment to enable a continuous workflow with less mode and context switching.

We developed Collection Objects (COs). COs embodies selections and groups as objects, which can themselves be directly manipulated using gestures. As such, selection is no longer a transient state of objects but a collection of objects that can be filtered, overlapped, and collectively manipulated. Further, a group is no longer a rigid and closed structure, but rather a set of objects that can be freely added, removed, navigated, and accessed directly.

Built upon Attribute Objects [44], COs consists of two sets of attributes: 1) attributes acting as expressive search filters to enable rapid expansion and contraction of the selection scope and 2) attributes enabling for meaningful visualization and the advanced manipulation of multiple objects within the collection. Complementary to the ***micro*** interaction with attributes of an object [44], our work, explores ***macro*** manipulation of multiple objects. We demonstrate how the various properties of COs can be coherently encapsulated to achieve continuous and fluid manipulation of multiple objects in a vector drawing application. We also present the results of an expert assessment, wherein professional illustrators used our drawing tool to create vector arts.

RELATED WORK

Our research draws from prior work on selection techniques for gesture-based interfaces, alternative selection mechanisms and grouping, the manipulation of multiple objects in GUIs, and the objectification of UI elements.

Selection Techniques in Touch and Pen based Interfaces

Selection is a key research problem in HCI. Significant work has investigated the efficiency of different input devices for pointing tasks [5, 12, 25]. Although relevant, the goal of the present work is to reduce the number of operations required to make and apply operations to selected groups of objects. This is intended to increase the efficiency of user input, which will save time and reduce fatigue and tedium. This is especially true for touch, which suffers from the "gorilla arm" (fatigue) [8] and "fat finger" (small target selection) problems [34].

The present work falls into the area of interaction techniques for direct-touch systems. A number of projects have examined selection for such devices. Accot and Zhai found that the performance of stylus crossing to select multiple targets depends on the layout and size of the targets [1]; similar results for touch input have also been found by Luo and Vogel [24]. Leitner and Haller further combined stylus crossing with area cursors to enable complex selections[22]. Strothoff et al. studied pin and touch gestures for efficiently grouping objects [36]. Tse et al. also explored gestural selection enabled by wrapping their hands around the objects to be selected, although this required more detail about user touch areas than most capacitive touch sensors report to software [39, 41].

Selection using pen-based UIs has also been widely explored [14, 22, 27]. Scriboli employs delimiters to phrase selection and action into one continuous pen stroke [14]. Recently, Hinckley et al. [15] advocated for a division of labor between pen and touch based on the strengths of each input modality: *pen writes and touch manipulates*, which built on findings from Brandl et al. [9]. Our work builds on these, with the selection and manipulation of many objects being achieved with direct touch manipulation gestures.

Recently, research has sought to ease the difficulties of selection by providing the user with system-interpreted selections. Suggero [23] and cLuster [29] employed Gestalt principles and various pre-trained selection perspectives to suggest possible selections for users based on their initial selection. Sloppy selection [21] and Lazy selection [45] refined users' selection based on user input and the underlying pattern of the screen content.

Our work is complementary to all the above techniques; we seek to provide a single selection mechanism, which can coherently encapsulate various selection techniques and allow users to fluidly compose, modify, and reuse a selection by manipulating a set of filter attributes.

We look beyond selection techniques, seeking to enable fluid selection-action flow which improves the efficiency and experience by reducing the number of tedious and unnecessary selection tasks.

Alternative Selection and Grouping Mechanisms

In a typical GUI dialog, a selection is created to indicate to the computer to which objects a command will apply [30]. Usually, when a new selection is made, the previously selected objects are deselected. It is common, however, that particular parts of content require frequent editing, resulting in the tedious repetition of selection tasks. To ease this problem, some commercial design applications, such as Adobe Illustrator, allow users to save a selection before it is replaced by a newly made one. However, this requires the user to foresee its usage and navigate through menus. Anecdotally, this has been referred to as a "hidden gem" of Adobe Illustrator [31].

Grouping is an alternative to reusing a previous selection. Typically, a user can group currently selected objects to transform the selection of multiple objects into a persistent aggregate object. As such, the selection of any object inside the group always selects the group as a whole. While this leads to easy reselection of the same set of objects, the rigid structure prevents fluid selection across groups which forces users to constantly group and ungroup objects [32].

Additionally, the hierarchical structure of groups prohibits the simultaneous existence of overlapping groups. To address this, Saund et al. proposed a flat lattice grouping structure to allow users to create overlapping groups [32]. A sequence of groups associated with one object can be cycled through by subsequent mouse clicks according to the most-recently-used order. Similarly, Rock & Rails [42] proposed creating offset proxy objects, where manipulations performed on the proxies were applied to both the proxies and their linked objects. Further, objects were able to belong to multiple groups simultaneously, by linking to multiple proxies. Our work combines hierarchical structure, which allows for meaningful organization of objects, and overlapping selection, which penetrates the hierarchical structure and allows for high flexibly of selection. We further reduce the rigidity of hierarchical structure by enabling easy and fast navigation of levels of hierarchy with direct bimanual gestural input.

Manipulation of Multiple Objects in GUIs

In a traditional toolbar UI, the values of a selection's attributes are displayed when one object is selected. However, when multiple objects are selected, only those shared values are displayed, and the visual representation for the remaining ones is ambiguously missing [19]. Prior work has sought to solve many of the problems of manipulating the attribute values of multiple objects [13, 16, 19, 33]. Hoarau et al. display all the attributes of the selected objects in a side panel to reveal the implicit structure of a selection [16]. Interactions with such values enables limited manipulation of the subsets of objects represented by the values. Kwon et al. provide a UI with both numeric and direct manipulation handles on surrogate objects [19]. Our work provides a novel UI solution to tackle this problem that is faster and a more direct means to accomplish such tasks, enable new ones, and avoid tedious interactions.

In a command-object system, one's experience manipulating multiple objects can be further enhanced with advanced commands. GACA employs a group-aware arrangement tool to reduce the number of alignment operations [45]. We support the typical workflow of interacting with multiple objects, such as sharing various attributes to a set of objects and editing individual objects without paying the penalty of switching selections, while preserving the space wherein advanced operations of each attribute can be embedded.

When interacting with multiple objects, users strategically plan their operations with respect to the given system for optimal performance [26]. As an example, marking menu favors object-oriented strategy: it is more efficient for users to issue multiple distinct commands on one object. The opposite, floating menus are more efficient when a user repeatedly issues the same command, favoring command-oriented strategy. While a common UI design approach is to favor one or another and let users adapt to it [30], users have to constantly shift between strategies based on the nature of tasks, their cognitive contexts, and individual preferences [26]. The mismatch between the user strategy and the interaction technique breaks user's continuous mental flow and results in lower task performance. Our approach supports both strategies: it enables users to change individual attributes of all selected objects, while it still provides the flexibility to change every attribute of individual objects within a selection without context switching.

Objectification of UI Elements

The present work seeks to enable complex editing while maintaining the direct physical manipulation paradigm. To do so, we introduce a new UI element which embodies the selection and grouping, and can be directly manipulated. This approach directly builds on several projects attempting to objectify UI elements.

Researchers have made several attempts to objectify interaction into GUI controls with the intention of leveraging the human experience with the physical world to interact with the digital one [35]. A traditional approach is to objectify tools or commands using graphical UI widgets such as buttons or menus. By providing an object-like representation to tools, they become objects that can be directly manipulated by users [2, 4, 7, 28]. While this led to interfaces with familiar elements borrowed from the physical world, one drawback is that such interactions are limited by their reliance on metaphors: the physical world provides no mechanism to interact with abstract content, such as the brightness or opacity of a photo. As an example, in most present systems, attributes are represented using numbers or text, and these attributes confine the interactions to basic control widgets, such as buttons and slide bars [3].

To extend the usage of direct physical manipulation in GUIs, Xia et al. [44] proposed *Attribute Objects* as an objectification of abstract attributes. Using a card-like representation, Attribute Objects can be moved, copied, linked, interpolated, and so on, using direct manipulation gestures. The prototype application, Object-Oriented

Drawing (OOD), demonstrated how complex drawing applications could be built without the need for complex, form-based UIs. Although OOD enables micro-manipulation of every attribute, a clear omission is the ability to macro-manage multiple objects. Our work builds on the concept of objectifying abstract content: each of our Collection Objects is the embodiment of the selection state and the group structure. We demonstrate how such an embodiment provides a set of powerful interactions with multiple objects.

COLLECTION OBJECTS

Despite the simplicity of the two step selection-action model of a GUI dialog, users encounter a number of difficulties when interacting with multiple objects. A selection, while being formed, may get lost due to its transient nature; it may also be incomplete or hard to complete as objects fall out of the viewport or hide under other objects. Objects can be grouped to maintain the structure or to reuse the selection, but the rigid group structure prohibits the selection of individual objects within it, resulting in repetitive ungroup-select-regroup procedures. Navigation and the manipulation of group structure is poorly supported, often causing a user to break her actions and seek help from other widgets (e.g., a layer panel). While in multi-selection, quickly copying or adjusting the style of an object within the selection requires a user to switch between multi-selection and single selection; thus, what is only one mental step for the user cannot be achieved without several selection-action cycles.

Collection Objects attempt to address all the above problems by providing a single coherent UI with the following properties.

It objectifies selection. It appears as an independent object on the canvas, which is persistent: it must be deleted or modified to end the selection. As such, existing selections will not get lost unless the user explicitly deletes them, resulting in a lower penalty for erroneous selection and easier reuse of a previous selection without creating rigid structure.

It can be composed and modified. Collection Objects coherently encapsulates various selection techniques as well as afford new ones using a set Attribute Object [44]. Attributes such as geometry and color can be used as selection filters to search for, and select, objects with the same style across the entire canvas. Attribute Objects of Collection Objects may be added, replaced, manipulated, or removed using simple direct manipulation gestures, enabling a rich set of selection techniques and rapid expansion and contraction of the selection scope.

It objectifies group structure. Objects in a collection can be grouped only for maintaining the structure. Because of objectification, the scope of a group can be trivially managed using the same techniques of composing selection, which eliminates indirect management with other widgets and context switching. Group structure is hierarchical to enable meaningful content organization. Yet, it can be quickly navigated using bimanual gestures to edit its subparts.

It integrates overlapping selection, which allows for simultaneous existence of meaningful and flexible selections, ***with open group structure,*** which further grants selection of objects across groups, while preserving the hierarchical structure.

It supports rich manipulation of multiple attributes. Tuned for the typical workflow with multiple objects, Collection Objects support the quick sharing of attributes to a collection and the manipulation of individual objects by quasi-moding the collection. By doing so, one can fluidly conduct a sequence of actions without switching between single selection and multi-selection.

It requires no context switching. By encapsulating the above functionalities, sequence selections and actions take place within one UI element.

Creating and Deleting Collection Objects

A Collection Object (Figure 2) is instantiated when the user wants to work with multiple objects simultaneously. This can be done by holding a finger on the canvas. Once initiated, *tapping* drawing objects while holding a Collection Object adds them to that CO. Alternatively, a user can expand from a single selection using the miniature CO (Figure 3) on every single object. The selection can be deleted by dragging the Collection Object off the canvas.

Identifying and Representing Collection Objects

Each Collection Object is represented by a diamond (Figure 2). Since several Collection Objects can co-exist on the canvas, it is important to differentiate each CO, as well as to be able to easily find a particular one. To do so, the border of the CO is color-coded. When manipulating one object, its existing Collection Objects, as well as the link between them, are highlighted using the corresponding color.

The diamond provides an anchor, where each of its four corners represent a different attachment. The left corner links to the drawing objects contained within the collection, visually linking the CO and its constituent objects. The top corner of the diamond attaches to the set of Attribute Objects which act as the attributes of the CO and define a filter for the selection. Additionally, another set of Attribute Object cards is located on the right corner of the diamond. These represent the *attributes of the objects* contained within the selection, similar to the toolbar in a traditional UI. Adding to, removing from, or changing Attribute Object cards in this set will result in changes to the selected objects. Finally, the bottom corner can be connected with another CO to spawn a child collection using Boolean operations.

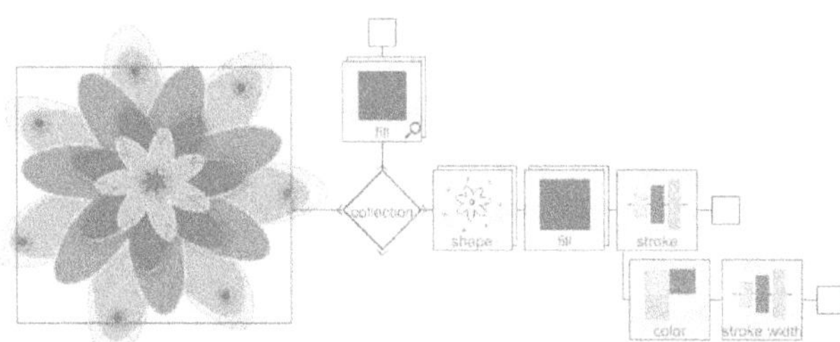

Figure 2. A drawing of a flower. Its red pedals have been collected in the Collection Object shown to the right. Two sets of Attribute Object cards are shown: Those of the Collection Object (top), and those of the selected objects (right).

SELECTION WITH COLLECTION OBJECTS

Replacing the transient selection state with a persistent embodiment, Collection Objects, enables safe iterative selection without the fear of accidentally losing it with an errant click. Just as important, it also allows for fluid cycles of selection-action units by reusing and modifying existing Collection Objects. In addition to simply holding the CO and tapping objects to be added into the collection, Collection Objects unifies various selection techniques, such as lasso/crossing selection, selection by attribute, suggestive selection, and fuzzy selection. Further, because selections are persistent, each may be used to iterate on the current selection.

Attributes of the Collection Object

Attributes of the Collection Object located on the top corner of the diamond act as filters to define the selection (Figure 2) A user can add filter attributes into the collection by dragging attribute cards into the filter list. Attributes in this set are applied to the selection using an "and" relationship, similar to the chain effect in Side Views [38]. A user can expand or shrink the scope of the selection by adding or removing Attribute Object cards to this set (Figure 3). We now describe the unique set of filter attributes of our Collection Objects and their effects on selection tasks.

Selection Boundary Attribute

Lasso selection and cross-to-select with pen input are common selection techniques in gesture-based interfaces [1, 14, 24]. To support this, each CO contains a boundary attribute, which enables both selection techniques. To create a boundary attribute, the user first holds the CO to put the system into a quasi-mode, where the paths drawn by the pen become selection boundaries rather than normal drawing paths. In this quasi-mode, as soon as the pen touches the screen, it creates a boundary attribute which is inserted into the CO. The shape of the boundary determines which drawing objects are selected: a closed (or nearly closed) boundary selects objects inside it (lasso selection), while an open boundary selects objects it crosses (crossing selection). A user can further edit the boundary by holding the attribute and modifying the paths, similar to [22].

Alternatively, the shape attribute of existing drawing objects may be used as a selection lasso to select all the drawing objects within its bounds. This reduces the need to create a selection boundary, which can be difficult in a crowded scene. Figure 3 shows an example utilization: to select all of the strokes comprising the alpaca's maw, the user simply opens the stack of Attribute Object cards for the outline of the maw. Similar to the original OOD, the user can make a copy of its shape attribute and drag it into the Collection Object defining a boundary. All objects contained within the boundary are selected immediately.

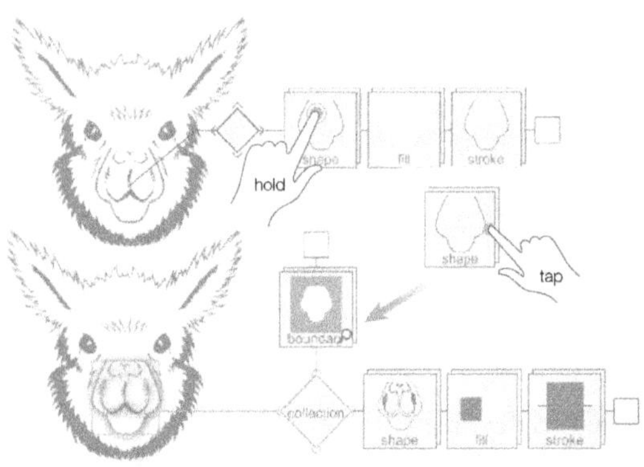

Figure 3. The user copies the "shape" attribute of the maw and drags it into a CO, which uses the shape as a kind of lasso, immediately selecting all drawing objects within it.

Style Attribute

Other attributes of existing objects may also be copied and inserted into the Collection Object to enable selection by attributes. For example, if a user wishes to select all objects with a particular fill color(s), she may copy the fill attribute of an existing object and insert it into the CO. Immediately, all drawing objects with that same fill color are selected (Figure 4 a,b). Similarly, in a night scene where the stars share a shape but not a color, a user can select all the stars by inserting a geometry attribute (i.e., a sub-attribute of a shape, regardless of size, orientation, or position) into the Collection Object. Instead of making a selection and editing the selected objects, a user can dynamically change the selection scope by manipulating the values of filters. The selection feedback of different attribute value reveals how attributes are used across the scene. In a floor plan example, a user can adjust a stroke width filter attribute to understand the load distribution on the wall.

Fuzziness Meta Attribute

With vector graphics, it is common that different drawing objects have attributes that are similar but not identical, such as color or stroke width. When an Attribute Object is inserted into the Collection Object, a fuzziness sub-attribute is automatically added to it. The fuzziness value indicates the tolerance associated to a filter and can be edited to handle similar but not identical attributes (Figure 4). For example, in a heat map, searching by a particular fill color with a certain tolerance allows the user to select objects whose fill is within the chosen range across the canvas. She can also adjust the tolerance to dynamically change the selection. This can be useful, if, she wishes to quickly locate similar objects and change them collectively.

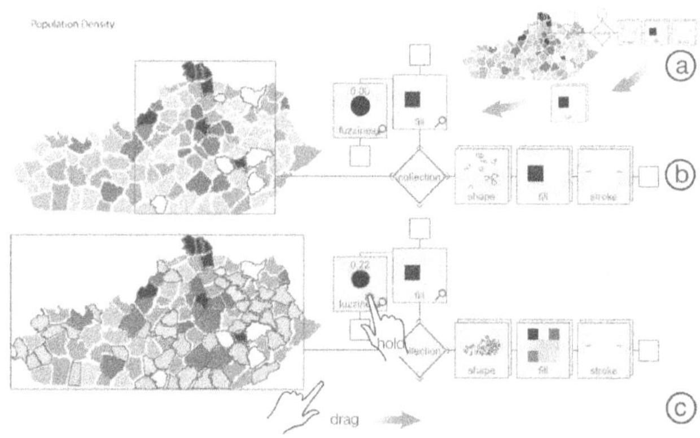

Figure 4. a) The user selects two objects with different fill colors b) and uses the fill to select objects with either color; c) she can then adjust the fuzziness sub-attribute to select objects with a similar but not identical color.

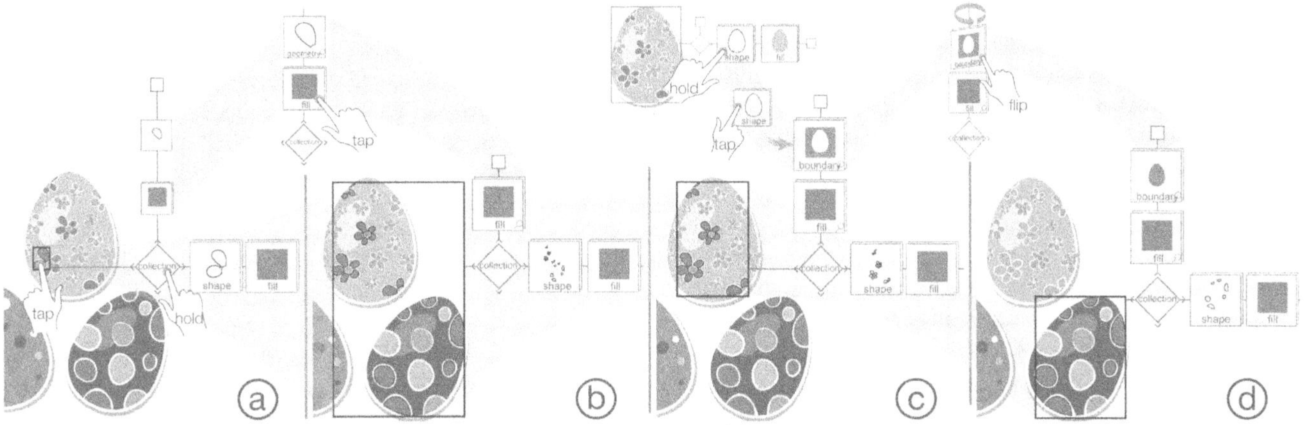

Figure 5. Selection sequence on one Collection Object. a) the user holds a CO and taps pedals to select them; the system automatically suggests possible filters; b) tapping the fill expands the selection to all red objects; c) she can copy the shape of the top egg and drag it into the CO to limit the selection; d) after changing the color, flipping the boundary card selects the red pedals in another egg.

Emergent Filter Attribute

In some cases, a user may start to select objects individually, without care for their attributes. This can be accomplished by holding the CO and either tapping the object to be added or lassoing a selection boundary. As the user adds objects, the tool will examine them for common attributes and then recommend the commonalities as possible criteria. These emergent selection filters appear briefly on the filter attribute list with a lower opacity. A single tap on the potential attribute adds it persistently to the collection and will expand the selection scope to include all objects with the same attribute value (Figure 5a,b). This technique augments previous suggestive selection techniques based on Gestalt theory [23, 29] by allowing the user to explicitly indicate what attributes she wants to search with.

Invert Filter Attribute

To exclude objects with a certain attribute from a selection, the user can invert the filter condition by performing a horizontal flip gesture on the filter card. In Boolean terms, that attribute will exist in an "*and not*" relationship with the other attributes in the set of filters. This expands the common "invert selection" command found in most drawing programs from spatial location to any other attribute type.

Compose and Reuse Selection with Filter Attributes

Performing a perfect selection is difficult and tedious. The key to an effective selection mechanism is to allow the user to compose selections with various techniques and reuse them in later tasks. Collection Objects enable users to freely combine and modify multiple attributes to achieve complex selections as well as reuse and modify existing COs without starting from an empty selection for every desired edit.

Imagine a user wants to select all the red petals within the top Easter egg (Figure 5a). She may simply hold a CO and tap to select the petals. While doing so, the system suggests possible attributes to her, such as the fill color and geometry (Figure 5a,b). Tapping the red fill color adds all the red petals into the CO, including ones in another egg. She can then copy the shape attribute of the top egg into the CO to constrain the selection within the specified boundary (Figure 5b,c). Then after changing colors , she can simply flip the boundary card switching to the red petals in another egg (Figure 5c,d).

In the floor plan example, the architect can also easily re-use the CO to select another set of lines with different stroke width by adjusting the value of the stroke attribute, which is being used as a search filter.

Compose Collection Object with Direct Manipulation

Objectifying selection allows users to physically manipulate Collection Objects directly, which further enables higher level composition of the scope of an existing selection.

Invert: Similar to flipping a filter attribute, to invert the search condition, existing CO can be horizontally flipped to transform to its inversion. Creating an empty CO and then flipping it allows a user to perform a *select all* operation.

Union, Intersection, and Subtraction: Holding two COs generates a new CO between the two. The user can then slide left or right to choose which Boolean operation he wants to use to generate this third new CO.

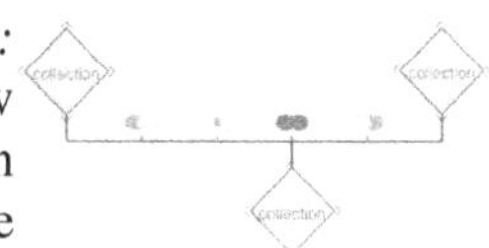

Figure 6 Boolean operation of COs

GROUPING WITH COLLECTION OBJECTS

In existing applications, a user can group selected objects to save the selection. However, this rigid structure also imposes difficulties for selecting objects within it. To select objects across groups, a user will have to first ungroup multiple times if they are maintained in a multi-level hierarchical structure. If she intends to save the group for later reuse, she will have to regroup them. Despite its rigid structure, grouping is still beneficial for forming meaningful structures. For example, a user can form a group of selected objects enabling operations such as scale, rotation, and alignment to be applied to the group instead of individual objects within the group. We seek to enable users to achieve such purposes while allowing quick navigation within the structure and preserving fast and fluid selection.

Creating a Group
A set of selected objects can be transformed into a group simply by flipping the CO vertically. Once the flip finishes, an icon appears within its diamond to indicate its grouped state. Flipping it again ungroups it. With CO, objects can still be freely added into or removed from the group using the selection techniques described above. By way of comparison, with existing applications, this has to be done either by ungrouping, reselecting, and then regrouping or using a layer panel to indirectly select objects by manually scrolling through a long list of items and visually matching them with graphical objects.

Hierarchical Structure vs. Lattice (Overlapping) Structure
Unlike the overlapping structure of normal Collection Objects, which is meant for high flexibility of selections, groups are organized in a tree structure. We choose the tree structure over the lattice structure (Figure 4 of [32]), as lattice grouping does not effectively reduce the number of objects to be managed and further a tree structure better matches users' understanding of the structure of a scene. These allow users to quickly navigate to the desired group with less mental effort. Contrarily, lattice structure, with which the flat groups are organized by most-recently-used order, requires the users to remember the sequence of when each group has been used [32].

Navigating the Tree Structure
A single tap of an object opens the Collection Object card of the group on the topmost level it belongs to (Figure 7a). If a user wants to access objects on the lower levels of the tree, she can hold the object she wants to navigate to and drag the diamond card (Figure 7). Immediately after her finger touches the diamond card, the levels associated with the held object appear underneath the finger, through which she can then drag the card vertically to navigate to different levels. While keeping her finger on the card, she can switch to hold another object to dive into a different branch of the tree.

Alternatively, she can hold the object and drag another finger vertically on the canvas to quickly navigate to the desired group. This allows her to rapidly navigate a multilevel tree structure with one hand in a local and bidirectional way, while adjusting the spatial attributes of the selected group with another hand.

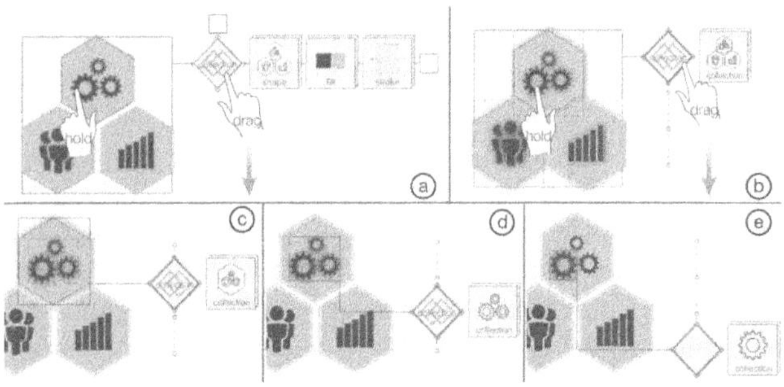

Figure 7 (a) Hierarchy of the group can be navigated by holding the object a user wants to navigate to and dragging the CO card vertically; (b) - (e) levels of held object updates as the user drags the card.

Selection of Objects Across Groups
One UI problem encountered when using grouping is that objects within a group or across groups cannot be easily selected. We solve this by keeping the group rigid to direct manipulation, easy to navigate, yet open to selection. When groups exist, they can be aggregated into a new CO by holding the CO and tapping on the groups. If a user wants to select objects within the group, she can touch her finger on the object she wants, drag down to navigate the level, as if it penetrates the structure, and release her finger at the level she wants to select the object. She can keep selecting objects in other groups simply by swiping down on the object as she becomes fluent with the gesture. Before releasing her finger to add a (sub-)group into the selection, she can swipe to the right, as in a marking menu, to add individual objects of the group into the selection rather than the group itself. Operations like alignment will be applied to the objects individually, instead of the group.

If a user flips this CO card, wishing to group an overlapping selection, a flip back animation will be played to indicate the current CO cannot be grouped because of the hierarchical structure.

ATTRIBUTES OF SELECTED OBJECTS
In addition to the filter attributes that define the selection, Collection Objects include an aggregation of the attributes present within the selected objects of the collection, similar to how a toolbar is updated to show common properties among selected objects in a WIMP UI. In this section, we describe how these Attribute Object cards may be manipulated to edit the selected objects.

Visual Representation
Given a collection of attributes, the UI displays all the values of attributes, similar to [16] but in a scalable way. For example, the stroke card shows strokes of different colors and widths. This representation is dynamically updated when attributes of the selected object are manipulated, Figure 9.

Showing Attributes: Iconic, Aggregates, or All
When a user first opens a Collection Object, an iconic representation of each of its attributes is shown on the Attribute Object cards, such as the color palette seen in Figure 8. The user is then able to expand the card to two levels. When the user first expands the card, an aggregate is shown. If the user continues to expand beyond this aggregate view, the complete set of values will appear.

Aggregates: When the user first expands the card with a vertical pinch gesture, an attribute-specific aggregate is shown, such as the gradient shown in Figure 8. For scalar values, such as x or y position, the max, min, and mean are shown. These aggregates allow the user to quickly find, copy, or change attribute values. As an example, if the user selects a group of objects and wishes to vertically align an unselected object with that group, she can quickly copy the "max" card from the "Y" attribute of the group to the new object; the object will immediately align with the top of the group. Alternatively, the user can also *replace* these cards.

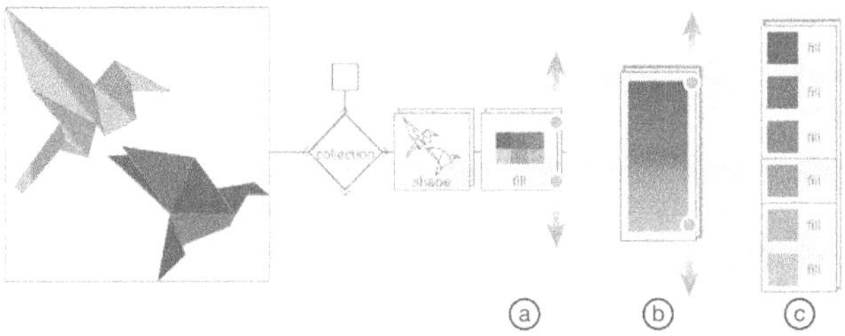

Figure 8. Example of three levels of expansion of attributes of objects in a collection: a) iconic; b) aggregate (in this case, a gradient), and c) a list of all values.

As an example, if she replaced the "min" Attribute Object card of the line thickness attribute with another value, all drawing objects whose line thickness was equal to the previous minimum would be updated.

All: If the user wishes to see all attribute values, she can continue to expand the card (Figure 8c). Additionally, each object within the collection will open its attribute object card in situ. This allows the user to copy or replace particular values within the set.

Direct Manipulation of Attribute Objects

In a traditional WIMP UI, the only possible operation on attributes of a selection of objects is assigning a single attribute value to all the selected objects. Conversely, with Attribute Objects, one can perform rich manipulation of attributes on selected objects.

In OOD [44], an attribute could be directly manipulated by holding its card and sliding another finger on the screen (e.g., holding the "drop shadow" card and dragging on the canvas translated the shadow to another position). We build on this by further using the landing object as a mode of touch input. Now, if the user holds the stroke attribute of the collection, and lands another finger on the canvas, moving her second finger will change the stroke width of all the objects in the collection. However, if she lands her finger on a particular object, only that object's stroke width will be changed. This allows users to quickly adjust the manipulation of an individual object or a collection of objects. Compared to the traditional form-filling paradigm and selection mechanism, this approach provides two important benefits. First, it allows the user to simultaneously manipulate attributes of several objects, without forcing them to change to the same value, as in traditional UIs. Second, the quasi-mode associated with the landing object can significantly reduce the need to switch between single selection and multi-selection. By doing so, one can fluidly conduct a sequence of actions without redoing complex selections or repeatedly grouping and ungrouping objects.

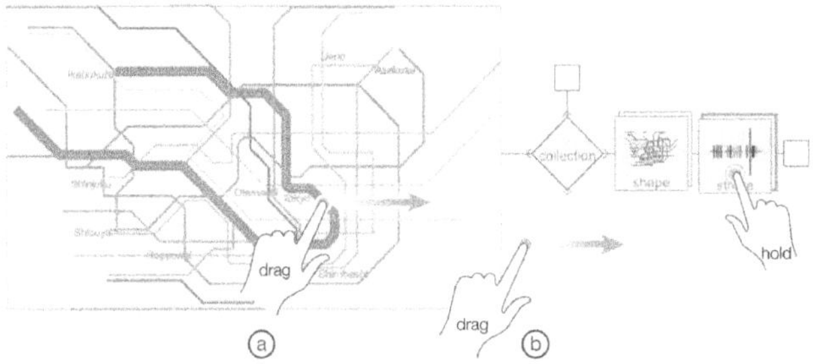

Figure 9. Example of direct manipulation of attributes. While holding the "stroke" card, the user can change the stroke thickness of a) an individual object within a collection by dragging their finger along the object or b) all thicknesses within the collection by dragging on the canvas.

Propagating Individual Values from the Collection

The traditional WIMP UI allows a user to set a value in a global widget to apply that attribute value to all the selected objects. However, even simple tasks using this functionality can require unreasonable effort. For example, to apply the fill color of one of the selected objects to all the others, the user will have to individually select the object, look up its fill attribute value, remember or copy the value, multi-select the other objects, and then set the value for the selection. With Collection Objects, this can be trivially achieved by holding the fill attribute of the collection of the objects and then tapping any other object to retrieve its fill color. Similarly, holding position attributes and tapping an object indicates he wants the whole collection aligned to it.

EXPERT EVALUATION

To validate whether Collection Objects is a useful replacement for the traditional way of working with multiple objects. We conducted an expert evaluation to gain feedback about the effectiveness and usefulness of Collection Objects. We were also interested in the utility of each individual interaction technique.

Apparatus

Our system is implemented as Win32 application in Windows 10 using OpenGL, running with 1920x1200px Wacom Cintq 24 HD display with capacitive finger touch and EMR pen hover + touch. Touch and stylus inputs can be simultaneously received and reliably differentiated.

Participants

We recruited 6 professional graphic designers (3 female, aged from 25 to 39) to evaluate our system. All participants have more than 5 years' experience using vector graphic tools, such as Adobe Illustrator and Inkscape. Participants were compensated $50 for a 90-minute session.

Procedure

Each expert review session consisted of the following stages:

Training on Collection Objects (25 - 30 minutes)

Participants were introduced to the concept of Collection Objects with a short verbal walkthrough of it techniques. Then, the experimenter trained the participant on the interface by having them complete a nine step drawing exploring all features of our system. During training, the experimenter described each interaction verbally to the participant and asked them to perform the actions. If the participant had difficulty performing the interaction, the experimenter would only then demonstrate it. We also kept each step of the drawing corresponding to each interaction technique simple, which allowed us to observe how the participants learned each technique and later applied them during the follow-up exercise part of the experiment.

Exercise and Freeform Usage (30 - 40 minutes).
Participants were then asked to practice the interaction techniques by replicating another drawing provided by the experimenter, this time without further guidance. After completing the tasks, participants were asked to explore the interface by creating their own illustrations.

Questionnaire and Interview (20 minutes)
After using the system, participants completed a questionnaire about Collection Objects. The questions addressed both the usefulness and usability of each technique using a 7-point Likert scale (1- Strongly disagree, 7- Strongly agree). Participants were then interviewed with open-ended questions to collect further feedback on utility and usability of Collection Objects and the workflow with COs, compared with traditional ways of working with multiple objects.

Results

Utility of Collection Objects
Participants were specifically asked to rate the usefulness of each of the interaction techniques. The results presented in Figure 10 show a common agreement among participants. This indicates that the interaction techniques enabled by Collection Objects are valuable and desired. As P3 commented: *The functions are fantastic. Especially with complex drawings, it can be so much more useful.*

Among the various techniques, participants strongly favored filtering by attributes, quick group navigation, and direct selection across groups (6/6 strongly agree), as they found these functions *powerful and unseen in other applications (P4)*. Particularly, they support basic and frequently used functionalities, which are *extremely useful (P1) and set apart actual user experience (P1)*, but *they (other applications) do fail on (P1)*. Our tool *really has the potential (P6)* to help them achieve tasks that were previously tedious or *impossible (P6)*.

Landing object as mode and sharing values to a CO were also acknowledged by participants (5/6 strongly agree, 1/6 agree), as they found *having so much control on what I select is really amazing. It makes the work process continuous and faster (P6)*.

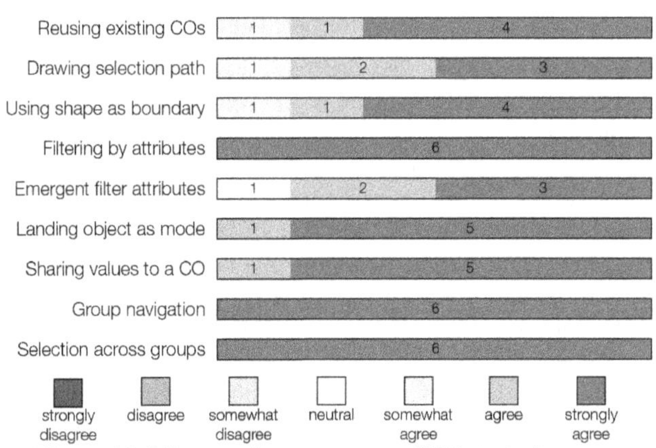

Figure 10. Likert-scale responses to "This technique was useful in my drawing tasks."

Other features also valued by participants included, the conventional selection using drawing paths, as well as the novel emergent filters only identified as *distracting* by P1.

Workflow vs Traditional Tools
Participants respond positively on the workflow with Collection Objects rating the statement "The experience of working with multiple objects in our system is fluid" as "strongly agree" (5/6) and "agree" (1/5). When interviewed, they attributed the fluidity to four features of our system:

1) less context switching with Collection Objects, since a series of selection, grouping, and manipulation of objects can be achieved through direct manipulation of one Collection Object and its two sets of attributes: *Having so many functionalities in this little thing [Collection Object] is great. You can just work with it (P2)*, as opposed to the existing applications where the users *have to go to the toolbar, the layer panel, and a bunch of other stuff; they are all over the places (P2).*

2) composing and modifying selection with filter attributes, since it frees the user from having to *search the whole canvas by myself (themselves) (P4).* It also reduces mental effort as the users can rely on the search filters to select the unseen objects: *It's very relaxing. Many times I missed the things I wanted to select. They were either underneath other objects or I simply didn't see them. Sometimes I double checked my selection...(P4)* but *your system can reliably find them for me (P4).* Being able to modify the selection allows the users to easily switch to a related selection, which fits the general workflow. *Because the changes are kind of related. If you have just changed the opacity, it's very likely that you will continue changing it (P4).*

3) the open group structure and quick navigation of groups, which reduces the effort of managing the structure of the drawing: *with Illustrator, half the time, I am managing groups. That's not designing, that's just managing.* It also enables direct, quick, and flexible selection *without changing groups; the sliding to get to the group, man, it's so fast (P3).*

4) the rich manipulation of the aggregated attributes of the selected objects, which *is really designed with the considerations of supporting complex designs (P5).* It also allows for spontaneous manipulation of the selection: *sometimes (in other applications) you really just want to change it and quickly try out something, and you have to give up your selection. That slows down my design process (P2).*

Grouping with Collection Objects
Comparing against existing tools, all participants positively acknowledged how COs seamlessly combine overlapping selections with hierarchical group structures. They also valued our preference on using trees over lattice structures, as they found overlapping structures confusing (P2, 4).

P4. *If you cross group all over the place, then things belong to everything else, that's kind of weird. If you are preventing from doing that, that would be best. Because otherwise, that would actually be a mistake. But the ease of selection within the groups is really important.*

Being able to easily change the scope of the group was found useful for maintaining a cleaner and flatter group structure, It reduces *unnecessary groups (P1), which are a nightmare for later changes (P1),* but usually created *to avoid the ungroup, select, and regroup procedure (P1).*

Features Suggested by Participants

Once the participants understood the concept, they started to explore the limits of our system and discovered features that had not been demonstrated. As P2 noted, *"The features are so rich. You see I was doing a lot more than your system has, that's because I understand it".*

Interesting behaviors and features were observed or suggested by our participants. After learning that the shape of an existing object could be used as the boundary of a selection, P1 tried to share the shape of the canvas to achieve a select all function. Having successfully done that, P1 then tried to select all the red objects on the top layer, by sharing the shape of the layer object. However, since our system does not provide a shape attribute for layer object, P1 then tried to share the whole layer object with a CO. Although this is not supported by the current system, it shows that the participant understood the concept that selection can be composed by setting up a boundary and then filtering it. Since the layer object is itself a container, it also reveals that existing COs could be used to define the scope of a new collection, further expanding the expressiveness of Collection Objects.

Learning Curve

Participants agreed that the techniques were easy to learn (5/6 strongly agree, 1/6 agree). We found them could learn the few simple rules which formed the basis of all interactions: top of the diamond is for searching and the right is for editing, holding an object indicates the interaction is bounded to it, and attributes are objects. We intentionally repeated these principles in the training, as we learned this is an effective way to teach how to use the system. Three of our participants also took part in study of [44] and they found the new interface uniform consistent with the original concept (3/3 strongly agree), as P1 commented: *it's like you have learned how to use a game controller, and then you can play all the games.*

Summary

The results of the expert evaluation suggest that Collection Object enables rich, advanced, and fluid manipulation with multiple objects, which were previously tedious or even impossible in existing applications.

DISCUSSION AND FUTURE WORK

While participants positively acknowledged the usefulness of Collection Objects, they also identified usability problems that can be addressed by future work. P1 found that the richness of features in our system is "overwhelming". As P1 noted, *"it has so many features, and sometimes I discovered something you hadn't shown me. I was worried there are some things in the system I don't know, and I may accidentally activate them."* This indicates that the usability can be improved by clearly communicating the capability of the system to the users. P6 found that having COs floating made the working area messier. Although, P4 noted the opposite as she found it useful to have them on the canvas for immediate access to previous selections, a future system can provide a side panel to organize Collection Objects.

One drawback of the direct manipulation paradigm, is selecting unseen objects, for example, objects may be simply out of the view, in a complex scene, or covered by other objects [13]. Bringing unseen objects into view requires extensive manual searching and visual comparisons [13]. Our select-by-search functionalities mitigate this problem, e.g., filters within one CO can be reversed individually, they can be chained together with an AND relationship, and OR relationship is partially supported within each attribute. To extend such features to different attributes, the chain metaphor can be augmented to allow each node of the chain to host more than one card and several chains to be parallel. As such, a search task can be done by spatially manipulating the attribute cards. It would also be interesting to explore whether this could achieve a regex complete complexity.

Future work can also explore the inclusion of other selection techniques into Collection Objects. For example, instead of using specific style attributes as search filters, Gestalt principles can be directly used as selection filters, with their weights accessible and adjustable through the fuzziness attribute. Potential selection results can be suggested directly to the user in a way similar to the emergent filter attributes.

One clear future step is to compare with existing WIMP tools. This may reveal the different strategies users may take to achieve a certain goal and the difference of performance, such as the amount of steps required.

The OOD system provides a micro view of objects by allowing the user to freely disassemble objects into smaller units – Attribute Objects. Complementary to it, Collection Objects explores the macro manipulation of a collection of objects, which provides the opportunity to explore interaction at a higher level. creating a large number of objects is itself difficult and time-consuming. Future work could explore how Collection Objects can enable easy and fast generation of multiple objects of certain patterns. This could be useful in the area of computer-aided design, data visualization [40], and texture-based drawing [18].

CONCLUSION

We have presented Collection Objects, the embodiment of the transient selection and the rigid group structure. The physical embodiment combined with direct physical manipulation gestures demonstrates the rich properties of Collection Objects, which not only enables a single quick selection-action operation, but also provides a coherent mechanism wherein a series of manipulation of multiple objects can be rapidly performed with no context switching. Demonstrated through expert evaluation, Collection Objects enables quick, flexible, fluid interaction with multiple objects. We hope Collection Objects will enable complex applications with direct physical input.

REFERENCES

1. Johnny Accot and Shumin Zhai. 1997. Beyond Fitts' law: models for trajectory-based HCI tasks. In *Proceedings of the ACM SIGCHI Conference on Human factors in computing systems* (CHI '97). ACM, New York, NY, USA, 295-302. DOI=http://dx.doi.org/10.1145/258549.258760
2. Robert St. Amant and Thomas E. Horton. 2002. Characterizing tool use in an interactive drawing environment. In *Proceedings of the 2nd international symposium on Smart graphics*(SMARTGRAPH '02). ACM, New York, NY, USA, 86-93. DOI=http://dx.doi.org/10.1145/569005.569018
3. Michel Beaudouin-Lafon. 2000. Instrumental interaction: an interaction model for designing post-WIMP user interfaces. In *Proceedings of the SIGCHI conference on Human Factors in Computing Systems* (CHI '00). ACM, New York, NY, USA, 446-453. DOI=http://dx.doi.org/10.1145/332040.332473
4. Benjamin B. Bederson, James D. Hollan, Allison Druin, Jason Stewart, David Rogers, and David Proft. 1996. Local tools: an alternative to tool palettes. In *Proceedings of the 9th annual ACM symposium on User interface software and technology* (UIST '96). ACM, New York, NY, USA, 169-170. DOI=http://dx.doi.org/10.1145/237091.237116
5. Xiaojun Bi, Yang Li, and Shumin Zhai. 2013. FFitts law: modeling finger touch with fitts' law. In *Proceedings of the SIGCHI Conference on Human Factors in Computing Systems* (CHI '13). ACM, New York, NY, USA, 1363-1372. DOI: http://dx.doi.org/10.1145/2470654.2466180
6. Eric A. Bier and Steven Freeman. 1991. MMM: a user interface architecture for shared editors on a single screen. In *Proceedings of the 4th annual ACM symposium on User interface software and technology* (UIST '91). ACM, New York, NY, USA, 79-86. DOI=http://dx.doi.org/10.1145/120782.120791
7. Eric A. Bier, Maureen C. Stone, Ken Pier, William Buxton, and Tony D. DeRose. 1993. Toolglass and magic lenses: the see-through interface. In *Proceedings of the 20th annual conference on Computer graphics and interactive techniques* (SIGGRAPH '93). ACM, New York, NY, USA, 73-80. DOI=http://dx.doi.org/10.1145/166117.166126
8. Sebastian Boring, Marko Jurmu, and Andreas Butz. 2009. Scroll, tilt or move it: using mobile phones to continuously control pointers on large public displays. In *Proceedings of the 21st Annual Conference of the Australian Computer-Human Interaction Special Interest Group: Design: Open 24/7* (OZCHI '09). ACM, New York, NY, USA, 161-168. DOI=http://dx.doi.org/10.1145/1738826.1738853
9. Peter Brandl, Clifton Forlines, Daniel Wigdor, Michael Haller, and Chia Shen. 2008. Combining and measuring the benefits of bimanual pen and direct-touch interaction on horizontal interfaces. In*Proceedings of the working conference on Advanced visual interfaces* (AVI '08). ACM, New York, NY, USA, 154-161. DOI=http://dx.doi.org/10.1145/1385569.1385595
10. Bill Buxton. Chunking and phrasing and the design of human-computer dialogues. *IFIP '86*, 475–480.
11. Fanny Chevalier, Pierre Dragicevic, and Christophe Hurter. 2012. Histomages: fully synchronized views for image editing. In *Proceedings of the 25th annual ACM symposium on User interface software and technology* (UIST '12). ACM, New York, NY, USA, 281-286. DOI=http://dx.doi.org/10.1145/2380116.2380152
12. Paul M Fitts. (1954). The information capacity of the human motor system in controlling the amplitude of movement.*Journal of experimental psychology*,*47*(6), 381.
13. David M Frohlich. The history and future of direct manipulation. *Behaviour & Information Technology* 12.6 (1993): 315-329. .
14. Ken Hinckley, Patrick Baudisch, Gonzalo Ramos, and Francois Guimbretiere. 2005. Design and analysis of delimiters for selection-action pen gesture phrases in scriboli. In *Proceedings of the SIGCHI Conference on Human Factors in Computing Systems* (CHI '05). ACM, New York, NY, USA, 451-460. DOI=http://dx.doi.org/10.1145/1054972.1055035
15. Ken Hinckley, Koji Yatani, Michel Pahud, Nicole Coddington, Jenny Rodenhouse, Andy Wilson, Hrvoje Benko, and Bill Buxton. 2010. Pen + touch = new tools. In *Proceedings of the 23nd annual ACM symposium on User interface software and technology* (UIST '10). ACM, New York, NY, USA, 27-36. DOI=http://dx.doi.org/10.1145/1866029.1866036
16. Raphaël Hoarau and Stéphane Conversy. 2012. Augmenting the scope of interactions with implicit and explicit graphical structures. In *Proceedings of the SIGCHI Conference on Human Factors in Computing Systems* (CHI '12). ACM, New York, NY, USA, 1937-1946. DOI=http://dx.doi.org/10.1145/2207676.2208337
17. Steve Jobs. Mac World Expo 2007: Keynote.
18. Rubaiat Habib Kazi, Fanny Chevalier, Tovi Grossman, Shengdong Zhao, and George Fitzmaurice. 2014. Draco: bringing life to illustrations with kinetic textures. In *Proceedings of the SIGCHI Conference on Human Factors in Computing Systems* (CHI '14). ACM, New York, NY, USA, 351-360. DOI: http://dx.doi.org/10.1145/2556288.2556987
19. Bum chul Kwon, Waqas Javed, Niklas Elmqvist, and Ji Soo Yi. 2011. Direct manipulation through surrogate objects. In *Proceedings of the SIGCHI Conference on*

Human Factors in Computing Systems (CHI '11). ACM, New York, NY, USA, 627-636. DOI=http://dx.doi.org/10.1145/1978942.1979033

20. David Kurlander and Eric A. Bier. 1988. Graphical search and replace. In *Proceedings of the 15th annual conference on Computer graphics and interactive techniques* (SIGGRAPH '88), Richard J. Beach (Ed.). ACM, New York, NY, USA, 113-120. DOI=http://dx.doi.org/10.1145/54852.378495

21. Edward Lank and Eric Saund. 2005. Sloppy selection: Providing an accurate interpretation of imprecise selection gestures. *Comput. Graph.* 29, 4 (August 2005), 490-500. DOI=http://dx.doi.org/10.1016/j.cag.2005.05.003

22. Jakob Leitner and Michael Haller. 2011. Harpoon selection: efficient selections for ungrouped content on large pen-based surfaces. In *Proceedings of the 24th annual ACM symposium on User interface software and technology* (UIST '11). ACM, New York, NY, USA, 593-602. DOI=http://dx.doi.org/10.1145/2047196.2047275

23. David Lindlbauer, Michael Haller, Mark Hancock, Stacey D. Scott, and Wolfgang Stuerzlinger. 2013. Perceptual grouping: selection assistance for digital sketching. In *Proceedings of the 2013 ACM international conference on Interactive tabletops and surfaces* (ITS '13). ACM, New York, NY, USA, 51-60. DOI=http://dx.doi.org/10.1145/2512349.2512801

24. Yuexing Luo and Daniel Vogel. 2014. Crossing-based selection with direct touch input. In*Proceedings of the SIGCHI Conference on Human Factors in Computing Systems* (CHI '14). ACM, New York, NY, USA, 2627-2636. DOI: http://dx.doi.org/10.1145/2556288.2557397

25. I. Scott MacKenzie, Abigail Sellen, and William A. S. Buxton. 1991. A comparison of input devices in element pointing and dragging tasks. In *Proceedings of the SIGCHI Conference on Human Factors in Computing Systems* (CHI '91), Scott P. Robertson, Gary M. Olson, and Judith S. Olson (Eds.). ACM, New York, NY, USA, 161-166. DOI: http://dx.doi.org/10.1145/108844.108868

26. Wendy E. Mackay. 2002. Which interaction technique works when?: floating palettes, marking menus and toolglasses support different task strategies. In *Proceedings of the Working Conference on Advanced Visual Interfaces* (AVI '02), Maria De Marsico, Stefano Levialdi, and Emanuele Panizzi (Eds.). ACM, New York, NY, USA, 203-208. DOI=http://dx.doi.org/10.1145/1556262.1556294

27. Thomas P. Moran, Patrick Chiu, and William van Melle. 1997. Pen-based interaction techniques for organizing material on an electronic whiteboard. In *Proceedings of the 10th annual ACM symposium on User interface software and technology* (UIST '97). ACM, New York, NY, USA, 45-54. DOI=http://dx.doi.org/10.1145/263407.263508

28. Ken Perlin and David Fox. 1993. Pad: an alternative approach to the computer interface. In*Proceedings of the 20th annual conference on Computer graphics and interactive techniques*(SIGGRAPH '93). ACM, New York, NY, USA, 57-64. DOI=http://dx.doi.org/10.1145/166117.166125

29. Florian Perteneder, Martin Bresler, Eva-Maria Grossauer, Joanne Leong, and Michael Haller. 2015. cLuster: Smart Clustering of Free-Hand Sketches on Large Interactive Surfaces. In *Proceedings of the 28th Annual ACM Symposium on User Interface Software & Technology* (UIST '15). ACM, New York, NY, USA, 37-46. DOI: http://dx.doi.org/10.1145/2807442.2807455

30. Jef Raskin. The Humane Interface: New Directions for Designing Interactive Systems. 2000.

31. Chun Russel. Adobe Flash Professional CC Classroom in a Book, Adobe Press. 2014.

32. Eric Saund, David Fleet, Daniel Larner, and James Mahoney. 2003. Perceptually-supported image editing of text and graphics. In *Proceedings of the 16th annual ACM symposium on User interface software and technology* (UIST '03). ACM, New York, NY, USA, 183-192. DOI=http://dx.doi.org/10.1145/964696.964717

33. Ben Shneiderman. The future of interactive systems and the emergence of direct manipulation ." *Behaviour & Information Technology* 1.3 (1982): 237-256.

34. Katie A. Siek, Yvonne Rogers, and Kay H. Connelly. 2005. Fat finger worries: how older and younger users physically interact with PDAs. In *Proceedings of the 2005 IFIP TC13 international conference on Human-Computer Interaction* (INTERACT'05), Maria Francesca Costabile and Fabio Paternò (Eds.). Springer-Verlag, Berlin, Heidelberg, 267-280. DOI=http://dx.doi.org/10.1007/11555261_24

35. Randall B. Smith. 1986. Experiences with the alternate reality kit: an example of the tension between literalism and magic. In *Proceedings of the SIGCHI/GI Conference on Human Factors in Computing Systems and Graphics Interface* (CHI '87), John M. Carroll and Peter P. Tanner (Eds.). ACM, New York, NY, USA, 61-67. DOI=http://dx.doi.org/10.1145/29933.30861

36. Sven Strothoff, Wolfgang Stuerzlinger, and Klaus Hinrichs. 2015. Pins 'n' Touches: An Interface for Tagging and Editing Complex Groups. In *Proceedings of the 2015 International Conference on Interactive Tabletops & Surfaces* (ITS '15). ACM, New York, NY, USA, 191-200. DOI: https://doi.org/10.1145/2817721.2817731

37. Ivan E. Sutherland. 1964. Sketch pad a man-machine graphical communication system. In*Proceedings of the SHARE design automation workshop* (DAC '64). ACM,

New York, NY, USA, 6.329-6.346. DOI=http://dx.doi.org/10.1145/800265.810742

38. Michael Terry and Elizabeth D. Mynatt. 2002. Side views: persistent, on-demand previews for open-ended tasks. In *Proceedings of the 15th annual ACM symposium on User interface software and technology* (UIST '02). ACM, New York, NY, USA, 71-80. DOI=http://dx.doi.org/10.1145/571985.571996

39. Edward Tse, Chia Shen, Saul Greenberg, and Clifton Forlines. 2006. Enabling interaction with single user applications through speech and gestures on a multi-user tabletop. In *Proceedings of the working conference on Advanced visual interfaces* (AVI '06). ACM, New York, NY, USA, 336-343. DOI=http://dx.doi.org/10.1145/1133265.1133336

40. Bret Victor. Drawing Dynamic Visualization. 2013.

41. Daniel Wigdor. 57.4 :*Invited Paper*: The Breadth—Depth Dichotomy: Opportunities and Crises in Expanding Sensing Capabilities. SID Symposium Digest of Technical Papers, 42: 845–848.

42. Daniel Wigdor, Hrvoje Benko, John Pella, Jarrod Lombardo, and Sarah Williams. 2011. Rock & rails: extending multi-touch interactions with shape gestures to enable precise spatial manipulations. In*Proceedings of the SIGCHI Conference on Human Factors in Computing Systems* (CHI '11). ACM, New York, NY, USA, 1581-1590. DOI=http://dx.doi.org/10.1145/1978942.1979173

43. Jacob O. Wobbrock, Meredith Ringel Morris, and Andrew D. Wilson. 2009. User-defined gestures for surface computing. In *Proceedings of the SIGCHI Conference on Human Factors in Computing Systems* (CHI '09). ACM, New York, NY, USA, 1083-1092. DOI=http://dx.doi.org/10.1145/1518701.1518866

44. Haijun Xia, Bruno Araujo, Tovi Grossman, and Daniel Wigdor. 2016. Object-Oriented Drawing. In*Proceedings of the 2016 CHI Conference on Human Factors in Computing Systems* (CHI '16). ACM, New York, NY, USA, 4610-4621. DOI: http://dx.doi.org/10.1145/2858036.2858075

45. Pengfei Xu, Hongbo Fu, Chiew-Lan Tai, and Takeo Igarashi. 2015. GACA: Group-Aware Command-based Arrangement of Graphic Elements. In *Proceedings of the 33rd Annual ACM Conference on Human Factors in Computing Systems* (CHI '15). ACM, New York, NY, USA, 2787-2795. DOI: http://dx.doi.org/10.1145/2702123.2702198

46. Pengfei Xu, Hongbo Fu, Oscar Kin-Chung Au, and Chiew-Lan Tai. 2012. Lazy selection: a scribble-based tool for smart shape elements selection. *ACM Trans. Graph.* 31, 6, Article 142 (November 2012), 9 pages. DOI=http://dx.doi.org/10.1145/2366145.2366161

IllumiPaper: Illuminated Interactive Paper

Konstantin Klamka, Raimund Dachselt
Interactive Media Lab Dresden
Technische Universität Dresden, Germany
{klamka, dachselt}@acm.org

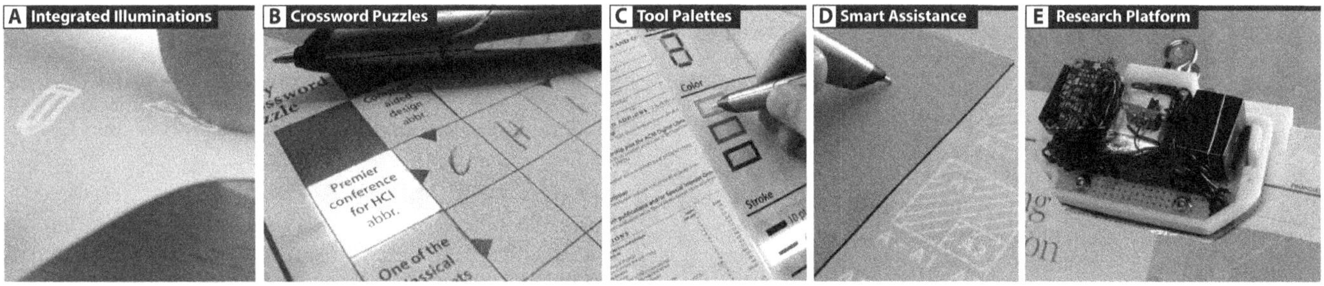

Figure 1. Our ILLUMIPAPER research platform (E) provides paper-integrated visual feedback without losing the sensory richness and flexibility of paper (A) and supports several applications including educational grid puzzles (B), interactive tool palettes (C) or even math exercise sheets (D).

ABSTRACT
Due to their simplicity and flexibility, digital pen-and-paper solutions have a promising potential to become a part of our daily work. Unfortunately, they lack dynamic visual feedback and thereby restrain advanced digital functionalities. In this paper, we investigate new forms of paper-integrated feedback, which build on emerging paper-based electronics and novel thin-film display technologies. Our approach focuses on illuminated elements, which are seamlessly integrated into standard paper. For that, we introduce an extended design space for paper-integrated illuminations. As a major contribution, we present a systematic feedback repertoire for real-world applications including feedback components for innovative paper interaction tasks in five categories. Furthermore, we contribute a fully-functional research platform including a paper-controller, digital pen and illuminated, digitally controlled papers that demonstrate the feasibility of our techniques. Finally, we report on six interviews, where experts rated our approach as intuitive and very usable for various applications, in particular educational ones.

Author Keywords
Digital pen and paper; electro-luminescence; pen interaction; visual feedback; Anoto; thin-film display; augmented paper.

ACM Classification Keywords
H.5.2. Information Interfaces and Presentation:
User Interfaces. - Graphical user interfaces, Input devices and strategies, Interaction styles, Prototyping

CHI 2017, May 06–May 11, 2017, Denver, CO, USA.

ACM ISBN/978-1-4503-4655-9/17/05...$15.00.
DOI: http://dx.doi.org/10.1145/3025453.3025525

INTRODUCTION
Over hundreds of years, the use of paper and writing has become a major cultural achievement and has maintained its importance until today's information age. The success of paper is based on its simplicity, sensory richness and versatility, which foster a widespread dissemination and ubiquitous availability. The affordances of paper for writing and sketching provide unique advantages over digital media [35, 34]. This becomes evident, for example, in active reading tasks when highlighting words, marking graphics or adding drawings. In addition, paper has been found to be the most direct, flexible and intuitive way to annotate documents [17]. Despite these advantages, the growing need of its digital integration into our daily life requires novel solutions. While maintaining the unique properties of paper, powerful software tools and computing functionality should be combined with real paper for added digital value.

The development of camera-based digital pens (e.g., with Anoto™ technology) or sensor-based versions laid the basis for recognizing and analyzing handwritten text on paper, but the provision of visual feedback, e.g., to communicate pen or system states, remains challenging. To address this problem, a wide range of modalities (cf. [55, 34, 59]), i.e., primarily visual feedback (e.g., [65]) as well as audio [44] and haptic [27, 28] or direct muscle feedback [33] have been investigated. However, until now visual feedback – while sometimes displayed on the pen or projected onto paper – is not *directly* integrated into the paper, which would allow providing feedback close to the ink and directly related to the content itself. This would eliminate the problem of visual inconsistencies between physically written content and digitally associated, but otherwise imperceptible information. Typical digital pen-and-paper applications which would benefit from this coexistence – besides many others – could be interactive educational exercise sheets, semantic layers in professional construction plans or simply adjustments of color, line thickness, etc. for writing or sketching in personal notepads.

Although ultra-thin high-resolution screens, such as flexible OLED or E-Ink displays, enable rich interactions [62] and will become available in the long term, we argue that these display types will perhaps always lack some of natural paper's properties (e.g., texture, tearing, folding) and might be too expensive and complex for replacing paper entirely.

In contrast, we see high potential in emerging printed electronics and displays technologies as an important enabling factor towards seamlessly integrated digital paper enhancements. Printed technologies provide ultra-thin, flexible and versatile input and output capabilities on standard paper, thereby preserve almost all unique paper properties and can even be produced in low-cost printing processes in large-scale [53, 60]. In our work, we aim to enable paper augmentation without additional projector setups or display devices, which often seem to be at odds with the flexibility and portability of paper and most of its natural advantages. Therefore, we focus on novel printed segment-based feedback technologies, which position themselves between simple feedback (e.g. LEDs) and next-generation displays (e.g. OLEDs, E-Ink) in their visual capabilities. Hence, our research questions are *where*, *how* and *when* paper-integrated, visual feedback can support user interactions in pen-and-paper user interfaces (PPUIs) and *which* interaction techniques and applications are suitable. Therefore, we examine these aspects in detail and contribute:

- **A systematic exploration** of combining digital pen-and-paper solutions with emerging, low-cost, paper-integrated thin display technologies to visually enhance common paper-related tasks along essential design dimensions.
- **A systematic feedback repertoire** for real-world applications including feedback components for paper widget controls, correctness checks, supporting layout and motion tasks as well as dynamic smart requests.
- **A fully-functional research platform** including a prototype that can be seamlessly clipped to digitally-enabled paper to get paper-based visual feedback in several different application scenarios. We introduce a set of interactive illuminated paper sheets, which demonstrate selected PPUI applications as representative examples.
- **A qualitative evaluation**, i.e., six semi-structured interviews in hands-on sessions with experts from the fields of psychology, education and HCI providing valuable insights.

The remainder of this paper is structured along these contributions: First, we sum up previous work to provide a systematic overview and position our own work. We then introduce our concept and contribute essential design dimensions for paper-integrated feedback along the axes position, type and time. Afterwards, we propose a systematic repertoire of generic feedback components. Subsequently, we describe the realization of our research platform and present a set of implemented applications that we evaluate in expert interviews. A discussion on challenges and future work will conclude our work. For illustrations, we use a color scheme that decodes visual feedback in **green** and user interactions in **blue**.

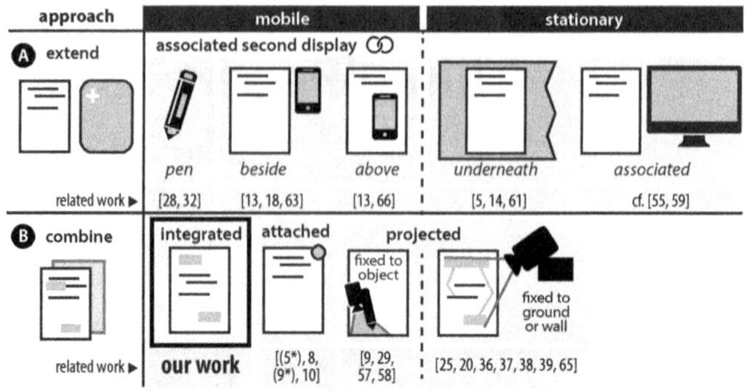

Figure 2. Visual feedback: Using additional screens (A); Combining a visual layer onto the paper itself (B). The overview considers only work that includes pen interaction, natural paper and active visual feedback.

BACKGROUND AND RELATED WORK

Since the objective of this paper is a synergistic approach that seamlessly bridges the gap between physical, handwritten content and virtual associated information, we focus on work that investigates visual augmentation approaches for pen-and-paper user interfaces as well as novel and promising paper-based technologies. Therefore, we group our related work section into visual feedback in PPUIs, paper-based electronics, and emerging thin-film display technologies that are suitable for a seamless paper integration.

Visual feedback in Pen-and-Paper User Interfaces (PPUIs)

The need for visual support in PPUIs has long been known and researchers introduced several approaches that are often based on new enabling technological developments, e.g., projectors, pico-projectors, tiny microcontrollers with LEDs, thin-film displays. Therefore, we classify visual feedback by the augmentation approach (see Figure 2, rows), which either *extends* the paper with dedicated displays (A) or *combines* a visual layer onto the paper itself (B). In addition, we consider the mobility of the approaches (see columns).

In order to visually *extend* a paper, additional screens have been used beside [14, 43], above [29] or underneath the paper. Personal mobile devices [13, 18, 66, 63] have been used to show additional information, and dedicated displays have been built into digital pens (e.g. small OLED screens [32], color-encoded LEDs [28, 32]), which provide simple feedback capabilities. This on-pen feedback is paper independent, enables the fast provision of generic information (e.g., scrolling text on an integrated OLED screen [32]), and uses electronics which are already integrated in digital pens. However, feedback is only provided on the pen and never directly on the paper, where it could be displayed position-dependently, e.g., for providing feedforward [64] and feedback information to the user at the right place. In contrast, stationary displays (e.g. monitors, tabletops [14, 61]) provide rich paper-associated feedback with a high information density, but lack a seamless integration and create a media break by physically separating input and output area.

Besides the extension of paper based on dedicated displays (A), a series of further augmentation approaches merge virtual information layers with physical paper directly (B). To *combine* paper with a visual augmentation layer, research has been primarily focused on *projection-based* approaches, which augment paper by wall-mounted [65, 37, 38, 36, 25, 39, 20], mouse-mounted [58], pen-mounted [57], mobile attachable [30] or even book-attached [9] projector and camera setups. The DIGITALDESK [65], VIDEO MOSAIC [37], ARIEL [38] and ENHANCEDDESK [25] are early examples of stationary projection-based workstations that consider the affordances of a real desktop and enable rich paper augmentation. Mackay et al. [36, 39] and Hurter et al. [20] also investigate the augmentation of flight strips for air traffic control. Song et al. [57, 58] examine spatially-aware mobile projection techniques and propose a design space including overlaid content layers, menus, 3D views and remote collaboration. While these approaches can provide dynamic and rich content overlays, they are limited in their seamless integration and miniaturization, since projectors basically require a minimal projection distance, cause image disorder by projected overlaps and mostly expect good lighting conditions.

Paper-Based Electronics

Since our work aims to integrate displays directly into the paper itself (see Figure 2, B), we use paper-based electronics as a basis to realize paper-integrated traces for illuminating elements and additional sensors by the application of conductive layers and tapes. Paper-based electronics utilize fabrication methods which include copper tapes [49], threads [8] and exposed [7] or vinyl cut [54] foils. Conductive microparticle pastes & pens [4, 12] enable circuit sketching, while nanoparticle inks [40, 42] can be printed instantly [24, 23]. To add functionality, capacitive and resistive sensing enables customizable [22], even cuttable [45], approaches for proximity, (multi-)touch and pressure recognition [16]. Utilizing the piezoelectric effect further provides pressure, temperature [51] and even deformation [52] detection. In addition, physical widgets have been integrated by crafting paper controls [48, 15] or attaching off-the-shelf components as soldered, clipped [47, 10, 21, 26, 22], adhesive [5, 19, 50] or magnetic [6, 11, 12] parts. As an alternative, thin-film technologies facilitate flexible components, that will be seamlessly integrated in the future. An emerging set of these components including soft batteries, paper speakers, membrane sensors, flexible controllers and thin-film displays are already available – the latter of particular importance for our work.

Thin-Film Display Technologies

In general, display technologies can be classified in pixel-addressable high-resolution displays (e.g. OLED, e-paper) and in segment displays, which highlight predefined shapes based on electrochromism (EC) [2], thermochromism (TE) [31] or electroluminescence (EL) [1, 46]. Although advanced display types, such as e-paper, have promising properties (e.g., preserving content without battery), we focus on lightweight, low-current-consuming, segment-based EL and EC displays, which are robust, inexpensive and easy to integrate with pen interaction. Previous work on EC displays investigated the manufacturing process [2], developed multi-layered color displays [41] and even demonstrated fast switching intervalls and high-contrast. Furthermore, flexible EL displays have been proposed by cutting segments from an EL film [1] or screen printing the substrate layers [46], which provides highly customizable printed displays. Olberding et al. [46] introduced a comprehensive design space of custom-printed EL displays and proposed application examples including interactive postcards, watchstraps and awareness plants. However, to the best of our knowledge, these display technologies have not been combined with digital pen interaction before.

CONCEPT: DESIGN OF VISUAL FEEDBACK

In this section, we first describe our *design goals*. Following this, we propose design dimensions for segment-based displays (being our technological basis), and identify *position*, *visual type* and *time* of feedback as important design criteria for the conception of paper-integrated feedback in PPUIs.

Design Goals

Our motivation drives us to develop a neat, robust and lightweight paper concept that builds on highly miniaturized, paper-thin emerging technologies to seamlessly integrate visual feedback in common natural paper sheets. To achieve this, we developed the following design goals:

(G1) **Utility:** The visual feedback should support users in their familiar work process and overcome inconsistencies between physically written and virtual content.

(G2) **Integration:** The advantages of normal paper (e.g. sensory properties) have to be preserved and the augmentation should be mobile, lightweight and subsidiary.

(G3) **Versatility:** A variety of applications should be supported by using specialized, domain-specific augmented papers or more generic papers addressing a wider range of tasks (e.g., paper buttons for annotations).

(G4) **Simplicity:** All augmentation techniques should be easy to use, not disturb established workflows and seamlessly work together in their application context.

Considering these design goals and currently available technologies, we decided to use segment-based, ultra-thin EL and EC displays, which basically consist of substrate layers that can be printed directly on standard paper and are able to illuminate (EL) or change color (EC) in predefined regions. Although segment-based displays are fixed in place and limited in their visual capabilities, we assume that their smart integration and use are a promising approach to support many simple paper tasks in a more ambient and casual style.

Where? – Feedback Position

Olberding et al. [46] introduce a five-dimensional design space for digital fabrication of printed displays concerning the fabrication process, shapes, substrates, input sensing and display primitives, thereby taking on a technical perspective. We extend the design space by the dimension of *feedback position*, which defines the spatial relation between user input and visual output respectively. We differentiate *in-place*, *close-by*, *page-related* and *book-related* feedback (see Figure 3), which we describe in the following.

In-place feedback (IP) provides an immediate visual response at the same physical position as its respective user input. This

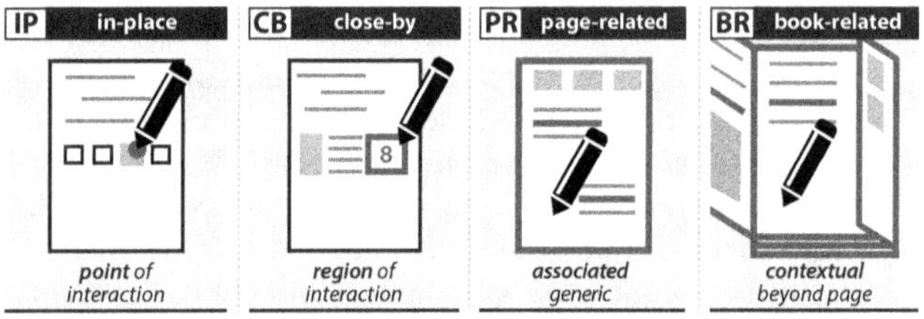

Figure 3. Visual Feedback Position: in-place (A), close-by (B), page- (C) and book-related (D). User feedback in green, interactions in blue.

feedback type requires predefined, visible interaction regions on the paper and is thereby suitable for applications with fixed placeholders (e.g., request forms, multiple choice tests) or paper control elements (e.g., buttons, sliders). The feedback can either support a state visualization (e.g., button on/off) or encode simple information (e.g., highlighting invalid fields). In-place visualizations afford a strong sense of system awareness for users, because input and output are linked directly.

Close-by feedback (CB) places illuminated elements in near proximity to task-related reference points, which are seamlessly linked to the semantic context (e.g., beside a task description). The loose coupling allows more flexible and greater interaction regions, which can be used for complex and area-based interactions. This could for example be an automatical correctness check of a calculation that displays the validity beside the task description after completion.

Page-related feedback (PR) elements are fixed in a well-arranged, clear layout position (e.g., page margins) and refer to dynamic interactions with the entire page. Thereby, they are typically not customized for a single task, but rather represent a visual encoding for more global information. Feedback can be of boolean type (e.g., content successfully saved), symbolic or numeric (e.g., average values or number of tasks solved on the page). Page-related feedback can be realized by means of reusable and flexible multi-segment displays.

Book-related feedback (BR) enables visual interaction capabilities beyond a single page and provides even more generic feedback. Therefore, the display must be visible for all pages. This may be done with foldable book flaps or flexible, attachable bookmarks, which provide additional augmented palettes, toolboxes or interactive color swatches. In addition, book-related feedback can also be integrated into a mobile clipboard, which let the display elements shine through paper. This could be especially beneficial for survey applications, which use a large amount of standardized form sheets.

Another important aspect is the side of the paper on which the display elements are printed. Illuminating elements, such as EL displays, can be printed either on the back (in a reverse substrate layer order) or directly on the front page. Back printed illuminations are invisible in a switched off state and shine through when they are turned on. Thereby, all overlaying paper regions can be printed and written on. Display elements that are printed on the front of a page are perceivable in any state, are non-writable and are thereby more present. Color-changing, non-illuminating elements, such as EC displays, must be printed at the front side – or at least the paper layer must be stenciled at this place (see Figure 1, C).

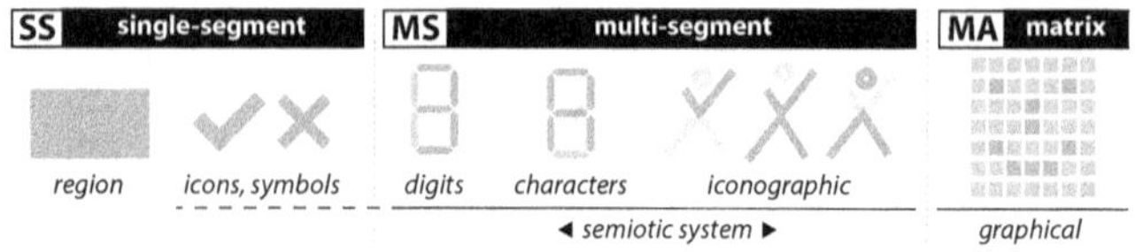

Figure 4. Visual Types: single-segment (SS), multi-segment (MU) and matrix (MA).

How? – Visual Types

In addition, the *visual type* of a segment display plays a central role in the design of integrated visual feedback since it specifies the visual capabilities in a decisive way. Basically, these displays can be classified along the axis of their addressable segments, spatial arangements and overall page coverage (see Figure 4). Therefore, we group the displays into the categories of *single-segment* (SS), *multi-segment* (MS) as well as *matrix* (MA) arrangements (cf. [46]). Single-segment displays can illuminate a specific action item with an icon or highlight predefined regions, while multi-segment displays are capable of providing more complex semiotic information, including glyphs, digits or even custom sets of iconographic symbols for specific application tasks. Matrix arrangements are basically a minimalist form of pixel addressable displays and facilitate low-resolution graphical information.

Besides the visual appearance (e.g., brightness, color, contour) of a display, *temporal animation pattern* allow for a further design dimension. By turning the segments on and off, it is possible to direct the user's awareness or even decode more complex information based on a frequency modulated blink pattern (e.g., frequency visualizing a time countdown).

When? – Feedback Time

Depending on the current interaction tasks, the provision of visual feedback can be needed before, during or after a user interaction. Therefore, we identify the *feedback time* as an important dimension in the design of paper-integrated visual feedback and propose to differentiate into feedforward, continuous feedback and post-feedback (see Figure 5).

Feedforward (FF) is shown before an action is executed (cf. [64]). An example could be the highlighting of all mandatory fields of a form before the user begins to fill out the fields.

Continuous feedback (CF) is displayed during an action and becomes necessary whenever a user performs a prolonged, continuous action (e.g., follows a path), which requires immediate visual feedback (e.g., for a potential correction).

Post-feedback (PF) is provided after a user action and often visualizes an analyzed state (e.g., rating, validity) of the previous action subsequently. For text input, post-feedback is the only suitable feedback because the interpretation mostly makes sense if the input is already finished.

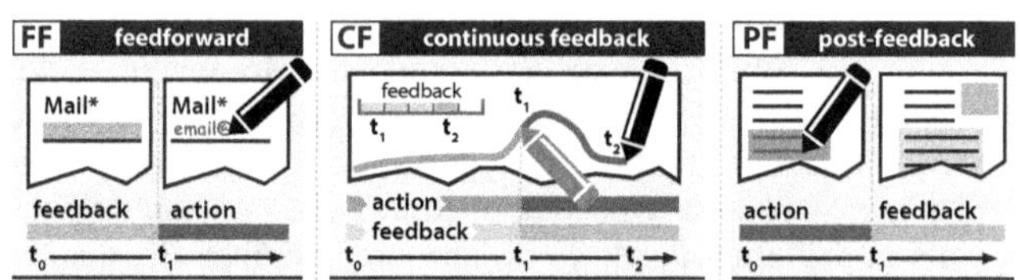

Figure 5. Visual feedback can be provided before (FF), during (CF) and after (PF) an interaction.

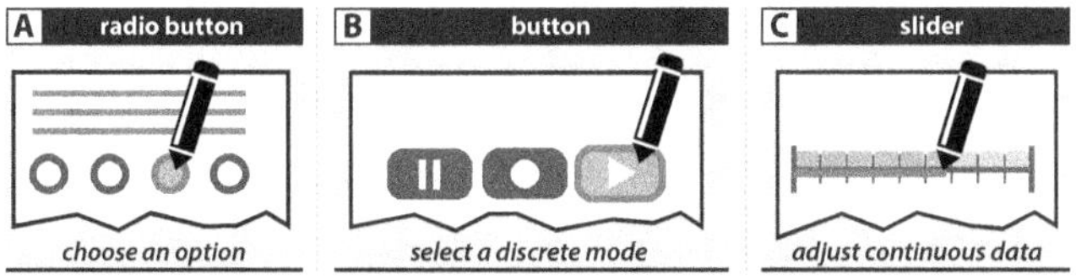

Figure 6. Controls and widget feedback: The active selection is highlighted exclusively (A). Each toggle button can indicate its state actively (B). Sliders provide a segment-based continuous feedback (C).

CONCEPT: FUNDAMENTAL FEEDBACK COMPONENTS

After we have discussed where, how and when feedback can be displayed directly on paper, in this section we describe, which typical interface tasks of PPUIs can benefit from dynamic feedback. We propose five fundamental visual feedback components using paper-integrated illuminations that can serve as basic building blocks for future ILLUMIPAPER applications. A wide range of generic interface components with dynamic feedback is introduced in the following, including paper widgets, validity control, smart requests, layout and motion sequence support.

1. Feedback for Controls and Widgets: Most currently available digitally-enabled notepads provide printed control elements at the header or footer to (de)activate specific functions such as capturing, tagging pages, sharing content or annotating slides [56]. A common problem of this interface design is the lack of clear system feedback that increases the risk of triggering incorrect actions (e.g., tap twice) since the user has no chance to recognize the state. To address this problem, we propose the use of immediate visual feedback for paper controls and widgets communicating the current state. Our visual feedback covers common control elements (see Figure 6) including radio buttons (A), functional buttons (B) and sliders (C). These and similar widgets can be easily used for graphical parameter control in existing digital pen notebook applications.

2. Validity Feedback: In many applications users might be interested in getting immediate (simple) validity feedback of their handwritten entries concerning a specific task (see Figure 7). This could for example be the proper completion of an application form (D) or the correct solution for a math calculation (E), multiple-choice question (F) or even a grid puzzle (see Figure 1, B and Figure 14, B2). Although these examples differ in their form and complexity, the underlying design principle remains the same: User's input in a predefined region is analyzed and compared to the correct answer, which might involve complex analysis algorithms. The result could be either visually decoded with a single segment display indicating (in)valid state or by using two separated or even a multi-segment display, which highlights both states actively. We assume that validity feedback works best when it is positioned in-place or close-by to the content and task at hand.

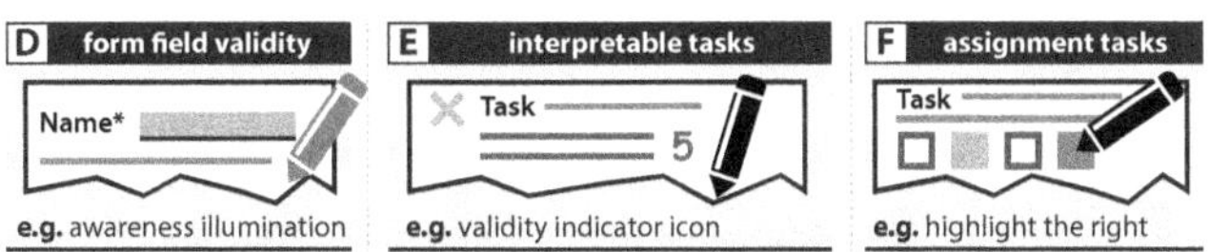

Figure 7. Validity feedback can be used to highlight invalid fields (D) and to visualize the correctness of different answer types (E, F).

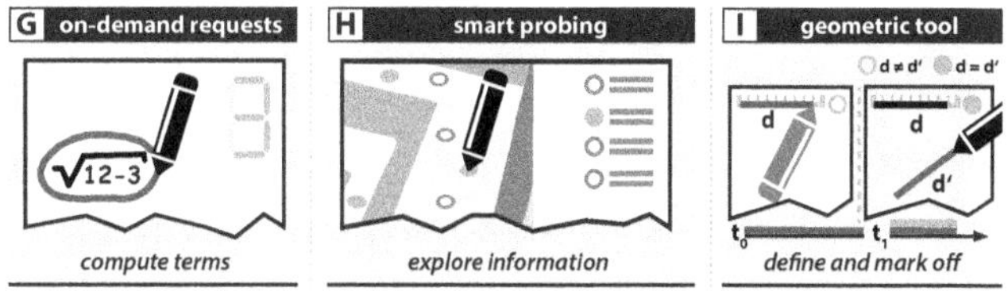

Figure 8. Smart requests comprise rich on-demand feedback (G), probing feedback (H) or even advanced visual tools (I).

3. Smart Request Feedback: To provide a paper tool repertoire including calculators, interactive graphics and rulers, we introduce the concept of smart requests (see Figure 8), which enables powerful paper-integrated analysis and visualization capabilities for a variety of tasks. We propose *on-demand requests* (G), *smart probing* (H) and a *geometric tool* (I) as promising interaction components taking advantage of our approach, creating added value (e.g., avoiding media breaks) and thereby simplifying common workflows.

On-demand requests (G) allow users to get seamlessly associated or even computed information by marking a written expression. For example, it is possible to compute complex, written mathematical terms directly on the paper by simply encircling a term. A paper- or notepad-integrated numeric display will show the results immediately (see also Figure 1, C, above the color widget). Thereby, the workflow will not be interrupted by switching to a calculator requiring to re-enter the whole term.

Smart probing (H) enables the fast perception of information associated with a point or region by using the pen as an exploration tool. For example, the smart probing can help to recognize tube or cable types in a construction drawing by simply moving the pen above. The paper legend key is linked to the associated section and illuminates immediately. Besides these predefined relationships, it is also possible to use the tool for dynamic probing. For example, a mathematical equation just written can be validated by touching the comparison operator with the pen.

Geometric tools (I) provide dynamic measurement capabilities. For example, if a user wants to draw a line with a specific length (e.g., 7 cm) with a digital pen, paper-integrated feedback can help to visualize the distance traveled. The current distance can either be visualized with multi-segment bars that show a linear progress of the achieved distance or with a single icon that uses a blink frequency to indicate the remaining distance. When the user reaches the desired distance, constantly illuminated feedback is provided until the user finishes the action. This feedback component allows to draw true to scale when a ruler is not available.

4. Layout Feedback: In addition to the previous feedback components, we introduce layout feedback (see Figure 9), which supports the user by providing on-demand *rulers* (J), different *grid systems* (K) or predefined design *templates* (L). All auxiliary layout illuminations can be enabled or disabled at any time, e.g., by tapping a paper button with the pen. Although these feedback components are simple and just provide visual guidance, we assume that they can enhance a variety of common tasks, such as writing properly, sketching perspectively, tracing templates or exercising geometry.

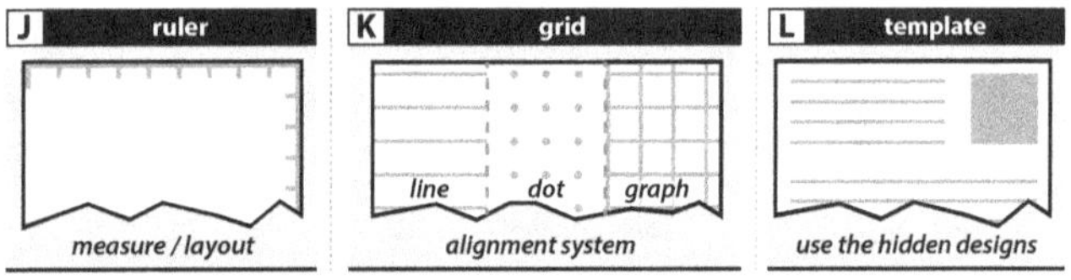

Figure 9. Layout feedback supports measurement & alignment (J), grid-based (K) and even template-based (L) layout tasks.

Figure 10. Direct feedback visualizes its validity in-place (M), while motion post-feedback displays the result after an interaction (N). In contrast, handling instructions (O) are used to indicate directions to take.

5. Feedback for Motion Sequences: PPUIs also provide further opportunities to analyze stylus motion patterns. The captured position data enables the comparison of spatial deviations to a given path or a predefined motion pattern concerning the accuracy, precision and speed. Exemplary application scenarios could include the training of handwriting (e.g., learning new characters and symbols) or the strengthening of physical capabilities with respect to dexterity (e.g., to combat a disease or a restricted range of motion). We propose the usage of multi-segment displays, which can visually encode more complex information caused by continuous values sampled during the motion. We devised the three motion feedback principles (see Figure 10) direct motion feedback (M), post motion feedback (N) and dynamic handling instructions (O).

Direct Motion Feedback (M) visually supports a user during her or his motion with regard to correctness. During a motion, we assume the user's awareness to be on the pen and the respective paper region. Multi-segment regions around the predefined path can be used, which illuminate when the user leaves the optimal path. In addition, we suggest to combine pen-integrated vibrotactile or even muscle feedback (cf. [33]) with visual feedback to address more sensory channels.

Post Motion Feedback (N) provides feedback after a motion sequence. Since motion sequences are basically not spatially bound, we propose the usage of page- or book-related semiotic displays, which provide some abstract feedback with regard to the success of the whole motion sequence.

Handling Instructions (O) provide visual feedforward information and can thereby support the user in sketching a path. Based on the current pen position and progress, future pen directions can be indicated. A multi-segment with eight radial navigation arrows can, e.g., display the next direction to take.

Extended Input: So far, we focused on single pen interaction to reduce complexity and gain a better understanding of the visual integration. However, it is possible to extended the input capabilities. In the following, we shortly discuss advanced input modalities that have the potential to work in concert with our introduced techniques.

Multiple pens allow collaborative interaction since most digital pens transmit unique identifiers. This enables user specific visual feedback, which can either support or even create novel applications. Depending on the usage context, for instance, different user roles (e.g., supervisor, student) can enable or limit interactions (e.g., result checking). Therefore, visual feedback can help visualizing this roles and respective interaction capabilities along a set of symbols or colors.

Another promising input modality is the *direct interaction with the paper itself*, enabled by smart paper-based electronics (cf. related work). As our techniques already require a conductive layer for the illuminating elements, we see a potential to extend the layer with *capacitive* and *resistive sensing* to further enrich the input side. Thus, one could bend a corner to bookmark a page or use touch input in combination with pen input, thereby supporting multimodal interaction.

ILLUMIPAPER PROTOTYPE

In order to apply and evaluate our previously introduced feedback components, we built a fully-functional research platform (see Figure 12, details 1-8). Technically, our setup consists of four components (see Figure 11 for details): A digital stylus (S), different augmented papers (P), a smart controller clip (C) and an Android device (D). We assume that the controller clip and Android application could become superfluous in the long term as a result of further miniaturization towards paper-thin microprocessors. In the following, we briefly describe each component in more detail, and refer for important design decisions to our design goals (G1-G4).

Digtal Stylus: We use an Anoto™-enabled Maxell DP-201 digital pen to stream its stroke and state data via Bluetooth to a server, which in turn forwards the data in the Open Sound Control (OSC) format via WiFi to our mobile device[1] (S►D).

Illuminated Paper: We build on standard paper (design goal G2) onto which we printed an Anoto™ Pattern to enable pen interaction. We also added a printed outline of the controller to indicate the smart clip position. Depending on the actual application (see below), graphical and textual content, e.g., multiple choice questions, are normally printed on top. In addition, we integrated all paper augmenting parts including EL segements (e.g., ✓, ✗), EC seven-segment displays, capacitive touch fields, a resistive paper identifier (Ω) and all necessary traces (≡) at the back. To investigate several designs, we used low-cost rapid prototyping methods (see Figure 13) instead of printing the necessary electronics directly on the paper. Therefore, we realized traces by sketching with a conductive pen [12]. All contacts (•) are strengthened with copper via an electrically conductive adhesive tape to prevent abrasion (Figure 13, C). The thin-film displays are created with off-the-shelf multi-contact EL foils, which we cut in suitable forms and covered each with a custom plotted stencil foil (Figure 13, A). This allows for fast, reliable and flexible design iterations (G3) with materials available to everyone. Already now, advanced fabrication methods (e.g.,

[1] Since Anoto™ introduced the commercial Android Live SDK, pens can be paired directly, which enable even faster mobile setups.

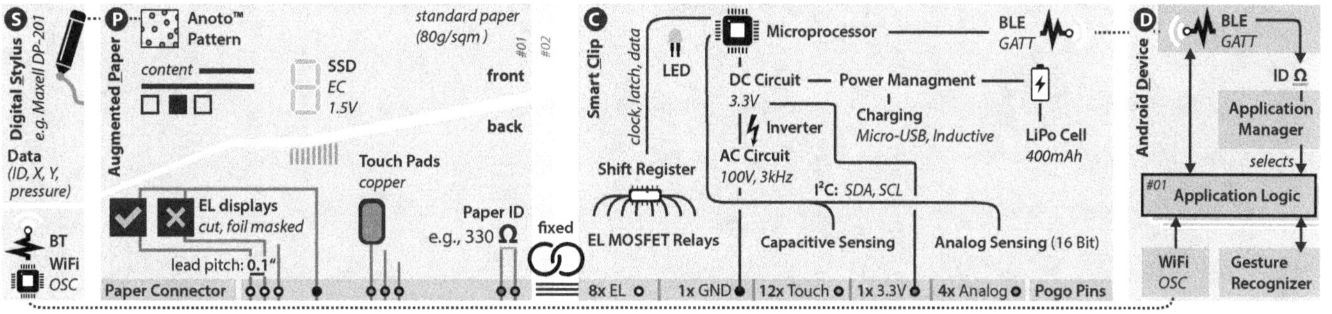

Figure 11. Technical schema: A digital stylus (S), different augmented paper sheets (P), a smart paper controller clip (C) and an Android device (D).

conductive inkjet printing [24] and EL screen-printing [46]) can be used to increase the degree of quality and integration. By completely printing our ILLUMIPAPERS with conductive tracks, illuminating substrates and inkjet content layers, scalability is facilitated and even potential mass-production can be achieved (cf. [53]).

Smart Clip: Our paper attachable controller basically consists of two electrical circuits. A low-voltage DC circuit powers the microprocessor including its associated logic parts, while a high-voltage frequency AC circuit is needed for the EL illumination. A battery provides electric power to both (see Figure 12, 2). The AC voltage is being generated by an inverter. We built in eight solid state relays, addressed by an 8-bit shift register, to switch the EL segments and handle the brief zero crossings (3). In addition, we used the I^{2}C bus to integrate twelve capacitive sensing channels for touch recognition as an additional modality and added four analog channels to identify paper sheets based on its unique resistance contact (cf. [39]) and to provide resistive sensing (G3). All signal traces are integrated inside a bulldog clip (1) that seamlessly establishes a physical connection (P≡≡C) to the conductive paper layer when it is closed (cf. [10, 21, 26, 22]) and is easy to use (G4). To avoid loose contacts caused by surface irregularities or lateral shifts, we propose the usage of 27 small spring-loaded pogo pins (7) and integrate a sideway limitation to ensure a safe contact and high robustness (G2). Further on, a built-in power management provides versatile charging capabilities (G4) via USB (1) or even with our integrated inductive wireless charging module (8). For data communication, we use the lightweight Generic Attribute Profile (GATT) over Bluetooth Low Energy (BLE). All components are built on breadboards, which are housed in a 3D printed case with a built-in clip mechanism (1, 7).

Figure 12. Our ILLUMIPAPER research platform and its components.

Android Device: Finally, we built an Android application, which receives digital pen data via OSC (S►D), handles the data for its application scenario and communicates respective state commands to the smart clip via BLE (C◄D). Therefore, we implemented the recognition of simple pen gestures (e.g., tap, hold), realized an intersection detection of predefined regions and integrated Vatavu et al.'s $P Point-Cloud Recognizer [3] to process character- and glyph-based input (G2). Based on a specified unique ohmic resistance (Ω) of each smart paper, our application selects the respective logical mapping for the encoded use case automatically (G3, G4).

Scalability: Our prototype demonstrates a variety of input and output capabilities using a exploratory configuration. However, we also pay attention to customization and scalability for further applications by using clock-driven components (e.g., shift register, I^{2}C parts) and tiny paper connectors. This allows us, for example, to control much more displays on a page by cascading additional shift registers. Furthermore, our augmented sheets can be taken to a next level by building an all-in-one production pipeline that prints the Anoto™ pattern, conductive and display layers at once.

Further details on the fabrication and additional technical resources are available on our research project website[2].

APPLICATIONS

In this section, we will illustrate how our ILLUMIPAPER concept and its prototypical realization can be practically applied to personal, educational and even professional daily-life activities. Out of the many possible applications, we describe five implemented real-world scenarios in more detail (see Figure 14, B), which fall into one of the three areas *multiple choice tests* (1), *grid puzzles* (2) and *mathematical applications* (3). These applications have also been used in our hands-on expert interviews. In addition, we provide an outlook to further application scenarios, which we have partly realized. All implemented applications make use of our previously introduced fundamental feedback components and use it in their specific application context.

[2] ILLUMIPAPER research website: `https://imld.de/illumipaper/`

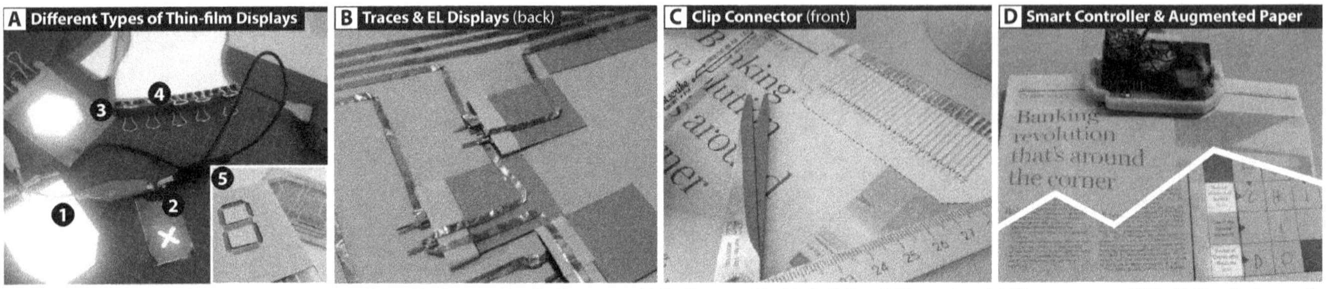

Figure 13. We considered several thin-film display technologies: cut (A1) & stenciled EL foils (A2), printed EL segments [46] (A3), elastomeric ELastoLite Panels® (A4) end printed EC SSDs [67] (A5). Finally, we used cut & stenciled EL foils in fast iterations. To realize paper traces we used combinations of copper (B) as well conductive tape with conductive ink (C). As a result, we came up with a 27 pin connector (C) for our smart clip (D).

Multiple Choice Tests: We implemented two multiple choice tests as a wide-spread method to examine knowledge (see Figure 14, B1). Our main idea was to improve current correction procedures (e.g., with solution templates) and to provide pupils or students with an interactive learning experience. We realized an application where the user can get the results of her answers immediately. For that, we extended traditional multiple choice tests by attaching EL foils at the back of each answer item (see also Figure 13, A1+B)[3]. We chose white colored regions to visualize correct and red ones to communicate incorrect or missing answer fields. The users can get the results either after finishing all questions or whenever a proof button is explicitly triggered. As examples, we chose a more generic geographic test including two questions with three possible answers each and an excerpt of an official driver's license test including two questions combining text and image. To discuss perception and interaction, we realized three variants. Our first variant highlights correct and incorrect fields, our second setting highlights only right answers and the last one illuminates wrong answers exclusively.

Interactive Grid Puzzles: As a second application, we realized a small picture and crossword puzzle with direct illuminated feedback (see Figure 1, B and Figure 14, B2). Such puzzles are not only entertaining, but help improving knowledge and even logical capabilities (e.g., sudoku). They are very popular in educational applications and among hobbyists. By touching the crossword with the digital pen, our ILLUMIPAPER controller is invoked. After a user has correctly solved a row or column, the respective question field illuminates immediately. As an alternative variant, we also implemented on-demand feedback. Thereby, feedback is only shown if the question field was explicitly triggered. For this application type, we see a high potential for classroom assessment techniques that are basically designed for self-study and -control.

Smart Mathematic Paper: In addition, we propose techniques to improve math exercises (see Figure 14, B3). Among them are *on-demand calculations*, *live result checking* and a set of *interactive exam tools* (e.g., time control, interim results, graphical hints, overall ratings) as important and recurring interaction tasks, which have the potential to take advantage of our visual feedback approach. Again, we aim to provide rich paper-integrated digital capabilities while preserving the unique paper properties. Workflows could be simplified, since additional calculators and corrections by supervisors or teachers might be superfluous.

On-demand calculations allow the user to compute complex written terms directly on the paper by simply encircling an expression. A paper- or notepad-integrated printed EC seven-segment displays will preview the results in real-time. Furthermore, it is often necessary to check single conversions in sequence to find a mistake. We propose *live result checking*, which provides instant visual feedback about the correctness of mathematical transformations and simplifications. Holding the pen on a comparison operator indicates its validity, which is visualized by a small green check mark or a red cross at the top of the page. Moreover, it is possible to utilize visual feedback for *interactive exam tools*, which include the visualization of the remaining time, the provision of interim results, the preview of graphical tips for a mathematical approach or an initial rating or grading tendency.

Further Applications: We briefly present two additional applications of interactive *paper forms* and *interactive tool palettes*, which are currently not completely implemented.

Standardized paper forms can be used for many applications, e.g., for medical records, industrial checklists or business purposes. They facilitate a fast and structured data collection and enable a simple as well as machine-friendly processing. Although automated checks can detect validity problems, it is often challenging for the user to fill out forms correctly without any assistance. This is due to the fact that users are unsure whether their input is valid, complete and interpreted correctly. We address this issues by proposing integrated visual feedback in forms and records applications. Based on our seamlessly integrated *validity feedback* components (see Figure 7) it becomes possible to highlight missing or invalid fields and visualize selection states. To highlight points of interest immediately and enable appropriate feedback, we decided to use region or symbolic illuminations, which can basically be positioned in or close-by the form field.

In addition, we propose *interactive tool palettes for educational scenarios* (see Figure 1, C). In this type of application supervisors and teachers comment or correct a text from a pupil or student using digital pen and paper. A foldable paper control column (cf. Figure 3, BR) can help them choosing the right graphical and didactical options. Colored and labeled check boxes or radio buttons can for example be used to define an annotation type (e.g., mistakes in red and comments in

[3]Please note that these tracks can be easily replaced by printed ones.

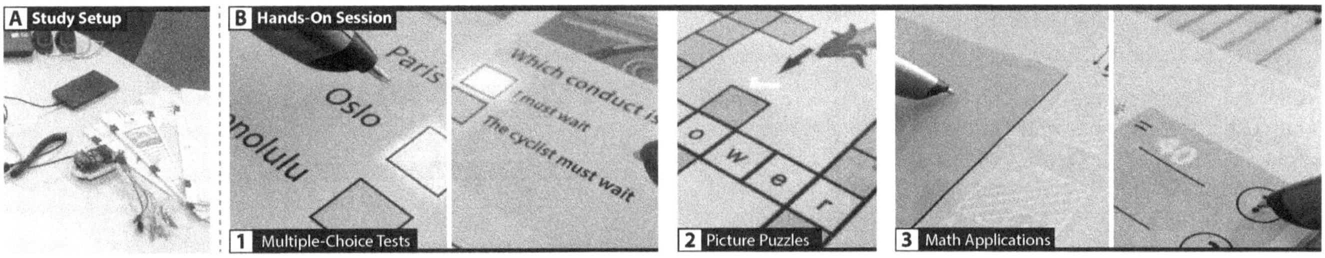

Figure 14. We conducted six expert interviews in our lab (study setup, A). Our hands-on session (B) consisted of five functional application scenarios, which are grouped into the three categories of *multiple choice tests* (1), *picture puzzles* (2) and *mathematical applications* (3).

green). The current selection is visualized with in-place EL feedback in the associated color for the teacher. Every annotation or correction is then stored with its type to be presented later on to the student using a computer system.

EXPERT INTERVIEWS

In order to evaluate our approach, we conducted a series of semi-structured expert interviews to gain a better understanding of how our paper-integrated feedback is assessed from *psychological*, *educational* and *HCI* perspectives.

Participants: We invited six interdisciplinary experts (3 female, 3 male) that split up into two masters in education (research associate + postdoctoral researcher with comprehensive teaching experiences), two psychologists (graduate assistant + postdoctoral researcher) and two HCI experts (research associates), which were recruited from our local university. Our participants are aged between 26 and 50 years (M = 32.83, SD = 8.79) and were unpaid.

Apparatus: To ensure a realistic evaluation in which participants can physically test multiple variants, we built a series of ILLUMIPAPER clipboards that can be used several times and require only the replacement of the paper layer itself. We integrated all display and trace layers into the clipboard and attached exchangeable paper sheets above. The clipboards are connected to our ILLUMIPAPER controller (see prototype section) via quickly exchangeable alligator clips and are controlled by our mobile application (see Figure 14, A).

Tasks & Procedure: Our participants were separately interviewed in a 60 minute hands-on session with five functional application scenarios, which cover a wide range of our proposed feedback components and are grouped into three categories (see Figure 14, B).

First, we demonstrated the digital pen system and introduced our experts to the topic. We pointed out possible inconsistencies between digital and physical properties. In addition, we presented ultra-thin display technologies to provide an overall understanding of our ILLUMIPAPER research platform.

In the main part of our evaluation, participants were asked to test our previously described applications (see Figure 14, B) and to comment on the usefulness, potential and also on possible problems of our paper-integrated feedback approach, including the applicability of features to their own everyday practices. Therefore, we first presented our generic multiple choice test with color-encoded in-place feedback and continued with a more specific application case of a driver's license test (1). Our second scenario was a picture puzzle (2) with symbolic close-by feedback and textual input. In the last category, we asked to solve two simple math applications (3), which support the user with numeric results on-demand or even provide graphical tips for the mathematical approach to solve a simple area calculation. Our experts received visual feedback as described in our feedback components and application sections. In addition, whenever appropriate, we discussed further ideas of our participants by using a contextual wizard-of-Oz simulation based on our mobile debug view that allowed us to switch on all illuminated elements manually.

Measures: To protocol our interview procedures and in-study observations, we made video recordings, kept the inscribed application papers, took notes during the interviews and used an additional secretary, who wrote a detailed record of the whole interview. All interviews were accompanied by questionnaires that include five-point scales (see Figure 15) and also a number of open questions to get qualitative feedback after each application category and at the end.

RESULTS & DISCUSSION

In the following, we provide insights into our promising findings (see Figure 15) and report on lessons we learned.

All experts were able to assess the validity of their multiple choice answers (see Figure 14, B1) with our proposed validity feedback. The experts in psychology felt that our in-place feedback techniques have clear advantages over traditional paper solution templates, which require in general a higher cognitive load to spatially associate and link items. In addition, one educational expert esteemed the capability of archiving interactive papers that could decrease the risk of lost knowledge (e.g., by an uninstalled e-learning application on a tablet) and is thereby beneficial for pupils, who want to look up already learned content. Moreover, we asked the experts to comment on our design. All participants agreed on our proposed solution that answers should be color-encoded (typically, green: correct answer; red: incorrect answer). They also should be displayed simultaneously to avoid any ambiguities, i.e., to highlight correct fields in green (or white) and at the same time wrong or inappropriate fields in red.

The provision of validity feedback for logical grid puzzles (see Figure 14, B2) became the subject of a controversial debate. Some HCI and psychology experts liked the idea to solve the puzzle without any assistance and argue that the design of a grid puzzle is already a suitable feedback mechanism. However, all experts did comment that they advocate the use of this application for educational purposes to support, for instance, children in preschool (see Figure 15, Q3).

In addition, one expert also suggested the illumination of single cells to support the exploration of spelling mistakes.

Our math applications (see Figure 14, B3) were rated by our experts as most useful (Q1) and applicable for education (Q4). However, two participants were frustrated with our interactive help system concerning the specific content of support feedback they received (Q4). The experts proposed more generic tips, similar to an extract of a mathematical table that supports alternative solution paths. In our math puzzle with substitutions, our HCI and educational experts suggested the additional support for touch input to reveal interim results, which our research platform already supports. Our participants commented that they sometimes felt uncomfortable to physically draw on a paper button and prefer touch interactions. Therefore, one HCI expert suggest the use of embossed or surface-treated paper buttons and mentioned as an example non-writable surface coats to support ink-free pen taps and sensory feedback for direct touch interactions in specific interaction regions. Furthermore, our educational experts contributed the idea of adjustable, personalized feedback options that can either be defined by the student or the teacher. Finally, we discussed our math live result checking. Overall, participants liked the technique and assumed that teachers can correct tests more quickly. Our educational experts value the idea of a correction assistant without losing control.

In general, our expert interviews revealed that our approach has been assessed as useful, intuitive and self-descriptive for several applications scenarios (see Figure 15, Q1+Q3). The most positive response received during these sessions was the promising potential for education as well as professional application contexts (Q6). In addition, all experts value the combination of natural paper properties with our integrated illuminations. Overall, participants liked the various interaction techniques that were realized, however, they also raised interesting questions and suggestions that need to be examined in a next iteration of our application cases.

LIMITATIONS AND CHALLENGES

We assume that paper-thin and flexible microprocessors will emerge and further display technologies will be made possible in the near future. However, our current research platform is limited in its form factor (dedicated clip), maximum addressable channels and even in the space-saving design of traces. We assume that next miniaturized and completely printed iterations will support a fully-integrated approach and the application of ILLUMIPAPER in more ubiquitous contexts.

Although the production costs of illuminated papers are much cheaper (cf. [46]) than emerging high-resolution OLED screens, their lifetime is actually shorter. Therefore, we currently recommend the conscious application of illuminated papers by using them for more long-term, recurring or important applications.

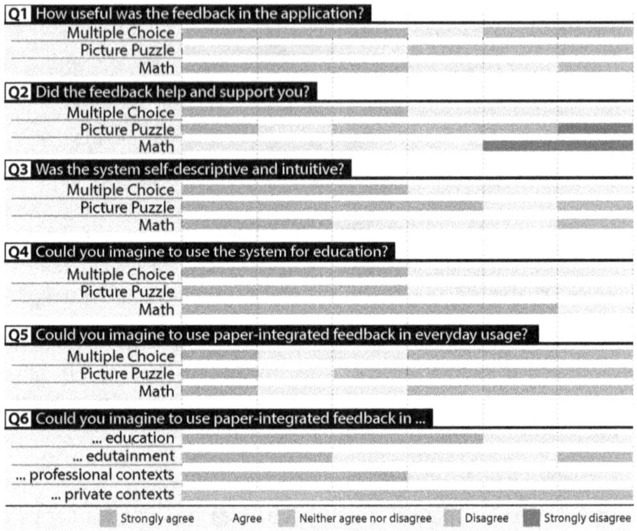

Figure 15. Survey results of questions scored on a five-point scale.

CONCLUSION AND FUTURE WORK

In this paper, we presented the idea of using emerging printed, segment-based display technologies to enhance PPUIs. We classified previous work along their used approaches for paper augmentation and positioned our own idea. As a main contribution, we introduced our concept of ILLUMIPAPER that seamlessly combines pen interactions with paper-integrated visual feedback. We described the essential design axes of position, visual type and feedback time for segment-based visual feedback and proposed a rich set of generic feedback components that address common interaction tasks in PPUIs. Starting from these interaction and feedback components, we have built a comprehensive, technical research platform that supports all of our introduced feedback components. Further on, we have shown the feasibility of our approach with several applications, which we have not only implemented, but also successfully reviewed in six expert interview sessions. Our observations and interviews let us suppose that our concept of ILLUMIPAPER has a sufficient potential to enhance several PPUIs for typical paper-related tasks and can bridge the gap between physical and virtual layers.

For future work, our ILLUMIPAPER system needs to be examined in additional studies, e.g. by comparing it to current on-pen feedback solutions. Furthermore, we would like to improve our existing paper sheets by using more sophisticated fabrication methods [24, 46] and investigate further thin-film technologies such as the integration of OLED segments. In addition, our prototypes need to be further miniaturized and technically extended (e.g., more addressable visual channels) to enhance user acceptance and to support more complex application scenarios. Finally, we plan to extend our set of applications and investigate them in a field study to confirm our promising results in professional application environments.

ACKNOWLEDGEMENTS

This work was in part funded by grant no. 03ZZ0514C of the German Federal Ministry of Education and Research (BMBF measure Twenty20 – Partnership for Innovation, project fast).

REFERENCES

1. Orkhan Amiraslanov, Jingyuan Cheng, Peter Chabrecek, and Paul Lukowicz. 2014. Electroluminescent based Flexible Screen for Interaction with Smart Objects and Environment. In *3rd IUI workshop on Interacting with Smart Objects*.
2. Peter Andersson, Robert Forchheimer, Payman Tehrani, and Magnus Berggren. 2007. Printable All-Organic Electrochromic Active-Matrix Displays. *Advanced Functional Materials* 17, 16 (2007), 3074–3082. DOI: http://dx.doi.org/10.1002/adfm.200601241
3. Lisa Anthony and Jacob O. Wobbrock. 2010. A Lightweight Multistroke Recognizer for User Interface Prototypes. In *Proceedings of Graphics Interface 2010 (GI '10)*. Canadian Information Processing Society, Toronto, Ont., Canada, Canada, 245–252. http://dl.acm.org/citation.cfm?id=1839214.1839258
4. Bare Conductive. 2014. Electric Paint. (2014). http://www.bareconductive.com/.
5. Florian Block, Michael Haller, Hans Gellersen, Carl Gutwin, and Mark Billinghurst. 2008. VoodooSketch: Extending Interactive Surfaces with Adaptable Interface Palettes. In *Proceedings of the 2Nd International Conference on Tangible and Embedded Interaction (TEI '08)*. ACM, New York, NY, USA, 55–58. DOI: http://dx.doi.org/10.1145/1347390.1347404
6. Leah Buechley, Sue Hendrix, and Mike Eisenberg. 2009. Paints, Paper, and Programs: First Steps Toward the Computational Sketchbook. In *Proceedings of the 3rd International Conference on Tangible and Embedded Interaction (TEI '09)*. ACM, New York, NY, USA, 9–12. DOI: http://dx.doi.org/10.1145/1517664.1517670
7. Varun Perumal C and Daniel Wigdor. 2015. Printem: Instant Printed Circuit Boards with Standard Office Printers & Inks. In *Proceedings of the 28th Annual ACM Symposium on User Interface Software & Technology (UIST '15)*. ACM, New York, NY, USA, 243–251. DOI: http://dx.doi.org/10.1145/2807442.2807511
8. Marcelo Coelho, Lyndl Hall, Joanna Berzowska, and Pattie Maes. 2009. Pulp-based Computing: A Framework for Building Computers out of Paper. In *CHI '09 Extended Abstracts on Human Factors in Computing Systems (CHI EA '09)*. ACM, New York, NY, USA, 3527–3528. DOI: http://dx.doi.org/10.1145/1520340.1520525
9. Raimund Dachselt and Sarmad AL-Saiegh. 2011. Interacting with Printed Books Using Digital Pens and Smart Mobile Projection. In *Proceedings of the Workshop on Mobile and Personal Projection (MP2) @ ACM CHI 2011*.
10. Christian Decker, Michael Beigl, Adam Eames, and Uwe Kubach. 2004. DigiClip: Activating Physical Documents. *2013 IEEE 33rd International Conference on Distributed Computing Systems Workshops* 3 (2004), 388–393. DOI: http://dx.doi.org/10.1109/ICDCSW.2004.1284059
11. Johannes Deich, Michael Markert, Jens Geelhaar, Martin Schied, Jens Hammerschmidt, and Gabriel Rausch. 2013. Form & Function Toolkit: Printed Electronics for Unconventional Interface. In *Proceedings of the 8th International Conference on Tangible, Embedded and Embodied Interaction (TEI '14)*. ACM, 365–368. DOI: http://dx.doi.org/10.1145/2540930.2567900
12. Electroninks. 2015. Circuit Scribe. (2015). http://www.circuitscribe.com/.
13. Berna Erol, Emilio Antúnez, and Jonathan J. Hull. 2008. HOTPAPER: Multimedia Interaction with Paper Using Mobile Phones. In *Proceedings of the 16th ACM International Conference on Multimedia (MM '08)*. ACM, New York, NY, USA, 399–408. DOI: http://dx.doi.org/10.1145/1459359.1459413
14. Katherine M. Everitt, Meredith Ringel Morris, A. J. Bernheim Brush, and Andrew D. Wilson. 2008. DocuDesk: An Interactive Surface for Creating and Rehydrating Many-to-Many Linkages among Paper and Digital Documents. In *Horizontal Interactive Human Computer Systems, 2008. TABLETOP 2008. 3rd IEEE International Workshop on*. 25–28. DOI: http://dx.doi.org/10.1109/TABLETOP.2008.4660179
15. Natalie Freed, Jie Qi, Adam Setapen, Cynthia Breazeal, Leah Buechley, and Hayes Raffle. 2011. Sticking Together: Handcrafting Personalized Communication Interfaces. In *Proceedings of the 10th International Conference on Interaction Design and Children (IDC '11)*. ACM, New York, NY, USA, 238–241. DOI: http://dx.doi.org/10.1145/1999030.1999071
16. Nan-Wei Gong, Jürgen Steimle, Simon Olberding, Steve Hodges, Nicholas Edward Gillian, Yoshihiro Kawahara, and Joseph A. Paradiso. 2014. PrintSense: A Versatile Sensing Technique to Support Multimodal Flexible Surface Interaction. In *Proceedings of the SIGCHI Conference on Human Factors in Computing Systems (CHI '14)*. ACM, New York, NY, USA, 1407–1410. DOI: http://dx.doi.org/10.1145/2556288.2557173
17. Wilfred J. Hansen and Christina Haas. 1988. Reading and Writing with Computers: A Framework for Explaining Differences in Performance. *Commun. ACM* 31, 9 (Sept. 1988), 1080–1089. DOI: http://dx.doi.org/10.1145/48529.48532
18. Felix Heinrichs, Daniel Schreiber, Jochen Huber, and Max Mühlhäuser. 2012. Toward a Theory of Interaction in Mobile Paper-digital Ensembles. In *Proceedings of the SIGCHI Conference on Human Factors in Computing Systems (CHI '12)*. ACM, New York, NY, USA, 1897–1900. DOI: http://dx.doi.org/10.1145/2207676.2208328

19. Steve Hodges, Nicolas Villar, Nicholas Chen, Tushar Chugh, Jie Qi, Diana Nowacka, and Yoshihiro Kawahara. 2014. Circuit Stickers: Peel-and-stick Construction of Interactive Electronic Prototypes. In *Proceedings of the SIGCHI Conference on Human Factors in Computing Systems (CHI '14)*. ACM, New York, NY, USA, 1743–1746. DOI: http://dx.doi.org/10.1145/2556288.2557150

20. Christophe Hurter, Rémi Lesbordes, Catherine Letondal, Jean-Luc Vinot, and Stéphane Conversy. 2012. Strip'TIC: Exploring Augmented Paper Strips for Air Traffic Controllers. In *Proceedings of the International Working Conference on Advanced Visual Interfaces (AVI '12)*. ACM, New York, NY, USA, 225–232. DOI: http://dx.doi.org/10.1145/2254556.2254598

21. Sam Jacoby and Leah Buechley. 2013. Drawing the Electric: Storytelling with Conductive Ink. In *Proceedings of the 12th International Conference on Interaction Design and Children (IDC '13)*. ACM, New York, NY, USA, 265–268. DOI: http://dx.doi.org/10.1145/2485760.2485790

22. Çağdaş Karataş and Marco Gruteser. 2015. Printing Multi-key Touch Interfaces. In *Proceedings of the 2015 ACM International Joint Conference on Pervasive and Ubiquitous Computing (UbiComp '15)*. ACM, New York, NY, USA, 169–179. DOI: http://dx.doi.org/10.1145/2750858.2804285

23. Yoshihiro Kawahara, Steve Hodges, Benjamin S. Cook, Cheng Zhang, and Gregory D. Abowd. 2013. Instant Inkjet Circuits: Lab-based Inkjet Printing to Support Rapid Prototyping of UbiComp Devices. In *Proceedings of the 2013 ACM International Joint Conference on Pervasive and Ubiquitous Computing (UbiComp '13)*. ACM, New York, NY, USA, 363–372. DOI: http://dx.doi.org/10.1145/2493432.2493486

24. Yoshihiro Kawahara, Steve Hodges, Nan-Wei Gong, Simon Olberding, and Jürgen Steimle. 2014. Building Functional Prototypes Using Conductive Inkjet Printing. *Pervasive Computing, IEEE* 13, 3 (July 2014), 30–38. DOI:http://dx.doi.org/10.1109/MPRV.2014.41

25. Hideki Koike, Oichi Sato, and Yoshinori Kobayashi. 2001. Integrating Paper and Digital Information on EnhancedDesk: A Method for Realtime Finger Tracking on an Augmented Desk System. *ACM Trans. Comput.-Hum. Interact.* 8, 4 (Dec. 2001), 307–322. DOI:http://dx.doi.org/10.1145/504704.504706

26. Daisuke Komoriya, Buntarou Shizuki, and Jiro Tanaka. 2015. *Task Specific Paper Controller that Can Be Created by Users for a Specific Computer Operation*. Springer International Publishing, Cham, 418–428. DOI:http://dx.doi.org/10.1007/978-3-319-20804-6_38

27. Johnny C. Lee, Paul H. Dietz, Darren Leigh, William S. Yerazunis, and Scott E. Hudson. 2004. Haptic Pen: A Tactile Feedback Stylus for Touch Screens. In *Proceedings of the 17th Annual ACM Symposium on User Interface Software and Technology (UIST '04)*. ACM, New York, NY, USA, 291–294. DOI: http://dx.doi.org/10.1145/1029632.1029682

28. Chunyuan Liao, François Guimbretière, and Corinna E. Loeckenhoff. 2006. Pen-top Feedback for Paper-based Interfaces. In *Proceedings of the 19th Annual ACM Symposium on User Interface Software and Technology (UIST '06)*. ACM, New York, NY, USA, 201–210. DOI: http://dx.doi.org/10.1145/1166253.1166285

29. Chunyuan Liao, Qiong Liu, Bee Liew, and Lynn Wilcox. 2010a. Pacer: Fine-grained Interactive Paper via Camera-touch Hybrid Gestures on a Cell Phone. In *Proceedings of the SIGCHI Conference on Human Factors in Computing Systems (CHI '10)*. ACM, New York, NY, USA, 2441–2450. DOI: http://dx.doi.org/10.1145/1753326.1753696

30. Chunyuan Liao, Hao Tang, Qiong Liu, Patrick Chiu, and Francine Chen. 2010b. FACT: Fine-grained Cross-media Interaction with Documents via a Portable Hybrid Paper-laptop Interface. In *Proceedings of the 18th ACM International Conference on Multimedia (MM '10)*. ACM, New York, NY, USA, 361–370. DOI: http://dx.doi.org/10.1145/1873951.1874001

31. Liyu Liu, Suili Peng, Weijia Wen, and Ping Sheng. 2007. Paperlike thermochromic display. *Applied Physics Letters* 90, 21 (2007). DOI: http://dx.doi.org/10.1063/1.2742781

32. Livescribe. 2007. Echo Smartpen. (2007). http://www.livescribe.com/.

33. Pedro Lopes, Doǎa Yüksel, François Guimbretière, and Patrick Baudisch. 2016. Muscle-plotter: An Interactive System Based on Electrical Muscle Stimulation That Produces Spatial Output. In *Proceedings of the 29th Annual Symposium on User Interface Software and Technology (UIST '16)*. ACM, New York, NY, USA, 207–217. DOI: http://dx.doi.org/10.1145/2984511.2984530

34. Paul Luff, Guy Adams, Wolfgang Bock, Adam Drazin, David Frohlich, Christian Heath, Peter Herdman, Heather King, Nadja Linketscher, Rachel Murphy, Moira Norrie, Abigail Sellen, Beat Signer, Ella Tallyn, and Emil Zeller. 2007. *Augmented Paper: Developing Relationships Between Digital Content and Paper*. Springer Berlin Heidelberg, Berlin, Heidelberg, 275–297. DOI: http://dx.doi.org/10.1007/978-3-540-72727-9_13

35. Paul Luff, Christian Heath, Moira Norrie, Beat Signer, and Peter Herdman. 2004. Only Touching the Surface: Creating Affinities Between Digital Content and Paper. In *Proceedings of the 2004 ACM Conference on Computer Supported Cooperative Work (CSCW '04)*. ACM, New York, NY, USA, 523–532. DOI: http://dx.doi.org/10.1145/1031607.1031695

36. Wendy E. Mackay, Anne-Laure Fayard, Laurent Frobert, and Lionel Médini. 1998. Reinventing the Familiar: Exploring an Augmented Reality Design Space for Air Traffic Control. In *Proceedings of the SIGCHI Conference on Human Factors in Computing Systems (CHI '98)*. ACM Press/Addison-Wesley Publishing Co., New York, NY, USA, 558–565. DOI: http://dx.doi.org/10.1145/274644.274719

37. Wendy E. Mackay and Daniele S. Pagani. 1994. Video Mosaic: Laying out Time in a Physical Space. In *Proceedings of the Second ACM International Conference on Multimedia (MULTIMEDIA '94)*. ACM, New York, NY, USA, 165–172. DOI: http://dx.doi.org/10.1145/192593.192646

38. Wendy E. Mackay, Daniele S. Pagani, L. Faber, B. Inwood, P. Launiainen, L. Brenta, and V. Pouzol. 1995. Ariel: Augmenting Paper Engineering Drawings. In *Conference Companion on Human Factors in Computing Systems (CHI '95)*. ACM, New York, NY, USA, 421–422. DOI: http://dx.doi.org/10.1145/223355.223763

39. Wendy E. Mackay, Guillaume Pothier, Catherine Letondal, Kaare Bøegh, and Hans Erik Sørensen. 2002. The Missing Link: Augmenting Biology Laboratory Notebooks. In *Proceedings of the 15th Annual ACM Symposium on User Interface Software and Technology (UIST '02)*. ACM, New York, NY, USA, 41–50. DOI: http://dx.doi.org/10.1145/571985.571992

40. Mitsubishi. 2015. NanoBenefit 3G Series: Silver Nano Ink and Silver Nano Inkjet Media. (2015). http://www.mitsubishiimaging.com/digital-imaging-diamond-jet-NANOINK.html.

41. Yoshihisa Naijoh, Tohru Yashiro, Shigenobu Hirano, Yoshinori Okada, SukChan Kim, Kazuaki Tsuji, Hiroyuki Takahashi, Koh Fujimura, and Hitoshi Kondoh. 2011. Multi-Layered Electrochromic Display. In *IDW*, Vol. 11. 375–378.

42. NanoPAINT. 2015. Piezoresistive and Piezoelectric Ink. (2015). http://www.nanopaint-tech.com.

43. Moira C. Norrie and Beat Signer. 2003. Switching over to Paper: A New Web Channel. In *Proceedings of the Fourth International Conference on Web Information Systems Engineering, 2003. WISE 2003*. 209–218. DOI: http://dx.doi.org/10.1109/WISE.2003.1254484

44. Moira C. Norrie, Beat Signer, Michael Grossniklaus, Rudi Belotti, Corsin Decurtins, and Nadir Weibel. 2007. Context-aware Platform for Mobile Data Management. *Wirel. Netw.* 13, 6 (Dec. 2007), 855–870. DOI: http://dx.doi.org/10.1007/s11276-006-9858-y

45. Simon Olberding, Nan-Wei Gong, John Tiab, Joseph A. Paradiso, and Jürgen Steimle. 2013. A Cuttable Multi-touch Sensor. In *Proceedings of the 26th Annual ACM Symposium on User Interface Software and Technology (UIST '13)*. ACM, New York, NY, USA, 245–254. DOI: http://dx.doi.org/10.1145/2501988.2502048

46. Simon Olberding, Michael Wessely, and Jürgen Steimle. 2014. PrintScreen: Fabricating Highly Customizable Thin-film Touch-displays. In *Proceedings of the 27th Annual ACM Symposium on User Interface Software and Technology (UIST '14)*. ACM, New York, NY, USA, 281–290. DOI: http://dx.doi.org/10.1145/2642918.2647413

47. Elin Rønby Pedersen, Tomas Sokoler, and Les Nelson. 2000. PaperButtons: Expanding a Tangible User Interface. In *Proceedings of the 3rd Conference on Designing Interactive Systems: Processes, Practices, Methods, and Techniques (DIS '00)*. ACM, New York, NY, USA, 216–223. DOI: http://dx.doi.org/10.1145/347642.347723

48. Jie Qi and Leah Buechley. 2010. Electronic Popables: Exploring Paper-based Computing Through an Interactive Pop-up Book. In *Proceedings of the Fourth International Conference on Tangible, Embedded, and Embodied Interaction (TEI '10)*. ACM, New York, NY, USA, 121–128. DOI: http://dx.doi.org/10.1145/1709886.1709909

49. Jie Qi and Leah Buechley. 2014. Sketching in Circuits: Designing and Building Electronics on Paper. In *Proceedings of the SIGCHI Conference on Human Factors in Computing Systems (CHI '14)*. ACM, New York, NY, USA, 1713–1722. DOI: http://dx.doi.org/10.1145/2556288.2557391

50. Raf Ramakers, Kashyap Todi, and Kris Luyten. 2015. PaperPulse: An Integrated Approach for Embedding Electronics in Paper Designs. In *Proceedings of the 33rd Annual ACM Conference on Human Factors in Computing Systems (CHI '15)*. ACM, New York, NY, USA, 2457–2466. DOI: http://dx.doi.org/10.1145/2702123.2702487

51. Christian Rendl, Patrick Greindl, Michael Haller, Martin Zirkl, Barbara Stadlober, and Paul Hartmann. 2012. PyzoFlex: Printed Piezoelectric Pressure Sensing Foil. In *Proceedings of the 25th Annual ACM Symposium on User Interface Software and Technology (UIST '12)*. ACM, New York, NY, USA, 509–518. DOI: http://dx.doi.org/10.1145/2380116.2380180

52. Christian Rendl, David Kim, Sean Fanello, Patrick Parzer, Christoph Rhemann, Jonathan Taylor, Martin Zirkl, Gregor Scheipl, Thomas Rothländer, Michael Haller, and Shahram Izadi. 2014. FlexSense: A Transparent Self-sensing Deformable Surface. In *Proceedings of the 27th Annual ACM Symposium on User Interface Software and Technology (UIST '14)*. ACM, New York, NY, USA, 129–138. DOI: http://dx.doi.org/10.1145/2642918.2647405

53. Bérenger Roth, Roar R Søndergaard, and Frederik C Krebs. 2015. Roll-to-roll printing and coating techniques for manufacturing large-area flexible organic electronics. In *Handbook of Flexible Organic Electronics*, Stergios Logothetidis (Ed.). Woodhead Publishing, Oxford, 171 – 197. DOI: http://dx.doi.org/10.1016/B978-1-78242-035-4.00007-5

54. Valkyrie Savage, Xiaohan Zhang, and Björn Hartmann. 2012. Midas: Fabricating Custom Capacitive Touch Sensors to Prototype Interactive Objects. In *Proceedings of the 25th Annual ACM Symposium on User Interface Software and Technology (UIST '12)*. ACM, New York, NY, USA, 579–588. DOI: http://dx.doi.org/10.1145/2380116.2380189

55. Beat Signer. 2006. *Fundamental Concepts for Interactive Paper and Cross-Media Information Spaces*. Ph.D. Dissertation. ETH Zürich. DOI: http://dx.doi.org/10.3929/ethz-a-005174378

56. Beat Signer and Moira C. Norrie. 2007. PaperPoint: A Paper-based Presentation and Interactive Paper Prototyping Tool. In *Proceedings of the 1st International Conference on Tangible and Embedded Interaction (TEI '07)*. ACM, New York, NY, USA, 57–64. DOI: http://dx.doi.org/10.1145/1226969.1226981

57. Hyunyoung Song, Tovi Grossman, George Fitzmaurice, François Guimbretiere, Azam Khan, Ramtin Attar, and Gordon Kurtenbach. 2009. PenLight: Combining a Mobile Projector and a Digital Pen for Dynamic Visual Overlay. In *Proceedings of the SIGCHI Conference on Human Factors in Computing Systems (CHI '09)*. ACM, New York, NY, USA, 143–152. DOI: http://dx.doi.org/10.1145/1518701.1518726

58. Hyunyoung Song, Francois Guimbretiere, Tovi Grossman, and George Fitzmaurice. 2010. MouseLight: Bimanual Interactions on Digital Paper Using a Pen and a Spatially-aware Mobile Projector. In *Proceedings of the SIGCHI Conference on Human Factors in Computing Systems (CHI '10)*. ACM, New York, NY, USA, 2451–2460. DOI: http://dx.doi.org/10.1145/1753326.1753697

59. Jürgen Steimle. 2012. *Pen-and-Paper User Interfaces: Integrating Printed and Digital Documents*. Springer Berlin Heidelberg. DOI: http://dx.doi.org/10.1007/978-3-642-20276-6

60. Jürgen Steimle. 2015. Printed Electronics for Human-computer Interaction. *interactions* 22, 3 (April 2015), 72–75. DOI: http://dx.doi.org/10.1145/2754304

61. Jürgen Steimle, Mohammadreza Khalilbeigi, Max Mühlhäuser, and James D. Hollan. 2010. Physical and Digital Media Usage Patterns on Interactive Tabletop Surfaces. In *ACM International Conference on Interactive Tabletops and Surfaces (ITS '10)*. ACM, New York, NY, USA, 167–176. DOI: http://dx.doi.org/10.1145/1936652.1936685

62. Aneesh P. Tarun, Peng Wang, Audrey Girouard, Paul Strohmeier, Derek Reilly, and Roel Vertegaal. 2013. PaperTab: An Electronic Paper Computer with Multiple Large Flexible Electrophoretic Displays. In *CHI '13 Extended Abstracts on Human Factors in Computing Systems (CHI EA '13)*. ACM, New York, NY, USA, 3131–3134. DOI: http://dx.doi.org/10.1145/2468356.2479628

63. Theophanis Tsandilas. 2012. Interpreting Strokes on Paper with a Mobile Assistant. In *Proceedings of the 25th Annual ACM Symposium on User Interface Software and Technology (UIST '12)*. ACM, New York, NY, USA, 299–308. DOI: http://dx.doi.org/10.1145/2380116.2380155

64. Jo Vermeulen, Kris Luyten, Elise van den Hoven, and Karin Coninx. 2013. Crossing the Bridge over Norman's Gulf of Execution: Revealing Feedforward's True Identity. In *Proceedings of the SIGCHI Conference on Human Factors in Computing Systems (CHI '13)*. ACM, New York, NY, USA, 1931–1940. DOI: http://dx.doi.org/10.1145/2470654.2466255

65. Pierre Wellner. 1993. Interacting with Paper on the DigitalDesk. *Commun. ACM* 36, 7 (July 1993), 87–96. DOI: http://dx.doi.org/10.1145/159544.159630

66. Ding Xu, Ali Momeni, and Eric Brockmeyer. 2015. MagPad: A Near Surface Augmented Reading System for Physical Paper and Smartphone Coupling. In *Adjunct Proceedings of the 28th Annual ACM Symposium on User Interface Software & Technology (UIST '15 Adjunct)*. ACM, New York, NY, USA, 103–104. DOI: http://dx.doi.org/10.1145/2815585.2815740

67. Ynvisible. 2015. Printoo. (2015). http://www.printoo.pt/.

Does Practice Make Perfect? Learning to Deal with Latency in Direct-Touch Interaction

Elie Cattan[1], Amelie Rochet-Capellan[2], Pascal Perrier[2], Francois Berard[1]

Univ. Grenoble Alpes, LIG[1] & GIPSA-lab[2]
F-38000, Grenoble, France
first.last@imag.fr[1]

CNRS, LIG[1] & GIPSA-lab[2]
F-38000, Grenoble, France
first.last@gipsa-lab.grenoble-inp.fr[2]

ABSTRACT

Touch latency has been shown to deteriorate users' performances at levels as low as 25 ms, but this was tested only in short experimental sessions. Real life usage of touchscreens covers much longer periods. It provides training which could lead to reduce the impact of latency.

We investigate users' ability to compensate for touch latency with training. Two groups of participants were trained on a tracking task during ten different days over two weeks with either high or low latency. The gap of performances between the two groups, observed at the beginning of the experiment, was reduced by 54 % after training. Users can thus compensate for latency, at least partially. These results nuance the negative effects of touch latency reported in previous work. They suggest that long-term studies could provide better insights on users' behaviors when dealing with touch latency.

ACM Classification Keywords

H.5.2 User Interfaces: Input devices and strategies (e.g., mouse, touchscreen)

Author Keywords

latency; direct-touch; learning; training; tracking task; user performances

INTRODUCTION

Touch latency, the delay between a user's touch input and the resulting feedback, has been shown to decrease users' performances at levels as low as 25 ms [5, 15]. Current commercial touchscreens exhibit latencies in the range of 50 – 100 ms [8], at which users' performance is still strongly affected. Touch interaction is yet more and more present in our everyday life on devices such as smartphones, tablets or larger interactive surfaces. This recurrent use of touchscreens with substantial levels of latency suggests that people may become used to a digital world that answers to their actions with delay. It is unclear, however, if they also learn to *compensate* for latency over time. In other words, after a prolonged use of lagging touchscreens, are people able to execute tasks at the same performance level as without latency?

The motor control literature provides insights into perturbation compensation in the context of visuomotor recalibration experiences. The human brain was shown to quickly compensate for different kinds of perturbation such as visual prism distortion and virtual force fields [30]. People also compensate for delayed visual feedback [6, 10, 21], but it is unclear how long it takes for this compensation to be efficient. These studies also focused on indirect interaction with the hand hidden from the participant's view. This situation is notably different from the direct touch situation in which both the hand and the delayed feedback are visible.

For direct touch, the HCI literature has recently provided several studies on the impact of touch latency on perception or performance [1, 5, 9, 15, 16, 24, 25]. Participants of these studies, however, are only exposed to latency for a short duration (usually less than an hour). In real life, people use their devices every day, during longer periods of time, repeating some tasks several times a day. Real-life usage, thus, offers much more training and opportunity to develop compensatory strategies to counteract the latency of the device. The detrimental effects of touch latency could then be different after heavy exposure than at first exposure.

In this work, we investigate the following questions:

- Do users compensate for latency with practice? If they do, is the compensation partial or total?
- How long does that take?
- How long does that last?
- Is this compensation limited to a specific task or can it be transferred to similar tasks?

We focus on a tracking task. Two groups of participants are trained on the task during 10 sessions spread on different days over two weeks. The *test* group deals with a latency comparable to that of current commercial devices while the *control* group is trained with an almost unnoticeable latency. Our goal is to evaluate if the test group, whose performances should be negatively impacted by latency at the beginning of the experiment, could catch up with the performances of the control group with training.

In order to better understand changes induced by long-term exposure to latency, we also test for transfer of learning to

CHI 2017, May 6-11, 2017, Denver, CO, USA.

ACM ISBN 978-1-4503-4655-9/17/05 ...$15.00.
http://dx.doi.org/10.1145/3025453.3025585

another trajectory. If the compensation is not specific, it would diminish greatly the negative influence of touch latency since users would be able to deal with the delayed feedback on a second task without a new learning phase. We also test for long-term retention to see how long the compensation last.

The presentation of our work is divided as follow. First, we introduce previous work on the detrimental effect of latency as well as on touch latency compensation and transfer of learning. We then explain the design choices of our user study, which was meant to assess the effect of touch latency after several days of training. Finally, we present and discuss the results of the study and their contribution to the understanding of the touch latency effect on users' behaviors.

RELATED WORK

Detrimental effects of latency on interaction

The effects of latency on users' performances were first studied for mouse interaction. MacKenzie and Ware showed that latency decreases users' performances for pointing tasks and that the effect increases with task difficulty [20]. When latency increased from 8 ms to 225 ms, movement time increased by 63 % and error rate more than tripled. They also observed a floor effect since no difference in performance was found between 8 ms and 25 ms. This result was recently refined in a study by Friston et al.[11]. They evaluated users' performances at various levels of mouse latency on both Fitts' and Steering tasks, and showed that mouse latency begins to affect performances at around 16 ms. The impact of latency with a mouse has also been studied for tracking tasks by Pavlovych and Gutwin and then by Ivkovic et al. who showed that above 50ms, latency significantly impacts the precision of the tracking [14, 26].

In direct touch interaction, the temporal delay translates into a spatial gap between the user's finger and the feedback (a cursor, or a dragged object for example). This makes latency more perceivable than in indirect interaction. Ng et al. and Deber et al. measured the Just Noticeable Difference (JND) that users were able to perceive when dragging a square on a touchscreen. They showed that, on average, users can detect latencies down to 6 ms when dragging a square [25] and that they are capable to perceive a latency improvement of 8.3 ms [9]. However, this perception is strongly dependent from the task. Deber et al. showed that the perception threshold is higher for tapping than for dragging [9]. Ng et al. and Annett et al. showed that tasks implying more cognitive load lead to higher thresholds of perception [1, 24]. Focusing on the effect of latency on *users' performances* rather than on the *JND*. Jota et al. showed that users' target acquisition time in direct touch interaction is affected at latency levels as low as 25 ms [15]. Contrary to mouse interaction, no evidence of a floor effect was found. These results were extended to higher task difficulties by Cattan et al. [5].

While latency has been shown to affect performances at levels as low as 25 ms, commercial touchscreens still exhibit latency values in the range [50-100] ms [8]. Software solutions based on prediction have been proposed to compensate for latency [5, 13, 22]. Users, however, by getting used to endure the latency of their devices, may also learn to develop themselves compensatory strategy by changing their behaviour when facing latency. We did not find any elements to confirm or refute this hypothesis in the HCI literature since all aforementioned studies report brief exposures to high latencies, i.e. less than an hour in a single session. Here, we investigate participants' ability to compensate for latency through an experimental paradigm involving a longer training.

Adaptation to delayed feedback

Adaptation to delayed feedback has been studied for a long time in the motor control literature. We review studies which provide some elements of answer to our questions, and in particular "do people compensate for latency?" and "how long does it take?"

Touch interaction can be divided in tapping actions and dragging actions. Adaptation to tap latency has been studied thoroughly in the motor control literature. Temporal Order Judgment or Simultaneity Judgment tasks enable to compute the Point of Subjective Simultaneity (PSS) between a tap from the user and a visual feedback. The PSS is naturally shifted in negative delay value: the feedback feels simultaneous only when appearing with some delay, a phenomena known as the negative asynchrony [2, 16]. This might partially explain why the latency in tapping interaction is less perceivable than in dragging [9]. When continuously exposed to larger delays, users' PSS shifts even more negatively than the natural negative asynchrony, showing an adaptation to the delay [17, 31]. Keetels and Vroomen observed that the temporal recalibration remains small (between 9.4 ms and 16.1 ms) compared to the experiment delay (100 ms asynchrony) [17]. They make the hypothesis that the PSS shift might become bigger with longer exposures.

Latency for visual feedback in tap interaction is not an important bottleneck in HCI because the latency of current devices is already close to the 69 ms perception threshold [9]. Moreover, people are able to recalibrate their perception when exposed to delayed feedback. We thus chose to focus on touch dragging, where latency appears as a notable hindrance for touch interaction.

Latency compensation for continuous actions, like moving an object or a cursor, has been studied in the motor control literature but for indirect interaction using a mouse or a joystick. Cunningham et al. studied feedback delay compensation using a mouse, doing one dimensional motion [6]. Participants had to play a game, moving a plane horizontally on the screen to avoid obstacles coming up. Participants were tested in a single session experiment with a low delay first and then trained with 235 ms delay. After training, participants were roughly as good as with low delay. This indicates a quick and complete compensation from the subjects. Foulkes and Miall also uncovered latency compensation when tracking a target with a joystick [10]. Three groups of participants with different latency levels (0 ms, 200 ms and 300 ms) were trained over 2-3 days on an unpredictable tracking task. A clear improvement was seen on both delayed groups, "roughly proportional to the magnitude of the delay". However, they expressed that the time required to compensate for latency was "very slow". They extrapolated that it would take about 5h of exposure to latency for a complete compensation. Miall and Foulkes extended their work in a new experiment with a similar design but with five 1h sessions over 5 days. They showed that 5h exposure was still not sufficient to see complete compensation [21].

Results about the time needed to compensate for the latency seem contradictory. Rohde et al. argue that the unpredictability of the tracking task used by Foulkes and Miall may be a factor in latency compensation [29]. Rohde et al. experimented with a predictable vs. unpredictable indirect tracking task in a single session. They showed that only the group in the predictable condition shows compensation with a decrease of the tracking error with time. In a more recent work, Rohde and Ernst argue that adaptation might occur only when feedback delay is unequivocally identifiable "from other perturbations that can produce superficially similar effects, such as inertial changes, spatial offsets, etc..." [28].

Our experiment tests if the compensation, uncovered in the case of indirect interaction, also occurs in the case of direct touch. In indirect interaction, the user sees a unique feedback and the studied inconsistency is between the proprioceptive feedback of the hand and the visual feedback of the cursor which represents the hand. With direct touch, the user can see both the hand (which is not delayed) and the feedback (a dragged object for example) which suffers from the system latency. The inconsistency is thus between the expected behavior of the dragged object and its actual behavior. In this situation, learning to compensate for latency could happen differently.

Previous work also demonstrated that learning can take different durations depending on the nature of the task, we thus designed an experiment spread over several days in anticipation of a potential long-term compensation.

Transfer of learning

We also question if the compensation for latency developed for a given task is specific, or if it can be used on another task. In the motor control literature, this phenomenon is studied through the *transfer of learning* paradigm.

Learning a task leads to skill improvement and these modifications might have an impact when performing another task. When an improvement of performances is observed on the other task, a "transfer of learning" has occurred [27]. In this paper, we study if latency compensation, through training on a particular task, can transfer to another task with the same amount of latency.

De la Malla et al. studied the transfer of learning of delay compensation between different interception tasks [7]. They showed that the learning can transfer to tasks with little variations from the training task (like a starting position displacement) but does not seem to transfer across different interception tasks, even if they seem similar. For example, there was no evidence of transfer between a "target interception" task and a "passing through a moving gap" task. In this experimental design, participant's hand is hidden and users only see a cursor on the screen. Transfer could be different in the case of direct touch where the hand is visible.

This specificity of the transfer of learning was also observed in a recent HCI study and was used as a behavioral metric of the sensorimotor similarity between different interactions in sequential pointing [3].

EXPERIMENT: DEALING WITH TOUCH LATENCY BEFORE AND AFTER PRACTICE

Experiment design

We design our experiment to test these two hypothesis:

- People can learn to deal with latency on a tracking task and, through practice, their performances become as good as when performing the task without latency.
- This learning can then be transferred to a similar task.

Participants perform a tracking task during ten practice sessions spread over two weeks. Our approach is to compare the effect of the latency on the task at first exposure and after the training. We expect to see an improvement of performances with practice. We also need to distinguish in this improvement which part accounts for the acquisition of skills specific to the task (learn the trajectory and speed of the target or how to track smoothly) and which part accounts for the compensation of latency. Thus, we used a *control group* trained on the same task but with minimal latency (i.e. 25 ms, as low as our system permits). The group dealing with latency is called the *test group*. During the practice sessions, the improvement of performances of the control group can only be due to the development of tracking skills. By making a difference with the test group, it enables to assess the improvement due to the learning of latency compensation. The test group, having to deal with latency, should show lower performances in the first session. Comparison between groups at the last session also enables to evaluate if latency can be totally compensated (performances of the test group finally catch up those of the control group), only partially or not at all.

The experiment imposes a between subject design: participants have to be tested in the same condition for two weeks, and their training then prevent their participation in another condition. The between subject design introduces a difficulty: the performance difference between the test and control group could be partly explained by a difference in the average participant performance of each group. We thus control the assignation of each participant to the test or control group by assessing their performances on a tracking task that they perform before the first session. The individual performance is computed on ten trials of tracking with the high level of latency used in the main sessions. We call this the *balancing task*. It is executed at the very beginning of the experiment. This procedure enables us to balance both groups in term of participant's abilities to track a target and to deal with latency.

The test group is trained with 75 ms of latency which approximates the latency of many current commercial devices [8]. In an ideal case, the control group should be trained with no or negligible latency. But a system offering touch interaction on a large surface with negligible latency has never been achieved. We approximate the zero latency condition by replicating the system of Cattan et al. [5]. This system uses a low latency

(a) Graphical output during a trial. The red disc is controlled by the participant's finger, the white disc (partially covered) is the target, which follows the ellipse path counterclockwise. Here, the target is not totally covered by the red disc and the crescent moon is in front indicating that the participant is late.

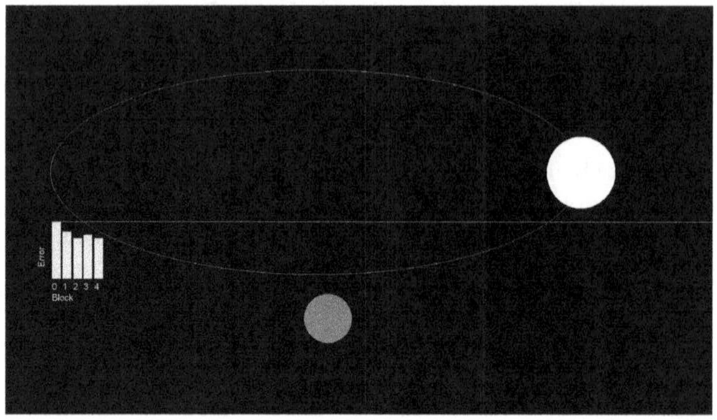

(b) At the end of a trial. The large white disc is the starting area for the next trial. A bar chart (displayed only between two trials) presents the results of the session's previous trials. The horizontal red line corresponding to the 0th trial is the averaged tracking error of the last session and sets a goal for participants.

Figure 1. The display at two different moments of a session

device coupled to a prediction technique (details are provided in the *Apparatus* section). We assume that the potential effect of the remaining latency in the control group is negligible compared to the effects of the 75 ms latency in the test group. For simplification purpose, in the remainder of this article we will refer to "with latency" for the test group, and to "without latency" for the control group.

To investigate if the compensation is task specific, the transfer of learning is assessed with a second tracking task, called the "transfer task". The transfer task follows a different path than the main task; it is performed on the first and on the last participant's session.

20 persons (5 females) participated in the study, all right-handed, with a mean age of 28 (range 23–37, sd = 3.74). Participants were mostly students coming from different labs/schools from our campus. Most of them own a smartphone and/or a tablet and use it every day.

Apparatus

Since we want to have a control group with participants performing the tracking task with a latency as small as possible, we need a touchscreen device that enables low latency. Literature introduces several examples of custom made devices with latency lower than current commercial devices [1, 5, 25]. The system used by Annett et al. and Ng et al. restricts the working area to a small surface of $24cm \times 16cm$ with a grayscale display only. We therefore choose to replicate the system used by Cattan et al. [5]. It implements touch detection on a regular screen using optical tracking. The system has a baseline touch latency of 25 ms that we regularly check using a predictive method [4]. Cattan et al. also used a linear prediction to virtually reduce the baseline latency of the system that we also replicate. This linear prediction is well suited for our tracking task since it implies no sudden change of speed. Cattan et al. extrapolate that with the prediction, the system is equivalent to a 9 ms or less latency system.

For the experiment, we use this 9 ms equivalent latency for the control group. For the test group, a 75 ms condition is simulated from the 25 ms baseline by adding 50 ms of idle time before dealing with received touch events.

Task

We choose a task difficulty that is high enough to allow some learning and performance improvement. We also choose a novel task so that all participants have no training on the task at the beginning of the experiment. In particular, we avoid the common "dragging an object to a target" task: most participants use touchscreens in their daily life, and thus they have various levels of training on this task with various levels of latency. A tracking task meets our requirements. In pilot tests, we observed that complex paths were not required to observe learning. Using a circle with constant speed, however, would not suit our objective. A constant speed translates to a constant spatial gap between the finger and the feedback. This is a special case which flaws the temporal nature of the latency and may, according to Rohde and Ernst [28], hide a learning effect. Therefore we choose an ellipse path with a target speed linked to the curvature by the 2/3 power law. According to Lacquaniti et al [19], this speed profile follows the natural motion of the hand.

Users control a red disc *object* (1.78cm radius) on the screen with the index finger. The screen displays the path followed by a white disc *target* (1.78cm radius). Displaying the path of the target ensures that the target motion is predictable which, according to Rohde et al. is a condition to have delay adaptation [29]. The target motion (position and speed) follows these equations:

$$\begin{cases} x(t) = 840 + 720 * cos(t) \\ y(t) = 640 + 270 * sin(t) \end{cases} \qquad \begin{cases} x'(t) = -720 * sin(t) \\ y'(t) = 270 * cos(t) \end{cases}$$

x and y are coordinates expressed in pixels for a screen size of 1920×1080 pixels, with a diagonal of 24 inches (pixel size=0.277mm), and with the origin at the bottom left. The time t is expressed in seconds. The target follows an ellipsoidal trajectory, making a complete cycle in 2π seconds. The ellipse is slightly off center to the top left to prevent that participants' right hand hits the bottom and right edges of the screen when performing the task.

Participants drag the object to a starting area at the rightmost point of the ellipse. The target area turns green to indicate that the object is inside. When the object is in the starting area for 0.5s, the target appears and begins its counterclockwise path on the ellipse. The participants' goal is to follow the target as close as possible. Since the target and the object have the same size, participant attempt to completely occlude the target with the object. A complete occlusion is difficult, and the target usually reveals itself as a white "crescent moon" under the red object, creating a clear visual feedback indicating if the participant is late (moon in front) or early (moon behind). The display during a trial is illustrated on Figure 1a.

During a *trial*, the target makes three laps. Error is not measured during the first lap to let the participant catch up with the target and get back the rhythm of the motion. During the two following laps, the tracking error is sampled at 120Hz: it is the distance between the disc center and the target center. A trial lasts around 20s ($3 \times 2\pi$). When the rightmost point of the ellipse is crossed at the end of the third lap, the trial ends. The trial error is recorded as the average tracking error over the two final laps. The system moves the object back to a fixed position at the bottom left of the screen, ready for the next trial.

We allow participants to follow their progress by displaying their trial error at the end of each trial, as illustrated on Figure 1b. The display is a bar chart where the first bar represents the participant's trial error averaged across the trials in his previous session. In the specific case of the first session, the first bar just indicates the first trial error. The first bar has always the same size on the different sessions and is emphasized by a horizontal red line. The following bars represent the error of the current session's trials. The size of each bar is computed relatively to the first one. Participants implicitly attempt to not exceed the red line: this means that they improved their performance compared to the previous session. The bar chart disappears as soon as the object is dragged to the starting area to begin the next trial.

We also define a second trajectory to study the transfer of learning. The study by De La Malla et al. indicated that transfer only occurs when tasks are very similar [7]. A task too dissimilar to the ellipse would thus certainly lead to a null transfer which would not be useful for interpretation. We prefer a very close task to see what amount of transfer can be observed in favorable transfer conditions. We choose the eight-shaped curve defined by the following equations:

$$\begin{cases} x(t) = 840 + 720 * cos(t) \\ y(t) = 640 + 405 * sin(2t)/2 \end{cases} \qquad \begin{cases} x'(t) = -720 * sin(t) \\ y'(t) = 405 * cos(2t) \end{cases}$$

The eight shape is interesting because the right side is very similar to the right side of the ellipse, the left side of the eight is similar to the ellipse but with the target going clockwise instead of counterclockwise. And finally, the center part is a diagonal trajectory in both directions that is not included in the ellipse. We thus can presume that the transfer of learning from the ellipse to the eight could be different on these different parts. The display during a trial for the transfer study is illustrated on Figure 2.

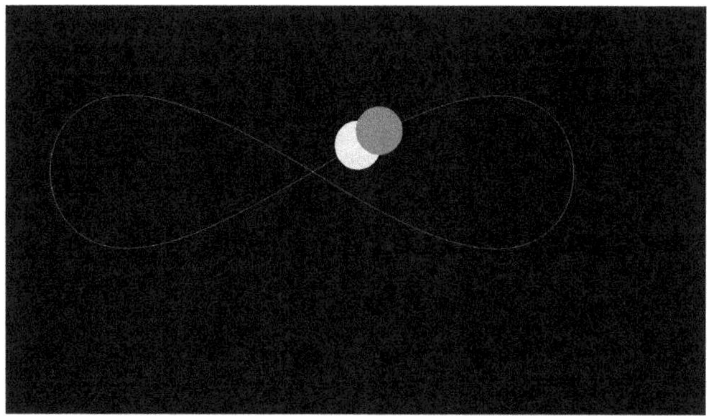

Figure 2. Graphical output during a trial of the transfer task.

Temporal distribution of training sessions

Sleeping has been shown to be an important factor in the improvement of motor skill performances [32]. We thus choose to spread our learning sessions on different days with the goal of observing clear learning effects. Gerbier et al. showed that an expanding schedule of repetition could optimize the retention [12] however we prefer to keep a rather flexible timetable for participants' convenience.

We choose to spread the complete training on the ellipsoidal tracking on ten sessions of sixty trials each. The session length is calibrated to last around half an hour. Pilot study showed that longer sessions may introduce a strong effect of fatigue. A semi-regular lapse of time between sessions is imposed: all sessions are done on different days (i.e. with at least a night of sleep between two sessions), two sessions cannot be separated by more than three days and the whole ten sessions have to fit within three weeks. In addition, participants perform their sessions around the same hour of the day. Eventually, due to schedule constraints, two participants of the test group did two of their ten sessions on the same day (separated by several hours). We do not observe any strong effect of the session distributions: the learning curves are similar between participants doing three sessions per week every other day and participants coming every day of the week (except week-ends).

During sessions, short pauses are *allowed* between each trial but longer 30s pauses are *imposed* every ten trials to prevent participants to rush through and be jaded for the last trials.

Our secondary objective is to study the potential transfer of learning between the ellipsoidal tracking and the eight-shape tracking. For this purpose, we measure the performance of participants on the eight-shape at the beginning of the first session and at the end of the last session. This is the *transfer task*. The distribution of sessions is summarized on Figure 3.

Measurement and analyzes

During the training part, 20 participants performed 10 sessions of 60 trials, totaling 12000 trials. From these, 34 trials (0.3 %)

Session	1			2	...	9	10	
Task	bal.	trans.	Training					trans.
Ctrl	10	10	60	60	...	60	60	10
Test	10	10	60	60	...	60	60	10

Figure 3. Summary of the temporal distribution of sessions depending on the group: control (Ctrl) or Test. "bal." is short for "balancing task" and "trans." for "transfer task". Numbers indicate the number of trials in each session. Grey cells are trials with latency, white cells are trials without latency. Sessions 2 to 9 are identical.

were removed as outliers due to optical tracking problems (the optical marker was somehow hidden during the trial).

We use the tracking error (i.e. the distance between the center of the dragged object and the center of the target) as the performance metric. We define *error*, the dependent variable of the experiment, as the average error per sample over all trials of a participant's session. *error* is used to assess improvement from training, but also for balancing the performances of the control and test groups, and for measuring the transfer of learning. In the case of the 10 trials, used to measure the transfer of learning in the first and last session, the 5 first trials are discarded because the abrupt switch from ellipse to eight shape results in very high *error*. We thus measure the transfer of learning after a quick (less than 2 min.) adaptation to the new shape.

We study the effect of two factors on *error*:

- SESSION is within-subject, with levels 1 to 10. In the specific case of the transfer of learning study, SESSION can only take two values, 1 and 10.
- GROUP is between-subject, with levels *control* and *test*.

RESULTS

Balancing task

Averaged *error* for the control group ($4.57mm \pm 0.63$) and the test group ($4.58mm \pm 0.70$) on the balancing task are very similar, indicating a good balance of user performance between the two groups. An unpaired t-test reveals a high probability of the NULL hypothesis ($t(18) = -0.04, p > .96$).

Training along sessions

error curves along sessions, averaged over groups, are presented in Figure 4.

There is a larger variability between participants in the test group than in the control group. It can be seen on Figure 4 with larger confidence intervals for the test group. Both groups showed approximately the same standard deviation between participants on the balancing task (0.63 vs. 0.70), hence this larger variability in the test group during the training demonstrates that people react differently when facing latency. Some of them have their performances badly impacted while others manage to compensate more quickly. On the contrary, in the control group, the participants followed more or less the same learning curve.

On the first session, performances are lower in the test group than in the control group, showing the negative influence of latency. There is a 18 % loss in performances due to latency

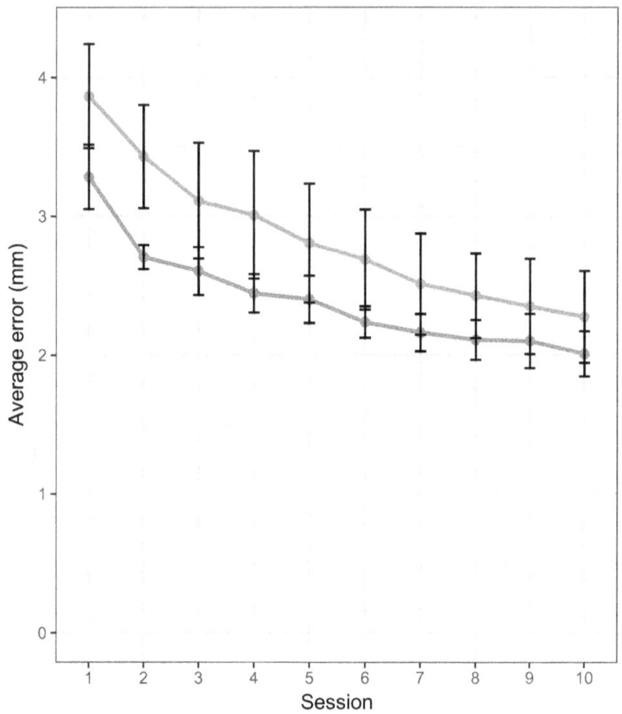

Figure 4. Tracking error in both control (red) and test (blue) groups averaged over the participants for each session.

(from 3.28mm to 3.86mm, a 0.58mm loss). While performance loss on target acquisition time has been well studied, this first result shows that latency also greatly impacts participants' tracking abilities.

On the ten practice sessions, a two-way ANOVA reveals a strong global effect of SESSION ($F_{9,162} = 125, p < .001$). We can see on Figure 4 that this effect is due to a continuous decrease of the tracking error with practice, showing the learning of new skills. All participants improve their performances after 10 training sessions: tracking error is significantly lower on the last session compared to the first session (paired t-test, $t(19) = 16, p < .001$). The intra session standard deviation (variation on the sixty trials of a single session) globally decreases from 0.51mm to 0.25mm showing that participants also improve their regularity through sessions. Participants do not have the same learning speed. Some of them present stabilized performances on the last three sessions whereas others are still making progress on the last session. Globally, 50 % of the decrease of *error* happens between the first and the third session. This is coherent with many previously observed learning curves, indicating that improvement becomes more difficult with time.

The ANOVA also uncovers an effect of GROUP on *error* ($F_{1,18} = 7.2, p = .015$). The test group, dealing with latency, has globally lower performances over the ten sessions. But the ANOVA reveals an interaction between GROUP and SESSION ($F_{9,162} = 3.7, p < .001$). We compare the performance difference between groups before and after the training. The 0.58mm performance loss due to latency, measured on the first day, decreases to 0.26mm on the last day. This is a 54 %

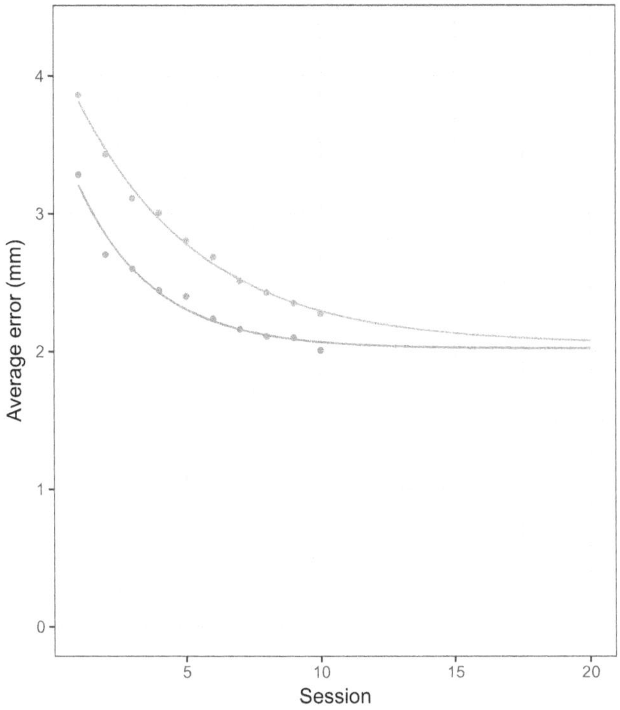

Figure 5. Extrapolation of the learning data for the control (red) and the test (blue) group with exponential models.

reduction. The negative influence of latency is thus more than halved in ten practice sessions. The test group is catching up progressively with the control group. As the only difference between groups is the presence of more latency in the test group, it shows that in addition to tracking skills, participants in the test group also develop specific mechanisms that enable them to compensate for latency.

We also run two post-hoc unpaired t-tests (with Bonferroni correction) on the first and last session which reveal a significant difference between the two groups in the first session ($t(18) = -2.98, p = .016$) but not in the last session ($t(18) = -1.64, p > 0.2$). These tests have to be interpreted cautiously though. The continuity of the curves shape in Figure 4 suggest that the difference in the last session is not random.

These results show that people can compensate at least partially for a delayed feedback on the tracking task. The strong negative influence of latency that is usually observed at initial exposure may not be as problematic as previously thought when considering long term exposure.

Curve extrapolation

The curves in Figure 4 did not reach a plateau. This suggests that more progress could be expected if participants had trained on more sessions. To get an idea of the final performances gap between the two groups, we experimented with curve extrapolations. Learning curves are known to be described by power or exponential laws [23]. After trying various models, we obtained a good fit with an exponential model.

Figure 5 shows the result of the exponential fit on the learning curves of both groups. The fit is done by a least square minimization of the error with the following equation (with three degrees of freedom): $y = Ae^{-Bx} + C$. The fit is very good in both conditions with $R^2 = 0.97$ for the control group and $R^2 = 0.99$ for the test group. With the models, the gap of performances between the groups continues to reduce after the tenth session until it reaches an asymptotic level. The convergence levels are 2.02mm and 2.05mm for the control and test groups, respectively. This extrapolation indicates that people dealing with latency are able, through practice, to almost entirely compensate for 75 ms of latency for a tracking task.

However, we tested fitting our model on a smaller number of sessions and we observed that the asymptotes of both groups systematically lower as we add further sessions in the fits. This indicates that despite the good fit, the exponential model may converge too quickly compared to the real learning curves. In other words, the model certainly still overestimates the actual asymptotes, even with 10 points for each group.

Transfer task

The results for the transfer task are illustrated on Figure 6.

We analyze *error* on the global eight-shaped trajectory in sessions 1 and 10 (Figure 6, "Global"). An ANOVA shows a strong effect of GROUP ($F_{1,18} = 25, p < .001$) meaning that the test group, dealing with latency, has a bigger *error*. It also shows a strong effect of SESSION ($F_{1,18} = 123, p < .001$) meaning that participants better perform the tracking task on the eight shape in the last session compared to the first.

In the control group, the averaged tracking error on the eight shape is reduced from 4.03mm on the first day to 2.88mm after the training on the ellipse. This 28 % reduction of the error is too large to be attributed only to the training offered by the 10 trials of the first session: the two sessions were separated by at least 10 days without training. Furthermore, the training between sessions 1 and 2 of the ellipse only leads to a 17.6 % improvement while offering six times more trials. Hence, this amplitude of improvement reveals a transfer of learning between the two tasks. The transfer appears as incomplete because the 28 % reduction is smaller than the 39 % error reduction that occurred on the ellipse (from 3.28mm to 2.01mm).

The ANOVA also uncovers an interaction between GROUP and SESSION ($F_{1,18} = 6.9, p = .017$) which indicates that the test group had more transfer than the control group. This indicates that not only the tracking skills are transferred, but also the skills which enable to compensate for the latency.

The error difference between groups, due to the latency, is 1.42mm on the first session (4.03mm and 5.45mm). It is larger than with the ellipse because the velocity profile on the eight shape is more variable and has higher peaks, which makes latency harder to tackle. The difference is reduced to 0.72mm (2.88mm and 3.60mm) in the last session. This is a 49 % reduction of the gap of performances between the two groups, similar to the 54 % found for the ellipse. This confirms that

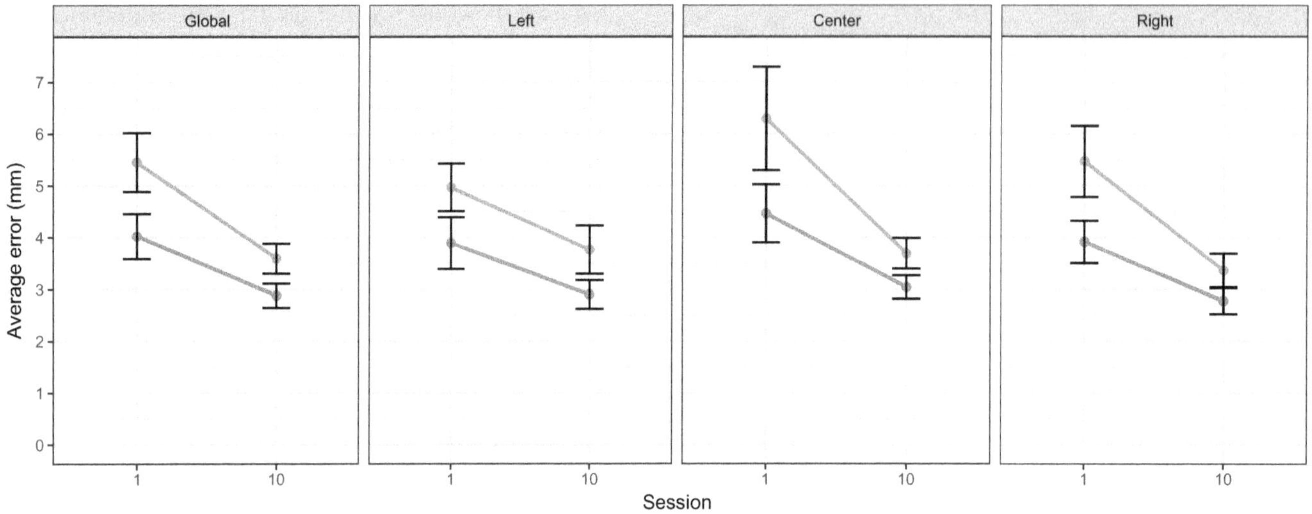

Figure 6. Transfer or learning. Tracking error in both control (red) and test (blue) groups averaged over the participants for the transfer task. The "Global" graph gives the transfer for the whole shape while the next graphs give the detailed transfer for different sections of the eight shape.

the ability to compensate for latency can transfer between the two tasks.

We tested our hypothesis that the transfer could be different on different sections of the eight shape. We cut the eight into three parts ($x < 600$, $600 < x < 1080$, $1080 < x$) and we included the factor EIGHT_PART with levels LEFT, CENTER and RIGHT. Figure 6, "Left", "Center" and "Right" shows the tracking error on the three parts for both groups in session 1 and 10.

In session 1, the tracking error is larger in the center part for both groups since in this area, the target is at its highest speed, making it harder to follow. In addition, participants of the test group had worse results on the right part compared to the left part: the position of the hand tends to hide the delayed feedback on the right part which makes the tracking more difficult.

The transfer of learning appeared to be strong for both groups in the center part, which is surprising since the trajectory is very different from the ellipse in this section. However, the amplitude of the tangential velocity is very similar. The ability to transfer tracking skills may thus be related to the velocity in a larger part than to the shape of the trajectory.

A triple interaction between GROUP, SESSION and EIGHT_PART indicates that the difference of transfer between the two groups is not the same for each eight part ($F_{2,36} = 3.5, p = .04$). The strong negative impact of latency in the test group on the center and right parts creates a lot of room for improvement, which may explain a bigger transfer in the test group than in the control group in these sections. On the center, the velocity of the target has also a bell-shaped profile, which is similar to the ellipse which certainly favors the transfer. On the contrary, on the left part, latency compensation does not seem to transfer: there is the same amount of transfer in both groups. This can be explained by the combination of two elements: a trajectory in an opposite direction compared to the ellipse and a velocity which cannot be found in the ellipse velocity profile.

These results indicate that the transfer of latency compensation for a tracking task can depend on both the trajectory shape but also the velocity profile of the target.

POST-EXPERIMENT: LEARNING RETENTION

Hypothesis and design

Our participants are able to greatly improve their performances after 10 training sessions on the course of 3 weeks. But would this persist over time? We ask to available participants of our study to come back between 7 and 9 weeks after their last training session. 12 participants (6 control - 6 test) are available for this post-experiment test. We check that, during this time, none of them had any exposure to tracking tasks similar to our experimental task. The task is equivalent to half a session of training (i.e. 30 trials). It is performed by participants in the same condition as in the training experiment.

On the control group, we expect participants' performances to drop a little compared to the tenth session due to the lack of practice. A similar drop is expected on the test group for the same reason. However, since latency is usually considered as a perturbation, our hypothesis is that the latency compensation would only be temporary. We expect participants of the test group to lose their ability to compensate for latency, and thus to observe a larger drop of performances than in the control group.

Since we need to compare the between-subject groups, we also verify that the two sub-groups of 6 participants are still balanced. The average errors of the two sub-groups are very close: 4.36 for the control group and 4.28 for the test group, the difference is not significant as revealed by an unpaired t-test ($t(10) = 0.3, p > .77$).

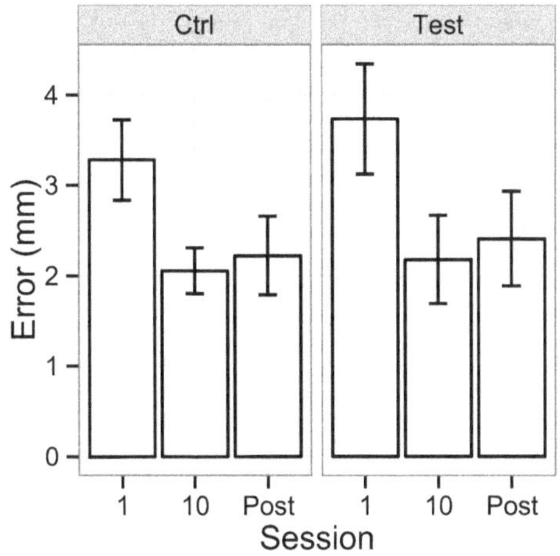

Figure 7. Error in sessions 1, 10 and in the Post-test for the Control (Ctrl) and Test groups.

Results

Since participants did not practice the task for at least seven weeks, the post session reveals a notable improvement during the session. We consider the first twenty trials to be a quick (less than 10min) re-familiarization with the task and we measure the tracking error on the ten last trials. Results are illustrated on Figure 7. An ANOVA is run to evaluate the effect of SESSION (10th vs. post-test) and GROUP on the error.

The tracking error on the post-session is significantly above the error level of the tenth session ($F_{1,10} = 6.39, p = .03$), but the loss of precision is minimal: +0.2mm. In particular, this is a small step back compared to the improvement achieved in the training ($-1.39mm$). There is no significant effect of GROUP ($F_{1,10} = 0.46, p > .5$) nor interaction between GROUP and SESSION ($F_{1,10} = 0.16, p > .69$). This means that participants are able, in less than 10 minutes, to reach a similar level of performances to that of their tenth training session. In addition, the drop of performance between the tenth and the post sessions is found similar in the two groups.

Our hypothesis of the temporary learning of latency compensation is thus invalidated: latency compensation allowed participant of the test group to acquire a sustainable amelioration of their baseline performance on the tracking task.

In the next section, we discuss the consequences of the results of the experiment and the post-experiment.

DISCUSSION

Latency compensation through practice

Considering only the control group, the results of the study show that, with practice, participants have learned skills related to tracking a target on a touchscreen. The tracking on the eight shape shows that these skills are not specific to the ellipse trajectory but are more general and can transfer to another trajectory with a different velocity profile.

The test group shows bigger improvements during the training, catching up progressively with the control group. This means that, in addition to skills related to tracking, participants of the test group also developed mechanisms specific to the presence of latency in order to compensate for it.

Different velocity profile on the ellipse and on the eight shape lead to different spatial gaps between the finger and the disc when dealing with latency. Relying only on visual feedback would give only spatial indications and thus would not lead to any transfer of latency compensation between the ellipse and the eight. The substantial transfer to the eight trajectory that we observed in the test group thus indicates that other mechanisms must have been developed by participants in the test group to integrate the temporal nature of the delay and to manage to apply them to another trajectory.

Latency seen as an inherent feature of touchscreens

Our experiment proved that users can learn to compensate for latency with practice. According to Krakauer, there are two different learning processes: "adaptation", and "skill learning" [18].

Adaptation is a modification of brain mechanisms in order to perform action accurately in the presence of a sensorial or mechanical perturbation. For example, it is well known that people adapt quickly their actions when facing a displacement of their field of view induced by prismatic glasses: with training, their performance in reaching or pointing tasks quickly attains pre-perturbation levels [30]. When the perturbation is removed, the observation of a negative after-effect shows that the user continues to behave as if the perturbation was still there. This after-effect is taken as an evidence of an adaptation: some visuomotor recalibration occurred in the users' brain.

"Skill learning" is defined as a shift in the speed-accuracy trade-off for a task when no systematic perturbation is present. In contrast to adaptation, which is the adjustment to a perturbation in order to get back to the pre-perturbation performances baseline, skill learning is the improvement of this baseline. Skill learning requires more time than adaptation. A more complete review of the learning processes can be found in Krakauer et al. [18].

Since touch interaction has been designed to mimic actions of the physical world, which does not suffer from latency, we assumed that a delay on a touchscreen device would be seen as a perturbation to which people could adapt. Participants indeed developed mechanisms to compensate for latency on our tracking task and their performances came close to those of a group trained with almost no latency. Adaptation, however, as defined in the motor control field, is certainly not the correct term to describe this progress. The learning retention experiment showed that the mechanisms developed to compensate for latency were still present after seven weeks without practice. This demonstrates that these mechanisms are more related to skill learning, i.e. the improvement of a baseline performance using a device with latency.

Considering the everyday use of touchscreens, when users deal with a laggy device, they may not see it as a perturbation, but rather as a tool that takes time to be accustomed with. In the motor control studies where the hand was not visible or the interaction indirect [6, 7, 10, 21], adaptation occurred. In the case of touch latency, the interaction is direct and it is as if the hand manipulates a (lagging) tool. Hence, observing skill learning is not surprising.

One way to consider latency is as an inherent feature of a touchscreen device. For an analogy, someone may learn to drive an old car with no power steering. This person may take more time to learn how to turn the steering wheel correctly compared to someone learning on a power steering car, but this will not be seen as a perturbation. And this person should be able to reach the same driving performance as the one who learned with power steering.

This view of latency is strengthened by the time required by the gap of performances to decrease. As stated by Krakauer, "Skill learning takes much longer than adaptation" [18]. In our study, the difference between the two groups did not disappear after one or two sessions but decreased progressively for the whole ten sessions. This may also explain some participants' comments found in Ng et al. [25]: they report that users can be unaware of latency as long as the comparison is not explicit. But once participants have tried a very low latency device ($\approx$1 ms), they find the latency of current devices "completely unacceptable". Before having experienced a better device, users may not have considered latency as a perturbation, but rather as an inherent feature of the touchscreen device.

Impact of touch latency on users performances

The development of new skills through 10 practice sessions resulted in the reduction of 54 % of the negative impact of latency on the tracking task. Furthermore, there is retention of these skills, even after more than seven weeks without training. Hence, our study indicates that the impact of touch latency on users' performances is less severe than what could be expected from previous work.

We chose an experimental task with a *predictable* trajectory, and a task in which latency cannot be confused with other perturbations (spatial or inertial). The goal was to favor learning [29, 28]. More common HCI tasks will have to be studied to assess the generality of our results. Target acquisition tasks include motions that are strongly erratic during the adjustment phase [5], hence compensating for latency on such motion should be more difficult than for the smooth trajectory used in our work.

The transfer of learning between different levels of latency would be another interesting investigation since users interact with many devices and applications that exhibit different levels of latency. Such study could tell if the skills developed to compensate for the latency in one condition could propagate easily to different activities, or if new learning phases would be necessary. A lack of transfer between different levels of latency would argue for systems and applications with identical latency levels.

Finally, although this work indicates that the impact of latency may be less harmful than previously thought, this should not restrain the development of low latency devices: learning to compensate for latency takes a lot of time, and may only transfer to very similar tasks. More importantly, compensating for latency may have a cost. Users dealing with latency may be able to reach performances similar as with no latency but this might imply more concentration and cognitive load and induce fatigue. These effects should also be objectively evaluated in future studies.

CONCLUSION

We presented a study aimed at getting a better insight on the negative effects of touch latency on users' performances. We demonstrated that users can learn new skills that enable them to compensate substantially for the negative influence of latency on a tracking task. The performance loss due to latency was more than halved with 10 half-hour training sessions. The retention of this skill was good more than seven weeks after the last training session. These results nuance the results of previous studies where the effect of latency was only tested on short sessions. Latency should still be considered as a major hindrance since learning to compensate for latency requires a sizable effort, it may not occur or transfer to every types of tasks, and it may have a high cognitive cost. All these will have to be studied in further experiments.

ACKNOWLEDGEMENT

This work has been partially supported by the LabEx PERSYVAL-Lab (ANR-11-LABX-0025-01).

REFERENCES

1. Michelle Annett, Albert Ng, Paul Dietz, Walter F. Bischof, and Anoop Gupta. 2014. How Low Should We Go?: Understanding the Perception of Latency While Inking. In *Proceedings of Graphics Interface (GI)*.
2. Gisa Aschersleben. 2002. Temporal control of movements in sensorimotor synchronization. *Brain and cognition* 48, 1 (2002), 66–79.
3. François Bérard and Amélie Rochet-Capellan. 2015. The Transfer of Learning as HCI Similarity: Towards an Objective Assessment of the Sensory-Motor Basis of Naturalness. In *Proceedings of the 33rd Annual ACM Conference on Human Factors in Computing Systems*. ACM, 1315–1324.
4. Elie Cattan, Amélie Rochet-Capellan, and François Bérard. 2015a. A Predictive Approach for an End-to-End Touch-Latency Measurement. In *Proceedings of the 2015 International Conference on Interactive Tabletops & Surfaces*. ACM, 215–218.
5. Elie Cattan, Amélie Rochet-Capellan, Pascal Perrier, and François Bérard. 2015b. Reducing Latency with a Continuous Prediction: Effects on Users' Performance in Direct-Touch Target Acquisitions. In *Proceedings of the 2015 International Conference on Interactive Tabletops & Surfaces*. ACM, 205–214.
6. Douglas W Cunningham, Vincent A Billock, and Brian H Tsou. 2001. Sensorimotor adaptation to violations of temporal contiguity. *Psychological Science* 12, 6 (2001), 532–535.

7. Cristina de la Malla, Joan López-Moliner, and Eli Brenner. 2014. Dealing with delays does not transfer across sensorimotor tasks. *Journal of vision* 14, 12 (2014), 8.
8. Jonathan Deber, Bruno Araujo, Ricardo Jota, Clifton Forlines, Darren Leigh, Steven Sanders, and Daniel Wigdor. 2016. Hammer Time!: A Low-Cost, High Precision, High Accuracy Tool to Measure the Latency of Touchscreen Devices. In *Proceedings of the 2016 CHI Conference on Human Factors in Computing Systems*. ACM, 2857–2868.
9. Jonathan Deber, Ricardo Jota, Clifton Forlines, and Daniel Wigdor. 2015. How Much Faster is Fast Enough?: User Perception of Latency & Latency Improvements in Direct and Indirect Touch. In *Proceedings of ACM CHI*.
10. Alexander J McC Foulkes and R Chris Miall. 2000. Adaptation to visual feedback delays in a human manual tracking task. *Experimental Brain Research* 131, 1 (2000), 101–110.
11. Sebastian Friston, Per Karlstrom, and Anthony Steed. 2014. The Effects of Low Latency on Pointing and Steering Tasks. (2014).
12. Emilie Gerbier, Thomas C Toppino, and Olivier Koenig. 2015. Optimising retention through multiple study opportunities over days: The benefit of an expanding schedule of repetitions. *Memory* 23, 6 (2015), 943–954.
13. Niels Henze, Markus Funk, and Alireza Sahami Shirazi. 2016. Software-reduced touchscreen latency. In *Proceedings of the 18th International Conference on Human-Computer Interaction with Mobile Devices and Services*. ACM, 434–441.
14. Zenja Ivkovic, Ian Stavness, Carl Gutwin, and Steven Sutcliffe. 2015. Quantifying and mitigating the negative effects of local latencies on aiming in 3d shooter games. In *Proceedings of the 33rd Annual ACM Conference on Human Factors in Computing Systems*. ACM, 135–144.
15. Ricardo Jota, Albert Ng Ng, Paul Dietz, and Daniel Wigdor. 2013. How Fast is Fast Enough? A Study of the Effects of Latency in Direct-Touch Pointing Tasks. In *ACM CHI*. ACM.
16. Topi Kaaresoja, Stephen Brewster, and Vuokko Lantz. 2014. Towards the temporally perfect virtual button: touch-feedback simultaneity and perceived quality in mobile touchscreen press interactions. *ACM Transactions on Applied Perception (TAP)* 11, 2 (2014), 9.
17. Mirjam Keetels and Jean Vroomen. 2008. Temporal recalibration to tactile–visual asynchronous stimuli. *Neuroscience letters* 430, 2 (2008), 130–134.
18. John W Krakauer and Pietro Mazzoni. 2011. Human sensorimotor learning: adaptation, skill, and beyond. *Current opinion in neurobiology* 21, 4 (2011), 636–644.
19. Francesco Lacquaniti, Carlo Terzuolo, and Paolo Viviani. 1983. The law relating the kinematic and figural aspects of drawing movements. *Acta psychologica* 54, 1 (1983), 115–130.
20. I Scott MacKenzie and Colin Ware. 1993. Lag as a determinant of human performance in interactive systems. In *Proceedings of ACM CHI*. 488–493.
21. RC Miall and JK Jackson. 2006. Adaptation to visual feedback delays in manual tracking: evidence against the Smith Predictor model of human visually guided action. *Experimental Brain Research* 172, 1 (2006), 77–84.
22. Mathieu Nancel, Daniel Vogel, Bruno De Araujo, Ricardo Jota, and Géry Casiez. 2016. Next-Point Prediction Metrics for Perceived Spatial Errors. In *Proceedings of the 29th Annual Symposium on User Interface Software and Technology*. ACM, 271–285.
23. Allen Newell and Paul S Rosenbloom. 1981. Mechanisms of skill acquisition and the law of practice. *Cognitive skills and their acquisition* 1 (1981), 1–55.
24. Albert Ng, Michelle Annett, Paul Dietz, Anoop Gupta, and Walter F. Bischof. 2014. In the Blink of an Eye: Investigating Latency Perception During Stylus Interaction. In *ACM CHI*. ACM, 1103–1112.
25. Albert Ng, Julian Lepinski, Daniel Wigdor, Steven Sanders, and Paul Dietz. 2012. Designing for low-latency direct-touch input. In *Proceedings of ACM UIST*. ACM, 453–464.
26. Andriy Pavlovych and Carl Gutwin. 2012. Assessing target acquisition and tracking performance for complex moving targets in the presence of latency and jitter. In *Proceedings of the 2012 Graphics Interace Conference*. Canadian Information Processing Society, 109–116.
27. David N Perkins, Gavriel Salomon, and others. 1992. Transfer of learning. *International encyclopedia of education* 2 (1992), 6452–6457.
28. Marieke Rohde and Marc O Ernst. 2016. Time, agency, and sensory feedback delays during action. *Current Opinion in Behavioral Sciences* 8 (2016), 193–199.
29. Marieke Rohde, Loes CJ van Dam, and Marc O Ernst. 2014. Predictability is necessary for closed-loop visual feedback delay adaptation. *Journal of vision* 14, 3 (2014), 4.
30. Reza Shadmehr, Maurice A Smith, and John W Krakauer. 2010. Error correction, sensory prediction, and adaptation in motor control. *Annual review of neuroscience* 33 (2010), 89–108.
31. Chess Stetson, Xu Cui, P Read Montague, and David M Eagleman. 2006. Motor-sensory recalibration leads to an illusory reversal of action and sensation. *Neuron* 51, 5 (2006), 651–659.
32. Matthew P Walker, Tiffany Brakefield, Alexandra Morgan, J Allan Hobson, and Robert Stickgold. 2002. Practice with sleep makes perfect: sleep-dependent motor skill learning. *Neuron* 35, 1 (2002), 205–211.

MarkPad: Augmenting Touchpads for Command Selection

Bruno Fruchard[1,2] **Eric Lecolinet**[1] **Olivier Chapuis**[2]

[1]LTCI, CNRS, Telecom ParisTech, Université Paris-Saclay F-75013 Paris, France

[2]LRI, Univ. Paris-Sud, CNRS, Inria, Université Paris-Saclay F-91405 Orsay, France

Figure 1: Tactile or visual marks on the touchpad help performing gestures: (Left) Dense configuration of tactile marks, (Middle) Light configuration with marks only on the borders, (Right) Example of a menu in novice mode. This menu and the selected shortcut on its right side correspond to the red area and the red gesture line in the middle picture.

ABSTRACT

We present MarkPad, a novel interaction technique taking advantage of the touchpad. MarkPad allows creating a large number of size-dependent gestural shortcuts that can be spatially organized as desired by the user. It relies on the idea of using visual or tactile marks on the touchpad or a combination of them. Gestures start from a mark on the border and end on another mark anywhere. MarkPad does not conflict with standard interactions and provides a novice mode that acts as a rehearsal of the expert mode. A first study showed that an accuracy of 95% could be achieved for a dense configuration of tactile and/or visual marks allowing many gestures. Performance was 5% lower in a second study where the marks were only on the borders. A last study showed that borders are rarely used, even when the users are unaware of the technique. Finally, we present a working prototype and briefly report on how it was used by two users for a few months.

Author Keywords

Gestural interaction; bezel gestures; tactile feedback; spatial memory; touchpad; user-defined gestures; Marking menus.

ACM Classification Keywords

H.5.2. Information Interfaces and Presentation (e.g. HCI): User Interfaces – Input devices and strategies

http://dx.doi.org/10.1145/3025453.3025486

INTRODUCTION

Users often perform the same actions when interacting with a computing device, such as executing favorite application commands and opening favorite applications, files or Web pages. These actions typically require using different interaction techniques such as menus (for commands), permanent or hidden toolbars (for opening applications) or favorite bars (for opening Web pages). Beside menus, most of these techniques only rely on recognition and do not provide an expert mode. Menus provide hotkeys but "simple" hotkeys, typically those using the first letter of the associated command, are in limited number and most of them are already used. Creating new hotkeys thus tend to require complex key modifier combinations. Marking and Bezel menus [21, 27] are another solution but they only support a limited number of shortcuts at a menu level.

In this paper, we propose a new technique called *MarkPad* (Figure 1) which takes advantage of the touchpad of laptop computers to perform any type of frequent action. MarkPad supports a large number of commands (680 in our experiment) and offers much flexibility for organizing them. It provides an homogeneous way of performing all these different actions and allows grouping them in a way that is meaningful for the user, whatever their type. For instance, one could gather all actions (applications, commands, scripts, Web pages, etc.) related to certain task, activity or project in a single group acting as a kind of conceptual area.

MarkPad both provides a novice and an expert mode and relies on simple gestural shortcuts that are identical in both modes. Its design extends Marking and Bezel menus [21, 27] by taking the size of the gestures into account, which considerably increases the number of possible gestures. In order to achieve sufficient performance, MarkPad relies on augmenting the touchpad by adding *visual* or *tactile* marks on it (Figure 1). This simple solution, which only requires cheap materials (e.g. paper stickers or adhesive tape) makes it possible to use the technique at virtually no cost on current devices.

MarkPad gestures start from the border of the touchpad to avoid conflict with standard interactions. More precisely, they start from user-defined areas (materialized by tactile or visual marks) that correspond to menus. Menu items are activated by performing a gesture starting from one of these areas and ending in another area located where the user wants on the touchpad (Figure 1). Each menu can contain a large number of items (34 in our experiment), which can be laid out in a way that is meaningful to the user by using spatial arrangements that highlight semantic relationships. As this design leverages spatial memory, it should also favor memorization [15, 35, 41]. Moreover, it avoids forcing users to arbitrarily dispatch related items in different menus because of their limited capacity, as with Marking and Bezel menus. Groupings relying on user-defined semantics, not only make it easier to discover or find again items [32] but should also improve learning and memorization [4, 10, 47].

After presenting the related work and describing the technique, we report on two lab studies showing that 95% accuracy can be obtained for a dense configuration of 680 gestural shortcuts and that marks can be removed at the center of the touchpad at the price of slightly lower performance (about 90% accuracy for the same challenging configuration). In a last study, we show that users rarely use the borders of the touchpad, even when they are unaware of the proposed interaction technique, and that the gestures we propose are likely less prone to involuntary activations than directional gestures. Finally, we present a working prototype and briefly report on how it was used by two users (authors of this article).

RELATED WORK

Command selection is one of the elemental actions when interacting with a GUI. Standard techniques include menus, toolbars, hotkeys and gestures. A large body of work in HCI proposes improvements of these techniques as well as adaptations to various contexts, such as mobile interaction. Considering the large number of studies, we focus on a few of them related to gestural interaction, spatial layout and tactile cues.

Gestural interaction and gestural menus. Using gestures for command selection has been proposed as an alternative to menus or hotkeys [3]. Most modern operating systems now allow performing gestures for activating commands. But they are usually specified by manufacturers and bound to specific actions that cannot be changed. Some applications, such as [29, 20] on the Mac, solve this problem by allowing users to define custom actions and gestures. However, few commands elicit gestural agreement, especially if they are of an abstract nature [48]. Providing a mechanism for *discovering* and *learning* gestures is thus of primary importance.

Marking menus [27] solve both problems by offering a novice mode that is similar to the expert mode. Users *discover* gestures by browsing menus and *learn* them through the force of repetition. But Marking menu only support a limited number of items at a given menu level, usually up to eight [27], which may force users or UI designers to employ awkward groupings of menu items [49]. Various derived techniques have been proposed, such as for instance Flower menus [5], which rely on curved gestures to increase capacity, Octopocus [7], which leverages discoverability using feedforward, Augmented letters [38], which combines handwriting and menus to improve memorization. Yet, these techniques do not provide the same capacity and the same flexibility for organizing commands as MarkPad and they require an appropriate activation mechanism because they conflict with other interactions such as drag and drop, drawing or text selection [26].

Spatial layout. Another approach is to use specific areas of the visual or motor space for interaction purpose. Bezel menus [21] avoid conflicting with standard gestures by using only gestures that start from the border of a touch screen, but they only support small menus and might suffer from involuntary activations. Similarly, bezels were used for performing gestures on smartwatches [25] but for a limited set of 16 possible gestures. Using several modalities as in BezelTap [43] (a bump on the bezel and a slide on the screen) prevents involuntary activation but requires slightly more complex gestures and the use of an accelerometer.

Although this tends to be replaced by two-finger gestures, some touchpads still have a dedicated scroll zone on one or several of their sides. Specific areas of the touchpad were used also for performing commands in [9]. This study proposed a set of one-finger and multitouch static gestures (with the `fn` key pressed and at least one finger touching the touchpad border) and dynamic gestures joining one border to another. While the present study also takes advantage of the touchpad borders, it does not rely on the same kind of gestures and proposes an unified technique both providing a novice and an expert mode. Finally, combining locations on a sensitive area and directional gestures was explored in Zone menus [49] for increasing the number of available commands in Marking menus. As other previous Marking menu-derived approaches, this technique conflicts with standard interactions and does not offer the capacity and the flexibility of MarkPad.

Computer systems often provide "hot" corners or hidden toolbars that either trigger commands or display menus when the mouse cursor reaches the corners or the borders of the screen (e.g., the Mac Dock or the Windows Charm Bar). Schramm et al. [42] proposed four techniques for improving hidden toolbars. Using several devices, they found a trade-off between completion time and error detection while using vision-free interfaces. Contrary to MarkPad, these techniques require moving the cursor as they do not rely on the motor space. Moreover they only support a limited number of commands.

Finally, the spatial layout can leverage spatial memory as in CommandMaps [40] that flattens the hierarchy of commands to improve performance, or in FastTap [18] and its adaptation to smartwatches [28] which rely on a static grid that allows fast command selection on tablets and small devices.

Tactile cues. Tactile sense plays an important role for eyes-free interaction or in multi-focus situations. For example, physical buttons or the border of a smartphone can help users to interact with a smartphone [11]. Helping users to alleviate the lack of vision through tactile cues was proposed in several studies. For example, Jansen et al. [22] used tangible widgets fixed on a tablet to interact with a wall display, Corsten et al. [14] used marks on the back of a mobile device to improve pointing on the device, and Harrison et al. [19] compared different types of tangible buttons. Haptic feedback can also be used for different purposes like guiding [17] or providing more information to users [23].

THE MARKPAD TECHNIQUE

Attributes and modalities. MarkPad gestures rely on the combination of several geometric attributes and modalities. While these gestures only depend on their starting and ending areas, users may also perceive them as the combination of a *position*, a *direction* and a *distance*. Touchpads also have a small bezel and four corners that act as *visual* and *tactile* landmarks, which is likely to help interaction [43] as well as the *visual* or *tactile* marks that augment the touchpad.

In a famous article, Miller pointed out that multidimensional stimuli improve absolute judgments [30]. Other studies in psychology and HCI suggest that combined stimuli, or the presence of contextual cues improve learning and memorization [4, 24, 35, 39], which should make our gestures easier to perform and to memorize. While the idea of combining locations and directions has already been proposed for improving Marking menus [49] and Bezel gestures [21, 43], using distance without a visual representation has rarely been studied and either the number of items was relatively small [18] or accuracy was limited [31]. This is because it may be difficult for users to draw strokes of a given length without any visual reference to provide a sense of scale [27, 49]. Our first study will show that *visual* or *tactile* marks (or, more precisely, *visuo-tactile* marks as tactile marks can be seen by the user) solve this problem, even for a dense configuration of a maximum of 680 gestural shortcuts that was used to test the limits of the technique.

Visual/tactile marks. Such marks only involve small modifications of the touchpad and can be unobtrusive. Visual marks can consist of small landmarks. Tactile marks can be almost invisible, for example by using transparent adhesive tape or by slightly changing the surface roughness. Their presence is not annoying on the borders of the touchpad because borders are seldom used, as our last study will show. However, they might be unpleasant in the center of the touchpad, especially during pointing tasks. One solution consists of having marks only in the border areas (Figure 1, middle), a case we will consider in our second study. Another solution would be to use dynamic tactile marks that are activated after the user initiates a gesture from the borders, using technologies providing tactile feedback in real time [1, 8, 12]. Such technology has for instance been used in Métamorphe [6] to promote hotkey usage.

Usage without marks. The technique can also work without marks provided that areas are large enough, thus not too numerous (e.g., 5 horizontally and 3 vertically on the borders [43]). In particular, for border areas, the user can take advantage of the bezel and the corners of the touchpad to position his finger.

Absolute vs. relative pointing. Importantly, MarkPad uses the touchpad as an *absolute* pointing device. This means that it does not conflict with interaction techniques such as active borders, hidden toolbars, charm bars, etc. because these techniques rely on the position of the *mouse cursor*, not on where the user touches the touchpad. In other words, we take advantage of the fact that the touchpad is normally used as an *relative* pointing device. Because we start gestures from the borders, both ways of using the touchpad (i.e. absolute or relative pointing device) do not conflict, except in the rare cases where the user touches the border involuntary. Moreover, the software can prevent cursor movement once a MarkPad gesture is initiated on the border.

Interaction. MarkPad provides three interaction modes (full-novice, expert and semi-novice) depending on user expertise. In *full-novice mode*, the user first holds the Function key (she could also double tap the border, touch it in a special area or use one of the methods described in [42]). The names of the available menus are then displayed on the borders of the screen. Their location correspond to those of the starting areas (or "menu areas") of the MarkPad gestures on the touchpad, which can be materialized by visual or tactile marks.

Once the desired menu is selected by touching the appropriate menu area, the names of the items contained in this menu are displayed on the screen, as well as lines indicating the gestures that must be done for activating these items (Figure 1, right). The menu is transparent, displayed in full-screen mode and superimposed on top of the applications running on the desktop. The user can then perform the desired gesture, which consists in moving his finger from the menu area to the item area. The associated action is triggered when the user releases his finger. The gesture can be canceled by moving the finger to an empty area, or back again to the menu area. All these operations can be performed without looking at the touchpad because the location of the finger touch is continuously displayed on the screen at the same relative location.

Expert mode occurs when the user already knows the gesture. He can then directly perform this gesture without holding the Function key. *Semi-novice mode* is an intermediate case when the user knows the menu area, but not the appropriate gesture. In this case he can double touch the desired menu area, or touch it for at least 500ms, to make this menu appear. This design relies on *rehearsal* [27, 42]. It allows fluid transition from novice to expert use as the same gestures are performed in all cases.

Areas and marks. Menu and menu item areas can either correspond to the tactile/visual marks on the touchpad or to the *absence* of such a mark between two marks (especially along the borders), a "no-mark" being in fact a kind of a mark. Menu areas must be located on the borders, but the

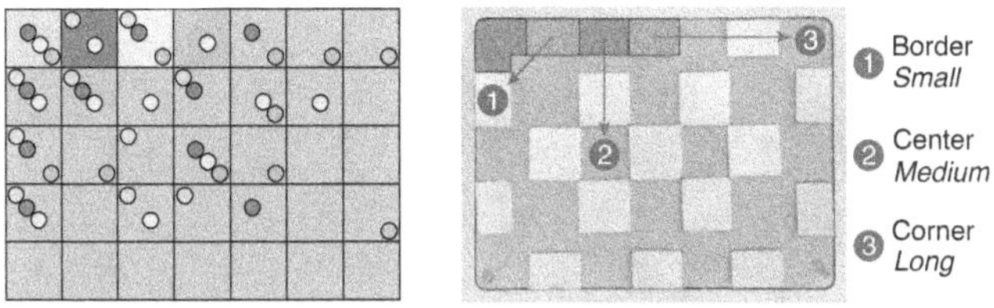

Figure 2: (Left) Evaluated gestures: the circles correspond to the ending areas and their color indicates their starting area (no colors were shown on the actual interfaces). (Right) Three examples of gestures shown on top of the actual *Tactile* interface.

user can place menu item areas wherever she wants. Areas can have various sizes (Figure 9) and can be larger than actual tactile/visual marks. For instance, corner areas do not need to be large, but large areas are beneficial in the center of the touchpad, especially if the technique is used without marks in the center of the touchpad.

As locations do not change, after some practice, users should be able to perform some of the gestures without looking at the touchpad in expert mode, especially when using tactile marks. This would let them focus on their main task by preventing to-and-fro head and eye movements between the screen and the touchpad.

COMMAND SELECTION IN EXPERT MODE

This first study aims at evaluating the performance of the technique in expert mode when visual or tactile marks are present on the touchpad. For this purpose, we built three versions of a plastic layer that we fixed on top of the touchpad (Figure 2-right). The first version had thin *Tactile* marks that the user could see and feel, and the second version *Visual* marks that could only be seen. The last version, called *Mixed*, combined the two previous cases: tactile marks were provided on the borders and visual marks in the center. We built this last version because we thought that while tactile marks might improve performance, they might be inconvenient in the center of the touchpad.

As shown on Figure 2, in this experiment, we used a grid layout containing a large number of rectangular areas ($7 \times 5 = 35$ areas). A valid gesture can start from one of the border areas and end in any area, except the area it was started from. Tactile and visual marks appear in light gray while other areas, which look darker, were left empty. Both types of areas (with or without marks) were used in the experiment. The prototypes were built using cheap materials (plastic sheets, paper stickers, adhesive tape, marker paint...) that anyone could use to customize his own touchpad.

We choose a 7×5 area configuration because 1) it allows for a large number of commands (20 starting areas $\times 35 - 1$ ending areas = 680 shortcuts); 2) according to [43] an odd number of border areas is preferable to an even number; 3) the size of all areas was in line with recommendations for interacting with touchscreens [33, 46]. Areas in the center were about 15×15mm. Border areas were a bit smaller in order not to occupy too much space. Their smallest side (i.e. their width for left/right border or their height for top/bottom borders) was 10mm. As can be noticed on Figure 2, there was a small dead zone of 5 mm between the border and center areas. As

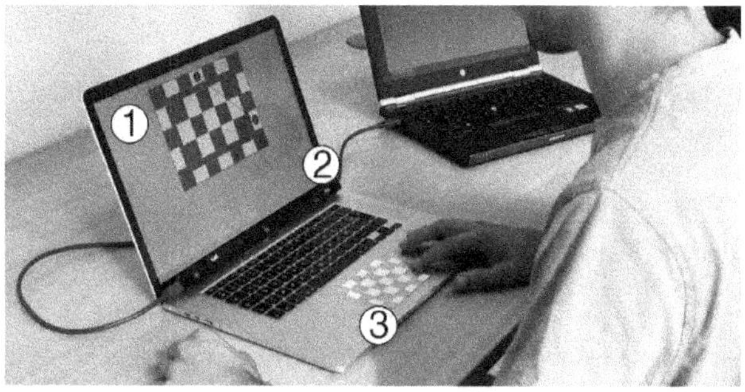

Figure 3: Experiment setup: 1) Stimulus shown during command selection tasks (two blue circles indicate the starting/ending areas), 2) Tobii EyeX device tracking users' gaze, 3) *Tactile* interface on the touchpad.

will be explained in the last study, this dead zone is intended to reduce involuntary activations. It was included for the sake of realism but has no or marginal impact on this study.

Experimental design

Hypotheses. We hypothesized that: (**H1**) all interfaces should provide sufficiently high accuracy, but that, because they provide more information, *Tactile* marks should (**H2**) offer better performance and (**H3**) require participants to take less time looking at the touchpad (and/or look at it less often).

As we could not test the performance of all 680 possible gestures, we chose a representative subset considering three characteristics: the type of the starting and ENDING areas and the LENGTH of the gesture. The starting areas were the top left corner, the top middle area (both easier to point at according to [16]) and the two areas between them, as shown on Figure 2. We chose neighboring areas because we thought they might lead to more confusions than areas that would have been far from each other. Moreover, these areas were representative of all the possible kinds of starting areas (corner, middle, between). The ENDING area was either a *Corner*, *Border* or *Center* area and LENGTH was the number of areas between the starting and ending areas (either 0 = *Small*, 1 = *Medium*, 2 = *Long*), as shown on Figure 2. We balanced these characteristics to obtain 14 *Small*, 14 *Medium* and 14 *Long* gestures (thus a total of 42 gestures), with 4 of them ending in a *Corner*, 19 in a *Border* and 19 in a *Center* area.

We used an AUXILIARY task to make the command selection task more realistic. The user had to do this task and then to perform a selection using the technique. The AUXILIARY was either a *Pointing* or *Key input* task. The participants had to place the mouse cursor inside a circle of 35 pixels, 250 pixels away in the first case, and to press the '5' and '7' keys on the keyboard in the second case. We expected that these tasks would impact performance and users' gaze.

Stimulus. After the participant performed the AUXILIARY task, the 7×5 grid was displayed on the laptop screen with a blue circle showing the starting area (Figure 3). When the participant touched the touchpad, the ending area appeared on the grid (also as a blue circle). She could then complete the gesture. We used this design to simulate an expert behavior where the user keeps looking at the screen while performing the gesture on the touchpad. We did not show both areas at

	Visual	*Mixed*	*Tactile*
Success rate (%)	95.64 ± 2.11	94.83 ± 1.84	95.63 ± 1.69
Task duration (in ms)	2013 ± 152	2061 ± 156	2100 ± 125
Execution time (in ms)	975 ± 89	1019 ± 78	1041 ± 67
Number of glances	1.84 ± 0.13	1.72 ± 0.16	1.74 ± 0.15
Glance duration (in %)	36.05 ± 2.4	32.38 ± 3.5	31.85 ± 3.1

Table 1: Summary of the main results for each interface. Mean with 95% Confidence Interval computed relatively to the participants mean.

once because we noticed in pretests that participants then systematically only looked at the touchpad to perform the gesture. This two steps procedure thus encourages participants to keep their focus on the screen.

No feedback was displayed on the screen *while* performing the gesture, but feedback was provided *after* this step. Once the participant released her finger, a line between the starting and ending areas she selected was displayed on the grid. This line was green and shown during 1 second in case of success, but red and shown during 2.5 s (as a penalty) in case of an error. The participant could then start the next trial by pressing the space bar.

Procedure. We asked 12 right-handed participants to perform our study (9 men, 3 women, aged from 22 to 35 years). The whole experiment lasted 30 to 40 minutes. We blocked by INTERFACE (*Tactile*, *Visual* and *Mixed*) and the presentation order was counter-balanced over participants. For each INTERFACE, participants had to perform a training block of 6 trials followed by an evaluation block of 84 trials. Participants performed each gesture two times, each time with a different AUXILIARY task (randomized). Finally, participants were asked to fill a questionnaire at the end of the experiment.

Apparatus. The experiment was performed on a 15" Macbook pro with a 2.2 Ghz Intel Core i7 processor. The size of the touchpad was 105×76 *mm*. We used a Tobii EyeX eye-tracking system [44] running on a Windows 7 computer to record users' gaze. Both computers were interacting through the UDP protocol. The INTERFACES used for the experiment were made of plastic sheets on which paper stickers were stuck to create tactile marks (Figure 3). Visual marks were drawn using a white Posca pen.

Results

We based our analysis on the following measures: the *success rate*, the *task duration* (total completion time of command selection), the *execution time* (time elapsed between touching and releasing the touchpad for performing the gesture), the *number of glances* at the touchpad and the *glance duration* (in percentage of the *task duration*). Table 1 provides a summary of the results. The main result is that all interfaces reached high accuracy.

ANOVA tests show no significant effect of the INTERFACE on *success rate* ($F_{2,22} = 0.43$, $p = 0.655$), *task duration* ($F_{2,22} = 0.57$, $p = 0.576$), *execution time* ($F_{2,22} = 1.54$, $p = 0.236$) or the *number of glances* ($F_{2,22} = 3.14$, $p = 0.063$). However, another ANOVA reveals a significant effect on the *glance duration* ($F_{2,22} = 9.83$, $p = 0.01$). A post-hoc t-test shows that the *Visual* interface required more time looking at the touchpad than the *Mixed*

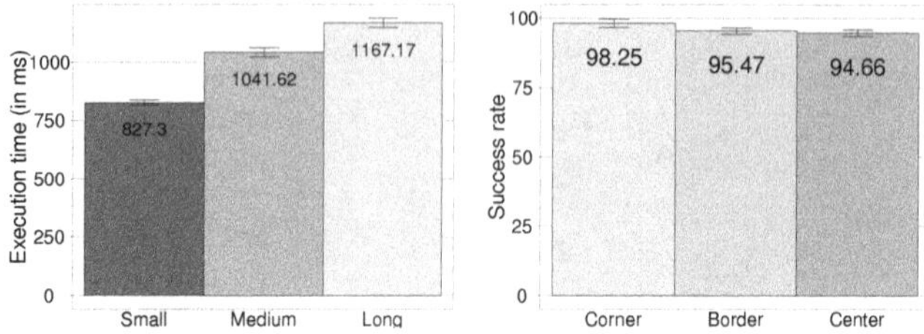

Figure 4: (Left) *Execution time* relative to LENGTH, (Right) *Success rate* relative to ENDING AREA.

($p = 0.014$) and *Tactile* ($p < 0.01$) interfaces[1]. While we expected this result, the *execution time* was not significantly different (its mean value was in fact slightly shorter for the *Visual* interface, Table 1). We also ran ANOVAs on the same measures to evaluate the effect of the AUXILIARY task preceding the command selection tasks, but we found no significant differences.

We also looked at the impact of the LENGTH and the ENDING AREA. ANOVAs reveal an effect for both of them on the *success rate* (respectively $F_{2,22} = 6.23$, $p < 0.01$ and $F_{2,22} = 11.32$, $p < 0.01$) and on the *execution time* (respectively $F_{2,22} = 7.04$, $p < 0.01$ and $F_{2,22} = 135.62$, $p < 0.01$). Post-hoc t-tests show that *Small* gestures are completed successfully more often than *Long* gestures (96.73% vs. 94.72%, $p < 0.01$). Unsurprisingly, smaller gestures were also performed significantly faster than longer ones (respectively 827ms, 1042ms, 1167ms, all p's < 0.01, Figure 4). Other t-tests reveal that gestures finishing on a *Corner* were completed successfully more often than others (98.25% vs. *Border* 95.47% and *Center* 94.66%, Figure 4) and that gestures finishing on a *Corner* or a *Border* area were quicker than the ones finishing in the *Center* (respectively 997ms, 978ms and 1049ms).

Finally, we wanted to evaluate when users looked at the touchpad (whether on *touch* or *release* of the gesture). An ANOVA for the *percentage of time* users looked at the touchpad when *releasing* their finger reveals an effect of the INTERFACE ($F_{2,22} = 3.83$, $p = 0.037$). A post-hoc t-test does not reveal any further difference, although *Visual* required users to look while releasing their finger 74% of all trials while *Mixed* and *Tactile* required respectively 65% and 64% of them.

Questionnaire. We asked participants to rank all interfaces from the least to most appreciated with possible ties (on a scale from 1 to 3, with 3 being the best). Small non significant differences were found between them (means: *Visual* 2.00, *Mixed* 2.17 and *Tactile* 2.33). Then we asked them to fill Likert-scales with levels from 1 to 7 about their perception of their *success rate*, their *confidence* level, how often they *looked* at the touchpad and on the *mental demand* required for each INTERFACE. The *Tactile* interface seemed to be better perceived in all cases but no significant difference was found. We also asked participants if they found that tactile marks were disturbing when performing the pointing task. A median value of 5 (slightly agree) was obtained on a scale from 1 to 7 (7 for "completely agree").

[1]All our t-tests are without Bonferroni adjustment for the reasons explained in [34]. However, they stay significant with Bonferroni-Holm adjustment.

Discussion

The main result of this experiment is that all interfaces reached a completion rate of about 95%, which satisfies (**H1**) and validates the feasibility of the technique. A limitation of the experiment is that, because of their large number (680), we only considered a subpart (42 gestures) of the overall possible gestures. However, we tested the technique under somewhat extreme conditions. Not only we used a very dense grid but we chose neighboring starting and ending areas. These two characteristics are likely to increase confusions because gestures were more similar to each other than if they were starting from large and distant areas. In real usage, most users will use less gestures, larger areas (especially in the center of the touchpad) and will favor the most convenient areas (as for instance, *Corner* and *Center* areas).

The *execution time* was about one second and the total *selection time* of about two seconds for all interfaces, which seems reasonably fast as all participants were using the technique for the first time. While comparing studies is uneasy because tasks and devices differ, these results seem in phase with previous research on shortcut techniques. For instance, *selection times* about 2200 ms were obtained for 3×8 hierarchical Marking menus and about 2000 ms for both 16×16 Zones and Polygons menus [27, 49]. Shorter times were obtained for smaller menus (e.g. about 1300 ms for 2×8 Marking menus [27] and 1517 ms for the Swipe technique in [42]), but these results are not comparable as we used a dense configuration with small areas close to each other. Times would probably be shorter for simpler configurations with large areas. As a possible indication, Bezel menus, which can approximately be seen as a kind of MarkPad menu with very large (infinite) areas, were found to have an *execution time* of 382 ms for trained users [21].

As expected, the 14 short gestures were faster (about 830 ms for the *execution time*) and should thus be favored for frequent commands. Gestures along the borders were also slightly faster and offered slightly better success rates. Again, we did not test all possible gestures but, in case some other gestures would be slower, this should not be a problem considering the large number of available gestures. Finally, it is worth noticing that *Key input* tasks were not disadvantaged comparing to *Pointing* tasks, although the fingers were not already on the touchpad in the first case.

Contrary to our expectations, the *Tactile* and *Mixed* interfaces did not provide better *success rate* or *execution time* than the *Visual* interface, which refutes (**H2**). We thought that participants would take less time looking at the touchpad (**H3**) and would thus perform gestures faster (**H2**). While they actually spent less time looking at the touchpad and seemed to make less glances ($p = 0.063$), the execution time was not significantly different. This might be because this setup was new for the participants, or because tactile marks slightly slowed their movements. Interestingly, in all conditions, participants were partly able to interact without looking at the touchpad. Given how the stimulus was displayed, they needed to look two times at the touchpad to see where were their fingers, but the mean *number of glances* was between 1.72 and 1.84 depending on the condition. A further analysis showed this was because they ended the gestures eyes-free in these cases.

Participants seemed to slightly prefer the *Tactile* interface but were also (slightly) concerned about the fact that tactile marks might be annoying, especially in the center of the touchpad. This suggests that the *Mixed* design might be the best alternative. Another option, that we studied in the next experiment, consists in using marks only on the border of the touchpad.

SIMPLIFIED INTERFACES

The goal of this second experiment was to evaluate whether sufficient performance could be achieved without *Visual* or *Tactile* cues in the center of the touchpad. For the sake of comparison, we compared 4 different conditions: *Full Tactile*, *Light Tactile*, *Light Visual* and *None*. *Full Tactile* uses the same *Tactile* interface as in the previous experiment, and serves as a baseline. We chose the *Tactile* rather than the *Visual* interface to gather more results about users feelings with tactile cues. *Light Tactile* and *Light Visual* are similar to the *Tactile* and *Visual* interfaces except they do not have marks in the center. Finally, *None* corresponds to the extreme case where the touchpad does not have any mark.

Experimental design

Procedure. The procedure was the same than in the previous experiment except that we ran the experiment with 16 right-handed participants (11 men, 5 women, aged from 23 to 38 years old, none participated to the previous experiment) and that had to perform a training block of 12 trials using the *Full Tactile* interface, so that they could get used to the technique.

Hypotheses. We hypothesized that (**H1**) the *Full Tactile* interface would lead to the best success rate and the *None* interface to the worst and (**H2**) that participants would take more time looking at the touchpad (and look at it more often) with *Light Tactile* and *Light Visual* than with *Full Tactile* as this interface should help them performing part of the task eyes-free.

Results

Table 2 shows the results for our main measures. We use similar ANOVAs as in the previous experiment. They reveal an effect of the INTERFACE on the *success rate* ($F_{3,45} = 45.30$, $p < 0.01$), the *number of glances* ($F_{3,45} = 10.48$, $p < 0.01$) and the *glance duration* ($F_{3,45} = 2.97$, $p = 0.042$). Post-hoc t-tests show (1) that the *None* interface leads to the worst results ($p < 0.01$ compared to all others) and *Full Tactile* to the best results ($p = 0.011$ vs. both *Light Visual* and *Light Tactile*); (2) that participants looked less often to the touchpad with the *None* interface ($p < 0.01$ vs. *Light Visual* and *Light Tactile*; $p = 0.023$ vs. *Full Tactile*), and less often with the *Full Tactile* than with the *Light Visual* interface ($p = 0.047$); (3) that *glances duration* is shorter for *None* than for *Light Visual* ($p < 0.01$, we found no other significant differences between the other interfaces).

The ANOVA also reveals a significant interaction between INTERFACE and ENDING AREA on *success rate* ($F_{6,90} = 3.32$, $p < 0.01$), see Figure 5. Indeed, post-hoc t-tests show that the *None* interface leads to the worst success rates for all the ENDING AREA (all p's < 0.02), but we find a significant difference between *Full Tactile* and both *Light Visual* and *Light Tactile* only for

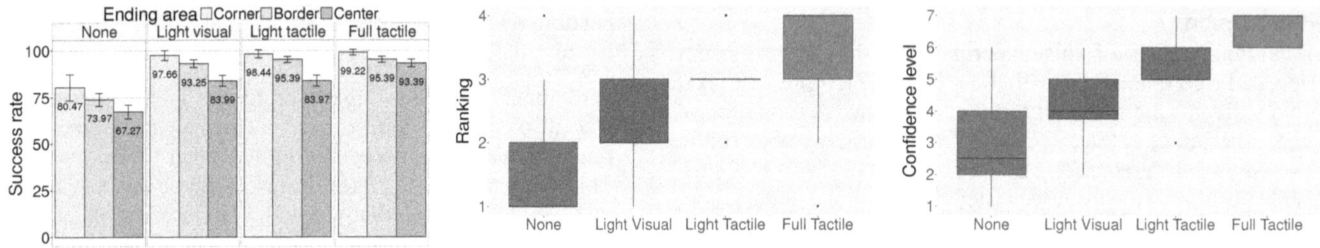

Figure 5: (Left) The *success rate* by ENDING AREA for each INTERFACE; (Middle) ranking of the INTERFACE on a scale from 1 to 4 (4 - best); (Right) participants confidence on the INTERFACE on a scale from 1 to 4 (7 - complete confidence).

	None	*Light Visual*	*Light Tactile*	*Full Tactile*
Success rate (%)	71.56 ± 5.9	89.49 ± 4.3	90.53 ± 3.5	94.85 ± 2.3
Task duration (ms)	2347 ± 284	2388 ± 337	2353 ± 220	2223 ± 161
Execution time (ms)	1161 ± 153	1215 ± 187	1232 ± 132	1144 ± 95
Number of glances	1.58 ± 0.22	1.91 ± 0.22	1.85 ± 0.19	1.76 ± 0.15
Glance duration (%)	30.88 ± 4.2	36.08 ± 4.0	34.28 ± 4.3	34.15 ± 3.6

Table 2: Summary of the results for each interface.

the *Center* area (93.39% for *Full Tactile* vs. 83.99% for *Light Visual* and 83.97% for *Light Tactile*, Figure 5).

We also evaluated *when* users were looking at the touchpad. An ANOVA on the percentage of trials for which users looked at the touchpad while *releasing* their finger shows an effect of the INTERFACE ($F_{3,45} = 9.51$, $p < 0.01$). A post-hoc t-test reveals that *None* requires less glances than the other interfaces when releasing the finger (48.13% of the trials vs. *Light Visual* 69.79%, *Light Tactile* 67.28%, and *Full Tactile* 68.33%, all p's < 0.01).

Questionnaire. A non-parametric Wilcox t-test reveals that the *None* interface was perceived as the worst (all p's < 0.01 except for *Light Visual* $p = 0.016$), as shown on Figure 5. More t-tests show differences for the perceived *success rate* and *confidence level*. *Full Tactile* achieves the best perceived *success rate* (vs. *None* and *Light Visual* $p < 0.01$, vs. *Light Tactile* $p = 0.024$) and *Light Tactile* is perceived as more successful than *Light Visual* ($p = 0.024$) and *None* ($p < 0.01$). A t-test on the *confidence level* shows that participants felt more confident with *Full Tactile* than with the other interfaces, and with *Light Tactile* than with *Light Visual* and *None* (all p's < 0.01), as shown in Figure 5.

Discussion

This experiment shows that marks are needed to obtain a good *success rate*, at least with a dense configuration, which validates (**H1**). While poor results are obtained with *None* (71.6%), they are lower but still acceptable with *Light Tactile* and *Light Visual* (about 90%). As the errors for the light interfaces mainly come from the gestures that end in the center, this suggests that these latter configurations would provide satisfactory success rates with less numerous and larger areas in the center of the touchpad.

Interestingly, the success rate is higher for the *Center* areas with *Light Tactile* and *Light Visual* than with *None* although these interfaces are identical (no marks) in the center. A likely reason is that the participants used the marks on the border in the first cases to guess the location of the areas in the center of the touchpad. Moreover, we noticed that the way they started the gestures was quite important. Marks on the border not only helped participants to start from the proper area but also to locate their finger in the center of this area. This reduces errors when moving the finger to the ending area because the finger tends to "drift". Hence, errors are less likely if the finger is well positioned at the beginning of the gesture.

Participants looked less often at the touchpad with *Full Tactile* than with *Light Visual* but there is no significant difference for the *glance duration* and the *execution time* although mean values show the same trend. Also, mean values slightly differ for *Full Tactile* vs. *Light Tactile* but no significant difference was found. Moreover, the interfaces with *tactile cues* were more comfortable for users since they felt more confident using them. As with the previous experiment, tactile marks seem to help users, which partly validates (**H2**), but a longitudinal experiment with experienced users would be needed to measure this effect more accurately.

Finally, participants looked at the touchpad significantly less often in the *None* condition, which is consistent with the fact that looking at it provided much less information than in the other conditions.

BORDER USAGE

Sensitive surfaces are primary designed for pointing. Bezel gestures [25, 37] and MarkPad are based on the hypothesis that users do not start pointing gestures from the border of the surface. However, they may accidentally touch the border from time to time. In particular, because of its location on the computer, they may inadvertently swipe at the touchpad when moving their hands to use the keyboard.

For this reason we conducted a study for estimating how frequently users perform gestures starting from the borders in real-life situations. Importantly, participants were not aware that an interaction technique might use borders for a specific purpose. As users would probably adapt their behavior in such a case, the results we obtained can be seen as an upper bound of the number of possible involuntary activations.

In addition to MarkPad gestures joining two different areas on the touchpad (here called *"Strokes"*), we also considered 8-directional Marking menu gestures (called *"Slides"*), all of them starting from the touchpad border. After collecting the data, we computed how many gestures would have been detected, depending on two varying factors: the *border width* (W on Figure 6) and the *minimal length* of the gestures.

Gesture minimal length (in mm)	Border width (in mm): 1	2	3	4	5	6	7	8	9	10	11	12	13	14	15
1	1.86	3.01	3.58	3.98	4.27	4.57	4.91	5.39	5.95	6.57	7.33	8.19	9.18	10.36	11.73
	0.71	0.94	0.98	1.07	1.15	1.25	1.42	1.71	2.06	2.48	3.03	3.66	4.38	5.22	6.22
3	0.65	1.14	1.44	1.69	1.88	2.11	2.37	2.79	3.27	3.82	4.50	5.26	6.15	7.22	8.47
	0.44	0.65	0.75	0.87	0.96	1.08	1.25	1.53	1.88	2.31	2.85	3.47	4.17	5.00	6.00
5	0.41	0.70	0.91	1.12	1.27	1.46	1.70	2.09	2.55	3.07	3.72	4.44	5.29	6.32	7.52
	0.34	0.54	0.65	0.77	0.86	0.97	1.14	1.43	1.78	2.20	2.73	3.33	4.03	4.86	5.84
7	0.34	0.56	0.71	0.87	1.00	1.18	1.41	1.79	2.23	2.72	3.34	4.03	4.85	5.84	6.99
	0.29	0.47	0.57	0.69	0.78	0.89	1.06	1.35	1.70	2.11	2.62	3.21	3.89	4.70	5.66
9	0.30	0.47	0.60	0.73	0.84	1.01	1.23	1.59	2.01	2.50	3.10	3.77	4.57	5.52	6.63
	0.27	0.42	0.52	0.64	0.72	0.84	1.01	1.29	1.63	2.03	2.54	3.11	3.79	4.58	5.53

Table 3: Detection of Slide and Stroke gestures depending on the *border width* and their *minimal length*.

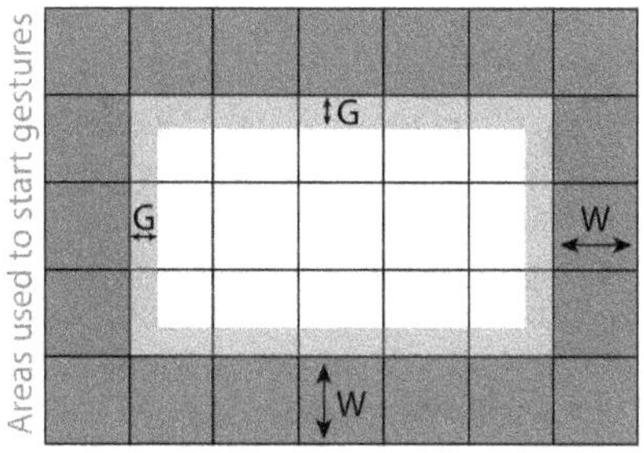

Figure 6: Touchpad configuration used for our study (W is the *border width*, G is the *gap*).

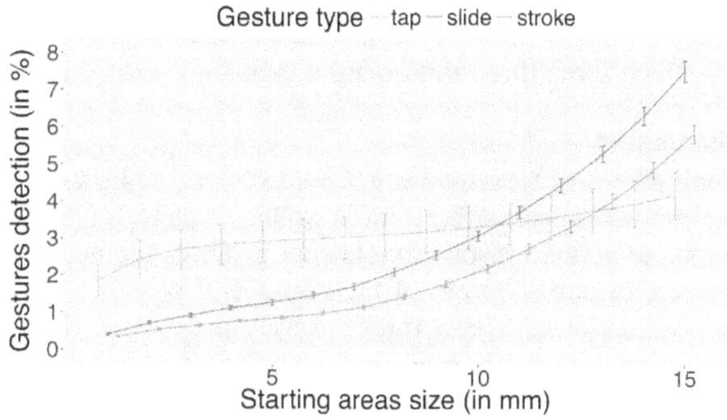

Figure 7: Percentage of Tap (blue), Slide (purple) and Stroke (orange) gestures depending on *border width* for a *minimum length* of 5mm.

We used the same $7 \times 5 = 35$ area configuration as in the previous experiments (Figure 6). The width of the 20 border areas (in blue in the figure), or their height for those on top and bottom borders, depends on *border width*. Directional *Slides* can start from any of these areas and end anywhere, provided they are longer than *minimal length*. Smaller gestures are ignored and would thus have no effect in real-life applications. The same rules apply for MarkPad *Strokes*, except that, by construction, they cannot start and end in the same area.

Procedure. We performed a study on 12 right-handed users (8 men, 4 women) that lasted one week. They all used their own Macbook with an integrated touchpad of 105×76mm. We implemented a logging software to detect all finger contacts when the computers were being used. The collected data included the number of finger touches, their locations and size. We collected a total of 1547680 gestures, with an average number of 128973 gestures per user (mean gesture duration was about 600ms).

Analysis. After collecting the data, we computed which gestures would have been detected as *Slides* or *Strokes* for a *border width* between 0 and 15 mm and a *minimum length* between 1 and 9 mm. The results are given as percentages of detected *Slides* or *Strokes* relatively to the total number of *"gesture"* on the touchpad. A *"gesture"* consisted of touch followed by a release. We only considered one-finger gestures in this study. For the sake of comparison, we also detected *Taps* occurring in the border area (with a tolerance of 1 mm and a maximum duration of 250 ms).

Results

As can be seen in Figure 7 and Table 3, few gestures were detected (at least for reasonable values of the *minimal length* and the *border width*) although the participants were not aware of the techniques. This means that users seldom use the touchpad borders, at least when the touchpad is relatively large (105×76 mm), a common trend on laptops.

MarkPad *Strokes* were less often detected that directional *Slides*. For instance, for a *minimal length* of 5 mm, the difference was about 20% for a *border width* of 1 mm, then reached a maximum of 50% for 6 mm and, finally decreased to reach 29% for a width of 15 mm. This difference (strongly) increases for smaller values of the *minimal length* and decreases for larger values. The reason for this difference is that *Strokes* cannot end in the area they started from, meaning they must *cross* the edges of their starting area. This reduces the probability of doing the gesture by chance (i.e. only a part of the gestures starting from a given area crosses its edges).

As can be expected, both the *minimal length* and the *border width* strongly impact results. Increasing the *minimal length* to reduce the number of detected gestures may be problematic because users may think the technique is unreactive or buggy if no action occurs. In this regard, a length of about 5 mm may be a reasonable compromise. Conversely, reducing too much the *border width* may lead to misdetections. Experienced users, who will perform the gestures quickly, without paying attention because they are focused on their main task, may not start the gestures from the very border of the touchpad and miss the active area. Hence, this value should probably depend on user habits and preferences. As will be explained in the next section, two users have been using the technique for a few months. After some testing, they chose values between 5.5 and 8.5 mm.

Further analyzing the data, we noticed that many detected gestures ended in the center, close to their starting areas. We thus added a *gap* between the border areas and the center areas (Figure 6) to see whether this would improve results. Fig-

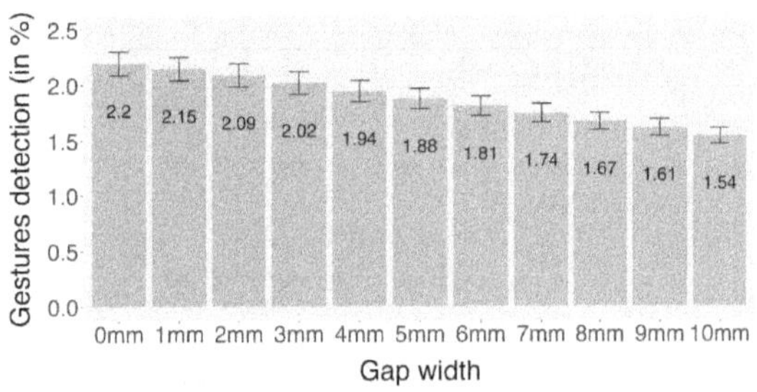

Figure 8: Gap impact on gestures detection (*border width* = 10mm).

ure 8 shows the results for a *gap* varying from 0 to 10 mm with a *border width* of 10 mm and a *minimal length* of 5 mm. As can be seen, this solution has a valuable effect.

Discussion

Our analysis of touchpad usage data shows that users seldom use the touchpad borders, even when unaware of the technique. For this reason, the detection rates obtained can be seen as an upper bound of the number of possible involuntary activations. These rates strongly depend on the *minimal length* and the *border width*. The *minimal length* should be small, to avoid making the interaction unpleasant, but not too small, to avoid involuntary activations. A length of about 5 mm seems a good compromise. Considering this, the detection rate for MarkPad *Strokes* was respectively of 0.34%, 0.86%, 2.20% for a *border width* of 1, 5, 10 mm. Using a *gap* of 10 mm, these values decreased to 0.22%, 0.61%, 1.54%. A gap requires longer Strokes, but only toward the center.

A very small *border width* may make the technique hard to use. Considering the values chosen by the two users who tested the technique, a value between 5 and 10 mm seems a reasonable choice. This is also in phase with recommendations for interacting with touchscreens (about 8 or 9 mm for optimizing accuracy) [33, 46]. Moreover, while we performed our two first experiments width a *border widths* of 10 mm, we noticed that, using the same data, the success rates where almost the same (about 1% lower) for a *border width* of 8 mm. This means that, although the visual/tactile marks were 10 mm large, participants almost only used 80% of their surface. Hence, 8 mm may be a good default value (the detection rate is then of 1.03% for a gap of 10 mm). However, the user should be allowed to customize this value.

Finally, MarkPad *Strokes* were noticeably less often detected that directional *Slides* although the ending areas were not taken into account (except that the ending area could not be the starting area). The difference in results strongly depends on the *minimal length* and the *border width* and can be rather large, especially for small *minimal lengths* (up to 3.7 times). This technique, or, more precisely, the fact it requires crossing the edges of the starting area [2], may thus provide a simple way for reducing involuntary activations when using Bezel menus [21].

PROTOTYPE AND ACTUAL USE

MarkPad has been implemented on MacOS and relies on various mechanisms (system calls, AppleScript, hotkey/event generation, private MacOS multitouch API) for performing all the different actions that have been mentioned so far. It is

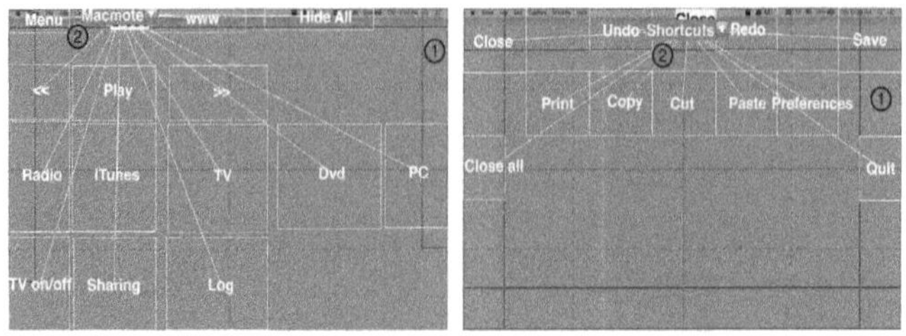

Figure 9: Menu examples for two different users. The (2) red cirles indicate the name of the currently selected menu. The (1) circles show where starting areas can be located (inside the blue rectangles), according to the preferences of each user. Note that the edges of the shortcut areas are only displayed in edition mode to avoid cluttering the display.

application agnostic in that sense that it can launch any application, execute almost any command and open any document (provided that an application allows displaying it). It can also send messages to other applications through a TCP/IP connection. The prototype works as a background task and consumes very little CPU and only when executing shortcut actions or when touching the touchpad (about 0.5-1% CPU charge on a MacBook Pro 3 GHz Core i7).

The prototype has been continuously used for 3 or 6 months by the two first authors while it was being developed. Interestingly, these two users used the prototype differently in many aspects. While they both created shortcuts and menus for accessing their favorite applications and documents (mainly Web pages) they did not organize them in the same way and did not put the focus on the same actions. For instance, as shown in Figure 9, one user created gestural shortcuts for replacing common hotkeys (copy, paste, etc.) which allowed fast keyboard-free copy-paste [13], while the other user continued using standard hotkeys. Conversely, the second user created a menu for controlling iTunes and his multimedia home environment.

Both users created a menu for opening the most frequently used applications. This menu was considered especially helpful because it allowed fast switching from an application to another. Moreover, activating an application twice in sequence makes it disappear, which allows "glancing" at an application (e.g. quickly looking at the calendar or the mail). Menus contained shortcuts either performing the same kind of system function (e.g. launching applications) or mixing them. For instance, the Multimedia menu shown in Figure 9 contains shortcuts for opening Web pages (a Web interface) and applications (iTunes), activating commands (play/pause, next/previous), or sending commands to a remote application (for switching on the TV, etc.). This highlights the fact that users should not be arbitrarily forced to use different interaction techniques for performing related actions just because they trigger different mechanisms.

Shortcuts areas were positioned in very different ways by the two users. For instance, one user liked using areas on the bottom border of the touchpad, but the other user found this inconvenient and never used such areas, probably because of his specific way of placing hands. Another difference, visible at Figure 9, is that one user liked using areas in the touchpad center, while the other user mainly used areas along or close to the borders. This figure also shows that users customized the sizes of the areas to improve interaction. Initially, the two users also used directional Slides (a possibility offered by the software) but eventually only used MarkPad gestures because they kept creating shortcuts and space was missing.

Both users used tactile marks on the border, but none in the center of the touchpad because they found them inconvenient. One user used almost invisible transparent tape while the other preferred white marks as those shown on Figure 1. Both users used the marks on the border to locate the other areas (i.e. areas without marks towards the center of the touchpad). They used different border widths (about 5.5 and 8.5 mm) and mainly used the expert mode, which is consistent with the fact they created their own shortcuts and menus. These different strategies highlight the numerous possibilities offered by the technique and the importance of customization.

We developed a shortcut editor which allows associating MarkPad Strokes (and directional Slides) with all the above-described actions (Figure 9). This editor can be invoked by clicking on the MarkPad icon on the MacOS menu bar or by pressing the mouse on a menu name while the Function key is held down. As said before, pressing this key shows all menu names. The user can then press the mouse on the desired menu name, then drag the mouse to create a new shortcut that is positioned where it is released. The editor is then automatically opened so that the user can specify the desired action. Various actions (such as generating common hotkeys) are predefined and only require selecting them in a menu. Opening applications, scripts or documents is almost as simple: the user just needs to select the corresponding action in a menu and paste or type the proper URL or command name. Help is provided for more complex commands.

As said above, this system allows for creating one's own customized vocabulary of gestures, but this may be too burdensome for novice users. A solution is to provide predefined sets of gestures activating common actions that the user would only customize if needed. More specialized sets of actions corresponding to functional themes could also be proposed. As the technique is especially useful for bookmarking Web pages and accessing them quickly, a functionality which is rarely offered by current software (or only for few items via a small favorite bar), it could be specially adapted for this purpose. As another direction, this system could also serve to implement some sort of a multiple-object clipboard that would allow users to easily store and access temporary content as in [36].

Finally, another important issue is the cost of mistakes (e.g. closing the wrong application), which may happen from time to time. This problem is already taken into account by quickly displaying the name of the activated command on the screen after performing a gesture, so that the user can know which command she triggered. However, a more sophisticated history mechanism may be useful to retrieve what gesture was fired, and, ideally, to undo undesired actions. Morever, the editing interface could guide the user to help him chose gestures that are very unlikely to be triggered unvoluntary for activating dangerous commands.

CONCLUSION AND FUTURE WORK

We presented MarkPad, a technique taking advantage of the touchpad to perform size-dependant gestural shortcuts. By taking the size of the gestures into account, which considerably increases the number of possible gestures, MarkPad supports a large number of commands and offers much flexibility for organizing them. MarkPad relies on augmenting the touchpad by adding visual or tactile marks on it, a simple solution that only requires cheap materials and allows using the technique at virtually no cost on current devices.

We reported on the results of two experimental studies evaluating command selection in expert mode with a dense configuration of 680 possible gestures, more than all existing techniques with a comparable input channel. Using a full tactile or visual interface to help selection, we obtained an accuracy of 95% and a completion time similar to well known techniques. Subjective results suggested that a mixed interface (borders with tactile marks and center with visual marks) was a promising solution. The accuracy reached 90% without marks at the center (without speed lost), but the results suggest that this simpler interface is viable when used with larger areas in the center of the touchpad. These studies also revealed that users need to look more at the touchpad using visual cues, which, interestingly, did not impede selection time.

We evaluated the usability of our design in everyday use with a study on 12 participants that lasted one week. It confirmed our assumption that borders are seldom used for pointing interaction, but still enough to trigger involuntary gestures. Our analysis highlighted 1) the impact of the width of the border areas, 2) that a gap between border and center areas reduces gesture detection, 3) that the gestures we propose are less prone to involuntary activation than directional slides. A MarkPad running prototype was finally presented along with two users feedback during a few months.

In future work, we plan to adapt the technique to touchscreens using technologies providing dynamic tactile feedback and to the mouse, using, for instance, a multitouch mouse [45]. Other ideas include (1) replacing the touchpad with a small touchscreen to dynamically display possible actions, (2) mapping the top border marks with the current application menus to allow accessing them directly without moving the cursor, (3) mixing MarkPad gestures with text entry (by pressing key(s) in sequence while touching a mark), thus creating a new type of hotkeys, (4) using new gestures, as for instance Augmented letters [38] starting from the borders. Finally, as the MarkPad design leverages spatial memory, it should also favor memorization, an aspect we also plan to study.

ACKNOWLEDGMENTS

This research was partially funded by Labex DigiCosme (ANR-11-LABEX-0045-DIGICOSME), operated by the French Agence Nationale de la Recherche (ANR) as part of the program "Investissement d'Avenir" Idex Paris-Saclay (ANR-11-IDEX-0003-02). The authors would like to thank Gilles Bailly and Sylvain Malacria for fruitful discussions, and the reviewers for their comments that helped improve the paper.

REFERENCES

1. Actronika. Tactronik. Retrieved January 2017 from http://www.actronika.com/
2. Georg Apitz and François Guimbretière. 2004. Crossy: A crossing-based drawing application. In *Proceedings of the 17th Annual ACM Symposium on User Interface Software and Technology (UIST '04)*. ACM, 3–12. DOI: 10.1145/1029632.1029635
3. Caroline Appert and Shumin Zhai. 2009. Using strokes as command shortcuts: Cognitive benefits and toolkit support. In *Proceedings of the SIGCHI Conference on Human Factors in Computing Systems (CHI '09)*. ACM, 2289–2298. DOI: 10.1145/1518701.1519052
4. A.D. Baddeley. 2013. *Essentials of Human Memory (Classic Edition)*. Psychology Press, East Sussex, UK.
5. Gilles Bailly, Eric Lecolinet, and Laurence Nigay. 2008. Flower menus: A new type of marking menu with large menu breadth, within groups and efficient expert mode memorization. In *Proceedings of the Working Conference on Advanced Visual Interfaces (AVI '08)*. ACM, 15–22. DOI: 10.1145/1385569.1385575
6. Gilles Bailly, Thomas Pietrzak, Jonathan Deber, and Daniel J. Wigdor. 2013. Métamorphe: Augmenting hotkey usage with actuated keys. In *Proceedings of the SIGCHI Conference on Human Factors in Computing Systems (CHI '13)*. ACM, 563–572. DOI: 10.1145/2470654.2470734
7. Olivier Bau and Wendy E. Mackay. 2008. Octopocus: A dynamic guide for learning gesture-based command sets. In *Proceedings of the 21st Annual ACM Symposium on User Interface Software and Technology (UIST '08)*. ACM, 37–46. DOI: 10.1145/1449715.1449724
8. Olivier Bau, Ivan Poupyrev, Ali Israr, and Chris Harrison. 2010. Teslatouch: Electrovibration for touch surfaces. In *Proceedings of the 23Nd Annual ACM Symposium on User Interface Software and Technology (UIST '10)*. ACM, 283–292. DOI: 10.1145/1866029.1866074
9. Mathieu Berthellemy, Elodie Cayez, Marwan Ajem, Gilles Bailly, Sylvain Malacria, and Eric Lecolinet. 2015. SpotPad, LociPad, ChordPad and InOutPad: Investigating gesture-based input on touchpad. In *Proceedings of the 27th Conference on L'Interaction Homme-Machine (IHM '15)*. ACM, Article 4, 8 pages. DOI: 10.1145/2820619.2820623
10. Gordon H. Bower, Michal C. Clark, Alan M. Lesgold, and David Winzenz. 1969. Hierarchical retrieval schemes in recall of categorized word lists. *Journal of Verbal Learning and Verbal Behavior* 8, 3, 323–343. DOI: 10.1016/S0022-5371(69)80124-6
11. Andrew Bragdon, Eugene Nelson, Yang Li, and Ken Hinckley. 2011. Experimental analysis of touch-screen gesture designs in mobile environments. In *Proceedings of the SIGCHI Conference on Human Factors in Computing Systems (CHI '11)*. ACM, 403–412. DOI: 10.1145/1978942.1979000
12. Géry Casiez, Daniel Vogel, Qing Pan, and Christophe Chaillou. 2007. RubberEdge: Reducing clutching by combining position and rate control with elastic feedback. In *Proceedings of the 20th Annual ACM Symposium on User Interface Software and Technology (UIST '07)*. ACM, 129–138. DOI: 10.1145/1294211.1294234
13. Olivier Chapuis and Nicolas Roussel. 2007. Copy-and-paste between overlapping windows. In *Proceedings of the SIGCHI Conference on Human Factors in Computing Systems (CHI '07)*. ACM, 201–210. DOI: 10.1145/1240624.1240657
14. Christian Corsten, Christian Cherek, Thorsten Karrer, and Jan Borchers. 2015. Hapticase: Back-of-device tactile landmarks for eyes-free absolute indirect touch. In *Proceedings of the 33rd Annual ACM Conference on Human Factors in Computing Systems (CHI '15)*. ACM, 2171–2180. DOI: 10.1145/2702123.2702277
15. Mary Czerwinski, Maarten Van Dantzich, George Robertson, and Hunter Hoffman. 1999. The contribution of thumbnail image, mouse-over text and spatial location memory to web page retrieval in 3D. In *Proceedings of INTERACT*, Vol. 99. ISO Press, 163–170. http://www.msr-waypoint.net/en-us/um/people/marycz/interact99.pdf
16. Jérémie Gilliot, Géry Casiez, and Nicolas Roussel. 2014. Impact of form factors and input conditions on absolute indirect-touch pointing tasks. In *Proceedings of the SIGCHI Conference on Human Factors in Computing Systems (CHI '14)*. ACM, 723–732. DOI: 10.1145/2556288.2556997
17. Tovi Grossman, Xiang Anthony Chen, and George Fitzmaurice. 2015. Typing on glasses: Adapting text entry to smart eyewear. In *Proceedings of the 17th International Conference on Human-Computer Interaction with Mobile Devices and Services (MobileHCI '15)*. ACM, 144–152. DOI: 10.1145/2785830.2785867
18. Carl Gutwin, Andy Cockburn, Joey Scarr, Sylvain Malacria, and Scott C. Olson. 2014. Faster command selection on tablets with FastTap. In *Proceedings of the SIGCHI Conference on Human Factors in Computing Systems (CHI '14)*. ACM, 2617–2626. DOI: 10.1145/2556288.2557136
19. Chris Harrison and Scott E. Hudson. 2009. Providing dynamically changeable physical buttons on a visual display. In *Proceedings of the SIGCHI Conference on Human Factors in Computing Systems (CHI '09)*. ACM, 299–308. DOI: 10.1145/1518701.1518749
20. Andreas Hegenberg. BetterTouchTool application. Retrieved January 2017 from https://www.boastr.net
21. Mohit Jain and Ravin Balakrishnan. 2012. User learning and performance with bezel menus. In *Proceedings of the SIGCHI Conference on Human Factors in Computing Systems (CHI '12)*. ACM, 2221–2230. DOI: 10.1145/2207676.2208376

22. Yvonne Jansen, Pierre Dragicevic, and Jean-Daniel Fekete. 2012. Tangible remote controllers for wall-size displays. In *Proceedings of the SIGCHI Conference on Human Factors in Computing Systems (CHI '12)*. ACM, 2865–2874. DOI: 10.1145/2207676.2208691

23. Yvonne Jansen, Thorsten Karrer, and Jan Borchers. 2010. Mudpad: A tactile memory game. In *ACM International Conference on Interactive Tabletops and Surfaces (ITS '10)*. ACM, 306–306. DOI: 10.1145/1936652.1936734

24. William P. Jones and Susan T. Dumais. 1986. The spatial metaphor for user interfaces: Experimental tests of reference by location versus name. *ACM Trans. Inf. Syst.* 4, 1, 42–63. DOI: 10.1145/5401.5405

25. Yuki Kubo, Buntarou Shizuki, and Jiro Tanaka. 2016. B2B-Swipe: Swipe gesture for rectangular smartwatches from a bezel to a bezel. In *Proceedings of the 2016 CHI Conference on Human Factors in Computing Systems (CHI '16)*. ACM, 3852–3856. DOI: 10.1145/2858036.2858216

26. Gordon Kurtenbach and William Buxton. 1991. Issues in combining marking and direct manipulation techniques. In *Proceedings of the 4th Annual ACM Symposium on User Interface Software and Technology (UIST '91)*. ACM, 137–144. DOI: 10.1145/120782.120797

27. Gordon Kurtenbach and William Buxton. 1993. The limits of expert performance using hierarchic marking menus. In *Proceedings of the INTERCHI '93 Conference on Human Factors in Computing Systems (INTERCHI '93)*. IOS Press, 482–487. http://dl.acm.org/citation.cfm?id=164632.164977

28. Benjamin Lafreniere, Carl Gutwin, Andy Cockburn, and Tovi Grossman. 2016. Faster command selection on touchscreen watches. In *Proceedings of the 2016 CHI Conference on Human Factors in Computing Systems (CHI '16)*. ACM, 4663–4674. DOI: 10.1145/2858036.2858166

29. MagicPrefs. Magic Trackpad application. Retrieved January 2017 from http://magicprefs.com

30. George A Miller. 1956. The magical number seven, plus or minus two: Some limits on our capacity for processing information. *Psychological review* 63, 2, 81. DOI: 10.1037/h0043158

31. Mathieu Nancel and Michel Beaudouin-Lafon. 2008. *Extending Marking Menus with Integral Dimensions: Application to the Dartboard Menu*. Technical Report Technical report 1503. LRI.

32. K. L. Norman. 1991. *The Psychology of Menu Selection: Designing Cognitive Control at the Human/Computer Interface*. Ablex Publishing Corp., Norwood, NJ, USA.

33. Pekka Parhi, Amy K. Karlson, and Benjamin B. Bederson. 2006. Target size study for one-handed thumb use on small touchscreen devices. In *Proceedings of the 8th Conference on Human-computer Interaction with Mobile Devices and Services (MobileHCI '06)*. ACM, 203–210. DOI: 10.1145/1152215.1152260

34. Thomas V. Perneger. 1998. What's wrong with bonferroni adjustments. *British Medical Journal* 316, 7139, 1236–1238. DOI: 10.1136/bmj.316.7139.1236

35. Simon T. Perrault, Eric Lecolinet, Yoann Pascal Bourse, Shengdong Zhao, and Yves Guiard. 2015. Physical loci: Leveraging spatial, object and semantic memory for command selection. In *Proceedings of the 33rd Annual ACM Conference on Human Factors in Computing Systems (CHI '15)*. ACM, 299–308. DOI: 10.1145/2702123.2702126

36. Jeffrey Pierce, Matthew Conway, Maarten van Dantzich, and George Robertson. 1999. Toolspaces and glances: storing, accessing, and retrieving objects in 3d desktop applications. In *Proceedings of the SIGCHI Conference on Human Factors in Computing Systems (CHI '99)*. ACM, 163–168.

37. Volker Roth and Thea Turner. 2009. Bezel swipe: Conflict-free scrolling and multiple selection on mobile touch screen devices. In *Proceedings of the SIGCHI Conference on Human Factors in Computing Systems (CHI '09)*. ACM, 1523–1526. DOI: 10.1145/1518701.1518933

38. Quentin Roy, Sylvain Malacria, Yves Guiard, Eric Lecolinet, and James Eagan. 2013. Augmented letters: Mnemonic gesture-based shortcuts. In *Proceedings of the SIGCHI Conference on Human Factors in Computing Systems (CHI '13)*. ACM, 2325–2328. DOI: 10.1145/2470654.2481321

39. Joey Scarr, Andy Cockburn, and Carl. Gutwin. 2012a. Supporting and exploiting spatial memory in user interfaces. *Foundations and Trends in Human-Computer Interaction* 6, 1, 1–84.

40. Joey Scarr, Andy Cockburn, Carl Gutwin, and Andrea Bunt. 2012b. Improving command selection with CommandMaps. In *Proceedings of the SIGCHI Conference on Human Factors in Computing Systems (CHI '12)*. ACM, 257–266. DOI: 10.1145/2207676.2207713

41. Joey Scarr, Andy Cockburn, Carl Gutwin, and Sylvain Malacria. 2013. Testing the robustness and performance of spatially consistent interfaces. In *Proceedings of the SIGCHI Conference on Human Factors in Computing Systems (CHI '13)*. ACM, 3139–3148. DOI: 10.1145/2470654.2466430

42. Katherine Schramm, Carl Gutwin, and Andy Cockburn. 2016. Supporting transitions to expertise in hidden toolbars. In *Proceedings of the 2016 CHI Conference on Human Factors in Computing Systems (CHI '16)*. ACM, 4687–4698. DOI: 10.1145/2858036.2858412

43. Marcos Serrano, Eric Lecolinet, and Yves Guiard. 2013. Bezel-tap gestures: Quick activation of commands from sleep mode on tablets. In *Proceedings of the SIGCHI Conference on Human Factors in Computing Systems (CHI '13)*. ACM, 3027–3036. DOI: 10.1145/2470654.2481421

44. Tobii Eyetracking. Tobii EyeX. Retrieved January 2017 from http://www.tobii.com/xperience/

45. Nicolas Villar, Shahram Izadi, Dan Rosenfeld, Hrvoje Benko, John Helmes, Jonathan Westhues, Steve Hodges, Eyal Ofek, Alex Butler, Xiang Cao, and Billy Chen. 2009. Mouse 2.0: Multi-touch meets the mouse. In *Proceedings of the 22nd Annual ACM Symposium on User Interface Software and Technology (UIST '09)*. ACM, 33–42. DOI: 10.1145/1622176.1622184

46. Daniel Vogel and Patrick Baudisch. 2007. Shift: A technique for operating pen-based interfaces using touch. In *Proceedings of the SIGCHI Conference on Human Factors in Computing Systems (CHI '07)*. ACM, 657–666. DOI: 10.1145/1240624.1240727

47. Julie Wagner, Eric Lecolinet, and Ted Selker. 2014. Multi-finger chords for hand-held tablets: Recognizable and memorable. In *Proceedings of the 32Nd Annual ACM Conference on Human Factors in Computing Systems (CHI '14)*. ACM, 2883–2892. DOI: 10.1145/2556288.2556958

48. Jacob O. Wobbrock, Htet Htet Aung, Brandon Rothrock, and Brad A. Myers. 2005. Maximizing the guessability of symbolic input. In *CHI '05 Extended Abstracts on Human Factors in Computing Systems (CHI EA '05)*. ACM, 1869–1872. DOI: 10.1145/1056808.1057043

49. Shengdong Zhao, Maneesh Agrawala, and Ken Hinckley. 2006. Zone and polygon menus: Using relative position to increase the breadth of multi-stroke marking menus. In *Proceedings of the SIGCHI Conference on Human Factors in Computing Systems (CHI '06)*. ACM, 1077–1086. DOI: 10.1145/1124772.1124933

Experimental Evaluation of Sketching on Surfaces in VR

Rahul Arora[1,2], Rubaiat Habib Kazi[2], Fraser Anderson[2], Tovi Grossman[2],
Karan Singh[1], George Fitzmaurice[2]
[1]DGP Lab, University of Toronto, Toronto, ON, Canada [2]Autodesk Research, Toronto, ON, Canada
{arorar, karan}@dgp.toronto.edu {firstname.lastname}@autodesk.com

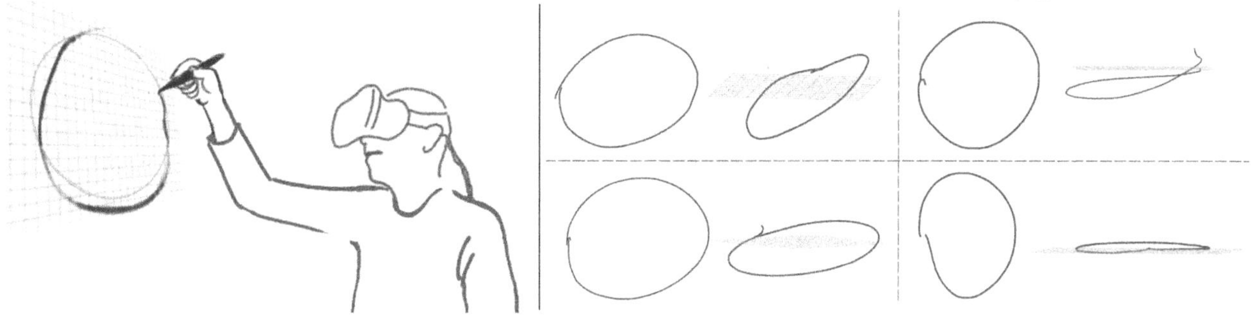

Figure 1. Virtual Reality affords the freedom to sketch in unconstrained 3D spaces (left). However, our study indicates that drawing accurately in VR is challenging. Inaccuracies in depth as well as the target planar projection (right) are common.

ABSTRACT
Sketching in immersive 3D virtual reality (VR) environments has great potential for a variety of interactive 3D design applications. Precisely sketching the intended strokes in mid-air, however, can be a challenge. In this paper, we present a set of controlled studies to analyze the factors affecting human ability to sketch freely in a 3D VR environment. In our first study, we directly compare traditional sketching on a physical surface to sketching in VR, with and without a physical surface to rest the stylus on. Our results indicate that the lack of a physical drawing surface is a major cause of inaccuracies in VR drawing, and that the effect is dependent on the orientation of the drawing surface. In a second experiment, we evaluate the extent to which visual guidance can compensate for the loss of sketching precision in VR. We found that while additional visual guidance improves positional accuracy, it can be detrimental to the aesthetic quality of strokes. We conclude by distilling our experimental findings into design guidelines for sketching tools in immersive 3D environments.

Author Keywords
Virtual reality; 3D drawing; motor ability; visual factors.

ACM Classification Keywords
H.5.1 Information interfaces and presentation (e.g., HCI): Artificial, augmented, and virtual realities.

CHI 2017, May 06-11, 2017, Denver, CO, USA
© 2017 ACM. ISBN 978-1-4503-4655-9/17/05…$15.00
DOI: http://dx.doi.org/10.1145/3025453.3025474

INTRODUCTION
Recent advancements in Virtual and Augmented Reality (VR/AR) devices have spurred considerable public interest in utilizing the technology for design applications. The availability of consumer-grade devices such as HTC Vive and Microsoft HoloLens has enabled development of mainstream and experimental tools for a variety of visual design tasks such as painting & sketching [43, 44], 3D modeling [44], storytelling [9], and conceptualization [21]. These tools have the potential to change how everyday objects are visualized and designed as they allow users to create, view and modify their designs in 3D at a real-world scale (see Figure 2).

Sketching is a basic task used in many visual design pipelines due to its freeform and expressive nature. Since freehand sketching provides an intuitive method of conceptualizing ideas, there has been considerable research [4, 10, 18, 34, 41, 42] into using freehand sketches to create three-dimensional artifacts by lifting 2D sketches into the third dimension. The HCI community has complemented this research by producing interfaces allowing sketching directly in 3D [15, 25, 36]. Prior works [20, 36] indicate that professional designers are excited by the possibility of using direct 3D input for sketching, but find it difficult, and get frustrated by the lack of control over their strokes (Figure 1). While there have been some quantitative studies exploring how 3D sketching capabilities improve with learning [40] and how force feedback affects precision [27], here has been limited work that evaluates and quantifies the factors which influence drawing in unconstrained, mid-air environments.

In this paper, we perform a set of formal experiments to study the human ability to draw in mid-air VR environments, and explore the impact that physical and visual guidance can have on 3D sketching accuracy. We first conduct a series of observational sessions with professional designers to understand how professionals approach mid-air sketching. Based on these sessions, we formulate an experiment aimed at quantifying drawing accuracy in VR compared to traditional 2D drawing by varying the presence of a physical drawing surface, in three canonical orientations. We then conduct a second experiment to observe how visual guidance provided by the drawing system in VR impacts drawing accuracy for both planar and non-planar curves, across a greater range of surface orientations.

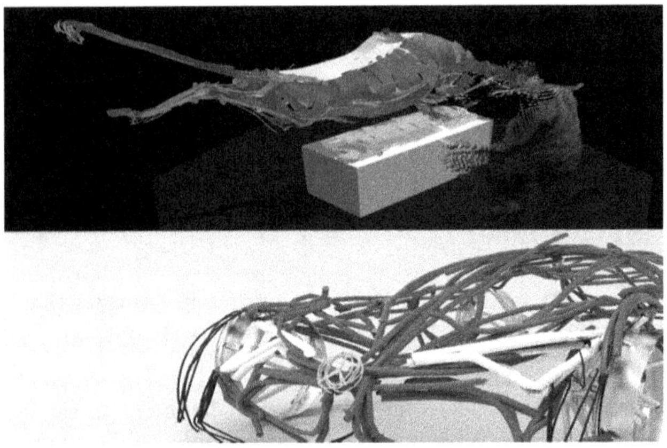

Figure 2. VR sketching using consumer-grade tools—Google Tilt Brush (top[i]) and Gravity Sketch (bottom[ii]).

Our first study showed that the mid-air drawing accuracy in VR, measured via the mean overall deviation from a target stroke, decreased by 148% compared to traditional 2D drawing. However, by including a physical drawing surface within a VR environment, the loss of accuracy was reduced to 20%. Our second study found that visual guidance can serve to improve mid-air sketching accuracy, but leads to worse aesthetic quality of strokes, as measured via curve fairness [12]. In both studies, surface orientation was a key factor of the above accuracy levels. Based on these results, we present a broad set of interaction guidelines that can help guide the future design of VR-based design tools.

RELATED WORK

Our work relates to existing literature on 3D curve creation, design using immersive displays, and drawing ability evaluations. We discuss each of these below.

3D Curve Creation

The traditional method for creating curves in 3D is by using a set of interface elements to specify multiple geometric constraints leading to the final 3D curve. Desktop modelling software allows users to drag control points in 3D space to create the desired curvature. Alternative interfaces in the research literature include specialized hardware such as Grossman et al.'s tape based system [16], or using software-based interfaces such as the one proposed by Bae et al. [4] to specify projection planes.

Closer to our topic of study is a class of 3D curve creation techniques that involve freehand 3D motion to specify curves. Due to the lack of 3D display technologies, early systems, such as the 3-Draw tool [33] were forced to use 2D displays. More recently, 3D display and head tracking technologies have enabled the creation of complex and high quality curve networks [27, 29, 39] using mid-air 3D motion as direct input. Notably, such systems have mostly been explored for generating freeform "organic" curves (Figure 2). We hypothesize that this is because of the innate difference in human drawing ability in 2D compared to 3D, and this forms an important motivation of the initial observation sessions presented in this paper.

Design using Immersive Display Technologies

Early graphics research produced a number of prototypes for design tools utilizing immersive hardware (displays covering a large field-of-view) [29, 39, 41]. Recent advancements in immersive display and spatial tracking technologies have led to a new spur in commercial, research, as well as hobbyist tools harnessing virtual reality for painting, drawing, and modelling tasks [9, 21, 43–45]. Demand for VR content has inspired the creation of novel VR interfaces for authoring storyboards [17] and animations [46].However, limited work has investigated the usability and human factors of such 3D design tools. To study designer preference for various UI interfaces, Israel et al. [20] conducted a luminary study involving focus groups of expert designers. While they collected subjective opinions on 3D drawing and sketching, there was no quantitative evaluation of how designers utilized these interaction techniques.

Drawing Ability Evaluation

There have been many studies on human drawing ability in the fields of motor control, psychology, and HCI. Cohen and Bennett [8] attributed the misperception of the target object as a major reason for drawing inaccuracies. Schmidt et al. [35] focused on expert performance in drawing simple curves in various different projections, and found that even expert artists fail to perceive and/or draw on 2D projections of 3D objects accurately. Fitzmaurice et al. [13] discussed how artists reach optimal orientations in pen-and-paper drawing by rotating the paper, and how digital interfaces for 2D drawing can support this interaction. Our study extends these findings to freehand 3D sketching.

In the VR domain, Keefe et al. [26, 27] studied the impact of force feedback on 3D sketching accuracy by utilizing a Phantom Omni haptic device. In contrast, we compare mid-air sketching to the natural, passive feedback provided by a physical surface, thus better mimicking the traditional drawing setting. Further, unlike a Phantom Omni, this does not limit input range. We also quantify the influence of various factors in isolation, and present novel results on surface-projected sketch accuracy. Jackson and Keefe [22] and Kühnert et al. [28] performed design studies to explore sketching over physical props for rapid prototyping. These works informed the visual guidance in our second study.

Perhaps the investigation closest in application to ours is that of Wiese et al. [40], who studied the learnability of mid-air sketching in a CAVE environment. Our research contributes new findings on how factors such as physical constraints, visual guidance, orientation, and scale affects mid-air drawing ability in a head-mounted VR environment.

Motor control studies, such as the one by Abend et al. [1], have studied the speed and position profiles of the human hand for various target motions. In the HCI community, various models for understanding speed and accuracy have been proposed for 2D gestures [7, 19], but work in 3D has been limited to low-level motor control evaluations [24].

INITIAL OBSERVATIONAL SESSIONS

Before conducting our two controlled experiments, we first directly observed artists working within a VR 3D sketching system. The goal of these sessions was to obtain feedback on the challenges and opportunities of 3D freehand sketching. The resulting observations would be used to guide the areas of focus for our quantitative evaluation.

We invited five expert designers (two industrial designers, two concept artists, and an architect) to participate in a design session using Tilt Brush [43] (version 5.4), a VR sketching application. An HTC Vive device was used for the sessions. Participants were asked to generate a 3D sketch of anything related to their domain and expertise in a 60-minute session.

Observations

In general, the participants were positive about the ability to draw in scale, directly in 3D, utilizing the immersive and freeform nature of VR sketching. Artists drew conceptual models of edge-heavy objects such as cars, an interior design of a room, as well as organic shapes such as shoes and humans. We observed that the drawing characteristics seemed to vary across various positions and orientations of the drawing plane. Participants did mention that accuracy and precision of the strokes in 3D VR environments were more critical, compared to its 2D counterparts:

"In 3D situations, line accuracy is more important than 2D situations, since you're conveying more information to the viewer. In 2D, the viewer needs to make a mental leap to go from 2D to 3D. On the contrary, in 3D, because you get more info, you're looking more precisely at the quality of the line" (P2)

In general, participants felt that is could be challenging to depict a desired shape, noting in particular that curves that were meant to be planar often ended up as convex (P2, P5). The participants also felt they could not always achieve the intended result due to inaccurate positioning (P1, P2). The designers unanimously agreed that they require more tools for precision and greater controls for meaningful design tasks in VR. Participants suggested having snapping tools (P2, P3), haptic feedback (P1, P4), and projection to existing planes and surfaces (P2, P3, P5). Participants (P2-P5) also reported that ergonomic issues such as neck and shoulder pain may occur when using VR over an extended period.

Our observations are consistent with those that can be made from existing repositories of VR sketching workflows [47]. While artists were able to design successfully, there were certainly struggles when trying to depict a desired curve accurately in 3D space. In the following sections, we present two controlled experiments to gain a better understanding the human limits of freehand drawing, which could eventually lead to design recommendations for such systems.

EXPERIMENT 1: VR VS. TRADITIONAL DRAWING

While the ability to draw non-planar curves makes mid-air sketching unique, planar curves play an integral role for both shape perception and within the 3D design process, as evidenced by numerous previous works [4, 30, 41], as well as our initial observational sessions. In the first experiment, we sought to investigate how mid-air drawing ability of planar curves in VR compares to traditional drawing on a flat surface. In particular, we wanted to study how the presence or absence of a physical drawing surface affects drawing of planar curves. To this end, the participants were exposed to three main experimental conditions. In the *traditional* condition, participants drew on a physical surface. In the *VR* condition, participants used a VR head-mounted display and drew in 3D space. In the *hybrid* condition, participants drew on a physical surface while using the same VR headset.

Experimental Design

The experiment was designed as a 3 x 3 x 3 x 3 within-subjects study, with independent variables of *Condition* (*traditional*, *hybrid*, *VR*), *Drawing Plane* (*horizontal*, *vertical*, *sideways*), *Shape* (*u-line*, *v-line*, *circle*), and *Size* (*small*: 10cm, *medium*: 30cm, *large*: 60cm). The three drawing plane configurations are illustrated in Figure 3a. All of these planes were located at a comfortable position [6, 32]. For each of these planes, we defined *U-V* coordinate axes that define the *u-line* and *v-line* orientations (Figure 3b).

Participants performed the experiment in a single session lasting 40-50 minutes. The order in which participants were exposed to each *condition* was counterbalanced by a Latin square. Within each condition, the order of the appearance of the drawing planes was again dictated by a Latin square per participant. For each plane orientation, the stroke shape order was randomized. For each stroke shape, participants had to complete three sets of trials, each of which was a random permutation of the three stroke sizes. Overall, each participant drew 243 strokes. For practice, participants drew a medium-sized stroke for each shape, before each condition.

Participants

In total, 12 able-bodied individuals (8 male, 4 female), aged 22 to 51, participated in the study. All participants were right-handed or ambidextrous, and used their right hand to draw. Participants were 164-183cm tall, and none had sketching experience using VR/AR devices, or professional drawing experience. Participants were paid for participating.

Apparatus

In the *traditional* condition, participants had access to a large (84") display, which displayed the target strokes and was used as a physical drawing surface. Drawing was performed using a dry-erase pen augmented with motion-capture markers (Figure 4a). However, strokes were only recorded when the participants pressed a trigger on a HTC Vive controller (Figure 4b) held in their left hand. In the *hybrid* condition, participants wore the HTC Vive HMD, and the large display was still used as the drawing surface. Simplified 3D models of the display and the tracked pen were rendered via the HMD. In the *VR* condition, no drawing surface was used or displayed, and a matte gray background was rendered. In all the three conditions, the pen position and orientation was tracked at 60 Hz using OptiTrack motion capture cameras. The HTC Vive display had a refresh rate of 90Hz. The software for the experiment was implemented in C# using Unity and SteamVR for rendering and interaction, and OptiTrack's Motive software for motion capture.

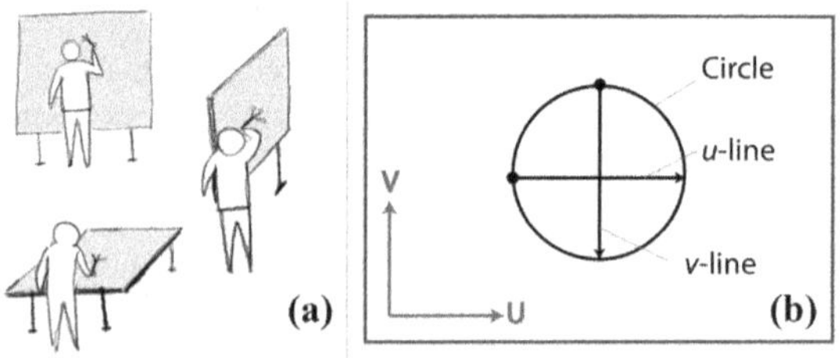

Figure 3. Alignment of the three *drawing planes* (a) clockwise from top: *vertical*, *sideways*, and *horizontal*; and arrangment of the three stroke shapes (b) in Experiment 1.

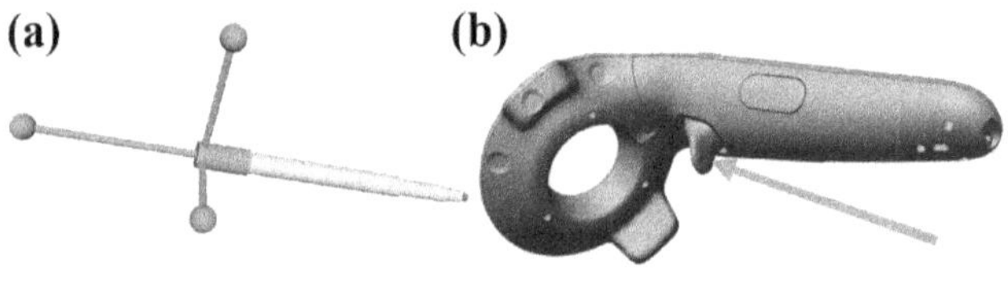

Figure 4. Apparatus: The motion-captured pen (a) and the HTC Vive controller (b) used for drawing.

Procedure

Participants were instructed to stand at a fixed spot before starting to draw in a new drawing plane to ensure controlled results. Without this constraint, participants would be able to change their orientation relative to the drawing surface, thereby confounding the results. For the *horizontal* orientation, the drawing surface was kept at a height of 1m, while for the other two orientations, the surface was arranged so that the center of the stroke was at a height of 1.4m. Following ergonomic guidelines [32], the target strokes were centered approx. 40cm in front of participants.

The trial started with the participant being shown the target stroke along with the starting point, both rendered in black. Participants were instructed to draw all circles in a clockwise direction, while the starting spots on lines were chosen so that the horizontal lines were drawn left-to-right or far-to-near, and the vertical lines top-to-bottom. The target stroke was shown until the participant pressed the trigger in their left hand to initiate drawing. Participants were told to execute the strokes as quickly and accurately as possible. Strokes were rejected automatically if any point on the input was over 20cm away from the target, and the trial was repeated.

For the *traditional* condition, the target strokes were shown on the large screen, and the marker left a visible ink trail. For the *hybrid* condition, the screen was tracked by motion capture markers, and rendered virtually at the same position in space so that participants actually drew on the physical surface. In the *VR* and *hybrid* conditions, participants used the same pen to draw, but the target and drawn strokes were shown via the HMD.

In the *traditional* condition, an experimenter erased the stroke drawn by the participant after each trial. In the *hybrid* and *VR* conditions, the input stroke was hidden 1 second after the participant finished drawing it.

Data Preparation

Strokes were recorded as sequences of 3D points sampled at 60Hz. The points were initially transformed to a local coordinate system defined relative to the target stroke. This is defined for lines such that the line starts at $(0, 0, 0)$ and ends at $(l, 0, 0)$, and for circles such that the target stroke is centered at $(0, 0, 0)$ and the starting point is at $(-l/2, 0, 0)$, where l is the value of the *size* variable. The local XY-plane for the stroke coincides with the drawing plane.

To preprocess the input data before error measures were computed, a median filter with a window size of 6 points (equivalent to 100ms) was applied to filter out any high frequency tracking noise. Some of the strokes in *traditional* and *hybrid* conditions had small tails sticking out of the plane at either ends of the stroke due to slight difference between the participants' intention of beginning/ending drawing and actually pressing/leaving the ON/OFF switch. These tails, found via deviation from mean z-coordinate of the stroke, were removed before further processing. Then, piecewise linear approximation of the stroke length was used to resample all input strokes to 100 equidistant points. Finally, all the strokes were translated such that the starting point matched the starting point of the target stroke. This was done to minimize the impact of positional error caused by participants misjudging the exact position of the target stroke, as well as equipment error such as minor inaccuracies in calibrating the coordinate axes of the motion capture system and the Vive. We denote a resampled and translated stroke S via the sequence of points $p_1, p_2, \dots, p_{100}$, where each point $p_i = (\mathrm{x}, \mathrm{y}, \mathrm{z})$ is represented as a 3-tuple.

Measurements

Repeated Measures-ANOVAs were performed to analyze various error measures. All post-hoc pairwise comparisons were performed using Bonferroni-corrected paired t-tests. The following measures were computed.

Mean Overall Deviation

Mean deviation is defined as the average distance of the (resampled) points of user-drawn stroke from the target stroke. Due to the resampling and positional correction in the pre-processing steps, this measure effectively computes the average distance of the drawn stroke from the target stroke. For a line, this is therefore defined as the average deviation from the local X-axis.

$$\overline{\text{OD}}_\text{L} = \frac{1}{n}\sum_{i=1}^{n}\sqrt{(p_i.y)^2 + (p_i.z)^2}$$

For circles, it is the average deviation from the target circle.

$$\overline{\text{OD}}_\text{C} = \frac{1}{n}\sum_{i=1}^{n}\sqrt{\left(\sqrt{(p_i.x)^2 + (p_i.y)^2} - l/2\right)^2 + (p_i.z)^2}$$

Mean Projected Deviation

Since two of the conditions involved a physical constraint that would eliminate any errors in the z direction, an informative measure of accuracy is also the deviation from the intended shape when the drawn shape is projected onto a plane. This can be computed by setting the z term in the mean overall deviation equations to zero. Note that for *traditional* and *hybrid* conditions, overall and projected deviations are equivalent, as $p_i.z$ is always zero.

Results

Mean Overall Deviation

The *condition* variable had a significant effect on the mean overall deviation ($F_{2,22} = 69.6, p < .001$). Statistically significant effects were also observed for *drawing plane* ($F_{2,22} = 8.09, p < .005$), *shape* ($F_{2,22} = 203, p < .001$) and *size* ($F_{2,22} = 169, p < .001$). The value for the *VR* condition ($M = 2.08\text{cm}, SD = 1.71\text{cm}$) was much higher than that for the *hybrid* ($M = 1.01\text{cm}, SD = 1.09\text{cm}$) and *traditional* ($M = 0.84\text{cm}, SD = 0.87\text{cm}$) conditions.

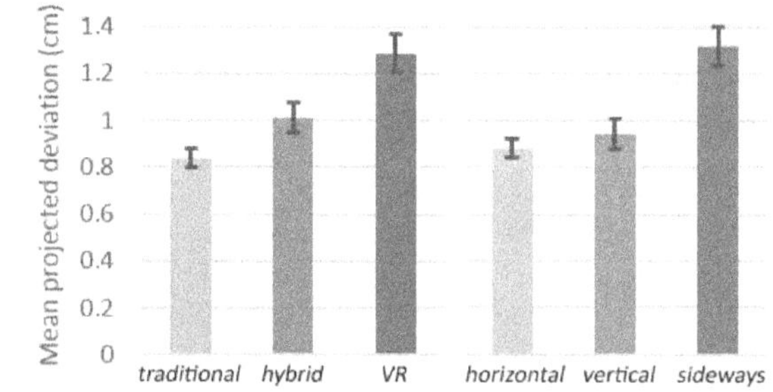

Figure 5. Main effects of *condition* (left) and *drawing plane* (right) for mean projected deviation.

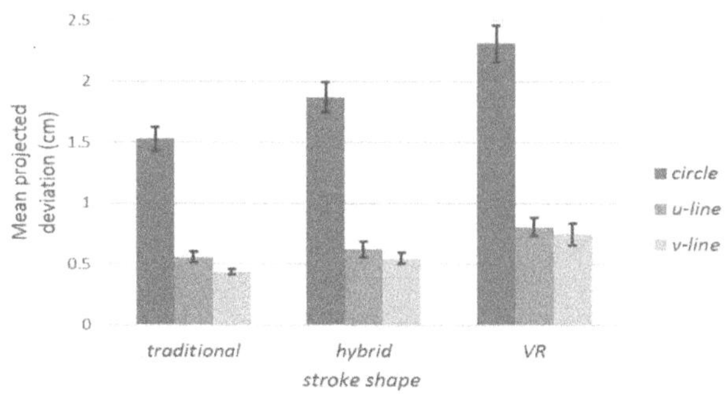

Figure 6. *Stroke shape* x *condition* interaction on mean projected deviation.

Post-hoc pairwise comparison showed that all three conditions were significantly different, with *VR* exhibiting over twice the inaccuracy of either of the other two conditions, showing that moving into the third dimension adds a large amount of inaccuracy. For brevity, we skip further discussion to focus on mean projected deviation.

Mean Projected Deviation

Significant main efects were observed for all four factors—*condition* ($F_{2,22} = 23.8, p < .001$), *drawing plane* ($F_{2,22} = 27.5, p < .001$), *shape* ($F_{2,22} = 173, p < .001$), and *size* ($F_{2,22} = 133, p < .001$). Interaction effects were observed for both *condition* x *shape* ($F_{4,44} = 6.89, p < .001$), *condition* x *size* ($F_{4,44} = 9.60, p < .001$), but not *condition* x *plane* ($F_{4,44} = 1.43, p = .24$).

The *VR* condition resulted in the highest deviation ($M = 1.29\text{cm}, SD = 1.32\text{cm}$) followed by *hybrid* ($M = 1.01\text{cm}$, $SD = 1.09\text{cm}$, and *traditional* ($M = 0.84\text{cm}$, $SD = 0.87\text{cm}$). Post-hoc pairwise comparison showed significant differences between all *conditions* ($p < .05$) (Figure 5, left).

Stated differently, there was a 20.2% decrease in accuracy by wearing an HMD and rendering the environment virtually, and a further 27.2% decrease by removing the supporting physical surface. These results demonstrate that the difficulty of in-air 3D sketching is two-fold, impacted by both motor and visual limitations. Visually, the user no longer has direct line of sight to their hand and pen, and must rely on virtual depth perception cues. From a motor standpoint, the lack of a physical surface introduces even further inaccuracies.

With respect to orientation, the *sideways* drawing plane had the largest mean projected deviation ($M = 1.32\text{cm}, SD = 1.30\text{cm}$), and was significantly different ($p < .01$) from both the *horizontal* ($M = 0.95\text{cm}, SD = 0.94\text{cm}$) and *vertical* ($M = 0.88\text{cm}, SD = 0.98\text{cm}$) planes which were not significantly different from each other (see Figure 5, right). The irregular movements required to draw on the *sideways* drawing plane likely contributed to these results.

Figure 6 shows the effects of *shape* for each condition. As one may expect, the *circle* caused the most difficulty, ($M = 1.90\text{cm}, SD = 1.38\text{cm}$) as compared to one-dimensional lines (combined $M = 0.62\text{cm}, SD = 0.62\text{cm}$). It can be seen that the effect is amplified in the *VR* condition, as indicated by the significant *condition* x *size* interaction. All values of *Size* were significantly different ($p < .001$), with the means following the order *small*: 0.54cm ($SD = 0.51\text{cm}$), *medium*: 0.94cm ($SD = 0.88\text{cm}$), and *large*: 1.65cm ($SD = 1.46\text{cm}$). This indicates that drawing a stroke of larger size is inherently more difficult, hinting at a trend similar to that observed by Cao and Zhai [7] for 2D gestures of much-smaller sizes. The trend is probably due to the increasing effect of the stroke being dictated by the natural arcs of arm movement.

Shape Trends

Beside aggregated measures of accuracy, it is also interesting to observe trends in deviation from target as participants progressed through the strokes. We visualize mean projected deviation trends for circles in Figure 7a. A noticeable effect is the consistency of the average circle across the *conditions*. In contrast, the average circles for the three *drawing planes* are visibly different (Figure 7b). This may be due to different muscle groups needed to draw on each of the planes.

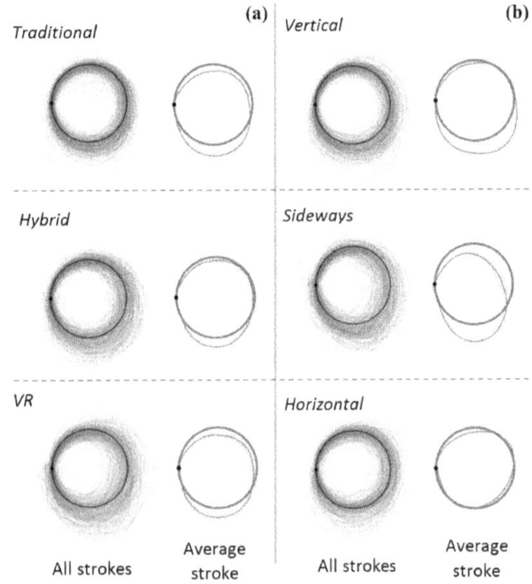

Figure 7. Visualization of projected deviation for *circles*. Circles drawn in different *conditions* (a), and *drawing planes* (b). For each row, all circles (left), and average circle with 95% confidence interval (right) are shown.

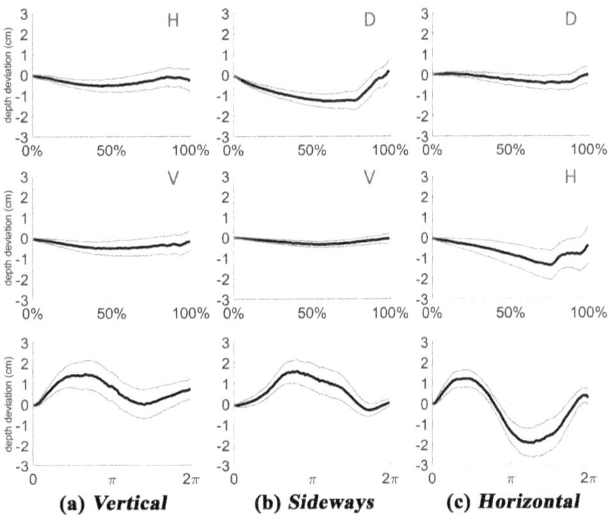

Figure 8. Depth deviation trends for different *drawing planes* and *shapes*. Row 1-2: lines, row 3: circles. Key for lines—H: horizontal left-to-right, V: vertical, and D: horizontal (depth) far-to-near.

For the *VR* condition, we can also look at the deviation in depth across the stroke progress. Figure 8 illustrates this effect of drift for each orientation and shape. In particular, it can be seen that the same lines drawn in different imaginary planes have very different characteristics. This may be an effect of pen grip, which was informally observed to change with the drawing planes, even in the *VR* condition.

EXPERIMENT 2: FACTORS OF VR DRAWING

Our first experiment showed that there are both motor and visual challenges involved with drawing in VR. In this second experiment, we focus on the VR drawing condition in greater depth, and determine if some of the challenges can be alleviated with enhanced visual guidance. Expanding on Experiment 1, we also examine a larger variety of plane orientations and the effect of drawing non-planar strokes.

Visual Guidance

A central challenge of working in 3D is being provided with adequate depth cues and visual feedback. We therefore explored combinations of two forms of visual guidance resulting in four visual guidance conditions (Figure 9).

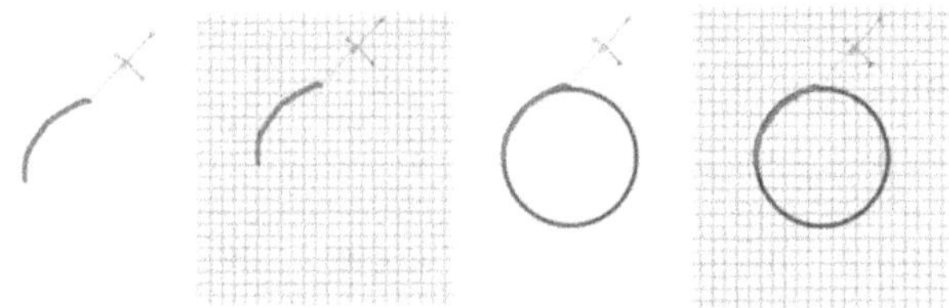

Figure 9. Visual guidance variants tested in Experiment 2. Left to right: *none*, *surface*, *stroke*, and *both*.

Surface Grid

Previous work in sketch-based modelling uses rendered surfaces to help users anchor their strokes in 3D [4]. We sought to examine the effect of visual guidance plane on the characteristics of sketched strokes. We use a grid line pattern as the rendered surface, as prior research [2, 5] suggests it as an effective texture for the perception of a surface.

Target Stroke

A more detailed form of visual guidance is to render and trace over the actual target stroke. In VR, this condition simulates drawing over virtual objects, inspired by existing literature [22]. Examples of this task include marking out boundaries of CT scan [23], or using an imported image or model as scaffolding to guide freehand strokes [15].

In addition to these two guidance conditions, we also test a condition that combined them (*both*), and a condition that provided no visual guidance (*none*).

Drawing Surface Orientations

To gain a deeper understanding of how the orientation of the drawing surface affects accuracy, we tested 13 different surface orientations. We positioned the drawing surfaces tangential to a hemisphere of radius 40cm, placed approx. 15cm in front of the participant's head. The orientation is defined using the pair of angles (φ, θ) by which the plane was rotated around the center of the hemisphere along the vertical (down-to-up) and horizontal (left-to-right) axes, respectively. Both φ and θ were defined to be zero for the vertical plane in front of the participant. The various orientations studied were (Figure 10a):

$$(\varphi = 0, \theta \in \{0, 45, -45, 90, -90\}),$$
$$(\varphi = 90, \theta = 0), (\varphi = -90, \theta = 0),$$
$$(\varphi = 45, \theta \in \{0, 45, -45\}), (\varphi = -45, \theta \in \{0, 45, -45\})$$

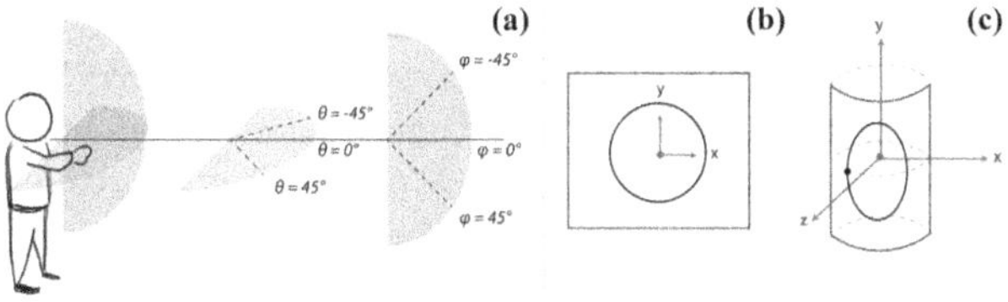

Figure 10. Orientations (a) and surface shapes—*flat* (b) and *curved* (c)—used in the Experiment 2.

Experimental Design

The experiment was designed as a 4x13x2 within-subject study. The independent variables were *visual guidance* (*none*, *surface*, *stroke*, *both*), *surface orientation* (see above) and *surface shape* (*curved* or *flat*). The curved surface consisted of a cylindrical surface of radius $R_0 = 15cm$ (Figure 10c). The target shape was fixed as a 30cm circle.

The experiment was divided into four blocks, one for each of the *visual guidance* conditions. The ordering of *visual guidance* was counterbalanced using a balanced Latin square. For each level of visual guidance, the participants were exposed to 13 orientations of the drawing surface, ordered randomly. For each of these orientations, they had to complete three sets of trials, each of which involved drawing two circular strokes—one on a planar surface (*flat*), and the other on the cylindrical surface (*curved*). The surface shapes were ordered randomly. Overall, each participant executed 312 strokes, in a single session lasting 50-80 minutes.

Participants

We recruited 12 able-bodied participants (8 male, 4 female), aged 22 to 53. None of the participants had experience using VR/AR for sketching, or professional experience sketching or painting. Participants were paid for their participation.

Procedure

Participants were instructed to stand at a fixed spot for the duration of the experiment, and to avoid moving their lower body as much as possible. The procedure was otherwise the same as the first experiment: participants used a trigger switch in their left hand to engage the pen, and the drawn stroke was shown to them in real-time. Each trial consisted of drawing a circle of diameter 30cm as a single stroke. The apparatus was the same as the first experiment, using an HTC Vive and OptiTrack system for display and tracking.

Data Preparation

The filtering procedure, as discussed in Experiment 1, was performed to remove tracking noise from the data. However, strokes were not translated to align their starting points, to observe how the presence or absence of certain visual guidance affects depth perception and positioning accuracy.

For comparing stroke characteristics for the two values of the *surface shape* variable, the circles drawn on the *curved* (cylindrical) surfaces were transformed to a planar circle by unwrapping the surface [3] such that it becomes the XY plane in the new coordinate system, while the Z direction remains the same. This unwrapping transforms curves drawn in the *curved* condition into an equivalent coordinates system as the curves drawn in the *flat* condition.

Measurements

The main measurement is mean projected deviation, as defined for Experiment 1, which represent the components of the overall deviation in the local XY plane. We also look at depth deviation (defined below), which represents the overall deviation in the local Z direction. We do not discuss overall deviation, as its trends were very similar to that of mean projected deviation. In addition to these accuracy levels, we also examine the aesthetic quality of the drawn strokes, and the stroke execution time.

Mean Depth Deviation

The mean depth deviation refers to mean deviation of the stroke from the target in local Z-direction ($^1/_n * \sum_{i=1}^{n} |p_i.z|$). This measure will help estimate the effectiveness of visual guidance to aid depth perception during the drawing task.

Mean Fairness Deviation

Fairness of a curve is an important measure of its aesthetic quality [12, 31], useful in many design applications. The fairness of a curve is defined using the smoothness of its curvature. We use a very simple approximation to compute this. Formally, if the curvature of the input curve at point p_j is C_j, then we define mean fairness deviation as:

$$\overline{\mathrm{FD}} = \left(\frac{1}{n-1}\right) \sum_{i=1}^{n-1} \frac{|C_{i+1} - C_i|}{\mathrm{avg}(C_i, C_{i+1})}.$$

Intuitively, this measure penalizes frequent curvature changes in the input stroke, which are undesirable in design applications. A perfect circle has a fairness deviation of 0.

Stroke Execution Time

Stroke execution time is the total time spent in executing a stroke. Measuring this allowed us to estimate the extent to which strokes were performed as rapid arm movements in contrast to participants correcting themselves mid-stroke.

Results

Mean Projected Deviation

Significant main effects were observed for *surface shape* ($F_{1,11} = 59.3, p < .001$), *visual guidance* ($F_{3,33} = 81.8, p < .001$), as well as for *surface orientation* ($F_{12,132} = 2.74, p < .01$). The *angle* x *surface shape* interaction was also significant ($F_{12,132} = 3.24, p < .001$).

For *visual guidance* conditions, the greatest error was with *none* ($M = 2.02$cm, $SD = 1.05$cm), followed by *surface* ($M = 1.67$cm, $SD = 0.72$cm), *stroke* ($M = 0.87$cm, $SD = 0.51$cm), and *both* ($M = 0.84$cm, $SD = 0.52$cm) (Figure 11, left). Post-hoc comparisons revealed that all pairs other than (*stroke*, *both*) were significantly different. This suggests that the drawing surface provides useful guidance for participants, and showing the target stroke helps even more.

However, showing the drawing surface when the target curve is already visible may not lead to additional accuracy.

For *surface shape*, mean projected deviation was higher for *curved* ($M = 1.63\text{cm}, SD = 0.97\text{cm}$), compared to *flat* ($M = 1.07\text{cm}, SD = 0.71\text{cm}$). This may be due to additional mental and motor overhead costs associated with drawing a non-planar stroke.

In contrast to the large effect of *drawing plane* observed in Experiment 1, the difference between various *surface orientations* was significant, but smaller. The maximum difference between any pair of surface orientation values was 0.32cm. This may be because the surfaces in this experiment were positioned to have projections of comparable sizes on the participants' eyes. Consistent with the first experiment, accuracy was greatest at the horizontal plane.

Mean Depth Deviation

The mean depth deviation was also significantly affected by *visual guidance* ($F_{3,33} = 23.8, p < .001$), *surface orientation* ($F_{12,132} = 4.52, p < .001$), and *surface shape* ($F_{1,11} = 8.75, p < .05$). Post-hoc comparisons revealed that *none* was significantly less accurate than each of the three visual guidance conditions. However, the three visual guidance conditions were not significantly different from one another (Figure 11, center). The exact values followed the order: *none* ($M = 2.11\text{cm}, SD = 1.02\text{cm}$), *surface* ($M = 1.37\text{cm}, SD = 1.11\text{cm}$), *stroke* ($M = 1.01\text{cm}, SD = 0.58\text{cm}$), and *both* ($M = 0.91\text{cm}, SD = 0.46\text{cm}$).

For *surface shape*, the mean depth deviation for *curved* surfaces ($M = 1.27\text{cm}, SD = 0.86\text{cm}$) was actually lower than for *planar* surfaces ($M = 1.43\text{cm}, SD = 1.04\text{cm}$). However, there was a significant interaction effect observed between *surface shape* and *visual guidance* ($F_{3,33} = 4.93, p < .01$). *Curved* surfaces exhibited higher depth deviation than *flat* ones when no visual guidance was provided, but lower depth deviation when any additional visual guidance was provided. This shows that with adequate visual feedback, users may be able to draw non-planar curves as accurately as planar ones.

The mean depth deviation trend for surface orientation is visualized in Figure 11, right. This data shows that sketching in the vertical plane is least accurate ($M = 1.66\text{cm}$, $SD = 1.35\text{cm}$), and accuracy gradually increases as the orientation moves away from the vertical plane in all directions. Consistent with the first study, accuracy is greatest at the horizontal plane ($M = 1.02\text{cm}, SD = 0.63\text{cm}$).

Mean Fairness Deviation

Both *visual guidance* ($F_{3,33} = 20.6, p < .001$) and *surface shape* ($F_{1,11} = 22.6, p < .001$) had a significant effect on Mean Fairness Deviation. Drawn curves were significantly fairer when the target curve was invisible when drawing ($M_{none} = 0.29$; $M_{surface} = 0.32$), as compared to when it was visible ($M_{stroke} = 0.37$; $M_{both} = 0.38$). This followed our informal observation, as participants focused on staying close to the target curve when that guide was displayed.

For surface shapes, we observed that circles drawn in *planar* condition ($M = 0.32, SD = 0.10$) were fairer than those on *curved* surfaces ($M = 0.36, SD = 0.09$). Lastly, *surface orientation* was found to be significant as well ($F_{11,132} = 7.73, p < .001$). In particular, drawing on the vertical plane ($(\phi, \theta) = (0, 0)$) produced the fairest curves.

Stroke Execution Time

Total time spent executing curves on the two *surface shapes* was significantly different ($F_{1,11} = 34.3, p < .001$). This is somewhat expected since the planar circles can be completed with a simple movement, while non-planar strokes on the *curved* surface require more careful manipulation of the arm. The level of *visual guidance* also significantly influenced ($F_{1,11} = 20.2, p < .001$) the curve execution time, with participants spending more time with increase in visual guidance ($M_{none} = 3.31s$, $M_{surface} = 4.11\text{s}$, $M_{stroke} = 5.58\text{s}$, $M_{both} = 6.02\text{s}$). All but the last two differences were statistically significant.

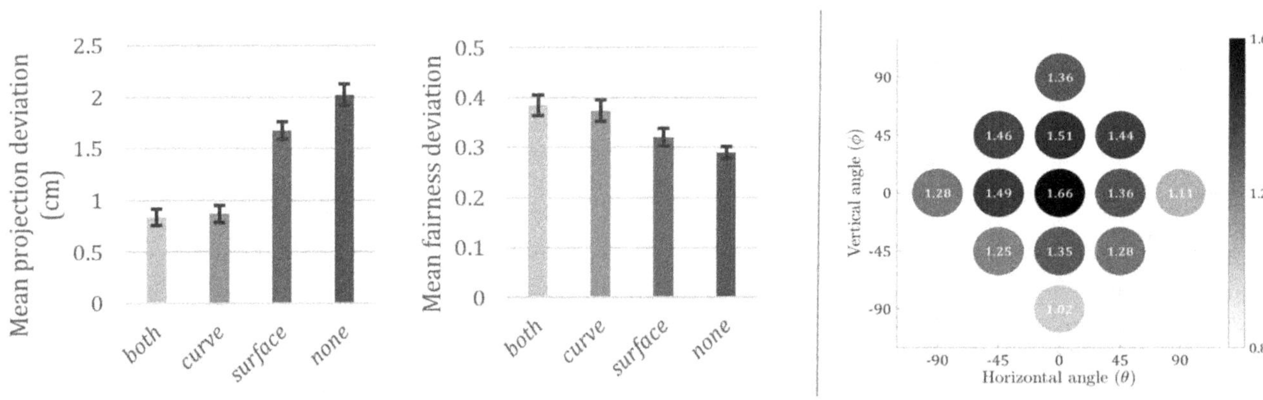

Figure 11. Main effects of *visual guidance* on mean projected deviation (left) and mean fairness deviation (center), and of *surface orientation* on mean depth deviation. The observed trend for *visual guidance* was exactly the opposite for projection and fairness deviations. Depth deviation improved when moving away from the vertical plane in front of the participants.

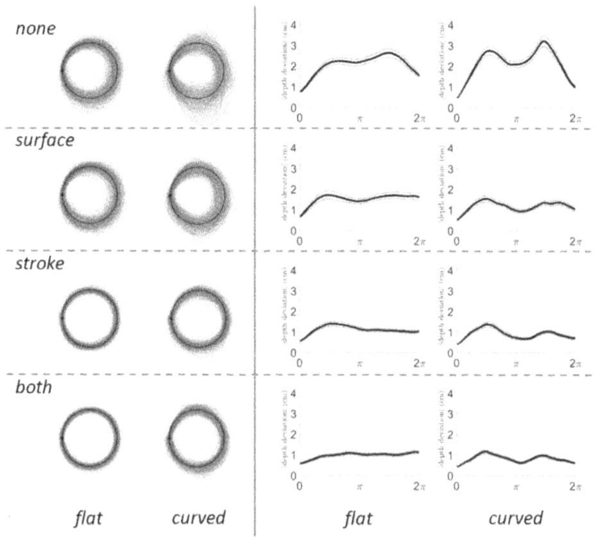

(a) Surface projections (b) |Depth deviation|

Figure 12. Effect of *visual guidance* and *surface shape*. Visualization of surface projections of all strokes (a), and trends of depth deviation with 95% confidence intervals (b). Notice the interaction effect between the two variables on the depth deviation measure.

While curve tracing was slower than drawing without any guidance, similar to Viviani and Terzuolo's [38] observation for curves on a plane, the magnitude of the difference was much smaller than the tenfold differencc thcy found.

Stroke execution time correlated strongly with mean fairness deviation ($r = .82, p < .001$), but negatively correlated weakly with mean overall deviation ($r = -.38, p < .001$). Contrary to the observed trend [7] for gestures, this indicates that spending more time on the stroke leads to marginally better accuracy. However, it leads to a high chance of poor curve quality. This is likely due to the difficulty in keeping a stylus stable during slow movements in 3D space.

Visual Trends

Similar to the first experiment, visualization of data reveals interesting trends in the drawing characteristics. We visualize the surface projections of all drawn circles in Figure 12a. In Figure 12b, we illustrate the associated depth deviations. This visualization reveals an interesting trend with respect to depth deviation: the maximum depth deviation lies around $\pi/2$ radians from the start, and the minimum occurs around π radians. For *curved* surfaces, another local maximum exists around $3\pi/2$ radians. A similar, albeit more noisy, trend of two characteristic jumps at $\pi/2$ and $3\pi/2$ radians was also seen for curvature. This leads to a hypothesis that participants followed an overly linear path for a quarter of the stroke before making a sudden direction change and continuing on towards linearity again, and repeated this process for the next half as well.

DISCUSSION AND FUTURE WORK

The initial pilot observation clearly points out that, while designers appreciate the freeform nature of 3D sketching in VR, precision and control is often required for meaningful design tasks. Designers expressed interest in switching back and forth between freeform and controlled sketching modes.

In our experiments, we observed that the lack of a physical drawing plane, surface position, shape and orientation, stroke size, and visual guidance were important factors affecting drawing ability in VR. While a physical drawing surface improves accuracy by 22% as compared to unguided mid-air drawing, a virtual surface itself, easily incorporated in many design applications, can improve accuracy by as much as 17%. In applications where the target curve is known a priori, showing that curve can further boost accuracy, but may lead to aesthetically poor strokes. It should be noted that our results characterize strokes drawn by amateurs with no prior VR-sketching experience. It is possible that mid-air drawing precision improves with practice and experience. Wiese et al. [40] reported encouraging results on learnability of freehand 3D sketching in a short-term study conducted on design students. Future work on VR sketching learnability can gain from our experience by benchmarking against our results.

While primarily targeted towards sketching applications, our results for conditions with no visual guidance could also be utilized for estimating user precision in performing 3D gestures in VR. Thus, these results could apply to a wide variety of use-cases, such as mode switches or command invocations, or navigation gestures. These use cases result in potential applicability of the results to a number of VR domains such as motor skill training [14], animation and modeling [44, 46], and data visualization [11].

Physical Surface

During our observational sessions, designers recommended projecting their strokes into desired virtual planes for greater accuracy. However, our experimental study indicates that, compared to accuracy achieved in traditional sketching, projecting to virtual planes in VR is 53% worse, while drawing on a physical surface in VR is only 20% worse. This is a strong motivation for devices combining existing drawing methods in VR. One potential approach is to hold a clipboard, or other rigid surface in the non-dominant hand to rest upon [33]. An alternative approach is dynamically configurable drawing surfaces actuated by robotic arms (Figure 13a). While the former potentially allows for higher mobility, the latter may be preferable in long design sessions where fatigue becomes a major factor. Such surfaces could potentially provide a more natural haptic feedback without limiting input range, unlike existing active haptic devices used to aid 3D sketching [27].

Visual Guidance

Our experimental results indicate that visual guides, such as grids and scaffolding curves, can help to position strokes more accurately, increasing accuracy by 17% and 57%, respectively. Visual guidance may be augmented by snapping techniques, such as the recently implemented "Guides" feature in Tilt Brush [43], which snaps strokes to nearby surface widgets. However, such guides should be used with caution. In particular, tracing over an existing curve adversely affects the drawing quality. Rendering a grid may provide the right balance between accuracy and aesthetics. These results are in contrast to assumptions for 2D sketching [37] for which curve smoothing algorithms are based. Therefore, novel stroke processing methods may be needed to account for the lack of curve fairness.

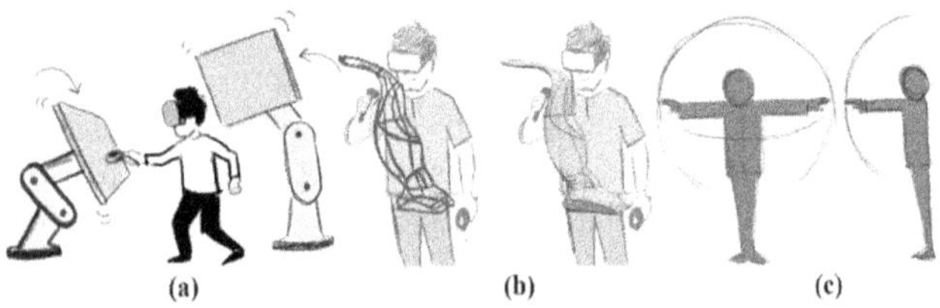

Figure 13: Examples of VR interface elements based on our design suggestions: use of an actuated physical support (a), automatic surfacing with semi-transparent rendering (b), and positioning strokes for maximum projection size (c).

Depth Perception

Depth perception is critical for VR design applications. Our hybrid condition from the first experiment validated that the difficulties of drawing in VR are not solely due to the lack of physical constraint, but also due to the visual impairments. For example, we observed that participants were not able to match the endpoint of their drawn circles to the starting point. Participants in our initial observation sessions had similar complaints about depth perception, more so when the scene had many curves. Advanced visual guides, beyond the approaches tested in our second experiment, could be explored. A common method employed in desktop-based modelling applications is fog rendering, to blur distant objects. In an immersive environment, depth may also be effectively conveyed via a 3D grid, which cannot be employed in 2D due to the resulting visual clutter. While drawing curve networks or concept sketches, automatic surfacing with semi-transparent rendering may also be useful for indicating relative depth (see Figure 13b).

Orientation, Position, and Navigation

The drawing plane orientation had a significant effect on accuracy in both experiments. In general, the familiar horizontal orientation was most accurate, with vertical orientations performing worse. The effect was most prominent in the first study when participants had to draw on the sideways plane that was centered with their body. In contrast, the planes in experiment 2 had approximately the same projection on the user's eyes, and all of them were at a comfortable motor distance. Bae et al. [4] defined the "sketchability" measure for 2D sketches, which states that a good view for sketching 2D strokes is one where the sketch surface has a large visible projection. The trend we observed hints that the same model applies for sketching in an immersive VR environment as well. Thus, it would be interesting to explore how VR design tools could equip designers with simple navigation tools that enable them to snap or project the drawing planes to positions and orientations with higher "sketchability" (Figure 13c).

Drawing Scale

Our experiments provide evidence that drawing in large scale leads to a sharp increase in drawing inaccuracies. This can be partly attributed to the tendency of the human arm to follow a natural arc. This might lead to the conclusion that, contrary to prior recommendations [20, 36], full-scale design in VR is not a good strategy, if precision is desired. Instead, we suggest that VR design tools allow users to draw in a small manageable scale to improve accuracy and comfort, while allowing users to quickly switch to full-scale view to utilize the visualization benefits afforded by VR [20, 36].

Non-planar Strokes

While a large number of design tasks can be performed using planar strokes only [10, 41], previous work suggests that non-planar strokes occur commonly in scenarios such as automobile design [15] and organic shapes [21]. Since our experiments indicate that drawing on planar surfaces produces more accurate and fair curves, we believe that mid-air design tools could often incorporate methods to allow planar curves to be projected onto curved surfaces. However, our results also showed that with adequate visual feedback, users may be able to accurately draw non-planar curves in mid-air. Previous work utilizing 2D displays have used orthographic projections of surfaces onto planes [15], or level set representations of 3D spaces around a surface [34]. How well these techniques relate to artist intent in VR is an interesting avenue to explore in the future. Finally, we only studied a fundamental set of non-planar strokes—circles projected onto a constant curvature convex surface. While the impact of factors studied here is likely independent of shape complexity, more complex 3D strokes are an interesting topic for future investigations. For instance, it is unknown how surface curvature and torsion affect stroke performance.

CONCLUSION

By taking away the flatness of paper, VR sketching tools enable artists and designers to dive in and create in free space without any constraints. While this offers immense freedom and expressiveness, our observations indicate that sketching precise curves for design tasks in VR is very challenging. Our paper quantitatively explores multiple factors affecting the imprecision in 3D sketching in VR, including scale, lack of physical surface, orientation, and planarity. We hope that this understanding would lay out the foundation for building tools to equip designers with the desired precision and controls. Based on our analysis, we also discuss a number of design and interaction guidelines that could potentially alleviate the precision problem for sketching in VR and warrant further investigation. However, further studies are required to understand the effectiveness of these solutions to respect artist intent and maintain fidelity. We hope that our work would take this medium forward by making it more receptive to the needs of creative design.

ACKNOWLEDGEMENTS

R.A. was funded in part by MITACS Accelerate IT07655.

REFERENCES

1. W. Abend, E. Bizzi, and P. Morasso. 1982. Human Arm Trajectory Formation. *Brain* 105, 2: 331–348. http://doi.org/10.1093/brain/105.2.331
2. George J. Andersen, Myron L. Braunstein, and Asad Saidpour. 1998. The perception of depth and slant from texture in three-dimensional scenes. *Perception* 27, 9: 1087–1106.
3. Tom M. Apostol and Mamikon A. Mnatsakanian. 2007. Unwrapping curves from cylinders and cones. *American Mathematical Monthly* 114, 5: 388–416.
4. Seok-Hyung Bae, Ravin Balakrishnan, and Karan Singh. 2008. ILoveSketch: as-natural-as-possible sketching system for creating 3d curve models. *Proceedings of the 21st annual ACM symposium on User interface software and technology*, ACM, 151–160. http://doi.org/10.1145/1449715.1449740
5. A. Bair and D. House. 2007. Grid With a View: Optimal Texturing for Perception of Layered Surface Shape. *IEEE Transactions on Visualization and Computer Graphics* 13, 6: 1656–1663. http://doi.org/10.1109/TVCG.2007.70559
6. Barbara Bradley. 2003. *Drawing People*. North Light Books, Cincinnati, Ohio.
7. Xiang Cao and Shumin Zhai. 2007. Modeling Human Performance of Pen Stroke Gestures. *Proceedings of the SIGCHI Conference on Human Factors in Computing Systems* (CHI '07), ACM, 1495–1504. http://doi.org/10.1145/1240624.1240850
8. Dale J. Cohen and Susan Bennett. 1997. Why can't most people draw what they see? *Journal of Experimental Psychology: Human Perception and Performance* 23, 3: 609.
9. Josh Constine. Oculus "Quill" Turns VR Painting Into Performance Art. *TechCrunch*. Retrieved September 20, 2016 from http://social.techcrunch.com/2016/01/26/oculus-quill/
10. Chris De Paoli and Karan Singh. 2015. SecondSkin: Sketch-based Construction of Layered 3D Models. *ACM Trans. Graph.* 34, 4: 126:1–126:10. http://doi.org/10.1145/2766948
11. C. Donalek, S. G. Djorgovski, A. Cioc, et al. 2014. Immersive and collaborative data visualization using virtual reality platforms. *2014 IEEE International Conference on Big Data (Big Data)*, 609–614. http://doi.org/10.1109/BigData.2014.7004282
12. Gerald Farin and Nickolas Sapidis. 1989. Curvature and the Fairness of Curves and Surfaces. *IEEE Comput. Graph. Appl.* 9, 2: 52–57.
13. George W. Fitzmaurice, Ravin Balakrishnan, Gordon Kurtenbach, and Bill Buxton. 1999. An Exploration into Supporting Artwork Orientation in the User Interface. *Proceedings of the SIGCHI Conference on Human Factors in Computing Systems* (CHI '99), ACM, 167–174. http://doi.org/10.1145/302979.303033
14. Anthony G. Gallagher, E. Matt Ritter, Howard Champion, et al. 2005. Virtual Reality Simulation for the Operating Room: Proficiency-Based Training as a Paradigm Shift in Surgical Skills Training. *Annals of Surgery* 241, 2: 364–372.
15. Tovi Grossman, Ravin Balakrishnan, Gordon Kurtenbach, George Fitzmaurice, Azam Khan, and Bill Buxton. 2002. Creating Principal 3D Curves with Digital Tape Drawing. *Proceedings of the SIGCHI Conference on Human Factors in Computing Systems* (CHI '02), ACM, 121–128. http://doi.org/10.1145/503376.503398
16. Tovi Grossman, Ravin Balakrishnan, and Karan Singh. 2003. An Interface for Creating and Manipulating Curves Using a High Degree-of-freedom Curve Input Device. *Proceedings of the SIGCHI Conference on Human Factors in Computing Systems* (CHI '03), ACM, 185–192. http://doi.org/10.1145/642611.642645
17. Rorik Henrikson, Bruno De Araujo, Fanny Chevalier, Karan Singh, and Ravin Balakrishnan. 2016. Multi-device storyboards for cinematic narratives in VR. *In proceedings of UIST 2016.*
18. Takeo Igarashi, Satoshi Matsuoka, and Hidehiko Tanaka. 1999. Teddy: A Sketching Interface for 3D Freeform Design. *Proceedings of the 26th Annual Conference on Computer Graphics and Interactive Techniques* (SIGGRAPH '99), ACM Press/Addison-Wesley Publishing Co., 409–416. http://doi.org/10.1145/311535.311602
19. Poika Isokoski. 2001. Model for Unistroke Writing Time. *Proceedings of the SIGCHI Conference on Human Factors in Computing Systems* (CHI '01), ACM, 357–364. http://doi.org/10.1145/365024.365299
20. J.H. Israel, E. Wiese, M. Mateescu, C. Zöllner, and R. Stark. 2009. Investigating three-dimensional sketching for early conceptual design—Results from expert discussions and user studies. *Computers & Graphics* 33, 4: 462–473. http://doi.org/10.1016/j.cag.2009.05.005
21. B. Jackson and D. F. Keefe. 2016. Lift-Off: Using Reference Imagery and Freehand Sketching to Create 3D Models in VR. *IEEE Transactions on Visualization and Computer Graphics* 22, 4: 1442–1451. http://doi.org/10.1109/TVCG.2016.2518099
22. Bret Jackson and Daniel F. Keefe. 2011. Sketching Over Props: Understanding and Interpreting 3D Sketch Input Relative to Rapid Prototype Props. *IUI 2011 Sketch Recognition Workshop*.
23. Peter Karasev, Ivan Kolesov, Karl Fritscher, Patricio Vela, Phillip Mitchell, and Allen Tannenbaum. 2013. Interactive medical image segmentation using PDE control of active contours. *IEEE transactions on medical imaging* 32, 11: 2127–2139.
24. Raghavendra S. Kattinakere, Tovi Grossman, and Sriram Subramanian. 2007. Modeling steering within above-the-surface interaction layers. *Proceedings of the SIGCHI conference on Human factors in computing systems*, ACM, 317–326. http://doi.org/10.1145/1240624.1240678

25. Daniel F. Keefe, Daniel Acevedo Feliz, Tomer Moscovich, David H. Laidlaw, and Joseph J. LaViola Jr. 2001. CavePainting: a fully immersive 3D artistic medium and interactive experience. *Proceedings of the 2001 symposium on Interactive 3D graphics*, ACM, 85–93. http://doi.org/0.1145/364338.364370
26. Daniel F. Keefe and David H. Laidlaw. 2007. Poster: Analysis of Performance in Precise 3D Curve Input Tasks in Virtual Reality. *IEEE Visualization (Best Posters Session)*.
27. Daniel Keefe, Robert Zeleznik, and David Laidlaw. 2007. Drawing on air: Input techniques for controlled 3D line illustration. *IEEE Transactions on Visualization and Computer Graphics* 13, 5: 1067–1081.
28. T. Kuehnert, S. Rusdorf, and G. Brunnett. 2011. Virtual Prototyping of Shoes. *IEEE Computer Graphics and Applications* 31, 5: 30–42. http://doi.org/10.1109/MCG.2010.81
29. Jung-hoon Kwon, Han-wool Choi, Jeong-in Lee, and Young-Ho Chai. 2005. Free-Hand Stroke Based NURBS Surface for Sketching and Deforming 3D Contents. In *Advances in Multimedia Information Processing - PCM 2005*, Yo-Sung Ho and Hyoung Joong Kim (eds.). Springer Berlin Heidelberg, 315–326.
30. James McCrae, Nobuyuki Umetani, and Karan Singh. 2014. FlatFitFab: Interactive Modeling with Planar Sections. *Proceedings of the 27th Annual ACM Symposium on User Interface Software and Technology* (UIST '14), ACM, 13–22. http://doi.org/10.1145/2642918.2647388
31. J. McCrae and K. Singh. 2008. Sketching piecewise clothoid curves. *Proceedings of the Fifth Eurographics conference on Sketch-Based Interfaces and Modeling*, Eurographics Association, 1–8. http://doi.org/10.2312/SBM/SBM08/001-008
32. Julius Panero and Martin Zelnik. 1979. *Human Dimension and Interior Space: A Source Book of Design Reference Standards*. Watson-Guptill, New York.
33. Emanuel Sachs, Andrew Roberts, and David Stoops. 1991. 3-Draw: A Tool for Designing 3D Shapes. *IEEE Comput. Graph. Appl.* 11, 6: 18–26. http://doi.org/10.1109/38.103389
34. Johannes Schmid, Martin Sebastian Senn, Markus Gross, and Robert W. Sumner. 2011. OverCoat: An Implicit Canvas for 3D Painting. *ACM SIGGRAPH 2011 Papers* (SIGGRAPH '11), ACM, 28:1–28:10. http://doi.org/10.1145/1964921.1964923
35. Ryan Schmidt, Azam Khan, Gord Kurtenbach, and Karan Singh. 2009. On Expert Performance in 3D Curve-drawing Tasks. *Proceedings of the 6th Eurographics Symposium on Sketch-Based Interfaces and Modeling* (SBIM '09), ACM, 133–140. http://doi.org/10.1145/1572741.1572765
36. Shun'ichi Tano, Shinya Yamamoto, Junko Ichino, Tomonori Hashiyama, and Mitsuru Iwata. 2013. Truly Useful 3D Drawing System for Professional Designer by "Life-Sized and Operable" Feature and New Interaction. In *Human-Computer Interaction – INTERACT 2013*. Springer Berlin Heidelberg, 37–55.
37. Yannick Thiel, Karan Singh, and Ravin Balakrishnan. 2011. Elasticurves: exploiting stroke dynamics and inertia for the real-time neatening of sketched 2D curves. *Proceedings of the 24th annual ACM symposium on User interface software and technology*, ACM, 383–392. http://doi.org/10.1145/2047196.2047246
38. P. Viviani and C. Ternuolo. 1982. Trajectory Determines Movement Dynamics. *Neuroscience* 7, 2: 431–7.
39. Gerold Wesche and Hans-Peter Seidel. 2001. FreeDrawer: a free-form sketching system on the responsive workbench. ACM Press, 167. http://doi.org/10.1145/505008.505041
40. Eva Wiese, Johann Habakuk Israel, Achim Meyer, and Sara Bongartz. 2010. Investigating the learnability of immersive free-hand sketching. *Proceedings of the Seventh Sketch-Based Interfaces and Modeling Symposium*, Eurographics Association, 135–142.
41. Baoxuan Xu, William Chang, Alla Sheffer, Adrien Bousseau, James McCrae, and Karan Singh. 2014. True2Form: 3D Curve Networks from 2D Sketches via Selective Regularization. *ACM Trans. Graph.* 33, 4: 131:1–131:13. http://doi.org/10.1145/2601097.2601128
42. Youyi Zheng, Han Liu, Julie Dorsey, and Niloy J. Mitra. 2016. SmartCanvas: Context-inferred Interpretation of Sketches for Preparatory Design Studies. *Computer Graphics Forum*, Wiley Online Library, 37–48.
43. Tilt Brush by Google. Retrieved January 8, 2017 from https://www.tiltbrush.com/
44. PaintLab VR - Paint and Sculpt in Virtual Reality. *PaintLab VR*. Retrieved September 20, 2016 from http://paintlabvr.com
45. DesignSpace. Retrieved September 20, 2016 from http://www.designspacevr.com/
46. Tvori—Anyone Can Tell a Story. Retrieved September 20, 2016 from http://tvori.co
47. Virtual Art Sessions. Retrieved September 20, 2016 from https://virtualart.chromeexperiments.com/

I Am The Passenger: How Visual Motion Cues Can Influence Sickness For In-Car VR

Mark McGill me@markmcgill.co.uk
Alexander Ng Alexander.Ng@glasgow.ac.uk
Stephen Brewster Stephen.Brewster@glasgow.ac.uk
Glasgow Interactive Systems Section, School of Computing Science, University of Glasgow, UK

ABSTRACT
This paper explores the use of VR Head Mounted Displays (HMDs) in-car and in-motion for the first time. Immersive HMDs are becoming everyday consumer items and, as they offer new possibilities for entertainment and productivity, people will want to use them during travel in, for example, autonomous cars. However, their use is confounded by motion sickness caused in-part by the restricted visual perception of motion conflicting with physically perceived vehicle motion (accelerations/rotations detected by the vestibular system). Whilst VR HMDs restrict visual perception of motion, they could also render it virtually, potentially alleviating sensory conflict. To study this problem, we conducted the first on-road and in motion study to systematically investigate the effects of various visual presentations of the real-world motion of a car on the sickness and immersion of VR HMD wearing passengers. We established new baselines for VR in-car motion sickness, and found that there is no one best presentation with respect to balancing sickness and immersion. Instead, user preferences suggest different solutions are required for differently susceptible users to provide usable VR in-car. This work provides formative insights for VR designers and an entry point for further research into enabling use of VR HMDs, and the rich experiences they offer, when travelling.

ACM Classification Keywords
H.5.m. Information Interfaces and Presentation (e.g. HCI): Miscellaneous

Author Keywords
In-motion; In-car; Automobile; Autonomous Car; Passenger; Virtual Reality; Mixed Reality; Motion Sickness; HMD;

INTRODUCTION
For many travellers, a long journey is not to be relished. Journeys can last for significant durations, for example car journeys in UK last on average 22 minutes [17], with commutes lasting 55 minutes [58]; in the USA, drivers spend 56 minutes a day on average in-transit [76]. These journeys can be repetitive (e.g. the commute to work), with travellers frequently noting that such trips are wasted time [24, 80]. Whilst collocated social interaction can offer some respite [33], journeys are often conducted without the physical presence of friends or family, with the car providing solitary personal space [24]. Entertainment and productivity options are limited to displays significantly smaller than those in the home or office (e.g. phones, tablets, laptops, dashboards and rear-seat systems [81]). In the specific case of car journeys, these issues will gain increasing prevalence given the arrival of fully autonomous cars, which would free drivers from the driving task, and consequently increase the occurrence of passenger experiences.

CHI 2017, May 06 - 11, 2017, Denver, CO, USA

ISBN 978-1-4503-4655-9/17/05...$15.00
DOI: http://dx.doi.org/10.1145/3025453.3026046

While autonomous cars will allow for radical redesign of the car interior (e.g. seating locations and internal display configurations [20]), passengers will still perceive themselves as being in a constrained space, with the physical limitations of the interior dictating what is possible to be rendered and displayed. Moreover, the passenger's visual perception of motion may be compromised by use of these displays, through changes in gaze angle (e.g. looking down/away from windows) and occlusion (presenting content over windows, or occluding windows to enhance immersion [43]). This has implications for motion sickness, which in-part arises from the sensory mismatch of visually and physically perceived motion [59, 85].

Many people become travel sick when watching TV, reading or working in vehicles, meaning that they cannot use the time productively. These problems will grow in number with the arrival of autonomous cars [20, 19, 71]; the act of driving stops many people from feeling sick due to the anticipatory cues of being the driver [75] and without these cues people who did not get sick will now do so. Consideration needs to be given to how entertainment and productivity can be supported whilst minimizing motion sickness. Virtual Reality (VR) and Augmented Reality (AR) Head Mounted Displays (HMDs) have the potential to significantly expand the display space, enabling immersive entertainment and workspaces that go beyond the physical limitations of the car interior. Problematically, VR HMDs also occlude visual perception of reality [44, 6] and thus the car's motion, and are likely to lead to sensory mismatch and, consequently, motion sickness. However, assuming the orientation and velocity of the vehicle can be tracked at low latency, HMDs have the potential to portray the vehicle motion virtually. Accordingly, for both VR HMDs, and passengers more generally, the problem of occluding the visual perception of motion, and the resultant sensory mismatch this causes, can be solved (as demonstrated in consumer VR rollercoasters which run over a known and precisely controlled route [77]). VR and AR HMDs are capable of conveying the motion of the vehicle at all times, from all viewing angles. Consequently, the problem is then: how should these dynamic and unpredictable physical motions be visually presented, and how can they be integrated into any virtual scene without reducing the immersion of the VR content.

This paper examines VR HMD use in-car, in-motion for the first time. Through a user study, we investigate whether consuming stationary 360° VR content in-car and in-motion induces motion sickness. We examine this both for existing consumer VR HMDs that interpret rotations of the car as rotations of the HMD, and future positionally-tracked HMDs that do not. We also examine to what extent motion sickness can be rectified by conveying motion peripherally, allowing for physical motion cues to be combined with any VR content. New baselines for VR motion sickness in-car are established and guidelines for future experimentation are provided, before we finally explore the further research required to enable comfortable VR HMD use in-motion.

RELATED RESEARCH

Motion Sickness

Motion sickness refers to illness arising from a person being within a motion environment, such as a moving vehicle [59]. Symptoms of motion sickness typically include cold sweat, dizziness and nausea/vomiting [52]. The predominant theory is that it arises due to sensory conflicts (also sensory re-arrangements or sensory mismatch), as first discussed by Reason and Brand [59]) between what Bertolini *et al.* describes as motion-sensitive input signals [3]. For example, if the motion perceived by the visual system conflicts with that perceived by other sensory systems there is a likelihood of motion sickness being induced. Reason and Brand [59] (as summarised by [5]) described there being two major categories of motion sickness, being derived from conflict between angular and linear vestibular systems (Canal-Otolith mismatch), and conflict between visual and vestibular systems (visual-vestibular mismatch).

The vestibular system (or inner ear) is essentially a human inertial motion sensor, able to detect rotational changes (equivalent to a gyroscope, sensed via the semicircular canals) and acceleration (equivalent to an accelerometer, sensed via the Otolith organs). This information is used alongside cues from the visual system and the somatosensory system (e.g. motor actions and proprioception) to determine a perception of self-motion. Reason and Brand suggested there were two types of conflict: type 1, where both systems signal contradictory motion information, and type 2, where one system signals motion whilst the other does not. The greater the discrepancy between the sensory information and the expected sensory information, the greater the chance of motion sickness occurring, and the greater the severity of the sickness [53, 5].

There are however other theories regarding the origins of motion sickness. The subjective vertical conflict theory [5] suggests that motion sickness arises from "situations where the determination of the subjective vertical, the internal representation of gravity, is challenged", meaning movements where the reference point of gravity changes, e.g. roll and pitch movements when seated, but not yaw movements (side-to-side). For example, "driving uphill at night along a winding road may provoke car sickness in the passengers in the back seat. The continuously changing gravitoinertial force vector, together with the inability of the semicircular canals to appropriately signal the angular motion because of the stable visual interior of the car... will subsequently provoke motion sickness." [5]. The ecological theory of motion sickness suggests that it occurs due to motion causing postural instability:

> "Animals become sick in situations in which they do not possess (or have not yet learned) strategies that are effective for the maintenance of postural stability (p. 195), and that postural instability... is necessary to produce symptoms" [60] from [8]

Indeed, studies have demonstrated that motion sickness can occur due to postural sway even without visual cues [54]. Postural sway has been considered as an indicator of the onset of motion sickness [12]. However, the fundamental causes of motion sickness are not yet fully understood, with suggestions that "an underlying central mechanism... driving both our posture and motion sickness symptoms" exists [8, 12].

Regardless of the underlying theory, it is well known that specific movements play significant roles in motion sickness. For example, Bles *et al.* noted that "linear acceleration and deceleration without appropriate view of the road ahead" induced sickness [5]. Lateral (bumps and undulations in a car ride) and vertical oscillations (at low frequencies, between 0.1 and 0.5Hz, peaking at 0.16Hz, e.g. the motion of a boat) both induce motion sickness [32]. The Coriolis or cross-coupling effect [30] is when nausea is provoked by head movements during yaw motion (i.e. where a conflict arises between the Canal-Otolith systems). Consider a car turning a corner, whilst a passenger additionally rotates their head. Depending on the directions of the rotation, the perceived rotational velocity may be very different to the actual rotational velocity. This is one of a number of effects experienced, particularly by pilots [55].

Finally, it is important to note that perception of motion is not uniform with respect to the field of view of the viewer:

> "Peripheral vision is relatively better at detecting motion than form. A moving object seen in the periphery is perceived as something moving, but it is more difficult to see what that something is... A person's ability to detect slow-moving stimuli decreases with eye eccentricity... For faster-moving stimuli, however, the ability to detect moving stimuli increases with eye eccentricity." [34] from [1] and [14]

Indeed, Keshavarz *et al.* [38] noted the impact of peripheral vision on perception of motion, showing that having peripheral vision of a projection screen displaying vehicle motion caused greater visually-induced motion sickness.

Occurrence and Prevalence

Motion sickness has three components: the characteristics of the stimulus, the susceptibility of the person, and the total time of exposure [59]. The result is that "anyone with a functional vestibular system can suffer from motion sickness, given the right prerequisites and if the exposure is continuous over a long period" [16] with studies showing that "virtually anyone with normal vestibular function when exposed to provocative physical body motion, disruption of vestibulo-ocular reflexes, or optokinetic stimulation can to some extent be made motion sick". [40]. Thus prevalence tends to be categorised by severity of affliction. It has been suggested that approximately one-third of the population are highly susceptible to motion sickness (becoming sick frequently when on any transport) ([49] from [40]), where ~5–10% of the population is extremely sensitive to motion sickness, ~5–15% relatively insensitive, and ~75% are subject to normal motion sickness (i.e. to a limited degree) [48], in line with observations based on the MSSQ-short motion sickness susceptibility questionnaire in a sample of 1711 members of the public [41].

Modes of transport, and their motions, also play a role in determining the severity of the experiences. All forms of transport create stimuli that will cause motion sickness for some given sufficient exposure. Seasickness typically has the most severe potential for sickness, given the strong stimuli involved, the length of exposure, and the frequent lack of matching visual stimuli, with one study reporting incidence on naval vessels of 62% [16]. For cars, passengers are particularly at-risk. For example, up to a quarter of co-drivers in rally cars were found to become motion sick if they were reading a book or sitting in the back seat [57]. But even public transport such as buses [29] or trains can cause significant problems [10, 13]. Generally, females [69] and children [31] have been shown to be more susceptible, with females showing greater variability in motion sickness over time than males [46, 42, 28].

Revisiting the sensory re-arrangement theory, consider a person suffering from motion sickness during a car journey. Their vestibular system can sense the accelerations/decelerations of the car being made by the driver, the lateral oscillations of the car resulting from a combination of the quality of the road and the ability of the driver, and the rotational changes made as the driver navigates and turns. Meanwhile, their visual system may or may not provide an awareness of motion (depending on the accessibility and visibility of external reference points such as the terrain, which can vary if the passenger decides to, say, read a book or is sitting in the back and unable to see out of the windows), and this awareness of motion may not align with what the vestibular system is suggesting regarding the magnitude of motion. Finally, other sensory capabilities (e.g. the somatosensory system) will only provide relevant feedback to the driver who is in control of the vehicle. Thus, there are many scenarios where sensory mismatches can occur, with motion sickness being the result.

The Future Of Motion Sickness In-Car

Car motion can be categorised as having lateral oscillations (rolls), rotational changes in direction (yaw), and vertical changes/oscillations (pitch), as well as accelerations/decelerations. These motions are influenced by the driver, and the road conditions, with the perception of these motions dictated by whether an individual is driving or is a passenger, where they are seated and what visual references of motion they are able to attend to. Of these, the primary contributor to motion sickness in cars is considered to be lateral oscillations (<0.5Hz) caused by variations in the road quality and driving style. This effect is compounded by seating position, with the rear seats increasing the magnitude of the oscillations [75].

The eventual adoption of autonomous cars is likely to change the primary contributor of motion sickness from oscillations to sensory mismatches. Firstly, it is feasible to suggest that the autonomous car could provide notice of actions [19], and drive in a style that minimizes oscillations, for example choosing high quality roads and gradual acceleration/decelerations.

Secondly, existing drivers will be freed from the driving task, reclaiming approximately 368 person hours per year spent by drivers in England alone [17]) for entertainment and productivity on-the-move, such as reading, working, consuming audio-visual media, gaming, etc. [67]. This would allow for the redesign of the internal environment of the car to better facilitate non-driving tasks (given that driving controls may be unnecessary) [21, 19], affecting both visual perception of motion and capability to anticipate motion. Indeed, proposals have been suggested to utilize the full space of the car for media consumption activities, such as a drop-down projector screen patented by Ford [15].

Thirdly, a network of autonomous cars could diminish car ownership and lead to increased incidence of car/ride sharing, guiding interior design toward privacy in a potentially shared resource [50]. This could lead to a greater variety of seating positions being utilized, with passengers in the rear more common, and seating becoming flexible and not necessarily front-oriented [20]. Consequently, a resurgence of interest in motion sickness treatments has been noted, specifically attributed to the use of displays in cars (termed *nauseogenic visual displays* [27]). Thus, whilst an autonomous vehicle might work to minimize motion sickness-inducing oscillations, the passengers may well undermine this effort by inducing motion sickness through their activities [20].

Mitigations, Treatments and Recovery

With respect to car travel specifically, minimizing lateral oscillations (e.g. reducing accelerations[75]) is effective [18]. Drivers have been shown to avoid motion sickness because of their engagement with other sensory systems (e.g. proprioceptive feedback) and their control of the motion aiding anticipatory actions. For example, lateral oscillation-based motion sickness is avoided through prediction of the oscillations as they depend upon the driving behaviour, which in turn allows for compensatory actions such as tilting the head [3, 27, 63]. When applied to passengers, this foreknowledge can diminish perceived motion sickness [78, 21].

For accelerations/decelerations and rotational movements, providing an artificial horizon can reduce motion sickness [74]. Bles *et al.* [5] suggested that this was due to "the fact that seeing the horizon helps to keep the sensed and subjective vertical aligned", framing this within their subjective vertical conflict theory. Stability has also been shown to diminish motion sickness, through aligning the body with changes in the environment [26, 27] and minimizing head movements [4]. As previously discussed, a growing body of evidence has suggested that postural stability, or lack thereof, can play a significant role in determining the severity of motion sickness [12]. Regarding longer-term approaches, habituation (providing sufficient exposure for adaptation to occur) is the primary means of treating motion sickness. However, "5% of the population never adapts to motion sickness triggering stimuli, given a fully functional vestibular system" [16], whilst the duration of car journeys, and overcoming initial sickness, may prevent habituation. Pharmacological approaches can be problematic in terms of effectiveness, availability and cost, and may have a negative affect on concentration. Behavioural approaches, such as controlled breathing or listening to calming music [84], can provide relief, but require that the individual devote focus on that activity rather than work or play.

Regarding recovery from motion sickness, there are three factors: sensitivity to stimulation, the rate of adaptation to stimulation, and the time constant of the decay of the elicited symptoms [40]. However, much as with the factors that induce motion sickness, there is a high degree of variability in each of these recovery factors, with "the decay of symptoms vary[ing] enormously across individuals... by 100-1" [40].

Vection & Visually Induced Motion Sickness In VR

When considering VR HMDs in-motion, visually perceived motion must be considered. Vection is often described as "illusory self-motion" [39]. This illusion of self-motion, in the absence of any congruent physically perceived motion, is primarily the cause of Visually Induced Motion Sickness (VIMS), often a significant component of simulator sickness / cybersickness [39]. For example, if the VR HMD wearer is stationary yet visually perceives their avatar walking or running through a virtual environment, this would have the potential to induce VIMS.

The problem of vection has been tackled in a number of ways, most pertinently by Fernandes and Feiner [22], who manipulated the visibility of mid-peripheral motion cues, resulting in decreased VIMS. As discussed , disparity between what is visually and physically perceived is likely to induce motion sickness, and VR HMD use in-motion offers up new ways in which this disparity might occur:

Motion sickness / inverse vection An illusion of stability where the VR user may physically perceive motion whilst visually perceiving a stable virtual environment;

Contradictory vection An illusion of self-motion conveyed through VR that contradicts perceived physical motion, e.g. moving left in VR whilst turning right in the car;

Magnitude of vection A portrayal of self-motion which matches the physically perceived motion but at a different magnitude, e.g. perceiving a car acceleration as a small, subtle movement instead of as absolute velocity, or increasing the visual magnitude of the acceleration to exhilarate.

Each of these disparities is likely to be compounded by the amount and type of movements performed by the VR user, e.g. viewing content which requires constant and rapid changes in gaze orientation, compared to content which is stable or whose orientation or position is physically manipulated by the user (e.g. reading a book, or physically grabbing and moving the world [47]). Thus, careful consideration must be given as to what particular form of motion conflict is examined, and how it is physically enacted.

Existing Support For VR HMD Use In-Motion

There has been little recent work looking at VR HMD use in-motion with the current generation of consumer headsets. Soyka *et al.* [73] as part of the *VR-Hyperspace* project examined the effect of turbulent motions on VR HMD users in a flight simulator, using an Oculus Rift DK 1 to prototype VR use as an aeroplane passenger as part of an examination of future entertainment options in-flight. They evaluated turbulence/oscillations through three turbulent episodes of 10 seconds, in two virtual motion environments: a virtual aeroplane and a magic carpet ride over tropical islands. They found that "brief exposure to turbulent motions [do] not get participants sick". Indeed, VR HMDs have seen recent deployment in real-world flights as standard, most notably by Qantas[64]. Once the plane is up to speed there are few turns or changes in acceleration to cause perception problems.

Currently, VR HMDs are heavily reliant on high frequency, low latency inertial measurement units (IMUs) to accurately track the wearer's head to provide dynamically updating displays. This is the case for both existing mobile HMDs (e.g. the Samsung Gear VR, which supports rotational movement only) and PC-based headsets (e.g. positionally tracked devices such as the HTC Vive and Oculus Rift). Gyroscopes are typically used as part of a sensor fusion approach, alongside accelerometers and magnetometers for accurate 3 DOF rotational tracking, external beacons and/or cameras for 6 DOF positional tracking [2], to track the movement of the headset.

This reliance on gyroscopes means that when used in-motion, viewing is influenced by orientation changes caused by transportation (e.g. a car turning a corner), which is interpreted in the same way as the user turning their head. This is a result of the current focus on delivering accurate, low latency tracking in stationary environments. However, positionally-tracked VR HMDs will in the future be able to maintain stable viewing in-motion, meaning the VR view of the world need only react to movement by the user, and not the vehicle. This can already be seen in highly controlled scenarios, where the external motion of the VR HMD is known in advance, such as in the case of VR rollercoasters where users experience synchronized virtual and physical representations of the ride [77]. Consequently, both existing VR HMDs (which interpret vehicle movements as head movements) and future positionally-tracked VR HMDs (which could ignore external movements) merit consideration with respect to sickness incidence in-motion.

Outcomes From Literature Review

Users of VR HMDs in motion, engaging in interactive environments where their visual perception of motion may not be aligned with their physically perceived motion, may exhibit some degree of motion sickness. This is likely to make HMDs very difficult to use in cars for many people and thus the benefits offered by autonomous vehicles cannot be taken advantage of. Given this, the first problem we investigated was motion sickness incidence due to VR HMD use in-motion to provide a baseline, which is missing from the literature. Specifically, we looked at both VR HMDs that interpret the turning of a vehicle as part of the user's head movement, and future VR HMDs that have a stable frame of reference with respect to vehicle movement. We then examined how motion cues could be delivered to users in combination with a virtual environment, utilizing the sensitivity of peripheral vision, to see what effect this might have on motion sickness and immersion. In this way, we aimed to provide a general solution for sensory conflict that could be used for any static VR content.

STUDY: IN-CAR VR HMD USE IN-MOTION

We examined the use of VR HMDs in-motion through an in-car study of passengers wearing VR HMDs watching 360° VR video content as they were driven around a city. We could recreate an ecologically valid driving experience, of particular relevance to autonomous cars and public transport, and examine the effects of real-world motion cues, specifically rotations and accelerations/decelerations, over a set route. Our aims were to examine:

- VR HMDs where all rotations affect VR viewing orientation, regardless of whether they occurred through user head movements or vehicle motion;
- Future positionally-tracked VR HMDs that can compensate, correct for or ignore external vehicle rotation;
- The utility of peripheral visual motion cues to give some sense of external vehicle motion.

Six conditions were defined. They evaluated the effect of providing a stable VR view relative to car motion (contrasting current VR HMDs in-motion and future VR HMDs that could ignore vehicle motion), and of re-incorporating some perception of vehicle motion through mid-peripheral vision. There were two baselines: ((1) VR video and (2) motion only), an additional Condition (3) to test the accuracy of our motion cues, and three Conditions (4–6) to examine these effects (V=Video, M=Motion)[1]:

1: VR Video Baseline simulator sickness. Users were stationary, wearing a VR HMD, watching 360° video. This was to get a baseline for standard simulator sickness;
2: Motion Only Baseline motion sickness. Users were in motion but not watching VR. This gave a baseline for motion sickness from just being driven in a car;
3: VR Motion Environment In-motion, wearing a VR HMD. The motion of the car was synchronously portrayed in VR, with the HMD user perceiving themselves moving through a basic landscape. This was to evaluate whether our sensing of motion matched what was physically perceived;
4: VR V+M In-motion, wearing a VR HMD, with all rotations (head movements and vehicle rotations) interpreted as head movements. **This conveyed turning of the car**;
5: VR V+M with compensation In-motion, wearing a VR HMD, with compensatory rotations of the video counteracting vehicle rotations. This provided a stable view in VR, **conveying no vehicle motion**;
6: VR V+M with peripheral feedback As Condition 5, with compensatory rotations of the video counteracting vehicle rotations, but with the motion environment of Condition 3 blended into the peripheral ±10° of the VR view. This was to evaluate the effectiveness of presenting motion cues mid-peripherally alongside existing VR content. **This conveyed turning and acceleration peripherally**.

Implementation

For the VR HMD, we used a Samsung Gear VR mobile HMD (SM-R322, 310 grams, 96° FOV, see Figure 1) paired with a Samsung S7 smartphone (VR framework version 11, service version 2.4.29, 60Hz). To have the capability to both convey the motions of the car in VR, and counteract the rotations of the car, a Nexus 5 smartphone was used. It was mounted to the car, with its gyroscope (sampled at 30Hz at a latency of ~40ms) providing bearing changes. It was also paired with an OBD2 device (OBDLink LX [72], ~14Hz at a latency of 100ms) for capturing car velocity in real-time. For communicating the car motion to the HMD, we used a SocketIO server over which both the Nexus 5 and S7-powered HMD communicated. The study was conducted in a 2015 model Vauxhall Insignia, chosen both to minimize oscillations (through a modern suspension system) and provide a fast OBD2 link.

[1]To see how conditions operated in-motion, view the attached video.

Figure 1. Left: Gear VR HMD used in study. Right: Peripheral blending of Condition 6, combining motion landscape and 360° video.

There were three software elements. Firstly, we created a motion environment synchronized to the car motion. An initial gyroscope bearing was taken with users looking straight ahead whilst wearing the headset. Subsequent changes in this bearing determined the direction of the forward vector in the motion environment, with velocity also portrayed. Secondly, we stabilized the VR view with respect to car motion. Given the black box sensor fusion of the VR HMD tracking, we chose to exploit the fact that 360° VR video is typically rendered on a sphere, using gyroscope readings to perform counter-rotations of the sphere. Pilot testing showed that readings taken every second frame, combined with linear interpolation to smooth transitions, provided the most comfortable and accurate counter-rotation, accounting for variance in the gyroscope readings. Thirdly, we blended the stabilized video content and the motion environment for the peripheral motion cues. For this we used a shader effect combined with raycasting to determine the current video fixation point, with alpha blending to combine the motion environment and the video.

It is important to note that this approach, whilst suited to a prototype system, had some drawbacks regarding gyroscope drift. A gyroscope is subject to drift over time and motion. In the case of the Gear VR, a combination of gyroscope, accelerometer and magnetometer are used to retain a relatively accurate bearing. However, magnetometer readings are unreliable in-motion, due to variances in the magnetic field and the environment. Thus, it was inevitable that drift would occur. We designed a mechanism to allow users to re-orient the system, taking a new bearing for the forward vector and resetting the Gear VR tracking. To do this, users interacted with the Gear VR touchpad, located on the right side of the headset. If any desynchronization was perceived, they were to look straight ahead and swipe downwards. The VR view then faded out and back in over the course of 2 seconds.

Demographics and Pre-Screening

Eighteen males (18<age<35) were recruited from University mailing lists/forums (mean age=25.1, SD=4.7). They were pre-screened on motion sickness susceptibility using MSSQ-Short [25] with selection based on having, at worst, only moderate susceptibility (all participants in the 75th%ile MSSQ with majority in the 50th%ile of slightly susceptible or less). This level was chosen as we did not have an understanding of the magnitude of the sickness effects of VR HMD use in motion and thus could not ethically examine more susceptible participants at this point. Participants were asked not to take anti-motion sickness medications, antihistamines, or alcohol immediately prior to the experiment, and to abstain from eating for at least an hour prior.

Measures and Experimental Design

For measuring motion sickness, during each condition we used a standard 7-point illness rating scale from [29] where the extreme indicated the participant was experiencing moderate nausea and wished to stop, at which point they would inform the experimenter and the condition would be stopped prematurely. Changes were indicated in real-time by participants using forward and backward swipes of the Gear VR touchpad, which would temporarily present the scale over the VR content. The Simulator Sickness Questionnaire (SSQ) [36] was used after each condition to measure both motion and simulator sickness, and duration was noted in the event of prematurely stopping a condition due to sudden onset of illness, or reaching the maximum point on the illness rating scale. Physiological measures were ruled out, as they are both weakly correlated with motion sickness [70], and their use would be confounded by other factors (e.g. immersion, excitation due to unexpected movements). For measuring presence, the iGroup Presence Questionnaire (IPQ) [68] was used. Finally, users were asked to rank the VR Video In-Motion conditions (4–6) in order of preference, before taking part in a short interview.

The experimental design was heavily influenced by pilot testing regarding both duration and ordering. Typically, motion sickness studies last for in excess of 15 minutes [5]. They are often conducted with extreme stimuli to provoke significant sickness effects [7]. However, these durations were problematic for our study given the unknown magnitude of sickness effects of VR HMD-use in motion. Instead, we evaluated each condition for 10 minutes of standard city driving and gave plenty of rest time between conditions. To provide consistent and ecologically valid motion stimuli, laps of a quiet, predominantly one-way road system with no traffic lights were undertaken. The acceleration profile can be seen in Figure 2. Each lap took ~2 minutes and featured 4 places where notable accelerations and decelerations occurred, meaning that each condition consisted of ~5–6 laps. Conditions started and ended at the entrance to a public park, allowing participants to leave the car for recovery, if required.

Through pilot testing, we determined that two separate ~1hr:15min sessions, with 3 conditions per session were sufficient to allow for both experimentation and as much recovery time as required by participants. The exception to this was Condition 5 (VR V+M w/ compensation), which was particularly problematic with respect to sickness and recovery time, with a high likelihood that participants would be unable to continue. Accordingly, this condition was evaluated last. The first session was counter-balanced for Conditions 3, 4 and 6. The second session evaluated the baselines (Conditions 1 and 2), again counter-balanced, and then finally Condition 5. Three VR video clips were used, chosen on the basis of containing no movement, portraying stationary events in 360° [51, 62, 79], and played in the same order for every condition.

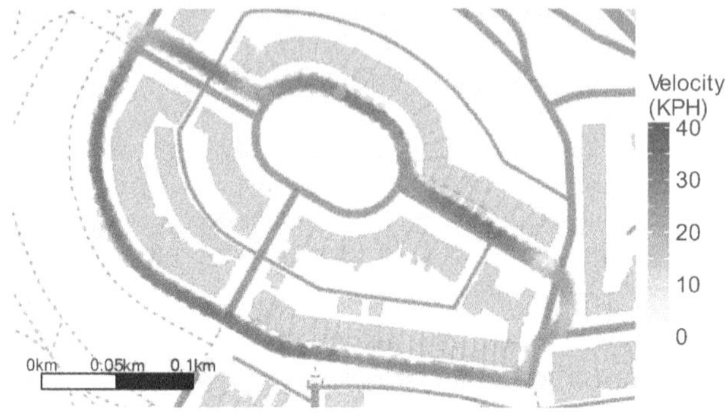

Figure 2. 0.86km test route velocity profile, as captured throughout the study across participants using GPS and OBD2 velocity.

RESULTS

Unless otherwise stated, for parametric tests a repeated measures ANOVA was performed using *lme()* in *R* as prescribed by [23], with likelihood ratios reported, and *post hoc* Tukey contrasts performed where applicable. For non-parametric tests (denoted NP) a Friedman's ANOVA was performed using *friedman.test()* in *R*, with *post hoc* pairwise Wilcoxon Rank Sum Tests performed where applicable.

Duration of Usage and Perception Of Motion

All of the VR in-motion conditions featured some early stoppages due to feelings of nausea, predominantly toward the end, as reflected in the mean duration of each condition, see Table 2. There were no statistical differences in terms of the subjective perceptions of rotations or motion, but the peripheral blending of Condition 6 significantly diminished participants' sense of acceleration. In general, perception of motion was not rated highly, indicating that rotations and accelerations alone do not convey the full breadth of experienced motion. The lack of positional tracking of the GearVR meant that oscillations (e.g. uneven roads) and positional movements (e.g. leaning forward or backward based on accelerations) were not incorporated into the visual representation of motion.

Sickness and Presence

Sickness on the SSQ scales showed a statistically significant increase in all the VR in-motion conditions compared to both baseline simulator and motion sickness, but there were no significant differences between the VR in-motion conditions. Mean presence (IPQ score) remained unaffected by the motion of the car and the means by which this motion was incorporated. The generally low presence scores suggest this metric was confounded by the relatively low presence of the Gear VR HMD and the 360° video content.

Rankings Against Susceptibility, Sickness & Presence

Broadly, there was little to discriminate between the in-motion conditions. However, user rankings (see Table 1) revealed differing preferences, with half of participants preferring some form of conveyance of motion. Examining motion sickness susceptibility scores against preferences hints at these preferences being aligned with susceptibility, as seen in Figure 3. An ANOVA on susceptibility scores showed a significant difference $F(2,15) = 4.12, p < 0.05$ on user preference, with *post-hoc* Tukey showing differences between preferring Conditions 4–6 ($p < 0.05$) but not 5–6 ($p = 0.09$) or 4–5 ($p = 0.69$), suggesting that those that preferred the peripheral blending condition featured a greater susceptibility to motion sickness.

Metric	4 VR Video+Motion	5 VR V+M w/compensation	6 VR V+M w/peripheral feedback
User preferences	4 (22%)	8 (44%)	6 (33%)
Excluding (4)	–	9 (50%)	9 (50%)

Table 1. Total of preferred conditions, and preferred conditions excluding (4) by taking second preferences.

Examining the real-time illness rating (Figure 4), we see how preferences were influenced by perceived sickness. For those that preferred Condition 4 (VR Video+Motion, with the view rotating as the car turned), the stabilized view of Condition 5 led to a steady and continual increase in sickness. Whilst this was somewhat diminished by the peripheral cues of Condition 6, the more overt presentation of rotation in Condition 4 was best suited to this group and matched their inherent motion sickness. For those that preferred Condition 5 (VR V+M w/ Compensation, with the rotations of the car not affecting viewing), the visual perception of motion in Conditions 4/6 appeared to make their symptoms worse, especially the combination of visual cues of Condition 6. With these participants, their sickness was minimized by not presenting motion. It appears that these individuals are particularly susceptible to visual discrepancies in motion, suggesting that our conveyance of motion was insufficiently synchronized, or that perceiving different conflicting cues is particularly problematic for them. For those that preferred Condition 6 (VR V+M w/ Peripheral Feedback), the peripheral cues appeared to slow the onset of sickness, however all conditions provoked a consistent level of sickness throughout.

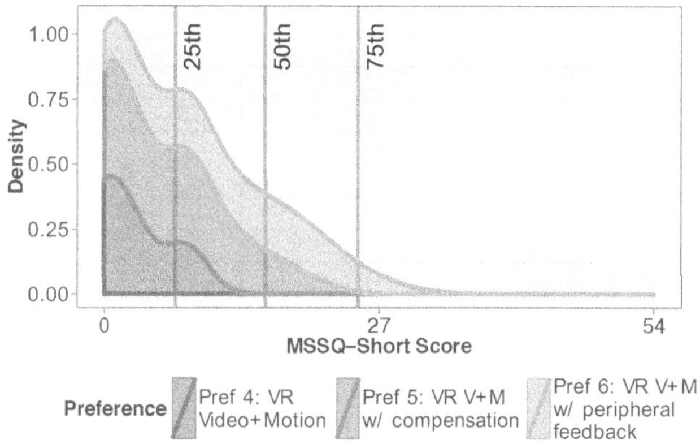

Figure 3. Stacked density plot (*geom_density* in R, using ..count.. and "stack") of motion sickness susceptibility against preferred condition (higher is more susceptible), with labels indicating susceptibility percentiles for the general population from [41]. 50th%ile is considered "slightly susceptible", and 75th%ile "moderately susceptible".

Examining SSQ total sickness against first preference and Condition, a two-factor ANOVA showed no main effects on Condition ($p = 0.37$) or preference ($p = 0.54$), but a significant interaction effect ($F(4,30) = 5.65, p < 0.01$), with contrasts showing an effect on Condition 4 versus 5 against preference for Condition 4 versus 5 ($b = -12.02, t(30) = -4.08, p < 0.01$), which can be seen in Figure 5. There was no significant con-

Metric	1 VR Video	2 Motion Only	3 VR Motion Env.	4 VR Video+Motion	5 VR V+M w/ Compensation	6 VR V+M w/ Peripheral Feedback	RM-Anova	Tukey *Post-hoc*
Mean Duration (sec)	600.0 (0.0)	600.0 (0.0)	569.9 (122.9)	563.5 (118.5)	567.2 (96.8)	555.4 (95.6)	$\chi^2(5) = 8.99, p = 0.1$	NA
Total Stopped early	0	0	2	3	3	5	$\chi^2(5) = 12.9, p < 0.05$	1-6, 2-6
IPQ Score	3.5 (0.9)	–	–	3.6 (0.9)	3.3 (0.9)	3.4 (0.8)	$\chi^2(3) = 2.54, p = 0.47$	NA
SSQ.N Nausea	9.0 (15.6)	8.5 (14.6)	39.2 (29.8)	53.5 (52.4)	58.8 (49.9)	60.4 (49.7)	$\chi^2(5) = 49.59, p < 0.01$	1-{3,4,5,6}, 2-{3,4,5,6}
SSQ.O Oculomotor	12.9 (16.5)	3.4 (9.1)	35.0 (28.0)	37.9 (33.7)	43.0 (37.3)	43.4 (35.3)	$\chi^2(5) = 51.83, p < 0.01$	1-{3,4,5,6}, 2-{3,4,5,6}
SSQ.D Disorientation	13.1 (26.3)	6.2 (10.9)	57.2 (62.4)	62.6 (71.5)	71.9 (72.1)	72.7 (71.4)	$\chi^2(5) = 44.8, p < 0.01$	1-{3,4,5,6}, 2-{3,4,5,6}
SSQ.TS Total Score	6.2 (10.4)	3.0 (5.0)	24.1 (23.1)	27.4 (28.6)	31.2 (28.9)	31.6 (28.0)	$\chi^2(5) = 49.80, p < 0.01$	1-{3,4,5,6}, 2-{3,4,5,6}
Rotation (NP)	–	–	4.1 (1.1)	3.9 (1.8)	–	3.3 (1.7)	$\chi^2(2) = 1.4, p = 0.5$	NA
Motion (NP)	–	–	4.1 (1.2)	–	–	3.4 (1.8)	$\chi^2(1) = 1.6, p = 0.2$	NA
Acceleration (NP)	–	–	4.5 (1.0)	–	–	3.4 (1.5)	$\chi^2(1) = 12, p < 0.01$	NA

Table 2. Statistics and questionnaire results. IPQ score 0–6, higher is more presence; SSQ score higher is more sickness (max 235); Ranking lower is better; Rotation/Motion/Acceleration 0–6 from strongly disagree to strongly agree that visual and physical motion cues were aligned. Green denotes $p < 0.05$, NP denotes non-parametric tests.

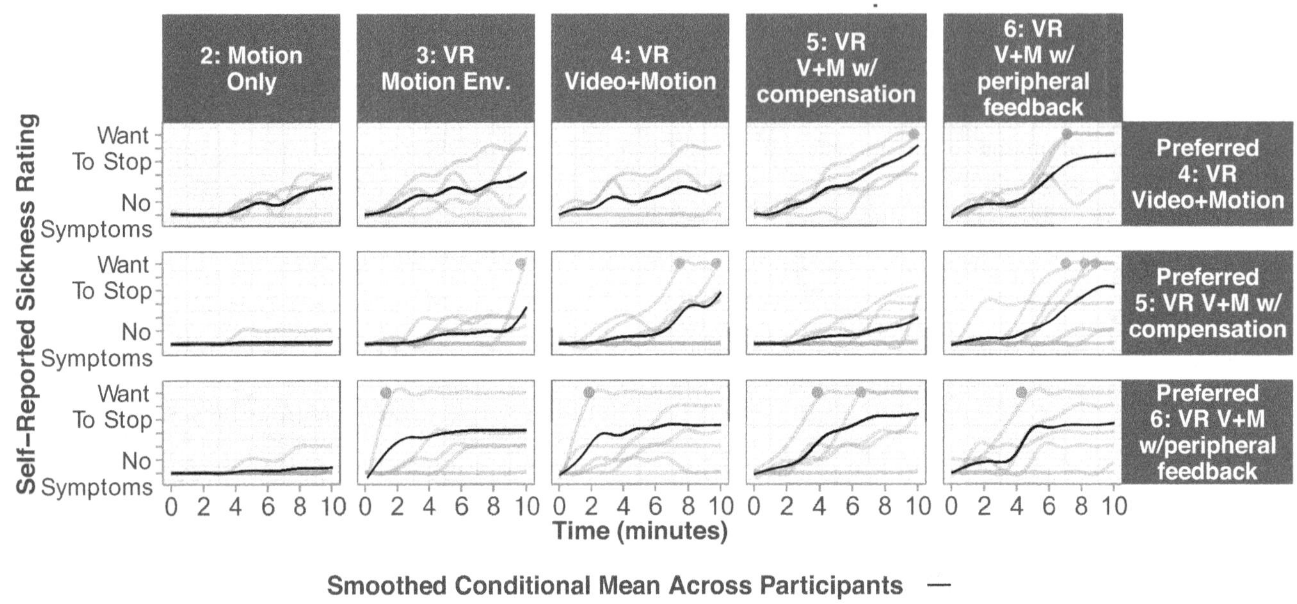

Figure 4. Plot of smoothed conditional mean real-time sickness ratings against condition and preference across participants (in black), with individual participants plotted (in colour) and if they stopped the condition prematurely (coloured circles show time stopped).

trast between Condition 5/6 against preference for Condition 5/6 ($b = -4.99, t(30) = -1.88, p = 0.06$). However, the interaction plot suggests a similar trend to that demonstrated in Figure 3, with sickness being in-part minimized by preference.

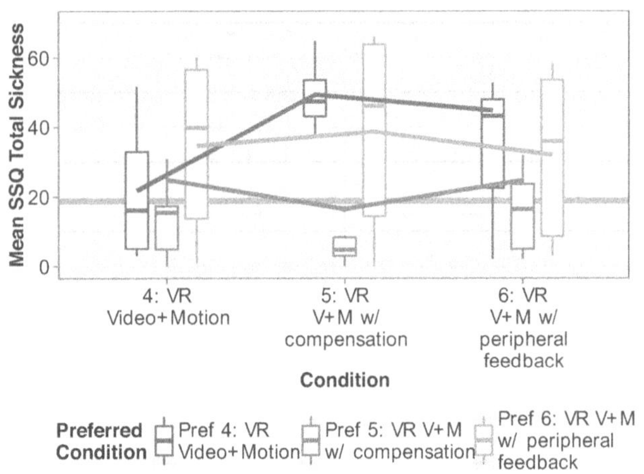

Figure 5. Interaction plot of SSQ total sickness score against condition and preference (higher is worse). Boxplots indicate the first and third quartiles (25th and 75th percentiles). Coloured lines indicate means. Grey background line indicates the sickness score of the *2F64C* flight simulator, suggested as indicating a problematic level of sickness [37].

Examining IPQ presence in VR against preference and Condition, a two-factor ANOVA showed no effect of Condition ($p = 0.33$) but a significant effect of preference ($F(2,15) = 4.8, p < 0.05$) with no interaction ($p = 0.52$). *Post-hoc* Tukey tests showed higher mean presence scores for those preferring Condition 4 versus Condition 6 ($p < 0.05$), but not 4–5 ($p = 0.69$) or 6–5 ($p = 0.09$).

Interviews

Interviews were loosely guided on the basis of reported preferences. Interviews were coded using Initial Coding, where participants' statements were assigned emergent codes over repeated cycles. These codes were then grouped using a thematic approach and reported based on frequency and interest (see [66]), with representative excerpts quoted.

Incorporating Rotations Of The Car "Like A Tour"

Six participants commented on the fact that Condition 4, where the view rotated with the car, aided exploration whilst feeling natural, allowing them to explore beyond the physical viewing constraints of the headset:

> *P1*: It was interesting because I saw stuff which would normally be behind me. You can look around in the car with the headset on, but it takes quite a lot of effort to see what's directly behind you.
> *P8*: Despite the car moving and shifting your perspective, it felt more like I'm in a cinema and... the camera is panning and focusing my attention on other things.

Conversely, 6 participants said they did not appreciate the "lack of control" (P11), noting "it was quite annoying if you were trying to focus on something and obviously the car is turning away" (P6). Attempting to compensate for this motion to continue looking at a particular point of focus caused one participant (P14) to note an onset of sickness.

Providing No Motion Cues Is Dichotomous

For 5 participants, Condition 5 was preferred because it allowed for more control over their viewing, which was in one case noted as "worth the slight discomfort" in comparison to other conditions (P9). However, 6 participants reported an intolerance to this lack of motion presentation:

> *P3*: I think the feeling was more intense compared to the others. I felt the stomach effect more in this particular one than the rest of them.
> *P14*: I could just tell that this was going to make me ill quite quickly... it was more immersive almost, but it just meant that especially if you were going faster or when there were bumps mid turns... I knew I was getting there with that one.

Peripheral Motion Provides Comfort For Some

For Condition 6, three participants specifically noted that perceiving peripheral motion provided comfort, with 7 participants noting some preference for peripheral cues:

> *P8*: You're very much aware that OK we are moving, we are turning, I'm very aware of what the car is doing. It's slightly comforting, because you have this sort of experience and feedback because you still have this contact with the real world.
> *P11*: The mixed image of the motion and video felt more comfortable. I could feel motion and I knew that there was motion happening in the vision, it made sense.
> *P14*: The peripheral one I thought was the best because it showed where I was going... I felt the least sick in this one, but then it wasn't quite as immersive... but I think having something in the visual field was better.

However, 6 participants noted that the peripheral cues either distracted from their immersion or were felt to be unnecessary. In 3 cases it made it difficult to focus on the VR content, whilst for 2 participants it provoked more nausea through the conflict of visual imagery. In addition, 2 participants noted that they struggled to or did not perceive the peripheral cues:

> *P6*: I preferred with no peripheral view because you can just focus purely on the video. Having the edges visible on the screen is just a distraction for no good reason.
> *P10*: My nausea felt more severe, the motion combined with the static images of the video maybe enhanced that somehow.

Discontinuities Are Disruptive

Two users noted that discontinuities between the VR motion environment and their perception of the physical world were particularly off-putting, with the VR content not adequately reflecting the changing environment around them:

> *P6*: When the sun did hit me, that was a bit confusing. The sun came out after I put the headset on, so I didn't actually realize there was going to be warm sunlight hitting my body.
> *P9*: It was a really strange disconnect between an overcast sky [in VR] and feeling sunlight on my skin. You start looking around subconsciously for the sun, and when you go behind a tree and there's no difference in temperature, you don't feel yourself going into the shade.

DISCUSSION

Our experimental conditions set a baseline for future work as they demonstrate, for the first time, the differences in motion sickness levels between seated VR and use in-car and in-motion. We also showed the effects of different visual presentations of motion on users, which we will now discuss.

No Universally Suitable Visual Portrayal of Motion

The results indicate that there was no universal solution for minimizing sickness. We evaluated three VR in-motion conditions: (4) conveyed rotations only, (5) conveyed no motion and (6) peripherally conveyed rotations and accelerations. Examining motion sickness susceptibility, perceived sickness, presence and real-time illness revealed few differences between conditions over the 18 participants. However, breaking these results down by preference suggests that different presentations may be required by different subsets of passengers, with the wrong type actually making people feel worse.

Preference For Conveyance Of Motion Was A Dichotomy

Preferences were split between conditions, with 4 participants preferring Condition 4, 8 preferring Condition 5 and 6 preferring Condition 6. Conveying rotations through Condition 4 confused matters somewhat, as these preferences were in-part based on the capability of this condition to allow for more exploration, with the view of the VR scene moving with the car. Excluding (4) and taking second preferences (see Table 1), half the participants preferred some presentation of motion, and half did not. This preference did not entirely align with susceptibility, sickness or immersion. However, for those with a higher susceptibility to motion sickness, peripheral conveyance of motion was in-part preferred, with feedback suggesting that peripheral presentation provided support.

VR That Ignores External Motion Was Useable For Some

For those that preferred the view of Condition 5, which compensated for the turns of the car, sickness scores were typically below the threshold given by Kennedy *et al.* [37] that denotes a level of sickness deemed problematic for simulator use. This suggests that, given a VR HMD that can counteract vehicle rotations, for these users VR in-motion is useable (albeit for the short duration examined). For these users, conveying or integrating motion into their experience appeared to increase their sickness, being both unnecessary, distracting and potentially introducing a subtle discrepancy in perceived motion to which these individuals were particularly attuned.

VR In-Motion Was Problematic For Many

For the majority of participants, sickness exceeded what would be considered acceptable for a motion simulator [37]. Our results demonstrate that there are significant problems regarding VR HMD use in-motion that need to be overcome to make VR in-motion usable for the general population.

Limitations and Guidelines For Further Experimentation

Our use of a compensatory gyroscope will have led to additional visual discrepancy, meaning it is possible that sickness was over-reported. The latency of the gyroscope and OBD2 link, the gyroscopic drift (~20° per min), the necessity for user resets of the forward vector (~once per lap, mean=4.9, SD=2.4) and the lack of conveyance of oscillations could all contribute to a, likely modest, increase in sickness. Consequently, we recommend that VR HMDs supporting positional tracking be used in-motion if possible. This would provide an accurate forward vector for car motion, as well as allow the conveyance of oscillations, a component of motion sickness we were unable to evaluate. Whilst other implementations could be considered (e.g. GPS and gyroscope, periodic resets of orientation, marker tracking), some form of positional tracking appears preferable. Problematically, consumer HMDs with positional tracking currently fuse both optical tracking and IMU data, meaning there is a reliance on gyroscopes which would make their immediate deployment in-car difficult.

There are also a number of factors upon which sickness is likely to vary that must be accounted for e.g. duration of stimulii; the effectiveness of interventions over time; characteristics of the route, vehicle and motion experienced; different forms of vection (see Section 2.2); differing motion and simulator sickness susceptibilities; the specifications of the HMD; age and user demographics; and the virtual content being experienced. For example, manipulating the workload demands of virtual content would be likely to have an impact, given that mental distraction has been shown to decrease sickness [9]). Future studies should consider these factors to determine whether our approach (e.g. a narrow demographic and a controlled real-world route) is suitable.

Evaluating VR in-car is also ethically challenging. Due to ethical and resource constraints, we evaluated multiple conditions per session, for durations of 10 minutes at a time (given the unknown magnitude of sickness that would be induced). Whilst counter-balancing was employed, and participants were given significant recovery breaks between conditions, there may be cumulative effects across a session. This design was acceptable given we were examining low-susceptibility individuals, however for a broader population, we would evaluate one condition per session over multiple days to rule out cumulative effects and allow for increased exposure time.

RECOMMENDATIONS FOR FURTHER RESEARCH

Peripheral Blending and Other Presentation Techniques

With respect to direct extensions of this study, peripheral blending of motion shows some promise for susceptible individuals. However, this implementation was limited by the technology. The Gear VR HMD has a field of view (FOV) of ~96°; of this, our peripheral display took over $\pm 10°$ from the edge. Whilst this is peripheral with respect to the HMD, this is not fully peripheral with respect to our visual field. Consequently, any expansion in VR FOV (e.g. HMDs with high FOV lenses [82] or sparse peripheral displays [83]) would allow for further exploration of the effectiveness of conveying motion through the mid-to-far periphery of the eye.

We used a basic VR landscape to portray motion to maintain 60Hz when rendered in conjunction with video content. Higher fidelity portrayals (e.g. based on real surroundings with discernible landmarks), or abstract cues (e.g. using environmental or shader effects to portray motion) could prove effective. Motion could be incorporated implicitly into VR (as with the Gear VR and Condition 4), by design (as part of a game), or generically for any content (e.g. peripheral blending) and could be incorporated dynamically based on the perceived sickness of the user. The magnitude of this presentation of real world motion could also be manipulated, with subtle conveyances potentially effective, for example visually perceiving small movements on the basis of larger accelerations and decelerations. Given foreknowledge of the route, motion could also be conveyed only when it occurs, for example showing a motion landscape for the duration of the car turning, or viewing could be restricted temporarily [22]. Initial user calibration will also be required to determine susceptibility and choose the best method of VR presentation.

Anticipatory Cues and Provoking Anticipatory Actions

Our literature review suggested a number of promising avenues. Firstly, having an understanding of impending motion might help users to compensate for, and anticipate, changes in velocity and acceleration. Manipulating the VR view to induce anticipatory actions might also help prevent motion sickness. In tilting trains it has been noted that "if head roll was initiated before the lateral acceleration, there was no motion sickness" [3, 35]. Asking car passengers to mimic the driver's head movements has noted a similar effect [3, 78]. As an example, a VR display that tilted content so users had to match the tilt to continue reading might mimic these results. Similarly, the conveyance and magnitude of oscillations could be altered in VR. Such effects might make VR HMDs, and notably also AR HMDs, ideally suited to facilitating entertainment and work whilst preventing motion sickness in autonomous cars and other transportation, where the environment might lead to sensory conflict and consequently motion sickness [20].

Vestibular Counter-Stimulation

Mitigations are also not limited to visual cues [27]. For example, Galvanic Vestibular Stimulation (GVS) [11] has the capability to alter our physical perception of motion and has been applied to the problem of vection [56], whilst other devices (e.g. inducing physically inducing vibrations) have also been suggested [7]. These could be used to counteract physically perceived motion. However, there are still significant difficulties to overcome regarding the practicality of delivery, adoption and effectiveness in the general population.

Social Acceptability And Safety

Willingness to use VR HMDs in-motion must be considered. For private spaces such as cars, provided there is sufficient trust [65] in the vehicle, then VR HMD use is more straightforward. However, for public transport, social acceptability, and issues of personal space and safety may inhibit adoption [61]. McGill *et al.* have begun to look at ways of bringing people into the VR world to address some of these issues [44, 6, 45]. AR HMDs may be more acceptable here and research into solutions across mixed-reality HMDs should be investigated.

CONCLUSIONS

As cars become autonomous, more passengers will need to fill more time on journeys. One way to do this is with VR and AR HMDs. These headsets have the potential to allow passengers to virtually escape the confines of their vehicle. Instead, they might spend their time in a virtual cinema with friends at-a-distance [45], or a virtual office, making more entertaining and productive use of travel time. However, a key drawback is motion sickness.

Given this motivation, this paper has, for the first time, examined the usability of VR HMDs in-car. Through an on-the-road study, we have established the extent to which motion sickness represents an obstacle to such usage in real world conditions. We have also examined how motion sickness can be diminished through differing visual presentations of motion in VR, aimed at minimizing sensory conflict. We found that there is no one best presentation with respect to sickness and immersion, with differently susceptible groups requiring different solutions, be they conveyance of rotations, peripheral conveyance of motion, or no conveyance of motion at all. Finally, based on both our results and the existing literature, we give suggestions for further experimentation, and describe what new research is required to arrive at AR and VR HMDs that are usable in-motion, providing an entry point for HCI to contribute to this problem. Our results suggest that there is, as-yet, no universal solution for minimizing sickness from VR HMD use in-motion, however we have begun to explore how different solutions can make VR HMDs usable in transit.

REFERENCES

1. Stuart Anstis. 1986. Motion perception in the frontal plane: Sensory aspects. *Handbook of perception and human performance.* 1 (1986), 16–1.
2. Ben Lang. 2013. An Introduction to Positional Tracking and Degrees of Freedom (DOF). (2013). http://www.roadtovr.com/introduction-positional-tracking-degrees-freedom-dof/
3. Giovanni Bertolini and Dominik Straumann. 2016. Moving in a Moving World: A Review on Vestibular Motion Sickness. *Frontiers in Neurology* 7 (2016), 14. DOI:http://dx.doi.org/10.3389/fneur.2016.00014
4. Alvah C. Bittner and John C. Guignard. 1985. Human factors engineering principles for minimizing adverse ship motion effects: Theory and practice. *Naval Engineers Journal* 97, 4 (1985), 205–213. DOI: http://dx.doi.org/10.1111/j.1559-3584.1985.tb01355.x
5. Willem Bles, Jelte E Bos, Bernd de Graaf, Eric Groen, and Alexander H Wertheim. 1998. Motion sickness: only one provocative conflict? *Brain Research Bulletin* 47, 5 (1998), 481 – 487. DOI: http://dx.doi.org/10.1016/S0361-9230(98)00115-4
6. Daniel Boland and Mark McGill. 2015. Lost in the rift. *XRDS: Crossroads, The ACM Magazine for Students* 22, 1 (nov 2015), 40–45. DOI: http://dx.doi.org/10.1145/2810046
7. JE Bos. 2015a. Less sickness with more motion and/or mental distraction. *Journal of Vestibular Research* 25, 1 (2015), 23–33. http://content.iospress.com/articles/journal-of-vestibular-research/ves00541
8. Jelte E. Bos. 2011. Nuancing the relationship between motion sickness and postural stability. *Displays* 32, 4 (2011), 189 – 193. DOI: http://dx.doi.org/10.1016/j.displa.2010.09.005
9. Jelte E. Bos. 2015b. Less sickness with more motion and/or mental distraction. *Journal of Vestibular Research* 25, 1 (2015), 23–33. DOI: http://dx.doi.org/10.3233/VES-150541
10. Claudio Braccesi, Filippo Cianetti, and Renzo Scaletta. 2015. The use of the PCT index in railway motion sickness incidence evaluation. *Proceedings of the Institution of Mechanical Engineers, Part F: Journal of Rail and Rapid Transit* 229, 4 (2015), 428–445. DOI: http://dx.doi.org/10.1177/0954409713514963
11. Michael J. Cevette, Jan Stepanek, Daniela Cocco, Anna M. Galea, Gaurav N. Pradhan, Linsey S. Wagner, Sarah R. Oakley, Benn E. Smith, David A. Zapala, and Kenneth H. Brookler. 2012. Oculo-Vestibular Recoupling Using Galvanic Vestibular Stimulation to Mitigate Simulator Sickness. *Aviation, Space, and Environmental Medicine* 83, 6 (2012), 549–555. DOI: http://dx.doi.org/10.3357/ASEM.3239.2012
12. Jean-Rémy Chardonnet, Mohammad Ali Mirzaei, and Frédéric Mérienne. 2015. Visually Induced Motion Sickness Estimation and Prediction in Virtual Reality using Frequency Components Analysis of Postural Sway Signal. In *ICAT-EGVE 2015 - International Conference on Artificial Reality and Telexistence and Eurographics Symposium on Virtual Environments*, Masataka Imura, Pablo Figueroa, and Betty Mohler (Eds.). The Eurographics Association. DOI: http://dx.doi.org/10.2312/egve.20151304
13. Bernard Cohen, Mingjia Dai, Dmitri Ogorodnikov, Jean Laurens, Theodore Raphan, Philippe MÃijller, Alexiou Athanasios, JÃijrgen Edmaier, Thomas Grossenbacher, Klaus StadtmÃijller, Ueli Brugger, Gerald Hauser, and Dominik Straumann. 2011. Motion sickness on tilting trains. *The FASEB Journal* 25, 11 (2011), 3765–3774. DOI:http://dx.doi.org/10.1096/fj.11-184887
14. Stanley Coren, Lawrence M. Ward, and James T. Enns. 1999. *Sensation and Perception.* John Wiley & Sons.
15. M.A. Cuddihy and M.K. Rao. 2013. Autonomous vehicle entertainment system US9272708 B2. (2013). https://www.google.com/patents/US9272708 US Patent 9,272,708.
16. Joakim Dahlman. 2009. *Psychophysiological and Performance Aspects on Motion Sickness.* Ph.D. Dissertation. Linköping University, Faculty of Health Sciences, Rehabilitation Medicine.
17. Department for Transport. 2016. National Travel Survey. (2016). https://www.gov.uk/government/statistics/national-travel-survey-2015
18. Cyriel Diels. 2014. Will autonomous vehicles make us sick. In *Contemporary Ergonomics and Human Factors.* Boca Raton, FL: CRC Press, 301–307.
19. Cyriel Diels and Jelte E. Bos. 2015. User Interface Considerations to Prevent Self-driving Carsickness. In *Adjunct Proceedings of the 7th International Conference on Automotive User Interfaces and Interactive Vehicular Applications (AutomotiveUI '15).* ACM, New York, NY, USA, 14–19. DOI: http://dx.doi.org/10.1145/2809730.2809754
20. Cyriel Diels and Jelte E. Bos. 2016. Self-driving carsickness. *Applied Ergonomics* 53, Part B (2016), 374 – 382. DOI: http://dx.doi.org/10.1016/j.apergo.2015.09.009 Transport in the 21st Century: The Application of Human Factors to Future User Needs.
21. M. Elbanhawi, M. Simic, and R. Jazar. 2015. In the Passenger Seat: Investigating Ride Comfort Measures in Autonomous Cars. *IEEE Intelligent Transportation Systems Magazine* 7, 3 (Fall 2015), 4–17. DOI: http://dx.doi.org/10.1109/MITS.2015.2405571
22. A. S. Fernandes and S. K. Feiner. 2016. Combating VR sickness through subtle dynamic field-of-view modification. In *2016 IEEE Symposium on 3D User Interfaces (3DUI).* 201–210. DOI: http://dx.doi.org/10.1109/3DUI.2016.7460053

23. Andy Field, Jeremy Miles, and Zoë Field. 2012. *Discovering Statistics Using R*. SAGE Publications. 992 pages. https://uk.sagepub.com/en-gb/eur/discovering-statistics-using-r/book236067

24. Benjamin Gardner and Charles Abraham. 2007. What drives car use? A grounded theory analysis of commuters' reasons for driving. *Transportation Research Part F: Traffic Psychology and Behaviour* 10, 3 (2007), 187 – 200. DOI:http://dx.doi.org/10.1016/j.trf.2006.09.004

25. John F. Golding. 2006. Predicting individual differences in motion sickness susceptibility by questionnaire. *Personality and Individual Differences* 41, 2 (2006), 237–248. DOI: http://dx.doi.org/10.1016/j.paid.2006.01.012

26. John F Golding and Michael A Gresty. 2013. Motion sickness and disorientation in vehicles. *Oxford textbook of vertigo and imbalance. Oxford University Press, Oxford* (2013), 293–306. DOI: http://dx.doi.org/10.1093/med/9780199608997.003.0028

27. John F Golding and Michael A Gresty. 2015. Pathophysiology and treatment of motion sickness. *Current opinion in neurology* 28, 1 (feb 2015), 83–8. DOI:http://dx.doi.org/10.1097/WCO.0000000000000163

28. John F Golding, Priscilla Kadzere, and Michael A Gresty. 2005. Motion sickness susceptibility fluctuates through the menstrual cycle. *Aviation, space, and environmental medicine* 76, 10 (oct 2005), 970–3. http://www.ncbi.nlm.nih.gov/pubmed/16235881

29. Michael J Griffin and Maria M Newman. 2004. Visual field effects on motion sickness in cars. *Aviation, space, and environmental medicine* 75, 9 (sep 2004), 739–48. http://www.ncbi.nlm.nih.gov/pubmed/15460624

30. F E Guedry and A J Benson. 1978. Coriolis cross-coupling effects: disorienting and nauseogenic or not? *Aviation, space, and environmental medicine* 49, 1 Pt 1 (jan 1978), 29–35. http://www.ncbi.nlm.nih.gov/pubmed/304719

31. Isadora Ferreira Henriques, Dhelfeson Willya Douglas De Oliveira, Fernanda Oliveira-Ferreira, and Peterson MO Andrade. 2014. Motion sickness prevalence in school children. *European journal of pediatrics* 173, 11 (nov 2014), 1473–82. DOI: http://dx.doi.org/10.1007/s00431-014-2351-1

32. M Hosseini and S Farahani. 2015. Vestibular findings in motion sickness. *Auditory and ...* (2015). http://avr.tums.ac.ir/index.php/avr/article/view/10

33. Ohad Inbar and Noam Tractinsky. 2011. Make a Trip an Experience: Sharing In-car Information with Passengers. In *CHI '11 Extended Abstracts on Human Factors in Computing Systems (CHI EA '11)*. ACM, New York, NY, USA, 1243–1248. DOI: http://dx.doi.org/10.1145/1979742.1979755

34. Jason Jerald. 2015. Perception of Space and Time. In *The VR Book: Human-Centered Design for Virtual Reality*. Association for Computing Machinery, Chapter 9. DOI: http://dx.doi.org/10.1145/2792790

35. Judith A. Joseph and Michael J. Griffin. 2007. Motion Sickness from Combined Lateral and Roll Oscillation: Effect of Varying Phase Relationships. *Aviation, Space, and Environmental Medicine* 78, 10 (2007), 944–950. DOI:http://dx.doi.org/10.3357/ASEM.2043.2007

36. Robert S. Kennedy, Norman E. Lane, Kevin S. Berbaum, and Michael G. Lilienthal. 1993a. Simulator Sickness Questionnaire: An Enhanced Method for Quantifying Simulator Sickness. *The International Journal of Aviation Psychology* 3, 3 (jul 1993), 203–220. DOI: http://dx.doi.org/10.1207/s15327108ijap0303_3

37. Robert S. Kennedy, Norman E. Lane, Kevin S. Berbaum, and Michael G. Lilienthal. 1993b. Simulator Sickness Questionnaire: An Enhanced Method for Quantifying Simulator Sickness. *The International Journal of Aviation Psychology* 3, 3 (jul 1993), 203–220. DOI: http://dx.doi.org/10.1207/s15327108ijap0303_3

38. B Keshavarz, H Hecht, and L Zschutschke. 2011. Intra-visual conflict in visually induced motion sickness. *Displays* (2011). http://www.sciencedirect.com/science/article/pii/S0141938211000539

39. Behrang Keshavarz, Bernhard E Riecke, Lawrence J Hettinger, and Jennifer L Campos. 2015. Vection and visually induced motion sickness: how are they related? *Frontiers in psychology* 6 (jan 2015), 472. DOI: http://dx.doi.org/10.3389/fpsyg.2015.00472

40. James R. Lackner. 2014. Motion sickness: more than nausea and vomiting. *Experimental Brain Research* 232, 8 (2014), 2493–2510. DOI: http://dx.doi.org/10.1007/s00221-014-4008-8

41. Steve Lamb and Kenny C. S. Kwok. 2014. MSSQ-Short Norms May Underestimate Highly Susceptible Individuals: Updating the MSSQ-Short Norms. *Human Factors: The Journal of the Human Factors and Ergonomics Society* (2014). DOI: http://dx.doi.org/10.1177/0018720814555862

42. Robert L Matchock, Max E Levine, Peter J Gianaros, and Robert M Stern. 2008. Susceptibility to nausea and motion sickness as a function of the menstrual cycle. *Women's health issues : official publication of the Jacobs Institute of Women's Health* 18, 4 (2008), 328–35. DOI: http://dx.doi.org/10.1016/j.whi.2008.01.006

43. Matt Kamen. 2016. Ford patents windshield movie screen for driverless cars. (2016). http://www.wired.co.uk/article/ford-patents-movie-window-for-driverless-cars

44. Mark McGill, Daniel Boland, Roderick Murray-Smith, and Stephen Brewster. 2015. A Dose of Reality: Overcoming Usability Challenges in VR Head-Mounted Displays. In *Proceedings of the 33rd Annual ACM Conference on Human Factors in Computing Systems - CHI '15*. ACM Press, New York, New York, USA, 2143–2152. DOI: http://dx.doi.org/10.1145/2702123.2702382

45. Mark McGill, John H. Williamson, and Stephen Brewster. 2016. Examining The Role of Smart TVs and VR HMDs in Synchronous At-a-Distance Media Consumption. *ACM Transactions on Computer-Human Interaction (TOCHI)* 23, 5, Article 33 (Nov. 2016), 57 pages. DOI: http://dx.doi.org/10.1145/2983530

46. K Meissner, P Enck, ER Muth, S Kellermann, and S Klosterhalfen. 2009. Cortisol levels predict motion sickness tolerance in women but not in men. *Physiology & behavior* 97, 1 (apr 2009), 102–6. DOI: http://dx.doi.org/10.1016/j.physbeh.2009.02.007

47. Mark Mine, Arun Yoganandan, and Dane Coffey. 2014. Making VR Work: Building a Real-world Immersive Modeling Application in the Virtual World. In *Proceedings of the 2Nd ACM Symposium on Spatial User Interaction (SUI '14)*. ACM, New York, NY, USA, 80–89. DOI:http://dx.doi.org/10.1145/2659766.2659780

48. Montavit. 2016. Causes and treatment of motion sickness. (2016). http://www.montavit.com/en/areas-therapy/causes-and-treatment-motion-sickness

49. JB Murray. 1997. Psychophysiological aspects of motion sickness. *Perceptual and motor skills* (1997). http://www.amsciepub.com/doi/pdf/10.2466/pms.1997.85.3f.1163

50. Elon Musk. 2016. Master Plan, Part Deux. (2016). https://www.tesla.com/blog/master-plan-part-deux

51. NBC Sports. 2016. Rio Olympics: 360 Tour of RIO. (2016). https://www.youtube.com/watch?v=Yv6zRv-qKmk

52. NHS Choices. 2014. Motion sickness symptoms. (2014). http://www.nhs.uk/conditions/motion-sickness/pages/introduction.aspx

53. Charles M Oman. 1990. Motion sickness: a synthesis and evaluation of the sensory conflict theory. *Canadian journal of physiology and pharmacology* 68, 2 (1990), 294–303.

54. Natalie Owen, Antony Graham Leadbetter, and Lucy Yardley. 1998. Relationship between postural control and motion sickness in healthy subjects. *Brain Research Bulletin* 47, 5 (1998), 471–474. DOI: http://dx.doi.org/10.1016/S0361-9230(98)00101-4

55. A. J. Parmet and W. R. Ercoline. 2008. Spatial Orientation in Flight. In *Fundamentals of Aerospace Medicine* (fourth ed.), Jeffrey R. Davis, Johnson Robert, and Jan Stepanek (Eds.). Lippincott Williams and Wilkins, Chapter 6. http://www.lww.com/Product/9780781774666

56. Paul James. 2016. Samsung's New Headphones Trick Your Inner Ear to Move You in VR. (2016). http://www.roadtovr.com/samsungs-new-headphones-trick-your-inner-ear-to-move-you-in-vr/

57. Philippe Perrin, Alexis Lion, Gilles Bosser, Gérome Gauchard, and Claude Meistelman. 2013. Motion sickness in rally car co-drivers. *Aviation, space, and environmental medicine* 84, 5 (may 2013), 473–7. http://www.ncbi.nlm.nih.gov/pubmed/23713212

58. Press Association. 2015. Millions of people spend two or more hours commuting a day. (2015). https://www.theguardian.com/money/2015/nov/09/million-people-two-hours-commuting-tuc-study

59. James T Reason and Joseph John Brand. 1975. *Motion sickness*. Academic press.

60. Gary E. Riccio and Thomas A. Stoffregen. 1991. An Ecological Theory of Motion Sickness and Postural Instability. *Ecological Psychology* 3, 3 (1991), 195–240. DOI:http://dx.doi.org/10.1207/s15326969eco0303_2

61. Julie Rico and Stephen Brewster. 2010. Usable Gestures for Mobile Interfaces: Evaluating Social Acceptability. In *Proceedings of the SIGCHI Conference on Human Factors in Computing Systems (CHI '10)*. ACM, New York, NY, USA, 887–896. DOI: http://dx.doi.org/10.1145/1753326.1753458

62. Roadshow. 2016. See where Tesla makes its cars in 360 degrees. (2016). https://www.youtube.com/watch?v=vmHvvZjV87U

63. A Rolnick and R E Lubow. 1991. Why is the driver rarely motion sick? The role of controllability in motion sickness. *Ergonomics* 34, 7 (jul 1991), 867–79. DOI: http://dx.doi.org/10.1080/00140139108964831

64. Qantas News Room. 2015. Qantas & Samung unveil industry-first virtual reality experience for travellers. (2015). http://www.qantasnewsroom.com.au/media-releases/qantas-samsung-unveil-industry-first-virtual-reality-experience-for-travellers/

65. Davide Salanitri, Chrisminder Hare, Simone Borsci, Glyn Lawson, Sarah Sharples, and Brian Water Fi Eld. 2015. Relationship between trust and usability in virtual environments: An ongoing study, Vol. 9169. Springer Verlag, 49–59. DOI: http://dx.doi.org/10.1007/978-3-319-20901-2_5

66. J Saldaña. 2015. *The coding manual for qualitative researchers*. https://uk.sagepub.com/en-gb/eur/the-coding-manual-for-qualitative-researchers/book243616

67. Brandon Schoettle and Michael Sivak. 2014. Public opinion about self-driving vehicles in China, India, Japan, the U.S., the U.K., and Australia. (oct 2014). http://deepblue.lib.umich.edu/handle/2027.42/109433

68. Thomas Schubert, Frank Friedmann, and Holger Regenbrecht. 2001. The experience of presence: Factor analytic insights. *Presence: Teleoperators and virtual environments* 10, 3 (2001), 266–281.

69. K Sharma and Aparna. 1997. Prevalence and correlates of susceptibility to motion sickness. *Acta geneticae medicae et gemellologiae* 46, 2 (jan 1997), 105–21. http://www.ncbi.nlm.nih.gov/pubmed/9492893

70. Avi Shupak and Carlos R Gordon. 2006. Motion sickness: advances in pathogenesis, prediction, prevention, and treatment. *Aviation, space, and environmental medicine* 77, 12 (2006), 1213–1223.

71. M Sivak and B Schoettle. 2015. Motion sickness in self-driving vehicles. (2015). http://deepblue.lib.umich.edu/handle/2027.42/111747

72. OBD Solutions. 2016. OBDLink® LX Bluetooth | OBDLink® | OBD Solutions. (2016). http://www.obdlink.com/lxbt/

73. F. Soyka, E. Kokkinara, M. Leyrer, H. Buelthoff, M. Slater, and B. Mohler. 2015. Turbulent motions cannot shake VR. In *2015 IEEE Virtual Reality (VR)*. 33–40. DOI: http://dx.doi.org/10.1109/VR.2015.7223321

74. D Tal, G Wiener, and A Shupak. 2014. Mal de debarquement, motion sickness and the effect of an artificial horizon. *Journal of Vestibular Research* (2014). http://content.iospress.com/articles/journal-of-vestibular-research/ves00505

75. M Turner and M J Griffin. 1999. Motion sickness in public road transport: the effect of driver, route and vehicle. *Ergonomics* 42, 12 (dec 1999), 1646–64. DOI: http://dx.doi.org/10.1080/001401399184730

76. U.S. Department of Transportation. 2009. Summary of travel trends. *National Household Travel Survey* (2009).

77. VR Coaster. 2016. Synchronized VR Rollercoasters. (2016). http://www.vrcoaster.com/

78. Takahiro Wada and Keigo Yoshida. 2016. Effect of passengers' active head tilt and opening/closure of eyes on motion sickness in lateral acceleration environment of cars. *Ergonomics* 59, 8 (2016), 1050–1059. DOI: http://dx.doi.org/10.1080/00140139.2015.1109713 PMID: 26481809.

79. Wall Street Journal. 2016. How Thousands of Pigeons Became Art (360 Video). (2016). https://www.youtube.com/watch?v=v9wWuKbnvyc

80. Laura Watts and John Urry. 2008. Moving methods, travelling times. *Environment and Planning D: Society and Space* 26, 5 (2008), 860–874. DOI: http://dx.doi.org/10.1068/d6707

81. David Wilfinger, Alexander Meschtscherjakov, Martin Murer, Sebastian Osswald, and Manfred Tscheligi. 2011. Are We There Yet? A Probing Study to Inform Design for the Rear Seat of Family Cars. Springer Berlin Heidelberg, 657–674. DOI: http://dx.doi.org/10.1007/978-3-642-23771-3_48

82. Will Mason. 2015. Wearality shows off a new 180-degree FOV lens for VR. (2015). http://uploadvr.com/wearality-180-degree-fov-lens-vr/

83. Robert Xiao and Hrvoje Benko. 2016. Augmenting the Field-of-View of Head-Mounted Displays with Sparse Peripheral Displays. In *Proceedings of the 2016 CHI Conference on Human Factors in Computing Systems (CHI '16)*. ACM, New York, NY, USA, 1221–1232. DOI: http://dx.doi.org/10.1145/2858036.2858212

84. Fleur D Yen Pik Sang, Jessica P Billar, John F Golding, and Michael A Gresty. 2003. Behavioral methods of alleviating motion sickness: effectiveness of controlled breathing and a music audiotape. *Journal of travel medicine* 10, 2 (2003), 108–11. http://www.ncbi.nlm.nih.gov/pubmed/12650654

85. Li-Li Zhang, Jun-Qin Wang, Rui-Rui Qi, Lei-Lei Pan, Min Li, and Yi-Ling Cai. 2016. Motion Sickness: Current Knowledge and Recent Advance. *CNS neuroscience & therapeutics* 22, 1 (jan 2016), 15–24. DOI: http://dx.doi.org/10.1111/cns.12468

VaiR: Simulating 3D Airflows in Virtual Reality

Michael Rietzler **Katrin Plaumann** **Taras Kräenzle** **Marcel Erath**
Alexander Stahl **Enrico Rukzio**
Institute of Mediainformatics, Ulm University, Ulm, Germany
firstname.lastname@uni-ulm.de

ABSTRACT
The integration of multi-sensory stimuli, e.g. haptic airflow, in virtual reality (VR) has become an important topic of VR research and proved to enhance the feeling of presence. VaiR focuses on an accurate and realistic airflow simulation that goes far beyond wind. While previous works on the topic of airflow in VR are restricted to wind, while focusing on the feeling of presence, there is to the best of our knowledge no work considering the conceptual background or on the various application areas. Our pneumatic prototype emits short and long term flows with a minimum delay and is able to animate wind sources in 3D space around the user's head. To get insights on how airflow can be used in VR and how such a device should be designed, we arranged focus groups and discussed the topic. Based on the gathered knowledge, we developed a prototype which proved to increase presence, as well as enjoyment and realism, while not disturbing the VR experience.

ACM Classification Keywords
H.5.2. User Interfaces: Haptic I/O; H.5.2. User Interfaces: Prototyping

Author Keywords
Virtual reality; airflow; presence; evaluation.

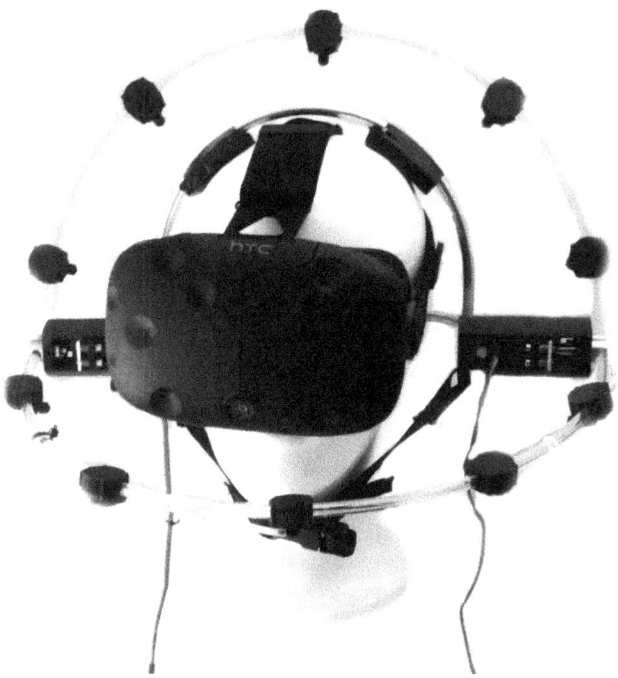

Figure 1. The VaiR Prototype worn in combination with a HTC Vive head mounted display. Fixed to frame mounted onto the Vive's straps are two bows. These bows are moved by two separate motors, allowing both bows to each rotate 135°. Fixes on each bow are five nozzles (each 36° apart), were the air streams come out. Several nozzles can be used at the same time. Due to the modular design, nozzles can be moved along the bows and changed as needed. That way, angle and dispersion of the air streams can be customized. VaiR is so designed that a container of pressurized air, valves, power source and an arduino controller can be worn as a backpack.

INTRODUCTION
Enhancing presence and immersion is one of the major goals of Virtual Reality (VR) research. The sense of *being there* [7] both occurs and can be supported in three dimensions: the personal, the environmental and the social forms of presence. The main focus of this paper is to enhance the personal feeling of presence. This can be achieved by simulating sensory stimuli as close as possible to the capability of a sensor regarding range and intensity. Appealing multiple senses amplifies the feeling of presence and immersion in VR applications [3, 6]. Besides the inherent integration of visual and audio [9, 13] in most VR systems, a large body of work exists to include further channels in the VR experience. Those channels include haptics [1, 19], warmth [4, 5] and smell [21, 20]. Regarding haptics, integration can be applied in different ways. In this paper, we focus on enriching haptics by simulating airflow accompanying visual and audio content.

Though simulating airflow, most of all in the form of wind, in VR has been researched in the past, little work regarding the conceptual side has been done. To fill this gap in knowledge, we conducted a series of three focus groups with participants of various VR literacy. In those focus groups we explored how, where, and in which situations air streams could be leveraged to enrich VR experiences. The discussions showed that airflow simulation can go far beyond the simulation of wind, reaching from realistic effects to unrealistic superpowers for gaming. Many desired applications need to be applied with less delay

CHI 2017, May 06 – 11, 2017, Denver, CO, USA

ACM 978-1-4503-4655-9/17/05...$15.00
DOI: http://dx.doi.org/10.1145/3025453.3026009

as possible and have to be precise or even animated in the three dimensional space.

The results of the focus groups led to the design of a prototype wearable on ones head. The proposed prototype, as shown in Figure 1, can easily be combined with current head mounted displays. It also allows three dimensional airflow simulation with a reaction time of less then 20 milliseconds until stimulus. Air streams are pneumatically generated, allowing a maximum air speed of around 25km/h. The advantages of using pneumatics translate in the size and weight of the prototype as well as the reaction time and maximum air speed that can be applied to the user. Prior systems either used a static wearable or a completely stationary approach, which both restricts the accurate animation of wind sources and do not support temporary effects like gusts due to too much delay.

The short reaction time of VaiR also offers new possibilities of staging a VR experience, since the duration of applied air pressure and its intensity is variable and responds within milliseconds to changes. This allows to use VaiR as both, an effect channel to directly support visual or auditive stimuli (e.g. the blast of an explosion), as well as a tool to simulate more steady conditions (e.g. wind at a coast). The movable bows on which the nozzles are mounted can rotate in angles of 270 degree of freedom, which can be e.g. used to follow animations of objects, like a helicopter flying over the user's head.

In a user study we analyzed how presence and enjoyment were affected by incorporating the wind models in four scenarios involving wind resulting form users' movements, static wind sources, a combination of both and air streams underlining certain effects. Our results on one hand support the results of prior works showing an increase of presence using airflow in VR. On the other side we could show that enjoyment is influenced even more.

The contributions of this paper can be summarized as conceptual, technical and empirical. First, the results of the focus groups provide conceptual insights in how diverse user groups could benefit from airflow simulation in VR. Second, the proposed prototype is the first mobile pneumatic airflow simulator designed for VR. We also introduce new features, including rotatable bows and short reaction times. And third, our empirical study, which showed how wind can enhance presence and enjoyment, including four different scenarios using different airflow sources and features.

RELATED WORK

There are several ways of generating air streams. The related work follows two major approaches: static sources placed around users, and systems mounted on users' head.

Static Sources

Deligiannidis et al. [2] used a stationary fan in front of the user to simulate the airflow of driving a scooter while traveling through a large scale virtual environment. They observed an increase of immersion when using the wind simulation. Moon et al. [16] presented WindCube, a wind display for VR applications. They used multiple fans placed in the users' surrounding to provide a three-dimensional wind experience. In their evaluation, participants could not distinguish wind sources having less gap than 45°. They also report a significant increase of subjective presence using wind.

Verlinden et al. [18] built a virtual sailing environment using eight static fans. Their evaluation results show an improved immersion when using wind. Participants suggested several improvements to the system, including higher airflow disparity, higher wind resolution, and reduction of noise. Pluijms et al. [17] used the same simulator to measure how good humans can distinguish different directions and strengths. The participants were expert sailors as well as non-sailors. Their results indicate, that the direction can be recognized more precise for frontal wind directions than for wind from behind. Wind was also perceived faster when impinged frontally.

Kulkarni et al. [12] enhanced a VR-cave with a very accurate wind simulation using vortices of airflow and applied a similar approach to their TreadPort Active Wind Tunnel (TPAWT) [11]. The TPAWT integrated locomotion interfaces as well as other sensory outputs like visual, auditory or olfactory. The design of the TPAWT allows each fan to produce a distributed full-body experience, similar to real wind.

Hüllsmann et al. [8] enhanced a cave by adding fans and lamps to simulate wind and warmth. Both influenced the subjective presence of participants. They also state a reaction time of their setup with around 3.1 seconds when turned on and 1.3 seconds when turned off.

Our prototype differs from the above mentioned work in three ways: First, we use pneumatic wind generation, leading to far less delay (below 2 ms). Second, our prototype is designed for mobile use. And third, through the movable bows our prototype allows more variable wind positions and even animations of wind wind sources.

Head Mounted Sources

Kojima et al. [10] described a wearable helmet that consists of four audio speakers that produce wind that is forwarded by tubes towards the user's ears, the region they found to be most sensitive. This wearable approach reduces the reaction times. They also state, that the region around the ear has a high spatial resolution of perception which would lead to a large number of wind sources. They evaluated the precision of wind localization of four participants, which indicated higher precision close to the ear.

Lehmann et al. [14] proposed both a stationary and a wearable approach of producing wind. Both approaches were implemented using two fans. As stated in other related work, the wind had in both cases a positive impact on presence. Yet, participants preferred the mobile over the stationary set-up.

Related work has proved, that a mobile wearable device can be build and is preferred by participants. Though there are no results on the implications and effects on immersive VR.

FOCUS GROUPS: ON THE USE OF AIRFLOW IN VR

We were interested in the potential knowhow on how to design airflow in VR. Especially since using air streams was regarded more as a technical challenge in prior work, we aimed at getting insights on potential application and use cases but also on technical requirements. Thus, we conducted a series of three focus groups, each consisting of participants from the VR user groups VR consumers, VR developers and VR researchers. In each focus group, we asked participants what potential they saw in airstreams in VR, which scenarios they imagined, and how such a device should be designed and implemented. Afterwards, the prototype was presented to each focus group. In an open discussion, the aforementioned topics regarding design and implementation as well as usage scenarios were revisited.

Participants

Participants were recruited through flyers and personal contact. For the VR consumer group, we recruited 5 participants. The average age was 23.8 years (2.45 SD), participants were students of computer science. VR consumers are mostly users of VR, without having developed VR applications. VR developers were participants who developed VR applications for at least a year on a regular basis, for examples games, without researching VR as such. We recruited 4 developers, with an average age of 26.5 (3.1 SD). The respective group included developers with focus on serious games, driving simulation and storytelling. Researching VR as such was a criterion for participants in the VR researcher group. Here, we recruited 5 participants (four of them HCI and one psychologist), at average 29.6 (7.23 SD) years old. All participants gave consent and received 5 €compensation. Each focus group took about one hour.

Results

The recordings of the focus groups were transcribed verbatim. Subsequently, three researchers performed an open coding on the transcript of the first focus groups (VR consumers). The codes were compared, conflicts were resolved with discussions and revisiting of the transcript. Following, the other two focus groups were coded in the same way. If agreed upon, codes from the first focus group were used, if not, new codes were created. Conflicts were solved through discussion and revisitation of transcripts. This way, we gained a codebook applicable to all three focus groups. Based on the initial codes, axial coding was performed to find themes and concepts. Namely, we identified the three categories: requirements, applications and experiences.

Requirements

Modelling the wind concerns either how wind should be rendered, but also how practitioners wished to be able to include it in their applications. Regarding the rendering of wind, it should be as realistic as possible, including dynamic aspects like gusts, precision, direction changes and reaction time. Developers expressed the need for a simple interface, preferably integratable in existing developing environments, and design guidelines covering how to provide the best experience.

Applications

Participants saw wide ranges of applications for wind in VR. Those applications ranged from realistic ones to unrealistic ones. Application areas covered entertainment, simulation,

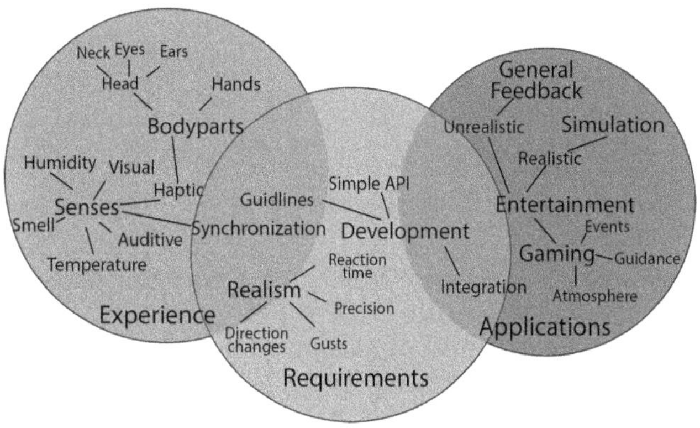

Figure 2. Overview of the focus group results.

and feedback. In case of applications falling in the entertainment area, participants liked both realistic and unrealistic air stream simulations. Realistic rendering of air streams could amplify events, examples mentioned by developers include pressure resulting from explosions as well as weather conditions. Unrealistic air streams could be leveraged as representations of super powers in games, or represent energy states of players. Air streams were further regarded useful when guiding users attentions, e.g. to make them aware of risks or points of interest, or to render elements were users could not see them, e.g. the breath of a monster behind a player. Generally, air streams were seen useful in games, to raise the experience.

Participants found air streams useful for enriching different simulations, covering simulations of environments like cliffs, seas, and deserts. Air streams could also be useful in sales simulations. Other types of simulations used air streams to underline the users movements, e.g. while riding a bicycle, driving in a convertible, riding a roller coaster or flying. Further, air streams were seen as useful for giving haptic feedback to users, e.g. for guiding users or simulating barriers as mentioned by one of the developers.

Experience of wind

Regarding the experience, focus group participants were concerned with the body part air streams are perceived most with as well as the synchronization with other channels. Regarding the body parts, most important were hands and head, were people usually do not wear cloths and thus feel real air streams more. Furthermore, head regions were of particular interest to participants. They explicitly mentioned several regions (neck, eye region, ears) of interest, since they were either important for certain use cases or seen as particularly sensitive for air streams. Additional to the region air streams were applied on, it was seen as important to synchronize them with other channels. Those channels covered especially audio, but also visual. During the discussion, other not yet implemented modalities like temperature, smell and humidity came up and were discussed by researchers and developers. Those were seen as closely linked with air streams, and could enrich and complete the experience even further. Examples for this included simulation of environments, like hot dry air in deserts, and humid and salty air at coasts. The researcher group also discussed

Figure 3. Examples of different nozzles to vary spray angle and intensity.

the potential problem of wearing VR glasses that mask large parts of the face. They suggested to use visual cues like a virtual character wearing glasses to enhance the experience. The same could also be done if the hands were not stimulated by airflow by having the character wearing gloves.

IMPLEMENTATION

The prototype consists of two main technical components, one being the head mount, and the second being a backpack including the logic board and valves to control the system. The software consists of two parts, a Unity plug-in that translates positions, angles and intensities into the the VaiR coordinate system and streams the respective data to the logic board (either via Bluetooth 4.0 Low Energy, or using the serial port). The prototype can therefore be used for sitting as well as mobile VR experiences.

Technical setup

Participants of the focus groups as well as related work suggest, that the region being most important for airflow application is the head region. Considering other found requirements like synchronization, fast reaction time and the possibility of simulating non constant airflow finally led to the desing of our pneumatic head mounted device. The use of fans, which have to be turned on and off takes too long would not meet the defined temporal requirements. To reduce the weight of the prototype, the setup mounted on the head was reduced to a minimum, consisting of two bows (each having 5 nozzles with an angular distance of 36°). We decided to use an angular distance of 36° instead of the proposed 45° since the latter would lead to a single nozzle pointing towards the ears. Since literature and related work emphasizes the importance of the ears for directional perception, the 36° arrangement enables to stimulate the ear region with nozzles per ear. We also designed a variety of nozzles with different spray angles as well as a different amount and diameter of holes. The different nozzles could be used to simulate different airflow sources. In our testing a triangular shape provided the best area to intensity ratio, which was important since hair blocked a fair amount of the wind intensity. The nozzles are mounted on the bows with a custom printed holder using threads to allow quick swapping for testing and to fit into the idea of a modular design. Some examples are shown in figure 3. The bows are rotated by two servo motors. To mount the setup on the user's head, a retainer which connects the components is located in the middle of the setup (see figure 4). The control unit is worn as a backpack for mobile scenarios, or can be placed anywhere within the user's reach. A Redbearlab Blend, a development board with BLE 4.0 support for mobile was chosen as central processing unit. The board controls the motors rotating the bows, as well as 14 valves, ten applied to the tubes attached to the nozzles on the bows and four as exhaust air valves to vary the pressure and

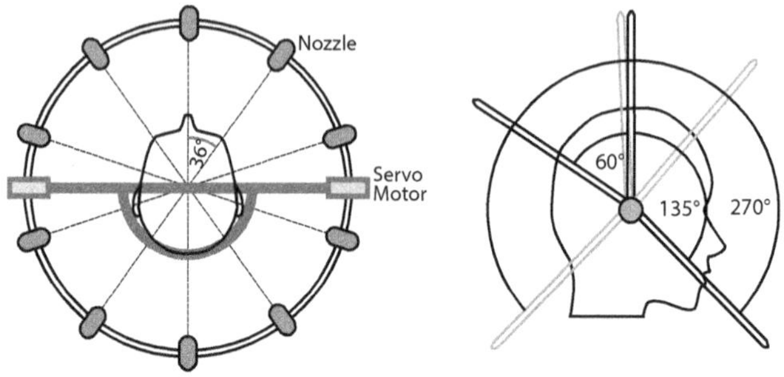

Figure 4. The VaiR setup: Two bows with nozzles having a angular distance of 36° and two servo motors to control the angle of each bow seperately (left). Each bow can be rotated 135°, overall 270° around the user's head and neck can be displayed (right).

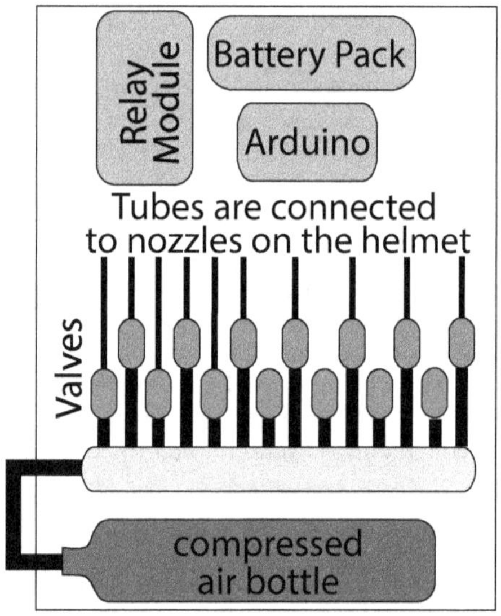

Figure 5. The Backpack consists of a compressed air bottle and 14 valves (ten for the nozzles, and four to vary the intensity) as well as the control unit.

therefore the air speed at the nozzles. The pressure of a maximum of 2 bar can be induced by e.g. compressed air bottles. The VaiR helmet is lightweight with around 766 g (compared to around 600 g of an HTC Vive), while the backpack currently weights about 4 kg. The current prototype consists of two heavy PVC sheets on which the electronics and valves are applied. The weights could though be reduced by using more lightweight components and by using valve blocks instead of single valves. The helmet's measures were kept as close as possible to a user's head wearing current VR glasses, which lead to a diameter of around 21 cm. The backpack currently measures 40 cm x 25 cm x 15 cm, but could be designed much smaller in a second iteration.

Unity3D Plug-In

The Unity3D plug-in consists of various airflow sources (static sources, effect sources and sources modeling the airflow of a moving user). A source can be configured by a set of attributes. These are e.g. the speed or the intensity of the modelled gusts, as well as the horizontal or vertical angles and a maximum distance.

Static sources can be used to model airflow of long term sources, which can be wind, a ventilator or a helicopter. Effect sources are triggered and the effect lasts for a defined time frame and are used as (repeated) short term sources, e.g. for firing a gun or support game effects like an explosion. All attributes can be staged by using scripts or animations.

For the calculation of the entry angle of airflow, the 3D coordinate system is split in two – a horizontal and a vertical angle. On hardware side, the horizontal angle is represented by the nozzles and the vertical one by the angle of the bows. The angular distance of the nozzles is 36°. Defining the origin of a nozzle as angle zero, each nozzle is used to simulate a source within an angular distance of $\pm 18°$. The horizontal entry angle is calculated by using the position of the source (P_S) and the position of the user (P_U) as well as the user's viewing direction as a quaternion (Q_U. The entry vector (V_E) and the horizontal and vertical angles (A_H, A_V) are calculated as follows:

$$V_E = Q_U^{-1} \cdot (P_U - P_S) \tag{1}$$

$$A_H = \arccos(\begin{bmatrix}0\\1\end{bmatrix} \cdot \begin{bmatrix}V_E.x\\V_E.z\end{bmatrix}) \cdot \frac{180}{\pi} \tag{2}$$

$$A_V = \arccos(\begin{bmatrix}0\\1\end{bmatrix} \cdot \begin{bmatrix}V_E.y\\V_E.z\end{bmatrix}) \cdot \frac{180}{\pi} \tag{3}$$

The horizontal angle is then mapped to the matching nozzle, and the vertical one is translated into the bow's coordinate system. If the speed is influenced by the distance, the loss of speed is interpreted as a linear mapping of distance to speed until reaching zero. Since the user will have to wear VR glasses, parts of the face are occluded and therefore no longer able to feel the stimulation of airflow. We therefore left out the respective angles. The bows keep resting on top of the glasses or below, depending on the calculated angle.

Design Space and applications

The short reaction time as well as the rotatable bows – allowing animated airflow sources as well as a 3D experience –, as well as the strong maximal wind speed of around 25 km/h makes the VaiR system suitable for a variety of applications and opens a large design space.

Static sources, like a global wind, that can be staged more realistic by simulating gusts, while even strong wind of over 25 km/h can be displayed. But also non static sources, like a rotatable ventilator can be simulated, by changing vertical angles by rotating the bows, or by changing horizontal angles by using different nozzles. A helicopter may fly over the user's head, where the gust property can be used to simulate turbulences of the rotor blades and the position of the helicopter is represented by the bow angles and the used nozzles.

Besides such sources which involve longer durations, it is also possible to apply short term effects. While playing a shooter for example, short blasts can support the feeling of shooting a gun, or simulate the shock wave of an explosion.

Since the VaiR system enables the simulation of two independent sources at a time, it is also possible to stage an experience with multiple effects, or a constant source with additional effects using short term blasts. When wearing the backpack, it is also possible to have a mobile experience using e.g. the HTC Vive.

EVALUATION

Since the main focus of the VaiR prototype is to enhance the feeling of presence and the enjoyment while consuming VR content, we focused our evaluation on these two factors. We developed four different Unity scenes, each of them having a focus on a different kind of airflow source. To exclude side effects which could arise by a user interacting in a different way, we decided to design the conditions passive only, with the user taking part as observer. This design ensured on one hand that the sequence of events was determined and equal for each participant and on the other hand excluded side effects on presence and enjoyment which could occur due to different behavior.

Participants

Overall 24 participants (20 male and four female, aged 20 to 36 – mean: 26) took part in our evaluation. Each of them was compensated with 10 €. We asked them to describe their previous experience with virtual reality on a five point Likert scale (from 0: no experience to 5: very experienced). The answers were evenly distributed with a mean of 2.7 and a standard deviation of around 1.5. There were as many novice VR users as experienced ones.

Scenes

We developed four different Unity3D scenes that allowed the participants to passively consume the VR content, without any distracting interactions. All scenes are shown in figure 6 and 7.

The first scene takes the participants to a cliff at the seaside. While standing right in front of the edge, the user can turn around facing the sea, where a static wind source is placed, which is simulating wind that blows from across the sea. The wind is modelled using weak gusts and an average wind speed of around 20 km/h. When turning one's back to the sea, a landscape with trees waving in the wind and small hills is presented.

In the second scene, the participants find themselves sitting in a fun ride in a fair scenario. The camera is placed in a cabin attached on the end of a rotating arm. The cabin, and therefore the participant's orientation was always horizontal to prevent sickness. The direction of the wind varied according to the cabin's movement, which was a circular one. The wind speed also varied according to the movement speed, with a maximum of around 25 km/h.

The third scene is staged in a windy and foggy area. The viewer sits in a golf cart, driving through the area. There are two different wind sources that can be felt at the same time. The first being the airstream of the moving cart blows in the inverse driving direction, while the second one is a static wind source located far behind the cart, on the right side. The far

Figure 6. The first and second scene used for the evaluation. a) The cliff scene looking towards the sea and b) view when turned around. c) The fair scene regarded from outside and d) the first person view. e) The golf cart scene from first person view.

Figure 7. The third and fourth scene used for the evaluation. a) The cart scene in first person view. b) The horror scene: bats flying over the head, c) a rotating saw runs through the viewer's neck and d) a Zombie appears.

distance allows the simulation of wind, with a constant global wind direction – independent of the actual position of the cart.

The last scene was the most complex one and most of all is based on the ideas gathered in the focus groups. The participants reported many use cases of airflow as an effect source and mentioned different examples in horror scenarios, like bats flying over the user's head, or non visual experiences including audio and airflow.
The scene starts at a foggy and gloomy place, with a wooden hut in the distance. There is a constant wind source blowing from behind, while a second wind source is used as an effect channel, supporting events. The first event is a group of bats flying from behind over the users head. The effect wind source starts behind the user and moves until coming from front. To simulate the strokes of the wings, this source has a high gust intensity. The wind therefore varies in speed and angle over time. The second event is a kind of zombie that comes closer in large steps, when he arrives directly in front of the user, a short and strong wind is applied to support the shocking moment. Then the virtual camera *runs* towards the hut. The movement is again supported by air stream, while the static wind source still blows from behind. When entering the hut, the visual image turns to black. Only the audio of a monster breathing from behind can be heard – and felt, since every breath is supported by airflow. The last event occurs, when the lights turn on again and a giant saw is rotating in front of the camera, which can be felt by a gusty airflow source. The saw starts moving directly under the camera, simulating to get the head cut off while the wind source of the saw moves towards the user's throat.

As discussed in the focus groups, potential application areas can be found in entertainment (realistic and unrealistic) or simulations. Two of the chosen scenes were discussed in the focus groups. First of all the cliff, as an example of an environmental simulation. The second discussed one was the horror scene, which is also an example of an unrealistic entertainment application. We furthermore wanted to cover different sources of airflow as discussed in the focus groups. External sources and ones induced by personal movements were both covered in the presented scenes. Since the fair covered the movements and the cliff scene the external one, the golf cart scene was chosen as combination of both, containing external wind as well as user's movements.

Method

We used a within subjects design, in which each participant was subjected to eight different treatments (four different scenes, either with the simulation of airflow or without). The sequence of the eight treatments was determined by a Latin Square to balance effects of adaption. To measure presence and engagement we used the E^2I questionnaire [15] without the items concerning the memory task, since they are not relevant for the presented conditions. The E^2I questionnaire has a separate presence and enjoyment score. While the presence score is determined by eight items, the enjoyment is the mean of four sub-scores.

Procedure

Each participant was welcomed and introduced to the subject of the evaluation and the procedure. Then the prototype was shown and the basic functionality described. After this, the participants signed a declaration of consent regarding the usage of the gathered information for scientific purposes and were then asked to complete a demographic questionnaire, including the items *age, gender* and *VR experience*. Afterwards, the participants were helped putting on the VaiR helmet, earphones and a Oculus Rift DK 2 as VR headset and started with the first treatment. Each sequence lasted for about 1.5 minutes. The participants completed the E^2I questionnaire after each condition until the end of the procedure. Finally, each participant filled out a final questionnaire, consisting of information regarding general interest in airflow simulation in VR, and how much each scene was influenced by the use of airflow. Each session lasted for about 40 minutes and the participants were thanked and compensated with 10 €.

Results

The results presented in the next sections are based on the questionnaire results raised as described.

Presence and Enjoyment

The E^2I Questionnaire includes eight items regarding the presence. We excluded two of them, since one is focused on a memory task, and a second, that compares two different systems. The presence score is calculated by the mean of all related items, while the distraction factor is inverted. The treatment using the VaiR helmet proved to have a significant positive impact on the felt presence of the participants (Wilcoxon signed-rank test: $Z=-2.362$, $p<.05$).

To calculate the enjoyment score, the mean of four different items is used. It consists of questions like how sad the participant felt when the experience was over, how much he enjoyed it, if he wanted to repeat it and how interesting it was. There was a significant increase of enjoyment using the wind treatment (Wilcoxon signed-rank test: $Z=-5.518$, $p<.05$). Interestingly, the mean improvements regarding enjoyment were much larger then the improvements of the presence score. When comparing each scenes separately to the respective control condition without VaiR the increase of enjoyment remained significant on the 5% level using the Wilcoxon signed-rank test (cart: Z= -2.858, cliff: Z = -3.698, fair:Z = -2.393, horror: Z= -1.770).

In a next step we regarded the difference between the scenes – by comparing all the control conditions and the VaiR conditions separately. Where the presence was not significantly different on the 5 % level ($p = .075$) without VaiR treatment, we observed significant differences when VaiR was used ($p = .009$) using the Friedman two way analysis of variance by ranks. We could find the difference between the horror scene compared to all others using a Bonferroni post-hoc test. We could find the increase of presence being highest in the horror scene, while the other scenes did not differ.

We could not observe any significant differences between the scenes regarding enjoyment. Since we assumed, that the increase of presence would also lead to an increase of enjoyment, we took a closer look on the horror scene and found a great variance regarding the perceived enjoyment between the users in the VaiR condition. While some rated the enjoyment as three times as high as without, there were participants stating only half the enjoyment. We assume that the high variance arised by the different affinity towards horror in general which will be considered in more detail in the *Discussion* section.

Distraction and Realism

We also regarded four items related to the subjective feeling of realism of the VR experience separately. Since the simulation of airflow is designed to increase the level of felt realism while consuming VR content, we compared the mean of the four sub-scores with and without VaiR. Again, the treatment with airflow simulation increased the perceived realism significantly (Wilcoxon signed-rank test: $Z=-2.967$, $p<.05$)

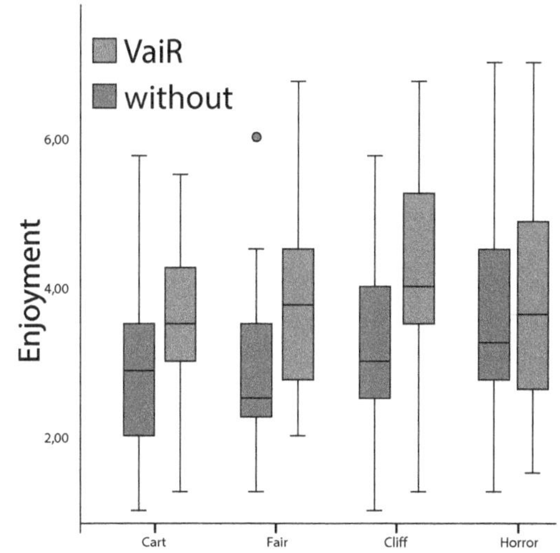

Figure 8. The results of the enjoyment scores per scene.

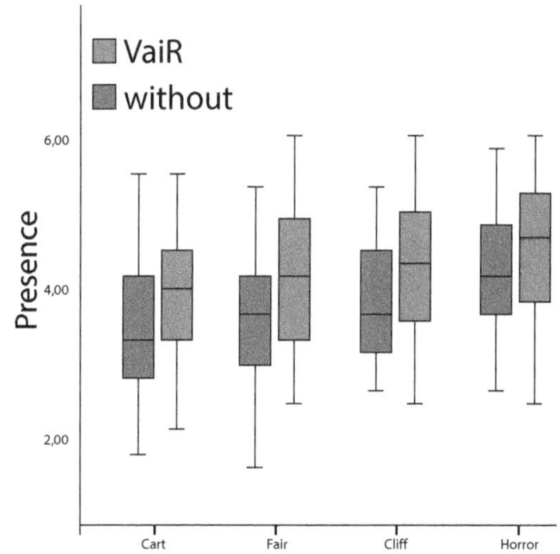

Figure 9. The results of the presence scores per scene.

The VaiR system is placed on the participant's head. This could lead to distractions when the bows move or the nozzles (being close to the ears) be heard. We therefore compared the distractions felt by the participants when using VaiR and when not. The E^2I questionnaire contains one item regarding the perceived distractions from outside VR. There could not be found any significant changes regarding the influence of VaiR on the perceived distractions (Wilcoxon signed-rank test: $Z=-0.468$, $p>.05$, mean (airflow) 2.89 vs 2.79 (no airflow)).

Participants preferences

At the end of the session, we asked the participants to complete one last questionnaire which contained more general questions regarding the consume of VR content with or without the proposed system. Only 2 of the 24 participants stated to prefer VR without VaiR, the same participants stated that they do not want to consume VR with any simulation of airflow at all. We also asked the participants if they had in general a stronger

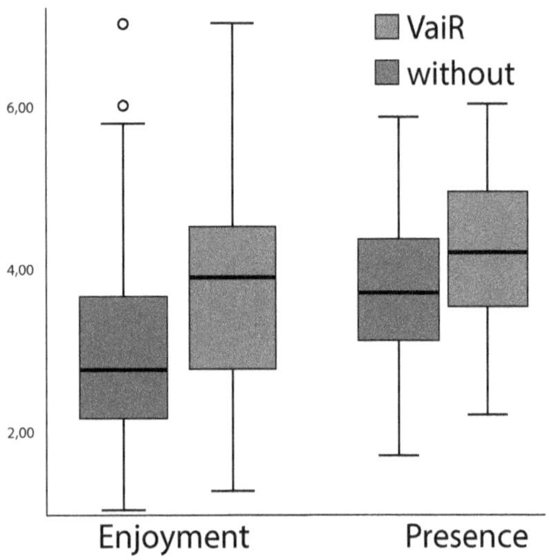

Figure 10. The results of the E²I presence and enjoyment scores.

feeling of being there while using VaiR, which was confirmed by all participants, except the two mentioned ones.

Discussion

Our results on one side confirm the results of previous works on the simulation of airflow in virtual reality to increase the felt presence. In addition, we could show that there is an even higher impact on the enjoyment while consuming VR content. We assume that enjoyment as well as presence could even influenced more in interactive gaming situations, when airflow events are related to an action.

Each scene was significantly enjoyed more when consumed with the simulation of airflow. While we could not find any significant differences between the respective scenes, except for the horror scene, presence and enjoyment increased for each scene when using VaiR. The horror scene was rated very controversial – most of all in the VaiR condition. While there was a very strong effect regarding the presence when compared to the other scenes, we could not find a significant effect for enjoyment. Since some participants stated, that the horror scene was too exciting and that the airflow simulation involved them even more in the scene (which was not perceived as positive for these participants), we assume, that the overall experience was very high in the horror scene, which was perceived as either very positive, or as negative – depending on the personal affection to horror.

Since the increase of perceived presence and enjoyment was highest in the horror and the fair scene, we assume that the fast reaction time and the possibility of simulating airflow in 3D had an high impact, since the respective scenes most of all used the named features.

Though VaiR is head-mounted and having nozzles close to the user's head, there were no additional distractions from outside VR.

Overall, 22 of the 24 participants would like to use VaiR in the context of VR, while the remaining two participants stated to prefer no airflow simulation at all.

CONCLUSION

In this paper we presented VaiR, a pneumatic head-mounted, mobile prototype design for the enhancement of presence and enjoyment in virtual reality (VR) by allowing precise animations of airflow in real-time. The conceptual insights of three different focus groups (including developers, users and researchers in the field of VR) were used for the design of our prototype and provided deep insights about the potential applications of airflow simulation in VR.

The developed pneumatic prototype allows the simulation of various effects, ranging from static wind over fully animated, moving object like a helicopter, to short term effects (e.g. shock wave of an explosion) in real-time. The prototype can display two independent sources simultaneously, which allows the staging VR experiences using e.g. static sources and an additional effect channel.

The insights of the focus groups, as well as some findings of related work suggest a mobile set-up. Our head-mounted system is low weighted and has a fast reaction time of under 2 ms between the raised event and the felt actuation. The two independent rotating bows additionally support mobility by not only reacting on animated airflow sources, but on user's virtual orientation.

We could confirm results of previous experiments, which showed that the treatment with wind enhances presence and could further show, that also the felt realism and most of all enjoyment is strongly influenced by airflow. Our findings strongly underline the great potential of three dimensional real-time airflow application.

We plan to further enhance the experience by the simulation of warmth by preheating the airflow and by adding olfactory cues to the air. It is also planned to test the effects in a mobile gaming scenario.

REFERENCES

1. Grigore C Burdea and Frederick P Brooks. 1996. *Force and touch feedback for virtual reality*. Wiley New York.

2. Leonidas Deligiannidis and Robert JK Jacob. 2006. The vr scooter: Wind and tactile feedback improve user performance. In *3D User Interfaces (3DUI'06)*. IEEE, 143–150.

3. H. Q. Dinh, N. Walker, L. F. Hodges, Chang Song, and A. Kobayashi. 1999. Evaluating the importance of multi-sensory input on memory and the sense of presence in virtual environments. In *Virtual Reality, 1999. Proceedings., IEEE*. 222–228. DOI: http://dx.doi.org/10.1109/VR.1999.756955

4. Jose Dionisio. 1997a. Temperature feedback in virtual environments. (1997). DOI: http://dx.doi.org/10.1117/12.266357

5. J. Dionisio. 1997b. Virtual hell: a trip through the flames. *IEEE Computer Graphics and Applications* 17, 3 (May 1997), 11–14. DOI:http://dx.doi.org/10.1109/38.586012

6. Julia Fröhlich and Ipke Wachsmuth. 2013. *The Visual, the Auditory and the Haptic – A User Study on Combining Modalities in Virtual Worlds*. Springer Berlin Heidelberg, Berlin, Heidelberg, 159–168. DOI: http://dx.doi.org/10.1007/978-3-642-39405-8_19

7. Carrie Heeter. 1992. Being there: The subjective experience of presence. *Presence: Teleoperators & Virtual Environments* 1, 2 (1992), 262–271.

8. Felix Hülsmann, Julia Fröhlich, Nikita Mattar, and Ipke Wachsmuth. 2014. Wind and Warmth in Virtual Reality: Implementation and Evaluation. In *Proceedings of the 2014 Virtual Reality International Conference (VRIC '14)*. ACM, New York, NY, USA, Article 24, 8 pages. DOI:http://dx.doi.org/10.1145/2617841.2620712

9. S Husung, R Mikalauskas, C Weber, and T Kästner. 2010. Modelling of sound propagation of technical systems for real-time VR-applications. *Mechanika* 4 (2010), 33–37.

10. Yuichiro Kojima, Yuki Hashimoto, and Hiroyuki Kajimoto. 2009. A Novel Wearable Device to Present Localized Sensation of Wind. In *Proceedings of the International Conference on Advances in Computer Enterntainment Technology (ACE '09)*. ACM, New York, NY, USA, 61–65. DOI: http://dx.doi.org/10.1145/1690388.1690399

11. S. D. Kulkarni, C. J. Fisher, P. Lefler, A. Desai, S. Chakravarthy, E. R. Pardyjak, M. A. Minor, and J. M. Hollerbach. 2015. A Full Body Steerable Wind Display for a Locomotion Interface. *IEEE Transactions on Visualization and Computer Graphics* 21, 10 (Oct 2015), 1146–1159. DOI: http://dx.doi.org/10.1109/TVCG.2015.2424862

12. S. D. Kulkarni, M. A. Minor, M. W. Deaver, E. R. Pardyjak, and J. M. Hollerbach. 2012. Design, Sensing, and Control of a Scaled Wind Tunnel for Atmospheric Display. *IEEE/ASME Transactions on Mechatronics* 17, 4 (Aug 2012), 635–645. DOI: http://dx.doi.org/10.1109/TMECH.2011.2113353

13. Pontus Larsson, Daniel Vastfjall, and Mendel Kleiner. 2001. Ecological acoustics and the multi-modal perception of rooms: real and unreal experiences of auditory-visual virtual environments. (2001).

14. A. Lehmann, C. Geiger, B. Woldecke, and J. Stocklein. 2009. Poster: Design and evaluation of 3D content with wind output. In *3D User Interfaces, 2009. 3DUI 2009. IEEE Symposium on*. 151–152. DOI: http://dx.doi.org/10.1109/3DUI.2009.4811231

15. JJ-W Lin, Henry Been-Lirn Duh, Donald E Parker, Habib Abi-Rached, and Thomas A Furness. 2002. Effects of field of view on presence, enjoyment, memory, and simulator sickness in a virtual environment. In *Virtual Reality, 2002. Proceedings. IEEE*. IEEE, 164–171.

16. Taeyong Moon and Gerard J. Kim. 2004. Design and Evaluation of a Wind Display for Virtual Reality. In *Proceedings of the ACM Symposium on Virtual Reality Software and Technology (VRST '04)*. ACM, New York, NY, USA, 122–128. DOI: http://dx.doi.org/10.1145/1077534.1077558

17. Joost P Pluijms, Rouwen Cañal-Bruland, Wouter M Bergmann Tiest, Fabian A Mulder, and Geert JP Savelsbergh. 2015. Expertise effects in cutaneous wind perception. *Attention, Perception, & Psychophysics* 77, 6 (2015), 2121–2133.

18. Jouke C Verlinden, Fabian A Mulder, Joris S Vergeest, Anna de Jonge, Darina Krutiy, Zsuzsa Nagy, Bob J Logeman, and Paul Schouten. 2013. Enhancement of presence in a virtual sailing environment through localized wind simulation. *Procedia Engineering* 60 (2013), 435–441.

19. Bernhard Weber, Mikel Sagardia, Thomas Hulin, and Carsten Preusche. 2013. *Visual, Vibrotactile, and Force Feedback of Collisions in Virtual Environments: Effects on Performance, Mental Workload and Spatial Orientation*. Springer Berlin Heidelberg, Berlin, Heidelberg, 241–250. DOI: http://dx.doi.org/10.1007/978-3-642-39405-8_28

20. T. Yamada, S. Yokoyama, T. Tanikawa, K. Hirota, and M. Hirose. 2006. Wearable Olfactory Display: Using Odor in Outdoor Environment. In *IEEE Virtual Reality Conference (VR 2006)*. 199–206. DOI: http://dx.doi.org/10.1109/VR.2006.147

21. Y. Yanagida, S. Kawato, H. Noma, A. Tomono, and N. Tesutani. 2004. Projection based olfactory display with nose tracking. In *Virtual Reality, 2004. Proceedings. IEEE*. 43–50. DOI: http://dx.doi.org/10.1109/VR.2004.1310054

Collaborative Map Making: A Reflexive Method for Understanding Matters of Concern in Design Research

Hee Rin Lee, Selma Šabanović
Indiana University
Bloomington, IN, USA
{hrl, selmas}@indiana.edu

Sonya S. Kwak
Ewha Womans University
Seoul, Republic of Korea
sonakwak@ewha.ac.kr

ABSTRACT
HCI researchers investigating the politics of technology design have recently focused on how design practice can tackle "Matters of Concern"—complex social issues perceived and experienced in multiple ways. These researchers suggest design research can generate *new* networks of human and non-human actors to express and act on these issues. Prior studies, however, tend to restrict their networks within traditional boundaries (e.g. existing organizations, local communities) and categories (e.g. human/nonhuman binary) without examining their significance for participants. We suggest collaborative map making as a reflexive method for understanding current Matters of Concern from the perspectives of diverse actors, not just researchers. As case studies of the method's use, we present two studies of domestic computing technologies in the US and South Korea, which show how collaborative map making allows salient networks to expand beyond the individual actors in the home to local and global power issues outside of boundaries (e.g. physical house) and categories (e.g. private/public space) commonly recognized in HCI. Our methodology provides HCI researchers with a way to understand existing Matters of Concern, so they can position themselves to address and act on these issues.

Author Keywords
Actor Network; Matters of Concern; Situational Analysis; Reflexivity; Home; Collaborative Mapping

ACM Classification Keywords
H.5.m. Information interfaces and presentation (e.g., HCI): Miscellaneous;

INTRODUCTION
Since 2011, more than 100 South Koreans, mostly pregnant women and infants, died after using a toxic disinfectant for humidifiers in their homes [1,4]. Figuring out the source of the problem took quite some time, as the individuals all looked for personal causes of the deaths, and there was no attempt for the group of people affected to share their problems and concerns. Eventually the real cause of the deaths was revealed, and it was clear that the accidents were the result of the actions of several actors in and beyond South Korea: the sterilizers were from Reckitt Benckiser, a British multinational consumer goods company, its sales were made possibly through deregulation policies in South Korea and advertisements for the products, and the effects were compounded by dry winter weather. Understanding this incident and preventing similar future occurrences requires exploring relations and power dynamics among the diverse and widespread actors participating in the technology's design and use.

In recent years, HCI researchers have studied the emergence of complicated sociopolitical issues (e.g. sustainability, immigration), and explored how design research can express and affect those issues [2,11,13,20]. Among these efforts, HCI researchers have been investigating Matters of Concern based on Actor Network Theory (ANT) [22], which has enabled researchers to study and design technology within broader social contexts (e.g. within the public sphere). Previous work in this vein has investigated the ability of computing technologies as nonhuman actors to bring together diverse human actors to share problematic situations and social issues in a *new* network. In this paper, we build on and also shift the focus of this research trajectory by suggesting *collaborative map making* as a participatory method to help HCI researchers scrutinize existing networks and Matters of Concern *before* constructing new networks around novel technical interventions. Collaborative map making involves three processes: 1) researchers select keywords related to the context and phenomenon being studied, 2) participants develop micro maps to express their everyday experiences and concerns related to the keywords, and 3) researchers make micro maps out of participants' micro maps.

To describe our method for exploring the political valence of the design and research process for computing technologies, we first present Latour's notion of Matters of Concern and ANT and describe how Matters of Concern and ANT have been studied in HCI. Secondly, we illustrate our proposed method—collaborative map making—by presenting two case studies of its use in US and South Korean homes. We focus on the home because it has not been a popular space in which to explore Matters of

CHI 2017, May 06-11, 2017, Denver, CO, USA
© 2017 ACM. ISBN 978-1-4503-4655-9/17/05…$15.00
DOI: http://dx.doi.org/10.1145/3025453.3025535

Concern in HCI, despite the political aspects of domestic technology use, as exemplified by the above incident. Finally, we explain the benefits of collaborative map making that enable HCI researchers to focus on exploring Matters of Concern beyond HCI's conventional categories (e.g. human/nonhuman) and boundaries (e.g. home/work) by actively engaging participants' perspectives. In conclusion, we propose HCI researchers can mediate between individuals' personal issues and policy by showing how they are closely tied in technology design and use.

RELATED WORK

Matters of Concern have been studied in HCI using ANT as the underlying theoretical framework. First, we discuss Matters of Concern and Actor Network Theory (ANT) as conceptualized by Latour, then explain how these concepts have been adopted within HCI, and finally explore how Participatory Design (PD) has been used as a methodology to study and address such sociopolitical issues.

Actor Network Theory (ANT) and Matters of Concern

In his book, "Reassembling the Social", Latour describes the concepts of ANT and Matters of Concern starting with a critique of how social scientists built their knowledge of society based on four uncertain beliefs [22]. The first uncertainty is about specific groups (e.g. family, organization) as the basic research units in social science. Although groups are not absolute but constructed based on social scientists' definitions and practices (e.g. groupings based on geographical location), social scientists investigate society mainly within group boundaries. Latour argued that researchers should not limit their investigations to predefined groups but seek to understand group formation, which can lead to the emergence of new types of groups. As the second and third uncertainty, Latour examined social scientists' overemphasis of the importance of (human) actions, at the expense of ignoring the agency of nonhumans as social actors.

Latour's final point of critique addresses the uncertainty of fact finding as the research goal of social science. In opposition to such Matters of Fact, he suggested a new research focus for social scientists: Matters of Concern. Latour proposed to flexibly *trace relations*, the network, of what matters to people as a humble cartographer, rather than to restrict knowledge of society within strong predefined boundaries (e.g. family) and categories (e.g. human/nonhuman) as an authoritative professional.

In our study, we describe a method for HCI researchers to explore Matters of Concern, without limiting their knowledge within existing boundaries or categories in HCI. As a case study, this paper particularly focuses on the home, which has been commonly defined by the physical boundaries of the house, and categorized as personal space in contrast to public space. Due to the boundaries and categories of the home within HCI [5,8,16,33,35], it has not been a popular context for studying Matters of Concern. We show how issues at home closely relate to more complex sociopolitical dynamics in societies all over the world, and how householders could be promising members of a group that technological interventions can bring together as an active public.

ANT and Matters of Concern in HCI

ANT to Illustrate Material Power of Computing Technologies

A growing number of HCI researchers have been using Latour's "Matters of Concern" and Actor Network Theory (ANT) to explore the role of design research for addressing socio-political issues [11,20]. These studies investigated how ANT envisions technologies not just as tools within certain locations, but as political actors enabling democratic action by bringing people together to collectively visualize and discuss shared issues. These studies have focused on the power of computing technologies as nonhuman actor interventions; one example shows how a smart phone app for sharing bicycles not only brought local citizens together but also provided evidence to enable transportation policy changes, thereby figuring as a social actor [20]. The research shows how computing technologies (or the design process) can facilitate a newly networked "public" [10] that can collectively express and discuss Matters of Concerns in freshly constructed and networked groups.

As in these previous studies, we consider technologies as nonhuman actors, but do not emphasize their agency. As a step before investigating new technology and the emerging networks around it, collaborative map making shows current situations in actor network form. Our study particularly pays attention to the *relational* components of the network, including previously unrevealed associations among diverse actors. Current arguments in HCI intensify the power of computing technologies and build networks centered on them. This simplifies HCI researchers' view of sociotechnical networks. As a result, other actors within the network who are not directly connected with technology, and the relationships among them, become invisible in research. Groups in previous HCI studies are mostly geographically bound (e.g. local community), which is an arguably limited way to generate networks. In our study, we aim to explore the complexity and multiplicity of networks by performing a relational analysis through collaborative map making. In the collaborative process, individual participants develop their own networks—micro maps—expressing their personal concerns, and we, researchers, develop macro maps by associating individuals' networks. At the same time, while making maps, both researchers and participants critically examine their own values and understanding of the situation.

ANT as a new frame for Politics in Participatory Design

Since its inception in the 1970s, the political aspects of design have been of utmost importance to PD researchers, in particular as a more democratic perspective on the design and adoption of technology [28]. PD has included minority groups, such as workers who could previously not participate when automating factories, and more recently other underrepresented users—such as homeless mothers and children [9], children within families [25]—in studies. Recent PD research has had a more limited expression of political issues within the design process, compared to the early days when PD practitioners aimed to democratize the work environment. Björgvinsson et al. found it difficult to express and affect power dynamics due to the situational complexity of computing technologies as computers entered into diverse parts of daily life [2]. When computers were mainly situated within the workplace, power dynamics were easier to figure out: workers were clearly the ones that PD researchers should support. However, current power issues do not reside within one context (e.g. the workplace) but fluidly tie into places across organizational and community boundaries (e.g. work and home). Thus, PD researchers have been developing different ways to act on politics in and through computing. One approach has been to design a "Thing," a network of people and technologies that deals with Matters of Concerns rather than to develop certain technologies for certain users (e.g. a living lab providing public space for people to gather and develop an agonistic public environment) [2].

Our study builds on these prior efforts to incorporate political issues into the design process. Specifically, we investigate a method for understanding existing networks in computing environments before building new ones through new computing technology. In previous studies, researchers determined the Matters of Concern from their assumptions and perspectives on what was important (e.g. air pollution [11], immigrants [2]). However, researchers are also actors who are part of the network and whose situated perspectives affect how they interpret the issues [32]. Socio-computational networks existed before researchers created new webs, and researchers enter into existing networks before making new ones. As researchers enter existing networks, they build relations to other actors. The researchers' position in the network determines their roles and standpoint, which then affect how they represent other actors [31] and constitute the new network. In previous studies, researchers' positions and their relations to other actors have rarely been inspected (e.g. researchers were facilitators but their positions were not thoroughly scrutinized) (see Figure 1 for differences between networks as expressed in previous studies and our current work.). Our proposed method, collaborative map making, will provide a way to understand the complexity of existing networks, and in turn allow researchers to take up suitable positions and relations with other actors in the networks.

COLLABORATIVE MAP MAKING INSPIRED BY SITUATIONAL ANALYSIS

Situational Analysis

Collaborative map making is inspired by Situational Analysis [6], a methodology that focuses on analyzing relations among actors developed by Clarke, a feminist STS scholar. Situational Analysis is a more reflexive version of Grounded Theory, originally developed by Strauss and

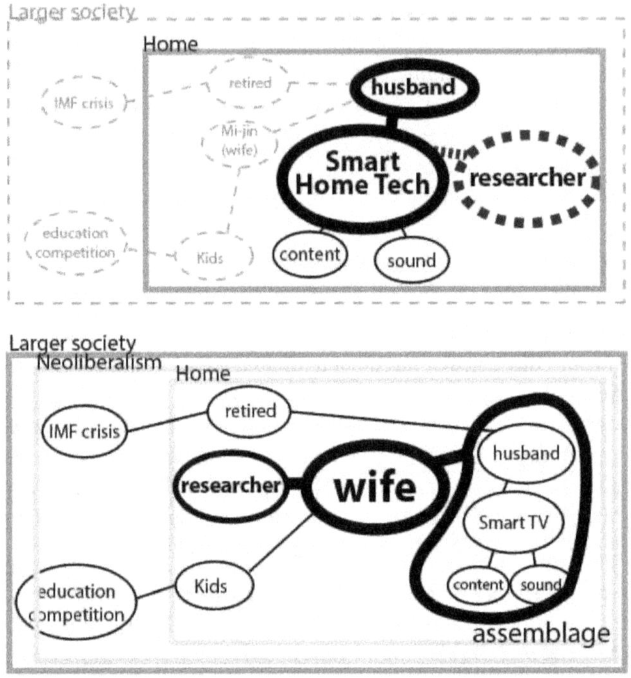

Figure 1 Top: A previous home study network where a researcher is focused on and closely tied to a certain technology, Bottom: Alternative home study network where a researcher positions themselves more closely to participants.

Glaser [14]. Early Grounded Theory was a systematic way of building sociological theories with qualitative data, in contrast to predominant quantitative methodologies. Situational Analysis enables researchers to be more self-reflexive: it helps researchers to avoid possible limitations of relating actors according to existing categories (e.g. human/nonhuman) or boundaries (e.g. conventional social hierarchy). Making situational maps is an essential analytical process in Situational Analysis, and the main point of map making is to understand the situation and concerns of actors involved in the situation. Situational maps are constructed based on matters that diverse social worlds or actors care about enough to fashion discourses and actions relating to them, similar to Latour's Matters of Concern [22]. Situational maps focus on relations among actors and social worlds sharing concerns, focusing on the conceptual and qualitative ties between them.

Collaborative Map Making

In this paper, we adapt situational maps to find Matters of Concern, the complex networks of existing issues. We borrowed core idea of Situation Analysis to relate actors dynamically, regardless of existing categories or boundaries based on concepts and disciplines in HCI. While situational maps were tools meant for researchers, our approach is to make maps with and for participants as well. The focus of our analysis is therefore also on the collaborative map-making *process* and actively including participants' perspectives into it. In this section, we explain 1) the main components of, 2) the essential materials for, and 3) the main features of the collaborative map making method.

Key components: keywords and micro/macro maps

Keywords: Keywords play the role of less obtrusive questions in interviews; they propose research directions to participants, but still give them enough room to lead the research. Researchers should carefully provide several keywords to participants that participants can use to develop their own micro maps. We do not recommend technical research terms as keywords, cultivated from the researchers' academic culture (e.g., Internet of Things (IoTs), assistive robots). Technical terms could forge a strong boundary between researchers and participants as those with and those without technical knowledge. This boundary could interfere with genuine collaborations between the two groups. For example, we found that traditionally marginalized groups within the technology design process, such as women, become passive in expressing their everyday issues when encountering technical terms [24]. Also, when participants perceive technology as a central concept, they tend to identify as users and talk about how they use technologies rather than their actual everyday issues.

Micro maps: Each participant makes a micro map. Micro maps reveal the participant's matters of concern in the form of a network. A micro map is composed of any words that participants think are related to the keywords; in our research they usually contained 15-20 words. Participants are asked to mark the words they find most important, to provide researchers with a guideline when interpreting micro maps from participants' perspectives. Each word is written on one post-it. Participants then categorize their words as they want, giving each group a title and defining relations to other groups. Importantly, participants should have as much control over the micro map making process as possible, flexibly changing their maps as they want.

Macro maps: Macro maps show interconnected matters of concern among participants. After finishing all micro map making, researchers build macro maps by connecting components of each participant's network. Researchers take the most important words from micro maps to the macro map and relate participants' issues. In some cases, researchers could triangulate the relations uncovered by their analysis with other literature (e.g. local news, anthropological scholarship). Although researchers develop macro maps, participants can make changes to macro maps if they want.

Research materials

Post-It note: The ubiquitous 1 3/8 in x 1 7/8 in Post-It is an essential material to facilitate flexibility in each map, as it allowed both participants and researchers to make changes to maps whenever and as they wanted.

Sketch pad: We used an 11 in x 14 in sketch pad to record micro maps. Participants categorized their Post-It notes on the sketch pad, wrote the names of each group, and explained relations among groups.

Photographic Camera: Since the process for map making is important, and maps could be flexibly updated, taking a photo of different map versions is useful for analysis.

Adobe Illustrator: When making macro maps, Adobe Illustrator software was useful for our research. Since we had many meaningful words (or statements) chosen by participants to work with, it was difficult to physically manage all the words. As Illustrator supports vector images, we could flexibly zoom in and out while building our maps throughout our analysis process. Any software based on vector graphics would work similarly to Illustrator.

Voice Recorder: The collaborative process and communications between researchers and participants are as, if not more, important than the physical maps themselves. Researchers recorded the process for analysis.

Etc: pen, markers, etc.

Essential features of collaborative map making

Reflexivity: Reflexivity is important in collaborative map making, as the map making process aims to help researchers to collaboratively explore participants' Matters of Concern. In our case studies, reflexivity about our relation to technology was essential, as we particularly wanted to understand participants' self-defined networks. When focusing on certain technologies, researchers could understand participants only as users. Technical components were therefore added into the research process after understanding participants' matters of concern from their perspectives first.

Flexibility: Although we propose collaborative map making as a method for understanding the interpretations, use, and consequences of technology related to broader Matters of Concern, the method also aims to explore ways to manage power dynamics between researchers and participants. Different researchers could develop or utilize micro and macro maps in diverse ways to examine their possible biases and understand participants' perspectives.

Multiplicity: Each map, either micro maps or macro maps, could be constructed in multiple ways, as the maps are contingent. For example, when utilizing micro maps for continuing sessions, we asked participants to alter their maps if needed. We assumed participants' issues might have changed as the follow-up session was performed a year after the first map making process.

TWO CASE STUDIES OF COLLABORATIVE MAP MAKING

We suggest *collaborative map making* as a method to help HCI researchers understand current situations participants face in the form of actor-networks. In particular, we chose domestic contexts in two countries to show how collaborative map making benefits HCI researchers to find Matters of Concern, without relying on existing categories and boundaries. We explain the detailed benefits—understanding Matters of Concern—of our proposed methodology through these two collaborative map making case studies. The cases also show how collaborative map making can be flexibly employed in HCI projects. We will explain the map making process through four steps: 1) selecting keywords, 2) micro map making, and 3) macro map making, and 4) utilizing map making results. To retain participants' individuality, we use pseudonyms for them.

Case study 1: Older Adults' Networks in the US

Step 1: Selecting keywords

The first step for map making is selecting keywords. The US study is part of a larger PD project exploring assistive robots for older adults. The project was initiated in 2014 in Bloomington, Indiana—a small town with several retirement communities. We first interviewed older adults about how they are using existing technologies in their everyday lives [23], and map making was conducted as a follow-up study. We recruited Baby Boomers, who have an important place in the global phenomenon of population aging [27] which inspires assistive technology studies [21, 34]. In the first study, we found assistive technology design incorporated stereotypes and biases about older adults, which is why we employed collaborative map making.

In summer 2015, we employed collaborative map making as a second study to understand older adults' lives from their perspectives. We had six Baby Boomer participants including three participants from the first study. This study aimed to avoid framing older adults from our (researchers') perspectives, which is likely to bring in stereotypes. We intended not to negatively relate "older adults" and "aging", focusing on aging as a disability. We wanted to see how older adults relate "me," "home," and "aging" in their own ways and let participants construct networks related to the three keywords. Although assistive technology is our main academic interest as technology design researchers, we did not use "assistive technology" as a keyword so as not to frame older adults only in relation to technology, which could impact their map making process.

Step 2: Micro map making

Participants wrote about 15 words without restriction on Post-Its, and then developed their situational maps (micro maps) explaining the relations among the words. Among six participants, we illustrate Pam's map-making process to show how the map making helped us to redefine the relation between older adults and aging. We focus on one participant to provide a nuanced description of participants and their maps.

Pam's micro map: Pam (female, 58 years old) is a freelance editor and writer. She has been living independently in a rented house. She has a noticeable disability in her left leg and half of her body. Pam was interviewed at a café near her house. Pam was a continuing participant from our first study, which helped researchers to build trust with the participants over time.

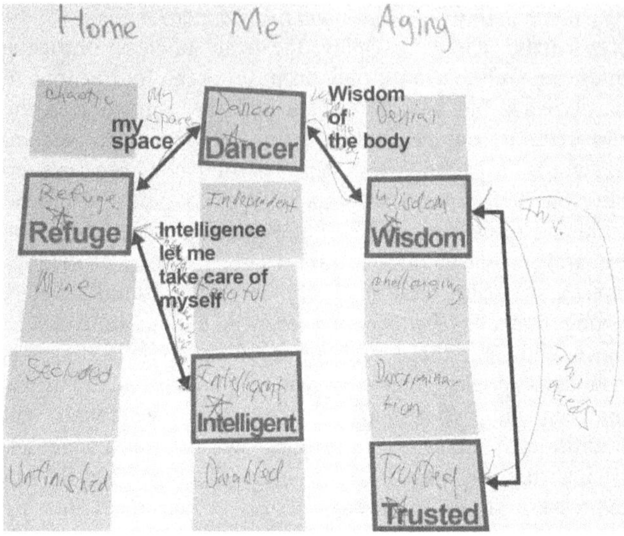

Figure 2 Pam's situational map (a micro map)

Pam wrote 15 words related to "home," "me," and "aging" (see Figure 2). In her map, she picked "refuge," "dancer," "intelligent," "wisdom," and "trusted" as the most important words. The five most important words illustrate how her ability is meaningful in her life. She explained her home as a *refuge,* since she can be herself at home, away from the pressures of the world and other people. As well as refuge, *dancer* was another important word, providing her own space. She has had prosthetics for about ten years and has difficulty controlling the left side of her body; however, she said "dancer" was the first word that came to mind when she thought about herself. "*Intelligent*" was also an important word for her, closely related to "refuge." Pam's intelligence let her take care of herself and keep her independence. Her identity as a dancer was closely tied to her "*wisdom*," which she attributed to her aging experience. Her wisdom comes together with being "*trusted.*" She explained that the older she gets, the more people trust her. She said her friends let her take care of their children due to this trust. Pam said she has been a writing tutor and friend to the 10-year-old daughter of a friend.

Following Pam's interpretation of her map and her focus on those five words, we tried to understand other words in relation to the five. Pam also spent considerable time telling us about issue-related words, such as "discrimination." Pam's five most important keywords indicate her identity with abilities (e.g. someone who could be a "dancer," and "intelligent" enough to take care of herself) and her issues come from the factors that interfere with that identity. However, Pam's "*disabled*" body was not the main factor causing her problems, in contrast to the assumptions behind most assistive robotic technology designs [21,23]. Pam explained the word "disabled" as one of facts about her body. Her disabled body posed difficulties, but was not her biggest issue. "Discrimination," a word in her map, explains her actual issues, which includes complex network of people and the larger social structure.

When describing *"discrimination,"* Pam explained her experience during her job search. Pam said that she has given up trying to find a job due to discrimination she experienced. She thinks that it is from people's stereotyped perspectives on her age. Several years ago, she found a job posting identical to her previous position, during which she had gotten to know the people in the company that posted the new job openings. Pam was glad to apply for the job. But, after a long wait, the company went dark. When Pam contacted them, they said she was not a good fit for the job. Pam asked why, because she had ample experience in that position, and they said they knew that but still did not want her. Pam thought this was a form of age discrimination. She filed an EEOC complaint against the company, but the manager lied to the officer, saying that Pam was late for an interview and did not answer correctly. The EEOC officer said she could sue personally, but the office could not help her anymore without evidence. Her voice as a potential employee was too small within the legal system, especially when she lacked the money to hire a lawyer. This experience made her stop applying for jobs, and she has had no regular income since. This explained how she sometimes wants to avoid the world and other people, as well as how her home became a "refuge" to her.

While explaining her map, Pam mentioned several technologies, such as the TV, a wheelchair, and a little electric car in a grocery store, in relation to her situation. Among them, she told us how her powered wheelchair caused issues relating to her discrimination experience and subsequently limited financial situation. Pam said:

I do have a powered wheelchair. The challenge with that is being able to afford having my home ramped so that I can take the wheelchair out, down the front step, and out. And then, I wouldn't be able to use my powered wheelchair anywhere but in the neighborhood right now, because I don't have a lift for the wheelchair. That's expensive.

Pam's micro map-making process showed us that her main issues originate from her relations to people and structures within society. To tackle her issues, she needs assistive technologies mediating between herself and the complex societal factors (e.g. legal systems) that relate to her issues, so that she can express her voice or show her frustration as a worker. In contrast, most assistive technologies mediate the relation between Pam and her body (e.g. a wheelchair letting her move around despite her disabled left leg). Without the map, we would never expect to hear that she identifies herself as a "dancer" and how the word relates to her issues. Without situational analysis, we might just think that she wants to focus on developing her abilities within the dichotomy between ability vs. disability and aim to design technologies equipped to tackle that, rather than her deeper issues.

As in this example, we started to construct networks from individuals and not from a certain community as the previous Matters of Concern studies in HCI. With a different method, we identified the complex relations among various actors, from Pam to managers in the company that she applied to and to EEOC officers, which also related to workers' rights and issues related to the legal system. Also, collaborative map making enabled us to find more users' perspectives than traditional questions. If we investigated assistive technologies with targeted interview questions, we might have asked about possible technologies. Then, we would probably design assistive technologies to relieve the participant's difficulties related to her mobility as her powered wheelchair. However, her Matters of Concern related to broader parts of society (e.g., legal systems for workers), which are not regularly part of HCI studies and interventions.

Step3: Macro map making

After the participants' map making process, we developed a macro map (see Figure 3). As we did for Pam's map, we tried to grasp each participant's network and issues. Then, we moved the most important words from micro maps to the illustrator to make macro maps. As participants did, we made groups of words as shown in Figure 3. As a result, we found four groups: 1) older adults' self-identities, 2) older adults' interpretations of aging related to their identities, 3) the meaning of home, and 4) older adults' frustrations. While exploring relations among the groups, we found that older adults' issues were an important component in understanding relations among the groups. We went back to the transcripts and found how our participants discussed their problems. We constructed our macro maps using words defining the issues and related words from participants' micro maps.

Throughout our process of exploring relations among the groups for macro map making, we recognized that issues often emerged when older adults had relations to actors and systems outside the home (or their aged bodies). Older adults were still themselves and viewing their aging as one of their life experiences. However, social systems outside the home do not interpret their aging as they do, which causes problems for them. As with Pam, other two female participants lamented people's stereotyped perspectives on old ladies and how they limited their employment. Richard (male, 63, a retired doctor)'s issue emerged from his relationship to the national insurance system. He said that taking 20 pills a day is not fun, but tolerable. His real issue is that he cannot afford the 20 pills without Obamacare, which might be repealed. Participants were aware that their issues are closely related to actors and systems outside the home (or their bodies). However, they blamed themselves for their troubles, saying they should have tried harder to save their money when they were young. Macro map making revealed that not only Pam, but older adults in general, need help to handle their relationships with other parts of society as citizens as well as aged technology users.

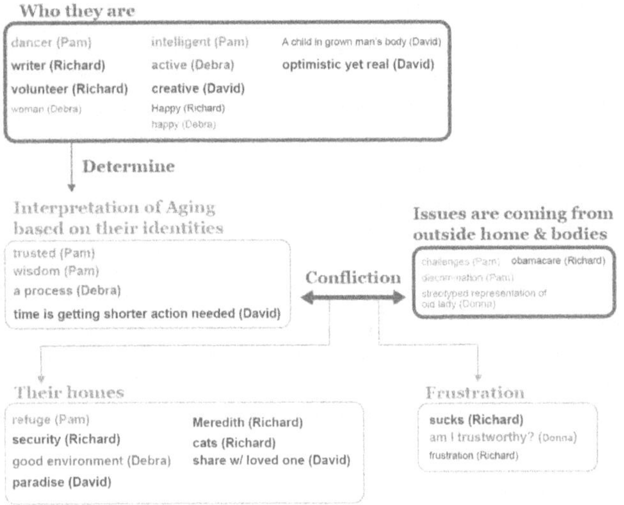

Figure 3 A macro map from the US study based on participants' individual maps

Step 4: Utilizing map-making results for design

Based on the findings of collaborative map making, HCI researchers could develop alternative types of technologies helping older adults to address their needs as citizens. Our participants acknowledged that their matters of concerns include not just themselves but other social actors. However, participants have limited ways to act on the social and welfare systems, which current technology design rarely takes into account.

Case study 2: Householders' Networks in South Korea

Step 1: Selecting keywords

The first step of map-making is selecting three keywords for micro map-making. In our previous studies at home in South Korea, we found that the use of smart home technologies was entangled with social dynamics at home [24]. Based on these findings, this project explores domestic technologies' possibilities as social interventions. Collaborative map making was performed during the project's first session in order to understand the existing network of householders reflecting their Matters of Concern from participants' perspectives. 7 families, including 11 householders, participated in the project.

As we were interested in social dynamics at home, our keywords were "me," "home," and "family." In the previous study, we found that focusing on certain technologies could distort the presentation of social dynamics at home, and we excluded smart home technologies as keywords. For example, female participants were not interviewed within recent smart home studies since researchers could not find females directly using the smart home technologies in which researchers were interested [5,33,35]. When researchers focus on technologies, people who do not have strong relationships with the technologies were excluded from study. In contrast, we investigate how participants' perspectives on their matters of concern through collaborative map making.

Step 2: Micro map making

We asked each participant to make their own maps as shown in Figure 4. we asked participants to write any 15 words related to our keywords, "me," "home," and "family"; then, we asked them to make maps by grouping and relating those words as they liked. Among our participants, we discuss Daewon's map as an example of micro map-making process.

Daewon's map: Daewon (male, 35 years old) is an apprentice at an Italian restaurant, which he started a year ago after quitting his job as a financial analyst at a large company. Daewon lives in a suburb of Seoul, the capital of South Korea, with his wife and daughter. His family moved from Seoul when the rent on their apartment increased. He worked for 10 hours every day as an apprentice with a 2-hour commute. There are no official weekends or holidays at this job, though he has four days off per month.

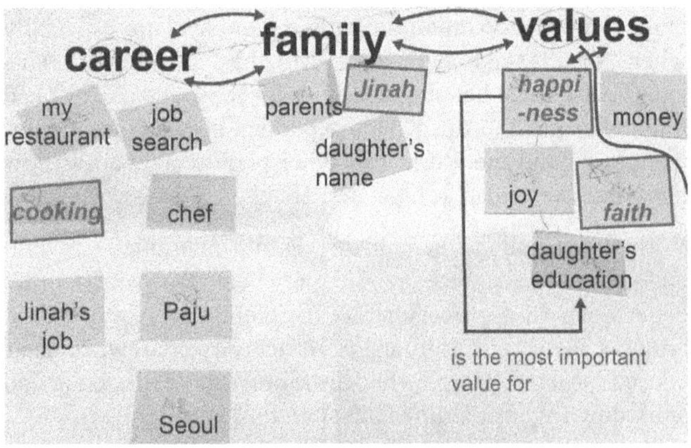

Figure 4 Daewon's situational map (a micro map)

Daewon wrote 15 words related to the three suggested keywords, "me," "home," and "family." In his map, he picked "cooking," "Jinah (wife)," "happiness," and "faith" as the most important words. The five most important words explain his issues relating to his recent career path change. He said that "happiness" is the most important word among the four, and all the words are closely interrelated. He said he decided to change his career path because of "*happiness.*" He described his life as an analyst as not very pleasant. Being an analyst could guarantee economic status and social position. However, the job was stressful, and he knew he would be forced to retire around the age of 45 like all other white-collar workers in South Korea. Considering that average life expectancy is heading toward 100 and South Korea has a limited pension system, he worried about his future years as the breadwinner for his family. His speculation about "happiness" led him to explore "*cooking*" as an alternative career direction, one in which he has been interested. Due to the career change, "*Jinah,*" his wife, should start her new full time job. He felt very sorry for his family, especially for Jinah, because of his limited income, but he could not find other ways to keep himself happy and his family economically stable in the long term. He said his "*faith*" in religion helps him greatly persevere through his currently rough and unstable situation.

Daewon's map-making process revealed how his issue includes various societal factors, including his status as a father, a worker in the flexible labor market, and the unstable pension system in Korea. Daewon chose early retirement, as companies can no longer guarantee lifelong employment. The labor market of South Korea became flexible after IMF economic crisis in 1997 (e.g., early retirement system, sharply increased numbers of non-regular workers [25]), and the South Korean national pension system is not stable [6]. His status as an unstable breadwinner saddens him because he sees providing for his family as his duty according to traditional Confucian gender roles [39]. The economic instability makes him lonely and stressed. As the head of his family, it is difficult for him to complain or share his difficulties with other family members.

We did not constrain our participants in thinking about their issues, especially with technical terms. Thus, Daewon could pay the most attention to issues not related to technologies, and at the same time, relate his issues to his experience with technologies. While explaining the map, he mentioned his internet TV as his least favorite object. Daewon usually watches TV alone in his living room after coming back from work around 1 AM. At that time, no one else in his family is awake. Silence makes his home seem cold, and the TV is the only thing that can talk. He often loses his sense of time, watching TV until 2 or 3 AM. He needs to leave for work at 7 AM. He wants to stop watching TV, but continues as it as the easiest way of relieving his stress.

Step 3: Macro map making

After each of our 11 participants in South Korea made their maps, we developed a macro map (see Figure 5). We first went through each participant's map as we did for Daewon. Then, we constructed a few statements explaining each participant's Matters of Concern. From the statements, we found a pattern among participants in the same gender and age groups (e.g. 30-something male participants suffer from flexible labor market policies). For example, as Daewon can't stop watching his TV, another participant Ji-eun (P3, female, 39, full time mother) explained her husband constantly watches TV in the home. Ji-eun said her husband suffered from long working hours and stressful working conditions in a large technology company. The stress made her husband keep watching TV when he is at home, decreasing communication between him and other family members. Also, we found different age groups with same gender were related to each other. For example, Eunja (P4w, female, 60, housewife)' complained her husband watches TV all day long, which started in his 30s. When he was in his 30s, he watched TV after work. Even after his retirement, watching TV is his main occupation. The limited time with family members due to long working hours limited husbands' communication ability with their families. Consequently, the 50 and 60-something husbands watched TV most of the time. Based on the groups that emerged, we searched through local South Korean anthropology, sociology, and gender studies' literature. The process was for triangulating our interpretations of the relationships among gender, age, and family dynamics in contemporary South Korea. The triangulation process helped us identify that Neoliberalism was a crucial theme to understand contemporary South Korea, especially after the IMF crisis in 1997, and to use that knowledge in our identification of main Matters of Concern.

The macro map making process in South Korea showed participants' seemingly personal issues in the homes were closely related to the South Korean socio-economic system. However, participants blamed themselves, saying that they failed to perform their roles efficiently. Based on the common patterns, we came up with the macro maps as below. The macro map clarified that our householders' issues stem from the Neoliberal system overemphasizing the importance of individual efforts. The macro map-making process visualized the notion that householders need help to perceive their issues as community's issues and as citizens in relation to actors outside the home.

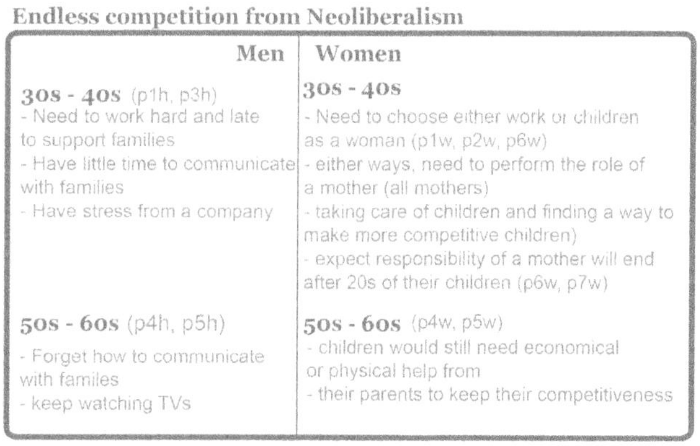

Figure 5 A macro map from South Korean study based on participants' individual maps (household 1 husband: p1h, household 2 wife: p2w)

Step 4: Utilizing map-making results for design

After the map making process, we added technical components into our research gradually so that we could construct alternative domestic technologies based on participants' network. For example, as a second step, we provided the participants with basic sensors so they could explore how technologies could affect their Matters of Concerns. While collaboratively designing technologies, we tried to visualize how participants' issues are not just personal but related to systemic issues. To raise participants' critical awareness, we showed participants our macro maps and how their concerns are interrelated with those of other participants. Also, we collaboratively developed Internet of Things (IoTs) prototypes with participants to share narratives of different participants' issues.

What we learned from the two case studies

Throughout the map-making process, we found that the entanglement of concerns connected participants' individual issues to local and global politics—the Matters of Concern. Homes were not just a private space separated from outside power dynamics, despite their framing as such in HCI [8,16,36]; also see [7,26] for a critique. The most interesting finding to us was that participants' ways of perceiving their issues were closely related to a Neoliberal ethos [12,29]: endorsing individualized selves and self-governing. When discussing their issues, participants believed that they could be in a better situation with more individual effort. If older adults tried harder to save money in their early years, they would be fine now; if fathers had better jobs and earned more money, the whole family situation will be better off; if mothers managed their children better, the children will be competitive and win the education race. Participants were most critical of their own inefficiency and individualized their issues; however, those issues were not only interconnected, but also strongly tied to systemic problems in society. Neoliberalism overemphasizes individuals' roles and minimizes the role of the government [3]. The US government, ever since the Reagan administration [18], and the South Korean government after the IMF in 1997 [29], have pursued Neoliberal deregulation policies encouraging individuals' self-governance. To counter this individualization, grouping people's issues and providing a technological platform for them to voice their societal concerns (e.g. education policy) is an essential step towards technology that can deal with Matters of Concern.

DISCUSSION

We have shown how collaborative map making can help us explore current situations in the context of existing Matters of Concern. Subsequently, we are going to discuss the advantages of employing our suggested methodology: 1) collaborative map making reflexively situates researchers within a network, 2) collaborative map making enables researchers to constitute the "public" from an individual's experiences from the private space of the home, 3) collaborative map making helps researchers focus on Matters of Concern, regardless of pre-existing categories such as human/nonhuman binary, and finally 4) collaborative map making deepens the current meaning of "situation" and context in HCI.

Collaborative map making raises the issue of perspectives when studying Matters of Concern. In our study, participants played essential roles in defining Matters of Concern; participants determined important actors (or actants) and their relations to each other that constitute Matters of Concern. Then, we as researchers created further ties by finding associations among participant' issues while keeping and valuing the original relations among actors. When we were making macro maps, we kept checking whether the original issues in the micro map reflected back to the macro map correctly to conserve participants' perspectives. Also, when we reported our results, participants' narratives were used to explain their primary concerns from their perspectives. In previous HCI studies, researchers have paid little attention to whose perspectives gain the most power when making networks. Researchers, as actors with power in the network, decided what are Matters of Concern from their perspectives, and researchers defined each actor in the network based on their own concerns. Although researchers extend their informants' contexts from a lab to an organization (or a home) and finally to the public sphere, power dynamics between researchers and the researched still exist.

The issue of perspectives within the network has been discussed as power flows among actors, where the ones with the most power can decide all other actors' representations [30]. HCI Researchers need to reflexively acknowledge their position and relations to other actors, and their existing pre-assumptions and biases while identifying old and making new networks. After all our efforts to collaborate with research participants, inevitably we as the researchers were the ones to finalize the macro maps, and decided whose narratives should be included in this paper. However, we hope our study opens the discussion of perspectives issues within studies exploring Matters of Concern in HCI.

Collaborative map making facilitates finding Matters of Concern, regardless of existing geographic boundaries. Previous studies have explained that Matters of Concern or the "public"—sharing the concerns and taking action—are not necessarily bound by geographical locations; however, most studies are performed in local communities [2], or with governments [11] who are geographically selected at the community level. In our study, we expand possible actors within the public not based on existing local organizations but from individuals who are seemingly unrelated to each other. Collaborative map making visualizes how an individual's experience with technology or issues at home—the private space—are entangled with state-level policies and globalized power dynamics. Although our participants in the US and in South Korea are geographically far from each other, their Matters of Concern are closely related to state-level (or national-level) policies; also, their seemingly personal concerns were public concerns which could be reflected in the policy making process. Thus, a future project could involve developing a Thing to detect those personal and individual issues, aggregate the issues, and reflect the issues back to participants and into the policy making process.

The strength of collaborative map making is analyzing Matters of Concern regardless of geographical locations, derived from Clarke's cartography used to make situational maps [6]. Clarke does not follow geographical space hierarchies (e.g., defining Chicago by the Chicago loop < Chicago city < Illinois < the US < Americas). Rather, depending on the issues, a home could be linked to national-level issues rather than at city level. Collaborative map making would help HCI researchers to find existing Matters of Concern by following research subjects' perspectives and by associating the concerns dynamically.

Collaborative map making sensitizes HCI researchers to the power of technologies beyond the category of human/nonhuman. Understanding the power of nonhuman actors is an important point of ANT, which is also important in HCI. However, ANT is also a critique on sociologists' research practices and categories, which limits their knowledge making. Thus, when HCI researchers adopt ANT, we could be reflexive and examine our existing research practices to be aware of how they limit us.

One of the common research features in HCI is that HCI researchers value computing technologies above other actors, due to the field's origins in Computer Science. Although HCI researchers have rarely analyzed computing technologies as meaningful actors as humans, computing technologies have been at the center of HCI studies. For example, in recent "in-the-wild" smart home studies, women became invisible actors because they were not the primary users of computing technologies [5,33,35]. The computing technologies researchers were interested in were granted power and the agency to define who should be in the studies or not. Considering the position of computing technologies at the heart of HCI research, HCI researchers need to be careful when focusing primarily on its power. Computing technologies, in the HCI context, have been not the ignored nonhuman actors of sociology, but special actors with significant power. Considering the power of technology in HCI, HCI researchers should carefully examine what relations computing technologies have to other actors and the power dynamics among them; collaborative map making can support such relational analysis.

Collaborative map making stimulates HCI researchers and participants to deeply situate their knowledge and issues. Situatedness has been an important issue in HCI ever since Suchman explained how the action of using technologies is different depending on the situations; she explained actions are mutually shaped between an actor and her environment. To situate the use of technologies, HCI researchers have investigated context; they employed various methodologies (e.g. ethnography, in-the-wild studies, participatory design) to reflect contextual knowledge into technology design and evaluation. Collaborative map making expands the meaning of situatedness by adding power issues between the researcher, as an action observer, and the research participant as an actor (who performs the action), to the analysis. Although a researcher observes how a user acts, the researchers' findings through observation are not enough to explain their situatedness; that is because a researcher has her own perspectives, and she cannot say she thoroughly understands her subject' situations just with observation.

Situatedness in collaborative map making is connected to Haraway's notion of situated knowledge [15], which HCI has discussed as an alternative epistemology [17]. As knowledge comes from researchers, who are located within a certain society, culture, and history, every piece of knowledge is derived from a certain perspective. Thus, knowledge cannot be seen as a universal truth or fact, but exists in multiple forms depending on the perspectives that constitute it. Research participants are also located within a certain society, culture, and history. When researchers study them, researchers cannot know them without understanding the complex relations that research participants have with other diverse actors within the network, which can be explored through collaborative map making. The map making process benefits participants as well; they can reflexively analyze their concerns and increase critical awareness related to systemic issues. After the micro map making in our two studies, participants said they had not known their issues are this complex, and some took pictures of their maps to share with other householders. When two householders participated in the session together, they liked to share their maps to understand each other' concerns. In addition, when we shared our macro map, participants were sometimes relieved that their issues were not entirely their fault, as their seemingly personal issues were closely tied to systemic issues; some participants then wanted to act on the systemic issues and policies if there is a way.

CONCLUSION

We introduced collaborative map making as a reflexive way to understand participants' in-depth situation with Matters of Concern. The method revealed complex connections of the homes to sociopolitical dynamics in the broader society. These connections showed a public can be constructed regardless of conventional boundaries defining social groups by characteristics like geography, kinship, etc. Also, in our two case studies, we found both US and South Korean participants live and interpret their experiences in the context of Neoliberal policies, which overemphasize the importance of individuals' efforts in society. Following the Neoliberal ethos, participants individualized their issues, believing increased efficiency of their lives will create desired improvements. A promising direction for HCI research could be enabling individualized people to collectively address their issues, despite their separation due to Neoliberal beliefs and individualism. The suggested method could also provide a way for HCI researchers to relate their design process to policy issues, which are of increasing importance and interest to HCI [19,37].

ACKNOWLEDGMENTS

We thank all the participants in our research, and Laura Foster, Erik Stolterman, David Hakken, and Hye Jung Cho-Han who provided helpful comments on previous versions of this document. We are also grateful to Rob Kling Center for Social Informatics (RKCSI) at Indiana University for funding this research.

REFERENCES

1. 2016. Reckitt Benckiser sold deadly sterilisers in South Korea. In *BBC*.
2. Erling Bjögvinsson, Pelle Ehn, and Per-Anders Hillgren. 2010. Participatory design and "democratizing innovation". In *Proceedings of the 11th Biennial Participatory Design Conference*, 41-50.
3. Ha-Joon Chang. 2014. *Economics: the user's guide*. Bloomsbury Publishing USA.
4. Saabira Chaudhuri. 2016. Reckitt Benckiser Apologizes for Disinfectant Deaths. In *Wall Street Journal*, Slough, England.
5. Marshini Chetty, Hyojoon Kim, Srikanth Sundaresan, Sam Burnett, Nick Feamster, and W. Keith Edwards. 2015. uCap: An Internet Data Management Tool For The Home. In *Proceedings of the 33rd Conference on Human Factors in Computing Systems*, 3093-3102.
6. Adele Clarke. 2005. *Situational analysis: Grounded theory after the postmodern turn*. Sage.
7. Ruth Schwartz Cowan. 1983. *More work for mother: The ironies of household technology from the open hearth to the microwave*. Basic Books.
8. Andy Crabtree and Tom Rodden. 2004. Domestic Routines and Design for the Home. *Computer Supported Cooperative Work (CSCW) 13*, 2: 191-220.
9. Christopher Le Dantec. 2012. Participation and publics: supporting community engagement. In *Proceedings of the SIGCHI Conference on Human Factors in Computing Systems*, 1351-1360.
10. Carl Disalvo. 2009. Design and the Construction of Publics. *Design issues 25*, 1: 48-63.
11. Carl Disalvo, Jonathan Lukens, Thomas Lodato, Tom Jenkins, and Tanyoung Kim. 2014. Making public things: how HCI design can express matters of concern. In *Proceedings of the 32nd annual ACM conference on Human factors in computing systems*, 2397-2406.
12. Virginia Eubanks. 2012. Digital dead end: Fighting for social justice in the information age. MIT Press.
13. Batya Friedman. 1996. Value-sensitive design. *interactions 3*, 6: 16-23.
14. Barney G Glaser and Anselm L Strauss. 1965. Discovery of substantive theory: A basic strategy underlying qualitative research. *American Behavioral Scientist 8*, 6: 5-12.
15. Donna Haraway. 1988. Situated Knowledges: The Science Question in Feminism and the Privilege of Partial Perspective. *Feminist Studies 14*, 3: 575-599.
16. Richard Harper. 2003. Inside the Smart Home: Ideas, Possibilities and Methods. In *Inside the Smart Home*, R. Harper (ed). Springer London, 1-13.
17. Steve Harrison, Phoebe Sengers, and Deborah Tatar. 2011. Making epistemological trouble: Third-paradigm HCI as successor science. *Interacting with Computers 23*, 5: 385-392.
18. David Harvey. 2007. *A brief history of neoliberalism*. Oxford University Press, USA.
19. Steven J. Jackson, Tarleton Gillespie, and Sandy Payette. 2014. The policy knot: re-integrating policy, practice and design in cscw studies of social computing. In *Proceedings of the 17th ACM conference on Computer supported cooperative work and social computing*, 588-602.
20. Tom Jenkins, Christopher A. Le Dantec, Carl Disalvo, Thomas Lodato, and Mariam Asad. 2016. Object-Oriented Publics. In *Proceedings of the 2016 CHI Conference on Human Factors in Computing Systems*, 827-839.
21. John Vines, Pritchard Gary, Wright Peter, Olivier Patrick, and Brittain Katie. 2015. An Age-Old Problem: Examining the Discourses of Ageing in HCI and Strategies for Future Research. *ACM Trans. Comput.-Hum. Interact. 22*, 1: 1-27.
22. Bruno Latour. 2005. *Reassembling the social: An introduction to actor-network-theory*. Oxford university press.
23. Hee Rin Lee, Haodan Tan, and Selma Šabanović. 2016. That robot is not for me: Addressing stereotypes of aging in assistive robot design. In *2016 25th IEEE International Symposium on Robot and Human Interactive Communication (RO-MAN)*, 312-317.
24. Hee Rin Lee and Selma Šabanović. 2013. Weiser's dream in the Korean home: collaborative study of domestic roles, relationships, and ideal technologies. In *Proceedings of the 2013 ACM international joint conference on Pervasive and ubiquitous computing*, 637-646.
25. Brenna Mcnally, Mona Leigh Guha, Matthew Louis Mauriello, and Allison Druin. 2016. Children's Perspectives on Ethical Issues Surrounding Their Past Involvement on a Participatory Design Team. In *the Proceedings of the 2016 CHI Conference on Human Factors in Computing Systems*, 3595-3606.
26. Christena E Nippert-Eng. 2008. *Home and work: Negotiating boundaries through everyday life*. University of Chicago Press.
27. Jennifer M Ortman, Victoria A Velkoff, and Howard Hogan. 2014. An aging nation: the older population in the United States, U.S.C. Bureau Ed.
28. Jesper Simonsen and Toni Robertson. 2012. *Routledge international handbook of participatory design*. Routledge.

29. Jesook Song. 2006. Family Breakdown and Invisible Homeless Women: Neoliberal Governance during the Asian Debt Crisis in South Korea, 1997-2001. *positions: east asia cultures critique 14*, 1: 37-65.
30. Susan Leigh Star. 1990. Power, technology and the phenomenology of conventions: on being allergic to onions. *The Sociological Review 38*, S1: 26-56.
31. Lucy Suchman. 1995. Making work visible. *Commun. ACM 38*, 9: 56-ff.
32. Lucy Suchman. 2002. Located accountabilities in technology production. *Scandinavian journal of information systems 14*, 2: 7.
33. Leila Takayama, Caroline Pantofaru, David Robson, Bianca Soto, and Michael Barry. 2012. Making technology homey: finding sources of satisfaction and meaning in home automation. In *Proceedings of the 2012 ACM Conference on Ubiquitous Computing*, 511-520.
34. Adriana Tapus, Maja J Mataric, and Brian Scassellati. 2007. Socially assistive robotics [Grand Challenges of Robotics]. *Robotics & Automation Magazine, IEEE 14*, 1: 35-42.
35. Rayoung Yang and Mark W. Newman. 2013. Learning from a learning thermostat: lessons for intelligent systems for the home. In *Proceedings of the 2013 ACM international joint conference on Pervasive and ubiquitous computing*, 93-102.
36. Nicola Yuill, Yvonne Rogers, and Jochen Rick. 2013. Pass the iPad: collaborative creating and sharing in family groups. In *Proceedings of the SIGCHI Conference on Human Factors in Computing Systems*, 941-950.
37. Amy X. Zhang and Scott Counts. 2016. Gender and Ideology in the Spread of Anti-Abortion Policy. In *Proceedings of the 2016 CHI Conference on Human Factors in Computing Systems*, 3378-3389

Toward Principles for the Design of Navigation Affordances in Code Editors: An Empirical Investigation

Austin Z. Henley, Scott D. Fleming, Maria V. Luong
Department of Computer Science
University of Memphis
Memphis, Tennessee, USA
{azhenley, Scott.Fleming, mluong}@memphis.edu

ABSTRACT

Design principles are a key tool for creators of interactive systems; however, a cohesive set of principles has yet to emerge for the design of code editors. In this paper, we conducted a between-subjects empirical study comparing the navigation behaviors of 32 professional LabVIEW programmers using two different code-editor interfaces: the ubiquitous tabbed editor and the experimental Patchworks editor. Our analysis focused on how the programmers arranged and navigated among open information patches (i.e., code modules and program output). Key findings of our study included that Patchworks users made significantly fewer click actions per navigation, juxtaposed patches side by side significantly more, and exhibited significantly fewer navigation mistakes than tabbed-editor users. Based on these findings and more, we propose five general principles for the design of effective navigation affordances in code editors.

ACM Classification Keywords

D.2.6 Software Engineering: Programming Environments; H.5.m. Information Interfaces and Presentation (e.g., HCI): Miscellaneous.

Author Keywords

Programming environments; navigation; design principles; visual programming languages; user study.

INTRODUCTION

Design principles have proven to be a key tool for designers of interactive systems. Principles help guide the design of a system by providing a set of heuristics and best practices, often based on empirical evidence. Moreover, such principles serve to inspire new design decisions and to facilitate the comparison of competing designs. Without principles, designers are left to rely on intuition, increasing the risk of wasting time and effort relearning which designs are effective and of repeating past mistakes. Design principles have been proposed to help designers in a variety of different contexts, including the design of mixed-initiative user interfaces [17], of web pages that support information foraging [47], of affordances for debugging machine-learning systems [28], of affordances to help end-user programmers learn enough to overcome barriers [19], and of games for computer science education [30].

One actively studied domain of interactive systems that has yet to benefit from a cohesive set of design principles is code editors. Numerous code-editor designs have been proposed over the years. Early designs emphasized a windowed paradigm in which each open code file was displayed in a separate window (e.g., Visual C++ 6.0). More recent development environments have favored tabbed editor interfaces (e.g., as in Eclipse and Visual Studio). Dissatisfied with the status quo, researchers have also proposed more radical designs. For example, canvas-based editors enable programmers to arrange open code fragments on a large 2D canvas (e.g., as in Self [46], Jasper [6], Code Canvas [12], and Code Bubbles [4]). Despite all this design exploration, a set of effective design principles for code editors has yet to be codified.

In this work, we aim to create a cohesive set of design principles targeting *navigation affordances* for code editors. Code navigation is a key concern in code-editor design. Studies have shown that programming tasks typically involve large amounts of information seeking. For example, one study found that programmers spent 50% of their time foraging for information during debugging tasks [40]. As a consequence of all this information seeking, navigation takes up a significant portion of the time programmers spend on tasks. One study found that programmers spent 35% of their time on the mechanics of navigation alone [23], and another found that programmers averaged over 5 navigations per minute during programming tasks [14]. Thus, navigation affordances can have a substantial impact on a programmer's time and effort on task.

Toward our goal of design principles, we have been exploring *Patchworks* [15], an experimental code-editor design. In contrast to tabbed editors, Patchworks is based on the idiom of a sliding grid strip of code fragments. In a preliminary evaluation [15], Patchworks users navigated significantly faster and made fewer navigation mistakes than users of a tabbed editor (Eclipse). A subsequent simulation study [16] also showed that Patchworks can significantly increase the number

CHI 2017, May 6–11, 2017, Denver, CO, USA.
© 2017 ACM ISBN 978-1-4503-4655-9/17/05...$15.00.
http://dx.doi.org/10.1145/3025453.3025645

of highly efficient *on-screen navigations* (i.e., navigations to code already visible on screen) that programmers make.

Although these preliminary evaluations of Patchworks showed promise, they had key limitations. The participants were CS graduate students, leaving the question of whether the results will generalize to professional developers. Moreover, the initial evaluation involved artificial navigation tasks that enabled precise recording of navigation times, but did not explore more natural development activities, such as debugging. In the second study, navigation logs of Java programmers were used to simulate the experience of a Patchworks user; however, Patchworks' effect on navigation decisions was not tested.

In this paper, we present a new empirical study that both addresses our goal of principles as well as overcomes the limitations of prior Patchworks evaluations. In particular, we performed an observational user study that compared the ubiquitous tabbed editor design with the experimental Patchworks design to inductively build a set of design principles. To address ecological validity, participants in our new study consisted of 32 professional programmers at a large software company, and the tasks they performed were more-naturalistic program-debugging tasks. The central goals of our study were

(1) to evaluate how well Patchworks achieves its goals,
(2) to investigate other navigation-related trends not specifically addressed by Patchworks, but relevant to the design of code editors, and
(3) to create a set of design principles based on our findings.

As our subjects of study, we selected experts and tasks in a visual dataflow programming language, LabVIEW [8]. Most prior research on programmer navigation has studied textual programming languages (especially Java). A key reason for choosing a visual dataflow language was that we seek to create a universal set of editor-design principles and to avoid overfitting the principles to the idiosyncrasies of a particular programming language or paradigm. Additionally, this choice afforded us the opportunity to compare the navigation characteristics of visual language programmers to those of textual-language programmers from prior research.

Based on this work, we make the following key contributions:

- Findings of the most ecologically valid evaluation of Patchworks to date.
- Five empirically grounded principles for the design of navigation affordances in code editors based on the findings.
- The first empirical comparison of navigation characteristics of visual dataflow language (LabVIEW) programmers and textual language (Java) programmers.
- An implementation of the Patchworks editor design for the LabVIEW development environment.

BACKGROUND

Programmer Navigation

The literature on programmer navigation can help shed light on the navigation affordances programmers will find effective. As mentioned above, programmers spend a considerable portion of their time on tasks navigating [14, 23]. One reason for this navigation is that programmers engage extensively in information foraging to locate task-relevant code [23]. This process typically involves traversing relationships between fragments of code (e.g., following control-flow dependencies) [22]. Due to the size and complexity of software projects, programmers may spend considerable time inspecting irrelevant code [23, 39], or even "getting lost" in the code [10, 11].

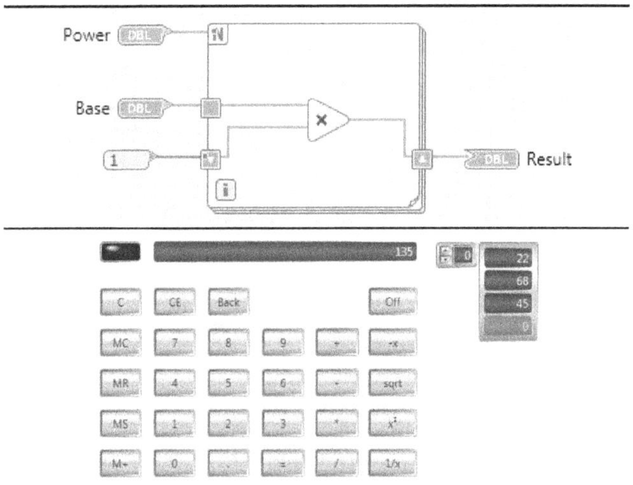

Figure 1. LabVIEW block diagram (top) and front panel (bottom).

One key pattern is that most navigations tend to revisit code the programmer recently visited. For example, studies of predictive models of programmer navigation have consistently found that one of the strongest predictors of which code method (i.e., subroutine) a programmer would click in next was how recently he/she had visited the method (i.e., more recently implies more likely) [10, 26, 29, 33, 38, 45]. Studies have also found that between 82% [16, 45] and 95% [33] of programmer navigations were to previously visited methods.

Recently, researchers have proposed novel interface designs to support revisiting. Tools such as Mylyn [21], Jasper [6], Code Bubbles [3, 4], Code Canvas [12], and Patchworks [15] enable programmers to collect and easily revisit code fragments. Other tools, such as Blaze [27] and Stacksplorer [20], provide visualizations that enable programmers to traverse code relationships. The designs of these tools range widely, and in this paper, we aim to distill key principles to help tool designers provide transformative navigation capabilities without sacrificing the essential navigation needs of programmers.

Visual Dataflow Languages

Most prior work on programmer navigation has focused on Java and Java-like programming languages, so we opted to focus our study on visual dataflow languages to mitigate the effects of Java's idiosyncrasies on our findings and to shed light on the navigation behaviors of visual dataflow programmers. Instead of textual source code, these languages are characterized by programs being made up of boxes (functions) and arrows (values), as illustrated at the top of Fig. 1. The execution of the program follows the dataflow via the arrows. Thus, visual dataflow languages have a radically different syntax than Java-like textual languages while still providing many of the same foundational features, such as modularity.

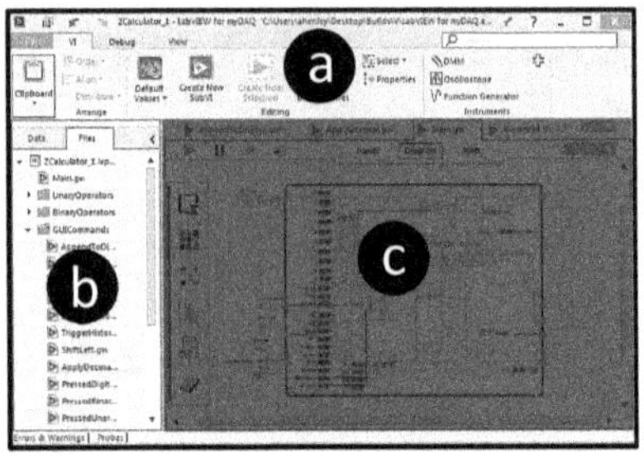

Figure 2. The LabVIEW IDE. The command ribbon (a) and the project explorer (b) were the same for all participants; however, the code editor (c) varied (tabbed vs. Patchworks).

In this paper, we focus on LabVIEW, a commercial visual dataflow programming environment that is one of the most widely used visual programming languages to date [49]. In LabVIEW, programs are composed of modules, called *Virtual Instruments* (VIs). Fig. 1 (top) illustrates the code for a VI, represented as a *block diagram*, that takes 3 inputs, performs a multiplication in a loop, then outputs the result. In LabVIEW, each block diagram is associated with a graphical user interface, called a *front panel*, as shown at the bottom of Fig. 1.

CODE EDITORS COMPARED

In our study, we compared the navigation affordances of two code-editor designs: the ubiquitous tabbed code editor and a research design, the Patchworks code editor [15]. Both editors were implemented within the LabVIEW integrated development environment (IDE) depicted in Fig. 2. The LabVIEW IDE provides features similar to those of other popular IDEs (e.g., Eclipse and Visual Studio), including a project explorer for opening VIs (Fig. 2b) as well as debugger and search tools accessible via the command ribbon (Fig. 2a).

Borrowing from information foraging theory [41], we assume a programmer's task environment to have a "patchy" structure, where a *patch* may be a code file, web page, or other interface that the programmer reads or edits as a unit. In LabVIEW, each VI is associated with two patches: its block diagram and its front panel. The programmer *navigates* by moving his/her attention from one patch to another.

All editors that we are aware of, including the two under study, maintain a set of "open" patches that the programmer has accessed (or *opened*). The tabbed and Patchworks editors differ mainly in the affordances they provide for displaying, organizing, and navigating among open VI patches, and we detail those differences below.

Tabbed Code Editor

Tabbed code editors are based on an interface paradigm similar to paper file folders, as shown in Fig. 3. Currently, they are by far the most popular code-editor interface. Tabbed editors default to a *single-patch display* in which the contents of one patch fill most of the editor's available space (Fig. 3c). Each open patch has a labeled "tab", like a paper file folder (Fig. 3a). The programmer may navigate among open patches by clicking on the tabs. If too many patches are open, some tabs are elided and made available via a drop-down menu (Fig. 3b). The programmer may reorder tabs by dragging and

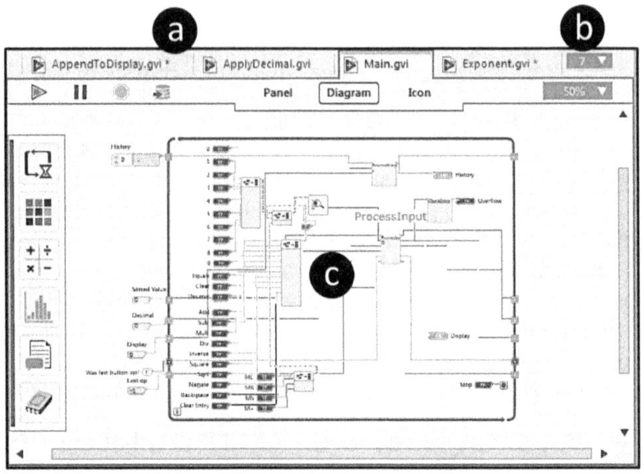

Figure 3. The tabbed code editor. Tabs (a) could be used to switch among open patches. If too many patches were open, some of the tabs were elided (b). This single-patch display (c) filled the rest of the pane with one VI patch.

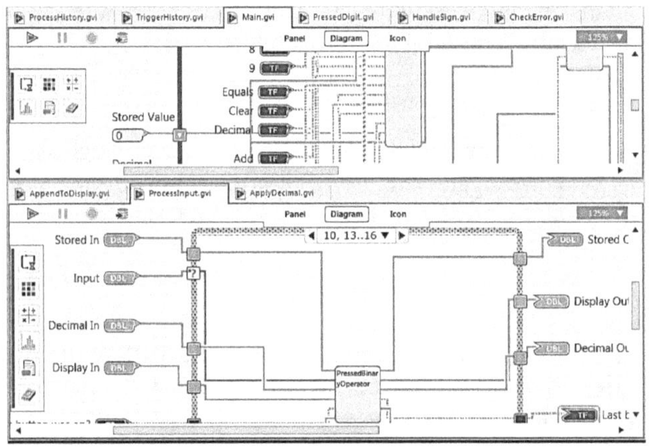

Figure 4. Tabbed editor manipulated into a multi-patch display, allowing two VI patches to be placed side by side.

dropping, and may close a patch by clicking a button on its tab. The programmer may also manipulate a tabbed editor into a *multi-patch display* (in which two patches are placed side by side) by splitting the editor pane into two panes, and dragging and dropping tabs between the panes, as illustrated in Fig. 4.

Patchworks Code Editor

The Patchworks code editor is an experimental design that aims to ease navigation among open patches. In this work, we focus on four key subgoals of the design:

- Reduce the cost of navigation (i.e., clicks per navigation).
- Facilitate the juxtaposition of patches (i.e., placing patches side by side on screen).
- Reduce navigation mistakes (i.e., accidentally navigating to the wrong patch).
- Enable efficient toggling between multi-patch and single-patch views.

As illustrated in Fig. 5, the Patchworks editor's main display consists of a *patch grid* with four fixed *patch cells*. Each patch cell may contain a VI block diagram or front panel. The choice of four patch cells was based on the typical size of a VI and the study-monitor size. (In contrast, the prior Patchworks editor

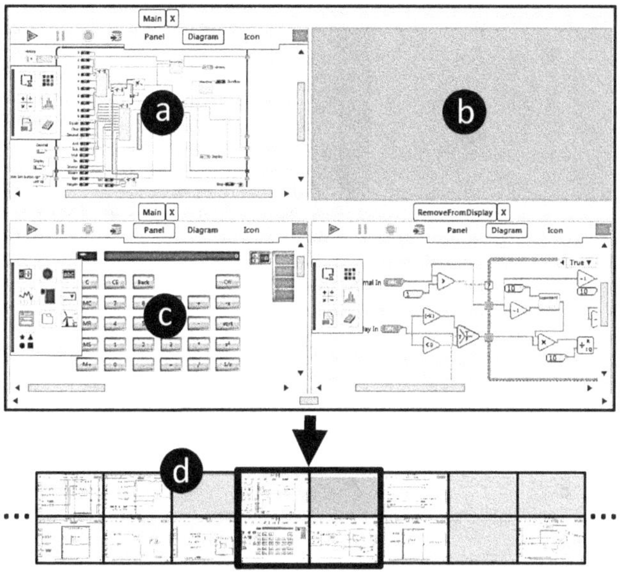

Figure 5. The Patchworks code editor. This multi-patch display divides the editor pane into a patch grid with four patch cells. Each patch cell may contain a block diagram (a) or front panel (c) for a VI, or it may be empty (b). The displayed patch grid is actually a view into a larger patch strip (d), and the programmer can navigate by sliding the view left or right along the patch strip.

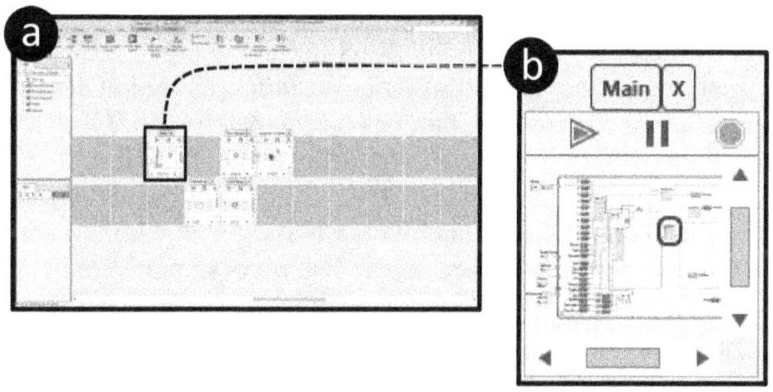

Figure 6. Patchworks' bird's eye view (a) enables the user to zoom out, and survey and organize his/her open patches. It represents each patch with a thumbnail (b).

for Java [15] had six patch cells.) This multi-patch display aims to facilitate juxtaposition of patches by emphasizing the presentation of more than one patch on screen at a time, while the fixed grid layout aims to reduce tedious window management. Patches can be efficiently moved and swapped between cells via dragging and dropping.

To enable navigation beyond the patches visible on screen, the patch grid is actually a view into a larger *patch strip*, illustrated by Fig. 5d. The programmer navigates among patches by sliding the view left or right along the patch strip using a keyboard shortcut or horizontal scrollbar. This 1-dimensional patch strip aims to reduce navigation mistakes by simplifying the space of possible navigation actions (slide left or right) and to facilitate efficient visual scanning of open patches. Additionally, the Patchworks editor enables toggling to a bird's eye view of the patch strip that shows a thumbnail of each open patch, as illustrated in Fig. 6. The programmer can rearrange patches from the bird's eye view via the same dragging and dropping interactions as in the patch-grid view, and can zoom back into the patch-grid view by clicking on a selected patch.

Patchworks also enables toggling a patch to a "blowup" view that takes up the entire editor space. To toggle into or out of the blowup view, the programmer double-clicks the selected patch's title label. In this way, Patchworks aims to enable efficient switching between multi-patch and single-patch display.

METHOD

To address our research goals, we conducted an observational laboratory study of professional LabVIEW programmers engaged in debugging. We divided the participants into two treatments, each using a different editor. The *Tabs Group* used an editor based on the ubiquitous tabbed interface to perform debugging tasks, whereas the *Patchworks Group* used the Patchworks editor.

Participants

Our participants consisted of 32 professional programmers from a large technology company (27 males, 5 females). All held bachelor's degrees in engineering, and five also held master's degrees. On average, they had 1.6 years of professional programming experience ($SD = 1.0$) and 2.1 years of LabVIEW experience ($SD = 1.8$). They all reported using LabVIEW on a daily basis for their jobs.

Code Base and Tasks

For our study, the participants worked on a calculator application, illustrated in Fig. 1 (bottom), written in LabVIEW, consisting of 34 VIs. The application was based on a publicly available sample application [7] written in an old version of LabVIEW, and we ported this sample application to the current version of LabVIEW. We also seeded the application with five bugs that we actually encountered during the porting process.

As tasks, each participant worked on fixing the five seeded bugs. The tasks were ordered from least to most difficult. For example, Task 1 required understanding mainly one VI, whereas Task 4 required understanding interactions between several. All participants did the tasks in the same order, and had to complete the current task before beginning the next.

Procedure

Prior to their study sessions, participants were randomly assigned to the Tabs and Patchworks Treatment Groups such that there were 16 participants in each group. Each session took roughly 1 hour. First, the participant filled out a background questionnaire. Next, the participant viewed a short presentation on the code base and the editor they would be using (tabbed or Patchworks, depending on treatment). The participant then practiced with the editor and code base for 10 minutes, answering questions about the source code. The participant then worked for 40 minutes on the debugging tasks. To better understand where participants placed their attention, we asked them to "think aloud" as they worked. At the end of the session, the participants took part in a semi-structured interview in which they discussed any issues they had and their thoughts on the editor. We recorded screen-capture video and audio of participant utterances throughout the session.

Qualitative Analysis

As our main analysis, we used qualitative coding methods to identify where the participants navigated—that is, on which patches they placed their attention—throughout each of their sessions. Following the coding rules from a prior study [16], we coded each time (accurate to a second) a participant moved his/her attention from one patch to another. Additionally, we coded navigation mistakes based on participants' utterances after a navigation, indicating if a navigation did not result in their intended destination.

To ensure the reliability of our analysis results, we applied a standard inter-rater reliability method in which two researchers independently code the same 20% of the data, and must achieve at least 80% agreement using the Jaccard index. When the researchers have reached this level of agreement, they may split up the remaining data to be coded individually. The two coders for our study achieved 88.9% agreement for 20% of the video data, and individually coded the remaining data.

RESULTS

To address our research goals, we collected and analyzed over 21 hours of video of our 32 professional programmers engaged in debugging, half using a tabbed editor and half using Patchworks. On average, participants completed 2.63 of the 5 tasks ($SD = 0.71$), with each completed task taking an average of 9.55 minutes ($SD = 7.24$). Although there was no significant difference in the rate of success or overall task time between the treatment groups, they did exhibit key differences with respect to navigation—the focus of our investigation.

In this section, we first report the results of our comparative evaluation of Patchworks' navigation affordances. Next, we describe empirical trends across our treatments that are relevant to the design of navigation affordances and that are not specifically addressed by Patchworks. We close the section with a comparison of our LabVIEW programmers' navigation traits with those of Java programmers in prior studies.

Patchworks Evaluation Results

Using our analysis data, we evaluated the extent to which Patchworks met each of its four main design goals.

Reducing Navigation Cost

To evaluate the goal of reducing navigation cost, we randomly sampled 10 navigations from each participant and counted the number of click actions the participant performed in making that navigation. Such actions mainly included tab clicks in the tabbed editor and patch-strip shift actions in Patchworks.

As Fig. 7 shows, navigations in Patchworks were considerably more efficient, requiring fewer clicks, than navigations in the tabbed editor. On average, Patchworks participants made less than half (40%) of the click actions that Tabs participants made per navigation. This difference was statistically significant (Mann–Whitney: $U = 22.5$, $Z = 3.96$, $p < 0.0001$).

Facilitating Patch Juxtaposition

Consistent with Patchworks' goal of facilitating juxtaposition, Patchworks participants juxtaposed patches more than Tabs participants. Every Patchworks participant juxtaposed patches

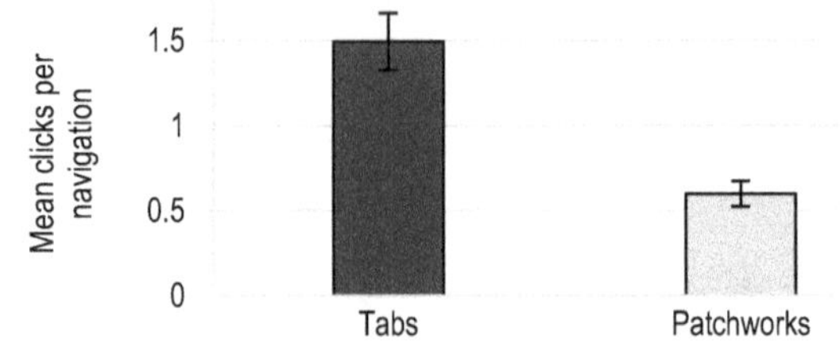

Figure 7. Patchworks participants performed significantly fewer click actions per navigation than did Tabs participants (smaller bars are better). Whiskers denote standard error.

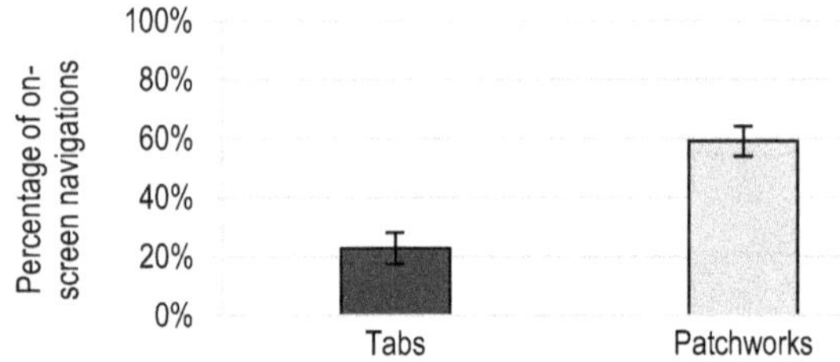

Figure 8. Patchworks participants made significantly more on-screen navigations than did Tabs participants. Whiskers denote standard error.

during their tasks. In contrast, only 10 of the Tabs participants (63%) juxtaposed patches. This difference was statistically significant (Fisher's exact test: $p < 0.01$).

Patchworks participants also rearranged their juxtaposed patches more than Tabs participants. In fact, only one Tabs participant, P15, rearranged his juxtaposed patches. In contrast, 11 of the 16 Patchworks participants had at least one episode of rearranging patches on the patch strip. Of these 11 participants, they dragged and dropped a patch from one grid cell to another an average of 4.9 times ($SD = 3.6$). Comparing just the Tabs and Patchworks participants who juxtaposed at all, significantly more of the Patchworks participants rearranged their juxtaposed patches than did the Tabs participants (Fisher's exact test: $p < 0.01$).

Following from Patchworks participants' greater tendency to juxtapose patches, they also made significantly more on-screen navigations than Tabs participants (Mann–Whitney: $U = 29$, $Z = 3.71$, $p < 0.0002$). Fig. 8 illustrates this difference. On-screen navigations are highly efficient because they require moving only one's eyes (no clicking). In one extreme case, Patchworks Participant P13 made over 80% of his navigations to patches already on screen.

The Patchworks participants' high rate of on-screen navigations had a considerable influence on their lower average cost of navigation; however, it was not the only contributor. Even if on-screen navigations were excluded from our cost analysis, Patchworks participants still made significantly fewer clicks per navigation (Tabs: $M = 1.80$, $SD = 0.58$; Patchworks: $M = 1.36$, $SD = 0.23$; Mann–Whitney: $U = 53.5$, $Z = 2.79$, $p < 0.003$).

Reducing Navigation Mistakes

Another reason that Patchworks participants made fewer clicks per navigation was that they made fewer navigation mistakes. Based on our qualitative analysis, no Patchworks participant ever indicated mistakenly navigating to a patch other than the one he/she intended. In contrast, Tabs participants made many

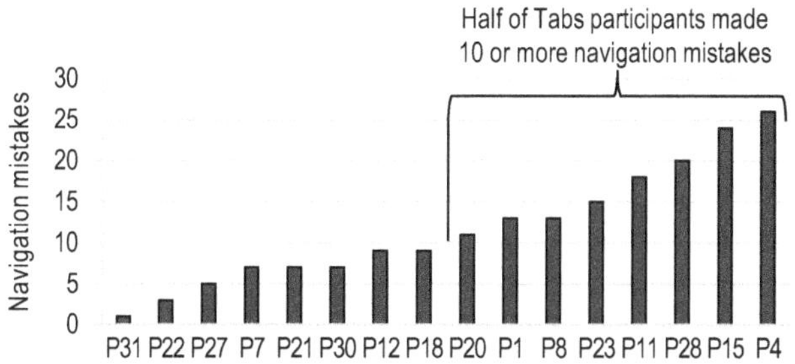

Figure 9. Tabs participants made numerous navigation mistakes in which they clicked on a tab other than the one they intended. All Tabs participants made at least one such mistake, and half of Tabs participants made 10 or more.

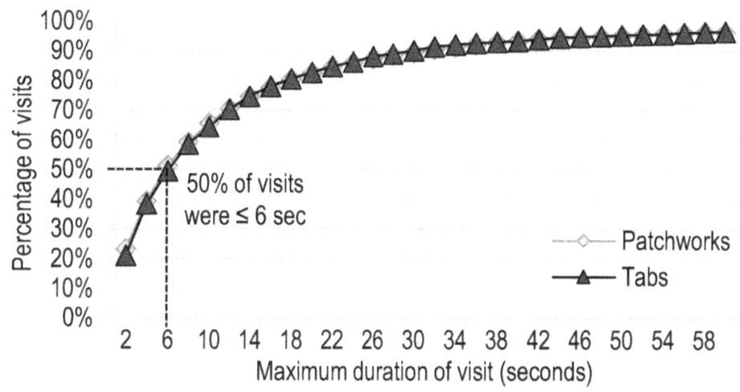

Figure 10. Participants often visited patches for very short intervals, which is consistent with quick scanning. In fact, half of visits lasted 6 seconds or less.

navigation mistakes in which they were seeking a particular patch and clicked the wrong tab to get there. As Fig. 9 shows, all Tabs participants made at least one navigation mistake, and on average, Tabs participants made 11.75 mistakes per session ($SD = 7.28$)—roughly one every 3 minutes. Because no Patchworks participant indicated making a navigation mistake, and every Tabs one did, the statistical difference between the treatments was highly significant (Fisher's exact test: $p = 0$).

Enabling Efficient Blowup View

To evaluate the goal of enabling efficient toggling between single-patch and multi-patch displays, we counted uses of Patchworks' blowup-patch feature to see whether participants used it consistently. We also checked whether the blowup view tended to complement the multi-patch view (as opposed to replacing it). In this evaluation, there was no comparison data, as the tabbed editor lacked an analogous feature.

A strong majority of Patchworks participants made use of the blowup view. All but three Patchworks participants toggled at least once, and nearly one third of all Patchworks participants blew up patches over 10 times. Moreover, the participants who used the feature did so an average of 15.5 times ($SD = 17.5$)—more than once for every 3 minutes.

For Patchworks participants, the blowup view complemented the multi-patch grid well. On average, participants did not stay in the blowup view very long during each use ($M = 33.5$ seconds, $SD = 20.9$), preferring to use it in combination with the patch grid. As a result, all Patchworks participants, except one, spent less than 50% of their sessions in the blowup view.

Trends across Treatments

In addition to evaluating Patchworks' design goals, we checked for three key trends in how programmers navigate and manage open patches. None of these trends were specifically addressed by Patchworks' design goals; however, they all pose relevant considerations in the design of navigation affordances for code editors.

Rapid Patch Scanning

One trend we tested for was rapid scanning of patches. In particular, we wanted to see if participants tended to make their visits to patches short, and if they tended to make series of short visits indicative of scanning patches.

Based on our navigation data, all participants, regardless of treatment group, did a considerable amount of rapid scanning of patches. One key indicator of this behavior was that most of the visits to patches that the participants made were quick. As Fig. 10 shows, half of the visits that participants made to patches lasted 6 seconds or less.

To see if participants were making these short navigations in clusters, we applied DBSCAN [13], a density-based clustering algorithm commonly applied to time-series data. We allowed for up to 5 seconds between navigations and a minimum of 3 navigations to be clustered.

The DBSCAN results showed that every participant engaged in quickly scanning across multiple patches. To illustrate, Fig. 11 visualizes the DBSCAN results for Participant P17, with his 14 clusters of quick navigations spread throughout his session. Overall, 44% of all navigations that participants made were part of a quick-navigation cluster. On average, participants had 17.3 such clusters ($SD = 8.6$) during their 40-minute sessions. No participant had fewer than 4 clusters, and one participant had 34.

Cleaning Up Open Patches

Another trend that we checked for was patch-cleanup behavior—the tendency to let open patches accumulate and then engage in bulk closing of the patches. To this end, we logged each time a participant closed a patch, and to detect bulk closures, we again used DBSCAN to identify clusters (10 seconds between closes, minimum of 3 closes per cluster).

Based on our data, nearly all participants engaged in cleanup, closing open patches throughout their sessions. The Tabs and Patchworks participants closed patches at similar rates: Tabs Participants averaged 14 closes per session ($SD = 6.8$) and Patchworks Participants averaged 16.1 ($SD = 8.9$). Our DBSCAN results showed that 63% of closes were part of clusters, and participants had an average of 3.4 clusters per session ($SD = 2.2$). The average number of closes in a cluster was 4.1 ($SD = 1.8$), which accounted for 69% of the open patches on average ($SD = 22$).

Navigations to Program-Output Patches

A final trend we tested for was the extent to which programmers navigate to program-output patches. Our LabVIEW-based editors differ from those of other popular IDEs in that they present the output (i.e., front panel) of the program under development in patches similar to the code patches. We included navigations to these program-output patches in our

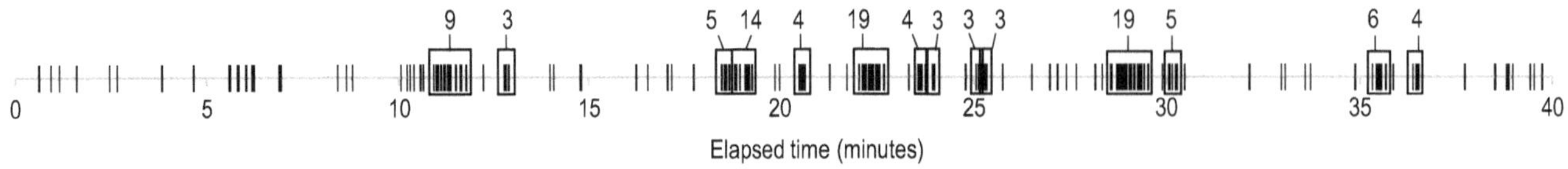

Figure 11. Navigation timeline for P17 with DBSCAN clusters highlighted and cluster size labeled.

Table 1. The textual-language programmer navigation data sets we compared with our visual dataflow language programmer data.

Data Set	Participants	Task Type	Task Time	Language	Size of Code
[14] Fritz et al. FSE'14	5 professionals, 4 CS students, 3 CS faculty	Feature modification	75 min	Java	14–53k LOC
[16] Henley et al. VL/HCC'14	14 CS students	Feature addition	120 min	Java	3–17k LOC
[36] Piorkowski et al. CHI'12	11 professionals	Debugging	70 min	Java	97k LOC
[37] Piorkowski et al. ICSME'15	11 CS students	Debugging	30 min	Java	99k LOC
This Study	32 professionals (16 Tabs + 16 Patchworks)	Debugging	40 min	LabVIEW	34 VIs

navigation coding, and analyzed the frequency of those navigations relative to the code ones.

Based on our data, all participants, regardless of treatment, made a considerable number of navigations to program-output patches. On average, Tabs Participants made 29.2% of their navigations to program-output patches ($SD = 7.5$) and Patchworks participants made 26.2% ($SD = 7.9$).

Visual Dataflow versus Textual Language Programmers

To compare the navigation behavior of textual language programmers and visual dataflow language programmers, we compared our data with results reported by four prior studies (i.e., [14, 16, 36, 37]). We focused our comparison on two key navigations traits: (1) how much the programmers navigated and (2) how much the programmers revisited patches. In the prior studies, the patches among which programmers navigated were Java methods. For our comparison analysis, we operationalized patches as VI block diagrams, which are analogous to methods. Table 1 describes each of the prior textual-language studies.

As Figs. 12 and 13 show, the visual dataflow language programmers exhibited similar navigation traits to the textual language programmers from prior studies. The rates of navigation for our participants were squarely in the middle of the range of navigation rates exhibited by textual language programmers from the literature (Fig. 12). Furthermore, our visual dataflow participants also revisited patches frequently—even more so than prior textual language programmers (Fig. 13).

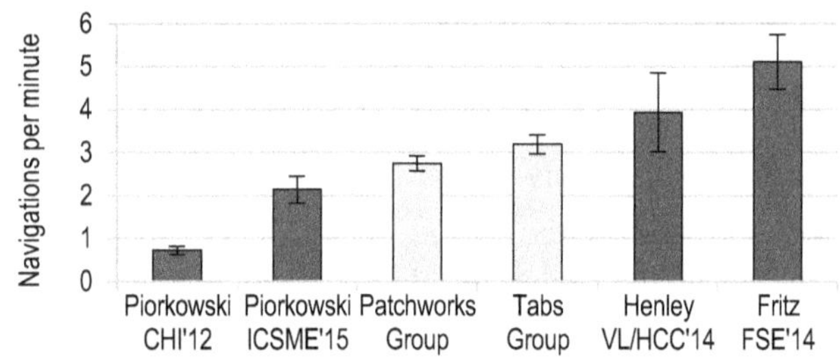

Figure 12. Our visual dataflow language programmers (light bars) navigated at rates similar to prior textual language programmers (dark bars). Whiskers denote standard error.

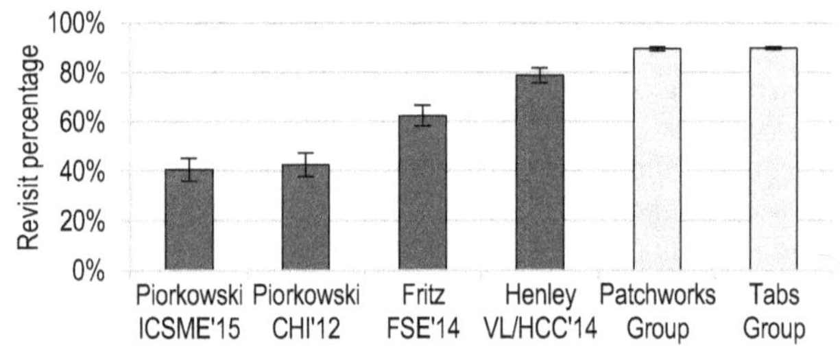

Figure 13. Like prior textual language programmers (dark bars), our visual dataflow language programmers (light bars) revisited patches frequently. Whiskers denote standard error.

DISCUSSION

Implications for Design: Principles

Toward our goal of design principles for code editors, we built upon our quantitative results with additional qualitative analyses of our think-aloud data. In particular, we mapped from quantitative data points to participant episodes, and examined those episodes in detail to help explain and expand upon our results. Informed by these quantitative and qualitative data, we inductively propose five principles, summarized in Table 2.

Table 2. Candidate design principles for code editors.

Name	Definition
Juxtaposition Principle	Enable efficient (re)arranging of multiple open patches side by side on screen at a time.
Signpost Principle	Thumbnails/summaries/labels of open patches must provide sufficient information to quickly make effective navigation decisions.
Blowup Principle	Enable efficient toggling of an open patch within a multi-patch display to an enlarged, possibly single-patch, display.
Cleanup Principle	Enable efficient closing of open patches that are not currently relevant and causing clutter.
Heterogeneity Principle	Apply the above principles to all types of frequently visited patches (not only code).

The Juxtaposition Principle

The Juxtaposition Principle emphasizes enabling programmers to efficiently (re)arrange multiple patches side by side on screen. Although both the Patchworks and tabbed editors support juxtaposing patches, the Patchworks editor better satisfies the Juxtaposition Principle's efficiency aspect. Patchworks' fixed grid of patch cells meant that juxtaposing was simply a matter of opening patches, each in its own cell. In contrast, the tabbed editor required the programmer to tediously split, position, and resize windows. As our results show, every Patchworks participant juxtaposed patches during their tasks, whereas six of the Tabs participants never juxtaposed at all.

The benefit of Patchworks' compliance with the Juxtaposition Principle was made clear by how many more navigations its users made to patches already on screen than did the tabbed-editor users (recall Fig. 8). Such on-screen navigations are highly efficient as they require only moving one's eyes.

The lack of juxtaposing by Tabs participants was not for lack of desire to do so, however:

> P15: "One useful feature might be to have the block diagram tile here [beside a front panel]... I want to see both at once."

> P31: Wanted to "look at a bunch of windows next to each other."

Moreover, all Tabs participants who did juxtapose expressed difficulty in doing so:

> P20: "It is difficult to have multiple VIs [patches] open at the same time and be looking at them at the same time."

> P21: "I don't have very many options in terms of how I can arrange these [patches]."

For example, P31 struggled for nearly 2 minutes with juxtaposing before arriving at a satisfactory configuration.

The ease of *rearranging* patches in Patchworks paid off for Patchworks participants by enabling them to set up long series of these on-screen navigations. For example, Patchworks Participant P9 rearranged his patches so that he could watch four VIs simultaneously while debugging. With this arrangement, he made 36 consecutive on-screen navigations. P3 also rearranged his patches effectively: he had three episodes of rearranging that yielded 25, 15, and 14 consecutive on-screen navigations, respectively. P5 clearly expressed his appreciation for rearranging in the Patchworks editor:

> P5: "The carousel [Patchworks] is nice because you have a lot of different options [to arrange]."

In lieu of juxtaposing, Tabs participants resorted to less-efficient clicking back and forth between tabs. For example, P7 made 164 of his 187 navigations in back-and-forth sequences. Another participant, P15, made a sequence of 27 navigations in less than 3 minutes flipping between the same two tabs. These navigation actions could have been eliminated if the patches were juxtaposed on screen.

The Signpost Principle

The Signpost Principle emphasizes the importance of having small, concise representations or summaries of open patches that provide sufficient information to quickly make effective navigation decisions. Tabs were the main form of such representations used in the tabbed editor. In contrast, Patchworks used code thumbnails to summarize the contents of VIs in the bird's eye view (recall Fig. 6b).

In many circumstances, tabs did not convey sufficient information for participants to make effective navigation decisions, and as a consequence Tabs participants made numerous navigation mistakes (recall Fig. 9). The problems with tabs were further reinforced in numerous episodes by Tabs participants. For example, P4 had two episodes of "losing" tabs.

> P4: "Where did I put it? ... I lost it."

> P4: "Way too many things open at this point ... Where did it go? ... Nope, I lost it. Now I can't go back because I don't know where I was."

Tabs Participant P18 further expounded on the difficulty of having too many tabs:

> P18: "If I have too many tabs, same issue if I have too many windows, it makes it really small and you can't see the name."

In contrast, Patchworks participants expressed positive impressions of the thumbnail patches in the bird's eye view.

> P25: "You can zoom out, and you can pan out to see what all you actually have open, so that's really helpful, so it resolves the getting-lost-in-a-thousand-VIs thing."

> P2: "I do like that you can zoom out and see everything that you are looking at... Definitely helps."

Two Patchworks participants even drew direct comparisons between the tabbed and the Patchworks designs:

> P5: "Hopefully you name your VIs well so that you can re-navigate [using tabs], but I think with the carousel [Patchworks] it would definitely be an improvement once you got used to it"

> P6: "This is excellent. I like this a lot better than having to go through the list of VIs you have open... It is definitely easier to navigate."

The Blowup Principle

The Blowup Principle emphasizes providing a programmer the ability to efficiently toggle a patch in a multi-patch display into an enlarged "blowup" view. Only the Patchworks editor contained a feature for toggling to a blowup view. Thus, the empirical support for this principle came entirely from the Patchworks participants.

As our empirical results showed, Patchworks participants made substantial use of the blowup-patch feature in tandem with the multi-patch display of the patch grid. For example, P26 toggled into the blowup view 40 times during his session, yet he spent only 26% of his session in this view. Likewise, another participant, P2, commented explicitly on liking to toggle back and forth between the patch grid and blowup view:

> P2: "Easy to zoom in, zoom out, bring it to be full sized [referring to the blowup view] ... It is nice to go back and forth [toggles and untoggles the blowup view repeatedly]."

One popular strategy was to use the blowup view for large, complex VIs. For instance, P26 repeatedly toggled the complex ProcessInput VI into blowup mode, while using the multi-patch display to visit smaller VIs. Similarly, P14 also used the blowup view when she needed to understand complex VIs. She toggled the complex Main VI into a blowup view several times during her session:

> P14: "I'm going to make it 100% of my screen so I can read into it... I'm trying to figure out what is going on in this Main VI."

The Cleanup Principle

The Cleanup Principle emphasizes helping programmers to efficiently close open patches that are cluttering the workspace and are not currently relevant to what the programmer is working on. Implicit in this principle is the idea that relevant patches should not be closed along with the irrelevant ones. Both the tabbed and Patchworks editors had only rudimentary features for closing individual open patches (clicking a button on the tab or patch-cell label, respectively). Thus, for all our participants, regardless of treatment, cleaning up open patches meant closing each selected patch individually.

As our results showed, participants tended to let open patches pile up, and then perform cleanup on groups of patches. For example, P4 became overwhelmed by the number of open patches, and began closing patches:

> P4: "Too many things open right now. I just need to clean it up a bit."

The importance of closing only irrelevant patches was made clear by episodes where participants inadvertently closed relevant ones. If participants closed all of their patches, they almost always began reopening a subset of the patches; however, they often had difficulty finding the right patches to re-open. For example, Tabs Participant P20 had started cleaning up, rapidly closing tabs, but then realized he had accidentally closed the one he wanted:

> P20: "I think I closed the VI by accident."

He then re-opened four of the patches he had just closed in a tedious search for the relevant patch. Thus, helping programmers to perform cleanup *without closing relevant patches* was an important consideration in the Cleanup Principle.

The Heterogeneity Principle

The Heterogeneity Principle emphasizes facilitating programmer navigation among a variety of patch types—beyond only code. In our study, both the tabbed and Patchworks editors treated program output (LabVIEW front panels) as first-class patches similar to the source code (block diagrams). Regardless of the editor used, participants made over a quarter of their navigations to those non-code patches.

A debugging strategy employed by all the Patchworks participants but one was to juxtapose code patches with program-output patches to observe the effect of code changes on run-time values. For example, P9 juxtaposed three block diagrams (code patches) and one front panel (program-output patch). He then repeatedly interacted with the front panel and watched the dataflow propagate through each of the block diagrams in an attempt to determine the cause of an incorrect value. Other Patchworks participants discussed similar strategies:

> P13: "I placed them side by side to see the front panel and diagram, mostly for the Main VI, to see where inputs were going through."

> P16: "I usually had the Main front panel and diagram up, and one or two other diagrams up."

Interestingly, this juxtaposing approach was popular among Tabs participants as well. Although Tab participants rarely juxtaposed, every one of the ten who did, did so to place a code patch alongside a program-output patch. For example, at first, P28 had his tabbed editor in the default single-patch display. He repeatedly switched back and forth between a block diagram (code) tab and a front-panel (program output) tab to observe how values were affected. He repeated this tedious process for nearly 6 minutes before becoming frustrated and reconfiguring his editor to juxtapose the two patches, enabling him to more efficiently navigate between them. Such empirical observations clearly motivate the Heterogeneity Principle's emphasis on non-code patches.

Triangulation with Prior Research

To enhance the credibility and validity of our candidate principles, we triangulated with prior research results. Although the principles were inspired by our empirical study, support for each one could also be found scattered throughout the literature.

Regarding the Juxtaposition Principle, there is support for the idea that programmers want to juxtapose code and doing so enhances their ability to navigate. For example, one study found that programmers expressed wanting to juxtapose code patches [2]; however, similar to our Tabs participants, they rarely do because of the tediousness of juxtaposing patches in tabbed editors, such as Eclipse [2, 4, 25]. In our previous study comparing editors with single-patch and multi-patch displays (Eclipse versus Code Bubbles and Patchworks), participants who used the multi-patch editors navigated significantly faster than those who used the single-patch editor—despite being experienced with the single-patch editor and unfamiliar with the multi-patch ones [15].

Furthermore, the importance of being able to rearrange patches efficiently in multi-patch displays has also been well motivated. For example, Plumlee and Ware [42] have argued convincingly about the inefficiencies of window management. In particular, they found that sizing and positioning windows on screen required users to devote inordinate amounts of time and attention. Efficiency of rearranging patches is of particular importance to programmers, because studies have found that their goals change rapidly during programming tasks [29, 36], thus, suggesting that they will need to rearrange often. However, in modern tabbed code editors, such rearranging is tedious, and as a consequence, programmers rarely do so [4, 25].

Prior research on recognition versus recall has clear implications for the Signpost Principle. It is well known that, in accessing a memory, recognition based on cues in the environment requires humans to do less mental processing than does recalling without such environmental support (e.g., [1]). The Signpost Principle is concerned with being able to quickly remember sufficient information about patches to make effective navigation decisions. Thus, it emphasizes providing programmers with effective opportunities for recognition. Consistent with our study results, prior works have critiqued tabbed editors for the lack of recognition support offered by tabs. For example, they have found tabs to not be representative of their associated patches, and thus, disruptive to associative memory [32, 35]. In fact, one study showed that programmers frequently had to check the content of patches associated with tabs because they could not infer the content from the labels on the tabs [44]. To overcome these issues, thumbnails, similar to those provided by the bird's eye view in the Patchworks editor, have been investigated. For example, thumbnails have been found to effectively support information retrieval by end users [43] and to help programmers navigate large code files and code bases [9]. Recently, such thumbnails have been incorporated into several popular code editors, including Visual Studio and Sublime Text.

In contrast to the above principles, we are unaware of any existing research related to the Blowup Principle; however, blowup-patch features have recently begun to appear in popular code editors. For example, both Eclipse and Visual Studio allow programmers to toggle editor patches to a blowup view. However, these editors are still based on single-patch tabbed editors. In their cases, the main benefit of the blowup view is to overcome the limited screen space afforded to the editor due to a multitude of other panels present in the development environment (e.g., package explorer, console output, outline view, etc.). In fact, the tabbed version of LabVIEW also had many views; however, its designers did not include a blowup feature for editor patches, suggesting that they could have benefited from the Blowup Principle.

Prior research has confirmed the Cleanup Principle, and in particular, the importance of helping programmers clean up only irrelevant code. For example, studies have shown that programmers often close all of their open patches to proceed from a clean slate [11, 34]. Many modern code editors provide "close all" features; however, wiping all tabs has also been found to be problematic, because programmers actually want to keep some of the patches open. For example, one study found that programmers wasted an average of 60 seconds to reopen the patches they wanted after closing too many of them [23]. Others have similarly reported on the costliness of recovering such state after suspending a task due to the loss of contextual cues [18]. However, despite this evidence, tools have yet to provide effective support for selective cleanup.

Support for the Heterogeneity Principle from prior research has mainly focused on the importance of facilitating navigation between code and program output. A primary benefit of enabling such navigation is that it potentially shortens a programmers' feedback loop of running the application, interacting with it, and observing the runtime behavior. For example, the Whyline programming environment allows a programmer to ask questions about a program's output and provides direct links to the relevant code [24]. Another tool, the Theseus programming environment, annotates JavaScript source code with runtime information, thus, combining program code and output into a single patch [31]. Still other tools have provided navigational links between code and other types of artifacts, such as emails and bug reports [48] and related code examples from the web [5]. Such tools further illustrate the potential benefits of considering heterogenous patch types in the design of code editors.

Limitations
Our study had several limitations to generalizability common to laboratory studies of programmers. For example, there is a question as to how well the sample of programmers and tasks in our study represent our target populations. Our participants were unfamiliar with the code base and were given a relatively short amount of time (less than 1 hour) to work; however, they were all professional programmers, increasing the likelihood that they were representative of expert programmers of visual dataflow languages. The code base was also relatively small; however, it was based on an open source example, and the seeded bugs were ones we actually encountered in practice. Finally, we studied only two editor designs, leaving the comparison of other designs for future work.

CONCLUSION
In this paper, we have presented an empirical study comparing the navigation behaviors of professional LabVIEW programmers using two different code-editor interfaces: the ubiquitous tabbed editor and the experimental Patchworks editor. Key findings of our study included the following:

- Patchworks users performed significantly fewer clicks per navigation than users of the tabbed editor.
- Patchworks users juxtaposed patches significantly more than users of the tabbed editor, and as a consequence, also made more highly efficient on-screen navigations.
- Patchworks users exhibited significantly fewer navigation mistakes than users of the tabbed editor.
- All programmers, regardless of editor, tended to let open patches pile up and then clean them up by closing them en masse; however, following such closings, they often had difficulty locating patches they had inadvertently closed.
- All programmers, regardless of editor, frequently navigated between code and program-output patches.
- Like textual language programmers in prior studies, the visual dataflow language programmers in our study exhibited high rates of navigation and frequently revisited patches.

Based on these findings, we proposed five principles for the design of effective navigation affordances in code editors.

Moving forward, we hope that the principles we proposed will help serve as an invaluable resource and foundation for the designers of code editors. There continues to be considerable enthusiasm for the design of new navigation affordances for code editors (e.g., [4, 12, 15, 20, 27]). However, prior to this work, a cohesive set of guidance on the design of these complex, multifaceted interfaces has been sorely lacking. Thus, our proposed principles help fill an important gap that should enable designers to explore imaginative new features while ensuring that the essential navigation needs of programmers continue to be met effectively.

ACKNOWLEDGMENTS
We give special thanks to Andrew Dove for his counsel on all things LabVIEW. This material is based upon work supported by National Instruments and by the National Science Foundation under Grant No. 1302117. Any opinions, findings, and conclusions or recommendations expressed in this material are those of the authors and do not necessarily reflect the views of National Instruments or of the National Science Foundation.

REFERENCES
1. John R. Anderson and Gordon H. Bower. 1972. Recognition and retrieval processes in free recall. *Psychol. Rev.* 79, 2 (March 1972), 97–123.
2. Andrew. Bragdon. 2009. *Creating Simultaneous Views of Source Code in Contemporary IDEs Using Tab Panes and*

MDI Child Windows: A Pilot Study. Technical Report CS-09-09. Brown Univ.

3. Andrew Bragdon, Steven P. Reiss, Robert Zeleznik, Suman Karumuri, William Cheung, Joshua Kaplan, Christopher Coleman, Ferdi Adeputra, and Joseph J. LaViola, Jr. 2010a. Code Bubbles: Rethinking the User Interface Paradigm of Integrated Development Environments. In *Proceedings of the 32nd ACM/IEEE International Conference on Software Engineering - Volume 1 (ICSE '10)*. ACM, New York, NY, USA, 455–464.

4. Andrew Bragdon, Robert Zeleznik, Steven P. Reiss, Suman Karumuri, William Cheung, Joshua Kaplan, Christopher Coleman, Ferdi Adeputra, and Joseph J. LaViola, Jr. 2010b. Code Bubbles: A Working Set-based Interface for Code Understanding and Maintenance. In *Proceedings of the SIGCHI Conference on Human Factors in Computing Systems (CHI '10)*. ACM, New York, NY, USA, 2503–2512.

5. Joel Brandt, Mira Dontcheva, Marcos Weskamp, and Scott R. Klemmer. 2010. Example-centric programming: Integrating Web search into the development environments. In *Proc. 28th Int'l Conf. on Human Factors in Computing Systems (CHI '10)*. ACM, New York, NY, USA, 513–522.

6. Michael J. Coblenz, Andrew J. Ko, and Brad A. Myers. 2006. JASPER: An Eclipse Plug-in to Facilitate Software Maintenance Tasks. In *Proceedings of the 2006 OOPSLA Workshop on Eclipse Technology eXchange (ETX '06)*. ACM, New York, NY, USA, 65–69.

7. National Instruments Corporation. 2008. LabVIEW Calculator. `http://www.ni.com/example/30779/` Accessed: 2017-01-06.

8. National Instruments Corporation. 2017. LabVIEW System Design Software. `http://www.ni.com/labview/` Accessed: 2017-01-06.

9. Robert DeLine, Mary Czerwinski, Brian Meyers, Gina Venolia, Steven Drucker, and George Robertson. 2006. Code Thumbnails: Using Spatial Memory to Navigate Source Code. In *Proceedings of the Visual Languages and Human-Centric Computing (VL/HCC '06)*. IEEE Computer Society, Washington, DC, USA, 11–18.

10. Robert DeLine, Mary Czerwinski, and George Robertson. 2005. Easing Program Comprehension by Sharing Navigation Data. In *Proceedings of the 2005 IEEE Symposium on Visual Languages and Human-Centric Computing (VL/HCC '05)*. IEEE Computer Society, Washington, DC, USA, 241–248.

11. Robert DeLine, Amir Khella, Mary Czerwinski, and George Robertson. 2005. Towards Understanding Programs Through Wear-based Filtering. In *Proceedings of the 2005 ACM Symposium on Software Visualization (SoftVis '05)*. ACM, New York, NY, USA, 183–192.

12. Robert DeLine and Kael Rowan. 2010. Code Canvas: Zooming Towards Better Development Environments. In *Proceedings of the 32nd ACM/IEEE International Conference on Software Engineering - Volume 2 (ICSE '10)*. ACM, New York, NY, USA, 207–210.

13. Martin Ester, Hans-Peter Kriegel, Jörg Sander, and Xiaowei Xu. 1996. A density-based algorithm for discovering clusters in large spatial databases with noise.. In *Proc. 2nd Int'l Conf. Knowledge Discovery and Data Mining (KDD '96)*. 226–231.

14. Thomas Fritz, David C. Shepherd, Katja Kevic, Will Snipes, and Christoph Bräunlich. 2014. Developers' Code Context Models for Change Tasks. In *Proceedings of the 22nd ACM SIGSOFT International Symposium on Foundations of Software Engineering (FSE '14)*. ACM, New York, NY, USA, 7–18.

15. Austin Z. Henley and Scott D. Fleming. 2014. The Patchworks Code Editor: Toward Faster Navigation with Less Code Arranging and Fewer Navigation Mistakes. In *Proceedings of the SIGCHI Conference on Human Factors in Computing Systems (CHI '14)*. ACM, New York, NY, USA, 2511–2520.

16. Austin Z. Henley, A. Singh, Scott D. Fleming, and Maria V. Luong. 2014. Helping programmers navigate code faster with Patchworks: A simulation study. In *Proceedings of the 2014 IEEE Symposium on Visual Languages and Human-Centric Computing (VL/HCC '14)*. 77–80.

17. Eric Horvitz. 1999. Principles of Mixed-initiative User Interfaces. In *Proceedings of the SIGCHI Conference on Human Factors in Computing Systems (CHI '99)*. ACM, New York, NY, USA, 159–166.

18. Shamsi T. Iqbal and Eric Horvitz. 2007. Disruption and Recovery of Computing Tasks: Field Study, Analysis, and Directions. In *Proceedings of the SIGCHI Conference on Human Factors in Computing Systems (CHI '07)*. ACM, New York, NY, USA, 677–686.

19. W. Jernigan, A. Horvath, M. Lee, M. Burnett, T. Cuilty, S. Kuttal, A. Peters, I. Kwan, F. Bahmani, and A. Ko. 2015. A principled evaluation for a principled Idea Garden. In *Proc. 2015 IEEE Symposium on Visual Languages and Human-Centric Computing (VL/HCC '15)*. 235–243.

20. Thorsten Karrer, Jan-Peter Krämer, Jonathan Diehl, Björn Hartmann, and Jan Borchers. 2011. Stacksplorer: Call Graph Navigation Helps Increasing Code Maintenance Efficiency. In *Proceedings of the 24th Annual ACM Symposium on User Interface Software and Technology (UIST '11)*. ACM, New York, NY, USA, 217–224.

21. Mik Kersten and Gail C. Murphy. 2006. Using Task Context to Improve Programmer Productivity. In *Proceedings of the 14th ACM SIGSOFT International Symposium on Foundations of Software Engineering (FSE '06)*. ACM, New York, NY, USA, 1–11.

22. Katja Kevic, Braden M. Walters, Timothy R. Shaffer, Bonita Sharif, David C. Shepherd, and Thomas Fritz. 2015. Tracing Software Developers' Eyes and Interactions for Change Tasks. In *Proceedings of the 2015 10th Joint Meeting on Foundations of Software Engineering (ESEC/FSE 2015)*. ACM, New York, NY, USA, 202–213.
23. Andrew J. Ko, Htet Aung, and Brad A. Myers. 2005. Eliciting Design Requirements for Maintenance-oriented IDEs: A Detailed Study of Corrective and Perfective Maintenance Tasks. In *Proceedings of the 27th International Conference on Software Engineering (ICSE '05)*. ACM, New York, NY, USA, 126–135.
24. Andrew J. Ko and Brad A. Myers. 2009. Finding Causes of Program Output with the Java Whyline. In *Proceedings of the SIGCHI Conference on Human Factors in Computing Systems (CHI '09)*. ACM, New York, NY, USA, 1569–1578.
25. Andrew J. Ko, Brad A. Myers, Michael J. Coblenz, and Htet Htet Aung. 2006. An Exploratory Study of How Developers Seek, Relate, and Collect Relevant Information during Software Maintenance Tasks. *IEEE Trans. Softw. Eng.* 32, 12 (Dec. 2006), 971–987.
26. Jan-Peter Krämer, Thorsten Karrer, Joachim Kurz, Moritz Wittenhagen, and Jan Borchers. 2013. How Tools in IDEs Shape Developers' Navigation Behavior. In *Proceedings of the SIGCHI Conference on Human Factors in Computing Systems (CHI '13)*. ACM, New York, NY, USA, 3073–3082.
27. Jan-Peter Krämer, Joachim Kurz, Thorsten Karrer, and Jan Borchers. 2012. Blaze: Supporting Two-phased Call Graph Navigation in Source Code. In *CHI '12 Extended Abstracts on Human Factors in Computing Systems (CHI EA '12)*. ACM, New York, NY, USA, 2195–2200.
28. Todd Kulesza, Margaret Burnett, Weng-Keen Wong, and Simone Stumpf. 2015. Principles of Explanatory Debugging to Personalize Interactive Machine Learning. In *Proceedings of the 20th International Conference on Intelligent User Interfaces (IUI '15)*. ACM, New York, NY, USA, 126–137.
29. Joseph Lawrance, Margaret Burnett, Rachel Bellamy, Christopher Bogart, and Calvin Swart. 2010. Reactive Information Foraging for Evolving Goals. In *Proceedings of the SIGCHI Conference on Human Factors in Computing Systems (CHI '10)*. ACM, New York, NY, USA, 25–34.
30. Michael J. Lee, Faezeh Bahmani, Irwin Kwan, Jilian LaFerte, Polina Charters, Amber Horvath, Fanny Luor, Jill Cao, Catherine Law, Michael Beswetherick, Sheridan Long, Margaret Burnett, and Andrew J. Ko. 2014. Principles of a debugging-first puzzle game for computing education. In *Proceedings of the 2014 IEEE Symposium on Visual Languages and Human-Centric Computing (VL/HCC '14)*. 57–64.
31. Tom Lieber, Joel R. Brandt, and Rob C. Miller. 2014. Addressing Misconceptions About Code with Always-on Programming Visualizations. In *Proceedings of the SIGCHI Conference on Human Factors in Computing Systems (CHI '14)*. ACM, New York, NY, USA, 2481–2490.
32. Chris Parnin and Robert DeLine. 2010. Evaluating Cues for Resuming Interrupted Programming Tasks. In *Proceedings of the SIGCHI Conference on Human Factors in Computing Systems (CHI '10)*. ACM, New York, NY, USA, 93–102.
33. Chris Parnin and Carsten Görg. 2006. Building Usage Contexts During Program Comprehension. In *Proc. 14th IEEE Int'l Conf. Program Comprehension (ICPC '06)*. 13–22.
34. Chris Parnin, Carsten Görg, and Spencer Rugaber. 2010. CodePad: Interactive Spaces for Maintaining Concentration in Programming Environments. In *Proceedings of the 5th International Symposium on Software Visualization (SOFTVIS '10)*. ACM, New York, NY, USA, 15–24.
35. Chris Parnin and Spencer Rugaber. 2012. Programmer information needs after memory failure. In *Proc. 20th IEEE Int'l Conf. Program Comprehension (ICPC '12)*. 123–132.
36. David Piorkowski, Scott Fleming, Christopher Scaffidi, Christopher Bogart, Margaret Burnett, Bonnie John, Rachel Bellamy, and Calvin Swart. 2012. Reactive information foraging: An empirical investigation of theory-based recommender systems for programmers. In *Proc. ACM SIGCHI Conf. Human Factors in Computing Systems (CHI '12)*. ACM, New York, NY, USA, 1471–1480.
37. David Piorkowski, Scott D. Fleming, Christopher Scaffidi, Margaret Burnett, Irwin Kwan, Austin Z. Henley, Jamie Macbeth, Charles Hill, and Amber Horvath. 2015. To Fix or to Learn? How Production Bias Affects Developers' Information Foraging during Debugging. In *31st IEEE International Conference on Software Maintenance and Evolution (ICSME '15)*. 11–20.
38. David Piorkowski, Scott D. Fleming, Christopher Scaffidi, Liza John, Christopher Bogart, Bonnie E. John, Margaret Burnett, and Rachel Bellamy. 2011. Modeling programmer navigation: A head-to-head empirical evaluation of predictive models. In *Proceedings of the 2011 IEEE Symposium on Visual Languages and Human-Centric Computing (VL/HCC '11)*. 109–116.
39. David Piorkowski, Austin Z. Henley, Tahmid Nabi, Scott D. Fleming, Christopher Scaffidi, and Margaret Burnett. 2016. Foraging and Navigations, Fundamentally: Developers' Predictions of Value and Cost. In *Proceedings of the 24th ACM SIGSOFT International Symposium on Foundations of Software Engineering (FSE 2016)*. ACM, New York, NY, USA, 97–108.

40. David J. Piorkowski, Scott D. Fleming, Irwin Kwan, Margaret M. Burnett, Christopher Scaffidi, Rachel K.E. Bellamy, and Joshua Jordahl. 2013. The Whats and Hows of Programmers' Foraging Diets. In *Proceedings of the SIGCHI Conference on Human Factors in Computing Systems (CHI '13)*. ACM, 3063–3072.

41. Peter Pirolli and Stuart Card. 1999. Information Foraging. *Psychological Review* 106, 4 (1999), 643–675.

42. Matthew D. Plumlee and Colin Ware. 2006. Zooming Versus Multiple Window Interfaces: Cognitive Costs of Visual Comparisons. *ACM Trans. Comput.-Hum. Interact.* 13, 2 (June 2006), 179–209.

43. George Robertson, Mary Czerwinski, Kevin Larson, Daniel C. Robbins, David Thiel, and Maarten van Dantzich. 1998. Data Mountain: Using Spatial Memory for Document Management. In *Proceedings of the 11th Annual ACM Symposium on User Interface Software and Technology (UIST '98)*. ACM, New York, NY, USA, 153–162.

44. Janice Singer, Robert Elves, and Margaret-Anne Storey. 2005. NavTracks: Supporting Navigation in Software Maintenance. In *Proceedings of the 21st IEEE International Conference on Software Maintenance (ICSM '05)*. IEEE Computer Society, Washington, DC, USA, 325–334.

45. Alka Singh, Austin Z. Henley, Scott D. Fleming, and Maria V. Luong. 2016. An Empirical Evaluation of Models of Programmer Navigation. In *IEEE Int'l Conference on Software Maintenance and Evolution (ICSME '16)*. 9–19.

46. Randall B. Smith, John Maloney, and David Ungar. 1995. The Self-4.0 User Interface: Manifesting a System-wide Vision of Concreteness, Uniformity, and Flexibility. In *Proceedings of the Tenth Annual Conference on Object-oriented Programming Systems, Languages, and Applications (OOPSLA '95)*. ACM, New York, NY, USA, 47–60.

47. Jared M. Spool, Christine Perfetti, and David Brittan. 2004. *Designing for the Scent of Information*. User Interface Engineering, Middleton, MA.

48. Davor Čubranić, Gail C. Murphy, Janice Singer, and Kellogg S. Booth. 2005. Hipikat: A Project Memory for Software Development. *IEEE Trans. Softw. Eng.* 31, 6 (2005), 446–465.

49. Kirsten N. Whitley, Laura R. Novick, and Doug Fisher. 2006. Evidence in Favor of Visual Representation for the Dataflow Paradigm: An Experiment Testing LabVIEW's Comprehensibility. *Int. J. Hum.-Comput. Stud.* 64, 4 (April 2006), 281–303.

Follow-My-Lead: Intuitive Indoor Path Creation and Navigation Using Interactive Videos

Quentin Roy [1], Simon T. Perrault [2], Shengdong Zhao [3], Richard C. Davis [4], Anuroop Pattena Vaniyar [1], Velko Vechev [3,5], Youngki Lee [1], Archan Misra [1]

[1] Singapore Management University, Singapore [2] Yale-NUS College, Singapore
[3] NUS-HCI Lab, National University of Singapore, Singapore
[4] Act8 Design Pte. Ltd., Singapore,
[5] Chalmers University of Technology, Gothenburg, Sweden

quentin@quentinroy.fr, simon.perrault@yale-nus.edu.sg, zhaosd@comp.nus.edu.sg, rcdavis@act8design.com, anurooppv@smu.edu.sg, velko.vechev@gmail.com, youngkilee@smu.edu.sg, archanm@smu.edu.sg

Anna is organizing a talk on her university's campus. | As she arrives, she records the path **leading** to the room using *FML*. | Bob arrives later. First, he is disoriented. | Then, he realizes Anna sent him an *FML* path. | He **follows** it and reaches the room quickly and easily.

Figure 1. *Follow-My-Lead* (FML) scenario. Drawings ©Marie Dorso.

ABSTRACT
We present *Follow-My-Lead*, an alternative indoor navigation technique that uses visual information recorded on an actual navigation path as a navigational guide. Its design revealed a trade-off between the fidelity of information provided to users and their effort to acquire it. Our first experiment revealed that scrolling through a continuous image stream of the navigation path is highly informative, but it becomes tedious with constant use. Discrete image checkpoints require less effort, but can be confusing. A balance may be struck by adding fast video transitions between image checkpoints, but precise control is required to handle difficult situations. Authoring still image checkpoints is also difficult, and this inspired us to invent a new technique using video checkpoints. We conducted a second experiment on authoring and navigation performance and found video checkpoints plus fast video transitions to be better than both image checkpoints plus fast video transitions and traditional written instructions.

CHI 2017, May 06-11, 2017, Denver, CO, USA
© 2017 ACM. ISBN 978-1-4503-4655-9/17/05...$15.00
DOI: http://dx.doi.org/10.1145/3025453.3025976

ACM Classification Keywords
H.5.2. User Interfaces (D.2.2, H.1.2, I.3.6): Interaction styles (e.g., commands, menus, forms, direct manipulation)

Author Keywords
Indoor Navigation; Mobile Computing; Smartglasses; Video; Wearable Computing; Leader-Follower; Egocentric Visual Navigation.

INTRODUCTION
Way-finding remains a complicated but essential task in many urban environments. Traditionally, users rely on maps and signs to orient themselves in unfamiliar outdoor environments, a task known to be difficult [16, 36]. Today, however, outdoor navigation has many viable commercial *You are Here* solutions, e.g. Google or Apple Maps, that offer fast and convenient guidance and have been universally adopted by mobile users [25].

In contrast, user-friendly indoor navigation continues to be a challenging problem, with commercial solutions being limited in scale and coverage. Google Indoor Maps, for example, currently covers about 10,000 locations, a tiny sliver of commercial buildings worldwide [54]. Indoor navigation poses two widely recognized challenges. First, GPS is less reliable indoors and localization requires additional infrastructure (e.g., WiFi APs or BLE beacons). Second, most buildings do not have up-to-date floorplans that are readily available [28].

Other challenges include the need for 3-D wayfinding [23] and the higher complexity of indoor vs. outdoor environments. Consequently, indoor navigation systems that show a user's location on a map are likely to be rare for some time.

We present *Follow-My-Lead* (*FML*), an alternative solution to indoor navigation. Unlike previous approaches, *FML* needs neither localization nor maps. Thus, it makes no assumptions about the user's environment or infrastructure support, does not require any particular data, and can be used anywhere. To meet this goal, *FML* relies on a leader-follower approach [43] and implements an *egocentric visual navigation* strategy [11,21]. A leader walks through the entire path once and captures what followers should see along the route. Followers navigate by comparing the views presented by *FML* (Figure 2) to what they see in the real world. The system is fully functional on a mobile phone, but it has been designed to be used with a head-mounted camera and display (i.e. smartglasses) controlled through a smartwatch or a smartphone in a cross-device fashion.

Though egocentric visual navigation has been investigated before, our work shows that the interaction design is not straightforward. On one extreme, scrolling through a continuous image stream – a technique we call *Continuous Flow* (*CF*) – allows followers to reach their destination with few errors, but it also requires continuous interaction and attention. This quickly becomes tedious and can make it difficult for followers to maintain proper situational awareness. At the opposite extreme, our results show that a succession of still images [5,11,21] – a technique we call *Image Checkpoints* (*IC*) – requires much less interaction and attention, but is hard to follow. To mitigate both drawbacks, we designed an intermediate solution that we call *Image Checkpoints + Fast Forwarding* (*IC+FF*). This third technique relies on image checkpoints, but illustrates transitions by playing the path video between checkpoints at high speed. This technique strikes a balance between the extremes, giving followers richer information while reducing their effort to acquire it. However, precise control remains required to deal with complicated segments.

Also, our investigations show that selecting the right set of checkpoints can be challenging for the leader, who must author this path. Consequently, we modified *Image Checkpoints + Fast Forwarding* to develop an alternative approach, called *Video Checkpoints + Fast Forwarding* (*VC+FF*). Using this technique, leaders have the ability to mark a segment of the path as a checkpoint. Video checkpoints ease the pressure on leaders to capture a single right image, and they turn out to be more helpful to followers as well.

To our knowledge, this is the first time that the development of egocentric visual paths has been studied from the perspective of both *authoring* and *following*. Our key contributions include:

1. An efficient indoor navigation system, based on egocentric visual guides, that works anywhere, requiring neither floor plans nor infrastructural support,
2. An exploration of four alternative egocentric visual navigation strategies and their trade-offs in terms of (1) fidelity of the leader's path to the follower's view, (2) effort required to follow paths, and (3) effort required to author paths.
3. Empirical evidence collected through two experiments: one with twelve participants and three tasks that shows the benefits of *IC+FF* for followers, and another with 18 participants and three tasks that shows the benefits of *VC+FF* for both leaders and followers.

RELATED WORK

Indoor Localization

In outdoor settings, localization is typically performed using either GPS [18] or via triangulation of cell tower signals [7]. Both approaches are highly unreliable indoors [50].

Strategically installing localization artifacts inside buildings is generally the most accurate strategy for indoor localization. Radio Frequency Identifier Description (RFID) [35,53] and infrared [1,49] tend to be used most often in the literature. Other systems make use of ultrasound [39,50], RF beacons [26,39], Bluetooth beacons [24,47] or even visual markers (e.g. barcodes) to be scanned [2,34,44]. As these approaches rely on enhancing the environment with new equipment, installing and maintaining this equipment can be expensive, and each organization (e.g. museum, airport, or university) must make its own investment.

Another approach is to record and process the signal of wireless local area networks (WLAN) to determine user location [3,17,56], e.g. RADAR [3]. However, the precision can vary, in particular due to multipath issues and signal similarity (i.e., *fingerprinting ambiguity*) [2,39,54].

Visual localization approaches make use of computer vision to correlate images taken from the pedestrian's device with localized reference images from a database [54,55,57]. However, reference images can easily be missed on the way, particularly if the user is not invested in the reference matching task. Visual localization user interfaces may need to be adapted to encourage users to help the system [31].

Finally, dead-reckoning solutions incrementally calculate users' location by aggregating the data of movement sensors (e.g. accelerometers or pedometers) since the last known location [19,28,42,43]. However, the sensor data is noisy and needs to be carefully processed [19]. Also, as the localization is an incremental process, errors accumulate over time (*drift* effect). As a result, these techniques often suffer from poor accuracy and landmark-based corrections are occasionally needed to recover from drift [48].

Despite more than a decade of research, indoor localization has still seen very limited deployment [54]. Our approach, based on the leader-follower paradigm, does not need underlying location support [4] and thus dispenses with the usual assumption that indoor localization will soon be widespread.

Indoor Navigation Guides

Maps are by far the most widespread outdoor navigation guides [1, 2, 25, 32], but they are sometimes difficult to read [16, 36], even when they indicate the user's location (*You-Are-Here* maps) [25]. Indoor navigation in single-floor buildings is often even more complicated [6,40], and the complexity grows when one has to move from floor to floor [23]. Moreover, floor plans are often not available: Google Indoor Maps, arguably the largest indoor maps database, only covers about 10,000 locations worldwide, which remains a "tiny fraction of millions of shopping malls, museums, and airports worldwide" [54], not to mention universities and office campuses.

Instructions, e.g. turn-by-turn instructions telling the user what he should see and do at each step [10], are another common navigation guide. Instructions are generally textual [5,20,21], pictographic [10,33] or audio [20,22]. Pure activity-based instructions (e.g. directions to take, distance to walk, stairs to climb, etc) [10,33] can sometime be automatically inferred by a computer from sensor data [10,41]. Instructions that include landmark clues (e.g. *Pass the door X23, cross the open-space*) [9,20] are preferred [30] but need to be created manually.

In addition, the use of vibrations to give instructions has been the focus of much research work. "Shoulder-tapping" approaches use the location of the vibration (e.g. left wrist) to induce the user to take a turn [8,45,46]. Pielot et al. instead used temporal patterns to indicate direction [38], which only requires one actuator. Vibrations are relatively unobtrusive compared to visual navigation: users remain free to concentrate their sight on their surroundings. However, vibrations have been found to be less-efficient than GPS-based personal navigation devices for pedestrians [37].

Egocentric visual navigation relies on giving users imagery of what they should be seeing along the way [5,11,12,17,21,51,55]. A major advantage of this approach is the visibility of landmarks [5,12], by far the most preferred type of navigation cues [30]. Many of these systems provide a sequence of images at strategic locations along the path [5,11,20]. Some systems adjust the visual perspective of landmark images automatically based on the orientation of users' mobile devices, but these approaches have been evaluated primarily outdoors and require manual curation of geotagged landmark image corpora [21]. Some use video instead of images [11,12], but since the video speed seldom matches users' preferred walking speed, many users view videos before starting to move. Wenig et al. addressed this by having users manually scroll through a stream of images displayed on a watch [51]. In studies, egocentric visual navigation has proven efficient for people with cognitive disabilities [11,27] and for aging populations [20]. Compared to maps without localization, egocentric visual navigation has been shown to be more useful, easier to use, less cognitively demanding, and less stressful for younger populations with no disability [55].

FOLLOW MY LEAD

The *Follow-My-Lead* (*FML*) project aims to develop a realistic indoor navigation tool that can be used today in any building. This implies that we cannot rely on new infrastructure (e.g. RF beacons) or new data (e.g. buildings maps, which are often unavailable).

Figure 2. ***Follow-My-Lead*'s display with the *Video Checkpoints + Fast Forwarding* technique. The blue areas on the progress bar at the top represent checkpoints.**

The scenario represented in Figure 1 illustrates a common situation in indoor navigation. Using *FML*, Anna can easily create a path to any meeting's location and distribute it to attendees, and Bob can find his way without additional assistance.

Approach

To meet these constraints, we opted for a leader-follower approach [43,57]: a *leader* creates a path and sends it to *followers* to help them reach the destination. We formulated two main design goals for *FML*:

1. A follower should be able to efficiently and easily follow a path.
2. A leader should be able to create a high-quality path quickly, ideally by walking the path only once.

Our work is inspired by previous work that leveraged images of landmarks to enhance navigation [5,11,21,55]. We pushed this concept to the extreme and rely exclusively on *egocentric visual navigation*: followers are provided with an interactive display of what they should be seeing all along the way. Hence, followers' navigation strategy is to follow the interactive display by comparing it to the real world. As our experiments will show, a careful balance of trade-offs in the design of this interactive display can make this approach easy and efficient for both leaders and followers alike.

Apparatus

We envision a future where wearable devices are widespread and interconnected, allowing cross-device interactions [13,14]. With this in mind, while our implementation is fully functional on a single smartphone, we designed both leader and follower interfaces to be viewed on smartglasses and controlled through smartphones or smartwatches. The camera of the smartglasses can accurately and effortlessly capture what leaders see along their path. In contrast, holding a smartphone at eye level while walking can be tiresome. For followers, manipulating a smartphone on the go usually means walking "head-down", which reduces awareness of their surroundings [8]. Instead, a head-mounted display enables them to rapidly switch their focus between the display and the real world without any head movement.

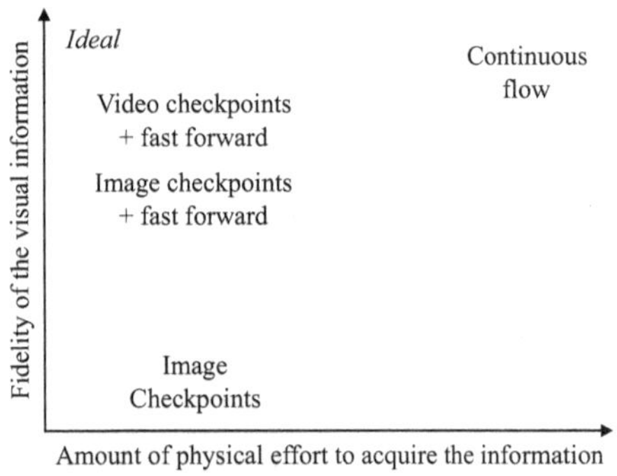

Figure 3. The fidelity / effort trade-off. Fidelity to the follower's view depends on the quantity of images shown, how informative those images are (assuming leaders select meaningful checkpoints), and when images appear. Physical effort is estimated by how much interaction a technique requires.

Design for Following: Fidelity versus Effort

Our early efforts focused on designing the information display for followers. Our prototypes and pilots revealed a relationship between two essential properties: the *fidelity* of the path information, and the *effort* needed to navigate through it. We say path information is high-fidelity if it is close to what a follower actually sees, and we say it is low-fidelity if visual imagery is sparse, poorly chosen, or shown at the wrong time. Similarly, navigation effort is low if it is automatic and high if it takes constant interaction. In the absence of automatic positioning, these properties are linked. For example, a continuous image stream of the leader's view provides high fidelity, but it requires high effort to synchronize the images with the follower's view. At the opposite extreme, a path with a few images may take little effort to step through, but it has such low fidelity to the follower's view that it may be hard to follow. To explore this trade-off, we designed our first two techniques at opposite ends of this design space (Figure 3): *Image Checkpoints* provide a low-fidelity path view and requires little user interaction, while *Continuous Flow* provides a full recording of the leader's view but requires continuous interaction while navigating. We then designed a third technique, *Image Checkpoints + Fast Forwarding*, as a compromise between the two.

All techniques are designed to be manipulable without the need to remove one's eyes from the route.

Image Checkpoints (IC)

Using image checkpoints to mark important steps on a route is a straightforward navigation solution proposed several times in the literature [5, 21, 27], though rarely as a self-sufficient navigation method [11]. Leaders can easily record checkpoints by taking snapshots as they walk. Following these checkpoints requires very little interaction: after reaching one checkpoint, followers switch to the next with a single action. However, the ease of finding the next checkpoint depends on how well the leader chose it. If the next checkpoint is not clearly visible from the current one, followers may get lost.

With our system, when a smartwatch is present, followers tap on the watch to go to the next checkpoint or press and hold for 330ms to go back to the previous one. When running on a smartphone, followers use the volume buttons (up = next, down = previous). This is similar to a technique from Chang et al. developed for cognitively impaired users, but we add simple controls to remove the need for localization technology [11].

Continuous Flow (CF)

At the opposite end of the spectrum, our second design displays the totality of the leader's view from beginning to end. Followers *scroll* through the entire image stream and can precisely adjust the progress of the video to their pace and exact location on the route.

Since recording the path requires no action other than walking the route, the quality of the path is less dependent on the leader. However, the information is raw and unfiltered, and some of it may be distracting (e.g. turning to greet someone) or uninformative (e.g. slow walks down long corridors). It is the follower's responsibility to find the most relevant segments, such as turns and intersections.

When using a smartwatch for input, followers scroll using circular gestures around the bezel of the watch, as in the Cyclostar approach [29]. When using a smartphone, followers scroll by dragging on the touch screen. (Note: While this paper was being written, Wenig et al. proposed a similar approach for smartwatches [52].)

Image Checkpoints + Fast Forwarding (IC+FF)

We designed *IC+FF* to be a compromise between the two other techniques. Like *IC*, it relies on a succession of checkpoints chosen by the leader. However, the transition between two checkpoints is shown as a high speed video. We empirically determined that playing the video at 15 times the original speed kept the transition short while ensuring that it was easily intelligible. With this design, followers receive all the information they received in *CF*, but with a greater focus on the parts that the leader believed to be most relevant. The fidelity of this display is only slightly lower than *CF*, while the ease of interaction for the follower is equivalent to *IC*. The controls for this design are also identical to *IC*.

IC+FF resembles another technique from Chang et al. [11], but our image flow is faster and we added controls. Our conceptual model is also slightly different: Chang et al. make use of series of video prompts while *IC+FF* is a single video of the path that is paused at strategic locations.

Display

In our experiments, we used the Epson Moverio BT-200 smart glasses, which puts the display at the center of the user's vision. Ideally, the display should appear at the bottom or the right [15]. However, most of today's mobile head mounted displays have a limited field of view and little or no control over the placement of the display. We expect the next generation to overcome this limitation. In case of discomfort, we allowed users to hide the display by tapping the watch with two fingers or or by pressing both of the phone's volume buttons simultaneously. However, our participants rarely used this feature in our experiments.

Design for authoring

Our later efforts focused on path creation. Our first experiment showed that the *IC+FF* technique was promising, but that choosing a good set of image checkpoints can be challenging. Choosing well is important, as previous work shows that poor choice of landmark images makes a path hard to follow [5,21, 27]. This problem inspired a fourth design.

Video Checkpoints + Fast Forwarding (VC+FF)

With *VC+FF*, instead of taking image snapshots for checkpoints, leaders can record a whole segment of the path as a video checkpoint. This recording can include audio, giving the leader an opportunity to point out important details by speaking. As with *IC+FF*, the follower's display will show less relevant segments of the route as high-speed (15×) videos, while the video checkpoints will be shown at normal speed. While video checkpoints may take slightly longer to watch and might slow down the follower, they provide more information and reduce pressure on the leaders to choose the right image. For example, instead of wondering when to put a checkpoint to represent a turn, a leader may record the whole turning movement as a video checkpoint. To our best knowledge, there are no techniques similar to *VC+FF* in existing literature.

Authoring

To create a path, a leader need only record the route and indicate where checkpoints should be. We designed *FML*'s authoring tool so that both are captured in parallel: leaders mark checkpoints while they walk the route. Hence, no post-processing is required, creating a path is fast, and the authoring interface is minimal.

When using a smartphone, we again relied on volume buttons so the interface could easily be used eyes-free. In the case of *IC* and *IC+FF*, a checkpoint is recorded when a button is released. In the case of *VC+FF*, checkpoints are recorded while a button is being pressed. When using a smartwatch, in the case of *IC* and *IC+FF*, a checkpoint is recorded with a tap on the display. In the case of *VC+FF*, a first tap starts the recording of a video checkpoint, and a second tap ends it.

EXPERIMENT 1: FOLLOWERS' CONTROL STRATEGY

In our first experiment, we explored the trade-off between fidelity to the follower's view and the effort needed to explore the path (see Figure 3). We compared the *Continuous Flow* (*CF*) and *Image Checkpoints* (*IC*) techniques, located at two different extremes of the scale, and the *Image Checkpoints + Fast Forwarding* (*IC+FF*) technique, an in-between design.

We hypothesized that *CF* would allow users to follow paths with minimal cognitive load, but would quickly become uncomfortable due to the constant interaction required. We also hypothesized that *IC* would be cognitively demanding, because it only provides partial information, though it requires little interaction. We thought *IC+FF* would be a good compromise between these two techniques.

Path Creation

Path creation was a critical step in our experimental design. Each participant can follow a path only once. Thus, we had to create equivalent paths in terms of length and difficulty.

Positioning checkpoints was another critical aspect, as bad checkpoint positioning has an impact on path difficulty [5,21, 27]. After multiple tests and pilots, we defined four following rules: (1) checkpoints should contain at least one salient feature (e.g. sign, window...); (2) it should always be possible to see the next checkpoint from the current checkpoint; (3) there should be one checkpoint before and after each turn, staircase or door; (4) there should be no more than 30 seconds between checkpoints.

We used pilots to assess the equivalence of the routes under each *Technique* and iterated to obtain a set of routes that met our criteria. The routes were created on the campus of the National University of Singapore (NUS). All were confined to pedestrian areas, mostly indoors, and approximately 250 meters long.

Participants

Twelve participants were recruited from Singapore Management University (SMU) students and staff (5 females) aged 18 to 30 years old ($M = 22.6$, $SD = 3.8$). They received the equivalent of 7.4 USD for their participation. They were all in good physical condition. The experiment was conducted on the campus of NUS, and all participants declared that it was their first time on campus.

Apparatus

The experimental software was run on Epson Moverio BT-200 smart glasses and a Huawei Watch. The watch was worn on the non-dominant wrist and participants used its touch screen to input commands to the system. Additionally, we used a Samsung Galaxy S7 Edge to connect the glasses and the watch together.

Task

Participants were asked to use our system to follow three different paths using the three different techniques. They were instructed to balance speed and accuracy to reach the destination as quickly as they could while still taking as few wrong turns as possible. They could walk rapidly but were not allowed to run (for safety reasons).

Procedure

Participants began the experiment by filling out a demographic questionnaire. We then described the whole experiment and led them to a training path, where participants tried each of the three techniques on different ~100 meter segments. After training, participants completed the three experimental paths, each with a specific technique. Finally, they filled out a post-experimental questionnaire where they gave subjective feedback.

The experiment was run during week days, and paths were not blocked. Crowd size was random and usually varied from 5 to 50 persons on the way.

Design

We used a within-subjects design with one independent variable: *Technique {CF, IC, IC+FF}*. Our design was fully counterbalanced: three paths were created, and each technique

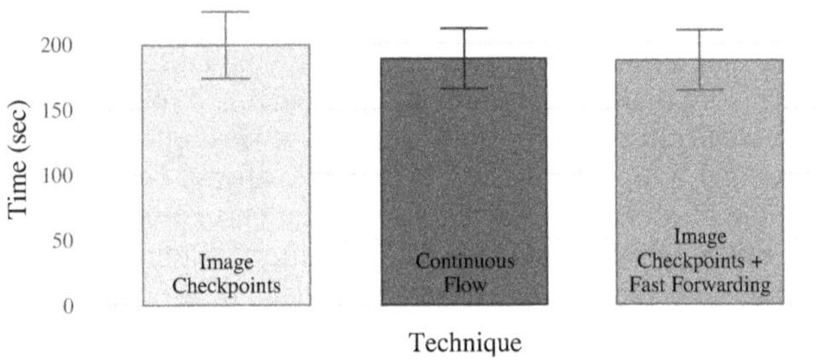

Figure 4. Total path time. Error bars show .95 confidence intervals.

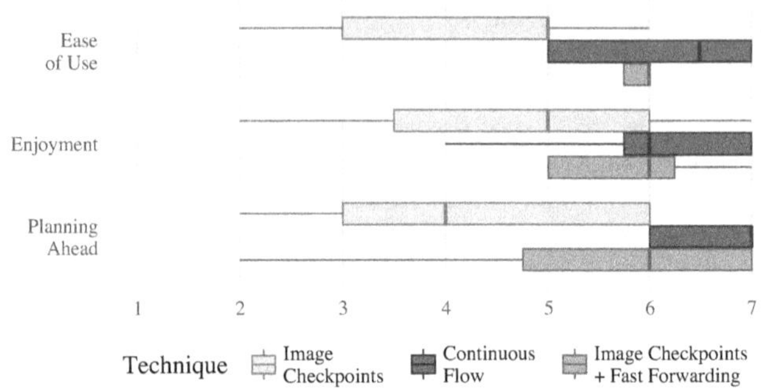

Figure 5. Subjective Feedback by Technique. Each box shows the 25th and 75th percentiles with the median as a bold line. The whiskers show min and max values.

was used on each path four times. We measured time and errors as dependent variables. Time was measured from when a participant started a path to when they reached the destination. Errors were counted if the user went the wrong way for more than two seconds. In case of such errors, participants were asked to correct their path.

Each participant took approximately 1 hour 30 minutes to complete the experiment. Participants were allowed to take breaks between each trial. We recorded 12 participants $\times$ 3 techniques = 36 trials.

Results

All measurements were taken manually by an experimenter following the participant. We recorded the total time to reach the destination, the number of hesitations and the number of errors (i.e. when a participant took a wrong direction). Note: for ANOVA, we applied Greenhouse Geisser correction when the sphericity assumption was violated.

Homogeneity of the Paths

Since our experiment required it, we checked to ensure that our three paths were equivalent in terms of length and completion time. The average path completion times were 192s, 195s, and 186s. A one-way ANOVA did not show any significant effect of *Path* on completion time ($p = .17$), suggesting that the three paths we created for this experiment were roughly equivalent.

Total time

Total path time results are shown in Figure 4. The average time to complete a path was 191 seconds, which suggests an average walking speed of 4.7 km/h. A one-way ANOVA showed a significant main effect of the *Technique* on Total Time ($F_{1.62,17.92} = 5.39, p = .019$). *IC+FF* was the fastest technique (M = 187s), closely followed by *CF* (M = 188 s) and *IC* (M = 199 s). Pairwise t-tests with Bonferroni corrections showed that *IC+FF* was significantly faster than *IC* ($p < .05$). No other significant differences were found.

Errors

As mentioned earlier, errors were counted when participants went the wrong way for more than two seconds, after which they were asked to correct their path. Overall, participants performed an average of 0.47 errors/trial, with 0.33 errors/trial for *IC+FF*, 0.42 for *CF* and 0.66 for *IC*. A Cochran Q test did not show any effect of *Technique* on the number of errors ($p > .05$).

Subjective Feedback

We asked our participants to rate their experience with each technique, using a 7-point Likert scale on (a) how easy they found the technique to use, (b) how much they enjoyed using it and (c) if they were able to plan ahead when using it. We performed statistical analysis on the results for each question using Friedman tests and pairwise Wilcoxon signed ranks tests with Bonferroni correction as a post-hoc test. The general feedback for each affirmation was very positive, with no technique scoring lower than 4.17 on average (see Figure 5).

Ease of Use. We observed a significant effect of *Technique* on participants' rating ($\chi^2(2) = 17.59, p < .001$). Post-hoc comparisons also showed a significant difference between *IC* ($M = 4.17/7$) and the two other techniques ($p < .01$ in both cases, $M = 6.17/7$ for *CF* and $5.75/7$ for *IC+FF*).

Enjoyment. Overall, participants enjoyed the three techniques ($M = 5.38/7$), and we observed a significant main effect of Technique on Enjoyment ($\chi^2(2) = 7.75, p = .02$). *CF* received the highest rating ($M = 6/7$), followed by *IC+FF* ($M = 5.58/7$) and *IC* ($M = 4.58/7$). *CF* received a significantly better rating than *IC* ($p < .05$).

Planning Ahead. On average, participants declared that they were able to plan ahead using our techniques ($M = 5.3/7$). *Technique* had an effect on the rating ($\chi^2(2) = 17.6, p < .0001$). *CF* received the best ($M = 6.25/7$), followed by *IC+FF* ($M = 5.5/7$). Both scored significantly better than *IC* ($M = 4.17/7$, both $p < .01$).

Feedback and Discussion

Based on objective and subjective measures, the *IC* technique appears weaker than the other two: it is slower and participants rated it lower. Participants reported that the technique suffers from a "*lack of details*" (P8) and that one "*can get lost easily as it doesn't show you how to get to the next checkpoint*" (P5). This validates our initial hypothesis, and we chose not to pursue this technique any further.

Our followers were overall faster with *IC+FF* and *CF*, and the subjective feedback does not significantly differ between the two. Thus, both seem viable.

In the light of the Effort/Information trade-off, the limited interaction using *IC+FF* was appreciated. P1 stated that *IC+FF* "*was much simpler for me and convenient as I do not have to continuously scroll on my smart watch (a simple tap would bring me a step forward) and it shows me a path to walk instead of just screenshots like the IC technique*". P4 also mentioned that it was "*a good balance between [IC] and [CF]*". However, participants reported that one "*might still get lost if the path is complicated*" (P5), e.g. when "*there are a lot of turns*" (P9). About *CF*, participants liked the "*possibility to look for details*" (P11) and that they were able to "*rewind the path and find [their] way easily*" when lost (P3). However, 7 out of 12 agreed that having "*to keep scrolling on the watch can be quite inconvenient*" (as stated by P5). It is likely that this issue will get worse if users' hands are full, e.g. with a bag. P9 also noted that it "*might not be that great of an idea especially when one is climbing down or up the stairs*" and P6 complained "*CF requires constant attention. I can't look at the road if I am staring at the screen all the time*". We also noted that one participant ran into a bench while using this technique. This may reveal safety issues with *CF*.

In summary, *CF*, the technique with highest fidelity to the follower's view, performed particularly well. But high fidelity is not the only important concern: participants were also concerned about the need for constant interaction with *CF*. *IC+FF* performed as well as *CF* but required much less interaction, which our participants appreciated. Thus, *IC+FF* looks like a good compromise in terms of Effort and Fidelity. However, *IC+FF* does lack *CF*'s precise control and the ability to slowly rewind, e.g. when a checkpoint is not well positioned. Hence, the best design seems to be a combination of techniques. *IC+FF* is a good choice for the common case, when less interaction is desirable, and *CF* is a good choice when precise control is required.

Finally, note that we focused on followers and carefully crafted the paths ourselves. Authoring for *CF* is trivial (one need only walk the route), while our experience and previous work indicate that choosing the right checkpoints for *IC+FF* is both difficult and critical for path quality [5, 21, 27]. Thus, our next experiment studied path authoring to assess the performance of techniques like *IC+FF* in real-life scenarios.

EXPERIMENT 2: PATH AUTHORING

In the first experiment, our followers performed well with *Image Checkpoints + Fast Forwarding* (*IC+FF*). However, we carefully crafted the path ourselves — with multiple iterations — to make them as close to optimal as possible. In a real-life scenario, leaders should be able to create high-quality paths quickly and painlessly, ideally just by walking the route one time. Hence, we designed a second experiment to investigate leaders' ability to author paths.

Our first experiment also taught us that choosing a good set of checkpoints could be challenging for an author. This problem inspired a fourth design, *Video Checkpoints + Fast Forwarding* (*VC+FF*), that allows authors to record a whole segment of the path as a video checkpoint instead of a single image.

For this second experiment, we wanted to compare the authoring experience with *Image Checkpoints + Fast Forwarding* (*IC+FF*) and *Video Checkpoints + Fast Forwarding* (*VC+FF*). To better validate our results, we also decided to include a baseline that does not rely on any technology: *Written Instructions* (*WI*). The discussion for our first experiment explains that *IC+FF* and *VC+FF* should ideally be combined with *Continuous Flow* (*CF*) to allow precise control during difficult situations. However, we did not make this combination in experiment 2, because it would benefit both *IC+FF* and *VC+FF* equally and would increase variance in time measurements (making analysis more difficult). Also, we were interested in the performance of these techniques in isolation. One may notice, though, that this put *IC+FF* and *VC+FF* at a slight disadvantage compared to *WI*.

To record a path, leaders need only indicate where checkpoints should be as they walk. Our authoring tools for *IC+FF* and *VC+FF* made use of physical volume buttons. Image checkpoints were captured when a button was released (*IC+FF*) and video checkpoints were recorded while a button was being pressed (*VC+FF*). Video checkpoints also captured audio, enabling authors to give special instructions.

For this experiment, we chose three new routes. As in experiment 1, all were at NUS, indoors, and approximately 250 meters long. As before, we took steps to ensure that the three routes had similar complexity.

Participants

We recruited two groups of participants, nine leaders and nine followers. For the leaders, we recruited nine students and staff from NUS (3 females), aged 25 to 44 years old ($M = 30, SD = 6.12$). All leaders were highly familiar with the environment. For the followers, we recruited nine students and staff from SMU (5 females), aged 25 to 33 years old ($M = 27.22, SD = 2.49$). None of the followers were familiar with the environment. All participants received the equivalent of 7.4 USD reward for their participation and were in good physical condition. The best performing leader and follower received the equivalent of 35.1 USD each as an extra incentive.

Apparatus

FML Trials. The apparatus in this experiment was similar to experiment 1. Both followers and leaders used the Epson Moverio BT-200 smartglasses as a display. Leaders' input device was an Epson trackpad with volume controls connected by wire to the smartglasses. (This device is equivalent to a smartphone for this study's purposes.) Followers wore a Huawei smartwatch on their non-dominant wrist and used this for input. Followers also carried a Samsung Galaxy S7 Edge in their pocket that managed communication between the watch and the glasses.

WI Trials. The apparatus was a clipboard with a sheet of paper. Leaders also had a pen to write with.

Tasks

Our experiment took place in two phases. In phase one, each leader authored three paths, one with each of the three different techniques. In phase 2, each follower tried to follow the three paths created by a single leader.

Each leader trial began with the experimenter taking the leader to the beginning of a route. The leader would then walk through the entire route once and was asked to remember it as accurately as possible. After reaching the end, the leader was asked to take the same route backwards to reach the starting point. After this, leaders recorded a path for one of the techniques. In all but one trial, leaders completed their paths in a single pass. In one trial, a leader went the wrong way and was allowed to restart. In *WI* trials, leaders used a clipboard to write instructions on paper along the way.

Followers had to follow the paths while trying to balance speed and accuracy, as in experiment 1.

Procedure

Participants began the experiment by filling out a demographic questionnaire. We then described the whole experiment to them and led them to a training route. During the training route, participants (both leaders and followers) tried each of the three techniques on a 100-meter segment. Leaders were given a chance to look at the *IC+FF* and *VC+FF* training paths that they authored. To save time, leaders did not actually write out full *WI* training paths, but they were shown example instructions written by two previous leaders. We also discouraged leaders from drawing maps in *WI* trials, because attempts to do this produced confusing results in pilot tests.

After training, participants authored or followed all three paths, each with a different technique. Finally, participants answered a post-experimental questionnaire in which they gave subjective feedback on all techniques. The experiment was run on week days and crowd size varied similarly to experiment 1.

Design

A within-subject design was used with one independent variable: *Technique {VC+FF, IC+FF, WI}*. We counterbalanced with a Latin Square, ensuring that each technique was used on each route three times for both groups.

Leaders. We measured authoring time as a dependent variable. Authoring time was the total time required for the leader to walk through the entire path while setting up checkpoints or writing instructions. As subjective feedback, we also measured the ease of use, enjoyment, and path quality (how easily they thought others could follow their path). Leaders performed the experiment in around 1 hour and 30 minutes and were able to take breaks between each trial.

Followers. We measured task time and errors as dependent variables. Task time was the total time required for the participant to reach the destination while following the entirety of the path. For this experiment, we counted an error if the user went the wrong way and was not able to recover from this error in 40 seconds. After 40 seconds, the experimenter would help the participant back to the path. As subjective feedback, we also measured ease of use, enjoyment and ability to plan ahead. Followers performed the experiment in around 1 hour and 10 minutes and were able to take breaks between each trial.

The total number of trials was 54 = (9 leaders + 9 followers) × 3 techniques.

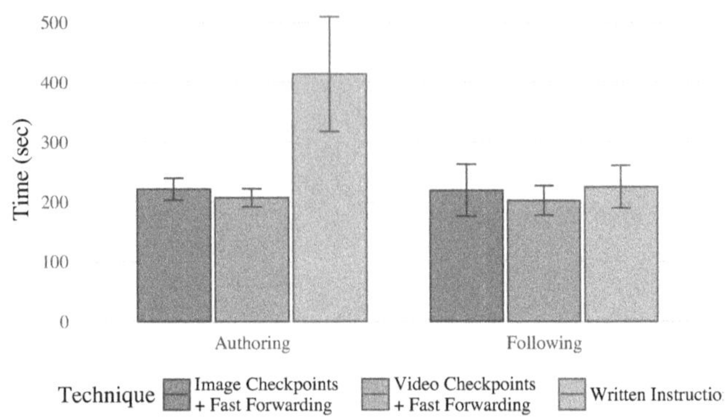

Figure 6. Authoring and Following time.

Results

We used ANOVA coupled with pairwise t-tests and Holm-Bonferroni correction to analyze time, a Cochran Q test to analyze errors, and Friedman's test with pairwise Wilcoxon signed ranks tests and Bonferroni correction for subjective feedback.

Leaders

Our main dependent variable for the leader phase was the time to author a path. The quality of the path itself is hard to evaluate but is reflected in the performance of the follower.

Authoring Time. A one-way ANOVA showed a significant main effect of Technique on authoring time ($F_{1.03,8.25} = 24.79, p < .001$, see Figure 6). Our participants were faster at creating paths with *VC+FF* ($M = 207$ s) than with *IC+FF* ($M = 221$ s) and *WI* ($M = 413$ s). Post-hoc comparisons showed significant differences between the three techniques (all three p<.05). The average walking speed of our leaders was 4.32 km/h for *VC+FF*, 4.05 km/h for *IC+FF* and 2.16 km/h for *WI*.

Subjective Feedback. Both *IC+FF* and *VC+FF* got good ratings (5.56/7 average). *WI* on the other hand received slightly negative feedback rating between 3/7 and 4.88/7 (Figure 7). We observed an effect of Technique on ease of use ($\chi^2(2) = 12.06, p < .01$), with *IC+FF* ($M = 5.88/7$) and *VC+FF* ($M = 6.67/7$) rating significantly better (both $p < .05$) than *WI* ($M = 3/7$). We found the same effect ($\chi^2(2) = 13.86, p < .001$) for enjoyment, with *WI* ($M = 3.56/7$) getting a significantly lower result than *IC+FF* ($M = 5.88/7$) and *VC+FF* ($M = 6.44/7$) (both $p < .05$). The trend continued with path quality ($\chi^2(2) = 15.77, p < .001$), with leaders giving a neutral rating to *WI* ($M = 4/7$), significantly lower than *IC+FF* ($M = 5.56/7, p < 0.5$) and *VC+FF* ($6.33/7, p < 0.5$).

Audio. All nine leaders used audio to give general directions (e.g. "turn left") or to highlight specific landmarks (e.g. "find the yellow trash bin").

Followers

Trial completion time was strongly dependent on the quality of the leader's path. Also note that we helped participants in the case of hard to recover errors, which lowers the time for conditions in which these errors occurred.

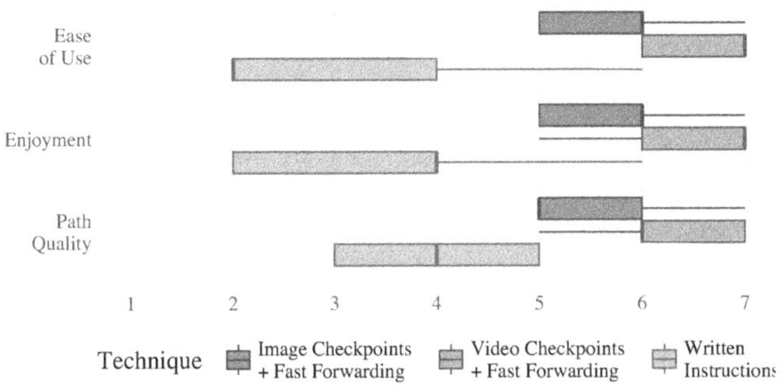

Figure 7. Leaders' Subjective Feedback.

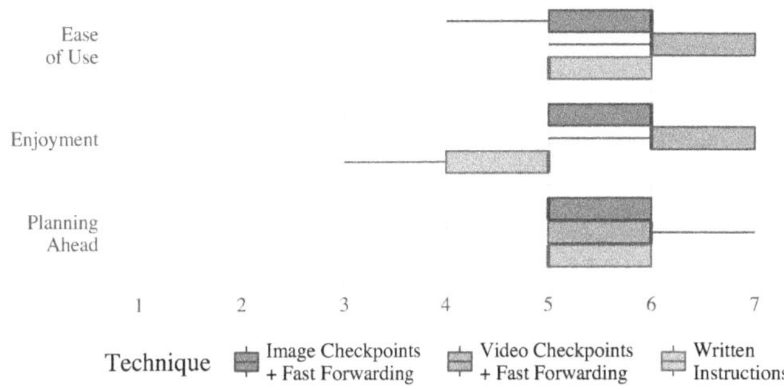

Figure 8. Followers' Subjective Feedback.

Time. The average time to complete a path was 215 s (Figure 6). An ANOVA did not show any significant main effect of Technique on time ($p = .61$). It took less time for our participants when they were using *VC+FF* ($M = 202$ s), followed by *IC+FF* ($M = 219$ s) and *WI* ($M = 225$ s), which suggests average walking speeds of 4.44, 4.11, and 3.99 km/h, respectively.

Errors. We counted a total of 5 hard to recover errors. Four were with *WI* and one was with *IC+FF*. For *WI*, errors would happen if the instructions were ambiguous or there was a missing step. The *IC+FF* error occurred outdoors when a leader's path showed a very fast turn with no checkpoint before or during the turn. A Cochran Q test did not show any significant main effect for *Technique* ($p = .71$).

Subjective feedback. Feedback from participants was positive overall (Figure 8). We observed no significant main effect of Technique on ease of use ($M = 5.3/7, p = .06$) but *VC+FF* was slightly higher than *IC+FF* and *WI*. For ability to plan ahead, the ratings are close (4.67 to 5/7, $M = 4.81/7$) without significance ($p = .41$). However, the technique had a significant effect on enjoyment ($\chi^2(2) = 14.21, p < .0001$). Our participants enjoyed using *VC+FF* ($M = 6.22/7$) significantly more than *IC+FF* ($M = 5.67, p < .001$) and *WI* ($M = 4.11/7, p < .001$). We also found a significant difference between *IC+FF* and *WI* ($p < .05$).

Audio. We also asked our participants to rate the following affirmation on a 5-point Likert scale: *I think I would have been able to find my way without audio.* The average score was 3.88/5 with only one participant giving a 2 (Somewhat Disagree) which suggests that our followers were confident that they could have used *VC+FF* even without audio. Audio was still appreciated, as P7 stated "I like audio [annotations] because it's almost as if I had someone walking with me".

Discussion

In this second experiment, our primary purpose was to investigate path authoring. Overall, creating a path with *VC+FF* is 6.3% faster than with *IC+FF* and 49.8% faster than with *WI*. Our subjective feedback showed that using *WI* made participants feel less confident in the quality of their paths, and they found it harder and less enjoyable to use. It is worth mentioning that all of our leaders were unfamiliar with the *VC+FF* and *IC+FF* techniques, and we believe that they could produce better paths with more training. However, the results are very encouraging and show that paths can be created quickly and accurately, even with minimal training.

Followers were also quite fast and usually accurate while following paths, as their average walking speed with *VC+FF* and *IC+FF* is respectively 4.44 and 4.11 km/h, slightly faster than *WI* (3.99 km/h). Our leaders' lack of confidence in their *WI* paths did not show itself in the followers' time, where we observed a mere 20-second difference (not significant). However, error rates did show problems with *WI*: 4/9 of our participants got lost when using *WI* and were unable to recover without external help. Another 1/9 got lost using *IC+FF* due to a lack of suitable checkpoints and low brightness in the video.

Overall, authoring times were shorter with *VC+FF*. The improvement over *IC+FF* is low (6.3%) but significant. In general, *VC+FF* also received slightly better subjective feedback. We believe that this difference is due to three factors. First, creating an image checkpoint requires more thought, since the choice of landmark and frame has to be carefully considered. Second, video checkpoints allow leaders to show the complete movement they are performing (e.g. a turn) instead of having to select a small set of relevant frames, as in *IC+FF*. A final advantage of *VC+FF* is the inclusion of audio commentaries, which were used by all 9 leaders. We believe this gave them more confidence, allowing them to go slightly faster. Interestingly, while audio was appreciated by followers, they were confident that they could have followed the paths without it.

DISCUSSION OF FOLLOW-MY-LEAD

Fidelity/Effort Trade-off for Followers

The different techniques we designed using the *Follow-My-Lead* approach represent different choices for the Fidelity/Effort trade-off. The *Continuous Flow* (*CF*) technique shows the most detailed information about the route at the cost of constant manual scrolling through the video. At the other end of the spectrum, *Image Checkpoints* (*IC*) requires minimal interaction effort at the cost of significantly reduced fidelity, showing important landmarks only. The results of our first experiment show that it was important for our participants to have access to most of this information. However, it was inconvenient and potentially dangerous to manually scroll through the whole interactive video using *CF*. As such, we believe that fast-forwarding–based techniques such as *Image Checkpoints + Fast Forwarding* (*IC+FF*) or *Video Checkpoints +*

Fast Forwarding (*VC+FF*) strike a better balance. However, followers may still occasionally need more details; therefore, complementing *IC+FF* and *VC+FF* with *CF*-like interaction is useful to handle difficult situations.

Authoring Paths

We designed *Follow-My-Lead* to allow quick path authoring with little or no practice. Our first experiment taught us that choosing the right path checkpoints is not as straightforward as it seems. This inspired us to invent the *Video Checkpoints + Fast Forwarding* (*VC+FF*) technique.

Our second experiment showed that leaders were able to create paths with both *IC+FF* and *VC+FF* just by walking the route once. However, it was faster, easier and more enjoyable with *VC+FF*. Compared to *WI*, our leaders were approximately twice as fast with *VC+FF* and *IC+FF*. The paths authored with *VC+FF* were easy to follow: followers using *VC+FF* paths quickly recovered from any errors. *IC+FF* achieved a good performance, but one follower was confused when a leader failed to put a checkpoint at a critical turn. These events confirm our hypothesis that the creation of discrete checkpoints can be complex and requires more training than video checkpoints.

Audio annotations were used by all nine of our leaders, making them more confident about the quality of their *VC+FF* paths. Interestingly though, our followers were confident (3.88/5) that they would have been able to follow the paths without these annotations. Audio can help to give additional contextual information, such as the floor to select in an elevator, the fact that a door needs an access card to open, or anything that may be hard to capture with a camera, e.g., pressing a small switch that is barely visible.

Improvements for Video Checkpoints + Fast Forwarding

Our authoring tool currently allows video checkpoints to be created only while walking a route, but leaders might go the wrong way while authoring a path. Allowing the leader to reshoot the last few seconds of a path would be an interesting improvement.

Limitations

While our experiments help to validate the *FML* prototype, we recognize that real-world usage scenarios raise additional issues that need further investigation. *FML* is susceptible to changes in the environment — e.g., storefronts seen in the leader's path may have changed since it was recorded and may no longer match the follower's view. This problem has bedeviled a wide variety of indoor localization technologies. We believe that this problem is more acute for other methods, such as WiFi-based localization, where radio signals fluctuate on timescales of seconds. In contrast, the majority of checkpoints used in our studies referred to *structural* characteristics (e.g., stairwells and turns) that are very likely to be stable.

Finally, while authoring paths with *Follow-My-Lead* requires a leader to walk through a route, some leaders may wish to provide path instructions from a remote location, such as a home or office. In such situations, leaders tend to write instructions from memory. However, our pilot studies indicate that such attempts are prone to oversights and imprecisions, even for someone who is highly familiar with a route.

CONCLUSION

We present *Follow-My-Lead*, a system for creating and following paths based on interactive videos captured by a leader. *Follow-My-Lead* is ideal for indoor wayfinding, because it needs neither localization technology nor floor plans.

In our first experiment, we investigated the Fidelity/Effort trade-off. We showed that our *Image Checkpoints + Fast Forwarding* technique strikes a better balance between fidelity to the follower's view and the interaction effort required to maintain this view. However, precise control of an interactive video – as enabled by the *Continuous Flow* technique – may still be helpful as a fall-back technique when leaders choose checkpoints poorly.

In our second experiment, we compared *Video Checkpoints + Fast Forwarding*, *Image Checkpoints + Fast Forwarding* and *Written Instructions*. We found out that authoring for *Video Checkpoints + Fast Forwarding* is faster and easier than *Image Checkpoints*, and both are much faster than creating *Written Instructions*. In the second part of the study, participants were able to follow these paths easily. While we did not find significant differences in terms following time, our followers made less hard-to-recover errors when using *Video Checkpoints + Fast Forwarding*. Participants also enjoyed *Video Checkpoints + Fast Forwarding* more than *Written Instructions*.

For future work, we would like to further investigate the relative usage of *Continuous Flow* and *Video Checkpoints + Fast Forwarding* when both are available to followers. We would also like to use devices' sensor data to automatically create checkpoints during the authoring process.

ACKNOWLEDGEMENTS

This work was partially supported by the Singapore Ministry of Education Academic Research Fund Tier 2 under research grant MOE2014-T2-1063 and National University of Singapore Academic Research Fund Tier 1 under research grant 251RES1617. All findings and recommendations are those of the authors and do not necessarily reflect the views of the granting agencies or the universities.

REFERENCES

1. Gregory D. Abowd, Christopher G. Atkeson, Jason Hong, Sue Long, Rob Kooper, and Mike Pinkerton. 1997. Cyberguide: A Mobile Context-aware Tour Guide. *Wireless Networks* 3, 5 (oct 1997), 421–433. DOI: http://dx.doi.org/10.1023/A:1019194325861
2. Masatoshi Arikawa, Shin'ichi Konomi, and Keisuke Ohnishi. 2007. Navitime: Supporting Pedestrian Navigation in the Real World. *IEEE Pervasive Computing* 6, 3 (jul 2007), 21–29. DOI: http://dx.doi.org/10.1109/MPRV.2007.61
3. Paramvir Bahl and V.N. Padmanabhan. 2000. RADAR: an in-building RF-based user location and tracking system. In *Proceedings IEEE INFOCOM 2000.*

Conference on Computer Communications. Nineteenth Annual Joint Conference of the IEEE Computer and Communications Societies (Cat. No.00CH37064), Vol. 2. Ieee, IEEE, 775–784. DOI: http://dx.doi.org/10.1109/INFCOM.2000.832252

4. Karolina Baras, A. Moreira, and F. Meneses. 2010. Navigation based on symbolic space models. In *2010 International Conference on Indoor Positioning and Indoor Navigation, IPIN 2010 - Conference Proceedings*. IEEE, IEEE, 1–5. DOI: http://dx.doi.org/10.1109/IPIN.2010.5646810

5. Ashweeni Kumar Beeharee and Anthony Steed. 2006. A Natural Wayfinding Exploiting Photos in Pedestrian Navigation Systems. In *Proceedings of the 8th Conference on Human-computer Interaction with Mobile Devices and Services (MobileHCI '06)*. ACM, New York, NY, USA, 81–88. DOI: http://dx.doi.org/10.1145/1152215.1152233

6. Gordon Best. 1970. Direction-finding in large buildings. *Architectural Psychology. London: RIBA Publications* (1970), 72–91.

7. Daniel G Borkowski, Hingsum F Fung, Hadi F Habal, Kenneth Chao, Sheng-roan Kai, and D Packard I I Robert. 1996. Cellular network-based location system. (1996).

8. Sal Bosman, Bas Groenendaal, J. W. Findlater, Thomas Visser, Mark de Graaf, and Panos Markopoulos. 2003. GentleGuide: An Exploration of Haptic Output for Indoors Pedestrian Guidance. In *International Conference on Mobile Human-Computer Interaction (Mobile HCI)*. Springer, 358–362. DOI: http://dx.doi.org/10.1007/978-3-540-45233-1_28

9. Nicholas A. Bradley and Mark D. Dunlop. 2002. *Understanding Contextual Interactions to Design Navigational Context-Aware Applications*. Springer Berlin Heidelberg, Berlin, Heidelberg, 349–353. DOI: http://dx.doi.org/10.1007/3-540-45756-9_37

10. A J Bernheim Brush, Amy K Karlson, James Scott, Raman Sarin, Andy Jacobs, Barry Bond, Oscar Murillo, Galen Hunt, Mike Sinclair, Kerry Hammil, and Steven Levi. 2010. User Experiences with Activity-based Navigation on Mobile Devices. In *Proceedings of the 12th International Conference on Human Computer Interaction with Mobile Devices and Services (MobileHCI '10)*. ACM, New York, NY, USA, 73–82. DOI:http://dx.doi.org/10.1145/1851600.1851616

11. Yao-Jen Chang and Tsen-Yung Wang. 2010. Comparing Picture and Video Prompting in Autonomous Indoor Wayfinding for Individuals with Cognitive Impairments. *Personal Ubiquitous Computing* 14, 8 (dec 2010), 737–747. DOI: http://dx.doi.org/10.1007/s00779-010-0285-9

12. Billy Chen, Boris Neubert, Eyal Ofek, Oliver Deussen, and Michael F Cohen. 2009. Integrated Videos and Maps for Driving Directions. In *Proceedings of the 22Nd Annual ACM Symposium on User Interface Software and Technology (UIST '09)*. ACM, New York, NY, USA, 223–232. DOI: http://dx.doi.org/10.1145/1622176.1622218

13. Xiang 'Anthony' Chen, Tovi Grossman, Daniel J Wigdor, and George Fitzmaurice. 2014. Duet: Exploring Joint Interactions on a Smart Phone and a Smart Watch. In *Proceedings of the 32nd annual ACM conference on Human factors in computing systems (CHI '14)*. ACM Press, New York, New York, USA, 159–168. DOI: http://dx.doi.org/10.1145/2556288.2556955

14. Pei-Yu (Peggy) Chi and Yang Li. 2015. Weave: Scripting Cross-Device Wearable Interaction. In *Proceedings of the 33rd Annual ACM Conference on Human Factors in Computing Systems (CHI '15)*. ACM, New York, NY, USA, 3923–3932. DOI: http://dx.doi.org/10.1145/2702123.2702451

15. Soon Hau Chua, Simon T Perrault, Denys J C Matthies, and Shengdong Zhao. 2016. Positioning Glass: Investigating Display Positions of Monocular Optical See-Through Head-Mounted Display. In *Proceedings of the Fourth International Symposium on Chinese CHI (ChineseCHI2016)*. ACM, New York, NY, USA, 1:1–1:6. DOI:http://dx.doi.org/10.1145/2948708.2948713

16. Roger M Downs and David Stea. 1973. *Image and environment: Cognitive mapping and spatial behavior*. Transaction Publishers.

17. Niklas Elmqvist, Morten Fjeld, David Axblom, Jonas Claesson, Joseph Hagberg, Daniel Segerdahl, Yan Tai So, Anders Svensson, Mattias Thorén, and Martin Wiklander. 2007. 3DVN: A Mixed Reality Platform for Mobile Navigation Assistance. In *ACM CHI2007 Workshop on Mobile Spatial Interaction*. 1–4.

18. Ivan Alexander Getting. 1993. The Global Positioning System. *IEEE spectrum* 30, 12 (1993), 36–38.

19. Andrew R. Golding and Neal Lesh. 1999. Indoor navigation using a diverse set of cheap, wearable sensors. In *Wearable Computers, 1999. Digest of Papers. The Third International Symposium on*. 29–36. DOI: http://dx.doi.org/10.1109/ISWC.1999.806640

20. Joy Goodman, Stephen Brewster, and Phil Gray. 2005. How can we best use landmarks to support older people in navigation? *Behaviour & Information Technology* 24, 1 (jan 2005), 3–20. DOI: http://dx.doi.org/10.1080/01449290512331319021

21. Harlan Hile, Radek Grzeszczuk, Alan Liu, Ramakrishna Vedantham, Jana Košecka, and Gaetano Borriello. 2009. Landmark-Based Pedestrian Navigation with Enhanced Spatial Reasoning. In *Proceedings of the 7th International Conference on Pervasive Computing (Pervasive '09)*. Springer-Verlag, Berlin, Heidelberg, 59–76. DOI: http://dx.doi.org/10.1007/978-3-642-01516-8_6

22. Simon Holland, David R Morse, and Henrik Gedenryd. 2002. AudioGPS: Spatial Audio Navigation with a Minimal Attention Interface. *Personal Ubiquitous Comput.* 6, 4 (jan 2002), 253–259. DOI: http://dx.doi.org/10.1007/s007790200025
23. Christoph Hölscher, Tobias Meilinger, Georg Vrachliotis, Martin Brösamle, and Markus Knauff. 2006. Up the down staircase: Wayfinding strategies in multi-level buildings. *Journal of Environmental Psychology* 26, 4 (dec 2006), 284–299. DOI: http://dx.doi.org/10.1016/j.jenvp.2006.09.002
24. Haosheng Huang, Georg Gartner, Manuela Schmidt, and Yan Li. 2009. Smart environment for ubiquitous indoor navigation. In *New Trends in Information and Service Science, 2009. NISS'09. International Conference on.* IEEE, 176–180.
25. Toru Ishikawa, Hiromichi Fujiwara, Osamu Imai, and Atsuyuki Okabe. 2008. Wayfinding with a GPS-based mobile navigation system: A comparison with maps and direct experience. *Journal of Environmental Psychology* 28, 1 (mar 2008), 74–82. DOI: http://dx.doi.org/10.1016/j.jenvp.2007.09.002
26. Anthony LaMarca, Yatin Chawathe, Sunny Consolvo, Jeffrey Hightower, Ian Smith, James Scott, Timothy Sohn, James Howard, Jeff Hughes, Fred Potter, Jason Tabert, Pauline Powledge, Gaetano Borriello, and Bill Schilit. 2005. Place Lab: Device Positioning Using Radio Beacons in the Wild. In *Proceedings of the Third International Conference on Pervasive Computing (PERVASIVE'05).* Springer-Verlag, Berlin, Heidelberg, 116–133. DOI: http://dx.doi.org/10.1007/11428572_8
27. Alan L. Liu, Harlan Hile, Henry Kautz, Gaetano Borriello, Pat A. Brown, Mark Harniss, and Kurt Johnson. 2006. Indoor wayfinding: Developing a Functional Interface for Individuals with Cognitive Impairments. In *Proceedings of the 8th international ACM SIGACCESS conference on Computers and accessibility (Assets '06).* ACM Press, New York, New York, USA, 95. DOI: http://dx.doi.org/10.1145/1168987.1169005
28. Markus Löchtefeld, Sven Gehring, Johannes Schöning, and Antonio Krüger. 2010. PINwI: Pedestrian Indoor Navigation Without Infrastructure. In *Proceedings of the 6th Nordic Conference on Human-Computer Interaction: Extending Boundaries (NordiCHI '10).* ACM, New York, NY, USA, 731–734. DOI: http://dx.doi.org/10.1145/1868914.1869016
29. Sylvain Malacria, Eric Lecolinet, and Yves Guiard. 2010. Clutch-free panning and integrated pan-zoom control on touch-sensitive surfaces. In *Proceedings of the 28th international conference on Human factors in computing systems (CHI '10).* ACM Press, New York, New York, USA, 2615. DOI: http://dx.doi.org/10.1145/1753326.1753724
30. Andrew J May, Tracy Ross, Steven H Bayer, and Mikko J Tarkiainen. 2003. Pedestrian Navigation Aids: Information Requirements and Design Implications. *Personal Ubiquitous Comput.* 7, 6 (dec 2003), 331–338. DOI: http://dx.doi.org/10.1007/s00779-003-0248-5
31. Andreas Möller, Matthias Kranz, Stefan Diewald, Luis Roalter, Robert Huitl, Tobias Stockinger, Marion Koelle, and Patrick A Lindemann. 2014. Experimental Evaluation of User Interfaces for Visual Indoor Navigation. In *Proceedings of the SIGCHI Conference on Human Factors in Computing Systems (CHI '14).* ACM, New York, NY, USA, 3607–3616. DOI: http://dx.doi.org/10.1145/2556288.2557003
32. Daniel R Montello. 2005. *Navigation.* The Cambridge handbook of visuospatial thinking, New York. 257–294 pages.
33. Alessandro Mulloni, Hartmut Seichter, and Dieter Schmalstieg. 2011. Handheld Augmented Reality Indoor Navigation with Activity-based Instructions. In *Proceedings of the 13th International Conference on Human Computer Interaction with Mobile Devices and Services (MobileHCI '11).* ACM, New York, NY, USA, 211–220. DOI: http://dx.doi.org/10.1145/2037373.2037406
34. Alessandro Mulloni, Daniel Wagner, Istvan Barakonyi, and Dieter Schmalstieg. 2009. Indoor Positioning and Navigation with Camera Phones. *IEEE Pervasive Computing* 8, 2 (apr 2009), 22–31. DOI: http://dx.doi.org/10.1109/MPRV.2009.30
35. Lionel M Ni, Yunhao Liu, Yiu Cho Lau, and Abhishek P Patil. 2004. LANDMARC: Indoor Location Sensing Using Active RFID. *Wirel. Netw.* 10, 6 (nov 2004), 701–710. DOI: http://dx.doi.org/10.1023/B:WINE.0000044029.06344.dd
36. Michael J O'Neill. 1991. Effects of signage and floor plan configuration on wayfinding accuracy. *Environment and Behavior* 23, 5 (1991), 553–574.
37. Martin Pielot and Susanne Boll. 2010. Tactile Wayfinder: Comparison of Tactile Waypoint Navigation with Commercial Pedestrian Navigation Systems. In *Proceedings of the 8th International Conference on Pervasive Computing (Pervasive'10).* Springer-Verlag, Berlin, Heidelberg, 76–93. DOI: http://dx.doi.org/10.1007/978-3-642-12654-3_5
38. Martin Pielot, Benjamin Poppinga, Wilko Heuten, and Susanne Boll. 2011. A Tactile Compass for Eyes-free Pedestrian Navigation. In *Proceedings of the 13th IFIP TC 13 International Conference on Human-computer Interaction - Volume Part II (INTERACT'11).* Springer-Verlag, Berlin, Heidelberg, 640–656. http://dl.acm.org/citation.cfm?id=2042118.2042179
39. Nissanka B Priyantha, Anit Chakraborty, and Hari Balakrishnan. 2000. The Cricket Location-support System. In *Proceedings of the 6th Annual International Conference on Mobile Computing and Networking (MobiCom '00).* ACM, New York, NY, USA, 32–43. DOI: http://dx.doi.org/10.1145/345910.345917

40. Martin Raubal and Max J Egenhofer. 1998. Comparing the complexity of wayfinding tasks in built environments. *Environment and Planning B: Planning and Design* 25, 6 (1998), 895–913. DOI: http://dx.doi.org/10.1068/b250895

41. Nishkam Ravi, Nikhil Dandekar, Preetham Mysore, and Michael L Littman. 2005. Activity Recognition from Accelerometer Data. In *Proceedings of the 17th Conference on Innovative Applications of Artificial Intelligence - Volume 3 (IAAI'05)*. AAAI Press, 1541–1546. http://dl.acm.org/citation.cfm?id=1620092.1620107

42. Günther Retscher and Michael Thienelt. 2004. NAVIO: A Navigation and Guidance Service for Pedestrians. *Journal of Global Positioning Systems* 3, 1&2 (dec 2004), 208–217.

43. Yuanchao Shu, Kang G Shin, Tian He, and Jiming Chen. 2015. Last-Mile Navigation Using Smartphones. In *Proceedings of the 21st Annual International Conference on Mobile Computing and Networking (MobiCom '15)*. ACM, New York, NY, USA, 512–524. DOI: http://dx.doi.org/10.1145/2789168.2790099

44. Asim Smailagic and Richard Martin. 1997. Metronaut: a wearable computer with sensing and global communication capabilities. In *Digest of Papers. First International Symposium on Wearable Computers*. IEEE Comput. Soc, 116–122. DOI: http://dx.doi.org/10.1109/ISWC.1997.629927

45. Koji Tsukada and Michiaki Yasumura. 2004. ActiveBelt: Belt-Type Wearable Tactile Display for Directional Navigation. In *UbiComp 2004: Ubiquitous Computing*. Springer, 384–399. DOI: http://dx.doi.org/10.1007/978-3-540-30119-6_23

46. Jan van Erp, Hendrik van Veen, Chris Jansen, and Trevor Dobbins. 2005. Waypoint navigation with a vibrotactile waist belt. *ACM Transactions on Applied Perception* 2, 2 (apr 2005), 106–117. DOI: http://dx.doi.org/10.1145/1060581.1060585

47. Philipp Wacker, Kerstin Kreutz, Florian Heller, and Jan Borchers. 2016. Maps and Location: Acceptance of Modern Interaction Techniques for Audio Guides. In *Proceedings of the 2016 CHI Conference on Human Factors in Computing Systems (CHI '16)*. ACM, New York, NY, USA, 1067–1071. DOI: http://dx.doi.org/10.1145/2858036.2858189

48. He Wang, Souvik Sen, Ahmed Elgohary, Moustafa Farid, Moustafa Youssef, and Romit Roy Choudhury. 2012. No Need to War-drive: Unsupervised Indoor Localization. In *Proceedings of the 10th International Conference on Mobile Systems, Applications, and Services (MobiSys '12)*. ACM, New York, NY, USA, 197–210. DOI: http://dx.doi.org/10.1145/2307636.2307655

49. Roy Want, Andy Hopper, Veronica Falcão, and Jonathan Gibbons. 1992. The Active Badge Location System. *ACM Transactions on Information Systems* 10, 1 (jan 1992), 91–102. DOI: http://dx.doi.org/10.1145/128756.128759

50. Andy Ward, Alan Jones, and Andy Hopper. 1997. A new location technique for the active office. *IEEE Personal Communications* 4, 5 (oct 1997), 42–47. DOI: http://dx.doi.org/10.1109/98.626982

51. Dirk Wenig, Johannes Schöning, Brent Hecht, and Rainer Malaka. 2015. StripeMaps: Improving Map-based Pedestrian Navigation for Smartwatches. In *Proceedings of the 17th International Conference on Human-Computer Interaction with Mobile Devices and Services (MobileHCI '15)*. ACM, New York, NY, USA, 52–62. DOI: http://dx.doi.org/10.1145/2785830.2785862

52. Dirk Wenig, Alexander Steenbergen, Johannes Schöning, Brent Hecht, and Rainer Malaka. 2016. ScrollingHome: Bringing Image-based Indoor Navigation to Smartwatches. In *Proceedings of the 18th International Conference on Human-Computer Interaction with Mobile Devices and Services (MobileHCI '16)*. ACM, New York, NY, USA, 400–406. DOI: http://dx.doi.org/10.1145/2935334.2935373

53. Scooter Willis and Sumi Helal. 2005. RFID Information Grid for Blind Navigation and Wayfinding. In *Ninth IEEE International Symposium on Wearable Computers (ISWC'05)*. IEEE, 34–37. DOI: http://dx.doi.org/10.1109/ISWC.2005.46

54. Han Xu, Zheng Yang, Zimu Zhou, Longfei Shangguan, Ke Yi, and Yunhao Liu. 2015. Enhancing Wifi-based Localization with Visual Clues. In *Proceedings of the 2015 ACM International Joint Conference on Pervasive and Ubiquitous Computing (UbiComp '15)*. ACM, New York, NY, USA, 963–974. DOI: http://dx.doi.org/10.1145/2750858.2807516

55. Qianli Xu, Liyuan Li, Joo Hwee Lim, Cheston Yin Chet Tan, Michal Mukawa, and Gang Wang. 2014. A Wearable Virtual Guide for Context-aware Cognitive Indoor Navigation. In *Proceedings of the 16th International Conference on Human-computer Interaction with Mobile Devices & Services (MobileHCI '14)*. ACM, New York, NY, USA, 111–120. DOI: http://dx.doi.org/10.1145/2628363.2628390

56. Zheng Yang, Chenshu Wu, and Yunhao Liu. 2012. Locating in Fingerprint Space: Wireless Indoor Localization with Little Human Intervention. In *Proceedings of the 18th Annual International Conference on Mobile Computing and Networking (Mobicom '12)*. ACM, New York, NY, USA, 269–280. DOI: http://dx.doi.org/10.1145/2348543.2348578

57. Yuanqing Zheng, Guobin Shen, Liqun Li, Chunshui Zhao, Mo Li, and Feng Zhao. 2014. Travi-Navi: Self-deployable Indoor Navigation System. In *Proceedings of the 20th Annual International Conference on Mobile Computing and Networking (MobiCom '14)*. ACM, New York, NY, USA, 471–482. DOI: http://dx.doi.org/10.1145/2639108.2639124

Mobility in Later Life – Appropriation of an Integrated Transportation Platform

Martin Stein[1,2], Johanna Meurer[1], Alexander Boden[2], Volker Wulf[1,2]

[1]Information Systems and New Media, University of Siegen, Siegen, Germany

[2]Fraunhofer Institute for Applied Information Technology (FIT), Sankt Augustin, Germany

{martin.stein; johanna.meurer; alexander.boden; volker.wulf}@[1]uni-siegen.de; [2]fit.fraunhofer.de

ABSTRACT

We present the results of a design case study focusing on supporting the daily transportation of elderly in Germany. We conceptualized, developed and studied the appropriation of a transportation information system intended to ease switching between different transportation modes. Based on a literature review and a context study with 21 interviews we explored routinized transport mode usage and barriers when switching between modes. Iteratively, we co-designed a transport platform accessible via a website, a mobile app, and an iTV app. We further looked at the appropriation of the platform into the daily lives of 19 persons. Studying the appropriation highlighted different factors that facilitate the adoption of alternative transport options. The factors included reducing uncertainty, complementing transport information with context information (e.g. weather) and providing informational access based on the user's preferences as well as fitting in with the situational needs (activity related).

Author Keywords

Transportation; Mobility; Elderly; Participatory Design; Qualitative Research.

ACM Classification Keywords

H.5.2 User Interfaces - User-centered design

INTRODUCTION

Mobility is an essential part of modern society and a prerequisite for autonomous living. In later life, this participation and autonomy are challenged by various factors such as diminished driving capabilities, reduced financial resources and shrinking social networks. This can force the elderly to deviate from previous routines. At the same time, combinations of existing and new modes of mobility may, while offering new possibilities, require an adjustment over time to establish new routines. When these transitions are forced upon people, adopting alternative transport options [33] can affect one's perceived wellbeing in later life [52]. For example, when people need to give up driving, switching instead to public transport: The fact that they have no knowledge of how to retrieve necessary schedule information [48] renders common activities such as accomplishing daily errands or visiting friends cumbersome. Of course, "the elderly" or "older adults", are a very heterogeneous group, with multifarious biographical, social backgrounds. The sample we present is not necessarily representative of all the problems encountered by this population. Works in gerontology or social science [48,77], HCI [33,47], and especially transportation research [52,59,63] have examined mobility choices; both preferences that influence adoption as well as the drawbacks of specific modes which prevent people from using particular options. Yet these studies often have a very rationalistic viewpoint, typically focusing on logistical and infrastructural influences on the pattern of mobility. In this paper, we try to understand transportation habits from a user's perspective; specifically, how they are embedded into everyday activities. Based on an intermodal transport information system [7,47,68], we want to understand the factors that facilitate the adoption of those transport options, potentially extending one's set of commonly used transport modes. By doing so, we hope to lower the impact of barriers encountered during aging, allowing older adults to maintain or even increase their wellbeing in later life.

Based on a literature review and an empirical context study, this paper provides a deeper understanding of how the elderly routinely use different modes of transportation and also how and when they diverge from these routines. Subsequently, we show the results of a long-term "in the wild" appropriation study of an intermodal transportation information system. The system design was informed by the insights from the context study and evolved from designing with participants of our study. We highlight both the necessity of, and potential for, integrating complementary, mode-independent information to support transportation in a situated, activity-oriented way. We argue that looking at transportation from this user perspective reduces uncertainty, fosters independence and autonomy and promises to facilitate the adoption of suitable transport alternatives.

CHI 2017, May 06 - 11, 2017, Denver, CO, USA

ACM 978-1-4503-4655-9/17/05…$15.00
DOI: http://dx.doi.org/10.1145/3025453.3025672

The paper is structured as follows: Section two highlights the challenges of switching between modes as well as the specifics of the elderly regarding transportation and is followed by the description of methods. Following the design case study approach [76], the rest of the paper describes an initial context study, the implementation and design of an intermodal transportation prototype and its appropriation study. We end the paper by discussing our results.

RELATED WORK

When it comes to elderly people, research typically emphasizes the general occurrence of physical impairments that coincide with aging [9]. It can be argued that focusing on these impairments and their consequences is a mistake [62] as older adults – even those in the upper range - tend to be in overall good health [62,71], which has led to more research on extending the wellbeing of the elderly [17] (e.g. in care settings [50], communities [49] and mobility [47,77]).

The Specifics of Older Adults' Mobility

The existing literature [47] highlights two other key aspects when it comes to the mobility preferences of older adults, namely "decisional autonomy" and "mobile independence". The first aspect highlights the fact that a transport mode not only needs to be able to address a concrete need (e.g. going to the theater every Thursday at 6 o'clock in the evening) but rather is assessed based on the opportunities it provides. The second deals with older adults seeking to maintain their independence when considering transportation opportunities. Independence means "being able to manage [the] daily mobility by utilizing [one's] own resources in accordance with one's abilities and without depending on others" [47]. The elderly, therefore, establish routines fostering their well-being in relation to these aspects. Nevertheless, transportation habits change in later life. Research in this regard highlights how mobility is affected by aging, based on the dimension of (a) quantified movement, (b) structural preconditions such as the availability of infrastructure, and (c) the before-mentioned focus on the physical status [77].

Regarding a), for example, one can see a decrease of trips after retirement, while in the US, the share of trips made using cars increases [62]. In Germany, senior citizens tend to continue to use the car and are generally more active [79]. Concerning infrastructure (b), Mollenkopf et al. argue that extended car usage is partly due to the fact that the proportion of older adults in western societies living in rural areas continues to increase, where access to public infrastructures and information about them is more problematic [48]. The paucity of this information additionally prevents elderly users from using alternatives to the car [24], which explains why the fear of losing their driver's license is common among older adults [63].

Habits and Transportation

HCI-research around transportation is mostly concerned with providing better access to certain transportation modes or assisting with specific tasks when engaging with one of these modes. Most of the common transportation modes have been researched, e.g. public transportation (PT) [21,27], walking [37], cycling [58], motorcycling [55], ridesharing (RS) and carpooling [12,29,47,54,69] and extensively car navigation (e.g. [28,38,41,42]). The focus of the studies within each mode varies greatly and it is beyond the scope of this paper to describe them all. Even so, several studies focusing on PT (e.g. [3,5,13,21,44,56,78]) deal with issues of payment [56], real-time information and waiting times [13,21,78], accessibility [44], and specific user needs [3] in order to increase the quality of service [59]. For example, Siira et al. [66] and Barham et al [6] demonstrate the possibilities inherent in integrating information about public transportation on a mobile device. Only a few studies exist in HCI which focus on behavioral change in transportation without being bound to a specific mode. Hasselqvist et al. [33] explore how people adopt more sustainable (car-free) transportation practices and Meurer et al. [47] identify motivations and barriers encountered by the elderly in using different modes, yet specifically focusing on RS. These studies highlight that understanding why and how transportation modes are routinized, how they can be effectively supported, and why they are difficult to change is of utmost importance [1,2,4,73] for supporting the appropriation of a new mode [30]. Typically, choices of transportation mode are closely tied to the respective travel goal [1] and to previous commitments (e.g. purchase of a car) [4]. New forms need to overcome established habits and provide extended benefits even when the person is predisposed to make use of the new form [73].

In this regard, people need to assess the appropriateness of transport opportunities. Several factors have been identified in literature such as shorter waiting times, reduced uncertainty, increased ease of use, willingness to pay, greater possibilities for the adjustment of travel behavior and more flexibility [18,20,21]. According to Redman et al. [59], those factors can be distinguished between "physical" and "perceived" attributes. The first mainly covers objective facts that can be easily observed or measured, such as reliability, the condition of vehicles, frequency, and accessibility. The latter category deals with the subjective experiences of the passengers such as experienced comfort, feeling of safety or perceived overall convenience. Redman et al.'s attributes are useful for understanding the attitude towards the adoption of PT as an alternative mode, and mode switching in general. For example, they suggest that monetary factors (e.g. free PT; increasing cost of private transportation) have an effect on the willingness to switch from private cars to PT initially [22], yet need to be complemented to sustain the transition [64,70], e.g. by increasing the level of convenience [15], shortening travel times and increasing the frequency of the services [19] or by providing live information [45]. Redman et al. [59] conclude that a superior level of service quality in certain dimensions of one mode is the main cause of lack of demand in other modes, such as RS (e.g. [14,32,57]).

By looking at a more specific set of users, we may better understand the appropriation of new, potentially beneficial, transportation options. To do so, we will present our findings on the design and appropriation of an intermodal transportation information system. While all the aforementioned studies highlight important factors, there are only very few design concepts dealing with multi- or intermodal solutions [31] and - to our knowledge – no studies in HCI reporting on the appropriation of such integrated multi- or intermodal solutions from a user's perspective (although appropriation more generally is widely discussed. See e.g. [16,23]).

METHOD

	Context Study	Evaluation Study
Number of participants	21	19
Age distribution	Min: 58 Max: 80 Average:69	Min:60 Max: 82 Average:71
Mode usage (multiple)	Car: 17 PT:5 Ridesharing: 9	Car: 15 PT: 5 Ridesharing: 7
Area	Rural:11 Urban: 10	Rural: 10 Urban: 9

Table 1: Details of user sample

Our study presents a design case study [76] and is based on a long-term Living Lab approach over a period of three years (February 2012 until January 2015). We define the Living Lab as a "user-centred, open innovation eco-system based on a systematic user co-creation approach integrating research and innovation processes in real life communities and settings" (openlivinglabs.eu; [8,26,53]). The basic point of Living Lab methodologies is to introduce new and innovative technologies into what are, as far as practicable, naturalistic settings. Typically, they are also associated with mixed methods. Although many studies of this kind have been centered on the home, there is no particular reason why research of this kind cannot be extended to the wider community (see e.g. [23]). Our study was part of a research project on the mobility practices of older adults in Germany (Figure 1) based on interviewing, observational work and Participatory Design principles [11]. Our interest is in designing tools to extend wellbeing in later life [62,71] and to learn from the specific case we look at.

Participants (see Table 1) came from a region that includes both urban and rural areas with approximately 280,000 inhabitants in total and 100,000 inhabitants living the main city. PT options in the region are the bus and the train (train is mainly used for inter-city travel). Bus services are limited in some rural areas which are mostly inhabited by older adults. The region is hilly with diverse terrain.

The participants were equipped with an Android-based Smartphone in May 2012. During weekly meetings, they received support in how to use the device for basic tasks (using it as a "daily device" for tasks such as calendar management, messaging, transportation, phone calls etc.). After this appropriation phase, the weekly meetings were mainly used to conduct co-design workshops (more than 40 workshops with 6-10 participants on average; see section "Iterative Design of System"). The iterative design phase ended in August 2014. Participants continued using the prototype until the end of 2014. We then conducted 19 evaluation interviews in conclusion.

Context Study and Evaluation

To collect data, we conducted 40 interviews in total. 21 interviews were conducted in participants' homes before (initial interview study) and 19 interviews after (appropriation interview study) we developed our prototype. Two participants of the initial interview study did not take part in the later phases (co-design, evaluation) of the project. A further two participants dropped out during the project and were replaced by others. The interviews were audio-recorded and transcribed verbatim afterward. After transcribing the interviews, we conducted a *content analysis* [46] to identify significant themes. The duration of interviews depended on the preferences of the interviewees and thus varied in length from 45 minutes to two and a half hours.

We conducted the initial interviews together with project partners, and analyzed focusing on diverse aspects, e.g. with regard to opportunities and obstacles of RS [47]. Our analysis was design-oriented and focused on how transportation is routinized, and analyzed the reasons people have for deviating from these routines. The interviews centered on problems regarding the transportation habits of

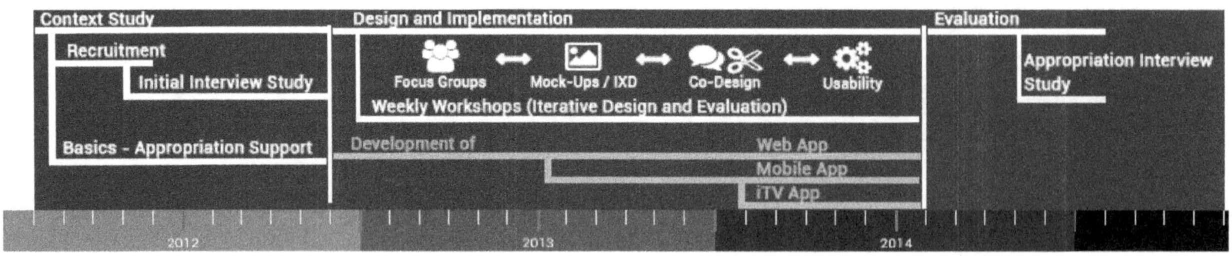

Figure 1: Long-term Living Lab Process

the elderly. We were especially interested in the organization and planning of the interviewees' daily transportation to understand their reasoning regarding transportation choices to reveal potentials for ICT-based support. The analysis resulted in different codes which were collectively clustered into several topics, like 'usage of transportation modes,' 'planning of transport,' 'cooperation in mobility', and 'self-perception of abilities in older age'. Based on this, we further developed the categories presented in the later section.

In the evaluative interview study focusing on the appropriation of the tool (Figure 1 - "Evaluation"), we focused on the integration of the prototype into the participants' daily lives. Although we already had the chance to see routine use developing at the weekly meetings (Figure 1 - "Design and Implementation"), we were iteratively developing the application and therefore conducted a second interview study at the end of 2014 in which we asked about the influence of the prototype from the participants' point of view. We identified the situations and tasks for which our application was deemed useful, as well as situations where participants stuck to their existing tools and routines or situations in which they made use of other tools that they had become aware of since the introduction of the smartphones. The users' long-term involvement in the design process allowed us to build a trustful relationship [51] and further enabled us to observe the appropriation of our (and other) application(s) over time. This in turn helped us to understand the situations and issues described by participants during the second study.

Figure 2: Participants design the iTV-interface

Iterative Design of the System

Between the two interview studies (Figure 1 - "Design and Implementation"), we engaged in over 40 co-design workshops with the participants in order to design a mobile (Figure 3 and Figure 4), a web and an iTV application for integrated transportation information services. After the "Basics - appropriation support" phase (Figure 1), we conducted workshops to understand how an integrated transport information system might be designed. In the beginning, the workshops focused on existing practices regarding different transportation modes. We further introduced available tools, such as flinc for RS or DB-Navigator for PT (official app of the German Railway System). Based on these steps, we first developed paper-based mockups that we discussed with participants. Due to the complexity of the system, in some cases we provided initial ideas and conceptual solutions, using their critique as a resource for further designs [74]. In other cases, we conducted workshops and asked users to design interfaces (Figure 1 - "Design and Implementation / Prototyping"). For example, we conducted a co-design workshop to design the layout and select the functionality of the iTV application (Figure 2), whilst another one tested different interaction prototypes to negotiate RS arrangements and a further workshop dealt with privacy, using card sorting to identify relevant information structures and sharing preferences.

CONTEXT STUDY – CURRENT TRANSPORTATION ROUTINES OF ELDERLY

In the following, we will outline the results of our context study. We structured our results according to two sets of criteria. The first deals with resources, knowledge, and skills that participants mentioned as relevant. The second deals with contextual factors influencing the reasoning. The study aimed to understand how older adults choose transportation options in their daily life, verifying and extending existing findings in the literature.

Resources and Knowledge at One's Disposal

To understand how people adopt different transportation modes in everyday life, it is necessary to understand the opportunities created by infrastructures and resources. Our participants described various aspects that show how transportation infrastructures (of different modes) are understood as mobility resources:

"As long as I can still walk to the bus stop, I'll use the bus, I'm happy. It's my independence. I'd like to stay independent actually. And for me, that means the bus. Not the car, because I don't own one." (Female1, 73, PT)

"I'm lucky to have my children around, at least some of them live here. And if I call them, they take me wherever I want if they are available." (Female3, 73, PT)

The quotes highlight the importance of resources, including a strong social network or the physical capability necessary for organizing one's mobility. These are typically strongly connected to individual situations. A lack of capability, for example, can render specific modes unusable. A comment by one of our participants highlights how he is not able to use PT but instead uses the car to reach certain destinations that are not in close proximity to a bus stop.

[Talking about the ticket fares of PT] For me the determining factor is, 'where does the bus stop?' and 'how far do I have to walk to my destination?', it's down to my problems with walking. I might walk 500 meters or even a kilometer but I think there is more to it. For me, walking is just getting worse." (Male1, 81, CAR)

The quote points to another important issue. To make use of certain travel opportunities, people need not only to be aware of the opportunities but also require certain knowledge to make use of the available options (*'where does the bus stop?'*). This knowledge becomes especially important when switching to new or unfamiliar modes. It consists of what we might call operational strategies. For example, one participant describes such a strategy regarding PT:

"The timetable often changes, just a couple of minutes, and when you're going out, you think 'Oh yes, you still have time' but then you see there is nobody standing at the bus stop anymore. And you think to yourself 'has the bus already left?'" (Female3, 73, PT)

Car owners often described a total absence of such knowledge with regard to PT. They pointed out that it prevents them from switching to PT in many situations. More generally, our participants highlighted issues with "translating" their knowledge into information that can be used in different transportation modes. Thus people often referred to personal landmarks when describing locations, referring to personally meaningful expressions such as "to my brother's place", "the supermarket" (having a specific or a set of specific supermarkets in mind) or names used locally names which were not officially documented. Other place references were personally or socially constructed and imply a certain understanding of destinations and activities (e.g. people mentioned "the computer club" when talking about a course on computers for senior citizens that takes place weekly in the area), like regular meeting points with friends, e.g. one participant referring to the gym by saying "doing sports".

It becomes obvious that the participants acquired knowledge and developed strategies for their daily routines and modes of choice. While participants wanted to maintain their familiar routines and available resources (especially car owners), they also described specific cases in which explicit factors led them to deviate from routines and switch modes. These situations are particularly interesting as they allow us to understand our participants' reasoning and identify factors that come into effect regarding the use or non-use of a transport option.

Reasoning on Transportation Options

In this section, we will explore the various situational influences when settling on a transport option. For instance, taking the bus to the city center eliminated the need to search and pay for a parking space. These advantages were often recognized spontaneously and triggered the rescheduling of activities. This was typically indicated by quotes such as "since I'm already in the city center" or "as I'm taking the car/bus anyway".

"If you're going on the bus anyway [instead of walking], you might as well buy groceries before you go home." (Female4, 73, PT)

Most participants reported that they would continuously (re-) compile their "personal schedules". This requires continual access to information to ensure that rescheduling is possible on the backdrop of the transport mode being used. Throughout this rescheduling, participants tried to align the activities' temporal and spatial conditions with the options provided by the various modes. A common issue is that certain activities cannot be precisely scheduled in advance as they imply vague restrictions on time and destination - they entail a certain degree of temporal flexibility.

"We can't do it all today, there isn't enough time. [...] You simply do the rest the next day. You plan things ahead and it works out. And even if it doesn't work out, you just say so – but we have more time than younger people anyway." (Female1, 73, PT)

"You can just sit in the bus shelter or whatever – you're sure to see a neighbor passing by, purely by chance. You strike up a conversation and time flies when you get chatting. [...] It sometimes happens that we're so immersed in conversation that you completely forget the time... And when that happens, I just catch the next bus." (Male3, 66, CAR/PT)

The quotes demonstrate that participants anticipate deviations from schedules. People engage in numerous activities which imply temporal constraints. For instance, the examples above describe very loose time constraints. Such activities can easily be incorporated into the schedule and can easily be rescheduled. The need to be temporally flexible goes hand-in-hand with the fact that some activities do not require a specific destination. Or from a practical point of view, certain activities might be carried out at diverse locations, resulting in an interchangeability of destinations:

"I just check out all the little stores and it doesn't matter to me what kind of store it is. As I said, I buy my groceries in the stores that I think stock what I need."(Female5, 75, CAR/PT)

This process of scheduling is summed up by a participant talking about activities with fixed times and places which nevertheless provide an opportunity to schedule in other activities:

"Sometimes things are already planned [in terms of having fixed appointments such as visiting the dentist]. You know you are going to a certain place, so you know things that can be done there. For example, at the town hall, I can drop things off there or whatever. It's natural to combine things like that." (Female1, 73, PT)

This respondent used the town hall as a reference point to consider possible activities. In this case, the town hall is located in the city center where several other stores and also the postal office where "one can drop things off" are located. This shows that spaces do not always determine activities or vice versa. For instance, instead of using one's usual post office, one may mail a package from a post office near the town hall in order to combine the mailing activity with the town hall errand. Owing to temporal and spatial flexibility, an activity may be associated with several directions and vice versa. In this regard, existing literature [47,54], stresses the importance of flexibility. Transport options need to provide a sufficient degree of flexibility (temporal and spatial) to be adopted. If options lack this degree of flexibility, people are unable to align their activities to the offered transportation services and thus are unlikely to switch to those modes [59].

Considerations for the Design of Systems Supporting Transportation

To provide new transportation opportunities for our participants, especially in areas where infrastructures such as PT are sparse (e.g. rural areas) or existing concepts such as Uber or flinc fail due to a lack of critical mass, we derived design implications from previously presented studies (see related work) and our complementary interview study. We outline the challenges and guiding themes for the design of our prototype in the following.

Awareness about available transport opportunities

One implication highlighted by Meurer et al. [47] and which has been further confirmed in the interview study is that older adults want to be aware of the opportunities available. Thus solutions need to incorporate different information sources to extend the user's options. For example, a system could provide the user with multi- / intermodal transport information to explore and compare all available opportunities. Even if the information on the various transport modes is not used, its availability might conceivably help to increase one's decision-making autonomy [47], and the integration of this information also addressed the issue of access to information on unfamiliar transport modes [24,48]. Generally, easy access to information on multiple modes makes the adoption of other transport options more likely [59].

Ability to make use of transport opportunities

The promotion of autonomy is an important aspect of the mobility of older adults. For this, being independent of others is a crucial requirement. As shown in our interview study, retrieving relevant transport information necessitates not only knowledge about existing opportunities but also operational knowledge regarding different transportation options. This is in line with the existing results for the specific case of the elderly [24,47,48] but also has more general implications with regard to access to relevant transport information [59]. Further, the steps to make use of a transport opportunity, e.g. payment, should be integrated [15]. Generally, information should be individualized to provide more benefits. Prior work on single modes has shown the necessity of features such as retrieving individual schedules in PT [21,34] or providing carpooling and RS opportunities based on similar whereabouts. See [10,60] who developed a system for PT for retrieving individual schedules.

Taking into account context and reasons for travel

The analysis showed that many decisions with regard to transportation are made taking into account a variety of information both contextual (e.g. the weather) and social (e.g. meeting people at the bus stop). Additionally, this decision-making often takes place prior to travel (e.g. considering activities which can be combined with fixed appointments and destinations), as well as spontaneously while traveling (e.g. finding suitable destinations close by, such as groceries). Thus, the user needs to be able to retrieve information relevant to his current situation and the service should therefore meet the requirements of the passenger's activity. For example, information about the frequency of travel opportunities (e.g. in PT [19]) can inform reasoning and allow rescheduling. Further personal preferences / requirements in terms of comfort and safety [59] should be taken into account as well as the situational implications of the intended activity (e.g. by integrating third party services and appropriate interaction mechanisms)

DESIGN AND IMPLEMENTATION

Based on derived implications we created a prototype. The development was twofold. The selection and integration of services were conducted in an iterative, co-design process [76]. We developed the necessary backend systems, which allow the integration of different transportation providers, event calendar sources and map services (including routing capability).

From a user perspective, the prototype is a platform allowing users to retrieve intermodal transportation information. The main goal of the prototype was the aggregation and combination of all available transport modes within a specific region. We included RS, PT, taxi services and special needs transportation services, the information about which could be retrieved using either a website, a mobile app or an iTV app. The inclusion of additional information, such as the event calendar or POI information was an exemplary result of the co-design process.

The interaction was designed in a way that it created awareness about transport opportunities nearby (Figure 3) by showing all the available options for a given location. The search interface provided unified access to information about all modes. The location was either entered by the user or automatically retrieved using GPS. The idea was that awareness about available transport opportunities would lower the barrier to certain modes whilst simultaneously allowing the experienced user of a mode (especially PT) to retrieve relevant information quickly, such as imminent departure times. As soon as the user entered a destination (Figure 4), the results showed different itineraries consisting of combinations of all available modes. The user can of course enter preferences, e.g. to exclude certain modes from the results, slower walking speeds (for connections within PT) or required space for luggage etc. The user can define default values, which can be adjusted for each search if necessary. The user can also make use of a classic click and text-based input. Further, they can use a map to choose locations or enter search requests via natural language voice input. In addition, point-of-interest (POI)-based and "event-based" destination inputs are provided. POI-based input allows users to choose from different venues using the foursquare API (https://developer.foursquare.com/). Event-based input allows users to browse upcoming events in the test region that were retrieved from a calendar of public events. When users looked up travel information for such events, the system automatically takes time and the destination of the event into account. The speech input function could parse natural language sentences by searching for tokens in the sentences, such as relative or absolute time inputs ("tomorrow", "in ten minutes", "at three o'clock"), addresses and venue types (e.g. "restaurants"). Various transportation modes were included to address users' awareness of available resources. This was further addressed by always showing nearby transportation modes whenever the app was started up. The map-based input, the generic search interface and other features (e.g. exploring POI databases or upcoming events) addressed the issue of lack of knowledge due to unfamiliarity. Our aim was to provide the user with the opportunity to access different kinds of transport information without the prerequisite of having specific mode-related (e.g. names of bus stops) or local (e.g. addresses of places) knowledge. We further took location into account by using GPS information and showing nearby facilities. Further, we provided features which allow the user to enter venue categories and then choose from available alternative destinations based on his or her intended activity.

Figure 3: Start screen without destination

Figure 4: Start screen with destination

APPROPRIATION OF THE PROTOTYPE

In this section, we outline aspects arising when participants used the prototype "in-the-wild". Users were free to use whatever tools they liked and we did not limit our observations to assessing the appropriation only of our prototype but also paid attention to the various tools and strategies that were evident. During the final year of the project, our prototype was used more than 500 times per month resulting in about 11,000 sessions in total. The monthly peak usage was 3,800 sessions due to local TV reports. Access was achieved 60% of the time using a mobile device and 40% using a desktop or the TV app (combined).

The study revealed blind spots in existing literature that stem from a strong focus on (mode-specific) transportation factors. The appropriation study helped us to understand the extent to which increased awareness and better access to relevant transport information as well as extended (contextual) information influenced the participants' willingness to adopt new or different transport options.

Reducing Uncertainty

Generally, the prototype was positively received. The participants especially liked the regional focus of the tool, which was mainly established by integrating a local event calendar as well as selected design elements (such as the header image) which resembled landmarks of the area. As most of the participants did not use any ICT-based tools to support their transportation before the project (except for car navigation systems), we were interested to discover in which situations and for which tasks they would use and adopt (transportation) tools. One interesting point was the time of usage and the specific incentive to use the app. We expected that users would appreciate the mobile app for getting information on the go, but to our surprise they pointed out that they use the mobile device for the careful planning of trips in advance:

"Occasionally I check departure times when I'm in bed late at night or early in the morning. I think you [addressing the interviewer] have a different way of doing that. Rather off the cuff." (Female4, 73, PT)

The quote illustrates that checking in advance was used as a means to reduce the uncertainty caused by a lack of experience with the device (as she points out, the interviewers are more capable of coping with the task spontaneously). Yet mobile access to such information also reduced uncertainty regarding one's mobility. For example, Female11 *(PT, 82 years)* compared two situations before and after familiarizing herself with different apps. Once, she found herself lost at an intermediate train station, helplessly trying to find an alternative connecting train after arriving late. Nowadays, she points out, *"the phone provides [her] with security"* when otherwise disoriented; anecdotally telling a story about how she managed to find the way back to her hotel using her phone to find an alternative route when some streets had been closed due to construction sites. Several participants outlined how easy access to information helped them to validate trips generally:

"Sometimes you have to change buses, and you can check if there is a better connection" (Female4, 73, PT)

It became clear that people appreciated the ease of information retrieval using ICT, which allows access to information *en route*. Yet the mobile app was also used within the users' existing routines for planning things:

"I won't always bring the smartphone in future. I don't need it. I'm happy to have it at home, especially for the internet and when I want to check things such as the buses. Or events.

That is the really great thing about our app." (Female7, 78, CAR/PT)

It was surprising how strongly the "always on" characteristic of the mobile devices was highlighted. The mobile phone and the app provided easy, spontaneous access to information related to transportation and was therefore used more than the desktop web application. Generally, by extending participants' access to information they felt more aware of opportunities and more confident of finding suitable options.

Situated Exploration of Opportunities

The introduction of the technology turned out to influence the participants' (perceived) flexibility. While the prototype sometimes blended in with existing routines, it also became clear that the appropriation of the tool(s) and the influence it had on existing routines was very different depending on one's prevalent transportation usage. Participants who mainly used PT for their daily trips reported greater benefits from using the technology as assistance. Even in the case of very regular PT users, the application helped to create better awareness of the available opportunities:

[Talking about search results containing different alternatives of going to the city center from the participant's home that had not been expected by the user]
Interviewer: Why do you think this result is wrong?
Female3: This connection doesn't head to the city. It ends up in [VillageName]. [Female3 recognized that this bus is just the first part of the whole trip]
Female3: ...Then I can board Line 555 in order to get to the cemetery. AND [recognizes that the connection is a suitable alternative] this is important to know, that there is an alternative to the main connections. It's really interesting that this information is programmed into the application. Very nice! (Female3, 73, PT)

With the prototype, users even established new ways of retrieving information, abandoning tools they had previously used such as writing down departure times before going somewhere. The prototype enabled more flexible scheduling within their daily tasks:

[Talking about information on PT]:
Interviewer: Did you use the printed timetable before?
Female3: Yes, I always wrote down the departure time before I went out.
Interviewer: And now, do you check the time on the move?
Female3: Yes, you do not necessarily know in advance when you will be going back. If you have an appointment or just stroll around the city.
Interviewer: And how did you deal with that before you had the phone?
Female3: I always wrote down several alternative departure times for the return journey. (Female3, 73, PT)

The two quotes highlight how the application helped to facilitate flexibility within daily activities - on the one hand by providing more information *("...this is important to know, that there is an alternative to the main connection...")* and on the other by facilitating access to this information (using a phone instead of writing down departure time in advance). This interest in information providing new opportunities in each situation was not limited to PT users but especially extended to car users. Even though car users rarely use other modes of transportation, they reported instances of information retrieval, such as looking for events to visit, POIs or PT connections and RS out of curiosity:

Male4: [Being asked if he uses the prototype for PT] Rarely, since we usually take the car. But that doesn't mean that I never use it. Just recently, we went to [CityName] and we liked it there. So I thought about going there again and checked out how to get there using buses and trains. [...] At that time I used the German railway system app because I knew it from the computer. But I used our app when we visited our children. I wanted to know what the PT-situation is over at their place. Even there [He emphasizes the fact that information is available because the children live in a very rural area] our app tells you where the next bus stop is and how to get there. (Male4, 71, CAR)

What makes this quote interesting is that the app allowed him to retrieve the information necessary to make use of PT in the situation he found himself in even though he was not actually using PT. We found that participants were generally interested in exploring all avenues of possibility, both in terms of available transport options as well as potential destinations. In this sense, the integrated calendar provided a strong incentive to use our app. Thus, the inclusion of "mode-independent" complementary information can serve as a starting point for becoming aware of other mobility options. All participants highlighted the prototype's event calendar in this sense. Most of our participants pointed out how they just opened the application to look for interesting events and simultaneously became aware of alternative transport options:

[When browsing events in the event calendar] "And the app provides me with alternatives for getting there and I can think about whether to take the bus or the car." (Female8, 65, CAR)

The extent to which the calendar was used and pointed to as a central part of the application was unexpected but shows how browsing for opportunities might lead to experimenting with unfamiliar transport opportunities. Thus while the integration of various transport information was necessary, additional information for certain activities can point at the suitability (or even advantages) of alternatives for a certain activity. For example, after familiarizing herself with our app, one user thought about using PT to visit her sister in hospital as parking spaces are limited. In this case, for example, the suitability of PT could be highlighted by providing timetables alongside the visiting hours of the hospital.

Integrating Transportation and Daily Activities

As exemplified above, participants of our study constantly described situations in which they made use of options because it was suitable for their intended activity. However, participants also described situations where the shortcomings of our prototype were evident:

[Talking about the provided details of a connection, one user demanded more information, yet the application did not provide any further information about the route at this point] "I wanted to see the whole route. See which way it goes. Because that would be interesting. For example, if I get on bus 333…it also goes to the city center…yet it takes a detour through another part of the city. If I take this one… tough luck! So it is interesting to know which route it takes." (Female7, 78, CAR/PT)

The quote highlights how the information required is not limited simply to the details that enable the interviewee to get to their destination, but that the information provided needs to support flexibility or provide additional opportunities for scrutiny. In this regard, PT users reported using different applications for different contexts, e.g. they used the official application of the German railway service for longer journeys, but our app for traveling within the city. Even though both applications provide the same PT information, they integrate different additional services (e.g. ticket reservation in the official app and POI services and local events in our app). The example of the event calendar showed that the information our participants made use of was not limited to "logistical" information bound to any mode. We expected POI information to have a similar incentivizing effect, yet the users cared much less about POI than about events. When we questioned this, it transpired that most of the categories within the POI databases consist of venues the users already knew. As a result, browsing the POIs was not such a great incentive to use the application as information about events was. Nevertheless, POIs turned out to be of value to the participants, with a very specific focus on the utility of places:

"So, I really would like to see information on toilets being integrated into the application. Information like this should be available. That's quite useful for elderly people like us. Some years ago, that issue was quite challenging in the city." (Female10, 63, CAR)

Here the situated value of information for transportation is highlighted and how it renders an infrastructure or destination suitable (the ones close to public or accessible restrooms). It becomes apparent that the availability of contextual information when deciding whether or not to consider a certain mode when engaging in a certain activity is crucial. In another example, a participant outlined which different modes she takes into account and how this is influenced by the availability of information:

Female7: „For example, when my sister visits, we usually go to Italian restaurants. And then I look where the closest Italian is."
Interviewer: "Do you look for the closest one?"
Female7: "If we walk, I look for the closest. But she has a car, so I can look for places we can drive to." […Talking about how to choose the best venue…] "I would choose the nearest venue. Or… I mean..., if it is easy to get to, why not catch the bus and walk a few meters. This thing [the app] is quite helpful." (Female7, 78, CAR/PT)

The quote describes how POI information can become useful when a sister's visits. In this case, she and her sister do not prefer a specific Italian restaurant and therefore several destinations are interchangeable. Compared to the example provided by Female10, which shows how information on specific POI (such as toilets) can render certain routes (and therefore modes fixed on those routes) dispreferred, the example of Female7 shows how information about the accessibility of POIs influences which destinations and modes people consider in the first place when deciding on trips. It becomes obvious that POI information (including its reachability) serves to allow participants to explore their options in terms of destinations and transportation.

This focus on the situational use of the system became even more critical for RS. The RS feature of the application was used only rarely, resulting in no matching of offers and requests even after the system was made available publicly. We asked for reasons why the feature within our app was not used. In many cases, people complained about the necessity of planning and entering trips in advance to publish the request or the offer. This caused issues of critical mass that rendered the RS feature not very useful.

"I seldom use the app. Sometimes I open it out of curiosity, but I've never needed it. I like the way it is designed and I can see the PT connections. But you only start using ridesharing when you are sure that someone will reply. It's a dead end right now". (Female9, 60, CAR)

In cases where we could observe RS (e.g. when people joined a ride to visit our weekly meetings), people preferred to use a messenger, as it allowed them to offer a ride more spontaneously. Utilizing an messenger as the tool of choice for RS highlights how participants sought to maintain flexibility while extending their RS network (which was previously limited to family members and close friends). We expected people to adopt RS because of the increased awareness facilitated by being presented alongside other options. Our concept for RS, however, was not always suitable for the users' everyday mobility. It mostly followed concepts of established long-distance RS platforms and hence was inappropriate for daily, short distance travel, as it requires people to plan in-advance, causing conflicts with users' independence and decisional autonomy [47].

DISCUSSION

Based on the literature and context study we expected our participants to appreciate the integration of different transport information into one system. As the literature [47,54,59] points out, the flexibility provided by a transport option is crucial to its adoption into daily life. Hence, we anticipated that the extended awareness about travel options provided by our tool would increase the participants' flexibility. In particular, we found that ubiquitous access to detailed information can reduce uncertainty, thereby fostering independence and increasing autonomy [47]. It allowed the participants to assess the suitability of transport options for certain activities and personal preferences (e.g. finding the shortest connections and not being "trapped" in a bus, forced to take detours). The example of our RS feature, which was largely rejected, highlighted the importance of this fact. Users saw greater potential in messengers for supporting their current RS practices (e.g. using group chats to offer rides). In this regard Wash et al. [75] have already argued in favor of informal RS communication. They allow users to easily negotiate details and spontaneously offer rides and can be easily integrated into daily routines [59]. Thus, they restrict one's decisional autonomy to a lesser extent [47] and allow for leverage of existing social structures [12].

Yet above all, our study highlights that fostering the adoption of new transport modes by dint of incorporating transportation information can be further enhanced by the addition of complementary situated and contextual information, e.g. the event calendar which provided up-to-date information about upcoming events. This information motivated participants to look for transportation options, tempting them to look at alternative modes of transportation. The recognition of alternative modes of mobility can be seen as the first step towards challenging routinized behavior [1,2,4,30,73]. The POI information, on the other hand, became relevant within a given situation where specific needs arise (e.g. finding the closest toilet or a restaurant). This is in line with arguments made by Redman et al. [59], stating that the ease of integrating an option into one's daily activities is of utmost importance for stimulating and sustaining adoption. It is also in line with existing findings regarding specific modes of transportation, such as PT [25,59] or RS [47,54,75].

The findings on the appropriation study help to illustrate the findings from the context study and prioritize them from a user's perspective. They indicate that it was not necessarily a question of being aware of all options (as shown in [24,48,59]), but rather of being aware of the information that highlights the *situated appropriateness of an option in a given context.* Focusing on a particular context instead of creating awareness about *all* options addresses a common problem of "mode-oriented" concepts that merely focus on infrastructural and logistical aspects. Modes are not simply interchangeable, but, as Hasselqvist et al. [33] showed, transportation routines are established in relation to specific activities (e.g. daily errands, visiting friends, etc.). The rejection of RS in favor of WhatsApp as well as the strong interest in the calendar highlighted that appropriation of transportation tools is highly contextual and "in-situ" studies are needed to understand "how technologies are 'domesticated'" [67,72,76]. Therefore, concepts aiming at the adoption of various modes need to support the establishing of new routines for certain activities instead of just providing alternative logistical information.

While existing concepts, focusing on single modes, start to reflect personal needs (e.g. in PT [25,35]) or provide more situational relevance (e.g. in RS [60]), they remain "mode-bound", mostly adapting the logistical information to the user's needs yet often neglecting unintended uses [36,39] or other interactional factors [40,61]. Our findings offer design opportunities and approaches for overcoming this shortcoming. Acknowledging the "turn to practice in HCI" [36,40,61,65], our study shows that tools establishing new transport routines [1,2,4,30,73] need to align relevant information with the context of a practice to transform it. We have argued here that understanding how these factors come to be integrated requires a long-term approach, one which is geared to understanding how users appropriate functionalities over time. In this manner, we go some way towards discovering what works and what does not. The major limitation of our study, we feel, is scalability. We do not know, as yet, whether the results we report here would be valid, for instance, for a large, urban, environment where complexities are multiplied.

CONCLUSION

In conclusion, we found support for the findings of our context study, namely increased awareness about options, the consideration of personal knowledge and ability (e.g. in terms of "personal information spaces" [25]) and the importance of 'local' reasoning (e.g. taking into account contextual information [34,43]). Yet the results of the appropriation study stress how the relevance of information for the user depends on his/her situational requirements. Based on the user's activity (or intention), the interplay of different kinds of information is required, including non-transport related information such as weather, alternative destinations or activity-related restrictions and implications (e.g. starting time when going to the cinema). In addition to existing studies which mostly highlight logistical information and transportation infrastructure, we argue for an integrated understanding of transportation and the user's practical intentions. Regarding the adoption of different transport options, understanding this intention serves two purposes: 1) It provides opportunities to create awareness about existing alternatives; and 2) it highlights the necessity of providing information allowing users to assess the suitability of options. Therefore future support for transportation needs might integrate activities, events, alternative modes and other contextual information in an even more detailed and sophisticated way. Methods for personalizing information resources of this kind would, we feel, be one such useful future direction.

ACKNOWLEDGMENTS

This research was supported by German Federal Ministry of Education and Research (Grant Number 16 SV 5674). We thank our colleagues from University of Siegen and Fraunhofer FIT who provided insight and expertise that greatly assisted the research and helped to sharpen discussion and conclusion of this paper.

REFERENCES

1. Henk Aarts and Ap Dijksterhuis. 2000. The Automatic Activation Of Goal-Directed Behaviour: The Case Of Travel Habit. *Journal of Environmental Psychology* 20, 1: 75–82. https://doi.org/10.1006/jevp.1999.0156
2. Henk Aarts, Bas Verplanken, and Ad van Knippenberg. 1997. Habit and information use in travel mode choices. *Acta Psychologica* 96, 1–2: 1–14. https://doi.org/10.1016/S0001-6918(97)00008-5
3. Paul André, Max L. Wilson, Alisdair Owens, and Daniel Alexander Smith. 2007. Journey planning based on user needs. In *CHI '07 Extended Abstracts on Human Factors in Computing Systems* (CHI EA '07), 2025–2030. https://doi.org/10.1145/1240866.1240944
4. David Banister. 1978. The influence of habit formation on modal choice —a Heuristic model. *Transportation* 7, 1: 5–33. https://doi.org/10.1007/BF00148368
5. Tonatzin Yutzin Baños, Emmanuel Aquino, Fernando David Sernas, Yazmín Regina López, and Roberto Carlos Mendoza. 2007. EMI: A System to Improve and Promote the Use of Public Transportation. In *CHI '07 Extended Abstracts on Human Factors in Computing Systems* (CHI EA '07), 2037–2042. https://doi.org/10.1145/1240866.1240946
6. Philip Barham, Stefan Carmien, and Ainara Garzo. 2015. The Assistant Project: Creating a Smartphone App to Assist Older People When Travelling by Public Transport. In *Proceedings of the ICT4AgeingWell 2015*, 20–22.
7. Michael Behrisch, Laura Bieker, Jakob Erdmann, and Daniel Krajzewicz. 2011. SUMO – Simulation of Urban MObility: An Overview. In *Proceedings of SIMUL 2011, The Third International Conference on Advances in System Simulation*. Retrieved August 16, 2016 from http://www.thinkmind.org/index.php?view=instance&instance=SIMUL+2011
8. Birgitta Bergvall-Kareborn, Marita Holst, and Anna Ståhlbröst. 2009. Concept Design with a Living Lab Approach. In *2009 42nd Hawaii International Conference on System Sciences*, 1–10. https://doi.org/10.1109/HICSS.2009.123
9. Andrew D. Beswick, Karen Rees, Paul Dieppe, Salma Ayis, Rachael Gooberman-Hill, Jeremy Horwood, and Shah Ebrahim. 2008. Complex interventions to improve physical function and maintain independent living in elderly people: a systematic review and meta-analysis. *Lancet (London, England)* 371, 9614: 725–735. https://doi.org/10.1016/S0140-6736(08)60342-6
10. Nicola Bicocchi and Marco Mamei. 2014. Investigating ride sharing opportunities through mobility data analysis. *Pervasive and Mobile Computing* 14: 83–94. https://doi.org/10.1016/j.pmcj.2014.05.010
11. Jeanette Blomberg and Helena Karasti. 2012. Positioning ethnogrpahy with Participatory Design. In *Routledge International Handbook of Participatory Design*. Routledge.
12. Margot Brereton, Paul Roe, Marcus Foth, Jonathan M. Bunker, and Laurie Buys. 2009. Designing participation in agile ridesharing with mobile social software. In *Proceedings of the 21st Annual Conference of the Australian Computer-Human Interaction Special Interest Group: Design: Open 24/7*, 257–260.
13. Carl Collins, Amy Grude, Matthew Scholl, and Robert Thompson. 2007. Txt Bus: Wait Time Information on Demand. In *CHI '07 Extended Abstracts on Human Factors in Computing Systems* (CHI EA '07), 2049–2054. https://doi.org/10.1145/1240866.1240948
14. Daniel. J. Dailey, Donald Loseff, and David Meyers. 1999. Seattle smart traveler: dynamic ridematching on the World Wide Web. *Transportation Research Part C: Emerging Technologies* 7, 1: 17–32. https://doi.org/10.1016/S0968-090X(99)00007-8
15. Joyce Dargay and Saara Pekkarinen. 1997. Public Transport Pricing Policy: Empirical Evidence of Regional Bus Card Systems in Finland. *Transportation Research Record: Journal of the Transportation Research Board* 1604: 146–152. https://doi.org/10.3141/1604-17
16. Paul Dourish. 2003. The Appropriation of Interactive Technologies: Some Lessons from Placeless Documents. *Computer Supported Cooperative Work (CSCW)* 12: 465–490.
17. Jeannette Durick, Toni Robertson, Margot Brereton, Frank Vetere, and Bjorn Nansen. 2013. Dispelling Ageing Myths in Technology Design. In *Proceedings of the 25th Australian Computer-Human Interaction Conference: Augmentation, Application, Innovation, Collaboration* (OzCHI '13), 467–476. https://doi.org/10.1145/2541016.2541040
18. Katrin Dziekan and Karl Kottenhoff. 2007. Dynamic at-stop real-time information displays for public transport: effects on customers. *Transportation Research Part A: Policy and Practice* 41, 6: 489–501. https://doi.org/10.1016/j.tra.2006.11.006
19. Lars Eriksson, Margareta Friman, and Tommy Gärling. 2008. Stated reasons for reducing work-commute by car. *Transportation Research Part F: Traffic Psychology and Behaviour* 11, 6: 427–433. https://doi.org/10.1016/j.trf.2008.04.001
20. Markus Fellesson and Margareta Friman. 2012. Perceived Satisfaction with Public Transport Service in Nine European Cities. *Journal of the Transportation Research Forum* 47, 3. https://doi.org/10.5399/osu/jtrf.47.3.2126
21. Brian Ferris, Kari Watkins, and Alan Borning. 2010. OneBusAway: Results from Providing Real-time Arrival Information for Public Transit. In *Proceedings of the SIGCHI Conference on Human Factors in Computing Systems* (CHI '10), 1807–1816. https://doi.org/10.1145/1753326.1753597

22. Carlo V. Fiorio and Marco Percoco. 2007. Would You Stick To Using Your Car Even If Charged? Evidence from Trento, Italy. *Transport Reviews* 27, 5: 605–620. https://doi.org/10.1080/01441640701322727
23. Tom Flint and Phil Turner. 2016. Enactive appropriation. *AI & SOCIETY* 31, 1: 41–49. https://doi.org/10.1007/s00146-015-0582-y
24. Stefanie Fobker and Reinhold Grotz. 2006. Everyday Mobility of Elderly People in Different Urban Settings: The Example of the City of Bonn, Germany. *Urban Studies* 43, 1: 99–118. https://doi.org/10.1080/00420980500409292
25. Stefan Foell, Reza Rawassizadeh, and Gerd Kortuem. 2013. Informing the Design of Future Transport Information Services with Travel Behaviour Data. In *Proceedings of the 2013 ACM Conference on Pervasive and Ubiquitous Computing Adjunct Publication* (UbiComp '13 Adjunct), 1343–1346. https://doi.org/10.1145/2494091.2499219
26. Asbjørn Følstad. Living labs for innovation and development of information and communication technology: a literature review. *The Electronic Journal for Virtual Organizations and ...*. Retrieved December 13, 2016 from https://www.academia.edu/949819/Living_labs_for_innovation_and_development_of_information_and_communication_technology_a_literature_review
27. Pin Sym Foong, Vincent Jr. Diaz, Aaron R. Houssian, Adam Huse, and Pornsuree Jamsri. 2007. EventStream: Integrated Transit Information System. In *CHI '07 Extended Abstracts on Human Factors in Computing Systems* (CHI EA '07), 2061–2066. https://doi.org/10.1145/1240866.1240950
28. Jodi Forlizzi, William C. Barley, and Thomas Seder. 2010. Where Should I Turn: Moving from Individual to Collaborative Navigation Strategies to Inform the Interaction Design of Future Navigation Systems. In *Proceedings of the SIGCHI Conference on Human Factors in Computing Systems* (CHI '10), 1261–1270. https://doi.org/10.1145/1753326.1753516
29. Mareike Glöss, Moira McGregor, and Barry Brown. 2016. Designing for Labour: Uber and the On-Demand Mobile Workforce. In *Proceedings of the 2016 CHI Conference on Human Factors in Computing Systems* (CHI '16), 1632–1643. https://doi.org/10.1145/2858036.2858476
30. Philip B. Goodwin. 1977. Habit and hysteresis in mode choice. *Urban studies* 14, 1: 95–98.
31. Martha V. Gukeisen, David Hutchful, Pieter Kleymeer, and Sean A. Munson. 2007. altVerto: using intervention and community to promote alternative transportation. In *CHI '07 Extended Abstracts on Human Factors in Computing Systems* (CHI EA '07), 2067–2072. https://doi.org/10.1145/1240866.1240951
32. Mark Haselkorn, Jan Spryidakis, Cathy Blumenthal, Susan Michalak, Brain Goble, and M. Garner. 1995. Bellevue Smart Traveler: design, demonstration and assessment. WA-RD 376.1. Retrieved March 17, 2014 from http://trid.trb.org/view.aspx?id=1168898
33. Hanna Hasselqvist, Mia Hesselgren, and Cristian Bogdan. 2016. Challenging the Car Norm: Opportunities for ICT to Support Sustainable Transportation Practices. In *Proceedings of the 2016 CHI Conference on Human Factors in Computing Systems* (CHI '16), 1300–1311. https://doi.org/10.1145/2858036.2858468
34. J Hightower. 2003. From Position to Place. In *In: Proc. of the 2003 Workshop on Location- Aware Computing*, 10–12.
35. Ricardo Hoar. 2008. Visualizing Transit Through a Web Based Geographic Information System. *International Journal of Environmental, Earth Science and Engineering* 2, 10: 2–7.
36. Victor Kaptelinin and Liam J. Bannon. 2012. Interaction Design Beyond the Product: Creating Technology-Enhanced Activity Spaces. *Human–Computer Interaction* 27, 3: 277–309. https://doi.org/10.1080/07370024.2011.646930
37. Aram Kim, Hyemi Kim, Hannah Baek, Seohyun Lim, Sungjin Hong, and Jinwoo Kim. 2016. Most of the Time, I Walk: A Guideline for the Elder's Walking Navigation Services. In *Proceedings of HCI Korea* (HCIK '16), 157–163. https://doi.org/10.17210/hcik.2016.01.157
38. Martin Knobel, Marc Hassenzahl, Josef Schumann, Melanie Lamara, Kai Eckoldt, and Andreas Butz. 2013. A Trip into the Countryside: An Experience Design for Explorative Car Cruises. In *CHI '13 Extended Abstracts on Human Factors in Computing Systems* (CHI EA '13), 565–570. https://doi.org/10.1145/2468356.2468456
39. Alina Krischkowsky, Bernhard Maurer, and Manfred Tscheligi. 2016. Captology and Technology Appropriation: Unintended Use as a Source for Designing Persuasive Technologies. In *Persuasive Technology* (Lecture Notes in Computer Science), 78–83. Retrieved December 13, 2016 from http://link.springer.com/chapter/10.1007/978-3-319-31510-2_7
40. Kari Kuutti and Liam J. Bannon. 2014. The Turn to Practice in HCI: Towards a Research Agenda. In *Proceedings of the SIGCHI Conference on Human Factors in Computing Systems* (CHI '14), 3543–3552. https://doi.org/10.1145/2556288.2557111
41. Joonhwan Lee, Jodi Forlizzi, and Scott E. Hudson. 2005. Studying the Effectiveness of MOVE: A Contextually Optimized In-vehicle Navigation System. In *Proceedings of the SIGCHI Conference on Human Factors in Computing Systems* (CHI '05), 571–580. https://doi.org/10.1145/1054972.1055051
42. Gilly Leshed, Theresa Velden, Oya Rieger, Blazej Kot, and Phoebe Sengers. 2008. In-car Gps Navigation: Engagement with and Disengagement from the Environment. In *Proceedings of the SIGCHI*

Conference on Human Factors in Computing Systems (CHI '08), 1675–1684. https://doi.org/10.1145/1357054.1357316

43. Jialiu Lin, Guang Xiang, Jason I. Hong, and Norman Sadeh. 2010. Modeling people's place naming preferences in location sharing. In *Proceedings of the 12th ACM international conference on Ubiquitous computing* (Ubicomp '10), 75–84. https://doi.org/10.1145/1864349.1864362
44. Yi-Tien Lin, Hsiao-Ching Su, I-Wen Lo, and Po-Lin Chou. 2016. BringUBus: Matching Buses to Passengers with Lower Mobility. In *Proceedings of the 2016 CHI Conference Extended Abstracts on Human Factors in Computing Systems* (CHI EA '16), 44–49. https://doi.org/10.1145/2851581.2890640
45. S. Maclean and Daniel Dailey. 2002. Wireless Internet Access to Real-Time Transit Information. *Transportation Research Record: Journal of the Transportation Research Board* 1791, 1: 92–98. https://doi.org/10.3141/1791-14
46. Philipp Mayring. 2000. Qualitative Content Analysis. *Forum Qualitative Sozialforschung / Forum: Qualitative Social Research* 1, 2. Retrieved June 30, 2016 from http://www.qualitative-research.net/index.php/fqs/article/view/1089
47. Johanna Meurer, Martin Stein, David Randall, Markus Rohde, and Volker Wulf. 2014. Social Dependency and Mobile Autonomy: Supporting Older Adults' Mobility with Ridesharing Ict. In *Proceedings of the SIGCHI Conference on Human Factors in Computing Systems* (CHI '14), 1923–1932. https://doi.org/10.1145/2556288.2557300
48. Heidrun Mollenkopf, Fiorella Marcellini, Isto Ruoppila, Pia Flaschenträger, Christina Gagliardi, and L Spazzafumo. 1997. Outdoor mobility and social relationships of elderly people. *Archives of gerontology and geriatrics* 24, 3: 295–310.
49. Claudia Müller, Dominik Hornung, Theodor Hamm, and Volker Wulf. 2015. Practice-based Design of a Neighborhood Portal: Focusing on Elderly Tenants in a City Quarter Living Lab. In *Proceedings of the 33rd Annual ACM Conference on Human Factors in Computing Systems*, 2295–2304. Retrieved April 4, 2016 from http://dl.acm.org/citation.cfm?id=2702449
50. Claudia Müller, Cornelius Neufeldt, David Randall, and Volker Wulf. 2012. ICT-development in residential care settings: sensitizing design to the life circumstances of the residents of a care home. In *Proceedings of the SIGCHI Conference on Human Factors in Computing Systems* (CHI '12), 2639–2648. https://doi.org/10.1145/2207676.2208655
51. Claudia Müller, Lin Wan, Martin Stein, and Cornelius Neufeldt. 2012. Experience of Giving and Receiving–Living Lab-based Technology Design with Elderly People. Retrieved January 9, 2016 from http://cci.drexel.edu/faculty/jrode/stein.pdf
52. Susanne Nordbakke and Tim Schwanen. 2014. Transport, unmet activity needs and wellbeing in later life: exploring the links. *Transportation*: 1–23. https://doi.org/10.1007/s11116-014-9558-x
53. Corinna Ogonowski, Benedikt Ley, Jan Hess, Lin Wan, and Volker Wulf. 2013. Designing for the living room: long-term user involvement in a living lab. In *Proceedings of the 2013 ACM annual conference on Human factors in computing systems* (CHI '13), 1539–1548. https://doi.org/10.1145/2466110.2466205
54. Fatih Kursat Ozenc, Lorrie F. Cranor, and James H. Morris. 2011. Adapt-a-ride: understanding the dynamics of commuting preferences through an experience design framework. In *Proceedings of the 2011 Conference on Designing Pleasurable Products and Interfaces* (DPPI '11), 61:1–61:8. https://doi.org/10.1145/2347504.2347571
55. Manoj Prasad, Paul Taele, Daniel Goldberg, and Tracy A. Hammond. 2014. HaptiMoto: Turn-by-turn Haptic Route Guidance Interface for Motorcyclists. In *Proceedings of the SIGCHI Conference on Human Factors in Computing Systems* (CHI '14), 3597–3606. https://doi.org/10.1145/2556288.2557404
56. Gary Pritchard, John Vines, and Patrick Olivier. 2015. Your Money's No Good Here: The Elimination of Cash Payment on London Buses. In *Proceedings of the 33rd Annual ACM Conference on Human Factors in Computing Systems* (CHI '15), 907–916. https://doi.org/10.1145/2702123.2702137
57. Steve Raney. 2010. San Francisco to Silicon Valley, California, Instant Ridesharing with Transfer Hub. *Transportation Research Record: Journal of the Transportation Research Board* 2143, 1: 134–141. https://doi.org/10.3141/2143-17
58. Sasank Reddy, Katie Shilton, Gleb Denisov, Christian Cenizal, Deborah Estrin, and Mani Srivastava. 2010. Biketastic: Sensing and Mapping for Better Biking. In *Proceedings of the SIGCHI Conference on Human Factors in Computing Systems* (CHI '10), 1817–1820. https://doi.org/10.1145/1753326.1753598
59. Lauren Redman, Margareta Friman, Tommy Gärling, and Terry Hartig. 2013. Quality attributes of public transport that attract car users: A research review. *Transport Policy* 25: 119–127. https://doi.org/10.1016/j.tranpol.2012.11.005
60. Michael Rigby, Antonio Krüger, and Stephan Winter. 2013. An Opportunistic Client User Interface to Support Centralized Ride Share Planning. In *Proceedings of the 21st ACM SIGSPATIAL International Conference on Advances in Geographic Information Systems* (SIGSPATIAL'13), 34–43. https://doi.org/10.1145/2525314.2525334
61. Markus Rohde, Peter Brödner, Gunnar Stevens, Matthias Betz, and Volker Wulf. 2016. Grounded design–A praxeological IS research perspective. *Journal of Information Technology*.

62. Sandra Rosenbloom. 2003. The mobility needs of older Americans. *Taking the High Road: A Transportation Agenda of Strengthening Metropolitan Areas*: 227–54.
63. Tim Schwanen, David Banister, and Ann Bowling. 2012. Independence and mobility in later life. *Geoforum* 43, 6: 1313–1322. https://doi.org/10.1016/j.geoforum.2012.04.001
64. Akshaya K. Sen, Geetam Tiwari, and V. Upadhyay. 2007. Should bus commuting be subsidized for providing quality transport services? — A case for Delhi. *Sadhana* 32, 4: 329–345. https://doi.org/10.1007/s12046-007-0028-4
65. Elizabeth Shove, Mika Pantzar, and Matt Watson. 2012. *The Dynamics of Social Practice: Everyday Life and how it Changes*. SAGE.
66. Erkki Siira and Samuli Heinonen. 2015. Enabling Mobility fot the Elderly: Design and Implementation of Assistant Navigation Service. In *Proceedings of the Transed 2015*.
67. Gunnar Stevens, Volkmar Pipek, and Volker Wulf. 2009. Appropriation Infrastructure: Supporting the Design of Usages. In *End-User Development*, Volkmar Pipek, Mary Rosson, Boris de Ruyter and Volker Wulf (eds.). Springer Berlin / Heidelberg, 50–69. Retrieved from http://dx.doi.org/10.1007/978-3-642-00427-8_4
68. Joseph S. Szyliowicz. 2003. Decision-making, intermodal transportation, and sustainable mobility: towards a new paradigm. *International Social Science Journal* 55, 176: 185–197. https://doi.org/10.1111/j.1468-2451.2003.05502002.x
69. Adi Tedjasaputra and Eunice Sari. 2016. Sharing Economy in Smart City Transportation Services. In *Proceedings of the SEACHI 2016 on Smart Cities for Better Living with HCI and UX* (SEACHI 2016), 32–35. https://doi.org/10.1145/2898365.2899800
70. John Thøgersen and Berit Møller. 2008. Breaking car use habits: The effectiveness of a free one-month travelcard. *Transportation* 35, 3: 329–345. https://doi.org/10.1007/s11116-008-9160-1
71. Cecilia Tomassini, Stamatis Kalogirou, Emily Grundy, Tineke Fokkema, Pekka Martikainen, Marjolein Broese van Groenou, and Antti Karisto. 2004. Contacts between elderly parents and their children in four European countries: current patterns and future prospects. *European Journal of Ageing* 1, 1: 54–63. https://doi.org/10.1007/s10433-004-0003-4
72. Manfred Tscheligi, Alina Krischkowsky, Katja Neureiter, Kori Inkpen, Michael Muller, and Gunnar Stevens. 2014. Potentials of the "Unexpected": Technology Appropriation Practices and Communication Needs. In *Proceedings of the 18th International Conference on Supporting Group Work* (GROUP '14), 313–316. https://doi.org/10.1145/2660398.2660427
73. Bas Verplanken, Henk Aarts, Ad van Knippenberg, and Anja Moonen. 1998. Habit versus planned behaviour: A field experiment. *British Journal of Social Psychology* 37, 1: 111–128. https://doi.org/10.1111/j.2044-8309.1998.tb01160.x
74. John Vines, Mark Blythe, Stephen Lindsay, Paul Dunphy, Andrew Monk, and Patrick Olivier. 2012. Questionable Concepts: Critique As Resource for Designing with Eighty Somethings. In *Proceedings of the SIGCHI Conference on Human Factors in Computing Systems* (CHI '12), 1169–1178. https://doi.org/10.1145/2207676.2208567
75. Rick Wash, Libby Hemphill, and Paul Resnick. 2005. Design decisions in the RideNow project. In *Proceedings of the 2005 international ACM SIGGROUP conference on Supporting group work* (GROUP '05), 132–135. https://doi.org/10.1145/1099203.1099228
76. Volker Wulf, Markus Rohde, Volkmar Pipek, and Gunnar Stevens. 2011. Engaging with Practices: Design Case Studies As a Research Framework in CSCW. In *Proceedings of the ACM 2011 Conference on Computer Supported Cooperative Work* (CSCW '11), 505–512. https://doi.org/10.1145/1958824.1958902
77. Friederike Ziegler and Tim Schwanen. 2011. "I like to go out to be energised by different people": an exploratory analysis of mobility and wellbeing in later life. *Ageing & Society* 31, 5: 758–781. https://doi.org/10.1017/S0144686X10000498
78. John Zimmerman, Anthony Tomasic, Charles Garrod, Daisy Yoo, Chaya Hiruncharoenvate, Rafae Aziz, Nikhil Ravi Thiruvengadam, Yun Huang, and Aaron Steinfeld. 2011. Field trial of Tiramisu: crowd-sourcing bus arrival times to spur co-design. In *Proceedings of the SIGCHI Conference on Human Factors in Computing Systems* (CHI '11), 1677–1686. https://doi.org/10.1145/1978942.1979187
79. 2010. *Mobilität in Deutschland - Ausgewählte Ergebnisse (Mobility in Germany - Selected Findings)*. ADAC, München. Retrieved August 2, 2016 from https://www.adac.de/_mmm/pdf/statistik_mobilitaet_in_deutschland_0111_46603.pdf

Gains from Participatory Design Team Membership as Perceived by Child Alumni and their Parents

Brenna McNally[1], Matthew Louis Mauriello[2], Mona Leigh Guha[1], Allison Druin[1]
Human-Computer Interaction Lab
College of Information Studies[1]; Department of Computer Science[2]
University of Maryland, College Park
{bmcnally, mattm401, mguha, allisond}@umd.edu

Figure 1. Adults and children working together on a PD team to prototype children's technologies. **Far left:** Paper prototyping a web-based survival game. **Middle left:** Using mobile devices and paper mockups to iterate a history game. **Middle right:** Presenting paper mockup ideas for a mobile mental health application. **Far right:** Presenting 3D prototyped ideas for a virtual reality game.

ABSTRACT
The direct gains children perceive from their membership on Participatory Design (PD) teams are seldom the focus of research studies. Yet, how HCI practitioners choose to include children in PD methods may influence the value participants see in their participation, and thereafter the outcomes of PD processes. To understand what gains former child members of a PD team perceive from their participation we conducted a two-part study. In Study 1 we surveyed and interviewed child alumni of a PD team to determine gains that are perceived first-hand. In Study 2 we obtained a secondary perspective by surveying and interviewing parents of alumni. We report on the perceived gains to former participants that were identified and described in these two studies—including *collaboration, communication, design process knowledge,* and *confidence*. We reflect on our findings through discussions of the continued applicability of gains, new opportunities, and implications for PD practitioners and methods.

ISBN 978-1-4503-4655-9/17/05...$15.00
DOI: http://dx.doi.org/10.1145/3025453.3025622

Author Keywords
Children; Participatory Design; Co-Design; Gains; Participant Perspective

ACM Classification Keywords
H.5.m. Information interfaces and presentation (e.g., HCI): Miscellaneous;

INTRODUCTION
Participatory Design (PD) is a design approach used in HCI research that provides practices and techniques to actively include users throughout the technology design process [21,36]. PD researchers have been motivated to involve diverse populations as active partners in the design process, expanding the possibilities of new ideas for innovation. This inclusive approach to developing new technologies also results in the development of new PD methods that specialize in facilitating feedback from specific populations— such as the elderly [17,30], persons with special needs [18,4,33], and children [14,24,28,42]. In the case of children, whom our research focuses on, not only have numerous new technologies been developed [9,37,39,40] but there has also been a need to design new PD techniques [12,23,35,44,45] that support the full inclusion of children in the design process. However, while the benefits HCI practitioners receive from working with children in PD can include developing more child-centric interfaces, spending less time on testing after a technology is developed, and finding surprising new innovations [36], research is less clear on the gains to child PD participants.

There has been some discussion within the research community on the indirect benefits to child PD participants: for instance, that they have contributed to a better technology, or that their voice has been heard in the design of a technology that they, as a member of the user group, are meant to use [7]. In addition to remaining aware of indirect benefits, there is a need to assess what direct gains may exist for the youth who are involved in PD. Specifically, if we uncover the benefits that youth on PD teams experience we can improve existing design techniques and devise new techniques that better support their paths to innovation. This could lead to better design recommendations from the PD process. In addition to potential improvements to the process, developing an understanding of participant gains would advance our community's ethical ambition to go beyond "preventing harm" to participants, as promoting direct gains builds upon themes that are central to PD: attention and care for users [8], mutual learning [2,7,25], and core PD values of democracy, emancipation, and quality of work [21,36].

In response to these potential benefits from PD processes, studies that aim to identify the direct gains to PD participants have emerged [7,8,19]. However, research has yet to determine what gains persist over time from the perspective of child PD participants. Understanding the gains resulting from children's participation in PD could be of mutual benefit to both researchers and child participants. Our work attends to the gains that child PD participants experience in an effort to 1) improve the PD process and PD techniques, 2) create better technologies from this improved process, and 3) enhance participant-researcher relationships. Perhaps most importantly, our efforts to shed light on the long-term effects of children's participation on PD team are grounded in the philosophy that PD activities should be *"meaningful within themselves"* [2, pg.167].

In this work we seek to understand what meaning former participants derived from their involvement on a PD team that has been active since 1998. We ask, "*What gains, if any, do former child participants and their parents perceive from children's involvement on a Participatory Design team?*" We address this question through an examination of the perspectives of child participant alumni and their parents, captured through surveys and interviews with both groups. In Study 1, we surveyed twelve former child participants of a PD team with 1-5 years experience on the team, and six were further interviewed. In Study 2, seventeen parents, who cumulatively had 21 children participate on the team, were surveyed and four participated in follow-up interviews. In this way we obtained two distinct viewpoints on gains to children from participation on a PD team: 1) the removed, and in some cases adult, views of the persons who personally experienced gains, and 2) the views of parents who could observe changes in the behaviors and attitudes of their children outside participation on the design team.

The results of this work uncover direct gains that child alumni and their parents perceive from participation on a PD team, including *collaboration*, *communication, design process knowledge,* and *confidence*. We also discuss the continued applicability of gains to child alumni, new opportunities, and the implications of this work for PD practitioners and methods.

BACKGROUND AND RELATED WORK

We first provide a background on how PD has been adapted for use with children and on the specific PD team discussed in this work. We then review previous works that have investigated participant gains from PD activities.

Participatory Design with Children

Participatory Design offers a set of practices and techniques to involve end-users of a technology a role in actively designing it [36]. Originally conceived in a democratic movement to give Scandinavian factory workers a role in designing technology they would use on the job [5,21,36], the success of PD has led to its extension beyond this sociopolitical context. PD is now used to design technologies with other user populations as active participants in the process, such the elderly [17,30,], persons with special needs [18,4,33], and children [8,15,28,42]. It has also inspired methods such as co-design; while the term co-design is sometimes used synonymously with PD, the co-design subset of PD differs in that it does not assume any one stakeholder's views or input are more important than another's [6]. Co-design methods involve children to surface the desires of these young people [15]. During co-design sessions, techniques are utilized that have been adapted to support design input from children (e.g., the *Bags of Stuff* 3D prototyping technique, the *Big Paper* paper-prototyping technique) [45].

Methods of PD with children differ in the degree of participation requested from children. Informant Design, for instance, allows for many children to participate in the design process for a relatively short period of time, giving other stakeholders feedback on the work being developed at critical points in the design process [41,42]. The method of Bonded Design goes a step further, and involves an intensive, intergenerational partnership between adults and children built on the belief that children should be included in the entire design process [28]. In Bonded Design, the team works on a single project over the course of several weeks. Similarly, within the Cooperative Inquiry (CI) method, children and adults work closely throughout the entire design process. However, CI requires a high degree of participation from children, that of a design partner (Figure 2) [15]. In the CI method, which most closely follows the co-design subset of PD, children participate on the design team for an academic year and work on numerous projects, and can choose to participate for multiple years [24]. This work is situated within the context of a CI team, further described below.

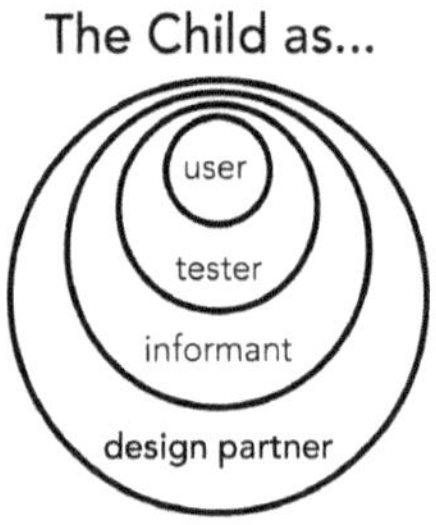

Figure 2. The relationships between the roles children can have in the design of technologies for children [15].

Kidsteam History
This work discusses a CI team called Kidsteam, which has met at the University of Maryland's Human-Computer Interaction Lab since 1998. During Kidsteam design sessions, 6-8 children ages 7-11 work with adults from diverse disciplinary backgrounds as design partners to design technologies for children. These 90-minute design sessions are held twice weekly throughout the academic year, and are preceded by a two-week summer program where the team learns design techniques and how to work together. At the end of each year, child participants are given a $100 budget to spend on a technology gift of their choice (with parents' approval), and have in the past selected items such as e-readers, robot dogs, and mini-drones, which they receive at the team's annual party.

Throughout the program's 18-year history, Kidsteam has worked on a wide variety of projects for academic, industry, and nonprofit groups. Projects have ranged in content area from educational to entertaining— such as second language learning [32], STEM topics [1,29,37], and interactive theatre [40]— and across platforms— including mobile, tangible, wearable, and web applications. There are currently 60+ Kidsteam child design partner alumni, and many former child members are now adults (18+ years old).

Gains from Participation in PD Projects
While much of the literature concerning PD involves the technological or design process outcomes of PD work, recent years have seen an increased interest in the gains of different stakeholders on PD teams. Most notably, two studies by Bossen, Dindler, and Iversen and a third by Garde et al. specifically analyze the "gains" of participants on PD teams [7,8,19]. In each of these studies, differences in gains from participation are discussed across different stakeholder groups. Through retrospective interviews investigating the long-term gains that four distinct participant groups—students in their teens, teachers, administrators, and a politician—Bossen et al. reported that:

> *"In this case, interdisciplinary communicative skills, knowledge, and experience with new technology, linked to their professional practices, were amongst the gains" [7, p.149].*

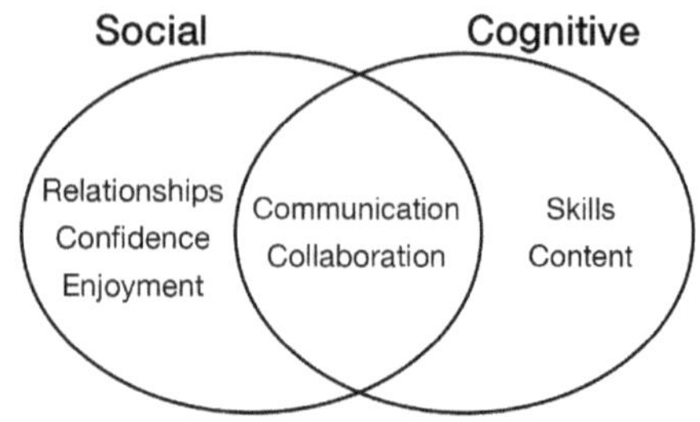

Figure 3. The social and cognitive experiences of child design partners [22].

Similarly, Garde et al discussed how most of their PD participants exhibited gains in the areas of technology learning, insights into work practices, feeling heard, and having a generally positive experience [19]. While gains of interdisciplinary, largely adult, PD teams have begun to receive attention, the gains of youth participants have received less attention, which our work begins to address.

Frustrations Impeding Gains. While participatory environments may foster gains from PD activities, conversely an environment that is rife with frustrations may obstruct gains. In looking at impediments to user gains, Bossen et al. identified three frustrations that seemed to impede gains: unresolved differences between aims, absence of a clear set-up for collaboration, and different conceptions of technology [8]. Despite the frustrations on the project, participant gains included technology access and cross-professional networking [8]. With regard to this work, while frustrations were discussed during participant interviews, and exist within PD with children [22,31], moving beyond identifying participant frustrations into a deeper understanding of how child frustrations impede gains is outside the scope of this work, which focuses on the identification and description of gains.

Gains of Children Who Participated on PD Teams
Despite seldom being the focus of research studies, gains to children can nonetheless be found throughout discussions and observations made by researchers in their descriptions of PD studies. Among the most commonly observed gains of child participants of PD teams are the related dimensions of collaboration and communication. Collaboration skills are a foreseeable benefit due to the nature of working on a design team, where the development of designs and prototypes requires collaborative efforts between team members [15,16]. Similarly, researchers describe how increases in communication skills, which generally emphasize children's ability to share their ideas during a collaborative design process, occur both between children [3] and between children and adults [26]. Another observed gain is content knowledge, as child designers are introduced to content knowledge that is relevant to design challenges. For instance, children designing a mobile application that incorporates thermography may gain content knowledge about heat transfer. Researchers acknowledge this fairly

often, both in regard to broad content learning [14,34] and learning curricular units in schools [3]. Additionally, as design is largely about solving problems, being part of a PD team may also help develop children's problem solving abilities [27]. Finally, a less specific gain to participants that researchers have noted is an increased understanding of technology through increased exposure to it [14,20,34]. While fewer researchers describe other participant gains from involvement in design processes, it is important to identify all areas that may be significant from the perspective of child participants. These less frequently cited benefits include designerly-ways-of-knowing (e.g., tackling ill-defined problems) [10], creativity [27], and fun [28].

In contrast to these works, whose primary concerns were outside the gains of their participants, two studies have discussed gains to child participants more directly. A study by Hansen & Iversen discussed the motivating factors of teenagers that participated in a PD project, and found motivations that included direct gains, such as encouragements (e.g., awards, lunch) and being endorsed as experts (e.g., respect, recognition) [25]. Work by Guha investigated the impacts that participating on a PD team had on children over the course of a year of participation [22]. Through observations of the children, artifact analysis, and interviews with the children and their parents, Guha uncovered impacts on child design partners in the areas of social and cognitive skill development (Figure 3) [22]. The next challenge—and the purpose of this study—is to return to former child PD team participants and their parents and discover what, if any, impacts of participation are perceived as gains after participation has ended.

STUDY 1: CHILD DESIGN PARTNER ALUMNI

To investigate the potential gains participation on a PD team can afford child participants, we conducted anonymous surveys with alumni of Kidsteam followed by interviews with a subset of survey participants. This work is part of a larger study, the first phase of which reported on the ethical implications of these surveys and interviews [31]. The method and analysis for the alumni data, while described in [31], are also described below.

Method

In Study 1, surveys and interviews were conducted with child participant alumni. The open-ended survey questions and interview transcripts were qualitatively analyzed.

Surveys

Participants. Child design partner alumni were recruited for an anonymous, online survey. Parents of the 56 eligible alumni were asked to forward a recruitment email to team alumni. Outdated contact information (e.g., defunct email addresses) prevented us from contacting approximately 23% of parents. A total of 12 alumni (3 male, 9 female) completed the survey. Their involvement on Kidsteam began between 1998 and 2013 and lasted for an average of 2.3 years (*SD*=1.3). Participants left the team an average of 6.4 years before the study (*SD*=4.1).

Procedure. The online surveys were distributed in spring of 2015 and were designed to take no more than 15 minutes. To begin the survey alumni had to indicate consent or, if under age 18, have a parent consent to participation and read an assent script to the alumni participant. The survey included open-ended, short answer questions as well as closed, 5pt likert-scale questions. Questions reviewed general experiences with the team, team relationships (e.g., respect), and topics related to participation (e.g. whether participants believed their ideas and opinions were important to the team). Participants were not compensated.

Interviews

Participants. Participants were recruited from those alumni who stated they were interested in being contacted for a follow-up interview at the end of the online survey. Of the seven volunteers, the six who best represented a range of years of participation, time since participation ended, and gender (one male, five female) were interviewed in fall of 2015 about their experiences and expectations. Participants were members of Kidsteam for an average of 2.0 years (*SD*=1.1), began participation on Kidsteam between 1998 and 2012, and three were currently adults (age 18+).

Procedure. The semi-structured interviews with child design partner alumni lasted 34 minutes (*SD*=16.8) on average and were held either on the University of Maryland's campus or via a videoconference (e.g., Skype). Interview questions began broadly (e.g., *"Tell me what it was like to be part of Kidsteam."*) and later included questions about areas of interest defined in the literature (e.g., positive/negative experiences, ability to participate). Participants did not receive compensation. Parents could be present during interviews with children under age 18 as long as they agreed not to engage in the interview. Participants consented and, as appropriate, assented to audio recording, which were transcribed for analysis.

Analysis

Our primary analysis consisted of qualitatively coding the open-ended survey question responses and the interview responses, which are supported by results of the likert responses where applicable. Following a method of coding prescribed by Straus and Corbin [35], a researcher began the analysis by open coding all responses to the open-ended survey questions. These data were then iteratively categorized through two coding checks with three members of the research team. An initial codebook was developed through combining the results of the coding checks with ideas drawn from research literature. The initial codebook contained 23 codes and their definitions, grouped under eight categories: *Relationships, Projects, Incorporation of Ideas, Security and Consent, Fun, Knowledge and Skills, Confidence,* and *Social Interactions.* The codebook went through an additional coding check with the research team to refine and clarify codes, resulting in 20 codes within the eight categories. The refined code set and definitions formed the final version of the codebook.

Inter-Rater Reliability was then computed between two researchers on a random selection of 20% of the short-response survey data and two randomly selected, transcribed interviews, coded at the sentence level. Researchers achieved a score of .92 using Cohen's Kappa, as calculated within NVivo software, considered *almost perfect agreement* (range: .81 to .99) [43]. Having reached agreement, one researcher independently coded the remaining open-ended survey response and interview data.

Findings

In this section we present findings on child design partner alumni's perceptions of the gains they received from their participation on a PD team and issues that may relate to gains. Quotes in this paper represent themes from the data, and are identified by participant group (i.e., A for alumni, and later P for parent), data source (i.e., S for survey and I for interview), and participant number (i.e., 3). For example, the third child alumnus to respond to the survey is identified as "AS3." This section begins with the results of an initial survey question about whether gains existed, and then goes on to detail the gains participants described in the entirety of their surveys and interviews.

Initial Responses on the Existence of Gains

Survey respondents were initially asked a binary question about whether they had learned anything from their participation on the team, with most (10) answering *yes*. One participant abstained from answering this question and another responded *no*. When the 10 survey participants who answered *yes* were subsequently asked a short-response question about what they learned, they described learning about design processes (9) (e.g., synthesizing ideas, brainstorming), conveying their ideas (4) (e.g., presenting), domain knowledge (3), and that their opinions mattered (3). These responses, in addition to other gains that participants described throughout the entirety of their surveys and interviews, are elaborated upon in the following sections.

Communication

Improvements to their ability to convey ideas to other people, including giving presentations, were observed by half of the interviewed alumni (3/6). These participants described how their ability to communicate with non-peers improved— both communicating with adults as a child or, in one case, communicating with children now that the participant is an adult. One of the interview participants described how presenting helped her overcome feelings of shyness, as being able to rely on her teammates to present with her created a safe space to learn how to communicate her ideas: *"One thing that helped was being in a group and presenting. I didn't always have to talk independently"* (AI1). Survey responses by some (2) alumni re-iterate the ideas that participation on the PD team helped them to, *"express my ideas to other people without feeling afraid"* (AS8), and to communicate with non-peer groups:

> *"I learned how to present and convey my ideas more effectively. I also think it helped me in my interactions with adults and expressing my ideas and concerns to them" (AS2).*

Collaboration

Collaboration skills, specifically the ability to work with teammates to produce and evaluate prototypes, were among gains noted by half of the alumni participants (5/12 survey, 4/6 interview). As participant AI6 described:

> *"I think the most important thing I gained from Kidsteam was working in a group. ...You had to work and learn how to mix people's ideas and make new things from that, and not overpower the group."*

This participant also went on to describe how this applied to current schoolwork, stating: *"They make me work in groups in school, so it's helpful to know how to not [only] be a leader but to help move the group forward which is what I felt like I did in Kidsteam."* Similarly, another participant described working with the group as a safe space to produce and combine ideas, *"Being able to give equal amount of support in designing something as the next person, and having those ideas be listened to without the fear of discrimination"* (AS10). In addition to mixing and combining ideas to make a single design prototype, collaboration was discussed in terms of facilitating brainstorming: "*Even if my thoughts were not used directly, all of the ideas bounce off each other and spark new trains of thought"* (AS3).

Confidence

During discussions about their experiences on the team, most alumni interview participants (5/6) described an increase in their confidence (i.e., their ability to handle design tasks) as being interrelated with impacts on self-esteem (4/6) (i.e., how they felt about themselves as a person). More specifically, alumni realized the *value of their opinions and ideas* (5/6), especially when working with partners outside the university, such as the White House: *"When we went to the White House I realized [our ideas] are probably going to be affecting the whole country"* (AI2). These ideas were reflected in the survey responses, through comments such as, *"I learned that my opinion mattered"* (AS1), or another participant who noted that, *"My ideas do matter as a child"* (AS3).

Material Benefit

Alumni participants described the benefits of receiving the end-of-the-year gift. When asked what they believed the purpose of the end-of-the-year gift was, survey participants (12) described it as: a thank you (6), a reward for hard work (3), a way to attract new members (3), and a way to inspire kids with technology (2). Interview participants (2/6) described how choosing technology gifts they wouldn't normally receive was motivational:

> *"[There was] the prospect of getting this thing at the end of the year when I was at a point in my life when other people are deciding what I would get. Ram sticks so I could play Lord of the Rings, Battle for Middle Earth?*

There was no possible way I could have gotten that besides Kidsteam" (AI5).

Participant AI1 similarly described the end-of-the-year gift: "*It was a $75 parrot robot. This was the most extravagant thing I ever owned... I remember thinking that it was something that we could have created at Kidsteam.*"

Design Process

Design process knowledge was one of the most common gains expressed by both survey participants (12/12) and interview participants (6/6). Alumni discussed the design process in three primary ways: 1) the design techniques that were used, 2) having new problem solving skills, and 3) insights into the complexity of the design process.

With regard to the design techniques used in the sessions, when referring to the Big Paper technique AS1 described how, *"I learned... it is also possible to draw something on a piece of paper and have it show up as a game on the computer."* Certain techniques were favored over others, as with AI1 who, *"hated journaling with a passion"* but, *"love[d] Bags of Stuff more than anything."*

Alumni also spoke about their understanding of design processes in terms of having new strategies to solve problems: *"I learned how to approach problems differently"* (AS6). Participant AI4 expanded on this idea, stating, *"It's not exactly like I could tackle problems I normally couldn't, it's about having a different strategy to solve the problem."* This ability to address problems in a different way applied to current creative interests and schoolwork of alumni. For example, participant AI4 described how creativity learned from Kidsteam helped with *"art and fiction writing"* that was done for fun, while Participant AI3 described how using design techniques learned on Kidsteam helped with schoolwork:

> *"When I'm doing a craft for a school project I kind of use the designing techniques that Kidsteam taught us. And also, I'm going to be taking Robotics Class. I'm pretty sure that's going to start helping. Even though we didn't really work with robots [on Kidsteam], the design factor is still there."*

Finally, alumni described how they navigate the complexity of designing technologies. In the words of AS3, part of the responsibility of being a designer is considering how technology will, *"work with many people"* and how designers, *"have to consider many points of view."*

Career Direction

The three alumni interview participants who were currently adults (age 18+) each described how their history with adult members of the PD team influenced their career paths. These alumni described how they had re-contacted adult design partners who were currently working with the team, and how these adult design partners had directly influenced the alumni's job prospects through helping them obtain internships and job opportunities. Two alumni participants also described how Kidsteam influenced their undergraduate course selection, such as participant AI5:

> *"Now I'm studying CS, trying to figure out how to take as many design classes as I possibly can... I don't think I ever would have gotten close to that career path if I hadn't been in Kidsteam, but that's definitely the stuff that Kidsteam does, and it's what I'm hoping to do."*

Factors Influencing Gains

Alumni participants discussed a number of factors that may influence the prevalence of gains or their ability to report gains from their participation on a PD team, including enjoyment, frustrations, and recall. As was also discussed in the first piece of this larger study, all survey participants (12/12) found the experience to be enjoyable [31], describing it as *"fun"* or *"very cool."* Participants also described their relationships with adults as being respectful and positive [31]. As participant AI4 summarized, *"I really liked the program."*

Alumni also cited frustrations, such as disliking a particular design technique, a recurring project, or not always *"getting along with"* the other child members of the team [31]. Finally, regarding recall, two interviewees (2/6) at one point responded that they did not remember the answer to a specific question very clearly.

STUDY 2: PARENTS OF ALUMNI

In study 2, we obtained an alternate perspective on the gains children on a PD team experience by surveying and interviewing their parents, who could observe changes in alumni attitudes and behaviors outside their participation on the team. The goal of this study was to corroborate and expand the results of Study 1.

Method

Study 2 presents an analysis of surveys and interviews that were conducted with parents of child design partner alumni.

Survey

Participants. As parents could have multiple children participate in Kidsteam, the 17 parents that were surveyed (4 male, 13 female) cumulatively had 21 children (10 male, 11 female) participate on the team. These alumni participated on Kidsteam between the years of 1998 and 2013, stayed on the team an average of 2.0 years (SD=1.3), and left the design team an average of 7.9 years prior to the start of the study (SD=4.9).

Procedure. Parents were recruited for the anonymous, online survey through email. The online surveys for parents of design partner alumni were designed to take no more than 10 minutes and included closed, likert-scale questions as well as open-ended, short answer questions. Questions began broadly (e.g., *"What were your expectations when your child joined Kidsteam?"*) before becoming more narrowly focused on topics identified from the literature across both the likert and open-ended questions. Parent participants did not receive compensation.

Interview

Participants. Parent interviewees were recruited in spring of 2016 from a pool of survey respondents who stated they were interested in participating in a follow-up interview. Four parents responded to the interview request (1 male, 3 female), and represented the experiences of 6 child alumni (5 male, 1 female) who participated on Kidsteam between the years of 1999 and 2013 for an average of 1.8 years (*SD*=.75). Participants left the design team an average of 9.0 years prior to the study (*SD*=5.4).

Procedure. All participants completed the follow-up interview at a location that was convenient to them, either at the University of Maryland's campus or via a videoconferencing service (e.g., Skype). Interview questions began with broad, open-ended questions— such as, *"In a few sentences, tell me about your overall experience with Kidsteam."*— and later included direct questions about areas of interest derived from the literature. The semi-structured interviews lasted an average of 23 minutes (*SD*=6.3). Participants agreed to be audio recorded during the interview; all recordings were transcribed for analysis. Interviewees did not receive compensation.

Analysis

To illuminate differences and similarities between the alumni and parent perspectives on gains from participation, analysis of the parent survey and interview data began with the codebook that was established in Study 1. The codebook was further refined after analyzing a randomly selected, transcribed interview with another member of the research team to refine, clarify, and discover any emergent codes. During this process a 9th category of *Fiscal Considerations* was added to the codebook.

Inter-Rater Reliability was then computed between two researchers on a random selection of 20% of the short response survey data and one randomly selected interview. A Cohen's Kappa score of .86 was achieved, as calculated within NVivo software, considered *almost perfect agreement* (range: .81 to .99) [43]. Having reached agreement, one researcher coded the remaining data.

Findings

In this section we present findings on the gains to child PD team alumni as perceived by their parents, as well as topics that relate to gains, (e.g., factors that may have influenced gains). The representative quotes presented in this section are identified by: participant group (i.e., P for parents), data source (i.e., S for survey, I for interview), and participant number (i.e., 3). For example, the second parent interview participant has the identifier "PI2."

Initial Responses on the Existence of Gains

When parent survey participants were initially asked a binary question about whether their child/children learned new skills from participating on the design team, 16/17 answered *yes.* While one participant answered *no,* he identified gains (e.g., confidence) in later questions. When respondents choosing *yes* were subsequently asked a short-response question about what their children learned, parent participants listed: design skill sets (9) (e.g., prototyping), group-work and collaboration (7), ability to convey their ideas (7), and comfort with technology (5). These and other gains discussed throughout the parents' surveys and interviews are discussed below.

Communication

When asked what impacts they noted from participating on a PD team, most (12/17) parent survey responses described how their children made improvements in communication, particularly with regard to giving presentations and communicating with adults. Parents described gains such as, *"presentation skills"* (PS8) and how participation on the team, *"has helped [my son] with advocating himself in school and with adults"* (PS16). Another parent survey participant (PS13) described how team events, such as speaking at a conference, contributed to improvements in her child's public speaking. In the follow-up interviews, a parent participant described how her children's team experiences might yet benefit them in the future:

> *"Also working remotely with people. The work [Kidsteam] did working with other teams far away will help [my son] because a lot of people work with others around the world" (PI2).*

Collaboration

Half of parent participants (11/17 survey, 3/6 interview) observed changes in their children's collaboration skills. Some parent participants discussed aspects of collaboration broadly in relation to working with teammates, such as the experience being, *"a good experience working with others"* (PS14) or, *"working within a group or team"* (PS1). Other parent participants were more specific regarding how their child had learned to work with others to design technologies, such as PS16:

> *"He is so good at working with a group of people. He understands preparation, he knows that when he makes a commitment to work with others that he needs to do his share, but he can step back and let others do what they need to do and not feel like he isn't doing his job."*

This ability to compromise was an aspect of collaboration that was also described by other parent participants, such as PS11, who stated, *"She learned more about working with groups and the necessary compromises"* (PS11).

Confidence

Parents of alumni (10/17 survey, 4/4 interview) described how their children gained in confidence during their participation on the PD team, partially attributing this to how participation illustrated to their children how important their ideas were. Parents described how, *"[Participating] made [my daughter] more confident,"* (PS3) and, *"My child gained self-confidence in general"* (PS8).

Frequently, parent participants connected this confidence to children speaking about or sharing their ideas. Parent participants described how their children gained in *self-esteem* by having their opinions valued:

> *"It was very positive from the self-esteem point of view—the, your opinions are valuable point of view. ...This is may be one of the few places where kids have their ideas seriously considered and discussed- and rejected or not, but in a real way" (PI3).*

Technology Exposure

Some parent participants (6/17 survey, 2/4 interview) described how their children gained *"computer skills"* (PS4) and became, *"more comfortable around new technology"* (PS3). Parent participants also noted that their children were *"exposed to interesting technologies"* (PS5) through participating on the design team, and that this exposure to new technologies fostered continued interest in working with computers.

Financial Benefits

While financial benefits were not covered in the surveys, all parent interview participants (4/4) discussed financial benefits of the PD team, some noting that these benefits could motivate facilitating children's participation on the team. These pragmatic gains included the facts that the program 1) was a free after-school activity, 2) included a free, 2-week summer program, and 3) offered a technology gift at the end of each year of participation.

Design Processes and Techniques

Design processes, such as *"brainstorming"* and *"applying specific prototyping techniques"* (PS8), were part of what parent participants (7/17 survey, 3/4 interview) discussed as an element their children had learned. Parent participants also described how their children still use specific design techniques in their schoolwork and professional lives, such as PI2 who described their child's use of Sticky Noting [28]: *"[My child] still loves his post-it notes."*

Respect in Relationships with Adults

Most (12/17) parent survey participants agreed that participating on the PD team changed perceptions of respect between their children and adults—both in terms of offering respect and expecting respect. As participant SP16 concisely explained, *"He affords [adults] respect and expects it in return."* Three of these participants specified that the PD team participation supported existing expectations of respect toward their children from adults, such as PS14 who stated, *"[It was] good to have adults model respect for him (but not saying it was a big change)."* Other participants discussed how the new expectations of their children contrasted with other adult relationships their children had:

> *"[My children] came to realize there were some adults who attended to what they were saying and to their ideas. They came to respect and like those adults[...] And when they went to school and had to deal with adults who had no interest in their ideas they could recognize OK this is an adult that doesn't do that. We could think it over and talk about it, and that became part of our conversation in dealing with their public schooling" (IP4).*

Attribution of Gains

While all participants were asked to focus on what gains they believed stemmed from membership on Kidsteam, parent participants often emphasized both why and to what extent they attributed the impacts they were discussing to participation on the PD team. As previously mentioned, some parents described how the PD team setting supported or enhanced existing expectations, such as SP11 who stated,

> *"[My child] was ...accustomed to having [her] thoughts and ideas taken seriously by adults... I think the Kidsteam environment further supported this belief."*

Others, such as PI2 who homeschooled her child while he was participating on the design team, credits participation on the team with cultivating certain gains entirely:

> *"I was getting him educational opportunities wherever they were. I know there is where he picked up some reasoning skills, there is where he picked up typing skills. ...I can ascribe [specific gains] to working with Kidsteam pretty firmly" (PI2).*

Factors Influencing Gains

Parent participants recounted two factors that may have influenced how they reported their children's gains: recall and enjoyment. Regarding recall, during interviews 2 of the 4 parent participants began descriptions of the experiences they and their children had by emphasizing that they were trying to recall events from many years ago, so it may be difficult to recall everything. The only parent interview participant who did not appear to have recall issues had a child who had left the team within two years of the interview. None of the survey responses (0/17) indicated issues of recall. Regarding enjoyment, parent participants observed that their children appeared to have fun on the PD team. *"He always complained to go to school every day but he was always very happy to come to Kidsteam"* (IP1). However, one parent recalled that their child said being on the team was, *"sometimes boring"* (PS15). Other parents explained how there was more excitement about attending on some days more than others, such as when the team was working on a particularly interesting project.

DISCUSSION

How participants are involved on PD teams matters. To continue to improve the PD process and techniques, and to create better technologies from this improved process, it is critical that HCI research goes beyond discussions of indirect benefits to participants by acknowledging that direct participant gains can be a part of PD outcomes (see Table 1). Here, we discuss the continued applicability of gains, new opportunities, and the implications of this work for PD practitioners and methods.

Continued Applicability of Gains

Within the findings of this study we learn that participants may actively benefit from their participation on PD teams. Participation on the design team influenced alumni's knowledge of the design process and how they engaged with technology, even after their participation on the team had ended and across the contexts of their schoolwork and their personal interests. What was further encouraging was that the parents of alumni largely agreed with the gains that the former participants described. We see these direct gains as enabling a way for HCI researchers to do more than "prevent harm" to child participants—to have an *attention and care* for participants such that they *actively benefit* from their participation in PD research programs.

However, it is important to note that the type of participation asked of alumni during their design team experience may have influenced the continued application of gains described in this study. In a number of ways, the CI method itself may create a "best case scenario" [7] for encouraging types of participation that could promote gains, such as its focus on relationship building and the long-term nature of participation. Alternatively, it may not be the case that such high degrees and durations of participation are required for children to experience direct gains. Future work should, therefore, consider what gains might emerge from other forms of PD with children.

Reflection on Obstacles to Gains

An essential step toward fostering participant gains is not only to identify and illustrate direct participant gains, but also to develop an understanding of obstacles to attaining gains. Prior work with adults in PD has identified how frustrations may be an impediment to participant gains [8]; while participants in this study described relatively few frustrations, this may have been influenced by an increased likelihood to respond to calls to participation if they had a positive experience on the team. Still, child PD alumni in this study as well as child PD participants in previous works have described frustrations that could impact gains [22,23]. To achieve a complete picture of gains from participation, and how to facilitate them, future work will need to examine what frustrations child participants encounter and how these frustrations may influence gains.

A Missing Gain: Content Knowledge

A noteworthy exception to the gains participants perceived in this work is *content* knowledge. The topics covered in design sessions (e.g., science inquiry, language learning) are a potential source of gains. Previous research suggested that content knowledge could be an expected outcome: *content* was a cognitive impact found in Guha's year-long case study evaluation of children on a PD team (Figure 3) [22], and *specific content* is one of three areas, along with *general* and *design* skills, where Barendregt posits PD could incorporate learning goals [2]. However, the gains described by participants in this research, while largely discussing the other topics within these two models, did not include content knowledge. This does not mean that content

Gains Described	Study 1: Alumni	Study 2: Parents	Differences and Similarities Between Study 1 and 2
Career Direction	✓		—
Collaboration	✓	✓	Both focused on teamwork and group compromise; alumni discussed its applicability to prototyping
Communication	✓	✓	Both focused on presentation skills. Parents focused on communication with adults and alumni on overcoming fears
Confidence	✓	✓	Both described knowing children's opinions matter; alumni also related this to self-esteem
Design Processes/ Techniques	✓	✓	Alumni focused on broader and process insights; parents on specific design techniques
Financial Benefits		✓	Both discussed end of the year gifts; parents also described the team as free after school and summer programs
Material Benefits	✓	✓	
Respect with Adults		✓	—
Technology Exposure		✓	—

Table 1. A summary of the gains children experienced through participating on a PD team that were described by child participant alumni and their parents.

knowledge was not part of participants' immediate gains, nor do we believe these gains are non-existent after participation has ended. Rather, we believe this points toward an opportunity to encourage participants to perceive the value of the content presented in PD sessions, and that this gap points toward the need for work such as [2,3,7] that make content goals explicit.

Toward 21st Century Educational Goals

While the team in this study meets outside of school hours, many methods of PD with children take place within classrooms. In considering this broader context of PD with children, researchers have suggested that the benefits of participation on PD teams should reflect the expectations of the schoolroom context that children are in (i.e., there should be learning involved) [2]. Despite not seeing content knowledge in the results of this study, other gains described do relate to modern educational goals. The Partnership for 21st Century Learning (P21) is the most, *"detailed and more widely adopted"* [11, p.4] of existing frameworks for 21st century skills [38]. Many specific skills are focused on within the P21 framework, including *Life and Career Skills*—among them Flexibility and Adaptability, Initiative and Self Direction, Social Skills, and Leadership—and *Learning and Innovation Skills*—covering Creativity and

Innovation, Critical Thinking and Problem Solving, and Communication and Collaboration. A number of these 21st century competencies overlap with the gains to child participants highlighted by this work, including confidence, technology knowledge, and presentation skills. The overlap of gains from PD and 21st century learning goals suggests that the PD process itself may help meet the educational expectations of child PD participants and their parents.

Implications of Gains from PD for Practitioners
Here we present several implications for PD practitioners who wish to encourage participant gains through their work. While we are not able to draw causal relationships from this study, there were a number of influencing factors that participants described alongside the gains that were being explained. We present these factors as prospective ways to foster gains in PD activities.

Safe Design Environments. A common PD goal is to maintain respectful, safe environments for taking design risks. Participants' descriptions of how safe design environments encouraged gains may make it critical to encouraging gains in intergenerational PD.

Discuss Impact. Certain project types (e.g., public-facing projects, projects iterated over multiple sessions) were described alongside a number of gains (e.g., confidence) as evidence of participants' influence. Practitioners should be explicit with children regarding their project impacts.

Technique Choice. Participants described their continued use or adaption of techniques they learned on the PD team (e.g., sticky noting, Bags of Stuff). Practitioners hoping to encourage gains may choose to incorporate these techniques when able.

Reflections on Method: Multiple Perspectives on Gains
Obtaining multiple perspectives on a phenomenon is a common methodological approach, and is one this study suggests is particularly relevant to researching gains from PD team participation. This work begins to build an understanding of distinctions between how gains are perceived from the perspectives of child PD team alumni and their parents. Parents of child participants can observe their child's behavioral and attitudinal changes outside team participation, and therefore offer a new perspective on gains to children that may enhance or differ from those of participants or researchers.

In this study, gains were either noted by both child PD team alumni and their parents, but emphasized differently, or only noted by one group or another (Table 1). Regarding the former, while *Communication*, *Collaboration*, *Confidence, Design Process/Techniques,* and *Material/ Financial Benefits* gains were found across both participant groups, each group had a slightly different perception of these gains. For instance, while both participant groups discussed gains in lasting knowledge about design processes, parent perceptions of gains in this dimension were largely focused on specific design techniques, while alumni participants described an increased holistic understanding of the technology design process. Gains noted by only one participant group were less common, though important. For example, while alumni described their relationship with the adult design partners on the team as being respectful [31], it was only parent participants—having observed differences in how their children offered and expected respect from adults outside the design team—who described *respect in relationships with adults* as something gained through participation on the design team. Given the existence of these distinctions, we note that asking diverse populations about gains from PD activities may be necessary to obtaining a complete picture of gains from PD. These distinctions situate this work and may inform studies looking to inspire more meaningful forms of participation by supporting direct gains from PD activities.

Limitations of the Study
The ability of participants in this study to recall information from their participation is the primary limitation of this work. Imperfect memories of events, particularly as the team has been active for 18 years, may have caused facts to be obscured or exaggerated over time; moreover, attributing gains to a particular experience can be a difficult task [7]. However, what a participant may recall in this regard may also be connected to what gains were most ingrained—particularly in the case of the child alumni. Additionally, as previously discussed, the gains described in this work likely relate to the high degree and duration of participation asked of participants. Finally, two potential limitations arise from the pool of participants: the participants were mostly female, and it is possible that parents and alumni who chose to participate in the study were more likely to do so because they recalled their experiences positively.

CONCLUSION AND FUTURE WORK
This paper contributes a new understanding of what gains former child members of a PD team experience and attribute to their participation. Our findings identify and describe the direct gains of alumni and have implications for how the PD process of developing new technologies can positively impact the participants who partake that process.

This research is part of a larger study investigating PD practices while working with children, and there are a number of avenues for future study. A next step would be to investigate whether gains can be firmly ascribed to participation on PD teams. Gains from other forms of PD with children should be explored, as should the value of content presented to participants during design sessions. Future work should investigate what frustrations child PD team participants encounter and how these frustrations may impact gains. Lastly, gains of adults who work on intergenerational PD teams should be better understood.

ACKNOWLEDGEMENTS
We would like to thank the participants who volunteered for this research, the HCIL members who supported this research, and the design partners of Kidsteam.

REFERENCES

1. June Ahn, Michael Gubbels, Jinyoung Kim, and Johnny Wu. 2012. SINQ: Scientific INQuiry learning using social media. In *CHI'12 Extended Abstracts on Human Factors in Computing Systems* (CHI '12).
2. Wolmet Barendregt, Tilde M. Bekker, Peter Börjesson, Eva Eriksson, and Olof Torgersson. 2016. Legitimate Participation in the Classroom Context: Adding Learning Goals to Participatory Design. In *Proceedings of The 15th International Conference on Interaction Design and Children* (IDC '16), 167-174.
3. Ahmet Baytak and Susan M. Land. 2010. A case study of educational game design by kids and for kids. In *Procedia-Social and Behavioral Sciences.* 2,2: 5242-5246.
4. Laura Benton, Hilary Johnson, Emma Ashwin, Mark Brosnan, and Beate Grawemeyer. 2012. Developing IDEAS: Supporting children with autism within a participatory design team. In *Proceedings of the SIGCHI Conference on Human Factors in Computing Systems* (CHI '12), 2599-2608.
5. Gro Bjerknes, Pelle Ehn, Morten Kyng, and Kristen Nygaard. 1987. *Computers and democracy: A Scandinavian challenge*. Gower Publishing Ltd.
6. Elizabeth Bonsignore, June Ahn, Tamara Clegg, Mona Leigh Guha, J. Yip, Allison Druin, and J. P. Hourcade. 2013. Embedding Participatory Design into Designs for Learning: An Untapped Interdisciplinary Resource? In *CSCL 2013 Conference Proceedings Volume 1 — Full Papers & Symposia* (CSCL 2013), 549–556.
7. Claus Bossen, Claus, Christian Dindler, and Ole Sejer Iversen. 2010. User gains and PD aims: assessment from a participatory design project. In *Proceedings of the 11th Biennial Participatory Design Conference* (PDC '10), 141-150.
8. Claus Bossen, Christian Dindler, and Ole Sejer Iversen. 2012. Impediments to user gains: experiences from a critical participatory design project. In *Proceedings of the 12th Biennial Participatory Design Conference* (PDC '12), 31-40.
9. Luca Colombo, Monica Landoni, and Elisa Rubegni. 2014. Design guidelines for more engaging electronic books: insights from a cooperative inquiry study. In *Proceedings of the 15th International Conference on Interaction Design and Children* (IDC '14), 281-284.
10. Nigel Cross. 2006. *Designerly ways of knowing.* Springer London.
11. Chris Dede. 2010. Comparing frameworks for 21st century skills: *21st century skills: Rethinking how students learn.* 20: 51-76.
12. Christian Dindler, Eva Eriksson, Ole Sejer Iversen, Andreas Lykke-Olesen, and Martin Ludvigsen. 2005. Mission from Mars: a method for exploring user requirements for children in a narrative space. In *Proceedings of The 2005 International Conference on Interaction Design and Children* (IDC '05), 40-47.
13. Betsy DiSalvo and Carl DiSalvo. 2014. Designing for Democracy in Education: Participatory Design and the Learning Sciences. In *Proceedings of the Eleventh International Conference of the Learning Sciences* (ICLS '14).
14. Allison Druin. 1999. Cooperative inquiry: developing new technologies for children with children. In *Proceedings of the SIGCHI Conference on Human Factors in Computing Systems* (CHI'99), 592-599.
15. Allison Druin. 2002. The role of children in the design of new technology. *Behaviour and Information Technology.* 21,1: 1-25.
16. Allison Druin and Carina Fast. 2002. The child as learner, critic, inventor, and technology design partner: An analysis of three years of Swedish student journals. *International Journal of Technology and Design Education.* 12,3: 189-213.
17. R. Darin Ellis and Sri H. Kurniawan. 2000. Increasing the usability of online information for older users: A case study in participatory design. *International Journal of Human-Computer Interaction* (IJ HCI). 12,2: 263-276.
18. Elizabeth Foss, Mona Leigh Guha, Panagis Papadatos, Tamara Clegg, Jason Yip, and Greg Walsh. 2013. Cooperative Inquiry extended: Creating technology with middle school students with learning differences. *Journal of Special Education Technology.* 28,3: 33-46.
19. Julia A. Garde and Mascha C. van der Voort. 2014. Participants' view on personal gains and PD process. In *Proceedings of the 13th Participatory Design Conference* (PDC'13), 79-82.
20. Franca Garzotto. 2008. Broadening children's involvement as design partners: From technology to "experience". In *Proceedings of the 7th International Conference on Interaction Design and Children* (IDC'08), 186-193.
21. Judith Gregory. 2003. Scandinavian approaches to participatory design. *International Journal of Engineering Education.* 19,1: 62-74.
22. Mona Leigh Guha. 2010. *Understanding the Social and Cognitive Experiences of Children Involved in Technology Design Processes.* PhD Dissertation. University of Maryland, College Park, MD.
23. Mona Leigh Guha, Allison Druin, Gene Chipman, Jerry Alan Fails, Sante Simms, and Allison Farber. 2004. Mixing ideas: A new technique for working with young children as design partners. In *Proceedings of the 2004 Conference on Interaction Design and Children* (IDC'04), 35-42.
24. Mona Leigh Guha, Allison Druin, and Jerry Alan Fails. 2013. Cooperative Inquiry revisited: Reflections of the past and guidelines for the future of intergenerational

co-design. In *International Journal of Child-Computer Interaction* (IJCCI). 1,1: 14-23.

25. Elin Irene Hansen and Ole Sejer Iversen. 2013. You are the real experts!: Studying teenagers' motivation in participatory design. In *Proceedings of the 12th International Conference on Interaction Design and Children* (IDC'13), 328-331.
26. Juan Pablo Hourcade. 2008. Interaction design and children. In *Foundations and Trends in Human-Computer Interaction.* 1,4: 277-392.
27. Yasmin B. Kafai. 2003. Children designing software for children: what can we learn?. In *Proceedings of the 2003 Conference on Interaction Design and Children* (IDC'03), 11-12.
28. Andrew Large, Valerie Nesset, Jamshid Beheshti, and Leanne Bowler. 2006. "Bonded design": A novel approach to intergenerational information technology design. In *Library & Information Science Research.* 28,1: 64-82.
29. Tak Yeon Lee, Matthew Louis Mauriello, June Ahn, and Benjamin B. Bederson. 2014. CTArcade: Computational thinking with games in school age children. In *International Journal of Child- Computer Interaction* (IJCCI). 2,1:v26-33.
30. Stephan Lindsay, Daniel Jackson, Guy Schofield, and Patrick Olivier. 2012. Engaging older people using participatory design. In *Proceedings of the SIGCHI Conference on Human Factors in Computing Systems* (CHI'12), 1199-1208.
31. Brenna McNally, Mona Leigh Guha, Matthew Louis Mauriello, and Allison Druin. Children's Perspectives on Ethical Issues Surrounding Their Past Involvement on a Participatory Design Team. *In Proceedings of the 2016 CHI Conference on Human Factors in Computing Systems* (CHI'16), pp. 3595-3606.
32. Brenna McNally, Mona Leigh Guha, Leyla Norooz, Emily Rhodes, and Leah Findlater. 2014. Incorporating peephole interactions into children's second language learning activities on mobile devices. In *Proceedings of the 2014 Conference on Interaction Design and Children* (IDC'14), 115-124.
33. Karyn Moffatt, Joanna McGrenere, Barbara Purves, and Maria Klawe. 2004. The participatory design of a sound and image enhanced daily planner for people with aphasia. In *Proceedings of the SIGCHI Conference on Human Factors in Computing Systems* (CHI'04), 407-414.
34. Jamie Montemayor, Allison Druin, Allison Farber, Sante Simms, Wayne Churaman, and Allison D'Amour. 2002. Physical programming: designing tools for children to create physical interactive environments. In *Proceedings of the SIGCHI Conference on Human Factors in Computing Systems* (CHI'02), 299-306.
35. Neema Moraveji, Jason Li, Jiarong Ding, Patrick O'Kelley, and Suze Woolf. 2007. Comicboarding: Using comics as proxies for participatory design with children. In *Proc. of the SIGCHI Conference on Human Factors in Computing Systems* (CHI'07), 1371-1374.
36. Michael J Muller. 2003. Participatory design: The third space in HCI. In *Human-Computer Interaction: Development Process.* 4235: 165-185.
37. Leyla Norooz, Matthew Louis Mauriello, Anita Jorgensen, Brenna McNally, and Jon E. Froehlich. 2015. BodyVis: A New Approach to Body Learning Through Wearable Sensing and Visualization. In *Proceedings of the Annual ACM Conference on Human Factors in Computing Systems* (CHI'15), 1025-1034.
38. Partnership for 21st Century Learning (P21). 2016. Framework for 21st Century Learning. Retrieved September 16, 2016 from www.p21.org
39. Alex Quinn, Benjamin B. Bederson, Elizabeth Bonsignore, and Allison Druin. 2009. StoryKit: Designing a Mobile Application for Story Creation By Children and Older Adults. Tech. rep. HCIL-2009-22, Human Computer Interaction Lab, University of Maryland, College Park.
40. Karen Rust, Elizabeth Foss, Elizabeth Bonsignore, Brenna McNally, Chelsea Hordatt, Meethu Malu, Bie Mei, and Hubert Kofi Gumbs. 2014. Interactive and live performance design with children. In *Proceedings of the 2014 conference on Interaction Design and Children* (IDC'14), 305-308.
41. Michael Scaife, Yvonne Rogers, Frances Aldrich, and Matt Davies. 1997. Designing For or Designing With? Informant Design for interactive learning environments. In *Proceedings of the ACM SIGCHI Conference on Human Factors in Computing Systems* (CHI'97), 343-350.
42. Mike Scaife, and Yvonne Rogers. 1999. Kids as informants: Telling us what we didn't know or confirming what we knew already. *The Design of Children's Technology,* 27-50.
43. Anthony J. Viera and Joanne M. Garrett. 2005. Understanding interobserver agreement: the kappa statistic. *Fam Med.* 37,5: 360-363.
44. Greg Walsh, Allison Druin, Mona Leigh Guha, Elizabeth Foss, Evan Golub, Leshell Hatley, Elizabeth Bonsignore, and Sonia Franckel. 2010. Layered Elaboration: A new technique for co-design with children. In *Proc. of the SIGCHI Conference on Human Factors in Computing Systems* (CHI'10), 1237-1240.
45. Greg Walsh, Elizabeth Foss, Jason Yip, and Allison Druin. 2013. FACIT PD: a framework for analysis and creation of intergenerational techniques for participatory design. In *Proc. of the SIGCHI Conference on Human Factors in Computing Systems* (CHI'13), 2893-2902.

Examining Adult-Child Interactions in Intergenerational Participatory Design

Jason C. Yip[1], Kiley Sobel[2], Caroline Pitt[1], Kung Jin Lee[1], Sijin Chen[1], Kari Nasu[1], & Laura R. Pina[2]
University of Washington - The Information School[1], Human Centered Design & Engineering[2]
Seattle, Washington, USA
{jcyip, ksobel, pittc, kjl26, sijinc, knasu13}@uw.edu; lpina@cs.washington.edu

ABSTRACT
Prior studies have focused on child interactions in participatory design (PD) with adults and children, but less is known about what specific adult-child interactions constitute a partnership. In this study, we unpack what constitutes an "equal partnership" in PD between adults and children. On the basis of prior literature, we created a new framework that examines the complementary roles between children and adults. Next, we analyzed a case study of a year-long intergenerational design team of children (ages 7-11) and adults. From this analysis, we determined that design partnerships are composed of four dimensions that span from unbalanced to balanced interactions: *facilitation, relationship building, design-by-doing,* and *elaborating together.* Finally, to demonstrate its utility, we analyzed two focal co-design sessions using our framework. Our analysis suggests that an equal partnership in PD is not a single static interaction but a development over time of design interactions influenced by context, experience, and participants.

Author Keywords
Participatory Design; Co-design; Cooperative Inquiry; Children; Design Methods; Youth

ACM Classification Keywords
D.2.10. Design: Methodologies

INTRODUCTION
Designing new technologies for children is no easy task. As adults, we cannot rely on our own childhood experiences to inform our technological designs for present and future children. Therefore, in the late 1990's, child-computer interaction researchers began employing participatory design (PD), a method focusing on engaging users in the design process and emphasizing a democratic and collaborative relationship between users and designers to create new technologies [3,15]. By providing agency and opportunities for users to contribute, PD attempts to ensure that users have an equal standing with designers in the design process [28]. Some researchers, while engaging and viewing children as active contributors in the process of PD, have described this interaction between adult designers and children as an *equal partnership* [8,15,16,26,32,41,44,51,52]. Both Druin [15,16] and Guha et al. [26] state that children can be "equal stakeholders" in design with adults. McNally et al. [32] explain that children can have an "equal voice" in the design process. However, among other researchers – because adults often set the agendas, choose the research project, and organize the design activities – there is a perspective that equal PD partnerships between children and adults are difficult to manage or are not as equal as they seem [30,39,42].

CHI 2017, May 06 - 11, 2017, Denver, CO, USA

ACM 978-1-4503-4655-9/17/05…$15.00
DOI: http://dx.doi.org/10.1145/3025453.3025787

Despite frequent use of the term equal partnerships in PD with children, very little knowledge exists as to how to analyze and explain what an adult-child design partnership is. Equality is assumed to take place in design partnerships by some researchers. However, it may take a more deliberate effort to set up these kinds of partnerships, and often these efforts have only been described implicitly in the literature. To help us understand adult-child partnerships better, our work delves into understanding the nature of equality in adult-child interactions. We explore the meaning of design partnerships through examining equitable interactions that occur in PD sessions. Our research questions are: (1) What range of interactions occurs between children and adults during co-design activities? (2) What practices and interactions occur in adult-child co-design that are equitable?; and (3) How does unpacking adult-child interactions help us to better conceptualize design partnerships in PD?

To answer these questions, we reviewed prior literature and developed a theoretical model that defines how adult-child roles intersect in the design of technologies. Next, we conducted an analysis of 36 co-design sessions over a period of one year. In these co-design sessions, six to ten ethnically diverse children (ages 7-11) designed children's technologies with four to seven adults. We found that design partnerships can be broken down into four dimensions: *facilitation, relationship building, design-by-doing,* and *elaboration*. Each of the dimensions varies along a spectrum of unbalanced and balanced interactions between children and adults (i.e., moments when participants dominate or work together). To demonstrate the utility of the dimensions, we provide a close analysis of two focal design sessions using the dimensions to examine equitable practices.

Our study highlights the nuances that exist in adult-child design interactions, provides common ground for researchers to discuss the extent to which equal adult-child partnership occurs, and contributes an analytical tool for researchers wanting to examine adult-child design partnerships. A close examination of what constitutes equitable practices can help HCI researchers determine how to support equality in other PD contexts and participants.

BACKGROUND

Equal (Equality) and Equitable (Equity)

Before we begin, the terms *equal (equality)* and *equitable (equity)* need to be defined for this study. Our approach stems from traditions in multicultural educational research that examines equality and equity between students, teachers, schools, and policies [2]. The term *equality (equal)* means "the same". Adults and children in PD partnerships can have *the same* opportunities to contribute to idea generation, design, and decision-making practices [15,16,26]. However, because adults have unequal access to power, influence, and knowledge compared with children [34], we recognize equality is not a given in these partnerships and that equity must be considered. *Equity (equitable)* emphasizes how people in power can allocate resources and commit effort to helping others overcome obstacles to find fairness and success [2]. In adult-child PD, overcoming unequal power dynamics is not a simple task [34]. Therefore, we focus on equitable partnership practices (e.g., guidance, scaffolding) when it comes to supporting children in the context of the design process [26].

When we examine *equal* PD partnerships and *equitable* practices in this study, we take the following perspective. First, everyone's contribution (e.g., ideas, opinions, artifacts, etc.) can be valued *equally*, but the engagements and interactions to make these contributions need to be *equitable*. Second, participants' expertise is *equally* important (e.g., knowledge of childhood, domain knowledge, etc.), but tools and techniques that emphasize *equitable* design interactions are needed (e.g., working with arts and crafts materials instead of highly technical prototyping tools). Finally, children and adults can be *equal* members of a PD group, but we need *equitable* practices to support participants' investments in the co-design group. While the literature points to these needs, less has been documented about how to define equitable interactions in design partnerships. Therefore, the goal of this study is to provide a deeper examination of equitable practices and develop an analytic framework to study design partnerships.

Supporting Democratic Practices in PD

Democratic practices are the foundation for equality in PD. On a theoretical level, Ehn [19] describes PD as a process of creating new "language-games" that make sense to both users and designers. Design tools mediate participants' interactions by providing ways for them to access their individual areas of expertise that relate to the shared design practice. Yet, "participation applies not only to users participating in the language-game of design, but perhaps more importantly to designers participating in use" (Ehn [19], p. 68). Similarly, Brandt, Binder, and Sanders [10] frame PD as a third space in which users and designers come together to "playfully participat[e] in a new practice that brings together means and ends in what one could call a new game of possible futures" (p. 171). In translating these ideas of democratic design participation as a shared game between users and designers, researchers have developed specific tools and techniques for PD that mediate their interactions and draw on their specific knowledge [10,47].

Child-computer interaction researchers have different perspectives from each other about what democratic PD interactions look like between adults and children. The *representative democracy* perspective of PD focuses on how children's ideas are included and represented [39]. In Read et al.'s [39] PD research, they often work with larger numbers of children (about 80 - 100) over shorter amounts of time. The priority in these groups is to emphasize appropriate fair democratic representation in PD. In contrast, we work with seven to ten children over longer periods of time. Therefore, our priority is examining closely how the adult-child interactions support *direct democratic* practices, in which choices and decisions are made directly together during design sessions.

Participatory Design Methods for Working with Children

Along these same lines, researchers who work with children have conceptualized design and interactions between adult designers and children with their own sets of methods and techniques [20,47]. On one end of the spectrum is Scaife et al.'s *Informant Design*, in which adults treat children as native informants [42]. Scaife et al. [42] are clear that adults do not treat children as equal partners. Here, children are considered experts at being children and design ideas can be developed from children, but they cannot contribute equally to the design process compared to adults.

Closer towards equal design partnerships, the ChiCI group works with local schools to run design workshop sessions with children [40]. In addition, the group developed a PD method called *MESS* (Mad Evaluation Session with Schoolchildren) Days in which classrooms of children come to the university to do design activities [27]. Teachers observe and researchers act as facilitators in the process. This method was developed on the basis of the notion that organizing design sessions with children is logistically difficult and that ensuring there is a "representative sample" of children in sessions is challenging [27]. Large et al.'s [30] *Bonded Design* emphasizes that children should play an active role in the design process, that both adults and children have their own expertise, and both adult and child are necessary to carry out design. However, Large et al. [30]

question the extent to which true equality can exist between participants in an intergenerational design team because adults generally lead and control the design session.

Most related to our current theoretical and methodological approach is Druin's [15,16] *Cooperative Inquiry* (CI), also known as co-design. CI is a PD method that focuses on children and adults working together as equal design partners on the iteration, elaboration, and design of new technology for children [15]. In CI, adults and children design technologies *for children, with children.* This method focuses on creating design partnerships in which children should have equal opportunities to contribute to the design process in any way they can [16]. Certain practices in CI are inherent to supporting equitable interactions, such as adults eating snacks together with children, wearing casual clothing, and sitting on the ground with children. However, past literature has not yet explored how these practices are equitable in supporting equal contributions in co-design.

Adult-Child Roles in Participatory Design

The majority of research conducted in this child-focused PD space emphasizes children's specific roles [15,16,24,25,29,51,52]. When children engage in PD, and specifically co-design, children are seen as domain experts in childhood [20]. They take on roles throughout the process that span from user to design partner [15,16]. Children are also learners throughout the design process [15,26,30]. By utilizing specific child co-design methods, children can partake in design activities through prototyping [15], brainstorming [24], critiquing [46], taking notes [15], utilizing subject domain knowledge [50,51], and even facilitating and leading co-design sessions [52].

For the most part, researchers have only incidentally noted adult roles in the design process as facilitators, caregivers, and design and idea contributors [24,26,36,41]. McNally et al. [32] surveyed former child co-designers about their experiences up to ten years after participating in their adult-child design partnerships. These former child co-design participants recognized that adults have different responsibilities than children during the process, such as organizing the co-design sessions and time management. Despite these different adult responsibilities, former child co-designers did not feel that this impacted their ability to have a legitimate influence on design outcomes.

Benton and Johnson [4] carried out an extensive literature review of PD design methods and techniques for adults working with children and disabilities. This review describes the different roles, extensive responsibilities, and complex activities of both child and adult participants in these technology design projects. In the cases they reviewed, adults acted as facilitators who clarified children's ideas; motivators for children to participate in the session; children's caregivers; proxies who participate in design on children's behalf; and as co-designers and design partners who generated individual ideas, scaffolded children's brainstorming, and integrated ideas with the children [4].

Overall, because most literature in this space has studied adult engagement as ancillary and secondary, especially in comparison with child roles, empirical studies are now needed that consider both children and adults. Our work begins to address this need for research by developing a dimensional framework on the basis of a deep case study analysis. This framework conceptualizes the equitable interactions and partnerships between children and adults over a long period of co-designing together.

WHAT IS A DESIGN PARTNER?

In technology design, Druin [16] identifies four roles that children take on (see Figure 1). As *users*, children are observed interacting with technology by adults. As *testers*, children try out technology prototypes and provide adults input on the basis of their tests. As *informants*, children answer questions, co-develop new ideas, and sketch and develop low-fidelity prototypes with adults. Finally, as *design partners*, children and adults are equal stakeholders throughout the entire process of designing new technology.

Figure 1. The roles children play in the design of children's technology [16].

On the basis of our literature review, we claim adults also have four corresponding roles when designing technologies with children. In our model, each adult role is the complement to each child's role: when the child is a *user,* the adult is an *observer* [11,37,38]; when the child is a *tester,* the adult is a *test facilitator* [17,31]; when the child is an *informant,* the adult is an *interpreter* [5,18,48]; and when the child is a *design partner,* the adult is also a *design partner* [16].

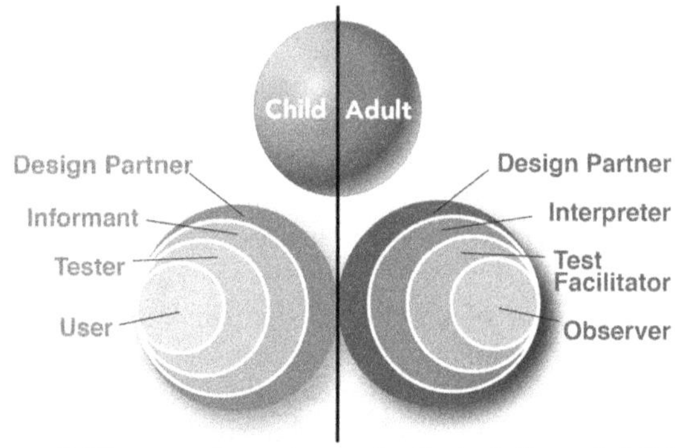

Figure 2. The complementary roles that adults and children play in the design of children's technologies.

Figure 2 shows the relationship between child roles and the corresponding roles we identify for adults. The sphere represents the entire engagement between children and adults in technology design. When the sphere is split open, the different roles between children (left side) and adults (right side) are shown. The circles are concentric as per Druin's [16] framework; each role includes aspects of those roles that historically have come before it. We have purposely created different distances between the complementary roles to indicate the amount of direct interaction necessary between the adults and children in these roles. We explain this distance for every role in the ensuing paragraphs.

The role of the *adult observer* is based on traditions in anthropology and educational psychology [11,37,38]. Observations of children can occur in naturalistic and laboratory settings [37]. Researchers attempt to understand how children as users of existing technologies react in these settings and what it says about the design of future technologies [16]. In Figure 2, we have placed the user-observer circles far apart because adults do not need to directly interact with children (e.g., adults can watch videos of children, observe from another room or far away, etc.).

The *test facilitator* role is based in traditions of cognitive psychology [17]. If children are testers of prototypes, the adults play the role of choosing the usability tests, determining the child participants, and facilitating the testing session [31]. In Figure 2, the circles are in closer proximity than user-observer roles; test facilitators can directly interact with children as testers, but the adults do not need to engage for very long or closely with the children.

When children are informants, the adult plays the role of the *interpreter*. The interpreter draws methods from anthropology, psychology, and sociology [5,18,48]. While children design, draw, and communicate as an informant, the adult interpreter co-constructs dialogue, listens closely, and learns from the child. The distance of the circles (Figure 2) between informants and interpreters is even closer but still they never touch. While adult interpreters can work alongside with children, they do not necessarily have to claim or strive for equality in partnership with children [30].

Finally, adults can take on the role of *design partner* in the process of designing technology with children. Most importantly, adults and children are *design partners* when they work with each other as equal stakeholders throughout the entire process of designing new technology [16]. To indicate this close partnership, the outer layers of both design partner roles are touching (Figure 2). In comparison with the other three adult-child roles (*user-observer, tester-test facilitator*, and *informant-interpreter*), less has been documented about specific interactions that constitute the design partner roles. There are equitable practices in co-design that are largely implicit; therefore, we need a framework that helps researchers understand equity and how to support equality in their intergenerational PD practices.

METHODS

Although we have defined our usage of the terms *equal* and *equitable* in adult-child design partnerships and have shown adult-child roles in technology design, we still need to examine real-world interactions to unpack these conceptions. Therefore, we employed the comparative case study method [33] to examine what equitable practices support equal contributions, expertise, and membership in design partnerships. This method allowed us to (1) closely examine what engagements and interactions happen in co-design sessions with adults and children over time and (2) develop a framework to conceptualize adult-child design partnerships. We illustrate the development of our framework through vignettes. Finally, we conduct a deep analysis of two focal co-design sessions to show the utility of our framework.

Context and Participants

We examined an intergenerational co-design group of design researchers and children called *KidsTeam UW*. *KidsTeam UW* consisted of ten children (ages 7-11) from October 2015 to May 2016. We chose ages 7-11 because this age is old enough developmentally to co-design but young enough to think as a child [24]. We recruited child participants through professional connections and word-of-mouth. We strove for diversity in socioeconomic status, gender, ethnicity, and age to promote multiple viewpoints [24]. Four of the children returned in August 2016 for a weeklong session with three new children (n = 7). Thus, 13 different children participated in the group over time. Adults in this group consisted of core members and project partners. The core members included undergraduates, graduate students, post-doctoral researchers, and one professor. The project partners consisted of librarians, non-profit organizations, and university researchers. Please see Table 1 for demographics information. From October 2015 to December 2015 and February 2016 to May 2016, *KidsTeam UW* met twice a week on a university campus in 90-minute sessions. In one week in August 2016, *KidsTeam UW* had six 90-minute sessions. The design sessions involved working on multiple research projects with university and non-profit partners, creating branding (i.e., logos, group website), and engaging in exploratory design practice.

Data Collection

Co-design sessions. Each of the 36 co-design sessions began with *snack time* (~15 minutes), in which children and adults ate and interacted with each other (e.g., drawing, playing games). In *circle time* (~15 minutes), children and adults gathered together in a circle on the ground to go over the 'question of the day' (to get everyone's thoughts on a particular topic) and the logistics of the co-design session. During *design time* (~45 minutes), adults and children interacted using PD techniques meant to foster collaborative design [47]. Finally, during *discussion time* (~15 minutes), children and adults all gathered together to go over the designs of the day and make final suggestions. A single video camera recorded each of these sessions and focused on adult-child interactions. The researchers photographed the activities and artifacts and afterward wrote analytical memos for each session. To analyze the videos, a primary viewer (an author) watched five to six videos and took notes on what the adults were doing with the children. Next, a secondary viewer (another author) watched the same videos and added to the primary viewer's notes.

Child name	Age	Gender	Ethnicity	Adult name	Age	Gender	Ethnicity
Gina	11	Female	Asian	Jason	36	Male	Asian
Aileen	11	Female	White	Caroline	24	Female	White
Athena#	7	Female	Asian/Black	Vivian	25	Female	White
Austin#	11	Male	Asian	Lili	30	Female	White
Riku#	9	Female	Asian/White	Oscar	30	Male	White
Anishinaabe	9	Female	Native	Kung Jin	26	Female	Asian
Animikiik	11	Male	Native	Kari	19	Female	Asian
Simon	9	Male	White	Kiley	26	Female	White
Marlene	7	Female	White	Sijin	19	Female	Asian
Winston#	7	Male	White	Laura	32	Female	Hispanic
Carmen*	9	Female	Asian/White	Edith	19	Female	White
Veritas*	9	Male	Native/Asian				
Martin*	7	Male	Hispanic				

Table 1. Demographics of the core co-designers. Names of all participants are pseudonyms, except authors. Asterisk* refers to children that came in August 2016 only. Hashtag# refers to children that attended all sessions.

Interviews. The lead author conducted two rounds of interviews with the children. The first interviews occurred in February 2016 (n = 9), and the second interviews occurred in May 2016 (n = 8). For both interview rounds, questions focused on children's perceptions of their interactions in the co-design group and what they thought of the adults. Interviews lasted roughly 10 minutes each. We chose not conduct interviews with the four children from the summer session because they had only been part of the team for one week. The lead author also conducted interviews with the core adult team members (n = 9) between July and August 2016. The interview questions focused on adults' perspectives of their interactions with children and their roles in the co-design group. Adult interviews lasted about 30 minutes. All interviews were audio recorded and transcribed.

Data Analysis

To develop a framework to understand what a design partnership between adults and children entails, we used a grounded theory approach with constant comparative analysis [14]. First, the same primary and secondary researchers that watched and took notes on the videos individually started the open coding process. Using a qualitative analysis web application called *Dedoose*, we open coded the adult and child interactions that occurred in each co-design session. From this process, we generated a codebook with the following codes: how adults facilitated the sessions and how children responded, how adults managed children's behavior, how the adults and children co-designed together, how the children and adults talked and interacted with one another, and the kinds of support children needed in design. Next, the primary and secondary researchers recoded their data (interviews, video notes) using this codebook. As we applied the coding scheme, we also made changes to the codebook when a new theme was identified. In a collaborative axial coding session, the researchers then compared and contrasted codes to identify the emerging themes from these co-design sessions. Generally, we placed codes referring to managing children's behavior, organizing the design sessions, and time management under *facilitation*. Friendship and playful behavior codes produced *relationship building*. Design critiques and participating together in design generated *design-by-doing*. Codes for idea suggestions and mixing ideas were grouped as *elaboration*. We further recoded the data to develop new codes on how adults scaffolded children's designs.

We triangulated our findings with our analytical memos, interviews, and photographs to make sure all pieces of evidence were mutually supportive [33]. To establish validity, we presented our analysis to two external reviewers not closely related to this project to ensure that our comparisons were representative of the ideas and design process of the adults and children. Finally, we engaged in a selective coding process. We developed diagrams to formalize the relationships of the themes and categorized the emergent themes around a set of core categories [14]. These core categories became the four dimensions of our framework.

FINDINGS

The first section examines what adult-child practices constitute a co-design partnership. We present four dimensions of adult-child interactions: *facilitation, relationship building, design-by-doing,* and *elaboration.* The range of the dimensions are according to Read et al.'s [41] concept of balanced design, which assumes an equal partnership between domain experts (children) and design experts (adults), both engaged in informing and creating their designs. We use the term *balanced* to refer to specific interactions in co-design that are equitable and lead to an equal amount of contributions from both adult and child (i.e., the right side of the dimensions). In contrast, *unbalanced* refers to moments in co-design when either the children or adults are dominating in their contribution, which leads to unequal contributions and inequitable interactions (i.e., the left side of the dimensions). To demonstrate the spectrum of each dimension, we present short vignettes of co-design sessions as examples. The second section of the findings presents a detailed analysis of two focal co-design sessions using the four dimensions. To denote pseudonyms between adults and children, we use superscript A (Name^{A}) to indicate adults and superscript C (Name^{C}) to indicate children.

Facilitation

The *facilitation* dimension examines how much support and mediation takes place between the adults and children (Figure 3). The facilitation dimension spans from unbalanced assistance when only adults facilitate the co-design session to balanced partnership when adult and child equitably facilitate together. Facilitation in co-design (by both adults and children) can include organizing and managing the flow of the co-design session, leading the group discussions, and summarizing the group's ideas [52]. However, adults often have the additional responsibility of refocusing children during co-design, which is an unbalanced interaction. The most common theme in the adult interviews emphasized the difficulty in refocusing children, managing their behavior, and motivating children to design. The following vignette is an example of unbalanced facilitation because only the adult is trying to get the children back on the design task.

Figure 3. The spectrum of adult-child facilitation dimension.

Towards Unbalanced Facilitation Vignette: Co-design session #13. *Children were learning how to collaborate in co-design by taking apart one group's low-tech prototype and remixing it into another design. The goal was to build technologies to help families engage in programming together. The children received a prior group's design of a rocket and a movie theater to remix. The children in the group, Gina^{C}, Animikiik^{C}, and Simon^{C} were distracted. Kiley^{A} asked the group, "Okay, wait, do you want to build on the theater, or do you want to build on the rocket?" Simon^{C} called out, "I don't know." Kiley^{A} told Simon^{C}, "You have to choose one." Simon^{C} answered, "I don't like either." Kiley replied to Simon^{C}, "How can we make something you do like?" During this time, Animikiik^{C} gathered his own materials to make his own robot while Gina^{C} created a magic wand with pipe cleaners.*

Adults and children can also work together equitably to organize and lead the interactions [52]. In the example below, moments of facilitation occurred when the child and adult work together to decide how to lead the presentation.

Towards Balanced Facilitation Vignette #1: Co-design session #21. *Children and adults used large paper and markers [24] to design how a Super Mario Maker™ video game could be used for library learning settings. Riku^{C} and Aileen^{C} worked with Kung Jin^{A} on their design. Riku^{C} directed Kung Jin^{A} how she wanted to present, "Okay, so when we present it [the design], pretend this [design] has its own big sheet of paper on the wall." Kung Jin^{A} responded, "I can hold it [the design] too, or you can put it back here," and pointed to a whiteboard. Riku^{C} reflected, "Actually, can we make it on the wall?" Kung Jin^{A} answered, "Yeah." Riku^{C} excitedly said to Aileen^{C}, "We can make it on the wall!" Kung Jin^{A} made another suggestion, "Or you can put it here [on a large cardboard sheet]. We can use this thing." Riku^{C} raised her arms in the air in agreement, "Oh yeah! Let's use that!"*

A third example demonstrates that children can, want to, and should be allowed to facilitate and that adults can and should help children contribute as facilitators.

Towards Balanced Facilitation, Vignette #2: Co-design session #36. *Carmen^{C} came to the large whiteboard in the room. The group was using a technique called Stickies to evaluate a children's programming tool [15]. In the Stickies session, adults typically put up the written notes of likes, dislikes, and design ideas on a large board in an affinity diagram. However, in this co-design session, Carmen^{C} wanted to place her own dislike comment on the board. Lisa^{A} (female visitor) worked with Carmen^{C} to decide where on the board this comment should be placed.*

Relationship Building

Children need to feel comfortable that adults take their ideas and designs seriously [16,26]. Our findings support that balanced relationships are a necessary component in design partnerships. The *relationship building* dimension examines how much social interaction occurs in the co-design group (Figure 4). This dimension runs from adults being socially distant from children to the establishment of closer relationships between adults and children.

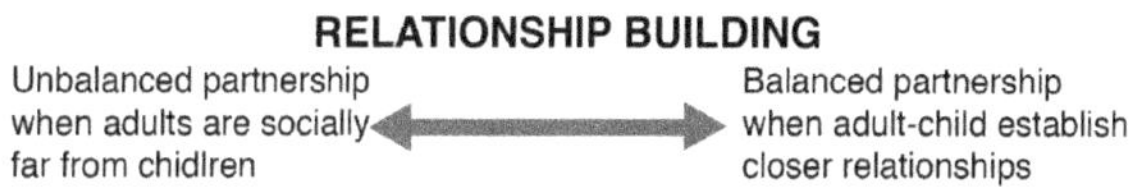

Figure 4. The spectrum of relationship building dimension.

When adults are socially far from children (i.e., when adults and children take quieter non-interactive stances), unbalanced interactions are more likely to occur. Many first time adult visitors have come to work with the team but did not always establish equitable relationships. For example, in the following vignette, a graduate student struggled to shift from a design expert to acting as partner in co-design, even though we invited her to join as an equal partner.

Towards Unbalanced Relationship Building Vignette: Co-design session #29. *A new graduate student (female, age 30) worked with our group to understand the relationship between value-sensitive design [23] and children's perceptions of the world and technology. The new student mostly sat on the ground but did not talk to the children. The graduate student later indicated that when working with the children, she was quiet because she had never actually worked closely with children before.*

In contrast, social closeness, represented by the right side of the spectrum, helps in relationship development. We identified two types of adult-child social interactions that lead toward more balanced co-design partnerships. First, children and adults often act silly together outside of co-design activities. Such examples in our data include adults playing with children and their toys, adults dancing with children, adults crawling around pretending to be cats, and adults playing games with children. These are genuine and unplanned interactions that cause children to feel more comfortable around adults and break away from traditional adult-child power structures. For instance, in interviews, children noted the adults are "fun" and "silly" and how important this friendly atmosphere was for participating in co-design. A second type of social interaction is developing strong appreciation and respect between adults and children during co-design. The example below illustrates this point.

Towards Balanced Relationship Building Vignette: Co-design session #10. *Riku[C] and Anishinaabe[C] presented their design ideas about a robot tutorial to the group. Because time was running out, Jason[A] told them that if they wanted to continue to share their ideas, they could do so after the session ended. Once we dismissed the children, immediately Riku[C] and Anishinaabe[C] came to Jason[A] to present their ideas, without the rest of the group listening. These two children wanted to continue co-designing even when they had the option to go home. Anishinaabe[C] in her interview noted that she liked the close "attention" from the adults because it made her feel "superior."*

Design-by-Doing Interactions

Design-by-doing refers to moments when design activities take place, such as building and evaluating prototypes, creating mockups, and developing scenarios. A design-by-doing approach emphasizes the participation in language games, that is, users and designers engage in a shared activity for better understanding and good design [19]. Here, design-by-doing activities and methods allow both users and designers to use practical skills when participating in design processes. An unbalanced partnership occurs when adults just observe how children engage in design-by-doing but do not participate together with the children. A balanced partnership occurs when adults and children engage together in design-by-doing (Figure 5).

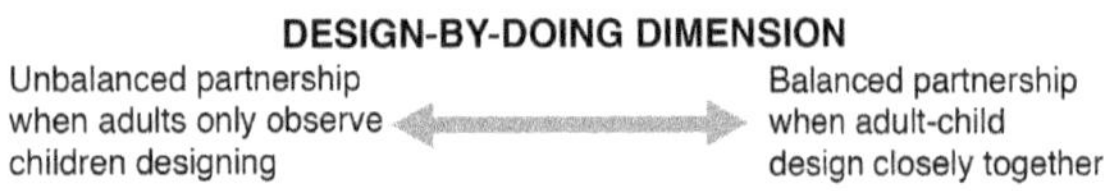

Figure 5. The spectrum of design-by-doing dimension.

The following vignette illustrates how adults can be present in a design-by-doing activity but not actively participate. Here, the adults were still learning how to engage in design-by-doing equitably with children.

Towards Unbalanced Design-By-Doing Vignette: Co-design session #10. *Kung Jin[A], Kari[A], and Edith[A] worked with Animikiik[C] and Aileen[C] on the robot tutorial. Animikiik[C] and Aileen[C] worked quietly while Kung Jin[A] and Kari[A] watched the group and Edith[A] took notes. The adults pointed to specific parts of the children's designs for clarification, and the children responded back to the adults. However, there was no collaboration in the process between adults and children.*

An equitable interaction between adults and children emphasizes balanced design-by-doing collaborations and exchanges in the process. The following vignette demonstrates how a child and adult collaboratively exchanged dialogue and designed together.

Towards Balanced Design-By-Doing Vignette: Co-design session #28. *Vivian[A] worked with Winston[C] to design learning activities around the technology of Little Bits™ (a snap-in-place electronic building blocks platform). In the dyad, Winston interacted with cardboard and Legos™ to combine them with the Little Bits™ electronics. To create his design, he told Vivian[A], "If we do this [put the Legos™ blocks together in a certain arrangement], but we do it for all of them [put them in that arrangement]." Vivian[A] leaned into Winston[C] and asked, "How should I build this [design]? Would you like me to do something else?" Winston took a piece of cardboard and said, "Well, we are going to use this one right now and we should cut out that piece." Vivian[A] took the cardboard piece and attempted to understand Winston[C]'s direction. Vivian[A] used a black marker and drew a series of lines on the cardboard and checked in with Winston[C] to see if what she did was okay. While Winston[C] put the Lego™ pieces together, Vivian[A] cut across the cardboard at the marks she made. She passed the cut cardboard to Winston[C] so he could tape together the Lego™ and cardboard for their design.*

Elaboration

Elaboration emphasizes adults and children generating and mixing ideas together (Figure 6). While ideation is part of design practice, and thus could be collapsed with *design-by-doing*, we created a distinct dimension for elaboration because of how consistently this theme occurred in our data, distinct from other design activities. An unbalanced partnership exists when children only tell adults what they want or vice versa—when only adults generate ideas.

Figure 6. The spectrum of elaboration dimension.

Towards Unbalanced Elaboration Vignette: Co-design session #8. *In this session children evaluated the video game Super Mario Maker™ using the Stickies technique [15]. Both children and adults could have presented their likes, dislikes, and design ideas. However, most of the adults spent significantly more time writing down what children were saying. Rather than coming up with their own ideas, adults asked children for design ideas and what they liked and disliked. Here, we did not observe collaborative ideation between adults and children.*

Balanced elaboration occurs when active idea exchanges occur between children and adults. Riku[C] noted in her interview that it was important for adults to help "build or give ideas" to children. For instance, children and adults consistently "mixed ideas" during the co-design sessions.

Towards Balanced Elaboration Vignette: Co-design session #10. *Javier[A] (male, age 50, community partner), Jason[A], and Caroline[A] worked with Simon[C] using large paper [24] to create a tutorial for programming a robot. Simon[C] excitedly talked about creating a "random button" on the robot that would sometimes help you or lead you astray. Jason[A] asked, "Why would that be helpful to anybody?"*

Simon^{C} insisted it would just be a fun idea. Javier^{A} pressed Simon^{C} to think more about whether his random button was helpful. Simon^{C} defended his idea, "Well, maybe it's helpful. Maybe it's not." Javier^{A} laughed, "So it's sorta like a game!" The adults started to mix Simon^{C}'s idea with the notion of an "I feel lucky" button from Google™.

In this vignette, adults and children worked together to elaborate on and mix their ideas together. The adults did not dismiss Simon^{C}'s ideas, but treated him maturely by asking him clarifying questions. The adults and children continued to build on the idea of randomness, fun, and gamification.

Focal Design Sessions

To illustrate the dimensions along their spectra, we chose two focal co-design sessions as contrasting cases for analysis [33]. Our goal in this is to not only clarify the dimensions, but to also demonstrate how to apply this framework. Our demonstration will help researchers use the framework in their own PD work. We chose an earlier (Fall 2015, session #9) and a later session (Spring 2016, session #30) to demonstrate how experience in co-design influences partnerships. Both co-design sessions specifically involved designing technology. The first sessions consisted of generating early design ideas, using the co-design technique Bags-of-Stuff (low-fidelity prototyping with arts and crafts materials) [15]. The second session, which took place later in the year, consisted of evaluating a higher-fidelity prototype with the Stickies technique [15].

As a summary of the interactions across the sessions, Figure 7 shows a visual comparison between co-design sessions #9 and #30 along the spectra of dimensions. Additionally, Figure 7 illustrates how a span of points along the spectrum of a dimension can be present in a single design session. It shows how co-design sessions can have diverse interactions, towards balanced *and* unbalanced, within one session. Each of these dimensions shows a continuum of interactions that occurred in the co-design session, as indicated by black (session #9) and grey (session #30) bars. Wider bars along a dimension horizontally indicate a wider range of balanced/unbalanced interactions. The narrower the bars horizontally, the more likely the dimension leans towards balanced or unbalanced for that session.

Focal Design Session 1: Museum Technology

Description. In co-design session #9, we conducted an exploratory activity focusing on how children view museums and what technologies can be designed for the space. Seven children and six adults attended. We divided the children and adults into four groups, where each group had at least one adult and one child. The two remaining adults (the lead facilitator, Jason^{A}, and a new researcher, Lili^{A}) moved between groups. The groups created low-fidelity prototypes of their museum ideas, using a variety of art supplies (Bags-of-Stuff) [15]. The groups then presented their designs to the entire group. Finally, the entire team briefly discussed major ideas that arose from the various designs, such as large touchscreens and expert teachers.

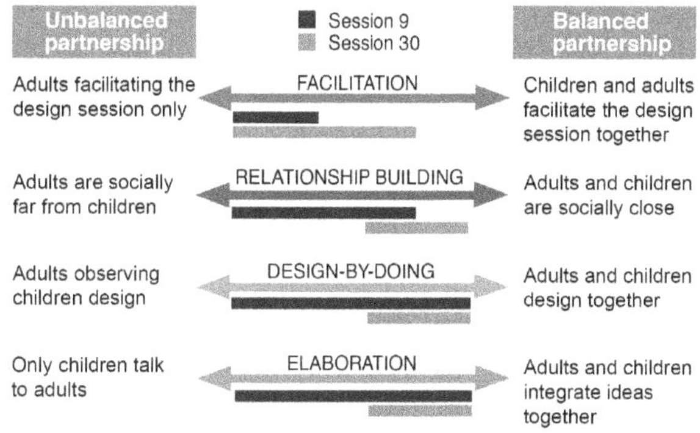

Figure 7. A visual comparison of co-design sessions #9 and #30 along the spectra of the dimensions.

Analysis with respect to dimensions. With respect to *facilitation*, we identified that adults tended to lead more than the children. Adults frequently reminded children to stay on the design task. For example, while designing a museum video game, Jason^{A} had to keep Winston^{C} and Simon^{C} from throwing arts and craft supplies at each other. While designing, Marlene^{C} and Athena^{C} started chasing each other and putting things in each other's hair. Vivian^{A} had to quickly intervene and get the girls to stop running around. During the group discussion, only adults led the design presentation by prompting the children to speak about the different features of their museum technologies at the appropriate time.

A wide range of *relationship building* interactions occurred in this session. Here, the variety of interactions are more in-between, rather than leaning towards balanced or unbalanced. Some interactions reflected social closeness while others were distant. Vivian^{A} and Athena^{C} talked about the USA cartoon *Charlie Brown*™, joking about how the teacher spoke in an indistinguishable voice. Other adults were quieter and interacted less with children. Lili^{A} (new member), worked with Aileen^{C} on her animal museum design, but they did not engage in conversation.

Design-by-doing also varied in this co-design session, indicating more in-between interactions. Some adults worked very closely with the children. While Winston^{C} and Jason^{A} were working together, Winston^{C} suggested that virtual reality (VR) should be included in their museum videogame. Jason^{A}, an expert with lots of experience in adult-child co-design, grabbed a piece of paper and put it on Winston^{C}'s head and asked him if this is how his VR should work. Jason^{A} continued to work closely with children by asking questions, and taking children's artifacts and adding designs to them. Edith^{A} and Lili^{A}, on the other hand, took a more passive role when working with Aileen^{C}. Edith^{A} and Lili^{A} provided Aileen^{C} with the supplies she needed to work on her animal museum technology, but did not participate in the design activity with her.

The *elaboration* dimension shifted from group to group between balanced and unbalanced. In Winston^{C} and Simon's^{C} group, Jason^{A} elaborated together with them on their idea to create a room in which museum patrons build video games. Jason[A] mentioned that this room could be composed of holograms. Simon[C] created a paper cube and Jason[A] discussed how this cube could project holographic images. Winston[C] jumped in and talked about how the cube could also project pictures. Within other groups, adults did not elaborate on children's ideas. The adults asked children specific questions about their designs, but no new ideas were generated and mixed together through this process.

Focal Design Session 2: Children's Programming Tool

Description. Co-design session #30 was the seventh session we had developing a children's programming tool for game design [1]. We worked with Ayush[A], a doctoral computer science student (age 35, male) and the lead designer. The children's task was to evaluate a story-based tutorial for this programming tool, using the Stickies evaluation technique [15]. We divided the eight children and four adults into four groups, and had the lead adult facilitator and Ayush[A] rotate groups. After the children evaluated the programming tool, the adults and children shared their ideas in a group discussion about how to make further improvements.

Analysis with respect to dimensions. The *facilitation* dimension still tended to lean more towards adult leading. For instance, adults set the pace of the activity, asked the children many questions about their evaluation of the programming tool, and led the presentation during the group discussion. However, moments of balanced adult-child facilitation did occur. For example, as Ayush[A] introduced the changes to the programming tool, children immediately directed the conversation. Aileen[C] asked if characters and sprites could appear instantly. Riku[C] suggested creating and deleting the sprites. As Ayush[A] discussed more about the sprites, Riku[C] jumped into the conversation about the magical items in the tutorial. Ayush[A] shifted the conversation to answer Riku[C]'s question. She continued, "And then on the characters the water, I saw water, the water blocks." Ayush[A] noted that she was asking about a feature she saw in the interface and said, "Yes, you call it water blocks." In this example, all the children's questions facilitated and directed the discussion of how the adult designer should discuss the features.

In terms of *relationship building*, because this was adults' and children's 30th co-design session together, their social distance was closer, both in friendship and design. For instance, during snack time, Athena[C] acted like a cat and Kiley[A] asked whether her "cat name" would be "Fidget." Aileen[C] and Caroline[A] played a smartphone game together. During the co-design evaluation, Winston[C] called Ayush[A] over and asked him to see and play his design from the programming tool. Athena[C] asked Kung Jin[A] to look at her design too. Both adults and children felt comfortable working and playing with each other.

Although session #30 focused on an evaluation technique, the adults and children also engaged in the *design-by-doing* dimension. Here, both the user (child) and designer (adult) expressed propositional knowledge and practical understanding of the technological tool [19]. Both the adult and child critiqued the design together in the activity by creating ideas for new features. For instance, Kiley[A] and Winston[C] evaluated the programming tool's tutorial. Kiley[A] critiqued the system's tutorial, "Could that be a rule? Like when you click something back, it [sprite] gets bigger, can you, like, resize it?" Winston[C] replied "Yeah, I think you might be able to [have that]. Yeah, totally." Kiley[A] replied, "I think that would be cool to teach resizing [in the tutorial]." Similarly, Kari[A] asked Riku[C] if an indicator about changing font usage would be helpful: "Maybe we can have, like, an indicator, saying, telling you which spot you are on." Riku[C] said, "Yeah, that'd be helpful," and Kari[A] wrote it on a sticky note. In both examples, adults were not worried about suggesting their ideas to the children.

Finally, for the *elaboration* dimension, children and adults mixed their ideas together during the larger group discussion. Jason[A] summarized the findings with respect to the likes, dislikes, and design ideas. Winston[C] soon commented that he wanted to see "invisible blocks" to help with the mechanics. Jason[A] clarified Winston[C]'s position, "Like a transparent block?" Ayush[A] added on, "Like a trigger, so when something moves through there, you can go to a new scene, something like that?" Winston[C] confirmed the clarification. Ayush[A] then asked the group how many would like to see a transparent block in the interface. All the children enthusiastically raised their hands. Aileen[C] called out loudly, "Invisible blocks would be cool, but it would be a lot easier if we [the sprites] could just jump." From these ideas, Jason[A] asked, "Would it help [in the tutorial] if Ayush[A] had a list of mechanics in the game?" The children all agreed with this mixed idea.

DISCUSSION AND IMPLICATIONS

We argue that deeper understanding of design partnerships requires an analysis of both designer (adult) and domain expert (child). Previous work tends to focus on the important role of children [15,16,24,25,29,51,52]. However, the adult designer is not an invisible partner to be ignored, but rather key and instrumental to how the partnership runs. It is of great importance for designers to self-reflect on their roles in PD [6,7]. We believe our framework of adult-child complementary roles (*user-observer, tester-test facilitator, informant-interpreter*, and *adult-child design partner*) (Figure 2) contributes to the field of HCI research because it represents design partnerships in a more holistic fashion. By augmenting Druin's [16] framework on children's roles with adults, we allow for deeper examination of both children and adults in PD (which we exemplified in this research). Because we conceptualized the adult-child roles as complementary, we focused our analysis on how both children and adults facilitated, socialized, designed, and elaborated together. This allowed us to theorize about what interactions constitute equitable practices in co-design.

Our work also shows that describing adult-child PD partnerships as either 'equal' or 'unequal' is too simplistic. Instead, the term 'equal partnership' for adult-child PD needs to be broken down into specific and observable equitable interactions. Our results illustrate how dimensions of adult-child interactions (*facilitation, relationship building, design-by-doing,* and *elaboration*) can range from unbalanced to balanced. Furthermore, the range of interactions along each dimension can exist in the same session among different groups, with different people, or at different times. Ultimately, our four dimensions allow researchers to refine their understanding of where equitable co-design practices manifest and where they do not.

We claim that the concept of equality in adult-child co-design is not static, but is rather dynamic, contextual, and participant sensitive [41]. Instead of describing PD partnerships as binary either-or, we believe it is more productive to discuss how adult-child PD partnerships are working towards equality as a goal along a spectrum. We believe the best way to explain equal adult-child partnerships in PD is to look at the overall trend of balanced and unbalanced partnerships through interactions within our dimensions. Design partnerships that have more balanced contributions in the dimensions are more likely to be demonstrating shifts towards equality. In contrast, more unbalanced interactions in the design partnership dimension mean that it is unlikely supporting equality. Describing interactions via these dimensions can aid in clarifying what researchers mean by "equal" design partnerships between children and adults.

However, equal partnerships and equitable practices do not occur instantly, even when there is an attempt to establish the necessary conditions. In our first focal case, following Guha et al. [26], novice adults struggled to have equitable interactions and to establish themselves as equal partners. Similarly, children need time to acclimate towards equitable practice. In the second focal case, children and adults had spent many sessions together. Thus they could work together to facilitate the session, demonstrate close ties in relationships, physically design together, and elaborate together without hesitation. More importantly, we now have a set of observable and explicit interactions that researchers can use to support new adults and children to engage in equitable practices. For instance, we can emphasize to novice adults the importance of design-by-doing or helping children find ways they can co-facilitate the sessions [52].

Finally, this study demonstrates that design partnerships cannot be described by one dimension or one type of interaction. We posit that the dimensions in our framework are tightly connected, and one dimension does not supersede another. For instance, if adults do not engage in *relationship building* with children, then it is unlikely the group will have equitable *facilitation*, *design-by-doing*, and *elaboration* practices. On the other hand, an adult and child may have a close relationship outside of the design sessions, but they might not know how to engage in *design-by-doing* or *elaboration* either; thus, they cannot be design partners. Our dimensions help triangulate and assess the state of co-design partnerships. For instance, if there are close *design-by-doing* interactions and strong *relationship building*, but there are fewer moments in *elaborating* together (e.g., adults quiet, children talking) and less shift towards helping children *facilitate* the co-design session (e.g., adults lead the sessions only), over time the sessions may become more playful design workshops, rather than fostering equality and equity in a co-design partnership.

LIMITATIONS

Our dimensions of adult-child design partnership are meant to be used as an analytic tool and not as a quantitative scale to measure if adult-child PD groups have reached or not reached equal partnership and equitable practices. Additionally, the framework is highly context-dependent. Therefore, we advocate that researchers from varying design philosophies working with children use our four dimensions as a contextual guide, rather than an objective measurement to determine if PD with children and adults lean towards equal partnership and equitable practices.

FUTURE WORK AND CONCLUSION

Our adult-child co-design partnership framework has strong potential for future HCI research. For instance, researchers can begin by examining how to adapt our framework to other contexts that have power imbalances in PD. Such PD contexts include design experts working with medical patients [13], office workers [35], teachers [12], senior citizens [9], families [49], people with impairments [43,45], neurodiverse children [21,22], and other stakeholders. Additionally, our framework may need to be examined on a scale of years to determine how equality in PD partnership evolves over time. Future work also needs to examine whether balance in our dimensions could be established within hours, days, or weeks. Furthermore, potential future research can determine the extent to which our framework's dimensions are related to each other and how it applies to other more diverse and complex interactions. Finally, our dimensions were developed in a case study of a co-design group of seven to ten children and four to six adults. Future research can examine how these dimensions may be utilized in analyzing differently sized groups in PD.

In conclusion, our study has provided a comprehensive model to better understand adult-child roles in technology design and a clear framework for researchers to examine equitable practices and equal contributions in co-design. These analytical tools give us better insight into what constitutes a design partnership. Furthermore, they will be useful to researchers interested in ensuring equitable practices and setting an equitable agenda in future PD work.

ACKNOWLEDGMENTS

Thank you to all the children and project partners in KidsTeam UW, the anonymous reviewers for their feedback, June Ahn and Brenna McNally for their analysis, and The Seattle Public Library and Juan Rubio for funding and supporting this work. Lastly, we acknowledge Mona Leigh Guha and Allison Druin for their sage advice.

REFERENCES

1. Rahul Banerjee, Jason Yip, Kung Jin Lee, and Zoran Popović. 2016. Empowering children to rapidly author games and animations without writing code. In *Proceedings of the The 15th International Conference on Interaction Design and Children* (IDC '16), 230–237. http://doi.org/10.1145/2930674.2930688
2. James A. Banks and Cherry A. McGee Banks. 2009. *Multicultural Education: Issues and Perspectives* (5th. ed.). John Wiley & Sons.
3. Mathilde Bekker, Julie Beusmans, David Keyson, and Peter Lloyd. 2003. KidReporter: A user requirements gathering technique for designing with children. *Interacting With Computers* 15, 2: 187–202.
4. Laura Benton and Hilary Johnson. 2015. Widening participation in technology design: A review of the involvement of children with special educational needs and disabilities. *International Journal of Child-Computer Interaction* 3-4: 23–40.
5. Hugh Beyer and Karen Holtzblatt. 1997. *Contextual Design: Defining Customer-Centered Systems*. Morgan Kaufmann, San Francisco, CA.
6. Jeanette L Blomberg and Austin Henderson. 1990. Reflections on participatory design: Lessons from the Trillium experience. In *Proceedings of the ACM CHI Conference on Human Factors in Computing Systems,* 353–360.
7. Jeanette Blomberg and Helena Karasti. 2012. Positioning ethnography within Participatory Design. *Routledge International Handbook of Participatory Design*: 86-116.
8. Elizabeth Bonsignore, Derek Hansen, Anthony Pellicone, et al. 2016. Traversing transmedia together: Co-designing an educational alternate reality game for teens, with teens. In *Proceedings of the The 15th International Conference on Interaction Design and Children* (IDC '16), 11–24. http://doi.org/10.1145/2930674.2930712
9. Eva Brandt, Thomas Binder, Lone Malmborg, and Tomas Sokoler. 2010. Communities of everyday practice and situated elderliness as an approach to co-design for senior interaction. In *Proceedings of the 22nd Conference of the Computer-Human Interaction Special Interest Group of Australia on Computer-Human Interaction*, 400–403.
10. Eva Brandt, Thomas Binder, and Elizabeth B.N. Sanders. 2012. Tools and techniques: Ways to engage telling, making and enacting. In *Routledge International Handbook of Participatory Design*, Jesper Simonsen and Toni Robertson (eds.). Routledge, New York, 145–181.
11. Urie Bronfenbrenner. 1979. Contexts of child rearing: Problems and prospects. *American Psychologist* 34, 10: 844–850.
12. John M. Carroll, George Chin, Mary Beth Rosson, and Dennis C. Neale. 2000. The development of cooperation: Five years of participatory design in the virtual school. In *Proceedings of the 3rd Conference on Designing Interactive Systems: Processes, Practices, Methods, and Techniques* (DIS '00), 239–251. http://dx.doi.org/10.1145/347642.347731
13. Jane Clemensen, Simon B. Larsen, Morten Kyng, and Marit Kirkevold. 2007. Participatory design in health sciences: Using cooperative experimental methods in developing health services and computer technology. *Qualitative Health Research* 17, 1: 122–130. http://doi.org/10.1177/1049732306293664
14. Juliet Corbin and Anselm Strauss. 2014. *Basics of Qualitative Research: Techniques and Procedures for Developing Grounded Theory*. SAGE.
15. Allison Druin. 1999. Cooperative Inquiry: Developing new technologies for children with children. In *Proceedings of the ACM CHI Conference on Human Factors in Computing System,* 592–599. http://doi.org/10.1145/302979.303166
16. Allison Druin. 2002. The role of children in the design of new technology. *Behaviour and Information Technology* 21, 1: 1–25. http://doi.org/10.1080/01449290110108659
17. Joseph Dumas and Jean Fox. 2009. Usability testing: Current practice and future directions. In *Human-Computer Interaction: Development Process*, Andrew Sears and Julie A. Jacko (eds.). CRC Press, 232–252.
18. Donna Eder and Laura Fingerson. 2002. Interviewing children and adolescents. In *Handbook of Interview Research: Context & Method*, Jaber F. Gubrium and James A. Holstein (eds.). SAGE, 181–202.
19. Pelle Ehn. 1993. Scandinavian Design: On Participation and Skill. *In Participatory Design: Principles and Practices,* Douglas Schuler and Aki. Namioka (eds.). CRC Press, 41–77.
20. Jerry Alan Fails, Mona Leigh Guha, and Allison Druin. 2012. Methods and techniques for involving children in the design of new technology for children. *Human–Computer Interaction* 6, 2: 85–166.
21. Christopher Frauenberger, Judith Good, and Wendy Keay-Bright. 2011. Designing technology for children with special needs - Bridging perspectives through participatory design. *CoDesign: International Journal of CoCreation in Design and the Arts* 7, 1: 1–28.
22. Christopher Frauenberger, Julia Makhaeva, and Katharina Spiel. 2016. Designing smart objects with autistic children: Four design exposès. In *Proceedings of the 2016 CHI Conference on Human Factors in Computing Systems* (CHI '16), 130–139. http://doi.org/10.1145/2858036.2858050
23. Batya Friedman, Peter Kahn Jr., and Alan Borning, 2008. Value sensitive design and information systems. In *The Handbook of Information and Computer Ethics*, K. Himma and H. Tavani (eds.), Wiley, Hoboken, NJ, 69-102.
24. Mona Leigh Guha, Allison Druin, Gene Chipman, Jerry Alan Fails, Sante Simms, and Allison Farber. 2004. Mixing ideas: A new technique for working with

young children as design partners. In *Proceedings of Interaction Design and Children*, 35–42.
25. Mona Leigh Guha, Allison Druin, Gene Chipman, Jerry Alan Fails, Sante Simms, and Allison Farber. 2005. Working with young children as technology design partners. *Commun. ACM* 48, 1: 39–42. http://doi.org/10.1145/1039539.1039567
26. Mona Leigh Guha, Allison Druin, and Jerry Alan Fails. 2013. Cooperative Inquiry revisited: Reflections of the past and guidelines for the future of intergenerational co-design. *International Journal of Child-Computer Interaction* 1, 1: 14–23.
27. Matthew Horton, Janet C. Read, Emanuela Mazzone, Gavin Sim, and Daniel Fitton. 2012. School friendly participatory research activities with children. In *CHI '12 Extended Abstracts on Human Factors in Computing Systems* (CHI EA '12), 2099–2104. http://doi.org/10.1145/2212776.2223759
28. Finn Kensing and Jeanette Blomberg. 1998. Participatory design: Issues and concerns. *Computer Supported Cooperative Work (CSCW)* 7, 3–4: 167–185. http://doi.org/10.1023/A:1008689307411
29. Monica Landoni, Elisa Rubegni, Emma Nicol, and Janet Read. 2016. How many roles can children play? In *Proceedings of the The 15th International Conference on Interaction Design and Children* (IDC '16), 720–725. http://doi.org/10.1145/2930674.2932222
30. Andrew Large, Valerie Nesset, Jamshid Beheshti, and Leanne Bowler. 2006. "Bonded design": A novel approach to intergenerational information technology design. *Library & Information Science Research* 28, 1: 64–82. http://doi.org/10.1016/j.lisr.2005.11.014
31. Panos Markopoulos and Mathilde Bekker. 2003. On the assessment of usability testing methods for children. *Interacting With Computers* 15, 2: 227–243.
32. Brenna McNally, Mona Leigh Guha, Matthew Louis Mauriello, and Allison Druin. 2016. Children's perspectives on ethical issues surrounding their past involvement on a participatory design team. In *Proceedings of the 2016 CHI Conference on Human Factors in Computing Systems* (CHI '16), 3595–3606. http://doi.org/10.1145/2858036.2858338
33. Sharan B. Merriam. 2009. *Qualitative Research: A Guide to Design and Implementation*. John Wiley and Sons, San Francisco, CA.
34. Virginia Morrow and Martin Richards. 1996. The ethics of social research with children: An overview. *Children & Society* 10, 2: 90–105.
35. Michael J. Muller. 2008. Participatory design: The third space in HCI. In *The Human-Computer Interaction Handbook (2nd ed.)*, A. Sears and J. Jacko (eds.). L. Erlbaum Associates, New York, NY, USA, 165–186.
36. Valerie Nesset and Andrew Large. 2004. Children in the information technology design process: A review of theories and their applications. *Library & Information Science Research* 26, 2: 140–161. http://doi.org/10.1016/j.lisr.2003.12.002
37. Anthony D. Pellegrini, Frank Symons, and John Hoch. 2014. *Observing Children in Their Natural Worlds: A Methodological Primer*. Routledge, New York, NY.
38. Jean Piaget. 1952. *The Origins of Intelligence in Children*. International Universities Press, New York, NY.
39. Janet C. Read, Daniel Fitton, and Matthew Horton. 2014. Giving ideas an equal chance: Inclusion and representation in participatory design with children. In *Proceedings of the 2014 Conference on Interaction Design and Children*, 105–114.
40. Janet C. Read, Stuart MacFarlane, S. Rebecca Kelly, Emanuela Mazzone, and Matthew Horton. 2006. The ChiCI Group. In *CHI '06 Extended Abstracts on Human Factors in Computing Systems* (CHI EA '06), 295–298. http://doi.org/10.1145/1125451.1125517
41. Janet Read, Peggy Gregory, Stuart MacFarlane, Barbara McManus, Peter Gray, and Raj Patel. 2002. An investigation of participatory design with children – informant, balanced and facilitated design. In *Proceedings of Interaction Design and Children International Workshop*, 53–64.
42. Michael Scaife, Yvonne Rogers, Frances Aldrich, and Matt Davies. 1997. Designing for or designing with? Informant design for interactive learning environments. In *Proceedings of the ACM SIGCHI Conference on Human Factors in Computing Systems*, 343–350.
43. Karin Slegers, Pieter Duysburgh, Helma van Rijn, and Niels Hendriks. 2012. Participatory design for users with impairments affecting cognitive functions and communication skills. In *Proceedings of the 12th Participatory Design Conference: Exploratory Papers, Workshop Descriptions, Industry Cases-Volume 2*, 141–142.
44. Mega Subramaniam, Claire Valdivia, Anthony Pellicone, and Zach Neigh. 2014. Teach me and trust me: Creating an empowered online community of tweens and parents. *iConference 2014 Proceedings*. Retrieved September 19, 2016 from https://www.ideals.illinois.edu/handle/2142/47292
45. Jelle Van Dijk, Niels Hendriks, Christopher Frauenberger, et al. 2016. Empowering people with impairments: How participatory methods can inform the design of empowering artifacts. In *Proceedings of the 14th Participatory Design Conference: Short Papers, Interactive Exhibitions, Workshops*, 2: 121–122.
46. Greg Walsh, Allison Druin, Mona Leigh Guha, et al. 2010. Layered elaboration: A new technique for co-design with children. In *Proceedings of the SIGCHI Conference on Human Factors in Computing Systems (CHI '10)*, 1237–1240. http://doi.org/10.1145/1753326.1753512

47. Greg Walsh, Elizabeth Foss, Jason C. Yip, and Allison Druin. 2013. FACIT PD: Framework for analysis and creation of intergenerational techniques for participatory design. In *Proceedings of the SIGCHI Conference on Human Factors in Computing Systems* (CHI '13), 2893–2902. http://doi.org/10.1145/2470654.2481400
48. Helen Westcott and Karen Littleton. 2005. ExpKaring meaning in interviews with children. In *Researching Children's Experience: Approaches and Methods*, Sheila Greene and Diane Hogan (eds.). SAGE, Thousand Oaks, CA, 141–157.
49. Jason C. Yip, Tamara Clegg, June Ahn, et al. 2016. The evolution of engagements and social bonds during child-parent co-design. In *Proceedings of the 2016 CHI Conference on Human Factors in Computing Systems* (CHI '16), 3607–3619. http://doi.org/10.1145/2858036.2858380
50. Jason C. Yip, June Ahn, Tamara L. Clegg, Elizabeth Bonsignore, Daniel Pauw, and Michael Gubbels. 2014. "It helped me do my science." A case of designing social media technologies for children in science learning. In *Proceedings of Interaction Design and Children*, 155-164. http://dx.doi.org/10.1145/2593968.2593969
51. Jason C. Yip, Tamara L. Clegg, Elizabeth Bonsignore, Helene Gelderblom, Emily Rhodes, and Allison Druin. 2013. Brownies or Bags-of-Stuff? Domain expertise in Cooperative Inquiry with children. In *Proceedings of Interaction Design and Children*, 201–210. http://dx.doi.org/10.1145/2485760.2485763
52. Jason C. Yip, Elizabeth Foss, Elizabeth Bonsignore, et al. 2013. Children initiating and leading Cooperative Inquiry sessions. In *Proceedings of Interaction Design and Children*, 293–296. http://dx.doi.org/10.1145/2485760.2485796

Participatory Evaluation with Autistic Children

Katharina Spiel[1], **Laura Malinverni**[2], **Judith Good**[3], **Christopher Frauenberger**[1,3]
[1] TU Wien (Vienna University of Technology), Austria
[2] University Pompeu Fabra, Barcelona, Spain
[3] University of Sussex, Brighton, United Kingdom
katharina.spiel@tuwien.ac.at laura.malinverni@upf.edu
j.good@sussex.ac.uk christopher.frauenberger@tuwien.ac.at

ABSTRACT
Participatory Design (PD) has become a standard methodology in HCI, however, the evaluation of the outcomes of participatory processes is often exclusively driven by researcher defined measures of success. Through our work with autistic children, who have radically different life worlds from our own, it became evident that their criteria for the success of a project are most likely also very different. In order to address the limitations of researcher defined and led evaluations in this context, we developed an approach for *participatory evaluation* called PEACE (Participatory Evaluation with Autistic ChildrEn). Using this approach, we were able to include autistic children in dedicated evaluation phases through the co-definition of goals and methods, joint processes of data gathering and the co-interpretation of results. We discuss three case studies in which we successfully applied our approach and conclude with a reflection on the novel insights created through participatory evaluation and researchers' roles in such a process.

ACM Classification Keywords
H.5.m. Information Interfaces and Presentation (e.g. HCI): Miscellaneous

Author Keywords
Children; Autism; Participatory Evaluation

INTRODUCTION
Participatory Design (PD) researchers include users in shaping the technologies with which they interact. Often, though, researchers' goals in PD projects define the success of the resulting prototypes, as well as the focus of evaluation [2]. Participants are reduced to providing data to support researchers' hypotheses. When the development of technology moves beyond the pragmatic evaluation of efficiency and efficacy, novel questions about what is worth evaluating come to the fore [21]. Expanding the role of research participants in the evaluation of technology further opens up perspectives beyond the safe space of researchers' expectations.

Action Research, a field in the Social Sciences with similar theoretical and moral underpinnings, already includes research participants in evaluation [22]. It allows for different stances that, when combined, deliver a richer description of agendas and use contexts than the researchers' perspective could provide on its own. Unfortunately though, participatory evaluation (PE) has received scant attention within Human Computer Interaction (HCI) – and even less when children are involved.

When working with autistic children[1] in particular, it is important to acknowledge that they perceive the world in which they live very differently compared to non-autistic, adult researchers [9]. In recent years, an increasing number of projects have involved autistic children in participatory design (e.g., [36, 17, 1, 34, 26]). However, their participation in the evaluation phase has been nearly non-existent because it is deemed very difficult to elicit concrete feedback from autistic children [15]. While communication with autistic children is indeed complex, it may be that a lack of methods offers a better explanation for why they have been included in co-design, but not in evaluation. PEACE – our approach to PE with autistic children, addresses this gap and, in addition, offers researchers working with neurodiverse [8] user groups in general a tool through which to engage them in evaluation processes.

After detailing current approaches for participatory evaluation and the unique challenges inherent in working with autistic children, we introduce PEACE, our approach to PE with autistic children. Through three case studies in the context of the OutsideTheBox project, we show how it can be successfully applied in very different ways to yield rich situated knowledge. We discuss our insights together with a critical reflection on the roles taken by children and formal researchers alike. Finally, we conclude with a view to the development of further versions of this approach.

CHI 2017, May 06 - 11, 2017, Denver, CO, USA

ACM 978-1-4503-4655-9/17/05...$15.00
DOI: http://dx.doi.org/10.1145/3025453.3025851

[1] We acknowledge that different individuals on the autism spectrum have different preferences when it comes to person-first (individuals with autism) vs. identity-first (autistic individuals) language. However, since there is an indication that identity-first is the predominantly self-chosen form (see [27]), we use it in this paper.

PARTICIPATORY EVALUATION

Participatory Evaluation has been sporadically used within and outside of HCI. However, participatory evaluation with autistic children requires a different approach to account for their uniquely situated way of perceiving, and making sense of, the world around them. To our knowledge, no framework or approach has so far addressed this issue.

History of Participatory Evaluation

The first conceptualisations of Participatory Evaluation (PE) date from the 1960s and 1970s [4], with initial applications in economic development [19] and patient centred health-care [7]. Three primary characteristics of PE play a role in the process, but can be configured differently: control of the evaluation (e.g., participants – researchers), stakeholder selection (e.g., individuals – group representatives) and depth of participation (e.g., determining goals and methods – gathering data) [7].

PE can be used pragmatically or with a transformative agenda. In the first form, PE is implemented because it yields richer knowledge, and results in greater acceptance by participants; in the second form, participants are invited to use PE as a platform for emancipation and empowerment [7]. Separating these two agendas makes sense in politically tense environments such as the implementation of policies in economic development contexts, but in technology contexts both agendas converge – especially with marginalised user groups.

There are several issues commonly discussed in PE contexts, among them ethical questions about data ownership and the definition of technical quality [7]. Relatedly, power differences between researchers and participants and protocols for interaction that aim to overcome these differences are considered in the literature [3]. Particularly marginalised user groups, such as autistic children, often face multiple power differences. In this specific case, non-autistic researchers have higher social status, are better equipped to function in a world with neurotypical demands and are not least physically taller, manifesting the power inequality through appearance. It is thus vital to the success of PE to reflect on existing power differences and ways in which they can be countered before conducting any participatory research, be it design or evaluation.

Participatory Evaluation in HCI

Participatory evaluation is not very prominent within HCI. The few cases in which it has been formalised include a cooperative work context [37] and a trauma resuscitation context [31].

The first context led to the development of the PETRA (participatory evaluation through redesign and analysis) framework, which states that one of the benefits of participatory evaluation within technological work settings is that viewpoints of theory-driven evaluators and design-based participants can be combined. In this way, evaluators gain access to the participants' perspective, and vice versa [37]. However, the framework focuses on the *evaluators'* goals and methods, and reduces the participatory aspect to the execution of the methodological approach, through which evaluators and participants co-construct meaning about the technology. In the end, researchers perform the final analysis by themselves.

In the second context, trauma resuscitation, initial research by Kusanaki and Saracenic suggests using participatory design methods for participatory evaluation [30], effectively merging phases of enquiry into the use context, design and evaluation [31]. They describe applications of their framework to projects where participatory evaluation could function as a way to include users who cannot or do not want to commit to a fully fledged participatory design process. To date, however, they have not published a final version of their framework.

Bossen et al. [2] propose seven questions for researchers conducting evaluation in participatory design processes: what is the purpose of the evaluation, who is conducting it, who is participating in it, who has the power to define evaluation criteria, which methods are used, who is the intended audience and what is expected of the evaluation. In participatory evaluation, these questions are not only asked of researchers, but mutually decided upon by research participants and formal researchers.

What is currently lacking, however, is a methodology that ties together both the participatory design and participatory evaluation aspects of a project in such a way that the same participants can co-construct the evaluation of a technology in a way that is meaningful to them.

Participatory Evaluation with Children

Involving children in PE, poses several challenges: it is important that a child can be met at the level of their abilities so that they can contribute in a way which is meaningful to them. Participating children must be able to express themselves, while researchers must attempt to ensure that they understand what has been expressed in a contextual way; much in the tradition of listening as 'an active process of communication involving hearing, interpreting and constructing meanings, not limited to the spoken word' [5]. This can be achieved through observation, interviews, questionnaires, structured activities (such as role-play with dolls/puppets or game activities), multi-sensory explorations [5], analysing children's photographs [13], interviews guided by these photographs [25], drawings/paintings [16], photo/video tours or journals [11].

Children already have different roles in technology research. Druin describes these roles as 'user', 'tester', 'informant' and 'design partner', implicitly indicating that this order also follows an order of participation and agency [12]. Participation along this categorisation seems to be limited to design phases only, however. As soon as technology is developed, children are relegated to the role of testers without any agency in defining what makes a technology successful and desirable or, conversely, a failure.

Initial approaches to participatory evaluation with neurotypically developing children fall back on a combination of heuristic evaluation tied into participatory design methods, which inherently have predefined goals and methods [42]. Hence, meaning is again constructed primarily by researchers through the input the children deliver, without the children being able to actively intervene or put their own interests forward.

Overall, a range of methods exist for accessing children's opinions, but none for structurally inviting them to participate directly in decisions about the goals and methods of an evaluation. They do not decide where, or how, to collect data, and their individual interests around the evaluation of a technology are not taken into consideration. Through more participatory approaches, children could be encouraged to reflect on the data acquired (be it quantitative or qualitative, from others or from themselves). Furthermore, given that they are also part of the user group, such an approach would ultimately yield additional knowledge about what they deem important.

EVALUATING TOGETHER WITH AUTISTIC CHILDREN

Most technologies for autistic children are grounded in an interventionist perspective (see [28] for an overview). As a consequence, their evaluation has generally been framed around the researchers' goals of functionally understanding their effectiveness with respect to behavioural outcomes. In both the development of such technologies and their evaluation, the perspective of autistic children becomes secondary. When co-creating technologies with autistic children, it became very apparent to us how necessary it is to include them in evaluation procedures from the start.

Starting with the definition of the goals of the evaluation, autistic children may already challenge researchers' pre-conceived expectations in terms of the purpose and evaluation criteria as well as the intended audience and the required methods. In classical researcher-driven evaluation, the selection of methods is generally derived from a combination of the research questions and the epistemological stance of the researchers (see [20]). However, when working in PE it becomes important to decide on methods based on the abilities of the participants, and with a view to ensuring that the resulting data are meaningful to all involved. By separating the definition of goals of participatory evaluation from the methods, we separate the questions of *what* is evaluated from *how* it is evaluated. Both parts inherit different aspects of meaning making, agency and participation – as we will detail in PEACE below.

When conducting participatory evaluation with autistic children, co-defining *what* to evaluate can be challenging due to the abstract nature of the task. In order to make it possible for the children to meaningfully participate in the evaluation procedure, some of these questions have to be asked via concrete illustrations. For example, when discussing how to find out more about the broader desirability of a technology, providing details of who those 'others' might be, and relating them to populations familiar to the child, such as classmates or 'children your age', helps them to process the abstract notion of the appeal of a technology.

Certain goals implicitly or explicitly include or exclude certain methods. If we want to know whether other people like a technology, or how useful it might be beyond its intended use case, observations of use are not sufficient. Similarly, if the goal is to better understand the reliability of a technology, it is less useful to interview others about the look and feel. However, each evaluation goal comes with a set of choices regarding data acquisition methods. If a method fails to address the way in which an autistic child makes sense of their environment, the participatory evaluation will be less successful.

Autism & Sense Making

Autism is a spectrum condition with a plethora of symptoms which can differ greatly for individuals with the same diagnosis. While the cause remains unclear, it is likely a combination of environmental and genetic factors [14]. Symptoms can include differences in reciprocal socio-communicative interaction with non-autistic people as well as repetitive interests and behaviours, which are also the main diagnostic criteria. As awareness increases, the condition is being recognised and subsequently diagnosed more frequently, and it is estimated that about 1 in 68 children are on the spectrum [38].

Autistic individuals experience the world around them differently and make sense of it in a different way [9]. The strategies that autistic individuals have for dealing with heightened sensory input include repetitive behaviours and self-stimulatory actions (also known as 'stimming'). Repetitive communication is often meaningful for an autistic individual, but not necessarily in a way a non-autistic person might expect. For example, the repetition of a fact like 'the door is open' can indicate distress (e.g., 'I want it closed'), worry (e.g., 'What if the cat runs out?'), something that pleases them and they want to share, or something that allows them to block out other sensory inputs in a stressful environment. Whenever non-autistic people interpret autistic behaviour and communication, this has to be done very carefully, and in a context dependent manner. Consequently, non-autistic researchers often shy away from explicitly including autistic modes of communication, since it is very difficult to ensure that expressions are interpreted and handled appropriately. This is even more true in the case of autistic children, as non-autistic researchers have several modes of relative power in societal hierarchies (such as age, social status, attributed agency and so on).

Insights from Participatory Design

Given that participatory evaluation has rarely been explored within HCI, we lack proven methods, particularly in the context of marginalised user groups such as autistic children. Fortunately, in the past few years, several projects have explored the participatory design space opened up by the collaboration with autistic children. The expertise which has developed around how to plan interactive sessions with autistic children and make their contributions count is invaluable when conceptualising participatory evaluation with them.

The IDEAS framework [1] emphasises structural features of participatory design sessions to involve autistic children. It is – to our knowledge – the most detailed and prominent approach for PD with autistic children. IDEAS consists of a set of seven guidelines which we have adapted for participatory evaluation with autistic children. We have retained the headlines, but re-situated their meaning to an evaluation context:

1. *Concept of Meaning*: ensure that children have a meaningful understanding of the goals and methods of an evaluation;
2. *Distractibility*: adapt to the child's hobbies and interests; include them when framing questions or offering methods;
3. *Concrete vs. Abstract Thinking*: present options clearly and unambiguously; favour contextual closed questions over abstract ones [15];

Stage	Child	Researcher
Setting Goals and Methods	Articulating goals	Offering different ways in which to discuss potential goals and methods
	Determining final goal rankings and methods for answering research questions	
Gathering Data	Taking the lead on gathering data	Prompting and supporting the child
	Coordinating data gathering	
Interpreting Results	Interpreting data	Pre-processing raw data
	Discussing all interpretations of data	

Table 1. Stages in PEACE together with children's and researchers' contributions alike.

4. *Organising and Sequencing/Visual vs. Auditory Learning*: provide visual identifiers for available options, e.g., goals or methods;
5. *Excessive Anxiety/Prompt Dependence*: always have a set of alternatives when planning to engage with the child;
6. *Strong Impulses*: build on the abilities of the child and refrain from demanding modes of interaction they dislike;
7. Involve several individuals when conducting sessions in order to flexibly provide assistance.

Additionally, providing a delicate balance between freedom and structure is essential when working with autistic children [32]. One way to achieve this is by providing a narrative frame in a freely explorable space [34], such that children are guided in their interaction by a background story which they can adhere to in their interaction or not. Malinverni et al. [33] also structured the evaluation activities of children, but left space for individually guided exploration of the technology being evaluated. By focusing their evaluation on aspects like the 'children's focus of attention' they allow for implicit participatory evaluation that is guided by how the children attend to the technology and what they find interesting about it. Ultimately, even methods designed to reflect on activities such as design exposés [17] can be useful in mapping out the potential evaluation space for and with autistic children. All of these concepts were influential in the development of our own approach to participatory evaluation with autistic children – PEACE.

PEACE – PARTICIPATORY EVALUATION WITH AUTISTIC CHILDREN

The PEACE framework comprises three stages, which roughly follow the PE phases identified in the principles of community engagement described in [35]. In our version the 'planning' stage became *setting goals and methods*, the 'implementation' stage became *gathering data*, while the 'completion' and 'dissemination' stages have been combined in *interpreting the results*. Throughout the description we reference the individual guidelines from the IDEAS framework [1], describing how they are relevant to a particular stage. Table 1 details these stages and the individual contributions of children and researchers alike.

Setting Goals and Methods

Since participatory evaluation is a process of collaborative meaning making, researchers also bring their evaluation goals to the table and are able to negotiate them with a child's ideas of evaluation. Contributions from researchers and children are addressed in the following way:

- Researchers' perspectives are part of the evaluation only if they *make sense to the child* as well;
- Children's perspectives are only disregarded if there is no way to answer them. No goal gets dropped, rather, researchers work to determine the intent behind the goal and then re-frame the question.

Following these principles, the child's perspective is privileged in order to counteract the traditional power dynamics of research projects. Researchers have the task of interpreting the child's communicative acts in a mindful way. Sometimes, goals might be hidden in a drawing or in the particular way that the child interacts with prototypes or classmates. Previously conducted participatory design sessions can also provide an indication of the evaluation goals that are meaningful to the children. These goals should be ranked by researchers and children together in order to establish which questions definitely need to be answered. This ranking of goals in order of mutual priority also allows the child to withdraw from the evaluation at the point where they feel satisfied that their goals have been met.

Given that many autistic children find it difficult to think in the abstract, questions about the goals of an evaluation should be grounded in the concrete. Goals can be identified through questions such as: "What does my family think about the technology?", "Is it still fun to interact with the technology after two months?" or "Could this technology be a commercial success?"[2].

If possible, methods should be adapted and re-framed so that the child feels competent in conducting part of the data gathering. Often, it helps to take a look at the hobbies or interests a child has and go from there. Not being able to adjust methods in a way that allows the child to participate in data gathering runs the risk that the child will feel and be less involved in the evaluation as a whole.

Gathering Data

The child can gather data on their own (e.g., recording the number of times they interacted with the object) or together with the researcher (e.g., interviewing other people). Often an evaluation has several goals, which are addressed by different

[2]While the latter is technically an extremely abstract question, in our experience the concept has been used as a stand-in for the desirability of a technology.

methods. Researchers should ensure that there are several options within a method available to the child. For example, if it's important to know what others think, researchers could suggest interviews or questionnaires. Within that there are different questions to specify and also different ways to conduct them (e.g., on the street with strangers or at home with family or anything between these two poles). Choices should be presented in a sequenced order so that the child is not overwhelmed.

Researchers can assist the child in carrying out the chosen method(s) by giving prompts and encouraging the child to go to the next step, e.g., the next question in an interview. If researchers are not present, they can give support and feedback on data gathering in evaluation meetings.

Interpreting Results

While some children might enjoy processing and interpreting the raw data, data should in most cases be pre-processed by researchers, and in a way which acknowledges individual children's preferences in terms of, for example, visual or auditory modalities. Even though every processing step adds a level of interpretation to the data, it also helps create opportunities for discussion with the child. With pre-processed data, and options for alternative interpretations, a child can make qualified judgements and challenge the presented research perspective on the data. For example, visualising which questions in interviews attracted the most attention (e.g., by length of answer) or at which times a technology was used and then debating the importance of that information gives the child the opportunity to acknowledge different angles from which to see their technology, but also gives the researchers insight into what the child deems important to know about a (co-designed) technology, and why. This step might, again, necessitate a non-verbal mode of communication, such as a Picture Exchange System, sign language, or spatial positioning and interpreted behaviour/reactions towards the pre-processed data.

CASE STUDIES

Within OutsideTheBox[3] we co-design technologies with autistic children that target their holistic well-being. The resulting technological artifacts range from small tokens to large body interaction devices. Over the span of at least one full school year, we met each child bi-weekly for an hour long session, usually at their school. The main purpose of the technologies we individually develop with the children is that they make sense in their lives and enable them to share the positive experiences they have with those technologies. Hence, our evaluation focuses on this high level goal from the researchers' perspective in all cases.

In the first year we attempted to evaluate outcomes in a more traditional manner in the sense that the goals and methods were decided solely by the research team. Data gathering processes were difficult and often unfruitful, because while they matched the families' abilities, they placed too high a cognitive load on them (e.g., remembering to fill out a questionnaire at regular intervals over a certain period of time) [40]. The three cases presented here are from the second year of OutsideTheBox, during which we attempted participatory evaluation with three different children: Quentin, Mia and Yvan[4].

Quentin

When we first met Quentin, he was nine years old and went to a mainstream school. Our collaboration spanned 16 months and 15 meetings overall, with large breaks in between due to summer vacation periods. Quentin was diagnosed with Aspergers when he was in pre-school. Tinkering and crafting were well-loved activities, but only for the purpose of creating a finished object that has a use (even if it is not necessarily obvious to outsiders).

Figure 1. Sound Cubes – developed together with Quentin

After a phase of Contextual Inquiry [23], we decided to use Digital Fabrication [18] as our design generating method. On our design journey, we mostly met in an empty classroom, although two sessions were conducted at the university, where 3D-printers, a laser printer, a CNC machine and several smaller fabrication tools are available. Inspired by the potential of these machines and a prototype from a different research project[5], we dove into the development of Sound Cubes (see Figure 1).

The Sound Cubes were realised as a pair, however it is technically feasible to create additional cubes such that any cube could function with any other. The cubes can record a sound message, replay it or move it to another cube. Every cube can also receive messages from any other and play these. Each side of the cube is dedicated to a different function: one for the speakers, one for the microphone and recording, one for message replay, one for receiving messages, one for dropping a message (via direct contact) and finally, one to place the cube on. The last surface can also be used to individualise

[3] http://outsidethebox.at

[4] All names have been changed.

[5] http://igw.tuwien.ac.at/sparkling

the cube so that e.g., each family member has their own, or opened to tinker with the technical components of the cube.

Setting Goals and Methods

Throughout our collaboration, Quentin was constantly making sure that he performed well. He asked about the quality of his work and – because he was quite aware of the research project and its context, and knew of other children we worked with – asked how his work related to that of others. Whenever he asked for feedback from his classmates, he presented what he had constructed in that session, but did not let them interact with the objects. These utterances and observations made it clear to us that it was important for Quentin that the cubes be *desirable to others* as well as *functional and reliable*. The latter point coincided with our own interest, as we also wanted to know *who would use the cubes, and how*.

Since Quentin was also an enthusiastic member of the 'Science Club' at his school, we decided on a data gathering method that could generate numerical data. That way, we could create visuals and data that was expected of a positivist approach, which is the dominant language through which *science* is represented in popular media. We expected that such data would be most meaningful to Quentin. Additionally, he had his own tablet device, which he liked interacting with. We developed a set of relevant questions together (see Table 2), which had the added benefit of giving us the opportunity to discuss with Quentin the different types of questions that can be used in questionnaires.

Question 7 was particularly important to him: "Others should want the device, but I will be the only one who has it!". Our questionnaire platform was QuickTapSurvey, which allowed Quentin to gather data on his own device while also giving the research team access to the questionnaire responses.

#	Question Type	Question
1	Binary	Did you use the Cubes yourself?
2	Number	How often did you use them so far?
3	Ranking	What attribute of the Cubes is most important to you?
4	Scale	How well do the Cubes function?
5	Text	What would you change about them?
6	Mult. Choice	What do you least like about them?
7	Binary	Do you want to have a Cube for yourself?
8	Text	Do you have an idea for a different name?

Table 2. Quentin's Questionnaire, showing specific questions and question type

Gathering Data & Interpreting Results

Our plan was that Quentin would gather data independently at home using the tablet version of the questionnaire and, if possible, gather more responses together with us at school. Unfortunately, there were strict rules imposed on using private tablets on school grounds, which rendered the second endeavour impossible. Additionally, Quentin did not collect any responses himself.

From this, we understood that there were two problems with our approach. While Quentin wanted to do science related activities, they focused on *constructing* physical objects rather than the general ideas behind scientific methods. The purpose of gathering answers to the questionnaires was ultimately not tangible enough for him to find it interesting. Additionally, it turned out that he did not really use the Sound Cubes, but instead wanted to show his idea and creation to others in order to gather positive affirmation. The evaluation methods we had planned together – even though jointly agreed upon – did not match this desire appropriately.

Quentin's case study illustrated the need to be more concrete and more situated in activities the children already enjoy when conducting participatory evaluation in order to make it fruitful and meaningful for everyone involved. Additionally, it encouraged us to reflect on the "tyranny of participation" [6] and how not every participant will be equally interested in every part of the design and evaluation process. However, by creating a space in which Quentin could have more power over outcomes if he chose to do so, we learnt more about the interaction between Quentin and the Sound Cubes. The joint formulation of questions helped us in particular to understand which aspects of the Sound Cubes were important to him.

Mia

Mia had recently been diagnosed with Autism Spectrum Condition when we met her. The nine-year old was aware of her diagnosis, but she and her family were still figuring out what it meant to them and their daily life. Mia's school acted as a supportive anchor in that it provided dedicated, additional teaching staff for her class on some days during the week. She loves everything related to the Super Mario games, with Toad and Yoshi being her favourite characters. She also likes playing outdoor sports and drawing, but dislikes handwriting.

Using the semantics of a Super Mario game world, we used theatre methods [39] and augmented them with playful elements to learn more about Mia's life context [41]. We established that she finds getting up in the morning extremely annoying and difficult – so difficult, in fact, that already during our second of 16 meetings, she suggested that we create a cushion that wakes her up by vibrating next to her instead of the disturbing sound made by her then-current alarm clock. Once we understood how important first impressions of a day are in creating a good mood, we also understood the potential positive impact of such a technology.

The Rattle Alarm System (see Figure 2) consists of three parts. At the core, there is an alarm clock module – aesthetically modelled after Toad's head – which displays the current time through blue lights on a NeoPixel light ring with 24 LEDs. The alarm time can be set through a light touch on top of the module and is displayed with a green light. When the alarm goes off, the Super Mario theme song plays in an endless loop and the cushion vibrates. The alarm can be stopped by getting up and stepping on the pressure mat, which functions as an off-switch. Shortly after the alarm turned off, the clock plays a little melody – different every day – which sets the mood of the day as a stand-in for a horoscope.

Figure 2. The Rattle Alarm System – Developed together with Mia – left: cushion, middle: alarm clock, right: pressure mat

Setting Goals and Methods

Most of our sessions with Mia took place at her school in an empty classroom adjacent to her own classroom. After each session, she had the possibility to show what she had accomplished that day to her teacher and afterwards to selected friends. During one of those after-sessions in class, one of her friends told us that Mia occasionally distributes her own newspaper with news for the class (albeit with not much text written in them). It was deemed desirable to belong to the group of people who were allowed to read the newspaper.

Figure 3. Announcement of the Rattle Cushion Alarm System

In order to co-establish goals for the evaluation, we asked Mia to create an advert of her technology that focuses on desired effects and how mornings are shaped with the Rattle Alarm System. Figure 3 shows the core part of her finished advert. All parts of the system are depicted with their functionality: the clock plays Super Mario music, the cushion rattles and the mat gives a horoscope. The text below reads (translated): "The way to get up happy!". In addition to giving us an idea about her own mental model of the functionality (e.g., placing the melody-as-horoscope functionality on the mat instead of the clock), the advert also tells us that one of her goals in the evaluations is to find out whether the system has *a positive impact on her morning routine*. The research team was interested in *how the technology could be truly integrated in Mia's life*.

Methodologically, we created a pool of methods with which we could answer these questions – all of them newspaper related.

- A *report* about how the Rattle Alarm System and who uses it. This would inform us about the elements and contexts of use that are important to Mia.
- A *review* of the Rattle Alarm System with an accompanying rating. This would give us an insight into what works well already and what has to be still improved in order to make the technology robust enough to be part of Mia's life. The review and report also potentially tell us about how the interaction shapes the morning routine.
- *Interviews* in which Mia asks others about their opinion of the system. The questions can tell us more about Mia's interests, the answers provide an understanding of others' interpretation of the system and the choice of interviewees also shows us whose opinion is important to Mia.
- An *illustration* of the system in actual use, which we could then use and compare to the advert to see how the two drawings relate to each other.

We also agreed that we would bundle all contributions together to create an issue of her newspaper that focuses solely on the Rattle Alarm System.

Gathering Data

Mia could either gather data on her own at home or during the sessions with support from a researcher – and she chose both, resulting in a report on the design process and two interviews.

The report about the design process was integrated into one of her usual newspaper issues, in which she picked up on daily news with her own take on the European Soccer Championships and the performance of the Austrian team on the front page as well as comics and jokes on the last page. On the pages in between she detailed the design process within its context of a research project with autistic children. She also made clear that she saw herself as an inventor of something that might be useful to others as well. "In an interview (sic!), [Mia] said: (...) I can understand that others have similar problems with getting up in the morning."

Several weeks after receiving the prototype to test out at home, we conducted an evaluation oriented meeting. In that meeting, Mia role played the situation in the mornings and gave critical feedback on the sensitivity of the top button, the structure of the cable connecting the mat and the alarm clock as well as the intensity of the vibration of the cushion. She then decided to interview her mother and a co-located researcher. She asked about the quality of the system and about what the interviewees felt should be changed. She also asked how many 'stars' on a scale of one to five the system would get, and enquired what they would invent if they were part of a similar project. During both interviews, she had a professional demeanour. One of the researchers prompted her to ask further questions when she appeared to be stuck. This additional structure enabled her to get through all questions without being required to read handwriting – a task she finds exhausting.

Interpreting Results

From the interview with her mother, Mia could establish that others indicated a positive influence of the design process and the technology on her life. During the session, she herself noted that she agreed with that assessment, even though she had so far only used the system occasionally.

We were also able to identify necessary improvements that would make the system more robust: a better protected and tighter connection between the alarm clock and the mat, more vibration power in the cushion as well as better distribution of the vibration next to an adjustment of the sensitivity of the top button on the alarm clock. We decided on further meetings to improve those open points. An actionable plan also shows all participants, formal researchers and child alike, what the effects of an evaluation can be and how to act on its results.

When asking for the star rating during the interviews, Mia's mother awarded five stars for the aesthetics and two for functionality (motivated by the lack of robustness). The other interviewee awarded four stars. Afterwards, Mia announced that she now had collected eleven stars and that she wanted to see how many stars she could earn in total. That way, she re-appropriated the interpretation of the rating and gamified the evaluation process on her own. Additionally, Mia's report indicated that the process and resulting prototype were having a positive and affirmative effect on her life.

From working with Mia, we learnt that data gathering methods can be interesting to a child, if framed correctly and if the child can assign a potential utility to the activity. Even if researchers and the child differ in their interpretation of a method – as seen with the stars – the child's interpretation is more important and more indicative of their own perspective on the technology to evaluate, but also the evaluation process as such.

Yvan

All things related to planets and space travel are of great interest to Yvan. The eight-year-old, diagnosed with Autism Spectrum Condition, talked at length about these topics whenever he could; not always considering whether his audience was actually interested in listening. At the beginning of our cooperation, which, to date, spans 13 sessions, Yvan was educated in a special needs class, but transitioned into a multi-age classroom later.

At the first couple of design workshops we conducted Contextual Inquiry [23]. That way, we not only learnt more about Yvan's core interests, but also how important his five year-old brother Hank is to him. During our ideation phases he constantly envisioned his brother in potential use contexts. Once we settled on the idea of a Time Machine, with which we could travel through time and space to different temporal stages and different planets, we explored the actualisation of this idea through means of Digital Fabrication [18]. While the Time Machine initially had the form of a pyramid and later followed the concept of a travel tower, we eventually decided that it would consist of two parts: an immersive light blanket and a navigation interface (see also, Figure 4).

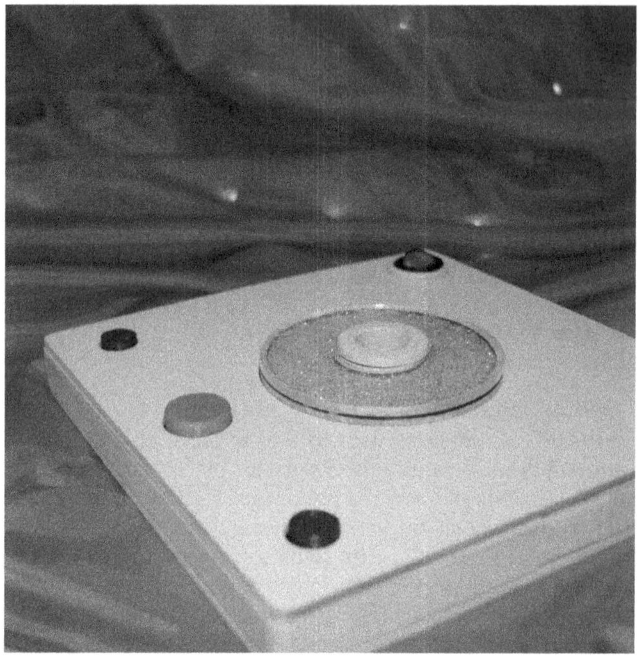

Figure 4. Time Machine – developed together with Yvan – foreground: navigation interface, background: immersive light blanket

While the technological parts of the Time Machine are comparatively simple, the smartness of the technology emerges in use. Through the navigation interface, a user can control different light patterns on the blanket. They only become meaningful through the narrative established between users. Yvan then tells elaborate stories in which he travels to different planets at different points in time. Once he 'lands', he steps out of the machine and grabs different things in the environment, but gives them a different meaning, appropriate to the time and place he travelled to. This type of pretend play is notoriously difficult for autistic children [24]. However, the Time Machine introduces just enough structure for Yvan to do so cooperatively. Another effect of the Time Machine is that it becomes a productive release for Yvan's specialised knowledge that engages the other person as well. They experience the immersive space together and can both shape the narrative. The specialised knowledge becomes part of a joint adventure instead of a one-sided lecture.

Setting Goals and Methods

Next to the evaluation goal – established through our collaboration – that *the Time Machine should be enjoyable for Hank as well*, we asked Yvan directly, what would define success for his technology, since he was using the concept himself previously. He stated that *others should deem the Time Machine as cool* and also, that *it should be really fast*. Since the speed of the time machine is virtually constructed by the given story context, we re-interpreted that goal and wanted to find out *whether the Time Machine suitably supports immersive narratives for Yvan*. Assessing the speed of the Time Machine remained part of the evaluation as a goal by itself.

Methodologically, we established a TV show called *Research with Yvan*, in which he presented the Time Machine and reported on trips undertaken with it. This was requested by Yvan himself, who was continuously fascinated by the camera which recorded all of our sessions together. We also set up a showcase of the Time Machine in Yvan's classroom and – somewhat impromptu in an evaluation session together with Hank – let both brothers create a drawing of the use context of the Time Machine.

Gathering Data

All data gathering was done jointly with the researchers. The TV show was filmed during a latter design session in order to evaluate how well the blanket idea and initial prototypes matched Yvan's expectations. He animatedly reported about a trip to Saturn and Jupiter that he had just undertaken with one of the researchers, detailing especially how fast the Time Machine was and what kinds of things they found on these planets during their trip.

When Yvan received the first fully functional prototype, we also showcased it in class. He presented photos from the design process and led some children under the blanket to take a trip to different planets. Unfortunately, a soldering seam became loose and the lights did not work properly. Many children were confused about what exactly was happening, although some were open to the frame of pretend play and talked about their own perspective on the time travel.

Figure 5. Drawing by both users of the Time Machine on how they interact with it – real name initials have been smudged

After several weeks in which they used the Time Machine in a home setting, Yvan and Hank created the drawing depicted in Figure 5. It shows both of them (drawn in each of their favourite colours with size following age) under a fully illuminated blanket with two different navigation boards, even though only one exists. On the upper left, there is an alien they encounter on the planets they visit (depicted at the top).

Interpreting Results

Yvan took the opportunity to reflect on the perceived speed of the Time Machine himself during the recording of *Research with Yvan*. He enthusiastically established that the machine was, indeed, really fast. Since he is the only person who can judge this, his opinion is the most important to consider when trying to answer this question. The research team also inferred from this that immersion was successfully supported.

Due to the malfunction of the blanket in the showcase, only a couple of classmates were enthusiastic about the invention. Yvan (and the formal researchers) had hoped for more success. While he was initially very excited about presenting his technology, he did not want to do another showcase once the short circuit was fixed. The research team would have liked to investigate this question further, however, it was answered for Yvan, therefore no further enquiries were undertaken.

Hank expressed being very happy with the Time Machine. While Yvan and Hank were drawing Figure 5, Hank said that he would like to play even more with it, but Yvan did not want to play as often. Yvan also reported that whenever they went on time travel, they did so together (which has also been confirmed by their parents). From this, we inferred that Hank enjoyed the Time Machine as much or even more than Yvan.

DISCUSSION

PEACE achieved what the original concept of PE set out to do: involve the primary stakeholders of an intervention or design directly in assessing its effect. Through this, we created a space in which researchers acknowledge the children's agency and meaningful interpretations of technologies and the ways in which they can be assessed. Pragmatically, this provides us with insights that were previously unattainable. Autistic children had control of the evaluation,and were individually involved and deeply engaged in conducting the evaluation. As such, all three characteristics [7] of PE are present. PEACE could allow for a range of use contexts and is adaptable for other user groups as well.

Each specific case provided us with unique insights which we could not have obtained without participatory evaluation. From Quentin, we learnt that methods must be chosen in tune with *activities* that the child likes. Mia showed us the necessity of carefully managing structures and freedoms to create a space in which she could perform evaluation. Finally, Yvan challenged our pre-conceived notion of the team always being able to reach agreement by interpreting a one-time failure as absolute whereas the researchers still saw it as an open question – and how researchers have to take their own agenda back in order to not accidentally override a child's interpretation.

In addition to these individual insights, we also learnt what is important to autistic children across these case studies. We discuss this as well as the roles and responsibilities of everyone involved in PEACE in this section.

Insights from Case Studies

Across the case studies, we understood that the success of a PE endeavour – as of any participatory project – relies on the interest that participants have in undertaking the action. Some participants are more interested in creating the outcomes of a participatory design project and do not feel the need to enquire more formally about the process or outcomes.

Furthermore, these cases showed us that it is important to understand that participants' goals do not necessarily have to be interesting to formal researchers or make sense to them. However, for participatory evaluation to earn its name, it is vital that we take these goals seriously, assign proper methods to evaluate them and create results that are meaningful to all. Those results should be reflected on together with the participant in order to ensure that they see their questions answered, especially if researchers interpret a goal differently.

When data is created, the same data can be interpreted differently. We saw this with the stars assigned to the Rattle Alarm System, where they became part of something that had to be earned in sum, or when the research team attributed others' lack of enthusiasm to a system failure, whereas the child was acknowledging a more generic failure and was no longer interested in further enquiring into that evaluation goal. Both interpretations must be seen as equally valid, with action being taken based on the child's agreement and interest, not solely motivated by researchers' agendas.

It was interesting to us to see that all children included some form of external validation within the evaluation procedure. They wanted their objects to be desirable to others as well, be it out of envy (Quentin), a desire to be meaningful for more people (Mia) or to make sure that a specific person benefits from the design as well (Yvan).

Roles & Responsibilities

When we started conceptualising PEACE, we thought carefully about the roles that researchers might take in Participatory Evaluation processes. After all, one could argue that the reason why researchers take over the evaluation of PD processes is because they possess the necessary skills to do so.

In PEACE, researchers facilitate the evaluation process and encourage autistic children to explore angles of their work they might not have explored otherwise. Through appropriate framing and structuring, they provide space for the children to answer the questions that interest them. In order to suitably support the child, researchers must not only know the child's interests and preferred activities well, they must also have a wide pool of evaluation methods from which they can draw. They choose a set of potentially useful methods, introduce them to the child and agree the final ones together. They must also have additional methods at the ready that they can flexibly switch to if a child shows decreased interest in the established one. Researchers' skills, competency and experience, together with the child's interests, focus and questions, are the ingredients of a successful participatory evaluation.

In some cases, researchers may have additional research questions which they are trying to answer that might be unimportant or meaningless to the child. While these questions cannot be addressed within the PEACE framework, we encourage researchers to augment the process with established modes of evaluation that can yield different types of knowledge. What PEACE offers, however, is a previously unexplored perspective on the experiences of autistic children with technologies: their own.

CONCLUSION

In this paper, we motivated participatory evaluation with autistic children and reflected on the concept in its historical context as well as considering how it has been previously discussed in HCI and with children. After presenting the parameters and particularities involved in participatory evaluation with autistic children, we presented the PEACE framework, which comprises three essential steps: defining goals and methods, gathering data and interpreting the results – all done in a participatory and evolving fashion. Three case studies provided us with insights into potential pitfalls, as well as insights that can be gained from unexpected outcomes, even if particular steps within the evaluation are not carried out according to plan. Finally, we discussed the implications for participatory evaluation across these case studies, and considered the role of researchers in such a process.

Despite all this, further work is needed in order to establish PEACE as a fully fledged research tool. For one, it would be useful to try out a range of different methods in order to create a methodological tool-set that is available to researchers. We also have yet to see how concepts from Participatory Design methods, such as narrative framing [10], temporal displacement [43] or the metaphor of magic [29] might transfer to participatory evaluation. Finally, our approach requires intimate knowledge of one child's abilities, interests and favourite activities. It is not yet clear how this transfers to a group of children, particularly a group with mixed abilities.

What we have delivered here is a proof of concept that it is possible to include autistic children actively in the evaluation of the technologies they co-design. PEACE is the first framework that allows researchers to conduct participatory evaluation with autistic children in a way that appropriately acknowledges their agency, needs and abilities.

ACKNOWLEDGEMENTS

This research is funded by the Austrian Science Fund (FWF): [P26281-N23] "OutsideTheBox - Rethinking Assistive Technologies with Children with Autism" project. Our deepest gratitude to Julia Makhaeva for being part of this research endeavour. Geraldine Fitzpatrick, Oezge Subasi, Matthias Wunsch, Francisco Nunez and anonymous reviewers helped refine earlier versions of this paper. Kearsley Schieder-Wethy assisted in proof reading and grammatical corrections.

We would also like to thank our participating families, schools and the local government, in particular the department for inclusion in public education which facilitated access to our participants. Above all, we thank the children who continue to inspire our work.

REFERENCES

1. Laura Benton, Hilary Johnson, Emma Ashwin, Mark Brosnan, and Beate Grawemeyer. 2012. Developing IDEAS: Supporting Children with Autism Within a Participatory Design Team. In *Proceedings of the SIGCHI Conference on Human Factors in Computing Systems (CHI '12)*. ACM, New York, NY, USA, 2599–2608. DOI: http://dx.doi.org/10.1145/2207676.2208650
2. Claus Bossen, Christian Dindler, and Ole Sejer Iversen. 2016. Evaluation in Participatory Design: A Literature Survey. In *Proceedings of the 14th Participatory Design Conference: Full Papers - Volume 1 (PDC '16)*. ACM, New York, NY, USA, 151–160. DOI: http://dx.doi.org/10.1145/2940299.2940303
3. Tone Bratteteig and Ina Wagner. 2012. Disentangling power and decision-making in participatory design. In *Proceedings of the 12th Participatory Design Conference: Research Papers - Volume 1 (PDC '12)*. ACM, Roskilde, Denmark, 41–50. DOI: http://dx.doi.org/10.1145/2347635.2347642
4. Sharon Brisolara. 1998. The history of participatory evaluation and current debates in the field. *New Directions for Evaluation* 1998, 80 (1998), 25–41. DOI: http://dx.doi.org/10.1002/ev.1115
5. Alison Clark*. 2005. Listening to and involving young children: a review of research and practice. *Early Child Development and Care* 175, 6 (2005), 489–505. DOI: http://dx.doi.org/10.1080/0300443050013l288
6. Bill Cooke and Uma Kothari. 2001. *Participation: The new Tyranny?* Zed Books, London, UK.
7. J. Bradley Cousins and Elizabeth Whitmore. 1998. Framing participatory evaluation. *New Directions for Evaluation* 1998, 80 (1998), 5–23. DOI: http://dx.doi.org/10.1002/ev.1114
8. Nick S. Dalton. 2013. Neurodiversity HCI. *interactions* 20, 2 (March 2013), 72–75. DOI: http://dx.doi.org/10.1145/2427076.2427091
9. Hanne De Jaegher. 2013. Embodiment and sense-making in autism. *Frontiers in Integrative Neuroscience* 7 (2013), 15. DOI:http://dx.doi.org/10.3389/fnint.2013.00015
10. Christian Dindler and Ole Sejer Iversen. 2007. Fictional Inquiry - design collaboration in a shared narrative space. *CoDesign* 3, 4 (Dec. 2007), 213–234. DOI: http://dx.doi.org/doi:10.1080/15710880701500187
11. Sue Dockett, Sarah Main, and Lynda Kelly. 2011. Consulting Young Children: Experiences from a Museum. *Visitor Studies* 14, 1 (April 2011), 13–33. DOI: http://dx.doi.org/10.1080/10645578.2011.557626
12. Allison Druin. 2002. The Role of Children in the Design of New Technology. *Behaviour and Information Technology* 21, 1 (2002), 1–25. http://hcil.cs.umd.edu/trs/99-23/99-23.html
13. Johanna Einarsdottir. 2005. Playschool in pictures: children's photographs as a research method. *Early Child Development and Care* 175, 6 (2005), 523–541. DOI: http://dx.doi.org/10.1080/03004430500131320
14. Marc Fakhoury. 2015. Autistic spectrum disorders: A review of clinical features, theories and diagnosis. *International Journal of Developmental Neuroscience* 43 (June 2015), 70–77. DOI: http://dx.doi.org/10.1016/j.ijdevneu.2015.04.003
15. Christopher Frauenberger, Judith Good, Alyssa Alcorn, and Helen Pain. 2013. Conversing Through and About Technologies: Design Critique as an Opportunity to Engage Children with Autism and Broaden Research(er) Perspectives. *International Journal of Child-Computer Interaction* 1, 2 (May 2013), 38–49. DOI: http://dx.doi.org/10.1016/j.ijcci.2013.02.001
16. Christopher Frauenberger, Judith Good, and Wendy Keay-Bright. 2010. Phenomenology, a framework for participatory design. In *Proceedings of the 11th Biennial Participatory Design Conference*. ACM, ACM, Sydney, Australia, 187–190.
17. Christopher Frauenberger, Julia Makhaeva, and Katharina Spiel. 2016. Designing Smart Objects with Autistic Children: Four Design Exposès. In *Proceedings of the 2016 CHI Conference on Human Factors in Computing Systems (CHI '16)*. ACM, New York, NY, USA, 130–139. DOI:http://dx.doi.org/10.1145/2858036.2858050
18. Christopher Frauenberger and Irene Posch. 2014. Exploring Future Technologies Through Digital Fabrication With Autistic Children. In *Participatory Design in Digital Fabrication workshop at FabLearn'14*. FabLearn'14, Stanford, CA, USA, Article 1, 4 pages. http://outsidethebox.at/files/fabwithasd.pdf
19. Gila B. Garaway. 1995. Participatory evaluation. *Studies in Educational Evaluation* 21, 1 (1995), 85–102. DOI: http://dx.doi.org/10.1016/0191-491X(95)00007-H
20. Egon G. Guba and Yvonna S. Lincoln. 1994. Competing Paradigms in Qualitative Research. In *Handbook of qualitative research*, Norman K. Denzin and Yvonna S. Lincoln (Eds.). Sage Publications, Inc., London, UK, 105–117.
21. Steve Harrison, Phoebe Sengers, and Deborah Tatar. 2011. Making epistemological trouble: Third-paradigm HCI as successor science. *Interacting with Computers* 23 (2011), 385–392. DOI: http://dx.doi.org/10.1016/j.intcom.2011.03.005
22. Gillian R. Hayes. 2011. The Relationship of Action Research to Human-computer Interaction. *ACM Transactions on Computer-Human Interaction* 18, 3 (2011), 15:1–15:20. DOI: http://dx.doi.org/10.1145/1993060.1993065
23. K. Holtzblatt and S. Jones. 1993. Contextual inquiry: A participatory technique for system design. In *Participatory design: Principles and practice*. Erlbaum, Hillsdale, NJ, USA, 180–193.

24. Christopher Jarrold. 2003. A Review of Research into Pretend Play in Autism. *Autism* 7, 4 (2003), 379–390. DOI:http://dx.doi.org/10.1177/1362361303007004004

25. Jane Jorgenson and Tracy Sullivan. 2009. Accessing Children's Perspectives Through Participatory Photo Interviews. *Forum Qualitative Sozialforschung / Forum: Qualitative Social Research* 11, 1 (2009), Art. 8. http://www.qualitative-research.net/index.php/fqs/article/view/447

26. Wendy E. Keay-Bright. 2007. The Reactive Colours Project: Demonstrating Participatory and Collaborative Design Methods for the Creation of Software for Autistic Children. *Digital Creativity* 1, 2 (2007), 7–16. http://ijg.cgpublisher.com/product/pub.154/prod.17

27. Lorcan Kenny, Caroline Hattersley, Bonnie Molins, Carole Buckley, Carol Povey, and Elizabeth Pellicano. 2015. Which terms should be used to describe autism? Perspectives from the UK autism community. *Autism* 20, 4 (July 2015), 1362361315588200. DOI: http://dx.doi.org/10.1177/1362361315588200

28. Julie A. Kientz, Matthew S. Goodwin, Gillian R. Hayes, and Gregory D. Abowd. 2013. Interactive Technologies for Autism. *Synthesis Lectures on Assistive, Rehabilitative, and Health-Preserving Technologies* 2, 2 (2013), 1–177. DOI: http://dx.doi.org/10.2200/S00533ED1V01Y201309ARH004

29. Mike Kuniavsky. 2007. Magic as a Metaphor for Ubiquitous Computing. *Ambidextrous Magazine* Spring (2007), 36–37.

30. Diana Kusunoki and Aleksandra Sarcevic. 2012. Applying Participatory Design Theory to Designing Evaluation Methods. In *CHI '12 Extended Abstracts on Human Factors in Computing Systems (CHI EA '12)*. ACM, New York, NY, USA, 1895–1900. DOI: http://dx.doi.org/10.1145/2212776.2223725

31. Diana S. Kusunoki and Aleksandra Sarcevic. 2013. A Participatory Framework for Evaluation Design. In *iConference 2013 Proceedings*. iSchools, Fort Worth, Texas, 860–864. DOI:http://dx.doi.org/10.9776/13439

32. Julia Makhaeva, Christopher Frauenberger, and Katharina Spiel. 2016. Creating Creative Spaces for Co-designing with Autistic Children: The Concept of a "Handlungsspielraum". In *Proceedings of the 14th Participatory Design Conference: Full Papers - Volume 1 (PDC '16)*. ACM, New York, NY, USA, 51–60. DOI: http://dx.doi.org/10.1145/2940299.2940306

33. Laura Malinverni, Joan Mora-Guiard, and Narcis Pares. 2016. Towards methods for evaluating and communicating participatory design: A multimodal approach. *International Journal of Human-Computer Studies* 94 (2016), 53 – 63. DOI: http://dx.doi.org/10.1016/j.ijhcs.2016.03.004

34. Laura Malinverni, Joan MoraGuiard, Vanesa Padillo, MariaAngeles Mairena, Amaia Hervás, and Narcis Pares. 2014. Participatory Design Strategies to Enhance the Creative Contribution of Children with Special Needs. In *Proceedings of the 2014 Conference on Interaction Design and Children (IDC '14)*. ACM, New York, NY, USA, 85–94. DOI: http://dx.doi.org/10.1145/2593968.2593981

35. CDC/ATSDR Committee on Community Engagement. 2011/Accessed July 14, 2016. Principles of Community Engagement. (2011/Accessed July 14, 2016). https://www.atsdr.cdc.gov/communityengagement/

36. Narcis Pares, Paul Masri, Gerard van Wolferen, and Chris Creed. 2005. Achieving dialogue with children with severe autism in an adaptive multisensory interaction: the "MEDIATE" project. *IEEE Transactions on Visualization and Computer Graphics* 11, 6 (Nov. 2005), 734–743. DOI:http://dx.doi.org/10.1109/TVCG.2005.88

37. Susi Ross, Magnus Ramage, and Yvonne Rogers. 1995. PETRA: participatory evaluation through redesign and analysis. *Interacting with Computers* 7, 4 (1995), 335–360. DOI: http://dx.doi.org/10.1016/0953-5438(96)87697-1

38. Ginny Russell, Stephan Collishaw, Jean Golding, Susan E Kelly, and Tamsin Ford. 2015. Changes in diagnosis rates and behavioural traits of autism spectrum disorder over time. *British Journal of Psychiatry Open* 1, 2 (2015), 110–115. DOI: http://dx.doi.org/10.1192/bjpo.bp.115.000976

39. Steve Sato and Tony Salvador. 1999. Methods & Tools: Playacting and Focus Troupes:: Theater Techniques for Creating Quick, Intense, Immersive, and Engaging Focus Group Sessions. *interactions* 6, 5 (Sept. 1999), 35–41. DOI:http://dx.doi.org/10.1145/312683.312715

40. Katharina Spiel, Christopher Frauenberger, Geraldine Fitzpatrick, and Eva Hornecker. 2017. When Empathy Is Not Enough:Assessing the Experiences of Autistic Children withTechnologies. In *Proceedings of the 2017 CHI Conference on Human Factors in Computing Systems (CHI'17)*. ACM, New York, NY, USA, tbd. DOI: http://dx.doi.org/10.1145/3025453.3025785

41. Katharina Spiel, Christopher Frauenberger, Julia Makhaeva, and Fares Kayali. 2016. Talking about Myself - Playful Inquiry into an Absent Life World. In *Workshop on Games as HCI Method at CHI'16.* ., San Jose, USA, Article 0, 4 pages.

42. Jean Lee Tan, Dion Hoe-Lian Goh, Rebecca P. Ang, and Vivien S. Huan. 2013. Participatory evaluation of an educational game for social skills acquisition. *Computers & Education* 64 (2013), 70–80. DOI: http://dx.doi.org/10.1016/j.compedu.2013.01.006

43. Giasemi Vavoula and Mike Sharples. 2007. Future technology workshop: A collaborative method for the design of new learning technologies and activities. *International Journal of Computer-Supported Collaborative Learning* 2, 4 (2007), 393–419. DOI: http://dx.doi.org/10.1007/s11412-007-9026-0

Co-Designing with Preschoolers Using Fictional Inquiry and Comicboarding

Alexis Hiniker[1,2] alexisr@uw.edu
Kiley Sobel[1,2] ksobel@uw.edu
Bongshin Lee[1] bongshin@microsoft.com
[1]Microsoft Research, Redmond, WA, USA
[2]Human Centered Design and Engineering, University of Washington, Seattle, WA, USA

ABSTRACT
In this case study, we describe a design workshop with 7 children age 4-6 using existing co-design techniques known to elicit design insights in older individuals. We found that our 5- and 6-year-old participants successfully generated design ideas using these methods, while 4-year-olds were unable to create solutions in a traditional format. However, these younger children enthusiastically offered opportunities where, with methodological guidance, the researcher could have followed the child's lead and shifted the design question to one that was potentially more meaningful for the participant. We propose future work to examine the effectiveness of giving these younger participants greater authority in defining and scoping the problem space.

Author Keywords
Design workshop, early childhood, participatory design, fictional inquiry, comicboarding.

ACM Classification Keywords
H.5.m. Information interfaces and presentation (e.g., HCI): Miscellaneous.

INTRODUCTION
Very young children are major consumers of digital media, with 97% of infants using a smartphone before their first birthday and 75% of children owning their own dedicated mobile device by the time they turn four [20]. Designing experiences that best serve these young children can be challenging, as a variety of prior work shows that design paradigms created for adults can break down when embedded in digital experiences for children [14]. Interface elements that are intuitive for adults are not always easy for children to understand [13,15], and children's needs, interests, and social attachments differ systematically from adults'.

This challenge is exacerbated by the fact that relatively few co-design methods exist for children under six as compared to other age groups. Though the post-modern conception of childhood recognizes that even very young children are independent agents, separate from their caregivers, with their own opinions and knowledge [22], surfacing their insights remains challenging. Young children are still acquiring the capacity to reflect on and articulate their impressions of the world [27,28] and are less likely to be aware of what they know. As a result, direct methods that require explicit knowledge—while often successful with adult users—are less likely to be effective with children [10].

CHI 2017, May 06 - 11, 2017, Denver, CO, USA

ACM 978-1-4503-4655-9/17/05...$15.00
DOI: http://dx.doi.org/10.1145/3025453.3025588

Several prior studies have found that co-designing with preschoolers can be productive and meaningful [9,12,26], although established techniques sometimes require modifications [9,11]. The purpose of this project was to document our experiences using specific co-design techniques with preschoolers that, to our knowledge, have not been tried with this age group. Though our ultimate goal was to generate design insights for an app that helps children plan out their play time, we also wanted to explore the effectiveness of these specific methods with both older and younger preschoolers.

Here, we describe our experiences during a two-hour co-design workshop with preschoolers and kindergartners age 4-6. We used two established participatory design techniques, fictional inquiry [4] and comicboarding [24], a construction activity, and traditional user testing to elicit design insights. We found that our 5- and 6-year-old participants were able to generate and articulate ideas that designers could easily understand and build on, while 4-year-olds generated less cohesive ideas and often shifted to another topic. The contribution of this work is to add to the small existing body of research that reports on co-designing with children under 6 by documenting the effectiveness of these specific co-design techniques and describing the differences we encountered between older and younger preschoolers.

RELATED WORK

Co-designing with Children
In the last decade, the Child-Computer Interaction community has increasingly come to value involving children in the design process. Druin developed a widely adopted model for evaluating the role that children play in the design of a system [5], providing designers with a framework for involving their young users and representing these users' interests in the design process. This framework has been highly influential, and a variety of systems have been created with children

as design partners and design informants [25]. However, like much research on interaction design and children [17], the majority of this work targets children age 6-12.

A smaller body of work has investigated co-designing with preschoolers in particular. Past research has shown that participatory design methods developed for school-age children can be effective with preschoolers, though they may need modifications [9]. Tikkanen et al. supported preschoolers in successfully generating design guidance for a novel musical toy using existing sketching, prototyping, and music-making techniques [29]. Separately, Borum et al. attempted to use the "Bags of Stuff" method [6] to design with 3-to-5-year-olds [2]. Though they concluded that typical prompts lacked sufficient backstory to engage children this age, they also hypothesize that further storyline development would make this technique accessible to young children.

Others have developed new co-design methods specifically with preschoolers in mind. For example, Guha et al. created Mixing Ideas [11], a technique for combining the design insights of multiple children, to specifically address preschoolers' egocentric struggles to collaboratively build on the ideas of others [21]. Einarsdottir et al. developed a technique for eliciting preschoolers' implicit knowledge by having them document their day with disposable cameras [8].

We build on this existing work by expanding the set of methods that have been studied as co-design tools for preschoolers. We also distinguish between older and younger preschoolers and describe how these methods differentially support these two different groups.

Design Methods

We employed four different types of design activities in our workshop, two of which are existing methods that have previously been evaluated with older users. *Fictional Inquiry* [4] entails creating an immersive fictional storyline and prompting participants to brainstorm within the context of this imagined reality. By creating a fictional context for individuals to develop ideas, this method attempts to reduce the constraints of reality and free participants to be more generative. Prior work has found fictional inquiry to be effective with adults [18] and with school-aged children [3].

Comicboarding [24] is a participatory design technique that provides the structure of comic strips and the scaffolding of partially completed content as a method for supporting individuals in coming up with novel ideas. By providing users with a framework for ideas rather than a blank slate, comicboarding provides a springboard for participation that is particularly valuable to populations with little experience brainstorming. Prior work has shown comicboarding to be effective in eliciting design insights from school-aged children with cancer diagnoses [30] and preteens on the autism spectrum [1], among others. As this technique was designed for novice brainstormers, it is theoretically well-matched to preschool co-designers. Here we explore its effectiveness with this age group in practice.

METHODS

We conducted a two-hour, four-part design workshop with 7 children. Three children were age 4 (4y0m - 4y3m) and four children were age 5 or 6 (5y6m - 6y2m). Four participants were female, three male. Parents identified all children as non-Hispanic White. All children were either in kindergarten or enrolled full-time in a daycare or preschool program. Participants were recruited through convenience sampling and each family was given a US$50 Amazon gift card for their participation. We divided participants into two groups by age (one with 4-year-olds, and one 5- and 6-year-olds); each group was paired with 2 adult facilitators.

Materials and Procedures

The design goal of our workshop was to generate insights to guide the creation of a system that allows children to plan out how they will spend their time with entertainment media. Children engaged in four design activities to help us generate design ideas for this app. The first activity was a fictional inquiry session, for which we created an original story titled *Happy Birthday R2D2!* (Figure 1). The story describes characters from Star Wars™ planning out activities for R2D2's birthday party and documenting their plan with an app they call "Star Play Memory Technology." After reading the story aloud as a group, children were asked to sketch the screens of the Star Play Memory Technology. Researchers facilitated the session and asked open-ended questions as children sketched, such as, "*Can you tell me about your picture?*" and "*Oh, and how does that help Luke remember the plan?*" The Stars Wars theme was of interest to all children, as determined by informal conversations with parents in advance.

After children completed these sketches, they participated in 3 different comicboarding exercises (e.g., Figure 2). Each comicboard was designed with panel-style scaffolding [24], such that the comic was complete except for a single missing panel for children to fill in. The comicboards extended the storyline of our fictional inquiry and brought in elements of planning that were not probed in the original story. When a child was ready, a facilitator read the comicboard out loud with the child, along with a prompt at the bottom of the page explaining the missing panel. Children sat with their age-defined group as they sketched but worked individually.

Figure 1: Storyboard for "Happy Birthday R2D2," our fictional inquiry storyline. R2D2 plans the play activities for his birthday party. When Luke tries to relay this information to Leia, he forgets the details and uses an app to recall the plan.

Figure 2: Comicboard with panel scaffolding.

After completing all three comicboards, children participated in a self-directed construction activity. A facilitator asked the child to think of something he or she would like to make and presented the child with a variety of construction materials, including art supplies and Lego blocks. The facilitator supported the child in identifying an end goal and then helped the child articulate a plan for achieving it. Each child then used an iPad to record a video of him or herself describing the construction plan. The child then had the opportunity to create the object, with adults facilitating as needed.

Finally, each child engaged in a series of user tests with a prototype iPad application. This application's interface allowed children to select and organize a set of icons representing different play activities (i.e., creating art, riding a bike, reading, etc.). Children tested a series of different versions of the interface and attempted to execute specific tasks, such as picking three activities to play and specifying the order in which to play them.

Data Analysis

All sessions were audio and video recorded. The research team transcribed these recordings into field notes that documented all dialogue as well as participant and facilitator behaviors and interactions. Our final data set was composed of these transcriptions and photographs of the artifacts children created. We used a holistic open-coding approach [16] to identify themes that were relevant to our design goal of understanding children's mental models of planning. We further identified themes relevant to the effectiveness of our design methods and the types of insights they generated. Codes were organized into categories of: 1) use of and relation to materials, 2) mental models, representations and symbols, and 3) interpretability and connection to prompts.

RESULTS AND ANALYSIS

Systematic Differences between Age Groups

We found that these techniques easily elicited on-topic ideas from our 5- and 6-year-old participants. For example, in the following exchange, a researcher (R) and child participant (P) discuss the child's plan for constructing an object of her choice. Though she initially is unable to articulate her plan, with scaffolding from the researcher, she is able to identify specific steps to follow.

R: *"What are you going to make?"*
P: "I am gonna make a hat."
R: *"Alright. And can you describe how you're gonna do it?"*
P: "I need to make it to see how to do it."
R: *"Ok. Do you remember any of the parts? Or any of the steps?"*
P: "I remember that first you tape a round thing around, a piece of paper around, like a crown."
P: "Then, I, um, put the top on it."
P: "And then I put a strip of paper on the top of it."

In contrast, a researcher had the following exchange with a 4-year-old participant engaged in the same activity. Despite prompts from the researcher, the child struggled to articulate actions that would lead to the desired end goal.

R: *"What are you going to make? Will it be a zoo? Or a house?"*
P: "A house!"
R: *"Alright, so think about all the steps you have to do, what do you have to do if you build a house?"*
P: "I don't know."
R: *"You don't know? Think about what you might do."*
P: "I don't know."
R: *"What are the different parts of a house? Does it have a roof?"*
P: "Yes."
R: *"What else does it have?"*
P: "Umm… a flashlight."

Similarly, all of our 5- and 6-year-old participants were able to create topical, easily interpretable design solutions to our fictional inquiry prompt (Figure 3, top). These participants described interfaces for planning a series of activities that stored a list of what to do, kept track of order, and assigned relative durations to each activity in the plan. They told us that their interfaces documented activities by "*tak[ing] pictures of different things,*" that a user changes the plan by "*exing out*" obsolete activities, and that the interface displays a star for each activity that a user completes.

In contrast, none of our 4-year-old participants created artifacts or solutions that designers could easily interpret with traditional methods (Figure 3, bottom). For example, these younger participants suggested "*Big circles,*" "*I'm gonna draw a cake,*" and, "*Break the window [of the rocketship]*" as techniques for keeping track of planned activities. Though facilitators used the same prompts and the same graduated scaffolding to break the design problem into smaller and smaller pieces, our younger participants were unable to articulate on-topic ideas in response to problems set up with fictional inquiry, comicboarding, or construction methods.

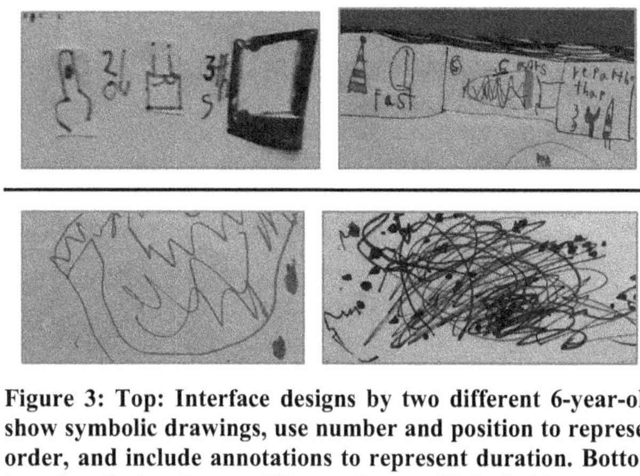

Figure 3: Top: Interface designs by two different 6-year-olds show symbolic drawings, use number and position to represent order, and include annotations to represent duration. Bottom: interface designs by two different 4-year-olds lack this structure.

Unlike these generative activities, we were able to extract useful findings from participants of all ages with our traditional usability tests. In this structured interface where children were locked into predefined interaction patterns, both older and younger children engaged with the interface in a way that revealed insights into their mental models of time, order, symbolism and magnitude. For example, one 4-year-old dragged out a set of icons, rearranged them, and then pointed to each from left to right when probed to explain the order in which he would perform them, suggesting that a left-to-right pattern is already meaningful to him.

Highly Suggestible Responses

We also saw that children in both groups were easily influenced by our ideas and materials. For example, one 6-year-old created a representation in which he ordered a series of activities by aligning their icons in left-to-right order (Figure 3, top left). He did so by first drawing them on paper in order, cutting out each one, and then taping them onto a new sheet of paper in the same order, suggesting his cutting and taping were inspired more by the materials than by his own goals.

Similarly, participants consistently incorporated literal details from the materials we used and from facilitators' comments, regardless of their relevance. One comicboard included pictures of a wrench and screws as superfluous details in the illustration. Several children filled in this comicboard with a solution that also contained a wrench and screws (Figure 4). In our user testing, multiple children specified the duration of an activity by pinching to make the icon for the activity very small and saying things like, "*Each one is gonna be for NO minutes!*" suggesting their behaviors were driven more by the options presented than by goal-directed choices.

Our results suggest that designers should anticipate children drawing on all aspects of their surroundings and context when generating ideas. Using fewer, more open-ended materials and interpreting children's solutions with this limitation in mind may lead to more fruitful sessions for this age group.

DISCUSSION AND CONCLUSION

Fictional inquiry, comicboarding, and constructing were all productive techniques for our 5- and 6-year-old participants. These children were able to construct novel solutions in response to our prompts and, with scaffolding from facilitators, broke down problems and engaged with them piece-by-piece. They understood the storyline we provided, asked questions that were pertinent to the topic, and articulated solutions that could be incorporated into our designs. One contribution of this work is the empirical demonstration that, within our small sample, these specific techniques are useful

Figure 4: Children add superfluous wrenches to their comicboards (middle, right) after seeing our wrench (left).

for soliciting design input from older preschoolers and involving them in the design process.

Our 4-year-old participants, however, responded to prompts from these methods with what we at first experienced as creative but wildly off-topic comments. Yet despite the fact that they could not present easily interpretable, traditionally packaged artifacts, these younger children remain experts on being children and have design insights that are not obvious to adults [5]. Had we supported our participants in creating a house made of a roof and a flashlight, or in designing an app to break the window of a rocket ship, we might have shifted from our preconceived design question to a question of greater meaning and relevance to the child.

Our very conception that these children's responses were "off-topic" presupposes the idea that adult facilitators are the authority on which topics are up for discussion. But as Iversen et al. explain, true design partnership with children requires that children have equal voice in defining and scoping design problems [19]. Probing to understand why the flashlight had high salience for our participant may have given us greater insight into her experience with and interest in this particular tool. Prior work shows that young children's playful interactions with the world have deeper meaning, though this meaning is not always obvious [23].

Though our results do not directly show that 4-year-olds can act as productive design partners, they reveal a systematic way in which we failed to accommodate them in partnership. This experience has led us to ask what might happen if we commit radically to following their lead in problem definition, and we intend to explore this further in future work. New methods to support facilitators in translating these design contributions would also be of great value.

Our study is limited in that we worked with a small set of children, addressing a specific design problem, during a one-day session, in one cultural context. We also chose a design problem (planning a sequence of play activities) that poses its own cognitive challenges for preschoolers. The age differences we saw may be specific to our small sample. Future work remains to understand if the gap between 4- and 5-year-olds is an important inflection point for these methods, or if the struggles of our younger participants were specific to the context in which we used them.

We found that older preschoolers used fictional inquiry and comicboarding prompts to generate design insights that were easy to understand and adopt, and children of all ages were easily influenced by their environment. Younger children offered solutions that, on the surface, appeared to be wild non-sequiturs but might, with a deeper commitment from facilitators to follow the child's lead, give us better insight into their experiences and values.

ACKNOWLEDGMENTS

We thank our participants for sharing their expertise on childhood and on design. Images have been lightly edited to remove visuals not licensed for commercial use.

REFERENCES

1. Laura Benton and Hilary Johnson. 2014. Structured approaches to participatory design for children: can targeting the needs of children with autism provide benefits for a broader child population? *Instructional Science* 42, 1, 47–65. http://doi.org/10.1007/s11251-013-9297-y
2. Nanna Borum, Eva Petersson Brooks, and Anthony Lewis Brooks. 2015. Designing with Young Children: Lessons Learned from a Co-creation of a Technology-Enhanced Playful Learning Environment. Springer International Publishing, 142–152. http://doi.org/10.1007/978-3-319-20889-3_14
3. Christian Dindler, Eva Eriksson, Ole Sejer Iversen, Andreas Lykke-Olesen, and Martin Ludvigsen. 2005. Mission from Mars. *Proceeding of the 2005 conference on Interaction design and children - IDC '05*, ACM Press, 40–47. http://doi.org/10.1145/1109540.1109546
4. Christian Dindler and Ole Sejer Iversen. 2007. Fictional Inquiry—design collaboration in a shared narrative space. *CoDesign* 3, 4, 213–234. http://doi.org/10.1080/15710880701500187
5. Allison Druin. 2002. The role of children in the design of new technology. *Behaviour & Information Technology* 21, 1, 1–25. http://doi.org/10.1080/01449290110108659
6. Allison Druin and Allison. 1999. Cooperative inquiry. *Proceedings of the 1999 conference on Human factors in computing systems - CHI '99*, ACM Press, 592–599. http://doi.org/10.1145/302979.303166
7. Pelle Ehn. 1993. Scandinavian design: On participation and skill. *Participatory design: Principles and practices*, 41–77.
8. Jóhanna Einarsdóttir. 2007. Research with children: methodological and ethical challenges. *European Early Childhood Education Research Journal* 15, 2, 197–211. http://doi.org/10.1080/13502930701321477
9. Allison Farber, Allison Druin, Gene Chipman, Dawn Julian, and Sheila Somashekher. 2002. How Young Can Our Technology Design Partners Be? *PDC*, 272–277.
10. M Elizabeth Graue and Daniel J Walsh. 1998. *Studying children in context: Theories, methods, and ethics*. Sage Publications.
11. Mona Leigh Guha, Allison Druin, Gene Chipman, Jerry Alan Fails, Sante Simms, and Allison Farber. 2004. Mixing ideas. *Proceeding of the 2004 conference on Interaction design and children building a community - IDC '04*, ACM Press, 35–42. http://doi.org/10.1145/1017833.1017838
12. Mona Leigh Guha, Allison Druin, and Jerry Alan Fails. 2013. Cooperative Inquiry revisited: Reflections of the past and guidelines for the future of intergenerational co-design. *International Journal of Child-Computer Interaction* 1, 1, 14–23. http://doi.org/10.1016/j.ijcci.2012.08.003
13. Alexis Hiniker, Kiley Sobel, Sungsoo (Ray) Hong, Hyewon Suh, India Irish, and Julie A. Kientz. 2016. Hidden symbols: How informal symbolism in digital interfaces disrupts usability for preschoolers. *International Journal of Human-Computer Studies* 90, 53–67. http://doi.org/10.1016/j.ijhcs.2016.03.006
14. Juan Pablo Hourcade. 2008. Interaction design and children. *Foundations and Trends in Human-Computer Interaction* 1, 4, 277–392.
15. Juan Pablo Hourcade, Benjamin B. Bederson, and Allison Druin. 2004. Preschool children's use of mouse buttons. *Extended abstracts of the 2004 conference on Human factors and computing systems - CHI '04*, ACM Press, 1411. http://doi.org/10.1145/985921.986077
16. Hsiu-Fang Hsieh and Sarah E Shannon. 2005. Three approaches to qualitative content analysis. *Qualitative health research* 15, 9, 1277–1288.
17. Sara Isola and Jerry Fails. 2012. Family and Design in the IDC and CHI Communitieis. *Proceedings of the 2012 conference on Interaction Design and Children -- IDC '12*, 40–49.
18. Ole Sejer Iversen and Christian Dindler. 2008. Pursuing aesthetic inquiry in participatory design. *Proceedings of the Tenth Anniversary Conference on Participatory Design 2008*, 138–145.
19. Ole Sejer Iversen and Christian Dindler. 2013. A Utopian agenda in child–computer interaction. *International Journal of Child-Computer Interaction* 1, 1, 24–29. http://doi.org/10.1016/j.ijcci.2012.08.002
20. Hilda K Kabali, Matilde M Irigoyen, Rosemary Nunez-Davis, et al. 2015. Exposure and Use of Mobile Media Devices by Young Children. *Pediatrics*, 136, 6, 1-7. http://doi.org/10.1542/peds.2015-2151
21. Richard M Lerner. 2001. *Concepts and theories of human development*. Psychology Press.
22. Berry Mayall. 2008. 5 Conversations with Children. *Research with children: Perspectives and practices*, 109.
23. Susan A. Miller, Ellen B. Church, and Carla Poole. Ages & Stages: Don't Forget to Laugh - The Importance of Humor. *Scholastic*. Retrieved from http://www.scholastic.com/teachers/article/ages-stages-dont-forget-laugh-importance-humor
24. Neema Moraveji, Jason Li, Jiarong Ding, Patrick O'Kelley, and Suze Woolf. 2007. Comicboarding. *Proceedings of the 2007 conference on Human factors in computing systems - CHI '07*, ACM Press, 1371. http://doi.org/10.1145/1240624.1240832
25. Valerie Nesset and Andrew Large. 2004. Children in the information technology design process: A review of

theories and their applications. *Library & Information Science Research* 26, 2, 140–161.

26. Hanna Niemi and Saila Ovaska. 2007. Designing spoken instructions with preschool children. *Proceedings of the 2007 conference on Interaction design and children - IDC '07*, ACM Press, 133-136. http://doi.org/10.1145/1297277.1297304
27. Jean Piaget. 1971. Psychology and Epistemology: Towards a Theory of Knowledge. trans. *Arnold Rosin. Markham: Penguin Books Canada.*
28. Jean Piaget. 1973. To understand is to invent: The future of education.
29. Ruut Tikkanen and Netta Iivari. 2011. The Role of Music in the Design Process with Children. Springer, Berlin, Heidelberg, 288–305. http://doi.org/10.1007/978-3-642-23765-2_21
30. Pontus Wärnestål, Petra Svedberg, Jens Nygren, Pontus Wärnestål, Petra Svedberg, and Jens Nygren. 2014. Co-constructing child personas for health-promoting services with vulnerable children. *Proceedings of the 2014 conference on Human factors in computing systems - CHI '14*, ACM Press, 3767–3776. http://doi.org/10.1145/2556288.2557115

Making Space for the Quality Care: Opportunities for Technology in Cognitive Behavioral Therapy for Insomnia

Haining Zhu
Pennsylvania State University
University Park, USA
hbz5037@psu.edu

Yuhan Luo
Pennsylvania State University
University Park, USA
ypl5142@ist.psu.edu

Eun Kyoung Choe
Pennsylvania State University
University Park, USA
echoe@ist.psu.edu

ABSTRACT
Insomnia can drastically affect individuals' overall well-being and work performance, with substantial costs to society and industry. Cognitive behavioral therapy for insomnia (CBT-I) is a psychotherapeutic treatment, which requires patients to track sleep and share the data with CBT-I clinicians. However, the number of specialists who can provide CBT-I limits the number of patients who can receive it. In this paper, we aim to identify opportunities to leverage technology to assist clinicians in delivering quality and effective CBT-I services to broader populations. Toward this goal, we conducted formative studies, including 11 CBT-I clinic observations and 17 semi-structured interviews, to understand the current workflow of CBT-I and associated challenges. We discuss how technology can assist clinicians and patients throughout the various steps of CBT-I workflow while addressing some of the identified challenges, and more broadly, how technology can make space for clinicians and patients to build quality therapeutic relationships.

Author Keywords
Cognitive Behavioral Therapy for Insomnia (CBT-I); self-monitoring data; patient-generated data; clinical workflow; observation; interview; patient engagement.

ACM Classification Keywords
H.5.2 [Information Interfaces and Presentation]: User-centered design: J.3 [Life and Medical Sciences]: Medical information systems.

INTRODUCTION
Chronic sleep and wakefulness disorders affect an estimated 50-70 million Americans, costing hundreds of billions of dollars in direct medical expenses and an estimated $150 billion yearly for businesses (e.g., from accidents, productivity losses, and employee nonattendance); furthermore, tired drivers, even without the influence of alcohol, account for nearly 20% of general population injuries from serious car crashes [23]. Cognitive Behavioral Therapy for Insomnia (CBT-I) is a safe and effective insomnia treatment [47, 63]. CBT-I attempts to treat the factors responsible for individuals sleep problems through behavioral modifications, rather than prescription medications; it has fewer known side effects and longer-lasting effects than drugs alone [41, 42].

CHI 2017, May 06-11, 2017, Denver, CO, USA

DOI: http://dx.doi.org/10.1145/3025453.3025549

CBT-I could help many insomnia patients if it can be employed in a scalable and effective way, but this is difficult in practice. CBT-I requires patients to capture sleep and contextual data and share them with clinicians, often using a paper-based diary, over several in-person visits [51]. As is the case for many CBT based treatments (e.g., depression [66], anxiety [44]), CBT-I often imposes heavy data collection burden on patients [51]. Despite numerous sleep tracking devices and applications developed both from academia (e.g., [19, 34, 40]) and industry (e.g., [5, 3]), the adoption of these technologies in real-world clinical practice has been notoriously slow and often faces resistance [20, 70]. Moreover, personal attention is the most important prognostic indicator for positive outcomes in CBT-I [30]. Significant work in patient-clinician communication literature emphasizes the importance of in-person communication, which serves as a channel to convey socio-emotional support, exchange information, and make treatment decisions [49, 57]. As quality communication and patients' satisfaction towards patient-clinician communication are positively related to patient compliance [49, 53], it is difficult to simply cut back the number of sessions, reduce the in-person time, or automatize the practice.

As such, finding a balance between clinician involvement and broader delivery of efficient care by leveraging technology is an important HCI research problem. The CBT-I context offers unique opportunities for us to reflect on the existing care practice, from which we can understand the value of in-person patient-clinician communication as well as existing pitfalls and design opportunities. To this end, we want to understand what aspects of in-person CBT-I can be successfully assisted by technology as opposed to remain to be accomplished by clinicians based on a proper understanding of CBT-I workflow [60]. Our research is thus specifically oriented toward answering the following three questions:

- RQ1: What is the current workflow of clinician-guided in-person CBT-I and associated challenges in each step?
- RQ2: In the context of CBT-I, how do clinicians engage patients in the care practice?
- RQ3: What are opportunities for technologies to support clinicians and patients in the CBT-I practice?

To answer these research questions, we conducted observational fieldwork in a sleep clinic, coupled with patient and clinician interviews. Our work offers the following three contributions: 1) a detailed account of in-person CBT-I workflow, as well as the associated challenges from the perspectives of both clinicians and patients; 2) identification of the aspects of CBT-I which can specifically be leveraged by technology versus in-person interaction; and 3) design implications for CBT-I technologies based upon and sensitive to individuals' differing needs and preferences. Our work provides an in-depth understanding of CBT-I practices, and our findings could help build better therapeutic relationships between patients and clinicians.

RELATED WORK

In this section, we provide related work on how technologies used in the hospital affect patient-clinician interaction, and background literature on CBT and CBT for Insomnia.

Technologies in the Hospital Setting

Technology in the hospital setting is a double-edged sword. Notably, electronic medical records (EMR) have unintentionally resulted in reductions in time spent directly with patients [50], tensions negotiating human contact and screen-sharing [16], system-induced errors [8], and communication challenges [27]. Researchers have conducted observation and interview studies (e.g., [43, 60, 69]) to systematically explore EMR adoption, clinical workflow, and associated challenges. For example, Unertl and colleagues examined the information flow of clinicians using EMR and categorized activities into *information access*, *information input*, and *communication* [61]; they noted that clinical informatics tools are not designed with workflow comprehension, which could result in decreased clinical efficiency, increased medical errors, and missed key or subtle data. As patient-clinician communication quality is significantly related to patients' care adherence and health outcomes [58], understanding clinical workflow and information behaviors is necessary when designing tools supporting patient-clinician interactions.

Technologies are also being designed to engage patients in their care [52, 62]. Interactive tabletops for non-directive play therapy, for example, could enhance therapy without interrupting processes or hindering patient-clinician relationships, although such technologies may lessen clinician engagement [53]. Patients reacted favorably to patient-centric mobile displays of medical information (e.g., progress reports, care plans, and care teams in Emergency Departments) [52, 65]. Empowering technologies and patient involvement in care practice, through encouraging information seeking or question asking, can positively affect health outcomes [29]. Recently, virtual and augmented reality (VR and AR) technologies have been used in exposure therapy for phobias [67]. Furthermore, physical artifacts that utilize sensors and display heart rate via light patterns, pre-recorded messages that reflect personally meaningful contents, and non-digital means of distraction show promise in promoting wellbeing in complex mental healthcare contexts [59].

Patients are also using self-tracking technologies in interactions with clinicians [21, 45, 70]. Health data can be captured at home and shared with clinicians between or during visits [15, 70]. Mobile devices are promising platforms for capturing and inferring behaviors. For example, sleep behaviors can be inferred from embedded smartphone sensors (e.g., [40]), and tools like Android's widgets can lower patients' data capture burden [19]. However, how to enable patients to share data with appropriate personnel (e.g., sleep clinician) was often beyond the scope of these works. Moreover, there is little organizational support for sharing patient-generated data [70]. Many patients share by bringing data collection tools into clinics, which can disrupt patient-clinician communication [20], or increase clinicians' workload. For these reasons, many clinicians and patients still cling to more familiar, traditional means of data collection and communication (e.g. pen and paper) [39].

To minimize negative consequences of novel technology, it is necessary to understand the contexts of use by engaging with clinicians and patients during the early phase of design [10]. Conducting ethnographic fieldwork is challenging for non-clinical researchers, but it is an effective method to understand healthcare practices and contexts [11, 28]. We thus adopt this approach in our research. While we build upon extensive prior patient-clinician interaction research, we specifically fill gaps by examining how clinicians engage patients in the care practice and aim to identify opportunities for self-care technologies to help balance clinician involvement and broader delivery of efficient CBT-I care.

Cognitive Behavioral Therapy

Cognitive behavioral therapy (CBT) refers to a broad set of psychotherapeutic approaches, which aim to help mental health patients understand how thoughts and cognition affect behaviors. CBT is grounded in the premise that certain psychological problems and mental disorders are encouraged by maladaptive cognitive factors, including beliefs and schemas [31]. Although CBT produces longer-lasting benefits than pharmaceuticals alone [42], CBT access is low [24]. Waiting times for appointments are often lengthy, in part owing to a shortage of qualified CBT clinicians [33], inconveniences of scheduling and attending appointments [55], and rising healthcare costs [32]. Even if patients have had access to CBT, they have historically been unable to utilize treatment because they could not successfully engage with necessary professional services [24, 46].

To address some of these problems and extend treatment availability, researchers developed Computerized-CBT (cCBT). However, cCBT faces several barriers, including low engagement indicated by low take-up rates and varying dropout rates. Systematic reviews examining cCBT for depression report that reported take-up rates are low (ranging 3.3% to 25%) [33]. cCBT systems users also have various dropout rates from 0% to 42.9% among different studies, with little explanation of the factors that contributed to participant motivations or continued engagement [68]. In HCI, researchers specifically examined how patients engage with cCBT in mental health contexts [25, 26, 36, 54]. Rennick-Egglestone and colleagues suggested that cCBT systems should help identify and remove users not suited for the

ID	Location	Age	Sex	Professional title	Expertise	Year of practice	Interview /observe
H1	PA	35	M	Licensed Psychologist, Assistant Professor of Psychiatry	Academic Sleep Research, Clinical Behavioral Sleep Medicine	10 years	I/O
H2	WI	51	F	Licensed Psychologist, Certified in Behavioral Sleep Medicine	Mental health, depression, anxiety, sleep related disorders	8 years	I
H3	IL	43	M	Counselor	Insomnia , delayed sleep phase syndrome, circadian rhythm disorders, sleep apnea	2 years	I
H4	NY	57	M	Psychotherapist	Relationship and social issues, sexual health, sleep related disorders, psychodynamic psychotherapy	3 years	I
H5	Australia	58	M	Provisional Psychologist	General Psychology, insomnia, sleep related disorders, anxiety, depression	3 years	I
H6	CO	29	F	Occupational therapist, research associate II	Cognitive behavioral therapy for insomnia, sleep related disorders	8 months	I
H7	PA	62	M	Licensed psychologist and Neuropsychologist	Anxiety, depression, sleep related disorders	20 years +	I
H8	CA	39	F	Licensed psychologist, Clinic Director and Faculty	Behavioral sleep medicine, sexual medicine	8 years	I
H9	PA	45	F	Medical Psychologist	Addiction, behavioral medicine, sleep related disorders	10 years	I
H10	DE	47	M	Licensed psychologist, Associate Director, Internship Coordinator	Sleep related disorders, depression, anxiety, substance abuse disorder	8 years	I

Table 1: Interview and observation participant demographics: Clinicians.

intervention, respond to mental health deteriorations, tailor information presentations to the user, and support user disengagement from the intervention [54]. In another study, Doherty and colleagues conducted design workshops with key stakeholders of CBT and suggested ways to encourage patient engagement by providing interactive and graphical exercises, support from clinicians and professionals, and opportunities for social interaction [26]. Researchers also explored a game-based CBT approach [25] and a clinician-moderated web-based application [36], both aimed toward adolescents who were reluctant to attend face-to-face interventions. Coyle and colleagues noted the significance of supporting patient-clinician relationships and again raised concerns that technological interventions may disengage clinicians from therapies; they also noted that personalization, flexibility, and multimodal interaction might best support cCBT [25]. Likewise, prior work discusses the role of technology for patient-clinician relationships within mental health treatment and provide implications for designing cCBT-based technologies, which may not be applicable to in-person CBT for Insomnia. They also lack guidance on how to enable efficient sharing and collaborative sensemaking of patient-generated data between patients and clinicians, which are key components of CBT for insomnia. Therefore, we attempt to fill the gaps of prior research by examining how both patients and clinicians can benefit from technologies that specifically aid in data tracking, data sharing, and patient-clinician communication in the context of CBT for Insomnia.

Cognitive Behavioral Therapy for Insomnia

Although CBTs for various domains share similar psychotherapeutic approaches, CBT for insomnia (CBT-I) includes several unique components. CBT-I generally consists of six to eight independent treatment sessions, beginning first with intake evaluation, followed by treatment initiation usually of stimulus control therapy (i.e., avoiding clock watching in the bedroom, restricting time spent awake and set of behaviors one can engage in while in the bed or bedroom) and sleep restriction therapy (i.e., patients are limited to spending exactly an equal amount of the time they sleep in their beds), then sleep titration (i.e., clinicians gradually, incrementally adjust sleep duration) and sleep hygiene, and ending with four additional sessions which adjust sleep titration depending upon patient response, with the final session also including discussions of relapse prevention [51]. CBT-I often requires expansive information seeking through surveys, interviews, and sleep diaries, as well as education related to sleep logging, sleep behavior modification, and sleep hygiene [18]. Currently, the majority of clinicians and patients still use pen and paper to collect data. However, these factors offer the unique opportunity for computing technologies to respond to efficiency and adherence.

Several technologies have been developed to help insomnia patients employ self-guided CBT-I (e.g., CBT-I Coach [4], CBTforInsomnia [2], Somnio [31], RESTORE [32], SHUTi [56]). Notably, researchers demonstrated web-based CBT-I technologies (e.g. Somnio, RESTORE, and SHUTi) help significantly improve insomnia patients' sleep behaviors if engagement is maintained [31, 32, 56]. However, similar to other Computerized-CBT technologies, engagement and high dropout rates remain concerns, with no clear explanations of why people disengage and how to better engage them. We therefore examined how sleep clinicians engage patients during in-person CBT-I to search for opportunities related to CBT-I technological delivery systems, and how HCI researchers can help clinicians create a sensitive, stepped-care system [64].

METHOD

We conducted 11 observations of CBT-I sessions and semi-structured interviews with 17 participants (7 insomnia patients and 10 CBT-I clinicians). This research was approved by the university's Institutional Review Board (IRB).

Observations

In previous studies, researchers used direct observation to understand clinic workflow and identify existing problems [14, 22]. We conducted direct observations in the Sleep Research and Treatment Center at a university-affiliated medical center located in the U.S. Mid-Atlantic region. For each session of observations, the observer sat in the corner of the exam room, taking detailed notes of the patient-clinician interaction and treatment process. Two researchers made 6 trips to the site, staying there from 9am till 4pm each time. The clinicians we

ID	Age	Sex	disease	Status	Observed	Current status	Occupation	Previous treatment	Interview /observe
P1	58	F	Chronic moderate insomnia, snoring	New Patient	twice	Done (5 sessions)	Work from home	Sleep study	I/O
P2	18	F	Hypersomnia, Depression	New Patient	once	Ongoing (4 sessions)	High school Student	melatonin	I/O
P3	71	F	Chronic insomnia	Return Patient	twice	Ongoing (3 sessions)	Retired English Teacher	Ambien, sleep study	I/O
P4	33	F	Insomnia, anxiety	New Patient	once	Ongoing (4 sessions)	Stay at home, on disability	CBT for anxiety	I/O
P5	>30	M	-	New Patient	once	-	-	-	O
P6	>20	F	-	New Patient	once	-	-	-	O
P7	29	M	Circadian rhythm disorder, fatigue, memory loss	New Patient	once	Ongoing (2 sessions)	Ph.D Candidate	Sleep study, Melatonin, Alteril	I/O
P8	74	M	Hypersomnia, Sleep apnea, restless legs	Return Patient	once	Ongoing (3 sessions)	Retired Government Agent	Provigil, Neurontin	I/O
P9	48	M	Chronic insomnia	New Patient	once	Ongoing (2 sessions)	Attorney	Ambien	I/O

Table 2: Interview and observation participant demographics: Patients

worked with decided whether to let the researchers observe the CBT-I session depending on the patients' case. For example, we did not observe patients with comorbid conditions (e.g., insomnia and depression) because observations would negatively affect the treatment. Due to the sensitive nature of the conversation, we did not record the audio. After observing 11 CBT-I sessions (9 new patients, 2 return patients), the observers noted the recurrence of similar themes in the patients' data from this particular site. Each observation lasted from 1 (return patient) to 2 (new patient) hours.

Interviews

Additionally, we conducted semi-structured interviews with CBT-I clinicians and insomnia patients for two reasons. First, we wanted to check for external validity of our observations by interviewing CBT-I clinicians from internal and external sites. Second, we wanted to follow up with the patients whom we observed to learn their perspectives and experiences with the CBT-I process. To thank the interview participants for their time and effort, we provided each clinician participant a $50 gift card and each patient participant a $30 gift card, which is a common approach in healthcare research.

Interviews with Clinicians

Clinician participants were recruited both by word-of-mouth referrals and through the American Board of Sleep Medicine (ABSM) website [1]. The inclusion criteria for clinicians necessitated that they have experience providing CBT-I, which requires highly specialized training. We interviewed 10 clinician participants (one from the observation site, nine from external sites). Clinician interviews were done either via phone (n = 9) or Skype (n = 1). Table 1 shows our clinician participants' demographic information. We designed the interview questions for clinicians to gain an understanding of their reasonings behind each step of the treatment process, personalized treatments for individuals, their attitudes towards technology, and current challenges they face. Interview questions for clinician participants included the following: (1) What is the typical diagnosis and treatment process (workflow) for a new patient and return patient? (2) What is the best use of in-person visit time? (3) What are the strategies clinicians use to motivate and engage patients in their care practice? (4) How might technology be used to enhance various aspects of CBT-I treatments? and (5) What types of patients are suitable to utilize self-guided CBT-I versus in-person CBT-I treatment?

Interviews with Patients

Our recruiting methods for patients were restricted to those patients from our initial observations. Among the 9 patients we observed, we obtained consent to conduct an interview with 7; one patient declined our interview request, and we lost contact with another patient. Patient interviews were conducted via phone (n = 6) or Skype (n = 1). Table 2 shows our patient participants' demographic information. We designed the interview questions to guide participants to discuss their experiences with CBT-I. Interview questions for patient participants included the following: (1) What motivated the patient to follow the sleep restriction? (2) What tools have the patient used to collect and store sleep data, and how do they reflect upon their sleep data? (3) How does the patient envision doing CBT-I remotely? (4) How was the patient's experience with the visit in terms of interacting with the clinician? and (5) What are the challenges with regard to the visit?

Dataset and Analysis

Upon clinicians' and patients' consent, we collected screenshots of patients' sleep diaries, the clinician's excel sheets for calculating the patients' sleep efficiencies (see Appendix), and the typical surveys clinicians used with their patients. We also digitized all the observation notes.

All interviews were audio-recorded and transcribed to facilitate analysis. Each interview lasted from 40 to 80 minutes. To ensure the confidentiality of participants, we assigned a unique participant identifier to refer the roles of the participant: H# to denote a clinician participant, and P# to denote a patient participant.

To develop the CBT-I workflow, we began with the clinical workflow categories reported by Ni and colleagues, who examined physical therapy consultation visits [43]. Their model consists of 3 high-level activities (i.e., *information seeking* during injury assessments, *education* during medical and treatment contexts, and *documentation* for injuries and patient progress). We further extended the model to better characterize the CBT-I workflow. For the themes relevant to RQ2 and RQ3, we used thematic analysis [12]. Two researchers analyzed transcripts from two patient interviews and two clinician interviews independently, and they used qualitative open coding to note prominent themes that were discovered across the data pool. Once the team agreed on the high-level themes identified, one researcher iteratively coded the data and updated the coding scheme. The research team gathered again to conduct axial coding to identify relationships among the high-level coding schemes.

RESULTS

In this section, we present the observation and interview results to report existing gaps and opportunities in CBT-I practices. We describe our results according to the three research questions (RQs) presented earlier.

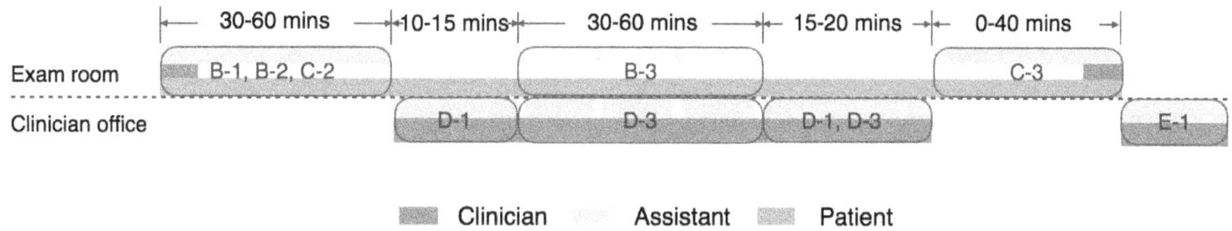

Figure 1: This figure shows a breakdown of the time and location individuals (e.g. red bars for clinicians, yellow for assistants, blue for patients) spend during different stages of workflow when clinicians see new patients. Note that new patients will spend significant amounts of time during their visits in the exam room waiting for clinicians to calculate patient survey/questionnaire scores. The labels correspond to the stages of workflow in Table 3.

RQ1: Clinical Workflow of CBT-I

Here, we describe the detailed workflow of CBT-I and differences across clinicians. We then present what we observed as the impediments to providing personalized and quality care.

Detailed Workflow of CBT-I

CBT-I practice involves patient in-home activities, clinician information seeking through surveys and interviews, sleep data sharing between clinicians and patients, intensive education components for patients to learn concepts as part of cognitive restructuring, and extensive patient documentation of sleep data. In Table 3, we describe high-level and sub categories that constitute the clinical workflow of CBT-I.

Most profoundly, CBT-I workflow extends to patients' homes, where they have to track sleep data (A-1) and follow sleep prescriptions as part of stimulus control and sleep restriction techniques (A-2). Our clinical workflow is distinguished from prior workflow models (e.g., [43, 60, 69]) by the inclusion of patients roles (i.e., patient in-home activities) and the bringing of them to the forefront of the CBT-I workflow. Information seeking includes the screening survey via semi-structured clinician interview schedule (B-1), contextual information gathering (B-2), and the pre-treatment assessment survey (B-3). Information sharing consists of sleep data review (C-1), during which a clinician and patient look at the sleep diary together and discuss progress. They also share personal experiences (C-2), bidirectionally expressing their personal emotions and stories. Patients need to learn background information about CBT-I (C-3) such as how to fill out the sleep diary, how to follow the sleep hygiene recommendation, and how to employ self-guided sessions. Clinicians also provide sleep prescriptions, which patients should precisely follow (C-4). Clinicians score patients' survey data (D-1), compute their sleep efficiency and total sleep time (D-2), evaluate patients' situations to prescribe (D-3), and document patients' visits on the electronic medical record (E-1). The workflow varied depending on whether the patient was a new patient or a return patient. For new patients, in-office activities include information seeking (B-1, B-2, B-3), information sharing (C-2, C-3), information assessment (D-1, D-3), and documentation (E-1) (Figure 1). The patient makes return visits consisting of a slightly different workflow pattern: for return patients, there were in-home activities (A-1, A-2, A-3), information seeking (B-3), information sharing (C-1, C-2, C-3, C-4), information assessment (D-1, D-2), and documentation (E-1) (Figure 2). The indicated duration of new patient visits was from 40 minutes to 2 hours, and the duration of return patient visits varied from 35 minutes to 1 hour. Treatment is terminated for a given patient depending upon his or her progress; a patient who closely follows his or her prescriptions will likely end treatment in fewer sessions than a patient who does not.

Activities	Sub-activities
A. Patient In-home Activities	A-1. Sleep Data Tracking A-2. Sleep Restriction and Stimulus Control A-3. Other Assignments
B. Information Seeking	B-1. Screening Survey B-2. Contextual Information Gathering B-3. Pre-treatment Assessment Survey
C. Information Sharing	C-1. Sleep Data Review C-2. Personal Experience Sharing C-3. Education C-4. Prescription
D. Information Assessment	D-1. Survey Data Scoring D-2. Sleep Data Scoring D-3. Pre-treatment Evaluation
E. Documentation	E-1. Patients' Record

Table 3: Activities and sub-activities in CBT-I workflow.

Differences Across Clinicians

Although most clinicians followed typical CBT-I processes, we learned from our observation and interview studies that the workflow is not completely the same across the clinicians due to variations in clinic settings and patient types. The observation of H1's practice allowed us to closely look at how clinicians access patients' data, interact with patients, and personalize treatments for different patients. We, however, complemented the observation data with interviews with 9 other clinicians (H2-H10), which helped us identify similarities and differences in CBT-I workflow (see Supplemental material). For example, because our observation took place at a training hospital, the clinician (H1) was training an assistant who helped him in collecting patients' information and documentation, which was not a typical situation for other clinicians we interviewed. The number of sessions also varied: among the 10 clinicians who participated in the study, 3 of them (H1, H4, H5) applied the standard 6-sessions of CBT-I to patients, 2 of them (H8, H9) applied 4 to 6 sessions, and for the other clinicians (H2, H3, H6, H7, H10), the number of sessions varied from 3 to 15 depending on the patients' situations (e.g., comorbidity).

In addition, there are other differences across the clinicians that are worthy of highlighting. For example, H3 asked his new patients to complete an hour-long online survey (B-1) before their first visits so that they could have efficient face-to-face sessions and save both the clinician's and patient's time. Similarly, H6 emailed all the questionnaires (B-1) and sleep diaries with handouts (C-3) and scored the data (D-1, D-2) using a digital system before a patient's visit. H4 did a brief phone consultation before the first session to make sure that a patient is qualified for CBT-I. H5 started the very first session by educating patients on the importance of sleep (C-3). H10 met with patients who already brought medical sleep evaluations and 2-week long sleep diaries to their first visits. Lastly, H7 was an outlier among the 10 clinician participants, who only talked with patients and never employed any sleep diary or questionnaire.

Current Impediments to the quality CBT-I care

Our observation and interview data suggests that many patients made progress with regard to sleep and expressed satisfaction with CBT-I. However, both clinicians and patients faced several challenges in the CBT-I practices which might discourage engagement or negatively affect treatment results. Below, we report these challenges according to the specific activities of the clinical workflow.

A. In-home activities: Impediments in this stage concern patient sleep data tracking and difficulties with following sleep restriction schedule. Two clinicians believed that requiring patients to maintain a sleep diary produces stress which is counterproductive to the goals of relaxation inherent to CBT-I. H9 mentioned, *"sleep diary seems like it's very burdensome or putting their [patients] focus on sleep in a way that exacerbates."* Furthermore, some patients found it difficult to answer certain questions asked in the sleep diary. For example, patients had difficulty answering questions regarding time to fall asleep, or number of awakenings experienced during a night. Patients often estimated answers, so diary data were often subjective. The subjective nature of the diary data was not a problem for clinicians because patient's own perception of their sleep was what they looked for. Sleep restriction was often difficult for patients to follow; it required incredible determination and self-control: *"I had a patient not too long ago who came in and they were engaged when they were with me but then they would go home and they would give up"* [H3]. However, some patients [P1, P3, P9] were very motivated to follow their sleep restrictions; they hoped that their clinicians would add extra sleep time during future sleep titration, and they usually tried to distract themselves to maintain wakefulness (e.g. by walking around, watching TV, etc).

Challenges can lead patients to forget to record their data, fabricate data, or make mistakes, leading to unreliable data which might interfere with a clinician's ability to make proper

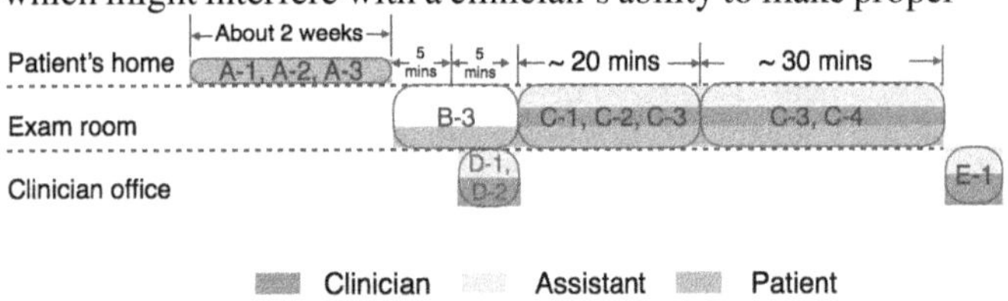

Figure 2: CBT-I workflow for return patients. The labels correspond to Table 3. Color legend can be found in Figure 1.

judgments. The first few weeks of CBT-I are a particularly difficult time for patients, as they have to adjust to the new sleep restriction schedule, which often means that they are getting a lot less sleep than before. Currently, clinicians are unable to remotely track patients' progress; at most, patients contact clinicians over email or phone call if they desperately need a clinician's help.

B. Information seeking: In this stage, patients and clinicians face various challenges regarding data capturing and sharing. Clinicians primarily retrieved patients' information through four means: surveys, sleep diaries, sensing devices, and polysomnography (sleep studies). Clinicians asked new patients to complete a Screening Survey and a Pre-Treatment Assessment during the first session. These surveys' efficacies are supported by research, but some of the questions confused patients. For this reason, H1's assistant's main job was to help some patients accurately fill out the surveys by sitting next to them and reading out the questions.

Patients typically started a sleep diary at the conclusion of the initial session, but if the clinician suspected that there were comorbid complications, such as circadian rhythm disorders, sleep apnea, or restless legs syndrome, then special devices were assigned to the patient. In such cases, clinicians trusted ActiGraph's (a validated wearable device that monitors human rest and activity; ActiGraph does not provide feedback to the patients) accuracy more than data from sleep diary. However, patients' information seeking endeavors have often been hindered by inefficient communication and contemporary practices. For example, patients lack access to their ActiGraph data, so clinicians must print the graphs to discuss results. P2 stated, *"It was a chart that he had printed out and he explained everything to me."* Some patients used mobile apps for their sleep diary, but clinicians who received this data had to manually input each data point. Clinicians also found it difficult to transfer or share patient generated data on different platforms. Because commercial sleep tracking technology did not support data exporting or sharing, many clinicians continued to use paper sleep diary.

C. Information sharing: CBT-I sessions are highly structured and precisely-designed. Clinicians followed the CBT-I manual and provided patients with the handouts that contain the same information regardless of applicability. Some patients felt that the charts and handouts involved are overly generalized. P3 remarked, *"she gave me a new one for cognitive restructuring [worksheets]. I'm having a little trouble seeing how relative that is to what I'm going through at this time. It doesn't seem to me that I need that."* Because of the lack of technological support, clinicians often printed and provided patients generic templates as examples. P7 noted, *"I think it might have been something from previous patient."* However, contrary to common patient perceptions, clinicians tended to personalize treatments in general. Our observation data suggests that the clinician and his assistant spent a great deal of time discussing proper prescriptions for patients with comorbid diseases, and that clinicians in all circumstances provided patients with a personalized sleep prescription. To find patients' ideal sleep durations, clinicians engaged patients over the course of multiple back-and-forth communications, utilizing the shared data to make gradual adjustments in sleep titration and sleep restrictions. These prescriptions often proved difficult for patients (*"I feel it's difficult to follow, cause it's out of my norm"* [P9].) Although, clinicians knew just how challenging this process was for most patients, patients could quickly lose motivation to continue participating; as H5 noted: *"...when [patients] were really struggling to stick with the prescription of their bed time. That would be the point at which they walk away."*

D. Information assessment: Current information assessment practices do not properly utilize electronic means of data collection and assessment, leading to missed opportunities for communication between patients and clinicians. The sleep diary is critical for most CBT-I clinicians to diagnose and evaluate patients. Clinicians use it to calculate sleep-efficiency and sleep duration, evaluate the patient's weekly progress, and decide if a patient needs to have further treatments. Paper-based sleep diaries offer many benefits over digitized versions. For example, paper-based sleep diaries allow for easy data recording, support self-reflection, and have detailed questions. However, we observed that clinicians usually spent an average of 5-10 minutes during the visit digitizing a patient's sleep diary for a single week to calculate various measures such as sleep efficiency. However, clinicians often did not share the digitized sleep diary (e.g., weekly progress, graph) with patients: *"I don't think I actually did [see the graph]. It was there on his computer I was listening to his interpretation of it"* [P8]. Even though data collection is critical for CBT-I, clinicians often provided prescriptions based on estimations, as H9 remarked, *"It's more impressionistic based on the diary because I think it [calculate the sleep efficiency] takes too much time."*

These inefficiencies and missed opportunities are not just present in information assessments for patient-generated data; they are built into current clinician practices and workflow. Surveys are commonly utilized by clinicians to screen patients who can most benefit from CBT-I. Patients required between ten minutes and an hour to complete these surveys. Once completed, clinicians returned to their offices and scored the surveys, while leaving patients in the exam room. As seen in Figure 1, patients can spend a long time waiting alone during these early information seeking processes. *"[I]t's like I'm just sitting here filling out questionnaires for like an hour. So I don't see any immediate benefit, but I'm assuming that there is a benefit in the future..."* [P7]. Because the questionnaires are handwritten, clinicians had to manually input patient data into an excel spreadsheet to calculate scores while the patient was waiting in the room. In-person visits lasted approximately one hour, but a great deal of work, including information seeking, information sharing, assessment, and education, needs to be completed in this short time. Clinicians must often make quick estimates of results instead of precise calculations. *"I'm not sure she even looked at more than a page or two of [sleep diary] for just a brief—she looks over them no more than two minutes"* [P3].

Other Challenges: Both observation and interview data indicated that scheduling an appointment with a CBT-I clinician is the most common challenge for patients. Some patients waited 2-3 months for their initial appointments. During this time, patients may experience fluctuations in their sleep conditions and might resort to continuing pharmaceutical treatments or unguided self-experimentation to ease their problems. Furthermore, scheduling problems often persisted throughout the treatment period. Our data indicated that periods between visits are typically between 2 and 4 weeks in duration. Despite the difficulty of scheduling an appointment, people commonly cancelled and dropped out of ongoing treatments once scheduled. We note that the high patient dropout rates and the shortage of qualified CBT clinicians are also common challenges in other CBT-based therapies.

We also found challenges specific to the CBT-I therapy. For example, technology is often a contributing factor in sleep problems [13]. Sufferers of insomnia also may have low motivation or may opt for easier pharmaceutical-based treatment options. Furthermore, some clinicians, especially primary care doctors, would not refer to clinicians who provide CBT-I because they still consider insomnia a secondary disease.

RQ2: Strategies for Encouraging Patient Engagement

Despite the impediments inherent to the in-person CBT-I (e.g., difficulty with scheduling due to the small number of qualified clinicians), a vast majority of patients and clinicians felt that in-person communication is irreplaceable in many situations. In this section, we describe what elements of CBT-I encourage patients to engage in the care practice.

Patients' Motivators (C-2, C-3)

Patient motivations for staying engaged after initial CBT-I sessions arise from several factors. The first factor is that of socially shared or personally experienced success. Stories about successful treatments and personally perceived improvements, whether from general feelings or trends in sleep diary data, are motivational. P2 noted: *"The fact that I'm going to feel better when I wake up motivates me because I'll do anything for that."* A patient's success can also be motivating for clinicians, as H5 noted, *"it was good experience for me as well... that's very rewarding to see how well it worked at the end of the treatment."* The second factor stems from motivational messages provided by clinicians. CBT-I sleep compression and sleep restriction prescriptions require determination and self-control to follow. Clinicians employed the motivational interview technique to promote patient engagement, which is illustrated in the following example: *"so instead of me telling them what they're doing and how they should change it, I try to elicit that from them as I find that they can tell me what they're doing and why that's impacting them in a negative way and why that should be changed"* [H6]. Lastly, a patient's own data collection practices, combined with the knowledge that their data would be shared with clinicians, empowered and motivated patients. Recording data in a sleep diary increases a patient's awareness of his/her own behaviors and makes him/her feel accountable for his/her actions. P9 stated that *"once I put in the data, I know that the doctor will ultimately see that. So it serves as a motivation or incentives to be compliant with the doctor's orders."* Patients are accountable to their clinicians for a sleep diary which contains a record of relevant actions; they may thus try to avoid negative clinician judgments by providing incomplete or false records, or they may foster feelings of pride when they successfully complete difficult prescriptions.

Personalization (B-2, C-2, C-4)
Clinicians demonstrate personalized approaches in various ways—by fine-tuning treatment, by building inter-personal bonds, and by assessing whether patients qualify for CBT-I treatment. Clinicians selectively choose and emphasize which aspects are more important than others, thus providing patients personalized and relevant information. Clinicians also personalize sleep prescriptions based on each patient's circumstances. For example, in employing sleep restriction, some clinicians may initially allow extra time on a bed to encourage patient retention, especially for resistant or comorbid patients. For example, recognizing P4's anxiety, H1 "negotiated" with P4 over her sleep schedule by allowing her to both initially have a fixed wake up time, and to only gradually shift her to-bed time. Not all clinicians agree with this negotiation methodology, including H3, who notes: *"So if you think about CBT-I as a dosage, if someone's not getting a strong enough dose of CBT-I, like if I'm giving them seven hours when they need six, then what's happening there is I'm under dosing them."*

Building alliances with patients makes them feel supported, which can increase engagement. Clinicians thus attempt to portray a collaborative relationship with patients. Patients also prefer the "personal touch" provided by clinicians in traditional in-person visitations, specifically during discussions, when asking questions and receiving answers, and when receiving explanations. P3 remarked, *"Having a personal relationship with someone really improves because I trust them more, because I understand them more"*. Clinicians have the ability to instantaneously provide feedback, the knowledge, and experience to direct necessary conversations, and the ability to build inter-personal bonds.

One strength of in-person CBT-I is the clinician's ability to diagnose insomnia comorbid with other conditions and interact with patients in a flexible manner: *"A certain number of people that I see are probably suffering from a more generalized anxiety disorders. Some of them may have depressional problems. Part of what I'm doing is trying to rule out other possibilities or at least to understand sleep problem in the context of a large difficulty"* [H7]. Clinicians were particularly sensitive to patients with comorbid conditions; sometimes, they referred those patients to another department because treating an underlying condition was necessary to treating insomnia.

Setting up expectations (A-2, C-3)
During the initial CBT-I session, clinicians tell patients what to expect: if they follow the prescription, treatment will be successful, but they will feel worse before they get better. Knowing what to expect often has profound effects on patients. Techniques taught to patients during visits likely persist in the patients' memories, and if a sleep disorder should arise later they will have the experience, knowledge, and confidence to solve the problem. P1 stated, *"It's educating me to think differently, and to identify triggers that might be inhibiting my sleep. There were relaxation techniques and things like that. Try to turn off those negative thoughts and the worry before bed, try to let things go, a lot of education about that."*

Reflection (C-1)
Recording and tracking sleep data using paper-based or application-based sleep diaries can help patients maintain engagement and awareness. Paper-based sleep diaries have a row labeled "comments," which affords patients the opportunity to record additional contextual information which may or may not have contributed to positive or negative sleep experiences. P3 stated, *"couple of nights ago we had like 60 miles an hour winds here. The whole house just like shook all night long. That definitely had an effect on me. I just wrote that in there so that he would know why I didn't have such great night."* This contextual information is also extremely important for clinicians, as it may change how particular data should be interpreted. *"There was one client who was really sick one day and I just deleted that data from that week, because it was going to distort all the figures"* [H5]. When compared to digitized sleep diaries, which usually have a small screen, paper-based sleep diaries often have a much larger physical form which allows some patients to easily see numbers and comment details. Three clinicians suggest that using pen and paper can give a patient an overall picture and facilitate patient reflection.

RQ3: Opportunities for Technology to Support CBT-I
Utilizing technology for in-person CBT-I could have both positive and negative effects on clinicians and patients. The patient could become accountable to the clinician and be less likely to drop-out of his or her treatment. Contrarily, technology could also invite problems with patient engagement and attrition if the patient perceives that he or she is receiving less clinician attention. Below, we provide workflow-based design opportunities for leveraging technology to preserve the gist of in-person CBT-I while easing clinicians' and patients' burdens with mundane tasks.

Support patient in-home activities
The patient's tracking of sleep data, such as by capturing sleep and contextual factors using pen and paper, is a significant part of in-home activities. Despite the existence of many available sleep tracking technologies—such as mobile [35] and consumer wearable technologies (e.g., [3]) as well as validated medical devices (e.g., [7]), we found that these technologies were rarely used in practice. Only one clinician (H1) had used Actigraph in one case to get data for comparison to a patient's sleep diary. In fact, all clinicians opposed the idea of utilizing automated capture of sleep data (e.g., wearable sensing or pressure sensing) in CBT-I because the patient's own perceptions of sleep and reflections upon sleep data are key components of CBT-I. We suspect that existing sleep tracking tools mainly focus on lowering people's capture burden without fostering self-awareness and reflection that occurs in paper-based sleep diary use. We therefore see opportunities in designing semi-automated sleep tracking tools [17], which leverage manual input for subjective measures (e.g., sleep quality) to enhance awareness, while simultaneously utilizing

sensing technology for capturing rich contextual information [34] and automatically calculating important measures such as sleep efficiency, which used to be calculated by hand in the clinician's office.

Semi-automated sleep diaries can provide many opportunities for patients to reflect on behaviors by providing opportunities to collect and review data. They can also allow clinicians to remotely monitor patients' progress and intervene to customize sleep prescriptions and treatments when necessary. Although we were worried about information overload, clinicians such as H3 expressed the desire to receive data when it becomes available: *"I absolutely want to get the data as quickly as possible because it makes it less likely that the patient will forget and then do the whole thing like the day before they come in to see me."* Reminders with encouraging messages can also be employed to alert people to track sleep and follow the sleep prescription. As H5 mentioned, *"Some fun technology just to pop up and say, 'Hey, you're doing great. Keep going.' Have that little, you know. Encouragement-type technology."* Furthermore, patient awareness that a clinician will view and utilize his/her logs will increase the patient's motivation to track, data accuracy, and accountability. Also, having timestamps of when the diary logs were entered can increase clinicians' trust of patient-generated data, thus making them confident in their assessments based on diary data. Finally, while allowing clinicians to remotely prescribe sleep regimens (e.g., wake up time and to-be time), we need to further examine how to balance personalizing remote treatment plans and in-person visits to increase patient motivation and engagement.

Support information seeking

Technology can also be used to support information seeking and assessment. Notably, for some patients, surveys can be filled out prior to patient visitations: *"Yeah, that would be ideal if we could have them have an interface where they were able to complete questionnaires in their sleep log, and it automatically dumps that into the EMR and then notify our clinicians of your patients completed their questionnaire"* [H8]. If patients can complete surveys or questionnaires on their own outside of the visitation times, clinicians benefit by having time to see more patients, which was a theme expressed by several clinicians. Patients will also benefit from having quality in-person time to discuss treatment options and rationale during those visitations instead of filling out the questionnaire or waiting in the room during the scoring and assessment. This approach however will not work for people with limited health literacy.

Support information sharing

One of the benefits that technology can provide in the current CBT-I workflow is the ways in which it can support information sharing across time and space [21, 38, 48]. Technology's ability to allow for asynchronous (not at the same time), distributed (not in the same location) data sharing between clinicians and patients to support patient in-home activities has been mentioned previously in this paper; such methods include the sharing of electronic sleep diary and environmental contextual data via web-based platform. Currently, some of our clinician participants kindly let patients share their weekly sleep data via email or over phone calls and promptly respond to patients' urgent needs (e.g., patient is having a very hard time falling asleep, difficulties with following sleep prescription) without compensation, but this altruistic model might not scale in the future. Additionally, there are various points in the CBT-I workflow where information sharing is needed during the in-person visit (C-1 through C-4). For example, automated data sharing and data visualizations could help both the patient and the clinician readily understand the patient's state and progress, while reducing the time a clinician spends digitizing the paper-based diary entries to calculate sleep efficiency and draw graphs.

Support information assessment

Once the patient and clinician have established a trusted partnership during the initial phase of CBT-I, the patient's treatment plans can be supported through technology, with potential for aspects such as automatic generation of the patient's sleep prescription and remote sending of prescriptions. However, it would be important for the clinicians to have an ability to fine tune the generated prescription based upon patients' individual needs. Furthermore, H8 suggested: *"maybe having modules the clinician can assign like having them do a breathing exercise, or having them do a worry log on the technology or something like that. Then assign these modules as it applies to that particular patient if it applies to that patient."* In both cases, clinician burden can be lessened and patients can receive personalized treatment plans especially when they are unable to visit in-person, or when they are making good progress such that they do not need to have an hour-long, in-person session with the clinician. To ensure treatment efficacy and improve patient accountability and adherence in the home, clinicians should be equipped with an ability to remotely monitor patients' involvement and progress, although such monitoring might pose privacy concerns [21], which might discourage some patients.

DISCUSSION

Here, we discuss what it means to "make space for the quality care" in CBT-I contexts; we focus on how to enhance therapeutic relationships between the clinician and the patient, and what aspects of in-person CBT-I care should be emphasized further with the help of technology.

Making Space for the Quality Care

Technology cannot suitably solve every issue in CBT-I care, but we argue that it should be used to address the inefficiencies of the current care practice. Utilizing technology in these circumstances could allow clinicians and patients to focus on important tasks such as building a trustful relationship and sharing and reflecting upon experiences. These activities are crucial for promoting the development of effective personalized treatments. To our knowledge, the bulk of research regarding sleep technology is focused on supporting patient in-home activities (e.g., sleep tracking). Some research in CBT-I specifically discusses how patients on waiting lists for in-person CBT-I therapy or with less severe cases of insomnia may utilize cCBT-I to sufficiently meet their needs [64]. Researchers can utilize our CBT-I workflow model (patient in-home activities; information seeking; information sharing;

information assessment; and documentation) to locate under-researched themes and tasks, and examine them deeply to find novel opportunities to utilize technology.

For example, supporting information sharing with technology in CBT-I care is one under-explored area. Clinician attitudes towards leveraging technologies for accessing patient-generated data appear to be mixed; while recognizing that summarization techniques and visual analytics could help them quickly identify insights from data and encourage data reflection, they also have concerns over having access to too much data in real time [70]. As the efficiency of sharing, quality of reflection, and patient satisfaction would largely depend on how the visualization tool is designed, it is therefore important to involve both patients and clinicians during the design process to create easily understandable visualizations that support their goals and priorities.

The ability for clinicians to provide personalized care throughout every CBT-I workflow stage for each patient, such as by allowing for flexibility in sleep times for new and return patients, was another strength of in-person CBT-I care. Recent studies suggest that personalization plays an important role in improving treatment efficacy [6, 9, 26]. Although Beun argues that a virtual mobile coach can exercise automated personalization (i.e., "adaptation") when providing sleep prescriptions to treat insomnia patients [9], our study suggests otherwise; our clinician participants provided structured CBT-I treatment in a personalized yet strict manner to ensure treatment efficacy. Alankus and colleagues also emphasized the role of clinicians in customizing key aspects of treatments—such as in adjusting difficulty levels of rehabilitation games for stroke patients [6]. We believe that clinicians' sensitivity to patients' unique and individual situations and personalization based on these contextual data are the keys in successful delivery of in-person CBT-I treatment.

Support Patients with Varying Levels of Motivation

Although our research concerns with improving the in-person CBT-I practice, some of our findings relate to Computerized CBT-I. As mentioned earlier, the high dropout rate is a known problem of Computerized CBT-I, and not everyone can benefit from it. Our clinician participants suggested that people who benefit most will have strong motivations, confidence, and both the willingness and capability to learn and act upon the CBT-I manual's instructions; this is consistent with findings in other literature [64]. Furthermore, our data suggests that self-employed Computerized CBT-I will require mental stability with few comorbid diseases and adequate technical aptitude. Our findings are consistent with Maclean and Pound [37] in that a clinician presence can positively affect patient motivation to complete therapy due to personalized treatment and rewards, clarification, and support especially during the initial treatment sessions. Participants believed that Computerized CBT-I would not provide as precise, individualized, and personal treatments as human clinicians. P9 described, *"Doctor would take into account my sleep history for the three years prior to starting the CBT-I... my job obligation and profession, height, weight, blood pressure—all those types of things and come up with an overall evaluation rather than just simply plotting information into a matrix and then giving a number kicked out by an equation."* Given the respective advantages and drawbacks of in-person and Computerized CBT-I, we envision a decision support system that helps clinicians at the earlier stage of care to identify those individuals who will most benefit from in-person CBT-I versus Computerized CBT-I. For example, based on survey instruments and in-person interviews, clinicians can assess patients' emotional, physical, and psychological states to identify those who are unmotivated or who have comorbidities (thus needing more face-to-face time with clinicians) versus those who are motivated and reliable (thus needing less face-to-face time with clinicians). Clinicians can then direct the motivated patients to the Computerized CBT-I solution and occasionally check their progress while offering more sensitive care and attention to those who desperately need the in-person supervision. In the long run, we see the potential for combining in-person CBT-I and Computerized CBT-I to accommodate diverse needs and varying comprehensive abilities of the patients, but future work remains to design how to best combine these two separate models to provide quality care in a scalable way.

Limitation

This study was conducted in the U.S. and as such, comments and discussion about the hospital billing mechanism might not apply, or will be less of a concern in other countries. We also note that we could not observe as many late-stage CBT-I sessions in comparison to the earlier sessions despite our visits to the hospital occurring over the course of 3 months. We therefore complemented our data with clinician interviews.

CONCLUSION

In this study, we described the clinical workflow of CBT-I practice and proposed ways that technology could be utilized to enhance the quality of in-person care. Our findings suggest that CBT-I workflow consists of the following five categories: patient in-home activities, information seeking, information sharing, information assessment, and documentation. Our work represents an expansion of the prior clinician workflow model [43], in which we uniquely incorporate the patient's roles and activities in a CBT-I context. These elements are significant for creating quality care, but as of yet have remained under-utilized in workflow models. In analyzing the CBT-I workflow, we identified several elements that make the in-person therapy effective, such as what encourages patient engagement (e.g., socially shared or personally experienced success, self-reflection) and how clinicians motivate patients (e.g., personalized treatment, motivational messages). We also identified challenges in the CBT-I practice that make therapy ineffective and exhausting. Based on the in-depth analysis of the CBT-I workflow, we provide workflow-based design opportunities for leveraging technology to help clinicians and patients build therapeutic relationships while easing their burdens with mundane tasks.

ACKNOWLEDGMENTS

The research presented in this article was funded by the National Science Foundation under awards CRII:CHS-1464382.

REFERENCES

1. 1978. American Board of Sleep Medicine. `http://www.absm.org/bsmspecialists.aspx`. (1978). Accessed: 2016-09-18.
2. 2005. CBT for Insomnia. `http://www.cbtforinsomnia.com`. (2005). Accessed: 2016-09-18.
3. 2007. Fitbit. `https://www.fitbit.com/`. (2007). Accessed: 2016-09-18.
4. 2013. CBT-i Coach. `https://cbticoach.org`. (2013). Accessed: 2016-09-18.
5. 2014. Withings Aura Sleep Sensor. `https://www.withings.com/fr/en/products/aura/sleep-sensor-accessory`. (2014). Accessed: 2016-09-18.
6. Gazihan Alankus, Amanda Lazar, Matt May, and Caitlin Kelleher. 2010. Towards customizable games for stroke rehabilitation. In *Proceedings of the SIGCHI Conference on Human Factors in Computing Systems*. ACM, 2113–2122.
7. S Ancoli-Israel, R Cole, C Alessi, M Chambers, W Moorcroft, and C Pollak. 2003. The role of actigraphy in the study of sleep and circadian rhythms. American Academy of Sleep Medicine Review Paper. *Sleep* 26, 3 (2003), 342–392.
8. Joan S Ash, Marc Berg, and Enrico Coiera. 2004. Some unintended consequences of information technology in health care: the nature of patient care information system-related errors. *Journal of the American Medical Informatics Association* 11, 2 (2004), 104–112.
9. Robbert Jan Beun. 2013. Persuasive strategies in mobile insomnia therapy: alignment, adaptation, and motivational support. *Personal and Ubiquitous Computing* 17, 6 (2013), 1187–1195.
10. Ann Blandford, Erik Berndt, Ken Catchpole, Dominic Furniss, Astrid Mayer, Helena Mentis, Aisling OKane, Tom Owen, Atish Rajkomar, and Rebecca Randell. 2012. Experiencing Interactive Healthcare Technologies: embracing'the wild'on its own terms. *Invited submission to ToCHIs special issue on The Turn to the Wild* (2012).
11. Ann Blandford, Erik Berndt, Ken Catchpole, Dominic Furniss, Astrid Mayer, Helena Mentis, Aisling Ann OKane, Tom Owen, Atish Rajkomar, and Rebecca Randell. 2015. Strategies for conducting situated studies of technology use in hospitals. *Cognition, Technology & Work* 17, 4 (2015), 489–502.
12. Virginia Braun and Victoria Clarke. 2006. Using thematic analysis in psychology. *Qualitative research in psychology* 3, 2 (2006), 77–101.
13. Cameron A Brick, Darbi L Seely, and Tonya M Palermo. 2010. Association between sleep hygiene and sleep quality in medical students. *Behavioral sleep medicine* 8, 2 (2010), 113–121.
14. Jane Carthey. 2003. The role of structured observational research in health care. *Quality and safety in health care* 12, suppl 2 (2003), ii13–ii16.
15. Yunan Chen, Karen Cheng, Charlotte Tang, Katie A Siek, and Jakob E Bardram. 2013. Is my doctor listening to me?: impact of health it systems on patient-provider interaction. In *CHI'13 Extended Abstracts on Human Factors in Computing Systems*. ACM, 2419–2426.
16. Yunan Chen, Victor Ngo, Sidney Harrison, and Victoria Duong. 2011. Unpacking exam-room computing: negotiating computer-use in patient-physician interactions. In *Proceedings of the SIGCHI Conference on Human Factors in Computing Systems*. ACM, 3343–3352.
17. Eun Kyoung Choe, Saeed Abdullah, Mashfiqui Rabbi, Edison Thomaz, Daniel A Epstein, Matthew Kay, Felicia Cordeiro, Gregory D Abowd, Tanzeem Choudhury, James Fogarty, Bongshin Lee, Mark Matthews, and Julie A Kientz. 2017. Semi-automated tracking: a balanced approach for self-monitoring applications. *Pervasive Computing* (2017).
18. Eun Kyoung Choe, Sunny Consolvo, Nathaniel F Watson, and Julie A Kientz. 2011. Opportunities for computing technologies to support healthy sleep behaviors. In *Proceedings of the SIGCHI Conference on Human Factors in Computing Systems*. ACM, 3053–3062.
19. Eun Kyoung Choe, Bongshin Lee, Matthew Kay, Wanda Pratt, and Julie A Kientz. 2015. SleepTight: low-burden, self-monitoring technology for capturing and reflecting on sleep behaviors. In *Proceedings of the 2015 ACM International Joint Conference on Pervasive and Ubiquitous Computing*. ACM, 121–132.
20. Chia-Fang Chung, Jonathan Cook, Elizabeth Bales, Jasmine Zia, and Sean A Munson. 2015. More than telemonitoring: Health provider use and nonuse of life-log data in irritable bowel syndrome and weight management. *Journal of medical Internet research* 17, 8 (2015), e203.
21. Chia-Fang Chung, Kristin Dew, Allison Cole, Jasmine Zia, James Fogarty, Julie A Kientz, and Sean A Munson. 2016. Boundary Negotiating Artifacts in Personal Informatics: Patient-Provider Collaboration with Patient-Generated Data. In *Proceedings of the 19th ACM Conference on Computer-Supported Cooperative Work & Social Computing*. ACM, 770–786.
22. Enrico Coiera and Vanessa Tombs. 1998. Communication behaviours in a hospital setting: an observational study. *Bmj* 316, 7132 (1998), 673–676.
23. Harvey R Colten, Bruce M Altevogt, and others. 2006. *Sleep disorders and sleep deprivation: an unmet public health problem*. National Academies Press.
24. David Coyle, Gavin Doherty, Mark Matthews, and John Sharry. 2007. Computers in talk-based mental health interventions. *Interacting with computers* 19, 4 (2007), 545–562.

25. David Coyle, Nicola McGlade, Gavin Doherty, and Gary O'Reilly. 2011. Exploratory evaluations of a computer game supporting cognitive behavioural therapy for adolescents. In *Proceedings of the SIGCHI Conference on Human Factors in Computing Systems*. ACM, 2937–2946.
26. Gavin Doherty, David Coyle, and John Sharry. 2012. Engagement with online mental health interventions: an exploratory clinical study of a treatment for depression. In *Proceedings of the SIGCHI Conference on Human Factors in Computing Systems*. ACM, 1421–1430.
27. Richard Frankel, Andrea Altschuler, Sheba George, James Kinsman, Holly Jimison, Nan R Robertson, and John Hsu. 2005. Effects of exam-room computing on clinician–patient communication. *Journal of General Internal Medicine* 20, 8 (2005), 677–682.
28. Dominic Furniss, Rebecca Randell, Aisling Ann OKane, Svetlena Taneva, Helena Mentis, and Ann Blandford. 2014. Fieldwork for healthcare: guidance for investigating human factors in computing systems. *Synthesis Lectures on Assistive, Rehabilitative, and Health-Preserving Technologies* 3, 2 (2014), 1–146.
29. Sheldon Greenfield, Sherrie Kaplan, and John E Ware. 1985. Expanding patient involvement in care: effects on patient outcomes. *Annals of internal medicine* 102, 4 (1985), 520–528.
30. Fjóla Dögg Helgadóttir, Ross G Menzies, Mark Onslow, Ann Packman, and Sue O'Brian. 2009. Online CBT I: Bridging the gap between Eliza and modern online CBT treatment packages. *Behaviour Change* 26, 04 (2009), 245–253.
31. Winni F Hofman, Anand Kumar, and others. 2010. Online treatment of insomnia using behavioral techniques. *Sleep Diagn Ther* 5, 3 (2010), 28–32.
32. M Holmqvist, N Vincent, and K Walsh. 2014. Web-vs telehealth-based delivery of cognitive behavioral therapy for insomnia: a randomized controlled trial. *Sleep medicine* 15, 2 (2014), 187–195.
33. Eva Kaltenthaler, Paul Sutcliffe, Glenys Parry, C Beverley, A Rees, and Michael Ferriter. 2008. The acceptability to patients of computerized cognitive behaviour therapy for depression: a systematic review. *Psychological medicine* 38, 11 (2008), 1521–1530.
34. Matthew Kay, Eun Kyoung Choe, Jesse Shepherd, Benjamin Greenstein, Nathaniel Watson, Sunny Consolvo, and Julie A Kientz. 2012. Lullaby: a capture & access system for understanding the sleep environment. In *Proceedings of the 2012 ACM Conference on Ubiquitous Computing*. ACM, 226–234.
35. Shaun Lawson, Sue Jamison-Powell, Andrew Garbett, Conor Linehan, Erica Kucharczyk, Sanne Verbaan, Duncan A Rowland, and Kevin Morgan. 2013. Validating a mobile phone application for the everyday, unobtrusive, objective measurement of sleep. In *Proceedings of the SIGCHI Conference on Human Factors in Computing Systems*. ACM, 2497–2506.
36. Reeva Lederman, Greg Wadley, John Gleeson, Sarah Bendall, and Mario Álvarez-Jiménez. 2014. Moderated online social therapy: Designing and evaluating technology for mental health. *ACM Transactions on Computer-Human Interaction (TOCHI)* 21, 1 (2014), 5.
37. Niall Maclean and Pandora Pound. 2000. A critical review of the concept of patient motivation in the literature on physical rehabilitation. *Soc Sci Med* 50, 4 (2000), 495–506.
38. Lena Mamykina, Elizabeth Mynatt, Patricia Davidson, and Daniel Greenblatt. 2008. MAHI: investigation of social scaffolding for reflective thinking in diabetes management. In *Proceedings of the SIGCHI Conference on Human Factors in Computing Systems*. ACM, 477–486.
39. Gabriela Marcu, Kevin Tassini, Quintin Carlson, Jillian Goodwyn, Gabrielle Rivkin, Kevin J Schaefer, Anind K Dey, and Sara Kiesler. 2013. Why do they still use paper?: understanding data collection and use in Autism education. In *Proceedings of the SIGCHI Conference on Human Factors in Computing Systems*. ACM, 3177–3186.
40. Jun-Ki Min, Afsaneh Doryab, Jason Wiese, Shahriyar Amini, John Zimmerman, and Jason I Hong. 2014. Toss'n'turn: smartphone as sleep and sleep quality detector. In *Proceedings of the SIGCHI Conference on Human Factors in Computing Systems*. ACM, 477–486.
41. Matthew D Mitchell, Philip Gehrman, Michael Perlis, and Craig A Umscheid. 2012. Comparative effectiveness of cognitive behavioral therapy for insomnia: a systematic review. *BMC family practice* 13, 1 (2012), 1.
42. Charles M Morin, James P Culbert, and Steven M Schwartz. 1994. Nonpharmacological interventions for insomnia. *Am J Psychiatry* 151, 8 (1994), 1172.
43. Tao Ni, Amy K Karlson, and Daniel Wigdor. 2011. AnatOnMe: facilitating doctor-patient communication using a projection-based handheld device. In *Proceedings of the SIGCHI Conference on Human Factors in Computing Systems*. ACM, 3333–3342.
44. Peter J Norton and Terri L Barrera. 2012. Transdiagnostic versus diagnosis-specific CBT for anxiety disorders: A preliminary randomized controlled noninferiority trial. *Depression and Anxiety* 29, 10 (2012), 874–882.
45. Francisco Nunes, Nervo Verdezoto, Geraldine Fitzpatrick, Morten Kyng, Erik Grönvall, and Cristiano Storni. 2015. Self-Care Technologies in HCI: Trends, Tensions, and Opportunities. *ACM Transactions on Computer-Human Interaction (TOCHI)* 22, 6 (2015), 33.
46. US Department of Health, Human Services, and others. 1999. Mental health: A report of the Surgeon General. (1999).

47. Isa Okajima, Yoko Komada, and Yuichi Inoue. 2011. A meta-analysis on the treatment effectiveness of cognitive behavioral therapy for primary insomnia. *Sleep and Biological Rhythms* 9, 1 (2011), 24–34.
48. Aisling Ann O'Kane and Helena Mentis. 2012. Sharing medical data vs. health knowledge in chronic illness care. In *CHI'12 Extended Abstracts on Human Factors in Computing Systems*. ACM, 2417–2422.
49. Lucille ML Ong, Johanna CJM De Haes, Alaysia M Hoos, and Frits B Lammes. 1995. Doctor-patient communication: a review of the literature. *Social science & medicine* 40, 7 (1995), 903–918.
50. Sun Young Park, So Young Lee, and Yunan Chen. 2012. The effects of EMR deployment on doctors work practices: A qualitative study in the emergency department of a teaching hospital. *International journal of medical informatics* 81, 3 (2012), 204–217.
51. Michael L Perlis, Carla Jungquist, Michael T Smith, and Donn Posner. 2006. *Cognitive behavioral treatment of insomnia: A session-by-session guide*. Vol. 1. Springer Science & Business Media.
52. Laura Pfeifer Vardoulakis, Amy Karlson, Dan Morris, Greg Smith, Justin Gatewood, and Desney Tan. 2012. Using mobile phones to present medical information to hospital patients. In *Proceedings of the SIGCHI Conference on Human Factors in Computing Systems*. ACM, 1411–1420.
53. Olga Pykhtina, Madeline Balaam, Gavin Wood, Sue Pattison, Ahmed Kharrufa, and Patrick Olivier. 2012. Magic land: the design and evaluation of an interactive tabletop supporting therapeutic play with children. In *Proceedings of the Designing Interactive Systems Conference*. ACM, 136–145.
54. Stefan Rennick-Egglestone, Sarah Knowles, Gill Toms, Penny Bee, Karina Lovell, and Peter Bower. 2016. Health technologies In the wild: experiences of engagement with computerised CBT. In *CHI'16 Proceedings of the SIGCHI Conference on Human Factors in Computing Systems*. Association for Computing Machinery.
55. Lee M Ritterband, Linda A Gonder-Frederick, Daniel J Cox, Allan D Clifton, Rebecca W West, and Stephen M Borowitz. 2003. Internet interventions: in review, in use, and into the future. *Professional Psychology: Research and Practice* 34, 5 (2003), 527.
56. Lee M Ritterband, Frances P Thorndike, Linda A Gonder-Frederick, Joshua C Magee, Elaine T Bailey, Drew K Saylor, and Charles M Morin. 2009. Efficacy of an Internet-based behavioral intervention for adults with insomnia. *Archives of General Psychiatry* 66, 7 (2009), 692–698.
57. Debra L Roter, Richard M Frankel, Judith A Hall, and David Sluyter. 2006. The expression of emotion through nonverbal behavior in medical visits. *Journal of general internal medicine* 21, S1 (2006), S28–S34.
58. Moira Stewart, Judith Belle Brown, Heather Boon, Joanne Galajda, Leslie Meredith, and Michelle Sangster. 1999. Evidence on patient-doctor communication. *Cancer* 25 (1999), 30.
59. Anja Thieme, John McCarthy, Paula Johnson, Stephanie Phillips, Jayne Wallace, Siân Lindley, Karim Ladha, Daniel Jackson, Diana Nowacka, Ashur Rafiev, and others. 2016. Challenges for Designing new Technology for Health and Wellbeing in a Complex Mental Healthcare Context. In *Proceedings of the 2016 CHI Conference on Human Factors in Computing Systems*. ACM, 2136–2149.
60. Kim M Unertl, Matthew B Weinger, and Kevin B Johnson. 2006. Applying direct observation to model workflow and assess adoption. In *AMIA Annual Symposium Proceedings*, Vol. 2006. American Medical Informatics Association, 794.
61. Kim M Unertl, Matthew B Weinger, Kevin B Johnson, and Nancy M Lorenzi. 2009. Describing and modeling workflow and information flow in chronic disease care. *Journal of the American Medical Informatics Association* 16, 6 (2009), 826–836.
62. David K Vawdrey, Lauren G Wilcox, Sarah A Collins, Suzanne Bakken, Steve Feiner, Aurelia Boyer, and S Restaino. 2011. A tablet computer application for patients to participate in their hospital care. In *AMIA Annu Symp Proc*, Vol. 2011. 1428–1435.
63. Norah Vincent and Samantha Lewycky. 2009. Logging on for better sleep: RCT of the effectiveness of online treatment for insomnia. *Sleep* 32, 6 (2009), 807–815.
64. Norah Vincent and Kate Walsh. 2013. Stepped care for insomnia: an evaluation of implementation in routine practice. *Journal of clinical sleep medicine: JCSM: official publication of the American Academy of Sleep Medicine* 9, 3 (2013), 227.
65. Lauren Wilcox, Dan Morris, Desney Tan, and Justin Gatewood. 2010. Designing patient-centric information displays for hospitals. In *Proceedings of the SIGCHI Conference on Human Factors in Computing Systems*. ACM, 2123–2132.
66. Nicola Wiles, Laura Thomas, Anna Abel, Nicola Ridgway, Nicholas Turner, John Campbell, Anne Garland, Sandra Hollinghurst, Bill Jerrom, David Kessler, and others. 2013. Cognitive behavioural therapy as an adjunct to pharmacotherapy for primary care based patients with treatment resistant depression: results of the CoBalT randomised controlled trial. *The Lancet* 381, 9864 (2013), 375–384.
67. Maja Wrzesien, Cristina Botella, Juana Bretón-López, Eva del Río González, Jean-Marie Burkhardt, Mariano Alcañiz, and María Ángeles Pérez-Ara. 2015. Treating small animal phobias using a projective-augmented reality system: A single-case study. *Computers in Human Behavior* 49 (2015), 343–353.

68. Robert Zachariae, Marlene S Lyby, Lee M Ritterband, and Mia S O'Toole. 2016. Efficacy of internet-delivered cognitive-behavioral therapy for insomnia–A systematic review and meta-analysis of randomized controlled trials. *Sleep medicine reviews* 30 (2016), 1–10.

69. Kai Zheng, Hilary M Haftel, Ronald B Hirschl, Michael O'Reilly, and David A Hanauer. 2010. Quantifying the impact of health IT implementations on clinical workflow: a new methodological perspective. *Journal of the American Medical Informatics Association* 17, 4 (2010), 454–461.

70. Haining Zhu, Joanna Colgan, Madhu Reddy, and Eun Kyoung Choe. 2016. Sharing Patient-Generated Data in Clinical Practices: An Interview Study. In *AMIA Annual Symposium Proceedings*, Vol. 2016. American Medical Informatics Association.

Prescribing 10,000 Steps like Aspirin: Designing a Novel Interface for Data-Driven Medical Consultation

Yoojung Kim[1], Eunyoung Heo[3], Hyunjeong Lee[1], Sookyoung Ji[1], Jueun Choi[1], Jeong-Whun Kim[2], Joongseek Lee[1], Sooyoung Yoo[3]
User Experience Lab, Seoul National University, Seoul, South Korea[1]
Department of Otorhinolaryngology, Seoul National University Bundang Hospital, Seongnam, South Korea[2]
Center for Medical Informatics, Seoul National University Bundang Hospital, Seongnam, South Korea[3]
{tendtoyj, emilyheo, hyunjeong.lee, purpler7, cje0520, kimemail, joonlee8, yoosoo0}@snu.ac.kr

ABSTRACT
Due to the prevalence of personal health tracking, cases of self-logged data being utilized in the clinic are gradually increasing. However, obstacles to clinicians' ability to further adopt such data-driven medical consultations in the existing workflow remain, such as lack of time and poor interoperability. In this paper, we conducted a workshop to design a clinician interface supporting the integration of data-driven consultation into the existing workflow and investigate the role of the interface in situ. After implementing the clinician interface designed based on the workshop results, we observed 32 cases of actual use within the clinical context. We found that our interface, *DataMD*, helped the clinician construct a new workflow, enhanced the clinician's counseling skills, and facilitated more in-depth conversation. This paper contributes to empirically identifying the role of a clinician interface through a user-centered design approach.

Author Keywords
Data-driven medical consultation; patient-generated data; self-logged data; clinician interface; design workshop.

ACM Classification Keywords
H.5.2. Information interfaces and presentation: User Interfaces; User-centered Design.

INTRODUCTION
It is difficult for clinicians to acquire a thorough understanding of their patients in the medical office. To understand patients, clinicians collect evidence by reviewing various kinds of lab data, such as vital signs and specific test results [18, 51]. In order to determine the correlation between the lab results and the symptoms patients report, clinicians often ask their patients additional questions. Based on these fragmented pieces of evidence and their prior knowledge, clinicians make medical decisions, such as which medicines to prescribe [47]. They also have to explain the type of medication and any side effects of the treatments to their patients. All these tasks should be done in as little as five to at most 20 minutes [14, 34]. This is a common problem in the hospital, and it is obvious that the doctor's office is a site where clinicians encounter information overload [17, 18, 54], which inhibits clinicians' ability to understand their patients completely.

It is extremely challenging to insert another process into this already dense workflow. It is even more difficult when the new process involves patient-generated data consultations. Previous studies and reports have already pointed out the obstacles of utilizing such patient-generated data within the medical setting [2, 14, 37, 44, 49, 53]. Many issues relate to data capture/access and further situational constraints in medical practices [53]. As mentioned above, situational constraints, such as lack of time [35, 49] and information overload [27, 54], have been pointed out as some of the most challenging and endemic obstacles.

Despite these challenges, major hospitals and healthcare providers are attempting to adopt data-driven consultation [52]. Quickly obtaining information on patients' everyday lives is more critical in specific clinical settings where overweight patients suffering from chronic diseases need regular visits to check their overall health conditions and receive advice from clinicians. It is crucial for clinicians to have a thorough understanding of their patients for precise diagnosis and proper treatment [1, 6, 33], especially in the case of chronic disease patients [8]. In the past, patients mostly provided their daily habits through verbal recall, which was time-consuming and forced doctors to make estimations. On the contrary, data-driven consultation helps clinicians gain a deeper understanding of their patients' behaviors and feelings [14] in a relatively short amount of time. In other words, if the data-driven consultation process is well integrated into the current workflow [38], the doctor–patient relationship can be improved despite the situational constraints [8, 14, 29].

However, it was not until recently that the integration of data-driven consultation, in which clinicians utilize self-logged data in the hospital, began to be researched. Chung et al. identified the feasibility, benefits, and challenges of

CHI 2017, May 06-11, 2017, Denver, CO, USA
© 2017 ACM. ISBN 978-1-4503-4655-9/17/05...$15.00
DOI: http://dx.doi.org/10.1145/3025453.3025570

data-driven consultation from the perspective of both healthcare providers [14] and patients [15]. West et al. [53] reviewed prior studies and examined clinicians using vignette-based roleplaying. These studies derived empirical findings by investigating how data-driven consultation aligns with current workflows and work practices. However, little research has been done on the role of actual clinician interfaces and the way in which such interfaces should be designed [8, 38].

Therefore, in this paper, we aim to help doctors understand patients quickly by designing a clinician interface that provides a set of clues for checkup conversations. To do so, we explore how the data-driven consultation interface should be designed and identify its role by in-situ observation. Given these objectives, the research questions are as follows:

- How should a clinician interface for data-driven consultation be designed?
- How does the newly designed clinician interface help the integration of data-driven consultation with the current routine?

In order to answer these questions, we conducted a 15-month-long user-centered design process with 18 stakeholders. Focusing on the first question, we set design goals based on the preliminary study. We found two issues clinicians encountered: (1) difficulty catching any distinctive events that caused dramatic changes in patients' behaviors when clinicians were not monitoring them and (2) difficulty discovering those events quickly and discussing them further with patients. To reflect on these issues, we conducted a design workshop and designed a dashboard interface for supporting conversations in the exam room. Then, we implemented the interface, DataMD, which can be integrated with the current electronic medical records (EMR) system. To answer the second question, we conducted a field study by observing 32 cases of actual use within the clinical context.

This study contributes to the HCI field by (1) providing design guidelines through a user-centered approach, (2) developing an interface that supports data-driven consultation, and (3) identifying the role of the clinician interface using patient-generated data in an actual clinical setting.

RELATED WORK

We reviewed previous work to understand the opportunities and challenges of data-driven consultation as well as the role of the clinician interface.

Benefits of Using Patient-Generated Data in Clinical Settings

Triggered by the advent of smartphones and wearable devices, and the *Quantified Self* movement [24], self-tracking has become a common habit [13]. According to [23], 70% of Americans—especially those suffering from chronic diseases—log at least one of their or their spouses' health indicators. Many studies have been carried out to investigate how these data could be useful for health management [16, 31, 32, 43]. While addressing the difficulties of interpreting such data [9], researchers further emphasized the necessity of expert interventions [12].

This led to recent studies on data-driven consultations in which clinicians utilize patient-generated data within the clinical setting [14, 34, 53]. It has been identified that using patient-generated data has many benefits. Chung et al. [14, 15] asserted that patient-generated data could offer supporting evidence for diagnoses and positively influence the doctor–patient relationship. Above all, it could enable clinicians to learn about and motivate their patients [38] and thus provide them with personalized treatment [22].

Challenges of Integrating Data-Driven Consultation into Existing Workflow

Despite its benefits, the challenges that hinder the integration of data-driven consultation mostly relate to situational constraints within the clinician's office, such as information overload and lack of time. Clinicians are responsible for multiple tasks, both behavioral and cognitive, and therefore need a high mental capacity [54]. Internally, numerous types of reference data are needed to support clinicians' decision making [27, 47]. Externally, some resources are displayed on the EMR, while others are presented in paper form [4, 11, 27]. Several studies report that clinicians encounter difficulty in appreciating the value of data-driven consultation due to such information overload [17, 54]. Furthermore, lack of time has come to the fore [20, 35, 48, 49]. Clearly, the adoption of data-driven consultation is challenging, as the existing workflow is already tight and dense.

The data itself has also been deemed an obstacle. Data gathered by patients is less standardized [30]; therefore, hospitals still have difficulties collecting data from diverse sources [25]. Recently, healthcare service providers released data platforms such as HealthKit [28] and Google Fit [26] to manage personal health data. In the near future, data recorded from individual tools will be supplied from health data platforms, and hospitals will obtain the data by accessing the platforms. In the end, the problem returns to how clinicians can utilize such data efficiently.

Role of Clinician Interface

A well-designed interface could be helpful for integrating data-driven consultation into the existing workflow [8, 38]. According to Kim et al. [34], showing patient-generated data on a standardized interface can help clinicians better understand their patients. When interpreted using the six activities suggested by West et al. [53], Kim et al.'s study implied that an interface can help clinicians overcome information overload by supporting the stages of discovery, evaluation, and initial hypothesis formation. The study also showed that the clinician interface's summary data allows clinicians to assess patients' status, and the detailed information enables them to discover abnormal points very quickly [34]. It implies that the role of the interface is important in overcoming the problem of insufficient time.

Data-driven consultation mediated by an interface could also affect the doctor–patient relationship. According to previous studies [35, 46], clinicians have difficulties counseling patients in the exam room due to a lack of confidence, information, and time. Taft et al. [50] found that an EHR helped physicians' communication skills in the exam room by assisting them with the reading and writing of medical information. The problem is, according to many studies [4, 11], that clinicians' focus on devices while reviewing medical data could cause exclusive viewing [11]. The same problem could arise during a data-driven consultation [4]. However, the characteristics of patient-generated data distinctively differ from those of medical data, since patients play a significant role in the acquisition of the data [7, 8]. Therefore, patient-generated data is more likely to lead to collaborative viewing [15, 29, 40]. According to Kim et al., patients showed great interest in self-logged data and were highly engaged with their medical treatment when reviewing their data on the interface with clinicians [34]. The studies mentioned above suggest that a well-designed interface might help to both improve clinicians' counseling skills and increase patient interest.

DESIGN PROCESS

To design the clinician interface, we employed a user-centered approach. The design process lasted 15 months and went through five stages: **preliminary study, design goal, design workshop, implementation,** and **field study**. A total of 18 participants—clinicians (4), healthcare informatics experts (3), healthcare service providers (3), a healthcare service developer (1), an EMR developer (1), a college student (1), and HCI researchers (5)—were involved in the design process. The long-term design process allowed us to explore various issues and more thoroughly develop the design.

In the preliminary study, we identified the current workflow and discovered opportunities to insert data-driven consultation. We conducted in-depth interviews with four clinicians with different specialties from Seoul National University Bundang Hospital: otorhinolaryngology (C1), family medicine (C2), rehabilitation medicine (C3), and urology (C4). The interviews consisted of two parts and took a total of 40 minutes. During the first part, we asked clinicians about their behavioral procedures in the examination room and their interaction points with the EMR system, paper reports, and nurses. During the second part, we investigated clinicians' opinions on how they would integrate data-driven consultation into the existing workflow based on the scenarios they wrote. After the interviews, we combined the journey maps of the existing workflow from each clinician into a unified journey map. Finally, we concluded with the final two journey maps that represented the current (as-is) and desired (to-be) workflows (Figure 1).

Secondly, we refined the requirements by observing actual data-driven consultations and conducting discussion sessions with clinicians. We derived three themes from the requirements, which were gathered from three types of data. The main data were transcripts containing 40 cases of six clinicians using patient-generated data [34], which were re-analyzed considering this paper's research questions. Other data were collected from clinician interviews and survey results. We asked clinicians about their thoughts on data-driven consultation and investigated their perceptions of the usefulness of each type of data through a survey. After extracting and listing several requirements from the data, we conducted a thematic analysis and elicited three themes.

Thirdly, we conducted a design workshop with 18 participants to make sketches of a concrete interface. The objectives of the co-creative design workshop were to (1) make sketches of a concrete interface with clinicians who were aware of the current workflow and (2) consider unexplored issues through the participation of various stakeholders. The participants were divided into four groups with various backgrounds. Every group contained a clinician or healthcare informatics expert.

The design workshop consisted of three sessions (structure, visualization, and paper prototyping), which took a total of five hours. Before the group activities, we explained the current workflow and essential requirements, and printed guides were distributed to each team to serve as reminders for participants. Most of the time was spent on teamwork, but there were presentations after each session. During the first session, we asked everyone to spend 30 minutes selecting an interface structure. The participants were provided with examples (e.g., dashboard, grid view). Afterward, they were asked to make a new structure for a clinician interface. In the second session, participants spent 80 minutes sketching ideas about data visualization. We handed out data samples in Excel-sheet format. In the last session, each group spent 70 minutes making a paper prototype. Finally, each participant had three votes to cast on the paper prototype components. A week after the workshop, we documented the results with a decision-making list. After all the participants attended charrettes, we shared the voting results and reached the final guidelines.

After finishing the design workshop stage, we implemented the interface, Data MD, on the actual EMR system. Then, we conducted a field study to observe the role of our interface. These two stages are described in the respective sections below.

PRELIMINARY STUDY

Before designing the interface, we investigated the current workflow and identified how data-driven consultation might integrate with it. As a result of the preliminary study, four behavioral tasks were identified: skimming lab data on the EMR system, asking patients follow-up questions, typing in comments on the EMR system, and orally

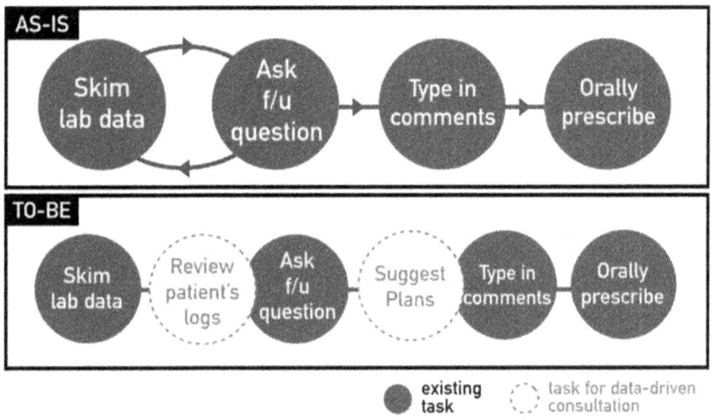

Figure 1. The two boxes are the current and desired workflows. Each circle represents a task and is ordered by time. The to-be workflow is what the clinicians want/expect in terms of change.

prescribing and explaining medications. Clinicians emphasized that data-driven consultations can aid in the betterment of the first two tasks, which involve iterative learning about patients through conversations. This provides the clinicians with the prerequisite information and allows them to approach critical questions without wasting time. This provides the clinicians an opportunity to plan behavioral changes with the patient.

Clinicians addressed the necessity of a uniform clinician interface that integrates patient-generated data from various individual tools, supporting the findings in previous studies [3, 8, 29]. Interestingly, clinicians emphasized that the new interface should be designed as a separate window from the existing EMR system. They pointed out that EMR data and patient-generated data differ in terms of reliability, validity, and medical value, as revealed in previous studies [19, 38, 49]. They clarified that patient-generated data has not yet been proven to have a clinical correlation with any diseases and that a separate window would help distinguish patient-generated data from medically verified data. Therefore, we decided to design it such that the patient-generated data was separate from the EMR system.

DESIGN GOAL

We refined the requirements of clinicians and derived three goals of the clinician interface design.

Helping Clinicians Skim Data Quickly

We found that the clinician interface should help clinicians skim trends from various types of data quickly so that they can discover distinctive points. Clinicians want to be able to review summarized data to understand patients effectively. C2 commented, *"To put it simply, I want to see my patients' status at a glance; that is, in as little time as it takes them to leave the exam room and enter my office."* Simultaneously, clinicians need to review data in detail to determine abnormalities. For example, clinicians often read the trends of the activity data (steps) and discover an unusual point when the number of steps taken suddenly decreases. They then need to scrutinize the data collected that day. These conflicting requirements imply that both summarized and detailed data are needed.

Supporting Collaboration of Clinicians and Patients

It is important for clinicians to read the data collaboratively and discuss them with their patients. Clinicians think they can answer critical questions quickly using patient-generated data and that discussing cases with patients can increase the quality of care. While patient-generated data is produced by the patients, lab data is generated at hospitals. Patients are interested in and knowledgeable of their data [7, 15]. Thus, an interface should be designed to facilitate doctor–patient collaboration and discussion [4, 11, 14].

Creating Procedures to Enable Clinicians to Have an Impact on their Patients

Clinicians highlighted that data-driven consultation was useful only when it included specific plans that could affect patients in the real world. This implies that not just reviewing data but actually setting goals creates therapeutic value [22], especially by motivating patients to modify their behaviors [15, 34]. Despite such importance, little research has been conducted on setting goals with patient-generated data. We observed that clinicians easily forget patients' unrecorded data. Since clinicians orally set goals, patients and clinicians cannot remember them with exactitude. To prevent goals from being lost, a clinician interface should be designed to record them and influence patients' lives.

DESIGN WORKSHOP

We explored how the three design goals can be reflected in the clinician interface through a design workshop.

All-in-one Interface with a Hierarchical Structure

The first design guideline was related to a desirable structure. The results showed that the information should be organized hierarchically on a single-page screen.

All-in-one Interface is More Efficient

Interestingly, all the groups proposed new types of structures in which all data were displayed on a single page. We expected that navigating separate pages would allow clinicians to read data faster, but the results indicated the opposite. Clinicians and health informatics experts argued that a single page is better for a holistic review. *"Clicking wastes time, so one screen is better for speed"* (C2). A single view was also beneficial for cross-referencing various types of data. One team's developer and designer preferred to distribute information across a few pages, but they changed their minds after hearing the clinician's opinion. Another group reported similar processes.

The legacy system, the existing EMR system, influenced clinicians' preferences for combining all the data in a single page. Clinicians were accustomed to the current EMR system, which runs on a 21-inch monitor. As they were used to reviewing heterogeneous data on a single-page view, it was natural for them to design the new interface in a similar way. *"I'd rather not design it too differently from the (current) EMR"* (C1). Two other clinicians (C2, C3) and an EMR developer made similar points.

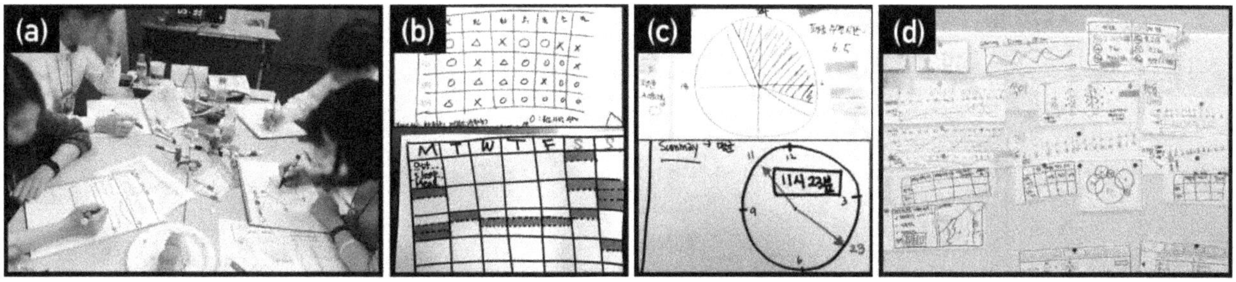

Figure 2. (a) is a scene of sketching ideas in the second stage of the workshop. (b) shows sketches of a calendar-style grid with O/X marks. (c) presents ideas that borrowed a schedule pie chart to represent wakeup time, bedtime, and sleep duration. (d) is an example of a paper prototype.

Hierarchical Structure for Skimming Data Quickly

Most groups discussed the issue of information overload caused by listing the data on a single page, and two groups proposed a hierarchical information structure to solve this issue. During this process, there was a discussion on the importance and characteristics of each data type. Clinicians suggested that each type should be distinguished, as they categorize weight, blood pressure, and stress as outcome data in their practices. The activity, food, and sleep data were considered primary data that affect the outcome data.

They suggested a three-level data summarization process involving a holistic summary, individual data summary, and detailed individual data. This could be connected to interpretation levels. For example, if a holistic summary were to represent the average quantity of activity, meals, and sleep, a clinician could think, "This patient did not exercise but ate a lot. No problem with sleeping." After that, the clinician might decide to review the individual data summary of activities and get a new interpretation: "S/he is usually active but only has inactive days on particular weekends." If needed, the clinician could look into the detailed individual data. This step-by-step sequence might improve effectiveness, because some information might not be necessary but could be selectively interpreted.

All the groups mainly dealt with a holistic summary, since it is essential to deciding the level of interpretation required. The two highest ranked components were a different type of representation of a holistic summary. One was a table with numeric values (e.g., averages) to help clinicians quickly comprehend each value. The other was a multi-line graph where the multiple lines overlapped to enable clinicians to compare various data trends. Clinicians supported its usefulness, stating that the current vital signs are visualized in the same way. For this reason, we agreed to adopt the overlay graph and test it in the field despite several issues with axis synchronization and its complexity of interpretation.

Line Graphs for Trends and Heat Maps for Distinctive Points

In this section, we mainly describe the result of the drawing session where participants discussed data visualization.

Easiest Visualization for Representing Trends

Participants agreed that an individual data summary could help clinicians scan trends effortlessly. That is, an individual data summary shows a span of data, while a holistic summary provides a snapshot of data. As for the voting results, the most popular individual summary visualization was the time-series line graph. There are two merits to using a line graph. Because line graphs are common, clinicians can quickly catch trends from them, and some values are displayed on line graphs. In addition, it is possible to visualize any time-series data with ease, whereas other new visualizations depend on the data type.

One of the groups argued the necessity of customized visualization techniques based on the different traits of each data type. Activity data could be represented on a calendar-style grid view with O/X marks, because whether patients achieve their goals is important (Figure 2-b). It would allow clinicians to check at a glance if their patients are exercising continuously. In the case of sleep, some borrowed a schedule pie chart to represent wakeup time, bedtime, and sleep duration (Figure 2-c). However, many participants were concerned that those visualizations required additional interpretation and did not show trends well.

After discussion, all participants agreed on the common formats, such as the line and bar graph formats, due to their familiarity. It reflects the conflicts between the needs and costs of using patient-generated data in the exam room. Clinicians were confident that using the data would be useful, but they had trouble anticipating the difficulties associated with the data. The cost, including misinterpretation of the data and learning system, influenced their preference for familiarity. Since clinicians did not want to take risks or have uncertainties, they were inclined toward common visualizations and various options (e.g., summary & details, reference values).

Heat Maps for Looking into Distinctive Points in Depth

Heat maps were chosen to express detailed individual data for the primary data (i.e., activity, food, and sleep). When clinicians discover a distinctive point, such as a sudden decrease in a line graph, they form initial hypotheses and want to verify them [53]. They want to know exactly what happened at that point. Many participants tried to represent the details of each data type by dividing a day into three

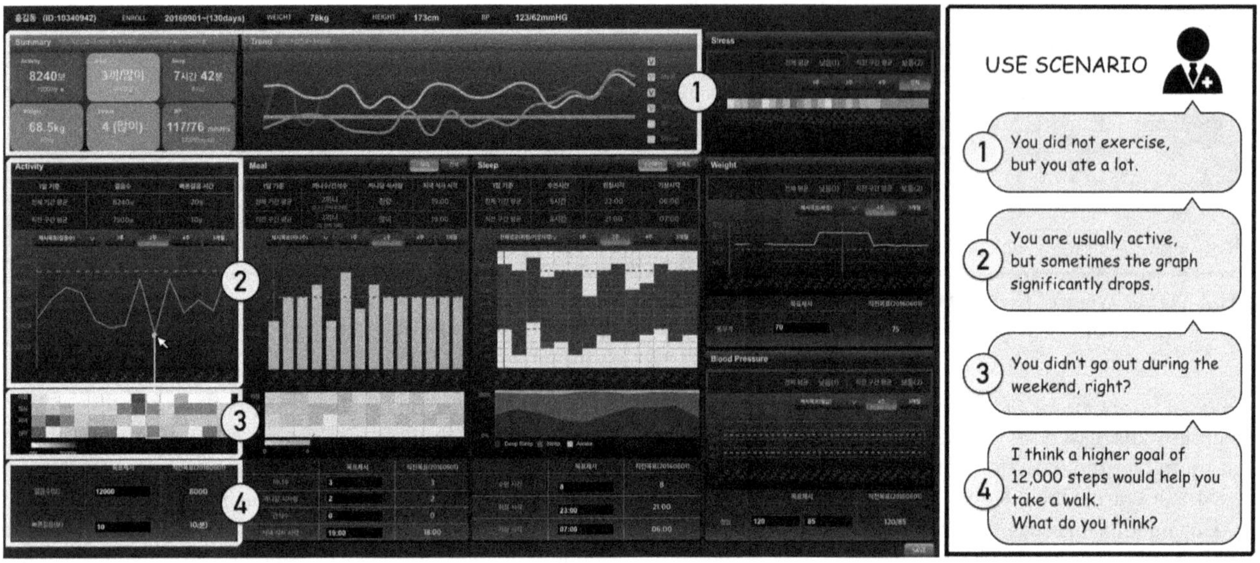

Figure 3. The view of the clinician interface is named *DataMD*. A clinician, the intended user, can: (1) skim patient-generated data via the numerical summary and graph with multiple trend lines (2) review a trend line for each data component, and discover abnormal points (3) if needed, look at the heat map to check for details (4) adjust the goal with his/her patient.

sections: morning, afternoon, and evening. It reflected the requirements that clinicians wanted to examine in-depth dimensions beyond daily quantities. It was also expected to promote communication between clinicians and patients. As the visualization was similar to the mental model of a daily routine—morning, afternoon, and evening—patients could talk about their status and feelings without difficulty.

During the charrette, the heat map was considered an appropriate format to visualize amounts in each time section. Adding an additional time section, night, was suggested to review problematic points. For example, many patients take a late-night meal impulsively, which would be dealt with separately from supper. In addition, a stacked bar graph was selected for sleep data due to the different structure of sleep quality data.

Multiple Numeric Input Fields for Prescribing Measurable Goals

The requirement of creating preset procedures to prescribe goals and therefore impact patients was emphasized. Clinicians desired to set goals as they would prescribe medication on the EMR system. One group suggested the idea of setting goals by entering exact numbers. The idea was popular with participants, especially clinicians. This simple interaction was expected to help clinicians compress a discussion with patients and integrate it into the workflow. An additional opinion that the history of the prescribed goals should be shown was also reflected.

To adjust and set specific goals, appropriate criteria were required. Clinicians noted that reference values are needed to make immediate decisions. Among many candidates, two values were selected: the average of an individual patient's data during the total logging period and the average during the interval between the last visit and the current visit. During the workshop, some participants commented that a similar group's average could be helpful. However, it was not reflected in the interface, because there would not be enough data to calculate in the early stage. The discussion of reference values changed frequently. Participants could not decide which reference values would assist clinicians' decision making. This implied that a field study should be conducted to identify the final reference value choices.

IMPLEMENTATION

We implemented the clinician interface, named DataMD, enabling clinicians to utilize patient-generated data based on the design guidelines. After developing the first prototype, we modified it five times based on the feedback from the workshop participants. We revised the graph scale, certain kinds of reference values, and the color of the graph and background. Considering the legacy system, we made a small button on the bottom right of the original EMR page to access the interface for patient-generated data. In response to the clinicians' request, we also chose a dark theme to maintain consistency with the existing system.

We confirmed the six types of data, which can be classified into two categories (primary and outcome data), as discussed in the section above. The primary data area includes activity, food, and sleep data, and the outcome data area includes stress, weight, and blood pressure data. Every data type has a unique color to prevent confusion (Figure 3). There had been save buttons placed on each goal, but we reduced it to just one button, reflecting clinicians' comments that it was too confusing.

Holistic Summary Area

The holistic summary area is located at the top left, which is expected to help clinicians skim data quickly and choose the level of interpretation.

- ***The profile*** is provided as a bar at the top. It contains patients' basic information, such as name, sex, age, disease, and body mass index (BMI).
- ***The numerical summary*** consists of six boxes, which represent the average or the latest value of each data type. For the primary data, average values are displayed to catch a snapshot of a patient: average number of steps, food portion size and eating frequency, and sleeping duration. All the data boxes include the last goal number in a small font.
- ***The graph with multiple trend lines*** represents the relative trends of each data type. Due to the axis synchronization issue, the axes are not displayed. Instead, we define the lowest data point as zero and the highest as 100. This component helps clinicians cross-reference and compare the six types of data so that they can discover correlations between them.

Primary Data Area

The primary data area contains three data components. Each data component has four elements, including an individual data summary, detailed individual graph, reference values, and numeric input fields for goal setting.

- In ***the activity data*** component, there is a trend line graph for grasping the total daily number of steps. The heat map in the activity data component represents the intensity of exercise during four predefined time sections: morning, afternoon, evening, and night. Two input fields are provided to insert a goal number for the daily step count and a required duration of a high-level exercise per day.
- In ***the food data*** component, there is a bar graph representing the average portion size per day. The heat map represents the portion size for each time section. Additionally, the frequency of snack intake is provided with another tab for the trend line graph. There are four input fields to input frequency of meals, portion size per meal, time of eating, and frequency of snack intake.
- ***The sleep data*** component is different from the other primary data. The total sleep duration and wakeup/bedtime are represented with a unique type of trend graph with a bar element. A stacked bar graph is used to visualize the quality of sleep based on the duration of light sleep, deep sleep, and awakening. There are three input fields to set the bedtime, wakeup time, and total sleep duration.

Outcome Data Area

The outcome data are different from the primary data. There is only a summary of each data type, because these data do not have qualitative dimensions. They are usually cross-referenced with the primary data, so we chose different graph forms.

- ***Stress data*** is represented in the heat map to emphasize a remarkable change. Since individuals cannot control stress levels, there is no input field to set a goal.
- ***Weight data*** is visualized as a line graph with a reference line of the previous goal weight. There is a numeric input field to set a goal weight.
- ***Blood pressure data*** is visualized in a line graph, similar to weight data. There are two lines, the highest and lowest values, with dotted reference lines.

FIELD STUDY

We investigated in situ how DataMD helps the integration of data-driven consultation into the existing workflow.

Case study. In the field study, we aimed to trace how clinicians interact with DataMD and how it encourages clinicians to change over time. We employed the case study method, since we focused on tracking the variations between each patient, as well as the internal change in the clinician, over experience. A total of 32 medical checkups were observed within a month.

Recruitment. Due to the strict consent policies of certain departments, only one clinician (C1, otorhinolaryngology) participated in the field study. The clinician recruited patients interested in weight management. Most of them were suffering from chronic diseases, such as hypertension, hyperlipidemia, and sleep apnea. After deciding to participate in the study at the clinician's office, patients were informed about the overall process outside the office. The patients were provided with Misfit devices to log their steps and sleep data and a logger app to collect food, stress, weight, and blood pressure data for a month. They were asked to visit every two weeks to check their status and receive advice from clinicians. We funded their blood tests and three consultation visits. They were also rewarded with a $15 coffee card.

Among the recruited patients, we observed 26 checkups of 18 patients with their consent. Among the patients, eight of them visited twice in a month. Therefore, we could identify the change in the clinician's use of the interface with the same patient. In addition, we examined six cases without using our interface to compare and therefore identify the distinct role of the clinician interface, DataMD.

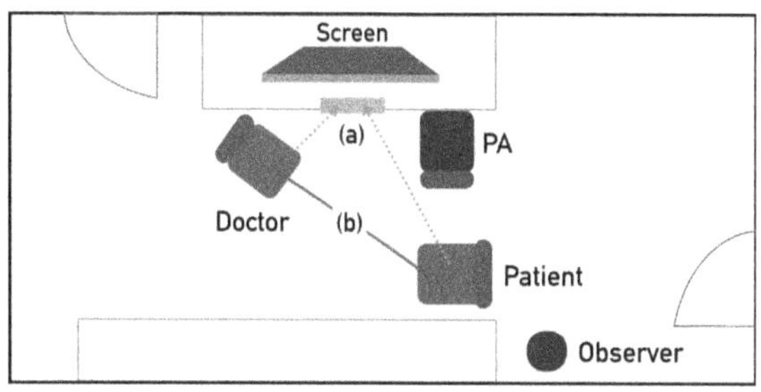

Figure 4. Layout of the observation site. The blue arrows (a) indicate line-of-sight if both patient and clinician want to. (b) infers an eye contact between patient and clinician.

Environment. The office was equipped with several medical machines. Patients sat on the prepared chair (Figure 4). A clinician and physician assistant (PA) were present in all cases. Researchers voice-recorded the conversations and counted the number of times the clinician and patient made eye contact, the clinician's interactions with the interface, and other nonverbal events.

Analysis. After transcribing all the voice-recording files and collecting field notes, we conducted a thematic analysis [10] using a supporting tool named Reframer [43]. We aimed to explore the roles of the interface based on the initial perspective. Thereby, the transcription and field notes were coded according to the three essential requirements.

Helping Clinicians Make a New Workflow Suitable for Data-driven Consultation

To our surprise, we observed that the physician created a new workflow around the interface. Three phases were identified: (1) skimming data, (2) asking questions, setting goals, and providing explanations, and (3) inputting goals.

The first step, skimming data, naturally integrated into the workflow. When the patient stepped into the medical office, the clinician engaged the patient in small talk and started using the interface to review self-logged data. When necessary, the clinician viewed lab reports or paper reports and briefly explained the results to the patient.

> ***Doctor:*** *Did you do a good job?*
> ***Patient:*** *I tried, but I was on vacation, so I couldn't take a lot of walks.*
> ***Doctor:*** *(while looking at the EMR) Your cholesterol levels were high, but the numbers are even higher than usual. (switches windows, looks at the numerical summary on DataMD) I see you wore the device every day; that's good. You don't exercise, you eat two meals on an average day, and you sleep pretty well. You have to look after your weight; it is excessive. Mainly, you need to walk more.*
>
> **— Case no. 1 (sex: male, age: 43, visit 2, duration: 09:12)**

The second phase was unique, because the clinician repeatedly asked questions, set goals, and provided explanations. After skimming information, the clinician asked for context, such as abnormal points or feelings. By doing so, the clinician set goals with the patient.

> ***Doctor:*** *(while looking at the line graph on the meal component) Your meal patterns aren't dramatic. I mean the pattern hasn't really changed from before. (clicks on the snack tab) Oh, I see that you've been munching a lot. (looks at patient)*
> ***Patient:*** *Snacks... Yeah, I feel a bit guilty. Well, I ate a lot of snacks during vacation.*
> ***Doctor:*** *Oh, I see, during vacation. But besides that, you're doing good. (looks at the heat map in the meal component) What about keeping our goal as before? Or maybe we can cut down on the snacks a bit? (looks at patient)*
> ***Patient:*** *Good, I'll cut my snacks in half.*
>
> **— Case no. 14 (sex: male, age: 37, visit 3, duration: 02:21)**

This process was repeated for each data type. However, goals were only set when the clinician decided that the patient needed behavior modification. By selectively setting goals, the clinician made effective use of the limited time.

During the third phase, the clinician did not type in the goals right away but waited until the end of the consultation and typed in all the goals at once, perhaps because typing during consultations would have hindered conversations with patients. This all-at-once behavior was possible, since the goals were simple numbers. The PA occasionally typed in comments in the EMR for the clinician. However, as for DataMD, the clinician took charge of setting goals and typing comments.

As a result, data reading and explaining integrated into the workflow as expected; however, goal setting did not. This conflict between DataMD and the existing EMR will be elaborated upon in the discussion section.

Improving Clinicians' Counseling Skills with Data

The clinician showed selective behavior with more experience with DataMD, which resulted in looking at the data he deemed important. This means that the clinician formed strategic approaches to read the data efficiently within a short period of time.

As the clinician's data-driven counseling skills improved, his overall strategy of using DataMD also changed. At first, he read the interface as intended by the designers. However, as time passed, he reduced the time spent on reading data and started to compare primary data and outcome data to interpret interrelations. The results of such interpretations were reflected in the goal setting.

> ***Doctor:*** *(while looking at the line graph in the activity component) Your activity graph drops significantly (looking at the line graph in the food component), but your food intake is high. Not just the food intake, but I think you should start working out. That's why you're not losing weight. I think you should walk about 10,000 steps a day... (looks at the patient)*
>
> **— Case no. 23 (sex: male, age: 39, visit 3, duration: 03:04)**

In addition, the data deemed important differed across patients. In the following case, the clinician interpreted high stress levels, along with changes in sleeping patterns, and recommended a medical test.

> ***Doctor:*** *Are you going through a lot of stress lately?*
> ***Patient:*** *Yes, the company isn't going well these days.*
> ***Doctor:*** *I see that your sleep satisfaction scores are lower than before. Is it because of the stress?*
> ***Patient:*** *I can't sleep these days, because of the pressure. I'm too tense.*
> ***Doctor:*** *First of all... I think you should find a way to lower the stress. Maybe you can take some walks... (while looking at the snack graph in the meal component) But you have to stop eating at night. Let's wait and see how the polysomnography goes.*
>
> **— Case no. 13 (sex: male, age: 35, visit 3, duration: 02:37)**

Data that was difficult to interpret, or which needed further experience, tended to be excluded. For instance, the trend summary was a relatively harder component to interpret. Therefore, the first two or three times, the clinician tried to read the trend summary graph as shown. However, after gaining experience, he excluded the trend summary graph and focused on interpreting other data. It implies that the clinician became skillful enough to manage his counseling time and select data content.

Facilitating In-depth Conversation

The DataMD interface supported and promoted doctor–patient communication within the medical office. The conversation naturally kicked off with the clinician asking the patient if they were logging data consistently. When the interface showed that the patient had diligently gathered data, the clinician would make eye contact with the patient and compliment them; otherwise, he would encourage them to do so.

> ***Doctor:*** *(looking at the whole screen) Overall, you're doing a great job on collecting data. You've been doing especially great on logging your meals (makes eye contact with patient). Great, this is amazing. (looks back at the screen) But I can see a few days are empty.*
>
> ***Patient:*** *Oh, I was a bit busy during the weekend. It's difficult to log everything.*
>
> **— Case no. 5 (sex: male, age: 39, visit 3, duration: 03:06)**

The DataMD interface became the center of attention, leading to the collaborative viewing of clinician and patient. Since the interface was on a fixed monitor screen, and the patient was sitting at a 45-degree angle (Figure 4), the interface was constantly viewable. The patients showed high interest in the fact that the doctor had reviewed the data that they had collected and actively asked questions.

> ***Doctor:*** *You're the best patient I've seen so far. (looking at the heat map in the meal component) You started to deliberately eat less at night compared to before you came to the hospital, right?*
>
> ***Patient:*** *Yes, yes. How did you know? (looks at the DataMD screen) Can you tell?*
>
> ***Doctor:*** *Yes, can you see? The colors are different. (looks at the patient) We can see it at a glance, because the color fades. You did a great job at eating less.*
>
> **— Case no. 3 (sex: male, age: 37, visit 2, duration: 04:40)**

The interesting point was that despite an additional screen (DataMD was used on top of the EMR), more eye contact was observed while using both systems compared to when the clinician only used the EMR. The clinician recursively asked patients questions, searched for new evidence, and tried to relate that to the medical values that appeared on the EMR. This shows that the use of an interface does not directly lead to less eye contact or human interaction. On the contrary, shorter appointments and less eye contact were observed in the existing workflow without DataMD. We also found that patients' responses were mostly short, such as yes/no, in the existing workflow. Therefore, it took longer to obtain the same context information (e.g., on vacations, lifestyle patterns). This result suggests that when appropriate data is shown, the doctor–patient relationship is enriched through increased eye contact and depth of conversation.

DISCUSSION

We now summarize and discuss the lessons learned from our design process.

Tensions Surrounding Data-driven Consultation

Our main objective was to design and explore the role of a comprehensive interface that connects data-driven consultation to existing workflows. In the process, we discovered that tensions surrounding workflow integration still remain. Even though a time-crunched clinician unfamiliar with patient-generated data was able to review many patients' data easily via the uniform interface, we found conflict between the new and old systems. We could not completely prevent the new interface from clashing with the existing system. For example, entering comments into the EMR and setting goals are similar tasks, yet they were separated in our implementation due to the differences in the reliability and completeness of lab data and patient-generated data. There has not been a proven correlation between patient-logged data and diseases, which makes patient-generated data less reliable [5, 19, 38]. In addition, clinicians chose not to view the two data types in the same window for the same reasons. In these circumstances, presenting patient-generated data with medically proven lab data may cause confusion among clinicians.

In short, this issue cannot be solved solely by designing an interface; rather, it requires collaboration among experts in both the medical and HCI fields. HCI researchers and medical experts can investigate whether patients' health could be improved by using patient-generated data.

DataMD as a Doctor–Patient Translator

The DataMD interface served to connect patients and clinicians like a translator. Specifically, the numeric input fields for setting goals promoted communication between patients and doctors. While setting goals, clinicians acquired a deeper understanding of their patients' behaviors and thoughts. We observed that adjusting and setting goals affected both clinicians and patients. Patients explained their status and expressed their opinions to adjust the goals, which motivated patients to achieve them [2, 33, 36, 41]. Further studies are needed on the patient side, as we were unable to conduct a deep inquiry into the patients.

We believe this observation provides several ideas for further research. First, the way in which patients are influenced by exam-room goal adjustments should be investigated. A one-sided order process, as in a conventional medical practice, can make patients too dependent on clinicians' instructions [34, 40]. Patients should be experts on their data and be able to adjust goals and change their habits independently [40]. Increasing goal type flexibility is strongly recommended to encourage patients to actively express their preferences and interest in their data. For example, the current goal of activity is only represented by steps, so patients cannot reflect their preferences, such as for swimming or cycling. It reduces not only patient interest but also their effort to adjust goals. Therefore, HCI researchers have to support both clinicians and patients by designing flexible clinician interfaces and self-tracking tools that promote in-depth conversations [29].

Second, it is necessary to consider how the adjusted goal in the exam room would be delivered to patients. We designed DataMD, where clinicians can simply enter numbers to set goals without wasting time. Conveying goals via numbers is much more precise and reliable, whereas natural language is much more expressive and easier to understand [9]. Both methods have trade-offs. Thus, patients' perceptions of, and preference for, the interaction type should be examined.

Potential Risks of Using Patient-Generated Data in Clinical Settings

In this paper, the clinician could understand patients' status and provide advice to them through our interface, DataMD. However, there are several ethical issues that cannot be ignored. The typical problem is the risk of data misinterpretation, which can cause clinicians to endanger patients unwittingly. No correlations have been identified between certain diseases or symptoms and patient-generated data. It means that although clinicians carefully analyze and interpret patient-generated data, there is always a risk of making an erroneous decision. Therefore, both the technology and hospital policies should provide a safety net to lower that risk. For example, on the technology side, inventing algorithms to avoid mistakes could be a solution. On the hospital policy side, hiring experts on analyzing patient-generated data or educating nurses and PAs could prevent clinicians from making mistakes.

Another problem is the side effects of managing health via data. Patients might focus on just collecting data even if they continue to engage in unhealthy behaviors, because clinicians judge patients' status based on the data alone. For example, some patients could skip meals for convenience rather than eating healthy food. Clinicians should consider this kind of risk and encourage patients to talk about their difficulties with changing behaviors. Providing personalized recommendations also encourages patients to engage in healthy behaviors. Further research needs to investigate possible factors affecting patients' attitudes, such as clinicians' usage of data and changes in prognosis.

Disparity between Expectations and Actual Use

We found that consistent visualizations improved the clinician's counseling skills. This still leaves some points on ways of visualizing the data open to discussion.

The graph with multiple trend lines, which was strongly suggested by clinicians, gradually became less used over consultations, because it required time and effort to read and interpret the data. It was explained that a similar graph containing many vital signs, such as blood pressure and body temperature, was currently in use, so reading a graph with six lines would not be a problem. This was, however, the least-used component. The gap between their expectations and actual use was caused by the unfamiliarity of patient-generated data [1, 2]. Clinicians have learned enough about vital signs in medical school and the hospital to be able to read patterns and discover unusual points without effort. In addition, vital signs do not fluctuate much from one individual to another, making them easy to identify. On the other hand, clinicians do not have enough knowledge of patterns represented in patient-generated data. Patient-generated data change dynamically, unlike vital signs, which increases the confusion in interpretation [9]. In short, this implies that the unique characteristics of patient-generated data should be identified through further study.

CONCLUSION AND FUTURE WORK

Although many studies have identified the benefits of using patient-generated data in clinical settings, obstacles to adopting data-driven consultation remain. In this paper, we aimed to design a clinician interface to support data-driven consultation and investigate the role of the interface in situ. However, there are several limitations of this study. Further research is to be conducted, as we found that data-driven consultation influenced both clinicians and patients. Because we focused on the clinician's perspective in this paper, we decided to exclude 15 patients' interview data. Future work will cover the patient's side. In addition, we did not observe various clinicians due to the lack of consent. Although the case study of one clinician with 32 cases provided several insights, it should be refined and enriched by other cases.

Despite these limitations, we expect that our findings will offer insights for healthcare providers, designers, and HCI researchers to design a clinician interface. For future work, we plan to investigate both patients and clinicians under data-driven consultation to broaden our perspective and enrich our findings.

ACKNOWLEDGMENTS

This research was supported by a grant of the Korea Health Technology R&D Project through the Korea Health Industry Development Institute (KHIDI), funded by the Ministry of Health & Welfare, Republic of Korea (grant number: HI14C3213).

REFERENCES

1. Manal Almalki, Kathleen Gray, and Fernando Martin Sanchez. The use of self-quantification systems for personal health information: big data management activities and prospects. *Health information science and systems* 3, 1 (2015): 1. DOI=http://dx.doi.org/10.1186/2047-2501-3-S1-S1

2. Jessica S. Ancker, Holly O. Witteman, Baria Hafeez, Thierry Provencher, Mary Van de Graaf, and Esther Wei. 2015. "You Get Reminded You're a Sick Person": Personal Data Tracking and Patients With Multiple Chronic Conditions. *Journal of medical Internet research*. 17, 8 (August 2015): e202. DOI=http://dx.doi.org/10.2196/jmir.4209
3. Jessica S Ancker, Holly O. Witteman, Baria Hafeez, Thierry Provencher, Mary Van de Graaf, and Esther Wei. 2015. The invisible work of personal health information management among people with multiple chronic conditions: qualitative interview study among patients and providers. *Journal of medical Internet research* 17, 6 (June 2015):137. DOI=http://dx.doi.org/10.2196/jmir.4381
4. Ole A. Andreas, Anita Das, and Dag Svanæs. 2012. Mobile health IT: The effect of user interface and form factor on doctor–patient communication. *International journal of medical informatics* 81, 1 (January 2012): 12-28. DOI=http://dx.doi.org/10.1016/j.ijmedinf.2011.09.004
5. Jessica S. Ancker, Holly O. Witteman, Baria Hafeez, Thierry Provencher, Mary Van de Graaf, and Esther Wei. 2015. The invisible work of personal health information management among people with multiple chronic conditions: qualitative interview study among patients and providers. *Journal of medical Internet research* 17, 6 (2015). DOI=http://dx.doi.org/10.2196/jmir.4381
6. Geoff Appelboom, Melissa LoPresti, Jean-Yves Reginster, E. Sander Connolly, and Emmanuel PL Dumont. 2014. The quantified patient: a patient participatory culture. *Current medical research and opinion* 30, 12 (December 2014): 2585-2587. DOI=http://dx.doi.org/ 10.1185/03007995.2014.954032
7. Stinne Aaløkke Ballegaard, Thomas Riisgaard Hansen, and Morten Kyng. 2008. Healthcare in everyday life: designing healthcare services for daily life. In *Proceedings of the SIGCHI Conference on Human Factors in Computing Systems* (CHI '08). ACM, New York, NY, USA, 1807-1816. DOI=http://dx.doi.org/10.1145/1357054.1357336
8. Stefan Becker, Talya Miron-Shatz, Nikolaus Schumacher, Johann Krocza, Clarissa Diamantidis, and Urs-Vito Albrecht. 2014. mHealth 2.0: experiences, possibilities, and perspectives. *JMIR mHealth and uHealth* 2, 2 (April-June 2014): e24. DOI=http://dx.doi.org/10.2196/mhealth.3328
9. Frank Bentley, Konrad Tollmar, Peter Stephenson, Laura Levy, Brian Jones, and Scott Robertson, Ed Price, Richard Catrambone, and Jeff Wilson. 2013. Health Mashups: Presenting Statistical Patterns between Wellbeing Data and Context in Natural Language to Promote Behavior Change. *ACM Trans. Comput.-Hum. Interact.* 20, 5, Article 30 (November 2013), 27 pages. DOI=http://dx.doi.org/10.1145/2503823
10. Virginia Braun and Victoria Clarke. 2006. Using thematic analysis in psychology. *Qualitative research in psychology* 3, 2 (January 2006): 77-101. DOI=
11. Yunan Chen, Victor Ngo, Sidney Harrison, and Victoria Duong. 2011. Unpacking exam-room computing: negotiating computer-use in patient-physician interactions. In *Proceedings of the SIGCHI Conference on Human Factors in Computing Systems* (CHI '11). ACM, New York, NY, USA, 3343-3352. DOI=http://dx.doi.org/10.1145/1978942.1979438
12. Eun Kyoung Choe, Bongshin Lee, Matthew Kay, Wanda Pratt, and Julie A. Kientz. 2015. SleepTight: low-burden, self-monitoring technology for capturing and reflecting on sleep behaviors. *In Proceedings of the 2015 ACM International Joint Conference on Pervasive and Ubiquitous Computing* (UbiComp '15). ACM, New York, NY, USA, 121-132. DOI=http://dx.doi.org/10.1145/2750858.2804266
13. Eun Kyoung Choe, Nicole B. Lee, Bongshin Lee, Wanda Pratt, and Julie A. Kientz. 2014. Understanding quantified-selfers' practices in collecting and exploring personal data. In *Proceedings of the 32nd annual ACM conference on Human factors in computing systems* (CHI '14). ACM, New York, NY, USA, 1143-1152. DOI=10.1145/2556288.2557372 http://doi.acm.org/10.1145/2556288.2557372
14. Chia-Fang Chung, Jonathan Cook, Elizabeth Bales, Jasmine Zia, and Sean A. Munson. 2015. More than telemonitoring: Health provider use and nonuse of life-log data in irritable bowel syndrome and weight management. *Journal of medical Internet research* 17, 8 (August 2015): e203. DOI=http://dx.doi.org/ 10.2196/jmir.4364
15. Chia-Fang Chung, Kristin Dew, Allison Cole, Jasmine Zia, James Fogarty, Julie A. Kientz, and Sean A. Munson. 2016. Boundary Negotiating Artifacts in Personal Informatics: Patient-Provider Collaboration with Patient-Generated Data. In *Proceedings of the 19th ACM Conference on Computer-Supported Cooperative Work & Social Computing* (CSCW '16). ACM, New York, NY, USA, 770-786. DOI=http://dx.doi.org/10.1145/2818048.2819926
16. Sunny Consolvo, David W. McDonald, Tammy Toscos, Mike Y. Chen, Jon Froehlich, Beverly Harrison, Predrag Klasnja, Anthony LaMarca, Louis LeGrand, Ryan Libby, Ian Smith, and James A. Landay. 2008. Activity sensing in the wild: a field trial of ubifit garden. In *Proceedings of the SIGCHI Conference on Human Factors in Computing Systems*

(CHI '08). ACM, New York, NY, USA, 1797-1806. DOI=http://dx.doi.org/10.1145/1357054.1357335

17. Martin Dawes and Sampson Uchechukwu. 2003. Knowledge management in clinical practice: a systematic review of information seeking behavior in physicians. *International journal of medical informatics* 71, 1 (August 2003): 9-15. DOI= http://dx.doi.org/10.1016/S1386-5056(03)00023-6
18. Neelima Deshpande, Mary Publicover, Harry Gee, and Khalid S. Khan. 2003. Incorporating the views of obstetric clinicians in implementing evidence-supported labour and delivery suite ward rounds: a case study. *Health Information & Libraries Journal* 20, 2 (June 2003): 86-94. DOI=http://dx.doi.org/ 10.1046/j.1471-1842.2003.00422.x
19. Manon L. Dontje, Martijn de Groot, Remko R. Lengton, Cees P. van der Schans, and Wim P. Krijnen. 2015. Measuring steps with the Fitbit activity tracker: an inter-device reliability study. *Journal of medical engineering & technology* 39, no. 5 (2015): 286-290. DOI=http://dx.doi.org/ 10.3109/03091902.2015.1050125
20. Glyn Elwyn, Adrian Edwards, and Paul Kinnersley. 1999. Shared decision-making in primary care: the neglected second half of the consultation. *Br J Gen Pract* 49, 443 (1999): 477-482.
21. Deborah Estrin and Ida Sim. 2010. Open mHealth architecture: an engine for health care innovation. Science 330, 6005 (2010): 759-760. DOI=http://dx.doi.org/ 10.1126/science.1196187
22. Caroline Free, Gemma Phillips, Louise Watson, Leandro Galli, Lambert Felix, Phil Edwards, Vikram Patel, and Andy Haines. 2013. The effectiveness of mobile-health technologies to improve health care service delivery processes: a systematic review and meta-analysis. *PLoS Med* 10, 1 (15 January 2013): e1001363. DOI=http://dx.doi.org/10.1371/journal.pmed.1001363
23. Susannah Fox and Maeve Duggan. Tracking for health. *Pew Research Center's Internet & American Life Project*, 2013.
24. Gary Wolf - The Quantified Self. Video. (June 2010). Retrieved September 22, 2016 from https://www.ted.com/talks/gary_wolf_the_quantified_self?language=en
25. Valerie Gay and Peter Leijdekkers. 2015. Bringing health and fitness data together for connected health care: mobile apps as enablers of interoperability. *Journal of medical Internet research* 17, 11 (November 2015). DOI=http://dx.doi.org/10.2196/jmir.5094
26. Google Fit. Retrieved 2016 form https://www.google.com/fit/
27. Amanda Hall and Graham Walton. 2004. Information overload within the health care system: a literature review. *Health Information & Libraries Journal* 21, 2 (June 2004): 102-108. DOI=http://dx.doi.org/ 10.1111/j.1471-1842.2004.00506.x
28. Healthkit Apple Developer. Retrieved from https://developer.apple.com/healthkit/
29. Alastair van Heerden, Mark Tomlinson, and Leslie Swartz. 2012. Point of care in your pocket: a research agenda for the field of m-health. *Bulletin of the World Health Organization* 90, 5 (2012): 393-394. DOI= http://dx.doi.org/10.2471/BLT.11.099788
30. Institute for Health Technology. Transforming Health Care Through Big Data: Strategies for leveraging big data in the health care industry. *Institute for Health Technology*. 2013
31. Nicholas Huba and Yan Zhang. 2012. Designing patient-centered personal health records (PHRs): health care professionals' perspective on patient-generated data. Journal of medical systems 36, 6 (2012): 3893-3905. DOI=http://dx.doi.org/ 10.1007/s10916-012-9861-z
32. Eun-Young Jung, Jonghun Kim, Kyung-Yong Chung, and Dong Kyun Park. Mobile healthcare application with EMR interoperability for diabetes patients. *Cluster Computing* 17, 3 (November 2014): 871-880. DOI=http://dx.doi.org/ 10.1007/s10586-013-0315-2
33. Sandra K. Joos, David H. Hickam, Geoffrey H. Gordon, and Laurence H. Baker. 1996. Effects of a physician communication intervention on patient care outcomes. Journal of general internal medicine 11, no. 3 (1996): 147-155. DOI=http://dx.doi.org/10.1007/BF02600266
34. Yoojung Kim, Sookyoung Ji, Hyunjeong Lee, Jeong-Whun Kim, Sooyoung Yoo, and Joongseek Lee. 2016. "My Doctor is Keeping an Eye on Me!": Exploring the Clinical Applicability of a Mobile Food Logger. In *Proceedings of the 2016 CHI Conference on Human Factors in Computing Systems* (CHI '16). ACM, New York, NY, USA, 5620-5631. DOI=http://dx.doi.org/10.1145/2858036.2858145
35. Rober F. Kushner. 1995. Barriers to providing nutrition counseling by physicians: a survey of primary care practitioners. *Preventive medicine* 24, 6 (1995): 546-552. DOI=http://dx.doi.org/10.1006/pmed.1995.1087
36. Ian Li, Anind Dey, and Jodi Forlizzi. 2010. A stage-based model of personal informatics systems. In *Proceedings of the SIGCHI Conference on Human Factors in Computing Systems* (CHI '10). ACM, New York, NY, USA, 557-566. DOI=http://dx.doi.org/10.1145/1753326.1753409

37. John Lynn. 2015. Fitbit Data in the EMR? Retrieved from http://www.emrandehr.com/2015/11/03/fitbit-data-in-the-emr/

38. Maulik D. Majmudar, Lina Avancini Colucci, and Adam B. Landman. The quantified patient of the future: Opportunities and challenges. In *Healthcare* 3, (3): 153-156. Elsevier, 2015.

39. Stephane Meystre. 2005. The current state of telemonitoring: a comment on the literature. *Telemedicine Journal & e-Health* 11, 1 (February 2005): 63-69. DOI= http://dx.doi.org/10.1089/tmj.2005.11.63.

40. Sonali R. Mishra, Shefali Haldar, Ari H. Pollack, Logan Kendall, Andrew D. Miller, Maher Khelifi, and Wanda Pratt. 2016. "Not Just a Receiver": Understanding Patient Behavior in the Hospital Environment. In *Proceedings of the 2016 CHI Conference on Human Factors in Computing Systems* (CHI '16). ACM, New York, NY, USA, 3103-3114. DOI=http://dx.doi.org/10.1145/2858036.2858167

41. Ira S. Ockene, James R. Hebert, Judith K. Ockene, Gordon M. Saperia, Ed Stanek, Robert Nicolosi, Philip A. Merriam, and Thomas G. Hurley. 1999. Effect of physician-delivered nutrition counseling training and an office-support program on saturated fat intake, weight, and serum lipid measurements in a hyperlipidemic population: Worcester Area Trial for Counseling in Hyperlipidemia (WATCH). *Archives of Internal Medicine* 159, 7 (April 1999): 725-731. DOI=http://dx.doi.org/10.1001/archinte.159.7.725.

42. Bernardine M. Pinto, Henry Lynn, Bess H. Marcus, Judith DePue, and Michael G. Goldstein. 2001. Physician-based activity counseling: intervention effects on mediators of motivational readiness for physical activity. *Annals of Behavioral Medicine* 23, no. 1 (February 2001): 2-10. DOI=http://dx.doi.org/ 10.1207/S15324796ABM2301_2

43. Mashfiqui Rabbi, Min Hane Aung, Mi Zhang, and Tanzeem Choudhury. 2015. MyBehavior: automatic personalized health feedback from user behaviors and preferences using smartphones. In *Proceedings of the 2015 ACM International Joint Conference on Pervasive and Ubiquitous Computing* (UbiComp '15). ACM, New York, NY, USA, 707-718. DOI=http://dx.doi.org/10.1145/2750858.2805840

44. Reframer. Retrieved from https://www.optimalworkshop.com/reframer

45. Coline W. Rhodes, 2015. Fitbit data in the EMR? I don't think so! Retrieved November 2 from https://healthcareit.me/2015/11/02/fitbit-data-in-the-emr-i-dont-think-so/

46. Nancy K. Russell and Debra L. Roter. 1993. Health promotion counseling of chronic-disease patients during primary care visits. *American journal of public health* 83, 7 (July 1993): 979-982. DOI=http://dx.doi.org/ 10.2105/AJPH.83.7.979

47. Line Silsand and Gunnar Ellingsen. 2016. Complex Decision-Making in Clinical Practice. In *Proceedings of the 19th ACM Conference on Computer-Supported Cooperative Work & Social Computing* (CSCW '16). ACM, New York, NY, USA, 993-1004. DOI=http://dx.doi.org/10.1145/2818048.2819952

48. Moira Stewart, Judith Belle Brown, Heather Boon, Joanne Galajda, Leslie Meredith, and Michelle Sangster. 1999. Evidence on patient-doctor communication. *Cancer* 25 (1999): 30.

49. Mark Sullivan. 2015. Guess what? Doctors don't care about your Fitbit data. Retrieved August 15, 2015 from http://venturebeat.com/2014/08/15/guess-what-doctors-dont-care-about-your-fitbit-data/

50. Teresa Taft, Leslie Lenert, Farrant Sakguchi, Gregory Stoddard, Caroline Milne. 2014. Effects of electronic health record use on the exam room communication skills of resident physicians: a randomized within-subjects study. *Journal of the American Medical Informatics Association*: amiajnl-2014. DOI= http://dx.doi.org/10.1136/amiajnl-2014-002871

51. Athanasios Tsoukalas, Timothy Albertson, and Ilias Tagkopoulos. 2015. From data to optimal decision making: a data-driven, probabilistic machine learning approach to decision support for patients with sepsis. *JMIR medical informatics* 3.1 (2015): e11. DOI=http://dx.doi.org/10.2196/medinform.3445

52. Chris Welch. 2015. Major Los Angeles hospital enables Apple's HealthKit for 80,000 patients. Retrieved April 27, 2015 from http://www.theverge.com/2015/4/27/8502929/apple-healthkit-cedars-sinai-hospital

53. Peter West, Richard Giordano, Max Van Kleek, and Nigel Shadbolt. 2016. The Quantified Patient in the Doctor's Office: Challenges & Opportunities. In *Proceedings of the 2016 CHI Conference on Human Factors in Computing Systems* (CHI '16). ACM, New York, NY, USA, 3066-3078. DOI=http://dx.doi.org/10.1145/2858036.2858445

54. Nathan Zeldes and Neil Baum. 2011. Information overload in medical practice. *The Journal of medical practice management: MPM*. 26, 5: 314.

Crafting a View of Self-Tracking Data in the Clinical Visit

Helena M. Mentis[1], Anita Komlodi[1], Katrina Schrader[2], Michael Phipps[2], Ann Gruber-Baldini[2], Karen Yarbrough[2], & Lisa Shulman[2]
[1]Department of Information Systems, University of Maryland Baltimore County, Baltimore, MD, USA
[2]University of Maryland School of Medicine, Baltimore, MD, USA
{mentis, komlodi}@umbc.edu {kschrader, mphipps, abaldin, kyarbrough, lshulman}@som.umaryland.edu

ABSTRACT
When self-tracking encounters clinical practices, the data is reshaped by goals and expertise that exist within a healthcare framework. To uncover these shaping practices, we provided a Fitbit Zip step-count sensor to nine patients with Parkinson's disease. Each patient wore the sensor for four weeks and then returned for a clinical visit with their neurologist. Our analysis focuses on this first clinical visit after four weeks of data had been collected. Our use of conversation analysis of both talk and action makes visible the practices engaged in by both collaborative members to 'craft a view' of the data toward shared decision making. Our findings reveal the deliberate guiding of attention to specific views and interpretations of the data through both talk and actions and we explain how our systematic analysis has uncovered tools for the mutually beneficial crafting practices of the clinician and patient.

Author Keywords
Activity tracker; quantified self; self-tracking; perception.

ACM Classification Keywords
H.5.m. Information interfaces and presentation (e.g., HCI): Miscellaneous.

INTRODUCTION
For those with difficult-to-manage chronic conditions, aligning self-tracking data with health goals is a crucial step in sustaining healthful behavior. As self-tracking data is increasingly being integrated into electronic health record (EHR) patient portals the potential is there for bringing this data into the clinical office visit [34,36]. These new tools offer the possibility for relating the information that is generated during doctors' visits with the information from people's daily lives. In a sense, self-tracking is blurring the line between the home and clinic [9], and a challenge for the design and use of self-tracking tools is how to design for this bridging moment. For instance, the US-based EHR provider, EPIC, is now supporting patients to upload certain self-tracking data through the patient portal. But there is no indication that clinicians nor patients know how to incorporate this data during routine clinical visits. Despite incentives under the U.S. Affordable Care Act to support more data-driven medicine, questions still remain about what practices and tools needs to be in place so self-tracking data can be integrated into patient records and used to monitor health in a patient-centered manner. Self-tracking data needs to move beyond the rhetoric of simply being there to "inform" as that will be greeted as more work by clinicians. And yet there is a lack of evidence in how to support the discussion and use of this data in order to integrate it into clinical management of chronic conditions.

CHI 2017, May 06 - 11, 2017, Denver, CO, USA

ACM 978-1-4503-4655-9/17/05...$15.00
DOI: http://dx.doi.org/10.1145/3025453.3025589

This is a challenging question if you consider that when self-tracking encounters clinical practices the data is reshaped by goals and expertise that exist within a healthcare framework [34]. One can not simply fold self-tracking data into established clinical practices without some work on the part of both the patient and the clinician. For one, the data differs from what is reflected upon at home. For instance, one's multiple blood sugar readings when at home have very different implications on care trajectories when discussed during the clinical visit [32]. This is because of how the data is shaped and co-interpreted by both the clinician and patient [1,19–21,37]: an object of scrutiny may take on many different forms as a result of each of the different actors' viewpoints [31]. Data is only understood via manipulation and interpretation based on context and experience. This means that data viewed by oneself may transform and take on an entirely different meaning in a collaborative viewing full of negotiation and interpretation [1,20,37].

In our research program, we were motivated to explore the practices that emerge by both the patient and clinician in utilizing that data within a clinical visit. Although self-tracking practices as well as the integration of self-tracking data into the clinical sphere have been of great interest to the HCI community, the studies to date have not explored the talk and actions that surround the use of the data within the clinical realm [2,22,46]. Our immediate questions are not whether self-tracking data will be used in clinical healthcare settings or if it has some measurable effect on health outcomes (although this is an interest of ours in the long term), but *rather how is the presentation and shaping of self-tracking data enacted via talk and actions.*

These questions translate to our focus on the work required to *shape the data to engage in the co-construction of knowledge and shared decision-making*. In this paper, we show that clinicians and patients do not simply look at the data, but they engage in *crafting a view* towards some mutually agreed upon understanding. By 'crafting' we are building on the work of Mentis, et al. [28] who described this collaborative data usage process as a deliberate execution on what view of the data is of importance to invoke a particular view of the body and actions on the body to be shared. The data is visualized and configured in such a way that it conforms to the needs of the collaborator and thus plays an important role in the way the visualized data is discussed and acted upon [19][37]. Interactions with the visualization of the data does not simply highlight data as much as actually produce a particular view of the body. Thus, through crafting a view of the data during discussion, each collaborator is disciplining the data leading to a particular presentation towards a particular aim. Typically, this aim is to argue towards a particular co-interpretation of the data. We are specifically discussing how the dialogue and actions enacted by both the clinicians as well as patients have a shaping effect on what is attended to in the data visualizations as well as how that data is interpreted.

We provided a Fitbit Zip activity tracker to nine patients with Parkinson's disease – a group of patients that could significantly benefit from a regular walking practice. Each patient wore the sensor for four weeks and then returned for a follow-up appointment with their neurologist. The analysis presented here focuses on this first clinical visit after four weeks of data had been collected. Our use of conversation analysis of both talk and action makes visible the practices engaged in by both collaborative members to make sense of the data towards a shared care decision. Our findings reveal the deliberate guiding of attention to specific interpretations of the data through both talk and actions. We also show the discrepancy between the clinicians' actions on the data and the patients' 'hands off' nature with the physical data objects. Finally, we explain how this analysis has uncovered suggestions for designs of shared data viewing tools in the clinic to support crafting.

BACKGROUND

Self-Tracking Data within the Clinical Health Context

Advances in self-tracking technologies and infrastructure including health monitoring sensors, EHR patient portal integration, and web-based self-management apps have the potential to transform how people with chronic conditions manage their care. Yet there is still very little known about how to harness these opportunities to meaningfully enhance quality of care and self-management within the clinical visit [32,34]. Both patients and clinicians perceive self-tracking technologies as an opportunity to improve communication [2,46], however patients and clinicians are uncertain of the data's role in disease management [23,45]. With time, though, self-tracking data will increasingly be integrated into EHR patient portals and web-based apps. For instance, the University of Maryland Medical System EHR provider, EPIC, recently began to support data uploading from FitBit and Apple HealthKit sensors and plans to expand to a larger range of accelerometers in their next release.

With this future integration in mind, there has been an interest in understanding how self-tracking data can be usefully integrated into the clinical health context [2,22,46]. Of note is the work by Chung et al [6] who adopted the framework of boundary negotiating artifacts [25] to investigate how patient-generated data was transformed into different physical or conceptual forms to support collaboration. Their specific notion of inclusion artifacts – the data patients bring to the clinic visit – is the type of object we are investigating in this study. Around that object, we are exposing the talk and actions by each party that shape that data into a meaningful artifact. Chung et al [6] also uncovered in their study that patients were frustrated with not being able to focus on their most pressing questions. The authors state that this was uncovered a design opportunity to create goal-oriented visualizations or summaries to help focus the collaborative review. With the following study, we argue that the visualization itself is not at issue; rather it is the mechanism with which a collaborator has to craft a view of the data in order to guide the other's gaze. With our study, we are uncovering how each collaborator currently guides the gaze of the patient-clinician pair on the data in order to focus on questions of interest.

Co-interpreting Self-Tracking Data towards Shared Decision-Making

As the clinical sphere moves towards embracing 'messy' life data for more meaningful clinical encounters, there is also a shift in the way that knowledge and power are manifest in the clinical realm. This is particularly important to address as there is often negotiation and interpretation of data in clinical decision-making [1,19–21,37]. Studies show that health data is not self-evident and work must be done in order to use the data in practice. Despite the trajectory of technological innovations to reveal more information about the body, assessing its health and functions is still a matter of negotiation and interpretation [3,20,37].

In collaborative contexts, this is especially true as different experiences can significantly affect one's ability to 'see' the same data interpretation as well as communicate about it [27]. A stimulus that is held constant can still evoke different interpretations due to it being embedded in a context as well as the experiences and knowledge one brings to bear on the perception of what is before them [15]. All seeing of data is interpretation – no matter if you are a patient on which the data is being collected or a clinician whose training provides medical explanation and data reading skills – and interpretations differ in how they are linked to past experiences, motivations, and the role of each person [31].

As self-tracking data begins to be more accepted in medical context, we are then at risk of blindly reproducing traditional disease-centric assumptions and power asymmetry in the discussion and use of that data [42]. A solution to sidestep that problem is to support the co-construction of knowledge [42]. Mentis et al [30] highlighted the iterative and constructive data interpretation acts that are reliant on an alignment of shared perceptions between clinician, patient, and lay caregiver – that which they termed *co-interpretation*. In their follow-up work [29] they further showed the changes that occur in clinical co-interpretive practice by the use of a simple movement sensing system in clinical practice. Some of these changes were of benefit such as the sensor validating the patient's felt experience and the clinician using the data as prompts for patients to further reflect and share their perceptions. However, there were also drawbacks to the introduction of a movement sensor to the co-interpretive practice, most notably the raising of the sensor data as embodying truth as well as the clinicians providing their own interpretation of the data before allowing for patients to form and articulate their perspective. These are both benefits and concerns we wished to observe within the context of self-tracking data – data collected outside of the clinic walls and of which the movements were not directly observed by the clinician.

Daily Walking for Patients with Parkinson's Disease

With this study, we are particularly interested in activity monitors and, in particular, those that provide a daily step-count. Numerous studies show the feasibility and benefits of step-count monitors across many chronic conditions [8,10–13,26,33,39,44]. The Parkinson's disease (PD) patient population can attain considerable health benefits from a daily walking practice. PD is the second most common neurodegenerative disorder and the incidence of PD is likely to increase as the proportion of older individuals within the population increases [43]. PD symptoms show individual differences, disease progression is variable, and the degree of disability can fluctuate over the course of a day. As the disease progresses, people with PD experience losses in mobility and independence and subsequently a strong negative impact on the quality of life of patients and their family caregivers. Daily walking for patients with Parkinson's disease is 1) pivotal to maintain independence, 2) improves diverse symptoms of chronic conditions and 3) is a key component of prevention – delaying disability and reducing risks of disease progression [5,41]. However, sedentary behavior and poor adherence to activity/exercise recommendations are overwhelmingly persistent problems [24,35].

METHODS

The fieldwork was performed at a neurology ambulatory center associated with the University of Maryland Medical System. We obtained Institutional Review Board approval from the University of Maryland Baltimore Office of Human Research Protections and participants consented before beginning the study. Currently, the neurologists in this center discuss the importance of regular activity and ask their patients about their activity levels, but the discussions are not substantial and the physicians are concerned that the patients are not aware of how little they are actually walking. The following study was an opportunity for the neurologists to have some real data during these discussions.

Study Design

Patients were recruited after their regularly scheduled clinic visits with their neurologist. If they expressed interest, they were provided with a Fitbit Zip (that they would keep as a thank you for participating in the study) and a thorough explanation and walkthrough by the research coordinator on how to use the activity tracker. The patient would log-on to the Fitbit website with their own email address and a self-assigned password, which they then would share with the research coordinator for her to use to download the data at the end of the study. At the end of this session the patients were also provided with a document explaining how to use the activity tracker and how to regularly sync the activity tracker data with their app or the web.

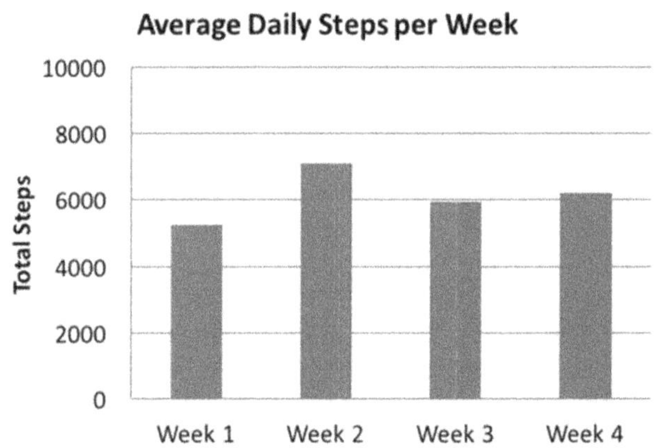

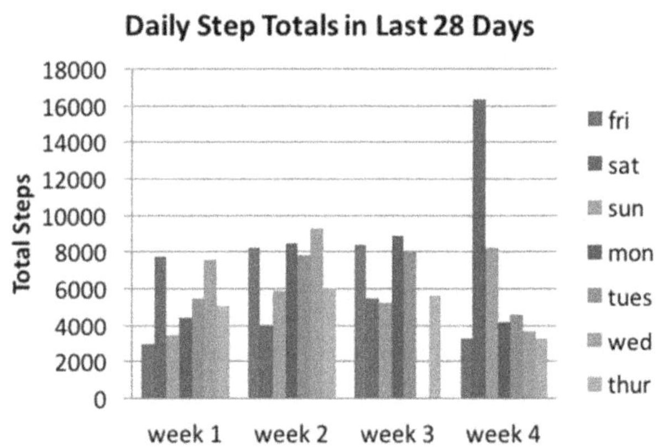

Figure 1. Weekly and Daily Step-count Graphs. Each clinician-patient session was provided these two graph views created from their downloaded Fitbit Zip data.

Table 1. Patient Demographics

	P1	P2	P3	P4	P5	P6	P7	P8	P9
Age	67	57	55	65	66	59	70	64	53
Gender	Male	Male	Male	Female	Female	Female	Male	Male	Female
Neurologist	DR1	DR1	DR2	DR2	DR2	DR1	DR2	DR2	DR2

For four weeks, the patients wore the activity monitor and had access to view their step count data on their personal tablet, phone, or computer of their choice. Patients then returned for an office visit with their neurologist to discuss the data. Due to the length of time between regularly scheduled meetings (typically a 3-6 months' time period), these 1-month follow-up office visits were scheduled for the sole purpose of discussing the activity tracker data. Thus, the office visits were scheduled for only 10 minutes.

During these visits, the clinician and patient were seated in a private clinic room and provided with two graphs that would be similar to planned presentations of self-tracking data within EMR systems such as EPIC: a daily step-count view and a weekly average step-count view (Figure 1). Although the patients had access to their data through the Fitbit apps or web interface, the neurologist had not seen the data prior to the office visit and neither the patient nor the neurologist had seen these specific aggregate graphs. The patient-clinician pair were presented with two copies of these graphs in cases where both the patient and clinician desired their own view.

Study Participants

The patient inclusion criteria for the study was: 1) Idiopathic Parkinson's disease diagnosed by a movement disorders specialist, 2) ability to walk with or without a cane, 3) optimization of anti-parkinsonian medications, 4) successful completion of the Evaluation to Sign Consent. The patient exclusion criteria included: 1) presence of aphasia, 2) patients requiring use of a walker or human assistance, 3) presence of active/unstable medical conditions, 4) non-fluent in English. A total of nine patients were recruited.

Two attending neurologists who specialized in PD were recruited for this study. This was a targeted recruitment as both neurologists see the most Parkinson's patients in the clinic and are interested in motivating their patients to increase their walking behavior. They had little experience, though, with including and discussing patient-generated data as their current patients either do not use self-tracking technologies or do not bring the data to their appointments.

Table 1 describes the patient demographics and which neurologist conducted the follow-up session. Throughout the findings, we refer to patients with the code PT#, referring to the patient number that is found in Table 1. Likewise, DR# refers to one of the two neurologist.

Data Collection

We employed observations, video recordings, and field notes for analysis. We also had the opportunity to ask questions of the clinicians following the assessments to further clarify and provide insight with what we observed during the clinical appointments. Video recordings were used for systematic action analysis. We positioned a video camera on a shelf over the desk pointing down to capture actions and talk while not capturing faces. Video recordings included discussions of the graphed Fitbit data between patients, clinicians, and any caregivers that may be present. As a further step in data collection and validation, we employed member-checking throughout the study by discussing our interpretations with the clinicians.

Data Analysis

For the evaluation of the captured videos, we followed the analytical practice outlined in detail in Heath, Hindmarsh, and Luff [16]. We began by conducting an ethnomethodologically-informed Conversation Analysis [18]. This entailed a detailed Conversation Analysis transcription that captured utterances, pauses, inflection, and overlap as well as a notation of visible conduct as outlined by Goodwin [14] and Heath & Luff [17].

We then engaged in an iterative open-coding method that categorized the resulting practices until clear themes were revealed. Our focus for this analysis was around uptake and use of the data as a resource for co-interpretation. We progressively refined and compared concepts to one another to gain internal coherency. We achieved this by focusing the analysis on how the clinicians, patients, and caregivers assessed and communicated about motor and functional ability based on the use of the data, talk and body language. The practices entailed by the clinicians were interpreted as needs for the data in care practices while the challenges identified were interpreted as opportunities for sensors in facilitating co-interpretation practices.

RESULTS

Despite the patient-clinician pair viewing the same data throughout the session, there were three different ways that the data was taken up and shaped to inform the conversation. Each of the following three sections corresponds to one of these three different crafting moments. As our motivation was to explicate the talk and action that come together in these uses of the data – this is not achieved with one quote, but rather a series of action and talk. Thus, we present our findings as vignettes from our observed data, each illustrating key moments for the co-interpretive process of self-tracking data use. The examples provided are indicative of these data use moments, but are by no means the only occurrences witnessed – these are clear trends seen across our data sample.

Co-Interpreting the Data Outliers

When presented with the data for the first time, it was understandable that the first characteristic the clinician would highlight in the dialogue were the data outliers. These were either high or low step counts that perceptually popped out. Thus, clinician typically began with the Daily Step-Count graph. This is the graph that presented the total step-count for every day in the prior four weeks. Oftentimes it revealed these outliers had nothing to do with the patient's motivation, or lack thereof, to walk. More often these anomalies were due to some intricacy of life. For instance, the following patient's high days were entirely due to the ebb and flow of his work.

1 DR1 ((Leans over graphs)) Let's see if there's any patterns that we can se::e at all_ (0.2) It seems like (0.2) on that one Saturday you >kind of took it a little< easier maybe(,) but otherwise it was >pretty consistent around< the 10,000 >which is the recommendation<(.) (0.2) [Wow this is amazing, here you reached 20,000 steps on one day(,)]
[((points to day with pen, hovers))] 2.0

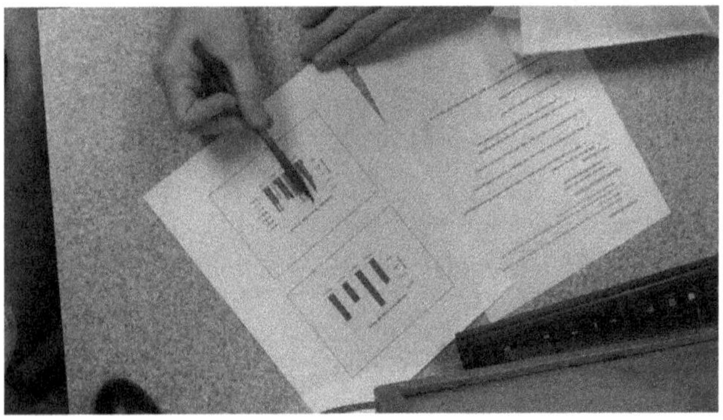

2 PT2 I know what day that was(.)
3 DR1 What was that(?)
4 PT2 We had a lot of deliveries that day, hospital beds and chairs_ I deliver medical supplies_ That one day there, we were pretty well swamped(.)
5 DR1 OK(.) So you did lots of walking clearly_
6 PT2 Yeah(.)
(2.0)
7 DR1 >That's right(.)< So you're still working full time right(?)
8 PT2 Yeah(.)

In the first half of this vignette, we see the clinician identifying a very high step count on one day and this revealed how the patient's job played an important part in the amount of walking he was achieving. Later in the session, the clinician had turned his attention to the Weekly Step-Count graph – this presents each of the four weeks as an average daily step-count. He is now beginning to see the impact of the patient's uneven work schedule on his walking behavior and brings into focus outliers in the averages asking how they are being affected by this factor.

50 DR1 [What do you think ((Points to Weekly Step-Count Graph))]

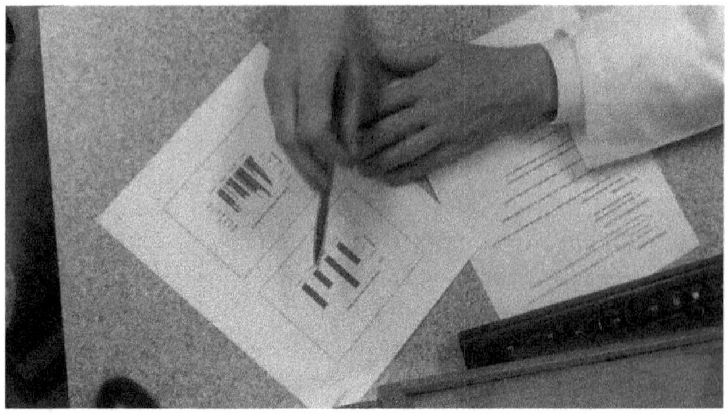

(1.5) were the factors that made you a little less active maybe in the third and the fourth week(?) Was it just not as busy [at work(?)]
51 PT2 [>Not as busy<], probably(.) That would almost have to be::e, it was slow for a few days(.) (0.2) It runs in spurts(.) Some weeks >we're really busy< and then other weeks we're not real busy it depends on what we've got to do_=
52 DR1 In your free time, unrelated to your work, how much physical activity do you do then?=
53 PT2 Mmm::mm Not a lot(.)

Here the outliers identified in the Daily Step-Count graph and the Weekly Step-Count graph came together to spur a discussion regarding activity outside of work – i.e. activity that is self-motivated by the need to maintain one's mobility due to the PD as opposed to required activity due to one's job. The patient was not consciously aware of how much he was walking overall, but, more specifically, he was not aware of the impact his job had on the amount of activity he was and was not getting. The clinician guided the review of the data by calling attention through both talk and action to the daily step count and then the weekly step count. Along with the conversation around the significant highs and lows that were evident in the presented data the patient was able to contribute his knowledge towards specific moments of interpretation to provide a better understanding of his walking behavior in the context of his life. What is important is that this guided use and co-interpretation of the data began to emerge for the clinician as well as the patient and highlighted a problem with the patient's activity level that might have been missed had they been simply discussing average over the week or month. Addressing one's self-motivated walking behavior early, while one is still fairly functional, is an important step in maintaining activity as the disease progresses.

Having one variable in one's life that would impact the data so noticeably was a bit of an anomaly for our data set. What we saw happen much more often was a mix of various life factors that had some fairly large step-count impacts. With the following patient, his low days were primarily linked to a vacation while his high days were due to being back into the routine of work and after work exercise.

```
29 DR1  Overa::ll >we can see that< there are
   some days that are (0.2) lower(,) Like
   [here green is (0.5) Thursday(.)]
   [((Points to Daily Step-Count graph))]
```

```
   But then the thi::rd week on Thursday is
   >your highest day in fact<. What is your
   explanation [for days that are a little
   lower or higher(?)
30 PT3          [Well, I can explain that easy
   enou::gh is week 2 ((Gestures to graphs))
   that very, very low Thursday, that was
   the drive day home(.) That accounts for
   being fairly sedentary in a vehicle and
   then when you do get home, you don't do
   too much to make up for that (0.2) or at
   least I didn't. Then u::m the previous
   Thursday ((Gestures to graphs)) on week
   1, was one of those days where I think
   largely, we did our fishing(.) That
   started with our little fishing trip, so
   I was out on a lake in a boat for a good
   part of the day and then when I wasn't, I
   was recuperating from being out in the
   boat because that takes it out of you,
   you know. You're in the sun all day.
   You're having fun, but nevertheless, all
   that stuff. Then that third week
   ((Gestures to graphs)) where Thursday was
   (0.5) higher than average days in
   general, I think was just a (0.5) typical
   work day along with some after work
   exercise or activities where we did some
   walking and running in addition to the
   routine of work(.)
```

At the start of this vignette the clinician called attention to specific days in the Daily Step-Count graph through both talk as well as explicitly pointing to the graph. This then subsequently set the stage for the patient to highlight his own experience for each of the days in question. Throughout this interchange, the patient is highlighting that it is not his internal motivation to walk or not, but the realities of leisure and work that had led to the outliers.

However, understanding of anomalies was not very informative with regards to devising walking strategies and goals. It only provided small snapshots of understanding that might not be very informative going forward. For instance, incidents we saw such as a vacation in August, a family death, forgetting one's Fitbit, or bad medication reactions are all singular life events that do not address how the patient is managing to integrate walking into their lives. What we see next is how the clinician begins to shape the way the conversing pair identify a walking *trend*.

Building Up the Story from Trends

After a review and discussion of data outliers, the clinicians would turn once more to the data and begin to look for trends. This might entail the Weekly Step-Count graph view at this point or still the Daily Step-Count graph. Whichever data they took up, this was typically led by the clinician who was seeing the data before them. But the process of co-interpretation was also engaged in by the patients who were adding their perception of what they sensed from their lived experiences as well as what they saw in the data.

In the following vignette we see the clinician begin to craft a view of a trend based on days of the week. Her use of the pen is meant to specifically guide the eye of the patient to see and confirm this day-based trend.

```
13 DR2  When we look at the day by da::y
   graphs the (0.2) one consistent thing
   that pops o::ut to me is that the
   [orange bars are consistently, even in
   recent weeks, >I don't know about the
   week five here, but in week three, week
   four, and week two, they're the low]
   [((Points to each orange bar on the Daily
   Step-Count graph))]
```

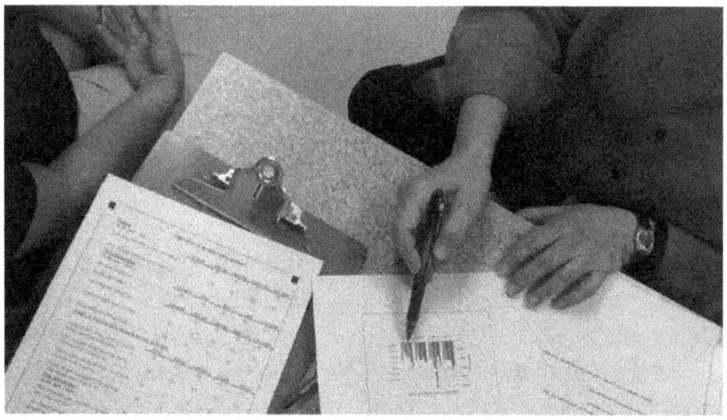

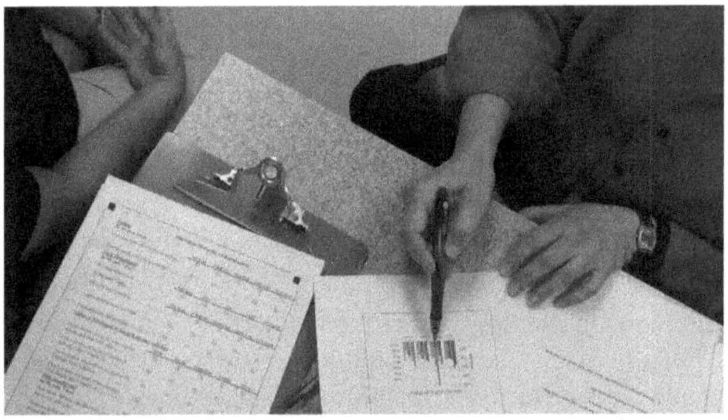

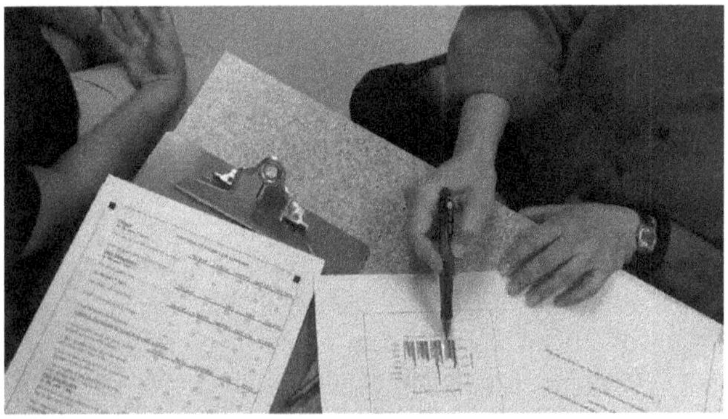

```
   and that's Sunday so Sunday was=
14 PT4  >I probably do< less on Sunday. I
   might read a lot or you know_
   DR2  I mean it's good to know that because
   here is the average ((Points to Weekly
   Step-Count graph))so even if we focused
   on days where you are low in order to try
   to   [focus on that(.)]
15 PT4  [Well there       ] ((Gestures to
   Weekly Step-Count graph)) are many days
   when I want to go out and wa::lk but when
   the medication wears off it's like I'm a
   little shaky and my right foot >kind of<
   like dra::g you know I'm like almost
   limping kind of(.) When I'm like that
   (0.5) there's not much I can do. I mean,
   I can do some things-
```

We first see in this vignette the clinician noticing a small pattern with Sundays being a low day. She points to each of the Sundays on the Daily Step-Count graph for the patient to see the relative difference. The patient adds that those are most likely low days due to her desire for leisure. The clinician then refers to the weekly averages stating that the Sundays may be having the unintended effect of an overall low average step-count. But this is where the patient moves the conversation in the direction of a barrier that is really causing the problem for her – her chronic illness and the ineffectiveness of her medication. This is a common problem when a patient has been on levodopa for a few years – the medication will not last as long as it had before and this requires a closer spacing of medication being taken or higher dose. This discussion again brings up that overall trends are not due to one's lack of motivation, but rather a problem associated with one's health condition. It was the change in shaping the way the data was viewed that is interesting here, though. Whereas the clinician wanted to see the trend in the daily total step count and deduce that as the cause of the low weekly averages, it is the patient who wanted to change the way the weekly averages were seen. She wanted to highlight how the weekly averages were due to her medication problems and that was a pervasive underlying problem not linked to any one day.

Identifying trends though was not an easy task. Anomalies 'popped' out and were usually better remembered. Trends is where the real work began between the patient and clinician. This required both parties to feel they had something to contribute to the conversation. It required both parties to be looking at the same data in the same manner. In the following vignette we see how difficult the identification of a trend can be for the patient that is aware of how many different life variables come into play, but has no way to organize them and share them with her clinician. Despite specific points of data called out and a trend beginning to emerge, the patient is still unable to link what she is seeing to what she is experiencing.

```
41 DR2  Then it looks like overall on your
   weekends, you tend to walk less(.) Do you
   think that that's accurate(?)
   [That's your orange bars-((Points to each
   orange bar on the Daily Step-Count
   graph))]
```

```
42 PT5  Right(.)
43 DR2  And the [blue before it(.)          ]
                [((Points to last blue bar on
   the Daily Step-Count graph))]
```

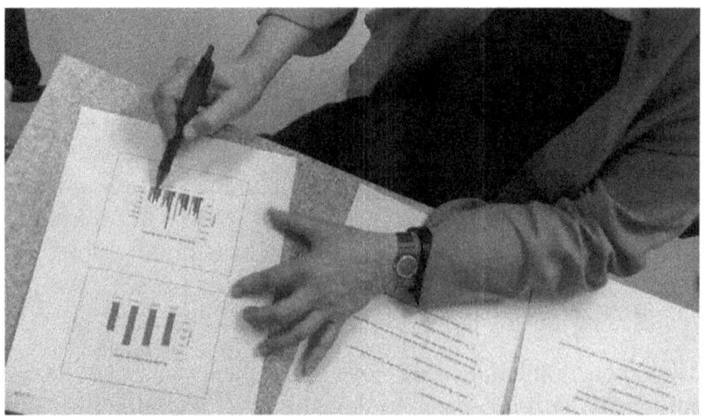

You see how those tend to be- Because out here is actually Tuesday(.) Tuesday could be quite low. So you see any patterns there or you just really can't make head nor tail out of it(?)
44 PT5 I don't really see a pattern^ Although I would like to. I'm a very (2.0) organized neat(.) I like repetition of things and all(.) I don't feel like I have my ducks in a row yet(?) For the summer(?) There's too many variables(.) With vacation and-
45 DR2 Also with your medicine problems(.)
46 PT5 With the medicine problems(.)

As we had seen with PT4, other factors get in the way of regular walking. Although the clinician used the same tactic as she had with PT4, pointing to each of the bars she wanted to highlight as a trend, the patient felt she had nothing to offer in terms of an understanding of that data trend. Instead this patient directly spoke of the challenges in seeing some patterns in her data; particularly as there were other life events occurring (i.e. vacation breaks) and health problems (i.e. a new medication making her feel ill) causing so many anomalies in her data. In fact, this was still very useful information as the trend was most likely not laying within the graphs, but rather a confluence of events that caused high and low walking days. This in turn changes the focus when discussing walking strategies.

Identifying a Walking Strategy

It is understandable that up to this point, the data has been called upon within the discussion – it has been the focus of their interaction and actions were directed towards shaping what graph or bars the pair would attend to. But there is a point in each of these visits where the conversation shifts to discussing potential strategies for increasing walking. This is a point in the conversation where the same old recommendations could be trotted out by the neurologist. What we see instead is the identification of walking strategies that are attuned to the evolving interpretation of the data while still actively shaping what aspects of the data are under scrutiny.

Based on their experience to date, identifying a suitable step-count goal was fairly difficult for most of the patients. They looked at a goal as a maximum as opposed to something that was regularly achievable and maybe even oftentimes passable every day. This was a good opportunity to refocus the attention of the patient on what the data is showing them so far.

For instance, we had a number of patients that had significant health issues that were preventing them from walking as much as they would like. In the following vignette, we continue with PT4 who had medication problems preventing her from walking long distances. Through a further discussion she also indicated severe pain preventing long bouts of walking. The strategy posed by the clinician took into account that even shorter walking sessions spaced out over the day was more feasible for her. Then, later in the session, we see this knowledge coming into play when devising a suitable daily step goal.

49 DR2 What would you say(,)- based on the fact that >I mean your high day is obviously< 10,000(.) Your [low da::y is below 2,000 on a Sunday over here(.)] ((Points to Daily Step-Count graph))
What would you think would be a reasonable goal for you, as an average for the week(?)
50 PT4 Steps(?)
51 DR2 Yeah(.) (3.0)
52 PT4 Seven or eight(,) Seven(?)
53 DR2 Seven would be really (0.2) great(.) I think that we should say five. Pick a practical goal for you that you could really with the pain-
54 PT4 That I would achieve in short-
55 DR2 That you could really achieve(.)
56 PT4 ((Leans over and looks at graphs)) Well, then I guess it would be five(.)
57 DR2 Five would be good. See five is over [here
[((Points to Y axis on Daily Step-Count graph))]

so still it's the minority of days(.) See (0.5) [if I put a line across here,]
[((Draws invisible line with retracted pen tip on the Daily Step-Count graph))]

it's the minority of days that you hit
five (0.5) you know so-

We begin this vignette with the clinician using talk and gesture to highlight the lowest daily step counts as a means to devise an attainable walking strategy. The patient, though, aims much higher than the clinician had in mind so her attempts at shaping the conversation had not been met. So he suggests another number which the patient agrees to as well. However, at this point, the clinician uses the data to highlight *why* this number is an attainable goal. She uses her pen to draw an imaginary line across the data at the goal they just agreed upon. This makes visible for the patient how the prior four weeks' data would fall within that goal.

Compared to our prior vignette, in the following vignette, both the clinician and the patient use the data to support their argument through both talk and gestures.

28 DR2 What do you think would b::e based on
your knowledge now- what do you think
would be a good goal for you to consider
for activity(?)
29 PT9 In terms of steps(?)
30 DR2 Yeah(.)(4.0)
31 PT9 Probably 15,000 steps a day would be
a good reach for me(.) >I think there's
one< or two days ((Gestures to Daily
Step-Count graph)) that I made 15,000
steps and I was very pleased with that(.)
32 DR2 That is a big goal(.)
33 PT9 I think all I would have to add to my
daily routine would be a serious walk
(0.5) every day(.)
34 DR2 It's always important when you set a
goal it has to be a realistic goal(.)
Otherwise, you (0.2) can be really (0.2)
disincentivized by really not reaching
your goal(.) Probably you want to do that
in phases-
35 PT9 Okay well shall we knock it down to
10,000 a day then(?)
36 DR2 Yeah(.) Yeah(.) Let's do that(.) But
if you reach 10,000 a day
37 PT9 [((Picks up shared graphs))]
38 DR2 [at least three days a week] (0.5) I
would think that that was quite good(.)
[((Picks up second copy of graph))]
[>Let's see what you're doing here.<]
This is the 10,000 mark(.) There was,
week two you did that. You reached 10,000
or more.
39 PT9 Mm-hmm^
40 DR2 Week four(.) Week three(.) Actually
you reached 10,000 three days a week
almost every week except for week one(.)

We begin this vignette by seeing the patient use the data as evidence of her ability to achieve a 15,000 step count. She uses both talk and gesture to call attention to these points on the graphs – lending evidence to be co-interpreted by the clinician. The clinician then provides her assessment of that number as being a large goal and perhaps a lesser number is more incentivizing. When they agree on 10,000 steps per day, the patient picks up the graphs to better read them based on their ongoing discussion. This was a unique moment that we did not see with our other patients. This then leads to the clinician picking up the second copy of the graphs and point out on the Weekly Step-Count graph that her average step count was above that step-count goal. She then continues to turn their attention to the Daily Step-Count graph and point out how each week had at least a few days of reaching that goal. This shared use and shaping of the data through talk and actions is how a walking strategy evolved in a co-interpretive practice.

DISCUSSION

In this study of self-tracking data use during clinical visits, we have foregrounded the talk and actions that bring various aspects of the data into focus for the collaborative pair to interpret and act upon together. We wanted to reveal the work that is conducted beyond simply looking at the data 'to be informed' in order to make the data clinically relevant. We showed that the same data comes into being three different ways towards achieving co-interpretation in the clinical visit. More importantly, we have shown how crafting a view of the data through talk or actions turns the data into a resource for these moments in order to be able to collaboratively identify health strategies and goals. This work constitutes the difference between simply looking at the data to one of co-construction and integration of the data.

It is important to note that all of our participants coincidently did not have prior experience with an activity tracker. Although we did not capture their engagement with the Fitbit app or website during the intervening four weeks, most participants mentioned they looked at their step count every day, but did not engage in looking at trends on their own via the app or website. This is important as this means the majority of the interpretation practices were conducted in the clinic. In this light, we are seeing an unequal distribution of crafting between the clinician and patient, both in terms of when data is brought in as evidence (e.g. "let's look at the data", "as you can see here") as well as how actions around the data shape the seeing practices of the pair (i.e. pointing or annotation). Despite the low-tech and equally available placement of the graphs, the interaction of the patients with the graphs was minimal beyond simply viewing. Crafting on that side entailed primarily talk. These moments were especially unique to the patient, though, as it was an opportunity for them to share their lived experiences to explain the data. On the clinician side, they had limited additional information to help co-construct the narrative, and so crafting involved talk around the data as well as physical actions to bring into focus what they saw in the data. In a longer study, we may see these trends change, though, as the patient or clinician may engage in trend analysis prior to the regularly scheduled clinical meetings.

Although this may seem like a effective and efficient idea, there is cause to not encourage that to occur. On the physician side, Anderssen et al [4] showed that the interpretation of implantable cardioverterdifibrillator data was a collaborative practice engaging both clinicians and patients and that, in a telemonitoring setup, much of that interpretation process could not be completed. In other words, the neurologists may not be able to do more than identifying outliers. As for patients, there is a danger to patients drawing incorrect conclusions from the data, which can be detrimental to their health[38]. However, there is some intervention that may be needed as we are seeing the same need for a patient to really look at and understand the data and form their own interpretation as was shown in Mentis, et al. [29]. Only then is the patient able to engage with the clinician in a co-interpretation process. We thought that the use of data that was captured outside of the clinic would have a more equalizing effect in the amount of time both parties needed to start creating their own understanding and so we would see an equal amount of crafting practices, but this turned out to not be so. We think these two studies are beginning to show a clear need for interventions that allow patients to craft a view of the data.

This is where we return to a discussion of the tools that bring the patient and clinician together into the practice of continually crafting a view of the data through actions and talk throughout the clinical session. Our analysis of the talk and actions used have uncovered mechanisms that could easily be enhanced through further interactive tools. In the following section, we explore two design opportunities for the presentation of self-tracking data in the clinical visit.

Tools for Crafting a View of Self-Tracking Data in the Clinical Visit

Our findings have led us to some clear design implications. However, by design, we do not entirely mean design of the visualization of data being reviewed during the clinical visit. The opportunity for changing the EHR interface is minimal. However, there are specific tools that would have an enhancing effect on the practices of crafting a view that we aim to support.

Annotation capability: Pointing and annotating were common actions taken up by both the clinician and patient. These are the tools that allow the data visualization to be disciplined. If these were interactive graphs, then we might expect further interactions such as zooming in or clicking on a week to highlight the week's days. However, the act of pointing and annotating should not be dismissed even in such interactive scenarios. Providing a digital pen for annotation and pointing allows for the display of these gestures on the graph as well as the capture and later review of these gestures. For instance, a patient could review what was circled or pointed to or where the line was drawn across on the graph when they returned home. Likewise, at the next follow-up visit, the clinician could review what they focused on last time and use those annotations to help craft a viewing of the newly collected data.

Personal views: Presenting personal and shared views is not a new concept for those within CSCW. However, we see this as a mechanism for facilitating patient access for data shaping through actions as well as talk. Providing the patient with a tablet, for instance, set to the patient portal view of the data, reduces the barrier for a patient to interact with the data. This would also likely reduce the patient being always led by the crafting of the clinician and instead allow the patient to shape the viewing practices at all. If also augmented by the annotation capability we outlined, such annotations on the tablet could then be transmitted to the clinician's view of the data and vice versa. Bringing these two functionality together would be a powerful opportunity to further investigate the changes in data crafting.

CONCLUSION

Many questions can to be debated around the usefulness of self-tracking data in clinical care, but we can not ignore that this data is indeed being brought into the clinical sphere and can have real value. This study took a systematic look at how *the presentation and shaping of self-tracking data is enacted via talk and actions* with an eye towards creating opportunities for fully co-constructive decision-making practices to emerge. Our data points to two tools that, although not technologically novel, may provide a needed support to the bridging between the mutually beneficial crafting practices of the clinician and patient.

REFERENCES

1. Margunn Aanestad. 2003. The Camera as an Actor Design-in-Use of Telemedicine Infrastructure in Surgery. *Computer Supported Cooperative Work (CSCW)* 12, 1: 1–20. http://doi.org/10.1023/A:1022492210898
2. Rikke Aarhus, Stinne Aaløkke Ballegaard, and Thomas Riisgaard Hansen. 2009. The eDiary: Bridging home and hospital through healthcare technology. In *ECSCW 2009*. Springer London, London, 63–83. http://doi.org/10.1007/978-1-84882-854-4_4
3. Morana Alac. 2008. Working with Brain Scans: Digital Images and Gestural Interaction in fMRI Laboratory. *Social Studies of Science* 38, 4: 483–508. http://doi.org/10.1177/0306312708089715
4. Tariq Andersen, Pernille Bjørn, Finn Kensing, and Jonas Moll. 2011. Designing for collaborative interpretation in telemonitoring: Re-introducing patients as diagnostic agents. *International Journal of Medical Informatics* 80, 8: e112–e126. http://doi.org/10.1016/j.ijmedinf.2010.09.010
5. Arlene S. Bierman. 2001. Functional status: the six vital sign. *Journal of general internal medicine* 16, 11: 785–6. http://doi.org/10.1111/j.1525-1497.2001.10918.x
6. Chia-Fang Chung, Kristin Dew, Allison M Cole, et al. 2016. Boundary Negotiating Artifacts in Personal Informatics: Patient-Provider Collaboration with Patient-Generated Data. In *Proceedings of the 19th ACM Conference on Computer-Supported Cooperative Work & Social Computing - CSCW '16*, 768–784. http://doi.org/10.1145/2818048.2819926
7. Terry Ellis, James T Cavanaugh, Gammon M Earhart, et al. 2011. Factors associated with exercise behavior in people with Parkinson disease. *Physical therapy* 91, 12: 1838–48. http://doi.org/10.2522/ptj.20100390
8. Terry Ellis, Nancy K Latham, Tamara R DeAngelis, Cathi A Thomas, Marie Saint-Hilaire, and Timothy W Bickmore. 2013. Feasibility of a virtual exercise coach to promote walking in community-dwelling persons with Parkinson disease. *American journal of physical medicine & rehabilitation / Association of Academic Physiatrists* 92, 6: 472-81–5. http://doi.org/10.1097/PHM.0b013e31828cd466
9. Brittany Fiore-Gartland and Gina Neff. 2015. Communication, Mediation, and the Expectations of Data: Data Valences Across Health and Wellness Communities. *International Journal of Communication* 9, 0: 19.
10. Claire F Fitzsimons, Graham Baker, Stuart R Gray, et al. 2012. Does physical activity counselling enhance the effects of a pedometer-based intervention over the long-term: 12-month findings from the Walking for Wellbeing in the west study. *BMC Public Health* 12, 1: 206. http://doi.org/10.1186/1471-2458-12-206
11. Lauren J. Frensham, Dorota M. Zarnowiecki, Gaynor Parfitt, Sharron King, and James Dollman. 2014. The experiences of participants in an innovative online resource designed to increase regular walking among rural cancer survivors: a qualitative pilot feasibility study. *Supportive Care in Cancer* 22, 7: 1923–1929. http://doi.org/10.1007/s00520-014-2177-4
12. Merrill Funk and E. Laurette Taylor. Pedometer-Based Walking Interventions for Free-Living Adults with Type 2 Diabetes: A Systematic Review.
13. Nicholas D Gilson, Guy Faulkner, Marie H Murphy, et al. 2013. Walk@Work: An automated intervention to increase walking in university employees not achieving 10,000 daily steps. *Preventive medicine* 56, 5: 283–7. http://doi.org/10.1016/j.ypmed.2013.01.022
14. Charles Goodwin. 1981. *Conversational Organization: Interaction Between Speakers and Hearers*.
15. Charles Goodwin. 1994. Professional Vision. *American Anthropologist* 96, 3: 606–633. http://doi.org/10.1525/aa.1994.96.3.02a00100
16. Christian Heath, Jon Hindmarsh, and Paul Luff. 2010. *Video in Qualitative Research*. SAGE Publications.
17. Christian Heath and Paul Luff. 2012. Embodied Action and Organizational Activity. In *The Handbook of Conversation Analysis*. John Wiley & Sons, Ltd, Chichester, UK, 281–307. http://doi.org/10.1002/9781118325001.ch14
18. Alexa Hepburn and Galina B. Bolden. 2012. The Conversation Analytic Approach to Transcription. In *The Handbook of Conversation Analysis*. John Wiley & Sons, Ltd, Chichester, UK, 57–76. http://doi.org/10.1002/9781118325001.ch4
19. Stefan Hirschauer. 1991. The Manufacture of Bodies in Surgery. *Social Studies of Science* 21, 2: 279–319. http://doi.org/10.1177/030631291021002005
20. Kelly Joyce. 2005. Appealing Images: Magnetic Resonance Imaging and the Production of Authoritative Knowledge. *Social Studies of Science* 35, 3: 437–462. http://doi.org/10.1177/0306312705050180

21. Bonnie Kaplan. 1995. Objectification and negotiation in interpreting clinical images: implications for computer-based patient records. *Artificial Intelligence in Medicine* 7, 5: 439–454. http://doi.org/10.1016/0933-3657(95)00014-W

22. Yoojung Kim, Sookyoung Ji, Hyunjeong Lee, Jeong-Whun Kim, Sooyoung Yoo, and Joongseek Lee. 2016. "My Doctor is Keeping an Eye on Me!" In *Proceedings of the 2016 CHI Conference on Human Factors in Computing Systems - CHI '16*, 5620–5631. http://doi.org/10.1145/2858036.2858145

23. Clemens Scott Kruse, Darcy A Argueta, Lynsey Lopez, and Anju Nair. 2015. Patient and provider attitudes toward the use of patient portals for the management of chronic disease: a systematic review. *Journal of medical Internet research* 17, 2: e40. http://doi.org/10.2196/jmir.3703

24. Lonneke ML de Lau and Monique MB Breteler. 2006. Epidemiology of Parkinson's disease. *The Lancet Neurology* 5, 6: 525–535. http://doi.org/10.1016/S1474-4422(06)70471-9

25. Charlotte P. Lee. 2007. Boundary Negotiating Artifacts: Unbinding the Routine of Boundary Objects and Embracing Chaos in Collaborative Work. *Computer Supported Cooperative Work (CSCW)* 16, 3: 307–339. http://doi.org/10.1007/s10606-007-9044-5

26. Suzanne M McDonough, Mark A Tully, Adele Boyd, et al. 2013. Pedometer-driven walking for chronic low back pain: a feasibility randomized controlled trial. *The Clinical journal of pain* 29, 11: 972–81. http://doi.org/10.1097/AJP.0b013e31827f9d81

27. Helena M. Mentis and Carolina Johansson. 2013. Seeing movement qualities. In *Proceedings of the SIGCHI Conference on Human Factors in Computing Systems - CHI '13*, 3375. http://doi.org/10.1145/2470654.2466462

28. Helena M. Mentis, Ahmed Rahim, and Pierre Theodore. 2016. Crafting the Image in Surgical Telemedicine. In *Proceedings of the 19th ACM Conference on Computer-Supported Cooperative Work & Social Computing - CSCW '16*, 742–753. http://doi.org/10.1145/2818048.2819978

29. Helena M. Mentis, Rita Shewbridge, Sharon Powell, Melissa Armstrong, Paul Fishman, and Lisa Shulman. 2016. Co-Interpreting Movement With Sensors: Assessing Parkinson's Patients' Deep Brain Stimulation Programming. *Human–Computer Interaction* 31, 3–4: 227–260. http://doi.org/10.1080/07370024.2015.1073592

30. Helena M. Mentis, Rita Shewbridge, Sharon Powell, Paul Fishman, and Lisa Shulman. 2015. Being Seen. In *Proceedings of the 33rd Annual ACM Conference on Human Factors in Computing Systems - CHI '15*, 511–520. http://doi.org/10.1145/2702123.2702342

31. Annemarie Mol. 2002. *The Body Multiple: Ontology in Medical Practice*. Duke University Press, Durham, NC.

32. Annemarie Mol. 2008. *The Logic of Care: Health and the Problem of Patient Choice*. Routledge, New York.

33. Marilyn L Moy, Nicole A Weston, Elizabeth J Wilson, Michael L Hess, and Caroline R Richardson. 2012. A pilot study of an Internet walking program and pedometer in COPD. *Respiratory medicine* 106, 9: 1342–50. http://doi.org/10.1016/j.rmed.2012.06.013

34. Gina Neff and Dawn Nafus. 2016. *Self-Tracking*. MIT Press, Cambridge, MA.

35. Marlies van Nimwegen, Arlène D. Speelman, Esther J. M. Hofman-van Rossum, et al. 2011. Physical inactivity in Parkinson's disease. *Journal of Neurology* 258, 12: 2214–2221. http://doi.org/10.1007/s00415-011-6097-7

36. Mitesh S. Patel, David A. Asch, Kevin G. Volpp, et al. 2015. Wearable Devices as Facilitators, Not Drivers, of Health Behavior Change. *JAMA* 313, 5: 459. http://doi.org/10.1001/jama.2014.14781

37. Amit Prasad. 2005. Making Images/Making Bodies: Visibilizing and Disciplining through Magnetic Resonance Imaging (MRI). *Science, Technology & Human Values* 30, 2: 291–316. http://doi.org/10.1177/0162243904271758

38. DA Redelmeier and A Tversky. 1996. On the belief that arthritis pain is related to the weather. *Proceedings of the National Academy of Sciences* 93, 7: 2895–2896.

39. Ronel Roos, Hellen Myezwa, Helena van Aswegen, and Eustasius Musenge. 2014. Effects of an Education and Home-Based Pedometer Walking Program on Ischemic Heart Disease Risk Factors in People Infected with HIV. *JAIDS Journal of Acquired Immune Deficiency Syndromes* 67, 3: 268–276. http://doi.org/10.1097/QAI.0000000000000299

40. Hanneke Schuurmans, Nardi Steverink, Siegwart Lindenberg, Nynke Frieswijk, and Joris P J Slaets. 2004. Old or frail: what tells us more? *The journals of gerontology. Series A, Biological sciences and medical sciences* 59, 9: M962-5. http://doi.org/10.1093/GERONA/59.9.M962

41. Lisa M. Shulman, Leslie I. Katzel, Frederick M. Ivey, et al. 2013. Randomized Clinical Trial of 3 Types of Physical Exercise for Patients With

Parkinson Disease. *JAMA Neurology* 70, 2: 183. http://doi.org/10.1001/jamaneurol.2013.646

42. Cristiano Storni. The politics of design in Sociotechnical dispositif. Reconciling Healthcare toward a future patient-centric perspective. In *Interact*.

43. Thomas Sue and Doug MacMahon. 2004. Parkinson's disease, palliative care and older people: part 2: by reading this article and writing a practice profile, you can gain ten continuing education points (CEPs). You have up to a year to send in your practice profile. Guidelines on how to write. *Nursing Older People* 16, 2: 22–28.

44. Jane E. Sullivan, Lauren E. Espe, Amanda M. Kelly, Laura E. Veilbig, and Mary J. Kwasny. 2014. Feasibility and Outcomes of a Community-Based, Pedometer-Monitored Walking Program in Chronic Stroke: A Pilot Study. *Topics in Stroke Rehabilitation* 21, 2: 101–110. http://doi.org/10.1310/tsr2102-101

45. Sara Urowitz, David Wiljer, Kourtney Dupak, et al. 2012. Improving diabetes management with a patient portal: a qualitative study of diabetes self-management portal. *Journal of medical Internet research* 14, 6: e158. http://doi.org/10.2196/jmir.2265

46. Peter West, Richard Giordano, Max Van Kleek, and Nigel Shadbolt. 2016. The Quantified Patient in the Doctor's Office. In *Proceedings of the 2016 CHI Conference on Human Factors in Computing Systems - CHI '16*, 3066–3078. http://doi.org/10.1145/2858036.2858445

What Happens to Digital Feedback?: Studying the Use of a Feedback Capture Platform by Care Organisations

Andy Dow[1], John Vines[3], Toby Lowe[1,2], Rob Comber[1] and Rob Wilson[2]

[1] Open Lab, Newcastle University, Newcastle upon Tyne, UK {a.r.dow; robert.comber}@ncl.ac.uk

[2] KITE, Newcastle University, Newcastle upon Tyne, UK {toby.lowe; rob.wilson}@ncl.ac.uk

[3] School of Design, Northumbria University, Newcastle upon Tyne, UK john.vines@northumbria.ac.uk

ABSTRACT

In this paper we report on a four-month long field trial of ThoughtCloud, a feedback collection platform that allows people to leave ratings and audio or video responses to simple prompts. ThoughtCloud was trialled with four organisations providing care services for people with disabilities. We conducted interviews with staff and volunteers that used ThoughtCloud before, during and after its deployment, and workshops with service users and staff. While the collection of feedback was high, only one organisation regularly reviewed and responded to collected opinions. Furthermore, tensions arose around data access and sharing, and the mismatch of values between 'giving voice' and the capacity for staff to engage in feedback practices. We contribute insights into the challenges faced in using novel technologies in resource constrained organisations, and discuss opportunities for designs that give greater agency to service users to engage those that care for them in reflecting and responding to their opinions.

Author Keywords

Feedback; social care; health; democracy.

ACM Classification Keywords

H.5.m. Information interfaces and presentation (e.g., HCI): Miscellaneous;

INTRODUCTION

The feeding back of opinions and experiences of service users to those who provide services is an integral feature of most service evaluation, improvement and commissioning processes. In addition, in certain domains—such as those where vulnerable or marginalised groups receive support for their health and care—the collection and response to feedback is also a mechanism whereby people can have their voices heard [41]. The desire to give voice to service users and actively involve them in the design of new services is often enshrined in the mission statements of care providers, especially those operating in community and not-for-profit contexts. Furthermore, in the United Kingdom (UK), government policy stipulates that those who access and use health and care services take a central role in determining the form that service provision should take [22]. Yet, despite this, many voices are still excluded [33] and, while feedback is routinely collected, it is often done so in a tokenistic fashion instead of contributing to meaningful user participation in service innovation [2].

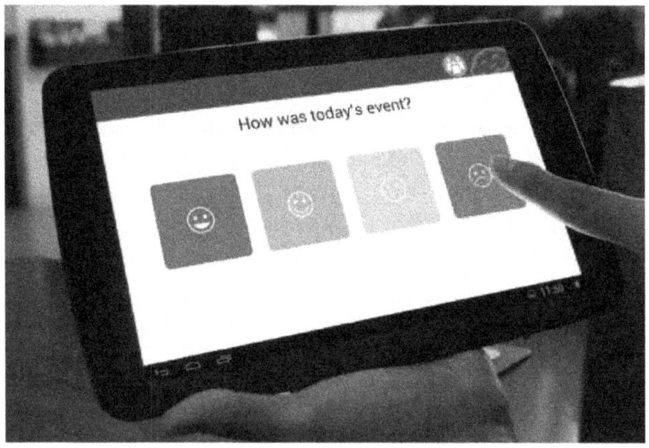

Figure 1. The ThoughtCloud feedback collection system.

The study of innovative digital technologies for capturing opinion is well established within HCI literature [8,13,20,21,27,37,42]. We build on this growing area of research, as well as extending our own prior work [14], to explore, in greater depth, the use practices emerging around an iterated version of an existing system, over a much longer period of time in a more diverse range of settings—investigating the roles simple feedback technologies play in care organisations. Our research was centered around a four-month field trial of ThoughtCloud, a tablet-based application that allows care staff to set prompts and questions which are then responded to via likerts and short audio and video recordings. This new version of ThoughtCloud also supported organisation staff to review and annotate collected feedback, respond to specific instances of feedback, and to post approved content to a public feed. Staff and volunteers at four care organisations were introduced to ThoughtCloud and used it to complement or replace traditional feedback gathering

CHI 2017, May 06-11, 2017, Denver, CO, USA
ACM 978-1-4503-4655-9/17/05.
http://dx.doi.org/10.1145/3025453.3025943

methods. Staff and service users were engaged throughout the study to understand how the technology aligned with organisational practices, as well as to study the practices that evolved around the ongoing use of ThoughtCloud. We offer two contributions to HCI discourse on designing for non-profit organisations in a care context. First, we build on prior work on feedback technologies to highlight challenges associated with aligning these systems with the values of non-profits driven by socially responsible principles. Second, we offer a number of implications for designing in this context going forward, emphasising issues related to embedding technologies within existing practices, and the ways these technologies relate to wider policy issues.

BACKGROUND

It is increasingly common for health and care service users to be consulted on and take a central role in the design, development and, more recently, the commissioning of services [17]. While critical to many private and commercial endeavours, the active involvement of service users in such processes has become a key feature of health and care sectors, especially in nations where such services are publically funded and state governed [35]. In the UK, where this research has been conducted, government policy stipulates that those who regularly use certain care and health services take a central role in determining the form that service provision should take [22]. Since 2007 the greater involvement both of the service user and the general public in service provision within the UK National Health Service [2] has been enshrined in policy as a duty for statutory bodies, and includes the gathering of views on local government social care services [22]. More recent acts of parliament—such as The Care Act and the Children and Families Act—have stipulated that information on local service provision should not only be collected in an easily accessible, up-to-date repository, but that some form of feedback should be collected around this information as well [23,24].

The UK is not alone in privileging service users as a valuable resource for consultation in the delivery of care planning, with a similar ethos found in Australia and advocated for by the World Health Organisation [5]. However, while official rhetoric identifies "patients as users whose voices should be listened to in order to ensure responsive services" [2:xxiii], in reality there is a lack of direction around how this might practically be achieved. This has led, in the UK at least, to an environment where, "despite this supportive policy context, progress to achieve greater involvement is patchy and slow and often concentrates at the lowest levels of involvement" [34:1].

The Ritual of Feedback in the Not-for-Profit Care Sector

Feedback, which we define as the collection of and responding to opinions and views of service users, can provide an opportunity for people to have their voices heard [41]. However, it has been argued that feedback is often used perfunctorily rather than contributing to meaningful user participation [2]. Tritter [40] draws a distinction between indirect involvement; where professionals gather information from the public, and direct involvement; where service users take an active role in decision making, with the former characterising the majority of involvement and the latter as the more desirable [1]. The latter is reflected in care organisations—especially those oriented towards the provision of care in the not-for-profit or community sector—where there is often a commitment to giving those citizens (who are vulnerable or marginalised) a voice [15]. Many such organisations are founded on and driven by values stemming from social justice in disability activism [35], demonstrating a commitment to lobbying for direct policy changes that ensure equality of access and opportunity. At the same time these organisations are often committed to a philosophy of being user-led, which in some cases means that service users are committee or board members, guiding service provision accordingly.

While it is often desired, direct participation can be challenging in settings where many service users have a physical or learning disability or significant care needs [15]. Furthermore, increasingly such services, even if charitable and not-for-profit in nature, operate within a competitive environment where many organisations are experiencing cuts to funding. Considering the often highly limited human and financial resources of such organisations [7], and their need to evidence metricised outcomes to report to and attract funders, indirect forms of engagement tend to take prominence [9,16], as these produce quantitative 'evidence' which commissioners demand [31]. However, such forms of engagement—like surveys, questionnaires, or interviews—can be quite problematic and exclusionary for many of the populations that rely on and use such services [19,36]. As such, despite the values of such organisations, limited time, resources and the need to acquire funds can lead to tokenistic involvement or the giving of feedback by a proxy [29].

HCI and the Care Sector

The care sector and care relationships have become increasingly important areas of enquiry in HCI in recent years. Prior work has extensively studied the role of technology in supporting new practices for informal (e.g. [48]) and formal (e.g. [38]) carers and to support interactions and relationships between carers and those in receipt of care (e.g. [47,49]). However, relatively little work has examined the issues of user voice and participation in these settings. An exception to this is Hook et al. [25], who investigated the role of video as a medium for capturing experiences of community care project events. They worked with individuals such as young people at risk of problem outcomes, unemployed adults, people with special educational needs, and people with health conditions to create video documentation of project activities to communicate what individuals gained from their involvement in the project. Hook et al. highlight how simple digital technologies can be used to evidence the invisible work that goes on in social care spaces, and highlight how user generated media can be used as part of service evaluation processes with funding agencies.

Our own prior work on the ThoughtCloud system [14] built on the research of Hook et al. We discuss this prior work, which this paper extends, in the following section.

PRIOR WORK ON THOUGHTCLOUD

ThoughtCloud is a simple, lightweight system designed for collecting feedback from people using an application (app) running on an Android tablet. It was designed with a not-for-profit care organisation to support and extend existing feedback practices. The app poses questions, defined by an organisation, allowing people to respond via simple likert ratings and audio or video messages. The tablet can be set-up at events in a range of ways, including being placed on a stand at 'entrance and exit' points, by being handed around to people or being placed in private spaces. The ThoughtCloud system was designed with the requirements of resource limited not-for-profit organisations in mind. The full design process, and the initial four week long field trials of the system, are reported in detail elsewhere [14].

ThoughtCloud was intended to respond to issues around the noted lack of capacity to collect feedback and the inappropriateness of traditional methods for certain populations of care service users. In our prior work, we reported on a short field trial whereby the system was used by two organisations working with people with disabilities and cognitive impairments. Findings highlighted enthusiasm for the technology, from service users and staff, for the simple way it enabled people to 'talk to' those who organise and oversee events, projects and services. It was found that the system made explicit practices of mediating feedback (by showing this in audio or video clips) and provided ways to observe individual service user gains over time. The study also highlighted the importance of timely responses to feedback, especially that of a sensitive nature, and defining specific roles and responsibilities for staff who administer, review and support others in the use of the system. Finally, the trials highlighted the importance of sharing feedback among staff and volunteers.

The study reported here extends this prior work, by investigating the use of a redesigned version of ThoughtCloud across a longer period of time (twelve weeks rather than four) and in collaboration with a larger number of diverse care organisations (four rather than two). There was therefore the opportunity to explore its use at many more sessions, in a variety of settings, examining in greater detail how ThoughtCloud supports existing and emerging practices of collecting and responding to feedback. In the next section we detail the key design decisions followed as the system was redesigned.

Redesigning ThoughtCloud

An initial priority was to develop features that facilitated the use of ThoughtCloud without the support of the research team. For the tablet app this focused on including functionality for system admins to create new feedback events, which would suggest default settings for questions to pose to users. An event editing panel was also introduced, allowing for a more flexible system that can be reconfigured while events were underway. Similarly, the application was redesigned to work offline, allowing it to be more portable. This was complimented with the introduction of a manual sync feature, allowing data collected on a tablet to be synced to a remote server when a Wi-Fi connection was available.

A further focus of redevelopment was on creating a website where feedback collected could be reviewed, shared with other staff and volunteers and, if appropriate, published online. Within the administration panel, a configuration panel was added that allowed users to create an account for their specific organisation, making them the 'system admin'. This had tiered access functionality, along with the ability to manage who else had access to ThoughtCloud data and the visibility of content. This was identified as important in the previous study since the potential for service users to leave sensitive information was observed. Managers therefore retained the power to grant access to others working in the organisation. It had also been identified that sharing with other staff members and volunteers within the organisation was desirable. This was made possible through admins being able to create accounts with a lower level of access to the system.

New ways of sorting and searching for feedback were created too: recurring events could be sorted by date and type, while a flexible tagging feature was added for video and audio feedback. These features, combined with secure data transfer between clients, servers and media repositories ensured that ThoughtCloud was a robust system, that was both usable and secure.

STUDY DESIGN

Since our earlier work highlighted the potential for systems like ThoughtCloud to support new and meaningful feedback practices in care organisations, we wished to study its use over a more extensive period of time. Furthermore, we were motivated to study how ThoughtCloud might be used across a more diverse range of care organisations operating at different scales and providing different types of services.

Four organisations took part in this study: 1) *SmartSkills* (SS): providing advocacy, referral, befriending services and leisure activities for people with various disabilities, and ages ranging from young people in their late teens to older adults; 2) *Bright Times* (BT), providing leisure and social activities to people with learning disabilities, aged from mid 30s to late 60s; 3) *Young People First* (YPF), working with young people (up to 25 years old) in care and with special educational needs; and 4) *Horizons* (H), a new organisation working in care homes with people with dementia. Each of these organisations were previously aware of our work with

Organisation	Staff & Volunteers	No. of Events	Ratings (Vids/Auds)	Website Logins
Smart Skills	35	41	169 (47/65)	12
Bright Times	4	15	79 (36/18)	4
Young People First	145	5	39 (5/6)	2
Horizons	1	27	92 (4/67)	17
Total	185	88	379 (92/156)	35

Table 1 Overview of organisations and their system use

ThoughtCloud, recognised feedback as vital to their everyday work with vulnerable service users, and had approached the research team with a request to use ThoughtCloud. Each of the organisations were of a different size (see Table 1), with most making use of volunteers in some capacity, ranging from nearly 150 staff and volunteers (TPF) to one person operations (H). Furthermore, the larger organisations worked primarily out of a central building where the majority of their activities and events take place (SS and YPF), and the smaller organisations (BT and H) conducted outdoor activities or ran sessions in different locations.

A primary contact at each organisation was identified to act as the system's administrator (hereafter system admin), taking responsibility for managing their organisation's account. They were taken through the steps of creating an account for their organisation on the ThoughtCloud website, as well as the relevant aspects of the system, including how to: use the tablet application; create an account and userID; setting passwords for access; and how to configure feedback collection events and review and share feedback with additional users. At this initial meeting events and activities were identified where the system would be used to collect feedback. Visits to groups using the system were arranged so the purpose of the system could be explained. This also presented an opportunity to observe the use of the tablet application by the organisation. Throughout the study, the research team checked collected data remotely, with permission, for sensitive submissions that may need to be flagged.

Qualitative Data Collection

Semi-structured interviews were planned and conducted at key stages of the study to understand more about the organisations and their use of ThoughtCloud. Initial interviews conducted prior to the trial starting were used to explore attitudes to feedback, as well as to get a clearer idea of how feedback was currently collected, how it was reviewed and used within the organisation and how they saw ThoughtCloud fitting into those processes. Following deployment, after two-weeks a member of the research team contacted the system admins individually to ensure that there were no problems with the system, to remind them to sync their tablets regularly and to log in to ensure that no data was lost. Further in-person interviews were conducted eight weeks into the trial, with questions based on observations of system use up until that point. At this stage an additional member of staff at one organisation, (SS), was identified as a 'champion' of the system and was interviewed to explore their motivations and experiences using it to collect feedback. Finally, exit interviews were conducted to review the totality of the system's use, exploring successes and ideas for future development. In total 15 interviews lasting between 30 minutes and 1hr 10mins were conducted with six different individuals, each paid members of staff from across the four organisations.

Two two-hour long workshops were also conducted following the end of the trial. The first was with 10 service users with a variety of learning disabilities who had given feedback using the system and made use of services from (SS) and (BT). This workshop involved a paper based feedback giving exercise, exploring service user understanding of feedback by creating 'feedback letters', and deciding to whom and about what they would give feedback on. The second workshop was with 8 staff and volunteers representing all participating organisations. Participants were asked to complete workbooks where they responded to feedback prompts drawn from example feedback collected from the trial. This explored both how feedback should be treated once collected using the current system, and how staff members would respond to provocative versions of a future redesign of ThoughtCloud.

System Data Collection

System use data was obtained from recording user interactions with the ThoughtCloud website, including: number of logins to the website; number of additional user accounts created; number of events created; amount of feedback collected; sharing or 'using' feedback; number of times frequency data was synchronised from the tablet application to the ThoughtCloud server. This data was analysed and used to determine interview questions, in order to explore emerging use practices and address barriers to using the system that were suggested by the use data.

Data Analysis

Given the nature of the data collected, we utilised a qualitative approach to incorporate the different data collection methods into one corpus comprising: interviews; field notes and workshops. All interviews and workshops were audio recorded and then transcribed. Thematic analysis [6] was used to examine the data collected from these disparate sources. Data was systematically summarised by textual codes and then into themes, guided by field notes collected at the participating organisations and the observed use of the system. These were further refined into the final themes, which we present in the following sections. Both participants and organisations are referred to using pseudonyms in line with the institutional ethics review procedure followed when designing the study.

Figure 2. Finding opportunities to use ThoughtCloud in the café of an exhibition centre at an annual event.

FINDINGS

Feedback was collected at a total of 88 events across the four participating organisations. It was used at recurring activities as well as one-off and annual events (Figure 2) attended by heterogeneous populations of service users: the youngest being 10 years old and having a behaviour disorder and the oldest being 95 with cognitive impairment. In most cases, service users were requested to leave feedback by a member of organisation staff or a volunteer and supervised as they did so. A total of 379 ratings were left by users across the entirety of the field trial. On 248 occasions users left an additional recorded message: 92 video and 156 audio comments (see Table 1 for summary).

The use of the tablet application was broadly consistent across all organisations, with each appearing committed to maximising opportunities for feedback collection. For the majority of those staff members and volunteers who used ThoughtCloud, their engagement with it was restricted to the tablet application to collect feedback. By contrast there was comparatively little engagement with the ThoughtCloud website where feedback collected can be reviewed. Overall, 35 logins were recorded across all of the organisations during the field trials. (YPF) recorded the fewest examples, with only two logins across the length of the study. Notably, it was the smallest organisation, (H), which reviewed feedback the most (17 logins, 49% total logins). Use data suggests certain feedback wasn't checked on regularly or in a timely manner.

In the following, we report the themes from our analysis of the data. For the purposes of clarity we have organised these themes into two sections: i) support for our prior work; and ii) novel findings that extend our prior work on ThoughtCloud. Through these sections we combine both transcribed interview and workshop data to highlight the differing practices and processes that evolved around the use of the ThoughtCloud system.

Supporting Prior Work

Initial motivations for collecting feedback

For each of the participating organisations ThoughtCloud was seen as having practical utility. It was seen as a way of 'evidencing' practice for funding: *"People give us money. They want to know that we are spending the money wisely and* [...] *it is having some kind of beneficial effect."* (Robbie). It also offered an opportunity to collect ideas to develop new services or to refine and replace existing ones: *"getting that feedback I guess to help us think about what we're doing and how we're doing it."* (Steve). For (H), which was a new organisation, feedback gathered by ThoughtCloud provided evidence to demonstrate their development: *"I want it to be more empirically-based, much more thorough, much more appropriate and effective."* (David). By all, ThoughtCloud was seen to be practical and accessible, which is particularly important for the populations that each of the organisations we worked with served: *"These are people with learning disabilities and anecdotally they can tell you stuff but if you want to measure stuff it is a little bit more difficult."* (Robbie) This is consistent with findings from our prior work in that our participating organisations were motivated by similar goals for feedback collection and use.

Training up and promoting use

As stated, our main contacts had the ThoughtCloud system demonstrated to them in order for them to take a role as system admins. At the three larger organisations it was intended that these admins would introduce the tablet app to colleagues so they could use it too. At (BT) and (YPF) there was a consensus that the feedback collection component of the system was easy to pick up and learn: *"That's the beauty of it, it is so straightforward."* (Robbie). At (YPF) in particular, an approach was taken where staff members were given short demonstrations of how to use the system: *"I've shown someone who facilitates one of the groups how to use it and that was fine.* [...] *everyone's picked it up pretty quickly."* (Hannah). However, as is common of community sector organisations, there was a huge diversity of skills and expertise when it came to using digital technologies. This was a particular issue at (SS), where one system admin (Alice) primarily explained how to use the system via emails sent to staff and volunteers: *"It wasn't being pushed* [...] *Alice has sent quite a few emails suggesting people use it and saying why it's important."* (Grace). As such, initially this organisation struggled integrating the new version of ThoughtCloud into daily practices: *"It was more just a suggestion it's there"* (Grace). There was an emphasis on asking and telling people to use ThoughtCloud, but less on actively demonstrating and promoting its use. This was underlined by another system admin reflecting that this was too passive: " [It's] *not enough. 'Good morning. How are you? Are you using ThoughtCloud today?' should be my morning greeting to all of my colleagues"* (Steve). This supports the prior findings that ThoughtCloud was both suited to its purpose and learnable, but suggests consideration be paid to how it could be more meaningfully appropriated in a context with less support from the research team.

Using ThoughtCloud at sessions and events

Although ThoughtCloud was designed with a specific use case in mind, operating on a tablet stand after events, as per our prior study, organisations were encouraged to adapt it as they saw fit. For example, for (YPF) it made sense to place the tablet on a stand in a kitchen where a drop-in session was being held for young people. At other times the tablet was taken along to outings for the youth participation group, where it was more practical to pass the tablet between people: *"It's good to have the stand, because I think that worked really well with the drop-in. I think if I had a stand with my group, they wouldn't probably figure it was there."* (Hannah). For (SS), however, operating out of a large building with multiple rooms on different floors, attempts were made to think through systemising the tablet's deployment: *"Maybe people who set up the rooms for a room booking can always put ThoughtCloud in the middle of the room … So, yes, you get the tables, the tea, the coffee, and ThoughtCloud."* (Steve)

For (BT) their services comprise a mix of outdoor activities such as gardening and cycling as well as in door group activities such as yoga or carpet bowls. On one occasion, the tablet on the stand had not been correctly set to feedback capture mode and the screen had timed out and shut off. When asked about this Robbie reflected: *"I prefer using it, holding it myself* [...] *I'm making sure their head's in the middle of the screen and I can prompt."* (Robbie) David from (H) had a similar preference, which he felt was more suited to his clients who were mostly people with dementia, *"Just getting them familiar with holding it and passing it around and not worrying about it at all."*

It should also be noted that, by far, the majority of the recorded feedback was overwhelmingly positive, with people praising the organisation collecting the feedback or, in many cases, praising specific individuals working for those organisations. In the case of (BT) where collection was supervised by Robbie, service users would at times address the camera using his name, as though they were speaking to him directly. It is possible to speculate that the presence of organisation staff or volunteers when giving feedback somewhat skewed the nature of the feedback services provided; however, we should note that the video and audio recordings themselves act as a means for evidencing situations where those giving feedback are being strongly guided by another person. Again, this echoes the findings of our prior work where veracity and transparency, especially of video feedback, was greatly appreciated.

Extending Prior Work

The values of care organisations and practitioners

Significantly, the participating organisations were primarily driven to collect feedback as a result of their underlying "user-led" values: *"As a user-led organisation, the view of disabled people, families and carers are important to us. We're driven by our values."* (Steve). All of the organisations, in different ways, were dedicated to providing opportunities for vulnerable or marginalised people to feel listened to, *"Giving people a voice … it's central to the whole philosophy of the organisation,"* (Alice); *"If people are listening to you, your sense of self and your confidence goes up."* (David). Therefore, there was a real sense that the collection of thoughts and opinion would enable disenfranchised groups to participate in civic life and be treated as an equal citizen:

"If disempowered people have had their voices taken away from them they can certainly fight for it back themselves [...] *other folks find that really difficult to do independently* [...] *we're all about amplifying the voice of disabled people."* (Steve)

The significance of these values to those working in these settings was particularly evident when approximately midway through the trial at (SS) one person started to promote ThoughtCloud's use despite having no structured training from the organisation. Grace had "*worked it out for herself.*" (Grace) This enabled her to show another staff member how to use the system as well. On another occasion she introduced it to a volunteer who ran a regular participation group, enabling them to use it after their sessions. She also identified new opportunities where it could be used, sometimes at activities with which she had no involvement or limited contact. Reflecting on this, she explained that as a trainee social worker she understood the value of feedback and the importance of listening to service users: *"For me personally it's to develop practice, that's something that's trained in."* (Grace). For her, the system spoke to personal and professional values around motivations to collect feedback.

Making the most of every opportunity

Although by the end of the trial feedback was being collected regularly across three of the organisations, staff would frequently refer to *"missed opportunities"*. At (SS) an expectation had emerged of almost continual use of ThoughtCloud borne out of the need to evidence the operations of the organisation. This led to disappointment around the actual volume that was being collected: "[It's] *not as much as we'd like.*" (Steve) However, as noted earlier, with no clear strategy for integrating the system into practices, at times it was forgotten: "*I had forgotten to bring it downstairs*" (Grace).

Similar concerns were raised at the other organisations. At (BT) the use of ThoughtCloud was often "*tacked on*" (Robbie) at the end of a session or event. A difficulty both (BT) and (H) faced was that sessions would be ran by one person and, having a number of different things to manage at once, would be easily forgotten. On one occasion Robbie took ThoughtCloud on a cycling trip to capture feedback throughout the day: "*it wasn't actually till the end of the day I went into me bag: 'Damn it's there'*" (Robbie). Interestingly, these missed opportunities sometimes led to service users being asked to do a 'second take', repeating an opinion that they had expressed in passing earlier for the camera to ensure that it was captured:

"We did a ride leader training the other day and one of our members finished the ride leader training and said: 'This is the best thing, it's really good.' I said: [...] *'Let's do this on the ThoughtCloud' So, he did."* (Robbie)

At (YPF) the administrator struggled to find opportunities where she was able use the tablet. She attempted to introduce it into sessions with other groups, run by other staff members and volunteers and, after a few limited and frustrating attempts, abandoned trying:

"It's been a little bit frustrating in the sense that I haven't had a lot of opportunities to use it myself … in terms of the drop-ins, maybe it needs a central person like Barry to promote it with maybe the four staff that would be involved and potentially accessing it." (Hannah)

For this organisation their feedback processes were stringently defined and adhered to: *"It's difficult. You know, and it does take time for that too you've got to chat to parents to explain to them what it is"* (Hannah). As a result having concerns around safeguarding for all of those under their care was commonplace and perhaps understandably fostered a natural suspicion of recording technology brought into such a regulated context.

It was notable, however, that while the organisation staff themselves were concerned about forgetting to collect feedback, over time service users still began complaining about having to give feedback time and time again. For example, Grace reported that a group she brought the tablet to complained: "*Oh doing this again? Did you not get enough the last time?"* (Grace). This complicates the notion of continual feedback collection reinforced by management at (SS), highlighting how such practices can cause a kind of 'feedback fatigue'. Further, it highlights a potential lack of value placed in feedback on the side of some service users—or at least a lack of knowledge of the importance placed on feedback by those organisations that rely on a mix of government contracts and private funding bids. Indeed from the workshop with service users, a picture emerged of feedback and opinion giving as opaque terms. This was acknowledged by Susan, observing that educating service users about this could be an important part of feedback processes: "[if] *they know that they're being heard and they're more likely to leave more feedback in the future, leading to your critical feedback, maybe?"* (Susan).

Challenges with administration

As noted earlier, while all of the organisations engaged in considerable amounts of feedback collection, there was a relatively limited amount of engagement with the ThoughtCloud website's admin panel by some of them. It became evident to us at an early stage that feedback was not being reviewed. This was further evidenced at the mid-point interviews where admins attempted to login and most struggled to remember UserIDs and passwords. Passwords had either been forgotten or written in notebooks or on scraps of paper left lying around in offices: "*I'm just trying to remember what my password was. I think it might be in my other notebook."* (Hannah). While the research team resolved these access difficulties, engagement with the admin panel was not seen to increase across the remainder of the study, and in fact most logins correspond with interviews being conducted by the researcher where the participant was explicitly instructed to login. In one example, (YPF), this accounts for all recorded system logins. Perhaps unsurprisingly the only organisation that did not require a new password was also that which used the review system the most, (H), since they were logging in on a regular basis to review feedback.

For those who didn't regularly use the admin panel, they had forgotten how to use it and asked to be reminded of how to complete simple operations. At (SS), Alice said, "*It's not routine and I'm IT phobic."* For Steve, however, he reflected about this lack of engagement, *"I'm not yet plugged into the value of doing it* […] *Before I do it the first time, that hasn't happened, I suspect."* (Steve). As such, although there was a strong belief at (SS) that ThoughtCloud should be used continuously to collect feedback, it was clearly challenging to embed the reviewing of this feedback into daily practices and routines, *"We haven't quite embedded using ThoughtCloud as a routine part of everything we do* […] *I'm not quite sure what that's for, but that is absolutely a kind of cultural thing again, isn't it?"* (Steve). In part, this suggests some of the organisations were unsure of the value of ThoughtCloud as a means for giving voice to their service users. The standard practice at both (SS) and (BT) was to use feedback as a means to promote or evidence their work for funding bodies and proposals. As Steve himself noted, it was desirable to *"hoover up feedback and drop it into* […] *board meeting reports and end-of-year reports, that sort of thing."* (Steve). Robbie from (BT) observed that he rarely checked in to review feedback because he's *"always there when they give it"*, referring back to his preferred practice of recording videos with the people who take part in his activities. However, the lack of reviewing of feedback was more problematic at (SS) due to its size, where multiple people were using the system, where it was more frequent for people to respond to questions on their own, and where none of the staff that regularly collected feedback had access to the administration panel. Reflecting on the overall lack of engagement, Alice suggested that perhaps "*it should be in somebody's job description*" to not just use ThoughtCloud at sessions but to regularly log in and checking what people say. Steve further suggested, *"Somebody should have an hour a week where they log in and review stuff."* (Steve).

Reviewing and using feedback

Despite the above difficulties, feedback collected was still valued. Perhaps unsurprisingly, the organisation evidencing the most logins was the newest organisation that was still developing the services that they provided. David from (H) used the videos collected via ThoughtCloud to support his, *"ongoing reflections"* on his practice. He explained how he would log in to ThoughtCloud's website after sessions, and expend a great amount of time and effort manually transcribing each of the recordings. Doing this, he engaged in a close viewing of the data and frequently reflected on how he acts. In one case, he stated:

"I wasn't giving any energy [in a session]. *Physically I wasn't standing up, I wasn't charging around* [...] *Archie says, 'What you need to do David is put more energy,' So really powerful feedback, thanks to that, from Archie, telling me what I should be doing."* (David)

As well as creating evidence to communicate how he was personally progressing, he also considered his transcribed notes as evidence for the regulator of health and social care: *"you need to get these ideas out and down* [on paper] *and a lot of people have said that from the care quality commission."* (David). At (BT) and (SS) feedback was used to get further funding, with transcribed audio feedback included as evidence in an application for funding for social activities: *"We've absolutely used it for funding for* [a leisure group] *at present."* (Steve). In terms of informally acquiring resources, following a session of cycling training, Robbie (BT) asked if there was a way to share feedback with a collaborating organisation to show them how much their contribution was valued:

"To pay back to people who have done stuff. I think that would be nice. To be able to turn round and say: 'Look we've got video footage of people saying how wonderful you are and your course.' And they're obviously very excited about that." (Robbie)

Robbie's comments here highlight how there was a desire to share feedback more widely beyond the organisation's boundary; however, as we note in the following theme, the sharing of feedback within and beyond organisations, and even beyond just key members of staff, was highly contested by some.

Complexities around sharing feedback

While in our previous studies, the sharing of feedback—within the organisation, with funders, and with the wider public—was seen to be important, this rarely happened across these longer studies. This was despite ThoughtCloud being redesigned to handle the sharing of content between designated staff and the publishing certain feedback online. This could, in part, be linked with concerns around the sensitivity of the data. Furthermore, in some cases, as at (SS), reviewing of feedback was mostly imagined to be an individual practice conducted by the staff running and overseeing an event. Alice explained how information is shared within (SS): *"confidentiality, in organisations like this, is on a need-to-know basis* [...] *it shouldn't be shared between one person and others in the team, unless they need to know."* (Alice). Alice further noted that, in its current form ThoughtCloud didn't offer a fine grain enough set of access permissions to allow for individuals to see some data and not others, *"So there's a choice of all or nothing, really?"* (Alice). As a result, specific people act as a barrier to sharing feedback; i.e., they don't devolve responsibility, perhaps because they don't realise they have to: *"To be honest, I don't think we have used it other than just informing Steve and I."* (Alice). Confronted with these barriers to staff members reviewing the feedback they collect—i.e., admins not giving others access rights—Steve reflected that such limits on internal data sharing be revoked: *"Why should Grace be worried that Janice can see what the people on the S&S course thought about the course that's been run by Grace? Why should that be an issue?"* (Steve).

While the value of sharing feedback with staff and volunteers was well understood, reticence to share publically remained. For those organisations working with people with cognitive impairments and young people, this was felt particularly acutely. At (H) the idea of sharing recorded feedback publically was treated cautiously: *"We could do it anonymously"*. For (YPF) the issue was how such a feature would enmesh with existing safeguarding policies: *"We'd have to get consent from the parents* [...] *We'd have to be quite careful about having that online* [...] *We've got to follow our data protection policy."* (Hannah).

Although the participating organisations were anxious about having feedback posted online, there was also a worry that there was a lack of "giving feedback" on the feedback. Robbie from (BT) said he tried to make sure those who give feedback get a chance to view the videos they create: *"What you will find, especially if people leave a video, they will want to watch it"* (Robbie). Alice at (SS) went further: *"morally, you should respond. If they give their views and nobody has heard that's worse"* (Alice). Here Alice demonstrates an awareness that the act of collecting feedback itself comes with a moral obligation to respond; yet clearly there is confusion about how best to do this. Indeed, our engagements with service users highlighted how there was a general lack of awareness of what was happening with the 'messages' they were recording, other than them being looked after by the person running the session. It was further acknowledged by some of the organisations that even if they were to publish the feedback collected, part of the problem would be the limitations for some of their service users in terms of access to online resources. The (SS) team thought around the problem by suggesting that they have a display permanently situated on their premises: *"In terms of the reception area, it would be great [...] even if it was just a laptop sized screen that people could notice."* (Alice). However, for (YPF) this would still remain problematic, with consent being foregrounded as a significant issue: *"We'd have to get consent from parents. It's not as simple as just saying yes from our point of view."* (Hannah).

DISCUSSION

This study highlights a number of challenges facing community care organisations embedding digital technology into established feedback practices, particularly regarding issues identified with the reviewing and actioning of service user opinion. Voida and colleagues [28,43–46] alert us to how community and not-for-profit organisations are deeply complex and offer many challenges for technology design. Through real-world use and non-use [3,4] of ThoughtCloud, we observed how technical literacy is a very clear, real-world barrier and how the chaotic nature of care environments often meant that ThoughtCloud would not be engaged with. We also experienced being drawn into the infrastructure, as has been observed by others [11,26], of not-for-profit care ourselves. As such, these are clearly highly dynamic contexts for technology design, where the situation of use and the primary users are continually shifting.

One reaction to this might be, as suggested by Steve, to engage in more top-down policing of the use of ThoughtCloud. However, this seems inappropriate for resource limited environments where most staff and volunteers are simply trying their best to care for people. Instead, we see the value in exploring the ways systems like ThoughtCloud might support more flexible and meaningful practices of promoting service user voice that align with the values of care organisations like those in our study. In the following closing sections of the paper, we discuss some opportunities and challenges associated with this approach.

Mismatching Values and Practices

One of the motivations for the organisations we worked with in using ThoughtCloud was that it was seen to speak directly to their values around giving their service users a voice. However, in practice we observed that the way in which ThoughtCloud was used contradicted these values. Certain members of the participating organisations still went to great lengths to collect feedback using ThoughtCloud, but in many of these instances the feedback they collected was not reviewed, explicitly responded to, or used in any way. Indeed, there was a great emphasis on the *"hoovering up of feedback"* and prioritising this as evidence for funding bids or to gain further resource from other organisations. Therefore, while the values underpinning participation in the study were around giving those with care needs an opportunity to be heard, it was rare to see this be actioned or accounted for. At best, this is disappointing. At worst, given the findings of our prior work [14], it's worrying that critical comments or the revealing of personal safety issues via ThoughtCloud might be left unaccounted for by organisational staff.

While low-level technical problems, such as those surrounding lost passwords, caused some problems, we found these to be attributable to a lack of engagement with the web based part of the system rather than an indication of issues relating to the system's design (they were quickly and easily resolved and often accompanied by apologies for not having had time to take a look). We acknowledge, however, that there is potential for the system to do more to hold admins to account, especially in relation to feedback that is not being viewed or actioned. For example, it would be a trivial matter for the system to report, perhaps via email, when new feedback has been uploaded, prompting system admins to review it or take action. Similarly, the system might enquire what action is to be taken regarding viewed feedback and suggest ways in which to progress the feedback. Of course, this might add further work to already overflowing inboxes in organisations where the priority is to answer directly to a service user. A balance may be found in the system reporting a weekly digest summarising the amount of feedback collected that week and, more crucially, reminding them regarding that which has not been responded to or actioned.

As we observed, only one organisation logged in to review collected feedback regularly. The others were unambiguous about their use of feedback as a means to provide evidence to funding bodies, with one in particular (BT) enthusiastic about their participation with the research project for its demonstration that they were engaged in 'novel monitoring' practices. Our study then highlights an attitude to feedback which is concerned with demonstrating the efficacy of existing practice rather than using that data to reflect on, and improve practice. This reflects literature on the public and voluntary sector, that highlights how outcome-based funding practices, prevalent in the not-for-profit sector, foster particular behaviours, where: "workers become focused on how to produce the required performance information." [31:5] The use practices we observed are examples of problems driven by structural issues relating to feedback practices. These structural issues encourage organisations to demonstrate user engagement in ways that appear to be legitimate but in reality affirm existing indirect and tokenistic approaches to involving users in service appraisal and (re)design. In executing user engagement in this manner, organisations then lose sight of the potential for service users to offer valuable input and opinion that might impact the services they provide.

An example of best practice, in relation to the existing system's use, was evidenced by Grace using ThoughtCloud to record herself. This had a two-fold benefit; first, it simply enabled her to demonstrate how it works and build confidence in using it to leave feedback; second, her practice of using ThoughtCloud on herself demonstrated its wider utility as a tool for reflection-on-practice. This sort of critical self-reflective practice has been shown to be invaluable in social work literature [18,39] and was a practice that David also participated in during his use of ThoughtCloud. Furthermore, it is something that many care and charitable organisations increasingly have to demonstrate engagement with and learning around [35]. Therefore, if the purpose of feedback in organisations like these is to support reflection on user experiences of services to iterate and refine, then building such technologies explicitly into entire practices of individual and group reflection on and documentation of work seems entirely sensible [10,32]; creating a 'culture of feedback' beneficial to the confidence and efficacy of staff and volunteers, which could then be passed on to service users themselves.

Feedback Sharing, Exchanging and Making Visible

A further set of issues from our study relate to how the data collected using ThoughtCloud can be operationalised, making the work of the organisation more visible, both to the populations served and to the wider community. Some of the reasons why the feedback was not engaged with once collected was due to two organisations being single person operations; but others were because of problems with access levels within organisations and a general lack of value seen in the current ways ThoughtCloud 'published' feedback online. The former issue demonstrates the inappropriateness of traditional access management methods, such as those associated with modern CMS systems, in this setting, and prompts creative thinking regarding how recorded information could be quickly and safely shared, both with service users and the relevant organisation members, to ensure maximum utility.

The latter issue of publishing feedback was particularly divisive with organisations with service users that did not have access to the web at home; therefore, they simply didn't see *"the point"*. While publishing feedback online was seen by us as a way of supporting engagement with external parties (and indeed friends, family and carers of people who use services) this was a clear oversight in the design that impeded engagement. However, through this oversight we learned that there was a desire for having feedback be 'more visible' both within organisations and between organisations they collaborated with. Elsewhere it has been shown that data presentation techniques have great value in fostering communication within local communities [12,27], as such, we might imagine a future version of ThoughtCloud that publically publishes use statistics showing, not just that feedback is being collected, but that it is being reviewed, responded to and meaningfully incorporated into service provision. Alternatively, organisations like (SS) and (YPF) could have simple, networked displays in their facilities where feedback, or summaries of feedback and how the origianisation will respond, can be 'pushed to' and made visible.

While using public and semi-public displays might make the collection and responding to feedback more visible, it doesn't deal with issues of acquiring consent to share media of individuals—a particular issue for two of our participating organisations who have safeguarding responsibilities for their service users. This raises questions of how safeguarding and consent should be appropriately managed, a problem with digital systems generally [30], but one which must be addressed lest voices are excluded [33]. A great strength, and characteristic of the community care sector is that many organisations know each other well, or at the very least are aware of each other and know specific individuals working within other organisations (as was the case between our collaborators). Leveraging the affordances of digital systems such as ThoughtCloud, we might imagine new forms of 'distributed consent giving' where consent to share is agreed upon by several trusted parties in a network of care, perhaps even drawn from these other care organisations. However, as some individuals require secure partitioning of their identifying information within organisations potentially working simultaneously with dangerous individuals connected to them [50], such an approach would require great care in applying into practice.

IMPLICATIONS AND CONCLUSION

In this paper, we have presented a 12 week field trial of ThoughtCloud, a feedback collection platform, with four not-for-profit and community sector care organisations. We have built on our previous shorter studies of an earlier version of this system by studying how the ThoughtCloud system is used over an extended period of time, examining how the technology is incorporated into the existing work practices of these organisations and supports them in both collecting and responding to the feedback and opinion of their service users. Our findings highlighted that, despite there being a huge amount of value seen in the principles of feedback collection and the technology itself, structural issues around technological literacy and performance management in this sector limited the meaningfulness of ThoughtCloud's use as a tool to support advocacy of service users. Our findings highlight how the design of future systems needs to:

- be designed to foster a culture of feedback where the value of ongoing collection is communicated to both those giving feedback (i.e., that it may influence future funding of services) and reviewing feedback (i.e., that it can be used to enable reflection on practice);
- hold organisations to account, feeding back their performance as feedback reviewers, and prompting them when feedback is waiting to be reviewed;
- make the practice of listening to service users visible to the wider community through publishing data related to, not just feedback collection, but also response rates and how it has shaped funding and service provision.

Despite the noted challenges, there are still clear opportunities for feedback technologies like ThoughtCloud to foster meaningful, direct participation with excluded groups. Our experience shows us, as has been demonstrated elsewhere [32], that funding driven feedback practices for accountability rather than learning effects the practices of organisations. New mechanisms to capture feedback by themselves are insufficient to overcome this challenge. In future the design challenge concerns, not just the configuration of systems like ThoughtCloud, but also how organisational performance management mechanisms are designed to include such systems, creating a culture of reflexivity and learning.

ACKNOWLEDGEMENTS

We'd like to thank SmartSkills, Young People First, Bright Times and Horizons (not their real names) as well as all of our participants for giving their time and support. This research was funded through the EPSRC CDT in Digital Civics (EP/L016176/1). Data supporting this publication is openly available under an 'Open Data Commons Open Database License'. Additional metadata are available at: http://dx.doi.org/10.17634/154300-38. Please contact Newcastle Research Data Service at rdm@ncl.ac.uk for access instructions.

REFERENCES

1. Sherry R. Arnstein. 1969. A Ladder Of Citizen Participation. *Journal of the American Institute of Planners* 35, 4: 216–224. http://doi.org/10.1080/01944366908977225
2. Marian Barnes and Phil Cotterell. 2011. *Critical perspectives on user involvement*. The Policy Press.
3. Eric P. S. Baumer, Jenna Burrell, Morgan G. Ames, Jed R. Brubaker, and Paul Dourish. 2015. On the importance and implications of studying technology non-use. *interactions* 22, 2: 52–56. http://doi.org/10.1145/2723667
4. Eric P.S. Baumer, Morgan G. Ames, Jed R. Brubaker, Jenna Burrell, and Paul Dourish. 2014. Refusing, limiting, departing. *Proceedings of the extended abstracts of the 32nd annual ACM conference on Human factors in computing systems - CHI EA '14*, ACM Press, 65–68. http://doi.org/10.1145/2559206.2559224
5. Penny Bee, Helen Brooks, Claire Fraser, and Karina Lovell. 2015. Professional perspectives on service user and carer involvement in mental health care planning: A qualitative study. *International Journal of Nursing Studies* 52, 12: 1834–1845. http://doi.org/10.1016/j.ijnurstu.2015.07.008
6. Virginia Braun and Victoria Clarke. 2006. Using thematic analysis in psychology. *Qualitative Research in Psychology* 3, 2: 77–101. http://doi.org/10.1191/1478088706qp063oa
7. Paul Breckell, Kate Harrison, and Nicola Robert. 2011. *Impact Reporting in the UK Charity Sector*. Retrieved August 24, 2015 from http://www.cfg.org.uk/resources/~/media/Files/Resources/Impact Reporting in the UK Charity Sector.ashx
8. Harry Brignull and Yvonne Rogers. 2003. Enticing people to interact with large public displays in public spaces. *In Proceedings of INTERACT*, 17–24. http://doi.org/10.1.1.129.603
9. Care Quality Commission. 2013. *RAISE building partnerships between CQC and voluntary & community sector organisations in the South East Summary of key points :* Retrieved September 20, 2015 from http://www.regionalvoices.org/sites/default/files/library/Final Report on CQC Focus Group - Summary version RAISE.pdf
10. A. L. Cunliffe. 2004. On Becoming a Critically Reflexive Practitioner. *Journal of Management Education* 28, 4: 407–426. http://doi.org/10.1177/1052562904264440
11. Hilary Davis, Sonja Pedell, Antonio Lopez Lorca, Tim Miller, and Leon Sterling. 2014. Researchers as proxies for informal carers: Photo sharing with older adults to mediate wellbeing. *Proceedings of the 26th Australian Computer-Human Interaction Conference, OzCHI 2014*, 2001: 270–279. http://doi.org/10.1145/2686612 2686652
12. Hilary Davis, Jenny Waycott, and Shou Zhou. 2015. Beyond YouTube. *Proceedings of the Annual Meeting of the Australian Special Interest Group for Computer Human Interaction on - OzCHI '15*: 579–587. http://doi.org/10.1145/2838739.2838771
13. Trien V. Do, Keith Cheverst, and Nick Taylor. 2015. Content analysis of a rural community's interaction with its cultural heritage through a longitudinal display deployment. *British HCI '15: Proceedings of the 2015 British HCI Conference*, 46–55. http://doi.org/10.1145/2783446.2783567
14. Andy Dow, John Vines, Rob Comber, and Rob Wilson. 2016. ThoughtCloud : Exploring the Role of Feedback Technologies in Care Organisations. *Proceedings of the 2016 CHI Conference on Human Factors in Computing Systems*, 3625–3636. http://doi.org/10.1145/2858036.2858105
15. Robert F. Drake. 1996. Charities, Authority and Disabled People: A qualitative study. *Disability & Society* 11, 1: 5–24. http://doi.org/10.1080/09687599650023290
16. Phil Edwards. 2002. Increasing response rates to postal questionnaires: systematic review. *BMJ* 324, 7347: 1183–1183. http://doi.org/10.1136/bmj.324.7347.1183
17. David H Evans, Roger J Bacon, Elizabeth Greer, Angela M Stagg, and Pat Turton. 2015. "Calling executives and clinicians to account": user involvement in commissioning cancer services. *Health Expectations* 18, 4: 504–515. http://doi.org/10.1111/hex.12051
18. A.G Fallis. The death of reflective supervision? An exploration of the role of relfection within supervision in a Local Authority Youth Offending Service. *The Journal of Research, Policy and Planning* 31, 2: 93–104. http://doi.org/10.1017/CBO9781107415324.004
19. Tony Gilbert. 2004. Involving people with learning disabilities in research: Issues and possibilities. *Health and Social Care in the Community* 12, 4: 298–308. http://doi.org/10.1111/j.1365-2524.2004.00499.x
20. Connie Golsteijn, Sarah Gallacher, Licia Capra, and Yvonne Rogers. 2016. Sens-Us : Designing Innovative Civic Technology for the Public Good. *Proceedings of the 2016 CHI Conference on Human Factors in Computing Systems*, 39–49.
21. Connie Golsteijn, Sarah Gallacher, Lisa Koeman, et al. 2015. VoxBox : a Tangible Machine that Gathers Opinions from the Public at Events. *Proceedings of TEI '15*, 201–208. http://doi.org/10.1145/2677199.2680588

22. Trisha Greenhalgh, Charlotte Humphrey, and Fran Woodward. 2010. *User involvement in Health Care*.
23. Department of Health. 2014. *Children and Families Act 2014*. Queen's Printer of Acts of Parliament. Retrieved July 18, 2015 from http://www.legislation.gov.uk/ukpga/2014/6/contents/enacted
24. Department of Health. 2014. *Care Act 2014*. Queen's Printer of Acts of Parliament. Retrieved September 15, 2015 from http://www.legislation.gov.uk/ukpga/2014/23/enacted
25. Jonathan Hook, Rachel Clarke, John Mccarthy, Kate Anderson, Jane Dudman, and Peter Wright. 2015. Making the Invisible Visible : Design to Support the Documentation of Participatory Arts Experiences. *Proceedings of CHI 2015*, 2583–2592. http://doi.org/10.1145/2702123.2702187
26. Ian G Johnson, John Vines, Nick Taylor, Edward Jenkins, and Justin Marshall. 2016. Reflections on Deploying Distributed Consultation Technologies with Community Organisations. *Proceedings of the 2016 CHI Conference on Human Factors in Computing Systems*: 2945–2957. http://doi.org/10.1145/2858036.2858098
27. Lisa Koeman, Vaiva Kalnikaitė, and Yvonne Rogers. 2015. "Everyone Is Talking about It!": A Distibuted Approach to Urban Voting Technology and Visualisations. *Proceedings of CHI '15*, 3127–3136. http://doi.org/10.1145/2702123.2702263
28. Matthias Korn and Amy Voida. 2015. Creating Friction: Infrastructuring Civic Engagement in Everyday Life. *Aarhus Series on Human Centered Computing* 1, 1: 12. http://doi.org/10.7146/aahcc.v1i1.21198
29. Biza Stenfert Kroese, Alinda Gillott, and Vicky Atkinson. 1998. Consumers with intellectual disabilities as service evaluators. *Journal of Applied Research in Intellectual Disabilities* 11, 2: 116–128.
30. Mark Lizar and Mary Hodder. 2014. Usable Consents. Tracking and Managing Use of Personal Data with a Consent Transaction Receipt. *Proceedings of the 2014 ACM International Joint Conference on Pervasive and Ubiquitous Computing: Adjunct Publication*, 647–652. http://doi.org/10.1145/2638728.2641681
31. Toby Lowe and Rob Wilson. 2015. Playing the Game of Outcomes-based Performance Management. Is Gamesmanship Inevitable? Evidence from Theory and Practice. *Social Policy and Administration*. http://doi.org/10.1111/spol.12205
32. Toby Lowe, Rob Wilson, and Sophie Boobis. 2016. The Performance Management of complex systems – enabling adaptation. *Performance Management Association*.
33. Timothy Milewa. 2004. Innovation or Fragmentation of a Universal Citizenship ? *Social Policy and Administration* 38, 3: 240–252.
34. Josephine Ocloo and Rachel Matthews. 2016. From tokenism to empowerment: progressing patient and public involvement in healthcare improvement. *BMJ Quality and Safety*, March: 1–7. http://doi.org/10.1136/bmjqs-2015-004839
35. Michael Oliver. 2012. *Social work with disabled people*.
36. Alzheimer Society. 2010. *My name is not dementia*. Retrieved September 20, 2015 from http://www.alzheimers.org.uk/site/scripts/documents_info.php?documentID=1339
37. Nick Taylor, Justin Marshall, and A Blum-Ross. 2012. Viewpoint: empowering communities with situated voting devices. *Proceedings of CHI '12*, 1361–1370. http://doi.org/10.1145/2207676.2208594
38. Anja Thieme, John McCarthy, Paula Johnson, et al. 2016. Challenges for Designing New Technology for Health and Wellbeing in a Complex Mental Healthcare Context. *Proceedings of the 2016 CHI Conference on Human Factors in Computing Systems*: 2136–2149. http://doi.org/10.1145/2858036.2858182
39. Neil Thompson. 2008. *The critically reflective practitioner*. Palgrave Macmillan.
40. Jonathan Q Tritter. 2009. Revolution or evolution : the challenges of conceptualizing patient and public involvement in a consumerist world. *Health Expectations* 12, 3: 275–287. http://doi.org/10.1111/j.1369-7625.2009.00564.x
41. Jonathan Quetzal Tritter and Alison McCallum. 2006. The snakes and ladders of user involvement: Moving beyond Arnstein. *Health Policy* 76, 2: 156–168. http://doi.org/10.1016/j.healthpol.2005.05.008
42. Vasilis Vlachokyriakos, Rob Comber, Karim Ladha, et al. 2014. Poster Vote : Expanding the Action Repertoire for Local Political Activism. *Proceedings of DIS '14*: 795–804. http://doi.org/http://dx.doi.org/10.1145/2598510.2598523
43. A Voida, Z Yao, and M Korn. 2015. (Infra) structures of Volunteering Volunteerism. *Proceedings of the 18th ACM Conference on Computer Supported Cooperative Work*. http://doi.org/http://dx.doi.org/10.1145/2675133.2675153
44. Amy Voida and Amy. 2011. Shapeshifters in the voluntary sector. *interactions* 18, 6: 27. http://doi.org/10.1145/2029976.2029985
45. Amy Voida, Ellie Harmon, and Ban Al-Ani. 2011. Homebrew databases. *Proceedings of the 2011 annual conference on Human factors in computing systems -*

CHI '11, ACM Press, 915. http://doi.org/10.1145/1978942.1979078

46. Amy Voida, Ellie Harmon, and Ban Al-Ani. 2012. Bridging between organizations and the public. *Proceedings of the 2012 ACM annual conference on Human Factors in Computing Systems - CHI '12*, ACM Press, 1967. http://doi.org/10.1145/2207676.2208341
47. Jayne Wallace, Anja Thieme, Gavin Wood, Guy Schofield, and Patrick Olivier. 2012. Enabling Self, Intimacy and a Sense of Home in Dementia: An Enquiry into Design in a Hospital Setting. *Proceedings of the SIGCHI Conference on Human Factors in Computing Systems*: 2629–2638. http://doi.org/10.1145/2207676.2208654
48. Jayne Wallace, Peter C. Wright, John McCarthy, David Philip Green, James Thomas, and Patrick Olivier. 2013. A design-led inquiry into personhood in dementia. *CHI '13 Extended Abstracts on Human Factors in Computing Systems on - CHI EA '13*, ACM Press, 2883. http://doi.org/10.1145/2468356.2479560
49. Jenny Waycott, Hilary Davis, Frank Vetere, et al. 2014. Captioned Photographs in Psychosocial Aged Care: Relationship Building and Boundary Work. *Proceedings of the 32nd annual ACM conference on Human factors in computing systems - CHI '14 Annual ACM Conference on Human Factors in Computing Systems*: 4167–4176. http://doi.org/10.1145/2556288.2557290
50. Rob Wilson, Mike Martin, Sarah Walsh, and Paul Richter. 2011. Re-Mixing Digital Economies in the Voluntary Community Sector? Governing Identity Information and Information Sharing in the Mixed Economy of Care for Children and Young People*. *Social Policy and Society* 10, 3: 379–391. http://doi.org/10.1017/S1474746411000108

Facade: Auto-generating Tactile Interfaces to Appliances

Anhong Guo[1], **Jeeeun Kim**[2], **Xiang 'Anthony' Chen**[1], **Tom Yeh**[2], **Scott E. Hudson**[1], **Jennifer Mankoff**[1], **Jeffrey P. Bigham**[1]

[1] Human-Computer Interaction Institute, Carnegie Mellon University, Pittsburgh, PA, USA
[2] Department of Computer Science, University of Colorado Boulder, Boulder, CO, USA

{anhongg, xiangche, scott.hudson, jmankoff, jbigham}@cs.cmu.edu,
{jeeeun.kim, tom.yeh}@colorado.edu

Figure 1. Facade is a crowdsourced fabrication pipeline that enables blind people to make flat physical interfaces accessible by independently producing a 3D-printed overlay of tactile buttons. From left to right, we demonstrate example applications including microwave, refrigerator door, copier, and another microwave. Insets shows close views of individual embossed buttons.

ABSTRACT

Common appliances have shifted toward flat interface panels, making them inaccessible to blind people. Although blind people can label appliances with Braille stickers, doing so generally requires sighted assistance to identify the original functions and apply the labels. We introduce *Facade*—a crowdsourced fabrication pipeline to help blind people independently make physical interfaces accessible by adding a 3D printed augmentation of tactile buttons overlaying the original panel. Facade users capture a photo of the appliance with a readily available fiducial marker (a dollar bill) for recovering size information. This image is sent to multiple crowd workers, who work in parallel to quickly label and describe elements of the interface. Facade then generates a 3D model for a layer of tactile and pressable buttons that fits over the original controls. Finally, a home 3D printer or commercial service fabricates the layer, which is then aligned and attached to the interface by the blind person. We demonstrate the viability of Facade in a study with 11 blind participants.

ACM Classification Keywords

H.5.2 Information interfaces and presentation: User Interfaces - *Input devices and strategies*; K.4.2 Computers and Society: Social Issues - *Assistive technologies*

DOI: http://dx.doi.org/10.1145/3025453.3025845

Author Keywords

Non-visual interfaces; visually impaired; blind; accessibility; crowdsourcing; fabrication; 3D printing; computer vision.

INTRODUCTION

Flat touchpads have proliferated on common appliances, making them inaccessible for blind people. The task of creating an appropriate tactile overlay to adapt to inaccessible appliances currently requires in-person sighted help and a labeling device that can print embossed labels. However, sighted assistance is not always available, and a labeling device doesn't solve issues such as layout and size of labels. Automatically generated tactile overlays could address both issues. We present an end-to-end crowdsourced fabrication pipeline that can be done independent of in-person sighted help, and costs less than $10 per appliance.

To identify the existing challenges of using inaccessible interfaces of home and work appliances, we conducted a formative study with six blind participants. We identified four design requirements for a system to augment physical interfaces for non-visual access: *(i)* the solution for tactile labeling should enable blind users to independently augment and access their appliances without in-person sighted assistance, *(ii)* the augmented labels should be customizable to address individual needs, *(iii)* the solution should allow for learning and memorization of the interface, and *(iv)* the tactile labels should support easy attachment and reproduction for repeated use.

We introduce *Facade*, a crowdsourced fabrication pipeline to make physical interfaces accessible by adding a 3D printed layer of tactile buttons overlaying the original panel (Figure 2). When a blind person encounters an inaccessible appliance for the first time, s/he uses the Facade iOS app to capture a

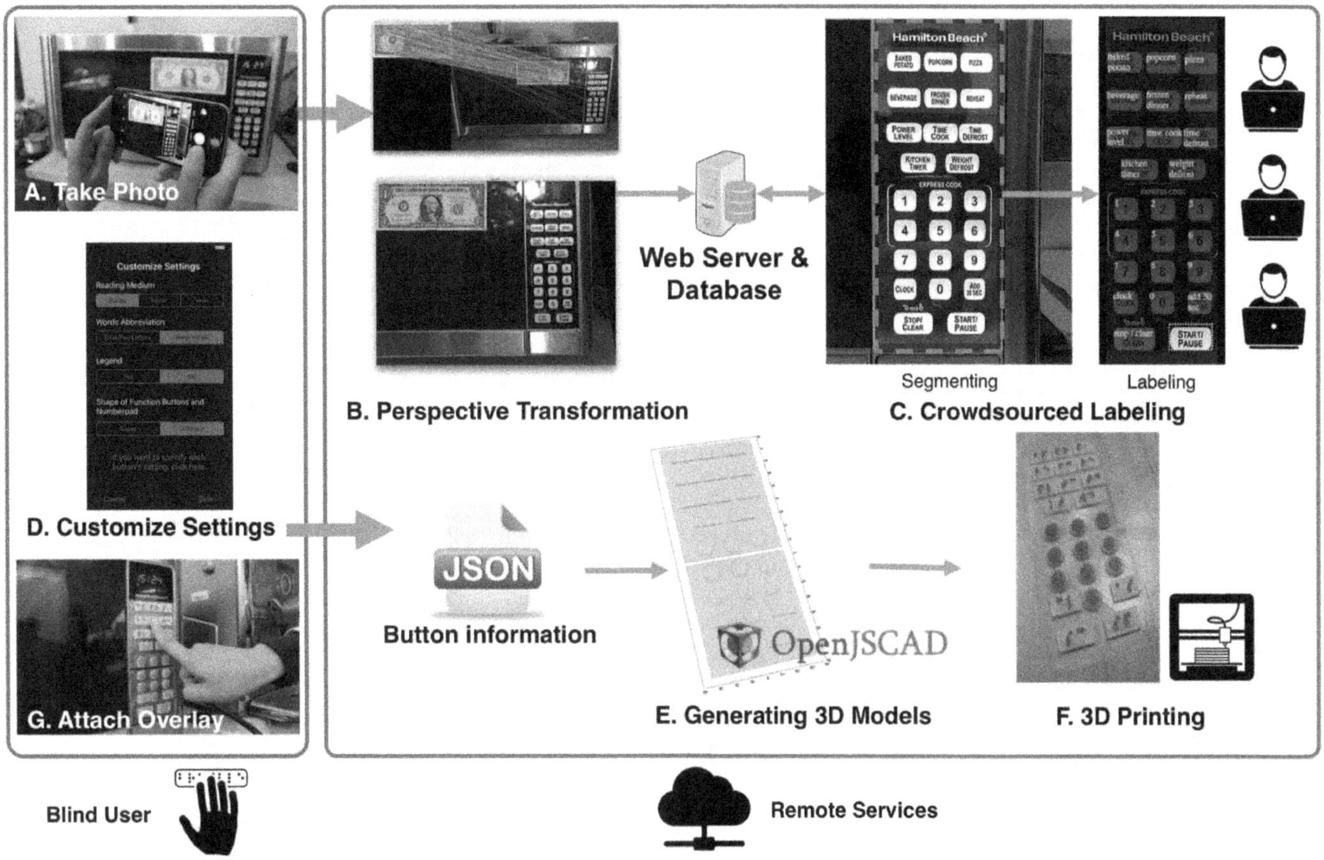

Figure 2. Facade users capture a photo of an interface they would like to use with a fiducial marker attached to it (we use a dollar bill). Using perspective transformation, the interface image is warped to the front view and absolute measurements are calculated. Then this image is sent to multiple crowd workers, who work in parallel to quickly label and describe elements of the interface. Blind users can then customize settings of the labeling strategy, and these labels and preferences are used to generate the 3D models of a tactile layer matching the original controls. Finally, an off-the-shelf 3D printer fabricates the layer, which is then attached to the interface using adhesives.

photo of the interface using a dollar bill as a fiducial marker for recovering size information (Figure 2A and B). Within a few minutes, crowd workers mark the layout of the interface, annotate its elements (*e.g.*, buttons or other controls), and describe each element (Figure 2C). These labels are then used to generate 3D models of a layer of tactile and pressable buttons matching the original controls (Figure 2E), which the blind users can customize by changing the shape and labels of the buttons using the Facade iOS app (Figure 2D). Finally, an off-the-shelf 3D printer can be used to fabricate the layer (Figure 2F). The printed button facade is designed to be easily aligned and attached to its appliance using adhesives (Figure 2G). Although consumer-grade 3D printers might not be readily available to blind people at home, many printing services are available from which a print can be mail-ordered. In addition, we can expect that consumer-grade printers will continue to improve in speed and robustness. Even with mail-order costs, Facade is an inexpensive ($10 from a service such as 3D Hubs[1]) and more accessible alternative solution.

[1]https://www.3dhubs.com

This paper makes the following contributions:

- In a user study, we identify existing challenges and design requirements for augmenting physical interfaces with tactile markers.
- We introduce Facade, a crowdsourcing and fabrication pipeline to augment inaccessible physical interfaces with overlaid 3D printed tactile buttons.
- Our validation shows that Facade enables blind people to independently augment appliance interfaces, and that fabricated overlays provide rich and usable tactile feedback for accessing otherwise inaccessible appliances.

RELATED WORK

Recent advances in consumer-grade 3D printers and the do-it-yourself (DIY) movement have changed the audience of 3D printing. It has already been established as a tool that enables amateurs to create a wide variety of assistive technologies [11, 12, 24, 31]. However, the barriers to entry for 3D modeling custom assistive technologies are high, which has lead to research on tools that can support amateurs without requiring mastery of modeling (*e.g.,* [16]). In addition, assistive technology must typically interoperate with existing objects in the real world, which brings new challenges such as attachment [15] and interoperation [36].

In terms of accessibility for blind users, 3D printing has been used to produce custom labels on 3D printed objects [37], generate tactile maps [10, 19, 20, 39], support literacy skills through the creation of tactile picture books [27], teach design [32], mathematics [13], programming [26] and deliver tactile visualizations [9, 38]. These applications of 3D printing share a focus on 3D representations that can be customized beyond what is possible with the current state of the art (thermal printing or Braille labeling). However, this body of work assumes a sighted person who designs and produces the 3D printed artifact, which may limit a blind person's ability to access 3D printed solutions as needed.

One potential way of reducing the barriers to accessing sighted assistance is to shift the work to a virtual crowd [3, 6]. A number of crowd-powered systems have been developed to make visual information accessible to blind people [7]. VizWiz lets blind people take a picture, speak a question, and get answers back from the crowd within approximately 30 seconds [4]. Chorus:View [29] pairs a user with a group of crowd workers using a shared video stream. "Be My Eyes"[2] matches users to a single volunteer over a shared video stream. VizWiz::LocateIt [5] allows blind people to ask for assistance in finding a specific object. RegionSpeak [46] enables spatial exploration of the layout of objects in a photograph using a touchscreen. VizLens [21, 22] fuses crowdsourcing and computer vision to robustly and interactively help blind people use inaccessible interfaces in the real world, similar to a screen reader. Recently, physical crowds have been organized to construct pre-designed large-scale structures [28]. However, crowds have not in the past been used to create custom 3D printed objects. Facade combines a crowd interpretation pipeline with an accessible 3D printing application [23].

Another approach is to create new devices that are accessible, but this is unlikely to make all devices accessible due to cost. As more and more devices are connected to the Internet and can be controlled remotely, the problem becomes one of digital accessibility, which is easier to solve. For example, users may bring their own smartphone with an interface that is accessible to them, and use it to connect to the device [17, 35, 41]. Facade handles the legacy of inaccessible devices, which neither approach does.

To summarize, 3D printing can produce customized physical augmentations, and crowdsourcing can release the constraints of in-person sighted help through online and always-available visual assistance. Both have been applied with success in the domain of accessibility, including addressing the needs of blind users. Facade's novel contribution is in bringing these threads of research together to solve the important problem of making everyday appliances accessible.

FORMATIVE STUDY

To better understand how blind people currently use and accommodate home and office appliances, we conducted a formative study with 6 blind participants (all female, age 34-73). Four of the participants were congenitally blind, and the other two had light perception. All were Braille readers.

Procedure

We first went to the home of a blind individual, and observed how she cooked a meal and used home appliances. We then conducted semi-structured interviews with all participants. We asked questions about home appliance use, whether these appliances were accessible, if not, the ways employed to use these appliances, and strategies to label them. The studies were documented with video and audio recordings, as well as handwritten notes. We extracted key quotes and themes that reflected participants' personal strategies and challenges.

Results: Design Considerations

Participants remarked that interfaces are becoming much less accessible as flat digital touch pads replace physical buttons, which can at least be easily found by fingers once the locations of different functions were memorized. Appliances mentioned by participants were very diverse, and their interfaces differed in size, label, type of functions and number of buttons.

We identified four design requirements for a system to generate augmented physical interfaces for non-visual access. We refer to the participants in our formative study as F1 - F6 below (and also include related comments gathered later from our evaluation study participants P1 - P11).

Independence

Blind users often depend on in-person sighted assistance to identify the original functions and apply the labels on home appliances. When they bought a new appliance, they needed to wait for sighted help before being able to use the appliance.

> *My brother let me and my husband know what buttons are, we decide what buttons matter for us. And we write the Braille to label them, he again help us to stick onto buttons.* (P2)

The problem of existing solutions of applying Braille stickers, is that blind people cannot independently make appliances accessible. To address this, our solution should enable blind users to independently augment appliance interfaces, without needing to wait for help from sighted people.

Custom Settings

Participants had their own preferences and strategies for labeling. Simple dots (which could easily be counted and felt at a glance) were a popular choice on number buttons. Although not identical to Braille numeric characters, Braille readers also liked this strategy and only used Braille labels on more complex features, such as soft/melt, cook time, reheat, defrost, cancel and start on the microwave.

However, participants said they don't need all the buttons to be labeled. Some of them put bump dots or easily recognizable marker on frequently used buttons.

> *I put bump dots on only the 'add 30 seconds' button that I frequently use.* (F1)

When all the buttons are labeled with the same Braille dots, it's harder for them to find the number pad. Some of them mark only one of the number buttons (*e.g.,* 0 or 5) as the reference to identify all others. F5 suggested that differentiating the number pad from other buttons could make interacting with the microwave faster.

[2] http://www.bemyeyes.org

Please indicate where the number starts, and that is enough. I can identify where other buttons are, it will make tasks quicker. (F2)

I do not need to mark the entire number pad. 0, left and right are enough to get where number buttons are. (F3)

Our solution should accommodate different preferred labeling strategies and reading mediums (Braille, printed letters, or dots). It should also use different shapes for functional buttons and number pads to reduce searching time.

Memorization Strategy

Since blind people were not familiar with the appliance functions, when using in-person sighted help for identifying the original functions and applying the labels, it was hard for them to remember the abbreviations and functions for more than a few buttons [33]. Therefore, they only tended to label a few buttons with only one or two Braille letters due to the limited size of the buttons, which limited their access to the appliances. There are also appliance interfaces that are hard to label. F1 reported making legend for a toaster oven since the buttons are hard to add labels on. Related to it, P5 stated:

I have an index card for a washer in my apartment, what normal hot and normal warm buttons are. I had my mom to help me to label when I moved in long time ago. (P5)

To address this, our solution should better support learning and memorization of the appliance functions through the use of in-app support, or physical legend.

Robustness

The Braille labels applied to the interface will wear out over time. When it happened, blind people lost access to the specific buttons, and required sighted help again to reapply the labels.

We use microwave in the kitchen with dirty hands. Braille stickers are so easily fall off. (P2)

To solve this problem, our solution should allow blind users to easily do the attachment independently. Furthermore, it should support easy reproduction and decrease the amount of effort required for the repeated work on the same appliance.

To summarize, our findings indicate that a solution for tactile labeling should allow blind users to independently augment and access their appliances. The solution should also support rich tactile feedback, diverse labeling strategies and preferences to address a wide range of individual needs. Furthermore, the solution should allow for learning and memorization of the interface, as well as easy attachment and reproduction.

FACADE

Assisted by the Facade iOS app, blind users capture a photo of an inaccessible interface with a readily available fiducial marker (a dollar bill) for recovering size information. The web server transforms the image to the front perspective then feeds this image to multiple crowd workers, who work in parallel to quickly label and describe elements of the interface. These labels are then used to generate a 3D model for a layer of tactile and pressable buttons matching the original controls, which blind users can customize by changing the shape and labels of the buttons using the Facade iOS app. Finally, a home 3D printer or service fabricates the layer, which is then aligned and attached to the interface by blind users. Facade works as a pipeline, and is fully automated. Users do not need to attend to its full complexity.

Capture and Perspective Transformation

The first time a user encounters an interface, s/he uses the Facade iOS app to take a photo of the interface with a dollar bill (Figure 2A), and sends the image to be processed and pushed to the crowd for manual labeling. The dollar bill is used to produced an image of the interface warped to appear as if from the front perspective, and to recover size information. We use a dollar bill as an example to demonstrate the utility of using currency bills as fiducial markers because of its ubiquity, its standard size and appearance, and its richness in details and texture to provide sufficient feature points for tracking. We expect that a deployed version of Facade would allow users to choose their preferred bill in their local currency.

Facade uses SURF (Speeded-Up Robust Features) [2] feature detector to compute key points and feature vectors in both the standard image of the dollar bill and the input image. Then the feature vectors are matched using FLANN (Fast Library for Approximate Nearest Neighbors) [34] based matcher. By filtering matches and finding the perspective transformation [44] between the two images using RANSAC (Random Sample Consensus) [18], our system is able to localize the standard dollar bill image in the input image, and warp the input image to the front perspective for further labeling. Figure 2B shows the results of perspective transformation using a dollar bill. Using a system similar to VizLens [22], the Facade app streams images to the backend server, which then localizes either side of the dollar bill in the image and provides real-time feedback on the aiming of camera relative to the dollar bill to blind users. By reading out instructions such as "not found", "move phone to left/right/up/down/further" and "aiming is good", the app guides the blind user to more easily take a photo from the front perspective, which will result in better warped image after the perspective transformation. The computer vision components are implemented using C++ and the OpenCV Library.

Facade only has knowledge of the dollar bill and provides guidance based on its location, without knowing where the interface is. Blind users use this guidance, combined with their knowledge of the relative location of the interface and the dollar bill, to aim the camera and take photos. However, if the appliance interface is partially cropped in the photo, in the next step, crowd workers will provide feedback to the user for taking another photo. Using a second marker could help, but appliances might not have enough space to fit two markers. In the future, we could use more advanced techniques for helping blind users take photos [25, 30, 42, 43, 45].

Crowdsourced Segmenting and Labeling

Facade uses a two-step workflow to label the area of the image that contains the interface and then label the individual visual elements (Figure 2C), similar to those in VizLens [22]. Crowd workers are first asked to rate the image quality, and segment the interface region. Results are combined using majority vote. To assist with later attachment, we ask crowd workers to segment the interface region aligned with the physical boundaries of the appliance interface, so that blind people can feel that boundary and align the overlay themselves.

Crowd workers are then instructed to draw bounding boxes around all of the individual buttons within the interface area, and provide a text annotation for each element (such as labeling buttons as 'baked potato', 'start/pause'). In this step, crowd workers work in parallel, and the worker interface shows labeled elements to other workers as they are completed.

Fabricating Accessible Augmented Layer

Labels are used to generate a 3D model for a tactile and pressable button layer, matching the original controls. After labeling by crowd workers, the blind user can use VoiceOver to customize the preferences for the tactile layer to be fabricated using the iOS app (Figure 2D). Blind users specify customizations using a virtual version of the interface displayed on their iPhone. Informed by our study, we allow individual buttons to be customized using Braille, embossed letters, or embossed symbols. Although embossed capital letters were not mentioned in our study, blind participants did mention using shared machines at home and at work with sighted people, which embossed letters allows for co-located access. Embossed letters also improve access for non-Braille readers, who can recognize capital letters almost as well as Braille readers recognize Braille [14]. Finally, users can customize the abbreviation strategy (*i.e.*, which letters are used to represent a word or phrase); request a legend; edit the tactile label of individual buttons; set which buttons to label or remain flat; and customize the shape of buttons (useful for differentiating special buttons such as numbers).

Based on the results from our formative studies, we decide by default to detect and use different shapes for function (rectangular) and number (spherical) buttons when generating the 3D tactile overlay. Following common numeric keyboard or button pad accessibility conventions [40], by default we only label number 5 with a dot on the spherical button for the numbers.

The settings and the crowd-generated labels are then passed to our automated design tool. We implemented an OpenJSCAD script to generate the final STL files of 3D models of the augmented buttons for printing (Figure 2E). The input to the program is a generated JSON object including the dimensions of the tactile overlay, average button size, as well as the dimensions, positions, labels and preferences of each button. With this data, the script first generates groups of labeled 3D buttons. We determine the depth of the buttons to be proportional to the size of the buttons. To get the scale factor for Braille and letters, we first divide the button width by two to situate two characters, and then divide each area to hold two columns and three rows of dots including spacing. Compared to the standard dot radius and spacing size [1], the proportion is defined by this scale factor, and applied to determine the size of letters and symbols.

If short acronyms are not provided for each button label, the program automatically generates the abbreviations. By default, when adding Braille on top of the buttons, we use two characters for each button due to the limited surface area and the size of Braille characters: a word (*e.g.*, 'Clock') is abbreviated by the first two letters (*e.g.*, 'CL'); and multiple words (*e.g.*, 'Power Level') are abbreviated by the initial letters of the first two words (*e.g.*, 'PL'). When requested, a separate

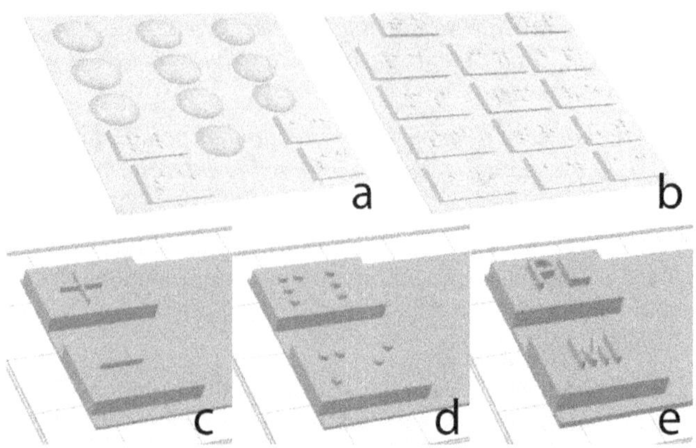

Figure 3. Shapes inform users of different functionalities. For example, half spherical buttons without Braille label indicates number buttons *(a)*, while rectangular buttons with Braille labels indicate function buttons *(b)*. Users are also able to change settings to use symbols *(c)*, Braille *(d)*, or embossed letters *(e)* for buttons labels such as plus and minus.

STL file is generated containing a legend (Figure 5e) detailing the abbreviations of the button labels, with the first column being acronyms, and the second column being the full words.

Our automated design tool then places buttons on top of a thin (2 layers in Gcode, 0.8mm) flat sheet, which creates a flat surface below the buttons that is easily attached to appliances with adhesives. Then, the program splits the tactile overlay into separate groups according to the 3D printer's print bed size limit, and combines all sheets, buttons and embossed labels in each group into one piece for printing. The script can also merge multiple pieces as one print job based on print bed size to reduce print time. Our system exports files in ready-to-print STL format, which can be printed at the blind user's home or through a commercial 3D printing service. An example 3D printed tactile overlay for a microwave is shown in Figure 2F. The overlay design in Figure 3 was finalized after several design iterations as we detail in the next section.

DESIGN ITERATIONS

To produce the most effectively functioning tactile overlay, we went through several design iterations. The microwave we chose as the testing device was a Hamilton Beach 1.1 Cu Ft Microwave (Figure 4c). Similar to most common microwaves, buttons on this microwave are flat and provide little (if any) tactile feedback. It contains some familiar buttons (0-9), and many that are likely to be less familiar (*e.g.*, time defrost, baked potato). All of our tactile overlays used in design iterations and user evaluations were produced with off-the-shelf consumer grade 3D printers using the FDM (fused deposition modeling) technique of 3D printing.

Iteration #1: Design Probe

To test the 3D printed Facade overlay, we first created a design probe—a 3D printed sheet in PLA plastic of buttons labeled with Braille acronyms, attached to the microwave (Figure 4). We used an inverted cone shape for buttons, with the radius of the top surface corresponding to the actual size of the original button, and the radius of the bottom surface smaller (Figure 4a). Thus, the design reduces the pressure required for blind users to press on the top surface to activate the original buttons on

Figure 4. A design probe tested with 6 blind participants. An augmented button set with Braille labels *(a)* is attached to the microwave *(c)*, and buttons are connected with thin bridges to facilitate pressing *(b)*.

the microwave. To minimize assembly time, we attached the buttons in a grid with connectors between buttons (Figure 4b), so that they could be batch printed, and also attached to the physical interface as a whole. We also made the connectors very thin so that the plastic buttons deform more easily when pressed. All of this design work was done by hand, but in a style that can be automatically generated for Facade.

We tested this design with the same participants from our formative study, and identified the following issues:

- Some unexpected 3D printed artifacts on the edges of the top surface made the Braille dots feel overly rough, reducing legibility.
- Duc to print resolution, Braille dots had different heights, reducing legibility.
- The plastic buttons were too hard to push.
- The button set did not attach to the microwave panel well and fell off after several times of use, due to the small contact regions.
- Because PLA does not deform, the connector bridges broke after pressing for a few times.

Iteration #2: Material Exploration

Informed by the participants' feedback to our initial design probe, we modified the design of the tactile overlay, and tested different combinations of materials (Figure 5a-d) to improve attacheability, legibility, and pressibility. Using a flat and thin sheet printed in flexible NinjaFlex[3] as the base of the overlay can make the augmentation much easier to attach to the appliance interface with adhesive.[4] The flexible material also made it much easier to press than using only PLA for the design probe.

While using NinjaFlex can improve attachability and pressability, it sometimes leaves undesired artifacts in the form of fine threads between Braille dots (think of melted cheese threads between pizza slices). These threads could reduce Braille legibility. One solution is to print Braille using hard material such as PLA (which we denote as Flex+PLA label), as shown in Figure 5b. A problem that occurred with this design is

Device	Material	Label
Hamilton Beach microwave	Flex*	Braille (Fig. 5a)
	Flex+PLA label	Braille (Fig. 5b)
	Flax+PLA cover	Braille (Fig. 5c)
	Flex+PLA cover	Letters (Fig. 5d)
	PLA legend	Braille (Fig. 5e)
Frigidaire Gallery microwave	Flex	Braille
Frigidaire fridge	Flex+PLA label	Braille
KitchenAid fridge	Flex	Letters + Symbol
Sharp microwave	Flex	Braille
Richo Alficio MP 6500 Copier**	Flex+PLA cover	Embossed letters Printed full words

Table 1. Interface, material and reading medium combinations used in design iteration 2 to improve attacheability, legibility, and pressibility.
* Flex refers to NinjaFlex or SemiFlex for flexible material printing
** Required manual intervention for raised buttons

that these Braille dots may become dislodged from the button surface over time, due to the combination of heterogeneous materials. Another solution for this is to print several layers of the button together with Braille dots in PLA, while printing the rest of the bottom layers in NinjaFlex, resulting in a larger contact area between the two materials to allow them to stick together nicely (which we denote as Flex+PLA cover). Table 1 summarizes our experiments on various printing mediums and material combinations for a wide variety of home appliances.

We then obtained formative feedback of the examples shown in Table 1 from one blind individual (female, 24 years old, college student). In three different settings (*i.e.*, pure NinjaFlex, Flex+PLA label, and Flex+PLA cover), the participant said all three testing material combinations were equally legible. Interestingly, she was most comfortable with reading the pure NinjaFlex version of the tactile overlay, despite the fine threads across dots. Unfortunately, both Flex+PLA label and Flex+PLA cover versions required her to press the button a lot harder to trigger the original interface. Overall, the NinjaFlex version of the tactile overlay had the best pressability and attachability among all material combinations we explored.

Iteration #3: Improved Legibility

Since the NinjaFlex version of printed Braille has enough detail and so is easily legible by a user, we printed the entire overlay in pure NinjaFlex including Braille. As guided by the user who tested our second design above, we also improved our design of the embossed letter version to make the letters thinner with larger gaps between letters for distinction.

For this improved design, we further tested the legibility of the Braille labels with two blind individuals (one female), both of whom provided formative feedback on the design. One suggested making the Braille dots more distinctive by raising the dots higher or reducing the button height. The other Braille expert, who works for a Braille publisher, suggested that Braille dots with a convex top are easier to read by touch than with a flat cylindrical top because convex tops provide a more salient separation between adjacent dots. Therefore, we changed the Braille dots from cylinders to domes, and finalized our design for the user evaluation we present next.

[3] https://ninjatek.com/products/filaments/ninjaflex/
[4] We used 3M removable double-sided Scotch Tape.

Figure 5. Example printed overlays and legends generated by Facade. ***(a)-(d)*** **demonstrate the different material combinations we tested in the design iterations (NinjaFlex with Braille, Flex+PLA Braille label, Flex+PLA Braille cover, and Flex+PLA embossed letter cover). Facade users can choose to print a legend for the abbreviations** ***(e)*****. If a user does not have a 3D printer at home, models can also be printed through commercial printing services and mail-ordered.** ***(f) and (g)*** **show two example prints ordered from 3D Hubs using PolyFlex and SemiFlex materials.**

USER EVALUATION

The goal of our user study was to evaluate whether Facade allows blind people to independently augment appliance interfaces, and how the fabricated overlay performs in assisting blind people accomplish realistic tasks that involve otherwise inaccessible interfaces. Our user evaluation included each step that the blind user needs to do in Facade.

Apparatus and Participants

We used the same inaccessible microwave as detailed in design iterations. The Facade iOS app was used in the study, installed on an iPhone 5c, runing iOS 9.3.4. For this particular evaluation, all the images were labeled by the experimenter as introducing the crowd would result in compounding factors. The tactile overlays used in the study were generated and 3D printed beforehand to save time. The quality of perspective transformation, crowdsourced labeling, and model production is presented in the next section ("Technical Evaluation"). We recruited 11 blind users (6 female, age 40-82). The demographics of our participants are shown in Table 2.

Procedure

Following a brief introduction of the study and demographic questions, participants were asked to attach a one dollar bill next to the interface with the goal of facilitating photo taking in the next step to include both the dollar bill and the complete interface into the field of view. Then, participants were asked to take five photos of the microwave control panel with the assistance of the Facade iOS app, followed by another five photos taken with the built-in camera app on iOS. After each photo was taken, simulated crowd feedback on image quality was provided. These images were used to evaluate the perspective transformation and crowdsourced labeling.

Next, the labels for the microwave were entered into the app to simulate it having been crowd labelled, and participants were asked to explore the customization interface for identifying their reading medium and other preferences. Then, based on the reading medium chosen by the participants, the fabricated overlay of the microwave was presented to the participants, and they were asked to attach the overlay onto the microwave with double-sided tapes by aligning the edges. Images of the attached overlay was taken, and experimenters tested individual buttons to evaluate whether the alignment was sufficient for activating the microwave controls.

Next, we used a sheet of Braille or embossed letters in randomized order to familiarize participants with the shape and feeling of the tactile labels. Then, participants were asked to identify and read out the label of each button of the microwave. Accuracy was recorded, and participants were told the meaning of each abbreviation, *e.g.*, BP for Baked Potato.

Next, participants were asked to complete 11 locating tasks and 4 simulated cooking tasks. For locating tasks, the participant was asked to locate a button with the assistance of the tactile overlay, and then push to trigger the button. Tasks included Power Level, Baked Potato, Frozen Dinner, Kitchen Timer, Clock, Popcorn, Time defrost, 0, 2, 4, and 8. For simulated cooking tasks, we designed more realistic tasks that involved a series of button presses. For example, a multi-button cooking task would require pressing a configure button (*e.g.*, weight defrost, time defrost, or time cook), followed by setting a time duration by pressing the number pads (*e.g.*, 2, 1, 0 for two minutes and 10 seconds, or two pounds and 10 oz), and finally pressing the 'Start' button. For both locating and simulated cooking tasks, we measured accuracy and time.

After performing tasks on the microwave with the tactile overlay using their reading medium preferences, we also tested overlays we printed out with other settings, such as the same microwave augmented with Braille or embossed letters, and a fridge interface augmented with embossed letters and symbols.

After each step of the study, we collected Likert scale ratings and subjective feedback from the participants. Finally, we ended the study with a semi-structured interview asking for the participant's comments and suggestions on the Facade system. The study took about one and a half hours and the participants were compensated for $50. The whole study was video and audio recorded for further analysis.

ID	Gender	Age	Occupation	Vision Level	Reading Medium	Smartphone Use
P1	Male	63	Retired	Blind, since birth	Braille, 60 years	iPhone, 7 years
P2	Female	68	Retired	Blind, since birth	Braille, 62 years	iPhone, 8 years
P3	Female	75	Retired	Light perception	Braille, 20 years	No
P4	Male	82	Retired	Blind, since 8 years old	Braille, 75 years	No
P5	Female	46	Unemployed	Blind, since birth	Braille, 42 years	iPhone, 2 months
P6	Male	40	IT professional	Light perception, tunnel vision	Mostly audio	iPhone, 10 months
P7	Female	42	AT consultant	Blind, since birth	Braille, 22 years	iPhone, 2 years
P8	Male	43	Rehab counselor	Blind, since birth	Braille, 36 years	Mostly iPhone, 10 years
P9	Female	58	Retired	Blind, since 1 year old	Braille, 50 years	iPhone, 5 years
P10	Female	61	Retired	Light perception, since birth	Braille, 35 years	iPhone, 6 years
P11	Female	68	Retired	Blind, since birth	Braille, 62 years	iPhone, 1.5 years

Table 2. Participant demographics for our user evaluation with 11 blind users.

Results

We now detail our user study results and summarize user feedback and preferences. For all Likert scale questions, participants were asked to rate along a scale of 1 to 5, where 1 is very negative and 5 is very positive, *e.g.,* 1 for very hard to perform, and 5 for very easy to perform.

Participants spent an average of 30.3 seconds ($SD = 19.1$) to attach the dollar bill and found it very easy to perform ($M = 4.8, SD = 0.41$). For taking photos assisted with the Facade mobile app, participants took an average of 33.6 seconds ($SD = 24.5$) to take each photo, and rated neutral for the difficulty of taking photos ($M = 3.2, SD = 1.3$). The reason why it was not easy was mainly because it required users to hold the device very stable, and there was no direct feedback of where the interface was. However, participants mentioned that after taking a few photos, feedback became easier to follow.

For applying the tactile overlay onto the microwave control panel, it took participants an average of 117.1 seconds ($SD = 83.0$) to attach the overlay, including 2 of the 11 participants failed to attach the overlay correctly (Figure 6). Participants rated it relatively easy to attach the overlay ($M = 3.8, SD = 1.9$). Participants applied the strategy of aligning from the top and using gravity to keep the overlay flat and align towards the bottom. P7 suggested that making the edge of the tactile overlay more distinctive can make it easier to align with the interface. Depending on the size of the buttons, slight offset will not affect using the appliance (such as Figure 6 P5). Furthermore, if the buttons are physically raised, they will also help with aligning the tactile overlay.

Identification Tasks

Ten out of 11 participants chose Braille as their primary reading medium and used our tactile overlay augmented with Braille labels, while P6 used the embossed letter version of tactile overlay. In order to compare participants' performance and report on our Braille quality, we only report the performance of the ten participants who used Braille. For identification tasks, it took participants an average of 112.6 seconds ($SD = 44.1$) to read through all 25 buttons of the microwave, with an accuracy of 98.3% ($SD = 0.018$). Errors happened to letters including C, D, and P. Participants rated reading the Braille as easy ($M = 4.2, SD = 0.92$). The errors were mostly caused by the limited resolution of the printer and some remaining artifacts on the print. We believe this will be further resolved with improvements in 3D printers and printing materials, as detailed in the survey of different materials and printing techniques in the next section. Participants also mentioned that when sitting in front of the microwave in our study, their hands needed to be flipped backward when reading the Braille, which affected the accuracy. This effect will be reduced when they place the microwave at the position they prefer, and as they get familiar with the functions over time as they use them.

Locating and Simulated Cooking Tasks

For locating tasks, it took participants an average of 6.7 seconds ($SD = 4.6$) to locate and push to activate each of the function buttons, while it all took less than 1 second for the number buttons. The overall accuracy was 97.3% ($SD = 0.044$). We asked participants to locate the number pad in a separate task to evaluate whether the different shapes of function and number buttons facilitate locating, and all participants rated it as very easy (5). Participants also found it very easy to remember the button name by acronyms ($M = 4.9, SD = 0.32$), locate the buttons ($M = 4.6, SD = 0.70$), push the buttons ($M = 4.5, SD = 0.53$), as well as operate the microwave with the tactile overlay ($M = 4.8, SD = 0.42$).

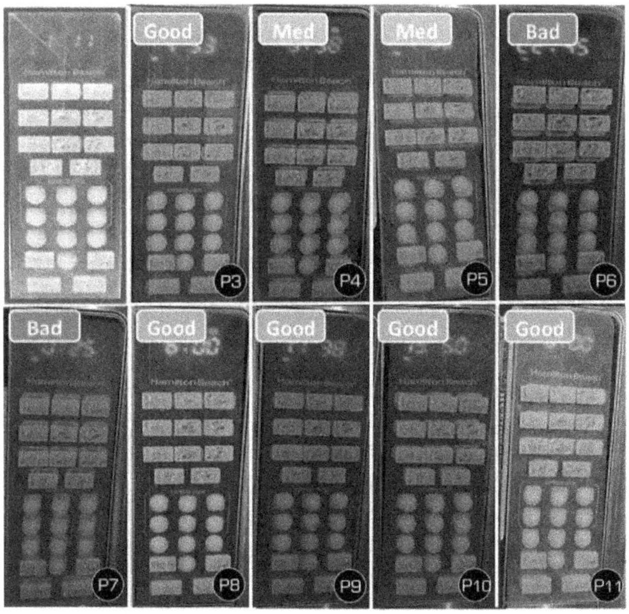

Figure 6. Examples of the attached overlay performed by the participants. For P4 and P5, slight offset did not affect using the appliance. An exact alignment is shown in the top left corner.

Specifically for pushing the buttons, we observed there were 6 times across all 110 locating tasks participants needed to push the button more than once to activate it. Participants commented that with the overlay, they needed to apply slightly more force to activate the button than the original microwave, but it was still very easy to perform. P3 suggested making the buttons thinner and closer to the interface to reduce the force required, similar to a Dymo label tape.

For simulated cooking tasks, it took participants an average of 17.2 seconds ($SD = 10.1$) to complete each sequence, with an accuracy of 92.5% ($SD = 0.169$).

Embossed Letters and Symbols

Though none of the participants use embossed letter or symbol as their primary reading medium, they have mostly encountered them in everyday lives, such as in elevators, doorways, hotel rooms, or restrooms.

For identification tasks on the embossed letter version of tactile overlay for the microwave control panel, it took participants an average of 218.1 seconds ($SD = 132.9$) to complete all 25 buttons. And for a fridge overlay that contains both embossed letters and symbols, it took them an average of 142.0 seconds ($SD = 76.0$) to read through 10 buttons.

Subjective Feedback

When asked which of the three reading medium they preferred (*i.e.*, Braille, embossed letter, symbol), all participants chose Braille, mostly because it aligns with their primary reading medium. P5 mentioned that if living with sighted people or people with partial vision, he could also accommodate with embossed letters.

When asked to compare Facade with the traditional method of applying Braille labels, participants commented *"I like [Facade] much better. I can do it myself, to me it's huge. I don't need to wait for someone to come over and label things for me. If template gets damaged, then I can create a new one. With the [traditional] labels I made, things start get peeled off soon. I think this is neat (P1)"*, and *"This makes a lot more sense. Dymo easily fall off. I like this better (P6)."*

Participants also provided suggestions to make Facade work with interface widgets of other shapes, such as circular knobs (P9). P8 suggested to add a simple/advanced mode in the customization interface in the mobile app for people who prefer labeling the complete panel versus only a small set of buttons. P1 suggested that the feedback provided in the app should be more specific, such as saying "dollar bill in focus", "images are too close", *etc.*

Overall, participants were excited about the potential of Facade and several asked when they can use it on their appliances.

TECHNICAL EVALUATION

We conducted a multi-part technical evaluation in order to understand how each component of the Facade pipeline performs across a range of interfaces and usage scenarios.

Interface Capture

We first evaluated how well the Facade iOS app performs in assisting blind people in capturing photos containing both the dollar bill and the interface of the device, and how well our perspective transformation component performs in warping images to a front view of the interface.

Figure 7. Examples for image localization and warping on photos taken by the participants using a dollar bill as the fiducial marker. Boxes show in green represents warping results that were good enough for generating a usable tactile overlay model, while those shown in orange and red represents failure cases.

We used photos of the microwave taken by the participants from our user evaluations (described in the previous section). Out of the 55 images taken when the Facade iOS app provided feedback, the perspective transformation component was able to identify the dollar bill and successfully warp the image to a front perspective for 34 cases (61.8%). In 4 of 55 cases, it identified the dollar bill, but the resulting warping was not suitable for further labeling and printing. In the remaining 17, the dollar bill failed to be localized. Pictures taken with the Camera app built into iOS were worse. Only 18 (32.7%) were successful, 3 were not ideal, and 34 did not localize the bill.

These image are then labeled by crowd workers, and labels are used to generate 3D models of the tactile overlay. Each segmenting task paid \$0.15 (~40sec of work, \$13.5/hr). Each labeling task paid \$.02 (<10sec, \$9/hr). We evaluated the crowdsourcing workflow, and generated analogous results to [22] as they share a similar crowdsourcing workflow. In prior work, the crowdsourcing labeling workflow was fast (8 minutes), accurate (99.7%), and inexpensive (\$1.15). Accuracy is high because tasks are simple, and we perform automatic and redundancy checks on button size, aspect ratios, and labels. For the 34 successful pictures taken using the Facade app, Facade was able to generate a usable tactile overlay model for 21 of them (61.7%). On the other hand, 16 out of 18 images taken with the built-in Camera app were able to generate a usable overlay model. Figure 7 shows examples for image localization and warping on photos taken by the participants.

The results show our Facade iOS app allowed participants to take better photos for generating the tactile overlay. It is important to note that since the Facade iOS app streams all images to the backend server when aiming the camera, we could configure our system to automatically pick several images where the dollar bill can be found before the user clicks the "take photo" button. This would also require adding another step in the crowdsourcing workflow for the crowd workers to select the best warped image.

Model Production

We next tested our pipeline on several other appliance interfaces, including three different microwaves, two refrigerators,

Material	Printer	Resolution	Price
NinjaFlex	Lulzbot TAZ5	Medium	$10.00
SemiFlex	Lulzbot TAZ5	Medium	$10.00
PolyFlex	Lulzbot TAZ5	Medium	$10.00
Nylon	ProJet 660 SLS	High	$31.40
Flexible Resin	FormLab SLS	High	$21.70

Table 3. We experimented with a variety of materials and printing techniques. Test prints were ordered from 3D Hubs.

and a printer, some of these are shown in Figure 1. In addition to varying appliances, we also experimented with a variety of printing techniques. Figure 5(a-d) shows tactile overlays printed with PrintrBot Simple Maker's kit (FDM) in our lab, each costs less than $5 (printed in 15% infill, 0.4mm layer thickness, 3 solid layers for top/bottom). Figure 5fg shows two example prints ordered from 3D Hubs using PolyFlex and SemiFlex materials. As shown in Table 3, we also tried out Nylon and Flexible Resin printed with SLS (selective laser sintering) printing technique, which generated much higher resolution Braille labels.

DISCUSSION AND FUTURE WORK

Facade enables blind people to access flat physical interfaces by auto-generating a tactile overlay. We focused on augmenting inaccessible buttons in this paper, while this concept can be extended to work with other types of interface elements. For example, for a mechanical knob, tactile markings can be attached to the main interface, leaving the knob area empty, and a separate pointer printed and attached. Another approach is to fabricate a knob that supports internal movement.

Once the original physical interface is covered by the tactile buttons, sighted users living with blind users, or external caretakers cannot easily identify the original functions [8]. We chose transparent filament to print the overlaid buttons to see through the background. Yet, the button had multiple layers, which reduced transparency. To address this, we can support both sighted and blind people to access the appliances by applying different colors of materials to make the text labels visually salient, similar to Figure 5b. For appliances where visual elements are not as cluttered as the examples we show, we could place the tactile labels around the interactive elements and leave a hole for the button to directly make them accessible to sighted people (similar to Thingiverse thing: 1415446). Other attachment strategies can also be investigated with mechanical structures, such as hinge, flip door, sliding, *etc.*

For buttons that are not flat, our current approach of using a flat sheet for attachment wouldn't work. As an initial investigation, we show in the copier example in Figure 1 that additional measurements are required for creating concave structures to fit the embossed buttons. We have implemented this feature as an input parameter in our fabrication design tool. However, more advanced approaches need to be integrated to support the acquisition of this value. For example, instead of asking the blind person to take a photo, using a depth camera could better capture the convex properties of the physical interface.

For interfaces or buttons that are too small or cluttered, putting tactile labels on top of the buttons wouldn't work due to the fixed size of Braille. To mitigate this problem, we could configure Facade to print an overlay with minimal markings to attach to the interface, while generating another legend detailing the interface layout and labels on the side.

Our 3D printed augmentation is designed to overlay an interface which is triggered by manual force. If the augmented sheet covers a capacitive touchscreen, it would likely disrupt operation of the interface. One possible solution to address this problem is to print the button with conductive material that connects human skin's conductivity through the 3D printed objects. While this is an interesting approach and needs to be investigated to expand the range of interface that Facade can support, we leave this for future work.

The cost of Facade is rapidly changing and it may soon be competitive with creating labels with tape. 3D printing material is quickly getting cheaper, and approaching that of embossed labels using Dymo tape. In our current pipeline, the interface layout and labels are generated from the crowdsourcing workflow. However, these could also be acquired from remote friends or family, provided by the appliance manufacturers, or automatically retrieved from online manuals. Collectively, labels for common appliances may also benefit a new user. Furthermore, similar approaches can be used for other tasks, such as for a sighted partner or a building manager to quickly collect images and automatically produce tactile labels and augmentations to make a space accessible, which is likely more efficient than manual labeling.

Our evaluation demonstrates the viability of Facade by deeply evaluating each component. This will guide us (and others) in future work to understand how each component is likely to work in deployment and how we might usefully improve the system (*e.g.*, using more advanced blind photography, using more robust crowd labeling workflows, applying other fabrication techniques or materials, *etc.*)

CONCLUSIONS

We have presented *Facade*, a crowdsourced fabrication pipeline for blind users to augment inaccessible physical interfaces by 3D printed tactile overlays. Our system empowers blind users to access physical interfaces in everyday lives in an independent and inexpensive way. We introduced the design of the system and its technical architecture, evaluated it in a user study with 11 blind participants, and evaluated each component separately to understand its limitations.

Compared with traditional embossed labelers, Facade does not require in-person sighted assistance, provides richer tactile feedback using different reading mediums and button shapes, and reduces memory load by providing a legend and in-app support: embossed labels do none of these. Our research envisions a future when 3D printers are faster and more ubiquitous in people's homes. Facade can benefit blind users by generating tactile overlays to home appliances in minutes, complementing or replacing in-home embossed labelers.

ACKNOWLEDGMENTS

This work has been supported by the National Science Foundation, Google, and the National Institute on Disability, Independent Living, and Rehabilitation Research (NIDILRR). We thank the blind participants and workers on Mechanical Turk who contributed to our studies.

REFERENCES

1. American Foundation for Blind 2016. Braille: Deciphering the code. http://braillebug.afb.org/braille_deciphering.asp. (2016).
2. Herbert Bay, Tinne Tuytelaars, and Luc Van Gool. 2006. SURF: Speeded up robust features. In *Proceedings of the 9th European Conference on Computer Vision - Volume Part I (ECCV'06)*. Springer-Verlag, Berlin, Heidelberg, 404–417. DOI:http://dx.doi.org/10.1007/11744023_32
3. Jeffrey P. Bigham, Michael S. Bernstein, and Eytan Adar. 2015. Human-computer interaction and collective intelligence. *Handbook of Collective Intelligence* 57 (2015).
4. Jeffrey P. Bigham, Chandrika Jayant, Hanjie Ji, Greg Little, Andrew Miller, Robert C. Miller, Robin Miller, Aubrey Tatarowicz, Brandyn White, Samual White, and Tom Yeh. 2010a. VizWiz: Nearly real-time answers to visual questions. In *Proceedings of the 23rd Annual ACM Symposium on User Interface Software and Technology (UIST '10)*. ACM, New York, NY, USA, 333–342. DOI: http://dx.doi.org/10.1145/1866029.1866080
5. Jeffrey P. Bigham, Chandrika Jayant, Andrew Miller, Brandyn White, and Tom Yeh. 2010b. VizWiz::LocateIt - Enabling blind people to locate objects in their environment. In *Computer Vision and Pattern Recognition Workshops (CVPRW), 2010 IEEE Computer Society Conference on*. IEEE, 65–72. DOI: http://dx.doi.org/10.1109/CVPRW.2010.5543821
6. Erin Brady and Jeffrey P. Bigham. 2015. Crowdsourcing accessibility: Human-powered access technologies. *Foundations and Trends in Human-Computer Interaction* 8, 4 (2015), 273–372. DOI: http://dx.doi.org/10.1561/1100000050
7. Erin Brady, Meredith Ringel Morris, Yu Zhong, Samuel White, and Jeffrey P. Bigham. 2013. Visual challenges in the everyday lives of blind people. In *Proceedings of the SIGCHI Conference on Human Factors in Computing Systems (CHI '13)*. ACM, New York, NY, USA, 2117–2126. DOI: http://dx.doi.org/10.1145/2470654.2481291
8. Stacy M. Branham and Shaun K. Kane. 2015. Collaborative accessibility: How blind and sighted companions co-create accessible home spaces. In *Proceedings of the 33rd Annual ACM Conference on Human Factors in Computing Systems (CHI '15)*. ACM, New York, NY, USA, 2373–2382. DOI: http://dx.doi.org/10.1145/2702123.2702511
9. Craig Brown and Amy Hurst. 2012. VizTouch: Automatically generated tactile visualizations of coordinate spaces. In *Proceedings of the Sixth International Conference on Tangible, Embedded and Embodied Interaction (TEI '12)*. ACM, New York, NY, USA, 131–138. DOI: http://dx.doi.org/10.1145/2148131.2148160
10. Emeline Brule, Gilles Bailly, Anke Brock, Frederic Valentin, Grégoire Denis, and Christophe Jouffrais. 2016. MapSense: Multi-sensory interactive maps for children living with visual impairments. In *Proceedings of the 2016 CHI Conference on Human Factors in Computing Systems (CHI '16)*. ACM, New York, NY, USA, 445–457. DOI:http://dx.doi.org/10.1145/2858036.2858375
11. Erin Buehler, Stacy Branham, Abdullah Ali, Jeremy J. Chang, Megan Kelly Hofmann, Amy Hurst, and Shaun K. Kane. 2015. Sharing is caring: Assistive technology designs on thingiverse. In *Proceedings of the 33rd Annual ACM Conference on Human Factors in Computing Systems (CHI '15)*. ACM, New York, NY, USA, 525–534. DOI:http://dx.doi.org/10.1145/2702123.2702525
12. Erin Buehler, Amy Hurst, and Megan Hofmann. 2014a. Coming to grips: 3D printing for accessibility. In *Proceedings of the 16th International ACM SIGACCESS Conference on Computers and Accessibility (ASSETS '14)*. ACM, New York, NY, USA, 291–292. DOI: http://dx.doi.org/10.1145/2661334.2661345
13. Erin Buehler, Shaun K. Kane, and Amy Hurst. 2014b. ABC and 3D: Opportunities and obstacles to 3D printing in special education environments. In *Proceedings of the 16th International ACM SIGACCESS Conference on Computers and Accessibility (ASSETS '14)*. ACM, New York, NY, USA, 107–114. DOI: http://dx.doi.org/10.1145/2661334.2661365
14. H. Burton, D.G. McLaren, and R.J. Sinclair. 2006. Reading embossed capital letters: An fMRI study in blind and sighted individuals. *Human brain mapping* 27, 4 (2006), 325–339. DOI: http://dx.doi.org/10.1002/hbm.20188
15. Xiang 'Anthony' Chen, Stelian Coros, Jennifer Mankoff, and Scott E. Hudson. 2015. Encore: 3D printed augmentation of everyday objects with printed-over, affixed and interlocked attachments. In *Proceedings of the 28th Annual ACM Symposium on User Interface Software and Technology (UIST '15)*. ACM, New York, NY, USA, 73–82. DOI:http://dx.doi.org/10.1145/2807442.2807498
16. Xiang 'Anthony' Chen, Jeeeun Kim, Jennifer Mankoff, Tovi Grossman, Stelian Coros, and Scott E. Hudson. 2016. Reprise: A design tool for specifying, generating, and customizing 3D printable adaptations on everyday objects. In *Proceedings of the 29th Annual Symposium on User Interface Software and Technology (UIST '16)*. ACM, New York, NY, USA, 29–39. DOI: http://dx.doi.org/10.1145/2984511.2984512
17. Adrian A. de Freitas, Michael Nebeling, Xiang 'Anthony' Chen, Junrui Yang, Akshaye Shreenithi Kirupa Karthikeyan Ranithangam, and Anind K. Dey. 2016. Snap-To-It: A user-inspired platform for opportunistic device interactions. In *Proceedings of the 2016 CHI Conference on Human Factors in Computing Systems (CHI '16)*. ACM, New York, NY, USA, 5909–5920. DOI: http://dx.doi.org/10.1145/2858036.2858177

18. Martin A. Fischler and Robert C. Bolles. 1981. Random sample consensus: A paradigm for model fitting with applications to image analysis and automated cartography. *Commun. ACM* 24, 6 (June 1981), 381–395. DOI: http://dx.doi.org/10.1145/358669.358692

19. Timo Götzelmann. 2016. LucentMaps: 3D printed audiovisual tactile maps for blind and visually impaired people. In *Proceedings of the 18th International ACM SIGACCESS Conference on Computers and Accessibility (ASSETS '16)*. ACM, New York, NY, USA, 81–90. DOI: http://dx.doi.org/10.1145/2982142.2982163

20. Timo Götzelmann and Aleksander Pavkovic. 2014. *Towards automatically generated tactile detail maps by 3D printers for blind persons*. Springer International Publishing, Cham, 1–7. DOI: http://dx.doi.org/10.1007/978-3-319-08599-9_1

21. Anhong Guo, Xiang 'Anthony' Chen, and Jeffrey P. Bigham. 2015. ApplianceReader: A wearable, crowdsourced, vision-based system to make appliances accessible. In *Proceedings of the 33rd Annual ACM Conference Extended Abstracts on Human Factors in Computing Systems (CHI EA '15)*. ACM, New York, NY, USA, 2043–2048. DOI: http://dx.doi.org/10.1145/2702613.2732755

22. Anhong Guo, Xiang 'Anthony' Chen, Haoran Qi, Samuel White, Suman Ghosh, Chieko Asakawa, and Jeffrey P. Bigham. 2016a. VizLens: A robust and interactive screen reader for interfaces in the real world. In *Proceedings of the 29th Annual Symposium on User Interface Software and Technology (UIST '16)*. ACM, New York, NY, USA, 651–664. DOI: http://dx.doi.org/10.1145/2984511.2984518

23. Anhong Guo, Jeeeun Kim, Xiang 'Anthony' Chen, Tom Yeh, Scott E. Hudson, Jennifer Mankoff, and Jeffrey P. Bigham. 2016b. Facade: Auto-generating tactile interfaces to appliances. In *Proceedings of the 18th International ACM SIGACCESS Conference on Computers and Accessibility (ASSETS '16)*. ACM, New York, NY, USA, 315–316. DOI: http://dx.doi.org/10.1145/2982142.2982187

24. Megan Hofmann, Jeffrey Harris, Scott E. Hudson, and Jennifer Mankoff. 2016. Helping hands: Requirements for a prototyping methodology for upper-limb prosthetics users. In *Proceedings of the 2016 CHI Conference on Human Factors in Computing Systems (CHI '16)*. ACM, New York, NY, USA, 1769–1780. DOI: http://dx.doi.org/10.1145/2858036.2858340

25. Chandrika Jayant, Hanjie Ji, Samuel White, and Jeffrey P. Bigham. 2011. Supporting blind photography. In *The Proceedings of the 13th International ACM SIGACCESS Conference on Computers and Accessibility (ASSETS '11)*. ACM, New York, NY, USA, 203–210. DOI: http://dx.doi.org/10.1145/2049536.2049573

26. Shaun K. Kane and Jeffrey P. Bigham. 2014. Tracking @Stemxcomet: Teaching programming to blind students via 3D printing, crisis management, and twitter. In *Proceedings of the 45th ACM Technical Symposium on Computer Science Education (SIGCSE '14)*. ACM, New York, NY, USA, 247–252. DOI: http://dx.doi.org/10.1145/2538862.2538975

27. Jeeeun Kim and Tom Yeh. 2015. Toward 3D-printed movable tactile pictures for children with visual impairments. In *Proceedings of the 33rd Annual ACM Conference on Human Factors in Computing Systems (CHI '15)*. 2815–2824. DOI: http://dx.doi.org/10.1145/2702123.2702144

28. Benjamin Lafreniere, Tovi Grossman, Fraser Anderson, Justin Matejka, Heather Kerrick, Danil Nagy, Lauren Vasey, Evan Atherton, Nicholas Beirne, Marcelo H. Coelho, Nicholas Cote, Steven Li, Andy Nogueira, Long Nguyen, Tobias Schwinn, James Stoddart, David Thomasson, Ray Wang, Thomas White, David Benjamin, Maurice Conti, Achim Menges, and George Fitzmaurice. 2016. Crowdsourced fabrication. In *Proceedings of the 29th Annual Symposium on User Interface Software and Technology (UIST '16)*. ACM, New York, NY, USA, 15–28. DOI: http://dx.doi.org/10.1145/2984511.2984553

29. Walter S. Lasecki, Phyo Thiha, Yu Zhong, Erin Brady, and Jeffrey P. Bigham. 2013. Answering visual questions with conversational crowd assistants. In *Proceedings of the 15th International ACM SIGACCESS Conference on Computers and Accessibility (ASSETS '13)*. ACM, New York, NY, USA, Article 18, 8 pages. DOI: http://dx.doi.org/10.1145/2513383.2517033

30. Roberto Manduchi and James M. Coughlan. 2014. The last meter: Blind visual guidance to a target. In *Proceedings of the SIGCHI Conference on Human Factors in Computing Systems (CHI '14)*. ACM, New York, NY, USA, 3113–3122. DOI: http://dx.doi.org/10.1145/2556288.2557328

31. Samantha McDonald, Niara Comrie, Erin Buehler, Nicholas Carter, Braxton Dubin, Karen Gordes, Sandy McCombe-Waller, and Amy Hurst. 2016. Uncovering challenges and opportunities for 3D printing assistive technology with physical therapists. In *Proceedings of the 18th International ACM SIGACCESS Conference on Computers and Accessibility (ASSETS '16)*. ACM, New York, NY, USA, 131–139. DOI: http://dx.doi.org/10.1145/2982142.2982162

32. Samantha McDonald, Joshua Dutterer, Ali Abdolrahmani, Shaun K. Kane, and Amy Hurst. 2014. Tactile aids for visually impaired graphical design education. In *Proceedings of the 16th International ACM SIGACCESS Conference on Computers and Accessibility (ASSETS '14)*. ACM, New York, NY, USA, 275–276. DOI: http://dx.doi.org/10.1145/2661334.2661392

33. George A. Miller. 1956. The magical number seven, plus or minus two: Some limits on our capacity for processing information. *Psychological review* 63, 2 (1956), 81. DOI: http://dx.doi.org/10.1037/h0043158

34. Marius Muja and David G. Lowe. 2009. Fast approximate nearest neighbors with automatic algorithm configuration. In *International Conference on Computer Vision Theory and Application VISSAPP'09)*. INSTICC Press, 331–340.
35. Jeffrey Nichols, Brad A. Myers, Michael Higgins, Joseph Hughes, Thomas K. Harris, Roni Rosenfeld, and Mathilde Pignol. 2002. Generating remote control interfaces for complex appliances. In *Proceedings of the 15th Annual ACM Symposium on User Interface Software and Technology (UIST '02)*. ACM, New York, NY, USA, 161–170. DOI:http://dx.doi.org/10.1145/571985.572008
36. Raf Ramakers, Fraser Anderson, Tovi Grossman, and George Fitzmaurice. 2016. RetroFab: A design tool for retrofitting physical interfaces using actuators, sensors and 3D printing. In *Proceedings of the 2016 CHI Conference on Human Factors in Computing Systems (CHI '16)*. ACM, New York, NY, USA, 409–419. DOI: http://dx.doi.org/10.1145/2858036.2858485
37. Lei Shi, Idan Zelzer, Catherine Feng, and Shiri Azenkot. 2016. Tickers and talker: An accessible labeling toolkit for 3D printed models. In *Proceedings of the 2016 CHI Conference on Human Factors in Computing Systems (CHI '16)*. ACM, New York, NY, USA, 4896–4907. DOI: http://dx.doi.org/10.1145/2858036.2858507
38. Saiganesh Swaminathan, Thijs Roumen, Robert Kovacs, David Stangl, Stefanie Mueller, and Patrick Baudisch. 2016. Linespace: A sensemaking platform for the blind. In *Proceedings of the 2016 CHI Conference on Human Factors in Computing Systems (CHI '16)*. ACM, New York, NY, USA, 2175–2185. DOI: http://dx.doi.org/10.1145/2858036.2858245
39. Brandon Taylor, Anind Dey, Dan Siewiorek, and Asim Smailagic. 2016. Customizable 3D printed tactile maps as interactive overlays. In *Proceedings of the 18th International ACM SIGACCESS Conference on Computers and Accessibility (ASSETS '16)*. ACM, New York, NY, USA, 71–79. DOI: http://dx.doi.org/10.1145/2982142.2982167
40. United States Access Board 2016. Advancing full access and inclusion for all. https://www.access-board.gov/guidelines-and-standards. (2016).
41. Gregg Vanderheiden and Jutta Treviranus. 2011. Creating a global public inclusive infrastructure. In *International Conference on Universal Access in Human-Computer Interaction*. Springer, 517–526. DOI: http://dx.doi.org/10.1007/978-3-642-21672-5_57
42. Marynel Vázquez and Aaron Steinfeld. 2014. An assisted photography framework to help visually impaired users properly aim a camera. *ACM Transactions on Computer-Human Interaction* 21, 5, Article 25 (Nov. 2014), 29 pages. DOI:http://dx.doi.org/10.1145/2651380
43. Samuel White, Hanjie Ji, and Jeffrey P. Bigham. 2010. EasySnap: Real-time audio feedback for blind photography. In *Adjunct Proceedings of the 23rd Annual ACM Symposium on User Interface Software and Technology (UIST '10)*. ACM, New York, NY, USA, 409–410. DOI: http://dx.doi.org/10.1145/1866218.1866244
44. Wikipedia. 2016. Homography (computer vision) — Wikipedia, The Free Encyclopedia. (2016). https://en.wikipedia.org/w/index.php?title=Homography_(computer_vision)&oldid=752434320 [Online; accessed 1-December-2016].
45. Yu Zhong, Pierre J. Garrigues, and Jeffrey P. Bigham. 2013. Real time object scanning using a mobile phone and cloud-based visual search engine. In *Proceedings of the 15th International ACM SIGACCESS Conference on Computers and Accessibility (ASSETS '13)*. ACM, New York, NY, USA, Article 20, 8 pages. DOI: http://dx.doi.org/10.1145/2513383.2513443
46. Yu Zhong, Walter S. Lasecki, Erin Brady, and Jeffrey P. Bigham. 2015. RegionSpeak: Quick comprehensive spatial descriptions of complex images for blind users. In *Proceedings of the 33rd Annual ACM Conference on Human Factors in Computing Systems (CHI '15)*. ACM, New York, NY, USA, 2353–2362. DOI: http://dx.doi.org/10.1145/2702123.2702437

People with Visual Impairment Training Personal Object Recognizers: Feasibility and Challenges

Hernisa Kacorri, Kris M. Kitani, Jeffrey P. Bigham, Chieko Asakawa
Carnegie Mellon University
Pittsburgh, USA
hkacorri@cmu.edu, kkitani@cs.cmu.edu, jbigham@cs.cmu.edu, chiekoa@cs.cmu.edu

ABSTRACT
Blind people often need to identify objects around them, from packages of food to items of clothing. Automatic object recognition continues to provide limited assistance in such tasks because models tend to be trained on images taken by sighted people with different background clutter, scale, viewpoints, occlusion, and image quality than in photos taken by blind users. We explore personal object recognizers, where visually impaired people train a mobile application with a few snapshots of objects of interest and provide custom labels. We adopt transfer learning with a deep learning system for user-defined multi-label k-instance classification. Experiments with blind participants demonstrate the feasibility of our approach, which reaches accuracies over 90% for some participants. We analyze user data and feedback to explore effects of sample size, photo-quality variance, and object shape; and contrast models trained on photos by blind participants to those by sighted participants and generic recognizers.

ACM Classification Keywords
H.5.m. Information Interfaces and Presentation (*e.g.*, HCI)

Author Keywords
blind; accessibility; photographs; object recognition; computer vision

INTRODUCTION
Blind people have been quick to adopt assistive technologies for identifying objects such as text readers, barcode readers, color readers, and crowd-powered object recognition applications. However, there are still many limitations that hold back their use for more independent living. For example, a barcode reader, *e.g.*, i.d. mate [9], may cost up to a few thousand dollars, and requires a readable barcode and an updated product database. Text readers, such as KNFBReader [15], work best on flat surfaces and printed materials and are thus not applicable for many object recognition tasks. Color readers such as Color Teller [22] typically used to help with outfit matching, can be very sensitive to lighting conditions, forcing the user to memorize color mappings to distinguish between clothes under different illumination. Applications that use the crowd to identify an object, such as BeMyEyes [3], BeSpecular [4] and TapTapSee [21], can obtain high recognition rates but often come with a per demand cost, require an Internet connection, raise privacy concerns [1], and assume crowd availability.

CHI 2017, May 06 - 11, 2017, Denver, CO, USA.

ACM 978-1-4503-4655-9/17/05..$15.00.
DOI: http://dx.doi.org/10.1145/3025453.3025899

Figure 1. Object instances that participants in our study chose to train their personal object recognizers on. Can you tell which two objects were trained by the same participant? (4,2) (2,2) .rewsnA

On the other hand, the development of assistive technologies that make use of a commodity smartphone's camera and on-board processing overcome many of the challenges listed above. Smartphones have been adopted by many people with visual impairments. Cameras can be used to capture both flat and 3D objects. By doing all processing on the device, the technology is not dependent on an Internet connection and naturally ensures privacy. Based on these observations, we are interested in examining the feasibility (and challenges) of a self-contained image-based object recognition algorithm trained specifically for and by people with visual impairments.

Benefits of Personalization. One of the key conditions for developing a robust real world assistive computer vision system, is to significantly constrain the imaging conditions of the recognition task. One such successful example for people with visual impairment are money readers, which work for a small number of object classes, *e.g.*, bills of different denominations. Conversely, building a super object classifier which can recognize all the possible object instances of interest for all visually impaired people, is not possible with current object recognition technology.

Assuming that we cannot train on all the possible object instances of interest to all visually impaired people, we suggest constraining the recognition task through *personalization*. We adopt the concept of a personal object recognizer, where people with visual impairment collect (sequentially) a small sample of photos from their object of interest and provide custom labels to train their personalized application. By limiting the recognition task to a single user, we not only constrain the number of object classes but also reduce the variability between training and testing images. This is natural since such an application would be trained and tested by the same person under similar conditions and subjected similarly to any idiosyncratic characteristics, as shown in Fig. 1.

Feasibility Study. While many blind people use Braille labels to annotate their objects, or some *ad hoc* organizing system, they might not be familiar with the concept of training a personal recognizer though photo taking. As Phase 1 of our study, we provid participants with a description of how our technology works along with some basic photo taking instructions. We solicit suggestions from users on how such technology might be used and ask them to photograph a few snapshots of objects in their homes over a one-week period.

Data collected in Phase 1 are analyzed to estimate the instance distribution for objects of interest, and confirm our intuition that object classes in our problem best fit within the scenario of finer grained sets of labels. We use observations from results in Phase 1 to compile a set of training instructions and invite the participants to our lab for a round of simulated training and testing under controlled conditions.

Experiments from Phase 2 demonstrate the potential of our approach, which reaches accuracies over 90% for some participants. Our error analysis, combined with observations from images and video recordings from Phase 2, uncovers user factors that can degrade the performance of a personal object recognizer and should be prioritized for robustness of a real world application. We also contrast our personal object recognizer with different approaches using recognizers trained by sighted people and a generic object recognizer to confirm the feasibility of our approach.

Contributions. We develop a framework for allowing people with visual impairments to train an image-based personalized object recognition algorithm and show that one can achieve high accuracy by constraining the task through personalization. Our feasibility study shows that personalization through fine-grained object recognition is in fact, a necessity for many people with visual impairments. Furthermore, our experiments with blind participants show that personalized object recognition algorithms have superior performance over generic state-of-the-art object recognition models.

RELATED WORK

Prior work in object recognition for people with visual impairment mainly spans two areas, crowd-powered and automatic object recognition. There are few cases in each area where image classifiers are trained on images captured by blind users. TapTapSee [21], a crowd-powered application, tries to automate the objection recognition process by training models on previously seen images with matching crowdsourced labels, while preserving a human-backed image recognition approach. Aipoly [2], a generic image recognition application, obtains "image–label" pairs from blind users by asking them to teach the application with image and description pairs. In both cases, training is neither immediate nor personalized. Images provided by one user may adversely affect the performance of the model for any other user.

The closest application to our work is LookTel Recognizer [16]. This application allows users to recognize objects given a library of training images. It requires "high-quality, well-framed images with ample lighting" captured with the assistance of sighted people. To our knowledge, our work is the first study of the feasibility of blind people training their own object recognizers. To understand differences due to photos taken by sighted people, we also compare models trained by blind versus sighted participants in our study.

Another line of research involves obtaining higher quality photos from blind users. Crowd-powered applications directly solicits camera positioning guidance from a crowd-worker until a good quality image is obtained. Researchers, *e.g.*, [25], have also investigated automated approaches for extracting good quality information-rich frames from continuous camera video streams. In both cases, a good quality photo is implicitly defined as one that is either interpreted properly by a sighted person or as one that maximizes the recognition from a model trained on images taken by sighted people.

We suspect that a high quality personal object recognizer can work with a looser notion of quality. For our approach, both training and testing images are provided by the same person, under similar conditions and for a bounded number of object classes. As a consequence, the image may not contain the entire object. Instead, an image is considered of good quality if there is enough consistency across training and testing images for any given object class, and there are sufficient discriminative characteristics to limit confusion between classes.

PERSONAL OBJECT RECOGNIZER

State-of-the-art image recognition trains machine learning models that achieve performance comparable to, or even exceeding, human recognition, with performance reported against ImageNet [19], an established benchmark for object classification with millions of images. Typically, thousands of examples are needed to train an image classifier. However, we can use transfer learning by leveraging fully trained recognition models, and adapting them to new image classification tasks using only a few samples. Transfer learning [13] applies knowledge from one model to solve a different but related problem. Here, the labels differ while the marginal distributions of data are related [14].

Baseline. As our baseline object recognizer, we use Inception-v3 network [20] (hereafter, ''Inception"), a state-of-the-art model from Google which achieves a 3.46% top-5 error rate[1] on ImageNet when classifying images into 1000 classes.

[1]Top-5 error rate indicates how often the model fails to give the correct answer in the top 5 guesses.

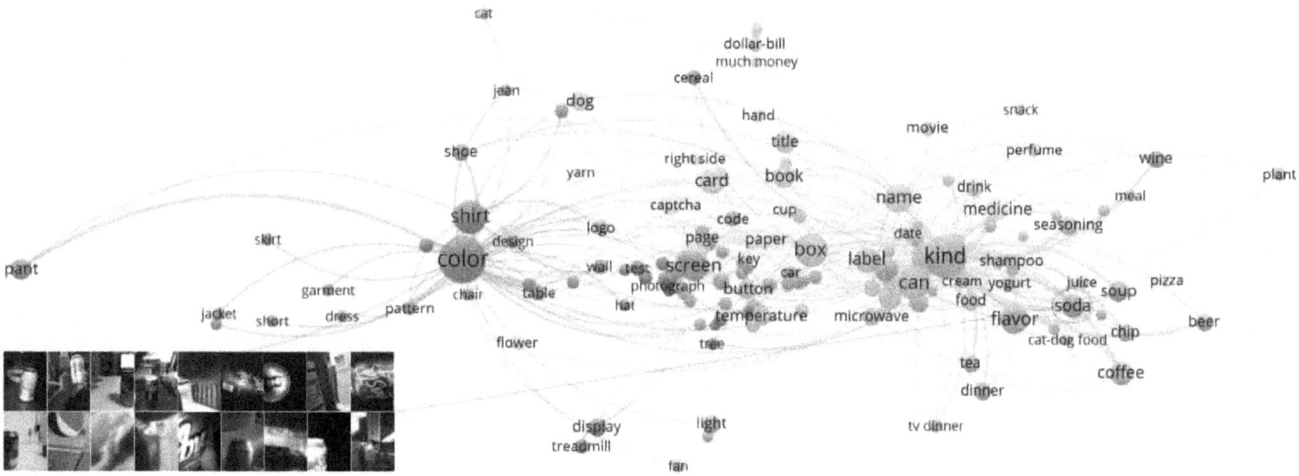

Figure 2. Term co-occurrence network for user questions in VizWiz dataset with sample images for the co-occurring terms 'soda' and 'kind'.

Our classifier. Google released a pre-trained Inception allowing researchers to build higher level machine learning layers. With transfer learning, an Inception model trained on ImageNet can be retrained or 'fine-tuned' for new image classes. The intuition is that lower layers in Inception's pre-trained model have learned generic low-level representations for distinguishing objects. Thus, these generic features can be re-purposed for other recognition tasks. To build a personal object recognizer, we load the pre-trained Inception, replace the top layer with a new (softmax) layer trained on the new user-defined classes. The new layer yields probabilities for each class. We take the class with the highest probability to be the network's classification for a given image. While our experiments process examples in batch mode, in a realistic scenario, photos for a new class would be processed one class at a time by adding a new node to the final layer.

A key challenge to our problem is that the sample size for training has to be limited to a practical small number. Our problem is an instance of *N-way k-shot learning*, where k is a small number of samples, *e.g.*, 1-20, and N is the number of object classes. Our approach follows recent research using a pre-trained Inception on ImageNet for k-shot learning tasks. For example, Vinyals et al. (2016) [24] showed that a pre-trained Inception on ImageNet is a competitive baseline for N-way k-shot learning, outperforming proposed state-of-the-art methods when the label distribution is fine grained. Similarly, prior work in fine-grained image classification, such as the LifeCLEF challenge [7], also used a trained GoogLeNet CNN (a prior version of Inception) on ImageNet and replaced its top layers as in our approach, achieving high performance. Therefore, transferring knowledge using a pre-trained Inception on ImageNet for N-way k-shot classification of a fine-grained dataset is a competitive approach.

We do not know *a priori* potential biases in object categories of interest for people with visual impairment. However, we hypothesize that object classes in our problem will better fit the scenario of fine grained sets of labels as in the previous works [24, 7]. Our intuition is that people with visual impairment are interested in distinguishing between objects with similar shape and texture, difficult to tell by touch. We examine this further in the following sections.

PRELIMINARY INSIGHTS FROM VIZWIZ DATASET

To gain better insights on our recognition task, we analyzed the publicly available VizWiz dataset[2], which includes questions and images from people with visual impairment accompanied by human-backed image recognition and answers provided by a sighted crowd. While an initial analysis classified these questions into identification, description, and reading categories [5], the focus of our analysis is to identify the types of object categories and characteristics being asked as well as their relationships.

Specifically, we apply VOSViewer text mining [23] to VizWiz users' questions, a total of 33,543 transcribed questions. We extract the most relevant terms and create a term co-occurrence network, as shown in Figure 2. There are a total of 163 terms occurring at least in 20 questions. Each term is visualized as a node and co-occurring terms are linked with an edge. Term occurrence and co-occurrence is denoted by node size and edge thickness. Terms with high relevance are grouped together into clusters, and each cluster may be seen as a topic governing the question.

The co-occurence network in Figure 2 allows us to make the observation that blind users often know the general object category such as shirt, bottle, can, soup, soda, coffee, medication but are interested in *specific* characteristics of those objects such as color, kind, flavor, label, brand, and name. This highlights the need of an instance object recognizer over generic image classification.

Zooming into one of the nodes in Figure 2 and examining the photos taken by blind users, we observe large variability not only in the instances of soda cans but also in the background clutter, scale, viewpoints, occlusion, and image quality. The diversity of the images indicates that it may be quite difficult to learn an image classifier that can be robust to such extreme intra-class variance.

[2] http://vizwiz.org/data/

STUDY AND DATA COLLECTION

The VizWiz dataset is rich with images taken by people with visual impairment but does not contain sequential photos of the same object taken by a given user. Thus, we are unable to use VizWiz to assess the feasibility of our approach. To understand the potential of learning with few examples given by blind people, we designed a two phase study. We recruited 8 blind participants (P1-P8) from the local community who were familiar with smartphones and asked them[3] to take photos of objects in their homes (Phase 1) and in our lab (Phase 2).

Table 1 shows participants' demographic information and period of smartphone usage. Fig. 3 reports their media and technology usage, and attitudes potentially affecting our task, based on the Rosen et al. questionnaire [17]. In open-end questions, P1 and P8 reported on home appliances using Braille labels, and P3-P7 reported on objects that are: easy to confusing, frequently used, big enough to accommodate labels, or in new visiting environments. Participants indicated that making Braille labels is time consuming and requires a lot of discipline. When possible, they use alternative strategies for distinguishing between similar objects based on touch (*e.g.* shape and size), sound (*e.g.*, shaking a jar), smell, weight, order (cans stacked based on flavors), and location (different cabinets). When these strategies failed, users would turn to technology, with the following applications and devices mentioned across 8 participants: BeMyEyes [3], BeSpecular [4], CamFind [6], Color Teller [22], Facetime (to ask family members and friends), i.d. mate Galaxy [9], KNFB Reader [15], Opticon [12], Talking Goggles [8], and TapTapSee [21].

ID	*Gender*	*Age*	*Blind (since)*	*Handedness*	*Smartphone*
P1	F	42	birth	right	2014
P2	M	40	birth (light)	right	2015
P3	F	68	birth	right	2008
P4	M	63	birth	left	2009
P5	F	46	birth	right	2016
P6	M	43	birth	right	2006
P7	F	61	birth (light)	right	2010
P8	F	58	10 months	right	2011

Table 1. Participants' demographics and smartphone use period.

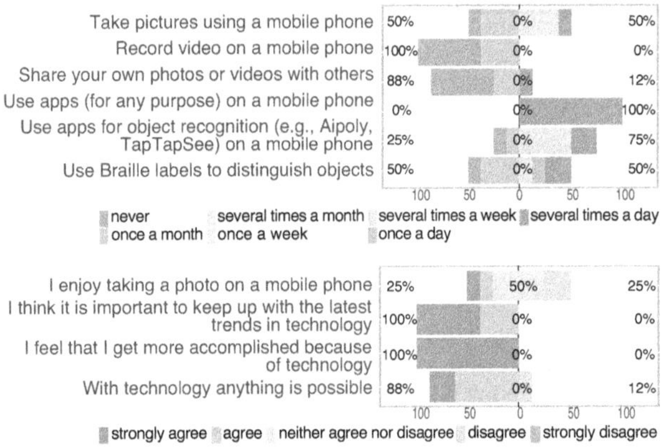

Figure 3. Technology experience and attitude responses.

[3]Under IRBSTUDY2015_00000052

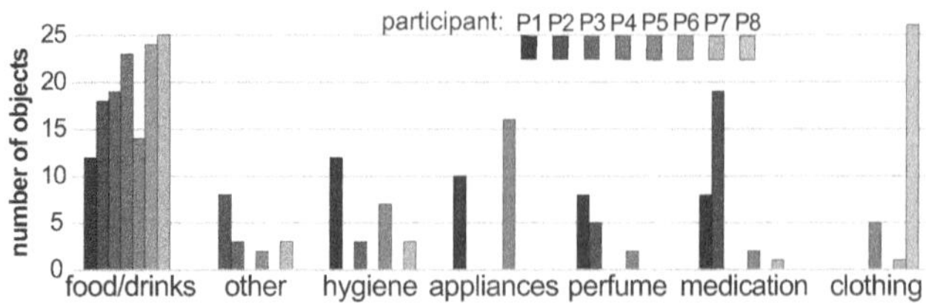

Figure 4. Distribution of object instances chosen by the participants.

Phase 1: In Situ

Over a week period, participants were asked to take photos of up to 50 objects of their choice, spending no more than 2 hours overall. Participants were asked to imagine that they are building a personalized phone application which uses the camera to recognize objects in *their* home. We further explained that the application is personalized in that it will work well only for the small number of objects on which it will be trained. Thus, they would have to choose the top 50 objects they would like their personalized application to recognize. Participants were instructed to label and take at least 5 photos for each of these objects on top of an empty table without surrounding objects. We suggested positioning the phone 8 to 12 inches from the object to ensure that it was within the scope of phone camera. Additional instructions on accessible photo taking were also included in the task description.

The goal of this phase was to allow participants time to process what a personal object recognizer entails before reporting their feedback about this technology, provide an estimate of the target domain with class distribution per classifier, and inform the characteristics and challenges of this task.

Observations and Findings in Phase 1

We received photos of 23 to 50 (average 35.12) distinct objects per participant with a total of 1,543 photos across participants. Figure 4 illustrates the distribution of the object instances that participants chose for training a personal recognizer. We observe that this distribution shares similarities with the term graph extracted from VizWiz users in Figure 2.

Drilling down within object groups, we observe that participants choose object instances typically falling under the same category such as "dove body wash winter" and "summer body wash dove"; and, "seasoned breadcrumbs" and "unseasoned breadcrumbs". Also of interest, we notice that for one of the participants, P8, all objects of interest are t-shirts with different patterns. This confirms our intuition that the classes of objects in our problem best fit within the scenario of finer grained sets of labels.

In our analysis of the *user-defined labels* for the selected objects, we observed:

Preference for personalized metadata. Beyond knowing brand, label, name, color, scent, flavor, as in the VizWiz data in Figure 2, participants would also like to record when and where they obtained the objects, washing instructions, cost, *etc.*. For example, one of the participants labeled some objects as ".... medals: Id race and year", "T-shirts: color, washing, where from and year".

Challenges in assigning labels to objects. Participants had a difficult time assigning labels to objects in their homes. This highlights the limitations of a personal object recognizer, which assumes that during training participants will have knowledge of object labels. For example, participant would label some of their objects as "box of cereal", "another box of cereal", "K cup, unknown flavor", "Pasta sauce, not sure what kind".

At the end of this study phase, we asked the participants to indicate some of their reasoning for choosing their objects. We believe that their responses, shown below, highlight user expectations from this technology:

> *"things I did not wanted to wait for a response", "things that take more time to figure out the other ways, time-based", "things that I thought would be interesting* e.g., *seasoned breadcrumbs versus non seasoned breadcrumbs", "things that I want to distinguish from others (brand and flavor).* e.g., *cookies, all of their boxes look similar and I don't want to open before", "things that I lost track of what they are", "cans and bottles that look similar", "things based on pretty much what I was doing those days (spice, cans, food) and a lot of those things are marked in Braille", "things that I would pull out of the draw and ask a family member or use the color identifier but it doesn't work. It was one of the things it would get mixed up easily".*

There are no previous datasets of sequential photos of objects taken by blind people for the purpose of training a classifier. Thus, we examined the *collected images* to identify interesting patterns and user behaviors that could be informative for the task at hand to drive Phase 2 of our study. We observed:

Distinct and consistent training strategies. Participants tend to develop distinct training strategies. Figure 1 illustrates photos of 8 products selected by 7 participants to train their personal object recognizer. Two products, rows 2 and 4 in the second column, are taken by the same participant. While not instructed to do so, participants tried to introduce some variation across the 5 images per object. And their perception of how to produce such variation for training also varied: different viewpoints, distances from the object, rotation, and visible side. However, it is interesting that each participant tended to be consistent given an object shape. If this consistency continues in the testing mode of a personally trained application it could lead to higher recognition rates.

Exaggerated or non-discriminative viewpoints. Some of the training images in the sequence of 5 include exaggerated viewpoints and scale in an attempt to provide a holistic view of the object rather than capture discriminative characteristics, *e.g.*, last photos of cylindrical objects tend to be from the top of the lid with no texture or visual characteristics. This could be an artifact of how training is perceived by the participants. We suspect one of the limitations of this approach to be the fact that images used for training are captured sequentially and in a different mode than testing. Typically, successful machine learning models are trained on images pulled from a similar distribution as in testing. Not only will the training images for a given object have limited background and light variation, since they are taken sequentially, but it could be that these exaggerated training images will not be observed in everyday usage, as noticed in the VizWiz dataset.

Pre-compiled set of instructions. Based on our observations from this phase of the study, we compiled a set of instructions for blind people to train a personal object recognizer. These instructions are used in Phase 2 of the study.

1. *Increase consistency across training and testing.* When taking training photos, imagine how your future self could be holding and taking a photo of that object to identify it.
2. *Limit background clutter.* Lay the object down in a table or any other flat surface. If it is a cylindrical shape it is okay to hold it to stabilize it, as long as your hand does not cover the object.
3. *Ensure that the object is in the camera scope*: feel where the camera is located in the phone and position the camera to the center of the object. Move away from the object upwards while holding the phone parallel to the desk.
4. *Ensure that most of the object is in the camera scope.* Distance the phone from the object relative to the object size (closer for smaller far way for larger).
5. *Obtain more discriminative photos.* Many products tend to avoid printing their labels where the seal is. If you can tell by touch where the seal, avoid taking photos on that side.

Phase 2: In Laboratory

We selected a subset of 15 object instances and asked Phase 1 participants to train and test a personal object recognizer in a lab setting. Object instances, shown in Figure 5, fall under the food/drink group which had the highest object occurrence across most participants in Phase 1 of the study. This is shown in Figure 4 and in agreement with the most relevant terms in the VizWiz network in Figure 2. The goal of this study was to collect data that will allow us to assess the feasibility of our approach and explore effects of photo-quality variance, sample size, and object characteristics. Our primary interest was understanding performance variation due to inherent differences in how blind users conceptualize and perform training tasks. We minimized variations in conditions, present in Phase 1, such as background, discriminative characteristics of objects, and lighting. We ensured that participants operated with a common understanding of how such an application would

Figure 5. Phase 2 objects: baking soda, cheetos, chewy bars, chicken broth, coca cola, diced tomatoes, diet coke, dill, fritos, lacroix apricot, lacroix mango, lay's, oregano, pike place roast, pike place roast decaf.

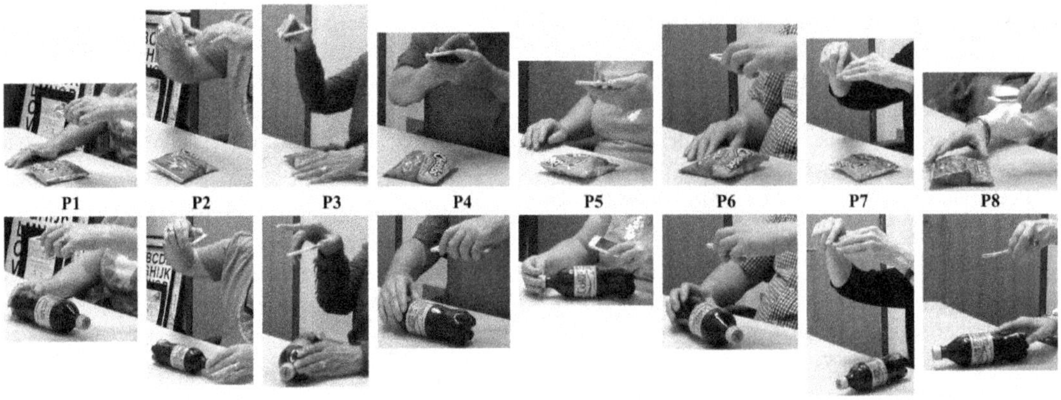

Figure 6. Idiosyncratic object and camera manipulation across participants during training.

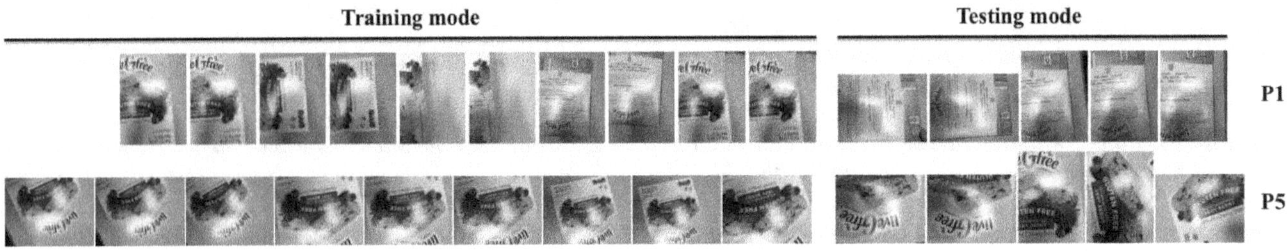

Figure 7. Training and testing images from P1 and P5 on "chewy bars" object illustrating distinct training strategies. (Images are uniformly sampled from the available 30 training images.)

work by providing them with the pre-compiled instructions, resulting from Phase 1, and feedback in a practice session with 3 distinct objects from Figure 5. We also controlled for variation in the order and way in which objects are passed to the user, e.g. randomized order and randomized up-side of objects, to simulate real-world scenarios. This allows us to not only compare performance variability across different participants but also to contrast models trained on photos by blind participants to those by sighted participants and generic recognizers.

Phase 2 has two main modes: training and testing. In the simulated training mode, participants were asked to take about 30 sequential photos of each of the 15 objects. In the simulated testing mode, participant were only able to take one photo of each given object to try and identify it. To minimize learning effects, objects were shuffled consistently across participants, in such a way that there were 5 photos for each object and two consecutive photos were never of the same object.

The lab setup was identical in practice, training, and testing modes for all participants. To ensure identical lighting conditions, a room without natural light was chosen. To take the photos, participants used VoiceOver on an iPhone 6 device and were recommended to use the volume buttons as in the practice mode. To draw insightful observations, each session was recorded on video.

In this phase, we also collected data from two sighted people. The first person (S1) is one of the authors of this paper, who is familiar with Inception and the transfer learning approach being adopted, serves merely as an upper baseline to the discriminative power of model for the 15 selected object instances and the background and lighting settings in this study. The strategy here was to collect high quality images, shown in Figure 5, with very limited variability, both during training and testing, while following the pre-compiled instructions as well as visual feedback from the camera. The results from S1 can be used to interpret results from other participants by excluding effects due to the particular task or experiment setting.

The second person (S2) is a sighted female, age 38, who is not familiar with Inception or other image classification tasks and machine learning. S2 serves as a second sighted person for an upper baseline of good quality images and received the same information about this experiment as the participants. Both S1 and S2 followed the practice, training, and testing modes as the blind participants under the same setting.

Observations and Findings in Phase 2

We collected a total of 4,120 photos in training mode and 661 in testing mode from our participants P1-P8. A participant spent on average 65 seconds to take about 30 training photos for an object (23 – 245[4], std: 35.2).

When looking at the participants' photos and video recordings of the sessions, we observed:

Presence of user's hand in training images. To take photos, participants used one hand (P1, P3, P5, P6, P8), two hands (P7), or interchanged between two hands (P2, P4) as shown in Figure 6. Excepting P8, all participants tend to include one hand in the training photos to either hold an object, or simply as a reference point to ensure that the object is in the photo. However, for very few participants, this

[4]The peek of 245 seconds was observed for the baking soda since the package was leaking and needed more care when rotating.

behavior was mirrored in the testing photos with P1, P2, and P6 being the most consistent. We expect these differences to be reflected in the performance of the personal object recognizer trained by each participant in our experiments.

Reinforced distinct and consistent training strategies. Our observations in Phase 1 about distinct training strategies were reinforced in Phase 2. With the option of more photos per object, 30 photos compared to 5 in Phase 1, participants introduced user-distinct variations that focused more on the visible face of the object, up side-down rotations, viewpoints, and distances from the object. Figure 7 illustrates the difference between the visible faces variation and distance variation introduced by P1 and P5.

Variation in training unobserved in testing. The exaggerated viewpoints and scale discussed in the observations of Phase 1 seem to hold here too. For example, independently of how the "chewy bars" box was passed to P1 in testing mode, the participant consciously avoided viewpoints from the narrow box opening side, while initially such a viewpoint was included many times towards the end of the training examples. Participants were instructed to increase consistency across training and testing by imagining how their future self would be taking the photos. However, many of them perceived the number of 30 examples as high and often interpreted it as an opportunity for variation and covering of edge cases.

Different training strategies among sighted participants. Interestingly, we also observed a big difference between sighted people S1 and S2. S1, aware that the highest accuracy is achieved with maximal consistency across training and testing images, introduced minimal variance in the training samples and preserved that consistency during testing, *e.g.*, taking photos from the front of the object to cover most of the phone screen. On the other hand, S2 introduced variation in viewpoints, sides, and distance from the object hoping to give the application "a more holistic view" of the object. We suspect that training strategies are affected by the way people perceive machine learning concepts, such as training a recognizer, and can thus make a difference in the classifier performance.

We are interested in gauging willingness of blind users to take the time of training their application and taking photos for this purpose. At the end of the study, we asked the participants to indicate whether training a personal object recognizer is feasible with responses shown in Figure 8. We also solicited comments on possible challenges they faced during simulated training and testing in Phase 2 of the study. We found that participants agreed with the feasibility of training a personal object recognizer from the blind user's perspective. Their main concerns were: knowing whether the photos were good, knowing the area of a package where the label or distinguishing information resides, obtaining feedback from the camera such as lighting conditions and number of photos taken, deciding on the distance between the object and camera lens. One of the participants stated "*the most challenging and most fun is training the person.*"

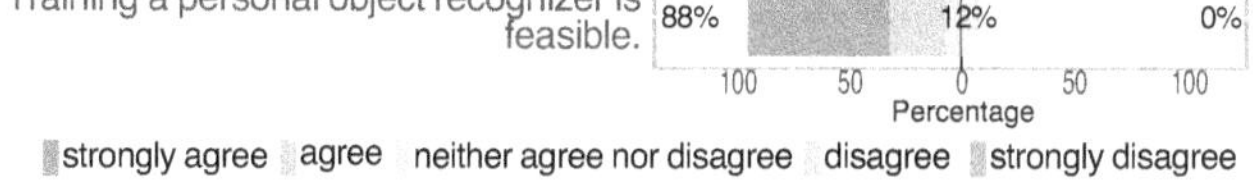

Figure 8. Subjective responses on the feasibility of our approach.

EXPERIMENTS AND RESULTS

To assess the proposed approach, we used data obtained in Phase 2 to build personal object recognizers for each participant (P1-P8 and S1-S2) and report their performance in terms of accurately predicting labels for the corresponding testing images belonging to 15 object classes in Figure 5. The hyperparameters for our models were: 1000 training steps, 0.01 learning rate, 2048-dimensional feature vector, and 299 x 299 input image. Training images were always pulled from the set of photos collected in training mode in Phase 2. Testing images included all images in testing mode, about 75 images per participant. Given that the image data were obtained from a controlled study, to avoid overfitting to characteristics of the data related to task and experiment settings, we did not perform any further fine tuning of the model parameters.

Model Performance

Figure 9 illustrates results from personal object recognizers trained and tested on data from P1-P8 and S1-S2. The number of training images obtained in Phase 2 varied slightly across objects and participants. For more comparable results, we randomly selected 20 images of each object per participant across all experiments. To account for randomness in the selection process and randomness inherent in the training process, we built 10 model attempts per object recognizer and controlled for random seeds for reproducibility throughout all experiments.

For blind participants P1-P8, the personal object recognizers achieved accuracies ranging from 50.7% up to 92% ($\mu = 75.95\%, \sigma = 13.29$). For comparison, a random prediction for a 15-way classification would yield about 7% accuracy, while a model trained on data from S1 a sighted computer scientist with understanding of the underlying algorithms achieved an average accuracy of 99.6%, and a model trained on S2, a sighted person unaware of the underlying methods, achieved an average accuracy of 96.9%.

As expected, S1, taking images with minimal variation across training and setting, achieved almost perfect scores and out-

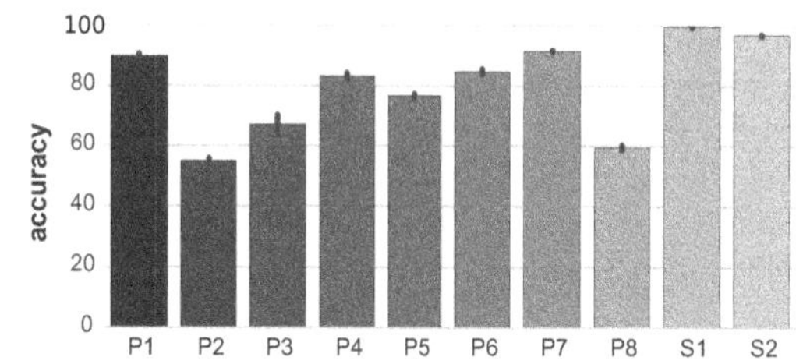

Figure 9. Results of a personal object recognizer trained and tested on images from each participant with 20 samples per object and error bars calculated over 10 random experiment runs.

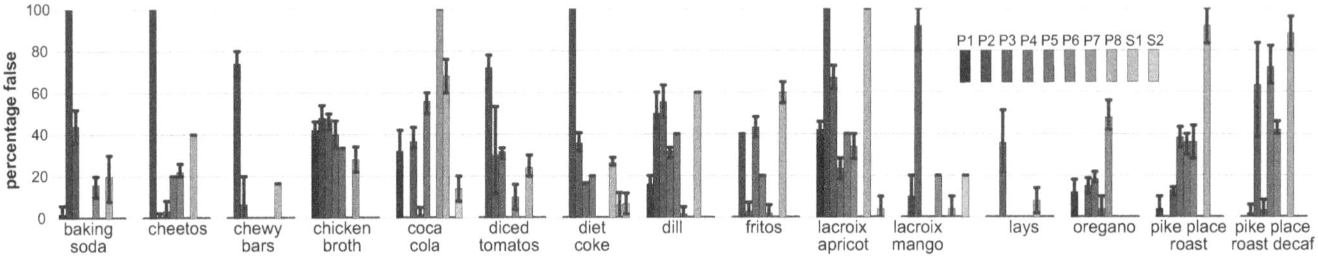

Figure 10. Percentage of misclassified images per object category across all participants indicating that difficult-to-recognize objects are not uniformly distributed across participants. (A 100% indicates that all 5 test images within that category were misclassified and error bars show variation over 10 random experiment runs.)

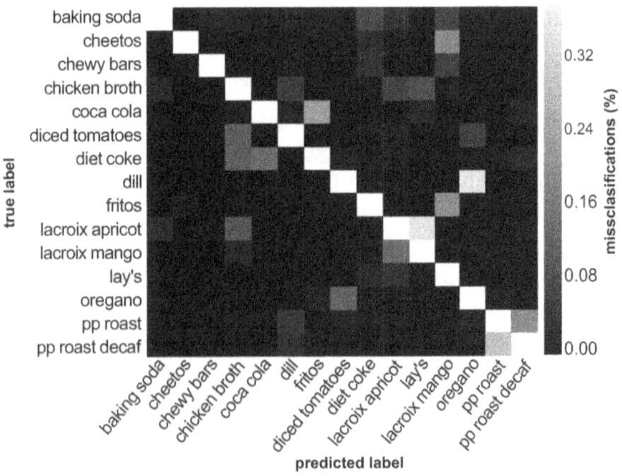

Figure 11. Most mislabeled objects over P1-P8 recognizers share shape and visual similarities. (Percentages are averaged over 10 random experiment runs.)

performed all participants. This serves as an upper baseline for the performance of our approach given the object stimuli, experimental setup of Phase 2, and the hyper parameters of our model. The fact that some of our participants P1 and P8 achieved performances comparable to those of a sighted participant S2 highlights the potentials of our approach.

Error Analysis

While the results on testing accuracy of Figure 9 allowed us to quickly grasp the potential of this technology, we looked deeper for how to improve upon it. In this section, we focus our attention on the errors and attempt to link them with prior observations from the study.

Figure 10 shows the percentage of misclassified images per object category, across all participants, with error bars calculated over the 10 trials. Our first observation here is that objects which are difficult to recognize are not uniformly distributed across participants. For example, focusing on P2 and P8, whose models achieve the lowest accuracies (seen in Fig 9), we observe P2's model consistently misclassifies baking soda, cheetos, diet coke, and lacroix mango, whereas P8's model consistently misclassifies lacroix apricot, pike place roast, and pike place roast decaf.

Examining the training and testing images for P2 and P8 on the highly misclassified objects, we find that their recognizers' performances vary for different reasons. Participant P2's strategy for introducing variation during training tended to be consistent with the variation in testing. The degradation in classifier performance was due to idiosyncratic characteristics of the participant. As shown in Figure 6, P2 tended to hold the camera at a higher distance from the object and with a slight tilt away from the object. As a result, the object is marginally included or excluded in many of the training photos. For example, none of the training data for diet coke included the object in the image frame. Thus, it is critical for a real world application to account and provide feedback for the presence of the object during training, either by detecting the tilt in users phone or by using computer vision techniques.

However, from participant's P8's images among highly misclassified objects, we observed that training images included exaggerated viewpoints, *e.g.*, the last photos of lacroix apricot tend to be from the top of the can and many of the last k-cup photos were taken from the side, while none of the testing photos for those objects where taken from those perspectives. Our models were trained on 20 randomly selected images from the participant's training pool, and we believe that more intelligent sampling techniques for selecting training data can be employed to build more robust models.

Figure 11 illustrates aggregated results on misclassified testing images across participants P1-P8 as a confusion heatmap. We observe that the highest confusions are: lacroix apricot as lacroix mango, dill as oregano, pike place roast decaf as pike place roast, coca cola as diet coke, fritos as lay's, and cheetos as lay's. These are all objects that were intentionally chosen due to shared shape and visual similarities. Interestingly, even for the sighted participant S2, the misclassified pairs were (lacroix apricot, lacroix mango) and (coca cola, diet coke). We suspect that there is room for better performance in our models orthogonal to the quality of photos taken by blind people, *e.g.* additional data, more training steps, and tuning of other parameters.

Effect of Order in Training Examples

Our initial results were obtained from personalized classifiers trained on 20 randomly sampled images per object from the available pool of participant's training images. However, training images for any given object are acquired sequentially from users. We wondered whether training on a batch of photos taken sequentially would affect performance. Further, would it make a difference where this sequential batch is taken from among the entire sequence? This could matter if participants modulate their photo-taking strategies as they manipulate the

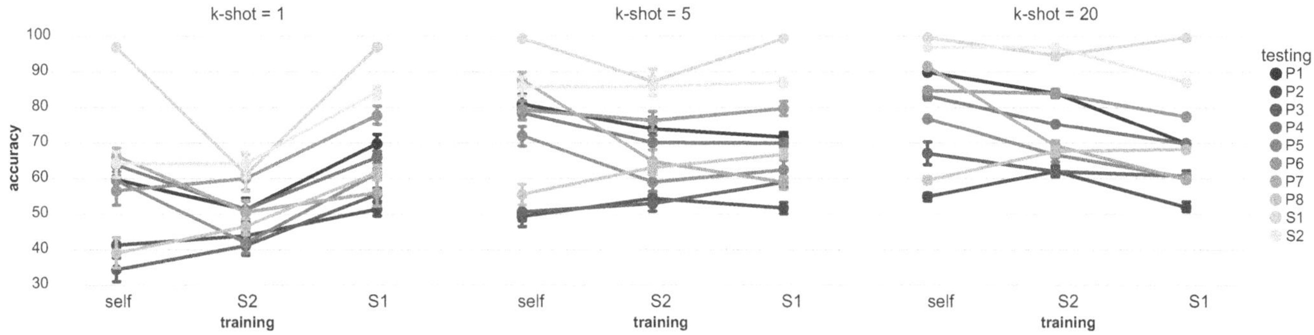

Figure 12. A personal object recognizer trained and tested on images from the same blind participant tends to outperform a recognizer trained on images from a sighted person S1 or S2 when the training size is bigger ($k\_shot = 20$).

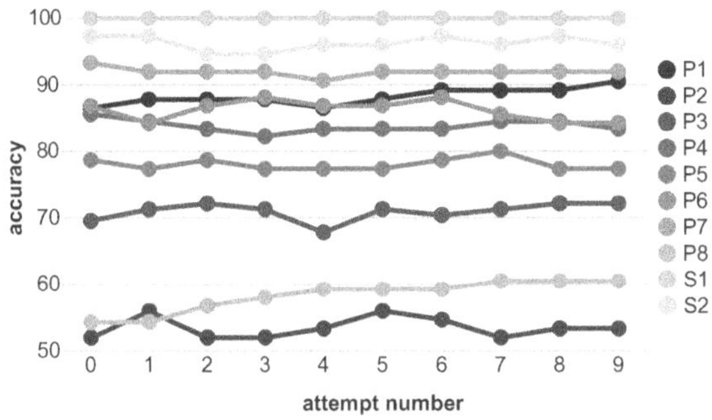

Figure 13. Selecting training samples through a sliding window did not have similar effect on recognizers' accuracy across participants.

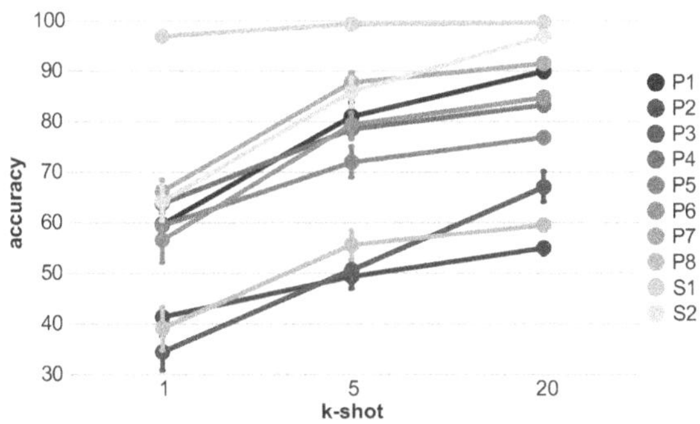

Figure 14. Recognizer's accuracy increases with the sample size, where $k = 1, 5, 20$.

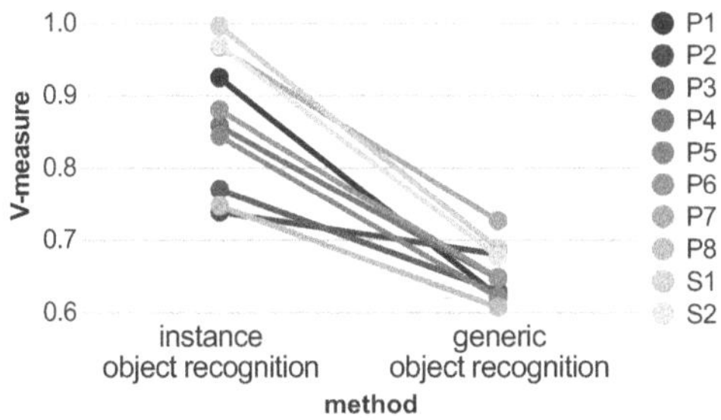

Figure 15. A personal object recognizer achieves higher desirable classification properties than a generic state-of-the-art object recognizer.

objects. To investigate this, we ran a set of experiments where the 20 samples were selected sequentially from the pool of available training images per object. For each participant's recognizer, we ran 10 attempts, where each attempt shifts the selected images by one. For example, in attempt 0, we train on the first 20 images, *i.e.* images $1, \ldots, 20$, in attempt 1, we train on images $2, \ldots, 21$, and so on. On comparing recognizers' performance on random versus sequential training images, we did not observe a consistent effect across all participants P1-P8. Moreover, we did not observe a common pattern when drilling down into achieved performance across participants per attempt in the sequential selection, shown in Figure 13. This may be because many of our stimuli objects were cylindrical or that participants develop different strategies to train their personal object recognizer. As above, we believe that more sophisticated approaches need to be investigated for selecting a good subset of training images.

Effect of Sample Size and Data Augmentation

One issue raised by the participants is how Braille labeling is time consuming and requires a lot of discipline. Even though we observed that participants were able to take, on average, 30 photos of an object over 65 seconds, we explored the potential of the proposed approach for training with highly limited sample sizes of 1 and 5 with k-shot learning [5]. Figure 14 illustrates the model accuracies across participants per value of k. In 1-shot learning, blind participants' recognizers achieved an average accuracy of 52.6% ($23.5\% - 73.3\%, \sigma = 12.7$) with P7's classifiers outperforming those of a sighted person, S2. Across all participants, higher k resulted in better accuracy.

The most minimal improvement was observed for S1, who serves as an upper baseline in these experiments, and for the blind participant P2. For S1, this can be explained by the fact that both training and testing images were high quality and introduced minimal variation by intention. However, for P2 this is as an effect of many training images which exclude the object, as discussed in the section on error analysis. We believe that presence of outlier images (i.e. unrepresentative of the object) in the training data can bias the solution, severely degrading classification performance in k-shot learning.

A common practice to improve the performance of machine learning models is to augment the original training data with

[5]Results in k-shot learning are typically reported for $k = 1, 5, 20$.

new data generated by applying different distortions on the original ones. To demonstrate the potentials of data augmentation for our approach we expanded the effective size of the training data by randomly cropping and scaling up to 20% of the image, and by applying up to 10% brightness to training images of participants P5, P6, and P7. By adding possible variation of the same images we could help the personal object classifier be more robust on distortions that can occur in testing. Initial results show that accuracy might be boosted by up to 10.7% ($\mu = 3.8\%, \sigma = 3.2$).

Contrast to Models Trained on Photos by Sighted People

As discussed in the related work section, LookTel Recognizer, the closest application to our work, requires training on high-quality and well-framed images taken by sighted people in the user's environment. While we cannot directly compare LookTel performance to our approach, we explore the benefits of having a sighted person training a blind user's personal object recognizer. Specifically, we compare the accuracy achieved by models trained and tested on images by the same person to the accuracy of models trained on images by S1 or S2 but tested on images from all all participants.

Results, shown in Figure 12, show that models trained on a single example ($k = 1$) perform best when the training image is taken by a sighted person, with better performance using S1's recognizer. However, for larger training samples, a personal object recognizer trained and tested on images from the same blind user tends to outperform a recognizer trained on images from a sighted person. Specifically, for $k = 20$ we observe that the accuracy of predicted labels drops for 6 out of 8 blind participants, with P2 and P8 as exceptions.

Contrast to Generic Image Recognition

While not a straightforward comparison, we wanted to explore how a personal object recognizer trained to recognize object instances performs relative to a generic image recognition model, the method used by most mobile applications for the blind. Since a generic recognizer is not trained on user-defined labels, an accuracy score cannot be calculated directly. Thus we cannot directly contrast its performance with our approach. However, we can compare desirable properties of the two, such as consistency of their predictions given images of the same object, and ability to distinguish between two different objects. For example, assume a blind user provides a photo to AppX, an imaginary mobile application with a fully trained Inception model, and receives the top-1 predicted label. The user is interested in distinguishing between the 'pike place roast' and the 'pike place roast decaf k-cups', shown in Figure 5 and has noticed that AppX recognizes the first as 'Petri dish' and the second as 'bottlecap'. If AppX consistently identifies 'pike place roast' as 'Petri dish' and the decaffeinated as 'bottlecap', then the user could learn a $1-1$ mapping and still benefit from AppX despite the confusion in actual object labels. Though such a solution is not scalable, its utility in limited scenarios led us to contrast it with our approach. For this comparison, we adopt the V-measure [18] metric from cluster evaluation, which is independent of the absolute values of the labels. Thus, it measures the agreement of two independent label assignment strategies on the same data. First, we calculate V-measures for each of the participants' recognizers in Fig 9 using true labels for testing images and the corresponding predicted labels as inputs. We average V-measures across the 10 experiment runs for each participant. To obtain the V-measure from a fully-trained Inception model, not adapted to the participants, we use true labels for testing images per participant against Inception's predicted labels belonging to 1000 possible classes (distinct from user-defined labels).

Figure 15 illustrates the obtained V-measures contrasted per each participant. We observe that for all the participants, our approach achieves higher V-measures, where a 100% accuracy would correspond to a V-measure 1.0.

CONCLUSION AND FUTURE WORK

We have presented a method that allows people with visual impairments to train a personal object recognition algorithm to differentiate between everyday objects specific to the user. By doing so, we have provided a solution for a very practical need for people with visual impairments – instance level object recognition. Additionally, by leveraging the constraints on the image data distribution through personalization, we were able to create image classifiers that can adapt state-of-the-art generic classifiers for user specific tasks using only a small number of examples.

Based on our observations and findings, our future work will explore user interface design and computer vision methods to increase robustness in training. This will involve automating and providing user feedback on some of the pre-complied set of instructions *e.g.* indicating detected background clutter based on image analysis and a tilting phone based on the accelerometer. We found that one of the main reasons for performance degradation is the absence of the object of interest from the training examples due to challenges in photo-taking by blind users. Based on our observation of the users tendency to use their hand as a guiding point of reference for the camera, we will incorporate elements from our prior work on first-person activity recognition [11] to select training examples where the object appears in the vicinity of the user's hand. Moreover, we will investigate intelligent sampling techniques for selecting representative and diverse subsets of training examples from discriminative viewpoints.

While there are many parameters that can still be evaluated (*e.g.*, incremental model learning, extreme illumination changes, video versus images), the more important remaining issue is one of scalability over long periods of time. Although we have shown success for a moderately sized dataset, what happens as the number of objects increase over time to hundreds or thousands of labels? We believe that this work has been instrumental in understanding the use of personalized object classifiers for a short duration of time (*i.e.*, 2 hour time frame) and hope that it serves as an impetus for large-scale long-term evaluation (*e.g.*, based on remote usage data [10]) to validate the longevity and utility of such technologies.

ACKNOWLEDGMENTS

This work has been supported by Shimizu Corporation. Kris Kitani is supported in part by JST CREST.

REFERENCES

1. Tousif Ahmed, Roberto Hoyle, Kay Connelly, David Crandall, and Apu Kapadia. 2015. Privacy Concerns and Behaviors of People with Visual Impairments. In *Proceedings of the 33rd Annual ACM Conference on Human Factors in Computing Systems (CHI '15)*. ACM, New York, NY, USA, 3523–3532. http://doi.acm.org/10.1145/2702123.2702334
2. Aipoly. 2016. Vision through artificial intelligence. (2016). http://aipoly.com/
3. BeMyEyes. 2016. Lend you eyes to the blind. (2016). http://www.bemyeyes.org/
4. BeSpecular. 2016. Let blind people see through your eyes. (2016). https://www.bespecular.com/
5. Erin L Brady, Yu Zhong, Meredith Ringel Morris, and Jeffrey P Bigham. 2013. Investigating the appropriateness of social network question asking as a resource for blind users. In *Proceedings of the 2013 Conference on Computer Supported Cooperative Work*. ACM, 1225–1236.
6. CamFind. 2016. Search the physical world. (2016). http://camfindapp.com/
7. Julien Champ, Titouan Lorieul, Maximilien Servajean, and Alexis Joly. 2015. A comparative study of fine-grained classification methods in the context of the lifeclef plant identification challenge 2015. In *CLEF 2015*, Vol. 1391.
8. Talking Goggles. 2016. A camera with speech. (2016). http://www.sparklingapps.com/goggles/
9. i.d. mate. 2016. Talking bar code scanners. (2016). http://www.envisionamerica.com/store
10. Hernisa Kacorri, Sergio Mascetti, Andrea Gerino, Dragan Ahmetovic, Hironobu Takagi, and Chieko Asakawa. 2016. Supporting Orientation of People with Visual Impairment: Analysis of Large Scale Usage Data. In *18th International ACM SIGACCESS Conference on Computers and Accessibility*. ACM.
11. Minghuang Ma, Haoqi Fan, and Kris M Kitani. 2016. Going Deeper into First-Person Activity Recognition. In *Proceedings of the IEEE Conference on Computer Vision and Pattern Recognition*.
12. Opticon. 2016. Handheld Scanner. (2016). http://www.opticonusa.com/products/handheld-solutions/
13. Sinno Jialin Pan and Qiang Yang. 2010. A survey on transfer learning. *IEEE Transactions on knowledge and data engineering* 22, 10 (2010), 1345–1359.
14. Novi Patricia and Barbara Caputo. 2014. Learning to learn, from transfer learning to domain adaptation: A unifying perspective. In *Proceedings of the IEEE Conference on Computer Vision and Pattern Recognition*. 1442–1449.
15. KNFB Reader. 2016. Access to print materials. (2016). http://www.knfbreader.com/
16. LookTel Recognizer. 2016. Instantly recognize everyday objects. (2016). http://www.looktel.com/recognizer
17. Larry D Rosen, Kelly Whaling, L Mark Carrier, Nancy A Cheever, and J Rokkum. 2013. The media and technology usage and attitudes scale: An empirical investigation. *Computers in Human Behavior* 29, 6 (2013), 2501–2511.
18. Andrew Rosenberg and Julia Hirschberg. 2007. V-Measure: A Conditional Entropy-Based External Cluster Evaluation Measure. In *Joint Conference on Empirical Methods in Natural Language Processing and Computational Natural Language Learning (EMNLP-CoNLL'07)*, Vol. 7. 410–420.
19. Olga Russakovsky, Jia Deng, Hao Su, Jonathan Krause, Sanjeev Satheesh, Sean Ma, Zhiheng Huang, Andrej Karpathy, Aditya Khosla, Michael Bernstein, Alexander C. Berg, and Li Fei-Fei. 2015. ImageNet Large Scale Visual Recognition Challenge. *International Journal of Computer Vision (IJCV)* 115, 3 (2015), 211–252.
20. Christian Szegedy, Vincent Vanhoucke, Sergey Ioffe, Jonathon Shlens, and Zbigniew Wojna. 2015. Rethinking the inception architecture for computer vision. *arXiv preprint arXiv:1512.00567* (2015).
21. TapTapSee. 2016. Mobile camera application designed specifically for the blind and visually impaired iOS users. (2016). http://www.taptapseeapp.com/
22. Color Teller. 2016. The Talking Color Identifier. (2016). http://www.brytech.com/colorteller/
23. Nees Jan Van Eck and Ludo Waltman. 2011. Text mining and visualization using VOSviewer. *ISSI Newsletter* 7, 3 (2011), 50–54.
24. Oriol Vinyals, Charles Blundell, Timothy Lillicrap, Koray Kavukcuoglu, and Daan Wierstra. 2016. Matching Networks for One Shot Learning. In *In Proceedings of the Conference on Neural Information Processing Systems (NIPS'16)*.
25. Yu Zhong, Pierre J Garrigues, and Jeffrey P Bigham. 2013. Real time object scanning using a mobile phone and cloud-based visual search engine. In *Proceedings of the 15th International ACM SIGACCESS Conference on Computers and Accessibility*. ACM, 20.

Jackknife: A Reliable Recognizer with Few Samples and Many Modalities

Eugene M. Taranta II
etaranta@gmail.com

Amirreza Samiei
samiei.amirreza@knights.ucf.edu

Mehran Maghoumi
mehran@cs.ucf.edu

Pooya Khaloo
pooya@cs.ucf.edu

Corey R. Pittman
cpittman@knights.ucf.edu

Joseph J. LaViola Jr.
jjl@cs.ucf.edu

University of Central Florida
Orlando, FL 32816, USA

ABSTRACT

Despite decades of research, there is yet no general rapid prototyping recognizer for dynamic gestures that can be trained with few samples, work with continuous data, and achieve high accuracy that is also modality-agnostic. To begin to solve this problem, we describe a small suite of accessible techniques that we collectively refer to as the Jackknife gesture recognizer. Our dynamic time warping based approach for both segmented and continuous data is designed to be a robust, go-to method for gesture recognition across a variety of modalities using only limited training samples. We evaluate pen and touch, Wii Remote, Kinect, Leap Motion, and sound-sensed gesture datasets as well as conduct tests with continuous data. Across all scenarios we show that our approach is able to achieve high accuracy, suggesting that Jackknife is a capable recognizer and good first choice for many endeavors.

ACM Classification Keywords

H.5.2 Information interfaces and presentation: User interfaces, input devices and strategies; I.5.5 Pattern recognition: Implementation, interactive systems

Author Keywords

Gesture Recognition; Dynamic Time Warping; Rapid Prototyping; Gesture Customization; User Evaluation.

INTRODUCTION

Although gesture recognition has been an active area of research for some time, it has become especially popular in the last decade with the introduction of several low-cost interactive devices, such as the Wii Remote, Kinect, and Leap Motion. To support gesture recognition on these devices, a flurry of techniques have been proposed and evaluated, many of which rely on domain specific knowledge to achieve competitive accuracy (above 90%). And unsurprisingly, support vector machines, hidden Markov models, conditional random fields, decision trees and random forests, as well as variants of these machine learning approaches are ubiquitous [16]. However, these popular approaches are also inappropriate for rapid prototyping or gesture customization given that either copious training data or advanced knowledge of machine learning are typically required.

For the rapid prototyping community, gesture recognition must be easily accessible[1] for development on new platforms, where best approaches have not been identified, or where libraries and toolkits may not yet be available and consumers are unfamiliar with machine learning. The $-family of recognizers [1, 2, 17, 35, 38] has been effective at addressing this issue for pen and touch, though attempts to generalize these techniques to higher dimensionalities have been less successful. For gesture customization, recognizers must work well with as little as one training sample per gesture class, as users may be unwilling to provide a plethora of samples for a variety of classes. Even when we relax these constraints, most research still only focuses on one domain or input device, *e.g.*, Kinect, Leap Motion, or Wii Remote for full body or hand gestures, and rarely does research consider general methods that might easily be adopted to any modality. Another common issue is that many researchers evaluate their methods using segmented data without addressing continuous data stream related issues. As a result, it remains unclear and confusing what might be a good starting point when one desires to incorporate gesture recognition into their work.

We begin to address these issues with Jackknife, a general recognizer for dynamic gestures that, much like a multitool, is a collection of techniques designed to handle various scenarios. Our recognizer is designed to be modality-agnostic, so that little domain specific knowledge is required, and competitive accuracy can be achieved with minimum training data. At the heart of Jackknife is dynamic time warping (DTW), an elastic dissimilarity measure suitable for handling large gesticulation variability. As DTW has repeatedly been shown to be a high quality recognizer in time series research, especially for nearest neighbor (NN) pattern matching, it is surprising to

[1] By easily accessible we mean self contained, easy to debug, and can be implemented without too much effort.

CHI 2017, May 06-11, 2017, Denver, CO, USA
 ISBN 978-1-4503-4655-9/17/05...$15.00
DOI: http://dx.doi.org/10.1145/3025453.3026002

us that this technique is not already the de facto go-to gesture recognition method. Still, since DTW itself was not designed explicitly for gesture recognition, we introduce several extensions that improve its base accuracy under various conditions.

While the main contribution of this paper is a general, device-agnostic dynamic gesture recognizer, several additional contributions are made to achieve this objective, which are that we promote and raise awareness that DTW is a powerful 1-NN gesture recognizer useful for rapid prototyping and custom gestures; demonstrate that the inner product of gesture path direction vectors is often a better local cost function for DTW as compared to the pervasive squared Euclidean distance, which to the best of our knowledge has not been explicitly evaluated; present new correction factors that modify the DTW score and help disambiguate certain gestures as well as further separate negative samples from positive sample; and introduce a new method to select a per class rejection threshold for gesture spotting in a continuous stream and evaluate this method with a new dataset collected from 40 participants. Finally, reference source code and our dataset is available at `http://www.eecs.ucf.edu/isuelab/research/jackknife`.

The rest of the paper is organized as follows. First, we present related works where we focus on what motivates Jackknife, after which we describe our recognizer in detail. With an understanding of the core methods in hand, we subsequently evaluate the various aspects of Jackknife by analyzing visualizations of score distributions, and by performing recognition tests with segmented and continuous data. Finally, we discuss our findings.

RELATED WORK

Since space precludes a comprehensive discussion of all gesture recognition work, we direct the reader to few surveys [12, 21, 25, 30, 31]. For a taste, Mitra and Acharya [21] discuss different gesture recognition methods such as hidden Markov Models (HMM), particle filtering and condensation, finite-state machines (FSM), and neural networks. As hand-based gesture recognition is a popular topic, Suarez and Murphy [31] look through recognition methods using depth images. These methods include common and customized approaches like Du's [8] classifier that counts the number of convex points in a hand silhouette for classification over a small set of static poses. Ibraheem and Khan [12] also discuss HMMs, neural networks, and histogram based feature and fuzzy clustering algorithm methods. Sarkar *et al.* [30] similarly report on both 2D and 3D methods for hand gesture recognition. It is worth noting that computer vision techniques such as those just mentioned are common in the gesture (and action) recognition literature; however, in this work we assume that gestures are a time series of trajectories through a multidimensional space.

A common theme of these works is that a large amount of training data is needed to train the recognizers. Another issue is that many approaches also require domain-specific knowledge to extract features useful for discriminating gesture classes, which in itself can be a very challenging problem to solve. Two clear advantages of DTW-based recognizers are that competitive accuracy is still possible with limited data and complex feature extraction is unnecessary.

Why DTW and Not Some Other Measure?

Gestures are naturally represented as time series, and it has long been known that DTW is an excellent measure for 1-nearest nearest (1-NN) pattern recognition in times series classification problems. As an example of its power, Giusti and Batista [10] compared 48 dissimilarity measures over 42 time series datasets and found that DTW and CIDDTW [4] (which is incorporated in this work) are among the top performing measures on average. More recently, Bagnall *et al.* [3] conducted an extensive evaluation of 18 recently proposed state-of-the-art classifiers over 85 datasets and found that many of the approaches do not actually outperform 1-NN DTW or Rotation Forest, and they also remark that DTW is a good base to compare against new work.

DTW has also already been used quite successfully in gesture recognition. Celebi *et al.* [6] implemented weighted DTW for Kinect to recognize 8 gestures with 28 samples per gesture. They weighted each skeleton joint differently by optimizing a discriminant ratio. Wu *et al.* [39] utilized DTW for user identification and authentication on Kinect. Their dataset consisted of 8 unique gestures, each repeated 5 times, collected from 20 individuals. Bodiroza *et al.* [5] used DTW on Kinect data to recognize 6 hand gestures performed 20 times by a single subject. Vikram *et al.* [36] developed a DTW-based recognizer for the Leap Motion sensor to recognize hand writing in the air. Their dataset consisted of both uppercase and lowercase alphabetical letters, and each letter was repeated 5 times by 100 participants. Not only do we see again that a large number of training samples are used, but also these works mostly utilize Euclidean distance as the local cost function for DTW. In our approach, we emphasize the inner product of gesture path direction vectors and show that this local cost function usually achieves higher accuracy.

What About Speed... I Hear It's Slow?

DTW is infamous for its sluggishness, which we believe is an unfair assessment. In its classic form, DTW is quadratic; however, Rakthanmanon *et al.* [23] demonstrated that DTW can be optimized to achieve search times faster than typical linear time Euclidean distance search algorithms. Further, even without optimizations, Vatavu [34] found that low sampling rates achieve high accuracy for Euclidean distance, angular, and DTW based 2D gesture recognizers. In this work, we resample gestures to $n = 16$ points; and by using a Sakoe-Chiba Band [29] (to control pathological warping) that constrains DTW's search window to $r = 2$, complexity drops to $\mathcal{O}(rn)$. It is also useful to compare DTW with \$P [35], a $\mathcal{O}(n^{2.5})$ recognizer: specially, we note that \$P is popular and in common use, suggesting that the algorithmic complexity of DTW should not be an issue for many applications.

How Can We Select a Rejection Criteria?

Liu and Chua [19] summarize three common approaches for rejecting negative samples: build a set of garbage models from a set of explicitly defined unwanted patterns, learn a cut off based on the distribution of scores between classes, or generate mixture models from positive samples to form a *universal background model* (UBM). These are general methods used across various fields and in particular the UBM approach stems from speaker recognition [26]. In all of these cases, there is a sufficient amount of training data to construct representative probability distributions, which is a not a luxury we have with only one or two training samples per gesture class. Our approach is most like UBM, where negative samples are synthetically generated from positive samples, although we do not generate an explicit background model. Instead we use the distribution of scored synthetic negative and positive samples to help select a rejection threshold. To increase the positive sample distribution, we synthetically generate new samples using a recently introduced technique, gesture path stochastic resampling [32].

JACKKNIFE

Jackknife is a multitool for gesture recognition equipped with the following functionalities: dynamic time warping using the inner product of gesture path direction vectors as the local cost function and squared Euclidean distance as a back up, correction factors that inflate the scores of dissimilar gestures, and a synthetic gesture generator for learning a rejection criteria. In practice, one will only need to implement the components required for their specific application.

In this work, we treat gestures as time series, an ordered set of points:

$$P = (p_i | i = 1..n), \tag{1}$$

where n is the number of points in the series and each $p_i \in \mathbb{R}^m$. Typical values of m for various modalities include $m = 2$ for pen or touch, $m = 21 \times 3$ for Kinect 2.0, and $m = 21 \times 3$ for Leap Motion. A gesture can also be represented as a set of unit length direction vectors through m-space, which we refer to as the *gesture path direction vectors*:

$$\vec{P} = \left(\vec{p}_i = \frac{p_{i+1} - p_i}{| p_{i+1} - p_i |} \,\middle|\, i = 1..n-1 \right). \tag{2}$$

Further, we denote a query sequence as Q and a template sequence as T, where a template is a time series representation of a specific gesture class. Jackknife employees 1-nearest neighbor classification, where a query is compared against all templates stored in a database, and the template whose measure against the query is least dissimilar is said to match the gesture class of the query. Formally, given a set of templates $\mathbb{T}$ and a query Q, the query's class is the gesture class of $T_i \in \mathbb{T}$ that minimizes their dissimilarity:

$$match = \underset{T_i \in \mathbb{T}}{\text{argmin}} \prod_{j=1}^{F} f_j(T_i, Q), \tag{3}$$

where f_1 is the DTW measure of T and Q, and $f_{2 \leq i \leq F}$ are correction factors. This approach is based on the complexity-invariant distance (CID) measure [4]. CID inflates a base distance measure, such as Euclidean distance or DTW, with a correction factor (CF) that is a measure of the complexity difference between a template and query. CF ranges from one to positive infinity such that time series similar in "complexity" score near one and the base distance measure remains relatively unchanged. Otherwise, the score is inflated. Our interpretation of CID is that a good CF is able to capture information about the dissimilarity of two time series for which the base distance measure is unable, though the CF measure does not necessarily need to relate to notions of complexity.

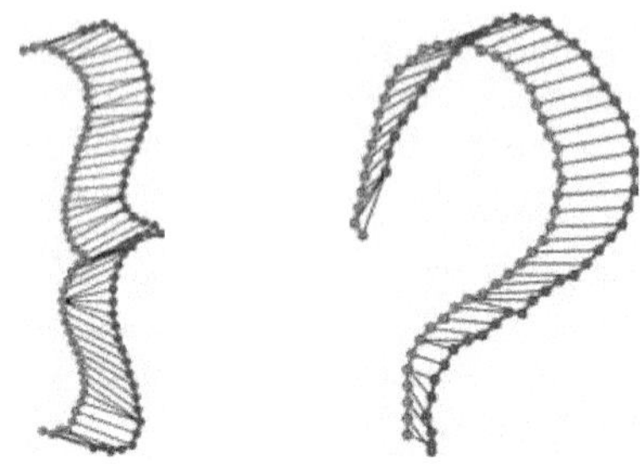

Figure 1: Visualization of the 2D alignment found by DTW between two right curly braces (left) and two unistroke question marks (right), from the $1-GDS dataset [38].

Dynamic Time Warping

Dynamic time warping (DTW) is a dissimilarity measure that allows local warping of time series in order to find the best alignment. Given two time series T and Q of length n and m, we construct an n-by-m cost matrix. Each element (i, j) in the matrix stores the minimum cumulative distance between the subsequences $t_1, ..., t_i$ and $q_1, ..., q_j$. This cumulative distance can be found efficiently with dynamic programming by solving the following recurrence:

$$\gamma(i, j) = d(t_i, q_j) + min \begin{cases} \gamma(i-1, j-1) \\ \gamma(i-1, j) \\ \gamma(i, j-1), \end{cases} \tag{4}$$

where $d(t_i, q_j)$ is a local cost function, discussed shortly. In other words, during the evaluation of element (i, j), the cumulative measure of three neighbors are considered, the minimum is taken, and the local cost of matching t_i to q_j is added to the minimum, which then becomes the minimum cumulative distance for the subsequences under evaluation. Once the matrix is fully evaluated, element (n, m) is the DTW score for T and Q. The path through the matrix that defines the minimum cumulative distance between the sequences is the optimal warping path, which is a set of alignments between T and Q. A visualization of the warping path between two different 2D gestures is shown in Figure 1.

Local Cost Function

The local cost function $d(t_i, q_j)$ in Equation 4 is most frequently the squared (or standard) Euclidean distance over z-score normalized sequences[2]: $d(t_i, q_j) = (t_i - q_j)^2$. Though, we find in gesture recognition that this cost function is not always the best option. An alternative that has received less attention is the inner product of a feature vector measure [20], which can also be applied to gestures. Instead of extracting feature vectors from a time series, we utilize the gesture path direction vectors (see Equation 2). Since the inner product is a similarity measure in $[-1, 1]$ for unit vectors, we convert this to a dissimilarly as follows:

$$d(\vec{t}_i, \vec{q}_j) = 1 - < \vec{t}_i, \vec{q}_j > \tag{5}$$

[2]Each sequence is z-score normalized independently.

where $1 \leq i < n$. This approach is inspired by the 2D Penny Pincher [33] gesture recognizer that also uses the inner product of direction vectors, an approach that proved to be empirically faster than alternative unistroke recognizers while remaining competitive in accuracy. When used as the local cost function, we will later demonstrate that the inner product measure (IP) is often superior to the squared Euclidean distance measure (ED) in gesture recognition problems.

Warping Window Constraint

With classic DTW, pathological warping can occur when a small part of one subsequence is inappropriately mapped to a large portion of another [24]. To prevent this issue, one can constrain the amount of warping allowed. A popular approach is the Sakoe-Chiba Band [29], which limits the maximum distance r the warping path can stray from the diagonal, where $|i-j| \leq r$. An additional benefit immediately apparent is that constraining the warping path can significantly speedup DTW as less of the cost matrix is evaluated. The optimal warping window varies per problem [24], but a very common constraint is 10% of the time series length, which also yields very good results in our testing.

Lower Bounding DTW

The cost of performing DTW is not much of a concern when working with segmented data at a low resampling rate as well as with a small number of gesture classes and training samples. However, when working with a continuous data stream where DTW evaluations are frequent and observational latencies are problematic, it can be useful to prune templates that will obviously not match a query. An efficient lower bound (LB) score, where $LB(T,Q) \leq DTW(T,Q)$, can be used to avoid a full evaluation in two cases: when the determined lower bound is worse than a predetermined rejection threshold or when a closer match has already been found. One such lower bound for DTW using ED is LB_{Keogh} [13], which envelopes a time series T with an upper (U) and lower (L) band based on a window constraint r:

$$U = \left(u_i = \max_{i-r \leq i \leq i+r} t_i\right) \quad L = \left(l_i = \min_{i-r \leq i \leq i+r} t_i\right). \tag{6}$$

Note that $\forall_i\ L_i \leq t_i \leq U_i$. To lower bound a query Q against a template T for DTW using ED, we define:

$$LB_{Keogh}(T,Q) = \sum_{i=1}^{n} \begin{cases} (q_i - U_i)^2 & \text{if } q_i > U_i \\ (q_i - L_i)^2 & \text{if } q_i < L_i \\ 0 & \text{otherwise} \end{cases}, \tag{7}$$

which is visualized in Figure 2.

A lower bound has also been derived for the inner product of posteriorgrams [40] based on the local cost function $d(t_i, q_j) = -log\langle t_i, q_j\rangle$. One issue with this inner product lower bound is that each component in a posteriorgram is non-negative, which is unlike gesture path direction vectors whose components can take on negative values, and hence a different lower bound is required. Our inner product lower bound is similar to LB_{Keogh}, where the upper and lower bands are calculated in the same way. However, the summation instead is based on the IP distance. If a component in the query vector is positive, then its similarity will be maximized when paired with the upper band

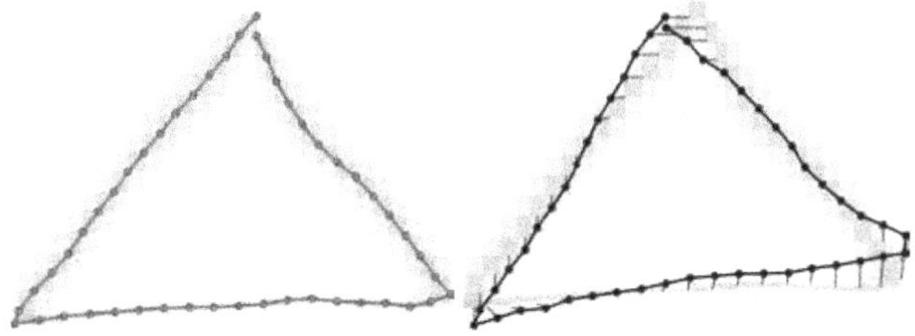

Figure 2: Visualization of a LB_{Keogh} lower bound in 2D for the triangle gesture from $1-GDS [38]. On the left, the combined upper and lower bands of a template form a light blue bounding box per point. On the right, the LB_{Keogh} lower bound is calculated for a query as the sum of the minimum squared Euclidean distance from each point in Q to the corresponding point boundary from T (shown as thin black lines).

component (if both signs are positive), but the dissimilarity is also minimized when paired with the upper band (if the signs are opposite). For the same reasons, if a component in a query vector is negative, pairing with the lower band will always produce the best possible result, which leads to the following IP lower bound:

$$LB_{IP}(T,Q) = \sum_{i=1}^{n} 1 - min\left[1, \max\left(-1, < lb_i, q_i >\right)\right]$$
$$lb_i^j = \begin{cases} U_i^j & \text{if } q_i^j j \geq 0 \\ L_i^j & \text{otherwise} \end{cases}, \tag{8}$$

where j indexes a vector's components ($1 \leq j \leq m$) and the template and query sequence are assumed to be unit length. This lower bound can be proved using the same techniques as in [13, 40].

Correction Factors

After the DTW score is calculated, correction factors are applied that inflate this score based on additional dissimilarities not as easily perceived by only time warping measures, a method that we adopted from CIDDTW [4]. Our correction factors, however, use the inverse inner product of normalized feature vectors:

$$f_i(T,Q) = \frac{1}{< g_i(T),\ g_i(Q) >}, \tag{9}$$

where $2 \leq i \leq F$ per Equation 3 and each g_i transforms the time series into a *normalized* vector whose dimensionality is greater than one (otherwise its normalization would simply result in a scalar equal to one). The vector must also comprise only non-zero components so that the denominator of Equation 9 falls in $(0,1]$ and the domain of f_i becomes $[1,\infty)$. Intuitively, times series that are similar should score near one so that DTW score inflation is minimized.

We now describe two correction factor transformations that are designed specifically for gestures and are inspired indirectly by Rubine's features for pen based gesture recognition [28]. In both cases, we focus on between-component information that is scale and position invariant. These latter attributes are important to ensure that differences between users do not appear as dissimilarities in their gesticulations. First, the component-wise absolute distance traversed by gesture P is given by:

$$g_{abs} = \sum_{i=1}^{n-1} |\vec{p}_i| . \tag{10}$$

Once g_{abs} is normalized, the components of this vector yield a relative measure of the total distance traveled by each component — this correction factor helps to ensure that the contributions to the gesture path for each component of two different samples are similar in measure.

Our second feature is based on the bounding box extents of the concatenated *unnormalized* direction vectors in $\mathbb{R}^m$ space:

$$\begin{aligned} g_{bb} &= bb_{max} - bb_{min}, \\ bb_{max} &= \left(bb_{max_j} = \max_{1 \le i < n} \sum_{i=1}^{n-1} p^j_{i+1} - p^j_i \right), \\ bb_{min} &= \left(bb_{min_j} = \min_{1 \le i < n} \sum_{i=1}^{n-1} p^j_{i+1} - p^j_i \right). \end{aligned} \tag{11}$$

Once normalized, we have the relative distances spanned by each component. We found this bounding box correction factor to be useful in compensating for gestures that are mostly similar, except in span. Consider two gestures: *climb ladder*, which is a hand over hand action, and *balance*, which is a seesaw-like action with arms extended [9]. In both cases, the hands, wrists, and elbows oscillate vertically. The only major difference is that one's arms are extended outward to perform the balance gesture. This extension, which occurs at the beginning of the action, represents only a small duration of the entire gesture and may be difficult to detect with either ED or IP, depending exactly on how a participant performs either gesture. However, the bounding box (span) of each gesture is very different, which is why using the bounding box as a correction factor can improve recognition accuracy.

Rejection

How one can determine an appropriate per template rejection threshold from only a minimum amount of training data remains a difficult problem. With sufficient amounts of training data, a recognizer can estimate within class score probability densities and select thresholds sufficiently low enough to prevent type II (false negative) errors. One can also use negative samples that are non-gesture sequences to help control type I (false positive) errors by ensuring that a rejection threshold is sufficiently high enough to prevent false positives. With access to both positive and negative samples, one can instead select a threshold that minimizes both error types, which is the strategy we adopt. However, in this work, we assume that only a minimum number of positive training samples are given, as little as one or two per gesture class. This limitation implies we need to somehow synthesize both negative and positive samples.

To create negative samples, positive samples are spliced together to create semi-nonsense, noise-like sequences. We favor this approach because we desire that negative samples have parts of real gestures embedded within to ensure that Jackknife can reject sequences that partially resemble but are not actually real gestures. To generate synthetic negative samples, we randomly sample k training samples and from each sample we randomly sample $(n-1)/k$ sequential direction vectors. These direction vectors are concatenated together to form a negative sample. We then compare each template with the negative sample using DTW and save the results per template. This process is repeated a number of times, after which the scores are z-score normalized per template.

The generation of synthetic positive samples requires a different approach. Gesture path stochastic resampling (GPSR) [32] is a new synthetic data generation developed specifically for 2D gestures and rapid prototyping. A gesture path is non-uniformly resampled to $n+x$ points, after which the distance between subsequent points is normalized to unit length, and finally x random points are removed. GPSR was shown to produce realistic results for pen and touch gestures; however, for our use, we do not require realism. Rather, we only need to be able to create a distribution of samples that when evaluated with DTW generates a score distribution similar to the true distribution, and we found GPSR works well for this purpose. For additional information on implemented details and pseudocode, we refer the reader to [32]. In Jackknife, we use GPSR to create synthetic positive samples that are scored with DTW against their seed samples. These within class scores are then z-score normalized using the mean and standard deviations generated from the negative samples evaluation above.

Now we are able to determine a rejection threshold. With the distribution of positive and negatives samples (all of which have been z-score normalized), a standard deviation λ is selected that minimizes the aggregate false and negative positive count. Since we trained with a noise-like pattern, our goal is to be able to reject idle-like motion[3]. The per template rejection threshold δ is then:

$$\delta_i = \mu_i - \lambda \sigma_i, \tag{12}$$

where μ_i is the mean of the negative sample scores relative to each template i and σ is its standard deviation. As we will show in an evaluation, this approach appears to select thresholds near the optimum.

EXAMINATION OF THE DISTRIBUTIONS

To examine the distribution of scores generated by Jackknife for a specific dataset, we do the following: For a given subject, a recognizer is trained with one random sample per gesture class. All z-score normalized synthetic scores generated as part of the training process are saved for analysis. An additional, but unique test sample per gesture class is subsequently evaluated, and the within class DTW score of each test sample, before and after correct factor inflation, are similarly z-score normalized and saved. Last, new synthetic negative samples are again generated, scored, and saved. This process is repeated 10 times per subject and all results are combined into a single set of distributions.

Results are shown in Figure 3, and we note a number of observations. First, the within class samples distribution is well

[3]To increase tolerance to higher energy patterns, the minimization can non-uniformly weight the importance of true and false positives.

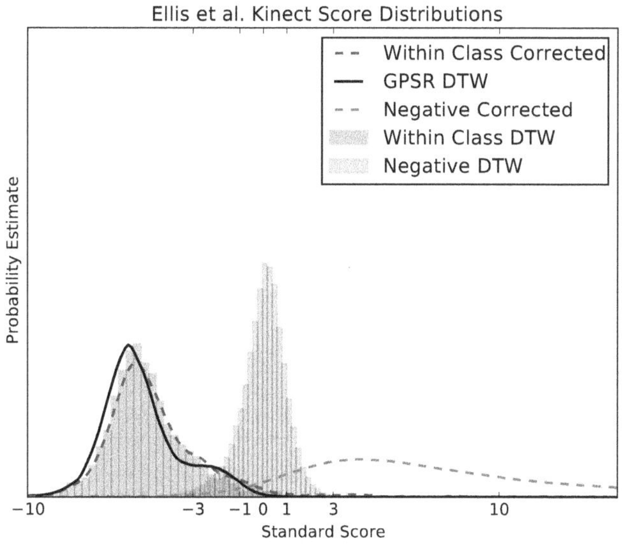

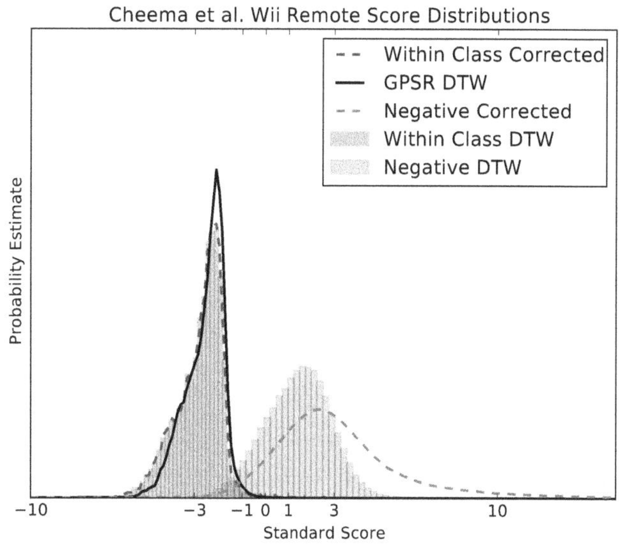

Figure 3: Normalized distributions of within class and negative samples before and after correction factors are applied, as well as the synthetic positive sample distribution for Ellis *et al.*'s [9] and Cheema *et al.*'s [7] datasets.

separated from the negative samples, having only a small amount of overlap, which we perceive as a desirable property for a noise pattern; a poor noise distribution would be far away from the within class samples and result in unreliable rejections thresholds (no false positives or false negatives). Second, the within class corrected DTW scores are remarkably close to the true distribution of the uncorrected DTW scores, whereas the distribution of negative samples are shifted right, away from the within class distribution. This observation suggests that the correction factors are doing their job, although further analysis in the next section will quantitatively confirm this. Finally, the positive samples generated using GPSR form a score distribution that is quite near the true distribution. This does not imply that the synthetic samples are realistic, but it does help build confidence that GPSR can be used to help find a reasonable rejection threshold when used in combination with synthetic negative samples.

EVALUATION OF SEGMENTED DATA

In order to evaluate Jackknife, we consider a number of publicly available gesture datasets that span a range of input modalities. Where appropriate, we compare our recognizer against alternative methods. In general, we start with low dimensional data and work our way into higher dimensions. We perform repeated measures full factorial ANOVA analysis to understand if there are statistically significant differences between the recognizer variants evaluated. However, because recognition error rates are often quite low, accuracy measures are often non-normally distributed and may also violate the homogeneity of variance assumption, which is why we utilize the Aligned Rank Transform method for ANOVA analysis [37]. In the ANOVA results tables, the measure factor is either euclidean distance (ED) or inner product (IP), and the correction factors (CF) are either disabled (False) or enabled (True). Further, $T = x$ specifies that x samples (templates) per gesture class are used for training.

Pen and Touch

Table 1 presents results for Jackknife variants on the $1-GDS pen and touch dataset [38]. This dataset contains 4800 samples of 16 pen gestures collected from 10 participants. Our results were obtained using a writer-independent protocol. The reason for focusing on writer-independence is that state-of-the-art recognizers already achieve near perfect recognition rates in writer-dependent tests on this dataset. Given a training participant, our writer-independent protocol randomly selects T samples per gesture class from that participant for training. Next, one sample per each gesture class is randomly selected from the pool of samples from all other participants, which is used as the test set. This sampling process is repeated 500 times, and all results for the training participant are combined into a single average accuracy value for that individual. This process is repeated for each participant, so that each is used to supply training data.

We observe that using inner products (IP) with gesture path direction vectors yields higher accuracy with significance, as does increasing the template count. Correction factors were not a significant factor; however we cannot say how the correction factors affect negative samples with this test. In Table 2 we compare the best Jackknife variant to $1 [38] and $P [35], two popular rapid prototyping $-family recognizers. The main observation is that Jackknife outperforms the alternative recognizers by a large margin and with significance.

Wii Remote

In Table 3, we report results for Jackknife variants on Cheema *et al.*'s Wii Remote dataset [7]. This dataset contains 15625 samples of gestures collected from 25 participants who individually provided 25 samples per gesture. This dataset is particularly interesting because as compared to other Wii Remote datasets, the gesture vocabulary is large at 25 classes and the Wii Remote traverses through various orientations. Our results were obtained using a user-dependent protocol

Measure	CF	T=1		T=2	
		μ	(σ)	μ	(σ)
ED	False	0.91	(0.03)	0.92	(0.03)
ED	True	0.91	(0.03)	0.92	(0.03)
IP	False	0.94	(0.02)	0.95	(0.03)
IP	True	0.94	(0.02)	0.95	(0.03)

Effect	$F_{1,63}$	$Pr(>F)$	η_p^2
Measure	412.65	< .001	.87 (L)
CF	0.33	.57	.01 —
Templates	86.8	< .001	.58 (L)
Measure × CF	0.0	.96	.00 —
Measure × Templates	10.84	< .01	.15 (L)
CF × Templates	0.13	.72	.00 —
Measure × CF × Templates	0.02	.88	.00 —

Table 1: Writer-independent mean accuracies for Jackknife variants on \$1-GDS [38], as well as ANOVA results with statistically significant effects highlighted and their effect size labeled: (L)arge, (M)edium, or (S)mall.

Recognizer	T=1		T=2	
	μ	(σ)	μ	(σ)
Jackknife	0.94	(0.02)	0.95	(0.03)
\$1	0.88	(0.02)	0.90	(0.01)
\$P	0.84	(0.02)	0.86	(0.02)

Table 2: Writer-independent mean accuracies for several recognizers on \$1-GDS [38]. There is a significant difference between recognizers with a large effect size ($F_{2,45}, p < .001, \eta_p^2 = .92$), and a post hoc analysis shows that all recognizers are significantly different from each other.

similar to the original work of Cheema *et al.* [7]. For each experiment in this protocol, T samples are selected at random from a participant for training and the remaining $25 - T$ samples are selected for testing, and this selection process is performed 500 times per each participant. We did not run a user-independent protocol because device orientation has a significant impact on the accelerometer signal data, and there is a great deal of variance in how the Wii Remote is held by each participant. However, applications that track device orientation can easily adjust the signals in order to support user-independence. To improve accuracy for the inner product (IP) Jackknife variant, the acceleration data was integrated into 3D position points per [15], but we found this was unhelpful for the squared Euclidean distance variant (ED). There was a significant difference between the ED and IP measures, where the IP measure gave higher accuracies. There was also a small positive effect when utilizing the correction factors; though, due to truncation, this cannot be seen in the table.

We next compared the best performing Jackknife variant against alternative domain-specific recognizers (DTW with quantization [18], \$3 [14], and Protractor 3D [15]), whose results are shown in Table 4. DTW with quantized accelerometer data performed slightly better than Jackknife, although accuracies were similar. We note that other than the common step to integrate acceleration samples into position trajectories, Jackknife did not require domain specific knowledge to achieve high accuracy. On the other hand, DTW with quantized data required an analysis of the accelerometer data and a selection of the quantization levels, which may be domain or device specific.

Measure	CF	T=1		T=2	
		μ	(σ)	μ	(σ)
ED	False	0.79	(0.05)	0.86	(0.04)
ED	True	0.80	(0.05)	0.86	(0.04)
IP	False	0.93	(0.03)	0.96	(0.02)
IP	True	0.93	(0.03)	0.96	(0.02)

Effect	$F_{1,168}$	$Pr(>F)$	η_p^2
Measure	1747.23	< .001	.91 (L)
CF	3.91	< .05	.02 (S)
Templates	314.67	< .001	.65 (L)
Measure × CF	2.23	.14	.01 (S)
Measure × Templates	44.05	< .001	.21 (L)
CF × Templates	0.17	.68	.00 —
Measure × CF × Templates	0.03	.86	.00 —

Table 3: User-dependent mean accuracies for Jackknife variants on Cheema *et al.*'s Wii Remote dataset [7], as well as ANOVA results with statistically significant effects highlighted and their effect size labeled: (L)arge, (M)edium, or (S)mall.

Recognizer	T=1		T=2	
	μ	(σ)	μ	(σ)
DTW (w/ quantization)	0.94	(0.03)	0.97	(0.02)
Jackknife	0.93	(0.03)	0.96	(0.02)
\$3	0.71	(0.06)	0.79	(0.06)
Protractor 3D	0.63	(0.06)	0.73	(0.06)

Table 4: User-dependent mean accuracies for various recognizers on Cheema *et al.*'s Wii Remote dataset [7].The recognizer main effect is significant with a large effect size ($F_{3,168} = 789.72, p < .001, \eta_p^2 = .93(L)$), and post hoc tests show that all recognizers are also significantly different from each other.

Kinect

In Table 5, results are presented for the Ellis *et al.* (Parkour) [9] Kinect dataset, which contains 1280 samples of 16 parkour actions, *e.g.* climbing and vaulting, collected from 16 participants using a Kinect sensor. We used the same user-dependent test protocol as reported in the last section. The local cost function was significant, where the Jackknife IP measure outperformed ED, and IP was able to achieve 99% accuracy with one training sample. The correction factors were are also significant and played a role in substantially driving down the error rates[4]. We also ran a user-independent variant of this test and found that IP with correction factors and T=2 achieved 96% accuracy, whereas ED with correction factors achieved 70%.

We also replicated Ellis *et al.*'s observational latency test [9] that evaluated recognizer accuracy when training and test data

[4]It is important to note that as accuracies reach high levels, seemingly small improvements in accuracy are actually large reductions in error rates.

Measure	CF	T=1		T=2	
		μ	(σ)	μ	(σ)
ED	False	0.88	(0.05)	0.93	(0.03)
ED	True	0.89	(0.05)	0.94	(0.03)
IP	False	0.97	(0.03)	0.99	(0.02)
IP	True	0.99	(0.02)	0.99	(0.01)

Effect	$F_{1,105}$	$Pr(>F)$	η_p^2
Measure	383.89	< .001	.79 (L)
CF	16.62	< .001	.14 (M)
Templates	80.36	< .001	.43 (L)
Measure × CF	1.73	.19	.02 (S)
Measure × Templates	35.86	< .001	.25 (L)
CF × Templates	3.38	.07	.03 (S)
Measure × CF × Templates	0.0	.96	.00 —

Table 5: User-dependent mean accuracies for Jackknife variants on the Parkour dataset [9], as well as ANOVA results with statistically significant effects highlighted and their effect size labeled: (L)arge, (M)edium, or (S)mall.

were truncated to varying frame counts in order to minimize the delay between when a user performs an action and when the time that action is recognized. If an action can be recognized before completion, observational latency can be reduced. In Table 6, we see that Jackknife with IP achieves the highest accuracy for all frame count levels.

Recognizer	10	15	20	25	30	40	60
Jackknife IP w/ CF	24	53	78	90	95	98	99
Ellis *et al.* [9]	14	37	65	82	91	95	96
Conditional Random Field	15	25	47	67	81	91	94
Bag of Words	11	21	44	68	83	92	94

Table 6: Recognition percentage accuracies for Jackknife and recognizers evaluated by Ellis *et al.* [9] (bottom three) for varying length video sequences. Both training and testing data are truncated to the specified number of frames.

Acoustic Gestures

Hand based gesture interactions with computers via Doppler shifted sound waves is presently gaining attention [11, 27]. Unlike other interface devices evaluated to this point, sound waves are especially subject to noise as extracting and detecting frequency changes over a large spectrum with low cost hardware still lacks robustness. Further, complex over-the-air hand gestures are prone to large variations in shape and speed, the later of which manifests itself uniquely in frequency distributions (unlike in 2D or 3D Euclidean space where speed alone does not change the observed trajectory). These issues make accurate gesture recognition difficult. To test whether Jackknife is suitable for this input modality, we collected a new dataset comprising eighteen dynamic hand gestures collected from 22 participants with a 5 speaker, 1 microphone setup based on [22] (see our project website for more details). The raw data is represented as a 33 frequency bin distribution per speaker, which results in an $m = 165$ component vector per frame. Jackknife results are shown in Table 7, which were obtained using the user-dependent protocol [7] described previously. In early testing, we learned that z-score normalization on the spectrum data was harmful; we believe this is because for some gestures, there is no motion through certain frequency bins, and so z-score normalizing those components only served to scale up noise. Therefore, ED- is also reported, which is the squared Euclidean distance measure on raw data without z-score normalization. While ED- is not formally part of Jackknife (as this result required an additional investigation and some domain knowledge), we feel that the reader should be aware of this result. Additionally, since the bounding box correction factor does not have meaning in this context, we only utilize the absolute distances traveled correction factor.

Measure	CF	T=1		T=2		T=4	
		μ	(σ)	μ	(σ)	μ	(σ)
ED	False	0.71	(0.08)	0.81	(0.08)	0.87	(0.07)
ED	True	0.75	(0.07)	0.83	(0.06)	0.89	(0.05)
ED-	False	0.83	(0.07)	0.90	(0.05)	0.94	(0.04)
ED-	True	0.84	(0.06)	0.91	(0.05)	0.94	(0.04)
IP	False	0.72	(0.07)	0.81	(0.06)	0.88	(0.06)
IP	True	0.75	(0.06)	0.84	(0.05)	0.90	(0.05)

Effect	F Value	$Pr(>F)$	η_p^2
Measure	$F_{2,483} = 491.46$	< .001	.67 (L)
CF	$F_{1,483} = 72.36$	< .001	.13 (M)
Templates	$F_{3,483} = 551.31$	< .001	.77 (L)
Measure × CF	$F_{2,483} = 10.02$	< .001	.04 (S)
Measure × Templates	$F_{6,483} = 11.41$	< .001	.12 (M)
CF × Templates	$F_{3,483} = 1.76$	.15	.01 (S)

Table 7: User-dependent accuracy results for Jackknife variants on the acoustic gesture dataset, as well as ANOVA results with statistically significant effects highlighted and their effect size labeled: (L)arge, (M)edium, or (S)mall. ED- indicates that sequences were not z-score normalized.

As is shown, the local distance measure and correction factor effects are significant. In a post hoc analysis, we found that ED- was significantly different from ED and IP, but the latter measures where not different from each other. Good accuracy ($\geq 90\%$) can be achieved with ED- with two templates, otherwise four templates are required with IP.

Performance

Over 10,000 iterations, we trained a C++ based Jackknife recognizer with our Kinect user study data (see next section), which is 63 components per point. The recognizer was trained with T=10 templates per gesture class, resulting in 140 templates (since there are 14 gesture classes). The recognizer was then used to evaluate one additional sample per gesture class and the evaluation time in *micro*seconds per sample was recorded. On a MacBook Pro, 2.2 GHz Intel Core i7 with 8GB DDR3 memory, the average time to execute a recognition test on a raw sample was 395 µs (std=90.2); or equivalently, the evaluation process took approximately 2.82 µs (0.64) per template, amortized.

EVALUATION OF CONTINUOUS DATA

To evaluate the effectiveness of our approach in rejecting non-gesture sequences from a continuous data stream, we collected

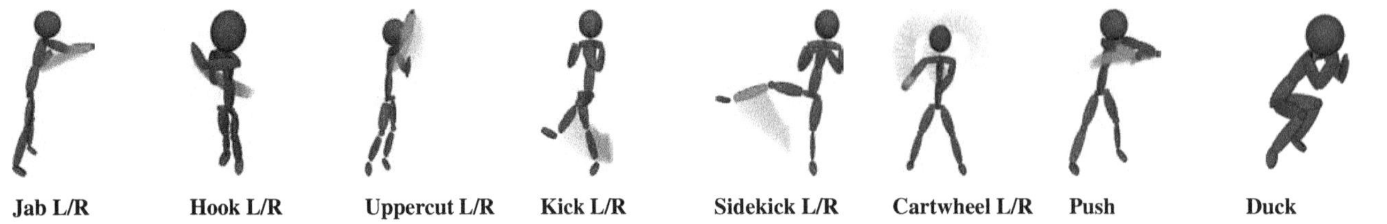

Table 8: List of 14 Kinect gestures used in our contiguous data study. Note that L/R indicates there is a left and right side version of the gesture.

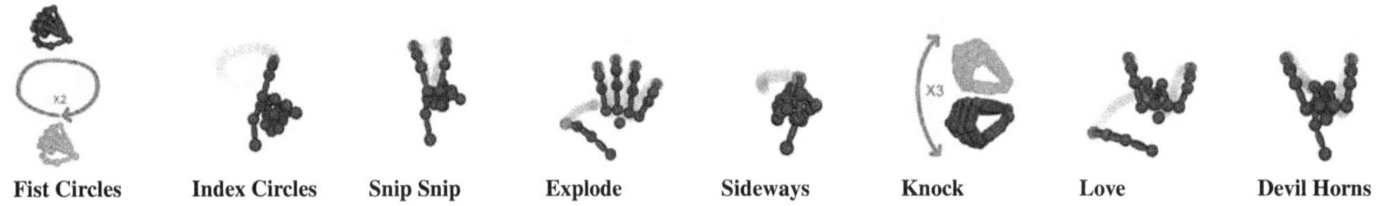

Table 9: List of 8 Leap Motion gestures used in our contiguous data study. Each gestures starts with one's hand in a first and ends in the same position.

λ	F_1 Score	Precision	Recall	FPR	Pruned
	$\mu(\sigma)$	$\mu(\sigma)$	$\mu(\sigma)$	$\mu(\sigma)$	$\mu(\sigma)$
1.5	95.7 (5)	95.4 (5)	96.1 (6)	0.3 (0)	89.2 (6)
1.75	96.0 (6)	96.0 (6)	96.1 (7)	0.3 (0)	90.1 (5)
2.0	96.9 (5)	97.3 (5)	96.5 (6)	0.2 (0)	90.9 (5)
2.25	96.4 (6)	97.5 (4)	95.5 (7)	0.2 (0)	91.7 (5)
2.5	95.9 (6)	97.5 (4)	94.5 (8)	0.2 (0)	92.6 (4)
2.75	95.1 (5)	97.5 (3)	93.0 (8)	0.2 (0)	93.3 (4)
1.98	96.4 (5)	96.8 (5)	96.1 (6)	0.2 (0)	90.8 (5)

Table 10: T=2 Percentage accuracy results for various rejection thresholds on the Kinect gesture dataset shown in Table 8. The last entry is the threshold that was automatically selected.

λ	F_1 Score	Precision	Recall	FPR	Pruned
	$\mu(\sigma)$	$\mu(\sigma)$	$\mu(\sigma)$	$\mu(\sigma)$	$\mu(\sigma)$
1.5	93.8 (5)	93.3 (7)	95.0 (7)	0.8 (0)	54.8 (7)
1.75	94.4 (5)	95.0 (5)	94.4 (8)	0.6 (0)	58.1 (7)
2.0	94.3 (5)	95.8 (5)	93.3 (8)	0.5 (0)	62.5 (7)
2.25	94.0 (7)	97.7 (3)	91.5 (11)	0.3 (0)	66.2 (6)
2.5	92.8 (8)	98.1 (3)	89.4 (13)	0.2 (0)	70.2 (6)
2.75	90.9 (10)	98.3 (2)	86.3 (15)	0.2 (0)	73.7 (5)
1.95	93.8 (6)	95.7 (5)	92.5 (9)	0.5 (0)	61.8 (8)

Table 11: T=2 Percentage accuracy results for various rejection thresholds on the Leap Motion gesture dataset shown in Table 9. The last entry is the threshold that was automatically selected.

test data from a pool of 40 students (30 male and 10 female) at the University of Central Florida, ranging in age from 18 to 28. The participants were divided into two groups where the first group worked with a Kinect and the second group worked with a Leap Motion. We collected segmented training data of the gestures shown in Tables 8 and 9 as well as a continuous, uninterrupted session of the sample gestures performed in random order with repetitions, which is discussed in detail below. Each participant took around 15 to 20 minutes to complete all tasks, including a pre-questionnaire to collect demographic information, and all were compensated $10 for their time.

The experimental setup comprised a 50 inch Sony Bravia HDTV and a Microsoft Kinect 2.0 or Leap Motion. The Kinect sensor was mounted above the HDTV using a mounting device and was kept stationary throughout all sessions. The Leap Motion sensor was mounted on a desktop in front of the television and was kept in place through a single session using tape, except in one case where the participant was left handed and the sensor's orientation was changed to accommodate for their comfort. Further, a box was placed between the participant and the device so one could rest their arm and avoid fatigue, which also helped to control the distance and orientation of a participant's hand during the study.

Data Collection

We developed a data collection utility with two modes using Unity 3D v5.4. The first mode allowed us to collect clean, segmented samples of each gesture for training. A participant was asked to perform a specific gesture that was initiated by a count down. The sequence was then resampled and replayed to ensure correctness. If an error occurred or the participant was unhappy with the replay, the sample was discard and recollected. This process was repeated twice so two training samples per gesture were collected. Note that all gestures were demonstrated to a participant before any data was collected. The second mode enabled us to collect a continuous stream of gesture articulations. Our application prompted the participant to perform a specific gesture selected at random, and once we confirmed the correct action was performed, we manually advanced the application to the next gesture. Otherwise, if an error occurred, *e.g.*, a malformed gesture or loss of tracking, the action was retried. A proper example of each gesture was collected three times so that there were a total of 14×3 valid Kinect gestures and 8×3 valid Leap Motion gestures included in the *unsegmented* stream.

We noticed the Kinect lost track of some participants more frequently than others, which may be related to the texture and colors of the participants clothing. In such cases the skeleton appeared jittery on the screen and gesture were repeated as necessary. The Leap Motion device also frequently lost tracking and detected incorrect hand poses, such as reporting that both the index and middle fingers were extended when, in fact, only the index was so. These problems were exacerbated with 5 participants who had smaller hands. Also, we actually collected data for 9 Leap Motion gestures, but found one gesture (not shown in Table 9) was difficult for participants to perform. This gesture was removed from our analysis.

Results

Using data collected from each participant, we trained Jackknife and replayed the participant's session. All classification results including true and false positives (tp and fp) as well as true and false negatives (fn and fn) were averaged into an overall result. Additional parameters were tuned as follows: the recognizer was run once every 10 frames using the last four seconds of buffered frame data[5]; once an action was detected, the buffer was cleared and the recognizer was suspended for 2 seconds, which we believe is sufficient time to prepare for the next gesture; and a gesture was considered as executed if Jackknife returned the same result twice in a row. Based on our experiences, these are fairly reasonable criteria, which can be tuned to match a practitioner's specific requirements.

We reran the above procedure several times for different levels of λ used to set the rejection threshold (see Equation 12). Table 10 shows results for our Kinect continuous data test, and Table 11 shows results for the Leap Motion test. The rejection threshold is important in balancing precision ($tp/(tp+fp)$) and recall ($tp/(tp+fn)$), and the F_1 score is the harmonic mean of these measures. Our goal is to therefore maximum F_1. In the Kinect test, we are able to achieve 96.9% at $\lambda = 2.0$, which is close to the automatically selected threshold $\lambda = 1.98$. Similarly, the maximum F_1 score of 94.4% for the Leap Motion test occurred at $\lambda = 1.75$, which again is near the automatically selected $\lambda = 1.95$. Recall that the automatic threshold is selected so that the false and true negatives generated from synthetic data is minimized, which appear to be appropriate for idle movement in between actions. However, λ can also be increased to allow for a larger variety of non-gesture actions to be performed at the expense increased false negatives. According to our results, the affect on the F_1 score is not too large, where the improvement in precision may well be worth the loss in recall for many applications. These results suggest that Jackknife is useful for working with continuous data.

DISCUSSION

Jackknife is designed to be a "go-to" recognizer for gesture interface development that can span multiple modalities and still achieve competitive accuracy. By combining DTW with concepts developed for 2D gesture recognition, for rapid prototyping and gesture customization, we believe our recognizer accomplishes its objective. There is no simple criterion by which one can judge a recognizer and determine that is it excellent or terrible. At best we can compare with other recognizers in a specific domain for a specific dataset when such is available and speak in relative terms. In this way, we see that Jackknife is very competitive. Examples include the $1-GDS pen and touch dataset where Jackknife with IP outperformed $1 and $P; Cheema *et al.*'s [7] Wii Remote datasets, where Jackknife was on par with the domain-specific quantized DTW; and Ellis *et al.*'s [9] Parkour dataset, where our recognizer achieved 99% accuracy with one training sample, and can be used to reduce observational latency. Even with atypical gesture data such as sound frequencies, Jackknife is able to reach greater than 90% accuracy with only two training samples per gesture. From another perspective, based on accuracy results reported for 36 3D gesture recognizers across different domains [16] (Table 1), one might expect a competitive recognizer to fall between 88—98% (93% ± 5.29%) accuracy. In all tests performed, Jackknife fell in this range.

However, a gesture recognizer can only be a go-to option if it can also support continuous data, which requires robust rejection. By using GPSR [32] to create synthetic positive samples that are combined with synthetic negative samples, we are able to learn a per template rejection threshold with only one training sample per gesture class. We were able to show through an evaluation of continuous data that this automatic process is able to derive a threshold near the optimum.

One Recognizer To Rule Them All?

No, while Jackknife has been demonstrated to be a versatile tool, we do not claim that our recognizer is appropriate for every situation or even that it is the best solution possible for any one situation, and some limitations are worth noting. First, Jackknife presently does not handle static poses. Motion into and out of a static pose can be detected, but a single frame pose does not constitute a time series appropriate for DTW treatment, a limitation of Jackknife we intend to address in future work. The techniques presented also do not generalize to arbitrary variability; for instance, a 3D hand gesture of a circle drawn counterclockwise does not automatically pair with a clockwise gesture without providing appropriate training samples. A last issue that requires attention is that the resampling rate n for GPSR has to be manually tuned. Similar to the optimal-n equation for synthetic 2D gestures, work needs to be done to find an equivalent for more complex data.

CONCLUSION

We have presented Jackknife, a general gesture recognizer suitable for rapid prototyping and gesture customization that works well with little training data as well as continuous data. Our recognizer uses DTW with an inner product local cost function on normalized gesture path direction vectors, which was shown to outperform the squared Euclidean distance alternative in most tests, although Jackknife can be equipped with either measure. We also introduced two new correction factors for DTW that help disambiguate certain gesture classes and inflate negative, non-gesture sample scores. Finally, we proposed a new method of automatically selecting a rejection criteria for continuous data that, according to our evaluation of online data, can select a threshold close to the optimum. Overall, we have demonstrated that Jackknife shows promise of being a capable and robust go-to gesture recognizer.

[5] We used four seconds because some gestures were performed slowly by some participants; though we could have used a shorter duration in most cases. Since the gesture paths are resampled to $n = 16$, idle frames do not significantly contribute to the shape of the action.

ACKNOWLEDGMENTS
This work is supported in part by NSF Award IIS-1638060, Lockheed Martin, Office of Naval Research Award ONR-BAA15001, Army RDECOM Award W911QX13C0052, and Coda Enterprises, LLC. We also thank the ISUE lab members at UCF for their support as well as the anonymous reviewers for their helpful feedback.

REFERENCES
1. Lisa Anthony and Jacob O. Wobbrock. 2010. A Lightweight Multistroke Recognizer for User Interface Prototypes. In *Proceedings of Graphics Interface 2010 (GI '10)*. Canadian Information Processing Society, Toronto, Ont., Canada, Canada, 245–252.
2. Lisa Anthony and Jacob O. Wobbrock. 2012. $N-protractor: A Fast and Accurate Multistroke Recognizer. In *Proceedings of Graphics Interface 2012 (GI '12)*. Canadian Information Processing Society, Toronto, Ont., Canada, Canada, 117–120.
3. Anthony Bagnall, Aaron Bostrom, James Large, and Jason Lines. 2016. The Great Time Series Classification Bake Off: An Experimental Evaluation of Recently Proposed Algorithms. Extended Version. *arXiv preprint arXiv:1602.01711* (2016).
4. Gustavo E.A.P.A. Batista, Xiaoyue Wang, and Eamonn J. Keogh. 2011. *A Complexity-Invariant Distance Measure for Time Series*. Chapter 60, 699–710.
5. Saša Bodiroža, Guillaume Doisy, and Verena Vanessa Hafner. 2013. Position-invariant, Real-time Gesture Recognition Based on Dynamic Time Warping. In *Proceedings of the 8th ACM/IEEE International Conference on Human-robot Interaction (HRI '13)*. IEEE Press, Piscataway, NJ, USA, 87–88.
6. Sait Celebi, Ali Selman Aydin, Talha Tarik Temiz, and Tarik Arici. 2013. Gesture Recognition using Skeleton Data with Weighted Dynamic Time Warping.. In *VISAPP (1)*. 620–625.
7. Salman Cheema, Michael Hoffman, and Joseph J. LaViola Jr. 2013. 3D Gesture classification with linear acceleration and angular velocity sensing devices for video games. *Entertainment Computing* 4, 1 (2013), 11 – 24.
8. Heng Du and TszHang To. 2011. Hand gesture recognition using Kinect. *Techical Report, Boston University* (2011).
9. Chris Ellis, Syed Zain Masood, Marshall F. Tappen, Joseph J. Laviola, Jr., and Rahul Sukthankar. 2013. Exploring the Trade-off Between Accuracy and Observational Latency in Action Recognition. *International Journal of Computer Vision* 101, 3 (Feb. 2013), 420–436.
10. Rafael Giusti and Gustavo E. A. P. A. Batista. 2013. An Empirical Comparison of Dissimilarity Measures for Time Series Classification. In *Proceedings of the 2013 Brazilian Conference on Intelligent Systems (BRACIS '13)*. IEEE Computer Society, Washington, DC, USA, 82–88.
11. Sidhant Gupta, Daniel Morris, Shwetak Patel, and Desney Tan. 2012. Soundwave: using the doppler effect to sense gestures. In *Proceedings of the SIGCHI Conference on Human Factors in Computing Systems*. ACM, 1911–1914.
12. Noor A. Ibraheem and Rafiqul Z. Khan. 2012. Survey on Various Gesture Recognition Technologies and Techniques. *International Journal of Computer Applications* 50, 7 (2012).
13. Eamonn Keogh and Chotirat Ann Ratanamahatana. 2005. Exact indexing of dynamic time warping. *Knowledge and information systems* 7, 3 (2005), 358–386.
14. Sven Kratz and Michael Rohs. 2010. The $3 recognizer: simple 3D gesture recognition on mobile devices. In *Proceedings of the 15th international conference on Intelligent user interfaces*. ACM, 419–420.
15. Sven Kratz and Michael Rohs. 2011. Protractor3D: a closed-form solution to rotation-invariant 3D gestures. In *Proceedings of the 16th international conference on Intelligent User Interfaces*. ACM, 371–374.
16. Joseph J LaViola. 2013. 3d gestural interaction: The state of the field. *International Scholarly Research Notices* 2013 (2013).
17. Yang Li. 2010. Protractor: A Fast and Accurate Gesture Recognizer. In *Proceedings of the SIGCHI Conference on Human Factors in Computing Systems (CHI '10)*. ACM, New York, NY, USA, 2169–2172.
18. Jiayang Liu, Lin Zhong, Jehan Wickramasuriya, and Venu Vasudevan. 2009. uWave: Accelerometer-based personalized gesture recognition and its applications. *Pervasive and Mobile Computing* 5, 6 (2009), 657 – 675. PerCom 2009.
19. Xiao-Hui Liu and Chin-Seng Chua. 2010. Rejection of non-meaningful activities for HMM-based activity recognition system. *Image and Vision Computing* 28, 6 (2010), 865–871.
20. Robert Macrae and Simon Dixon. 2010. Accurate real-time windowed time warping. In *in ISMIR, 2010*. 423–428.
21. S. Mitra and T. Acharya. 2007. Gesture Recognition: A Survey. *IEEE Transactions on Systems, Man, and Cybernetics, Part C (Applications and Reviews)* 37, 3 (May 2007), 311–324.
22. Corey Pittman, Pamela Wisniewski, Conner Brooks, and Joseph J. LaViola Jr. 2016. Multiwave: Doppler Effect Based Gesture Recognition in Multiple Dimensions. In *Proceedings of the 2016 CHI Conference Extended Abstracts on Human Factors in Computing Systems*. ACM, 1729–1736.

23. Thanawin Rakthanmanon, Bilson Campana, Abdullah Mueen, Gustavo Batista, Brandon Westover, Qiang Zhu, Jesin Zakaria, and Eamonn Keogh. 2012. Searching and mining trillions of time series subsequences under dynamic time warping. In *Proceedings of the 18th ACM SIGKDD international conference on Knowledge discovery and data mining*. ACM, 262–270.

24. Chotirat Ann Ratanamahatana and Eamonn Keogh. 2004. Everything you know about dynamic time warping is wrong. In *Third Workshop on Mining Temporal and Sequential Data*.

25. Siddharth S. Rautaray and Anupam Agrawal. 2015. Vision based hand gesture recognition for human computer interaction: a survey. *Artificial Intelligence Review* 43, 1 (2015), 1–54.

26. Douglas A Reynolds, Thomas F Quatieri, and Robert B Dunn. 2000. Speaker verification using adapted Gaussian mixture models. *Digital signal processing* 10, 1 (2000), 19–41.

27. Wenjie Ruan, Quan Z Sheng, Lei Yang, Tao Gu, Peipei Xu, and Longfei Shangguan. 2016. AudioGest: enabling fine-grained hand gesture detection by decoding echo signal. In *Proceedings of the 2016 ACM International Joint Conference on Pervasive and Ubiquitous Computing*. ACM, 474–485.

28. Dean Rubine. 1991. Specifying Gestures by Example. *SIGGRAPH Computer Graphics* 25, 4 (July 1991), 329–337.

29. Hiroaki Sakoe and Seibi Chiba. 1978. Dynamic programming algorithm optimization for spoken word recognition. *IEEE transactions on acoustics, speech, and signal processing* 26, 1 (1978), 43–49.

30. Arpita R. Sarkar, G. Sanyal, and S. Majumder. 2013. Hand Gesture Recognition Systems: A Survey. *International Journal of Computer Applications* 71, 15 (2013).

31. J. Suarez and R. R. Murphy. 2012. Hand gesture recognition with depth images: A review. In *2012 IEEE RO-MAN: The 21st IEEE International Symposium on Robot and Human Interactive Communication*. 411–417.

32. Eugene M. Taranta, II, Mehran Maghoumi, Corey R. Pittman, and Joseph J. LaViola, Jr. 2016. A Rapid Prototyping Approach to Synthetic Data Generation for Improved 2D Gesture Recognition. In *Proceedings of the 29th Annual Symposium on User Interface Software and Technology (UIST '16)*. ACM, New York, NY, USA, 873–885.

33. Eugene M. Taranta II, Andrés N. Vargas, and Joseph J. LaViola Jr. 2016. Streamlined and accurate gesture recognition with Penny Pincher. *Computers & Graphics* 55 (2016), 130 - 142.

34. Radu-Daniel Vatavu. 2011. The Effect of Sampling Rate on the Performance of Template-based Gesture Recognizers. In *Proceedings of the 13th International Conference on Multimodal Interfaces (ICMI '11)*. ACM, New York, NY, USA, 271–278.

35. Radu-Daniel Vatavu, Lisa Anthony, and Jacob O. Wobbrock. 2012. Gestures As Point Clouds: A $P Recognizer for User Interface Prototypes. In *Proceedings of the 14th ACM International Conference on Multimodal Interaction (ICMI '12)*. ACM, New York, NY, USA, 273–280.

36. Sharad Vikram, Lei Li, and Stuart Russell. 2013. Writing and Sketching in the Air, Recognizing and Controlling on the Fly. In *CHI '13 Extended Abstracts on Human Factors in Computing Systems (CHI EA '13)*. ACM, New York, NY, USA, 1179–1184.

37. Jacob O. Wobbrock, Leah Findlater, Darren Gergle, and James J. Higgins. 2011. The Aligned Rank Transform for Nonparametric Factorial Analyses Using Only Anova Procedures. In *Proceedings of the SIGCHI Conference on Human Factors in Computing Systems (CHI '11)*. ACM, New York, NY, USA, 143–146.

38. Jacob O. Wobbrock, Andrew D. Wilson, and Yang Li. 2007. Gestures Without Libraries, Toolkits or Training: A $1 Recognizer for User Interface Prototypes. In *Proceedings of the 20th Annual ACM Symposium on User Interface Software and Technology (UIST '07)*. ACM, New York, NY, USA, 159–168.

39. J. Wu, J. Konrad, and P. Ishwar. 2013. Dynamic time warping for gesture-based user identification and authentication with Kinect. In *2013 IEEE International Conference on Acoustics, Speech and Signal Processing*. 2371–2375.

40. Yaodong Zhang and James R Glass. 2011. An inner-product lower-bound estimate for dynamic time warping. In *2011 IEEE International Conference on Acoustics, Speech and Signal Processing (ICASSP)*. IEEE, 5660–5663.

Ubiquitous Accessibility for People with Visual Impairments: Are We There Yet?

Syed Masum Billah* **Vikas Ashok*** **Donald E. Porter+** **IV Ramakrishnan***

*Department of Computer Science, Stony Brook University, NY, USA
{sbillah, vganjiguntea, ram}@cs.stonybrook.edu
+Department of Computer Science, University of North Carolina at Chapel Hill, NC, USA
porter@cs.unc.edu

ABSTRACT

Ubiquitous access is an increasingly common vision of computing, wherein users can interact with any computing device or service from anywhere, at any time. In the era of personal computing, users with visual impairments required special-purpose, assistive technologies, such as screen readers, to interact with computers. This paper investigates whether technologies like screen readers have kept pace with, or have created a barrier to, the trend toward ubiquitous access, with a specific focus on desktop computing as this is still the primary way computers are used in education and employment. Towards that, the paper presents a user study with 21 visually-impaired participants, specifically involving the switching of screen readers within and across different computing platforms, and the use of screen readers in remote access scenarios. Among the findings, the study shows that, even for remote desktop access—an early forerunner of true ubiquitous access—screen readers are too limited, if not unusable. The study also identifies several accessibility needs, such as uniformity of navigational experience across devices, and recommends potential solutions. In summary, assistive technologies have not made the jump into the era of ubiquitous access, and multiple, inconsistent screen readers create new practical problems for users with visual impairments.

Author Keywords

Ubiquitous accessibility; visually impaired users; multiple screen readers; remote access; mobile computing.

ACM Classification Keywords

K.4.2 Computers and Society: Social Issues

INTRODUCTION

Nearly all aspects of modern life now incorporate computing. The nature of computing has also shifted, from a user owning a single, dedicated PC to the modern era where users commonly own multiple devices, including desktops, phones, tablets, and laptops. As internet access has connected these devices, software has given users the ability to interact with data and apps on any of these devices at any time, from anywhere. For instance, users commonly work from home, using remote desktop technology, run applications for different operating systems (OSes) in a virtual machine, or interact with other programmable devices. This concept, called **ubiquitous access**, has fundamentally changed how users interact with computers, unlocking new opportunities in business, education, and health care. Although ubiquitous access has not been fully realized (e.g., one cannot access smartphone apps remotely from a laptop, and the "internet of things" is still in its infancy), users no longer use a single computer and OS; work, education, and other circumstances require users to move among different computer systems as part of daily life.

Related to ubiquitous access is the concept of **Ubiquitous Accessibility** (UA) [30], wherein *assistive technologies,* which help users with disabilities use computers, also become ubiquitously available. We define UA relatively broadly: users with disabilities should be able to interact as easily as any other user with multiple devices, or multiple applications that may be running on a cloud or remote system. This paper focuses on users with visual impairments. For these users, the predominant assistive technology is a Screen Reader (SR), which narrates the on-screen text, and provides keyboard shortcuts for efficient navigation of the content. Current SRs are not portable across OSes because of the heterogeneity of accessibility APIs [2, 10, 22, 23], creating potential barriers for users with visual impairments.

As computing platforms proliferate, so do SRs. This paper seeks to understand the impact of this trend on users. Different SRs have different navigation models; learning or regularly switching between different SRs can lead to cognitive load and frustration. Specifically, the paper examines potential accessibility issues when visually-impaired people interact with (i) applications on multiple devices, possibly with different operating systems, and (ii) applications hosted on remote and cloud-based systems.

This paper summarizes the results of a user study with 21 visually-impaired participants. The study involved using screen readers in remote access scenarios; switching screen readers on different types of computers; and open-ended

CHI 2017, May 6–11, 2017, Denver, CO, USA.

ACM 978-1-4503-4655-9/17/05...$15.00.
DOI: http://dx.doi.org/10.1145/3025453.3025731

discussion about the users' experience with using computers at home, workplace and school. We focus on desktop computing, as this is still the primary way computers are used in education and employment, but with some mobile device activities and a focus on the increasing need for users to incorporate multiple devices, OSes, and software packages into their daily routine. Questions for participants included: *What difficulties did they face in switching between different devices? How often do they need to access a computing device that is not their own (e.g., computers in public libraries and universities), and the difficulties experienced in this process?*

The study reveals several practical obstacles to education and employment that users face today; these problems will only be exacerbated as different types of devices proliferate. For instance, screen readers on the same OS do not support applications equally well; several study participants reported losing employment after routine software upgrades broke accessibility. Similarly, remote access technology often renders assistive technology unusable; another participant reported failing a college course because required course software was deployed on a virtual desktop system, which did not interoperate with the student's SR.

A common theme from these interviews is that uniformity of experience is essential—whether it is from having the same SR installed on every device, or simply consistent navigation models and shortcuts across SRs. Our participants agreed that it would be useful to be able to carry one screen reading device with them, such as using their smartphone as a terminal to other computers.

RELATED WORK

The term *ubiquitous accessibility* [30] was coined by Vanderheiden to describe the goal of extending assistive technologies to the new models of interaction enabled by ubiquitous computing. Vanderheiden proposed "pluggable interfaces" for the computing devices at hand, and recommended that these interfaces should be available online for use anywhere. Several papers [8, 11, 20, 29] explore ubiquitous accessibility within a model where all user interface (UI) elements and their relationships are represented in a high-level user interface description language, such as UIDL [7, 18], and, to adapt to a user's disability, these interfaces are adapted according to a set of rules derived from the user's profile, interaction history, and the specific kind of disability.

Our motivation for conducting this study was a surprising dearth of holistic studies of end-to-end issues in accessibility, especially as end-user technology trends are shifting towards ubiquitous access. In other words, we wanted to know the most important accessibility problems computer users faced, so we could focus our own research agenda. A number of previous user studies have investigated usability issues in accessibility in specific domains. Specifically, prior studies have identified usability and accessibility issues in JAWS SR [28], exercise tracking devices [26], and in particular applications, including social media, email clients, and course management systems [15, 24, 31, 32]. Ahmed et al. study issues in privacy and security facing blind users [9].

Given the amount of content that is moving to the web, there is a reasonable argument that the browser will effectively become the OS. Web accessibility [12] is a special case of UA, which focuses on making the Web accessible. We agree that web accessibility is essential, but also note that there is a long "tail" of software, essential to education and employment, that has not yet moved to the web, which must become accessible.

Sinter [13] addresses the problem of integrating screen readers with remote desktop technologies—a rapidly growing technology [34]. Sinter works with clients and servers running different OSes. Similarly, Hahn et al. describe an application of remote desktop technologies for online, collaborative training of low-vision screen magnifier users [33]. The work of Dixon et al. that interprets User Interface elements from pixels can possibly be adapted to address inaccessibility problems in cross-platform computing [16]. Although tools like Sinter may be useful building blocks for accessibility solutions, this study identifies important, open problems that should be solved.

METHODS

The IRB-approved study was conducted at Lighthouse-Guild in New York City [5]. The 21 visually-impaired participants were from the New York metropolitan area, including New Jersey and Connecticut, and were recruited through email advertisements. Participants were required to have some experience with college education (not necessarily completing a degree), and some degree of familiarity with two or more screen readers. Users were both interviewed and asked to complete some screen reading tasks. The interviews were semi-structured and in-person, to facilitate open-ended discussion of issues we may not have anticipated in advance.

Interview Preparation and Process

Two interviewers conducted the study – one interacted with the participant, while the other recorded and transcribed the interviews. Following completion of the first five interviews, the interviewers analyzed the transcripts using an iterative coding process with initial coding and identified concepts [14], categorized them, framed new questions for subsequent interviews, and updated the concept list.

For the interactive part of the study, the interviewers used two laptops (Mac and Windows), two smartphones (iPhone and Android), and two full-size, standard, external keyboards (one Windows, one Mac). The Windows computer with dual boot capability (Win7, Win10) had the following applications installed: major screen readers (JAWS [27], NVDA [25], SuperNova [17], Windows-Eyes [21], and System Access [1]); popular internet browsers (IE, Firefox, Chrome with ChromeVox [3]); remote access tools (Microsoft RDP, NVDARemote [6] and System Access-2-Go); Office 2015; and NEWT [35] network emulator. The

Profession	Expert	Inter.	Beginner
Musician		P1	P2
Transcriber		P3, P4	
IT/Tech	P5, P6	P7	
Teacher		P8	P9
Info. Dispatcher			P10, P11, P12
Student	P13, P14, P15	P16	
Self-employed	P17	P18	
Radio-host			P19
Service Industry			P20
Unemployed			P21

Table 1. Participants' IDs and screen reading skills (expert, intermediate, and beginner) grouped by professions.

Mac laptop included its built-in VoiceOver screen reader, and a VirtualBox virtual machine running Windows 7 and the same applications listed above. The two computers were directly connected to each other via an Ethernet cable; NEWT was used to emulate different network types (Wi-Fi, WLAN, Cellular) between the computers. All computers and phones had internet access.

Participants were asked to perform tasks within simulated ubiquitous access scenarios, such as (a) browsing file directory with: (1) VoiceOver on Mac using Finder, and (2) JAWS on Windows using Windows Explorer; and (b) editing Word documents on a local Windows computer and editing Word documents on a remote Windows computer. For tasks involving interaction with remote applications, the network speeds were varied using NEWT. Participants used these simulated scenarios to demonstrate specific accessibility issues they faced in their daily lives, and as a starting point for open-ended conversation during the interview. All participants utilized the full 3 hours, with a 5-minute break after 1.5 hours. Each participant was compensated $75.

Interview Protocol

We began by asking participants to introduce themselves, their educational and professional background, history of visual impairment, and their use of assistive technologies.

Our interview questions were designed to elicit feedback on UA. The topics were preselected; however, questions under each topic were adapted somewhat to each participant's expertise and profession. The topics explored were: (1) Difficulties in switching from one device or platform or screen reader to another. A sampler of questions under this topic included: (a) *What motivated you to become familiar with the other SRs?* (b) *Do you customize your SR?* (c) *What difficulties did you face in learning a new SR?* (e) *Would you prefer your smartphone's SR over your desktop's?* (2) Accessing remote applications and devices. Sample questions in this category included: (a) *Are you aware of any remote access technologies?* (b) *What was your experience in using them?* (c) *Will you use them in the future?* (3) Usability of computers and accessible technologies at school and work. Example questions were as follows: (a) *Do you bring your own screen reader for use at school and/or at work (why or why not)?* (b) *How do you handle software that is not fully usable with your screen reader?* (c) *How frequently does your application software gets updated?* (d) *How familiar are you with SRs at your school or at work?*

We also discussed potential solutions to problems that participants experienced, and, if applicable, told participants about additional accessibility technologies they were unaware of. The interview process culminated with participants making suggestions and recommendations.

Participant Demographics

The 21 participants included 11 men and 10 women, all with college experience. Participants varied in age from 22 to 63 (mean=43, median=37). 18 were blind and 3 had very low vision. They had varying amount of expertise in screen reading, and came from diverse professional backgrounds as shown in Table 1. The table lists unique IDs (P1, P2, etc.) for the participants.

FINDINGS

This section reports our findings, supplemented with corroborating comments from the participants. Block quoted, italicized passages are direct quotes from participants.

Switching Devices, Platforms, and Screen Readers

All participants who were college students or recent graduates, described the following accessibility issues they frequently experienced with computers on campus: (i) absence of SRs; (ii) having to use a different SR than the SR they were familiar with; (iii) using a different OS platform than the one they prefer; (iv) dealing with different versions (Win10 vs. Win7) of a familiar platform; (v) not having appropriate privileges for customizing SR settings; and (vi) losing their customized SR settings following the termination of their current session.

Although sighted users also experience unfamiliarity when switching devices/platforms, the problem is compounded for blind users, because different SRs offer different navigation strategies with overlapping and sometimes conflicting shortcuts. For example, P5, a recent college graduate, who could not use her preferred SR at school, had this to say:

> *The settings of JAWS at University is different from the settings of NVDA that I am used to. It makes it more difficult because you have to spend time to figure out what works. You cannot use your custom strategies on the school computer, and it slows you down -- a lot of key presses and efforts in vain.*

6 participants reported severe difficulties using their preferred SR at school because of different OS versions – Win10 vs Win7. Version changes are disruptive, e.g., the simple, up/down navigation on the start menu in Win7

becomes confusing on the grid-layout of Win10, because of non-uniform sizes and irregular alignment of grid cells. Quoting P16:

> *Windows 10 has too many grids, that it is a hassle to navigate. It gets stuck up and I have to restart my PC each time by pressing reboot button. And then I lose my custom JAWS settings.*

All participants agreed that it would be useful if their preferred SR and settings were portable – i.e., easily installed on workplace and school computers. However, two participants (P13, P14) who had previously used a portable version of NVDA SR on a flash-drive and the cloud-based System-Access-to-Go, said that these worked only on Windows OS, and, thus, could not be used on the Macs in their university libraries. Moreover, they felt that these portable screen readers were slow and had poor usability.

Switching between screen readers on the same platform

13 participants who were JAWS users had also learned to use at least one other Windows-specific SR. Their motivation was economic: a single JAWS license costs around $1,000/annually, whereas NVDA is free and both Windows-Eyes and System Access are affordably priced. The hidden cost of switching to these no-cost or low-cost SRs is a disruptive, inefficient, and frustrating learning experience. P8, a teacher at a disability center, shared her experience:

> *Knowledge of knowing one screen reader is not transferrable. Every screen reader works somewhat differently. It's like putting a lot on my plate.*

For P17, an expert in JAWS, the problem he had in learning Window-Eyes was that of the fast shortcuts:

> *The basic shortcuts are same, but the fast ones are different. To learn that, you need to take classes.*

Usually, a SR's 'fast' shortcuts are application-specific, designed to improve navigation. The richness and efficiency of these 'fast' shortcuts distinguish SRs from each other.

Participants also noted that user experience varies for similar applications even when using the same SR. For example, NVDA provides a better browsing experience with Firefox than with IE. Moreover, they reported that SRs were not robust and prone to software crashes. Quite often participants were faced with the need to use an unfamiliar SR at school or at work, as the contracted IT vendor for these institutions didn't provide any alternatives. P6, an IT professional, said:

> *I usually use JAWS at work. But when I need to work with SPSS software, SPSS crashes with JAWS. So I have to switch to another screen reader called Super Nova. In Super Nova, the key commands are different. So I use Super Nova only when I use SPSS. When I'm done with SPSS, I have to switch back to JAWS. And the pain comes in when I'm using SPSS, and I have to IM somebody, I have to switch back and forth [between two screen readers]. And you can't run two screen readers at a time. Because the commands confuse each other. Every time, I turn off a screen reader software, and switch to another one, there is always a risk that the computer will crash. When I'm running the survey dataset in the background, it's like I'm praying and praying and praying, please, don't crash.*

Switching screen readers across platforms

All participants indicated that it would be very hard and disruptive to learn a new SR on an unfamiliar platform. 7 participants had tried learning VoiceOver, Mac's free, built-in SR. Only two (P14 and P15) succeeded, and it took them 3-4 months to become reasonably proficient. P15 had this to say about her switching experience:

> *Switching between Windows and Apple was highly inconvenient, because of the differences in keyboard, shortcuts, and navigational strategies [flat vs. hierarchical].*

E.g., JAWS on Windows explores an application roughly from left-to-right, top-to-bottom (flat), whereas navigation on VoiceOver follows a logical, tree hierarchy (analogous to Folder Tree in Windows Explorer, as explained by P1).

P14, another participant who switched from Windows to Mac, still uses JAWS inside a Virtual Machine running Windows, for browsing the Web with IE and for editing MS Word docs. P14 reported that running two SRs still leads to occasional confusion. To avoid such problems, after buying a Mac laptop, P4 installed Windows using Boot Camp.

Participants' reported a reluctance to switch SRs because of the time, effort, and financial burden to train on a new SR. They summarized the training process as memorizing numerous shortcuts, navigational strategies, and building muscle memory through practice. The net effect is that having been trained in one SR, they preferred not to go through the training process for a new SR without compelling reasons to do so.

Switching Screen Readers due to Software updates

8 participants reported that they worried about their employment security, particularly when the software at work was updated or new applications were introduced. 5 (P3, P7, P12, P20, P21) stated that they lost full-time employment because upgraded versions of required software did not interoperate as well with their current SRs. They were then required to use a different, unfamiliar screen reader that worked with these upgrades. P3 and P7, whose SR expertise was between intermediate and expert level, decided to quit instead of retraining on a new SR; P12, P20, and P21, who were beginners, tried to adapt but were let go because they were less productive than before. At the time of this study, P21 was still unemployed.

3 participants (P5, P9, P10) reported knowing someone who had lost a job for similar reasons.

Accessing Remote Devices and Cloud Applications

Remote access technologies, such as Microsoft RDP or Citrix are commonly used for telecommuting and deploying educational software. Yet, these technologies operate by relaying pixels from the remote display to a client application, and are not accessible from an SR on the client [13]. The alternatives are to relay audio from a screen reader on the remote system, or to synthesize audio locally as it is done in NVDA-Remote [6] and JAWS-Tandem [4].

With the exception of P9, P10, and P20, all other 18 participants were aware of the existence of remote-access technologies. However, only 6 had actually used Microsoft RDP and JAWS-Tandem remote-access technology. 3 of them (P5, P6, P17) had used JAWS-Tandem only for the purpose of training and troubleshooting. They reported that JAWS-Tandem requires the same SR and OS on both the remote and local system, reducing flexibility. In fact, 15 participants had misconceptions about the use of remote access technologies; they believed these technologies were only for an IT vendor or an instructor to provide technical support over the internet.

Telecommuting

10 participants, who were all employed, would prefer to work from home, especially on bad weather days. They were, however, skeptical of existing RDP technology. 3 of these 10 (P3, P4, P11) had tried Microsoft RDP with audio being relayed by the remote SR. They found the user experience restrictive, slow, and frustrating. The other 7 were either dissuaded by friends' negative experiences, or did not know how to set them up. For example, P12 said the following:

> *I do know that you can access other computers from your personal laptop, but I don't know what software to use for that purpose.*

Accessing academic institutional resources from home

Educational institutions commonly place course materials on remote servers that are accessed via virtual desktop clients, such as Citrix. 4 participants reported the latency of relaying SR audio over remote desktop, especially over WLAN, rendered the solution unusable. P14 failed a course because the course software hosted on the school's Citrix server didn't work well with the SR installed on that server.

DISCUSSION

Our findings revealed that the participants found it difficult to switch SRs regardless of the underlying platforms, because of the differences in shortcuts and navigational models. Intuitively, blind users build a mental model of where items are in the UI, not necessarily how they appear on the screen, but where things are in the logical navigation order. When this ordering changes due to (i) software updates (e.g. ribbon replaces classical menu in MS Word) or (ii) switching SRs, the user has to relearn a new mental model which is tedious and disruptive. The participants reported that such changes can cause navigational confusion, and often they have to abort and restart applications, which has also been observed by Tavares et al. [28].

With regard to remote access, extant technologies are inflexible and have been found to have poor usability with SRs. Moreover, visually-impaired people need help setting up these tools, such as remote access client, virtual private networks, and portable screen readers.

In the open-ended discussion, participants suggested ideas that can serve as the basis for future ubiquitous accessibility research. A sampler of these ideas are as follows:

Uniformity of interaction experience. A consistent theme from our interviews was the need to have uniform interaction experience across different screen readers and platforms. One suggestion was to standardize screen-reader shortcuts across platforms. Although keystrokes can be remapped relatively easily, encapsulating the heterogeneity of different platforms and navigation models is an open problem. Another suggestion was to have uniformity of UI elements across platforms. Harris [19] advocates the use of standardized UI description languages for this purpose.

Universally portable screen reader. All participants expressed a desire to carry their screen reader and all personal customizations with them, plugging it into any computer they need to use in the course of their day. However, assistive technologies are generally OS-specific; the differences in the underlying accessibility APIs create barriers to SR portability. Sinter [13] has taken a step towards addressing this problem

Smartphone as a "portable" screen reader. 19 participants owned smartphones. They had learned to use the SR on their smartphones with some proficiency and carry their smartphones everywhere. If any other device or application could appear to the smartphone SR as an accessible app, using some remote access protocol over a network or local wireless protocol like Bluetooth, this would meet their accessibility needs. We note that several projects are investigating building blocks for this direction of ubiquitous accessibility [8, 29].

CONCLUSION

Usability issues in current screen readers create significant barriers to employment and education for users with visual impairments. Some of these issues are because not all applications that run on an OS are accessible on a screen reader for that OS. Other issues are the product of the move toward ubiquitous accessibility; remote and virtual desktop infrastructure are widely used, yet interact poorly with current assistive technologies. Until users have a consistent screen reading experience across a range of devices, applications, and operating systems, the vision of ubiquitous access will be thwarted. One promising direction is using the smartphone as a primary, portable interface to other devices.

Acknowledgments: We thank Yevgen Borodin, the anonymous reviewers, and our shepherd for their insightful feedbacks. Part of this work was completed while Porter was at Stony Brook University. This research was supported in part by NSF: IIS-1447549, CNS-1161541, CNS-1405641; National Eye Institute of NIH: R01EY026621; NIDILRR: 90IF0117-01-00, and VMware.

REFERENCES

1. System Access. Available from: http://www.serotek.com/systemaccess.
2. GNOME Accessibility Architecture (ATK and AT-SPI). Available from: https://developer.gnome.org/accessibility-devel-guide/stable/dev-start-5.html.en.
3. Introducing ChromeVox. Available from: http://www.chromevox.com/.
4. JAWS Tandem. Available from: http://www.freedomscientific.com/JAWSHq/JAWSTandemQuickStart.
5. LightHouse GUILD, Available from: http://www.lighthouseguild.org/.
6. NVDA Remote brings free remote access to the blind. Available from: http://nvdaremote.com/.
7. OASIS User Interface Markup Language (UIML). Available from: https://www.oasis-open.org/committees/uiml/.
8. Julio Abascal, Amaia Aizpurua, Idoia Cearreta, Borja Gamecho, Nestor Garay-Vitoria, Raúl Miñón. 2011. Automatically generating tailored accessible user interfaces for ubiquitous services *The proceedings of the 13th international ACM SIGACCESS conference on Computers and accessibility*, ACM, Dundee, Scotland, UK, 187-194.
9. Tousif Ahmed, Roberto Hoyle, Kay Connelly, David Crandall and Apu Kapadia. 2015. Privacy Concerns and Behaviors of People with Visual Impairments *Proceedings of the 33rd Annual ACM Conference on Human Factors in Computing Systems*, ACM, Seoul, Republic of Korea, 3523-3532.
10. Apple. NSAccessibility. Available from: https://developer.apple.com/reference/appkit/nsaccessibility.
11. Matthew Tylee Atkinson, Matthew J. Bell and Colin H. C. Machin. 2012. Towards ubiquitous accessibility: capability-based profiles and adaptations, delivered via the semantic web *Proceedings of the International Cross-Disciplinary Conference on Web Accessibility*, ACM, Lyon, France, 1-4.
12. Jeffrey P. Bigham, Craig M. Prince and Richard E. Ladner. 2008. WebAnywhere: a screen reader on-the-go *Proceedings of the 2008 international cross-disciplinary conference on Web accessibility (W4A)*, ACM, Beijing, China, 73-82.
13. Syed Masum Billah, Donald E. Porter and I. V. Ramakrishnan. 2016. Sinter: Low-bandwidth Remote Access for the Visually-impaired. in *Proceedings of the Eleventh European Conference on Computer Systems*, New York, NY, USA, ACM, 27:21-27:16.
14. Alan Bryman, Bob Burgess and others. 2002. *Analyzing qualitative data*. Routledge.
15. Rocío Calvo, Ana Iglesias and Lourdes Moreno. 2013. Accessibility barriers for users of screen readers in the Moodle learning content management system. *Universal Access in the Information Society*, 13 (3). 315-327. 10.1007/s10209-013-0314-3
16. Morgan Dixon, Daniel Leventhal and James Fogarty. 2011. Content and Hierarchy in Pixel-based Methods for Reverse Engineering Interface Structure. in *Proceedings of the SIGCHI Conference on Human Factors in Computing Systems*, New York, NY, USA, ACM, 969-978.
17. Dolphin. SuperNova Screen Reader, Available from: http://www.yourdolphin.com/productdetail.asp?id=1.
18. Josefina Guerrero-Garcia, Juan Manuel Gonzalez-Calleros, Jean Vanderdonckt and Jaime Munoz-Arteaga. 2009. A Theoretical Survey of User Interface Description Languages: Preliminary Results *Proceedings of the 2009 Latin American Web Congress (la-web 2009)*, IEEE Computer Society, 36-43.
19. Kip Harris. 2006. Challenges and solutions for screen reader/I.T. interoperability. *SIGACCESS Access. Comput.* (85). 10-20. 10.1145/1166118.1166120
20. Michael Heron, Vicki L. Hanson and Ian W. Ricketts. 2013. ACCESS: a technical framework for adaptive accessibility support *Proceedings of the 5th ACM SIGCHI symposium on Engineering interactive computing systems*, ACM, London, United Kingdom, 33-42.
21. GW Micro, Window-Eyes. Available from: http://http//www.gwmicro.com/Window-Eyes/.
22. Microsoft. Microsoft Active Accessibility: Architecture. Available from: https://msdn.microsoft.com/en-us/library/windows/desktop/dd373592(v=vs.85).aspx.
23. Microsoft. UI Automation Overview. Available from: http://msdn.microsoft.com/en-us/library/ms747327.aspx.
24. Meredith Ringel Morris, Annuska Zolyomi, Catherine Yao, Sina Bahram, Jeffrey P. Bigham and Shaun K. Kane. 2016. "With Most of It Being Pictures Now, I Rarely Use It": Understanding Twitter's Evolving Accessibility to Blind Users. in *Proceedings of the 2016 CHI Conference on Human Factors in Computing Systems*, New York, NY, USA, ACM, 5506-5516.
25. NVAccess. NV Access: Home of the free NVDA Screen Reader. Available from: http://www.nvaccess.org/.

26. Kyle Rector, Lauren Milne, Richard E. Ladner, Batya Friedman and Julie A. Kientz. 2015. Exploring the Opportunities and Challenges with Exercise Technologies for People who are Blind or Low-Vision. *Proceedings of the 17th International ACM SIGACCESS Conference on Computers & Accessibility*, ACM, Lisbon, Portugal, 203-214.

27. Freedom Scientific. JAWS Screen Reader. Available from: http://www.freedomscientific.com/downloads/jaws.

28. Kristen Shinohara and Josh Tenenberg. 2007. Observing Sara: a case study of a blind person's interactions with technology *Proceedings of the 9th international ACM SIGACCESS conference on Computers and accessibility*, ACM, Tempe, Arizona, USA, 171-178.

29. Joãa Tavares, Jorge Barbosa, Cristiano Costa, Adenauer Yamin and Rodrigo Real. 2012. Hefestos: A Model for Ubiquitous Accessibility Support. in *Proceedings of the 5th International Conference on PErvasive Technologies Related to Assistive Environments*, New York, NY, USA, ACM, 27:21-27:28.

30. Gregg C. Vanderheiden. 2008. Ubiquitous Accessibility, Common Technology Core, and Micro Assistive Technology. *ACM Transactions on Accessible Computing*, 1 (2). 1-7. 10.1145/1408760.1408764

31. Violeta Voykinska, Shiri Azenkot, Shaomei Wu and Gilly Leshed. 2016. How Blind People Interact with Visual Content on Social Networking Services. *Proceedings of the 19th ACM Conference on Computer-Supported Cooperative Work & Social Computing*, ACM, San Francisco, California, USA, 1584-1595.

32. Brian Wentz, Harry Hochheiser and Jonathan Lazar. 2013. A survey of blind users on the usability of email applications. *Univers. Access Inf. Soc.*, 12 (3). 327-336. 10.1007/s10209-012-0285-9.

33. Thomas Hahn, Hidayat Ur Rahman, Richard Segall, Christoph Heim, Raphaela Brunson, Ankush Sharma, Maryam Aslam, Ana Lara-Rodriguez, Md. Sahidul Islam, Neha Gupta, Charles S. Embry, Patrick Grossmann, Shahrukh Babar, Gregory A. Skibinski, and Fusheng Tang. 2016. Remote Access Programs to Better Integrate Individuals with Disabilities. *In Proceedings of the 18th International ACM SIGACCESS Conference on Computers and Accessibility (ASSETS '16)*. ACM, New York, NY, USA, 245-250. DOI: https://doi.org/10.1145/2982142.2982182.

34. Visiongain, "The Cloud-Based Virtual Desktop Infrastructure (VDI) Market 2013-2023." Available from: https://www.visiongain.com/Report/1160/The-Cloud-Based-Virtual-Desktop-Infrastructure-(VDI)-Market-2013-2023.

35. Network Emulator Toolkit. Available from: https://blog.mrpol.nl/2010/01/14/network-emulator-toolkit/.

BIGnav: Bayesian Information Gain for Guiding Multiscale Navigation

Wanyu Liu[1,2] **Rafael Lucas D'Oliveira**[3,1] **Michel Beaudouin-Lafon**[2] **Olivier Rioul**[1]

[1]LTCI, CNRS, Telecom ParisTech, Université Paris-Saclay, F-75013, Paris, France

[2]LRI, Univ. Paris-Sud, CNRS, Inria, Université Paris-Saclay, F-91400, Orsay, France

[3]Applied Mathematics, University of Campinas, Campinas, Sao Paulo, Brazil

{wanyu.liu,olivier.rioul}@telecom-paristech.fr, mbl@lri.fr, rgldoliveira@gmail.com

ABSTRACT

This paper introduces BIGnav, a new multiscale navigation technique based on Bayesian Experimental Design where the criterion is to maximize the information-theoretic concept of mutual information, also known as information gain. Rather than simply executing user navigation commands, BIGnav interprets user input to update its knowledge about the user's intended target. Then it navigates to a new view that maximizes the information gain provided by the user's expected subsequent input. We conducted a controlled experiment demonstrating that BIGnav is significantly faster than conventional pan and zoom and requires fewer commands for distant targets, especially in non-uniform information spaces. We also applied BIGnav to a realistic application and showed that users can navigate to highly probable points of interest on a map with only a few steps. We then discuss the tradeoffs of BIGnav—including efficiency vs. increased cognitive load—and its application to other interaction tasks.

ACM Classification Keywords

H.5.2. [Information Interfaces and Presentation]: User Interfaces-Interaction styles; I.3.6 [Computer Graphics]: Methodology and Techniques-Interaction techniques

Author Keywords

Multiscale navigation; Guided navigation; Bayesian experimental design; Mutual information

INTRODUCTION

Multiscale interfaces are a powerful way to represent large datasets such as maps and deep hierarchies. However, navigating these spaces can be frustrating and inefficient. Most applications, such as Google Maps, only support pan-and-zoom [22]. Others, such as the DragMag [32], use focus+context techniques. In both cases they leave the user in complete control of navigation, leading to frustrating situations such as getting "lost in desert fog" [17].

CHI 2017, May 06-11, 2017, Denver, CO, USA

DOI: http://dx.doi.org/10.1145/3025453.3025524

A few techniques assist navigation by taking advantage of the system's knowledge of the information space: topology-aware navigation [21], visual saliency mediated navigation [16], object pointing [11] and semantic pointing [3] "steer" users towards potential targets, therefore reducing the risk of getting lost. Other techniques interpret users' intentions to guide navigation: SDAZ [14], for example, adjusts the zoom level according to the user-controlled velocity. While these approaches have proven effective, we believe we can do better by combining them into a more general framework.

We introduce *BIGnav*, a guided navigation technique that uses both the a priori knowledge of the information space and the progressively acquired knowledge of the user's intention. *BIGnav* guides navigation through a three-step process:

1. The system interprets user input as an intention revealing what the user is and is not interested in;
2. The system then updates a probabilistic model of the information space to take into account this intention;
3. Finally the system navigates to a new view such that the subsequent user input will maximize the expected information gain of the system.

BIGnav uses Bayesian Experimental Design [19], an approach where the system "runs experiments" on the user to maximize an expected utility. This utility is information gain, a concept from information theory [28, 29] that represents the amount of information obtained about a variable, here the intended target, from another variable, here the user's input. In other words, *BIGnav* is a form of human-computer partnership where user and system cooperate to achieve a common objective.

The rest of the paper is organized as follows. After a review of related work and a short introduction to Bayesian Experimental Design, we introduce *BIGnav* in detail. We describe a 1D simulation to show how the system can guide navigation to a target using only a few commands. We then report on a controlled experiment with 16 participants comparing standard pan-and-zoom navigation with *BIGnav*. Finally, we describe a real-world application for navigating maps and conclude with directions for future work.

RELATED WORK

BIGnav uses a human-computer partnership to guide navigation. We therefore discuss related work in assisted multiscale navigation and human-computer collaboration and adaptation.

Assisted Multiscale Navigation

Pan and zoom are the canonical navigation commands in multiscale interfaces. Panning lets users change the position of the view while zooming lets them modify the magnification of the viewport [8, 22]. Navigation tasks consist in acquiring or pointing a specific target, characterized by a position and size. It generally involves view navigation, whereby the user must first bring the target into view, at a scale where it can be selected. Despite being quite different from traditional pointing, Guiard & Beaudouin-Lafon [10] have shown that Fitts' law [6] applies to multiscale pointing. Therefore we adopt Fitts' paradigm and use the index of difficulty (ID) in our controlled experiment to assess pointing performance.

Much work has explored effective pan-and-zoom navigation. Furnas & Bederson [7, 8] introduced space-scale diagrams to better understand navigation trajectories in multiscale interfaces. Igarashi & Hinckley [14] proposed Speed-Dependent Automatic Zooming (SDAZ), where the zooming factor depends on the user-controlled velocity so that users do not need to directly control zooming. By contrast, Appert & Fekete [1] created Orthozoom, a 1D scroller where users control zooming by moving along the scroller's orthogonal dimension, improving navigation in very large documents. *BIGnav* uses a different approach: it assists navigation by interpreting classical pan-and-zoom commands to calculate a new view according to an information gain criterion.

Other approaches assist navigation by exploiting features of the information space. GravNav [16] uses visual saliency to combine standard pan and zoom with an attention vector. Topology-aware navigation [21] guides panning movements along the links of a node-link structure. Content-aware scrolling [15] uses the content of the document to control the direction, speed and zooming factor. In a similar vein, Galyean [9] assists 3D navigation by pulling users along a pre-computed path, while still letting them deviate slightly from it. Similar to these approaches, *BIGnav* takes advantage of the structure of the information space to guide navigation, but uses a probabilistic model to represent its knowledge.

Collaboration and Adaptation

While the notion of cooperative interaction between humans and computers is quite ancient [18], the concept of human-computer collaboration has emerged in HCI more recently [31]. In human-computer collaboration, two agents, a human and a computer, work together to achieve shared goals. A key aspect of collaboration is communication, for example to define goals, negotiate how to proceed and determine who will do what. Similar ideas can be found in *mixed-initiative design* [12], *human-computer partnership* [27] and *continuous uncertain interaction* [33]. All these approaches suggest that great opportunities lie between systems that provide automatic services [13] and systems where users are in direct control [30]. *BIGnav* applies this general framework to multiscale navigation, which to our knowledge has not been done before.

Several approaches have used the notion of information to guide navigation and pointing. Pirolli & Card [25, 26] have introduced the concept of *information foraging*, whereby people adapt their navigation strategies to increase information in an information seeking task. An important difference with our work is that in information foraging, users do not know where the information is located. In addition, information foraging is based on Optimal Foraging Theory while *BIGnav* is based on Bayesian Experimental Design [19]. Williamson & Murray-Smith [34] use control theory and an entropy-based method where agents "run 'experiments' on the user" to let the user select a target without pointing. This work is closest to ours, however the proposed system used randomized stimuli while *BIGnav* maximizes the expected information gain.

Finally, Mackay [20] has proposed the concept of *co-adaptation* between people and technology to describe how users adapt to technology but also adapt technology to their needs. However, as with information foraging, co-adaptation comes from the users, not the system. In *BIGnav*, the system adapts to user's input and navigates to the view such that the user's subsequent input will provide maximum information. In other words, the system both adapts to the user and seeks valuable information from the user.

BACKGROUND: BAYESIAN EXPERIMENTAL DESIGN

This section provides background on Bayesian Experimental Design and Information Theory. Readers familiar with these two concepts can skip this section. Only formulas (1) and (4) are used in the rest of the paper.

Consider a scientist who wants to determine some parameter θ of nature. He can choose to perform an experiment x that will provide an observation y. A probabilistic model is used where Θ, X and Y are the random variables corresponding to θ, x and y, respectively. Bayesian Experimental Design [19] provides a framework to optimize the choice of the experiment x by maximizing an expected utility, commonly defined in terms of the information gained about the parameter θ by the experiment x. The utility may also involve factors such as the financial (or other) cost of performing the experiment.

To optimize the choice of the experiment, the scientist needs two pieces of information, or *priors*:

1. A prior probability distribution $P(\Theta = \theta)$ for all values of θ, which expresses the scientist's knowledge about the random variable Θ before the experiment; and
2. A conditional probability distribution[1] $P(Y = y \mid \Theta = \theta, X = x)$ of the observation Y given the actual value of the parameter θ and the chosen experiment x.

After an experiment x is performed and an observation y is obtained, the scientist updates his knowledge about the parameter θ through Bayes' theorem:

$$P(\Theta = \theta \mid X = x, Y = y) = \frac{P(Y = y \mid \Theta = \theta, X = x)P(\Theta = \theta)}{P(Y = y \mid X = x)} \quad (1)$$

where $P(Y = y \mid X = x) = \sum_{\theta'} P(Y = y \mid \Theta = \theta', X = x)P(\Theta = \theta')$.
This new probability distribution serves as the new prior, on which the scientist can perform another experiment.

[1] The conditional probability $P(A = a \mid B = b)$ reads "the probability of $A = a$ given $B = b$".

The goal of an experiment is to reduce the uncertainty about Θ. As a measure of this uncertainty we use Shannon's entropy function[2] [28, 29]. Initially, the scientist's uncertainty about Θ is given by $H(\Theta)$. After performing an experiment $X = x$ and having observed $Y = y$, the scientist's uncertainty about Θ is given by $H(\Theta|X = x, Y = y)$. The *information gain* is the difference between these two uncertainties:

$$IG(\Theta|X = x, Y = y) = H(\Theta) - H(\Theta|X = x, Y = y). \quad (2)$$

It is generally not possible to know a priori how much information a specific experiment will give[3]. However, for each experiment one can calculate the *expected* information gain[4]:

$$IG(\Theta|X = x, Y) = H(\Theta) - H(\Theta|X = x, Y). \quad (3)$$

To calculate the expected information gain, the scientist uses Bayes' theorem for entropies to convert equation (3) to:

$$IG(\Theta|X = x, Y) = H(Y|X = x) - H(Y|\Theta, X = x). \quad (4)$$

where the first term is given by

$$\sum_y P(Y = y|X = x)\log_2 P(Y = y|X = x).$$

and the second one by

$$\sum_{y,\theta} P(\Theta = \theta)P(Y = y|\Theta = \theta, X = x)\log_2 P(Y = y|\Theta = \theta, X = x).$$

All the elements in these terms are given by the two priors given to scientist. The scientist can therefore calculate the expected information gain for each possible experiment and choose the experiment that he expects to be most informative.

BIGNAV: BAYESIAN INFORMATION GAIN NAVIGATION

The key idea of our approach is to have the system "run experiments" on the user in order to gain information about the user's goal, i.e., the intended target. *BIGnav* uses Bayesian Experimental Design as follows (Fig. 1a):

- The system plays the role of the scientist;
- The unknown parameter θ is the intended target (known only to the user);
- The experiment x is the view that the system shows to the user after each input; and
- The observation y is the user input after seeing x.

Scenario

Before describing the process in detail, we illustrate how it works through a brief scenario introducing Lucy.

Lucy is a HCI student exploring how BIGnav *works on a 1D map featuring isolated islands. To navigate to a particular island, she issues a series of commands to go left, go right or zoom in. With only two islands on the map, a single input is sufficient for* BIGnav *to determine the intended target and update its probability distribution of most likely target. With three islands, all to the left of Lucy, the first input will go to the most likely island if* BIGnav *has some prior knowledge about what Lucy wants. Otherwise, it will show the island in the middle and wait for Lucy's next input, because in this configuration the next input (left, right or zoom in) will uniquely specify the target. If Lucy makes a mistake, her next input will let* BIGnav *dynamically update its knowledge of Lucy's interest. With the more difficult task of navigating among 50 islands,* BIGnav *interprets each command, updates its knowledge and shows Lucy a view where her next command is most likely to maximize the reduction of uncertainty (or information gain) about the intended target. Figure 1(b) shows a case where* BIGnav *guides Lucy to her target in 4 steps.*

Detailed Description

We now describe in detail how *BIGnav* uses Bayesian Experimental Design and information gain to guide navigation. The three key random variables are:

- Θ represents any point of interest, i.e., possible intended target. For each target θ, and the probability that it is the actual intended target is $P(\Theta = \theta)$. These probabilities constitute the a priori knowledge that the system has about the user's interest, and is updated as the user navigates.
- X represents any possible view provided by the system. $X = x$ is a particular view shown to the user. Note that the number of possible views is potentially very large.
- Y represents any particular command y issued by the user. The possible input commands are: move towards a direction, zoom in or click on the target when it is big enough to be clickable. Note that zooming out is not required in this framework: if the target is out of view, the user should indicate in which direction it is rather than zooming out.

We now describe the three-stage navigation process.

(1) Interpreting user input: Given the view x shown to the user and the user's intended target θ, $P(Y = y|\Theta = \theta, X = x)$ is the probability that the user provides an input command $Y = y$ given θ and x. This probability distribution is the system's interpretation of the user's intention when giving this command. For instance, if island B is to the left of Lucy, what is the probability of Lucy giving the left command when knowing that island B is located to her left? $P($*go left* | *island B is the intended target, island B is located to the left of the current view*$) = 1$ if Lucy is completely confident about what she is doing. But maybe Lucy is not accurate all the time. Say she is only correct 95% of time, then we need to consider that she makes errors. For instance, $P($*go left* | *island B is the intended target, island B is located to the left of the current view*$) = 0.95$ and $P($*go right* | *island B is the intended target, island B is located to the left of the current view*$) = 0.05$. $P(Y|\Theta = \theta, X = x)$ is a priori knowledge that must be given to the system. In the implementation section, we describe how we define it in 1D and 2D situations respectively.

(2) Updating system's knowledge: Given the view x shown to the user and the user reaction y to that view, the system can update its estimate $P(\Theta|X = x, Y = y)$ of the user's interest with equation (1). If the system has no prior knowledge about the

[2] The Shannon entropy of a random variable V that takes n possible values, the i-th value of which has probability p_i, is given by $H(V) = -\sum_{i=1}^{n} p_i \log_2 p_i$. Entropy is usually measured in bits and can be interpreted as the level of uncertainty about a variable. It is maximal when all possible values of the variable have the same probability.

[3] Information gain might be negative but is positive on average.

[4] Also known as the mutual information $I(\Theta; Y|X = x)$, which in contrast to equation (2), is always positive.

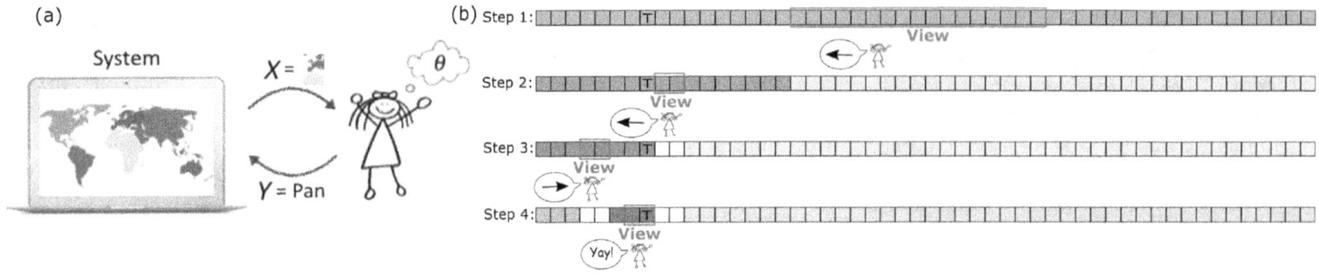

Figure 1. (a) *BIGnav*: The system is a scientist experimenting on the user (Lucy). θ is the intended target in Lucy's mind. X is the view provided by the system. Lucy provides an input Y given what she sees in the view (X) and what she wants (θ). (b) Lucy navigates to a particular island (T) among 50 others with *BIGnav*. The color gradient shows the probability of each island being Lucy's target. The redder, the higher the probability.

user's intended target, e.g., at the beginning, each θ has the same probability of being the target and $P(\Theta)$ is uniform. As the user issues commands, the system gains knowledge about the likelihood that each point of interest be the target, reflected by the changes to the probability distribution. This is done, for each point of interest, by taking its previous probability, multiplying by the above user input function $P(Y = y|\Theta = \theta, X = x)$, and normalizing it so that the sum of the new probabilities over all the points of interest equals one.

(3) Navigating to a new view: With the new probability distribution after receiving user input, *BIGnav* then goes over each view $x \in X$, calculates its expected information gain with equation (4) and picks the view for which it is maximal. To maximize equation (4), *BIGnav* looks for a trade-off between two entropies. To maximize the first term, the view should be such that all user commands given that view are equally probable (for the system). To minimize the second term, the view should provide the user with meaningful information about the points of interest. Maximizing a difference does not necessarily mean to maximize the first term and minimize the second, so the maximum information gain is a trade-off between these two goals. For example, showing only ocean will increase the first term but will also increase the second term. After locating the view with maximal information gain, *BIGnav* navigates there and waits for user's next input.

IMPLEMENTATION

We now describe our implementation of *BIGnav*. We first go through the 1D case with the last example in scenario (Fig. 1b), then show the implementation of the 2D case.

BIGnav in 1D

The 50 islands are the points of interest, therefore $\Theta = \{1,2,\ldots,50\}$. The system does not have prior knowledge about Lucy's intended target island, so the initial distribution is $P(\Theta_1 = i) = \frac{1}{50}$.

The view presented to Lucy at each step is defined by $X = \{[a,b] \subseteq [1,50]\}$. The maximum zoom factor is such that a view cannot be smaller than two blocks ($b - a \leq 2$). Since it is a 1D map, Lucy can go to the left, go to the right, zoom in or select the target if the view is at the maximum scale. We note these commands $Y = \{\leftarrow, \rightarrow, +\text{ (zoom in)}, \bullet\text{ (click target i)}\}$.

We start by modeling Lucy's behavior. We consider that Lucy makes some mistakes when panning and zooming, but will not miss the target when it is shown in the view and clickable:

$$P(Y = \rightarrow \mid \Theta = \theta, X = [a,b]) = \begin{cases} 0.9 & b < \theta \\ 0.05 & a < \theta \\ 0.05 & a \leq \theta \leq b \text{ and } b - a > 2 \\ 0 & a \leq \theta \leq b \text{ and } b - a \leq 2 \end{cases}$$

$$P(Y = \leftarrow \mid \Theta = \theta, X = [a,b]) = \begin{cases} 0.05 & b < \theta \\ 0.9 & a < \theta \\ 0.05 & a \leq \theta \leq b \text{ and } b - a > 2 \\ 0 & a \leq \theta \leq b \text{ and } b - a \leq 2 \end{cases}$$

$$P(Y = + \mid \Theta = \theta, X = [a,b]) = \begin{cases} 0.05 & b < \theta \\ 0.05 & a < \theta \\ 0.9 & a \leq \theta \leq b \text{ and } b - a > 2 \\ 0 & a \leq \theta \leq b \text{ and } b - a \leq 2 \end{cases}$$

$$P(Y = \bullet \mid \Theta = \theta, X = [a,b]) = \begin{cases} 1 & a \leq \theta \leq b \text{ and } b - a \leq 2 \\ 0 & \text{otherwise.} \end{cases}$$

In Figure 1b, the islands are represented by square boxes and colored in shades of red indicating the degrees to which the system believes the island is the target, i.e., island i is darker than j if $P(\Theta = i) > P(\Theta = j)$. Island 8 has a **T** indicating that it is the target. The blue rectangle is the view that the system shows to Lucy. After seeing the view, Lucy provides an input command y to the system.

We can now show *BIGnav* in action.

Step 1: Since the initial distribution is uniform, the system's uncertainty about Lucy's target is $H_1 = H(\Theta_1) = \log_2 50 = 5.64$ bits.

The system then goes over every image $[a,b]$, finds that $[18,34]$ maximizes the expected information gain and displays the corresponding initial view to Lucy. In this case the expected information gain from Lucy's next action is $IG(\Theta_1 \mid X = [18,34], Y) = 1.08$ bits.

Lucy inputs $\leftarrow$ after seeing $[18,34]$. The system then updates its knowledge with equation (1) and ends up with a new distribution Θ_2 given by $P(\Theta_2) = P(\Theta_1 \mid X = [18,34], Y = \leftarrow)$. Using Bayes' theorem we have:

$$P(\Theta_2 = i) = \begin{cases} 0.05 & i < 18 \\ 0.002 & i \geq 18. \end{cases}$$

The updated uncertainty is $H_2 = H(\Theta_2) = 4.65$ bits, resulting in an actual information gain $H_1 - H_2 = 0.99$ bits, very close to the expected information gain of 1.08 bits.

Step 2: The system now searches for the best view using the new distribution $P(\Theta_2)$, finds that it is $[9,10]$ with an expected information gain of $IG(\Theta_2 \mid X = [9,10], Y) = 1.24$ bits and displays it to Lucy. She then inputs $\leftarrow$ after seeing $[9,10]$. The system then updates Θ_2 to Θ_3 as follows:

$$P(\Theta_3 = i) = \begin{cases} 0.12 & i < 9 \\ 0 & 9 \leq i \leq 10 \\ 0.006 & 10 < i < 18 \\ 0.0003 & i \geq 18. \end{cases}$$

The entropy of Θ_3 is $H_3 = 3.36$ bits, so the actual information gain for this step is $H_2 - H_3 = 1.29$ bits, higher than the expected information gain of 1.24 bits.

Step 3: With the same process, the best view is now $[4,5]$ with an expected information gain of $IG(\Theta_3 \mid X = [4,5], Y) = 1.58$ bits. Lucy inputs $\rightarrow$, leading to the updated distribution

$$P(\Theta_4 = i) = \begin{cases} 0.01 & i < 4 \\ 0 & 4 \leq i \leq 5 \\ 0.28 & 5 < i < 9 \\ 0 & 9 \leq i \leq 10 \\ 0.015 & 10 < i < 18 \\ 0.0007 & i \geq 18. \end{cases}$$

The entropy of Θ_4 is $H_4 = 2.70$ bits, so the actual information gain is $H_3 - H_4 = 0.66$ bits, compared to the expected information gain of 1.58 bits.

Step 4: The best view is now $[7,8]$ with an expected information gain of $IG(\Theta_4 \mid X = [7,8], Y) - 1.84$ bits. Lucy sees that the target island is in the view and happily clicks on it. The updated distribution is updated to

$$P(\Theta_5 = i) = \begin{cases} 1 & i = 8 \\ 0 & \text{otherwise}. \end{cases}$$

The entropy of Θ_5 is $H_5 = 0$ bits since there is no more uncertainty about the target. The actual information gain is $H_4 - H_5 = 2.7$ bits, while the expected gain was 1.84 bits.

Lucy finds her target island in only 4 steps. At step 1, *BIGnav* divides the map in 3 so that the three commands (left, right and zoom in) have equal probability. It does not consider a click as the view is still far from being fully zoomed-in to select the target. At step 2, one would expect it to divide the left third of the map in 3 again so that the view would be about 5 boxes wide. However, since it is close to the maximum scale, and it knows that Lucy never misses her target when it is in the view and is clickable, showing a 2-box zoomed-in view will give *BIGnav* extra information: if this is the target, Lucy will click on it; if it is not and Lucy moves away, the probabilities of these two boxes become 0. Step 3 and step 4 work similarly.

We ran 200 simulations with 50 islands and a uniform initial distribution and found that it required 3.3 steps on average.

BIGnav in 2D

We implemented *BIGnav* in a 2D application using Java 1.8 and the open source ZVTM toolkit [23]. As for the 1D case, we need to define Θ, X and Y:

Θ represents points of interest in the multiscale information spaces. Each point θ_i is defined by a triplet (x_i, y_i, p_i) where (x_i, y_i) is the coordinate of point i and p_i is the dynamic probability that point i is the user's intended target.

X represents views that the system can show to the user. A view is defined by a triplet (vx, vy, z) where (vx, vy) is the center of the view and the zoom level z determines the view size. A view is fully zoomed in when $z = 1$. In traditional multiscale navigation, the system can pan and zoom continuously, leading to a huge number of possible views. With *BIGnav*, we need to calculate the information gain corresponding to every single view $X = x$, which would incur an enormous computational cost if views could be centered at any pixel and have any size. We therefore discretize the set of views by using tiles and discrete zoom factors. The tiles are 200×150 pixels each, and each tile can contain at most one point of interest. When $z = 1$, the view is composed of 4×4 tiles. Each successive value of z increases the number of tiles (5×5, 6×6, etc.).

Y represents input commands that the user can provide. In many pan-and-zoom applications, users can pan in any direction by a range of distances, and zoom in and out by fixed amounts. As for the views, we reduce this set of commands to make computation tractable in our prototype. We slice the view into nine regions representing eight panning directions and a central zooming region (Fig. 2). The eight panning regions have a 45° angle, and the zooming region is half the size of the view. A single movement of the mouse wheel movement triggers a zoom while a drag action triggers a pan. The angle between the mouse-down and mouse-up points of the drag determines the panning direction. The last input is a click on the target, available only when zoom level $z = 1$.

We now describe our implementation of the navigation steps.

(1) Interpreting user input: To interpret user input, we need to define $P(Y = y \mid \Theta = \theta, X = x)$, i.e., the probability of each command given a target and a view, e.g., $P($*pan East* | *target (5, 7), view (4, 4, 2)*$)$. If the user were perfectly reliable, we could assign a probability of 1 to the correct command for each target θ and each view x, and 0 to the others. But we know that users make errors. To model the error rate, we collected data during a calibration session. The goal was to determine how confident participants were when issuing commands. The task was to indicate in which direction the target was in a set of views. A set of concentric circles, identical to those used in the experiment below, showed the direction of the target when it was not within the view (Fig. 3a).

We tested all ten input commands Y (8 pan operations, zoom in and click on the target) with 5 repetitions each, resulting in 50 trials per participant ($N = 16$). The results (Table 1) show that 90% of panning commands are correct and 4% are in one of the adjacent directions (Fig. 2). For zooming commands, 95% of the commands are correct while for clicking on the target, 100% of the commands are correct.

(2) Updating system's knowledge: We use equation (1) to update the probabilities p_i of each point of interest being the target given the current view x:

For all points of interest θ_i, the new p_i' is the previous p_i multiplied by the user expected behavior $P(Y = y \mid \Theta = \theta_i, X = x)$ divided by the normalization over all points of interest.

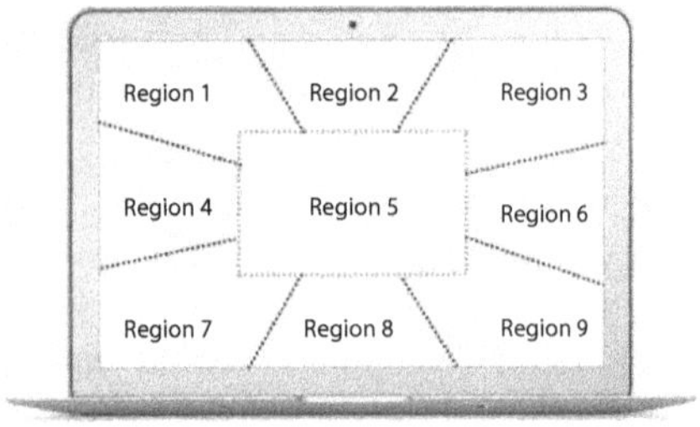

Figure 2. Nine regions representing user input, delimited by dotted lines. Panning regions also include the space outside the current view.

Command	*Main Region*	*Adjacent Regions*	*Other Regions*
Pan	0.90	0.04	0.0033
Zoom	0.95	0.00625	0.00625
Click	1	0	0

Table 1. Calibration results used as prior knowledge about the user behavior $P(Y = y|\Theta = \theta, X = x)$.

(3) Navigating to a new view with maximum expected information gain: For each view x and each user input y, the expected information gain is the difference between two uncertainties:

Uncertainty before user input y =
minus the sum of $p_i \times log_2 p_i$ *over all points of interest*
Uncertainty after user input y =
minus the sum of $p'_i \times log_2 p'_i$ *over all points of interest*

We then calculate the new view:

For all possible views x, calculate expected information gain with equation (4). Return the view $(vx_{max}, vy_{max}, z_{max})$ *with maximum information gain and display it.*

EXPERIMENT

Our goal is to study the performance of *BIGnav* in what Javed et al. call *micro-level navigation*, when the user has decided on a destination and needs to navigate to it [16]. This is different from searching [24] or wayfinding [5] tasks where the user does not know where the target is located.

We conducted a controlled experiment where participants have to navigate towards a known target. Based on the theoretic analysis, we formulate four hypotheses:

H1: *BIGnav* is faster than *STDnav* for distant targets;

H2: *BIGnav* performs better in non-uniform information spaces, i.e., when the system has prior knowledge of users' interest;

H3: *BIGnav* outperforms *STDnav* in terms of number of commands and rate of decreasing uncertainty;

H4: *STDnav* is preferred by users, more comfortable and intuitive.

Participants

Sixteen participants (3 female), age 24 to 30 (mean = 25.9, σ = 1.7), were recruited from our institution and received a handful of candies for their participation. All of them were right-handed, had normal or corrected-to-normal vision, and were familiar with WIMP interfaces. Participants were instructed to navigate to the target as fast as they could but were not informed of the condition they used.

Apparatus

The experiment was conducted on a MacBook Air with a 1.4 GHz processor and 4 GB RAM. The software was implemented in Java with the ZVTM toolkit [23]. The window was 800×600 pixels, centered on a 13-inch screen set to 1440×900 resolution. A standard mouse was used with the same sensitivity for all participants.

Procedure

We use a full-factorial within-participants design with a main factor: navigation technique (TECH); and two secondary factors: distribution of targets (DISTR), index of difficulty (ID).

Navigation Technique (TECH)

We compare *BIGnav* with standard pan-and-zoom:

- *BIGnav*: our guided navigation technique. The ten user commands (eight pan, zoom in, select target) and error rates are as described in the previous section.
- *STDnav*: the standard pan and zoom technique, used as baseline. A left mouse drag pans the view in world space proportional to the number of pixels dragged in screen space, and the mouse wheel zooms around the center of the view.

In order to compare information gains between the two conditions, we make the same computations as for *BIGnav* in the *STDnav* condition, except for the display of the new view.

Distribution (DISTR)

In order to compare different types of information spaces, we compared six distributions of points of interest by combining three spatial distributions (*Grid*, *Random* and *Cluster*) with three probability distributions (*Uniform*, *Random*, *Cluster*) of the a priori likelihood of each target. Since not all combinations are meaningful, we selected six of them. The first three have a uniform probability distribution, i.e., all points of interest have equal probability of being the target, and different spatial distributions:

- *Grid+Uniform*: points of interest are arranged in a grid, providing a strong visual pattern.
- *Random+Uniform*: points of interest are placed randomly.
- *Cluster+Uniform*: points of interest are organized in clusters, which is typical of geographical maps [4], where a central city is surrounded by smaller towns. We used 5 clusters of 10 targets.

The other three distributions use a non-uniform probability distribution of being the target:

- *Grid+Random*: points of interest are on a grid with random probabilities of being the target. These probabilities are bounded by *Uniform* and *Cluster*.
- *Random+Random*: points of interest are randomly distributed and have random probabilities.
- *Cluster+Cluster*: points of interest are clustered and the probability of the center of each cluster is ten times higher than that of the surrounding points of interest.

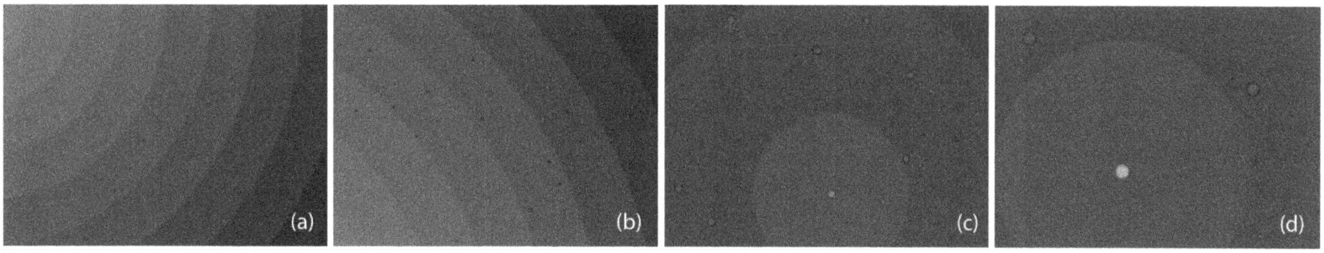

Figure 3. (a) Calibration: participants were asked to give a direction that indicates where they think the target is located (here: north-west). (b-c) Experimental condition with the target indicated in red. (d) Last step in the experimental condition: the target becomes green when it is clickable.

The first three configurations are meant to demonstrate that *BIGnav* works well even without prior knowledge about potential targets. The other three configurations are meant to assess the added advantage, if any, of using such prior knowledge. In particular, the last distribution is typical of, e.g., maps.

Index of Difficulty (ID)

The ID is related to the distance between the initial position of the view and the target to navigate to. Using Fitts' definition of the ID [6], the distance D to travel is $D = 2^{ID} \times W$, where W is the (constant) target width. We adopted the same large IDs as in other multiscale navigation studies [1, 16]: 10, 15, 20, 25 and 30 bits.

We used a $[2 \times 6 \times 5]$ within-subject design: we tested 2 TECH for 6 DISTR and 5 ID conditions. Each condition was replicated 5 times, so that each participant performed 300 trials. We blocked the conditions by TECH. Half the participants started with *STDnav* and the other half with *BIGnav*. Within each block, we systematically varied the order of DISTR and ID combinations across participants using a Latin square so as to reduce the influence of learning effects. For each condition, the targets were drawn randomly according to the probability distribution of the DISTR condition. All participants used the same target in the same DISTR × ID × Replication condition.

Task

The task is a multiscale pointing task: starting from a fully zoomed-out view, the participant must navigate towards the target until it is fully zoomed in and click on it. The target is surrounded by concentric circles so that it is always possible to tell in which direction and how far it is (Fig. 3).

The information space contains 50 points of interest: 49 are distractors and displayed in blue, one is the target and displayed in red. The ID is used to compute the scale of the initial view so that it contains all the points of interest. The target becomes green and clickable only when the view is fully zoomed in.

Participants first receive general instructions about the session and performed several practice trials with each technique. After the session, they answer a questionnaire asking them for feedback and comments on the experiment and the techniques. A typical session lasts 60 minutes, including training.

Data Collection

For each trial, the program collects the task completion time (TCT), the commands that the participants issued, the uncertainty and position of the view at each step and the information gain after each command. We collected 2 TECH × 6 DISTR × 5 ID × 5 Replications × 16 Participants = 4800 trials in total.

RESULTS

For our analyses, we first removed 23 missed trials (about 0.5%) and then 54 outliers (about 1.1%) in which TCT was 3 standard deviations larger than the mean. We verified that misses and outliers were randomly distributed across participants, techniques and conditions.

Task Completion Time

Table 2 shows the results of a repeated-measures full factorial ANOVA on TCT. All main effects are significant, as well as two interaction effects: TECH × DISTR and TECH × ID.

Figure 4 shows the interaction effect between TECH and ID for task completion time (TCT). On average, *BIGnav* is 24.1% faster than *STDnav* across all ID. A post-hoc Tukey HSD test reveals a robust interaction effect: *BIGnav* is significantly faster than *STDnav* when ID > 15 ($p < 0.0001$), significantly slower when ID = 10 ($p < 0.0001$) and not significantly different for ID = 15 ($p = 0.99$). These results support **H1**: *BIGnav* is 22.3% faster than *STDnav* for $ID = 25$ and 35.8% faster for $ID = 30$.

The ANOVA also reveals an interaction effect between TECH and DISTR. A post-hoc Tukey analysis shows that for *STDnav*, DISTR does not affect TCT. *BIGnav*, however, shows a larger advantage in non-uniform information spaces (13.7% faster, $p < 0.01$) than in uniform ones, with *Cluster+Cluster* being the fastest (Fig. 5), supporting **H2**. However, there is no significant difference within probability distribution conditions. For non-uniform distributions: *Cluster+Cluster* (6.51 ± 1.71s), *Random+Random* (6.74 ± 1.55s) and *Grid+Random* (6.62 ± 1.67s). For uniform distributions: *Grid+Uniform* (7.70 ± 1.60), *Random+Uniform* (7.83 ± 1.58s), and *Cluster+Uniform* (7.70 ± 1.62s).

We then further compare *BIGnav* and *STDnav* when ID > 15 in all DISTR conditions with a post-hoc Tukey HSD test. The results indicate that *BIGnav* is significantly faster than *STDnav* for distant targets especially in non-uniform information spaces. Particularly, when $ID = 25$, *BIGnav* is 16.9% faster than *STDnav* in uniform distributions ($p < 0.001$) and is 27.6% faster in non-uniform ($p < 0.0001$). When $ID = 30$, *BIGnav* is 31.7% faster than *STDnav* in uniform distributions ($p < 0.0001$) and is 40.0% faster in non-uniform ($p < 0.0001$).

Factors	*df, den*	*F*	*p*
TECH	1, 15	4948.94	< 0.0001
DISTR	5, 75	38.32	< 0.0001
ID	4, 60	5363.35	< 0.0001
TECH × DISTR	5, 75	47.23	< 0.0001
TECH × ID	4, 60	955.19	< 0.0001
DISTR × ID	20, 300	1.26	= 0.2
TECH × DISTR × ID	20, 300	0.72	= 0.8

Table 2. Full-factorial ANOVA on TCT.

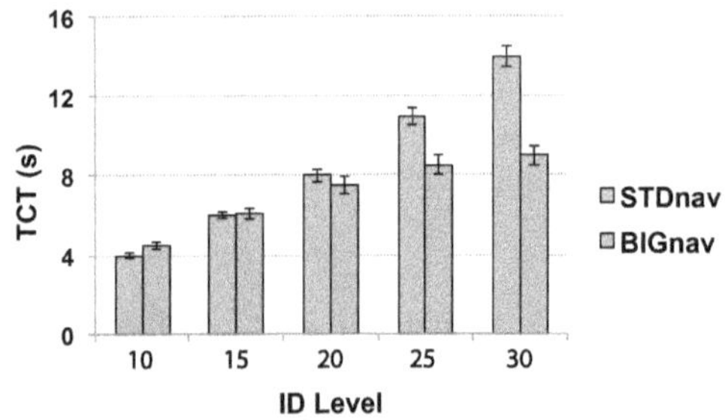

Figure 4. Means and confidence intervals of TCT by ID.

In summary, these results support hypotheses **H1** and **H2**: *BIGnav* is faster than *STDnav* for distant targets and especially in non-uniform information spaces. *BIGnav* is also not significantly different from *STDnav* for close targets (ID = 15).

Number of Commands

In order to get a sense of the differences in control strategies across conditions, we compare the number of user commands issued by the participants. Because of the continuous control in the *STDnav* conditions, we aggregate the mouse and wheel events as follows: we count one panning command per sequence from a mouse down to a mouse up, and one zooming command per series of mouse wheel with less than 300ms between them.

We perform a TECH × DISTR × ID full-factorial ANOVA on the number of commands issued (Table 3) and find that while TECH and ID significantly affect the number of commands used, DISTR has a non-significant effect. The ANOVA also indicates that the TECH × ID interaction effect is significant. A post-hoc Tukey HSD confirms that while the number of commands progressively increases with ID in *STDnav*, it is barely

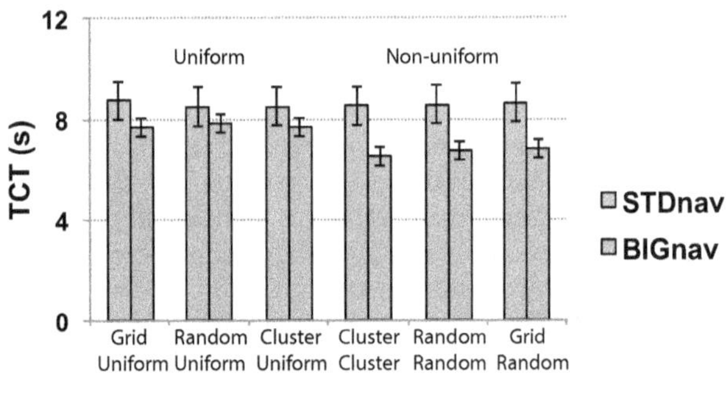

Figure 5. Means and confidence intervals for TCT by DISTR.

Factors	*df, den*	*F*	*p*
TECH	1, 15	364818.2	< 0.0001
DISTR	5, 75	0.99	= 0.4
ID	4, 60	10636.43	< 0.0001
TECH × DISTR	5, 75	0.23	= 0.9
TECH × ID	4, 60	11783.96	< 0.0001
DISTR × ID	20, 300	0.65	= 0.9
TECH × DISTR × ID	20, 300	0.71	= 0.8

Table 3. Full-factorial ANOVA on the number of commands.

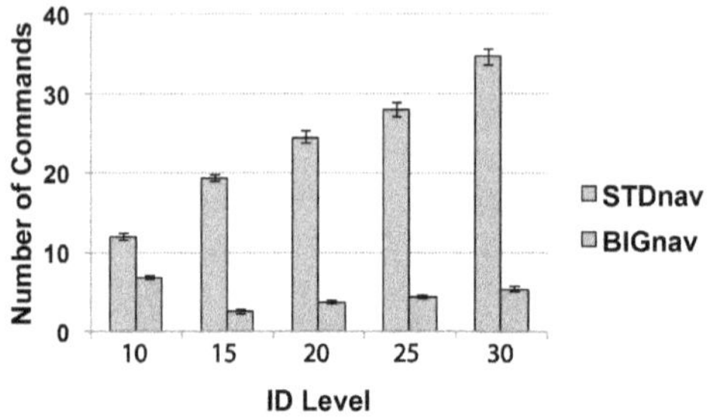

Figure 6. Means and confidence intervals for # of commands by TECH.

affected by ID in *BIGnav* (Fig. 6). For instance, when ID = 25, *STDnav* requires 28.1 commands on average whereas *BIGnav* requires 4.4 commands. When ID grows to 30, *STDnav* requires 34.5 commands on average whereas *BIGnav* requires only 5.8 commands.

Interestingly, *BIGnav* results in more commands for ID = 10 than for larger distances. Although it still outperforms *STDnav*, it requires significantly more commands for ID = 10 than for the other ID except = 30. The reason may be that the target falls into the view very quickly but *BIGnav* tends to move it away to gain more information, because it does not know it is the target. Some participants got frustrated by this behavior and started to issue arbitrary commands.

Regarding the ratio between pan and zoom commands, we find that in *STDnav*, 79.33 ± 2.03% of the commands are zooming commands vs. 20.67 ± 2.51% for pans, but the proportions are reversed for *BIGnav*: 26.74 ± 4.46% for zooming vs. 73.26 ± 3.87% for panning. This is because with *BIGnav*, zooming is only needed when the target is within the view, and panning commands most often result in a new view with a different level of zoom.

Uncertainty and Information Gain

Since the essence of *BIGnav* is to maximize the expected information gain at each command, we compare the actual information gain between *STDnav* and *BIGnav*. In both cases, the uncertainty that the system has about the users' intended target drops to zero gradually.

In *STDnav*, sometimes a command does not make a difference in uncertainty, i.e., the information gain is null. This is typically the case when the system is certain of what users are going to do. For example, when completely zoomed out, users must zoom in. Similarly, if a view contains 99% of the probability distribution, users will almost certainly zoom in.

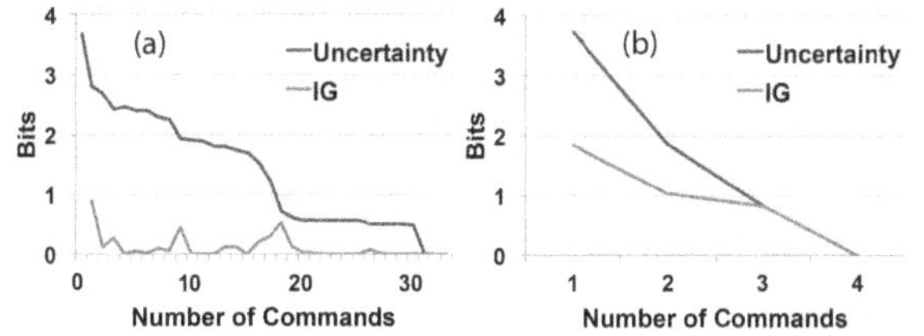

Figure 7. Uncertainty decrease and information gain for each successive command in (a) ***STDnav*** **and (b)** ***BIGnav*****.**

By contrast, with *BIGnav*, the system gains information at each step, therefore uncertainty drops to zero much faster and with many fewer commands. In our data, 40.4% of the commands in *STDnav* do not reduce uncertainty. The rest of the commands reduce uncertainty by 0.26 bits on average. In *BIGnav*, all commands reduce uncertainty by 0.88 bits on average. Figure 7 shows typical plots of uncertainty reduction for the two techniques and the same other conditions (*Random+Uniform* and *ID* = 30). These results support **H3** that *BIGnav* outperforms *STDnav* with much lower command usage and much higher rate of decreasing uncertainty.

Trajectory in Multiscale Worlds

Another way to look at the navigation strategies is to plot the reduction in ID over time. As participants pan and zoom, they get closer (most of the time) to the target and therefore the ID progressively decreases from the initial level to 0. Figure 8 shows typical plots for two trials by the same participant in the same condition (*Random+Uniform* and *ID* = 30). With *STDnav*, the reduction of ID is globally steady while with *BIGnav* we see sudden drops and long plateaus as well as occasional increases of the ID.

ID increases may occur for example when the view is close to the target and there is a cluster of points of interest further away in that direction. To maximize the expected information gain, *BIGnav* may choose to move towards the cluster and end up further away from the target. Another cause for ID increase is when the user makes a mistake.

The long plateaus represent waiting time and confirm the qualitative results reported below: that *BIGnav* incurs a higher cognitive load. This is probably due in part to our implementation of *BIGnav*, which skips to the new view after each input command rather than transition to it with an animation. But it is also probably the case that the user has to interpret the new location to plan the next move, whereas with *STDnav* the user can anticipate the system response.

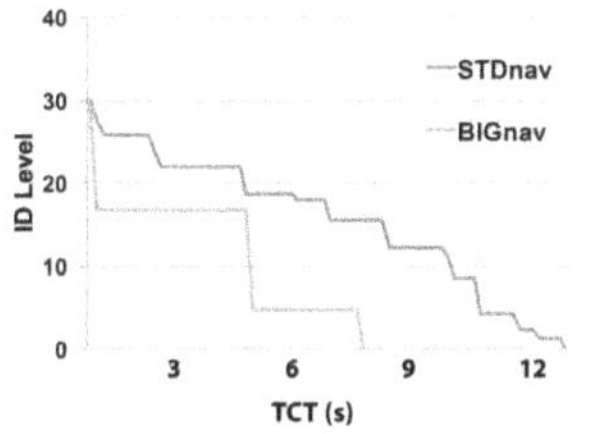

Figure 8. Time plot of the decrease in ID in the ***STDnav*** **and** ***BIGnav*** **conditions, for two trials with the same other conditions.**

Qualitative Results

The post-hoc questionnaire provides self-evaluation of performance and comfort level as well as subjective preference for the two techniques. Regarding performance and comfort level, assessed on a five-point Likert scale, we find no significant differences.

While we expected participants to dislike *BIGnav* because of its unusual and possibly counter-intuitive mode of operation despite its efficiency (**H4**), we were surprised that half the participants liked it better than *STDnav*: *"with one direction, it combines zoom and pan, which was faster than doing it by hand"*, *"The way it navigates is quite interesting. For most of the cases, only 2,3 actions are needed to find the target"*, and *"I like the interaction part. Somebody is guessing what I'm doing"*. The eight participants who preferred *STDnav* found it *"more comfortable, doesn't require that much attention"*, *"more intuitive as I can anticipate what I would see next"* and *"I'm already used to it"*. These results indicate that *BIGnav* can be a practical technique for efficient navigation.

APPLICATION: BIGMAP

To demonstrate a realistic application of *BIGnav*, we implemented a map application with a 80000 × 60000 high-resolution map of Europe using the ZVTM toolkit [23] (Fig. 9). It features the top 50 largest urban areas[5] and uses their population as probability distribution. This corresponds to the *Random+Random* distribution of the controlled experiment.

We conducted several pilot studies where participants had to navigate to specific cities from a completely zoomed-out view down to the maximum scale, where the city labels are readable (*ID* = 25). Since this task relies on cognitive skills such as the participants' geographical knowledge, we concentrated on observing users and collecting subjective evaluation feedback.

Most participants could navigate to the target city very quickly, in a few steps, especially for cities with large population, hence higher probability, such as London and Paris. One of the participants referred to *BIGnav* as *"3 steps to Paris"*. For smaller cities such as Helsinki (rank 50), participants can still navigate efficiently. Most of them feel comfortable with *BIGnav* as they are familiar with the map of Europe and can reorient themselves rapidly. However, they get frustrated when the target is already in the view but *BIGnav* moves away from it in order to gain information. One participant mentioned that *"it would be nice if we could change between pan and zoom and this one (*BIGnav*) freely so that it can help us get through all the zooming at the beginning, but once I see the target, maybe I'll switch back to pan and zoom for the last few steps"*.

BIGmap illustrates how to derive a probability distribution from external data, here the population of the cities. More generally, the distribution should reflect the targets' degree of interest, which is typically application-dependent. The distribution can also integrate usage data, such as most popular cities. Finally the results of a search can be turned into a distribution according to the ranking of the results, therefore integrating searching and navigation into a single paradigm.

[5]https://en.wikipedia.org/wiki/Larger_urban_zone

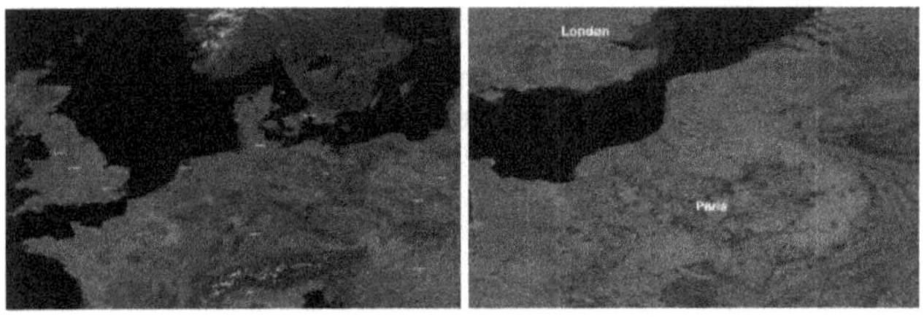

Figure 9. (a) Part of the map of Europe used by *BIGmap*. (b) Navigating towards Paris from the previous view.

DISCUSSION

We have shown that *BIGnav* is an effective technique, especially for distant targets and non-uniform information spaces. The most efficient distribution condition in the experiment was *Cluster+Cluster*, which corresponds to the small-world structures found in many datasets, showing that *BIGnav* is a promising approach for real-world applications. However, both the experiment and the *BIGmap* prototype exhibit some shortcomings, especially for small-ID tasks. We now discuss how to make *BIGnav* more comfortable to use, and then address the wider notion of human-computer partnership.

Comfort in Navigation

In standard pan-and-zoom interfaces, users can navigate the space in a continuous manner and constantly anticipate the system response. This gives them a sense of control and makes for a smooth user experience. By contrast, *BIGnav* uses discrete steps and the system's response can be difficult to anticipate and even frustrating, in particular when getting close to the target. This results in long idle times between commands (Fig. 8) and a higher cognitive load as users reorient themselves and decide on their next move. In a sense, this proves the success of the technique, since it is designed to maximally challenge the user at each step.

Yet there must be a way to improve user experience and make navigation smoother. First, we could use animations to smooth transitions and help users stay oriented. Research has shown that one-second animations are sufficient and do not slow down expert users [2]. Second, we could combine *BIGnav* with standard pan-and-zoom according to user input: large panning and zooming movements would use *BIGnav*, smaller ones traditional pan and zoom. Finally we could reduce the size of the grid and increase the number of panning directions to provide finer control, however this requires heuristics or optimizations of the computational cost.

Navigation Partnership

BIGnav is a collaborative approach as system and user work together to achieve a common objective [27, 31]. Whereas current multiscale navigation systems have leveraged either information in the multiscale world [15, 16, 21] or the users' intentions [14], *BIGnav* combines these two sources of information. Like mixed initiative systems [12], *BIGnav* optimizes decision under uncertainty. However, the use of Bayesian Experimental Design turns these systems on their head: rather than finding the action that best responds to the user, *BIGnav* challenges the user to give it useful information.

BIGnav also relates to the notion of adaptation [20, 25]. In *Information foraging* [25], users adapt their strategy to gain valuable information from the system, whereas in *BIGnav*, the systems prompts users for valuable information.

Our approach leads to a reverse form of co-adaptation [20]: While co-adaptation is about users adapting to new technology and also adapting it to their own needs, *BIGnav* adapts to users through its prior knowledge, which could change over time, and adapts users to its needs by prompting them constantly for information. This creates a more balanced partnership than the random changes used by Williamson & Murray-Smith [34], which challenge the user but without the long-term reward of system adaptation to the user.

CONCLUSION AND FUTURE WORK

BIGnav is a new multiscale navigation technique based on Bayesian Experimental Design with the criterion of maximizing the information-theoretic concept of mutual information. At each navigation step, *BIGnav* interprets user input, updates its estimate of the user's intention, and navigates to a view that maximizes the expected information that will be gained from the user's subsequent input.

We ran a controlled experiment comparing *BIGnav* with standard pan and zoom for different levels of difficulty and different distributions of the information space. Our main result is that *BIGnav* is up to 40.0% faster than the baseline for distant targets and non-uniform information spaces.

To the best of our knowledge, *BIGnav* is the first attempt at introducing an information-theoretic and Bayesian approach to multiscale navigation. Our next goal is to reduce users' cognitive load while still ensuring *BIGnav*'s efficiency. We also want to improve the computational cost of the technique in order to support more input commands and a finer grid.

Beyond navigation, we are interested in applying this approach to other tasks, such as searching. Indeed, the model can be framed in terms of human-computer interaction as follows:

- X can be any system feedback, e.g., visual, auditory, haptic;
- Y can be any human input, e.g., touch input or gaze;
- $P(\Theta)$ can model many kinds of prior knowledge about users' goals, as well as reflect their interaction history.

The paradigm shift from "responding to user input" to "running experiments on the user" is a novel perspective on the notion of human-computer partnerships, and the Bayesian Information Gain model opens the door to a wide range of "BIG" applications.

ACKNOWLEDGMENTS

We thank the reviewers, our participants and our colleagues Yves Guiard and Wendy Mackay. This research was partially funded by Labex DigiCosme (ANR-11-LABEX-0045-DIGICOSME), operated by the French Agence Nationale de la Recherche (ANR) as part of the program "Investissement d'Avenir" Idex Paris-Saclay (ANR-11-IDEX-0003-02), by European Research Council (ERC) grant n° 695464 ONE: Unified Principles of Interaction, and by CNPq (Brazilian National Research Council) grant n° 201545/2015-2.

REFERENCES

1. Caroline Appert and Jean-Daniel Fekete. 2006. OrthoZoom Scroller: 1D Multi-scale Navigation. In *Proceedings of the SIGCHI Conference on Human Factors in Computing Systems (CHI '06)*. ACM, New York, NY, USA, 21–30. DOI: http://dx.doi.org/10.1145/1124772.1124776
2. Benjamin B Bederson and Angela Boltman. 1999. Does animation help users build mental maps of spatial information?. In *Information Visualization, 1999.(Info Vis' 99) Proceedings. 1999 IEEE Symposium on*. IEEE, 28–35.
3. Renaud Blanch, Yves Guiard, and Michel Beaudouin-Lafon. 2004. Semantic Pointing: Improving Target Acquisition with Control-display Ratio Adaptation. In *Proceedings of the SIGCHI Conference on Human Factors in Computing Systems (CHI '04)*. ACM, New York, NY, USA, 519–526. DOI: http://dx.doi.org/10.1145/985692.985758
4. Stephen J Carver. 1991. Integrating multi-criteria evaluation with geographical information systems. *International Journal of Geographical Information System* 5, 3 (1991), 321–339.
5. Mark Evers, Mariët Theune, and Joyce Karreman. 2007. Which Way to Turn?: Guide Orientation in Virtual Way Finding. In *Proceedings of the Workshop on Embodied Language Processing (EmbodiedNLP '07)*. Association for Computational Linguistics, Stroudsburg, PA, USA, 25–32. http://dl.acm.org/citation.cfm?id=1610065.1610069
6. Paul M Fitts. 1954. The information capacity of the human motor system in controlling the amplitude of movement. *Journal of experimental psychology* 47, 6 (1954), 381.
7. George W. Furnas. 1997. Effective View Navigation. In *Proceedings of the ACM SIGCHI Conference on Human Factors in Computing Systems (CHI '97)*. ACM, New York, NY, USA, 367–374. DOI: http://dx.doi.org/10.1145/258549.258800
8. George W. Furnas and Benjamin B. Bederson. 1995. Space-scale Diagrams: Understanding Multiscale Interfaces. In *Proceedings of the SIGCHI Conference on Human Factors in Computing Systems (CHI '95)*. ACM Press/Addison-Wesley Publishing Co., New York, NY, USA, 234–241. DOI: http://dx.doi.org/10.1145/223904.223934
9. Tinsley A. Galyean. 1995. Guided Navigation of Virtual Environments. In *Proceedings of the 1995 Symposium on Interactive 3D Graphics (I3D '95)*. ACM, New York, NY, USA, 103–ff. DOI: http://dx.doi.org/10.1145/199404.199421
10. Yves Guiard and Michel Beaudouin-Lafon. 2004. Target Acquisition in Multiscale Electronic Worlds. *Int. J. Hum.-Comput. Stud.* 61, 6 (Dec. 2004), 875–905. DOI: http://dx.doi.org/10.1016/j.ijhcs.2004.09.005
11. Yves Guiard, Renaud Blanch, and Michel Beaudouin-Lafon. 2004. Object Pointing: A Complement to Bitmap Pointing in GUIs. In *Proceedings of Graphics Interface 2004 (GI '04)*. Canadian Human-Computer Communications Society, School of Computer Science, University of Waterloo, Waterloo, Ontario, Canada, 9–16. http://dl.acm.org/citation.cfm?id=1006058.1006060
12. Eric Horvitz. 1999. Principles of Mixed-initiative User Interfaces. In *Proceedings of the SIGCHI Conference on Human Factors in Computing Systems (CHI '99)*. ACM, New York, NY, USA, 159–166. DOI: http://dx.doi.org/10.1145/302979.303030
13. Eric Horvitz, Jack Breese, David Heckerman, David Hovel, and Koos Rommelse. 1998. The Lumiere project: Bayesian user modeling for inferring the goals and needs of software users. In *Proceedings of the Fourteenth conference on Uncertainty in artificial intelligence*. Morgan Kaufmann Publishers Inc., 256–265.
14. Takeo Igarashi and Ken Hinckley. 2000. Speed-dependent Automatic Zooming for Browsing Large Documents. In *Proceedings of the 13th Annual ACM Symposium on User Interface Software and Technology (UIST '00)*. ACM, New York, NY, USA, 139–148. DOI: http://dx.doi.org/10.1145/354401.354435
15. Edward W. Ishak and Steven K. Feiner. 2006. Content-aware Scrolling. In *Proceedings of the 19th Annual ACM Symposium on User Interface Software and Technology (UIST '06)*. ACM, New York, NY, USA, 155–158. DOI: http://dx.doi.org/10.1145/1166253.1166277
16. Waqas Javed, Sohaib Ghani, and Niklas Elmqvist. 2012. GravNav: Using a Gravity Model for Multi-scale Navigation. In *Proceedings of the International Working Conference on Advanced Visual Interfaces (AVI '12)*. ACM, New York, NY, USA, 217–224. DOI: http://dx.doi.org/10.1145/2254556.2254597
17. Susanne Jul and George W. Furnas. 1998. Critical Zones in Desert Fog: Aids to Multiscale Navigation. In *Proceedings of the 11th Annual ACM Symposium on User Interface Software and Technology (UIST '98)*. ACM, New York, NY, USA, 97–106. DOI: http://dx.doi.org/10.1145/288392.288578
18. J. C. R. Licklider. 1992. Man-Computer Symbiosis. *IEEE Ann. Hist. Comput.* 14, 1 (Jan. 1992), 24–. http://dl.acm.org/citation.cfm?id=612400.612433
19. Dennis V Lindley. 1956. On a measure of the information provided by an experiment. *The Annals of Mathematical Statistics* (1956), 986–1005.
20. Wendy E Mackay. 2000. Responding to cognitive overload: Co-adaptation between users and technology. *Intellectica* 30, 1 (2000), 177–193.

21. Tomer Moscovich, Fanny Chevalier, Nathalie Henry, Emmanuel Pietriga, and Jean-Daniel Fekete. 2009. Topology-aware Navigation in Large Networks. In *Proceedings of the SIGCHI Conference on Human Factors in Computing Systems (CHI '09)*. ACM, New York, NY, USA, 2319–2328. DOI: http://dx.doi.org/10.1145/1518701.1519056

22. Ken Perlin and David Fox. 1993. Pad: An Alternative Approach to the Computer Interface. In *Proceedings of the 20th Annual Conference on Computer Graphics and Interactive Techniques (SIGGRAPH '93)*. ACM, New York, NY, USA, 57–64. DOI: http://dx.doi.org/10.1145/166117.166125

23. Emmanuel Pietriga. 2005. A toolkit for addressing hci issues in visual language environments. In *2005 IEEE Symposium on Visual Languages and Human-Centric Computing (VL/HCC'05)*. IEEE, 145–152.

24. Emmanuel Pietriga, Caroline Appert, and Michel Beaudouin-Lafon. 2007. Pointing and Beyond: An Operationalization and Preliminary Evaluation of Multi-scale Searching. In *Proceedings of the SIGCHI Conference on Human Factors in Computing Systems (CHI '07)*. ACM, New York, NY, USA, 1215–1224. DOI: http://dx.doi.org/10.1145/1240624.1240808

25. Peter Pirolli and Stuart Card. 1995. Information Foraging in Information Access Environments. In *Proceedings of the SIGCHI Conference on Human Factors in Computing Systems (CHI '95)*. ACM Press/Addison-Wesley Publishing Co., New York, NY, USA, 51–58. DOI: http://dx.doi.org/10.1145/223904.223911

26. Peter Pirolli and Stuart Card. 1999. Information foraging. *Psychological review* 106, 4 (1999), 643.

27. Jens G Pohl. 1997. Human-Computer Partnership in Decision-Support Systems: Some Design Guidelines. *Collaborative Agent Design (CAD) Research Center* (1997), 36.

28. Claude E Shannon. 1948. A mathematical theory of communication. 27 (1948), 379–423, 623–656.

29. Claude E Shannon and Warren Weaver. 1949. The mathematical theory of communication. (1949).

30. Ben Shneiderman. 1987. Designing the User Interface Strategies for Effective Human-computer Interaction. *SIGBIO Newsl.* 9, 1 (March 1987), 6–. http://dl.acm.org/citation.cfm?id=25065.950626

31. Loren G Terveen. 1995. Overview of human-computer collaboration. *Knowledge-Based Systems* 8, 2 (1995), 67–81.

32. Colin Ware and Marlon Lewis. 1995. The DragMag Image Magnifier. In *Conference Companion on Human Factors in Computing Systems (CHI '95)*. ACM, New York, NY, USA, 407–408. DOI: http://dx.doi.org/10.1145/223355.223749

33. John Williamson. 2006. *Continuous uncertain interaction.* Ph.D. Dissertation. University of Glasgow.

34. John Williamson and Roderick Murray-Smith. 2004. Pointing Without a Pointer. In *CHI '04 Extended Abstracts on Human Factors in Computing Systems (CHI EA '04)*. ACM, New York, NY, USA, 1407–1410. DOI: http://dx.doi.org/10.1145/985921.986076

Design and Evaluation of a Handheld-based 3D User Interface for Collaborative Object Manipulation

Jerônimo Gustavo Grandi[1], Henrique Galvan Debarba[23], Luciana Nedel[1] and Anderson Maciel[1]
[1]Federal University of Rio Grande do Sul, Institute of Informatics
[2]École Polytechnique Fédérale de Lausanne, Immersive Interaction Group
[3]Artanim Foundation, Geneva, Switzerland
{jggrandi,nedel,amaciel}@inf.ufrgs.br, henrique.debarba@artanim.ch

ABSTRACT
Object manipulation in 3D virtual environments demands a combined coordination of rotations, translations and scales, as well as the camera control to change the user's viewpoint. Then, for many manipulation tasks, it would be advantageous to share the interaction complexity among team members. In this paper we propose a novel 3D manipulation interface based on a collaborative action coordination approach. Our technique explores a smartphone – the touchscreen and inertial sensors – as input interface, enabling several users to collaboratively manipulate the same virtual object with their own devices. We first assessed our interface design on a docking and an obstacle crossing tasks with teams of two users. Then, we conducted a study with 60 users to understand the influence of group size in collaborative 3D manipulation. We evaluated teams in combinations of one, two, three and four participants. Experimental results show that teamwork increases accuracy when compared with a single user. The accuracy increase is correlated with the number of individuals in the team and their work division strategy.

ACM Classification Keywords
H.5.2. User Interfaces: Input devices and strategies; H.5.3. Group and Organization Interfaces: Computer-supported cooperative work

Author Keywords
3D User Interfaces; Collaborative Manipulation; User Studies.

INTRODUCTION
The accomplishment of spatial tasks in 3D virtual environments (VE) involves a complex coordination of virtual manipulations, such as translation, rotation and scale [27]. Each of these transformations refers to independent degrees of freedom (DOFs). While these manipulations are fundamental to any 3D virtual environment, performing them freely demands a highly cognitive effort to coordinate the possible transformations [25]. 3D user interfaces (3DUI) try to reduce the mental overhead by mapping natural gestures and movements into the corresponding action in the VE. However, create effective interfaces for 3D virtual systems is challenging [24]. Many 3DUI techniques have been proposed to allow natural, precise and fast interaction with virtual environments [5]. Techniques are typically designed for specific purpose applications. Some of them have become relatively common due to the easy access to the market, such as gaming console interfaces. Nevertheless, as of today, research in the 3D object manipulation field mainly focus on single-user interaction.

Figure 1: Three users simultaneously driving the object through the virtual environment. The colored rectangles indicate the position and orientation of each user in the VE. The three windows at the right-side show the three personal views.

One alternative towards 3D manipulations efficiency is to share the work and solve the task in a parallel and collaborative manner. Collaborators may wish to split the different aspects of the manipulation among them. Thus, perhaps, accomplishing the assignment faster, more accurately and with less fatigue. Teamwork, in turn, involves considerable negotiations [6] and, as team members vary, team strategies and task accomplishment processes change as well. Modeling such human interactions raises novel collaborative concepts compared to those typically grounded in a single-user scenario [19]. An effective design of a collaborative 3DUI for virtual environments has to take into account perceptual, cognitive and social issues. Researchers in the social and cognitive field have demonstrated that a wide

CHI 2017, May 6-11, 2017, Denver, CO, USA.
Copyright © 2017 ACM ISBN 978-1-4503-4655-9/17/05 ...$15.00.
http://dx.doi.org/10.1145/3025453.3025935

range of tasks are better performed in collaborative groups than by individuals alone [13], but there is a lack of this kind of study in the collaborative 3D manipulations field.

One of the main advantages of having a collaborative interface is that it provides users with an individual action perspective of the same scene, which may also include shared and individual viewpoints. In 3D, because of the occlusions, it is impossible to be precise when working from a single perspective (egocentric or allocentric). The accomplishment of simple 3D manipulation tasks, such as a docking, requires constant movement of the user to check occluded parts. This is tedious, especially when the objects' shape is complex. Collaboration between multiple users, in this case, can help in precision and time performances.

In this work, we introduce and assess a novel 3D user interface for collaborative object manipulation. Our technique explores the advantages of smartphones as an interface for 3D interaction. Smartphones are portable, lightweight, wireless and ubiquitous in our contemporaneous life. Most current devices include inertial sensors and a touchscreen, from which one can retrieve the device orientation and multi-touch gestures. The transformation actions we exploit are consolidated in the everyday tasks when interacting with mobile apps and games, such as touch and slide to translate, device orientation to rotate, and pinch and spread to scale the virtual object. Our approach accepts simultaneous connection of multiple smartphones, allowing users to collaborate by simultaneously controlling any manipulation DOFs. This produces equal participation, individual responsibility and positive interdependence, which are necessary features in a collaborative task.

We first assessed the interface with four informal user experiments on docking and obstacle crossing tasks with teams of two users. These experiments were used to refine the interaction, ergonomics and user experience. Then, we conducted a controlled study to understand the influence of group size in collaborative 3D manipulation. We evaluate teams in combinations of one, two, three and four participants. We hypothesize that the team's overall performance increases accordingly to the number of members in the team.

RELATED WORK

Smartphone as 3DUI

The use of smartphones as 3DUI input devices for an external computing environment has already been explored to some extent. Here, we focus on works that use mobile devices to perform 3D manipulations of distant objects displayed on a second screen.

Early work have explored the orientation of a mobile device to intuitively rotate an external object. Katzakis et al. [11] showed a gain in time with the 1:1 mapping of device and virtual object orientation as compared to mouse and touchscreen input. Song et al. [23] used the orientation of a mobile device to rotate a slicing plane in a medical volume data. The mobile device is placed close to a large projection, and the slicing plane extends from the edges of the device. Debarba et al. have explored inertial sensors combined with touchscreens to provide coarse + fine-grained 3D selection [7, 8]. The former reference also includes 2D translation and uniform scaling of distant objects.

Berge et al. [4] have designed a smartphone-based overview+detail interface to interact with 3D public displays. They focus on solutions for the translation of the smartphone detailed view on the overview public screen. They evaluated three interaction techniques to control the movements of the detailed view: classical touchscreen pad, mid-air movements of the mobile device and around the device mid-air hand. Mid-air techniques performed better than touchscreen input, and mid-air phone is most suitable in usual public conditions. In another work [3], Berge et al. extend the mid-air hand into an "Around the smartphone" (ASP) approach to manipulate 3D elements on a second screen. They evaluated the technique against an existing tangible and a tactile implementations in two user studies. Both ASP and tangible performed similarly and better than the tactile technique. Rotation tasks were statistically better performed with the tangible technique. In this technique the rotations follow the wrist movements of the user in a 1:1 mapping. They used a tracking device for rotation calculations instead of the smartphone sensors.

Liang et al. [14] investigated the easiest and most intuitive sensory inputs to use in a tablet, and the most natural interactions to perform in such devices. Although the authors have evaluated the interactions with a tablet, they point out that smaller devices would perform better in motion gestures. A tablet was also the interface for Lopez et al. [15] for their touch-based navigation of 3D visualizations in stereoscopic large displays.

The way we perform the translation transformations is similar to the plane-casting technique presented by Katzakis et al. [12]. Their technique covers rotations and selection as well. They also performed an evaluation compared with an implementation of WAND, classical 6-DOF user interface. They report a significant advantage on translation time using the plane-casting when compared with a wand technique. The smartphone rotation is also explored in Tiltcasting [17], which uses a virtual plane to select 3D objects in crowded virtual environments, and in MobiSweep [26] for creating, modifying, and manipulating 3D shapes in a second screen.

Collaborative Manipulation of 3D Objects in 3DVEs

The demand for spatial collaborative virtual manipulations emerges when single-user tasks become too difficult to perform due to the many degrees of freedom involved and when the task requires the participation of multiple users. It may happen in many application fields, such as simulation and training, and data exploration [20]. A study conducted by Aguerreche et al. [2] compares three main approaches for collaborative 3D objects manipulation in VE: collaborative tangible device, proposed by themselves [1], DOF separation [18] and mean average of the actions [9].

A tangible user interface (TUI) is designed to give a physical form the power to control virtual objects. A TUI can be non-reconfigurable – the physical object cannot be modified, or configurable, where the shape can change. Aguerreche et al. [1] designed a configurable tangible device (CTD) that can be manipulated by single or multiple users to control

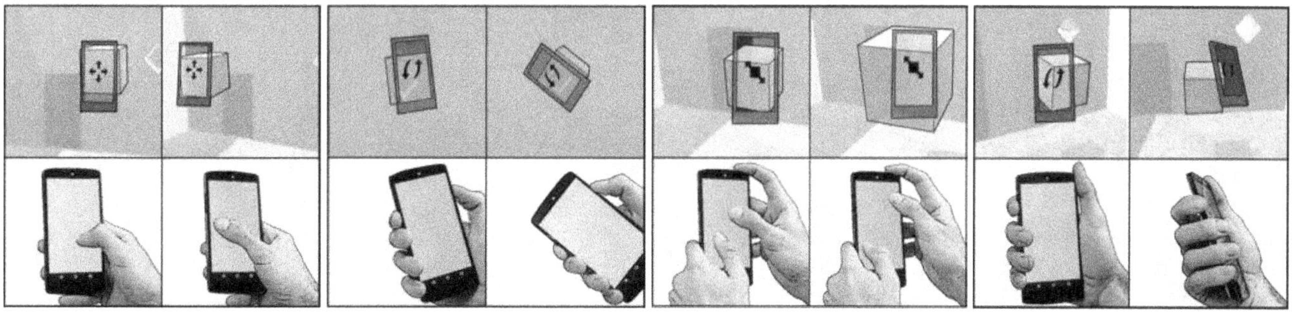

(a) Object translation (b) Object rotation (c) Object scale (d) Camera rotation

Figure 2: Walkthrough of manipulations that a mobile phone cursor can perform over the selected object: (a) translation can be applied by touching the mobile phone screen and sliding the point of contact, the object translates on the plane defined by the mobile device orientation; (b) by holding the volume down button and rotating the phone one can rotate the object likewise; (c) scale is applied by touching the screen with two fingers and producing a pinch/spread gesture; (d) the camera orientation can be controlled by holding the volume up button and rotating the mobile phone.

a virtual object in a VE. In a similar manner, Salzmann et al. [21] propose to use a non-reconfigurable tangible device for two-user collaborative interactions. They also compare their technique with a virtual method in an assembly task. Both authors report that a prop-based interaction improves task performance and collaboration because of the link between the two users provided by the tangible device.

DOF separation consists in splitting the tasks among users. In this case, the number of DOFs that each user can access and control is limited: one user controls rotation of the object, while the other one is limited to translation. Pinho et al. [18] explore this approach to demonstrate that the use of cooperative interaction techniques can be more efficient than two users working in parallel using single-user interaction techniques.

The mean technique, in turn, combines user's actions by averaging positions and orientations that they provide. The SkeweR [9] technique enables multiple users to simultaneously grab any part of a virtual object through special points called "crushing points". To determine the translation and the rotation of a grabbed object, SkeweR considers positions of these points and average the 3D object final position. Ruddle et al. [20] propose symmetric and asymmetric solutions to combine two users movements to obtain the virtual object final position.

There are two main differences between previous works and ours. First, we do not restrict the DOFs per participant in the group, but they can organize themselves to split the work. Second, participants' actions are not averaged but summed up in the final object transformation. More details are given in Section *Managing Concurrent Transformations*.

3D MANIPULATION INTERFACE

Graphical Representation

The representation of each mobile phone in the VE includes two elements: (i) a smartphone 3D model that orbits around the selected object following the phone orientation (Figure 2). When the user rotates the device, the virtual cursor (virtual representation of the smartphone) follows, assuming the same orientation and (ii) a picture-in-picture (PIP) camera containing the point of view of the orbiting phone model, positioned at the top right corner of the display (Figure 1). The PIP camera is meant to provide additional depth cues, which are rather limited when the display is shared among multiple users. Each connected device is labeled with a color. The user interface includes a global camera and display, which are shared by all collaborating users. All mobile phones are calibrated with respect to the screen position.

We also render icons on the virtual phone representation indicating the transformation being performed by each user, so that collaborating users can be aware of each other's actions without the need of verbal communication. The icons can indicate that a mobile phone is either performing a translation, rotation or scale on the selected object (Figure 2a-c).

We chose to not use the device display for visualization. It avoids the focus changing between the main screen and the device display that can lead to the losing of context.

Manipulation Mapping

Our 3D manipulation interface uses the mobile phone physical orientation, the touchscreen, and the physical volume buttons to manipulate a total of 7 DOFs of a selected 3D object. More specifically, there are 3 DOFs for translation, 3 DOFs for rotation and 1 DOF for uniform scale.

We use the sensors fusion capability provided by the Android API to retrieve the device orientation. The fusion uses the accelerometer, gyro, and magnetometer to provide an orientation in the 3D space. A calibration action is used once to provide a 1:1 mapping. To translate the selected object, a plane is defined using the device orientation (1:1 mapping). This plane is aligned to the touchscreen and, as the thumb (or any other finger) starts to touch and slide on the screen, a corresponding translation is applied to the object (Figure 2a). The object translation rate is constant and equivalent to 1 unit in the VE for each 333 pixels of sliding over the device's screen. The cube has initial side of 1 unit. The selected object is rotated by pressing and holding the volume down button. Throughout

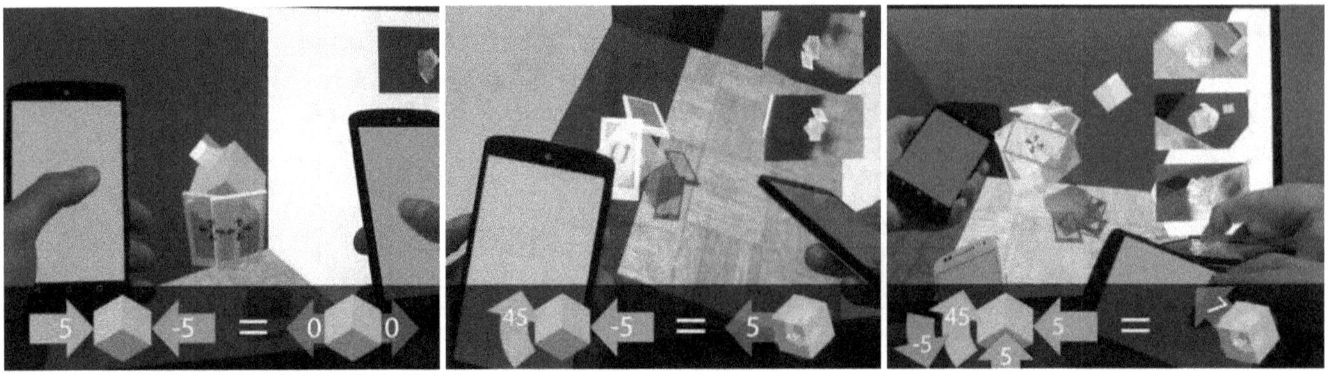

(a) Forces cancellation (b) Transformations merge (c) Concurrent access to the same DOF

Figure 3: Concurrent access to transformations. Every action performed by each user counts as a transformation step. At the bottom of the image we show the applied forces and the resulting transformation.

the time the button is pressed, the virtual object will rotate following the orientation of the phone (Figure 2b). Thus, during a rotation action, the manipulated object follows a 1:1 mapping with the physical device. We do not allow changes in the rotation rate in order to preserve this absolute mapping. Clutch can be usedto reach a total rotation beyond wrist limits (i.e. perform object rotation, reposition the mobile phone, then perform a new object rotation). Uniform scale is performed by pinch and spread gestures with two fingers on the touchscreen (Figure 2c). The scale is obtained by dividing the current distance between the fingers by their initial distance. Finally, the main camera (shared among users) follows the selected object at a fixed distance. If a user wishes to change the camera orientation, this can be done using the volume up button in a similar manner as the virtual object rotation action (Figure 2d). The virtual shared camera can be only rotated in the pitch and yaw axes. If users wish a personalized point of view, they can use the embedded PIP camera.

A user can perform any transformation action isolated or two by two: rotation and translation, scale and rotation, camera rotation and translation, scale and camera rotation.

GENERALIZING FOR COLLABORATIVE 3D MANIPULATION

Managing Concurrent Transformations

We do not impose limits on the number of simultaneous users. All users have access to all available functions. While working in groups, collaborating users may wish to split the different aspects of the manipulation among them. For instance, while the first user translates an object, the second user could rotate this same object.

All user actions are stored in a matrix representation and sent through the network to the server. Every action performed by each individual user counts as a transformation step. Action matrices are multiplied by the transformation matrix of the virtual object. Therefore, every contribution from each user is summed up into the final object's transformation without restrictions or weights. Therefore, if two users move the object in opposite directions, the position of the object will not change (Figure 3a). On the other hand, if they manipulate the different transformations in parallel, the transformations are merged (Figure 3b). Figure 3 shows the concurrent access of same transformations by three users.

Since all the users' actions are applied directly to the manipulated virtual object, we smooth the movements with an exponential moving average filter [22] to minimize the undesired flickering. It was chosen because it only needs the previous values to filter the signal. In this work, the filter is in the format: $NewValue = PrevValue * (1 - C) + CurrentSignal * C$. Where C is the filter constant. We fixed $C = 0.5$.

COLLABORATIVE 3D MANIPULATION ASSESSMENT

We conducted four public demonstrations of our collaborative user interface prior to the user study presented below. In these demonstrations we proposed different 3D manipulation tasks: object docking, and obstacle crossing. In the former, the users had to manipulate 7-DOF of selected objects in order to stack them by precisely docking one on top of the other. In the latter, the users had to manipulate a selected cube to take it from an initial to a destination position. The cube had to be carried through a sequence of walls with openings while avoiding collisions but occupying the maximum volume possible. Surface constraints were used to prevent the interpenetration between the cube and the obstacles. Over a hundred people have tested our technique in the demonstrations. We collected users' feedback to refine the interaction, ergonomics and user experience.

The obstacle crossing task was then used for a formal experiment to assess the effect of group size on manipulation time and accuracy. Three tasks are part of the obstacle crossing experiment. The first task is a wall with a square opening scaled down but aligned to the axes of the manipulated cube. The second is a wall with a both scaled and rotated square opening. The third is a winding tunnel with cross sections that vary in width and orientation (Figure 4). Each task starts after a three seconds count down and finishes when the object reaches the destination area at the end of the obstacle. The first two walls are used for training and the tunnel is used for the evaluation.

The evaluation consists in calculating the time and the accuracy to transpose the tunnel. We calculated the time from the start to the end of the task and the accuracy through a checkpoint system. The checkpoints are objects identical to the manipulated object (yellow cubes in Figure 4). We placed eight checkpoints along the tunnel path with a static position, orientation and scale so as to occupy the maximum volume at that location. To perform the task with high accuracy the users had to occupy the maximum volume of these checkpoints with the manipulated cube while completing the circuit. To calculate the error between the manipulated object m and a checkpoint c, we take the minimum distance from a vertex m_i to all vertexes in c. Thus, the error for each checkpoint is the maximum distance among the minimum distances previously calculated. For each task, we compute the error median for the eight checkpoints.

To the best of our knowledge, there is no well established interface for 3D collaborative manipulation (translation, rotation and scaling) to permit a comparison with our technique. We are aware of slightly distinct input-output mappings of mobile input for some of these transformations in a single user mode, though, from very good results regarding precision and comfort [7, 8]. We used these previous results to justify our design choices and decided to focus on the evaluation of the collaborative aspects of our technique.

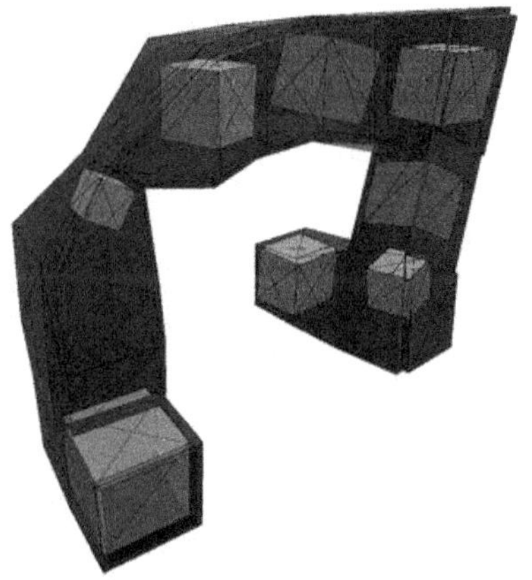

Figure 4: Checkpoints in the obstacle crossing task.

USER STUDY

Design and Procedure

We aim to investigate the relationship between group sizes and the time and accuracy to complete the tasks. Furthermore, we intend to understand the influence of work distribution balance and work division in the performance of each group combination. Thus, the experiment follows a between subject design with *Group size* as the only independent variable, with one, two, three or four participants. Dependent variables collected were *time* to complete the task and *accuracy* of the group, and *transformation actions* (translation, rotation, scale or camera rotation), including duration and magnitude of the action performed by each individual subject. The accuracy is measured as described before in Section *Collaborative 3D Manipulation Assessment*.

Participants answered a characterization form before the experiment. They also watched an informative 2 minutes video about the technique and the task. Then, we handed the mobile devices already connected in the virtual environment to the participants. We demonstrated the calibration steps and, after that, we started with the training session. The training session began with an individual exercise and continued with the group practice. The session finished when all participants were satisfied, without time restrictions. Then, users recalibrated the devices (when needed) and we started the test. Between the trials, users could recalibrate the devices as well. We asked participants to prioritize accuracy over time. The test ends with a post-experiment questionnaire. In average, the experiment sessions lasted 30 minutes.

Our first hypotheses are:

- H1. Groups with more than one member complete the tasks faster
- H2. Groups with more than one member complete the tasks with more accuracy
- H3. For the tested group size range, if groups increase in members, the time to complete tasks drops proportionally
- H4. For the tested group size range, if groups increase in members, the accuracy to complete tasks increase proportionally

If the hypotheses are confirmed, we can assume that our interface provides a significant gain in performance through collaborative work.

Task

We used the obstacle crossing game with three wall configurations, as described in Section *Collaborative 3D Manipulation Assessment*. The training sessions consist of the first two walls. The test session is formed by one trial for each practice wall and two trials for the tunnel. In all trials, the selected object starts 4 units distant from the walls. After the obstacle, the object has to be carried to a finishing wall distant 4 units.

The Section *Results* reports only the two trials in the tunnel task for the statistical analysis.

Subjects

Sixty subjects participated voluntarily in this experiment (nine female), aged 24 years in average (SD=3.6). They were all Computer Science students with no movement restrictions on wrists and arms. Thirteen of the individuals had never used gestural interactions with Kinect, Wiimote or mobile devices. We arranged the participants in 5 groups of one, 7 groups of two, 7 groups of three and 5 groups of four individuals.

Experimental Setup

Our setup is composed of mobile devices, a server computer, a projection screen and a WiFi router. An app on the phone communicates with the server that manages the client's data and the virtual environment. In the experimental setup, the same screen was shared by all the users.

Although we used diverse handheld devices, all of them were Android-based smartphones with the 5.0+ version of the operating system and had WiFi connection. They had physical volume buttons placed on the side of the device, touch screen, and gyroscope and accelerometer sensors. The same compilation of the application was installed on all devices.

The server application runs on a PC and is developed on Unity 3D. It renders the virtual environment, manages the connections with the mobile phones, and the manipulation of the transformations to be performed. Communication between server and phones is via a dedicated WiFi router and uses TCP network protocol to ensure that the packets will arrive in the correct order.

The projector is a Sharp with 1024x768 resolution. It is placed at 225 cm above the participants and 260 cm far from the projection screen. The projected image has 143x110 cm in size. The participants are placed next to each other at a distance of 220 cm from the screen. Figure 5 shows the physical space setup.

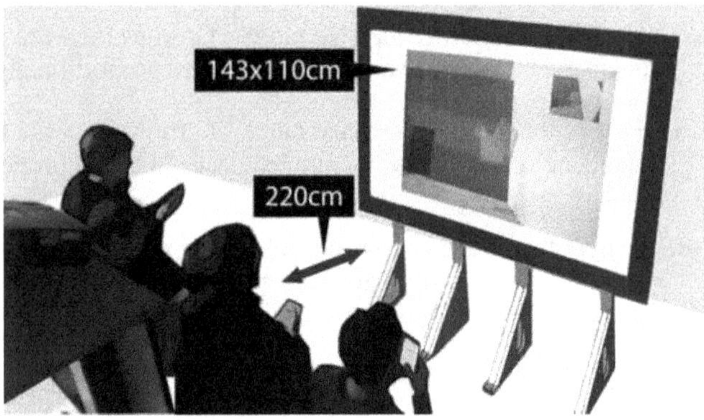

Figure 5: Physical setup of the experiments. Participants are placed next to each other at a distance of 220 cm from the screen. Each of them has its own device.

RESULTS

Group Size vs. Time and Accuracy

Figure 6 shows the time and accuracy that each group configuration achieved in the evaluation. For the statistical analysis, we first verified if the relation between the independent (group size) and the dependent variables (time and accuracy) could be evaluated using ANOVA. We fitted a linear regression and tested the normality of the residuals (Shapiro-Wilk test). Residuals were not normally distributed on both comparisons. Although Norman [16] suggests that ANOVA is robust when residuals are not normally distributed, we made a conservative choice by using non-parametric tests as these make claims about the difference of medians instead of the average.

We conducted a Kruskal-Wallis test, which can determine if a statistically significant difference exists between the levels of *group size* without assuming residuals to follow the normal distribution. Post-hoc was conducted using paired Dunn tests with Holm-Bonferroni correction.

Group Size vs. Task Completion Time

The Kruskal-Wallis test failed to reject equality of medians across different group sizes for task completion time ($H(3) = 2.1834$, $p = 0.54$), thus we reject H1 and H3. See Figure 6a.

Group Size vs. Task Accuracy

As we hypothesized in H2, the Kruskal-Wallis test revealed significant effect of group size on task accuracy median ($H(3) = 21.3522$, $p < 0.0001$). The post-hoc Dunn test indicates that significant accuracy increase occurs between group sizes 1 and 3 ($p = 0.0486$), 1 and 4 ($p < 0.0001$), 2 and 4 ($p = 0.0024$) and 3 and 4 ($p = 0.0226$). This result confirms H4. No significant difference was measured between group sizes 1 and 2, and between group sizes 2 and 3. See Figure 6b.

Groups vs. Work Division

Accuracy vs. Work Distribution Balance

For a more complete understanding on how the various group sizes affect accuracy, we analyzed the balance of the work distribution among members of teams with different sizes. Our hypothesis is that the balance of work distribution affects the task accuracy. The work distribution balance is a value between zero and one, where zero is the minimum work distribution and one is the maximum work distribution.

Before the work distribution evaluation, we performed an analysis to assess the workload of each team members for all group sizes. Each participant's workload was quantitatively measured dividing the user's active time by the group's active time. The Kruskal-Wallis test revealed a significant effect in the workload when group sizes vary ($H(3) = 79.0784$, $p < 0.0001$). The Dunn post-hoc indicates significant decrease in workload between groups size 1 and 2 ($p < 0.0006$), 1 and 3 ($p < 0.0001$), 1 and 4 ($p = 0.0031$), 2 and 3 ($p < 0.0007$), 2 and 4 ($p < 0.0001$) and 3 and 4 ($p = 0.0303$).

Then, we computed the work distribution balance. We calculated the group variance using each individual workload previously calculated. We adjusted the results by multiplying the variance by the respective group size. In this test, only groups with two, three and four members were evaluated, since the work distribution in groups with one participant is zero. However, the Kruskal-Wallis test failed to reject equality of medians across different group sizes for work distribution balance ($H(2) = 4.482$, $p = 0.11$). This hinders our intent of correlating accuracy with overall work distribution balance directly. Nevertheless, this result permitted us to focus on action division patterns, as detailed next.

Groups vs. User Roles

The work distribution balance omits the group action division by calculating a single distribution score for the whole group. Here, we analyze each team member individually to find a work division pattern. Our hypothesis is that the groups that divide actions among members are more accurate than the groups that do not divide. The time series on Figure 7 shows the different strategies adopted by two groups with four participants, each with similar work division balance (A = 96.4%, B = 95.5%) but with different action strategies and accuracy. To

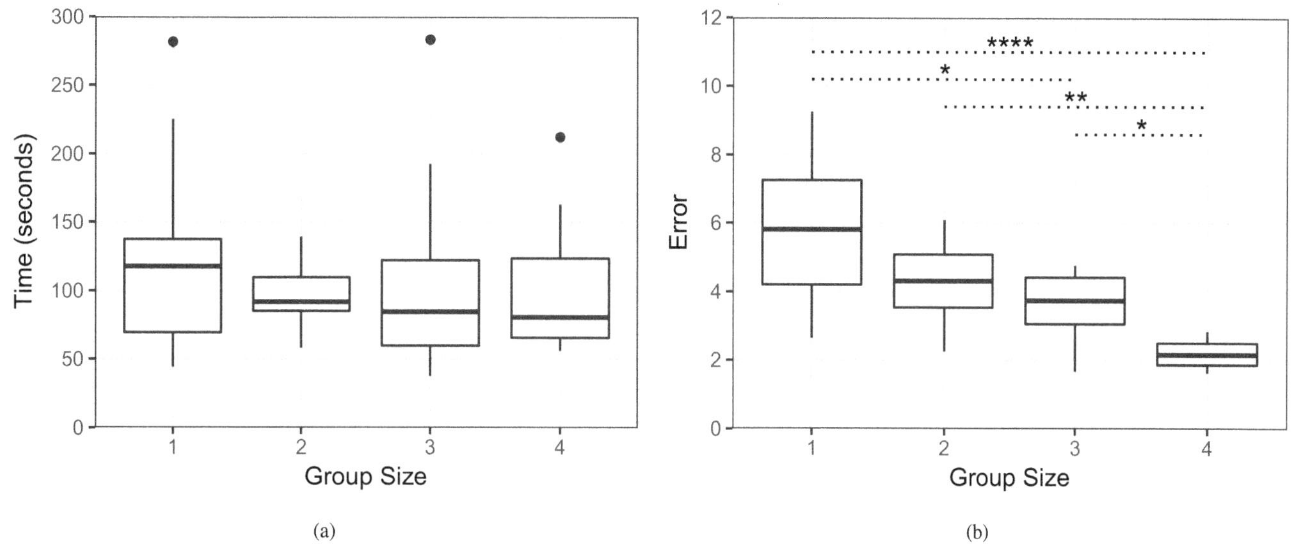

Figure 6: (a) There was no significant difference in time to complete the tasks between groups. (b) Group size 4 is the most accurate (Mdn = 2.16, SD = 0.44), followed by size 3 (Mdn = 3.74, SD = 0.94), size 2 (Mdn = 4.31, SD = 1.18), and size 1 (Mdn = 5.81, SD = 2.16).

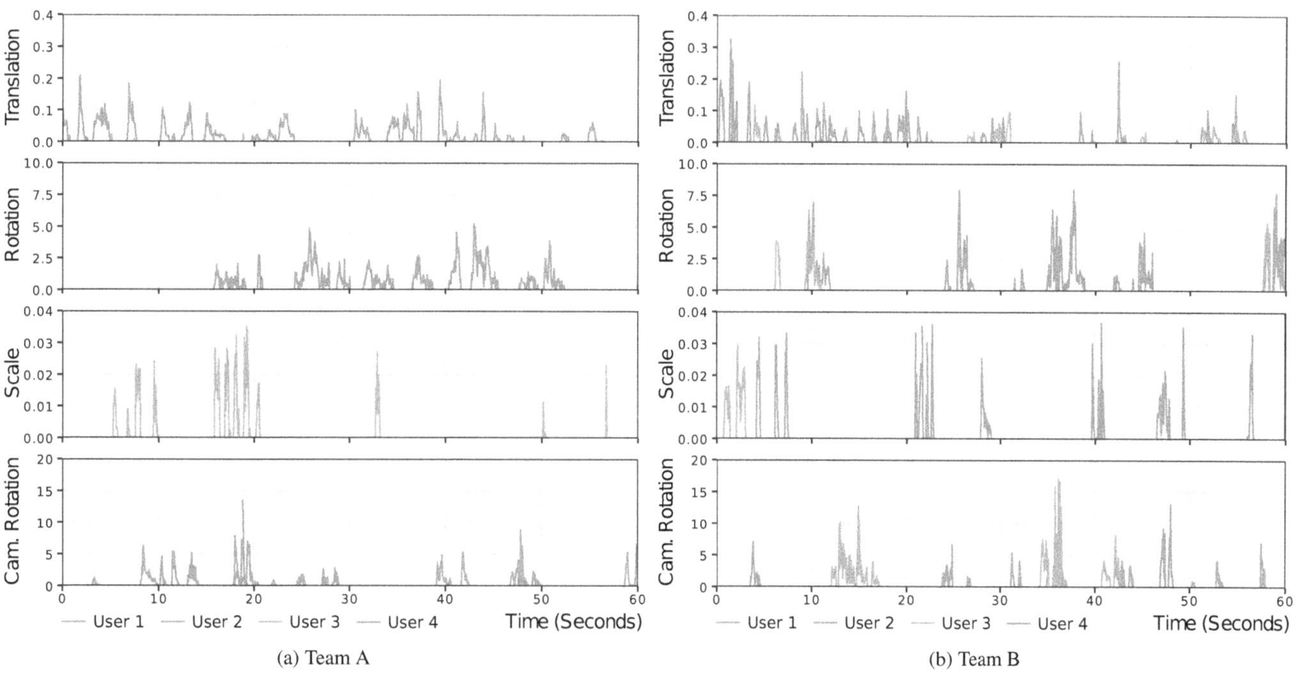

Figure 7: Time series of one task showing the collaboration strategy adopted by Team A and B with four participants. Both teams have similar work division balance (A = 96.4%, B = 95.5%) but different strategies. Team A splitted the transformations among the participants in such a way that, on average, all team members performed 3.25 roles swap. They completed the task in 60.7 seconds and with 1.85 errors. Team B adopted a division strategy, on average all team members performed 15 roles swap. They completed the task in 63.9 seconds (the last 3.9s are omitted in the plot) and with 2.78 errors.

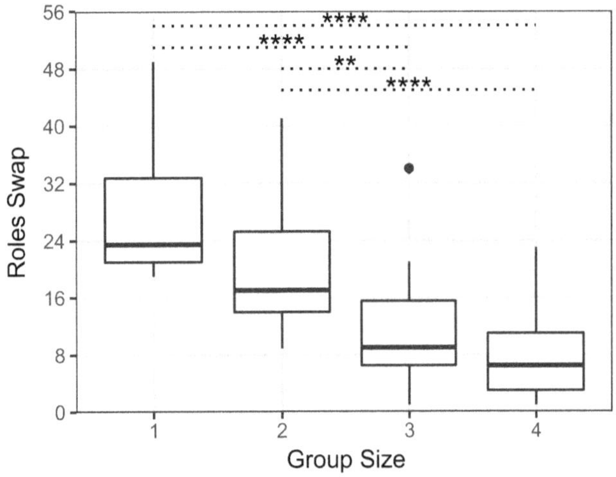

Figure 8: Individuals in groups with four members swap roles less often (Mdn = 6.5, SD = 6.26), followed by groups with size 3 (Mdn = 9, SD = 7.21), size 2 (Mdn = 17, SD = 10.22) and size 1 (Mdn = 23.5, SD = 10.71).

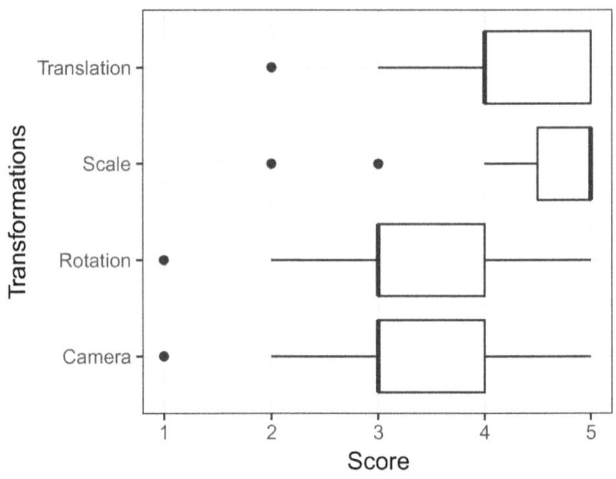

Figure 9: User's opinion about the technique comfort for each transformation. The results are reported in the Likert scale where 1 is very uncomfortable and 5 is very comfortable. Translation (Mdn = 4, SD = 0.73), scale (Mdn = 5, SD = 0.65), rotation (Mdn = 3, SD = 0.94) and camera rotation (Mdn = 3, SD = 1.08).

extract the division of actions between the groups, we identified the frequency users change between actions (translation, rotation, scale). We call this change a *role swap*.

The Kruskal-Wallis variance analysis revealed significant effect between groups and user roles changes ($H(3) = 40.1615$, $p < 0.0001$). The post-hoc Dunn test indicates that significant action division occurs between groups size 1 and 3 ($p < 0.0001$), 1 and 4 ($p < 0.0001$), 2 and 3 ($p = 0.0031$) and 2 and 4 ($p < 0.0001$). Groups size 1 and 2, 3 and 4 do not differ significantly (see Figure 8).

Accuracy vs. User Roles

Since the accuracy and the action division have similar behaviors, we hypothesized that the two variables were related. The Pearson correlation revealed a significant effect between error and user roles changes ($r = -0.3957$, $p < 0.0001$).

Learning Between Trials

In Figure 10, we measured the learning effect between the two trials. We assessed the time and accuracy for all groups together. The Wilcoxon signed rank test indicated no significant increase in accuracy between trials ($Z = 144$, $p < 0.5879$) and a significant effect in time between trials ($Z = 214$, $p = 0.0032$).

User Comfort

In Figure 9, we report the user responses to comfort when performing the transformations. Most users reported that the translation and scale actions are very comfortable to perform. Object and camera rotations had mostly neutral or positive opinions. They have almost the same comfort level according to users, being slightly but clearly below the other two transformations.

DISCUSSION

Technique Performance

The findings in our study indicate that handheld devices are powerful tools for 3D collaborative tasks. We observed that team arrangements with two, three and four members solve the tasks significantly more accurately than individuals (groups with one member). Interestingly, the accuracy increases faster with larger group sizes. For group sizes of one and two, there is only significant increase when compared with groups with two or more additional members. However, between group sizes 3 and 4, the accuracy increases significantly. No significant difference in completion time is reported, which may have been influenced by the instruction to prioritize accuracy over time in our experiment.

To understand the causes for accuracy increasing with larger group sizes, we investigated whether it was caused by the way teams balance the actions among team members. The statistical analysis revealed no significant increase. Thus, we further explored the accuracy effect by analyzing the team's work division. We observed a significant drop in the swap of roles of the team members on larger groups. It indicates that users tend to specialize in one transformation, consequently better dividing the tasks. The behavior between accuracy and work division follows the same trend, as observed in Figure 6b and Figure 8. We correlated the two variables, and the results indicate that the work division strategy is related to the error drop.

We also investigated the learning effect between the two repeated trials. We report a significant drop in time to complete the tasks without affecting accuracy. It indicates that with more training, groups tend to perform the task faster while keeping equivalent accuracy.

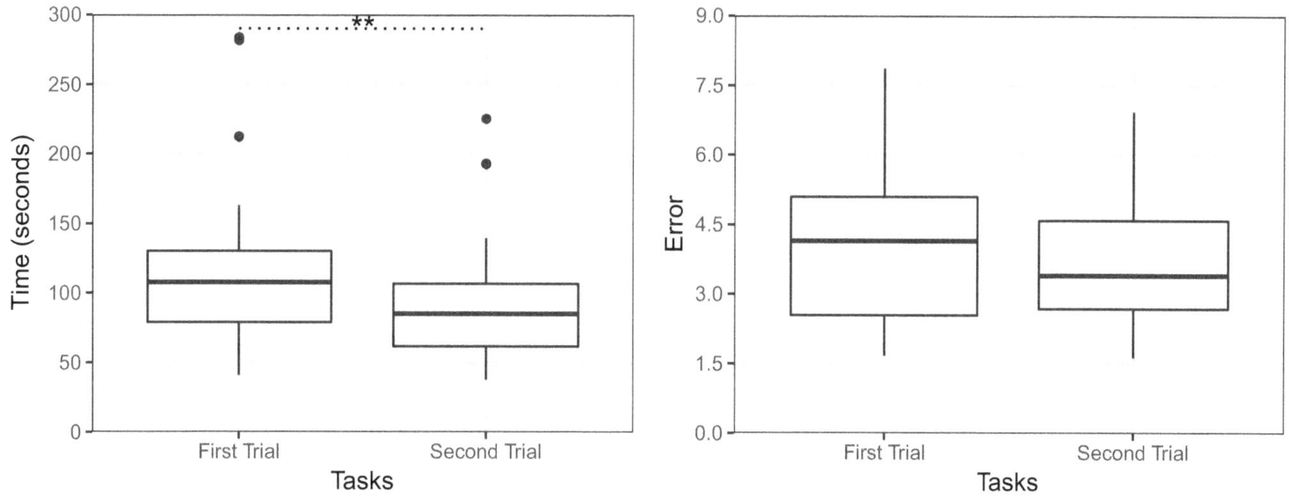

(a) (b)

Figure 10: (a) Groups complete the task significantly faster in the second trial (Mdn = 85.12, SD = 44.81) than the first (Mdn = 107.59 , SD = 65.58). (b) There is no significant accuracy effect between the first (Mdn = 4.14, SD = 1.74) and the second (Mdn = 3.59, SD = 1.83) trials.

Technique Comfort

The results shows that the technique is comfortable. We observed that translation and scale receive better scores than both object and camera rotations. It is known that actions performed by small muscle groups, such as fingers tend to be more comfortable than larger muscle groups, such as wrist and arm [28]. This may explain why the rotation actions were ranked one step below the others, even if still well ranked. Nevertheless, we exchanged comfort for affordance in our design. We believe that the use of direct mapping for rotations is more natural than rotations with the fingers, as the user indirectly holds the virtual object.

Ringelmann Effect

The Ringelmann Effect states that the addition of new coworkers in a collaborative task (the original was a rope pulling task) leads to a linear decrement in the member's performance. Ingham et al. [10] reproduced the effect with teams of 1 to 6 participants. They report a significant drop in individual performance in groups with more members. Even though our experiment was not designed to test the effect, in Section *Accuracy vs. Work Distribution Balance*, we found a correlation between workload and group size. It suggests that, in virtual collaboration, team members tend to work less in larger groups as previously demonstrated in the real world collaborative tasks.

CONCLUSION

In this paper, we presented the design of a novel 3D user interface for collaborative object manipulation in 3D virtual environments. The technique is based on smartphones and uses the touchscreen and the inertial sensors as a 3DUI. The technique has proven to be intuitive and robust. More than a hundred participants have tested it and could provide data and feedback about its usability. In several informal tests, users were invited to download the app in their own smartphones and to join an on-going manipulation session. We tested it with teams composed of more than ten members using smartphones of different models. All of them easily and quickly understood the purpose and mechanics of the technique, indicating a high affordance.

Smartphones, being versatile and ubiquitous devices, conveniently adapt as input devices to be used in combination with an external or wearable display. While we evaluated our interaction technique using a large screen (integrating a shared+personal view) as display device, the technique is friendly to other display form factors such as HMDs or CAVEs. Changing the view to VR HMDs or augmented reality HMDs (e.g. Hololens) could provide greater individual perspective, while the input manipulations would not change much.

In formal user experiments, we demonstrated that the technique design is suitable to be used by teams. Teams with more members performed more accurately than smaller groups. In larger groups, members could better divide the basic tasks, assuming roles and, as a consequence, decreasing the workload. Speed was not the goal in our experiments, but we also observed that speed increases from the first use of the system to the second one without affecting accuracy, demonstrating that the users learn fast. However, more tests should be done regarding the technique learning curve.

In this study, we aimed at understanding how groups behave in a situation where users have freedom to perform any transformation at any time. In a future work, we plan to focus on different levels of controlled labor division in a way that each user will be responsible for only one specific type of transformation. We expect that, by forcing the role division between the peers, the accuracy could be increased for all the groups.

ACKNOWLEDGMENTS

We thank all the users that volunteered for the experiment. Thanks are also due to Iago Berndt for his help with the implementation and Victor Adriel de Jesus Oliveira for his help with the text and analysis revision. We finally acknowledge the funding from CAPES, CNPq (305071/2012-2), and FAPERGS (2283-2551/14-8).

REFERENCES

1. Laurent Aguerreche, Thierry Duval, and Anatole Lécuyer. 2010. Reconfigurable Tangible Devices for 3D Virtual Object Manipulation by Single or Multiple Users. In *Proceedings of the 17th ACM Symposium on Virtual Reality Software and Technology (VRST '10)*. ACM, New York, NY, USA, 227–230. DOI: http://dx.doi.org/10.1145/1889863.1889913
2. Laurent Aguerreche, Thierry Duval, and Anatole Lécuyer. 2011. Evaluation of a reconfigurable tangible device for collaborative manipulation of objects in virtual reality. In *Theory and Practice of Computer Graphics*. 81–88.
3. Louis-pierre Bergé, Emmanuel Dubois, and Mathieu Raynal. 2015. Design and Evaluation of an "Around the SmartPhone" Technique for 3D Manipulations on Distant Display. In *SUI15*. 69–78. DOI: http://dx.doi.org/10.1145/2788940.2788941
4. Louis-Pierre Bergé, Marcos Serrano, Gary Perelman, and Emmanuel Dubois. 2014. Exploring Smartphone - Based Interaction with Overview + Detail Interfaces on 3D Public Displays. *MobileHCI 2014* (2014), 125–134. DOI: http://dx.doi.org/10.1145/2628363.2628374
5. Doug A Bowman, Ernst Kruijff, Joseph J LaViola, and Ivan Poupyrev. 2004. *3D User Interfaces: Theory and Practice*. Addison Wesley Longman Publishing Co., Inc., Redwood City, CA, USA.
6. Elizabeth F Churchill and Dave Snowdon. 1998. Collaborative virtual environments: an introductory review of issues and systems. *Virtual Reality* 3, 1 (1998), 3–15.
7. Henrique Debarba, Luciana Nedel, and Anderson MacIel. 2012. LOP-cursor: Fast and precise interaction with tiled displays using one hand and levels of precision. *IEEE Symposium on 3D User Interfaces 2012, 3DUI 2012 - Proceedings* (2012), 125–132. DOI: http://dx.doi.org/10.1109/3DUI.2012.6184196
8. Henrique G. Debarba, Jerônimo G. Grandi, Anderson Maciel, Luciana Nedel, and Ronan Boulic. 2013. Disambiguation Canvas: A Precise Selection Technique for Virtual Environments. In *Lecture Notes in Computer Science (including subseries Lecture Notes in Artificial Intelligence and Lecture Notes in Bioinformatics)*. Vol. 8119 LNCS. 388–405. DOI: http://dx.doi.org/10.1007/978-3-642-40477-1_24
9. Thierry Duval, Anatole Lécuyer, and Sébastien Thomas. 2006. SkeweR: A 3D interaction technique for 2-user collaborative manipulation of objects in virtual environments. In *3DUI 2006: IEEE Symposium on 3D User Interfaces 2006 - Proceedings*, Vol. 2006. 69–72. DOI: http://dx.doi.org/10.1109/VR.2006.119
10. Alan G Ingham, George Levinger, James Graves, and Vaughn Peckham. 1974. The Ringelmann effect: Studies of group size and group performance. *Journal of Experimental Social Psychology* 10, 4 (1974), 371–384.
11. Nicholas Katzakis and Masahiro Hori. 2009. Mobile phones as 3-dof controllers: A comparative study. In *Dependable, Autonomic and Secure Computing, 2009. DASC'09. Eighth IEEE International Conference on*. IEEE, 345–349. DOI: http://dx.doi.org/10.1109/DASC.2009.76
12. Nicholas Katzakis, Robert J Teather, Kiyoshi Kiyokawa, and Haruo Takemura. 2015. INSPECT: extending plane-casting for 6-DOF control. *Human-centric Computing and Information Sciences* 5, 1 (dec 2015), 22. DOI: http://dx.doi.org/10.1186/s13673-015-0037-y
13. Patrick R. Laughlin. 2011. *Group Problem Solving*. Princeton University Press.
14. Hai Ning Liang, Cary Williams, Myron Semegen, Wolfgang Stuerzlinger, and Pourang Irani. 2013. An investigation of suitable interactions for 3D manipulation of distant objects through a mobile device. *International Journal of Innovative Computing, Information and Control* 9, 12 (2013), 4737–4752.
15. David Lopez, Lora Oehlberg, Candemir Doger, and Tobias Isenberg. 2016. Towards An Understanding of Mobile Touch Navigation in a Stereoscopic Viewing Environment for 3D Data Exploration. *IEEE Transactions on Visualization and Computer Graphics* 22, 5 (may 2016), 1616–1629. DOI: http://dx.doi.org/10.1109/TVCG.2015.2440233
16. Geoff Norman. 2010. Likert scales, levels of measurement and the "laws" of statistics. *Advances in health sciences education* 15, 5 (2010), 625–632.
17. Krzysztof Pietroszek, James R. Wallace, and Edward Lank. 2015. Tiltcasting: 3D interaction on large displays using a mobile device. *Proceedings of the 28th Annual ACM Symposium on User Interface Software & Technology - UIST '15* (2015), 57–62. DOI: http://dx.doi.org/10.1145/2807442.2807471
18. Marcio S Pinho, Doug A Bowman, and Carla M Dal Sasso Freitas. 2008. Cooperative object manipulation in collaborative virtual environments. *Journal of the Brazilian Computer Society* 14 (2008), 54–67. http://www.scielo.br/scielo.php?script=sci
19. Mike Robinson. 1993. Designing for Unanticipated Use.... In *ECSCW '93*. 187–202. DOI: http://dx.doi.org/10.1145/958217.958218
20. Roy A Ruddle, Justin C D Savage, and Dylan M Jones. 2002. Symmetric and asymmetric action integration during cooperative object manipulation in virtual environments. *ACM Transactions on Computer-Human Interaction (TOCHI)* 9, 4 (2002), 285–308.

21. H. Salzmann, J. Jacobs, and B. Froehlich. 2009. Collaborative interaction in co-located two-user scenarios.. In *Proc. of JVRC 2009 (Joint Virtual Reality Conference of EGVE - ICAT - EuroVR)*. 85–92.

22. Steven Smith. 2013. *Digital signal processing: a practical guide for engineers and scientists*. Newnes.

23. Peng Song, Wooi Boon Goh, Chi-Wing Fu, Qiang Meng, and Pheng-ann Heng. 2011. WYSIWYF: Exploring and Annotating Volume Data with a Tangible Handheld Device. In *Proceedings of the 2011 annual conference on Human factors in computing systems - CHI '11*, Vol. D. ACM Press, New York, New York, USA, 1333. DOI: http://dx.doi.org/10.1145/1978942.1979140

24. Wolfgang Stuerzlinger and Chadwick A. Wingrave. 2011. The value of constraints for 3d user interfaces. *Virtual Realities: Dagstuhl Seminar 2008* (2011), 203–223. DOI: http://dx.doi.org/10.1007/978-3-211-99178-7_11

25. Manuel Veit, Antonio Capobianco, and Dominique Bechmann. 2009. Influence of degrees of freedom's manipulation on performances during orientation tasks in virtual reality environments. *Proceeding VRST '09 Proceedings of the 16th ACM Symposium on Virtual Reality Software and Technology* 1, 212 (2009), 51–58. DOI: http://dx.doi.org/10.1145/1643928.1643942

26. Vinayak, Devarajan Ramanujan, Cecil Piya, and Karthik Ramani. 2016. MobiSweep: Exploring Spatial Design Ideation Using a Smartphone as a Hand-held Reference Plane. In *Proceedings of the TEI '16: Tenth International Conference on Tangible, Embedded, and Embodied Interaction - TEI '16*. ACM Press, New York, New York, USA, 12–20. DOI: http://dx.doi.org/10.1145/2839462.2839490

27. Shumin Zhai and Paul Milgram. 1998. Quantifying coordination in multiple DOF movement and its application to evaluating 6 DOF input devices. *Proceedings of the SIGCHI conference on Human factors in computing systems - CHI '98* (1998), 320–327. DOI: http://dx.doi.org/10.1145/274644.274689

28. Shumin Zhai, Paul Milgram, and William Buxton. 1996. The influence of muscle groups on performance of multiple degree-of-freedom input. *Proceedings of the SIGCHI conference on Human factors in computing systems common ground - CHI '96* (1996), 308–315. DOI: http://dx.doi.org/10.1145/238386.238534

TDome: A Touch-Enabled 6DOF Interactive Device for Multi-Display Environments

Houssem Saidi[1], Marcos Serrano[1], Pourang Irani[2], Emmanuel Dubois[1]

[1] University of Toulouse – IRIT
Toulouse, France
{first_name.last_name}@irit.fr

[2] University of Manitoba
Winnipeg, Canada
Irani@cs.umanitoba.ca

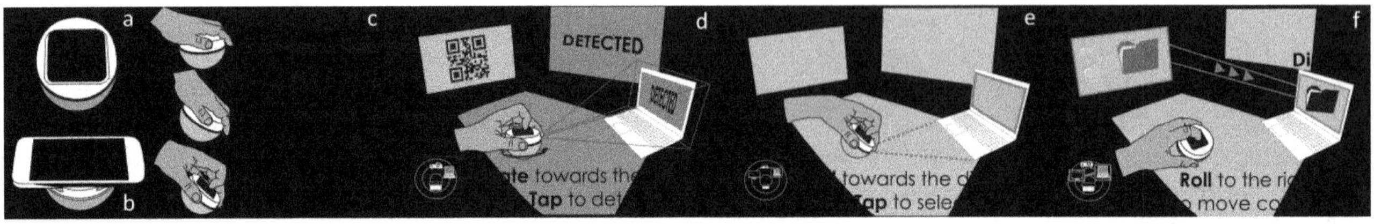

Figure 1. TDome combines a small (a) or large (b) touchscreen with a dome-like mouse [23]. TDome supports performing combined gestures (c), i.e. a 6 DOF physical manipulation followed by a touch input. TDome facilitates several common tasks in MDEs, such as d) display registration using its embedded camera, e) device selection and f) cross-display data transfer.

ABSTRACT

The rapid evolution of multi-display environments (MDEs) has created a vacuum in need of novel input devices to optimize interaction in MDEs. In this paper, we propose TDome, a novel touch-enabled 6DOF input and output device to facilitate interactions in MDEs. TDome offers a private display as output, and multiple degrees of freedom as input by combining touch gestures on the display with physical rotation, roll and translation manipulations of the device. TDome allows versatile interactions that address major MDE tasks, which we illustrate through various proof-of-concept implementations: detect surrounding displays, select one display, transfer data across displays, reach distant displays and perform private interactions. We explore TDome's usability and suitability for MDEs through three user studies. First we explore combined *physical+touch* gestures from which we discard uncomfortable combinations. We experimentally validate their feasibility and come up with a set of 71 combined gestures that can be easily performed and efficiently detected. Finally, we collect user feedback to identify natural mappings between gestures and MDE interactions.

Author Keywords

Multi-display environments; input device; touch input; rolling device.

CHI 2017, May 06-11, 2017, Denver, CO, USA
© 2017 ACM. ISBN 978-1-4503-4655-9/17/05...$15.00
DOI: http://dx.doi.org/10.1145/3025453.3025661

ACM Classification Keywords

H.5.2. Information interfaces and presentation (e.g., HCI): Interaction.

INTRODUCTION

Multi-displays environments (MDEs), combining vertical and horizontal displays of varying shapes and forms, have shown significant value for interacting with heterogeneous data sources and in multiple contexts such as 3D exploration [7], collaborative scenarios [12], crisis management [14] and scientific data visualisation [33]. MDEs offer numerous advantages for organizing information across displays, for enhancing individual and group work, for providing support to peripheral information and for extending the interaction space. The incidental emergence of MDEs has resulted in a device vacuum: to our knowledge no device has been specifically implemented for optimizing interactions in such spaces.

Researchers have mainly proposed adapting existing devices to tackle individual MDE tasks, such as the mouse for multi-monitor pointing [5], or smartphones for cross-display data-transfer or distant pointing [11,22]. However such adaptations can result in undesirable side effects: mice are not appropriate when the user is standing [22] and smartphones held in mid-air can be tiring and cumbersome for long interactions [16]. Recent research has demonstrated the use of wearable devices to perform cross-device interactions [18,32]. However, current wearables lack proper input mechanisms and mainly serve private purposes. If MDEs are to become the office of the future, as envisioned by many [26,28], can we design a device specifically tuned for such an environment? Adopting a unique device would avoid the homing effect when switching from one device to another, enhance privacy in such environments through personal data control and visualization, lead to a coherent set of interactions with the varied MDE applications, and ultimately contribute to a more fluid task flow, a key element in MDEs [4].

To this end we present a novel touch-enabled device, TDome, designed to facilitate interactions and address a range of tasks in MDEs [9,32]. TDome is the combination of a touchscreen, a dome-like Mouse [23] providing 6 DOF, and a camera that can sense the environment. TDome thus inherits properties of other existing mouse-like devices but includes many novel features to tackle the needs of common MDE tasks [9,32]: TDome identifies the spatial layout of displays (Figure 1-d); facilitates distant interaction and data transfer across displays (Figure 1-ef); and enables personal interactions by using the touchscreen as a private output medium. In our work we designed and implemented different techniques employing two versions of TDome (small and large touchscreen) to address these MDE tasks.

In this paper we address two major challenges for applying TDome in MDEs: first, the device's usability, which demands the user to coordinate a physical manipulation with a touch gesture (we refer to as combined gestures - see Figure 1-c); second, the mapping between TDome gestures and MDE tasks. To validate TDome's usability and suitability for MDEs, we conducted three user studies. We first carry out a formative study to discard gestures deemed too uncomfortable. We followed this with a controlled system validation in which we identified the success rate and performance of combined gestures. Results show that users can comfortably and precisely perform 54 combined gestures with TDome when it is equipped with a large touchscreen and 17 when it has a small touchscreen. Finally, using this set of gestures, we collected user feedback on the best mappings from TDome gestures to common MDE tasks. Results reveal that users take benefit of the semantics of TDome gestures to easily map them to certain tasks, such as rolling the device to view private information, or performing a Drag on the touchscreen to send content across displays.

We offer two contributions. (i) We introduce TDome, a novel device aimed directly at facilitating MDE interactions and discuss its properties with regards to MDE common tasks. (ii) We introduce a diverse range of MDE interaction possibilities with our prototypes. To validate these contributions, we identify the most usable TDome interactions. We then obtain qualitative feedback on mappings from TDome features to MDE tasks.

RELATED WORK

We present a range of techniques designed to support interaction in MDEs. In most cases, a new technique was implemented using an already existing device.

Early multi-display interaction techniques

While mouse input is suited for interactions with multiple desktop monitors [5], such a device does not adapt well to multi-display environments (MDEs), where displays may be scattered within the physical space [34]. One of the earliest solutions, Pick'n Drop [27], proposes the use of a stylus to transfer information from one device to another. The stylus has also been used for pointing [20], a particularly difficult task when displays are large or far from the user. However, due to the limited DOF of such devices, these solutions focus on specific interaction techniques but do not cover the broad set of MDE tasks.

Adapting mobile and wearable devices for MDEs

Performing physical gestures with mobile devices leverages significantly more DOF than those available with existing devices, such as mice. The main reason is that such devices combine a number of sensors that expand the input/output space (e.g. touch, tilt). Examples include the use of mobiles for pointing [22], for continuous map navigation [10,21], for copy-and-paste operations [30] or for interacting with distant 3D content [8]. The camera on the mobile device has been used to transfer data between MDE displays [11,13]. Another common approach is to use mobile devices for multi-display overview+detail tasks [3,7]. However, holding a mobile device in mid-air can be tiring [16], especially as mid-air manipulations lack precision. To overcome this problem, mobile devices can be actuated [31,19], which poses new limitations (robustness, speed).

Researchers have recently proposed the use of wearable devices for MDE operations, such as data transfer [18, 32]. For instance, Gluey [32] is a user interface based on the combination of a head-worn-display with a camera, which facilitates seamless input transitions and data movement across displays. Such devices offer mostly personal capabilities in MDEs.

Roly-Poly Mouse

A number of multi-DOF input devices have been proposed in the literature. Although they were not specifically designed in the context of MDEs, their capabilities are related to those of TDome. TDome's rounded shape allows tilting the device, similar to the Rockin' Mouse [2] or the VideoMouse [17], and is directly inspired by a more recent device, the Roly-Poly Mouse (RPM) [23]. Using a completely rounded bottom as RPM has been shown to provide larger amplitude of movement than previous tilting devices, and it also enables compound gestures (see Table 1 in [23] for a summary on the differences between RPM and previous tilting and multi-DOF mice).

While the rounded dome-like shape of RPM offers multiple degrees of freedom, it hinders the device's stability. Unintended physical manipulations (e.g. Roll during Translation) are common on devices with such a form factor (cf. study 1 in [23]). In our work we correct this problem by combining physical manipulations with touch gestures, to ensure the robustness of TDome interactions.

The use of a touchscreen coupled with an input device is an approach already adopted in the design of the LensMouse [36]. Other mice have also proposed the use of multi-touch [6]. However, all of them coupled a 2D mouse with a touchscreen, while the TDome uses a 6D mouse. This brings a new challenge in terms of device usability that we address in this paper through two user studies.

TDOME OVERVIEW

TDome is a touch-enabled multi-DOF input device that embodies features and a form factor that facilitate MDE interactive tasks. This unique device results from the composition of a touchscreen with a dome-like Mouse, providing rotation, Roll, Translation and Lift-Up motions (6 DOF). The device also includes a camera that can sense the environment. We present an illustrative usage scenario with TDome prior to presenting its features.

Usage scenario

Harry is an engineer working on a smart campus project that monitors data collected by multiple sensors on the university. To visualize and interact with the large datasets of energy consumption, the university has set up a multi-display environment composed of several displays, a large projection wall and two TDome devices.

As Harry enters the room to start his daily supervision of the energy data, he grabs one TDome and uses it to initialize the multi-display environment by simply pointing at each active display. He then selects the wall projection by rolling the device toward the wall. Harry decides to Spread the data visualisation across two displays: he selects both displays with TDome and transfers the visualizations from one to the other with a TDome gesture. As he wants to look closer at information on the second display, he grabs TDome and walks towards the display, using the device in mid-air to perform a zoom on the data for a closer look.

Later that day, Mary enters the room and grabs the second TDome. They have a meeting to explore the university map to mark points of interest. Harry and Mary take their personal smartphones and couple them with each TDome to benefit from personal interactions. Each smartphone shows a personal view of the projected map, which allows them to add and access personal annotations. Before ending, Harry wants to log onto the campus website and upload his annotations: he rolls TDome towards himself to display a virtual keyboard on the device's touchscreen and enter his personal password discreetly on the login page, displayed on the tabletop.

This scenario illustrates how TDome allows users to detect surroundings displays arrangement, select one display, move content between displays, reach to content at distant displays and perform personal interactions on TDome.

Device Manipulation

Interacting with TDome requires the explicit combination of a physical manipulation with a tactile gesture on the touchscreen. The sequential combination of both actions acts as a delimiter whose accidental activation is unlikely, as demonstrated in our controlled evaluation (below). This approach reduces the risk of issuing a command after performing a physical manipulation inadvertently and improves the robustness of the device. As illustrated in Figure 2, four different physical manipulations (Translations, Roll, Rotation and Lift-Up) can be combined with four different touch gestures (Tap, Drag, Pinch, Spread) for using TDome.

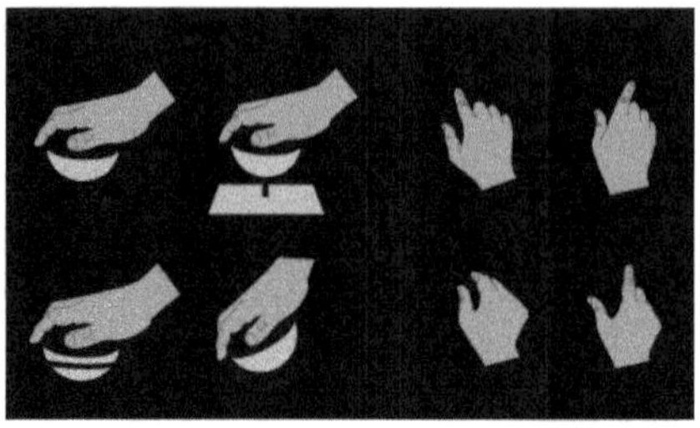

Figure 2. TDome allows performing combined gestures, i.e. a physical manipulation followed by a touch gesture

Initially, we favoured a one-handed interaction where the dominant hand was used to perform the physical manipulation on the device and the touch gestures on the display. But our preliminary tests revealed that some gestures were easier to perform in a bimanual mode, thus extending the touch vocabulary.

TDome versions: small and large touchscreen

We implemented two design variations of TDome resulting from different device composition alternatives [24]: one with a small touchscreen inserted into the spherical shell (Small version) and one with a larger touchscreen laid on top of the spherical shell (Large version). As these two versions were meant to be complementary, we favoured the possibility of rapidly switching them as opposed to having two separate devices. This opens interesting possibilities, such as switching to the large touchscreen when a larger display is needed.

IMPLEMENTATION

TDome core elements

We used the RPMouse [23] design guidelines to define the dimension of our device: a diameter of 8cm (~ 3.15in) was the easiest to handle and manipulate. As with the original RPMouse, we weighted the device with putty so that the device returns to its initial upright position when released (roly-poly toy principle).

Regarding the touchscreens, we implemented both the Small and Large versions. To restrict our device to the selected size, we had to limit the small screen size to less than 8cm. To create the Small version, we removed the bracelet from an Android smartwatch SimValley AW-414 (63g, 45x44x14mm, 28x28mm touchscreen) and enclosed the smartwatch into TDome. To implement the Large version, we used a Galaxy S4 smartphone (5 in, 134g, 137x70x8mm). We used the smartwatch's camera, which is situated on the edge of the watch, to provide TDome with a horizontal camera view. The camera has a 3MP sensor and a resolution of 1728x1728 pixels.

To support device modularity, the interchange of both touchscreens had to be easy and quick. We thus 3D printed two plastic adaptors that can be adjusted on a 3D printed base: the first one holds the watch while the second one fixes the phone using a magnet (Figure **3**). The two plastic adaptors are very rapidly interchangeable. Altogether, the Small version, involving a smartwatch, weighted 207g in total and the Large version, involving a smartphone, weighted 297g. We used TCP sockets over a local Wifi network to connect the watch to the main computer.

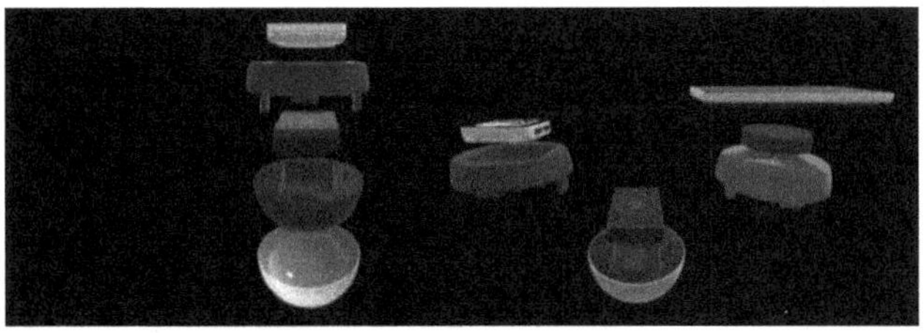

Figure 3. Arrangement of TDome elements for the Small version (left). Both TDome versions are rapidly interchangeable (right).

Physical manipulation detection

The spherical shell holds an x-IMU of x-io Technologies (48g, 57 × 38 × 21 mm) to detect the Roll and Rotation of the device in 3D. The IMU is composed of a triple-axis gyroscope, accelerometer and magnetometer. The refresh rate of the sensors goes up to 512Hz and we used Bluetooth to connect the IMU with the computer. The IMU offered an angular precision of 1°. We 3D printed a holder to fit the IMU in a horizontal position inside the TDome (Figure **3**).

To detect the displacement of the device, we used an infrared bezel (Zaagtech, 42") that generated TUIO events. We implemented a filtering process to discard touch events that were detected when fingers touched the surface around the device. Thresholds were also empirically defined to avoid the detection of unwanted Translations, Rolls or Rotations: user's physical manipulations must reach a minimum amplitude to be detected (5cm for Translation, 30° for Roll, 45° for Rotation). Lift-Up was detected as soon as TDome was no longer in contact with the table.

SUITABILITY OF TDOME FOR MDES

One of the key characteristics of Multi-Display Environments (MDEs) is their heterogeneous nature. For the majority, MDEs are composed of displays offering different properties (size, orientation, input capabilities), which have led to a set of major interaction requirements [9,32]: *input redirection* (i.e. redirect input channels to different displays), *output redirection* (i.e. move content between displays), *physical relationship* (i.e. possess high-level information on the spatial layout of the displays), *reachability* (i.e. interact with a distant display) and *personal data management* (i.e. personal input and output interaction). TDome properties suit these interaction requirements.

Spatial sensing

TDome physical manipulations allow performing 3D pointing in the surrounding space. Combined with the on-board camera, it allows sensing the environment. This can be used to detect and locate nearby displays, creating a spatial layout of the MDE displays represented through a radar-view (*physical relationship*).

Input interaction

TDome allows up to 3 types of 2D pointing: by moving the device, by rolling it or by interacting with the touchscreen. These ranges of positioning facilitate *input redirection.* This also offers input that best suits a given display, such as a cursor for precise tasks, or touch input for coarser input.

Output interaction

The touchscreen display can be used as a visual buffer to move data among displays in MDEs (*output redirection*). It may also be useful to display a zoomed-in version of a selected area on a distant display (*reachability*). The built-in vibratory capabilities are an alternative to discretely provide the user with private information (*personal data management*).

Through the easy interchange of the Small and Large TDome versions, the user can adopt the most appropriate display for each task; e.g., to visualize large graphs, the user can choose the Large version, but to display the compact radar-view (i.e. a view of the MDE spatial layout), a smaller display is more appropriate (*output redirection*).

Mid-air interaction

Two of TDome's physical manipulations (Roll and Rotate) can be used in mid-air, thus facilitating physical displacements to interact with distant displays (*reachability*). It also offers more flexibility to the user to ensure the privacy for some of its tasks (*personal data management*).

Form factor

TDome's tilting capabilities facilitate orienting the device towards oneself for private input and output interaction (*personal data management*); and attaching their personal smartphone to TDome's base allows users to access their personal applications and data (*personal data management*).

TDOME MDE INTERACTION TECHNIQUES

We now introduce a set of proof-of-concept prototypes illustrating how the previous properties contribute to facilitate interaction in MDEs.

Display layout registration

To fulfil the physical relationship and arrangement requirement, we implemented a semi-automatic acquisition of the displays layout in the MDE. This technique allows detecting the displays and building a radar view interface of them, which can be later exploited to interact with the displays of the environment.

During the detection phase, TDome detects a QR code ascribed to each display (better recognition algorithms may not necessitate codes for detection as demonstrated by HuddleLamp [25]). The user orients TDome toward each display successively, so that the device's on-board camera detects the QR codes (Figure 4 – left). Once the QR code is recognized, the user taps the touchscreen to terminate the identification: the detected display is assigned a position in the environment thanks to the incorporated IMU.

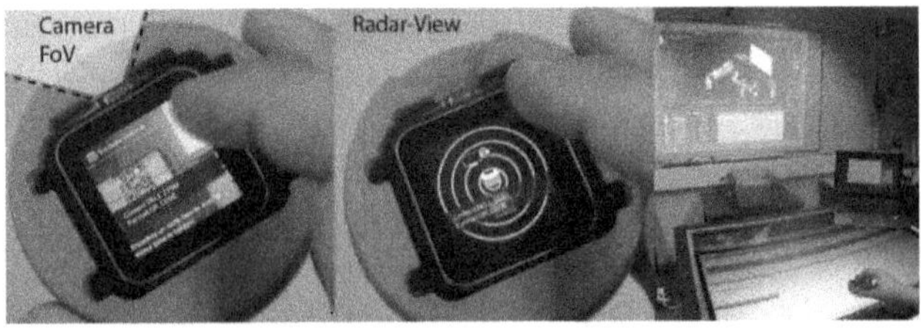

Figure 4: TDome's on-board camera detects displays (left) and creates a radar-view of the spatial layout (center). Then the user can select a display by Rolling + Tapping towards it (right).

The user progressively creates a radar view describing the relative position of all detected displays, with TDome in its center (Figure 4 – center). The user can manually adjust the distance of each display to TDome on the radar view. Once created, the radar view can be used with a Roll + Tap on TDome to select a specific display, by rolling TDome in the direction of the display and tapping on the touchscreen to validate (Figure 4 – right).

Input redirection

One recurrent need in MDEs is to manage input redirection. In addition to changing focus from one display to another, TDome offers an input interaction that matches the input possibility to the display it is connected to. TDome can be used as a touch input device through its embedded touchscreen, as a mouse with its translation capability and as a 3D Mouse with its rotation and tilting capabilities depending on the input capability of the display it is redirected to.

For instance, to interact with a map on a distant touchscreen, the user can perform a Roll + Drag on TDome to pan, and a Lift-Up + Pinch on TDome to zoom. Both touchscreen gestures (Drag and Pinch) are the same than what would be used on the distant touch display. While using only TDome's touchscreen gestures would be possible, using them in combination with the physical gestures (Roll or Translate) ensures a high recognition rate, prevents false positives, as demonstrated by our controlled study presented below and offers additional controls: the Roll angle may impact the panning speed.

Moving content between displays

We developed two interaction techniques to move content from one display to another. The Translation + Pinch/Spread technique combines a physical manipulation of TDome to select a display and a gesture on the touchscreen to grab or place some content on the selected display (Figure 5). In our implementation, Translation + Pinch grabs the application of the screen selected by the translation's direction, and displays it on the tabletop; while Translation + Spread sends the tabletop application to the screen situated in the translation's direction. Usually, Pinch and Spread are two well-established gestures for zooming in map or photo applications. Therefore, we plan to design appropriate feedback to avoid any confusion.

Figure 5. A Translation + Spread gesture sends the tabletop content (left) to a secondary display (right).

We implemented a second technique using the radar view on TDome to create a virtual information tunnel between two displays (Figure 6-left). The user creates the tunnel by sequentially selecting two displays on the radar view. Once the tunnel is defined, the user can move content along the tunnel with a Roll + Tap on TDome: rolling is performed in the spatial direction of the second display (i.e. a Roll to the right if the display is on the right of the first one); a Tap gesture finalizes the transfer.

Figure 6: Using the virtual tunnel technique to transfer information between displays.

Mid-air interaction

To support the reachability requirement, TDome provides support to interact with distant displays, i.e. beyond the user's reach. Given the size, shape and wireless design of TDome, the user can physically move to the distant display and perform mid-air interactions with TDome (Figure 7 - left).

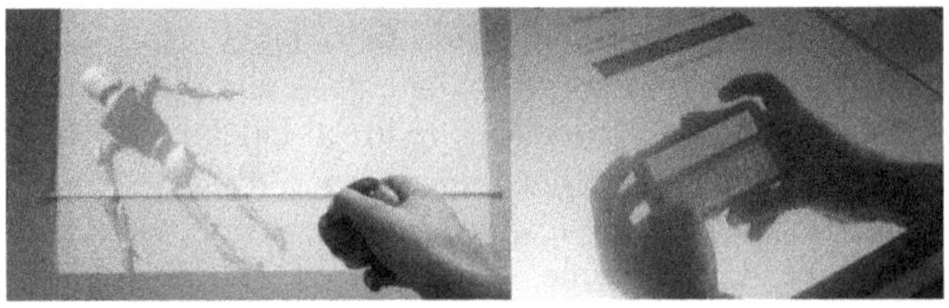

Figure 7: Illustrating mid-air interaction with TDome (left) and privacy conservation when typing a password (right).

Password input

To preserve confidential information, the user can roll the device towards himself or lift the device to visualize and input content privately. For instance, TDome's large touchscreen can be used as a private virtual keyboard to input a password on a surrounding display (Figure 7 – right). TDome can also be used to visualize a private detailed view of a public context.

Other techniques

Beyond effectively supporting essential interactions in MDE, TDome can be used for other common tasks such as controlling a pie menu on a distant display, supporting multi-clipboard copy and paste, and pointing on distant displays. We implemented all these interaction techniques using different combinations of physical manipulations and touch gestures.

Resulting challenges for TDome usage

These techniques illustrate how TDome contributes to the execution of relevant interactive situations in MDEs and how it is useful and sufficient to address major MDE interactions. Using a single device contributes to a more fluid interaction in MDEs by maintaining the user in the flow of her activity [4].

Informal tests also provided some early feedback on the importance of precision and on the required number of available gestures: a precise control of the device is important to perform spatial interactions, such as rolling to select a display; and the user requires a wide set of gestures to cover the multiple set of controls and interactions across displays. Therefore, conferring the highest usability level to TDome is essential to ensure MDEs will take full advantage of the device properties.

For these reasons, we first focused on exploring the usability of the device itself. To this end we performed a user experiment dedicated to identifying the set of most precise and robust TDome gestures.

EXPLORATORY STUDY ON TDOME GESTURES

The goal of this exploratory study was to inform the implementation of input gestures combining physical manipulations with touch input, by studying only their comfort and collecting initial user feedback. Ultimately we wanted to discard gestures that would be deemed too uncomfortable. While literature on physiology could be anticipatory, it would not help in identifying all the appropriate combinations of wrist gestures and multi-touch finger input. For this reason, we did not want to discard any gesture immediately and ran this exploratory study to reduce the initial gesture design space.

Protocol

We carried this exploratory study with 4 participants (all right-handed) from the local university. We instructed participants to manipulate the TDome with their dominant hand. During the experiment they were confronted with the two different versions of TDome (Small and Large). In both settings, they tested three physical manipulations (Roll and Translate in 8 different directions, Rotate in two directions, Lift-Up) in combination with four touch gestures (Tap, Drag, Pinch, and Spread). Pinch and Spread gestures being more complex to perform, participants repeated these gestures twice: once with the dominant hand and once with the non-dominant hand (e.g. in a bi-manual setting).

Participants performed 2 TDome versions × 19 physical manipulations × 6 touch gestures = 228 combined gestures per participant. We asked participants to repeat each combined gesture 3 times, i.e. each participant performed 684 trials. We asked them to rate each gesture combination from 1 (comfortable) to 5 (uncomfortable) to help them verbalize their opinion and comment on their ratings. We report on their qualitative comments.

Results

Participants were very positive about performing the following gestures both with the Small and Large versions of TDome:

- Tap and Drag combined with any physical manipulation (Translation, Rotation, Roll or Lift-Up).
- Pinch and Spread in a bi-manual setting (one hand manipulates the rolling device while the other touches the display) when combined with a Translation, Rotation or Lift-Up.

However some other gestures seemed too uncomfortable to be performed:

- Performing Pinch and Spread with a single hand was always deemed very uncomfortable when combined with any physical gestures and for both TDome versions (Small and Large).
- Performing Pinch and Spread in a bi-manual setting in combination with a Roll gesture was perceived to be very uncomfortable.

We decided to remove these uncomfortable gestures (Pinch and Spread with a single hand or in combination with Roll) from our subsequent work.

CONTROLLED EXPERIMENT

The goal of this controlled experiment was to validate the feasibility of combined gestures, i.e. physical manipulation + touch input. We hypothesize that certain touch gestures could be difficult to perform on the Small version, on which certain combinations could lead to errors.

Combined Gestures

From the previous exploratory study, we decided to use two touch gestures with one hand: Tap and Drag. Gestures using two fingers, i.e. Spread and Pinch, were performed with two hands: one hand held the device while the other performed the touch gesture. These touch gestures were used in combination with a Translation, a Roll, a Rotation and a Lift-Up of TDome.

Task

Participants were required to perform each gesture, following a visual indication on a tabletop display. TDome was placed in an initial position at the center of the surface, indicated by a visual feedback. We let users hold the device as they pleased. We asked participants to perform the gestures as fast as possible with high accuracy. We provided continuous visual feedback indicating the state of the device (position, Roll and Rotation) as well as touch gestures on the display. We provided them with knowledge of result and in case of error we indicated which gesture (physical manipulation and/or touch gesture) had been erroneously performed. Each trial started when the user pressed a button on the tabletop, which displayed the instructions, and ended when a combined gesture had been recognised.

Participants

We recruited 12 participants (3 female), aged 27.5 years on average (SD=4.89) from the local university. 11 of them were right-handed and 3 of them took part in the exploratory study.

Apparatus

We used the TDome implementation described earlier. The device was used on a tabletop display (96×72cm) of 102 cm height thus requiring the user to stand during the experiment. We used the display in an area limited to the size of the infrared bezel (42 inches, 1920×1080px).

Design and protocol

The experiment followed a 2x4x4 within-subjects design, with Display (Small, Large), Physical manipulation (Translate, Roll, Rotate and Lift-Up) and Touch gesture (Tap, Drag, Pinch and Spread) as factors. We did not test the condition combining Roll with Pinch/Spread, as this combination appeared to be highly uncomfortable in our pre-study. We also decided to study one random translation direction to limit the experiment length: previous studies on RPM [36] showed that all translation directions were as easy to perform. For the other physical manipulations, participants performed eight Roll directions and two Rotations (left/right).

Our pre-study also showed that Pinch and Spread gestures seemed more difficult than Tap and Drag. Therefore, we paired Tap with Pinch, and Drag with Spread to balance the different blocks length and difficulty. Trials were grouped in four blocks: one block corresponded to one Display and two touch gestures (Tap/Pinch or Drag/Spread).

The four blocks were counterbalanced across participants using a 4x4 Latin Square. For each block, we ordered touch by difficulty: first Tap or Drag, then Pinch or Spread. For each set of trials corresponding to one touch gesture, the physical manipulations were ordered in a predefined way (Lift-Up, Translation, Roll and Rotation) because a random sorting would have made the instructions difficult to follow. Each combined gesture was repeated three times. Completing the four blocks took approximately 25 minutes.

The study started with a training set made of the same four blocks than in the experiment. The training consisted of 94 trials and took approximately 20 minutes. After the training, each participant performed 192 trials:

- 144 trials for the Tap and Drag: 2 Displays x 12 Physical Manipulations (1 Translation + 8 Rolls + 2 Rotations + 1 Lift-Up) × 2 Touch gestures × 3 repetitions.
- 48 trials for the Pinch and Spread: 2 Displays x 4 Physical Manipulations (1 Translation + 2 Rotations + 1 Lift-Up) × 2 Touch gestures × 3 repetitions.

We collected 192 × 12 participants = 2304 trials in total, which took approximately 45 minutes for each participant.

Collected Data

We logged all gestures from start to finish. We calculated success rates, completion time from instruction onset to validation, unintended touch gestures on the Display and amplitude of the physical manipulations. We classified errors in three categories according to the gesture that had been erroneously performed: physical, touch or both. Finally, we asked participants to rate each condition on a 1-5 Likert scale on perceived difficulty.

RESULTS

A Shapiro-Wilk test established that the data was not normal and we could not normalize it. Therefore we used a Friedman test (we report χ_2 and p) to compare more than 2 conditions, and Wilcoxon tests otherwise (we report p value). Where appropriate, we used a Bonferroni correction. We first discuss the success rate for the Small and Large versions separately as a Wilcoxon test showed a significant effect of Display on success rate ($p<.001$).

Success rate: Large version

When using the Large version, we found no significant effect of Touch gestures (Friedman: $\chi_2=3.87$, $p=0.2$) or Physical manipulations (Friedman: $\chi_2=4.1$, $p=0.2$) on success rate. Overall, success rate with the Large version was 94.44%. Errors were distributed among Physical Manipulations (2.52%) and Touch gestures (2.86%).

A Friedman test reveals a significant effect of Touch gesture on success rate when performing a Rotation ($\chi_2=13.32$, $p=.003$): a Wilcoxon test reveals a significant difference between Tap and Drag (81.94% vs. 98.61%; $p=.022$) and between Tap and Pinch (81.94% vs. 97.22%; $p=.045$).

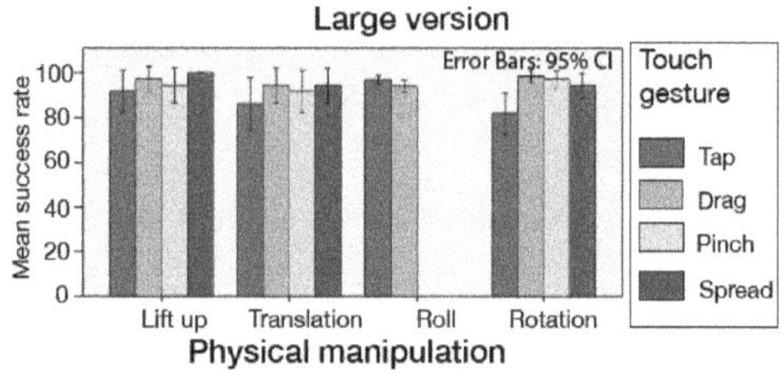

Figure 8. Mean success rate for each combination of Physical manipulation and Touch gesture when using the Large version.

We observed that when instructing participants to perform a Rotation + Tap combined gesture, 91% of the erroneously detected touch gestures are Drag gestures. Performing a Rotation induces a wrist distortion that may affect the user's ability to precisely tap the display without swiping the finger: this may explain why a Drag is easier to perform than a Tap. Spread and Pinch are not affected by the wrist rotation since they are performed in a bi-manual setting (Figure 8).

Success rate: Small version

When using the Small version, a Friedman test revealed a significant effect of Physical Manipulation (χ_2=17.46, p<.001) and Touch gestures (χ_2=33.56, p<.001) on success rate. We analyse the success rates for each combined gesture, i.e. the combined Physical manipulation and Touch gesture.

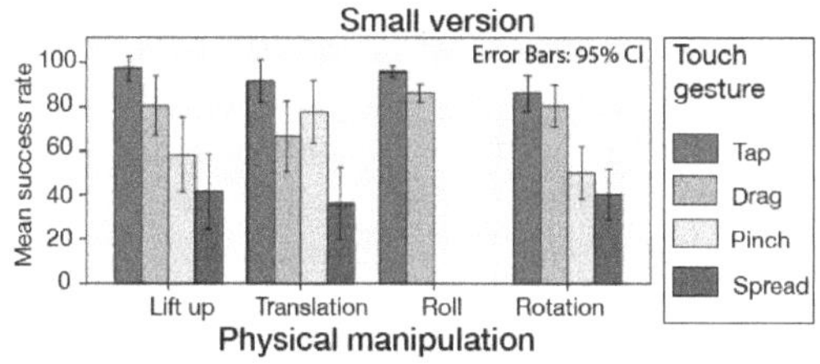

Figure 9. Mean success rate for each combination of Physical manipulation and Touch gesture when using the Small version.

A Friedman test reveals a significant effect of Touch gestures on success rate when performing a Lift-Up (χ_2=16, p=.001), a Translation (χ_2=15.75, p=.001), a Roll (χ_2=6.4, p=.01) or a Rotation (χ_2=21.6, p<.001):

- Lift-Up: a Wilcoxon test reveals a significant difference between Tap and Spread (92.22% vs. 41.67%; p=.001) and Tap and Pinch (92.22% vs. 58.33; p=.04). Success rate with Drag is 80.56%.
- Translation: a Wilcoxon test reveals a significant difference between Tap and Spread (91.67% vs. 36.11%; p=.001) and between Pinch and Spread (77.78% vs. 36.11%; p=.02). Success rate with Drag is 66.67%.
- Roll: a Wilcoxon test reveals a significant difference between Tap and Drag (95.83% vs. 86.11%; p=.04).
- Rotation: a Wilcoxon test reveals a significant difference between Tap (86.11%) / Drag (80.56%) and Spread (40.28%) / Pinch (50.0%; p<.02).

Completion time

A Wilcoxon test shows no difference between the Small and the Large versions (p=.08). Overall, it took participants 2.5 seconds to perform a combined gesture. While we found some differences across gesture combinations, all of them are compatible with the micro-interactions concept [1], i.e. fast interactions that take less than 4s completion: all times ranged between 2.1s and 2.7s.

Unintentional touches

We recorded unintended touches on the Small and Large versions. Overall, results were similar for both versions: we detected unintentional touches in 2% of the trials. These touches did not necessarily raise errors. The sequential use of a touch interaction after a physical gesture prevents from launching a command unintentionally.

Subjective feedback

When considering the physical manipulations, results show that with the Small version, more than 50% of the participants found easy or very easy (4 or 5 on Likert scale) to perform a combined gesture involving a Roll, Translation or Lift-Up. In the case of the Large version, more than 75% of participants rated these gestures as easy or very easy.

When considering the touch gestures, we observed that with the Small version more than 50% of participants found difficult or very difficult (1 or 2 on Likert scale) to perform a combined gesture involving a Spread or Pinch. With the Large version, 60% or more of the participants found easy or very easy to perform combined gestures involving any kind of touch gesture.

Summary

Results reveal differences between the Small and Large versions (Figure 10). With the Small version, the experiment reveals that 17 combined gestures can be comfortably and efficiently performed: those based on the combination of a Roll (8 directions), a Translation (8 directions) or a Lift-Up with a Tap gesture (with a success rate of 95.83%, 91.67% and 92.22% respectively).

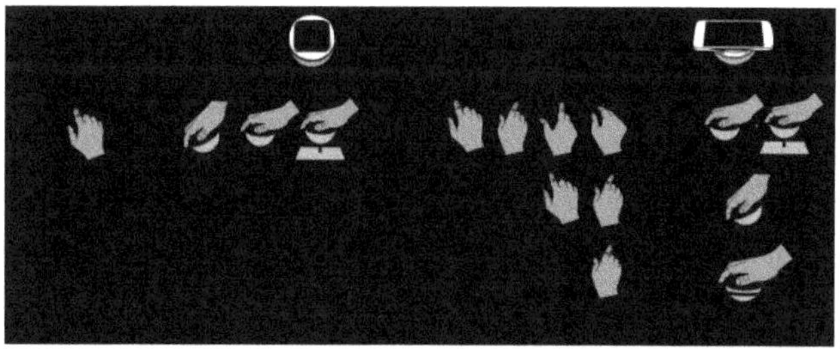

Figure 10. Summary of the 17 (Small) + 54 (Large) combined gestures which offer a good usability and performance.

With the Large version, the experiment reveals that 54 combined gestures can be comfortably and efficiently performed: 16 results from the combination of a Roll (95.49% success rate) with Tap or Drag gesture, 36 result from the combination of a Translation (91.67% success rate), or Lift-Up (95.83% success rate) with one of the four touch gestures (Tap, Drag, Pinch, Spread) and 2 results from the combination of a Rotation with a Drag (98.61% success rate).

MAPPING TDOME GESTURES TO MDE TASKS

We elicited user input through a user study to explore how the selected set of gestures from our previous experiment can be mapped to MDE interactive tasks.

Overview and rationale

We asked users to choose, for each TDome task, one gesture from the set of gestures selected in the controlled experiment.

MDE tasks considered

From our scenarios, we considered the following 7 tasks: pointing on a distant display; zooming on a distant display; displacing a window from one display to another (horizontal tunnel, vertical tunnel); sending a window from Tabletop/TDome (user position) to a distant display and vice-versa; selecting an icon on the radar view; panning and zooming a focused view of a distant context; and typing on a private keyboard.

Participants

12 (1 female) students and researchers from the local university volunteered for this study. They were aged 31.9 years on average (SD=9). Five of them took part in the previous studies.

Procedure

Participants were given the two TDome versions (Small and Large) and were situated in an MDE environment comprised of a tabletop, 4 displays and 1 video-projection. We familiarized our participants with TDome capabilities by showing them a video illustrating the combined gestures (without showing any interactive task). For each combined gesture, we asked participants to perform it themselves with both versions of TDome. Then, we asked participants to select and justify, for each task and each TDome version, which gesture they preferred. The session took about 15 minutes.

Collected data

Every user generated one sheet with a summary of the gestures chosen for each task and TDome version. We recorded users' verbal comments.

Results

Amongst all available combined gestures, only one was never used in our study (Lift-Up + Drag). Overall, participants took advantage of the gestures diversity to match the different tasks. The agreement scores [36] of the combined gestures (Physical manipulation + touch gestures) range between 0.3 and 0.6. These scores are in line with previous studies [36]. For the sake of clarity, we detail separately for each task the choice of physical manipulations and touch input.

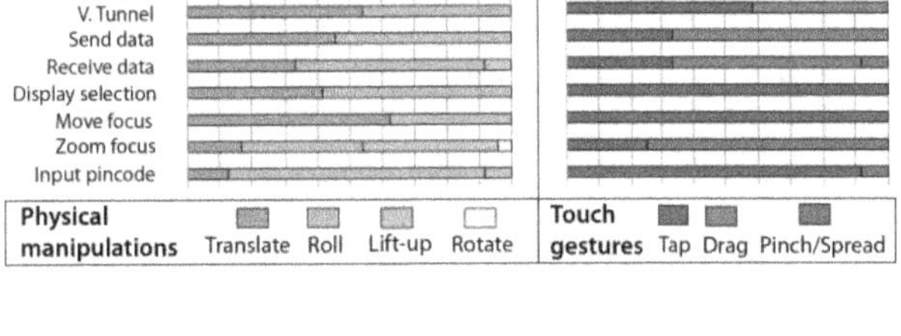

Figure 11. Percentage of users that chose each physical gesture on both versions of TDome (left) and each touch gesture on the Large version (right) for MDE tasks.

Physical manipulations

Our results were similar for the Small and Large versions concerning which physical gesture to use. Thus we report both results together (i.e. 24 gestures per task).

Two physical gestures were used more often: Translate and Roll (Figure 11-left). For some tasks, one was preferred over the other: *Translation* for panning (17/24), or for moving a focus (15/24); *Roll* for private pincode input (19/24). For other tasks, such as redirecting data using the tunnel, output redirection or display selection, there was no clear preference for one of these two gestures.

The Lift-Up gesture was used for zooming 13 times (i.e. lifting up the device activates zoom mode). Rotation was used only one time for each of our zooming tasks.

Touch gestures

While only the Tap gesture is feasible on the Small version, users selected different gestures on the Large version according to the task (Figure 11-right). For instance, Pinch and Spread were preferred for zooming (10/12), and Drag was preferred for sending content from the tabletop to other displays (8/12). Taping was the preferred gesture for map panning (12/12), display selection (12/12) or pincode input (11/12).

DISCUSSION AND PERSPECTIVES

TDome benefits

We presented two versions of TDome: a Small version with an integrated touchscreen and a Large version based on attaching a smartphone. TDome's unique features offer several advantages to interact with MDEs:

- TDome supports performing multiple combined gestures involving a physical manipulation of the device (Translation, Roll, Rotation or Lift-Up) followed by a touch gesture on the touchscreen (Tap, Drag, Pinch or Spread). Such a combination prevents from unintended activations due to parasite touches on the touchscreen;
- The combined gestures from our final set represent good candidates to support rapid access to interactive commands;
- The two TDome versions are easily interchangeable and offer complementary functionalities: the Small version is useful to rapidly launch shortcuts, while the Large version offers a larger display area and supports multi-touch gestures (Pinch and Spread);
- Rolling TDome can be used to interact with multi-dimensional data through continuous physical gestures, as demonstrated earlier [23];
- The embedded display can be used as a personal display area to augment output visualisation, such as in overview + detail techniques [29];

- The embedded display can also be used to show feedback of the TDome interactions, such as displaying a copied object for the copy/paste technique.

Guidelines for mapping TDome gestures to MDE tasks

We propose a set of guidelines to map TDome gestures to MDE tasks based on our mapping study as well as on our experience developing TDome interaction techniques:

- TDome offers a diversity and large number of possible gestures of which users can take advantage as illustrated in our mapping study. Some of these gestures have natural mappings with MDE tasks, such as Rolling towards oneself to display private information, Pinch and Spread for zooming or dragging for sending data to another display. Appropriately combined with a physical manipulation or a touch gesture, these should become the "default" combined gestures with TDome on MDEs.
- While some mappings are obvious and have a large consensus, others are sometimes split between two types of gestures (usually Roll or Translation): this suggests that using TDome in an MDE could benefit from a device personalization step wherein the user defines his preferred mapping, especially for output redirection.
- Interacting in an MDE involves system tasks (i.e. tasks related to the environment, such as display selection) and application tasks. Since these tasks could be assigned to the same TDome gestures, there is a need for a mode switching gesture. The Lift-Up manipulation combined with touch input, is a good candidate as it was considered for switching between pan and zoom tasks in our mapping study

Memorability of a large number of gestures

TDome offers a large set of usable combined gestures. This diversity of available controls is particularly relevant to tackle tasks in MDEs. However, increasing the amount of controls might make them hard to memorize. The physical nature of these combined gestures can help cluster them according to the physical manipulation, as shown in our mapping study. Further experiments are required to identify how such clustering can improve gestures or command memorization.

Collaboration

MDEs are naturally designed to support collaboration. We can envision multiple TDome like devices, each controlled by the MDE's users. However, in such cases input and output redirection mechanisms would need to be effectively controlled. Control mechanisms have been proposed by others [14] to handle synchronization, locking and input conflicts, and future iterations of TDome will adapt or build on such proposals.

Future work

In this paper we focused on the suitability of TDome capabilities for MDE tasks and the feasibility of its combined gestures. TDome interaction techniques still need to be fine tuned and future work should compare their performance with a baseline for each MDE task. Theoretically, since TDome integrates the same capabilities as existing MDE devices, we hypothesise that it can perform similarly for each individual MDE task. For instance, TDome can perform translations like a mouse, and has the same touch and mid-air capabilities as a smartphone. Moreover, since TDome is a unique device that supports a range of core MDE tasks, it should improve the overall performance by reducing homing transition times and promoting the interaction flow. Therefore, beyond individual controlled comparisons, it would be interesting to carry a longitudinal study. We leave these studies for future work.

Beyond these aspects, we plan to focus on user expertise of TDome techniques: most menu or command techniques consider novice and expert modes as well as the transition from novice to expert [15]. In our work we focused on how the combined gestures are performed. It will be interesting to design techniques that efficiently support both novice and expert users and the transition from one group to the other, as done with the Marking Menus [37].

We also plan to investigate the extension of our physical manipulation gestures by adding thresholds. For instance, each Roll gesture could launch two different commands according to the Roll amplitude (under or over 42° according to our study results). Technical alternatives also need to be investigated to replace the infrared bezel used to detect the TDome translations. We are currently exploring the application of conductive paint on the external surface of TDome, which will allow using the device on any capacitive surface.

CONCLUSION

We presented TDome, a device designed for interactions in MDEs. We designed two TDome prototypes: a Small version with an integrated touchscreen and a Large version based on attaching a smartphone. We explored combined gestures involving a physical manipulation (Translation, Roll, Rotation or Lift-Up) followed by a touch gesture (Tap, Drag, Pinch or Spread) through a 3-steps process. First, an exploratory study focusing on comfort established that 60 combined gestures could be comfortably performed. Second, a controlled experiment evaluated the user's performance as well as the subjective perceived difficulty. Results revealed that the number of gestures that can be precisely and easily performed is 17 with the Small version, and 54 with the Large version. Finally, a user survey explored the mappings between these gestures and MDE tasks. Results show that some combined gestures are more prone to be used in specific tasks than other. In general, we find participants are able to match TDome features to MDE tasks

ACKNOWLEDGEMENTS

This work is funded by the neOCampus project of the University Paul Sabatier (Toulouse, France) and part of the AP2 project (research grant AP2 ANR-15-CE23-0001).

REFERENCES

1. Daniel L. Ashbrook. 2010. *Enabling Mobile Microinteractions*. Ph.D. Dissertation. Georgia Institute of Technology, Atlanta, GA, USA. Advisor(s) Thad E. Starner. AAI3414437
2. Ravin Balakrishnan, Thomas Baudel, Gordon Kurtenbach, and George Fitzmaurice. 1997. The Rockin'Mouse: integral 3D manipulation on a plane. In *Proceedings of the ACM SIGCHI Conference on Human factors in computing systems* (CHI '97). ACM, New York, NY, USA, 311-318. DOI=http://dx.doi.org/10.1145/258549.258778
3. Dominikus Baur, Sebastian Boring, and Steven Feiner. 2012. Virtual projection: exploring optical projection as a metaphor for multi-device interaction. In *Proceedings of the SIGCHI Conference on Human Factors in Computing Systems* (CHI '12). ACM, New York, NY, USA, 1693-1702. DOI=http://dx.doi.org/10.1145/2207676.2208297
4. Benjamin B. Bederson. 2004. Interfaces for staying in the flow. *Ubiquity* 2004, September (September 2004), 1-1. DOI=http://dx.doi.org/10.1145/1074068.1074069
5. Hrvoje Benko and Steven Feiner. 2005. Multi-monitor mouse. In *CHI '05 Extended Abstracts on Human Factors in Computing Systems* (CHI EA '05). ACM, New York, NY, USA, 1208-1211. DOI=http://dx.doi.org/10.1145/1056808.1056878
6. Hrvoje Benko, Shahram Izadi, Andrew D. Wilson, Xiang Cao, Dan Rosenfeld, and Ken Hinckley. 2010. Design and evaluation of interaction models for multi-touch mice. In *Proceedings of Graphics Interface 2010* (GI '10). Canadian Information Processing Society, Toronto, Ont., Canada, Canada, 253-260.
7. Louis-Pierre Bergé, Marcos Serrano, Gary Perelman, and Emmanuel Dubois. 2014. Exploring smartphone-based interaction with overview+detail interfaces on 3D public displays. In *Proceedings of the 16th international conference on Human-computer interaction with mobile devices & services* (MobileHCI '14). ACM, New York, NY, USA, 125-134. DOI: http://dx.doi.org/10.1145/2628363.2628374
8. Louis-Pierre Bergé, Emmanuel Dubois, and Mathieu Raynal. 2015. Design and Evaluation of an "Around the SmartPhone" Technique for 3D Manipulations on Distant Display. In *Proceedings of the 3rd ACM Symposium on Spatial User Interaction* (SUI '15). ACM, New York, NY, USA, 69-78. DOI=http://dx.doi.org/10.1145/2788940.2788941
9. Boring, S. 2007. Interacting in Multi-Display Environments. In DC Ubicomp'07. ACM.
10. Sebastian Boring, Marko Jurmu, and Andreas Butz. 2009. Scroll, tilt or move it: using mobile phones to continuously control pointers on large public displays. In *Proceedings of the 21st Annual Conference of the Australian Computer-Human Interaction Special Interest Group: Design: Open 24/7* (OZCHI '09). ACM, New York, NY, USA, 161-168. DOI=http://dx.doi.org/10.1145/1738826.1738853
11. Sebastian Boring, Dominikus Baur, Andreas Butz, Sean Gustafson, and Patrick Baudisch. 2010. Touch projector: mobile interaction through video. In *Proceedings of the SIGCHI Conference on Human Factors in Computing Systems* (CHI '10). ACM, New York, NY, USA, 2287-2296. DOI=http://dx.doi.org/10.1145/1753326.1753671
12. Christophe Bortolaso, Matthew Oskamp, T.C. Nicholas Graham, and Doug Brown. 2013. OrMiS: a tabletop interface for simulation-based training. In *Proceedings of the 2013 ACM international conference on Interactive tabletops and surfaces* (ITS '13). ACM, New York, NY, USA, 145-154. DOI=http://dx.doi.org/10.1145/2512349.2512792
13. Tsung-Hsiang Chang and Yang Li. 2011. Deep shot: a framework for migrating tasks across devices using mobile phone cameras. In *Proceedings of the SIGCHI Conference on Human Factors in Computing Systems* (CHI '11). ACM, New York, NY, USA, 2163-2172. DOI=http://dx.doi.org/10.1145/1978942.1979257
14. Olivier Chapuis, Anastasia Bezerianos, and Stelios Frantzeskakis. 2014. Smarties: an input system for wall display development. In *Proceedings of the SIGCHI Conference on Human Factors in Computing Systems* (CHI '14). ACM, New York, NY, USA, 2763-2772. DOI=http://dx.doi.org/10.1145/2556288.2556956
15. Andy Cockburn, Carl Gutwin, Joey Scarr, and Sylvain Malacria. 2014. Supporting Novice to Expert Transitions in User Interfaces. *ACM Comput. Surv.* 47, 2, Article 31 (November 2014), 36 pages. DOI: http://dx.doi.org/10.1145/2659796
16. Juan David Hincapié-Ramos, Xiang Guo, Paymahn Moghadasian, and Pourang Irani. 2014. Consumed endurance: a metric to quantify arm fatigue of mid-air interactions. In *Proceedings of the SIGCHI Conference on Human Factors in Computing Systems* (CHI '14). ACM, New York, NY, USA, 1063-1072. DOI: http://dx.doi.org/10.1145/2556288.2557130
17. Ken Hinckley, Mike Sinclair, Erik Hanson, Richard Szeliski, and Matt Conway. 1999. The VideoMouse: a camera-based multi-degree-of-freedom input device. In *Proceedings of the 12th annual ACM symposium on User interface software and technology* (UIST '99). ACM, New York, NY, USA, 103-112. DOI=http://dx.doi.org/10.1145/320719.322591

18. Steven Houben and Nicolai Marquardt. 2015. WatchConnect: A Toolkit for Prototyping Smartwatch-Centric Cross-Device Applications. In *Proceedings of the 33rd Annual ACM Conference on Human Factors in Computing Systems* (CHI '15). ACM, New York, NY, USA, 1247-1256. DOI: http://dx.doi.org/10.1145/2702123.2702215
19. Chang-Min Kim and Tek-Jin Nam. 2015. G-raff: An Elevating Tangible Block for Spatial Tabletop Interaction. In *Proceedings of the 33rd Annual ACM Conference on Human Factors in Computing Systems* (CHI '15). ACM, New York, NY, USA, 4161-4164. DOI: http://dx.doi.org/10.1145/2702123.2702444
20. Miguel A. Nacenta, Dzmitry Aliakseyeu, Sriram Subramanian, and Carl Gutwin. 2005. A comparison of techniques for multi-display reaching. In *Proceedings of the SIGCHI Conference on Human Factors in Computing Systems* (CHI '05). ACM, New York, NY, USA, 371-380. DOI=http://dx.doi.org/10.1145/1054972.1055024
21. Mathieu Nancel, Julie Wagner, Emmanuel Pietriga, Olivier Chapuis, and Wendy Mackay. 2011. Mid-air pan-and-zoom on wall-sized displays. In *Proceedings of the SIGCHI Conference on Human Factors in Computing Systems* (CHI '11). ACM, New York, NY, USA, 177-186. DOI=http://dx.doi.org/10.1145/1978942.1978969
22. Mathieu Nancel, Olivier Chapuis, Emmanuel Pietriga, Xing-Dong Yang, Pourang P. Irani, and Michel Beaudouin-Lafon. 2013. High-precision pointing on large wall displays using small handheld devices. In *Proceedings of the SIGCHI Conference on Human Factors in Computing Systems* (CHI '13). ACM, New York, NY, USA, 831-840. DOI: http://dx.doi.org/10.1145/2470654.2470773
23. Gary Perelman, Marcos Serrano, Mathieu Raynal, Celia Picard, Mustapha Derras, and Emmanuel Dubois. 2015. The Roly-Poly Mouse: Designing a Rolling Input Device Unifying 2D and 3D Interaction. In *Proceedings of the 33rd Annual ACM Conference on Human Factors in Computing Systems* (CHI '15). ACM, New York, NY, USA, 327-336. DOI: http://dx.doi.org/10.1145/2702123.2702244
24. Gary Perelman, Marcos Serrano, Mathieu Raynal, Celia Picard, Mustapha Derras, and Emmanuel Dubois. 2016. DECO: A Design Space for Device Composition. In *Proceedings of the 2016 ACM Conference on Designing Interactive Systems* (DIS '16). ACM, New York, NY, USA, 435-446. DOI: http://dx.doi.org/10.1145/2901790.2901893
25. Roman Rädle, Hans-Christian Jetter, Nicolai Marquardt, Harald Reiterer, and Yvonne Rogers. 2014. HuddleLamp: Spatially-Aware Mobile Displays for Ad-hoc Around-the-Table Collaboration. In *Proceedings of the Ninth ACM International Conference on Interactive Tabletops and Surfaces* (ITS '14). ACM, New York, NY, USA, 45-54. DOI=http://dx.doi.org/10.1145/2669485.2669500
26. Ramesh Raskar, Greg Welch, Matt Cutts, Adam Lake, Lev Stesin, and Henry Fuchs. 1998. The office of the future: a unified approach to image-based modeling and spatially immersive displays. In *Proceedings of the 25th annual conference on Computer graphics and interactive techniques* (SIGGRAPH '98). ACM, New York, NY, USA, 179-188. DOI: http://dx.doi.org/10.1145/280814.280861
27. Jun Rekimoto. 1997. Pick-and-drop: a direct manipulation technique for multiple computer environments. In *Proceedings of the 10th annual ACM symposium on User interface software and technology* (UIST '97). ACM, New York, NY, USA, 31-39. DOI=http://dx.doi.org/10.1145/263407.263505
28. Jun Rekimoto and Masanori Saitoh. 1999. Augmented surfaces: a spatially continuous work space for hybrid computing environments. In *Proceedings of the SIGCHI conference on Human Factors in Computing Systems* (CHI '99). ACM, New York, NY, USA, 378-385. DOI=http://dx.doi.org/10.1145/302979.303113
29. Houssem Saidi, Marcos Serrano, and Emmanuel Dubois. 2016. Investigating the effects of splitting detailed views in Overview+Detail interfaces. In *Proceedings of the 18th International Conference on Human-Computer Interaction with Mobile Devices and Services* (MobileHCI '16). ACM, New York, NY, USA, 180-184. DOI: http://dx.doi.org/10.1145/2935334.2935341
30. Dominik Schmidt, Corina Sas, and Hans Gellersen. 2013. Personal clipboards for individual copy-and-paste on shared multi-user surfaces. In *Proceedings of the SIGCHI Conference on Human Factors in Computing Systems* (CHI '13). ACM, New York, NY, USA, 3335-3344. DOI: http://dx.doi.org/10.1145/2470654.2466457
31. Julian Seifert, Sebastian Boring, Christian Winkler, Florian Schaub, Fabian Schwab, Steffen Herrdum, Fabian Maier, Daniel Mayer, and Enrico Rukzio. 2014. Hover Pad: interacting with autonomous and self-actuated displays in space. In *Proceedings of the 27th annual ACM symposium on User interface software and technology* (UIST '14). ACM, New York, NY, USA, 139-147. DOI=http://dx.doi.org/10.1145/2642918.2647385
32. Marcos Serrano, Barrett Ens, Xing-Dong Yang, and Pourang Irani. 2015. Gluey: Developing a Head-Worn Display Interface to Unify the Interaction Experience in Distributed Display Environments. In *Proceedings of the 17th International Conference on Human-Computer Interaction with Mobile Devices and*

Services (MobileHCI '15). ACM, New York, NY, USA, 161-171. DOI=http://dx.doi.org/10.1145/2785830.2785838

33. Nicole Sultanum, Sowmya Somanath, Ehud Sharlin, and Mario Costa Sousa. 2011. *"Point it, split it, peel it, view it"*: techniques for interactive reservoir visualization on tabletops. In *Proceedings of the ACM International Conference on Interactive Tabletops and Surfaces* (ITS '11). ACM, New York, NY, USA, 192-201. DOI=http://dx.doi.org/10.1145/2076354.2076390
34. Manuela Waldner, Ernst Kruijff, and Dieter Schmalstieg. 2010. Bridging gaps with pointer warping in multi-display environments. In *Proceedings of the 6th Nordic Conference on Human-Computer Interaction: Extending Boundaries* (NordiCHI '10). ACM, New York, NY, USA, 813-816. DOI=10.1145/1868914.1869036 http://doi.acm.org/10.1145/1868914.1869036
35. Jacob O. Wobbrock, Meredith Ringel Morris, and Andrew D. Wilson. 2009. User-defined gestures for surface computing. In *Proceedings of the SIGCHI Conference on Human Factors in Computing Systems* (CHI '09). ACM, New York, NY, USA, 1083-1092. DOI=http://dx.doi.org/10.1145/1518701.1518866
36. Xing-Dong Yang, Edward Mak, David McCallum, Pourang Irani, Xiang Cao, and Shahram Izadi. 2010. LensMouse: augmenting the mouse with an interactive touch display. In *Proceedings of the SIGCHI Conference on Human Factors in Computing Systems* (CHI '10). ACM, New York, NY, USA, 2431-2440. DOI=http://dx.doi.org/10.1145/1753326.1753695
37. Shengdong Zhao and Ravin Balakrishnan. 2004. Simple vs. compound mark hierarchical marking menus. In *Proceedings of the 17th annual ACM symposium on User interface software and technology* (UIST '04). ACM, New York, NY, USA, 33-42. DOI=http://dx.doi.org/10.1145/1029632.1029639

A Field Experiment of Spatially-Stable Overviews for Document Navigation

Carl Gutwin[1], Andy Cockburn[2], and Nickolas Gough[1]

[1]Department of Computer Science
University of Saskatchewan
Saskatoon, Canada
gutwin@cs.usask.ca

[2]Computer Science and Software Engineering
University of Canterbury
Christchurch, New Zealand
andy@cosc.canterbury.ac.nz

ABSTRACT

Finding (and re-finding) locations in text documents is a common activity for most computer users – but tools for document navigation are still limited in many ways. Previous research has shown that a spatially-stable overview of the entire document can be substantially faster than any other navigation technique – particularly when revisiting previous locations. However, the overview technique has only been tested in a limited laboratory study, so little is known about whether it works in more realistic contexts. To answer this question, we developed a PDF viewer that incorporates several document-navigation techniques, and carried out two studies. First, we ran a field experiment in which users carried out search tasks using an overview and other techniques – on their own computers in a non-laboratory environment. Second, we ran a smaller field study in which people used our viewer (with choice of navigation techniques) for their own PDF tasks. In the field experiment, the overview was significantly and substantially faster than other techniques, and in the field study, the technique was frequently used for a wide variety of documents. Our work provides confirmation of the value of spatially stable overviews as a basis for document navigation.

Author Keywords

Document navigation; space-filling thumbnails; scrolling.

ACM Classification Keywords

H.5.m. Information interfaces and presentation (e.g., HCI).

INTRODUCTION

Finding and re-finding locations in text documents is a common activity for most computer users. There are many ways for people to navigate in documents – such as scroll bars, scroll wheels, touch-based flick scrolling, rate-based drag scrolling, page up/down keys, arrow keys, thumbnail views, outline views, "go to page number" controls, and

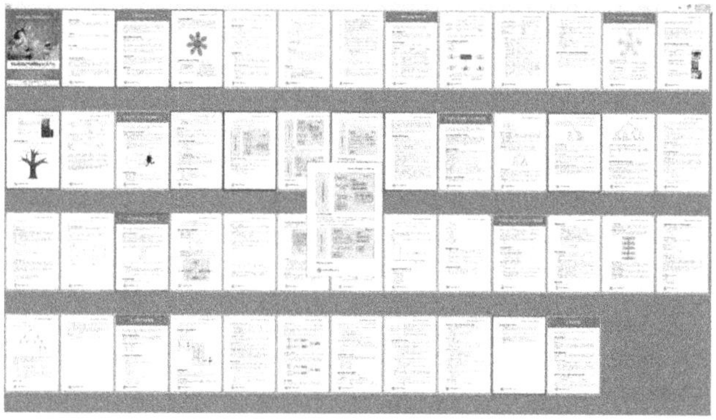

Figure 1. A document overview, showing all document pages at once: the current page is outlined blue, recently visited pages red. Hovering on a thumbnail magnifies the page.

"Find" dialogs. Despite this range of techniques, the tools provided in most document viewers have two limitations.

First, it can be difficult to do *visual search for a target page*. In many situations, users remember visual features of a page, rather than its page number or text heading. For example, people may remember a picture on the page (e.g., "the page with the picture of an octopus") or the overall layout (e.g., "the page where the bottom half was empty"). Pages have distinctive "page shapes," and people have considerable perceptual expertise in visual pattern-matching – but current systems do not provide a good way for users to conduct efficient visual search. While some viewers provide a sidebar column of thumbnails that shows 5-10 pages at a time, considerable scrolling is still required.

Second, it can be difficult to *revisit a page*. Going back to previously-visited locations is a common activity (often accounting for a large percentage of page visits [2, 3]). In these situations, users often think of the page in terms of their visitation history (e.g., "the page I was just at"). Current document viewers, however, do not record interaction history, so there are no tools to help users revisit recent (or frequent) pages. Although research on interaction history is now more than 25 years old (e.g., [16]), and although it has been implemented in research prototypes [4], real-world viewers do not make use of this valuable information.

Previous research suggests that thumbnail overview interfaces can address these problems. These interfaces provide two views of a document – an ordinary page view,

CHI 2017, May 06 - 11, 2017, Denver, CO, USA

ACM 978-1-4503-4655-9/17/05…$15.00
DOI: http://dx.doi.org/10.1145/3025453.3025905

and a spatially-stable full-screen overview of the entire document (e.g., Figure 1). The user brings up the overview with a control action (e.g., a right-click); to go back to the page view, the user clicks on any of the thumbnails in the overview (and that is the page shown in the page view).

Overviews have several valuable properties for document navigation. An overview treats a document as a 2D map, whereas scrolling is based on the metaphor of a long 1D piece of paper. The overview therefore provides an *absolute* representation of the document, rather than a relative one. The two key advantages of absolute representations are that they are inherently stable (which facilitates formation of spatial memories), and that they permit direct access to document regions using predictable methods (e.g., clicking on a page thumbnail that lies at a consistent location). Relative document navigation, in contrast, is inherently *un*stable, impeding formation of a spatial document model [22, 23]; in addition, the mechanisms used to acquire specific document regions are unpredictable because they can vary depending on the current document location.

Overviews support visual search because they concurrently show thumbnails of all pages in the document, arranged in a grid. The overview presentation preserves the main visual features of each page (including color, layout, pictures, and whitespace), enabling visual search based on "page shapes." As shown by Figure 1, pages are clearly differentiable even in miniature. Overviews also implicitly support revisitation because of their spatially-stable arrangement – a particular page is always in the same place in the grid, so users can go directly to a page by clicking on its position in the overview.

More than ten years ago, a previous implementation and study of the overview representation – called Space Filling Thumbnails (SFT) – showed the advantages of the overview approach [7]. The overview technique was faster than six other navigation methods, particularly when revisiting pages. Although the previous study provided strong evidence of the value of SFT, the study was limited in four ways: first, it was conducted in a lab setting, which can lead to artificial results; second, it only used mock-ups of the different views, rather than implementing the technique in a real viewer; third, it used tasks that only revisited locations once, whereas more frequent revisitation is common; and fourth, it did not explore the reasons why the overview was faster than the main competitor (a thumbnail sidebar).

To provide a second and more thorough investigation of document overviews, we carried out two studies that examined overviews in more realistic settings. We added several navigation techniques to an open-source PDF viewer, and carried out two studies with 25 people who installed our document viewer on their own computers for one month. The first study was a field experiment [19] which asked people to carry out controlled tasks, but in their everyday computing environment. Participants searched for target pages using one of three interfaces: scrolling (i.e., the scrollbar, scroll wheel, and keyboard navigation), scrolling plus a thumbnail sidebar, and the overview as described above. We used documents of 10, 50, 100, and 200 pages.

The field experiment showed that overviews were significantly faster overall for the three longer documents (50, 100, 200 pages), with a substantial advantage when tasks involved page revisitation. Overall, search times with the overview were 11.3 seconds, compared to 18.7 seconds for scrolling with thumbnails, and 28 seconds for scrolling. In addition to these quantitative results, we also gathered qualitative data about how and why the techniques differed.

Our second analysis was a small field study that ran concurrently with the field experiment. We asked some of the participants to use our custom PDF viewer for their own documents and their own tasks, and we logged their interaction with these documents. In this study, participants could choose to use any of the navigation mechanisms built into the viewer. The log data provides additional evidence that overviews can be a successful technique for real tasks: people used the overview for 31% of the more than 550 page visits, showing that the technique is feasible for real use.

Overall, our studies provide a useful triangulation of earlier laboratory evaluations. Our results add new evidence about the effectiveness of spatially stable overviews, their ability to work in a broad range of usage environments, the underlying design principles that can explain their performance, and their feasibility for real-world tasks.

RELATED WORK

Two main areas of research have influenced our work on spatially stable document overviews: improved methods for scrolling, and spatially stable interfaces.

Improved methods for scrolling

Scrolling has been a fundamental part of interaction since the first visual editors [30], and a wide range of input and output methods have been developed to improve user performance and experience in moving through documents. The comparative efficiency of alternative scrolling methods will be influenced by the nature of the user's navigational task. It is therefore unlikely that one method will be the best for all scrolling activities. For example, if the user finds a particular page number in an index, the most efficient method for moving to that area in the document might be to type the target page into a "go to" field. Alternatively, if the user needs to center the document in the page for reading comfort, the scroll wheel may provide the most convenient method; and manipulating the scroll-thumb might be a suitable method for moving to the start or end of the document.

Hill and Hollan [16] proposed adding "edit wear and read wear" marks into the otherwise blank scroll-trough, which would allow users to see the document regions that are most frequently used. Alexander et al. [4] implemented and evaluated a related method in their 'footprints' scrollbar, which left marks in the scroll-trough to demark regions most recently visited by the user. Their evaluation showed that when the system correctly inferred the document regions that were of interest to the user, footprint marks significantly reduced scrolling time by providing direct shortcuts to document regions. However, they offered little assistance to users when their target region was not selected for explicit marking. Wightman et al. [31] described a related 'TouchMark' system for easing document navigation on touchscreen devices, including support for revisitation.

Many researchers have examined input methods that allow faster and more accurate control over scroll-based target acquisition. The method used to evaluate these techniques typically involved showing a target destination to the user (via highlighting in the scroll-trough and in the document itself), then asking them to move as quickly as possible to the target line in the document. Hinckley et al. [17] showed that Fitts' law [13] accurately models scroll-based target acquisition of this form, with both position-control input devices (such as a scroll wheel) and with rate-control input (such as an isometric joystick, or middle mouse-button dragging). More recently, researchers have scrutinised the transfer functions that translate user actions with an input device into scrolling outcomes [24]: Cockburn et al. [8] proposed and evaluated a transfer function that adapted the scroll wheel's gain based on document length; Quinn et al. [25] examined touch-scrolling transfer functions; and Aceituno et al. [1] examined edge-based transfer functions in which scroll speed depends on the distance that the user drags beyond the window edge.

Spatial memory

When users interact with physical or electronic documents, they build up a spatial understanding of the location of document features [22, 23]. While people find ways to mark salient document regions when using physical documents (e.g., folding a dogear into a page, or using a finger as a temporary bookmark), analogous methods are relatively poorly supported in electronic documents.

Space-Filling Thumbnails (SFT) was proposed to improve users' ability to form and exploit spatial memory for document regions [7]. The technique allows users to toggle between two full-window views of a document – a view that displays a single document page, and a thumbnail view that shows all pages in the document in spatially stable locations. Clicking on a thumbnail immediately shows that page in the main view. The thumbnail view is accessed by pressing a control key. A lab-study evaluation showed that SFT was faster than a variety of other scrolling methods, particularly when tasks involved revisitation.

Although not directed at document navigation, CommandMaps [26, 27] use a similar approach to provide rapid access to all of the commands in an interface via a spatially stable presentation of all commands at once. Traditional interfaces divide commands between different menus or toolbars, reducing a user's ability to form and exploit spatial memory (due to spatial overloading) and requiring extra mechanical actions to traverse through the command hierarchy. Evaluations demonstrated that users quickly learn the correspondence between spatial locations and commands, enabling CommandMaps to reduce command selection times compared to other methods. The studies of CommandMaps progressed from an initial lab-based study of a prototype system [28] to a field study of an actual system used for realistic work.

DESIGN OF DOCUMENT-NAVIGATION OVERVIEWS

The main design objectives proposed for Space-Filling Thumbnails [7] were spatial stability and the visual display of all pages. We summarize these here and add several other factors including the problem of changing window size, how to best support visual recognition, the differences between overviews and general zoom capability, and the choice of a full-screen overview rather than a multi-window view. These design issues guided our implementation of a fully-functional PDF viewer (described below).

Spatial stability and changing window sizes

Previous research clearly shows the value of stability in the development of location memory. When data organization changes from task to task, the time to find an item increases linearly with the number of candidate items, but when data locations are stable, performance quickly improves to a logarithmic function of the number of items [6]. This change occurs because once items are well known, their locations can be retrieved from memory, which follows the logarithmic Hick-Hyman law of choice response [6, 18, 29].

Maintaining perfect spatial stability, however, is almost impossible in a real-world document viewer – for example, when the user moves the viewer to a different monitor, they translate the entire overview to a new location; when they resize the window, the original overview may no longer fit into the available space.

Previous work on this issue, however, provides us with an appropriate design path. Scarr and colleagues studied the resilience of spatial memory to various transformations (i.e., once a spatial arrangement is learned, what is the effect of translating, scaling, or rotating the arrangement) [28]. They found that only rotation caused any substantial loss of performance, suggesting that moving the viewer application within the user's display environment will not be a major problem. Scarr and colleagues also looked at the issue of changing window aspect ratio – they examined user performance after "reflowing" items into a new arrangement, and compared it with performance after scaling the arrangement to fit the new window (maintaining relative spatial locations). The results of this test clearly showed that scaling was much better because it allowed users to continue to use their spatial memory.

As a result, we maintain the layout of our document overview across window-size changes. The grid is set up based on the user's window size when the document is first opened, and these grid dimensions are kept stable; if necessary, the thumbnails are scaled to be able to present the grid in the available space. Of course, the user can request that the grid be re-created, (e.g., if they are switching permanently from a portrait to a landscape monitor setup).

Finally, the overview presents a rich visual space that provides a wide variety of potential landmarks for the user's memory – the graphical elements in a document overview gives a much more memorable visual field than other representations (such as scrollbars).

Supporting recognition and search with "page shapes"

As described above, a main way that users look through documents is by searching for remembered visual characteristics of a page. The SFT system [7] provided thumbnails that showed the overall layout of the page, but small details were often lost – leading to questions, for example, about whether the overview could be used for visual pattern-matching in documents longer than 200 pages.

With advances in display resolution, however, it is now possible to provide high-quality thumbnail images that allow much more detailed visual recognition. For example, Figure 2 shows the actual size of a thumbnail from a 100-page document; on a high-DPI laptop screen such as Apple's Retina Display, it is relatively easy to identify the details of the diagram on the page, and to read the main headings. In our experience with overview-based document navigation, these high-resolution thumbnails can be important, because the success of a user's visual search depends on how many other pages have similar visual attributes to the target. When the number of candidate pages is large, high resolution displays can help to by allowing users to use finer-grained detail as additional search criteria.

As with the earlier implementation of SFT, our overview also provides an enlarged pop-up thumbnail, displayed when the user hovers over any page in the overview. The increased size of the pop-up provides an intermediate way for users to inspect a page without committing to the selection – particularly useful when candidate pages have been identified by a more general visual scan. The pop-up size can be configured by the user, but is not dependent on the document length – therefore, precise page details can be seen even with long documents.

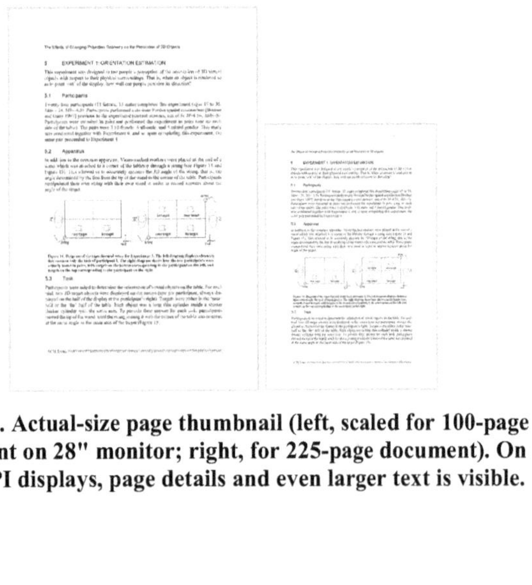

Figure 2. Actual-size page thumbnail (left, scaled for 100-page document on 28" monitor; right, for 225-page document). On high-DPI displays, page details and even larger text is visible.

Another new feature in our view is that it marks recently-visited pages with a red border, as shown in Figure 1 – this is a form of "read wear" described earlier [16]. In our implementation, we mark both the pages that have been inspected using the pop-up (in orange) and pages that have been selected (in red). The highlights are cleared once the user leaves the overview for more than one minute (these times can be set by the user).

Fixed overviews vs. arbitrary zoom

Our approach relies upon two fixed levels of zoom – the overview (i.e., zoomed out all the way), and the main page view (i.e., zoomed in all the way). By hard-coding these two levels into the design, we gain important simplicity that allows performance improvements (other controls remain available to configure zoom level of the page display). Variable levels of zoom provide useful utilities for the user, but they address a different purpose to the overview (such as scrutinizing a particular document feature). Providing a shortcut to a fully-zoomed-out view (i.e., the overview) is intended to promote the benefits described earlier – enhanced visual search and improved revistitation through support for spatial memory formation and exploitation.

Full-screen overview vs. multiple views

Some systems provide semantic overviews as secondary views beside or inset into the main page view. This is a useful representation for some tasks – in particular, the task of understanding your current location in relation to the overall structure of the document. However, there are two reasons why a multiple-view solution would be less effective in a document-navigation system.

First, the screen real estate available for document thumbnails is a critical resource that can greatly change the success of visual search based on page shapes. An inset overview would not be able to provide the level of detail needed for visual pattern-matching in longer documents. Second, our observations of document navigation suggest that there are few if any user tasks that require both the detailed view and the overview at the same time. It is more likely that users want to carry out a navigation action (e.g., choose a new location for inspection), and then carry out a task that uses the detail view (e.g., read text on the page). Given the serialized nature of these tasks, it makes sense to multiplex the available window space and give maximal area to the overview.

Overviews as a base representation

One of the main advantages of absolute and stable document representations is that their structure and meaning can be learned and relied upon. As mentioned above, this enables people to use spatial memory as a shortcut to finding previously-visited pages, and provides a landmark-rich substrate on which memory can be anchored. Once the base representation is learned, however, other information can be encoded in the overview. Our visualizations of the user's current page and recent pages are an example, and other information is also possible (e.g., in a collaborative document space, the overview can show others' locations).

Working together with other document-navigation tools

Different document-navigation tools provide solutions to different kinds of user tasks. We are not suggesting that overview-based navigation will solve all search needs – rather, that overviews can support certain common tasks that are currently unsupported. Overviews do not provide support for local and linear navigation (e.g., reading across a page boundary), and we do not suggest that users should go to the overview to move by a single page.

The overviews presented here, however, need not displace other navigational techniques – users are already capable of understanding several different methods for moving around in documents, and it is likely that overviews could be added to current document viewers without disrupting current practices. In addition, other methods for improving existing techniques' support for tasks like revisitation (e.g., marks in the scrollbar to indicate recent visits [4]) can be used in conjunction with an overview approach.

A CUSTOM PDF VIEWER WITH OVERVIEW NAVIGATION

We built a custom viewer based on the open-source IcePDF Java PDF system (www.icesoft.com/icepdf/). The viewer is shown in Figures 1 & 3 (left), and contains most of the main features of commercial PDF viewers (including zooming, rotating, annotating, and printing). The existing viewer also supports several types of document navigation: scrolling (with scroll bar and scroll wheel), keyboard navigation (arrow keys and PageUp/PageDown keys), a Find dialog, and a basic thumbnail sidebar view (Figure 3).

Figure 3. Thumbnail sidebar view in our viewer (left) and the Adobe Acrobat viewer with default thumbnail size (right).

We added an overview navigation system to the basic viewer, and we also enhanced the thumbnail sidebar view. The overview provides a full-screen grid of thumbnails that shows the entire document, as discussed above. Users show the overview by pressing the right mouse button; once the overview is visible, users can go back to the page view either by left-clicking on a page (which opens that page in the main view) or right clicking (which returns them to the page they were on when they opened the overview). In the overview (Figure 1), the current page is highlighted with a blue border, and recently-visited pages are highlighted with a red border. Pages that have been recently inspected (with the enlarged popup shown on hover) have an orange border.

The thumbnail sidebar view works consistently with commercial viewers – the thumbnails can be scrolled independently of the main view, and clicking on a thumbnail takes the main view to that page. We augmented the existing thumbnail sidebar with the "current page" and "recently visited" border highlights. We also added code to the custom viewer to control the presentation of experimental tasks (described below) and to log all navigation actions (both during experimental tasks and during everyday use).

STUDY METHODS

We carried out two experiments with the custom PDF viewer – a field experiment that involved controlled manipulation of conditions in a field setting, and a related field trial in which the PDF viewer was used for the participants' own work, substantially without experimental controls. Here we describe the methods for the field experiment (the setting and apparatus for the field trial was the same). Our main goal in the field experiment was to examine the performance of overview-based document navigation in comparison to regular scrolling and thumbnail-enhanced scrolling – when installed on a wide variety of computers and monitors in people's ordinary usage environments. A second goal was to find out more about the reasons for the performance characteristics of different navigation methods.

Participants, Procedure, and Apparatus

24 participants were recruited by e-mail from two university communities (9 women, 15 men, mean age 28.1 years). All participants were highly experienced with mouse-and-windows computers (more than two hours use per day) and with document viewers (more than 30 minutes use per day).

Participants joined the study by visiting a web page with instructions and links to an informed consent form and a demographics questionnaire. Participants downloaded and installed our custom PDF viewer on their own computer, and sent their e-mail address to us for communication during the study. During the following month, we sent messages to the participants asking them to carry out tasks with the viewer.

When asked to carry out an experimental task, participants selected that task from a "Search Tasks" menu in the viewer. Each task loaded a specific document with a specific length (included with the viewer) and asked the participant to find a series of target pages using one of the three study interfaces (Scrolling, Scrolling+Thumbnails, or Overview). Target pages were shown at the top right of the screen (at 50% size). The experiment tasks are shown for the three interface conditions in Figures 4-6. The test documents were edited to remove page numbers, and the "Find" functionality was turned off for the search tasks. In addition, the recent-visits highlights were turned off for the Overview and Scroll+

Thumbnails conditions, to prevent these visualizations from providing an easy way to find the targets.

Once the participant found the page, they clicked on it in the main page view, and the system went on to the next search task for that interface. There were four target pages, which were revisited different numbers of times: two pages were revisited four times, and two pages were revisited twice (for a total of 12 search trials per task). Once the task was complete, the participant was directed to visit a web page with a post-task effort survey (based on the NASA-TLX).

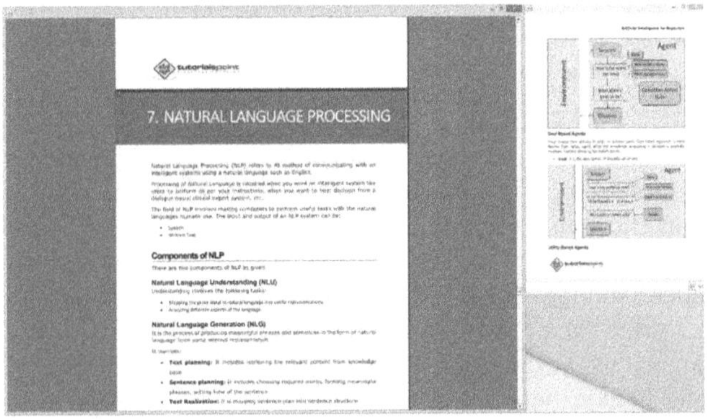

Figure 4. Search task in the Scrolling interface.

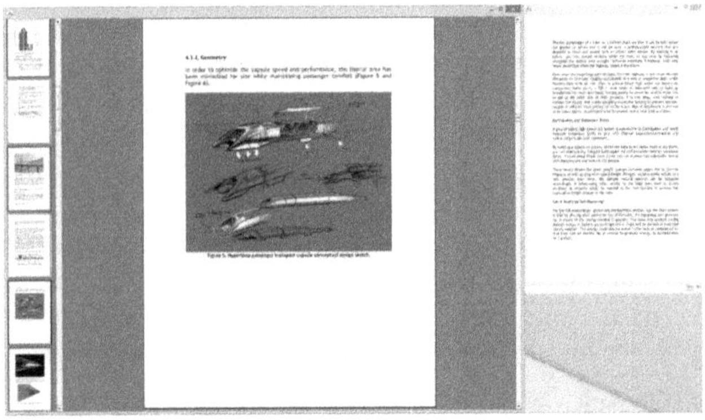

Figure 5. Search task in the Scroll+Thumbs interface.

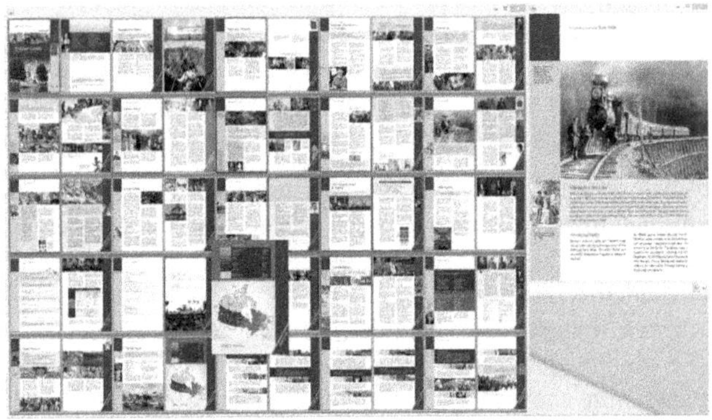

Figure 6. Search task in the Overview interface; participants could move back and forth from overview to page view.

Participants carried out tasks with each interface and with four different document lengths (10, 50, 100, and 200 pages). The e-mail messages asked participants to carry out the tasks for a particular length, for all interfaces. Participants were allowed to choose the order of the interfaces, and the time of day when they completed the tasks. To ensure that each specific document was used equally with all interfaces, the assignment of documents to interfaces was manipulated remotely during the study. Performance data was recorded by the viewer and sent back to a secure web server for collection and analysis. Participants were asked to do the tasks at approximately one-week intervals; therefore, the four tasks were completed over about one month.

Experimental Conditions

The three interfaces used to carry out the tasks were:

- *Scroll* (Figure 4), using the normal page view and any of the built-in scrolling mechanisms (scrollbar, scroll wheel, PageUp/ PageDown keys).
- *Scroll+Thumbnails* (Figure 5), using both the scrolling mechanisms above plus the thumbnail sidebar. These thumbnails had their own scrollbar.
- *Overview* (Figure 6), using the grid view described above. Scrollbars were removed from the page view, but the scroll wheel and keyboard navigation were available.

Easy vs. Hard Page Shapes

Our experience with document overviews suggested that some pages would be more difficult to find than others when using visual pattern-matching. We therefore chose two types of targets for each search task: "easy" targets had obvious visual characteristics that were not frequently repeated among the pages of the document; "hard" targets had visual characteristics that were common to many pages. Figure 7 shows examples of easy (top row) and hard (bottom row) targets: the targets are the leftmost image, and representative other pages from the document are shown to the right.

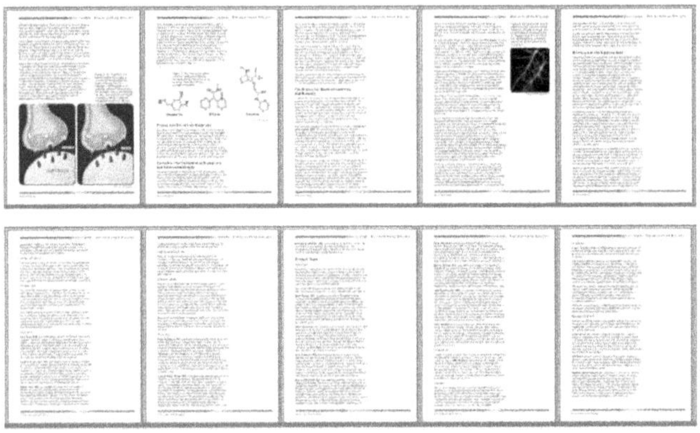

Figure 7. Above: "easy" target (leftmost) with representative other pages from the document to its right. Below: "hard" target (leftmost) and other pages to its right.

Study Design and Data Analysis

The in-the-wild nature of the field experiment meant that some participants did not complete all of the tasks. The incomplete mapping between participants and conditions prevents the creation of a standard linear model for ANOVA. In order to make use of all of the participants' data, we used a Hierarchical Mixed Model (HMM), which allows a similar analysis but accommodates missing data from some participants [10]. The analysis was carried in R using the *nlme* library, using participant as a random factor.

The study therefore used a mixed between/within repeated-measures design, with three factors:

- *Interface*: Scrolling, Scroll+Thumbnails, Overview
- *Document Length*: 10, 50, 100, or 200 pages
- *Visit*: first, second, third, or fourth
- *Target Difficulty*: "easy" or "hard" as described above

The dependent measure was search completion time; for subjective responses, the measures were responses to the NASA-TLX.

Participants' Computing Environments

Participants were asked to provide details of their computing environments. 16 stated that they completed tasks using a desktop computer+monitor arrangement, 5 reported using a laptop, 2 a laptop+monitor, and 1 gave no answer. Three types of operating system were reported, with 9 using some version of Microsoft Windows, 4 using Mac OS X, and 8 using a version of Linux; 3 gave no answer. Display sizes ranged from 16 to 28 inches. Several display resolutions were also reported: 1440×1080 (2), 1680×1050 (7), 1080p (9), 2800×1800 (2) and 3200×2000 (1); 3 gave no answer.

Variations in hardware setup, and other demographic variables such as age, sex, and computing experience, had no discernable effect on the results reported below.

RESULTS (FIELD EXPERIMENT)

Task Performance

Overall, there were substantial differences in search time for different interfaces, different document lengths, and different visits to a target. Analysis using the Hierarchical Mixed Model (HMM, see Data Analysis above) showed strong main effects of *Interface* ($F_{2,2303}$=15.62, p<.0001), *Length* ($F_{3,2303}$=36.20, p<.0001), *Visit* ($F_{3,2303}$=13.36, p<.0001), and *Difficulty* ($F_{1,2303}$=7.13, p=.0076) on search time.

These data are shown in Figures 8-10. Overall, the Overview was fastest (11.28s per search, s.d. 19.2), followed by Scroll+Thumbnails (18.73s, s.d. 38.4) and Scrolling (28.07s, s.d. 51.2). However, these differences must be interpreted in light of the significant interactions described below.

The HMM showed significant interactions between *Interface* and *Length* ($F_{2,2303}$=6.44, p=.0016), between *Interface* and *Visit* ($F_{6,2303}$=2.21, p=.040), and between *Length* and *Visit* ($F_{3,2303}$=6.54, p=.0002). These interactions are illustrated in Figure 10. For the 10-page document, there is little difference between the interfaces, but the difference increases with document length. In addition, the figure shows that revisitation saves proportionally more time as documents grow longer.

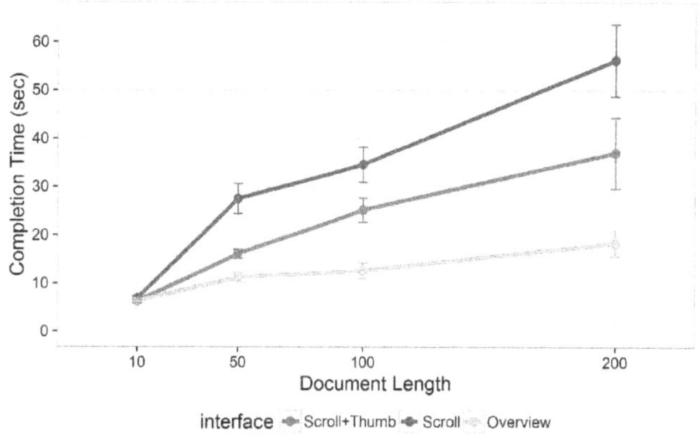

Figure 8. Completion time (±s.e.) by interface and length.

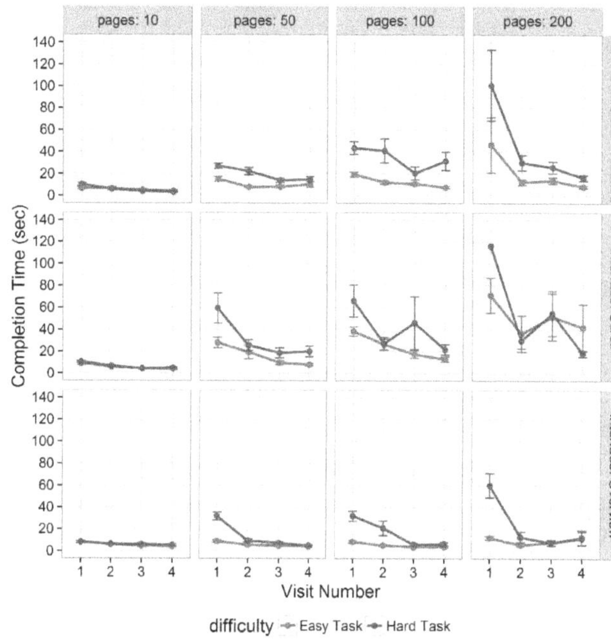

Figure 9. Completion time (±s.e.) by interface (rows), length (columns), visit number (x-axis), and difficulty (color).

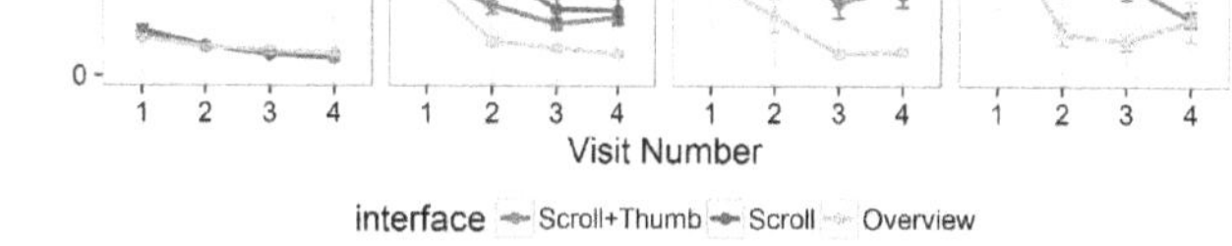

Figure 10. Completion time (±s.e.) by doc length (columns), interface (color), and visit number (x-axis).

Perception of Effort

After each task (interface and document length), participants filled out an effort questionnaire based on the NASA-TLX. Mean response scores are shown in Figure 11. Effort scores approximately follow the performance results above: there are few differences between interfaces for 10-page documents, but larger differences for longer documents. In particular, the Overview is consistently scored as requiring lower effort and as causing less frustration than Scrolling or Scroll+Thumbnails.

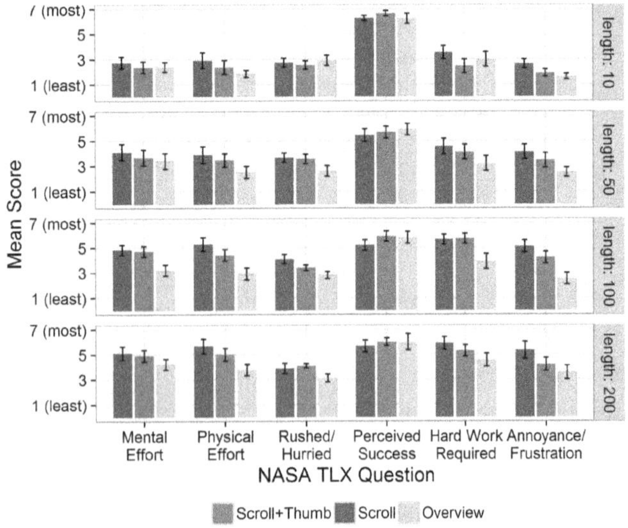

Figure 11. Mean TLX Scores (±s.e.) by interface and length.

Search Strategies and Participant Comments

Participant comments and discussions over the course of the study revealed strategies used with the different interfaces, and difficulties in these conditions.

Scroll+Thumbnails supports page matching, but helps less with revisitation

Participants had mixed comments about the Scroll+ Thumbnails interface. First, it was clear that the thumbnails helped users carry out visual matching – for example, one person said: "I used the scrolling thumbnails bar to scroll through pages. I remembered the specific features of a target page, and looked for that feature while scrolling through the interface with mouse." The limited number of thumbnails, however, was seen as a problem: as one person stated, "For the large documents, it was annoying to use the thumbnails because you could see so few of them at one time. It still felt like scrolling to me."

Interestingly, participants used similar language to describe their solution strategies for revisitation searches with Scroll+ Thumbnails, and none of them mentioned using a different strategy when finding pages for the third or fourth time. For example, one participant said as an overall comment about this interface "When there were lots of pages, it took a while to find the desired page;" another stated "I found it difficult with large files and specially, in target pages where there were limited features to focus on."

Scrolling poorly supports page matching and revisitation

Participants were consistently negative about their experiences with the regular Scrolling interface. There were several expressions of frustration with this method for the longer documents – for example, "When it came to the 100 and 200 pages experiment, it was hard to finish since I had to scroll most of the pages in that experiment to find the target page;" "I found it most difficult in large documents when my current location was too far from the target page. It was so frustrating to scroll through so many pages".

Participants mentioned several strategies that they adopted to try and find or re-find pages with the Scrolling interface. Although people tried to use visual pattern-matching (e.g., "I tried to see what could be easier to spot in that page, for instance, picture etc."), this became difficult with longer documents (e.g., "When there were a lot of pages, you sometimes passed the correct page because you were scrolling fast in an attempt to get through it quicker"). Several participants also stated that they attempted to remember the location of the scroll thumb for a particular page (e.g., "I also tried to keep track of a page's location in the scroll bar. It took me close to target page then I used scrolling"). Other participants mentioned using the background image on their desktop as a marker to help them remember these locations – as described below, maintaining this memory of scrollbar locations was sometimes difficult.

In some cases, participants were forced to use the content of the document in order to help them find a target. For example, one participant said that "Most documents had chapters or sections, so I tried to remember which section each page was in." This strategy was not mentioned for either of the other techniques.

It is difficult to remember page locations in linear views

As mentioned above, several people stated that they tried to remember the location of the scroll thumb when they found a page for the first time. This was not easy to do, since there are few landmarks or visual textures in the scrollbar to help form an accurate memory (as the participant above noted, this strategy was only useful as an approximation). In addition, several participants related instances where they simply forgot to fix the location in their memory before going on to the next task – and once the scroll thumb had moved, the opportunity to remember the previous location was lost. This problem occurred both in the main page view and in the thumbnail sidebar.

Overview supported both pattern-matching and revisitation

Comments were generally very positive for the Overview representation. Participants clearly indicated that they were able to carry out both visual pattern-matching and spatial-memory-based revisitation. Commenting on their strategy for finding a page for the first time, one person stated that the Overview "was super easy and comfortable. I did not have to scroll through lots of pages just to find one page. When in this interface, all the pages were shown at a time, which actually saved me a lot of browsing time." Another person said "you can see all the pages in one view" as the reason why this interface was effective for finding targets.

Participants also recognized that they were able to remember page locations for revisitation, instead of having to carry out another visual search. For example, one person remarked on the value of the overview's richer visual representation: "I remembered the relative position of the target page with reference to other pages, and notable features like colors, image, bold texts etc. to quickly revisit that page." Another participant said that they remembered the pages based on their "physical position in a two dimensional plane."

"Hard" targets are difficult, and require different strategy

Targets where the page shape of the target was not unique in the document were seen as more difficult for all three interfaces – for example, participants disliked targets where there were "limited features to focus on," such as targets that were "just a page full of text."

When faced with these targets, participants stated that they had to adapt their strategy for visual page search. Whereas with an "easy" target people could look for the most obvious visual features of the page, "hard" targets required people to consider a second level of visual detail. For example, if a target page looked superficially similar to many pages, participants had to start looking for other features – such as where bold words appeared in the paragraph, the length of a paragraph, or the shape of the right edge of the text block.

RESULTS FROM FIELD TRIAL OF EVERYDAY USE

We asked participants from the field experiment to also try using the custom PDF viewer for their everyday document viewing in addition to the experimental tasks. There was no restriction or requirement on how they should use the tool, and all interfaces were available at all times. Fourteen of the study's participants used the system for at least one of their own tasks over the one-month period. A summary of this use is shown in Table 1.

Table 1. Summary of non-experiment use of the viewer

Document Length	# Opened	# People	Total Page Visits	Scrollbar, Wheel, Keys	Overview	Thumbs
1..9	38	11	202	134	68	0
10..19	14	5	74	59	15	0
20..49	7	4	45	40	5	0
50..99	8	4	117	72	36	9
100..199	6	4	90	57	33	0
200..250	1	1	28	13	15	0
	74	**14**	**556**	**375**	**172**	**9**

Although this is only a small amount of data, some initial patterns of use emerged that could be followed up in a larger field trial. First, people did use the overview interface – the fraction of page visits accounted for by the overview interface was higher than expected (31% of the 556 page views). This total may be artificially high due to participant interest in a novel interface – but given the low rates of adoption that are often seen in studies where users are already familiar with an existing interface, we see this willingness to use the overview as a positive sign. In addition, people used the overview in all document lengths – although we were surprised that there was not a greater proportion of overview use in long documents. Third, there was very little use of the thumbnail sidebar (the nine page visits were all from one user).

The real-world use of the viewer, however, showed that there are a wide variety of document tasks that people carry out, and that these affect the interface features that people use. For example, several participants mentioned that they often opened documents just to print a particular page, or to cut and paste a quotation – and these tasks did not involve the kinds of search and revisitation that we included in the earlier study tasks, and were usually easy to accomplish using only the standard scrollbar and scrollwheel. In addition, one participant also noted that when he opened a document to read it, the linear document model worked well, and he did not need to navigate in a random-access fashion. When participants did use the overview, however, they saw it as valuable – one participant stated that he used the overview almost exclusively for his own work, but only after realizing its benefit from the study tasks. Finally, three participants mentioned their use of the read-wear marks (and one commented that these would have been very helpful in the study tasks where revisitation was more frequent).

The main practical conclusion that we draw from the everyday use of the system is that the overview interface worked well enough for people to be able to use it for a large number of page visits. This shows that the approach is feasible and usable in real-world use over a wide variety of implemented systems and real document lengths.

DISCUSSION

Results of the field experiment and field study support the findings of the SFT lab study conducted a decade ago [7]. The overview allowed users to complete document navigation tasks much more quickly than other methods, particularly when revisiting document regions.

Importance of replication and experimental triangulation

Research in most scientific fields is incremental. Scientists carefully replicate their colleagues' studies, seeking to understand their generality and boundaries of application. Computer Science is a somewhat anomalous field in that the word '*incremental*' is often used as a criticism – the implication is that instead, we should be seeking paradigm shifts in our research; an objective that Meyer [20] characterized as a 'mania'.

Our results agree with those of the earlier lab study, and they did so even though participants were using their own machines in their own homes (or offices). Prior to conducting the field study, the agreement between studies was far from certain. For example, Fitchett et al. [11] conducted a field evaluation (like ours) seeking to replicate findings of an earlier lab study [12]. Yet their findings differed substantially – an interface feature that had large performance advantages and strongly positive subjective assessments in the lab was more-or-less ignored when evaluated in the field. Many other researchers have noted concerns regarding discrepancies between experimental outcomes when investigating the same interfaces using different methodologies [5, 9, 21], leading to recommendations for methodological triangulation [14, 15].

Future empirical work might seek further triangulated evidence of SFT's performance when different experimental methods are used to cue the users' page retrieval. Our field study, like previous lab studies of SFT, used images of the target page to the retrieval, and these images were continually available to the user during the task. While we believe this task cuing method is appropriate (particularly for page revisitation, where users have a memory for the visual shape of page content), method triangulation could provide further evidence of the techniques' relative strengths.

Why does SFT work?

Traditional scrolling mechanisms (with the exception of 'goto page') are all *relative* means for attaining a target region in a document. Therefore, the user's input to acquire any particular document region differs dependent on where they initiate their action. The scroll thumb does provide an absolute *depiction* of the location of the current view within the document (e.g., when the thumb is in the middle of the scroll trough, the view is at the middle of the document). However, it is difficult to use this depiction for absolute location selection – the behavioral outcome of clicking on any particular location in the scroll trough depends on the relative location of the thumb (the document is scrolled towards its start if the thumb is below the click; and towards its end if the click is above). Even zoom controls are predominantly relative (e.g., control-scroll wheel, or zoom-in/out keys and buttons).

We believe that the dominance of relative methods for document navigation causes the problems that users have in forming an understanding of the spatial location of document features, as observed in prior studies [22, 23].

Overviews, in contrast, provide a consistent and *absolute* method for viewing and acquiring document features. A user who wishes to navigate to a particular page can display the overview, find the target page, point to it and click on it at a certain x, y coordinate in the view. For any subsequent navigation to that page, clicking in the same x, y location will retrieve the same page. This facilitates rapid spatial decisions, and predictable anticipatory actions by the user.

Deployment issues

Although the results for the overview are promising, there are some important issues to understand and address prior to any practical deployment. First, like the previous lab studies of SFT, our studies only examined static documents in which content does not change. Real documents, in contrast, can change in length as new pages are added or deleted. Further studies are needed to examine how performance with overviews degrades when editing changes cause a lack of stability in thumbnail locations. We suspect that the combination of consistent spatial vicinity plus visual cues from the thumbnails' appearance will allow overviews to outperform other scrolling methods in the presence of editing changes, but this requires validation.

Second, there are related issues to address in adapting overview presentations to substantial changes in aspect ratios when windows are resized or mobile devices are reoriented (between landscape and portrait display modes). The homescreen icon layout on mobile devices encounters a similar design problem – if the spatial layout is consistent across orientations, users gain from spatial predictability, but the aesthetics may be compromised by blank spaces and malformed icons; conversely, if the spatial layout is inconsistent, icon locations may be unpredictable (slowing performance), but the aesthetics may be improved. As mentioned earlier, Scarr [28] examined related issues, noting strong performance advantages for spatial stability.

Third, a critical deployment issue concerns consistency with existing scrolling behaviors. Obviously, users can only benefit from overviews if they use them, and the benefits increase with level of use because spatial memories develop with experience. However, users are extremely familiar with scroll wheels, scrollbars, and touch-scrolling gestures, and the more users rely on these well-practiced and habitual utilities, the less they will experience the potential benefits of overviews. Overcoming stasis in interaction paradigms is highly challenging, but it can and does occur – for example, the now-ubiquitous scroll wheel was first popularized by the Microsoft IntelliMouse in 1996, more than a decade after the widespread introduction of the mouse; and touch-scrolling (with disappearing scrollbars) was popularized by the iPhone in 2007, more than a decade later. The frequent use of the overview in our small field study, however, can be interpreted as providing an initial indication that the benefits of the overview may help it overcome the "interface inertia" typically seen in real-world deployment.

CONCLUSIONS

Efficient methods of document navigation are essential for effective office work. Current document applications support a broad range of utilities for scrolling and traversing through documents, but the behavior of nearly all of them is relative to the user's current document location. As a result, current scrolling interfaces provide little support for two main ways that users navigate – visual page searching, and revisitation. Prior research and lab-study findings have suggested that document overviews may improve the efficiency of navigation, particularly when revisiting document regions. The research presented in this paper deepens the analysis and understanding of the main design principles underlying document overviews; it also introduces new overview features, and through two field evaluations, it extends and supports prior findings on the efficiency of overviews. Our work contributes to the now-strong case for including overview displays in commercial document applications.

REFERENCES

1. Aceituno, J., Malacria, S., Quinn, P., Roussel, N., Cockburn, A. and Casiez, G. The design, use, and performance of edge-scrolling techniques. *International Journal of Human-Computer Studies 97* (2017), 58--76.
2. Alexander, J. Understanding and Improving Navigation within Electronic Documents *PhD Thesis. Computer Science and Software Engineering*, University of Canterbury, Christchurch, 2009.
3. Alexander, J. and Cockburn, A. An empirical characterisation of electronic document navigation. in *Proceedings of Graphics Interface (GI 2008)*, Canadian Information Processing Society, (2008), 123-130.
4. Alexander, J., Cockburn, A., Fitchett, S., Gutwin, C. and Greenberg, S. Revisiting Read Wear: Analysis, Design, and Evaluation of a Footprints Scrollbar. in *Proceedings of CHI'09: ACM Conference on Human Factors in Computing Systems*, ACM Press, (2009), 1665-1674.
5. Chiasson, S., Biddle, R. and Oorschot, P.C.v. A second look at the usability of click-based graphical passwords *Proceedings of the 3rd symposium on Usable privacy and security*, ACM, Pittsburgh, Pennsylvania, USA, 2007, 1-12.
6. Cockburn, A. and Gutwin, C. A Predictive Model of Human Performance with Scrolling and Hierarchical Lists. *Human-Computer Interaction 24*, 3 (2009), 273-314.
7. Cockburn, A., Gutwin, C. and Alexander, J. Faster Document Navigation with Space-Filling Thumbnails. in *Proceedings of CHI'06 ACM Conference on Human Factors in Computing Systems*, ACM Press, (2006), 1-10.
8. Cockburn, A., Quinn, P., Gutwin, C. and Fitchett, S. Improving Scrolling Devices with Document-Length-Dependent Gain. in *Proceedings of CHI'12: ACM Conference on Human Factors in Computing Systems*, ACM, (2012), 267-276.
9. Duh, H.B.-L., Tan, G.C.B. and Chen, V.H.-h. Usability evaluation for mobile device: a comparison of laboratory and field tests. in *Proceedings of the 8th conference on Human-computer interaction with mobile devices and services*, ACM, (2006), 181-186.
10. Field, A., Miles, J. and Field, Z. *Discovering Statistics with R*. Sage, 2012.
11. Fitchett, S., Cockburn, A. and Gutwin, C. Finder Highlights: Field Evaluation and Design of an Augmented File Browser. in *Proceedings of the SIGCHI Conference on Human Factors in Computing Systems*, ACM, (2014), 3685-3694.
12. Fitchett, S., Cockburn, A. and Gutwin, C. Improving Navigation-Based File Retrieval. in *Proceedings of the SIGCHI Conference on Human Factors in Computing Systems*, ACM, (2013), 2329-2338.
13. Fitts, P.M. The Information Capacity of the Human Motor System in Controlling the Amplitude of Movement. *Journal of Experimental Psychology 47* (1954), 381-391.
14. Greenberg, S. and Buxton, B. Usability Evaluation Considered Harmful (Some of the Time). in *Proceedings of CHI'08: ACM Conference on Human Factors in Computing Systems*, ACM Press, (2008).
15. Hertzum, M. User Testing in Industry: A Case Study of Laboratory, Workshop, and Field Tests. Kobsa, A. and Stephanidis, C. eds. *Proceedings of the 5th ERCIM workshop*, 1999, 59-72.
16. Hill, W., Hollan, J., Wroblewski, D. and McCandless, T. Edit Wear and Read Wear. in *Proceedings of CHI'92 ACM Conference on Human Factors in Computing Systems*, (1992), 3-9.
17. Hinckley, K., Cutrell, E., Bathiche, S. and Muss, T. Quantitative Analysis of Scrolling Techniques. in *Proceedings of CHI'02 ACM Conference on Human Factors in Computing Systems*, (2002), 65-72.
18. Hyman, R. Stimulus information as a determinant of reaction time. *Journal of Experimental Psychology 45* (1953), 188-196.
19. McGrath, J. Methodology Matters: Doing Research in the Behavioral and Social Sciences. in Baecker, R.a.G., J and Buxton, W and Greenberg, S ed. *Readings in Human-Computer Interaction: Towards the Year 2000*, 1995.
20. Meyer, B. Incremental research vs. paradigm-shift mania. *Commun. ACM 55*, 9 (2012), 8-9.
21. Nielsen, C.M., Overgaard, M., Pedersen, M.B., Stage, J. and Stenild, S. It's worth the hassle!: the added value of evaluating the usability of mobile systems in the field *Proc. Nordic conference on HCI*, ACM, 2006, 272-280.
22. O'Hara, K. and Sellen, A. A comparison of reading paper and on-line documents. in *Proceedings of CHI'97 ACM Conference on Human factors in Computing Systems*, (1997), 335-342.
23. O'Hara, K., Sellen, A. and Bentley, R. Supporting Memory for Spatial Location While Reading from Small Displays. in *Extended Abstracts of CHI'99 Conference on Human Factors in Computing Systems*, (1999), 220-221.
24. Quinn, P., Cockburn, A., Casiez, G., Roussel, N. and Gutwin, C. Exposing and understanding scrolling transfer functions. in *Proceedings of the 25th annual ACM symposium on User interface software and technology*, ACM, (2012), 341-350.
25. Quinn, P., Malacria, S. and Cockburn, A. Touch scrolling transfer functions. in *Proceedings of the 26th annual ACM symposium on User interface software and technology*, ACM, (2013), 61-70.
26. Scarr, J., Cockburn, A., Gutwin, C. and Bunt, A. Improving command selection with CommandMaps. in *Proceedings of the SIGCHI Conference on Human Factors in Computing Systems*, ACM, (2012), 257-266.
27. Scarr, J., Cockburn, A., Gutwin, C., Bunt, A. and Cechanowicz, J. The Usability of CommandMaps in Realistic Tasks. in *Proceedings of ACM CHI 2014 Conference on Human Factors in Computing Systems*, ACM, (2014).

28. Scarr, J., Cockburn, A., Gutwin, C. and Malacria, S. Testing the robustness and performance of spatially consistent interfaces. in *Proceedings of the 2013 SIGCHI Conference on Human Factors in Computing Systems*, ACM, (2013), 3139-3148.
29. Seow, S.C. Information Theoretic Models of HCI: A Comparison of the Hick-Hyman Law and Fitts' Law. *Human-Computer Interaction 20*, 3 (2005), 315-352.
30. Sutherland, I. Sketchpad: A Man-Machine Graphical Communication System. in *AFIPS Spring Joint Computer Conference*, (1963), 329-346.
31. Wightman, D., Ginn, T. and Vertegaal, R. TouchMark: flexible document navigation and bookmarking techniques for e-book readers *Proceedings of Graphics Interface 2010*, Canadian Information Processing Society, Ottawa, Ontario, Canada, 2010, 241-244.

Imagined Connectivities: Synthesized Conceptions of Public Wi-Fi in Urban India

Nithya Sambasivan and Paul M. Aoki
Google Inc.
Mountain View, CA, USA
nithyasamba@google.com, aoki@acm.org

ABSTRACT
India and other economies in the Global South are undergoing a proliferation in public Wi-Fi, with large-scale deployments from industry and government. In this paper, we report on a qualitative study on public Wi-Fi conceptions as held by urban Indians, prior to connecting to a network. Our findings show that prior public Wi-Fi users and non-users alike raised a surprising range and depth of conceptions—ranging from suspicion of operators' intentions to monetize, to concerns about sexual image morphing, to fears of phone wipeouts, to aspiration—which were informed by popular media, Bluetooth cultures, and social learning. We found these conceptions of Wi-Fi networks to significantly influence adoption of public Wi-Fi. With enormous investments in public Wi-Fi initiatives, we call for network providers to address these deep conceptions among emerging users; by suggesting ways to build public awareness, better user experiences, and business model innovation.

ACM Classification Keywords
H.5.2. Information Interfaces and Presentation (e.g. HCI): User Interfaces

Author Keywords
ICTD, HCI4D, Internet, access, Public Wi-Fi, India, media studies, imaginaries

INTRODUCTION
India lags behind many other countries in terms of Internet access at an estimated 22% [53]. India's size, population, and emerging economy with stubbornly high poverty rates mean that truly ubiquitous deployment of high-speed infrastructure networks will not be economically sustainable any time soon.

In light of these realities, affordable public Wi-Fi is viewed as the democratic access solution for high-speed connectivity [44]. Accordingly, there have been several recent investments for large-scale public Wi-Fi deployments. For example, Google's partnership with Indian Railways and Railtel [52], Facebook's Express Wi-Fi [36], and Microsoft's TV whitespaces trials [34]. Similarly, the national government has committed to public Wi-Fi access for citizens through Digital India, the national infrastructure initiative that aims to connect 250,000 villages to optical fiber. Over 67 billion USD has been pledged for this initiative from companies within India alone [37]. India is not alone in this regard—public Wi-Fi is being deployed across the Global South, for example, México Connectado in Mexico [2] and DoST in the Philippines [19]. These public Wi-Fi initiatives remain free or low-cost in order to be accessible to a majority of people in emerging economies.

Communities in the Global South have been shown to seek out low cost or free-of-cost alternatives due to price-consciousness, lower affordability, and cultural norms. Users invest significant effort in improvising workarounds for low costs; examples of which include side-loading, piracy, and delayed access [51, 54, 66, 74]. However, in a qualitative study with middle-class urban Indians, we found that despite the economic incentive, even free and relatively higher speed service was not enough to motivate our participants to adopt public Wi-Fi. Many participants had tried and dismissed public Wi-Fi, or had refrained from trying it at all.

In contrast with the adoption pattern in the Global North, where Wi-Fi use became widespread before 3G/4G was widely affordable, all of our Indian participants already had access to mobile Internet (i.e., were *mobile-first* users [18]) before the introduction of public Wi-Fi. Public Wi-Fi was often perceived as superfluous in our study. Several participants would instead continue to use 2G/3G because it was "enough" for their needs. Some switched back to 2G/3G when they encountered poor experiences and negative conceptions of public Wi-Fi.

Despite Wi-Fi being in its nascent stages, participants in our study encountered public Wi-Fi with preconceptions from other sources, unlike earlier technological waves of the mobile phone or telecenters. The conceptions of public Wi-Fi connectivity drew not only on practical experience, Bluetooth cultures, and second-hand experiences but also, crucially, on meanings communicated through popular media. In common with anthropologist Arjun Appadurai's 'imagination as social

CHI 2017, May 6-11, 2017, Denver, CO, USA.
ACM ISBN 978-1-4503-4655-9/17/05.
http://dx.doi.org/10.1145/3025453.3025545

practice' [1] [6], our participants invoked received notions of public Wi-Fi imaginaries from news media and popular culture. These conceptions were surprisingly rooted in real fears, deep insights, and specifics, whether firsthand or synthesized.

In this paper, we trace the user conceptions around free public Wi-Fi in India. We interviewed 2G/3G mobile Internet users who were occasional- or non- users of public Wi-Fi in Mumbai and Hyderabad. We found two factors that impeded connecting to public Wi-Fi.

- A complex depth of conceptions around unclear value propositions; fears of sexualization of identity, hacking of devices, incurring financial costs, and radiation risks of public Wi-Fi. Yet, there was an aspirational and 'modern' image of public Wi-Fi.
- Among those who had experienced public Wi-Fi, cumbersome and intrusive connection processes, regulatory requirements, and poor network qualities in practice led to frustration and abandonment of the networks.

We argue that public Wi-Fi initiatives should consider these conceptions while designing networks in order to influence adoption and uptake.

The research contributions of the paper are twofold. Our first contribution is a thematic description of these synthesized conceptions of public Wi-Fi, as assembled by participants from manifold sources. A second contribution is a set of suggestions for how public Wi-Fi providers and designers can cater to these conceptions through interaction designs and their associated business models.

This paper is organized as follows. We first describe the background of public Wi-Fi and our research approach. Next, we describe the Wi-Fi imaginaries, from the abstract aspirations to the specific threats. Then we describe the practical experiences of public Wi-Fi from prior experience and responses to our design provocations. Finally, we provide some suggestions for the design, policy, education, and business models around public Wi-Fi initiatives.

RELATED WORK

Prior research on public Wi-Fi

Scholarly research on the usage of public Wi-Fi is not yet extensive. From the literature on community wireless networks, there are a number of retrospective histories and experience reports (e.g., guifi [8]) as well as numerous traffic measurement studies (e.g., [3]). However, these studies provide only general information on user adoption and network usage. Our research focuses on the broader state of public Wi-Fi in India and specific conceptions that affect the trajectory of use or non-use of public Wi-Fi.

Qualitative user research of public Wi-Fi use in the USA and Europe (*e.g.*, Forlano on community Wi-Fi [28]; Hampton and Gupta on public Wi-Fi [31]; and Sanusi and Palen on coffee shop Wi-Fi [60]) frequently highlight two tensions. First, public Wi-Fi enables 'escape' from home or work. The escape is to a noisy, crowded 'third place' lacking physical privacy, but evades co-habitants/co-workers and their interruptions. Second, establishing clear legitimacy of users' claims to physical and non-physical hotspot resources [60] whether the network is free, paid, or an amenity for paying customers is often quite difficult for both users and venues. A general reluctance to pay for Wi-Fi [28] seems to motivate many to free-ride and take advantage of the fact that venue enforcement is often spotty and normative rather than technical. Qualitative user research in Cuba points to re-configurations in time and space planning due to the high costs of access [22]. The focus in these studies is generally on users who are motivated to take advantage of the infrastructure. In this paper, we extend these discussions by providing an account of how both Wi-Fi users and non-users make meaning out of public Wi-Fi, in a context where its penetration is nascent, but prior mobile data familiarity exists.

Security and privacy research documents a general lack of understanding of Wi-Fi and its security features, often leading to risky behaviors (*e.g.*, Kang *et al.* on Internet mental models [39] and Klasnja *et al.* on general Wi-Fi understanding among users [41]). Specifically, these studies show that Wi-Fi risks were ill-understood even in high-tech regions of USA, but practical details were well known. Less attention is paid to the choice of Wi-Fi non-use that might result from such misunderstandings; however, see [13]). In contrast to previous research in the west on user understanding, in our research, we find in-depth user conceptions of threats and poor experiences that led to a pause or reluctance to connect to public Wi-Fi.

We attend to the particularities of the Indian context, documenting TV, print, and social media around Wi-Fi; national policy; socio-cultural milieu; and infrastructural context. These conditions may apply elsewhere, for example, growing Wi-Fi, a healthy media, celebrity adulation, or government infrastructural efforts may give rise to versions of these conceptions.

Media and Wi-Fi

Media analysis has highlighted the incoherence of meaning associated with Wi-Fi by the public. Not only does Wi-Fi have multiple narratives favored by different stakeholders (e.g., 'openness and sharing' vs. 'security and convenience' [45]), but it continually acquires new meanings from other sources—every deployment site, implementing product, or monetization strategy comes with its marketing tropes and symbolic associations. One can relate these layers of meaning to Lefebvre's ideas on (schematic) representations of space and (symbolic) spaces of representation [33] and apply them to networks [21]. Here, we will limit ourselves to description, noting the connections drawn by participants between public meaning and their own views and behaviors.

[1] Our goal here is not to characterize imaginaries at societal scale, such as historical national identities (as in Anderson's imagined communities [5]) or sociotechnical futures. It is more in line with Appadurai's 'imagination as social practice' [6] and, in particular, his use of technoscapes and mediascapes to analyze individual agency within landscapes of technology diffusion and media narrative and imagery. Appadurai believes that global diffusion and new technologies have loosened the coherence of the Northern ideology in which these concepts were originally held together. Fact and fiction blur into each other. The scapes are disjunctive, deploying differently in each cultural setting, giving it different local meanings.

Internet access in the Global South

We briefly share the broader context of Internet access in order to situate the meaning of public Wi-Fi in emerging economies. Prepaid methods are used by a vast majority of mobile subscribers, as many as 95% in India [70]. Prepaid allows financial flexibility in top ups, made possible by ubiquitous top-up shops. Internet access is generally characterized by slow speeds and high costs (as a proportion of income) [35]. Internet usage is, therefore, rationed and deliberate [18, 59, 74], with a 'metered mindset' [18] and a range of strategies to keep costs low [49, 59]. Low-cost and low-end smart phones, primarily on Android OS, are on the rise [23], although gifting, sharing, second-hand phones, and hand-me-downs are common [54]. Public Wi-Fi co-exists with this constrained space, providing higher speeds at lower costs.

THE LANDSCAPE OF PUBLIC WI-FI

Basics of public Wi-Fi

By public Wi-Fi we mean Wi-Fi access networks intended to serve users in public places. We do not assume that public Wi-Fi networks are public in the sense of being owned by the public (e.g., a municipal government), operated by the public (e.g., community Wi-Fi), openly accessible to the general public (e.g., unsecured), or free-of-charge to the public—though they may be any of these.

From a global network design perspective, Wi-Fi spectrum is usually unlicensed and can therefore be very cost-effective.

There are a number of common payment models for public Wi-Fi. Access may be free-of-charge, offered as an amenity or with ads. Access may be billed to the user's mobile data or charged directly. Similarly, there are several ways to access public Wi-Fi [27]. Most common is the captive portal, in which the user enters information into a web page to get access. Some venues, especially smaller ones, offer unsecured or pre-shared-key-secured networks (PSK). And a few venues offer carrier Wi-Fi, where mobile network credentials are used to authenticate the customer and bill their mobile data.

Public Wi-Fi in India

The rising number of smartphones, ease of deployment of Wi-Fi, and low fixed line penetration motivate telecom and government alike to provide high-speed connectivity in public locations [44]. India appears to be at the cusp of public Wi-Fi growth with massive investments from industry and government. Unlike the west, community or municipal Wi-Fi has not taken off in India and public Wi-Fi remains a venue-based service [44].

All public Internet access in India, including hotspots and cybercafés, are required to follow the Know Your Customer (KYC) protocol of identity verification after the 2008 Mumbai terror attacks [38]. Captive portals are commonly used for KYC login by big venues. Mobile phone numbers are 'traded' for a verification code to confirm the identity of the device/user, which is used to login to the network. Due to its cumbersome steps, detrimental effects on user experience, and panopticon-like enforcement of revealing personal identities, the KYC process has met with dissent in India [62].

A note on the Indian technological context is imperative. As of 2016, India has a population of 1.28 billion, out of which 306 million use mobile Internet [1]. 2G is the dominant network due to coverage and affordability. GSMA expects 50% of Indian subscribers to stay on 2G even in the year 2020 [61]. In an Ericson survey, 88% of respondents felt 3G was too expensive [23]. Only 19.8 million households have access to fixed-line broadband [70]. Public Wi-Fi, while growing, is still in the early stages at an estimated 31,000 hotspots nation-wide [44].

METHODOLOGY

Participants

Semi-structured interviews were conducted in the cities of Hyderabad and Mumbai, India during July-September 2015 for a design ethnography project [56] intended to inform a public Wi-Fi initiative. Participants were recruited through an external recruitment firm, to which screening criteria were provided. We interviewed thirty-six people altogether, eighteen men and eighteen women. Participants were recruited across a diverse range of ages (19-64), low- to middle-income socioeconomic groups, and occupations including college students, homemakers, working professionals, retirees, service workers and unemployed people. As the research was intended to inform a new, access-broadening Wi-Fi initiative, the focus was on nascent users, although public Wi-Fi itself is recent in India. All participants owned a mobile phone—typically a low-end Android smart phone, though a few owned feature-phones—and all had access to prepaid mobile data, though most used the data intermittently. Nine participants had access to fixed-line or mobile broadband Internet in the home as well. Most (26) had no prior experience with public Wi-Fi and the rest (10) had used public Wi-Fi at least once; 16 had prior first-hand experience with Wi-Fi at home or work.

Method and analysis

Interviews lasted two hours each. Interviews were conducted in Hindi, Telugu, and English. Interviews were conducted by the first author; the second author partnered on analysis and synthesis. No personally identifying details were collected. All data were transcribed securely online. Pseudonyms are used when discussing participants below.

The interviews were conversational in style, but covered a fixed set of questions around Internet and Wi-Fi use. Questions focused on the awareness, discovery and attitudes around Wi-Fi; device and app use; behaviors on Wi-Fi networks including non-public Wi-Fi networks; contextual factors in venues; and pain points on networks located in venues. After the in-depth interviews, low-fidelity design provocations for captive portals were shown for feedback. The design included a simple multi-step login process following KYC, abstracted from currents models of captive portals (described later in the 'practical experiences' section; see Figure 3). The provocations were printed on paper to remove technological intimidation and to create room for comfort and scribbles. Questions around the provocations were centered on value, attitudes and perceptions around the wireless technologies and the connection process. The goal was not to evaluate the usability of the design, but to shed light on prior connection experiences and high-level architecture of the design components.

Interview data were analyzed using a general inductive approach [68]. Our evaluation objective was to elicit factors to inform the design of public Wi-Fi systems. Next, transcripts were read multiple times, affinity clusters were developed, and key themes were derived and iteratively refined. Forty-four codes were developed, for example, security and place-based behaviours, which were developed into themes discussed here. We focused on characterizing the experiences and understandings of public Wi-Fi.

Sites

Hyderabad and Mumbai were chosen as the sites of study, to understand public access in metro cities of two sizes. Mumbai, state capital of Maharashtra is the financial capital of India with a population of 18m. Ethnically diverse, Mumbai has global wealth and local poverty at once [7], with a vibrant commercial culture, including banking and Bollywood, and a thriving shadow economy [54]. Hyderabad, state capital of Andhra Pradesh and Telengana, is home to pharmaceutical and technology companies, including Google and Microsoft development offices. The city is more traditional in lifestyle and cultural attitudes than Mumbai.

WI-FI IMAGINARIES

Technologies are envisioned, translated, resisted or consumed in relation to their socio-cultural contexts. In our study, the imaginaries of public Wi-Fi as held by participants drew from an assortment of local news media, national policy, popular culture, carryover notions from prior technologies like Bluetooth, and personal experiences. Public Wi-Fi, then, goes from an invisible connectivity technology to a material medium with pre-existing values, anxieties, expectations, and experience attributes. Similar to Dourish, we approach public Internet in light of its social and cultural effects, but also maintaining a focus on its material realities [20].

In this section, we present the various imaginaries of public Wi-Fi as held by participants in our study. As such, each person spoke of several different conceptions of Wi-Fi. The multilineal conceptions co-existed with each other. Many of these motivated them to try Wi-Fi, whereas others were discouraging. Taken together, they forged a more calculated, speculative, and hesitant experience with public Wi-Fi. First, we illustrate the aspirational aspects of public connectivity circulated by media and welfare policies. The introduction of Wi-Fi as part of civic life invoked images of modernity, national development, pride, and social connectedness among our participants. These positive conceptions were relatively abstract frames for the desire to connect to public Wi-Fi.

Next, we highlight the conceptions around fears and concerns. In contrast with the abstract positive conceptions, these conceptions related to direct and specific threats: privacy and personal safety, security, personal health, financial implications. The threats were derived from scientific, biological, sociological, financial and experiential sources. Like positive conceptions, these conceptions drew extensively on media reports and public discourse as well; but personal experiences were understood in light of such information, making them seem more damaging to real life. While several of these conceptions may be found worldwide, the magnitude, legitimacy and consequences of these fears are much more nuanced and severe in the Indian context, which we elaborate later.

Development, modernity, and 'fashion'

Public Wi-Fi imaginaries were painted with broad strokes of socio-economic development, modernity, and trendiness by national policy and media. First, the discourse of the grand national infrastructure projects had a remarkable influence on awareness and imagination around Wi-Fi in our study. The Digital India campaign produces high visibility announcements, state visits, and public-private partnership launches that are widely covered in news media [55]. The Indian Prime Minister, titled 'India's first cyber premier', colors citizens' technology perceptions with his pro-technology stance and regular use of social media [50]. At the state level, provision of public Wi-Fi is often a part of electoral manifestos, modeled on programs in global cities such as Shanghai and Singapore [26]. The rollout of public Wi-Fi is viewed as a part of the continuum of India's technological emergence; depicted by media as placing the country on the 'information superhighway' [69].

In our interviews, participants, including non-users, were highly aware of public Wi-Fi initiatives in their cities. Public Wi-Fi was broadly viewed as a public amenity for the welfare of tax-paying citizens, a program for national and urban development, not just as venue-based services. All participants knew from media reports of locations where it was being set up, including parks, public squares and private establishments. However, Wi-Fi availability was not predictable in public places due to its early stages.

Our participants often described Wi-Fi, particularly in the public sphere, as 'fashion,' a term signifying its trendy and modern associations. The Internet has long been a signifier of modernity and progress. Larkin notes that infrastructure does not just operate on the technical level, but also on the level of fantasy and desire [43]. In our interviews, the convenience of accessing Internet and being connected to any part of the world was described as 'modern'. The spatial and situated nature of access from places where participants wanted to be seen in, such as Starbucks, Café Coffee Day or InOrbit Malls, made the Wi-Fi more coveted and turned it into social currency. In more mundane places like bus stops and train stations, the presence of Wi-Fi was viewed as a positive delight, "elevating the experience". Even with mobile data being available in most places, Wi-Fi as an amenity for customers or citizens was seen as exclusive. The material aspects of public Wi-Fi presented it as an icon of status and modernity in the public spaces, similar to Spitulnik's observation of radio sets in Zambia [67]. Nisha, 27, a beautician, observed how high speed Wi-Fi invokes pride, and how the national capital enjoys more benefits:

"It's fashion. College students and teens like to use Wi-Fi in our age group. The students and youth want to share their pics and their feelings immediately. If Wi-Fi is faster than mobile data, you can be proud of using it, you can tell your friends you are using Wi-Fi. In Delhi they have a road. They did a study on it, I saw on Google called 'Wi-Fi Road' or something.

We also should have it, not like Necklace Road, where the speed is pathetic. Hyderabad should become modern."

Second, independently of government announcements, the media carry a thriving discourse on technologies in India. Kavoori and Chaddha argue that the process of appropriation of technologies in the Global South occurs not through Internet media, but through mass media like televisions, newspapers, and magazines [40]. Front-page and full-page newspaper ads for the latest gadgets are commonly found in India. Physical marketing collateral, like billboards and posters, for technologies can be found in most urban and some rural areas. Indeed, twenty one participants described wide media coverage as the first test of credibility.

Third, another influencer of public awareness of technology was the film industry. Popular films exert an enormous influence on public culture, politics, ideologies and lifestyles in India [16]. Unsurprisingly, the advertising industry leverages the public adulation and goodwill vested in film celebrities to sell products. Not only are celebrities brand ambassadors for popular products; less well-known and upcoming brands are also endorsed by them to increase brand value (see an account of how the public image of a celebrity actor affected app installs [25]). Sapna, 41, a homemaker, connected film actors with public honesty:

"It would be better if a hero I admire like Amitabh [Bachchan], or someone my daughter admires, like Varun Dhawan, did an ad for new Wi-Fi in the city. They will not lie to us."

Finally, word-of-mouth played a huge role in diffusion of new technologies. Social intermediation for first-time Wi-Fi users from their friends and family had helped them navigate the connection process and get on the network for the first time [58]. Word-of-mouth and credibility through social networks were also noted to be factors in trying out new services. Harish, 35, a factory supervisor noted:

"I will wait until other people use Wi-Fi and give reviews. I really trust my friends and family members. If they confirm it's good, then I try it. They tell me where it's free and good."

To sum up, public Wi-Fi was portrayed and perceived as nation-building infrastructure, social currency, and a vision of global modernity. Yet, specific fears often trumped these aspirations and desires, moving and shaping reluctance with public Wi-Fi. We now turn to a description of these perceived risks.

Sexualization and spam

Public Internet access in India must be understood in the context of a few social themes relating to privacy. For domestic security, all public Internet providers must follow the KYC protocols (see above). Implementations of KYC results in two main concerns, often rooted in experience. First, that personal information is not well protected by those who collect it. Second, sexual harassment of women, wide reporting of harassment and sexual violence cases (*e.g.*, [65]) that resulted from simply appearing in the public sphere, gave female participants pause about revealing any identifying or personal information to strangers. In this section, we describe the various personal information fears expressed by our participants as they relate to public Wi-Fi login and usage.

Participants reported experiences with Wi-Fi access provided through captive portals, password-secured networks, and unsecured networks. Recall that in India, mobile phone numbers are required in the online registration process, with one-time passwords sent via SMS to confirm the validity of the collected number. However, in our study, three of the Wi-Fi users reported logging in to unsecured venue-based networks, which presumably violates regulatory requirements. The obvious user experience issues and the need to deploy software infrastructure for captive portals may motivate venues to provide simpler password-secured and unsecured networks. Due to the slow login process with OTPs, sometimes as long as 10 minutes, ten participants reported often logging in to a better experience with unsecured networks.

In giving out the phone number for login, participants reported being spammed with marketing messages and apparent selling of personal information to telemarketers. These experiences did not instill confidence in captive portals. In addition to requiring mobile number entry for verification, several captive portals presented additional fields for personal information, such as full name, e-mail address and home address. Even though these fields were marked as optional, most participants in our study did not pay attention to the optional tag; instead, they reported feeling uncomfortable and intruded upon. Thirteen participants had enabled 'Do Not Disturb' (DND), a service to block unsolicited SMS that is widely used in large cities [64]. Others, more ambivalent about marketing, did not. Ram, 41, a manufacturing executive says:

"AP [Andhra Pradesh state] government introduced Wi-Fi in public places like trains, but it takes so much time. They are asking for your number, only if you give your number then they give you the password. It was taking 30 minutes to get the OTP. Then they will sell the data to marketing companies. But I have not enabled DND because sometimes I get calls or coupons, like they asked me and my wife to come and collect a gift. We didn't go. If a place asks for a password, you just leave it. Never put a phone number."

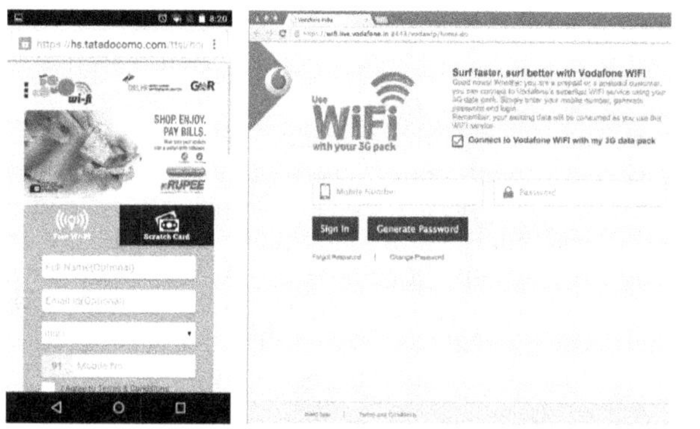

Figure 1. Sample captive portals mentioned in the study.

While provision of personal information caused discomfort for most, this was particularly acute among women. Fears included using phone numbers for prank calls, using personal information for stalking, and morphing profile photos into pornographic content, a reputational attack that occurs in other regions as well [14]. While public sexual harassment is a worldwide problem (see [17]), it is much more visible in the public sphere in India since the gruesome 2012 Nirbaya rape incident [65]. For example, rape assaults are regularly covered by national news media. In turn, the public discourse around harassment may have led to a more pronounced consciousness around personal safety.

In particular, captive portals seeking personal information such as phone numbers, full name, or zip code were considered intrusive by female participants among both Wi-Fi users and non-users. Incidents of personal information misuse and its devastating consequences on women led to a recognition of the side effects of data trails online. Online fears are tied to offline consequences, such as physical stalking and groping, in South Asia [4]. As an example, a 21-year old female committed suicide after her Facebook profile picture was morphed into a nude image [24]. A less damaging experience mentioned by eight participants was being stalked online or receiving friendship requests from strangers.

Although technically captive portals cannot abuse profile pictures, such fears were profound among female participants and seven even reported abandoning Wi-Fi logins to avoid entering their phone number. Five female participants reported sharing only their secondary or tertiary SIM numbers or their spouse's phone number for public services. Anu, 34, homemaker, says:

"I don't like if they ask me for my number when connecting. They can misuse. We are ladies, we face more harassment problems. You are always thinking: will they send us a message like a dirty message? Or take our profile pic? Women only give details to people they know. If the person asking is a good person I will give, but how do I know? I'll give other people but I won't give to Wi-Fi. Why do they need name, phone number, address and all these personal details? What are they going to do?"

While the collection of identifying information no doubt seems prudent to officials concerned with domestic security, a widespread concern that unknown parties will abuse this data can be seen in non-use patterns in our study.

My 2G is good enough

Since the vast majority of India does not have access to a high-speed connection, public Wi-Fi is a preferred route for broadband networks in India [44]. Despite its purported higher speeds and relatively low costs, public Wi-Fi did not always offer clear benefits in comparison to mobile data or home broadband to our participants. In this section, we highlight how existing mobile data connectivity felt superior to public Wi-Fi to many participants in our study.

Wi-Fi was generally associated with "free," "fast," and "reliable", imagined as the fastest technology, followed by 3G and 2G. Still, 2G was seen as adequate for Internet needs. Similarly, in spite of the general association between Wi-Fi and "free," i.e., being cheaper than mobile data, cost savings were described as a minor motivating factor in trying public Wi-Fi. Instead, participants portrayed surprisingly complex reasons for whatever interest they had in public Wi-Fi.

Nine non-users of Wi-Fi stated a preference to use their 2G data plans instead of hotspots. There are many reasons for this. High speeds were seen as more relevant for IT professionals and tech-savvy users. Sambasivan *et al.* [57] report a similar observation for wired networks. While 2G mobile data provided limited speeds, popular lightweight limited activities, such as social media, were seen as acceptable on the networks. High-bandwidth activities, such as streaming and gaming, had limited occurrence or achieved through side-loaded means. Public Wi-Fi was not associated with enrichment, convenience, or high-quality experiences, unlike in other contexts where Wi-Fi is used in public venues.

Here, Kiran, a 36-year-old secretary who did basic tasks online explains her hesitation to try free public Wi-Fi. Note Kiran's comfort with terms like 'MBs' and '2G net pack,' data plan concepts that were familiar and regularly used by other participants as well:

Kiran: *"I don't know what is this Wi-Fi. My children and neighbors talk about it, but I don't know much. I already have MBs from my 2G net pack, so why would I use it? They are not going to give my MBs back. I have 2G. It works for me. Even if it is free, I will not use W-Fi."*

Kiran characterized her net pack purchase as a sunk cost and did not see how using free Wi-Fi would benefit her. Given the cost-consciousness in this context [49], the hesitation to connect to a network at no or low cost is surprising.

Viruses and wipeouts

Being connected to a public, shared network led to an acute sense of vulnerability in our study. Hacking, receiving or sending malicious content, and phone wipeouts were consistently brought up as concerns when connecting to public Wi-Fi, issues not generally raised in western world studies (*e.g.*, [39, 41]). In this section, we describe the various conceptions as they relate to the 'public' nature of public Wi-Fi networks.

Concerns of hacking were focused on device hacking and content deletion, rather than misappropriation of account information, unauthorized transactions or sharing private data; in terms of Wash's folk model of viruses, "mischievous" rather than "criminal" [72] (which contrasts with most other findings, *e.g.*, [12, 41]).

In many cases, concerns appeared to be a form of transfer learning from more familiar wireless networks—notably Bluetooth—to Wi-Fi. Bluetooth was adopted for sharing and side-loading of previously downloaded media content (*e.g.*, movie songs and photos) in the days of feature phones. Wireless sharing with friends, family and bare acquaintances has become widespread social practice [66]. By downloading and side-loading content through multiple hops, media and file content are prone to virus infections. Six participants narrated personal experiences and anecdotal stories of getting viruses from sharing offline content, leading to slowing down of phones or resetting the OS (although these instances could result from low-end phones with overloaded RAM crashing, similar to [66]). With causality of phone wipeouts being difficult to point to, there was general anxiety and caution with connecting to public networks, from carryover fears. Yamuna, 28, reported how her entire phone was wiped out, including beloved selfies, a large contact list and carefully curated song collection, just after receiving a song from her neighbor on Bluetooth. She then took her phone to a repair shop to restore and set up, now with anti-virus software. Any network with sharing, according to her, then became insecure; Yamuna refused to connect to any public Wi-Fi network because she wanted "no chance of risking my phone again."

While the security concerns brought anxiety to Wi-Fi users, they did not always prevent them from connecting wirelessly. Seven prior Wi-Fi users expressed "many people are connected", concerned that networks could be vulnerable to strangers reading their data bits. In some cases, the relationship between wireless networks may not have been clear, let alone which networks were more likely to spread infected content. Bhanu, 35, a lawyer narrates:

"Trust factor is very low. My husband connected to the Wi-Fi at CCD and he got some requests because the Bluetooth was on and he was connected to the network. He transferred a few songs and a movie and he got a virus. He had to reformat his phone. It was too much. My friend had to reformat her laptop. She blames the Wi-Fi for getting the virus. So many of my friends tell me not to use public Wi-Fi."

Low personal awareness of technology and its consequences was also cited as a reason to not use public Wi-Fi. The perspective here was to avoid a new technology because of too many security unknowns. Vaibhav, 44, a corporate trainer narrated:

"I have a friend that refuses to use Wi-Fi, he still uses the wires. I think, 'This is a smart guy, and I am a stupid fool. I think he knows something. Am I going too far with this technology?' So many hackers are there. Who knows if my phone will get hacked if I use Wi-Fi?"

Other concerns raised around seamlessness were control over network selection, owner of the data brands or networks and personal information misuse (see above).

As an illustrative aside, Wi-Fi in the home was viewed as very different from public Wi-Fi due to the ability to set private network passwords, analogous to [12, 39]. The ability to assign one's own password, as opposed to one generated by a source of limited trust, or being authenticated by strangers running a captive portal enabled a feeling of control over the network. Mobile Internet was also viewed as a secure connection. Four users viewed public networks with KYC logins and PSK passwords were viewed as more secure (recall that some venues provide unsecured Internet access without captive portals or passwords).

The participants' conceptions of Wi-Fi intermixed public discourse on online safety (hackers attacking wireless networks, strength of passwords) with personal experience (prevalence of viruses), confusions (conceiving of Wi-Fi as more risky than other types of networks) and social norms (expectations of response to sharing requests).

Personal health

Health concerns from Wi-Fi emissions were seriously regarded in our study. Electromagnetic fields (EMF) from mobile networks and devices receive regular press and government attention around the world [73]. In our study, radiation risks regularly surfaced in TV, news and social media, leading to limited use or apprehensions about using public Wi-Fi.

Seven participants in Hyderabad mentioned viewing a recent television news feature on Wi-Fi health risks. The program discussed the radiation risks of using Wi-Fi with scientific-sounding facts and real-world examples of corporeal damage through cancer, brain damage or animal and bird deaths. Ahmed, the nutritionist was one of the viewers of the program. Here he talks about the credibility of a feature on national television; since viewing the program, he switched off his phone at nights and avoided using Wi-Fi in public places. In Ahmed's view, using the Wi-Fi was a "dose of radiation, you use very less or don't use at all."

"Wi-Fi causes health problems. I have seen it on TV, NDTV or Aaj Tak. They did a special show on Wi-Fi. My daughters and I got very scared. We shut off our Wi-Fi for two days. It can cause mental disorder or cancer. They showed that sparrows can die. It was on national television, so they can't fake it. They advised us to shut off the Wi-Fi router when we are not using it. In public places we can't shut it so I avoid completely. If you keep any mobile in your pocket with Wi-Fi, you will feel the rhythm of your heartbeat changing."

Ahmed was one of the few participants who avoided public Wi-Fi due to health concerns. Seven prior users expressed worries about Wi-Fi radiation and self-capped their usage.

Social sharing of news items through WhatsApp, Facebook and regional magazines reinforced these messages. Often these messages carried weighty qualifiers, such as international news, health or astronomy organizations; severe health risks that cannot be dismissed easily; and emotional significance in sharing the health warnings to close ones. Burrell, in a study of rumors in Ghana, notes that they at once combine vague animosity or threats, attached to concrete events and times and institutional responsibility [11]. Chitra, a 35-year old banker, showed us a recent forward on NASA- and BBC-approved phone radiation warnings she received (which has circulated since 2010 in Ghana and been declared a hoax (see Figure 2) [9]). She forwarded the message to three of her relatives. Public Wi-Fi to Chitra was part of a larger class of radiation prone technologies, indistinguishable from mobile phones.

The risks of Wi-Fi were perceived not only in public Wi-Fi networks, but also in home networks; in fact, five participants unplugged routers at home, motivated by frugality as well as health reasons (also noted in [57]). As Swapna, 39, a homemaker, reflected on the inadvertent connection of her phone to her neighbor's Wi-Fi, even when she unplugged her router. Eventually she switched off her phone Wi-Fi toggle:

"Wi-Fi can give you headaches... At night we switch off the Wi-Fi network in the home. But our tenants live downstairs in 50m radius. Sometimes my phone connects to their Wi-Fi at night. Then we told them to switch it off. After 11, no Wi-Fi."

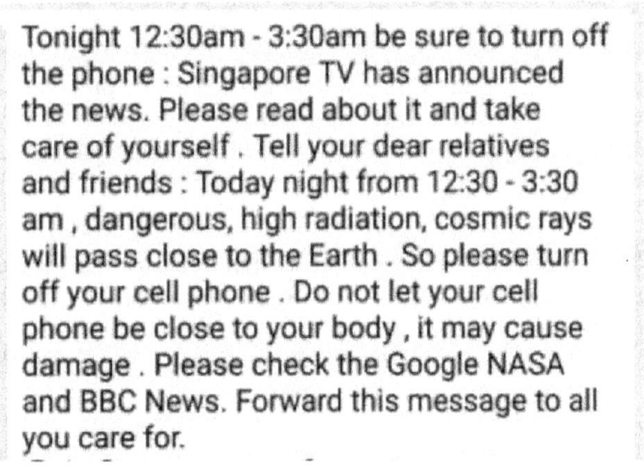
Tonight 12:30am - 3:30am be sure to turn off the phone : Singapore TV has announced the news. Please read about it and take care of yourself . Tell your dear relatives and friends : Today night from 12:30 - 3:30 am , dangerous, high radiation, cosmic rays will pass close to the Earth . So please turn off your cell phone . Do not let your cell phone be close to your body , it may cause damage . Please check the Google NASA and BBC News. Forward this message to all you care for.

Figure 2. A Whatsapp forward received by a participant.

In their concern about EMF, these participants are no different from any number of concerned citizens worldwide; cancer fears concern British elders [42] and cause Kenyan and Zambian farmers to switch off their phones [73] as well. What is notable here is the attribution of physical effects, real or not, to EMF from Wi-Fi but not from mobile networks and the focused discourse on the risks at national and social levels. For example, neither informant speaks of 2G handset emissions, which are at much higher peak power levels [71]. Indeed, notice that the way that Swapna detects her tenants' Wi-Fi is by the fact that her smartphone connects to it.

It is the "new" technology that is singled out in public discourse of news and social media, in personal concerns (fear), in corporeal sensitivity and in concrete response (non-use). As in earlier responses to mobile towers (*e.g.,* [10]), the focus is not on fully removing the infrastructure in use, but on the *control* of infrastructure coming into use. As in ubicomp research on off-the-grid "disconnectors", disconnection from infrastructure is selective rather than total and irreversible [46].

Financial fears

News stories, government announcements, and commercial advertisements had created an expectation among all participants that free-of-charge use was the norm for public Wi-Fi. When asked if they had ever paid for Wi-Fi access, participants resoundingly replied in the negative: "*Never! If you have to pay then why do I have mobile data?*" Given this, it may seem strange to characterize cost as a specific threat of public Wi-Fi.

As is often noted in studies in developing regions, a key issue for prepaid telecom users is direct control over costs [49, 59]. Acquisition of prepaid data packs involves meticulous planning around the amount of data, validity, and cost. Lack of clarity around how usage is billed in public Wi-Fi threatens users' control over meeting their communication needs under a constrained telecom budget. Non-users expressed suspicions that Wi-Fi advertised as "free" would turn out to cost something after all. Here the distinct entities of time on Wi-Fi networks and mobile networks were viewed as fungible, boundary-less monetary units. Two non-users expressed that free-of-cost usage still did not clearly indicate to them whether their mobile data balance would be cut off.

Confidence had been established in their operators' billing rates and practices given their current usage. It was not a small thing to abandon the familiar data pack for an unknown entity (public Wi-Fi operators), even one that promised free use and potential for high-speed use cases.

PRACTICAL EXPERIENCES OF PUBLIC WI-FI

Up to this point, we have mainly discussed the conceptions held by participants about public Wi-Fi that steered them toward or away from adoption, or at least experimentation. We now turn to the practical experience of accessing public Wi-Fi. We summarize participants' responses to our design provocations and recollections of prior experiences with captive portals (see Figure 3). Note that in order to be displayed, captive portals require a user to open any http URL on a browser or open a phone notification.

Confusion with captive portals

Participants found captive portals to be confusing and error-prone; connecting was not an obvious process. First, twenty-one participants, including public Wi-Fi non-users and even a few self-identified users mentioned that upon connecting to an unsecured network, they would go straight to application use. That is, the intermediate step of opening the captive portal page to sign in did not fall within the natural course of expected actions. Fifteen participants expressed that unsecured networks need no further step. In practice, the individual would not be connected to the network.

Second, in walking through the captive portal process, there were drop-offs. The KYC process was not clearly understood, hence these individuals did not expect to receive or check SMS. Twelve participants, especially women, expressed privacy issues of refusal to enter phone numbers and other personal information (see above). A common touchpoint for determining whether one was finally online was when social media messages started flowing into applications. Five participants forgot their access code from SMS by the time they toggled to the browser. Of these, three wondered if they should send a reply to the SMS received. Prior Wi-Fi users had a clearer understanding of the KYC captive portal process that non-users; but not uniformly since some had connected to open networks or PSK-protected networks (see above).

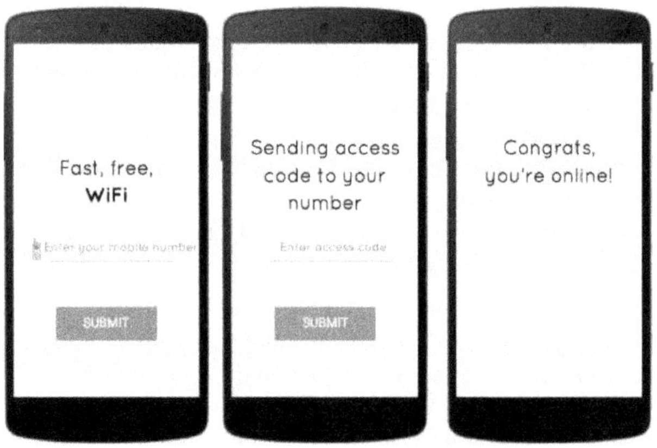

Figure 3. Design provocations used in the study.

Slow speeds

As mentioned above, Wi-Fi as a concept was associated with "free, fast, and reliable," but in public places it was considered slow by those who had actually used it (in practice, poorly provisioned Wi-Fi can be as slow as 2G). Not only was the actual connection reported to be slow, but the KYC login on captive portals was also reported to take a while. Six participants reported abandoning the connection process when they did not receive an access code in a few seconds.

Due to the unpredictability of availability at a future locale, of actual speeds, and so on, public Wi-Fi was never the go-to network for doing things online in our study. Rather, it was used for low-priority browsing. Mobile data, even 2G, was viewed as a lot more dependable. Fourteen prior Wi-Fi users connected to public Wi-Fi to find an alternative when mobile data was exhausted or running low. On low balance, their intent to connect surfaced not because a Wi-Fi network was available and one was habituated to a continuous connection, but because an activity arose that required online access.

Discovery of Wi-Fi

The process of getting connected to a public Wi-Fi network was involved and resource-intensive. Notification alerts for local Wi-Fi networks did not appear for most, as a majority (twenty-six) of our participants (even prior users) kept their phone Wi-Fi turned off. Eight of those with home Wi-Fi also turned off Wi-Fi when outside. This mirrored the widespread practice of turning off mobile data to save battery power and prevent background data usage by applications [49]. Instead, discovery of public networks was accomplished through physical posters and word-of-mouth.

Discovery was characterized by gendered concerns. Studies have documented gender gaps in phone access in South Asia (women are 38% less likely to own phones in India) [30]. Six female participants wanted to run new technology by their spouses for approval. Among them, technology adoption decisions were deferred to men. Three female participants expressed concerns about being intimidated by seeking help from male staff, the social consequences of conversing with males, and mis-trusting strangers. Ameya, 29, a tailor, reflects:

> *"I would come home and talk about Wi-Fi, if I see it. My husband would ask me, 'why did you talk to someone [the agent], why do you trust this person'. He says people do make a fool out of wives, but not husbands."*

DISCUSSION

Based on the experiences of participants in our study, we note that public Wi-Fi is approached with a complex set of imaginaries, from multiple sources. In the words of Malinowski, '*myths are not merely stories told, but realities lived...myth, is not merely symbolic, but a direct expression of subject matter*' [47]. Despite the aspirational leanings, the conceptions largely encompassed deep-rooted fears and risks, impacting the adoption and usage of public Wi-Fi.

How does a new technology co-exist or conflict with the social practices and material properties of existing technologies? Infrastructure studies underscore that infrastructures are formed when several technological systems combine to form a union: light bulbs succeeded not due to the mere innovation in bulb design, but from linking many underlying financial, technical and administrative systems [43, 32]. As a recent network technology, public Wi-Fi was surrounded by hype in national development, urban modernity, and media advertisements. Yet, points of friction from previous technology cultures surfaced in phone wipeouts fears, or when relevancy of Wi-Fi seemed low compared to 2G. With a fallback option of 2G, many participants did not want to make the effort to switch, or converted back when fears or frustrations with Wi-Fi arose.

While a public hotspot can be set up by any establishment by lighting up an access point, our research points to a non-trivial number of aspects to get right for adoption. If the network is not well provisioned; the login process difficult; the value of using public Wi-Fi over mobile data unclear; or the fears and concerns unaddressed; public Wi-Fi may not feel inviting to many. However, these factors are not insurmountable and successes are starting to emerge. The recent deployment of Wi-Fi in train stations by the Google partnership with Indian Railways and RailTel had 5 million users as of Dec 2016 by providing a spam-free, high-speed, simple login experience with several branding touch points [48].

With the data above in mind, we can now develop some general points relevant to the idea of Internet ubiquity in India.

Public Wi-Fi as approachable networks

We can expect that public Wi-Fi access will continue to expand, due to government and industry interest in providing infrastructure to the public. The contours of Wi-Fi continue to shift, as it evolves as a technology and more people encounter it in India. As an infrastructure gains prevalence and prominence over time, fears and concerns may diminish or transform [10].

If public Wi-Fi were to be truly democratic, the design of these infrastructures need to consider less resourced individuals who may get marginalized due to the embedded politics [43]. Designing experiences that do not reinforce existing socio-economic privelages, such as literacy, gender, affordability, or social class, by making the experiences safe, intuitive, low cost and inclusive. Experience providers should clearly state cost implications of connections, to avoid user confusion about using up mobile credit or bank balances. Since open networks were associated with compromised security, any measures of security from captive portals are paramount. Health concerns around radiation risks or eye problems from using Wi-Fi networks could be clarified through legitimate TV shows, radio programs or social media forwards from carriers.

At the same time, awareness initiatives around the connection itself may help make systems more usable, draw relevance and remove fears around Wi-Fi. Guided walkthroughs on user devices may make the networks seem more relatable and help users assess the quality firsthand. Human agents and kiosks are widely employed in India and other emerging economies to introduce new concepts and were considered easily approachable in our study [66].

Public Wi-Fi as infrastructure for the public

Public Wi-Fi operates in public space and was imagined much like a public space: locational, shared, and subject to overuse, unlike mobile networks that were perceived as pervasive, private, and consistent. The shared network often created a feeling of vulnerability. Many KYC implementations requested more information than needed. Intrusive implementations of KYC led to concerns about personal identity misuse and sexual harassment, leading to refusal to connect.

Minimal information should be collected to improve user trust and sign-in flows. Captive portals in our study that collected optional personal information for marketing purposes were met with abandonment, low trust, or user annoyance. Care should be taken to address why the information is collected and what will be done with it. Personally-identifying information could be stored with trusted entities in order to maximize user trust in safeguarding the information [15].

Female participants in our study expressed higher comfort levels with seeking help to learn about the networks, but some expressed reservations with male members. Initiatives that have strong female representation in providing access, such as Internet Saathi's agents [29], could provide a welcoming experience for women.

As a cautionary note on ubiquitous public Wi-Fi access, some of the underlying fears discussed here could be actualized or exacerbated, such as women's safety online; cybercrime; or fraud. Policy makers and regulators would have to pro-actively consider the effects of unregulated and accelerated expansion of access in an effort to digitize the nation.

Public Wi-Fi as reliable experiences

High-latency and unreliable performances and unintuitive login processes characterized the practical experience of public Wi-Fi access in our study. Captive portals offer the most inclusive legal solution to public access since they work with any browser-capable devices and place no burden on users to install special-purpose software. However, captive portals need to be made usable to be accessible to a wider range of new users and meet regulatory requirements. Easy, secure, and rapid connection experiences provide welcoming experiences to those who seek to connect.

Reliable and high-speed networks are at the core of the network experience. As noted in a study of broadband speeds among Indian families [57], speed is experiential and not necessarily an aspiration- or desire-based driver to a network. Those who did experience good quality networks recalled them as delightful episodes in a sea of spotty networks. While bandwidth is particularly expensive in emerging economies, free but poor quality access did not seem adequate to drive adoption to new network infrastructures. As noted above, many people have other options they already understand and rely upon, even if it means using slow, personal 2G data plans.

Public Wi-Fi as "free" infrastructure

As we have seen, participants had clearly been party to the overwhelming discourse of "free" public Wi-Fi. In the Global North, institutions have a modest obligation to provide amenity service, at a reasonable level of quality and security, to the extent that even normatively illegitimate users routinely take advantage of free Wi-Fi service if they can. In India, we were surprised by the degree to which making service free-of-charge was not enough to convince participants that it was worth taking up.

Public Wi-Fi came with affective costs. There is pleasure in receiving something for free [63], but the frustrations of lack of relevancy, lack of ubiquity, unpredictable performance, and complex user experience relative to the familiar use of purchased mobile data more than balanced it. Public Wi-Fi came with perceived risks—security threats, privacy threats, reputation threats, and health threats. Saving money was not always enough to justify use.

Today's networks are heterogeneous, and the assemblages we rely upon to deliver ubiquitous services now span many technologies and operating entities. As designers we often find we must accept physical 'seams' in infrastructure [21], but the idea that networks themselves might be associated with wildly differing levels of trust and selectively avoided is seen as an idea accepted by only a few studies [13]. This was not the case in our data. While multiple networks now exist in India of today, it still remains a messy, resistant counter to the 'anytime, anywhere' vision [21].

From a socio-economic development point of view, it is unusual to find that 2G mobile data might be seen as preferable to "free, fast" Wi-Fi in developing regions. In some cases, this could be attributed to participants seeing public Wi-Fi as "not free" or "not fast"; but in any case, we can see this as another example of users constructing a "digital repertoire" [18] of usage patterns, suited to their particular circumstances.

CONCLUSION

Indian Internet users are largely familiar with the idea of Wi-Fi, but public Wi-Fi infrastructure is certainly not pervasive and efforts to make it more widely available are significant. We wanted to study users' and non-users' conceptions so that we could understand how likely it was that urban middle-class Indians would instantly take advantage of new Wi-Fi opportunities. What we found is that despite the recent introduction, people came to public Wi-Fi with conceptions shaped by media, popular culture, prior technology cultures and personal or second-hand experiences. As such, these received notions led to vague interest but also reluctance due to specific threats around personal safety, credit balance, health, and device security. Poor experiences further deterred interest. Even prior users of public Wi-Fi expressed concern with connecting to these networks.

While one might assert that the conceptions described here will prove to be ephemeral, it is through action—public awareness, better user experiences, public education, service demonstrations, business model innovation—that they will be changed.

ACKNOWLEDGEMENTS

Our sincere thanks to Vaishali Jain for research support. We thank our participants, the Google Station team, Jose Faleiro, Asif Baki, and our ACs and reviewers.

REFERENCES

1. 2016. IAMAI report. https://goo.gl/Ku53n4. (Feb 2016).
2. 2016. Mexico Connectado website. http://mexicoconectado.gob.mx/. (Sep 2016).
3. Mikhail Afanasyev, Tsuwei Chen, Geoffrey M Voelker, and Alex C Snoeren. 2010. Usage patterns in an urban WiFi network. *ACM Trans. Netw.* 18, 5 (2010), 1359–1372.
4. Syed Ishtiaque Ahmed, Steven J Jackson, Nova Ahmed, and others. 2014. Protibadi: A platform for fighting sexual harassment in urban Bangladesh. In *CHI*. ACM, 2695–2704.
5. Benedict Anderson. 2006. *Imagined Communities: Reflections on the Origin and Spread of Nationalism*. Verso.
6. Arjun Appadurai. 1996. *Modernity at Large*. Univ. Minnesota Press.
7. Arjun Appadurai. 2000. Spectral housing and urban cleansing: Notes on millennial Mumbai. *Public Culture* 12, 3 (2000), 627–651.
8. Roger Baig, Ramon Roca, Leandro Navarro, and Felix Freitag. 2015. guifi.net: A network infrastructure commons. In *ICTD*. 27.
9. BBC. 2010. Ghana text hoax predicting earthquake prompts panic. https://goo.gl/kFb6uk. (Jan 2010).
10. Adam Burgess. 2004. *Cellular Phones, Public Fears, and a Culture of Precaution*. Cambridge Univ. Press.
11. Jenna Burrell. 2013. The materiality of rumor. In *Materiality and Organizing: Social Interaction in a Technological World*, Paul M. Leonardi, Bonnie A. Nardi, and Jannis Kallinikos (Eds.). Oxford Univ. Press, 315–332.
12. Jay Chen, Michael Paik, and Kelly McCabe. 2014. Exploring Internet security perceptions and practices in urban Ghana. In *SOUPS*. 129–142.
13. Erika Chin, Adrienne Porter Felt, Vyas Sekar, and David Wagner. 2012. Measuring user confidence in smartphone security and privacy. In *SOUPS*. 1.
14. Elisabetta Costa. 2016. *Social Media in Southeast Turkey*. UCL Press.
15. Rachna Dhamija and Lisa Dusseault. 2008. The seven flaws of identity management: Usability and security challenges. *IEEE Security & Privacy* 6, 2 (2008), 24–29.
16. Sara Dickey. 1993. The politics of adulation: Cinema and the production of politicians in South India. *J. Asian Stud.* 52, 02 (1993), 340–372.
17. Jill P Dimond, Michaelanne Dye, Daphne LaRose, and Amy S Bruckman. 2013. Hollaback!: The role of storytelling online in a social movement organization. In *CSCW*. 477–490.
18. Jonathan Donner. 2015. *After Access: Inclusion, Development, and a More Mobile Internet*. MIT Press.
19. DoST. 2016. DoST Wi-Fi. https://goo.gl/bNwGVD. (July 2016).
20. Paul Dourish. 2015. Not the Internet, but this Internet: How othernets illuminate our feudal Internet. In *Aarhus Conf.* Aarhus Univ., 157–168.
21. Paul Dourish and Genevieve Bell. 2007. The infrastructure of experience and the experience of infrastructure. *Environ. Plan. B* 34, 3 (2007), 414–430.
22. Michaelanne Dye, David Nemer, Laura Pina, Nithya Sambasivan, Amy Bruckman, and Neha Kumar. 2017. Locating the Internet in the parks of Havana. In *CHI*. ACM.
23. Ericson. 2015a. The Changing Mobile Broadband Landscape. http://goo.gl/Lwgpwk. (Mar 2015).
24. Ericson. 2015b. Girl commits suicide after morphed pics appear on Facebook. http://goo.gl/UGZyfi. (Jun 2015).
25. Firstpost. 2016a. It's business, not personal. http://goo.gl/HbnG10. (Mar 2016).
26. Firstpost. 2016b. Will make Delhi a WiFi city in a year. http://goo.gl/fPd0cK. (Mar 2016).
27. Rob Flickenger. 2003. *Building Wireless Community Networks*. O'Reilly.
28. Laura Forlano. 2009. WiFi geographies: When code meets place. *The Info. Soc.* 25, 5 (2009), 344–352.
29. Google. 2016. Internet Saathi. http://goo.gl/7SDwk2. (Jun 2016).
30. GSMA. 2016. Bridging the Gender Gap. http://goo.gl/517XPf. (Mar 2016).
31. Keith N Hampton and Neeti Gupta. 2008. Community and social interaction in the wireless city: Wi-Fi use in public and semi-public spaces. *New Media & Society* 10, 6 (2008), 831–850.
32. Andrew B Hargadon and Yellowlees Douglas. 2001. When innovations meet institutions: Edison and the design of the electric light. *Adm. Sci. Q.* 46, 3 (2001), 476–501.
33. Lefebvre Henri. 1991. *The Production of Space*. Oxford Univ. Press.
34. HT. 2016. Microsoft CEO in India, to focus on cloud, net connectivity. https://goo.gl/0dR3o5. (2016).
35. IE. 2015. Measuring the Information Society Report. https://goo.gl/efTaaV. (Mar 2015).
36. IE. 2016. Facebook may soon launch cheap WiFi in India. http://goo.gl/poUhL3. (Mar 2016).
37. DNA India. 2015. Digital India: CEOs commit to invest Rs 4.5 trillion. https://goo.gl/xM7smT. (Jul 2015).
38. IT. 2008. IT amendment act. . (July 2008).

39. Ruogu Kang, Laura Dabbish, Nathaniel Fruchter, and Sara Kiesler. 2015. 'My data just goes everywhere': User mental models of the Internet and implications for privacy and security. In *SOUPS*. 39–52.
40. Anandam Kavoori and Kalyani Chadha. 2006. The cell phone as a cultural technology: Lessons from the Indian case. In *The Cell Phone Reader*, Anandam Kavoori and Noah Arceneaux (Eds.). Peter Lang, 227–239.
41. Predrag Klasnja, Sunny Consolvo, Jaeyeon Jung, and others. 2009. 'When I am on Wi-Fi, I am fearless': Privacy concerns and practices in everyday Wi-Fi use. In *SOUPS*. 1993–2002.
42. Sri Kurniawan. 2006. An exploratory study of how older women use mobile phones. In *UbiComp*. Springer, 105–122.
43. Brian Larkin. 2013. The politics and poetics of infrastructure. *Annu. Rev. Anthropol.* 42 (2013), 327–343.
44. LiveMint. 2015. Future of public Wi-Fi hot spots in India. `https://goo.gl/efTaaV`. (Aug 2015).
45. Adrian Mackenzie. 2005. Untangling the unwired: Wi-Fi and the cultural inversion of infrastructure. *Space and Culture* 8, 3 (2005), 269–285.
46. Scott D Mainwaring, Michele F Chang, and Ken Anderson. 2004. Infrastructures and their discontents. In *UbiComp*. Springer, 418–432.
47. Bronislaw Malinowski. 1926. *Myth in primitive psychology*. Norton.
48. Mashable. 2016. Google's free Wi-Fi is now available at 100 railway stations in India. `https://goo.gl/epHBKr`. (Dec 2016).
49. Arunesh Mathur, Brent Schlotfeldt, and Marshini Chetty. 2015. A mixed-methods study of mobile users' data usage practices in South Africa. In *UbiComp*. ACM, 1209–1220.
50. Joyojeet Pal. 2015. Banalities turned viral: Narendra Modi and the political tweet. *Television & New Media* 16, 4 (2015), 378–387.
51. Alex Pentland, Richard Fletcher, and Amir Hasson. 2004. Daknet: Rethinking connectivity in developing nations. *IEEE Computer* 37, 1 (2004), 78–83.
52. Sundar Pichai. 2016. Bringing the Internet to more Indians. `http://goo.gl/P9E9Z3`. (Mar 2016).
53. Nandagopal Rajan. 2016. Internet Trends 2016. `http://goo.gl/ByYKF2`. (Mar 2016).
54. Nimmi Rangaswamy and Nithya Sambasivan. 2011. Cutting Chai, Jugaad, and Here Pheri: Towards UbiComp for a global community. *PUC* 15, 6 (2011), 553–564.
55. Reuters. 2015. Modi revives campaign for digital India. `http://goo.gl/7HvbQ5`. (2015).
56. Tony Salvador, Genevieve Bell, and Ken Anderson. 1999. Design ethnography. *Des. Manage. Rev.* 10, 4 (1999), 35–41.
57. Nithya Sambasivan, Gulzar Azad, Paul M Aoki, and Saswati Saha Mitra. 2016. We call it Hi-Fi: Exposing Indian households to high speed broadband wireless Internet. In *ICTD*. ACM, 3.
58. Nithya Sambasivan, Ed Cutrell, Kentaro Toyama, and Bonnie Nardi. 2010. Intermediated technology use in developing communities. In *CHI*. ACM, 2583–2592.
59. Nithya Sambasivan, Paul Lee, Greg Hecht, and others. 2013. Chale, how much it cost to browse?: Results from a mobile data price transparency trial in Ghana. In *ICTD*. ACM, 13–23.
60. Alena Sanusi and Leysia Palen. 2008. Of coffee shops and parking lots: Considering matters of space and place in the use of public Wi-Fi. *CSCW* 17, 2-3 (2008), 257–273.
61. Debhasis Sarkar. 2016. 5 reasons why 4G is not able to excite India. `http://goo.gl/fvtWC`. (Feb 2016).
62. Ajay Shah. 2012. What security? Costs of KYC outweigh the benefits. `https://goo.gl/SQaGSi`. (May 2012).
63. Kristina Shampanier, Nina Mazar, and Dan Ariely. 2007. Zero as a special price: The true value of free products. *Mark. Sci.* 26, 6 (2007), 742–757.
64. Vijay Sharma. 2013. Phone Numbers in DND directory. `http://goo.gl/usZ751`. (Mar 2013).
65. Smriti Singh. 2016. Delhi gang rape. `http://goo.gl/CCrDbZ`. (Mar 2016).
66. Thomas N Smyth, Satish Kumar, Indrani Medhi, and Kentaro Toyama. 2010. Where there's a will there's a way: Mobile media sharing in urban india. In *CHI*. ACM, 753–762.
67. Debra Spitulnik. 2002. Rethinking reception through Zambian radio culture. In *Media worlds*, Faye D. Ginsburg, Lila Abu-Lughod, and Brian Larkin (Eds.). Univ. Calif. Press, 337–354.
68. David R Thomas. 2006. A general inductive approach for analyzing qualitative evaluation data. *Amer. J. Eval.* 27, 2 (2006), 237–246.
69. TOI. 2015. A digital dream to put India on information superhighway. `https://goo.gl/CxYC2u`. (May 2015).
70. TRAI. 2016. The Indian Telecom Services Performance Indicators: January - March 2016. `https://goo.gl/vmP1ZX`. (Mar 2016).
71. Peter A Valberg, T Emilie van Deventer, and Michael H Repacholi. 2007. Base stations and wireless networks. *Environ. Health Pers.* (2007), 416–424.
72. Rick Wash. 2010. Folk models of home computer security. In *SOUPS*. ACM, 11.
73. Susan P Wyche, Melissa Densmore, and Brian Samuel Geyer. 2015. Real mobiles: Kenyan and Zambian smallholder farmers' current attitudes towards mobile phones. In *ICTD*. ACM, 9.
74. Susan P Wyche, Thomas N Smyth, Marshini Chetty, Paul M Aoki, and Rebecca E Grinter. 2010. Deliberate interactions: Characterizing technology use in Nairobi, Kenya. In *CHI*. ACM, 2593–2602.

Agency in Assistive Technology Adoption: Visual Impairment and Smartphone Use in Bangalore

Joyojeet Pal[1], Anandhi Viswanathan[2], Priyank Chandra[1], Anisha Nazareth[3], Vaishnav Kameshwaran[1], Hariharan Subramonyam[1], Aditya Johri[4], Mark S. Ackerman[1], Sile O'Modhrain[1]

[1] University of Michigan, Ann Arbor, Michigan, USA - {joyojeet, prch, vaikam, harihars, ackerm, sileo}@umich.edu

[2] Independent Researcher, Bangalore, India - anandhi.viswanathan@gmail.com

[3] International Institute of Information Technology, Bangalore, India - anisha.nazareth@iiitb.org

[4] George Mason University, Fairfax, Virginia, USA - johri@gmu.edu

ABSTRACT

Studies on technology adoption typically assume that a user's perception of usability and usefulness of technology are central to its adoption. Specifically, in the case of accessibility and assistive technology, research has traditionally focused on the artifact rather than the individual, arguing that individual technologies fail or succeed based on their usability and fit for their users. Using a mixed-methods field study of smartphone adoption by 81 people with visual impairments in Bangalore, India, we argue that these positions are dated in the case of accessibility where a non-homogeneous population must adapt to technologies built for sighted people. We found that many users switch to smartphones despite their awareness of significant usability challenges with smartphones. We propose a nuanced understanding of perceived usefulness and actual usage based on *need*-related social and economic functions, which is an important step toward rethinking technology adoption for people with disabilities.

Author Keywords

Accessibility; India; Mobile Phones; Android; Bangalore; iOS

ACM Classification Keywords

H.5.m.: Miscellaneous. K.4.2 Social Issues: Assistive technologies

INTRODUCTION

Theories on technology adoption or acceptance among people with disabilities have for more than two decades been influenced by work on technology *abandonment*. Such work has at its center the technological artifact and the factors that impact its use, or more typically lack thereof. Outside the accessibility domain, work on technology adoption is largely dominated by *technology acceptance models* (TAM), which emerged out of management information systems (MIS) research. Unlike abandonment models, these models lay emphasis on the intrinsic and extrinsic factors that influence technology use.

In the last two decades, the line between technology designed specifically for people with disabilities — i.e. *assistive technology* (AT) — and mainstream technology is increasingly blurred. This is because devices built for mainstream markets have begun to support accessibility features that make them usable by people with disabilities. A prime example is the smartphone, which offers the capability of several AT devices or software that used to be separately purchased (e.g., screen readers, magnifiers, voice recorders). In addition, the app ecosystem supports a range of AT functions.

For blind users, adopting smartphones has meant adapting to the touchscreen interface, the app universe, and the use of internet services. Agency on the part of visually impaired mobile users to accept or reject this new model of mobile interaction is undercut by the fact that older keypad-based feature phones with separately installed AT software are being eased out of circulation [32].

Additionally, while a smartphone enables a range of digital services including access to media, location-based services, and online commerce, access to the full gamut of smartphone affordances depends in part on the network infrastructure, device capabilities, and individuals' ability to effectively navigate the interfaces. This has made technology adoption a moving target because the technology per se is part of an ecosystem of technologies, making it difficult to isolate the acceptance of one object of analysis away from a broader whole. Consequently, technology adoption research needs to go beyond solely whether or not individuals buy and use devices to understand the nuances of how people switch from devices and platforms.

CHI 2017, May 06 - 11, 2017, Denver, CO, USA

ACM 978-1-4503-4655-9/17/05…$15.00
DOI: http://dx.doi.org/10.1145/3025453.3025895

Using a survey of 81 mobile users with visual impairments in Bangalore, India, we show that an understanding of the functions that technologies enable, along with user experiences, helps create a more complete picture of technology adoption in accessibility settings. We present a description of what people use their mobile phones for, and how that differs across classes of devices that people can afford. We present qualitative data highlighting users' perspectives of the roles that mobile phones play in enabling and supporting various functions in their lives. Finally, we examine these data against the user experiences of things that do not work, to understand what people are willing to adapt and work around in the interest of maintaining their digital being.

We propose a move away from reductionist approaches (abandonment) and technology adoption models, which all suggest a binary answer to whether a technology is adopted or abandoned. Instead we argue that human agency may need to be understood within the necessity of adopting certain mainstream devices, such as mobile phones.

RELATED WORK

Management Information Systems Approaches to Technology Adoption

The technology acceptance model (TAM) [12] has been at the heart of an influential movement around thinking about the conditions under which individuals accept and continue to use information technology. TAM proposes two key constructs around factors influencing technology adoption. The first is "perceived usefulness," which is defined as "the degree to which a person believes that using a particular system would enhance his or her job performance" [12]. The second factor, "perceived ease of use," is defined as the "degree to which a person believes that using a particular system would be free of effort" [12, p. 320].

While previous research has focused on these two core constructs and their operationalization through questionnaires, subsequent refinements have examined other factors that influence adoption. These include motivation, which probes the extent to which a person desires to perform an activity as "it is perceived to be instrumental in achieving valued outcomes that are distinct from the activity itself, such as improved job performance, pay, or promotions." [13 p.1112] Motivations are seen either intrinsically (from one's own sense of value in a technology) or extrinsically (from the value attributed socially by its use) [13]. Other work has looked at the role of affect, which refers to the ways in which intrinsic emotions or feelings of gratification are invoked by the adoption or continued use of a technological artifact [35].

Synthesizing these and other constructs to study technology adoption, Venkatesh et al. [36] proposed the Unified Theory of Acceptance and Use of Technology (UTAUT), which puts forth four constructs, three of which examine use intent: performance expectancy, effort expectancy, and social influence; the fourth, facilitating conditions, is a determinant of use behavior. This work has been influential in business studies around technology adoption, and variants of the constructs have been used to examine technology adoption in organizational and industrial settings including banking [38], e-government [2], social media [11], and health records [4], as well as with specific population groups such as doctors [37], students [1], public relations professionals [3], veterans [8], and police officers [7]. Related strands of work include studies of the diffusion of innovations that take a macro view of which technologies do and don't make it in societies, and the various actors involved [31], and work on technology appropriation that goes beyond the idea of adoption to how people incorporate technology into their lives [5].

HCI Approaches to Technology Adoption in Accessibility

The traditional focus of technology adoption in accessibility research on abandonment has been attributed to a range of market and design factors [16, 29, 33]. Key among these has been a history of impairment-centric AT products that have found their way to users through innovators' desire to solve disability with technology or through welfare funding for accessibility, rather than as marketable products designed with user research [15, 28]. Kintsch and DePaula [20], proposing a framework for AT adoption, suggest four factors — the desire for changes in function, frustration tolerance, lack of stigma, and willingness to incorporate into daily routine — as factors in understanding individuals' abandonment behavior. More recent work has looked specifically at using TAM to frame the role of digital accessibility in the adoption of e-government and Section 508 guidelines [17]. Djamasbi et al. [14] proposed the extension of TAM to include information accessibility as a determinant of the traditionally used ease of use and usefulness metrics.

With the advent and widespread use of mobile devices with advanced capabilities, research started to examine smartphones as central to individuals' accessibility environments. Kane et al. [19], in their study of people with visual and motor disabilities, found that despite device inaccessibility, people adopted various strategies to adapt and use devices for their purposes. Work on web interfaces likewise showed that faced with inaccessible artifacts and digital information, users come up with a range of workarounds in adopting technology [6]. Yet, with increasing mobile penetration, the notion of AT as an irreplaceable artifact in one's daily functioning has made constant access to the mobile device critical [34].

At the device level, TAM-related research has suggested that the rapid adoption of smartphones in the mainstream market is explained through its confirmation of the model's ease of use and usefulness metrics [26, 27], as well as its fulfilling hedonic and utilitarian purposes [10]. Design research has likewise suggested the ease of visual swipe-based interactions [22]. However, for people with visual impairments the initial transition to smartphones was difficult until later innovations in tap and swipe functions made them more accessible [18].

Fears around the movement from keypad-based phones to touchscreen-based phones continue to be a deterrent to technology adoption [9]. Rodrigues et al. [30], conducting primary research in the wild, have shown that gaining proficiency in smartphone use is daunting a priori, and continues to present significant challenges in early use, leading to workarounds or limited use of device capabilities by users trying to stay within their comfort zone. These works bring to fore the centrality, and in many cases inevitability, of smart devices and their interfaces to our everyday experience.

Our work here deals with AT adoption in a Global South setting — where the comparative lack of access to resources, network infrastructure, and location-based services, as well as a lack of user-base for AT and the adoption of technologies typically designed for users in the West — creates an additional layer of challenges around the adoption and use for people with disabilities [23]. Related work on accessibility has studied smartphone adoption from the perspective of urban living, technical transition challenges, and community support for visually impaired smartphone users [25].

METHODOLOGY

Survey Instrument

We conducted a survey of 180 questions, administered to 81 respondents, along with a semi-structured interview with a subset of 26 respondents. Eleven follow-up interviews were conducted among 26 interviewees following the first analysis of transcripts, and the follow-up interviews focused on UX issues that were brought up during the first round of interviews. The research was conducted between July 2015 and April 2016 in Bangalore, starting with the surveys and followed by first- and second-round interviews. Because perceived usefulness — and specifically the income and economic participation within that concept — was part of our study, we restricted our sample to working-age adults. Respondent ages ranged from 21 years to 61 years (male μ=29, female μ=32). Two thirds of the sample was age 25–39 years. Table 1 describes the gender and device make-up of the interviewees and survey respondents. Table 2 describes the degree of vision impairment and length of smartphone use in the sample. Most respondents (88.9%) were employed. Top occupations were clerical (43.2%), executive (21.0%), teaching (11.1%), and tech (9.9%).

The 180 survey questions were divided into demographics, technology ownership and use history, affordance use, purchase behavior, repair behavior, transit behavior, AT comfort, and constructs (see Table 3).

The respondents for the first round were recruited through local disabled people's organizations (DPOs) and we thereafter worked outward by snowball sampling. All surveys and interviews were conducted using one of three languages — Kannada, English, or Tamil. All respondents were adults who were employed or actively seeking employment. Use of assistive technology such as a screen reader or magnifier on a mobile device was a prerequisite for participation in the study; therefore, we excluded anyone who did not use mobile phones or had only basic phones without AT installed. This in part explains the relative under-sampling of people who started using mobile phones within the last 5 years, who tend to be a younger or relatively lower-income populations using starter phones without AT capability.

Platform	Survey respondents		Interviewees	
	Male	Female	Male	Female
Android	24	14	7	10
iOS	9	2	5	1
Symbian	21	9	2	1
Other	1	1	0	0
Total	55	26	14	12

Table 1. Survey and Interview Sample Description by Platform

Top brands in our survey sample were Nokia (38.3%) Samsung (24.7%), Moto (14.8%), and Apple (13.6%). We classified the devices as smart/feature according to specifications on GSMArena. All primary devices, including feature phones, had internet capability. Besides phones, the commonly owned technologies among respondents were laptops (62%), desktops (47%), and voice recorders (21%). For interviews, we selected a subset of respondents from the survey sample to represent feature phones (3), low-end android (Pre-KitKat: 8), high-end android (9), and iOS (6) users. We oversampled users with newer phones because they had wider device experience and had dealt with multiple transitions.

Sight / **Years using mobile**	Moderate vision loss	Severe vision loss	Profound vision loss	No light perception
0–5 years	1	3	3	1
5–10 years	7	12	23	14
>10 years	2	2	4	9

Table 2. Survey sample by sight and years using mobile phone

The vast majority (71) of surveyed individuals were legally blind (20/200+) and primarily used audio interfaces for managing the mobile interaction. Of 10 sampled individuals who had vision of up to 20/160 (moderate vision loss), 8 used a magnifier as their primary AT (Table 2). Of the total sample, 22 people (27%) had lost sight after age 10.

Constructs

The construct formation for our research was informed by the studies of technology adoption in MIS and HCI rather than a strict interpretation of TAM. The first set of constructs included derivatives of "perceived usefulness," using the UTAUT framework [36]. We operationalized elements of the social infrastructure that might provide facilitating conditions for technology use as well as direct intrinsic motivations around device use.

We gave users seven constructs in the survey to agree or disagree with on a Likert scale of 5, adapted from a questionnaire used in a global study of mobile use [23]. The questions were phrased as follows: "The mobile phone has increased my: (1) sense of independence, (2) safety, (3) productivity, (4) economic participation, (5) income, (6) social circle, and (7) mobility" (Table 3).

Construct	Explanation to respondent
Independence	Feeling of being able to manage one's own affairs
Safety	Feeling of physical safety during various activities
Economic participation	Feeling of being able to take part in activities like banking and shopping
Income	Earnings potential
Productivity	Feeling of mobiles increasing productivity at personal or professional endeavors
Social circle	Feeling of mobiles positively impacting one's size of social connections
Mobility	Feeling of being able to navigate public spaces

Table 3. Constructs for studying perceived usefulness

The second thread of technology-adoption-related survey questions was around usage, extending "perceived ease of use" constructs to include usability experiences. Here, we did not use TAM-based attitudinal questions; instead we measured people's actual use of various functions on their mobile devices such as music, radio, news, e-books, browsing, email, apps, camera, global positioning system (GPS), connecting to a computer, installing apps, using apps, social media, and camera. We created a construct, high-function mobile use (HFMU), which was a composite of all these, counting all respondents who counted more than six uses for their primary mobile device.

Qualitative research

Interviews lasted 30–60 minutes and were transcribed verbatim. The interviews were carried out by researchers who were also involved in the surveys, thus themes from the survey analysis played an important role in the direction of the interviews. Interview questions included descriptions of daily activities and technology use on mobile and desktop, purchase and device transition behavior, and descriptions of the impact of the mobile on constructs from Table 3. All interviews were allowed to thread based on topics that were interesting to us and we wished to probe further. All surveys and interviews were conducted in person by authors, and took place at respondents' homes or places of work. The interviews were used to provide in-depth descriptions of experiences and attitudes related to tech adoption. The interviews were open-coded by two researchers; the researchers conducted a second round of reading the transcripts to focus on usability discussions.

Limitations

We focused on people with access to mobile devices capable of AT, thus we over-sampled more affluent individuals within the population of people with visual impairments in Bangalore. With many TAM-related studies, analysis of perceived usefulness depends on Likert scale measurements of self-reported data on independence and economic participation, for example, and these self-reports might differ from individuals' actual behavior.

FINDINGS

Cost

We found that there is a fairly high cost associated with any technology switch because of the price of phones. People spend a reasonably high share of their monthly income on their mobile device, and this share increases for respondents in lower income brackets. Devices cost more than 70% of a family's pre-tax monthly household income (Table 4).

Income bracket [1]	Mean Cost of phone (US$)	Cost of device as share of monthly HH income	Cost of device as share of monthly personal income	Mean years using mobile device	Mean years using smart-phone
Low (13)	129.86_{a} (101.06)	$.71_{a}$ (.59)	$.71_{a}$ (.64)	7.00_{a} (2.73)	0.56 (.76)
Middle (38)	193.47_{ab} (137.85)	$.31_{b}$ (.23)	$.52_{a}$ (.42)	9.32_{b} (2.05)	1.4 (1.53)
High (15)	312.00_{b} (269.32)	$.15_{b}$ (.17)	$.42_{a}$ (.66)	9.40_{b} (2.54)	1.4 (1.27)
F	4.157**	11.062***	0.778	5.336***	2.049

Table 4. Cost of mobile devices by median household income of respondents. Standard deviations are in parentheses. ** = p < .05, *** = p < 0.01. Means that do not share subscripts differ by p < .05 according to Tukey's post-hoc test. *HH* household

With respect to cost of the phone as a share of monthly household income, there was a statistically significant difference between groups as determined by one-way analysis of variance (ANOVA): ($F(2,62) = 11.062$, $p < .001$). A Tukey post-hoc test revealed that the cost of a phone is statistically significantly higher for low-income respondents ($.71 \pm 0.59$) than middle-income ($.31 \pm .23$, $p < .001$) and high-income ($.15 \pm .17$, $p < .001$) respondents.

With respect to device longevity, we found that on average, people had used their most recent device for approximately 19 months, but there were significant differences between HFMU users (14 months) and non-HFMU users (19 months). We found a very significant difference in mean age of current device between smartphones (~13 months) and feature phones (~32 months). This is likely to be a result of the relatively recent shift to smartphones in India, but we can also conclude that users switching from feature

[1] Low-income defined as monthly household income of Rs. 20,000 (US$300) or less, middle-income as Rs. 20,000-100,000 and high income as over Rs. 100,000 monthly

phones were typically using their current devices to the end of their usable lives. In some cases, respondents reported replacing the external casings multiple times to keep a feature phone going. We found in our sample that almost all the used phones (9 of 10) were Nokia models with Talks installed.

We found that respondents with lower income were also less likely to cohabit with another significant wage-earner, thus earning a majority share of their household income. This made device purchase largely the financial responsibility of the individual with a disability. The data in Table 4 also show that on average, smartphones are relatively new in Bangalore, even though the vast majority of our respondents had spent 9 or more years using mobile devices. iOS users in our sample tended to be on average wealthier than those who opted for Android devices, who in turn tended to have higher household incomes than those who had mobile devices running on other platforms. Wealth also impacts individuals' technology environments — smartphone users were more likely to carry laptops than feature phone users, which suggests a greater physical contact with technology.

Respondents relied on others within the community of people with visual impairments for information on models, as well as second-hand devices. All 10 owners of used devices in our sample were male, reaffirming earlier research that showed men had better access to used phones because of their larger social networks, partly from fewer restrictions on their movements than women [24]. We also find that disabled persons' organizations (DPOs) and non-governmental organizations (NGOs) play a role in tech adoption because they had been a source of discounted bundled Talks software on Symbian phones and moreover played a role in encouraging people with visual impairments to use mobile technology by including AT-related subjects as part of technical training and independent-living sessions. With the integration of accessibility features into the device with smartphones, NGOs reduced their role in actual procurement but were still a source for tech support and offered introductory classes for Android and iOS for visually impaired users.

Perceived Usefulness

Using the constructs from Table 3, we examined perceived usefulness on social and economic metrics. When asked about perceived usefulness, respondents were told to evaluate impacts related to their current device; however, the influence of past and recent devices is potentially likely. All but one person in our smartphone sub-sample had owned a feature phone with separately installed AT. Smartphone users had a median of five past devices before their current one, whereas the median number of past mobile devices owned by a current feature phone user was 3.5. Smartphone users (66.0%). were significantly more likely than feature phone users (16.1%) to be HFMU; there were no gender differences.

Intrinsic Motivators: Social Functions

The UTAUT models cover some facets of facilitating conditions and social influences in understanding technology acceptance. Our questions around social usefulness interrogate four elements — mobility, social access, safety, and independence — in which the individual exerts different levels of direct control themselves, versus reliance on facilitating conditions in their social environments. For instance, on the function of social access, respondents report feeling relatively empowered to make new social media contacts and maintain casual connections through smartphones. On the other hand, physical mobility presents a function in which the facilitating conditions of the society around them — thus the physical infrastructure, reliance on sighted guides to access transportation, etc., are critical for access.

	Physical Mobility	Social circle	Safety	Indepe-ndence
Male (55)	42.33	41.41	37.82	41.60
Female (26)	38.19	40.13	47.73	39.73
Mann-Whitney U	642.0	692.5	540.0**	682.0
Smartphone(50)	36.96	40.99	40.63	43.47
Feature phone(31)	47.52	41.02	41.60	37.02
Mann-Whitney U	573.0**	774.5	756.5	651.5*
Non-HFMU (43)	42.62	42.35	44.00	38.81
HFMU (38)	39.16	39.47	37.61	43.47
Mann-Whitney U	747.0	759.0	688.0	723.0

Table 5. Survey and Interview Sample Description by Platform. Mann-Whitney test - individual cells report mean rank. * = $p < 0.1$, ** = $p < 0.05$, *** = $p < 0.01$

All four social metrics scored between *agree* and *strongly agree*, and independence ranked highest among all. Because the dependent variables were ordinal but not normally distributed, we compared mean ranks instead of means. The test indicated that the sense of safety attributed to mobiles was greater for females than for males ($U = 540.00$, $p < 0.05$). Additionally, people who kept a backup device reported higher impacts of safety and independence (.05%). Males (25.5%) and females (26.9%) were equally likely to have second devices, so the relationship between safety and independence held across gender. The second devices were typically used for two reasons — during device transitions, or as an emergency device. The most common backup mobile was a Nokia N series phone.

One apparently counter-intuitive finding is that the feature phone users perceived a greater sense of access to public spaces (mobility) than those using smartphones. We attribute this to the underwhelming transit-related affordances of smartphones in Bangalore, where GPS-based navigation on maps or rideshare applications do not work well as a result of technical and street-naming issues. On the other hand, the feature phones provide users with a basic but reliable tool for mobility — that of being able to call someone for directions.

Intrinsic Motivators: Economic Functions

Income consistently ranked lowest among all populations (and technology platforms) in terms of the mobile's perceived value. Income was the metric that people felt mobile phones gave them the least control over, because getting a job depended on extraneous factors such as employers' accessibility awareness (Table 6).

	Productivity	Economic participation	Income
Male (55)	42.11	45.43	43.14
Female (26)	38.65	38.65	36.48
Mann-Whitney U	654.00	471.50***	597.50*
Smartphone (50)	42.52	45.26	40.63
Feature phone (31)	38.55	34.13	41.60
Mann-Whitney U	699.00	562.00**	765.50
Non-HFMU (43)	39.19	30.83	42.77
HFMU (38)	43.05	52.51	39
Mann-Whitney U	739	379.50***	741.00

Table 6. Survey and Interview Sample Description by Platform. Mann-Whitney test. Individual cells report mean rank. * = $p < 0.1$, ** = $p< 0.05$, *** = $p< 0.01$

Economic effects are a significant part of TAM-related studies, particularly those that relate to individuals' sense of greater work productivity or ability to earn. In our survey, we probed both factors alongside economic participation, use of banking, and commerce. From among the economic factors related to adoption, we found that one, productivity, can be relatively more controlled by the individual, whereas economic participation and income require some form of extrinsic influence, such as investment into facilitating participation or access to jobs.

Some effects related to economic participation result from developments in recent years that allow for greater management of finances through smartphones. Independently accessing and managing banking prior to digital banking was a challenge for blind people, and even getting credit cards was difficult because of individual banks requiring physical signatures (despite no reserve bank stipulations) for account operation. Several respondents cited using or browsing FlipKart, a leading online marketplace, which prioritizes mobile devices as its primary sale platform and has been relatively accessible on the screen reader ShinePlus and iOS VoiceOver, and more recently on TalkBack.

We found that respondents consistently ranked productivity highest among economic benefits. People indicated they can better manage their processes and respond to communications because of the access to their mobile phones. In all settings, productivity's positive impact ranked between *agree* and *strongly agree*. Economic participation was rated highly overall, but there was much variation among groups (Table 6): men indicated more economic participation than women (Mann-Whitney $U = 471.50$, $p < 0.01$), smartphone users tended to rate economic participation higher than feature phone users ($U = 562.00$, $p < 0.01$), and those who have a high number of functions on their mobile phones tended to very significantly feel a higher sense of economic participation ($U = 379.50$, $p < 0.01$). In comparison, influence on income was rated poorly across all groups, with no group scoring significantly above a neutral rating.

To probe device attachment, we asked respondents to comment on how long they felt they could go without their mobile devices if needed. There was no difference on the self-perception of dependence on the device based on the number of years using a device, or based on gender. However, respondents who had high-function mobile use reported higher dependence ($p <.05$).

The perceived usefulness of the mobile device, however, showed no apparent impact on the use of the other main digital information device — the computer. First, while email and browser use were preferred on a desktop, social media were equally used on both platforms, and smartphone users were more likely to carry a laptop daily.

Usage

TAM frameworks, while helpful in understanding some of the broader social drivers of adoption, are less valuable with issues of actual usage and usability. Technology adoption studies in HCI are relevant in understanding what specific functions are being performed on the devices and how these differ across technologies.

Device capability and use

We found that technology adoption varies in terms of the number and extent of applications used, even within groups of respondents who used the same devices. We found, for instance, relatively high use of media such as books, radio, and music on feature phones and that these carried over to smartphones, suggesting that it is worth measuring entertainment as a perceived usefulness function. Table 7 shows that a majority of feature phone users used their phones for listening to and storing music. Several respondents reported challenges with media storage with moving to iOS (unfamiliarity with iTunes) and Android (naming structures for media files).

The use of internet-based services changed fundamentally once an individual switched to a smartphone. Even though the feature phones had browsers, email, and social media, we found that their rate of use rose with smartphones. While it is likely that there was an impact of early adopter behavior — i.e. individuals more likely to try new technologies move to smartphones first — interviews suggest that switching to smartphones was more related to regular phone update cycles than a desire to try something new.

Interviews revealed that the distinction between those who voluntarily adopt new technology and those for whom the switch is mandatory because of extraneous factors impacts attitude toward the new device, primarily in terms of fear of the interface and to some extent annoyance. However, our survey data show that there is no significant difference between device use among early smartphone adopters vs. more recent adopters.

When measuring the use of various functions on smartphones (Table 7), we were unable to measure whether access to other interfaces, specifically computers, impacted the adoption of these functions, because the overwhelming majority of our respondents (76) were also regular computer users. We also found no relationship between years of computer use with the number of functions used on a smartphone. For browsing, social media, and email, the three domains where it is possible to look comparably at which device is preferred, we found that email and browsing were used on both a desktop and the mobile. Here, the survey data were inconclusive on what was preferred (with the exception of Facebook, which was significantly preferred on desktop by regular users). However, the interview data offered us useful insights into the distinctions. Interviews revealed that smartphones were preferred for output, e.g., reading emails and basic browsing, whereas desktops were preferred for input such as composing emails and internet searches.

	Smartphone (50)		Feature phone (31)	
	Used at least once on current mobile	Used Daily	Used at least once on current mobile	Used daily
Email	41**	31***	5**	3***
Browser	36**	26**	11**	7**
Music	45	26	25	11
Radio	27	15	15	10
Books	18	8	11	6
WhatsApp	45***	39**	9***	8**
GPS	19	1	5	2
News	36	28	17	15
Games	8	3	2	0
Facebook	33***	22	9***	4
Twitter	9	1	2	1
LinkedIn	6	1	1	0
Chat Client	46***	38***	11***	8***
Audio Chat	39***	16**	7***	3**

Table 7. Survey and Interview Sample Description by Platform (significance within group of modality of use). * = $p < 0.1$, ** = $p < 0.05$, *** = $p < 0.01$

While our question on social circles in our examination of perceived usefulness showed no self-reported difference between smartphone and feature phone users, we found that WhatsApp and chat clients are by far the most widely used apps. Interviews suggested that access to social media like WhatsApp helped users maintain more regular contact with existing social networks rather than expanding into new networks. On the other hand, GPS-related use was extremely limited among study participants — only 1 of 19 smartphone users who had installed GPS used it regularly. GPS is a major draw for accessibility — navigation using a smartphone is among the commonly cited reasons for people wanting to adopt them — but respondents report that GPS is functionally unusable as a result of the poorly labeled streets, widespread use of informal landmarks, difficulties locating what side of the street one is on (a problem when boarding rideshare services), and general issues with audio output of location information. Device capability was also an issue because many users had phones with older versions of Android and had limited memory, with which data-heavy apps did not work.

In the past, at the very least one expected to pay about Rs. 9000 (~ US$150) for a feature phone with legal screen-reading software such as talks. Alternatively, people either purchased used phone or acquired pirated software, which could come with problems of its own. Typically, someone who used a used or low-end feature phone without legal software could for the cost of their old device upgrade to a basic Android with in-built, legal software. But the majority of the Android phones in the sub-US$100 range had less capacity, necessitating that users repeatedly delete apps (as voice-based apps and media take more memory) and clear cache, sometimes to where the phone was reduced to a voice-calling device because it was out of memory.

> *If a sighted person buys a phone, especially from a low-income group, he might possibly buy a phone that costs him say 2500 because Android phones pretty much start from 2500 to 3000. But the point there is people don't understand that correspondingly if you want to have a great deal of accessibility features in the phones it is definitely going to cost you more than 7500-8000.... See that used to be the problem with Microsoft. You have to invest on the laptop; on top of it, you have to invest on the screen reader. That is a pain, it's an absolute pain because you know we are talking about a section of the community which is sort of not economically that well off.*
>
> *Male, 42, journalist, iPhone 4S*

Usability adoption mismatch

We found that the basic TAM premise of ease of use aligning with whether a device gets adopted needs more nuance. Fears of adopting a touchscreen device were almost universally expressed in interviews about the initial move to smartphones; invariably the idea of a smartphone was used interchangeably with the idea of a touchscreen-only device. Interaction with touchscreens itself was not new — a third of the sample of non-smartphone users had some experience using touchscreens through access to others' devices or to hybrid touchscreen/keypad devices like Nokia N97. The real fear was about giving up keypad interaction entirely, even though we found that over time respondents preferred the smartphone and were highly likely to make it a primary device.

> *[The keypad phone] was quite easy to learn. I just needed to know basic key combinations — like the position of the Talks button, menu button, arrow keys, etc. — the rest was easy to learn. I don't think I had any kind of major*

difficulty that I could not solve on my own. Very rarely I had to take help from friends. In case of the touch phone, it was the reverse in the beginning. I needed help even to understand the screen and the location of icons on the screen. I had to take support from my friends and VI colleagues. ... I have become more interested in technology after starting to use touch phone. Earlier my usage of the phone was limited to basic purposes like talking and messaging. I was using computer for sending emails or browsing the internet. After starting to use the smartphone, it has become very exciting. First, there are so many apps. I like checking out new apps and installing whatever I find to be very useful.

Male, 28, clerical worker, Samsung Galaxy

Technology adoption studies have also not adequately addressed users building redundancies into their technology environments. In interviews, respondents stated that unlike sighted mobile users in their networks, they did not swap SIM cards into new devices when they switched. Getting a new phone often meant getting a new SIM, typically with a prepaid connection, and continuing to operate the old one in case of failures. Users would eventually transition their contact information, but would expect to have a period, frequently several months, with two or more active devices. We had five respondents who (at the time of the research) still used a feature phone as their primary device, even after obtaining a smart device. But we also found that redundancies are generally built into all mobile use across the spectrum of phone users — those with feature phones were in fact even more likely to continue to have a second basic calling device. In interviews it emerged that Symbian-based devices had a reputation of crashing, thus having a failsafe device was a strategy that many respondents had internalized over time.

The difficulty of the initial adoption process aside, not a single one of our respondents had entirely abandoned the new smartphone after switching, although 10 of our 50 smartphone users continued to use a keypad phone daily. On average, they had been using the smartphone for 9 months while continuing to use another device. However, the usage findings in Table 7 suggest that applications that were already available on feature phones appear to be more used with smartphones. This suggests that adopting a smartphone makes the person do more with their devices over time.

The quality of use of certain affordances can change when moving from one interface to another. Social media, for instance, was commonly noted as a motivation for moving to smartphones. Yet the actual interaction on social media sites changed to more consumption than contribution after moving from feature phones to smartphones as users struggled with input. Tap-release and double-tap typing were challenging both in early adoption but also for more advanced touchscreen users, and voice typing was mostly untenable because of poor voice recognition. Editing mid-sentence on touchscreens was a common concern: The design of Android devices around Google meant that replicating contacts and drives posed usability concerns.

I could [add contacts] easily in the Nokia C5. I am finding it very difficult to [on Android]. First of all, opening contacts is a long procedure. First I have to open the apps folder, then the contacts folder, then I have to search for contacts and then type the name of the contact on the touch screen. Then I have to open the contact and read out the number.... Saving numbers is even more difficult. I have to type the number on the dial keyboard. This keyboard is very sensitive, even while dragging from key to key, numbers I don't wish to select also get selected. I have to keep checking in the edit box to see if the number is getting typed correctly ... the entire number has to be typed again.

Female, 30, clerical worker, Samsung J1

Adapting to the visual optimization

When measuring perceived usefulness, it was difficult to construct means of estimating how people felt about interfaces that would evolve the needs of a user population different from themselves in needs and capabilities. The notion of control emerged in interview discussions around technology, and not just over specific interfaces but over the environment in which people operated.

Moving from Symbian-based devices to smartphones changed the support environment for users. The old environment relied on expertise with software such as Talks, which was internal to the community of people with visual impairments. DPOs and a community of well-connected AT users in Bangalore have traditionally provided tech support. With smartphones, we found that users take troubleshooting assistance from sighted users. Soft keypads present a number of problems, some of which require sighted intervention. An example is using interactive voice response (IVR) menus, which many users struggled with. Proximity sensors turn off the voice and deactivate the buttons on the screen, making it difficult for a blind person to navigate while trying to listen for IVR options and type on the soft keypad. Relying on the social grapevine or Google groups for tech support could offer solutions, but sometimes their complexity was such that reverting to a sighted intermediary was the only real option.

The technique is to use commas between numbers. It works like this: in the dial edit box, first enter the number that has to be called; follow the number with 10 – 15 commas without spaces (this is to bridge over the time taken by the IVR to read out the menu options); follow the comma with the number from the menu that has to be selected; follow again with 10 – 15 commas for the next menu – continue the process. I have used this technique to enter a call conference on Sabsebolo. It works, but it is very tedious. Also, this method can be used only on IVR menus where the options are already known; on fresh

IVR numbers, this might take a number of attempts before the required section can be reached.

Female 35, self-employed, Samsung Galaxy

Sighted users have the option of switching to speakerphone mode with a soft keypad, which did not work for the respondents. There are several comparable examples. In our survey, we asked respondents for examples of technology or options they would have liked on their devices. We found that usable GPS is the single most desired, followed by keypads, optical character recognition, and better voice recognition. All of these capabilities were available in people's devices, but they were mostly unusable, mostly because of design choices that optimized the functions for sighted users. The issues noted with poor GPS could be mitigated by sighted users following the visual, turn-by-turn navigation despite the lack of street names, but this did not work for our respondents. With voice recognition, services in India are optimized for people who either can afford data or can be quick to switch between data and local WiFi, which respondents had trouble with because adding oneself to wireless networks is slower without a sighted interface.

I found that voice typing does not work if internet connectivity is not there because every time the voice needs to connect with Google for recognition. Since I don't have a regular net connection, I prefer to type and keep messages ready so they can be sent when connection resumes.

Female, stenographer, Nokia N97

Other challenges with adopting a primarily visual interface include managing media in folders, which for Android devices is again optimized for sighted users, who can recognize on thumbnails what a media item contains. Also, the range of bundled software typically sold on branded Android devices pushes ads that can be easy to get rid of for sighted users, but frequently cause unintended click-throughs for people using tap and swipe navigation.

Finally, relatively straightforward fixes that could be applied with minor setting changes are sometimes a source of prolonged annoyance. Visual-orientation settings like auto-switching screen orientation from portrait to landscape were a consistent problem, despite it being a relatively well-known problem that many users faced. Several respondents reported problems with monitoring battery usage and device memory, and reported referring to sighted intermediaries to help manage these.

DISCUSSION

Based on these findings, we suggest three enhancements to research in technology adoption related to accessibility.

First, AT adoption work in HCI has only recently started moving toward general-purpose devices after a longer history of examining technologies specifically designed for people with disabilities. The success or failure in the market of such devices depended on the uptake of one population — that of people with disabilities. This no longer applies. While this has been partially true with adoption of general-purpose devices like personal computers in the past, the focus of accessibility research there was generally on mediating the technology, such as the screen-reading environment, between the individual and the device. Smartphones represent a distinct problem in that they are part of the digital being of people and are central to a range of daily practices above and beyond communication and information access.

In MIS approaches to AT adoption, people's expectation of a technology being useful or easy to use is a central point of analysis. As we find here, the users of the feature phones rank the usefulness of their devices at par or higher than those who use smartphones, even though the smartphone users use their devices for a more varied set of tasks. Adoption of these devices or platforms by people with visual impairments is then moot — they have no choice. Rather, the new question becomes how people adapt, what they successfully adapt, and what they don't. More important, the new environment for mobiles is evolving to the needs and standards of sighted people.

There is scope to learn from both the MIS and HCI approaches: Kintsch and DePaula's [20] work on abandonment, which deals with factors like frustration tolerance and routinization, and work in TAM that seeks to understand extrinsic motivations in adopting a new technology. The case of GPS use provides us an example of this — the TAM models would suggest that the high demand for mapping and navigation services pushes up the perceived usefulness of the technology. We were often told by respondents that wayfinding was one of the main drivers of switching to smartphones However, we know from studying the user experience how and why GPS is not actionable, yet smartphones remain in use because GPS is only one among a range of services. Yet, to understand this in more granularity for what may make this untenable, we need to first identify GPS within the functional need for mobility, and understand that there are no other technological options for blind people — thus the failure of the device to provide this service does not push the user toward another device. The smartphone user defaults to the "feature phone way" of wayfinding — i.e. calling someone.

Second, we propose that in both the human–computer interaction and the management communities, technology adoption has been framed in binary terms. Technologies like mobile phones no longer allow for such analysis, because one would have to reframe the unit of analysis as the adoption of one or another specific element within the device rather than the device itself, which in turn may influence the decision to switch devices. To some extent, the flip side of this is also true, where the smartphone is seen as a single monolithic entity. While people do think of iOS devices as special and apart from the rest of the smartphone universe, those shifting from feature phones to basic Android devices often have expectations for the device based on hearsay on higher-end models that define what people think a smartphone can do. This frequently serves up a surprise to users who find out, for instance, that their in-built RAM is too small to support a range of apps. Here, we don't see any specific "inhibitor" to adoption per se; instead we find that the individual using a device with such restrictions functions at a lower level of capability because of a mismatch between their expectation of device affordances and what their device can actually do. This problem is arguably greater in the accessibility field because people don't have the same ability to test or research devices that sighted individuals may.

Technology adoption studies need to capture the functions that people use their devices for. We propose the functions — independence, safety, productivity, economic participation, income, social circle, and mobility — as useful metrics going forward because they allow a granular means of studying adoption and allow us to ask the right questions for deeper study. Here, for instance, we found that poor results on perceived usefulness function with regard to income can be studied through looking at social questions of labor market inequities for people with disabilities, whereas on perceived usefulness on productivity, a deeper user experience study into uses of input could be helpful.

Third, both bodies of work on technology adoption underestimate the role of social infrastructures. While Bangalore is a single case with its unique characteristics, the overarching structural factors found in our sample are relevant to other urban parts of the Global South as well. More than a third of our sample (25/81) first used assistive technology at a non-profit, which emphasizes both the lack of domestic resources to access AT and the important role that non-government actors play in people's access to technology, and as previous research has shown, elsewhere in low- and middle-income countries [21]. The result, however, is that DPOs have an vital role in enabling the choices that people make with regard to their technology use and access to maintenance infrastructures. In these, the function of access and repair are assisted if not regulated by the institutions that enable technology use.

CONCLUSION

In the last two decades work in CHI, especially HCI4D, has highlighted an increase in technology adoption challenges for various marginalized populations that may not have the agency to have their preferences represented in the technologies they eventually use. In this study, we argue that traditional studies of technology adoption have not adequately addressed several key elements that define the use of accessible technologies by people with disabilities, particularly in a Global South setting. Some of these, such as the imagination of adoption or abandonment as a binary, are high level, and others, such as specifics of input interfaces, are more specific to the daily experience of accessible technology use.

These frameworks do not consider the history of use, or a user's trajectory through various technologies. Nor for that matter do they consider adoption as an ever-evolving state. A crucial element of study is the issue of agency within technology adoption. For studies of technology adoption, the agency of the individual to choose to use a technology is an important defining element of its success or lack thereof. As more technologies become part of a daily environment of digital being, this may no longer be a choice.

The timing is important for accessibility studies because the smartphone ecosystems are evolving around a mainstream sighted paradigm. And yet, in parallel, the smartphone has the potential to be the primary gateway for visually impaired users to access the larger context of IOT devices, where accessibility through a smartphone app could be the only means of gaining independent access to all sorts of smart devices from washing machines to thermostats. These may seem a while away in parts of the Global South where a number of basic infrastructure challenges still exist, but getting the underlying systems right is important for a future in which access to similar technology moves towards greater affordability.

While much is known in HCI and MIS alike about assistive technology adoption and rejection, the extant knowledge is driven by our understanding of individual preferences and choices in largely non-mandatory technology use settings. Broadening adoption investigations to include functions of usefulness can help in understanding exactly where technology is working and where we need more effort. What matters in technology adoption then is not whether a technology is adopted, but rather how it is — and what that can tell designers and practitioners about the needs of users.

REFERENCES

1. Muneer Mahmood Abbad, David Morris and Carmel de Nahlik. 2009. Looking under the bonnet: Factors affecting student adoption of e-learning systems in Jordan. *The International Review of Research in Open and Distributed Learning* 10, 2.

2. Suha AlAwadhi and Anne Morris. 2008. The use of the UTAUT model in the adoption of e-government services in Kuwait. In *Proceedings of the 41st Annual Hawaii International Conference on System Sciences.* IEEE, Washington, DC, 219.

3. Ozlem Alikilic and Umit Atabek. 2012. Social media adoption among Turkish public relations professionals: A survey of practitioners. *Public Relations Review* 38, 1, 56-63.

4. Corey M. Angst and Ritu Agarwal. 2009. Adoption of electronic health records in the presence of privacy concerns: The elaboration likelihood model and individual persuasion. *MIS Quarterly* 33, 2, 339-370.
5. Francois Bar, Matthew S. Weber and Francis Pisani. 2016. Mobile technology appropriation in a distant mirror: Baroquization, creolization, and cannibalism. *new media & society*, 1461444816629474.
6. Yevgen Borodin, Jeffrey P. Bigham, Glenn Dausch, and I.V. Ramikrishnan. 2010. More than meets the eye: A survey of screen-reader browsing strategies. In *Proceedings of the 2010 International Cross Disciplinary Conference on Web Accessibility (W4A)*. 2010. ACM, New York, NY.
7. Harry Bouwman, Lidwien van de Wijngaert and Henny de Vos. 2008. Context-sensitive mobile services for police officers: A re-assessment of TAM. In *Proceedings of the 2008 7th International Conference on Mobile Business*. IEEE, Washington, DC, 191-200.
8. Gary L. Boykin and Valerie J. Rice. 2015. Exploring the use of technology among US Military service members and veterans. In *Proceedings of the Human Factors and Ergonomics Society Annual Meeting*. SAGE Publications.
9. Maria Claudia Buzzi, Marina Buzzi, Barbara Leporini and Amaury Trujillo. 2014. Designing a text entry multimodal keypad for blind users of touchscreen mobile phones. In *Proceedings of the 16th international ACM SIGACCESS Conference on Computers & Accessibility*. ACM, New York, NY, 131-136.
10. Heasun Chun, Hyunjoo Lee and Daejoong Kim. 2012. The integrated model of smartphone adoption: Hedonic and utilitarian value perceptions of smartphones among Korean college students. *Cyberpsychology, Behavior, and Social Networking* 15, 9, 473-479.
11. Lindley Curtis, Carrie Edwards, Kristen L. Fraser, Sheryl Gudelsky, Jenny Holmquist, Kristin Thornton and Kaye D. Sweetser. 2010. Adoption of social media for public relations by nonprofit organizations. *Public Relations Review* 36, 1, 90-92.
12. Fred D. Davis, 1986. *A technology acceptance model for empirically testing new end-user information systems: Theory and results*. Ph.D/Sc.D. Thesis. Massachusetts Institute of Technology, Cambridge, MA. URI: http://hdl.handle.net/1721.1/15192
13. Fred D. Davis, Richard P. Bagozzi and Paul R. Warshaw. 2006. Extrinsic and intrinsic motivation to use computers in the workplace. *Journal of Applied Social Psychology,* **22,** 14, 1111-1132.
14. Soussan Djamasbi, Thomas Tullis, Matthew Girouard and Michael Terranova. 2006. Web accessibility for visually impaired users: Extending the Technology Acceptance Model (TAM). In *Proceedings of the 12th Americas Conference on Information Systems (AMCIS 2006),* Acapulco, Mexico, 367.
15. Alan Foley and Beth A. Ferri. 2012. Technology for people, not disabilities: Ensuring access and inclusion. *Journal of Research in Special Educational Needs*, 12, 4, 192-200.
16. Marion Hersh and Michael A. Johnson Eds.). 2008. *Assistive technology for visually impaired and blind people* (1st ed.). Springer-Verlag, London, UK.
17. Paul Jaeger and Miriam Matteson. 2009. E-government and technology acceptance: The case of the implementation of section 508 guidelines for websites. *Electronic Journal of e-Government*, 7, 1, 87-98.
18. Shaun K. Kane, Jeffrey P. Bigham and Jacob O. Wobbrock. 2008. Slide rule: making mobile touch screens accessible to blind people using multi-touch interaction techniques. In *Proceedings of the 10th International ACM SIGACCESS Conference on Computers and Accessibility (Assets '08)*. ACM, New York, NY, 73-80.
19. Shaun K. Kane, Chandrika Jayant, Jacob O. Wobbrock and Richard E. Ladner. 2009. Freedom to roam: A study of mobile device adoption and accessibility for people with visual and motor disabilities. In *Proceedings of the 11th International ACM SIGACCESS conference on Computers and Accessibility (ASSETS'09)*. ACM, New York, NY, 115-122.
20. Anja Kintsch and Rogerio DePaula. 2002. A framework for the adoption of assistive technology. *SWAAAC 2002: Supporting Learning through Assistive Technology*, 1-10.
21. Helen Meekosha and Karen Soldatic. 2011. Human rights and the Global South: The case of disability. *Third World Quarterly* 32, 8, 1383-1397
22. Tom Page. 2013. Usability of text input interfaces in smartphones. *Journal of Design Research* 11, 1, 39-56.
23. Joyojeet Pal, Priyank Chandra, Terence O'Neill, Maura Youngman, Jasmine Jones, Ji Hye Song, William Strayer, Ludmila Ferrari. 2016. An accessibility infrastructure for the Global South. In *Proceedings of the Eighth International Conference on Information and Communication Technologies and Development*. ACM, New York, NY, No. 24.
24. Joyojeet Pal and Meera Lakshmanan. 2015. Mobile devices and weak ties: A study of vision impairments and workplace access in Bangalore. *Disability and Rehabilitation: Assistive Technology*, 10, 4, 323-331.

25. Joyojeet Pal, Anandhi Viswanathan and Ji-Hye Song. 2016. Smartphone adoption drivers and challenges in urban living: Cases from Seoul and Bangalore. In *Proceedings of the 8th Indian Conference on Human Computer Interaction (IHCI '16)*. ACM, New York, NY, 24-34.

26. Namkee Park, Yong-Chan Kim, Hae Young Shon and Hongjin Shim. 2013. Factors influencing smartphone use and dependency in South Korea. *Computers in Human Behavior* 29, 4, 1763-1770.

27. Yangil Park and Jengchung V. Chen. 2007. Acceptance and adoption of the innovative use of smartphone. *Industrial Management & Data Systems* 107, 9, 1349-1365.

28. Betsy Phillips and Hongxin Zhao. 1993. Predictors of assistive technology abandonment. *Assistive Technology* 5, 1, 36-45.

29. Marti L. Riemer-Reiss and Robbyn R. Wacker. 2000. Factors associated with assistive technology discontinuance among individuals with disabilities. *Journal of Rehabilitation* 66, 3, 44.

30. André Rodrigues, Kyle Montague, Hugo Nicolau and Tiago Guerreiro. 2015. Getting smartphones to TalkBack: understanding the smartphone adoption process of blind users. In *Proceedings of the 17th International ACM SIGACCESS Conference on Computers & Accessibility*. ACM, New York, NY, 23-32.

31. Everett M. Rogers. 2003. *Diffusion of innovations* (5th ed.). Simon and Schuster, New York, NY.

32. Rajeev Kumar Saxena and Neelu Tiwari. 2016. A study on mobile subscription, penetration and coverage trend in Indian mobile sector. *IJSRST* 2, 3.

33. Marcia J. Scherer. 1996. Outcomes of assistive technology use on quality of life. *Disability and Rehabilitation* 18, 9, 439-448.

34. Kristen Shinohara and Jacob O. Wobbrock. 2011. In the shadow of misperception: Assistive technology use and social interactions. In *Proceedings of the SIGCHI Conference on Human Factors in Computing Systems (CHI '11)*. ACM, New York, NY, 705-714.

35. Ronald L. Thompson, Christopher A. Higgins and Jane M. Howell. 1991. Personal computing: Toward a conceptual model of utilization. *MIS Quarterly* 15, 1, 125-143.

36. Viswanath Venkatesh, Michael G. Morris, Gordon B. Davis and Fred D. Davis. 2003. User acceptance of information technology: Toward a unified view. *MIS Quarterly* 27, 3, 425-478.

37. Viswanath Venkatesh, Xiaojun Zhang and Tracy A. Sykes. 2011. "Doctors do too little technology": A longitudinal field study of an electronic healthcare system implementation. *Information Systems Research* 22, 3, 523-546.

38. Tao Zhou, Yaobin Lu and Bin Wang. 2010. Integrating TTF and UTAUT to explain mobile banking user adoption. *Computers in Human Behavior* 26, 4, 760-767.

Money, God, and SMS: Explorations in Supporting Social Action Through a Bangladeshi Mosque

Md. Rashidujjaman Rifat
Information Science
University of Colorado
Boulder, Colorado, USA
rashidujjaman.rifat@colorado.edu

Jay Chen
Computer Science
New York University
Abu Dhabi, UAE
jay.chen@cs.nyu.edu

Kentaro Toyama
School of Information
University of Michigan
Ann Arbor, Michigan, USA
toyama@umich.edu

ABSTRACT
Religious institutions hold a significant place in daily life for the vast majority of people in the world, especially in developing countries. Yet despite their social prominence, and despite HCI's emphasis on the social context of technology, organized religion is neglected in both the HCI and ICTD literature. This paper explores the relationship that mosques in Bangladesh have with their constituencies and with technology, with an eye toward the integration of technology with existing religious institutions as a way to achieve positive social ends. We first describe a qualitative exploration of several mosque communities in Bangladesh, where we find that skepticism and pragmatism about modern technology interact in a complex way that nevertheless leaves room for technical interventions. We then describe a randomized controlled trial to study the relative value of SMS messages infused with overtly religious or secularly altruistic frames for the purpose of mosque fundraising. We find that SMS messages increase donations overall, but that their framing is significant. Messages with secular altruistic framing increased donations by 9.5%, while those with religious sentiment increased donations by 57.3%. Our findings demonstrate how technologies like SMS amplify underlying religious forces and suggest the possibility of working with religious institutions in applying positive ICT interventions.

Author Keywords
ICT4D; religion; techno-spirituality; SMS; donation

ACM Classification Keywords
K.4 Computers and Society; H.1.2 User/Machine Systems

INTRODUCTION
Organized religion plays a significant role in the lives of a great majority of the world's population [26], and religiousness is known to be inversely correlated with wealth [12]. Meanwhile, there is a vast literature in HCI and information science asserting that social institutions in socio-technical systems are critical in ensuring that technologies have their intended impact [7, 15, 44]. A subset of this literature focusing on international socio-economic development further suggests that impact is dependent on institutional capacity [62, 64]. Together, these propositions suggest that religious institutions ought to be a primary site of interest for those seeking to cause socio-economic impact in the developing world through technology. Yet, religious and spiritual institutions, and specifically their relationship to information communication technology (ICT) rarely appear in the literatures of HCI, information systems, and ICT for development (ICTD).

ACM 978-1-4503-4655-9/17/05...$15.00
DOI: http://dx.doi.org/10.1145/3025453.3025960

Some research on ICTs in religious contexts exists. Researchers in the early days of the Internet examined how ICTs were being used in religious organizations for daily operational purposes (e.g., accounting or email) [41]. Other work considered resistance to change in certain religious communities [49], the relationship between religion and technology [3, 39], and implications for design and theory [68]. However, there is little work on technology use by religious institutions in developing countries [68].

This paper takes early steps toward understanding how computing technology could be applied in collaboration with religious institutions in the developing world to achieve positive social goals. We studied the practices of several mosque communities in Bangladesh and considered how technology could be used to help one particular institution. After several months of dialogue and engagement, we gained insight into the mosque's organizational structure, its relationship with the surrounding community, its nuanced attitude toward modern technology, and its various goals. We then incrementally assisted the mosque with several technology-focused improvements to mosque operations, as a way to gain trust and further understanding. Finally, we designed and implemented a more ambitious intervention to increase mosque donations through SMS messages in a way that we believe simultaneously satisfied values held by the mosque and ourselves. Through a sixteen-week randomized controlled trial, we tested (a) whether SMS messaging can be used by a mosque to increase donations, and (b) whether appeals to religious sentiment or secular altruism in SMS messaging led to greater donations.

Our work informs the HCI community with respect to several questions: What relationship do developing-world religious organizations have with digital technology? What kind of technology interventions might make sense both to the leadership of a developing-world mosque and to those with more secular values? How do different kinds of very brief, SMS-constrained messages affect rates of giving among a religious constituency? And more broadly, could religious institutions be meaningful partners in attempts to cause positive social change? To the best of our knowledge this is the first study both to explore a developing-world religious organization's relationship to ICT and to experiment with the effect of religious versus secular altruistic messaging for fundraising in the context of a religious institution.

RELATED WORK

Three areas of related research frame and influence our work: religion and HCI; SMS-based ICT interventions; and fundraising technology.

Religion and HCI

Prior work has emphasized the importance of working with established institutions to achieve technological impact [7, 15, 64], but thus far religious institutions have been neglected in the HCI literature. Religious organizations have many of the same features as other large actors in international development, but they also have unique elements. They transcend national and linguistic boundaries; they comprise a wide range of socio-economic strata; and they often control very significant financial resources. Yet, they have value systems that can be at odds with modern secular values; they tend to act as federations of small, locally autonomous organizations, even when there is a strong, centralized hierarchy; and, they have wide-ranging and deep relationships with many of the intended beneficiaries of development efforts. Indeed, over 80% of people in the world are religious [26], and in developing countries, the figure frequently exceeds 95% [26].

Despite religion's prevalence, however, research on religion within HCI and ICTD has been sparse [11]. Muller et al. [43], and later Bell [6] speculated that there could be inherent tensions between technology and religion. Bell coined the term and elaborated upon a "techno-spiritual" framework for the study of this research space. Since then, several studies have documented the practices of mediated prayers and discussion of religious content online [6, 8, 10, 41, 71, 70]. A few papers have also explored the potential techno-spritual design space [24], which includes tools for online meditation [29], mobile phones for religious participation [56], mobile applications for prayer [69], and home automation during Sabbath [67]. Of the literature, the work most closely related to ours is Wyche et al.'s discussion on the connection between secular and religious aspects of life in the United States and Kenya [68]. But where other work describes existing appropriations of technology for religious purposes, or designs of applications to assist in spiritual practices, our goal is to consider how technology might be incorporated into existing religious institutions for the sake of positive social ends.

SMS Reminders

SMS-based systems are an established tool for clinical and health behavior interventions [65]. Within healthcare SMS-based reminders have been used for improving medication adherence [13, 57], clinical management [37, 54], and health-related behavior modification [47]. Information and education interventions through voice and SMS reminders have been demonstrated to improve health outcomes [40]. Due to the lack of high-tech networked and communications infrastructure in developing regions, SMS-based systems lower the barriers for entry for applications such as healthcare [9, 30]. In the HCI literature, Perrier et al. [48] showed how a hybrid SMS messaging system can leverage the capabilities of both human and computer in a healthcare application. Other applications for finance such as SMS-based mobile banking are also growing in popularity [32, 51, 61], and recent mobile marketing strategies have used SMS as a platform for real-time communication with mobile consumers [35, 52].

The effectiveness and user acceptance of SMS-based services in relation to the SMS content has been widely discussed. One study of an SMS-reminder system for blood donations found a significant positive relationship [23]. However, the study also reported that such relationships are affected by socially accepted norms. The role of user attitudes in their adoption of ICTs has also been explored extensively [19, 63]. Densmore [16] found that SMS messages could be used to establish communications for health financing in Uganda, but SMS alone was not enough to maintain effective relationships. Our work differs from previous research in its focus on working with religious organizations, and on the differential impact of SMS messages with religious or secular framing.

Fundraising Technology

Motivations, inspirations, and deterrents in fundraising activities have been also discussed widely across different disciplines both from fundraisers' and donors' perspectives. Weisbrod and Dominguez's traditional economic model of fundraising states that donors' contributions are determined by price, the organization, and quality of the information [66]. Gerber et al. [20] and other works [50] described the motivations for crowdfunding activities including helping others and being a part of the community. Klein discusses fundraising for social change as a grassroots collective practice [38].

Specific to nonprofits and community organizations, Goecks et al. [22] outlined six roles that technology plays in fundraising. Three of these roles interact with our work. First, the organization communicates with donors through technology channels regarding its activities, goals, and impacts. Second, technology is used by the leadership to provide information regarding the organization's activities and improves trust regarding financial practices. Third, direct exposure to technology can change attitudes of the organization toward technology. Similar to our work, Merkel et al. [42] described challenges of and methodological approaches to sustainable IT management practices in community non-profit organizations and stresses the understanding of socio-technical dynamics in relation to IT use and adoption in community organizations. We conduct an exploratory study to first understand the existing dynamics surrounding fundraising and ICTs in an effort to cope with these challenges when designing our intervention.

EXPLORATORY STUDY

To better understand the mosque context, we conducted an exploratory field study in both rural and urban communities in and around Dhaka, Bangladesh, one of the most densely populated cities in the world [45]. With more than 1,900 mosques, it is popularly known as the 'City of Mosques' [31]. Though there are many mosques of historical import, every neighborhood community has a community mosque of its own. In most cases, community mosques are part of a larger complex that includes an orphanage, a *madrasah* (a school for Islamic education), and a religious learning center for children. These community mosques function as a commons for social interaction [31].

Method

In April, 2015, one of us (the first author) began an exploratory study in the rural Mymensingh area where a local Islamic cleric helped us reach five different mosques and two madrasahs. Raised Muslim in Bangladesh, the first author was well aware of the challenges of engaging with religious organizations [11] and convincing them to agree to a decidedly secular research agenda.

For nearly three months we conducted a qualitative study of these communities that consisted of weekly visits to the mosques. We conducted unstructured interviews with mosque affiliates and participant observation in mosque rituals and activities. Participants were chosen by purposive snowball sampling. We spoke with the *imam* of the mosque, the clerics, students in attached *madrasahs*, the management committees, and the members of the mosque community who come to pray.

The themes were high-level at the beginning: existing religious practices of the mosque, the integration of those practices with the civic goals of the greater community, the form and nature of the mosques' relationship with their surrounding communities, and the mosque constituents' relationship to ICTs. Toward the end of our study, we concentrated our attention on one specific mosque in Dhaka, the Sabujkanan Mosque, where the first author has been a moderately active member for eight years. As we began focusing on this mosque, some portion of our time was also spent performing light technical assistance for the mosque leadership, which we describe below. Once it became clear that our primary mosque was most interested in help with fundraising, we further concentrated our interviews and observations around fundraising and the mosque's financial organization. Upon deciding to work with the fundraising of the mosque, we converged upon more focused predetermined themes: the mosque management committee and their roles in fundraising, the madrasah and orphanage activities and their funding sources, the community engagement in the fundraising and overall mosque activities. IRB approval was obtained for all phases of our research.

As requested by mosque leaders and clerics, we did not record the interviews and avoided shooting photographs or video. All primary data was thus recorded as handwritten notes by the interviewer. A few additional sources, including mosque-generated record books and donation journals were also used.

Since we had an interventionist goal in mind, our analysis was based on the general inductive method [60] with few a priori expectations about what we would discover. Similar to a grounded theory approach [58], we considered sections of our notes by theme, and recorded brief thematic summaries of related portions of the data. These themes were discussed by all authors in bi-weekly conversations which also often resulted in new or confirmatory questions that were asked and answered in subsequent visits to the field. For the purposes of this paper, we discarded data that did not contribute to an understanding of the mosque's general goals and operations, technology-related topics, or opportunities for partnership.

Findings

Our exploration yielded a significant body of notes and insights that went well beyond the issues of mosque goals and relationship to technology. Below, however, we focus on those topics that illuminte potential areas for collaboration on social programs, issues related to technology, and issues related to fundraising.

Mosque Rituals

Among Muslims, the most salient activity is prayer. As is widely known, Muslims pray five times a day, at dawn, midday, afternoon, sunset, and evening. Each prayer session is preceded by a melodious call to prayer that is broadcast using several electrically powered loudspeakers around the mosque. These are loud enough to be heard throughout the local community. Attendance at mosque prayers varies by time and occasion. Attendance is greater during the sunset and evening prayers when people are home from work. Attendance also increases severalfold during *Ramadan*. After the evening prayer, some devotees stay for and additional 15 to 20 minutes to discuss Islamic rules in religious practice and in daily life. Toward the end of these sessions, the assembly discusses more practical problems in the neighborhood along with possible solutions.

Another well practiced Islamic ritual is the weekly *jummah*, or Friday prayer, that occurs during midday. Attendance at jummah is typically eight to ten times that of other prayers. Many people come to the mosque only once a week for jummah. During jummah, there is a special session called the *khutbah* where the imam delivers a speech on a selected topic, typically discussing Islamic regulations and community practices. Khutbah can be fraught. As one imam informed us, *"We have to be careful of our speech during khutbah so that it cannot be interpreted either to go against the government or to inspire Islamic militants."* Sometimes, government or philanthropic announcements related to healthcare, local security, and disaster preparedness are also conveyed to the community in khutbah. Such announcements, along with occasional emergency announcements, are also broadcast via the external loudspeakers.

In addition to the loudspeakers, the mosques we interacted with used other ICTs such as calculators for accounting, digital clocks to keep time, an internal public announcement system to amplify the imam's speeches, and video monitors for public announcements.

Mosque Leadership

Every mosque has a management committee that is selected by the people within the local community during an open meeting. The committee comprises a general chair, 3 to 5 secretaries, and 8 to 10 general members. Serving on the committee is voluntary and uncompensated. Committee members thus tend to be retirees or local landlords who can afford the time. Sometimes, local political leaders join the committee. All are elected based on their perceived integrity and credibility among the local community. The main responsibilities of the management committee include recruiting employees both for the mosque and the madrasah; collecting and coordinating funds; utilizing the fund to pay the mosque staff; and expanding mosque facilities. Besides managing the mosques, the committees also work to contribute to local social activities and services. For example, we found some mosques that perform waste management for their communities.

The mosque management committee hires the imam in the mosque. The committee pays the imam a monthly salary and provides accommodation, utilities, and other amenities. The committee and the imam do not, however, have a strictly manager-employee relationship. The imam is more visible and venerated by the community than the committee members, and also ensures that any administrative decisions made by the committee do not conflict with Islamic law. On the hand, the committee has the authority to replace the imam, if the imam violates mosque rules.

Because the imams and committee members tend to be of higher socio-economic status, they all have mobile phones. Many committee members have smartphones, though their use tends to be limited to voice calls, texts, FM radio, and the occasional taking of photos. The committee members we spoke with sometimes also used a personal computer at work and many had one at home, though home PCs tended to be used by younger members of their families.

Social Services

Mosques often deliver social services, with two kinds of madrasahs being among the most common forms in Bangladesh. *Alia* madrasahs are registered, funded, and regulated by the government, and they include modern general education alongside Islamic education [4]. Apart from such alia madrasahs, many mosques have an attached *qawmi* madrasah, which are not affiliated with the government and focus only on religious training. Unlike alia madrasahs, many qawmi madrasahs also manage an orphanage. These madrasahs recruit students and take on orphans from inside and sometimes outside the local community. The madrasah arranges food, accommodation, basic healthcare, and educational expenses for the students and orphans. Usually, the madrasahs are funded from the internal fund of the mosque, which is separate from the greater mosque organization. Funding for the madrasahs is mostly raised through donations from community members.

For approximately 50% of students and orphans, food is arranged by lodging them in a community member's house where they receive three meals a day. The community members who receive these students are not financially compensated. The mosque leadership works hard to make arrangements for as many students as possible, but funds and space are both limited. Students in the madrasahs also voluntarily contribute to different community activities such as fundraising for medical support, repairing potholes, or taking part in social functions.

We also found some mosques that performed vaccinations for local children, oversaw community waste management (by hiring individual waste collectors), and ran neighborhood watch programs where burglaries occurred.

Relationship with the Community

The mosque committees that we engaged with valued strong relationships with the communities they served, because community support is required for the mosque to survive. However, mosque leaders found it challenging to build and maintain trust with their communities. This point was emphasized several times by our respondents. Specific priorities mentioned by the mosque leaders include presenting a clear image of the community members and staff; delivering information about the activities undertaken by the mosque to those who do not attend regularly; communicating the costs of mosque activities transparently; and devising proper ways of approaching community members for donations. As one mosque leader explained,

"Look, many people only come to say their prayers. They need to know who is on the committee so that when we ask them for donations they don't doubt committee members' backgrounds or the use of the funds. We have many dependable people in the committee who are serving the mosque with their heart and soul. They also have good academic and financial backgrounds that can help earn the trust of the people. People in the community may already know them, but just don't know that they are on the committee."

Fundraising

Despite potential collaborations in education and healthcare, it became clear that the Sabujkanan Mosque which we ultimately partnered with was most interested having us support efforts to raise revenue. Having witnessed the various pro-social activities of the mosque, we felt that increasing the mosque's capacity to deliver such services was in line with our own values, though not as directly focused on them as we would like.[1] As we focused on increasing donations to the mosque, we sought to understand the mosque's fundraising strategy and tactics, and where in the fundraising process we could most have impact.

The mosque maintains a central bank account that serves as the locus of all financial management. The finance secretary of the committee performs all transactions and informs other committee members about each transaction. All donations are recorded in a single registry book. According to the committee, the mosque has established a trustworthy and transparent financial management system. We found that community

[1]The mosque, for example, was also in the process of building a new structure, and much of the funds raised were for that purpose. This, however, seemed no different from large non-profits and development agencies spending a portion of their donations on impressive buildings in Geneva or Washington, DC.

mosques and associated madrasahs employ four main strategies to collect donations:

Pledged giving. The biggest part of a mosque's funds comes from individual donations. The mosque maintains a registry containing individual gifts pledged along with phone numbers. A mosque representative calls the numbers of people who have pledged. People go to the mosque and give the pledged funds to the imam, a committee member, or other staff member working in the donation booth near the mosque. The mosque maintains a *donation log* to keep track of these donations. The donation log records the donor's name, address, phone number, and the amount of money donated. A copy of this information in the form of a receipt is given to the donor.

Donation booth. Mosques often have a permanent donation booth set up at a busy nearby road. A mosque employee is stationed at the booth for two sessions a day. The employee uses a small loudspeaker and continuously recites from the *Quran* or sings religious songs, and asks passers-by to donate money (see Figure 1). Donor information is not recorded for gifts made at the booth.

Staff and committee collections. Mosque committee members, the imam, and the mosque staff often tap their friends and acquaintances for gifts. These relationships may go beyond the local community and include professional connections, hometown connections, and connections abroad. Several committee members are also landlords and will approach their tenants. As with individual donations, receipts are maintained for such donations as well.

Jummah box. The mosque collects donations during jummah each Friday using a number of locked collection boxes. The boxes are passed down each row and people insert donations. After jummah, the mosque staff collects the boxes and records the total collected amounts in the main registry. The money is then deposited into the mosque's account. Donor information is not recorded.

Figure 1. A mosque's donation booth and employee on the loudspeaker.

Mosques occasionally employ methods other than the above four. Many mosques place locked donation boxes in busy places (e.g., in a market, at a busy intersection) with written requests for donations. Another strategy is for students to sit by the side of a road with a loudspeaker and small table during festivals to recite from the Quran and explain the benefits of donating. Finally, mosques sometimes print leaflets and distribute them locally and in other localities.

Techno-Spiritual Tensions

Information communication technologies are not always welcome or compatible with religious ideas and beliefs. Some interpretations of Islam explicitly prohibit watching movies, listening to recreational music, or interacting with members of the opposite sex outside of marriage. In Bangladesh as in other developing countries, these interpretations are common, though not absolute [28]; they are more strictly followed by mosque leaders, but not by all community members. This tension has been explored to some extent in previous work [6], but few designs have successfully mediated this tension [11].

It was, therefore, unsurprising that some of the initial comments and questions we received were hostile and suspicious. One imam said to us, *"Television is Satan's box."* That imam did not watch television and forbidded his family (his sons and wife) as well because he believed that television programs distract youth from Islam. Other mosque leaders told us that they only used their mobile phones for talking, even though many owned feature phones with some multimedia capabilities. When we asked a madrasah teacher about mobile phones, he told us, *"Mobile phones will destroy our students."* This teacher discouraged students from using mobile phones even for emergencies. In general, teachers are concerned that students may be using the phones for entertainment and other activities prohibited by the mosque. When we expressed our interest in working with the mosque committee on a technology project, the committee members asked us, *"Are you a blogger?"* Around that time, several non-religious bloggers had been killed by Islamic militants [53], which increased tensions around the mosque. All of the mosque leaders we spoke with were careful with respect to technology; they believed subversive bloggers used the Internet, and thus, the Internet was not to be trusted. Although nearly all of the committee members held bachelor's degrees, we received many questions that indicated hostility toward or ignorance of technology. However, technology apprehensions were not uniform. A few young committee members enthusiastically suggested using a Facebook page for the mosque to help reach the community easily and quickly spark discussions about the mosque, but they also anticipated some challenges:

"I was thinking of opening a Facebook page for the mosque, but then I realized that I am too busy. I have a job you know; most of the committee members have jobs as well. The imam and other staff could have time to maintain a Facebook page, but they won't do it as there are women's profiles on the Facebook and it is forbidden to be on the same platform as women and communicate with them."

Changing Technology Perceptions

The mosque community's generally suspicious attitude towards technology made our efforts to suggest a technology project challenging. But Islam has no specific prohibitions against technology use, per se, so we tried to see whether there were uses of technology that the mosque leaders would approve. Through ongoing discussions over multiple visits, we were able to unpack some of the fears and eventually change attitudes. Our approach was to raise awareness, educate, and demonstrate the potential benefits to the mosque.

For example, given the mosque's interests in engagement with the community, we suggested that we could help the mosque setup a website, but they initially refused. We showed them the websites of several other mosques to try and convince them, but as one senior community member explained, *"We cannot introduce a blog for our mosque. You know what is happening. Some bloggers have been killed recently."* But in a later meeting, one junior committee member brought up an example of a fishermen's village that raised money using a website and social media to build a school. Eventually, these and other discussions managed to convince the clerics and senior committee members to setup a mosque website. In a series of meetings during which we set up the website, the mosque committee was exposed to and trained to use basic content-development software. Later, as we prepared to launch the site, one committee member commented, *"If we can provide this information on the website, then we can earn [the community members'] faith."*

Another example also involved efficient communication. Mosques are always looking for opportunities to invite people from organizations who might make large donations. During the courting process, a mosque needs to maintain good communication with the organization, but correspondence is traditionally delivered through direct mail. The mosque leaders consulted with us to develop a faster and more formal communication strategy. We thus helped them open an email account and taught them how to use email not only for maintaining connections with donors, but also for collaboration within their committee. Since then, the staff has been using email as an important component of the mosque's communications. We also taught staff members to use common computer applications including spreadsheets to keep donation information, PowerPoint for printing banners, and applications to share donation records with others online. Over the course of our engagement with the mosque staff they gradually developed more positive attitudes toward technology.

Intervention Possibilities

As our engagement intensified, we started looking for potential technology interventions that could benefit the mosque community while also achieving secular socio-economic development goals. The mosque leaders eventually invited two young mosque members who had experience with technology to participate in these discussions and to advise. Through these discussions, we identified three major concerns. First, around the time we started our study, Bangladesh had witnessed several incidents involving the killing of online activists. Additionally, extremists had begun threatening sacred institutions of other religions and a Buddhist temple was located nearby. These extremist threats caused dramatic increases in government security forces surveilling the area. Second, the imam and his assistant clerics were responsible for ensuring that technology engagements did not violate Islamic laws. To satisfy this requirement, every possible intervention had to be discussed with the imam in the presence of one or more committee members and the appointed members with technological knowledge. Third, as the mosque and the attached madrasah are community funded and driven, the mosque leadership wanted to make sure that our intervention was approved of by the community.

The leadership asked us to help find technology solutions that would increase revenue and community engagement. We considered each of the following.

Mobile media. We found widespread use both among mosque leadership and members, of mobile media for recording and spreading religious speech. Community members and leaders frequently attend religious conventions arranged by mosques and other religious organizations. At these gatherings, people recorded religious speeches on their smartphones and shared them with others. Since only a few people in these communities own smartphones, these recordings are often played and discussed in a group setting. One young committee member spoke with us about the possibilities of using such recording technology for madrasah education. The committee member's idea was to introduce recordings to help students reciting the Quran identify their mistakes and at the same time reduce the workload of the imam. However, while the teacher of the madrasah believed it would be useful, the senior members considered the costs of the technology and content production prohibitive.

Mobile money. Over the past few years, mobile money has been adopted in many countries due to its convenience and efficiency in personal and business financial transactions [5, 33, 17], and Bangladesh's bKash is among the world's most used mobile money services. In our meetings with the committee, we asked for their opinion on introducing mobile money so that potential donors could send their donations directly to the mosque. There were objections to this idea, but they were notably non-religious. The chair of the committee commented,

> *"Yes, mobile money transactions can be easy, but it can also create problems. We have two common [bank] accounts where we have simultaneous access for some committee members. So, when any money transaction occurs, others know about it. It is easy to coordinate. But if you create a bKash account for the mosque, someone has to carry that number. If [bKash] does not show any record of transaction, other members will not know about how much came in a day. It might create distrust among committee members."*

SMS-based donation reminders. The leadership believed that they could increase donations by making regular broadcast calls (through their public speaker system) to all community members. We suggested instead an SMS-based reminder system rather than broadcast audio, and this idea was eventually adopted by the leadership for three reasons. First, given the mosque's concerns and strict adherence to proper processes, SMS was the least intrusive intervention. Second, since there were many existing mechanisms for collecting donations, it seemed more useful to complement existing channels than to introduce a new collection mechanism. Third, the ubiquity of SMS and ease of deployment was high compared to other technology options such as voice calls or smartphone applications.

RANDOMIZED CONTROLLED TRIAL

To make the best use of an opportunity to apply a technology intervention with the mosque, we ran an experiment to understand what kind of messaging would impact donations. In particular, we noticed that the mosque used references to Islamic sacred texts – the Quran and Hadiths – to convince people to donate, so we were curious about whether religious framing was an effective practice compared with, say, appeals to altruism. Our hypotheses were that SMS reminders from a trusted mosque would indeed increase donations, and that given the mosque context, religious appeals would be more effective than appeals to altruism. For our randomized controlled trial (RCT), we designed, implemented, and evaluated an SMS-based system intended to increase donations to the mosque. The system prototype was developed between June and September, 2015, and its roll-out and evaluation took place between October, 2015 and March, 2016.

Study Site

We continued to work with the Sabujkanan Mosque for this phase of our study. At the time, the mosque was going through a renovation process to accommodate its growing community. The estimated funding needed to complete the renovation was more than 10 million taka ($\sim$130,000 USD), mostly from individual donors. Mosque committee members also went to both private and government organizations to collect funding for the renovation. By the beginning of our RCT, a quarter of the total construction work was completed, costing more than 3 million taka ($\sim$39,000 USD).

We discussed our research plan with the mosque committee in the beginning of August, 2015. The mosque committee wanted us to ensure that the research would not violate any Islamic rules. In particular, Islamic law prohibits participation in games of chance, and an RCT includes an element of chance. So, we explained our proposal in detail with the Imam and other clerics who gave us their approval and conveyed their opinion to the mosque committee.

Participants

To gather participants for our RCT, we collected the mobile phone numbers of people in the mosque community. No other personal or identifying information about the participants was collected. We collected numbers through three sources: We collected 77 phone numbers from the pledge log. We collected 31 phone numbers from the donation log. Finally, landlords on the committee were requested to talk to their tenants about using their mobile numbers to remind them about donating. They managed to collect 120 phone numbers. In total, 228 phone numbers were collected.

Procedure

Our 228 participants were divided into four groups of 57. We employed a RCT with a 2x2 factorial design with three treatment groups and one control group: The *religious* group received only SMS messages with religious sentiment, the *non-religious* group received secular SMS messages appealing to altruism, the *both* group received both the religious and secular messages separated by five minutes, and the control group received no messages.[2] The order of non-religious and religious messages sent to the 'both' group was reversed each week. We randomly assigned members from our participant pool to each of the groups [36]. Groups were stratified by the source of the phone numbers (i.e., the various logs), as well as by their past donation history and frequency of mosque attendance where known.

We prepared a set of four secular and four religious messages. The complete set of messages are included in the supplementary materials. Each of the four secular messages contained a few words focused on secular goals of the mosque community (e.g., youth empowerment, local security, healthcare, elementary education), with no religious sentiment. An example of a secular SMS message:

Regularly meeting with your neighbors strengthens our community. When people see each other regularly, trust develops and there is an opportunity to discuss and solve problems together. Supporting institutions that build community helps ensure social security in the neighborhood. Support institutions that allow neighbors to gather together to strength social bonds. Let's donate to Sabujkanan Jame Mosque.

Each of the religious messages began with a verse from the Quran or the Hadiths. The verses were related to the worldly and otherworldly benefits of giving. The verses are followed by few words to encourage donations. An example:

Rasulullah (SM)[3] says, "People say that my wealth is mine. Yet wealth used only in three cases is his wealth: What he has finished eating, what he has wasted wearing, and what he has deposited donating. He will leave the rest of his wealth, people will take away that." (Muslim)[4] So, donate for the building of Sabujkanan Mosque, deposit your very own wealth for afterlife, for you and for your parents.

Both types of messages were two text SMS messages in length. The SMS messages were written in Bengali, the native language in Bangladesh, and initially transliterated into English characters. All messages were approved by the mosque committee. A mosque secretary made announcements every two weeks at jummah about the SMS reminders, so that participants knew they might receive such messages. In addition, the name of the mosque was included in every message so that recipients would not ignore the messages as spam. We requested at jummah that participants report any problems regarding SMSs, but no complaints were voiced.

After splitting the participants into groups and finalizing SMS messages, we prepared an automatic SMS messaging gate-

[2]Each week the *both* group received *two* messages, i.e. both a religious and non-religious message. In retrospect, this was not ideal, as we cannot attribute the differences in the *both* group to the fact of additional messages or the combination of messages. However, sending only one religious or non-religious message each week to the *both* group would also have had limitations.

[3]A common shorthand for "sallallahu alaihi salam" (may Allah send prayers and peace upon him)

[4]"Muslim" is one collection of Hadith

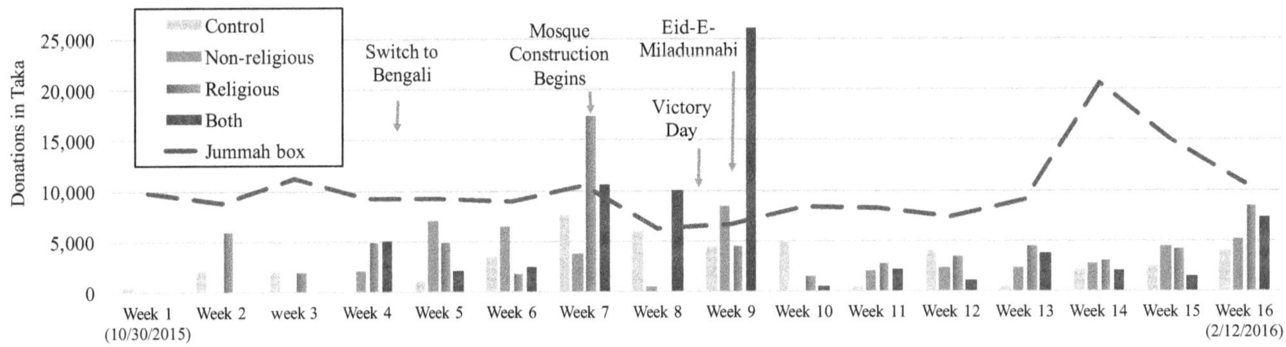

Figure 2. Weekly donations per group over the sixteen week RCT.

way and started sending messages to the participants on October 24, 2015. We continued to send SMS messages each week until February 5, 2016. Since the jummah collection box was anonymous, we were unable to collect data on donation behavior through that source. To minimize the impact of this on our study, we scheduled the sending of messages on Saturdays at 11:00am (the day after after jummah). Saturdays are a government holiday in Bangladesh and sending SMS messages on Saturdays enabled participants to be reminded to bring money during their prayer that day.

The same set of four messages were sent once a week in sequence in four rounds. Each round was four weeks long. In the first round, the messages were sent in Bengali language using English characters because of the widespread practice of using English fonts in short messages. Starting the second round, and following a suggestion by the mosque committee that most mobile phones supported Bengali fonts, we used Bengali for the rest of the study.

Prior to sending any messages we met several times with the mosque committee to remind them to continue to keep track of the individual donation records. Keeping track of the donation log was straightforward; the mosque committee collected the donors' mobile phone numbers and gift amounts. The staff working in the street-side donation booth was also instructed by the mosque committee to note down the the phone numbers of donors who donated more than 30 taka (~0.40 USD). We also requested the committee landlords to note down the phone numbers and amounts donated by their tenant donors. We could not come up with a method to keep track of individual donations to the jummah box, but we tracked total gifts each week. We continued to collect donation records until May 2016 (approximately 3 months after our study period) to minimize the possibility of missing any delayed records. We rejected approximately 10% of the collected donation records due to lack of phone number information indicating a donor as a study participant.

Results

Figure 2 illustrates the total donation amounts per group over the period of our sixteen week RCT. Since the donations each week are highly variable, we used a four week sliding window over the sixteen week period to reduce this effect and conducted a two-way ANOVA. The two factors of the ANOVA are the 'non-religious SMS messages' and 'religious SMS messages'. The two-way ANOVA shows that a statistically significant difference exists between the groups ($F = 5.20$ and $p < 0.01$). Tukey's post hoc tests were conducted on all pairs of groups given the statistically significant ANOVA. All pairs of groups were found to be significantly different. Our results show that while secular SMS reminders increased donations by 9.5% over no reminders at all, religious SMS reminders increased donations by 57.3%. Furthermore, sending both reminders increased donations by 77.5%, suggesting a super-linear effect of including both kinds of messages. These differences correspond to total increases in donations of 57 USD, 341 USD, and 461 USD, respectively. About one third of our participants made gifts in a traceable way during our trial, so this comes to increases per donor (not per participant) of approximately 0.99 USD, 5.99 USD, and 8.10 USD, respectively, over the 16-week period – considerable for a group whose income we heard to be between 10,000 and 30,000 taka (130 – 390 USD) per month. On top of the control group average donation of 803 taka (10.45 USD) and standard deviation 2,136 taka (27.77 USD), this represents increases in donations of 0.035, 0.21, and 0.29 standard deviations, respectively – quite high for the groups receiving religious messages.

The weekly donation records followed a positive trend in terms of the amount of total donation over time in all of the four groups. While the overall trend is increasing for each group, the donations all increased during the second round from week five to week eight likely due to the switch from transliterated Bengali to Bengali script along with two Islamic events. There were also a few dips in donations corresponding to national and international holidays, and the end of the year. According to the mosque committee, donations decrease during the start of a new year because people become busy with work and pay less attention to the mosque.

In addition to the donation amounts, the number of people who donated per week increased over time. The number of donors was lowest at the beginning of the study for every group. Gradually, the total number of donors per week increased until the end of ninth week. As with the total donation amount, from the beginning of the tenth week, there is a decrease in the number of donors corresponding to the end of the year. The number of donors slowly began to increase again following the tenth week until the end of the study.

DISCUSSION

Religious-Secular Collaboration

Our findings suggest that mosques can be a viable partner for ICT projects that seek positive social goals, and much in the way we hypothesized: Where religious and secular goals align, a mosque serves as an institution trusted by the local community, and whose efforts technology can amplify.

We discovered several advantages to working with mosques, as well as challenges not found with non-religious organizations. One of the advantages is that at least in Bangladesh, mosques are already seen by the government and by citizens as a provider of some public services. In some cases, this means they receive public funds to provide social services. On the other hand, decision-making remains local and largely autonomous, so negotiations can occur relatively swiftly – even in spite of initial resistance – without the obstacles of a rule-bound bureaucracy. In addition, mosque leaders are in contact with other leaders of other mosques, so there is also potential for any practice adopted by one mosque to spread to others by word of mouth. As we saw in our engagement, the activities of one mosque can serve as inspiration to others.

Several advantages were unexpected. One was mosque leaders' skeptical stance toward technology, which meant they were inherently focused on the practical outcome of any technical intervention; they were not tempted by shiny gadgets for their own sake. Another advantage was that because Islam is open about its goals and directives, it was straightforward to identify points of alignment as well as of conflict. Unlike other development actors which can be opaque or coy about their motives, we found mosque leaders to be direct about what they wanted in a collaboration.

Among the challenges is that projects must comply with a host of religious rules and guidelines, not all of which are immediately apparent. A related issue is that some compromise is required to achieve secular ends – in our case, our impact on the community was indirect at best, with any increase in mosque revenue likely to be diluted among multiple projects, not all having socio-economic impact. Also, the time required to establish mutual understanding and trust is arguably greater in a religious-secular partnership than among collaborators which share a secular outlook. Our project was facilitated by a long-time member of the mosque community, but even so, it took months of discussion and negotiation to reach a point where we could discuss meaningful collaborations. It is not at all clear that an outsider could have achieved the same results.

The tradeoff between these advantages and disadvantages is difficult to gauge, at least with our limited scope. Nevertheless, we found that the mosque itself benefited from and appreciated our efforts. Four notable changes were reported to us or observed anecdotally. First, among the mosque leaders there was increased discourse surrounding technology as they were convinced that it could be appropriated in useful and religiously compatible ways. Second, the younger members of the committee had greater opportunity to voice their ideas in the mosque's decision-making processes, as they were seen as more knowledgeable about ICTs. Third, the community members learned more about the mosque and engaged in more activities and decisions. Fourth, technology began to play a role in fundraising, record keeping, and communications. Taken together, the mosque constituents began working together to improve their community through technology adoptions appropriate to their religious considerations.

The increased donations achieved through our intervention were appreciated by mosque leadership. The mosque committee applauded the increase after the RCT for two reasons beyond the increased fundraising output. First, the SMS reminders helped them easily and consistently reach the the majority of people in their community. After our RCT, the committee felt that SMS messaging was an easy way to convey other mosque messages and increase community engagement. Second, though our study was limited to the local community, it provided a basis for the mosque leadership to imagine other ways of using the introduced technologies. For example, one idea that the committee suggested was to combine SMS messaging with a link to the newly launched website to reach distant donors. By the end of our study, the committee was considering the purchase of a computer so that they could be more technologically self-sufficient.

Community Engagement

Community participation and collaboration are often crucial in addressing social and economic issues [14, 55, 18]. On many occasions organization-community relationships have been demonstrated to benefit both parties [2, 1, 25]. Thus, increasing community connectedness with formal community organizations can be instrumental in solving local problems. By building on the existing social interests and political structures, technology can be an effective tool for introducing additional services [62].

Beyond expanding the technology discourse, our engagement with the mosque community led to other forms of engagement. Specifically, long-term SMS messaging in the mosque community led to reports of increased community engagement in mosque activities. Many of the participants included in the study were not regular mosque attendees. These regular SMS message reminders created a sense of connectedness to the mosque even though they were largely absent. The mosque committee informed us that they received a greater response from the younger community members in their madrasah programs who later wished to volunteer to help with fundraising. A number of community members began visiting the madrasah and orphanage and spoke with students there. Community members mentioned that the mosque was 'active' and 'more than a prayer hall'. Some of the secular messages provided up-to-date information about mosque construction, madrasah education, and community security. The mosque committee mentioned that many participants spoke with mosque clerics, staff, and the committee regarding these issues during the period of the study. The imam's appreciation of our efforts was expressed indirectly:

"People used to spend much more time in the mosque. It was the center of governance activities and rules were made here.

Now, times have changed and the mosque has become unimportant. If you can make the mosque the center of the community without violating Quran and Sunnah with your [technological intervention], then you will be blessed."

Trust and Transparency

Prior to our study, the mosque used several different ways to increase transparency including announcing the collected sum from the jummah boxes in the previous week and occasional announcements of the collected amounts of the past months. While these announcements were useful, they were unable to reach the majority of their constituents. A similar issue of legitimacy is examined in recent work that describes the importance of making information visible in charitable organizations so as to establish stronger personal connections with their donors [59]. After the mosque website was online, the committee requested that we include the weekly donation log and appointed a committee member to work with us to figure out the proper format.

Outside the local community, as the mosque began construction the committee attempted to reach out to several ministries for donations. Before doing so, they asked us to upload several documents on the mosque website, which included the detailed design of the mosque and an estimate of the costs from the construction firm. One committee member said,

"The good thing for our mosque is that we have a website now so anyone can see what's happening and what we need. As you can see, we are stuck in the middle of the construction because we don't have funds to complete it. ... We are planning on approaching [our connections] for gifts because they usually donate to such causes, but they don't have time to come visit the mosque. If we can put all the required information on the website, they may be convinced to give."

The relationship between trust and transparency also surfaced during our discussions with mosque leadership about the introduction mobile money for donations. In the literature, complex service charges [27] and security threats [46] in mobile money have been examined in prior work, but there are further opportunities to study and improve the transparency of modern digital services, especially mobile financial services. These questions surrounding transparency of ICT-based tools, particularly for financial transactions, have also been noted in other developing contexts [21].

Limitations and Future Work

There are several limitations to the generalizability of our study. For one thing, we engaged with only five mosques in Bangladesh and only one with significant depth. We believe that most of our findings hold for a broad range of community mosques in Bangladesh, but no comprehensive generalizations can be made, and certainly not outside of Bangladesh.

Another limitation is the degree to which religious messages might have impact in other contexts. We designed the study under the hypothesis that religious messages would do well when coming from a trusted religious organization, so it is not clear whether similar results would be obtained in other contexts, even if they are religious in nature. Additional factors likely tilted our pool of participants toward the more religious (and therefore, more likely to be swayed by religious messages): Announcements about the project were made during jummah, but regular jummah attendees are among the more religious members of the community. And, the sources of participant phone numbers meant that they were all people who had donated at least once before. Though these biases in the total sample reduce the external validity of our work, they are within the scope of the theory that technology amplifies underlying human forces. Nothing we found suggests that the technology caused people to do things they were not already inclined to do. It would be interesting to confirm the degree to which similar results hold outside of a religious organization, or completely outside a religious context.

Another major limitation of our study is with gender. Almost all of our participants were male. Even though women make donations to the mosque, they do so through male family members with few exceptions. This bias is not unusual given how women's participation is inhibited otherwise in the community we worked with, as well as in other religious and developing contexts [34]. Nevertheless, there is scope for future research to make women's participation in religious institutions more visible.

We encountered other challenges that constrained our study. For example, we would have liked to have asked how users felt about the SMS messages, but that would have required further testing the rapport we had with the mosque leadership. Given the sensitive nature of our intervention, we hesitated to push the leadership for this level of access. Instead, we relied on indirect feedback we heard from committee members. Longer engagement with the mosque might allow us to interact more directly with community members, unmediated by the mosque leadership.

CONCLUSION

This paper presented an exploratory qualitative study and RCT conducted with mosque communities in Bangladesh. We found that despite challenges and initial hesitation, it was possible to run an ICT project with outcomes that supported both the mosque and our own non-religious socio-economic development goals. Selectively applied, technology can amplify existing inclinations in a religious organization that also tend toward secular objectives. Moreover, we experienced distinct advantages to working with community religious organizations that are not always present with secular development institutions. We believe this research opens up a range of future work that engages with religious organizations and communities for the sake of causing positive, secular social change.

ACKNOWLEDGEMENTS

We thank the mosque communities we worked with for their time and the Sabujkanan Mosque leadership for their openness and partnership. We also thank our anonymous reviewers for helpful comments; special thanks go to an anonymous shepherd who provided iterative feedback.

REFERENCES

1. Laura S Abrams and Jewelle Taylor Gibbs. 2000. Planning for school change school-community collaboration in a full-service elementary school. *Urban Education* 35, 1 (2000), 79–103.
2. Dawn Anderson-Butcher, Hal A Lawson, Jerry Bean, Paul Flaspohler, Barbara Boone, and Amber Kwiatkowski. 2008. Community collaboration to improve schools: Introducing a new model from Ohio. *Children & Schools* 30, 3 (2008), 161–172.
3. Greg G Armfield and R Lance Holbert. 2003. The relationship between religiosity and Internet use. *Journal of Media and Religion* 2, 3 (2003), 129–144.
4. Mohammad Niaz Asadullah, Nazmul Chaudhury, and Syed Rashed Al-Zayed Josh. 2009. Secondary school madrasas in Bangladesh: incidence, quality, and implications for reform. *Human Development Sector, The World Bank. Retrieved from: http://siteresources. worldbank. org/EXTDEVDIALOGUE/Resources/BangladeshMadrasa ReportFinal. pdf* (2009).
5. Bangladesh Bank. 2012. Mobile financial services in Bangladesh: An overview of market development. *Bangladesh Bank Policy Paper, July* (2012).
6. Genevieve Bell. 2006. No more SMS from Jesus: ubicomp, religion and techno-spiritual practices. In *International Conference on Ubiquitous Computing*. Springer, 141–158.
7. Robert P Bostrom and J Stephen Heinen. 1977. MIS problems and failures: A socio-technical perspective. *MIS Quarterly* 1, 3 (1977), 17–32.
8. Brenda E Brasher. 2001. *Give Me That Online Religion*. John Wiley & Sons, Inc.
9. Suzana Brown and Timothy X Brown. 2013. Value of mobile monitoring for diabetes in developing countries. In *Proceedings of the Sixth International Conference on Information and Communication Technologies and Development: Full Papers-Volume 1*. ACM, 267–273.
10. Elizabeth Buie and Mark Blythe. 2013a. Meditations on YouTube. In *Proceedings of the 6th International Conference on Designing Pleasurable Products and Interfaces*. ACM, 41–50.
11. Elizabeth Buie and Mark Blythe. 2013b. Spirituality: there's an app for that!(but not a lot of research). In *CHI'13 Extended Abstracts on Human Factors in Computing Systems*. ACM, 2315–2324.
12. Pew Research Center. 2007. World publics welcome global trade – but not immigration. *The Pew Global Attitudes Project* (2007). `http://www.pewglobal.org/2007/10/04/world-publics-welcome-global-trade-but-not-immigration/`
13. Mihail Cocosila, Norm Archer, R Brian Haynes, and Yufei Yuan. 2009. Can wireless text messaging improve adherence to preventive activities? Results of a randomised controlled trial. *International Journal of Medical Informatics* 78, 4 (2009), 230–238.
14. Gary Craig and Marjorie Mayo. 1995. *Community Empowerment: A Reader in Participation and Development*. Zed Books.
15. James N Danziger, William H Dutton, and K.L. Kraemer. 1982. *Computers and Politics: High Technology in American Local Governments*. New York: Columbia University Press.
16. Melissa Densmore. 2012. Experiences with bulk SMS for health financing in Uganda. In *CHI'12 Extended Abstracts on Human Factors in Computing Systems*. ACM, 383–398.
17. Kevin Donovan. 2012. Mobile money for financial inclusion. *Information and Communications for Development* 61 (2012), 61–73.
18. Kathleen Coulborn Faller and James Henry. 2000. Child sexual abuse: A case study in community collaboration. *Child Abuse & Neglect* 24, 9 (2000), 1215–1225.
19. Marcelline Fusilier and Subhash Durlabhji. 2005. An exploration of student internet use in India: the technology acceptance model and the theory of planned behaviour. *Campus-Wide Information Systems* 22, 4 (2005), 233–246.
20. Elizabeth M Gerber and Julie Hui. 2013. Crowdfunding: Motivations and deterrents for participation. *ACM Transactions on Computer-Human Interaction (TOCHI)* 20, 6 (2013), 34.
21. Ishita Ghosh, Jay Chen, Joy Ming, and Azza Abouzied. 2015. The persistence of paper: a case study in microfinance from Ghana. In *Proceedings of the Seventh International Conference on Information and Communication Technologies and Development*. ACM, 13.
22. Jeremy Goecks, Amy Voida, Stephen Voida, and Elizabeth D Mynatt. 2008. Charitable technologies: Opportunities for collaborative computing in nonprofit fundraising. In *Proceedings of the 2008 ACM conference on Computer supported cooperative work*. ACM, 689–698.
23. Harry Gombachika and Maganizo Monawe. 2011. Correlation analysis of attitudes towards SMS technology and blood donation behaviour in Malawi. *Journal of Health Informatics in Developing Countries* 5, 2 (2011).
24. Carma R Gorman. 2009. Religion on demand: Faith-based design. *Design and Culture* 1, 1 (2009), 9–22.
25. Robert Gronski and Kenneth Pigg. 2000. University and community collaboration experiential learning in human services. *American Behavioral Scientist* 43, 5 (2000), 781–792.

26. Conrad Peter Hackett and Brian J Grim. 2012. The global religious landscape: A report on the size and distribution of the world's major religious groups as of 2010. Pew Research Center, Pew Forum on Religion & Public Life.

27. Md Mehedi Hasan and Md Rayhanul Islam. 2013. Assessing service quality of mobile money transfer in Bangladesh: A case study on bKash. *International Journal of Innovative Research and Development—— ISSN 2278–0211* 2, 7 (2013).

28. Carole E Hill, Karen D Loch, Detmar Straub, and Kamal El-Sheshai. 1998. A qualitative assessment of Arab culture and information technology transfer. *Journal of Global Information Management (JGIM)* 6, 3 (1998), 29–38.

29. Michelle Hlubinka, Jennifer Beaudin, Emmanuel Munguia Tapia, and John S An. 2002. AltarNation: interface design for meditative communities. In *CHI'02 Extended Abstracts on Human Factors in Computing Systems*. ACM, 612–613.

30. Amber Houssian, Mohammad Kilany, and Jacob Korenblum. 2009. Mobile phone job services: Linking developing-country youth with employers, via SMS. In *2009 International Conference on Information and Communication Technologies and Development (ICTD)*.

31. Abu H Imamuddin, Ara Hessian Shamim, and Sarkar Debashir. 1985. Community mosque–A symbol of society. *REGIONALISM IN ARCHITECTURE. Sem Aga Khan/ed. R. Powell. Singapore* (1985).

32. Md Subrun Jamil and Fouzia Ashraf Mousumi. 2008. Short messaging service (SMS) based m-banking system in context of Bangladesh. In *Computer and Information Technology, 2008. ICCIT 2008. 11th International Conference on*. IEEE, 599–604.

33. Beth Jenkins. 2008. Developing mobile money ecosystems. *Washington, DC: International Finance Corporation and Harvard Kennedy School* (2008).

34. Naila Kabeer. 2005. Gender equality and women's empowerment: A critical analysis of the third millennium development goal 1. *Gender & Development* 13, 1 (2005), 13–24.

35. Petros Kavassalis, Ntina Spyropoulou, Dimitris Drossos, Evangelos Mitrokostas, Gregory Gikas, and Antonis Hatzistamatiou. 2003. Mobile permission marketing: Framing the market inquiry. *International Journal of Electronic Commerce* 8, 1 (2003), 55–79.

36. J Kendall. 2003. Designing a research project: randomised controlled trials and their principles. *Emergency Medicine Journal* 20, 2 (2003), 164.

37. Hee-Seung Kim. 2007. A randomized controlled trial of a nurse short-message service by cellular phone for people with diabetes. *International Journal of Nursing Studies* 44, 5 (2007), 687–692.

38. Kim Klein. 2011. *Fundraising for Social Change*. Vol. 21. John Wiley & Sons.

39. Lily Kong. 2001. Religion and technology: Refiguring place, space, identity and community. *Area* 33, 4 (2001), 404–413.

40. Santosh Krishna, Suzanne Austin Boren, and E Andrew Balas. 2009. Healthcare via cell phones: a systematic review. *Telemedicine and e-Health* 15, 3 (2009), 231–240.

41. Elena Larsen and L Rainie. 2001. Cyberfaith: How Americans pursue religion online. *December* 23 (2001), 21.

42. Cecelia Merkel, Umer Farooq, Lu Xiao, Craig Ganoe, Mary Beth Rosson, and John M Carroll. 2007. Managing technology use and learning in nonprofit community organizations: methodological challenges and opportunities. In *Proceedings of the 2007 Symposium on Computer Human Interaction for the Management of Information Technology*. ACM, 8.

43. Michael J Muller, Ellen Christiansen, Bonnie Nardi, and Susan Dray. 2001. Spiritual life and information technology. *Commun. ACM* 44, 3 (2001), 82–82.

44. Bonnie A Nardi. 1995. Studying context: A comparison of activity theory, situated action models, and distributed cognition. *Context and consciousness: Activity theory and human-computer interaction* (1995), 69–102.

45. Newgeography.com. 2012. Evolving Urban Form: Dhaka. *Evolving Urban Form: Dhaka — Newgeography.com* (2012). `http://www.newgeography.com/content/003004-evolving-urban-form-dhaka`

46. Jin Nie and Xianling Hu. 2008. Mobile banking information security and protection methods. In *Computer Science and Software Engineering, 2008 International Conference on*, Vol. 3. IEEE, 587–590.

47. Jami L Obermayer, William T Riley, Ofer Asif, and Jersino Jean-Mary. 2004. College smoking-cessation using cell phone text messaging. *Journal of American College Health* 53, 2 (2004), 71–78.

48. Trevor Perrier, Nicola Dell, Brian DeRenzi, Richard Anderson, John Kinuthia, Jennifer Unger, and Grace John-Stewart. 2015. Engaging pregnant women in Kenya with a hybrid computer-human SMS communication system. In *Proceedings of the 33rd Annual ACM Conference on Human Factors in Computing Systems*. ACM, 1429–1438.

49. Howard Rheingold. 1999. Look who's talking. *Wired Magazine* 7, 1 (1999).

50. Scott I Rick, Cynthia E Cryder, and George Loewenstein. 2008. Tightwads and spendthrifts. *Journal of Consumer Research* 34, 6 (2008), 767–782.

51. Emmanuel Rotimi, Oludele Awodele, and Olutayo Bamidele. 2007. SMS banking services: A 21st century innovation in banking technology. *Issues in Informing Science and Information Technology* 4 (2007), 227–234.

52. Arno Scharl, Astrid Dickinger, and Jamie Murphy. 2005. Diffusion and success factors of mobile marketing. *Electronic Commerce Research and Applications* 4, 2 (2005), 159–173.
53. Ryan Shaffer. 2015. Crisis in Bangladesh: Secularists Killed by Extremists and Under Legal Threat from Government. *Crisis* (2015).
54. Jennifer R Shapiro, Stephanie Bauer, Ellen Andrews, Emily Pisetsky, Brendan Bulik-Sullivan, Robert M Hamer, and Cynthia M Bulik. 2010. Mobile therapy: Use of text-messaging in the treatment of bulimia nervosa. *International Journal of Eating Disorders* 43, 6 (2010), 513–519.
55. David G Simmons. 1994. Community participation in tourism planning. *Tourism Management* 15, 2 (1994), 98–108.
56. Rhiannon Sterling and John Zimmerman. 2007. Shared moments: opportunities for mobile phones in religious participation. In *Proceedings of the 2007 Conference on Designing for User eXperiences*. ACM, 15.
57. Ulla Strandbygaard, Simon Francis Thomsen, and Vibeke Backer. 2010. A daily SMS reminder increases adherence to asthma treatment: a three-month follow-up study. *Respiratory medicine* 104, 2 (2010), 166–171.
58. Anselm Strauss and Juliet Corbin. 1998. *Basics of Qualitative Research: Techniques and Procedures for Developing Grounded Theory* . Sage Publications, Inc.
59. Katie G Tanaka and Amy Voida. 2016. Legitimacy Work: Invisible Work in Philanthropic Crowdfunding. In *Proceedings of the 2016 CHI Conference on Human Factors in Computing Systems*. ACM, 4550–4561.
60. David R Thomas. 2006. A general inductive approach for analyzing qualitative evaluation data. *American Journal of Evaluation* 27, 2 (2006), 237–246.
61. Dube Thulani, Njanike Kosmas, Manomano Collins, and Chiriseri Lloyd. 2011. Adoption and use of SMS/mobile banking services in Zimbabwe: An exploratory study. *Journal of Internet Banking and Commerce* 16, 2 (2011), 1.
62. Kentaro Toyama. 2015. *Geek Heresy: Rescuing Social Change from the Cult of Technology*. PublicAffairs.
63. Viswanath Venkatesh. 2000. Determinants of perceived ease of use: Integrating control, intrinsic motivation, and emotion into the technology acceptance model. *Information Systems Research* 11, 4 (2000), 342–365.
64. Mark Warschauer and Morgan Ames. 2010. Can One Laptop per Child save the world's poor? *Journal of international affairs* (2010), 33–51.
65. Jin Wei, Ilene Hollin, and Stan Kachnowski. 2011. A review of the use of mobile phone text messaging in clinical and healthy behaviour interventions. *Journal of Telemedicine and Telecare* 17, 1 (2011), 41–48.
66. Burton A Weisbrod and Nestor D Dominguez. 1986. Demand for collective goods in private nonprofit markets: Can fundraising expenditures help overcome free-rider behavior? *Journal of Public Economics* 30, 1 (1986), 83–96.
67. Allison Woodruff, Sally Augustin, and Brooke Foucault. 2007. Sabbath day home automation: it's like mixing technology and religion. In *Proceedings of the SIGCHI Conference on Human Factors in Computing Systems*. ACM, 527–536.
68. Susan P Wyche, Paul M Aoki, and Rebecca E Grinter. 2008a. Re-placing faith: reconsidering the secular-religious use divide in the United States and Kenya. In *Proceedings of the SIGCHI Conference on Human Factors in Computing Systems*. ACM, 11–20.
69. Susan P Wyche, Kelly E Caine, Benjamin Davison, Micheal Arteaga, and Rebecca E Grinter. 2008b. Sun dial: exploring techno-spiritual design through a mobile islamic call to prayer application. In *CHI'08 Extended Abstracts on Human Factors in Computing Systems*. ACM, 3411–3416.
70. Susan P Wyche, Kelly E Caine, Benjamin K Davison, Shwetak N Patel, Michael Arteaga, and Rebecca E Grinter. 2009. Sacred imagery in techno-spiritual design. In *Proceedings of the SIGCHI Conference on Human Factors in Computing Systems*. ACM, 55–58.
71. Susan P Wyche, Gillian R Hayes, Lonnie D Harvel, and Rebecca E Grinter. 2006. Technology in spiritual formation: an exploratory study of computer mediated religious communications. In *Proceedings of the 2006 20th Anniversary Conference on Computer Supported Cooperative Work*. ACM, 199–208.

Negotiating Absent Practices and Dormant Features: Discourse as a Means of Shaping the Implementation of a Global Enterprise System to Meet Local Work Culture

George Kandathil
Indian Institute of Management
Ahmedabad, India
gmk@iima.ac.in

Erica L. Wagner
School of Business
Administration
Portland State University, USA
elwagner@pdx.edu

ABSTRACT
The introduction of a new enterprise system to an organization often necessitates the accommodation of standardized practices, which may be in conflict with local users' practices and their work culture. We explore such a conflict in an India-based multinational organization using an eight-month interpretive case study. Based on grounded analysis, we present a narrative account of how consultants, on contract for managing the deployment and making necessary adjustments, used discourse as a means of shaping user understanding about the features and practices embedded in the underlying system, which were not initially realized through the interface. Sustained user resistance to this shaping led to a negotiated compromise and adaptation of the system to incorporate local work culture. Our findings allow us to explore the under-theorized role of discursive power within an implementer-user-technology trio, and illustrate the feedback utility of user resistance in developing culturally-inclusive designs.

Author Keywords
HCI; affordance; appropriation, culture; discursive; Enterprise system; HCI4D; critical design; cross-cultural design; workplace studies; CSCW.

ACM Classification Keywords
H.5.m. Information interfaces and presentation: User Interfaces—Theory and methods.

INTRODUCTION
Technology appropriation has been a major focus of CSCW studies and Information System studies for decades [32, 36]. It is the process through which technology is evaluated by people over time and adopted, adapted and incorporated into their work practices [8, 9]. Adoption involves a decision to use a technology to support one's practices. Adaptation is the process of modifying either users' needs and their existing practices to suit the artifact (i.e., user adaptation) or conversely, the artifact to suit users' needs and their existing practices (i.e., artifact adaptation), or both (i.e., mutual adaptation), entailing artifact redesign. Thus, appropriation seems to complete the design of technology through use – a point that warrants more attention [8, 9, 36]. Scholars across fields have investigated appropriation during software implementation calling for the acknowledgment of post-implementation modification to software and work practices of user organizations as part of appropriation for which businesses should plan and budget [25, 33, 58]. Rather than interpreting such mutual adaptation as a design failure, it may better be interpreted as productive steps toward creating a 'working system' [57]. After all, the alternative is non-use of technology [40].

As we shift to supporting the mutual adaptation process within software projects, we must study how users as a collective, rather than individual [53], come to appropriate the software and what modifications to the artifact are required as part of that appropriation [19, 32, 36, 50, 51, 57]. We focus on the first issue by presenting detailed evidence of a collective cognitive shift in how users thought about a standardized software package embedded with quite a different approach to work than the users had been accustomed to. We examine how system implementers, called "consultants", discursively shape users' collective understanding of software functionality and the underlying changes to local work practices that would accompany the implementation of a ubiquitous IT, an Enterprise System (ES).

Recent CSCW studies consider ES as an information infrastructure – a standardized integrated system that needs embedding in settings for which it is not explicitly designed [32]. Embedding often entails conflicts between the practices and culture that the artifact embodies (along with its supporters) and the local practices and work culture (along with its proponents). The resolution of such conflicts through artifact adaptation make the system generic, giving it the characteristic of an infrastructure [36, 45]. The

CHI 2017, May 6–11, 2017, Denver, CO, USA.

ACM ISBN 978-1-4503-4655-9/17/05...$15.00.
http://dx.doi.org/10.1145/3025453.3026039

discursive dynamics and the cultural underpinnings of these conflicts in developing the standard ES design into an infrastructure are less understood [29, 32, 37, 43], and scarcely studied within CSCW stream, although ES has become a ubiquitous collaboration technology [32, 36]. Similarly, while highlighting the point that appropriation and adaptation are ongoing processes as technology affordances emerge in context and through discourse, recent HCI affordance studies call for exploring discursive power, agency, and user voice within implementer-user-technology trio [19, 47, 53]. By addressing these issues, this study helps understand design as a process complete through use. These are our first set of contributions.

Drawing on the interactionist-relational view of affordance in HCI field, we coined the term "Technology Non-Affordance" (TNA) to highlight the relevance of features and practices that were not included in the standard design and were this not afforded. Here, discursive dynamics was central to (1) the attempts to impose a culturally exclusive design, perpetuated as the gold standard, on user communities, and (2) users' opposition to realize the potential for the system to be adapted. Our eight-month long interpretive case study in an India-based Western multinational company (MNC) captures the emergence of the TNA-related conflicts between consultants and user groups and among user groups over artifact adaptation versus user adaptation. Sustained user resistance resulted in a negotiated compromise to accommodate local practices and work culture into the standard design. Thus, we address challenges in creating culturally inclusive designs and in incorporating organizational needs in a developing country—two important issues for HCI community [1, 48]. Specifically, we show the feedback utility of user resistance in developing culturally inclusive design, questioning the ethics of undermining user resistance which will be interesting to ethical HCI design [1, 48] – our second contribution.

THE INTERACTIONIST-RELATIONAL VIEW

During the past few decades, HCI literature has been witnessing a gradual shift from a cognitivist approach, which considers affordances as individual user's perception of action possibilities based on the properties of the artifact, to an Interactionist-Relational approach. The latter conceptualizes affordances as dynamically emerging properties of the interaction between users and their environment including the artifact [17, 55]. The interaction is influenced by the sociocultural context in which the interaction occurs, and involves adaptation [21]. This situated nature suggests that designers and their intermediaries (e.g., system implementers) can influence the ongoing process of emergence and adaptation [17, 34]. They can thus shape user understanding of affordances which are created through technology use [21, 47].

For such shaping, often, cultural means are used since they mediate human actions like technology use and adaptation [22]. One such significant cultural means is discourse [48] between relevant actors, such as implementers and users. By definition, discourse provides the conventions and range of reproducible meanings through which actors find possibilities to make sense of social situations. Creation of discourse, thus, is an exercise of power to the extent it draws boundaries of possible interpretations, excluding alternatives. Hence, affordance is redefined thus: "The action possibilities posed by an artifact in use and associate the artifact with practices. They emerge as the material [the capabilities that afford or constrain users' action as they interact with the artifact] and the discursive are fused together during technology use" [47]. In other words, affordances arise when users' discursively constructed meaning and habituated use (part of practice) of technology meet their experience of technology features as they use or appropriate the features. Yet, in HCI affordance studies, with its focus tied on the micro level and individual users, the immediate context, the role of discursive power and articulated user voice are under-explored [19, 47, 53].

This paper presents a case study that draws on the interactionist-relational perspective but applies it in a context where features are not afforded but left dormant or absent based on discursive justification. In such contexts, the consultants' discourse related to both affordance and non-affordance gains weight. Non-affordances are action impossibilities posed by an artifact-in-use, an understanding of which is shaped through discourses, particularly on system limitations or constraints. For example, the consultants suggest that certain features or practices (which needs connections between features) cannot be accommodated because the underlying system does not support them – even if it does. Such discourses influence user beliefs and understanding about what system can and cannot support [2, 24]. Subsequently, user experience of system limitations and constraints, as users interact with the technology, may reinforce their discursively shaped beliefs and understanding about what system cannot do. These discourses are more likely to be significant in a context where users are unfamiliar with the technology, and the technology is too complex for them to develop quick visibility into it or understand it on their own. Thus, users may find it difficult to perceive dormant features embedded in the standard design and figure out useful features and practices absent in the design.

Consequently, users would have to lend credibility to the perceived experts', such as consultants', discourse on system capability and limitations, even when they do not accurately reflect what the system is actually capable of. Users' belief in system incapability or constraints, which rest on the consultants' discourses, may motivate them to self-limit request for redesigning the system to suit their needs. Thus, users could be forced to adopt the standard design, muffling articulated user voice. On the other hand, as users grow familiar with the technology, they may oppose implementers' discourse, creating conflicts, as the

MIS implementation literature shows [2, 20, 57]. This shift in the discursive power can trigger negotiation for resolving conflicts. Thus, overall, discourse becomes a central means of negotiating adaptation of the system over time.

With their focus anchored on enabling aspects of affordance, HCI affordance literature and CSCL studies tend to ignore these constraining aspects of affordance, the related role of the implementers' discursive power over users and their use of technology, and the ensuing processes [19, 22, 50, 51]. We aim to address these issues of technology appropriation and the role of discourse in the context of implementing an ES – an information infrastructure.

RESEARCH AIMS: TECHNOLOGY APPROPRIATION AND DISCOURSE IN ES IMPLEMENTATION

Our research aims are to explore the following: (a) How do ES consultants discursively shape user community's understanding of ES functionality and the underpinning changes to work practices during the implementation? and (b) How do users respond to it as they appropriate the technology, and with what implications?

Our focus on ES is important for CSCW studies, particularly, that adopt an information infrastructure perspective. The collaborative technologies that are developed within short time across a few sites have been dominating both early and late CSCW scholarship [27, 36]. Unlike them, collaborative technologies such as ESs are shaped and used across many sites, span decades, and accommodate evolving heterogeneous user practices. Their development and implementation involve interconnections of numerous modules/systems, dynamically evolving portfolios of systems and shaping by an installed base of existing systems and practices. Hence, they are characterized as information infrastructure [14, 32, 36].

ESs, one class of packaged work process-oriented global software applications, are large integrated systems with slight design differences depending on the industry package that is being sold. ES vendors typically divide their software packages into standardized application "modules" such as production, accounting, and human resources. Organizations hire vendor-certified "system implementers" who claim to tailor the system to client organizations' specific needs. Vendors integrate implementation experience with various clients not just to identify requirements but to incorporate the difference between the practices embedded in the standard design and the clients' local practices into the standard design. Such incorporations make the standard design more generic – a process called generification - within which design extends into the implementation and use of the system [32, 37]. This stretching makes the design process a 'continuing design in use' [13]. Thus, design is completed by intermediaries, such as implementers, through incorporation (or its lack) of local practices into the standard design as well by users via appropriation or 'improvised use' [34] in response to affordances [60] and non-affordances.

During implementation, the globally founded generic nature of ES occasions conflicts between the software embedded standardized practices and the specific unique local work practices. As a recent review highlights, the ES and related studies across a range of traditions show that such conflicts are hard to reconcile as they involve cultural and political dynamics [32, 36]. Yet, "an infrastructure occurs when the tension between local and global is resolved" [45, p. 114]. Hence, a cultural-political understanding of these conflicts and their resolution is important [15, 23]. However, such examinations are scarce within CSCW studies [29, 32], although a review of early CSCW studies had pointed to this need [27].

The MIS implementation studies that examine this process typically attribute these conflicts and the difficulties to resolve them to the misfit between the standardized generic needs embedded in the package and the user organization's specific needs, both bearing cultural roots [44, 46]. The user organization's needs typically stem from the way an organization would have been operating for years [44], in other words, patterned work practices that are built on shared norms, values, and beliefs, which interactively form organization's work culture [41, 54]. Similarly, in the case of ES, its standardized needs rest on its inscribed-culture as explained next.

Explicit structures such as functionality and data are given material form in the ES as coded transactions (i.e., data), and tables and relations (i.e., functionality). Both are instantiated in the system as explicit scripts. The way these structures are designed creates technological affordances (and non-affordances) that enable and constrain roles, control structures, and organizational culture - latent structures of the system [46] that are not perceptible to users. In this sense, ES is inscribed (implying the latent nature) with a work culture, which is accepted as an integral element of the artifact that exists as part of the delivered package separate from its use [42, 46]. Hence, the conflict in accommodating local work practices can stem from the contrast between the ES-inscribed culture and the user organization's prevalent work culture, if such a conflict exists. Thus, to understand the cultural underpinnings of potential conflictual discursive interaction between consultants and users during ES appropriation, we need to examine the ES-inscribed culture vis-à-vis the user community's work culture. Therefore, we begin our research with the following question: (a) How does the focal user community's work culture compare with the ES-inscribed culture? We follow it up with the questions we raised at the beginning of this section.

METHOD

We conducted an exploratory longitudinal in-depth case study in an India-based MNO, WestIndia (pseudonym), which had an ongoing ES implementation.

Case Background

From inception in 1996 until the take-over of WestIndia by another Western business group in 2006, the responsibility for developing organizational practices was largely rested with the Indian managing director. Within two years of operation, WestIndia became the market leader with a reputation for customer responsiveness. However, from 2002 onwards there was increased market competition. WestIndia responded by increasing the number of specialty products from 10 to 100, of which nearly 70% were custom-made. To facilitate this high level of customization, managers and their subordinates (below managers, staff comprising engineers and officers (e.g., accountants) and below them supervisors) were given significant decision autonomy. They were expected to improvise to meet customer needs and manage the uncertainties involved in unexpected customer demands.

In February 2007, the new owners asked WestIndia to implement an ES to get an integrated view of the firm. Sales presentations by various consultants followed, and the contract was awarded to a non-Indian firm that had successfully implemented ES in neighboring countries.

Data Creation and Analysis

Our field immersion started in July 2007, when the first module was implemented. The field research was designed to gain access to individual interpretations of reality by collecting and analyzing language and actions related to the ever-changing perceptions of technology. This subjective reality is accessed through the articulations of participants as they assign meaning to what is said and done. This indicates an interpretive approach [59, 56].

The first author, hereafter Field Researcher (FR), conducted the field investigation and analysis as part of his doctoral dissertation. During data collection, he related with the organizational members as a doctoral researcher. Primary data came from 70 semi-structured in-person face-to-face interviews each lasting 60 minutes or more (see Table 1) and participant observation (including participation in ten meetings) spanning eight continuous months.

# of interviewees	# of times interviewed (# of person* # of times)
3 consultants	1*1+1*5+1*3
9 managers	4*3+2*2+3*1
14 engineers/officers	3*3+8*2+3*1
9 supervisors	5*2+4*1
Total # of interviewees: 35	Total # of interviews: 70

Table 1: Details of primary data collection

The interviews were conducted at-the-time, as the system was rolled out in the company, and either on the company premises or the interviewee's residence as per interviewees' comfort. Interviewees were selected through snowball sampling. To track changes in an individual's interpretations, FR conducted systematic repeat interviews (see Table 1). The interview was loosely structured around two broad themes: the meaning and expectations that the actors attribute to the packaged software; and any anticipated or actual changes in the software/firm perceived by the interviewee to be noteworthy. This interview approach was devised to encourage uninterrupted storytelling related to issues of central importance to the interviewee [56].

Supplementary data from other sources included WestIndian company documents, group discussions, minutes of ES-related meetings and reports provided to WestIndia by ES consultants, and researcher's field notes. The group discussion was not focused and orchestrated. Instead, when engineers and supervisors came together (typically in plant office) or managers and engineers got together (typically in the canteen), FR would raise some questions which created the discussion. We used the constructivist version of grounded theory for analysis [10]. During fieldwork, we started exploratory coding, grouped related codes, and created focused themes, for example, 'ES design', 'culture', 'discourse' and 'system limitations'. Based on the feedback from key actors and their narratives, FR refined codes, groups, and their assignment to themes. Key actors were identified based on FR's ongoing assessment of direct and indirect influence that the person seemed to exert. They included two consultants, six managers, two officers, four engineers, and three supervisors. They were repeatedly interviewed. Besides ongoing feedback, near the end of the fieldwork, FR sought oral feedback on his analysis which he narrated to them one-on-one.

This feedback-refinement cycle was continued until these analytic elements formed a coherent story. From these themes, we considered literature on affordance and coined TNA as a way to explain the political dynamics around system limitations. Since discourse was another major theme that emerged in our cyclic analysis, we focused on it in relation to non-affordances. Hence, we captured various discourses through creating narrative accounts. The focus on non-affordance-discourse relationship helped understand the political interactions that emerged in the implementer-user-technology trio during the encounter between ES-inscribed culture and local work culture.

FINDINGS

The contrast between ES culture and WestIndian culture

Prior to the ERP implementation, without systematically checking the availability of materials and machines, WestIndia used to accept all customer orders. Subsequently, the managers would negotiate with each customer to fix the customer delivery dates that were orally expressed and treated as guidelines rather than deadlines. The confirmed sequence and details of customer orders and the corresponding delivery dates in the form of a weekly production schedule would be issued for production. Subsequently, and many times as the delivery date (promised to customers) approached since some orders would not have sufficient machines or material for production, WestIndia managers would negotiate with customers to get an extension on delivery dates. This negotiation strategy continued for a long time. The result was that some customers would start pressing the managers to expedite delivery. Managers would "push in" these "emergency" orders for production, stopping and replacing other ongoing production.

Since the pushed-in customer orders would not have allocated production materials, the materials reserved for ongoing orders would be diverted to these emergency orders. Employees called this practice material diversion. The reallocation of materials was usually recorded later at the employee's convenience and sometimes it was not recorded at all, indicating a lack of time-bound action. The result was an incorrect record of material consumption. It led to poor estimates of material requirements, and in turn, a shortage of production materials at the point of production. The results were production schedule slippage and delayed production, which were normalized. Whenever the schedule slipped, the managers would again negotiate with the customers and the cycle would repeat, reproducing and reinforcing the underlying temporal norms and meanings, which conflicted with the ES-inscribed culture.
The objective of ES is to maximize profit through improving efficiency. Inscribed templates are designed to achieve efficiency by fostering procedural adherence at the cost of improvisation by forcing time-bound actions. For example, the technical ES documentation at WestIndia stated: "for better control and efficiency…user has to strictly follow steps..and [standard] procedures ..and make real time [data] input". Consistent with this statement, if users deviated from standard procedures or did not provide real-time input, the software would raise red flags and error messages. Moreover, compared to the local practice, ES demanded rigid temporal order. For instance, in contrast with customer push-in, in the standard ES at WestIndia, after the confirmation and issue for production, the order and the dates were unchangeable within the Customer Order table.

Below is a summary of this analysis vis-a-vis aspects of the ES-inscribed culture, highlighting the contrast between the two.

Aspects of Culture	WestIndian Culture	ES-inscribed Culture
Production related value	Adaptation to local and customer needs through improvisation	Consistency of products and processes through standardization
Procedure-related value	Local autonomy resulting in process variations	Standard operating procedures with rigid adherence
Norms	Flexible temporal order Temporal imprecision Schedule slippage	Rigid temporal order Temporal precision Schedule adherence
Belief	Time as flexible Time as less bound	Time as rigid Time as more bound

Table 2: WestIndian culture versus ES-inscribed culture

The Role of Discursive Power, Emergence of Non-Affordance, and User Community's Response

We present below a narrative account of consultants' discursive shaping of user understanding of ES functionality and the underpinning changes to work practices and users' response, which was contingent on their experience of non-affordances. While presenting this account, we use the following notations: (1) source of data is mentioned except for interview excerpts, and (2) FR=interviewer, M=manager, O=officer, E= engineer, S=supervisor, and C=consultant.

Phase 1: Discursive Creation of inherently constrained ES and the First Opposition (Jun 07 – Sep 07)

In the sales presentation, ES was portrayed as flexible. Although this point was not a major selling point, it caught audience imagination. Consequently, many organizational members understood ES as a technology which could be tailored to the organization's needs:
E6: *Many of us felt that there was a best practice technology, standard, but customizable to our needs.*

However, three months later, in the first implementation meeting the consultants highlighted the ES's inflexibilities. As one manager recalled:
M4: *It seemed the only way for us was just fall in line (adopt the standard ES). They (consultants) repeatedly highlighted that they could do nothing that would disturb the [ES] core…since the system is so complex and has some in-built constraints.*

All managers, officers, and engineers attended this meeting. Most interviewees had similar recall of this meeting:
O3: *The takeaway (of the meeting) was 'better you guys change since [ES] cannot change much'.*

After two weeks the second implementation meeting took

place. In this meeting, the consultants repeatedly highlighted the constraints built into the standard ES. However, some employees, particularly, a manager (M1), opposed the 'mere adoption', and suggested that ES must incorporate WestIndia's best practices. Many interviewees recalled this meeting as 'M1 vs. consultants':

E2: *That (meeting) was a fight. They (consultants) repeated the need for adoption and the in-built constraints...They rejected M1's most suggestions, saying such changes were impossible to make (since) ES by its very nature required some standard integrated links and formats.*

Meanwhile, as the minutes of ES meeting reveals, the consultants had noticed that delays and lack of efficiency (employees' and processes') were serious issues that bothered WestIndia. Subsequently, the consultants presented adopting standard ES as a solution to these problems:

C1: *As we did in your (FR's) presence, we've been telling them [ES] implementation would solve their problems: inefficiencies and delays. For this, they should use its best practices, replacing their local practices.*

When many users accepted this discourse, the consultants extended it adding that the adoption of the standard ES would only result in delay reduction and efficiency increase. They also linked this to the need for accepting 'inherent system constraints that make certain changes impossible':

C2: *If you want to be more efficient with no delays, you should accept the system's constraints as well. Isn't it natural that every benefit comes at a cost? We aren't hiding that cost (in project meeting 4).*

Most managers bought into this discourse resulting in a shared localized meaning of ES: a delay reducer and an efficiency increaser with built-in constraints:

M3: *It's like [ES] comes, and the company has to fall in line...The result is delay reduction and efficiency increase...you can't anyway change (standard practices) much; the system won't allow, so adopt them for your good.*

However, a few engineers and officers informally inspired by M1 had a different view although they shared the same localized meaning of ES:

O7: *[ES] can reduce delays and increase efficiency better by accommodating our best procedures, for example, material diversion...not mere adoption. These technologies can accommodate some modifications. (in an informal conversation with FR)*

Thus, while accepting the situated meaning of ES as a delay reducer, this group challenged the consultants' discourse around the meaning of ES as a largely non-modifiable product. Further, while the consultant categorized some modification suggestions as technically infeasible due to inherent system constraints, the opposing group categorized them as feasible. An example from a testing session that further illustrates this struggle over categorization follows:

E7: *In cargo, we face unexpected strikes and so lose time and money...[ES] should capture this variation.*

C2: *It will disturb the master tables..they are linked to payment, creating problems there too. This system does not allow modifying the master table this way.*

E7: *There can be some things the system won't permit, but my request does not appear that huge. Why don't you try?*

This opposing discourse favoring customization, however, did not mobilize a significant number and was ignored by the consultants and others. Consequently, WestIndia went ahead adopting the standard design and started the trial use.

Phase 2: Users' Initial Experience of Non-affordances (Sep 07–Nov 07)

By now, as this section shows, through trial use, users came to two realizations: (1) The main action possibility that ES provides is delay reduction; realization of which warrants using the standard ES practices on a daily basis, and (2) the consultants' claim of ES functionality constraints are true as the users' frequent use of the new system showed them. Illustrations follow.

E10: *I tried getting in logistic variations by using workarounds. But, the system needs some high level of standardization to create efficiency. If you don't enter standard input, it outputs junk! So, you got to act as the system prescribes; standards alone aren't the full story.*

M5: *There is a big difference between what ES contains and what we've been doing for a long time...we aren't time bound. Delays are normal and fine. Due dates are flexible guidelines; we skip SOP sequence. But, in ES, due dates are rigid, you should adhere to sequence and act on time...these reduce delays, making you more efficient.*

The consultants had also realized this contrast between the ES's temporality and WestIndian temporality (see Table 2). The consultants anticipated that this contrast could potentially result in significant requests for customization. Below is an excerpt from an informal conversation with the consultants:

C2: *Huge work ahead (referring to the contrast). Buckle up to fight your way out or use the trick of the trade.*

FR: *What is the trick of the trade?*

C2:*..tell them it (user suggested modification) is technically infeasible, and make them buy it.*

Thus, categorizing users' customization request as technically infeasible was the consultants' intentional strategy to reduce customization, and hence was political in nature. This discursive control gradually undermined the articulated opposing voices.

Simultaneously, in coalition with some managers and linking to the issues of user discipline, the consultants created another discourse, which suggested that the standard ES design had the potential to bring about desirable discipline, for example, temporal discipline

around workflow:
M5: *We don't have proper records and time sensitivity..we need discipline. As [consultants] rightly say, [ES] helps here. I realized this in my daily use. [ES] can discipline and make us efficient…We (managers) have been helping them (non-managerial employees) understand it.*

Thus, the affordance of delay reduction and temporal behavioral discipline emerged in trial use as users were guided by delay reduction and discipline discourses. These affordances also confined interpretation of ES to delay reducer and discipliner and constrained user appropriation of ES features for meeting local needs. They also implied the need for the change in users' temporal workflow, local work practices, norms, and values. As a result, the local work culture would change for the better. Consequently, users did not pursue any of their modification suggestions once the consultants categorized them as technically infeasible, accepting this point. Illustrative excerpts follow:
O4: *If you are not doing the job the way system demands, it will catch you with warnings and errors…I realized that, as they (consultants) say, certain actions like clustering are impossible…so, we stopped wasting time on suggestions.*

E3: *Now, time runs out...we've to finish in time; it's the system forcing us to do so…we become more efficient.*

Thus, users experienced a quick change in their work culture – a shift to ES-inscribed culture (see Table 2) which made certain actions that they used to perform regularly, now, impossible. This TNA experience reinforced the credibility of consultants' discursive creation of TNA. Gradually, non-affordances became the cost one pays for experiencing certain new affordances while realizing the valued benefit - "increased efficiency". Hence, in users' cost-benefit analysis, the discursively privileged highly beneficial efficiency increase justified perceived system constraints and thus further enhanced the credibility of the consultants' TNA discourse. Then, whether the technology design was factually non-modifiable was irrelevant because the discourse itself was powerful enough to convince but for a limited time as the next two phases show.

Phase 3: Recurring Non-affordances and the Second Opposition (Nov 07 – Jan 08)

As the trial period progressed, the users experienced that the ES subjected them to more elaborate systems of recordkeeping and accountability (than the existing ISs did). This realization led to the second round of opposition to consultants' discursive creation of ES as a beneficial inherently non-modifiable product. Thus, while the manager-consultant coalition portrayed the ES as a beneficial discipliner favoring adoption, based on their experience and prior understanding, a group comprising some officers, engineers, and supervisors articulated ES as a disciplinary constraint that is detrimental to WestIndia and individual employees. Illustrative examples follow starting with an excerpt from a group discussion:

S8: *Also due to integration, ES doesn't allow you to violate procedures…it forces you to do things in time…We lost the freedom to decide on the fly...that flexibility had been cherished here.*

E4: *Efficiency at the cost of quality and flexibility, the hallmarks of WestIndia...Adoption brings more stress…In our system, we deviate from procedures; no one questions. It gives us...flexibility that we are losing now. In ES, others can see the violations; that makes us more monitorable.*

Next is an interview quote.
S5: *We can't deviate from the standard procedures as we used to do…It's not that the (ES) standards can't be modified. In some cases, it's possible but [consultants] just label them impossible; guys here buy that.*

This group realized the loss of a valued action possibility – the possibility to skip procedural steps, which allowed exercise of their decision autonomy. They found this action impossible within the ES. However, since they were suspicious of the consultants' categorization and believed that ES could accommodate local practices, instead of creating workarounds or appropriating partially, resumed challenging the consultants' discourse and categorization discursively. In certain instances, the opposition was explicit. An example from purchase module discussion follows:
M5 to M1: *When you suggest modifications, you should keep in mind the technical limitations of [ES].*

C2: *Look, I repeat, the system is pretty much complex…with accumulated limitations. Database and the language have its limitations and constraints; no one can do anything.*

(The argument between purchase staff and the consultants went on for half an hour and finally)

C2: *I can make the due date field editable; you vary the date depending on the vendor. But it's always better to standardize…it's not that we are reluctant to modify, but the system doesn't permit, it just cannot (permit).*

M4: *What we are asking is not that terribly basic..It can't be that impossible.*

Meanwhile, M1, whom many took as the informal leader of the opposing voices, was terminated from employment. This signaled a threat to the opposing group, and subsequently, the public opposition waned. Yet, in private conversations, many users grew skeptical of consultants' TNA discourse and categorization, although they had experienced non-affordances.

Phase 4: The Third Opposition and the incorporation of the local culture (Jan 08 – April 08)

Although the consultants' political strategy of discursively shaping user experience of affordances and non-affordances to consultants' advantage had largely been successful so far, a significant number of users now started believing that the ES was modifiable:

M6: *Initially I believed that it (ES) can't be customized due to system limitations. Now, that belief is changing. I don't mean there aren't any system constraints. But, when we persist and pressure [consultants], their standpoint changes. So, there's this hope: we can get [ES] customized.*

As this excerpt indicates, this group that had so far been in coalition with the consultants, believing in consultants' justification of technical infeasibility for not incorporating user suggestions, now, noticed consultants yielding to some persistent demands. Hence, they started suspecting the credibility of consultants' TNA related discourse and believing in the opposing group's discourse:

M5: Perhaps, they [the opposing group] have some points…Sure [M1], with his long experience, knew a lot.

Meanwhile, in the [ES], the users had been searching for more features, which they had repeatedly been using as part of their existing work practices, such as a utility to do the what-if scenario analysis and perform customer push-in. The standard design did not support or include them. Hence, the consultants had to agree that the current version of ES was limited in its features. Users labeled these limitations as *system deficiencies* that needed improvement rather than as system constraints. Hence, managers in unison suggested incorporating certain local practices as a way to enhance the ES's functionalities. An illustrative example follows.

M6: *Here, we have a number of variables, which the [ES] is unable to factor in. It has limited features and is deficient in what-if-analyses, job clustering, dynamic scheduling, etc…If the system could dynamically self-rectify based on our feedback, we could've relied on it, avoided customer push-in and sorts* (in a meeting with the consultants).

Simultaneously, following trial use, the group that had initially sided with the consultants, along with a manager and officers/engineers who had been opposing the consultants' discourse, reflected on their interaction with the ES and the opposing discourse. Subsequently, they realized that by accepting the standard design, they were losing their decision autonomy and customer responsiveness. They decided to use these criteria for selecting the local practices for incorporation and to compel the consultants to yield to their demands pointing to the potential loss of customer responsiveness. The management had considered customer responsiveness as WestIndia's competitive advantage, and hence it had significant import. Gradually, the group mentioned above started citing the potential loss of customer responsiveness and the absence of certain features as the two grounds to demand incorporation of these local practices such as customer push-in, material diversion, and job clustering:

M3*: Adopting (ES) procedures will reduce our flexibilities. We've to rather completely rely on the system. This [ES] doesn't have many (design) features that we need…so, better we retain our flexibilities. If we don't, we will lose customers. This is our standpoint now.*

These employees created a new localized meaning for the ES, a flexibility reducer, an argument that was raised in the second round of opposition. In this new discourse, flexibility meant the capability to respond to customer needs dynamically that is enabled by certain local practices, freedom to make changes, and the skill to respond creatively to unexpected variations. As mentioned in the case background, these were valued aspects of WestIndian work culture. Illustrative examples follow.

M2*: Efficiency is good...but we also need exploration provisions...that skill to manage the unexpected is flexibility...these have been our traditional competencies.*

E3: *(standard) [ES] almost eliminates our flexibilities… soon we'll be at the system's mercy. (Chat between engineers and officers, field journal notes).*

Given that the previously opposing group had raised flexibility reduction (but not in terms of customer responsiveness), this discourse rapidly picked up momentum. The consultants kept warning WestIndia that incorporation of such local practices would significantly change the ES design, and reduce potential benefits for WestIndia. However, simultaneously, consultants started making a cost-benefit analysis of the customization and discussed this idea with the vendor over two months. Finally, apprehending the intensity of user opposition and a consequent potential contract revoke, the consulting firm agreed to develop a more flexible ES for meeting WestIndia's needs and work culture. In return, they asked WestIndia to be the consultants' service ambassador in India. Users demanded for incorporating customer push-in, material diversion, job clustering, what-if-scenario analysis, and pre-batch processing. However, the consultants informed that they could incorporate the practices that would retain customer responsiveness and would not take more than three months to complete. Users found these criteria satisfactory on the following grounds: (1) customer responsiveness was their main concern and the practices related to customer responsiveness retained their decision autonomy to reasonable extent, (2) the top management was getting concerned about time overrun. Thus, the conflict between users and consultants was finally resolved through a negotiated compromise.

The redesign included the development of user interfaces that linked the sales, production and materials modules, and a number of changes that enabled users to (a) push-in customers manually, (b) material diversion: re-allocate material reserved for job orders to fill emergency orders, and (c) enter output data from their spreadsheet-based what-if analyses into the ERP. The first change had been users' demand from the beginning of phase 4. The second demand was initiated by M1 and others in phase 1 and re-appeared in phase 3 and phase 4. The third was a compromise move: although users demanded incorporation of what-if-scenario analysis, they realized that it would take more than three months. Hence, users agreed to consultants' suggestion.

These changes required both activation of dormant features, inclusion of new features, and interconnection of features to create new work practices. Consequently, the temporal rigidity of the ES schedules was reduced. Still, in other modules, time-bound action was maintained. By adapting the standard ES design, WestIndia appropriated the system that embodied contrasting temporalities: rigidity (i.e., the culture inscribed in standard design) and flexibility (an aspect of the local culture). This adaptation created a culturally inclusive design that is sold widely as a generic product with work flexibility as a distinctive feature.

DISCUSSION

This study presents a narrative account of how discourse is used as a means of shaping user understanding about the underlying features and practices in an ES which are not perceptible to the users. The study maps the entailing conflict between the proponents of global, standardized work practices embedded within the ES (demanding user adaptation) and supporters of locally valued work practices (suggesting artefact adaptation). Our in-depth case study explains how power relationships within implementer-user community-technology trio manifest in active discursive creations of situated meaning of technology through consultants on the one hand and local meaning that unfolds and changes through continuous user opposition on the other. The sustained user resistance led to a negotiated compromise. These contributions are important since HCI literature and CSCW technology appropriation literature have rarely examined such discursive power relationships and conflict resolution process closely [22, 26, 47, 48], while they are crucial to the process of completing design through use [36, 37] and to understand its ethical underpinning [3, 4].

The study shows how, despite initial resistance from a user group, consultants used discursive creation of TNA and supportive situated meanings of technology which compelled users to self-limit their suggestions to modify the standard design – one that was presented to them as the gold standard. Hence, attending to TNA may reveal the process of imposing a culturally exclusive design and perpetuating it as the gold standard – a common concern of ethical and culturally sensitive design [48], cross-cultural design [1, 47], and post-colonial studies [4, 18].

However, the perpetuation may not last long, if there is sustained meaningful user opposition, as our study illustrates. If users reflect upon their co-workers' sustained resistance along with their multiple interactions with the technology, the consultants' discursive shaping, and their yielding to the opposition, the initial resistance may mobilize others to the extent that the resistance is value-based rather than person-based [52]. Such collective user resistance can lead to the emergence of a culturally inclusive design that incorporates local practices. Following the perspective that is dominant in organizational change studies [52], recent ICT4 D and HCI4D studies consider user resistance to adoption of the standard design as a bottleneck to overcome [e.g., 39]. Our study argues for a shift from this approach to understanding user resistance as productive [12] - a potentially useful feedback for creating a culturally inclusive design. This shift would help advance the design goal of "pluralism" that the third wave of HCI research pursues [5], given pluralism comes from thinking significantly different from way the dominant perspective prescribes. Although technology appropriation studies describe an alternate way of resisting, a passive resistance of non-use [40] or a non-evaluative approach to resistance [8], not all contexts may allow non-use. For example, often, in developing countries, work systems, which claim to replace traditional local practices with modern globally best practices, bring with it the impetus to adopt to these ways of working because one is paid to do so.

As technology appropriation literature, particularly from the information infrastructure perspective, suggests, design is an ongoing process that is complete through implementation and habitual use [7, 8, 36], which indicates the need to design for appropriation. The appropriation studies argue that informing designing-for-appropriation requires an understanding of how users attribute functional values to software [37]. Our study shows that functional values such as delay reduction that users attribute to the artifact, in the beginning, may depend significantly on the situated meaning of artifact that the consultants discursively create due to lack of user perceptibility of the underlying system. This dependence, however, can change as users grow familiar with the technology through repeated use, and as they start questioning the consultants' discourses based on their technology use, making their own collective meaning of the artifact. Beneath the expressed functional value and collective meaning lies the cultural value (which users may become cognizant of in due course). For example, while delay reduction privileged the cultural value of efficiency inscribed in the ES, customer responsiveness and dynamic customer prioritization privileged the cultural value of flexibility that underpinned local work practices. Hence, to the extent technology appropriation is a process of meaning making that involves cultural expressions, in short, cultural appropriation, [26] designing for appropriation should involve an understanding of cultural appropriation. This cultural appropriation, as our study illustrates, is inherently political since it encapsulates the question of whose cultural values count.

When designing for appropriation, designers should identify the adaptation means to be offered to users [40, 51]. Considering designing as a cultural engagement may help designers in this process since as our study shows, the requirement for adaptation of the standard design and related tension often arise from the mismatch between the artifact-inscribed culture and the users' existing work culture. Such a step would facilitate development of culturally sensitive design. Finally, if technology appropriation is considered as an interaction between the local culture of the user-community and designer community's culture, an ethical approach to design for appropriation may privilege local culture in case of irresolvable conflict between the two cultures. This is because, finally, it is not designers but the user community who has to live with the technology. Of course, it raises a question of which user culture should designers privilege, in the case where conflicting subcultures exist within the user community.

Within our case, cultural inclusion via artifact adaptation indicated generification, since subsequent to the adaptation the incorporated cultural practices became a distinctive feature of the artifact in vendor packaging. Hence, this study shows the fine-grained political work that stemmed from TNA experiences which led to a specific generification strategy – cultural appropriation. While the existing information infrastructure studies focus mostly on generification prior to diffusion of the artifact [36, 43], our study details post-diffusion generification. Together these insights suggest that generification is an ongoing multistage process.

Regarding the fine-grained political work, this study highlights shifts in user discourses from supporting to opposing the consultants' discourse and the consequent negotiated compromise that involved not only persuasion but also perceived coercion (e.g., consultants' apprehension of contract revoke). Such nuanced understanding is necessary to advance the scholarship on the work involved in accommodating and developing information infrastructure [32, 36]. We further show how users form different interest-based groups and shift their interest over time, breaking away from the discursive coalition with consultants later to form a new coalition with other user groups. This dynamic account enriches the less-nuanced picture, which is prevalent in the extant literature, of pitting single user group with unvarying interest against consultant in developing information infrastructure and global software [36, 37].

Overall, this study argues for two expansions to broaden our current understanding of technology appropriation and connect it to related HCI scholarship: (1) conceptualize the dialogical interaction [49] between designers/ system implementers and users as a cultural-political engagement, rather than merely as appropriation, in which users' right to dissent is enshrined. Such a broad conceptualization fits within the suggestion of postcolonial designers to explore design as culture [28]. This step could transform the interaction into a democratic process that is ethically sensitive – a goal within the HCI4D scholarship [31]. (2) Explore the conflicts related to development/implementation of information infrastructures as not merely issues of knowledge integration [30, 38, 43], but as a cultural-political dynamic that entails ethical considerations beyond a cost-benefit based negotiated compromise.

CONCLUSION

This study urges HCI scholars to examine designers/implementers as political actors who struggle to advance their self-interest using cultural means such as discursive creation of TNA with ethical implications for culturally sensitive designs. We thus show how attending to the emergence of non-affordances can become useful for developing culturally inclusive design.

We advocate a dialogical design process [49] to integrate action and meaning in cross-cultural design, which would make work systems usable, ethical and meaningful to those tasked with effectively utilizing the system. The key aspect of this approach is to consider user resistance as productive and a process valuable at par with the exercise of power by change agents such as implementers. Such a design approach could facilitate user empowerment and development of a critical reflective perspective, one of the stated objectives of critical HCI scholarship [4] and postcolonial computing [5].

ACKNOWLEDGMENTS

We thank the shepherd, the anonymous reviewers, and the ACs for providing helpful comments on previous versions of this document. This paper benefitted substantially from the shepherd's prompt and useful comments. Author 1 is deeply grateful to Prof. Mohan Turaga for his continuous support and feedback on various drafts of this paper, and to Ms. Debaparna Mukherjee, for her sincere assistance. Author 1 acknowledges the grant from IIMA R & P unit.

REFERENCES

1. Yaw Anokwa, Smyth N. Thomas, Ramachandran Divya, Sherwani Jahanzeb, Schwartzman Yael, Luk Rowena, Ho Melissa, Moraveji Neema, and DeRenzi Brian.. 2009. Stories from the field: reflections on HCI4D experiences. *Information Technologies and International Development* 5, 4: 101–115.
2. Bijan Azad, and Faraj Samer. 2011. Social power and information technology implementation: a contentious framing lens. *Information Systems Journal* 21, 1: 33-61.
3. Shaowen Bardzell. 2010. Feminist HCI: taking stock and outlining an agenda for design. *In Proceedings of the SIGCHI Conference on Human Factors in Computing Systems* (ACM), 1301–1310.
4. Shaowen Bardzell, Bardzell Jeffrey, Forlizzi Jodi, Zimmerman John, and Antanitis John. 2012. Critical design and critical theory: the challenge of designing for provocation. *In Proceedings of the Designing Interactive Systems Conference* (ACM*)*, 288–297.
5. Susanne Bødker. 2006. When second wave HCI meets third wave challenges. *In Proceedings of the 4th Nordic conference on Human-computer interaction: changing roles* ACM, 1–8.
6. Chet Bowers A. 1988. *The cultural dimensions of educational computing: Understanding the non-neutrality of technology.* Teachers College Press.

7. Jennie Carroll. 2004. Completing design in use: closing the appropriation cycle. *In Proceedings of the 12th European Conference on Information Systems*, ECIS.
8. Jennie Carroll and Fidock Justin. 2011. Beyond resistance to technology appropriation. In *System Sciences (HICSS), 2011 44th Hawaii International Conference on* IEEE, 1-9.
9. Jennie Carroll, Howard Steve, Peck Jane, and Murphy John. 2002. A field study of perceptions and use of mobile telephones by 16 to 22 year olds, *Journal of Information Technology Theory and Application* (JITTA) 4, 2: 49-62.
10. Kathy Charmaz. 2006. *Constructing Grounded Theory: A Practical Guide Through Qualitative Analysis.* SAGE Publications, New Delhi.
11. Paul Dourish. 2003. The appropriation of interactive technologies: Some lessons from placeless documents. *Computer Supported Cooperative Work 12:* 465–490.
12. Jeffrey Ford, Laurie Ford, and Angelo D'Amelio. 2008. Resistance to change: The rest of the story. *Academy of management Review* 33, 2: 362-377.
13. Joan Greenbaum and Morten Kyng. (eds.) 1991. Design at Work: Cooperative Design of Computer Systems, Hillsdale, NJ: Lawrence Erlbaum Publishers.
14. Ole Hanseth and Nina Lundberg. 2001. Designing work oriented infrastructures. *Computer Supported Cooperative Work* (CSCW) 10, 3-4: 347-372.
15. Ole Hanseth, Eric Monteiro, and Morten Hatling. 1996. Developing information infrastructure: The tension between standardization and flexibility. *Science, Technology and Human Values*21, 4: 407–126.
16. Steve Harrison, Deborah Tatar , and Phoebe Sengers. 2007. The three paradigms of HCI. *Presented at conference on Human Factors in Computing Systems* (CHI).
17. Ian Hutchby. 2001. Technologies, texts and affordances. *Sociology 35*, 2: 441–456.
18. Lilly Irani, Janet Vertesi, Paul Dourish, Kavita Philip, and Rebecca Grinter. 2010. Postcolonial computing: a lens on design and development. *In Proceedings of the SIGCHI Conference on Human Factors in Computing Systems* (ACM), 1311–1320.
19. Chris Jones, Lone Dirckinck-Holmfeld, and Berner Lindtröm. 2005. CSCL-The Next Ten Years: A View from Europe. *In Proceedings of the 2005 Conference on Computer Support for Collaborative Learning: learning: the next 10 years!,* 237-246.
20. George Kandathil, Erica Wagner, and Sue Newell. 2011. Translating ES-Embedded Institutional Logics through Technological Framing: An Indian based Case Example. *ECIS Proceedings* 47, 1, 1.
21. Victor Kaptelinin and Bonnie Nardi. 2012. Affordances in HCI: toward a mediated action perspective. *In Proceedings of the SIGCHI Conference on Human Factors in Computing Systems*, ACM , 967–976.
22. Victor Kaptelinin. 2003. Learning with artefacts: integrating technologies into activities. *Interacting with Computers* 15, 6: 831-836.
23. Helena Karasti, Karen S. Baker, and Florence Millerand. 2010. Infrastructure time: Long-term matters in collaborative development. *Computer Supported Cooperative Work* 19, 3-4: 377–415.
24. Paul M. Leonardi. 2011. When flexible routines meet flexible technologies: Affordance, constraint, and the imbrication of human and material agencies. *MIS quarterly 35*, 1 147–167.
25. Ben Light. 2001. The maintenance implications of the customization of ERP software. *Journal of Software Maintenance Evolution* 13: 415–429.
26. Silvia Lindtner, Ken Anderson, and Paul Dourish. 2012. Cultural appropriation: information technologies as sites of transnational imagination. *In Proceedings of the ACM 2012 conference on computer supported cooperative work. (*ACM), 77-86.
27. Kalle J. Lyytinen, and Ojelanki K. Ngwenyama. 1992. What does computer support for cooperative work mean? A structurational analysis of computer supported cooperative work. *Accounting, Management and Information Technologies* 2, 1: 19-37.
28. Henry Mainsah and Andrew Morrison. 2014. Participatory design through a cultural lens: insights from postcolonial theory. *In Proceedings of the 13th Participatory Design Conference*, 2, (ACM)83-86.
29. David Martin, Mark Hartswood, Roger Slack , and Alex Voss . 2006. Achieving dependability in the configuration, integration and testing of healthcare technologies. *Computer Supported Cooperative Work*15, 5–6:467–499.
30. Stina Matthiesen and Pernille Bjørn. 2015. Why replacing legacy systems is so hard in global software development: An information infrastructure perspective. *In Proceedings of the 18th ACM Conference on Computer Supported Cooperative Work & Social Computing* (ACM), 876-890.
31. Samantha Merritt and Shaowen Bardzell. 2011. Postcolonial Language and Culture Theory for HCI4D. *In Proceedings of the CHI'11 EA*, 1675-1680.
32. Eric Monteiro, Neil Pollock, Ole Hanseth, and Robin Williams. 2013. From artefacts to infrastructures. *Computer supported cooperative work* (CSCW), 22(4-6), 575-607.
33. Mari K. Oja, Sue Newell, Erica Wagner, and Robert Galliers. 2015. Coping with Information Technology: Mixed Emotions, Vacillation and Non-conforming Use Patterns. *MIS Quarterly 39,* 2 367-392.

34. Wanda J. Orlikowski. 1996. Improvising Organizational Transformation over Time: A Situated Change Perspective, *Information Systems Research* 7, 1: 63-92.
35. Wanda J. Orlikowski. 2002. Knowing in Practice: Enacting a Collective Capability in Distributed Organizing. *Organization Science* 13, 3: 249-273.
36. Neil Pollock and Robin Williams. 2010. e-Infrastructures: how do we know and understand them? Strategic ethnography and the biography of artefacts. *Computer Supported Cooperative Work*19: 521–556.
37. Neil Pollock and Robin Williams. 2008. *Software and Organisations.* Routledge.
38. Lene Pries-Heje and Yvonne Dittrich. 2009. ERP implementation as design. *Scandinavian Journal of Information Systems* 21: 27-58.
39. Divya Ramachandran, John Canny, Prabhu D. Das, and Edward Cutrell. 2010. Mobile-izing health workers in rural India. *In Proceedings of the SIGCHI Conference on Human Factors in Computing Systems* (ACM), 1889–1898.
40. Christine Satchell and Paul Dourish. 2009. Beyond the user: use and non-use in HCI. In *Proceedings of the 21st Annual Conference of the Australian Computer-Human Interaction Special Interest Group: Design*: *(ACM).*
41. Edgar H. Schein. 1990. Organizational culture. *American Psychological Association* 45, 2: 109.
42. Siew K. Sia and Christina Soh. 2007. An assessment of package– organisation misalignment: institutional and ontological structures. *European Journal of Information Systems* 16, 5: 568-583.
43. Line Silsand and Gunnar Ellingsen. 2014. Generification by translation: designing generic systems in context of the local. *Journal of the Association for Information Systems* 15, 4: 177.
44. Christina Soh, Siew K. Sia, and Joanne Tay-Yap. 2000. Enterprise resource planning: cultural fits and misfits: is ERP a universal solution? *Communications of the ACM* 43, 4: 47-51.
45. Susan L. Star and Karen Ruhleder. 1996. Steps toward an ecology of infrastructure: Design and access for large information spaces. *Information Systems Research* 7, 1: 111-134.
46. Diane M. Strong and Olga Volkoff. 2010. Understanding organization-enterprise system fit: a path to theorizing the information technology artifact. *MIS quarterly 34*, 4 731–756.
47. Huatong Sun and William F. Hart-Davidson. 2014. Binding the material and the discursive with a relational approach of affordances. *In proceedings of the 32nd annual ACM conference on Human factors in computing systems* (ACM), 3533–3542.
48. Huatong Sun. 2012. *Cross-cultural technology design: Creating culture-sensitive technology for local users.* Oxford University Press,
49. Huatong Sun. 2009. Designing for a dialogic view of interpretation in cross-cultural IT design. In *Proceedings of HCI International 4:* 108-116.
50. Daniel D. Suthers. 2005. Technology affordances for intersubjective learning: A thematic agenda for CSCL. In *Proceedings of the 2005 conference on Computer support for collaborative learning: learning 2005: the next 10 years!* 662-671.
51. Pierre Tchounikine. 2016. Contribution to a theory of CSCL scripts: taking into account the appropriation of scripts by learners. *International Journal of Computer-Supported Collaborative Learning*, 1-21.
52. Robyn Thomas, Leisa D. Sargent, and Cynthia Hardy. 2011. Managing organizational change: Negotiating meaning and power-resistance relations. *Organization Science 22*, 1: 22–41.
53. Gefion Thuermer, Silke Roth, Markus Luczak-Rösch, and Kieron O'Hara. 2016. Internet use, in-and exclusion in decision-making processes within political parties. In *Proceedings of the 8th ACM Conference on Web Science* (ACM), 205-214.
54. Harrison M.Trice and Janice M. Beyer 1993. *The cultures of work organizations* Englewood Cliffs, NJ: Prentice Hall. 419-420.
55. Dhaval Vyas, Christina M. Chisalita, and Gerrit C. Van Der Veer. 2006. Affordance in interaction. In *Proceedings of the 13th European conference on Cognitive ergonomics: trust and control in complex socio-technical systems*, ACM, 92– 99.
56. Erica Wagner and George Kandathil. 2016. Narrative Methodologies in Information Systems Literature: Illuminating Interconnectivity and Change over Time. *Communications of the Association for Information System* 39, 555.
57. Erica Wagner and Sue Newell. 2006. Repairing ERP Producing Social Order to Create a Working Information System. *The Journal of Applied Behavioral Science* 42, 1: 40-57.
58. Erica Wagner and Sue Newell. 2007. Exploring the Importance of Participation in the Post-implementation Period of an ES Project: A Neglected Area. *Journal of the AIS,* 8(10), article 32.
59. Geoff Walsham. 1993. *Interpreting information systems in organizations.* John Wiley & Sons, Inc.
60. Robin A. Williams, James K. Stewart, and Roger Slack. 2005. Social Learning in Technological Innovation: Experimenting with Information and Communication Technologies, Edward Elgar.

Hybrid HFR Depth: Fusing Commodity Depth and Color Cameras to Achieve High Frame Rate, Low Latency Depth Camera Interactions

Jiajun Lu[2,1], Hrvoje Benko[1], Andrew D. Wilson[1]

[1]Microsoft Research
Redmond, WA, USA
benko@microsoft.com,
awilson@microsoft.com

[2]University of Illinois
Urbana, IL, USA
jlu23@illinois.edu

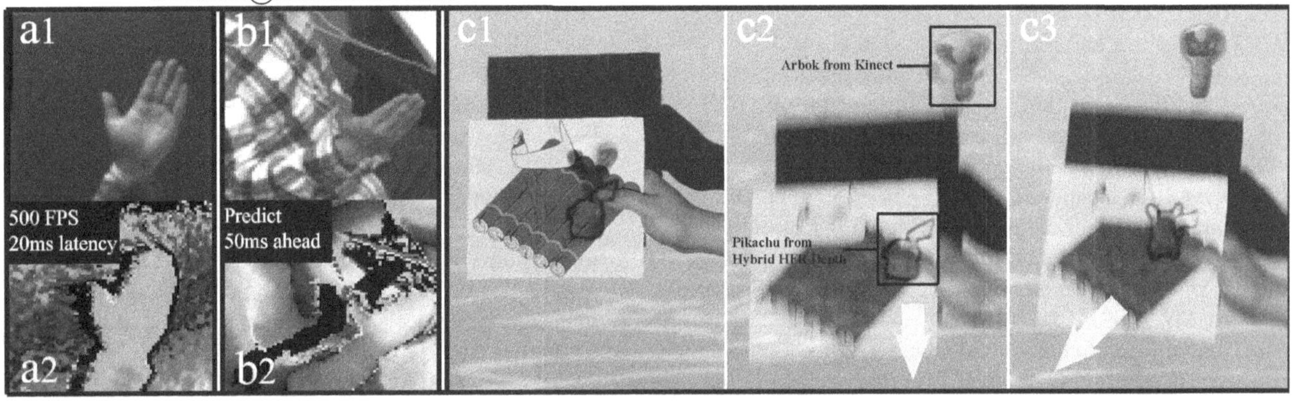

Figure 1. Hybrid HFR Depth is a high frame rate, low latency, configurable dept h camera solution built from a Kinect and a color camera. Depth output is 500 frames per second (maximum) and 20 milliseconds latency in (a1-2), and depth is predicted 50ms into the future in (b1-2). Our high frame rate, low latency depth solution supports applications sensitive to lag and framerate: (c1-3) illustrates interactive projection mapping, where Arbok and Pikuchu are projected onto the raft using either standard Kinect depth stream (Arbok) or Hybrid HFR Depth stream (Pikachu) to track the projection surface. (c1) Arbok and Pikachu are projected on the raft when hand is still. (c2) (c3) Arbok is off the raft and Pikachu is on the raft when hand is moving.

ABSTRACT

The low frame rate and high latency of consumer depth cameras limits their use in interactive applications. We propose combining the Kinect depth camera with an ordinary color camera to synthesize a high frame rate and low latency depth image. We exploit common CMOS camera region of interest (ROI) functionality to obtain a high frame rate image over a small ROI. Motion in the ROI is computed by a fast optical flow implementation. The resulting flow field is used to extrapolate Kinect depth images to achieve high frame rate and low latency depth, and optionally predict depth to further reduce latency. Our "Hybrid HFR Depth" prototype generates useful depth images at maximum 500Hz with minimum 20ms latency. We demonstrate Hybrid HFR Depth in tracking fast moving objects, handwriting in the air, and projecting onto moving hands. Based on commonly available cameras and image processing implementations, Hybrid HFR Depth may be useful to HCI practitioners seeking to create fast, fluid depth camera-based interactions.

CHI 2017, May 06 - 11, 2017, Denver, CO, USA

ACM 978-1-4503-4655-9/17/05...$15.00
DOI: http://dx.doi.org/10.1145/3025453.3025478

Author Keywords

depth camera; Kinect; latency; frame rate; configurable

ACM Classification Keywords

H.5.2. Information interfaces and presentation (e.g., HCI): Input devices and strategies (e.g., mouse, touchscreen)

INTRODUCTION

Consumer depth cameras such as Microsoft Kinect have been useful in various HCI applications. But the frame rate (30Hz) and high latency (at 60-80 milliseconds) of such cameras can limit their use in interactive applications sensitive to lag and framerate. Low frame rates can complicate tracking, particularly for fast moving, flexible objects like hands. High latency during interaction can confuse or even nauseate users, particularly in AR and VR applications, or when overlaying graphics on physical objects that move unpredictably.

In the absence of commercially available high frame, low latency depth sensors, we explore solutions involving commodity depth sensors and commonly available color cameras. We demonstrate a *hybrid high frame rate depth* (Hybrid HFR Depth) camera solution, which registers a Kinect v2 to a Point Grey Grasshopper 3 camera, a commercially available configurable, high frame rate, high resolution and low latency color camera. With the two cameras aligned, we calculate optical flow over a small region of interest (ROI) of the color camera. The frame rate and latency of CMOS cameras such as the Point Grey camera is related to the size of the ROI, with small ROIs obtaining high frame rate (500Hz) and low latency. We apply the resulting flow field to warp the depth samples in the image plane. Our experiments demonstrate that the errors in measurement resulting from our approach are small. Our approach also allows a small amount of prediction to further reduce latency.

We demonstrate three applications of Hybrid HFR Depth. Our applications are chosen to expose the benefits of high frame rate, and low or negative latency. We show Hybrid HFR Depth tracking a ping pong ball with dense, accurate samples of depth. We use Hybrid HFR Depth to track a fingertip, producing an accurate, dense trace useful for rendering and gesture recognition. Finally, we show that Hybrid HFR Depth is well-suited to interactive projection mapping applications. High latency in a projection mapping system can cause projected graphics to slide or shift on fast moving objects. Hybrid HFR Depth's high frame rate and latency reduction allows projection mapping onto a moving hand.

By utilizing inexpensive, commonly available cameras, and common computer vision image processing routines (OpenCV) we hope Hybrid HFR Depth enables HCI practitioners to create fast, fluid depth camera-based interactions.

RELATED WORK

There are a variety of previous works that seek to increase the frame rate and reduce the latency of depth cameras. They include a range of approaches including simple prediction using a dynamical model, modifications of existing depth image computation algorithms possibly involving exotic hardware, and highly specialized hardware.

Prediction by Dynamical Models

Dynamical models allow a degree of prediction in software, thereby reducing latency. Xia et al. [19] sought to find a camera and software-based approach to reduce the latency of touchscreen interaction. Based on collected training data, Xia et al. estimated touch down locations and triggered device interactions in advance. Knibbe et al. [8] used a Kalman Filter to predict the motion of a ball in flight. Kitani et al. [7] placed a camera inside a ball and used image processing to determine its speed of rotation, triggering the camera at precise moments to capture the scene below. At low frame rates, such dynamical models must be very accurate to make helpful predictions, limiting the utility of the approach.

Specialized Depth Processing

Other related works improve performance of depth cameras by exploiting low-level properties of how depth is computed. Such approaches tend to rely on exotic components, modifications of existing components, and intimate knowledge of how depth is computed on today's depth cameras. The focus of these works is on improving frame rate; improvements in latency are not discussed.

Schmidt et al. [15] presented a method to implicitly calibrate multi-tap 3D Time of Flight sensors, increasing the frame rate by a factor of two. Their prototype is a proof-of-concept written in Matlab.

Stuhmer et al. demonstrated that a modified Kinect v2 operating at 300Hz can track a fast moving ping pong ball accurately [17]. They modified the Kinect depth sensor to capture raw infrared images, and performed model-based tracking against these raw captures. The method requires models for both object and motion, and so works only for rigid simple shapes in simple motion. In contrast, our method obtains high frame rate and low latency depth map for a region of interest under general motion.

Fanello et al. [3] combined an exotic high-frame rate full-frame camera with a Kinect v1 structured light projector to obtain depth frames at 375Hz. They contribute a machine learning approach to optimize the Kinect v1 computation of disparity to keep up with the high frame rate camera.

Increasing Frame Rate by Specialized Hardware

Specialized hardware may be used to reduce latency and increase frame rate for a particular application. Papadakis et al. [14] minimized latency in head-tracking immersive simulations by reducing buffering latency in their display hardware, achieving a 50% reduction in overall system latency. Lumospheres [9] presented a hardware optimization approach to accurately project on balls under projectile motion. Okumura et al. [13] introduced a low latency camera with a series of saccade mirrors for ball tracking technology. Their system is purely vision based (no depth), so it can only track visually salient objects.

Customized hardware generates impressive results, but the expense of such approaches put them out of reach of typical HCI practitioners. In contrast, our method uses off-the-shelf, affordable hardware.

Hybrid Cameras

Lu et al. [11] demonstrated improving the spatial resolution of the depth stream by calibrate the Kinect with a color camera. They used an edge map and optimization-based interpolation and optical flow to aggressively upsample depth. Their work demonstrated that depth is not hard to interpolate accurately; that current optical flow estimates are accurate enough to support depth interpolations; and registering a depth sensor with color camera can produce an improved depth stream.

In contrast to previous work, our approach shows that color camera can empower depth camera in all aspects. Our approach combines off-the-shelf hardware by vision algorithms to reduce latency and increase frame rate. It is a compromise between exotic and expensive customized hardware approaches and limited software-based approaches.

OVERVIEW AND CONTRIBUTIONS

Our Hybrid HFR Depth approach combines an off-the-shelf Xbox Kinect v2 and Point Grey Grasshopper 3 camera (see Figure 2(a)), and uses computer vision algorithms to create configurable high frame rate and low latency depth images. Our Grasshopper 3 GS3-U3-51S5M-C Mono supports configuration of region of interest, frame rate, resolution, shutter speed and so on. It features a Sony IMX250 CMOS, 2/3" imager, running at 75Hz at full 2448x2048 resolution, and at 500Hz with a 256×256 region of interest (ROI).

Table 1 compares Hybrid HFR Depth with the individual sensors used in our system. As the table shows, Hybrid HFR Depth inherits characteristics of both Point Grey camera and Kinect v2.

	Kinect v2	Point Grey	Hybrid HFR
Frame Rate	30Hz	75-500Hz	75-500Hz
Latency	60-93ms	10ms	22ms
Full frame	512×424	2448×2048	410×340
Min ROI	21×21	126×126	21×21
Max ROI	170×170	1020×1020	170×170

Table 1. Specifications of Hybrid HFR Depth and the two sensors used. Hybrid HFR Depth full frame dimensions are less than that of Kinect due to Kinect having a slightly wider field of view than Point Grey camera.

A main contribution of this paper is to use off-the-shelf cameras to create a practical, affordable and easily accessible high frame rate, low latency depth image solution. Compared to customized hardware [9, 13, 14] and software-only approaches [3, 7, 8, 15, 17, 19], it is hybrid in nature. We evaluate high frame rate depth qualitatively and quantitatively and demonstrate the usefulness of our Hybrid HFR Depth in three application scenarios.

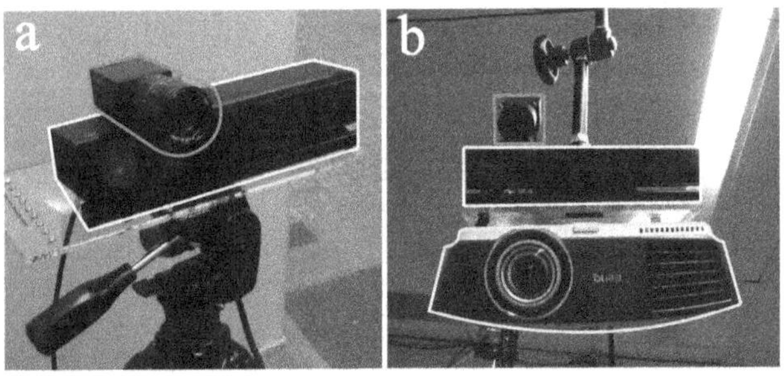

Figure 2. (a) Our Hybrid HFR Depth uses off-the-shelf Point Grey camera and Kinect v2. (b) Our projection mapping system adds an off-the-shelf projector.

METHOD

Hybrid HFR Depth combines Kinect v2 and Point Grey RGB camera by vision algorithms. We first briefly introduce the pipeline and then include details of each part. First, we rigidly mount the two sensors together and calibrate them (Figure 2a). The Point Grey camera has about 6 times higher pixel count in each dimension than Kinect depth frames, so we down sample the color frames and align them with the depth frames. Second, we estimate the delay of each sensor to accurately align the two data streams in time to perform our vision algorithms. Third, we use GPU implementation of the Brox optical flow [2] to estimate the flow from Point Grey color images. This flow field is used to warp the Kinect v2 depth data in XY direction. Because the depth samples not only move in XY direction, but also move in Z direction (as depth value changes), we use linear extrapolation to predict movement in the Z direction. We can further reduce the latency due to the Point Grey camera and image processing. Because we have reliable high frame rate depth stream, we find a simple acceleration model works well to reduce or eliminate latency or predict future depth frames.

Sensor Calibration

We find that a simple, fast calibration modeling only lens distortion and affine transformation works well. First, we use OpenCV's camera calibration routines to estimate the lens distortion of Kinect IR camera and Point Grey color camera. Then, we use RANSAC to estimate the affine transformation matching corresponding points in color images and IR images.

Alignment in Time

Kinect v2 and Point Grey cameras have very different latencies. To align the sensors in time to perform vision algorithms and understand the latency of the system, we measure the latency of each sensor. Point Grey camera latency is measured by recording the time between sending an image request and receiving an image, around 10ms (varies slightly according to the image size). Kinect's latency is more difficult to measure. Instead we measure its latency relative to the Point Grey camera. We swing a scissor in circles like a clock (scissor is the hour hand of clock), and continuously take images with both Point Grey camera and Kinect. For each Kinect image, we find the image from Point Grey camera that best matches the clock (scissor in same rotation angle). Because all images have time stamps, it's easy to find that the relative latency is 50ms. Since the Point Grey camera has absolute latency of 10ms, the actual latency of each Kinect frame is about 60 milliseconds. Kinect generates depth frames every 33 milliseconds (30Hz), so the actual latency is between 60 and 93ms. With sensor latencies and time stamps for both data streams, we can accurately align Kinect depth frame and Point Grey color frame. We align depth frame D_k at time k to color frame at time $t = k - 50ms$.

Our Hybrid HFR Depth obtains a minimum 20ms latency, which is the sum of Point Grey camera latency and image processing time. Our depth stream can be as fast as 500Hz, so the actual minimum latency, without further prediction, is 20+2 milliseconds.

Region of Interest (ROI)

A common CMOS camera can run very fast (high frame rate and low latency) by reducing the region of interest (ROI). We exploit this feature by calculating our fast depth stream on a moving ROI, focusing on the object of interest. This strategy greatly increases effective frame rate while reducing computation cost. We crop the Kinect depth image to the corresponding ROI in software, and configure the Point Grey ROI using the camera's API. Determining the ROI in an application is generally easy, because we need only low frame rate Kinect depth to determine the position of fast moving objects of interest. For example, if we want to focus on the right hand, we can use the Kinect depth to find the center of the right hand at 30Hz and update the Point Grey ROI continuously to track the center of the hand. If the full size depth stream is needed, we can copy the calculated ROI depth back to the full size Kinect depth image. This full frame obtains high framerate and low latency inside the ROI and usual Kinect performance elsewhere.

Generating High Frame Rate Depth Images

High frame rate depth images are computed by warping the latest Kinect depth image by dense optical flow of high frame rate Point Grey images. From color images I_t and I_{t+1} we obtain the flow field $F_{t,t+1}$ and define an image warping function $I_{t+1} \approx warp_{F_{t,t+1}}(I_t)$. A high frame rate depth image H_{t+1} is obtained by warping the latest Kinect depth image D_k by the flow field: $H_{t+1} = warp_{F_{t,t+1}}(D_k)$. Subsequent frames $H_{t+i}, (i > 1)$ are not computed by warping the previous frame H_{t+i-1} but by updating the previous flow field so that it models all motion since the latest depth image. For $i > 1$:

$$F_{t,t+i} = warp_{F_{t,t+i-1}}(F_{t,t+i-1}) + F_{t+i-1,t+i}$$

$$H_{t+i} = warp_{F_{t,t+i}}(D_k)$$

where $F_{t+i-1,t+i}$ is the output of optical flow computation on the two latest color frames.

We use OpenCV's GPU implementation of Brox's algorithm [2]. However, even with GPU acceleration, the flow calculation is slow (maximum 150Hz) compared to our Point Grey camera (maximum 500Hz). We find that the relation between flow calculation time and image size is not linear: the flow calculation time increases much more slowly than image size. We can use batch processing to compute flow over multiple pairs of images to speed up computation at a small cost in latency (refer to Figure 4, increasing batch size by one will increase minimum 2ms latency). For example, with a batch size of n, we concatenate n Point Grey images, run optical flow on this large image, and then split the result into n small flow images. This approach allows Hybrid HFR Depth to run as fast as the Point Grey camera.

The warping process described above operates over the spatial domain of the image but does not model changes in the depth values themselves (e.g.; an object moves closer or further away from the camera). To calculate accurate depth values for H we linearly extrapolate the Z component of Kinect depth images. We find the most recent two Kinect depth images D_{k-1} and D_k and their corresponding color images I_{t_1} and I_{t_2}. Assuming that change in depth is constant over a small period, we update the Z component of H_t as:

$$Z_t = warp_{F_{t_2,t}}(D_k + (D_k - warp_{F_{t_1,t_2}}(D_{k-1}))\frac{t - t_2}{t_2 - t_1})$$

This relationship is depicted in Figure 3.

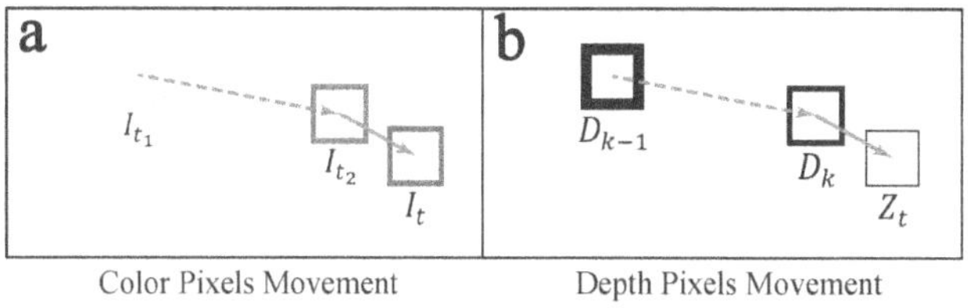

Figure 3. Generating high frame rate depth images. (a) Optical flow is used to estimate motion in the color images from I_{t_1} and I_{t_2}, which correspond to Kinect depth images D_{k-1} and D_k. High frame rate depth image H_t is generated by warping D_k by the flow I_{t_2} to I_t. (b) depth values Z are determined by linear extrapolation of the change in depth from D_{k-1} to D_k, following the motion in the color image.

Prediction

Because they are densely sampled in time, the high frame rate depth frames can be used to predict future frames using a second order model of motion. We estimate accurate velocity and acceleration with 30 samples, and assume the acceleration is constant during prediction. With the flow estimation and the acceleration model, we can predict future flows and future depth frames. We can use this approach to reduce latency, possibly to zero or even negative values. Aggressive prediction will naturally affect depth image accuracy, especially around discontinuities in the depth image. Applications that are less sensitive to inaccuracies around object boundaries in the depth image (e.g., object tracking) may benefit from significant prediction.

CONFIGURATION DETAILS

In this section, we consider various implementation details of the Hybrid HFR Depth approach. These can be configured to suit a given application.

Hybrid HFR Depth specification

There are four quantities that relate to the performance of the proposed technique: ROI, batch size, frame rate, and latency. *ROI* can be configured from 40 pixels in each dimension, enough to capture the whole hand, to 170 pixels in each dimension, enough to capture the whole upper body. As noted above, our implementation may compute optical flow over several images. *Batch size* indicates the number of images included in this computation. Changing batch size trades off latency and framerate. The relation between optical flow calculation time and batch size is not linear. For example, when the ROI is 50 pixels in each dimension and batch size is 1, the frame rate is around 100Hz. If batch size is 8, the frame rate is around 400Hz. In general, the *frame rate* varies from around 100Hz to 500Hz, depending on ROI and batch size, and can be configured to target a given application. *Latency* in our system is the sum of Point Grey camera latency and processing latency (greater with larger batch sizes). When prediction is used, latency can be reduced to zero or even become negative. We illustrate the relationship between frame rate and latency without prediction under different ROIs and batch sizes in Figure 4.

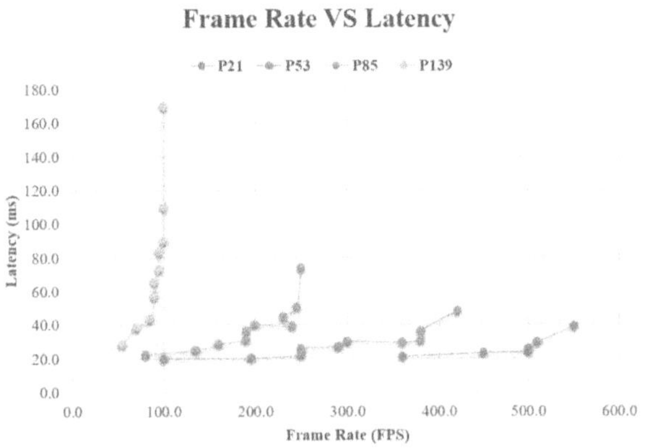

Figure 4. Batch processing optical flow calculations impacts frame rate and latency: when batch size increases, both frame rate and latency increase at a rate that depends on the size of the ROI. We illustrate the empirical relationship between frame rate and latency for four ROI sizes (P21, e.g., denotes an ROI 21 pixels in each direction). The first point along each curve indicates a batch size of one (no batching). Each point thereafter indicates a batch size of one more frame. In general, larger ROI size causes greater latency, higher frame rates correspond to greater latency (due to batch processing), and latency increases slowly with batch size, at first.

We give the configurations of three example applications we present later in Table 2. The basic principle is to tune the most critical aspect of configuration for a given application. In hand writing, for example, frame rate is the most important factor. In tracking, both higher frame rate and lower latency is desirable. In projection mapping, frame rate similar to projector refresh rate (60Hz) is adequate, while aggressive prediction is needed.

	ROI Size	Batch Size	Latency	Frame Rate
Writing	85×85	6	40ms	200
Tracking	75×75	4	30ms	200
Mapping	106×106	1	22 (-70)ms	70

Table 2. Hybrid HFR Depth configurations for the three example applications presented in this paper. With projection mapping, if no prediction is used, the latency is 22 milliseconds. If prediction is used, the latency is -70 milliseconds.

Other Configuration Options

Increased Field of View: Fixing the ROI while down sampling the input depth image sacrifices spatial resolution but significantly increases the effective field of view without impacting computation time. For example, resizing the depth image to 25% increases the field of view fourfold. This can be useful for applications that require larger field of view.

Increased Accuracy: Optical flow calculations are subpixel in nature, but its accuracy is related to the resolution of the input images. Higher resolution images yield more accurate optical flow. In order to increase accuracy, we can use color images with resolution four times that of the depth image to more accurately estimate optical flow, and then down sample the flow. This approach will generate higher accuracy high frame rate depth at the cost of lower frame rate and higher latency.

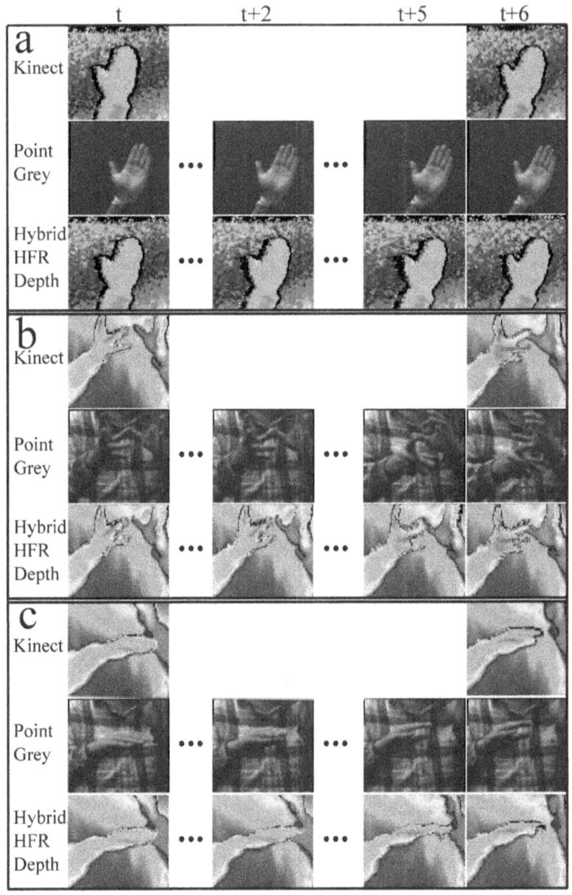

Figure 5. Example sequences of hand movement illustrate the quality of high frame rate depth images. Hybrid HFR Depth images have higher frame rate, lower latency (hands move ahead of Kinect depth) and quality similar to the input Kinect depth images.

EVALUATION

Figure 5 illustrates the quality of the high frame rate depth image on examples of hand motion. The accompanying video gives further examples and gives a better sense of the quality of the generated sequences. Depth direction hand motion example is not visually obvious, so we only include a quantitative example in Table 3.

Quantitative Evaluation

To evaluate the quality of the Hybrid HFR Depth images we would like to compare the generated 300Hz high frame rate depth image to an equivalently 300Hz high frame rate ground truth depth image. Because we have no such 300Hz high frame rate ground truth available, we instead use the 30Hz Kinect depth image stream as ground truth, and take every tenth Kinect depth image as 3Hz input. This essentially slows down the sequence by a factor of 10. During usage, we speed up both depth streams 10 times to simulate 300Hz ground truth and 30Hz input to the Hybrid HFR Depth algorithm (see Figure 6). In recording test sequences, we may take some care in producing motions that are approximately slowed down by a factor of 10.

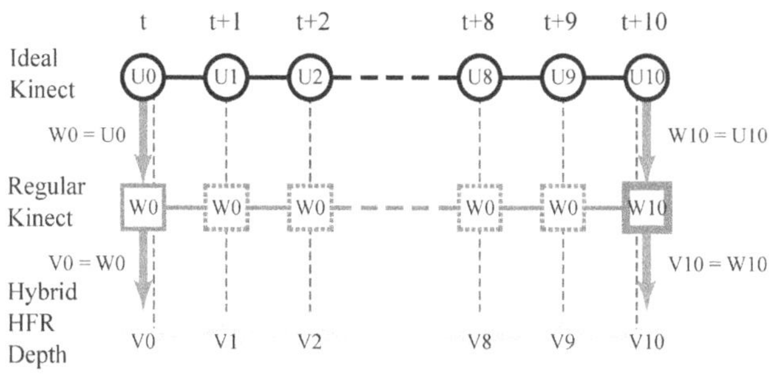

Figure 6. Illustration for quantitative evaluation. "Ideal Kinect" is simulated by capturing slow motion with Kinect (30Hz). "Regular Kinect" frames are meant to simulate the standard Kinect stream before the 10x slow simulation and are held for 10 frames. "Hybrid HFR Depth" takes as input every tenth Kinect frame. Symbols inside sample point (circle, rectangle and star) means the depth frames. Red dash line indicates comparisons reported in the text.

Dataset

We collected seven sequences of hand motions: three simple hand motions S1-3 (similar to first row of Figure 5), three more complex hand motions C4-6 (similar to second row of Figure 5) and one hand motion only in depth direction D7 (scene is similar to first row of Figure 5 and hand moves in depth). In each sequence, the subject moved their hands in approximately one tenth normal speed. We save only frames that have both Kinect depth and Point Grey images, so we get a sequence of normal hand moving speed, and each Point Grey color image has a corresponding depth images. When these sequences are processed, we feed every Point Grey image and one out of ten "Ideal Kinect" depth images into the system, to simulate the different frame rates of two sensors. During evaluation, "Ideal Kinect" depth images are used as ground truth.

Metrics

To compare the generated depth image against "Ideal Kinect" ground truth, we calculate average absolute per pixel difference across the image (threshold the absolute per pixel error to maximum 500mm), ignoring pixels that have no value (black pixels in our figures).

Results

Pixel noise around discontinuities in depth can be large. For example, Figure 7(f) and (g) illustrate two successive Kinect frames when the subject is not moving. Figure 7(h) depicts the absolute value. In this example the average absolute per pixel difference is 15mm. Table 3 shows the error for the seven test sequences. In this table, "Regular Kinect" refers to simply using the "Regular Kinect" stream described earlier as the high frame rate depth image. This serves as a simple baseline measure of performance if one were to naively upsample the Kinect depth image.

As expected, the "Hybrid HFR" and "Hybrid HFR w/ prediction" errors are substantially reduced from that of naive upsampling. "Hybrid HFR w/ prediction" refers to the high frame rate depth image generation with prediction to reduce latency to zero. This results in a slight increase in error compared to the regular "Hybrid HFR" which is synchronized with the Point Grey camera (no prediction).

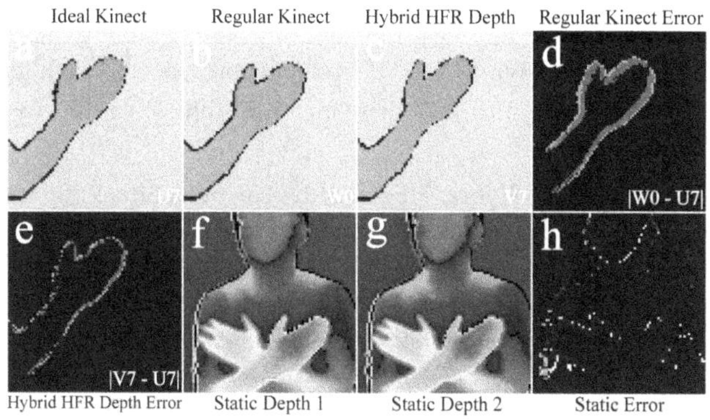

Figure 7. Depth errors are large around depth boundaries. (a-e) corresponds to Figure 5a: (a) is ground truth depth U7 of the example from "Ideal Kinect", (b) is the corresponding "Regular Kinect" depth W0, seven frames before the ground truth image, (c) is Hybrid HFR Depth image V7, (d) shows the per pixel error for "Regular Kinect", compared to ground truth, (e) is the same for Hybrid HFR Depth. We evaluate the Kinect sensor noise in (f-h). (f) is a Kinect depth frame at time t, (g) is a Kinect depth frame at time t+1, (h) is the absolute difference between the two depth frames.

Sequence	"Regular Kinect"	Hybrid HFR	Hybrid HFR w/ prediction
S1	14.4mm	10.3mm	10.8mm
S2	23.6	14.2	14.8
S3	24.4	15.6	16.5
C4	25.5	17.6	17.9
C5	18.0	14.9	15.3
C6	25.0	18.9	19.6
D7	46.9	38.3	39.2

Table 3. Average per pixel error in millimeters (threshold to maximum 500mm) between calculated depth image and ground truth depth image. S1-S3 are simple sequences, C4-C6 are more complex sequences, D7 includes motion in depth. "Regular Kinect" is described in Figure 6. "Hybrid HFR" refers to our high frame rate depth image with no prediction (minimum latency 20ms), while "Hybrid HFR w/ prediction" includes prediction to reduce latency to zero.

APPLICATIONS

Hybrid HFR Depth benefits a variety of applications that work better with high frame rate and/or low latency sensing. We show three important and representative tasks to demonstrate the usefulness of our system. First, we demonstrate that our low latency and high frame rate depth stream can be used to track fast moving objects. Then, we demonstrate that the high frame rate depth stream can be used in small gesture control and hand writing interfaces. Finally, we demonstrate using prediction to reduce latency in interactive projection mapping.

Object Tracking

Tracking moving objects is a fundamental task in computer vision. Kinect can be very useful in object tracking, particularly when the object moves against a known background depth. However, the low frame rate of Kinect can make tracking fast moving objects accurately more difficult. Our Hybrid HFR Depth can provide robust high frame rate and no latency object tracking, even for fast moving objects.

To demonstrate Hybrid HFR Depth in an object tracking, we give a simple but informative example of tracking a bouncing ping pong ball, which moves relatively quickly and changes direction quickly when it bounces. Tracking the ping pong ball throughout the bouncing motion is relatively easy with the high frame rate and low latency depth map. We record the ping pong ball bouncing events with Kinect, Hybrid HFR Depth and Point Grey cameras. From Figure 8, we find that Hybrid HFR Depth produces high quality depth images with high frame rate and low latency.

Figure 8. A ping pong ball is tracked with both Kinect v2 and Hybrid HFR Depth. The Hybrid HFR Depth image exhibits lower latency than Kinect. The high frame rate depth image is far ahead of the Kinect image but is slightly behind the Point Grey image (due to computation time).

Small Gesture Input

The Kinect sensor has been popularly applied to gesture recognition and control interfaces. Many existing systems either require the users to perform large scale hand gestures or require the users to be near to the controller. Our system enables the capture of small gestures imaged from a long distance (1.5m to 4m). By accurately detecting fast fingertip gesturing and writing, we can give commands to the remote computer or write on the screen.

High frame rate is particularly important for hand tracking systems, because fingers are flexible and fast, making them especially hard to track. The best open source hand tracker (by Oikonomidis et al.; [12]) still suffers from periods of lost tracking due to high computation cost and low frame rate. Sharp et al. introduced a new pipeline that estimates hand pose per frame [16]. However, tracking is performed at low frame rate.

We can find the fingertip in each depth frame to obtain a trace of the fingertip. It often suffices to find the closest point in the region of the hand. A high quality trace can be difficult to obtain when the frame rate is low (i.e., the fingertip moves a lot between two frames) and the depth noise is high (i.e.; closest point is not always the fingertip). To combat noise, we can smooth the fingertip trace using a Kalman filter. However, such smoothing alters the shape of the trace in undesirable ways. Figure 9 shows a number of gestures as recorded by Hybrid HFR depth, and the regular Kinect image with and without smooth. The traces show that users can reliably draw simple gestures with small finger motions in the air at a distance of 1.5m to 4m. With a gesture recognizer such as the "$1 gesture recognizer" [18], traces can be converted to corresponding commands for a remote interface. This could allow for a user to control their Xbox with small finger movement while lying on the sofa, for example.

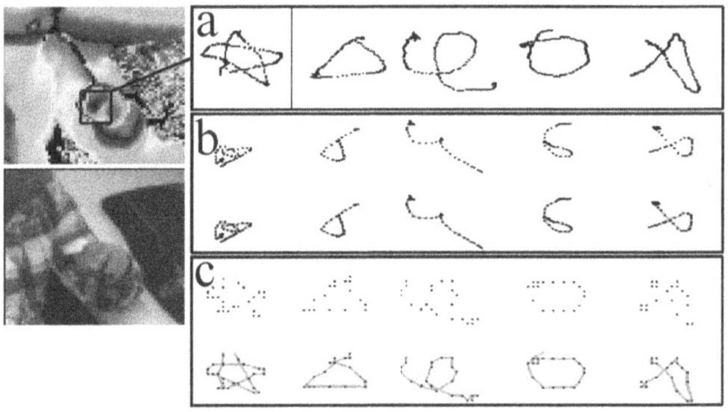

Figure 9. The user may draw simple shapes in the air to control a remote interface. (a) shows fingertip trace captured by Hybrid HFR Depth, with Kalman Filter applied. (b) is the same motion captured by Kinect, with Kalman Filter applied. In this case the Kalman filter alters the shape of the input gesture because of aliasing. (c) is the trace of Kinect skeleton hand tip without a Kalman Filter. Clearly high frame rate and subpixel accuracy improves writing in the air.

Besides drawing simple shapes, users may write words in about 2 meters away. This is a challenging task because only high frame rate and accurate depth stream can preserve all the sharp curves, small circles and other details during fast finger movement. Figure 10 demonstrates writing a phrase, using the same three techniques as above. The algorithm for Hybrid HFR Depth and Kinect depth hand writing are identical. When the finger moves slowly, the differences between these methods are small. However, when the finger moves quickly we find that Hybrid HFR Depth tracks the fingertip more reliably, and the resulting trace looks better.

Figure 10. We demonstrate the advantages of hand writing with Hybrid HFR Depth. (a)(b)(c) are generated from the same motion sequence. The task is challenging because writing words involves many sharp turns and curves, requiring high frame rate and high accuracy. (b) illustrates using the regular Kinect depth stream (closest point), and (c) illustrates the trace of the Kinect skeleton hand tip. (a) illustrates Hybrid HFR Depth trace, which is of noticeably higher quality due to greater sampling frequency.

Interactive Projection Mapping

Projector-camera systems afford various interaction possibilities, combining both natural and mixed-reality 3D interaction. Jones et al. [4] introduced a system to augment the area surrounding a television with projected visualizations to enhance traditional gaming experiences. RoomAlive [5] transformed a room into an immersive, augmented entertainment experience through the usage of video projectors. Later, Benko et al. [1] proposed a spatial augmented reality system that uses dynamic projection mapping to support interaction with 3D virtual objects. However, in current projection mapping systems, accumulated latency from the depth sensor, image processing, graphics rendering and projection introduces errors in alignment in dynamic scenes. Projected graphics can seem to slip from its expected position, adversely impacting on the immersive experience. Recently, Knibbe et al. [8] and Koike et al [9] used software-based prediction to reduce the system latency. However, they only work with rigid objects in projectile motion. Our Hybrid HFR Depth can be used to track arbitrary motions and objects.

A custom hardware approach such as that of Koike et al [9] can reduce latency, typically with some expense and complexity. Using fast touch sensors rather than cameras, Jota et al. [6] describe a custom hardware-based projection-based drawing system that demonstrates that users are sensitive to surprisingly small amounts of latency (approximately 1ms) in direct manipulation settings such as that of interactive projection mapping.

To make projection mapping work reliably for moving objects with non-customized hardware, we can use our high frame rate and no latency Hybrid HFR Depth stream. While systems such as [8] must predict up to 110ms + 33ms to eliminate constant latency and latency due to camera frame rate, our system can reduce the time to 70 + 4ms (10ms Point Grey camera latency, 10ms optical flow calculation latency and 50ms projection mapping system latency), making prediction easier. Moreover, the higher frame rate can result in higher quality prediction to further reduce latency.

Calibration

We use RoomAlive toolkit [5] to calibrate our projector-camera setup (see Figure 2(b)). By applying extrinsic and intrinsic camera parameters, a point in depth image space can be transformed to projector space. A low or zero latency depth image can be used to render virtual objects into a similarly low-latency projection.

Combating Latency

To obtain the best interactive experience with our projection mapping system, we aim to completely eliminate latency, so that graphics projected onto moving objects appear to stay on the object. Operating system, rendering and projector latencies combine to an approximate total of 50ms. Given the 20ms minimum latency of the Hybrid HFR Depth approach, we must apply a prediction of approximately 70ms.

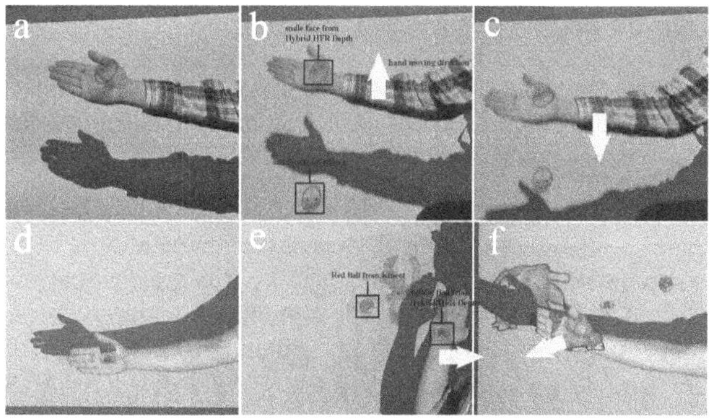

Figure 11. We compare dynamic projection mapping results with Kinect v2 and our Hybrid HFR Depth. We use Kinect v2 depth to project a sad face or a red ball onto the hand, and use Hybrid HFR Depth to project a happy face or a yellow ball onto the hand. In (a) and (d), hand is still, in others, hand is moving in the direction of the yellow arrow. In (f), hand is moving very fast, and yellow ball is off the hand, but still ahead of the red ball. In general, the Hybrid HFR Depth based methods stick graphics to moving hand better.

Figure 11 shows projection mapping results with Hybrid HFR Depth and Kinect v2. To numerically evaluate how our system works, we count the number of frames in which the projected graphics is fully on the hand, fully off the hand, or partially on the hand, as in [8]. We count these frames manually by analyzing videos of the system in operation, and compare the performance of the standard Kinect depth stream with Hybrid HFR Depth. Table 4 shows these counts as a percentage of the test sequences for three speeds of motion.

	Kinect			Hybrid HFR Depth		
	All on	Partially off	Fully off	All on	Partially off	Fully off
Slow	18.6%	23.2%	58.2%	71.1%	28%	0.9%
Medium	13.7%	20.4%	65.9%	63.3%	35.6%	1.1%
Fast	9.5%	16.7%	73.8%	44.2%	44.8%	11%

Table 4. Percentage of test frames for which projected graphics is fully on, partially off, or fully off the user's hand. We manually count the percentage from three 900 frame sequences of slow, medium and fast motions.

LIMITATIONS

Our Hybrid HFR Depth system has a number of limitations. First, the system requires good, stable lighting. Dim or very strong lighting, or rapidly changing lighting will affect the quality of the optical flow-based motion estimation and therefore impact Hybrid HFR Depth quality. The high frame rate of the Point Grey camera limits the effective exposure time and light gathering capability of the camera; for example, 500Hz capture leaves only 2ms to collect light. In our projection mapping example, rapidly changing graphics might significantly affect the result quality. In this case it may be possible to use infrared imaging, though some care must be taken to avoid the narrow-band illumination of the Kinect's time-of-flight imager.

Second, optical flow has other limitations that can impact Hybrid HFR Depth quality. For example, optical flow can fail when there is a lack of texture, repeating textures, or strong reflections in the scene.

Third, OpenCV's optical flow implementationis still computationally expensive on today's hardware. Our current Hybrid HFR Depth prototype optionally employs batch processing of optical flow, potentially creating an undesirable tradeoff between latency, frame rate and ROI size (see Figure 4). Recently, Kroeger et al. [10] demonstrated a fast optical flow algorithm, which runs at 300-600Hz on a single CPU core with high resolution images. This may remove the need for batch processing, help obtain greater than1000Hz frame rate through multi-core scheduling, decrease depth latency and enlarge ROI.

Fourth, the specification of the Point Grey camera used in our prototype is another limitation. With Hybrid HFR Depth, we can reach the maximum frame rate of the Point Grey camera in most ROI size by manipulating batch size. A better color camera might allow a higher frame rate.

Finally, latency-sensitive applications such as projection mapping may require as much as 70ms of prediction. Our prediction model uses a simple acceleration model and is optionally further smoothed by a Kalman filter. Prediction is typically adequate because our inputs have higher frame rate and less time needs to be predicted. However, during sharp turns and accelerations, predictions are likely to be inaccurate. We still observe that our predictions will return to correct values faster than Kinect depth. More sophisticated data-driven approach to prediction is likely to improve the results.

FUTURE WORK

Hybrid HFR Depth could be improved in a number of ways to make it more powerful and useful.

One interesting direction of future work is to further exploit the complementary nature of the two cameras by creating real time super resolution depth images. This would help in applications where Kinect struggles to deliver adequate resolution. For example, when at a distance of 4m, an adult hand may be 15 pixels wide, making it difficult to resolve individual fingers. Meanwhile, our prototype's color image has about six times more pixels in each dimension. Combining depth information from Kinect with the color information from Point Grey camera, we can potentially generate a depth map six times that of Kinect.

While exploiting faster and more exotic cameras may enable higher frame rates, lower latency and a larger ROI, we also see the value in limiting our implementation to cameras that use inexpensive, commodity imagers, such as common web cameras. Employing an inexpensive common camera might broaden the appeal of the Hybrid HFR Depth approach among practitioners, much as the original Kinect did for interactive applications. CMOS imagers continue to rapidly advance in technology, with many smartphones able to record 240Hz videos.

Regarding applications, Hybrid HFR Depth might be particularly useful in Augmented Reality and Virtual Reality systems, where higher frame rate and lower latency are important factors in rendering stable, accurately aligned graphical augmentation, and in improving user comfort.

CONCLUSION

This paper proposes an approach to combine off-the-shelf hardware to create a high frame rate, low latency configurable depth stream. Hybrid HFR Depth is more powerful than a purely software-based approach, and less demanding than a customized hardware approach. We presented detailed specifications of Hybrid HFR Depth to demonstrate the capability and flexibility of the system needed to address a variety of applications. Our evaluation of Hybrid HFR Depth shows that the quality of the generated depth image is good enough to benefit three demonstrated interactive applications.

REFERENCES

1. Hrvoje Benko, Andrew D. Wilson, and Federico Zannier. 2014. Dyadic projected spatial augmented reality. In Proceedings of the 27th annual ACM symposium on User interface software and technology, pp. 645-655. ACM, 2014. DOI: http://doi.org/10.1145/2642918.2647402
2. Thomas Brox, Andrés Bruhn, Nils Papenberg, and Joachim Weickert. 2004. High accuracy optical flow estimation based on a theory for warping. In European

conference on computer vision, pp. 25-36. DOI: http://doi.org/10.1007/978-3-540-24673-2_3

3. Sean Ryan Fanello, Christoph Rhemann, Vladimir Tankovich, A. Kowdle, S. Orts Escolano, D. Kim, and S. Izadi. 2016. Hyperdepth: Learning depth from structured light without matching. In CVPR, vol. 2, p. 7. 2016.
4. Brett R. Jones, Hrvoje Benko, Eyal Ofek, and Andrew D. Wilson. 2013. IllumiRoom: peripheral projected illusions for interactive experiences. In Proceedings of the SIGCHI Conference on Human Factors in Computing Systems, pp. 869-878. DOI: http://doi.org/10.1145/2470654.2466112
5. Brett R. Jones, Rajinder Sodhi, Michael Murdock, Ravish Mehra, Hrvoje Benko, Andrew Wilson, Eyal Ofek, Blair MacIntyre, Nikunj Raghuvanshi, and Lior Shapira. 2014. RoomAlive: magical experiences enabled by scalable, adaptive projector-camera units. In Proceedings of the 27th annual ACM symposium on User interface software and technology, pp. 637-644. DOI: http://doi.org/10.1145/2642918.2647383
6. Ricardo Jota, Albert Ng, Paul Dietz, and Daniel Wigdor. 2013. How fast is fast enough?: a study of the effects of latency in direct-touch pointing tasks. In Proceedings of the SIGCHI Conference on Human Factors in Computing Systems (CHI '13). ACM, New York, NY, USA, 2291-2300. DOI: http://dx.doi.org/10.1145/2470654.2481317
7. Kris Kitani, Kodai Horita, and Hideki Koike. 2012. BallCam!: dynamic view synthesis from spinning cameras. In Adjunct proceedings of the 25th annual ACM symposium on User interface software and technology, pp. 87-88. DOI: http://doi.org/10.1145/2380296.2380335
8. Jarrod Knibbe, Hrvoje Benko, and Andrew D. Wilson. 2015. Juggling the Effects of Latency: Motion Prediction Approaches to Reducing Latency in Dynamic Projector-Camera Systems. Microsoft Research Technical Report MSR-TR-2015--35. DOI: http://dx.doi.org/10.1145/2815585.2815735
9. Hideki Koike, and Hiroaki Yamaguchi. 2015. LumoSpheres: real-time tracking of flying objects and image projection for a volumetric display. In Proceedings of the 6th Augmented Human International Conference, pp. 93-96. DOI: http://doi.org/10.1145/2735711.2735824
10. Till Kroeger, Radu Timofte, Dengxin Dai and Luc Van Gool. 2016. Fast Optical Flow using Dense Inverse Search. In Proceedings of the European Conference on Computer Vision (ECCV). DOI: http://doi.org/10.1007/978-3-319-46493-0_29
11. Jiajun Lu, and David Forsyth. 2015. Sparse Depth Super Resolution. In IEEE Conference on Computer Vision and Pattern Recognition (CVPR), pp. 2245-2253. DOI: http://doi.org/10.1109/CVPR.2015.7298837
12. Iason Oikonomidis, Nikolaos Kyriazis, and Antonis A. Argyros. 2011. Efficient model-based 3D tracking of hand articulations using Kinect. In BMVC, vol. 1, no. 2, p. 3. DOI: http://dx.doi.org/10.5244/C.25.101
13. Kohei Okumura, Hiromasa Oku, and Masatoshi Ishikawa. 2011. High-speed gaze controller for millisecond-order pan/tilt camera. In Robotics and Automation (ICRA), 2011 IEEE International Conference on, pp. 6186-6191. DOI: http://doi.org/10.1109/ICRA.2011.5980080
14. Giorgos Papadakis, Katerina Mania, and Eftichios Koutroulis. 2011. A system to measure, control and minimize end-to-end head tracking latency in immersive simulations. In Proceedings of the 10th International Conference on Virtual Reality Continuum and Its Applications in Industry, pp. 581-584. DOI: http://doi.org/10.1145/2087756.2087869
15. Mirko Schmidt, Klaus Zimmermann, and Bernd Jähne. 2011. High frame rate for 3D Time-of-Flight cameras by dynamic sensor calibration. In ICCP 2011, pp. 1-8. DOI: http://doi.org/10.1109/ICCPHOT.2011.5753121
16. Toby Sharp, Cem Keskin, Duncan Robertson, Jonathan Taylor, Jamie Shotton, David Kim, Christoph Rhemann et al. 2015. Accurate, robust, and flexible real-time hand tracking. In Proceedings of the 33rd Annual ACM Conference on Human Factors in Computing Systems, pp. 3633-3642. DOI: http://doi.org/10.1145/2702123.2702179
17. Jan Stuhmer, Sebastian Nowozin, Andrew Fitzgibbon, Richard Szeliski, Travis Perry, Sunil Acharya, Daniel Cremers, and Jamie Shotton. 2015. Model-Based Tracking at 300Hz using Raw Time-of-Flight Observations. In ICCV, pp. 3577-3585. DOI: http://doi.org/10.1109/ICCV.2015.408
18. Jacob O. Wobbrock, Andrew D. Wilson, and Yang Li. 2007. Gestures without libraries, toolkits or training: a $1 recognizer for user interface prototypes. In Proceedings of the 20th annual ACM symposium on User interface software and technology, pp. 159-168. DOI: http://doi.org/10.1145/1294211.1294238
19. Haijun Xia, Ricardo Jota, Benjamin McCanny, Zhe Yu, Clifton Forlines, Karan Singh, and Daniel Wigdor. 2014. Zero-latency tapping: using hover information to predict touch locations and eliminate touchdown latency. In Proceedings of the 27th annual ACM symposium on User interface software and technology, pp. 205-214. DOI: http://doi.org/10.1145/2642918.2647348

Understanding the Aesthetic Evolution of Websites: Towards a Notion of Design Periods

Wen Chen **David J. Crandall** **Norman Makoto Su**
School of Informatics and Computing, Indiana University
Bloomington, Indiana, USA
{wc23, djcran, normsu}@indiana.edu

ABSTRACT
In art and music, time periods like "classical" and "impressionist" are powerful means for academics and practitioners to compare and contrast artifacts that share aesthetics or philosophies. While web designs have undergone changes for 25 years, we lack theories to describe or explain these changes. In this paper, we take a first step towards identifying and understanding the design periods of websites. Drawing from humanistic HCI methods, subject experts of web design critically analyzed a dataset of prominent websites whose lifetimes span over a decade. These informed judgments reveal a set of key *markers* that signal shifts in design periods. For instance, advances in display technologies and changes in company strategies help explain how design periods demarcated by particular layout templates and navigation models arise. We suggest that designers and marketers can draw inspiration from website designs curated into design periods.

ACM Classification Keywords
H.5.m. Information Interfaces and Presentation (e.g. HCI): Miscellaneous

Author Keywords
Design periods; interaction design criticism; websites; art

INTRODUCTION
From Google's iconic, minimalistic search page, to The New York Time's white, newspaper-like layout, to Reddit's retro, text-heavy format, it is clear that our experience of a website and its creator is due in part to its visual design [30]. Website design has evolved dramatically over the last 25 years, from the simple static pages of text on gray backgrounds of the mid-1990s to the visually-rich, interactive, "responsive" designs of today. Various design styles have come and gone, driven in part by changes in technology (e.g., HTML frames in the late 1990's, mobile devices in the 21st century) and audiences (e.g., as the web has become mainstream).

ACM ISBN 978-1-4503-4655-9/17/05 ...$15.00.
http://dx.doi.org/10.1145/3025453.3025607

To describe the historical narrative of art, historians and critics have developed rich notions of "periods" or "movements" that describe time intervals when artists and their work have shared a particular aesthetic style or philosophy (e.g. classical, romantic, impressionist) [22, 31, 32]. Although the analogy is not perfect—changes on the web may be driven more by evolution in technology than in changes in aesthetic style, for example—identifying "periods" of online design may nevertheless be useful to better understand its evolution over time. Periods enable critics to coherently compare and contrast works according to their particular qualities (e.g., impressionist art emphasizes tone color and atmosphere). By defining a period, techniques (e.g., screen printing), styles (e.g., cubism), tools (e.g., camera obscura), and vocabulary (e.g., found art) are identified, and become portable concepts that are appropriated, built-upon, and even rejected (e.g., impressionist music as a reaction to romantic music) by future artists. Periods posit a definition of art that is institutional [3]; in other words, art is created not in isolation but are "joint products of all the people who cooperate via an art world's characteristic conventions to bring works like that into existence" [6, p.35]. Thus artists must work within the social context, conventions, and histories of critics, galleries, the public, and other members of the art world so that what they do can be legitimately regarded as art.

Just as artists find periods useful in stimulating their own work, researchers in human-computer interaction have argued that designers should be aware of the designed artifacts that surround them, using tools like annotated portfolios of designed artifacts to compare, contrast, and describe the characteristics, aesthetics, and uses of existing designs [9, 18]. By amalgamating artifacts into various categories or designs, these portfolios help HCI practitioners see particular "styles" of design that arise from a single organization. In fact, Gaver and Bowers [18] argue that annotated portfolios resonate with HCI designers because they replicate practices that artists use to articulate and motivate their work. Portfolios not only inform designers of the landscape of interactive artifacts, but can also "inspire...as a reference point for future design work" [18].

Some work has suggested examining design styles from a historic perspective, for example looking at past designs (e.g. patents) to help reflect on what it means to have or design an innovative prototype [11, 37]. Past designs also reveal old interaction styles that gave rise to rich experiences or sensations that have been lost, and interaction designers may find inspiration by reviving these experiences in today's users [25, 39].

Thus it may be worthwhile to holistically reflect upon multiple design styles over time, similar to how artists may reflect on or respond to multiple styles and periods.

Meggs et al. [23] provide an expansive history of graphic design from Egyptian cuneiform to web and interactive design. Yet, unlike in art, we are not aware of any formal effort to describe or characterize design periods of the web, despite its 25-year history. Indeed, as Bardzell and Bardzell [5, p.18] note, "[m]any HCI systems are presented with little to no reference to their own historical genealogies...Yet other design fields...do have significant histories, and practicing designers know how to use them." We see a need to understand the patterns of change in web design, to explain how and why certain designs have stayed while others have faded, and to provide insight into past, present, and future design practices. Analogous to annotated portfolios, we believe that characterizing and capturing online design periods could be valuable to website designers. For example, designers could search for websites belonging to the same design period as Apple's, or find sites that embrace the hacker aesthetic of Reddit. Marketers could draw from design periods that have proven successful in the past. We also imagine design periods to be useful beyond HCI. Organizational scholars could examine the relationship between innovation and design: e.g., are companies that are trend setters in the "art world" of web design (by starting new web design periods) more innovative? Political scientists could examine whether design periods represent particular values (e.g., conservatism vs liberalism).

In this paper, we draw from methods of Humanistic HCI [5] to take first steps towards developing a concept of design periods for websites. We assembled a dataset of nearly 14,000 snapshots of 9 prominent websites over a 13 year period using the Internet Archive [2]. We then created posters showing each website's appearance at regular temporal intervals. Blending think-aloud [24] and interview techniques [36] with interaction criticism [4], we facilitated sessions asking recruited experts—web designers and developers and visual artists—to offer a critical analysis of the website designs, guiding them to identify design periods (as they judged them), to describe similarities and differences of periods across time, to articulate potential period names, and to form justified positions on the forces that drove shifts from one period to another.

Our findings make three key contributions towards the notion of design periods. Although preliminary and based on a small sample of websites and experts, these findings nevertheless lay the groundwork for the longer-term goal of understanding how web design has evolved over time. First, our findings suggest that there are several key *markers* of web design periods. Our experts identified differences in visually-identifiable properties of websites that served to separate design periods from one another, specifically information architectural models (the underlying navigation model afforded by the design), visual flavors (aesthetic qualities of the design), and media composition (ratios of different types of media like video and text). A shift in marker (e.g., highlighting search bars over navigation bars) suggested a shift in design periods. Second, drawing from our experts' responses and experiences with web design, we identify possible factors that suggest why these markers instigated new design periods. Increased information density requirements, new technological innovations, changing company strategies, and design fashions helped create new design periods. Third, we take a preliminary step towards describing the history of the web according to *global design periods*, suggesting four periods in particular: Rudimentary, Chaos, Formative, and Condensation (using names suggested by our experts). We close by discussing implications and limitations of our research in understanding web design periods.

RELATED WORK

Science and technology studies, particularly studies on the social construction of technology (SCOT) [26], have emphasized the historical nature of design and that the social, cultural, and institutional context of artifacts has a key role in shaping the function, intent, and look of designs. The evolution of technologies such as lighting [8] and automobiles [20] have been probed through the lens of SCOT. These studies have revealed the sometimes surprising role that humans have in the designs and uses (e.g., uses that are both unintended or perhaps subtly intended [38] by the designers themselves) of technology.

In HCI, there have been calls to examine the history of interactive designs. Wyche et al. [39] examined patents and popular literature archives to derive cultural themes in domestic technologies. Leahu et al. [21] reviewed challenges in AI's history and how solutions to such challenges might also apply to ubiquitous computing. Buxton gives a historical account of touch screens [11], observing that this approach can "shed light on the nature of innovation." The Buxton Collection [1] is a website featuring historical collections of designs (e.g., computer mice), but does not present them in any systematic fashion nor offer any analysis of the designs.

Two particular lines of work examining style have direct relevance to our own interest in design periods. Øritsland and Burr's [25] research seeks to understand the concept of style over time by focusing on physical products with small displays and limited buttons (e.g., thermostats). Looking at product lines from a single company, experts were able to identify distinct interaction style periods based on how they differed on three properties: new technological innovations, company spirit, and current societal trends. We refer to and build upon some of these attributes of style periods in our own findings. Bertelsen and Pold [7] present an interaction criticism guide to interrogate interaction designs. Through use of the guide, they examined how students in multimedia education both identify and find motivations behind interaction styles of applications such as Microsoft Word and a web-based calendar system that draw from baroque and renaissance architecture. While our work does not explicitly use this guide, we similarly facilitated sessions with experts to draw out their skilled judgments on what counts for design periods in digital artifacts.

While the web is arguably the most encountered interaction design today, little work has systematically examined the evolution of its design. Visualization tools have been developed to see how webpage *content* has changed (e.g., in Wikipedia [35]). Similar to how past work has examined visualizing the evolution of web ecologies [13], we are also concerned with the evolution of design ecologies (trends spanning multiple websites). Our methods find inspiration from work that uses visualizations as a method to elicit rich feedback from users [12,34].

Lastly, a body of work examines the relation of websites' particular visual qualities to factors such as visual appeal and cultural dimensions. Work by Reinecke et al. [29] has made great strides in operationalizing the aesthetic qualities of a website. They found that image metrics such as text/non-text areas and colorfulness significantly impact the perception of visual complexity, and that visual appeal dropped with increased complexity. We hope to build upon Reinecke et al.'s work by adding new factors that may help operationalize the visual qualities of websites. In a later study, Reinecke and Gajos [28] examined website preferences from around the world, finding, for example, that visitors from Finland preferred less colorful websites. They found that older participants preferred more complex websites and speculate that "older users might simply be more used to text-heavy 'web 1.0' designs." This web 1.0 design, we argue, could be regarded as a distinct design period. While not a rigorous study, Cook and Finlayson [14] conduct a study similar to ours that examines qualitative differences of websites, in particular examining how design aspects map to cultural constructs like individuality. They suggest that particular images that take up prominent space reflect on a society's individualism or lack thereof. We similarly ask our informants to identify important aspects of websites, but in the context of identifying components that mark off design periods.

INTERACTION DESIGN CRITICISM SESSIONS

We sought to take a first step towards understanding what it might mean to talk about periods of design for websites. While a humanistic approach would prioritize our own sensibilities as academics actively engaged in modes of criticism such as discourse analysis and close reading, we felt a need to explicitly incorporate the expertise of practitioners. Practitioners and researchers are often mentioned as the beneficiaries of research results, but, when viewed as experts, they provide different but complimentary ways to understand how to situate a work within a notion of periods—*our approach blends our abilities to do and facilitate interaction criticism [4] with the designers' long-term honed, practical knowledge of designing websites*. For instance, we reason that designers who have worked in industry can judge the underlying organizational motivations behind design periods better than academics.

We give voice to the judgments of our practitioners via what we call *interaction design criticism sessions*. We generated large posters that chronologically showed a website's appearance over time. Practitioner experts were guided by the authors, experts in criticism, to treat the poster as a gallery of art pieces. In essence, these galleries were *collections* of technological artifacts subject to interaction criticism, or close readings of designs [4]. We facilitated these sessions by introducing stylistic periods as conventionally taught in humanities (e.g., music appreciation [31,32]) and engaging in practices of interaction criticism relevant to periods such as explicating an artifact's position in history, reception, designers, interface qualities, social context, subject matter, and exemplars. We strove to create an egalitarian environment where dialogue between academic and practitioner is discursive, interpretative, and evolving.

Bardzell and Bardzell [5, p.52–53] discuss a humanistic methodology in HCI by which critical and social scientific approaches are *blended*. The examples they provide "blend" by doing critical analysis of empirical data. Analogously, our interaction design criticism sessions represent a blend of empirical data collections methods—semi-structured interviews [36] and think-aloud techniques—with interaction design criticism. We differ in that our analysis is also grounded in the critiques proffered by our subject experts, practitioners with extensive experience in web development, design, and art.

Subject Expert Recruitment

From September to December 2015, we recruited 10 practitioners from four categories of expertise—web designer, web developer, user interface developer, visual artist—to seek diverse viewpoints on the aesthetic evolution of web design. These categories reflect our interest in critiques from experts to interpret aesthetic qualities of websites, websites as a visual art form, or the web's underlying technologies. All experts had at least two years of professional experience (see Table 1).

Posters

Our experts did close readings of large posters (about 1m wide by 2m tall) that chronologically showed a subset of snapshots of a website's appearance over time. We used the Internet Archive's Wayback Machine [2] as the source of our snapshots. This service hosts over 150 billion archived pages, dating back as early as 1996, though its archives are not complete and contain errors (e.g., some images hosted on external sites have disappeared). We manually identified a diverse set of 9 major websites which have been sufficiently popular to be representative of mainstream design across time and for which reasonably complete, long-term archives existed. We downloaded all available HTML snapshots for each page, averaging about 4,000 archives per site. We then rendered each HTML page to a PDF using an automated script. Finally, we manually reviewed the PDFs, removing renderings that appeared grossly incorrect (e.g., missing major components). This yielded 13,963 high quality snapshots of nine web pages, summarized in Table 2. Our posters represent a variety of different types of sites, including media (AOL, MSN, Yahoo), financial (Bloomberg), science (SLAC, the Stanford Linear Accelerator Center), technology (Cisco, Sun), government (White House), and entertainment (IMDB). We do not claim that this set of 9 pages is statistically representative of the entire web—it is focused on English corporate and government websites, for example, and a much larger set of sites that were more methodically sampled would be needed to assess its generality, but it nevertheless includes a reasonably diverse set of popular websites, consistent with the goal of taking first steps towards understanding the evolution of web design.

Our large posters allowed experts to view each page in detail and to compare different years of design; this gave experts both a local and global view of a page's evolution. The posters were hung on a wall, and our experts were encouraged to sketch on the posters directly to help them organize, record,

ID	Occupation (Years)	Education	Gender	Age Range	First use of Internet	Reviewed website posters
W1	web designer (2)	Master	M	25 - 34	1996	bloomberg.com, slac.stanford.com, whitehouse.gov
W2	web designer (12)	Ph.D	M	35 - 44	1995	yahoo.com, imdb.com, msn.com
W3	HCI designer (6)	Ph.D	M	25 - 34	1996	cisco.com, bloomberg.com
U1	UX developer (4)	Ph.D	M	25 - 34	2006	imdb.com, msn.com
U2	UX developer (10)	Ph.D	F	25 - 34	2000	aol.com, yahoo.com
D1	web developer (3)	Master	F	18 - 24	2003	cisco.com, sun.com
D2	web developer (6)	Master	M	18 - 24	2003	aol.com, sun.com, slac.stanford.com
D3	web developer (10)	Master	M	25 - 34	1999	slac.stanford.com, whitehouse.gov
A1	glass artist	Bachelor	F	45 - 54	1998	whitehouse.gov, bloomberg.com
A2	studio art graduate	Master	F	18 - 24	2002	sun.com, aol.com

Table 1. Recruited experts in our study.

Webpage	Date range	No. of snapshots	Mean snapshots/yr
aol.com	2000–2012	1,746	134.3
bloomberg.com	2000–2013	2,169	154.9
cisco.com	1999–2013	1,279	85.3
imdb.com	2001–2013	933	71.8
msn.com	1999–2013	2,802	200.1
slac.stanford.edu	1999–2013	843	56.2
sun.com	1997–2010	1,071	76.5
whitehouse.gov	2000–2010	1,320	120.0
yahoo.com	1999–2013	1,800	120.0

Table 2. Snapshots collected for our posters.

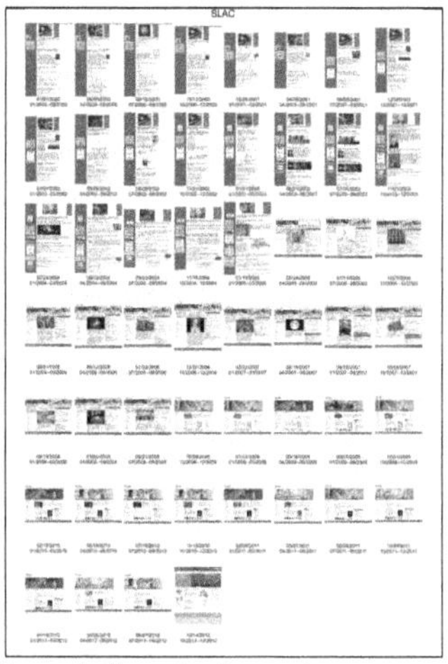

Figure 1. Sample of one of our posters.

and articulate their critiques. We archived these marked-up posters after the interviews. An example of a poster is shown in Figure 1. For each poster, we showed a subset of screenshots for a given website along with the date, spaced 3 months apart. When pages were not available on the required day, we showed the closest page within 7 days, or if no screenshot was available at all for that week, we showed the words "No Data." We randomly assigned two or three posters to each expert such that each of the 9 sites was viewed by at least two experts.

Session Procedure

We began our interaction design criticism sessions by defining our terminology, including a broad explanation of design periods by analogy with art history terms. For each of their assigned websites, we asked the subject expert to critically interpret our poster and to draw on their experience and practices to skillfully identify and group together periods of similar design. We paid close attention to eliciting experts to articulate, reason about, and judge the qualities that were shared by each website design in each period, and then how each period was different from its neighbors. This allowed experts to consider periods as local, independent entities, while also considering their globally dependent nature on other periods. Lastly, we asked our experts to give a descriptive name for each period.

We also asked follow up questions such as: what makes a design endure, why do certain patterns appear and disappear, how did one period influence the next, do you had a favorite period and why, and predict the future designs for each website. We closed by asking our experts whether they could identify any "global" design patterns or periods that seemed to apply to the broader web and not just to each individual site.

FINDINGS

Our study shows that experts identified common themes on how web design has changed over time and the forces that have driven these changes. It also provided insight that might lead to a first step towards a notion of web design periods.

Key Markers of Web Design Periods

Our experts described web design periods in terms of particular attributes, which we call *markers* because they serve as useful ways to characterize the differences between other periods. Three specific types of markers came up repeatedly in our sessions: (1) information architecture models, or the ways in which websites afford navigation, (2) visual flavor, or the aesthetic and visual design elements of the website, and (3) the media composition, or the extent to which certain media such as text, images, and video make up a website's content. We now discuss findings for each of these markers in detail.

Information Architecture Models

We found that many design changes were driven by the changing navigation models that websites emphasized over time. In other words, particular elements on websites give cues to users on the best ways to navigate and absorb information. All of our experts mentioned that the types of browsing behavior intended by these elements was a key marker of a site's design period. In fact, W2 felt that information architecture models were the strongest general marker of design periods

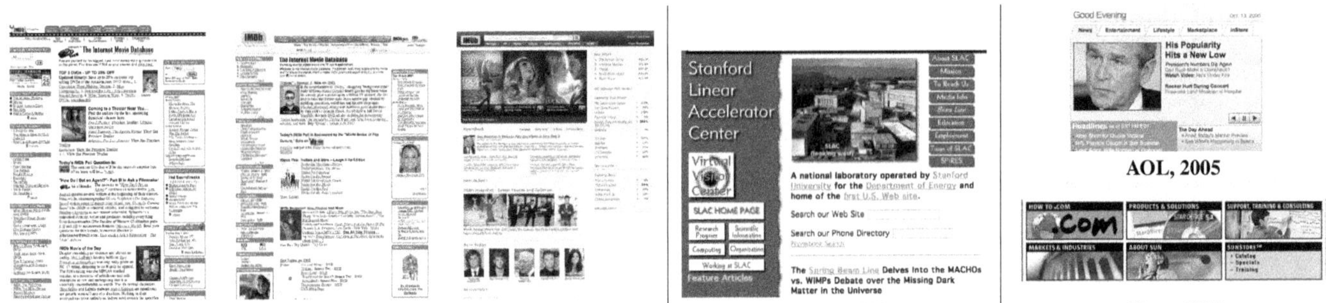

2001 2007 2012 (a) IMDB | SLAC, 2000 (b) | AOL, 2005 Cisco, 2000 (c)

Figure 2. Examples of information architecture models highlighted by our experts: (a) evolution of navigation bars on IMDB over time, (b) SLAC page as of 2000, showing prominent menu of links in the upper right, and (c) examples of card- and grid-based navigation systems.

across websites (i.e., independent of a particular website's company strategy or specific visual style). Participants identified the menus used for navigation and for search as two specific web elements that are critical for conveying information architecture models across nearly any design period. Changes in the relative prominence of these two elements seem to reflect changes in both the nature of website content and user expectations over time.

The navigation bar is an organized list of the site's main content, and conveys the information architecture model of the website. Nine of our participants mentioned changes in navigation, and five explicitly identified navigation bars as the *primary* marker for grouping design periods. D2 stated that navigation bars made websites clearer and less wordy. W2 explained the importance of the navigation bar when examining the snapshots of IMDB, a subset of which is shown in Figure 2(a). He pointed out that the 2001 design featured very prominent navigation menus that occupied most of the left, top, and right areas of the page. By 2007, the search bar had been moved to a larger, more prominent position at the top of the page. By 2012, most of the navigation menus were hidden, with the search bar occupying an even more prominent position. He explained:

The form of the navigation would be the main feature. To me, it changes the periods. You see, [the yellow navigation bar on the top in 2001] is kind of similar with [the bar on top of the 2007 design]. They basically provide the links to the information. And the website removed the navigation at the end [in 2012 design]...Here [the form of navigation] is ...how the website is defined.

Our experts described "failed" attempts at navigation bars before 2005. D2 and D3 thought the navigation of SLAC in the early 2000s (shown in Figure 2(b)) was poorly designed. D2 felt the position and orientation of the navigation bar limited its scalability, so that new links could not be easily added, because the height of the bar had to match the height of the photo next to it. Better-designed bars are usually located horizontally either below the main logo or at the bottom of the page, vertically on the left or right sidebar, or in a table near the center of the page. Card-like designs with tabs were common as well, as shown in Figure 2(c). Among these variations, six experts (W1, D1, D2, D3, U1, U2) preferred the left sidebar, while the center was the the least preferred position of navigation because it was easily overlooked. We can see this consensus of the experts is also widely used in current web designs.

Search bars appeared in eight of our nine websites around the year 2000. Experts noticed that after 2010, many websites enlarged the search bar and moved them to a prominent position at the top (e.g., for IMDB in Figure 2(a)). W2 commented that the search bar has become a crucial design element:

I don't care [about] the information on the main page. I used to look at some [of the] "recommended" information pushed to me on YouTube, but now I even don't look at them. When I want to know something, for example, a director or a movie, I go to IMDb and search. So what I expect is, the website can give me the information that I search for and then I browse after that, not before.

D2, who worked as a web developer from 2008 to 2014, shared his first-hand knowledge on the prevalence of search bars. He noted how web templates that were widely used by companies then generally had a Google search bar on the top. D3 shared his view that searching has evolved into a dominant manner of finding information, necessitating that web designers emphasize search bars over navigation:

[In 2000], people have no idea how to look up information so you should provide a super nice structure. But [in late 2000s], you don't care about structure anymore, and you only search for the information you are looking for. So those navigation bars become less important, and search becomes a thing.

Other signals of information architecture models were also mentioned by our subjects. Experts suggested that website architectures have over time reduced the content on the main page, simplifying them to emphasize a few key products or messages. A *highlight* component (e.g., the large image in the 2012 IMDB site of Figure 2(a)) is now a common approach to quickly convey the spirit, tone, and main message or product of the website, as explained by D1:

The main feature (representing their current main product) is highlighted...other information on the main page are (text) links. Those large images (representing the main feature) are designed to be very appealing. You know, we may not read the text but we remember the pictures subconsciously.

Experts noted that the highlight can take various forms, including a prominent image banner or a group of images without much text. Recent designs of AOL and MSN in Figure 5 use an image with a short caption for highlighted news stories, while stories of secondary importance just have text links.

Visual flavor

As we might suspect, experts identified the aesthetic properties of websites as a strong indicator of design periods. Our artist subgroup was quick to notice even minor visual changes of websites over time. Three elements were each mentioned by at least three experts: (1) color scheme, (2) overall layout, and (3) quality or refinement of visual elements.

Color schemes portray a certain feeling of style and aesthetics to users. For example, *flat design* [27], which makes heavy use of white space and embraces a sense of minimalism, is currently quite popular (as of 2016). Designs in the early 2000s also had flat elements with simple color schemes, but typically did not share the minimalistic sense (e.g., compare 2000 and 2013 for Bloomberg in Figure 3(a)). W3, D3, U1, A1, and A3 indicated that color scheme changes were especially important for identifying design periods. W3 even proposed naming design periods after colors; for Bloomberg in Figure 3(a), for example, he named 2004 the "Blue period" and 2008 the "Media-consumer black" period. U1 thought colors play an important role in humans' pre-attentive processing, so uniquely colored sections "pop out" immediately. Alternating color schemes can help users discriminate between distinct parts of a page, as he explained for MSN in Figure 3(b):

I think the key factor to divide the period is how the website is colored, what kind of color schemes it uses. [In 2004] you can see the blue and green, and [in 2011] you can see it completely flat. The color really easily catches people's attention. Color is not the emphasis; the content is the emphasis. Color may highlight the borders and add emphasis. That's why the color scheme is important.

Layout templates in web design are usually horizontally or vertically oriented. Five experts mentioned that modern websites had obviously better layouts than earlier designs and that a good layout was necessary for an aesthetically pleasing website. U1 thought a good layout kept web page elements distinct and organized even when the page had few solid borders. While overall layout has definitely changed over time, our experts did not explicitly articulate specific criteria of what constitutes a good layout. D2 explained:

The number of possible web structures is few: horizontal, vertical or some combination of them. The design fashions change and never come back, but web structure [layout] seldom changes.

The layouts from early 2000s to the present are especially resilient and do not have much variability. D1 gave one possible reason: the improvement in text alignment technology in layout templates allowed a clean look even when the amount of text information increased.

Visual element quality refers to the complexity or sophistication of images, videos, text, and other visual page elements. Experts did not view this as vital as other criteria for distinguishing design periods, but several experts did observe that it had improved with time. A1 noted the logo on whitehouse.gov had subtly changed over time (Figure 4), with later designs being higher-resolution and more sophisticated.

Media Composition

Text, images, and videos are used to disseminate information on a web page, and the proportions and compositions of these have changed over time. All experts noted that web developers in the early 2000s used text-heavy designs on the main page, whereas modern developers believe wordy pages lose users. D1 used the Cisco page (Figure 3(c)) as an example:

[Design in early 2000s] only provides a bunch of links, there is actually no information on the page. Then later, they use some pictures, icons, and something appealing to users. And the 2008 Cisco design is not much different from 2004, having the same links but using less words. When we compare these two, the 2004 one has lots of information here [the lower part of the page], but users may be confused by the abundant text.

D2 noted that hyperlinks have been partially replaced by images and videos:

Now there are more videos. People don't like to read text. I guess that is the reason the text hyperlinks go down [in] their number. You can see more videos than just the text hyperlinks. When I see the hyperlinks, for example...in 2000, I just read the link but don't want to go in and see what is in the link.

Explaining Design Periods

As described in the last section, our interaction design criticism sessions revealed that people identified information architecture models, visual flavor, layout templates, and media composition as key markers of design. Now we describe how our experts explained these markers. In other words, why did web pages change these markers? What led to these design periods? Øritsland and Buur describe how changes in design are due to technological innovations, a company's spirit (rhetoric), and societal trends [25]. While drawing from these factors as critical reasons for web design markers, our study also suggests other forces at work.

Increased Information Density

Experts observed that over time, the density of information of websites has increased, which has forced designers to think about how to organize so much information. For example, W1 and D1 pointed out that it was not time consuming for early web users to browse and understand websites because there simply was not much content to trawl through. By the mid-2000's, however, pages had become much more information-rich, and users could easily get lost if pages were not well organized. As a result, the markers of information architecture models and the layout templates evolved to meet such needs. Increasingly powerful search functions can be regarded as responses to this sort of information overload, for example. D3 explained the move from menus to search features: *"The*

(a) bloomberg.com

(b) msn.com

(c) cisco.com

Figure 3. Some examples of the evolution of visual flavor highlighted by our experts, including (a) bloomberg, (b) msn, and (c) cisco.

menus implicitly are structured as a tree. It can be a long path from the main page to my destination page."

Technological Innovation

However, information density does not fully explain the rise of search bars, which became popular in the early 2000s even among small websites. Eight of our experts identified innovations in web technologies as a key driver of design change. W1 mentioned that easy-to-use search components led many websites to add them around 2000, even for sites that did not need them. Other technological developments have included image formats like SVG for high-resolution and responsive graphics, scripting technologies like JavaScript and Flash, and improved back-ends that enable dynamic, customized pages. Two particular forms of innovation were mentioned: hardware and web technology.

Hardware technology improvements have included both network and display technology, and several experts identified both of these as driving new design periods. Faster networks have enabled transmitting larger files, such as high-resolution images and video, while better displays have led designers to take advantage of their capabilities. U1 explained:

The better resolution and tonal range makes...modern web pages [look good] even though they have a minimum number of colors. Imagine if we still used the monitors from the 1990s. Those monitors have low resolution and small color space. [If] we browse current web pages from those monitors, [they would] look awful.

The rise of mobile devices significantly affected web design, and mobile devices are now used more than PCs to access the Internet [15, 19]. Responsive designs are widely used to adapt the size and position of UI components to a device's display. Three subjects (D2, U1, U2) said the widespread adoption of sidebars was due to these devices. U2 explained:

Around 2010, people frequently browse websites from the mobile phone, but the screen of mobile is much smaller than the computer monitor. We use something maybe called "flows"

Figure 4. Progression of the whitehouse.gov logo from 1999–2015.

to make the layout for the main content adapt to the devices, and keep a kind of constant size of sidebar on one side of the screen. Users maybe can hide the sidebar in some websites. In this way, users can quickly target the sections they are looking for.

Web technology refers to the tools to design and develop websites. With web technologies constantly evolving, designers and developers have had increasing flexibility in their designs over time. Past research has found that certain innovations in web technology have been directly responsible for popularizing the Internet. For example, the graphical browser in 1993 led to dramatic growth in online use [33]. Although our experts did not examine the code of websites, they did mention that web technologies were likely the cause of certain changes, including visual elements such as typeface and image quality. When asked to identify design periods, W2 said:

To me, [web technology] is the real distinction. I cannot say just by looking at the screenshots of the websites. That is not enough. We should review the HTML code. But we still can tell some of them from the poster. Back to 2000, they are table-based. And in 2010, they are CSS-based.

Web techniques also made websites faster and more dynamic. For example, D1 pointed out that the use of animations has evolved over time. Animation became common with the adoption of GIFs and Flash, but after 2012, HTML5 animations gradually replaced them due to their lighter-weight code and higher quality. Another example is Ajax, which pre-fetches content and gives websites a dynamic feeling. It can update information (e.g., hourly top 10 articles) in dynamic components without reloading static visual components, which brings a smoother experience for web users.

Lastly, new practices of quickly prototyping and designing websites have had an influence. D1, D2 and D3 mentioned their use of web templates, which prescribe current visual flavors and information architecture models. Popular templates have had a direct influence on propagating particular markers of web design across many domains.

Company Strategies

The way in which information is presented by a company is a powerful symbol [16] of its progressiveness and rhetoric. W1, W2, D1, and D2 noted that changes in design period markers could be attributed to the company wishing to convey a certain spirit. MSN was brought up as one particular example. Before 1998, msn.com was a domain operated by Microsoft as an online service provider. When msn.com switched to being used by Microsoft's Interactive Media Group, its content switched to be more media-related, and this was reflected in its visual style and layout (see Figure 3(b)). As we look back at the designs across MSN's history, D2 stated that we found its visual flavor reflected the visual flavor of Microsoft's products over that time. In other words, the design periods of msn.com are intertwined with the user interface design changes of Microsoft's software products.

More broadly, the information organization of a web page often serves a marketing purpose. For example, web pages put currently promoted products in a prominent position, and if the company has many products, the main page has a more complex layout. The website owner may also change the layout of the web page to suit third party advertisements. In the 2000s, many websites put their advertisements on large floating windows, which web users could not miss. In addition, D2 mentioned the use of the left sidebar as a "dark pattern" [10]:

Now we mostly stick the navigation bar on the left, not having to be static [i.e., so the navigation can be hidden], and put the main story on the right side. Because most web users are right-handed, users prefer keeping their mouse at the right side of the page. Then users have higher possibility to click the highlight [the links in the right main part of the pages, e.g., advertisements]. Also, if they want to get the navigation, move mouse directly to it, which is easy.

Design Fashions

Design fashions changes the visual flavor of websites on a large scale. W1, D1, and D2 all mentioned that since the late 2000s, many websites have had a common layout from top to bottom: a horizontal navigation bar, a large banner, the main content of the page, and a footer (e.g., the 2012 Cisco design in Figure 3(c)). Several experts mentioned that this horizontally-dominant layout avoids the need for users to scroll vertically in order to access the most important content of the page. D1 worked in a IT consultancy company around 2010, and mentioned that his company routinely used this same template to develop the websites for many small companies. Similarly, W1 mentioned the large horizontal banner is very popular and widely used in all kinds of websites.

Design fashions may also be driven by the widespread use of some popular technological elements. For instance, in 2014 Vishal Gaikar popularized the web element for infinite scroll loading [17], and three of our experts (W1, D1, D2) mentioned these elements are now widely used, especially on news websites. As another example, W1 said that in the late 1990s, many websites added search boxes, even though many sites were not complex enough to need them. In his opinion, these elements were added largely to keep up with the current design fashion as opposed to being useful components.

Global Design Periods

Although our dataset and subject pool are not large or representative enough to develop a holistic "theory" of evolution of the broader web, we nonetheless explored whether our subjects could help suggest rough "global" web design periods. We asked our experts to reflect on the web design periods they noticed across our set of websites and on the broader web, instead of just on the particular sites we showed them. We sought to understand the extent to which design changes may be dependent on the context of particular sites, versus more global changes that are observed on the web at large.

Experts noted that one could discern whether websites were on the leading edge of design periods. W1, D1 and D3 thought media websites such as bloomberg.com readily adopted more progressive design periods, while government and education websites lagged behind. For example, in our dataset we found that media websites adopted flat designs an average of about 3 years before other websites (e.g., AOL in 2010, Bloomberg in 2009, MSN in 2010, but Cisco in 2015, SLAC in 2009, and White House in 2014).

Our experts did identify some consistent patterns in the design periods across our websites. It should be emphasized that not all design periods happen at the same time (e.g., some lag as mentioned before), nor do they look identical across websites. For websites of the same genre, global design periods are somewhat more readily identifiable. For example, media websites often quickly leveraged new standard frameworks and web techniques and therefore ended up having similar layouts on their web pages (see Figure 5).

We looked for agreement across our subjects on what the major general design periods of the web might be. Eight of our experts thought we could divide periods into four rough categories (using names suggested by experts):

- **Rudimentary (U1), Simplicity (U2), or Informational (U3) period.** Experts used words like "naive" to describe the designs of the late 1990s and the early 2000s. Pages at that time were functional and informational (text-heavy), and lacked a balanced design. W1 mentioned that websites of the 1990s were arranged like digital versions of the front page of a newspaper, where the structure revolves around "headlines" that are links to other pages, with short "articles" or abstracts on the main page.
- **Chaos, Gradient (U1), Light (W1), or Rise of the Image (W2) period.** From 2000 to 2005, websites seemed to try to formulate and integrate web-specific design principles, and many foundational web elements were introduced during this period. Yet many of our subjects used words like "terrible," and "overused, garish, colorful backgrounds" (W3) for this period. Four of our subjects thought the image elements that became popular during this period were just decorative and did not offer any function. Images were often shaded, giving a 3D look. The amount of content sharply increased and made some websites look crowded.
- **Formative (U1) or Cinematic (W3) period.** This period begins around 2007 when Web 2.0 became popular. Basic layouts for websites of different genre were established, which give well-organized layouts for many websites. Five of our experts (W1, D1, D2, D3, U2) thought new web technologies brought large visual changes to web designs in this period. W3 thought the banner became eye-catching and popular in this period (see cisco.com 2008 or 2012 design in Figure 3(c)), leading to his "cinematic" term.
- **Condensation (U1), Sci-Fi (A2), or Flat (W3) period.** This period started around 2011, with an emphasis on refined designs with clear information architecture models. Flat designs are popular and websites make heavy use of various media types (text, image, video, animation). Adaptive UIs and responsive design elements are widely adopted.

msn.com aol.com

Figure 5. Comparison of msn.com on December 22, 2012 (left) with aol.com (right) on December 9, 2012. Although msn.com is column-dominant and aol.com is row-dominant, they present similar visual experiences compared to the websites in other categories such as IT services.

W1 contributed an interesting opinion on the evolution of web design from a pure web designer's perspective:

The layout [in late 1990s] is sort of weird. It looks like it just wants some things there. I think this form is just when people were learning how to setup layout properly before it becomes actually possible. Around 2005, people start thinking there are too many links on the pages and they don't have enough space for them. So they need search. Then they started considering the usability. Some websites used to be very usable websites, but became heavy with some techniques. What are the particular advantages of them [techniques]? So for some reason, they are something that really struck people. So they bring us back and make us think about the answer.

W1 also mentioned "bringing back" older technologies, and W3 thought it might be similar to something in art history:

In terms of art history, when a period evolved to another. Again because [designers] were seeking the truth in a different way, they acted against the move that came before.

DISCUSSION

Our findings support the factors that compose visual complexity found by Reinecke et al. [29]. That work found that visual complexity was a strong predictor for a website's initial visual appeal. Our markers for design periods cover many of the markers that make up Reinecke et al.'s model of visual complexity: ratios of text and non-text areas are related to media composition, and colorfulness and hue are related to visual flavor. However, visual complexity does not capture some of the nuances we found in our markers, such as the information architecture model—the tension between search and browse affordances. While colorfulness was found by Reinecke et al. to play a minor role in appeal, our results suggest that it is highly indicative of design periods.

Of course, the relationship between visual appeal and design periods is complex. Reinecke and Gajos [28] found that user age influenced perceptions of visual appeal, with older people favoring text-heavy pages. This suggests that visual appeal is not an obdurate measure. As suggested by several of our experts, people tend to like the designs that immediately surround them. This may mean that some websites may avoid more progressive designs because it may be beneficial to portray an image of stability or conservatism.

As with most technology, we find that both technological determinism and the social construction of technology play a key role in website design. New technological innovations like JavaScript bring about new design periods, but shifting societal concerns like changing company spirits or messages also help to shape them.

When we asked our experts about the utility of our concept of web design periods, some mentioned that they would indeed find some inspiration from the past. D3 described wanting to use shaded navigation bar icons on a web design, but could not find many such icons on the modern web. By going back in time, he might discover that shaded icons were popular in the mid 2000s, using those pages as exemplars of such icons. In fact, we found that experts were perhaps already implicitly using their own notion of design periods to predict future designs. For example, D1 predicted that there would be a restoration of different shades of colors in a few years, as a reaction against the flat and minimal designs that are currently popular. D1 thought this kind of design is overused and makes current web designs drab. She especially mentioned that designs with solid borders have advantages:

As a user, I will be more attracted by the information in a solid frame. Like [sun.com in 2008] puts several pieces of information (like the title) in the right curved block. I will notice that but I won't read all information there. Then [in 2010], it uses solid border for each information. I will be caught, I may quickly scan each of them.

She thought there should be a renaissance of a design period featuring the visual flavors of solid borders and shading, although it would not be an exact duplication of that past period. From here, we might suggest that examining the *demise* of design periods would be useful—at what point does a certain marker of design period become tired and in need of change (a saturation point)?

LIMITATIONS AND FUTURE WORK

We acknowledge that our dataset is small and not statistically representative of the broader web (e.g., no non-English sites), so our study does not lead to comprehensive conclusions about the markers and causes of design evolution. Instead, we view the changes, forces, and design periods we suggest here as a starting point for further studies with a broader variety of pages (e.g., non-English, non-western, less popular, short-lived, etc.). Similarly, this preliminary study relied on a small pool of people, and future studies should include a broader set of expertise. For example, although our experts were qualified to interpret aesthetic qualities of websites, most did not have the same depth of critical and socio-cultural-historical analytical skills that a professional art historian or critic would. Future work should include these voices to develop a more systematic theory of web design. Finally, we believe that other critical methods (e.g., analysis and argumentation) would be conducive to the study of web design periods and should be incorporated into follow-up studies.

One way to make a larger-scale study practical would be to create tools that automatically detect major changes in visual features over time, allowing participants to focus on these change points as opposed to having to examine thousands of daily screenshots for each website. Such a tool may also be useful in its own right; four of our experts (W2, W3, U1 and D3) thought it would useful for web designers to explore historical changes through such a tool, and eight experts believed it would have a place in education and research. W3 opined that such a tool would foster a dialogue on the evolution of websites and allow people to view exemplars of design periods.

CONCLUSION

Similar to artistic domains, we imagine the development of a web design period theory will offer a systematic way to advance the study of historical web designs. Our paper is a first step towards understanding how and why web designs have changed over time. We conducted interaction design sessions in which we asked a diverse group of experts to critically interrogate changes in web design and the forces behind them. We hope that our concept of and initial findings on web design periods may eventually lead to theories and practical tools for understanding how web design changes over time, such as annotated repositories of historical designs that future designers and researchers will be able to explore.

ACKNOWLEDGMENTS

This work was supported in part by the National Science Foundation through CAREER grant IIS-1253549.

REFERENCES

1. 2016. The Buxton Collection. http://research.microsoft.com/en-us/um/people/bibuxton/buxtoncollection/default.aspx. (2016).

2. 2016. Internet Archive: Wayback Machine. (2016). https://archive.org/web/
3. Thomas Adajian. 2016. The Definition of Art — The Stanford Encyclopedia of Philosophy. http://plato.stanford.edu/archives/sum2016/entries/art-definition/. (2016). [Online; accessed 19-September-2016].
4. Jeffrey Bardzell. 2011. Interaction criticism: An introduction to the practice. *Interacting with Computers* 23, 6 (Nov. 2011), 604–621. DOI: http://dx.doi.org/10.1016/j.intcom.2011.07.001
5. Jeffrey Bardzell and Shaowen Bardzell. 2015. Humanistic HCI. *Synthesis Lectures on Human-Centered Informatics* 8, 4 (Sept. 2015), 1–185. DOI: http://dx.doi.org/10.2200/S00664ED1V01Y201508HCI031
6. Howard S. Becker. 2008. *Art Worlds* (25th anniversary, updated and expanded ed.). University of California Press, Berkeley, CA, USA.
7. Olav W. Bertelsen and Søren Pold. 2004. Criticism As an Approach to Interface Aesthetics. In *Proceedings of the Third Nordic Conference on Human-computer Interaction (NordiCHI '04)*. ACM, New York, NY, USA, 23–32. DOI: http://dx.doi.org/10.1145/1028014.1028018
8. Wiebe E. Bijker. 1992. *The social construction of fluorescent lighting, or how an artifact was invented in its diffusion stage*. MIT Press, Massachusetts.
9. John Bowers. 2012. The Logic of Annotated Portfolios: Communicating the Value of 'Research Through Design'. In *Proceedings of the Designing Interactive Systems Conference (DIS '12)*. ACM, New York, NY, USA, 68–77. DOI:http://dx.doi.org/10.1145/2317956.2317968
10. Harry Brignull. 2016. Dark Patterns: fighting user deception worldwide. http://darkpatterns.org/. (2016).
11. Bill Buxton. 2010. A touching story: A personal perspective on the history of touch interfaces past and future. In *SID Symposium Digest of Technical Papers*, Vol. 41. Wiley Online Library, 444–448. http://onlinelibrary.wiley.com/doi/10.1889/1.3500488/abstract
12. Stuart K. Card, Jock Mackinlay, and Ben Shneiderman. 1999. *Readings in Information Visualization: Using Vision to Think*. Morgan Kaufmann, San Francisco, Calif.
13. Ed H. Chi, James Pitkow, Jock Mackinlay, Peter Pirolli, Rich Gossweiler, and Stuart K. Card. 1998. Visualizing the Evolution of Web Ecologies. In *Proceedings of the SIGCHI Conference on Human Factors in Computing Systems (CHI '98)*. ACM Press/Addison-Wesley Publishing Co., New York, NY, USA, 400–407. DOI: http://dx.doi.org/10.1145/274644.274699
14. Jack Cook and Mike Finlayson. 2005. The impact of cultural diversity on web site design. *Advanced Management Journal* 70, 3 (July 2005), 15–23. https://ritdml.rit.edu/handle/1850/7707
15. Susmita Dasgupta, Somik Lall, and David Wheeler. 2001. *Policy Reform, Economic Growth, and the Digital Divide: An Econometric Analysis*. Vol. 2567. World Bank Publications.
16. Martha S Feldman and James G March. 1981. Information in Organizations as Signal and Symbol. *Administrative Science Quarterly* 26, 2 (1981), 171–186.
17. Vishal Gaikar. 2014. The 10 Hottest Web Design Trends of 2014. (2014). http://www.tricksmachine.com/2014/07/the-10-hottest-web-design-trends-2014.html
18. Bill Gaver and John Bowers. 2012. Annotated Portfolios. *Interactions* July + August (2012), 40–49. https://interactions.acm.org/archive/view/july-august-2012/annotated-portfolios
19. Friedhelm Hillebrand. 2002. *GSM and UMTS: the Creation of Global Mobile Communication*. John Wiley & Sons, Inc.
20. Ronald Kline and Trevor Pinch. 1996. Users as Agents of Technological Change: The Social Construction of the Automobile in the Rural United States. *Technology and Culture* 37, 4 (Oct. 1996), 763–795.
21. Lucian Leahu, Phoebe Sengers, and Michael Mateas. 2008. Interactionist AI and the promise of Ubicomp, or, how to put your box in the world without putting the world in your box. In *Proceedings of the International Conference on Ubiquitous Computing (UBICOMP '08)*. ACM Press, New York, NY, USA, 134–143. DOI: http://dx.doi.org/10.1145/1409635.1409654
22. Victor Margolin. 1989. *Design discourse: History, Theory, Criticism*. University of Chicago Press.
23. Philip B Meggs and Alston W Purvis. 2016. *Meggs' History of Graphic Design*. John Wiley & Sons.
24. Janni Nielsen, Torkil Clemmensen, and Carsten Yssing. 2002. Getting Access to What Goes on in People's Heads?: Reflections on the Think-aloud Technique. In *Proceedings of the Second Nordic Conference on Human-computer Interaction (NordiCHI '02)*. ACM, New York, NY, USA, 101–110. DOI: http://dx.doi.org/10.1145/572020.572033
25. Trond Are Øritsland and Jacob Buur. 2000. Taking the Best from a Company History – Designing with Interaction Styles. In *Proceedings of the 3rd Conference on Designing Interactive Systems: Processes, Practices, Methods, and Techniques (DIS '00)*. ACM, New York, NY, USA, 27–38. DOI: http://dx.doi.org/10.1145/347642.347658
26. Trevor J. Pinch and Wiebe E. Bijker. 1987. The Social Construction of Facts and Artifacts: Or How the Sociology of Science and the Sociology of Technology Might Benefit Each Other. In *The Social Construction of Technological Systems: New Directions in the Sociology and History of Technology*. MIT Press.
27. António Pratas. 2014. *Creating Flat Design Websites*. Packt Publishing.

28. Katharina Reinecke and Krzysztof Z. Gajos. 2014. Quantifying Visual Preferences Around the World. In *Proceedings of the SIGCHI Conference on Human Factors in Computing Systems (CHI '14)*. ACM, New York, NY, USA, 11–20. DOI: http://dx.doi.org/10.1145/2556288.2557052

29. Katharina Reinecke, Tom Yeh, Luke Miratrix, Rahmatri Mardiko, Yuechen Zhao, Jenny Liu, and Krzysztof Z. Gajos. 2013. Predicting Users' First Impressions of Website Aesthetics with a Quantification of Perceived Visual Complexity and Colorfulness. In *Proceedings of the SIGCHI Conference on Human Factors in Computing Systems (CHI '13)*. ACM, New York, NY, USA, 2049–2058. DOI: http://dx.doi.org/10.1145/2470654.2481281

30. David Robins and Jason Holmes. 2008. Aesthetics and credibility in web site design. *Information Processing & Management* 44, 1 (Jan. 2008), 386–399. DOI: http://dx.doi.org/10.1016/j.ipm.2007.02.003

31. Charles Rosen. 1998a. *The Classical Style: Haydn, Mozart, Beethoven* (expanded ed.). W. W. Norton & Company, New York.

32. Charles Rosen. 1998b. *The Romantic Generation* (fifth ed.). Harvard University Press, Cambridge, MA, USA.

33. Ronald J. Vetter, Chris Spell, and Charles Ward. 1994. Mosaic and the World Wide Web. *Computer* 27, 10 (1994), 49–57.

34. Fernanda B. Viégas, Scott Golder, and Judith Donath. 2006. Visualizing Email Content: Portraying Relationships from Conversational Histories. In *Proceedings of the SIGCHI Conference on Human Factors in Computing Systems (CHI '06)*. ACM, New York, NY, USA, 979–988. DOI: http://dx.doi.org/10.1145/1124772.1124919

35. Fernanda B. Viégas, Martin Wattenberg, and Kushal Dave. 2004. Studying Cooperation and Conflict Between Authors with History Flow Visualizations. In *Proceedings of the SIGCHI Conference on Human Factors in Computing Systems (CHI '04)*. ACM, New York, NY, USA, 575–582. DOI: http://dx.doi.org/10.1145/985692.985765

36. Robert Stuart Weiss. 1995. *Learning from Strangers: The Art and Method of Qualitative Interview Studies*. Simon and Schuster, New York.

37. Mikael Wiberg and Erik Stolterman. 2014. What Makes a Prototype Novel?: A Knowledge Contribution Concern for Interaction Design Research. In *Proceedings of the 8th Nordic Conference on Human-Computer Interaction: Fun, Fast, Foundational (NordiCHI '14)*. ACM, New York, NY, USA, 531–540. DOI: http://dx.doi.org/10.1145/2639189.2639487

38. Steve Woolgar. 1990. Configuring the User: the Case of Usability Trials. *The Sociological Review* 38, S1 (1990), 58–99.

39. Susan Wyche, Phoebe Sengers, and Rebecca E. Grinter. 2006. Historical Analysis: Using the Past to Design the Future. In *Proceedings of the International Conference on Ubiquitous Computing (UBICOMP '06)*. Springer-Verlag, Berlin, 35–51. http://dx.doi.org/10.1007/11853565_3

Understanding Blind People's Experiences with Computer-Generated Captions of Social Media Images

Haley MacLeod[1], Cynthia L. Bennett[2], Meredith Ringel Morris[3], Edward Cutrell[3]

[1]School of Informatics & Computing
Indiana University
Bloomington, IN, USA
hemacleo@indiana.edu

[2]Human Centered Design & Engineering
University of Washington
Seattle, WA, USA
bennec3@uw.edu

[3]Microsoft Research
Redmond, WA, USA
{merrie, cutrell}@microsoft.com

ABSTRACT

Research advancements allow computational systems to automatically caption social media images. Often, these captions are evaluated with sighted humans using the image as a reference. Here, we explore how blind and visually impaired people experience these captions in two studies about social media images. Using a contextual inquiry approach (n=6 blind/visually impaired), we found that blind people place a lot of trust in automatically generated captions, filling in details to resolve differences between an image's context and an incongruent caption. We built on this in-person study with a second, larger online experiment (n=100 blind/visually impaired) to investigate the role of phrasing in encouraging trust or skepticism in captions. We found that captions emphasizing the probability of error, rather than correctness, encouraged people to attribute incongruence to an incorrect caption, rather than missing details. Where existing research has focused on encouraging trust in intelligent systems, we conclude by challenging this assumption and consider the benefits of encouraging appropriate skepticism.

Author Keywords

Automatic image captioning; alt text; accessibility; blindness; social media; Twitter.

ACM Classification Keywords

K.4.2. Social issues: Assistive technologies for persons with disabilities.

INTRODUCTION

Thanks to advances in AI, computational systems are now capable of automatically generating captions describing objects, people, and scenery in images (e.g., [9,12,27]). While these systems vary in accuracy, they are prominent enough that we are beginning to see them integrated into social media platforms (e.g., [33]). One group that stands to benefit from these advancements are blind and visually impaired people (BVIP), who have expressed frustration with increasingly visual content on social media [22,29,32]. Knowing the content of images in social contexts allows BVIPs to more fully participate in social conversations, get more information from news, and enjoy entertainment or humor [22]. Automatic captioning tools have the potential to empower BVIPs to know more about these images without having to rely on human-authored alt text (which is often missing [4,13,26]) or asking a sighted person (which can be time consuming or burdensome [3,5,6]).

Because AI systems used for image captioning were not designed with BVIP use as a primary scenario, they have been evaluated by measuring the similarity between a machine's output and that of a sighted human [16,23]. Sometimes this is done through user studies where sighted people are asked to rate the quality of a caption for a given image [25,27] or choose the best from a series of captions [9]. This does not take into account the experiences of BVIPs, who cannot use the visual image as a reference point and would be experiencing these captions outside of a controlled experimental context.

In this paper, we explore how blind and visually impaired people experience automatically generated captions on social media. We focus specifically on Twitter, since it is heavily used by BVIPs [5] to access a range of types of content (news, humor, etc.) across different relationships (personal, professional, strangers) [22]. Using a contextual inquiry approach, we find that BVIPs place a great deal of trust in these captions, often filling in details to resolve differences between a tweet's text and an incongruent caption (where the image caption does not seem to match the content or context of the tweet). We build on these findings by conducting an online experiment to explore this phenomenon on a larger scale and investigate the role of caption phrasing in encouraging trust or skepticism. Our findings suggest that captions worded in a way that emphasize the probability of error, rather than correctness, encourage BVIPs to attribute incongruence to an incorrect caption rather than to missing details. The specific contributions of this work are:

1) A description of blind people's experiences with automatically generated image captions.
2) An evaluation of the role of phrasing on a blind person's trust in a caption.
3) Recommendations for automated captioning systems and further areas of research.

CHI 2017, May 06 - 11, 2017, Denver, CO, USA

ACM 978-1-4503-4655-9/17/05…$15.00
DOI: http://dx.doi.org/10.1145/3025453.3025814

RELATED WORK

Social Media & Visual Impairments

Social media use continues to be popular, and this is also true among BVIPs [5,22,29,32]. Specifically, previous work has explored BVIP experiences on Facebook and Twitter. Wu and Adamic [32] found many similarities between blind and sighted Facebook users, but noted that while visually impaired users post more status updates, they post and engage with fewer photos. Voykinska et al. [29] explored this phenomenon further, focusing on how blind people interact with visual content on Facebook. They describe blind users' interest in participating in common Facebook activities such as posting a photo or commenting on a friend's photo, alongside a fear of getting something wrong and a frustration with the lack of useful contextual information. The authors outline strategies people use to interpret visual content, finding that author-generated descriptions, when available, were considered the most useful. More recently, Facebook released an automatic image captioning tool that provides a list of objects and scenes identified in a photo [33].

In Brady et al.'s [5] study of how BVIPs use social media sites, they found that blind people are especially active on Twitter because of its simple, text-based interface. In June 2011, Twitter added capabilities for photo sharing [11] and Morris et al. [22] described the impact this change had on BVIPs. Their study highlighted challenges with the increasing prevalence of images. Since this time, Twitter added the ability to include alt text descriptions of images with a tweet [19], but this setting must be enabled explicitly.

Automatic Image Captioning

While existing research has examined ways of generating better captions manually [21], an interesting new approach to addressing the lack of descriptions for social media images is to generate these alt text captions automatically. Research in this area has generally been focused on the necessary artificial intelligence advancements (particularly in computer vision and natural language generation) to be able to accomplish such a task with a reasonable level of accuracy [10,17,23,25,27,34]. Recent successes have resulted in the deployment of such tools in a variety of applications, including as part of social platforms [33].

These solutions are typically evaluated using standardized metrics measuring the similarity between a machine's output and that of a sighted human [16,23]. These metrics help compare various algorithms when they are run on common datasets. Researchers also often conduct user studies, asking sighted individuals to rate the quality of a caption for a given image [25,27], or asking them to choose the best of a series of captions [9] to assess the quality difference between human-authored captions and machine-generated captions. This makes sense given that most work on automated captioning is not focused on generating alt text for BVIPs, but rather is motivated by scenarios like providing metadata to improve image search. The evaluation criteria for caption quality and the cost/benefit tradeoffs for different types of errors are different than they would be if designed with accessibility as the primary scenario. The fact that such systems are now being repurposed for accessibility purposes (as in [33]) requires a reexamination of their fundamental assumptions, such as what makes a good caption or what the relative risks are in the precision/recall tradeoff.

In this work, we build on previous research on BVIP experiences with visual content on social media and focus specifically on automatically generated captions. We explore how these captions are experienced *in situ* by blind users who cannot see an image and therefore do not have the same frame of reference for the quality of the caption as the sighted people that have historically evaluated these algorithms. We contribute to understanding how to adapt existing caption generation tools to accessibility scenarios.

Framing Effects

Previous research has shown that BVIPs appreciate hearing captions provided as complete sentences, rather than as a list of keywords [33]. This requires not only advanced computer vision and deep learning techniques but also advanced techniques for converting those results to natural language. As such, some implementations (such as on Facebook [33]) choose to provide a list of keywords to better prioritize accuracy. Other implementations do integrate the captions into full sentences (such as in Microsoft's Cognitive Services Computer Vision API [36]), but little is known about the implications of the way in which these captions are worded.

We turn to research from psychology on framing effects [28] to explore different ways of wording captions to give people a more accurate sense of how reliable they are. Work on framing effects discusses how people react to information when it is framed differently, and the impact this has on decision making. Commonly this is done as a study of positive versus negative framing. For example, Marteau [20] compared differences in a decision to undergo surgery between people presented with either the phrasing "X% chance of dying" (negative framing) or "Y% chance of surviving" (positive framing), finding that people tended to be more risk-averse in the negative framing scenario and more risk-tolerant in the positive framing scenario.

Framing effects are also sometimes studied by comparing natural language and numeric risk descriptors. Young et al. [35] compared participants' perceptions of risk when presented with semantic descriptions (i.e., plain English) and with numeric values, finding that people tend to overestimate the likelihood of low probability events when provided with natural language descriptions.

Framing effects have been studied in many different contexts, and have been used to inform the design of persuasive technology within the HCI community [7,8,14,18]. In our work, we explore the application of framing to image captioning as a way of communicating confidence in the accuracy of a caption.

CONTEXTUAL INQUIRY ON EXPERIENCES WITH IMAGE CAPTIONS IN THE TWITTER FEED

In the first phase of our research, we used contextual observations and interviews with a small number of blind Twitter users (n=6) to better understand their current experiences navigating images in their Twitter feed. We also introduce captioned images into the Twitter feed to gauge responses to the automatically generated captions.

Method

Recruitment & Participants

We targeted Twitter users for our study, so we recruited participants primarily through Twitter and additionally through snowball sampling. We sent tweets from our personal and organizational accounts using hashtags relevant to our target demographic, such as *#blind* and *#a11y* (a general hashtag related to accessibility). We purchased advertising on Twitter to promote our tweets, targeting our ads to Twitter users in our geographic area who had previously used hashtags relating to accessibility or visual impairments, and had interests similar to accounts relating to blindness (e.g. advocacy organizations or services used by people who are visually impaired).

To be eligible for our in-person study, participants had to be at least 18 years old and use Twitter on an iOS device using the VoiceOver screen reader. This VoiceOver screen reader converts on-screen information to aural speech. In the case of a mobile Twitter app, VoiceOver will read out loud the tweet author, the tweet text, descriptions of any emojis, any alt text associated with an image, and the number of likes or retweets. Participants were instructed to bring their personal iOS device to the study, so they could easily use their preferred settings (such as a comfortable speed for VoiceOver). Each participant received a $150 VISA gift card as gratuity. Information about the six participants who took part in this study can be found in Table 1.

Procedure

To ground our understanding of blind people's experiences on Twitter, we began by asking participants to open their preferred Twitter application and use it as normal. We asked them to think out loud, describing what they were doing. We used example tweets and images from their personal feeds to ground conversations around their experience with images in the feed and with Twitter as a whole.

#	Gender	Age	Visual Impairment	App
P1	F	57	Blind since birth	Twitterific
P2	M	34	Blind since birth	Twitterific
P3	F	56	Blind since birth	Twitterific
P4	M	24	Blind since birth	Twitterific
P5	M	35	Minimal light perception since birth	Twitter
P6	F	52	Minimal light perception for past 7 years.	Twitter

Table 1:. Contextual Inquiry Participant Demographics.

We then directed participants to a specific Twitter account we created. This account consisted of 14 tweets, each with an image and an alt text caption. The tweets in this account were collected from hashtags that were trending during the period leading up to the study (e.g., *#ThrowbackThursday, #MyUnOlympicEventWouldBe, #AlwaysMakesMeSmile, #WhenIWasYoung*) as well as from popular Twitter accounts (e.g., Ellen DeGeneres, Buzzfeed, The New York Times). We selected tweets to represent a range of topics including memes, humor, news, politics, and celebrities.

We used the Microsoft Cognitive Services API's [37] to automatically generate captions for the images. These captions are full sentence descriptions of objects and known celebrities in the image. We also used Optical Character Recognition (OCR) to transcribe text in images that were text-heavy. An important note is that these captions ranged substantially in their accuracy: some captions were mostly accurate and complete (6 captions), some were correct but were missing some important information (4 captions), and some were completely wrong (4 captions). The Microsoft Cognitive Services Computer Vision API [36] provides a confidence measure of the caption results, and Microsoft's CaptionBot.ai tool [38] integrates these into the full sentence descriptions, typically in the form "I'm not really sure but I think it's…" or "I'm 98% sure that's…".

We asked participants to search for this Twitter account and go through these tweets, again thinking out loud. We told participants that the images' alt text came from a computer algorithm, and explained that phrasing like "I'm not really sure but I think…" or "I'm 98% sure that is a picture of …" would give them a sense of how confident the algorithm was in the caption it had generated. We warned them explicitly that captions would sometimes be wrong.

After participants reviewed these tweets, we asked questions about their experience with the captions and what they found useful. We then asked how much they trusted the accuracy of the captions and whether there were any captions they thought were wrong or incomplete. We revealed some of the tweets that had entirely incorrect captions and provided more accurate descriptions of the images. We additionally asked how they would behave had these tweets shown up in their regular news feed, and whether they preferred more information (even if it was sometimes wrong) or less information (but have it be more reliable).

Analysis

We recorded audio and video of our observations and interview sessions with participants. Each study session took approximately one hour. We iteratively analyzed these sessions using open and axial coding

Findings

Participants tended to trust the captions, commenting *"I felt pretty confident about them being accurate"* (P2). P1 explained, *"I have to trust them because I don't have any form of reference…Unless somebody sighted were saying 'I*

Figure 1: Image tweeted by Hillary Clinton used as a probe. The tweet text reads, *"Some on the other side may say our best days are behind us. Let's prove them wrong."* The computer generated caption says, *"I am not really confident, but I think it's a man is doing a trick on a skateboard at night."* The image is actually a black and white photo of Hillary Clinton walking onto a stage with a crowd of people in the background.

Figure 2: Image tweeted by the New York Times used as a probe. The tweet text reads, *"Why isn't Italy kinder to gays?"* The computer generated caption says, *"I'm not really confident, but I think it's a person holding a tennis racquet and she seems neutral face."* The image is actually of two copies of the statue of David digitally altered so one has his arm around the other and they are looking at each other.

don't know why they said that, that's not what it is at all...' You know if somebody were sitting beside me and said 'That's not a dog, that's a something else'...then I would have to say 'well gee, somebody wrote that incorrectly'"

Some participants expressed skepticism when asked about trust in captions in general, but this was not reflected in their behavior during the think-aloud protocol. For example, P3 claimed that she was only 50% trusting of the captions and said that she normally confirms the content of an image with her daughter before taking an action. She explains, *"if I'm going to retweet something, I want to know that I'm retweeting what I think it is... I definitely wouldn't retweet that without somebody looking at it first. And after all these years my daughter is getting to the point where's she's like 'mooooommmmm' 'Oh just tell me! Minimum words! I know you can do it in 145 characters!' and I'll go 'okay, I'm going to retweet that to people I know'. So I don't retweet a photo unless I truly know."* Yet, when it came to specific examples from our set of tweets (in this case, the Hillary Clinton tweet from Figure 1) she expressed, *"I probably would have just retweeted it thinking it was a photo of a skateboarder."* This could have potential social consequences for her: *"I would have been so in trouble by my friends...People would be like, 'I thought we don't talk about politicals...', 'I thought we keep this clean....', 'Are you supporting her?' I'd be all like 'calm down, calm down I thought it was this.'"*

Resolving Dissonance

Participants described assessing the accuracy of the caption based on how well it matched their expectations given the tweet text. P4 explained that his trust varied depending on this mismatch: *"When it made sense, I tended to trust it. When it didn't make sense or I couldn't see how it related, I was like 'where does this come from?' Maybe I don't trust it."* Yet when participants were reviewing the tweets (after they had been warned captions *could* be wrong, but before they had been told which ones *were* wrong), they resolved this dissonance not by suggesting that the caption was wrong, but by describing scenarios or explanations that would connect an unexpected image to the tweet text. In one example, P2 reviewed the tweet in Figure 2 and resolved this dissonance with the explanation, *"Okay, so it's a tennis player. Who, if I recognized tennis players, maybe she's gay."* Similarly, P3 explained the incongruence in Hillary Clinton's tweet in Figure 1 by filling in a detail about it being an *older* man on a skateboard: *"If you say, there's an older man on a skateboard at night that would make more sense. That's the way I take 'our best days are behind us' because I'm an old lady...which is not true because I've seen people in their 90s do amazing things."*

P5 didn't have a resolution for the dissonance, but instead thought the answer might be found in the linked article and was curious to find out more: *"Like huh. Why is a tennis racket involved in this story? ... like the way pictures are eye catching to people, it would engage a different side of my perception. Saying, oh tennis racket. I don't play tennis, but maybe that's even more interesting than I thought. Because, why is there a tennis racket involved in this story?"*

Awareness of Disclaimers

Participants showed signs of at least being aware of the disclaimers and confidence warnings, sometimes stopping to comment on them. P1 stopped after a tweet to remark *"That's funny..."* explaining, *"Just their comment, 'I think it's a tree but I'm not sure.' It's like, okay, whatever."* P3 was similarly amused by the captions, mimicking *"He THINKS it's a plate of pasta and broccoli? You don't know????? How bad is that picture...?"* P5 told us that the confidence levels were the least useful of all the information that had been presented to him, stating that *"Me personally I know, and I think most people would understand, that it is a computer algorithm."*

Expertise on Computer Vision

Participants worked hard to explain the failings of the captioning algorithm or described how they imagined it worked. Several participants brought up some background they had in software development or some familiarity with technology that they credited for this understanding. As P4 described, *"I don't see how a table looks like another guy at all. Or a tree looks like an infographic. I mean it's got text it should be able to recognize that. I'm a software developer for a living so I'd say my opinions are kind of educated."*

Even participants who did not mention any expertise in technology worked to understand how a caption might be wrong, often either personifying the algorithm or referring to a programmer that was responsible for the captions. P3 reviewed an image that the algorithm had labelled as pasta with broccoli and asked, *"Is [the image] fuzzy? Is it not clear enough to know the difference between a green and a tan colored food?"* After we described the food as linguini with spinach, she concluded, *"No wonder he was confused it might be broccoli. Greenness kind of confuses people who don't know vegetables. It's green right?"*

When describing their understanding of the limitations of such algorithms, some participants still underestimated how wrong a caption could possibly be. Before receiving the accurate description of the image in Figure 2, P5 stated, *"I would understand if it turned out to be a beach ball or something whatever looks like a tennis racquet. Or a badminton paddle or something. A racquetball racquet. I would understand if it turned out to be different."*

Risk Tolerance

Participants varied in their willingness to encounter wrong captions from time to time (in exchange for more information) as opposed to having limited information (that was consistently correct). P2 preferred some risk, feeling that *"most of the time it's going to be fairly accurate"* whereas P3 expressed that *"even if it was less information but it was what it was, I would have more confidence in retweeting it."*

P4 was trusting of the captions before hearing descriptions of the images but quickly stated, *"It doesn't really give me confidence if it can be THAT wrong"* after he heard accurate descriptions of some images. And yet when asked about the tradeoff between correctness and detail, he still said *"I think I'd rather have more information that could be wrong. I can make that decision whether I want to trust it or not."*

Summary

Overall, our observations suggested that participants believed many incorrect captions, despite their self-reported double-checking strategies and abilities to correctly assess the accuracy of a caption. Rather than suspect a caption was wrong, they filled in details to resolve incongruences between a tweet's text and its caption.

Limitations

It can be challenging to recruit BVIPs for in-person studies, and our sample size from this first study is accordingly limited. However, these exploratory contextual inquiry sessions with BVIPs revealed a number of challenges with automatically generated captions. Even when we explicitly, deliberately primed participants (telling them the captions came from algorithms, warning them the captions might be wrong, explaining how to interpret the confidence disclaimers) issues of trust rose to the surface. Being aware of these issues made it possible for us to construct a second study (our online experiment) to explore this phenomenon on a larger scale online.

Additionally, we are conscious that behaviors and perceptions communicated in this lab study, particularly those about behaviors in response to captions and anticipated social consequences, may not be reflective of *in situ* interactions. This is a challenging area to study in the wild, because so few images on Twitter currently have any image descriptions, and to our knowledge none are automatically generated. This may be an interesting area of future study as captioning systems become more widely used.

Finally, although we did not explicitly collect data about education or employment from participants in this study, several participants referred to a background in software engineering or some relevant technical field during our discussions with them. These were people who seemed to have high numeracy skills, and we were unsure whether responses to disclaimers like "I'm 98% sure that's…" might be different for different levels of education or numeracy. It's also possible that people with strong technical backgrounds might understand captioning systems differently from people without that same experience. In our second study, we explicitly asked about education level and technical proficiency of participants and found these items were not predictive of trust in captions.

EXPERIMENT ON THE IMPACT OF CAPTION PHRASING ON TRUST AND SKEPTICISM

Building from our interview results, we conducted an online experiment to explore themes of trust in incongruent captions on a larger scale. We additionally explored ways of phrasing the captions to encourage a higher level of distrust in captions that intuitively seem off. This experiment was designed to answer three main research questions:

1) To what extent are our findings from the contextual inquiry study consistent on a larger scale?
2) Is research on positive and negative framing effects relevant in constructing captions to direct trust?
3) Is there a difference between a caption phrased using numeric values and a caption phrased using natural language with respect to directing trust?

Method

Recruitment & Respondents

As in our contextual interviews, we recruited through Twitter using the *#blind* and *#a11y* hashtags. We again purchased advertising on Twitter, targeting users in the United States who had previously used hashtags relating to accessibility or visual impairments with interests similar to accounts relating to blindness. Participants had to be at least 18 years old, living in the U.S., with a visual impairment, and use Twitter. Each respondent received a $5 Amazon gift card as gratuity.

	Positive Framing	Negative Framing
Natural Language Framing	*"I'm really confident that's a cat sitting on a counter next to a window."*	*"There's a small chance I could be wrong, but I think that's a cat sitting on a counter next to a window."*
Numeric Framing	*"There's an 80% chance that's a cat sitting on a counter next to a window."*	*"There's a 20% chance I'm wrong, but I think that's a cat sitting on a counter next to a window"*

Table 2: Four different framings of a caption.

We received 100 valid responses to our experiment. Participants ranged in age from 20 – 66 (M=33.8). 30% identified as female and 69% as male. They had been experiencing their visual impairment for 1 – 66 years (M=12) and 21% had experienced their visual impairment since birth. Respondents had tweeted a median of 3,918 tweets (mean 19,653). They had a median of 270 followers (mean 707) and were following a median of 379 accounts (mean 1,812). Participants had varied educational and professional backgrounds; 38% had completed college, and 44% had a career involving technology in some capacity.

Procedure

We designed an online experiment using the SurveyGizmo tool, and pilot-tested the experimental questionnaire with a range of screen readers to ensure accessibility. There were four parts to this instrument:

1) ***Background questions***: Description and length of visual impairment, age, gender, education, skill level and background in technology, frequency of Twitter use, Twitter client(s) used, and Twitter handle (used to look up number of tweets posted, number of followers, and number of accounts followed).
2) ***Tweets and understanding:*** We provided ten tweets (in random order). As in the first study, we warned participants that the captions were generated by a computer algorithm and may not always be accurate. For each tweet, participants heard the tweet author, the tweet text, and a computer-generated caption describing the tweet's associated image attachment. After each tweet, we asked participants to rate on Likert scales the extent to which the caption improved their *understanding of the image* and their *understanding of the tweet as a whole.* Drawing from research on Bayesian Truth Serum [24] (a method for eliciting truthful subjective data where objective truth is unknowable), we also asked the extent to which the caption would *be helpful to other visually impaired people*.
3) ***Overall trust:*** After having reviewed all ten tweets, respondents rated how much they *trusted the captions overall* and whether they thought *other visually impaired people could trust the captions*. We also asked them to rate *the intelligence of the computer algorithm* that had generated the captions.

Confidence	Positive Framing	Negative Framing
>85%	*I'm absolutely sure*	*There's no way I'm wrong*
61% - 85%	*I'm really confident*	*There's a small chance I could be wrong*
26% - 60%	*I'm pretty sure*	*I'm not completely sure*
<=25%	*I'm only sort of confident*	*I have absolutely no idea but my best guess is*

Table 3: Captions in four natural language bins.

4) ***Request for further information:*** We asked respondents which of the images they would like more information on and why/why not. Options for why/why not included being *interested/disinterested* in the tweet, *trusting/distrusting* the caption, finding the caption to be *sufficiently/insufficiently detailed*, or a write in option.
5) ***Optional debriefing:*** At the end of the questionnaire, respondents had the option to click a link that took them to accurate, human-authored descriptions of the images.

Respondents were randomly assigned to four possible study conditions. We varied *framing* [whether the confidence measure accompanying each caption was framed *positively* (i.e., how confident the algorithm was that the caption was correct) or *negatively* (i.e., how confident the algorithm was that the caption was incorrect)], and we varied *abstraction* [whether the confidence measure was presented as an exact *numeric* value (i.e., a percentage amount) or in a *natural language* frame (i.e., using words)], resulting in four possible variants (2 framings x 2 abstractions), as shown in Table 2. In the natural language conditions, the percentage values were grouped into four bins (Table 3). The captions and confidence values were taken from Microsoft's Cognitive Services Computer Vision API [36]. The caption text (the description of the image that follows the confidence warning) was consistent across study conditions.

The tweets in the study were taken from popular hashtags or Twitter accounts, across a range of topics. We selected images that would allow for a range of *congruence* with the tweet (i.e., how well the caption matches expectations based on the tweet), with a focus on the extreme cases; we included four tweets with *high congruence*, four tweets with *low congruence*, and two tweets in the middle.

We also selected tweets with images that would allow for a range of *confidence* (as reported by the Cognitive Services API), again focusing on the extreme cases; we included four tweets with low reported accuracy *(low confidence)*, four with high reported accuracy *(high confidence)*, and two in the middle (one on each side of 50%).

Note that these two taxonomies (confidence and congruence) overlap partially, but not entirely, and that the API's reported confidence level does not always match what a sighted human might assign as an accuracy score. The tweets used in this study, as well as our classifications of congruence and confidence can be found in Table 4.

	Tweet author and text	Confidence Disclaimers	Caption Text	Image	Human-Authored Description
High Congruence	ALensOnAmerica. Share your best wildlife photo from a national park and get feedback from @chamiltonjames. #YourShot.	There's a 25% chance that's… There's a 75% chance I'm wrong, but I think that's… I'm only sort of confident that's… I have absolutely no idea, but my best guess is that it's…	…a bear is swimming in the water.		The image shows two otters floating on their backs in the water. One is sleeping and the other has its mouth open as though it's smiling.
	The Bloggess. I feel like I'm intruding in my own kitchen. "I'll just see myself out. I didn't know this room was reserved."	There's an 80% chance that's… There's a 20% chance I'm wrong, but I think that's… I'm really confident that's… There's a small chance I could be wrong, but I think that's…	…a cat sitting on a counter next to a window.		There are three cats sitting on the counters in a kitchen staring somewhat menacingly at the camera.
	Buzzfeed. 19 of the most disrespectful sandwiches ever made.	There's a 52% chance that's… There's a 48% chance I'm wrong, but I think that's… I'm pretty sure that's…. I'm not completely sure, but I think that's…	…a close up of a sandwich.	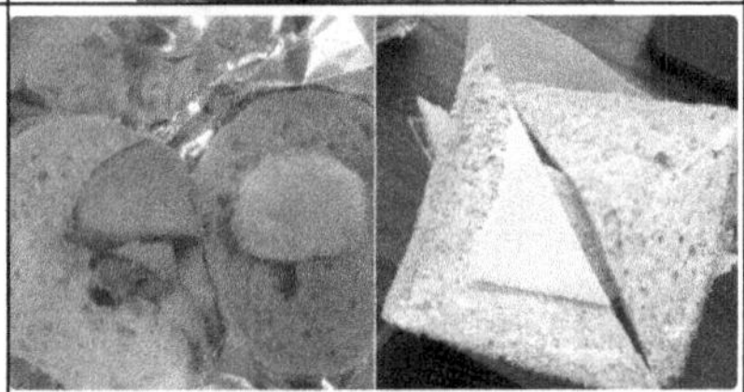	The image is two photos of open faced sandwiches. The first is an English muffin with a tiny piece of ham on one half and a tiny fried egg on the other half. The second is two slices of bread and one tiny piece of cheese on one half.
	Whole Foods Market. Ready for #summer entertaining? Plan w/ special diets in mind. #glutenfree #paleo #vegan	There's a 94% chance that's… There's a 6% chance I'm wrong, but I think that's… I'm absolutely sure that's… There's no way I'm wrong about this. It's…	…a plate of food with broccoli.		The image shows a plate of pasta with a green pesto sauce and fresh basil leaves mixed in.
Medium Congruence	Fizzington Womack. For the last time, quit pointing that thing at me. I am not a Pikachu! #PokemonGo	There's a 99% chance it's … There's a 1% chance I'm wrong, but I think it's a… I'm absolutely sure it's… There's no way I'm wrong about this. It's…	…a cat sitting on a couch.		It's a cat sitting on a couch.
	Harvard Business Review. 3 psychological principles to help us interpret recent political events — and be better at predicting future outcomes.	There's a 99% chance that's… There's a 1% chance I'm wrong, but I think it's… I'm absolutely sure it's… There's no way I'm wrong about this. It's…	… a table topped with plates of food and Donald Trump.		The image shows a dinner table with plates and cutlery all set out. Near the middle of the table there's an image of Donald Trump's head. It sort of looks like it was printed on paper and cut out and placed on the table.

Table 4. Tweets used in the online experiment **(continued on next page).**

Table 4: Tweets used in the online experiment (continued from previous page).

Low Congruence	Hillary Clinton. Some on the other side may say our best days are behind us. Let's prove them wrong.	There's a 23% chance that's... There's a 67% chance I'm wrong, but I think that's... I'm only sort of confident that's... I have absolutely no idea but my best guess is that it's...	...a man doing a trick on a skateboard at night.		The image shows Hilary Clinton walking onto a stage in front of a large crowd of people.
	The New York Times. Why isn't Italy kinder to gays?	There's a 10% chance that's... There's a 90% chance I'm wrong, but I think that's... I'm only sort of confident that's... I have absolutely no idea, but my best guess is that it's...	...a person holding a tennis racquet.		The image shows two nude, male statues (both are the Statue of David) next to each other over a bright pink solid background.
	Seattle Police Department. Bank robber arrested after abandoning pants.	There's a 5% chance that's... There's a 95% chance I'm wrong, but I think that's... I'm only sort of confident that's... I have absolutely no idea, but my best guess is that it's...	...a person on a surf board in a skate park.		The image shows text from a poem by Shel Silverstein called Something Missing. The poem goes like this: I remember I put on my socks, I remember I put on my shoes. I remember I put on my tie that was printed in beautiful purples and blues. I remember I put on my coat, to look perfectly grand at the dance. Yet I feel there is something I may have forgot—What is it? What is it?...
	ESPN. A massive gator interrupted a group's golf round ... in Florida, of course.	There's a 98% chance that's... There's a 2% chance I'm wrong, but I think that's... I'm absolutely sure that's... There's no way I'm wrong about this. That's...	......a horse standing on top of a lush green field.		The image shows a golf course with an alligator walking across it.

Analysis

In our analysis, we primarily considered two independent variables, each with two levels: 1) *framing* of the caption (positive vs. negative) and 2) the *abstraction* of the caption (numeric vs. natural language). Additionally, we sometimes considered 3) the *congruence* of the caption (high vs. low) or 4) the *confidence* reported in the caption (high vs. low). When we consider congruence, we exclude tweets with medium congruence as these are cases that did not fit cleanly into either the high or the low category (or could arguably fit into either). We similarly exclude the tweets with medium confidence when looking for differences by confidence level.

We focused our analysis on a number of different dependent variables. From part two of the experimental instrument we collected three Likert scale ratings for **understanding** *("This caption improved my understanding of the image," "This caption improved my understanding of the tweet as a whole," "I think other visually impaired people would find this caption helpful")*. We will refer to these three questions of **understanding** as U1, U2, and U3 throughout our findings. These questions were five-point scales answered for each tweet.

From part three, we collected three Likert scale ratings relating to **overall trust** (*"Overall, I trust these captions," "I think other visually impaired people could reasonably trust these captions," and "How intelligent do you think the computer algorithm that came up with these captions is?")*. We will refer to these three five-point **overall trust** scales as OT1, OT2, and OT3.

From part four, we collected data for whether or not a given caption was *sufficiently* ***detailed*** and whether or not participants had ***trust*** *that the caption is correct*. We refer to these three-point scales as D for **detailed** and T for **trust** throughout the findings. As in part two, these questions were answered for each tweet.

FINDINGS

To explore the findings from our initial study (i.e., the contextual inquiry) on a larger scale we explored the extent to which a participant's self-reported trust in the captions overall aligned with how useful they found each specific caption (and whether this changed depending on how the caption was phrased). Implicit in this comparison are two assumptions: 1) at least one part of finding a caption to be useful in situ is believing it to be true, and 2) believing a caption to be useful may influence a decision about an image (such as whether to retweet it or not).

Overall Trust in Captions vs. Perceived Utility of Captions

For the questions about overall trust in the captions (OT1 – OT3) we found that respondents were fairly trusting of captions overall; Likert scale responses were slightly skewed towards the upper part of the five-point scale (OT1 M=3.9, SD=0.8; OT2 M=3.7, SD=0.9; OT3 M=3.8, SD=0.8). We conducted Mann-Whitney's U tests to compare differences in trust overall (OT1 – OT3) and found no significant differences between study groups, which suggests that caption phrasing did not make a difference to one's assessment of the captioning technology's trustworthiness overall; participants reported that, as a whole, they found the captioning system to be trustworthy.

For responses to questions about the usefulness of specific captions (U1 – U3) we found that respondents found the captions to be helpful overall. As with trust, Likert scale responses were slightly skewed towards the upper part of the scale (U1 M=3.7, SD=0.9; U2 M=3.6, SD=0.9; U3 M=3.7, SD=0.9). We similarly conducted Mann-Whitney's U tests for U1 – U3 and found no significant differences between groups for these questions, suggesting that phrasing did not make a difference to one's assessment of usefulness overall.

Differences in Trust by Caption Type

Next, we were interested in whether there were differences in trust for *different kinds* of captions. In particular, we were interested in cases of extreme (in)congruence. Tweets with *high congruence* were cases where the image caption was closely related to the tweet's context (i.e., the tweet text and author). Tweets with *low congruence* were cases where the caption was unexpected or weird, given the tweet text. These assignments were made manually by the research team and informed by our observations in the contextual interviews. Our goal by altering phrasing of tweets was to encourage BVIPs to respond to these cases of low congruence with more skepticism, considering the possibility the caption might be wrong rather than assuming it was correct and building unsupported narratives to fill in missing details.

We were also interested in cases where the caption was either *highly confident* or *highly uncertain*. In some cases, the confidence estimations were incorrect (e.g., *"There's a 98% chance that's a horse standing on top of a lush green field"* when there is actually an alligator in the image, not a horse), but we are nonetheless interested in understanding the extent to which these confidence estimations play a role in one's trust or distrust of a given caption.

Congruence. We conducted a Wilcoxon Signed-rank test for each of the dependent variables (D, T, U1, U2, U3). We found significant differences between congruence levels for trust and all three understanding questions (Table 5). There was no significant difference in detail. (People found tweets with high congruence to be more trustworthy (M=2.0 vs. 1.9, three-point scale for T) and more helpful (3.9 vs. 3.6 for U1, 3.7 vs 3.5 for U2, 3.8 vs. 3.6 for U3, five-point scales).

T	Z=-2.59	p<0.01	r=0.13
U1	Z=-4.62	p<0.01	r=0.23
U2	Z=-2.88	p<0.01	r=0.14
U2	Z=-2.73	p<0.01	r=0.14

Table 5: Results of Wilcoxon Signed-rank test showing significant differences in congruence for trust, understanding.

We also examined *subsets* of tweets (only high congruence tweets and only low congruence tweets) to consider whether there were significant differences between conditions (i.e., simple effects for positive vs. negative framing or for numeric vs. natural language abstraction for the two levels of congruency). We conducted a Mann-Whitney's U test for each of the dependent variables in the two subsets of the data.

When we looked only at tweets with low congruence, we saw significant differences in trust (mean ranks of positive and negative framing were 214 and 191, respectively; respectively; U=17194, Z=-3.37, p<0.01, r=0.17 for T); people who received negatively framed captions trusted incongruent captions *significantly less often* than people who received positively framed captions (M=1.8 vs. 2.0 for T, three-point scale). ***This would suggest that people faced with negative framing are more distrusting of incongruent captions.*** There was no difference in trust when congruence was high.

We also saw significant differences in understanding. Understanding of the image (U1) was significantly different both when the tweets were highly congruent (mean ranks of positive and negative framing were 185 and 211, respectively; U=16870, Z=-2.36, p<0.02, r=0.12 for U1) and highly incongruent (mean ranks of positive and negative framing were 220 and 187, respectively; U=16076, Z=-3.19, p<<0.01, r=0.16 for U1). People who received negatively framed captions found the captions with high congruence to be more helpful to understanding the image (M=4.0 vs. 3.8 for U1, five-point scale) and the captions with low congruence to be less helpful (M= 3.4 vs. 3.8 for U1, five-point scale). This is ideal, as our goal is to encourage BVIPs to rely less on a caption that might be incorrect. People who received positively framed captions found captions with low congruence to be more helpful. This suggests that people who received positively phrased captions felt these mismatched captions added to their understanding of the image. Given that all four of our incongruent captions were at least partially wrong, it could be dangerous for an individual to make a decision off the provided caption alone. ***Negatively phrased captions better encouraged a lower level of reliance on incongruent captions, and a higher level of reliance on congruent captions.***

Confidence. We again conducted a Wilcoxon Signed-rank test for each of the dependent variables (D, T, U1, U2, U3) and only found a significant effect of confidence on trust ($Z=-2.26$, $p<0.03$, $r=0.11$). People trusted tweets with high reported confidence *significantly more* than tweets with low reported confidence ($M=2.0$ vs. 1.96). This makes intuitive sense, although we note again that the reported confidence and the actual accuracy of a caption may not always be well matched.

We also examined subsets of tweets by confidence, using Mann-Whitney's U tests. For tweets with low confidence, we found a significant difference in detail depending on the framing of the caption (mean ranks of positive and negative framing were 183 and 212, respectively; $U=16633$, $Z=-2.86$, $p< 0.01$, $r=0.14$ for D). When tweets reported low confidence, people found negatively framed captions significantly more detailed than positively framed captions ($M=2.0$ vs. 1.8).

DISCUSSION

In our contextual inquiry, we saw that BVIPs are trusting of automatically-generated captions, even when they don't make sense. They filled in details or built unsupported narratives to resolve these differences, rather than suspect that captions might be wrong, even when we warned them the captions were authored by a fallible computer algorithm. We conducted an online experiment where we learned that a) our findings from the contextual inquiry study are consistent across a larger sample size and b) negatively framed captions are more appropriate for encouraging appropriate skepticism in uncertain captions (i.e., where congruence and/or confidence are low).

Thus, we recommend that automatically generated captions be phrased in a way that reinforces the possibility the caption might be wrong (negative framing). As there were no significant differences in results between the natural language and numeric groups, we leave decisions of abstraction up to the designers.

Negatively framed captions help BVIPs rely more on their intuition about a caption, rather than unquestioningly trusting a caption and making decisions based off misinformation. This may encourage people to seek a second opinion on the content of an image before taking an action (e.g., retweeting) and risking social embarrassment if they are wrong. While getting a second opinion for *every* image might be burdensome or inconvenient, the results of our experimental online study suggest that negatively framed captions help encourage skepticism most in situations where that second opinion is most important; where congruence and/or confidence are low and the risk of incorrectness is high.

There is a broader implication here, as well; while there is a great deal of current research on modelling uncertainty in intelligent systems, there is very little on *communicating* that uncertainty. In fact, there is even research on how to encourage people to have *more* trust in these intelligent systems (e.g., [1,2,15,30]). The problem here is that even the best intelligent systems or agents do make mistakes, and when there is complete trust in these systems there can also be consequences, be that social embarrassment from retweeting an image because of false information or even safety risks in the case of self-driving cars. While we, of course, encourage researchers to continue working toward improving the accuracy of these systems, we also stress the importance of being able to effectively communicate uncertainty to users so they can more appropriately decide how to behave or how much trust to place in a system. In our work, we took an initial step toward investigating ways of engendering skepticism in situations of uncertainty, recognizing that there are many other contexts where a similar investigation would be valuable.

CONCLUSION

We conducted a small contextual inquiry where we learned that blind and visually impaired people are very trusting of even incorrect AI-generated captions, filling in details to reconcile incongruencies rather than suspecting the caption may be wrong. They described being skilled at detecting incorrect captions and as being consistent about double-checking, but this was not reflected in their behaviour. We then conducted an online experiment to validate these findings on a larger scale. Through this study, we additionally learned that negatively framed captions are best suited to encouraging distrust in incongruent or low confidence captions.

This work provided the first evaluation of full sentence algorithmically generated image captions with blind and visually impaired people, and our results have implications towards how to better adapt existing captioning systems for accessibility scenarios, such as describing social media images. This was also an initial step toward investigating ways of encouraging distrust in cases of uncertainty by intelligent systems, and we encourage researchers to pursue these questions of effective communication of that uncertainty in other domains as well.

REFERENCES

1. Stavros Antifakos, Nicky Kern, Bernt Schiele, and Adrian Schwaninger. 2005. Towards Improving Trust in Context-aware Systems by Displaying System Confidence. In *Proceedings of the 7th International Conference on Human Computer Interaction with Mobile Devices &Amp; Services* (MobileHCI '05), 9–14. https://doi.org/10.1145/1085777.1085780
2. Johannes Beller, Matthias Heesen, and Mark Vollrath. 2013. Improving the driver–automation interaction an approach using automation uncertainty. *Human Factors:*

The Journal of the Human Factors and Ergonomics Society 55, 6: 1130–1141.

3. Jeffrey P. Bigham, Chandrika Jayant, Hanjie Ji, Greg Little, Andrew Miller, Robert C. Miller, Robin Miller, Aubrey Tatarowicz, Brandyn White, Samual White, and Tom Yeh. 2010. VizWiz: Nearly Real-time Answers to Visual Questions. In *Proceedings of the 23Nd Annual ACM Symposium on User Interface Software and Technology* (UIST '10), 333–342. https://doi.org/10.1145/1866029.1866080
4. Jeffrey P. Bigham, Ryan S. Kaminsky, Richard E. Ladner, Oscar M. Danielsson, and Gordon L. Hempton. 2006. WebInSight:: Making Web Images Accessible. In *Proceedings of the 8th International ACM SIGACCESS Conference on Computers and Accessibility* (Assets '06), 181–188. https://doi.org/10.1145/1168987.1169018
5. Erin L. Brady, Yu Zhong, Meredith Ringel Morris, and Jeffrey P. Bigham. 2013. Investigating the Appropriateness of Social Network Question Asking As a Resource for Blind Users. In *Proceedings of the 2013 Conference on Computer Supported Cooperative Work* (CSCW '13), 1225–1236. https://doi.org/10.1145/2441776.2441915
6. Michele A. Burton, Erin Brady, Robin Brewer, Callie Neylan, Jeffrey P. Bigham, and Amy Hurst. 2012. Crowdsourcing Subjective Fashion Advice Using VizWiz: Challenges and Opportunities. In *Proceedings of the 14th International ACM SIGACCESS Conference on Computers and Accessibility* (ASSETS '12), 135–142. https://doi.org/10.1145/2384916.2384941
7. Eun Kyoung Choe, Jaeyeon Jung, Bongshin Lee, and Kristie Fisher. 2013. Nudging People Away from Privacy-Invasive Mobile Apps through Visual Framing. In *Human-Computer Interaction – INTERACT 2013: 14th IFIP TC 13 International Conference, Cape Town, South Africa, September 2-6, 2013, Proceedings, Part III*, Paula Kotzé, Gary Marsden, Gitte Lindgaard, Janet Wesson and Marco Winckler (eds.). Springer Berlin Heidelberg, Berlin, Heidelberg, 74–91. Retrieved from http://dx.doi.org/10.1007/978-3-642-40477-1_5
8. Eun Kyoung Choe, Bongshin Lee, Sean Munson, Wanda Pratt, and Julie A. Kientz. 2013. Persuasive Performance Feedback: The Effect of Framing on Self-Efficacy. *AMIA Annual Symposium Proceedings* 2013: 825–833.
9. Jacob Devlin, Hao Cheng, Hao Fang, Saurabh Gupta, Li Deng, Xiaodong He, Geoffrey Zweig, and Margaret Mitchell. 2015. Language Models for Image Captioning: The Quirks and What Works. In *ACL – Association for Computational Linguistics*, 100.
10. Jeff Donahue, Lisa Anne Hendricks, Sergio Guadarrama, Marcus Rohrbach, Subhashini Venugopalan, Trevor Darrell, and Kate Saenko. 2015. Long-term recurrent convolutional networks for visual recognition and description. 2625–2634. https://doi.org/10.1109/CVPR.2015.7298878
11. Jack Dorsey. 2011. search+photos. *Twitter Blogs*. Retrieved August 12, 2016 from https://blog.twitter.com/2011/searchphotos
12. Hao Fang, Saurabh Gupta, Forrest Iandola, Rupesh K. Srivastava, Li Deng, Piotr Dollar, Jianfeng Gao, Xiaodong He, Margaret Mitchell, John C. Platt, C. Lawrence Zitnick, and Geoffrey Zweig. 2015. From captions to visual concepts and back. In *Computer Vision and Pattern Recognition (CVPR), 2015 IEEE Conference on*, 1473–1482. https://doi.org/10.1109/CVPR.2015.7298754
13. Morten Goodwin, Deniz Susar, Annika Nietzio, Mikael Snaprud, and Christian S. Jensen. 2011. Global Web Accessibility Analysis of National Government Portals and Ministry Web Sites. *Journal of Information Technology & Politics* 8, 1: 41–67. https://doi.org/10.1080/19331681.2010.508011
14. Jan Hartmann, Antonella De Angeli, and Alistair Sutcliffe. 2008. Framing the User Experience: Information Biases on Website Quality Judgement. In *Proceedings of the SIGCHI Conference on Human Factors in Computing Systems* (CHI '08), 855–864. https://doi.org/10.1145/1357054.1357190
15. Tove Helldin, Göran Falkman, Maria Riveiro, and Staffan Davidsson. 2013. Presenting System Uncertainty in Automotive UIs for Supporting Trust Calibration in Autonomous Driving. In *Proceedings of the 5th International Conference on Automotive User Interfaces and Interactive Vehicular Applications* (AutomotiveUI '13), 210–217. https://doi.org/10.1145/2516540.2516554
16. Ting-Hao Kenneth Huang, Francis Ferraro, Nasrin Mostafazadeh, Ishan Misra, Aishwarya Agrawal, Jacob Devlin, Ross Girshick, Xiaodong He, Pushmeet Kohli, Dhruv Batra, and others. 2016. Visual Storytelling. In *Proceedings of the 2016 Conference of the North American Chapter of the Association for Computational Linguistics: Human Language Technologies*.
17. Andrej Karpathy and Li Fei-Fei. 2015. Deep visual-semantic alignments for generating image descriptions. In *Computer Vision and Pattern Recognition (CVPR), 2015 IEEE Conference on*, 3128–3137. https://doi.org/10.1109/CVPR.2015.7298932
18. Young-Ho Kim, Jae Ho Jeon, Eun Kyoung Choe, Bongshin Lee, KwonHyun Kim, and Jinwook Seo. 2016. TimeAware: Leveraging Framing Effects to Enhance Personal Productivity. In *Proceedings of the 2016 CHI Conference on Human Factors in Computing Systems* (CHI '16), 272–283. https://doi.org/10.1145/2858036.2858428
19. Todd Kloots. 2016. Accessible images for everyone. *Twitter Blogs*. Retrieved August 12, 2016 from https://blog.twitter.com/2016/accessible-images-for-everyone
20. Theresa M. Marteau. 1989. Framing of information: Its influence upon decisions of doctors and patients. *British*

Journal of Social Psychology 28, 1: 89–94. https://doi.org/10.1111/j.2044-8309.1989.tb00849.x

21. Valerie S. Morash, Yue-Ting Siu, Joshua A. Miele, Lucia Hasty, and Steven Landau. 2015. Guiding Novice Web Workers in Making Image Descriptions Using Templates. *ACM Transactions on Accessible Computing* 7, 4: 1–21. https://doi.org/10.1145/2764916
22. Meredith Ringel Morris, Annuska Zolyomi, Catherine Yao, Sina Bahram, Jeffrey P. Bigham, and Shaun K. Kane. 2016. "With Most of It Being Pictures Now, I Rarely Use It": Understanding Twitter's Evolving Accessibility to Blind Users. In *Proceedings of the 2016 CHI Conference on Human Factors in Computing Systems* (CHI '16), 5506–5516. https://doi.org/10.1145/2858036.2858116
23. Nasrin Mostafazadeh, Ishan Misra, Jacob Devlin, Larry Zitnick, Margaret Mitchell, Xiaodong He, and Lucy Vanderwende. 2016. Generating Natural Questions About an Image. *Proceedings of the 54th Annual Meeting of the Association for Computational Linguistics*.
24. D. Prelec. 2004. A Bayesian Truth Serum for Subjective Data. *Science* 306, 5695: 462–466. https://doi.org/10.1126/science.1102081
25. Krishnan Ramnath, Simon Baker, Lucy Vanderwende, Motaz El-Saban, Sudipta N. Sinha, Anitha Kannan, Noran Hassan, Michel Galley, Yi Yang, Deva Ramanan, Alessandro Bergamo, and Lorenzo Torresani. 2014. AutoCaption: Automatic caption generation for personal photos. In *Applications of Computer Vision (WACV), 2014 IEEE Winter Conference on*, 1050–1057. https://doi.org/10.1109/WACV.2014.6835988
26. Y. Shi. 2006. E-Government Web Site Accessibility in Australia and China: A Longitudinal Study. *Social Science Computer Review* 24, 3: 378–385. https://doi.org/10.1177/0894439305283707
27. Kenneth Tran, Xiaodong He, Lei Zhang, Jian Sun, Cornelia Carapcea, Chris Thrasher, Chris Buehler, and Chris Sienkiewicz. 2016. Rich Image Captioning in the Wild. *Proceedings of CVPR 2016.*
28. Amos Tversky and Daniel Kahneman. 1985. The Framing of Decisions and the Psychology of Choice. In *Environmental Impact Assessment, Technology Assessment, and Risk Analysis: Contributions from the Psychological and Decision Sciences*, Vincent T. Covello, Jeryl L. Mumpower, Pieter J. M. Stallen and V. R. R. Uppuluri (eds.). Springer Berlin Heidelberg, Berlin, Heidelberg, 107–129. Retrieved from http://dx.doi.org/10.1007/978-3-642-70634-9_6
29. Violeta Voykinska, Shiri Azenkot, Shaomei Wu, and Gilly Leshed. 2016. How Blind People Interact with Visual Content on Social Networking Services. In *Proceedings of the 19th ACM Conference on Computer-Supported Cooperative Work & Social Computing* (CSCW '16), 1584–1595. https://doi.org/10.1145/2818048.2820013
30. Michael Wagner and Philip Koopman. 2015. A Philosophy for Developing Trust in Self-driving Cars. In *Road Vehicle Automation 2*, Gereon Meyer and Sven Beiker (eds.). Springer International Publishing, Cham, 163–171. Retrieved from http://dx.doi.org/10.1007/978-3-319-19078-5_14
31. Jacob O. Wobbrock, Leah Findlater, Darren Gergle, and James J. Higgins. 2011. The Aligned Rank Transform for Nonparametric Factorial Analyses Using Only Anova Procedures. In *Proceedings of the SIGCHI Conference on Human Factors in Computing Systems* (CHI '11), 143–146. https://doi.org/10.1145/1978942.1978963
32. Shaomei Wu and Lada A. Adamic. 2014. Visually Impaired Users on an Online Social Network. In *Proceedings of the SIGCHI Conference on Human Factors in Computing Systems* (CHI '14), 3133–3142. https://doi.org/10.1145/2556288.2557415
33. Shaomei Wu, Jeffrey Wieland, Omid Farivar, and Jill Schiller. 2017. Automatic Alt-text: Computer-generated Image Descriptions for Blind Users on a Social Network Service. In *Proceedings of the 20th ACM Conference on Computer Supported Cooperative Work and Social Computing*. https://doi.org/10.1145/2998181.2998364
34. Kelvin Xu, Jimmy Ba, Ryan Kiros, Kyunghyun Cho, Aaron Courville, Ruslan Salakhudinov, Rich Zemel, and Yoshua Bengio. 2015. Show, Attend and Tell: Neural Image Caption Generation with Visual Attention. In *Proceedings of The 32nd International Conference on Machine Learning*, 2048–2057.
35. Sean Young and Daniel M. Oppenheimer. 2009. Effect of communication strategy on personal risk perception and treatment adherence intentions. *Psychology, Health & Medicine* 14, 4: 430–442. https://doi.org/10.1080/13548500902890103
36. Microsoft Cognitive Services - Computer Vision API. Retrieved August 24, 2016 from https://www.microsoft.com/cognitive-services/en-us/computer-vision-api
37. Microsoft Cognitive Services. Retrieved August 24, 2016 from https://www.microsoft.com/cognitive-services
38. CaptionBot - For pictures worth the thousand words. Retrieved August 24, 2016 from https://www.captionbot.ai/

Time Travel with One Click: Effects of Digital Filters on Perceptions of Photographs

Yilang Peng
Annenberg School for Communication
University of Pennsylvania
Philadelphia, PA
ypeng@asc.upenn.edu

ABSTRACT
Today's digital photographs are being heavily "filtered." By simple clicks on mobile apps like Hipstamatic and Instagram, users can easily apply digital filters to their pictures to create effects such as faux-vintage and light leaks. To understand the potential impacts of photo filters, we conducted an online experiment and investigated how the use of the black-and-white and film-style photo filters changed viewers' perceptions and descriptions of photographs. We found that photo filters substantially increased viewers' perceived temporal distances to photographs. Participants also tended to describe analogue-style photos more interpretively and tentatively than unfiltered ones, indicating an increase in construal levels. We suggest that the widely used photo filter is not just a tool to change aesthetics; it also adds a layer of history, meaning, and defamiliarization to photographs, allowing users to construct a mental distance in images that deviates from everyday experiences. We offer insights into the psychology of visual styles and implications for designing filter apps and photo-sharing platforms.

Author Keywords
Digital filter; construal level theory; visual style; mobile app; computational text analysis

ACM Classification Keywords
H.5.m. Information interfaces and presentation (e.g., HCI): Miscellaneous.

INTRODUCTION
Today's visual culture is characterized by the widespread use of digital photo filters. With filter apps like Instagram or VSCOcam, users can easily apply interesting effects to their pictures, for example, simulating the look of analogue photography or transforming a picture into a sketch (Figure 1). It is estimated that about half of the photos uploaded to Instagram have been processed by one of its retro filters [30]. According to a parenting website, millennial parents are even naming their babies after Instagram filters [5].

Figure 1. Photos processed by different mobile filter apps, with specific filter names in brackets.

As a technological innovation and a cultural phenomenon, the photo filter has invited a lot of discussion in the media [2, 9, 14]. Some have celebrated that filter apps provide ordinary users with convenient ways of exercising creativity and producing shareable images, while others have questioned whether the prevalence of photo filters encourages the visual sameness in photography or harms the credibility in photography by adding a fake layer of history and sentiment to pictures [2, 9, 14]. Despite the HCI's community's long-standing interest in photographic practices (e.g., [29]), not many studies have empirically tested the effects of photo filters. A few existing studies have so far mainly focused on filters' aesthetical appeal or users' motivations to use filters [6, 31, 35]. Some important aspects of the digital filter, for instance, its resemblance to analogue photography and its link to nostalgic consumption, are noticeably understudied.

Drawing inspiration from photography, psychology and art theories, we conducted a pioneering experimental study and investigated the impacts of photo filters from multiple perspectives. First, we propose that digital photo filters, by imitating the look of analogue photography and distorting the original color in photographs, can defamiliarize our experiences of ordinary objects and increase viewers' psychological distances to images. In addition, we use computational text analysis to compare viewers'

CHI 2017, May 06 - 11, 2017, Denver, CO, USA

ACM 978-1-4503-4655-9/17/05...$15.00
DOI: http://dx.doi.org/10.1145/3025453.3025810

descriptions of different versions of photos and argue that the use of photo filters can increase viewers' construal levels, leading them to perceive images more abstractly and interpretatively. At last, this study also takes participants' individual differences into account and question if they moderate filters' effects. In sum, this study provides fresh insights into the psychology of the digital filter, a popular feature of today's social media design, and offers implications for designing future photo-editing and photo-sharing technologies.

RELEVANT WORK

Aesthetic appeal

Previous research on the effects of photo filters has mainly focused on aesthetical appeal and visual engagement. Given the popularity of filters, one may simply assume that photo filters should make a picture more attractive. Users have expressed that filters allow them to improve the aesthetic quality of photos, adjust contrast, exposure or color, and make photos look fun and unique [6, 31]. However, people may prefer the original photo under certain circumstances: For example, the original photo is of good quality or the filter is so bold that it may distract viewers from the photo itself [6]. The hashtag #nofilter has also gained popularity on Instagram, signaling a user's claim that the accompanying photo has not been processed by filters [2].

Empirical studies have so far reached no decisive conclusions regarding filters' visual appeal. One study that experimentally examined the effects of three popular Instagram filters—Earlybird, Hefe, XProII—on people's aesthetical ratings of photographs found that people actually preferred unfiltered photos over filtered versions [35]. Another experiment that investigated non-photorealistic rendering—which transformed photographs into stylized paintings—showed that this technique actually had detrimental effects by reducing viewers' emotional responses to images and producing more confusion and distraction [32]. However, an analysis of Flickr photos revealed that filtered photos were 21% more likely to be viewed and 45% more likely to be commented on by viewers [6]. Specifically, filters that increased warmth, exposure or contrast, as well as those creating a vintage effect, made photographs more attractive to users. In contrast, filters that produced photographic artifacts or loss of highlight details were less engaging [6]. Given the inconsistency in previous studies, we propose a research question whether filtering photos impacts their visual appeal in this study.

RQ1: How does the use of photo filters impact the visual appeal of photographs?

Defamiliarization

The photo filter is not just an aesthetic tool; it also distorts the depicted reality in photographs. Some scholars argued that with filter apps users could create random and serendipitous effects in their photos, and aestheticize the imperfections embedded in analogue-look filters, thus countering the flawlessness of digital photography [12]. A comparative analysis of Instagram users and analogue photographers showed both groups used these technologies to escape from the stark reality created by digital cameras, and to give meanings and celebration to their daily experiences [31].

Such findings echo with some art theorists' claim that the defamiliarization of ordinary objects plays an important role in the production of art [38]. By presenting common things in an unusual way, the technique of defamiliarization primes viewers to pause and wonder at objects that are otherwise taken for granted, producing an artistic experience of the routinely seen. As Susan Sontag put, "the photographer is always trying to colonize new experiences or find new ways to look at familiar subjects—to fight against boredom" [40]. From this perspective, the photo filter more than changes photographs' look; it provides users with convenient and fun ways to distance their pictures from the reality as well as to elevate otherwise mundane moments.

Construal level theory

As analogue photo filters resemble an aesthetic from the past and create a deviance from the reality in photographs, a theory that particularly deals with our perceptions of distance—construal level theory (CLT)—should be relevant here. Psychologists and HCI researchers have applied the framework of CLT to study the impacts of various visual media, such as images versus words [4], teleconference [23], 3D panoramas [27], and virtual immersive environment [1]. Different communication mediums can effectively change our perceptions of distance and consequently how we think about things.

As CLT posits, the way an individual perceives an object or an event is influenced by psychological distance, which specifies how far away one feels the stimuli is from the here, now and the self. Objects or events are perceived in four dimensions of psychological distance: temporal (now vs. past or future), spatial (here vs. remote locations), social (self vs. others), and hypothetical (reality vs. counterfactual or unlikely events) [25, 44].

CLT posits that psychological distances impact how we see things. For events or objects at the far end of psychological distances, we think about them in abstract ways (high construal level). In contrast, for things at the near end of psychological distances, we perceive them in a more concrete and detailed way (low construal level). In addition, changing construal level can also influence people's perceptions of psychological distances. For example, thinking about actions in an abstract instead of a concrete way leads people to estimate the actions would happen in the more distant future [24].

Color vs. black-and-white

Research has shown that B&W and color photography

impact our perceptions of content in different ways [19, 21, 22, 41]. Particularly, previous research has shown that B&W photography is linked to more abstract, superordinate construal, while color photography is associated with more concrete, detail-oriented construal [21], which may offer us some insights into the effects of photo filters. The link between monochrome imagery and high construal level may have several explanations.

First, B&W photography completely removes the color from the original photos, creating a monochrome world that is not familiar to the naked eye [21]. The loss of color and the defamiliarization of the depicted objects in B&W photographs can make it more difficult for viewers to recognize and process the content in the photographs [22, 41]. Meanwhile, as people generally associate distant objects with difficulties to observe and apprehend, cognitive disfluency can increase psychological distance and construal level. For instance, subjects assigned to a questionnaire printed in an illegible font wrote more abstract answers than those seeing an easily readable font [3]. Therefore, by raising the level of disfluency, B&W photography is able to increase viewers' construal level.

The temporality embedded in B&W imagery may also account for the increase in psychological distance. Since color photography replaced B&W photography as the prevailing form of photography around the 1960s–1970s, people may associate monochrome imagery with a more distant past. Movies like *American History X* (1998) and *The Phantom of the Opera* have exploited the temporal connotation in B&W imagery and used it to represent the scenes that happened before the scenes in color. Photographers also argue that B&W pictures have a more timeless look than colored ones [34]. For instance, the World Press Photo of the Year 2015 was awarded to a B&W photograph, as "it's a very classical photo, and at the same time it's timeless" [47].

In addition, monochrome photos highlight the depicted objects' overall shapes and forms, while color photos facilitate attention to details and local features [21]. Compared to a B&W version, colored presentation of messages often draw people's attention to more peripheral, irrelevant and detailed information [19], reflecting low-level construal. In summary, the defamiliarization of reality, the loss of color and details, and the unique visual style associated with a certain time period, may all link B&W imagery to high construal level.

Photo filters and construal levels

Similar to the effects of monochrome imagery, analogue photo filters may also increase psychological distance and construal level by distorting the original photographs and creating a visual style that deviates from the reality. Without the aid of original colors, people might need additional efforts to retrieve and process the messages conveyed in filtered photographs. In addition, different aesthetic styles of photography are often linked to different time periods. The transition from film photography to digital photography happened around the 1990s and 2000s [26]. Studies also linked the use of photo filter apps to a nostalgic desire to connect with the past [12, 31]. Therefore, we should expect that filters that imitate certain historical styles of photography should influence how viewers construct the temporal distance of photographs.

H1: Compared to the original version, the use of B&W and film-style photo filters increases viewers' perceptions of temporal distance to photos.

As CLT posits, people experience different psychological distances—whether it is temporal, spatial, interpersonal or hypothetical—through similar mental mechanisms [7, 44]. Things perceived as distant or close in one dimension are also likely to be perceived similarly in other dimensions. If photo filters can increase perceived temporal distance, this effect should also extend to perceived spatial distance.

H2: Compared to the original version, the use of B&W and film-style photo filters increases viewers' perceptions of spatial distance to photos.

Construal level also impacts how people construct and describe events or objects. People tend to use more abstract and interpretative language to describe people or events that are psychologically far away [15, 25]. Based on previous research, we expect that different construal levels should be reflected in the following linguistic features:

Articles and numbers. Articles (e.g., "a," "the") are often used to refer to concrete objects or events, and numbers are used to specify the quantity. These two features may signal a high level of linguistic concreteness [33]. In one study, articles and numbers negatively correlated with the level of interpretation and linguistic abstraction in participants' descriptions of photographs [8].

Tentative words. Linguistic abstraction is related to the level of interpretation [8]. When construal level increases, people tend to make assumptions about events, instead of describing what they directly see. In one study, when describing a place, subjects' use of tentative words positively correlated with their estimation of the physical distance of that place [27]. As photo filters may increase psychological distance and construal level, we expect that subjects use fewer articles or numbers but more tentative words (e.g., *maybe*, *perhaps*, *or*, *guess*) for filtered photographs.

H3: Compared to the original version, viewers describe the B&W and film-style filtered photos in a more abstract and interpretative manner, which is manifested in (a) fewer articles and numbers, and (b) more tentative words.

Individual characteristics

At last, a few individual factors may impact how one sees and interprets photographs, moderating the impacts of photo filters. As many photo filters imitate visual styles from certain periods, age should play a role here as people of different age cohorts may differ in their exposure to various photographic aesthetics and technologies. People from the older generations might have witnessed how photographic aesthetics changed over decades, either from B&W to color photography or from film to digital photography. The younger generations might have less memory of the history of photography while being more familiar with widely accessible photo-filtering apps that can easily change the look of photographs.

In addition, people's knowledge of photography and involvement in photography can also influence whether they can recognize the potential manipulation in photographs and how they use digital filters. In one experiment, exposure to the technique of photographic manipulation led participants to regard news images less believable [39]. Interviews of filter users suggested that casual users often applied filters to substantially change the look of their photos with bold effects and visual artifacts, whereas serious amateurs who had experiences with professional cameras and post-editing software tended to use filters to do tasks like color correction and prefer more subtle effects [6]. However, previous studies have rarely examined the roles of individual differences, so this study proposes a research question regarding the potential moderating roles of participants' age and photographic knowledge in the effects of photo filters.

RQ2: Do viewers' age and photographic knowledge moderate the impacts of photo filters?

METHOD

Participants

A total of 201 participants located in the United States were recruited from the crowdsourcing platform Amazon Mechanical Turk [11]. Some demographic characteristics of the participants were obtained, including gender (56.7% female), age (M = 36.2, SD = 12.4), and education attainment (high school graduate or less = 13.4%, some college = 27.9%, college degree = 46.8%, and postgraduate = 11.9%).

Procedure

Participants were randomly assigned into three conditions (between-subjects): original (N = 72), B&W (N = 63) and film-style (N = 66). Each participant was exposed to ten photos and instructed to describe each photo as well as answer several questions about it. One subject in the film-style condition was removed from the dataset as he/she was repeating the same sentence in the descriptions of different photos, which resulted in a sample size of 200.

Stimuli

Ten photographs—referred as P1–P10 in the paper—were used in the study, which covered a wide range of topics, such as war, celebrity, festival and environmental pollution. All the photos featured some people with actions and a moderate amount of details so viewers could potentially engage in some levels of interpretations about these people's intentions or behaviors. These photos were also linked to some kind of event or remote places since participants were asked to estimate when and where the photo was taken in the study. All the photos were cropped and displayed in the same size (width 730px, ratio 3:2). Photos were processed with two filters (B1 and P8) from the mobile photo-editing app VSCOcam, which gave them a B&W, or a film-style, instant Polaroid look, respectively. Figure 2 illustrates how the same photo differs across the three conditions.

Figure 2. Examples of photos across three conditions.

Measures

Visual appeal. We constructed the scale based on previous research on the interestingness of news photographs [16]. The scale had four five-point items (α = .839): *the photo is of good quality*; *the photo draws my attention*; *the photo provokes emotions in me*; *I would like to know the story behind the photo*. Participants' ratings of the ten photographs were averaged.

Perception of temporal distance. On a scale from 1980 to 2016, participants indicated in which year they thought the photo was taken. Participants' perceived temporal distance was calculated by subtracting their averaged estimates of the ten photographs from 2016.

Perception of spatial distance. One a scale from 0 to 10000 miles, participants estimated how far away each photo was taken from where they were. To give them a reference point, participants were told that the distance between New York and San Francisco was about 2500 miles. In CLT literature, estimation of distance has been conventionally used as a proxy for psychological distance [3, 27]. Participants' estimates of the ten photographs were averaged.

Linguistic features. For each photo, participants were asked to describe the photo in a few sentences. In this study, we chose the software Linguistic Inquiry and Word Count (LIWC) to computationally analyze subjects' descriptions of photographs. LIWC is a program that categorizes words into psychologically meaningful categories, which has been widely used in the field of psycholinguistics [43]. Given that the average length of participants' descriptions was very short (M = 21.4 words, SD = 11.5), we used the averaged numbers of words belonging to the *article*, *number*, and *tentative* categories as dependent variables instead of LIWC's default metrics (percentage of words), as percentage measures tended to be unstable when divisors were small [20]. The length of participants' descriptions did not significantly vary by condition, $F(2, 197) = 0.91$, n.s.

Photographic knowledge. On five-point scales ranging from *no understanding* to *full understanding* (α = .942), participants indicated how familiar they were with the following terms: *exposure*, *aperture*, *white balance*, *depth of field* and *HDR* (M = 2.50, SD = 1.12).

ANALYSIS AND RESULTS

For R1, H1, H2, and H3, we conducted a series of ANOVA tests and planned contrasts that compared the means of the two filtered conditions to the original condition. Table 1 provides the correlations among the dependent variables examined in the study.

	temporal distance	spatial distance	article	number	tentative
visual appeal	−.115	.003	−.032	−.073	−.067
temporal distance		−.016	.001	−.041	.024
spatial distance			−.059	−.084	.001
article				.652*** (.064)	.599*** (−.407***)
number					.404*** (−.240***)

Table 1. Correlation matrix of dependent variables. Partial correlations among linguistic features controlled for the length of descriptions are provided in brackets. N = 200. ** p < .01, *** p < .001.

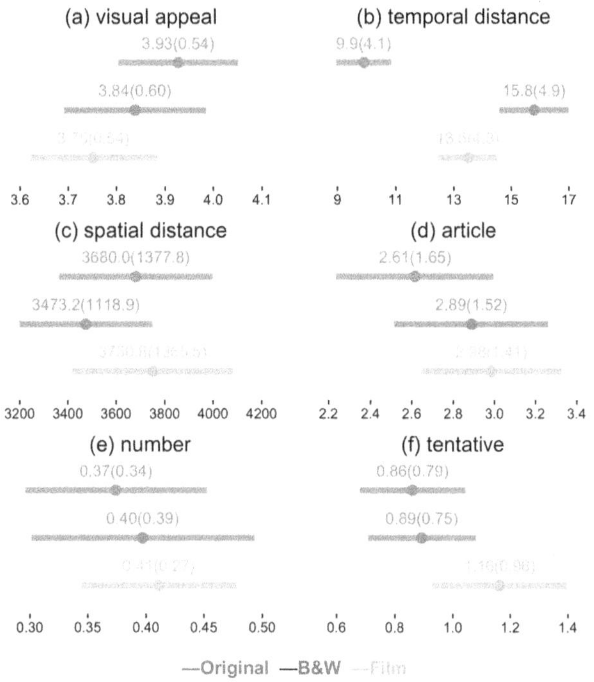

Figure 3. Means and standard deviations in brackets for dependent variables across three conditions. Error bars represent 95% confidence intervals.

Impacts on visual appeal

RQ1 asked whether the photo filters influenced photographs' visual appeal. There were no significant differences among the three conditions, $F(2, 197) = 1.69$, n.s. (Figure 3a). Additional planned contrasts, however, indicated that film-style filter might decrease photographs' visual appeal, though this trend was only approaching statistical significance, $p = .068$, Cohen's $d = 0.33$.

Impacts on psychological distances

H1 predicted that the B&W and the film-style filters increased viewers' perceptions of temporal distance, which was supported by the results (Figure 3b). There were significant differences among the three conditions in terms of participants' average estimation of temporal distances, $F(2, 197) = 30.74$, $p < .001$, partial $\eta^2 = .238$. According to participants' estimates, B&W and film-style filtered pictures were taken 5.90 ($p < .001$, $d = 1.31$) and 3.60 years ($p < .001$, $d = 0.86$) earlier on average than the original version.

H2 predicted that the two photo filters impacted people's perceptions of spatial distance, which was not supported by the results. No significant differences were found, $F(2, 197) = 0.79$, n.s. (Figure 3c).

Impacts on LWIC linguistic features

H3 looked at how different photo filters impacted the linguistic features of people's textual descriptions of the photographs. In terms of articles and numbers (H3a), ANOVA tests and planned comparisons showed no differences, $F(2, 197) = 1.09$ and 0.21, respectively, n.s. (Figure 3d, 3e).

The differences among participants' use of tentative words (H3b) were approaching statistical significance, $F(2, 197) = 2.60$, $p = .077$, partial $\eta^2 = .026$. Planned contrasts revealed that the film-style filter led subjects to use 0.30 more tentative words on average in each description, which was statistically significant ($p < .05$, $d = 0.34$), but B&W filter did not have a significant effect (n.s.) (Figure 3f).

Table 2 provides some examples of participants' descriptions that differ in the use of tentative words. Under low construal levels, subjects described the photo in

	Photo	Low tentative	High tentative
P1		A group of children smile up at the camera with their hands outstretched.	A group of African children. They appear rather healthy and vibrant. It appears that they are playing a game, most likely football with a home made ball.
P2		A new born baby is being weighed, checked, and wrapped. In comparison to everybody in the picture's hands then the baby is extremely small.	This is a baby is some sort of trauma. It may have been born prematurely or the mother may be hurt in some way. Doctors are trying to help the baby.
P4	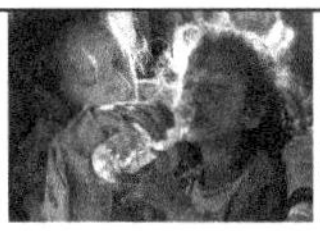	An American soldier is giving water to a young girl. The girl has a number 2 on her forehead.	The little girl is a survivor from some sort of traumatic event or natural disaster. It is very endearing to see the soldier comforting her and taking care of her.
P6		A helicopter has just dropped of US troops in the desert. The solder's form a circle on the ground with their guns drawn pointing outwards. Their packs besides them.	Looks like location is somewhere in the desert, possibly middle east. Soldiers are defending a landing zone for possible evacuation.
P7		This is a man holding a small turtle above a fishing net. The man is wearing a dirty white outfit and the sleeves are duck taped shut. He is standing on a boat with this turtle.	An oil covered turtle being held by a worker in a white coverall. This seems to be part of an environmental recovery and rescue attempt, probably after some kind of oil spill.

Table 2. Examples of participants' descriptions differing in the use of tentative words (underscored).

concrete details and used few tentative words. In contrast, subjects under high construal levels made inferences or hypotheses about the situation and people's intention, which led to an increase in tentative words (e.g., *or*, *some*, *possibly*).

Individual characteristics

RQ2 asked whether individual characteristics moderated the impacts of photo filters. We used a regression-based approach to better detect the interactions between categorical and continuous variables while retaining the moderators' effects on the outcomes [46]. Using effect coding, the analysis treated the original condition as the

	visual appeal	temporal distance	spatial distance	article	number	tentative
B&W	.026	$.439^{***}$	−.093	.042	−.001	−.084
film	$-.153^{+}$	.060	.067	.088	.052	$.205^{*}$
age	$.162^{*}$	$-.192^{**}$	.039	.055	−.073	.061
PK	$.211^{**}$	−.016	.074	−.119	−.089	$-.183^{*}$
age × B&W	.025	.088	.040	.023	−.051	−.139
age × film	$-.139^{+}$	$-.136^{+}$	−.095	−.063	.055	.079
PK × B&W	−.077	−.111	.008	−.062	.032	$-.173^{*}$
PK × film	$.145^{+}$	.026	−.006	.134	−.007	.108

Table 3. Regression analysis with interaction effects between individual characteristics and experimental conditions. Standardized coefficients are shown. PK = photographic knowledge. $^{+}p < .10$, $^{*}p < .05$, $^{**}p < .01$, $^{**}p < .001$.

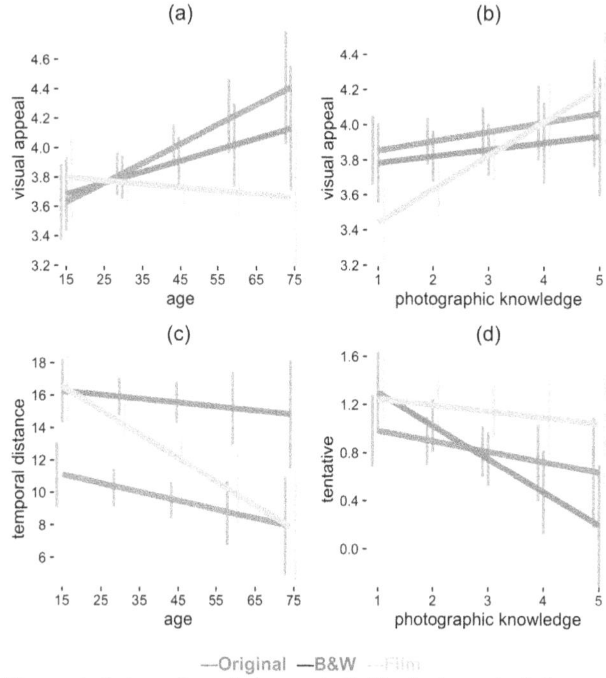

Figure 4. Interactions between individual characteristics and experimental conditions. Error bars represent 95% confidence intervals.

reference level and recoded the other two conditions as B&W (original = −1, B&W = 1, film = 0) and film (original = −1, B&W = 0, film = 1). We created four interaction terms that multiplied moderators (mean-centered) by experimental conditions.

As summarized in Table 3, one interaction term (photographic knowledge × B&W) was significant ($\beta = -.173$, $p < .05$) in predicting linguistic tentativeness, while three interaction terms were approaching statistical significance—age × film ($\beta = -.139$, $p = .095$) and photographic knowledge × film ($\beta = .145$, $p = .087$) in predicting visual appeal, and age × film in predicting temporal distance ($\beta = -.136$, $p = .067$).

We further illustrated the interaction patterns in Figure 4. Both age ($\beta = .162, p < .05$) and photographic knowledge ($\beta = .211, p < .01$) had positive impacts on visual appeal. However, while the younger generation found different versions of photographs equally appealing, the film-style filter decreased photos' visual appeal for older viewers (Figure 4a). In addition, while viewers who were knowledgeable about photography liked all three versions, less knowledgeable participants particularly found the analogue-style photographs unappealing (Figure 4b). Age also decreased perceived temporal distance ($\beta = -.192, p < .01$). The B&W filter increased perceived temporal distance among participants across all age groups, but the use of film-style filter only impacted the younger participants (Figure 4c). At last, the more knowledgeable about photography people were, the less tentative they were in the descriptions ($\beta = -.183, p < .01$). This trend was most prominent in the B&W condition (Figure 4d).

Post-hoc analysis of linguistic features

As an exploratory step, we also applied a text mining technique to investigate other potential ways of how photo filters might impact participants' language use—specifically, what linguistic features could best differentiate the three experimental conditions. The analysis used participants' descriptions as text input and the three experiment conditions as the labels to be predicted. We then extracted terms that had the strongest correlations with each condition—in other words, terms subjects used disproportionately more in one condition versus the other two [28]. Given the effects of photo filters are not widely examined in previous research, this data-driven approach in linguistic analysis—sometimes referred as the "open-vocabulary approach"—should generate new insights that might not be captured by pre-defined word categories and present a more comprehensive picture of digital filters' effects, providing directions for future research [37].

Figure 5 summarizes the results for each photograph. We only looked at unigrams (single words) that appeared at least 5 times in the descriptions. We also retained all the words that passed the significance test of $p < 0.05$ without further adjusting p-levels. It is important to acknowledge that this section of analysis is exploratory and might produce spurious positives. Other studies that adopt a similar approach often use a more stringent significance level corrected for the number of features examined (e.g., [37]). However, compared to those studies using big data, this study had an extremely small dataset ($N = 200$), and doing so would substantially reduce our power to detect potential differences. Future studies are needed to corroborate the following interpretations.

Based on the analysis, we can notice several trends:

Tentativeness. Consistent with our previous findings, participants used more words that indicate tentativeness for analogue-style filtered images, including P1 (*probably*, *seems*, *or*), P2 (*perhaps*, *appears*, *maybe*), P4 (*sort*), P5

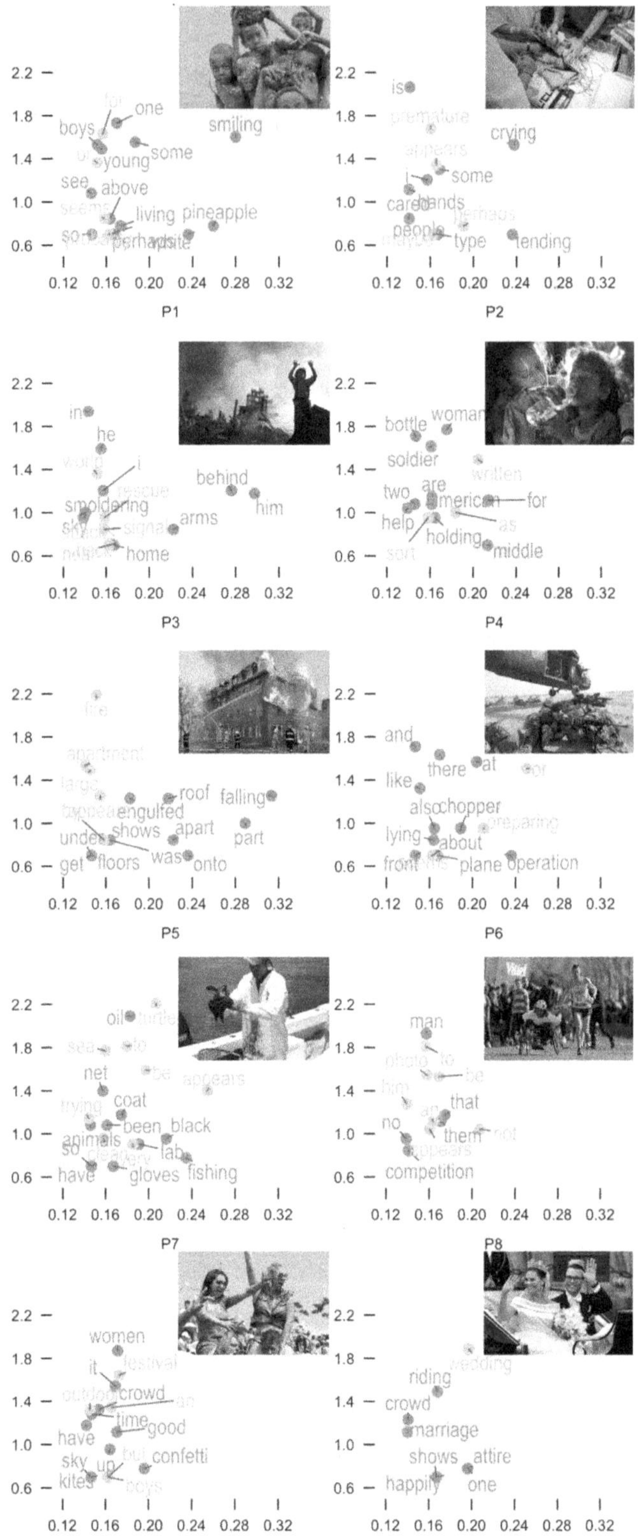

Figure 5. Terms used by participants that best differentiate the three conditions (original, B&W, and film) in each photo. Horizontal axes represent correlation coefficients and vertical axes represent log-transformed frequencies.

Credit: P1, IamNotUnique/Flickr; P2, Israel Defense Forces/Flickr; P5, Sylvain Pedneault/Wikipedia; P7, NOAA; P8, Marie-Lan Nguyen/Wikipedia; P9, Stinkie Pinkie/Flickr; P10, Holger Motzkau/Wikipedia; Others in Public domain.

(*appears*), P6 (*or*, *seems*), P7 (*appears*, *trying*), and P8 (*appears*). B&W filter also led participants to use more tentative words in P1 (*some*, *perhaps*) and P2 (*some*). Interestingly, participants also used more "I" when describing P2 and P3. Further inspection of participants' use of first-person pronouns suggested that this often signaled expressing personal interpretations (e.g., "I am guessing...," "I presume...," "I think...") or uncertainty (e.g., "I cannot tell if...," "I could be wrong...") in the sample. These trends corroborated the claim that the use of photo filters might lead to tentativeness and analytic thinking, indicating an increase in construal level.

Accuracy. The use of B&W photo filter might lead subjects to incorrectly identify the objects in pictures. For example, in P1, subjects in the B&W condition were more likely to say that one child was holding a *pineapple*, though the object was actually a handmade ball. In P6, subjects tended to see the helicopter as a *plane* in the B&W version, instead of a *chopper* in the original version. In P9, participants tended to see the small objects flying in the sky as *confetti*, but they were actually *kites*, noted by viewers who saw the unfiltered version. This trend seemed to indicate that by removing the original color in photos, B&W filters might make it more difficult for viewers to recognize the content in images, which could lead to more errors.

Details. Subjects seeing the original version seemed to be more likely to mention details in the background or objects in the periphery. For example, subjects noticed a *fishing net* shown at the bottom of P7, the *kites* flying in the background in P7, and mentioned the *sky* more in P3 and P9. They also noted that the person on the left in P4 was an *American soldier*—possibly due to the mark on her clothes—while participants in the B&W condition simply referred her as a *woman*. Meanwhile, B&W pictures seemed to highlight the contrast between black and white regions, making objects that were originally in black or white more prominent to viewers. For example, participants in the B&W condition tended to point out the white *lab coat* and black *gloves* in P7, and the B&W wedding *attire* in P10. Participants also seemed to pay more attention to the people in B&W photographs, as they mentioned more the *young boys* in P1, the *woman* in P4, the *man* in P8, and the *women* in P9—though this might also due to people in B&W used more vague and abstract terms to refer to people.

Emotion. Participants were more likely to mention the emotional expression in B&W photographs. They were more inclined to say that the children were *smiling* in P1, the baby was *crying* in P2, the girls were having a *good time*, and the couple were behaving *happily* in P10. This observation seemed to echo with some photographers' claim that B&W could accentuate emotional expressions in photographs [34].

DISCUSSION

With the wide availability of camera phones and online photo-sharing platforms, more and more people are practicing photography. A variety of photo filter apps have also changed the way of photo-editing, providing average users with easy and fun ways of reworking their photos. This work probes into this technocultural phenomenon and demonstrates how the use of photo filters could shape our perceptions and interpretations of images. The findings have implications in multiple aspects.

Understanding affordances of photo filters

Available HCI studies on the effects of photo filters have so far mainly focused on visual engagement and yielded contradictory results [6, 32, 35]. In this study, the film-style filter might actually decrease visual appeal, though this effect did not reach the conventional level of statistical significance. In addition, this research brought the concepts of defamiliarization and psychological distance into our understanding of visual styles. People found both B&W and film-style filtered photographs more distant than unfiltered ones on the temporal dimension, and the effect sizes were quite large. People also used more tentative words when describing film-style filtered images—which appeared as a medium-size effect—indicating an increase in personal interpretation and construal levels.

The post-hoc analysis of linguistic features not only corroborated the finding that using the digital filter increased linguistic tentativeness but also provided some new insights. Particularly, the use of B&W filters might highlight the emotional expressions in photos but make it more difficult for viewers to correctly identify the objects, while unfiltered photos made participants notice more background details that might be easily ignored in filtered versions. These findings seemed to suggest that photo filters did increase construal levels by decreasing cognitive fluency and shifting viewers' attention from local details to global themes in pictures. Nevertheless, future studies are needed to further examine these claims generated from the exploratory analysis.

The two filters studied also had distinct effects. Compared to the film-style filter, the B&W filter evoked a stronger sense of past but failed to statistically significantly influence visual appeal or linguistic tentativeness. Interestingly, the trend that photographic literacy decreased tentativeness was most salient in the B&W condition (Figure 4d). This might be due to that B&W photography has been long and commonly practiced among amateur photographers—especially in documentary photography and portrait photography [14, 34, 47]—thus not being seen as a novel or unfamiliar visual style by photographically knowledgeable participants. While the B&W filter substantially distorts the look of a photo by completely removing its color, it might have less defamiliarization effect to provoke higher levels of mental construal than the film-style filter.

In combination, this study highlights filters' potential multi-sided effects. A visually unfamiliar filter might make an image more difficult to process and less appealing.

However, the digital filter may also defamiliarize objects that are often seen as banal and commonplace, and help users construct a temporal distance in their photos. The defamiliarization might also provoke mental activities of high construal levels, such as imagination, contemplation, and interpretation, which are essential in creating artistic experiences.

Design photo filters and visual interfaces

This study indicates that digital filter is more than an aesthetical tool and app designers might construct different filters that fulfill certain purposes. For users who want to distance their photos from the reality, designers might provide a visually unfamiliar filter that imitates the look of analogue photography—like the one used in this study—to evoke a sense of time as well as more contemplation and analytic thinking among viewers. For users who want to candidly record the moments they capture in photos, designers might provide filters that do not substantially distort the original look of photos.

When designing visual aesthetics, practitioners should also take the characteristics of the users into account. For example, in the results, the analogue-look filter was not popular among people who were older and who had less knowledge about photography, while the younger generation and more knowledgeable viewers appreciated filtered and unfiltered versions almost equally (Figure 4). Therefore, photo-editing apps might be improved by being tailored to different types of users. For example, social media apps like Instagram might change their default order of photo filters for different people and recommend certain filters to users that they might most appeal to.

It might also be interesting to design features that allow users to preview the potential effects of applying different filters before they publish their photos to online social networks. For example, the linguistic analysis in the study implies that textual data like comments on photographs can be a rich source of discovering potential patterns of digital filters' effects. One might use the huge amount of social media data or findings from crowdsourcing experiments like this study to develop algorithms that can reliably predict the social feedbacks a photo might receive if processed by one particular filter. As some computer vision works have already started to use computationally calculated visual features to predict images' popularity and users' emotional status [36, 45], this should be a promising direction for future research and design.

The HCI community has also been interested in how to better visualize temporal data in different interfaces (e.g., [17]). This study suggested that the impacts of digital filters on perceived temporal distances were quite prominent. Therefore, it might be possible for designers to use different filters to visualize temporal data while simultaneously producing the psychological feelings of time. For example, in a newsfeed that predominantly features images and videos, using photo filters might be an easy way to effectively convey temporal information to viewers. Additionally, future studies might also examine what exact visual components of photo filters—for example, a change in saturation or a warm hue—that contribute to their effects on our perceptions of images and see if these effects also extend to abstract color schemes or visual artifacts that can be more widely applied in design.

The results may also indicate that some levels of distortion and defamiliarization in visual communication design might be valuable as they can reshape users' experiences of the familiar and the ordinary. As previous research has indicated, people take photos not only to document moments of their lives and share them within their social networks but also to elevate these special moments from their everyday experiences [18, 29]. Filter apps might allow users to add an additional layer to the documented, to rework the present as a potential past, and to distance their pictures from the mundane and the realistic. Future research may wish to examine how visual styles might impact our involvement with other types of visual media, such as videos and virtual environments.

Construal level theory and application

This study also contributes to our understanding of CLT. The use of B&W and film-style indeed increased perceived temporal distance, though the effect did not extend to the spatial dimension as hypothesized. The correlation between perceived temporal distance and spatial distance was also not statistically significant (Table 1), which seemed to contradict CLT's claim that all psychological distances are correlated. One explanation might be that the heterogeneity in participants' locations might add too much statistical noise to the analysis. Based on IP addresses, additional analysis that only included participants located in the contiguous United States ($N = 193$) and controlled for their states and geographic coordinates, however, still revealed no significant differences. Another explanation might be that participants were unable to translate psychologically felt distances to estimates of concrete numbers. Nevertheless, some previous research did point out that priming distance on the temporal dimension did not always influence people's perception of spatial distance, arguing that the spatial dimension is more primary than the temporal one [10, 48]. Further studies may use participants located in one location and photos of the same location—for instance, a famous landmark—with more subjective measures of spatial distance to see if filters impact perceptions of spatial distance.

Future studies can also examine the exact mechanism of how an analogue-style filter shapes people's interpretation of photographs. In this study, subjects' perceived temporal distance did not correlate with the linguistic features in their description (Table 1), which seemed to indicate that it was not the temporal distance that mediated the impacts of visual styles on viewers' construal levels. Thus, other mechanisms, such as color distortion, cognitive disfluency, and defamiliarization might play a role in the process, which suggests arenas for future research. In addition, the number of tentative words used did negatively correlate with the number of articles ($r = -.407$, $p < .001$) and numbers ($r = -.240$, $p < .001$) used, when the average length of descriptions was controlled for (Table 1). This seems to suggest that the use of articles and numbers could still signal higher certainty and lower construal level, but was not sensitive enough to reveal the effects of photo filters on language use in this study.

As psychological distance and construal level can shape people's attitudes and behaviors, the HCI community has been increasingly interested in applying CLT in designing persuasive messages and technologies (e.g., [42]). An increase in construal level can lead people to focus on more primary features of objects, think about actions in terms of goals instead of means, and interpret people's behaviors based on dispositions rather than specific situations [25]. Therefore, we can also use different visual styles to effectively change how people perceive things and their subsequent attitudes and behaviors. In an experiment, the use of B&W photography led people to focus more on the primary function of a product rather than its secondary features [21]. The photo filter might serve as a convenient tool for us to engineer attitudinal and behavioral changes via changing construal level.

Limitations

The current study has several limitations. First, only ten photos were used in the study and the photos chosen might be too specific to represent all genres of photographs. Future studies can further our investigation by looking at other categories of images, such as landscape, portrait and food. In addition, the photos used in the study were generally of good quality: viewers gave them an average rating of 3.84 on a 5-point scale of visual appeal. Future research may examine how filters impact more amateurish, technically flawed or low-quality pictures. The effects of photo filters might not be consistent across different kinds of photos. Future studies might also wish to look into the potential moderating roles of photos' characteristics.

As many images are viewed, edited and circulated on mobile screens these days, future studies might wish to ask participants to view photographs on mobile phones instead of computers. Previous research suggests that different photo sizes can impact people's aesthetical evaluation of photographs [13], and it would be interesting to see if the screen size moderates the impacts of filters. We also used between-subjects design in this experiment in order to prevent subjects from recognizing the presence of filters and consequently adjusting their answers. But this strategy might not fully simulate users' experience of picking up one filter from multiple options on their mobile apps, and future research can also explore this direction.

At last, the study only examined two filters in this study. In addition to distorting colors, mobile filters can also change the photograph by adding grains, scratches, vignette, frames and light leaks, or even transforming it into a painting (Figure 1). Given the diversity in today's photo filters, future studies might further investigate the effects of other types of filters as well as different components of filters.

CONCLUSION

We examine how the widely used photo filters impact people's perceptions and interpretations of photographs, inspired by defamiliarization theory and construal level theory. We showed that the use of two photo filters—one B&W and one analogue-style—substantially increased viewers' perceived temporal distances to photographs, but not spatial distance. Subjects also tended to describe analogue-style filtered photos more interpretively and tentatively than unfiltered ones, indicating an increase in construal level. Individual characteristics like age and photographic knowledge moderated the impacts of filters. We offer insights into visual styles, photographic practices and construal level theory, and provide implications for designing photo filters and visual interfaces.

REFERENCES

1. Ahn, S. J. 2015. Incorporating immersive virtual environments in health promotion campaigns: A construal level theory approach. *Health Communication* 30, 6: 545–556.

2. Alper, M. 2014. War on Instagram: Framing conflict photojournalism with mobile photography apps. *New Media & Society* 16, 8: 1233–1248.

3. Alter, A. L. and Oppenheimer, D. M. 2008. Effects of fluency on psychological distance and mental construal (or why New York is a large city, but *New York* is a civilized jungle). *Psychological Science* 19, 2: 161–167.

4. Amit, E., Algom, D., and Trope, Y. 2009. Distance-dependent processing of pictures and words. *Journal of Experimental Psychology: General* 138, 3: 400–415.

5. BabyCenter. 2015. Hottest baby name trends of 2015. Online article. (December 2015). Retrieved May 2, 2016 from: http://www.babycenter.com/0_hottest-baby-name-trends-of-2015_10408983.bc

6. Bakhshi, S., Shamma, D. A., Kennedy, L., and Gilbert, E. 2015. Why we filter our photos and how it impacts engagement. In *Proceedings of the International AAAI Conference on Web and Social Media* (ICWSM '15), 12–21.

7. Bar-Anan, Y., Liberman, N., and Trope, Y. 2006. The association between psychological distance and construal level: Evidence from an implicit association test. *Journal of Experimental Psychology: General* 135, 4: 609–622.

8. Beukeboom, C. J., Tanis, M., and Vermeulen, I. E. 2013. The language of extraversion: Extraverted people talk more abstractly, introverts are more concrete.

Journal of Language and Social Psychology 32, 2: 191–201.

9. Bevan, K. 2012. Instagram is debasing real photography. Online article. (19 July 2012). Retrieved December 1, 2015 from: http://www.theguardian.com/technology/2012/jul/19/instagram-debasing-real-photography
10. Boroditsky, L. 2000. Metaphoric structuring: Understanding time through spatial metaphors. *Cognition* 75, 1: 1–28.
11. Buhrmester, M., Kwang, T., and Gosling, S. D. 2011. Amazon's Mechanical Turk: A new source of inexpensive, yet high-quality, data?. *Perspectives on Psychological Science* 6, 1: 3–5.
12. Chandler, L., and Livingston, D. 2012. Reframing the Authentic: photography, mobile technologies and the visual language of digital imperfection. In *Proceedings of the Global Conference, Visual Literacies: Exploring Critical Issues*, 1–15.
13. Chu, W. T., Chen, Y. K., and Chen, K. T. 2013. Size does matter: How image size affects aesthetic perception? In *Proceedings of the ACM International Conference on Multimedia*, 53–62.
14. Estrin, J. 2012. Ben Lowy: Virtually unfiltered. Online article. (2 May 2012). Retrieved May 2, 2016 from http://lens.blogs.nytimes.com/2012/05/02/ben-lowy-virtually-unfiltered/
15. Fujita, K., Henderson, M. D., Eng, J., Trope, Y., & Liberman, N. 2006. Spatial distance and mental construal of social events. *Psychological Science* 17, 4: 278–282.
16. Halonen, R. 2014. *From Photographers to Viewers– What Makes Editorial Photos Interesting?*. Licentiate thesis. Aalto University, Espoo, Finland.
17. Heer, J., Kong, N., and Agrawala, M. (2009). Sizing the horizon: the effects of chart size and layering on the graphical perception of time series visualizations. In *Proceedings of the SIGCHI Conference on Human Factors in Computing Systems* (CHI '09), 1303–1312.
18. Ito, M., and Okabe, D. 2003. Camera phones changing the definition of picture-worthy. *Japan Media Review*, August 29, 2003.
19. Katzman, N., and Nyenhuis, J. (1972). Color vs. black-and-white effects on learning, opinion, and attention. *AV Communication Review* 20, 1: 16–28.
20. Kim, H. S. 2015. Attracting views and going viral: how message features and news-sharing channels affect health news diffusion. *Journal of Communication*, 65, 3: 512–534.
21. Lee, H., Deng, X., Unnava, H. R., and Fujita, K. 2014. Monochrome forests and colorful trees: The effect of black-and-white versus color imagery on construal level. *Journal of Consumer Research* 41, 4: 1015–1032.
22. Lee, K. J. and Perrett, D. 1997. Presentation-time measures of the effects of manipulations in colour space on discrimination of famous faces. *Perception* 26, 6: 733–752.
23. Lee, M. K., Fruchter, N and Dabbish, L. 2015. Making decisions from a distance: the impact of technological mediation on riskiness and dehumanization. In *Proceedings of the ACM Conference on Computer Supported Cooperative Work & Social Computing* (CSCW '15), 1576–1589.
24. Liberman, N., Trope, Y., McCrea, S. M., and Sherman, S. J. 2007. The effect of level of construal on the temporal distance of activity enactment. *Journal of Experimental Social Psychology* 43, 1: 143–149.
25. Liberman, N., and Trope, Y. 2008. The psychology of transcending the here and now. *Science* 322, 5905: 1201–1205.
26. Lucas, H. C., and Goh, J. M. 2009. Disruptive technology: How Kodak missed the digital photography revolution. *The Journal of Strategic Information Systems* 18, 1: 46–55.
27. Marlow, J., and Dabbish, L. 2014. When is a picture not worth a thousand words? The psychological effects of mediated exposure to a remote location. *Computers in Human Behavior* 30, 824–831.
28. Mayfield, E., and Rosé, C. P. 2012. LightSIDE: Text mining and machine learning user's manual. Manual. (Spring 2012). Retrieved from http://www.cs.cmu.edu/~emayfiel/LightSIDE.pdf
29. Miller, A. D., and Edwards, W. K. (2007). Give and take: a study of consumer photo-sharing culture and practice. In *Proceedings of the SIGCHI conference on Human factors in Computing Systems* (CHI '07), 347–356.
30. Miller, J. 2013. What your Instagram filter says about you. Infographic. (19 March 2013). Retrieved May 4, 2016 from http://blog.marketo.com/2013/03/what-your-instagram-filter-says-about-you-infographic.html
31. Morlot, E. 2013. *Nostalgic Consumption Behaviours among Young Generations in Photography: A Comparative Approach of Instagram and Analogue Photography*. Master thesis. Umeå University, Umeå, Sweden.
32. Mould, D., Mandryk, R. L., and Li, H. 2012. Emotional response and visual attention to non-photorealistic images. *Computers & Graphics*, 36, 6: 658–672.
33. Pennebaker, J. W., and King, L. A. 1999. Linguistic styles: language use as an individual difference.

Journal of Personality and Social Psychology 77, 6: 1296–1312.

34. Price, N. Undated. Color vs black and white photography—What makes sense and when? Retrieved May 10, 2016 from http://www.photographyvox.com/a/color-vs-black-and-white-photography/
35. Redi, J., and Povoa I. 2014. Crowdsourcing for rating image aesthetic appeal: Better a paid or a volunteer crowd? In *Proceedings of the International ACM Workshop on Crowdsourcing for Multimedia*, 25–30.
36. Reece, A. G., and Danforth, C. M. 2016. Instagram photos reveal predictive markers of depression. Online manuscript. (13 August 2016). Retrieve September 1, 2016 from http://arxiv.org/abs/1608.03282
37. Schwartz, H. A., Eichstaedt, J. C., Kern, M. L., Dziurzynski, L., Ramones, S. M., Agrawal, M., ... and Ungar, L. H. 2013. Personality, gender, and age in the language of social media: The open-vocabulary approach. *PLOS ONE*, 8, 9: e73791.
38. Shklovsky, V. 1965. Art as technique. In *Russian Formalist Criticism*, Lemon, L. T., and Reis, M. J. (eds.). University of Nebraska Press, Lincoln, NE, 3–24.
39. Snyder, S. R. 1991. *Are Emerging Technologies Affecting the Credibility of Photographs? An Experimental Study in Photographic Believability*. Master thesis. Texas Tech University, Lubbock, TX.
40. Sontag, S. 1977. *On Photography*. Dell/Delta, New York, NY.
41. Spence, I., Wong, P., Rusan, M., and Rastegar, N. 2006. How color enhances visual memory for natural scenes. *Psychological Science* 17, 1: 1–6.
42. Suh, M. M., and Hsieh, G. 2016. Designing for future behaviors: Understanding the effect of temporal distance on planned behaviors. In *Proceedings of the CHI Conference on Human Factors in Computing Systems* (CHI '16), 1084–1096.
43. Tausczik, Y. R. and Pennebaker, J. W. 2010. The psychological meaning of words: LIWC and computerized text analysis methods. *Journal of Language and Social Psychology* 29, 1: 24–54.
44. Trope, Y. and Liberman, N. 2010. Construal-level theory of psychological distance. *Psychological Review* 117, 2: 440–463.
45. Totti, L. C., Costa, F. A., Avila, S., Valle, E., Meira Jr, W., & Almeida, V. 2014. The impact of visual attributes on online image diffusion. In *Proceedings of the ACM conference on Web science*, 42-51.
46. West, S. G., Aiken, L. S., & Krull, J. L. 1996. Experimental personality designs: Analyzing categorical by continuous variable interactions. *Journal of Personality* 64, 1: 1-48.
47. World Press Photo. 2016. World Press Photo of the Year 2015 goes to Warren Richardson. Online article. (18 February 2016). Retrieved May 10, 2016 from http://www.worldpressphoto.org/news/2016-02-18/world-press-photo-year-2015-goes-warren-richardson
48. Zhang, M., and Wang, J. 2009. Psychological distance asymmetry: The spatial dimension vs. other dimensions. *Journal of Consumer Psychology* 19, 3: 497–507.

ForgetMeNot: Active Reminder Entry Support for Adults with Acquired Brain Injury

Matthew Jamieson[1], Brian O'Neill[2], Breda Cullen[1], Marilyn Lennon[3], Stephen Brewster[1], Jonathan Evans[1]

[1] University of Glasgow, Glasgow, United Kingdom {First.Last@glasgow.ac.uk}

[2] The Disabilities Trust, Graham Anderson House, United Kigdom {Brian.ONeill@thedtgroup.org}

[3] University of Strathclyde, Glasgow, United Kingdom{Marilyn.lennon@strath.ac.uk}

ABSTRACT

Smartphone reminding apps can compensate for memory impairment after acquired brain injury (ABI). In the absence of a caregiver, users must enter reminders themselves if the apps are going to help them. Poor memory and apathy associated with ABI can result in failure to initiate such configuration behaviour and the benefits of reminder apps are lost. ForgetMeNot takes a novel approach to address this problem by periodically encouraging the user to enter reminders with unsolicited prompts (UPs). An *in situ* case study investigated the experience of using a reminding app for people with ABI and tested UPs as a potential solution to initiating reminder entry. Three people with severe ABI living in a post-acute rehabilitation hospital used the app in their everyday lives for four weeks to collect real usage data. Field observations illustrated how difficulties with motivation, insight into memory difficulties and anxiety impact reminder app use in a rehabilitation setting. Results showed that when 6 UPs were presented throughout the day, reminder-setting increased, showing UPs are an important addition to reminder applications for people with ABI. This study demonstrates that barriers to technology use can be resolved in practice when software is developed with an understanding of the issues experienced by the user group.

Author Keywords

Assistive technology; memory rehabilitation; smartphone reminding; acquired brain injury; *in situ* study; field study

ACM Classification Keywords

J.3 LIFE AND MEDICAL SCIENCES; K.4.2 Assistive technologies for persons with disabilities

CHI 2017, May 06-11, 2017, Denver, CO, USA

© 2017 ACM. ISBN 978-1-4503-4655-9/17/05...$15.00

DOI: http://dx.doi.org/10.1145/3025453.3025888

INTRODUCTION

Acquired brain injury (ABI) includes trauma to the brain arising from a head injury (e.g. road traffic accidents and falls), cardiovascular events (e.g. stroke), illnesses or diseases (e.g. brain tumour or encephalitis). In the UK, there were 348,934 hospital admissions for ABI in 2013-14 [14]. Research from the USA indicates that males between the ages of 18 and 45 are at the highest risk of a head injury [27]. Prospective memory (PM), which involves forming, maintaining and carrying out future intentions, is often impaired after brain injury [37]. Other common problems include difficulties with planning and self-monitoring, and switching between or initiating tasks [6]. This can make it difficult for people to remember to carry out everyday tasks like taking medication and attending appointments, and to perform everyday activities such as personal care and shopping.

Smartphones are ubiquitous and are relatively low cost devices that offer applications that can support memory. Such technology is particularly suited to supporting PM problems using time-based alerts and reminders. Reminding apps are often designed as digital calendars or diaries into which reminders or alerts can be entered. Smartphone reminding software has been shown to be effective in helping people to compensate for memory difficulties [13,16]. They have an advantage over traditional memory aids such as paper diaries because they can actively prompt people ahead of their intended activities [30]. Most work in this area has focussed on the efficacy of the output of reminding devices (e.g. timely prompts) [7, 10, 19, 40], rather than the issues surrounding the accurate input of the reminders so that the user can receive the prompts [3].

It may be difficult for people with memory impairments following ABI to remember to set reminders in the first place. Additionally, if people have poor insight into memory difficulties, they may fail to set a reminder because they believe they will remember a future intention unaided. One solution to this is to have a caregiver or a family member set reminders. However, it may not be possible or desirable for a third party to enter reminders on behalf of the person with ABI [31]. For example, there could be issues with privacy or simply because events come up which caregivers do not know about (e.g. a spontaneous change of plan). Furthermore, setting and abiding by one's own schedule is an important part of independent living and is one of the goals of neuropsychological rehabilitation [7,42].

In this paper, we use an *in situ* field study approach to investigate the actual issues impacting the use of a smartphone reminder app for people with memory impairments after severe ABI. We report observations and participant feedback that provides novel, real-world insights for designers and researchers developing mobile memory aid technology. To tackle the issue of initiating reminder setting behaviour we introduce unsolicited prompting as a feature in a bespoke smartphone reminder app (ForgetMeNot). Unsolicited prompts are simply periodic prompts that ask, 'Do you need to set any reminders?'. During the field study, participants set significantly more reminders when receiving UPs than when not receiving them. Feedback about the acceptability of the UPs informs the future development and use of UPs in mobile reminding software.

RELATED RESEARCH

Prompting Technology

Studies that investigated the use of prompting technology in a rehabilitation setting for people with ABI have tended to focus on efficacy of timely prompts rather than the barriers preventing independent use and reminder entry [3,10,40]. Studies that have investigated the barriers to independent assistive technology use and reminder entry for have done so using focus group or lab-based experimental studies [4, 17, 29]. The observational field study reported in this paper took place *in situ* within a rehabilitation centre which gives novel insights into the issues that prevent the use of smartphone reminding technology over a number of weeks.

Efficacy studies

Jamieson *et al.* performed a systematic review and meta-analysis of studies investigating the efficacy of reminding technologies for people with ABI. Their analysis found that the use of prompting technology was more effective (large effect size $d = 1.27$, N = 147) when compared to practice as usual or the use of a paper diary or calendar [16]. Only 5 of the 9 group studies included in this analysis had participants entering their own reminders. In the others, reminders were set by a third party such as a caregiver or the experimenters. This means that a large proportion of the evidence that prompting technology is useful for people with ABI has only investigated the output stage of reminding.

These studies reported positive user experiences and usability findings, For example, McDonald and colleagues reported that the majority of participants (9 out of 12) preferred using Google Calendar on a PC to a paper diary [19] and Svoboda and colleagues [30] found that the participants continued to use a mobile phone as a reminder up to a year after their study was completed. However, these studies offer little depth as participants were not asked for feedback during the trials when using the technology. Furthermore, there may have also been a selection bias towards recruiting participants who were keen to use technology for memory compensation. Unless the issues that impact perceived usability and acceptance of technology prior to use are investigated further, it will be difficult to tell if smartphone reminding software would be used spontaneously by people with ABI, if they would find it acceptable, or continue to use it without substantial training.

Barriers to Use

Baldwin and colleagues found four main themes after interviews discussing assistive technology use with people with memory impairments after ABI (n = 8): 1) Emotional barriers (e.g. feeling like others will evaluate you negatively for using memory aids); 2) Reverse effects (using the technology has the opposite effect to the intended one, e.g. becoming so fed up with continually being reminded that you stop wanting to complete the intended task); 3) Beliefs about memory (believing that relying on technology will impair your ability to remember) and; 4) 'it's not in my nature' (the idea that technology is not for you) [2].

De Joode *et al.* used a lab study approach to investigate the difficulties 15 participants with ABI had while entering reminders onto calendar software on a PC. Their findings echoed many of the themes described in other research, describing the internal factors such as cognition and emotion. They also described external factors such as software and environmental distractions that influence information processing and task execution. Analysis of errors showed that while people with ABI made the same kinds of errors as healthy controls, they made them more often and made a higher number of negative emotional comments during use [4].

A focus group study that investigated the issues which prevent the use of smartphone reminding apps reported that apathy (failing to initiate the use of memory aids and strategies in the first place), and poor insight and memory (not realising that they are likely to forget) were important barriers [17]. These issues present a particularly challenging problem for clinicians hoping to encourage a client to use any form of memory aid. Even if the client has received substantial training and is capable of using the memory aid, he/she may still forget to use it, or not appreciate that it is needed. In this paper, we test an app with unsolicited prompting, a feature designed to help people with memory difficulties , insight and motivation by prompting them to enter reminders.

Unsolicited Prompting

An advantage of technologies such as smartphone reminding apps over pencil and paper memory aids is that they can actively alert attention and aid memory with well-timed and relevant prompts [10]. After reminders have been entered into the device (e.g. a weekly schedule), the technology will alert the user (at a relevant time) to the events or tasks that they intended to perform. It is also possible to create software that will prompt the user prior to any input. This kind of alerting is unsolicited by the user and so these types of prompts are referred to in this paper as Unsolicited Prompts (UPs). One difficult challenge with UPs is sending reminders about specific events before any information has been provided about the user's schedule. This problem might be solved by predicting the user's upcoming events based on previous input or by sensing the environment and prompting based on this information. For example, Google Now takes information from several synced applications such as email, weather forecasts and traffic updates to give relevant reminders. The Microsoft Band senses inactivity and prompts the user accordingly. These types of prompts, if accurate and timely, could be very useful for prompting people to perform everyday activities that they might otherwise forget.

In this paper, we focus on a different type of UP – one that periodically prompts participants to enter reminders into a smartphone reminder app asking, 'Do you need to set any reminders?'. This, like the UPs included in Google Now or Microsoft Band, could help overcome issues with insight and motivation which prevent the setting of reminders. However, this type of UP also has the additional advantages of a) not requiring the computation of additional information within the software to predict the content of the reminder and b) encouraging people to think about their memory tasks and manage their own schedule, which is a key part of neuropsychological rehabilitation after ABI [42]. If someone with memory difficulties after an ABI took note of a Doctor's appointment while on the phone, but became distracted and forgot to enter it into the app, a general prompt from the app could be enough. If later they made a mental note of a task they needed to do that evening, but did not believe they would forget it, the same UP from the reminder app might get them to set the reminder (especially if the prompt gave them the option to open the app).

Interruptions

One problem with a smartphone app providing UPs is that they may become annoying, which may lead people to stop using software. Prompts and 'push' notifications from mobile devices have become ubiquitous. Pielot *et al.* reported that 15 healthy smartphone users received on average 63.5 notifications per day and rated this as 'normal' [24]. However, the majority of these notifications were social messages that may be responded to in a different way to a prompt from a reminder app to actually do something. Shirazi and colleagues reported a large-scale study of mobile users' responses to different notifications [26]. They found that social notifications were generally responded to within 30 seconds and these social apps were unlikely to be 'blacklisted' by the user (so that notifications were prevented from appearing on the device).

Prompts from Calendar apps, the closest equivalent to the prompting app used in our study, were responded to after around 5 minutes and were blacklisted more often. This may be because non-social prompts were considered less important and therefore more irritating. Paul and colleagues used a one-word-response method to investigate the emotional experiences of receiving notifications [22]. They found that while people described receiving a social notification (e.g. an email or text from another person or a social media notification) with more positive words than negative, notifications which were not social were described with a similar number of positive and negative words. Of the negative words used, the most common was 'annoying'. These findings suggest that users may not necessarily attend or positively react to UPs in all cases.

The perceived usefulness of the content of the notification is also important; Felt and colleagues found that if apps which are not perceived as useful keep sending messages then users become annoyed and more likely to delete those apps [8]. This may be a bigger issue for people with ABI as they often lack insight into their memory difficulties and so may not find a UP useful even when they do have something to remember. These issues may hinder the effectiveness and acceptability of UPs. However, these studies looking at mobile phone interruptions have been carried out with high functioning, healthy people who use a mobile phone regularly. Little is known about how interruptions are perceived by people with ABI. Rehabilitation researchers highlight the low employment rates [37] and social isolation of people with ABI [5] so this may not be a group who already receive high volumes of notifications. It is possible that users receiving a low volume of notifications may find unsolicited interruptions more acceptable than those already receiving many notifications throughout the day.

Study Aims

Using an *in situ* field study, we investigated the issues that impact the use of a smartphone reminder system by people with cognitive impairment including memory difficulties after acquired brain injury. We also evaluated the impact of unsolicited prompting on reminder setting and acceptability.

METHOD

Participants and setting

The study involved three adults with self-reported memory difficulties after ABI. It took place within a 25 bed post-acute rehabilitation hospital in the UK for people with severe ABI. This is a living environment with 24-hour support, staffed by nurses, support workers, psychologists, speech and language therapists, occupational therapists and physiotherapists. Each service user has his/her own room, there are two communal lounge areas, two dining room areas, a laundry room, exercise studio and a kitchen. Difficulties in carrying out future intentions (prospective memory difficulties) are extremely common amongst the group. Between 23 and 25 service users were living in the unit during the study. This study setting was ideal because it allowed close observation of service users living in their normal environment where they have to remember several everyday tasks (e.g. medication, laundry, their daily rehabilitation schedule). University of Glasgow ethics committee and ethical approval from the rehabilitation organisation involved was granted for this study on 02.03.15 and 03.03.15 2014 respectively. All participants provided informed consent before taking part in the study. Two participants owned mobile phones (KT an iPhone and CD owned a feature phone). Before the study, KT reported previously using a calendar app to set reminders.

LE

LE is a 45 year old man who sustained brain damage after a fall in 2013 and has a history of previous injuries including a stroke, a traumatic brain injury (TBI) and recurrent seizures. He has difficulties with controlling his behaviour and with functional abilities such as self-care, cooking and cleaning. These have improved since admission to the unit. He has recently begun a vocational placement and has independent access outside the unit. He finds it difficult to initiate new behaviours which are not established habits. He also has difficulty maintaining his intentions and goals over more than a few minutes and so he is strongly driven by his environment. He has little insight into his difficulties and often does not understand the need for safety procedures or cognitive interventions. Staff reported that a reminder app could be helpful because he requires frequent prompting about activities.

KT

KT is 37 and sustained a severe TBI in a road traffic accident when he was 17. He has social skill deficits, disinhibition and psychiatric symptoms. Rehabilitation efforts have focused on his initiation of activities (morning routine and time keeping) and memory difficulties. He requires prompting to get out of bed in the morning and to ensure he is ready for rehabilitation sessions and vocational placements. Staff noted that KT sometimes requires prompting about everyday tasks such as doing the laundry. KT's memory difficulties, lack of motivation and apathy are issues that may benefit from prompting technology. He expressed that he dislikes being asked by staff members to do everyday tasks and so it was hoped that he might find prompts from technology more acceptable.

CD

CD is a 55 year old man who sustained a skull fracture in 2014 which led to left–sided brain injury. CD has severe memory difficulties, poor working memory and anxiety about his memory difficulties. He writes many notes because he is anxious about missing activities. However, he is also disorganized and has impaired short-term memory, so his notes often get lost or covered up leading to him forgetting things. A memory app could help because it would allow him to store his reminders in a phone which could alert him at the correct time. During the study period, CD had a rehabilitation goal of reminding the nurse about his medication, with the aim of moving to self-medicating safely.

Materials

ForgetMeNot app

ForgetMeNot is a simple smartphone reminder application designed and developed specifically for this study (Figure 1). The requirements for this design were developed by the research team in order to answer the research questions and complement the chosen methodology. The design requirements were a) that the app allows the user to set reminders for a specific time, b) that the app alerts the user at this time with an audio and visual prompt, c) that the app could be altered by the experimenter to include unsolicited prompts (UPs), d) that the app automatically logs the reminders set by participants and the participants' responses to the prompts.

The interface of the app was designed to be easy to read with large (the maximum text size which could allow all of the content to stay on one page), high contrast text (white and yellow text on a cyan background, and black text on white backgrounds). The home screen gave a choice of 6 types of reminders to set and no keyboard entry was required. Once the reminder has been chosen, a time can be selected for the alert to go off for that reminder. A standard Samsung time selector widget was chosen for the time selection screen. When the alert goes off, the text flashes continuously and a beep sounds along with a vibration every 30 seconds until the 'Done it!' button is pressed and the reminder is acknowledged. The reminders set for the day are logged automatically by the app (event selected and time) and can be seen by the user by selecting 'check today's reminders' at the top right of the reminder selection screen (seen on the top two screenshots of Figure 1). There is also the (hidden) option to allow a user to set prompts throughout the day. These are the unsolicited prompts (UPs) and, in the case of this study, the researcher set these at the beginning of the appropriate experimental phase. When the UP prompt activates it asks, 'Do you need to remember anything?' and flashes, beeps and vibrates every 30 seconds until an option is selected; 'YES' to this question allows a reminder to be set, and 'NO' closes the app. The participants' responses to this YES / NO question were logged automatically by the app and could be viewed by the experimenter. The event reminder and unsolicited prompts were programmed to override the volume controls on the phone so they would flash, beep and vibrate even if the volume on the phone was muted or in vibrate mode.

The design of the ForgetMeNot app was not intended to be a solution to all smartphone reminder usability difficulties for this group. Rather, it was intended to be a usable and learnable platform that would allow us to study the use of reminding technology in a rehabilitation setting and test the impact of UPs on reminder entry. If UPs were found to be useful, then they could be added to other reminding software.

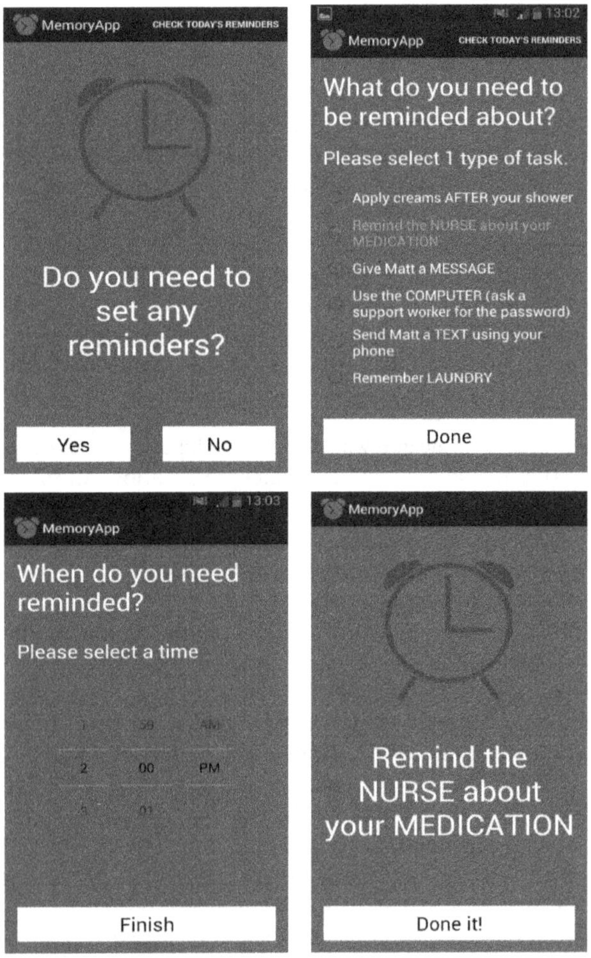

Figure 1. ForgetMeNot app. Top left: Unsolicited Prompt (UP) Top right: Task selection screen. Bottom left: Time selection screen. Bottom right: Specific reminder prompt. The task selections shown were the ones created for LE. KT and CD had slightly different tasks (see Table 1).

Hardware

ForgetMeNot is an Android app and it was provided on a Samsung Galaxy S3 smartphone (running Android version 4.3). Participants were free to use the phones for purposes separate from memory prompting (e.g. access Internet and make phone calls) and £10 of credit was given with each phone to cover text costs. We decided to provide phones for this study because two of the participants could not download the app onto their own phones. Furthermore, the experimenter had to manually enter the unsolicited prompts into the phone prior to the UP phase and so using participants own phones for this may have been perceived as intrusive.

Neuropsychological Tests

Several standardized tests were given to participants as part of their stay in the rehabilitation centre. These tests offer an overview of the participants' cognitive profile compared to the general population, in the domains of memory, executive functioning, attention, insight into their impairment and likely cognitive ability prior to their injury. Tests performed were the Wechsler Adult Intelligence Scale version 4 (WAIS-IV) [34], Test of Pre-morbid Functioning (TOPF) [35], the Behavioural Assessment of the Dysexecutive Syndrome (BADS) [41], the Cambridge Test of Prospective Memory (CAMPROMPT) [43] and the Rivermead Behavioural Memory Test (RBMT) [38].

Procedure

An observational *in situ* field study was carried out. ForgetMeNot app was provided to the participants for four weeks. At the beginning of the study memory tasks that participants often forgot to carry out were identified by the experimenter by talking to staff, asking the participants or referring to neuropsychological reports. Table 1 gives details of these activities. Additionally, we asked participants to pass a message to the experimenter and text the experimenter at a different time every day to create a larger set of reminders.

Initials	Daily tasks
LE	• Apply creams after shower • Ask to use the computer • Remember laundry • Remind the nurse about medication
KT	• Check schedule for vocational appointment • Have breakfast before leaving for a vocational appointment • Go to a rehabilitation session • Remind the nurse about medication
CD	• Ask to play a board game • Ask to use the computer • Remember laundry • Remind the nurse about medication

Table 1. Participants' daily tasks.

The study included two phases that each lasted two weeks during which the participants were given S3 Galaxy phones with the ForgetMenot app. The UP feature was included in one two-week phase and not the other. The order of the UP condition was randomly assigned for each participant using a coin flip. KT and LE had UPs for the first two-week phase and CD had UPs during the second two-week phase. The UPs were set by the experimenter to go off at six semi-random times during the day. The times were not completely random because we did not want to disturb people during their scheduled rehabilitation sessions (scheduled between 10am-11am, 11.30am-12.30pm, 1.30pm-2.30pm and 3pm-4pm on a weekday). The reminding tasks in the study only took place on weekdays between 9am and 8pm, although participants were free to set their own reminders for any time.

Participants were given a demonstration of how to use the app, during an hour-long session at the beginning of the study. This covered how to enter the app from the home screen, set a reminder task and time, check today's reminders, respond to prompts and how to respond to a UP. The main experimenter attended the rehabilitation centre every day during the study to collect the data. He helped with any other issues to do with phone use such as keyboard use for text messaging, phone charging and screen navigation, throughout the study.

The experimenter met with participants in nine hour-long study sessions: one prior to the beginning of the study to gather information about which memory tasks to set prompts for; two near the beginning of each phase to ensure people understood how to use the phone; four on different days during study to interview participants about their use of ForgetMeNot; and two sessions at the end of the study to administer further neuropsychological tests when necessary.

Each reminder that was entered into the app was logged and accessed by the experimenter at the end of the study. This log was used to tally the number of reminders set by each participant. This was the primary outcome variable. A potential limitation to simply logging the number of reminders set by participants was that participants could set reminders in the UP condition within three button presses (pressing 'YES' in response to the UP, then 'DONE' and 'FINISH'). This could lead to reminders being set thoughtlessly in a desire to dismiss the UPs. Using the reminder logs and information about what time each intended task was supposed to be completed, we were also able to develop a tally of 'fidelity checked' reminders. This variable was developed as a check that participants were thinking through the reminders they set. A fidelity checked reminder was defined as a) a reminder set for an event that the participant did have to do that day and b) was set for between half an hour before and 5 minutes after the event.

Daily reminders – study and app design

Only six different daily tasks could be set using the app and reminders could only be set for the current day. We recognize that setting reminders for longer-term events (e.g. 'meeting tomorrow' or 'appointment next week') is a useful function of most reminder apps. However, participants in this study received their rehabilitation plans daily and had few longer-term activities to remember. The ForgetMeNot app and experiment were designed to allow accurate measurement of the effectiveness of UPs in an everyday setting. Whether the memory task is to be performed later in the day or in a month's time, the user still needs to remember to enter it into the calendar application. Furthermore, unexpected events that were not planned at the beginning of the week may occur daily and require revision of the initial plan and extra reminders to be added. This app and study allowed us to investigate everyday reminder setting and to test whether or not UPs are an effective and acceptable way to increase this reminder setting behaviour.

RESULTS

Neuropsychological Profile

Table 2 summarises the cognitive profile on each of the neuropsychological tests for the participants.

Test	LE	KT	CD
WAIS-IV verbal comprehension score (description)	98 (average)	Not available	70 (Borderline impaired)
WAIS-IV full scale IQ (summary)	89 (Low average)	91 (Average)	74 (Borderline impaired)
TOPF predicted full scale IQ (description)	98 (Average)	115 (Above average)	89 (Low average)
RBMT percentile rank (95% CI) (description)	<0.1 (<0.1- 0.7) (Impaired)	0.5 (<0.1 - 3) (Impaired)	1 (0.2 – 6) (Impaired)
CAMPROMPT score (description)	8 (Borderline impaired)	6 (Impaired)	8 (Borderline impaired)
BADS age corrected score (description)	63 (Impaired)	81 (Low average)	73 (Borderline impaired)

WAIS-IV = Wechsler Adult Intelligence Scale version 4 [26]

TOPF = Test of Pre-morbid Functioning [27]

RBMT = Rivermead Behavioural Memory Test [30]

CAMPROMPT = Cambridge Test of Prospective Memory [34]

BADS = Behavioural Assessment of the Dysexecutive Syndrome [32]

Table 2. Cognitive profile on tests of intelligence, memory and executive function for the study participants.

Reminder Setting

Table 3 shows the average number of reminders and 'fidelity checked' reminders set by participants each day categorised by whether or not they were receiving UPs. The table shows that when not receiving Ups, LE set less than one reminder per day (mean = 0.7 reminders), KT set less than one reminder per week (mean = 0.1 reminders) and CD set 2.5 reminders per day. This increased markedly during the UP condition to a mean of 2.5, 1.7 and 6.3 reminders per day for LE, KT and CD respectively. The table also shows that this increase in reminder setting is also clear when only fidelity checked reminders were included. This confirms that the UPs were not just leading to an increase in reminder setting because thoughtless reminders were being set in order to dismiss the UPs.

Intervention Phase	Mean (SD) no. of reminders set per day LE	KT	CD
With UPs	2.5 (1.7)	1.7 (1.5)	6.3 (2.6)
With UPs (fidelity checked)	1.9 (1.1)	1.2 (1.0)	2.5 (1.3)
Without UPs	0.7 (0.9)	0.1 (0.3)	2.5 (1.8)
Without UPs (fidelity checked)	0.7 (0.9)	0.1 (0.3)	1.2 (0.8)

Table 3. Mean number of reminders and fidelity checkedreminders set per day in each intervention phase for each participant.

Field Observations

Phone Use

Participants did not set a large number of reminders, especially when they were not receiving the UPs (Table 3). Field note analysis also offers some insights into why this might have been.

In many of their comments KT and LE allude to their belief that they did not have much to be reminded about, either because they did not believe that they had anything to remember or because they did not believe they would forget. It was also the case that the rehabilitation centre where the study took place had a very set schedule and there was little chance that participants would experience very negative consequences of forgetting. For example KT said,

> *"Eh... Well I don't really have a chance to forget because I've got a timetable. I've got various things that remind me and that". KT*

Additionally, as part of their rehabilitation, service users in the unit were provided with, trained and prompted to use pencil and paper memory aids and memory aid strategies. For example LE said,

> *"Well I like my diary, I like keeping my diary 'cos I put everything in there" and, "...I write everything down. It's just... I don't really need that (points to phone) I write it all down". LE*

If other memory techniques were being used (for example LE using his diary and prompts in his room) then these may have contributed to performance of memory tasks, perhaps meaning that participants were supported with their memory as well as they could be with memory aids separate from ForgetMeNot. Additionally, especially in the cases of LE and KT, there were indications that they may have stopped using or ignored the phone, during at least some of the intervention days. For example, KT put the phone off for a day during the first week of the UP phase and LE stated that he put it away in his drawer at one stage preventing him from perceiving the prompts saying,

> *"I've put it in my drawer so I might hear a faint beep". LE*

LE was often observed to have put the phone in a drawer, saying that he was keeping it safe. He had to be prompted to keep the phone in his pocket a number of times during the first week of use.

Finally, CD also used pencil and paper memory aids and used his own phone to make notes of future events, though these did not prompt at set times. An unusual aspect of CD's use of ForgetMeNot, especially during the UP phase, was the number of reminders which he set that did not pass the fidelity check. He was observed to be setting several reminders per day on ForgetMeNot, all of which had the same content, namely to remind the nurse about medication. The majority of these were not 'fidelity checked' reminders because this memory task only had to be completed a maximum of two times per day. In spite of these reminders he repeatedly forgot to remind the nurse at the right time. When asked about this he revealed that he was setting this reminder in order to receive the auditory notification at the set time. However, he was entering different content into his own feature phone to match these reminders. When the ForgetMeNot notification fired it would remind him that he had something to do and he would look at the notes on his phone to find out what the task was. In the following conversation he describes this method,

> *"See when I get my diary of what I've got on today, where is it? Oh it's just in there. Ok so that's all the things I've got on. Putting that (paper diary) in that (phone). But it's all under..." CD*
>
> *"The sort of options that you get?" Experimenter*
>
> *"Aye it's under your medication. I just write it all in and put it in there as I know it's a basic whatever..." CD*
>
> *"And then you use that phone (his own feature phone) to back it up?" Experimenter*
>
> *"Yeah. I've not put it all in regularly but normally I do." CD*

The tasks he would input into the phone did not match the events that he was entering into his feature phone. For example, he would remind himself about going food shopping, attending rehabilitation sessions and going to the betting shop. Therefore, the way that CD used the app was to remind himself about his own tasks outside the research study, using prompts about the experimental tasks. He did not always carry out these experimental tasks but the prompts did remind him to check his schedule.

The insights which can be gained from field notes taken during this lengthy trial testing the efficacy of ForgetMeNot and UPs highlight the advantages of single case experimental design studies with embedded involvement from the researcher. The rich details that can be obtained can be used to help interpret and understand the findings and can inform future research in this area. For example, the insights described here highlight the importance of cognitive factors (such as insight into memory difficulties) and the environment and context (a highly structured rehabilitation setting) which influence the use of a technological memory aid intervention.

Unsolicited Prompts

During the weeks in which UPs were received, participants were asked what they thought about the UPs and why, as well as how they felt about the frequency and timing of the UPs. When first asked about the UPs after they had been introduced, KT reported that he had noticed them but usually pressed the 'no' option. He said,

> *"Well they (the UPs) all say the same thing. Presumably you'd have to go and check the phone but eh... I don't know I just always press no". KT*

The next week he was observed to have put the phone off and stated that this was because, 'it kept going off. It was annoying.' When asked if he ever found it useful to press the 'yes' option to set reminders he said, "No because I did press 'yes' a couple of times and it just came up with the same options. Unless I sent you a million texts, I didn't have anything to remember". He then agreed that he didn't think that he had enough to remember to justify it going off all the time, though this did not seem to be specific to the events entered into the phone. For example, he went on to say,

> *"There is just not enough going on here for me to have to remember anything to merit a device like that, you know". KT*

This may be interpreted to mean that KT did not feel that he needed to remember very much within the rehabilitation centre and this was why he chose to respond to the UPs by pressing 'no'. During the study period staff noted that KT did forget many events including tasks for which he could have used ForgetMeNot to set a reminder for. For example, he would often fail to check the schedule for vocational appointment or have breakfast before leaving for a vocational appointment. Therefore, it seems that KTs lack of insight fed into his lack of motivation; he did not perceive his memory failures and so did not believe he had anything to use the app for. Alternatively, he may have had insight into his memory difficulties but not believed that the tasks he needed to perform in the rehabilitation centre were important enough to merit setting a reminder. Whether caused by lack of motivation or insight, it was this perceived lack of need for reminding that made the UPs annoying to KT.

When interviewed in the first week of the UP condition, LE stated that he did not find the UPs annoying saying,

> *"No it's not annoying beeping me, no. I've put it in my drawer so I might hear a faint beep." LE*

However, at a later time he did report feeling frustrated with the notification, "No my memory is fine. I get to stage when that goes 'beep' I think not again!" This quote echoes comments made by KT indicating that UPs were annoying when they were not perceived as necessary either because he believed he would remember, or because he did not believe there was anything to remember. For LE, his belief was highlighted when he said,

> *"right, so when it goes in my pocket that's the alarm going off to tell me to take my medicine. But I don't do medicine, it gets brought to me. So the alarms for the medicine is not really my problem. The staff give me my medicine. I can't go... give me the meds!" LE*

This comment also highlights the fact that LE did not believe he was required to ask the nurse for medication even though this task was communicated to him at the beginning of each study phase. If LE forgot to ask the nurse for medication, the nurse would bring the medication to him at the end of their medication round. The structured environment of the rehabilitation centre, and LE's lack of insight into his memory difficulties meant that he had little motivation to complete this task even if he received a prompt to do it.

In contrast to LE and KT, CD had a positive attitude towards the UPs throughout the UP phase. He indicated that he did not find the UPs annoying and when asked about the number of prompts he said,

> *"There's never too many you know. If you need them, it's just if you've got them and done it all – but it's nothing against it you just don't need it. I just press no. As you say just press no. Ah I'm just, it's new to me so I'm amazed". CD*

This did not change throughout the two weeks of the UP phase, and CD indicated that he felt the prompts from the app could help to compensate for memory impairment, though he did feel anxious when using the phone in general. For example,

> *"I think yeah it's terrific. I'm still lacking that confidence with it but that's me, it's nothing to do with the phone, I've nothing against the phone at all. Yeah I can see, I can see how handy it can be. In fact, I'll end up probably I need, that's my brain there, my thoughts". CD*

The difference in attitudes towards the UPs between participants illustrates the importance of understanding insight into memory difficulties and motivation for rehabilitation, and the influence this can have on the acceptability of prompts. For example, KT and LE indicated that they did not set reminders because they did not believe they had anything to remember and reported that they felt their memory was fine. As a consequence, the UPs were occasionally perceived as annoying by these participants, especially into the second week of the UP condition. In contrast, CD was anxious about his memory, motivated to remember his schedule and appreciated that the app could really help with this. He was very happy to receive the UPs and perceived them as helpful.

When asked about the frequency of the UPs, KT and CD both stated that they thought the number of UPs was about right. CD was happy with the semi-random firing of the UPs, while KT indicated that, 'first thing in the morning, before my brain has engaged' would be the best time to be prompted. He elaborated by saying,

> *"You could just set the alarm and it goes off. Now normally you'd just remember, but... no it helps to let you know. It's like you wrote a letter to yourself (from) last night you know". KT*

DISCUSSION

Unsolicited prompts

The number of reminders set per day increased markedly with the introduction of UPs. This was also the case when only fidelity checked reminders were included in the analysis. This shows that all participants noticed the prompts and used them to open the app and set reminders. The setting of timely reminders, that passed the fidelity check to prompt a future intention was considerably more frequent when prompted by an UP than when they had to initiate this action with no prompt.

Overcoming the Barriers to Use

The field notes illustrated several barriers to the use of smartphone scheduling software in ABI rehabilitation. For example, LE left the phone charging in his drawer throughout the day because he wanted to keep it safe and because he did not feel like he needed the reminders. KT turned the phone off because he found it annoying and did not think it was useful. CD was initially concerned about using the phone because he felt he might break it. These barriers are difficult to overcome, however the success of the UPs in increasing the use of the device (Table 3) even amongst participants who were observed to have low motivation for using the software and little experience using smartphone technology is very encouraging. The increase in use of the app occurred for all three participants and this suggests that UPs which prompt people to enter reminders at random intervals during the day may be useful for overcoming some of the barriers to the use of prompting technology. This increase in use during the UP condition was especially prominent for CD who had good insight into his memory impairment and was highly motivated to use the device, indicating that other users with good insight into their difficulties, who are motivated, may also particularly benefit from UPs.

The ages of the participants may also have been a barrier. The participants were 37, 45 and 55 and the two older participants had very little experience with smartphones. It is likely that younger people with ABI would be more used to owning and using smartphones and this might mean they would find them easier to use and be less likely to have negative user experiences (such as worrying that they will break the device or that it will be stolen).

Methodological Considerations

Small N case studies such as this can have real value in HCI for health, especially when investigating hard to reach populations. For example, Wilson *et al.* (N = 1 with ABI) was an influential study that foreshadowed an RCT of the NeuroPage prompting device, and many subsequent studies testing reminding technology in clinical practice [39]. The Archipel [1] (N=1) and GUIDE assistive technologies [21] (N=2) have also been further developed and researched following small case studies. In the current paper, a rich contextual longitudinal study is reported with 3 people with severe ABI in an acute rehabilitation centre with very distinct cognitive profiles and behavioural issues. Close observation of their use of a reminder app during their on-going rehabilitation allowed those difficulties to be linked to the use of the app. For clinicians, the insights are extremely useful because they can recognise similar difficulties and traits in their own clients. This is one argument for the use of single case experimental design and case study methods in clinical research [32]. For both researchers and designers, this study design is valuable. In this case, it allowed us to detail issues that occur for people with specific difficulties, in specific settings. This offers insights for the future not always available when studying heterogeneous populations grouped by disease aetiology.

Future Research

When to prompt

The purpose of our study was to investigate the impact of UPs, rather than to investigate when or how to present UPs. The UPs were received at semi-random times, within the hours possible given the participants' rehabilitation schedules. ForgetMeNot is limited as it requires a carer, clinician or researcher to enter UP times. However, UPs could also be programmed to prompt randomly, or even predict when to prompt based on environmental cues. Decision making algorithms which are informed by sensors could also help determine the best times to interrupt. For example, Fischer and colleagues showed that people reacted faster to notifications if they were delivered after finishing a call or reading a text message [9]. Ho and Intille suggest that notifications may be received more positively if they occur between two physical activities (e.g. walking or sitting) [15]. Alternatively, an algorithm could mute users' phones in a personalized way in order to avoid unwanted interruptions [25], which would allow notifications to be sent at any time without fear of an embarrassing disturbance. The present study has shown that UPs do lead to increased reminder entering. This effect could be enhanced if algorithms can predict and select the most opportune times to send UPs.

How to prompt

ForgetMeNot's notifications including the UPs were designed to be highly noticeable because we wanted to be sure that participants received the prompts. The UPs beeped and flashed every 30 seconds if unanswered and this is likely to be more intrusive than the ideal UP. Future studies could test UPs which would balance nuisance with timely prompting.

For example, some modalities of notification may be less disruptive than others [20, 33]. It is telling that, despite two participants reporting that the UPs were annoying, they still entered more reminders into the app during the UPs phase compared to the non-UPs phase. It seems that being annoyed with the app did not put people off using it or negatively impact the efficacy of its use during the two weeks in which users received the UPs. This echoes previous research by Mehrotra and colleagues [18] who suggest that people find notifications annoying/disrupting even when they acknowledge that they are useful.

We found that low motivation linked to a lack of insight into memory difficulties was an important barrier to use and to acceptability when the UPs increased use. The mismatch between perceived and actual memory ability has been reported by previous researchers in the context of reminder setting amongst the general population. Gilbert and colleagues found that both subjective confidence in memory ability and actual memory ability influenced reminder setting behaviour, even though the two were uncorrelated [12].

In rehabilitation settings, improving insight into memory difficulties is often a key goal [42]. This is a difficult thing to do, especially if people have difficulties remembering (and therefore learning from) their experiences [17]. The literature on software for behaviour change offers potential solutions to improving people's engagement with apps. Different techniques that might work include using prompts linking behaviours to their positive outcomes [11], or drawing on social comparison or social modelling [23]. Future research will help us understand what content UPs could prompt with to be more effective (e.g. 'you'll be on time if you set a reminder.' Or 'your friend has set a reminder for an event, do you want to?') Alternatively, habit formation techniques could allow people to compensate for scheduling difficulties sustainably, in cases where insight cannot be improved [28].

Our aim when designing ForgetMeNot and UPs was to make the UI simple (sacrificing flexibility/functionality) to reduce potentially confounding usability issues when investigating the impact of UPs. Ideally, an app would be designed to flexibly set any reminder with ease, not just pre-set ones. It could be the case that people will need more support and training to use more complex reminding apps and that reminding apps should be designed to be accessible. Research on how best to train use in rehabilitation, how best to design the UI of reminding apps for this group, and how best to support people to initiate reminding behaviour (e.g. UPs) should be combined to understand the optimal conditions for successful scheduling.

CONCLUSION

An *in situ* observational study in a rehabilitation centre demonstrated the barriers to reminding technology use in this context and showed that UPs can markedly increase reminder setting. The participants recruited in this study are representative of people with severe memory and executive impairments after ABI and the results offer some insight into how effective and acceptable UPs would be for this group in real world settings.

Smartphone users may receive high numbers of unsolicited notifications, often referred to as pro-active or 'push' notifications. In 1991, Weiser imagined future technology as quiet and invisible servants which create calm [36]. Phones which offer frequent notifications, especially ones which were not solicited by the user, are anything but quiet and invisible. In this study, we demonstrated the positive impact that such notifications can have, in this case increasing use of a memory aid app in a rehabilitation setting. Useful notifications may put people off using technology if they become a nuisance, and nuisance notifications may increase people's use of technology. With user-centred research it is possible to overcome the barriers to technology use to create solutions that are useful and acceptable for all users.

People with ABI often have cognitive difficulties including poor prospective memory which can be supported by reminder apps. However, PM difficulties can make it difficult for this group to remember to enter reminders in the first place. Unsolicited prompting from the reminding software is a potential solution to this problem. In this study in-situ observational methodology was used to test the impact of unsolicited prompts from a reminder app on reminder setting and user experience for people with memory impairments after ABI. It was found that UPs increased the number of reminders set. Reminding technology has great potential in memory rehabilitation and UPs could be a useful solution to a problem which people with memory impairments face when using this technology.

REFERENCES

1. Arab, F., Bauchet, J., Pigot, H., Giroux, A., & Giroux, S. (2014, September). Design and assessment of enabling environments for cooking activities. In *Proceedings of the 2014 ACM International Joint Conference on Pervasive and Ubiquitous Computing: Adjunct Publication* (pp. 517-526). ACM.

2. Baldwin, V. N., Powell, T., & Lorenc, L. (2011). Factors influencing the uptake of memory compensations: A qualitative analysis. Neuropsychological Rehabilitation, 21, 484-501.

3. Boman, I-L., Bartfai, a, Borell, L., Tham, K., & Hemmingsson, H. (2010). Support in everyday activities with a home-based electronic memory aid for persons with memory impairments. *Disability and rehabilitation. Assistive technology*, *5*(5), 339–50.

4. De Joode, E. A., Van Heugten, C. M., Verhey, F. R. J., & Van Boxtel, M. P. J. (2012). Effectiveness of an electronic cognitive aid in patients with ac-

quired brain injury: A multicentre randomised parallel-group study. Neuropsychological Rehabilitation 23(1) 133-156.

5. Douglas, J. M. (2013). Conceptualizing self and maintaining social connection following severe traumatic brain injury. Brain injury, 27(1), 60-74.
6. Evans, J. (2003). Rehabilitation of executive deficits. In *Neuropsychological rehabilitation: theory and practice. In series Studies in neuropsychology: development and cognition,* ed., B Wilson, 54-55. New York/Amsterdam: Swets and Zeitlinger.
7. Evans, J. J., Emslie, H., & Wilson, B. A. (1998). External cueing systems in the rehabilitation of executive impairments of action.. *Journal of the International Neuropsychological Society*, *4*, 399-407.
8. Felt, A. P., Egelman, S., & Wagner, D. (2012, October). I've got 99 problems, but vibration ain't one: a survey of smartphone users' concerns. In Proceedings of the second ACM workshop on Security and privacy in smartphones and mobile devices (pp. 33-44). ACM.
9. Fischer, J. E., Greenhalgh, C., & Benford, S. (2011, August). Investigating episodes of mobile phone activity as indicators of opportune moments to deliver notifications. In *Proceedings of the 13th international conference on human computer interaction with mobile devices and services* (pp. 181-190). ACM.
10. Fish, J., Evans, J. J., Nimmo, M., Martin, E., Kersel, D., Bateman, A., Wilson, B. a, et al. (2007). Rehabilitation of executive dysfunction following brain injury: "content-free" cueing improves everyday prospective memory performance. *Neuropsychologia*, *45*(6), 1318–30.
11. Gardner, R. M., Bird, F. L., Maguire, H., Carreiro, R., & Abenaim, N. (2003). Intensive positive behavior supports for adolescents with acquired brain injury: Long-term outcomes in community settings. *The Journal of head trauma rehabilitation*, *18*(1), 52-74.
12. Gilbert, S. J. (2015). Strategic use of reminders: Influence of both domain-general and task-specific metacognitive confidence, independent of objective memory ability. Consciousness and Cognition, 33, 245–260.
13. Gillespie, A., Best, C., & O'Neill, B. (2012). Cognitive function and assistive technology for cognition: a systematic review. *Journal of the International Neuropsychological Society : JINS*, *18*(1), 1–19.
14. Headway (2015) Brain Injury Statistics. Retrieved September 19, 2015 from https://www.headway.org.uk/brain-injury-statistics.aspx
15. Ho, J., & Intille, S. S. (2005, April). Using context-aware computing to reduce the perceived burden of interruptions from mobile devices. In Proceedings of the SIGCHI conference on Human factors in computing systems (pp. 909-918). ACM.
16. Jamieson, M., Cullen, B., McGee-Lennon, M., Brewster, S., & Evans, J. J. (2014). The efficacy of cognitive prosthetic technology for people with memory impairments: A systematic review and meta-analysis. Neuropsychological Rehabilitation, 24, 419-444.
17. Jamieson, M., McGee-Lennon, M., Cullen, B., Brewster, S., & Evans, J. (2015, October). Issues influencing the Uptake of Smartphone Reminder apps for People with Acquired Brain Injury. *In Proceedings of the 17th International ACM SIGACCESS Conference on Computers & Accessibility* (pp. 339-340). New York, USA: ACM.
18. Mehrotra, A., Pejovic, V., Vermeulen, J., Hendley, R., & Musolesi, M. (2016). My Phone and Me: Understanding People's Receptivity to Mobile Notifications. In Proc. CHI 2016.
19. McDonald, A., Haslam, C., Yates, P., Gurr, B., Leeder, G., & Sayers, A. (2011). Google Calendar: A new memory aid to compensate for prospective memory deficits following acquired brain injury. *Neuropsychological rehabilitation*, *21*(6), 784-807.
20. McGee-Lennon, M., Smeaton, A., & Brewster, S. (2012). Designing Home Care Reminder Systems: Lessons Learned Through Co-Design with Older Users. *Proceedings of the 6th International Conference on Pervasive Computing Technologies for Healthcare*, 49–56.
21. O'Neill, B., Best, C., Gillespie, A., & O'Neill, L. (2013). Automated prompting technologies in rehabilitation and at home. *Social Care and Neurodisability*, *4*(1), 17-28.
22. Paul, C. L., Komlodi, A., & Lutters, W. (2011). Again?!! the emotional experience of social notification interruptions. In Human-Computer Interaction–INTERACT 2011 (pp. 471-478). Springer Berlin Heidelberg.
23. Paul, L., Wyke, S., Brewster, S., Sattar, N., Gill, J. M., Alexander, G., ... & Dybus, A. (2016). Increasing physical activity in stroke survivors using STARFISH, an interactive mobile phone application: a pilot study. *Topics in stroke rehabilitation*, *23*(3), 170-177.

24. Pielot, M., Church, K., & de Oliveira, R. (2014, September). An in-situ study of mobile phone notifications. In Proceedings of the 16th international conference on Human-computer interaction with mobile devices & services (pp. 233-242). ACM.

25. Rosenthal, S., Dey, A. K., & Veloso, M. (2011). Using decision-theoretic experience sampling to build personalized mobile phone interruption models. In Pervasive Computing (pp. 170-187). Springer Berlin Heidelberg.

26. Shirazi, S. A., Henze, N., Dingler, T., Pielot, M., Weber, D., & Schmidt, A. (2014, April). Large-scale assessment of mobile notifications. In Proceedings of the SIGCHI Conference on Human Factors in Computing Systems (pp. 3055-3064). ACM.

27. Sosin DM, Sniezek JE, Thurman DJ. (1996) Incidence of mild and moderate brain injury in the United States, 1991. *Brain Injury, 10,* 47–54.

28. Stawarz, K.M., Cox, A.L. & Blandford, A. (2015). Beyond self-tracking and reminders: Designing smartphone apps that support habit formation. In Proc. CHI 2015.

29. Sutcliffe, A., Fickas, S., Sohlberg, M. M., & Ehlhardt, L. A. (2003). Investigating the usability of assistive user interfaces. *Interacting with computers*, *15*(4), 577-602.

30. Svoboda, E., Richards, B., Leach, L., & Mertens, V. (2012). PDA and smartphone use by individuals with moderate-to-severe memory impairment: Application of a theory-driven training programme. *Neuropsychological rehabilitation*, *22*(3), 408-427.

31. Szymkowiak, Andrea, Kenny Morrison, Peter Gregor, Prveen Shah, Jonathan Evans, and Barbara Wilson. "Memojog-Successes and Limitations of a Memory Aid System." *Brain Impairment* 5, no. 1 (2004): 98.

32. Tate, R. L., Perdices, M., Rosenkoetter, U., Wakim, D., Godbee, K., Togher, L., & McDonald, S. (2013). Revision of a method quality rating scale for single-case experimental designs and n-of-1 trials: The 15-item Risk of Bias in N-of-1 Trials (RoBiNT) Scale. *Neuropsychological Rehabilitation*, *23*(5), 619-638.

33. Warnock, D., McGee-Lennon, M., & Brewster, S. (2013). Multiple notification modalities and older users. In Proceedings of the SIGCHI Conference on Human Factors in Computing Systems (pp. 1091-1094). ACM.

34. Wechsler, D. (2008). *Wechsler adult intelligence scale-fourth*. San Antonio, TX: Pearson

35. Wechsler, D. (2011). *Test of Premorbid Functioning. UK Version (TOPF UK)*. London, UK: Pearson Corporation.

36. Weiser, M. (1991). The computer for the 21st century. Scientific american, 265(3), 94-104.

37. Wilson, B. A. (1991). Long-term prognosis of patients with severe memory disorders. Neuropsychological Rehabilitation, 1(2), 117-134.

38. Wilson, B. A., Cockburn, J., & Baddeley, A. D. (1991). *The Rivermead behavioural memory test.* Bury St Edmunds, UK: Thames Valley Test Company.

39. Wilson, B. A., Emslie, H., Quirk, K., & Evans, J. (1999). George: Learning to live independently with NeuroPage®. *Rehabilitation Psychology*, *44*(3), 284.

40. Wilson, B. A, Emslie, H. C., Quirk, K., & Evans, J. J. (2001). Reducing everyday memory and planning problems by means of a paging system: a randomised control crossover study. *Journal of neurology, neurosurgery, and psychiatry*, *70*(4), 477–82.

41. Wilson, B. A., Evans, J. J., Alderman, N., Burgess, P. W., & Emslie, H. (1997). Behavioural assessment of the dysexecutive syndrome. In P. Rabbitt (Ed.), *Methodology of frontal and executive function* (pp. 239-250). London, UK: Psychology Press.

42. Wilson, B. A., Gracey, F., & Evans, J. J. (2009). *Neuropsychological rehabilitation: Theory, models, therapy and outcome*. Cambridge University Press.

43. Wilson, B. A., Shiel, A., Foley, J., Emslie, H., Groot, Y., Hawkins, K., & Watson, P. (2005). Cambridge test of prospective memory (CAMPROMPT). San Antonio: Pearson Assessment.

Interaction Proxies for Runtime Repair and Enhancement of Mobile Application Accessibility

Xiaoyi Zhang[1*], Anne Spencer Ross[1*], Anat Caspi[1,2], James Fogarty[1], Jacob O. Wobbrock[3]
[1] Computer Science & Engineering, [2] Taskar Center for Accessible Technology, [3] The Information School
DUB Group | University of Washington
{xiaoyiz, ansross, caspian, jfogarty}@cs.washington.edu, wobbrock@uw.edu

ABSTRACT
We introduce interaction proxies as a strategy for runtime repair and enhancement of the accessibility of mobile applications. Conceptually, interaction proxies are inserted between an application's original interface and the manifest interface that a person uses to perceive and manipulate the application. This strategy allows third-party developers and researchers to modify an interaction without an application's source code, without rooting the phone, without otherwise modifying an application, while retaining all capabilities of the system (e.g., Android's full implementation of the TalkBack screen reader). This paper introduces interaction proxies, defines a design space of interaction re-mappings, identifies necessary implementation abstractions, presents details of implementing those abstractions in Android, and demonstrates a set of Android implementations of interaction proxies from throughout our design space. We then present a set of interviews with blind and low-vision people interacting with our prototype interaction proxies, using these interviews to explore the seamlessness of interaction, the perceived usefulness and potential of interaction proxies, and visions of how such enhancements could gain broad usage. By allowing third-party developers and researchers to improve an interaction, interaction proxies offer a new approach to personalizing mobile application accessibility and a new approach to catalyzing development, deployment, and evaluation of mobile accessibility enhancements.

Author Keywords
Interaction proxies; accessibility; runtime modification.

ACM Classification Keywords
H.5.m. Information Interfaces and Presentation (e.g., HCI); K.4.2. Assistive Technologies for Persons with Disabilities.

INTRODUCTION
Mobile devices and their applications (apps) have become ubiquitous in daily life. Ensuring full access to the wealth of information and services provided by such apps is a matter of social justice [39], but for the estimated 15% of the world population with a disability [60], many capabilities and services offered by apps remain inaccessible. Pursuing more complete access requires contributions from researchers, from developers of mobile platforms (e.g., Apple, Google), and from the developers of thousands of individual apps.

Although individual apps can improve their accessibility in many ways, the most fundamental is adhering to platform accessibility guidelines. For example, the Android Accessibility Developer Checklist guides developers to "*provide content descriptions for UI components that do not have visible text*" [1]. This in turn allows the Android TalkBack screen reader to provide meaningful feedback to a person using the screen reader to interact with the app. Unfortunately, many apps fail to implement accessibility guidelines, including flagship corporate apps (e.g., as of August 2016, this paper finds missing metadata in current Android apps for Wells Fargo and Yelp that makes key functionality inaccessible). The problem is analogous to developer failure to provide alternative text for images on the web [6] or to implement accessibility guidelines in desktop applications [28].

When an app fails to implement fundamental accessibility support, people seeking to use that app often have few or no options for resolving the failure. An app's developer may lack awareness or knowledge needed to implement a fix. They may delay a fix due to competing development priorities (e.g., prioritizing new features), and other app updates may even introduce new accessibility failures. Alternatively, it might be difficult or impossible to obtain updates if original development of an app was contracted out or if the app is otherwise abandoned by its developer. A new approach to deploying accessibility enhancements could allow individuals or communities to quickly address accessibility failures that an app's original developer is unable or unwilling to address.

Finally, mobile platforms also face significant challenges and tradeoffs in prioritizing, designing, and implementing potential platform-level accessibility improvements. Although the impact of built-in platform support can be large, many promising techniques never make it to platform-level adoption. At the same time, researchers cannot reasonably rebuild a platform's entire accessibility infrastructure as part of exploring a new approach, so research is often limited to prototype apps. A new approach to deploying accessibility enhancements could both: (1) improve research by enabling

CHI 2017, May 06 - 11, 2017, Denver, CO, USA

ACM 978-1-4503-4655-9/17/05…$15.00
DOI: http://dx.doi.org/10.1145/3025453.3025846

* The first two authors contributed equally to this work.

deployment and evaluation of potential techniques, and (2) accelerate the impact of research by allowing promising accessibility enhancements to reach more people.

This paper introduces *interaction proxies* as a strategy for runtime repair and enhancement of mobile app accessibility. Interaction proxies are inserted between an app's original interface and the manifest interface [14] that a person uses to perceive and manipulate that app (e.g., the interface exposed by a screen reader like Android's TalkBack). As a strategy for third-party accessibility enhancements, interaction proxies therefore contrast with both: (1) fixes in individual apps (which can only be made by an app's developer), and (2) platform-level enhancements (which can only be made by the platform developer). The strategy is analogous to web proxies that modify a page between a server and a browser (including web proxies that modify pages to improve their accessibility [6,8,53]), but extended to address the design and implementation challenges of mobile app accessibility.

We demonstrate interaction proxies on Android, modifying interactions without an app's source code, without rooting the phone or otherwise modifying an app, while retaining all capabilities of the system (e.g., Android's full implementation of the TalkBack screen reader). Our implementations achieve this by modifying selected interactions using an accessibility service that creates overlays above an app while listening to and generating events to coordinate an interaction.

We then present a set of interviews with blind and low-vision people interacting with prototype interaction proxies, discussing their experiences and thoughts regarding such enhancements. As we will emphasize throughout this paper, our contribution is not intended to be any one specific accessibility enhancement. Rather, we aim to demonstrate the potential of interaction proxies as a *strategy* to support a variety of repairs and enhancements to the accessibility of mobile apps.

The specific contributions of our work therefore include:

- We introduce *interaction proxies* as a strategy for runtime repair and enhancement of the accessibility of mobile apps.
- We explore a design space of interaction re-mappings that can be implemented by an interaction proxy. This provides a framework for considering the design and implementation of mobile accessibility repairs and enhancements.
- We present a set of techniques for implementing interaction proxies and demonstrate implementations on Android without rooting the phone or otherwise modifying an app. A set of proof-of-concept Android implementations of interaction proxies demonstrate a range of technical techniques that developers and researchers can employ in implementing, deploying, and evaluating accessibility improvements.
- We present two sets of interviews with blind and low-vision people who use screen readers, first exploring accessibility barriers they encounter in apps and then exploring their reactions to using prototype interaction proxies as well as their thoughts on the potential of interaction proxies for enhancing the accessibility of mobile apps.

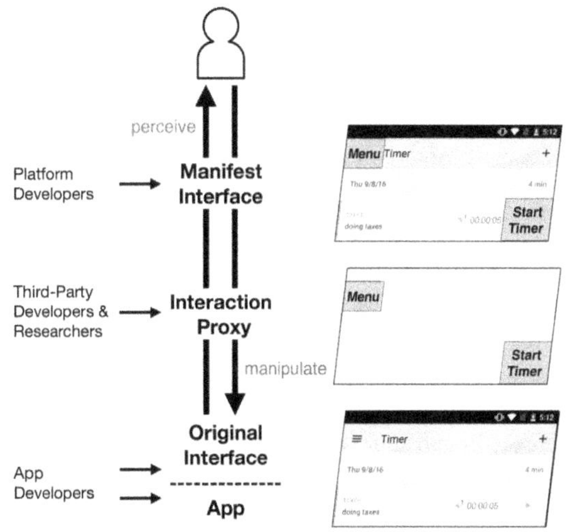

Figure 1. Interaction proxies are inserted between an app's original interface and the manifest interface a person uses to perceive and manipulate that app. This allows third-party developers and researchers to modify the interaction.

INTERACTION PROXIES

Effective interaction requires bridging both the gulf of evaluation (i.e., *perceiving and understanding* the state of an app) and the gulf of execution (i.e., *manipulating* the state of an app) [30]. These gulfs are bridged using an *interface*. For many people without disabilities, that interface is the original touch screen display. But it is important to clarify that *people commonly use different interfaces to access the same underlying app*. Many blind or low-vision people choose a *screen reader interface* (e.g., Slide Rule [34], Android's TalkBack, iOS's VoiceOver), which re-maps touch to support navigation separate from activation and may completely disable visual display of an app. Many people with motor impairments choose a *scanning interface*, which relies on visual perception but re-maps manipulation by scanning through potential targets that a person then activates using a switch. Even attaching an external keyboard or an additional display to a device can be considered a change in the interface used for interaction.

Borrowing from Cooper [14], we refer to the interface a person directly perceives and manipulates as the *manifest interface*. We contrast this with the *original interface* created by an app developer. For many people, the manifest interface may be the same as the original interface. However, many people with disabilities elect an alternative manifest interface. Conceptually, interaction proxies are inserted between an app's original interface and the manifest interface a person uses to perceive and manipulate that app, as illustrated in Figure 2.

We adopt the term "proxy" to be analogous to the web, where proxies can modify webpages between a server and their rendering in a browser (including web proxies with a purpose of improving web accessibility [6,8,53]). However, mobile app architectures do not allow the same approach to directly modifying the underlying representation of an interface prior to its rendering. Inserting an interaction proxy therefore aims to improve interaction by modifying how an app is perceived or

Figure 2. This interaction proxy repairs accessibility metadata than an app provides to a platform screen reader. (a) Toggl is a popular time-tracking app. (b) Its interface includes elements with missing or inappropriate metadata, which a screen reader manifests as "Navigate Up" and "One, Unlabeled". (c) Our third-party interaction proxy repairs the interaction with appropriate metadata for each element, so a screen reader manifests these elements as "Menu" and "Start Timer".

manipulated, without actually modifying the app. Key benefits are: (1) this does not require modifying the app, and (2) this does not require modifying the renderer of a manifest interface (e.g., a person continues to use Google's full implementation of Android's TalkBack screen reader). Figure 1 illustrates insertion of an interaction proxy to implement repairs of accessibility metadata in Figure 2. Using floating windows and other methods we detail in this paper, the interaction proxy provides corrected accessibility metadata. This can be implemented by a third-party developer or researcher, and the interaction proxy's modifications are then presented as part of the interface that is manifested by the platform screen reader.

There is significant overall promise in interaction proxies, which we examine in implementing several proof-of-concept enhancements and in interviews with blind and low-vision people interacting with those prototypes. But the interaction proxy strategy also has limitations. Specifically, the strategy is limited to interactions where a proxy can integrate itself into perception and manipulation of an app via a particular interface. A proxy must support both: (1) perception and understanding of the underlying app and the proxy's modifications via the manifest interface (e.g., Figure 1's upward arrow), and (2) manipulation of the underlying app and the proxy's modifications via the manifest interface (e.g., Figure 1's downward arrow). Proxies may simplify this by targeting only small portions of an interaction, leaving most of the original interaction unmodified. But care is required in developing an interaction proxy, as any seams or failures introduced by an interaction proxy can create new barriers to bridging the gulfs of evaluation and execution.

RELATED WORK

Our current work builds upon and is informed by prior research in mobile accessibility implementation, in accessibility repair and enhancement, and in runtime interface modification.

Mobile Accessibility Implementation

Designing and implementing support for mobile accessibility requires diverse contributions. One example can be seen in the design, adoption, and implementation of support for screen readers that make mobile apps more accessible to blind and low-vision people. Motivated by the research challenge of supporting blind people in using touch screens, Slide Rule introduced techniques for re-mapping gestures to support navigating and exploring the screen separately from activating targets in an interface [34]. These techniques were adopted by developers of screen readers for major mobile platforms (e.g., Android's TalkBack, iOS's VoiceOver), and now improve accessibility of apps on those platforms [42]. However, accessibility of apps on those platforms remains critically dependent upon the many developers of individual apps [1]. It is best for apps to be designed and developed to be broadly accessible [58], but third-party interaction proxies provide a complementary strategy when apps fall short of this goal.

One key requirement of the developers of individual apps is to provide metadata needed to support platform accessibility enhancements such as screen readers. Developers often fail to provide metadata for a variety of reasons (e.g., being unaware they should, lacking knowledge of how to do so, or failing to prioritize accessibility). This problem has been most studied on the web (e.g., with missing image alternative text [6]). Despite education and improved testing (e.g., [12,31,47]), such accessibility failures remain common on the web [25].

The same underlying challenge occurs in mobile and desktop interfaces, with individual app developers failing to implement platform accessibility support. The extent of the problem is difficult to measure, due to a relative lack of testing tools. Hurst et al. found roughly 25% of desktop elements are completely missing from the accessibility implementation of common desktop interfaces [28]. Milne et al. examined the accessibility of apps provided with mobile health sensors, finding none appropriately implemented platform accessibility standards [43]. The greater maturity of education and tooling in web accessibility makes it likely that mobile and desktop accessibility implementations are at least as poor as on the web, and blind and low-vision interview participants in this paper report missing accessibility metadata is a frequent barrier.

Accessibility Repair and Enhancement

Prior work repairing accessibility failures generally focuses on the web, where the representation rendered by a browser is available and can be directly modified. We use the term "proxy" to be analogous to prior research using web proxies to improve web accessibility [6,8,53], but our implementation mechanisms are quite different. Some accessibility repairs can be automated, such as attempting to automatically identify sources of alternative text for web images [6] or automatically increasing font size to improve readability [4]. Other approaches emphasize social annotation, wherein people contribute accessibility repairs that benefit additional people who encounter the same accessibility failure [37]. Such research has examined collaborative authoring of missing image alternative text and other metadata [51,54,55], sharing of scripts to implement site-specific repairs [7], and more recent work focusing on crowdsourcing contributions [27].

In addition to work on visual accessibility, many people with motor impairments choose accessibility techniques that modify how they manipulate an interface. SUPPLE modifies interface elements according to personal motor abilities [23,58]. Other systems leave interface layout unchanged, but apply techniques to ease pointing. Examples include making targets "sticky" [29,59], dynamically modifying cursor behavior according to a person's movement profile [57], and breaking a pointing interaction into multiple interactions that disambiguate the intended target [22,33,63]. Other research has explored alternative pointing for physically large devices [36].

Prior research examines how people adapt to accessibility barriers in mobile devices and how devices can enhance access in the physical world [35]. VizWiz examines supporting blind people in using a mobile device to take a picture and ask a crowd a question about that picture [5,11]. Extensions examine conversational interaction with the crowd [41] and soliciting volunteer assistance in social networks [9,10]. Related insights have been applied to supporting deaf students through real-time captioning for classroom activities [40].

There has been much less research in repairing or enhancing the accessibility of mobile apps. Notable examples include supporting macros motivated by accessibility needs [48] and implementations of pointing enhancements [63]. The SWAT framework examines system-level instrumentation of content and events to support developer creation of accessibility services [49], but requires rooting a device, which is a significant security risk and presents a technical expertise barrier. Our work explores a larger design space of re-mappings while working within the Android accessibility and security model. We thus extend the spirit of prior work in repair and enhancement, while developing new techniques for third-party accessibility enhancements in mobile apps.

Runtime Interface Modification

We also extend prior research in runtime modification of desktop interfaces. Such work employs different approaches than on the web, necessitated by a lack of ability to directly access or modify an interface's internal representation. Early work replaced a toolkit drawing object and intercepted commands (e.g., *draw_string*) [21,46]. More recently, Scotty examined runtime toolkit overloading, developing abstractions for implementing modifications in code injected directly into the interface runtime [20]. Complementary work explores input-output re-direction in the window manager [56], using information from the desktop accessibility API to make changes in an interface façade [52]. To overcome limitations of the desktop accessibility API and incomplete implementations of that API, recent work examines interpretation of interface pixels [28]. Runtime modification can be implemented using only pixel-level analysis [15,16,17,18,19,61] or in combination with information from an accessibility API [13]. Such approaches can allow authoring more specialized or accessible manifestations of underlying application functionality [62].

Our work builds on insights from the desktop, but the mobile app context does not allow prior approaches (i.e., does not allow direct modification of interface internals, nor surface modification via window manager redirection). We develop a new approach (i.e., using floating windows while coordinating perception and manipulation in the manifest interface), and we explore implications for mobile accessibility modifications.

RE-MAPPING INTERACTION

We now present a design space for supporting researchers and developers in the *design* of interaction proxies, considering *implementation* abstractions in the next section. Recall from Figure 2 that an interaction proxy helps a person to bridge the gulf of evaluation and/or the gulf of execution. A proxy achieves this by modifying: (1) perception in an interaction, (2) manipulation in an interaction, or (3) both. We consider such modifications in terms of how a proxy re-maps existing interaction into new interaction. This section considers each of five identified patterns of re-mapping and discusses potential interaction proxies in that region of the design space.

Although many potential enhancements fit cleanly into this design space, we note that some enhancements are better thought of as a combination of several interaction proxies, each of which re-maps an interaction according to this space.

From Zero to One

A re-mapping from *zero to one* adds a new interaction where there was none. By definition, this adds new information or functionality to a manifest interface, and we contrast it with later examples that correct or replace an existing interaction. Re-mappings might integrate new information obtained from an outside service or restore elements of an original interface that are inaccessible in a person's chosen manifest interface.

Figure 3 shows an example of adding information from an outside service. In interviews presented in this work, blind and low-vision people report they often do not have ready access to information about an app's accessibility prior to attempting to use the app. If a third-party service rated app accessibility, it would be preferable to make ratings available directly at the time that information is needed. Figure 3's proof-of-concept shows how a third-party interaction proxy could add a button for accessing such accessibility ratings from within the app store itself. Google's Accessibility Scanner app similarly inserts a floating button that allows invoking an accessibility checker for the current screen [24], but it targets developer inspection of an app rather than end-users seeking information about the accessibility of potential apps.

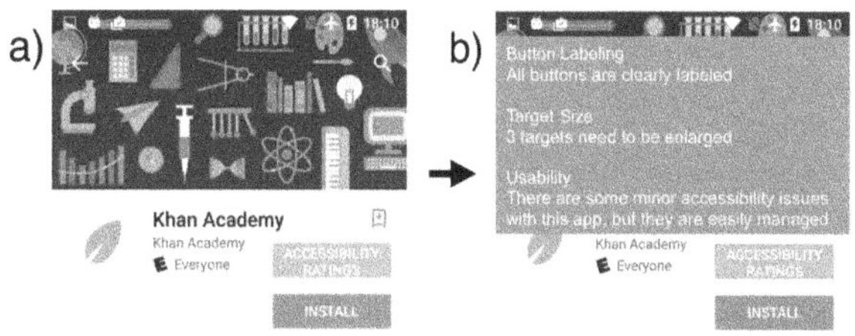

Figure 3. This interaction proxy adds third-party accessibility ratings directly within the app store. (a) An "Accessibility Ratings" button is added in empty space. (b) Selecting it shows third-party accessibility information for that app.

Later sections discuss Figure 7, an example of zero-to-one re-mappings that restore functionality missing in an interface manifested by a screen reader. Specifically, the Wells Fargo app fails to expose several of its interface elements, leaving them inaccessible to a person manifesting the interface with a screen reader. An interaction proxy repairs this, restoring access to each of the menu items from the original interface. Figure 8 presents the same problem occurring with the stars on Yelp's rating page. Inaccessible when using a screen reader, an interaction proxy restores these to the manifest interface.

From One to Zero

A re-mapping from *one to zero* removes an interaction. Examples include: (1) modifying a manifest interface to remove information or functionality from the original interface, and (2) modifications to correct or improve undesirable interactions introduced by a person's chosen manifest interface. For example, stencils-based tutorials remove access to much of an interface by limiting interaction to the current step in the tutorial [26,38]. iOS's Guided Access feature similarly allows disabling a phone's motion detection or disabling touch in a region of an interface [3]. Additional examples can include removing interactions that provide no value or are problematic in a person's chosen manifest interface (e.g., advertising, interstitial screens, spurious animations that generate distracting notifications with a screen reader).

From One to One

A re-mapping from *one to one* replaces an existing interaction with another. Figure 1 shows an example of elements with missing or incorrect accessibility metadata, which are therefore inappropriately manifested by a screen reader (e.g., presented as "One, Unlabeled"). Manipulation thus works as desired, but elements are difficult to correctly perceive. A third-party interaction proxy can correct this (e.g., presenting the button as "Start Timer"), proxying any manipulation to the underlying original interface. Although such a correction could also be considered a combination of a one-to-zero re-mapping (i.e., removing the incorrect data) and a zero-to-one re-mapping (i.e., adding the correct data), it is more straightforward to consider such direct replacement of an existing interaction as a one-to-one re-mapping.

Alternatively, an interaction proxy can modify manipulation while leaving information in individual elements unchanged. For example, our blind and low-vision interview participants report needed functionality can sometimes be difficult to reach when manifested by a screen reader. Because swiping gestures traverse elements serially, an example difficulty is when a screen reader manifests a target at the end of a list that must be traversed to access it (e.g., Toggl's "Create Timer" button prominently floats above the interface but the screen reader manifests it after all existing timers, Yelp's search box is readily available in the original interface but the screen reader manifests at the end of a list). Later sections discuss Figure 8 and our implementation of interaction proxies to modify navigation order in such interfaces.

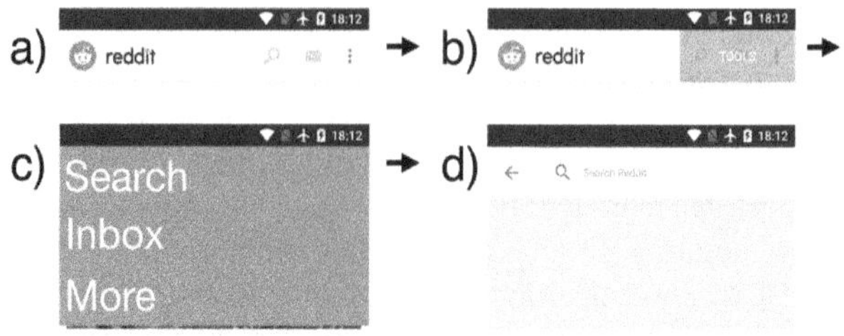

Figure 4. This interaction proxy replaces one interaction with a sequence of two interactions. (a) An interface contains several small adjacent targets. (b) Replaced with a single larger "Tools" button. (c) Selection displays a menu of the original targets. (d) A selected item is activated.

We note existing platform support for re-mapping interaction tends to be strongest for one-to-one re-mapping (e.g., both Android and iOS support interactively labeling elements that are missing screen reader metadata). But interaction proxies further allow third-party developers and researchers to develop, deploy, and evaluate new approaches (e.g., neither Android nor iOS provide integrated support for social annotation approaches to crowdsourcing accessibility text, as has been proposed and examined in web-based systems [27,51,54,55]).

From One to Many

A re-mapping from *one to many* replaces a single interaction with multiple interactions. This is often because the original interaction makes ability assumptions that are inaccessible to some people, such as fine-grained motor assumptions [58]. Unpacking such an interaction into a sequence of interactions can make it more accessible to more people. This generally requires designing for both perception and manipulation, as a person must navigate the new sequence of interactions. For example, prior work explores two-stage selection of small targets [22,33,63]. Figure 4 shows an interaction proxy that replaces a set of small adjacent targets with a single larger target that invokes a menu for choosing among them.

From Many to One

A re-mapping from *many to one* replaces multiple interactions with a single interaction. For example, prior work has explored this in accessibility macros [48]. Such macros can provide a new method for manipulating an app through a sequence of interactions that might otherwise be difficult or laborious (e.g., interfaces that rely upon timing constraints or active modes that are difficult for a person with a motor impairment to perform). A macro might also be invoked using a different modality, as with CoFaçade's support for configuring devices so an older adult can access functionality with on-screen buttons, with physical buttons, or with physical gestures like scanning an RFID tag [62]. In contrast to many-to-one re-mapping of manipulation, many-to-one re-mapping of perception can be implemented by summaries. For example, a home automation app might contain many visual indicators of devices, which a screen reader manifests by serially scanning through each device and its status, but a proxy could add support for a summary of which devices are currently on.

Composing Multiple Re-Mappings in an Enhancement

Apps and potential enhancements to those apps are composed of many interactions. In applying this design space to consider current and potential enhancements, it is helpful to consider enhancements as composed of many re-mappings, each of which is characterized by one of these five patterns.

A simple case is when an enhancement applies the same type of re-mapping to multiple interactions (e.g., modifying screen reader metadata on multiple elements, modifying navigation order among multiple elements, disabling multiple elements as part of a stencils-based tutorial). But complex enhancements can also be understood as compositions of many re-mappings. Later sections discuss personalized interface layout in Figure 10, as motivated by SUPPLE's generation of interface layouts adapted to an individual's motor abilities [23,58]. Considering such a complex enhancement in terms of its underlying re-mapping of many interactions can provide a useful framework for approaching its design and implementation.

IMPLEMENTATION IN ANDROID

The prior section provides a framework for considering *design* of interaction proxies. We now present a set of *implementation* abstractions and how each is implemented in Android. Our abstractions are sometimes similar to prior examinations of runtime interface modification (e.g., [20,52]), so we focus on details for interaction proxies in Android. Abstractions provide a higher-level language for discussing enhancements and convey what is needed to achieve these behaviors on other platforms. After introducing the primary abstractions, we discuss their composition to coordinate perception and manipulation over the course of modifying an interaction. Maintaining this coordination of the interaction is critical for an effective proxy.

Our interaction proxies are installed as Android accessibility services. This provides a proxy with some ability to inspect and manipulate other apps using privileged Android APIs. Installing an accessibility service requires explicit consent, and none of our enhancements require rooting the phone or otherwise modifying the operating system, as we believe it is inappropriate to require a person to compromise basic security of their device to access an app. Nevertheless, protecting against malicious accessibility services is an important topic for additional security research [32]. Prior research has explored composing interfaces from mutually distrustful elements [50], and the development of effective abstractions is important to improving the security of accessibility enhancements.

Abstractions for Android Interaction Proxies

Our basic strategy is to minimize the scale and complexity of an interaction proxy by intervening as little as necessary in an interaction. We achieve this using a combination of *floating windows* with the *introspection* and *automation* capabilities of an accessibility service. We note the percentage of Android devices on which each of the core requirements are available, reporting availability as of December 2016 [2]. Some capabilities are limited to more recent versions of Android, which have more limited market share. These will become more available as people transition to newer devices.

Floating Windows: Our interaction proxies intervene between an app's original interface and the manifest interface by creating floating windows that the interface manifests instead of the underlying app. Similar to overlapping windows on the desktop, floating windows sit above the app in z-order (e.g., Facebook Messenger's floating chat heads allow reading and replying to messages from the context of other apps). The floating windows capability has been included since Android 1.0 and is therefore available on all Android devices.

We further define a *Full Overlay* as a floating window that occludes the entire underlying app, and a *Partial Overlay* as occluding one or more elements while leaving other interactions unmodified. Enhancements composed of multiple re-mappings will often coordinate multiple partial overlays within an app.

Event Listeners: Some enhancements require detecting events in the underlying app (e.g., to trigger an update in an overlay). Android allows an accessibility service to listen to interface accessibility events (e.g., a button click, a text field focus, a view update, an app screen switch, a device app switch). Although limited to accessibility events that are invoked by the app, many necessary events are implemented by the default Android tools. This capability has been included since Android 1.6 and is available on 99.9% of Android devices [2].

Content Introspection: Some enhancements require knowledge of the content of elements in an underlying app. Proxies can inspect the app accessibility service representation. This provides a tree describing an app, where each node provides information about an element (e.g., content, size, state, possible actions), though we have noted that apps do not always expose correct or complete information via this representation. This capability has been included since Android 4.1 and is available on 97.5% of Android devices [2].

Automation: Some enhancements require manipulating an underlying app. Accessibility service automation support allows programmatic invocation of common manipulations of elements exposed via the accessibility service representation (e.g., click, long press, select, scroll, or text input directed to a node in the tree). This has been included since Android 4.1 and is currently available on 97.5% of Android devices [2].

Screen Capture: Some enhancements require information or presentation details not available through content introspection. This can include details of a view that the corresponding accessibility representation does not include in its model (e.g., pixel-precise positioning of content). The accessibility metadata provided by an app may also be incomplete or incorrect. Screen capture allows application of pixel-based methods developed in prior work (e.g., [13,15,16,17,18,19]), though some apps intentionally disable screen capture (e.g., banking apps). Screen capture has been included since Android 5.0 and is available in 60.7% of Android devices [2].

Gesture Dispatch: Some enhancements require simulating a gesture or touch. This can be because the automation events are not expressive enough for an enhancement to obtain a desired behavior, or it can be because an enhancement needs to manipulate an element that is not properly exposed by the accessibility representation. Gesture dispatch allows simulating a gesture or touch at any screen location. This capability is new in Android 7.0, but we have noted such capabilities will become more common as people transition to newer devices.

Current Implementation Limitations: We focus on Android, but support for these abstractions in other mobile platforms should similarly enable interaction proxies. We have also identified a few limitations of Android's current support. First, Android does not provide a robust unique identifier for each screen within an app. Similarly, the field used for differentiating among elements within a screen is optional and often not specified by developers. It can therefore be challenging to reason about the state of an app. Our current proxies use signatures computed from the tree exposed for content introspection. Pixel-based methods for annotation of interface elements could also be valuable [19]. Second, although an accessibility service can observe events, it cannot consume them (i.e., cannot redirect or prevent an event from occurring). The next section presents one implication of this in coordinating perception and manipulation. Finally, we have noted that accessibility services rely on app developers providing necessary events and metadata. Default tools provide this automatically whenever possible, but it is often missing. Our inclusion of screen capture and gesture dispatch provide additional options for interaction proxy implementation.

Coordinating Perception and Manipulation

A person perceives and manipulates the manifest interface, but that interaction must be re-mapped to the underlying original interface. Coordination of perception and manipulation in a re-mapping is critical to the illusion of the manifest interface remaining seamless (i.e., the interaction proxy being perceived as part of the interface, as opposed to itself being disruptive). The complexity of this coordination will vary according to the nature of the interaction and how it is re-mapped.

We have found that *direct* interaction is generally most straightforward to coordinate, as illustrated in Figure 5. Proxy implementation using floating windows means an interface is composed of layers. Projecting these into the display (i.e., flattening the layers along the z-axis) naturally results in interaction proxies occluding anything below. Manipulation is similarly straightforward. Figure 5 (left) shows selecting a button in the manifest interface, with Figure 5 (right) showing that hit-testing finds nothing at that location in the proxy layer and so selection passes to the underlying original interface. This straightforward coordination similarly extends to other *direct* interaction in the flattened interface. For example, the expected elements are naturally presented by Android TalkBack's exploration mode (i.e., as a person moves a finger around the screen to browse an interface with the screen reader, the expected element is naturally presented).

Coordination can be more challenging for *indirect* interaction. Figure 6 presents an example of a gesture-based interaction (i.e., swiping right to the next element in the navigation order). The manifest interface includes a button with correct metadata

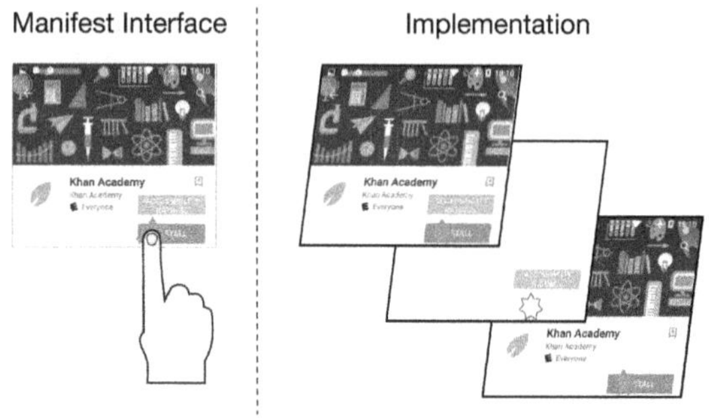

Figure 5. Direct interaction is generally straightforward to coordinate, with interface layers behaving as expected in their occlusion and in mapping input to the appropriate element.

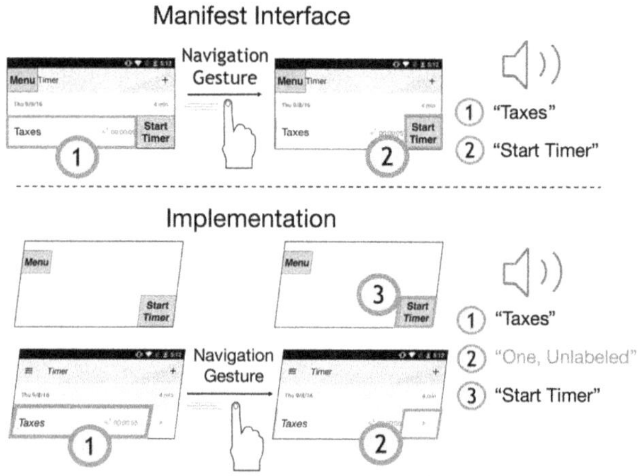

Figure 6. Indirect interaction can require more coordination. Here a gesture-based navigation requires an event listener to watch for "One, Unlabeled" to get focus and then immediately gives focus to "Start Timer". Perception in the manifest interface is seamless because the screen reader truncates reading of "One, Unlabeled", but this illustrates the type of coordination an interaction proxy may need to implement.

(i.e., "Start Timer") inserted to replace an original interface button that lacked metadata (i.e., "One, Unlabeled"). Figure 6 (top) illustrates the interaction experienced, swiping right to hear Android's TalkBack read "Start Timer". Figure 6 (bottom) reveals the navigation gesture is received by the original interface, which is unaware of the interaction proxy and gives focus to "One, Unlabeled". The proxy detects this using an event listener and immediately gives focus to "Start Timer", which is read aloud. In the instant that "One, Unlabeled" has focus, the screen reader begins to read it. However, this is imperceptible because focus moves to "Start Timer" and the screen reader aborts the prior reading (by design, ensuring prompt perception of interaction state during rapid navigation). The illusion of the manifest interface is therefore maintained. Although we do not present all of our interaction proxy implementations in this same detail, this example is intended to illustrate a typical coordination of an indirect interaction.

DEMONSTRATION IMPLEMENTATIONS

Prior sections have introduced several demonstration interaction proxies as part of conveying the strategy, design space, and implementation abstractions. This section presents additional details and demonstrations. All of our demonstrations were developed as proof-of-concept prototypes. By showing and explaining their key technical approaches, we aim to inform future development of the interaction proxy strategy. Details of these proof-of-concept implementations can also be found in their code, available at: https://github.com/appaccess.

Adding or Correcting Accessibility Metadata

Developers often fail to provide appropriate accessibility metadata for interface elements (e.g., labels for text fields). Although default tools provide this automatically whenever possible, people often encounter apps that have incomplete or incorrect metadata. Platforms have begun to support interactive correction, allowing a person to apply a custom label. But support is limited (e.g., Android only supports custom labels for elements with a `ViewIDResourceName`, which is itself optional and often not specified by app developers). Interaction proxies offer a strategy for third-party developers and researchers to develop and explore new approaches (e.g., social annotation approaches that have been proposed and examined in web-based systems [27,51,54,55]).

Figure 1 shows an example from Toggl, a popular time tracking app. The "Start Timer" button is missing metadata (i.e., the screen reader announces it as "One, Unlabeled") and the menu button has metadata resulting from an implementation artifact (i.e., is read as "Navigate Up"). Figure 7 shows a similar example in the Wells Fargo banking app (i.e., the label "Hamburger Button" is an implementation term better presented as "Menu"). Our interaction proxies identify these failures through *content introspection*, then obtain an image of the element using *screen capture*. Captured images can be used to obtain content descriptions (e.g., our proof-of-concept prototype uses a local database, envisioning social annotation mechanisms in future systems). Each failure is then repaired using a *floating window* to create a *partial overlay* that replaces the element in the manifest interface. Any manipulation of the element in the floating window is proxied to the original interface using *automation* to activate the appropriate element.

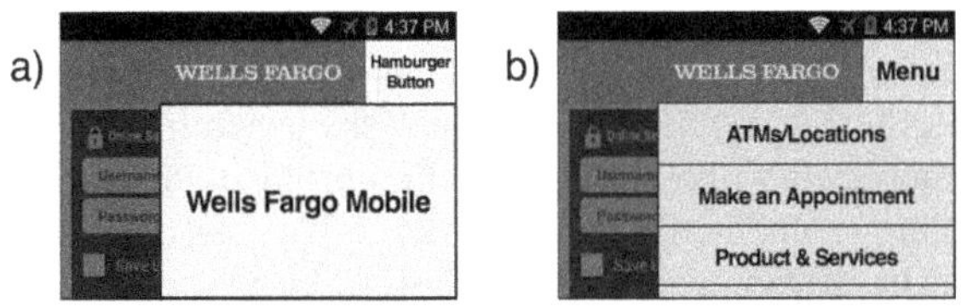

Figure 7. This interaction proxy corrects a "Menu" label and repairs interaction with the app's dropdown menu, which is otherwise completely inaccessible with a screen reader.

Figure 8. The Yelp app manifests its five-star rating system as a single element that cannot meaningfully be manipulated using a screen reader, and its navigation order using a screen reader makes it needlessly difficult to access "Search".

Restoring Missing Interactions

Figure 7 also illustrates repairing a similar but more severe failure in the Wells Fargo banking app. The original interface's dropdown menu includes several important functions, but does not correctly present itself to accessibility services. It therefore manifests as a single large element, is read as "Wells Fargo Mobile", and activates whatever menu item is in its physical center (e.g., "Make an Appointment"). Figure 8 shows a similar flaw in the Yelp app, which exposes its five-star rating system as a single element that cannot be meaningfully manifested by a screen reader. An interaction proxy repairs these using *screen capture*, a *floating window*, and *content introspection*. The proxy cannot use *automation* to manipulate underlying items, as this will again activate whatever item happens to be in the physical center of the erroneously monolithic element. The proxy instead activates the correct underlying item using *gesture dispatch* (i.e., sending a two-finger touch to the correct screen coordinate, which is consumed by the screen reader, generating a touch in the underlying original interface).

Modifying Navigation Order

Navigation order is a significant aspect of an interface, and optimal navigation may differ for different manifest interfaces (e.g., parallel visual scanning, touch-based exploration using a screen reader, serial navigation using a switch interface). Inappropriate orders can also result from an implementation failure, similar to other incorrect accessibility metadata. Figure 8 shows an example where an implementation error means the Yelp search box visually appears before the scrolling list of businesses, but is manifested after that list in a screen reader (i.e., making it difficult to access via serial navigation). Toggl similarly includes a "Create Timer" button that visually floats above the list of existing timers for easy and prominent access, but is manifested to a screen reader at the end of the list of existing timers. Our interaction proxies modify these navigation orders, moving the appropriate elements to the beginning of the manifest interface, using *content introspection*, *event listeners*, and *automation*, coordinating the interaction similar to the manner discussed in association with Figure 6.

Fully-Proxied Interfaces

Our prior interaction proxies have been minimal, emphasizing the ability to repair or enhance the accessibility of an interaction without needing to re-implement unrelated portions of the original interface. Such targeted re-mappings also highlight challenges of coordinating an interaction so that it blends in to the surrounding interface. Our same abstractions can also be applied in enhancements that proxy the entire interface, more completely changing the interface's manifestation.

Figure 9 shows an example of re-mapping interaction to implement stencils-based tutorials, a technique designed to help guide and focus a person through an interaction using "*translucent colored stencils containing holes that direct the user's attention to the correct interface component and prevent the user from interacting with other components*" [26,38]. Stencils could complement features like iOS Guided Access, providing additional capabilities, and enabling third-party development of different potential guides for varying needs

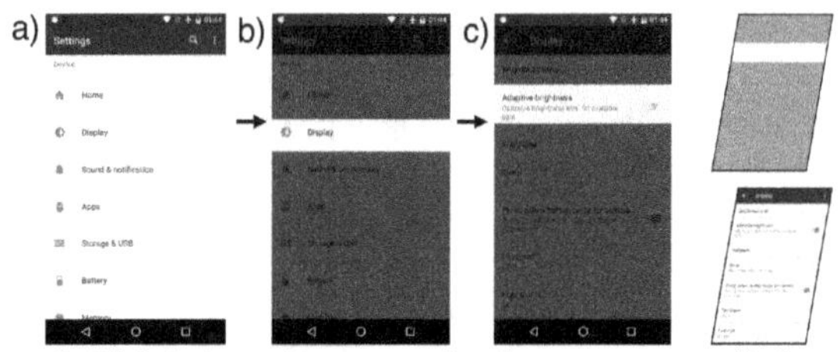

Figure 9. This interaction proxy implements a stencils-based tutorial. At each tutorial step, only the appropriate element is available. All other elements are obscured and disabled.

Figure 10. Motivated by research in personalized interface layout, this interaction proxy creates a completely new personalized layout for interacting with the underlying app.

(e.g., stencils in Figure 9 guide a person to a device setting). Our proxy is implemented using a *floating window* to create a *full overlay*, displayed as a translucent overlay and capturing all input. For each tutorial step, it uses *content introspection* to determine the bounds of elements that should be visible through the overlay (i.e., holes in the stencil), then *automation* to proxy manipulation of those elements. An *event listener* ensures the proxy's prompt response to interface changes, as when the interface advances between each step in the tutorial.

Figure 10 shows an example of a personalized interface layout, motivated by SUPPLE's approach to arranging entire interfaces to match an individual's motor abilities [23,58]. Although such personalization is promising for many accessibility needs, adoption of such methods is limited by a need for interfaces to be re-written as abstract specifications [45]. We instead propose an interaction proxy could re-map an original interface into an abstract specification which is then used to generate a personalized interface. As a proof-of-concept, our interaction proxy pictured in Figure 10 re-maps the original interface for Lose It! (a popular food journaling app) into model-level variables, then manifests those in a new interface. The new interface uses a different layout strategy to support larger text and buttons, and it presents underlying functionality differently (e.g., replacing a small sliding widget toggle with a larger checkbox element). Full implementation of this strategy is future research, but our proof-of-concept demonstrates the necessary combination of a *floating window* as a *full overlay*, perceiving the original interface using *content introspection* with *event listeners*, and manipulating it using *automation*.

INTERVIEWS REGARDING INTERACTION PROXIES

We conducted two sets of interviews with blind and low-vision people who use screen readers. Interviews were overall focused on: (1) accessibility barriers and the contexts in which they are encountered, (2) the experience of using an interface with an interaction proxy, (3) usefulness and potential of interaction proxies, and (4) potential for adoption of such enhancements.

Method

Our first set of interviews included eight people who are blind or low-vision and use a screen reader. We discussed what types of accessibility barriers these participants encounter in apps, how they navigate the barriers, how barriers could be addressed, and specific apps in which barriers are encountered. These interviews informed many of the interaction proxies developed in this paper. Specifically, participants identified three common barriers that potentially could be addressed with interaction proxies: mislabeled elements, inaccessible functionality, and challenging navigation. Participants also identified three major categories of app to be of interest: community engagement, productivity, and banking apps. Our proof-of-concept demonstrations and our second set of interviews therefore focused on these needs and opportunities.

Our second set of interviews included six people who are blind or low-vision and use a screen reader (including two from the first set). We developed three proof-of-concept enhancements to present to participants in support of these interviews: (1) Yelp: As illustrated in Figure 8, we repaired the stars on the business rating page to make it possible for a person using a screen reader to rate a business and repaired the navigation order to make the search box easier to reach. (2) Toggl: As illustrated in Figure 1, we repaired missing screen reader labels for elements associated with each existing timer. We also repaired navigation order to make the "Start New Timer" button easier to reach. (3) Wells Fargo: As illustrated in Figure 7, we repaired the items in the dropdown menu to be accessible with a screen reader and repaired the label of the menu button.

Interviews with these participants focused on the potential of interaction proxies to support accessibility enhancements. We asked each participant to use the Android Talkback screen reader to interact with the above three apps (on a Google Nexus 6P with Android 7.0). For each app, participants first completed simple tasks while our interaction proxy applied its repairs, then again with the screen reader manifesting the original interface. We chose this approach (e.g., instead of counterbalancing), in part because tasks generally could not be completed without the interaction proxy. Our focus was therefore on qualitative reactions rather than task metrics, and asking participants to begin with a task we knew was impossible would have undermined the interview. Participants discussed the feeling of the interaction with the interaction proxy active, how well it addressed accessibility barriers, and their ideas for the potential of accessibility enhancements. Interviews were transcribed and then analyzed using open coding.

Participants primarily reported using an iPhone, the more popular choice for people in the United States who use accessibility services [44]. Two reported using Android. Interaction with iOS's VoiceOver screen reader is similar to Android's TalkBack, and the barriers within apps are similar between platforms. We therefore believe these participants provided useful insight into the interaction proxy strategy.

Results

Interview participants reported our proof-of-concept prototype interaction proxies worked well for improving the accessibility of interactions. P3 said "*I think in every case [the enhancement] made it a much better experience than it would normally be*", while P5 said "*I think the enhancements have made it better*".

One goal for participant interaction with our prototypes during interviews was to examine seamlessness of the interaction (i.e., an interaction proxy being perceived as part of the interface, as opposed to itself being disruptive). Interviews explicitly probed this, in part by having participants first interact with the enhanced interface and then the app with its underlying accessibility failures. Participants ideally would not be able to distinguish between a natively accessible interface versus an interface that had been repaired or enhanced by an interaction proxy, and several participants commented that interactions were seamless. P3 said "*[the enhancements] made it behave as I would expect it to. I think, when the enhancements were on, I generally didn't have any trouble completing the tasks, which definitely means it's working*", while P2 said "*[the enhanced Yelp app] acted the way I would expect it to act*".

Two participants commented on swipe-based navigation when using a proxy that repairs metadata by changing screen reader focus (as discussed with Figure 6). P1 described "*lagginess*", and we did note the app and enhancement were unusually slow for this participant. P2 described "*oversensitivity*" that made it more difficult to use swipe-based navigation to select a target without skipping it. However, P2 also explicitly noted that the value provided by the enhancement was enough to outweigh "*oversensitivity*". Even when prompted, participants did not mention any other unusual or bothersome interactions.

Participant responses to the specific enhancements we showed were varied. For example, all participants agreed it was an improvement for the Wells Fargo app menu to be accessible, but all felt the "Forgot Password" item was still difficult to find because the app hid it in the dropdown menu. Even when an interaction proxy improves accessibility of an interface, there can still be usability barriers due to poor interface design choices.

All participants described how the types of enhancements we demonstrated could be made to address barriers they encounter, and all expressed interest in using such enhancements. P1 said "*In email…forward and reply all are at the very bottom of the message and if it's a really long message, it's really a pain to have to scroll all the way to the bottom of the message*". P5 said "*[an enhancement] would definitely be a value to be able to get the Greyhound app accessible so that I could be able to purchase tickets and look at the schedules and so forth*".

In discussions regarding the potential for broad deployment, all participants said they would be willing to submit apps needing repair or enhancement if they thought it was likely the enhancement would be created. P3 is a software developer and indicated he would be willing to create enhancements if good tools were available. P3 and P5 also expressed concern over whether enough people would contribute enhancements. P6 was more optimistic about participation, saying "*I do think that people would be very interested in it, and I think people would want to help contribute to the actual programming, and then people would also be interested in making suggestions.*" Finally, participants discussed their trust of third-party enhancements. They reported that primary factors in whether they would trust an enhancement enough to download it are the reputation of the source, endorsements from known organizations (e.g., the National Federation for the Blind), and feedback from other people who use screen readers.

DISCUSSION AND CONCLUSION

We have introduced interaction proxies as a strategy for runtime repair and enhancement of the accessibility of mobile apps. Inserted between an app's original interface and a manifest interface, an interaction proxy allows third-party developers and researchers to modify an interaction without an app's source code, without rooting the phone or otherwise modifying an app, while retaining all capabilities of the system. We have examined the interaction proxy strategy through a design space of interaction re-mappings, by defining and developing key implementation abstractions, and in Android implementations of proof-of-concept interaction proxies. Details of these proof-of-concept implementations can also be found in their code, available at: https://github.com/appaccess.

These conceptual and technical contributions are our primary contributions, and our interviews with blind and low-vision people who use screen readers provide support for further developing this strategy. Participants were enthusiastic for the strategy, based on our proof-of-concept prototypes repairing accessibility failures in popular real-world apps. Including these prototypes in our interviews provided a real-world context for discussing the potential of interaction proxies, and participants used this as a starting point for discussing other apps in which they have encountered accessibility barriers that might be addressed. Participants saw a need and potential for third-party enhancements, expressing interest in the value they could provide even if a repaired interaction was not quite seamless.

Our ultimate goal is to help catalyze advances in mobile app accessibility. Where contributions have previously been limited to developers of individual apps or the underlying mobile platform, interaction proxies open an opportunity for third-party developers and researchers to develop and deploy accessibility repairs and enhancements into widely-used apps and platforms. P1 motivated a multi-faceted approach by saying "*I mean I think what you did is great, to make some more improvements, but also how we can work with community people and ideally Google and [app] developers*". Interaction proxies therefore provide an additional tool that complements efforts to educate and support developers in improving the accessibility of their apps, as well as improvements in platform accessibility support.

ACKNOWLEDGEMENTS

We thank our participants for their contributions, and reviewers for their feedback on an earlier draft of this paper. This work was supported in part by the National Science Foundation under awards IIS-0811063 and IIS-1053868.

REFERENCES

1. Android Open Source Project. Accessibility Developer Checklist. http://developer.android.com/guide/topics/ui/accessibility/checklist.html#requirements
2. Android Open Source Project. Dashboards. http://developer.android.com/about/dashboards/index.html
3. Apple Inc. Use Guided Access with iPhone, iPad, and iPod touch. https://support.apple.com/en-us/HT202612
4. Jeffrey P. Bigham. (2014). Making the Web Easier to See with Opportunistic Accessibility Improvement. *Proceedings of the ACM Symposium on User Interface Software and Technology (UIST 2014)*, 117–122. http://doi.org/10.1145/2642918.2647357
5. Jeffrey P. Bigham, Chandrika Jayant, Hanjie Ji, Greg Little, Andrew Miller, Robert C. Miller, Aubrey Tatarowicz, Brandyn White, Samuel White, and Tom Yeh. (2010). VizWiz: Nearly Real-time Answers to Visual Questions. *Proceedings of the ACM Symposium on User Interface Software and Technology (UIST 2010)*, 333–342. http://doi.acm.org/10.1145/1866029.1866080
6. Jeffrey P. Bigham, Ryan S. Kaminsky, Richard E. Ladner, Oscar M. Danielsson, and Gordon L. Hempton. (2006). WebInSight: Making Web Images Accessible. *Proceedings of the ACM Conference on Computers and Accessibility (ASSETS 2006)*, 181–188. http://doi.org/10.1145/1168987.1169018
7. Jeffrey P. Bigham and Richard E. Ladner. (2007). Accessmonkey: a Collaborative Scripting Framework for Web Users and Developers. *Proceedings of the International Conference on Web accessibility (W4A 2007)*, 25–34. http://doi.acm.org/10.1145/1243441.1243452
8. Jeffrey P. Bigham, Craig M. Prince, and Richard E. Ladner. (2008). WebAnywhere: a Screen Reader On-the-Go. *Proceedings of the International Workshop on Web Accessibility (W4A 2008)*, 73–82. http://dx.doi.org/10.1145/1368044.1368060
9. Erin L. Brady, Yu Zhong, Meredith Ringel Morris, and Jeffrey P. Bigham. (2013). Investigating the Appropriateness of Social Network Question Asking as a Resource for Blind Users. *Proceedings of the Conference on Computer Supported Cooperative Work (CSCW 2013)*, 1225–1236. http://dx.doi.org/10.1145/2441776.2441915
10. Erin Brady, Meredith Ringel Morris, and Jeffrey P. Bigham. (2015). Gauging Receptiveness to Social Microvolunteering. *Proceedings of the ACM Conference on Human Factors in Computing Systems (CHI 2015)*, 1055–1064. http://doi.acm.org/10.1145/2702123.2702329
11. Erin Brady, Meredith Ringel Morris, Yu Zhong, Samuel White, and Jeffrey P. Bigham. (2013). Visual Challenges in the Everyday Lives of Blind People. *Proceedings of the ACM Conference on Human Factors in Computing Systems (CHI 2013)*, 2117–2126. http://doi.org/10.1145/2470654.2481291
12. Jim A. Carter and David W. Fourne. (2007). Techniques to Assist in Developing Accessibility Engineers. *Proceedings of the ACM Conference on Computers and Accessibility (ASSETS 2007)*, 123–130. http://dx.doi.org/10.1145/1296843.1296865
13. Tsung-Hsiang Chang, Tom Yeh, and Robert C. Miller. (2011). Associating The Visual Representation of User Interfaces with their Internal Structures and Metadata. *Proceedings of the ACM Symposium on User Interface Software and Technology (UIST 2011)*, 245–256. http://doi.acm.org/10.1145/2047196.2047228
14. Alan Cooper. (1995). *About Face: The Essentials of User Interface Design*. John Wiley & Sons, Inc., New York, NY.
15. Morgan Dixon and James Fogarty. (2010). Prefab: Implementing Advanced Behaviors Using Pixel-Based Reverse Engineering of Interface Structure. *Proceedings of the ACM Conference on Human Factors in Computing Systems (CHI 2010)*, 1525–1534. http://doi.acm.org/10.1145/1753326.1753554
16. Morgan Dixon, James Fogarty, and Jacob O. Wobbrock. (2012). A General-Purpose Target-Aware Pointing Enhancement using Pixel-Level Analysis of Graphical Interfaces. *Proceedings of the ACM Conference on Human Factors in Computing Systems (CHI 2012)*, 3167–3176. http://doi.acm.org/10.1145/2207676.2208734
17. Morgan Dixon, Gierad Laput, and James Fogarty. (2014). Pixel-Based Methods for Widget State and Style in a Runtime Implementation of Sliding Widgets. *Proceedings of the ACM Conference on Human Factors in Computing Systems (CHI 2014)*, 2231–2240. http://doi.acm.org/10.1145/2556288.2556979
18. Morgan Dixon, Daniel Leventhal, and James Fogarty. (2011). Content and Hierarchy in Pixel-Based Methods for Reverse Engineering Interface Structure. *Proceedings of the ACM Conference on Human Factors in Computing Systems (CHI 2011)*, 969–978. http://doi.acm.org/10.1145/1978942.1979086

19. Morgan Dixon, A. Conrad Nied, and James Fogarty. (2014). Prefab Layers and Prefab Annotations: Extensible Pixel-Based Interpretation of Graphical Interfaces. *Proceedings of the ACM Symposium on User Interface Software and Technology (UIST 2014)*, 221–230. http://doi.acm.org/10.1145/2642918.2647412

20. James R. Eagan, Michel Beaudouin-Lafon, and Wendy E. Mackay. (2011). Cracking the Cocoa Nut: User Interface Programming at Runtime. *Proceedings of the ACM Symposium on User Interface Software and Technology (UIST 2011)*, 225–234. http://doi.org/10.1145/2047196.2047226

21. W. Keith Edwards, Scott E. Hudson, Joshua Marinacci, Roy Rodenstein, Thomas Rodriguez, and Ian E. Smith. (1997). Systematic Output Modification in a 2D User Interface Toolkit. *Proceedings of the ACM Symposium on User Interface Software and Technology (UIST 1997)*, 151–158. http://doi.org/10.1145/263407.263537

22. Leah Findlater, Alex Jansen, Kristen Shinohara, Morgan Dixon, Peter Kamb, Joshua Rakita, and Jacob O. Wobbrock. (2010). Enhanced Area Cursors: Reducing Fine-Pointing Demands for People with Motor Impairments. *Proceedings of the ACM Symposium on User Interface Software and Technology (UIST 2010)*, 153–162. http://doi.org/10.1145/1866029.1866055

23. Krzysztof Z. Gajos, Daniel S. Weld, and Jacob O. Wobbrock. (2010). Automatically Generating Personalized User Interfaces with SUPPLE. *Artificial Intelligence*, *174*(12–13), 910–950. http://doi.org/10.1016/j.artint.2010.05.005

24. Google Inc. Accessibility Scanner. https://play.google.com/store/apps/details?id=com.google.android.apps.accessibility.auditor

25. Vicki L. Hanson and John T. Richards. (2013). Progress on Website Accessibility? *ACM Transactions on the Web*, *7*(1), 2:1-2:30. http://dx.doi.org/10.1145/2435215.2435217

26. Kyle J. Harms, Jordana H. Kerr, and Caitlin L. Kelleher. (2011). Improving Learning Transfer from Stencils-Based Tutorials. *Proceedings of the International Conference on Interaction Design and Children (IDC 2011)*, 157–160. http://dx.doi.org/10.1145/1999030.1999050

27. Yun Huang, Brian Dobreski, Bijay Bhaskar Deo, Jiahang Xin, Natã Miccael Barbosa, Yang Wang, and Jeffrey P. Bigham. (2015). CAN: Composable Accessibility Infrastructure via Data-Driven Crowdsourcing. *Proceedings of the Web for All Conference (W4A 2015)*, 1–10. http://dx.doi.org/10.1145/2745555.2746651

28. Amy Hurst, Scott E. Hudson, and Jennifer Mankoff. (2010). Automatically Identifying Targets Users Interact With During Real World Tasks. *Proceedings of the International Conference on Intelligent User Interfaces (IUI 2010)*, 11–20. http://dx.doi.org/10.1145/1719970.1719973

29. Amy Hurst, Jennifer Mankoff, Anind K. Dey, and Scott E. Hudson. (2007). Dirty Desktops: Using a Patina of Magnetic Mouse Dust to Make Common Interactor Targets Easier to Select. *Proceedings of the ACM Symposium on User Interface Software and Technology (UIST 2007)*, 183–186. http://doi.acm.org/10.1145/1294211.1294242

30. Edwin L. Hutchins, James D. Hollan, and Donald A. Norman. (2009). Direct Manipulation Interfaces. *Human–Computer Interaction*, *1*(4), 311–338. http://dx.doi.org/10.1207/s15327051hci0104_2

31. IDI Web Accessibility Checker : Web Accessibility Checker. http://achecker.ca/checker/index.php

32. Yeongjin Jang, Chengyu Song, Simon P. Chung, Tielei Wang, and Wenke Lee. (2014). A11y Attacks: Exploiting Accessibility in Operating Systems. *Proceedings of the ACM Conference on Computer and Communications Security (CCS 2014)*, 103–115. http://doi.org/10.1145/2660267.2660295

33. Alex Jansen, Leah Findlater, and Jacob O. Wobbrock. (2011). From The Lab to The World: Lessons from Extending a Pointing Technique for Real-World Use. *Extended Abstracts of the ACM Conference on Human Factors in Computing Systems (CHI 2011)*, 1867–1872. http://doi.org/10.1145/1979742.1979888

34. Shaun K. Kane, Jeffrey P. Bigham, and Jacob O. Wobbrock. (2008). Slide Rule: Making Mobile Touch Screens Accessible to Blind People Using Multi-Touch Interaction Techniques. *Proceedings of the ACM Conference on Computers and Accessibility (ASSETS 2008)*, 73–80. http://doi.acm.org/10.1145/1414471.1414487

35. Shaun K. Kane, Chandrika Jayant, Jacob O. Wobbrock, and Richard E. Ladner. (2009). Freedom to Roam: A Study of Mobile Device Adoption and Accessibility for People with Visual and Motor Disabilities. *Proceedings of the ACM Conference on Computers and Accessibility (ASSETS 2009)*, 115–122. http://doi.org/10.1145/1639642.1639663

36. Shaun K. Kane, Meredith Ringel Morris, Annuska Z. Perkins, Daniel J. Wigdor, Richard E. Ladner, and Jacob O. Wobbrock. (2011). Access Overlays: Improving Non-Visual Access to Large Touch Screens for Blind Users. *Proceedings of the ACM Symposium on User Interface Software and Technology (UIST 2011)*, 273–282. http://dx.doi.org/10.1145/2047196.2047232

37. Shinya Kawanaka, Yevgen Borodin, Jeffrey P. Bigham, Darren Lunn, Hironobu Takagi, and Chieko Asakawa. (2008). Accessibility Commons: A Metadata Infrastructure for Web Accessibility. *Proceedings of the ACM Conference on Computers and Accessibility (ASSETS 2008)*, 153–160. http://doi.org/10.1145/1414471.1414500

38. Caitlin Kelleher and Randy Pausch. (2005). Stencils-Based Tutorials: Design and Evaluation. *Proceedings of the ACM Conference on Human Factors in Computing Systems (CHI 2005)*, 541–550. http://dx.doi.org/10.1145/1054972.1055047

39. Richard E. Ladner. (2015). Design for User Empowerment. *Interactions*, *22*(2), 24–29. http://dx.doi.org/10.1145/2723869

40. Walter Lasecki, Christopher Miller, Adam Sadilek, Andrew Abumoussa, Donato Borrello, Raja Kushalnagar, and Jeffrey Bigham. (2012). Real-Time Captioning by Groups of Non-Experts. *Proceedings of the ACM Symposium on User Interface Software and Technology (UIST 2012)*, 23–34. http://dx.doi.org/10.1145/2380116.2380122

41. Walter S. Lasecki, Phyo Thiha, Yu Zhong, Erin Brady, and Jeffrey P. Bigham. (2013). Answering Visual Questions with Conversational Crowd Assistants. *Proceedings of the ACM Conference on Computers and Accessibility (ASSETS 2013)*, 18:1–18:8. http://doi.org/10.1145/2513383.2517033

42. Jonathan Lazar, Daniel F. Goldstein, and Anne Taylor. (2015). *Ensuring Digital Accessibility through Process and Policy*. http://www.elsevier.com/books/ensuring-digital-accessibility-through-process-and-policy/lazar/978-0-12-800646-7

43. Lauren R. Milne, Cynthia L. Bennett, and Richard E. Ladner. (2014). The Accessibility of Mobile Health Sensors for Blind Users. *International Technology and Persons with Disabilities Conference Scientific/Research Proceedings (CSUN 2014)*, 166–175. http://doi.org/10211.3/133384

44. J. Morris and J. Mueller. (2014). Blind and Deaf Consumer Preferences for Android and iOS Smartphones. In *Inclusive Designing*. Springer International Publishing, Cham, 69–79. http://doi.org/10.1007/978-3-319-05095-9_7

45. Brad Myers, Scott E. Hudson, and Randy Pausch. (2000). Past, Present, and Future of User Interface Software Tools. *ACM Transactions on Computer-Human Interaction 7*, 3–28. http://doi.org/10.1145/344949.344959

46. Dan R. Olsen, Jr., Scott E. Hudson, Thom Verratti, Jeremy M. Heiner, and Matt Phelps. (1999). Implementing Interface Attachments Based on Surface Representations. *Proceedings of the ACM Conference on Human Factors in Computing Systems (CHI 1999)*, 191–198. http://doi.acm.org/10.1145/302979.303038

47. Elaine Pearson, Chrstopher Bailey, and Steve Green. (2011). A Tool to Support the Web Accessibility Evaluation Process for Novices. *Proceedings of the Conference on Innovation and Technology in Computer Science Education (ITiCSE 2011)*, 28–32. http://dx.doi.org/10.1145/1999747.1999758

48. André Rodrigues. (2015). Breaking Barriers with Assistive Macros. *Proceedings of the ACM Conference on Computers and Accessibility (ASSETS 2015)*, 351–352. http://dx.doi.org/10.1145/2700648.2811322

49. André Rodrigues and Tiago Guerreiro. (2014). SWAT: Mobile System-Wide Assistive Technologies. *Proceedings of the International BCS Human Computer Interaction Conference (British HCI 2016)*, 341–346. https://dl.acm.org/citation.cfm?id=2742991

50. Franziska Roesner, James Fogarty, and Tadayoshi Kohno. (2012). User Interface Toolkit Mechanisms for Securing Interface Elements. *Proceedings of the ACM Symposium on User Interface Software and Technology (UIST 2012)*, 239–250. http://doi.acm.org/10.1145/2380116.2380147

51. Daisuke Sato, Hironobu Takagi, Masatomo Kobayashi, Shinya Kawanaka, Chieko Asakawa, and Asakawa Chieko. (2010). Exploratory Analysis of Collaborative Web Accessibility Improvement. *ACM Transactions on Accessible Computing (TACCESS)*, *3*(2), 5:1-5:30. http://doi.acm.org/10.1145/1857920.1857922

52. Wolfgang Stuerzlinger, Olivier Chapuis, Dusty Phillips, and Nicolas Roussel. (2006). User Interface Façades: Towards Fully Adaptable User Interfaces. *Proceedings of the ACM Symposium on User Interface Software and Technology (UIST 2006)*, 309–318. http://doi.acm.org/10.1145/1166253.1166301
53. Hironobu Takagi and Chieko Asakawa. (2000). Transcoding Proxy for Nonvisual Web Access. *Proceedings of the ACM Conference on Assistive Technologies (ASSETS 2000)*, 164–171. http://doi.org/10.1145/354324.354371
54. Hironobu Takagi, Shinya Kawanaka, Masatomo Kobayashi, Takashi Itoh, and Chieko Asakawa. (2008). Social Accessibility: Achieving Accessibility Through Collaborative Metadata Authoring. *Proceedings of the ACM Conference on Computers and Accessibility (ASSETS 2008)*, 193–200. http://doi.acm.org/10.1145/1414471.1414507
55. Hironobu Takagi, Shinya Kawanaka, Masatomo Kobayashi, Daisuke Sato, and Chieko Asakawa. (2009). Collaborative Web Accessibility Improvement: Challenges and Possibilities. *Proceedings of the ACM Conference on Computers and Accessibility (ASSETS 2009)*, 195–202. http://doi.acm.org/10.1145/1639642.163967
56. Desney S. Tan, Brian Meyers, and Mary Czerwinski. (2004). WinCuts: Manipulating Arbitrary Window Regions for More Effective Use of Screen Space. *Extended Abstracts of the ACM Conference on Human Factors in Computing Systems (CHI 2004)*, 1525–1528. http://doi.acm.org/10.1145/985921.986106
57. Jacob O. Wobbrock, James Fogarty, Shih-Yen (Sean) Liu, Shunichi Kimuro, and Susumu Harada. (2009). The Angle Mouse: Target-Agnostic Dynamic Gain Adjustment Based on Angular Deviation. *Proceedings of the ACM Conference on Human Factors in Computing Systems (CHI 2009)*, 1401–1410. http://doi.acm.org/10.1145/1518701.1518912
58. Jacob O. Wobbrock, Shaun K. Kane, Krzysztof Z. Gajos, Susumu Harada, and Jon E. Froehlich. (2011). Ability-Based Design: Concept, Principles and Examples. *ACM Transactions on Accessible Computing (TACCESS)*, *3*(3), 1–27. http://doi.org/10.1145/1952383.1952384
59. Aileen Worden, Nef Walker, Krishna Bharat, and Scott E. Hudson. (1997). Making Computers Easier for Older Adults to Use: Area Cursors and Sticky Icons. *Proceedings of the ACM Conference on Human Factors in Computing Systems (CHI 1997)*, 266–271. http://doi.acm.org/10.1145/258549.258724
60. World Health Organization. (2011). World Report on Disability. http://www.who.int/disabilities/world_report/2011/report/en/
61. Tom Yeh, Tsung-Hsiang Chang, and Robert C. Miller. (2009). Sikuli: Using GUI Screenshots for Search and Automation. *Proceedings of the ACM Symposium on User Interface Software and Technology (UIST 2009)*, 183–192. http://doi.acm.org/10.1145/1622176.1622213
62. Jason Chen Zhao, Richard C. Davis, Pin Sym Foong, and Shengdong Zhao. (2015). CoFaçade: A Customizable Assistive Approach for Elders and Their Helpers. *Proceedings of the ACM Conference on Human Factors in Computing Systems (CHI 2015)*, 1583–1592. http://doi.org/10.1145/2702123.2702588
63. Yu Zhong, Astrid Weber, Casey Burkhardt, Phil Weaver, and Jeffrey P. Bigham. (2015). Enhancing Android Accessibility for Users with Hand Tremor by Reducing Fine Pointing and Steady Tapping. *Proceedings of the Web for All Conference on (W4A 2015)*, 29:1-29:10. http://dx.doi.org/10.1145/2745555.2747277

SUGILITE: Creating Multimodal Smartphone Automation by Demonstration

Toby Jia-Jun Li[1], Amos Azaria[2], and Brad A. Myers[1]
[1] Human-Computer Interaction Institute, Carnegie Mellon University
[2] Computer Science Department, Ariel University
{tobyli, bam}@cs.cmu.edu, amos.azaria@ariel.ac.il

ABSTRACT
SUGILITE is a new programming-by-demonstration (PBD) system that enables users to create automation on smartphones. SUGILITE uses Android's accessibility API to support automating arbitrary tasks in any Android app (or even across multiple apps). When the user gives verbal commands that SUGILITE does not know how to execute, the user can demonstrate by directly manipulating the regular apps' user interface. By leveraging the verbal instructions, the demonstrated procedures, and the apps' UI hierarchy structures, SUGILITE can automatically generalize the script from the recorded actions, so SUGILITE learns how to perform tasks with different variations and parameters from a single demonstration. Extensive error handling and context checking support forking the script when new situations are encountered, and provide robustness if the apps change their user interface. Our lab study suggests that users with little or no programming knowledge can successfully automate smartphone tasks using SUGILITE.

Author Keywords
Programming by demonstration; smartphone automation; end-user development.

ACM Classification Keywords
H.5.2. Information interfaces and presentation (e.g., HCI): User Interfaces - *Interaction styles*.

INTRODUCTION
In smartphone usage, many common tasks are repetitive and tedious. Some also require a large number of actions, or navigating through a complex user interface (UI) structure. For instance, the current version of the Starbucks app for Android requires 18 taps to order a venti Iced Cappuccino with skim milk, and even more if the user does not have the account information stored. For those tasks, the users would often like to have them automated [2,26,38], for example, to have them performed by an intelligent software agent on their behalf [18]. In a motivating survey we conducted with 65 participants, 62.7% reported that they were interested in having a way to automate their repetitive tasks.

CHI 2017, May 06 - 11, 2017, Denver, CO, USA.

ACM 978-1-4503-4655-9/17/05…$15.00
DOI: http://dx.doi.org/10.1145/3025453.3025483

Intelligent agents like Siri, Cortana and Google Now can be activated by voice commands to perform various tasks, including device control, communication, web search, and calendar management. Such agents allow the user to focus on the specifications of the task while the agent performs the low-level actions [25], as opposed to the usual direct manipulation UI, in which the user must select the correct objects, execute the correct operations and control the environment [40]. However, prevailing smartphone intelligent software agents have limited functionality. They can only invoke built-in apps (e.g. Phone, Message, Calendar, Music etc.) and a few integrated external apps and web services (e.g. Search, Weather, Wikipedia). They lack the capability of controlling arbitrary third-party apps and services.

Companies like Apple are opening up the APIs to enable the third-party apps to integrate into their agents and to be activated from voice commands [45]. However, due to the cost and effort required, it is most likely that only some apps will be integrated and only some of the most popular tasks in those apps will be supported. Even for the supported apps, end users will still not be able to create automations for their personalized tasks and to integrate their personal requirements into the current smartphone agents. For example, most existing agents can invoke the music player, but they cannot incorporate the user's personal preferences in the automation, like applying a specific equalizer for an artist, or setting the volume to a pre-specified level before playing. Enabling personalization and customization is particularly important for modern smartphone users because they have very diverse patterns in what apps they use and how they use them [44].

Programming by Demonstration (PBD) is a promising technique to enable end users to automate their activities without necessarily requiring programming knowledge. It allows users to program in the same environment in which they perform the actions [11,24,30]. This makes PBD particularly appealing for many smartphone users, who have little knowledge of conventional programming languages, but are familiar with how to perform the tasks they wish to automate using the existing smartphone apps.

In this paper, we describe the design and implementation of SUGILITE[1], a PBD system that enables users to create task automations on smartphones and perform the tasks through a conversational interface. SUGILITE allows users to create generalized automation for tasks in arbitrary third-party mobile apps by simply demonstrating the procedure of performing the task using the regular app UI. SUGILITE is named after a purple gemstone, and stands for: **S**martphone **U**sers **G**enerating **I**ntelligent **L**ikeable **I**nterfaces **T**hrough **E**xamples. Our approach addresses the following three problems and limitations of other approaches:

Applicability: Many existing PBD systems [5,9,26] and mobile end-user development (EUD) systems [16,17] require the apps involved in the tasks to either use a special framework or library, or to provide an open API for their functionality. This limits the applicability of those systems – they can only be used to automate a small subset of tasks.

In contrast, SUGILITE can automate tasks using *any* third-party Android app (with a few exceptions noted in the Technical Limitation section), and can even create scripts that automate tasks across *multiple* apps. This makes PBD on smartphones much more useful, given nowadays an average U.S. smartphone user spends 90% of their mobile device time on apps [20], and uses 26.7 different apps [37].

Generalizability: Some previous macro-recording tools [39] do not suffer the applicability issues above. They can record a sequence of input events and replay the same actions at a later time. However, these scripts cannot be generalized, and will only perform the exact same tasks but not tasks with variations or different parameters. Other PBD systems (e.g. [27,32]) support generalization, but require multiple examples with different values for the parameters from the user. Prior studies have shown that end users often have a hard time giving meaningfully different examples for script generalization [12,28].

Our system has a multi-modal interface where the user can give a verbal command to execute an automation through a voice conversational interface, while making demonstrations and editing existing scripts using direct manipulation. In the background, SUGILITE detects the apps' UI hierarchy structures for all the activities that users visit. Then, SUGILITE combines the voice command, the actions recorded and an analysis of the app's structures to infer generalizations of the script. This allows SUGILITE to learn a generalized task from a single demonstration. In addition, if the recorded script encounters a new situation at runtime, then SUGILITE will allow the user to demonstrate new steps, which can either replace the original script (e.g., if the app has permanently changed the UI, or the users change what they want to do), or else can form a *fork*, and further generalize the script to work in the new situation. Finally, advanced users can manually generalize, review and edit the script through SUGILITE's editing interface.

Usability: Some mobile EUD systems (e.g. [38,46]) require users to program automations using a visual programming language or a textual scripting language. This imposes a significant learning barrier and prevents users with limited programming knowledge from using these systems.

In contrast, SUGILITE users can create automations by demonstrating the procedure using the familiar UIs of the actual apps involved. In our lab study, most participants were able to successfully automate tasks through SUGILITE, regardless of their prior programming experience.

Contributions

To summarize, the contributions of this paper are:

- SUGILITE, a mobile PBD system that enables the user to create an automation for arbitrary tasks across any or multiple third-party smartphone apps and to execute automated tasks through a multi-modal (speech) interface.
- A PBD script generalization mechanism that leverages the verbal command, the recorded actions, and recorded information about the UI hierarchy structures of the third-party apps to create a generalized program from a single demonstration. The system also has a representation of the recordings that allows users to manually edit scripts if necessary.
- An error checking and handling mechanism that improves the system's robustness when the underlying apps change, and also supports further generalization of the scripts to handle new situations as they arise.
- A lab study that showed users with different levels of programming experience were able to use our tool to create automation for four tasks derived from real-world scenarios with an 85.5% completion rate, plus subjective feedback showing they like and would want to use a tool like SUGILITE.

RELATED WORK

In this section, we discuss prior work in four areas related to our system: PBD in general, PBD generalization, instructable intelligent agents, and mobile end-user development (EUD) systems that use techniques other than PBD.

Task Automating by Demonstration

There have been many PBD systems to help people automate tasks [11,24]. However, PBD systems often require access to the internal data of the software where the demonstration happens. This limits the reach of those systems. For example, the CHINLE system [9] only works with interface generated by the SUPPLE framework [14], and DOCWIZARDS [5] only records actions performed on SWT widgets within Eclipse. Some PBD system focus on automating a specific type of task like file manipulation [29], photo manipulation [15], web tasks [23], or interactive interface construction [13,27]. Much work also has been done on PBD for human-robot interaction (e.g. [3,6,35])

[1] The source code is available at http://www.toby.li/sugilite_repo

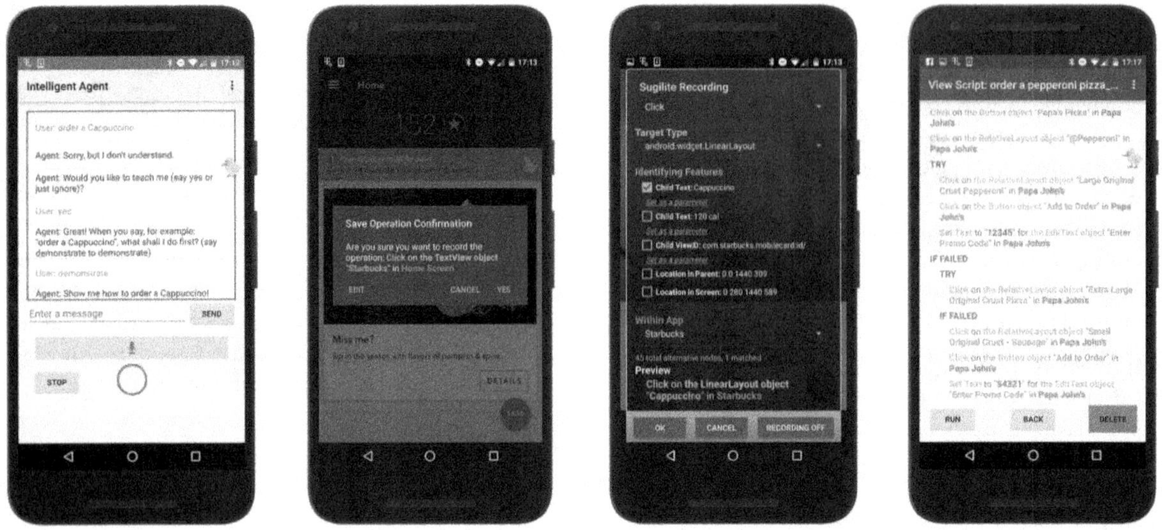

(a) (b) (c) (d)

Figure 1. Screenshots of SUGILITE: (a) the conversational interface; (b) the recording confirmation popup; (c) the recording disambiguation/operation editing panel and (d) the viewing/editing script window.

Very few PBD systems exist on smartphones. KEEP DOING IT [26] derives IF-THEN automation rules from the user's demonstration. But it can only invoke system functions like turning on Wi-Fi, setting the ringer to silent, etc. It does not have the ability to control arbitrary third-party apps on the phone like SUGILITE does. To our knowledge, SUGILITE is the first PBD system to allow the automation of arbitrary tasks on any third-party app on a smartphone.

However, there are macro-recording tools on smartphone like [39] that can record a sequence of input events and replay them later. A major limitation of such tools compared to SUGILITE is that they are too literal. They can only replay exactly the same procedure that was demonstrated, without the ability to generalize the demonstration to perform similar tasks. They are also brittle to any UI changes in the app.

Script Generalization

A major challenge for any PBD-based automation tool is script generalization [11,24,33] to support performing a *similar* task, but not necessarily the identical task [11]. Many approaches have been used in generalizing PBD scripts, including removing details (e.g. [19]), heuristics (e.g. [22,31,34]) and using multiple examples (e.g. [27]). SUGILITE uses a different approach, as discussed below.

Verbal Instruction

SUGILITE also uses verbal instructions in creating the automation. Prior works like [1,4,8,42] enable the users to instruct the agent to perform tasks using commands in natural language. A weakness of that approach on smartphone automation relates to efficiency – it can be slower to describe a smartphone operation in natural language than to simply tap on the screen. While we do not seek to make contributions in enabling better comprehension of verbal instructions, we leverage the current state-of-art work in comprehending verbal instructions to enhance the SUGILITE script generalizations.

End-User Development on Smartphone

Task automation is an important application for mobile EUD [36]. Besides PBD, there are other approaches to enable the end users to create automation on smartphones. Some approaches (e.g. [16,17,47]) use the "trigger-action" model, in which an "action" will be performed when the trigger happens. Compared with SUGILITE, these tools can only be applied on apps or services with open APIs available. The simple structures of their automation model also limit their uses in automating more complex tasks.

Alternatively, other systems like [38,46] allow the user to create automation with more complicated control structures (e.g. conditions, loops, exceptions). However, these suffer in usability compared with SUGILITE because they demand that users work with visual programming languages or textual scripting languages in unfamiliar interfaces.

EXAMPLE USAGE SCENARIO

This section presents an example scenario of a user interacting with SUGILITE. This example demonstrates our system's ability to learn generalized tasks with third-party applications from a user's single demonstration.

Order Starbucks Coffee[2]

Smartphone users can order a wide range of products through the apps provided by merchants. In our motivating survey, respondents reported that many such tasks required them to navigate through a complicated multi-level menu in the app to locate the desired offering, which would be especially annoying the same task is performed frequently.

[2] This scenario is also shown in the accompanying video.

Automating repetitive activities is a key motivation for SUGILITE. In this scenario, we show an example of how a user automates ordering Starbucks drinks using SUGILITE.

The user first gives SUGILITE a voice command, "Order a Cappuccino." using the conversational voice interface (Figure 1a), for which SUGILITE answers "Sorry but I don't understand. Would you like to teach me? Say 'demonstrate' to demonstrate." The user then says, "demonstrate" and starts demonstrating the procedure of ordering a Cappuccino using the Starbucks app.

She first clicks on the Starbucks icon on the home screen, taps on the main menu and chooses "Order", which is exactly the same procedure as what she would do if she is ordering manually through the Starbucks app. (Alternatively, she could also say verbal commands such as "Click on Starbucks", etc.) After each action, a confirmation dialog from SUGILITE pops up (Figure 1b) to confirm that the action has been recorded, and which also serves to slow down the user to make sure that the Android accessibility API has time to record the action.

The user continues the Starbucks "Order" procedure by clicking on "MENU", "Espresso Drinks", "Cappuccinos", "Cappuccino", "Add to Order" and "View Order" in sequence, which are all exactly the same steps that she would do without SUGILITE. In this process, the user could also demonstrate customizing the size, flavor, etc. according to her personal preferences. SUGILITE pops up the confirmation dialog after each click, except for the one on "Cappuccino", where SUGILITE is confused and must ask the user to choose from two identifying features on the same button (explained in the Implementation section): "Cappuccino" and "120cal" (Figure 1c). When finished, the user clicks on the SUGILITE status icon and selects "End Recording".

After the demonstration, SUGILITE analyzes the recording and parameterizes the script according to the voice command and its knowledge about the UI hierarchy of the Starbucks app (details in the Implementation section).

This parameterization allows the user to give the voice command "Order a [DRINK]", where [DRINK] can be any of the drinks listed on the Starbucks app's menus. SUGILITE can then order the drink automatically for the user by manipulating the user interface of the Starbucks app. Alternatively, the automation can also be executed by using the SUGILITE graphical user interface (GUI) or invoked externally by a third party app using the SUGILITE API.

Additional Examples

To exhibit the generalizability and customizability of SUGILITE, we list some other example tasks that we have successfully taught SUGILITE to execute:

- (American Express) *"Pay off my credit card balance."*
- (Venmo) *"Send [AMOUNT] dollars to [NAME]."*
- (Fly Delta) *"Find the flights from [CITY] to [CITY] on [DATE]."*
- (CHI 2016) *"Show me the papers by [NAME]."*
- (Transit) *"When is [BUS LINE] coming?"*
- (Pokémon Go) *"Collect my coins in the shop."*
- (GrubHub & Uber) "Request an Uber to the nearest *[TYPE]* restaurant

THE SUGILITE SYSTEM

Key Design Features

Multi-Modal Interface

To provide flexibility for users in different contexts, both creating the automation and running the automation can be performed through either the conversational voice interface or the GUI. In order to create an automation, the user can either give a new voice instruction, for which SUGILITE will reply "... Would you like to teach me?" or the user can start a new demonstration using SUGILITE's GUI.

When teaching a new command to Sugilite, the user can use verbal instructions, demonstrations, or a mix of both in creating the script. Even though in most cases, demonstrating app operations through direct manipulation will be more efficient, we anticipate some useful scenarios for instructing by voice, like when touching on the phone is not convenient, or for users with motor impairment.

The user can also execute automations by either giving voice commands or by selecting from a list of scripts. Running an automation by voice allows the user to give a command from a distance. For scripts with parameters, the parameter values are either explicitly specified in the GUI, or inferred from the verbal command when the conversational interface is used (see the Generalization section for details).

During recording or executing, the user has easy access to the controls of SUGILITE through the floating duck icon (See Figure 1, where the icon is on the right edge of the screen). The floating duck icon changes the appearance to indicate the current status of SUGILITE – whether it is recording, executing, or tracking in the background. The user can start, pause or end the execution/recording as well as view the current script (Figure 1d) and the script list from the pop-up menu that appears when users tap on the duck. The GUI also enables the user to manually edit a script by deleting an operation and all the subsequent operations, or to resume recording starting from the end of the script. Selecting an operation lets the user edit it using the editing panel (Figure 1c).

The multi-modality of SUGILITE enables many useful usage scenarios in different contexts. For example, one may automate tasks like finding nearby parking or streaming audible books by demonstrating the procedures in advance by direct manipulation. Then the user can perform those tasks by voice while driving without needing to touch the phone. A user with motor impairment can have her friends or family automate her common tasks so she can execute them later through the voice interface.

Script Generalization

Verbal Commands and Demonstrations*:* As shown in the example usage scenario, SUGILITE can automatically identify the parameters in the task and generalize the scripts from a single demonstration. After the user finishes the demonstration, SUGILITE first compares the identifying features of the target UI elements and the arguments of the operations against the verbal command, trying to identify the parameters by matching the words in the command. For example, for the verbal command "find the flights from New York to Los Angeles", SUGILITE identifies "New York" and "Los Angeles" as two parameters if the user typed "New York" into the departure city textbox and "Los Angeles" into the destination textbox during the demonstration.

This parameterization method provides users control over the level of personalization and abstraction in SUGILITE scripts. For example, if the user demonstrated ordering a venti Cappuccino with skim milk by saying the command "order a Cappuccino", we will discover that "Cappuccino" is a parameter, but not "venti" or "skim milk". However, if the user gave the same demonstration, but had used the command, "order a venti Cappuccino." then we would also consider the size of the coffee ("venti") to be a parameter.

For the generalization of text entry operations (e.g. typing "New York" into the departure city textbox), SUGILITE allows the use of any value for the parameters. In the checking flights example, the user can give the command "find the flights from [A] to [B]" for any [A] and [B] values after demonstrating how to find the flights from New York to Los Angeles. SUGILITE will simply replace the two city names by the value of the parameters in the corresponding steps when executing the automation.

In order to support generalization over UI elements, SUGILITE records the set of all possible alternatives to the UI element that the user operates on. SUGILITE finds these alternatives based on the UI structure, looking for those in parallel to the original target UI element. For example, suppose the user demonstrates "Order a Cappuccino" in which an operation is clicking on "Cappuccino" from the "Cappuccinos" menu that has two options "Cappuccino" and "Iced Cappuccino". SUGILITE will first identify "Cappuccino" as a parameter, and then add "Iced Cappuccino" to the set as an alternative value for the parameter, allowing the user to order Iced Cappuccino using the same script. By keeping this list of alternatives, SUGILITE can also differentiate tasks with similar command structure but different values. For example, the commands "Order Iced Cappuccino" and "Order cheese pizza" invoke different scripts, because the phrase "Iced Cappuccino" is among the alternative elements of operations in one script, while "cheese pizza" would be among the alternatives of a different script. If multiple scripts can be used to execute a command (e.g., if the user has two scripts for ordering pizza with different apps), the user can explicitly select which script to run.

App UI Hierarchy Structure: A limitation of the above method in handling alternative elements is that it can only generalize at the leaf level of a multi-level menu tree. For example, the generalized script for "Order a Cappuccino" cannot be used to order drinks like a Latte or Macchiato because they are on other branches of the Starbucks "Order" menu. Since the user did not go to those branches during the demonstration, SUGILITE could not know the existence of those options or how to reach those options in the menu tree. This is a challenge of working with third-party apps, which will not expose their internal structures to us nor can we traverse the menu structures without invoking their app on the main UI thread.

To address this issue, we created a background tracking service that records all the clickable elements in apps and the corresponding previous actions taken to reach each element. This service can run all the time, so SUGILITE can learn about all parts of an app that the user visits. Through this mechanism, we can construct the path to navigate the menu structure to reach a UI element. The text labels of all such elements can then be added to the sets of alternative parameter values for the scripts. This means that we can allow the user to order drinks that are not an immediate sibling to Cappuccino at the leaf level of the Starbucks order menu tree from a single demonstration.

This method has its trade-offs. First, it brings in false positives. For example, there is a clickable node "Store Locator" in the Starbucks order menu. The generalizing process will then mistakenly add "Store Locator" to the list of what the user can order. Second, running the background tracking affects the phone's performance. Third, SUGILITE cannot generalize for items that were never viewed by the user. Lastly, many participants expressed privacy concerns about allowing background tracking to store text labels from apps, since apps may dynamically generate labels with personal data like an account number or balance.

Error Checking and Handling

Error checking and handling has been a major challenge for many PBD systems [21]. SUGILITE provides error handling and checking mechanism to detect when a new situation is encountered during execution or when the app's UI changes after an update.

When executing a script, an error occurs when the next operation in the script cannot be successfully performed. There are many possible reasons for an execution error. First, it is possible that the app has been updated and the layout of the UI has been changed, so SUGILITE cannot find the object specified in the operation. Second, it is possible that the app is currently in a different state than it was during the demonstration. For example, if a user demonstrates how to request an Uber cab during normal pricing, and then uses the script to request a cab during surge pricing, then an error will occur because SUGILITE does not know how to handle the popup from the Uber app that asks for surge price confirmation. Third, the execution can also be interrupted by an external event, like a phone call or an alarm.

In SUGILITE, when an error occurs, an error handling popup will be shown, asking the user to choose between three options: keep waiting, end executing, or fix the script. The "keep waiting" option will keep SUGILITE waiting until the current operation can be performed. This option should be used in situations like prolonged waiting in the app or an interrupting phone call, where the user knows that the app will eventually return to the recorded state in the script, which SUGILITE knows how to handle. The "end executing" option will simply end the execution of the current script.

The "fix the script" option has two sub-options: "replace" and "create a fork", which allow the user to either demonstrate a procedure from the current step that will *replace* the corresponding part of the old script, or create a new alternative *fork* in the old script. The "replace" option should be used to handle permanent changes in the procedure due to an app update or an error in the previous demonstration, or if the user changes her mind about what the script should do. The "create a fork" option (Figure 1d) should be used to enable the script to deal with a new situation. The forking works similarly to the try-catch statement in programming languages, where SUGILITE will first attempt to perform the original operation, and then execute the alternative branch if the original operation fails. (Other kinds of forks, branches, and conditions are planned as future work.)

The forking mechanism can also handle new situations introduced by generalization. For example, after the user demonstrates how to check the score of the NY Giants using the Yahoo! Sports app, SUGILITE generalizes the script so it can check the score of any sports team. However, if the user gives a command "check the score of NY Yankees", everything will work properly until the last step, where SUGILITE cannot find the score because the demonstrations so far only show where to find the score on an American football team's page, which has a different layout than a baseball team's page. In this case, the user creates a new fork and demonstrates how to find the score for a baseball team. Details about how SUGILITE finds items on the screen is described below in the Implementation section.

Manual Script Editing

For advanced users, we provide an interface to manually edit and manually generalize the script (Figure 1d). In this interface, users can delete operations, create forks, or resume recording to add more operations to an existing script. They can also manually generalize the scripts to better reflect their intentions. For example, for the action "Click on 'Chile Mocha Frappuccino in Starbucks 'Featured' menu", the user can override the heuristic-generated identifying feature (see the Recording Handler section in Implementation for details) to use the screen location of the item instead of the text label of the item so the script will click on the *top item* on the "Featured" menu instead of always choosing the Chile Mocha Frappuccino.

Lastly, the user can manually create parameters. SUGILITE supports the use of a simple markup language. For the action "Set the text of the textbox 'Message' to 'The bus is delayed, I'll be home by 6PM'", the user can manually modify the text to "@*transportation* is delayed, I'll be home by @*time*" so she can reuse the script in similar scenario by only providing the values for the parameters instead of the whole text. Similarly, the user can set a parameter with the value or label of one UI element (e.g., the result of a search), which can be used for a later operation.

Implementation

In this section, we discuss the implementation of the SUGILITE components and how they are integrated with each other. SUGILITE is an Android application implemented in Java. Scripts and tracking data are stored locally on phone in an SQLite database. SUGILITE does not require jailbreaking/root access to the phone and should work on any phone running Android 4.4 or above.

Conversational Interface

The conversational intelligent agent we used in SUGILITE is built using the Learning by Instruction Agent (LIA) [4]. When the user gives a voice command, the audio is first decoded into text using Google's Speech API. Then LIA uses a Combinatory Categorial Grammar (CCG) parser to parse the verbal command. Based on the parsing result, LIA can initiate a new recording or execute a SUGILITE script. Details on LIA can be found in [4].

Background Accessibility Service

The SUGILITE background service registers as an Android accessibility service. It listens to AccessibilityEvent[3] and distributes the events to the recording handler or the execution handler based on the current mode of the system. The service receives an AccessibilityEvent through the listener whenever a view on the screen is clicked on (or long-clicked on), selected or focused. The service will also receive an AccessibilityEvent if the text on a view has changed, the state of the current window has changed, or the content of the current window has changed.

Recording Handler

The recording handler receives the AccessibilityEvent from the background service during the demonstration. It consumes the event if the event is for a user action (click, long click or text entry). From the AccessibilityEvent object, the handler gets meta-data features (text labels, screen locations, accessibility labels, view ID) for the target UI element on which the action was performed. It also includes all the other elements in the hierarchy of the entire current screen (the UI layout), which SUGILITE saves for error checking and generalization. SUGILITE also saves the child features (i.e. element has a child element that…) and the parent features of the target UI element.

[3] https://developer.android.com/reference/android/view/accessibility/AccessibilityEvent.html

SUGILITE applies the following rule-based heuristics to determine a subset of the features to be used in identifying the current screen and the current target UI element. SUGILITE first looks for the text or accessibility label in the UI element. If it has one, the system will verify that this feature is unique among all the UI elements on the screen. If this fails, SUGILITE seeks to find a unique second-level feature like view ID or label of a child element. If SUGILITE fails to find a feature to uniquely identify the element on the screen, it will use the screen coordinates of the element's bounding box. The chosen subset of features needs to (1) uniquely identify the UI layout of the screen and the specific target UI element on that screen, and (2) still work for future runs of the application to identify the same element.

If the handler determines that the heuristic-generated feature set can fulfill the above two requirements, the confirmation popup (Figure 1b) will be shown. Otherwise the disambiguation panel (Figure 1c) will be shown to ask the user to manually disambiguate what features should be used in the script. After this, SUGILITE generates and saves an operation to the current recorded script. The operation also stores identifiers for all the unique UI layouts and all the alternative UI elements that are structurally in parallel with the target UI element. After the demonstration, SUGILITE will use these when parameterizing and generalizing the script, as described earlier.

Execution Handler

The execution handler will be activated when an AccessibilityEvent is sent from the background accessibility service, which happens when the screen changes, or when the user takes any action. The execution handler will try to match the current UI layout to the stored one in the script, then it tries to find the required target UI element on the screen, and then it will try to perform the operation as specified in the current operation. In the SUGILITE UI, the floating icon of a duck will also move to the target UI element to signify the operation. If the current screen specified in the AccessibilityEvent was not among the recorded ones for the current operation, the error handling pop-up will be shown, signifying that the state of the current app does not match what was demonstrated for the operation.

If the current operation is successful, the execution handler will then proceed to handle the next operation. The error handling mechanism (described earlier) will be activated in case of an error.

SUGILITE API

SUGILITE has an API that allows external apps to utilize its recording, tracking and executing functionality. Scripts can be exported for editing/sharing or imported for executing in JSON format. Currently several research projects, both internal and external, are building upon or invoking SUGILITE.

Technical Limitations

Web-based Application: Because of the limitation of the Android accessibility mechanism, SUGILITE cannot record actions performed inside of browsers or in web-based applications. In the future, we can solve this by incorporating techniques used to access the HTML document object model (DOM) in existing web automation tools (e.g. [7,23]).

Graphical Icons: While many major apps are adding alternative texts to the icons to be more accessible, the icons in some popular apps remain unlabeled. For the icons with no text label or accessibility alternative text, the only way SUGILITE can identify them is by using the screen location, which is unreliable and not consistent across devices. For future work, we plan to use visual references similar to SIKULI [43] to identify the graphical elements in the script.

Gestures, Sensory Inputs and Text Entry: Due to the limitation of the Android accessibility mechanism, SUGILITE cannot record gestures or inputs from phone sensors (camera, accelerometer, gyroscope, etc.) during the demonstration. We can get access to the raw touch events and the raw sensor data with root permission of the phone, but that would lose SUGILITE's compatibility with unmodified phones. For the same reason, SUGILITE cannot record text typed directly into third-party apps using the on-screen keyboard. Instead, for text entry, users need to double tap on the textbox and type into a popup shown by SUGILITE.

Semantics in the Demonstration: In the current generalization mechanism of SUGILITE, we are treating the identifying features of elements and the parameters as strings, but SUGILITE does not attempt to understand their semantics or meaning. This means that in order to have proper generalization, the parameters in the user's verbal command have to match exactly the features of the target UI elements or the arguments of the operations. For example, if the user says "show me the flights to L.A. today" but demonstrates typing "Los Angeles" into the destination textbox in the Fly Delta app, then the script will not be automatically generalized. To address this, we are collaborating with researchers in natural language processing, who are working on understanding the semantics in verbal commands and smartphone apps [10,41]. This will enable SUGILITE to perform better script generalization from verbal commands.

EVALUATION

To assess how successfully users with various levels of prior programming experience can use some features of SUGILITE, we conducted a lab study where we asked the participants to teach SUGILITE new tasks for four given scenarios. (These tasks focus on recording "straight-line" scripts, and future work will evaluate the understandability of error handling and other control structures.)

Participants

19 participants aged 20-30 (mean = 24.2, SD = 2.55) were recruited from the local university community. The participants were required to be 18 or order, be active smartphone users and be fluent in English. All recruited participants were university students.

In the recruiting form, participants rated their own programming experience on a five-point scale from "no experience" to "experienced programmer". We specifically selected participants across a range of prior programming experience. In Table 1, we show the description used for each category and the number of participants in each.

Group - Programming Experience	*#*
1 – I've never done any computer programming	3
2 – I've done some light programming (e.g. Office macros, excel functions, simple scripts)	4
3 – Beginner programmer (experience equivalent to 1-2 college level computer science classes)	5
4 – Intermediate programmer (1-2 years of programming experience)	3
5 – Experienced programmer (2+ years of programming experience)	4
Total	19

Table 1. Number of participants (#) grouped by programming experience

Tasks

We chose five tasks for the study based on the common repetitive task scenarios from our motivating survey. The first task was used as a tutorial, where the experimenter showed the participant how to teach SUGILITE to complete the example task and explained how to operate SUGILITE. The other four tasks were given to the participants in random order. All the participants used the same Nexus 6 phone with SUGILITE and relevant apps installed.

Before each task, the participants were given time to get familiar with the involved apps (Uber, Starbucks, Yahoo! Sports and Gmail), so they were all proficient at performing the tasks using direct manipulation. We first asked the participants to perform the task directly without SUGILITE, and then asked them to teach SUGILITE the same task by demonstration. During the task, we would not answer questions on how to use SUGILITE (but we responded to the requests for clarification on the task specifications).

Below are the descriptions for each task, together with the SUGILITE components and commands used.

Tutorial Task: Pizza Ordering

In this task, we demonstrated the procedure of ordering a large pepperoni pizza for carryout at the nearest Papa John's store using the Papa John's app. The script was then automatically generalized so it can be used to order any of the three basic pizzas (pepperoni, cheese and sausage). There were one "SET_TEXT" and 9 "CLICK" operations in the script. Among them, two "CLICK" operations required manual disambiguating of the identifying features.

Task1: Get an Uber

The specification given to the participants was *"You should teach the agent how to use the Uber app to request an Uber X cab to the current location."* The standard procedure for this task had two "CLICK" operations, none of which required manual disambiguation of the identifying features. The participants were told to not confirm sending the Uber request to avoid being charged.

Task2: Check Sports Score

The specification given to the participants was *"You should teach the agent how to use the Yahoo! Sports app to show you the latest score of Pittsburgh Steelers."* The standard procedure for this task had four "CLICK" operations and one "SET_TEXT" operation, none of which required manual disambiguation of the identifying features. The parameter for the "SET_TEXT" operation is automatically generalized so the script can be used to check the score for any football team in Yahoo! Sports.

Task3: Order Coffee

The specification given to the participants was *"You should teach the agent how to use the Starbucks app to order a cup of Cappuccino." The* standard procedure for this task had 11 "CLICK" operations. Among them, one "CLICK" operation required manual disambiguation of the identifying features. This script is automatically generalized so it can be used to order any drink from the Starbucks app. The participants were told to not submit the final order to avoid being charged.

Task4: Send an Email

The specification given to the participants was *"You should teach the agent the command 'Tell Joe that I will be late because my car is broken.' by demonstrating how to send a new email to 'joe@example.com', with the subject 'I will be late' and body 'I will be late because my car is broken."* The standard procedure for this task had four "CLICK" operations and three "SET_TEXT" operations, none of which required manual disambiguation of the identifying features. This script is automatically generalized so it can respond to "Tell [NAME] that [SOMETHING] because [SOMETHING]"

Procedure

The study took about 1 hour per participant. After signing the consent form, the participant received the tutorial through the experimenter walking through the tutorial task. The tutorial took about 5 minutes. Following the tutorial, the experimenter gave the first task to the participant. Then the participant began to do the tasks as specified in the previous section. After performing the tasks, the participant filled out a usability questionnaire on their experiences interacting with SUGILITE. Finally, the experimenter conducted a brief semi-structured interview with the participant based on the questionnaire responses and the experimenter's observations during the study. Participants were compensated $15 for their time.

Results

Overall, 65 out of 76 (85.5%) scripts created by the participants ran and performed the intended task successfully. 8 out of the 19 (42.1%) participants succeed in all four tasks.

10 (52.6%) succeeded in three tasks and 1 (5.3%) succeeded in only two tasks. All participants completed at least two tasks successfully. A Pearson's chi-squared test was performed and no significant relationship was found between task completion and the level of prior programming experience ($X^2(4) = 4.15, p = 0.39$).

For each successful task, we measured the task completion time from when the voice command was successfully received until the participant ended the recording. We then used a one-way ANOVA to compare the task completion time of each task for participants grouped by their programming experience. No significant difference between the five groups as described in Table 1 based on task completion time was found for any of the tasks. The average task completion time of each task by group is shown in Figure 2. All times are in seconds.

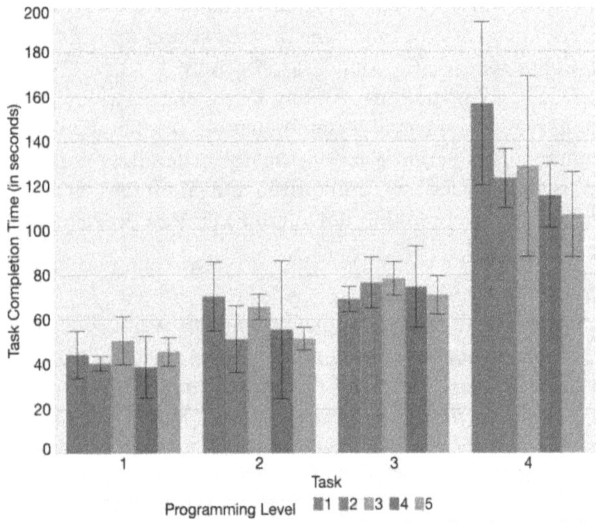

Figure 2. The average task completion time for the participants grouped by their programming experience. Shorter bars are better. Error bars show the standard deviations.

Task 1: All but one participant completed this task (94.7%). That participant "double clicked" (i.e. clicked twice in a row without waiting for the confirmation pop-up in between), which caused the system to fail to record the first action.

Task 2: 15 participants out of 19 (78.9%) completed this task. Four participants failed by entering the text directly into textboxes (they were supposed to double tap on the textbox and type into a pop-up due to the limitation discussed in the Technical Limitation section).

Task 3: 17 participants out of 19 (89.5%) completed this task. A participant erroneously "double clicked" and another participant recorded a click when the Starbucks app had not finished loading, which would cause the execution to block when this click is to be performed.

Task 4: 14 participants out of 19 (73.7%) completed this task. Five participant failed by entering the text directly into textboxes.

Time Trade-off

For each of the four tasks, we also calculated an average "break-even" point at n, for which if a task needs to be performed for at least n times, then the total time needed for automating the task and executing the script for n times is shorter than the time needed to do the tasks manually for n times. We use n as a rough measure for the time trade-off of using SUGILITE to automate tasks. In plain words, if a user needs to perform a task for more than n times, then automating the task with SUGILITE can save her time.

Using the average time it took to create the automation ($\bar{t}$), the average time it took to perform the task manually ($\overline{t_m}$) and the time it took to execute the automation (t_0), we calculate the average break-even value of n for each task, shown in Table 2.

Task	$\bar{t}$	$\overline{t_m}$	t_0	n
Task 1	44.47s	13.71s	3.35s	5
Task 2	58.61s	15.15s	5.12s	6
Task 3	74.29s	26.47s	7.34s	4
Task 4	125.25s	50.25s	6.14s	3

Table 2. Average time to automate the task ($\bar{t}$), average time to perform the task manually ($\overline{t_m}$), time to run the automation (t_0), and the "break-even" point (*n*) for the four tasks.

Statement	*Score*
"It's easy to learn how to use this system."	6.17
"My interaction with the system is clear and understandable"	6.00
"I'm satisfied with my experience using this system."	5.94

Table 3. Average scores on usability questions from the post- questionnaire (on a 7-point scale).

Statement	*Score*
"I find the system useful in helping me creating automation."	6.39
"I find automating tasks with the system is efficient"	6.11
"I would use this system to automate my tasks."	6.06

Table 4. Average scores on usefulness questions from the post-questionnaire (on a 7-point scale).

Subjective Feedback

Overall, SUGILITE received positive feedback on both usability and usefulness from the participants.

On the post questionnaire, the participants were asked to rate their agreement with statements related to their experience interacting with SUGILITE on a 7-point Likert scale from "Strongly Disagree" to "Strongly Agree." Table 3 shows the average score for the usability-related items on the questionnaire. Table 4 shows the average score for the usefulness-related questions.

In a semi-structured interview after the questionnaire, the participants were asked whether they found anything unclear or confusing in their interaction with SUGILITE. Most complaints were on the demonstration of text entry, where the user needs to type into a SUGILITE popup instead of the textbox in the original app. Participants found this to be unnatural and easy-to-forget. Some also reported information overload on the disambiguation panel (Figure 1c). It contained too much information, which made it hard to locate where they needed to read and make selections.

DISCUSSION

The outcome of the evaluation suggests no significant difference based on the level of programming experience of participants for all four tasks in either task completion rate or task completion time. The groups with no programming experience (Group 1) and only light programming experience (Group 2) completed 25 out of 28 (89.3%) tasks. The results indicate that end users with little or no programming experience can successfully use SUGILITE to automate smartphone tasks.

Looking at the "break-even" point for each task, we learn that for the four example scenarios, the user can save time with SUGILITE if they are to perform the tasks for more than 3 to 6 times. This implies that the efficiencies of many repetitive tasks could potentially benefit from automating through SUGILITE, because the overhead of creating automation using SUGILITE is small.

After the study, we asked the participants to describe scenarios from their own smartphone usage where SUGILITE would be helpful. Some of the scenarios involved using apps that are not likely to ever be integrated into existing agents, like the customized apps made for the university community to check the shuttle location, dining menu, meeting room availability, etc. Many organizations or communities have made such apps to serve the information needs of their members. Due to the limited engineering resources available and the small user base for those apps, they are unlikely to get integrated into the intelligent software agents for automation without EUD. But for the users of those apps, they often use the apps frequently and repetitively, so they wish to have their common tasks automated.

The participants commented that although some apps have already been integrated in the prevailing agents like Siri, some specific tasks they want are not supported. An example is that for the music player, users cannot change the equalizer settings or download the current song using voice commands. They also wished to incorporate personalized settings into the automation (e.g., setting the volume before playing a song).

They also proposed scenarios for creating SUGILITE automation beyond single apps. Users often perform a set of tasks in a row (e.g. check the weather, the traffic information and book a cab when waking up) so Sugilite can be used to create a single voice command for multiple tasks. Another example is a command "request an Uber to the nearest (sushi restaurant, pharmacy, grocery store…)", SUGILITE can first use Google Maps to retrieve the address of the nearest desired entity, then use the Uber app to request a cab with the destination filled in.

Besides the scenarios mentioned above, which SUGILITE is already capable of handling, participants also inspired us on potential directions for future work such as multi-device interaction, cross-user script sharing, smart device integration and enhanced accessibility support.

FUTURE WORK

From our experiences in the lab study, SUGILITE has been shown to be reliable and robust. For the next step, we plan to conduct a longitudinal field study of SUGILITE usage to help us understand how users use SUGILITE to help them on tasks in real life contexts. We plan to monitor what tasks they choose to automate, how they interact with SUGILITE in different modalities in different contexts, how they handle errors, and how much benefit SUGILITE can provide in real smartphone usage. Eventually we plan to release SUGILITE for general use by the public.

For future development, we plan to first solve the usability issues in text entry and the disambiguation panel raised in our lab study. We will develop a customized on-screen keyboard with keystroke recording to replace the default keyboard in the SUGILITE demonstration mode. This will enable SUGILITE to record what users type during the demonstration. We also plan to redesign the disambiguation panel to only display the most relevant information to avoid information overload. Finally, we hope to address the issues described in the Technical Limitation section and throughout this paper to expand the applicability of SUGILITE.

Two major concerns about our system are privacy and security. While we have not particularly focused on them in this paper, we do have plans for future work. In addition to the common practices like encryption and authentication, we are interested in detecting the "crucial steps" in a demonstration, such as the steps that are not undo-able (e.g. submit order, confirm deletion) or those that the user would like to review to ensure correctness. Once SUGILITE can successfully detect the crucial steps, it can then ask the user for confirmation by voice or in the GUI during execution.

CONCLUSION

Even though there have been many years of research on programming by demonstration and speech interfaces, SUGILITE is the first PBD system to show how they can successfully be put together on a smartphone to enhance the capabilities of both. We look forward to future collaborations between HCI and AI researchers for improved multimodal intelligent PBD user interfaces.

ACKNOWLEDGEMENTS

This work was supported in part by Yahoo! InMind project and by Samsung under GRO grant #A017479.

REFERENCES

1. James Allen, Nathanael Chambers, George Ferguson, et al. 2007. Plow: A collaborative task learning agent. In *Proceedings of the National Conference on Artificial Intelligence*, 1514.
2. V. Antila, J. Polet, A. Lämsä, and J. Liikka. 2012. RoutineMaker: Towards end-user automation of daily routines using smartphones. In *2012 IEEE International Conference on Pervasive Computing and Communications Workshops (PERCOM Workshops)*, 399–402. http://doi.org/10.1109/PerComW.2012.6197519
3. Brenna D. Argall, Sonia Chernova, Manuela Veloso, and Brett Browning. 2009. A survey of robot learning from demonstration. *Robotics and autonomous systems* 57, 5: 469–483.
4. Amos Azaria, Jayant Krishnamurthy, and Tom M. Mitchell. 2016. Instructable intelligent personal agent. In *Proc. The 30th AAAI Conference on Artificial Intelligence (AAAI)*.
5. Lawrence Bergman, Vittorio Castelli, Tessa Lau, and Daniel Oblinger. 2005. DocWizards: A System for Authoring Follow-me Documentation Wizards. In *Proceedings of the 18th Annual ACM Symposium on User Interface Software and Technology* (UIST '05), 191–200. http://doi.org/10.1145/1095034.1095067
6. Aude Billard, Sylvain Calinon, Ruediger Dillmann, and Stefan Schaal. 2008. Robot programming by demonstration. In *Springer handbook of robotics*. Springer, 1371–1394.
7. Michael Bolin, Matthew Webber, Philip Rha, Tom Wilson, and Robert C. Miller. 2005. Automation and customization of rendered web pages. In *Proceedings of the 18th annual ACM symposium on User interface software and technology*, 163–172.
8. David L. Chen and Raymond J. Mooney. 2011. Learning to Interpret Natural Language Navigation Instructions from Observations. In *AAAI*, 1–2.
9. Jiun-Hung Chen and Daniel S. Weld. 2008. Recovering from Errors During Programming by Demonstration. In *Proceedings of the 13th International Conference on Intelligent User Interfaces* (IUI '08), 159–168. http://doi.org/10.1145/1378773.1378794
10. Yun-Nung Chen, Ming Sun, and Alexander I. Rudnicky. 2015. Matrix factorization with domain knowledge and behavioral patterns for intent modeling. In *NIPS Workshop on Machine Learning for SLU and Interaction.*
11. Allen Cypher and Daniel Conrad Halbert. 1993. *Watch what I do: programming by demonstration*. MIT press.
12. Martin R. Frank and James D. Foley. 1993. Model-based User Interface Design by Example and by Interview. In *Proceedings of the 6th Annual ACM Symposium on User Interface Software and Technology* (UIST '93), 129–137. http://doi.org/10.1145/168642.168655
13. Martin R. Frank and James D. Foley. 1994. A Pure Reasoning Engine for Programming by Demonstration. In *Proceedings of the 7th Annual ACM Symposium on User Interface Software and Technology* (UIST '94), 95–101. http://doi.org/10.1145/192426.192466
14. Krzysztof Gajos and Daniel S. Weld. 2004. SUPPLE: automatically generating user interfaces. In *Proceedings of the 9th international conference on Intelligent user interfaces*, 93–100.
15. Floraine Grabler, Maneesh Agrawala, Wilmot Li, Mira Dontcheva, and Takeo Igarashi. 2009. Generating Photo Manipulation Tutorials by Demonstration. In *ACM SIGGRAPH 2009 Papers* (SIGGRAPH '09), 66:1–66:9. http://doi.org/10.1145/1576246.1531372
16. Ting-Hao Kenneth Huang, Amos Azaria, and Jeffrey P. Bigham. 2016. InstructableCrowd: Creating IF-THEN Rules via Conversations with the Crowd. 1555–1562. http://doi.org/10.1145/2851581.2892502
17. IFTTT. IFTTT. *IFTTT / Connect the apps you love.*
18. Jiepu Jiang, Ahmed Hassan Awadallah, Rosie Jones, et al. 2015. Automatic Online Evaluation of Intelligent Assistants. In *Proceedings of the 24th International Conference on World Wide Web* (WWW '15), 506–516. http://doi.org/10.1145/2736277.2741669
19. Ken Kahn. 1996. Toontalk TM—an animated programming environment for children. *Journal of Visual Languages & Computing* 7, 2: 197–217.
20. Simon Khalaf. Seven Years Into The Mobile Revolution: Content is King… Again. *Yahoo Developer Network.*
21. Tessa Lau. 2009. Why Programming-By-Demonstration Systems Fail: Lessons Learned for Usable AI. *AI Magazine* 30, 4: 65.
22. Tessa A. Lau and Daniel S. Weld. 1999. Programming by Demonstration: An Inductive Learning Formulation. In *Proceedings of the 4th International Conference on Intelligent User Interfaces* (IUI '99), 145–152. http://doi.org/10.1145/291080.291104
23. Gilly Leshed, Eben M. Haber, Tara Matthews, and Tessa Lau. 2008. CoScripter: Automating & Sharing How-to Knowledge in the Enterprise. In *Proceedings of the SIGCHI Conference on Human Factors in Computing Systems* (CHI '08), 1719–1728. http://doi.org/10.1145/1357054.1357323
24. Henry Lieberman. 2001. *Your wish is my command: Programming by example*. Morgan Kaufmann.
25. Pattie Maes. 1994. Agents That Reduce Work and Information Overload. *Commun. ACM* 37, 7: 30–40. http://doi.org/10.1145/176789.176792
26. Rodrigo de A. Maués and Simone Diniz Junqueira Barbosa. 2013. Keep Doing What I Just Did: Automating Smartphones by Demonstration. In *Proceedings of the 15th International Conference on Human-computer Interaction with Mobile Devices and Services* (MobileHCI '13), 295–303. http://doi.org/10.1145/2493190.2493216
27. Richard G. McDaniel and Brad A. Myers. 1997. Gamut: Demonstrating Whole Applications. In *Proceedings of the 10th Annual ACM Symposium on User Interface Software and Technology* (UIST '97), 81–82. http://doi.org/10.1145/263407.263515

28. Richard G. McDaniel and Brad A. Myers. 1999. Getting More out of Programming-by-demonstration. In *Proceedings of the SIGCHI Conference on Human Factors in Computing Systems* (CHI '99), 442–449. http://doi.org/10.1145/302979.303127
29. Francesmary Modugno and Brad A. Myers. 1994. Pursuit: Graphically Representing Programs in a Demonstrational Visual Shell. In *Conference Companion on Human Factors in Computing Systems* (CHI '94), 455–456. http://doi.org/10.1145/259963.260464
30. Brad. A. Myers. 1986. Visual Programming, Programming by Example, and Program Visualization: A Taxonomy. In *Proceedings of the SIGCHI Conference on Human Factors in Computing Systems* (CHI '86), 59–66. http://doi.org/10.1145/22627.22349
31. Brad A. Myers. 1990. Creating user interfaces using programming by example, visual programming, and constraints. *ACM Transactions on Programming Languages and Systems (TOPLAS)* 12, 2: 143–177.
32. Brad A. Myers. 1991. Graphical techniques in a spreadsheet for specifying user interfaces. In *Proceedings of the SIGCHI Conference on Human Factors in Computing Systems*, 243–249.
33. Brad A. Myers and Richard McDaniel. 2001. Sometimes you need a little intelligence, sometimes you need a lot. *Your Wish is My Command: Programming by Example. San Francisco, CA: Morgan Kaufmann Publishers*: 45–60.
34. Brad A. Myers, Brad Vander Zanden, and Roger B. Dannenberg. 1989. Creating graphical interactive application objects by demonstration. In *Proceedings of the 2nd annual ACM SIGGRAPH symposium on User interface software and technology*, 95–104.
35. Shin 'ichiro Nakaoka, Atsushi Nakazawa, Fumio Kanehiro, et al. 2007. Learning from observation paradigm: Leg task models for enabling a biped humanoid robot to imitate human dances. *The International Journal of Robotics Research* 26, 8: 829–844.
36. A. Namoun, A. Daskalopoulou, N. Mehandjiev, and Z. Xun. 2016. Exploring Mobile End User Development: Existing Use and Design Factors. *IEEE Transactions on Software Engineering* PP, 99: 1–1. http://doi.org/10.1109/TSE.2016.2532873
37. Nielsen. 2015. So Many Apps, So Much More Time for Entertainment.
38. Lenin Ravindranath, Arvind Thiagarajan, Hari Balakrishnan, and Samuel Madden. 2012. Code in the Air: Simplifying Sensing and Coordination Tasks on Smartphones. In *Proceedings of the Twelfth Workshop on Mobile Computing Systems & Applications* (HotMobile '12), 4:1–4:6. http://doi.org/10.1145/2162081.2162087
39. André Rodrigues. 2015. Breaking Barriers with Assistive Macros. In *Proceedings of the 17th International ACM SIGACCESS Conference on Computers & Accessibility* (ASSETS '15), 351–352. http://doi.org/10.1145/2700648.2811322
40. Ben Shneiderman, Catherine Plaisant, Maxine Cohen, Steven Jacobs, Niklas Elmqvist, and Nicholas Diakopoulos. 2016. *Designing the User Interface: Strategies for Effective Human-Computer Interaction*. Pearson, Boston.
41. Ming Sun, Yun-Nung Chen, and Alexander I. Rudnicky. 2016. HELPR: A Framework to Break the Barrier across Domains in Spoken Dialog Systems. In *International Workshop on Spoken Dialog Systems*.
42. Jesse Thomason, Shiqi Zhang, Raymond Mooney, and Peter Stone. 2015. Learning to interpret natural language commands through human-robot dialog. In *Proceedings of the Twenty-Fourth international joint conference on Artificial Intelligence (IJCAI)*.
43. Tom Yeh, Tsung-Hsiang Chang, and Robert C. Miller. 2009. Sikuli: Using GUI Screenshots for Search and Automation. In *Proceedings of the 22Nd Annual ACM Symposium on User Interface Software and Technology* (UIST '09), 183–192. http://doi.org/10.1145/1622176.1622213
44. Sha Zhao, Julian Ramos, Jianrong Tao, et al. 2016. Discovering Different Kinds of Smartphone Users Through Their Application Usage Behaviors. In *Proceedings of the 2016 ACM International Joint Conference on Pervasive and Ubiquitous Computing* (UbiComp '16), 498–509. http://doi.org/10.1145/2971648.2971696
45. SiriKit - Apple Developer. https://developer.apple.com/sirikit/
46. Automate - everyday automation for Android. LlamaLab. http://llamalab.com/automate/
47. Workato - Connect your apps. Automate your work. *Workato*. https://www.workato.com/

Automated Detection of Facial Expressions during Computer-Assisted Instruction in Individuals on the Autism Spectrum

Alex A. Ahmed & Matthew S. Goodwin
Northeastern University
Boston, Massachusetts

ABSTRACT

It has been suggested that computer-assisted instruction (CAI) is a promising method for educating students on the autism spectrum. We aimed to determine whether automated recognition of facial expressions aided in predicting CAI engagement and learning performance. Seven youth with autism (mean age = 12.7, SD = 4.2) interacted with a CAI program, TeachTown Basics, for 15 consecutive sessions. Video recordings of the participants' faces were collected during these sessions and facial expressions from these videos were analyzed using CERT, an algorithm that automatically outputs intensity values for each facial action unit (AU). Using these data, we attempted to operationally define two engagement indices: (1) behavioral engagement, the proportion of time a participant had their face oriented to the computer screen; and (2) emotional engagement, the activation of AUs previously associated with CAI. Our results suggest that both indices strongly correlated with one another, but that emotional (not behavioral) engagement predicted test performance. CAI knowledge domain, participant sex, and developmental age also contributed to the prediction.

Author Keywords

Emotion/Affective Computing; Education/Learning; Quantitative Methods; Computer Vision; Individuals with Disabilities & Assistive Technologies

ACM Classification Keywords

K.4.2 Social Issues: Assistive technologies for persons with disabilities

INTRODUCTION

Engagement, Learning, and CAI

Current research on student academic engagement defines it as a multifaceted construct including both emotional and behavioral components. Behavioral engagement refers to observable skills required to achieve positive learning outcomes, such as participation and attendance. Emotional engagement refers to a student's feelings in reaction to the learning process [9]. Although the link between engagement and learning has been well established, it is less clear how engagement interacts with and influences achievement outcomes, especially during CAI [11].

Craig et al. [5] assessed facial affect in neurotypical undergraduate students during CAI. Participants verbalized their affective states while video of their faces was simultaneously recorded. Videos were coded using the Facial Action Coding System (FACS), which categorizes 46 anatomical facial movements as distinct "action units" (AU) [6]. The authors reported that frustration, confusion, boredom, and eureka (the "joy of discovery") were most prominently expressed and that AU activations coincided with these self-reported emotions. AUs 1 (outer brow raise), 2 (inner brow raise), and 14 (dimpler) were associated with *frustration*; 4 (brow lowerer), 7 (lid tightener), and 12 (lip corner puller) with *confusion*; and 45 (eye closure) with *boredom*.

Computer Expression Recognition Toolbox

Although FACS allows observers to reliably identify fine-grained facial movements, manual coding is time-intensive. The Computer Expression Recognition Toolbox (CERT) is a computer vision tool that detects the presence of a face, and the intensity of AUs within it, from video data [17]. Although CERT was trained on adult faces, it has also been used to collect meaningful data from children [29]. Grafsgaard [7] used CERT to analyze facial expressions of neurotypical undergraduates as they interacted with a CAI tool. They reported that AUs 1, 2, 4, 7, and 14 were most commonly expressed in their sample, which was consistent with previous findings based on manual coding [5]. Interestingly, they also demonstrated that self-report of performance was positively predicted by AU14 activation, and that objective performance (student differences in pre- and post-test scores) were positively predicted by AU14 and negatively predicted by AU2. Henrie [9] has further suggested that the expression of positive and negative emotions can indicate engagement and disengagement, respectively. However, these results imply that negative emotions can accompany engaged and productive learning

CHI 2017, May 06 - 11, 2017, Denver, CO, USA

ACM 978-1-4503-4655-9/17/05…$15.00
DOI: http://dx.doi.org/10.1145/3025453.3025472

as well. Additional work is needed to characterize the relationship between emotional engagement and learning in CAI, not only in the general population, but especially in populations who cannot easily self-report their affective states [13,14,30].

CAI and Autism

Autism is a lifelong neurodevelopmental condition associated with difficulties in social interaction and communication, and repetitive or stereotyped behaviors [2]. Despite these common diagnostic characteristics, there is great heterogeneity in the clinical presentation of autism [18]. Carnahan [4] noted that many children with autism experience more difficulty in social situations, including traditional learning environments. Thus, their engagement in learning may require specialized support. Reviews of the current literature have highlighted how CAI programs can support individuals with autism by focusing attention, increasing motivation, bypassing potentially stressful social contexts, and providing a more structured learning environment [20,22,23,25,28].

Furthermore, a meta-analysis of technology-based interventions for autism reported that the proposed efficacy of CAI in this population is supported, but that individuals with average or above average IQ were overrepresented, comprising 67.8% of study participants [8]. Additional work is needed to expand the autism CAI literature to include more severely impacted individuals, especially those who cannot verbalize their learning processes.

Prior work has indicated that children with autism produce emotional facial expressions spontaneously, but that they may be infrequent or ambiguous relative to typically developing children's expressions [21]. Prior work has also demonstrated that children with autism have reduced capacity to self-report their emotional states [14]. Given the above, we sought to determine whether computational measures could be used to assess engagement and learning processes in those who have trouble self-reporting emotional states, with the longer-term goal of producing better CAI learning outcomes for all specialized learners. The current study used TeachTown Basics (http://web.teachtown.com/products/teachtown-basics), a commercially available CAI program whose efficacy as a teaching tool for students with autism has been previously demonstrated [31,32]. That is, children with autism who interacted with the program showed statistically significant gains in language and cognitive skills relative to those in a control group.

The present study sought to determine whether computationally-derived computer vision measurements of engagement were predictive of CAI learning outcomes in severely impacted youth with autism. The specific research questions examined were: How can we quantitatively characterize engagement in a CAI learning task? Is engagement, as we measured it, related to test performance? What factors moderate CAI learning performance in severely impacted youth with autism?

METHOD

Sample

Seven youth with autism (4 male, 3 female) with a mean age of 12.7 (range = 8-19 years) were recruited from a day program serving children with developmental disabilities. Diagnoses were confirmed by a licensed psychologist familiar with autism using DSM-IV guidelines, the Childhood Autism Rating Scale (CARS), and previous psychiatric reports [18]. Participant cognitive abilities as assessed by standardized intelligence measures (Stanford-Binet-IV, Leiter) or scales of cognitive development (Bayley Scales) ranged from 24-38 (M = 31) and 5-24 months, respectively. Scores on the CARS ranged from 31.5-43.5 (M = 39), placing our participants in the moderately to severely autistic range. Five of the youth were white, and two were African American/Black.

Procedure

All participants interacted with TeachTown Basics, and completed its self-contained academic lessons (discrete trials). Trials consisted of multiple-choice questions with 3 to 8 possible answers. The subject matter of the trials varied between 5 learning domains: adaptive skills, cognitive skills, language arts, language development, mathematics, and social and emotional skills. TeachTown Basics also presents learners with interactive reward games for 15-45 seconds between discrete trial tasks as reinforcement. In the present study, trials of the same type were grouped into tests. Every participant worked through several tests within a session, which lasted approximately 30 minutes each.

Each participant repeated their interaction with TeachTown Basics for at least 15 sessions. Although some participants had more than 15 sessions, only the first 15 were included in the present analysis to establish data consistency. Sessions were less than a week apart and often took place on consecutive days. The learning domain tested and number of tests administered varied across sessions.

Data Collection

Video

During each session, video of the participants' faces were recorded at approximately 30 frames per second. The camera was positioned above the computer screen, directly facing the participants.

Performance and Timing Information

TeachTown Basics produces a detailed, time-stamped report of each session, including all learning activities and responses that take place. We focused specifically on two activities, discrete trials (learning tasks) and interactive games (animated reward sequences displayed upon completion of a test). The software also reports the percentage of trials answered correctly for each test.

Facial Expression Recognition

Video from the first 15 sessions for each participant was passed through CERT, which produced a frame-by-frame analysis of AU intensity levels. We extracted AUs 1, 2, 4, 6, 7, 12, 14, 17, and 45 based on prior work implicating them in engagement during CAI [5,7]. Intensity levels for each frame of video were subtracted from each AU's session-wide average to allow for between-participant comparisons, because baseline AU activation can vary across individuals [7]. CERT-generated intensity levels of 0.25 or higher have been shown to indicate a threshold level of activation that reasonably avoids false-positives [7]. Thus, we calculated AU frequency scores by taking proportion of segment times when AU intensities were above threshold levels. These scores were defined as computational proxy indices of emotional engagement.

We also attempted to define a metric for engagement related to gross physical behavior. CERT outputs an empty value for a frame of video if it cannot detect the components of a face required to measure AU activations, including the eyes and mouth. We calculated the proportion of frames with empty values to characterize how much time participants' faces were oriented toward the screen, which was defined as a proxy index of behavioral engagement.

CERT results were segmented based on the activities reported from TeachTown Basics, such that for each discrete trial and reward video we obtained emotional and behavioral engagement index scores as described above. Additionally, for each test, we obtained the learning domain and the percentage of trials answered correctly, along with engagement scores for the duration of that test. We also considered chronological age, developmental age, and sex of the student participants as covariates.

RESULTS

Engagement Measures

Correlation

We sought first to investigate how the two quantitative engagement scores we defined were related. Spearman's correlations were performed between the mean frequency score of each AU of interest ("emotional engagement") and the mean percentage of time participants had their faces oriented toward the screen ("behavioral engagement") during activities. Data for all participants and for all 15 sessions were combined for this analysis.

Nine correlations were performed, resulting in a Bonferroni-corrected significance threshold of $p = 0.05/9 = 0.0055$. Four AUs significantly correlated with behavioral engagement after threshold correction ($p < 0.0055$): AU2 (rho = -0.19), AU4 (rho = -0.41), AU7 (rho = -0.28), and AU45 (rho = -0.19).

Linear Mixed Model Analysis

We specified a model to determine whether behavioral engagement was predicted by emotional engagement while also considering individual differences and the effect of time. Additionally, we sought to identify whether and how the categorical variable "activity" (learning trial or reward video) influenced behavioral engagement scores. A linear mixed model was defined with participant ID and session number as fixed effects, and with CAI activity, AU2, AU4, AU7, AU45, chronological age, developmental age, and sex as random effects.

Predictor	Estimate (Std. Error)	Chi-sq (df = 1)	p
AU4	-2.09 (0.34)	31.93	4.06E-09
AU7	-1.52 (0.91)	3.56	0.091
Chr. Age	0.03 (0.006)	11.30	0.00077
Dev. Age	0.11 (0.019)	7.16	3.78E-05
Sex	0.10 (0.023)	10.15	0.0014

Table 1. Model statistics and likelihood ratio tests for a model predicting behavioral engagement scores.

To reduce the model to its most parsimonious state, we calculated the Akaike Information Criterion (AIC) [1]. AIC is a measure of a model's information loss; when comparing models, the preferred model is that which has the minimum AIC (lower is better). We calculated the second-order "corrected AIC" (AICc), which factors in an increased penalty for extra parameters. This was done for the full model, and for the model with each of its predictors removed separately [10,19].

Removing AU45 and CAI activity parameters had a negative effect on AICc, and therefore a positive effect on goodness-of-fit. We removed these parameters from further consideration, which reduced AICc from -100.7 to -105.6. Additionally, removing AU4 had a substantially greater positive effect on AICc relative to other predictors.

We then performed likelihood ratio tests to gauge each predictor's contribution to the model (Table 1). Each predictor was removed individually and tested against the full model. All predictors except AU7 significantly influenced model likelihood at a threshold of $p < 0.05$.

Emotional engagement indices (AU4 and AU7) yielded a negative model estimate, indicating that increases in the frequency of those AUs decreased behavioral engagement prediction. The demographic covariate estimates showed that increasing age resulted in an increase in the prediction, but to a much smaller degree.

Test Performance

We specified a linear mixed model to identify factors moderating test performance. The initial model included a subset of AUs selected based on prior work [5,7]. Behavioral engagement, developmental age, chronological age, knowledge domain of the test, and sex were included as random effects. Test performance – the percentage of correct answers – was set as the outcome variable.

As in the prior section, a model selection procedure based on AICc comparisons was performed and the parameters AU1, 2, 7, 14, 17, 45, behavioral engagement, and age were removed.

Predictor	Estimate (Std. Error)	Chi-sq (df = 1)	p
Domain	-	12.1	0.0335
AU4	29.97 (14.9)	3.82	0.051
AU6	-42.04 (11.96)	12.59	0.00039
AU12	33.7 (9.20)	13.54	0.00023
Dev. Age	-8.37 (2.24)	10.5	0.0012
Sex	20.44 (6.10)	9.33	0.0023

Table 2. Model statistics and likelihood ratio tests for a model predicting test performance. Model estimates for the learning domain predictor are addressed in the main text.

Likelihood ratio tests revealed that all remaining predictors, except AU4, significantly influenced model likelihood (Table 2). The model estimates indicate that AU6 and AU12 had a negative and positive influence, respectively, on predicted test performance. Within the knowledge domain predictor, the "Social and Emotional" category had the largest effect on the prediction (-8.94, SE = 3.44), while the effects of the other domains were negligible (the estimates +/- their standard errors overlapped zero).

DISCUSSION

Using computer vision, we sought to define automated quantitative proxy indices of emotional and behavioral engagement with CAI and evaluate their relative contributions to learning outcomes in severely affected youth with autism. Four out of the nine AUs that comprised our emotional engagement index correlated with behavioral engagement. Of these, only AU4 (brow lowerer) survived model selection and likelihood ratio testing. AU4 negatively affected the prediction of behavioral engagement. This finding echoes prior work that associated AU4 activation with negative learning outcomes, such as finding a learning session not worthwhile [7].

We also found that knowledge domain, sex, developmental age, and AUs 6 (cheek raise) and 12 (lip corner puller) were influential in a model predicting test performance. However, our proxy measure of behavioral engagement did not improve model fit. This result indicates that head orientation towards the CAI program was not as closely linked to participants' successful learning as was their emotional experiences measured by facial expressions contingent on learning materials. Increased AU6 frequency led to a decrease in predicted test performance, while increases in AU12 led to an increase. AU12 produces smiling expressions [3,15,12]. AU6 raises the cheeks and narrows the eye openings, and has been associated with both smiles [3] and pain [16].

Limitations and Future Work

It is important to note that AUs are not singly correlated to discrete emotions. Emotions are often associated with multiple AUs activating in concert, and each AU can play a role in many emotional expressions. Future work is needed to further assess relationships among AUs in addition to their individual effects on student CAI outcomes.

A significant drawback of focusing solely on automated facial expression recognition is loss of contextual information surrounding AU activations. Although prior work has demonstrated the validity and accuracy of CERT in identifying facial expressions in children and adults (during CAI and in other contexts) [7,29,33], we recognize that false positives can be expected even after activation thresholding.

Critically, we acknowledge that our proxy measure of behavioral engagement lacks corroboration from manual coding or self-report in this study. CERT may have failed to detect a face despite a student being engaged; for example, due to the occlusion of facial features. Interestingly, however, students with more severe forms of autism may intentionally use a "looking away" strategy to reduce visual stimulation and better concentrate [26], suggesting a need for more sensitive metrics in this population.

Research involving minimally verbal individuals on the autism spectrum is constrained by idiosyncratic behaviors and severe deficits in communication [13,24,30]. This often precludes obtaining ground truth labels from self-report questionnaires, or from observers without clinical expertise. We hope that our preliminary findings inspire collaborative research between clinical psychologists and computing researchers to collect multimodal data. Developing prediction models of CAI engagement using these data would be especially useful for understanding and supporting the learning processes of students who cannot reliably provide self-reports.

CONCLUSION

We believe our study is the first to translate theoretical constructs of engagement to quantitative indices of facial orientation and expression, including their associations with CAI learning performance. Additionally, we demonstrated feasibility for automated emotion recognition (via CERT) in youth with more severe forms of autism. Most work in autism focuses exclusively on "high-functioning" populations. We found that facial expressions were strong predictors of test performance in our sample, but that facial orientation towards the screen was not. This result differentiates between behavioral and emotional components of student engagement in CAI, and may thus provide a useful measure for future studies of CAI in more severely affected youth with autism.

ACKNOWLEDGMENTS

The authors would like to sincerely thank the participants and families who gave their time and energy to this work.

REFERENCES

1. Hirotogu Akaike. 1998. Information Theory and an Extension of the Maximum Likelihood Principle. In *Selected Papers of Hirotugu Akaike*, Emanuel Parzen, Kunio Tanabe and Genshiro Kitagawa (eds.). Springer New York, New York, NY, 199–213. http://doi.org/10.1007/978-1-4612-1694-0_15
2. American Psychiatric Association. 2013. *DSM 5*. American Psychiatric Association.
3. Nigel Bosch, Sidney K D'Mello, Jaclyn Ocumpaugh, Ryan S Baker, and Valerie Shute. 2016. Using Video to Automatically Detect Learner Affect in Computer-Enabled Classrooms. *Acm Transactions on Interactive Intelligent Systems* 6, 2. http://doi.org/10.1145/2946837
4. Christi Carnahan, Shobana Musti-Rao, and Jody Bailey. 2015. Promoting Active Engagement in Small Group Learning Experiences for Students with Autism and Significant Learning Needs. *Education and Treatment of Children*, 32, 1: 37–61.
5. Scotty D. Craig, Sidney D'Mello, Amy Witherspoon, and Art Graesser. 2008. Emote aloud during learning with AutoTutor: Applying the Facial Action Coding System to cognitive–affective states during learning. *Cognition & Emotion* 22, 5: 777–788. http://doi.org/10.1080/02699930701516759
6. Paul Ekman and Wallace V. Friesen. 1978. *Facial Action Coding System.* Consulting Psychologists Press.
7. Joseph F. Grafsgaard, Joseph B. Wiggins, Kristy Elizabeth Boyer, Eric N. Wiebe, and James C. Lester. 2013. Automatically recognizing facial expression: Predicting engagement and frustration. *International Conference on Educational Data Mining*.
8. Ouriel Grynszpan, Patrice L. (Tamar) Weiss, Fernando Perez-Diaz, and Eynat Gal. 2014. Innovative technology-based interventions for autism spectrum disorders: A meta-analysis. *Autism* 18, 4: 346–361. http://doi.org/10.1177/1362361313476767
9. Curtis R. Henrie, Lisa R. Halverson, and Charles R. Graham. 2015. Measuring student engagement in technology-mediated learning: A review. *Computers & Education* 90: 36–53. http://doi.org/10.1016/j.compedu.2015.09.005
10. Clifford M. Hurvich and Chih-Ling Tsai. 1989. Regression and time series model selection in small samples. *Biometrika* 76, 2: 297–307. http://doi.org/10.1093/biomet/76.2.297
11. Michel Janosz. 2012. Part IV Commentary: Outcomes of Engagement and Engagement as an Outcome: Some Consensus, Divergences, and Unanswered Questions. In *Handbook of Research on Student Engagement*, L Sandra Christenson, L Amy Reschly and Cathy Wylie (eds.). Springer US, Boston, MA, 695–703. http://doi.org/10.1007/978-1-4614-2018-7_33
12. Takeo Kanade, Jeffrey F. Cohn, and Yingli Tian. 2000. Comprehensive database for facial expression analysis. *Proceedings Fourth IEEE International Conference on Automatic Face and Gesture Recognition (Cat. No. PR00580)*: 46–53. http://doi.org/10.1109/AFGR.2000.840611
13. Connie Kasari, Nancy Brady, Catherine Lord, and Helen Tager-Flusberg. 2013. Assessing the minimally verbal school-aged child with autism spectrum disorder. *Autism Research* 6, 6: 479–493. http://doi.org/10.1002/aur.1334
14. Jasna Legiša, Daniel S. Messinger, Enzo Kermol, and Luc Marlier. 2013. Emotional responses to odors in children with high-functioning autism: Autonomic arousal, facial behavior and self-report. *Journal of Autism and Developmental Disorders* 43, 4: 869–879. http://doi.org/10.1007/s10803-012-1629-2
15. James Jenn-Jier Lien, Takeo Kanade, Jeffrey F. Cohn, and Ching-Chung Li. 2000. Detection, Tracking, and Classification of Action Units in Facial Expression. *Robotics and Autonomous Systems* 31, 3: 131–146.
16. Gwen C. Littlewort, Marian Stewart Bartlett, and Kang Lee. 2009. Automatic coding of facial expressions displayed during posed and genuine pain. *Image and Vision Computing* 27, 12: 1797–1803. http://doi.org/10.1016/j.imavis.2008.12.010
17. Gwen C. Littlewort, Jacob Whitehill, Tingfan Wu, et al. 2011. The computer expression recognition toolbox (CERT). *IEEE International Conference on Automatic Face and Gesture Recognition and Workshops, FG 2011*: 298–305. http://doi.org/10.1109/FG.2011.5771414
18. Catherine Lord, Ann Wagner, Sally Rogers, et al. 2005. Challenges in Evaluating Psychosocial Interventions for Autistic Spectrum Disorders. *Journal of Autism and Developmental Disorders* 35, 6: 695–708. http://doi.org/10.1007/s10803-005-0017-6
19. Marc J. Mazerolle. 2016. AICcmodavg: Model selection and multimodel inference based on (Q)AIC(c). R package version 2.0-4. http://CRAN.R-project.org/package=AICcmodavg.
20. David Moore and Jill Taylor. 2000. Interactive Multimedia Systems for Students with Autism. *Journal of Educational Media* 25, 3: 169–177. http://doi.org/10.1080/1358165000250302
21. Heather J. Nuske, Giacomo Vivanti, and Cheryl Dissanayake. 2013. Are emotion impairments unique to, universal, or specific in autism spectrum disorder? A comprehensive review. *Cognition & Emotion* 27, 6: 1042–1061. http://doi.org/10.1080/02699931.2012.762900

22. Samuel L. Odom, Julie L. Thompson, Susan Hedges, et al. 2015. Technology-Aided Interventions and Instruction for Adolescents with Autism Spectrum Disorder. *Journal of Autism and Developmental Disorders* 45, 12: 3805–3819. http://doi.org/10.1007/s10803-014-2320-6

23. Robert C. Pennington. 2010. Computer-Assisted Instruction for Teaching Academic Skills to Students With Autism Spectrum Disorders: A Review of Literature. *Focus on Autism and Other Developmental Disabilities* 25, 4: 239–248. http://doi.org/10.1177/1088357610378291

24. Kathleen Ann Quill. 1995. *Teaching Children with Autism: Strategies to Enhance Communication and Socialization*. Delmar Publishers.

25. Sathiyaprakash Ramdoss, Wendy Machalicek, Mandy Rispoli, Austin Mulloy, Russell Lang, and Mark O'Reilly. 2012. Computer-based interventions to improve social and emotional skills in individuals with autism spectrum disorders: A systematic review. *Developmental Neurorehabilitation* 15, 2: 119–135. http://doi.org/10.3109/17518423.2011.651655

26. Deborah M. Riby, Gwyneth Doherty-Sneddon, and Lisa Whittle. 2012. Face-to-face interference in typical and atypical development. *Developmental Science* 15, 2: 281–291. http://doi.org/10.1111/j.1467-7687.2011.01125.x

27. Eric Schopler, Robert J. Reichler, and Barbara R. Renner. 1986. *The childhood autism rating scale (CARS): for diagnostic screening and classification of autism*. Irvington, New York.

28. Frederick Shic and Matthew S. Goodwin. 2015. Introduction to Technologies in the Daily Lives of Individuals with Autism. *Journal of Autism and Developmental Disorders* 45, 12: 3773–3776. http://doi.org/10.1007/s10803-015-2640-1

29. Karan Sikka, Alex A. Ahmed, Damaris Diaz, et al. 2015. Automated Assessment of Children's Postoperative Pain Using Computer Vision. *Pediatrics* 136, 1: 1–8. http://doi.org/10.1542/peds.2015-0029

30. Helen Tager-Flusberg, Daniela Plesa Skwerer, Robert M. Joseph, et al. 2016. Conducting research with minimally verbal participants with autism spectrum disorder. *Autism*: 1362361316654605. http://doi.org/10.1177/1362361316654605

31. Christina Whalen, et al. 2006. Positive behavioral changes associated with the use of computer-assisted instruction for young children. *Journal of Speech and Language Pathology and Applied Behavior Analysis* 1, 1: 11–26.

32. Christina Whalen, Debbie Moss, Aaron B. Ilan, et al. 2010. Efficacy of TeachTown: Basics computer-assisted intervention for the Intensive Comprehensive Autism Program in Los Angeles Unified School District. *Autism: the international journal of research and practice* 14, 3: 179–197. http://doi.org/10.1177/1362361310363282

33. Jacob Whitehill, Zewelanji Serpell, Yi-Ching Yi-Ching Lin, Aysha Foster, and Javier R. Movellan. 2014. The Faces of Engagement: Automatic Recognition of Student Engagementfrom Facial Expressions. *IEEE Transactions on Affective Computing* 5, 1: 86–98. http://doi.org/10.1109/TAFFC.2014.2316163

Comparing Touchscreen and Mouse Input Performance by People With and Without Upper Body Motor Impairments

Leah Findlater[1], Karyn Moffatt[3], Jon E. Froehlich[2], Meethu Malu[2], Joan Zhang[2]

[1,2]Human-Computer Interaction Lab
[1]College of Information Studies | [2]Dept. of Computer Science
University of Maryland, College Park, MD
leahkf@umd.edu, {jonf, meethu}@cs.umd.edu, joan.r.zhang@gmail.com

[3]ACT Research Group
School of Information Studies
McGill University, Montreal, QC
karyn.moffatt@mcgill.ca

ABSTRACT

Controlled studies of touchscreen input performance for users with upper body motor impairments remain relatively sparse. To address this gap, we present a controlled lab study of mouse *vs.* touchscreen performance with 32 participants (16 with upper body motor impairments and 16 without). Our study examines: (1) how touch input compares to an indirect pointing device (a mouse); (2) how performance compares across a range of standard interaction techniques; and (3) how these answers differ for users with and without motor impairments. While the touchscreen was faster than the mouse overall, only participants without motor impairments benefited from a lower error rate on the touchscreen. Indeed, participants *with* motor impairments had a *three-fold increase* in pointing (tapping) errors on the touchscreen compared to the mouse. Our findings also highlight the high frequency of spurious touches for users with motor impairments and update past accessibility recommendations for minimum touchscreen target sizes to at least 18mm.

Author Keywords

Human performance; motor impairments; accessibility; input devices; touchscreen; mouse.

ACM Classification Keywords

H.5.m. Information interfaces and presentation (e.g., HCI): Miscellaneous; K.4.2. Social issues: assistive technologies for persons with disabilities.

INTRODUCTION

Mobile devices can increase independence and provide a sense of empowerment for people with motor impairments [1,7,11]. While the shift to touchscreens has provided some benefits to motor-impaired users, such as requiring little force to register a tap and offering the flexibility to use alternative body parts (*e.g.*, a knuckle) [16], many accessibility challenges exist, ranging from simply pulling out the device [11] to being able to tap precisely without slipping [16].

CHI 2017, May 06-11, 2017, Denver, CO, USA
© 2017 ACM. ISBN 978-1-4503-4655-9/17/05…$15.00
DOI: http://dx.doi.org/10.1145/3025453.3025603

Figure 1. Cropped screenshots of the four study tasks, showing a range of orientations, target widths, and amplitudes.

Despite the above body of work, controlled studies of touchscreen input performance for people with upper body motor impairments are relatively sparse. Studies have compared novel techniques (*e.g.*, swabbing [17]) to a control condition such as tapping [9,10,17,20], but do not shed light on more general questions related to device comparisons (*e.g.*, touchscreen *vs.* mouse) and user groups. Other studies have compared tapping input performance for users with and without motor impairments, but using vertical touchscreen kiosks (*e.g.*, [6,14]), where the large target size and device orientation do not directly translate to mobile touchscreens.

The most comprehensive evaluations come from Trewin *et al.* [16] and Guerreiro and colleagues [3,12]. The former [16] evaluates a range of native interaction techniques within existing mobile apps, which is useful for ecological validity but did not allow for precise quantification of performance. The latter [3,12] provides a more precise measurement of speed and accuracy for users with and without motor impairments across common interactions (pointing, crossing, directional swiping), separately analyzing the data for each task and each group. However, the lack of direct comparisons and the use of non-standard input tasks (*e.g.*, as opposed to [5]) leads to an incomplete understanding of the inherent tradeoffs of different touchscreen interaction techniques for users with and without motor impairments. Neither evaluation included a mouse comparison.

Addressing these gaps, we conducted a controlled lab study to understand: (1) how touch input compares to indirect pointing devices (*e.g.*, a mouse); (2) how input performance compares across a range of standard interaction techniques; (3) how these answers differ for users with and without motor impairments. Thirty-two participants (16 with and 16 without motor impairments) completed a set of basic input tasks with both a mouse and a touchscreen tablet: *crossing*, *dragging*, *pointing*, and *steering*. We found a high error rate for touchscreen pointing (tapping) compared to mouse pointing for users with motor impairments, and, relatedly, a disparity in how direct touch benefits users with and without motor impairments. Secondarily, we provide a more detailed comparison of users with and without motor impairments in terms of two facets of touchscreen input accuracy: the impacts of target size and spurious touch frequency.

METHOD

Our method was largely consistent with past work [2].

Participants

This study included 16 participants with upper body motor impairments (WithMI) and 16 without (NoMI). The WithMI group was on average 42.0 years old (SD = 16.8), with 11 females and 5 males. They reported using computers daily (N = 9), a few times a week (5), or a few times a month (2), and using touchscreen devices daily (N = 13), a few times a week (1) or never (2). More detail on the WithMI group is in the Supplemental Materials, but reported medical conditions included cerebral palsy (N = 5), multiple sclerosis (4), C5 spinal cord injury (1), essential and orthostatic tremor (1), sports injury (1), arthritis (1), stroke (1), and traumatic brain injury (1).[1] The NoMI group was on average 19.8 years old (SD = 1.1), with 10 females and 6 males; all reported daily use of computers and touchscreen devices. [2]

Apparatus

The experimental testbed was written in JavaScript, HTML, and PHP. For the mouse condition, the testbed was loaded in a Chrome browser on a Mac laptop running OS X and connected to an external monitor with 1280×1024 resolution and a Logitech M310 wireless optical mouse. For the touchscreen, the testbed was loaded in Safari on an Apple iPad 3 in portrait orientation. The testbed guided participants through the four input tasks (crossing, steering, pointing, and dragging), each implemented based on the ISO 9241-9 circle 2D Fitts' law task standard [5]. We fully crossed amplitudes (A) of {250px, 500px} with widths (W) of {32px, 64px, 96px}, removing the combination (A=500px, W=96px) as it did not fit on the iPad screen with enough padding to allow a $2W$ overshoot of the target (the iPad is only 768px wide and the task canvas had to be square for the ISO task). The five $A \times W$ combinations thus provide an *Index of Difficulty (ID)* range of 1.9–4.1, where *ID* is the ratio between the distance to the target and its width and where higher values indicate greater input difficulty [15]: $ID = \log_2(A/W+1)$. On the iPad, the smallest target width, 32px, corresponds to a 6mm target.

Procedure

The procedure took up to one hour for the NoMI group and 90 minutes for the WithMI group, but otherwise was exactly the same for both. The iPad was placed flat on the table, but participants could adjust its specific location. Mouse speed was set to the OS X default. Participants could raise/lower the table before starting, necessary for some wheelchair users. The mouse and touchscreen were presented in counterbalanced order, with the crossing, dragging, pointing, and steering tasks randomly ordered for each device.[3] For each task, participants completed 5 practice trials (which they could opt to repeat once) and 55 test trials. Each trial began by activating a circular start target by tapping/clicking (pointing and dragging tasks) or holding/hovering for 300ms (crossing and steering tasks); see Figure 1. Spatial outlier trials, that is, where the movement distance was less than half of A or the endpoint was more than $2W$ away from the target center [8], were automatically redone by appending them to the end of the set of trials. Short breaks were offered midway through each task, between tasks, and mid-session. Background information was collected between tasks.

Experiment Design, Data, and Analysis

We used a 2×2×4 mixed factorial design: *Group* (WithMI *vs.* NoMI) × *Device* (mouse *vs.* touchscreen) × *Task* (crossing, dragging, pointing, steering). Order of presentation for *Device* was counterbalanced, while *Task* was randomized. As mentioned above, participants repeated spatial outlier trials, consistent with prior work [8,19]. Doing so assumes, however, that a spatial outlier is spurious in some way—perhaps an accidental touch or lift off when the participant is momentarily distracted. While this assumption may be reasonable for users without motor impairments [8,19], our WithMI group had a relatively high incidence of spatial outliers: 4.5% of trials *vs.* only 0.5% for the NoMI group. As such, we consider these trials to be valid; for both groups, we ignore the appended trials and only analyze the first attempt of each trial. Our dataset includes 14080 trials in total.

Our primary speed and error rate analysis includes all three factors in our experimental design. We use parametric tests (*e.g.*, ANOVAs, t-tests) for speed, and non-parametric alternatives (*e.g.*, Aligned Rank Transform ANOVAs [18], Wilcoxon signed ranks tests) for most other measures as they did not meet the normality assumption of parametric tests. When the degrees of freedom are fractional for ANOVAs, a Greenhouse-Geisser adjustment has been applied to account for sphericity violations. Posthoc pairwise comparisons were protected against Type I error using a Bonferroni adjustment.

RESULTS

We first compare the touchscreen and mouse before focusing specifically on issues with touchscreen accuracy.

Touchscreen versus Mouse

Speed. Overall speed results are shown in Figure 2, with detailed ANOVA results in Table 1. As expected, all three main effects (*Group*, *Device*, and *Task*) were significant: the WithMI group was slower than the NoMI group, the touchscreen was faster than the mouse, and tasks impacted speed differently. There were also significant interaction effects of *Group* × *Task* and *Device* × *Task*. Focusing on the interaction effect involving *Group*, our primary factor of

[1] One participant's response was unclear.

[2] The NoMI data was collected, in part, for a different study with 30 participants. We randomly selected 16 of these 30 NoMI participants to ensure equal sample sizes with the WithMI group.

[3] On the iPad, these primary tasks were optionally followed by pinch and zoom, which only half of the WithMI group completed due to ability and/or time. Thus, we do not report on pinch/zoom.

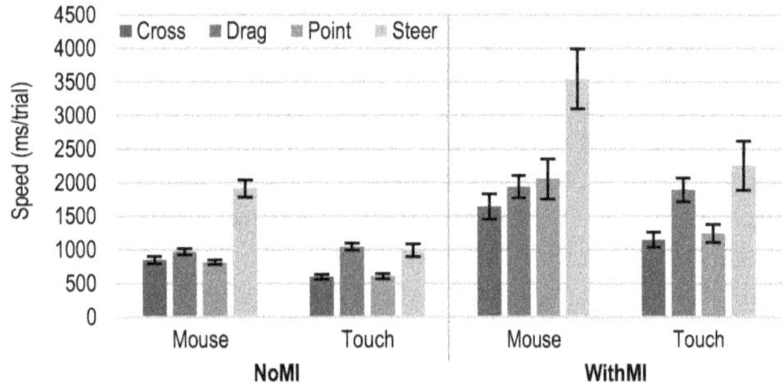

Figure 2. Average trial speed for participant groups without and with motor impairments ($N = 32$; error bars show standard error). Lower values are better.

Effect	Result		
Group	$F_{1,30} = 29.91$	$p < .001$	partial $\eta^2 = .50$
Device	$F_{1,30} = 25.12$	$p < .001$	partial $\eta^2 = .46$
Task	$F_{1.83,54.94} = 29.91$	$p < .001$	partial $\eta^2 = .56$
Group × Device	$F_{1,30} = 2.85$	$p = .102$	partial $\eta^2 = .09$
Group × Task	$F_{1.83,54.94} = 4.14$	$p = .024$	partial $\eta^2 = .12$
Device × Task	$F_{1.55,46.58} = 14.00$	$p < .001$	partial $\eta^2 = .32$
Group × Device × Task	$F_{1.55,46.58} = 0.70$	$p = .467$	partial $\eta^2 = .02$

Table 1. Three-way (*Group × Device × Task*) repeated measures ANOVA results for speed.

interest, we conducted posthoc pairwise comparisons of each of the four tasks within each group. For the WithMI group, steering fared the worst, at 2,901ms ($SD = 1{,}301$) per trial; it was significantly slower than all three other tasks (all $p < .05$). Dragging was also relatively slow, being significantly slower than crossing ($p < .05$). For the NoMI group, steering was significantly slower than crossing and pointing (all $p < .05$), but not different from dragging.

Overall, the *relative* performance of the four tasks was largely similar across the two groups for speed. For the most part, the WithMI group was simply slower, by on average about double the time. This is the case for both devices and all four tasks, with the possible exception of dragging versus crossing for the WithMI group.

Errors. The error rate results (Figure 3) are more complex. While Table 2 includes all detailed results from the ANOVA with ART, here we focus on the main effect of *Group* and interaction effects involving *Group* × *Device*, our primary and secondary factors of interest.

The NoMI group's average error rate was 6.1% ($SD = 4.3$) with the mouse and 3.2% ($SD = 2.2$) with the touchscreen. In contrast, the WithMI group had a significantly higher error rate, at 21.1% ($SD = 19.7$) with the mouse and 25.1% ($SD = 21.0$) with the touchscreen—in the latter case, almost *eight times as high* as the NoMI group. These patterns translated into a significant main effect of *Group* and a significant *Group* × *Device* interaction. Based on the interaction, posthoc pairwise comparisons using Wilcoxon signed ranks tests showed that the touchscreen resulted in significantly lower error rates than the mouse for the NoMI group ($p < .05$); no similar benefit was seen for the WithMI group.

Finally, there was a significant *Group* × *Device* × *Task* interaction. Pairwise comparisons showed that for NoMI participants, crossing and steering were more accurate with

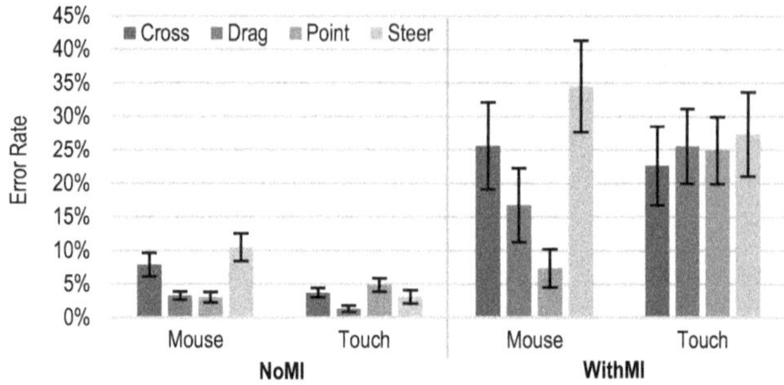

Figure 3. Average error rate for participant groups without and with motor impairments (N = 32; error bars show standard error). Lower values are better.

Effect	Result		
Group	$F_{1,30} = 14.81$	$p = .001$	partial $\eta^2 = .33$
Device	$F_{1,30} = 3.11$	$p < .001$	partial $\eta^2 = .09$
Task	$F_{3,90} = 22.03$	$p < .001$	partial $\eta^2 = .42$
Group × Device	$F_{1,30} = 22.70$	$p < .001$	partial $\eta^2 = .43$
Group × Task	$F_{3,90} = 11.00$	$p < .001$	partial $\eta^2 = .27$
Device × Task	$F_{2.35,70.56} = 28.98$	$p < .001$	partial $\eta^2 = .49$
Group × Device × Task	$F_{2.29,68.63} = 9.79$	$p < .001$	partial $\eta^2 = .25$

Table 2. Three-way (*Group × Device × Task*) repeated measures ANOVA with ART results for error rate.

the touchscreen than the mouse ($p < .05$), but no differences were found between the two devices for dragging or pointing. For WithMI participants, in comparison, pointing was the only task with significant differences between the two devices ($p < .05$). Here, the error rate was 24.9% ($SD = 20.0$) with the touchscreen versus only 7.4% ($SD = 11.3$) with the mouse. This finding has important practical implications for accessibility as pointing (tapping) is by far the most common touchscreen interaction technique.

A Closer Look at Touchscreen Errors

Following the disparity in how the touchscreen impacted errors for the two user groups, we conducted more detailed error analyses to examine target size and spurious touches.

Target size. Past work has recommended 12mm as an appropriate touchscreen target size for supporting users both with and without motor impairments based on seeing no further error reduction at larger sizes [12]. To revisit this finding and to directly compare the effects of target size for the NoMI and WithMI groups (unlike [12]'s separate analyses), we analyzed error rate based on the three target sizes in our task: 6mm, 12mm, and 18mm. Figure 4 shows the overall results. A 2×3 (*Group* × *Target Size*) ANOVA with ART showed that there were significant main effects of both *Group* ($F_{1,30} = 35.76, p < .001, \eta_p^2 = .54$) and *Target Size* ($F_{1.48,60} = 67.16, p < .001, \eta_p^2 = .69$) on average error rate.

More interesting, however, was a significant *Group* × *Target Size* interaction effect, showing that target size impacted the WithMI group differently than the NoMI group ($F_{1.40,60} = 67.16, p < .001, \eta_p^2 = .58$). The WithMI group had an average error rate of 42.1% ($SD = 29.2$) with the smallest target size (6mm), which dropped to 7.0% ($SD = 11.3$) for the largest size (18mm). For NoMI participants, error rates were close to zero for the larger two target sizes, but jumped to 7.4% on average ($SD = 4.7$) for the smallest targets—comparable to

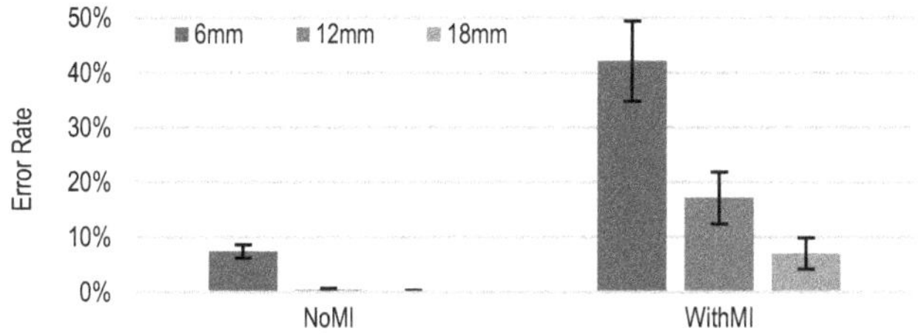

Figure 4. Touchscreen error rates by target size, collapsed across all four tasks (N = 32; error bars show standard error).

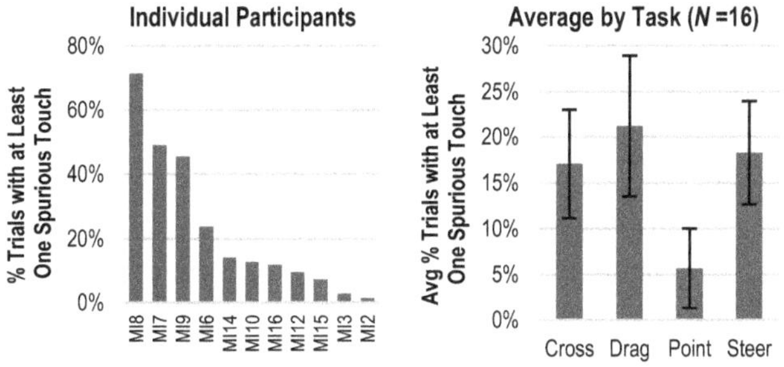

Figure 5. Spurious touches for the WithMI group (the NoMI group made almost no spurious touches): by participant (left) and by task (right). MI1, MI4, MI5, MI11 and MI13 made no spurious touches, thus are not shown in the individual chart.

the largest target size for WithMI participants. Pairwise comparisons based on the interaction effect emphasize these results: for the WithMI group, the smallest targets caused significantly more errors than the other two sizes, and the medium targets caused more errors than the largest ones (all $p < .05$). For the NoMI group, the smallest targets caused significantly more errors than the other two sizes ($p < .05$); there was no difference between the medium and large targets. The NoMI results are consistent with past work [4] and a recommended target size of ~9mm [13].

Spurious touches. While spurious touches are ignored in typical Fitts task (as in our earlier analysis), they can create problems in real systems, for example, causing an intended tap to result in a multi-finger gesture like zoom. While Mott *et al.* [10] report on the number of touchpoints on the screen during tapping tasks, participants in that study tapped in a "comfortable and natural" way, rather than under standard conditions. To our knowledge, spurious touches have not been reported in detail for users with motor impairments. Thus, we logged spurious touches for posthoc analysis.

Spurious touch rates for the WithMI group are shown in Figure 5. For this group, on average 5.7% of pointing trials (SD = 17.4) had one or more spurious touches, rising to 21.3% (SD = 30.8) for dragging trials. Spurious touches were also much more of a problem for some WithMI participants than others. Five of the 16 participants made no spurious touches at all, while participant MI8 made at least one spurious touch in 71% of trials. For comparison, only two NoMI participants made *any* spurious touches, for a total of four touches that all occurred in the dragging task.

Due to the lack of variance in the data from the NoMI group, we did not conduct a factorial analysis comparing the two groups. However, a Friedman test with the single factor of *Task* for the WithMI group was statistically significant ($\chi^2_{3,N=16} = 15.84, p < .001$). This result is not surprising, given that crossing, dragging, and steering require continuous touching during the trial, therefore increasing the chance of additional spurious touches compared to pointing.

DISCUSSION AND CONCLUSION

While our study shows that there is an overall speed advantage to the touchscreen over the mouse, touchscreen error rates were only lower than the mouse for users *without* motor impairments. Indeed, for users *with* motor impairments, touchscreen tapping (*i.e.*, pointing) errors were more than three times as high with the touchscreen than with the mouse. Tapping is by far the most common touchscreen interaction technique, which emphasizes the importance of efforts to improve tapping accuracy (*e.g.*, [10,20]).

Our results also update Nicolau *et al.*'s [12] recommended minimum touchscreen target size for users with upper body motor impairments. Their suggestion of 12mm was based on seeing no improvement from 12mm to 17mm, but error rates were over 20% for both sizes—likely unacceptably high for real use and potentially due to their participants being much less experienced with touchscreens than ours. Our results suggest that touchscreen targets should be at least 18mm to be accessible for users with a range of upper body motor impairments. Even at 18mm, our error rate was 7%, so future work should examine at what point the rates level off.

Nicolau *et al.* [12] also concluded that swipes were inaccessible for users with motor impairments, which is contradicted by Trewin *et al.* [16]. Our findings support Trewin *et al.*'s conclusion that swiping is accessible: relative to other tasks, steering (the closest of our tasks to swiping, and arguably more difficult) was not disproportionately hard for users with motor impairments compared to those without.

While spurious touches were a non-issue for participants without motor impairments, they were common for many users *with* motor impairments. Future work should investigate why spurious touches are a problem for some people with motor impairments and not others, as well as the extent to which these touches interfere with more realistic tasks that include multiple on-screen targets and where multitouch gestures are also available. For users with a high rate of spurious touches (*e.g.*, above 40% of trials) the ability to disable multitouch input may be useful.

Finally, our participants without motor impairments were much younger than those with motor impairments. While an age-matched study would better isolate the effects of motor impairment from general age-related effects, our control group likely offers a baseline of near-optimal human input performance. Moreover, our findings contrast work showing that older adults are both faster and more accurate with the touchscreen than the mouse [2]. This contrast emphasizes the influence of motor impairment in our study and the importance of considering these two user groups distinct.

ACKNOWLEDGMENTS

This project was funded by NSF grant IIS-1350438.

REFERENCES

1. Lisa Anthony, YooJin Kim, and Leah Findlater. 2013. Analyzing user-generated youtube videos to understand touchscreen use by people with motor impairments. In *Proceedings of the SIGCHI Conference on Human Factors in Computing Systems (CHI '13)*, 1223–1232. http://doi.org/10.1145/2470654.2466158
2. Leah Findlater, Jon E. Froehlich, Kays Fattal, Jacob O. Wobbrock, and Tanya Dastyar. 2013. Age-related differences in performance with touchscreens compared to traditional mouse input. In *Proceedings of the SIGCHI Conference on Human Factors in Computing Systems (CHI '13)*, 343–346. http://doi.org/10.1145/2470654.2470703
3. Tiago Guerreiro, Hugo Nicolau, Joaquim Jorge, and Daniel Gonçalves. 2010. Towards accessible touch interfaces. In *Proceedings of the ACM SIGACCESS Conference on Computers and Accessibility (ASSETS'10)*, 19–26. http://doi.org/10.1145/1878803.1878809
4. Christian Holz and Patrick Baudisch. 2011. Understanding Touch. In *Proceedings of the SIGCHI Conference on Human Factors in Computing Systems*, 2501–2510. http://doi.org/10.1145/1978942.1979308
5. International Organization for Standardization. 2002. *Ergonomic requirements for office work with visual display terminals (VDTs)—Requirements for non-keyboard input devices.*
6. Curt B Irwin and Mary E Sesto. 2012. Performance and touch characteristics of disabled and non-disabled participants during a reciprocal tapping task using touch screen technology. *Applied ergonomics* 43, 6: 1038–43. http://doi.org/10.1016/j.apergo.2012.03.003
7. Shaun K Kane, Chandrika Jayant, Jacob O Wobbrock, and Richard E Ladner. 2009. Freedom to roam: a study of mobile device adoption and accessibility for people with visual and motor disabilities. In *Proceedings of the ACM SIGACCESS Conference on Computers and Accessibility (ASSETS'09)*, 115–122. http://doi.org/10.1145/1639642.1639663
8. I. Scott MacKenzie and Poika Isokoski. 2008. Fitts' throughput and the speed-accuracy tradeoff. In *Proceedings of the SIGCHI Conference on Human Factors in Computing Systems (CHI'08)*, 1633–1636. http://doi.org/10.1145/1357054.1357308
9. Kyle Montague, Vicki L Hanson, and Andy Cobley. 2012. Designing for individuals: usable touch-screen interaction through shared user models. In *Proceedings of the ACM SIGACCESS Conference on Computers and Accessibility (ASSETS'12)*, 151–158. http://doi.org/10.1145/2384916.2384943
10. Martez E Mott, Radu-Daniel Vatavu, Shaun K Kane, and Jacob O Wobbrock. 2016. Smart Touch: Improving Touch Accuracy for People with Motor Impairments with Template Matching. In *Proceedings of the 2016 CHI Conference on Human Factors in Computing Systems*, 1934–1946. http://doi.org/10.1145/2858036.2858390
11. Maia Naftali and Leah Findlater. 2014. Accessibility in Context: Understanding the Truly Mobile Experience of Smartphone Users with Motor Impairments. In *Proceedings of the ACM SIGACCESS Conference on Computers and Accessibility (ASSETS '14)*, 209–216. http://doi.org/10.1145/2661334.2661372
12. Hugo Nicolau, Tiago Guerreiro, Joaquim Jorge, and Daniel Gonçalves. 2014. Mobile touchscreen user interfaces: Bridging the gap between motor-impaired and able-bodied users. *Universal Access in the Information Society* 13: 303–313. http://doi.org/10.1007/s10209-013-0320-5
13. Pekka Parhi, Amy K Karlson, and Benjamin B Bederson. 2006. Target size study for one-handed thumb use on small touchscreen devices. In *Proceedings of MobileHCI '06*, 203–210. http://doi.org/10.1145/1152215.1152260
14. M. E. Sesto, C. B. Irwin, K. B. Chen, A. O. Chourasia, and D. A. Wiegmann. 2012. Effect of Touch Screen Button Size and Spacing on Touch Characteristics of Users With and Without Disabilities. *Human Factors: The Journal of the Human Factors and Ergonomics Society* 54, 3: 425–436. http://doi.org/10.1177/0018720811433831
15. R. William Soukoreff and I. Scott MacKenzie. 2004. Towards a standard for pointing device evaluation, perspectives on 27 years of Fitts' law research in HCI. *International Journal of Human-Computer Studies* 61, 6: 751–789. http://doi.org/10.1016/j.ijhcs.2004.09.001
16. Shari Trewin, Cal Swart, and Donna Pettick. 2013. Physical accessibility of touchscreen smartphones. In *Proceedings of the 15th International ACM SIGACCESS Conference on Computers and Accessibility (ASSETS '13)*, 1–8. http://doi.org/10.1145/2513383.2513446
17. Chat Wacharamanotham, Jan Hurtmanns, Alexander Mertens, Martin Kronenbuerger, Christopher Schlick, and Jan Borchers. 2011. Evaluating Swabbing: a touchscreen input method for elderly users with tremor. In *Proceedings of the SIGCHI Conference on Human Factors in Computing Systems (CHI'11)*, 623–626. http://doi.org/10.1145/1978942.1979031
18. Jacob O Wobbrock, Leah Findlater, Darren Gergle, and James J Higgins. 2011. The Aligned Rank Transform for Nonparametric Factorial Analyses Using Only Anova Procedures. In *Proceedings of the SIGCHI*

Conference on Human Factors in Computing Systems (CHI '11), 143–146. http://doi.org/10.1145/1978942.1978963

19. Jacob O Wobbrock, Kristen Shinohara, and Alex Jansen. 2011. The effects of task dimensionality, endpoint deviation, throughput calculation, and experiment design on pointing measures and models. *Proceedings of the 2011 annual conference on Human factors in computing systems (CHI '11)*: 1639. http://doi.org/10.1145/1978942.1979181

20. Yu Zhong, Astrid Weber, Casey Burkhardt, et al. 2015. Enhancing Android Accessibility for Users with Hand Tremor by Reducing Fine Pointing and Steady Tapping. In *Proceedings of the 12th Web for All Conference*, 29. http://doi.org/10.1145/2745555.2747277

Designing Cultural Values into Interaction

Reese Muntean[1], Alissa N. Antle[1], Brendan Matkin[1], Kate Hennessy[1], Susan Rowley[2], and Jordan Wilson[2]

[1]Simon Fraser University
Surrey, Canada
rmuntean, aantle, bmatkin,
hennessy_kate @sfu.ca

[2]University of British Columbia
Vancouver, Canada
susan.rowley@ubc.ca,
jordanphwilson@gmail.com

ABSTRACT

In this paper, we highlight possibilities for designing intangible cultural values into interactions with technologies in heritage spaces. We do this specifically through the design of *ʔeləw̓kʷ — Belongings,* an interactive tangible table installed in a cultural heritage museum. The tabletop was collaboratively designed to communicate complex and narrative information and values about Musqueam culture. Rather than focusing only on content and interface design, we wanted visitors to also experience Musqueam values through their interactions with the system. We describe our value-sensitive design process, present five interdependent design goals, discuss the design strategies that enabled us to meet these goals, and evaluate our approach through a user study. From our design process and evaluation we offer recommendations for designing values into interactions more generally and for tangible interactions specifically in ways that support visitors' experience and understanding of specific cultural values through technology.

Author Keywords

Intangible cultural heritage; indigenous heritage; museums; tangibles; digital tabletops; value sensitive design.

ACM Classification Keywords

H.5.2. Information interfaces and presentation (e.g., HCI): User Interfaces, Evaluation/Methodology.

INTRODUCTION

Researchers are increasingly exploring how human values take shape in our digital technology (e.g. [19, 21, 44]). While initially these explorations examined universal values, culturally specific values can also be designed into digital systems and our interactions with these systems [10]. At the same time, museums continue to incorporate technology into exhibits, allowing visitors to engage with information in different ways and in greater depth. Digital technologies are also being used to move beyond a focus on tangible heritage objects to address the challenges of safeguarding intangible cultural heritage—the traditions or living cultural expressions that are passed on from generation to generation [43, 62]. In this paper we highlight possibilities for designing intangible cultural values into interaction in heritage spaces. We do this specifically through the design of an application for a multi-touch tangible table. Much of the work in this area has been focused on how and what visitors learn through interaction with tabletops (e.g. [2, 3, 4, 14, 15, 34]), how to design to support visitor engagement (e.g. [5, 8, 40]), and issues around initiating and sustaining interaction in public spaces (e.g. [23, 35, 37]).

The intersection of these research domains remains largely unexplored, yet holds great potential for using interaction design to convey cultural values and presenting intangible elements of culture in interactive museum exhibits. How do we design to convey and allow others to experience intangible cultural ideas, such as values?

In this paper we explore how collaborative interaction design could covey such values, driven by our research question: *What are effective design strategies that enable visitors to directly experience cultural values while they interact with Indigenous knowledge using a tangible tabletop system?* We examine the design goals, our design strategies related to each goal, and the evaluation of *ʔeləw̓kʷ — Belongings*, an interactive tangible tabletop at the Museum of Anthropology (MOA) at the University of British Columbia (UBC) which uses replicas of belongings from c̓əsnaʔəm (an ancient village site where modern day Vancouver, Canada is now located) with Musqueam intangible cultural knowledge and was part of the *c̓əsnaʔəm, the city before the city* exhibition exploring this history through the voices of Musqueam community members. From our analysis we offer generalizable design recommendations that can be used by researchers and designers of tangible interaction who want to support users in experiencing intangible elements of culture.

We will introduce ourselves here to situate ourselves as the authors, curators, researchers, and designers. We, the authors and faculty members and students from UBC and Simon Fraser University (SFU), comprised the core development team. Rowley at the time was co-head of the

CHI 2017, May 06-11, 2017, Denver, CO, USA

ACM 978-1-4503-4655-9/17/05···$15.00
DOI: http://dx.doi.org/10.1145/3025453.3025908

Department of Anthropology at UBC, Associate Professor, and Curator of Public Archeology at MOA. She has significant experience working collaboratively with the Musqueam Indian Band, and she and Wilson, a Master's student at UBC and a member of the Musqueam Indian Band, were the co-curators of MOA's exhibit. Our SFU team included Hennessy, an Assistant Professor with a background in anthropology whose own work is focused on the collaborative development of culturally specific new media applications and installations, and Antle, an Associate Professor who has expertise in tangible computing and embodied interaction. Matkin was a Master's student under Antle, and Muntean was a Master's student under Hennessy and the project manager of the tabletop. Our team also included two undergraduate students who had previously completed work with Antle. While the UBC team provided the content and museum-related support, the SFU members focused on the technical aspects of development, interaction design, fabrication of the physical aspects of the tangible interface, and the programming of the tabletop. All team members participated in the overall activity design of the table.

We begin this paper with a summary of related work, then outline our five interdependent design *goals* and describe the design *strategies* we employed to achieve these goals. Next we present our visitor study along with our results and design *recommendations* derived from what we have learned about designing cultural values into interaction.

RELATED WORK

Our work is situated in the areas of Value Sensitive Design, collaborative design with Indigenous communities, cultural heritage in human-computer interaction, and museum tabletop exhibits.

Value Sensitive Design

Value Sensitive Design (VSD), developed by Friedman, Khan, and Borning [19, 21], considers how human values are embedded within technologies and how these technologies can in turn shape values. Instead of the original, universal "values of human import" of VSD [20], here we look at certain cultural values that the design team carefully considered before the specific and specialized system was developed. Le Dantec et al. called for such an extension of VSD [44], recognizing that the classification of values was limiting and the "ex post facto value analysis" allowed for examining how systems affect users but not for informing system design. Borning and Muller later reflected on the next steps for VSD [10]. In this paper we take up three of the four topics discussed: addressing the universal vs. culturally specific values issue as an empirical one, strengthening Musqueam voice in publications, and making our own voices as researchers and designers more clear. Durrant et al. drew upon concerns from VSD in their research on values in curating videos in a human rights archive [18]. They noted a particular challenge for interaction designers is to enhance cultural engagement with sensitive archive materials while supporting empathic interactions, a challenge we take up in a different context here.

Collaborative Design with Indigenous Communities

Designing with Indigenous communities has similarities to and divergences from theories of participatory design and co-creative experiences (e.g. [7, 39, 40, 55, 58]). We see our collaborative process as more closely related to ideas of post-colonial computing as examined by Irani et al. and its response to uneven economic and power relations and cultural epistemologies [38]. The authors mention examples of information management systems as an intersection of cultural understandings and technology [61, 63] while grappling with issues of cultural property ownership (e.g. [11]), and we see our work as extending these ideas of creating technologies that communicate traditional cultural knowledge and allow for multiple ontologies and worldviews (e.g. [13, 48, 60]). The collaborative models displayed by museums and Indigenous communities (often in developing databases for cultural heritage) (e.g. [29, 31, 32, 33, 53, 54, 57]) informed our design process, though our work here explores new technologies for communicating this cultural information to the public.

Intangible and Digital Cultural Heritage in HCI

While the study of cultural heritage is an established domain in HCI research (e.g. [16, 22, 28, 46, 66]), the study of intangible and digital heritage remains underexplored in HCI (see [9]). This is not to say that no one is conducting such research. There are authors discussing new media and museums in the digital age (e.g. [41, 51]), looking at the digitization and safeguarding of cultural heritage [1, 45, 47, 52], technology for the museum space [27, 42], and connecting different forms of heritage such as natural, tangible, and intangible [24, 30]. Giaccardi and Palen explain how evolving information and communications technology can allow multiple media and interactive technologies to work together for users to experience and think about cultural heritage differently [25]. Multimodal or cross-media interaction can facilitate the exploration of tangible and intangible aspects of heritage together and allow new ways to engage with specific cultural values. Indeed, there are many examples of collaborations with Indigenous communities on multimodal projects that allow for archiving, storytelling, and interacting with intangible cultural heritage (e.g. [37, 56]). Our work contributes to this space by exploring how we can use the unique features of tangible touch tables in particular to convey both tangible and intangible cultural heritage to museum visitors.

Tangibles and Tabletops in Museums

Researchers are studying the design and use of tangibles in museums for both navigating the museum itself (e.g. [12, 65]) or information in interactive exhibits (e.g. [17, 49]). One example by Horn describes an approach to tangible interaction in which designers can evoke "social constructions or conventions", cultural forms such as counting systems, games, or currencies that often involve a physical artifact (Horn suggests that a high fidelity reproduction of the original cultural form is necessary) [34]. Horn and others have shown that cultural forms can be used for interaction design to utilize users' cognitive, physical, and emotional resources to increase usability and create meaningful experiences for users and observers [5, 34, 36, 59]. We extend this work, using cultural forms for interaction and experiencing values.

Mapping Place is an exhibit that introduces cultural concepts through the combination of a multi-touch table and an interface of physical objects [14]. It is based on a culturally specific storytelling device that utilizes beads, shell fragments, and carvings on a wooden board to guide stories and record history. The activity teaches the Luba peoples' mapping practices and perspectives through embedded cultural logic and structure, though Chu et al. found that participants who received a lesson before interacting with the exhibit showed better conceptualization and utilization of abstraction and symbolism in ways more similar to the Luba [14]. We wanted create this type of background lesson in the system itself, thus preparing visitors to experience values through their interactions.

Hornecker presents a field study of the *Tree of Life*, an interactive multi-touch tabletop exhibit that allows visitors to access information through a question-answer dialogue [35]. The question-answer format did not engage users as deeply as hoped and there were not enough layers to allow users to delve deeper. Others have recommended design approaches that may alleviate these issues such as presenting activities that initiate construction and testing of hypotheses, discovery, and meaning making (e.g. [15, 35, 64]) and reward visitors for early successes as well as for persistence in exploring further content [2, 15, 23, 35]. A balance between drawing visitors in and enabling them to persist and gain deeper understandings is key [15, 23, 35].

DESIGN REQUIREMENTS AND GOALS

The *ʔeləw̓kʷ — Belongings* project emerged in the context of the long-term collaboration between MOA and the Musqueam Indian Band (described in greater detail in [50]) and was designed in conjunction with members of the Musqueam community. Our collaborative design process and focus on values was a result and continuation of this relationship.

During our first design meeting, we developed nine main goals for the project, including highlighting Musqueam voices which was central to the overall exhibition. This session allowed us to see where our personal goals (and values) were as curators, designers, and researchers. Our team's interactions with the Musqueam Indian Band included representation at the Exhibit Advisory Committee meetings with Musqueam elders, visits to Musqueam reserve land to collaborate with community members on creating the photographic imagery, and incorporation of Musqueam language and values in our process. The Exhibit Advisory Committee was integral to ensuring that Musqueam's voice and values drove the exhibitions. Rowley and Wilson were members of this committee and attended the weekly meetings, reporting on our work and asking questions on behalf of our *ʔeləw̓kʷ — Belongings* design team. Many images on the tabletop were taken by community members, but Muntean also visited Musqueam to take photographs. For example, Muntean and Wilson worked with the Musqueam Fisheries Commission to photograph the fish preparation process and develop the main tabletop image.

The development team worked to incorporate Musqueam cultural values, and even their hən̓q̓əmin̓əm̓ language, in the design process including all related documentation and communications, such as using Musqueam's approved abbreviation for c̓əsnaʔəm, *csnm*, in file names and even in the code written for the tabletop application. Another example of this focus on values is evident in the use of the term "belongings" in the title of the tangible table and throughout this paper. While belongings excavated from c̓əsnaʔəm are more commonly referred to as "objects" or "artifacts", the Musqueam see them as still belonging to the hands that created them. As such, we adopted the term ʔeləw̓kʷ, a hən̓q̓əmin̓əm̓ term meaning belongings, to discuss what has been removed from c̓əsnaʔəm.

This collaborative design with cultural partners and the reflection upon cultural values throughout the process were so important that we consider them to be requirements for the design process. It is through this process that our goals and design recommendations developed. From the beginning of this process it was evident that Musqueam values and traditional knowledge were important to convey. Yet we wanted to move beyond descriptions of values and enable people to directly experience these values. Our commitment to this direction emerged early in the process and was likely a result of wanting to honor Musqueam's intentions for the exhibition and representation of their culture [26] and our own desire as designers and researchers to push the boundaries of design. In addition to these two requirements, we agreed upon five interrelated design goals that we hoped, when met, would enable visitors to experience cultural values through their interaction with a tabletop system.

Design Goal 1 [DG1]: Draw in People

In line with previous work (e.g. [3, 37]) our first goal was to draw in people to the space and initiate interaction with the table. Since the table was to be placed in a small alcove that was part of the larger exhibition, we needed a way to attract visitors into the space and encourage them to engage with our system.

Design Goal 2 [DG2]: Learn about Musqueam Culture

At the simplest level, we wanted people to learn something new about the Musqueam people, culture, and identity both past and present. The curators noted that by displaying ancient belongings, visitors might mistake material culture to be the same as culture, resulting in a false impression that

Musqueam culture is only about the past. Our learning goal was for visitors to understand that Musqueam is a contemporary society that has existed in the region for thousands of years.

Design Goal 3 [DG3]: Understand Richness of Belongings
Building on the basic knowledge in DG2, we also wanted visitors to understand the richness of information about the belongings, including how they were used and how common they were. In line with trends designing exhibitions for cultural heritage (e.g. [25]) and the notion of cultural forms [34], we wanted to display the belongings in such a way that people could interact with them physically rather than passively view them behind glass.

Design Goal 4 [DG4]: Understand Complexity of Stories
Building on DG2&3 and addressing issues raised in [35] about lack of depth and the importance of understanding the complexity of value-laden content [3], we wanted visitors to understand some of the complexity of information related to belongings excavated from c̓əsnaʔəm. We envisioned visitors learning some of the many stories related to each belonging.

Design Goal 5 [DG5]: Experience Cultural Values
Rather than telling visitors about culture values, our goal was to have visitors experience values through their interaction, adding cultural specificity to ideas from previous work that showed how enabling visitors to make their own interpretations about values through interaction had a greater impact than simply telling them about values [6]. Learning basic information about Musqueam culture through DG1-4 would provide context for visitors to experience values through interaction, similar to the prior lesson in [14]. We determined the values we wanted to focus on during the development process working with the curator and representatives of the Musqueam Indian Band. The most important value we wanted visitors to experience was that Musqueam cultural knowledge should be treated with respect. Other values included the importance of hən̓q̓əmin̓əm̓ language, the acknowledgment of belongings as still belonging to the ancestors who created them, and that access to culture knowledge is not given freely but should be earned. Our goal was for visitors to experience these four values through their interactions with the table.

SYSTEM DESCRIPTION AND DESIGN STRATEGIES

ʔeləw̓k̓ʷ — Belongings comprises a Samsung SUR40 table, three monitors, twelve replicas, and two activator rings. The physical installation occupies part of the exhibition space with three walls, with one monitor on each wall (See Figure 1). One monitor plays a series of photographs detailing the process of cleaning a fish. The remaining monitors are each associated with one of the ring tools. The table itself sits in the center of the space, displaying an image with a top-down view of a fish-cutting table. A rolling museum cart is nearby with twelve physical belongings for use on the table: six ancient belongings (celt, slate blade, cedar bark, net weight, decorated piece, and harpoon) and six contemporary belongings (Coke can, ice cube, quarters, keys, status card, and tide chart).

The monitors are intended to contribute to our goal of bringing people into the space [DG1]. The main monitor facing the gallery incorporates rich visuals with the slide show of a fish being cut and cleaned. The two side monitors display an image with all twelve belongings and play videos of Musqueam community members when visitors unlock special stories by exploring the belongings, thereby connecting tangible and intangible heritage.

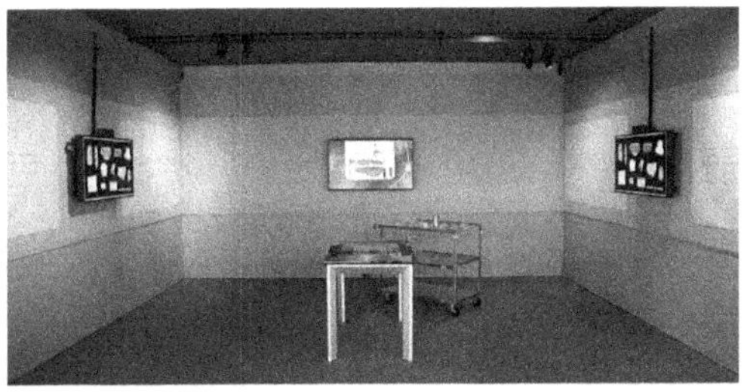

Figure 1. Museum setup ©Reese Muntean

Salmon fishing is used as an overall theme for the table, because it has been part of the Musqueam way of life for thousands of years, supporting DG1 and DG2. The image on the table shows a fish cutting table surrounded by related contemporary tools. Different items appear in the image including the bloody fish, fish fillets, knives, an axe, a woodpile, an iPhone, an oilcan, a gas can, a fishing net, boots, pavement, and a tote of fish. While the image serves to bring people over to the tabletop and offer a sense of Musqueam identity, each of these areas of the image also matches one of the physical belongings.

The belongings sit next to the tabletop on the cart. Like cultural forms [34], the replicas of ancient belongings were designed to look and feel as similar to the originals as possible [DG3]. However by allowing visitors to learn about the ancient belongings by directly handling them physically we break with traditional social practices around museum artifacts, which are typically behind glass.

Because they would be handled, we made sure that the look, texture, and weight were as close as possible to that of the original belongings. With permission from the Musqueam Indian Band, molds of the original belongings in MOA were made and replicas cast. The molds and material allowed us to approximate the texture and weight of the originals. The replicas were hand painted to match the details and colour variations of the originals. For the modern belongings we used the actual items coated in resin or sealer. Using the belongings as system inputs required the use of fiducial markers on each belonging, so we modified them to be small enough that they would not distract from the belonging or hinder the use of the belongings on the table. The cart, too, was incorporated as part of this dedication to representing the belongings accurately. In museum storage, artifacts are kept in small plastic zip lock bags. On the cart, we placed the belongings on top of zip lock bags containing a slip of paper with an image of the replica and its name in hən̓q̓əmin̓əm̓.

The two wooden rings sit on the table and are painted to match the specific monitors. There are four hən̓q̓əmin̓əm̓ terms etched around the rings, which serve as activators for the belongings. The hən̓q̓əmin̓əm̓ is included here to reiterate the importance of traditional language as included in our goals, DG2 and DG5.

Instructions are positioned on two sides of the table. The instructions include an illustration that shows how to put a belonging in the ring and text that explains the four hən̓q̓əmin̓əm̓ categories on the ring. These categories are *stem tə ʔi ?* (What is this?), *tatəlʼət* (Understanding it), *snəw̓eyəł* (Teachings since childhood), and *cyəθəs* (Having stories). When a belonging is placed in a ring on the table, a digital ring with the English translations of the hən̓q̓əmin̓əm̓ etchings appears on the table around the physical ring.

To access each category, visitors must complete different interactions, akin to small matching puzzles. The categories reveal different layers of information about the belongings as a way to convey the complexity of the stories that these belongings can embody [DG4]. This information appears on the table in the form of quotes from Musqueam community members, images, text, and historic documents. The activities required for each category take time and thought, and the correct answers are not always obvious. This was intended as a way for visitors to earn cultural knowledge and spend time engaging with Musqueam values. Once visitors complete the first three categories, they unlock a video of a Musqueam community member sharing their culture, stories, and lived experiences [DG5].

USER SCENARIO

We will now walk through each of these categories to explain the interactions involved and give examples of specific belongings and the information connected to them.

stem tə ʔi ? *(What is this?)*

To access basic information about a belonging's function, a user must place a belonging in an activator ring on the tabletop. This activation of the belonging brings up cards on the table that explain what the belonging is and what it was used for. This simple interaction brings people into the activity [DG1] and communicates information about the physicality of the belonging [DG3]. Handling the belonging and accessing the basic information meets the goal of understanding the use and place of the belongings in everyday life. With the small stone belonging, visitors feel the weight and texture of the rock and learn that it is a net weight that was used to place fishing nets in the river. Once visitors have basic knowledge they can explore *Understanding it* or *Teachings* which add different layers to the information about the belongings [DG2-4]

tatəlʼət *(Understanding it)*

When visitors touch the *Understanding it* section of the digital ring, dotted lines appear around hotspots on the table that correspond to particular belongings. The visitor must move the belonging and ring over the correct spot on the image to access information about a belonging's importance and place in Musqueam life.

Some connections are more obvious than others, e.g. the slate blade and the modern knife are both used for cutting. Other connections are more abstract and do not relate directly to the belonging's use, like the Indian status card that pairs with the tote of fish because of the fishing regulations imposed on First Nations by the Indian Act. The information cards in this case explain how the fishing tradition of the Musqueam people has changed with the laws that have been imposed upon them.

snəw̓eyəł *(Teachings since childhood)*

Visitors can learn more about the belongings in the *Teachings* category by matching an ancient belonging to its contemporary counterpart. Rather than connecting a belonging to the underlying image, here visitors are asked to make connections between the ancient and modern physical belongings. Through this activity visitors learn about continuity of Musqueam culture.

When a visitor touches the category on the digital ring, a black circle appears just outside the ring. Visitors place the matching belonging in the circle. The Coke can matches to the celt, representing extensive trade networks. The Coke can actually represents the global market economy, and the celt tells the story of Musqueam's history of trade. Ancient Musqueam people, too, had far-reaching trade routes that enabled them to acquire resources—like the nephrite from which this celt was crafted—that were unavailable in the region.

cyəθəs *(Having stories)*

When visitors touch *Having Stories*, a progress bar (specific to that belonging) appears to show how much more of the belonging they need to explore before they can unlock the video, encouraging them to spend more time with the information [DG5]. Once a visitor successfully completes the interactions for the first three categories, the progress bar becomes a button, allowing them to play a video clip with a Musqueam community member sharing his or her own personal narrative relating how they learned certain aspects of Musqueam culture and knowledge, relating intangible cultural knowledge to belongings.

USER STUDY

We conducted a field study of our *ʔeləw̓kʼʷ — Belongings* in the gallery space at MOA to address our research question: *What are effective design strategies that enable visitors to directly experience cultural values while they interact with Indigenous knowledge using a tangible tabletop system?* The study consisted of observations and open interviews with 24 visitors. Two researchers conducted this study in the gallery space over the course of two weeks. We collected data for 11 men and 13 women ranging in age from 18 to over 50 years old.

Researchers observed visitors interacting with the table. When a visitor had spent at least 2 minutes with the table and successfully put a belonging in a ring to access *What is this?*, a researcher would ask them to participate. We settled on this time and interaction milestone method of visitor selection as the one with the least bias. We drew from Block et al.'s study [8] on fluid grouping at tabletop exhibits, excluding those who the researchers characterized as *Shoppers* and *Joiners*. If the visitor agreed to participate, the researcher would step aside as they continued their exploration of the table. When visitors had finished using the tabletop, they filled out a brief questionnaire with demographic information and completed a structured interview lasting 10-20 minutes.

Data Collection

Our observational notes provide evidence that addresses how visitors entered the space and began interaction [DG1]. We designed our interview questions to explore visitor experience related to our other design goals [DG2-5]. We asked about visitor experiences in order of the goals (from entering/engaging to basic learning to deeper learning and the experience of values).

We began the interview with questions on what visitors learned about Musqueam culture and how they learned this (e.g. *What was something that surprised you about Musqueam culture that you didn't know before?)* [DG2].

To gauge visitors' understanding of the belongings and their stories [DG3&4], we asked questions about what they thought the objects represented, why they thought we called them belongings and if they saw any relationships between the four categories on information for each belonging (e.g. *While using the table, you placed different objects in the ring. What do you think those objects represent?*).

We asked visitors questions about what they learned of the values of Musqueam people [DG5] (e.g. *Can you describe what you learned about Musqueam values that you didn't know before? How did you learn this?*). We followed up by explicitly telling them that one Musqueam value is that culture knowledge should be treated with respect and then asked visitors to describe if/how they might have experienced that with the tabletop. We also asked if there were any other values that might have be reflected in what they were doing with the belongings on the table. We followed up by explicitly mentioning each value and asking visitors to describe if/how they might have experienced that with the tabletop (e.g. *A central Musqueam value is that cultural knowledge should be treated with respect. Can you describe any ways you might have experienced this value in the exhibit by what you did?*).

Analysis

Interviews were audio-recorded and transcribed. In our analysis we looked at data from each interview question separately. In order to address the interdependent nature of our design goals we also looked across data sources to explore how our inter-related strategies impacted visitor experience. Three researchers individually analyzed the transcriptions using open coding to identify emergent themes. The researchers individually went through two passes of the interview transcripts alongside observational notes. In the first pass we each identified themes, in particular looking for themes that related design features with visitor responses or behaviours. We looked for themes that were common, interesting, unexpected or indicated problems with the design. In the second pass we each fine-tuned our description of the themes and looked for inter-relationships between them. Then the three researchers worked as a group and compared themes. We had inter-rater agreement on all themes except one, for which we discovered we had used different terms to describe the same elements. While this level of coherence was unexpected, it gave us confidence in the reliability of our coding.

RESULTS

Our analysis provides evidence for validation of our approach of using inter-related goals and design strategies to enable museum visitors to experience Musqueam cultural values through interaction, and highlights areas where we need further refinement or exploration.

While acknowledging that our consent protocol influenced the time spent with the table, our participants interacted with the table for at least 4 minutes, with an average of 8.8 minutes and a median of 6.5 minutes. One participant spent 40 minutes using the table. Participants overall enjoyed the experience and left with new information about Musqueam culture.

We also note that while our participants logged a total of 212 minutes with the tabletop, no one was able to access a video by exploring all four categories of information. User interface issues were a factor here, and we addressed these issues in a software upgrade (which is not reported in this paper), drawing on insights from this user study.

Engaging and Learning about Musqueam Culture

We found that three design features contributed to achieving our goals that people would enter the space, interact with the table, and learn something new about Musqueam culture. The visually interesting salmon cutting slide show and the fish cutting image on the tabletop were successful in attracting people into the space and conveying basic information about Musqueam life. The cart of physical belongings also drew people in and immediately informed them visually about the culture due to their display in this particular exhibit context as well as the inclusion of both ancient and modern belongings. All participants understood that the Musqueam people were a fishing society in the past, and that they still live in Vancouver today and carry on the fishing tradition of their ancestors.

"I learned that obviously fish is a big part of it, or else that whole graphic wouldn't be there, and they're using nets...

They have to pay attention to the tides when they're fishing." – P22

The combination of the monitors along with the instructions, the rings, and the belongings—specifically the Coke can—all worked towards enticing people to interact. People picked up the belongings and rings from the cart and placed them on the table with little more than an illustration. The Coke can was a particularly interesting belonging that caught the eye of many participants. It motivated them to interact with the other belongings. Thirteen participants commented on this explicitly.

"I put the Coke bottle in there I just laughed at the description of it. It seems like just lacking of culture subject to all of our modern marketing and immediacy of our consumerism and all of that." – P16

Similarly, the combination of the belongings, the ring tool, and the *What is this?* information cards worked as an entry point to interacting with the table. Although *What is this?* was an entry into the complex information available, this activity was valuable in itself as it gave basic information about the belongings that people might not be familiar with.

"I spent most of the time exploring What is it? *rather than stories." – P17*

People learned new things about Musqueam's fishing culture and the tools they used. Seventeen participants were able to explicitly describe a new piece of information about Musqueam culture that they accurately learned. They did this through their interactions with the ring, which enabled them to access information cards, as well as through directly handling belongings as physical forms. One participant described seeing a harpoon in a display case elsewhere, but actually learning more about it from interacting with it on the tabletop.

"I've seen those, it's the harpoon? I've seen those in a couple display cases on my way here, and never knew what it was and what it would be used for, so it was kind of interesting to see what that was about." – P03

Richness and Stories about Belongings

Our second two design goals were about visitors reaching deeper understandings: the richness of information represented by belongings (beyond the identity and simple function) and the complex stories related to belongings. We found that three design features helped us to achieve these goals. These features were the selection of both ancient and modern belongings, the fidelity of the replicas, and the complexity of the four inter-related activities.

Ancient and modern belongings

Thirteen participants expressed that they understood the continuity of Musqueam culture in their interview responses, referencing the history of Musqueam people and their community today. The design feature of using ancient belongings with contemporary items worked well to get people thinking about cultural continuity.

"They're a changing culture. It's sort of something I gleaned just by looking at the objects on the table in the first place. When you approach it and you see a harpoon and a Coke can together, you almost don't need the table." – P22

"This goes back again to the idea of the old object and the new object co-existing, in the sense that there's hardly ever a distinct line between "Oh, this is the culture before, there's the culture now." – P18

The belongings, although they were physical objects, also represented intangible elements such as the complexity of their stories. As one participant expressed it,

"Obviously Coca-Cola is not just Coca-cola." – P11

Three participants overlooked the modern items, choosing to focus on the unfamiliar belongings. Their curiosity was satisfied by discovering what the ancient belongings were and what they were used for simply by accessing *What is this?* However, they missed some of the rich stories about the modern objects, and because they did not pair ancient and modern belongings, they missed learning about how traditions had evolved or remained the same (*Teachings*).

"I didn't end up putting anything like the Coke can or the keys in there, I put all the little things that I didn't know what they were for on the table." – P03

Belonging Physical Fidelity

The fidelity of the belongings, our careful considerations of how realistic they should look and feel, and the choice of displaying everyday belongings were important in having visitors understand that they were of utility and value. Eight participants described the importance of the ability to handle the belongings and how it allowed for a better understanding of them.

"It was just nice to have something in your hand. It gives you a little bit better perspective in maybe how it was used and how in relation to the other objects and giving you a little more perspective in that way." – P16

"I was using a knife... I kind of felt like the modern day knife, what we're used to now, is very different than what they had, but that's what they had. It's what they were using, and it's easy to understand how these tools were used and how these tools were created." – P04

The fidelity of the belongings also affected other aspects of interaction and impressions about values, which we will discuss in the Values section below.

Activity Complexity

The belongings and physical-digital ring were designed to enable visitors to trigger four different activities, each with a different kind of information about the belongings. Participants clearly understood that there was more information available about the objects, even if they could not understand how to interact with all four categories. For example, our design decision to place duo-language labels of the four categories of information on the ring tool enabled visitors to realize there was more information available. As one participant explained,

"It seemed almost like an intricate web. On the onset, it seems like they're four separate things that you kind of click on, and then after while you play around with it a little bit, and you start realizing that no, they're all connected. In order to fully understand it, you have to spend a considerable amount of time and mental effort to actually go through each of these little links and each of these little webs to actually get to that full understanding of how they're connected." – P18

The *Understanding it* task of matching belongings to the underlying image was effective in getting people to think about the continuity of culture as well as context. Visitors found that the ancient tools such as the slate blade and celt had more obvious connections to their modern day versions: the knife and the axe. By using some recognizable ancient tools and pairing them with modern counterparts, we enabled many visitors to understand the continuous and long history of Musqueam culture.

"Because the background was the modern objects, so to connect what is the possession of the belonging and how does it connect to a modern object that is still used today." – P20

Our decision to have belongings used on a tabletop display of a fish-cutting table provided context for the belongings. This decision enabled visitors to visually understand that the belongings and their stories related to one another, the belongings were embedded in complex stories [DG4] and the belongings showed how the Musqueam live today. For example, one visitor said,

"It's to give the object a place in the context so it isn't just an object in isolation. It's an object that connects to other objects, like the people, other functions. It has a functional reason for being there. It doesn't exist in isolation. It exists in context so it's trying to give context." – P06

"It's good to know what something does, but there's so much more to it than just what it does and what's involved in actually using it... how long it takes to do things and there're other pieces involved in using it and the engineering that goes behind it. There's so much more involved than just what it is. It adds another dimension to the object." – P16

The *Teachings* category, even though fewer people successfully accomplished that activity, still aided in achieving DG4 by showing the richness and complexity of information.

"(Matching ancient belongings to ancient belongings) would be important to understand how they're still used the same way and how those uses have changed. That would be important. How perhaps we've left behind some of the ancient uses or we rely on newer ways of learning in ... new contemporary ways of fishing." – P19

The four categories together on the ring, along with the status bar aided visitors' understanding that there was more to the story. When asked the relationship among the four categories, participants responded,

"Sort of different levels of depth to the conversation, right, so one was just a description of the object or belonging and then an application of it, how it was used and then how it connected to something else." – P17

"It seems like something can be a tool, but there's something deeper behind it. It gives a little bit more layers to the piece and it makes it less of just an object. It gives you a little bit more insight into the culture and pieces together." – P16

Values

The values we focused on were: treating cultural knowledge with respect, the importance of the hən̓q̓əmin̓əm̓ language, the notion that belongings still belonged to the ancestors, and that cultural knowledge should be earned. Without meeting our first four goals, it seems unlikely visitors would experience values through interactions. Once visitors entered the space, interacted with different objects, learned about Musqueam people, and began to see the complexity of information available [DG1-4], they were cued to experience values. We found that these interrelated design strategies enabled visitors to experience values.

For example, we purposefully broke the tradition of displaying belongings behind glass, placing replicas on a museum cart (See Figure 2) where they would normally only be accessible to museum staff. Seven participants noticed respect reflected in the way they carefully handled and returned the belongings to their proper places. Even the contemporary belongings were treated with some reverence, due to social cues as some participants noted.

"I knew that I needed to put (the belongings) back where I found them in order to leave it for someone else to be able to follow me and do the table. In that way, that's teaching me to be respectful for the display itself." – P05

"I treated them carefully. Actually the Coke can you treat it a bit like a cultural artifact, but I think that's because of the... social rules." – P06

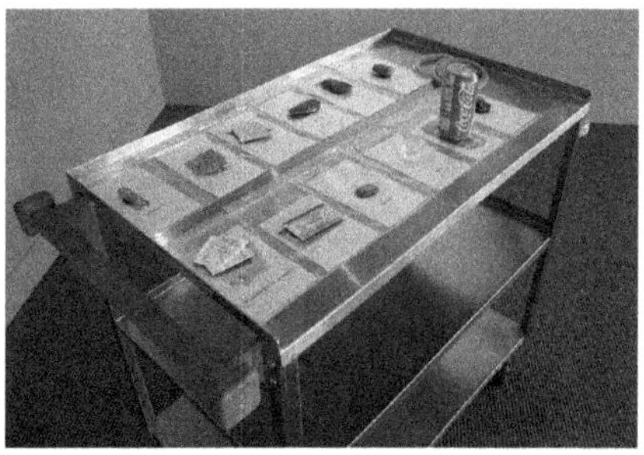

Figure 2. Belongings cart ©Reese Muntean

We also identified the physical-digital activity categories using both the hən̓q̓əmin̓əm̓ language and English, which created depth of content through non-linear layers (rather than linear game levels) and showed progress each time a belonging was placed in a ring. People were able to recognize values in their interactions, specifically in terms of the time and effort spent with the table.

Participants engaged with the table for an average of almost nine minutes, which illustrates the success of our choice to create complex interaction possibilities with inter-related activities and twelve different tangible belongings to use. Many visitors recognized that spending time to learn about this information was a way of respecting Musqueam culture.

"By taking the time to look at it... I'll walk up and actually read more of what I'm looking on other than just looking at something. Definitely, taking the time to digest what I read and think about it from a different person's place." – P08

"I think in that way it's giving your undivided attention as a way of showing respect." – P15

"This is interesting. It's subtle, but the value is having the respect to stay with something no matter what the situation is. My respect would have gone longer if it was a human. My respect was shorter because it was technology. That reflects on culture. If it is a human passing down traditions, it is longer term than to go back and just put out a book and try to teach it from a book. That's a huge lesson that I surreptitiously got, but no one spelled it out for me." – P21

The tabletop was a complex system, and people did not necessarily discover its full functionality. However, they did understand that making the effort was a sign of respect and earning knowledge.

DISCUSSION

In this paper we ask "*What are effective design strategies that enable visitors to directly experience cultural values while they interact with Indigenous knowledge using a tangible tabletop system?*" Yet key aspects of our collaborative approach extend beyond the tangible tabletop form. Our design process involved the close collaboration among team members with varying values and perspectives and our cultural partners. Through this collaboration we developed our goals for this project, including the desire to communicate values through interactions, the values that would be communicated, and the design strategies to meet these goals in a cultural tabletop exhibit by moving from basic engagement to deeper learning, then to the experience of cultural values.

From this process we introduce six recommendations for such designs. We generalize our findings so that other designers of technology for cultural heritage can support visitors in their experience of cultural values, through tangible interactions or interactions more broadly. We reiterate that these design recommendations exist within the context of collaboration with Indigenous partners in the design process and reflection on cultural values throughout.

Design Recommendations

1. *Cultural Forms.* Use both physical forms and the social practices around the forms to reflect values. Unusual or intriguing representations of cultural forms can draw people in. For example, the unusual images of fish and the high fidelity of the physical belonging replicas brought people into the space and enticed them to interact with the table, supporting Hornecker's concept of access points and entry points [37] and Horn's cultural forms [34]. Furthermore, the design of the physical properties can highlight values. In the case of the production of the belonging replicas, great care was taken to create replicas that shared the look and feel of the originals. These replicas took weeks to make, highlighting that ancient belongings were hand crafted and important. Social practices can also guide interaction and communicate tangible and intangible knowledge, such as values. Interaction design can mimic, mirror or reverse such practices. We played on traditional museum storage practices and in doing so both utilized and broke social practices around (not) handling artifacts in ways that enabled visitors to experience respect for the objects.

We do see a missed opportunity in this work to connect the social practices of the ancient belongings back to the physical cultural forms of the replicas. For example, we imagine visitors moving the slate blade in a cutting action as part of their interactions with the system.

2. *Accessible Information.* Create opportunities for immediate interaction and access to basic information. Placing a belonging in a ring marked with hən̓q̓əmin̓əm̓ provides a very simple form of access allowing visitors to interact immediately, quickly learn basic information, and gain exposure to the value of language. Furthermore, obtaining the basic *What is This?* information was simple, in line with the idea of apprehendability [4], offering the early successes [2, 15, 23], encouraging visitors to continue, priming them to understand more complex concepts [14], and offering multiple layers of information [35].

We designed for access, as others have recommended, yet we also designed deeper layers of information that required time and effort to access, reflecting values of earning knowledge and treating cultural knowledge with respect. We ensured access, but the structure and activities of how further information was accessed reflected a cultural value.

The complexity of the system along with our decisions to give little instruction or feedback were intended to slow visitors down to take time with the information. This did work, yet we were hoping visitors would be able to access more content than they actually did. While some visitors did uncover the multiple layers of information available from the different categories, which can enable richer interactive experiences [15, 23, 35], most did not reach this level of understanding.

For *Understanding it*, many participants understood from the dotted line what they were supposed to do but were still unable to do so. This was a combination of technical issues (e.g. accidental touches changing the category on the digital ring) as well as interaction design issues leaving participants confused about how to complete the task. For *Teachings*, visitors were uncertain as to what they should do or assumed the table was malfunctioning. These activities need clear instructions on the table or salient feedback to help visitors access the information. In our post-study revisions to the system, we improved usability of the *Teachings* and *Understanding it* activities, which may enable more visitors to reach the *Having Stories* content.

While we do see these issues of instruction and feedback as an area in which we can improve the design, it also speaks to the success of the interactions in helping visitors understand the complex stories and values we wanted to convey. *ʔeləw̓kʷ — Belongings* is rich with content that tells specific stories about the belongings of the Musqueam people and their continuing culture, but visitors were able to grasp information about Musqueam culture and identity, complex meanings behind the ancient and contemporary belongings, and even the specific value of earning and respecting knowledge without actually accessing much of the content.

3. *Connect.* Connect the exhibit to visitors' lives. The contemporary belongings provide connections from the exhibition to visitors' personal worlds. This provides a comparative foundation that may encourage visitors to connect cultural values to their own values. The juxtaposition of ancient and contemporary belongings encouraged visitors to think about the combination of objects, mentally engaging with the belongings before even physically interacting with them.

4. *Contextualize.* Provide context through different modalities. We found that, as suggested by Giaccardi and Palen [25], the multimodal information and the multimodal forms of interaction aided the exploration of tangible and intangible cultural heritage and allowed for new ways of engaging with specific cultural values. The tabletop fish cutting table image, the belongings, and the hən̓q̓əmin̓əm̓ language on the rings provided immediate context for visitors (before ever accessing the informational content) Visual and physical elements of our design immediately convey the strong fishing tradition of the Musqueam. The pairing of modern and ancient belongings creates a contextual timeline, connecting past and present.

5. *Hands on values.* Design the physical properties of tangible objects to convey cultural values in such a way that visitors can immediately perceive those values as they view and handle the objects. Visitors viewed and carefully handled lifelike replicas of belongings, and then placed them back in their marked location on the cart. Because of the replicas' high-fidelity form and their presentation, visitors directly experienced reverence and respect for these belongings, and by extension for the culture. There are many possibilities for reflecting values in physical forms. For example, the value of recycling could be communicated by low-fidelity, easily decomposable forms.

6. *Non-linear explorations.* Allow for different pathways for exploring information. We used four non-linear but inter-related activities that enabled visitors to engage with belongings in a variety of different ways, all of which conveyed complexity of information and reflected values without forcing visitors to explore all content. In other tabletop designs, tangible objects often trigger only simple pieces of information (e.g. [35]) or have single-use functions (e.g. magnifying glass). We suggest that a single belonging can enable a series of interrelated non-linear activities, providing a rich interactional experience. Individually these non-linear activities can appeal to visitors in different ways, with some people preferring basic information and others enjoying more puzzle-like activities. Taken together, these activities help to convey complex information and can be used to embody cultural values. While visitors could explore as much or little of the content they liked, the number of belongings and the ring's belonging-specific status bar hinted at the depth of information available and conveyed values around taking time, care, and effort to understand Musqueam culture. The specifics of activity designs will necessarily change based on the cultures, values, and exhibitions -- providing rich opportunities for new research.

CONCLUSION

In this paper we explore how cultural values can be communicated though interactions with a digital system, illustrating how values can be made tangible through a collaborative design approach to an interactive tangible tabletop museum exhibit. We see that experiencing cultural values through interactions is possible as a result of a collaborative process with a careful consideration of cultural values, physical and digital content design that lays a foundation for conveying values, and value-sensitive interaction design. We describe how we communicated cultural values by embodying them in tangible objects, playing on social practices, embedding them in activities that together with digital content creating opportunities for visitors to experience values through their interactions. We offer six design recommendations that may benefit designers of other culturally specific heritage applications and exhibits.

We found that tangible and embodied forms of interactions can be effectively used to support a greater understanding of values, Indigenous heritage, and continuity of culture in a museum setting. Overall, we hope our process and design can further the discourse around technology and values. We see our work as a successful contribution in understanding how to engage with cultural values during the design process and how to ensure that values are communicated through interactions with the resulting system.

ACKNOWLEDGEMENTS

Special thanks to the Musqueam Indian Band, Museum of Anthropology at the University of British Columbia, Maia Jensen at the SIAT Solid Space Fabrication Lab, SSHRC, and Grand NCE.

REFERENCES

1. Alonzo Addison. 2008. The Vanishing Virtual: Safeguarding Heritage's endangered digital record. In *New heritage: New media and cultural heritage*. Routledge, 27–39.
2. Sue Allen. 2004. Designs for learning: Studying science museum exhibits that do more than entertain. *Science Education* 88, 1: S17-S33.
3. Alissa N. Antle. 2014. Scratching the surface: Opportunities and challenges from designing interactive tabletops for learning. In *Learning Technologies and the Body: Integration and Implementation in Formal and Informal Learning Environments*. Routledge.
4. Alissa N. Antle, Allen Bevans, Josh Tanenbaum, Katie Seaborn, and Sijie Wang. 2011. Futura: design for collaborative learning and game play on a multi-touch digital tabletop. In *Proceedings of the Fifth International Conference on Tangible, Embedded, and Embodied Interaction* (TEI '11), 93–100.
5. Alissa N. Antle, Joshua Tanenbaum, Allen Bevans, Katie Seaborn, and Sijie Wang. 2011. Balancing act: enabling public engagement with sustainability issues through a multi-touch tabletop collaborative game. In *IFIP Conference on Human-Computer Interaction*, 194–211.
6. Alissa N. Antle, Joshua Tanenbaum, Anna Macaranas, and John Robinson. 2014. Games for change: Looking at models of persuasion through the lens of design. In *Playful User Interfaces*. Springer, 163–184.
7. Erling Björgvinsson, Pelle Ehn, and Per-Anders Hillgren. 2010. Participatory Design and "Democratizing Innovation." In *Proceedings of the 11th Biennial Participatory Design Conference*, 41–50.
8. Florian Block, James Hammerman, Michael Horn, Amy Spiegel, Jonathan Christiansen, Brenda Phillips, Judy Diamond, Evans E. Margaret, and Shen Chia. 2015. Fluid Grouping: Quantifying Group Engagement around Interactive Tabletop Exhibits in the Wild. In *Proceedings of the SIGCHI Conference on Human Factors in Computing Systems* (CHI '15), 867–876.
9. Maria Bonn, Lori Kendall, and Jerome McDonough. 2016. Preserving intangible heritage: Defining a research agenda. In *Proceedings of the Association for Information Science and Technology*, 1–5.
10. Alan Borning and Michael Muller. 2012. Next steps for value sensitive design. In *Proceedings of the SIGCHI Conference on Human Factors in Computing Systems* (CHI '12), 1125–1134.
11. Michael F. Brown. 2009. Exhibiting indigenous heritage in the age of cultural property. In *Whose Culture? The Promise of Museums and the Debate over Antiquities*. Princeton University Press, 147–165.
12. Francesco Cafaro, Leiah Lyons, Joshua Radinsky, and Jessica Roberts. 2010. RFID localization for tangible and embodied multi-user interaction with museum exhibits. In *Proceedings of the 12th ACM International Conference Adjunct Papers on Ubiquitous Computing* (Ubicomp '10), 397–398.
13. Fiona Cameron. 2010. Museum collections, documentation, and shifting knowledge paradigms. In *Museums in a Digital Age*. Routledge, 80–95.
14. Jean Ho Chu, Paul Clifton, Daniel Harley, Jordanne Pavao, and Ali Mazalek. 2015. Mapping Place: Supporting Cultural Learning Through a Lukasa-inspired Tangible Tabletop Museum Exhibit. In *Proceedings of the Ninth International Conference on Tangible, Embedded, and Embodied Interaction* (TEI '15), 261–268.
15. Luigina Ciolfi and Liam J. Bannon. 2003. Learning from museum visits: Shaping design sensitivities. In *Proceedings of HCI International*, 63-67.
16. Robert Davison. 2002. Cultural Complications of ERP. *Communications of the ACM*, *45*(7), 109–111.
17. Daniele Duranti, Davide Spallazzo, and Raffaella Trocchianesi. 2016. Tangible interaction in museums and temporary exhibitions: embedding and embodying the intangible values of cultural heritage. In *IFDP`16*, 160-171.
18. Abigail C. Durrant, David S. Kirk, and Stuart Reeves. 2014. Human values in curating a human rights media archive. In *Proceedings of the SIGCHI Conference on Human factors in Computing Systems* (CHI '14), 2685–2694.
19. Batya Friedman. 1996. Value-sensitive design. *Interactions* 3, 6: 16–23.
20. Batya Friedman and Peter H. Kahn Jr. 2003. Human values, ethics, and design. In *The Human-Computer Interaction Handbook*. L. Erlbaum Associates Inc., 1177–1201.
21. Batya Friedman, Peter H. Kahn Jr., Alan Borning, and Alina Huldtgren. 2013. Value sensitive design and information systems. In *Early engagement and new technologies: Opening up the laboratory*. Springer, 55–95.
22. Athanasios Gaitatzes, Dimitrios Christopoulos, and Maria Roussou. 2001. Reviving the Past: Cultural Heritage Meets Virtual Reality. In *Proceedings of the 2001 Conference on Virtual Reality, Archeology, and Cultural Heritage*, 103–110.

23. Ben Gammon. 2010. Visitors' Use of Computer Exhibits: findings from five gruelling years of watching visitors getting it wrong. In *Museums in a Digital Age*. Routledge, 281-290.
24. Elisa Giaccardi. 2008. Cross-media interaction for the virtual museum: Reconnecting to Natural Heritage in Boulder, Colorado. In *New Heritage: New Media and Cultural Heritage*. Routledge, 112–131.
25. Elisa Giaccardi and Leysia Palen. 2008. The Social Production of Heritage through Cross-media Interaction: Making Place for Place-making. *International Journal of Heritage Studies* 14, 3: 281–297.
26. Julie Gordonk. 2006. *Musqueam: A Living Culture*. Musqueam Indian Band.
27. Isaac Gwyneira. 2008. Technology Becomes the Object: The Use of Electronic Media at the National Museum of the American Indian. *Journal of Material Culture* 13, 3: 287–310.
28. Tim Hawkins, Jonathan Cohen, and Paul Debevec. 2001. A Photometric Approach to Digitizing Cultural Artifacts. In *Proceedings of the 2001 Conference on Virtual Reality, Archeology, and Cultural Heritage*, 333–342.
29. Kate Hennessy. 2009. Virtual Repatriation and Digital Cultural Heritage: The Ethics of Managing Online Collections. *Anthropology News* 50, 4: 5–6.
30. Kate Hennessy, and Natasha Lyons. 2016. Representing Natural Heritage: The Inuvialuit Smithsonian Project. In *Shifting Interpretations of Natural Heritage*. Boydell & Brewer, London, 279–292
31. Kate Hennessy, Natasha Lyons, Stephen Loring, Charles Arnold, Mervin Joe, Albert Elias, and James Pokiak. 2013. The Inuvialuit Living History Project: Digital Return as the Forging of Relationships Between Institutions, People, and Data. *Museum Anthropology Review* 7, 1-2: 44–73.
32. Kate Hennessy, Ryan Wallace, Nicholas Jakobsen, and Charles Arnold. 2012. Virtual Repatriation and the Application Programming Interface: From the Smithsonian Institution's MacFarlane Collection to Inuvialuit Living History. In *Proceedings of Museums and the Web 2012.*
33. R. Eric Hollinger, Edwell John, Jr., Harold Jacobs, Lora Moran-Collins, Carolyn Thome, Jonathan Zastrow Adam Metallo, Günter Waibel, and Vince Rossi. 2013. Tlingit-Smithsonian Collaborations with 3D Digitization of Cultural Objects. *Museum Anthropology Review* 7, 1-2: 201–253.
34. Michael S. Horn. 2013. The Role of Cultural Forms in Tangible Interaction Design. In *Proceedings of the 7th International Conference on Tangible, Embedded and Embodied Interaction* (TEI '13), 117–124.
35. Eva Hornecker. 2008. "I don't understand it either, but it is cool" - visitor interactions with a multi-touch table in a museum. In *3rd IEEE International Workshop on Horizontal Interactive Human Computer Systems,* 113–120.
36. Eva Hornecker and Jacob Buur. 2006. Getting a grip on tangible interaction: a framework on physical space and social interaction. In *Proceedings of the SIGCHI Conference on Human Factors in Computing Systems* (CHI '06), 437–446.
37. Eva Hornecker, Paul Marshall, and Yvonne Rogers. 2007. From entry to access: how shareability comes about. In *Proceedings of the Conference on Designing Pleasurable Products and Interfaces*, 328-342.
38. Lilly Irani, Janet Vertesi, Paul Dourish, Kavita Philip, and Rebecca E. Grinter. 2010. Postcolonial computing: a lens on design and development. In *Proceedings of the SIGCHI Conference on Human Factors in Computing Systems* (CHI '10), 1311–1320.
39. Ole Sejer Iversen, Kim Halskov, and Tuck W. Leong. 2012. Values-led participatory design. *CoDesign* 8, 2-3: 87–103.
40. Soojin Jun and Hyun-Kyung Lee. 2014. Dialogue and carnival: understanding visitors' engagement in design museums. *Digital Creativity* 25, 3: 247–254.
41. Yehuda Kalay, Thomas Kvan, and Janice Affleck. 2007. *New Heritage: New Media and Cultural Heritage*. Routledge.
42. Kenderdine, S., Shaw, J., Del Favero, D., & Brown, N. 2007. Place-Hampi: Co-Evolutionary Narrative & Augmented Stereographic Panoramas, Vijayanagara, India. In *New Heritage: New Media And Cultural Heritage*. Routledge, London, 275-293.
43. Richard Kurin. 2004. Safeguarding Intangible Cultural Heritage in the 2003 UNESCO Convention: a critical appraisal. *Museum International* 56, 1-2: 66–77.
44. Christopher A. Le Dantec, Erika Shehan Poole, and Susan P. Wyche. 2009. Values as lived experience: evolving value sensitive design in support of value discovery. In *Proceedings of the SIGCHI Conference on Human Factors in Computing Systems* (CHI '09), 1141–1150.
45. Brett Leavy, Theodore C. Wyeld, James Hills, Chris Barker, and Stephan Gard. 2007. Digital Songlines: Digitising The Arts, Culture And Heritage Landscape Of Aboriginal Australia. In *New Heritage: New Media And Cultural Heritage*. Routledge, 294-303.
46. Marc Levoy, Kari Pulli, Brian Curless, Szymon Rusinkiewicz, David Koller, Lucas Pereira, Matt Ginzton, Sean Anderson, James Davis, Jeremy Ginsberg, Jonathan Shade, Duane Fulk. 2000. The

Digital Michelangelo Project: 3D Scanning of Large Statues. In *Proceedings of the 27th Annual Conference on Computer Graphics and Interactive Techniques*, 131–144.

47. Peter Lyman, and Howard Besser. 2013. Defining the Problem of Our Vanishing Memory: background, current status, models for resolution. In *Museums in a Digital Age*. Routledge, 336-343.
48. Natasha Lyons, David M. Schaepe, Kate Hennessy, Michael Blake, Clarence Pennier, John R. Welch, Kyle McIntosh, Andy Phillips, Betty Charlie, Clifford Hall, Lucille Hall, Aynur Kadir, Alicia Point, Vi Pennier, Reginald Phillips, Reese Muntean, Johnny Williams Jr., John Williams Sr., Joseph Chapman, and Colin Pennier. 2016. Sharing deep history as digital knowledge: An ontology of the Sqewlets website project. *Journal of Social Archaeology*, 16, 3: 359–384.
49. Mark T. Marshall, Nick Dulake, Luigina Ciolfi, Daniele Duranti, Hub Kockelkorn, and Daniela Petrelli. 2016. Using Tangible Smart Replicas As Controls for an Interactive Museum Exhibition. In *Proceedings of the Tenth International Conference on Tangible, Embedded, and Embodied Interaction* (TEI '16), 159–167.
50. Reese Muntean, Kate Hennessy, Alissa Antle, Susan Rowley, and Jordan Wilson, and Brendan Matkin. 2015. ʔeləw̓k^{w} – Belongings: Tangible Interactions with Intangible Heritage. *Journal of Science and Technology of the Arts* 7, 2: 59-69.
51. Ross Parry. (Ed.). 2010a. *Museums in a Digital Age*. Routledge.
52. Ross Parry. 2010b. The Practice of Digital Heritage and the Heritage of Digital Practice. In *Museums in a Digital Age*. Routledge, 1-7.
53. Susan Rowley. 2013. The Reciprocal Research Network: The Development Process. *Museum Anthropology Review* 7, 1-2: 22–43.
54. Susan Rowley, Dave Schaepe, Leona Sparrow, Andrea Sanborn, Ulrike Tadermacher, Ryan Wallace, Nicholas Jakobsen, HannahTurner, and Tristan Goffman. 2010. Building an on-line research community: The Reciprocal Research Network. In *Proceedings of Museums and the Web 2010.* http://www.archimuse.com/mw2010/papers/rowley/rowley.html
55. Elizabeth B.-N. Sanders and Pieter Jan Stappers. 2008. Co-creation and the new landscapes of design. *CoDesign* 4, 1: 5–18.
56. Guha Shankar and Cordelia Hooee. 2013. Zuni Cultural Heritage Materials in the American Folklife Center: The Potential of Return. *Museum Anthropology Review* 7, 1–2: 74–84.
57. Moira G. Simpson. 2012. *Making Representations: Museums in the Post-Colonial Era*. Routledge.
58. Rachel Charlotte Smith and Ole Sejer Iversen. 2014. Participatory heritage innovation: designing dialogic sites of engagement. *Digital Creativity* 25, 3: 255–268.
59. Tess Speelpenning, Alissa N. Antle, Tanja Doering, and Elise van den Hoven. 2011. Exploring how tangible tools enable collaboration in a multi-touch tabletop game. In *IFIP Conference on Human-Computer Interaction*, 605–621.
60. Ramesh Srinivasan, Katherine Becvar, Robin Boast, and Jim Enote. 2010. Diverse knowledges and contact zones within the digital museum. *Science, Technology & Human Values* 35, 5: 735–768.
61. Ramesh Srinivasan, and Katie Shilton. 2006. The South Asian web: an emerging community information system in the South Asian diaspora. In *Proceedings of the Ninth Conference on Participatory Design: Expanding Boundaries in Design*, 125–133.
62. UNESCO Culture Sector - Intangible Heritage - 2003 Convention. Retrieved February 15, 2017, from http://www.unesco.org/culture/ich/en/convention
63. Helen Verran and Michael Christie. 2006. Digital Technologies and Aboriginal Knowledge Practices. Retrieved February 15, 2017 from http://www.cdu.edu.au/centres/ik/pdf/DigTech_IndigPlaceAust.pdf
64. Dirk vom Lehn, Jon Hindmarsh, Paul Luff, and Christian Heath. 2007. Engaging Constable: Revealing Art with New Technology. In *Proceedings of the SIGCHI Conference on Human Factors in Computing Systems* (CHI '07), 1485–1494.
65. Ron Wakkary and Marek Hatala. 2006. ec(h)o: Situated Play in a Tangible and Audio Museum Guide. In *Proceedings of the 6th Conference on Designing Interactive Systems* (DIS '06), 281–290.
66. Rafal Wojciechowski, Krzysztof Walczak, Martin White, and Wojciech Cellary. 2004. Building Virtual and Augmented Reality Museum Exhibitions. In *Proceedings of the Ninth International Conference on 3D Web Technology*, 135–144.

Kinecting with Orangutans: Zoo Visitors' Empathetic Responses to Animals' Use of Interactive Technology

Sarah Webber[1], Marcus Carter[1], Sally Sherwen[2], Wally Smith[1], Zaher Joukhadar[1], Frank Vetere[1]

[1]Microsoft Research Centre for SocialNUI
University of Melbourne, Parkville, Australia
{s.webber, marcusc, wsmith, zaher.joukhadar, f.vetere}@unimelb.edu.au

[2]Zoos Victoria
Parkville
Australia
ssherwen@zoo.org.au

ABSTRACT
Animal conservation organisations occasionally harness depictions of animals using digital technology to inspire interest in, and concern for animals. To better understand the forms of empathy experienced by people observing animal-computer interaction, we designed and studied an interactive installation for orangutans at a zoo. Through collaborative design we established an understanding of zoos' objectives and strategies related to empathy in the zoo context. We deployed a prototype installation, and observed and interviewed visitors who watched orangutans use the installation. Analysis of observations and interviews revealed that visitors responded with *cognitive, affective* and *motor* empathy for the animals. We propose that these empathetic responses are prompted by the visibility of orangutans' bodily movements, by the 'anthropic frame' provided by digital technology, and by prompting reflection on animals' cognitive processes and affective states. This paper contributes new evidence and understanding of people's empathetic responses to observing animal-computer interaction and confirms the value of designing for empathy in its various forms.

Author Keywords
Empathy; zoos; primates; conservation; animal-computer interaction.

ACM Classification Keywords
H.5.m. Information interfaces and presentation (e.g., HCI): Miscellaneous.

INTRODUCTION
Modern zoos aim to inspire visitors' concern for animals and conservation through engaging encounters with other species [23,48]. Zoos' presentations of animals are not simply educational, but also aim to be enjoyable and memorable. As part of this work, zoos draw

CHI 2017, May 06-11, 2017, Denver, CO, USA
© 2017 ACM. ISBN 978-1-4503-4655-9/17/05…$15.00
DOI: http://dx.doi.org/10.1145/3025453.3025729.

Figure 1. Interactive projections powered by a Microsoft Kinect in use by Dewi (6).

on and reinforce emotional responses to animals and foster a sense of "connection" with them [15].

Zoos use a range of strategies to create emotionally engaging experiences which motivate people to care about the natural world [16:111]. Many such strategies aim to elicit empathy, in various forms, towards animals. For example, naturalistic enclosures and enrichment (stimulating activities, habitats and toys) allow observation of natural behaviours at close proximity [25], fostering interest in animals' thoughts and feelings. Interpretive presentations often make connections between animals' and humans' behaviours, encouraging a sense of "shared identity" [15].

Several conservation organisations have identified the public appeal of animals using digital technology. Highly-publicised initiatives show animals using iPads [53,57], touchscreens built into zoo enclosures [47], motion sensitive cameras [12], and portable video cameras [59]. Though motivated by animal wellbeing (see, for example, [11,14,64]) or research objectives (for example, [41,50]), such initiatives have considerable potential to support visitor engagement. On the other hand, digital technology for animals could potentially attract controversy, in the context of shifting social attitudes towards animal displays [2], and critical voices which challenge more broadly zoos' animal-keeping practices (see, for example [37]).

Despite this, the impacts of animal-computer interaction on perceptions of animals have received little academic attention. This paper explores responses to animals' use of digital technology through a study of zoo visitors' perceptions of orangutans using an interactive installation which enables them to interact with digital games projected into their enclosure. We report on a trial of this installation conducted at the orangutan exhibit on several occasions over a period of one month.

The primary contribution of this paper is an understanding of zoo visitors' empathetic responses to orangutans which emerge in their reflections on the animals' use of interactive technology. Through visitor interviews we identify several forms of empathy for the animals. These findings indicate that digital technology could play a role in promoting zoo visitors' empathetic connections with animals. We conclude with insights on designing for empathy towards animals.

BACKGROUND

Conceptions of Empathy

Empathy has been broadly defined as "an emotional reaction in an observer to the affective state of another individual" [9:699]. However, research into empathy has been a site of considerable debate. Some have sought an explanation of empathy as a single mechanism which results in a range of psychological states and behaviours (including, for example, sympathy and prosocial behaviours) [52]. Others contend that the term *empathy* is used to refer to numerous separable, but allied psychological phenomena [4,9].

Throughout these debates, it has been commonplace to make distinctions between cognitive and emotional dimensions of empathy [9,19,52]. *Cognitive empathy* has been described as an intellectual response which allows one to understand others' points of view, or imagine the thoughts and feelings of others [4,9]. It is thus a concept closely related to *Theory of Mind*: the ability to conceive of others' thoughts, intentions, knowledge and affective states [9]. *Emotional empathy* includes affective responses to others' emotional states, which may result in the related phenomenon of *emotional contagion* [9]. Emotional empathy is also understood by many to include concepts such as *sympathy*, or compassionate responses to others' suffering [52].

Recent developments in neuroscience have resulted in increasing attention to a third major category of empathetic response: *Motor Empathy* [9,10]. The term *motor empathy* has been used to denote the response that leads people to mimic or represent internally others' movements, postures and facial expressions. The discovery of the Mirror Neuron System (MNS), neural systems which are activated not only when performing but also when observing an action [9,28,56], provides new foundations for understanding empathetic responses to others' movements and observable emotions. These insights also provide new scientific foundations for related concepts such as *embodied empathy* (a "body-oriented perspective" understanding of human interactions, emerging from psychotherapy [20]), and *kinaesthetic empathy* (an understanding of observers' bodily experience of others' movements developed in dance studies [24]). The relevance of these concepts to interaction design has been signalled by a small body of research (e.g. [17,24,26]). It has also been demonstrated that this form of response is elicited by observing non-human entities, such as robots performing complex actions [28]. However, to date HCI has failed to engage with the potential power of interactive technology to evoke bodily empathy in people observing system users.

Empathy for Animals

Empathy for animals has been studied primarily in terms of its impacts on attitudes and behaviours relevant to animal welfare [30,51], and its association with empathy for humans [18,49,58]. Such studies have focused on emotional components of empathy, particularly sympathy for animals in distress. It has been argued that interspecies empathy is a foundation of concern for animals' wellbeing [51:47]. In some studies, such as [30], *empathy for animals* is taken to be equivalent with attitudes to animal welfare.

Cognitive dimensions of empathy for animals have to a lesser extent been explored in research into the effects of *belief in animal mind* (BAM) - "beliefs about the extent to which animals have awareness, thoughts, and feelings" [31] - as a factor in people's attitude to animal use and welfare [34]. Belief in animal minds has been found to be a strong predictor of attitudes towards animals [34], and to have some association with empathy for animals (though this association is moderated by other factors) [31]. It should be noted that the concept of BAM does not assume the existence (or non-existence) of animal minds, but rather investigates people's attitudes on this matter, as one dimension of people's perceptions of animals.

The *perceived similarity* of animals to humans has also been found to predispose people to empathetic responses towards animals [13,31]. Several researchers and organisations have shown that people's empathy for animals, and support for animal rights and animal welfare, can be engendered through initiatives that anthropomorphise animals, for example by emphasising the human-like characteristics of animals through language or anecdotes [13].

Empathy in Human-Computer Interaction

In the field of human-computer interaction, empathy is considered primarily in the sense of *empathetic design,* as a resource to understand stakeholders and motivate design (see for example [65]). However, some researchers have turned their attention to the potential for digital technology to support empathy for others. Belman and Flanagan examine video games which aim to foster empathy between social groups, identifying guiding principles for design of such games [5]. The authors propose, for example, that games need to engage both cognitive and emotional empathy to impact on players' understanding of the world. Others have proposed mechanisms to support empathy between remote collaborators, for example through configuring systems to improve visibility of body language [46], or incorporating computational detection of others' facial expressions [42]. Huck and colleagues consider how empathy between members of a community can be enhanced through design which draws on and represents practices associated with church rituals [32]. In this paper however, we extend these approaches by arguing for increased attention to opportunities for designing interactive systems which foster *observers'* empathy for the users.

Empathy and Animal-Computer Interaction

The field of animal-computer interaction (ACI) maintains a keen focus on issues of animal wellbeing and ethics [38]. Animal-centred design work confronts the challenge of viewing the problem situation, and potential solutions, from the animal's perspective [38]. Interaction design approaches aiming to include the voice of the animal in the design process include the development of personas representing animals [27], and human-animal play (e.g. [33,62]). In this design project, we draw extensively on the knowledge and expertise of human participants (orangutan keepers) with close, long-standing relationships with individual animals in a specific context, an approach previously adopted in ACI research and design work (for example [39,40,54]).

Much ACI work attends to contexts in which human empathy for animals may play an important role in enabling communication and effective cooperation. For example, ACI research has investigated dog handlers' relationships with service dogs [54] and cancer detection dogs [39]. Other ACI interventions have sought to collect and present data representing animals' behaviour, aiming to increase people's ability to interpret animals' internal states and intentions, in initiatives that could support cognitive empathy. This approach has been applied to support adoption of shelter animals [1] and help owners' to understand their pets' needs [45]. However, some researchers have cautioned against quantification initiatives, highlighting the potential risks to animal welfare and human-animal relationships [35].

Other researchers have examined playful approaches to promoting people's affective responses and sense of connection with animals. For example, *Playing with Pigs* [22] presents a system which provides touchscreen installation for pigs at a farm, which people can interact with remotely. However, much research remains to be done to understand both the potential role of ACI in fostering empathy, and observers' empathetic responses to animals' use of interactive technology.

Empathy in Connections with Zoo Animals

To shape community conservation attitudes and behaviours, modern zoos build on visitors' desire to connect with animals [15], fostering visitors' *sense of connection* with animals through engaging encounters [15,23]. Visitors' emotional responses to animals are seen as an important dimension of conservation education which can lead to the formation of enduring memories [2,3]. The field of conservation education pays growing attention to the concepts of perceived similarity, BAM, empathy and related affective responses towards animals [7,16,55] as potentially significant mechanisms in conservation education and developing environmental attitudes [6,8,16]. In the context of the zoo, Myers et al. [43] explore three forms of response to animals which overlap with emotional and cognitive dimensions of empathy: the ability to imagine what it is like to be the animal; wondering about an animal's thoughts or feelings; and caring about saving the animal.

Digital Technology for Zoo Encounters

Zoos are beginning to make use of interactive technology, including screens to display digital media which can extend and augment the animal encounter; interactive systems to support educational experiences; and technology-based animal enrichment [61].

Of particular interest to zoos is the opportunity for technology to support educational, engaging encounters between animals and groups of visitors, while ensuring animal wellbeing and visitor safety. Indeed, any intervention in the zoo setting needs to take account of potential impacts on zoo visitors. Despite this, little is known about the effects of watching animals using digital technology. A study of touchscreen enrichment for orangutans at Zoo Atlanta found that seeing the screen in use increased visitors' perceptions that orangutans might benefit from using technology, and had no negative impacts impact on the visitor experience [50]. Viewers of a BBC documentary 'filmed' by chimpanzees at Edinburgh Zoo felt that they had learned about chimpanzee cognition and enrichment needs through the film [29]. Together, these studies suggest that such interventions might draw observers' attention to the animals' cognitive abilities and the implications for animal welfare, thereby contributing to empathy for animals.

Depictions of animals using digital technology have considerable appeal, and have been deployed by a number of conservation organisations to engage the public. The *Apps for Apes* program, which has provided iPads for orangutans at numerous zoos, aims at public engagement as well as cognitive enrichment for orangutans [57]. The international mainstream press regularly covers stories such as penguins' use of iPads [53] and animals taking 'selfies' [12]. The public engagement power of these depictions is evidenced by their popularity in online news and media aggregation platforms. Despite the apparent impact of these depictions on the viewer's curiosity and emotional responses towards the animals, these effects are not well understood. To investigate this phenomenon, this paper presents a novel interactive installation designed to explore zoo visitors' empathetic responses to orangutan technology use.

DESIGNING FOR EMPATHY AT THE ZOO

This research was conducted at Melbourne Zoo, Australia ("the Zoo"), in collaboration with its parent organisation Zoos Victoria. Melbourne Zoo houses six orangutans: an infant female (Dewi), her mother (Maimunah) and father (Santan) housed as a family group, an adolescent male (Malu), an older adult female (Kiani) and her adult daughter (Gabby).

We developed contextual understandings of the Zoo, and of the role of empathy in visitors' encounters with animals, through meetings and workshops with Zoo personnel (staff with responsibilities for animal welfare, animal keeping and visitor experience), and contextual inquiry with keepers at the orangutan enclosure. We also drew on observations and interviews researching digital technology at Melbourne Zoo (reported in [61]). Design concepts emerging from workshops were developed into visual prototypes which were refined with Zoo personnel. The Zoo's animal welfare specialist took a leading role in the collaboration, ensuring that the wellbeing and enrichment of the orangutans remained central to the project's objectives and methods.

Generating Empathy at the Zoo

Our initial investigations at Melbourne Zoo revealed the important role of empathy in the zoo visit, and how emotional responses to animal encounters responses are generated and managed. Like many long-established zoos, Melbourne Zoo has seen significant transformations in the keeping of animals. Consistent with broader trends, the Zoo has moved away from the focus on entertainment and reinvented itself as a conservation organisation, a change which has largely been driven by shifts in public attitudes towards animal welfare and use of animals [2]. The continuing popularity of the zoo visit means that Zoos Victoria, along with other modern zoos worldwide, has great potential to make significant contributions to conservation awareness in the community at large [2].

To achieve these conservation outcomes, the Zoo aims to encourage a connection between humans and animals, drawing on understandings that a zoo visit can result in an emotional connection to particular species, and that this connection can promote empathy and concern for the species' wellbeing [2,15]. These connections are facilitated in a range of settings, including 'close encounter' or 'behind the scenes' experiences, which allow visitors to meet the animals and talk with their keepers.

At Melbourne Zoo, animals' natural behaviours and capabilities are showcased through presenting enrichment or training. Enrichment is designed principally to provide animals with stimulation and variation in their environment and give them opportunities to express motivated behaviours, with the ultimate aim of enhancing animal welfare. Enrichment for orangutans, for example, often includes ropes to swing on, poles to climb and food puzzles to exercise cognitive abilities. Guided by Zoos Victoria's '*Connect, Understand, Act*' model for conservation education [36], scheduled presentations are delivered at animal enclosures, providing engaging explanations of animals' behaviours and traits, as well as conservation messages. Presenters aim to elicit emotional and empathetic connections with animals through techniques such as including personal narratives about individual animals, or encouraging visitors' playful mimicry of animals' behaviours. However, the Zoo aims to ensure that these presentations focus on an the animals' natural behaviour.

Empathetic Foundations for Design

In this work, we have adopted an conceptual frame of empathy for animals which seeks to integrate notions of cognitive and emotional empathy with zoos' techniques for eliciting visitor empathy. Accordingly, we consider *cognitive empathy* for animals (imagining how the animals would feel and think, and reflection on animal minds) as well as *emotional empathy* (evidence of emotional contagion, sympathy, concern about animals' welfare, or affective responses to observing the animals' state). As part of these, we also consider *perceived similarity* between animals and humans, (identifying similarities and differences, as well as drawing links between human behaviour and that of non-human species). This frame provided a foundation for design of an interactive installation aiming to foster visitor empathy for animals.

KINECTING WITH ORANGUTANS

In order to further explore how the use of digital technology by animals can generate empathetic responses in visitors we designed, developed and deployed a novel digital enrichment system for the orangutans at Melbourne Zoo. The development of this system followed an in-depth collaborative design process with a variety of stakeholders, and included several prototypes.

As part of the *Apps for Apes* program, the orangutans at Melbourne had prior experience with tablet computers. Observations of their use of the tablets during the design process highlighted their interest in digital sensory enrichment, but for safety reasons their access to the technology was very limited. Zoo keepers held the tablet such that the orangutan could only reach the device with their fingertips, stretched through metal bars. This was an extremely un-orangutan way to interact with something; affording only limited movements and investigations, and constricting play.

Our new system used a Microsoft Kinect sensor and projector to create a large 'touchscreen' style interface on the floor of the orangutan enclosure (see Figure 1). To afford the orangutans the ability to interact the way they wanted to, we developed our own touch-detection software, building on the approach of Wilson et al. [63], which was responsive to the variety of ways orangutans 'touch'; with whole hands, feet, faces and with objects. Both the data projector and the Kinect sensor operated through a glass wall of the orangutan enclosure. This design placed hardware outside of the animal enclosure, significantly reducing safety risk, and allowing the orangutans as much freedom as possible in their interactions. The installation was positioned at a glass corner of the orangutans' enclosure, so as to be readily visible to visitors entering the exhibit area.

Designing for Empathetic Responses

Through our design workshops we had identified three specific strategies for evoking empathetic responses:
(1) enable visitors to observe animals' natural behaviours at close proximity; (2) make visible to visitors the orangutans' cognitive capabilities; and (3) allow visitors to observe differences between individual animals' behaviours and preferences.

Using these strategies, we developed four applications that utilized our Kinect system in response to orangutans' existing enrichment and to foster empathetic responses. *Burst* (Figure 1) and *Sweep* (coloured tiles that disappear when touched) were highly responsive designs which introduced the interactivity of the system to the orangutans through visually interesting movement. They encouraged the natural, playful behaviour of sweeping, and allowed for a wide variety of interaction strategies, revealing cognitive capabilities such as using objects as tools for interaction.

In addition, two more complex applications, *Painting* and *Gallery*, were developed. *Painting* (Figure 2) replicated the experience of painting with a brush on a canvas (a regularly used form of enrichment). Touches left coloured marks, and five buttons on the side allowed the active colour to be changed. *Gallery* presented six images or videos, and when touched ('selected'), the content expanded to fill much of the projection. Videos played for 15 seconds. Orangutans could interact with the content creating a water-ripple effect. Both of these applications attempt to make visible the differences between the orangutans, in terms of their creativity (*Painting*) and preference towards content (*Gallery*). Simultaneously, these applications highlight their relevant cognitive capabilities, desires and intentions. An anecdote often recounted in live presentations at Melbourne Zoo refers to orangutan Kiani's love of photos of herself, and her habit of displaying visible preference when shown images on a tablet computer. *Gallery* attempts to make visible these kinds of individual preferences, but also the cognitive capability of the orangutans to recognise themselves in photographs (and display a preference towards them), as well as the other orangutans and their keepers.

RESEARCH METHOD

The system was installed at the orangutan enclosure on

Figure 2. Gabby (35) using the *Painting* application.

several occasions (for periods of 2-3 hours) over the course of 4 weeks. Orangutans' behaviour in the enclosure was video recorded while the system was active, from a static camera and a handheld camera. Debriefing meetings were conducted by researchers with the orangutan keepers and animal welfare specialist to support iterative refinement of the applications.

Semi-structured interviews were conducted with 25 visitors who observed the system in use. We approached adult visitors who were at the orangutan exhibit for at least 30 seconds while the installation was in place, and were seen to have observed the system in use. Interviews were conducted at the orangutan enclosure. Though our protocol allowed for interviewing groups of visitors (including children accompanied by adults), respondents all chose to take part in interviews individually. Participants were representative of adult visitors to the Zoo in terms of age distribution, and the majority were accompanied by young children. We developed a semi-structured interview protocol in which visitors were prompted to talk about:

- any interaction with the orangutans, or opportunities to view them up close;
- what they had learned at the orangutan exhibit that day;
- how the visit had affected their perceptions of orangutans;
- what they thought of the orangutan enclosure;
- what they thought of the installation, and what they thought its purpose was.

Interview numbers were constrained by the fact that the Zoo also wanted to capitalize on the potential of the installation to engage wider audiences through mass media: some sessions were therefore closed to the public to allow for professional filming.

Data Analysis

Recordings of meetings and visitor interviews were transcribed and analysed. Videos of animals' use of the system were reviewed by researchers, and memos created noting animals' salient behaviours and observable responses from visitors, where visible in the field of view. We reviewed these alongside memos from debriefing meetings, researchers' observations on orangutans' use of the system, and visitors' reactions to the installation. Through an iterative coding process, key concepts related to emotive responses to the animals and the technology were identified and categorised. In this analysis, we sought to identify the forms of empathy experienced by visitors who watched orangutans using the installation. Accordingly, in our development of codes we drew on the concepts of empathy for animals outlined above: cognitive empathy, including reflections on animals thoughts, intentions and desires; emotional empathy, including compassion and concern about animal welfare; and perceived similarity of orangutans to humans. This process resulted in the themes presented below.

RESULTS

In this section we describe the kinds of empathy experienced by visitors in response to orangutans' varied forms of engagement with the installation. We show how these forms of use were reflected in visitors' consideration of animals' cognitive processes and intentions, their affective states and their welfare needs.

Cognitive Empathy

An important aim of our system, consistent with the Zoo's goal of inspiring visitors' admiration for animals, was to make orangutans' cognitive capabilities visible to visitors. Watching the orangutans use the installation, many visitors' responses indicated close reflection on orangutans' mental states, including their intentions, desires and learning processes.

Reflections on Intentions

From the outset, orangutans approached and interacted with the installation directly, without encouragement from keepers. This was apparent to visitors, prompting them to reflect on the animals' intentions and the ways in which they were attracted by the installation. Several visitors observed that the orangutans were using the technology voluntarily [P04, P09, P12]. Some described how the orangutans were "*curious*" [P09] and wanted to "*explore*" [P13] the technology. This was seen as a positive aspect of the system, and one which had implications for reflections on animal wellbeing, discussed below. One respondent affirmed:

"*they're not being rewarded for interacting with the technology. So in that way it's a good thing because it's more free exploration, not sort of training to use it*" [P09].

This exploratory, unstructured use of the system seemed to lead visitors to reflect on the animals' intentions, concluding that they were determining for themselves what they wanted to achieve. One visitor noted how the installation was "*letting him* [adolescent orangutan] *explore what he can do with the computer*" [P13], while another described how the young female orangtan was "*trying to catch the patterns*" [P04].

Other participants attributed specific goals or intentions to the animals, and appraised the animals' use of the system accordingly:

"*I think he's struggling to choose the colours, get the concept - but I think he'll get the hang of it over time.*" [P11].

These assessments of orangutans' ability or inability to perform specific tasks were recorded principally when orangutans were using the *Painting* application.

Reflections on Desires

Initially, many of the orangutans explored the interface with their mouth and nose. Some of the orangutans seemed to attend more to the play of the lights from the projector on their body than to the projected images on the floor. On several occasions, orangutans positioned themselves in the light from the projector, moving limbs and body parts slowly as they watched the coloured light on their fur or skin. When interacting with the projections on the floor, the orangutans generally adopted forms of bodily interaction which were not consistent with human use of a touchscreen. For example, they commonly used the backs of their hands, forearms or other body parts to interact with the projections. Visitors interpreted these interactions as exploratory, and saw them as indicators of the orangutans' desire to engage with the system, commenting for example:

"*What's really interesting is that they're using the back of their hands to play with the patterns and she's obviously intrigued*" [P04].

Orangutans' more active engagement with the system included rolling and spinning on the projections. The two younger orangutans both made use of blankets or cloths to interact with the projections on the floor while swinging from the bars overhead. The combination of the Kinect sensor with projection display allowed orangutans to integrate their interactions with their habitual forms of play and whole-body movements. This seemed to contribute to visitors' sense that interacting with the system was a positive experience for the orangutans.

"*they seem to enjoy it*" [P01].

"*I think it's pretty impressive, yeah, just seeing them react and all that yeah, it's really impressive*" [P03].

Reflections on Learning and Intelligence

Several visitors commented on the orangutans' use of the system as a learning process:

"*it worked out - it was doing it with the sheet at first - and then thought, no I can actually do it with my feet and hands.*" [P05].

During the course of interviews, many respondents explicitly described how their perceptions of the orangutans had been impacted by seeing them using the installation. Many of the visitors stated that the experience confirmed their perception of the animals as intelligent, although some of these comments were very brief in nature. Several visitors commented that seeing the orangutans use the technology increased their appreciation of the animals' abilities:

"*Maybe they're smarter than I thought that they were*" [P15].

"*They can do a lot more than I thought, especially I didn't think they could do things with technology.*" [P11].

"*It reminds me that they're probably a lot more intelligent than the general public think they are and yeah, just, yeah just reminds me that there's more to animals than we think, which is pretty exciting*" [P16].

Over time, the orangutans seemed to gain familiarity with the system: keepers reported that the animals quickly learned what the installation could do and how to use it. This was noticed by some visitors:

"*I was interested to know how quickly they would get used to the software and it would just become another thing in there, just like 'aah, whatever' and it seems to be a bit like that, so it's another toy.*" [P06].

Several visitors felt it was likely that orangutans would rapidly habituate to the games provided, and novel stimulation and more challenging activities would need to be continually devised for them.

"*the challenge of the program is trying to work out a variety of things, they'll always have to be reviewing this, because I would say, with most animals, if they can solve certain problems they will be able to get to a level and once they get there they'll get bored*" [P12].

These comments indicate a thoughtful, reflective engagement with the animals, and an interest in the animals' inner world. For some visitors, this seemed to go deeper than the forms of wonderment and respect for animals' impressive abilities that zoos aim to inspire.

Perceptions of Orangutans' Similarity to Humans

People's perception of animals' similarity to humans plays an important role in empathy for animals. Reflecting on the animals' use of the technology, over half of the respondents mentioned the similarity between orangutans and humans, or drew comparisons between orangutans and human children.

Many respondents drew on their knowledge of children to interpret orangutans' cognitive engagement with the interactive technology. When assessing the potential benefits of technology for animals, some drew on their experience of keeping young children entertained:

"*I know trying to entertain a toddler,[...] anything that can distract or stimulate or keep concentration for a little while, it's brilliant*" [P01].

One interviewee drew on her knowledge of teaching children to conclude that the games needed to be made more challenging in order to maintain the orangutans' interest [P12]. A few explicitly considered children's engagement with technology when evaluating the technology:

"*'Well they seem to enjoy it, so I don't think there's anything wrong with it. I mean it's like having a toddler and people say, 'oh you shouldn't give them technology', but why not, it's just what we do now, so yeah. If my toddler gets to play with an iPad then I don't see why not*" [P01].

Emotional Empathy

Visitors' positive emotional responses to orangutans were evident in many of the interviews. There were some indications that these attitudes towards the animals contributed to, and were reinforced by, people's perceptions of the technology and its potential benefits for the orangutans:

"*I'm a bit in love with them anyway. So, anything that is provided that can help them and improve them and make their lives interesting, I think is fascinating.*" [P04].

Consideration of Animal Welfare

Concern for animal welfare is an important dimension of emotional empathy for animals, and this theme was salient in visitor interviews. Prominent in many visitors' responses was close consideration of animal wellbeing, and the potential impacts of the installation for animal welfare. When asked about their perceptions of the installation, most visitors gave primary consideration to the potential impact on orangutans' wellbeing. A majority deemed that innovative use of technology could be stimulating for the animals.

Visitors who made similar assessments described the installation as "*exciting*" [P05] or "*a clever concept*" [P18], with one stating that he would be happy to pay more to support this form of animal enrichment [P06].

Other visitors were more hesitant in their assessment of the potential benefits for orangutans' wellbeing. For some, the fact that orangutans were not encouraged or rewarded for using the installation was an important factor. Sited in the corner of one of the orangutans' indoor enclosures, the installation allowed orangutans to engage casually, as they moved around the enclosure. As part of their habitual patterns of movement through the space, orangutans regularly entered and left the area where the installation was located. This was noted favourably by visitors:

"*if they don't want to... but if they want some space they can move away, and yeah it's up to them*" [P10].

However, the interviewer recorded that one observer, who declined to participate formally in the research, expressed strong negative opinions on digital technology for zoo animals.

It is noted that our findings related to animal welfare attitudes entail a risk of social desirability bias, in that zoo visitors speaking with researchers may be likely to emphasise their interest in animal welfare and conservation. Therefore, we consider that the zoo context itself might be a factor which directs visitors' attention to questions of animal wellbeing.

In contrast to the attention given to animal wellbeing impacts, only 5 of the 25 respondents mentioned visitor education and engagement when evaluating the installation. observing for example that the intervention could be "*good for the kids, to let them see what [the orangutans] are capable of*" [P14]. It had been anticipated that visitors would give more attention to matters of visitor education and entertainment, particularly because most respondents were accompanied by small children. Despite this, visitors indicated that the installation provided good visibility of the orangutans and their behaviours.

"*The idea is really good, I think it's different* [...] *and the setup is good so we can see*," [P10].

"*It's been really... it's been amazing because they've all come up. Like we've actually seen more than we would on a normal day*" [P01].

This indicates that the installation design, as well as the siting and configuration of components, played a role in enabling visitors to closely observe, and reflect on orangutans' use of the system.

Motor Empathy

As the findings above suggest, visitors' engagement with the installation seemed to be enhanced not only by the visibility and dynamic nature of the installation itself, but also by the visibility and dynamic nature of orangutans' interactions. This seemed to allow for observers to respond directly to the physical movements of the orangutans. Many visitors commented on their goal-oriented movements:

"*I was at both windows and watching them hit, I saw two of them hit the dots for a while, so that was pretty impressive*" [P03].

"*she's trying to catch the patterns and in fact seeing an 18 month old child observing he's probably wanting to do the same sort of thing.*" [P04].

As this comment suggests, many children responded to the orangutans' movements and interactions in ways which suggested that they were attracted to these movements and interpreted them as forms of play. Some children were seen running, bouncing or crouching at the glass wall which separated them from the orangutans and the installation. (Figure 3).

Figure 3. The system was configured to allow visitors to observe the orangutans' use in close proximity. Many respondents drew comparisons between the play of Dewi (6), and similar aged human children.

DISCUSSION

Responding to zoos' interest in engaging audiences through depictions of animal-computer interaction, we have explored observers' empathetic responses to animals using an interactive technology. *Kinecting with Orangutans* has allowed us to study zoo visitors' responses to orangutans' use of an interactive installation. In this work, we have adopted a broad understanding of empathy for animals which incorporates cognitive and emotive dimensions, attending to perceived similarity between animals and humans, and the potential role of motor empathy.

Interviews with zoo visitors reveal responses consistent with empathy for animals, in accordance with our design strategies and theories of empathy. Visitors considered orangutan's cognitive abilities and affective states, were prompted to consider the similarities (and fine-grained differences) between humans and orangutans, and attended to the installation's impact on animal wellbeing.

In the following discussion we interrogate these findings further to explore how empathy can be evoked by watching animals using interactive technology. We explore the anthropic framing effects of digital technology, the role of interactivity in prompting reflection on animal minds, and motor empathy responses to watching animals' physical movements. We conclude by discussing the contributions of this work to animal-computer interaction and HCI more broadly, noting limitations of the study and proposing avenues for future research.

Anthropic Framing

Despite long-standing use of digital technology for primate research (see, for example [60]), computers are generally thought of, by the public at large, as tools used by humans alone. Seeing animals using interactive technology therefore creates a human frame of reference. It invites the observer to interpret the animals' behaviours through the lens of what one knows about one's own (or other people's) behaviour and cognition. This 'anthropic framing' effect is seen in interviewees' comments refering to the orangutans' similarities to humans. As previously discussed, this effect of emphasising orangutans' similarity to humans may contribute to empathy towards the animals [13].

On the other hand, an installation which exactly replicated technology designed for humans would perhaps not have been well received. Visitors' tendency to evaluate the installation in terms of its benefit to animals' wellbeing reflects a rejection of exhibits in which animals perform human-like behaviours for entertainment (consistent with prior work which reports zoo visitors' attention to matters of animal welfare and exploitation [2]). In addition, visitors noted approvingly that the *Kinecting with Orangutans* installation allowed for orangutans' preferred forms of interaction (such as using the back of the hand, feet, and objects), rather than requiring the animals to adopt human forms of interaction. Visitors' positive appraisal of the installation as appropriate for orangutans might in fact depend on the fact that neither the applications or interface look *quite* like any system they have seen used by humans.

Previous technology-based interventions for orangutans have made use of familiar technology designed for humans, notably iPads [57]. In contrast, *Kinecting with Orangutans* depends on a novel configuration of hardware. This prevented visitors from making assumptions about 'correct' forms of interaction. Visitors' observations were largely characterised by an attitude of curiosity, rather than appraisal. On the other hand, the *Paint* application replicated conventions which might have been familiar from drawing applications for touchscreen devices: this prompted two visitors to voice assumptions about the way that orangutans would want to use the application, leading them to believe the animal had failed in its attempt.

These findings have important implications for addressing concerns that providing digital enrichment might be seen as exploitative, in encouraging animals to perform 'human' activities. Our study suggests that technology which provides a familiar, anthropic frame encourages observers to perceive animals' similarities to humans, which has the potential to contribute to empathy for animals [13]. However, it also indicates that use of familiar conventions in the design of the technology should be balanced with (a) visitors' expectations that zoo enrichment should prioritise animals' natural behaviours, rather than coercing animals to perform for entertainment, and (b) the risk of prompting visitors to view animals' behaviours in terms of an ability (or failure) to replicate human interactions.

Revealing Animal Minds

Visitors' reflections on the orangutans' use of the installation indicated that a majority of respondents attributed thoughts and feelings to the orangutans. This indicates a belief in animal minds, which has demonstrated links with empathy for animals [31,34]. Our observations suggest that visitors' ability to watch and make sense of the animals' actions, and make inferences about the animals' intentions and cognitive processes depended on several related features of the installation. The capacity for full-body interaction enabled by the Kinect sensor, the relatively large dimensions of the projection area, and the use of brightly coloured, dynamic game interfaces contributed to the visibility of the installation itself and of orangutans' interactions with the system.

The recognisable appearance of the installation, discussed above in terms of its impact on perceptions of similarity, also allowed observers to draw on their own experience of using comparable systems (such as touchscreen displays), or prior observation of other people using such systems. This enabled them to assess the level of complexity involved, and to make inferences about the learning processes and potential difficulties faced by the orangutans. Observers' prior knowledge of comparable tasks provided a basis for people to be impressed by orangutans' ability to use interactive technology, but also enabled them to take the perspective of the orangutan user.

The visibility of the installation and the familiar frame of reference in which to interpret usage also enabled visitors to notice differences in the way individual orangutans interact with the system. By allowing orangutans to interact in a wide variety of ways, the installation revealed the animals' individual preferences and interests in a form which visitors could readily interpret to draw inferences about animal personalities.

This demonstrates some success in our design strategies of making visible to visitors the animals' natural behaviours, their cognitive capabilities and individual preferences. However the challenges of this approach are revealed by that fact that some interviewees' responses were limited to relatively superficial observations, such as comments about the "intelligence" of orangutans.

Motor Empathy

In addition to cognitive and emotional forms of empathy, there were also indications in our observations of visitors' responses which might be categorised as *motor empathy* or *kinaesthetic empathy*. Physical responses and bodily experience evoked by the physical movements of the orangutans were particularly evident in children's playful reactions to the installation, which were observed by researchers and evidenced by visitors' comments regarding children's desire to "do the same sort of thing" as the orangutans. Children's physical responses to orangutans' use of the installation is consistent with the tendency for young zoo visitors to play at the orangutan enclosure windows, mirroring and responding to the behaviours of the infant orangutan in particular (e.g. Figure 3).

This finding provides further support for the approach of enabling orangutans to explore and use their preferred forms of interaction, and catering to full-body movement. It also points to opportunities for interactive technology to support zoos' strategy of encouraging people to act out animals' behaviours in order to build connections with wildlife. This indication of the potential role of motor empathy in visitors' responses also suggests the need for further HCI attention to observers' felt, bodily experience of watching others use interactive systems [24].

Together, these understandings of people's responses to watching bodily movements provide a resource for animal-computer interaction design which has not been exploited to date. Furthermore, this points to the power of watching others use technology, and the potential for HCI to respond to this in the design of social and persuasive systems. More research is needed to understand the role of motor empathy in observing technology use by both animals and humans.

Limitations

These findings must be interpreted with some caution. Firstly, it seems reasonable to assume that zoo visitors' responses may be affected by a social desirability bias; in particular, this phenomenon might have increased respondents' consideration of animal wellbeing. This possibility is supported by studies of family zoo visits which have found that visitors' behaviours involve elements of performance enacted for other members of the public [21]. Secondly, despite the surprising depth of consideration given by many respondents to orangutans' cognitive processes, several visitors showed relatively superficial engagement with the animals, with comments limited to brief observations that orangutans are "intelligent". Thirdly, this study has been conducted with orangutans, the species considered to be humans' closest living relatives, and which are readily anthropomorphised. It is unclear how these findings might generalize to species which are less similar to humans or have less charismatic appeal, such as snakes [44]. Finally, further work is required to validate the impacts of specific design choices on zoo visitors' empathetic responses to animals.

Contributions and Future Work

The findings of this study provide a basis to further investigate how digital technology for animals can support emotionally engaging encounters with humans. This work suggests an important role for animal-computer interaction in the care and presentation of animals in zoos, which, despite critiques from some academic and public spheres, maintain broad popularity and a position of social and cultural significance in many countries. We find that observing animals using technology evokes responses commensurate with a 'close encounter' with an animal. These findings suggest a role for interactive installations in promoting empathetic encounters with animals in captive and non-captive settings. Further research is in progress to validate the impacts of digital enrichment in terms of animal wellbeing.

The above discussion provides new insights into the anthropic framing effects of digital technology, and design tactics relevant to specific forms of empathy. This work suggests opportunities for HCI to engage with the empathetic potential of watching others' use of technology as a resource for design, and as a resource for understanding the impacts of technology in social contexts.

CONCLUSION

This paper explores the forms of empathy experienced by people observing orangutans' use of a novel interactive system. Our study responds to representations of zoo animals using interactive technology, publicised by zoos to foster people's interest in wildlife. In collaboration with zoo personnel we investigated the zoo context, and developed an interactive installation for orangutans, drawing on zoos' tactics for fostering empathetic responses to animals. Visitor interviews conducted during trials of the installation indicate that observers responded to the animals with *cognitive empathy*, including reflections on animals' intentions, desires and perceptions of similarity to humans; *emotional empathy*, such as consideration of animals' wellbeing and needs; and revealed some responses consistent with *motor empathy*. We contend that digital technology establishes an anthropic frame in which to interpret animals' interactions, but that it may be important to moderate this through design which caters to species-specific behaviours, and to avoid replicating familiar human computer interfaces. We also find that animals' cognitive states and intentions are made apparent by a system which allows full-body interactions and is to some extent familiar to human observers. Finally, the indication that motor empathy may be evoked by watching physical forms of interaction has important implications for both ACI and HCI research and design. Overall, this study contributes new understanding of designing computer interactions to engender observers' empathy for animals and highlights the potential value of designing for empathy.

ACKNOWLEDGMENTS

This work was conducted in partnership with Zoos Victoria. The team would like to thank the individuals who generously shared their time and experience, and those who provided organisational and practical support for this research. Sarah Webber was supported by an Australian Government Research Training Program Scholarship and a Top-Up Scholarship from the Microsoft Research Centre for SocialNUI at The University of Melbourne.

REFERENCES

1. Joelle Alcaidinho, Giancarlo Valentin, Stephanie Tai, Brian Nguyen, Krista Sanders, Melody Jackson, Eric

Gilbert, and Thad Starner. 2015. Leveraging Mobile Technology to Increase the Permanent Adoption of Shelter Dogs. In *Proceedings of the 17th International Conference on Human-Computer Interaction with Mobile Devices and Services* (MobileHCI '15), 463–469. https://doi.org/10.1145/2785830.2785861

2. Roy Ballantyne, Jan Packer, Karen Hughes, and Lynn Dierking. 2007. Conservation learning in wildlife tourism settings : lessons from research in zoos and aquariums. *Environmental Education Research* 13, 3: 367–383. https://doi.org/10.1080/13504620701430604
3. Roy Ballantyne, Jan Packer, and Lucy A. Sutherland. 2011. Visitors' memories of wildlife tourism: Implications for the design of powerful interpretive experiences. *Tourism Management* 32, 4: 770–779. https://doi.org/10.1016/j.tourman.2010.06.012
4. C. Daniel Batson. 2009. These things called empathy: Eight related but distinct phenomena. In *The social neuroscience of empathy*, J. Decety and W. Ickes (eds.). MIT Press, Cambridge, MA, 3–15.
5. Jonathan Belman and Mary Flanagan. 2010. Designing games to foster empathy. *International Journal of Cognitive Technology* 15, 1: 11.
6. Jaime Berenguer. 2007. The Effect of Empathy in Proenvironmental Attitudes and Behaviors. *Environment and Behavior* 39, 2: 269–283. https://doi.org/10.1177/0013916506292937
7. Sarah M. Bexell, Olga S. Jarrett, and Xu Ping. 2013. The Effects of a Summer Camp Program in China on Children's Knowledge, Attitudes, and Behaviors Toward Animals: A Model for Conservation Education. *Visitor Studies* 16, 1: 59–81.
8. Sarah Marie Bexell. 2006. Effect of a Wildlife Conservation Camp Experience in China on Student Knowledge of Animals, Care, Propensity for Environmental Stewardship, and Compassionate Behavior Toward Animals. Retrieved August 21, 2016 from http://scholarworks.gsu.edu/ece_diss/1/
9. R. J. R. Blair. 2005. Responding to the emotions of others: Dissociating forms of empathy through the study of typical and psychiatric populations. *Consciousness and Cognition* 14, 4: 698–718. https://doi.org/10.1016/j.concog.2005.06.004
10. Danielle M. A. Bons, Floor E. Scheepers, Nanda N. J. Rommelse, and Jan K. Buitelaar. 2010. Motor, Emotional and Cognitive Empathic Abilities in Children with Autism and Conduct Disorder. In *Proceedings of the 7th International Conference on Methods and Techniques in Behavioral Research* (MB '10), 4:1–4:5. https://doi.org/10.1145/1931344.1931348
11. Helen Boostrom. 2013. Problem-solving with orangutans (Pongo Pygmaeus and Pongo Abelii) and chimpanzees (Pan Troglodytes): Using the iPad to provide novel enrichment opportunities. Texas A&M University. Retrieved July 1, 2015 from http://oaktrust.library.tamu.edu/handle/1969.1/150918
12. Karin Brulliard. 2016. Los Angeles Zoo animals are showing off some strong selfie skills. *Washington Post.* Retrieved September 19, 2016 from https://www.washingtonpost.com/news/animalia/wp/2016/03/10/los-angeles-zoo-animals-are-showing-off-some-strong-selfie-skills/
13. Max E. Butterfield, Sarah E. Hill, and Charles G. Lord. 2012. Mangy mutt or furry friend? Anthropomorphism promotes animal welfare. *Journal of Experimental Social Psychology* 48, 4: 957–960. https://doi.org/10.1016/j.jesp.2012.02.010
14. Andrea W. Clay, Bonnie M. Perdue, Diann E. Gaalema, Francine L. Dolins, and Mollie A. Bloomsmith. 2011. The use of technology to enhance zoological parks. *Zoo Biology* 30, 5: 487–497. https://doi.org/10.1002/zoo.20353
15. Susan Clayton, John Fraser, and Carol D. Saunders. 2009. Zoo experiences: conversations, connections, and concern for animals. *Zoo Biology* 28, 5: 377–397. https://doi.org/10.1002/zoo.20186
16. Susan Clayton and Gene Myers. 2015. *Conservation Psychology: Understanding and Promoting Human Care for Nature*. Wiley-Blackwell, Chichester, UK.
17. Shannon Cuykendall, Ethan Soutar-Rau, Karen Cochrane, Jacob Freiberg, and Thecla Schiphorst. 2015. Simply Spinning: Extending Current Design Frameworks for Kinesthetic Empathy. In *Proceedings of the Ninth International Conference on Tangible, Embedded, and Embodied Interaction* (TEI '15), 305–312. https://doi.org/10.1145/2677199.2680567
18. Beth Daly and L. L. Morton. 2006. An investigation of human-animal interactions and empathy as related to pet preference, ownership, attachment, and attitudes in children. *Anthrozoös* 19, 2: 113–127. https://doi.org/10.2752/089279306785593801
19. Mark H. Davis. 1983. Measuring individual differences in empathy: Evidence for a multidimensional approach. *Journal of Personality and Social Psychology* 44, 1: 113–126. https://doi.org/10.1037/0022-3514.44.1.113
20. Mathias Dekeyser, Robert Elliott, and Mia Leijssen. 2011. Empathy in psychotherapy: Dialogue and embodied understanding. In *The Social Neuroscience of Empathy*, Jean Decety and William Ickes (eds.). MIT Press, Cambridge, MA, 113–124.
21. Marjorie L. DeVault. 2000. Producing Family Time: Practices of Leisure Activity Beyond the Home.

Qualitative Sociology 23, 4: 485–503. https://doi.org/10.1023/A:1005582926577

22. Clemens Driessen, Kars Alfrink, Marinka Copier, Hein Lagerweij, and Irene van Peer. 2014. What could playing with pigs do to us? Game design as multispecies philosophy. *Antennae*, 30: 79.
23. John H Falk, Eric M Reinhard, Cynthia L Vernon, Kerry Bronnenkant, and Nora L Deans. 2007. *Why Zoos & Aquariums Matter : Assessing the Impact of a Visit to a Zoo or Aquarium*. Association of Zoos and Aquariums. Retrieved from https://www.aza.org/uploadedFiles/Education/why_zoos_matter.pdf
24. Sarah Fdili Alaoui, Thecla Schiphorst, Shannon Cuykendall, Kristin Carlson, Karen Studd, and Karen Bradley. 2015. Strategies for Embodied Design: The Value and Challenges of Observing Movement. In *Proceedings of the 2015 ACM SIGCHI Conference on Creativity and Cognition* (C&C '15), 121–130. https://doi.org/10.1145/2757226.2757238
25. Eduardo J. Fernandez, Michael A. Tamborski, Sarah R. Pickens, and William Timberlake. 2009. Animal–visitor interactions in the modern zoo: Conflicts and interventions. *Applied Animal Behaviour Science* 120, 1–2: 1–8. https://doi.org/10.1016/j.applanim.2009.06.002
26. Maiken Hillerup Fogtmann, Jonas Fritsch, and Karen Johanne Kortbek. 2008. Kinesthetic Interaction: Revealing the Bodily Potential in Interaction Design. In *Proceedings of the 20th Australasian Conference on Computer-Human Interaction: Designing for Habitus and Habitat* (OZCHI '08), 89–96. https://doi.org/10.1145/1517744.1517770
27. Jessica Katherine Frawley and Laurel Evelyn Dyson. 2014. Animal Personas: Acknowledging Non-human Stakeholders in Designing for Sustainable Food Systems. In *Proceedings of the 26th Australian Computer-Human Interaction Conference on Designing Futures: The Future of Design* (OzCHI '14), 21–30. https://doi.org/10.1145/2686612.2686617
28. V. Gazzola, G. Rizzolatti, B. Wicker, and C. Keysers. 2007. The anthropomorphic brain: The mirror neuron system responds to human and robotic actions. *NeuroImage* 35, 4: 1674–1684. https://doi.org/10.1016/j.neuroimage.2007.02.003
29. Elizabeth S. Herrelko. 2011. An assessment of the development of a cognitive research programme and introductions in zoo-housed chimpanzees. University of Stirling. Retrieved May 14, 2015 from http://dspace.stir.ac.uk/handle/1893/3654
30. Harold A. Herzog Jr., Nancy S. Betchart, and Robert B. Pittman. 1991. Gender, Sex Role Orientation, and Attitudes toward Animals. *Anthrozoös* 4, 3: 184–191. https://doi.org/10.2752/089279391787057170
31. Adelma M. Hills. 1995. Empathy and Belief in the Mental Experience of Animals. *Anthrozoös* 8, 3: 132–142. https://doi.org/10.2752/089279395787156347
32. Jonny Huck, Paul Coulton, David Gullick, Philip Powell, Jennifer Roberts, Andrew Hudson-Smith, Martin De-Jode, and Panagiotis Mavros. 2015. Supporting Empathy Through Embodiment in the Design of Interactive Systems. In *Proceedings of the Ninth International Conference on Tangible, Embedded, and Embodied Interaction* (TEI '15), 523–528. https://doi.org/10.1145/2677199.2687892
33. Ida Kathrine Hammeleff Jørgensen and Hanna Wirman. 2016. Multispecies methods, technologies for play. *Digital Creativity* 2016, 1: 1–15. https://doi.org/10.1080/14626268.2016.1144617
34. Sarah Knight, Aldert Vrij, Julie Cherryman, and Karl Nunkoosing. 2004. Attitudes towards animal use and belief in animal mind. *Anthrozoös* 17, 1: 43–62. https://doi.org/10.2752/089279304786991945
35. Shaun Lawson, Ben Kirman, Conor Linehan, Tom Feltwell, and Lisa Hopkins. 2015. Problematising Upstream Technology Through Speculative Design: The Case of Quantified Cats and Dogs. In *Proceedings of the 33rd Annual ACM Conference on Human Factors in Computing Systems* (CHI '15), 2663–2672. https://doi.org/10.1145/2702123.2702260
36. Rachel Lowry. 2009. Visitor based conservation campaigns at Zoos Victoria. *International Zoo Education* 45: 11–14.
37. Randy Malamud. 2015. The Problem with Zoos. In *The Oxford Handbook of Animal Studies*, Linda Kalof (ed.). Oxford University Press, Oxford, UK. https://doi.org/0.1093/oxfordhb/9780199927142.013.006
38. Clara Mancini. 2011. Animal-computer Interaction: A Manifesto. *Interactions* 18, 4: 69–73. https://doi.org/10.1145/1978822.1978836
39. Clara Mancini, Rob Harris, Brendan Aengenheister, and Claire Guest. 2015. Re-Centering Multispecies Practices: A Canine Interface for Cancer Detection Dogs. In *Proceedings of the 33rd Annual ACM Conference on Human Factors in Computing Systems* (CHI '15), 2673–2682. https://doi.org/10.1145/2702123.2702562
40. Clara Mancini, Janet van der Linden, Jon Bryan, and Andrew Stuart. 2012. Exploring Interspecies Sensemaking: Dog Tracking Semiotics and Multispecies Ethnography. In *Proceedings of the 2012 ACM Conference on Ubiquitous Computing* (UbiComp

'12), 143–152.
https://doi.org/10.1145/2370216.2370239

41. Christopher Flynn Martin, Rahul Bhui, Peter Bossaerts, Tetsuro Matsuzawa, and Colin Camerer. 2014. Chimpanzee choice rates in competitive games match equilibrium game theory predictions. *Scientific Reports* 4. https://doi.org/10.1038/srep05182
42. Katsutoshi Masai, Kai Kunze, Maki sugimoto, and Mark Billinghurst. 2016. Empathy Glasses. In *Proceedings of the 2016 CHI Conference Extended Abstracts on Human Factors in Computing Systems* (CHI EA '16), 1257–1263. https://doi.org/10.1145/2851581.2892370
43. Olin Eugene Myers and Carol D. Saunders. 2002. Animals as links toward developing caring relationships with the natural world. In *Children and nature: Psychological, sociocultural, and evolutionary investigations*. MIT Press, Cambridge, MA, 153–178.
44. Olin Eugene Myers, Carol D. Saunders, and Andrej A. Birjulin. 2004. Emotional Dimensions of Watching Zoo Animals: An Experience Sampling Study Building on Insights from Psychology. *Curator: The Museum Journal* 47, 3: 299–321. https://doi.org/10.1111/j.2151-6952.2004.tb00127.x
45. Jonathan K. Nelson and Patrick C. Shih. CompanionViz: Mediated platform for gauging canine health and enhancing human–pet interactions. *International Journal of Human-Computer Studies*. https://doi.org/10.1016/j.ijhcs.2016.04.002
46. David T. Nguyen and John Canny. 2009. More Than Face-to-face: Empathy Effects of Video Framing. In *Proceedings of the SIGCHI Conference on Human Factors in Computing Systems* (CHI '09), 423–432. https://doi.org/10.1145/1518701.1518770
47. Jordan Owen. 2016. Snow monkey at Lincoln Park Zoo names her baby by touchscreen. *Chicago Sun-Times*. Retrieved September 19, 2016 from http://chicago.suntimes.com/news/snow-monkey-at-lincoln-park-zoo-names-her-baby-by-touchscreen/
48. Patricia G. Patrick, Catherine E. Matthews, David Franklin Ayers, and Sue Dale Tunnicliffe. 2007. Conservation and Education: Prominent Themes in Zoo Mission Statements. *The Journal of Environmental Education* 38, 3: 53–60. https://doi.org/10.3200/JOEE.38.3.53-60
49. Elizabeth S. Paul. 2000. Empathy with Animals and with Humans: Are They Linked? *Anthrozoös* 13, 4: 194–202. https://doi.org/10.2752/089279300786999699
50. Bonnie M Perdue, Andrea W Clay, Diann E Gaalema, Terry L Maple, and Tara S Stoinski. 2012. Technology at the zoo: the influence of a touchscreen computer on orangutans and zoo visitors. *Zoo Biology* 31, 1: 27–39. https://doi.org/10.1002/zoo.20378
51. Clive Phillips. 2009. Empathy Towards Animals. In *The Welfare of Animals*. Springer Netherlands, 47–54. https://doi.org/10.1007/978-1-4020-9219-0_3
52. Stephanie D. Preston and Frans B. M. de Waal. 2002. Empathy: Its ultimate and proximate bases. *The Behavioral and Brain Sciences* 25, 1: 1-20-71.
53. Mark Prigg. 2015. P-P-P-Pick up an iPad: Zoo unveils app penguins play with their beak. *Daily Mail Online*. Retrieved September 19, 2016 from http://www.dailymail.co.uk/sciencetech/article-2897908/P-P-P-Pick-iPad-Zoo-unveils-latest-treat-penguins-app-play-beak.html
54. Charlotte Robinson, Clara Mancini, Janet van der Linden, Claire Guest, and Robert Harris. 2014. Canine-centered Interface Design: Supporting the Work of Diabetes Alert Dogs. In *Proceedings of the SIGCHI Conference on Human Factors in Computing Systems* (CHI '14), 3757–3766. https://doi.org/10.1145/2556288.2557396
55. P. Wesley Schultz. 2000. Empathizing With Nature: The Effects of Perspective Taking on Concern for Environmental Issues. *Journal of Social Issues* 56, 3: 391–406. https://doi.org/10.1111/0022-4537.00174
56. Simone G. Shamay-Tsoory. 2011. The Neural Bases for Empathy. *The Neuroscientist* 17, 1: 18–24. https://doi.org/10.1177/1073858410379268
57. Julian Smith. 2011. Apps for apes: Orang-utans want iPads for Christmas. *New Scientist* 212: 69–71. https://doi.org/10.1016/S0262-4079(11)63173-4
58. N. Taylor and T. D. Signal. 2005. Empathy and attitudes to animals. *Anthrozoös* 18, 1: 18–27. https://doi.org/10.2752/089279305785594342
59. Matt Walker. 2010. Movie made by chimpanzees to be broadcast on television. *BBC Earth News*. Retrieved September 19, 2016 from http://news.bbc.co.uk/earth/hi/earth_news/newsid_8472000/8472831.stm
60. D. A. Washburn. 2015. The four Cs of psychological wellbeing: Lessons from three decades of computer-based environmental enrichment. *Animal Behavior and Cognition* 2, 3: 218–232.
61. Sarah Webber, Marcus Carter, Wally Smith, and Frank Vetere. 2016. Interactive Technology and Human-Animal Encounters at the Zoo. *International Journal of Human-Computer Studies* 98: 150–168. https://doi.org/10.1016/j.ijhcs.2016.05.003
62. Michelle Westerlaken and Stefano Gualeni. 2013. Digitally Complemented Zoomorphism : a Theoretical Foundation for Human-Animal Interaction Design. In

Proceedings of the 6th International Conference on Designing Pleasurable Products and Interfaces. https://doi.org/10.1145/2513506.2513527

63. Andrew D. Wilson. 2010. Using a Depth Camera As a Touch Sensor. In *ACM International Conference on Interactive Tabletops and Surfaces* (ITS '10), 69–72. https://doi.org/10.1145/1936652.1936665

64. Hanna Wirman. 2014. Games for / with strangers - Captive orangutan (pongo pygmaeus) touch screen play. *Antennae*, 30: 104–112.

65. Peter Wright and John McCarthy. 2008. Empathy and Experience in HCI. In *Proceedings of the SIGCHI Conference on Human Factors in Computing Systems* (CHI '08), 637–646. https://doi.org/10.1145/1357054.1357156

Reconsidering Nature: The Dialectics of Fair Chase in the Practices of American Midwest Hunters

Norman Makoto Su and EunJeong Cheon
School of Informatics and Computing
Indiana University Bloomington
{normsu, echeon}@indiana.edu

ABSTRACT
In this paper, we describe an ethnographic study consisting of 14 interviews with hunters and participant observations in the American Midwest. We find that the ethos of "fair chase" serves to unite an eclectic group of hunters under a single moral compass. Fair chase posits, for example, that hunters must not have an improper advantage over animals. The actual practices of hunters in different communities (e.g., communities revolving around different weapons or professions), however, reveals a series of opposing points of view among hunters at large on what actually constitutes fair chase. We suggest that an understanding of fair chase and its dialectics can constructively problematize nature for human-computer interaction.

ACM Classification Keywords
H.5.m. Information Interfaces and Presentation (e.g. HCI): Miscellaneous

Author Keywords
Hunting; hunters; fair chase; nature; rural; values; ethics; dialectics

INTRODUCTION
It is difficult now to find a subculture in which technology is absent. Researchers have sought to investigate how both traditional and modern subcultures or milleux have had to contend with technology [1, 8, 40, 38, 13]. A central debate surrounding technology in such spaces [39] is whether it erodes our goals and values or whether such technologies can be leveraged to improve the good of humanity.

One popular strain of this rhetoric involves the need for modern society to better engage with *nature*. This rhetoric is not new and, in the United States, one of its strongest proponents was President Theodore Roosevelt who argued for a sort of self-reliance that could be best learned by toughing it out with nature and, more precisely, by hunting [29]. Roosevelt presciently warned that "[t]he chase is the best of all national pastimes and...a mere source of weakness if carried on in an unhealthy manner, or to an excessive degree, or under over-artificial conditions." Since then, Roosevelt's concept of *fair chase* has become standard teaching material for all hunters. It is the moral compass with which all hunters are guided by.

This notion of "over-artificial conditions" has been expounded upon in hunting. The insidiousness of "gadgetry" in hunting was a problem identified as early as the 1940s by Aldo Leopold, a founder of the wildlife management discipline. Leopold warned of the influence of gadgeteers [24]:

> He has draped the American outdoorsman with an infinity of contraptions, all offered as aids to self-reliance, hardihood, woodcraft, or marksmanship, but too often functioning as substitutes for them. Gadgets fill the pockets, they dangle from neck and belt...Each item of outdoor equipment grow slighter and often better, but the aggregate poundage becomes tonnage...But what of cultural values?

Leopold was not a Luddite; he believed technology could enhance the experience of hunting but also saw its potential as destroying the cultural value of hunting. He posited that hunting was "a contrast-value": a contrast between the world of mechanization and nature.

The intersection of nature and HCI has recently gained traction [19]. For instance, a body of research on birding, archery, and, indeed, hunting have been subject to fieldwork and subsequent design interventions [18, 11, 43]. While these studies have elucidated the detailed practices and interactions of those engaged in nature, both human and non-human, they do not focus on the intertwining of values and ethics with our practices in nature that Leopold refers to. Certainly, hunting and its ethos are inseparable precisely because the stakes seem higher—it involves the taking of a life.

In this study, following calls from design approaches such as value sensitive design [16, 23] and designing for authenticity [39] that argue for deep examination of the values embedded in subcultures and their practices, we describe an ethnographic study over two years involving participant observations and interviews with 14 hunters in Midwest America. Drawing from the notion of the dialectic from Hegel, we show

CHI 2017, May 06 - 11, 2017, Denver, CO, USA

ISBN 978-1-4503-4655-9/17/05...$15.00
DOI: http://dx.doi.org/10.1145/3025453.3025966

that hunters as a whole embrace the ethical code of fair chase, but when describing the practices they do to live out this ethos, they do it in terms of opposing forces. In other words, when hunters talk about how bows and arrows help them hunt ethically, they do it by describing how rifle hunters do not reach the same level of ethics. We argue that by identifying these tensions, we can reach a better understanding of how we might sensitively approach design for nature. Our approach takes a holistic approach to hunters, regarding them not as one single group, but consisting of multiple social worlds [37], each with their own practices and thereby anxieties with other hunters and actors.

This study makes the following contributions. First, we show that hunters embrace the normative ethos of fair chase that includes giving advantage to the animal, showing respect when harvesting animals, and communing with nature; however, this ethos is practiced in different ways by the diverse hunters in nature. Second, we draw from Hegel's dialectic analysis to describe opposing practices in the hunt and the land between stakeholders: different weapon users, non-hunters, hunters, state officials, scientists, long-time hunters, newcomers, and gadget users. We show how these tensions, or dialectics, often revolve around technological artifacts and that use of these artifacts reveal subtleties in interpreting fair chase. Third, we describe how these dialectics—different truths about fair chase—can elucidate design for HCI and nature. In sum, our work problematizes nature by questioning the notion of a uniform user-of-nature prevalent in HCI. Instead, HCI should consider opportunities to make bare the heterogeneity of value systems (and their practices) in nature.

RELATED WORK

Technologies for Communing with Nature

Recently, there has been growing attention in HCI to design technologies for enhancing our experiences with nature and supporting outdoor activities. A CHI 2016 workshop entitled *NatureCHI* [19] examined how technologies can promote our experience with nature by mediating interactions with plants or natural phenomenon (e.g., snowflakes), supporting diverse spaces of nature (e.g., zoos and graveyards), and facilitating outdoor recreational activities (e.g., skiing and climbing). The content of the workshop was organized around "the challenge of designing unobtrusive technology usage and user experiences in nature." Similarly, over the years, educational mobile tools [34, 30, 46, 33, 44] have been developed for users to learn about and engage with the surrounding nature.

However, NatureCHI and similar work typically do not examine the values of their users. Rather, by treating nature as an environment for homogeneous users, they focus on technologies as solving problems [5] and challenges in nature. For example, NatureCHI features mobile applications to support outdoor activities like skiing, interfaces that address issues with technology use in harsh weather conditions, and discussion on how existing technologies have disrupted people's experience with nature—thus, it is argued, there is a need to make unobtrusive technologies for nature. As a workshop, NatureCHI is a laudatory start to thinking about nature and HCI, and we hope to add nuance to the discussion by complicating users, values, and technology in nature. For instance, our findings show that technology, aside from sometimes being intrusive, is also purposefully utilized to increase both challenge and engagement with nature.

Hunting is a traditional activity that remains an avenue for humans to commune with nature and the wild. While a wide range of hunting technologies have been commercially developed to support hunting, there are relatively few HCI studies examining hunting practices and technologies. Deer hunting activities have been explored by Juhlin and Weilenmann to gain insight on designing online collaborative games [21, 7]. The authors studied a rifle hunting team by recording radio talk during the hunt, observing the actual hunt, and conducting informal interviews with the hunters. They found that seeking pleasure in hunting was as important a part of the activity as was bagging game for hunters. Radio allowed hunters not only to understand the progress of hunting but also to have fun by involving them in radio talk (e.g., sitting at the stand by themselves, but not being lonely because they could still collaborate with others remotely, which allowed them to relax between highly intense moments of the hunt).

Another focus of interest that studying hunting brings is human-animal interactions—for example, how technologies mediate interacting with dogs [2, 32, 43]. To understand the actual practices with existing technologies for communicating with dogs, Paldaninus et al. [32] conducted interviews with hunters who use dog-tracking systems during their hunt. In these studies, current GPS-based systems were perceived by hunters as useful tools to monitor the real time processes of hunting and managing their dogs. Building on this 2011 study, Weilenmann and Juhlin [43] examined how dog holders in a hunting team used GPS and suggested that designing technologies for interaction with non-human beings goes beyond a dyadic framework (that of the animal and the computer) to address the complex contexts which lay in technologies, humans, and animals. Another study by Aspling and Juhlin [2] used an actor-network theory lens to understand how hunters and boars carried out different strategies in hunting sites where technologies, such as trail cameras, were involved. While this paper does not examine the use of hunting dogs, this work on human-animal interactions provides useful insight on going beyond examining a single kind of nature user.

Alongside these studies on hunting, traditional archery [18, 17] and birding [11, 10] have also been investigated in HCI for the purpose of developing technologies to make such outdoor activities available in virtual environments. Geiger and colleagues attended traditional archery classes to phenomenologically understand how the body engages with the bow (e.g., sequences of drawing and releasing bow) and developed an archery simulator to detect the motions of users. In the aforementioned studies on birding, participant observations of birding practices and bird walks informed the design of an online, crowdsourced system for annotating bird calls.

Our research finds inspiration from Bidwell and Browning's [3] profound themes on designing for "natural places." We follow their lead in considering the dichotomy between

ID	Occupation	Hunting Experience
P1	Wildlife biologist*	Since 12 years old
P2	Lecturer at university	30 years
P3	HCI student	Since 9 years old
P4	Deer research biologist*	Beginner
P5	Wildlife biologist*	3 years
P6	Restoration biologist*	4-5 years
P7	IT admin	5-6 years
P8	IT program director	50+ years
P9	Laborer at DNR*	30+ years
P10	Bowhunter magazine writer	35 years
P11	Auto business facilities director	Since junior high
P12	President of bow company	Since college
P13	Full-time firefighter, Part-time bow maker	Since childhood
P14	Production chemist	Since 12-13 years old

bold = avid bowhunter, * = affiliated with the DNR

Figure 1. Informant Demographics

local and non-local as well as urban and rural. Their insights on, for example, public media portrayal of rural technology use, the apparent authority of technology mediated data, the "nitty-gritty of ordinary rural life," technology's potential to both recede and reveal nature, and the interplay of values and morality with technology in nature are salient to this paper's findings.

Hunting Ethics

While the scope of this paper limits our discussion, hunting ethics is an on-going discussion crossing many fields such as environmental ethics and sport philosophy. Each has its own interpretation and stance on the moral codes of hunting (e.g., whether hunting is justifiable, regardless of its benefits [26] to whether hunting ethics should belong to sport ethics [25]). We take to heart Fischer et al.'s [15] appeal to consider the perspectives of multiple stakeholders (e.g., non-hunters and critics of hunting) on the morality and legitimacy of hunting. Some consider hunter ethics as an individual obligation and thus self-governing (self-imposed) actions are necessary, while others put ethics in a broader context by emphasizing a variety of relevant agents alongside hunting. For example, according to Norton [28], ethical hunters are defined in terms of not merely exemplified practices but respectful attitudes towards a wide range of stakeholders (e.g., land, landowner, fellow, non-hunter, and the game they hunted). In particular, the virtue of "fairness" has been emphasized through the expectation that hunters abide by the principle of *fair chase* [41]. The basic idea of fair chase is to not put an animal's natural ability to survive at a disadvantage (a detailed explanation will be discussed later). Another widely recognized hunting ethic called the "Sportsman's Code" has also adapted the fair chase principle as one of their six codes [26]. Philosophically, in terms of judging what good hunting is, some hunters and environmental ethicists [35, 24] have suggested three standards: lowering hunters themselves to a community of nonhuman beings, following community virtues shaped by tradition and rituals, and respect for the biotic community (e.g., understanding the ecology of their community and being aware of land citizenship).

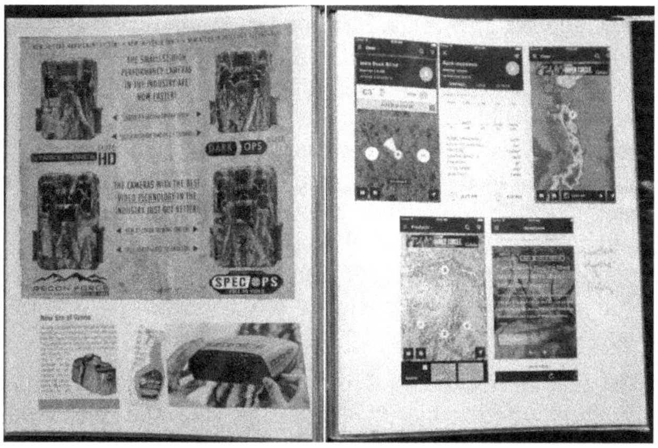

Figure 2. Hunter Equipment Scrapbook (L: equipment, R: hunting app)

METHODS

Over two years, we conducted ethnographic fieldwork in an American Midwest state consisting of 14 semi-structured interviews (ranging 50 minutes to two hours) with hunters of various species and participant observations of workshops run by the Department of Natural Resources (DNR). The DNR is a forward facing state agency for the conservation of public lands, wildlife and fish. The DNR engages with the public by fielding questions, educating the public (e.g., workshops on hunting, fishing, and birding), and creating and enforcing regulations on proper use of the state's resources. We interviewed hunter "citizens" to get a perspective into the everyday practices of hunters, many of whom were never formally taught hunting. In addition, we interviewed hunters who were also employed by the DNR to get a perspective of how hunting practices are formally discussed and regulated by institutions. All interviews were recorded and transcribed. Photos and field notes were taken during participant observations. Our study can be seen in light of a Value Sensitive Design approach that develops "a grounded analysis of values from the context" [23] for describing the value of "fairness" in nature and hunting.

Informants were recruited via snowball sampling. We had no prior relationship with the informants nor experience with hunting. Our informants were mostly experienced hunters with a variety of species and weapons. Figure 1 illustrates the detailed demographics of our informants. In interviews, semi-structured questions centered about themes of demographics, past experience hunting (e.g., first involvement with hunting), current practices, community and profession (e.g., membership in hunting organizations or clubs), and personal ethics or philosophy on hunting.

In addition to our interview protocol, we also created a hunting equipment scrapbook (Figure 2) containing image heavy advertisements and articles from popular magazines on hunting species prominent in Midwest America (American Waterfowler, Outdoor Life, Field & Stream, North American Whitetail, and Bowhunter) as well as screenshots of popular hunting apps. Scrapbooks have been shown to be effective in respecting the expertise of informants and stimulating rich stories about artifacts [45]. Images were chosen to convey a wide range of equipment such as weapons and their accessories (e.g., scopes, arrows), scent removers, camouflage, all-terrain vehicles, trail cameras, and decoys. In interviews, we asked our informants to flip through our scrapbook and reflect on the use of such equipment in their and other hunters' practices. We also asked informants to think about the ethical dimensions of the equipment in our scrapbook. This study takes a broad interpretation of technology from duck decoys to trail cams. Don Ihde's [20] post-phenomenological lens into technology similarly examined how our use of technologies from eyeglasses to video games influences our perception of the world.

The first author took a hunter education course (lessons on firearms, safety, ethics, wilderness survival and conservation required for those under 17 years old to obtain a hunting license) and enrolled in wild turkey hunting, whitetail deer hunting, and mourning dove hunting classes run by the DNR. Archival material such as pamphlets, handbooks, and maps were collected in these classes. He also accompanied one hunter on a deer hunt (six hours) and another hunter on a mourning dove hunt (five hours). The lead author gained hands-on experience scouting, harvesting, tracking, and field dressing animals. He also visited a bow making company and several fish and wildlife areas in the state. Interviews were mostly conducted in the residences or workplaces of our informants. In these visits hunters were often eager to show us their hunting paraphernalia (e.g., hunting trophies, weapons, books, photos). These activities represent an ethnographic approach to "understand another life world using the self or as much of it as possible as the instrument of knowing" [36, p.42]. We stopped our interviews at 14 because we had reached data saturation regarding hunter concerns of fair chase.

We adopt a constructivist grounded theory approach of inquiry [9] in analyzing our qualitative data. By adopting a constructivist stance, we are interested in not only the practices of hunters, but how what they do is constructed as legitimate actions in their social worlds. This suggests that how hunters themselves interpret their own actions with respect to the values and philosophies they adhere to is important. Moreover, we pay careful attention to how these actions are situated in the context of larger social, cultural, and institutional structures. Both authors iteratively developed our coding scheme together as we found emergent and common themes. First, both authors proceeded to open code in a line-by-line manner to capture emergent themes. As we coded and discussed our codings, a shared codebook was generated from which we did focused coding [9, p.57] around themes of fair chase, hunting practices, and the tensions between different actors in reifying fair chase through practices. Data collection and analysis informed each other; the interview protocol and informant pool were adjusted based on our iterative analysis. Our codes and memos form the genesis of the findings of our paper.

THE ETHOS OF FAIR CHASE

The ethos of "fair chase" was the moral compass upon which our hunters guided their practices. Fair chase was mentioned during all our interviews and observations. Hunter education classes teach its students to follow fair chase to be an ethical hunter. To set the stage, we will first discuss contemporary, formal definitions of fair chase by two of the most popular organizations that were mentioned: The Boone and Crockett Club and The Pope & Young Club.

While there are many formal definitions of fair chase, most are similar to a definition [41] by The Boone and Crockett Club (B&C Club), the oldest wildlife conversation organization in North America: "the ethical, sportsmanlike, and lawful pursuit and taking of any free-ranging wild, native North American big game animal in a manner that does not give the hunter an improper advantage over such animals." While The B&C Club is remarkably nuanced in acknowledging that ethics is a complex and personal matter, it nonetheless advocates for fair chase *standards*; these standards include obeying state laws and giving the animal every opportunity to elude the hunter. The Pope & Young Club notes that the "fair chase concept does, however, extend beyond the hunt itself; it is an attitude and a way of life based in a deep-seated respect for wildlife, for the environment, and for other individuals who share the bounty of this vast continent's natural resources" [42].

In our fieldwork, we found hunters similarly described the proper pursuit of animals as important. The rhetoric of hunters was to level the playing field, as much as they could, between themselves and the animal. Importantly hunters "gave" this to animals; they had to make decisions in their own hunting practices to allow animals a fighting chance: "*Fair chase is essentially an ethical framework and if I were to describe it, you use the minimum amount of advantage possible to get success*" (P6).

This give and take of animals represents a need for the hunter to have a challenge, to not "cheat" (P8) the animal. It has been commented on [31] that fair chase is really about the hunter's interests, not the animal's welfare and conservation. Indeed, without a challenge the hunt is not enjoyable. The challenge comes from, for example, understanding and overcoming the innate skills of animal species—deer have relatively poor eyesight but an excellent sense of smell, whereas turkey have the opposite, excellent eyesight but a poor sense of smell. In the latter case, hunters rely on turkey decoys to get them within range precisely because approaching turkeys is difficult.

Fair chase also requires respecting the harvesting of animals. Simply put, harvesting describes the activities surrounding an attempt to kill an animal and the subsequent actions thereafter. These activities include shooting, tracking (following a wounded animal), field dressing (gutting the animal for consumption), and transporting an animal. For instance, our hunters reported practices that honor an animal's body after it has been harvested.

Last, but not least, fair chase also means being submerged within nature, what Ortega y Gasset calls "being *within* the countryside" [31, p.124, emphasis in original]. Here fair chase means experiencing nature both viscerally and spiritually. Our hunters described fair chase as a way to return back to nature. The practices of being within the countryside mean, for some hunters, a way to exercise their *country competence* [12]—skills that they have honed from growing up in the country. Desmond used the term in his ethnography of wildland firefighters to motivate why firefighters chose their line of work and how they identified themselves in opposition to "city boys."

Broadly spoken, our hunters all talked about the need to gain a challenge in hunting by giving some advantage to animals, respecting the harvesting of animals, and a needed communion with nature. While hunters agreed that these aspects were necessary to achieve fair chase, their discourse on fair chase was elicited, implicitly and explicitly, dialectically.

THE DIALECTICS OF FAIR CHASE PRACTICE

The doctrine of fair chase unites hunters together but their practices to make fair chase happen differ. Our data shows that the continual attempt to reach a resolution of what constitutes fair chase by hunters can be best viewed as a series of oppositions. Hunters frame their practices in a *dialectic* manner. When hunters hunt on public land, they must do so with other actors: other hunters, state officials, animals, etc. Hunters frame their practices by setting them in opposition to the practices of other groups; such practices reveal contradictory points of views on fair chase that must be reconciled. Hegel's notion of the dialectic is a triadic process in which unity (initial, naive harmony) gives way to disunity (conflict), but resolves to unity [27]. This relationship between oppositions and their resolution is highlighted in the dialectic. Hegel argues that morality is not ingrained in our conscience, devoid from everyday experience. Rather, our actions are guided by an external social ethic, or *Sittlichkeit*, in which laws and customs have been established [22, p.xxi].

Below, we will describe the practices of fair chase among our hunters. In broad swipes, we will separate our findings into *the hunt*—the pursuit, with the intent to harvest, of the animal—and *the land*—the management and surveying of species and land to ensure a fruitful pursuit. Fair chase is typically defined as the pursuit [41], separate from any "conservation ethic." Yet, through our interviews, both the hunt and the land were mentioned in the same breath when speaking of fair chase. While we conceptually separate the two below, we emphasize that they are necessarily and messily intertwined. We show how these practices of fair chase are rhetorically framed by our hunters in terms of oppositional forces. Interviews have been anonymized and are identified by an ID number (Figure 1).

THE HUNT

Key to the pursuit of animals are practices inscribed in the weapons a hunter chooses and the harvest of animals (scouting, killing, field dressing, and tracking). Each set of practices have a number of dialectical elements (some involving technology) which reflect opposing ways of realizing fair chase.

Weapon Choice

In our Midwest State, shotguns, rifles with legal cartridges, muzzleloaders (modern re-creations of so-called primitive firearms such as flintlocks and percussion cap guns), crossbows, archery equipment (long bows, recurve bows, compound bows) and handguns are allowed in particular hunting seasons determined by the DNR. Deer hunting is the most iconic and popular species hunted in the state and is divided into weapon seasons—archery, firearms, and muzzleloader seasons. Our interviews revealed that the choice and use of a weapon signaled a particular brand of fair chase that sometimes was in opposition to those that chose other weapons.

Muzzleloaders

Weapons are a way to ensure challenge when hunting. The muzzleloader for instance can only fire one shot at a time and is cumbersome to load, requiring the hunter to pour black powder and insert the bullet into barrel of the gun. For some, the limitations of the muzzleloader made it attractive. The muzzleloader typically works best in dry conditions because rain or snow can make the powder wet. There is also the increased chance of misfire. P1 described how, "*...there's a lot of days when you're out there, and you'll see the deer...and it misfires or it doesn't fire.*"

Muzzleloaders are set in opposition to rifles. Modern muzzleloaders are accurate like rifles, but help some hunters reinforce the fair chase ethic that the animal is harvested ethically. Fair chase dictates that the hunter should only make a shot that they are confident will kill the deer quickly and humanely. When compared with rifles that are semi-automatic and have magazines, muzzleloaders force hunters to make each shot count. P11 recounts an ethical pact he made with his friends regarding weapon choice:

> A couple of us made the decision that one shot of higher velocity, higher effective range, was more important than multiple shots at a lower, closer range... If it's a high percentage shot,...it's going to be a ethical, clean, fast kill...It's just [a] little more pressure that you got one opportunity.

Crucially, P11 is describing how weapon choice makes the shot more *ethical*. Muzzleloaders present challenges in its operation and limited magazine capacity.

Bow and Arrows

In opposition to muzzleloaders and rifles, which are long-range and accurate, the decreased *proximity* needed to hunt is what bowhunters argue sets them apart. By getting so close to the animal, hunters are deliberately exposing themselves to the animal's natural defenses, possibly spooking the animal. Even if they are successful getting within distance, bowhunters need to comport their body to make an ethical shot. P8 explains, "*I still have to draw that bow back. I still have to anchor and shoot, right? Eight out of ten times, this is where you're going to lose the game. They're going to see you*" (P8). Bowhunters must be willing to not harvest any deer for the challenge. Here "*they've taken a more fair chase attitude because they're a lot more interested in the method than they are in the result.*" Fair chase is more than the challenge of harvesting but also the challenge of simply learning to shoot a new (old) way.

Rifles allow hunters to "snipe" an animal from nearly 400 yards away. As P7 put it, you are "*shooting an animal that doesn't have a clue that you're even in the same country versus getting close and being so close that, at any point in time, the slightest error is going to result in going home empty handed.*" In contrast, the skill necessary to get close to an animal and make an ethical, accurate shot with an arrow is markedly higher for bowhunters. Bowhunters need to put in "*much more of a commitment in terms of practice*" (P12). A gun allows the hunter to target the chest area, "*versus a bow you really need to hit the lungs*" (P14). They are "*choosing to limit*" (P8) themselves by shooting with a bow.

Certainly, many hunters take up bowhunting because there is a dedicated archery season for deers and turkeys; this allows people to continue hunting in some form as long as possible. One of the most contentious issues among bow and arrow (e.g., compound and recurve bows) hunters is the inclusion of crossbows in the archery season. Hunters disparagingly refer to crossbows as "crossguns." Aesthetically crossbows looks like a gun; P7 and P11 note it has bolts, not arrows, has a trigger, and a stock. Functionally, P10 explains how it acts like a gun: "*With a crossbow, I see a deer coming. He crosses that creek. I put the telescopic sight on him. I'm holding this like a gun. He gets close, he walks up, he turns broadside...and I do this [draws and locks an imaginary crossbolt]. That's the only movement*" (P10). Muscle power is not needed to draw the crossbow (P7). Crossbows are corrupting what should be a pure archery season. It provides a loophole (P11) for hunters to pretend they are adopting the archery ethic.

Within the bow and arrow community, there are "traditional" bowhunters. These bowhunters rely on recurve bows. Compound bows allow the hunter to easily draw back. Here, fair chase is about hunting by almost primitive means. P12 and P7 note that traditional equipment allows one to shoot instinctively, judging distance without lasers or sights and pins (mechanical aids on compound bows that allow bowhunters to accurately aim at varying distances). Traditional bowhunters argue that compound bows, similar to target archery, can be fixated on accuracy: "*I don't want to say that accuracy's not important to us, but pinpoint accuracy is not that big a deal...These guys with compounds, it's like kicking in the dirt and wrap the bull around a tree because they miss that little tiny bulls eye in there. Ease up man*" (P13). This methodical approach to shooting with compound bows is not a purist, atavist notion of fair chase for traditional bowhunters. In the wild, we need to rely on our instincts.

The issue of mixing different weapon "communities" together is also an issue of mixing hunters with different notions of fair chase together. In general, bowhunters also feel safer when hunters around them are using the same weapons. Bowhunters are weary of gun users who "*don't pay attention to what's behind the thing they're shooting [at]*" (P1). P11 sums up the ethereal experience of an ideal archery season as one with only real bowhunters where there are "*less people in the woods, less spooking of the game, less intrusiveness.*"

The Snapshot

If proximity is a key challenge provided by weapon choice, then why not simply take close pictures of wildlife? When asked how often he hunts, P10 answered, "*I hunt with a camera practically every day.*" P10 no longer feels the need to harvest many deer, and instead will take a picture of "*the one I passed up.*" However, P5 makes an opposing point that taking pictures and hunting involve a different level of commitment. In other words, taking pictures is ultimately a passive action, while hunting gives you a connection to the natural world by "*participating in the lifecycle.*" The use of decoys, calls, camouflage, and blinds are in service to the pursuit of animals: "*These little song birds were two, three feet from me, because I'm just camo'd up and hunkered down in this little thicket...They're just all around you. They don't know you're there...It's participating in nature.*" For P5, this experience of being immersed in nature would not be possible via observational means.

The Harvest

Harvesting an animal involves preparing the shot, the actual ethical shot, tracking the animal (if necessary), and field dressing (gutting the animal for consumption). As referred to earlier, the "ethical hunter" aims for one shot, one kill, or as P10 put it, "*If you draw blood, your hunt is over.*" This ensures that the animal does not suffer. When asked if they ever violated their own hunting philosophy, by far the most common narrative was when they wounded an animal or, worst yet, failed to track a wounded animal. For hunters these moments weighed heavily on them. P1 recalls a deer he did not recover at the age of twelve:

> I remember one back to when I was 12 years old when I wounded and didn't recover. It's just those one stick with you. Those are the aspects where you feel like you didn't live up to the ethic of hunting when you lost that animal.

For these hunters, it was not necessarily the act of losing the animal (and thus, not being to harvest the animal). Rather, it was their moral responsibility as an ethical hunter to make sure that the animal did not suffer. By wounding and then losing the animal, this meant that first, it was an unethical shot (e.g., a shot that was beyond one's skill level, a shot in the animal's gut), second, the animal was most likely in pain, third, there was an added responsibility now for the hunter to track the animal and then end its suffering, and lastly, loss of meat (sustenance). When P7 told us how he wounded a deer and tracked it, he said, "*I owe it to him.*" Some hunters spend "weeks" tracking deer. *Resolution* of a wounded deer is personally important for hunters.

Just as scouting for deer, learning its habits and routes demonstrate a sense of country competence [12], tracking also demonstrated country competence. While at the same time describing a failure of ethics, P12 noted a positive side of practicing tracking, "*[I]t disappeared...but I think the more experience that we have, you learn how to be more effective in tracking animals in terms of what to look for and the habits of big game.*"

Fair chase in harvesting came in conflict with "other hunters." When informants described other hunters they were often telling stories of strangers or people they did not know well. P2 describes his worst experiences hunting:

> When we're with other people and they don't kill the deer right away and then you have to track the deer...One of my brothers brought a guest...They shot a deer and they didn't hit it very well...we spent four hours at night trying to track the deer through the woods...Wherever they hit it, it must have been enough that blood came out but it was just bleeding. We're sure the deer lived because after

about four hours...blood started slowly disappearing and the deer kept on going.

Here, the other hunter is following fair chase practices in tracking, but perhaps ethically should not have attempted the shot in the first place. More blatantly, some other hunters disregarded fair chase altogether. P10 described one encounter: "*There was a guy that had hit a deer and lost it. He just said no big deal...Some people just have this attitude, 'It's just a deer. There are plenty of deer. I'll get another one.' That just rubs me the wrong way.*" P13 related a case when a bowhunter tried shooting a buck but was unwilling to traverse difficult terrain to track the deer—thus this other hunter violated fair chase because "*the opportunity to shoot it came up without any regard as to whether or not he could retrieve it or wanted to retrieve it.*"

Once an animal is harvested—killed—hunters may treat the body respectfully. During participant observations of a mourning dove hunt, after we retrieved the body of a dove we shot, our mentor told us, "*Don't just throw the dove onto the dirt into a big pile of bodies like some hunters do. Gently place the body onto the dirt.*" He explained later that this was to show respect for the sacrifice the birds made. Part of this respect also means properly field dressing animals for sustenance. P3 told us he no longer hunts with his cousins. After taking five geese on their land, "*we said, 'That's plenty of meat, we're good.' As we were leaving we saw them toss their geese in a ditch...there were probably a dozen geese. We were just appalled...We said, 'What are you doing?' And they said, 'Oh, our freezer's full, we don't have any room,' so they were shooting them for fun and we don't like that.*" The killing of animals purely for fun did not fit P3's conception of fair chase.

This respect for animals is set in opposition to other hunters, but it is also done for the sake of the public perception of hunting, especially non-hunters. Photos and videos disseminated online may perpetuate practices that are not fair chase for hunters. P11 disparaged of a video posted online where a traditional bowhunter made a shot too far to be ethically sound. Hunter-related videos posted on Facebook that showed excessive guts, blood, kicking (spasms), etc. could offend non-hunters. P12 admonished photos of braggadocio: "*They're laying on top of the animal. They've got their feet up on its antlers, just like, 'I'm the man.'*" Our hunters carefully framed their photos to portray respect for animals by, for instance, cleaning the blood off and putting water in the eyes to prevent shrinking. Many of our informants were cognizant of the "redneck" stereotype that some public had of hunters and sought to show their ethics—respect for animal and land—to counter these views. P14 told us about those that glorify killing instead of hunting: "*I don't think we need to flaunt it like put the dead animal on the hood of your car and drive down the road. We need to be courteous to people who don't care to see that.*"

THE LAND

Fair chase also involves practices that lead to some understanding of the interactions between species behavior and the land they reside and traverse in. The dialectical elements here reflect the nature of this understanding and how it is achieved. What constitutes the normative ethic of being with nature in hunting is oppositionally understood by different groups.

Decoys and Calls

While decoys and calls are thought in terms of pursuing animals, hunters spoke of this equipment in terms of understandings and misunderstandings of the land and its wildlife. With decoys, the challenge lies in the hunter's ability to fool the animal into believing the decoy or call is a real animal. P9 describes his satisfaction in outsmarting ducks:

> You go through all this work. You plan your decoys. You get the set up that you want. You do a good job of calling...a flock of ducks or geese into you and you completely got them fooled to where they come...and set right in the decoys. That's your satisfaction right there.

P7 recalls jumping for joy the first time he called a turkey and brought him within range (despite not getting a good shot). Bird calling can be done via a number of different mechanisms—vocally, whistles/flutes, boxes, or slates—and is considered a different skill to master. There are a number of national turkey calling competition. P7 believes that calls improves one's understanding of animals: "*Not only do you have to learn how to use a call, but...when to use the call. You have to learn why the animals make certain sounds, so you're educating yourself.*'

The user and non-use of decoys and calls also reflects opposition between non-scientist and scientist notions of fair chase. P5, an avid waterfowl hunter and biologist, uses not only country competence but *scientific knowledge* to successfully harvest ducks. He says, "*I use 24 [decoys] and I try to mimic the species composition that I see in the area [of the lake] at the time. Most people don't...but that's what I do.*" He is disdainful of "robo-ducks," ducks which have motors and emulate wing movement. Robo-ducks are problematic for P5 because juvenile ducks are particularly susceptible to them; this may have unintended consequences from a biological point of view (discourages ducks from breeding).

Birds also get acclimated to the use of calls and decoys. P1 notes the effect of "over-calling," saying that birds get used to it and can determine what is really a bird call or not. As birds hear more and more calls in areas with many hunters, hunters are forced to use more elaborate call devices to fool birds. Ducks older than 1-year are wary of decoys (P9). Interestingly, P5 believes that when birds outsmart the decoy—outsmart the hunter—it deserves to get away: "*If a duck lands in decoys, most hunters will stand up, it'll jump up and they'll shoot it. Once it lands in my decoys I've said, 'That bird got by me. It's on base. It gets to go away. I'm not going to shoot at it.'...It seems fair to me. It beat me*" (P5). He does not believe in the second chance to harvest the duck that other hunters do.

Those who do not revel in the challenge of decoys cause a phenomena P9 called "pass shooting." In essence, hunters who do not strategically shoot through the careful use of decoys, camouflage, "*don't let the birds work in. They just stand and shoot at stuff flying around*" (P9). Waterfowl hunters are often in close vicinity of each other. As a result of the gun blast from neighboring shooters, hunters are forced to shoot birds scared off by the sound of guns. The lack of fair chase with other hunters forces the hunter to adopt that same, less ethical, strategy if they want any hope of harvesting birds.

The Lay of the Land

Part of fair chase involves being submerged within nature. Hunters who grew up around a tradition of hunting have gotten to know the land around them intimately. They have put the time in over the years to understand how animals interact with the land. P2 was taught wayfinding skills as a child so that he "*always had a visual concept of what the land looked like and where you're at and things like that. It helped you understand where you were hunting.*" P3 below describes how he searches for deer paths and hunting locations by spending time to know the lay of the land:

> [W]e...spend...time...looking for deer trails, looking for bedding or droppings...because often we'll want to set up a stand...so we'll scout and like,"These are some good trees and it's overlooking this water, so that could be good."...Let's say there's a trail that the deer normally walk and we find a way to avoid that and walk a different way.

When waterfowl hunting, P9's knowledge of the land he grew up hunting in and now helps manages is almost "cheating." Unlike other hunters that rely on gear like drapes (camo blinds), he knows where the natural vegetation is and can "brush it in" to camouflage himself. Hunters also share their land knowledge with each other and online; P14 relies on his uncle who has "*walked those hills and ravines since he was a kid*" to let him know the opportune time and place for hunting around his uncle's area.

Ways to skip the work to get the lay of the land were disparaged. All but one hunter were highly against the use of drones to scout for animals. P3 thought the intimate process of knowing the area is lost with drones when you could easily spot a herd.

Long-time hunters contrasted themselves with newcomers. P4 surmised, "*[N]ewer hunters...want to...be able to just hike into the woods...hike in for a quarter of a mile, sit down, wait for a couple of hours and be able to get a deer.*" Putting her biologist cap on, she continued, "*The kind of population levels that deer managers are concerned with keeping the population at is usually lower than what a hunter who wants to be able to get a deer with very little effort is going to be able to be satisfied.*" Thus, while the experienced, "fair chase" hunters feels joy in knowing the land in which they would hunt, the modern, busy professional, the "*opening weekend hunters*" (P7) who hunts only when the season opens needs to maximize their time on such excursions. Hunters such as P12 acknowledge why technology is alluring, "*It's about time management...I don't have time to go sit in the tree and not know that there's going to be an opportunity for a big deer, so I'm going to control the variables, isolate the location where my odds are better. That's technology use to my advantage to get that deer.*"

Country competence with land also entails what we call *country toughness*, a willingness to tough it out to achieve fair chase. Country toughness is not embraced by many hunters; this is particularly evident in the behavior of deer near public land parking lots. In workshops we attended and in interviews, we were told that deer were more skittish and scarce within a hundred yards of parking lots. P4 noted that during hunting season deer typically stick to areas where hunters do not go. The use of all-terrain vehicles is seen as violating country toughness. They allow hunters to easily access remote, difficult to reach locations that typical automobiles could not reach.

Interestingly, we saw oppositions between country competence and scientific knowledge. Put simply, those with country competence had self-confidence over the lay of the land. When the DNR institutes new regulations based on their own, scientifically-based (e.g., surveys) methods, they often collide with this self-confidence. P1 described the situation when someone questioned his reduction of the rabbit season:

> He's like, "Well, I've got rabbits everywhere. Why are you changing the season?" I said, "Overall in the state, we don't." I said, "You may have your little paradise, but if you look at the habitat as a whole, that's not sustainable."

Trail cams, mentioned later, help bolster hunters' self-confidence on their lay of the land. For the DNR, many hunters have views that are fixed locally in time and place, while they—as scientists—have a global view informed by ecology and biology; they understand for instance how movement of populations of one species can effect other species in the state.

Trail Cams

Trail cams are time and/or motion activated cameras deployed on land by hunters to collect data on movement and habits of various species. Some cams require hunters to manually return back to them to retrieve video, while newer models can wirelessly transmit photos or alert hunters of new data.

For some hunters, trail cams violate the spontaneous, fortuitous character of nature. Rather than relying on a deep knowledge of deer—for example, scouting and tracking—cameras allow hunters to be far removed from the country. P1 explained a new behavior exhibited by deer hunters relying on trail cams:

> They're seeing these big bucks come in at night on these cameras, and they'll go the entire season and not shoot a deer because they're waiting for that one animal now...They name the deer...[T]hey're almost thinking that those are their animals. They see them every day on their camera. That they're not moving off the property...Most of the time, these cameras are catching these animals at night. A lot of those bucks are nocturnal. You're never going to shoot that buck.

There are a number of remarkable points made in this quote. First, trail cams are a means for hunters to survey public land. Second, they encourage hunters to target specific bucks (each season, hunters are limited in the number of deer they can harvest), those with large antlers (the belief is larger antlers means a wiser, more challenging deer to harvest). Hunters obsess over that "monster" buck (P5) or see bucks "develop all summer long" (P6) and begin to feel that they own particular wildlife. Third, the bucks they most desire and see in the trail cams may be nearly impossible to kill. Some hunters refer to these deer as "ghost" deer (P10). Other hunters refer to the cam-sighted deers as their "hit list" (P11). Lastly, while conservation officers told us that the American ethos of fair chase dictates that no one can "own" wildlife, trail cams encourage the exact opposite.

Some of our hunters however believe that general knowledge of the wildlife inhabiting their local hunting grounds can make hunting more informed (which trails to go to, which animals are around) and enjoyable. For one, it can give hunters hope that there are deer in the area. Some hunters reported nearly giving up on hunting because the situation seemed hopeless with no recent sightings. P14 remarked that other hunters like to be able to watch deer grow and being able to recognize when their favorite deers are pregnant, have children, etc. to see that the deer population is healthy (ensuring more future hunts). Thus trail cams can help hunters enjoy hunting itself by informing them about future, exciting possibilities of the land they occupy. Many hunters remarked that those who simply lacked the time (e.g., those that live in the city) to actively scout and track deer found the trail cam useful to manage what little time they had in the country best.

At the same time, trail cams were also seen by some hunters as replacing country competence and corrupting nature. With cameras, traditional means of looking for deer are substituted. Without tracking skills—looking for scrapes, signs, and tracks—hunters are now "*tracking all the movement based on cameras. They're not having to think about patterns and where the deer are at and doing a lot of pre-scouting. They just go set their cameras up, and that's it.*" (P1). P11 related how the very maintenance of cameras also disturbs nature because the hunter is "*constantly going out in the woods to go check his cameras, which is leaving more scent, more disturbing the wildlife, and it can hurt you later on when you go to hunt.*"

HCI & NATURE: WORLDS OF OPPOSITION

We have shown that hunters rhetorically describe their practices of the hunt and in the land dialectically—in terms of oppositional forces. Explaining why they do what they do for fair chase is rendered more evident when set against practices they do not approve. Crucially, this dialectic illustrates that hunters are not simply one group but rather composed of multiple social worlds [37]. For instance, though bowhunters can be thought of as inhabiting their own social world, they are nonetheless cognizant that in nature they will coincide with social worlds which encapsulate the values and practices of hunters skilled in other weapons. Each social world encompasses a set of particular practices that, when set in opposition of another social world's practices, simultaneously unify and reify their notion of fair chase. Such dialectics reinforce the fact that the practices of hunters cannot be separated from their values. The potential outcome of their actions—the death of a living being—and the scrutiny they face from others make this community especially sensitive to their values.

We suggest that designing technologies for nature and its inhabitants must address the confluence of normative values and the diverse practices that reflect a heterogeneity of values. Fair chase as a moral signpost can be readily explained by all hunters as proper challenge with game, respect of the harvest, and communion with nature; nevertheless, by doing fair chase, the social worlds of hunters interpret fair chase, and, by doing it differently, embody variegated beliefs. In the following subsections, we have labeled the various guises in which the dialectics of fair chase arose in our findings. These dialectics yield sensitizing concepts [4] for HCI practitioners and researchers to incorporate when designing technologies for subcultures of nature.

Weapon Communities

Oppositional views on weapons (rifles vs. muzzleloaders, guns vs. bows, bows vs. crossbows, bows vs. traditional bows, DNR vs. bowhunters) centered about debates on the role of weapons in creating a proper challenge when hunting game. We saw how technologies are intertwined with differing views of engaging fairly with nature—encouraging development of skills (one shot, one kill) via handicaps, prioritizing proximity to nature, tying values with technology choice (crossbow vs. bows), and engaging passively vs. actively with nature. This dialectic suggests that design needs to consider how technologies can serve to purposefully limit the capabilities of the user, changing the power relationship between users and nature. Rather than technology acting as a mediator for nature—making it easier to engage or deal with nature—it may make it harder to be with nature. This brings into question the meaning of engagement. If engagement also means commitment and treating each encounter with nature as special, rather than mundane, then technologies that draw out the rarity and spontaneity of engagement with nature should be designed. This needs to be balanced with the desire to easily track and survey nature with technology [3]. Past HCI studies of hunting have argued that the challenge of hunting (e.g., tracking animals, shooting with low visibility at a stand) adds to the satisfaction of the hunting experience. Yet, we have shown that there is no single conception of what makes something a "challenge"—to what degree and when does technology need to handicap or make each interaction count to make something a challenge?

Non-Hunter vs. Hunter

Oppositional views between non-hunters and hunters revolved around debates of respecting animals via hunting vs. observing wildlife (e.g., wildlife photography). Design opportunities exist to allow both parties to learn and experience the commitment choices each mode of animal interaction entails. Fair chase was also a symbol hunters needed to maintain for public (citizens and legislators), often non-hunter, perception that was disseminated online through photos and videos. Those who choose not to engage with nature may get a glimpse of those that do. As designers create technologies for those invested in nature, they may need to consider the forward-facing effects of their designs. For example, does the technology create nature lovers whose values are compatible with those of non-nature goers? Just as non-hunters expect a romanticized notion of hunting that hunters need to be aware of when taking photos posing with their harvest, designers need to consider how to properly glorify success in nature with technology.

The "Other" Hunter

Oppositional views between ethical vs. "other," non-ethical (or less ethical) hunters were brought out when discussing the harvesting of animals, especially with regards to ethical shooting and the wounding and tracking of animals. Hunters are always cognizant of the kind of environment created by "other" hunters. This dialectic suggests that interacting with nature, even if not done collaboratively, is always done in the presence of others. We saw that there is a desire for some hunters to commune indirectly with like-minded hunters (e.g., bowhunters with other bowhunters but not crossbow hunters); we might consider whether designs can somehow ensure an instantiation of nature that users desire to experience—one inhabited with actors of certain value. This dialectic also brings to the forefront whether technologies for nature should consider dealing with non-ethical behavior in nature and how designed technologies may eventually be appropriated for non-ethical behavior. For instance, our study found that hunters were sometimes forced to adopt practices they found unethical. Those ethical and more skillful hunters have learned how to immerse themselves in nature, emulating nature (e.g., with decoys and calls). Thus designers may need to think about avoiding a shallow engagement with nature that non-ethical users may have; designs should consider how users can gain a competence in understanding and even becoming an animal. Because what it means to violate fair chase is debatable, opportunities for design exist to bridge an understanding of why particular fair chase practices are frowned upon by some but deemed acceptable by other hunters. A particularly interesting application could teach hunters how other hunters create their own practices of "fairness" by giving a voice to animals (e.g., P5's story about letting ducks who land live).

Steeped in Country Competence

Oppositional views between those with vs. those without country competence often came up when talking about those who had grown up in a tradition of hunting in their local land vs. "weekend" hunters or newcomers. Country competence comes from years of communing with nature, for example, taking advantage of winds (P12) to identify the right spot for turkey hunting; such skill is tacit knowledge that technology may not offer. Often coupled with country competence, country toughness was set in opposition of those relying on technology, bypassing real immersion into nature. Designers may need to reveal the harshness of nature and the benefits of commitment (e.g., hunting farther away from parking lots can lead to better harvest). Country competence can possibly exclude early onset adult hunters—how might technologies bridge old-timers and newcomers with nature? Many new hunters, those from the city or working professionals, will never have a lay of the land—what role can technologies play in enabling newcomers without altogether destroying country competence? This tension suggests that designs should consider how technologies may supplant traditional practices with nature. Designers need to also consider how country competence informs the side-effects that maintaining technology has on nature (e.g., humans leaving a scent). This sustainability issue requires systems that help us understand how animals themselves become aware and wary of both humans and technology. Lastly, we saw that a different sort of country competence with animals arose with trail cams—people became intimately familiar with deer and grew up with them. Designs have potential to give users the "lay of the animals."

Scientific vs. Country Knowledge

Finally, the oppositional views between those with country competence vs. scientific knowledge frames those with handed-down, well-honed knowledge of the land and in hunting as problematic for those (e.g., the DNR) with scientific knowledge. This dialectic suggests that designs for nature need to reconcile scientific expertise with knowledgeable amateurs [14]. Technology that bridges the two perspectives should engage with varied perspectives into the ecology of nature—for instance the local vs. global views of nature. When building technologies to educate non-experts about nature, designs need to leverage the expertise of different parties (e.g., past work has involved biologists and landscape architects [34, 11, 10]). Country competence is usually done in rural areas—areas not often taken seriously in HCI as places for innovation and real crafting; future designs should not only take scientific knowledge seriously (which it already does so well) but rural or country knowledge as well. Opportunities may exist for designs to create greater empathy between these two social worlds.

These dialectics are not exhaustive nor are they clean-cut distinctions. Weapon communities have much to do with the tensions between hunters and "other" hunters *and* the tensions between those with and without country competence (e.g., bowhunters may say they have more country competence than rifle hunters). The reader is encouraged to develop their own dialectics and sensitizing concepts from our findings. We have emphasized that the dialectics yield design opportunities but opportunities that are always coupled with caveats. Hence, designing for nature will always be about acting between—balancing, bridging, converting, committing, and so on.

CONCLUSION

Our approach seeks to strengthen "the voice of the participants" when writing about and conducting a VSD investigation [6]. We take seriously the rationale our hunters gave for the practices they do in the name of fair chase. The discourse of the hunters themselves, in a way, establishes a coexistence of what Borning and Muller [6] identify as universal and culturally-specific values. In the hunting subculture, fair chase embodies a set of canonical values, yet the details of how hunters accomplish these values reveals a set of opposing interpretations—and thus their *own* values—of what fair chase means. Therefore, canonical values serve a rhetorical function to unify social worlds but differing practices belie the variegated social worlds of hunters. We emphasize that our hunters, as they would readily acknowledge, are not paragons of virtue—they all have experience violating their (ever-changing) notion of fair chase. Nonetheless, they know their ideals and, significantly, what values *others*, in their oppositional social worlds, hold. In such dialectics, we presented sensitizing concepts that complicate the design for "users" of nature. As experts of nature, our informants not only inspire designs for hunting but allow us to reconsider nature in general.

REFERENCES

1. Claudio Aporta and Eric Higgs. 2005. Satellite Culture: Global Positioning Systems, Inuit Wayfinding, and the Need for a New Account of Technology. *Current Anthropology* 46, 5 (Dec. 2005), 729–753. DOI: http://dx.doi.org/10.1086/432651
2. Fredrik Aspling and Oskar Juhlin. 2017. Theorizing Animal–Computer Interaction as Machinations. *International Journal of Human-Computer Studies* 98 (February 2017), 135–149. DOI: http://dx.doi.org/10.1016/j.ijhcs.2016.05.005
3. Nicola J. Bidwell and David Browning. 2010. Pursuing Genius Loci: Interaction Design and Natural Places. *Personal and Ubiquitous Computing* 14, 1 (Jan. 2010), 15–30. DOI: http://dx.doi.org/10.1007/s00779-009-0217-8
4. Herbert Blumer. 1954. What is Wrong with Social Theory? *American Sociological Review* 19, 1 (1954), 3–10. DOI:http://dx.doi.org/10.2307/2088165
5. Mark Blythe, Kristina Andersen, Rachel Clarke, and Peter Wright. 2016. Anti-Solutionist Strategies: Seriously Silly Design Fiction. In *Proceedings of the SIGCHI Conference on Human Factors in Computing Systems (CHI '16)*. ACM, New York, NY, USA, 4968–4978. DOI: http://dx.doi.org/10.1145/2858036.2858482
6. Alan Borning and Michael Muller. 2012. Next Steps for Value Sensitive Design. In *Proceedings of the SIGCHI Conference on Human Factors in Computing Systems (CHI '12)*. ACM, New York, NY, USA, 1125–1134. DOI: http://dx.doi.org/10.1145/2207676.2208560
7. Barry Brown and Oskar Juhlin. 2015. *Enjoying Machines*. MIT Press, Cambridge, MA.
8. Nicholas Carr. 2014. *The Glass Cage: Automation and Us* (1 edition ed.). W. W. Norton & Company, New York.
9. Kathy Charmaz. 2006. *Constructing Grounded Theory: A Practical Guide Through Qualitative Analysis*. SAGE Publications Ltd, London.
10. Mark Cottman-Fields, Margot Brereton, and Paul Roe. 2013. Virtual Birding: Extending an Environmental Pastime into the Virtual World for Citizen Science. In *Proceedings of the SIGCHI Conference on Human Factors in Computing Systems (CHI '13)*. ACM, New York, NY, USA, 2029–2032. DOI: http://dx.doi.org/10.1145/2470654.2466268
11. Mark Cottman-Fields, Margot Brereton, Jason Wimmer, and Paul Roe. 2014. Collaborative Extension of Biodiversity Monitoring Protocols in the Bird Watching Csommunity. In *Proceedings of the Participatory Design Conference (PDC '14)*. ACM, New York, NY, USA, 111–114. DOI: http://dx.doi.org/10.1145/2662155.2662193
12. Matthew Desmond. 2008. *On the Fireline: Living and Dying with Wildland Firefighters*. University of Chicago Press.
13. Lindsay Ems. 2014. Amish Workarounds: Toward a Dynamic, Contextualized View of Technology Use. *Journal of Amish and Plain Anabaptist Studies* 2, 1 (April 2014), 42–58. http://hdl.handle.net/1811/59690
14. Gary Alan Fine. 1998. *Morel Tales*. Harvard University Press, Cambridge, MA.
15. Anke Fischer, Vesna Kereži, Beatriz Arroyo, Miguel Mateos-Delibes, Degu Tadie, Asanterabi Lowassa, Olve Krange, and Ketil Skogen. 2013. (De)legitimising Hunting – Discourses Over the Morality of Hunting in Europe and Eastern Africa. *Land Use Policy* 32 (May 2013), 261–270. DOI: http://dx.doi.org/10.1016/j.landusepol.2012.11.002
16. Batya Friedman. 2004. Value Sensitive Design. In *Berkshire Encyclopedia of Human-Computer Interaction*. Berkshire Publishing Group LLC, Great Barrington, MA, 769–773.
17. Christian Geiger, Simon Thiele, Laurid Meyer, Stefan Meyer, Lutz Hören, and Daniel Drochtert. 2013. Goin' Goblins - Iterative Design of an Entertaining Archery Experience. In *Proceedings of the International Conference on Advances in Computer Entertainment Technology (ACE '13)*. Springer-Verlag, New York, 284–295. DOI: http://dx.doi.org/10.1007/978-3-319-03161-3_20
18. Sebastian Göbel, Christian Geiger, Christin Heinze, and Dionysios Marinos. 2010. Creating a Virtual Archery Experience. In *Proceedings of the International Conference on Advanced Visual Interfaces (AVI '10)*. ACM, New York, NY, USA, 337–340. DOI: http://dx.doi.org/10.1145/1842993.1843056
19. Jonna Häkkilä, Keith Cheverst, Johannes Schöning, Nicola J. Bidwell, Simon Robinson, and Ashley Colley. 2016. NatureCHI. In *Proceedings of the SIGCHI Extended Abstracts on Human Factors in Computing Systems (CHI EA '16)*. ACM Press, New York, NY, USA, 3574–3580. DOI: http://dx.doi.org/10.1145/2851581.2856495
20. Don Ihde. 1990. *Technology and the Lifeworld: From Garden to Earth*. Indiana University Press, Bloomington, IN.
21. Oskar Juhlin and Alexandra Weilenmann. 2008. Hunting for Fun: Solitude and Attentiveness in Collaboration. In *Proceedings of the SIGCHI Conference on Computer Supported Cooperative Work (CSCW '08)*. ACM, New York, NY, USA, 57–66. DOI: http://dx.doi.org/10.1145/1460563.1460575
22. Søren Kierkegaard. 2006. *Kierkegaard: Fear and Trembling*. Cambridge University Press, New York. Edited by C. Stephen Evans and Sylvia Walsh.

23. Christopher A. Le Dantec, Erika Shehan Poole, and Susan P. Wyche. 2009. Values As Lived Experience: Evolving Value Sensitive Design in Support of Value Discovery. In *Proceedings of the SIGCHI Conference on Human Factors in Computing Systems (CHI '09)*. ACM, New York, NY, USA, 1141–1150. DOI: http://dx.doi.org/10.1145/1518701.1518875

24. Aldo Leopold and Charles Walsh Schwartz. 1970. *A Sand County Almanac: With Other Essays on Conservation from Round River*. Oxford University Press.

25. Charles J. List. 2004. On the Moral Distinctiveness of Sport Hunting. *Environmental Ethics* 26, 2 (2004), 155–169. DOI: http://dx.doi.org/10.5840/enviroethics200426227

26. Brian Luke. 1997. A Critical Analysis of Hunters' Ethics. *Environmental Ethics* 19, 1 (1997), 25–44. DOI: http://dx.doi.org/10.5840/enviroethics199719137

27. John Mullen. 1981. The Discreet Charm of the Bourgeoisie. In *Kierkegaard's Philosophy: Self Deception and Cowardice in the Present Age*. The New American Library, Inc., New York, 23–33.

28. Bob Norton. 2007. *The Hunter: Developmental Stages and Ethics*. Riverbend Publishing, Helena, MT.

29. Edward of Norwich. 2005. *The Master of Game*. University of Pennsylvania Press, Philadelphia, PA. Foreword by Theodore Roosevelt.

30. Yutaro Ohashi and Makoto Arisawa. 2006. Nature Talk: A Proposed Audible Database System for Environmental Learning. In *Proceeding of the SIGCHI Conference on Interaction Design and Children (IDC '06)*. ACM, New York, NY, USA, 167–168. DOI: http://dx.doi.org/10.1145/1139073.1139077

31. José Ortega y Gasset. 1972. *Meditations on Hunting*. Macmillan Publishing Company, New York. Translated by Howard B. Wescott.

32. Mikko Paldanius, Tuula Kärkkäinen, Kaisa Väänänen-Vainio-Mattila, Oskar Juhlin, and Jonna Häkkilä. 2011. Communication Technology for Human-Dog Interaction. In *Proceedings of the SIGCHI Conference on Human Factors in Computing Systems (CHI '11)*. ACM, New York, NY, USA, 2641–2650. DOI: http://dx.doi.org/10.1145/1978942.1979329

33. Y. Rogers, S. Price, G. Fitzpatrick, R. Fleck, E. Harris, H. Smith, C. Randell, H. Muller, C. O'Malley, D. Stanton, M. Thompson, and M. Weal. 2004. Ambient Wood: Designing New Forms of Digital Augmentation for Learning Outdoors. In *Proceedings of the SIGCHI Conference on Interaction Design and Children (IDC '04)*. ACM, New York, NY, USA, 3–10. DOI: http://dx.doi.org/10.1145/1017833.1017834

34. Kimiko Ryokai, Lora Oehlberg, Michael Manoochehri, and Alice Agogino. 2011. GreenHat: Exploring the Natural Environment Through Experts' Perspectives. In *Proceedings of the SIGCHI Conference on Human Factors in Computing Systems (CHI '11)*. ACM, New York, NY, USA, 2149–2152. DOI: http://dx.doi.org/10.1145/1978942.1979254

35. Paul Shepard. 1997. *The Others: How Animals Made Us Human*. Island Press, Washington, DC.

36. Sherry B. Ortner. 2006. *Anthropology and Social Theory: Culture, Power, and the Acting Subject*. Duke University Press Books, Durham, NC.

37. Anselm Strauss. 1982. Social Worlds and Legitimation Processes. *Studies in Symbolic Interaction* 4 (1982), 171–190.

38. Norman Makoto Su. 2013. The Social Life of Tunes: Representing the Aesthetics of Reception. In *Proceedings of the European Conference on Computer Supported Cooperative Work (ECSCW '13)*. Springer-Verlag, London, 207–228.

39. Norman Makoto Su and Erik Stolterman. 2016. A Design Approach for Authenticity and Technology. In *Proceedings of the SIGCHI Conference on Designing Interactive Systems (DIS '16)*. ACM, New York, NY, USA, 643–655. DOI: http://dx.doi.org/10.1145/2901790.2901869

40. Norman Makoto Su and Lulu Wang. 2015. From Third to Surveilled Place: The Mobile in Irish Pubs. In *Proceedings of the SIGCHI Conference on Human Factors in Computing Systems (CHI '15)*. ACM, New York, NY, USA, 1659–1668. DOI: http://dx.doi.org/10.1145/2702123.2702574

41. The Boone and Crockett Club. 2016. The Boone and Crockett Club on Fair Chase. (Sept. 2016). https://www.boone-crockett.org/pdf/On_Fair_Chase.pdf

42. The Pope and Young Club. 2016. Rules of Fair Chase. (2016). https://pope-young.org/fairchase/

43. Alexandra Weilenmann and Oskar Juhlin. 2011. Understanding people and animals. In *Proceedings of the SIGCHI Conference on Human Factors in Computing Systems (CHI '11)*. ACM, New York, NY, USA, 2631–2640. DOI: http://dx.doi.org/10.1145/1978942.1979328

44. Danielle Wilde, Eric Harris, Yvonne Rogers, and Cliff Randell. 2003. The Periscope: Supporting a Computer Enhanced Field Trip for Children. *Personal and Ubiquitous Computing* 7, 3-4 (July 2003), 227–233. DOI: http://dx.doi.org/10.1007/s00779-003-0230-2

45. Susan Wyche, Phoebe Sengers, and Rebecca E. Grinter. 2006. Historical Analysis: Using the Past to Design the Future. In *Proceedings of the International Conference on Ubiquitous Computing (UBICOMP '06)*. Springer-Verlag, Berlin, 35–51. http://dx.doi.org/10.1007/11853565_3

46. Ron Yeh, Chunyuan Liao, Scott Klemmer, François Guimbretière, Brian Lee, Boyko Kakaradov, Jeannie Stamberger, and Andreas Paepcke. 2006. ButterflyNet: A Mobile Capture and Access System for Field Biology Research. In *Proceedings of the SIGCHI Conference on Human Factors in Computing Systems (CHI '06)*. ACM Press, New York, NY, USA, 571–580. DOI: http://dx.doi.org/10.1145/1124772.1124859

Exploring Seasonality in Mobile Cultural Heritage

David McGookin[1], Koray Tahiroğlu[2], Tuomas Vaittinen[1], Mikko Kytö[1], Beatrice Monastero[1], Juan Carlos Vasquez[2]

[1]Department of Computer Science
Aalto University
Espoo, Finland
firstname.lastname@aalto.fi
www.davidmcgookin.net

[2]Department of Media
Aalto University
Espoo, Finland
firstname.lastname@aalto.fi
sopi.aalto.fi

ABSTRACT
We present results of an investigation into the role of seasonality in mobile cultural heritage applications. 45 participants in 26 groups used one of two applications when visiting the Finnish recreational island of Seurasaari. Each provided summer and winter content, but varied in how this was presented. We uncovered how users consider seasonality in content, seasonal preferences, as well as how different media becomes more or less interesting if shown in or out of season. We present design considerations for future researchers to consider seasonality in cultural heritage applications.

Author Keywords
Cultural Heritage; Seasonality; Location-Based Interaction; Mixed Reality; Outdoor Heritage Site; Open-Air Museum

ACM Classification Keywords
H.5.1 Multimedia Information Systems: Artificial, augmented, and virtual realities; H.5.2 User Interfaces: Auditory (non-speech) feedback, Prototyping

INTRODUCTION AND BACKGROUND
Recently, there has been increasing study into the digital augmentation of outdoor cultural heritage sites. Such work focuses on communicating the lived experience - how people, their activities and events from the past can be experienced by visitors in the present. Although research has focused on a range cultural heritage sites [7, 8, 6, 11, 12, 1], work often uses similar techniques, with digital content geo-located in specific areas of a site, and accessed *in-situ* via a device the user carries or wears (such as a smartphone [7]) [10, 15, 2].

Commonality in solutions is largely due to the identified importance of fitting digital content into the environmental context [3, 4]. As noted by Smith [14]: *"heritage is not the historic monument, archaeological site, or museum artefact, but rather the activities that occur at them"*. Without considering such fit (both spatially and semantically), the relationship between digital and physical can be confusing, unconvincing or lost (e.g. GPS errors showing content in the wrong place).

CHI 2017, May 06 - 11, 2017, Denver, CO, USA

ACM 978-1-4503-4655-9/17/05...$15.00
DOI: http://dx.doi.org/10.1145/3025453.3025803

Figure 1. Left: An overview of the island, illustrating key features. Map image ©OpenStreetMap contributors. Right: The festival grounds in winter and summer, illustrating the significant seasonal variation.

Whilst work has considered how to fit content to the physical environment, there has been little consideration of how dynamic changes in that environment should affect content. For example, the environment and activities at McGookin *et al's* rural Roman hill fort [7] and Ciolfi and McLoughlins' open-air museum of 19th century life [2] would change significantly between summer and winter. However, they did not consider how digital content should change in response. Only O'Keefe *et al.* [9], in their framework on location-based storytelling, briefly discuss the 'volatility' of the environment, suggesting different stories should be used in summer and winter. However, they provide no study of this. Switching digital content to reflect seasons is a practical solution. However, such changes in a site are also part of its cultural heritage. Visitors may only visit a site once, so would gain no understanding of how it changes over a year.

There is a lack of research on how to both incorporate and reflect such seasonality to visitors. More importantly, we know nothing of how visitors would wish to consider it. Should only the current season be presented? Would visitors want to access out of season content, and if so, how? We take a first step in this by studying a seasonally enabled cultural heritage application for the Finnish island of Seurasaari.

SEURASAARI ISLAND

Located in central Helsinki, Finland, Seurasaari Island was founded as a recreational park in the 1800's. It is permanently open and free. It is significant in both natural and cultural heritage, mostly forested, and a habitat for a wide range of wildlife. The park has significant cultural heritage itself, with buildings dating from its founding as a park that house a cafe and restaurant, as well as the boathouse used by visitors to reach the island by steamboat before a bridge was built in the 1970's. In addition, the island contains an open-air museum, with traditional buildings (such as a farm, church) relocated from other parts of Finland. Whilst the museum grounds are part of the park, entering the buildings requires an entrance fee. The island is popular with both locals and tourists, and has significant seasonal variation. Temperatures usually vary between -20 to +20 °C between winter and summer, and daylight can vary by a maximum of 12 hours. Activities taking place in summer (such as numerous folk dancing and music events, and the major midsummer celebrations) are very different in winter (with fewer events and a generally quieter feel) (see Figure 1). The impact of seasonality is also found in the cultural history of the island. For example, steamboats to ferry passengers to the island couldn't run in winter, so a bridge across the frozen sea was laid.

EXPLORE

We worked with Seurasaarisäätiö [5] - who manage the island - to develop a mobile Android 'app' to support understanding Seurasaari's cultural heritage during a visit. During discussions, the importance of seasonality was highlighted, as was the 'app' avoiding distraction from the environment, and supporting free exploration of the island, rather than constraining visitors to a tour route (e.g. [6]).

Our final design, called Explore, primarily augmented 6 areas (see Figure 1) - although some content was placed outside these. Images and videos from the foundation's archive (both with text descriptions), as well as audio vignets describing something about the activities of a place, were geo-located at relevant locations in each area. Each content item was triggered as a user walked within 10-30m (determined via GPS). A standard Android notification (using a custom sound, vibration and icon) was presented (so the device screen did not need to be on). A dialog was also presented when the screen was turned on (see Figure 2 (A)). Responding to the notification presented the content, which was also marked on a map for later access (Figure 2 (B and C)).

To explore seasonality two sets of content were created. One represented a summer perspective (current season - since the study was run in summer), and another that represented a winter perspective (other season). Two variants of Explore were created to present these. Explore Switchable (ES) allowed participants to explicitly select between content sets via an icon on the app's toolbar (see Figure 2 (B)). Only content in the selected season could be discovered or viewed, but users could switch between the two at any time. The default was set to summer. Explore Combined (EC) made both winter and summer content available at all times. I.e. both content sets were treated as one. Different icons and notification sounds

(A) (B) (C)

Figure 2. Cropped screenshots illustrating both variants of Explore. A: A notification and dialog were presented when new content was found. B: The map view for Explore Switchable, note the icon in the toolbar to change seasons. C: The map view for Explore Combined. Note the different icons used to indicate seen winter and summer content.

were used to indicate which season content was from (see Figure 2 (C)). Our objective with both Explore versions was to encourage participants to consider how they would wish to consider seasonality, rather than designing one as a 'best' option. Explore Switchable (closest to the proposal of O'Keefe *et al.* [9]), allows users to focus on only one season (including the current one), whilst Explore Combined illustrates the differences between the seasons as a primary feature.

STUDY DESIGN

Our study ran over 5 days in June 2016. 45 participants (aged 15-79, mean 44.7 years, 24 female) in 26 groups (10 individuals, 11 groups of two, 4 groups of three and 1 group of four) took part. 10 groups were composed of locals, 15 were composed of tourists (either Finnish or Foreign), 1 was a mixture. Each participant received a movie ticket or Moomin mug (∼11 Euro) as compensation. We recruited groups as they arrived on the island via the bridge (see Figure 1). Participants completed a consent form and questionnaire. Each group was given an Android smartphone running one version of Explore. 11 used Explore Combined and 16 Explore Switchable (further discussed in Explicit Seasonal Changes). As participants often focus on the screen if the device is carried in the hand [10], each had a lanyard so it could be worn around the neck. Groups could use Explore as much or little as they wanted. Devices were collected as each group left the island at the end of their visit, and an interview conducted.

RESULTS

Group interviews were transcribed and coded using a framework approach [13], with differences between the two versions and views on season content used as initial codes. These were supplemented with on-device interaction logs.

Overall Use

Visit length was similar in both versions but varied widely between participants, reflecting the different purposes and time constraints of their visit (Explore Switchable (ES) M=108min S.D.=78min, Explore Combined (EC) M=107min, S.D.=53min). Tourists focused on the open-air museum area, either leaving afterwards but more often exploring another part of the island. Locals mostly came for a particular purpose (e.g. to walk around the coast). Whilst they walked through the open-air museum grounds (as it lies on the main path) they did not visit the buildings.

Groups stated they visited areas they already intended to visit. Explore did not change those plans, rather it helped inform participants of interesting content in those areas. The majority of groups used the lanyard, and participants only interacted with the device as a result of notifications. On average there was one interaction per group that was not the result of a notification. Most notifications were responded to ((ES) M=74.2%, (EC) M=87.6%). Common reasons for not responding included talking to someone else in the group or being engaged in another activity. Participants agreed that they felt their focus was on the environment (ES M=2.4 S.D.=1.3, EC M=2.9 S.D.=1.5, 7-point Likert), and were neutral to slightly disagree that the device distracted them from the environment (ES M=4.7 S.D.=1.6, EC M=4.4 S.D.=1.8). Whilst participants often did respond to notifications, they did not feel under pressure to do so.

Explicit Seasonal Changes

The first 12 Explore Switchable groups had summer as the default season (ESs). However, interaction logs showed only 2 groups changed season, so most saw no winter content. To investigate why we ran the final 4 groups with winter as the default season (ESw) (which is why the number of ES and EC groups is different). Only 6 of the 16 Explore Switchable groups changed season (a total of 10 season change events), 4 of these to summer from a winter default. Two main reasons for participants not switching seasons were identified.

Firstly, participants forgot about the ability to switch seasons. As interaction was driven by the notifications, it was easy to miss the opportunity to switch. However, participants often regretted not having done so. PG8 (ESs): *"I completely forgot about it and that was a pity because I thought I would have enjoyed it"*. PG4 (ESs): *"To be honest, I completely forgot. In retrospect, it bothers me. I should have looked at the winter photos too."*.

Secondly, was the preference for the content of a particular season. Overall this was for summer, as this best fitted the current environment: PG9 (ESs): *"no, we kept it on summer because we figured that was where we were"*. Two groups using the summer default versions tried winter for a short time but soon switched back, whilst 3 of the 4 groups who started with a default of winter either immediately changed or ended in summer. PG25 (ESw): *"I changed it to summer because it is summer"*. The overall view of these participants was that content should be season appropriate. PG9 (ESs): *"the idea was to keep it on summer because that's where we were and that people came in winter would put on winter."*. Although a minority, the opposite view was also expressed, where participants changed to winter because it was different. PG1 (ESs): *"I think that the more interesting thing is that it is different so it is winter. For me"*.

Related to this were perceived issues that trying to view more than one season would cause, encouraging a preference. For example, PG5 (ESs) felt he did not have enough time to view winter as well: *"If I would have much more time, why not."*, and wanted to avoid having too much content to view *"not too overflowing with all the information at once, so I just do summer"*. PG21 (ESs) noted they avoided switching as they didn't want interaction with the device to distract from the environment: *"we just want more to experience the nature, we don't want to play with the phone all the time"*.

Explore Combined Use

In comparison to Explore Switchable, Explore Combined raised relatively few comments. The majority of participants had no issue in distinguishing between summer and winter content, even though these were mixed. The variation in notification sounds was found to be effective. PG2 (ES): *"You almost heard it already from the sounds. Once you got the notification.... It became obvious through that."*. Other participants didn't need to rely on the notification sounds, finding that the content itself was obvious once viewed. PG19 (ES): *"when we realised that the images are -...- different, what plays during winter and summer"*. However, a small number did find mixing seasonal content confusing. PG3 (ES): *"It was actually a bit confusing. I was wondering why it shows winter... until (daughter's name) said that maybe its nice for some tourists to know how it looks like in the winter."*.

Some participants found notifications to be too frequent, in comparison to Explore Switchable participants who did not raise the issue. Due to all content being available, Explore Combined participants received more notifications (EC M=42.9, S.D.=17, ES M=31.3, S.D.=15). However, the impact of this is disproportionate, as some areas have a high amount of both winter and summer content (e.g. the open-air museum area - see Figure 1), whilst others (such as the festival grounds - see Figure 1) have more summer than winter content. This meant that in some places combining content led to a small increase in notifications, where in other areas combining seasons led to a significant increase. For some participants this resulted in the device requiring too much attention. PG3 (EC) *"maybe since the places the app played had something to show, they were quite concentrated... ... now it was maybe a bit too much info at the same time"*.

Viewing Out of Season Content

As Explore Switchable participants often didn't switch seasons, the majority of out of season viewing came from using Explore Combined. Such content often enhanced participants' understanding of the island. One member of PG14 (EC), who were tourists, noted how his assumptions about winter had been changed by Explore: *"when it is weather like today you can't even imagine, oh in winter it's cold and nobody on the island. It was interesting that people come in winter here to walk through the island. I thought it's closed and nobody is here."*. This view also extended to locals. PG12 (EC): *"I found it interesting because I don't usually visit Seurasaari, and when I do it's usually summer. So I don't get to see the place during winter."*. Visitors found this new perspective enhanced their visit, and to some extent supported the feeling of exploring in winter. PG23 (ESw), with two tourists, used the Switchable version in winter mode: *P1: "We saw winter the whole time.. ... It was fascinating. I mean we liked the photos, it was nice to - again, that's where it said this is 20 to 30 degrees below in winter." Interviewer: "did it make you feel somehow, help you to feel like winter or -". P2: "Yeah". P1: "Definitely"*. In this way out of season content supported some understanding of how the island changed for participants that could not visit in multiple seasons.

Impact of Media Type

The type of media presented also impacted the value of out of season content. In particular, images that showed the current scene participants could see, but from a winter perspective, were always highlighted as interesting, showing the difference between the seasons. PG7 (EC): *"I was by these buildings that were used to store hay, I think, and the image showed that in the winter people would attach straw to the roofs so birds could eat it. I thought that helped me understand the role of the building better"*. In contrast, images of the current scene participants could see, but from a summer perspective, were often uninteresting. PG7 (EC): *"If I'm looking at something in the summer I probably don't need to see a picture of it in the summer as well"*. This perspective on images was in contrast to audio recordings, where the summer recordings often enhanced the current view of participants, where winter recordings could jar. For example, a person describing taking part in a winter activity, and what it was like, was seen as odd in comparison to a similar recording of a summer activity.

Seasonal Preferences

In considering their preference between winter and summer content, responses were evenly split between two alternatives: current season and opposite season. Current season participants wanted content that fitted the current environment. PG19 (EC): *"probably the summer would have been more interesting since it's the summer now."*. However, participants did not want to exclude winter content altogether, rather limit it to a few key aspects to highlight variations. PG16 (EC): *"more of the summer things but yeah. Picture or two of winter it's not bad ..... 'cause it's like now and I'm visiting the island now"*. This adds to the discussion by Explore Switchable participants on why they stayed in summer, and reflects the importance of a close integration between the physical environment and digital content from prior work [3, 4].

Conversely, opposite season participants wanted more winter content as this was different to the current season. PG12 (EC): *"Maybe winter, because winter I don't get to see it at all."*. There were more comments from Explore Combined than Explore Switchable participants towards opposite seasons. As Explore Switchable participants often didn't switch seasons this is not surprising. But it may be that until visitors view out of season content, they don't see a value in it. The one group PG23 (ESw) who did use the Switchable version in winter noted their preference as: *"it was nice to have winter. Cause it added a different dimension. If we were here in winter it'd be nice to know about the summer."*.

DISCUSSION

We have uncovered new insight into how visitors consider seasonality in outdoor cultural heritage applications. Our discussion focuses around a set of design considerations that should be considered when incorporating seasonality.

There is value in showing out of season content. The importance of congruency between digital content and the environment, highlighted from prior work [3, 4], would argue content should reflect the current season. Yet, participants found out of season content often to be more engaging and interesting, offering new insight and deeper understanding to the heritage of the island. Some Explore Combined participants would have preferred out of season content to be the default option. However, out of season content may be most useful when it highlights the difference between the seasons. Whilst content relevant to the current season is a valuable default, relevant out of season content should also be presented. Though this should avoid overloading users with content.

Participants might need to be provoked to view out of season content. Explore Switchable participants only viewed summer (current) season content, even when winter was set as default season. Without being exposed to out of season content (as Explore Combined participants were) they failed to see value in viewing it, with a clear preference Explore should reflect the current season. Participants may therefore need to be provoked to view out of season content before seeing its value. How best to do this remains an open question.

Content should be tailored based on being in or out of season. Images of summer scenes that participants could currently see were often described as uninteresting, whilst winter images from the same perspective were discussed as being most interesting. Similarly, audio media that described activities in winter jarred with participants when presented in summer. We would expect a similar issue with such content presented in winter. Content needs to be tailored differently when it is presented in, and out of, season.

FUTURE WORK AND CONCLUSIONS

Although there is a lack of work considering seasonality in cultural heritage, that work argues content should fit to the current season [9]. However we found how visitors value and interpret seasonality is much richer. Both versions of Explore supported visitors to think about seasonality, yet neither can be considered as a good final solution. Our goal was primarily to understand how users thought about seasonality using a relatively well understood existing technique to augment cultural heritage sites, rather than try to design without that understanding. As our study was run in summer, we do not know if the preference for current season content would be the same if we ran the study in winter. Would participants want to 'escape' to a summer perspective? More widely, how different should seasons be before it is valuable to incorporate that difference? Our variation was more defined than many sites, and in some ways more predictable (summer is usually warm, and winter is usually cold), supporting a fairly low fidelity (two season) representation. However sites may also change more dynamically or less predictably. By incorporating our findings into new approaches to combine winter and summer content, and studying these in places with different seasonal variations, we will further explore and inspire the use of seasonality in outdoor cultural heritage applications.

ACKNOWLEDGMENTS

We thank Seurasaarisäätiö and Jutta Jaakkola for their assistance in developing content. The Aalto University Digitisation fund contributed to this study.

REFERENCES

1. Steve Benford, John Bowers, Paul Chandler, Luigina Ciolfi, Martin Flintham, Mike Fraser, Chris Greenhalgh, Tony Hall, Sten Olof Hellström, Shahram Izadi, Tom Rodden, Holger Schnädelbach, and Ian Taylor. 2001. Unearthing Virtual History: Using Diverse Interfaces to Reveal Hidden Virtual Worlds. In *Proceedings of the 3rd International Conference on Ubiquitous Computing (UbiComp '01)*. Springer-Verlag, London, UK, UK, 225–231. http://dl.acm.org/citation.cfm?id=647987.741334
2. Luigina Ciolfi and Marc McLoughlin. 2011. Challenges for the Technological Augmentation of Open-Air Museums : Bridging Buildings, Artefacts and Activities. *Nordisk Museologi* 1 (2011), 15–34.
3. Luigina Ciolfi and Marc McLoughlin. 2012. Designing for Meaningful Visitor Engagement at a Living History Museum. In *Proceedings of the 7th Nordic Conference on Human-Computer Interaction: Making Sense Through Design (NordiCHI '12)*. ACM, New York, NY, USA, 69–78. DOI: http://dx.doi.org/10.1145/2399016.2399028
4. Alessandro E Foni, George Papagiannakis, and Nadia Magnenat-Thalmann. 2010. A Taxonomy of Visualization Strategies for Cultural Heritage Applications. *Journal of Computing and Cultural Heritage* 3, 1 (July 2010), 1:1–1:21. DOI: http://dx.doi.org/10.1145/1805961.1805962
5. Seurasaari Foundation. 2016. Seurasaari Foundation Homepage. http://www.seurasaarisaatio.fi. (2016). [Online; accessed 20-September-2016].
6. Mark T. Marshall, Daniela Petrelli, Nick Dulake, Elena Not, Michele Marchesoni, Elisa Trenti, and Anna Pisetti. 2015. Audio-based narratives for the trenches of World War I: Intertwining stories, places and interaction for an evocative experience. *International Journal of Human-Computer Studies* (2015), 1–13. DOI: http://dx.doi.org/10.1016/j.ijhcs.2015.08.001
7. David McGookin, Yolanda Vazquez-Alvarez, Stephen Brewster, and Joanna Bergstrom-Lehtovirta. 2012. Shaking the Dead: Multimodal Location Based Experiences for Un-stewarded Archaeological Sites. In *Proceedings of the 7th Nordic Conference on Human-Computer Interaction: Making Sense Through Design (NordiCHI '12)*. ACM, New York, NY, USA, 199–208. DOI: http://dx.doi.org/10.1145/2399016.2399048
8. Marc McLoughlin and Luigina Ciolfi. 2011. Design Interventions for Open-air Museums: Applying and Extending the Principles of 'Assembly'. In *Proceedings of the SIGCHI Conference on Human Factors in Computing Systems (CHI '11)*. ACM, New York, NY, USA, 553–556. DOI: http://dx.doi.org/10.1145/1978942.1979019
9. Brian O'Keefe, David Benyon, Gaurav Chandwani, Madhav Menon, and Randy Duke, II. 2014. A Blended Space for Heritage Storytelling. In *Proceedings of the 28th International BCS Human Computer Interaction Conference on HCI 2014 - Sand, Sea and Sky - Holiday HCI (BCS-HCI '14)*. BCS, UK, 90–99. DOI: http://dx.doi.org/10.14236/ewic/hci2014.10
10. Daniela Petrelli, Luigina Ciolfi, Dick van Dijk, Eva Hornecker, Elena Not, and Albrecht Schmidt. 2013. Integrating material and digital. *Interactions* 20, 4 (2013), 58–63. DOI: http://dx.doi.org/10.1145/2486227.2486239
11. Tom Pfeifer, Paul Savage, and Bronwen Robinson. 2009. Managing the Culloden Battlefield Invisible Mobile Guidance Experience. In *Proceedings of the 6th International Workshop on Managing Ubiquitous Communications and Services (MUCS '09)*. ACM, New York, NY, USA, 51–58. DOI: http://dx.doi.org/10.1145/1555321.1555333
12. Josephine Reid, Erik Geelhoed, Richard Hull, Kirsten Cater, and Ben Clayton. 2005. Parallel Worlds: Immersion in Location-based Experiences. In *CHI '05 Extended Abstracts on Human Factors in Computing Systems (CHI EA '05)*. ACM, New York, NY, USA, 1733–1736. DOI: http://dx.doi.org/10.1145/1056808.1057009
13. J Ritchie and L Spencer. 1993. Qualitative Data Analysis for Applied Policy Research. In *Analysing Qualitative Data*, A Bryman and R Burgess (Eds.). Routledge, London, 173–194.
14. Laurajane Smith. 2011. The 'Doing' of Heritage: Heritage as performance. In *Performing Heritage: Research, Practice and Innovation in Museum Theatre and Live Interpretation*, A. Jackson and J. Kidd (Eds.). Manchester University Press, Manchester, 69–81.
15. Danae Stanton, Claire O'Malley, Kher Hui Ng, Mike Fraser, and Steve Benford. 2003. Situating Historical Events Through Mixed Reality: Adult-Child Interactions in the Storytent. In *Proceedings of the International Conference on Computer Support for Collaborative Learning 2003*. Springer, Netherlands, Bergen, Norway, 293–302. http://doi.acm.org/10.1007/978-94-017-0195-2_37

Where No One Has Gone Before: A Meta-Dataset of the World's Largest Fanfiction Repository

Kodlee Yin, Cecilia Aragon, Sarah Evans, Katie Davis
University of Washington, Seattle, USA
kodlee@fru1t.me, {aragon,sarahe,kdavis78}@uw.edu

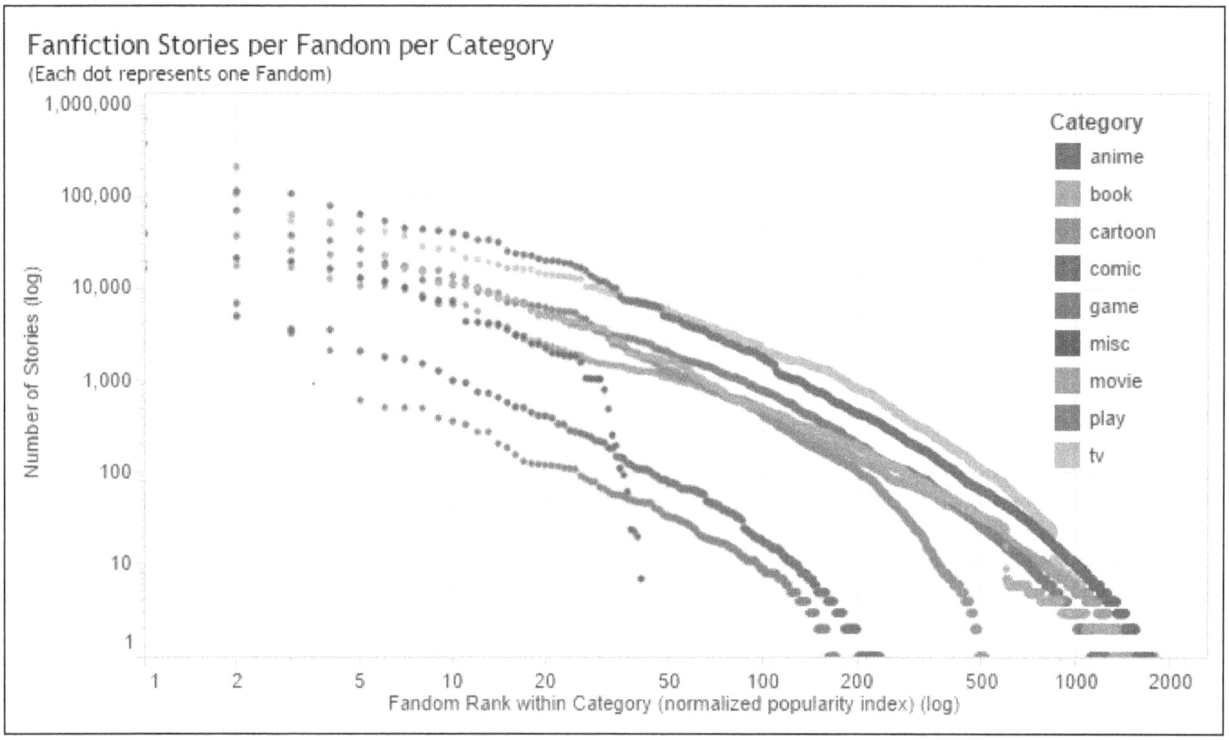

Figure 1. An overview of fanfiction story metadata by fandom/category. The category Books contains the most popular fandom (Harry Potter) by number of stories, but the category Anime is much deeper, with multiple fandoms generating more stories.

ABSTRACT

With its roots dating to popular television shows of the 1960s such as Star Trek, fanfiction has blossomed into an extremely widespread form of creative expression. The transition from printed zines to online fanfiction repositories has facilitated this growth in popularity, with millions of fans writing stories and adding daily to sites such as Archive Of Our Own, Fanfiction.net, FIMfiction.net, and many others. Enthusiasts are sharing their writing, reading stories written by others, and helping each other to grow as writers. Yet, this domain is often undervalued by society and understudied by researchers. To facilitate the study of this large but often marginalized community, we present a fully anonymized data release (via differential privacy) of the metadata from a large fanfiction site (to protect author privacy, story, profile, and review text is excluded, and only metadata is provided). We use visual analytics techniques to draw several intriguing insights from the data and show the potential for future research. We hope other researchers can use this data to explore further questions related to online fanfiction communities.

CHI 2017, May 6–11, 2017, Denver, CO, USA.

ACM ISBN 978-1-4503-4655-9/17/05...$15.00.
http://dx.doi.org/10.1145/3025453.3025720

Author Keywords

Fanfiction; online communities; youth.

ACM Classification Keywords

H.5.3 Group and organization interfaces: Web-based interaction.

INTRODUCTION

Writing, sharing, and discussing fanfiction is a hugely popular online activity, and the site we call Fanfics.com (anonymized to comply with terms of service) is a vast online fanfiction repository. As of June 5, 2016, there were 6,402,752 stories, 166,739,153 story reviews, and 1,455,952 authors on the site. To put this last figure in context, there were 113,000 active editors on English Wikipedia on the same date. Yet the number of ACM papers published on Wikipedia far exceeds the number of papers studying fanfiction: 1,581 Wikipedia papers compared to a handful of papers that deal with fanfiction. We do not claim that fanfiction has had the impact or importance of Wikipedia; nevertheless, the phenomenon of fanfiction is clearly an understudied online context relative to its popularity.

It is not simply its popularity that makes fanfiction worthy of investigation; it is what people are doing on these sites—and how they are benefiting—that merits empirical inquiry. Authors (often young people) are publishing stories that are several hundred thousand words in length, sometimes exceeding the length of the original works on which they were based. Readers are offering encouragement and constructive feedback on stories, which authors use to improve their writing [5,9]. All of this happens in a positive, supportive community atmosphere that stands in stark contrast to the negativity and even hate speech that is found on so many online sites (e.g., Reddit, 4chan, comments posted on news sites).

Previous work has documented the benefits that people gain through their participation in online fanfiction communities. Authors experience mentorship from the community, grow as writers, gain recognition for their work, and form meaningful connections with other fans [2-5,9-18]. Most existing research on fanfiction has consisted of relatively small-scale, ethnographic investigations. These studies offer valuable insight into users' experiences and interactions in online fanfiction communities. However, they cannot provide a comprehensive view of the full scope of activity on a fanfiction repository. The current study provides such a view, constituting the first fully anonymized data release of a fanfiction site's complete metadata, consisting of six million stories across ten thousand fandoms. Previous work that undertook quantitative analysis only sampled the data [7,19,21]. We utilize differential privacy [8] for the data release so that researchers can explore questions related to online fanfiction communities without violating the privacy of the authors. A secondary contribution of this work is the demonstration of a visual analytics approach to draw insight from this vast corpus of human-generated data.

PREVIOUS WORK AND BACKGROUND

History of Fanfiction

Fanfiction is a type of transformative work in which fans of a variety of different media—including television shows, movies, comic books, anime, and video games—write stories that are based on the original media but expand upon or alter it. Fanfiction authors may consider plot trajectories different from the original story, explore the untold background stories of characters, or place the characters in an "alternate universe" that is completely different from the original setting. Fanfiction stories can vary in length from "one shots" of less than 1000 words to novel-length stories.

Fanfiction developed within the context of popular television shows of the 1960s, such as Star Trek and The Twilight Zone [11]. Yet, one might go considerably further back in history and regard the works of Shakespeare and Virgil as early examples of fanfiction. Well-known works of contemporary fanfiction include *Wicked: The Life and Times of the Wicked Witch of the West* (based on Baum's *The Wonderful Wizard of Oz*), *Pride and Prejudice and Zombies* (based on Austen's *Pride and Prejudice*), and *The Wind Done Gone* (based on Mitchell's *Gone with the Wind*). For every popular example of fanfiction, however, there are thousands more fanfiction stories that are unknown to the general public.

Research on Fanfiction

Research on fanfiction began nearly 25 years ago with Jenkins' seminal investigation of fan culture [11]. This work was pivotal in countering negative stereotypes of fans and fan culture by describing fan communities as rich sites of participatory culture. Jenkins challenged the common view that fanfiction was unoriginal, derivative work, instead positioning fanfiction stories as highly creative acts of manipulating and extending source material in unexpected, boundary-pushing ways.

Since Jenkins' foundational work, research on fanfiction has addressed issues of legality [20,22,23], identity [1,3,14], sexuality [11,24], and educational value [4,6,9,12,15-18]. For example, Black [2,3,4] explored English Language Learners' (ELL) participation in online fanfiction communities, focusing in particular on language acquisition and identity formation. More recently, Campbell et al. [5] conducted an in-depth nine-month ethnographic investigation of Fanfiction.net and FIMFiction.net, which included participant observations and interviews with authors. In a follow-up study, they conducted a thematic analysis of 4,500 reader reviews on Fanfiction.net [9].

Selecting ten original canonical works from Fanfiction.net, Milli and Bamman [19] employed natural language processing (NLP) methods to investigate differences in the characters emphasized and the treatment of gender in fanfiction stories compared to the original works. They found that secondary characters tended to be mentioned more frequently than primary characters in fanfiction stories. In addition, they found a small but significant increase in the proportion of female character mentions in fanfiction stories compared to the original works. This investigation represents the first to apply computational methods to the study of fanfiction data, illustrating the potential to derive empirical insights from such an approach. However, the data used by Milli and Bamma

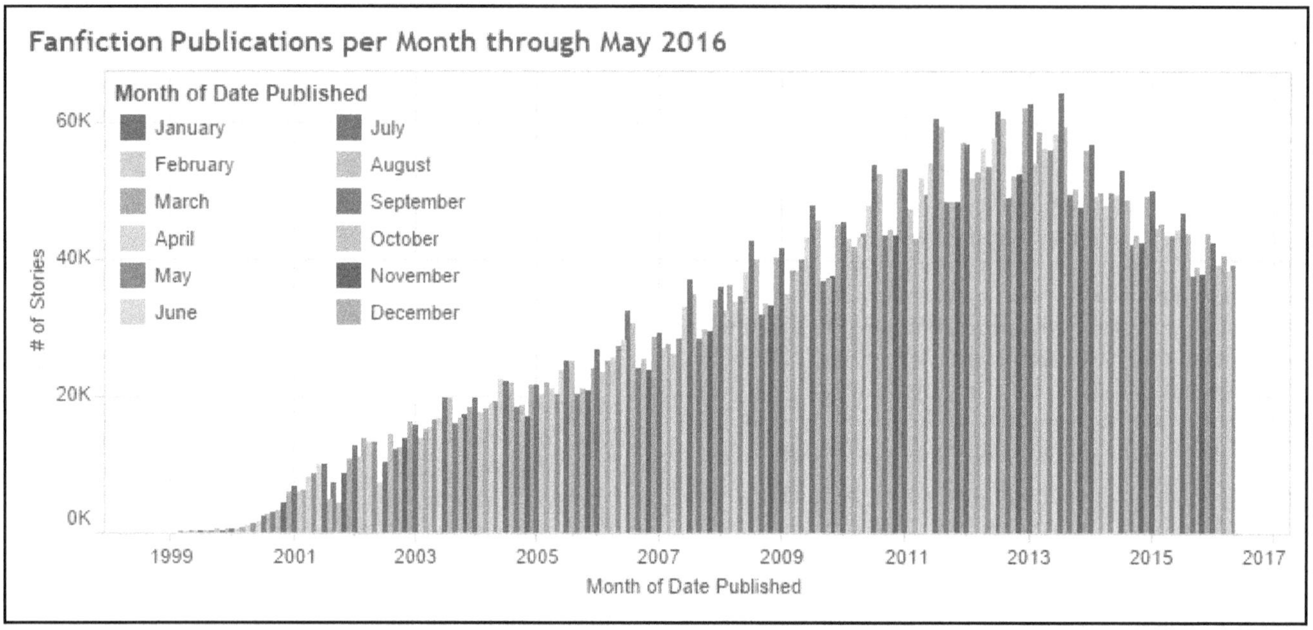

Figure 1. Story publication by month. Note the uptick in posting during northern hemisphere summer months.

constituted a fairly small proportion of the total corpus of fanfiction published on the site. The authors called for more quantitative analyses of fanfiction texts, and we hope that by making a large set of story metadata publically available and demonstrating its richness, we will be encouraging this type of research.

METHODS

Fanfics.com has various views for its website, none of which provide a complete snapshot. The site is organized hierarchically; the top-level subdivision is into nine *categories*: Anime/Manga, Books, Cartoons, Comics, Games, Misc, Movies, Plays/Musicals, and TV Shows. Each category is subdivided into *fandoms* (e.g. in the *Books* category, *Harry Potter* and *Twilight* are the two most popular fandoms). Finally, within each fandom, paginated lists of 25 stories per page, which we call *fandom pages*, provide the title, synopsis, author, content rating, language, and genre(s) (e.g., Romance, Drama) of each story, alongside statistics about each story such as word count, number of chapters, reviews, number of favorites and followers. Optional data includes the last time the story was updated, and characters from the fandom used in the story. Collectively, we define this information as the Fanfics.com *metadata*. It does not contain the story texts themselves, but is a rich and dynamic repository of information about the millions of writers and readers of fanfiction on this site.

We collected the data via a combination of Apache HttpComponents and jsoup. The list of fandoms was stored in a MySQL relational database. We processed the paginated fandom pages and stored the raw HTML results as-is for later processing. In total, we scraped and processed 10,339 fandoms on Sunday November 20, 2016. The data was stored in a normalized MySQL database with appropriate tables such as “genre,” “story,” “story_genre.” Variables were aggregated and Laplacian noise added to ensure differential privacy even among outliers.

FINDINGS

The dataset is accessible at **http://research.fru1t.me**. It contains metadata describing 6,807,100 stories across 1,516,335 authors in 44 languages. Each row contains an anonymized user ID, story ID, six quantitative, and six categorical variables as documented on the release site. The stories span 10,294 fandoms and use 46,337 unique characters 9,308,807 times. The 20 genres were applied on 6,159,491 stories, leaving 647,609 uncategorized.

The largest categories were Anime/Manga, TV Shows, and Books with 1,905,055, 1,553,815, and 1,442,290 stories each, respectively. The top genres were Romance, Humor, and Drama with 3,423,862, 1,296,042, and 1,147,377 stories each, respectively. Finally, the top fandoms were *Harry Potter*, *Naruto*, and *Twilight* with 713,814, 387,218, and 212,929 stories, respectively.

We have provided graphs and Tableau visualizations of a few of our most interesting findings. Figure 1 illustrates the differing “shapes” of fandom popularity within categories. Although the category Books contains the single most popular fandom (*Harry Potter*) by number of stories, the category Anime is much deeper, with multiple fandoms generating more stories overall.

We also observe that the hypothesis, based on our previous ethnographic investigations, that a significant portion of the authors on this site are English-speaking students, appears to be confirmed by the uptick in posting during the northern hemisphere summer months, with a brief blip in late December (Figure 2). Note the steady growth until 2013; we have no explanation for the drop-off after that year, and further research is encouraged.

Category	Stories	Authors	Avg Words	Median Words	Words StDev.	Avg. Chptrs	Median Chptrs	Chptrs StDev.	Avg. Reviews	Median Reviews	Reviews StDev.
anime	1,876,647	500,902	8,838	2,379	24,639	3.79	1	7.29	24.3	7	93.4
book	1,422,285	488,670	10,009	2,287	27,586	4.56	1	8.32	39.7	7	217.5
cartoon	453,925	138,790	8,885	2,412	25,003	4.23	1	7.28	20.4	7	59.8
comic	52,267	24,924	7,117	1,935	22,021	3.39	1	6.59	12.9	4	52.2
game	634,519	231,497	9,814	2,372	29,887	4.11	1	8.36	14.7	4	91.1
misc	207,563	101,161	7,544	1,929	37,524	3.83	1	8.26	12.0	3	48.1
movie	291,075	117,251	9,579	2,528	24,178	4.70	1	8.31	23.9	7	77.1
play	60,227	17,958	6,319	2,371	12,908	2.79	1	4.28	41.4	11	132.7
tv	1,404,244	299,347	8,867	2,296	24,040	4.18	1	8.56	23.8	7	79.7

Table 1. Per category information for the fanfiction database. Note that Anime is the most popular overall category, but each Anime fanfiction story receives fewer reviews on average than Book fanfiction.

	Adventure	Angst	Comfort/Hurt	Crime	Drama	Family	Fantasy	Friendship	Horror	Humor	Mystery	Parody	Poetry	Romance	Sci-Fi	Spiritual	Supernatural	Suspense	Tragedy	Western
Adventure	0	1061	324	55	3663	1341	2871	2437	205	3836	2008	131	42	13140	182	60	673	707	273	4
Angst	1061	0	3496	48	8741	2072	222	1312	612	994	367	123	1223	25148	11	186	247	356	3876	2
Comfort/Hurt	324	3496	0	25	1656	5231	154	3727	72	395	113	22	219	11924	1	87	82	85	1292	2
Crime	55	48	25	0	84	34	17	29	24	49	49	6	7	100	1	1	8	25	45	0
Drama	3663	8741	1656	84	0	2121	749	1449	435	3409	973	148	427	31054	21	141	354	799	1896	2
Family	1341	2072	5231	34	2121	0	338	2783	64	3219	175	32	104	5823	16	63	92	99	954	5
Fantasy	2871	222	154	17	749	338	0	593	52	896	301	68	66	2826	97	33	281	152	122	0
Friendship	2437	1312	3727	29	1449	2783	593	0	32	3973	192	37	78	12769	15	64	73	82	431	0
Horror	205	612	72	24	435	64	52	32	0	341	167	54	59	538	21	18	143	148	271	1
Humor	3836	994	395	49	3409	3219	896	3973	341	0	603	7375	525	46213	52	50	221	209	278	17
Mystery	2008	367	113	49	973	175	301	192	167	603	0	31	33	2511	12	21	145	305	117	2
Parody	131	123	22	6	148	32	68	37	54	7375	31	0	110	607	2	7	18	21	50	7
Poetry	42	1223	219	7	427	104	66	78	59	525	33	110	0	1971	1	42	22	15	392	1
Romance	13140	25148	11924	100	31054	5823	2826	12769	538	46213	2511	607	1971	0	80	251	765	1018	4943	15
Sci-Fi	182	11	1	1	21	16	97	15	21	52	12	2	1	80	0	5	16	11	6	0
Spiritual	60	186	87	1	141	63	33	64	18	50	21	7	42	251	5	0	53	8	127	2
Supernatural	673	247	82	8	354	92	281	73	143	221	145	18	22	765	16	53	0	84	51	1
Suspense	707	356	85	25	799	99	152	82	148	209	305	21	15	1018	11	8	84	0	129	0
Tragedy	273	3876	1292	45	1896	954	122	431	271	278	117	50	392	4943	6	127	51	129	0	0
Western	4	2	2	0	2	5	0	0	1	17	2	7	1	15	0	2	1	0	0	0

Table 2. Combinations of genres in the Harry Potter fandom. Humor/Romance is the most popular combination.

A simple table of category-aggregated metrics (Table 1) reveals interesting facts at a glance: Anime is the most popular category, but stories in Books and Plays receive more reviews per story on average, indicating, as has been shown in previous research [5, 9], more engagement and support of authors in those categories. Stories are significantly longer in the Books category than they are in any other category.

We extracted multiple visualizations from the data, only a small fraction of which are reproduced here due to space constraints. We found a classic power-law distribution in the word counts of stories with a peak under a thousand words. A matched-genre heat map table for the *Harry Potter* fandom (Table 2) reveals both understandable and intriguing correlations. It is not surprising that Romance contains more stories than any other genre, but it is intriguing that Western has the least. It is also interesting that Humor/Romance was the most popular combination of genres, comprising 7% of all *Harry Potter* stories out of 400 possible combinations.

CONCLUSION

With this work, we hope to make generally available a fully anonymized, rich dataset about a highly popular but understudied phenomenon. Even a cursory glance through the data uncovers fascinating details about differences among fandoms, varying proportions of stories between categories, how genre types vary by language, and more. We hope this dataset will pique researchers' curiosity and spur further study of this topic.

ACKNOWLEDGMENTS

We thank the reviewers for their helpful comments.

REFERENCES

1. Ayşegül Kuglin Altintaş. 2013. A New Hermione: Re-Creations of the Female Harry Potter Protagonist in Fan Fiction. *Z Anglist Am* 61, 2: 155–173.
2. Rebecca W. Black. 2006. Language, culture, and identity in online fanfiction. *E–Learning* 3, 2, 170-184.
3. Rebecca W. Black. 2007. Digital design: English language learners and reader reviews in online fiction. In *A new literacies sampler*, Michele Knobel and Colin Lankshear (eds.). Peter Lang, New York, NY, 115-136.
4. Rebecca W. Black. 2008. *Adolescents and Online Fan Fiction*. Peter Lang, New York, NY.
5. Julie Campbell, Cecilia Aragon, Katie Davis, Sarah Evans, Abigail Evans, and David Randall. 2016. Thousands of positive reviews: distributed mentoring in online fan communities. In *Proceedings of the ACM Conference on Computer Supported Cooperative Work* (CSCW '16). http://dx.doi.org/10.1145/2818048.2819934
6. Kelly Chandler-Olcott and Donna Mahar. 2003. Adolescents' *anime*-inspired "fanfictions": An exploration of multiliteracies. *J Adolesc Adult Lit.* 46, 7, 556-566.
7. Abigail De Kosnik, Laurent El Ghaoui, Vera Cuntz-Leng, Andrew Godbehere, Andrea Horbinski, Adam Hutz, Renee Pastel, and Vu Pham. 2015. Watching, creating, and archiving: Observations on the quantity and temporality of fannish productivity in online fan fiction archives. *Convergence: The International Journal of Research into New Media Technologies,* 21, 1:145-164.
8. Cynthia Dwork. A firm foundation for private data analysis, *Communications of the ACM*, vol. 54, 2011.
9. Sarah Evans, Katie Davis, Abigail Evans, Julie Campbell, David Randall, Kodlee Yin, and Cecilia Aragon. 2017. More than peer production: fanfiction communities as sites of distributed mentoring. In *Proceedings of the ACM Conference on Computer Supported Cooperative Work* (CSCW '17). http://dx.doi.org/10.1145/2998181.2998342
10. Casey Fiesler, Shannon Morrison, and Amy S. Bruckman. 2016. An archive of their own: a case study of feminist HCI and values in design. In *Proceedings of the 2016 CHI Conference on Human Factors in Computing Systems* (CHI '16). https://doi.org/10.1145/2858036.2858409
11. Henry Jenkins. 1992. *Textual Poachers: Television Fans & Participatory Culture.* Routledge, New York, NY.
12. Henry Jenkins. 2006. *Convergence Culture: Where Old and New Media Collide*. New York University Press.
13. Shannon Fay Johnson. 2014. Fan fiction metadata creation and utilization within fan fiction archives: Three primary models. *Transform Work Cultures* 17.
14. Soomin Jwa. 2012. Modeling L2 writer voice: Discoursal positioning in fanfiction writing. *Computers and Composition* 29, 4: 323-340.
15. Jayne Lammers. 2013. Fangirls as teachers: Examining pedagogic discourse in an online fan site. *Learning, Media and Technology* 38,4: 368-386.
16. Jayne Lammers. 2016. "The Hangout was serious business": Leveraging participation in an online space to design Sims fanfiction. *Res Teach Engl.* 50,4: 309-332.
17. Jayne C. Lammers and Valerie L. Marsh. 2015. Going public: An adolescent's networked writing on fanfiction.net. *J Adolesc Adult Lit.* 59, 3: 277-285.
18. Kerri Mathew and Devon Adams. 2009. I love your book, but I love my version more: Fanfiction in the English language arts classroom. *ALAN Review* 36, 3: 35-41.
19. Smitha Milli and David Bamman. 2016. Beyond canonical texts: a computational analysis of fanfiction. In *Proceedings of the Empirical Methods on Natural Language Processing Conference* (EMNLP '16).
20. Mollie E Nolan. 2006. Search for original expression: Fan fiction and the fair use defense. *SIU Law J* 30, 3: 533-571.
21. Charles Sendlor. 2011. Fan Fiction Demographics in 2010: Age, Sex, Country. Retrieved September 17, 2016 from http://ffnresearch.blogspot.com/2011/03/fan-fiction-demographics-in-2010-age.html
22. Leanne Stendell. 2005. Fanfic and fan fact: How current copyright law ignores the reality of copyright owner and consumer interests in fan fiction. *SMU Law Rev* 58: 1551.
23. Rachel L Stroude. 2010. Complimentary creation: Protecting fan fiction as fair use. *Marquette Intellect Prop Law Rev* 14, 1: 191.
24. Catherine Tosenberger. 2008. Homosexuality at the online Hogwarts: Harry Potter slash fanfiction. *Child Lit* 36, 1: 185–207.

Illumination Aesthetics: Light as a Creative Material within Computational Design

Cesar Torres, Jasper O'Leary, Molly Nicholas, Eric Paulos
Electrical Engineering and Computer Sciences
University of California, Berkeley
{cearto, j.oleary, molecule, paulos}@berkeley.edu

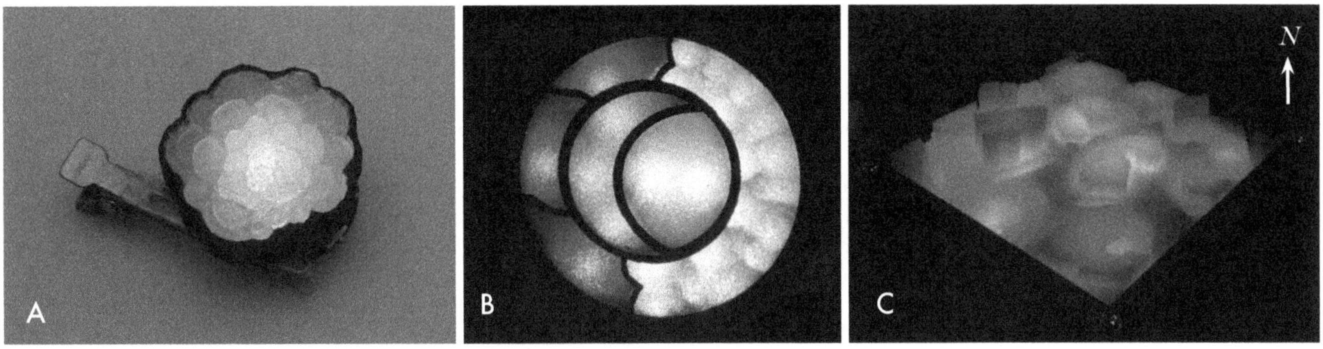

Figure 1. a) an illuminated hairpin (1 led); a tactile flexible diffuser cast with small glass beads creates diffusion and shadow, b) a sun-moon light art piece (25 leds); a computationally generated reflector controls light rays to form soft and hard edges to blend colored lights, c) a dynamic tactile map of an urban center (16 leds); volumetric diffusers indicate building locations; buildings light up in succession to indicate pathways.

ABSTRACT
Recent digital fabrication tools have enabled new form-giving using a wide range of *physical* materials. However, *light as a first class creative material* has been largely ignored within the design of our electronic objects. Our work expands the illumination design space by treating light as a physical material. We introduce a digital design tool that simulates and visualizes physical light interactions with a variety of materials for creating custom luminaires. We further develop a computational design and fabrication process for creating custom secondary optics elements (SOEs), which provides additional handles for users to physically shape and redirect light to compose, fill, and evenly diffuse planar and volumetric geometries. Through a workshop study with novice electronic designers, we show how incorporating physical techniques to shape light alters how users view the role and function of LEDs and electronics. We produce example pieces that showcase how our approach expands the electronics aesthetic and discuss how viewing light as material can engender novel, expressive artifacts.

Author Keywords
New Media; displays; lighting; luminaire; digital fabrication

CHI 2017, May 06–11, 2017, Denver, CO, USA
ACM 978-1-4503-4655-9/17/05.
http://dx.doi.org/10.1145/3025453.3025466

ACM Classification Keywords
H.5.m. Information interfaces and presentation: User Interfaces - Interaction Styles; D.2.2 Design Tools and Techniques: User interfaces

INTRODUCTION
Light is a rich, expressive medium that has enabled a tremendous amount of creativity and innovation in engineering, art, and design. This design space is quickly evolving with the introduction of smart Light Emitting Diodes (LEDs) (e.g. NeoPixels, dotStars) and electroluminescent materials (e.g. EL wire, OLED). These components are becoming easier to program, attach, and control, supporting a new ecology of devices appearing in increasingly diverse contexts and uses. However, most of these fundamental lighting elements were never intended to be used within such designs. In fact most manufactured electronic lighting components are produced for architectural lighting (39%), display backlighting (18%), and commercial signage (12%) [1]. Even worse, the most prevalent LED form-factors constrain the LED to the characteristic electronic point-light aesthetic. For many electronic projects, this limits the function of LEDs to simple status indicators. Even as the cost of the LED shrinks, the role, function, and control of LEDs in electronic devices has remained limited to blinking, flashing, and color changing via digital manipulation. The physical properties of the LED and light get omitted from the design conversation which unfortunately almost completely ignores the rich, expressive value that light can play when treated as a material.

How might we expand the different expressions of light and the LED to enable new *Illumination Aesthetics* — the expansion of light manipulation techniques to produce novel visual effects,

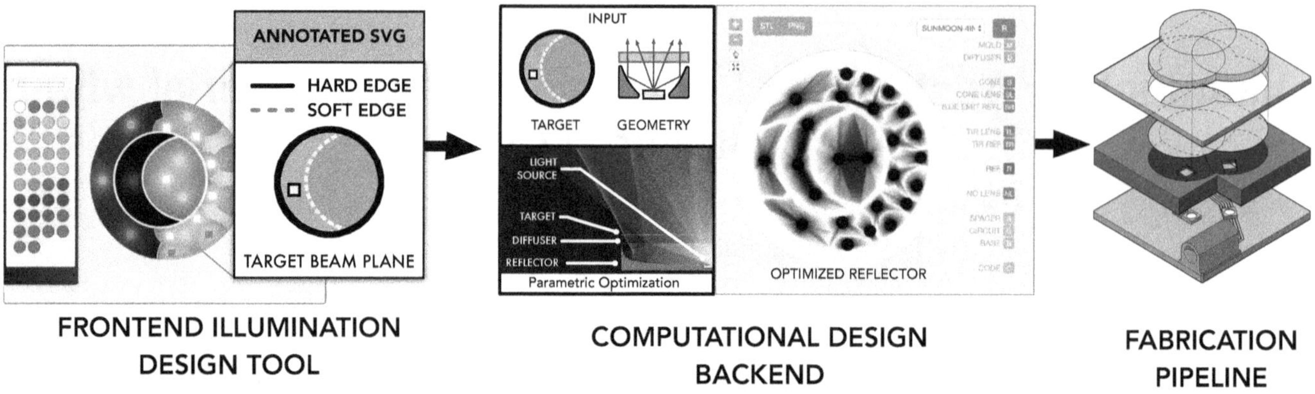

Figure 2. Luminaire Creation Pipeline. a) Given an SVG graphic, our luminaire design tool aids users with laying out LEDs, visualizing light interactions, and specifying target areas to fill with light. In the callout, an LED is specified to fill a moon-shape. b) A computational design backend generates an optimal secondary optics system to achieve the desired design using ray tracing to guide a simulated annealing search. All files for 3D printing geometries and milling circuits are produced by the backend, c) an instruction set guides the user to assemble the luminaire.

sensations, and interactions? Lighting designer Brad Hindson suggests four concepts for envisioning light as a material: light as sharp and diffuse, light as refractive and reflective, light as shadow creator, and light as dynamic element [11]. However within this expressive design landscape we lack accessible tools to readily manipulate and creatively form light.

In order to foreground light as an equal actor with other physical materials, this work develops techniques for creatively and computationally designing and fabricating secondary optics elements (SOEs). SOEs such as reflectors, diffusers, and lenses are commonly used to manipulate light emitted from a source such as an LED. Such secondary optics are commonly used in the lighting industry for applications like collimating LED rays to extend the distance a bicycle headlamp can travel, or for combining beams from multiple light sources to appear as one. However techniques for making, purchasing, or configuring appropriate materials to control light remains a tacit practice. This work aims to provide an accessible, generalizable fabrication technique for creating secondary optics to empower users to control and manipulate light and expand the electronic aesthetic.

To explore Illumination Aesthetics, we constructed a pipeline for creating luminaires — a device that produces, controls, and distributes light. The Illuminating Engineering Society (IES) [13] defines luminaires as consisting of: one or more lamps or LEDs, optical devices designed to distribute light, sockets for supplying electric power, and the mechanical components required to support or attach the housing.

Specifically, in this paper we present two contributions:

- A novel and accessible luminaire design tool for use by nonexpert electronic designers to visually design, simulate, and fabricate non-trivial illumination within physical objects.
- A computational design pipeline comprising the entire physical, electronic, and optical design of materials necessary to fabricate and realize the final desired luminaire.

We evaluated the design tool in a formal user study where participants designed their own luminaire. Each of the participant's luminaires were fabricated and used to gauge perceptions of the function and aesthetic of LEDs with the expanded abilities of our technique. Furthermore, through a set of example luminaires (Figure 1), we show how this fabrication technique enables a novel set of interactive interfaces which place light as a prime citizen in design.

RELATED WORK

Diverse communities have explored the potential of light and optics for creating interactive, aesthetically pleasing, and sensing artifacts. Below, we describe work that explores light as a physical material and medium.

Light as Medium

There exists a large body of work within the arts and design community that utilized light as an artistic medium, exploring material-specific optic properties to create engaging, critical work. Utilizing projected light, James Turrell influences a viewer's depth perception by simulating 3D forms on 2D spaces (*Shallow Space Constructions*) [27]. In *Exploded Views*, Jim Campbell creates three-dimensional animated shadows by controlling the intensity of several light sources suspended in a dense irregular grid [3]. Utilizing the subtle reflective properties of wood, Daniel Rozin's *Wooden Mirror* actuated a grid of small wooden "pixels" to different orientations to create changes in value and form images [25]. Eliasson's *The Weather Project* made use of light's refractive qualities, adding a fine mist to materialize moving weather formations indoors [6]. Notably, these works demonstrate a material and space-driven exploration of light.

Dynamic light has been explored in early work such as László Moholy-Nagy's *Light-Space Modulator* which spun reflective geometries to create visceral moving light installations [19]. Through long-exposure photography, the persistence of light was captured as a drawing and painting medium in influential works like Gjon Mili's *Picasso draws a centaur* [9]. Light has also been explored conceptually; most well known in this space, Dan Flavin created light objects that function as systems of investigation [7]. Pierce et al. further described other phenomenological dimensions of light in electronic objects as tied to the object, its material, and its source [23]. Our work particularly explores the design dimensions of illumination afforded through the optical manipulation of light.

Light as Interaction and Information

As an interactive medium, the active, changing nature of light affords playful, information rich interactions. Harrison et al. surveyed the design space of point lights in modern devices, notably linking common actuation behaviors ("On w/ Bright Flash") to functional evaluations ("Notification") [10]. Light has been shown to afford emotional reactions and interpretations in objects such as luminaires [12]. Design work in this space has also explored light as an active patina, assigning visual light patterns to recorded user interaction history and activity with a tabletop surface [8]. While previous work specifically looked at light that is dynamic and computationally controlled, this work foregrounds the physical design space of light and addresses the aesthetic development of illumination beyond the point-light.

Interactive Potential of Secondary optics

Although digital fabrication technology for optics is in its nascent stage, its potential for creating unique interactive experiences and objects has been explored. WonderLens, a system of magnet-embedded optical lenses coupled with magnetic sensing, demonstrated a wide range of tangible interactions with printed images [15]. In a computational design process, Papas et al. fabricated lenses with refractive geometries to hide, reveal, and obfuscate images placed directly underneath [21]. This process utilized simulated annealing to optimize facet geometries to refract light in a pre-described manner. Similarly, our work optimizes geometries to refract and reflect light to adhere to user-supplied illumination designs. Work in optics has demonstrated the large potential of materials and geometries to efficiently transport light (e.g. optic fiber), micro-array lenses to homogeneously diffuse light [26], or double-cylindrical lenses to shape light into rectangular beams [4]. Interactive objects have also been enabled by sensing changes in light through embedded optomechanics [2, 22, 28]. We see our technique working in tandem with optomechanical sensing, although we focus on expanding illumination aesthetics to enable even richer interactions.

Printed Secondary Optics

Early work in manipulating light leveraged fiber optics to transfer an image from projecters onto specific geometries using adjustable wide-angle lenses with short focal lengths [16]. Willis et al. [28] further demonstrated the feasibility of 3D printing light pipes and lenses within geometries to channel light and create novel illumination and sensing capabilities. By bundling light pipes and routing them through a structure, this technique has been shown to create screens on both spherical geometries [2] and arbitrary geometries [22]. The resolution of this display technique is largely dependent on the density of light pipes. Ultimately, each individual light pipe terminates and forms a pixel. While this allows generalizable image creation through programmatic control of the light pipe matrix, this type of screen is bound to the digital aesthetic where the expression of light is limited to pixel-based interactions and misses the opportunity to consider light as a material.

For reflective properties, Matusik et al. [18] demonstrated the feasibility of matching Bidirectional Reflectance Distribution Functions (BRDFs) with linear combinations of reflective inks. In order to expand our control of light and its visual properties, our approach builds on these printable optics techniques by exploring methods of controlling light using diverse materials in a user-centered design system. We leverage the interactive potential of secondary optics to enable users to explore a broader set of techniques to work with light.

AESTHETIC ILLUMINATION DESIGN OBJECTIVES

For novice electronic designers, the LED is often seen as an atomic design element with a rich digital design space – a key factor influencing the adoption of the LED as a staple component of electronic maker culture, art, and education.

We chose to build a design tool for making luminaires since the design space is concentrated around using light in its purest state. This is in contrast to interactive devices that prioritize a different set of interaction goals centered around user experience. The LED is also a principle entry point into electronics design for many users; by making this experience more expressive, we see a pathway for users to gain a deeper familiarity with materials and broaden participation in STEM.

From our personal experience teaching electronic device design and our survey of online project tutorials, the most common techniques for manipulating physical light from LEDs are using the device housing as a diffuser, shielding the light with a material, or even placing the LEDs on the non-user facing side of a device so as to create an ambient glow. We focus this work on expanding physical manipulation of light with the objective of aiding a user population consisting of novice interactive device designers.

Such an objective prioritizes a material-centric workflow which we define as a process which utilizes both abstract and physical interactions with materials. Under this lens, light should be represented as a responsive element, adhering to the physics of light and convey light's interactions with different materials. Materials and techniques for manufacturing need to be inexpensive and easy-to-use. Furthermore the tool should support an iterative design process, fit into existing practice with tools used by designers, and provide enough creative freedom for users to specify minute design parameters (e.g. bolt placement, led placement, enclosure shape), but offset tedious design tasks (e.g. aligning holes, routing traces, sizing mechanical and electrical components) to the tool.

We will describe how we designed such a design tool to allow users to creatively and expressively create luminaires that treat light as a material, and then describe the implementation of a computational design backend which produces digital design files and instructions for users to digitally fabricate secondary optic elements (SOEs) and assemble luminaires.

FRONTEND LUMINAIRE DESIGN TOOL

Our luminaire design tool was designed for users familiar with vector graphics and built as a web application (Figure 2). The web application allows a user to specify high-level luminaire design specifications such as LED placement, LED color, and target areas for the LED to fill. The tool uses the paper.js

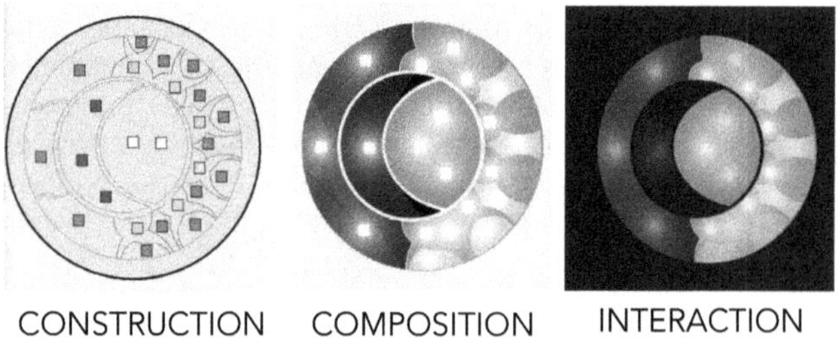

Figure 3. Illumination views. Each view can be toggled by a user when composing their design to showcase different illumination concerns. Each light source interacts with neighboring geometries and shows light interactions such as mixture and shadow creation.

vector graphics scripting framework [14] which enables common vector editing operations and backwards compatibility[1] with vector graphics applications. A computational backend, described in the next section, produces the digital fabrication files needed to fabricate the end design. An instruction set is provided to aid with post-processing and assembly.

From an initial vector graphic, the tool allows the user to specify whether paths block light (hard edge) or allow light to pass through (soft edge). Users can then place, remove, and relocate LED elements in a scene. Otherwise, all interactions with the design take place in an external vector graphic editor (e.g. Adobe Illustrator) in order to leverage user's knowledge of and expertise with existing graphic design tools. Depicted in Figure 3, we exposed different views to the user to prioritize different illumination aesthetic concerns. In a *construction view*, users are provided a clear view of housing elements (e.g. placement of nuts and bolts). This view allows a user to specify the shape to fill for each LED. In a *composition view*, white rays are radially emitted from each LED and interact with geometries, displaying the distribution of light in a scene as well as casting shadows when light blocking elements intersect with rays. An *interaction view* allows users to assign a unique color to track specific LED contributions in the overall illumination. Lastly, a *"lights-out"* toggle controls the background luminance to simulate a lit or unlit scene.

COMPUTATIONAL DESIGN BACKEND

To support a wide variety of luminaire designs, we built a computational backend to design custom secondary optical elements (SOEs) that diffuse, redirect, or focus light and the fixtures to appropriately configure and house them. For instance, an SOE can be designed to redirect light rays to run parallel to each other maximizing the lumens over a given area (i.e. collimating lens). Appropriately configured, this lens is the driving technology that allows bike lights to be visibile from a distance and evenly illuminate the path in front them. While such systems are readily available in consumer products, almost all manufactured SOEs shape light beams into circular areas; we expand this to include shape-optimized SOEs that can redistribute light to diffusely fill arbitrary shapes.

To leverage these new illumination capabilities, our approach intergrates these computationally designed components with

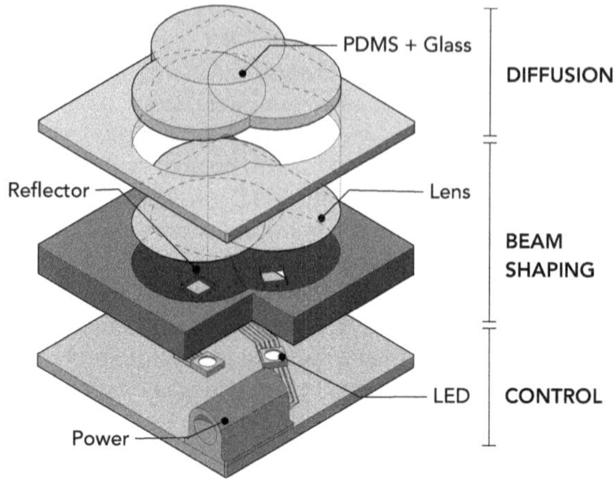

Figure 4. The luminaire consists of a light source powered through an external power supply; its rays are captured and redirected upward by a reflector, an optional lens is used to further shape the light beam; at the topmost layer, a PDMS-Glass diffuser scatters light evenly.

fluid interactions within our design tool to allow creative control of illumination; control is separated into three different layers which house, redirect, and diffuse one or more LEDs:

- DIFFUSION (3-5 mm): consists of materials with light scattering properties that can diffuse or produce an even distribution of light.
- BEAM SHAPING (10 mm): shapes light emitted from an LED using computationally-designed SOEs made with refractive or reflective materials.
- CONTROL (1.5 mm): composed of LEDs, a microcontroller, and a power connector on a printed circuit board (PCB).

One of the most powerful and useful parts of our approach is that it automatically generates digital design files needed to construct each layer of the luminaire. Depicted in Figure 4, these files produce a stacked assembly of components consisting of: 1) the 3D enclosure model, 2) a model to cast or print a diffuser, 3) a 3D reflector model, 4) a printed circuit board (PCB) design and microcontroller code. We can additionally specify whether the assembly functions as standalone (with a power supply and microcontroller), or as a component (with breakout pins) that can be integrated into more complex electronic designs.

Instructions are provided to assist the user with assembly, specifically: casting procedures, specifying appropriate material concentrations and estimated curing time to achieve the different effects specified in their design; printing procedures, providing assistance on the optimal parameters to set for different printing techniques (FDM/SLA); and post-processing procedures including sanding and finishing. In the following section, we describe how the diffuser, beam-shaping, and control layers are designed, fabricated, and evaluated to build custom luminaires.

DIFFUSER DESIGN

The purpose of a diffuser in a secondary optics system is to scatter light uniformly to control the luminous intensity of LEDs. A desirable quality of a diffuser is to optimize the amount of light transmitted through the diffuser (referred to as transparency). Haze, or the measure of scattered light

[1] Backwards compatability with custom paper.js applications and SVG editors was enabled by encoding application-specifc data in the SVG `data` attribute as a `JSON` string.

due to imperfections on the surface of the diffuser, is also commonly used to describe diffusers. Frosting surfaces, a standard technique for diffusing light, produces non-smooth micro-geometries that scatter light. While this is a effective technique for hard materials like acrylic, it also restricts interactions to a limited range of haptics. Our approach described below uses silicone doped with refractive materials to create flexible, tactile diffusers. In our evaluation section, we show how our diffusers outperform standard diffusing techniques.

Flexible diffusers

We introduce a technique for fabricating flexible diffusers for 2D geometries. These diffusers are cast from 3D printed molds using translucent platinum-cured PDMS (silicone) doped with high-refraction glass beads[2](Cole, 150 Micron). This silicone mixture is maker-friendly: it cures quickly in about 2 hours, is particularly forgiving in the demolding processs even with complex molds, and its low viscosity is useful for injection molding. Furthermore, glass beads are readily available in different sizes (from 0.1 mm to 3.0 mm) and can be used to produce different light textures. Figure 1 luminaires were fabricated with 840 micron beads, while Figure 9 were fabricated with 150 micron beads.

To find the optimal mixture ratios, we doped disks (⌀ 30mm x 3mm) with concentrations from 0% to 50%[3] glass by mass mixtures in 5% increments. We extracted luminosity plots from photographs, and found that 40% glass by mass produced the highest diffusion and transmission rates. We leveraged this property to fabricate several tactile and volumetric diffusers (Figure 1a,c), which produce visually-pleasing light effects.

While a good diffuser is a key component to a successful luminaire, its effectiveness relies on the shape of the light beam itself. For this reason, diffusers such as frosted acrylic require a large distance between the diffuser and light source to light up larger areas (see Figure 5, SPACER).

BEAM SHAPER DESIGN

To better control the shape of the light beam, or the distribution of light emitting from one or more light sources, we utilized computationally designed reflectors and lenses. Our approach uses a custom ray tracer to simulate how a beam is manipulated by these geometries. The process first extracts an entropy metric that describes how well a geometry shapes a beam to a desired output to guide a stochastic search through the parametric space of the geometry until an optimal geometry is found. The resulting geometry is then fabricated for use in a luminaire.

Parametric Models

Reflectors and lens designs were derived from commonly used SOE geometries and materials used in industry. We constructed models of each geometry as a vector graphic, parametrizing bezier curves to adhere to geometric design constraints depicted in Figure 5 and described below:

[2]Glass beads are commonly used in reflective street paint and signs.
[3]Mixtures with glass concentrations above 50% by mass suffered from curing issues.

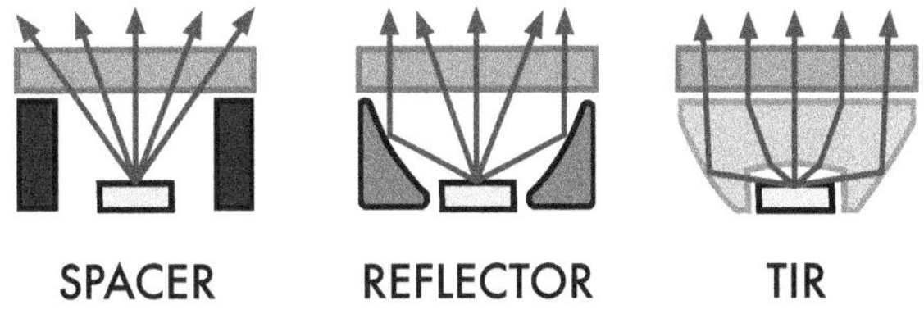

Figure 5. Secondary optics parametric models. A scene is constructed with a light source (yellow), reflective materials (red), non-reflective materials (black), refractive material (light blue), and diffusive material (green). LED light rays are modeled and traced with respect to different geometries. Three metrics, efficiency, coverage, and directionality, are used to characterize these geometries.

- SPACER. Adding a air gap between the light source and diffuse material is the most basic geometry for achieving diffusion. It is highly subject to the light source beam angle: although it works well for small diffusion targets, it requires a greater distance for large target diffusion areas limiting the range of possible applications.
- REFLECTOR. Parabolic reflectors utilize reflective geometries to bounce light towards a specific direction. They are generally inefficient, but are the most ubiquitous in lighting applications.
- TIR. If light traveling from a denser material (glass) escapes into a less dense material (air), and hits this interface at an angle greater than a critical angle, the light is reflected. This phenomena, known as Total Internal Reflection (TIR), is commonly used to efficiently transfer light (e.g. fiber optics). Lenses which utilize this phenomena typically have a cavity above the light source for rays of light to enter the lens medium at critical angles and achieve TIR (Figure 5c).

These paramterized models guide our procedure for generating SOEs for custom illumination designs.

Generating Shape-Optimized Secondary Optics

We decompose the procedure for generating shape-optimized SOEs into four stages: 1) profile extraction, 2) scene construction and ray tracing, 3) simulated annealing, and 4) geometry construction. A visual guide is depicted in Figure 2.

Input and Profile Extraction

After a user finishes their luminaire design, the tool exports an annotated SVG file. It contains the LED position information and the user-specified shape to fill, henceforth referred to as the beam plane. For each beam plane, we extract a set of cross-sections, or profiles. A circular beam plane for instance would have a single profile. Given a specific parametric model, we then compute the best geometry for each profile. In our user study, we chose to use a reflector model (Figure 5) for its relative ease to fabricate, although more complex secondary system setups and materials can be used.

Scene Construction and Ray Tracing

For each profile, we perform ray tracing by casting rays from the LED out into the materials and geometries described by the beam-shaping parametric model. This model may include diffusers, reflectors, and/or lenses. Each ray is encoded with an intensity value that diminishes based on transmission rates of materials, and adheres to light physics (Snell & Fresnel

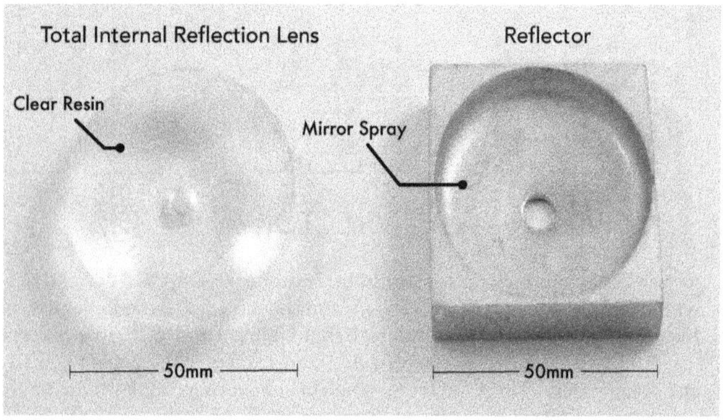

Figure 6. Fabricated reflectors. A total internal reflection (TIR) reflector printing in clear resin (left). Light enters through an air cavity above the LED and is reflected internally, spreading light throughout the lens. A parabolic reflector printing in clear resin, with a coat of mirror spray and acrylic coating (right).

Laws). We computed a metric to describe the quality of exiting light: *coverage*, or the amount of area covered by the light; *directionality*, or the deviation of the light's exiting direction to the surface normal; and *efficiency*, or the ratio of exiting intensity versus the initial intensity of all the rays. These metrics are used to select optimal geometries in a stochastic search.

Simulated Annealing

A powerful part of our technique is the use of a computational design backend engine to iteratively improve the luminaire designs within a complex higher-dimensional solution space. Using simulated annealing, we find acceptable solutions in our non-linear search space as follows: we initially generate a random geometry that satisfies the model's optical properties. Following the similated annealing metaphor, we extract an annealing factor α representing the relative temperature of the system. A "neighbor" geometry is produced by computing a neighborhood of size α around the each parameter in the model, and then choose a random position within that neighborhood. An annealing factor of 1 would span the full parametric space, while an annealing factor approaching 0 would pick a nearby parameter configuration. During each time step, we compute the energy of the system from the ray tracer light metrics which determine whether a geometry is stored as an optimal solution.

Geometry Construction

Unlike circular beam planes with a single profile curve, we require stitching together a hybrid geometry. We do this by treating each profile as an "elevation". We then make a 2.5D geometry by creating level sets which act as a heightmap. This ensures that all geometries are moldable and produce the least amount of artifacts from the printing process.

Fabrication

Once the digital modeling files are produced, they are printed using various 3D printing techniques (Figure 6). In our case, a Type A FDM printer at 0.1mm resolution was used for most luminaires. When higher quality reflection or refraction was required, a Form 1+ SLA printer at 0.025mm resolution was used with clear resin. Resolution is an important factor since ridging artifacts from stereolithography can cause low quality

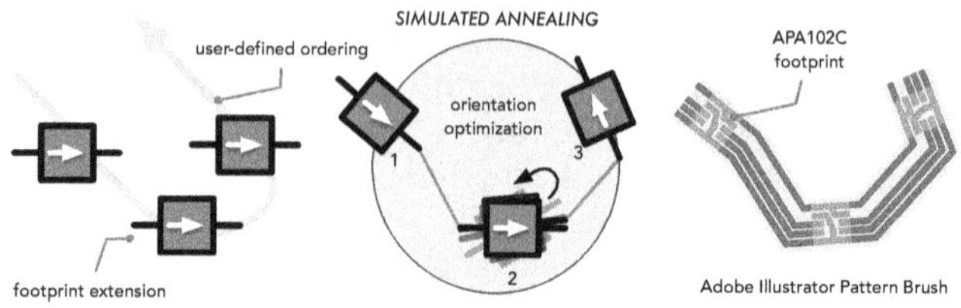

Figure 7. Trace assistance routine. a) user annotates SVG, b) positions are extraced and LED orientation is optimized, c) optimal path is extracted, d) design files produced for several processes, e) different substrates can be used to create rigid or flexible PCBs.

SOEs and uneven diffusion. Our pipeline alerts the user of luminaire quality issues when the LED density of the luminaire reaches a threshold above a reflector's efficiency. Since 3D printing with reflective materials is currently not achievable with commercial digital fabrication tools, we created reflective geometries by spraying 3D prints with a coat of Mirror Spray (Rust-Oleum 267727). This provided a low-cost approach to achieving the desired reflectance.

CONTROL LAYER DESIGN

While powering and controlling one LED is a relatively trivial task, as the number of LEDs increases, so does the circuit complexity. Such designs do not scale well since each LED requires an individual control wire or a special LED driver chip that usually enforces a matrix layout. We leverage an advancement in LED technology — dotStar (APA102C) RGB LED — that allows both simplified routing, individual RGB control of each LED, and uses the 5050 SMD package which is still large enough for hand-soldering. With the right circuit footprint, routing devolves to connecting each LED as links on a single strip.

We aid users by providing a trace-assistance mechanism which produces appropriate configurable files for PCB milling, etching, or sketching, custom to their luminaire design. This mechanism automates the PCB design process connecting LEDs using a "strip" routing algorithm. The strip can be represented as the shortest route that passes through each LED once and only once. As additional graph drawing constraints, LED orientation is unconstrained, no path overlaps can exist, and no acute turns should exist. Our trace assistance mechanism requests the user draw a path that connects all LEDs (Figure 7b). From this we obtain an ordering schema; to prevent LEDs from resting on a curve or turn, we extend the LED footprint to rest on parallel tracks (Figure 7a). To optimize LED orientation, we stochastically explore different orientations and utilize simulated annealing to find the design which minimizes overall strip length. The routine produces an editable path that allows users to add additional anchors and correct overlapping segments highlighted by our tool. Using Adobe Illustrator's Pattern Brush, we then convert this trace into the circuit footprint required by the LED specification (Figure 7c). For logical control, we add a footprint for an 8-pin socket to hold an ATTiny85 microcontroller (DIP) and a 3.1mm DC barrel jack for external power at the start of the strip. This is then milled, hand-soldered, and assembled to form the final luminaire. A certain degree of experience is needed to solder SMD LEDs; we found that once the technique is learned,

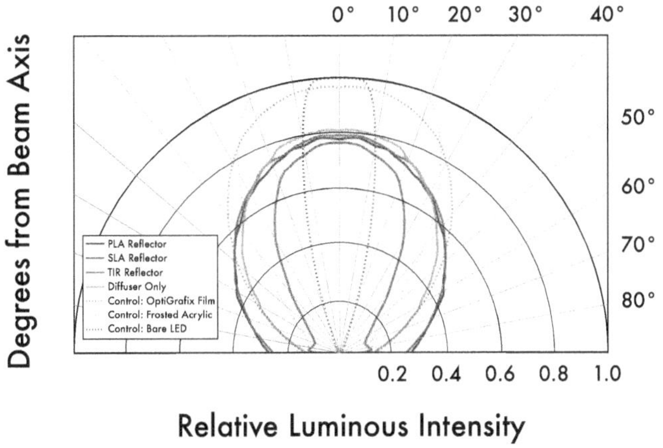

Figure 8. Polar Luminous Intensity Graph. The diagram indicates the distribution of relative luminous intensity of the luminaire. Control systems are marked with dashed lines.

one can comfortably solder 10 LEDs in 10-20 minutes. Solder paste techniques also exist which would greatly speed up and simplify the process, although the actual paste is a more hazardous material.

The hardware address of each LED is relative to the position from the microcontroller on the strip. We use this information to produce code for programming the LEDs to display user-defined colors and brightness. In particular, we translate spatial and hardware indexes, extract associated RGB values for each LED, convert the values into appropriate API command for the dotStar LED specification, and populate a code template that uses an ATTiny85 to send the appropriate signal.

EVALUATION: SECONDARY OPTICS SYSTEM

In order to quantify the effectiveness of our design tool and fabrication technique, we quantitatively evaluated our secondary optic systems against established material and diffusion techniques. We also invited 11 participants (described in the next section) to provide qualitative feedback on the overall look and feel of the diffusers and reflectors.

Setup

We constructed 7 secondary optic systems to assess luminaire quality. Each system had a circular beam plane 50 mm in diameter, positioned 10 mm above a 1 watt LED (APA102C) with a 120° viewing angle. The systems varied by the following conditions: (control) a bare uncovered LED; (control) a 3mm acrylic diffuser hand-frosted with 300 grit sandpaper; (control) two layers of 120 micron OptiGrafix Light Diffuser Film. The remaining four systems each had a 3 mm PDMS glass diffuser with: no reflector, a 0.1 mm resolution PLA reflector; a 0.005 mm resolution SLA reflector, and a 0.005 mm resolution SLA TIR reflector.

Each system was photographed in a dark room at ISO200 18mm f/11 1/100 sec; a 10 px Gaussian smoothing filter was applied to a 500 x 500 px downsampled grayscale image. A luminosity plot was constructed from the image's relative luminosity values relative to the angle from the beam axis.

Results

Figure 8 depicts the resulting luminosity plot for each system. While frosted acrylic and diffuser film do distribute luminosity (diffuse the LED), our optical systems were able to distribute more luminosity to the extreme angles (at 60°, 0.43 (PLA) compared to 0.3 (Acrylic)), and reduce glare at the beam axis (0°, 0.74 for TIR). We expect fabrication limitations to have caused lower efficiency and a bright halo in the outer regions of the TIR lens.

Participants in our study ranked the perceived diffuseness of each optical system, excluding the TIR system. Due to a small sample size, we report descriptive statistics and summarize results in Table 1:

0.005 mm SLA	**0.10 mm PLA**	**Diffuser Only**
$1.4 \pm .56$	2.1 ± 1.1	2.7 ± 0.71
OptiGrafix	**Frosted Acrylic**	**Bare LED**
3.8 ± 1.1	4.9 ± 0.3	6 ± 0

Table 1. Qualitative Ranking of Diffusement by Participants.

Notably, the system printed at the highest resolution (0.025 mm) was ranked as the most diffuse; the perceived difference between SLA and PLA printed reflectors, although quantitatively similar, was subject to stronger discrimination by participants (1.4 versus 2.1, rank). Frosted acrylic, while it only did better than an uncovered LED, had an aesthetic that many participants enjoyed. Furthermore, the tactile qualities of the PDMS-Glass diffusers were perceived as playful and interactive. Many participants desired the ability to design around these haptic features.

EVALUATION: DESIGN TOOL + LUMINAIRE

We also invited the 11 participants to design their own luminaires. The main goal of this user study was to obtain qualitative feedback on how the design tool facilitated luminaire design. We were especially interested in understanding a user's mental model of light, and what functions and aesthetic choices this understanding would afford.

Participants

We conducted the study with eleven participants who had previously used LEDs and had experience with vector graphic design. Participants were recruited from university mailing lists in Art, Architecture, and Design. The average age of participants was 22 ± 3 (7 female). Participants were selected based on self-reported expertise with vector graphic design and previous exposure working with LEDs and electronic device design. Most users reported limited experience with 3D printing or digital fabrication tools.

Procedure

Each user participated in a 1 hour workshop and 30 minute followup interview and was compensated $40. Each session resulted in a completed luminaire which was given to the user.

Workshop Each workshop consisted of an electronics background questionnaire, a showcase of luminaires, a diffuser ranking task, a design tool tutorial, and a 40 minute design task. Each participant was tasked with creating a luminaire graphic with 5-7 LEDs not to exceed a 5" x 5" area. Participants were also asked to reflect aloud on the example luminaires, the design tool, and their design process. Due to fabrication time limitations, each luminaire was fabricated by the investigators after the workshop; some degree of experience is needed to solder surface mount components, although components are relatively large (>5mm) and with practice easily hand-solderable. Additional steps were taken to demystify the process during the followup.

Followup After the luminaire was constructed, participants were invited back to reflect on the final design. To avoid blackboxing the process, participants were given a tour of the fabrication machines and provided an explanation of the materials and techniques involved in producing their luminaire. We asked users a series of questions regarding their experiences with the design tool, as well as the final fabricated devices.

RESULTS: DESIGN TOOL + FINAL LUMINAIRE

All participants successfully completed their designs; some designs are represented in Figure 9. We first report survey responses, then present qualitative results from participant interactions with the luminaire design tool during the workshop, and finally discuss interview responses once participants received their fabricated luminaires. We synthesize these findings into common themes and insights for future physical design tools.

Barriers of Entry to LED Design

In our survey, participants reported experience with through-hole component LEDs, while a few had interacted with addressable LED strips. The majority of users (8 of 11) had not worked with smart LEDs. Prior to being introduced to our tool, users described their projects involving LEDs in simple, binary terms. Their LEDs were used for behaviors like flashing and fading. Even for more hardware and software-proficient users, the language used to talk about light was limited to the binary "on/off". Other difficulties included hardware-to-design translation issues, especially in more complex designs like arranging LEDs in a circle:

> **Participant 170:** I remember it being tricky to address the LEDs ... we wanted the level of the circle to go up ... there was endless debugging with the strips.

Users cited the cost of smart LEDs and the difficulty to program complex behaviors as the primary barriers to LED usage.

Perceptions of the LED Aesthetic

Functionally, participants reported that LEDs used in personal projects were mostly used to indicate status. Aesthetics was the principle reason limiting LEDs to this specific use case. A majority of our participants mentioned that the aesthetics of LEDs, even in strip form, were unpleasant, and physically painful: "they hurt your eyes if you look directly at [them]." Users universally criticized the "characteristic look" of LEDs and how their overpowering presence and salience in designs forced their user to focus on the mechanics of the light rather than the design or overall experience:

> **Participant 160:** You look at them and you think "those are LEDs"... I don't like the characteristic look of LEDs. And I don't want to look at something and go "there's an LED inside that's making that light up."

Participants also described uncertainty relating to how their designs would appear in the final state, having difficulty prototyping and testing out various options:

> **Participant 169:** Sometimes LEDs just don't look that good. It's hard to know what they're going to look like to the user ... I'd love to make something that just diffused all of the lights together so that I could make a really nice transition between colors.

One participant so disliked seeing the mechanics of the LEDs that she took the opportunity to design in physical barriers to her luminaire to obfuscate the light source (Figure 9 #134), opting for an edge/rim light that emphasized the silhouette, despite the fact that our luminaires have built-in diffusers:

> **Participant 134:** [I don't want to] have that effect of seeing that bright LED directly. I feel like [seeing the LED underneath] reveals too much about how it functions.

Many participants never considered placing anything over the LEDs to affect the production of light. Some had attempted maneuvering around the bright lights by diffusing them with opaque or semi-transperent sheets, a plastic enclosure, or pre-fabricated lampshades. Despite strong negative experiences, users quickly warmed to the illumination aesthetic of the show-case luminaires:

> **Participant 179:** It's very aesthetically pleasing. And I like...the blend of colors that goes through it. It kind of reminds of seeing cities at night.

User Designs

Even in a brief workshop-style experience with limited exposure to the tool and this method of working with light, users readily generated unique light interactions. User-designed luminaires ranged from figurative to abstract (Figure 9). Several participants motivated their design decisions to elicit surprise, hiding elements in their design that would only be discoverable when power was supplied to luminaire (**#150**, **#179**, **#163**, and **#199**). Others used the design task as a sandbox, for example using a Venn diagram to explore color interactions (**#134**). Overall participant's assessment of their experience is summarized in Table 2. In particular, participants associated their perception of creative freedom with the tool (4.3) tied to the tool incorporating software (e.g. Adobe Illustrator) and design patterns that they are already familiar with.

	Creative Freedom	Object Quality	Agency
Rating	4.3 ± 1.0	3.9 ± 1.2	4.3 ± 0.7

Table 2. Qualitative Assessment Luminaire Design Tool and Fabricated Luminaire Objects. Responses are semantically anchored on a 5-point Likert scale, positive responses = 5.

Expanded Vocabulary Mirrors New Understanding

In our tool workflow, participants had to create and annotate their design geometries in an external vector graphics editor. Once a base design was created, our tool would load their graphics and apply treatments to more clearly indicate physical and conceptual geometries. Participants did have difficulty conceptualizing these distinctions in the abstract, however direct manipulation of light sources grounded their mental model of how the design tool worked:

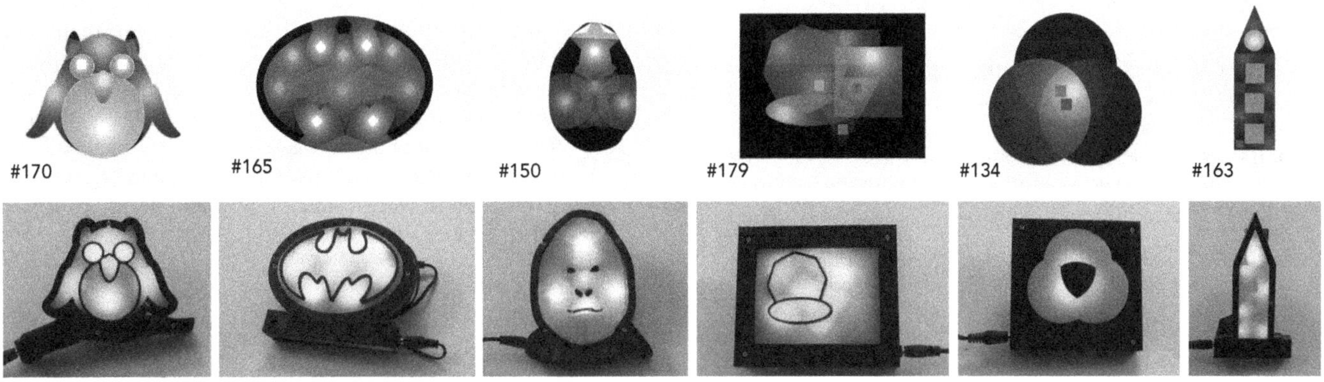

Figure 9. Luminaires fabricated from user designs: (top) simulated results from the luminaire design tool, (bottom) the final physical luminaire.

> **Participant 170:** I'm thinking about the way the light is going to work. I wanted to define shapes and I wanted to play with where the light was going to be placed.

One assumption we made was that participants would prioritize an arrangement of LEDs such as to produce a diffuse luminaire. However, for some, the light ray interactions became a formal element to consider. User #179 wanted to place LEDs in an arrangement that would create new shapes and forms from shadow and color interaction.

> **Participant 179:** There might be some leakage, if the [rays] intersect [geometries] at an interesting angle.

This approach exposed the positive and negative spaces that arose from the shadows created from different geometries. As users gained familiarity with the new capabilities afforded by the tool, they frequently returned to edit their base vector file, further developing their understanding of what effects their choices would have, and beginning to conceptualize light as a physical medium:

> **Participant 170:** I'm noticing the other shape that you made, these sides were different, so I could direct it to this edge, or this edge only. Instead I'm kind of diffusing it through the whole thing. I want to make one edge that encapsulates the shape but then also allows me to direct the light wherever I want.

For expert users, the largest amount of design time was spent on examining light interactions with geometries. We saw different light aesthetic concerns arise from the different simulated views. The composition view influenced more thinking around light decay/falloff.

> **Participant 169:** Also you can see a difference in the light intensity based on how concentrated the light beams are. I'm surprised that the light spreads so clearly in this [white ray view].

whereas the interaction (colored ray) view elicited more thinking about blending and LED color interactions:

> **Participant 170:** A second ago, the light was down here and it was covering more space but it wasn't really blending. So it's helpful to see that there might be some blending up here if I put the light up here...

Participants verbalized a new consideration of the physical factors of the LED. A shift in vocabulary reflected this new understanding of the aesthetic potential of light. All participants conceded they had never really thought about light interactions before, and the tool represented a new engaging type of thinking that they were eager to pursue in future designs.

Followup Reactions

In the followup, participants shared a new awareness of LEDs in their daily life. Diffusion was a particularly salient trait that began to take form in new design projects.

> **Participant 134:** I'm trying to make a tube of light ... I was thinking about what kind of considerations I have to make to get the light to spread all around.

Even participants sensitive to the LED aesthetic were motivated by the diffusion of their luminaires:

> **Participant 134:** I previously hadn't even thought about incorporating LEDs, but now I'm thinking about how we might incorporate LEDs to make things more user friendly.

Expectations from the tool's simulated results and the final physical luminaire formed a hard contract with user's end perception of the tool. Notably, participants were satisfied with the fidelity of the tool to the fabricated design results of their design (3.9). Specifically, users responded positively to the texture and flexibility of the diffusers. Users were intrigued with the way the tool allowed emergent shapes to appear, and expressed interest in the construction process. Some physical luminaires failed to meet expectations:

> **Participant 179:** I can't really tell the different shapes that were initially in the design ... besides the hard sharp boundaries. It is interesting [that] these cut off on each other a lot harder than I expected, like the yellow meeting the blue there's a sharp line of contrast – I thought there would be more of a mixing zone.

Despite this, participants reported feeling agency (4.3) to integrate their designs into more domain-specific projects upon understanding the limitations of the tool.

Renewal of Light as a Medium

Participants began to consider light as a physical medium over which they could wield control. Users emphasized blending and mixing of colors to achieve novel effects and indicated a desire to "paint with light", rather than simply add LEDs:

> **Participant 160** I've never even tried blending LED colors together so this facilitates a little more advanced thinking: I don't want to

just use LEDs separately; I want to blend them together to use color effects and make them brighter.

The tool allowed users to rapidly prototype their concepts, visualizing how the final piece would appear with the LEDs in place. Users readily incorporated soft and hard edges, mixing colors and delineated conceptual boundaries in their designs; users expressed a desire to play around with the tool more and discover new light interactions.

Participant 169: I'd play around more with hard edges and soft edges, to see if I could get some nice mixing. I'd love to see how the color is actually changing and change it with more intention.

DISCUSSION

Although this work discusses, explores, and expands the role of light in design, we see these insights and principles guiding the design of future tools for physical making.

LED as Hybrid Practice

Viewing and working with light as material presents a possible hybrid practice, or the conversation that arises from working with both digital and physical processes. This type of practice often strikes a tension largely motivated by traditional media's nearness-of-hand and digital media's distributed, fast, and random access. We see such a tension manifest in a common critique that electronics in visual design are overpowering, distracting from any other visual elements. On the other hand, this saliency has been largely leveraged by interaction designers to engage and captivate audiences. Often, this "tacking on of media" [20] limits the exploration of the physical design space to instead focus on designing through digital manipulation. This line of thinking aligned with the mental model and LED interaction patterns of participants in our workshop. This work provides an alternative viewpoint that positions a medium so closely aligned with the digital-aesthetic and provides handles to explore physical characteristics and interactions with light. The sun-moon artifact in Figure 1b demonstrates one such break in the digital aesthetic – the hard edge characteristic of graphic display; by allowing an analog mixture of light sources in the sun flames, a richer more organic aesthetic can arise. We envision this physical approach used in concert with digital exploration of smart materials.

LED Media Architectures

The demand for an expanded LED aesthetic is present and growing. As flexible electronics develop, LEDs can be integrated as tattoos on skin using maker-friendly processes [17]. In its most subversive role, low-cost LED "throwies" [24] have gained traction as urban graffiti. LEDs may also make their way into clothing and wearables should it be able to operate in a design space of ambiguity, slowness, and other physical characteristics [5]. For instance, with the wearable luminaire headpin depicted in Figure 1a, we might be able to have greater synergy with the complex texture of hair and clothing with the shadows cast by a tactile diffuser. This work supports these diversifying uses of the LED, providing handles to manipulate the LED as a material and expand the electro-aesthetic. Our fabrication technique, although bound by bed size, results in a final cost of 5" x 5" display component with 10 LEDs in the \$6-7 price range; as a standalone device, logical control and power bring the cost to \$12. Study participants all confirmed that design opportunities well deserved the cost; many cited access to fabrication facilities as the main issue to adoption. In this work, we described an approach for designing light emitted from the more ubiquitous and low-cost LED. We envision our tool as supporting a wider ecology of materials, including electroluminescence (EL) wire and panels, and organic polymer LEDs [29], to foreground the physical design of light in interactive devices, wearables, and urban architecture.

LIMITATIONS

In this work, we showed that we can generate geometries that more effectively diffuse a point light across a shape. However, our technique needs at least (5 mm) above the light source to be effective. We see our technique used in conjunction with light pipe structures that can transport light more efficiently that could reduce the footprint currently required to illuminate luminaires with large surface areas and complex geometries (i.e. twists-and-turns). Current 3D printing resolution still introduces artifacts into fabricated lenses; an efficient transfer of light would be possible with smooth surfaces, however we found aesthetically acceptable results using SLA printing techniques. As printing resolution improves, we foresee our tool as a preliminary step to designing custom non-imaging secondary optics for illumination design.

FUTURE WORK

While this work explores light's properties of diffusion, several opportunities exist for expanding Illumination Aesthetics. For instance, more advanced optics geometries such as side-emmision or phase masks can be used to finely redirect light to specific locations and produce expressive inteference patterns [30]; other techniques might incorporate motorized, high-powered, or architectural elements to produce interactive urban lighting. We touch on this with our tactile illumination map in Figure 1c, where an urban area is modelled using a 3D diffuser; buildings can be selectively illuminated to provide directions or materialize hidden energies from geophysical data feeds. While the work focuses on physical design, exploring the intersection of physical and digital control of light and other actuators could greatly expand electronic aesthetics.

CONCLUSION

In *Illumination Aesthetics*, we expanded a user's ability to physically manipulate and shape light through computational design and fabrication of secondary optics. We demonstrated that our computational design pipeline can support a wide range of geometric configurations. In our workshop study, we fabricated 11 custom luminaires designed by our participants found that our tool altered existing perceptions of the role and function of the LED in interactive objects and displays. We contribute design principles for supporting the expanding ecology of illumination design in order to fully leverage light as an expressive medium.

ACKNOWLEDGMENTS

We thank Ryan Kapur, Niraj Rao, Jacqueline Garcia for their aid with early design, implementation, and fabrication, and the anonymous reviewers for their valuable feedback. This research was supported by funding from Adobe and Nokia.

REFERENCES

1. 2015. *LED Lighting in the US*. Dossier. Statista.
2. Eric Brockmeyer, Ivan Poupyrev, and Scott Hudson. 2013. PAPILLON: Designing Curved Display Surfaces with Printed Optics. In *Proceedings of ACM Symposium on User Interface Software and Technology (UIST '13)*. ACM, New York, NY, USA, 457–462. DOI: http://dx.doi.org/10.1145/2501988.2502027
3. Jim Campbell. 2011. Exploded Views. (2011).
4. Hsi-Chao Chen, Jun-Yu Lin, and Hsuan-Yi Chiu. 2013. Rectangular illumination using a secondary optics with cylindrical lens for LED street light. *Optics Express* 21, 3 (Feb. 2013), 3201. DOI: http://dx.doi.org/10.1364/OE.21.003201
5. Laura Devendorf, Joanne Lo, Noura Howell, Jung Lin Lee, Nan-Wei Gong, M. Emre Karagozler, Shiho Fukuhara, Ivan Poupyrev, Eric Paulos, and Kimiko Ryokai. 2016. "I Don't Want to Wear a Screen": Probing Perceptions of and Possibilities for Dynamic Displays on Clothing. In *Proceedings of ACM SIGCHI Human Factors in Computing Systems (CHI '16)*. ACM, New York, NY, USA, 6028–6039. DOI: http://dx.doi.org/10.1145/2858036.2858192
6. Olafur Eliasson. 2003. Olafur Eliasson the Weather Project. (2003). http://www.tate.org.uk/whats-on/exhibition/unilever-series-olafur-eliasson-weather-project/olafur-eliasson-weather-project
7. Dan Flavin. 1963. Diagonal of May 25, 1963. (1963). http://www.themodern.org/collection/Diagonal-of-May-25-1963/1126
8. William Gaver, John Bowers, Andy Boucher, Andy Law, Sarah Pennington, and Nicholas Villar. 2006. The History Tablecloth: Illuminating Domestic Activity. In *In: DIS*.
9. Gjon Mili. 1949. Picasso draws a centaur. (1949).
10. Chris Harrison, John Horstman, Gary Hsieh, and Scott Hudson. 2012. Unlocking the expressivity of point lights. In *Proceedings of ACM SIGCHI Human Factors in Computing Systems*. 1683–1692. http://dl.acm.org/citation.cfm?id=2208296
11. Brad Hindson. 2013. Light as Material – Rethinking How We Use Light. (2013).
12. Jettie Hoonhout, Lillian Jumpertz, Jon Mason, and Tom Bergman. 2013. Exploration into Lighting Dynamics for the Design of More Pleasurable Luminaires. In *Proceedings of Designing Pleasurable Products and Interfaces (DPPI '13)*. ACM, New York, NY, USA, 185–192. DOI: http://dx.doi.org/10.1145/2513506.2513526
13. Illuminating Engineering Society. 2011. Discover Lighting: An Introduction to Lighting Basics. (2011). http://www.ies.org/lighting/sources/luminaires.cfm
14. Juerg Lehni and Jonathan Puckey. 2011. Paper.js. (2011).
15. Rong-Hao Liang, Chao Shen, Yu-Chien Chan, Guan-Ting Chou, Liwei Chan, De-Nian Yang, Mike Y. Chen, and Bing-Yu Chen. 2015. WonderLens: Optical Lenses and Mirrors for Tangible Interactions on Printed Paper. In *Proceedings of ACM SIGCHI Human Factors in Computing Systems (CHI '15)*. ACM, New York, NY, USA, 1281–1284. DOI: http://dx.doi.org/10.1145/2702123.2702434
16. Gordon E. Liljegren and Eugene L. Foster. 1990. Figure with back projected image using fiber optics. (Dec. 1990). http://www.google.com/patents/US4978216 U.S. Classification 353/28, 353/74; International Classification G09F19/00, G09F19/18, G09F19/08, A63H33/22, G03B21/00, A63H3/36, G09F19/02, G03B21/62; Cooperative Classification G09F19/02, G09F19/18, G09F19/08, G09F2019/086, G09F19/00, G09F2019/088; European Classification G09F19/18, G09F19/08.
17. Joanne Lo, Doris Jung Lin Lee, Nathan Wong, David Bui, and Eric Paulos. 2016. Skintillates: Designing and Creating Epidermal Interactions. In *Proceedings of Designing Interactive Systems (DIS '16)*. ACM, New York, NY, USA, 853–864. DOI: http://dx.doi.org/10.1145/2901790.2901885
18. Wojciech Matusik, Boris Ajdin, Jinwei Gu, Jason Lawrence, Hendrik P. A. Lensch, Fabio Pellacini, and Szymon Rusinkiewicz. 2009. Printing Spatially-varying Reflectance. In *ACM SIGGRAPH Asia 2009 Papers (SIGGRAPH Asia '09)*. ACM, New York, NY, USA, 128:1–128:9. DOI: http://dx.doi.org/10.1145/1661412.1618474
19. László Moholy-Nagy. 2016. Moholy-Nagy, László: Light-Space-Modulator. (Sept. 2016). http://www.medienkunstnetz.de/works/licht-raum-modulator/
20. Michael Nitsche, Andrew Quitmeyer, Kate Farina, Samuel Zwaan, and Hye Yeon Nam. 2014. Teaching Digital Craft. In *CHI '14 Extended Abstracts on Human Factors in Computing Systems (CHI EA '14)*. ACM, 719–730. DOI: http://dx.doi.org/10.1145/2559206.2578872
21. Marios Papas, Thomas Houit, Derek Nowrouzezahrai, Markus Gross, and Wojciech Jarosz. 2012. The Magic Lens: Refractive Steganography. *ACM Trans. Graph.* 31, 6 (Nov. 2012), 186:1–186:10. DOI: http://dx.doi.org/10.1145/2366145.2366205
22. Thiago Pereira, Szymon Rusinkiewicz, and Wojciech Matusik. 2014. Computational Light Routing: 3D Printed Optical Fibers for Sensing and Display. *ACM Trans. Graph.* 33, 3 (June 2014), 24:1–24:13. DOI: http://dx.doi.org/10.1145/2602140
23. James Pierce and Eric Paulos. 2013. Electric Materialities and Interactive Technology. In *Proceedings of the SIGCHI Conference on Human Factors in Computing Systems (CHI '13)*. ACM, New York, NY, USA, 119–128. DOI:http://dx.doi.org/10.1145/2470654.2470672

24. Evan Roth and James Powderly. 2006. LED Throwies. (2006).

25. Daniel Rozin. 1999. Wooden Mirror. (1999).

26. Peter Schreiber, Serge Kudaev, Peter Dannberg, and Uwe D. Zeitner. 2005. Homogeneous LED-illumination using microlens arrays, Vol. 5942. 59420K–59420K–9. DOI:http://dx.doi.org/10.1117/12.618747

27. James Turrell. 1968. Shallow Space Constructions. (1968).

28. Karl Willis, Eric Brockmeyer, Scott Hudson, and Ivan Poupyrev. 2012. Printed Optics: 3D Printing of Embedded Optical Elements for Interactive Devices. In *Proceedings of ACM Symposium on User Interface Software and Technology (UIST '12)*. ACM, New York, NY, USA, 589–598. DOI: http://dx.doi.org/10.1145/2380116.2380190

29. Tomoyuki Yokota, Peter Zalar, Martin Kaltenbrunner, Hiroaki Jinno, Naoji Matsuhisa, Hiroki Kitanosako, Yutaro Tachibana, Wakako Yukita, Mari Koizumi, and Takao Someya. 2016. Ultraflexible organic photonic skin. *Science Advances* 2, 4 (2016). DOI: http://dx.doi.org/10.1126/sciadv.1501856

30. Qiang Zhou, Wenzheng Yang, Fengtao He, Razvan Stoian, Rongqing Hui, and Guanghua Cheng. 2013. Femtosecond multi-beam interference lithography based on dynamic wavefront engineering. *Optics Express* 21, 8 (April 2013), 9851. DOI: http://dx.doi.org/10.1364/OE.21.009851

Transformative Appetite: Shape-Changing Food Transforms from 2D to 3D by Water Interaction through Cooking

Wen Wang[1,2*], Lining Yao[1*], Teng Zhang[3], Chin-Yi Cheng[1], Daniel Levine[1], Hiroshi Ishii[1]

[1]MIT Media Lab
Cambridge, USA
(wwen, liningy, chinyich, dvlevine, ishii)
@media.mit.edu

[2]Chemical Engineering,
MIT, Cambridge, USA
wwen@mit.edu

[3]Mechanical and Aerospace
Engineering, Syracuse
University,
Syracuse, USA
tzhang48@syr.edu

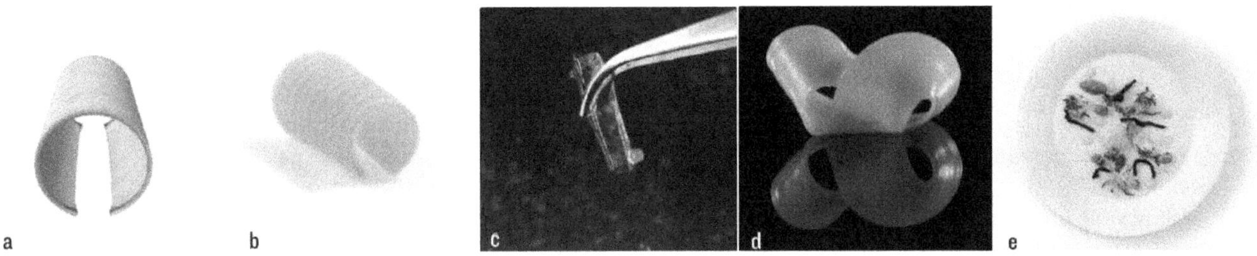

Figure 1. (a-b) Bending simulation of edible film and its corresponding actual sample; (c) self-wrapping water sushi; (d) 3D food from flat 2D film; (e) dish design with squid ink flavored twisting noodle.

ABSTRACT
We developed a concept of transformative appetite, where edible 2D films made of common food materials (protein, cellulose or starch) can transform into 3D food during cooking. This transformation process is triggered by water adsorption, and it is strongly compatible with the 'flat packaging' concept for substantially reducing shipping costs and storage space. To develop these transformable foods, we performed material-based design, established a hybrid fabrication strategy, and conducted performance simulation. Users can customize food shape transformations through a pre-defined simulation platform, and then fabricate these designed patterns using additive manufacturing. Three application techniques are provided - 2D-to-3D folding, hydration-induced wrapping, and temperature-induced self-fragmentation, to present the shape, texture, and interaction with food materials. Based on this concept, several dishes were created in the kitchen, to demonstrate the futuristic dining experience through materials-based interaction design.

∗The first two authors contributed equally to this work.

CHI 2017, May 06 - 11, 2017, Denver, CO, USA

ACM 978-1-4503-4655-9/17/05…$15.00
DOI: http://dx.doi.org/10.1145/3025453.3026019

Author Keywords
Transformable food; water interaction; 2D-to-3D; autonomous shape-changing; anisotropic swelling; interactive edibles; dish design

ACM Classification Keywords
Design

INTRODUCTION
The concept of 'flat packaging' was coined by IKEA, a Swedish furniture company, which manufactures 2D furniture segments for assembly into 3D furniture by people in their own homes. This concept enables the company to benefit from low shipping costs due to compactness of the 2D segments while maintaining the desired function and appearance of the 3D end products.

Here we propose a similar concept for the food industry, where edible materials are manufactured into highly compact 2D segments and transformed in the kitchen or on the dining table into 3D structures, which bring different textures and eating experiences to diners. We combine material science, computer-aided design and additive manufacturing to enable autonomous transformations in pre-defined ways, which liberates users from tedious cooking tasks. Specifically, through three techniques and dish examples, we aim to demonstrate that the 2D-to-3D transformation via hydration process is good for 1) creating unique mouth feel textures and shapes to enrich the eating experiences; 2) achieving programmable food transformations; and 3) save space during shipping and storage.

We believe that this concept and the technologies we developed for enabling food transformation via hydration will contribute to the evolution of more cost-effective food manufacturing and futuristic dining cultures. We feel that their most immediate applications will be found in upgrading quality of compact foods that are widely used in outdoor activities.

CONTRIBUTION

Design through Edible Material Innovation

- Characterized hygromorphic behaviors of three major food materials: gelatin (protein), agar and cellulose (fiber), as well as starch (carbohydrate), for designing bi-layer edible films.
- Explained the bending mechanism and simulated the sequential bending behaviors through finite element analysis.

Fabrication Practice and Computer-Aided Design

- Established a simplified simulation platform that combines material mechanics and geometric design, to enable users to design different shape transformations.
- Proposed a material fabrication strategy to create controllable transformation geometries.

Food Design

- Proposed autonomous shape-changing food that reduces shipping costs, enriches eating experiences, and saves storage space.
- Presented a new way to enhance interactions between diners and food through shape transformations from 2D-to-3D in the kitchen.

RELATED WORK

Material Based Shape-Changing Interfaces

Researchers in HCI have increasingly been working on material aspects of shape-changing interfaces, envisioning the embedded programmability through the design of material composition and structure, or, 'computational' materials with pre-programmed interactivities [1-4]. Rasmussen et al. [5] proposed a set of novel interaction modalities enabled by shape-changing interfaces, including functional aims (dynamic affordances, communication and force feedbacks) as well as hedonic aims (emotional experience and aesthetics). Coelho et al. further pointed out a material-based approach to design shape-changing interfaces [6]. In their paper, they described transformative materials that respond to different stimuli types. Our work contributes to this vision by introducing this approach to the application of food.

Water-Triggered Shape Transformation

Recently, materials that can change shape through interaction with water have been commonly used in many research domains, including drug delivery systems [7], interactive architecture [8, 9], smart household objects [4], motor generators [10] and biomimetic morphologies [11]. These smart materials exhibit different shapes when adsorbing or desorbing water, accompanied by swelling or shrinking with volume or structure change. To achieve high programmability of the final shape, they use either rigid shape constraints (e.g. fibrils or hinges) or uneven stress distribution (e.g. material geometry alignment) [12] through anisotropic swelling. All of these actuation system use synthetic materials as key components, which prevent them from being safe for consumption in the food industry - to our knowledge, we have not found, to date, any system completely made of edible, natural materials.

Shape-Changing Food and Digitally Fabricated Food

Food shape is an important factor for both the cooking and dining experience. Traditionally, shape change in food materials is observed and sometime used as a cooking indicator. For instance, ravioli (an Italian pasta) begins to inflate during boiling (due to starch hydration accompanied by vapor generation inside pasta), and floating signifies the complete boiling of the pasta. Recently, the design of interactive food has become an important research topic [13], and has been demonstrated within the context of HCI, where stimuli such as pH [14], lighting [15], and food cost [16] were used to enhance the interactivity between a diner and food materials. In particular, Kan et al. developed a series of edible organic sensor-actuators that respond to pH and transform in shape, color and odor [14]. Their paper envisions the wide use of such organic materials in material-mediated interaction design including food. It described shape-programmable pasta triggered by pH, and introduced a few use scenarios where shape-transformable pasta can be valuable: flavor and sauce retention, sensory augmentation, and user-based customization. Moreover, digital gastronomy [17] was proposed as a vision of how food can be prepared with property customization via a variety of digital fabrication machines including 3D printers and CNC machines. We are inspired by this domain of research, and propose a deeper investigation into the transformation triggered by hydration processes instead of pH, with hope that more stimuli types can be included to trigger shape -programmable food; in addition, we focus on investigating a practical use scenario - flat packed food - to save shipping and packaging cost.

MATERIALS EXPLORATION

Edible Materials Interact with Water

Cooking processes can be divided into two categories: hydration and dehydration. Each may cause shape transformation. These phenomena have been widely observed in kitchen during cooking. For example, noodles grow thicker as they are boiled or steamed, while potato strips inflate as they are baked or fried. In this paper, we focus on the hydration process and quantify the transformation of food materials during water adsorption.

We found most of the food gels hydrate and change volume when absorbing water through hydrophilic interaction within their molecular or intermolecular structure. One way to quantify a material's ability to hydrate is to use the swelling index (I_s), which is defined in Equation 1, where W_s is the weight of the swollen food material, and W_d is the weight of the dry food material.

$$I_s(\%) = \frac{W_s - W_d}{W_d} \times 100 \qquad \text{(Equation 1)}$$

We measured swelling index of a few major edible components (Figure 2), which showed that protein (gelatin), carbohydrate (starch), and soluble fiber (agar) can all absorb about five times its own weight within ten minutes (in film form), while insoluble fiber (ethyl cellulose film) cannot absorb any water. This finding is the basis of designing shape transformation through volume change by introducing anisotropic swelling behavior within the food's composite structure.

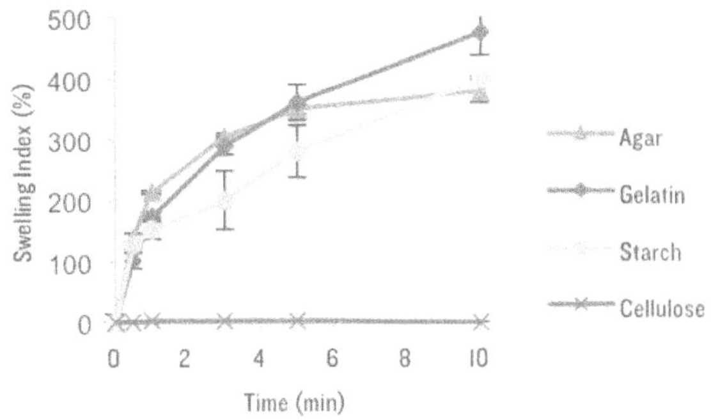

Figure 2. Comparison of swelling index of four different edible materials at 20°C.

Material Selection Rationale

In this paper, we focused on gelatin, and studied the shape-change behavior of gelatin-cellulose composite films during hydration through cooking. Our reasons for focusing on gelatin are multifold. First, gelatin dissolves well in solution before the gelation process, ensuring uniformity of the food gel before drying. Second, gelatin materials at different molecular weights (or Bloom numbers) are commercially available, enabling us to easily and precisely control their chemical and physical properties. Third, there are different sources of gelatin (e.g. from porcine skin, cattle bones), to suit diners' specific needs. Fourth, comparing with other edible materials (such as starch), it is much easier to prepare a flat film, due to the high flatness of the gelatin-air surface and its low attachment to the supporting holder (e.g. petri dish).

To form a composite structure, we choose ethyl cellulose as the water barrier, based on its low water adsorbing capacity and high alcohol solubility. The unique properties of ethyl cellulose compared with other types of cellulose (e.g. methylcellulose) enables high-precision digital printing and large-scale screen printing, by which ethyl cellulose fiber can be easily deposited through solvent evaporation. In literature, tensile stress of cellulose fiber is a well-known parameter and can be used to manipulate shape constraint effect and obtain a well-controlled transformation.

Temperature Dependent Swelling/Melting

While temperature modulation in cooking is commonplace, we have not found previous work using temperature modulation for controlling and manipulating food shape transformation. We aim to use temperature as a parameter to change swelling and melting of edible materials. To achieve this, we first studied the swelling behavior of these edible materials at different temperatures in water. As expected, at high temperature, edible films can absorb water at a faster rate than in cold water (Figure 3). This can be explained by Fick's law (Equation 2), where diffusion flux (J) is dependent on both diffusion coefficient (D) and the concentration at certain location ($\frac{\partial \varphi}{\partial x}$), where the diffusion coefficient (D) is a function of temperature (T) and proportionality constant (D_0) (material specific). E_A and k are constant.

$$J = -D\frac{\partial \varphi}{\partial x} = -(D_0 e^{-E_A/(kT)})\frac{\partial \varphi}{\partial x} \qquad \text{(Equation 2)}$$

Gelatin has a very low melting point, which becomes an important parameter in our design. High molecular weight gelatin begins to melt at ~40°C, and low molecular weight gelatin begins to melt at ~20°C. By adjusting hydration temperature, we can switch physical status of gelatin from a solid state to a liquid state. With these methods, we are able to prepare a composite structure and create temperature-sensitive hinges using low molecular weight gelatin to achieve programmable breakage due to melting.

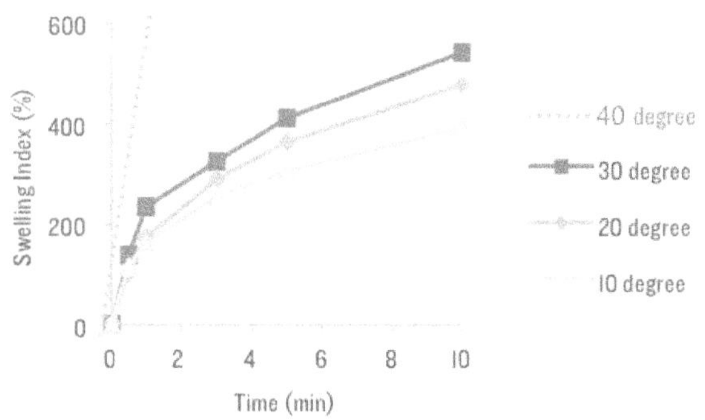

Figure 3. Temperature dependent swelling of gelatin.

COMPOSITE MATERIALS DESIGN

Designing Substrate Film

In order to design different physical transformations, we need to prepare a film with density distribution. We found that when preparing a film in a petri dish and evaporating water only from the top of that film, the desired density heterogeneity could be achieved (Figure 4).

The solid-air boundary contains a higher concentration of gelatin, due to surface aggregation of the solids towards the interface. After forming a dried top layer, water evaporation in lower portion of the film becomes restricted. This results in the formation of gelatin film with a dense top layer and a loose, porous bottom layer. We validated this hypothesis by scanning electron microscope (SEM) characterization (Figure 4), where the top layer of the film is much denser than the bottom layer.

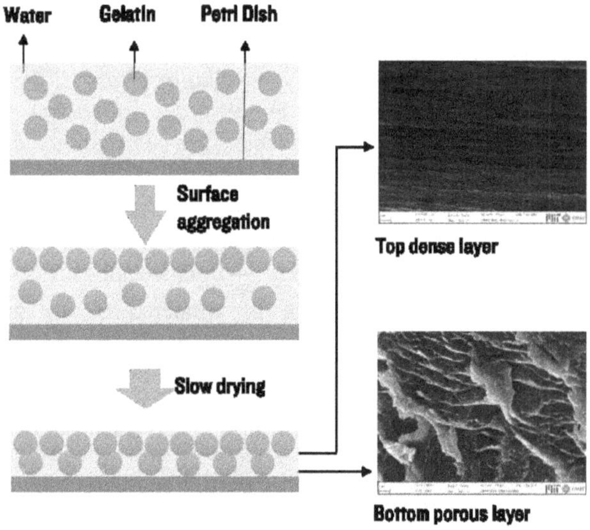

Figure 4. Formation of heterogeneous gelatin film.

Adding Shape Constraints/Water Barriers

In order to achieve a controllable bending behavior, we introduce ethyl cellulose strips as both shape constraints and water barriers on top of the gelatin film. This semi-rigid strip structure helps regulate the binding direction and create dynamic shape changes by modulating the top surface's water adsorption rate (mostly due to decreased water adsorption area).

MECHANISMS OF SHAPE TRANSFORMATION

Bending Analysis

When immerging the gelatin film with cellulose strips into water, the bottom layer exhibits a higher water adsorption rate than the top gelatin layer initially, due to a relatively larger water contact area. This initial upward bending direction is always along the longitude direction of the cellulose strip, because it is hard to compress a synergistic swollen top gelatin layer in the direction perpendicular to the cellulose strip (high expansion freedom).

Gelatin film is composed of a top layer (dense structure) and a bottom layer (porous structure) with a thickness ratio about 1:1 (based on SEM images). Thus, the overall water adsorption capacity of the top layer is higher than the bottom layer. After a specified duration, the folding direction reverses and the whole film bends downwards; the top layer has a greater capacity to absorb water (and swell) albeit at a slower rate than the bottom layer. The specific duration depends on the water adsorption rate, which can be controlled by designing the coverage of the cellulose on the gelatin surface, as well as the density of the cellulose strips (Figure 5).

During the hydration process, the gelatin film changes from glassy to a rubber-like state synchronized with water adsorption. The direction of bending depends on the stiffness of the cellulose strips at that time point. When cellulose is thick and stiff (shape constraint dominant), the film will bend towards the direction perpendicular to the cellulose strip. Otherwise, the film will prefer to bend along the direction of cellulose (flexible skeleton).

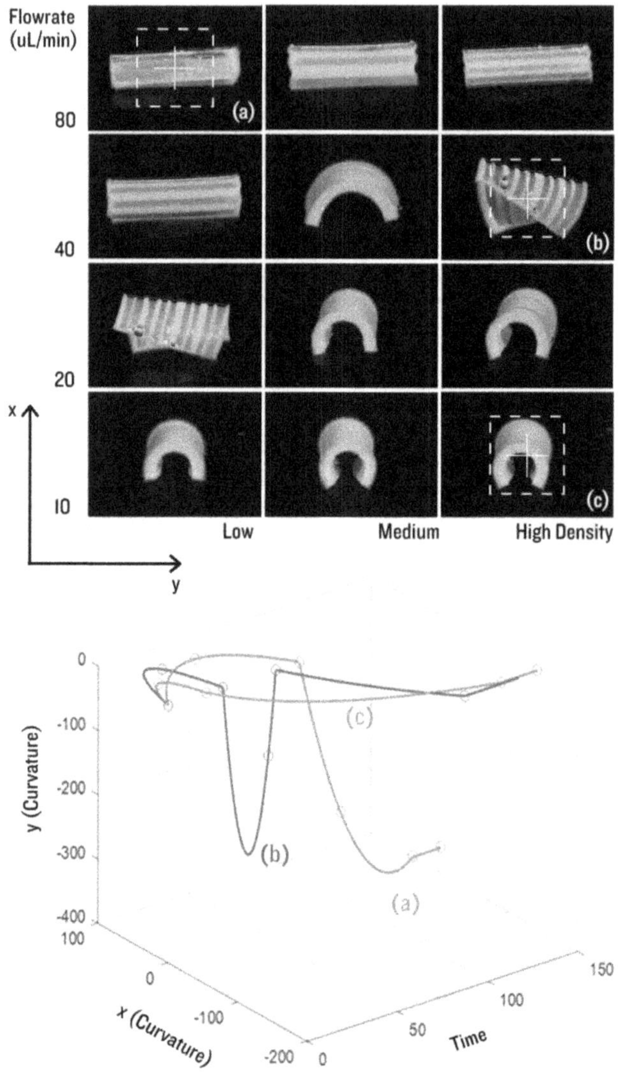

Figure 5. Bending curvature design by cellulose thickness and surface coverage density.

Mechanics Analysis

In short, we hypothesize that the cellulose strip has a dual role in controlling shape change of the whole structure. First, cellulose layer can be seen as a barrier for water diffusion, which modifies swelling behavior of the gelation film beneath of it. Second, the cellulose layer is also a mechanical constraint and can be used to tune the bending deformation of the structure. To verify this, we performed finite element (FE) simulations with software ABAQUS. Gelation and cellulose are each modeled as Neo-Hookean material in Equation 3, where μ is the shear modulus, $\lambda_i, i = 1,2,3$ the principle stretch ratio. The shear modulus of the bottom gelation layer is taken as the unit value ($\mu_1 = 1$) and the modulus of the top gelation layer is set to be $\mu_2 = 5$, as the density of the top film is higher than the bottom layer (SEM in Figure 4).

$$U = \frac{1}{2}\mu(\lambda_1^2 + \lambda_2^2 + \lambda_3^2 - 3) \qquad \text{(Equation 3)}$$

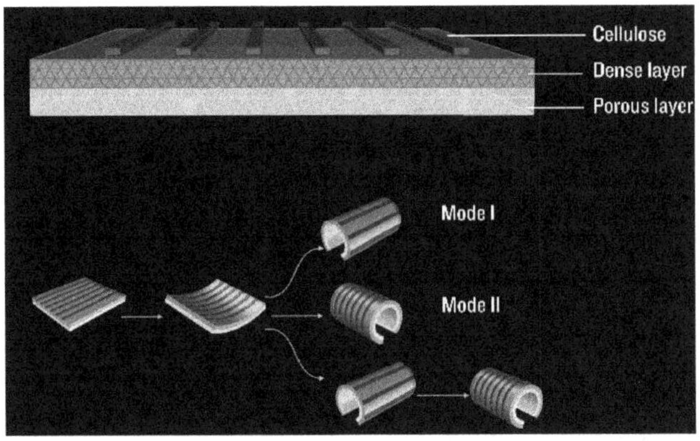

Figure 6. Diagram of three layer film and its sequential bending behavior.

To test the mechanical constraint effect of the cellulose, two set of simulations are carried out with a shear modulus of cellulose as $\mu_2 = 10$ and 25, respectively. The geometry of the structure is: thickness of bottom gelation film $h_1 = 35\,\mu m$; thickness of top gelation film $h_2 = 35\,\mu m$; thickness of cellulose layer $h_3 = 10\,\mu m$; the width of the structure is 15 mm and the height of the structure is 13.8 mm; the cellulose lines are shown in Figure 6. Our FE simulations clearly show that the structure with soft cellulose will choose bending mode I, while the structure with stiff cellulose will choose bending mode II (Figure 7).

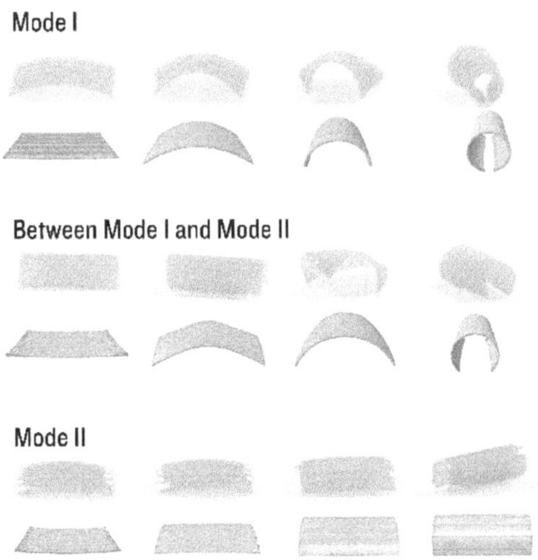

Figure 7. Comparison between actual transformation and simulation using finite element in ABAQUS.

FOLDING DESIGN

Beyond using straight lines as shape constraints to achieve one-dimensional folding, we have also developed two-dimensional folding by using either 2D constraints or distributing 1D constraints within 2D surface (Figure 8). By using curved lines or surface constraints, complex structures such as the flower shape, saddle shape, and cone shape were obtained. This folding principle provides us a basic grammar to design more complex shape transformations by simply manipulating geometry and constraints.

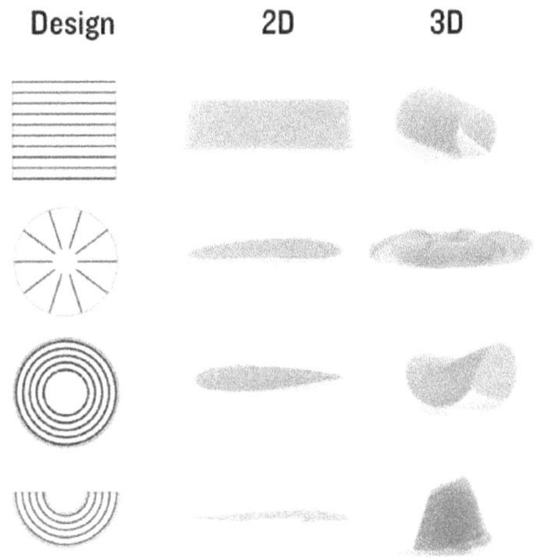

Figure 8. Design primitives (black lines indicate fiber location).

SIMULATION INTERFACE

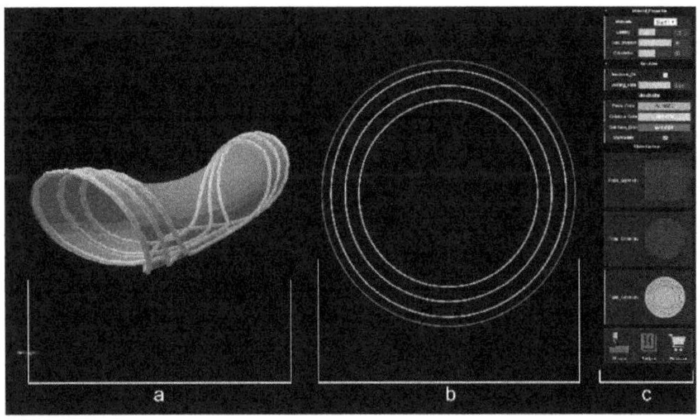

Figure 9. Illustration of user interface: a) transformation preview; b) cellulose constraints preview; c) variable sliders and options.

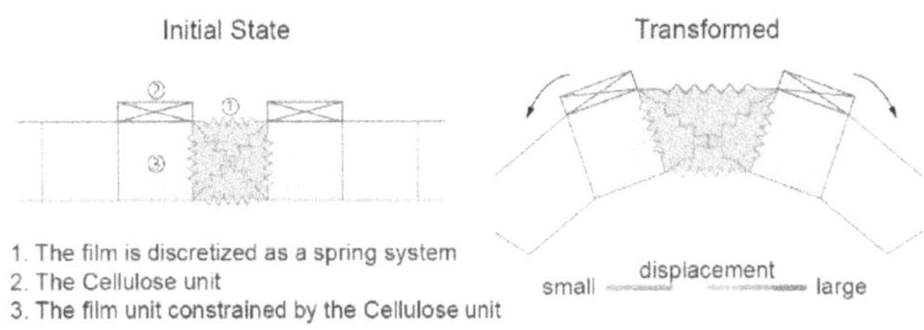

Figure 10. Simulation model units.

To facilitate design and predict the shape transformation of these edible films, we built a digital material design and simulation interface (Figure 9) with JavaScript, Rhinoceros, and Grasshopper. The platform can aid in the design process and interact with the user through the following steps. First, the user can select a variety of shapes for the substrate film. Second, our platform will automatically create the cellulose constraints based on the assigned shape. The user can tune the density, orientation, and thickness of the constraints by dragging sliders. After the constraints are defined, the user can preview the transformation immediately. When the users are satisfied with their design results, they can export support structure to G-code for printing.

To create a real-time preview, we pre-calculated a shape dataset in Rhino and Grasshopper, using a relatively simplified model (Figure 10) compared to our mechanics analysis. By interpolating the pre-calculated shapes in the database, the interface can visualize the result with virtually no computation costs. However, the capability of the design interface is limited by the dataset because the user cannot design shapes which we have not pre-calculated. For the current version, we only have the rectangle, saddle and flower shapes in our dataset.

FABRICATION STRATERGY

We combined wet lab material preparation with digital fabrication to achieve controllable food shape transformations. In doing so, we leverage the advantages of both methods to obtain a scalable and flexible fabrication strategy.

Materials

We procured PerfectaGel Gold gelatin sheets (200g Bloom) from Amazon.com. Low molecular weight gelatin (50-80 g Bloom, from porcine skin, Cat# 48720), ethyl cellulose (48.0-49.5% w/w ethoxyl basis, Cat# 46070) were purchased from Sigma-Aldrich. Food grade ethanol (95% w/v) was purchased from a local liquor store. Screen printing tools were purchased from Blink Art Supply. All other material science equipment was purchased from VWR and all other mechanical tooling was purchased from McMaster Carr. Traditional food materials were purchased from local supermarket.

Preparing Films

Edible films with heterogeneous density distribution were prepared by using plastic large petri dishes (diameter 15 cm) as containers in a wet lab. This method ensures one-directional water evaporation and a controllable density distribution. First, the solid edible materials (either gelatin or starch) were dissolved at a certain concentration (3-12% w/v) at room temperature for complete hydration (about 15 min). The solution was further transferred to a hotplate at ~60°C to ensure total melting of the solids in aqueous solution. We found this procedure could also be performed in a microwave (high heat for 1-2 min, avoid overheating). Conventionally, we use water to prepare a transparent and flavorless film. For adding flavors to the film, we found fruit punch, vegetable juice, and seafood extract can also be added into the mixture or as substitutes for water. Afterwards, varying amounts (12-60 mL) of solution were transferred into petri dish by pipet, to form different thicknesses of gel. The gel was cured at room temperature for about 5 min, and transferred to a windy area with fans to allow one-directional water evaporation (12-18 hours).

Preparing Cellulose Solution

Ethyl cellulose solution was used to create shape constraints on top of dried gelatin films, which control the bending direction during the hydration process due to the rigidity of the printed cellulose fiber. As ethyl cellulose does not absorb water, it can be used as a water barrier to decrease the top surface water adsorption rate. This will also create sequential shape transformations, where bending is firstly upwards (higher surface exposure in the bottom layer), and then downwards (higher overall expansion capacity). The printing solutions were prepared by dissolving ethyl cellulose solid materials in 95% food-grade ethanol (5-30% w/v), in a slightly heated water bath (~50°C).

Digital Printing through xPrint

With the purpose of increasing fabrication precision and customizability, we adapted a the digital printing platform xPrint [18] to deposit the cellulose on top of the gelatin films by an adjustable dispenser mounted on a CNC platform (Figure 11). Several parameters were tuned during printing, including cellulose concentration (5-30% w/v), line gap (1-5 mm), solution deposition speed (5-300 μL/min), gap between dispensing tip and gelatin film (0.1-0.5 mm), and tip diameter (0.008" to 0.024"), to achieve desired cellulose line thickness, height, and area coverage. Compared to previous materials used in xPrint, cellulose prepared in ethanol can easily solidify, potentially clogging the dispenser system.

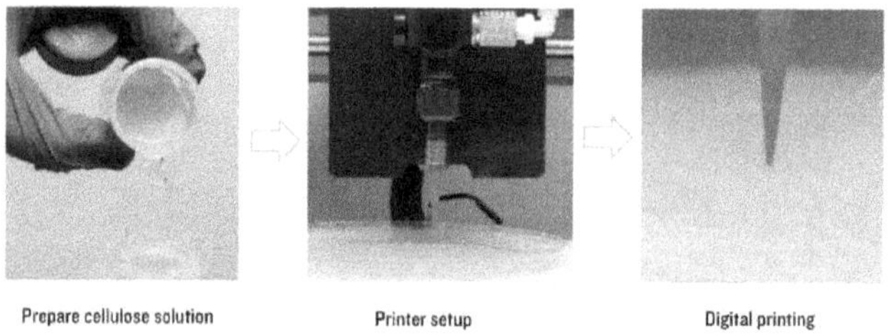

Figure 11. Digital printing process.

We found this was due to the evaporation of the ethanol in the windy fume hood. To reduce clogging, a seal cap with a long tubing outlet was attached on top of the solution reservoir connected with the dispenser. Before each printing, pre-extrusion at high flow rate (50 μL/min) was performed to ensure printing efficacy. Regular cleaning using 95% w/v ethanol was also used to clean the system between runs on different days.

Screen Printing

Beyond digital printing, we also applied screen printing to deposit cellulose, in order to demonstrate the scalability of our method (Figure 12). Similar to traditional screen printing, we substituted the base material with a flat gelatin film, and placed the mask on top of the screen mesh.

Cellulose concentration (5-30% w/v) was adjusted to achieve a desired viscosity, and a squeegee was used to spread the materials to form a thin layer. The height of cellulose depends on the total distance between top surface of mask and the film. This process can be easily scaled up for high volume manufacturing due to high efficiency. Since the cellulose will solidify on the mesh and it is tedious to clean, we also developed a simplified screen printing method without the mesh. Instead of sticking the cut mask by vinyl cutter on the mesh, the mask was directly pasted on the gelatin film. A tiny amount of cellulose solution (< 200 μL) was further spread using squeegee. Rapid peeling of the mask before complete solidification of cellulose is crucial to avoid unintentional removal of the cellulose strips.

Figure 12. Screen printing process.

FOOD INTERACTION TECHNIQUES

With the above-mentioned fabrication and simulation platform, we developed three techniques to demonstrate the customizability of achieving fragmentation, shape, texture, and interaction of food materials through shape transformation.

2D-to-3D Film

We fabricated different shapes of edible films through modulating both gelatin sheet geometry (e.g. disk, oval shape, S-shape) and shape constraint properties (e.g. cellulose density and thickness, line gap, total coverage). By adjusting these parameters, the rigidity of shape constraints and water diffusion rate can be modulated. We are able to match these fabricated shapes with the traditional molded pasta shapes (Figure 13 a-h), providing an exciting potential solution for making transformable 3D food. In the meantime, we also created new special shapes (Figure 13 i-k) that offer potential for novel dish development.

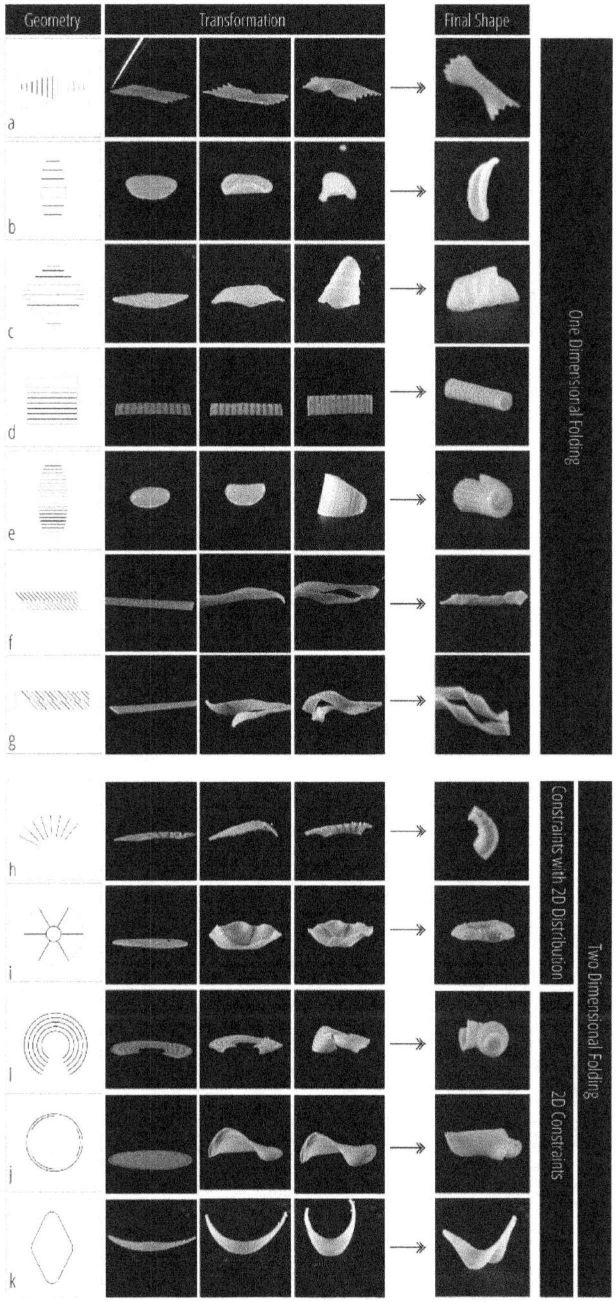

Figure 13. Folding Algorithm.

Self-wrapping Films

Intrigued by interaction between these 2D films and other edible materials, we developed a transparent edible film that wraps fish caviar when immersed in water (Figure 14). We control this transformation by engineering the geometry and thickness of the gelatin film, folding curvature, water temperature (hydration speed), and density of caviar suspended in water.

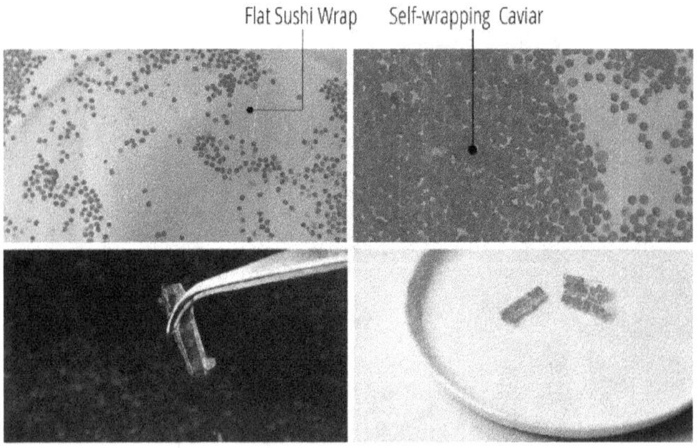

Figure 14. Self-wrapping water sushi.

Temperature Responsive Strips

We made film with two-layer composite structure - the top layer is formed by high Bloom number gelatin, while the bottom layer contains low Bloom number gelatin. When cooking at relative low temperature (~25°C), the linkage formed by high Bloom number gelatin will maintain solid state and hold the long thread shape of the noodle. In contrast, at higher cooking temperature (~40°C), the linkage between segments will be dissolved and noodles will form shortened and twisted segments (Figure 15). In addition, the wrapping direction can be controlled by adding another layer of cellulose on top. We also demonstrated the same idea using starch-gelatin composites.

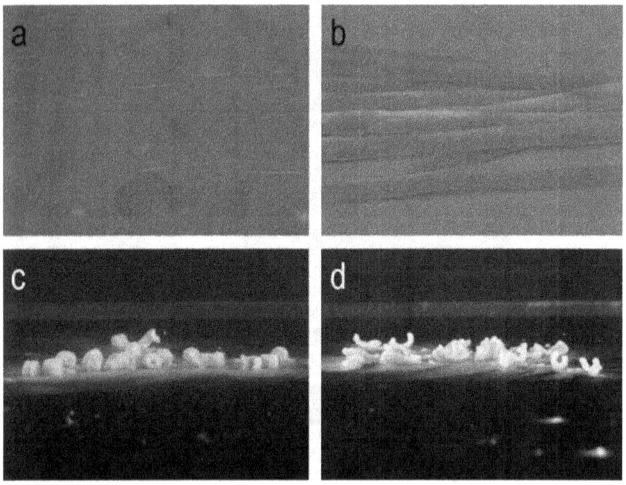

Figure 15. Temperature responsive noodle (a) prepared composite film; (b) strips. Self-chopped pieces in water (c) twisted along edge; or (d) twisted along diagonal.

DISH DESIGN

Co-developed with a chef, we applied the above-mentioned three techniques for designing edible and interactive food that can be served in a restaurant or at home.

Cold Pasta Salad

Considering starch consumption might be regulated for those who suffers from diabetes or obesity, we created transformable fruity pasta out of gelatin and cellulose, which are major components of proteins and fibers, as a heathier food substitute (Figure 16).

Recipe: Prepare edible gelatin gel (6% w/v) with flavored liquid (squid ink, potato extract, or seaweed) in a flat-bottom dish. Dry the film in kitchen with a fan for 12 hours. Digitally print cellulose solution (30% w/v) on gelatin film with the following parameters: line gap (based on geometry), solution deposition speed (20 μL/min), gap between dispensing tip and gelatin film (0.3 mm), and tip diameter (0.010"). Cut the film into different shapes and immerge into water at 30°C. The transformation should occur within 2 minutes.

Figure 16. Cold pasta salad design (a) Helix noodle with Point Judith squid, confit egg yolk and white hoisin; (b) Phytoplankton pasta salad with heirloom tomatoes and wild sorrel; (c) Flowering pasta with west coast foraged mushrooms and fermented burgundy truffle.

Cavier Cannoli

Cannoli excellently represents of interactions among multiple edible materials that have distinct flavors, especially in the contexts of taste and flavor. We hope to utilize our current transforming food methods to create a new dish - self-wrapping cavier cannoli, to demonstrate multiple food materials interactivity through designed shape transformation upon hydration. This design also enhances the interactivity between the diner and food itself, and offering new possibilities for the dining environment (Figure 17).

Figure 17. Transparent cavier cannoli with celery and crème fraiche.

Recipe: Prepare edible gelatin gel (6% w/v) in drinkable water in a flat-bottom dish. Screen print cellulose solution (15% w/v) on the gelatin film: line thickness (1 mm), line gap (3 mm). For a comfortable texture in-mouth, prepare a composite film of gelatin-agar without cellulose strips. Cut into square shape (2×2 cm) and emerge it into water with caviar at 35°C. Stir solution to have caviar present on both sides of the film. The transformation should occur within 2 minutes.

Self-chopped Noodle

Noodles have long and thin thread shapes. In a large family, it is often hard to accommodate everyone's requirement when serving noodles as the primary carbohydrate intake. For instance, kids may require soft noodles with shorten lengths for the ease of chewing and digestion, while adults may want longer noodles with chewy textures. So we propose the use of temperature responsive edible materials to meet the different diners' requirements (Figure 18).

Recipe: Prepare a gel with high Bloom gelatin (6% w/v) in seaweed extract. Dry it and cut it into small rectangular shapes (1×2 cm). Afterwards, prepare another gel with low Bloom gelatin (6% w/v) in a seaweed extract as well. Assemble the rectangular high Bloom pieces on the newly prepared wet low Bloom gelatin gel. Dry it for 18 hours. Print cellulose in lines with the following parameters: line thickness (1 mm), line gap (3 mm). Cut into long strips. Prepare a chicken soup at 37.5°C. Dip the strips into the soup and transformation should occur within 5 minutes.

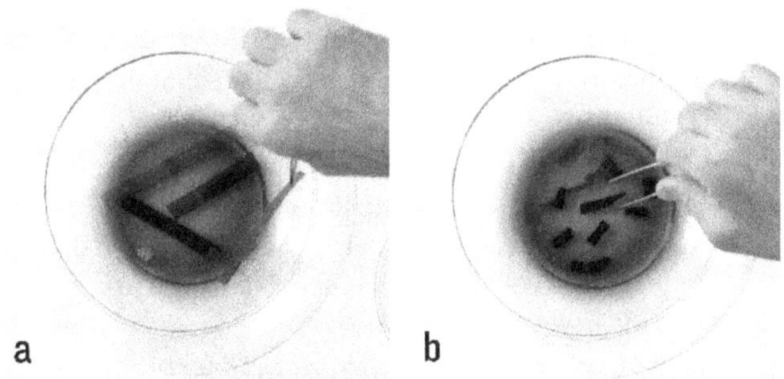

Figure 18. Chicken soup with self-chopped noodle.

DISCUSSION AND FUTURE WORK

Flat-packed Food Challenges and Opportunities

In modern society, food produced locally has become scarce. Much of the food in urban regions is produced remotely and shipped to customer, resulting in pollution to the air due to the emissions of greenhouse gases to the environment [19]. The flat-packed food proposed in this paper, may partially alleviate pollution, by reducing the amount of air shipped during food transport.

Take a package containing short macaroni pasta as an example, the densest packing of tubes (side view of the pasta) in the plane is the hexagonal lattice of the bee's honeycomb (Figure 19) [20]. The packing density (θ) can be calculated in Equation 4. If r = 0.8R, so θ = 67.3%, which means 67.3% of volume in the package is air. If instead we are able to flat-pack pasta, and transform it into 3D shapes during cooking, more than half of the space during shipping and storage will be saved.

$$\theta = \frac{\sqrt{3}R^2 - \frac{1}{2}\pi R^2 + \frac{1}{2}\pi r^2}{\sqrt{3}R^2} \qquad \text{(Equation 4)}$$

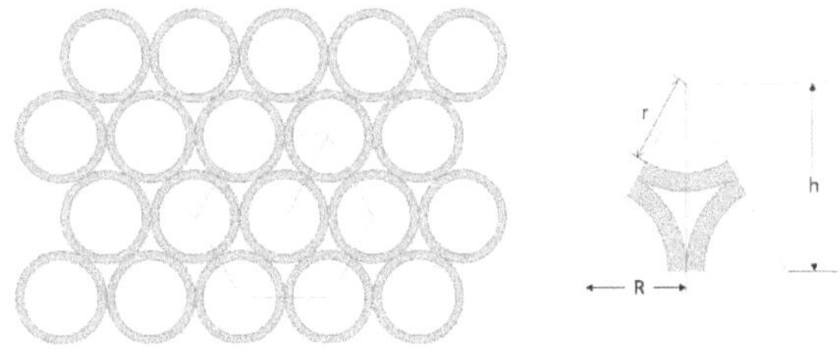

Figure 19. Macaroni pasta by hexagonal packing.

Future Fabrication Techniques

As a further step for our fabrication of shape-changing edible films, we aim to create a platform that will enable individual creation and customization of transforming edible films using off-the-shelf components.

As an example of such, we assembled a twin syringe desktop 3D printer for biological materials using the open source 3Drag printer chassis with Choco syringe extruders from Futura Group Srl. The printer design includes a small refrigeration system to rapidly solidify warmed substrate during printing. Use of the two syringes enables us to print two materials at a time - gelatin and cellulose simultaneously. The temperature control module on the syringe enables maintaining high temperature (50°C) of unprinted gelatin, and it can rapidly cooled down on the cooling panel after printing, to achieve layer by layer printing. The chassis uses a Velleman 8400 control board using Marlin firmware (http://marlinfw.org/). We operate the printer using Repetier-Host client software from Hot-World GmbH & Co with the GCode generator Slic3r from slic3r.org.

To print edible films, we first create two separate stl files for the encapsulating substrate and support substrate. These two files map to the film materials (e.g. agar and cellulose) and we generate G-code from these files using Slic3r. Upon printing, the temperature of each syringe is heated close to its material's glass transition temperature and extruded through the syringe at a target rate set by the firmware and G-code. The cooling system rapidly cools each layer of substrate to a solid state upon deposition, enabling layering of both materials to form the thin film. To date, we have run only preliminary tests for printing our materials using this method. We believe it offers considerable promise for desktop design and fabrication of transforming edible films.

Collaboration between CHI and Material/Food Science

Shape-changing interfaces based on material innovation is an emerging field in HCI. Beyond using non-edible materials that can change shape, stiffness, color, conductivity, and transparency, using edible materials provide new opportunities for HCI designers due to its low barriers to entry, high reproducibility, and safe consumption. In general, the design process is composed of three major steps. First, designers together with scientists predict the tangible outcome and analyze the theoretical feasibility. Second, scientists work closely with designers to test the material performance to develop a proof-of-concept design. They may re-adjust their goal based on the initial test results. Third, designers further improve the fabrication process and simulate the performance. Compared to conventional material-driven design, food material has low knowledge barrier and requires less hands-on training, enabling the high involvement of CHI designers in the whole process, from material discovery to the final design. The availability of the food materials will also provide other CHI researchers to enter into this research field easily, and reproduce previous design prototypes.

CONCLUSION

In this paper, we proposed a new concept - transformative appetite - that transforms 2D edible films to into 3D shapes by anisotropic swelling through cooking. Based on simulation using finite element analysis, a simplified geometry expansion model was built into a user interface, allowing users to create various design shapes, simulate transformation and fabricate transformable dishes. The underlying principles for more complex shape transformation were further applied to create innovative dining experience, enhancing the interactivity between food and cooking conditions, and between food and users.

ACKNOWLEDGEMENT

The work is financially supported by the MIT Media Lab and Food + Future (SIG 6933857). We thank Chef Matthew Delisle (L'Espalier) for helping create the dish, Amos Golan who suggested us the screen printing method, Kevin Leonardo for helping set up the dual-nozzle digital printing platform; Viirj Kan and Jifei Ou for their previous work as our source of inspiration and their lead on ideation around food and shape-changing pasta previously at the Tangible Media Group, MIT Media Lab; Brent Overcash and Greg Shewmaker for their industry insight and support on video production; Michael Indresano Production for helping with photography, Texture Technologies Corp for providing a texture analyzer to measure the food mechanical properties, Daniel I.C. Wang for providing wet lab space, Rohit Karnik, Pierre-Thomas Brun, Douglas Holmes, Matteo Pezzulla and Elisabetta A. Matsumoto for mechanical and mathematical insights, Kang Zhou for proofreading, and lastly Chengyuan Wei for initial experimental exploration and figure preparation.

REFERENCES

1. Vallg, A. et al. 2007. Computational composites. *SIGCHI '14, ACM*: 513-522.
2. Ishii, H. et al. 2012. Radical atoms: beyond tangible bits, toward transformable materials. *Interactions*. 19(1): 38-51.
3. Yao, L. et al. 2013. PneUI: pneumatically actuated soft composite materials for shape changing interfaces. *UIST '13, ACM*: 13-22.
4. Yao, L. et al. 2015. BioLogic: natto cells as nanoactuators for shape changing interfaces. *CHI '15, ACM*: 1-10.
5. Rasmussen, M. K. et al. 2016. Sketching Shape-changing Interfaces: Exploring Vocabulary, Metaphors Use, and Affordances. *CHI '16, ACM*: 2740-2751.
6. Coelho, M. and J. Zigelbaum. 2011. Shape-changing interfacesl. *UbiComp '11. ACM*: 15 (2): 161-173.
7. Zhang, S. Y. et al. 2015. A pH-responsive supramolecular polymer gel as an enteric elastomer for use in gastric devices. *Nat Mater* 14(10): 1065-1071.
8. Tibbits, S. 2014. 4D Printing: Multi-Material Shape Change. *Architectural Design* 84(1): 116-121.
9. Correa, D. et al. 2015. 3D-Printed Wood: Programming Hygroscopic Material Transformations. *3D Printing and Additive Manufacturing*. 2(3): 106-116.
10. Ma, M. et al. 2013. Bio-inspired polymer composite actuator and generator driven by water gradients. *Science* 339(6116): 186-189.
11. Gladman, A. S. et al. 2016. Biomimetic 4D printing. *Nat Mater* 15(4): 413-418
12. Erb, R. M. et al. 2013. Self-shaping composites with programmable bioinspired microstructures. *Nat Commun* 4: 1712.
13. Comber, R. et al. 2012. Food and interaction design: designing for food in everyday life. *CHI-EA '12, ACM*: 2767-2770.
14. Kan, V. et al. 2016. Organic Primitives: Synthesis & Design of pH-Reactive Material InterfacesMaterials with Organic Molecules for Biocompatible I/O. *arXiv preprint arXiv:1605.01148.*
15. Gronsky, S. 2007. Lighting food. *SIGGRAPH '07, ACM*: 34-44.
16. Schraefel, m. c. 2013. Green food through green food: a human centered design approach to green food technology. *UbiComp '13 Adjunct, ACM*: 595-598.
17. Mizrahi, M. Et al. 2016Digital Gastronomy: Methods & Recipes for Hybrid Cooking. *UIST '16, ACM*: 541-552
18. Wang, G. et al. 2016. xPrint: A Modularized Liquid Printer for Smart Materials Deposition. *CHI '16, ACM*: 5743-5752.
19. Miles, F. 2007. How Far Your Food Travels Has Serious Consequences for Your Health and the Climate, *Rep. Natural Resources Defense Council.*
20. Steinhaus, H. 1999. *Mathematical Snapshots*, Dover Publications.

Emotion Actuator: Embodied Emotional Feedback through Electroencephalography and Electrical Muscle Stimulation

Mariam Hassib[1,2,*], Max Pfeiffer[3,4,*], Stefan Schneegass[2,*], Michael Rohs[3], Florian Alt[1]

[1]LMU Munich, Ubiquitous Interactive Systems Group – {first.last}@ifi.lmu.de
[2]University of Stuttgart, VIS – {first.last}@vis.uni-stuttgart.de
[3]University of Hannover – {first.last}@hci.uni-hannover.de
[4]University of Münster– {first.last}@uni-muenster.de
[*] *Contributed Equally*

Figure 1. Embodied emotional feedback involves implicitly sensing emotions and displaying them by actuating the recipient's body.

ABSTRACT

The human body reveals emotional and bodily states through measurable signals, such as body language and electroencephalography. However, such manifestations are difficult to communicate to others remotely. We propose *EmotionActuator*, a proof-of-concept system to investigate the transmission of emotional states in which the recipient performs emotional gestures to understand and interpret the state of the sender. We call this kind of communication *embodied emotional feedback*, and present a prototype implementation. To realize our concept we chose four emotional states: amused, sad, angry, and neutral. We designed *EmotionActuator* through a series of studies to assess emotional classification via EEG, and create an EMS gesture set by comparing composed gestures from the literature to sign-language gestures. Through a final study with the end-to-end prototype interviews revealed that participants like implicit sharing of emotions and find the embodied output to be immersive, but want to have control over shared emotions and with whom. This work contributes a proof of concept system and set of design recommendations for designing *embodied emotional feedback* systems.

Author Keywords

Affective computing; affect display; emotion; emotion sharing; EMS; EEG.

ACM Classification Keywords

H.5.2 Information Interfaces and Presentation: User Interfaces – Input devices and strategies; Haptic I/O.

DOI: http://dx.doi.org/10.1145/3025453.3025953

INTRODUCTION

More and more people are living in long-distance relationships – often because people cannot easily find workplaces in the same city or are sent abroad temporarily [36]. In such situations couples struggle with maintaining social connectedness, typically by relying on text messages, social media, and voice communication [15]. Exchanging intimate information about one's emotions is an important maintenance behavior in long-distance relationships [42]. New ways of sharing and communicating emotions between long-distance partners has been the focus of recent research projects that increase empathy and overcome the drawbacks of traditional and current communication technologies [18, 41, 45].

This work focuses on exchanging information about emotions over a distance. The human body reveals affective states through measurable signals, such as heart rate, blood pressure, skin conductivity, muscle tension, facial expressions, pupil diameter, voice, body movements and posture, and brain activities (e.g., [9, 10, 11, 27, 43, 68]). We propose a system that measures the affective states of one partner and lets the recipient perform an emotional gesture representing the sender's affective state. In this way partners can experience similar sensations of the affective state and get emotionally connected. This may lead to an awareness of the affective state of the other person, which we explore in this work as a proof of concept. We call this kind of setup *embodied emotional feedback*: The recipient's own body is actuated to portray the emotional state of the sender. The recipient interprets his or her own movement and thereby gains knowledge about the emotional state of the sender. If the communication of affective states is set up in a bidirectional way a feedback loop emerges, with mutual effects on both partners.

We present a proof-of-concept implementation realizing *embodied emotional feedback* using electroencephalography (EEG) on the sending side and electrical muscle stimulation

(EMS) on the receiving side. EEG has been used to implicitly detect emotional states with good reliability [7, 37, 44]. EMS is a method adopted from physiotherapy and has been used successfully in HCI to actuate the human body [34, 38, 40, 50, 51, 62]. Combined, these are promising technologies to realize emotional awareness between two persons without needing explicit intervention of verbal or textual communication. In particular, we obtain information about a user's emotional state, for example, whether getting amused, sad, or angry, and use this information to actuate the receiving user such that he or she performs a certain gesture.

To evaluate our concept, we implemented an initial system and evaluated it in three studies. First, we focused on the input side (EEG). We created a classifier capable of differentiating emotional states such as amused, sad, or angry. Second, on the output side (EMS), we developed two gesture sets representing the emotional states and compared them with regard to the best fit to each emotion. We use natural expressions of emotional states which we elicit from the literature and gestures derived from the American sign language (ASL). Third, we combined the findings from the first two studies to assess its ability to create a sense of connectedness between two persons. Therefore, pairs of participants used our system in the context of a scenario taken from the real world.

The results show that participants performed better in distinguishing sign language gestures than natural gestures. These gestures serve as a basis that can be personalized in future implementations so as to reflect individual gestures of the partner. Interviews revealed that participants like implicit sharing of emotions and find the embodied output more immersive than common text notifications. However, they want to stay in control over which emotions to share, e.g., only positive emotions with friends, and both positive and negative emotions with one's partner.

CONTRIBUTION STATEMENT

We contribute the concept of *embodied emotional feedback*, a new way of sharing emotions. Over a distance it implicitly senses emotional states using EEG, communicates them to another person, and actuates the recipient's body using EMS with gestures as a result of these states. We present *emotion actuator*, a prototype to realize this idea, and three initial studies to evaluate the concept.

RELATED WORK

Prior research presents various approaches to achieve emotional communication and connectedness. Lottridge et al. [41] explore what remote couples lack from existing communication technologies and what they want to share and how. They identify *empty moments* (waiting, walking, waking up) as a design opportunity for sharing emotions. Dey and Guzman [17] discuss the design of presence displays for awareness and connectedness. Hassenzahl et al. [28] review design concepts and technologies that aim to create relatedness. They present six strategies for creating a relatedness experience: awareness, expressivity, physicalness, gift giving, joint action, and memories. We focus on awareness and expressiveness to enhance emotion communication between partners.

Explicitly sharing emotions has been studied in the context of MobiMood, a mobile system for sharing emotions among friends [12]. Emotishare [67] is a platform for sharing and responding to explicitly reported emotional states among friends. Social media are commonly used to share emotions [6]. People tend to restrict intense and negative emotions to private channels and share positive emotions more widely. This observation is supported by our findings.

Explicitly sharing emotions through emojis, text or speech can impose a burden on the provider. Here we focus on implicitly detecting and sharing emotions. Implicit emotion sharing has been explored by Perttula et al. [48] who present an EEG-based prototype for mood sharing on a public map among visitors of a large-scale event. Various projects aimed at augmenting mobile phones by an emotion channel. Cui et al. [13] use front-camera recordings of emotional reactions to received content to implicitly capture and transmit emotions. The system does not try to recognize the emotion but just captures it and returns it to the sender. The *Poke* system [45] uses an inflatable surface on the phone that receives finger pressure input from the back of another phone. A long-term study found that users developed vocabularies for expressing and understanding emotions.

Looking at emotion input, prior work investigated different ways for detecting emotions. Strohmeier et al. [60] found a relation between deforming an object and the represented emotion. Höök [30] investigated bodily persuasion through *affective loop* experiences, which employ physical, emotional interactions. In particular gestural interactions with a doll (for example, shaking it back and forth) influenced the emotion of a game character (e.g., anger). It was found that the experience of performing the gesture and the game character's feedback also have an effect on the user's emotion, leading to an *affective loop*. In our work, the recipient's body is actuated through implicitly sensed emotions rather than active gestural input.

Fagerberg et al. [22] draw from theories of movement and emotional expression to design a set of affective gestures for emotion input. Sundström et al. [61] propose *eMoto*, a system in which a user can explicitly input emotional states using pressure on a handheld token and the amount of movement of that token. Pressure is mapped to the valence axis while movement is mapped to the arousal axis. In contrast to these works, we use movement as an output modality.

For the emotional output modality beyond the regular displays and mobile phones, previous work looked into various wearables and tangible objects. *United-pulse* [66] are rings worn by a couple that play the heartbeat of the partner. Gooch and Watts [25] present a robotic grasping hand, that supports hand holding over a distance. Tsetserukou and Neviarouskaya [63] reproduce emotions of another person through a haptic device worn on the chest.

Researchers also investigated tangible pairs of objects for input and output. These include lights [1], picture frames [33], beds [18], and teddies [23] for communicating emotions.

EMBODIED EMOTIONAL FEEDBACK

Embodied emotional feedback involves implicitly sensing emotional state changes and displaying them by actuating the recipient's body. The approach involves recognizing emotions from physiological data and transmitting them from the sender to the receiver. Roles of sender and receiver may change depending on the direction of information flow over the bidirectional channel. In the literature there are examples of explicit and implicit forms of emotion input. Implicit emotion sensing has the advantage of not interfering with the emotional experience, yet it lowers control. Another aspect of implicit emotion sensing is that it is not necessary to verbalize the experienced emotion. The recipient becomes the output device of the sender's emotion. We hypothesize that this leads to a stronger sense of immersion, intensity and, possibly, a more intuitive understanding of the received emotion, compared to other output modalities. One reason for this expectation is that it has been shown that gestures are closely linked to emotions. Performing a gesture may increase or even evoke a particular emotion [16, 35]. When a person is more involved in a situation (e.g., in a partnership) empathy and resulting feeling of the other person can increase. In the following we describe the components of embodied emotional feedback.

Measuring Emotions

In a first step the emotions to be shared are measured. Different methods exist and the selection of a recognition method depends on the targeted theory of affect, the emotions of interest, context, as well as the intended goal of the evaluation [24]. These methods can be either subjective or objective.

Subjective methods include structured and non-structured questionnaires and self-assessments. Examples are the Positive and Negative Affect Schedule (PANAS) [65] and the Self-Assessment Manikin (SAM) [8]. These methods cover a large set of possible emotions. However, they depend on affective states that the participants are consciously aware of as well as being biased by language and culture [24].

Objective methods employ physiological and non-physiological sensors. A popular method is using cameras and image analysis to detect facial expressions based on Ekman's theory of emotion [20], which suggests a link between facial expressions and affective states [68]. Additionally, electromyography (EMG) recordings are used to recognize emotions from facial expressions [10]. Other methods measure heart rate [5, 29], skin conductance [58], respiration rate [29], pupil response [46], or electroencephalography signals (EEG) [24, 44] to recognize emotions. Although objective methods overcome some drawbacks of subjective ones, the physiological responses of individuals vary and are sometimes not easy to interpret. Also, the prior emotional state is usually not considered. Rather the emotional change is compared to a baseline or calibration phase. However, Picard argues that a universal solution to this issue is not required if a user-dependent solution is possible [52].

Current research efforts show that classifying emotions from facial expressions can achieve accuracies up to 80–90% under controlled conditions [9]. Psychology explicitly separates physiological arousal, the behavioral expression (affect), and the conscious experience of an emotion (feelings) [7]. Facial expressions and voice are related to the behavioral expression, which can be consciously changed or adapted and its interpretation is not objective [7]. EEG can implicitly and objectively measure the emotional state of the user. Therefore, we focus in this work on EEG for emotion measurement.

Linking Emotions and Movement

Emotions are closely linked to body posture, movement and body language [19, 21, 54]. We conducted a literature review to gain insight into which movement is *naturally* linked to which emotion, focusing on *anger*, *sadness*, and *amusement*. We chose these three emotions since they are basic emotions and well distributed in Russel's model of affect [55]. From the literature review we elicited movements that represent each emotion. Out of this movements we designed a single gesture for expressing each emotion (called *natural gesture*). These gestures are culture and person-depended but we believe that the selected gestures form a valid basis which can be well understood. In addition, we looked into the *American Sign Language*[1] (ASL) and picked the gesture corresponding to each emotion. Even though ASL is an abstract language, the signs representing emotions are chosen so that they are easy to link to the emotion and, thus, are easy to remember.

Although facial expressions are closely linked to emotions [21] we do not actuate the face for emotion output, because attaching EMS pads to the face is socially problematic and may compromise the user's safety. Rather we follow common safety practices to apply EMS to the limbs and the torso [53]. Note that in the future, transcranial magnetic stimulation (TMS) may be used to directly manipulate the motor cortex and thus move arms [3], fingers [32], or lips [59]. However, currently this technology is complex and bulky to use. The TMS coil has to be placed very precisely to actuate specific motor regions and hence cannot be used HCI contexts.

Amusement

The gesture related to amusement is described as an open gesture that extends the body [64]. This emotion is mostly linked to lifting up both arms [19] and keeping the hands high [27]. Thus, we designed the natural gesture so that the user lifts both hands and keeps them up (Table 1, top). In ASL, the gesture consists of making a fist with the right hand and then open and close the index and middle finger while lifting the lower arm up to the face (Table 1, bottom).

Anger

Anger is an emotion that is linked to violence [11] and aggressive forward positioning of the body [14]. In most literature, the core part of the gesture that is related to anger is clenching one's fist [19]. This gesture is sometimes described in combination with shaking the fist [64] or keeping the fist low or at the waist [27]. Based on this we designed the gesture as making a fist with both hands that is slightly lifted (Table 1, top). The related gesture in the ASL is to form a claw with the right hand in front of the face (Table 1, bottom).

[1] ASL: `https://www.signingsavvy.com/sign/`

	Emotion	Gesture	Movement	Timing	Muscle
Natural	Amusement		Hand up (5), lower arm up (2), upper arm up (1) (left and right)	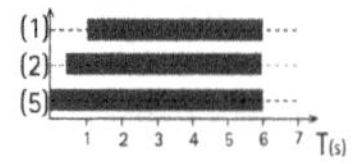	Extensor digitorum muscle (5), biceps brachii muscle (2), and deltoid muscle (1)
	Anger		Hand up (5) claw hand (3), hand down (4) (left and right)	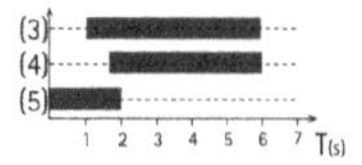	Extensor digitorum muscle (5), flexor digitorum superficialis muscle (3), flexor digitorum profundus muscle (4)
	Sadness		Lower arm up (2) (left and right)	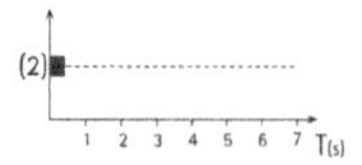	Biceps brachii muscle (2)
American Sign Language	Amusement		Lower arm up (2), claw hand (3), tow finger down (6), two finger up (7)	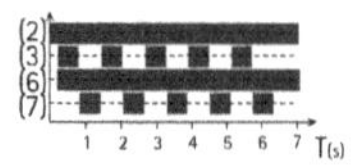	Biceps brachii muscle (2), flexor digitorum superficialis muscle (3), flexor digitorum profundus muscle inside (6), extensor digitorum muscle inside (7)
	Anger		Hand up (5), claw hand (3), lower arm up (2)	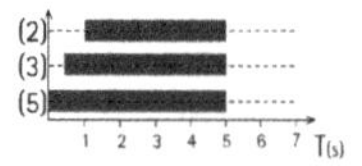	biceps brachii muscle (2), flexor digitorum superficialis muscle (3), extensor digitorum muscle (5)
	Sadness		Lower arm up (2)	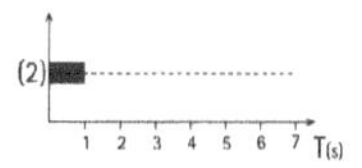	Biceps brachii muscle (2)

Table 1. Linking emotions to gestures and elementary movements. Different muscles are used to evoke certain movements with a specific timing so that the combination of the different muscle movements results in a gesture. The *movement*, *timing*, and *muscle* columns also depict the numbers of the actuated muscles between brackets which are further illustrated in Figure 4

Sadness

Sadness is characterized as a lack of body tension [19, 64]. It also includes subtle movements of the hands by either folding them in the lap [19] or putting them into the pocket [14]. However, the movements are performed rather slowly and gently [64]. Thus, we designed the gesture such that the user folds both hands on the lap (Table 1, top). In ASL, the gesture consists of moving the right hand up in front of the upper body and slowly sliding it down the chest (Table 1, bottom).

Creating Movements using EMS

From the above-mentioned gestures we isolated elementary muscle movements that can be evoked by EMS (Table 1). EMS delivers an electrical signal to the human body via non-invasive surface electrodes. As soon as the signal stimulates motor nerves, the corresponding muscle contracts and performs the intended movement, for example, lifting the arm. Related work shows examples of supporting interaction by actuating fingers [39], hands [62], arms [26] and legs [50].

Since the muscle position is user-dependent, the electrodes need to be placed at slightly different positions for each user. Even small changes in position can result in a different movement. To achieve a realistic movement, the EMS signal strength needs to be calibrated individually. As the muscle contracts, it changes its form, thereby shifting the relative positions of electrode and muscle. Therefore, the calibration process needs to take the intended movement into account. Furthermore, the timing has to be controlled thoughtfully.

THE EMOTION ACTUATOR

To investigate *embodied emotional feedback*, we created the *emotion actuator* system, which senses emotion changes and creates embodied feedback. The system consists of two main components, namely the *sensing* component, recognizing specific emotions, and the *actuation* component.

Sensing Component

We used the Emotiv EPOC[2] EEG device, which has 14 saline-based felt electrodes and two reference electrodes following the 10–20 electrode positioning system. The EEG signals are transmitted wirelessly to a laptop computer. The EPOC device provides both raw EEG data as well as affective and facial expression information. We used three main affective scores that are provided by the EPOC: *excitement*, *engagement*, and *frustration*. Engagement is the general cortical activation elicited through a stimulus. It is characterized by high EEG beta wave activity and related to heightened cognitive and affective states [43]. Excitement is a feeling of physiological arousal following an external stimulus. Frustration is the cortical activity related to cognitive and affective processes while trying to cope with negative emotional states [43]. The relation between these affective scores and our chosen emotions is not one-to-one. However, following the valence/arousal model of affect [55], amusement is positive valence and high arousal, sadness is negative valence and low arousal, and anger is negative valence and high arousal. We also utilized the EPOC's facial expression information to develop the features for the classifier. We utilized were *smile*, *clench*, and *laugh*. Literature has assessed the feasibility of emotion classification using the EPOC EEG data [2, 37, 47] and facial expression information [4].

Filtering and Feature Extraction

The EPOC comes with built-in notch filters and noise filtering. However, the signal quality varies, in particular for participants with lots of hair and due to some participants fidgeting in their seats during the recording. Thus, we applied an additional filter for further smoothing of the signal [56]. Data was divided into windows of three seconds and features were

[2]Emotiv EPOC: www.emotiv.com

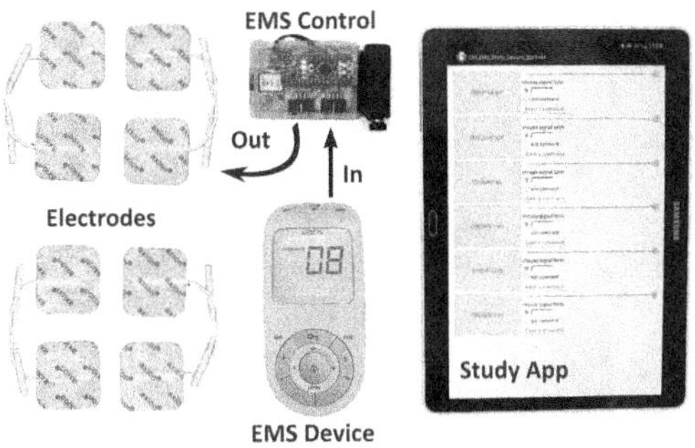

Figure 2. EMS control modules with two galvanically isolated circuits.

extracted per window. Since changes in the affective information evoked by the external stimulus (i.e., movie) are short term (a few seconds), we used windows of three seconds.

For simplicity, we based the features of the classifier on EPOC's affective and facial expression information. A score > 0.3 was counted as a smile/laugh/clench to avoid false positives. By examining the data prior to feature extraction, we found that clench scores were highest in movies with negative valence (sad/angry), whereas smile and laugh scores were highest in amusement movies. Our 18-dimensional feature vector includes the minimum, maximum, mean, median, and standard deviation of the excitement, engagement, and frustration scores as well as smile, laugh, and clench scores > 0.3. A random forest classifier with 100 trees was used to classify the data based on the defined features.

Actuating Component

To realize the actuating component, we use an EMS-based toolkit, which is composed of an off-the-shelf EMS-based massage device, a control board, and an Android app as described in [49]. The toolkit is available open source[3]. In total six EMS/TENS devices (Breuer Sanitas SEM 43) generate the signals for the twelve actuated muscles (Figure 4). As signal EMS parameters we used an electrical current of 10–30 mA, a the pulse width of 100 μs, and a pulse frequency of 100 Hz. These devices are connected to six autonomous modules which are controlled by the Android app via Bluetooth LE (Figure 2). The control module allows turning on/off and adjusting the intensity of the two EMS channels (each of which connects to two electrodes). Each module has two galvanically isolated circuits – one for handling the communication and one for the electrodes attached to the human body.

For composing the different gestures we developed an Android app that connects to multiple control modules. The app can control each muscle individually via a one-to-one mapping of button to muscle. As long as the button is pressed the muscle is being actuated. In addition, the intensity of the EMS signal is controlled through a slider for each muscle. Individual activation and intensity adjustment enable fine-grained calibration. The app allows a precise timing of the gestures. The application is also able to *replay* complete gestures by consecutively actuating muscles using a predefined timing. This is used after calibration to replay gestures.

[3]Let Your Body Move Toolkit `https://bitbucket.org/MaxPfeiffer/letyourbodymove/`

Emotion	Movie	Scene Description
Amusement	Benny&Joone	Benny plays the fool in a coffee shop
	A Fish Called Wanda	One of the characters is found naked
Anger	Schindler's List	Commander randomly shoots prisoners
	American History X	A neo-Nazi kills a man
Sadness	The Dead Poets Society	A schoolboy commits suicide
	Philadelphia	Andrew describes the pain& passion felt by the opera character

Table 2. The movies used in the study to evoke a certain emotion.

STUDY I: DETECTING EMOTIONS THROUGH EEG

In a first study, we investigated how accurately we could classify emotions using EEG data. Emotions can be evoked using different sensory stimuli such as visual or audio stimuli. In psychology, many different emotion eliciting databases exist [68] where audiovisual stimuli in the form of movies were successfully used to elicit emotions. For our study, we selected movies from the "FilmStim" movie clips database [57]. The database offers 70 movie scenes that were rated by 364 participants on 24 classification criteria. For each of the three emotions (anger, sadness, and amusement) we chose two movie clips that were ranked among the top ten movies on the discrete emotion criteria and on the perceived arousal and valence criteria [57]. The duration of each movie clip is 2–4 minutes. Table 2 provides a short description of each movie clip. Additionally, two neutral videos of 2–3 minutes each were used to elicit a neutral state (i.e., a state in which our system does not trigger feedback regarding the emotion). These movies were not part of the "FilmStim" movie database.

Study Design

Each participant watched each movie clip in Table 2. We collected EEG data and measured how strongly each video evoked the intended emotion through a questionnaire.

Procedure

Ten participants took part in the study (3 female, M=27, SD=4.8 years). As participants arrived at the lab they were briefed about the purpose of the study and asked to sign a consent form and fill out a demographics questionnaire. We equipped them with the EPOC device after applying saline solution to each of the electrodes. Using the EPOC control panel we ensured an optimal fit of the electrodes close to the scalp and in direct contact with the skin.

Participants were seated in a dark room in front of a 30 inch screen on which the chosen movie clips were shown. We first presented a neutral movie clip to establish a baseline for the device and to ensure signal stability. The clip showed a stationary image of a harp and light harp music. After that we showed the movies in randomized order. After each movie the participants provided two subjective ratings of the movie: A 7-point Likert scale rating for each of the three emotions and a 9-point Self-Assessment Manikin (SAM) score [8] for measuring arousal and valence of the emotion they felt during the movie. Both questionnaires were thoroughly explained to the participants before the study and a sample was shown.

Results

We labeled each movie with the emotion that received the highest score from the self-assessment. This was done to avoid inconsistencies between the experience of participants and the supposed category of the video. If the first rating was

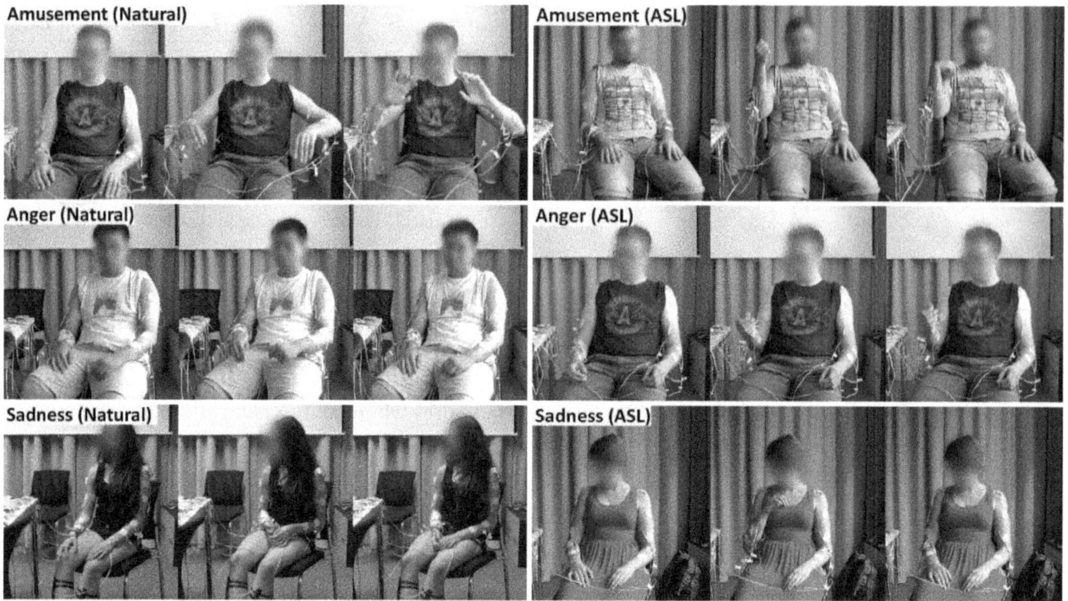

Figure 3. Snapshots of the different gestures performed in Study II. Each participant performed each of these six gestures.

Participant	Classes	Classification Accuracy(%)
1	AM,REL,SAD,ANG	67.7
2	AM,REL,SAD,ANG	59.4
3	AM,REL,SAD,ANG	67.3
4	AM,REL,SAD,ANG	70.8
5	AM,REL,ANG	89.2
6	AM,REL,SAD,ANG	81.3
7	AM,REL,SAD,ANG	66.9
8	AM,REL,SAD,ANG	70.1
9	AM,REL,SAD,ANG	82.9
10	AM,REL,SAD	77.0

Table 3. Per participant classification using a Random Forest classifier.

ambiguous, the arousal and valence values measured through the SAM were used. One participant rated an *angry* movie as *sad* (P10) and another participant rated a *sad* movies as *angry* (P5). We excluded the particular class from the evaluation for these two participants. Finally, instances in which both scoring systems were ambiguous were removed from the dataset. This happened in one case (P5).

Overall, we achieved an accuracy of 72.6% (*SD*=9.5%). Table 3 depicts the results of our participant-dependent classification which was done using Weka[4]. Results show that classification using features from the EPOC affective suite and facial expressions is possible, with accuracies between 59.4% and 89.2%. For P2, getting a consistent high quality contact between the electrode and the scalp was not always possible due to the participant's hair, which degraded signal quality and could be a reason for the low classification score.

STUDY II: COMPOSING A GESTURE SET

In a second study we explored how well the elicited body movements fit the detected emotions, as judged by participants. We compare the *natural gestures* to *ASL* gestures, ultimately selecting one gesture per emotion for the subsequent concept exploration study. We also collected user feedback in interviews. In particular we were interested whether the played emotions are easy to understand.

[4]Weka: `http://www.cs.waikato.ac.nz/ml/weka/`

Study Design

We again used a repeated-measures study design in which participants compare two gestures for each emotion. The independent variable was the gesture played via EMS, with these levels (see Table 1, *Gesture* column): natural amusement gesture, ASL amusement gesture, natural anger gesture, ASL anger gesture, natural sadness gesture, and ASL sadness gesture. We used a Latin squared order of gestures to prevent sequence effects. After experiencing a gesture, participants had to rate on a 7-point Likert scale how well they felt each gesture represented the three emotions amusement, anger, and sadness. In addition we collected interview responses.

Procedure

We invited 8 participants (4 female) aged 20–28 years (*M*=22.4, *SD*=2.7) to our lab. We recruited them from our institutional mailing lists.

When a participant arrived we first explained the purpose of the study. Then the participant filled out a consent form and a demographic questionnaire. We introduced the EMS system and tested whether the participant was comfortable with the sensation caused by the EMS actuation by applying EMS output to the extensor digitorum muscle (Figure 4, pad 5). We then equipped them with the electrodes required to actuate the muscles for the intended movements and calibrated each muscle individually. The current was increased step-by-step until we got the expected movement. In case the current got uncomfortable or we got an unintended movement we replaced the electrodes as described in [49]. We avoided to actuate complete gestures so participants would experience each emotion gesture for the first time in the study. We also did not show a depiction of the gestures to the participants. The whole calibration process took about 60 minutes. Then, participants performed the gestures in random order. Each gesture was performed up to 4 times to let the participants focus on the movements and get used to the actuation. When the participants were familiar with a gesture we asked

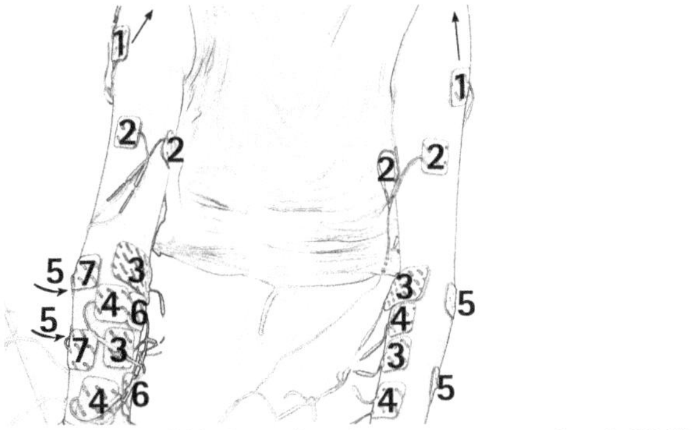

Figure 4. Placement of 12 electrode pairs to actuate muscles via EMS. The numbers refer to the muscles shown in Table 1, right.

them to rank this gesture according to the degree of agreement to the statement "this gesture fits the emotion amusement/anger/sadness" (1=strongly disagree, 7=strongly agree). We also asked participants what they (dis)liked and how they would describe each gesture.

Results

Quantitative Results

In general, the defined gestures conveyed the emotions in the intended way. As can be seen in Figure 5, the intended emotion received the best ranking in all cases except for the natural anger gesture. Looking more closely at this gesture, we found that the natural anger gesture was misinterpreted as representing amusement by participants P7 and P8.

Qualitative Results

We were particularly interested in how the participants experienced the different gestures.

Amusement. Participants described the natural gesture exciting (P1, P6). At the same time, P1 said that he found the gesture somewhat hectic. Some participants mentioned that raising their hands very high made them feel kind of funny, but not very natural. In contrast, the ASL gesture that focused mainly on the actuation of the biceps was also characterized as exciting (P6) but considered to be much more natural (P8).

Anger. Subjective feedback suggests that both the natural as well as the ASL gesture were overall perceived as a good fit. P1 disliked that the natural gesture felt cramped. P5 said that the natural gesture resembled shadow boxing. With regard to the ASL gesture, P1 and P7 said that the gesture created a kind of defensive, almost aggressive attitude, hence well reflecting the emotion. P3 stated that the gesture resembled dancing, since the arm rotates inwards.

Sadness. For the natural gesture, participants felt the gesture was defensive (P6), made them look puzzled (P8), and felt like waving at somebody (P8). P7 said that the ASL gesture made them feel thoughtful, thus nicely reflecting sadness. P8 felt the gesture could be confused with anger.

General feedback by the participants suggested that people did not actively interfere with the actuation but let the system control the movement. P3 mentioned that it was quite uncommon to be externally controlled, but soon got used to it. P7 mentioned that they felt the muscles, rather than the current. Only P2 felt that the actuation was artificial.

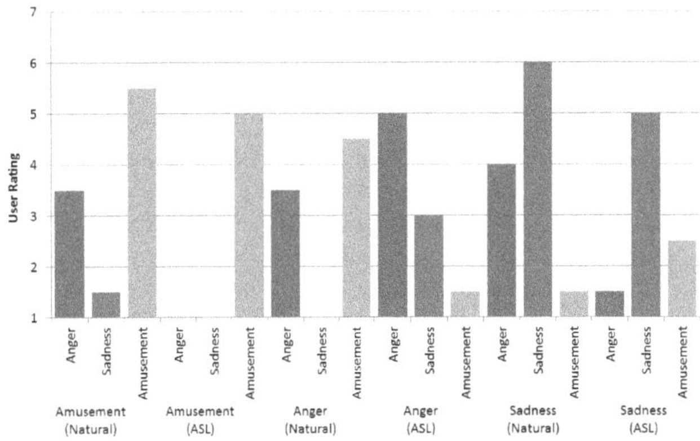

Figure 5. Median rating of how well the gesture fits the emotion for amusement, anger, and sadness on a 7-point Likert scale.

Selection of the Final Emotion Gesture Set

The qualitative feedback indicated that overall the gestures fit the emotions well – in particular the ASL gestures – even though there were some misinterpretations for both types of gestures. We believe that these mainly stem from the fact that people have different ways of expressing emotions. Apart from the qualitative feedback, an important criterion on which we based the decision for the final gesture set was the distinctiveness of a gesture. Thus, we looked at the maximum difference between the top and second rated emotion for the two gestures. In the end, there was a tendency towards the ASL gestures, which not only managed to convey each emotion correctly, but were distinctive and favored by participants.

Deriving Timings for Actuating Gestures

After the study, we derived the timings for each gesture based on the video recordings. We analyzed the individual movements of each participant regarding which timing each muscle needs to perform the gestures in an optimal way.

The automated ASL amusement gesture takes in total 7.2 s. The biceps brachii muscle (Figure 4, pad 2) was actuated from the beginning for the full 7.2 s, followed by the flexor digitorum profundus muscle (6) inwards, and the extensor digitorum muscle (7) inside with a delay of 0.25 s for 7.1 s. The extensor digitorum muscle (7) and flexor digitorum superficialis muscle (3) were alternatingly actuated for 0.4 s in total five times. The biceps lifts the arm up and as soon as the arm starts lifting, the flexor digitorum profundus muscle is actuated inside which closes the hand except for the index finger and middle finger. The extensor digitorum muscle (7) lifts the index and middle finger up and the flexor digitorum superficialis muscle (3) pushes the finger down again.

The automated ASL anger gesture takes 5 s. The biceps brachii muscle (2) is actuated the whole time, then the extensor digitorum muscle (5) is actuated with a delay 0.3 s for 4.7 s, and the flexor digitorum superficialis muscle (3) with a delay of 0.5 s for 4.5 s. First, this lifts the lower arm up, followed by the hand, and finally claws the fingers.

The ASL sad gesture only takes 1 s. The biceps is actuated for 1 s and pushes the lower arm up to the chest where it slides down the chest.

LIMITATIONS

While we used off-the-shelf massage devices and BCIs for creating *EmotionActuator*, we envision a usable and wearable system in the future. Particularly, setting up the actuation component in its current form is time consuming and intrusive due to the placement and calibration of self-adhesive electrodes [49]. The integration of these electrodes in smart garments will increase the usability and wearability of our system (cf. Keller and Kuhn [31]). The user will simply put on clothes with integrated electrodes and the system will be able to actuate the user without extensive prior calibration.

STUDY III: CONCEPT EXPLORATION

A qualitative evaluation of the emotion actuator concept was conducted with groups of two users. We obtained information on the emotional state of one of the participants via EEG and then conveyed it through EMS actuation to the other participant. The purpose of the study was to understand how well our approach helped people to feel connected and in witch situations they would like to use embodied emotional feedback. To create a realistic scenario, both participants were given different tasks. Whereas senders watched the same videos as in Study I, the receivers were asked to play a game on a tablet computer as a distraction task. We chose a non-emotional, non-time critical game called "Find the Difference 38"[5].

Apparatus

We connected the sensing (EEG) and the actuating components (EMS) of the system.The EEG input side involved the Emotiv EPOC connected to a PC. It sends data to the PC which computes features and determines the emotional state. The state is then sent wirelessly to the EMS side. Information on the emotional state of the sender is conveyed either through a standard text notification on the Android tablet[6] on which the participant played the game or through ASL gestures described above. Text notifications served as a baseline, as they are a common way of conveying emotional information. We chose short and easy-to-understand sentences. In particular, the messages stated "I am {angry | sad | amused}." In addition to the visual feedback the tablet computer vibrated twice when a notification was received.

In this study, we used the automated ASL gestures with the timings that were identified in Study II. Table 1, column *Timing*, summarizes the sequence and length of each actuation for the different muscles. For creating the gestures that represent the different emotions we used the same EMS control modules and calibration process as in Study II.

Study Design

The study followed a mixed design in which the sender (EEG) and receiver (EMS) is a between-subjects variable (i.e., a participant was either a sender or a receiver), whereas the feedback channel (EMS vs. textual) is a within-subject variable (i.e., each recipient received both EMS and textual notifications). We focused on qualitative feedback. The goal was to gather a deeper understanding of how people felt connected and involved depending on the kind of feedback.

[5]Find Difference 38 `https://play.google.com/store/apps/details?id=free.find.difference38`

[6]Android Notification `http://developer.android.com/guide/topics/ui/notifiers/notifications.html`

Procedure

For the study we recruited 8 participants (6 male, mean age 25.6, *SD* = 4.4 years) from a student mailing list and from our lab. Two of them were a married couple (P1, P2), two had been friends since childhood (P3, P4), two were colleagues (P5, P6), two did not know each other (P7, P8).

As participants arrived at the lab, they received an introduction on the purpose of the study. They were then divided randomly and assigned to one of the two groups – either the EEG group or the EMS group. Both were then led to separate rooms and were not informed about the task of their partner. People in the EEG group were quipped with the Emotiv EPOC and after that shown the neutral movie for calibration, before showing them the same set of movies (two per emotion) as in the first study (Table 2). During each movie, information on the respective emotional state was measured by the EEG device and directly sent to the other participant. Note that we checked each detected emotion before it was passed on to the receiver, because we could not guarantee that people responded to the movies in the intended way or the emotion was correctly recognized. An unexpected emotion happened twice, when participants responded with *anger* to a *sad* video. Our approach ensured that the intended emotion was transmitted to the receiver. The videos were played in a counterbalanced order and took 2–3 minutes each. The introduction and calibration took about 45 minutes. The participants watched approximately 20 minutes of video or played the game. Six emotion responses were sent during that time.

Participants assigned to the EMS group were first introduced to EMS. As in Study II, one muscle was actuated so that they could get used to the sensation and the strength be adjusted. After that, electrodes were attached to the muscles required to perform the gestures and the system was calibrated (Table 1). We let the participants experience each gesture and told them about their meaning. We then handed the tablet to the participants and asked them to play the game. Furthermore, we explained them that they would receive either a text notification on the tablet or would be actuated via EMS while playing the game. Participants were asked to name the received emotions.

After the study, one researcher removed the BCI and EEG equipment. Both participants were brought to the same room and a semi-structured interview was conducted.

Results

We clustered the statements and comments participants made during the interview according to different themes that were discovered during the analysis process.

Emotion Reception: Intensity and Immersion

First we were interested in how intensive and immersing the gestures were, compared to the text notifications. P4 stated that he found "emotions conveyed through motion much stronger than the textual emotions". P4 added, though, that he was not sure whether this increased strength stems from the gestures or his surprise that the approach indeed works. P6 pointed out that "electrical feedback is much more haptic" and added that it is "much more emotional if the body reacted compared to when you just look." He also felt that more brain activity was involved. P2 stated that "[the feedback] happens within the body and it somehow feels as that the emotion is inside the body." P8 said that with "EMS you feel the emotion [...], the text message you can just neglect." P4 explained that in the case of the text message he was more involved in the game than connected to the other person. P4 pointed out that he could feel the anger and amusement for the EMS feedback, but not sadness. Asked about what they (dis)liked, P4 responded that "it [EMS] is more expressive, that is an advantage." "It [EMS] is much more immersive than text." (P6)

Gesture Set

Participants said that it would have helped to know ASL. P4, P6, and P8 would have liked the gestures to more strongly differ from each other and that they could be more natural. "Apart from the fact that the gestures did not differ too much, they were quite nice" (P4). We asked P8 whether she expects facial gestures to work better than the proposed gestures. P4 felt that they might not be diverse enough and added "smiling and opening my mouth could work." When asked about how they liked the movement caused by EMS, P6 answered that it was "just normal – neither negative or positive." Furthermore he said that it "was quite funny to see the arm alone go up without this being caused by the brain."P4 was happy and surprised that it works so well. Furthermore, P4 said that despite being able to feel it without looking, he would have liked a notification to be "aware of that something is going to happen." P4 also suggested to repeat the gesture.

Sharing Emotions

We were interested with whom people would like to share emotions through the presented system. There was agreement among participants, that they would mostly share this information with close friends, family, or partners. P3 stated that this would be appropriate for "friends and people I am close to." P5 felt that his girlfriend "would be happy about that" and that his parents would be very interested in receiving this kind of information ("Parents! Oh parents are interested in that"). However, he also pointed out that it depends on the emotions themselves as well as on the granularity of the emotions.

We found a tendency that participants would share negative emotions with close friends only, whereas it would be okay with them to share positive emotions with a wider audience. P5 stated that "the last scene was very dark [...] happy information would have been nicer." He added that he would prefer sharing only nice or positive emotions like "how well I was feeling" to a broad audience and even social media. "Bad emotions are more for people that are close."

Some participants explicitly mentioned that they would like to stay in control of what is shared with whom by being allowed to select specific emotions to share as well as by constraining specific emotions to a specific audience. P6 said "I would like to select which information would be transmitted." P7 mentioned that "it depends on the context." He would not share emotion in that way "if you feel that you will be judged by people, knowing about that specific emotion that are you feeling" for instance "if you enjoy a particular scene that others might think is [bad]" or "misinterpret the emotion."

Emotion Provisioning: Implicit vs. Explicit

A lot of the feedback focused on whether people would favor providing emotional feedback implicitly or explicitly. Participants had mixed views. On one hand, participants clearly liked to stay in control of what would be conveyed (P3: "I would like to stay in control of what I give away"), on the other hand, participants also stated that they think they would probably not share emotions unless this happened in an automated way. P5: "Feedback should be given implicitly." He mentioned that he is lazy and finds it hard to talk about his feelings. He also added "I would never write, 'Oh, hey sweetheart, I feel ...' [...] But when I can engage my girlfriend with it, wonderful." Similarly, P3 emphasized that he also would not share such information in case he would need to do this explicitly. He said that "[it] would have been really great if somebody else was made aware of that I saw something bad". He mentioned that he would have had a hard time to formulate his emotions. He added that "when the system does it, it would be much easier." When asking P7 in which cases he would like to share his emotion implicitly he answered "[...] if I am busy [...] or if I am focused on something."

Application Areas

Participants had a number of ideas on further applications of emotion sharing with our approach. P6 would like to apply the concept to *video calls* to enhance the experience. P5 said that he would like to share emotions he had during *sports* activities. Participants suggested to use an emotional connection at *work* or in *lectures* to communicate cases in which they were overloaded or not being challenged enough (P5, P6, P7, P8). P5 and P6 could imagine emotions as a *complementary communication channel* between friends to implicitly share when they were bored. P7 mentioned that emotions could not only be transmitted to a remote person, but it could also used for *self-reflecting* his own emotion. He said "one might benefit from knowing more about oneself." In line with this comment, P8 added that she would find it helpful to get to reflect: "I often tend to be unfocused and am not aware of that. But the system could help me to get my focus back."

Finally, participants saw potential of the approach in cases where two people do not speak the same language or one person is disabled (deaf and mute) (P4). P6 mentioned he could imagine a number of places where this would be annoying: "it needs to be context aware. [...] I would not use it in a car."

DESIGN RECOMMENDATIONS

We focused on testing a prototype and understanding how people would share and perceive emotions in an immersive way through embodied emotional feedback. We discuss the implications of our findings on creating embodied emotional feedback systems and provide design recommendations.

Implicit and explicit sharing

Sensed emotions could be implicitly or explicitly shared. Explicit sharing allows senders to control when and what she/he shares. This induces effort and interrupts the sender. Several participants stated that they would only share if the process was automated with low effort (P3) and that they otherwise find it hard to talk about emotions explicitly (P5). Implicit sharing does not involve the sender and is seamless.

Design Recommendation: Depending on the situation, senders should have the possibility to decide between implicit and explicit sharing of the emotional state.

Providing Senders Control over What to Share

We found that there are situations in which the sender would like to stay in control as to when to share and which affective state should be shared (P3, P5 and P7). As mentioned before, senders would like to share positive emotions more then negative ones with certain recipients.

Design Recommendation: Senders should be provided the opportunity to specify which emotion to share with whom. For example by preselecting groups of emotions that are sent to a specific group of receivers. The time and context should be selectable, as mentioned by P5, emotions during a sport event would be shared more than emotions of a private moment.

Emotion Granularity and Information Overload

Some emotions are felt momentarily whereas others persist longer. For example excitement in a roller-coaster is a short experience compared to the bad mood after a separation in a relationship. Additionally, emotions are not categorical, they can be strong or weak on the arousal/valence scale [55]. In an everyday life system for affective communication, the frequency, timing, and granularity of transmitted information is relevant. It is probably annoying to continuously be made aware of a person's affective state, as mentioned by P6. Thus, embodied feedback could be constrained to strong affective states or changes, or be guarded by contextual factors.

Design Recommendation: Embodied emotional feedback systems need to consider the granularity of emotional changes. The thresholds of emotional responses triggering embodied feedback need to be defined to transmit *important* emotions. Users should have ultimate control of the amount and intensity of emotions transferred and received so as to balance immersion, consider context, and avoid information overload. For example, the output can vary between visual or tactile feedback to a full actuated posture or gesture.

Considering the Context of the Recipient

Affective information is privacy sensitive. There may be situations where the receiver is not alone and hence information on the affective state of the sender should not be disclosed. At the same time, in certain situations sharing emotions might be inappropriate or even dangerous (e.g., while driving).

Design Recommendation: Before providing embodied feedback, the receiver's context should be considered. As personal and environmental sensors allow information on a user's location, activity and people in the vicinity to be obtained, feedback should not be provided in situations where people maybe put at risk as well as in situations where private information may not be disclosed.

Future work could look at how to cope with such situations. Strategies include not delivering the information at all or postponing it. Yet, mechanisms are required that notify the sender about this, in particular in cases where an immediate response is expected. In addition, senders could be provided the opportunity to'force' the emotion to be transmitted in certain situations, for example, as others are present.

FUTURE WORK

The presented studies investigated unidirectional communication of affective information. In a real application, bidirectional exchange of emotions would be necessary. This would close the feedback loop. An important question for future work is how this feedback loop influences the emotional state of the connected persons: Will received sadness result in sadness in the recipient, which when played back will lead to a downwards spiral? Will received amusement cheer a sad person up? Another question is how and when the affective channel should be escalated to other forms of communication such as text or voice communication. Will the exchanged affective information be a "ticket to talk" – a reason to start a conversation around the causes of the other person's emotion? These questions require long-term studies with couples and more practical sensing and output technologies.

We presented an interpreted embodied emotional output through ASL gestures. The question is whether the sensory input necessarily needs to be classified into affective states. It is also conceivable to just replay the sender's bodily state with the recipient: For example, if an EMG sensor detects muscle tension, that muscle tension could be played back on the recipient using EMS without the need for interpretation on the system's side. Interpretation could be completely left to the recipient. Participants of Study I remarked that the body's expression of emotion and the recipient's interpretation differ among individuals. The gestures that partners usually perform given a certain emotion could be transmitted.

CONCLUSION

This work focuses on fundamental aspects of communicating emotions between two people remotely. Emotions are sensed with an EEG system, classified as amused, angry, sad, or neutral, sent and played back using EMS to actuate the recipient's body. The presented studies showed that EMS actuation may lead to an embodiment of emotional states, contributing to an intuitive understanding, immersion, and empathy.

Two different sets of playback movements have been investigated. The output is based on natural movements related to emotions and emotion-related sign language gestures (ASL). The ASL gesture set was shown to be more intuitive than gestures selected from the literature. One reason could be that we only considered gestures and body posture, but not facial expressions. Facial expressions play a crucial role in the judgment of emotion [21]. Open questions include how to determine opportune moments of sending embodied emotional feedback, how bidirectional feedback influences the states of the partners, and how and when the emotional feedback channel should be escalated to other forms of communication.

ACKNOWLEDGMENTS

This work was partly conducted within the Amplify project which received funding from the European Research Council (ERC) under the European Union's Horizon 2020 research and innovation programme (grant agreement no. 683008).

REFERENCES

1. Leonardo Angelini, Maurizio Caon, Denis Lalanne, Omar Abou khaled, and Elena Mugellini. 2015. Towards an Anthropomorphic Lamp for Affective Interaction. In *Proceedings of the Ninth International Conference on Tangible, Embedded, and Embodied Interaction (TEI '15)*. ACM, New York, NY, USA, 661–666. DOI: http://dx.doi.org/10.1145/2677199.2687914
2. V. H. Anh, M. N. Van, B. B. Ha, and T. H. Quyet. 2012. A real-time model based Support Vector Machine for emotion recognition through EEG. In *2012 International Conference on Control, Automation and Information Sciences (ICCAIS)*. 191–196. DOI: http://dx.doi.org/10.1109/ICCAIS.2012.6466585
3. MJ Asmussen, AZ Bailey, PJ Keir, J Potvin, T Bergel, and AJ Nelson. 2015. Combining Multiple Data Acquisition Systems to Study Corticospinal Output and Multi-segment Biomechanics. *Journal of Visualized Experiments* 107 (2015). DOI: http://dx.doi.org/10.3791/53492
4. Peter Aspinall, Panagiotis Mavros, Richard Coyne, and Jenny Roe. 2013. The urban brain: analysing outdoor physical activity with mobile EEG. *British Journal of Sports Medicine* (2013). DOI: http://dx.doi.org/10.1136/bjsports-2012-091877
5. Armando Barreto, Jing Zhai, and Malek Adjouadi. 2007. Non-intrusive Physiological Monitoring for Automated Stress Detection in Human-Computer Interaction. In *International Workshop on Human-Computer Interaction*. Vol. 4796. Springer, Berlin Heidelberg, 29–38. DOI: http://dx.doi.org/10.1007/978-3-540-75773-3_4
6. Natalya N. Bazarova, Yoon Hyung Choi, Victoria Schwanda Sosik, Dan Cosley, and Janis Whitlock. 2015. Social Sharing of Emotions on Facebook: Channel Differences, Satisfaction, and Replies. In *Proceedings of the 18th ACM Conference on Computer Supported Cooperative Work (CSCW '15)*. ACM, New York, NY, USA, 154–164. DOI: http://dx.doi.org/10.1145/2675133.2675297
7. Danny Oude Bos. 2008. EEG-based emotion recognition: The Influence of Visual and Auditory Stimuli . http://hmi.ewi.utwente.nl/verslagen/capita-selecta/CS-Oude_Bos-Danny.pdf. (2008). [Online; accessed 19-Jan.-2016].
8. Margaret M. Bradley and Peter J. Lang. 1994. Measuring emotion: The self-assessment manikin and the semantic differential. *Journal of Behavior Therapy and Experimental Psychiatry* 25, 1 (1994), 49 – 59. DOI: http://dx.doi.org/10.1016/0005-7916(94)90063-9
9. Carlos Busso, Zhigang Deng, Serdar Yildirim, Murtaza Bulut, Chul Min Lee, Abe Kazemzadeh, Sungbok Lee, Ulrich Neumann, and Shrikanth Narayanan. 2004. Analysis of Emotion Recognition Using Facial Expressions, Speech and Multimodal Information. In *Proceedings of the 6th International Conference on Multimodal Interfaces (ICMI '04)*. ACM, New York, NY, USA, 205–211. DOI: http://dx.doi.org/10.1145/1027933.1027968
10. John T Cacioppo, Richard E Petty, Mary E Losch, and Hai Sook Kim. 1986. Electromyographic activity over facial muscle regions can differentiate the valence and intensity of affective reactions. *Journal of personality and social psychology* 50, 2 (1986), 260. DOI: http://dx.doi.org/10.1037/0022-3514.50.2.260
11. Ginevra Castellano, Loic Kessous, and George Caridakis. 2008. Affect and Emotion in Human-Computer Interaction. Springer-Verlag, Berlin, Heidelberg, Chapter Emotion Recognition Through Multiple Modalities: Face, Body Gesture, Speech. DOI: http://dx.doi.org/10.1007/978-3-540-85099-1
12. Karen Church, Eve Hoggan, and Nuria Oliver. 2010. A Study of Mobile Mood Awareness and Communication Through MobiMood. In *Proceedings of the 6th Nordic Conference on Human-Computer Interaction: Extending Boundaries (NordiCHI '10)*. ACM, New York, NY, USA, 128–137. DOI: http://dx.doi.org/10.1145/1868914.1868933
13. Yanqing Cui, Jari Kangas, Jukka Holm, and Guido Grassel. 2013. Front-camera Video Recordings As Emotion Responses to Mobile Photos Shared Within Close-knit Groups. In *Proceedings of the SIGCHI Conference on Human Factors in Computing Systems (CHI '13)*. ACM, New York, NY, USA, 981–990. DOI: http://dx.doi.org/10.1145/2470654.2466125
14. Nele Dael, Marcello Mortillaro, and Klaus R Scherer. 2012. Emotion expression in body action and posture. *Emotion* 12, 5 (2012), 1085–1101. DOI: http://dx.doi.org/10.1037/a0025737
15. Marianne Dainton and Brooks Aylor. 2002. Patterns of communication channel use in the maintenance of long distance relationships. *Communication Research Reports* 19, 2 (2002), 118–129. DOI: http://dx.doi.org/10.1080/08824090209384839
16. Alwin de Rooij and Sara Jones. 2015. (E)Motion and Creativity: Hacking the Function of Motor Expressions in Emotion Regulation to Augment Creativity. In *Proceedings of the Ninth International Conference on Tangible, Embedded, and Embodied Interaction (TEI '15)*. ACM, New York, NY, USA, 145–152. DOI: http://dx.doi.org/10.1145/2677199.2680552
17. Anind K. Dey and Ed de Guzman. 2006. From Awareness to Connectedness: The Design and Deployment of Presence Displays. In *Proceedings of the SIGCHI Conference on Human Factors in Computing Systems (CHI '06)*. ACM, New York, NY, USA, 899–908. DOI: http://dx.doi.org/10.1145/1124772.1124905

18. Chris Dodge. 1997. The Bed: A Medium for Intimate Communication. In *CHI '97 Extended Abstracts on Human Factors in Computing Systems (CHI EA '97)*. ACM, New York, NY, USA, 371–372. DOI: http://dx.doi.org/10.1145/1120212.1120439

19. Sandra E Duclos, James D Laird, Eric Schneider, Melissa Sexter, Lisa Stern, and Oliver Van Lighten. 1989. Emotion-specific effects of facial expressions and postures on emotional experience. *Journal of Personality and Social Psychology* 57, 1 (1989), 100–108. DOI: http://dx.doi.org/10.1037/0022-3514.57.1.100

20. Paul Ekman. 1992. An argument for basic emotions. *Cognition & emotion* 6, 3-4 (1992), 169–200. DOI: http://dx.doi.org/10.1080/02699939208411068

21. Paul Ekman and Wallace V Friesen. 1967. Head and body cues in the judgment of emotion: A reformulation. *Perceptual and motor skills* 24, 3 (1967), 711–724. DOI: http://dx.doi.org/10.2466/pms.1967.24.3.711

22. Petra Fagerberg, Anna Stahl, and Kristina Höök. 2003. Designing Gestures for Affective Input: An Analysis of Shape, Effort and Valence. *MUM 2003 : proceedings of the 2nd International Conference on Mobile and Ubiquitous Multimedia, 10-12 December, 2003, Norrköping, Sweden* 57-65 (2003), 57–65.

23. Allan Fong, Zahra Ashktorab, and Jon Froehlich. 2013. Bear-with-me: An Embodied Prototype to Explore Tangible Two-way Exchanges of Emotional Language. In *CHI '13 Extended Abstracts on Human Factors in Computing Systems (CHI EA '13)*. ACM, New York, NY, USA, 1011–1016. DOI: http://dx.doi.org/10.1145/2468356.2468537

24. Gary Garcia-Molina, Tsvetomira Tsoneva, and Anton Nijholt. 2013. Emotional Brain-computer Interfaces. *Int. J. Auton. Adapt. Commun. Syst.* 6, 1 (Dec. 2013), 9–25. DOI: http://dx.doi.org/10.1504/IJAACS.2013.050687

25. Daniel Gooch and Leon Watts. 2012. YourGloves, Hothands and Hotmits: Devices to Hold Hands at a Distance. In *Proceedings of the 25th Annual ACM Symposium on User Interface Software and Technology (UIST '12)*. ACM, New York, NY, USA, 157–166. DOI: http://dx.doi.org/10.1145/2380116.2380138

26. Erik Grönvall, Jonas Fritsch, and Anna Vallgrda. 2016. FeltRadio: Sensing and Making Sense of Wireless Traffic. In *Proceedings of the 2016 ACM Conference on Designing Interactive Systems (DIS '16)*. ACM, New York, NY, USA, 829–840. DOI: http://dx.doi.org/10.1145/2901790.2901818

27. Hatice Gunes and Massimo Piccardi. 2007. Bi-modal Emotion Recognition from Expressive Face and Body Gestures. *Journal of Network and Computer Applications* 30, 4 (Nov. 2007), 1334–1345. DOI: http://dx.doi.org/10.1016/j.jnca.2006.09.007

28. Marc Hassenzahl, Stephanie Heidecker, Kai Eckoldt, Sarah Diefenbach, and Uwe Hillmann. 2012. All You Need is Love: Current Strategies of Mediating Intimate Relationships Through Technology. *ACM Trans. Comput.-Hum. Interact.* 19, 4, Article 30 (Dec. 2012), 19 pages. DOI: http://dx.doi.org/10.1145/2395131.2395137

29. J. A. Healey and R. W. Picard. 2005. Detecting stress during real-world driving tasks using physiological sensors. *Trans. Intell. Transport. Sys.* 6, 2 (June 2005), 156–166. DOI: http://dx.doi.org/10.1109/TITS.2005.848368

30. Kristina Höök. 2008. Affective Loop Experiences — What Are They?. In *Proceedings of the 3rd International Conference on Persuasive Technology (PERSUASIVE '08)*. Springer-Verlag, Berlin, Heidelberg, 1–12. DOI: http://dx.doi.org/10.1007/978-3-540-68504-3_1

31. Thierry Keller and Andreas Kuhn. 2008. Electrodes for transcutaneous (surface) electrical stimulation. *Journal of Automatic Control* 18, 2 (2008), 35–45. DOI: http://dx.doi.org/0.2298/JAC0802035K

32. L Kiers, Didier Cros, KH Chiappa, and J Fang. 1993. Variability of motor potentials evoked by transcranial magnetic stimulation. *EEG and Clinical Neurophysiology/Evoked Potentials Section* 89, 6 (1993), 415–423. DOI: http://dx.doi.org/10.1016/0168-5597(93)90115-6

33. Jina Kim, Young-Woo Park, and Tek-Jin Nam. 2015. BreathingFrame: An Inflatable Frame for Remote Breath Signal Sharing. In *Proceedings of the Ninth International Conference on Tangible, Embedded, and Embodied Interaction (TEI '15)*. ACM, New York, NY, USA, 109–112. DOI: http://dx.doi.org/10.1145/2677199.2680606

34. Ernst Kruijff, Dieter Schmalstieg, and Steffi Beckhaus. 2006. Using Neuromuscular Electrical Stimulation for Pseudo-haptic Feedback. In *Proceedings of the ACM Symposium on Virtual Reality Software and Technology (VRST '06)*. ACM, New York, NY, USA, 316–319. DOI: http://dx.doi.org/10.1145/1180495.1180558

35. James D Laird. 1984. The real role of facial response in the experience of emotion: A reply to Tourangeau and Ellsworth, and others. 47, 4 (1984), 909–917. DOI: http://dx.doi.org/10.1037/0022-3514.47.4.909

36. Irene Levin. 2004. Living Apart Together: A New Family Form. *Current Sociology* (2004), 223–240. DOI: http://dx.doi.org/10.1177/0011392104041809

37. Y. Liu, O. Sourina, and M. K. Nguyen. 2010. Real-Time EEG-Based Human Emotion Recognition and Visualization. In *2010 International Conference on Cyberworlds*. 262–269. DOI: http://dx.doi.org/10.1109/CW.2010.37

38. Pedro Lopes, Alexandra Ion, Willi Mueller, Daniel Hoffmann, Patrik Jonell, and Patrick Baudisch. 2015a. Proprioceptive Interaction. In *Proceedings of the 33rd Annual ACM Conference on Human Factors in Computing Systems (CHI '15)*. ACM, New York, NY, USA, 939–948. DOI: http://dx.doi.org/10.1145/2702123.2702461

39. Pedro Lopes, Patrik Jonell, and Patrick Baudisch. 2015b. Affordance++: Allowing Objects to Communicate Dynamic Use. In *Proceedings of the 33rd Annual ACM Conference on Human Factors in Computing Systems (CHI '15)*. ACM, New York, NY, USA, 2515–2524. DOI: http://dx.doi.org/10.1145/2702123.2702128

40. Pedro Lopes, Doăa Yüksel, François Guimbretière, and Patrick Baudisch. 2016. Muscle-plotter: An Interactive System Based on Electrical Muscle Stimulation That Produces Spatial Output. In *Proceedings of the 29th Annual Symposium on User Interface Software and Technology (UIST '16)*. ACM, New York, NY, USA, 207–217. DOI: http://dx.doi.org/10.1145/2984511.2984530

41. Danielle Lottridge, Nicolas Masson, and Wendy Mackay. 2009. Sharing Empty Moments: Design for Remote Couples. In *Proceedings of the SIGCHI Conference on Human Factors in Computing Systems (CHI '09)*. ACM, New York, NY, USA, 2329–2338. DOI: http://dx.doi.org/10.1145/1518701.1519058

42. Marion L. Chapman M. Carole Pistole, Amber Roberts. 2010. Attachment, relationship maintenance, and stress in long distance and geographically close romantic relationships. *Journal of Social and Personal Relationships* 27, 4 (6 2010), 535–552.

43. Maurizio Mauri, Valentina Magagnin, Pietro Cipresso, Luca Mainardi, Emery N Brown, Sergio Cerutti, Marco Villamira, and Riccardo Barbieri. Psychophysiological signals associated with affective states. In *Engineering in Medicine and Biology Society , 2010 Annual International Conference of the IEEE (EMBC)*. 3563–3566. DOI: http://dx.doi.org/0.1109/IEMBS.2010.5627465

44. Dan Nie, Xiao-Wei Wang, Li-Chen Shi, and Bao-Liang Lu. EEG-based emotion recognition during watching movies. In *2011 5th International IEEE/EMBS Conference on Neural Engineering (NER)*. 667–670. DOI: http://dx.doi.org/10.1109/NER.2011.5910636

45. Young-Woo Park, Kyoung-Min Baek, and Tek-Jin Nam. 2013. The Roles of Touch During Phone Conversations: Long-distance Couples' Use of POKE in Their Homes. In *Proceedings of the SIGCHI Conference on Human Factors in Computing Systems (CHI '13)*. ACM, New York, NY, USA, 1679–1688. DOI: http://dx.doi.org/10.1145/2470654.2466222

46. Timo Partala, Maria Jokiniemi, and Veikko Surakka. 2000. Pupillary Responses to Emotionally Provocative Stimuli. In *Proceedings of the 2000 Symposium on Eye Tracking Research & Applications (ETRA '00)*. ACM, New York, NY, USA, 123–129. DOI: http://dx.doi.org/10.1145/355017.355042

47. M. Perakakis and A. Potamianos. 2012. Affective evaluation of a mobile multimodal dialogue system using brain signals. In *2012 IEEE Spoken Language Technology Workshop (SLT)*. 43–48. DOI: http://dx.doi.org/10.1109/SLT.2012.6424195

48. Arttu Perttula, Antti Koivisto, Riikka Mäkelä, Marko Suominen, and Jari Multisilta. 2011. Social Navigation with the Collective Mobile Mood Monitoring System. In *Proceedings of the 15th International Academic MindTrek Conference: Envisioning Future Media Environments (MindTrek '11)*. ACM, New York, NY, USA, 117–124. DOI: http://dx.doi.org/10.1145/2181037.2181057

49. Max Pfeiffer, Tim Duente, and Michael Rohs. 2016. Let Your Body Move: A Prototyping Toolkit for Wearable Force Feedback with Electrical Muscle Stimulation. In *Proceedings of the 18th International Conference on Human-Computer Interaction with Mobile Devices and Services (MobileHCI '16)*. ACM, New York, NY, USA, 418–427. DOI: http://dx.doi.org/10.1145/2935334.2935348

50. Max Pfeiffer, Tim Dünte, Stefan Schneegass, Florian Alt, and Michael Rohs. 2015. Cruise Control for Pedestrians: Controlling Walking Direction Using Electrical Muscle Stimulation. In *Proceedings of the 33rd Annual ACM Conference on Human Factors in Computing Systems (CHI '15)*. ACM, New York, NY, USA, 2505–2514. DOI: http://dx.doi.org/10.1145/2702123.2702190

51. M. Pfeiffer and W. Stuerzlinger. 2015. 3D virtual hand pointing with EMS and vibration feedback. In *2015 IEEE Symposium on 3D User Interfaces (3DUI)*. 117–120. DOI: http://dx.doi.org/10.1109/3DUI.2015.7131735

52. Rosalind W Picard and Roalind Picard. 1997. *Affective computing*. Vol. 252. MIT press Cambridge.

53. David Prutchi and Michael Norris. 2005. *Design and development of medical electronic instrumentation: a practical perspective of the design, construction, and test of medical devices*. John Wiley & Sons. 344 pages.

54. John Riskind and Carolyn Gotay. 1982. Physical posture: Could it have regulatory or feedback effects on motivation and emotion? *Motivation and Emotion* 6, 3 (1982). DOI: http://dx.doi.org/10.1007/BF00992249

55. James A. Russell. 1980. A circumplex model of affect. 39, 6 (1980), 1161–1178. DOI: http://dx.doi.org/10.1037/h0077714

56. Abraham Savitzky and Marcel JE Golay. 1964. Smoothing and differentiation of data by simplified least squares procedures. *Analytical chemistry* 36, 8 (1964). DOI: http://dx.doi.org/0.1021/ac60214a047

57. Alexandre Schaefer, Frédéric Nils, Xavier Sanchez, and Pierre Philippot. 2010. Assessing the effectiveness of a large database of emotion-eliciting films: A new tool for emotion researchers. *Cognition and Emotion* 24, 7 (2010). DOI: http://dx.doi.org/10.1080/02699930903274322

58. Yu Shi, Natalie Ruiz, Ronnie Taib, Eric Choi, and Fang Chen. 2007. Galvanic Skin Response (GSR) As an Index of Cognitive Load. In *CHI '07 Extended Abstracts on Human Factors in Computing Systems (CHI EA '07)*. ACM, New York, NY, USA, 2651–2656. DOI: http://dx.doi.org/10.1145/1240866.1241057

59. Magdalena W Sliwinska, Sylvia Vitello, and Joseph T Devlin. 2014. Transcranial magnetic stimulation for investigating causal brain-behavioral relationships and their time course. *Journal of Visualized Experiments* 89 (2014). DOI: http://dx.doi.org/10.3791/51735

60. Paul Strohmeier, Juan Pablo Carrascal, Bernard Cheng, Margaret Meban, and Roel Vertegaal. 2016. An Evaluation of Shape Changes for Conveying Emotions. In *Proceedings of the 2016 CHI Conference on Human Factors in Computing Systems (CHI '16)*. ACM, New York, NY, USA, 3781–3792. DOI: http://dx.doi.org/10.1145/2858036.2858537

61. Petra Sundström, Anna Sthl, and Kristina Höök. 2007. In Situ Informants Exploring an Emotional Mobile Messaging System in Their Everyday Practice. *Int. J. Hum.-Comput. Stud.* 65, 4 (April 2007), 388–403. DOI: http://dx.doi.org/10.1016/j.ijhcs.2006.11.013

62. Emi Tamaki, Takashi Miyaki, and Jun Rekimoto. 2011. PossessedHand: Techniques for Controlling Human Hands Using Electrical Muscles Stimuli. In *Proceedings of the SIGCHI Conference on Human Factors in Computing Systems (CHI '11)*. ACM, New York, NY, USA, 543–552. DOI: http://dx.doi.org/10.1145/1978942.1979018

63. Dzmitry Tsetserukou and Alena Neviarouskaya. 2010. World's First Wearable Humanoid Robot That Augments Our Emotions. In *Proceedings of the 1st Augmented Human International Conference (AH '10)*. ACM, New York, NY, USA, Article 8, 10 pages. DOI: http://dx.doi.org/10.1145/1785455.1785463

64. Harald G. Wallbott. 1998. Bodily expression of emotion. *European Journal of Social Psychology* 28, 6 (1998), 879–896. DOI: http://dx.doi.org/10.1002/(SICI)1099-0992(1998110)28:6<879::AID-EJSP901>3.0.CO;2-W

65. David Watson, Lee A Clark, and Auke Tellegen. 1988. Development and validation of brief measures of positive and negative affect: The PANAS scales. 54, 6 (1988).

66. Julia Werner, Reto Wettach, and Eva Hornecker. 2008. United-pulse: Feeling Your Partner's Pulse. In *Proceedings of the 10th International Conference on Human Computer Interaction with Mobile Devices and Services (MobileHCI '08)*. ACM, New York, NY, USA, 535–538. DOI: http://dx.doi.org/10.1145/1409240.1409338

67. Matthew John Willis and Christian Martyn Jones. 2012. Emotishare: Emotion Sharing on Mobile Devices. In *Proceedings of the 26th Annual BCS Interaction Specialist Group Conference on People and Computers (BCS-HCI '12)*. British Computer Society, Swinton, UK, UK, 292–297. http://dl.acm.org/citation.cfm?id=2377916.2377954

68. Zhihong Zeng, Maja Pantic, Glenn Roisman, Thomas S Huang, and others. 2009. A Survey of Affect Recognition Methods: Audio, Visual, and Spontaneous Expressions. *IIEEE Transactions on Pattern Analysis and Machine Intelligence* 31, 1 (2009), 39–58. DOI: http://dx.doi.org/10.1109/TPAMI.2008.52

Understanding the Role Fluidity of Stakeholders During Assistive Technology Research "In the Wild"

LouAnne E. Boyd[1], Kyle Rector[2], Halley P. Profita[3], Abigale Stangl[4], Annuska Zolyomi[5], Shaun K. Kane[3], Gillian R. Hayes[1]

[1]Department of Informatics
UC Irvine, Irvine, USA
{boydl, hayesg}@uci.edu

[2]Department of Computer Science
University of Iowa, Iowa City, USA
kyle-rector@uiowa.edu

[3]Department of Computer Science
[4]ATLAS Institute
University of Colorado, Boulder, USA
{halley.profita, abigale.stangl, shaun.kane}@colorado.edu

[5]Information School
University of Washington, Seattle, USA
annuska@uw.edu

ABSTRACT

Deploying novel technologies requires the coordinated efforts of the research team, research participants, and a variety of community members and project stakeholders. To ensure that the project is completed successfully, these disparate groups of people engage in articulation work, which is the meta-work that supports the use of collaborative systems. In this paper, we examine the articulation work surrounding the deployment of systems that have found limited long-term adoption: assistive technology. Specifically, we examine three research deployments of a collaborative game for children with autism. Analysis of the articulation work performed during these studies demonstrates how research deployments of technologies create conditions in which stakeholders must take on additional roles to make the deployment work. By understanding the articulation work surrounding deployment studies engendered in this role fluidity, we can improve both research design and the analysis of data emergent from these studies.

Author Keywords

Deployment; articulation work; collaboration; assistive technology; role fluidity; autism

ACM Classification Keywords

H.5.3 Group and Organization Interfaces *Computer supported cooperative work,* K.4.2 Social Issues *Assistive technologies for persons with disabilities*

CHI 2017, May 06-11, 2017, Denver, CO, USA
 ISBN 978-1-4503-4655-9/17/05...$15.00
DOI: http://dx.doi.org/10.1145/3025453.3025493

INTRODUCTION

Researchers focusing on the uptake and use of assistive technology "in the wild" have found limited long-term adoption, partly due to the complexity, required adaptations, and social acceptability of these systems [7,19,28]. To the degree that they are adopted at all [7], assistive technology use is surrounded by an additional factor—the need for support from others, often in the form of articulation work [26,35].

Articulation work is the meta-work surrounding collaborative technology systems to make them work [36], typically including a *"set of activities required to manage the distributed nature of cooperative work"* [36]. The articulation work of supporting users with disabilities requires their caregivers to engage with assistive technology as secondary users [14,18] and as "IT support" [5,7]. In research studies, this phenomenon can be even more profound, with the research team themselves doing additional work to support the deployment of a system and interacting with participants, their family members or teachers, and other community members. In considering research deployments as cooperative work, articulation work refers to the ways in which a wide variety of actors influence when, where, how, and who engages with a research system.

Although articulation work is well studied in collaborative work contexts (*e.g.,* [27,34]), it has not yet been examined in light of the deployment of assistive technologies as we do here. Field deployments have increasingly become central to assistive technology research, because they provide important data about the context within which an assistive system might be taken up. Field deployments "provide rich data about how closely a concept meets the target population's needs and how users accept, adopt, and appropriate a system in actual use over time" [29]. Given the challenges in adopting assistive technology, these approaches are promising for understanding the adaptation and appropriation processes around assistive technologies that might make their adoption possible. However, they are not without their own challenges. As researchers who have conducted numerous deployment studies previously [4,16,19,24,25,32] and written about their advantages [29], we find it essential to look critically at the work that surrounds this method and the ways in which such work might influence our findings. Specifically, we examine the articulation work surrounding the deployment of Zody, a collaborative assistive and therapeutic game for teaching social skills to children with autism.

Field deployments require researchers to accomplish a variety of types of articulation work, such as "adjusting the data collection, study plan, or other factors"[29]. Negotiating the terms of research projects evolves in practice. In this work, we highlight how the negotiated and competing roles each stakeholder group played impacted the practices and outcomes of the deployment studies, which in turn invoke important considerations for study design and analysis of resulting data.

In our reflection on three deployments of Zody, we saw substantial articulation work that is often overlooked as a critical part of assistive technology evaluation and adoption. We also observed the impact the surrounding articulation work (*i.e.,* teachers encouraging students to play together when students wanted to play alone) had on the children's experiences with the technology and on the results we saw from the deployments.

Deployment studies by their nature require substantial buy-in from community partners and other collaborators who are not professional researchers. However, what is interesting here is the way in which these same people—including the children—must take on different roles simultaneously to accomplish the work of running a smooth deployment study. Maintaining multiple simultaneous roles requires fluid transition from one role to another as the context of the setting shifts between research to the usual day-to-day activities. Therefore, we suggest a new concept, *role fluidity,* as a previously unconsidered form of *articulation work* that surrounds the work of a deployment study. For example, the children morph from students to research participants and back again with varying levels of rights, autonomy, and engagement in each of those roles to meet the demand of the current moment. Likewise, researchers move from scientific observers to technical support to instructor in the space of minutes to benefit the study. Role fluidity demonstrates that each stakeholder assumes the shape of the current role they are expected to be in a given moment or activity, shifting back to another role when the most immediate need changes.

This paper contributes to discussions of both the deployment of novel technologies as a research method and articulation work as a practice surrounding assistive technology by explicitly examining the articulation work around the use of assistive technologies in field deployments. The concept of role fluidity extends our understanding of articulation work and highlights the importance of considering the impact of changing roles during research studies in the wild. A better understanding of role fluidity can lead us toward the goal of more robust research deployments and valid analysis of the research outcomes as well as deeper understanding of the ways in which assistive technology systems are often inherently collaborative.

RELATED WORK

This research touches on two important and overlapping areas, articulation work and collaborative games for children with autism. First, we provide an overview of research related to collaborative children's games designed to facilitate cooperation between users with autism during the use of a system. Then, we broadly discuss articulation work and related concepts around technologies that require collaboration to put or keep a system in use. We then relay challenges in articulation work to research practices.

Collaborative Games for Children with Autism

Collaboration is a common target behavior for children with autism because collaborative activities provide the opportunity to work on social interaction, comprised of understanding social norms, turn-taking, joint attention, etc. The children's social interaction skills can be supported by innovative technology leveraging mechanisms of collaborative technologies, such as supporting collocated users simultaneously using a single device. Several technology projects have addressed social relationship skills by developing tools for collaboration in which multiple students share the same device (*e.g.,* [3,13,14,17,23,30]). Touchscreens and other shared interactive surfaces "allow face-to-face interaction and multiple simultaneous inputs from individuals acting independently or as part of a group" [23], making them particularly compelling as platforms. Because of their inherently collaborative features, touchscreens have been used in research studies to teach a variety of social skills to children with autism. In particular, the high levels of structure that can be imparted using touchscreens have been shown to improve student performance in joint activities [13,17]. For example, Piper *et al.* developed and evaluated a tabletop system to support the teaching of turn-taking called SIDES [23]. By using a closed system in which behavior choices were prescribed and limited to a few options, clear visual directions, and consistent feedback, SIDES not only encouraged turn-taking during the game but improved social skills overall for participants. Although these large-screen projects are promising, at this time such hardware is not cost effective for most schools and clinics.

With the advent of the tablet and other mobile shared surfaces, smaller scale collaborative technologies are much more likely to be used beyond research settings. Additionally, these devices' small size might force children to become more comfortable with close physical proximity, a challenge for many students with autism. One such project, the Open Autism Project, focused on using multi-touch tablets to encourage social interactions "through creative, expressive, and collaborative activities" [18].

One way to scaffold children's collaborate play is through technology enforcement. Technology enforcement requires a certain action by children that demonstrates collaboration before enabling certain features. Examples of technology enforcement include the requirement to play using cooperative gestures before making progress, such as requiring two people to be in a photo before enabling the camera button. The developers of Incloodle , a camera taking application, found that requiring two faces be in the same picture frame before enabling the camera button helped children play with one another if they needed scaffolding. Additionally, previous studies have found that children wanted more enforcement from technical systems [3] and performed better than with human enforcement . However, the articulation work that went into the research study to create such productive deployments around assistive technologies for collaboration remains unstudied.

Articulation Work

When working on a project with multiple stakeholders, division of labor and clear articulation of the rights for each stakeholder limit the kind of natural imbalances that can emerge on teams with different levels of power and prestige [35]. When considering the composition of deployment teams—particularly those that include children and people with disabilities—these issues of power, prestige, and preconceived notions of competency for the other stakeholders [20] become even more central. Tensions emerge around the provenance of ideas, the distribution of effort, and conflicting values. "Articulation work" enables teams to overcome these challenges, but does so through the addition of overhead [27] in the form of analysis of the culture and politics of the work [34].

Coordination among stakeholders to make collaborative work successful results in patterns in articulation work that have often been described in binary groupings (i.e., local and global levels; inter and intra organization level; formal or *ad hoc*; routine or non-routine [1]). In the Abraham and Reddy inter- and intra-departmental coordination model, decisions at the global level (i.e., administration decides to go live with a new technology) may prove to be disruptive at the local level (i.e., staff is not yet trained on the tools). Decisions made by one party to "temporarily solve" an issue can result in further problems and "re-coordination of activities" for the other department [1]. These inter departmental conflicts or "cross boundary breakdowns" have bearing on innovative technology deployments in the wild as research activities are shared across organizations and stakeholders. In this work, we see articulation work carried out between stakeholder groups, but within each stakeholder who takes an additional role created by the work of participating in research.

As HCI researchers, we must acknowledge the articulation work that goes into creating, using, and researching technology [27]. Articulation work affects the research process. Similar challenges in organizations regarding both within and between group dynamics occur in research processes, yet not always delineated in the same way such as by differences in stakeholder group. Dachtera *et al.* (2104) found that different perspectives across research collaborators are not necessarily a "simply academic vs. industry dichotomy," but rather tensions that take rise from individual stakeholder group attitudes toward a research approach and differing research interests or expectations toward the research project [6]. Negotiated terms of project management occur more formally at the onset of a partnership, as a first order of business—"first order articulation work" [36]. First order articulation work here refers to "the planning and coordinating of who will be doing what, when, where and how etc., before the actual project begins [36].

Although many tensions can be addressed through first order articulation work, other challenges arise at the point the collaborative technology is put into use—called second order articulation work [36]. This work consists of handling missed responsibilities, re-delegation of unfinished jobs and all the crucial moves during the project that are necessary so that the project doesn't break down, or managing situations when technology does break down, as well as how the uptake of a collaborative technology differs in the wild form the expected trajectory.

Understanding how researchers navigate the challenges presented once a technology is put into place is essential to understanding the context of adaptation and adoption as well as ensuring that the inherent influence of researcher -led articulation work is accounted for in our research findings. As part of the research team, researchers have a variety of paths they can take in understanding their place in their work, such as: introspection, inter-subjective reflection, mutual collaboration, social critique, and discursive deconstruction [12]. Here, we provide details of our path by reflecting on the articulation work across three deployments.

We explored the articulation work of each stakeholder group (including the research team) around the use of Zody, an iPad application that encourages collaboration and social interaction between children with autism. In our work, not only were the children enlisted to cooperate during the collaborative play activity; children were also actors in the articulation work that occurred around deployment. As children were the intended primary users of the system, their needs and wants were in conversation with the roles of the other stakeholders and researchers, resulting in a negotiated deployment configured to multiple stakeholders' needs. Furthermore, the teachers and therapists negotiated the conditions under which the fieldwork was conducted, to meet the aims of research as well as the needs of their classrooms. Echoing the "dual nature" of articulation work that occurs at both local and global levels [1,11], we build on prior work by focusing on the articulation work of three different stakeholder groups (*i.e.,* researchers, teachers, children) during three different deployments to illuminate field deployments' complexities in the wild and the challenges that occur during the process, thus impacting the results. We ask: 1) How do multiple stakeholder negotiate field deployments, and 2) How do deployments create a need for role fluidity?

STUDY SETTINGS AND METHODS

Over the course of one year, we deployed Zody at three sites with 49 children and 12 adult caregivers. In this section, we describe the three sites of deployment, technology deployed, methods of setting up and conducting the three deployments, and our approach for analyzing the dynamic, context-specific articulation work that we observed. We describe the reflection on articulation work observed during these studies and demonstrate how this work indicates the need for and presence of role fluidity in the deployment of technological systems.

Collaborative Tech: Zody Experimental System

Zody is a prototype collaborative iPad game that supports cooperation in real time. The goals of this game design were to support collaboration and cooperation, and to demonstrate the development of better social reciprocity, social communication, and problem-solving through relationship-based interventions [33].

Several combinations of cooperative gestures support two players engaging in an action to realize a shared goal.

Zody employs different two-player "cooperative gestures," through which the system interprets the gestures of more than one user as contributing to a single, combined command" [21]. In this tablet game, cooperation and collaboration are supported through mechanics, such as simultaneous finger presses, differing player roles, or encouraging discussion to support social interactions. This structure created a role for each player as well as, recommending that players work together. The Zody game notably focuses on co-located players, making a video game social in face-to-face space. Additionally, the game provides options for cooperative play that are predictable (game mechanics provide options instead of a teacher prompting the same behavior) in a preferred modality (video game). The researcher selected the technology because collaborative play is a frequent target skill for children with autism, and an iPad game is a preferred mode of play.

Site Descriptions

The same version of Zody was used across three unrelated field sites. Each site provided a unique research setting, with different personnel. The first and last authors were involved in the design of each empirical study. At each site, use of the Zody game varied substantially, providing a diverse dataset through which to understand articulation work and its role in deployment studies (see Table 1).

Public School

Zody was first deployed at a special day class in a US public school, with children with mild to moderate learning

Site	Users	N	Facilitators and Materials	Procedure
Public School	Children ages 8-12; All participants had educational and parent-reported medical diagnoses of Autism-Spectrum Disorder (ASD).	8	• 1 Special Education Classroom Teacher • 2 School Psychologists/Research assistants • 1 Researcher • 3 dedicated iPads • 3 dedicated Lego sets • 3 cameras	• Facilitation of the deployment by researcher/school consultant; coordinated with the teacher and school psychologists • Introduction of Zody Game and Study orientation to students • Partner assignment of students • 4 Weeks of collaborative play (alternating weeks between iPad game and Lego build sets for 3 times a week for 10 minutes) • Participant pairs played with Zody a total of six, 10-minute sessions with data collection and video recording. • 30 minutes of free play time during orientation to the study
Private Summer School	Children ages 6-9, All participants had educational and parent-reported medical diagnoses of Autism-Spectrum Disorder (ASD) and/or ADHD.	35	• 1 School Director (oversight) • 1 School Psychologist (oversight) • 4 Staff members with teaching credentials training • 1 Researcher	• Facilitation of the deployment by researcher and director of summer school • Introduction of game to staff and children • Researcher downloaded iPad on 50 school devices • Free use during 3 weeks of summer school activities • Researcher invited to observe 10 minutes per grade once a week
Private Summer Camp	Children ages 6-12; All participants had educational and parent-reported medical diagnoses of Autism-Spectrum Disorder (ASD).	6	• 1 camp leader • 6 Staff members with behavioral training • 1 Researcher • 1 camera	• Facilitation of the deployment by researcher and leader of a 3 week summer camp • Researcher downloaded game on 10 camp devices • Video recording of Probing • Free use during 3 weeks of summer camp • Researcher present daily for 1 hour

Table 1. The site, users, facilitators, and procedure for each of the three deployments of Zody.

challenges and autism. The self-contained special education classroom activities were based on the individual education plans of its current students. Instruction was provided across individual, small group, and whole group activities. Eight children, ages 8-12, consented to play together with an assigned partner for 10 minutes three times a week across four weeks. In this study, iPad play was compared across the randomly assigned pairs to building Lego play sets, which occurred during alternating weeks.

Private School
The second site was a private, university-affiliated special school for children with learning and behavioral challenges (namely autism and ADHD) for first through fifth grade. The school's behavioral approach promotes self-awareness and self-control by providing explicit rewards for self-monitoring and for maintaining expected behaviors. The study was conducted during the summer school session. The summer program was run as a typical school day, with blocks of academics and social skill practice as well as recess and breaks. Thirty-five children, ages 6 to 9, were provided the option to play at break time across 3 weeks, if they earned "good behavior" points.

Summer Camp
The third site was a summer camp for children with autism. As a summer camp was primarily focused on social skills, this camp provided another type of opportunity to explore the use of Zody in a less academic, yet therapeutic, setting. Participants attended the full day camp for fifteen days. During a typical day at the summer camp, campers would rotate through thirty-minute group activities aimed at playing together (*e.g.,* field games such as kickball, relay races, balloon toss, dancing, water play, and indoor games like board games, Legos, cars, arts and crafts). Therapists prompt social skills such as initiating, maintaining, and ending activities smoothly between campers, and supported conversation between campers. Six campers, ages 6 of 12, consented to participate in technology probes with a partner during one of the daily free choice play breaks.

During deployments, we collected substantial observational data, logs, self-report or teacher reports to examine outcomes related to socialization and collaborative play. Results of in game use from the first study appear in [4]. However, when we analyzed the data across these studies collectively, we found evidence of a large amount of articulation work worthy of additional reflection.

Analysis

In this section, we describe our reflective approach for applying articulation work to understand the processes and practices surrounding three deployment studies. Here, we describe both the first and second order articulation work observed across the three deployment studies.

To begin our analysis, the first and last authors first reviewed interviews, videos, evaluation questions, and field notes from each deployment individually and discussed them in relation to each project alone. Based on preliminary results from this analysis, the first author then crafted a detailed description of each study and its results to serve as common ground for the rest of the research team. She then collected and combined the empirical data and shared these along with the site summaries with the remainder of the research team.

The entire team then reviewed and analyzed the data using constant comparative technique to identify patterns in the data [9] and view in comparison to existing articulation concepts, resulting in evidence of the planning and coordination of the deployment (first order articulation work), how breakdowns of both the technology and processes were handled (second order articulation work) [27,34] and a previously unconsidered strategy--role fluidity.

FINDINGS

Across these three sites, the first order articulation work to set up the studies resulted in three distinct research study designs. In this section, we present the first order articulation work that reveals the shaping of these arrangements. Secondly we discuss how formal roles negotiated at the outset (first order articulation work) morph, change, and conflict during the implementation of the study (secondary articulation work)—resulting in the need to move fluidly among dynamic roles. These roles shifted because of the different conceptualizations each stakeholder group had around the purpose of the technology and the need to incorporate the researcher's conceptualization into their behavior during specific research tasks.

First Order Articulation Work

Across the sites, the formal work of making the initial contact with sites began similarly. Either the first or last author had previous communications with the director at each field site, facilitating an initial email to gauge potential interest in a new project. Each director then invited the researchers to provide a staff orientation to the project. The study design evolved across each site as the use of the technology was negotiated. For example, the public school site agreed to a four-week quasi experiment (see[4] for in-game results) that included the support of three researcher facilitators and research materials *(i.e.,* lead research and two school psychologists all employed by the district) to implement the study procedures; the private school site requested that researcher upload the iPad game and visit the site for brief check ins; and the camp welcomed the researcher to probe daily during free play. Participant selection also varied. In the public school setting, consented participants were randomly assigned to a partner by the lead researcher whereas in the private school, the teachers permitted the children's play the game only if they turn points and picked a partner, and at the camp, after consenting, the therapists identified pairings of campers to put together. Lastly, the coordination of technology use was discussed before deployment and varied from only being used in the presence of the researcher in the public school setting to earned use at the private schools where the teachers decided it should be earned for collaborative use during a play break, finally to the camp where the game was available during the multiple free break times and partners where suggested by staff during the times the researcher was present. Data collection methods varied. In the public school setting, two researchers set up video cameras collecting minute-by-minute data that was also used by the staff for the student assessment. At the private school, staff permitted the collecting field notes reflecting 10 minutes per week drop in visits to observe, meet with teachers, and at the end of three weeks, and survey the teachers. Lastly, at the campsite, the lead researcher video recorded and collected field notes and made observations during the time allotted for technology probes at camp.

Second Order Articulation Work

Second order articulation work consists of handling missed responsibilities, re-delegation of unfinished jobs and all the necessary moves during the project that are necessary so that the project doesn't break down, or managing situations when technology does break down. By analyzing three research deployments of the same technology, we can see not only the wide variety of study designs form first order articulation work but also a nuanced type of second order articulation work. In particular, these findings highlight a new kind of second order articulation work—role fluidity—that results from the necessity for people to occupy multiple roles in support of a single research deployment. Acknowledging and understanding this type of articulation work is essential for complete assessment of outcomes of deployment studies.

Resolving Tensions through Role Fluidity

The second order articulation work surrounding these deployments had the incidental effect of creating a secondary role for many of the stakeholders. The deployment created unaddressed work, unexpected tasks, or tensions around different conceptualizations of the system that required stakeholders to move fluidly from their regular work to the work created by the research. In this section, we describe some of the most common dual roles and the resolutions of these roles in practice.

Teacher Becomes Research Facilitator

Teachers served as community partners in the research alongside their primary roles as instructors, who work to maintain positive and productive educational environments. A "paradox of participation"--when researchers seek a collaborative experience yet can not escape that they are the driving force behind the work [2]—occurred in the case of the private school where the school's mission was to provide highly individualized and systematic instruction and earned rewards yet the research task was to explore collaborative play. The mis-match in mission created by the deployment created tension that is apparent in the comment from a first grade teacher who said *"not all of my kids got the game loaded on the iPad (there were technical problems) which I think was a big reason why the game didn't catch onto much in our class."* The technical challenges he describes were related to his concern that adding a new game might impact the existing software on the iPads for his class, as relayed to the researcher later through the school psychologist. However, in the interests of maintaining the relationship and the collaboration, in the interview he described these as technical challenges. In other words, in his role as a teacher he gave priority to the existing classroom setup but in his role as a research collaborator he reported the problem as technical.

Similar tensions occurred in the public-school study—which was by far the most structured of the three studies in its design—the teacher reported promising the children they could complete the Lego set after the study ended. Here the teacher reconciled the desire of her students to keep playing with the researcher's request to keep the materials separate until the study was completed. There is some limited evidence to suggest she also allowed the children to play with the Legos between sessions during the study. However, she did not share this directly with the research team; the reports came from the children. These stories potentially indicate how she not only moved fluidly between the roles but also may have actively altered the study design and reported potentially inaccurate study data in the interests of satisfying her goals as both a teacher and a research collaborator. The lack of explicit knowledge about this from her also provides insight into the fine line that researchers must walk between gathering important contextual information and potentially offending research partners.

Thus, in field deployments of assistive technology, collaborative research teams must identify choices that the other stakeholders may make related to their primary roles, how these could potentially affect the research, and consider how to balance these. Additionally, safe spaces must be engendered to ensure that discussion of these choices is open and honest.

Student Becomes Research Participant

One might imagine that the research participants themselves, especially when children, do not particularly engage in work to make the deployment study work. However, our analysis indicates that users and research participants do in fact engage in second order articulation work during the study if not first order leading up to it. Specifically, in our case, children juggle the roles of research participant and young student. The research participants in the study were aware of the researcher's intention to observe their behavior in order to understand how children collaborate while playing the game so they behaved in they way the think the researcher expected. For example, a researcher asked participants at the public school to describe who began the play.

Figure 1: Photos of one summer camper showing the other camper how to use the cooperative gestures built into the iPad game.

Researcher: Who started playing?

Jesus[1] (age 10): You

Researcher: Right. After I said "start," then what happened?

Jesus: And then we build.

- Observational Notes from the Public School Study

Here the researcher is trying to delineate the start of play *after* her indication that playtime could begin. She is asking the participants to describe who—of the two of them—began playing first and why. Jesus makes a point to answer the researcher's question literally that the researchers cannot ignore her impact on their play. Next, Jesus described how he played with Legos beyond the researcher's gaze. We found these roles—participant and student—elicited different play behaviors as evidenced by his commented: *"before Miss (researcher's name) told us to build the cars, we used to build our own little gadgets."* His comment provides insight into the difference in their private versus prescribed play.

Perhaps the most apparent articulation work by the children is visible when they need to communicate the need to work together during the study. For example, when a camper missed the first day group orientation meeting, he quickly became confused about the collaborative game and his partner's insistence that they play together (see Figure 1). In responding to the question, "How did you like the game?" Brian, age 12, from the summer camp claimed:

"I didn't really like it, it didn't really fit my interest. It's kind of hard to figure out how to play. Well, my partner is kind of hard to cooperate (with). When it's moving that fast, It's hard to cooperate with him. Then [he] just got frustrated and [he] walked away stomping. He kept on saying 'just keep on playing.'"

In Brian's case, the work to smooth out his experience started with the child coaching him and then involved the researcher backtracking to explain the game mechanics during the session while the therapist assisted his partner in returning to play.

While playing a game with a friend might be enjoyable to many children this age, developing improved social skills was an explicit goal for each of the children in this study. Notably, this goal is not necessarily one the children share with those who set the goal for them. Thus, the children often asked to play by themselves, for example Jack said *"I just played by myself because it's more fun, but easier to (win) with two people. I think it's more fun alone because I get to control the mover, and throw".*

Another child from the public school study, Juan, also became frustrated with the collaborative activity. He occasionally left the table and walked to the other side of the room. On one occasion, he walked toward the door and the research assistant/school psychologist directed him to come back into the room. His partner explained at the end of the study that he left the table because he didn't want to throw the iPad. Here we see the children doing articulation work to maintain their participation in the study, as Tasha, age 9 said:

"Nobody wants to play alone in Zody. We don't want someone to walk away...They don't want to throw the iPad. They'll damage it. He wanted to play alone. You need partner to play together."

A common observation at the public school site, where game play was reserved to the research session, was the negotiation to gain first access to the iPad. At this site, the negotiation to participate in the research is not so hidden as the children tug for the iPad as if vying for ownership of the iPad--just before the session begins, to be the one who choses which mini-game and role to play at the to start of the session. Research staff also engaged in articulation work around this issue as we discussed outside of the sessions to resolve how to address this behavior and concluded that the device would be placed between the pairs on the table and no further intervention would occur, as seen in Figure 2.

[1] All names are pseudonyms

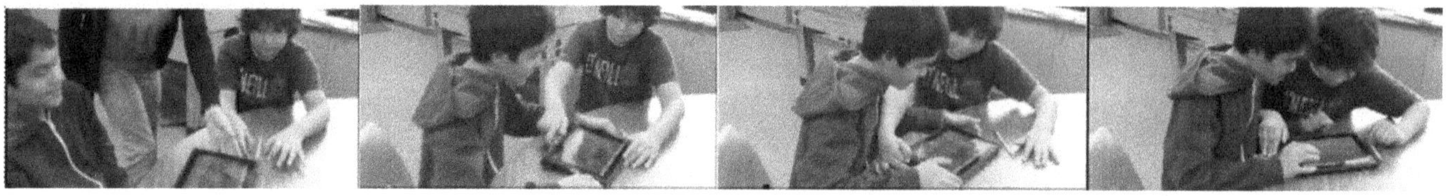

Figure 2: Two students from public school negotiated ownership once the staff releases the iPad for their joint use during the session.

Thus, we saw a variety of ways the children did articulation work to maintain their participation and collaboration in the study. The students engaged in hidden work to maintain their role as research participants. Their effort provides insight into alternative uses of the technology that may be more natural in the school context and more likely to persist in that context beyond a research study. This finding has implications for how any data regarding the tool's efficacy are interpreted, given that the student's engagement with the technology can shift based on what role that are playing at the moment of observation.

Evaluator Becomes Community Collaborator

Lastly, researchers also must balance between the role of community research partner and unbiased evaluator of the technology, which presents its own ethical challenges [22]. Juggling these multiple roles created tension around the conceptualization of the system, ultimately impacting how the system was used to meet each goal. We found in the environment of a research study, researchers also may have variable priorities. How do they present the project to each site? How do they appeal to all stakeholders? A fun game is more likely to score well on user satisfaction measures, to collect happy, publishable quotes from the children during interviews, and so on. At the same time, effectiveness of an intervention is fundamental to publishing research, as there exists well-documented bias against studies that publish negative results [10,31].

Perhaps unsurprisingly, when faced with a game, children tend to want the game to be fun regardless of any therapeutic purpose. At the same time, teachers and other caregivers are more likely to hope for therapeutic effectiveness. Here the researchers vacillate between portraying Zody as a game and teaching tool as she addresses teachers and students simultaneously. Students are increasingly savvy to the "chocolate-covered broccoli" of the educational game industry. For example, in the private school, upon first introducing the game to the students, one asked: *"Is this an educational game or a fun game?"* To which the researcher replied, "*both, I hope*." This exchange highlights the tension the researcher felt when describing the same piece of technology to students and teachers. Here the researcher plays three roles: partner to the teacher, researcher, and fun-game-bringer for the children.

In summary, the articulation work that surrounds deployments may lead us to overestimate the appeal of our research systems. Unconscious bias can seep in when community partners are heavily invested in the relationship and in the outcomes of the study. This is not to say that we should seek to eliminate this type of bias or change these engagements. Deployment studies are often the only way to see certain phenomena and understand the impacts of the designs in practice. However, recognizing and incorporating this kind of work into our analysis can give us a clearer picture of the practices and outcomes we observe.

DISCUSSION

Articulation work has been used to consider global and local [1,11] or intra and inter-organization, formal and *ad hoc*, routine and non-routine [1] work surrounding collaborative technologies. In this research, we build on these concepts to understand the articulation work that surrounds research deployments and uses of assistive technologies. The work we observed in these deployments goes beyond that which has been previously described. In this work, stakeholders actively and fluidly shift and manage multiple roles in response to and in support of this additional work, a concept we term *role fluidity*. By explicitly engaging with this articulation work surrounding deployments, we can see how formal roles negotiated at the outset (first order articulation work) morph, change, and conflict during the implementation of the study (secondary articulation work)—resulting in the need to move fluidly among dynamic roles.

Role fluidity highlights how stakeholders manage the demands of the research with day-to-day life. Uncovering role fluidity, as early in the process as possible, could result in understanding a greater diversity of needs per stakeholder and prepare not only for the work of the deployment but also for a more complete analysis of the results. Thus exploring the benefits of the technology per each role; how the benefit changes in the presence of other stakeholders; may reveal how the immediate needs may conflict with research activities. Lastly, we discuss how these conflicts are resolved or what trade-offs are made to have a deployment be successful.

Multi-Role Probing Regarding Perceived Benefits

One inherent challenge to conducting community-based research projects, such as deployment studies, is the limited knowledge the researchers may have of the context they are entering and the community partners may have of research procedures. Thus, the various team members may greatly struggle to predict what roles they may undertake and subsequently what activities they may undertake within those roles.

By explicitly engaging role fluidity early, research teams can turn this second order work into pre-emptive first order work.

For example, team members might read case studies of similar past projects and the roles undertaken. Alternately, they may brainstorm together or individually all the possible roles that might be expected on this project. Once a set of roles is established, even if incomplete, the research team can then explore scenarios and explicitly probe responses by role. This allows the stakeholders to move between possible roles in relation to hypothetical scenarios before the project fully begins.

By no means do we imagine that moving some of the work we observed during deployment to the planning stage would eliminate all of the challenges of deployment studies and the articulation work that surrounds them. Rather, this kind of effort is most likely to make for a space for discussion, reflection, and analysis. Similarly, during the study itself, parallel role-playing scenarios may shed light on the context of use and provide key empirical data. For example, in our work, to probe the relationship of the experiences to different roles, we might have asked the children to answer questions specifically thinking of themselves as a child or peer, a student, and as a research participant. This kind of approach has been used with child design teams to empower children to see themselves as "designers" rather than "children" or "research participants"[8]. By making explicit that which is currently fluid and implicit, we could uncover key empirical and design research considerations. However, more work is needed to understand the potential for this kind of approach.

Detecting conflict between and within roles

Additionally, seeking to understand the immediate needs of the teacher as well as the long-term goals of the research project could reveal conflicts. For example in the case of installing the game at the private school, being asked not to install it for some as an indicator there's a conflict between an immediate benefit of the tool and the long-term goal of the project. While problem solving through these "technical difficulties" this is a point for the researcher to be reflective bout each role each stakeholder is playing. Although it's difficult for teachers to change research put into motion by an administrator and an outsider, there could be opportunities to conduct different activities that would better suit the teacher's needs—for example having students do a one-time probe on a designed iPad and asking students and teachers to give "tester" feedback. This brief activity may minimize the need to for a teacher to take on additional roles.

Reflecting on researchers' multiple roles as trade offs

Researchers must reflect on their own immediate needs as community partners and longer-range needs as professionals that impact the trade-offs made in the final study design. For example, in this work, the lead author traded off exploring how long students might naturally engage with the game by meeting the need of the sites to have a well-rationalized recommendation for the amount of playing time desired by the researcher (*e.g.,* set at an estimated the minimal viable duration of 10 minutes). By acting as a community partner, we relay on our past experience in the field of special education that has yielded an understanding of the balancing act required in school settings. To meet the special education mandated services with this new research activity—a not yet proven intervention—decisions must be made based on the sites' needs rather than the researchers needs. For example, a researcher may be interested in pursuing a particular type of game play that is at odds with how end-users play the game when the researcher leaves the room. This change in behavior could lead researchers to explore what constitutes failure for different stakeholders.

Role fluidity requires reflection on the roles of multiple stakeholders as well as the need to account for different stages of deployment to understand the long-term impact that this technology can serve in the wild. This, ultimately, may lead to development iterations to inform software that can also support these *differing* roles and movement among them.

In deployment studies, researchers count on positive results, and though we try to maintain our objectivity in data collection, we often hope for positive results to serve as a foundation to build upon. At the same time, both the researchers and the community members with whom we have partnered for the deployment can be heavily invested in making the relationship work. In contrast to many other types of field work, deployments are interventions that require explicit action from multiple actors [29], and as seen in this work, a variety of articulation work and movement among roles to make deployment work.

Role Fluidity, part of the invisible work of deployment studies could possibly bias results by enabling interactions that would not occur without this extra work in the absence of a research study. Thus, failing to take into account these variables can lead to misinformed interpretations. For example, "the game was not played because of technical issues" could be easily dismissed as a common problem with technology deployment or it could reveal a tension the teacher was experiencing that indeed would be experienced even with more robust technologies. Encountering a "technical difficulty" could be a polite way for a teacher to maintain participation in the research even when they do not want to add the additional tasks to their existing program. We cannot fully consider the impact of role fluidity without explicitly making it visible and considering it in our analyses. Therefore, developing strong rapport with stakeholders, or establishing connections early and postulating how fluid one's role will be may reveal the hidden tensions of a study in the wild.

No particular study design will satisfy the tensions between all roles in one setting. Indeed, many tensions may not be identifiable prior to deployment and can be seen only through the articulation work that emerges around the study. Therefore, researchers engaged in deployment studies, particularly around assistive technologies, should be proactive in reporting how roles change amongst stakeholders with respect to their specific deployment. Collectively, we can then contribute to the body of knowledge around deployments as a method as well as articulation work as a concept for collaborative technology engagements. Furthermore, we as a community can differentiate tensions amongst different types of settings, relationship strength, and the design of both technologies and the studies we use to evaluate them.

CONCLUSION

This paper is a first step toward a larger discussion of the need for deep and explicit consideration for competing roles and expectations of each stakeholder during deployment studies. The work of deploying research technologies—including the work done by participants—should be considered in the design of deployment studies. In particular, a more fluid concept of stakeholder roles allows researchers to better account for the changing power dynamics inherent to research studies, even those that are heavily community based and participatory [15].

This work expands the considerations for articulation work to include the concept of *role fluidity as articulation work,* an emergent concern surrounding the introduction of research technologies. Further, we contribute to the methodological discussions surrounding deployment studies as an approach to understanding design and technological innovation by pointing out the need to consider articulation work in the design, implementation, and analysis of research studies.

Regardless of the final research design, consideration for the articulation work by participants embedded in that design and in the deployment of the technology should make for ethical, reliable, and productive scholarly practice. Allocating time and resources to account for articulation work could create a smoother road to technology adoption after the research phase. In the future, researchers in the wild should deeply consider the additional roles and potential conflicts created by their presence in the wild.

ACKNOWLEDGMENTS

Robert and Barbara Kleist supported this work. We thank the STAR group at UCI for reviewing early drafts of this paper. We would like to thank Katie Pine for shirn gher knowledge of computer supported cooperative work and Judith Gregory for expanding our understanding of organizations. And importantly, we thank the participants and their school for helping with this study.

REFERENCES

1. Joanna Abraham and Madhu C. Reddy. 2013. Re-coordinating Activities: An Investigation of Articulation Work in Patient Transfers. In *Proceedings of the 2013 Conference on Computer Supported Cooperative Work* (CSCW '13), ACM, New York, NY, USA, 67–78. DOI:http://dx.doi.org/10.1145/2441776.2441787
2. Daniella Arieli, Victor J. Friedman, and Kamil Agbaria. 2009. The paradox of participation in action research. *Action Research* 7, 3(Sep 2009), 263–290. DOI:https://dx.doi.org/10.1177/1476750309336718
3. A. Battocchi, F. Pianesi, D. Tomasini, M. Zancanaro, G. Esposito, P. Venuti, A. Ben Sasson, E. Gal, and P. L. Weiss. 2009. Collaborative Puzzle Game: A Tabletop Interactive Game for Fostering Collaboration in Children with Autism Spectrum Disorders (ASD). In *Proceedings of the ACM International Conference on Interactive Tabletops and Surfaces* (ITS '09), ACM, New York, NY, USA,197–204. DOI:http://dx.doi.org/10.1145/1731903.1731940
4. LouAnne E. Boyd, Kathryn E. Ringland, Oliver L. Haimson, Helen Fernandez, Maria Bistarkey, and Gillian R. Hayes. 2015. Evaluating a Collaborative iPad Game's Impact on Social Relationships for Children with Autism Spectrum Disorder. *ACM Transactions on Accessible Computing* 7,1, Article 3 (June 2015),18 pages. DOI:http://dx.doi.org/10.1145/2751564
5. Albert M. Cook and Janice Miller Polgar. 2014. *Assistive Technologies: Principles and Practice.* Elsevier Health Sciences.
6. Juri Dachtera, Dave Randall, and Volker Wulf. 2014. Research on research: design research at the margins: academia, industry and end-users. In *Proceedings of the SIGCHI Conference on Human Factors in Computing Systems* (CHI '14). ACM, New York, NY, USA, 713-722. DOI: http://dx.doi.org/10.1145/2556288.2557261
7. Melissa Dawe. 2006. Desperately seeking simplicity: how young adults with cognitive disabilities and their families adopt assistive technologies. In *Proceedings of the SIGCHI conference on Human Factors in computing systems*, (CHI '06), ACM, New York, NY, USA, 1143–1152. DOI:http://dx.doi.org/10.1145/1124772.1124943
8. Allison Druin. 2002. The role of children in the design of new technology. *Behaviour & Information Technology* 21, 1 (2002) 1–25. DOI: http://dx.doi.org/10.1080/01449290110108659
9. Yvonne D. Eaves. 2001. A synthesis technique for grounded theory data analysis. *Journal of Advanced Nursing* 35, 5 (Sep. 2001),654–663. DOI:http://dx.doi.org/10.1046/j.1365-2648.2001.01897.x
10. Gunther Eysenbach. 2004. Tackling Publication Bias and Selective Reporting in Health Informatics Research: Register your eHealth Trials in the International eHealth Studies Registry. *Journal of Medical Internet Research* 6, 3, (2004),35. DOI: http://dx.doi.org/10.2196/jmir.6.3.e35
11. Louise Færgemann, Teresa Schilder-Knudsen, and Peter H. Carstensen. 2005. The Duality of Articulation Work in Large Heterogeneous Settings — a Study in Health Care. In *ECSCW 2005*, Springer Netherlands, (2005),163–183. DOI:http:dx./10.1007/1-4020-4023-7_9
12. Linda Finlay. 2002. Finlay, Linda. "Negotiating the swamp: the opportunity and challenge of reflexivity in research practice." Qualitative research 2.2 (Aug. 2002): 209-230. *Qualitative Research*, 2.2: 209–230.

13. Eynat Gal, Nirit Bauminger, Dina Goren-Bar, Fabio Pianesi, Oliviero Stock, Massimo Zancanaro, and Patrice L. (Tamar) Weiss. 2009. Enhancing social communication of children with high-functioning autism through a co-located interface. *Ai & Society* 24, 1 (Aug. 2009),75–84. DOI:http://dx.doi.org/10.1007/s00146-009-0199-0
14. Leonardo Giusti, Massimo Zancanaro, Eynat Gal, and Patrice L. Tamar Weiss. 2011. Dimensions of collaboration on a tabletop interface for children with autism spectrum disorder. In *Proceedings of the SIGCHI Conference on Human Factors in Computing Systems*, (CHI '11). ACM, New York, NY, USA, 3295–3304. DOI:http://dx.doi.org/10.1145/1978942.1979431
15. Gillian R. Hayes. 2011. The relationship of action research to human-computer interaction. *ACM Trans on Compur-Hum Interact.* 18, 3, Article 15 (Aug. 2011), 20 pages. DOI:http://dx.doi.org/10.1145/1993060.1993065
16. Gillian R. Hayes and Gregory D. Abowd. 2006. Tensions in designing capture technologies for an evidence-based care community. In *Proceedings of the SIGCHI conference on Human Factors in Computing Systems* (CHI '06), ACM, New York, NY, USA, 937–946. DOI:http://dx.doi.org/10.1145/1124911
17. Juan Pablo Hourcade, Natasha E. Bullock-Rest, and Thomas E. Hansen. 2012. Multitouch tablet applications and activities to enhance the social skills of children with autism spectrum disorders. *Personal and Ubiquitous Computing* 16, 2 (Feb. 2012), 157–168. DOI:http://dx.doi.org/10.1007/s00779-011-0383-3
18. Juan Pablo Hourcade, Stacy R. Williams, Ellen A. Miller, Kelsey E. Huebner, and Lucas J. Liang. 2013. Evaluation of tablet apps to encourage social interaction in children with autism spectrum disorders. In *Proceedings of the SIGCHI conference on Human Factors in Computing Systems* (CHI '13). ACM, New York, NY, USA, 3197–3206. DOI:http://dx.doi.org/10.1145/1639642.1639663
19. Shaun K. Kane, Chandrika Jayant, Jacob O. Wobbrock, and Richard E. Ladner. 2009. Freedom to roam: A study of mobile device adoption and accessibility for people with visual and motor disabilities. In *Proceedings of the 11th International ACM SIGACCESS Conference on Computers and Accessibility* (Assets '09), ACM, New York, NY, USA, 115–122. DOI:http://dx.doi.org/10.1145/1639642.1639663
20. Simon B. Larsen and Jakob E. Bardram. 2008. Competence articulation: alignment of aompetences and responsibilities in synchronous telemedical collaboration. In *Proceedings of the SIGCHI Conference on Human Factors in Computing Systems* (CHI '08), 553–562. DOI:http://dx.doi.org/10.1145/1357054.1357144
21. Meredith Ringel Morris, Anqi Huang, Andreas Paepcke, and Terry Winograd. 2006. Cooperative gestures: multi-user gestural interactions for co-located groupware. In *Proceedings of the SIGCHI conference on Human Factors in Computing Systems* (CHI '06), ACM, New York, NY, USA,1201–1210. DOI:http://dx.doi.org/10.1145/1124772.1124952
22. Cosmin Munteanu, Heather Molyneaux, and Susan O'Donnell. 2014. Fieldwork with vulnerable populations. *Interactions* 21, 1(Jan. 2014) 50–53. DOI:http://dx.doi.org/10.1145/2543579
23. Anne Marie Piper, Eileen O'Brien, Meredith Ringel Morris, and Terry Winograd. 2006. SIDES: a cooperative tabletop computer game for social skills development. In *Proceedings of the 2006 20th anniversary conference on Computer supported cooperative work* (CSCW '06). ACM, New York, NY, USA, 1–10. DOI:http://dx. doi.org/10/1145/1180875.1180877
24. Halley Profita, Reem Albaghli, Leah Findlater, Paul Jaeger, and Shaun K. Kane. 2016. The AT Effect: How Disability Affects the Perceived Social Acceptability of Head-Mounted Display Use. In *Proceedings of the 2016 CHI Conference on Human Factors in Computing Systems* (CHI '16). ACM, New York, NY, USA, 4884–4895. DOI:http://dx.doi.org/10.1145/2858036.2858130
25. Kyle Rector, Lauren Milne, Richard E. Ladner, Batya Friedman, and Julie A. Kientz. 2015. Exploring the Opportunities and Challenges with Exercise Technologies for People Who Are Blind or Low-Vision. In *Proceedings of the 17th International ACM SIGACCESS Conference on Computers & Accessibility* (ASSETS '15). ACM, New York, NY, USA, 203–214. DOI:http://dx.doi.org/10.1145/2700648.2809846
26. Kjeld Schmidt. 1994. Cooperative work and its articulation: requirements for computer support. *Le Travail Humain* 57, 4: 345–366.
27. Kjeld Schmidt and Liam Bannon. 1992. Taking CSCW seriously. In *Proceedings of Computer Supported Cooperative Work (CSCW '92)* 1, 1-2: 7–40. DOI:http://dx.doi.org/10.1007/BF00752449
28. Kristen Shinohara and Jacob O. Wobbrock. 2011. In the Shadow of Misperception: Assistive Technology Use and Social Interactions. In *Proceedings of the SIGCHI Conference on Human Factors in Computing Systems* (CHI '11), ACM, New York, NY, USA, 705–714. DOI:http://dx.doi.org/10.1145/1978942.1979044
29. Katie A. Siek, Gillian R. Hayes, Mark W. Newman, and John C. Tang. 2014. Field Deployments: Knowing from Using in Context. In *Ways of Knowing in HCI*, Judith S. Olson and Wendy A. Kellogg (eds.). Springer New York, 119–142. DOI:http://10.1007/978-1-4939-0378-8_6
30. Greis F. Mireya Silva, Alberto Raposo, and Maryse Suplino. 2014. Exploring Collaboration Patterns in a Multitouch Game to Encourage Social Interaction and Collaboration Among Users with Autism Spectrum Disorder. In *Proceedings of Computer Supported Cooperative Work* (CSCW '14) 24, 2-3, 149–175. DOI:http://dx.doi.org/10.1007/s10606-014-9214-1

31. Robert J. Simes. 1986. Publication bias: the case for an international registry of clinical trials. *Journal of Clinical Oncology* 4, 10 (Oct. '86) 1529–1541.
32. Kiley Sobel, Kyle Rector, Susan Evans, and Julie A. Kientz. 2016. Incloodle: Evaluating an Interactive Application for Young Children with Mixed Abilities. In *Proceedings of the 2016 CHI Conference on Human Factors in Computing Systems* (CHI '16). CM, New York, NY, USA, 165–176. DOI:http://dx.doi.org/10.1145/2858036.2858114
33. Richard Solomon, Jonathan Necheles, Courtney Ferch, and David Bruckman. 2007. Pilot study of a parent training program for young children with autism The PLAY Project Home Consultation program. *Autism* 11, 3 (May '07), 205–224. DOI:http://dx.doi.org/10.1177/1362361307076842
34. Susan Leigh Star and Anselm Strauss. 1999. Layers of Silence, Arenas of Voice: The Ecology of Visible and Invisible Work. In *Proceedings of Computer Supported Cooperative Work (CSCW '99)* 8, 1-2, 9–30. DOI:http://dx.doi.org/10.1023/A:1008651105359
35. Anselm Strauss. 1985. Work and the Division of Labor. *Sociological Quarterly* 26, 1(1985), 1–19. DOI:http://dx.doi.org/10.1111/j.1533-8525.1985.tb00212.x
36. Anselm Strauss. 1988. The Articulation of Project Work: An Organizational Process. *Sociological Quarterly* 29, 2: 163–178. DOI:http://dx.doi.org/10.1111/j.1533-8525.1988.tb01249.x

Video Consumption Patterns for First Time Smartphone Users – Community Health Workers in Lesotho

Maletsabisa Molapo
University of Cape Town
Cape Town, South Africa
mmolapo@cs.uct.ac.za

Melissa Densmore
University of Cape Town
Cape Town, South Africa
mdensmore@cs.uct.ac.za

Brian DeRenzi
University of Cape Town
Cape Town, South Africa
bderenzi@cs.uct.ac.za

ABSTRACT
There is already strong evidence that mobile videos are a good vehicle for public health information dissemination, but there remain open questions around sustainability, appropriate target users, consumption patterns, content, and usage models. We analyse log and interview data of 42 community health workers (who were first time smartphone users) from a longitudinal 17-month deployment to better understand how the utility of mobile videos played out over time in rural Lesotho. During the study period, videos were viewed at an average of 170 times per month, for a total of 2898 views. Through this data we draw these primary findings: a) pausing is not contextually necessary, b) age is not a barrier to usage, c) the primary predictor of popularity of a given video is topical relevance and national campaigns, d) there is no apparent relationship between video length, popularity and completion rates, and e) new videos have only a short-lived novelty effect. Furthermore, we affirm that regular engagement with CHWs has an impact on continued usage, in addition to being important for reducing attrition due to technical issues.

Author Keywords
Community Health Workers; Lesotho; Mobile Health Video; Consumption Patterns; Understanding Users.

ACM Classification Keywords
H5.m. Information interfaces and presentation (e.g., HCI): Miscellaneous.

INTRODUCTION
There continues to be an alarming number of preventable deaths in rural areas in sub-Saharan Africa. The problem is complex and multifaceted, but one primary cause continues to be limited health knowledge [25]. Many people fail to prevent infection and manage their ailments with low-cost or freely available treatments because they are not aware of, or fail to understand, correct healthcare practices. These challenges are more pronounced in rural areas that do not have adequate access to healthcare professionals who provide health education, diagnosis and support.

Health education and health promotion efforts targeting these areas have been shown to reduce misconceptions, encourage citizens to access healthcare facilities, and educate the rural public towards leading healthier lives [1,5,11]. One such project is the Bophelo Haeso (BH) project in Lesotho [18]. BH supports the creation of local multimedia content to address health challenges faced by youth, men and women in hard-to-reach rural areas. In the BH model, rural-based nurses create health education content in the form of mobile videos that Community Health Workers (CHWs) use in their communities to help educate the public. The BH project has found that health education content delivered in video formats can reach patients who cannot read in these areas, changing behaviours and influencing health decisions [18]. Beyond the BH project, there are several studies that have reported improved community health education when CHWs are equipped with mobile videos for dissemination in rural areas [11,17,21,27].

However, despite reported successes of mobile videos for public health education, most studies are short term, and we still have limited understanding of critical questions around the sustainability of these programs. In this paper we analyse the logs generated by 17 months of usage in the BH project, supplementing this data with interviews with the CHWs. This longitudinal study enables us to look at patterns of usage: whether video views are sustained and how viewing rates are affected by researcher visits, introducing new content and other factors. We consider natural and technical attrition, seeking to understand underlying causes of decreased usage of the videos over time. We expect that this study will contribute to understanding the factors and design choices that are entailed in similar projects. The remainder of this paper presents background on Lesotho CHWs and what we have already learned from other video-based health education initiatives. From there we detail the BH project and describe the app used for viewing the videos. We then present our research methodology, findings, and conclude with discussion and implications for design.

CHI 2017, May 06-11, 2017, Denver, CO, USA
© 2017 ACM. ISBN 978-1-4503-4655-9/17/05…$15.00
DOI: http://dx.doi.org/10.1145/3025453.3025616

RELATED WORK

Our work forms part of a growing area of research that explores the use of mobile multimedia for community health education in low-resource settings. Initially, mobile multimedia had been used as an educational resource even outside community health education, such as in the Digital Green Project [8], Digital Study Hall [22] and the Story Bank Project [7]. These works demonstrated the potential of mobile multimedia in delivering non-textual educational resources while taking advantage of the ubiquity of the mobile phone. Projects such as Video Kheti took research on multimedia use in rural settings further by finding new ways of supporting low literate information consumers in locating and managing media on mobile devices [2].

The ASHA Assist [21] project first provided evidence that videos on phones could be used by CHWs as a counselling tool with their clients, often expectant mothers. However, this study was only done in an experimental setting over a period of 8 weeks. The Projecting Health project has seen much longer real-world evidence for the benefits of video for health education [11], including a further study that demonstrated that CHWs are the most effective channel for disseminating health videos for community education [28]. Building on this work, we sought to understand how, over a longer period of time, the trends of CHWs' video dissemination and consumption would change.

BACKGROUND

Community Health Workers

In remote villages in the highlands of Lesotho, the nearest health centre (clinic) can be up to a four-hour walk away. People who live in these communities do not have regular access to mainstream radio, television, or the Internet; they are cut off from regular methods of health education. Unsurprisingly, these remote areas have some of the highest rates of HIV infections, untreated tuberculosis, and maternal/neonatal mortality. To help alleviate this problem, public health facilities employ CHWs—residents of rural villages who receive monthly training to serve as the face of healthcare in their home villages. They provide basic healthcare services in the villages when needed, and are responsible for motivating people in their communities to adopt healthy lifestyles and make use of freely available services at health facilities. CHWs in Lesotho serve on an almost voluntary basis, with the majority receiving a stipend of about 22 USD per month. In some cases, CHWs are paid only once yearly, and there are CHWs who have never been paid at all. Despite little financial rewards, the CHWs in Lesotho continue to serve in their communities and attend monthly training meetings at the health centres.

The BH project works with two groups of CHWs, operating out of two separate health centres, designated in this paper as Health Centre 1 (HC1) and Health Centre 2 (HC2). At each health centre, there are one or more nurses responsible for training and monitoring CHWs. Nurses are in charge of identifying the information needs of the surrounding villages, and equipping CHWs to deliver the correct health education in their villages. At both HC1 and HC2, the nurses serve as the main healthcare providers – there are no doctors assigned to these centres, and this is the case for the majority of the rural clinics. Nurses are therefore seen as the 'doctors' of the community, and are greatly respected in the villages surrounding the health centres.

The BH Learning Model

BH uses a feedback-integrated multimedia health education model with emphasis on local content creation and elicitation of village-to-clinic feedback. CHWs are equipped with educational videos on mobile phones to assist with health education. The videos are authored by the nurses based at the rural health centres using the computer-based authoring tool developed by Molapo and Marsden [18] and are loaded onto the CHWs' devices offline using USB cables or Bluetooth. The BH project includes a feedback mechanism that allows CHWs to capture and submit feedback in the form of audio reports to give nurses insight into the status of people's health practices in the villages, and to inform the creation of future videos.

The BH Mobile Application

For the project phase reported in this paper, CHWs consumed (watched, showed to patients, shared with others) the health content from the BH app on Nokia Lumia smartphones (running Windows Phone OS Version 8.1). The BH app serves as a dedicated gallery for BH videos, a customized video player, and a feedback collection tool. The main benefit of having a mobile app for all BH activities is that it helps separate the BH multimedia from the rest of the personal files on CHWs' devices, for easy and quick access in the field; and that it enables the logging of CHWs' usage of the BH content. Deeper rationale for the design and features of the BH app is well-documented by Molapo et al [15], and outside the scope of this paper.

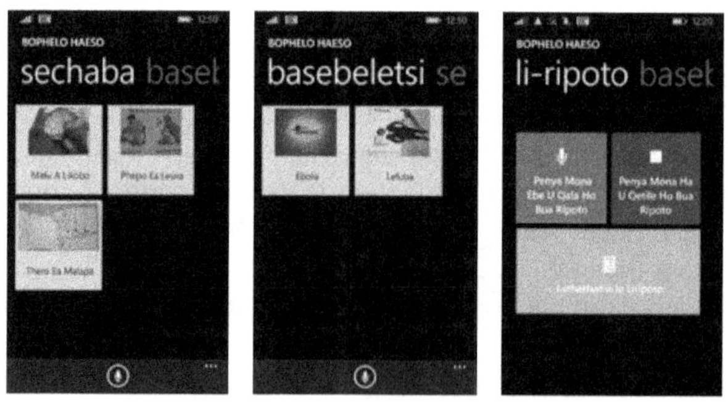

Figure 1 - Screenshots of the BH app showing the CHW Video List, Public Video List, and Reporting Page

The BH app has three pages, which users swipe left or right to cyclically navigate between. The first two pages are the BH gallery: videos meant for public consumption on Page 2, and videos meant for CHWs only on Page 1. In the period reported in this paper, however, the videos on the CHWs' list were also applicable to the public. The videos are displayed in a grid using thumbnails. Below a video thumbnail is the name of the video in Sesotho (the native language in Lesotho). The third page of the app is used for recording feedback, where CHWs record 'audio diaries' of their experiences and interactions in the villages.

The BH Project Timeline

The BH project consisted of three sequential phases. In the first phase (six months), CHWs consumed BH videos on Nokia Asha feature phones, and starting from Phase 2, CHWs used Nokia Lumia smartphones. Phase 2 (six months), the Exploratory Phase, allowed CHWs to acclimate to the smartphone devices through exploration Following exploration, the CHWs entered into Phase 3 (17 months), consuming BH content from the smartphone app.

In October 2014, when smartphones were deployed, none of the 54 CHWs had used a smartphone before. To give them the opportunity to explore and learn at their own pace, the CHWs were given six months with the phones and the app in the field, during which they were encouraged to *play* with the devices [24]. The devices, at launch, were simplified for the CHWs by removing unnecessary apps from the devices' home screen (e.g., maps, games, etc.), leaving only the BH app and five of the most useful tiles. While unnecessary apps were disabled from the home screens, we did find that approximately 20 CHWs (48%) installed custom applications of their preference (e.g., the Bible, radio, and meme-creating apps). A detailed analysis of this use is beyond the scope of this paper. Midway through the exploration period, the researchers released two videos to further encourage CHWs to explore the devices. The first video focused on the basic understanding of how the Internet, data connections, data bundles, and WhatsApp work on the devices, and the second on the navigation of the BH app.

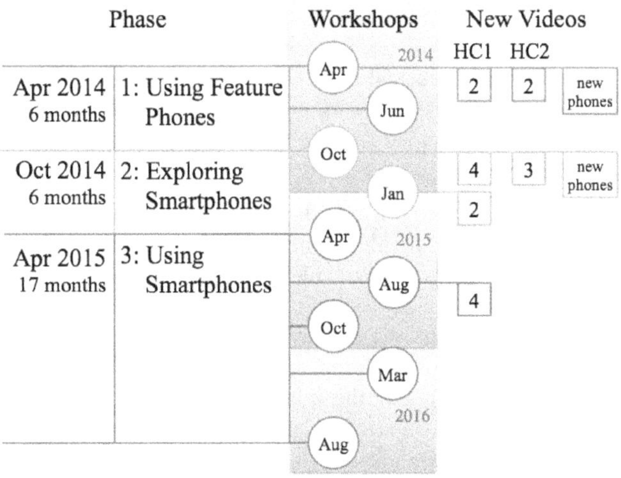

Figure 2 - Timeline of BH Activities

Most CHWs (70%) said they learned how to use the smartphones by a combination of personal exploration and receiving guidance from children and grandchildren, typical of older first-time smartphone users [9,20,23]. Only 20% said they learned entirely on their own, and 10% said they learned by exploring the devices with friends. Following the exploration phase, CHWs entered the active usage phase reported in this study. Throughout exploration and into the active use phase, all CHWs showed excitement and pride regarding the new devices, and that led to their enthusiasm to learn and explore.

BH Multimedia Content

By April 2015 when the evaluation of CHWs' consumption patterns began, the HC1 group had eight nurse-authored videos released to the CHWs, and HC2 had five. The dates for initial release per video are included in Table 1 and Table 2. At HC1 only, four new videos were released in August 2015. HC1 videos with the same names as some HC2 videos were indeed the same videos created by HC2 nurses but also deployed at HC1.

Title of Video	Duration (mm:ss)	First Released	Created By
Tuberculosis	04:44	Jun 2014	HC2 Nurse
STIs	03:15	Jun 2014	HC2 Nurse
Infant Nutrition	03:07	Oct 2014	HC2 Nurse
Family Planning	04:37	Oct 2014	HC2 Nurse
Ebola	01:55	Oct 2014	HC2 Nurse

Table 1. Videos released at HC2

Title of Video	Duration (mm:ss)	First Released	Created By
Tuberculosis	04:44	Jun 2014	HC2 Nurse
STIs	03:15	Jun 2014	HC2 Nurse
Ebola	01:55	Oct 2014	HC2 Nurse
Overall Family Health	04:20	Oct 2014	HC1 Nurse
Maternal and Newborn Health	05:20	Oct 2014	HC1 Nurse
Pregnancy Health	13:22	Oct 2014	HC1 Nurse
HIV Status	07:45	Jan 2015	HC1 Nurse
HIV Testing	06:06	Jan 2015	HC1 Nurse
Immunisations	10:50	Aug 2015	HC1 Intern
Traditional Remedies in Pregnancy	06:20	Aug 2015	HC1 Intern
Pregnancy Warning Signs	04:39	Aug 2015	HC1 Intern
True Signs of Labour	05:27	Aug 2015	HC1 Intern

Table 2. Videos released at HC1

BH USAGE OVER 17 MONTHS

Our objective, from April 2015 to August 2016 (17 months) was to study how CHWs would use the BH videos in their respective villages, asking the following research questions.

Research Questions

- RQ1: How frequently do CHWs play the BH videos, and how do consumption patterns change over time?
- RQ2: What video content is more popular in terms of sustained frequency of play?
- RQ3: How common is it for CHWs to pause and resume video playback when engaging with patients?
- RQ4: What attributes and attitudes of CHWs affect individual usage rates?
- RQ5: In what scenarios is the BH content used?

We expected to see a novelty period, as reported in related work [3], where the initial introduction of the application and subsequent new content causes a spike in the number of plays, which decreases over time (RQ1). We sought to understand three things: (1) the duration of the initial spike in interest when the videos were introduced, (2) the rate of decay in video plays, and (3) the frequency of video plays during the steady state period when the decay stabilizes. Additionally, we anticipated an increase in video usage after researchers met with the CHWs. We also sought to understand the properties of health videos that make them more or less popular among CHWs and their communities, and measure the ratio of partial to complete plays (RQ2). We hypothesised that short videos (less than 2 minutes) would be watched to completion more frequently than long videos (over 5 minutes). Our assumptions were that CHWs would pause videos often during playback to engage with patients (RQ3). Looking at individual CHWs, we sought to understand how CHWs compare to one another, looking at attributes or attitudes that affect individual usage rates (RQ4). Lastly, to interpret the trends observed, we aimed to further understand the scenarios where BH content is used and the interactions between CHWs and the public (RQ5).

Participants

We began with 54 CHWs during the exploration phase in October 2014. There were 24 CHWs from HC1 and 30 from HC2. The 54 CHWs ranged from 29 to 70 years old, with the mean age of 55.1 (*SD*=11.7). All but one CHWs are female. 7 (12%) completed varying levels of high school, 31 (58%) have primary school education only, and 16 (30%) did not complete primary school. All CHWs can read and write in Sesotho—the national language in Lesotho—although the older CHWs generally write very slowly. About 11 (20%) can read basic English with difficulty.

CHWs did not receive regular financial compensation from the project during the study, but were given $3-5 USD for transport and lunch during workshops with the research team. The smartphones, however, served as incentives for the CHWs, as they were also used for personal purposes. None of the CHWs had previously owned a smartphone, with only four having had some exposure to smartphones because their children owned smartphones. However, all CHWs had owned feature phones (provided by the project and self-acquired) and used the phones for SMS and calling, and 25 (60%) had also used their Nokia Asha feature phones for WhatsApp.

Procedure

During the 17-month period, the BH app logged CHWs' usage. The app generated logs that recorded the date and time every video was opened, the length of play and all pause activity: whether the video was paused, if the playback was resumed, and if resumed, the length of the pause. Analysis was limited to nurse-authored videos. The app also recorded actions such as sharing a video with another device via Bluetooth. The usage logs were collected over the 17 months and quantitatively analysed to answer the research questions above.

To complement the usage logs, qualitative data around the CHWs' experiences were collected multiple times during the study. This included semi-structured interviews with CHWs, focus groups, observations where CHWs would be asked to demonstrate how they use the BH app, and skits where CHWs demonstrated scenarios of BH use in their villages using drama [16], all conducted in Sesotho. All quotes included in this paper have been translated from Sesotho to English by the first author, a native Sesotho speaker.

Of the 54 CHWs originally enrolled in the study, data from 42 (21 from HC1 and 21 from HC2) was used for analysis. 12 CHWs were excluded from analysis because they had missing or incomplete logs because either the CHW died (1), moved to another country (1), the CHW's phone was stolen (1), the instrumented version of the app was not installed at the start of the study, i.e., they worked with an old version with no logging feature (4), or the CHWs were moved from active CHW duty in the villages to work full-time as assistants at the health centres (5).

At the beginning and end of the study (April 2015 and August 2016), we conducted user tests and interviews with CHWs to understand how they used BH content and to assess their proficiency of the BH app. In April 2015, all 42 CHWs were tested and interviewed. However, in August 2016, only 36 of the 42 CHWs attended the workshop and were tested and interviewed. In user tests conducted both at the beginning and end of the study, we sat with CHWs one-on-one. For each, the CHW was asked to find the BH app, launch it, play a specified video on page 2 of the app (e.g., the STIs video), abort the video playback, return to the gallery, play another video on page 1 of the app (e.g., the Tuberculosis video), etc. In the workshop held at the end of the study, we also asked the CHWs to each tell us the video they played the most during the 17 months, and give reasons why that video was the one they played the most.

Data Cleaning

Firstly, 10% of the raw records were removed: we removed all records with invalid timestamps (8% of total raw records), which was the result of the phone battery being removed and the clock being reset to the default time of a January 2014 date. We also removed all records for play events recorded on training and workshop dates (2% of total raw records). For the quantitative analysis, a "video view" means that the video was played for at least 10% of the video length, and "barely opened" means the video was played for less than 10% of the video length. We wanted to exclude records where the video was opened for only a few seconds (e.g. for demonstration purposes rather than content consumption), during which no health message would have been heard. For all the videos, at 10% into playback, the nurse has covered at least one main point on the topic at hand, indicating that a message was heard. The average length of the videos is 05:23 (323 seconds), meaning the average 10% of video length is 32.3 seconds.

RESULTS

In this section we report on our investigations into each of the research questions posed earlier.

RQ1: Consumption Patterns

For this research question we used the logs to identify patterns of how often videos were played by the CHWs, and we hypothesized that researcher visits and new videos would cause increased use that would decay quickly.

Frequency of Play and Effect of Researcher Visits (RQ1)

Figure 3 shows the mean number of BH video views per CHW by health centre over the 17-month period. The means are based on the number of CHWs who viewed videos that month.

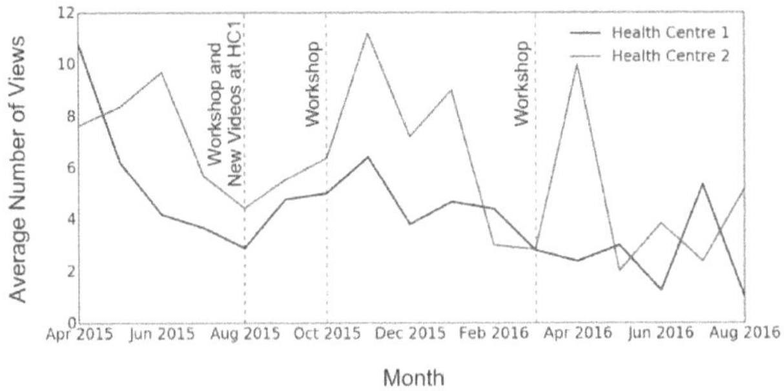

Figure 3 - Average number of views over 17 months

In the 14 of the 17 months, HC2 had more video views than HC1. Over the months, usage rates at both centres went up by 33% - 72% in the months following workshops with researchers, with the exception of HC1 after the March 2016 workshop, where instead a slight decrease in usage occurred after the workshop. In all other cases, after the workshop-induced spike in usage, a decline was seen until the next workshop when usage spiked again. When workshop 'excitement' subsided, usage settled at approximately 2-6 views per CHW per month. By the end of the study period, the average number of views per month had declined from 11.9 (HC1) and 7.6 (HC2) in April 2015 to 1.5 (HC1) and 5.8 (HC2) in August 2016 - declines of 87% and 24% respectively.

Newly Released Videos vs Old Videos (RQ1, RQ2)

At HC1, four new videos were introduced five months into the study. Figure 4 compares the usage of the four new videos against the eight old videos at HC1. This graph depicts the mean number of views per video in each set for CHWs that viewed at least one video in each given month. For the new videos, a steady increase in use was seen in the three months following release, reaching a peak on the third month after release. For two months, starting a month after the release of the new videos, new video usage surpassed old video usage; but in the next month after the usage rate of the new videos peaked, it declined by 81%. After the initial peak and decline, the new videos then joined the standard usage pattern of occasionally increasing and declining usage, but never rising as high as in the three months after initial release.

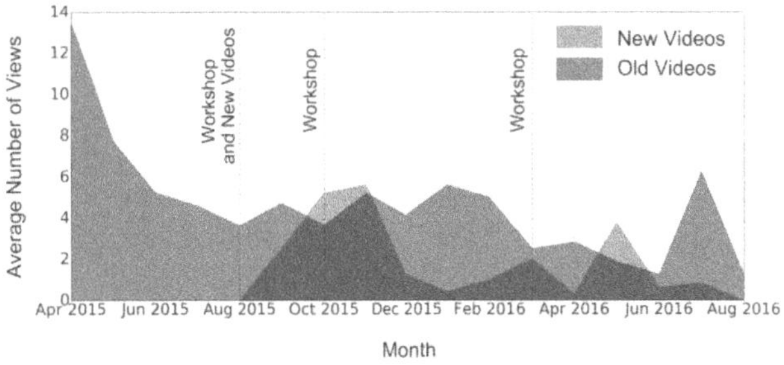

Figure 4 - Newly released videos vs old videos at HC1

RQ2: Video Popularity

As shown in Figure 4, video popularity due to novelty wears off after three to four months. In this section, we further examine factors that lead to sustained popularity.

Factors Affecting Popularity According to CHWs (RQ2)

When we asked CHWs which video they showed most often, 31 (74%) of CHWs said TB, 5 (12%) said STIs, 4 (9%) said topics relating to pregnancy and new-born health, and 2 (4%) said HIV-related topics. The primary reason for TB's high use is that they view TB as an epidemic in their communities, based on the number of TB-related deaths and rates of infection among the young and old. CHWs said many patients show TB symptoms, yet remain reluctant to test for TB and dismiss the symptoms as the flu or common cold. CHWs believe this is generally caused by a lack of knowledge about TB. Additionally, the TB video is the only video in which the nurse from HC2 can be seen. Seven HC2 CHWs mentioned that the appearance of the nurse helped them in their persuasion. One CHW reported a client said:

> *"We thought you are lying to us, but now we can see this is true, the nurse is here talking about this matter **in person.**"* – Reported by CHW 24, HC2

HIV is as much a crisis in rural Lesotho as TB. We asked CHWs and nurses why HIV videos were not as popular as the TB video. The nurses said that as part of the current national fight against TB, CHWs are tasked to identify suspected TB cases, encourage them to visit health centres for tests, then assist them through treatment to ensure adherence. Nurses believe that because of this specific mandate on TB, CHWs use the TB video more often. With HIV, they are expected to teach and support the public, but national campaigns are not as rigorous. Additionally, CHWs mentioned that HIV is now more accepted, whereas many people still deny the existence of TB as a medically treatable disease and blame witchcraft for deaths caused by TB.

Similarly, during the Ebola outbreak in West Africa in 2015, the Ebola video was used at high rates because there there was a national campaign launched to educate communities on Ebola. CHWs showed the Ebola video frequently in that period, but when it appeared there would be no outbreaks in Southern Africa, the national top-down push for Ebola education subsided, as did the CHWs' frequency of showing the Ebola video. The video on STIs was also popular among other CHWs, who stated that the video was known for its explicit graphic imagery of STI infected genitalia. Many people in CHWs' villages had never seen such images, or been exposed to the reality of STIs, so CHWs said they preferred to show the video to demonstrate that STIs are real. Figure 5 compares videos at HC2, confirming the usage patterns described by CHWs, with TB being the most used video, followed by Ebola in 2015 and early 2016, and then by STIs.

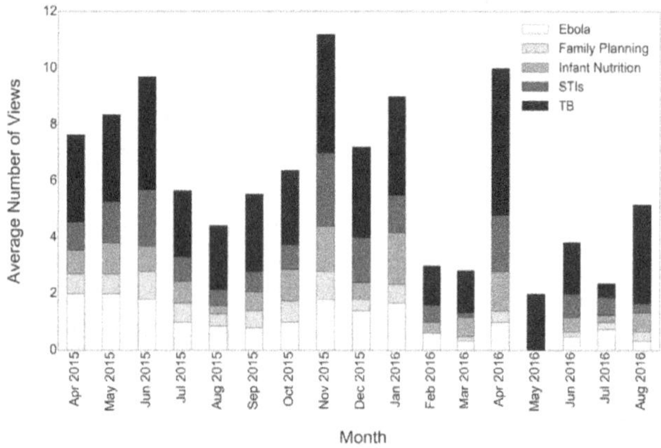

Figure 5 - Comparing per-video performance at HC2

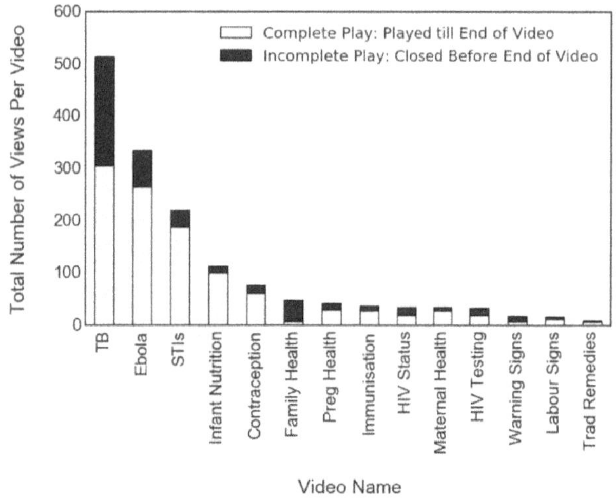

Figure 6 - Video Total Views Showing Completion Rates

Popularity, Frequency of Play and Completion Rates (RQ2)

Looking at the total number of times all videos were played in the 17-month period (2898), 37% of the time (1081 times), the videos were watched till the end, 15% of the time (448 times), the videos were not completed, but were watched beyond 10%, and 47% of time (1369 times), the video playback was terminated before reaching 10% of the video length. Figure 6 shows the total views per video for views longer than 10% of the video length, showing the ratio of complete to incomplete plays per video. Further, we wanted to understand if the most frequently viewed videos were also more likely to be watched till the end, and if shorter videos were more likely to be watched till the end. We found very weak correlation between number of video views and completion rate (Figure 7a, Pearson's $r(12)=0.09$, $p=0.75$) and between video length and completion rate (Figure 7b, Pearson's $r(12)=0.03$, $p=0.91$). In these plots, video popularity is the mean number of views for the video, and video completion is the ratio of completed video plays to total video plays for each video.

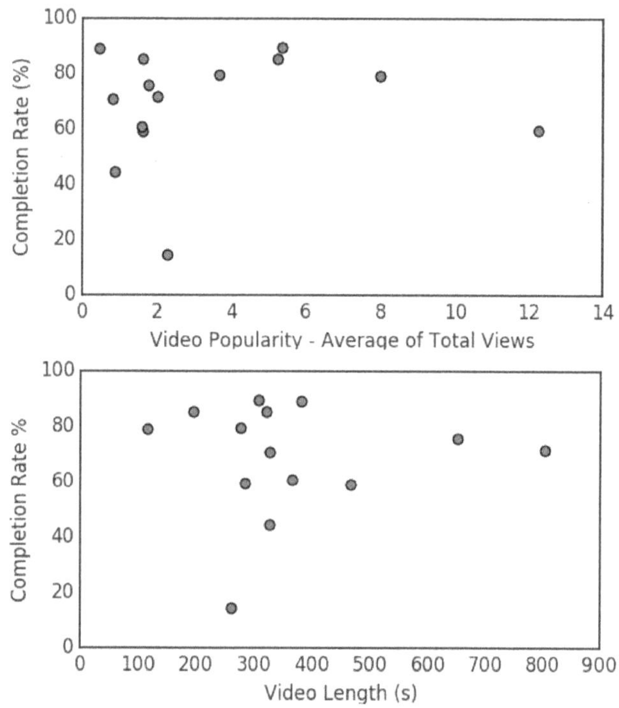

Figure 7 – (a) Video Popularity vs Video Completion Rates, (b) Video Length vs Video Completion Rate

RQ3: Pausing and Conversations

Ramachandran et al. [21] suggested that active pausing and discussion during a video would lead to greater behaviour change. Indeed, in early versions of the BH app, Molapo et al. [15] implemented a feature so CHWs could pause and add audio annotations at particular points in the video. This feature was later removed because it was found by the CHWs to be confusing and largely unused [15]. In the 17 months of the study, playback was paused during only 14% of video views. Of the pauses, playback was resumed only 25% of the time. The remaining 75% of the time, the app was closed, or the user returned to the video gallery. Where playback was resumed, pauses lasted an average of 8 seconds, with the longest pause being 27 seconds. In interviews with the CHWs, 90% confirmed that they rarely paused the videos when they showed them to the public or individual patients, saying that they preferred to let a video play till the end, and then have a discussion about it afterwards. When asked what they do if the audience have a question as the video plays, and one CHW said:

"I tell them to watch the rest of the video, and then we'll discuss. If they seem impatient and not willing to wait for the video to play till the end, I just close the app and allow them to talk." – CHW 9, HC1

RQ4: Characterizing Community Health Workers

We recognize that not every CHW used the application in the same way. In this section we examine some of the factors that we hypothesized might lead to different individual usage rates and styles.

CHW Smartphone and BH App Competence (RQ4)

As we launched into the active study phase, user tests and interviews were held with 42 CHWs to determine their familiarity and competence with the devices after the exploratory phase, and the same were held with 36 CHWs at the end of the 17-month period. In user tests done at the beginning and end of the study, all the CHWs could easily find the BH app, launch it, and arrive at page 1 of the video gallery. In both workshops, all CHWs could play a BH video from the BH gallery. However, at the beginning of the study, four CHWs struggled to understand how to play a specific video; they appeared to play any video without first looking at the thumbnail or label.

The four CHWs who struggled at the beginning of the study were present at the tests done at the end of the study, and two of them still struggled with finding a specified video after 17 months, though they could now navigate easily between the two pages of the app, one said she normally played all the videos for a few seconds, sequentially, until she found the one she was looking for. Two of the four CHWs who struggled at the beginning had improved and could navigate the app and play correct videos as easily as the rest of the CHWs. The rest of the CHWs correctly found the videos by reading the names of the videos and being guided by the thumbnails. The struggling CHWs received further training and guidance after both sessions.

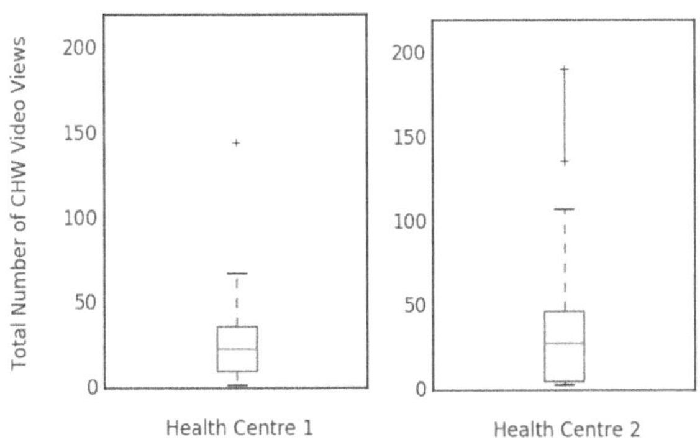

Figure 8 - Distribution of CHWs' accumulated total views

Total Views Accumulated Per CHW (RQ4)

At Health Centre 1 (*n*=21 CHWs), the mean number of total accumulated views in 17 months per CHW is 31.0, Median 23.0, Range 2 to 145 views, and *SD* = 31.6. At Health Centre 2 (*n*=21 CHWs), the mean number of total accumulated views in 17 months per CHW is 41.9, Median = 28.0, Range 3 to 191 views, and *SD* = 49.7. Figures 8 and 9 show the distribution of the total views accumulated per CHW in each of the CHW groups. The majority of CHWs (80% at HC1, 67% at HC2) viewed less than 50 videos in the 17 months, 13% at HC1 and 13% at HC2 viewed between 50 and 100 videos and 7% at HC1 and 20% at HC2 viewed over 100 videos in 17 months. HC1 had one outlier with a total of 145 total views, more than double the views of the next highest CHW who had 68 total views. HC2 had three similar outliers, with total views of 191, 136, and 108, followed by 74.

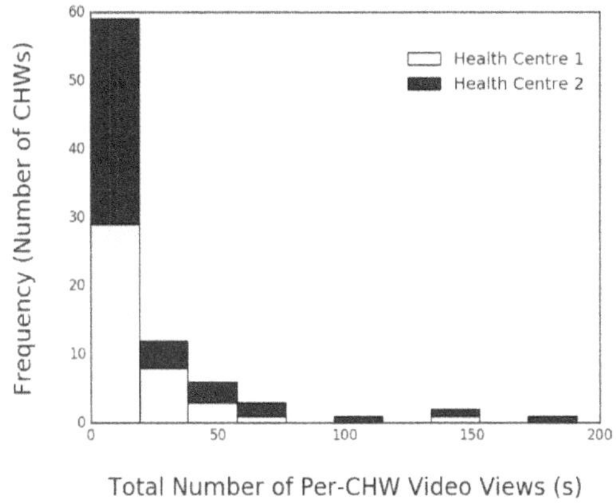

Figure 9 - Histogram of the CHWs' accumulated total views

Usage Patterns of Individual CHWs (RQ4)

To further understand the patterns of CHWs' use of BH videos, we looked at the usage patterns of a subset of individual CHWs. From each health centre group, we picked two CHWs with the highest number of total views, two with the lowest number of total views and two at the median of total views, closely examining 12 CHWs as seen in Figure 10. High-use CHWs did not necessarily watch videos at a steadily high rate across all the months on record. For each of the CHWs, there are one to two months in the 17 months when the CHW did not show any videos (6% - 12% of the time), but each had spikes of high usage in varied months, going as high as 30 video views a month. Three of the four high-use CHWs are some of the oldest CHWs (aged 70,66,62). Average-use CHWs consumed BH videos in 6 to 9 of the 17 months, with usage peaks going up to 10 - 12 video views a month. During the user tests in August 2016 (end of the study), Low User 1 and Low User 2 (they originate from both centres) were the only two CHWs (out of 36 tested) who could not find the required video by opening the app, swiping to Page 2 and playing the specified video. Our conclusion from watching their interaction with the app was that they used it rarely, and the logs confirm this as Low User 1 played only two videos (beyond 10% of the video length) during the entire 17-month period, and Low User 2 played only 11 videos (in only 3 of the 17 months). Low User 3 and 4 could easily navigate the app, made no errors and were able to perform all given tasks. We do not have an explanation for Low User 3's low usage rates, but while she showed few videos per month, she logged usage in nine months. Low User 4 was only 29 at the end of the study - she was one of the youngest CHWs. When asked about her performance, the nurse at her health centre said:

"I am not surprised. This one CHW is only interested in entertainment multimedia and using the BH-provided phone for personal uses only. She always has headsets on - playing music, funny videos, etc." – HC2 Nurse

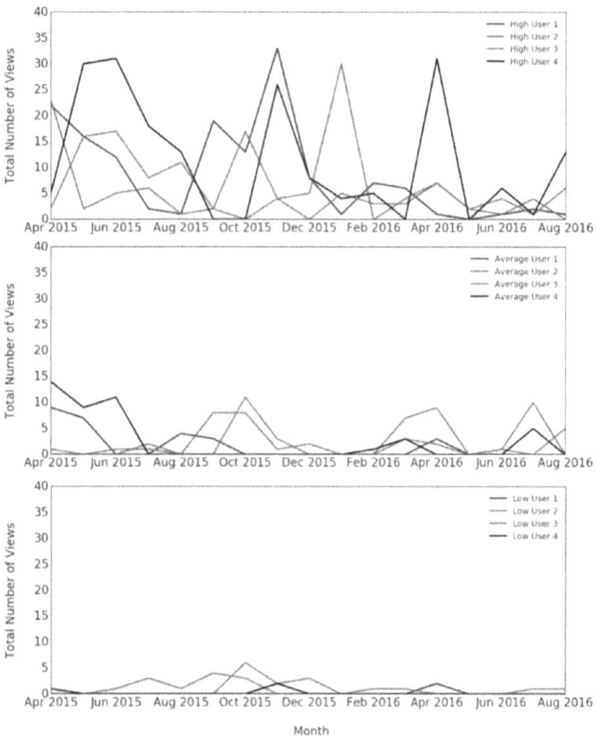

Figure 10 - (a) Usage patterns of four 'high users', (b) Usage patterns of four 'average users', (c) Usage patterns of four 'low users'

RQ5: Scenarios of Use

From interviews with CHWs, we discovered eight scenarios in which CHWs use the BH content.

1) CHWs take advantage of being among a group of people and show several videos for the general education of the group:

"As we sit and chat with my friends or neighbours, I normally bring out the phone and choose a video or multiple videos to show to them...normally I will begin with TB or STIs." – CHW 11, HC1

"During family events with my extended family, I will play one video to my relatives. They get amused and ask for more...At our family's Christmas feast, we watched all the videos in my phone." – CHW 26, HC2

2) When engaged with a specific user group, CHWs select a topic or topics of most relevance to the group:

"When I come across a group of young people, I show them the STIs videos."- CHW 5, HC1

"My daughter in law has a hair-dressing salon. I go there sometimes and make the girls waiting on the queue watch a few videos...I often show them the Family Planning video."- CHW 9, HC2

3) Members of the public occasionally request that CHWs show videos, without specifying a specific topic:

"Sometimes when we have just dispersed from a village meeting, one will ask me to show 'my interesting videos' and then I will choose one to play. Then people will gather and watch. I may end up showing three of four in that sitting." – CHW 12, HC1

4) Some members of the pubic request a specific video:

"At times I meet someone and they say – Hey, please show me that scary STIs video again!" – CHW 26, HC2

5) A CHW responds to perceived insufficient knowledge on a subject by playing the relevant video on the topic:

"Sometimes I listen to someone talk about a topic like Ebola or STIs, and realise how far from accurate their knowledge or assumptions are. Then I just pull out the video and show them what is correct."- CHW 2, HC1

6) CHWs also use videos as tools to convince patients to pursue recommended healthcare practices, using the nurse's voice to increase the credibility of their teachings.

"This is especially true for TB. I see someone with TB symptoms. I go and try to encourage him to go for a TB test. When he doesn't believe what I am telling him, I produce the TB video so the nurse can back-up what I am teaching"- CHW33, HC2

7) CHWs use videos as counselling material in home visits.

"When I have gone into a home to check on a patient, I will choose a video that I know will either persuade the patient to seek medical help, adhere to treatment, or be assured that their condition can be treated...In home visits, sometimes I play videos to caretakers more than to the patient." – CHW 30, HC2

8) At the instruction of the village chief, sometimes the village population is gathered for the CHW to address.

"Addressing the public at a 'Pitso' is very common. I talk to them about any relevant topic, based on my observations or because the nurse has instructed us to teach people on a certain topic. Sometimes at the Pitso, I will play a video and let the population listen to the nurse directly." – CHW 14, HC1

A *Pitso* is a gathering of the village public called by the chief. The *Pitso* usage scenario was one of the first that we learned from CHWs, and halfway through the 17-months study, we provided them each with a portable loud speaker that they could connect to their phones via audio jack or Bluetooth. We thought that the loud speakers would help CHWs in those outdoor settings when playing a video for large crowds. At the end of the study, however, only five of the 36 CHWs we interviewed confirmed they used the speakers.

DISCUSSION

This discussion is structured into two sections: first our improved understanding of CHWs as a result of this longitudinal study, and secondly, our observations and analyses of usage trends as observed from CHWs' logs.

Improved Understanding of CHWs

Community-Based Health Education in Practice

We found that CHWs use BH content in varying contexts and scenarios, which are beyond what we initially imagined. Due to varying contexts of use beyond the traditional house visits, CHWs have periods of high use followed by low use, e.g., when a CHW shows all the videos on her phone in one day at a family gathering, and then shows the next video two weeks later to new mothers when they bring their infants to her house for growth monitoring. We also found that CHWs play videos to large groups more often than to individuals, a phenomenon that has also been observed with Accredited Social Health Activists in India in a study by Ramachandran et al. [21].

However, in contrast to their findings, our CHWs preferred to play videos to completion and discuss the content after, rather than pausing to comment and clarify in the middle of playback. CHWs felt that by pausing to engage, they would be interrupting the nurse speaking in the video and it was more respectful to let the nurse finish. Pausing for discussion before playback was complete had the added effect of reducing interest in watching the rest of the video after a long discussion. While the first version of the app was designed to encourage pausing and engagement, CHWs found the pausing to be inconsistent with their preferred natural flow. In their interactions, CHWs and their clients often engage in long discussions that cannot be easily incorporated into a brief pause, as found by Kumar at al. [11] and Fiore-Silfvast et al. [6].

Simplicity for Confidence

Apart from their preferred flow, CHWs expressed a preference for simplicity as a reason for not pausing during video playback, in order to confidently manage the viewing sessions. They felt they wanted to conduct as simple a play session as possible, to avoid 'pressing so many buttons that they would end up confused and looking incompetent in front of their community members' [15]. It is for this reason that 60% of the CHWs did not seek video positions during playback, and why those who did, only moved the video forward, never backwards.

We also observed that this preference for avoiding errors led to CHWs' reluctance to use the supplied portable audio speakers. Many CHWs did not use the speakers. They did admit that they saw their utility, but they preferred not to carry any extra equipment that could potentially fail and embarrass them. Looking confident and technically competent was important to CHWs, to keep up the elevated status they received in their communities when they began using mobile phones for their work.

The Role of CHW Attitudes and Attributes in Usage Patterns

We interviewed the nurses to discuss the varying consumption patterns of the CHWs, and found that the common attribute of all high-use CHWs is that they are highly committed in general, even outside the BH project. For these CHWs, the technology was just an amplifier of prior intent [26]. Most of these CHWs happened to be the older CHWs, many of whom have done CHW work for more than 20 years, with commitment. One of the nurses said:

> *"At the end, we found that what is important is to have CHWs who are truly committed to their work. The ones who have high usage rates in BH were already very active CHWs..."* – Nurse at HC2

However, not all the committed CHWs were high users in the BH project, but only those who were also open to learning and leveraging technology for their work. We also found previously inactive CHWs whose commitment to community work was ignited by their excitement for the technology. Commitment to community work and openness to learn and explore the technology are certainly attributes and attitudes of CHWs that seemed to affect their usage rates.

Age Is Not a Limiter of Use

At the beginning of the BH project, nurses suspected that old CHWs (over the age of 60) would not be effective in the project because it would be hard for them to get accustomed to using mobile phones in their work. However, based on previous work on the studies with technology for the elderly and low-literate [19], when participatory and empowered design principles are applied [13], older people can get empowered and interested enough to learn and use technology. We decided to work with all CHWs, to study if CHWs of all ages and literacy could be empowered to learn to a point of using technology in their work.

From the usage logs 17 months later, we found that 72% of the high-end users are CHWs over the age of 55, with the highest users at the two health centres being 70 and 66. While the data does not suggest that old CHWs are more effective at mobile-supported health education than young CHWs, we found that old and committed CHWs can still be effective with technology when given the opportunity to learn the technology and when the design of the mobile application is considerate of limitations such as literacy, prior exposure to technology and failing eyesight. Our results also point to the importance of intermediaries like children and younger peers, as already discovered in other contexts in ICT4D work [9,10,20,23]; but also include lessons of the importance of allowing self-exploration. Some of the older CHWs preferred to explore and learn by themselves.

CHWs on Touch-Screen and English Interfaces
At the beginning of the study, 95% of the CHWs agreed that consuming the BH videos from the easily accessible BH app on the smartphone was quicker and simpler than navigating menus on a feature phone. The CHWs felt that interactions on a touch screen device were easy and fitting for their type of work, especially for the BH app where they did not need to type anything. One said:

> *"...with these phones, it's a quick tap, swipe, tap and the video is playing. It's so easy,* ***I think touch screen devices were created for old people*** *like us who need things to be right there when you open your phone."* – CHW 15, HC1 (Top User, Aged 70)

The challenge with smartphones and CHWs is limited English literacy [4]. Six CHWs, at different times in the study, uninstalled the BH app by mistake and when asked, one admitted that:

> *"Sometimes the phone brings up English messages I do not understand [asking to confirm an uninstall, for example], so I just press whatever I can press to remove that English message [then uninstall unaware]."*- CHW 30, HC2

On the devices used by CHWs, there was no Sesotho language option, and even if there were, we had previously found that the Sesotho translations on the phones are incomprehensible and confusing to CHWs. The feature phones previously used by CHWs had a Sesotho language option, but CHWs preferred to use English because the Sesotho version was too confusing. The difference between these native OS translations and the BH Sesotho interface, is that in BH we did not directly map English words into Sesotho equivalents: we made all Sesotho labels fully descriptive in a way the CHWs would understand.

Regular Engagement with CHWs
We found that after BH-focused workshops, CHWs remained motivated to use BH videos at increased rates, but that the initial enthusiasm after meetings eventually wore off and caused the frequency of plays to return to a lower, stable rate. We recommend regular engagement with CHWs, not only to keep them motivated to use the content, but also to encourage exploration of the technology and to counteract technical attrition [24]. Engagement with CHWs does not have to be by the researchers alone, but discussions and activities around CHWs' digital content can form part of their monthly meetings.

Analyses of Usage Trends

Topical Relevance Begets Video Popularity
Our expectation was that interest in videos would decay over time, with older videos losing popularity in favor of newer videos [14]. However, after 17 months, the two most watched videos were TB and STIs, which CHWs found to be the most relevant to their work based on their assessments of their clients' health information needs. TB remained the most viewed video because it assisted CHWs in their primary mandate under the current national TB campaign. The STI video was popular because it facilitated discussion on a highly prevalent issue that was otherwise taboo for discussion. Thus the primary retrospective indicator of a video's popularity is its topical relevance rather than any other features such as length, authorship, style or novelty.

Novelty Usage Spikes
Our results show an initial usage spike for all videos the CHWs had at the beginning of the study, and a spike in usage when new videos were introduced, showing temporary initial excitement over new content, but lasting no longer than three to four months. Novelty spikes can be leveraged for introducing new topics to the community, such as Ebola. However, in absence of sustained interest or extrinsic motivation, as with the TB videos, new videos must be introduced every few months.

Engaging Imagery: Explicit Content
Of all the BH videos, the STI video has the most explicit imagery, in part because it has images of genitalia, which are not commonly seen by many, and also because it shows scary images of untreated genital warts in males and females. The nurses wanted to communicate the importance of seeking medical attention as soon as one observes signs of an STI, emphasising that treatment is easily accessible, but also showing how dire the infections can be if left untreated. Of all the videos deployed in the 17 months in which we ran this study, the STI video was the most "talked about," having stimulated great interest and initiated dialogue among many in the CHWs' villages. Those who saw the video and were frightened by the images referred their friends to the CHWs to also watch the video. Those who requested to see the video would end up watching several others. The usage of this graphic video confirms the role of engaging or provocative imagery [12] in health education.

CONCLUSION

We worked with 54 CHWs, who were first-time smartphone users, and studied their use of multimedia content for community health education over 17 months. We enquired on the diffusion and use of the content over this period, seeking to understand the attributes of the content itself and the practices of the CHWs that affected patterns of consumption. We demonstrated that CHW engagement and topical relevance of the health videos affect rates of use the most, and presented lessons applicable to projects seeking to deploy multimedia content in rural settings over long periods of time.

ACKNOWLEDGEMENTS

We are grateful to the Schlumberger Foundation and the Hasso-Plattner-Institut for funding this research, as well as the nurses and community health workers who form part of the Bophelo Haeso Project.

REFERENCES

1. N. Campbell, E. Schiffer, A. Buxbaum, E. McLean, C. Perry, and T. M. Sullivan. 2014. Taking knowledge for health the extra mile: participatory evaluation of a mobile phone intervention for community health workers in Malawi. *Global Health: Science and Practice* 2, 1: 23–34. http://doi.org/10.9745/GHSP-D-13-00141

2. Sebastien Cuendet and Edward Cutrell. 2013. VideoKheti : Making Video Content Accessible to Low-Literate and Novice Users. *Proceedings of the SIGCHI Conference on Human Factors in Computing Systems*, ACM, 2833–2842.

3. Brian DeRenzi, Benjamin Birnbaum, Leah Findlater, et al. 2012. Improving community health worker performance through automated SMS. *Proceedings of the Fifth International Conference on Information and Communication Technologies and Development - ICTD '12*, ACM Press, 25. http://doi.org/10.1145/2160673.2160677

4. Pankaj Doke and Anirudha Joshi. 2015. Mobile Phone Usage by Low Literate Users. *Proceedings of the 7th International Conference on HCI, IndiaHCI 2015 - IndiaHCI'15*, ACM Press, 10–18. http://doi.org/10.1145/2835966.2835968

5. Susan M Dray, Ann Light, Andrew M Dearden, et al. 2012. Human Computer Interaction for Development: Changing HCI to Change the World. In *The Human-Computer Interaction Handbook: Fundamentals, Evolving Technologies and Emerging Applications. Human Factors and Ergonomics*, Andrew Sears and Julie A Jacko (eds.). Taylor and Francis Group, 1370–1391.

6. Brittany Fiore-Silfvast, Carl Hartung, Kirti Iyengar, et al. 2013. Mobile video for patient education: The midwives' perspective. *Proceedings of the 3rd ACM Symposium on Computing for Development - ACM DEV '13*, ACM Press, 1. http://doi.org/10.1145/2442882.2442885

7. David Frohlich, Dorothy Rachovides, Kiriaki Riga, et al. 2009. Storybank: Mobile Digital Storytelling in a Development Context. *Proceedings of the 27th international conference on Human factors in computing systems - CHI '09*, ACM Press, 1761. http://doi.org/10.1145/1518701.1518972

8. Rikin Gandhi, Rajesh Veeraraghavan, Kentaro Toyama, and Vanaja Ramprasad. 2007. Digital Green: Participatory video for agricultural extension. *2007 International Conference on Information and Communication Technologies and Development*, IEEE, 1–10. http://doi.org/10.1109/ICTD.2007.4937388

9. Ntwa Katule and Melissa Densmore. 2016. Leveraging Intermediated Interactions to Support Utilization of Persuasive Personal Health Informatics. *Proceedings of the Eighth International Conference on Information and Communication Technologies and Development*, ACM.

10. Neha Kumar and Richard J. Anderson. 2015. Mobile Phones for Maternal Health in Rural India. *Proceedings of the 33rd Annual ACM Conference on Human Factors in Computing Systems - CHI '15*, ACM Press, 427–436. http://doi.org/10.1145/2702123.2702258

11. Neha Kumar, Pallavi Lal, Richard Anderson, et al. 2015. Projecting Health: Community-Led Video Education for Maternal Health. *Proceedings of the Seventh International Conference on Information and Communication Technologies and Development - ICTD '15*, ACM Press, 1–10. http://doi.org/10.1145/2737856.2738023

12. Glenn Leshner, Paul Bolls, and Erika Thomas. 2009. Scare' Em or Disgust 'Em: The Effects of Graphic Health Promotion Messages. *Health Communication* 24, 5: 447–458. http://doi.org/10.1080/10410230903023493

13. Gary Marsden. 2008. Toward Empowered Design. *Computer* 41, 6: 42–46. http://doi.org/10.1109/MC.2008.207

14. Meeyoung Meeyoung Cha, Haewoon Haewoon Kwak, P. Rodriguez, Yong-Yeol Yong-Yeol Ahn, and Sue Sue Moon. 2009. Analyzing the Video Popularity Characteristics of Large-Scale User Generated Content Systems. *IEEE/ACM Transactions on Networking* 17, 5: 1357–1370. http://doi.org/10.1109/TNET.2008.2011358

15. Maletsabisa Molapo, Melissa Densmore, and Limpho Morie. 2016. Designing with Community Health Workers : Enabling Productive Participation Through Exploration. *Proceedings of the 1st African Conference on HCI (AfriCHI)*.

16. Maletsabisa Molapo, Melissa Densmore, and Limpho Morie. 2016. Apps and Skits:Enabling New Forms of Village-To-Clinic Feedback for Rural Health Education. *Proceedings of the 7th Annual Symposium on Computing for Development - ACM DEV '16*, ACM Press, 1–10. http://doi.org/10.1145/3001913.3001922

17. Maletsabisa Molapo and Gary Marsden. 2012. Health Education in Rural Communities with Locally Produced and Locally Relevant Multimedia Content. *Proceedings of the 3rd ACM Symposium on Computing for Development - ACM DEV '13*, 3–4.

18. Maletsabisa Molapo and Gary Marsden. 2013. Software support for creating digital health training materials in the field. *Proceedings of the Sixth International Conference on Information and Communication Technologies and Development Full Papers - ICTD '13 - volume 1*, ACM Press, 205–214. http://doi.org/10.1145/2516604.2516632

19. Michael J. Muller and Allison Druin. 2012. Participatory Design: The Third Space in Human-Computer Interaction. In *The Human-Computer Interaction Handbook: Fundamentals, Evolving Technologies and Emerging Applications. Human Factors and Ergonomics*, Andrew Sears and Julie A Jacko (eds.). Taylor and Francis Group, 1125–1153.

20. Tapan Parikh and Kaushik Ghosh. 2006. Understanding and Designing for Intermediated Information Tasks in India. *IEEE Pervasive Computing*.

21. Divya Ramachandran, John Canny, Prabhu Dutta Das, and Edward Cutrell. 2010. Mobile-izing health workers in rural India. *Proceedings of the 28th international conference on Human factors in computing systems - CHI '10*, ACM, 1889. http://doi.org/10.1145/1753326.1753610

22. Wang Randolph, Urvashi Sahni, Sumeet Sobti, et al. 2005. The Digital StudyHall. *Computer Science Department, Princeton University, Tech Rep. TR-723-05*.

23. Nithya Sambasivan, Ed Cutrell, Kentaro Toyama, and Bonnie Nardi. 2010. Intermediated technology use in developing communities. *Proceedings of the 28th international conference on Human factors in computing systems - CHI '10*, ACM Press, 2583. http://doi.org/10.1145/1753326.1753718

24. Ariel Schwartz, Mohini Bhavsar, Edward Cutrell, Jonathan Donner, and Melissa Densmore. 2013. Balancing burden and benefit: Non-Prescribed Use of Employer-Issued Mobile Devices. *Proceedings of the Sixth International Conference on Information and Communications Technologies and Development Notes - ICTD '13 - volume 2*, ACM Press, 140–143. http://doi.org/10.1145/2517899.2517911

25. Margaret Shangase, Supa Pengpid, Karl Peltzer, et al. TRADITIONAL BIRTH ATTENDANTS AND HIV / AIDS IN SOUTH AFRICA. *Health (San Francisco)*.

26. Kentaro Toyama and Kentaro. 2011. Technology as amplifier in international development. *Proceedings of the 2011 iConference on - iConference '11*, ACM Press, 75–82. http://doi.org/10.1145/1940761.1940772

27. Derek Treatman and Neal Lesh. 2012. Strengthening Community Health Systems with Localized Multimedia. *Proceedings of M4D 2012*, February.

28. Aditya Vashistha and Richard Anderson. 2016. Mobile Video Dissemination for Community Health. *Proceedings of the Eighth International Conference on Information and Communication Technologies and Development*, ACM.

Experiences of Delivering a Public Health Data Service

Emma Simpson, Rob Comber, Andrew Garbett, Ed Ian Jenkins, Madeline Balaam
Open Lab, Newcastle University,
Newcastle upon Tyne, UK
{emma.simpson, robert.comber, a.garbett, edward.jenkins, madeline.balaam}@ncl.ac.uk

ABSTRACT
The turn to in-the-wild within HCI has given rise to an increasing concern around designing technologies which are available at large scale. Uniquely, at the intersection of public health and HCI, our work has supported the deployment of a mobile application, FeedFinder, over the last three years. We delineate the ground-work that was required to sustain this mobile application over the long-term. Focussing in particular on efforts made to engage institutions in taking ownership over FeedFinder and the data it provides, we reflect on the tensions that arose between users and civic institutions, particularly around 'what matters'. We provide a reflection on key requirements when designing a health data service and provide three lessons learnt which can guide researchers toward their own successful and productive long-term research deployments.

Author Keywords
User-centred design; public health; breastfeeding; citizen-led data;.

ACM Classification Keywords
H.5.m. Information interfaces and presentation (e.g., HCI): Miscellaneous;

INTRODUCTION
The turn to-the-wild in HCI focusses on how communities engage with and make sense of technology for their everyday use [19,26,27,51]. More recently, research on in-the-wild deployments has seen a shift in discourse around understanding technologies in situ – not only for the short trajectory of a research project but for the extended engagement over the long term. This shift in discourse has presented new ways of thinking and reporting on designing for prolonged use and larger scale deployments [39,50–52], where typically, this information would be absent from publications [51]. The notion of prolonged use, and large (even global deployments) is increasingly important within HCI, particular when prototypes or tools have been developed to support political activism, community engagement, or health-related behaviours. We provide a substantive contribution to this field and particularly draw attention to the neglected human and social work needed in place to promote the success of these technologies. In particular, we attend to the work undertaken to engage public service providers in the long-term sustainable use of a digital civic service, in this case a public health data service. We focus our attention on 'what matters' to both users and civic institutions. In doing so, we highlight the tensions that arose and provide some key reflections to help guide the design and development of other health data services; *designing for action*, *designing for negotiation* and *designing for monetization*. In contrast, our lessons learnt delineate what support is needed from a research perspective for a successful and longer term deployment.

CHI 2017, May 06-11, 2017, Denver, CO, USA
ACM 978-1-4503-4655-9/17/05.
http://dx.doi.org/10.1145/3025453.3025881

Our work is situated at the intersection of Public Health and HCI, and based upon a mobile application that has been used in-the-wild for over three years. FeedFinder [1] is a free mobile application, available on iOS and Android. It was developed with the intention of creating a supportive health technology around which women could make the decision to breastfeed in public. It allows users to find and review venues for their breastfeeding friendliness on a map. Launching in July 2013, FeedFinder has been running at time of writing for over 36 months and has seen an uptake of almost 10,000 users worldwide. The data within the application has been contributed by the breastfeeding community, leaving around 3000 reviews across 3200 different venues. FeedFinder is thus situated alongside a range of crowdsourcing tools, enabling collective civic intelligence that empower citizens to take an active role in decision making and influence services they receive [2,26]. FeedFinder has continued to sustain user registrations and contributions over the last three years, and as it has continued to grow we routinely hear positive stories about its impact from women, businesses and the institutions that support it. But, clearly this has not just 'happened', and one of the goals of this paper is to illustrate and discuss the work involved in maintaining a successful research prototype and growing it into a digital civic service. To do this we reflect on the last 13 months of research and engagement activity around FeedFinder, predominantly focusing on engagement with public service providers and support staff, discussing the research and the 'other' work we have done to sustain FeedFinder and its community. We contribute a qualitative understanding of how a breastfeeding public health service used FeedFinder data to inform their services and a set of principles for supporting a 'public health data service'. We finish by describing a set of lessons we have learnt through the successful and long-term deployment of our research product, FeedFinder.

RELATED WORK

Recently there has been a surge in research aimed at exploring the role of such technologies in influencing city infrastructures and services [7,27,34,45,50] . Collaboration between citizens and civic workers through the medium of technology is on the rise. The ubiquity of mobile technology has enabled citizens to actively take part in new forms of civic engagement - involving city planning [7], providing opinion [50] influencing city maintenance [16,30], commissioning of their own location-based review apps [18], and becoming involved in political decisions [57]. Yet, despite this growing interest, there are still limitations with this work. In particular, a review of protocols around data-use suggests that often the data are used in relatively controlled research environments with little reflection on the prolonged engagement beyond a research project [7,27,34,50]. Traditionally, the use of apps and sensing technologies is at the heart of this research but app-oriented projects often suffer from longevity and sustainability issues [34]. A lack of funding and resource constraints, including technical support can often lead to an application becoming unsupported once a project comes to an end. At other times, without sufficient researcher engagement an application just ceases to be used. As [26] notes, any concept of prolonged engagement and visions of civic authorities and citizens acting as partners is far from yet achieved.

Data and Public Health

Advances in social computing and social media technologies have significantly changed the landscape of public health [5,25,49]. Communities are now able to create and share credible knowledge-based experiences of dealing with or responding to public health issues while increasing community wellbeing [1,5,17,21,22,25,28,41,42,49]. Coined 'Public Health 2.0' – this movement could enable open and collaborative efforts between health experts and specific communities to tailor public health services and interventions to the specific local needs of a community. Central to the success of the Public Health 2.0 endeavor is the vested interest from community members to act responsibly, participating and creating good quality content based on the common values and needs they share. There has been a growth in recent research aimed at understanding how communities in online forums such as PatientsLikeMe [44] are taking charge of their own health through sharing their lived experiences of living and dealing with their health conditions with one another. The premise of online health communities has confirmed that users often feel empowered, more confident, better informed and more likely to 'feel a sense of control over their future' while increasing confidence of interacting with healthcare providers [35,41,55]. Similarly, other online platforms are enabling citizens to advocate for better services based on reviewing their experiences with a particular practitioner, practice or hospital service [43]. This approach has been used predominantly in the US where healthcare is provided at a cost, and therefore patients want to ensure they are receiving the best possible care and treatment for their money. More recently in the UK, this approach has been harnessed by 'Patient Opinion' [43]. Ran as a social enterprise, the website boasts over 600 registered health services that are automatically sent feedback from the website when citizens leave a review. The review process is tracked and change documented, with a reported 10% of the reviews resulting in a positive change [43]. These new forms of engagement are shifting the move from what would traditionally be transactional to a more relational service model, reconfiguring power relations between communities and their service providers [58]. Despite this, little focus has been given to the impact of these new forms of communication and interaction on local public health service provision.

Although there is little academic research in this area, we also look to commercial reviewing services such as TripAdvisor [54] and Yelp [59] as inspiration for how something similar might operate within a public health context. There are however, clear contrasts between what would be a public health data service and that of comparison in the commercial sector. With the latter providing a platform for dialogue between businesses and the public, whereas a public health data service we would consider to be much more complex. In a public health context, multiple stakeholders would have an ability to act on potentially damaging reviews (e.g. affecting well-being of mothers/infant), but are also bound by certain factors such as local authority service level agreements [38], legislation or policy [15]. In a commercial review site, a business is likely to engage with a negative review to maintain footfall and reputation, but with breastfeeding for example, businesses seemlingly have less motivation to be engaged.

In the wider context of Public Health and HCI, conversations around the benefit of 'Big Data' are often shrouded in doubt [29,32,37]. 'Big Data' and citizen-led data collected through social computing channels has been discussed as a proxy for disease outbreak surveillance [32] but research in this area is very much in its infancy. On a smaller scale (i.e. at a local level) there is scope for citizen-led data to be used in practice to influence the type and quality of public health services that are received, perhaps in the guise of 'little data'.

Data in Collective Action

Social media technologies have been considered an instrumental and significant resource for collective action and social change [14]. In the wake of the crisis mapping phenomenon, scholars have reported how these applications have provided a vehicle for empowerment and better still-'saved lives' [2]. The appropriation of CrowdMap [6] to Ushahidi [40,60] and HarrassMap [23,24] has enabled citizens to become active agents in collective action and change the response to reporting disasters and crime. Scholars have recently turned to understand how these technologies can be re-appropriated for community development [2]. The difference being that the crises mapping tends to be of a short temporal nature, whereas in community development (e.g. crises such as housing, poverty) the applications require more persistent use and over a long period of time. Researchers have described how those working in community development can leverage the crisis mapping platforms and tap into tacit community knowledge while creating greater ownership over the process and data collected to influence organised interventions within the community [2]. Similar to other projects [7] these studies often recruit contributors to input data, incentivising the contribution of data by informing study participants that the data will be used to influence decision-making.

Other work in HCI has expressed the importance of translating data and designing to express matters of concern within a community [11,21,31]. DiSalvo et al [11] describe the notion of designing for 'publics' around environmental matters of concern. In recent years, Dewey's notion of 'publics' has been restored and renewed through shared interests across disciplines (namely social science and HCI) [7,8,11] and we consider these theoretical underpinnings are transferrable to the context of public health and HCI. Where constructed 'publics' is described as groups of diverse stakeholders brought together by identifying and expressing a social condition [7,9,10,12] – we can apply this to the context of breastfeeding. Where technology supports the formation of publics and occurs at the intersection of the socio-technical interactions between negotiating expression of issues and supporting the action taken in response [8,9]. A challenge for us then, is designing for 'communities-in-practice' where common social objectives already exist and are supported by 'relatively stable infrastructures' [13,31] The question is, how do we get them to adopt a change in their practice in this digital era?

FEEDFINDER: WHERE ARE WE NOW?

FeedFinder was launched in July 2013, and since this time, has received over 12,500 downloads of the app (67% on iOS), of which almost 10,000 have led to registered users adding near to 3,200 individual places, and over 3,000 reviews (see Figure 1). The service has been primarily used in the UK, however a growing number of venues and reviews have been added in the USA, Western Europe, Australia and Asia. The breastfeeding community are able to find, rate and review places in their locale based on their breastfeeding friendliness. Co-designed with breastfeeding mothers [1], the app contains criteria which are considered important for meeting their breastfeeding needs. Since the launch there have been a number of updates to the application, with new features added. This includes a better search functionality, users being able to upload image of a venue, 'like' other reviewers' and comments as well as share their review or other reviews onto different social media platforms, i.e. Facebook and Twitter. During this time, we have made some efforts to attract users and sustain our community, including the use of print materials, attendance at 'breastfeeding picnics', and facebook advertisements. Nevertheless, the majority of our users hear about FeedFinder through word-of-mouth.

Given its reported role in supporting women in some communities breastfeeding outside the home, we have made substantial efforts to sustain FeedFinder and work with local civic institutions who are at the forefront of breastfeeding support services. Quantitative analysis of user interactions with FeedFinder [1] highlight that users will typically engage with FeedFinder over a three-month period. As such, there is a need to continuously raise awareness of the application among new and expectant mothers to ensure the FeedFinder map is kept up-to-date and relevant. We understood that breastfeeding support services, based on their outreach, networks and activism would be well placed to support the promotion of FeedFinder over the long-term. We also believed that a number of organisations might have a vested interest in the data FeedFinder collects. We hoped in particular that the organisations would be motivated to act on reviews on the FeedFinder map, i.e. contacting businesses who had received negative comments, or low star-rating and commending businesses who were receiving consistently good ratings. This, we imagined would enable women to graduate from simply having a voice about breastfeeding services within the community, to having a say [47], through impacting on the delivery of services.

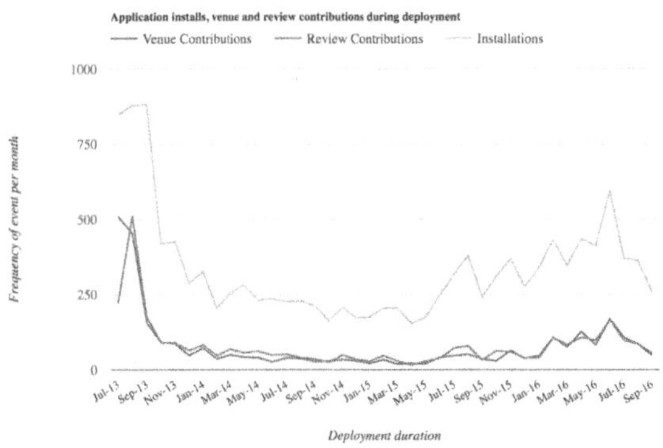

Figure 1: Application Installs, Venue and Review Contributions during Deployment

The commissioning of local breastfeeding support services is part of a wider agenda by Local Authorities to improve public health. A contract (Service Level Agreement – SLA) between the Local Authority Public Health department and community breastfeeding peer support services determines their responsibilities Currently, within the UK many breastfeeding peer support services are responsible for working toward gaining accreditation from the UNICEF Baby Friendly Initiative [56]. In short, meeting specific criteria set out by UNICEF will provide an award in receipt of recognition. Part of this criteria includes a 7-point plan aimed at sustaining breastfeeding in the community.

Particularly relevant to FeedFinder is point 7, *co-operation with the local community*. We considered that FeedFinder provided a tool through which breastfeeding services could co-operate with the local community to understand a wide range of local women's experiences of breastfeeding, as well as act on the reviews (where necessary).

CONTEXT, METHOD AND ANALYSIS

This paper reflects on 13 months of work supporting FeedFinder, from April 2015 to May 2016. When data collection began for this study, FeedFinder had been in continuous deployment for 2 years. Much of this work is situated in Newcastle upon Tyne within the North East UK, a city chosen specifically because of FeedFinder's dense use, and the local government's prolonged support of the project. UK-wide breastfeeding rates vary significantly between regions [4,33]. On average, 46% of all babies are exclusively breastfed at 1 week and 1% by 6 months [33]. Differences are seen across the UK but the North East of England has the lowest rates of exclusive breastfeeding compared to other regions at one week and 6 months, 36% and less than 1%, respectively. Society has a collective responsibility to provide a supportive and enabling environment for women who want to breastfeed [46]. The recent transition of public health services from the primary care sector to Local Authority has already exerted considerable financial and resourceful strain on services, with an additional call to cut £32 million to Newcastle City Council services in the coming year [38].

As motivated in the previous section, a great deal of our focus has been on establishing relationships with breastfeeding support services and developing a service design which would enable them to incorporate FeedFinder into their service provision. Over the last 13 months we had conversations with multiple stakeholders working in breastfeeding support - some of which proved successful, leading to further collaborative work and promotion of FeedFinder, while others were without fruition. In addition, the authors interviewed FeedFinder users (12) to understand how they use the application, as well as their experiences of use. We have held meetings with two managers of a breastfeeding support team, a midwife, an infant feeding coordinator and midwifery research nurse and attended a number breastfeeding support working group meetings (including children's centre staff, health visitors, physical activity coordinators, midwives, breastfeeding peer support workers and volunteers). The first and last author have given talks at a range of regional and national events about FeedFinder, and its impact on breastfeeding support. The first author set-up a Twitter account in an attempt to raise the profile of FeedFinder more generally. We established a longer-term working relationship with a breastfeeding support service in the city who are commissioned by the Local Authority to provide city wide breastfeeding support. The first author attended local breastfeeding support groups meeting peer supporters and breastfeeding women. Over the course of a year we attended the monthly meetings of the breastfeeding support services and kept in touch via email during the periods in between.

Through these conversations (interview, focus group and email) we identified a myriad of issues and strain on the breastfeeding support services. Firstly, most of the service providers we have spoken to haven't been able to monitor breastfeeding support in the community, and as such are not fulfilling a key part of the UNICEF baby friendly initiative described earlier. In addition, while service providers have attempted to provide print materials and resources for breastfeeding women, particularly on 'breastfeeding friendly venues', these have quickly become outdated and redundant without scope for any replacements. In addition, we have discovered that there is no universal breastfeeding policy that they can provide for businesses to ensure consistency in the community. Finally, although many of the support workers had heard about FeedFinder, they hadn't used it themselves, or seen it used in practice. Promoting the application was part of their service delivery plan, but none of the team had the app installed on their own mobile phones or were aware of how the app worked.

We report data from interviews, working group meetings, focus groups, field notes and observations. All instances of recorded data were transcribed verbatim and we adopted an inductive thematic analysis approach [3]. Each transcript was manually coded and NVivo 10 used to group codes into hierarchical themes which we present in this paper.

FINDINGS

Our goal was to understand the ways in which FeedFinder could become part of a public health data service for breastfeeding support services. We wanted to explore the potential uses of the data in practice, how this data should be made available as part of a service, as well as the ways in which the support service could work with us to help sustain the FeedFinder community. Throughout each monthly meeting the first author discussed the group's use of FeedFinder, their efforts at promoting it, and in addition an exploration of the 'live data'. The live data included free-text reviews on venues within their locale, star ratings for the venues (based on the criteria within the app, namely hygiene, privacy, comfort and baby facilities) and looking together at the FeedFinder map. We were particularly interested in whether and how the service thought they could use the data. We present the findings here under the following themes: accessing and unravelling the data, institutional and professional support, adding to the map and encouraging use, and finally, 'Whose job is it anyway?'

Accessing and Unravelling the Data

We set out to explore what it would mean for breastfeeding support services to have better access to data that could potentially impact on their service provision. It was immediately clear that access to the data was troublesome for the support service. Few had FeedFinder on their phone, but even when they did it was evident that the mobile application itself did not provide the required regional overview, or necessary filtering options. As currently designed, support workers would have to investigate all individual places and reviews to find opportunities for action. In addition, it was virtually impossible for the support service to identify recently added places or reviews. This gave rise to the necessity to develop a web-based interface for the data which would give a higher level view of the data collected by FeedFinder.

As we discussed further the needs of the breastfeeding support teams in accessing and acting upon FeedFinder data, the ability to compare data across administrative areas of the city (known as 'Super Output Areas') became a significant requirement. This enabled them to monitor areas of lower socio-economic status where it was expected by the support teams to be less common to see a breastfeeding woman in public. As Marie details: *"I think if you're looking at super output areas...like at the moment we're focusing on the west...obviously we're working there so we can look and if one of our areas is a two [breastfeeding friendliness rating] then we can look at it and one of our goals could be can we get it up [breastfeeding friendliness rating]?"*

While we began the design and development of this interface, the first author became responsible for trawling the application on a monthly basis to identify and gather reviews, using her discretion, that were in need of discussion, and presenting these to the support service. However, on presenting reviews - aimed at provoking a detailed response to how they would act quickly – the group became entangled in much more nuanced debates about the contextual factors. Using their own experiences to compare, they debated at length whether the data would actually warrant any action in response. At times, they described the evidence as 'weak' and called for a process where they could retrieve further information from both the women and or the business owner for confirmation and to look at it from a *'factual point of view'*.

Kate: but that's the thing isn't it, I mean it says 'not a great place to feed not enough room' but again they might have twins or they might have a child and then two other toddlers.

Marie: I think whatever they write you...

Kate: have to read between the lines a bit...

When discussing the data, they described how it became a matter of subjectivity and proposed numerous questions they would ask the woman who left the review. In response to this, they proposed ways we might further improve FeedFinder to be a useful resource for them. They suggested a social element, where they are able to respond to the women and ask for further information.

Marie: so that one there I would say, ok, not a nice place to feed, not enough room, I would pick out the bunch of all of these [reviews] and if the lady has left the name and contact number [imaginary scenario] and then you can get a bit more detail, what do you mean by not enough room,...because it could be arms on the chair, it could be the door opens inwards so you can't get your buggy in and shut the door, or it could be I've got twins, you know, so it is reading between the lines, but that is a potential option for a person to leave their [contact details]

It is notable that most of the dialogue around the data was framed in this way – seeking out the social and contextual factors which could have contributed to a woman's experience, and the possibility that a woman may have made a misjudgement which could be further clarified by speaking with them or with the business.

Marie: *"staff skirted around the subject of breastfeeding so we didn't receive a clear answer", so she obviously asked, but what was the questions...*

Jodie: *"maybes a telephone call to the Centre X or you know, its whether actually she asked...they might have actually given her somewhere else, she might have assumed that this is where I need to sit when actually that chair might have been for a toddler..."*

As they suggested ways in which the app could be further developed to allow for contacting the women to clarify their experience, they also desired to let women know their review was valid and had been taken care of *"would you then, say if you sent that email to say Store X or whatever would you then comment underneath about what you had done"* and further *"I think to reply to a comment to say 'hello we will look into this' or something is great, you know, to show that something is happening"*.

However, we observed differences between the idea of what's important and 'valid' when breastfeeding in public, with contrasting views from the breastfeeding women and those who provide support. In the context of breastfeeding and changing facilities, Fiona, a FeedFinder user and breastfeeding mother described *"I do tend to share, kind of, baby changing and feeding facilities because they often go hand-in-hand"*. While in contrast, the breastfeeding support team overlooked much of the data that made reference to changing facilities and were more interested in whether a venue was welcoming of breastfeeding, regardless of the changing facilities. Talking about amendments to the FeedFinder app to help guide women to talk less about facilities was mentioned by Jodie... *"that's what you want to know, whether they are breastfeeding welcome but if we're going right oh well that says about the baby facilities but we don't want to know about that but we're asking them to star it, so I would scrap that and have 'is it breastfeeding welcome'* [instead of baby facilities]." At times, they explicitly described how they were *'not interested in a place being child friendly'* but rather *'are they able to breastfeed'*. This was also reinforced when they questioned a woman's choice of venue after she reported that the place wasn't child friendly, however they also suggest a business has a right to respond.

Jodie: "*the thing is with this, because whether or not you, because it is Franco Bollo, whether or not there is some sort of email that goes to them or another establishment that says 'just to let you know we have received a review, blah blah blah'. and I do feel quite strongly you have got to give them the right to reply [the business], so they have to know, well they might say our staff, well I don't know...*"

Marie: "*but then Franco Bollo there's a flight of stairs but there's seats downstairs*"

Jodie: *there is but that's not our issue, our issue is not about being child friendly, it's about breastfeeding*

Marie: "*I think the issue here is she is saying it was happy for breastfeeding, the other issues are about the stairs and position next to a large group sometimes that is way out of our hands, we can't, that is their choice of venue, they have chosen a venue that has got a flight of stairs and no lift so it's not baby friendly but they are not saying it's not breastfeeding friendly*"

However, there were times when the breastfeeding support staff looked beyond their service level agreements and unpicked the data from the perspective of having been a breastfeeding mother. Drawing on their own experiences to sympathise when places don't provide the space to change and feed separately, Jodie recalls "*the baby changing is the toilet for babies so why would you make that the feeding room? it causes bad feelings for people waiting to change their babies because if you're feeding in there and there's a queue of people waiting to change then you come out, because I've experienced it, people will be glaring at you.*"

Interestingly, some of the conversations around the data were contradictory. We discussed the implications of a well-known health department store having directed a woman to an outside disabled toilet in order to feed, with Jodie (breastfeeding support) questioning whether the review was correct: "*there is, they have got, ah I might not have been in that one, but most [of the stores] have got a feeding room*". A similar response from a DIY store where a woman was shown to a ladies' toilet and given a stool to sit on was applauded, rather than chastised for encouraging a child to be fed in a place where previously they questioned: "*when somebody says oh you can go to the toilet and breastfeed would you go and eat your dinner there?*" rather than "*well done not just you know, what's that like a s**t sandwich, well done for doing this, the place was awful but??*" This rhetoric around breastfeeding reflects other research within the field of breastfeeding qualitative work [53].

Institutional and Professional Support

We take the position that an institutional seal of approval will likely help in promoting FeedFinder, and have discussed FeedFinder at a range of National Health Service events, raising its profile among breastfeeding activism groups (such as the National Childbirth Trust and La Leche) with varying levels of success. These concerns around what it means to provide support for such an application are well illustrated by our conversations with the breastfeeding support service and other FeedFinder users over the last 13 months. In some cases, support workers disagreed with the premise of the application, and suggested they could not endorse it. They suggested, for instance, that a 1 star review in the application would suggest that somewhere was not breastfeeding friendly – in direct contradiction to UK policy on breastfeeding. Concerns were also aired when the support services realized that their right to anonymity was waivered depending on their chosen user name when registering in the account on the FeedFinder app. This prompted dialogue around whether or not they would want to be identified by their own name when acting as a professional.

Jen: "*nobody would know like my name for example, you don't have to put your full name, do you, like JC or jenc, but no one would really know that is me as a person, especially if you don't put a picture, if you don't make a full profile, if I made a profile to say I'm from City X breastfeeding support, blah blah, then you know... I don't think I would put a picture on, and I've left a few reviews at different places that I have been which aren't related to work but I've thought it would be nice here [to breastfeed]*"

Here, Jen is concerned that 'outing' herself as a breastfeeding support worker might have implications for how her reviews are received and understood by the community, and potentially also businesses. She both doesn't want to be a target, or be concerned that everything she adds to the FeedFinder map is viewed in this 'official' capacity. This was also the case for some of the breastfeeding mothers we interviewed. In particular, one of our breastfeeding women was a General Practitioner (family doctor) and because her username on FeedFinder was her full name, this meant she would be identifiable – preventing her from leaving reviews around the place where she practiced, for fear of people assuming it was her professional view. As she describes, "*There was just one thing I did. When I logged on it says, "Have a username," and I'd actually just used my name. Then I can't change it. So I thought people would know who I am. Not that it's a huge problem for up here, but I'm a GP down in City A and so I wouldn't want people in City A knowing I'd left the review...so it's trying to keep that anonymity. Especially with maybe some of the smaller places you might leave a review for, they might know who you are. I can't change it now so I have to keep that. So that might stop people putting reviews down for, like, little local cafes if they've actually put their name down as their...*

We also explored the potential of sharing reviews on social media. As a new feature, we see this as an opportunity to open up the data for discussion online, but again, anonymity was a contributing factor which would inhibit a woman's decision to share reviews. As Katrina (breastfeeding mother) describes: "*I think again, it's a professional thing that you're told, you know, as teachers or doctors to be very careful about what you put on. If I shared something, but somebody had put on a really out-there review then I might be seen to be promoting that. So I'd be very careful about that.... I probably wouldn't share it on social media, because then I'd be seen to be promoting it. I mean, promoting breastfeeding is a great thing but if somebody's written a dodgy review and I hadn't read it, you know, just for those kinds of reasons.* Such views are not unique to Katrina. There is much concern across many of the institutions we have spoken to about FeedFinder which have focussed on the uncontrollable nature of social media, and user-generated content. As such, many of the conversations we have had with institutions have concluded that it would be necessary to view and agree with every review added to the map before institutional support for FeedFinder could be provided.

Additionally, the idea of a mobile application which supports breastfeeding is problematic for some members of the public health community. There were clear contrasts in the views posed by both the breastfeeding women and the breastfeeding support services. As Marie (breastfeeding support) noted, *"we discourage women from using their phones when nursing as it is a distraction and they should be bonding with the baby"*. This conflicts sharply with modern parenting practice [20], as described by one of our FeedFinder users: *"Yes, it's usually if I'm feeding him or something...like lots of people I'm glued to my iPhone...I think where I've been, yes, I do it in blocks [add reviews]"*.

Adding to the Map and Encouraging Use

As we have mentioned, the support team often questioned the data from the women in FeedFinder. In doing so, they raised doubts on the legitimacy of some of the data which resulted in them seeking to find out further information before considering a response. One way in which they did act however, was to populate the FeedFinder map with the women at weekly breastfeeding peer support groups. They also discussed the idea of incentivizing the volunteers to take on the role of reviewing places and inputting into the FeedFinder app. To encourage them to carry this out the staff discussed the idea of providing a 'prize' for the most reviews left or the best review.

Marie: *"something that we could do is get the volunteers to go out there and try different parks and then say to them on top of that go and put your review on FeedFinder"*

Jen: *is it worth me emailing all of our volunteers that we know have got a baby, sorry or breastfeeding or pregnant and saying it's like a little project for them?"*

Marie: "*we could send an email out to volunteers to generate interest again about [FeedFinder] or if they are finding it difficult or if they haven't, or they don't do apps and things if they forward the information we can put it on for them"*

Jodie: *"We could even put on a little prize for who gets the most increase of reviews or best..."*

Jen: *"I definitely see where volunteers fit into this, I mean because asking them to go out and about in their particular area to review establishments and or spread the word, obviously some of them are still breastfeeding, I just think it would be a nice volunteering opportunity for them without...it feeling like they have to do it... apart from that it's good from this point of view on this side too of trying to raise standards and raise numbers, so..."*

In addition, the breastfeeding support team, alongside multiple other organisations, requested paper-based promotional materials to help the breastfeeding support teams to promote FeedFinder. In response, we have designed and printed a range of different 'marketing' material to help partners and organisations promote FeedFinder on our behalf. We have been told that stickers are useful for putting on 'baby books' (an NHS record resource for a child given to mothers after they give birth) when health visitors or breastfeeding peer workers first met with a woman after giving birth. Leaflets and cards have also been requested by other service providers over the last 13 months to be used alongside conferences, meetings and breastfeeding picnics to help raise awareness of FeedFinder among healthcare workers, volunteers, and new and expectant mothers.

As we talked about promoting FeedFinder within the local community it became clear that regional competition could also function as a very poignant motivation for local service providers. Breastfeeding support workers often talked about 'doing better' than the adjacent cities in terms of breastfeeding rates and breastfeeding community support was an important sense of achievement *"oh we have got to beat City Y and City Z"*. This became of such importance to the breastfeeding service that we worked with that we agreed to incorporate a unique tracking link (for the service provider) on the leaflets and stickers we produced for them so that they would be able to track their 'download' rate in comparison to other services.

Whose Job is it Anyway?

In many cases, although the support workers had good intentions, any actions they would consider were either delegated to the role of a volunteer or directed toward the first author '*you* could just draft two standard emails', '*you* could contact businesses', '*you* could ask the women for further information'. There was a particular onus on us to take responsibility for the actions around the data. We had envisaged this to be a useful resource which would enable the service provider to monitor community support, opening up access to information which they were lacking previously. Instead, we were reminded frequently with reference to their contract (Service Level Agreement), any actions would be beyond their scope of work. Through working together the responsibility for action was pushed back to the researchers or when money came into the equation – on the business to pay to receive their services.

Jodie: "*So could we not just like, draft a letter?"*

Marie: "*No, its capacity for our team when it's not in our SLA."*

Kate: *"Unless someone is going to give us some money?"*

Jen: *"Do the businesses know this exists [FeedFinder], they should do."*

Jodie: *"I mean just a letter, not send it out but give it for {researcher} to send out."*

Jen: *"But what you going to put in that letter to improve on their services?"*

Marie: *"You can't just say – "I don't know if you would like to discuss it more and like a bit more understanding" I'm happy to use the central line for them to ring us but we can't offer them any training we haven't got the capacity and we don't get paid for it."*

Kate: *"But it's you [the researcher] that would do that?"*

Jodie: *"...we could get them to pay us for it, get the business to pay for it...come in and we deliver a session for £10 all your staff. You know, you would get a certificate at the end of it to put in the window to say we have all been trained."*

Despite considering that FeedFinder could provide the support service with easy access to data which they would need to fulfil elements of their service level agreements, how the organisation would use it in practice opened up a range of issues which were considered to increase the workload of the service. The disjoint between how the breastfeeding community wanted to rate, describe and share their experiences, versus the means by which the support service construed a positive breastfeeding experience, meant the service felt they would need to further clarify women's comments before action could be taken, further increasing demand on their time.

DISCUSSION

We have presented in this paper experiences of running a longer-term research project involving a sustained, three year long, in-the-wild deployment. Our documented experiences over the last 13 months of supporting FeedFinder, and in particular a year-long engagement with one breastfeeding service provider in the city, has identified the necessity for a web-based interface to allow better access to the FeedFinder data. We have identified key service design requirements that would enable this data to lead to real-world impact, and ultimately an improvement in services by multiple stakeholders (i.e. not just breastfeeding women). We are also concerned with making FeedFinder sustainable and passing ownership from us the 'researchers' to the communities and institutions that FeedFinder serves. Women see the benefit of FeedFinder in describing the public breastfeeding context but there's not enough resource to affect change [1]. We need the engagement of other key stakeholders and to influence policies to make that happen. We are currently in the process of designing and developing the web-based tool with a number of local service providers. Here we reflect on the requirements for a 'public health data service', finishing by presenting three lessons learnt which can be used by researchers working in the field to guide future long-term deployments.

A Public Health Data Service

Public health service providers have the option to engage with citizen-led data or not. Technology acts as an enabler for the collection of large datasets which would typically be difficult to collect and manage in a public health setting. A salient and often unanswered question when working with citizen-led data is 'how do we design to transform data for use in practice?' Citizen-led data can be messy, unpredictable and the challenge we are faced with is how to design interfaces that increases access to the data while visualizing it in a way that is beneficial, reduces labour and is a useful resource [2]. In addition, we have to consider the possibilities of designing for those with limited technical expertise, making it simple, engaging and intuitive as well as practical for those working in the field.

Designing for Action

In positioning FeedFinder as a 'DingPolitik' [1] we frame FeedFinder as a technology through which lived experiences of political conditions can be better known, and acted upon. While we recognise FeedFinder as an application which offers women a voice in sharing their experiences, it doesn't necessarily offer a 'say' [47]. Over the last three years we have witnessed some users utilising our dataset to create change in their community, but these have been in a minority [1]. As a result, we have created a condition, where women can voice concerns and experiences, but few institutions or organisations appear to be listening or acting. As found elsewhere there are challenges to working with communities bound by contracts and infrastructures [13,31]. In our case, working with a breastfeeding support service over the last year has emphasised the lack of time and resource these services have, particularly when delivering on anything but non-essential frontline services. In many ways, this is unlikely too different to the situation and experiences of a new mother, who similarly will struggle to find time for anything but the essentials.

A 'public health data service' should enable action. Taking inspiration from social platforms for change, such as Change.org, we have learnt that time for action is limited, and that taking action should be as simple as clicking a button. We consider, that alongside providing relatively standard review, search and filtering features, a data interface should automatically highlight places where action may be required. Similarly, other health data services such as [7] could also enable action - it could allow health professionals to identify areas where more support for physical activity is required. Other review based health data services like [43] provoke action among service providers where the quality of care is lacking. In our case, for example, we can identify places where venues are on a downward or upward trend (in terms of breastfeeding friendliness), areas within a locality where number of users is waning, or gaining momentum. Much like the support service whom we engaged with suggests, the data service should provide templates of emails, leaflets and posters which users (whether they be breastfeeding activists, breastfeeding support workers, or otherwise) can quickly download, adapt, print and circulate.

Designing for Negotiation

In discussing reviews with support services we were intrigued by the level of meaning making undertaken by the group. An experience shared by an individual was rarely taken at face-value, but instead dissected to identify whether action was necessary, or whether the women's experience was as should be expected. We found the support service providers regularly drew on their own experiences, as well as an institutional perspective on breastfeeding friendliness, to assess the legitimacy of a review. Similarly, to [2,7] we have found that the service providers own values and experience shape how the data is interpreted and ultimately how it is acted upon. Complex disputes and issues around data interpretation and analysis have been reported elsewhere [34]. A resolution suggested by the authors and what we agree with, is that specific criteria must guide the collection of data if it is to prove to be sufficiently useful to an outsider (i.e. those who didn't devise the data collection initially). Moreover, [50] highlights the issues that may arise by looking at data through an 'anti-perspectivist lens', explaining that such a data-as-truth view could cause damage or lead to a troublesome outcome if data is acted upon - without considering the ethical implications.

A 'public health data service' must thus enable negotiation of data collected, as well as negotiation of the criteria around which experiences are reported. In our case, the rating criteria for FeedFinder were established through a series of user-centred design workshops with breastfeeding women, where we privileged a woman's breastfeeding experience, over outcomes, practices or policy understood from an institutional perspective. Consequently, factors such as baby change facilities (which are part and parcel of intimate care of a young baby, alongside feeding), were selected as a crucial criterion for rating venues. But, such a criterion, according to the support services we have worked with, has nothing to do with breastfeeding friendliness. By designing to enable negotiation we envisage a scenario where breastfeeding support workers could propose alternative criteria to the community, based on their needs for the data. These new criteria could be voted on, and where appropriate incorporated into the application for women to use going-forward. Platforms such as App-Movement [18] could incorporate such phases of re-design into applications, when for example operating systems require updates to existing applications. Ongoing dialogue around what constitutes useful data could enable the end-users of the system to understand the value of their voice, leading to further motivation for use.

Trust and moderation of content continue to be an issue for institutions and private end-users, considering reputation to be at stake, if for example FeedFinder was found to contain libellous, or inflammatory reviews. As suggested, an interface which enables support services, businesses and other women to explicitly respond to reviews would provide an opportunity for negotiation of meaning, and appropriate action, akin to review services such as TripAdvisor and Yelp. Commercial services like these provide a platform where diaglogue can occur between the consumer and the business operator, allowing space for negotiation and potential reconcilary action (if need be). Such opportunities to respond may also help to increase confidence in the reliability and trustworthiness of the collected data.

Designing for Monetization

McMillan [34] highlights that it is often challenging to get service providers to take on additional work such as managing and analysing data without monetary incentives for their team. Neff [37] similarly discusses the implications of data driven work within a healthcare context whereby doctors do not see data as a source of value but rather costly and risky additional work. We experienced the same hesitancy, where the support services were unable to act on the data without extra funding or integration into their working contract by the Local Authority. Working in the context of breastfeeding over the last three years we have become increasingly aware of the lack of policy (national, regional and local) that support businesses, venues and places in being breastfeeding friendly, i.e. clearly specify what this means in terms of facilities available. This hinders service providers' ability to act on businesses which are not supporting breastfeeding (or receive negative reviews), as there are no clear guidelines about what should be in place.

This brings forth an opportunity which the FeedFinder dataset, and the 'public health data service' can provide. FeedFinder is in a unique position to evidence what makes for a good public breastfeeding experience based on a content analysis of women's reviews [48]. Such analysis can be translated into evidence-based policy and services, which in themselves have monetizing potential. For example, services could encourage businesses to sign-up to a 'FeedFinder Breastfeeding Scheme', for which businesses would pay a small fee to receive training based on policy, along with promotional materials and publicity. In tandem, women's use of FeedFinder allows services to keep track of businesses services, without increasing a service's workload extensively. This allows the service to keep-up-to-date with the extent to which businesses are upholding the policy (and potential need for re-training), as well as identify new businesses to include within the scheme.

Lessons Learnt

Finally, after supporting the deployment of a mobile application for three years (and running), we offer three lessons learnt which we consider to have enabled this unique long-term and engaged deployment within HCI.

Make Yourself Useful

Over the last three years we have presented FeedFinder at multiple NHS and council run events, discussing in particular the user-centred design process, along with how the application works, and what kind of dâta we have collected. These presentations have led to multiple meetings where stakeholders have wanted to discuss how they might make use of FeedFinder, or indeed persuade us to develop different kinds of location-based rate and review applications for other contexts [see 19]. These meetings do not always lead to concrete collaborations, but they do increase the visibility of the application and the work you are doing.

In FeedFinder, we have created an entirely unique dataset, which offers all kinds of interesting lenses on women's experiences of breastfeeding, geographical differences in these experiences, an evaluative tool for measuring more traditional 'interventions', through to a dataset which describes the structure of uptake and use of grass-root data movements. By finding ways to translate your data into meaningful tools for others (whether this be policy, new methods of evaluation), you can ultimately sustain interest in the application in ways which allow you to continue to support and update it as a product.

Have Assets to Hand

Throughout the deployment and interactions with external partners, local organisations, and media outlets we find ourselves time and time again communicating the values and affordances of the FeedFinder service. Being contacted by a media outlet, asked to present at an event, or engage with a local organisation has required that, as a team, we develop a common language and branding around the FeedFinder project. This has led to the creation and sharing of key assets, beyond those needed for third-party dissemination, in particular high-quality photographs and logos as well as text based materials (paper-based promotional materials, short overview statements, longer descriptive texts for different academic, healthcare worker, external organization purposes) between team members. These are crucial to delivering a consistent message behind the project but also in responding to opportunities for engaging with potential project partners and organizations to support these forms of services. Perhaps most importantly, What we have come to realise is that these promotional materials are just as much for the service-providers as they are for women themselves. Many of the individuals involved in supporting breastfeeding do not consider themselves to be technical, or interested in technology. In addition, these resources allow us to respond quickly and efficiently to inquiries about FeedFinder. Being rapid in our responses helps to give the impression that FeedFinder is a product, and that the team supporting it are trustworthy and responsive.

We recommend you think early on about a website, a hashtag, a logo and professional photographs related to your product / service. All these assets are key to communicating with your audience.

Think about the Service, Not Just the Application

Much of the time our focus has been on the design, development and re-development of the FeedFinder application. We have focussed on our immediate users, knowing for example, that they value baby-changing facilities as an intrinsic part of breastfeeding in public. This focus has been to the detriment of 'making ourselves useful' to wider services, which may have implications for the longevity of the application. Having now spent considerable time engaging with individuals providing services to communities, we realise that the data FeedFinder collects is not made available to them in ways which are at all feasible given their existing time pressures. We also know that the type of data collected does not always meet their specific needs.

Having only one point of access to data about your application causes bottlenecks. Not enabling every member of the research team to find for themselves how many downloads, how many users, how many reviews, etc, is limiting. We recommend you think early about the wider ecosystem which surrounds your application, identifying opportunities for how the data might be used not only by your research project, but also other key stakeholders. Tools such as Rich Pictures [36] may help here to illustrate all the ways in which different stakeholders might want to engage. Once you know how useful your data is, and the ways in which people will want to use it, implement tools and pipelines that provide access.

CONCLUSION

This paper has presented a rich description of the work involved in sustaining a successful technology in the wild. We set out to understand how we could encourage local service providers to take greater ownership of the user-generated data from FeedFinder to potentially impact on their service provision. We found tensions in achieving this, not least in negotiating 'what matters'.

Ultimately, what we want for FeedFinder is for it to translate into a 'public health data service' so that we can ensure this application continues to be made available to women for as long as necessary. We look to develop a service that is not commercially profitable but rather a sustainable service. The principles developed through our engagements with breastfeeding support services over the last 13 months are our intial steps in this process.

ACKNOWLEDGMENTS

We would like to thank the breastfeeding community for their continued support of FeedFinder. We also owe gratitude for the local services who have allowed us to work closely with them. David Oyeku who developed a prototype web-based interface for his masters thesis. This research was funded through the EPSRC Centre for Doctoral Training in Digital Civics (EP/L016176/1). Data supporting this publication is openly available under an 'Open Data Commons Open Database License'. Additional metadata are available at: http://dx.doi.org/10.17634/154300-40.

REFERENCES

1. Madeline Balaam, Rob Comber, Ed Jenkins, Selina Sutton, and Andy Garbett. 2015. FeedFinder : A Location-Mapping Mobile Application for

Breastfeeding Women. *Proceedings of the 33rd Annual ACM Conference on Human Factors in Computing Systems (CHI '15)*, 1709–1718. http://doi.org/http://dl.acm.org/citation.cfm?id=2702123.2702328

2. Ana. Brandusescu, Renee. E. Sieber, and Sylvie. Jochems. 2015. Confronting the hype: The use of crisis mapping for community development. *Convergence: The International Journal of Research into New Media Technologies*: 1–17. http://doi.org/10.1177/1354856515584320
3. V Braun and V Clarke. 2006. Using thematic analysis in psychology. *Qualitative research in psychology*. Retrieved January 4, 2016 from http://www.tandfonline.com/doi/abs/10.1191/1478088706qp063oa
4. Amy E Brown, Peter Raynor, David Benton, et al. 2010. Indices of Multiple Deprivation predict breastfeeding duration in England and Wales. *European journal of public health* 20, 2: 231–5. http://doi.org/10.1093/eurpub/ckp114
5. Wen-ying Sylvia Chou, Abby Prestin, Claire Lyons, and Kuang-yi Wen. 2013. Web 2.0 for health promotion: reviewing the current evidence. *American journal of public health* 103, 1: e9-18. http://doi.org/10.2105/AJPH.2012.301071
6. Crowdmap. 2016. Crowdmap. Retrieved from https://crowdmap.com/welcome
7. Christopher A. Le Dantec, Mariam Asad, Aditi Misra, and Kari E Watkins. 2015. Planning with Crowdsourced Data: Rhetoric and Representation in Transportation Planning. *Proceedings of the 18th ACM Conference on Computer Supported Cooperative Work & Social Computing - CSCW '15*: 1717–1727. http://doi.org/10.1145/2675133.2675212
8. Christopher A. Le Dantec and Carl DiSalvo. 2013. Infrastructuring and the formation of publics in participatory design. *Social Studies of Science*. Retrieved January 11, 2016 from http://sss.sagepub.com/content/43/2/241.short
9. Christopher Le Dantec. 2012. Participation and publics: supporting community engagement. *Proceedings of the 2012 ACM annual conference on Human Factors in Computing Systems - CHI '12*, ACM Press, 1351. http://doi.org/10.1145/2207676.2208593
10. Carl DiSalvo. 2009. Design and the Construction of Publics. *Design issues*. Retrieved January 8, 2016 from http://www.mitpressjournals.org/doi/pdf/10.1162/desi.2009.25.1.48
11. Carl DiSalvo, Jonathan Lukens, Thomas Lodato, Tom Jenkins, and Tanyoung Kim. 2014. Making public things: how HCI design can express matters of concern. *Proceedings of the SIGCHI Conference on Human Factors in Computing Systems (CHI '14)*, ACM Press, 2397–2406. http://doi.org/10.1145/2556288.2557359
12. Carl DiSalvo, Jeff Maki, and Nathan Martin. 2007. MapMover: A Case Study of Design-Oriented Research into Collective Expression and Constructed Publics. *Proceedings of the SIGCHI conference on Human factors in computing systems - CHI '07*, ACM Press, 1249. http://doi.org/10.1145/1240624.1240813
13. Pelle Ehn. 2008. Participation in design things. 92–101. Retrieved January 11, 2016 from http://dl.acm.org/citation.cfm?id=1795234.1795248
14. Nahed Eltantawy and Julie B. Wiest. 2011. The Arab Spring| Social Media in the Egyptian Revolution: Reconsidering Resource Mobilization Theory. *International Journal of Communication* 5, 0: 18.
15. Equality and Human Rights. 2010. Equality Act 2010. *The Equality Act*. Retrieved November 20, 2015 from http://www.calderstones.nhs.uk/media/files/Equality and Diversity/Equality Act 2010.pdf
16. FixMyStreet. FixMyStreet. Retrieved from https://www.fixmystreet.com/
17. Jeana H Frost and Michael P Massagli. 2008. Social uses of personal health information within PatientsLikeMe, an online patient community: what can happen when patients have access to one another's data. *Journal of medical Internet research* 10, 3: e15. http://doi.org/10.2196/jmir.1053
18. Andy Garbett, Rob Comber, Ed Jenkins, and Patrick Olivier. 2016. App Movement: A Platform for Community Commissioning of Mobile Applications. *Proceedings of the 2016 CHI Conference on Human Factors in Computing Systems - CHI '16*: 26–37.
19. William Gaver, Liliana Ovalle, Andy Boucher, et al. 2016. The Datacatcher: Batch Deployment and Documentation of 130 Location-Aware, Mobile Devices That Put Sociopolitically-Relevant Big Data in People's Hands: Polyphonic Interpretation at Scale. *Proceedings of the 2016 CHI Conference on Human Factors in Computing Systems - CHI '16*: 1597–1607. http://doi.org/10.1145/2858036.2858472
20. Lorna Gibson and VL Hanson. 2013. Digital motherhood: how does technology help new mothers? *Proceedings of the SIGCHI Conference on Human Factors in Computing Systems - CHI '13*, ACM Press., 313–322.

21. Andrea Grimes, Martin Bednar, Jay David Bolter, and Rebecca E. Grinter. 2008. EatWell: Sharing Nutrition-Related Memories in a Low-Income Community. *Proceedings of the ACM 2008 conference on Computer supported cooperative work - CSCW '08*, ACM Press, 87. http://doi.org/10.1145/1460563.1460579
22. Andrea Grimes, Brian M. Landry, and Rebecca E. Grinter. 2010. Characteristics of shared health reflections in a local community. *Proceedings of the 2010 ACM conference on Computer supported cooperative work - CSCW '10*, ACM Press, 435. http://doi.org/10.1145/1718918.1718992
23. HarassMap. Sexual Harassment in Greater Cairo: Effectiveness of Crowdsourced Data. Towards a Safer City. Retrieved June 29, 2015 from http://harassmap.org/en/wp-content/uploads/2013/03/Towards-A-Safer-City_full-report_EN-.pdf
24. HarassMap. Reconceptualizing Sexual Harassment in Egypt: A Longitudinal Assessment of el-Taharrush el-Ginsy in Arabic Online Forums and Anti-Sexual Harassment Activism. Retrieved June 29, 2015 from http://harassmap.org/en/wp-content/uploads/2013/03/Reconceptualizing-Sexual-Harassment-in-Egypt.pdf
25. Michael Hardey. 2008. Public health and Web 2.0. *The Journal of the Royal Society for the Promotion of Health* 128, 4: 181–189. http://doi.org/10.1177/1466424008092228
26. Mike Harding, Bran Knowles, Nigel Davies, and Mark Rouncefield. 2015. HCI, Civic Engagement & Trust. *Proceedings of the 33rd Annual ACM Conference on Human Factors in Computing Systems - CHI '15*: 2833–2842. http://doi.org/10.1145/2702123.2702255
27. Ian G Johnson, John Vines, Nick Taylor, Edward Jenkins, and Justin Marshall. 2016. Reflections on Deploying Distributed Consultation Technologies with Community Organisations. *Proceedings of the 2016 CHI Conference on Human Factors in Computing Systems*: 2945–2957. http://doi.org/10.1145/2858036.2858098
28. Rachel Keller. 2011. Using web 2.0 applications to increase local community wellbeing. *Proceedings of the 25th BCS Conference on Human-Computer Interaction (BCS-HCI '11)*: 485–490. Retrieved January 14, 2015 from http://dl.acm.org/citation.cfm?id=2305316.2305404
29. Muin J Khoury and John P A Ioannidis. 2014. Medicine. Big data meets public health. *Science (New York, N.Y.)* 346, 6213: 1054–5. http://doi.org/10.1126/science.aaa2709
30. Stephen F King and Paul Brown. 2007. Fix My Street or Else: Using the Internet to Voice Local Public Service Concerns. *Proceedings of the 1st international conference on Theory and Practice of Electronic Governance*: 72–80. http://doi.org/10.1145/1328057.1328076
31. Bruno Latour and Peter Weibel. 2005. *Making Things Public: Atmospheres of Democracy*. MIT Press. Retrieved July 20, 2015 from http://philpapers.org/rec/LATMTP
32. Michelina Mancuso, Xiaoquan Yao, Dan Otchere, et al. 2016. Proof of Concept Paper: Non-Traditional Data Sources for Public Health Surveillance. *Proceedings of the 6th International Conference on Digital Health Conference - DH '16*, ACM Press, 91–92. http://doi.org/10.1145/2896338.2896369
33. F McAndrew, J Thompson, and L Fellows. 2012. Infant feeding survey 2010. *Leeds: Health and ....* Retrieved August 18, 2015 from http://www.hscic.gov.uk/catalogue/PUB08694/Infant-Feeding-Survey-2010-Consolidated-Report.pdf
34. Donald McMillan, Arvid Engström, Airi Lampinen, and Barry Brown. 2016. Data and the City. *Proceedings of the 2016 CHI Conference on Human Factors in Computing Systems - CHI '16*, ACM Press, 2933–2944. http://doi.org/10.1145/2858036.2858434
35. P. K H Mo and Neil S. Coulson. 2010. Empowering processes in online support groups among people living with HIV/AIDS: A comparative analysis of "lurkers" and "posters." *Computers in Human Behavior* 26, 5: 1183–1193. http://doi.org/10.1016/j.chb.2010.03.028
36. Andrew Monk and Steve Howard. 1998. Methods & tools: the rich picture: a tool for reasoning about work context. *Interactions* 5, 2: 21–30. http://doi.org/10.1145/274430.274434
37. Gina Neff. 2013. Why Big Data Won't Cure Us. *Big data* 1, 3: 117–123. http://doi.org/10.1089/big.2013.0029
38. Newcastle City Council. 2016. *Newcastle City Council Budget 2016-2017*.
39. William Odom, Ron Wakkary, Youn-kyung Lim, Audrey Desjardins, Bart Hengeveld, and Richard Banks. 2016. From Research Prototype to Research Product. *Proceedings of the 2016 CHI Conference on Human Factors in Computing Systems - CHI '16*: 2549–2561. http://doi.org/10.1145/2858036.2858447
40. Ory Okolloh. 2009. Ushahidi, or "testimony": Web 2.0 tools for crowdsourcing crisis information. *Participatory Learning and Action* 59, January: 65–70.

41. Andrea G. Parker and Rebecca E. Grinter. 2014. Collectivistic health promotion tools: Accounting for the relationship between culture, food and nutrition. *International Journal of Human-Computer Studies* 72, 2: 185–206. http://doi.org/10.1016/j.ijhcs.2013.08.008

42. Andrea Parker, Vasudhara Kantroo, Hee Rin Lee, Miguel Osornio, Mansi Sharma, and Rebecca Grinter. 2012. Health promotion as activism. *Proceedings of the 2012 ACM annual conference on Human Factors in Computing Systems - CHI '12*, ACM Press, 99. http://doi.org/10.1145/2207676.2207692

43. Patient Opinion. 2015. Patient Opinion. Retrieved from https://www.patientopinion.org.uk/

44. PatientsLikeMe. Live better, together! | PatientsLikeMe. Retrieved July 23, 2015 from https://www.patientslikeme.com/

45. Tim Regan, David Sweeney, John Helmes, Vasillis Vlachokyriakos, Siân Lindley, and Alex Taylor. 2015. Designing Engaging Data in Communities. *Proceedings of the 33rd Annual ACM Conference Extended Abstracts on Human Factors in Computing Systems - CHI EA '15*, ACM Press, 271–274. http://doi.org/10.1145/2702613.2725432

46. NC Rollins, N Bhandari, and N Hajeebhoy. 2016. Why invest, and what it will take to improve breastfeeding practices? *The Lancet*. Retrieved February 5, 2016 from http://www.sciencedirect.com/science/article/pii/S0140673615010442

47. Jesper Simonsen and Toni Robertson. 2013. *International Handbook of Participatory Design*. Routledge.

48. Emma Simpson, Andrew Garbett, Rob Comber, and Madeline Balaam. 2016. Factors important for women who breastfeed in public: a content analysis of review data from FeedFinder. *BMJ open* 6, 10: e011762. http://doi.org/10.1136/bmjopen-2016-011762

49. Robert Steele and Dan Dumbrell. 2012. Putting the public into public health information dissemination. *Proceedings of the Seventeenth Australasian Document Computing Symposium on - ADCS '12*, ACM Press, 135–138. http://doi.org/10.1145/2407085.2407104

50. Alex S. Taylor, Siân Lindley, Tim Regan, et al. 2015. Data-in-Place: Thinking through the Relations Between Data and Community. *Proceedings of the 33rd Annual ACM Conference on Human Factors in Computing Systems - CHI '15*, ACM Press, 2863–2872. http://doi.org/10.1145/2702123.2702558

51. Nick Taylor, Keith Cheverst, Peter Wright, and Patrick Olivier. 2013. Leaving the wild: lessons from community technology handovers. *Proceedings of the SIGCHI Conference on Human Factors in Computing Systems - CHI '13*, ACM Press, 1549–1558.

52. Nick Taylor, Justin Marshall, and A Blum-Ross. 2012. Viewpoint: empowering communities with situated voting devices. *Proceedings of the SIGCHI Conference on Human Factors in Computing Systems - CHI '12*: 1361–1370. http://doi.org/10.1145/2207676.2208594

53. Gill Thomson, Katherine Esbich-Burton, and Renee Flacking. 2014. Shame if you do, Shame if you don't: Women's experiences of infant feeding. *Maternal And Child Nutrition*. Retrieved August 18, 2015 from http://clok.uclan.ac.uk/12089/3/12089_Thompson.pdf

54. TripAdvisor. 2017. TripAdvisor. Retrieved from https://www.tripadvisor.co.uk/

55. C F van Uden-Kraan, C H Drossaert, E Taal, B R Shaw, E R Seydel, and M A van de Laar. 2008. Empowering processes and outcomes of participation in online support groups for patients with breast cancer, arthritis, or fibromyalgia. *Qualitative Health Research* 18, 3: 405–417. http://doi.org/18/3/405 [pii]\r10.1177/1049732307313429

56. UNICEF. Baby Friendly Initiative. Retrieved from http://www.unicef.org.uk/babyfriendly/

57. Vasilis Vlachokyriakos, Rob Comber, Karim Ladha, et al. 2014. PosterVote. *Proceedings of the 2014 conference on Designing interactive systems - DIS '14*, ACM Press, 795–804. http://doi.org/10.1145/2598510.2598523

58. Vasilis Vlachokyriakos, Clara Crivellaro, Christopher A. Le Dantec, Eric Gordon, Pete Wright, and Ol. 2016. Digital Civics : Citizen Empowerment. *CHI Extended Abstracts on Human Factors in Computing Systems*: 1096–1099.

59. Yelp. 2017. YELP. Retrieved from https://www.yelp.co.uk

60. Matthew Zook, Mark Graham, Taylor Shelton, and Sean Gorman. 2010. Volunteered geographic information and crowdsourcing disaster relief: a case study of the Haitian earthquake. *World Medical & Health Policy* 2: 7–33. http://doi.org/10.2202/1948-4682.1069

Understanding Volunteer AT Fabricators: Opportunities and Challenges in DIY-AT for Others in e-NABLE

Jeremiah Parry-Hill[1] jlpetc@rit.edu
Patrick C. Shih[2] patshih@indiana.edu
Jennifer Mankoff[3] jmankoff@cs.cmu.edu
Daniel Ashbrook[1] daniel.ashbrook@rit.edu

[1]Golisano College of Computing and Information Sciences Rochester Institute of Technology
[2]School of Informatics and Computing Indiana University Bloomington
[3]HCI Institute Carnegie Mellon University

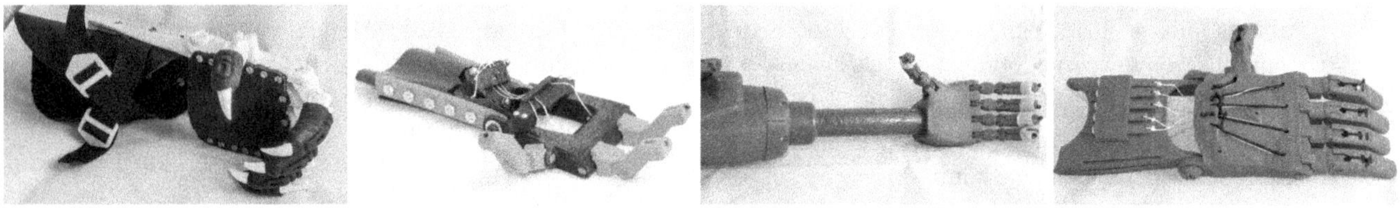

Figure 1. A variety of 3D-printed upper-limb assistive technology devices designed and produced by volunteers in the e-NABLE community. Photos were taken by the fourth author in the e-NABLE lab on RIT's campus.

ABSTRACT

We present the results of a study of e-NABLE, a distributed, collaborative volunteer effort to design and fabricate upper-limb assistive technology devices for limb-different users. Informed by interviews with 14 stakeholders in e-NABLE, including volunteers and clinicians, we discuss differences and synergies among each group with respect to motivations, skills, and perceptions of risks inherent in the project. We found that both groups are motivated to be involved in e-NABLE by the ability to use their skills to help others, and that their skill sets are complementary, but that their different perceptions of risk may result in uneven outcomes or missed expectations for end users. We offer four opportunities for design and technology to enhance the stakeholders' abilities to work together.

ACM Classification Keywords

H.5.3. Group and Organization Interfaces: Computer-supported cooperative work; K.4.2. Computers and society: Social issues—Assistive technologies for persons with disabilities.

Author Keywords

Accessibility; Assistive Technology; DIY; Limb Difference; Prosthetics; 3D Printing; Digital Fabrication; Making

INTRODUCTION

Do-It-Yourself Assistive Technology (DIY-AT) is an emerging phenomenon based on a vision of easily available, inexpensive customized assistive technology [19]. In addition to many of the examples of DIY-AT in the literature [7,16,18], DIY-AT as a form of volunteering has recently appeared: volunteer-based production of assistive devices on behalf of distant strangers. We term this activity "DIY-AT for Others." One prominent example of this activity is the e-NABLE community, the largest extant volunteer community focused on fabricating upper-limb assistive technology. e-NABLE is a loosely knit global community of volunteers—comprising, among others, AT designers, fabricators, coordinators, and recipients—that represents a coordinated effort to make 3D-printed upper limb AT available for free to those in need.

While compelling in principle, the practical realities of the vision of DIY-AT for Others have not been explored in depth, leaving many open and important questions. What are the optimal motivations for sustaining volunteer participation? What are the barriers to volunteer success? What do recipients want from DIY-AT produced from them, what factors increase utility and reduce abandonment? And finally, what are the clinical implications of volunteer-produced AT, and how can volunteers best leverage clinical expertise to increase safety and utility and reduce risk?

We present a study of the e-NABLE community that attempts to answer these questions through interviews with two groups of stakeholders: the fabricators who 3D print, assemble, and deliver the AT, and outside clinicians, such as prosthetists, who have expert knowledge, but often do not participate directly in e-NABLE activities. Our investigation revealed a complex, shifting landscape of motives and ideals that has not been heretofore described. Our findings center on describing the gaps between the stakeholders, adding evidence to prior research on prosthetic device users [2] and the limitations to collaboration between clinicians and makers [15].

CHI 2017, May 06 - 11, 2017, Denver, CO, USA

ISBN 978-1-4503-4655-9/17/05...$15.00

DOI: http://dx.doi.org/10.1145/3025453.3026045

As a social phenomenon, e-NABLE is surprisingly difficult to describe succinctly. It blends a personal fabrication community of practice, a support community for limb difference, a repository of resources for STEM educators, and more. The website of the Enable Community Foundation[7], an organizing body that performs fundraising and outreach activities, describes e-NABLE as "an international network of passionate volunteers using 3D printing technology and STEM education to develop and deploy hyper-affordable prosthetic devices to children and other underserved populations around the world in a safe, sustainable manner." Figure 1 illustrates some examples of the wide variety of upper-limb assistive technology designed and fabricated by e-NABLE volunteers.

The terminology we use in this paper is in keeping with that of the e-NABLE community: we use the term "limb difference" to refer to any reduction in the size of a limb, whether due to trauma, medical amputation or a congenital condition, and "device" or "assistive device" rather than "prosthesis" to refer to the products of the fabrication activities we studied.

In the next section, we briefly introduce e-NABLE in comparison to other volunteer groups providing AT, and then step up a level to explore relevant literature on motivations for volunteerism, the maker movement, and DIY assistive technology production. The section following introduces e-NABLE and the devices it produces. Next, we present our study's goal—answering questions about stakeholder roles, motivations, and difficulties that stakeholders face—along with our interview and analysis methods. Our findings section introduces the three main categories of interviewees—fabricators, designers, and clinicians—and highlights their complementary concerns and needs. Finally, we discuss opportunities for design around topics such as case management, multi-stakeholder co-design, and followup.

BACKGROUND

e-NABLE is an instance of volunteerism, specifically volunteer fabrication. Many volunteer organizations—both partially and entirely online—are dedicated to fabricating assistive devices for people with disabilities (*DIY-AT for Others*). Groups such as the US-based Adaptive Design Association[1] and the UK-based REMAP[2] coordinate volunteers who lend their skills to make assistive technology for people in need on a case-by-case basis. The ramps.org website[3] maintains a list of programs—many volunteer-based—which build free wheelchair ramps for those in need.

More specific to upper-limb difference, similar organizations to e-NABLE include The Victoria Hand Project[4], which focuses on creating sustainable systems to fabricate upper-limb devices in the developing world, and the Helping Hands Foundation[5], a group that provides support and information to families of children with affected upper limbs.

[1] http://www.adaptivedesign.org

[2] http://www.remap.org.uk/volunteering/making-equipment-for-people-with-disabilities

[3] http://www.ramps.org/free-ramps.htm

[4] http://victoriahandproject.com

[5] http://helpinghandsgroup.org

e-NABLE stands out from among these groups because of its exponential growth, the attention it has received in the media, and its relative lack of top down management and clinical expertise. It is a mostly bottom-up volunteer fabrication community in which participants use 3D printing to create affordable prosthetic devices for children and under-served populations around the world. Below, we highlight some open questions about how motivations for volunteerism and making play out in the case of DIY-AT for Others, as well as the definition and meaning of useful assistive technology.

Varied Drives for Volunteerism

Volunteer communities depend on a steady supply of new volunteers, as well as extended participation by seasoned volunteers. For both, it is important to understand what motivates volunteers to participate over time. Motivation to volunteer may be both *collective* (driven by a sense of obligation to the whole group) and *reflective* (driven by a desire for self-realization by fulfilling personal goals) [21]. These motivations are mutually compatible, and vary in their importance for each volunteer. Individual differences in expertise, empathy, reciprocity, obligation, and impact shape both willingness to volunteer and the style of volunteering in different ways for different volunteers [34].

One special category of volunteerism takes place online [10], most prominently in the context of free and open source software (FOSS) development [12, 25, 35]. Similar to other types of volunteering, volunteerism in FOSS projects may be sustained by intrinsic factors such as personal learning [36], to implement some personally desired functionality [31], or reasons such as fun, enjoyment, and the feeling of making a positive contribution [31].

In the case of DIY-AT, studies to date have focused on recipients (e.g., [2]), individuals creating DIY-AT for immediate family members [16], and maker communities encompassing those creating AT for their own use, as a personal challenge, for research purposes, and for universal purposes other than disability [6]. Little is known about the motivations driving volunteers to design and fabricate for others, as is the case for e-NABLE.

Motivations for and Barriers to Making

In contrast to online communities focused on knowledge capture [22], the sharing of code [11], or programming knowledge [26], volunteers creating assistive technology are making a physical artifact. Although creating artifacts by hand is a process as old as human history [5], we are in the midst of what has been called "the new industrial revolution" [1], fueled by inexpensive and easily available technologies such as 3D printers. This "maker" revolution has democratized the act and means of production [33], and is buttressed by a shift in DIY culture from the individual workshop to online web communities [29]. For example, Thingiverse[6] is an online community of amateur makers focused on sharing digital designs for physical objects. Online DIY communities tend to share an ethos of openness and knowledge sharing, where participation is motivated by creative expression and skill acquisition [23].

[6] http://thingiverse.com

While such online communities convey many benefits to makers, the dual physical/virtual nature of DIY practice poses a challenge: sharing a virtual object is much easier than sharing a physical one, but *instantiating* the virtual object as a physical one requires access to technology, material, and skills. This characteristic has given rise to physical makerspaces or hackerspaces [24]: offline spaces where enthusiasts come together to share tools, ideas, and techniques around constructing physical artifacts. In many cases, however, extra support is required for nascent makers. For example, in a study of a repair clinic in California, Rosner and Ames found that even within systems that attempt to empower non-expert users to make functional objects, skilled experts often must be involved [30]. Hudson et al. found that casual makers are deeply dependent on print center operators throughout the process—from bootstrapping their 3D printing workflow, to seeking help and troubleshooting, to verifying their outputs [17].

The creation of DIY-AT—often undertaken via 3D printing—is a small but important component of what occurs in DIY maker communities. DIY makers face difficulties in sustaining their effort due to a lack of basis for assessing the lasting impact of their creations [6], an especially troubling issue in a field where about one in three users abandon the AT they are given [27]. In contrast, non-technical caregivers (e.g., parents providing DIY-AT to children) may question whether they have the ability to produce AT that has a positive impact. These caregivers are concerned about their ability to fabricate assistive technologies, for reasons including social and technical barriers, self-confidence in their own practical ability, hesitation to invest time without the guarantee of a useful outcome, concerns regarding the aesthetics of the devices, and issues related to robustness and safety [16]. Open questions for DIY-AT include whether e-NABLE volunteers have similar motivations and skills to other makers, what barriers they face, and how a community whose stated purpose is AT production navigates the question of AT utility.

The Utility and Safety of DIY Assistive Technology

Abandonment describes the phenomenon of a user ceasing to use an AT device, and is a serious problem for assistive technologies in general [27] and for upper limb prosthetics in particular [4, 28]. Reasons for abandonment may include unattractive appearance of a device, comfort—including device fit and weight—and lack of functional gain, including feeling more functional without a device. DIY assistive technology has advantages in terms of aesthetics, specificity to the task at hand, and customizability. Such benefits can allow fabricated AT to meet new needs, such as addressing social aspects of accessibility including self-expression and identity formation [2, 32].

An advantage particular to 3D-printed assistive technology is its lightweight nature, in terms of both cost and heft, both of which are positively associated with successful outcomes [4, 28]. While 3D-printed devices such as those produced by e-NABLE may not facilitate as wide a range of tasks and activities as conventional prosthetics, they can support psychosocial development, whether that means "standing out" with a unique appendage, or "fitting in" with an anthropomorphic hand [8]. Additionally, DIY-AT for Others has the potential to support a participatory design process, allowing the recipient to help author solutions that meet their needs across both aesthetic and task specific settings (e.g., [13, 20].

One drawback to DIY-AT, however, is that it lacks oversight, a concern that is particularly visible in the context of large and public communities such as e-NABLE. In a recent summit report authored by e-NABLE volunteers, clinicians, and assistive technology researchers, many specific concerns about safety and practicality of 3D-printed substitutes for traditional upper limb prosthetics were raised [15]. However, this report leaves open questions about how e-NABLE volunteers and clinicians navigate these tensions and what the broader e-NABLE community thinks about them.

THE E-NABLE COMMUNITY

e-NABLE is a community of volunteers dedicated to designing, customizing, printing, and delivering 3D-printed assistive technology to those with upper-limb differences. Organized via two web sites (the Enable Community Foundation website[7] and e-NABLE community website[8]), a private Google+ community, a separate web forum, and various other forms of social media, e-NABLE's members exchange open hardware source files, advice, and support around this activity. The main locus of activity is the Google+ community, with over 9,000 members at the time of this writing.

e-NABLE's web sites characterize its mission as, "To enable any child or adult to receive a free or very low cost experimental upper limb prosthetic,"[7] and as "a global network of volunteers who are using their 3D printers, design skills, and personal time to create free 3D-printed prosthetic hands for those in need—with the goal of providing them to underserved populations around the world."[8]

How e-NABLE is Organized

e-NABLE's volunteers can choose among a wide set of roles. As itemized on the volunteer intake form, these include: fabricating devices, developing devices, blogging, writing documentation, being a regional "matcher" (connecting device fabricators to device recipients), producing media (primarily video and photographs), participating in the organizational team, training others, and translating documents. The volunteer intake form also identifies external roles: commercial sponsors, non-commercial partners, and teachers.

In practice, most volunteers begin as fabricators, the role that is also most prominent on the website, on social media, and in the Google+ community. The fabricator role exists because of the need for the organization to instantiate the software-based AT designs as physical objects that can be distributed to recipients. Fabricators print and assemble e-NABLE devices, which are typically mailed into a distribution center. They may optionally—depending on skill and interest—also interact with recipients, in which case they often personalize (decorate) or customize (change size or even slightly modify) the device and deliver it personally—though not usually *in* person—to the

[7] `http://enablecommunityfoundation.org`

[8] `http://enablingthefuture.org`

recipient. To be officially matched with a recipient, fabricators must first pass a test, producing a high quality hand that is vetted by volunteers.

The developer role differs from that of e-NABLE designer/developer, although many participants engage in multiple activities. While the role of developer might be seen as analogous to that of a developer in a FOSS community, in e-NABLE's this role comprises more of an engineering than a programming activity. Developers collaborate on adapting or creating new functionality, evaluating and improving the printability of devices, and devising ways to work better with the many and various 3D model files involved in different projects.

Another common role is 'teacher,' who works with students to fabricate and assemble devices. e-NABLE has an active education initiative, including funding to produce curricular material that is used in scout groups and schools.

It is unclear how often volunteers take on the other roles mentioned on the intake form, which are typically represented in the community by a small number of very dedicated volunteers. Thus, we will describe only the most relevant of these to our study—the "medical professional," meaning prosthetists, orthotists, and physical and occupational therapists. The exact tasks associated with this role are not specified on the community websites. As we discovered in our interviews, medical professionals are not directly involved in fabrication or design, in part due to concerns about incurring legal liability by "treating" recipients.

e-NABLE Devices

There is no single "e-NABLE device;" rather, the e-NABLE community uses a constantly evolving array of upper-limb assistive devices (e.g., Figure 1). Most of these devices share the mechanical property of providing basic grasp assistance and the aesthetic property of appearing—at least to a certain extent—like a human hand. Some advantages of e-NABLE devices over traditional prostheses include personalized aesthetics and lighter weight, both of which are positively associated with successful outcomes [4, 28]. Disadvantages include limited functionality and often the lack of a professionally fit socket (the part of the device that comes into direct contact with the user's body). As a result, e-NABLE's preference is to refer to the hands as *devices* rather than *prostheses*.

The popular perception of an e-NABLE device is that of a prosthesis that changes the recipient's life by virtue of its functionality:

> ...another child who now has an option that she would have never had before.[9]

> ...and can do things that she couldn't do before, like peel potatoes, pick up objects, and catch a ball.[10]

[9] http://enablingthefuture.org/2015/11/24/e-nabling-aruba-%E2%80%A2-a-3d-printed-hand-for-zizi/

[10] http://magazines.scholastic.com/kids-press/news/2016/01/A-Helping-3-D-Hand

Although 3D printing is the primary method of producing devices, many e-NABLE designs include a significant portion of non-printed parts. These can include elastic bands, specialized screws, hook-and-loop fasteners, leather, foam padding, and gel fingertips. Not all of these components are available in all parts of the world.

Because the design files are openly available in various venues, it is difficult for e-NABLE to track the number of devices that have been fabricated for recipients. One community member (V03) estimated at least 800 direct device deliveries to recipients with upper-limb difference had taken place over e-NABLE's lifetime.

STUDY

We conducted a study of e-NABLE volunteers over a period of twenty-two months. The goal of our study was to answer questions about the roles of different stakeholders in the community with respect to motivation for and barriers to participation.

At the inception of the study, the e-NABLE Google+ community had approximately 3,000 registered members, which grew to approximately 9,000 over the duration of our study. To better understand the community, we joined the Google+ community, followed members' posts, and observed e-NABLE's open-invitation video conferencing meetings (including a general "town hall"' meeting, and other open-invitation meetings of research and development groups). We also read through public news articles published about e-NABLE. One of the authors is an active e-NABLE volunteer, and multiple authors have participated in e-NABLE events. Although these forms of participation were motivated by goals separate from this paper, it has helped us to build rapport with a variety of e-NABLE's members including multiple types of stakeholders. Because the e-NABLE Google+ community is not public (requiring a sign-up to access), we do not directly quote from the community, only interviewees and news articles.

Method

Based on our correspondence with the local and online e-NABLE community, we designed a survey to give us a baseline understanding of the skills and motivations of participants in the community and to identify participants for interviews. The survey included questions about self-identified role(s) in e-NABLE, fabrication successes, background and experience with 3D printing, general challenges as an e-NABLE community member, perceived benefits of participation, and demographic information such as time since joining e-NABLE, occupation and age.

In February 2015, we posted an invitation in the Google+ community to complete the online survey, open to all e-NABLE community members. At the time of the invitation, the Google+ community had about 4,000 registered members. We received 63 responses to the preliminary survey. Thirty-nine respondents self-identified as current or aspiring fabricators of assistive devices for e-NABLE.

We used the findings from the survey, along with our review of the literature and study of the online community, to develop a semi-structured interview protocol that could provide deeper insight into the experiences of e-NABLE community members. The interviews began by establishing common ground through questions about how members and volunteers were introduced to the community. We then explored motivations for participation, interactions with various stakeholders, successes and barriers encountered during fabrication, impressions of use and maintenance of a device, and the personal benefits of participating in e-NABLE.

We conducted fourteen interviews. Six interviewees were survey respondents (V01, V02, V05, V07, C02, and C03 in Table 1); the rest were recruited via snowball sampling and direct communication. Our aim was to recruit a representative sample of e-NABLE stakeholders including fabricators, designers and medical professionals (which we refer to as "clinicians"). Our final sample includes a variety of roles within these categories, as highlighted in Table 1. Although our data includes a range of roles and perspectives, an important limitation of our study is a lack of data about recipients and how they use e-NABLE hands: e-NABLE has not released any information on this topic, and recipients are not typically members of the e-NABLE community, making access difficult. While Bennett et al. interviewed five adult e-NABLE recipients [2], and our participants include two volunteers who also use e-NABLE devices, the majority of e-NABLE recipients are minors who are not included in our, or any other public, data.

Nine of the interview sessions took place face-to-face, as permitted by geographic proximity to the researchers. We conducted the remaining five interviews via web conferencing or by telephone. We recorded a total of 14 hours, 10 minutes of interview sessions over the course of the study. The average length of an interview session was 61 minutes. We audio-recorded all of the interviews and transcribed the recordings for analysis.

Data Analysis

We performed analysis continuously throughout the data collection process, using iterative open coding [9]. We began with descriptive coding for each observation, and as our data accumulated, the focus of our analysis continued to evolve. We revised, merged, and broke down codes as the analysis evolved and more data were collected. We also used findings from the analysis to revise the topic of focus in subsequent interviews. In the end, we collated the products of our analysis in the form of codes and notes from the survey, interview, and online community studies. We analyzed this aggregated data using an affinity diagram [3], to find emerging themes, similarities, and differences. During the affinity diagramming process, we grouped a total of 587 quotes into 83 clusters spanning across 11 major intermediate themes. We iteratively refined these intermediate themes into the themes represented in the findings of this paper. Table 1 summarizes the demographics of our participants.

FINDINGS

The findings reported in this section primarily focus on two groups of stakeholders and the overlaps and disconnects between them. The first is *volunteers*: e-NABLE fabricators and designers, as well as other prominent community members involved in facilitating device production. The second is *clinicians*: medical professionals associated with e-NABLE. We describe each group's motivations for participating in e-NABLE, the skills they exercise, the barriers they encounter to participating, and their perceptions of the risks inherent in the project.

ID	*Gender*	*Age*	*Occupation*	*Role*
V01	F	25	Plastics engineer	Community member
V02	M	71	Ergonomics engineer	Designer, Fabricator
V03	M	62	Researcher	Community member
V04	F	21	Student (engineering)	Designer, Fabricator
V05	F	22	Student (engineering)	Designer, Fabricator
V06	F	42	Student (neurotech.)	Fabricator
V07	M	65	Semi-retired IT	Fabricator
V08	M	34	3D print shop tech.	Fabricator
V09	M	40	CAD technician	Fabricator
V10	M	20	Student (undeclared)	Fabricator
V11	F	43	Logistics coordinator	Community member
C01	M	33	Occupational therapist	Clinician
C02	F	24	Prosthetics student	Clinician in training
C03	F	30	Prosthetist	Clinician

Table 1. Interview participants; a prefix of V indicates "Volunteer" and C indicates "Clinician."

Volunteers

Fabricators told us that they participate because they feel that they are able to pursue challenging, meaningful work that impacts someone directly. Although most e-NABLE volunteers do not have personal experience with limb difference, many e-NABLE volunteers are motivated by a one-to-one, personal connection with those they are serving. The ultimate reward for an e-NABLE volunteer's hard work is exhibited in popular videos and press items showing the "unboxing" of hands and the thrilled reactions of the recipients[11]:

> We were able to give [an e-NABLE device] to a little girl, and [the volunteer fabricator] was there to give it to her ... Seeing things like that, and the smile on the faces, it's worth a million dollars. (V11)

In interviews, several volunteers reported "seeing smiling faces" as the ultimate aim of participating in e-NABLE. It is this personal connection of giving a gift that forms one of the cornerstones of volunteering for our interviewees, in line with Hustinx and Lammertyn's reflexive volunteer model [21]

Another reflexive motivation is the satisfaction of technical accomplishment. Similar to Shah's hobbyist-style open-source software developers [31], many e-NABLE volunteers relish the opportunity to develop their technical skills, especially around 3D modeling and printing, and to solve challenging technical problems:

> For me, personally, there's some kind of a self-esteem satisfaction related to solving a problem that nobody's ever solved before, creating something that nobody's ever seen before. The more difficult it is to make something work, the more excited I get, because the more likely it is that other people have given up before they solved all

[11] e.g., `https://youtu.be/I3cf49c_WjE`

> the problems. And probably it's never been done before. (V02)

Whether pursuing the distinction of solving novel puzzles, or simply attempting to print and assemble multi-part devices, a common thread of technical self-challenge runs through volunteers' motivations to participate in this form of volunteering. The Google+ forums are full of posts about new technological advances or requests for 3D printing or modeling advice.

One of the most common areas of technical knowledge needed amongst e-NABLE volunteers is the ability to manipulate, before printing, the digital designs for the AT devices, both from a fitting standpoint—"*Every individual recipient is different, and everything needs to be adjusted for them.*" (V09)—and for aesthetic customization. To properly adjust the size of the community-provided designs to fit the recipient, for example, a fabricator must clear a number of technical hurdles related to file formats and design software: there is no single standard for 3D CAD file formats or design software used in e-NABLE.

Aside from manipulating 3D files for sizing, many volunteers embrace the challenge of customization, "theming out" (V08) the hands by making aesthetic customizations (e.g., Figure 1):

> I'm actually building [the recipient's] new hand right now ... he loves playing the army games and Call of Duty, so I'm sending him an army-themed, you know, green and brown. (V08)

Although obtaining colored printer filament imposes an unanticipated additional cost for some volunteers, fabricators accepted this as a necessary expense of providing highly personalized devices with a high chance of adoption.

Once files are prepared for printing, volunteers must negotiate the "hocus pocus" (V02) necessary to operate a 3D printer for high-quality results, and then engage in assembling the parts to make a complete, working device:

> It's only $45 worth of materials, to make a hand, but, it's like, you know, 24 hours of babysitting a printer that may fail during that time, and you've got to spend another few hours to assemble it. (V02)

This emphasis on engineering is built into the structure of e-NABLE itself, both culturally and procedurally: a prospective volunteer's first contact may be with one of the e-NABLE websites, which prominently feature links to "Build a Hand." One of the first steps to be undertaken before being matched with a potential recipient is fabricating a test hand to prove technical skill.

As technical skills are emphasized in the implicit value system of e-NABLE, other factors are necessarily less emphasized. As an endeavor that is primarily about engineering, volunteers lack knowledge about assistive technology in general, participatory design, and the medical background necessary to enact true clinical care. Despite these gaps, in designing, customizing, printing, and delivering the AT, e-NABLE volunteers *are* working with recipients, creating custom assistive devices, and aware of possible safety issues.

For example, V01 describes a device customized not only for aesthetic but also practical purposes:

> They wanted to put a MIG [welder] wire feeder [into an e-NABLE arm], so it would feed the wire through the hand, so it would come out the fingertip. (V01)

The example above epitomizes an orientation toward problem solving that sets amateur fabricators apart from clinicians, who have a primary orientation toward risk management. The exercise of problem solving and creativity are areas where e-NABLE volunteers shine: although sometimes stymied by technical issues—file formats, modeling challenges, and 3D printing—they are able to exercise their skills to contribute to the community.

At the same time, volunteers we spoke with are aware that they lack the knowledge possessed by prosthetists and other clinicians:

> I do [have safety concerns], especially because I don't have any training in medicine or devices like that. I'm worried about hyperextension and pinch points, and pressure points. (V04)

Another volunteer described the expectation for recipients to pursue clinical care on their own:

> It's in the paperwork, in the pamphlets that the recipients' families have to sign. That we highly recommend getting involved with an occupational therapist as soon as possible. ... anything different that can add challenges to life, you know, seeing an occupational therapist is very important. So we stress that as important. (V08)

In summary, e-NABLE volunteers are committed to doing social good through the exercise of engineering expertise. While they understand that the involvement of clinical professionals is important, and worry about possible injury to recipients, the acquisition and exercise of technical skills is often the main focus of their activities.

Clinicians

Given their engagement with e-NABLE—which, as an organization is only just beginning to be visible in mainstream clinical venues—the clinicians we interviewed may not be representative of all professional prosthetic device experts. However, the three clinicians we spoke with shared a common, guarded opinion of e-NABLE. They do not represent converts to the movement; if anything, they are an "advance guard," both assessing e-NABLE as a potential threat to their profession while lending their insights in an abstract, informative fashion, to indirectly influence positive patient outcomes.

While volunteers are motivated by the acquisition and exercise of technical skill in an altruistic setting, clinicians are motivated by patient care in their everyday practice. Helping patients manage their greatest perceived loss is a basic tenet of the profession. Because of these differences, clinicians expressed the desire to add their clinical knowledge to help e-NABLE volunteers think beyond just the engineering of devices. This desire manifested in interviews as attempts at end user advocacy:

> Sometimes you have to remind engineers that the end product is for a person. You're not just making a cool thing! What [does the recipient] want it to do? (C02)

Clinicians also reported lending their expertise to e-NABLE by critiquing works-in-progress, rather than becoming involved directly in cases:

> If you want to be safe, you have to look at some of these contraindications, and potential hazards and dangers. ... So that's kind of where I'm at right now, is to kind of be the crybaby. (C01)

Whereas e-NABLE volunteers take pleasure in enacting aesthetically themed devices for children, such as "superhero hands," clinicians understand that aesthetic customization is nuanced, is personal, and that recipients of all ages benefit from expert counseling around aesthetic considerations:

> You can talk about "How important is how it looks to you?" And that has to come with a disclaimer: It's okay to say that [aesthetics are] important. It's a big deal. And sometimes that takes convincing, because people don't want to sound like they're vain. (C03)

Clinical interactions with a patient, including ongoing needs assessment, are necessarily more complex than simply dispensing a prosthesis. C02 discusses this need in the context of everyday clinical practice:

> ...every person needs a different one. [For example,] you don't just give [elderly] people the same foot. Some older people like to walk, or they have hills they need to go up, and you actually need pretty good ankles for that. While other people, you might just give them a regular leg because they feel more comfortable. (C02)

In short, whereas e-NABLE volunteers' expertise is engineering-focused, clinicians are trained medical practitioners. In their professional capacities, their motivation is to ensure long-term successful outcomes and safety for their patients. Technical skills are a subset of the range of skills clinicians bring to bear on patient care, alongside patient management. In addition, clinicians' technical skills are more specialized than those of e-NABLE volunteers. One area of deep expertise is fabricating the socket that attaches the prosthesis to the residual limb:

> The prosthetist, knowing anatomy, they're going to pad in all the right places. They know to particularly protect those [bony landmarks]: lateral condyles, medial condyles, the styloid processes on the wrists, if they have a wrist. (C01)

Clinicians know that the idea of a device "working" for a patient goes beyond pure functionality. Device comfort, safety, and relevance to the patient's needs, as proven by use, are primary concerns for the clinician. An uncomfortable experience may lead to potential injuries or device abandonment.

Clinicians also have a variety of nontechnical skills focused on continuing care. They reported that observing patient satisfaction at the moment of device provisioning is nearly guaranteed; true measures of satisfaction must be made over time. To ensure that patients are truly obtaining positive results with their device, clinicians emphasized the importance of followup visits:

> Things are going to change. People are going to encounter things they didn't expect. It's going to be a rare patient that walks out of the office and is wonderfully happy and never comes back for anything and they're still using it all that time. So the only way to make it successful is to have that kind of follow-up. (C03)

Since e-NABLE volunteers do not always possess medical knowledge of how to properly fit a device based on a patient's anatomy or have the ability to provide continuing care after device delivery, clinicians worried that an unsuccessful experience with an e-NABLE device might dissuade recipients from trying other prosthetic devices in the future (including traditional devices):

> If the experience was bad for whatever reason, they don't come back. They don't necessarily see another prosthetist. It's actually more common for them not to use the prosthesis and to have formed this idea that prostheses aren't for them. (C03)

C01 perceived the media stories about e-NABLE device deliveries as playing into the risk of expectation mismatch leading to abandonment:

> If people have a bad experience with an assistive technology device, especially one that's being built up by the media as being miraculous, but then they get the device and something goes wrong, they're disappointed. Then they might not be as likely to try other AT devices in the future. (C01)

For this reason, clinicians tend to be more skeptical of the trial-and-error approach that is often embraced by technologists, and they are less flexible and willing to experiment than the typical e-NABLE volunteer. C03 framed a clinician's aversion to brainstorming as a consequence of an orientation toward risk management:

> So, [if engineers] try to brainstorm something [with us], or you know, proof of concept, discuss things, all of the prosthetists are probably going to respond as if you're going to try to put it on a patient tomorrow. (C03)

Some clinicians hope to contribute to e-NABLE by providing a guideline to educate volunteers on the various device types and when to best introduce them, depending on the individual conditions of the patients:

> What I want to do with the community, eventually, is to set up those standardized tests of hand designs to see how well they work or do not work. (C02)

In summary, as medical professionals, clinicians are focused on patient well-being as their primary concern. Technical skills are a subset of the talents they bring to bear on helping patients address their greatest perceived loss; other professional competencies include expectation management and followup care. The clinicians we interviewed involved themselves in e-NABLE in the hopes of using their knowledge to steer the project toward the areas of most productive positive impact.

Self-fabrication

Two of the e-NABLE volunteers in our interviews are also limb-different e-NABLE device users who actively participate in the device design process, and fabricated their own devices. To maintain their anonymity, we do not attribute their quotes. Because they are not typical e-NABLE device recipients—as adults and highly skilled volunteers—we use their comments as a starting point to try to understand the factors influencing the meanings that recipients attach to e-NABLE and its devices.

These users do not value e-NABLE hands for functional reasons alone. One of the primary functions of prosthetic devices can be for self-expression rather than solely prosthesis, consistent with findings from Bennett et al. [2]: the aesthetic value of such a device is to manage stigma [14] and can influence self-presentation. As one self-fabricating user reported:

> Although the functionality isn't really that great for me, I feel far comfier wearing it than not wearing it when in public. It gives me more confidence.

One self-fabricator described a personal ideal of developing fabrication skills in order to maintain his own body parts without relying on others:

> This is a part of me, it's a work in progress; *I* am a work in progress. It's this idea of seeing yourself as something to work on, something that's worthy of improving, and making better, and maintaining.

In spite of that ideal, though, there is nuance around who is capable of making their own assistive technology. The same skill base that makes a volunteer fabricator successful is required of fabricator-recipients. Not everyone is equipped to operate a 3D printer, or to design printable parts.

Beyond personal fabrication skills, a recipient may not have all of the the clinical knowledge needed for correct device selection and personal outcome management. This professional knowledge can provide perspectives on potential benefits that recipients might not realize through self-experimentation alone.

While we would ideally like to know more about recipients who are not fabricators, this group, particularly the younger recipients who receive the most media attention, is nearly invisible to both e-NABLE itself and the literature. We did not include minors in the scope of this study, nor have any other researchers to date. However, our results are consistent with the only other study including adult e-NABLE recipients [2].

Discussion

Our interviews demonstrate that e-NABLE volunteers and clinicians have much in common. They are both motivated by a desire to use their skills to help people in need. Clinicians by their very nature perform their work in a non-virtual, one-on-one setting. Despite the distributed nature of e-NABLE, volunteers were also highly motivated by the idea of serving a particular individual. These common aspects of motivation, however, do not necessarily translate to shared practices. The number of clinicians involved in e-NABLE is small, and they are inclined to be wary of legal and medical issues; therefore, the clinicians we spoke to aimed to influence e-NABLE community practices, rather than engaging with particular recipients. The volunteers, on the other hand, emphasize the experimental nature of the devices e-NABLE produces, acknowledge their shortcomings in the clinical realm, and encourage recipients to seek out clinicians.

Both groups possess strong sets of skills. The skills of volunteers are engineering-focused: they see the opportunity to solve problems on a large scale through technical know-how, and are willing to expend great effort to prototype and test solutions. The Google+ community forum is full of experiments, technical questions, and stories of success and failure in 3D printing. Clinicians have deep technical skills as well, but are much more tightly focused on prosthetic practice, and may be wary of new and untested proposed technology. They understand sockets, fitting, safety, and long-term use. They also have the non-technical skill set of counseling—helping their patients to identity and articulate their needs, and empowering patients to make decisions that have the highest probability of a successful outcome. These two disparate sets of skills are complementary; the challenge is in how to couple the distributed engineering abilities of volunteers with the localized, in-person techniques of clinicians.

The volunteers acknowledge that there are risks around e-NABLE devices. They worry about factors such as breakage, injury, and improper use, but having less overall experience than clinicians, they—in essence—don't know what they don't know. Clinicians consider the same risks as volunteers, but add factors such as strain on different kinds of tissue and overuse of the unaffected limb. To operationalize this deep knowledge in the context of e-NABLE, however, remains a challenge. The current approach, of trying to impart some of this knowledge into e-NABLE—or, in C01's words, "*To be the 'bad guy,' pointing out the flaws; that we can make these amazing devices even better*"—may meet some success, but may also fail to capture the interest of a sufficiently large group of volunteers.

One of the largest areas of overlap between the e-NABLE volunteer and the e-NABLE-involved clinician is in the lack of concrete information about how the devices are being used. Although there is anecdotal evidence from adult recipients, volunteers' contacts with their own recipients, and stories in the news media, there is no information about the longer-term use of these devices. Both groups are aware of this lack of systematic use information, and both suggest that the solution is to encourage recipient engagement with clinicians.

OPPORTUNITIES FOR DESIGN

In this study, we have described a form of AT provision that has heretofore not been possible: people with affected upper limbs receiving rapidly produced low-cost body-powered prosthetic devices. Our findings identified differences in stakeholder motivations, skills, and perceptions of the risks of 3D-printed prosthetic devices. As with many complex social structures addressing large-scale societal issues, the e-NABLE community presents many opportunities for technological intervention, but at the same time resists quick and easy solutions. In this section, we sketch potential ways in which e-NABLE might sustain itself long-term while positively impacting those it seeks to serve.

We suggest four areas in which attention from researchers might yield fruit: incorporating some clinical expertise into the current framework for bringing device recipients into the e-NABLE system; a unified system to allow for co-design of devices with the involvement of volunteers, clinicians, and recipients; increasing volunteers' non-technical skills in support of improved recipient outcomes; and incorporating sensors for usage patterns into e-NABLE devices in order to inform clinicians and compensate for the lack of post-delivery followup.

Support Systems for Case Management

As we learned in our interviews, there are a wide variety of areas in which clinical expertise is important; however, the number of clinicians involved in e-NABLE is relatively small. Additionally, e-NABLE serves recipient populations who have no easy access to external clinical support. One possibility is to amplify clinical expertise through a "case management" system that encodes knowledge from clinicians about the advantages and disadvantages of devices, as well as encouraging volunteers to follow a more complete process (including follow up, for example). Such a system could also alert volunteers and recipients about situations where clinical input would be most valuable. Such a system would provide volunteers and recipients with a firmer grounding for making informed choices, make them aware of potential risks, and hopefully increase the likelihood of device success.

Platforms for Co-design

Each instance of customized AT for a recipient is an opportunity to design a unique instance of a device. However, design benefits from an ongoing, fluid dialogue, something that is difficult to achieve between fabricators and recipients even when they are co-located. Indeed, although one of the areas of greatest enthusiasm about e-NABLE devices is the ability to create recipient-specific aesthetic customizations, none of our interviewed volunteer fabricators discussed engaging in any sort of iterative dialogue about those customizations with recipients.

The difficulty of designing asynchronously at a distance could be addressed by a platform to engage volunteers and recipients in a co-design process, allowing the recipients to express their desires and preferences, and the volunteers to bring their technical and artistic skills to bear. Any such system, however, would have to be respectful of the mostly underage nature of e-NABLE recipients, as well as the constraints on time and energy that parents operate under.

A second area of opportunity for co-design is between volunteers and clinicians. This opportunity assumes the availability of significant clinical expertise, in contrast to the clinically grounded case management system suggested above. In the case of device co-design, volunteer designers could help with the design of new devices, or task-specific end effector designs intended to be used by multiple people. Clinicians could help to vet these devices and identify risks and safety concerns.

Alternatively, in the case of device provision, as suggested by Hofmann et al. [15], volunteer fabricators could focus on personalization, while clinicians could help to create professionally made sockets. Such a collaborative approach would allow volunteers to maintain the one-on-one relationship with recipients that is so important to their volunteering motivation, while allowing clinicians to have a role in co-creating meaningful solutions for recipients.

Increased Knowledge Sharing Between Stakeholders

The work of e-NABLE requires a wide variety skills from the volunteer. Many parts of our interviews with volunteers reflected the acquisition of skills related to the mysteries of 3D printing, mechanical engineering, and 3D CAD tools. Our clinician interviewees, however, revealed that helping a patient make an informed decision about prosthesis use involves a wide array of non-technical skills that are not apparent in the fabricators we interviewed. As e-NABLE grows, then, there may be an opportunity to use volunteers' enthusiasm for learning to involve them in discussions around clinical matters—understanding the limitations of different mechanical configurations, testing devices to ensure safety, and even helping potential recipients specify prostheses that reflect their individual contexts of use.

Quantified Usage Data

The lack of information about outcomes at the organizational level was also evident at the personal level in our interviews. This situation is not unique to e-NABLE; followup in mainstream prosthetics happens at a lower rate than clinicians wish for. While case management can help with this problem, e-NABLE also has a unique opportunity to collect fine grained, possibly even real-time data about device use. Because e-NABLE custom-manufactures each device, though, there is potential to build in instrumentation to track how and when the devices are used, or trigger follow up when it is most needed. Sensors and radios have been sufficiently miniaturized and optimized for low power that some modern-day smartwatches incorporate accelerometers, magnetometers, gyroscopes, and Bluetooth, and can last for nearly two weeks powered by a small battery. By using similar sensors and power optimizations—or by simply using a smartwatch modified to add a larger battery—researchers could begin tracking how e-NABLE devices are used. Such a data corpus could help volunteers and clinicians find patterns of use (e.g., is the device only used on weekdays?), postulate about how different device characteristics such as weight are a factor in use or non-use, and understand what kinds of questions to ask if and when followup happens.

LIMITATIONS

As time passes, the e-NABLE community continues to grow and evolve. Our research is a snapshot in time of the community, and hence only reflects the attitudes, opinions, skills, motivations, and goals of fourteen community members at a specific moment in time. Some current efforts, for example, attempt to move away from the completely distributed method by which e-NABLE currently operates towards a more-centralized and in-person method of designing and fabricating the devices. In addition, like any study dependent on volunteer participants, our results reflect self-selection bias. In particular, the e-NABLE volunteers we interviewed were people who were very active in e-NABLE and were mostly located in the United States, and our clinician interviewees may hold opinions divergent from professionals who have chosen not to engage with e-NABLE. Future research could benefit from including more voices from outside e-NABLE as well as a wider variety of e-NABLE participants.

CONCLUSION AND FUTURE WORK

In this study, we described e-NABLE, a community that has emerged to provide low-cost and personalized assistive technology to limb-different users. We presented the results of fourteen interviews with different stakeholders in e-NABLE, comprising volunteers and clinicians, and analyzed their overlaps and differences in terms of their motivation to participate in e-NABLE, the skills they bring to the project, and their perceptions of the risks inherent in the project. We found that both groups are motivated to use their skills to help people in need, their skill sets are complementary, and volunteers acknowledge the need for clinician involvement. However, their differing perceptions of the risks of providing experimental devices to limb-different recipients may result in uneven outcomes or missed expectations for end users.

We suggested four opportunities for design: creating a case management system to amplify sparsely available clinical expertise; supporting co-design between recipients and volunteers, or volunteers and clinicians; using volunteers' natural desire for skill acquisition to help them understand and integrate clinical concerns into their work; and augmenting deployed hands with sensors to gain knowledge of how they are used to inform future designs and trigger follow up as needed.

While our work focused on e-NABLE, our results have implications for other volunteer communities whose products may involve risk outside the scope of volunteer knowledge, as well as other communities that involve the production of physical devices for remote recipients.

ACKNOWLEDGMENTS

We thank Jon Schull and Shaun Kane for their feedback and advice on our study. This work was supported in part by the National Science Foundation under grant IIS-1464377.

REFERENCES

1. Chris Anderson. 2014. *Makers: The new industrial revolution*. Crown Business.
2. Cynthia L Bennett, Keting Cen, Katherine M Steele, and Daniela K Rosner. 2016. An intimate laboratory?: Prostheses as a tool for experimenting with identity and normalcy. In *CHI '16: Proceedings of the 2016 CHI Conference on Human Factors in Computing Systems*. ACM, New York, NY, USA, 1745–1756.
3. Hugh Beyer and Karen Holtzblatt. 1999. Contextual Design. *Interactions* 6, 1 (Jan. 1999), 32–42.
4. Elaine A Biddiss and Tom T Chau. 2007. Upper limb prosthesis use and abandonment: A survey of the last 25 years. *Prosthetics and Orthotics International* 31, 3 (2007), 236–257.
5. Leah Buechley and Hannah Perner-Wilson. 2012. Crafting technology: Reimagining the processes, materials, and cultures of electronics. *Transactions on Computer-Human Interaction (TOCHI)* 19, 3 (Oct. 2012).
6. Erin Buehler, Stacy Branham, Abdullah Ali, Jeremy J Chang, Megan Kelly Hofmann, Amy Hurst, and Shaun K. Kane. 2015. Sharing is caring: Assistive technology designs on Thingiverse. In *Proceedings of the 33rd Annual ACM Conference on Human Factors in Computing Systems*. ACM, New York, NY, USA, 525–534.
7. Erin Buehler, Shaun K. Kane, and Amy Hurst. 2014. ABC and 3D: Opportunities and obstacles to 3D printing in special education environments. In *Proceedings of the 16th International ACM SIGACCESS Conference on Computers & Accessibility (ASSETS '14)*. ACM, New York, NY, USA, 107–114.
8. Matthew B Burn, Anderson Ta, and Gloria R Gogola. 2016. Three-dimensional printing of prosthetic hands for children. *The Journal of Hand Surgery* 41, 5 (2016), e103–e109.
9. Juliet Corbin and Anselm Strauss. 2014. *Basics of qualitative research: Techniques and procedures for developing grounded theory*. SAGE Publications, Thousand Oaks, CA, USA.
10. Jayne Cravens. 2000. Virtual volunteering: Online volunteers providing assistance to human service agencies. *Journal of Technology in Human Services* 17, 2-3 (Oct. 2000), 119–136.
11. Laura Dabbish, Colleen Stuart, Jason Tsay, and Jim Herbsleb. 2012. Social coding in GitHub: Transparency and collaboration in an open software repository. In *Proceedings of the ACM conference on Computer Supported Cooperative Work*. ACM, New York, NY, USA, 1277–1286.
12. Jennifer L Davidson, Umme Ayda Mannan, Rithika Naik, Ishneet Dua, and Carlos Jensen. 2014. Older adults and free/open source software: A diary study of first-time contributors. In *Proceedings of The International Symposium on Open Collaboration*. ACM, New York, NY, USA, 5–14.
13. Lieven De Couvreur, Walter Dejonghe, Jan Detand, and Richard Goossens. 2013. The role of subjective well-being in co-designing open-design assistive devices. *International Journal of Design* 7, 3 (2013), 57–70.
14. Erving Goffman. 1963. *Stigma: Notes on the management of spoiled identity*. Prentice-Hall, Eaglewood Cliffs, NJ, USA.
15. Megan Hofmann, Julie Burke, Jon Pearlman, Goeran Fiedler, Andrea Hess, Jon Schull, Scott Hudson, and

Jennifer Mankoff. 2016. Clinical and maker perspectives on the design of assistive technology with rapid prototyping technologies. In *ASSETS '16: Proceedings of the 18th International ACM SIGACCESS Conference on Computers & Accessibility*. ACM, New York, NY, USA, 1–6.

16. Jonathan Hook, Sanne Verbaan, Abigail Durrant, Patrick Olivier, and Peter Wright. 2014. A study of the challenges related to DIY assistive technology in the context of children with disabilities. In *DIS '14: Proceedings of the 2014 Conference on Designing Interactive Systems*. ACM, New York, NY, USA, 597–606.
17. Nathaniel Hudson, Celena Alcock, and Parmit K. Chilana. 2016. Understanding newcomers to 3D printing: Motivations, workflows, and barriers of casual makers. In *Proceedings of the 2016 CHI Conference on Human Factors in Computing Systems (CHI '16)*. ACM, New York, NY, USA, 384–396.
18. Amy Hurst and Shaun K. Kane. 2013. Making "making" accessible. In *IDC '13: Proceedings of the 12th International Conference on Interaction Design and Children*. ACM, New York, NY, USA.
19. Amy Hurst and Jasmine Tobias. 2011. Empowering individuals with do-it-yourself assistive technology. In *Proceedings of the 16th International ACM SIGACCESS Conference on Computers & Accessibility*. ACM, New York, NY, USA, 11–18.
20. Sofia Hussain, Elizabeth B N Sanders, and Martin Steinert. 2012. Participatory design with marginalized people in developing countries: Challenges and opportunities experienced in a field study in Cambodia. *International Journal of Design* 6, 2 (2012), 91–109.
21. Lesley Hustinx and Frans Lammertyn. 2003. Collective and reflexive styles of volunteering: A sociological modernization perspective. *Voluntas: International Journal of Voluntary and Nonprofit Organizations* 14, 2 (2003), 167–187.
22. Aniket Kittur and Robert E Kraut. 2008. Harnessing the wisdom of crowds in wikipedia: Quality through coordination. In *Proceedings of the ACM Conference on Computer Supported Cooperative Work*. ACM, New York, NY, USA, 37–46.
23. Stacey Kuznetsov and Eric Paulos. 2010. Rise of the expert amateur: DIY projects, communities, and cultures. In *NordiCHI '10: Proceedings of the 6th Nordic Conference on Human-Computer Interaction: Extending Boundaries*. ACM, New York, NY, USA, 295–304.
24. Silvia Lindtner, Garnet D Hertz, and Paul Dourish. 2014. Emerging sites of HCI innovation: Hackerspaces, hardware startups & incubators. In *CHI'14: Proceedings of the SIGCHI Conference on Human Factors in Computing Systems*. ACM, New York, New York, USA.
25. Audris Mockus, Roy T Fielding, and James D Herbsleb. 2002. Two case studies of open source software development: Apache and Mozilla. *ACM Transactions on Software Engineering and Methodology* 11, 3 (2002), 309–346.
26. Seyed Mehdi Nasehi, Jonathan Sillito, Frank Maurer, and Chris Burns. 2012. Harnessing the wisdom of crowds in wikipedia: quality through coordination. In *Proceedings of the IEEE conference on Software Maintenance*. IEEE, New York, NY, USA, 25–34.
27. Betsy Phillips and Hongxin Zhao. 2010. Predictors of assistive technology abandonment. *Assistive Technology* 5, 1 (Oct. 2010), 36–45.
28. K Postema, V Van der Donk, J Van Limbeek, R AJ Rijken, and MJ Poelma. 1999. Prosthesis rejection in children with a unilateral congenital arm defect. *Clinical rehabilitation* 13, 3 (1999), 243–249.
29. Daniela Rosner and Jonathan Bean. 2009. Learning from IKEA Hacking: "I'm not one to decoupage a tabletop and call it a day.". In *Proceedings of the SIGCHI Conference on Human Factors in Computing Systems (CHI '09)*. ACM, New York, NY, USA, 419–422.
30. Daniela K. Rosner and Morgan Ames. 2014. Designing for repair?: Infrastructures and materialities of breakdown. In *Proceedings of the 17th ACM Conference on Computer Supported Cooperative Work and Social Computing (CSCW '14)*. ACM, New York, NY, USA, 319–331.
31. Sonali K Shah. 2006. Motivation, governance, and the viability of hybrid forms in open source software development. *Management Science* 52, 7 (July 2006), 1000–1014.
32. Kristen Shinohara and Jacob O. Wobbrock. 2011. In the shadow of misperception: Assistive technology use and social interactions. In *Proceedings of the SIGCHI Conference on Human Factors in Computing Systems (CHI '11)*. ACM, New York, NY, USA, 705–714.
33. Joshua G Tanenbaum, Amanda M Williams, Audrey Desjardins, and Karen Tanenbaum. 2013. Democratizing technology: Pleasure, utility and expressiveness in DIY and maker practice. In *CHI '13: Proceedings of the SIGCHI Conference on Human Factors in Computing Systems*. ACM, New York, New York, USA.
34. Amy Voida, Zheng Yao, and Matthias Korn. 2015. (Infra)structures of Volunteering. In *18th ACM Conference on Computer-Supported Collaborative Work*. 1704–1716.
35. Jing Wang, Patrick C Shih, and John M Carroll. 2015. Revisiting Linus's Law: Benefits and challenges of open source software peer review. *International Journal of Human-Computer Studies* 77, May 2015 (May 2015), 52–65.
36. Yunwen Ye and K Kishida. 2003. Toward an understanding of the motivation of open source software developers. In *Software Engineering, 2003. Proceedings. 25th International Conference on*. IEEE, 419–429.

VITA: Towards Supporting Volunteer Interactions with Long-Term Care Residents with Dementia

Pin Sym Foong[1], Shengdong Zhao[1], Kelsey Carlson[2], and Zhe Liu[1]
[1]NUS-HCI Lab,
National University of Singapore, Singapore
pinsym@u.nus.edu, zheliu1992@gmail.com,
zhaosd@comp.nus.edu.sg
[2]Ludwig-Maximilians-Universität,
Munich, Germany
kelsey.leigh.carlson@gmail.com

ABSTRACT
Volunteers are an important resource at long-term care homes because they can supply services, such as engagement activities, that over-burdened care staff struggle to provide. However, volunteers without sufficient training are often challenged in responding to dementia-linked behaviors, which can lead to frustrating difficulties during interaction. Additionally, short-staffed care homes have difficulties in training and maintaining volunteers. To better support volunteers in providing engagement activities for people with dementia without a high training burden, we created VITA, a tablet-based system that supplies carefully designed profiling and guidance using our dementia-appropriate engagement activity kit. Our evaluation indicated that the instructional guide supplied by VITA significantly improves volunteers' ability to facilitate engagement activities with people with dementia, approaching the level of engagement achievable by professional therapists.

Author Keywords
Engagement activity; tablets; dementia; nursing homes; volunteers; dementia care.

ACM Classification Keywords
H.5.m. Information interfaces and presentation (e.g., HCI): Miscellaneous.

INTRODUCTION
Volunteers can play an important role in nursing homes – they serve as a source of extra help because they provide services that understaffed nursing homes find difficult to supply [14]. Over the years, in many countries, volunteers have been recruited for a variety of service programs, such as reminiscence activities (Hong Kong) [4], friendly visiting (Canada) [12], and art activities (US) [24].

'Engagement activities' is an occupational therapy term for the activities provided in these types of service programs. The term is defined as any activity that can provide social and cognitive stimulation for residents, with the goal of improving psychosocial wellness. For people living with dementia, these engagement activities are critical, because the impairments stemming from the disease result in the loss of the ability for the person to seek out, plan for and engage in such activities on their own [8]. Nursing homes strive to supply such activities because studies show that the lack of such engagement can lead to the increase of undesirable behavior [5, 26], apathy [23], and depression [3] among people with dementia (henceforth referred to as "clients").

However, using volunteers in dementia care presents its own set of challenges. Volunteers are often inexperienced in responding to dementia-linked behaviors [17, 33, 39], and they are generally unfamiliar with the individual needs of the client [12,15,17,18], which can lead to frustrating difficulties during interactions [12,15]. These challenges can demotivate volunteers, who are unlikely to return as a result of disappointing interactions [13,15]. Consequently, nursing homes are required to invest already scarce resources to specially train volunteers [30] to interact with individuals with dementia.

Thus, we were motivated to address the problem of improving volunteer expertise when supplying engagement activities to clients, while minimizing burden to the long-term care home. To understand the practice of volunteering within the organizational constraints of the nursing home, we partnered with a local nursing home to observe and participate in volunteer activities. We also studied the nature of expertise among occupational and physical therapists who supply engagement activities, in order to identify appropriate ways to improve the expertise of volunteers. Our studies suggested that we might improve the level of expertise of volunteers by pre-packaging activities and client-customizing instructions for volunteers.

As a result, we developed VITA: Volunteer Interactions via Tablet-based Activities. It is comprised of a client Profile module, an Activity Kit module and a personalized Activity Guide. The Activity Kit contains a set of pre-packaged activities, each featuring a commercially available app with

CHI 2017, May 06-11, 2017, Denver, CO, USA

DOI: http://dx.doi.org/10.1145/3025453.302577

accompanying instructions for volunteers to facilitate client engagement with the app.

For example, if a client named Karen enjoys crafts, an employee of the nursing home can use VITA to create a tailored Profile for Karen that includes these activities. Then, when a new volunteer arrives and is assigned to engage Karen, the volunteer is given a tablet containing Karen's simplified biography and instructions on how to interact with her using these activities. Since Activity Guides are unique to each client, volunteers are more effective and time is saved for both volunteers and nursing home staff.

Using a mixed-methods study, we evaluated the effect of volunteers using VITA's Activity Guide on engagement of clients. We compared engagement outcomes against a control condition with no facilitation instructions, and also against the ideal scenario of one-to-one facilitation by an experienced therapist.

We found that volunteers using VITA's Activity Guide could facilitate engagement at significantly higher levels compared to those in the control condition. In addition, these results were comparable to therapist-interaction outcomes, with a stronger effect observed when used with clients with more severe dementia. Our findings indicate that this approach of providing volunteers with client biographical information that is supplemented with facilitation instructions enhances client engagement.

The contributions of this paper include the following:

1) Qualitative contextualized studies to derive user requirements for a computer-supported program for volunteers.
2) The provision of VITA, a tablet-based system that enables volunteers to facilitate engagement activities for individuals with dementia without a high training burden. VITA's central proposition is pre-packaged, volunteer-friendly activities that are easily customizable to client needs.
3) An empirical evaluation that shows the effectiveness of VITA, with findings that point to the importance of analysis of outcomes by dementia severity.

RELATED WORK

In this section, we review computer-supported ways to enhance engagement in dementia, and look also at volunteer-specific research.

In dementia care, there exists a large body of work focused on supplying clients with engagement activities [e.g. 14,29]. The key guideline derived from these physical engagement studies is to offer activities are customized to the individuals – by abilities [34], personal interests [22] or even personality [22]. Although such methods are possibly applicable to digital activities, there were no previous studies that have attempted customization of computer-based activities for engagement.

Digital apps have been studied as cognitive training programs [e.g. 26], but not as engagement activities that are targeted toward psychosocial wellness. Other studies, using custom-built multimedia devices for engagement, show that devices can be very effective as a focal point when interacting with people with dementia. Depending on the content it supplies, the device can help improve conversation via the supply of personal history [12] or cohort-based prompts [1], or improve the caregivers' understanding of the personality and preferences of the person with dementia via holistic health records [25], multimedia presentations [37], personalized art installations [35] and personal interactive jewelry [36].

While these devices are useful for clients and their caregivers, we could not directly apply them to the goal of this paper: improving volunteer expertise when interacting with clients. The studies mentioned above are targeted at clients and their primary caregivers (e.g. family and care workers), who are often already familiar with dementia care. We are not aware of any digital engagement artifacts designed specifically for use by volunteers, although volunteers may have been incidental participants in some cases [25,37]. Therefore, we expanded the scope of the literature review to volunteer training programs.

Training Programs for Volunteers

From our review of previous studies, we saw that the information requirements for volunteers have some similarities with primary caregivers, but also some important differences. Both groups share a need for better understanding of dementia itself [4,12,15,31]. Primary family caregivers want information on burden coping mechanisms [31,32] and alternative care services [32,33] for their loved ones, while volunteers have thus far expressed none of these information needs. Instead, they have expressed a variety of requests such as access to biographical history, preferences, recently conducted activities and even medical histories of the individuals with dementia [12,15,18]. The studies suggest that they want this information in order to build empathy and to connect with the client [15,18]. It appears that due to their unfamiliarity with the client, volunteers have information needs that revolve around basic 'getting-to-know-you' content.

Interestingly, although quite a few studies have reported what volunteers ask to know, to our knowledge there have been no studies that implement the delivery of such information, or subsequently assess the effects of sharing such information on volunteer efficacy. Thus, our first research question was to determine the nature and type of biographical information that a volunteer-support system should supply, in order to increase a volunteer's ability to engage with clients.

Another reported way to enhance the ability of volunteers to engage clients is to supply training - often a combination of knowledge about the disease and coping methods and information on conducting the target activity. Many studies report on the success of such activity-specific training programs [e.g. 4,17,18], indicating that volunteer training is a reliable method to improve volunteer efficacy.

At the same time, these studies report ongoing issues in the *supply* of volunteer training. They suggest that further work is needed to reduce volunteer drop-out [29], improve volunteer commitment [4], and reduce the duration of training [12]. Furthermore, some studies point out the need for creating a system for ongoing support post-training, via volunteer supervisors [14,24]. These difficulties are consistent with research on the difficulties of long term care facilities in general, where volunteer recruitment and management requires a significant use of resources [14,15,30].

Overall, the related work indicates that there is a research gap in knowing what type of information to offer volunteers to improve their interaction with clients. At the same time, there is a need to ensure that solutions implemented to support volunteers do not further strain the ability of long-term facilities to provide such systems.

DESIGN AND DEVELOPMENT OF VITA

As HCI researchers, we approached this challenge as an example of task support research. What behaviors should volunteers have in order to improve their efficacy with clients? How do experts, such as occupational therapists, behave with clients? Can we identify computer-supported methods to improve the ability of volunteers to attain these same behaviors? How do we design a system to minimize the maintenance burden to care staff?

To answer these questions, we first conducted an exploratory participant-observer [21] study at a local care home to gather insight into the practice of volunteering and volunteer management. Based on the findings of the first study, we drafted initial system concepts. We brought these concepts to a focus group consisting of long-term care staff with experience in supplying engagement activities. The feedback of the participants expanded our understanding of therapeutic expertise, and in turn informed our user requirements for the system.

Participant-Observation Study

We partnered with a 250-bed, subsidized long-term care facility in Singapore. As with half of nursing homes in this country the care center is run by a voluntary welfare organization[1] [39]. Detailed findings of this study are documented elsewhere [15], so we only summarize the key points below.

Strained Resources

We affirmed the aforementioned link between care staff shortage and the role of volunteers in a nursing home. At this nursing home, there was approximately 1 care staff to every 8 residents, which is far below government guidelines of 1 staff to 3.5 residents [39]. To alleviate the burden, the home's Volunteer Coordinator arranges an average of 2 group volunteer visits a month, each consisting of approximately 10–20 persons from a large variety of schools and welfare organizations.

Makeup of volunteers

Although this number was not small, we also learnt that the pool of volunteers was characterized by constant shifts in number and abilities. Almost all the volunteers were single visit volunteers, coming from various social organizations, companies and schools. The few long-term volunteers we encountered performed instrumental services, such as haircuts and administration. The home's Volunteer Coordinator explained, "*A regular commitment over a year is extremely difficult to negotiate with our partner schools. They have their own schedules too, so we just accept when we can, and try to request for help when we need it.*"

Types of engagement activities

Our next observation was that the physical constraints of the home strongly influenced the types of engagement activities the staff felt they could undertake. As with many long-term care facilities in metropolitan Asia, limited space was an issue. The home had shifted two years ago from a 5-story building with garden space to a new 9-story building with scarce surrounding land. With the new layout, staff had to adapt activities to involve fewer residents at one time, take up less space, involve less equipment, and require less movement between floors for residents with mobility difficulties..

Challenges of tablet-based activities

One example of a possible solution was the introduction of 'tablet therapy' as an engagement activity. The value of tablet technology in this setting comes from it being a single piece of equipment that has many interaction options, is portable, and has the potential for promoting interactions in smaller groups. We observed and interviewed single-visit volunteers with tablets who visited residents with dementia. While volunteers generally found the tablet to be a useful device for mediating conversations with the clients, they also experienced awkwardness and difficulty with the communication abilities and the dementia-linked behaviors of the clients they met. Many of them were also at a loss at how to engage these clients.

As a result of this study, we identified a design opportunity to support volunteers' information and expertise needs via the use tablets, due to the following reasons: 1) tablets were already in use, and volunteers found it useful to help facilitate activities with clients; 2) unlike physical activities, which often require an assortment of equipment and larger activity areas, tablets allow a wide variety of applications, catering to different interests, to be stored on a compact device. It also requires much less space to use.

[1] The remaining half are private homes

Focus Group Study

To better understand how to design tablet-based engagement activities, we conducted a focus group study with long-term care workers who were familiar with organizing engagement activity programs with volunteers.

Participants

We recruited an occupational therapist, a physiotherapist, a long-term care nurse, and a community care therapist (age mean=28.2, all female, average years in long-term care = 3.8). One co-author and a research student facilitated the focus group.

Materials and Method

Materials used during the focus group sessions were video footage of a tablet therapy session, early workflow sketches, and commercially available apps for dementia activities. We chose CleverMind [40] and GreyMatters [41] from the App Store's top 10 recommendations as they are specifically designed for clients, offering biographical information and a variety of game and engagement content.

Focus Group Results

The participants found that CleverMind and GreyMatters seemed to have cognitive game content (e.g. card matching) that suited the needs of clients, but they still would not choose to use such apps to facilitate engagement in their work due to the following reasons.

Firstly, the participants indicated that the content of the dementia-specific apps were too culture-specific. For example, CleverMind's music content was exclusively comprised of American music from the 1950's, which may not be familiar to local clients. Therapists explained that they often favor local music, sung in local dialects, as stimuli for engagement.

Secondly, the cognitive game content of the apps did not pre-customize the activities to the client's abilities. Therefore, some trial and error may still be needed in order to find the appropriate game and game level for a particular client. Participants mentioned that volunteers who are unfamiliar with either dementia or the client may interpret errors made during this search process as failures. Instead the physiotherapist suggested that volunteers be given 'booster activities', activities that are already known to succeed with each client, in order to boost the volunteer's confidence and quickly capture the client's attention.

When queried about how they think volunteers should use apps with clients, participants pointed out that many freely available apps can be re-purposed. In essence, activities around existing apps can be modified to become dementia-friendly. As mentioned by the occupational therapist, *"Most tasks can be broken into smaller tasks - with some prompting and cueing from a facilitator, often the clients can still complete these tasks."* For example, a client's self-dressing activity can be broken down into steps by laying out the clothing in the order of dressing on a bed. In the same way, the operation of an app can be presented in smaller steps in order to facilitate client participation and engagement. For example, using a coloring book app can be broken into the steps of choosing a color, applying a color, and choosing another color.

It was a new insight for us that even if an app were not designed to be dementia-appropriate, it could be re-purposed by presenting it to the client in smaller, more achievable steps. The occupational therapist explained further that this strategy is called 'activity modification' [34] and is often applied to physical engagement activities for clients. The basic premise of activity modification is that a therapist uses her familiarity with the client's abilities and interests to adjust an activity to match the level of remaining ability.

From Insights to User Requirements

The discovery of activity modification was a key insight on how to support non-expert activity facilitators such as volunteers. To enable these volunteers to modify and deliver activities, they should be able to 1) know a client's abilities and interests, 2) select appropriate apps and 3) provide app-based activities according to the client's abilities. Each of these user requirements generated sub-tasks that had to be addressed before we could meet these needs.

Firstly, information about a clients abilities and interests is usually, but not always available in therapy reports and daily interaction logs in the nursing home. However, these reports are not suitable for volunteers to use as they contain professional terms and sensitive health data, such as the patient's mental status and critical medical events. Therefore, another related design requirement of a support system is that it should be able to present the appropriate amount of information about the client, shown in ways that can be quickly understood.

Secondly, one way to enable volunteers to have appropriate apps is to pre-identify a set of dementia-friendly applications, preferring those that are cohort- or culture-appropriate. We also saw that the app re-purposing approach had the advantage of less maintenance via the utilization of already available content as existing apps may provide a ready supply of free and updated content for app-based modified activities. Despite these potential benefits, there remained a challenge to identify methods to effectively repurpose these apps. There is no previous dementia care research on how to do this for digital activities. Thus, there was an additional task of developing a replicable approach for selecting good candidate apps, and then modifying the app-based activities via the ability-specific instructions.

Thirdly, even if a volunteer were given the profile information of a client, and a collection of dementia-friendly apps, s/he may not know how to utilize this information to select the appropriate app and use it in an effective way to interact with the client. For example, if a

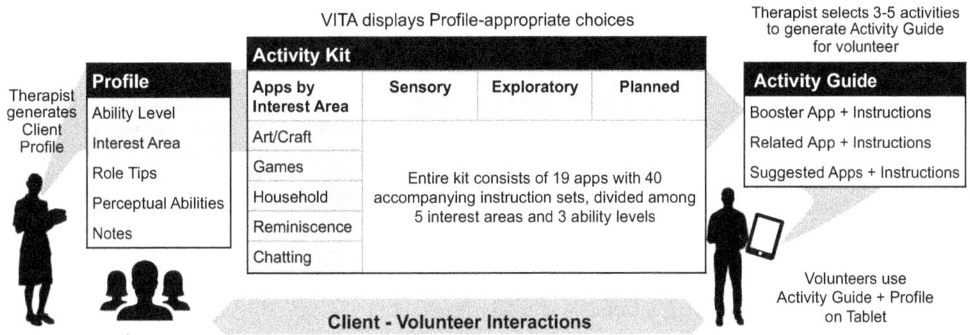

Figure 1: VITA System Components: Profile (left), Activity Kit (center, with Apps & Instructions) and Activity Guide (right)

volunteer knows that a client has low ability to communicate, will she be able to select and present content in a way that is stimulating but does not necessitate verbal response?

Thus, this led us to the third sub-task: not only should the client's profile should be provided, it should also be *pre-translated* into specific instructions on what apps to use and how to use the app in a way that caters to the remaining abilities of the client.

IMPLEMENTATION

To meet these requirements, we conceptualized the VITA prototype (see Fig. 1) as having 3 linked components:

1. Client Profile: This contains a set of simplified and glanceable biography of a client for volunteers to read before the engagement activity. This includes the client's overall ability level (e.g. *Exploratory*), interests (e.g. *Art/Craft*,) detailed perceptual abilities (e.g. *Hearing: fair*), volunteer role description (e.g. *Give instructions one step at a time*) and notes (e.g. *Prompt often*)

2. Activity Kit: This contains pre-packaged activities for volunteers. It has two major components.

2.1 The first component is a grid of apps categorized by client ability levels and interests.

2.2 The second component is the accompanying instructions on how to use a particular app when interacting with a client of a particular ability level.

3. Personalized Activity Guide: This contains the overall plan on how to interact with a particular client during an engagement session (e.g. *1. Introduce yourself, 2. Begin with "Polly Bubble Tea Maker": Let the resident...*). See bottom of Table 1 for the full example.

In our system, the therapist fills a web-based form so that the system can generate the client's Profile. Based on the stated ability level and interest(s), the system recommends a shortlist of interest- and ability-matched apps from the Activity Kit. Therapists select 3-5 of these activities, and these become the Activity Guide as a visit plan for the volunteer. The volunteer uses all three components to facilitate engagement activities with clients.

Activity Kit Development

To ensure the activity kit suits the needs of clients, we collaborated with an occupational therapist with more than 3 years of experience in creating and delivering engagement activities to form the development team. The following section describes the procedure for developing the kit.

First, we defined the types of interests and abilities that the contents of the Kit would cater for. For interest areas, we selected 5 interest areas based on previous literature [16]: reminiscence, household-linked activities, games, arts and crafts, and chatting,

For ability categorization, we looked at several available tools that can used to categorize clients ability levels (e.g., Allen's Cognitive Levels), and selected Pool Activity Levels (PAL) [42] as it is a well-established framework and has been previously utilized by other customized engagement activity programs [e.g.17,33]. PAL describes four ability levels. These are activities that require planning (Planned), activities that are only exploratory in nature (Exploratory), activities that are selected for their sensory (sound, sight) qualities (Sensory), and activities that trigger reactions (Reflexive). We excluded Reflexive activities because these require the use of direct physical stimulation to raise self-awareness levels of clients, and were therefore less appropriate for volunteers. Examples of these activities are stroking a person's arm or food tasting, which can be risky or too invasive for non-experts [28], as clients at this level of severity are often frail or uncommunicative. Combining the chosen interests and ability levels, we had a grid of 5 (interests) x 3 (ability levels) in our Activity Kit.

Next we looked for apps that would fit into this grid. We reviewed more than 80 apps and shortlisted 38 apps. With these, we began drafting app-specific facilitation instructions based on the abilities of the client in each ability level (Fig. 1, center). With the collaborating therapist, we wrote instructions to help volunteers understand *how* to modify tasks, *when* to prompt for responses, and *what* overall goal of the activity was. As we wrote the instructions, we obtained client input by testing these apps and instructions with clients at the nursing home.

	Sensory Level Abilities	Exploratory Level Abilities	Planned Level Abilities
Persona of client	Client may be easily distracted or demonstrate poor attention span, requiring plenty of guidance during activity.	Client may have moderate attention span and can be encouraged to participate more actively.	Client may have only mild impairments, may express preferences, and require only light guidance in order to sustain activity.
Client Attention Span	Write activities that do not require linking of steps from one action to the next.	Write activities that support client to follow 1-2 step instructions.	Write activities that support client to follow 2-3 step instructions or make own choices.
Client Problem Solving	Write activities that have no requirement for choice-making or problem-solving.	Write activities that have no requirement for problem-solving but prompts for client's choice.	Write activities that offer some problem-solving tasks and encourage clients to make choices.
Gameplay Objective of App	Choose apps with little gameplay objective – purely for sounds or visual appeal.	Choose apps with game objective or scoring system present.	Choose apps with objective or scoring system present.
Example App	*Fireworks Arcade*	*Polly Bubble Tea Maker*	*Polly Bubble Tea Maker*
Example App-based Instruction	*Use 'Start Show' option. Talk about fireworks, celebrations, and childhood memories.*	*Let the resident try to follow each instruction. When needed, help to read the instructions or point out the correct place to tap. Encourage and praise each step.*	*Let the resident lead. Only if needed, Help to read the instructions only if needed. Encourage resident to complete the task on their own.*

Table 1 Method of Developing Activities for the Activity Kit. Each activity is made up of an app and instructions for facilitation of engagement. The top section describes the type of apps to pick, and how to write facilitation instructions for a client's particular ability level. The bottom section provides examples. Note that the same app with different instructions can be used for different ability levels (e.g., *Polly Bubble Tea Maker* is used for both the *Exploratory* and *Planned* ability levels).

Apps were removed from the shortlist if clients found them too difficult despite the task breakdown, or if they were found to have practical problems such as not functioning on the target device, needing a consistent Wi-Fi signal, or having too many disruptive advertisements. For the final list of 19 apps, we created and tested 40 activities (apps and their instructions). Our method of creating these activities is presented in Table 1.

Profile Development

As mentioned earlier, we needed to present profile information effectively. Our early paper prototype, which contained the information requested by volunteers in our related work, had too much information. During pilot studies with 10 nursing home volunteers, we found that the volunteers retained only 3–4 Profile elements. Based on this feedback, we further reduced the Profile to what is seen on the left of Fig. 1 - client's interest area(s) and ability level, general instructions on the volunteer's conduct when interacting with clients at a particular PAL ability level are condensed to a maximum of four bullet points. The client's perceptual abilities are presented as a glanceable icon set focusing on the most salient characteristics (hearing, sight, speech, and manual dexterity with a tablet). Finally, there are some written notes from the collaborating therapist regarding the client (e.g., *"prompt often")*. In this way, we balanced the information delivered to a non-primary caregiver (volunteer) with the ability of the caregiver to process and use the information.

Formative Testing

Since the Activity Kit as a whole was developed with one collaborating occupational therapist, we decided to validate it with an unrelated group of experts to give feedback on the Kit. We asked three community care therapists to give feedback on the Activity Kit (n=3, all female, age mean=29.3, total years in dementia care=15). Overall the therapists concurred that the Kit would be useful for their work, the activity associated with each app was easy to understand. They provided some specific suggestions such as shortening some instructions further and adding instructions to ensure that the tablet volume is turned up sufficiently high. These suggestions have been incorporated in the kit.

We also pilot tested the Activity Guide. Our early prototypes contained 3 suggested activities from the Activity Kit, presented in order of execution. Participants in the pilot tests felt constrained by the too-strict activity prescription. We concluded that extreme specificity worked against the purpose of the Activity Guide, which was to enable volunteers to be proficient in interacting with the client. Subsequently, we limited the plan to the first two activities, but for the remaining activity slot, we encouraged the volunteer to actively choose from a suggested list of up to three activities. By permitting leeway, we wanted to encourage the volunteer to take a pro-active role in the engagement facilitation process.

At the end of the development process, we had a glanceable client Profile that helped to quickly introduce salient information on a client to a volunteer. The Activity Kit contained 19 apps and 40 instruction sets, of which 10 were for Sensory Activities, 18 for Exploratory Activities, and 12 for Planned Activities (Fig. 1). Therapists could use the client ability level and interest area to locate appropriate activities in the Activity Kit in order to generate customized Activity Guides. Activity Guides consisted of 1–2 known successful activities as the initial activity (Booster), followed by a second related activity (Related). Finally, there would be a few alternative activities (Suggested). With the content of VITA iterated to a reasonable point of

	Control Condition	VITA Condition	Therapist Condition
Client Profile	Yes	Yes	Yes
Activity Kit Apps	Yes	Yes	Yes
Activity Kit Instructions	No	Yes	No
Activity Guide	No	Yes	No

Table 2 Evaluation Conditions

development, we turned to a summative evaluation to confirm the usefulness of VITA.

EVALUATION

We conducted a study to investigate how VITA compares against the current practice of tablet-based engagement activities (Control Condition) and with the best-case scenario, a one-on-one, therapist-delivered tablet-based engagement activity (Therapist Condition).

Participants

Client Participants

We recruited client participants from our partner nursing home. The inclusion criterion was a documented diagnosis of dementia. The exclusion criteria were: the client had an accompanying diagnosis of bipolar disorder or schizophrenia, had no dexterity or movement in either hand, could not be seated in a chair/wheelchair, had a MMSE (Mini Mental State Exam) score of 23 or above, or was younger than 60 years of age.

Fourteen potential participants were identified. Three of the potential study participants' next-of-kin could not be reached for consent. One client refused to participate in the activity, and another was unwell. Replacements were purposively sampled in order to have clients for each ability level represented in the study. This resulted in 9 clients for our study (male n=5; age *M*=84.3, *SD*=8.6; MMSE *M*=13.4, *SD*=6.4). Ethnic representation of the participants included 6 Chinese, 1 Indian, and 2 clients of Eurasian origin. There were 3 participants at each ability level.

The home's occupational therapist profiled these participants to determine their PAL ability level, interests, and perceptual abilities with regard to tablets (visual, auditory, speech, and manual dexterity). These elements became the contents of the client's Profile. The time between Profile creation and the completion of evaluation was less than three weeks.

Volunteer Participants

Volunteer participants were students recruited from three tertiary institutions who were already visiting the home for service learning projects. Participants were compensated for their travel costs with a grocery voucher.

In all, 18 volunteer participants were recruited (male n=9; *M*=21.1, *SD*=4.2). Participants completed a pre-session questionnaire for control information on any prior experience with dementia, and languages spoken for matching with the clients. None of the volunteer

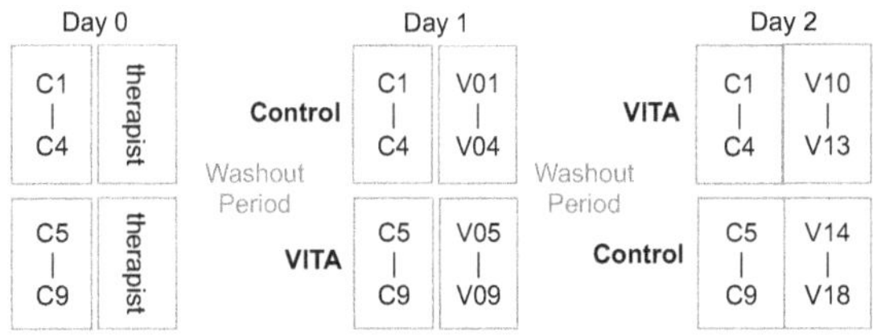

Figure 2 Study Design Showing Counterbalancing Order for Control and Test with Clients (C) and Volunteers (V)

participants reported any dementia-care training or having lived with older adults with dementia.

Apparatus

Our application launcher was loaded onto 4 Samsung Tab Pro 10.1 Tablets, running Android v. 4.4.2. For recording video, we used 4 Sony HDR-XR550E cameras with shotgun microphones attached to increase sound quality.

Method

Study Design

Our study involved 2 factors: Content delivery method and client's ability level. Content delivery method had three levels Control, VITA and Therapist. The client's ability level had three levels (Sensory, Exploratory, and Planned). Content for each condition is listed in Table 2. The Control condition mimics current practice where volunteers are given apps selected by care staff with general instructions. In the VITA condition, volunteers have the additional access to the facilitated instruction supplied by the Activity Kit. In the Therapist condition, a Therapist facilitates engagement as an expert, using just the Activity Kit apps.

Our study comprised of two sets of participants: clients and volunteers. To avoid potential interference between the test conditions, it would have been preferable to use a between-subject design for the delivery method factor for both types of participants.

However, due to the difficulties we had recruiting suitable clients, we were only able to conduct between-subjects testing for volunteers. Thus, the volunteers were randomly assigned to Control or Test, but met the same clients for all experimental conditions (within-subject for the clients).

The study design is detailed in Fig. 2. While involving the same clients in multiple test conditions may risk learning effects, in practice, the risk is largely reduced for these clients due to memory impairments [5]. To further reduce any risk, we applied a washout period of 6 days between conditions. At the same time, within-subjects testing for clients is particularly useful, as it helps to account for variance introduced by each client's unique set of abilities. Such study designs are not uncommon, especially for studies with caregiving dyads [e.g. 26].

All testing took place in the morning between 9 am and 11 am when the clients are the most alert. Volunteer participants were given 15 minutes to familiarize themselves with the Profile, Activity Guide and the pre-loaded apps on the tablet.

Testing Setup

Figure 2 Testing Setup

Subsequently, they were briefly introduced to the client in the testing room and were asked to offer the activities "based on the Profile and Guide", for up to 30 minutes. If the client indicated that they wanted to stop, they could do so. A video camera was set up for a medium, frontal view of the volunteer and the client (Fig. 3).

Measures

Client Engagement Measure

Since clients cannot self-report on their level of engagement, we selected a behavioral observational scale as the measuring instrument. Cohen-Mansfield's Observational Measure of Engagement (OME) was created specifically to measure engagement behavior. The OME is a validated method for measuring engagement and has been widely used at nursing homes [8]. For full psychometric properties of the OME, see [6].

In the OME, a trained observer uses a scored checklist to determine client *attitude* and *attention* during engagement. The method converts the observed behaviors into a numerical score between 2 to 34. A maximum score would require the client to be very attentive, to the point of being proactive, and maintain a very positive attitude, laughing and interacting continuously. On the other hand, the theoretical minimum would require a completely inattentive client who was disruptive or distracted most of the time, with a highly negative attitude.

To ensure objective scoring, two research assistants were trained on a 15-minute sample video of clients interacting with tablets. Discussion of the OME coding followed, as feedback for their coding choices. After training, they coded the client-volunteer interaction videos independently. Cohen's κ showed high agreement between the two coder's observations (0.82, p<0.01). Since the value was consistent with previously reported OME values [7], the scores were averaged to arrive at the final client engagement scores.

Volunteers' Measure

We constructed a post-session 14-item questionnaire to measure the following responses: usability of the system (6 items), usefulness of the client Profile (2 items) and activity guide (2 items), satisfaction with the apps used (2 items), and the amount of information presented (2 items). Items were graded on a 5-point Likert scale, which resulted in a score of 10 for each segment.

RESULTS

Client Engagement

Since the delivery method was a within-subject factor for clients, but client ability level was a between-subject factor, we conducted a two-way mixed ANOVA to compare the effect of the three delivery methods and three client ability levels on engagement scores. However, since the sample size was relatively small and the data was non-parametric, we used Aligned Rank Transform (ART) [38] as the statistical test. Fig. 4 (left) presents the engagement scores by clients' ability level and delivery method.

We found a significant main effect on the delivery method ($F_{2,12}$=8.00, p=.006). Pairwise t-Tests with Tukey corrections showed that the engagement measure score of both the VITA (M=25.7) and Therapist (M=26.1) delivery methods are significantly better than that of Control method (M=21.8) (all $p < .05$). No significant difference was found between the engagement measure of VITA (M=25.7) and Therapist (M=26.1) delivery methods (p=.99).

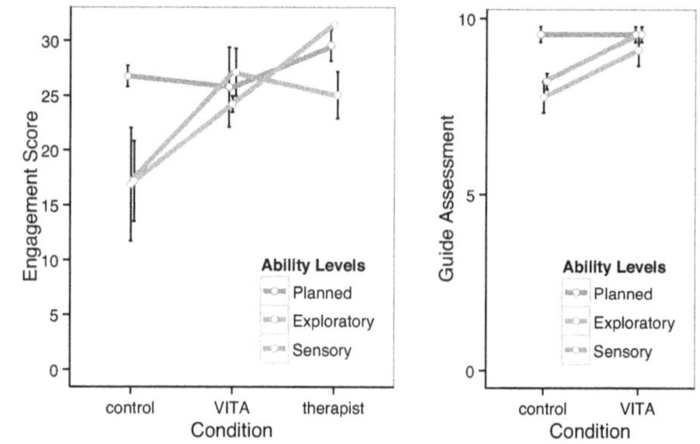

Figure 4 Clients' Average OME Score (standard error) (left) and Volunteer Guide Assessment by Delivery Method and Clients' Ability level (right)

These results have two implications. Firstly, volunteers in the VITA condition had a significantly higher client engagement score than in the Control condition, with an average increase of 18%. Cohen's effect size for client engagement (0.838) suggests a high practical difference between control and VITA delivery methods. Secondly, with the use of the Activity Guide, volunteers could achieve levels of client engagement comparable to an expert's.

Volunteers' Assessment of the Activity Guide

Unlike the previous analysis, the delivery method for volunteers is a between-subject factor with only two levels. Therefore, using ART again, we carried out a two-way ANOVA to compare the effect of the delivery methods and client ability level on the volunteers' assessment of the Activity Guide. In Fig.4 (right) the chart shows the volunteers' assessment of the Activity Guide component of VITA across delivery methods and client levels.

We found a significant main effect on delivery method ($F_{1,6}$=12.56, p=.01), indicating that overall, volunteers perceived VITA to be useful. However, there was also a significant main effect on ability level ($F_{2,6}$=5.69, p=.04), and a marginal significance on the interaction term ($F_{2,6}$=3.71, p=.09). A visual examination of the interaction plot Fig. 4 (right) suggests it was the Planned Level data that was the source of the interaction effect. When we removed the data from Planned Level clients, and ran the ANOVA again, there was only a significant effect of the condition ($F_{1,4}$ =19.3, p=.01), and no main effect from the Ability Level ($F_{1,4}$=1.6, p=.27).

These findings suggest that volunteers interacting with Planned Level residents had a different perception of the utility of VITA, as compared to those with Sensory and Exploratory residents. In other words, the results suggest that volunteers interacting with clients at the lower levels of ability (Sensory and Exploratory) perceived the Activity Guide to be more useful, even though the actual difference in Resident outcomes was not large.

As might be expected, there were no other significant differences among volunteers' ratings of the Profile content (M= 8.56, SD=1.46), quality of apps used (M= 8.22, SD=1.35), amount of information (M= 8.22, SD=1.26), and system usability (M= 23.50, SD=3.01).

Qualitative Findings

To explain the findings, we examined the videos of volunteers' usage of the Activity Guide provided in VITA and report also their post-session verbal feedback. In the Control condition videos, we observed volunteers having to spend more time experimenting and briefly testing some apps before finding an appropriate app for the client. In contrast, volunteers in the VITA condition appeared more confident of their choices and spent more of their time explaining the content of the applications and consequently engaging the client. Post-session interviews with volunteers shed light on this observation. Volunteer P8 (VITA condition) said this of the system: *"Easier way to get to know elderly because of Profile. (The) recommendations were great, and guide was very good. (The) information was adequate, nothing else was needed"*.

Volunteers also appeared more confident in leading the client. This might have been the result of having the activity 'booster' which improved the likelihood that the client would be interested. One of the reported benefits of using the Activity Guide was to help to specify the choices of engagement activities. Volunteer P1 (VITA condition) said that the customized instructions helped her to "*...select only what was important for the apps. Otherwise there were too many and I didn't know what he wants."* The list of activities also acted as a backup plan. When encountering disinterest in the 'booster' activity, Volunteer P11 (VITA condition) related her coping experience: *"Some apps were not appropriate. Even though I started with Float Free, the resident got bored, so (I) try (sic) other things... Water Colors was better."*

In contrast Volunteer P3 (Control condition) said: *"Enough info – yes, it's mainly information for starting to know about elderly. More information would be nice if...if elderly have used system before, show information about their preference and interest! You should recommend apps for each one."*

Finally, the videos show that volunteers in the VITA condition gave instructions more slowly, in a step-wise manner. This was in accordance with the instructions to offer single step guidance to the more severely impaired clients. The effectiveness of this behavior aligns with Jost et. al. [20]'s finding which suggested training dementia care volunteers to 'match pace' with the client. On the whole, the Activity Guide was functioning as intended in supplying appropriate content and instructions.

However, the volunteers who were paired with Planned Level clients expressed a conflicting wish. When shown both Guides, Volunteer P7 (VITA condition) preferred having fewer instructions: *"Variety was good to have. (The) Profile helps to start communicating, but Guide B is more preferred, even though Guide A (VITA) had more detail."* She felt it gave her more flexibility to respond to the client.

Another volunteer in the Control condition, P9, preferred the Guide version she was given, and reported thinking that she should *"hold back more during the session, to let the client direct it."* It seemed that less specificity was preferred when interacting with Planned Level clients.

DISCUSSION

Overall, both qualitative and quantitative findings lead us to conclude that VITA, composed of recommended apps and ability-customized facilitation instructions, can be used by volunteers to improve efficacy in engaging residents with dementia, with possibly a stronger perceived value among volunteers engaging clients with lower abilities. In addition to the main findings, we also have a few learning points, which we elaborate below.

Differential Results by Dementia Severity

A handful of previous work on engagement stimuli studies [9, 10] showed that higher functioning clients may have differing responses when compared to lower functioning clients, but little explanation was offered beyond having a longer attention span. In the case of this study, our Planned Level clients appeared to retain the ability to express preferences and maintain conversation with the facilitating partner. Since volunteers could get direct and immediate feedback from the clients, the verbal exchange was likely the most effective form of communication. This reduced the value of additional instruction, as indicated by the feedback from volunteers who used Activity Guides for Planned Level clients.

However, for clients who had lower abilities, just providing the pre-selected apps and Profile information to volunteers was not enough. It may be that this segment of the client population has more impaired communication, and inexperienced volunteers lack the ability to compensate for this loss. In this case, simple trial and error with the client did not work well, as it is difficult for the volunteers to get the needed feedback so that s/he can adapt his/her behavior to the situation. More specific guidance seemed to be appreciated by the volunteers.

These differential results may have implications for other dementia engagement researchers, as it raises the importance of analyzing intervention outcomes by client impairment severity, which is not often done. Such analyses will enable a better understanding of how interventions may be targeted. Considering that dementia is a progressive disease, understanding the effect of interventions over different stages of the disease will help the design of systems that should adapt to changes in the target user over time.

Improving Information for Volunteers

In our design, we took pains to iteratively and consultatively develop the Profile. We attempted presenting more types of background information (e.g. family history), but volunteers still appeared unable to process the information toward improving their interactions with people with dementia. Consequently, the design of the resulting Profile preferred glance-ability and ease of understanding over depth of information.

The process of Profile development uncovered a discrepancy between what volunteers have previously expressed an interest in and what volunteers can actually utilize. This is an important learning point for future work in client information systems for volunteers: even when volunteers express a specific need for information, the delivery of such information needs to be carefully balanced with how it can be digested and applied.

This did not mean that Profile content was of no use in the process of improving volunteer efficacy. Profiling for interest and ability levels formed the basis by which the Activity Guide, which *was* effective, was created. Thus, while our findings affirm related work on the importance of profiling, this study additionally suggests that inexpert caregivers should be helped in closing the knowledge-behavior gap by efficiently *translating and presenting* such information as appropriate instructions for interacting with each individual with dementia.

Reducing effort to maintain volunteer programs

VITA has the potential to reduce the amount of work needed to maintain an engagement activity program. Together, the profiling (up to 30 minutes), activity selection and guide generation (up to 20 minutes) result in a total customization time of less than an hour. Similar physical activity customization programs require about 8 hours of therapist time to customize activities for each client and train each caregiver [16]. According to the home's therapist, each Profile can be valid for about 6 months. Training time for volunteers was set at 15 minutes in this assessment, which is far less than the previously mentioned studies that place volunteer training at a minimum of 5 hours. Therefore, despite the initial time investment to curate an Activity Kit (which is highly re-useable), VITA can result in significant time savings.

Summary of VITA development

As mentioned in the development section of this paper, localized, culture- and cohort-specific content is an important element of engagement among clients. Thus, we present here the process of creating the VITA (Fig.5) for other care centers wishing to implement a tablet-based engagement activity program that utilizes the services of non-expert facilitators.

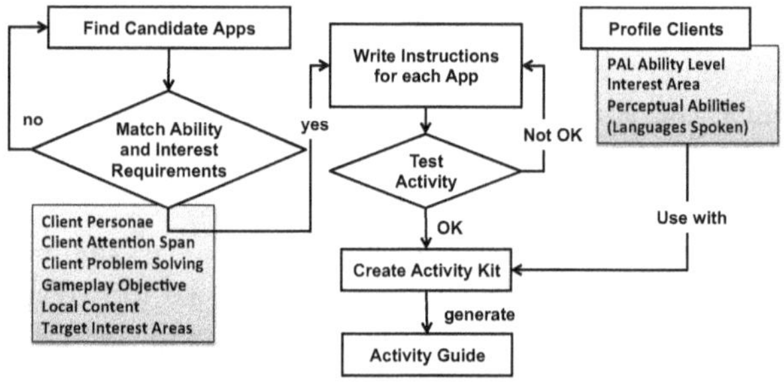

Fig. 5 VITA Creation Workflow

Limitations and Future Work

Although the result of our study is promising, a longer-term evaluation is needed to examine other related outcomes such as a reduction in negative psychosocial behaviors and impacts on the nursing home's management of volunteers. A longer-term study would enable increased understanding of sustainability and viability of VITA in the community, while unpacking further how to meet the different needs of clients with milder impairments.

CONCLUSION

The goal of our work was to meet an observed need for systems to support volunteer interactions when facilitating engagement activities to clients. In our evaluation, we found that VITA, the artifact resulting from our iterative design process could improve engagement outcomes for clients, by translating biographical information into actionable activities for untrained volunteers. In so doing, the system benefits nursing homes via the creation of a potentially stable resource for engagement activities out of a non-expert, transient volunteer population, and by saving time in deploying a volunteer expertise improvement program. In enabling more effective caregiving by volunteers, VITA represents advancement toward improving the quality of life for nursing home residents living with dementia.

ACKNOWLEDGEMENTS

This research is supported by the NUS Academic Research Fund T1 251RES1617. We thank all our participants and the staff of Villa Francis Home of the Aged who shared their valuable time and experience with us.

REFERENCES

1. Arlene J. Astell, Maggie P. Ellis, Lauren Bernardi, Norman Alm, Richard Dye, Gary Gowans, and Jim Campbell. 2010. Using a touch screen computer to support relationships between people with dementia and caregivers. *Interacting with Computers* 22, 4: 267–275. https://doi.org/10.1016/j.intcom.2010.03.003
2. Linda L. Buettner. 1999. Simple Pleasures: A multilevel sensorimotor intervention for nursing home residents with dementia. *American Journal of Alzheimer's Disease and Other Dementias* 14, 1: 41–52. https://doi.org/10.1177/153331759901400103
3. Sheung-Tak Cheng, Pizza K. Chow, Edwin C. S. Yu, and Alfred C. M. Chan. 2012. Leisure activities alleviate depressive symptoms in nursing home residents with very mild or mild dementia. *The American Journal of Geriatric Psychiatry: Official Journal of the American Association for Geriatric Psychiatry* 20, 10: 904–908. https://doi.org/10.1097/JGP.0b013e3182423988
4. Jenny C. C. Chung. 2009. An intergenerational reminiscence programme for older adults with early dementia and youth volunteers: values and challenges. *Scandinavian Journal of Caring Sciences* 23, 2: 259–264. https://doi.org/10.1111/j.1471-6712.2008.00615.x
5. J J Claus, E Mohr, and T N Chase. 1991. Clinical trials in dementia: learning effects with repeated testing. *Journal of Psychiatry and Neuroscience* 16, 1: 1–4.
6. Jiska Cohen-Mansfield, Maha Dakheel-Ali, and Marcia S. Marx. 2009. Engagement in persons with dementia: the concept and its measurement. *The American journal of geriatric psychiatry : official journal of the American Association for Geriatric Psychiatry* 17, 4: 299–307. https://doi.org/10.1097/JGP.0b013e31818f3a52
7. Jiska Cohen-Mansfield, Maha Dakheel-Ali, Khin Thein, and Marcia S. Marx. 2009. The impact of stimulus attributes on engagement of nursing home residents with dementia. *Archives of Gerontology and Geriatrics* 49, 1: 1–6. https://doi.org/10.1016/j.archger.2008.04.002
8. Jiska Cohen-Mansfield, Marcia S. Marx, Laurence S. Freedman, Havi Murad, Natalie G. Regier, Khin Thein, and Maha Dakheel-Ali. 2011. The Comprehensive Process Model of Engagement. *The American journal of geriatric psychiatry : official journal of the American Association for Geriatric Psychiatry* 19, 10: 859–870. https://doi.org/10.1097/JGP.0b013e318202bf5b
9. Jiska Cohen-Mansfield, Marcia S. Marx, Khin Thein, and Maha Dakheel-Ali. 2011. The Impact of Stimuli on Affect in Persons With Dementia. *The Journal of clinical psychiatry* 72, 4: 480–486. https://doi.org/10.4088/JCP.09m05694oli
10. Jiska Cohen-Mansfield, Khin Thein, Maha Dakheel-Ali, and Marcia S. Marx. 2010. The underlying meaning of stimuli: Impact on engagement of persons with dementia. *Psychiatry Research* 177, 1–2: 216–222. https://doi.org/10.1016/j.psychres.2009.02.010
11. Masashi Crete-Nishihata, Ronald M. Baecker, Michael Massimi, Deborah Ptak, Rachelle Campigotto, Liam D. Kaufman, Adam M. Brickman, Gary R. Turner, Joshua R. Steinerman, and Sandra E. Black. 2012. Reconstructing the Past: Personal Memory Technologies Are Not Just Personal and Not Just for Memory. *Human–Computer Interaction* 27, 1-2: 92–123. https://doi.org/10.1080/07370024.2012.656062
12. Thecla Damianakis. 2007. Volunteers' experiences visiting the cognitively impaired in nursing homes: a friendly visiting program. *Canadian Journal on Aging = La Revue Canadienne Du Vieillissement* 26, 4: 343–356. https://doi.org/10.3138/cja.26.4.343
13. M. H. Davis, J. A. Hall, and M. Meyer. 2003. The First Year: Influences on the Satisfaction, Involvement, and Persistence of New Community Volunteers. *Personality and Social Psychology Bulletin* 29, 2: 248–260. https://doi.org/10.1177/0146167202239050
14. Paul P. Falkowski. 2013. Volunteer programming impact on long-term care facilities. *Thesis*. Retrieved December 27, 2015 from http://digitalcommons.unl.edu/cehsdiss/169/
15. Pin Sym Foong and Shengdong Zhao. 2016. Design Considerations for Volunteer Support in Dementia Care. In *Proceedings of the International Symposium on Interactive Technology and Ageing Populations* (ITAP '16), 54–63. https://doi.org/10.1145/2996267.2996273
16. Laura N. Gitlin, Laraine Winter, Tracey Vause Earland, E. Adel Herge, Nancy L. Chernett, Catherine V. Piersol, and Janice P. Burke. 2009. The Tailored Activity Program to Reduce Behavioral Symptoms in Individuals With Dementia: Feasibility, Acceptability, and Replication Potential. *The Gerontologist* 49, 3: 428–439. https://doi.org/10.1093/geront/gnp087
17. Sara Raquel Costa Guerra, Sara Holtum Demain, Daniela Maria Pias Figueiredo, and Liliana Xavier Marques De Sousa. 2012. Being a Volunteer: Motivations, Fears, and Benefits of Volunteering in an Intervention Program for People With Dementia and Their Families. *Activities, Adaptation & Aging* 36, 1: 55–78. https://doi.org/10.1080/01924788.2011.647538
18. Wallis Jansson, Britt Almberg, Margareta Grafström, and Bengt Winblad. 1998. The Circle Model—support for relatives of people with dementia. *International Journal of Geriatric Psychiatry* 13, 10: 674–681. https://doi.org/10.1002/(SICI)1099-1166(1998100)13:10<674::AID-GPS840>3.0.CO;2-D
19. A. Jost, E. Neumann, and K.-H. Himmelmann. 2010. Synchronized communication between people with dementia and their volunteer caregivers. A video-based explorative study on temporal aspects of interaction and the transfer to education. *Current Alzheimer Research* 7, 5: 439–444.

20. Annemarie Jost, Eva Neumann, and K.-H. Himmelmann. 2010. Synchronized Communication Between People with Dementia and their Volunteer Caregivers. A Video-Based Explorative Study on Temporal Aspects of Interaction and the Transfer to Education. *Current Alzheimer Research* 7, 5: 439–444.
21. Barbara B. Kawulich. 2005. Participant Observation as a Data Collection Method. *Forum Qualitative Sozialforschung / Forum: Qualitative Social Research* 6, 2. Retrieved September 5, 2016 from http://www.qualitative-research.net/index.php/fqs/article/view/466
22. Ann Kolanowski and Linda Buettner. 2008. Prescribing Activities that Engage Passive Residents. An Innovative Method. *Journal of gerontological nursing* 34, 1: 13–18.
23. Elsa Leone, Audrey Deudon, Julie Piano, Philippe Robert, and Arnaud Dechamps. 2012. Are Dementia Patient's Engagement Using Tailored Stimuli the Same? The Apathy Dilemma in Nursing Home Residents. *Current Gerontology and Geriatrics Research* 2012: e942640. https://doi.org/10.1155/2012/942640
24. Elizabeth Lokon, Jennifer M. Kinney Kinney, and Suzanne Kunkel Kunkel. 2012. Building Bridges Across Age and Cognitive Barriers Through Art: College Students' Reflections on an Intergenerational Program With Elders who Have Dementia. *Journal of Intergenerational Relationships* 10, 4: 337–354. https://doi.org/10.1080/15350770.2012.724318
25. Neil Maiden, Sonali D'Souza, Sara Jones, Lars Müller, Lucia Pannese, Kristine Pitts, Michael Prilla, Kevin Pudney, Malcolm Rose, Ian Turner, and Konstantinos Zachos. 2013. Computing Technologies for Reflective, Creative Care of People with Dementia. *Commun. ACM* 56, 11: 60–67. https://doi.org/10.1145/2500495
26. Kristin Martin-Cook, Linda Hynan, Paul K. Chafetz, and Myron F. Weiner. 2001. Impact of family visits on agitation in residents with dementia. *American Journal of Alzheimer's Disease and Other Dementias* 16, 3: 163–166. https://doi.org/10.1177/153331750101600307
27. Simon McCallum and Costas Boletsis. 2013. A Taxonomy of Serious Games for Dementia. In *Games for Health*, Ben Schouten, Stephen Fedtke, Tilde Bekker, Marlies Schijven and Alex Gekker (eds.). Springer Fachmedien Wiesbaden, 219–232. Retrieved October 27, 2015 from http://link.springer.com.libproxy1.nus.edu.sg/chapter/10.1007/978-3-658-02897-8_17
28. Nan D. Musson, Jean Kincaid, Pat Ryan, Betty Glussman, Litha Varone, Nydia Gamarra, Reba Wilson, William Reefe, and Michael Silverman. Nature, nurture, nutrition: Interdisciplinary programs to address the prevention of malnutrition and dehydration. *Dysphagia* 5, 2: 96–101. https://doi.org/10.1007/BF02412651
29. Joseph Nagel, Peter Cimbolic, and Margie Newlin. 1988. Efficacy of elderly and adolescent volunteer counselors in a nursing home setting. *Journal of Counseling Psychology* 35, 1: 81–86. https://doi.org/10.1037/0022-0167.35.1.81
30. Eva S. van der Ploeg, Tapiwa Mbakile, Sandra Genovesi, and Daniel W. O'Connor. 2012. The potential of volunteers to implement non-pharmacological interventions to reduce agitation associated with dementia in nursing home residents. *International psychogeriatrics / IPA* 24, 11: 1790–1797. https://doi.org/10.1017/S1041610212000798
31. E. Rosa, G. Lussignoli, F. Sabbatini, A. Chiappa, S. Di Cesare, L. Lamanna, and O. Zanetti. 2010. Needs of caregivers of the patients with dementia. *Archives of Gerontology and Geriatrics* 51, 1: 54–58. https://doi.org/10.1016/j.archger.2009.07.008
32. Marén Schorch, Lin Wan, David William Randall, and Volker Wulf. 2016. Designing for Those Who Are Overlooked: Insider Perspectives on Care Practices and Cooperative Work of Elderly Informal Caregivers. In *Proceedings of the 19th ACM Conference on Computer-Supported Cooperative Work & Social Computing* (CSCW '16), 787–799. https://doi.org/10.1145/2818048.2819999
33. Matthieu Tixier and Myriam Lewkowicz. 2015. Looking for Respite and Support: Technological Opportunities for Spousal Caregivers. In *Proceedings of the 33rd Annual ACM Conference on Human Factors in Computing Systems* (CHI '15), 1155–1158. https://doi.org/10.1145/2702123.2702563
34. Maranda A. Trahan, Julie Kuo, Michelle C. Carlson, and Laura N. Gitlin. 2014. A Systematic Review of Strategies to Foster Activity Engagement in Persons With Dementia. *Health Education & Behavior* 41, 1 suppl: 70S–83S. https://doi.org/10.1177/1090198114531782
35. Jayne Wallace, Anja Thieme, Gavin Wood, Guy Schofield, and Patrick Olivier. 2012. Enabling Self, Intimacy and a Sense of Home in Dementia: An Enquiry into Design in a Hospital Setting. In *Proceedings of the SIGCHI Conference on Human Factors in Computing Systems* (CHI '12), 2629–2638. https://doi.org/10.1145/2207676.2208654
36. Jayne Wallace, Peter C. Wright, John McCarthy, David Philip Green, James Thomas, and Patrick Olivier. 2013. A Design-led Inquiry into Personhood in Dementia. In *Proceedings of the SIGCHI Conference on Human Factors in Computing Systems* (CHI '13), 2617–2626. https://doi.org/10.1145/2470654.2481363
37. Gemma Webster and Vicki L. Hanson. 2014. Technology for Supporting Care Staff in Residential Homes. *ACM Trans. Access. Comput.* 5, 3: 8:1–8:23. https://doi.org/10.1145/2543577
38. Jacob O. Wobbrock, Leah Findlater, Darren Gergle, and James J. Higgins. 2011. The Aligned Rank Transform for Nonparametric Factorial Analyses

Using Only Anova Procedures. In *Proceedings of the SIGCHI Conference on Human Factors in Computing Systems* (CHI '11), 143–146. https://doi.org/10.1145/1978942.1978963
39. Intermediate and Long-term Care in Singapore | Ministry of Health. Retrieved August 23, 2016 from https://www.moh.gov.sg/content/moh_web/home/Publications/information_papers/2006/intermediate_andlong-termcareinsingapore.html
40. Clevermind. *Clevermind.* Retrieved September 7, 2016 from http://myclevermind.com/
41. GreyMatters: Reaching Beyond Dementia. *App Store.* Retrieved September 7, 2016 from https://itunes.apple.com/us/app/greymatters-reaching-beyond/id900645661?mt=8
42. Jackie Pool Associates. Retrieved September 16, 2015 from http://www.jackiepoolassociates.org/

Micro-Versioning Tool to Support Experimentation in Exploratory Programming

Hiroaki Mikami
The University of Tokyo
Tokyo, Japan
mhiroaki@is.s.u-tokyo.ac.jp

Daisuke Sakamoto
The University of Tokyo
Tokyo, Japan
d.sakamoto@acm.org

Takeo Igarashi
The University of Tokyo
Tokyo, Japan
takeo@acm.org

ABSTRACT
Experimentation plays an essential role in exploratory programming, and programmers apply version control operations when switching the part of the source code back to the past state during experimentation. However, these operations, which we refer to as *micro-versioning*, are not well supported in current programming environments. We first examined previous studies to clarify the requirements for a micro-versioning tool. We then developed a micro-versioning tool that displays visual cues representing possible micro-versioning operations in a textual code editor. Our tool includes a history model that generates meaningful candidates by combining a regional undo model and tree-structured undo model. The history model uses code executions as a delimiter to segment text edit operations into meaning groups. A user study involving programmers indicated that our tool satisfies the above-mentioned requirements and that it is useful for exploratory programming.

ACM Classification Keywords
H.5.2 Information Interfaces and Presentation (e.g., HCI): User Interfaces; D.2.6 Software Engineering: Programming Environments

Author Keywords
Develpment environment; micro-versioning; version control system

INTRODUCTION
Experimentation is an essential part of exploratory programming; programmers write an experimental code fragment, test it, and discard the fragment frequently during programming [2, 13, 23]. During the iterations of this process, programmers often have to switch the part of the source code back to the past state. For example, they may sometimes restore a past code because the new code does not work as expected. Programmers use and modify different versions of source code when they revert the source code. These behaviors can be regarded as a series of small-scale version control operations, which we refer to as *micro-versioning*.

CHI 2017, May 6-11, 2017, Denver, CO, USA.

ACM ISBN 978-1-4503-4655-9/17/05 ...$15.00.
http://dx.doi.org/10.1145/3025453.3025597

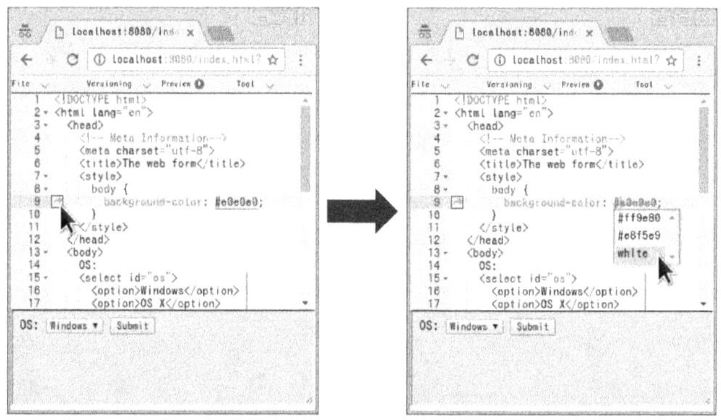

Figure 1. Screenshot of our prototype tool. It works in text editor to support micro-versioning. Our current implementation is designed for development of web page using HTML, CSS, and JavaScript. Bottom part shows preview of web page being developed.

A linear undo tool is widely used for micro-versioning. However, it causes various problems because it cannot undo edits if they are not the latest. Programmers need to manually maintain consistency if multiple separate parts of the code need to be undone together. For example, a programmer has to conduct linear undo operations twice to restore a deleted button widget and an associated listener code if she wants to restore the button widget. The button widget will not work if she forgets to restore the associated listener code.

Version control systems (VCSs), e.g., Git [9], are tools to support advanced operations such as commit and revert. However, they are designed to support version control operations during large-scale, collaborative software development and are not suitable for micro-versioning. These tools prevent users from conducting rapid micro-versioning operations because of the heavyweight of their user interfaces, that is, programmers have to open separate dialogs, find a specific edit, and select it to apply a versioning operation.

Yoon et al. reported that nearly 30% of micro-versioning operations are conducted by rewriting a source code directly [24]. However, a direct rewrite sometimes causes inappropriate text edits [23]. This suggests that programming environments require micro-versioning features that are better suited than the current tools. Therefore, we propose a micro-versioning tool that provides appropriate support in terms of the user interface and edit history.

We refer to version control operations *during exploratory programming* as micro-versioning. The granularity of the micro-versioning operations is between *backtracking* [23, 24] and version control operations conducted using VCSs. Backtracking focuses on only one region of a source code. On the other hand, versioning conducted using VCSs affects multiple regions and is often a large-scale, collaborative task involving multiple programmers. Micro-versioning also handles multiple regions of a source code; however, it is a small-scale, personal task. In this study, we used code executions as a delimiter to separate edit history into a meaningful set of edit operations [10]. This is based on an assumption that the user would execute a code after implementing a meaningful set of edits but would not execute it in the middle of a sequence of related edits.

We examined previous studies [21, 23, 24] to identify the following requirements for a micro-versioning tool. 1) It should have a lightweight user interface; 2) provide the user with visual information of operation; and 3) have an appropriate history model that proposes a limited amount of applicable micro-versioning features. We then developed a micro-versioning tool based on this analysis (Figure 1). The tool displays a candidate list, which is inspired by the auto-completion feature of integrated development environments (IDEs), to conduct micro-versioning. The tool visually represents locations where version control operations can be conducted. It also visualizes the operation in a code editor. We present our novel history model based on an current selective undo model [25]. Our model can extract meaningful micro-versioning operations from an edit history, eliminating inappropriate candidates. Finally, we report the results of a user study we conducted involving five participants to evaluate the usability of our tool and history model. We found that our tool satisfies the above requirements.

The main contributions of this study are as follows.

- We clarified the requirements for micro-versioning features based on previous research and developed a tool that contains the following two components.
- We developed a user interface to allow users to conduct micro-versioning operations in the main code editor without using separate dialogs.
- We constructed a history model that can extract meaningful micro-versioning operations from an edit history.
- We conducted a user study that demonstrated the usability of our tool and the effectiveness of our history model.

RELATED WORK

Linear Undo and Commenting Out

Programmers mostly conduct micro-versioning in two ways. The first involves using a linear undo tool [24], which can undo the latest edit (this is known as the shortcut-key `Ctrl+Z` in Windows and `Command-Z` in Mac OS). The second is based on commenting out [23], which is a feature of a programming language. These tools' capabilities are limited, but they and the features are widely used. For example, a linear undo tool cannot undo edits if they are not the latest. In addition, commenting out is problematic when multiple separate parts of the code need to be commented out or uncommented out together because programmers need to manually maintain consistency.

Extended Undo Tools

There are various extensions of linear undo tools because such tools are widely used and present many problems. Some text editors, such as Emacs [7], provide regional undo features that allow users to undo the latest edit in the selected region. These features solve the limitations of linear undo tools to some extent, but several problems remain. First, these tools do not provide visual representations, so they are often composed of a hidden feature. Second, they cannot apply edits to separate multiple parts of the source code at the same time. Finally, they cannot be used for all typical micro-versioning situations. For example, they cannot restore some previous text if there are undone text edits. Gundo [12] and Undo Tree [20] allow users to restore any previous texts by using tree-structured histories. However, these tools use complex user interfaces and cannot conduct regional undo operations, which are the most popular micro-versioning operations [25].

Several researchers have proposed selective undo tools that can undo any edits [18, 25], but they also use complex user interfaces. For example, when programmers selectively undo a specific edit in the simplest way, they are required to 1) open the history view, 2) find the edit they want to undo in the history view, and 3) undo the edit. Previous research has shown that many programmers tend to prefer lightweight user interfaces such as keyboard shortcuts (e.g., Quick Assist in Eclipse) rather than complex user interfaces such as dialogs and menus [21].

These tools [18, 25] sometimes generate inappropriate candidates as a result. The algorithm proposed by Yoon et al. [25] is used to attempt to generate appropriate candidates by considering regional conflicts. However, it still fails to eliminate inappropriate candidates in some cases. For example, suppose that a programmer sets a variable to `1.0`, changes the variable to `2.0`, undoes the previous edit, and finally changes the variable from `1.0` to `3.0`. If the user redoes the second operation, the algorithm generates `2.03.0`, which is inappropriate as a code. Our history model addresses these problems.

Version Control Systems

Version control systems are used often in programming. Many IDEs provide extensions that allow users to use VCSs [6] inside; however, they use complex user interfaces. Lee et al. proposed an IDE extension that embeds the information from VCSs into the code completion features [15]. This exetension allows users to complete the current method name using the method name of a previous version that exists in the program. However, this extension is not suitable for micro-versioning because such tools require that users commit manually, which is a heavy-weight process for micro-versioning.

Many IDEs have local history-keeping features that save the source code when a programmer saves a file, which allows the user to restore it later [5]. However, these features involve complex user interfaces such as dialogs and menus, and most only support linear undos, so they are also not suitable for micro-versioning. Steinert et al. proposed an IDE extension that suggests version information to users based on the difference between versions of abstract syntax trees (ASTs) and the success rate of unit tests [19]. The usability for programmers was not tested, but this extension helps users to understand the versions of a program.

History Management Models

Several studies have proposed history models that allow users to manage and manipulate a history more efficiently. Nancel et al. proposed a conceptual model of interacting with a history, which uses information related to the target content of a history (e.g., texts and images), application, and commands made by the user [17]. However, this model cannot conduct regional undo operations and apply text edits to multiple separate parts of a source code at the same time, although both this model and that of our proposed tool are for simulating a tree structure within a linear history model. Cass et al. proposed a selective undo algorithm and model, which use a process-programming language to define the dependencies for a task [4]. Their model and our model are for eliminating inappropriate candidates from the result of selectively undoing, but their model cannot apply text edits to multiple separate parts of a source code at the same time. In addition, it is unrealistic to always expect the definition of a task model for programming because programming is a complex task, and there are many types of tasks in programming. Hayashi et al. proposed a tool that enables the refactoring of the edit history [14]. Both this tool and our model are for obtaining the edit history that is useful for version control operations; however, the tool requires a user to refactor the edit history manually.

Git [9] allows the user to revert a commit selectively by using the `git revert` command. The history model used by Git does not directly support regional undo operations, although it has the characteristics of both tree-structured history models and selective undo history models. This model is not suitable for micro-versioning because regional undo operations are popular in micro-versioning [25]. Git also allows the user to selectively revert the region of the source code to the previous commit by using the `git checkout -p` command. It enables a user to conduct all micro-versioning operations; however, a user has to manually maintain consistency. The history model of Git does not contain the information when the user conducts the `git checkout -p` command.

LITERATURE SURVEY TO ELICIT MICRO-VERSIONING TOOL REQUIREMENTS

We investigated previous studies to better understand the problems that programmers encounter during micro-versioning and to elucidate the requirements for efficient micro-versioning tools. First, we investigated previous studies on *backtracking*, which is a user's action during micro-versioning, to better understand some of the problems of micro-versioning. These studies show that programmers often use linear undo tools or commenting out for micro-versioning and that these tools and features have various problems [23, 24]. Programmers sometimes cannot use linear undo tools because nearly 10% of all *backtracking* operations are selective [24]. In addition, programmers often make mistakes when they comment or uncomment out multiple separate parts of a source code at the same time [23]. This indicates that a micro-versioning tool requires a history model that can propose typical micro-versioning operations.

We also investigated previous studies on automated refactoring tools. Several studies indicate that an automated refactoring tool should have a simple, minimal, and lightweight user interface, which allows users to conduct refactoring rapidly because programmers tend to prefer these user interfaces [16, 21]. In addition, several studies indicate that refactoring tools should provide information 1) to support decision making and 2) prevent the tool from being a hidden feature [16, 21].

These previous studies took into account automated refactoring tools, but we believe the same issues affect micro-versioning tools; micro-versioning tools should have the same requirements as automated refactoring tools. A micro-versioning tool should have a lightweight user interface and provide visual information.

Based on our literature survey, we established the following requirements for a micro-versioning tool.

- A tool should have a lightweight user interface that allows the user to conduct micro-versioning operations rapidly. Thus, it should not use separate dialogs or user interfaces that are similar to these dialogs.
- It should provide users with visual information to make them aware of a tool and support decision making. It should always display visual representations and information about micro-versioning operations that are applicable.
- Finally, it should use a history model that proposes applicable micro-versioning operations.

OUR MICRO-VERSIONING TOOL

We designed our micro-versioning tool based on the requirements described above. The tool's user interface is lightweight and provides the user with visual information about micro-versioning operations. As described in the next section, the history model used with the tool can conduct typical micro-versioning operations and eliminate inappropriate candidates.

Our tool works inside a text editor and can be used for any textual programming language. The user can use both our tool and traditional methods (e.g., linear undo tools and commenting-out) because our tool is integrated in a typical text editor.

Example Scenario

Suppose a programmer creates a web-form. The web-form gathers information about a user's operating system (OS). She first uses the text field to input the name of the OS (Step 1 in Figure 2). She then replaces the user interface of the web-form from the text filed to the dropdown list because there are only a few OSes (Step 2 in Figure 2). Note that this edit affects multiple locations in the code. She then modifies the background color of the web-form (Step 3 in Figure 2). She presses the preview button after each change to see the result. Our proposed tool records all these edit operations.

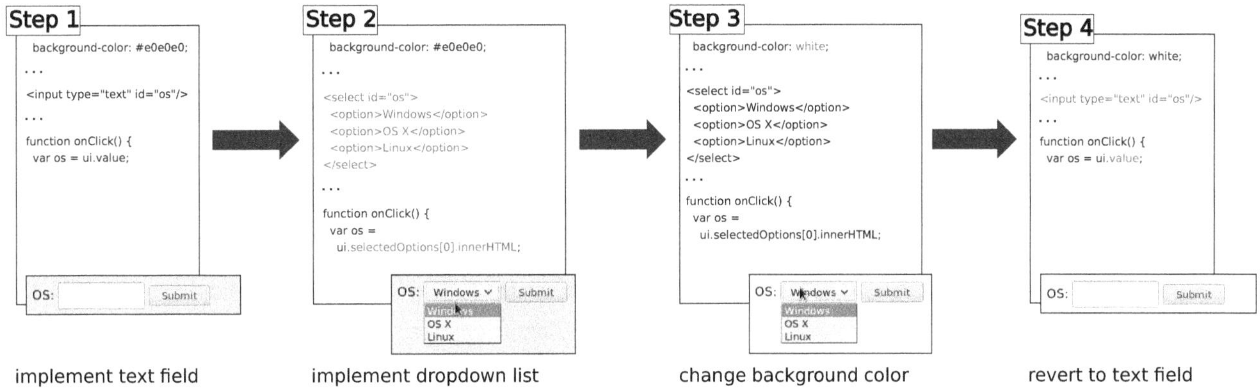

Figure 2. Example scenario of micro-versioning.

She notices that the dropdown list is unsuitable for the web-form because some users have several PCs. She wants to revert the change in the user interface. She sees *a marker* (Figure 5 A) and *indicator* (Figure 5 B), which are displayed with our tool, and notices that she can conduct micro-versioning operations related to the `select` tag by using our tool. The indicator and marker are generated by the recorded edit history.

She clicks the marker to conduct a micro-versioning operation. Our tool displays *a candidate list* (Figure 5 C) and *edit details* (Figure 5 D and E). She understands that the operation shown in the candidate list will revert the change in the user interface and the JavaScript program, which are required in order to use the text field. She clicks the operation shown in the candidate list because the operation matches her purpose. Finally, our tool conducts the micro-versioning operation, and the web-form uses the text field (Step 4 in Figure 2). Note that multiple lines including separated ones are appropriately reverted together.

Lightweight User Interface

We designed the proposed tool so users can conduct all the basic operations related to micro-versioning inside the text editor without separate dialogs. The tool displays all the user interface elements in a text editor and displays indicators as visual representations. Four types of indicators (Figure 3) are used. The type (i) indicator, which is a vertical line located to the right of a text, is used when the tool must delete or replace lines of the text. The type (ii) indicator, which is a triangle located to the left of a text, is used when it is necessary to insert lines. The type (iii) indicator, which is a text underline, is used when it is necessary to delete or replace words. Finally, the type (iv) indicator, which is a triangle located at the bottom of the line, is used to insert words.

The tool displays markers to allow easy access by a user because the indicators are small and difficult to click. The location of a marker depends on the corresponding text. If the corresponding text is composed of less than one line, a marker is located near the gutter of the text editor, which displays line numbers (Figure 4 A); otherwise, the marker is located to the right of the text (Figure 5 A). The candidate list is displayed when a user clicks on a marker or indicator or uses

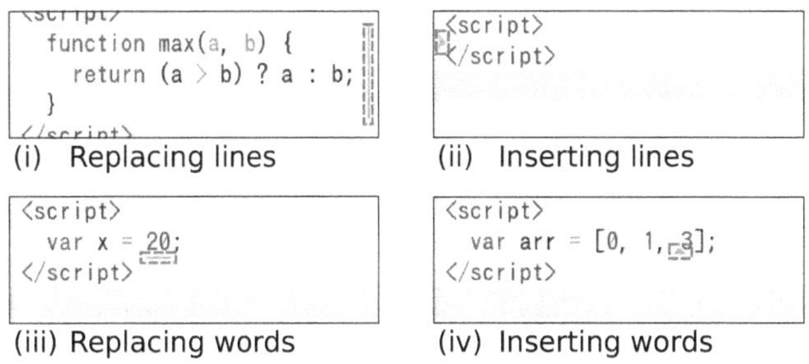

Figure 3. Four types of indicators.

the keyboard shortcut (`Ctrl+Space` by default). There are two types of candidate lists. The drop-down list (Figure 4 B), which is located below the text, is used when the related indicator type is (iii) or (iv); otherwise, the second (Figure 5 C) is used, which is located to the right of the text. Edit details are displayed either within the text editor or on the scrollbar (Figure 5 D and E). In addition, the user can use a mouse and keyboard to interact with our tool, such as opening a candidate list and conducting a micro-versioning operation.

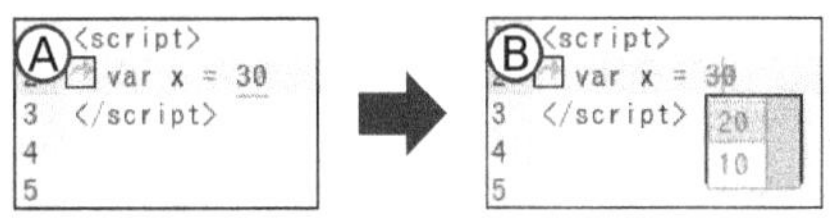

Figure 4. A) Example of marker and indicator. B) Example of candidate list, which is located below text.

Visual Information

Our tool always displays indicators to enhance the user's awareness of micro-versioning operations. A marker is displayed if the caret of the text editor is positioned on the corresponding text, which provides the user with information about the micro-versioning operations that are applicable to the focused text.

In addition, edit details and candidate lists provide information about a micro-versioning operation, such as text inserted and deleted by the micro-versioning operation. Edit details in the scrollbar show information regardless of whether the micro-versioning operations are displayed onscreen. If an

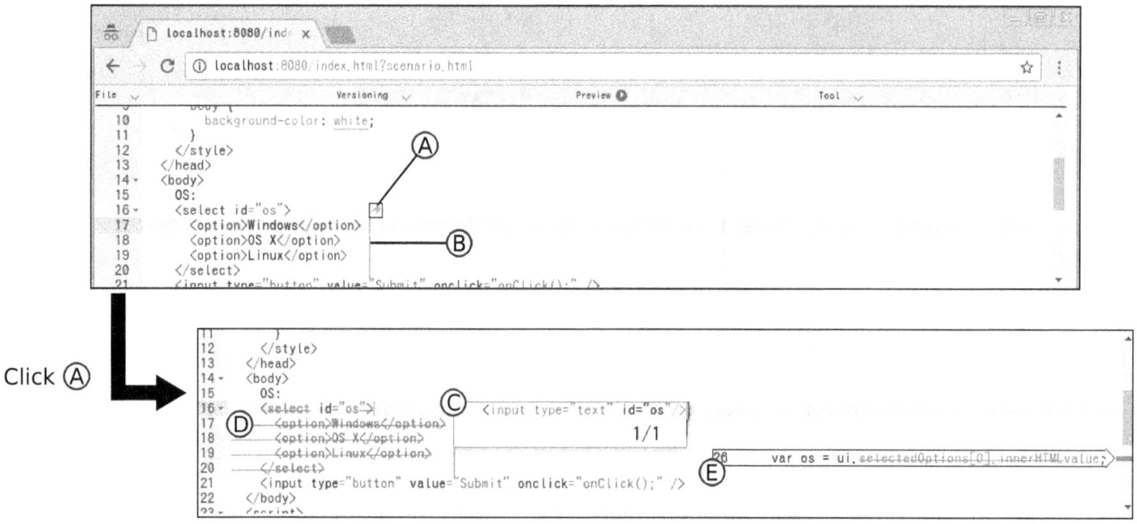

Figure 5. Lightweight user interface for micro-versioning. (A) Marker, (B) indicator. (C) candidate list, and (D and E) editing details

operation affects a large part of the source code, some edits are not visible on the screen. Thus, users are unable to follow what occurs when some edits are not displayed onscreen. We addressed this issue by displaying edit details that show the line numbers and the difference between texts on the scrollbar. The user can understand the outcomes of a micro-versioning operation by observing the edit details, so it is expected that they can conduct more accurate micro-versioning operations by using our tool compared with using linear undo tools or commenting-out. The text deleted by the operation appears as struck-out red text, whereas any text inserted by the operations is represented as blue text in edit details (Figure 5 D and E) and candidate lists (Figure 5 C).

Search Feature

The tool implements a feature that allows the user to search through all the recorded versions using text (Figure 6). The tool shows only recent operations inside the main text editor view to prevent confusion (described in the next section), however, this search feature will search for all the versions stored in the tool. The user opens the search bar, types text in it, and clicks the find button in the search bar. The tool then opens a candidate list and focuses on the operation that includes the typed text. If the user clicks the find button once more, the tool shows another operation that includes the text. This search feature is particularly useful when the user does not remember the location of the target micro version, but remembers the text included in the version.

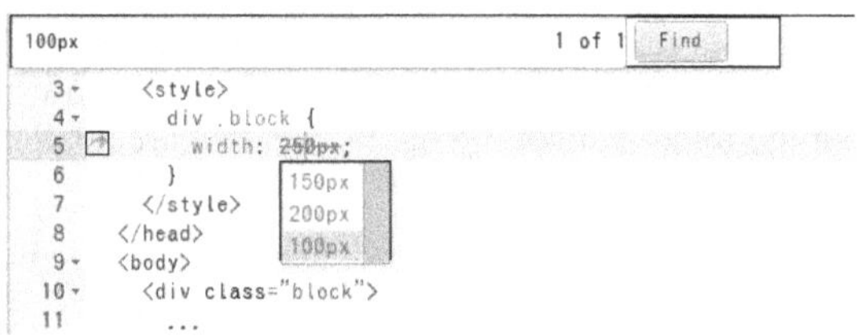

Figure 6. Search feature

HISTORY MODEL

Our history model extends the selective undo model [25] so that it can generate meaningful micro-versioning operations from an edit history. Specifically, our model supports the following four novel features: 1) regional redo, 2) exclusive edits, 3) grouping of separate edits, and 4) redo propagation. Before explaining these extensions, we first describe the basic building blocks of our model.

The original selective undo model aggregates collocated text edit operations (deletion, insertion, and replacement) into one and uses it as a basic unit. We call this an *atomic edit*. Our model also uses atomic edits but introduces a novel structure called *edit fragment* on top of them and uses it as a basic unit. An edit fragment wraps an atomic edit (called *representative edit*) and stores the following four additional pieces of information associated with the representative edit.

First, each edit fragment contains a flag indicating whether it is currently enabled or disabled. Second, each edit fragment stores timestamps when it was toggled (enabled or disabled) in the past. This is used to calculate its score when the system enumerates the candidates. Third, each edit fragment stores all the atomic edits caused by its last toggle. This information (called *affected edits*, AE) is necessary to undo these atomic edits when the edit fragment is toggled again. Finally, each edit fragment stores all the edit fragments that were disabled when it was disabled last time. This information (called *affected fragments*, AF) is used to support redo propagation.

Our model also stores *dependency relation* among edit fragments (this corresponds to *conflicts* among atomic edits in [25]). We define an edit fragment f2 *depending on* f1 when f2 is later than f1 and f2's representative edit overlaps that of f1 (Figure 7). Our model propagates disablement and enablement following the dependency relationship as in [25]. When f2 is enabled, f1 is automatically enabled. When f1 is disabled, then f2 is automatically disabled.

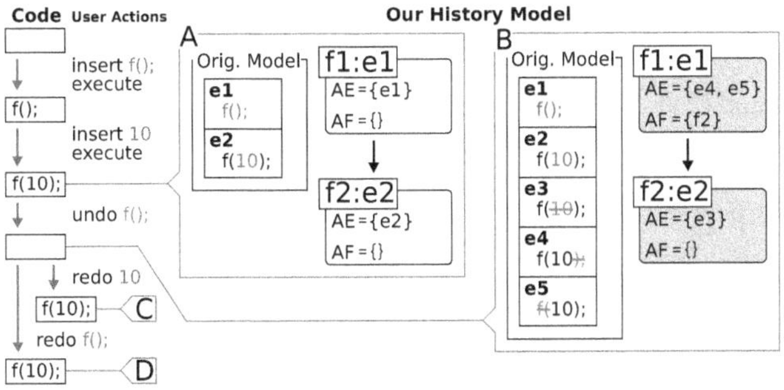

Figure 7. Regional undo and redo propagation. Our model wraps original model. e1 to e5 are atomic edits. f1 and f2 are edit fragments. Gray fragments are disabled. Black arrows represent dependency between edit fragments.

1) Regional Redo

The original model supports regional undo but does not fully support regional *redo*. Consider the situation shown in Figure 7. If the user undoes `e1` after Figure 7 A, the original model appropriately undoes `e2` as well (regional undo). However, if the user redoes `e2` after Figure 7 B (which corresponds to undoing `e3` in their model), the result becomes `10`, which is inappropriate. Ideally, the result should be `f(10)`.

Our model addresses this problem using the dependency relation among edit fragments. When the user redoes `e2` after Figure 7 B, it is recognized as enabling `f2` in our model. Since the model determines that `f2` depends on `f1`, it also enables `f1`. Enabling `f2` undoes `e3` and enabling `f1` undoes `e4` and `e5`, resulting in `f(10)` as expected (Figure 7 C).

2) Exclusive Edits

The original model fails to properly handle exclusive edits. Consider the situation shown in Figure 8. Since `e2` and `e3` replaced the same text, they should not coexist. However, if the user redoes `e2`, the original model is not aware of the relation and produces `x=2.03.0`, which is inappropriate.

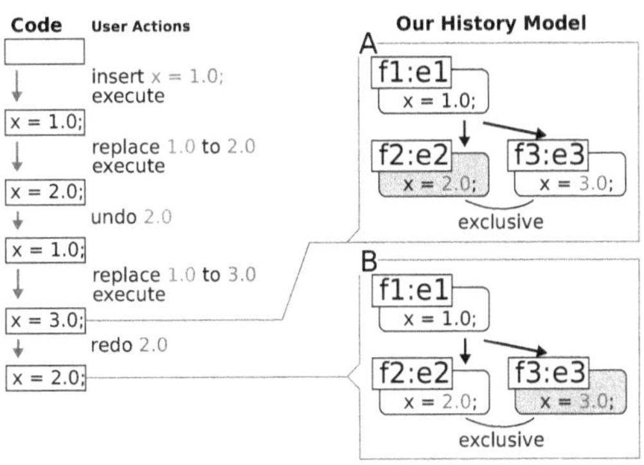

Figure 8. Example of model structure that contains *exclusive* relation.

Our model addresses this problem by simulating a tree-structured undo model by introducing an *exclusive* relation among edit fragments. We define that two edit fragments are *exclusively* related if they delete the same part of a text. When the user enables an edit fragment `f`, it automatically disables edit fragments that are *exclusively* related to `f`. For example, `f2` and `f3` in Figure 8 are *exclusively* related because both delete `1.0`. If the user enables `f2` after Figure 8 A, it disables `f3`, producing `x=2.0` as expected (Figure 8 B).

3) Grouping Separated Edits

The original model fails to handle separated, but related edits properly. Suppose that the user inserts `x=10;` and `print(x);` in distant locations in a code. If the user undoes `x=10;` then the system should also undo `print(x);` because `print(x);` becomes inappropriate without `x=10;`. However, the original model cannot support this.

Our model supports grouping of such separate edit fragments by using code executions as delimiter. The edit fragments created between the same two code executions are put into the same group [10]. If the model toggles an edit fragment `f`, it also toggles all the edit fragments in the same group. Consider the situation shown in Figure 9. If the user disables `f1`, the model disables `f2` because they are in the same group.

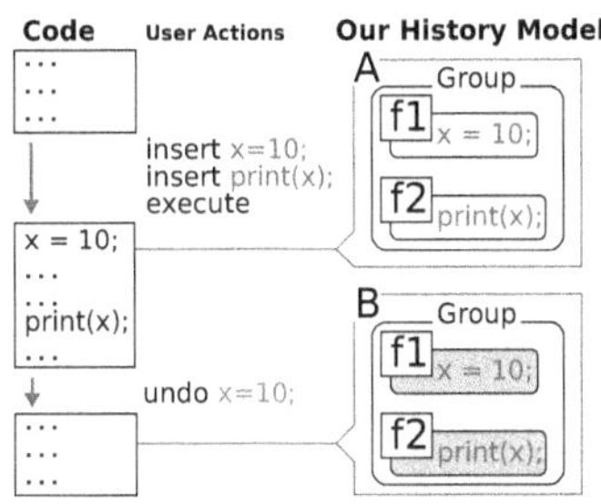

Figure 9. Example of model structure that contains separated but related edit fragments. Edit fragments f1 and f2 are put in same group.

4) Redo Propagation

If the user undoes an operation and redoes it later, the original code before undo should be restored. However, the original model fails to support this. Consider the situation shown in Figure 7. The original state is `f(10)` at Figure 7 A. When the user undoes `e1`, the original model also undoes `e2` because `e2` is dependent on `e1` (Figure 7 B). However, when the user redoes `e1` later, it does not redo `e2`, resulting in `f()`, which is different from the original state `f(10)`.

Our model uses the affected fragments stored in each edit fragment to address this problem. When the user enables an edit fragment, it also enables its affected fragments. Suppose that the user enables `f1` after Figure 7 B. The system automatically enables `f2` because `f2` is recorded as an affected fragment of `f1`. This successfully restores the original state `f(10)` (Figure 7 D).

Enumeration of Candidates

Our history model needs to enumerate candidate micro-versioning operations to show them in the code editor. First, the model calculates a score for each edit fragment by using an evaluation function found in an existing bug prediction algorithm [11] to generate candidates. The algorithm scores each edit fragment based on how many times the edit fragment was toggled, as well as their recentness. Second, it extracts the edit fragments with the highest N scores. We use $N = 5$ in our current implementation. It then toggles each edit fragment. Our model toggles other edit fragments related to the edit fragment as described above. The resulting code becomes a candidate of micro-versioning operations. Identical candidates are unified, so the number of candidates is less than N.

For example, the model extracts `f1` and `f2` in Figure 7 A in the case in which $N = 2$. The system generates an empty text as a result of disabling `f1` (disabling `f2` as well as a side effect), and generates `f()` as a result of disabling `f2` (no side effect).

IMPLEMENTATION

We implemented our micro-versioning tool as an extension of the Ace text editor[1], which works inside a web browser. The user interface of the micro-versioning tool was written in JavaScript, and the history model was implemented in Scala. The implemented tool is a text editor for coding HTML, CSS, and JavaScript. In addition to this micro-versioning tool, we implemented typical features of text editors, such as opening and saving a file. Our tool can also display the preview of the HTML opened in the text editor. Our current implementation is a proof-of-concept prototype and is missing important features to be used as a full-fledged coding environment. First, our current implementation only supports the edit of a single document (source code), and does not support the development of a system consisting of multiple documents. Second, our current implementation is built on a plain text editor and does not provide advanced supports seen in standard IDEs such as code completion and error highlighting.

The output of the history model is a set of candidate source codes, each of which corresponds to a candidate micro-versioning operation enumerated with the model. The system generates visual elements for each candidate source code as follows. The system first calculates the word-level differences between the current source code and the candidate source code using `dwdiff -P` command[2]. The tool also calculates the line-level difference by using the histogram diff algorithm[3], which is the algorithm used in EGit [6]. A collocated set of word-level and line-level differences is called a *delta*.

Indicators and candidate lists are created from either word-level or line-level deltas. If a word-level delta spans multiple lines, the system uses a corresponding line-level delta. Otherwise, it uses a word-level delta. Indicator and candidate lists are merged if they overlap. For example, indicator B and candidate list C in Figure 5 are created from the line-level delta because the word-level delta (replacing `">...</select>` with `"/>`) spans multiple lines. The candidate list in Figure 6 is created from the word-level delta.

Edit details are generated from the word-level difference. When the user focuses on a candidate, all the related edit details are shown, whereas other edit details are hidden. Our tool saves the edit history using the JSON format.

[1] https://ace.c9.io/

[2] http://linux.die.net/man/1/dwdiff

[3] http://download.eclipse.org/jgit/docs/jgit-2.0.0.201206130900-r/apidocs/org/eclipse/jgit/diff/HistogramDiff.html

USER STUDY

We conducted a small-scale user study to evaluate our tool and history model. The user study was composed of two parts. In the first part, participants tested our tool and evaluated its usability by completing questionnaires. The second part identified what users expect of micro-versioning candidates by showing several examples of typical micro-versioning situations to the participants.

We recruited five participants who were graduate or undergraduate students in our computer science department, all males aged 22 to 23 years. They each had over two years experience in programming and experienced with JavaScript and HTML.

Part I: Evaluation of Overall Tool

The aim of the first part of the study was to evaluate our tool. We examined whether our user interface satisfied the requirements determined in this study. First, the participants were asked to complete a training task in about 10 minutes using our proposed tool. Next, they were asked to complete a feature-adding task within about 1 hour. We observed and noted the behavior of the participants and their comments during the experiments. After finishing the tasks, we asked the participants to complete a questionnaire about our tool and micro-versioning tasks. The system usability scale (SUS) [3] was used in the questionnaire.

We prepared a training task to allow the participants to become familiar with our proposed tool so they could conduct micro-versioning operations. In the training task, a participant wrote a code to add an HTML button and its event listener first, before changing the behavior when clicking the button, then removed the button. The last change could be conducted by applying undo using our tool.

We prepared a paint program written in HTML, CSS, and JavaScript as the base code for the study, which contained 174 lines of code. Participants were asked to add a thickness control feature by using a text field and to re-implement the same by using a slider. Next, they were asked to add a preview of the thickness. Finally, they were asked to delete the preview feature. The paint program written in Java has been used in other studies [8, 23], and a thickness control feature was used to collect the *backtracking* behavior of programmers [23]. These studies showed that the Java program is sufficiently simple to understand and that is can be modified within a short amount of time, while implementing the thickness control feature requires some micro-versioning operations. Thus, we decided to use these programming tasks in our study. A previous study [23] also indicated that the behavior of most programmers was not affected by knowing that they might conduct a micro-versioning operation later. Thus, the participants were asked to do only one programming task in this study.

All the participants used a laptop computer (Core i5-5200U and 8GB RAM) on which our tool operated in Firefox 44.0.2. They used two full HD (1920 $\times$ 1080 pixels) displays and a mouse. The participants were told that they could use any resources available to write the program and for debugging. They mainly used Google to find JavaScript functions and

#	Question	P1	P2	P3	P4	P5
1	I thought it was easy to use	6	5	6	6	5
2	I thought it was suitable for programming	6	6	4	6	5
3	I felt very confident using the tool	3	3	1	6	3
4	I would imagine that most people would learn to use the tool very quickly.	6	3	2	6	3
5	I needed technical support to use it	4	2	7	2	5
6	I had to concentrate to use it	4	2	7	2	6
7	I would like to use the tool frequently	7	5	4	6	5

Table 1. Results of post questionnaire on seven-point Likert scale

	P1	P2	P3	P4	P5
Update preview	17	21	14	34	13
Open candidate lists	2	8	4	3	2
Conduct operations using our tool	1	3	3	1	2
Search operations	1	1	0	0	1
Revert operations manually	1	0	0	2	0

Table 2. Number of operations conducted during main task

HTML elements, and the Web console in Firefox for debugging.

Results

All the participants successfully completed the training and main tasks. The main task required 46.2 minutes on average (SD = 19.6 minutes). The results of the post-questionnaire analysis are listed in Table 1. A score was positive when it was higher than 4 for Q1–4 and Q7, but vice versa for Q5 and Q6. Table 2 lists the participants' actions related to micro-versioning during the main task.

All the participants agreed that our tool was easy to use (Q1). Three participants also responded that they would be able to write source code faster using our tool. Four participants responded negatively to Q3 because they were not familiar with our tool. One participant (P2) said that: *"I sometimes cannot predict the results of my operation. However, I think I will feel confident because the results were intuitive in the user study."* There were no negative responses to Q2 and Q7, but one participant (P3) was neutral. This participant also responded negatively to Q4–6. His neutral or negative responses were found to be related to his programming method, in which he wanted to manually write or rewrite each source code to check changes. Thus, he felt anxiety when he used our tool because several parts of the source code were changed simultaneously.

Visual information displayed by tool: All the participants said that the information displayed by the tool was useful. One participant (P1) said that: *"By using this tool, I could understand the location where I made changes at a glance."* Another (P4) said that *"I could understand the details of the proposed candidate by observing the information displayed by the tool."* During programming, all the participants observed a candidate list and edit details to find a desired micro-versioning operation before they decided their next actions. If they found a desired micro-versioning operation, it was applied. If not, they closed the candidate list and opened another list.

However, two participants complained that the information was not sufficient in several cases. One participant (P1) noted that it was sometimes difficult to understand the outcomes when the micro-versioning operation was complex. The right figure shows the edit details and candidate list that P1 said were complex. Another (P4) said that the indicators should display more information, such as the importance of micro-versioning operations. In addition, two participants (P1 and P4) ignored indicators when they reverted an extremely small operation and manually reverted the source code. For example, P1 changed the parameter from 1 to 10 then rewrote it from 10 to 1 without using our tool.

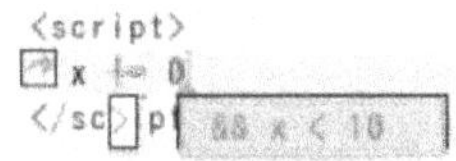

Complex visual information

Candidates proposed by tool: All the participants agreed that almost all the candidates proposed by the tool were appropriate. However, two participants (P2 and P3) said that the tool should not propose an operation for deleting the entire source code. They said that deleting all the source code was inappropriate, and it disrupted them when they tried to find a desired operation.

Other possible applications using tool: Three participants suggested that the proposed tool would also be useful for other applications. Two participants (P2 and P4) said that it might be useful for various types of creative activities, such as writing a novel, writing lyrics, composing music, and drawing pictures. One participant (P2) said *"My friend sometimes writes novels, and often conducts experiments. My friend would like to save and use the history of his experiments."* Another (P4) said that the proposed tool might be useful for programming education. He considered that novices often encounter problems while programming and that the proposed tool might be useful because it improves user experience when problems occur. One participant (P1) said that he would use the proposed tool when using document editing software such as Microsoft Word. Another (P2) considered that the tool might be useful when editing his schedule.

Performance: Our tool took several tens of milliseconds to add a new edit fragment during the experiment, and it is empirically linear time. It took 8.3 msec when the number of edit fragments was 10 on average and 54 msec when the size was 44.

Part II: Evaluation of History Model

The aim of the second part of the study was to evaluate our history model and compare it with other history models, such as linear undo and selective undo. Thus, we aimed to understand 1) whether the model can propose candidates that meet the expectations of users, and 2) whether it can eliminate inappropriate candidates. In this study, we investigated previous research [24, 25] to prepare the example situations for micro-versioning and found seven *backtracking* situations that are similar to the typical situations encountered during micro-versioning (Table 3) [23]. Second, a linear undo tool, which is the most common tool for micro-versioning, does not work well when multiple situations (e.g., refactoring and fixing small mistakes) occur simultaneously or when some text edits are undone [25].

The selective undo model may generate too many candidates when an example contains many text edits. Thus, we reduced the number of text edits by separating the example into four micro-versioning situations in which these four examples represent micro-versioning situations. Each example contained either multiple typical micro-versioning situations or text edits undone by a programmer (*A*, *B*, and *C* contained multiple situations and *D* contained an undone text edit). The programming tasks used in these examples were extracted from previous programming studies [22, 24, 25, 1, 23].

First, we showed the participants each example of an edit history and the candidate of micro-versioning operations generated using the selective undo model [25]. We used the selective undo model because the candidates it generated were composed of a superset of those generated using the extended undo models and our model. Figure 10 shows an edit history and the candidates for *D* in Table 3. We then asked the participants to select the candidates that could be considered as results after reverting a source code change. We also required explanations when a participant's selection differed from the result obtained with our model.

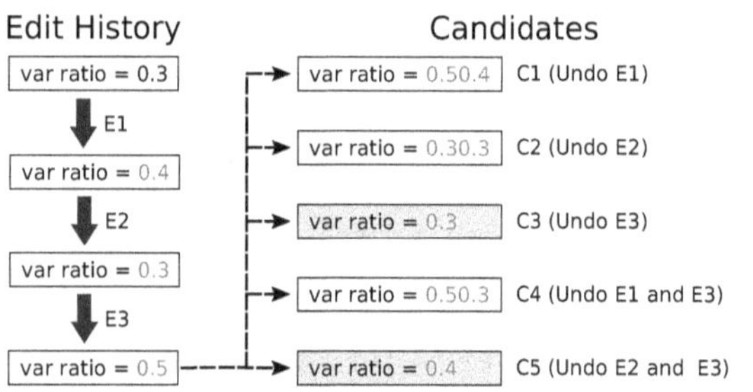

Figure 10. Edit history and candidates for *D* in Table 3. Gray candidates are those generated with our tool.

Results

Our history model generated a total of eight candidates from all edit histories. The participants correctly selected 7.4 of these on average (SD = 0.89). However, they selected 2.2 of the 14 candidates that could not be generated with our model on average (SD = 1.30). Table 4 lists the candidates that participants selected and those that our model generated for *D*. One participant (P3) selected C5, which could be generated with our model; however, he did not select C3, which could also be generated with our model.

We confirmed that all the candidates selected by the participants can be generated by combining several regional undo operations or one tree-structured undo operation. We also confirmed that none of the participants selected all the candidates generated with the selective undo model, indicating that the selective undo model generated several inappropriate candidates. These results indicate that our underlying assumptions regarding our model are reasonable. However, the sets of candidates selected by the participants were all different, except for *B*. This indicates that a history model cannot generate candidates that exactly match the expectations of all users.

We investigated the explanations given by the participants for the cases in which their answers differed from the output of our history model and identified the following two problems with our model. First, the expectations of the participants sometimes depended on the semantics of the program under development. For example, most participants (three out of five) answered that reverting several steps should be considered as a reverting operation in *A*, but all the participants answered that reverting several steps should not be considered as a reverting operation in *B*. All the participants said that *B*-2 and *B*-3 appeared to be totally different text edits and answered that they should not be reverted simultaneously. Likewise, all the participants answered that restoring an API name (*C*-2) should be considered as a reverting operation, but two participants (P1 and P5) said that restoring a typo (*A*-3) should not be considered as a reverting operation. They said that: *"I do not think that fixing a typo should be part of the edit history. Thus, I did not select restoring typo as a reverting operation."*

The second problem is concerned with reverting the last text edit, which is similar to a linear undo operation, and it differed according to the participant. Three participants (P1, P3, and P4) responded that reverting the last text edit should be considered as a reverting operation regardless of whether the reverted program could be compiled. However, two participants responded that a reverted program should be capable of being compiled.

DISCUSSION

The results of the first part of the user study indicate that our tool was useful and easy to operate. The participants agreed that our tool satisfied the requirements described above. In addition, we found that the user interface of the proposed tool might be useful for several tasks in addition to programming, such as creative activities and programming education. The results of the second part indicate that our history model could combine two extended undo models, show that appropriate individual reverting operations are different and that no history model can support all micro-versioning operations in all situations.

The possible extensions proposed by the participants were related to various targets such as writing novels, drawing pictures, and writing music, although our tool was designed for text-based programming. This shows that trial and error is a common task because a user encounters many problems during these iterative processes. Our findings also indicate that the defined requirements are important in various domains in addition to programming. However, providing micro-versioning tools in various domains would present many challenges, but identifying the specific requirements and using the proposed tool could help address these challenges.

User Interface of Micro-Versioning Tool

Our tool successfully displayed useful information. However, our results suggest that a more sophisticated visualization method is required, which should 1) be capable of generating

Case	Situation	Edit Summary	#Candidates	References
A	• refactoring • fix typo or small mistakes	(1) Write program with magic number (2) Introduce new variable to remove magic number. (3) Fix typo in name of variable.	7 (2)	[1, 22]
B	• try to find appropriate algorithm • fix code that was just added because it is not working	(1) Implement `factorial` method using recursion (2) Fix method (3) Implement `factorial` method using tail recursion	3 (2)	[1]
C	• understand use of new API • test various user interface designs	(1) Modify HTML using `innerText` variable (2) Change `innerText` to `innerHTML`. (3) Modify user interface from slider to text field	7 (2)	[23, 25]
D	• tune parameters	(1) Change parameter from 0.3 to 0.4 (2) Undo it (3) Change it to 0.5	5 (2)	[24]

Table 3. Examples of typical micro-versioning situations. Numbers in parentheses are those of candidates that can be generated with our history model.

Case *D*	C1	C2	C3	C4	C5
P1			✓		✓
P2			✓		✓
P3					✓
P4			✓		✓
P5			✓		✓

Table 4. Results of *D*. Checked cells were selected as reverting operations by participant. Gray cells can be generated with our model.

an understandable visualization of a complex operation and 2) provide all of the information related to a micro-versioning operation. Our tool limited the number of candidates, however, it can easily show more candidates by adding a "see more candidates" button, for example.

Displaying the behavior of the source code after the micro-versioning operation in a separate dialog sometimes provides a user with useful information, but it makes the user interface complex. We did not implement this feature because a micro-versioning tool should have a lightweight user interface. However, one participant reported that he experienced anxiety when he used the proposed tool and previewing the behavior of software might help reduce anxiety. However, a previous study indicated that many programmers did not observe a preview of the source code [21]. Thus, we cannot be certain whether previewing the behavior of software is helpful.

Extracting Appropriate Candidates

Another issue is that the appropriate candidates differ according to the programmers. There are several approaches to solve this issue. One approach is displaying many indicators so that all users can find their appropriate candidates by using the micro-versioning tool. However, this approach increases the number of inappropriate candidates and makes the user interface complex. Another approach is using a more sophisticated history model. Such a model may decrease the number of candidates that the user wrongly wants to revert to (e.g., the user overlooks the syntax error of the candidate). Yet another approach is changing the behavior of the history model according to the user. How to address this issue will be addressed in future research.

Limitations

Our history model uses code executions as delimiters, but this does not always work. For example, a programmer makes a button and the event listener of the button (edit *A*). She then executes the program. Finally, she adds the extra listener of the button (edit *B*). The relation between edits *A* and *B* cannot be extracted with our current implementation.

Using an AST can relax this restriction because it contains the syntax relation between edit fragments. However, there are several types of relations between fragments that cannot be extracted using an AST. For example, the font size of a title and that of a subtitle are related; thus, a programmer sometimes wants to update two parameters in sync. However, there is no relation between two parameters at the AST level. Our tool worked well in the user study; however, it and an AST should be combined to support more efficient micro-versioning.

We used the artificial programming tasks and edit histories in the user study without the related context of exploratory programming. We designed the tasks and histories based on common backtracking situations and previous programming studies to prevent them from being too artificial. All the participants were recruited from our university. However, previous studies showed that both university students and professional programmers frequently conduct exploratory programming and backtracking [23]. Our user study was small-scale and it is insufficient to quantitatively prove the practical usability of the system. Formal studies with a sufficient number of participants and comparison are necessary for this purpose.

CONCLUSION

We referred to the version control operations during exploratory programming as micro-versioning. We analyzed the problems that programmers encounter during micro-versioning processes and defined the requirements for a tool to support micro-versioning tasks. We also proposed a tool based on these requirements. The interface of the tool displays markers, indicators, candidate lists, and edit details in a text editor. Users can select an option from the candidate list to do micro-versioning tasks. The results of our user study indicate that our tool satisfies the requirements we identified, and that it is useful for programming and other tasks.

REFERENCES

1. Kent Beck. 2003. *Test-driven development: by example*. Addison-Wesley Professional.
2. Joel Brandt, Philip J Guo, Joel Lewenstein, Scott R Klemmer, and Mira Dontcheva. 2009. Writing Code to Prototype, Ideate, and Discover. *Software, IEEE* 26, 5 (2009), 18–24. DOI: http://dx.doi.org/10.1109/MS.2009.147
3. John Brooke. 1996. SUS-A quick and dirty usability scale. *Usability evaluation in industry* 189, 194 (1996), 4–7.
4. Aaron G Cass and Chris ST Fernandes. 2007. Using task models for cascading selective undo. In *Task Models and Diagrams for Users Interface Design*. Springer, Hasselt, Belgium, 186–201. DOI: http://dx.doi.org/10.1007/978-3-540-70816-2_14
5. Eclipse 2016. Eclipse - The Eclipse Foundation open source community website. (31 July 2016). Retrieved July 31, 2016 from http://www.eclipse.org/.
6. EGit 2016. EGit. (31 July 2016). Retrieved July 31, 2016 from http://www.eclipse.org/egit/.
7. emacs 2016. Emacs. (31 July 2016). Retrieved July 31, 2016 from https://www.gnu.org/software/emacs/.
8. James Fogarty, Andrew J Ko, Htet Htet Aung, Elspeth Golden, Karen P Tang, and Scott E Hudson. 2005. Examining task engagement in sensor-based statistical models of human interruptibility. In *Proceedings of the SIGCHI conference on Human Factors in Computing Systems (CHI 2005)*. ACM, Portland, Oregon, USA, 331–340. DOI: http://dx.doi.org/10.1145/1054972.1055018
9. git 2016. Git. (31 July 2016). Retrieved July 31, 2016 from https://git-scm.com/.
10. Max Goldman, Greg Little, and Robert C Miller. 2011. Collabode: collaborative coding in the browser. In *Proceedings of the 4th international workshop on Cooperative and human aspects of software engineering (CHASE 2011)*. ACM, Waikiki, Honolulu, HI, USA, 65–68. DOI:http://dx.doi.org/10.1145/1984642.1984658
11. Google Bug Prediction 2016. Google Bug Prediction. (24 July 2016). Retrieved July 31, 2016 from http://google-engtools.blogspot.jp/2011/12/bug-prediction-at-google.html.
12. gundo 2016. Gundo - Visualize your Vim Undo Tree. (29 March 2016). Retrieved July 31, 2016 from http://sjl.bitbucket.org/gundo.vim/.
13. Björn Hartmann, Loren Yu, Abel Allison, Yeonsoo Yang, and Scott R Klemmer. 2008. Design as exploration: creating interface alternatives through parallel authoring and runtime tuning. In *Proceedings of the 21st annual ACM symposium on User interface software and technology (UIST 2008)*. ACM, Monterey, CA, USA, 91–100. DOI: http://dx.doi.org/10.1145/1449715.1449732
14. Shinpei Hayashi, Daiki Hoshino, Jumpei Matsuda, Motoshi Saeki, Takayuki Omori, and Katsuhisa Maruyama. 2015. Historef: A tool for edit history refactoring. In *2015 IEEE 22nd International Conference on Software Analysis, Evolution, and Reengineering (SANER 2015)*. IEEE Computer Society, Montreal, QC, Canada, 469–473. DOI: http://dx.doi.org/10.1109/SANER.2015.7081858
15. Yun Young Lee, Sam Harwell, Sarfraz Khurshid, and Darko Marinov. 2013. Temporal code completion and navigation. In *35th International Conference on Software Engineering (ICSE 2013)*. IEEE Computer Society, San Francisco, CA, USA, 1181–1184. DOI: http://dx.doi.org/10.1109/ICSE.2013.6606673
16. Erica Mealy, David Carrington, Paul Strooper, and Peta Wyeth. 2007. Improving usability of software refactoring tools. In *Australian Software Engineering Conference (ASWEC 2007)*. IEEE Computer Society, Melbourne, Australia, 307–318. DOI: http://dx.doi.org/10.1109/ASWEC.2007.24
17. Mathieu Nancel and Andy Cockburn. 2014. Causality: A conceptual model of interaction history. In *Proceedings of the SIGCHI Conference on Human Factors in Computing Systems (CHI '14)*. ACM, Toronto, ON, Canada, 1777–1786. DOI: http://dx.doi.org/10.1145/2556288.2556990
18. Atul Prakash and Michael J Knister. 1994. A framework for undoing actions in collaborative systems. *ACM Transactions on Computer-Human Interaction (TOCHI)* 1, 4 (1994), 295–330. DOI: http://dx.doi.org/10.1145/198425.198427
19. Bastian Steinert, Damien Cassou, and Robert Hirschfeld. 2012. Coexist: Overcoming aversion to change. *ACM SIGPLAN Notices* 48, 2 (2012), 107–118. DOI: http://dx.doi.org/10.1145/2384577.2384591
20. undotree 2016. EmacsWiki: Undo Tree. (31 July 2016). Retrieved July 31, 2016 from http://www.emacswiki.org/emacs/UndoTree.
21. Mohsen Vakilian, Nicholas Chen, Stas Negara, Balaji Ambresh Rajkumar, Brian P Bailey, and Ralph E Johnson. 2012. Use, disuse, and misuse of automated refactorings. In *34th International Conference on Software Engineering (ICSE 2012)*. IEEE Computer Society, Zurich, Switzerland, 233–243. DOI: http://dx.doi.org/10.1109/ICSE.2012.6227190
22. YoungSeok Yoon and Brad A Myers. 2011. Capturing and analyzing low-level events from the code editor. In *Proceedings of the 3rd ACM SIGPLAN workshop on Evaluation and usability of programming languages and tools (PLATEAU 2011)*. ACM, Portland, OR, USA, 25–30. DOI:http://dx.doi.org/10.1145/2089155.2089163
23. YoungSeok Yoon and Brad A Myers. 2012. An exploratory study of backtracking strategies used by developers. In *Proceedings of the 5th International Workshop on Co-operative and Human Aspects of*

Software Engineering (CHASE 2012). IEEE Computer Society, Zurich, Switzerland, 138–144. DOI: http://dx.doi.org/10.1109/CHASE.2012.6223012

24. Young Seok Yoon and Brad A Myers. 2014. A longitudinal study of programmers' backtracking. In *IEEE Symposium on Visual Languages and Human-Centric Computing (VL/HCC 2014)*. IEEE Computer Society, Melbourne, VIC, Australia, 101–108. DOI:http://dx.doi.org/10.1109/VLHCC.2014.6883030

25. Young Seok Yoon and Brad A Myers. 2015. Supporting selective undo in a code editor. In *the 37th International Conference on Software Engineering-Volume 1 (ICSE 2015)*. IEEE Computer Society, Florence, Italy, 223–233. DOI:http://dx.doi.org/10.1109/ICSE.2015.43

Codeon: On-Demand Software Development Assistance

Yan Chen[1], Sang Won Lee[2], Yin Xie[1], YiWei Yang[2], Walter S. Lasecki[2,1], and Steve Oney[1,2]
School of Information[1], Computer Science & Engineering[2], University of Michigan, Ann Arbor
{yanchenm,snaglee,xieyin,yanyiwei,wlasecki,soney}@umich.edu

ABSTRACT
Software developers rely on support from a variety of resources—including other developers—but the coordination cost of finding another developer with relevant experience, explaining the context of the problem, composing a specific help request, and providing access to relevant code is prohibitively high for all but the largest of tasks. Existing technologies for synchronous communication (e.g. voice chat) have high scheduling costs, and asynchronous communication tools (e.g. forums) require developers to carefully describe their code context to yield useful responses. This paper introduces Codeon, a system that enables more effective task hand-off between end-user developers and remote helpers by allowing *asynchronous* responses to on-demand requests. With Codeon, developers can request help by speaking their requests aloud within the context of their IDE. Codeon automatically captures the relevant code context and allows remote helpers to respond with high-level descriptions, code annotations, code snippets, and natural language explanations. Developers can then immediately view and integrate these responses into their code. In this paper, we describe Codeon, the studies that guided its design, and our evaluation that its effectiveness as a support tool. In our evaluation, developers using Codeon completed nearly twice as many tasks as those who used state-of-the-art synchronous video and code sharing tools, by reducing the coordination costs of seeking assistance from other developers.

Author Keywords
Development support; intelligent assistants; crowdsourcing

ACM Classification Keywords
H.5.m Information Interfaces and Presentation (e.g. HCI): Miscellaneous; K.6.1 Management of Computing and Information Systems: Software Development

INTRODUCTION
Software developers rely heavily on support from external resources while programming. Although search engines and Community Question-Answering (CQA) websites (such as StackOverflow [33]) are the most popular resources for developers, the best support is often provided by other developers [31, 20, 12]. Unlike web-based resources, expert developers can provide personalized help, high-level advice, and project-specific code segments, and can often help identify and overcome bugs that are difficult for a single developer to find on their own [35]. However, it is often prohibitively difficult to find other developers willing to help, particularly for developers working outside of a large organization.

Recently, a small set of paid services began connecting developers with remote expert developers [23, 21], who can provide personalized feedback. These services use a *synchronous*, one-on-one model of communication where developers connect to a remote expert, make a request, and communicate via video chat and a shared editor. However, there are several drawbacks to this synchronous model [12]. There is a coordination cost of finding an expert who is available to help at the right time. If the first expert does not have sufficient expertise (which they cannot know until *after* they connect), there is a further cost—in both time and money—to finding a new expert. One-on-one mentoring also requires that the developer be attentive to the remote helper throughout the session. Although this is suitable for teaching-oriented requests where a back-and-forth conversation between developers and helpers is desirable, it is less helpful for tasks that can be handed off entirely to the helper, such as requests for short code snippets.

On-Demand Programming Assistance with Codeon
In this paper, we propose an *asynchronous* on-demand help seeking model for programmers who need support that can be more efficiently provided by remote expert developers than existing methods. We implement and evaluate this model in Codeon, a system that allows developers to request assistance as easily as they can through in-person one-on-one communication, and tracks helpers' responses, directly in the developer's Integrated Development Environment (IDE). As we will show, Codeon makes remote collaboration more practical by reducing coordination costs while still enabling rich communication between developers and helpers. Unlike previous asynchronous collaboration solutions (such as code repositories), Codeon is request-oriented: it makes it easy for developers to make sufficiently detailed requests and send to other developers, making the process quick and effective. Further, Codeon's asynchronous model is more scalable for multiple helpers than synchronous support tools because it allows multiple helpers to work in parallel with the developer. As our evaluation demonstrates, Codeon supports new forms of par-

CHI 2017, May 06-11, 2017, Denver, CO, USA.
Copyright © 2017 ACM ISBN 978-1-4503-4655-9/17/05$15.00.
DOI:http://dx.doi.org/10.1145/3025453.3025972

allel collaboration that make remote help-seeking more effective for developers. In this paper, we contribute the following:

- an effective approach for integrating external, parallelizable expert assistance into a developer's on-going process,
- tools and techniques that efficiently capture developers' requests' contexts and mediate communication between end users and remote developer helpers,
- evaluations of the trade-offs between speed and accuracy for system components in different help seeking stages,
- a system (Codeon) that instantiates our approach to improve development help-seeking tools, and
- evidence that Codeon helps developers solve more tasks in a given time span than current approaches.

We begin this paper with a discussion of related work. We then discuss how we designed and evaluated our system, followed by limitations and future work.

RELATED WORK

Our work builds on previous research into pair programming, developer help-seeking, distributed programming, and communication support tools.

Help Seeking in Software Development

Community Question Answering

Many CQA websites, such as Stack Overflow [33], provide online asynchronous support that allows software developers to post questions to a large community. These sites also accumulated these questions and answers that they received to form a large database of questions and answers for later reference. Prior work [2, 3] studied building an "organizational memory" through a growing database of questions and answers. These CQA sites have a number of limitations such as long waiting times to receive an answer after posting the requests and the face that answers are not personalized. In addition it takes significant time and effort to compose a question with enough context and explanation for other programmers to be able to provide an answer [5]. Codeon enables speech and content selecting modalities, and also provides on-demand expert support that allows developers to describe the requests as if the helpers were physically nearby. They can select a code snippet, verbally ask "what does this mean?", hand off execution of planned coordination to the system, and receive a meaningful response within minutes.

Commercial support platforms, such as Code Mentor [21] and hack.hands() [23], provide more personalized help for software developers. These sites allow developers to create requests and connect them (or let them self-select) with experts, and provide a shared code editor and text/voice communication channel. These sites represent the state of the art for seeking remote help from experts and use synchronous one-on-one communication. In our system evaluation, we show that on-demand support yields similar one-on-one support results while also having the benefit of being parallelizable.

Pair programming

Codeon is related to pair programming [14], a method that allows developers to work together in real-time more effectively. In particular, it is most related to distributed pair programming, which is a derived version of pair programming, allows remote participants to contribute to the same codebase simultaneously [6, 38]. Although the distributed pair programming approach removes many issues in real-time remote collaboration [32], it can still be difficult to coordinate and maintain context in distributed pairs. Our system instead aims to automate coordination by temporarily incorporating helpers into a task long enough for them to assist and then move on.

Information Needs for Developers

Researchers have summarized the types of questions that developers ask in different contexts. Sillito et al. categorized 44 types of questions developers ask when evolving a large code base [39]. Ko et al. explored six types of learning barriers in programming systems for beginners and proposed possible solutions from programming system sides [26], and also documented communication among co-located development teams [25]. Guzzi et al. analyzed IDE support for collaboration and evaluated an IDE extension to improve team communication [18].

Whereas these studies of information needs focused on existing team structures, our paper introduces a new path for information seeking via on-demand expert support, and the studies present qualitatively different data and implications. Unlike existing team structures, our paper proposes a team structure where a project stakeholder requests remote help from experts who are not stakeholders. This difference has significant implications for team trust, communication preferences, and context sharing.

Collaborative Development

Systems like Codeopticon [16] and Codechella [17] provide ways that helpers (i.e., tutors/peers) can efficiently monitor the behavior of multiple learners and provide proactive on-demand support. Version control systems such as git are often used in programming collaboration because they help developers in distributed teams synchronize source code. However, version control systems also require that developers manually push and pull changes and resolve merge conflicts. Collabode [15] introduced an algorithm that addressed the issue of breaking the collaborative build without introducing the latency and manual overhead of version control. Codeon fetches developers' latest code before helpers can send their code responses back and lets helpers handle all the conflicts if exists.

Communication tools like Slack or Skype make collaboration more effective by supporting conversational interaction, but it is often challenging to capture the code context within these tools. Commercial IDE tools such as Koding [40], and Cloud9 [22] enable users to code collaboratively online in real-time. Although these systems reduce many of the barriers developers face when working at a distance [32] and time spent on environment configuration, they do not support the case when developers are actively seeking help [41]. Codeon allows developers to create requests at any time by speaking their questions while the system automatically captures the problem's context.

IDE-Integrated Help Finding Tools

Codeon is a kind of Recommendation System in Software Engineering (RSSE) [37], which, unlike most CQA websites, often provides relevant information within an IDE. Prior work on RSSEs has used knowledge of how developers seek information to develop systems to provide semi-automated support [10, 11]. Blueprint [9] allows developers to rapidly search for a query in an embedded search engine in their local IDE. Seahawk [34] heuristically filtered search results to automatically increase the reliability of search results within an IDE. Hartmann et al. [19] also explored ways to aid developers in recovering from errors by collecting and mining examples of code changes that fix errors. These in-IDE approaches allow developers to save time by minimizing the change in task context associated with requesting information. Recently, Chen et al. [12] found that even with the state-of-the-art communication tools, such as Skype and JSBin, developers and helpers still face communication challenges when it comes to integrating answers into a codebase.

Tools that support developers using the crowd provide a way to potentially receive more personalized feedback than automated systems can do. CrowdCode [30] allows developers to make requests to the crowd with self-written specifications of the desired function's purpose and signature. But this approach is limited in how much it can reduce developers' time expenditure since making a request requires a detailed problem specification. Real-time crowdsourcing techniques have enabled on-demand interactive systems, which have been shown to be able to improve the efficiency of accomplishing complex tasks [27, 28, 29].

Human Expert Computation

In this paper, we leverage crowdsourcing to make our system available on demand and scalable. By using expert crowd platforms like Upwork [1], which have thousands of developers with a wide range of language and framework expertise, we can hire as many experts as needed to field a developer's set of requests. This allows Codeon to parallelize as much as the end user developer may want to.

Prior work has explored how to use a priori tasking and guidance to automate the coordination and task management process. Foundry [36] provided an interface for composing expert workflows for large tasks. Foundry was used to create *Flash Teams*—dynamic, expert crowd teams—to complete tasks faster and more efficiently than self-organized, or crowd-managed groups. In our work, we focus on similarly-focused tasks with well-scoped hand-offs, but do not assume that developers know the high-level composition of tasks in advance, instead allowing developers to define tasks on-the-fly as they discover and generate them.

CODEON

Codeon's design is based on the feedback we collected over the course of user studies of the three primary stages of help-request interactions: Stage 1) making a request, Stage 2) writing a response, and Stage 3) integrating the response (Figure 1). The design goal per stage is as follows: *(G1)*: to simulate the in-person communication in seeking for help, *(G2)*: to provide ways for a helper to associate responses with the working code context, and *(G3)*: to make the code integration as effortless as possible

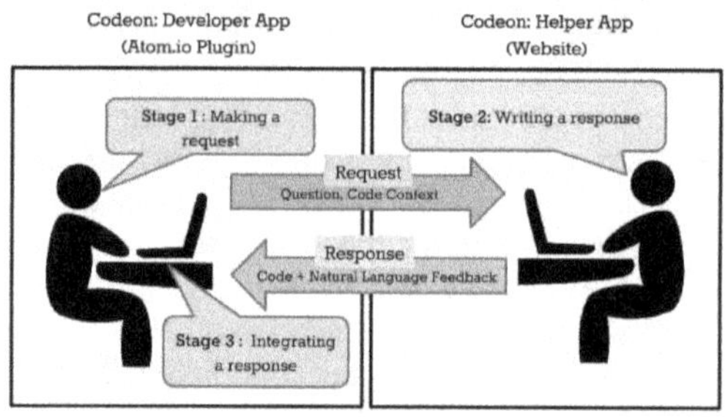

Figure 1: Asynchronous interactions between developers and helpers can occur in three stages: making a request (S1), writing a response (S2), and integrating the response (S3). In Codeon, developers use an IDE plug-in to make requests (S1) and integrate responses (S3), and helpers use a web-based IDE to view content and generate responses (S2).

Separating the workflow into three stages makes the communication asynchronous so that a question can be presented to multiple workers and routed to a worker that has right expertise for the scalability reason. These three studies aimed to help us better understand the trade-offs across different methods and features. To minimize the effects of varying prior expertise among participants, all preliminary studies used a synthesized programming language.

Codeon's developer interface is implemented as a plug-in for Atom.io—a widely used code editor—that allows them to make requests (S1) and visualize different formats of responses and integrate responses (S3) within Atom. For helpers, Codeon provides a web IDE that allows them to see a list of developers' requests and respond to them (S2).

Stage 1: Making a Request

User Study: Asking a Good Question

With the primary goal of improving the productivity, we designed this stage with two sub-goals in mind: 1) the speed of request making needs to be fast, and 2) the request needs to contain sufficient context to be understood. With these goals, we compared three modalities for describing requests: 1) speaking the request verbally (Voice), 2) typing the request (Text), and 3) selecting a request from a computed set of categories (Multiple Choice). We derived these categories from common query types observed during a previous study [12].

As prior work showed the importance of context in code request [12], we combined these modalities with three alternative methods for specifying the context of a given request:

Modality	Voice	Text	Multiple Choice
Highlight	11.0 / 2.6	45.5 / 25.4	15.0 / 13.1
Click	14.0 / 3.7	37.5 / 23.1	27.8 / 18.0
None	21.5 / 8.4	33.9 / 17.4	25.1 / 9.5

Table 1: Time to make a request per condition (avg./s.d.)

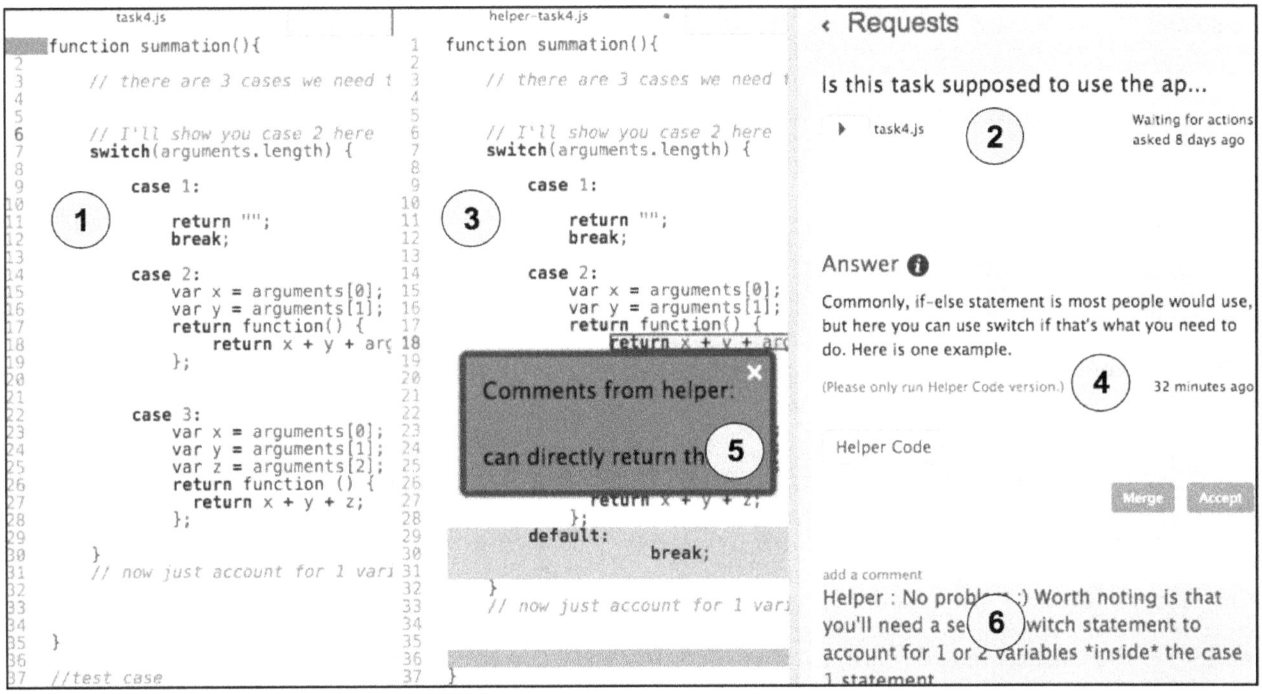

Figure 2: Codeon interface where the requests and responses are on the right panel(2). Developer's code(1) and helper's code(3) are side by side for better comparison. Other responses includes explanation(4), annotation(5), and comments(6)

1) selecting a region of content (Highlight), 2) pointing to one location in the content (Click), and 3) a control condition (No selector). Combining these request modalities and context selectors, we formed a 3×3 condition matrix for our experiment. We recruited 30 workers from Upwork to test the conditions and recorded the duration, content, and user activities of each request.

After removing the unanswerable requests (e.g. those that did not contain enough context), we found that, on average, voice requests were the fastest method for specifying requests, and text input was the slowest (Table 1). In the text condition, participants spent more time carefully crafting requests, whereas in the voice condition participants tended to speak more informally. The performance on the multiple choice option varied based on participants' familiarity with the options. However, we found in a subsequent evaluation of the questions' understandability that the multiple choice specifications were too vague to be understandable by helpers.

Codeon Design: Voicing Requests

As a result of our preliminary studies, we chose to use the speech modality for making requests. When developers make a request, Codeon records their voice, synchronized with their interactions with the editor (typing, highlighting, file switching, and scrolling), which serve as the content selectors. As a request in voice is a dynamic signal, the content selector can also be dynamic so that one request can have an animation of not only the activity of content selection, but also some other informative actions such as typing or viewport changes. This way, a developer can speak and highlight code corresponding to the request, which can be replayed in the helper's interface. This simulates a pair-programming condition where a developer is asking a question from the person who is co-located by speaking and pointing to content on the screen. In addition, as a result of pilot studies with Codeon, we also added a feature that allows developers to add an optional text title for each request for later reference.

Stage 2: Writing a response

User Study: Response Modalities

In this stage, we want to design features that allow helpers to provide different kinds of response format effectively and efficiently. We conducted a user study with participants responding to a simulated request. One response can have multiple parts and can be written in three different forms: 1) to select a segment of the code and to write an annotation that is associated with the highlighted segment (Code Annotation) 2) to write an explanation in a text box outside of the editor (Explanation), 3) to directly add and modify the code editor (Code Inline), and 4) the combination of all three types (All). We recruited 12 participants and recorded their performance on this task. Based on the common requests that participants had in Stage 1, we created three requests that each participant responded to. We measured the frequency of each answer type and conducted a post-study interview.

Our major high-level finding from this study is that participants' choice of response type depends on the request type, and each response type can well support one or more types of response formats. Overall, we concluded that these three different forms complement each other, and the usage frequency of each type varied based on both the request type and the helper's preference. Table 2 details the trade-offs we found between different response formats in this study in terms effectiveness and efficiency.

Condition	Advantages	Disadvantages	Design Takeaways
Code Annotation	• Preserves original code • Strong connection with the code context	• If the number and the length of annotations increase, they look littered and occlude the main code editor.	• Scalability needed while keeping high visibility
Explanation	• Preserves original code • Better suited for a long conceptual answer	• No connection between code and explanation	• Flexible and accessible
Code Inline	• Quick integration	• Possible merge conflicts • Low visibility	• High visibility necessary

Table 2: Advantages, disadvantages, and design takeaways for three response formats from developers and helpers' perspectives).

Codeon Design - Response Generation
In order to allow helpers to easily view, understand, and respond to each request, the helpers' side of Codeon is built as a web application where a helper can browse a list of developers' requests. Figure 3 illustrates the helpers' web interface. Once specific request is selected, the web application provides a programming environment that shows the files relevant to that request (files that were open in the developer's editor at the time of request generation). As mentioned earlier, a helper is able to not only play the audio that contains the question, but also see the developer's interactions with the Atom editor (e.g., text selection, scrolling, and content editing). Although the request might be involved only part of the original code base, all the scaffolding code are sent along with the request which makes the code executable.

Note that Codeon does not support voice response because we want the system to be scalable such that not only can one worker supports multiple developers but also multiple workers can work on one question. Multiple voice responses will make the response review process time consuming which violates our efficiency design goal. In our study, helpers used all three response types: code annotation, code inline, and explanation. In Codeon, helpers can choose and/or combine different types of answers based on their preference and the question's characteristics.

Stage 3: Integrating a response

User Study: Exploring Response Integration
The last step of the workflow is to review helpers' responses and make changes in the original code. For this step, we want to make sure that the three answer forms (code annotation, explanation, and code inline) can be integrated accurately and quickly by developers. With these two sub-goals in mind, we ran a user study of how developers integrate the same responses presented in different formats. The experiment was composed of four conditions (one condition for each individual response form and one condition with all response forms) with three tasks. We measured the time and accuracy of code integration in each condition.

To make sure a response in different formats contains the equivalent information, we converted an answer in one form to another with specific rules. For example, when converting annotation and code inline to explanation, we specify line numbers to associate the content with specific line numbers of the code. We recruited eight participants with two for each condition, and we recorded their screen during the study, and conducted a post-task interview.

While we cannot generalize the findings due to the sparse number of participants, we can find that explanation took the longest for code integration and the code inline took the shortest. Similar to the conclusion from the second study, the post-interview indicated that there was no strong preference for one of the three types. Rather, participants expressed the trade-off between the types of answers and how each type of answer can be desirable and not desirable in some ways. For example, code annotation is desirable in a way that the textual content can have strong connection with a certain part of the code, complementing the explanation format (which makes it difficult to map the content to the code snippets). Additionally, participants preferred code annotation, as it preserves the helper's original code (and does not add new lines like code inline would). However, it is often seen as being appropriate only for short answers since it is overlaid code editor, meaning that it scales poorly as the number and/or length of annotations increase.

Similarly, explanation format was desirable because it does not corrupt the original code, and it works well for both long and short responses. Compared to annotation and explanation, inline code allowed participants to finish the task more quickly on average. While this is desirable to make the integration process efficient, another challenge is that a participant may miss the code inline added by a helper. This naturally led us to design measures to keep track of a helper's code inline, similar to the Code Diff application which will highlight the new code added. We summarized the advantages and disadvantages for each response format and drew design implications from the results that facilitate future system development (Table 2).

Codeon Design: Response View & Integration
Codeon implements the response panel on the right side of the Atom.io editor. As there can be multiple requests and multiple formats per response, the scalable design is essential. The

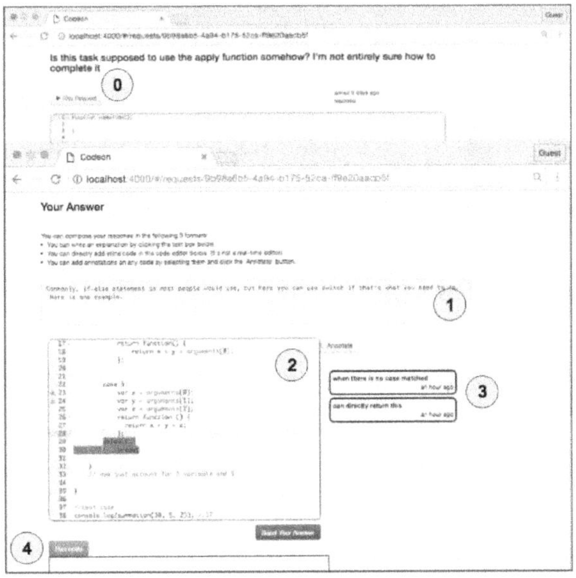

Figure 3: The helper side of Codeon is an interactive webpage that allows helpers to replay the request(0) and run the code(4). Helpers can respond to it with explanation(1), and inline code(2), and annotation(3).

view consists of two hierarchical levels: the requests view and the response detail view (Fig. 2).

The request view has a list of requests where each menu shows the brief summary of the request (title, associated file name, audio replay button) so the developer can keep track of multiple requests. Once a request is selected, the side panel shows the full information of the request and the most recently received response. In addition, if the response contains annotation or inline code, Codeon plugin will automatically split into a two-editor view with the developer's and the helper's code side by side. The region with annotation in the helper's code will be highlighted. When the 'Code Diff' button is clicked, Codeon will display a color-coded difference between the developer's and the helper's code, similar to the 'diff' functionality in modern version control systems (e.g. Git).

Finally, one important goal of the response is to support efficient code integration. With the support of color-coded diff, integration of new code submitted by a helper to the original code can be done in one button click. In addition, for the common issue of the merge conflict in collaborative programming—when more than one person modifies the same content — Codeon is designed to pull the most recent code (if there is any difference) to helper's side by default before helpers sending the responses. This is to reduce the workload of code merge for the developer. Lastly, to support conflict resolution and flexible integration, Codeon generates clear annotated conflict markers for developers, allowing them to automatically merge the helper's code or to restore the original copy.

Iterative Design of the End-To-End System

We iteratively designed the complete Codeon system based on the feedback from 19 developers who used Codeon for a series of small programming tasks. In the initial Codeon version, we found that developers could not 1) efficiently identify the code that responses corresponded to, 2) understand the differences between the original code and the helper's edits, and 3) merge results from helpers into a consistent and functioning solution. The final version of Codeon allows developers to: 1) better connect the content and the request by color mapping the line number and request panel, 2) better integrate helpers' response by refining the code merge strategy, and 3) more easily view and compare to helpers' responses with a side-by-side "Code Diff" tool.

EXPERIMENTAL SETUP

We conducted a laboratory study to better understand how Codeon affects developers' help-seeking behaviors.

Method

Codeon is built for any developers who seek programming support from remote experts. We recruited 12 students from authors' university as developers with the requirement of at least six months JavaScript experience. We also hired three professional programmers as helpers from Upwork (upwork.com), an online freelancer platform, who self-reported multi-year JavaScript experience. The three helpers participated in multiple trials because we found little learning effect in our pilot study and to ensure that the helpers we used met our expertise criteria. We ran an hour and a half training session with each helper to familiarize them with the system and the study. We prepared two JavaScript task sets with each set containing four programming problems. These problems are independent on each other, and their answers cannot be easily found online. To ensure the two sets of tasks were as equally challenging as possible, yet conceptually different, we asked two professional JavaScript developers to balance the tasks. Every developer solved a series of JavaScript tasks in two conditions: a "control" condition and a "Codeon" condition.

In the control condition, developers communicated with helpers via Skype (for real-time synchronous voice communication) and Codepen.io (for real-time synchronous code sharing). The control condition's features are representative of the communication mechanisms that code mentoring sites use [21, 23]. In the Codeon condition, Skype and Codepen.io were disabled, and the developer was instructed to use Codeon to make requests. Both conditions allowed developers to search for online materials. We collected audio and screen recordings during the study to capture the behaviors of the participants, and their responses to our follow-up questions. To minimize learning effects, we randomized the order of conditions (Codeon, control) and the task sets (A, B).

We also instructed participants to finish the tasks as fast as they could by using any resource they were given (online materials and a remote helper), but did not explicitly suggest any strategies. Each study lasted one and a half hour, including training for developers (15 min), the two conditions (30 min per each), and the interview (15 min).

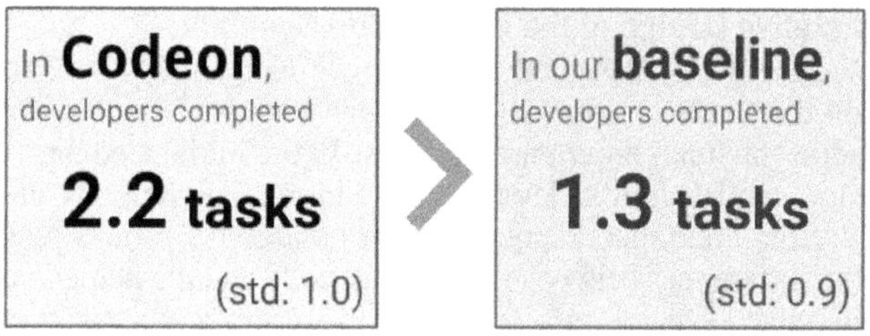

out of 4 programming tasks in 30 minutes, ***p-value =0.03***

Figure 4: Overall result: The # of completed tasks is significantly more in Codeon condition(avg./s.d.).

Hypotheses

We designed our study to evaluate four hypotheses:

$H_{\textbf{Performance}}$: Codeon can help developers to be more productive in development tasks than the control system could.

$H_{\textbf{SystemTime}}$: Time that developers spend with Codeon to ask for and get help is less than that in the control system.

$H_{\textbf{Interruptions}}$: Developers get interrupted less often in Codeon than in the control system.

$H_{\textbf{Parallelization}}$: Developers can better parallelize their efforts in Codeon than they can in the control system.

RESULTS

Overall Performance

The productivity of each condition was measured by counting the number of completed tasks (out of four tasks per condition given 30 minutes cutoff time). Figure 4 shows that the average number of completed tasks within the given time in the Codeon condition is significantly more than it is in the control condition (two-tailed paired-samples Students T-Test, $p = 0.03$), which supports our hypothesis $\text{H}_{\text{Performance}}$. To understand *why* developers were more effective with Codeon, we further analyzed our user data and described in the following sections.

Individual Task Performance

To understand the advantages of Codeon, we unpacked our data to investigate participants' performance on each task. As Table 3 shows, participants spent less time in completing task

	Codeon	Control	Time Increase(%)
Time spent per completed task	10.57	11.32	7.1%
Time spent per incomplete task	8.49	9.15	7.8%
Time spent per incomplete task in non-tail condition	6.84	8.47	23.7%

Table 3: The average time (in minutes) spent per task. Participants spent longer in the control condition, on both completed and incomplete tasks. Tasks in tail condition is the task that are stopped by the researchers by the time constraints (30 min). Note that, by definition, there cannot be complete task in the tail condition.

name	Codeon	Control	p-value
Avg. # of requests per completed task	1.71(1.41)	2.18(1.54)	0.45
system active time(sec) per completed task	165.8(106.3)	344.4(249.5)	0.05

Table 4: The # of requests made per completed task is not significantly different. The average system active time per completed task in Codeon is longer than in the control condition (avg./s.d.).

on average when using Codeon condition, although the difference is not significant. While Codeon may help developers to complete task quicker than the control model, the difference is not significant enough to account for outperforming. Meanwhile developers may waste more time on a task when they get stuck with it in the control condition. The time spent per incomplete task also support this conjecture. Especially if we exclude the incomplete tasks that were stopped by the researchers for 30 minutes ("tail condition"), we can observe a 23% time increase in the control group. As the time spent on the incomplete tasks were determined by an external factor (the time constraint), not by the developer's intention, we believe this measure better reflects the time spent on incomplete tasks for the comparison purpose. While we cannot calculate the statistical significance for these three measures as samples in each condition are part of the entire data set (e.g. complete tasks in Codeon are different from the complete tasks in the control condition), the results indicate that the improvement in overall productivity potentially comes from wasting less time when the developer cannot solve the problem in Codeon. We hypothesize ($\text{H}_{\text{Parallelization}}$) that the asynchronous nature of Codeon workflow encourages developers to hand off their work to a helper and to move on to the next task, whereas, in the pair-programming session, two developers typically work on the same task at a time. In the next section, we evaluate if developers parallelize work efforts during the experiments.

As we do not find strong evidence in developer completing tasks faster in Codeon, we further analyze how actively developers utilize the assistance system when they were able to complete tasks so as to give an account of the increase in overall performance. The average number of requests and *system active time* per complete task is reported in Table 4. System active time is the time that a developer spent on the assistance system (Codeon or the control system) to make requests to a helper and to receive assistance from the helper. System active time thus includes any time that would not have been needed if there was no helper, for example, watching the helper programming (in CodePen), creating a request, reviewing responses from the helper, or interacting with the helper (via Skype, CodePen or Codeon). The result shows we cannot see a significant difference in the number of requests made per complete task ($p = 0.45$). The system active time per completed task in Codeon, on the other hand, is less than the one in the control condition ($p = 0.05$), which shows a tendency to significance for our hypothesis $\text{H}_{\text{SystemTime}}$. Based on our self-assessment from the video annotation process, we notice that the cost of extra time in the control condition may come from the nature of synchronous communication

name	Codeon	Control
Avg. # of alerts	6.1(3.0)	1.9(2.2)
Avg. # of interruptions	2.5(1.6)	1.9(2.2)
Ave. of interruption/alert	0.48(0.3)	1.0(0)

Table 5: # of interruptions, alerts, and average of individual ratio of interruption/alert(Avg. / S.D.).

name	Codeon	Control
Avg. # of parallelization per developer	2.1(1.2)	0.3(0.6)
Total time(s) of parallelization	281.9(243.5)	2.4(5.7)
Avg. time(s) of parallelization per occurrence	114.2(80.5)	1.9(4.8)

Table 6: Time spent and the number of parallelization behavior in two conditions (Avg. / S.D.).

between two ends. For example, a remote pair-programming session may cost additional time coming from social norms, real-time typing process, additional out-of-context questions (or feedback) [13] that may not contribute to the overall performance and does not exist in the Codeon model. This aligns with our belief that Codeon is more efficient in seeking for and receiving help from a remote assistant. The efficiency in Codeon can potentially cause an overall increase in the performance by expediting completion time or giving the developers more time to complete.

Interruptions and Parallelization

Studies have shown that interruptions can be costly to programmers [24]. As Codeon follows the asynchronous collaboration model, we analyze the occurrences of a helper interrupting a developer and evaluate if it has any advantage of being less disruptive to the developers. Annotating the screen recordings of each experiment, we count the number of alerts and interruptions. An *alert* is a message from a helper that initiates a conversation, which gets an attention from the developer or notifies the developer that a response/comment is received. Receiving an alert does not necessarily mean that the developer needs to take action immediately or is interrupted. For example, in Codeon, a developer can see the notification of a helper's response and review the response later, once the work being carried out is done, or, in the control condition, the developer can ask the helper to wait a little while. In addition, the task that the developer was currently working on may be directly relevant to what the helper responded so that the interrupted task not needed to be resumed. We say an alert causes an *interruption* if the two following conditions are satisfied: i) the alert makes the developer immediately stop what they are working on in order to review or respond to the helper's message, and ii) the stopped task needed to be resumed later. Table 5 shows the absolute numbers of both alerts and interruptions are greater in the Codeon condition. This is because in Codeon, one comment is counted as an alert, whereas in the control condition, the developer and the helper constantly communicate so that they have a smaller chance to be interrupted as they are working together. However, when a helper alerts a developer in the conference call, the developer has to stop the current task 100% of the time. In the meantime, in Codeon, they were interrupted (immediately respond to the helper and later resumed the task) only half of the time (48%), and otherwise they could keep working on their task until the point that they finish the current activity (e.g. finishing the line that was being written, finishing reading online materials that were being read). Even when developers were interrupted in Codeon, we observed that most of the interruptions did not require a significant context switch in the developer's mental model as the interrupted task was relevant to the response from the helper. We did not choose to evaluate this as it can be subjective. If we look further detail for individual, 5 out of 12 developers chose to wait to review responses and, on average, they spent 18.1 seconds to finish the ongoing activity. Potentially, this tendency can scale once the system is deployed and is constantly used by developers. Indeed, using Codeon, developers can have better control over their workflow by having a smaller number of interruptions ($H_{\text{Interruptions}}$) whereas, in synchronous collaboration, the workflow will be determined by the pair otherwise the developer will be interrupted.

As briefly mentioned, another benefit of asynchronous collaboration can come from a developer parallelizing the task by handing off subtasks to helpers. To confirm the possible benefit in Codeon, we annotated the video to see if developers parallelize their work while waiting for responses from helpers. We present the number of parallelization and the time that the developers parallelize their tasks in Table 6. Table 6 presents that developers parallelized their work 2.1 times on average when they hand off their work to the helper ($mean = 2.1$) in Codeon condition, whereas in the control condition this behavior occurred close to zero ($mean = 0.3$). In addition, their time spent on parallelization is much longer in the Codeon condition. Furthermore, the two developers with parallelization behavior in control condition were instantly interrupted ($mean = 1.9s$) by helpers when they attempted to work on different tasks. We found that 11 out of 12 developers parallelized their work when using Codeon, but only two when using the control system. Thus we can assume the parallelization is natural in the setting of Codeon. The result supports our hypothesis $H_{\text{Parallelization}}$ that Codeon supports the distributed workflow. This potentially account for the improvement performance.The evidence and analysis above provide us with insights on the overall performance of two systems. Next, we review developers' feedback and screen recording to facilitate the qualitative analysis.

Post Interview and Developer Feedback

Parallelization

Nearly every developer (11/12) parallelized their efforts. We discovered two patterns of parallelization behavior from both post-interviews as well as our observations. After sending a request or comment, developers would either 1) review a different task, or 2) work on another part of the same task. The first pattern is more common, and some developers used it directly after they read the problem. The second pattern often happened in those tasks with multiple requirements. Developers would divide the task into a few subtasks and distribute some to helpers. For example, one task asks to remove the duplicates of an array and then sort it. One developer (P4) asked his helper to write a function to remove the duplicates. While waiting for a response, he started to code the sort method. Another developer (P9) moved on to a search task after making requests about writing a method and code debugging.

"I was able to kinda break down the tasks into subtasks, and kind of, things I can ask him to help with, and things I can work myself. (P9)"

In general, we observed that developers consistently showed a tendency to parallelize their work, regardless of the condition. However, we found that Codeon allows them to accomplish the distributed workflow.

Interruption

The post-interview also supports our hypothesis $H_{Interruptions}$ by having five participants directly mention the interruption issues in the control system (none in Codeon). There are two types of interruptions we noticed. One is direct interruption which we defined in the previous section, and the other is more subtle distraction coming from the conference call itself. For example,

"When using Skype, he kept asking me about clarifying things that I asked him, I couldn't do anything at the same time, like I had to pay my attention to what he's asking and make sure that whatever I'm asking him, he understood properly. (P9)"

Three developers in the control condition, although working on other tasks while waiting for helpers, were interrupted by their helpers (e.g. asking for confirmation, requesting to check for answers). The helper regularly asked for confirmation such as "you see this?", which force the developer to switch applications back and forth to interact with the helper until they eventually decided to solve this problem together.

CODEON FOR NON-PARALLELIZABLE TASKS

Our results demonstrate that Codeon can help developers complete more tasks when there is the possibility of parallelizing tasks. However, there may remain a subtle but important trade-off: if the success of Codeon is contingent on the amount of parallelism possible for a given problem, then there may be a "minimum" amount of task parallelism below which the baseline condition outperforms Codeon. Intuitively, predicting how parallelizable a future request will be in order to select the most effective system is highly impractical for developers. Fortunately, we found no evidence that this is ever necessary with Codeon.

To test if there exist any such cases where the baseline outperforms Codeon, we ran a study with 14 pairs of programmers (separate from those used in our primary study). We chose the hardest possible case for Codeon: program with an unfamiliar language with no potential parallelism between tasks. To make parallel tasks infeasible, developers were required to have no experience with the language used in the task (AngularJS). Because of unfamiliarity and all the tasks required some levels of understanding to finish, real time communication would provide stronger support.

Even comparing to an earlier version of Codeon, we found no evidence that the control condition outperformed Codeon ($p > 0.50$), even in this most challenging scenario. While we cannot conclusively prove these two cases are not different (i.e., disprove the null hypothesis), the lack of evidence of a difference in this study, and our anecdotal experience observing participants suggests no reason to expect a trade-off between the two systems to exist. Therefore, our data shows that Codeon can perform at least as well as the control system.

Additionally, we observed that 74.17% of the time a developer was engaged with the helper on average, versus 44% with Codeon (mean=0.44, s.d.=0.158, $p < 0.0005$). This further affirms the efficiency observations in our results.

DISCUSSION

Codeon User Interface

Almost all the developers (11/12) in the experiment gave positive feedback on Codeon's user interface, that supports our design decisions retrieved from the series of user studies.

For example, participants mentioned that making requests by using multimodal interaction (voice + code context) allows them to "give context easier" (P4). Furthermore, participants were generally in favor of the way in which Codeon integrates code-based responses. For example, the pop-up notification and the alert sound coming with the new message helped developers to be notified more quickly.

"..the notifications that it gave me are very good... comparing to only have text, add sound can help me to... when i look at the left i can still know what happens on the right.(P5)"

Codeon also prevents developers from "missing something that a helper wrote", and helps them better understand the code by allowing them to "compare two code files simultaneously" (P7). Two developers mentioned that they could not follow where the helper was typing in the control condition because, unlike Codeon, the interactions cannot be replayed nor easily recorded.

"In Codepen, the helper is changing in another window (other than Atom) that I have no idea what he did. In Skype, if I have a question I just say it but there is no history. (P3) "

Effects of Social Norms

Previous research shows that lower social burden on asynchronous communication activity than synchronous [4]. We also found that developers in the control condition expressed the challenge in real-time communication: phrasing the requests, or explaining the code. With the study setup of having a remote helper available in real-time via a conference call, four developers addressed that they were less comfortable and felt more pressure because they felt they "have to ask something" (P11), and less comfortable when having someone just "sitting there" (P11, P4). The rest of them felt little pressure and relied on helpers more to solve the problem. On the other hand, no one expressed similar concerns for Codeon. Codeon offers a more independent environment with little social pressure and the full control over code and the assistance pipeline.

"In Skype, but I also felt like, not that he's interrupting me, but like I can just hear him in the background, its kind of, not intimidating, but like, make me feel like I had to ask questions, even though I wanted to do stuff on my own. (P11)"

Potential of Codeon

One of the limitations of our study is that there are only four tasks, which limits Codeon's potential to support parallelization better and may lead to a larger difference in productivity. For example, there is one developer finished all four tasks in the Codeon condition within 30 minutes. Also, we found that the developers, who only have one task left before the session ended, cannot parallelize their effort(as they could before) because there are no other tasks left. Instead, after making a request for one task, they would continue working on that same task which creates redundancy.

In contrast, many developers expressed concerns on the control system for the synchronous nature of the collaboration. For example, as two developers are sharing an editor, the editor can be a limited resource that blocks a developer's interaction. Participants expressed that they felt limited for various reasons: being "stuck watching" (P12) the helper's typing, being distracted with the other "hear him in the background" (P11), or "delete my code and directly add his code" (P7). Especially given the social barrier in which a developer is put to work with a remote stranger, the pair programming model revealed some challenges for developers in engaging with the helpers in a short time.

Generalizing Codeon's Approach

Our target audiences are programmers who need support that can be more efficiently provided by remote expert developers than existing methods. This remote assistance model can be useful in many contexts including education and distributed teams. We focus on developers' communication, which is important in all of these use cases, regardless of team size or incentive. The three stages of Codeon system we have discussed before fit into a more general model that Codeon advances. Specifically, tools for generating sub-tasks in the current context of work (S1), making it easy for helpers to 'rehydrate' that context (S2), and providing tools for quickly and effectively integrating contributions (S3), can be used across various domains, for example, using software made for professionals (e.g. Photoshop or Final Cut Pro) Exploring how to effectively recreate this approach in other settings is future work beyond the scope of this paper.

LIMITATIONS AND FUTURE WORK

Codeon is an early step towards always-available, crowd-powered developer assistance. As such, there are several limitations to the current system, but also many exciting directions of future work that we hope to bring light to in the HCI, software engineering, and crowdsourcing communities.

Input Modalities

Based on observations and feedback, we found that more than half of participants prefer to have some of their requests made only in text. This is either because they are "used to typing questions" (P6), or they feel it is "hard to speak their questions clearly with one recording", or it is just because "typing is more convenient"(P6) for some cases. Indeed, three developers phrased their requests in the request title and did not record any audio. This suggests that we could enable both text and voice request modalities in future systems.

New Hiring Models for Expert Crowds

On-demand hiring models in prior work have mostly focused on non-expert workers (e.g. [8, 7]). These models assume a workflow that does not validate specific expertise, and usually involve a posted request that includes instructions in details. Future work will explore methods for ad hoc team formation and new expert-sensitive recruiting strategies, and will be able to leverage Codeon as a platform for testing these methods in the wild.

Team-Based Support of Requests

Not only may we be able to recruit individual expert helpers to field requests in parallel, but also we can begin exploring how teams can be formed around these tasks. This line of work shares many of the motivations of the prior work on Flash Teams [36]—quick assembly of efficient, scalable expert teams—but also aims to accomplish this without a priori knowledge of task structure. In place of a priori knowledge, we may be able to leverage what the system can understand about the structure and interplay of the user's existing codebase to find subtasks and even critical skill sets that may be hard to find individual expert helpers to completely address. We believe that Codeon provides an ideal platform for research such as this.

Longitudinal Deployment Studies

Using new tools in the software development process (or any expert workflow) requires time to acclimate to observe the true final effect. People become more comfortable with the tool, more knowledgeable in how to best use it in their work, and begin to plan out their tasks in the context of having the tool at their disposal. While our initial results in this paper show tremendous promise for Codeon, future work will study how developers' processes (both individual and collaborative) change with long-term use of the tool in team and for-hire settings. We are already starting to partner with development organizations, but conducting such a long-term evaluation is beyond the scope of this paper.

CONCLUSION

In this paper, we introduced Codeon, an in-IDE tool that allows software developers to get asynchronous on-demand assistance from remote programmers with minimal effort. Our results showed that developers using Codeon are able to complete nearly twice as many tasks as they could using state-of-the-art synchronous video and code sharing tools, by reducing the coordination costs of seeking assistance from other developers. We have already begun using Codeon in our research group to get external help, as well as efficiently collaborate within our own teams. In the future, in-IDE assistance can be used to further improve productivity, reduce interruptions, and even leverage a combination of human and machine intelligence to aid developers.

ACKNOWLEDGEMENTS

Thanks to Aaron Tatum, Zelin Pu, Gabriel Matute, and Jaylin Herskovitz for their feedback on the system design and data. This work was supported by the University of Michigan.

REFERENCES

1. Upwork inc. (formerly odesk), https://www.upwork.com, 2015. Accessed: April, 2016.
2. Ackerman, M. S. Augmenting organizational memory: a field study of answer garden. *ACM Transactions on Information Systems (TOIS) 16*, 3 (1998), 203–224.
3. Ackerman, M. S., and McDonald, D. W. Answer garden 2: merging organizational memory with collaborative help. In *Proceedings of the 1996 ACM conference on Computer supported cooperative work*, ACM (1996), 97–105.
4. Almaatouq, A., Alhasoun, F., Campari, R., and Alfaris, A. The influence of social norms on synchronous versus asynchronous communication technologies. In *Proceedings of the 1st ACM international workshop on Personal data meets distributed multimedia*, ACM (2013), 39–42.
5. Asaduzzaman, M., Mashiyat, A. S., Roy, C. K., and Schneider, K. A. Answering questions about unanswered questions of stack overflow. In *Proceedings of the 10th Working Conference on Mining Software Repositories*, IEEE Press (2013), 97–100.
6. Baheti, P., Gehringer, E., and Stotts, D. Exploring the efficacy of distributed pair programming. In *Extreme Programming and Agile MethodsXP/Agile Universe 2002*. Springer, 2002, 208–220.
7. Bernstein, M. S., Brandt, J., Miller, R. C., and Karger, D. R. Crowds in two seconds: Enabling realtime crowd-powered interfaces. In *Proceedings of the 24th annual ACM symposium on User interface software and technology*, ACM (2011), 33–42.
8. Bigham, J. P., Jayant, C., Ji, H., Little, G., Miller, A., Miller, R. C., Miller, R., Tatarowicz, A., White, B., White, S., et al. Vizwiz: nearly real-time answers to visual questions. In *Proceedings of the 23nd annual ACM symposium on User interface software and technology*, ACM (2010), 333–342.
9. Brandt, J., Dontcheva, M., Weskamp, M., and Klemmer, S. R. Example-centric programming: integrating web search into the development environment. In *Proceedings of the SIGCHI Conference on Human Factors in Computing Systems*, ACM (2010), 513–522.
10. Brandt, J., Guo, P. J., Lewenstein, J., Dontcheva, M., and Klemmer, S. R. Two studies of opportunistic programming: interleaving web foraging, learning, and writing code. In *Proceedings of the SIGCHI Conference on Human Factors in Computing Systems*, ACM (2009), 1589–1598.
11. Brandt, J., Guo, P. J., Lewenstein, J., Klemmer, S. R., and Dontcheva, M. Writing code to prototype, ideate, and discover. *Software, IEEE 26*, 5 (2009), 18–24.
12. Chen, Y., Oney, S., and Lasecki, W. Towards providing on-demand expert support for software developers. In *Proceedings of the SIGCHI Conference on Human Factors in Computing Systems*, ACM (2016).
13. Chong, J., and Hurlbutt, T. The social dynamics of pair programming. In *29th International Conference on Software Engineering (ICSE'07)*, IEEE (2007), 354–363.
14. Cockburn, A., and Williams, L. The costs and benefits of pair programming. *Extreme programming examined* (2000), 223–247.
15. Goldman, M., Little, G., and Miller, R. C. Real-time collaborative coding in a web ide. In *Proceedings of the 24th annual ACM symposium on User interface software and technology*, ACM (2011), 155–164.
16. Guo, P. J. Codeopticon: Real-time, one-to-many human tutoring for computer programming. In *Proceedings of the 28th annual ACM symposium on User interface software and technology*, ACM (2015).
17. Guo, P. J., White, J., and Zanelatto, R. Codechella: Multi-user program visualizations for real-time tutoring and collaborative learning. In *Visual Languages and Human-Centric Computing (VL/HCC), 2015 IEEE Symposium on*, IEEE (2015).
18. Guzzi, A., Bacchelli, A., Riche, Y., and van Deursen, A. Supporting developers' coordination in the ide. In *Proceedings of the 18th ACM Conference on Computer Supported Cooperative Work & Social Computing*, ACM (2015), 518–532.
19. Hartmann, B., MacDougall, D., Brandt, J., and Klemmer, S. R. What would other programmers do: suggesting solutions to error messages. In *Proceedings of the SIGCHI Conference on Human Factors in Computing Systems*, ACM (2010), 1019–1028.
20. Herbsleb, J. D., Klein, H., Olson, G. M., Brunner, H., Olson, J. S., and Harding, J. Object-oriented analysis and design in software project teams. *Human–Computer Interaction 10*, 2-3 (1995), 249–292.
21. Inc., C. Code mentor, https://codementor.io/, 2014. Accessed: April, 2016.
22. Inc., C. I. Cloud9 ide, https://c9.io, 2010. Accessed: April, 2016.
23. Inc, H. Hack.hands(), https://hackhands.com/, 2015. Accessed: April, 2016.
24. Iqbal, S. T., and Horvitz, E. Disruption and recovery of computing tasks: field study, analysis, and directions. In *Proceedings of the SIGCHI conference on Human factors in computing systems*, ACM (2007), 677–686.
25. Ko, A. J., DeLine, R., and Venolia, G. Information needs in collocated software development teams. In *Proceedings of the 29th international conference on Software Engineering*, IEEE Computer Society (2007), 344–353.
26. Ko, A. J., Myers, B., Aung, H. H., et al. Six learning barriers in end-user programming systems. In *Visual Languages and Human Centric Computing, 2004 IEEE Symposium on*, IEEE (2004), 199–206.

27. Lasecki, W., Miller, C., Sadilek, A., Abumoussa, A., Borrello, D., Kushalnagar, R., and Bigham, J. Real-time captioning by groups of non-experts. In *Proceedings of the 25th annual ACM symposium on User interface software and technology*, ACM (2012), 23–34.
28. Lasecki, W. S., Kim, J., Rafter, N., Sen, O., Bigham, J. P., and Bernstein, M. S. Apparition: Crowdsourced user interfaces that come to life as you sketch them. In *Proceedings of the 33rd Annual ACM Conference on Human Factors in Computing Systems*, ACM (2015), 1925–1934.
29. Lasecki, W. S., Wesley, R., Nichols, J., Kulkarni, A., Allen, J. F., and Bigham, J. P. Chorus: a crowd-powered conversational assistant. In *Proceedings of the 26th annual ACM symposium on User interface software and technology*, ACM (2013), 151–162.
30. LaToza, T. D., Towne, W. B., Adriano, C. M., and van der Hoek, A. Microtask programming: Building software with a crowd. In *Proceedings of the 27th annual ACM symposium on User interface software and technology*, ACM (2014), 43–54.
31. LaToza, T. D., Venolia, G., and DeLine, R. Maintaining mental models: a study of developer work habits. In *Proceedings of the 28th international conference on Software engineering*, ACM (2006), 492–501.
32. Olson, G. M., and Olson, J. S. Distance matters. *Human-computer interaction 15*, 2 (2000), 139–178.
33. Overflow, S. Stack overflow, https://stackoverflow.com/, 2015. Accessed: April, 2016.
34. Ponzanelli, L., Bacchelli, A., and Lanza, M. Seahawk: Stack overflow in the ide. In *Proceedings of the 2013 International Conference on Software Engineering*, IEEE Press (2013), 1295–1298.
35. Raymond, E. S. *The Cathedral and the Bazaar*, 1st ed. O'Reilly & Associates, Inc., Sebastopol, CA, USA, 1999.
36. Retelny, D., Robaszkiewicz, S., To, A., Lasecki, W. S., Patel, J., Rahmati, N., Doshi, T., Valentine, M., and Bernstein, M. S. Expert crowdsourcing with flash teams. In *Proceedings of the 27th annual ACM symposium on User interface software and technology*, ACM (2014), 75–85.
37. Robillard, M. P., Walker, R. J., and Zimmermann, T. Recommendation systems for software engineering. *Software, IEEE 27*, 4 (2010), 80–86.
38. Schenk, J., Prechelt, L., and Salinger, S. Distributed-pair programming can work well and is not just distributed pair-programming. In *Companion Proceedings of the 36th International Conference on Software Engineering*, ACM (2014), 74–83.
39. Sillito, J., Murphy, G. C., and De Volder, K. Asking and answering questions during a programming change task. *Software Engineering, IEEE Transactions on 34*, 4 (2008), 434–451.
40. Sinan Yasar, D. Y. Koding, 2012. Accessed: April, 2016.
41. Steinmacher, I., Silva, M. A. G., and Gerosa, M. A. Barriers faced by newcomers to open source projects: a systematic review. In *Open Source Software: Mobile Open Source Technologies*. Springer, 2014, 153–163.

PFIS-V: Modeling Foraging Behavior in the Presence of Variants

Sruti Srinivasa Ragavan[1], Bhargav Pandya[1], David Piorkowski[1, 2], Charles Hill[1], Sandeep Kaur Kuttal[3], Anita Sarma[1], Margaret Burnett[1]

[1]Oregon State University
Corvallis, OR, USA
{srinivas, pandyab, hillc, anita.sarma, burnett}@oregonstate.edu

[2]IBM Research
Yorktown Heights, NY, USA
david.piorkowski@ibm.com

[3]University of Tulsa
Tulsa, OK, USA
sandeep-kuttal@utulsa.edu

ABSTRACT
Foraging among similar variants of the same artifact is a common activity, but computational models of Information Foraging Theory (IFT) have not been developed to take such variants into account. Without being able to computationally predict people's foraging behavior with variants, our ability to harness the theory in practical ways—such as building and systematically assessing tools for people who forage different variants of an artifact—is limited. Therefore, in this paper, we introduce a new predictive model, PFIS-V, that builds upon PFIS3, the most recent of the PFIS family of modeling IFT in programming situations. Our empirical results show that PFIS-V is up to 25% more accurate than PFIS3 in predicting where a forager will navigate in a variationed information space.

Author Keywords
Variants; Information Foraging Theory.

ACM Classification Keywords
H.5.m. Information interfaces and presentation (e.g., HCI): Miscellaneous

INTRODUCTION
When engaged in computer-supported creative tasks—such as graphic design, creating a presentation, exploratory programming, or writing this CHI paper—people often need to build upon and compare multiple ideas, fit them together and save the intermediate steps [1]. One effect of such exploration can be the creation of *many*, *many* variants of the same artifact (e.g., image with different colors) [2, 12, 45].

People need to find (or re-find) and compare these earlier variants of the artifact, especially when things go wrong, they reach a dead-end, or they want to opportunistically harvest specific bits and pieces of prior work. For example, working in such ways with multiple variants is especially common in exploratory programming, where programmers—novices and experts—experimentally blend writing new code with reusing bits and pieces of code from different resources, including earlier variants [1, 2, 18, 27, 47].

Finding one's way to the right information in a large information space is difficult—even without the presence of multiple variants. For example, one study reported programmers spending about 35% of their time on just the mechanics of navigating a single variant of source code [19], and another study reported that, when other aspects of information seeking were also taken into account, programmers spent an average of 50% of their time navigating [34].

Information Foraging Theory (IFT) [36] helps explain how people spend their time in their information seeking activities. IFT proposes that a person seeking information follows the "information scent" perceived from the signposts ("cues") to locations of potentially useful information (patches), similar to the way predatory animals in the wild follow the scent to their prey. Since foraging in the presence of multiple variants *adds* a need for the forager to cognitively discern differences among very similar cues and patches, it stands to reason that the cost to foragers in a variationed information space will be higher than when patches and cues are more unique and distinctive.

Indeed, a recent study observed that foragers in a variationed information space adopted additional foraging mechanisms and strategies in the presence of multiple, similar variants [41]. These initial observations suggest the need for a deeper understanding of how well IFT can explain people's behavior in such a foraging situation, and how we might then harness IFT to build tools to support variations foraging. Computational models allow us to do this: they help researchers empirically validate concrete hypotheses derived from study observations and guide tool-building.

Toward this end, we present a new computational model of foraging that is able to account for multiple similar variants in an information space. Our new model, called PFIS-V (PFIS for Variation Space), builds on the PFIS (Programmer Flow by Information Scent) family of predictive IFT models for programming situations [32]. We chose programming as our domain because, as mentioned earlier, variations are a commonly-occurring phenomenon in this already information-seeking-intensive domain; however,

CHI 2017, May 06-11, 2017, Denver, CO, USA
 ISBN 978-1-4503-4655-9/17/05...$15.00
DOI: http://dx.doi.org/10.1145/3025453.3025818

the theoretical foundations should apply to other domains (e.g., web design, text documents, slide decks, etc.) as well.

We begin by modeling the properties of variants—such as similarities and differences—that users attended to during their variations foraging, leading us to our first RQ:

RQ1: How can we account for variants in computationally modeling programmers' foraging behavior?

We then empirically investigate the effectiveness of our computational model using the data collected from a prior study on variations foraging [41] to answer:

RQ2: How effective is our new computational model?

BACKGROUND AND RELATED WORK

Variants

Working with variants is a common phenomenon in exploratory, creative tasks. Researchers have built several tools to support variants in both non-programming (such as graphic design [11, 12, 45], personal information management [16]) as well as programming domains (e.g., web design [18, 20], professional software development [6], end-user programming [22, 13]). However, none of these tools (except [13]) support variations in exploratory programming.

Prior work on programmers reusing code from other variants during exploratory programming defined a program *variant* as a "*syntactically valid program that occurs together with other similar, related programs*" [41]. For example, if a programmer took the source code of a website and modified the background color of the home page, the resulting new program is a variant of the original program. The results, grounded in Information Foraging Theory (IFT), explain programmers' foraging behavior while seeking the right variant (and the relevant code snippets within) to reuse. We build on this prior work and use IFT to computationally model programmers' variations foraging.

Information Foraging Theory (IFT)

Information Foraging Theory is a theory of how people engaged in information-intensive tasks seek information. IFT is based on optimal foraging theory that explains how predators hunt for their prey in the wild [36]. The theory was first developed to explain people's information-seeking behavior in large document collections. Since then, it has been applied to explain user behavior in several other domains like web browsing and programming.

IFT borrows constructs from the optimal foraging theory: a person seeking information in an information environment (e.g., programmer searching for a code snippet in an IDE) is similar to a predator seeking prey in a foraging ground (*predator* = person, *prey* = information, *foraging ground* = information environment). The prey might be present in locations in the information environment called *patches* (e.g., files, classes or methods) and the patches might be connected to each other via *links* (e.g., IDE shortcut to go from one method to another). The network of patches and links together is called the *topology*.

Associated with the links is information that acts as *cues* for the predator: a cue tells the predator what might be at the other end of the link, thereby, becoming signposts to their prey. For example, the words in a method name act as cues about what the method does. The predator uses the scent emanating from these cues to reach the information they seek, just like animals sniff their way to their prey.

One of the ways in which IFT has been applied is to computationally model user behavior during different information-seeking tasks [3, 4, 10, 23, 37, 38, 39]; such models have informed the design of tools and interfaces for people engaged in information-intensive tasks. For example, the WUFIS [3] model uses the structure and content of web sites to predict which page a user would navigate to; this in turn helped lay the foundations for layout and information design in websites [43] and web-search engines [28].

Recently, IFT has been applied to programming tasks such as requirements tracing, debugging, maintenance and IDE design [9, 21, 23, 25, 29, 34, 35, 40, 31]. Researchers have built computational models to predict, and thus explain programmers' navigation in source code. The first such model, namely PFIS [24], used source code and task descriptions to predict which classes a programmer, working on a given task, would navigate to. PFIS was then extended to PFIS2 (and later refined to PFIS3 [32]) to model "reactive IFT" [26], that accounted for the evolving foraging goals of programmers as they perform their task. Piorkowski et al. used these models to build a system that recommends parts of code relevant to the current foraging goals (and sub-goals) [33]. However, the PFIS family so far has only accounted for a single program variant and is insufficient to explain foraging in a variationed information space.

Predicting programmer navigations

Navigating source code is nontrivial [19]: one of the ways researchers have attempted to help programmers navigate source code is by recommending source-code locations that the programmer might want to navigate next. To make their recommendations, these tools use different heuristics. Several tools use the historical activity of the programmer (e.g., past visited locations) to make a prediction [8, 14, 17, 30] while others use textual similarity (to bug report or current location), structure of the program (such as method invocations) [7, 15, 42, 44] or a combination of these [33]. However, none of these tools consider the case of a programmer navigating through multiple program variants.

MODELING PROGRAMMER NAVIGATIONS

Computational models serve two purposes: (i) they provide a way to validate hypotheses about programmers' foraging behavior, and (ii) the models can be directly used for theory-based tool building. We build on an existing family of predictive models, namely PFIS (Programmer Flow by Information Scent) [24], that model programmer's foraging in a *single* program variant. We chose PFIS because it is grounded in IFT, which is the underlying theory for several computational models of user behavior in several domains

[3, 10, 23], including programming activities like debugging [25] and maintenance [24].

PFIS3: Before we describe PFIS3 (the most recent model in the PFIS family), note that predictive models contain two parts: (i) the data model representing the program—its methods, words and links, and (ii) the algorithm that uses the data model to predict programmers' navigations in the program. In the rest of this paper, we use following terminology: *predictive model* refers to any model that predicts programmer navigations; *data model* refers to the underlying representation of the program; and the *algorithm* is responsible for making predictions using the data model (Predictive Model = Data Model + Algorithm).

PFIS3's data model operationalizes the topology of the information space (network of patches and links) as a graph. The information patches (here, methods) are represented as nodes (called *patch nodes)* while links between patches are represented by edges. A link between two patches exists when a programmer can go from one patch to another in a single-step IDE action (e.g., following an IDE shortcut to go to method definitions, scrolling to adjacent methods). The words in patches are modeled as nodes (called *word nodes*), while edges between patch nodes and word nodes indicate that the patch contains the word.

Figure 1 shows a program (left) represented in the data model (right). For each method (patch) in the program (e.g., `sum`, `count`, `average`), there is a patch node (blue ellipse) in the graph, and for every word in the program except reserved keywords (e.g., `numbers`, words in method names), the graph contains a word node (red square).

The method `average` calls methods `sum` and `count`, and a programmer can navigate between these methods using IDE shortcuts; therefore, these patches are linked via an invocation edge (labeled "*inv*"). Similarly, a programmer can navigate from the method `count` to the methods `sum` and `average` by scrolling; therefore, these patches are linked via adjacency edges (labeled "adj"). Thus the links in the graph model the environment's navigation affordances.

Let us look at the method `average`: the patch contains words like average (its name), numbers (parameter), and its content (calls to `sum, count`); these words in the patch serve as cues for a programmer foraging in this patch. The dashed edge (---) between the patch node *average* and the word node *numbers* indicates that the patch contains the word. Since the word `numbers` is also found in patches `sum` and `count`, the *numbers* word node is also connected to *sum* and *average* patch nodes via dashed edges (---).

The PFIS3 algorithm uses the data model to predict programmers' between-patch navigations. It does so by computing the "scent" of links from the programmer's current patch to all other patches the programmer has seen thus far. First, the algorithm activates some patches with initial weights based on the programmer's current location. The algorithm then spreads this activation to other patches based on source-code cues (words), the programmer's past navigation history, and the topology of the information space. The patches are then ranked by their resultant weights, and the algorithm returns the patch with the lowest rank as its prediction for the programmer's next navigation [33].

Let us look at an example (based on Figure 1) of the algorithm's working. Consider a programmer currently in method `count.` Although both `sum` and `average` are *adjacent* patches to `count`, the PFIS3 algorithm spreads higher activation to `average` than `sum`. This is because (a) there is an additional *invocation* link between `count` and `average`, and (b) the patch *`average`* has more words (*numbers, count*) in common with `count,` than `sum` (only *numbers*). Therefore, the algorithm predicts a navigation from `count` to `average`. Note that PFIS3 also takes pro-

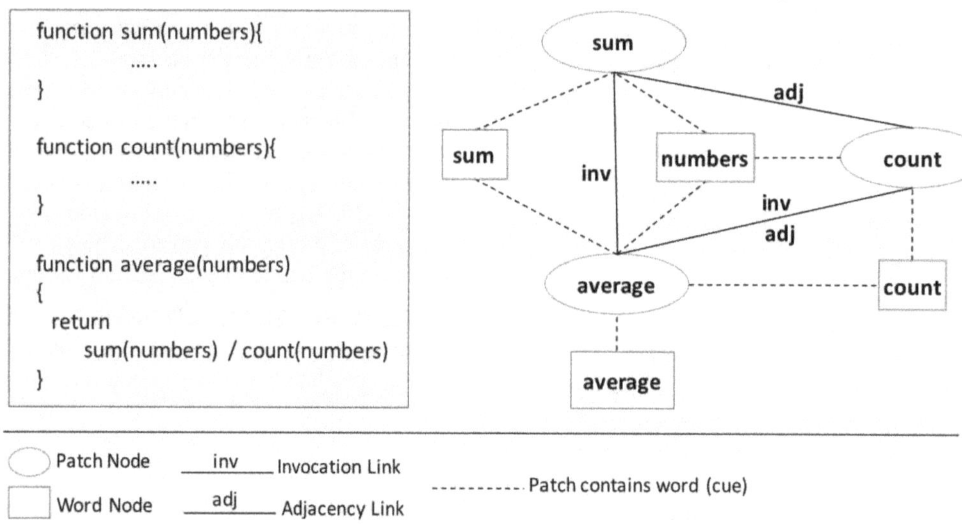

Figure 1. The PFIS3 data model operationalizes IFT: patches (methods) and words in source code are represented as nodes while links between patches and "patch contain word" relationships are represented by edges.

grammers' navigation history into account for making predictions, which we ignore here for illustration purposes.

While PFIS3 or other IFT models predict user behavior in a single variant of an artifact, none of them consider multiple variants. This leads us to our first research question:

RQ 1: How can we account for variants in computationally modeling programmers' foraging behavior?

We answer RQ1 in two stages: RQ 1a addresses representation of variants in data models, and RQ 1b focuses on algorithms that account for variants while making predictions.

RQ 1a: How do we represent variants to computationally model foraging in the presence of variants?

The PFIS3 data model can represent a *single* variant of a program. We extend this data model to represent *multiple* variants in *four* different ways, each making different assumptions about programmers' foraging among variants.

Variant-unaware data model

The *variant-unaware* data model is very similar to the PFIS3 data model: it represents patches (along with associated cues and links) from multiple variants in the same way PFIS3 represents a single variant of a program (Recall that a variant is an *entire copy* of a program). Such a data model is unaware of the properties of variants (such as the similarities and differences between variants), which programmers are aware of, and use in their foraging [41].

Figure 2(a) shows the variant-unaware representation of a program with four variants. We represent methods in the program using letters A, P, Q, R and S: nodes represent patches and edges represent links between them. A programmer starts with the first variant and makes changes to method R (whereby, $R' = R + \Delta R$) to create a new variant (and subsequently creates other variants too). While a programmer may be aware that patches R, R', and R" (or all of P) are similar, related patches across different variants, the variant-unaware model is unaware of these properties.

Since this data model captures the navigation affordances currently available in IDEs (and our study environment [41]), we use it as the baseline for our comparisons.

Variant-aware data model

One property of variants is that they have similar patches: prior results showed that programmers capitalized on this property while foraging [41]. We modeled this property by introducing "*variant-of*" links between *similar* patches across variants, thereby making it "variant-aware". We define two patches (in different variants) to be *similar*, if they have the *same fully-qualified names* (folder, file, class and method names) relative to the variant that contains them.

See the variant-aware data model in Figure 2(b): the "variant-of" links (dotted lines) between all patches P, or R, R', and R" indicate similar patches across different variants.

Variant and equivalence aware data models

Often, a small change in one variant (such as font color and size) might result in a new variant of a program. This leads to a lot of not just similar, but *identical* (exactly the same) patches among temporally close variants [41]. In a programming context, this means that methods can have the same fully-qualified names (folder, file, class *and* method names), as well as *exactly the same content* (parameter names, definition and words) across different variants.

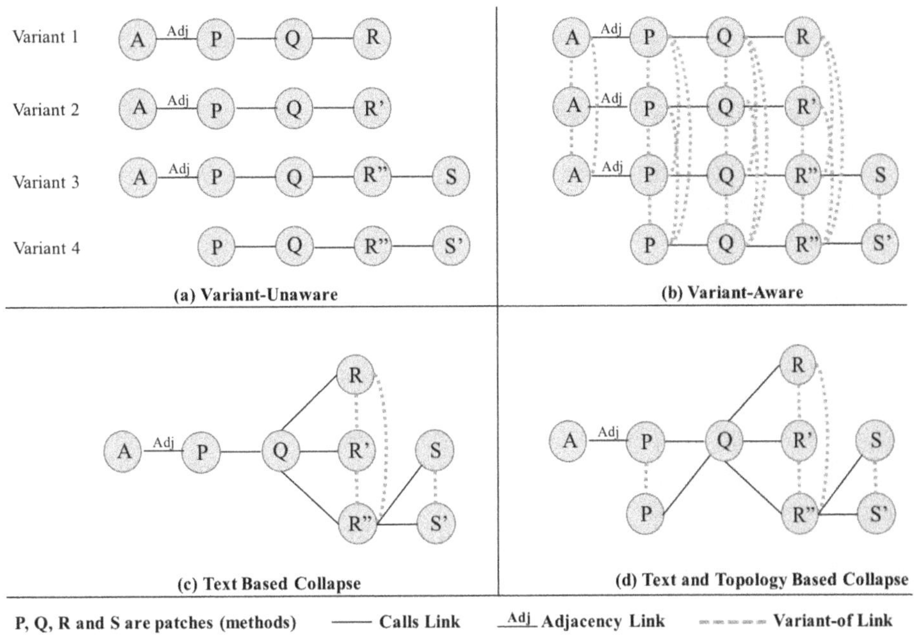

Figure 2. In order to introduce variant-awareness, we added "variant-of" edges (dotted lines) between similar patches in different variants (b). Further, we collapsed equivalent patches based on text-based similarity (c), or text-and-topology-based similarity (d).

From a foraging perspective, this means that the cues and the scent from these identical patches are also the same; hence, it does not matter which of these identical patches a programmer forages in. Since these patches are all equivalent to the programmer, we call them "*equivalent*" patches.

From a modeling perspective too, it does not matter which one of these equivalent patches a predictive algorithm predicts. Therefore, we collapse multiple equivalent patches into one super-patch to form a variant-and-equivalence-aware data model. We do this in two ways:

In *text-based equivalence* (denoted by suffix t), we call two patches equivalent if their contents are identical, i.e., they have exactly the same text. From a forager's perspective, this models the case where a programmer *does not* differentiate between patches (and treats them as equivalent) as long as they have the same content.

However, programmers *might* differentiate patches across variants even though they might have the same content! Consider the following scenario: two variants of a program contain identical patches P. In the first variant, there is a patch A that is right above (adjacent) to P, while there is no adjacent patch A in the second variant. In some situations, a programmer foraging in the two variants might perceive the two patches as different. In fact, prior studies on programmer navigation have shown that source-code structure is an important factor in modeling programmer navigations [32]. This leads us to an alternate definition for equivalence:

In *text-and-topology-based equivalence* (denoted by suffix t,t), two patches are equivalent if: (a) they have exactly the same content, *and* (b) their neighbors (patches linked by invocation and adjacency links) in the topology are *similar* (not necessarily identical).

See Figure 2 (b): patch P has links to patch A in the first three variants, but not in the last variant. The variant-and-equivalence-aware(t) only considers text similarity; therefore, patch P from all variants are collapsed into one single patch in Figure 2(c). On the other hand, the variant-and-equivalence-aware(t,t) considers similarities in both text as well as topology: therefore, it collapses the patch P in the first three variants (having same neighbors A and Q) alone into one node, while excluding the patch P in the last variant (since it has no neighbor A).

Notice that in both cases the variant-and-equivalence-aware data models preserve the notion of similar patches (variant awareness), denoted by the "variant-of" links between similar patches in both Figure 2(c) and (d).

One concluding remark about the two variant-and-equivalence-aware data models is that they represent variations to an artifact by only capturing the differences between the variants. This is unlike the variant-unaware or variant-aware data models which also capture redundant, similar patches. For example, in Figure 2, both variant-unaware and variant-aware data models retains four copies of patch Q, even though Q has not changed across variants (there is no Q'), whereas the two variant-and-equivalence-aware representations contain only one patch Q. This result can be directly applied in practical cases where variants need to represented or stored.

Having thus addressed the data modeling problem for program variants (RQ 1a), we next focus on the predictive algorithm (RQ 1b). Before we proceed to develop a new algorithm to predict programmer navigations in a variationed information space, we first modify PFIS3 to predict programmer navigations using the above four data models.

PFIS3 models foraging in a single program variant where a patch node in the data model represents a single patch in the program; therefore, the PFIS3 algorithm does not distinguish between patches and patch nodes. However, the PFIS3 approach fails for variant-and-equivalence-aware data models where one patch node might represent many equivalent (collapsed) patches. Therefore, we tweaked PFIS3 to distinguish between patches and patch nodes, and predict *patch nodes* in the graph instead of *patches* in the program. With this tweak, PFIS3 can predict programmer navigations in four configurations using the four data models; these serve as our baseline for comparisons.

Although PFIS3 can now predict using data models representing variants, its algorithm does not consider the properties of variants that programmers capitalize on, during their foraging [41]. Therefore, we extend the PFIS3 algorithm to account for these properties of variants in order to accurately model programmer behavior.

RQ 1b-How can we predict programmer navigation in a variationed information space?

PFIS3 models programmers' navigations to only patches that s/he has already visited (or seen): all other navigations are considered "*unknown*" because the programmer has never seen them. However, in the presence of variants, even though a programmer has not seen a particular patch, s/he might know about it if s/he has already seen a similar patch in a different variant. We therefore extend PFIS3 to PFIS-V (PFIS for Variants) to model this phenomenon that is unique to variations foraging.

Consider a programmer – let us call her Alice – foraging in a method `count` in variant V1 of a program. She then navigates to a different variant V2 and again sees a method `count` in V2. Even before Alice makes a decision to navigate to, or forage in the method `count` in V2, she already has some prior knowledge about the method; therefore, the method `count` is not entirely unknown to Alice. IFT assumes that an information forager makes rational decisions [37]; therefore, when Alice does decide to navigate to the method `count` in variant V2, it stands to reason that she has one of the two expectations: the method `count` in the two variants are identical, or, they are both different (depending on her foraging goal).

Definitions:

- Patch set P: set of all patches in the topology that the programmer has seen so far.
- Word set W: set of all words in all patches in P.
- Graph $G = (N_p \cup N_w, E_p \cup E_w)$, where,
  - N_p: set of nodes representing patches in P (a patch node can represent a single non-collapsed patch or multiple equivalent patches when collapsed).
  - N_w: set of nodes representing the words in W.
  - E_p: set of edges between two patch nodes, when the patches are linked by an adjacency, invocation or a "variant-of" link.
  - E_w: set of edges between a word node and a patch node, where the patch contains the word.
- Navigation history H: sequence of patches to which the programmer has navigated so far.

Steps to predict the (k+1)th patch in H:

- If programmer has not seen exact patch earlier:
  If programmer has seen a similar patch P_s: assume content of $(K+1)^{th}$ patch is exactly similar to P_s.
  Else, return "unknown"
- Set activation for each node in $G \to 0$.
- For the k^{th}patch p in H and $|H| - \delta < k$,
  - Increment activation for patch node for p by $0.9|H| - k$.
- Spread activation ($\propto = 0.85$, edge weights=1) such that only word nodes receive activation.
- Spread activation ($\propto = 0.85$, edge weights=1) such that only patch nodes receive activation.
- Rank the patch nodes in the decreasing order of activation.
  - If t patch nodes are tied at rank r, assign $rank = [r + \frac{t-1}{2}]$ to all t patch nodes.
- Return the rank for the node representing the $(k+1)^{th}$ patch.

Figure 3. The PFIS-V's algorithm. (Lines in blue indicate the differences from PFIS3)

Indeed, prior results showed that programmers looked for similarities and differences (based on their foraging goals) while foraging among similar patches in different variants [41]. From the perspective of modeling such programmer's behavior, there is no way of knowing what difference the programmer expects to find (between similar patches in different variants); hence the cues and scents for such a navigation cannot be modeled until the programmer actually navigates to the patch. Therefore, PFIS-V assumes and models the case that the programmer expects the two similar patches to be identical, as shown in Figure 3.

Recall that PFIS-V (and PFIS3) can predict programmer navigations in four configurations (using the four data models): we refer to these configurations using the notation "PFIS-V / data model", e.g., PFIS-V/variant-unaware.

EVALUATION

Methodology

We evaluated PFIS-V using the data containing over 650 click-based navigations [32], collected in our prior study with seven novice programmers [41]. Participants in the study made changes to a JavaScript-based game called Hextris, working in Cloud9, a web-based IDE, on a programming task that lasted 50 minutes. Participants' IDE actions as well as their screen interactions were recorded using Cryolite, a Cloud9 logger [48] and screen capture software.

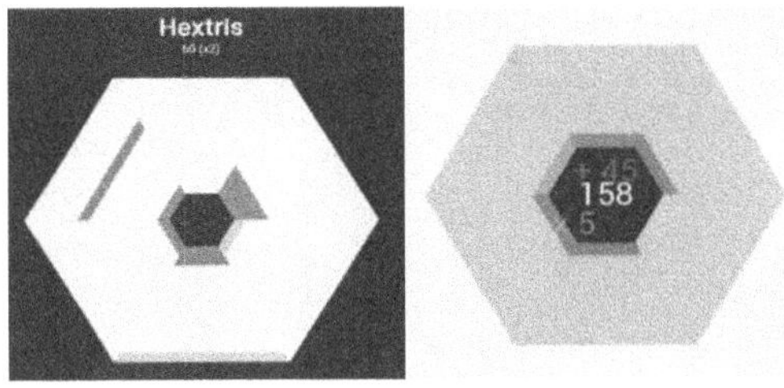

Figure 4. Participants were asked to move the score and multiplier above the hexagon, "like it was before" (Left: Before, Right: After)

The participants were asked to make the following changes to the latest version of the game (Figure 4(a)): (i) move the score indicator above the hexagon, (ii) move the score multiplier above the hexagon, and (iii) change the score color; all "like it was before" (Figure 4 (b)). The phrase "like it was before" was used in order to avoid explicitly mentioning that the solutions to the tasks were present in earlier variants. There were over 700 variants.

PFIS-V evaluation

We evaluated PFIS-V by predicting the *between-patch* navigations (navigations between methods)—within or across variants—that were made by participants during the programming task in the above-said study. We then analyzed the accuracy of these predictions, thus answering RQ2:

RQ 2: How effective is our new computational model, namely PFIS-V?

We answered this question by considering two aspects:

Unknown rates

Recall that models like PFIS3 and PFIS-V cannot predict programmer navigations in all cases; in some cases, they return "Unknown". The *unknown rate* is the percentage of navigations for which a model returns "Unknown". For example, an unknown rate of 60% means that the model *failed* to predict 60% of all programmer navigations.

Figure 5(b) compares the unknown rates of PFIS-V (blue) and PFIS3 (yellow): PFIS-V had lower unknown rates than PFIS3 for all seven participants (Note that lower is better). In other words, in the presence of variations, PFIS-V could predict (and hence model) programmer navigations in cases *where PFIS3 failed to make a prediction.* On an average, PFIS-V predicted 9.25% more navigations than PFIS3; for individual participants this number was as high as 20.19% (P07). Note that while the unknown rate indicates how often a model fails to make a prediction, it does not measure the accuracy of the predictions.

Hit rates

Hit rate, on the other hand, can measure the accuracy of predictions. Recall that the PFIS family returns the rank at

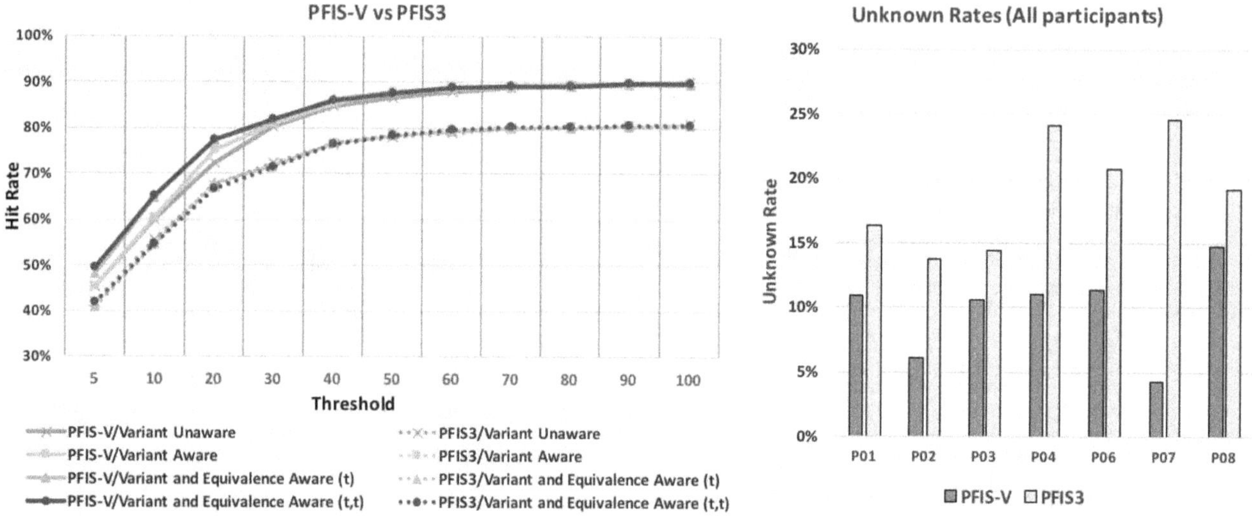

(a) (b)

Figure 5. Not only can PFIS-V predict navigations that PFIS3 cannot, PFIS-V also does so with a higher accuracy than PFIS3.

which the algorithm predicts the navigation (to be) made by a programmer (as shown in Figure 3). $Hit\ rate\ (N = k)$ read as "hit rate with threshold k", refers to the percentage of navigations that a model predicts at $rank \leq k$. In other words, a "hit rate (N=10) of 60%" means that for 60% of the navigations, the actual navigation made by the programmer was in the top 10 predictions made by the model.

In order to compare the accuracy of predictions made by two models, we compare their hit rates. Following the work of Piorkowski et al. on PFIS3 [32, 33], we generally use hit rate (N=10), unless specified otherwise. See Figure 5(a): the graph is a plot of average hit rates (across all participants) yielded by the different configurations of PFIS3 and PFIS-V, for different thresholds. Irrespective of the underlying data model (line colors), we see that on an average, *PFIS-V (solid lines) had higher average hit rates than PFIS3 (dotted lines)*, suggesting that programmers did capitalize on their knowledge of prior variants, as modeled by PFIS-V.

Although we found that the increase in hit rates when averaged across all participants was modest (about 10%), we saw a much higher increase in accuracy in predictions from PFIS3 to PFIS-V for individual participants. In the case of participant P07, PFIS-V had an increase of 25% accuracy as compared to PFIS3 (PFIS-V modeled with an accuracy of 65%, while PFIS3 attained a 40% accuracy). Further, PFIS-V could model individual participants' navigations with an accuracy as high as 83% (participant P01) [46]. Note that our results are based on only one study in a specific environment; further studies are needed to generalize these results. We now unpack the results of our evaluation further.

PFIS-V configurations

Recall that PFIS-V can predict in four different configurations, using four different data models. Each of the four data models make different assumptions about the programmers' mental model of the variationed information space and their foraging behavior. To empirically validate our assumptions about programmers' foraging behavior, we further investigated the four PFIS-V configurations.

In Figure 5(a), the different colored solid lines show the average accuracy (hit rates) of PFIS-V for different data model configurations. Focusing only on PFIS-V, we see that the variant-aware (yellow) configuration yielded higher hit rates than the variant-unaware (orange) one, while the variant-and-equivalence-aware configurations (overlapping green and brown solid lines) yielded even higher accuracy than the previous models. Thus, *PFIS-V/variant-and-equivalence-aware(t,t) made the most accurate assumptions about programmers' variations foraging.*

However, further analysis revealed that the above result does not hold for *all* participants: in fact, there existed *two* groups of participants. See Figure 6: the average accuracy of PFIS-V varied with the data models for Group-1 participants (lines do not overlap), while no such differences were observed for Group 2 (the four lines almost overlap).

Before we reason about the differences between these two groups, let us first review the foraging activities of the programmers in the study. Participants had to find and reuse snippets of code from an earlier variant, which included multiple foraging activities: (i) find the right "source" variant from over 700 variants, (ii) forage within that source variant to find the task-relevant patches, and (iii) make changes to the variant containing the latest version of the code ("destination" variant). In IFT terminology, foraging for the right variant from among several variants is called *between-variant foraging*, while foraging within *a* variant to find relevant patches is called *within-variant foraging*. In both these kinds of foraging, participants used different types of *cues* to lead them to their prey [41].

Partici-pant	Variant-unaware			Variant-aware			Variant-and-equivalence aware(t)			Variant-and-equivalence aware(t,t)		
	Patch Nodes	Edges	Variant-of Edges	Patch Nodes	Edges	Variant-of Edges	Patch Nodes	Edges	Variant-of Edges	Patch Nodes	Edges	Variant-of Edges
P04	276	623	0	276	817	194	261	752	159	263	756	163
P07	326	821	0	326	2288	1467	218	996	443	291	1780	1032

Table 1. For Group-1 participants, the graphs for the variant-and-equivalence-aware are smaller (lesser number of nodes and edges) than the other data model graphs.

Between-variant foraging: two behaviors

Let us now revisit the two participant groups: the primary difference between the two groups of participants is that they used different types of cues for their between-variant foraging. In order to find a right variant for reuse, Group-1 participants (2 out of 7) predominantly looked for differences in the source code between variants, while Group-2 participants (5 out of 7) exclusively used the variants' timestamp, changelogs or differences in the game's output. In IFT terms, Group-1 participants foraged in source-code patches using source-code words as cues, whereas Group-2 participants foraged extensively in non-source-code patches (like output, changelog) and used both textual and non-text-based (visual) cues. Both groups of participants, then, primarily used words in source-code as cues to locate the right patches within the variant (within-variant foraging).

Ideally, a computational model like PFIS-V should aim to model both within- and between-variant foraging of programmers, irrespective of the types of cues they might use or the types of patches they might forage in. Currently, PFIS-V can very well model within-variant foraging, where participants foraged in source-code patches and used as cues words in the source code.

However, in the case of between-variant foraging, PFIS-V modeled the foraging behavior of Group-1 participants (who used the text-based source-code words as cues) very well, but failed to model non-source-code patches and cues (like game's output), which Group-2 participants heavily used. This is because the current state of IFT-based computational models only account for text-based patches and cues in both their data models as well as algorithms. Significant additional work is needed to investigate accounting for non-source-code patches and cue types in IFT-based computational models; we leave this for future work.

Since PFIS-V can only completely model foraging in source code patches, using source-code-inspired cues, we focus our further evaluation of PFIS-V to such foraging behavior, i.e., for Group-1 participants.

PFIS-V: Modeling foraging in source-code patches

Figure 6 compares the average hit rates of the different PFIS-V configurations for the two groups of participants. The graph for Group 1 shows four distinct lines: the (average) accuracy of PFIS-V differed across the data models. The accuracy of different PFIS-V configurations were as follows: variant-and-equivalence-aware(t,t) > variant-and-equivalence-aware(t) > variant-aware > variant-unaware.

This indicates that the PFIS-V/variant-and-equivalence-aware(t,t) model was the most accurate model of programmers' foraging behavior, thereby validating the assumptions of that data model: (i) participants recognized and were aware of the similarities in patches between variants (variant-awareness), (ii) participants made comparisons between similar patches in different variants (equivalence-aware), and (iii) they compared similar patches between variants in terms of both their content and code structure (t,t).

The PFIS-V/variant-and-equivalence-aware(t,t) model has another advantage too. Table 1 shows the size of the graphs for the different data models for the two Group-1 participants: the size of the graph (number of nodes and edges) for the variant-and-equivalent-aware data models was found to be smaller than the other two data models. However, note

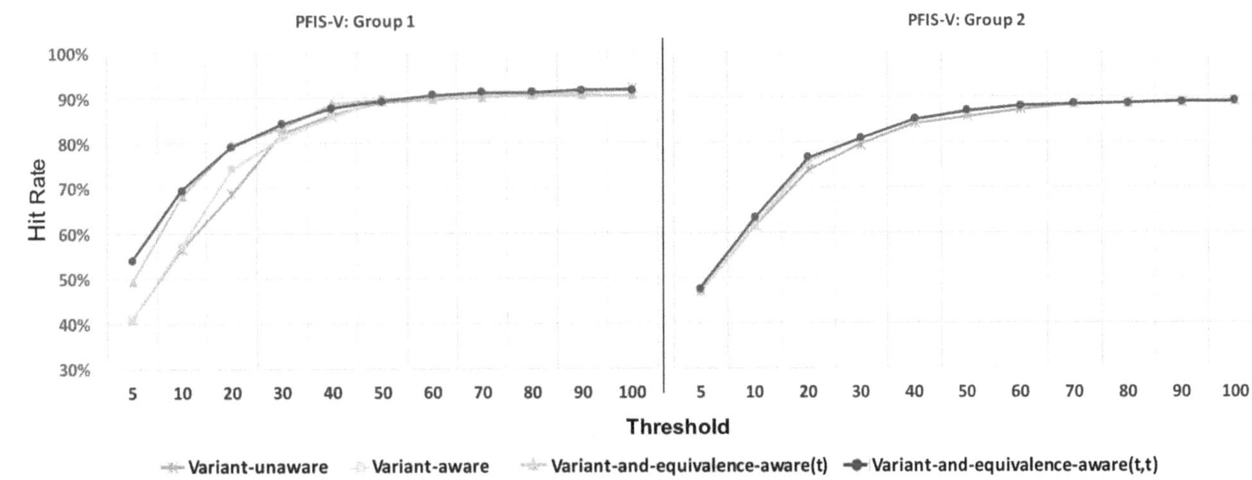

Figure 6. While the accuracy of PFIS-V varied with the different data models for Group-1 participants, no such differences existed in Group-2 participants.

that the size of variant-and-equivalence-aware(t,t) was *slightly* larger than variant-and-equivalence-aware(t).

This result about PFIS-V configurations finds its application in tool design: an operationalization of the variant-and-equivalence-aware(t,t) data model might be a compelling option for any tool that supports a large number of variants, especially for text-based artifacts (Group-1 situations). The smaller memory footprint of this model suggests that a similar representation of variants can be space-efficient, while the high modeling accuracy implies that the resultant tool can better address programmers' foraging requirements in an exploratory programming context.

The results of our evaluation of PFIS-V thus answers our second research question (RQ2) on the effectiveness of PFIS-V in predicting navigations: PFIS-V predicted more navigations than PFIS3, for all participants. Particularly PFIS-V modeled Group-1 participants more accurately in both between- and within-foraging scenarios, whereas it failed to model the between-variant foraging of Group-2 participants. These results uncover implications (discussed later) for both IFT-based modeling as well as tool design.

PFIS-V factors

An important aspect of models predicting programmer navigations, such as PFIS, is the *predictive factors* (heuristics) of the model. For example, a *recency* factor model predicts navigations based on how recently the programmer has visited that location. Piorkowski et al. identified seven such *factors* (based on prior literature) that can help predict programmer navigations [32].

PFIS-V is a *multi-factor* model: it combines three factors to make predictions, while a *single-factor* model uses only one. The three factors in PFIS-V are: (i) *recency* (did the programmer visit the patch recently?), (ii) *text similarity*, (is the patch similar to bug report or current patch?) and (iii) *source topology* (is the patch linked to current patch?).

PFIS-V combines these component factors by assigning them specific weights. The p and $\propto$ in the PFIS-V algorithm in Figure 3 are indeed weights assigned to different factors: note that the weights are the same as in PFIS3. Studying the predictions made by individual factors can provide insights for tuning these weights in PFIS-V, thereby improving predictive accuracy. To this end, we study the predictions for one Group-1 participant (P07), in the variant-and-equivalence-aware(t,t) configuration (since it yielded highest accuracy, as discussed in RQ2).

Figure 7(a) compares the hit rates (Y-axis) of PFIS-V with its constituent single-factor models. Consistent with Piorkowski et al.'s results in single variant situations [32], we see that *PFIS-V (blue) is a more accurate predictor of programmer navigations than its constituent single factors*.

To see how each factor contributes to PFIS-V's accuracy, consider a scenario where a programmer navigates to a new (earlier unvisited) patch by scrolling to an adjacent method. Since the programmer has *never* navigated to the patch earlier, the recency single-factor model returns "Unknown". However, the source-topology factor that considers adjacent patches can predict this navigation. Similarly, in variations foraging scenario, the "variant-of" links (source topology) or text similarity can predict navigations to similar patches in different variants. Thus, when one factor fails to predict, another factor fills in the gap and makes a prediction: PFIS-V can make accurate predictions due to such synergy.

See Figure 7: for P07, recency yields higher hit rates (which is good) as well as has higher unknown rates (a limitation). On the other hand, although text similarity and source topology yield lower hit rates, they predict navigations where

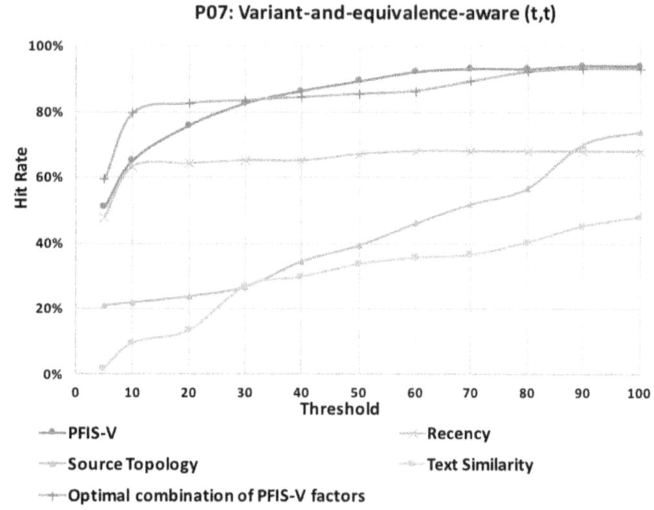

(a)

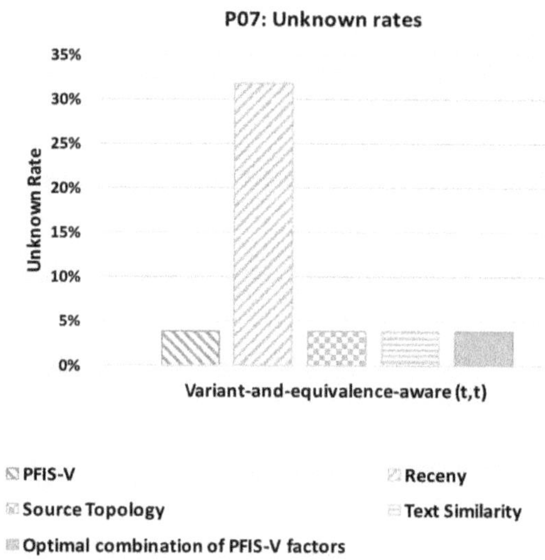

(b)

Figure 7. PFIS-V combines three factors (recency, source topology, text similarity): a synergy of these three factors leads to better predictive accuracy (higher hit rates (a), lower unknown rates (b)) than that of the individual factors.

recency cannot. Thus, *no single factor* in PFIS-V outperforms others in predicting programmer's navigations.

Given that a combination of factors in PFIS-V results higher predictive accuracy than just individual factors, we estimated the maximum accuracy that can be obtained by combining them: this serves as a benchmark for PFIS-V. We did this by computing the predictions made by an optimal combination of the three PFIS-V factors. For each attempted prediction, an optimal combination model yields the best prediction made by its component models. For example, if the three PFIS-V factors predicted a navigation with ranks 4, 20 and 30 respectively, their optimal combination model returns 4; therefore, at threshold N=10, it yields a hit (though only one constituent model yields a hit).

Figure 7(a)'s grey line shows the hit rates from such an optimal combination model (for P07). At threshold N=10, the hit rate of the optimal combination model is 60%, while that of PFIS-V is 51%. Further, the two models have the same unknown rates (Figure 7(b)). The marginal difference in hit rates between the two models is an indicator of PFIS-V's success, given that the optimal combination model is only a *theoretical ideal* while PFIS-V is a *practical model*.

DISCUSSION

Designing for variants

The presence of variants in large information spaces, such as programs, adds additional cognitive load as people have to forage for differences among *similar* variants. Modern software tools that represent variants (such as Git, a version control system) aim to support this foraging behavior by considering the *equivalence* among variants in their interfaces, i.e., these tools minimize cognitive load on users by leaving out whatever is similar, and only showing the differences between consecutive variants. However, from an IFT perspective, there are missing aspects in these tools. For example, the navigation affordances in tools that support variants are constrained, e.g., the absence of links from one patch to a similar patch across different variants [5].

Our model allows researchers and tool builders to evaluate hypotheses of programmers' foraging behavior in their environment. For example, one can posit that a programmer treats a method as different if the method got moved within a file. Such a hypothesis can be validated by comparing the modeling accuracies of PFIS-V while using text-based and text-and-topology-based similarity.

Our work also has several implications for tools. For example, the higher accuracy of variant-aware data models reveals the importance of navigation affordances between similar patches across variants ("variant-of" links). Similarly, the comparison results of the four data models reveals that the variant-and-equivalence-aware(t,t) model makes the closest assumptions about programmers' foraging. Therefore, tools aiming to support variation foraging can directly import this data model as their underlying data structure to represent variants.

Non-source code cues

Almost all IFT-based predictive models in programming thus far only model foraging among source-code patches, thereby only considering source-code-word cue types for predicting navigation. This is especially true for the PFIS family of models. However, our study participants used non-source-code patches and cues for their between-variant foraging, in exploratory programming scenarios [41].

In fact, our evaluations showed that there were two distinct types of foragers. Group 1 used source-code cue types and PFIS-V was able to accurately model foraging. However, Group 2 used non-source code cue types (e.g., output and changelogs) during their between-variant foraging, which PFIS-V does not capture in its model. This interfered with PFIS-V's ability to model Group 2's foraging behavior, thereby also limiting our ability to harness the model to understand (and predict) these programmers' foraging.

This reveals a gap in current IFT models—for programming as well as other variationed information spaces. For programming, modeling only source code cue types is insufficient in the context of multiple variants. Expanding to other types of information patches, such as outputs with visual content, mixed-media patches, semantic use of color, etc., can lead to significant new thought about comparing variants. Therefore, IFT-based computational models need to be extended to account for such patches. However, computing similarities and differences between output or test results patches between variants is a non-trivial problem, let alone modeling programmers' foraging behavior heavily involving such visual comparisons, as in our study [41]. We consider this to be an important new research opportunity in the area of computationally modeling variations foraging.

CONCLUSION

In this paper, we present a new computational model (PFIS-V) to model people's foraging behavior through an information space with variants. Our evaluation shows that PFIS-V predicted up to 20% more navigations than PFIS3, the latest of the PFIS family of models. Further, PFIS-V's predictions were up to 25% more accurate than PFIS3.

Such a computational model provides two benefits to HCI: researchers can use the model to gather evidence to support or refute hypotheses about variations foraging, and the model can guide as well as be directly imported to tools.

Finally, our results point to a challenging open research problem for predicting people's foraging behaviors over variationed information space with multiple types of information patches. We posit that it is time that IFT-based models account for such foraging behavior, which is especially important in variations foraging situations.

ACKNOWLEDGMENTS

We thank the reviewers for their feedback and our participants for their help. This work was funded in part by NSF 1253786, 1302113, 1314384 and 1559657 and David Piorkowski's IBM PhD fellowship.

REFERENCES

1. Joel Brandt, Philip J. Guo, Joel Lewenstein, Mira Dontcheva, and Scott R. Klemmer. 2009. Two studies of opportunistic programming: Interleaving web foraging, learning, and writing code. In *Proceedings of the SIGCHI Conference on Human Factors in Computing Systems (CHI '09), 1589-1598.*
2. Margaret M. Burnett, and Brad A. Myers. 2014. Future of end-user software engineering: Beyond the silos. In *Proceedings of the on Future of Software Engineering*, 201-211.
3. Ed H. Chi, Peter Pirolli, and James Pitkow. 2000. The scent of a site: A system for analyzing and predicting information scent, usage, and usability of a web site. In *Proceedings of the SIGCHI Conference on Human Factors in Computing Systems* (CHI '00), 161-168.
4. Ed H. Chi, Peter Pirolli, Kim Chen, and James Pitkow. 2001. Using information scent to model user information needs and actions and the Web. In *Proceedings of the SIGCHI Conference on Human Factors in Computing Systems* (CHI'01), pp. 490-497.
5. Mihai Codoban, Sruti Srinivasa Ragavan, Danny Dig, and Brian Bailey. 2015. Software history under the lens: a study on why and how developers examine it. In *Proceedings of the International Conference on Software Maintenance and Evolution (ICSME'15),* pp. 1-10.
6. Paul Clements and Linda Northrop. 2001. *Software Product Lines: Patterns and Practice.* Addison-Wesley Professional.
7. Davor Cubranic, Gail C. Murphy. 2003. Hipikat: Recommending pertinent software development artifacts. In *Proceedings of the 25th International Conference on Software Engineering* (ICSE '03), 408-418.
8. Robert DeLine, Amir Khella, Mary Czerwinski, George Robertson. 2005. Towards understanding programs through wear-based filtering. In *Proceedings of the ACM Symposium on Software Visualization*, 183-192.
9. Scott D. Fleming, Chris Scaffidi, David Piorkowski, Margaret Burnett, Rachel Bellamy, Joseph Lawrance, and Irwin Kwan. 2013. An information foraging theory perspective on tools for debugging, refactoring, and reuse tasks. In *ACM Transactions on Software Engineering and Methodology*, 22,14: 41 pages.
10. Wai-Tat Fu, and Peter Pirolli. 2007. SNIF-ACT: A cognitive model of user navigation on the World Wide Web. *Human Computer Interaction* 22.4 (2007): 355-412.
11. Björn Hartmann, Loren Yu, Abel Allison, Yeonsoo Yang, and Scott R. Klemmer. 2008. Design as exploration: Creating interface alternatives through parallel authoring and runtime tuning. In *Proceedings of the 21st Annual ACM Symposium on User Interface Software and Technology* (UIST '08), 91-100.
12. Björn Hartmann, Sean Follmer, Antonio Ricciardi, Timothy Cardenas, and Scott R. Klemmer. 2010. D. note: Revising user interfaces through change tracking, annotations, and alternatives. In *Proceedings of the SIGCHI Conference on Human Factors in Computing Systems*, 493-502.
13. Austin Z. Henley, and Scott D. Fleming. 2016. Yestercode: Improving code-change support in visual dataflow programming environments. *In IEEE Symposium on Visual Languages and Human-Centric Computing (VL/HCC'16).*
14. William C. Hill, James D. Hollan, Dave Wroblewski, Tim McCandless. 1992. Edit wear and read wear. In *Proceedings of the SIGCHI Conference on Human Factors in Computing Systems* (CHI '92), 3-9.
15. Mikkel R. Jakobsen, Kasper Hornbaek. 2006. Evaluating a fisheye view of source code. In *Proceedings of the SIGCHI Conference on Human Factors in Computing Systems* (CHI '06), 377-386.
16. Amy K. Karlson, Greg Smith, and Bongshin Lee. 2011. Which version is this? Improving the desktop experience within a copy-aware computing ecosystem. In *Proceedings of the SIGCHI Conference on Human Factors in Computing Systems* (CHI '11), 2669-2678.
17. Mik Kersten and Gail C. Murphy. 2005. Mylar: A degree-of-interest model for IDEs. In *Proceedings of the 4th International Conference on Aspect-Oriented Software Development* 159-168.
18. Scott R. Klemmer, Michael Thomsen, Ethan Phelps-Goodman, Robert Lee, and James A. Landay. 2002. Where do web sites come from? Capturing and interacting with design history. In *Proceedings of the SIGCHI Conference on Human factors in Computing Systems* (CHI '02), 1-8.
19. Andrew J. Ko, Brad A. Myers, Michael J. Coblenz, and Htet Htet Aung. 2006. An exploratory study of how developers seek, relate, and collect relevant information during software maintenance tasks. In *IEEE Transactions on Software Engineering.* 32, 12: 971-987.
20. Ranjitha Kumar, Jerry O. Talton, Salman Ahmad, and Scott R. Klemmer. 2011. Bricolage: Example-based retargeting for web design. In *Proceedings of the SIGCHI Conference on Human Factors in Computing Systems* (CHI '11), 2197- 2206.
21. Sandeep Kaur Kuttal, Anita Sarma, Gregg Rothermel. 2013. Predator behavior in the wild web world of bugs: An information foraging theory perspective. In *IEEE*

Symposium on Visual Languages and Human Centric Computing (VL/HCC'13), 59-66.

22. Sandeep K. Kuttal, Anita Sarma, and Gregg Rothermel. 2014. On the benefits of providing versioning support for end users: an empirical study. In *ACM Transactions on Software Engineering and Methodology* 21, 2:9.
23. Joseph Lawrance, Rachel Bellamy, Margaret Burnett. 2007. Scents in Programs: Does information foraging theory apply to program maintenance? In *IEEE Symposium on Visual Languages and Human-Centric Computing* (VL/HCC 2007), 15-22.
24. Joseph Lawrance, Rachel Bellamy, Margaret Burnett, and Kyle Rector. 2008. Using information scent to model the dynamic foraging behavior of programmers in maintenance tasks. In *Proceedings of the SIGCHI Conference on Human Factors in Computing Systems* (CHI '08), 1323-1332.
25. Joseph Lawrance, Christopher Bogart, Margarett Burnett, Richard Bellamy, and Kyle Rector. 2009. How people debug, revisited: An information foraging theory perspective. In *IEEE Transactions on Software Engineering*, 117-124.
26. Joseph Lawrance, Margaret Burnett, Rachel Bellamy, Christopher Bogart, and Calvin Swart. 2010. Reactive information foraging for evolving goals. In *Proceedings of the SIGCHI Conference on Human Factors in Computing Systems* (CHI '10), 25-34.
27. Brad A. Myers, YoungSeok Yoon, and Joel Brandt. 2013. Creativity support in authoring and backtracking. In *Proc. Workshop on Evaluation Methods for Creativity Support Environments at CHI (CHI '13)*, 40-43.
28. Jakob Nielsen. 2003. Information foraging: Why Google makes people leave your site faster. *Jakob Nielsen's Alertbox*.
29. Nan Niu, Anas Mahmoud, and Gary Bradshaw. 2011. Information foraging as a foundation for code navigation (NIER track). In *Proceedings of the 33rd International Conference on Software Engineering* (ICSE '11), 816-819.
30. Chris Parnin and Carsten Gorg. 2006. Building usage contexts during program comprehension. In *14th IEEE International Conference on Program Comprehension* (ICPC'06), 13-22.
31. Alexandre Perez and Rui Abreu. 2014. A diagnosis-based approach to software comprehension. In *Proceedings of the 22nd International Conference on Program Comprehension* (ICPC'14).
32. David Piorkowski, Scott D. Fleming, Christopher Scaffidi, Liza John, Christopher Bogart, Bonnie E. John, Margaret Burnett, and Rachel Bellamy. 2011. Modeling programmer navigation: A head-to-head empirical evaluation of predictive models. In *IEEE Symposium on Visual Languages and Human-Centric Computing* (VL/HCC'11), 109-116.
33. David Piorkowski, Scott Fleming, Christopher Scaffidi, Christopher Bogart, Margaret Burnett, Bonnie John, Rachel Bellamy, and Calvin Swart. 2012. Reactive information foraging: An empirical investigation of theory-based recommender systems for programmers. In *Proceedings of the SIGCHI Conference on Human Factors in Computing Systems* (CHI '12), 1471- 1480.
34. David Piorkowski, Scott D. Fleming, Irwin Kwan, Margaret M. Burnett, Christopher Scaffidi, Rachel K.E. Bellamy, and Joshua Jordahl. 2013. The whats and hows of programmers' foraging diets. In *Proceedings of the SIGCHI Conference on Human Factors in Computing Systems* (CHI '13), 3063-3072.
35. David Piorkowski, Scott D. Fleming, Christopher Scaffidi, Margaret Burnett, Irwin Kwan, Austin Z. Henley, Jamie Macbeth, Charles Hill, and Amber Horvath. 2015. To Fix or to Learn? How production bias affects developers' information foraging during debugging. In *IEEE International Conference on Software Maintenance and Evolution* (ICSME '15), 11-20
36. Peter Pirolli, and Stuart Card. 1995. Information foraging in information access environments. *Proceedings of the SIGCHI Conference on Human Factors in Computing Systems* (CHI '95), 51-58.
37. Peter Pirolli. 1997. Computational models of information scent-following in a very large browsable text collection. In *Proceedings of the ACM SIGCHI Conference on Human Factors in Computing Systems* (CHI '97), 3-10.
38. Peter Pirolli, Wai-Tat Fu. 2003. SNIF-ACT: A model of information foraging on the World Wide Web. *User modeling. Springer Berlin Heidelberg*, 45- 54.
39. Peter Pirolli, Wai-tat Fu, Ed Chi, and Ayman Farahat. 2005. Information scent and web navigation: Theory, models and automated usability evaluation. In *Proceedings of HCI International.*
40. Peter Pirolli. *Information Foraging Theory: Adaptive Interaction with Information*. 2007. Oxford University Press.
41. Sruti Srinivasa Ragavan, Sandeep Kaur Kuttal, Charles Hill, Anita Sarma, David Piorkowski, and Margaret Burnett. 2016. Foraging among an overabundance of similar variants. In *Proceedings of the 2016 CHI Conference on Human Factors in Computing Systems* (CHI '16), 3509-3521.
42. Vineet Sinha, David Karger, and Rob Miller. 2006. Helping users manage context during interactive exploratory visualization of large codebases. In *Visual*

Languages and Human-Centric Computing (VL/HCC'06), 187-194.

43. Jared M Spool, Christine Perfetti, David Brittan. 2004. Designing for the scent of information, *User Interface Engineering*.

44. Margaret-Anne Storey, Casey Best, Jeff Michaud, Derek Rayside, Marin Litoiu, Mark Musen. 2002. In *Extended Abstracts on Human Factors in Computing Systems* (CHI EA '02), 520-521.

45. Michael Terry and Elizabeth D. Mynatt. 2002. Side views: Persistent, on-demand previews for open-ended tasks. In *Proceedings of the 15th Annual ACM Symposium on User Interface Software and Technology* (UIST '02), 71-80.

46. Sruti Srinivasa Ragavan. PFIS-V. 2016. Retrieved on Dec 27, 2016 from http://web.engr.oregonstate.edu/~srinivas/pfis-v.html

47. YoungSeok Yoon and Brad A. Myers. 2014. A longitudinal study of programmers' backtracking. In Visual Languages and Human-Centric Computing (VL/HCC '14), 101- 108.

48. Natural Programming. Retrieved on August 21, 2016 from http://www.cs.cmu.edu/~NatProg/cryolite.html.

Improving Communication Between Pair Programmers Using Shared Gaze Awareness

Sarah D'Angelo
Northwestern University
Evanston, Illinois USA
sdangelo@u.northwestern.edu

Andrew Begel
Microsoft Research
Redmond, Washington USA
andrew.begel@microsoft.com

ABSTRACT
Remote collaboration can be more difficult than collocated collaboration for a number of reasons, including the inability to easily determine what your collaborator is looking at. This impedes a pair's ability to efficiently communicate about on-screen locations and makes synchronous coordination difficult. We designed a novel gaze visualization for remote pair programmers which shows where in the code their partner is currently looking, and changes color when they are looking at the same thing. Our design is unobtrusive, and transparently depicts the imprecision inherent in eye tracking technology. We evaluated our design with an experiment in which pair programmers worked remotely on code refactoring tasks. Our results show that with the visualization, pairs spent a greater proportion of their time concurrently looking at the same code locations. Pairs communicated using a larger ratio of implicit to explicit references, and were faster and more successful at responding to those references.

ACM Classification Keywords
H.5.3. Information Interfaces and Presentation (e.g. HCI): Group and organizational interfaces - collaborative computing, computer-supported collaborative work

Author Keywords
Eye-tracking; collaboration; pair programming

INTRODUCTION
Remote work is becoming increasingly popular because it supports a flexible lifestyle, and helps people avoid a long commute. Technological advances have improved remote work, however we still lose some important physical affordances of collocated work, such as non-verbal cues and gestures. This especially impacts the ability to understand where your partner is looking in a shared workspace. However, recent work using dual eye tracking technology has addressed this problem in the context of remote collaborative work [27]. The dual eye tracking solution enables tool builders to share eye gaze information with each worker and incorporate non-verbal cues into remote work.

CHI'17, May 06–11, 2017, Denver, CO, USA

ISBN 978-1-4503-4655-9/17/05...$15.00
DOI: http://dx.doi.org/10.1145/3025453.3025573

In our work, we apply this method to pair programming. Pair programming is a commonly practiced method of programming that allows two programmers to work together on a single project [49]. This method is popular at many technology companies, but often occurs only in teams that make it their standard practice. It requires scheduled co-presence during the work week along with special computer setups [4]. Previous work has demonstrated the effectiveness of this method and the perceived value by the participants [6, 12, 16, 23, 39]. For example, pairing demands a high level of attention and focus from the partners because they are continuously working with someone else and avoiding distractions [10, 46].

Pair programming is an appropriate task for studies of shared gaze awareness because it is tightly coupled, synchronous, and collaborative. These factors discourage people from working remotely when they are part of a pair programming team. Extending the reach of pair programming to support remote collaboration can improve flexibility of work location, accessibility, enable geographically distributed work, and accommodate the needs and preferences of a diverse workforce. A survey we conducted (reported in Section 3) found that developers would like this flexibility, but current tools for remote pair programming fail to recreate an effective pairing experience.

General tools for remote work, such as the use of Skype with screen sharing, lack the ability to share non-verbal cues that facilitate communication between collocated pairs [15]. Special purpose tools, such as Saros, a distributed IDE [43], support limited communication of mouse-based gestures. However, pairs still cannot make eye contact or see gestures that are not drawn on screen. The absence of these features makes disambiguating references difficult [22]. In a remote setup, pairs sometimes have to use many explicit references to coordinate with their partner on a specific location in code, often resorting to speaking line numbers. In this work, we aim to support synchronous collaboration in remote settings with a shared workspace. We designed a novel, shared gaze awareness visualization that reduces the effort required to communicate about specific locations in code by showing a collaborator where in the source code his/her partner is looking.

We evaluate our design for sharing gaze awareness in a study of pair programmers working in a simulated remote setting. Our design is subtle and accounts for noise in the eye tracking signal to avoid the negative effective of distracting displays that can mislead partners [13]. We conducted a within-subjects experiment to evaluate the visualization and understand how sharing gaze information affects the way pair programmers communicate about specific locations in code.

Our results show that when programmers can see where their partner is looking, they concurrently look at the same code more often. With the visualization, they are able to communicate about locations in the code more successfully, efficiently, and effectively. Thus, the design serves as a helpful aid for coordinating remote work. And, the same design could easily be integrated into many other forms of collaborative document editing.

We discuss the role of shared gaze awareness in remote pair programming and offer implications for the design of shared gaze awareness in computer-supported collaborative work.

RELATED WORK

Eye movements provide valuable information about how pairs communicate. For example, before speakers refer to an object, they look at it [20]. Listeners look at objects soon after they are referred to [1]. This relationship is important for coordination and developing common ground between partners [41, 42].

Remote work is challenging because it lacks important features of collocated work, such as knowing where your partner is looking. *Sharing gaze awareness*, or displaying where your partner is looking on your screen, is one potential intervention to help facilitate conversation and coordination. For example, listeners can use the speaker's gaze to help disambiguate similar objects [22].

Dual eye tracking studies have begun to explore how sharing gaze in real time between two remote partners influences coordination [27]. For example, remote collaborators can find a target in a image faster when shown their partner's gaze on screen [7]. Additionally, in a collaborative learning task, shared gaze information improved gains in learning and increased the partners' joint attention [44]. Sharing gaze also affects how partners communicate by allowing them to make use of more *deictic* references (i.e. this or here) using a gaze representation as a referential pointer [3, 13].

Pair programming is an interesting application space for sharing gaze awareness because it requires a high level of shared understanding [48]. Knowing what someone is looking at in code can provide insights for problem solving. For example, when novices were shown an expert programmer's gaze pattern in code review, it helped them identify bugs faster [47]. Additionally, in real-time gaze sharing between expert and novice, watching an expert's gaze as they explained an algorithm reduced the variability of gaze patterns in novices [38, 5].

Shared gaze is typically represented as a single point on screen that reflects the gaze coordinate stream interpreted from the eye tracker [3, 7, 13, 44]. However, alternative designs have explored depicting gaze in the periphery to subtly direct attention to specific areas in an image [2, 32]. Additionally, Stotts et al. displayed a head overlay on the screen to share gaze information and facial expressions [21]. Related work in collaborative document editing has also investigated unobstrusive indicators to signal where partners are working [36, 29]. We contribute to this space by evaluating a simple and transparent design for displaying gaze awareness in documents.

We can also analyze the relationship between two gaze streams during a collaborative task to evaluate effective coordination in pairs. The relationship between reference forms and gaze overlap can be a useful indicator of understanding between pairs [18]. Sharing cues, such as highlighting text, increases the amount of time pairs spend looking in the same place together [28, 45]. Additionally, gaze location can be predicted based on conversational content and actions in the shared workspace [34]. We investigate gaze overlap and the relationship between reference form and acknowledgments (both verbally and based on gaze).

Recreating the ability to see what your partner is looking at in remote collaborative work has many possible applications, ranging from pair programming [5] to remote physical tasks [17, 24]. We contribute to this space by evaluating a novel design for sharing gaze awareness to support effective communication in tightly-coupled tasks.

SURVEY

To motivate this work, we randomly selected 500 software developers at a large, technology company and asked them to respond anonymously to a survey about pair programming. We received 159 complete responses for a 32% response rate. 52.7% reported that they had pair programmed before. Consistent with previous work [6, 12, 16, 39], a majority of the respondents who have pair programmed say that they enjoy pairing and believe that it is effective.

In our work, we are particularly interested in expanding the capabilities for pair programming to effectively support remote pair programming. So we asked survey respondents whether they might take advantage of working remotely if they could. Our survey revealed that if they had no constraints, our respondents would like to spend over 11 hours per week (out of a 40 hour work week) working remotely. Respondents explained that working remotely would allow them to avoid a long commute, work in a place with fewer distractions, and adjust their schedule to accommodate personal needs. For example, one respondent said that working remotely would allow him/her to *"spend time with my 2-year-old son during the day, and then work in the evening more after he has gone to sleep."* Remote work can accommodate a wide range of lifestyle preferences and allow for new opportunities that may not have happened otherwise. At large companies with offices in many countries, effective remote work could improve and prompt new international collaborations.

Despite this desire to work remotely, those who pair program (usually on teams that practice pair programming religiously) rarely engage in remote pair programming. Our survey revealed that only 18.9% of the 87 respondents who said they had ever pair programmed had pair programmed remotely. Those that did pair remotely said they liked its convenience and flexibility. It allowed developers to work with people who are not in the same location, and was "necessary if the subject matter expert was not local."

Of the remaining 81.1% who had never tried remote pair programming, 40.3% considered it, but some worried that the technology and management would present barriers to success. One respondent said "I don't think our technology would support it enough to be effective." The most common tool used by our respondents is Skype with desktop sharing, which has no specific features designed for collaborative editing/programming.

We believe that the benefits of pair programming should not come at the expense of the ability to work remotely. Guided by our survey responses, we undertake a study to test the effectiveness of a novel, remote pair programming support tool.

PILOT OBSERVATIONS

We observed 3 teams at the same large technology company to gain an understanding of how they practice pair programming. Each video-recorded observation lasted one hour in the team's primary office space. Two researchers were present during the observations and taking notes.

Each of the three teams practiced a different form of pair programming. The first pair employed a special hardware setup using a single computer with two mirrored sets of dual monitors. They spent the hour planning a refactoring of the code that one of them had written with a different partner the week before. The second pair operated in a traditional driver/navigator role structure in front of one of the pair's dual monitor computer. The driver spent the hour explaining to the navigator the functionality of a particular code abstraction he had written by himself an hour before we observed them, when his partner was out at a meeting. The third team practiced "mobbing," in which they had four people in front of one computer with a large 50-inch monitor. One person, who was facile with source control commands, worked the keyboard, while the others sat around him. They spent their hour debugging a problem that had shown up in the nightly build of their web service.

As we observed each team, we were on the lookout for aspects of collocated pair programming that would not be well-supported in remote work. We found three: first, remote pairs would not be able to make eye contact, something that was frequently practiced in all three teams. From an outside observer's perspective, pair programming looks more like a social, conversational activity than an activity purely about the program on the monitor.

Second, the members of the teams made numerous hand gestures both at the screen and at one another, which would simply not be visible in a remote setting. Sometimes these gestures merely supported the on-going conversation (i.e. body language), but sometimes the person making the gesture was pointing at something on the screen to get the other person to notice it. The remote tools our survey respondents talked about having used would definitely not support resolving this kind of gesture.

Third, the teams made constant verbal and gestural references to specific locations on the screen, something that would be difficult to impossible to disambiguate while working remotely. The mobbing team demonstrated this acutely; even in their collocated setting, the "driver" experienced numerous difficulties interpreting the code locations at which his teammates were pointing. One pair was successful at using mouse-based selection to indicate the part of the code the other was supposed to pay attention to, but the other pairs experienced difficulty distinguishing between verbally called out functions with similar names, or where there were multiple calls to the same function in a single document.

We decided to focus primarily on the issue of referring to locations on screen by transforming the partners' gaze locations into on-screen visualizations.

GAZE VISUALIZATION

In this work, we investigate the effect of displaying gaze information to remote pair programmers in an unobtrusive and transparent way. We designed a novel, shared gaze visualization to indicate where in the code your partner is looking when programming together on a shared display. We conducted a within-subjects experiment in which pair programmers are asked to complete two refactoring tasks together, with and without our shared gaze visualization. We evaluate the effectiveness of our design by investigating where pairs are looking and how they communicate about specific locations on the screen. Additionally, we conducted post-task surveys and semi-structured interviews with our participants to understand the perceived utility of shared gaze awareness. Our results show that with shared gaze awareness, pairs spend more time looking at the same locations, are faster to acknowledge references, and use more implicit language when making references.

Design Process

Much of the previous literature on displaying gaze information uses a small, rapidly-moving point to illustrate where the eye is looking at the screen. This type of visualization moves too fast and can obscure the information on screen, both of which are distracting [13]. The single point representation is also inaccurate because the imprecision caused by noise and microsaccades that is inherent in current eye tracking technology results in biases in the returned screen coordinates [8, 35].

To avoid these problems, we initially focused on line-based text designs that could make the gaze visualization move more slowly. Our first design highlighted the background of an entire row of text, but initial pilot tests revealed that this to still be too distracting; too many pixels had to change color as the eye moved rapidly up and down the screen. First, we shrank the highlight rectangle horizontally. We started with a 10 pixel wide rectangle, but we found it to be too subtle in our pilot tests. So we increased it to 20 pixels, which was perceived as noticeable, but not distracting. Next, we tried illustrating the user's focus by increasing the saturation of the highlight color the longer the user looked at a particular line, but the subtle color change went unnoticed by our study participants. Finally, we tried changing the number of lines in

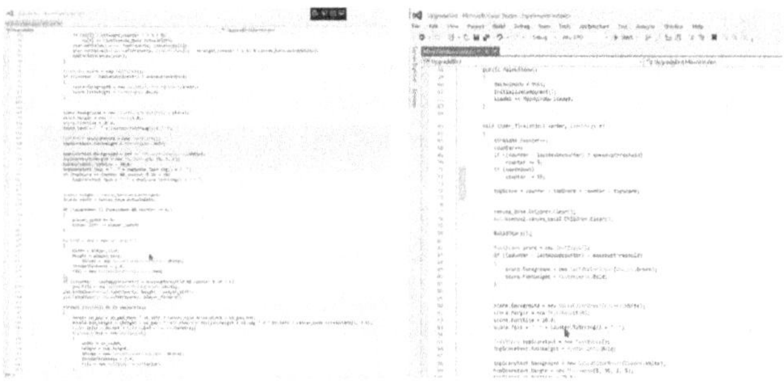

Figure 1. Screen Captures with First Iteration of Gaze Visualization (left) and Final Design (Right)

the highlighted rectangle to show the current range of lines at which the user was looking. However, when the eye moved rapidly around the screen, the rectangle would change size a lot. Also, with only 20-30 lines typically visible in the editor, the rectangle too often covered most of the screen, making the visualization useless.

In the end, we fixed the vertical span of the rectangle to 5 lines, colored it with a single pair of semi-saturated colors (chosen for maximal contrast with the default font colors used in Visual Studio), and moved it to the left margin of the text where the participants were already looking, so as to not attract their attention to irrelevant screen locations (e.g. blank spaces on the right side of the editor).

Gaze Visualization Design

Our final design is a 5-line high, 20 pixel wide, filled, colored rectangle displayed on the left margin of the other programmer's code editor (and vice versa), centered on the Y coordinate returned by the eye tracker (see Figure 1). The X coordinate is ignored, since in C#, there is rarely more than one code concept per line. Reducing the shared space to a 5-line span of code circumscribes the referential domain, allowing participants to use less specific language when reference to locations in code [30].

Similar to the hysteresis effect employed by a thermostat, if the eye moves within the lines circumscribed by the rectangle, the rectangle stays still to minimize the quick jumping movements typical to many visual gaze visualizations. If the eye moves outside the box a line or two up or down, the rectangle smoothly scrolls with it. When the eye jumps to a completely disjoint line, the box is re-centered on the new location. In addition, the rectangle drawn in our visualization changes colors. Normally, it is yellow, but becomes green when participants are looking at the same thing (defined as when their rectangles vertically overlap). This signal is designed to support shared intentionality (and shared attention) [48] by letting both programmers know that they are looking at the same part of the code at the same time.

STUDY METHOD

Participants

Twenty-four software developers from a technology company who were comfortable programming in C# participated in this study. Participants were recruited through emailed announcements on Agile development mailing lists at the company. All participants were consented and received USD$50 compensation for participating. For the study, pairs of participants were asked to work together in remote pair programming teams.

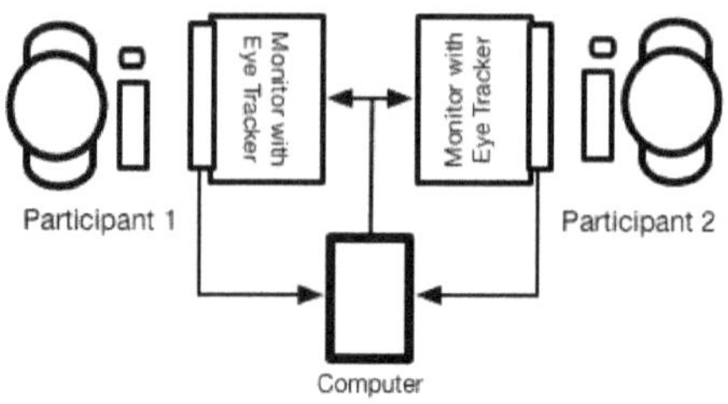

Figure 2. Experiment Setup

Setup

From our survey, we found that the most common pairing setup was a single computer with a single, shared display. When survey respondents paired remotely, they created this environment using a Skype call with simultaneous screen sharing. Since our study intended to evaluate a visualization that looked different on each person's computer, we could not use Skype. Instead, we simulated a Skype call using a single computer with two displays placed back-to-back, so that the participants could each work at their own station without seeing one another, yet still talk aloud to communicate (see Figure 2).

Each of the two participants had their own display (Monitor 1 (TX300): 23" 1920x1080, and Monitor 2 (EyeX): 24" 1920x1200, both at 96 DPI), mouse, keyboard, and an attached remote eye tracker (a Tobii TX300 (around USD$45,000) and a Tobii EyeX (USD$139)) running at 30Hz.[1] We used TeamPlayer4 [14] software to enable each participant to see and manipulate their own independent mouse cursor on the single experimental computer. A GoPro Hero 3 camera was set up to the left of each participant to record their facial expressions as they worked. Both displays were screen-captured and merged with their respective GoPro video feed into a single 2x2 MP4 format movie (see Figure 3).

To simulate screen sharing and support our gaze visualization, we created a Visual Studio 2015 extension. The extension displays the project code simultaneously in two code editor windows whose text (Consolas, 13 pt) and user interface are slaved to one another, but are displayed on the two separate monitors. When one participant scrolls his/her window, the other window scrolls to the same place. If a participant highlights text on their window it is also highlighted on their partner's window. If the participant switches editor windows, an identical window would open on the other screen. The extension captures eye tracking information from two eye trackers simultaneously. It renders the gaze visualization in both code

[1] We would have liked to use two of the much cheaper Tobii EyeX trackers, but it is not possible to put more than one EyeX on a computer.

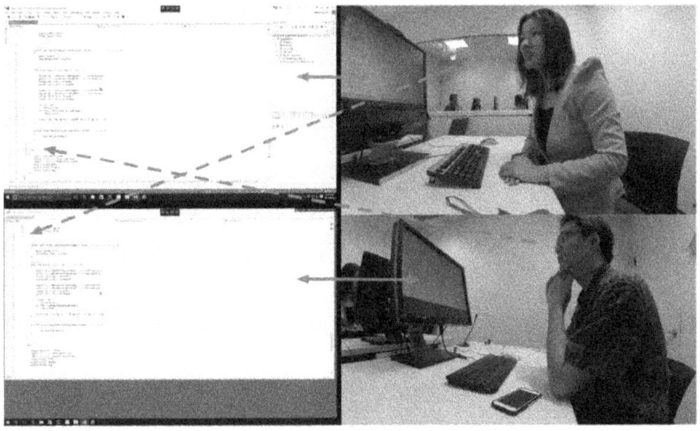

Figure 3. Combined Videos: Screen capture paired with monitor (indicted by horizontal arrows) and gaze of participant represented on the screen of their partner (indicated by diagonal arrows.)

editor windows (the only thing that is not duplicated between the code windows) and logs eye tracking data to disk.

Tasks

We employed a 2x2 counterbalanced (gaze awareness and task), within-subjects experimental design. Participants worked on two refactoring tasks intended to "clean up" the C# code for a Flappy Bird-like game [40] (see Figure 4), with our gaze visualization turned on and off. The two tasks were equivalent in difficulty (pilot tests helped us fine-tune this) and took about 15 minutes each.

To introduce the participants to the code, they were asked to collaborate with one another to make small changes to the game, e.g. changing the sizes of the bird or obstacles. This task was unmeasured. Then, the participants worked together to accomplish two refactoring tasks while being recorded and logged.

After completing each task, each participant filled out a 13-question Likert-scale questionnaire about their feelings about their performance on the task. The survey questions were adapted from McCroskey and McCain [31] on task attractiveness and from Begel and Nachiappan [6] on the qualities of good pair programming partners. Each question asked the participant to state the extent to which they disagreed or agreed with statements about how they worked with their partner. For example, "I felt like my partner and I were on the same page most of the time," or "I felt that I did more work than my partner." At the end of the study, the pair was interviewed informally about their impressions of the gaze visualization to subjectively evaluate its design and utility.

Video Analysis

To understand how the gaze awareness visualization influenced communication between the pair, all videos were coded for references and acknowledgments. Every time a participant made a reference or verbally acknowledged a reference, the time was logged, the type was recorded (reference or acknowledgement), and it was given a description code. The description code indicated the form of the reference, and ranged from implicit (deictic) to explicit (text selection). See Figure 5 for a complete list and Table 1 for code descriptions. The acknowledgment description indicated a "yes" if the reference was verbally understood, or "confused" if recipient did not follow the reference.

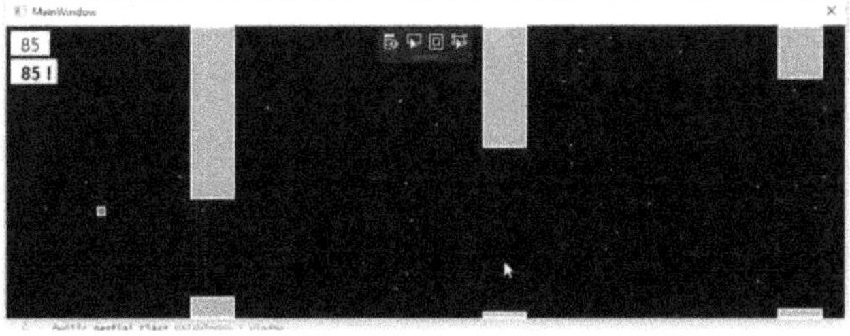

Figure 4. Example of Flappy Bird Game

Code	*Description*
Deictic	When a participant uses a deictic reference such as: this, that, or here. For example, *"I think it's this one over here."*
Abstract	When a participant uses an abstract concept or broader category to refer to an object. For example, *"We need to change the variable."*
Gaze	When a participant directly refers to the gaze visualization to refer to an object. For example, *"Right where I am looking."*
Specific	When a participant uses a specific word or name to describe an object. For example, *"I think it is called in Update Score."*
Typing	When a participant is referring to the text that they are currently typing in the shared window. For example, *"You just made a typo."*
Line Num	When a participant uses a line number to refer to a location. For example, *"Fix the error on line 139."*
Select	When a participant highlights a word or section of text to direct their partner to it, usually this reference is paired with a deictic reference. For example, *"This section right here (highlighting code)."*

Table 1. Reference Codes and Descriptions

Gaze Analysis

The main signal we analyzed from our log data was a *gaze overlap* signal. This is true if the two participants were looking at the same thing at the same time. Each participants' view area is defined as a sequence of five visible lines in the code editor, vertically centered on the participant's last eye gaze location. In each recorded sample, if any of the first partic-

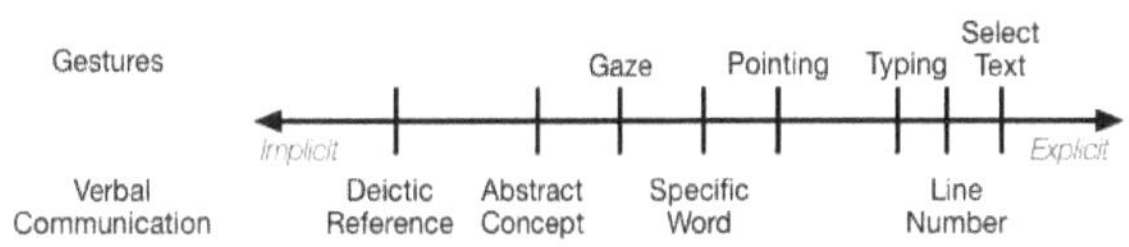

Figure 5. Reference Categories

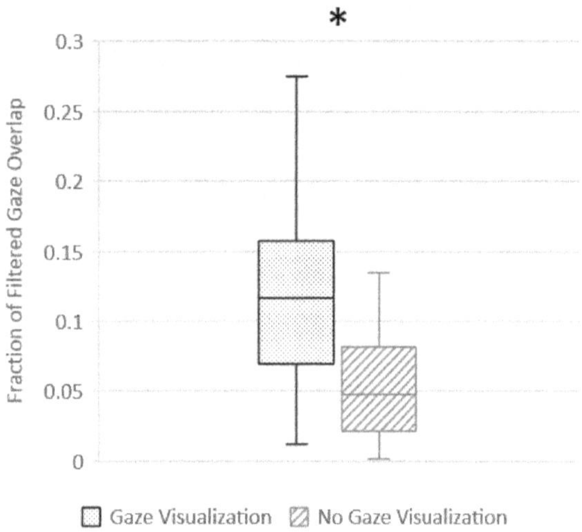

Figure 6. Fraction of gaze overlap in each pairs' tasks in the two experimental conditions. The ∗ indicates that the two conditions are statistically significantly different from one another.

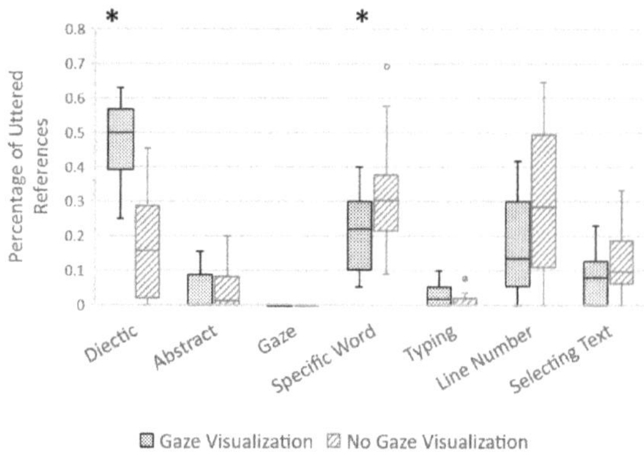

Figure 7. Fraction of references of each type uttered by the pair in the two experimental conditions. An ∗ is shown above reference types that are statistically significantly different from one another.

ipant's view area's lines overlapped the second participant's view area, we said that the gaze overlap was true. However, we filtered out gaze overlaps that lasted less than 100 ms to avoid spurious indications of gaze overlaps when the eye jumped around a lot. All of the results in Section 7 use this filtered gaze overlap measure.

Next, we measured the time from a person's utterance of a reference to a location on the screen to when that reference was verbally acknowledged by the other person. However, since the goal of the visualization is to help the participants look something when the other person referred to it, this analysis also considers shared gaze as an form of acknowledgment. When there was no explicit verbal acknowledgement, we defined the first filtered gaze overlap within 10 seconds as an implicit acknowledgement of the reference.

In addition to determining whether or not a reference was acknowledged, we recorded the time it took for that implicit or explicit acknowledgement to occur. If neither implicit or explicit acknowledgement was found, we considered that reference to be unacknowledged and unsuccessful.

RESULTS

In this section, we present the results of our data analysis. We looked at three questions.

1. How much time did the participants spend concurrently looking at the same thing?
2. What kinds of references were used by the participants?
3. How successful were references to locations in the code?

Timing

The basic premise of this work is that pairs that spend more time looking at the same thing work better together. For each pair of participants, we counted the total amount of time spent looking at the same thing (i.e. sum of filtered gaze overlap time) and divided it by the total time spent on each task to produce the fraction of time spent looking at the same thing. This is shown in Figure 6. Using JMP, we computed a one-way ANOVA to compare the effect of the gaze visualization on the fraction of filtered gaze overlap time, both with and without the gaze visualization. The mean score for the gaze visualization (M = 11.9%, SD = 0.6%) was significantly greater than without the gaze visualization (M = 5.9%, SD = 0.6%) [$F(1,35) = 58.243$, $p < 0.0001$]. This result suggests that in each task, participants spent 6% more time looking at the same things when using the gaze visualization.

Prior work has shown a similar effect in a primarily visual collaborative learning task [44]. Related studies suggest that pairs perform collaborative tasks better the more that they attend to the same things at the same time [9, 18, 33]. To further understand how this affect communication and coordination, we check that the increased gaze overlap is correlated with a *functional* improvement in collaboration.

References

As each person worked together on the refactoring tasks, each had to repeatedly make references to locations in the code to signal to their partner where to find or place some relevant code. These 470 total references span a continuum of the explicitness of the grounding inherent in the utterance (as shown in Figure 5). We counted the number of utterances of each reference type made by participants as they completed their tasks. Since each pair performed the same set of tasks, we normalized the values to produce the fraction of each utterance type made by participants over their tasks. The distribution of these ratios, divided by experimental condition, can be seen in Figure 7.

A oneway ANOVA indicates that the fraction of *deictic* references is significantly greater with the gaze visualization turned on (M = 46% SD = 4%) than when turned off (M = 18% SD = 4%) [$F(1,11) = 24.9663$, $p = 0.0004$]. The fraction of more explicit, *specific word* references is lower with the gaze visualization (M = 21% SD = 3%) than when it was not avail-

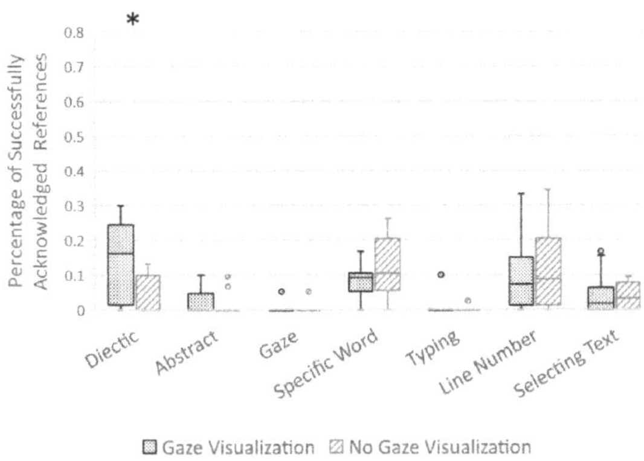

Figure 8. Fraction of *successfully* acknowledged references of each type uttered by the pair in the two experimental conditions. An ∗ is shown above reference types that are statistically significantly different from one another.

able (M = 34% SD = 3%) [F(1,11) = 7.1602, p = 0.0216]. This means the pairs were more comfortable using the more implicit, deictic references when they knew that they were able to see where the other was looking.

Acknowledged References

The reference fractions shown in Figure 7 show *all* the references that were attempted by the pairs, regardless of whether they were successfully understood and acknowledged. Over all reference types, there are many unsuccessful references. Only 37% of the attempted 249 references without the gaze visualization were acknowledged successfully. With the gaze visualization, 7% more (44%) of the 221 attempted references were. We now take a closer look at the overall 190 *successful* references to see if the gaze visualization helped the participants to communicate more effectively or efficiently.

In Figure 8, we show the distribution of successful references of each type, divided by condition. A one-way ANOVA shows that the proportion of successful deictic references is significantly higher when the participants saw the gaze visualization (M = 14.3% SD = 2.1%) than without it (M = 3.6% SD = 2.1%) [F(1,11) = 12.3214, p = 0.0049]. The other reference types show no significant differences between conditions. This means that people not only made more deictic references with the gaze visualization, but they were also 19% better at communicating them successfully.

Finally, we look at the time it took to communicate a reference to see whether the gaze visualization had an impact on making references quicker to acknowledge. Across all references, a one-way ANOVA shows that successful references were acknowledged more quickly with the gaze visualization (M = 1.7 sec SD = 0.11 sec) than without it (M = 2.1 sec SD = 0.1 sec) [F(1, 417) = 7.6624, p = 0.0058]. Surprisingly, when we split the data by reference type, deictic references are not significantly faster, but line number and specific name references are. A one-way ANOVA shows that line number references are faster with the gaze visualization (M = 1.9 sec SD = 0.3 sec) than without it (M = 2.5 sec SD = 0.2 sec) F(1,186) = 3.9073, p = 0.0496]. It also shows that specific name references are faster with the gaze visualization (M = 1.4 sec SD = 0.2 sec) than without it (M = 2.3 sec SD = 0.2 sec) [F(1,212) = 7.7144, p = 0.0060]. The other reference types are not significantly faster or slower between the two conditions.

In summary, our quantitative results showed that participants used more deictic references with the gaze visualization, suggesting that they are using the visualization as a referential pointer. This is consistent with prior work [3, 13]. Our study adds to this body of knowledge by showing that deictic references are successfully acknowledged more often with the gaze visualization, and that references are acknowledged faster, suggesting that it is useful aid for coordination.

Completion Time

There was no significant different in completion time between the gaze visualization and no gaze visualization conditions. Each pair was allotted 15 minutes to complete the coding task and all pairs used the entire time and were stopped by the researcher to change tasks. One explanation for the lack of difference is our sample population. We believe that the pairs worked for the entire allotted time because of their own personal quality standards as professional developers. Additionally, our informal instructions were intended to encourage natural collaboration and may have contributed to the continued effort to "clean up" the code after the basic refactoring task was completed.

Post-Task Questionnaire

A oneway ANOVA on the results from our post task survey indicate that when the gaze awareness visualization was displayed, participants said that their partner was able to focus more on the task (M = 4.57 SD = 0.05) compared to without the visualization (M = 4.42 SD = 0.05) [F(1,25) = 4.54, p = 0.04]. This suggests that participants were looking at the gaze visualization to gain insight about what their partner was attending to. Similarly, each partner knew when the other was looking at the document since the visualization was only displayed at that time. Participants might have been using this information to infer that their partner was on task, compared to without the visualization in which that added information is not available.

None of responses to the other questions were significantly different between conditions, though they may be subject to experimental bias. This suggests that the addition of the gaze awareness visualization might not influence the perceived quality of interaction between pair programmers. The benefits of shared gaze awareness are subtle, and might need to be used for extended periods of time before the perceived value is apparent.

Interview Results

At the end of the study, our interviews with the participants revealed that when they were aware that they were making use of the visualization, they used it to help communicate about locations in the and establish a shared understanding of what the other person is looking at.

> "I can get a context of where he is looking at the time, so it's a replacement for pointing." (Pair 3 — Participant 2)

Participants told us that they typically resort to using line numbers when talking about locations in code, but that they preferred to use our gaze visualization because it was easier. This is reflected in our quantitative analysis of references, which showed that participants used more deictic references with the gaze visualization, but more specific word references without it. This suggests that the visualization assisted coordination by allowing pairs to use deictic references and communicate without grounding on items first [11, 13, 19].

Participants also found the color changing to be a useful indicator that both partners were on the same page.

> "It was nice when it was green because we know we are looking at the same line...talking about the same line of code." (Pair 4 —Participant 1)

Participants spent more time looking at the same areas of code with the gaze visualization, suggesting that they were tightly coordinated and attended to the same information at the same time.

Participants said that the gaze visualization helped them to understand what their partner was talking about and attending to. None of the pairs expressed experiencing any difficulty interpreting the visualization, suggesting that a 5-line range of code is a sufficient range for assisting communication through successfully circumscribing the referential domain.

Interestingly, half of the participants expressed that they did not notice the visualization, stating that, *"I think I just forgot about it!"* (P7S2). Although they might not have been explicitly aware of the gaze visualization or how it was affecting their work, we did see changes in behavior. This result is not surprising when we realize that in collocated collaboration, gaze is a subtle signal, and we designed our gaze visualization to reflect that.

DISCUSSION

The addition of gaze awareness to remote collaborative work is a useful aid for coordination. The novel gaze visualization described in this work helped remote pair programmers communicate more effectively. These pairs used more deictic references which were more successfully acknowledged with the gaze visualization, suggesting that pairs used gaze awareness to effectively ground on items in the code. Pairs were faster to acknowledge references with the gaze visualization, suggesting that they understood what their partner was referring to. This may be due to faster grounding, or they could have already been in sync with their partner and were already looking at the same location when their partner communicated with them.

While we applied our tool to the pair programming domain, it could easily be extended to work with other types of documents. Our left-aligned visualization would work well with other types of text based documents. Additionally, the type of visualization evaluated here could be re-imagined to fit into a scroll bar, similar to visualizations explored by Hill and colleagues [25]. This would enable the visualization to work for documents whose contents are mirrored, but whose UI is not.

The effectiveness of the novel representation of gaze that we evaluate in this work demonstrates that gaze visualization design should take task structure into account. In the the context of pair programming, a non-obtrusive and non-distracting representation was appropriate for the task and well received by our participants. After the experimental session, when participants told us their subjective thoughts about the gaze visualization, they recognized that sometimes they wanted the visualization to show up only when they were intentionally trying to communicate a location to their partner.

> "I think the bigger thing for me is not where is he looking all the time but where does he want to have me look." (Pair 6 — Participant 2)

Future designs may consider a representation whose visibility is tied to the conversation between the partners. Using deictic references to inform the display of gaze awareness could provide more intentional cues and filter out non-signalling eye movements.

While eye trackers have become very inexpensive, they are not yet ubiquitous. However, the pair programming teams we observed were not shy about asking their employers for other specialized equipment to support pairing that cost many thousands of dollars. We can easily imagine remote pair programmers intent on making their programming experience more effective and efficient spending a few hundred dollars to do so.

Shared gaze awareness is a way to enhance the remote collaboration experience by providing people with an on-screen representation of where their partner is looking. This work fine-tunes gaze awareness with a simple and unobtrusive design that effectively supports coordination and communication. Our work aims to integrate novel and practical features into remote work in ways that have the potential to make it even better than collocated work [26].

Threats to Validity

All experiments contain tradeoffs in the design and implementation that affect their internal and external validity. The eye trackers we used are inherently inaccurate devices. In ideal situations, they can be accurate to 0.5 degrees, but as participants move around, the accuracy degrades. In this experiment, we had to rely on the participants to tell us when they believed the accuracy had degraded enough to require recalibrating the eye trackers. This happened to only 3 out of 24 participants in the study, and was done in between tasks. Based on our past experiences with eye trackers, we designed our gaze visualization to be five lines tall to account for the vertical inaccuracy we have seen in "perfectly" calibrated trackers.

Furthermore, we are using two different eye trackers in this experiment. Ideally, we would have used two inexpensive eye trackers to model an affordable system, however given the technical constraints imposed by tracker manufacturer, we had to use two different models from the same company. Both eye trackers are advertised to be accurate to within 0.5 degree, and we used them at the same sampling rate so they should be comparable. However, this more complex experimental setup is a limitation [37].

In this experiment, we simulated a remote work environment with a single computer and multiple monitors instead of the commonly used Skype with screen sharing to test out our theories behind the gaze awareness visualization. Our simulation performs better than the alternative because there is no latency in the audio (participants could just speak to one another in the same room) or the display (since they use the same computer). We did this because we could not make Skype's screen sharing show different displays to each participant. Latencies do cause some communication problems that we did not observe in our experiment. A future implementation of our tool would have to take into account these latencies to accurately assess when the participants are looking at the same thing at the same time.

Finally, we studied *remote* pair programming, not *distributed* pair programming. In remote pair programming, both partners use mirrored displays and look at same things together. Distributed pair programming loosens the mirroring requirement, supporting programmers working on the same codebase, but each having their own unique view of the system. Our visualization is based on a mirrored display, so it would not easily generalize to a distributed pair programming setup.

CONCLUSION

In this paper, we describe a study of remote pair programming. Through observations, we identified that remote pairs would have significant difficulties communicating about on-screen code locations. We took advantage of cheap eye tracking technology to develop a novel, dual eye tracking, gaze awareness visualization that helps pairs to see what the other person is looking at in a code document. We evaluated the visualization in an experiment in which pair programmers refactored source code while working in a simulated remote work environment. When the programmers used the visualization, they were more likely to look at the same thing at the same time. They were both faster and more successful at communicating using implicit, deictic references, and used them more frequently compared with references to explicit line number or specific words on the screen. Most participants recognized the value of the visualization, though some were not even consciously aware that the visualization had changed their behavior and helped them communicate efficiently.

Remote collaboration remains difficult for many people, especially when adapting a working style that originated and is typically practiced in collocated settings. When two people work together to create and edit code, the perceived and real challenges of communicating effectively and efficiently can inhibit them from taking advantage of the flexibility and accessibility affording to them by remote work. Our gaze awareness visualization takes us a step closer to removing those barriers.

ACKNOWLEDGEMENTS

We would like to thank the members of the VIBE research team and the software developers who participated in our study. This work was supported by Microsoft Research.

REFERENCES

1. Paul D Allopenna, James S Magnuson, and Michael K Tanenhaus. 1998. Tracking the time course of spoken word recognition using eye movements: Evidence for continuous mapping models. *Journal of memory and language* 38, 4 (1998), 419–439.
2. Reynold Bailey, Ann McNamara, Nisha Sudarsanam, and Cindy Grimm. 2009. Subtle gaze direction. *ACM Transactions on Graphics (TOG)* 28, 4 (2009), 100.
3. Ellen Gurman Bard, Robin L Hill, Mary Ellen Foster, and Manabu Arai. 2014. Tuning accessibility of referring expressions in situated dialogue. *Language, Cognition and Neuroscience* 29, 8 (2014), 928–949.
4. Kent Beck, Mike Beedle, Arie Van Bennekum, Alistair Cockburn, Ward Cunningham, Martin Fowler, James Grenning, Jim Highsmith, Andrew Hunt, Ron Jeffries, and others. 2001. Principles behind the Agile Manifesto. (2001). http://agilemanifesto.org/principles.html
5. Roman Bednarik, Andrey Shipilov, and Sami Pietinen. 2011. Bidirectional gaze in remote computer mediated collaboration: Setup and initial results from pair-programming. In *Proceedings of the ACM 2011 conference on Computer supported cooperative work.* ACM, 597–600.
6. Andrew Begel and Nachiappan Nagappan. 2008. Pair Programming: What's in It for Me?. In *Proceedings of the Second ACM-IEEE International Symposium on Empirical Software Engineering and Measurement (ESEM '08).* ACM, New York, NY, USA, 120–128.
7. Susan E Brennan, Xin Chen, Christopher A Dickinson, Mark B Neider, and Gregory J Zelinsky. 2008. Coordinating cognition: The costs and benefits of shared gaze during collaborative search. *Cognition* 106, 3 (2008), 1465–1477.
8. Teresa Busjahn, Roman Bednarik, Andrew Begel, Martha Crosby, James H. Paterson, Carsten Schulte, Bonita Sharif, and Sascha Tamm. 2015. Eye Movements in Code Reading: Relaxing the Linear Order. In *Proceedings of the 2015 IEEE 23rd International Conference on Program Comprehension (ICPC '15).* IEEE Computer Society, Washington, DC, USA, 255–265.
9. Mauro Cherubini, Marc-Antoine Nüssli, and Pierre Dillenbourg. 2008. Deixis and gaze in collaborative work at a distance (over a shared map): a computational model to detect misunderstandings. In *Proceedings of the 2008 symposium on Eye tracking research & applications.* ACM, 173–180.
10. Jan Chong and Rosanne Siino. 2006. Interruptions on Software Teams: A Comparison of Paired and Solo Programmers. In *Proceedings of the 2006 20th Anniversary Conference on Computer Supported Cooperative Work (CSCW '06).* ACM, New York, NY, USA, 29–38.
11. Herbert H Clark and Susan E Brennan. 1991. Grounding in communication. *Perspectives on socially shared cognition* 13, 1991 (1991), 127–149.

12. Alistair Cockburn and Laurie Williams. 2001. Extreme Programming Examined. Addison-Wesley Longman Publishing Co., Inc., Boston, MA, USA, Chapter The Costs and Benefits of Pair Programming, 223–243.

13. Sarah D'Angelo and Darren Gergle. 2016. Gazed and Confused: Understanding and Designing Shared Gaze for Remote Collaboration. In *Proceedings of the 2016 CHI Conference on Human Factors in Computing Systems*. ACM, 2492–2496.

14. Dicolab. 2016. Dicolab - multi-user, multi-cursor collaboration. (2016). `https://www.dicolab.com/products_teamplayer.html`

15. Jörg Edelmann, Philipp Mock, Andreas Schilling, and Peter Gerjets. 2013. Preserving Non-verbal Features of Face-to-Face Communication for Remote Collaboration. In *International Conference on Cooperative Design, Visualization and Engineering*. Springer, 27–34.

16. Ilenia Fronza, Alberto Sillitti, and Giancarlo Succi. 2009. An Interpretation of the Results of the Analysis of Pair Programming During Novices Integration in a Team. In *Proceedings of the 2009 3rd International Symposium on Empirical Software Engineering and Measurement (ESEM '09)*. IEEE Computer Society, Washington, DC, USA, 225–235.

17. Susan R Fussell, Leslie D Setlock, and Elizabeth M Parker. 2003. Where do helpers look? Gaze targets during collaborative physical tasks. In *CHI'03 Extended Abstracts on Human Factors in Computing Systems*. ACM, 768–769.

18. Darren Gergle and Alan T. Clark. 2011. See What I'M Saying?: Using Dyadic Mobile Eye Tracking to Study Collaborative Reference. In *Proceedings of the ACM 2011 Conference on Computer Supported Cooperative Work (CSCW '11)*. ACM, New York, NY, USA, 435–444.

19. Darren Gergle, Robert E Kraut, and Susan R Fussell. 2013. Using visual information for grounding and awareness in collaborative tasks. *Human–Computer Interaction* 28, 1 (2013), 1–39.

20. Zenzi M Griffin and Kathryn Bock. 2000. What the eyes say about speaking. *Psychological science* 11, 4 (2000), 274–279.

21. Karl Gyllstrom and David Stotts. 2005. Facetop: Integrated semi-transparent video for enhanced natural pointing in shared screen collaboration. 15 (May 2005), 1–10.

22. Joy E Hanna and Susan E Brennan. 2007. Speakers' eye gaze disambiguates referring expressions early during face-to-face conversation. *Journal of Memory and Language* 57, 4 (2007), 596–615.

23. Jo E Hannay, Tore Dybå, Erik Arisholm, and Dag IK Sjøberg. 2009. The effectiveness of pair programming: A meta-analysis. *Information and Software Technology* 51, 7 (2009), 1110–1122.

24. Keita Higuch, Ryo Yonetani, and Yoichi Sato. 2016. Can Eye Help You?: Effects of Visualizing Eye Fixations on Remote Collaboration Scenarios for Physical Tasks. In *Proceedings of the 2016 CHI Conference on Human Factors in Computing Systems*. ACM, 5180–5190.

25. William C. Hill, James D. Hollan, Dave Wroblewski, and Tim McCandless. 1992. Edit Wear and Read Wear. In *Proceedings of the SIGCHI Conference on Human Factors in Computing Systems (CHI '92)*. ACM, New York, NY, USA, 3–9.

26. Jim Hollan and Scott Stornetta. 1992. Beyond Being There. In *Proceedings of the SIGCHI Conference on Human Factors in Computing Systems (CHI '92)*. ACM, New York, NY, USA, 119–125.

27. Patrick Jermann, Darren Gergle, Roman Bednarik, and Susan Brennan. 2012. Duet 2012: Workshop on dual eye tracking in CSCW. In *Proceedings of the ACM 2012 conference on Computer Supported Cooperative Work Companion*. ACM, 23–24.

28. Patrick Jermann and Marc-Antoine Nüssli. 2012. Effects of sharing text selections on gaze cross-recurrence and interaction quality in a pair programming task. In *Proceedings of the ACM 2012 conference on Computer Supported Cooperative Work*. ACM, 1125–1134.

29. Sasa Junuzovic, Prasun Dewan, and Yong Rui. 2007. Read, write, and navigation awareness in realistic multi-view collaborations. In *International Conference on Collaborative Computing: Networking, Applications and Worksharing*. IEEE, 494–503.

30. Robert E Kraut, Darren Gergle, and Susan R Fussell. 2002. The use of visual information in shared visual spaces: Informing the development of virtual co-presence. In *Proceedings of the 2002 ACM conference on Computer supported cooperative work*. ACM, 31–40.

31. James C. McCroskey and Thomas A. McCain. 1974. The measurement of interpersonal attraction. *Speech Monographs* 41, 3 (1974), 261–266.

32. Ann McNamara, Reynold Bailey, and Cindy Grimm. 2009. Search task performance using subtle gaze direction with the presence of distractions. *ACM Transactions on Applied Perception (TAP)* 6, 3 (2009), 17.

33. Marc-Antoine Nüssli, Patrick Jermann, Mirweis Sangin, and Pierre Dillenbourg. 2009. Collaboration and abstract representations: towards predictive models based on raw speech and eye-tracking data. In *Proceedings of the 9th international conference on Computer supported collaborative learning-Volume 1*. International Society of the Learning Sciences, 78–82.

34. Jiazhi Ou, Lui Min Oh, Susan R Fussell, Tal Blum, and Jie Yang. 2008. Predicting visual focus of attention from intention in remote collaborative tasks. *IEEE Transactions on Multimedia* 10, 6 (2008), 1034–1045.

35. Christopher Palmer and Bonita Sharif. 2016. Towards Automating Fixation Correction for Source Code. In *Proceedings of the Ninth Biennial ACM Symposium on Eye Tracking Research & Applications (ETRA '16)*. ACM, New York, NY, USA, 65–68.

36. Mauro C Pichiliani, Celso M Hirata, Fabricio S Soares, and Carlos HQ Forster. 2008. Teleeye: An awareness widget for providing the focus of attention in collaborative editing systems. In *International Conference on Collaborative Computing: Networking, Applications and Worksharing*. Springer, 258–270.

37. Sami Pietinen, Roman Bednarik, Tatiana Glotova, Vesa Tenhunen, and Markku Tukiainen. 2008. A method to study visual attention aspects of collaboration: eye-tracking pair programmers simultaneously. In *Proceedings of the 2008 symposium on Eye tracking research & applications*. ACM, 39–42.

38. Sami Pietinen, Roman Bednarik, and Markku Tukiainen. 2010. Shared visual attention in collaborative programming: a descriptive analysis. In *proceedings of the 2010 ICSE workshop on cooperative and human aspects of software engineering*. ACM, 21–24.

39. Laura Plonka and Janet van der Linden. 2012. Why developers don't pair more often. In *Proceedings of the 5th International Workshop on Co-operative and Human Aspects of Software Engineering (CHASE '12)*. IEEE Press, Piscataway, NJ, USA, 123–125.

40. George Powell. 2016. Flappy Clone. (2016). `https://github.com/georgepowell/flappy_clone`

41. Daniel C Richardson and Rick Dale. 2005. Looking to understand: The coupling between speakers' and listeners' eye movements and its relationship to discourse comprehension. *Cognitive science* 29, 6 (2005), 1045–1060.

42. Daniel C Richardson, Rick Dale, and Natasha Z Kirkham. 2007. The art of conversation is coordination common ground and the coupling of eye movements during dialogue. *Psychological science* 18, 5 (2007), 407–413.

43. Stephan Salinger, Christopher Oezbek, Karl Beecher, and Julia Schenk. 2010. Saros: An Eclipse Plug-in for Distributed Party Programming. In *Proceedings of the 2010 ICSE Workshop on Cooperative and Human Aspects of Software Engineering (CHASE '10)*. ACM, New York, NY, USA, 48–55.

44. Bertrand Schneider and Roy Pea. 2013. Real-time mutual gaze perception enhances collaborative learning and collaboration quality. *International Journal of Computer-Supported Collaborative Learning* 8, 4 (2013), 375–397.

45. Kshitij Sharma, Patrick Jermann, Marc-Antoine Nüssli, and Pierre Dillenbourg. 2013. Understanding collaborative program comprehension: Interlacing gaze and dialogues. In *Computer Supported Collaborative Learning (CSCL 2013)*.

46. Alberto Sillitti, Giancarlo Succi, and Jelena Vlasenko. 2012. Understanding the Impact of Pair Programming on Developers Attention: A Case Study on a Large Industrial Experimentation. In *Proceedings of the 34th International Conference on Software Engineering (ICSE '12)*. IEEE Press, Piscataway, NJ, USA, 1094–1101.

47. Randy Stein and Susan E Brennan. 2004. Another person's eye gaze as a cue in solving programming problems. In *Proceedings of the 6th international conference on Multimodal interfaces*. ACM, 9–15.

48. Josh Tenenberg, Wolff-Michael Roth, and David Socha. 2016. From I-Awareness to We-Awareness in CSCW. *Computer Supported Cooperative Work* 25, 4-5 (Oct. 2016), 235–278.

49. Laurie A Williams and Robert R Kessler. 2000. All I really need to know about pair programming I learned in kindergarten. *Commun. ACM* 43, 5 (2000), 108–114.

Author Index

Abdelrahman, Yomna 3751
Abdolrahmani, Ali 4158
Abe, Kaho 465
Abouzied, Azza 6672
Abowd, Gregory D. 430
Ackerman, Mark S. 5929
Adams, Phil 1065
Adar, Eytan 3187
Agapie, Elena 1674, 6876
Aggarwal, Deepti 3916, 6593
Agnihotri, Meeshu 5245
Ahire, Shashank 2059, 5184
Ahlbrand, Benjamin 2940
Ahlström, David 679
Ahmed, Alex A. 6050
Ahmed, Syed Ishtiaque 906, 4741
Ahn, June 4863
Akkiraju, Rama 3506
Al Islam, A. B. M. Alim 531
Al Maimani, Ahmed 2440
Al Zayer, Majed 4063
Alakärppä, Ismo 4424
Alavi, Hamed S. 3856
Alexa, Marc 3954
Alfieri, Felicia 3775
Alha, Kati 2493
Alicea, Tyler Richard 6645
Alkhatib, Ali 4599
Allemandi, Gianluca 7005
Almeida, Teresa 2078
Alper, Basak 5485
Alperovich, Jeffrey M. 965
Alt, Florian 2239, 3751, 4254, 4640, 5114, 6133
Alvarado Garcia, Adriana 4585
Ambard, Alexander 4370
Ambe, Aloha Hufana 6632
Ambike, Satyajit 3328
Amershi, Saleema 2334
Amir, Amnon 6825
Ammi, Mehdi 1831, 4727
Amores, Judith 28
Anand, Anushka 2648
Andalibi, Nazanin 85, 1781, 3377
Andersen, Erik 541, 937, 960, 1431, 4911
Anderson, Bonnie Brinton 2215
Anderson, Fraser 2583, 5643
Anderson, Richard 1855
Andrist, Sean 2571
Angell, Linda 2805
Anstead, Edward 2264
Antle, Alissa N. 1805, 6062
Antoine, Axel 3281
Aoki, Paul 3138
Aoki, Paul M. 5917
Appert, Caroline 3741
Aragon, Cecilia 6106
Aramaki, Eiji 158
Araujo, Bruno 5592
Arawjo, Ian 4911
Arazy, Ofer 6381
Argelaguet, Ferran 5117
Arora, Rahul 5643
Artzi, Yoav 6475
Arya, Ali 1053
Asad, Mariam 2295, 6304
Asakawa, Chieko 5839
Ashbrook, Daniel 497, 6184
Ashok, Vikas 5862
Athukorala, Kumaripaba 1295
Atkinson, Mark 1339
Auffenberg, Frederik 1595
Augustine, Vinay 61
Aung, Maung 3775
Avci, Emre 828
Avellino, Ignacio 6718
Avle, Seyram 472
Avrahami, Daniel 3595
Ayobi, Amid 6889
Azaria, Amos 6038
Azenkot, Shiri 4170
Baber, Chris 1205
Babic, Teo 2617
Babinski, Maxim 5284
Bach, Benjamin 1397
Back, Jon 3390
Bagroy, Shrey 1634
Bai, Jing 965
Bailey, Brian P. 736, 3201, 4454, 4627, 5580
Bailly, Gilles 1307, 3741, 4715
Bak, JinYeong 893
Bakewell, Lyndsey L. 1339
Balaam, Madeline 1078, 5439, 6171
Balasubramanian, Ayshwarya 3187
Balestra, Martina 6381
Balestrini, Mara 2282
Ballard, Kacey 1726
Banovic, Nikola 4229, 6683
Bardot, Sandra 550
Bardzell, Jeffrey 1714, 6523
Bardzell, Shaowen 1714, 6523
Bar-Hillel, Aharon 1887
Barkhuus, Louise 1781, 4850
Barnett, Julie 1339, 2252, 3488
Barowy, Daniel W. 2347
Barreto, Manuela 1339
Barrios-Arciga, Odaris 195
Barry, Marguerite 2708
Bartindale, Tom 1078, 1688
Bartram, Lyn 1364
Bastin, Grace 1660
Bateman, Scott 1352, 1978
Bates, Jo 6620
Bates, Oliver 5361, 6986
Baud-Bovy, Gabriel 4146
Baudisch, Patrick 977, 1471, 2606
Bauer, Lujo 3775, 3787
Baumer, Eric P. S. 6291
Beaudouin-Lafon, Michel ... 4242, 5053, 5869, 6718, 6730
Bechtold, Oskar 3293
Begel, Andrew 6245
Beheshti, Elham 1583
Bellotti, Victoria 4370
Benedikter, Sebastian 4034
Benford, Steve 2091, 4302, 6948
Benko, Hrvoje 3718, 5966
Bennett, Cynthia L. 5988
Bennett, Paul N. 568
Bentley, Frank 85
Berard, Francois 4396, 5619
Beresford, Alastair R. 5361
Berger, Emery D. 2347
Bergstrom-Lehtovirta, Joanna 1497
Bernstein, Michael S. 73, 3523, 4599
Berry, Andrew B. L. 5257
Bertel, Sven 5123
Bertini, Enrico 5462
Beruscha, Frank 2845
Besançon, Lonni 1831, 4727
Beschastnikh, Ivan 3810
Bevilacqua, Frederic 4009
Bezerianos, Anastasia 5475
Beznosov, Konstantin 387, 3810
Bhattacharya, Arpita 1483, 3057

Bi, Xiaojun 705, 4216
Bian, Yulong 5016
Bianchi, Andrea 3106
Bianchi-Berthouze, Nadia 3903
Bichard, Jo-Anne 435
Bigham, Jeffrey P. 1867, 4617, 5826, 5839
Billah, Syed Masum 5862
Billinghurst, Mark 4045
Binns, Reuben 5208
Birbeck, Nataly 146
Bird, Jon 1131, 1756, 3557
Birk, Max V. 5271
Birk, Morten Henriksen 7029
Birnholtz, Jeremy 3163
Bjorn, Daniel 2215
Bjørn, Pernille 6487
Bläsius, Thomas 2606
Bloom, Noam 1887
Blythe, Mark 5400
Bobba, Rakesh B. 387
Boden, Alexander 5716
Bogers, Sander 1408
Boll, Susanne C.J. 667
Bonneau, Joseph 3787
Bonsignore, Elizabeth 2029
Bopp, Chris 810, 3608, 7015
Borchers, Jan 4654
Borges, Luciane Aguiar 773
Boring, Sebastian 1497, 3891
Borland, Ron 3045
Boukhelifa, Nadia 3645
Bousquet, Bruno 949
Bowen, Simon 6317
Bowey, Jason T. 1530
Boy, Jeremy 5462, 5485
Boyd, LouAnne E. 2865, 6147
Boynton, G.R. 4507
Bradford, Mark 3916
Bragg, Jonathan 1867
Brandes, Peter 5318
Brandt, Joel R. 6330
Branham, Stacy 4158
Brehm, Maximilian 2606
Brereton, Margot 6461, 6632
Brewer, Robin N. 568, 1867
Brewster, Stephen A. 1743, 2845, 4146, 5655, 6012
Briggs, Jo 797, 2320
Briggs, Pam 4935, 6425
Brittain, Katie 2163
Britton, Lauren M. 2499
Brooker, Phillip 2252, 3488
Brostow, Gabriel J. 6569
Brown, Barry 416, 3582, 4331
Brown, Erica Brown 1768
Brubaker, Jed R. 6291
Bruckman, Amy S. 3867, 6912
Brühlmann, Florian 5087
Bucci, Paul 3681
Buchanan, George R. 1131, 1756
Bulinski, Maximilian 2511
Bullek, Brooke 3833
Bulygin, Denis 2054
Buman, Matthew 6837
Burger, Christian 3632
Burgermaster, Marissa 4097
Burleson, Winslow 1843, 6837
Burnett, Margaret 6232, 6658
Burrell, Jennifer O. 2306
Burrows, Susannah 1193
Buschek, Daniel 2239, 4640
Buxton, Bill 3227, 3254
Byrne, Virginia 2029
Cakmak, Maya 5197
Caldeira, Clara 1647
Caltenco, Hector 4146
Camargo, Kasia 7005
Cambo, Scott A. 3595
Campbell, Jon 2890
Campbell, Neill D. F. 6569
Candau, Yves 5171
Candello, Heloisa 3476
Cang, Xi Laura 3681
Canioni, Lionel 949
Cao, Nan 2916
Cao, Xiang 4326
Cao, Yuanzhi 965
Car, Josip 2708
Carlson, Kelsey 6195
Carpenter, Christopher J. 6925
Carrascal, Juan Pablo 4417
Carriço, Luís 3810
Carter, Marcus 6075
Casiez, Géry 3281, 5117
Caspi, Anat 6024
Castelli, Nico 853, 1620
Castellucci, Steven J. 4194
Cattan, Elie 5619
Cauchard, Jessica R. 3120, 6794
Cecchinato, Marta E. 3557
Cetinkaya, Emine 6559
Chakraborty, Tusher 531
Chamberlain, Alan 4302, 6948
Chan, Gerry 1053
Chan, Liwei 3106, 5452
Chancellor, Stevie 3213
Chandra, Deepak 3972
Chandra, Priyank 4741, 4765, 5929
Chandrasegaran, Senthil 6581
Chandrasekharan, Eshwar 3175, 6912
Chandwani, Rajesh 4069
Chang, Christie 6683
Chang, Chunlei 1397
Chang, Joseph Chee 2334
Chang, Riley 2648
Chang, Victoria 6765
Chang, Yung-Ju 2535
Chantler, Mike J. 815
Chapuis, Olivier 5630, 6730
Chatting, David 435, 5386, 6398
Chauhan, Apoorva 3151
Chen, Chen 3551
Chen, Chenhui 2814
Chen, Fang 2814
Chen, Hsiang-Ting 2606
Chen, Jay 5941, 6511
Chen, Kaiyuan 109
Chen, Ko-Le 2078
Chen, Sijin 5742
Chen, Tianying 5221
Chen, Weixuan 989
Chen, Wen 5976
Chen, Xiang 'Anthony' 5826
Chen, Xiuli 1205
Chen, Yan 6220
Chen, Yu 1647
Chen, Yunan 880, 1647, 4520, 6889
Chen, Zikun 5452
Cheng, Alan 541
Cheng, Chin-Yi 6123
Cheng, Hsien-Tzu 2535
Cheng, Lung-Pan 1471, 3718
Cheng, Peng 2672
Cheng, Yunnuo 430
Cheon, EunJeong 6089
Cheshire, Coye 6381
Chetty, Marshini 6765
Chevalier, Fanny 4715, 5485
Chiticariu, Laura 6672
Cho, Daeki 893
Choe, Eun Kyoung 5773
Choi, Jueun 5787
Choi, Mina 325
Choi, Yi-King 3693
Christin, Nicolas 2202, 3775

Christy, Andrew 109
Chu, Sharon Lynn 109
Chuang, Lewis L. 2998
Chundury, Pramod 6765
Chung, Chia-Fang 1674, 4875
Churchill, Elizabeth F. 2189
Cila, Nazli 448
Clark, Gradeigh D. 374
Clarke, Rachel 2078
Clear, Adrian K. 6936
Clegg, Tamara 2029
Clough, Paul 6620
Cockburn, Andy 208, 3843, 5905, 6742
Cohn, Gabe 3293
Coleman, James 3657
Colley, Ashley 1179, 4424
Colnago, Jessica 3775
Comber, Rob 1078, 1688, 3352, 5813, 6171, 6960
Connelly, Kay 1660, 4924
Consolvo, Sunny 2189
Cooper, Seth 5034
Cooperstock, Jeremy R. 255
Corander, Jukka 1295
Corley, Christopher 61
Cornelio Martinez, Patricia 2426
Correia, Nuno N. 1093
Correll, Michael 1387
Corsten, Christian 4654
Coulton, Paul 265
Coveney, Ashley 208, 6742
Coventry, Lynne 6425
Cox, Anna L. 3557, 6889
Crabtree, Andy 5226
Cramer, Emily S. 1805
Crandall, David J. 5976
Cranor, Lorrie Faith 3775, 3787, 6973
Cranshaw, Justin 2382
Creus, Javi 2282
Crivellaro, Clara 3126
Cross, Jennifer 1607
Cuevas, Ángel 3799
Cuevas, Rubén 3799
Culbertson, Gabriel 1431
Culbertson, Heather 4972
Cullen, Breda 6012
Curmi, Franco 2359
Cutrell, Edward 2890, 5988
Dachselt, Raimund 2639, 5605
Daehlmann, Bjoern 4654
Dahlstedt, Palle 2814
Dai, Guozhong 4326
Dalvi, Girish 2059
D'Angelo, Sarah 6245
Darrah, Charles 5373
Das, Sauvik 3764
Das, Srijita 3838
Dasgupta, Aritra 1193
Dasgupta, Sayamindu 919, 3620
Daskalova, Nediyana 85
Davidson, Neil Alexander 1078
Davidson, Patricia 4097
Davis, Hilary 6960
Davis, Katie 35, 6106
Davis, Richard C. 5703
Dawes, Robert 4468
De Araujo, Bruno 15
De Choudhury, Munmun 170, 1634, 3213
De Pirro, Silvana 2426
de Vries, Roelof A. J. 336
Debarba, Henrique Galvan 5881
Debelius, Justine 6825
Deber, Jonathan 15
Deckers, Eva 1408
Degraen, Donald 1179
Deleris, Yannick 6742
Dell, Nicola 906, 2770
Deloatch, Robert 736
Demkova, Kamila 4370
Deng, Jia 1877
Deng, Zhigang 3011
Densmore, Melissa 6159
Depping, Ansgar E. 1040, 1530, 5271
DeRenzi, Brian 2770, 6159
Despard, Jessica 4585
DeVito, Michael A. 3163
Dey, Anind K. 4229, 6683
Dey, Arindam 4045
Dey, Sanorita 2376
Deza, Arturo 220
Dezfuli, Niloofar 1001
Di Marco, Chrysanne 1015
Dias, Beatrice 1607
Diedrick, Kate 2295
Dierk, Christine 6754
Dillahunt, Tawanna R. 2757
Dille, Paul 1607
Dillenbourg, Pierre 2449
Dimara, Evanthia 5475
Ding, Bolin 2904
Ding, Yu 3011
DiVerdi, Stephen 5428
Dixon, Henry 3775
Do, Ellen Yi-Luen 1731
Doherty, Gavin 2708
Doherty, Kevin 2708
D'Oliveira, Rafael Lucas 5869
Dombrowski, Lynn 4585
Dommaraju, Sandeep 6412
Dong, Mingda 5016
Dorr, Michael 3034
Doshi, Tulsee 3523
Dove, Graham 278
Dow, Andy 5813
Dow, Steven P. 4454, 4627, 5545, 5580
Dowell, John 2264
Dragicevic, Pierre 5475
Dreiser, Marc 3034
Druin, Allison 4948, 5730
Du, Fan 2916, 5498
Dubois, Emmanuel 5892
Durrant, Abigail C. 435, 5386, 6398
Dwyer, Tim 1397
Dye, Michaelanne 3867
E, Ilene L. 6794
E, Jane L. 6794
Eagan, James 3645
Eardley, Rachel 4680
Easley, William 4158
Ebert, David S. 2940
Ebner, Natalie 6412
Ecanow, Gabrielle 1583
Echtler, Florian 1518
Eckstein, Miguel P. 220
Edasis, Caroline 2149, 2175
Edrah, Aisha 1702
Edwards, Isabelle 2976
Edwards, W. Keith 6912, 5412
Eiband, Malin 4254
Eiglsperger, Philipp 5114
Eikey, Elizabeth V. 642
El Ali, Abdallah 667
Eleta, Irene 4430
Elfenbein, Michael 1065
Ellis, Donovan 6412
Elmqvist, Niklas 2940, 6581
Elsden, Chris 435, 5386, 6398
Elwany, Emad 2382
Emami Naeini, Pardis 3775
Emerson, John 5462
Emmadi, Nagraj 2059
Emmerich, Katharina 5284
Epstein, Daniel A. 6850, 6876

Erath, Marcel 5669
Erete, Sheena 2306
Eriksson, Elina 773
Etemad, S. Ali 1053
Evain, Andéol 5117
Evans, Abigail C. 35
Evans, Jonathan 6012
Evans, Sarah 6106
Evers, Vanessa 336
Fafard, Dylan Brodie 3943
Fakourfar, Omid 4501
Fan, Chengdiao 73
Fan, Min 1805
Fan, Xiangmin 4887
Farr-Wharton, Geremy 6960
Faste, Haakon 3403
Fdili Alaoui, Sarah 4009, 5171
Fei-Fei, Li 1877
Feinberg, Melanie 2952
Feit, Anna Maria 1118
Feltwell, Tom 2252, 3488
Feng, Wenxin 4326
Fennell, Chris 2228
Ferdous, Hasan Shahid 6960
Ferrario, Maria Angela 2359
Ferreira, Denzil 3569
Feuchtner, Tiare 5145
Feustel, Clayton 5245
Feuston, Jessica L. 182
Fiannaca, Alexander 2890
Figueiredo, Flavio 3476
Findlater, Leah 6056, 6813
Fink, Daniel 1899
Fischer, Patrick Tobias 1518
Fischman, Benjamin 1179
Fisher, Danyel 2904
Fitzmaurice, George 1290, 1817, 5643
Fitzpatrick, Geraldine 2696, 2853
Fjeld, Morten 3551
Flatla, David R. 519, 1352
Fleck, Stéphanie 949
Fleming, Scott D. 5690
Fleury, Cédric 6718
Flynn, Emma 2320
Fogarty, James 35, 1674, 4703, 6024, 6850, 6876
Follmer, Sean 5075
Folmer, Eelke 4063
Fong, Allan 2405
Foong, Eureka 4454
Foong, Pin Sym 6195
Foote, Jeremy 6376
Ford, Colin M. 1935
Forlines, Clifton 15
Forlizzi, Jodi L. 278, 1028
Foster, Jeffrey S. 362
Foth, Marcus 2826
Fourney, Adam 568
Francis, Patrick 61
Franciszkiewicz, Lukas 3972
Françoise, Jules 4009, 5171
Franczak, Patrick 1577
Fraser, C. Ailie 1817
Fraser, Mike 1923
Frauenberger, Christopher 2696, 2853, 5755
Freedman, Daniel 1887
Freeman, Euan 4146
Frens, Joep 1408
Frey, Jeremy 1459
Friday, Adrian 5361
Fridman, Lex 2805
Friedman, Batya 460
Fritz, Nicole 2371
Fritz, Thomas 61
Froehlich, Jon E. 133, 1768, 2029, 6056, 6813
Frommel, Julian 4021
Fruchard, Bruno 5630
Fu, Wai-Tat 2376, 3201, 5580
Fuelling, Sarah 3241
Fuhl, Wolfgang 2594
Funakoshi, Kotaro 3501
Furió, David 949
Fussell, Susan R. 760
Gai, Wei 5016
Gajos, Krzysztof Z. 1882, 4097
Gander, Delia 4838
Gao, Ge 760
Gao, Xianyi 5346
Garbett, Andrew 2163, 5386, 6171
Garboski, Stephanie 3833
Garncarz, Tom 4627
Gaston, Jacqueline 5034
Gay, Geri 1065
Gearig, Carolyn 3187
Gebru, Timnit 1877
Gerber, Elizabeth M. 810, 4454, 4627, 5580
Gerendasy, Samuel 2137
Gergle, Darren 3163, 6376
Gerling, Kathrin 1352
Gershenfeld, Neil 3657
Gervais, Renaud 1459
Ghosh, Sanjay 2059
Giaccardi, Elisa 448
Gianni, Rory 2964
Giannisakis, Emmanouil 4715
Gil, Hyunjae 3879
Gilbert, Eric 3175
Gill, Steve 4680
Giraud, Frédéric 5006
Girotto, Victor 1843
Girouard, Audrey 1447
Gleicher, Michael 2571
Goesele, Michael 5098
Gogia, Sumit 6330
Goh, Geon-il 2988
Goldman, Shelley 2792
Goldstein, Daniel G. 2347
Goncalves, Jorge 3569
Gong, Jun 5331
Gonzales, Amy 289, 2371
González Cabañas, José 3799
Good, Judith 5755
Goodwin, Matthew S. 6050
Gori, Julien 260
Gorkovenko, Katerina 2269
Gorman, Benjamin M. 519
Gough, Nickolas 5905
Gouscos, Dimitris 3126
Grandi, Jerônimo Gustavo 5881
Grauman, Kristen 3511
Gray, Colin M. 1441
Green, David Philip 1078, 4753, 6317
Greenberg, Saul 2583
Greenhalgh, Chris 4302
Greis, Miriam 828
Grenbæk, Jens Emil 6449
Griggio, Carla F. 727, 4266
Grinter, Rebecca E. 5412, 6912
Grisoni, Laurent 5006
Grønbæk, Jens Emil 7029
Grosse-Puppendahl, Tobias 3293
Grossman, Tovi 1817, 2583, 5643
Gruber-Baldini, Ann 5800
Grubert, Jens 3966
Grusky, Max 6475
Gu, Yizheng 4479
Guerra-Reyes, Lucia 4924
Guerreiro, Tiago 3810
Gugenheimer, Jan 4021, 4034
Guha, Mona Leigh 5730
Guha, Shion 906
Gui, Xinning 1647, 4520
Guiard, Yves 260

Guillet, Jean-Paul 949
Guimbretière, François 4911
Guo, Anhong 5826
Guo, Philip J. 1136, 7070
Guo, Yufan 3506
Gurari, Danna 3511
Gurvich, Ilya 1887
Guthe, Stefan 5098
Gutwin, Carl 208, 3843, 5905, 6742
Haag, Maren 6658
Haas, Nico 1577
Habib, Hana 3775
Hachet, Martin 949, 1459
Haimson, Oliver L. 48, 3377
Häkkilä, Jonna 1179, 4424
Hakulinen, Jaakko 3426, 6993
Haldar, Shefali 867
Hale, Scott A. 4430
Hall, Andrew 6352, 6902
Haller, Michael 2617
Halskov, Kim 278
Hammer, Jessica 5545
Han, Gyeol 484
Han, Kyungsik 1193
Hanafi, Maeda F. 6672
Haque, Md. Romael 906
Harlow, John 3071
Harmon, Ellie 3608, 7015
Harnett, C. K. 2024
Harrison, Chris 1, 3986, 4000
Hartzler, Andrea L. 5257
Hasan, Khalad 679
Hashash, Shafeka 4170
Hassan, Carolyn 2282
Hassib, Mariam 2239, 5114, 6133
Hattori, Kazuki 158
Hautea, Samantha 919
Hayes, Gillian R. 2865, 3377, 6147
Hazas, Mike 5361, 6986
Hazzard, Adrian 4302
He, Fang 937
He, Liang 133
He, Shuang 5568
Heath, Christian 5295
Hecht, Brent 1154, 1167, 1179, 6352
Hedman, Anders 2685
Heer, Jeffrey 1387, 2628, 2648
Heimonen, Tomi 3426, 6993
Hekler, Eric B. 3071
Hekler, Eric B. 6837
Henley, Austin Z. 5690
Hennessy, Kate 6062
Henry Riche, Nathalie 3241
Hentschel, Jasmine 748, 4069
Henze, Niels 1577, 5114
Heo, Eunyoung 5787
Herbsleb, James D. 655
Hertzmann, Aaron 5428
Hettinger, A. Zachary 2405
Heuten, Wilko 667
Heylen, Dirk 2462
Higuchi, Keita 6536
Hill, Benjamin Mako 919, 3620
Hill, Charles G. 6232, 6658
Hinckley, Ken 3227, 3241, 3254
Hiniker, Alexis 1483, 5767
Hinrichs, Uta 841
Hirata, Keiji 158
Hirose, Michitaka 5313
Hirsch, Tad 5257
Hjorth, Larissa 6593
Hnin, Wint Yee 1105
Hoang, Thuong 1419, 3916
Hoashi, Keiichiro 1142
Hock, Philipp 4034
Hoddy, Shaun 7005
Hodges, Steve 3293
Hoffman, Guy 580
Hoggan, Eve 3582
Höjer, Mattias 773
Holz, Christian 3293, 3718
Hong, Jason I. 3764
Hong, Matthew K. 5245
Hook, Jonathan 6317
Horn, Michael S. 1583
Hornbæk, Kasper 1497, 4994, 5040
Hornecker, Eva 1518, 2853
Hornof, Anthony 2137
Hornung, Dominik 7057
Horodniczy, Daniel 255
Horvath, Amber 1265
Hoshi, Takayuki 4314
Hoskyn, Maureen 1805
Hou, Youyang 2511
Houben, Steven 3929
Howe, Bill 2648
Howes, Andrew 1205, 1295, 1307
Hoyle, Roberto 3838
Hristov, Rumen 2116
Hsu, Chen-Yu 2116
Hsu, Yen-Chia 1607
Hu, Danielle 5545
Hu, Hou-Ning 2535
Hu, Michele 4170
Hu, Yongtao 6559
Huang, Chi-Wen 2535
Huang, Michael Xuelin 2546
Huang, Yifeng 4617
Huang, Yun 4617, 6777, 6789
Hubbard, Sarah 5197
Huber, Bernd 1882
Huber, Jochen 1001
Hudson, Scott E. 497, 5826
Hughes, Amanda L. 3151
Hughes, Janette 96
Huh, Jun Ho 387
Hull, Carmen 1217
Hullman, Jessica 1375, 2628, 3187
Hummels, Caroline 1408
Hupfeld, Annika 4443
Huron, Samuel 3645
Hurst, Amy 4158
Hurvitz, Aviv 1887
Hussien Ahmed, Mahmoud Mohamed 4960
Hussmann, Heinrich 4254
Hutson, Jevan Alexander 6645
Hwang, Jeong-in 6705
Hwang, Maria L. 4082
Hyde, Embriette R. 6825
Hyrskykari, Aulikki I. 3022
Ichinco, Michelle 1105
Igarashi, Takeo 6208
Ikeda, Kazushi 1142
Ilincai, Emilia-Stefania 3538
Ilinkin, Ivaylo 722
Ilisescu, Corneliu 6569
Im, Eunji 893
Im, Seunggyu 3879
Inkpen, Kori 2394
Ion, Alexandra 977
Iqbal, Shamsi T. 392
Irani, Pourang 679, 4405, 5892
Isbister, Katherine 465
Isenberg, Tobias 1831, 4727
Ishii, Hiroshi 989, 3669, 6123
Issartel, Paul 4727
Istance, Howell 3022
Iten, Glena 5087
Ito, Takayuki 6438
Jaakkola, Elisa 4424
Jabbar, Karim 6487
Jack, Margaret 6511
Jackson, Steven J. 4776, 6511
Jacobs, Jennifer 6330

Jacucci, Giulio 2064, 4534
Jad, Hussein Aly 2782
Jahanbakhsh, Farnaz 3201
Jahani, Jeiran 6475
Jain, Arushi 2233
Jain, Pravar 1731
Jakobi, Timo 853, 1620, 7057
Jalal, Ghita 5053
Jamieson, Matthew 6012
Jang, Sujin 3328
Jansen, Arne 2127
Janssen, Christian P. 392
Javornik, Ana 4838
Je, Seungwoo 3106
Jelen, Ben 4924
Jenkins, Edward Ian 6171, 2163
Jenkins, Jeffrey 2215
Jensen, Nanna 4875
Jetter, Hans-Christian 4548
Ji, Sookyoung 5787
Jia, Yuan 1949
Jiang, Xinlong 2865
Jiao, Alexander 133
Jin, Yanfeng 6683
Jo, Jaemin 2660
Johal, Wafa 2449
Johns, Mishel 405, 2840
Johnson, Daniel 2826
Johnson, Ian G. 2320
Johnson, Isaac 1167, 1726
Johnson, Noah 3775
Johri, Aditya 5929
Joinson, Adam 3821
Jokinen, Jussi P. P. 4203, 6993
Jones, Matt 3126, 5184
Jonsson, Martin 121
Jorge, Joaquim 4057
Joshi, Anirudha 2059, 5184
Joshi, Manjiri 2059
Jota, Ricardo 15
Jouffrais, Christophe 550
Joukhadar, Zaher 1419, 6075
Ju, Wendy 405, 2840
Jun, Eunice 6800
Jung, Daekyoung 6705
Jung, Jingun 2416
Jung, Malte 1431
Jung, Merel 3681
Kaasinen, Eija 6993
Kabelac, Zachary 2116
Kacorri, Hernisa 5839
Kacprzak, Emilia 1277
Kakehi, Yasuaki 989, 2106, 3669
Kalantidis, Yannis 3213
Kalkofen, Denis 6547
Kamalzadeh, Mohsen 2928
Kamar, Ece 2334
Kameswaran, Vaishnav 2757, 4069, 5929
Kan, Viirj 989
Kanaci, Halil Aytac 6569
Kandathil, George 5954
Kane, Shaun 1118
Kane, Shaun K. 6147
Kang, Bo 4692
Kang, Jennifer H. 6876
Kang, Seokbin 2029
Kang, Sungjoon 4561
Kangasrääsiö, Antti 1295
Kapadia, Apu 3838
Karahalios, Karrie 2376, 3201
Karamagioli, Evika 3126
Karkar, Ravi 6850
Karlesky, Michael 465
Karmon, Kfir 1887
Karolus, Jakob 2998
Karusala, Naveena 3340
Karvonen, Hannu 6993
Karwita, Shienny 1731
Kasahara, Shunichi 6438
Kaski, Samuel 1295
Kasneci, Enkelejda 2594
Kasuga, Shoko 6438
Kasunic, Anna 1973
Katabi, Dina 2116
Katzen, Monica 2029
Kaufman, Geoff 1973
Kaul, Oliver Beren 3729
Kavan, Ladislav 1794
Kawano, Taiki 5307
Kay, Matthew 6837
Kayali, Fares 5123
Kazemitabaar, Majeed 133
Kazi, Rubaiat Habib 5643
Kelleher, Caitlin L. 1105
Kelley, Christina 629
Kelly, David 1419
Kery, Mary Beth 1265
Keskinen, Tuuli 6993
Khairuddin, Irni Eliana 6499
Khaloo, Pooya 5850
Khamis, Mohamed 3751, 4254
Khan, Taslim Arefin 531
Kharrufa, Ahmed 5556
Khelifi, Maher 867
Khot, Rohit Ashok 6593
Khovanskaya, Vera 5373
Kientz, Julie A. 1483, 3057, 6850, 6864, 6876
Kim, Auk 4561
Kim, Bohyoung 6705
Kim, David 1583
Kim, Hyoungshick 387
Kim, Jeeeun 5826
Kim, Jeong-Whun 5787
Kim, Ji Tae 3365
Kim, Jinyoung 4948
Kim, John 893
Kim, Junhong 893
Kim, Junhyeok 679
Kim, Sunghee 722
Kim, Wonjae 6705
Kim, Yea-Seul 1375
Kim, Yoojung 2523, 5787
Kim, Younghoon 2628
King, Martha 2282
Kirk, David S. 435, 2078, 5386, 6398
Kirlik, Alex 736
Kirman, Ben 3488
Kirwan, Brock 2215
Kitani, Kris M. 5839
Kjeldskov, Jesper 6608
Klamka, Konstantin 5605
Klasnja, Predrag 3071
Kleinschmidt, Vanessa M. 4924
Klemmer, Scott 73, 6825
Klokmose, Clemens N. 4548
Knierim, Pascal 1577
Knight, Rob 6825
Knouf, Nicholas A. 1544
Ko, Andrew J. 4703
Kobayashi, Kazuki 3501
Kocielnik, Rafal 2382
Koedinger, Kenneth 1028
Koesten, Laura M. 1277
Kofinas, Nikolaos 362
Kokkalis, Nicolas 73
Komatsu, Takanori 3501
Komlodi, Anita 5800
Kommana, Yannis 2606
Konno, Keina 6438
Korhonen, Hannu 2493
Korinek, Elizabeth V. 3071
Kornfield, Rachel 325
Korsgaard, Henrik 7029
Kosciolek, Tomasz 6825

Koskinen, Elina 2493
Koskinen, Hanna Maria Kaarina 6993
Kostakos, Vassilis 3569
Kou, Yubo 4520
Kovacs, Robert 977, 2606
Krafft, Peter 2976
Kraft, Nicholas 61
Kralj, Christoph 2928
Kranz, Matthias 3966
Kränzle, Taras 5669
Krause, Jonathan 1877
Krause, Markus 4627
Kraut, Robert 6363
Krautter, Wolfgang 2845
Krekhov, Andrey 5284
Kristensson, Per Ola 4194
Krogh, Peter Gall 7029, 6449
Kröse, Ben 448
Kross, Sean 931
Krüger, Antonio 1571, 3126
Krüger, Jens 5284
Krupka, Eyal 1887
Kubota, Ayumu 2202
Kudo, Takashi 158
Kuehl, Kate 1154, 1179
Kuhl, Scott 5457
Kulkarni, Anand 1867
Kulkarni, Harish 1118, 2878, 2890
Kumar, Neha 748, 2792, 3340, 3867, 4069
Kumaraguru, Ponnurangam 1634
Kurzhals, Kuno 6559
Kuttal, Sandeep Kaur 6232
Kuzuoka, Hideaki 158, 5295, 5307
Kwak, Sonya S. 5678
Kwon, Sae bom 2523
Kwon, Sujin 3538
Kymäläinen, Tiina 6993
Kytö, Mikko 6101
Laaksolahti, Jarmo 2019
Laing, Mary 3352
Lalanne, Denis 3856
Lampe, Cliff 2511
Lampinen, Airi 3582, 4331
Landay, James A. 3120, 6794
Landwehr Sydow, Sophie 121
Lank, Edward 244, 5109, 6760
Laput, Gierad 1, 3764, 3986, 4000
Lasecki, Walter S. 6220
Lau, Timothy 5197
Lauridsen, Bjarke M. 6608
Laurier, Eric 416
LaViola Jr., Joseph J. 4692, 5850
Lawson, Shaun 146, 1339, 2252, 3126, 3488, 4935
Lazar, Amanda 2149, 2175, 7042
Lazem, Shaimaa 2782
Le, Huyen T. 4507
Le Dantec, Christopher A. 2295, 6304
Le Moignan, Effie 4935
Lecolinet, Eric 5630, 6730
Lécuyer, Anatole 5117
Ledo, David 2583
Lee, Adam J. 3838
Lee, Bokyung 484
Lee, Bongshin 629, 2660, 5767, 6705
Lee, DoYoung 3879
Lee, Geehyuk 2416
Lee, Hee Rin 5678
Lee, Hyunjeong 5787
Lee, Jin Ha 1483
Lee, Jisoo 6837
Lee, Jongin 893
Lee, Joonbum 2805
Lee, Joongseek 5787
Lee, Kung Jin 5742
Lee, Kwan Hong 893
Lee, Kyung ho 893
Lee, Kyung-Ryong 2988
Lee, Matthew L. 3595
Lee, Min Kyung 3365
Lee, Nicole B. 6876
Lee, Sang Won 6220
Lee, Scott 2770
Lee, Taeyoung 2523
Lee, Uichin 3538, 4561
Lee, Woohun 2488
Lee, Youngho 4045
Lee, Youngki 5703
Lee Hong, Anita 6461
Leichter, Ido 1887
Leigh, Darren 15
Leiva, Luis A. 4182
Lennon, Marilyn 6012
Leong, Hong Va 2546
Leong, Joanne 2617
Leong, Tuck Wah 6386
Lerner, Sorin 195
Lesh, Neal 2770
Lessel, Pascal 1571
Levi, Margaret 4599
Levine, Daniel 6123
Levine, John M. 6363
Levis, Sergio 7005
Li, Bochao 5457
Li, Boyang 61
Li, Haibo 2685
Li, Jamy 336
Li, Jessie 1867
Li, Jiajia 2546
Li, Lan 5331
Li, Linfeng 2757
Li, Toby Jia-Jun 6038
Li, Wilmot 6695
Li, Yunyao 6672
Liakata, Maria 3632
Liccardi, Ilaria 5208
Licoppe, Christian 5295
Light, Ann 797
Lim, Catherine 5257
Lin, Allen Yilun 1154, 1179
Lin, Cheng 5016
Lin, Tian 6412
Lin, Yen-Chen 2535
Lin, Yilun 6352
Lin, Yu-Ru 2916
Lindlbauer, David 3954
Lindley, Joseph 265
Lindqvist, Janne 374, 5346
Lindtner, Silvia 472
Linehan, Conor 4899
Liu, Can 374, 6730
Liu, Christine 2116
Liu, Feng 5428
Liu, Juan 5016
Liu, Leslie S. 1660
Liu, Min 965
Liu, Wanyu 1307, 5869
Liu, Xiaoxing 4278
Liu, Yikun 1949
Liu, Yuchen 2116
Liu, Yunhao 1961
Liu, Zhe 3506, 6195
Lizarondo, Leah 3365
Lockerbie, James 7005
Lomas, J. Derek 1028
Long, Kiel 1339, 2252, 3488
Lopes, Daniel Simões 4057
Lopes, Pedro 1471
Louis, Thibault 4396
Lowe, Toby 5813
Loyalka, Prashant 2792
Lu, Jiajun 5966
Lu, Le 348
Lu, Nannan 509

Lu, Yichen 6993
Ludman, Evette 5257
Luff, Paul K. 5295
Luger, Thomas 4548
Lukoff, Kai 4966
Luo, Hengliang 4479
Luo, Wencan 4887
Luo, Yuhan 5773
Luong, Maria V. 5690
Luria, Michal 580
Lyckvi, Sus Lundgren 2814
L'Yi, Sehi 2660
Lyu, Fei 4326
Ma, Haiwei 6902
Ma, Xiao 1781
Ma, Xiaojuan 556, 5568
MacDonald, Alistair 2320
Machover, Noa 989
Machulla, Tonja 828
Maciejewski, Ross 2940
Maciel, Anderson 5881
MacKay, Bonnie 1702
Mackay, Wendy E. 727, 4242, 4266, 5053, 6718
Mackinlay, Jock 2648
MacLean, Karon E. 3681, 6742
MacLeod, Haley 1660, 4924, 5988
Maes, Pattie 28, 3669
Maezawa, Akira 4290
Maghoumi, Mehran 5850
Magnor, Marcus 5098
Magnusson, Charlotte 4146
Mahoney, Jamie 4935
Maiden, Neil 7005
Makatura, Liane 1794
Mäkelä, Ville 3426
Malacria, Sylvain 3281, 4715
Malaka, Rainer 716
Malik, Abish 2940
Malinverni, Laura 5129, 5755
Malloch, Joseph 4266
Malu, Meethu 6056
Mamykina, Lena 4082, 4097
Mandl, David 6547
Mandryk, Regan L. 1040, 1530, 5271
Manikonda, Lydia 170
Mankoff, Jennifer 497, 4229, 5826, 6184, 6683
Mannonen, Petri 6993
Manthorne, Cori 2189
Manuel, Jennifer 1688, 2320
Marcano Belisario, Jose 2708
Marcus, Noah 195
Marino, David 3681
Marinov, Darko 3201
Markussen, Anders 3891
Marquardt, Nicolai 3929
Marques, Diogo 3810
Marriott, Kim 1397
Marsden, Nicola 6658
Marshall, Joe 4899
Marshall, Paul 2282, 6889
Marshall-Fricker, Charlotte G. 182
Martelaro, Nikolas 405
Martín-Albo, Daniel 4182
Martinez Plasencia, Diego 4383
Maruyama, Keita 5307
Marwecki, Sebastian 1471
Marzo, Asier 1923
Masden, Christina A. 6912
Matejka, Justin 1290
Matela, Nuno 4057
Matkin, Brendan 6062
Matthews, Tara 2189
Matthies, Denys J.C. 1911
Matulic, Fabrice 3267
Maudet, Nolwenn 5053
Mauriello, Matthew Louis 1768, 5730
Maya, Julian 5129
Mayra, Frans 2493
Mazmanian, Melissa 3377, 5373
Mazurek, Michelle L. 362, 931
McArthur, Victoria 5029
McCarthy, John 1326
McGill, Mark 5655
McGookin, David 6101
McGregor, Moira 3582
McGrenere, Joanna 2137, 4242, 4266
McIntosh, Jess 1923
McLachlan, Ross 4284
McMahon, Connor 1167
McMillan, Donald 3582
McNally, Brenna 4948, 5730
McNaney, Roisin C. 1313, 1339
McNeill, Andrew R. 6425
McPeak, Jason 133
McPherson, Andrew P. 6948
McReynolds, Emily 5197
McRoberts, Sarah 6352, 6902
Mech, Radomir 6330
Mehler, Bruce 2805
Meinel, Florian 2606
Mejova, Yelena 4507
Mekler, Elisa D. 5087, 5109
Melicher, William 3775
Mendes, Daniel 4057
Mendez, Chris 6658
Méndez, Gonzalo Gabriel 841
Meng, Xiangxu 5016
Meng, Xiaojun 3551
Mentis, Helena M. 5800
Mercer, Jamie 1313
Methven, Thomas S. 815
Meurer, Johanna 5716
Mexter, Leon 1313
Meyer, André N. 61
Meyer, Jochen 667
Michaelis, Joseph E. 301
Micinski, Kristopher 362
Mikami, Hiroaki 6208
Miller, David 2840
Miller, Matthew K. 2394, 5271
Minamizawa, Kouta 5452
Mir, Darakhshan J. 3833
Mishra, Sonali R. 867, 1674, 3071
Misra, Archan 5703
Miyashita, Homei 232, 5065
Mizouni, Rabeb 3538
Mochizuki, Takayoshi 5313
Moffatt, Karyn 6056, 6813
Mohamed Hussien Ahmed, Mahmoud 2672
Mohr, Peter 6547
Mok, Brian 2840
Molapo, Maletsabisa 6159
Möller, Torsten 2928
Monastero, Beatrice 6101
Moncur, Wendy 6398
Mondada, Francesco 2449
Monk, Andrew 6398
Monroy-Hernandez, Andrés 2382
Morales González, Rafael 3741
Moreno, Alejandro 2462
Moritz, Dominik 2648, 2904
Moro, Giulio 6948
Morreale, Fabio 6948
Morris, Meredith Ringel 568, 1118, 1867, 2558, 2878, 2890, 5988
Morrison, Cecily 2708
Morrissey, Kellie 146, 1326, 2163
Moseley, Braon 15
Moser, Carol 4344, 4358, 4966, 5221
Mott, Martez E. 2558
Moukperian, Melissa 497
Mousas, Christos 1794
Moutinho, Ana 4838

Moyer, Ilan 3657
Mueller, Florian 'Floyd' 2473, 6593
Mueller, Jörg 3954, 5145
Mühlhäuser, Max 1001
Müller, Claudia 7057
Müller, Jens 6481
Müller, Willi 2606
Munson, Sean A. 1674, 3057, 4875, 6850, 6876
Muntean, Reese 6062
Muradoglu, Melis 6412
Murnane, Elizabeth L. 1065
Musabirov, Ilya 2054
Mustafa, Maryam 5098
Mutlu, Bilge 301, 325, 2571
Myers, Andrew C. 4911
Myers, Brad A. 1265, 6038
Naaman, Mor 1781, 4284, 6475
Nacenta, Miguel A. 841
Nacke, Lennart E. 1015, 5109
Naing, Han Min 348
Nakano, Mikio 3501
Nakarai, Akihiro 2202
Nancel, Mathieu 244
Narumi, Takuji 5313
Nassir, Soud 6386
Nasu, Kari 5742
Nazareth, Anisha 5929
Nebeling, Michael 4574
Nedel, Luciana 5881
Nelimarkka, Matti 4534
Nemer, David 3867
Neustaedter, Carman 313, 1805
Newhart, Veronica Ahumada 342
Newman, Todd 2382
Ng, Alexander 2845, 5655
Ng, Sarah 6523
Ngai, Grace 2546
Ngo Quang, Hung 5318
Nguyen, Cuong 5428
Nguyen, David H. 7042
Nicholas, Molly 6111
Nielsen, Becky 2295
Nishi, Tsubasa 6438
Nishida, Jun 3316
Nisi, Valentina 1179
Nissen, Bettina 4825, 5386
Nittala, Aditya Shekhar 3095
Niu, Chengjie 5016
Norasikin, Mohd Adili 4383
Normark, Maria 4850
Norooz, Leyla 2029, 4948
Nourbakhsh, Illah 1607
Nousu, Hannu 6993
Nouwens, Midas 727
Nov, Oded 5462, 6381
Nunes, Nuno Jardim 1179
Oakley, Ian 3879
Obata, Koichi 1508
Oben, Mathias 716
Ochiai, Yoichi 4314
Oehlberg, Lora 96,2583
Ofek, Eyal 3718
Ogonowski, Corinna 853, 1620
Oguamanam, Vanessa 2029
Oh, Changhoon 2523
Oh, Jeungmin 3538
O'Hara, Kenton 6449, 6960
Okamura, Allison M. 3115, 4972
Okopny, Paul 2054
O'Leary, Jasper 6111
O'Leary, Kathleen 2189
Oleson, Alannah 6658
Oliveira, Daniela 6412
Oliveira, Nigini 6800
Olivier, Patrick 146, 1078, 2163, 3126, 4753, 5556
Olson, Judith S. 342
Olwal, Alex 716, 2617, 3095, 3972, 5075
O'Modhrain, Sile 5929
O'Neill, Brian 6012
Oney, Steve 6220
Oogjes, Doenja 4489
Opwis, Klaus 5087
Oriola, Bernard 550
Orji, Rita 1015
Orzech, Kathryn 6398
Osadchiy, Timur 5556
Östling, Ulrika Gunnarsson 773
Otsuki, Mai 5307
Otterbacher, Jahna 6620
Ou, Jifei 3669
Ouf, Nada 1794
Ouk, Felix 2648
Oulasvirta, Antti 1295, 2064, 3891, 4203, 5040
Outing, Thomas 133, 2029
Owaki, Richi 6438
Özgür, Ayberk 2449
Paavilainen, Janne 2493
Paay, Jeni 6608
Padilla, Stefano 815
Pahud, Michel 3227, 3254
Pal, Joyojeet 4741, 5929
Palanque, Philippe 6742
Palen, Leysia 2042
Pan, Serena 989
Panabaker, Sheri 3241
Pandey, Anshul Vikram 5462
Pandey, Vineet 6825
Pandya, Bhargav 6232
Pantidi, Nadia 1326
Paradiso, Ann 1118, 2890
Pares, Narcis 5129
Pargman, Daniel 773, 786
Park, Hyung Kun 2488
Park, Jundong 484
Park, Sangkeun 3538
Park, SoHyun 2523
Park, Sun Young 880
Park, Young-Woo 2988
Parker, Andrea G. 5232
Parry-Hill, Jeremiah 6184
Parsons, Paul 1441
Parzer, Patrick 2617
Patel, Nirmal 1028
Patel, Shwetak N. 6864
Patel, Tushita 5271
Pater, Jessica A. 3213
Patra, Abhisekh 1364
Paulo, Soraia 4057
Paulos, Eric 6111, 6754
Pearman, Sarah K. 6973
Pearson, Jennifer 5184
Peck, Evan M. 3833
Pederson, Claudia 1544
Peek, Nadya 3657
Peiris, Roshan Lalintha 5452
Pellicone, Anthony J. 4863
Peng, Wei 5452
Peng, Yilang 6000
Pennings, Ryan 6593
Perrault, Simon T. 5703
Perrier, Pascal 5619
Perrin, Marc-Emmanuel 3645
Peserico, Enoch 6943
Peters, Jeffrey R. 220
Petersen, Marianne Graves ...7029, 6449
Petralito, Serge 5087
Petridis, Ioannis 2252
Pfeiffer, Max 6133
Pfeil, Ulrike 1899
Pfeuffer, Ken 3254
Phang, Xiao-Shen 4194
Phelan, Chanda 4358

Phillips, Carol 1923
Phipps, Michael 5800
Pietriga, Emmanuel 3741
Pina, Laura R. 3867, 5742, 6850, 6864, 6876
Pine, Kathleen H. 4520
Pinhanez, Claudio 3476
Piorkowski, David 6232
Piper, Anne Marie 182, 2149, 2175
Pitt, Caroline 5742
Pittman, Corey R. 5850
Piumsomboon, Thammathip 4045
Piya, Cecil 6581
Pizza, Stefania 3582
Plaisant, Catherine 5498
Plane, Angelisa 2029
Plank, Thomas 4548
Plaumann, Katrin 5669
Ploderer, Bernd 3045, 3916, 6960
Pohl, Henning 5318
Pollack, Ari H. 867
Poonwala, Nikhil 1028
Pope, Vanessa C. 4468
Popiak, Alexander 2606
Poppe, Ronald 2462
Porter, Donald E. 5862
Porter, Emily 810
Porter, Joel 3821
Poupyrev, Ivan 3972
Prabhakar, Annu Sible 4924
Pratt, Wanda 867
Preibusch, Sören 3821
Prescott, J.J. 2511
Preston, Anne 5556
Pritchard, Gary 4753
Procter, Rob 3632
Profita, Halley P. 6147
Pschetz, Larissa 2964
Puri, Rohan S. 3972
Puussaar, Aare 6936
Pywell, Jake 6425
Qian, Kun 1961
Qu, Zening 2648
Quek, Francis 109
Quigley, Aaron 4194
Rader, Emilee 2228
Rädle, Roman 4548, 6481
Rae, Irene 313
Ragavan, Sruti Srinivasa 6232
Raghavan, Barath 786
Rahmati, Negar 3523
Raitor, Michael 4972
Ralston, James D. 5257
Ramakrishnan, I.V. 5862
Ramani, Karthik 965, 3328, 6581
Ramos, Julian 6683
Ranasinghe, Nimesha 1731
Randall, David William 3632
Rangale, Swati 2059
Rantala, Jussi 3681
Rao, Varun 4229
Rapley, Tim 146
Raptis, Dimitrios 6608
Rasch, Philip J. 1193
Rasche, Nancy 1441
Raskar, Ramesh 3972
Ratwani, Raj M. 2405
Ravichandran, Ruth 6864
Rawassizadeh, Reza 3569
Rayala, Swathi S.V.P. 387
Rector, Kyle 6147
Reddy, Madhu C. 642
Redmiles, Elissa M. 931
Reeves, Stuart 1558, 2091
Reidsma, Dennis 2462
Reilly, Derek 1702
Reimer, Bryan 2805
Reinecke, Katharina 1375, 1882, 4358, 6800
Reinoso, Martin 1419
Reiterer, Harald 1899, 4548, 6481
Rekik, Yosra 5006
Remy, Christian 6986
Ren, Gang 3693
Ren, Ruqin 6342
Ren, Xiangshi 2672, 3746, 4203, 4960
Resnick, Paul 4344, 4358
Retelny, Daniela 3523
Reynolds, Matthew S. 3293
Rho, Eugenia Ha Rim 3377
Riche, Nathalie Henry 5485
Riche, Yann 3241
Rietzler, Michael 5669
Rifat, Md. Rashidujjaman 906, 5941
Rigoll, Gerhard 3034
Rioul, Olivier 260, 5869
Rivera, Michael L. 497
Rix, Sally 5556
Robb, David A. 815
Robinson, Simon 5184
Rocha, Harold 6412
Rochet-Capellan, Amélie 5619
Roe, Paul 6461, 6632
Roesner, Franziska 5197
Rogers, Jon 2269
Rogers, Yvonne 2282, 4838
Rohs, Michael 3729, 5318, 6133
Roith, Johannes 73
Romagnoli, Matteo 6569
Rong, Xin 568
Roo, Joan Sol 1459
Rooney, Brendan 3106
Rosé, Carolyn P. 655
Rosenblat, Tanya 2757
Ross, Anne Spencer 6024
Rossitto, Chiara 4850
Roto, Virpi 6993
Roudaut, Anne 2440, 4405, 4680
Rouncefield, Mark 3632
Roussel, Nicolas 5117
Rowland, Duncan A. 4935
Rowley, Susan 6062
Roy, Quentin 5703
Ruder, Eric V. 6608
Rukzio, Enrico 4021, 4034, 5669
Saakes, Daniel 484
Saariluoma, Pertti O. 6993
Šabanović, Selma 5678
Saha, Manaswi 1768
Sahdev, Sidharth 15
Sahibzada, Hasibullah 1518
Sahoo, Deepak Ranjan 3705, 5184
Saidi, Houssem 5892
Sailaja, Neelima 5226
Sakamoto, Daisuke 6208
Saksono, Herman 5232
Salehzadeh Niksirat, Kavous 2672, 4960
Salovaara, Antti 2064, 4534
Salt, Karen 2320
Sambasivan, Nithya 3867, 5917
Samiei, Amirreza 5850
Samory, Mattia 3175, 6943
Sanders, Steven 15
Santini, Thiago 2594
Saraf, Aditya 5197
Saravanan, Abinaya 4229
Sarcar, Sayan 4203
Sareen, Harpreet 3669
Sargent, Randy 1607
Sarma, Anita 6232, 6658
Sarracino, John 195
Sarsenbayeva, Zhanna 3569
Sas, Corina 6499
Sato, Munehiko 3972

Sato, Yoichi 6536
Sato, Yuka 3083
Satterthwaite, Margaret 5462
Savage, Saiph 1867
Sawaya, Yukiko 2202
Schaekermann, Mike 5109
Schaper, Marie-Monique 5129
Scheme, Erik 1352
Schenk, Simon 3034
Schiller, Stephen 6695
Schiphorst, Thecla 4009, 5171
Schlegel, Rebecca 109
Schlesinger, Ari 5412, 6912
Schmalstieg, Dieter 6547
Schmidt, Albrecht 828, 2998, 5114
Schmidt, Ryan 2583
Schmitz, Martin 1001
Schneegass, Stefan 3751, 5114, 6133
Schneider, Oliver S. 3681
Schoenebeck, Sarita Y. 4344, 4966, 5221
Schofield, Guy 4753
Schofield, Tom 2252, 6398
Schöning, Johannes 716, 1154, 1167, 1179, 3126
Schorr, Samuel B. 3115
Schrader, Katrina 5800
schraefel, m.c. 1595
Schroeder, Jessica 1674, 6850, 6876
Schroeter, Ronald 2826
Schwartz, Josh 6475
Schweiger, Florian 4468
Schwind, Valentin 1577
Sciuto, Alex 5545
Scofield, Jeffrey 6850
Seaman, Sean 2805
Semaan, Bryan 2499, 4534
Sen, Shilad 6352
Sengers, Phoebe 5373
Seo, Jinwook 2660, 6705
Seppelt, Bobbie 2805
Serrano, Marcos 550, 4405, 5892
Sethi, Pooja 1855
Seufert, Anna 2606
Sezgin, Metin 5485
Shadbolt, Nigel 5208
Shaer, Orit 1544
Shafiq, Zubair 4507
Shamma, David A. 3213
Shannon, Amy 5545
Sharif, Mahmood 2202
Sharlin, Ehud 96
Sharma, Sumita 3426
Shaw, Aaron 6376
Sheikh, Alia 4468
Shelton, Martin 2189
Shen, Chia 5016
Shen, Solace 1431
Shepherd, David 61
Sherugar, Samyukta Manjayya 4069
Sherwen, Sally 6075
Shi, Shaoyun 5568
Shi, Weinan 4216
Shi, Yuanchun 692, 705, 4216, 4479, 5568
Shih, Patrick C. 6184, 3669
Shklovski, Irina A. 4875, 7057
Shneiderman, Ben 5498
Shodhan, Sharan 1028
Shorey, Paden 1447
Shu, Zhenyu 1794
Shulman, Lisa 5800
Siek, Katie A. 1660, 4924
Sien, Sang-Wha 6864
Silpasuwanchai, Chaklam 2672, 4203, 4960
Silverman, Max 5245
Simoneaux, Stephen F. 5245
Simperl, Elena 1277
Simpson, Emma 6171
Singh, Aneesha 3903
Singh, Karan 5643
Singh, Ranjit 4776
Singh, Vivek K. 2233
Sinha, Vibha 3506
Sirkin, David 405
Sirotkin, Alexander 2054
Skov, Mikael B. 6608
Sleeper, Manya 2189, 6973
Slegers, Karin 2127
Slovák, Petr 2696
Smit, Iskander 448
Smith, Joshua R. 3293
Smith, Nancy 1714
Smith, Wally 3045, 6075
Smolin, Yoni 1887
Snipes, Will 61
Snow, Stephen 1595
Sobel, Kiley 1483, 2890, 5742, 5767
Soden, Robert 2042
Soliman, Adam 6412
Somanath, Sowmya 96
Song, Hyunjoo 6705
Song, JiaoJiao 4627
Soni, Sandeep 2382
Sorcar, Piya 2792
Soro, Alessandro 6461, 6632
Sosik, Victoria Schwanda 1726
Sousa, Mario Costa 96
Sousa, Maurício 4057
Southern, Caleb 430
Speed, Chris 2964, 4443
Spelmezan, Daniel 3705
Spence, Jocelyn 4825
Spiel, Katharina 2853, 5123, 5755
Spiro, Emma S. 2976
Sprain, Leah 2042
Spring, Neil 5498
Sridhar, Srinath 3891
Srinivasan, Anirudh 3175
Srinivasan, Padmini 4507
Stahl, Alexander 5669
Staiou, Eleni-Revekka 3126
Stangl, Abigale J. 6147
Starbird, Kate 2976
Starke, Sandra Dorothee 1205
Stavness, Ian 3943
Steimle, Jürgen 1001, 3095
Stein, Martin 853, 5716
Steinberger, Fabius 2826
Stemasov, Evgeny 4021
Stenros, Jaakko 2493
Stenton, Phil 5226
Stevens, Gunnar 853, 1620
Stevens, Rock 362
Stone, Maureen 1364
Strasnick, Evan 3120, 5075
Strauber, Benjamin 2792
Strecker, Bernhard A. 1911
Striebel, Jonathan 2606
Strohmayer, Angelika 3352
Strohmeier, Paul 4994
Studd, Karen 4009
Stuerzlinger, Wolfgang 232, 3328
Sturdee, Miriam 265
Su, Norman Makoto 5976, 6089
Subramanian, Sriram 2426, 3705, 4383, 5184
Subramonyam, Hariharan 5929
Such, Jose M. 3821
Suh, Bongwon 2523
Sun, Emily 4284
Sun, Ke 692
Sun, Min 2535
Sun, Mingfei 556
Sun, Xiaoying 3746

Surale, Hemant Bhaskar 3267
Surana, Amit 220
Suri, Siddharth 2347
Sutherland, Marah 2137
Sutton, Selina 1078, 3488
Suzuki, Ippei 4314
Suzuki, Keita 5313
Suzuki, Kenji 3316
Suzuki, Yusuke 5307
Swearngin, Amanda 4703
Tabard, Aurélien 4242
Tabor, Aaron 1352
Tahiroğlu, Koray 6101
Takahashi, Haruki 5065
Takayama, Leila 325
Takeshita, Akiko 6438
Tallyn, Ella 2964
Tan, Joshua 3787
Tanaka, Atau 1093
Tang, Anthony 1978, 4501
Tang, John C. 48, 2394
Tanikawa, Tomohiro 5313
Tanner, Kesler 5075
Tao, Ye 509
Taranta II, Eugene M. 5850
Tasci, Cagri 1577
Tatzgern, Markus 6547
Tauscher, Jan-Philipp 5098
Taylor, Grant S. 220
Taylor, Jennyfer Lawrence 6461
Taylor, Nick 2269
Taylor, Robyn 4825
Taylor, Samuel Hardman 6645
Tchernavskij, Philip 5053
Teevan, Jaime 2382
Tekin, Burak S. 1558
Tennison, Jenifer F. A. 1277
Terveen, Loren 6352
Tewell, Jordan 1131, 1756
Thebault-Spieker, Jacob 1179, 6352
Theobalt, Christian 3891
Tholander, Jakob 121
Thomas, Geb W. 4278
Thomas, Jeremy 3787
Thomas, Vanessa 6986
Thompson, Stephen 4680
Thorpe, Rowan 3126
Tian, Feng 4326
To, Alexandra 3523
Tokuda, Yutaka 4383
Tokuhisa, Satoru 1508
Toledo, Arturo 1118
Tolley, David 1731
Tolmie, Peter 3632
Tomico, Oscar 5158
Tong, Hanghang 2916
Tong, Stephanie Tom 6925
Torres, Cesar 6111
Towne, W. Ben 655
Toyama, Kentaro 5941
Toyoda, Heishiro 2805
Trask, Catherine 6742
Tregillus, Sam 4063
Trujillo Pisanty, Diego 6398
Truong, Khiet P. 336
Tseng, Lucia 3681
Tu, Xiao 3227
Tuncer, Sylvaine 5295
Turner, Anna 2189
Turner, Dan 4370
Turunen, Markku 3426, 6993
Tzairi, Yuval 1887
Uddin, Md. Sami 3843
Ueoka, Ryoko 3083
Umapathi, Udayan 3669
Ur, Blase 3775, 3787
Urban, Bodo 1911
Ushiba, Junichi 6438
Ushigome, Yosuke 3972
Usmani, Wali Ahmed 3810
Vaittinen, Tuomas 6101
Valair, Anasazi 3681
Valente, Dan 6475
Valentine, Melissa A. 3523
Valez, Rafael 2029
Vallgårda, Anna 5158
van Berkel, Niels 3569
van Delden, Robby 2462
van der Heiden, Remo M.A. 392
Van Kleek, Max 5208
van Kollenburg, Janne 1408
Van Mechelen, Maarten 2127
Vance, Anthony 2215
Vance, Gillian 1078
Vaniea, Kami 3838
Vaniyar, Anuroop Pattena 5703
Vargo, Emma 989
Vashistha, Aditya 1855
Vasileiou, Konstantina 1339
Vasquez, Juan Carlos 6101
Vatavu, Radu-Daniel 4182, 4667
Veas, Eduardo 6547
Vechev, Velko 5703
Vega Galvez, Tomás 6754
Velt, Raphael 2091
Venolia, Gina 2394
Verma, Himanshu 3856
Vertanen, Keith 5457
Vertegaal, Roel 4417
Vetere, Frank 1419, 3916, 6075, 6960
Vezzoli, Eric 5006
Vi, Chi Thanh 2426
Vielhauer, Alexander 1571
Vigar, Geoff 1688
Vilardaga, Roger 3057, 6850
Vinayak 6581
Vines, John 1078, 1313, 1339, 2252, 2320, 3488, 5386, 5813
Vinnikov, Alon 1887
Visuri, Aku 3569
Viswanathan, Anandhi 5929
Vitale, Francesco 4242
Vlachokyriakos, Vasillis 3126
Voelker, Simon 4654
Vogel, Daniel 3267, 5331
Vogl, Anita 2617
Voida, Amy 810, 3608, 7015
Voida, Stephen 1949
von Bauer, Philipp 1899
von Zadow, Ulrich 2639
von Zezschwitz, Emanuel 4254
Vorvoreanu, Mihaela 1441
Votipka, Daniel 362
Wacksman, Jeremy 2770
Wadley, Greg 3045
Waern, Annika 3390
Wagemakers, Andrew John 3943
Wagner, Edward H. 5257
Wagner, Erica L. 5954
Wakkary, Ron 4489
Walker, Brendan 4825
Walker, Erin 1843, 6837
Walker, James 5457
Walker, Julie M. 4972
Wall, Ludwig 977, 2606
Wallace, James R. 6760
Wang, Anqi 6683
Wang, Cheng-Yao 4911
Wang, Chi 2904
Wang, Guanyun 509
Wang, Hongan 4326
Wang, Jingtao 2411, 4887
Wang, Lu 5016
Wang, MinJuan 2814
Wang, Qinglong 3746

Wang, Shuhan 937
Wang, Wen 6123
Wang, Wenping 3693, 6559
Wang, Yang 6777, 6789
Wang, Yiting 960
Wang, Yuntao 692, 5568
Wang, Zhenxin 4203
Warner, Jeremy 1136
Wash, Rick 2228
Wasmann, Merlin 667
Waterman, Amanda 4370
Wauck, Helen 5580
Webber, Sarah 3045, 6075
Wehbe, Rina R. 5109
Weigel, Martin 3095
Weingarten, Ariel 6760
Weir, Devon 6412
Weiskopf, Daniel 6559
Weitzner, Daniel J. 5208
Welsh, Daniel 1313
Wen, Hongyi 692
Wenig, Dirk 716, 1179
Wenig, Nina 1179
Westendorf, Lauren 1544
Wethington, Elaine 1065
White, Walker M. 960
Whitehead, Anthony 1053
Whiting, Emily 1794
Whitman, Haley 2137
Whittle, Jon 2359
Widdicks, Kelly 5361
Wiedermann, Ben 195
Wigdor, Daniel 15, 5592
Wilcox, Lauren 629, 5245
Wilde, Danielle 5158
Wilkinson, Gerard 2394
Willett, Wesley 1217, 3138
Williams, Amanda CdeC 3903
Williams, Kaiton 472
Williams, Michele 4158
Williams, Sarah 3241
Williams, Shane 1118, 2558
Williamson, John 3414
Williamson, Julie R. 3414
Wilson, Andrew D. 3718, 5966
Wilson, Graham 1743, 4146
Wilson, Jordan 6062
Wilson, Michael 1339
Wilson, Rob 5813
Wimmer, Raphael 3293
Windlin, Charles 2019
Winnemöller, Holger 6695
Wisniewski, Pamela 4692
Wobbrock, Jacob O. 35, 2558, 6024
Woelfer, Jill Palzkill 2189
Wong Sak Hoi, Geraldine 3632
Wongsuphasawat, Kanit 2628, 2648
Wood, Gavin 2252, 5439
Wood, Matthew 2078, 5439
Woodruff, Allison 3138
Woźniak, Paweł W. 2239, 2998
Wright, Pete 3126, 2163, 4753, 4825, 6317, 6936
Wu, Chenshu 1961
Wu, Chi-Jui 3929
Wuertz, Jason 1978
Wulf, Volker 853, 1620, 5716, 7057
Xia, Haijun 3227, 5592
Xia, Huichuan 6777, 6789
Xiao, Dan 1647
Xiao, Meihua 3011
Xiao, Robert 4000
Xiao, Xiang 2411
Xie, Jun 6695
Xie, Yin 6220
Xu, Anbang 3506
Xu, Panpan 2916
Xu, Tianyin 348
Xu, Weijie 705
Xue, Na 4617
Yamada, Akira 2202
Yamada, Seiji 3501
Yamada, Tomohiro 5313
Yamamoto, Kazuhiko 4290
Yamanaka, Shota 232
Yamaoka, Junichi 2106
Yamashita, Naomi 158, 5295
Yan, Bei 6342
Yan, Yukang 692
Yang, Chenglei 5016
Yang, Diyi 6363
Yang, Huizi 6412
Yang, Jackie 5075
Yang, Lei 541
Yang, Xing-Dong 5331
Yang, YiWei 6220
Yang, Yongliang 3693
Yang, Zheng 1961, 4479
Yao, Cheng 509
Yao, Lining 6123
Yao, Yaxing 6777, 6789
Yarbrough, Karen 5800
Yarosh, Lana 2993
Yarosh, Svetlana 6902
Yasu, Kentaro 4983
Yeh, Tom 5826
Yellapragada, Baladitya 3138
Yen, Yu-Chun (Grace) 5580
Yeo, Hui-Shyong 4194
Yi, HyeonBeom 2488
Yi, Xin 705, 4216, 4479
Yin, Kodlee 6106
Ying, Fangtian 509
Yip, Jason C. 1483, 2029, 5742
Yokoyama, Masanori 5313
Yonetani, Ryo 6536
Yoo, Daisy 460
Yoo, Sooyoung 5787
Yoshida, Shigeo 5313
Yoshino, Koichi 1508
You, Sijing 1471, 2606
Youn, Eunhye 2416
Young, Damon 2473
Young, Tony 1313
Yu, Bowen 2382
Yu, Chun 692, 705, 4216, 4479, 5568
Yu, Xing 1949
Yuan, Fengpeng 5346
Yue, Ya-Ting 3693
Yung, Marcus 6742
Yurman, Paulina 435
Zachos, Konstantinos 7005
Zaga, Cristina 336
Zagermann, Johannes 1899
Zave, Pamela 2993
Zhang, Caowei 509
Zhang, Cheng 430
Zhang, Jiawei 2940
Zhang, Joan 6056, 6813
Zhang, Teng 6123
Zhang, Weiyi 3916
Zhang, Xiaolian 509
Zhang, Xiaolong (Luke) 3693, 4326
Zhang, Xiaoyi 2878, 6024
Zhang, Yang 1, 3986, 4000
Zhang, Yankai 5568
Zhang, Yunbo 965
Zhang, Yuting 3011
Zhao, Jun 5208
Zhao, Peijun 5568
Zhao, Shengdong 3551, 5703, 6195
Zhao, Yuhang 4170
Zhao, Zhao 1053
Zhao, Zhenjie 556
Zheng, Yue 1961

Zhou, Huiyuan 1702
Zhou, Kaitlyn 2976
Zhou, Rui 748
Zhou, Rui 4069
Zhou, Yuanyuan 348
Zhou, Zimu 1961
Zhu, Bin 2685
Zhu, Haining 5773
Zhu, Jasmine 195
Zhu, Yeshuang 5568
Zia, Jasmine 6850
Zilles, Craig 736
Zimmerman, John 278
Zolyomi, Annuska 6147
Zubiaga, Arkaitz 3632
Zuckerman, Oren 580
Züger, Manuela 61

NOTES

NOTES

NOTES

NOTES

NOTES

NOTES

NOTES

NOTES

NOTES

NOTES

NOTES

NOTES

NOTES

NOTES

NOTES

NOTES

NOTES

NOTES

NOTES

NOTES

www.ingramcontent.com/pod-product-compliance
Lightning Source LLC
LaVergne TN
LVHW080105011026
849160LV00013B/1036
* 9 7 8 1 4 5 0 3 5 4 6 8 4 *